The Royal Horticultural Society

ENCYCLOPEDIA of GARDENING

The Definitive Practical Guide

The Royal Horticultural Society

ENCYCLOPEDIA of GARDENING

The Definitive Practical Guide

Editor-in-Chief
CHRISTOPHER BRICKELL

DK

LONDON, NEW YORK, MUNICH, MELBOURNE, DELHI

FIRST EDITION 1992

Managing Editor Jane Aspden
Managing Art Editor Ina Stradins
Senior Editor Kate Swainson
Senior Art Editor Lynne Brown
Editors Claire Calman, Alison Copland, Annelise Evans,
Helen Partington, Jane Simmonds; Judith Chambers, Katie John,
Teresa Pritlove; Jackie Bennett, Carolyn Burch, Joanna Chisholm,
Allen Coombes, Heather Dewhurst, Angela Gair, Lin Hawthorne,
Jonathan Hilton, Jane Mason, Ferdie McDonald, Andrew Mikolajski,
Christine Murdock, Lesley Riley
Designers Gillian Shaw; Gillian Andrews, Johnny Pau,
Vicky Short, Chris Walker; Rhonda Fisher, Bob Gordon,
Sally Powell, Steve Wooster
Photography Peter Anderson (with Steve Gorton and
Matthew Ward)
Illustrations Karen Cochrane, Simone End, Will Giles,
Vanessa Luff, Sandra Pond, John Woodcock; Andrew Farmer,
Aziz Khan, Liz Peperall, Barbara Walker, Ann Winterbothom

THIRD EDITION 2007

Senior Editor Helen Fewster
Senior Art Editor Joanne Doran

Editors Caroline Reed, Jane Simmonds,
Joanna Chisholm, Katie Dock
Designer Elly King
DTP Designer Louise Waller

Managing Editor Anna Kruger
Managing Art Editor Alison Donovan

Picture Research Mel Watson
Media Resources Lucy Claxton
Production Luca Frassinetti
Index Dorothy Frame

DORLING KINDERSLEY (DELHI)
Project Manager, Hi-res Workflow Pankaj Sharma
DTP Designers Harish Aggarwal, Tarun Sharma

This edition published in 2010
First edition published in Great Britain in 1992 by
Dorling Kindersley Limited, London

This revised and expanded edition published in Great Britain
in association with The Royal Horticultural Society by
Dorling Kindersley Limited, 80 Strand, London WC2R 0RL
A Penguin Company

2 4 6 8 10 9 7 5 3 1

A CIP record for this book is available from the British Library

ISBN 978-1-4053-6189-7

Colour reproduction by Colourscan, Singapore
Printed and bound by Toppan, China

Discover more at
www.dk.com

CONTENTS

INTRODUCTION 2

PART ONE: CREATING THE GARDEN

HOW TO APPLY THE PRINCIPLES OF DESIGN, AND CREATE AND PLANT GARDEN FEATURES

1 GARDEN PLANNING AND DESIGN 13

2 ORNAMENTAL TREES 53

3 ORNAMENTAL SHRUBS 89

4 CLIMBING PLANTS 123

5 ROSES 147

6 PERENNIALS 171

7 ANNUALS AND BIENNIALS 207

8 BULBOUS PLANTS 225

9 ROCK, SCREE, AND GRAVEL GARDENING 253

10 WATER GARDENING 281

11 CONTAINER GARDENING 305

12 CACTI AND OTHER SUCCULENTS 337

13 INDOOR GARDENING 353

14 THE LAWN 385

15 GROWING HERBS 403

16 GROWING FRUIT 417

17 GROWING VEGETABLES 491

PART TWO: MAINTAINING THE GARDEN

PRACTICAL ADVICE ON TOOLS AND EQUIPMENT, GREENHOUSES, AND BUILDING MATERIALS AND TECHNIQUES; UNDERSTANDING SOIL TYPE AND CLIMATE, HOW PLANTS GROW AND REPRODUCE, AND HOW BEST TO DEAL WITH PROBLEMS

1 TOOLS AND EQUIPMENT   550

2 GREENHOUSES AND FRAMES   566

3 STRUCTURES AND SURFACES   584

4 CLIMATE AND THE GARDEN   606

5 SOILS AND FERTILIZERS   616

6 PRINCIPLES OF PROPAGATION 629

7 PLANT PROBLEMS   639

8 BASIC BOTANY   674

Glossary of Terms   677

Index   683

Acknowledgements   751

SPECIAL FEATURES

Hardy Palms and the Exotic Look   60
Dwarf Conifers   62
Topiary   76
Hedges and Screens   84
Willow Walls   87
Bamboos   96
Shrubs for Ground Cover   101
Fuchsias   120
Clematis   138
Roses for Display and Exhibition   153
Perennials for Ground Cover   180
Irises   182
Hostas   186
Chrysanthemums   188
Ferns   194
Carnations and Pinks   196
Pelargoniums   204
Sweet Peas   214
Tulips and Daffodils   232
Dahlias   234
Lilies   251
Alpine Houses and Frames   277
Water Lilies   286
Waterside Decking   296
Balconies and Roof Gardens   312
Water Gardens in Containers   331
Conservatory Gardening   356
Bromeliads   362
Orchids   368
Pinch Pruning   377
Meadow Gardening   401
The Bed System   496
Frost and Wind Protection   612
Water Conservation and Recycling   614

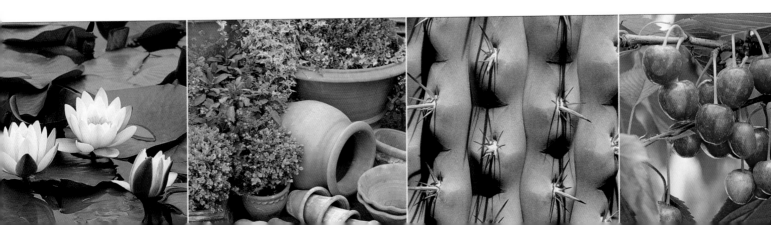

THE EDITOR-IN-CHIEF

CHRISTOPHER BRICKELL began his career with the Royal Horticultural Society in 1958, becoming Director of Wisley Garden in 1969. From 1985 until his retirement in 1993 he was Director General of the Society, representing its interests all over the world. He is the author of several books, has contributed to a number of horticultural and botanical reference works, and is Editor-in-Chief of Dorling Kindersley's *Encyclopedia of Plants and Flowers* and *A–Z of Garden Plants*, both also published in association with the Royal Horticultural Society. Christopher Brickell has since 1976 held the Society's prestigious Victoria Medal of Honour, and in 1991 was made a CBE for his services to horticulture. He is Chairman of the International Commission for the Nomenclature of Cultivated Plants, and is a past President of the International Society for Horticultural Science.

THE CONTRIBUTORS

ROGER AYLETT *DAHLIAS*

BILL BAKER *LILIES*

LARRY BARLOW (WITH **W.B. WADE**) *CHRYSANTHEMUMS*

CAROLINE BOISSET *CLIMBING PLANTS*

DENI BOWN *GROWING HERBS*

ALEC BRISTOW (WITH **WILMA RITTERSHAUSEN**) *ORCHIDS*

ROY CHEEK (WITH **GRAHAM RICE** AND **ISABELLE VAN GROENINGEN**) *PERENNIALS*

TREVOR COLE (WITH **MICHAEL POLLOCK**) *FROST AND WIND PROTECTION*

KATH DRYDEN AND **CHRISTOPHER GREY-WILSON** (WITH **JOHN WARWICK**) *ROCK, SCREE, AND GRAVEL GARDENING; ALPINE HOUSES AND FRAMES*

JACK ELLIOTT *IRISES; BULBOUS PLANTS; TULIPS AND DAFFODILS*

COLIN ELLIS (WITH **MERVYN FEESEY**) *BAMBOOS*

RAYMOND EVISON *CLEMATIS*

JOHN GALBALLY (WITH **EILEEN GALBALLY**) *CARNATIONS AND PINKS*

JIM GARDINER *ORNAMENTAL TREES; DWARF CONIFERS; TOPIARY; HEDGES AND SCREENS; ORNAMENTAL SHRUBS*

MICHAEL GIBSON (WITH **PETER HARKNESS**) *ROSES, ROSES FOR DISPLAY AND EXHIBTION*

GEORGE GILBERT *GROWING FRUIT*

RICHARD GILBERT *HYDROCULTURE*

WILL GILES *HARDY PALMS AND THE EXOTIC LOOK*

RUPERT GOLBY *GARDEN PLANNING AND DESIGN*

DEENAGH GOOLD-ADAMS (WITH **RICHARD GILBERT**) *INDOOR GARDENING*

DIANA GRENFELL *HOSTAS*

JOHN HACKER (WITH **GEOFF STEBBINGS**) *THE LAWN*

ANDREW HALSTEAD AND **PIPPA GREENWOOD** (WITH **CHRIS PRIOR** AND **LUCY HALSALL**) *PLANT PROBLEMS*

LIN HAWTHORNE *MEADOW GARDENING*

ARTHUR HELLYER (WITH **GRAHAM RICE**) *ANNUALS AND BIENNIALS*

CLIVE INNES (WITH **TERRY HEWITT**) *CACTI AND OTHER SUCCULENTS;* (WITH **RICHARD GILBERT**) *BROMELIADS*

DAVID JOYCE *CONTAINER GARDENING, BALCONIES AND ROOF GARDENS, WATER GARDENS IN CONTAINERS*

TONY KENDLE *SOILS AND FERTILIZERS*

HAZEL KEY (WITH **URSULA KEY-DAVIS**) *FERNS, PELARGONIUMS*

JOY LARKCOM (WITH **MICHAEL POLLOCK**) *GROWING VEGETABLES*

KEITH LOACH (WITH **DAVID HIDE**) *PRINCIPLES OF PROPAGATION;* (WITH **MICHAEL POLLOCK**) *BASIC BOTANY*

BILL MAISHMAN (WITH **JEFF BRANDE**) *SWEET PEAS*

PETER MARSTON *CONSERVATORY GARDENING*

PETER MCHOY (WITH **GEOFF STEBBINGS**) *TOOLS AND EQUIPMENT; GREENHOUSES AND FRAMES; STRUCTURES AND SURFACES*

MICHAEL POLLOCK *CLIMATE AND THE GARDEN; THE BED SYSTEM*

DAVID PYCRAFT *WEEDS*

PETER ROBINSON *WATER GARDENING; WATER LILIES; WATER CONSERVATION AND RECYCLING; WATERSIDE DECKING*

DON TINDALL *TENDER VEGETABLES AND FRUITS*

ISABELLE VAN GROENINGEN *PERENNIALS FOR GROUND COVER*

JOHN WRIGHT (WITH **GEORGE BARTLETT**) *FUCHSIAS*

WILLOW WALLS: TEXT AND PICTURES COURTESY OF *THE GARDEN* MAGAZINE

PREFACE

THE ROYAL HORTICULTURAL SOCIETY's *Encyclopedia of Gardening* was first published fifteen years ago. Over that period it has gained a reputation as the definitive guide to all aspects of practical gardening and for meeting the needs of both the home gardener and the horticultural student. It has also been regularly updated, and has now sold almost 1.75 million copies worldwide.

The revisions have enlarged this encyclopedia significantly over the past to include the latest trends and techniques in garden design, the growing of plants in containers, and contemporary tastes in plants. This latest revision explores many new issues relating to the choice of plants for a changing climate and matters affecting the environment, including water-related concerns, and methods of encouraging wildlife.

All these improvements have been made to ensure the *RHS Encyclopedia of Gardening*, now published in its third edition, continues to fulfil the Society's commitment to make the best of gardening information readily available to all who seek it. On behalf of the RHS, I would like to thank the Editor-in-Chief, Christopher Brickell, the other contributors, and the publishers for their continuing support in the publication of this work.

Peter Buckley
President, The Royal Horticultural Society
London, April 2007

INTRODUCTION

EVERY GARDENER keeping an eye on the weather will be aware of the gradual changes to the climate that have occurred over the last few decades. There is little, if any, doubt that extreme weather events of recent years – storms, periods of drought, and floods – are a consequence of global warming, due primarily to higher levels of greenhouse gases such as carbon dioxide in the atmosphere.

Climate change is a continuous process and, as plants are often sensitive to altered conditions, it is likely to present us with both challenges and opportunities. We may have to adapt both our plant choices, and our techniques, in order to maintain our gardens in the hot, dry summers and warm, wet winters that scientists predict. Adventurous gardeners may enjoy experimenting with an expanded range of plants, but lovers of tradition may struggle to maintain the perfect lawn.

Gardeners should not, however, be discouraged: the oxygen released into the atmosphere as a by-product of photosynthesis (the process by which green plants take in carbon dioxide and release oxygen to generate the energy for needed for growth) will help to alleviate some of the effects of global warming. Therefore simply by growing more plants and encouraging tree planting in local communities we can help to address the impact of global warming. And if we adopt more organic practices, perhaps reducing or avoiding the use of harmful chemicals, we can reap wider environmental benefits as we continue to pursue our most pleasurable national hobby – no matter what the weather.

How the dry garden grows
A combination of grey-leaved plants and bulbs defeat drought in the less-than-hospitable conditions of Beth Chatto's Gravel Garden in Essex. It demonstrates how careful plant choices can result in joyful late spring colour: plants such as yucca and echinops – which come from dry climates – associate well with the structure provided by drought-tolerant evergreens and conifers. The bulbous alliums and irises have low water requirements as they enter their dormant period soon after their flowers appear.

What is organic gardening?

The term "organic gardening" is often used rather simplistically to describe the cultivation of gardens without the aid of synthetically produced fertilizers, pesticides, or other chemicals to manage the soil and produce healthy, vigorous plants. This approach relies instead on using manures and fertilizers derived only from plant or animal residues to improve and maintain soil fertility.

However, the term also encompasses a wider holistic approach that not only stresses the avoidance of polluting activities (including bonfires), but also takes account of other environmental needs. These range from conserving scarce resources – for instance by saving and storing water, and recycling, reusing, or composting as much waste as possible – to being aware of the source and treatment of wood used for decking or furniture, or avoiding peat-based potting composts. Completely organic gardeners also prefer not to use natural materials – such as coir-based composts – if they have been transported vast distances when more local alternatives are available. The result is a natural, more sustainable way of gardening that recognizes the importance of biological and genetic diversity, advocates preventative methods for pest and disease control, and encourages wildlife.

Implementing completely organic principles can be a considerable challenge, and is a matter of choice. However, using synthetic products and chemicals to grow ornamentals, fruit, and vegetables does not rule out adopting other organic practices such as composting and integrated pest management.

Ways without chemicals
Deploy marigolds as companion plants to help deter soil pests; welcome ladybirds into the garden to control aphids; discourage bird pests like pigeons with improvised bird-scarers; and hoe lightly and regularly to keep weeds down.

Organic soil management and composting

The key to successful organic gardening is in the management of a well-structured and biologically active soil, supplemented as required by incorporating bulky materials such as composts, animal manures, leaf mould, or green manures. These organic soil improvers help to feed the soil organisms which break them down, providing plants with essential foods and trace elements. If necessary, natural fertilizers such as bonemeal, blood, fish and bone, seaweed meal, and rock phosphate may be applied when and where appropriate.

Dedication is required to develop and maintain a high level of soil fertility, and ensure that the soil structure, which allows the free passage of air and water through the soil particles, is not impaired. Heavy soil in particular may become compacted, restricting airflow and drainage, if walked on during cultivation, especially during cold, wet weather. Always use a board to spread your weight when planting.

Although digging breaks up compaction, helps improve drainage and root penetration, aerates the soil, and provides an opportunity to incorporate bulky manures, it is often best to keep this to a minimum. Some organic gardeners prefer not to dig at all: undisturbed soil loses less moisture through evaporation, provides a good environment for beneficial organisms, and may help to preserve soil structure. Regular mulching with organic soil improvers insulates the soil surface against water evaporation, improves the structure, and suppresses weeds.

Garden compost acts both as a soil improver and as a source of environmentally-friendly plant food, and a compost bin is an excellent recycling facility for kitchen, garden, and other organic waste: no garden should be without at least one heap. As well as supporting a community of microbes and soil organisms, the heap provides shelter for creatures like hedgehogs and grass snakes – which eat slugs.

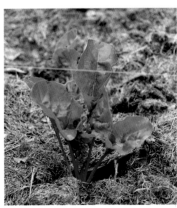

Waste not, want not
Every garden has room for a compost bin to provide a free mulch, and some bins can be quite attractive. Compost may be forked into the soil, but other organic soil improvers such as hay should only be applied as a mulch.

Making wildlife work
Attracting wildlife is a very satisfying method of pest control. A pond may reward you with hungry amphibians, a pile of logs or leaves is enough for a hedgehog, and both will compete for a slug dinner. Nectar-rich flowers draw bees and butterflies, as well as other beneficial pollinating insects.

Wildlife gardening

By their nature, gardens provide numerous habitats where wildlife can flourish. With the increase in urban development and changing agricultural practices taking their toll, these garden refuges are more important than ever. The presence of birds, butterflies, honey and bumblebees, moths, and hoverflies enhances the garden, and attracting wildlife is a very effective method of controlling pests. Natural predators and pollinating insects are much more likely to visit plants and be more active in gardens where no pesticides are used.

There are many ways of making your garden attractive to wildlife. For example, planting beds and borders with ornamentals that provide food like nectar, pollen, seeds, and fruits will encourage bees, ladybirds, lacewings, blue tits, and other birds that also feed on insect pests like aphids. Wildlife-attracting planting should also include species that provide birds with fruits or seeds in autumn and winter; for example, sunflowers, ornamental thistles, echinaceas, and rudbeckias will produce ample winter fare for seed-eating birds.

Water and shelter are also important for wildlife: water features, however small, add to the biodiversity of the garden by encouraging slug- and snail-eating amphibians to spawn, as well as providing birds and small mammals with the water they need daily. Birds, mammals, and insects will appreciate areas where they can live and breed; hedges and climbing plants provide excellent habitats, but purpose built boxes for hedgehogs, frogs, and even bats can also be installed to add to the range of wildlife and help to alleviate the loss of biodiversity in our countryside.

Naturalistic and meadow styles

Developing an area of a garden to emulate the richly diverse flora that occurs naturally in meadows, downland, and alpine pastures has considerable attractions for gardeners, particularly those who wish to provide habitats for wildlife. Even in relatively small gardens it is often possible to have a designated area of grass where wild flowers are encouraged to flower and seed naturally, to the benefit of bees, butterflies, and other insects, as well as small mammals and seed-eating birds. For ease of access, it may sometimes be convenient to identify pathways through meadow-like areas by maintaining a long grass/short grass regime. Meadow gardens are often devoted to growing native species, but you can extend the season and create a longer span of interest by naturalizing early- and late-flowering bulbs such as spring and autumn crocuses, snake's head fritillaries, and colchicums in the meadow area.

A recently developed "naturalistic" gardening style attempts to recreate, on a smaller scale, landscapes and habitats seen in various parts of the world as features in gardens. This concept is beginning to gain popularity, particularly among those who have witnessed the extraordinarily colourful displays of wild plants in parts of South Africa, California and Australia, and countries bordering the Mediterranean. Here, predominantly sandy areas are ablaze, usually in spring, with a kaleidoscopic range of annuals, perennials and bulbs that repeat their colourful displays annually. Reproducing the conditions in which these species grow is not always easy or realisitic, but it is possible to blend species with similar requirements from different areas of the world to create attractive displays. These may then self-seed to flower again the following year.

Relaxed meadow style
Drifts of annuals and perennials – including purple loosestrife, fennel, campanulas, and ox-eye daisies – appear to roam through grassland to create a flowering meadow. The result looks entirely natural but in fact is carefully contrived to achieve a pleasing mix of colour, and ensure that no one species dominates. Later in the year, dramatic seedheads add a beauty of their own.

Sustainable gardening

With the effects of climate change becoming more apparent it is important that as gardeners we consider seriously the sustainability of the way in which we use natural resources, and the effects that fertilizers and other chemicals have on the environment as a whole. The use of peat in horticultural products is a well-publicized example. Historically used as a base for potting composts, as a soil improver, and for mulching, we are now aware that commercial extraction has depleted unique wildlife habitats which will take thousands of years to recover. Gardeners who prefer to avoid peat-based products might wish to try alternatives such as leaf mould, composted bark, or – if no alternatives are available – coir (coconut-fibre).

Ways with water

As climate change results in seasonal temperatures and rainfall patterns becoming more variable it is probable – perhaps inevitable – that hotter summers and autumns with lower rainfall and more frequent periods of drought will lead to serious water shortages. It is essential that we counter the adverse impact this will have on our ability to maintain our gardens successfully (particularly with the most water-dependent crops and plants) by introducing water-saving techniques as standard gardening practice.

The most obvious way to ensure you have a good supply of water for the garden during periods of drought or hosepipe bans, is to collect and store rainwater running off the house, shed, and greenhouse roof in waterbutts and other covered containers. "Grey water" siphoned from washing machines or baths may be another source on a small scale, provided it does not contain high levels of cleaning or cosmetic products; it is not, however, suitable for use on edible crops.

It is also worth adopting various simple cultivation techniques to reduce the evaporation of water from the soil surface – for example, by preparing beds during autumn and winter, rather than in spring or summer when warm temperatures increase evaporation, or spreading mulches after rain to retain moisture. Prioritize the garden's needs – it is not necessary to water the lawn in a drought – and water thoroughly but less often, as this is more beneficial than a light sprinkling. Keep on top of weeds: they compete with garden plants for precious water.

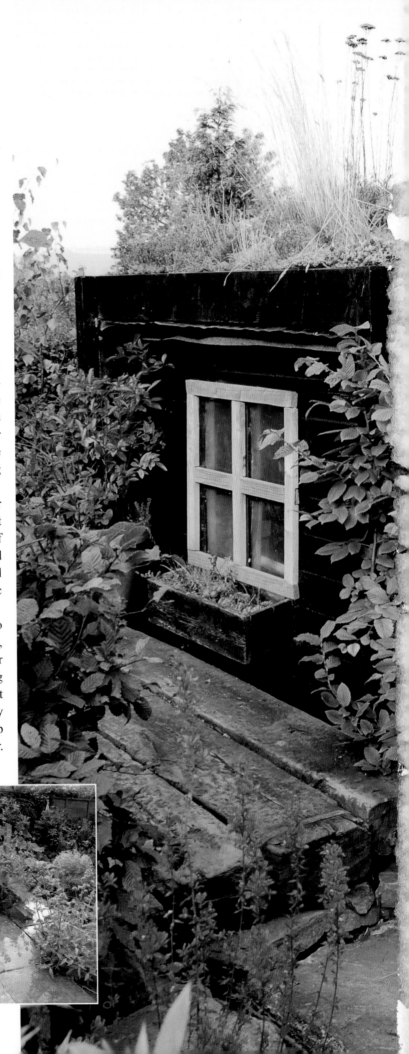

Water, water everywhere
Covered water butts and storage tanks help keep the garden watered in time of drought, but we also need strategies to cope with rainfall that delivers so much water so quickly that it causes flooding and water-logging. A "green roof" may absorb as much as 90 per cent of the water that falls on its surface, easing the strain on drainage systems, and providing all the benefits associated with plant growth.

The ethical approach

Re-using and recycling materials can play an important role in conserving resources as part of a sustainable gardening regime. Where possible vegetative material – prunings, lawn mowings, leaves, and vegetable waste – should be composted and used to improve soil structure, feed plants, and as a mulch. Avoid burning such waste, as this releases greenhouse gases. You can also develop an ethical approach to gardening by ensuring wood used for sheds, greenhouses, or furniture comes from a sustainable source: look for forest certification scheme labelling. Alternatively consider using reclaimed or recycled timber. Avoid applying wood-preserving treatments or paints containing volatile, air-polluting compounds – labels should identify them.

Although roof gardens have for many years been popular in urban situations, a more innovative approach – roof greening – is now being promoted on a wider scale. It has a high amenity value, particularly in crowded cities where "green roofs" increase biodiversity, providing birds with nesting and foraging sites and places for insects to breed. Green roofs also absorb rainwater that would otherwise disappear into the drainage system, insulate buildings by reducing heat loss, as well as benefiting the surrounding environment.

Conserving our plant heritage

Many ornamental plants are now endangered in the wild, partly due to over-collection, and gardeners are advised to check the origins of any plants they aquire. It is important to purchase plants and seeds that are of known cultivated origin to help stop any illegal trade in plants that are listed under the Convention on International Trade in Endangered Species of Wild Fauna and Flora (CITES) regulations – including popular groups of plants such as cacti, orchids, snowdrops (*Galanthus*), cyclamen and cycads.

It is, however, vital that we conserve older plants raised in gardens in the past, many of which have been replaced by newer cultivars. Old garden varieties are valuable for breeding new flowers, fuits, and vegetable crops; they can also pass on resistance to pests and diseases.

In a world with a changing climate, who knows what new challenges we might face? As gardeners, working close to nature, we are in a unique position to rise and respond to them.

Endangered species
It may seem astonishing that plants at risk of extinction in the wild include popular garden favourites such as Cyclamen repandum *(above) as well as orchids like* Lycaste deppei *(above, right). You can help to discourage the practice of over-collection from the wild by ensuring that your plants come from cultivated sources.*

CREATING THE GARDEN

HOW TO APPLY THE PRINCIPLES OF DESIGN, CHOOSE AND CULTIVATE
EVERY TYPE OF PLANT, AND CREATE AND PLANT GARDEN FEATURES

CHAPTER

1

GARDEN PLANNING AND DESIGN

To NURTURE a garden over a period of time – seeing it develop and mature through the seasons – is a rewarding experience for its creator. For a garden to be successful, however, it needs careful and considered thought from the very beginning. A garden with simple lines and a natural flow, effortlessly summoning up a relaxed charm, may appear to have received little design input, yet it is almost certainly underpinned by intelligent planning. The design process is conspicuous in a garden of geometric formality, but the same input is required for seemingly artless informal plantings if they are to combine the essential qualities of unity, balance, and proportion, and be in sympathy with their surroundings.

Why do we garden?

WHERE does the motivation come from to cultivate a piece of ground, altering its appearance for our own benefit? Perhaps we still have an instinctive need to grow food to survive, or to mark out a territory that defines a specific area as our own, or to raise a defensive boundary around it. Once within the garden gate, we can leave behind our working lives and retreat to the safety of our private space. Whatever the underlying motivation, that first small spark of interest can easily grow into a lifelong passion and a source of real enjoyment.

Climate and surroundings
In the majority of cases a garden will surround a house, creating fundamental practical requirements to tame the environment. The need for entry by foot and by vehicle will mean making clear paths and drives that allow easy access to the house in all weathers throughout the year. Similarly basic is the need for light: plant growth near windows and doors must be kept in check.

At a greater distance, planting a windbreak of trees and shrubs can provide invaluable protection against damaging winds, sheltering both buildings and less robust plantings. Such shelter-belts of trees will also prevent snow drifting into the garden on the prevailing wind. Conversely, in hot climates, trees and shrubs bring shade and coolness to the house and its immediate surround-

ings. Strategic, appropriate plantings of shrubs and trees can also help to preserve soil, by preventing erosion by wind and water.

The garden setting
The garden should never be viewed in isolation, removed from its context and setting. Garden boundaries define and protect our private space, limiting the influence of the outside world on the place we call home. They make it possible to screen, and thus "lose", unsightly features on adjacent land, as well as increasing privacy. Conversely, if your garden backs onto fields, boundaries can be designed to open up the view and bring the countryside into the garden, while still keep grazing animals at bay. Garden hedges and trees can also baffle noise from a neighbouring property or busy road.

A garden retreat can be used as an extension to the living areas within the home, making an imperceptible transition from house to garden. Paved terraces, plant-covered structures, and open-fronted verandas all blur the hard interface between inside and outdoors. They create safe outdoor play areas for children – especially welcome in a modestly sized house – as well as providing space for enjoying meals *al fresco*.

Enhancing our environment
Beyond the fulfilment of our basic living requirements, there is of course one obvious role that a garden

Defining boundaries
Land adjoining a garden may not need to be screened for privacy, or for protection. Make the most of an attractive rural view and incorporate it visually to blend with and extend your garden.

Harmonious setting
This beautifully planted cottage garden is perfectly in keeping with the style of the house. Pleasing colours, *textures, and shapes blend delightfully, blurring the boundaries between house and garden.*

Environmental concerns

Gardening according to environmentally sound principles is a goal that many today are contemplating. To exclude all harmful chemicals from the garden is a valiant first step towards running a garden that is in sympathy with the wider natural habitat.

There are also many other gardening practices that enhance and protect the environment rather than depleting and destroying it. Water conservation, recycling organic matter to produce garden compost, collecting autumn leaves to make leaf mould, using peat-free potting mixtures, and buying nursery stock (particularly bulbs) that have been raised in cultivation rather than collected from the wild are all relatively easy measures to adopt.

If you would like to develop your garden further along environmentally sound lines, consider creating a wildlife-friendly garden that includes plants that are food sources for birds and insects, shrubs and trees for nesting, and water for aquatic creatures. By avoiding the use of chemicals, you will also encourage more pollinating insects to visit your garden, generally improve plant performance and productivity, and thus considerably enrich the garden environment.

performs, and that is to improve the appearance of the house, whether for our own private enjoyment or to enhance the street or neighbourhood we live in. Community spirit is not, however, incompatible with a competitive tendency between neighbours, often generating passions and levels of gardening expertise rarely seen in professional horticulture.

To create a beautiful garden around the confines of a house and use the spaces to maximum effect is a challenge that many gardeners relish. Draw inspiration from the period of your house and its construction materials, and let your planting complement the style. The ultimate goal is to achieve a harmonious whole. This may look effortless, but those directly involved can appreciate the hard work, vision, and imagination that went into it.

Planning and designing a garden is a real opportunity to express your creativity, and to allow your personality to come through in the concept, design, colour, and plant combinations. Unlike interior design or painting a picture, a garden is a living thing that constantly changes, and each passing season will present new rewards and challenges. Although hard work, the practical nature of the majority of the tasks and the visual rewards so readily offered, make gardening a great tonic for those who spend the majority of their time working indoors or in an office.

Softening the landscape
Plants, especially flowering herbaceous ones like this yellow Achillea *and blue* Delphinium*, bring intense colours, natural forms, and seasonal change to the built surroundings, and provide a valuable haven for wildlife in harsh urban environments.*

Home-grown produce

A garden does not have to be large to be productive; even a modest plot can provide a variety of vegetables, fruit, and herbs for the kitchen as well as an abundance of flowers for the home. Traditionally, the garden always incorporated a good-sized vegetable plot for reasons of economy and to guarantee a steady supply of fresh food. Today, despite year-round availability of fruit and vegetables, many people are concerned about the over-use of pesticides and fertilizers and prefer to grow their own produce using organic methods. Although the yield from an organically grown crop may be slightly lower, many consider the taste and quality to be superior, and there is frequently less waste.

Security and access

The safety and security of your home can be improved significantly by the way the garden is designed and laid out. Open spaces around a house prevent unseen access, and are particularly important if you have security cameras, which require a clear vision around all sides of a building. Footsteps are readily heard on gravel surfaces – a great deterrent to burglars, especially when a dog is alerted by the noise. Impenetrable hedges of prickly and thorny material, such as hawthorn (*Crataegus monogyna*), holly (*Ilex aquifolium*) and firethorn (*Pyracantha*), are also very effective. Climbing plants and wall shrubs that offer easy access to first-floor windows should be avoided. For visitors and deliveries, the everyday accessibility of a house can be greatly improved by the careful planning of the garden, the avoidance of too many level changes, a comfortable width of paths, and the provision of vehicular access to at least one external door of the house.

The importance of garden design

The term "garden design" has connotations of formality and, for many, implies the application of rigid rules and formulae. Fortunately, this is not the case, but there is one overriding principle – adequate thought and consideration of all the alternatives are needed well ahead of any intended works. Many beautiful gardens have been and are created without the implementation of grand planning schemes. They have developed organically from a starting point: a favourite tree planted in an open place; a natural path between road and house; or from a previous owner's layout. Evolving year after year, possibly in a rather haphazard way with much left to chance, a garden of great charm can indeed come about, but opportunities may have been missed and a lack of cohesion is all too often apparent.

Design awareness

We live in a designed society. There is today a great awareness and appreciation of well-designed products, and gardens have not escaped the attentions of designers or the media. Beautifully illustrated books and magazines as well as informative television programmes have created a growing interest in styles, products, and plants, reaching a wider audience than ever before. For the first time, designers have been able to demonstrate visually the advantages of planning a garden, and then to communicate clearly, using photographs of each stage, the development of a design.

A designer's fresh and experienced eye can realize the potential of a plot, draw out its strengths, while respecting and taking inspiration from the site. Most importantly, a good designer will not impose his or her own ideas on the garden without also

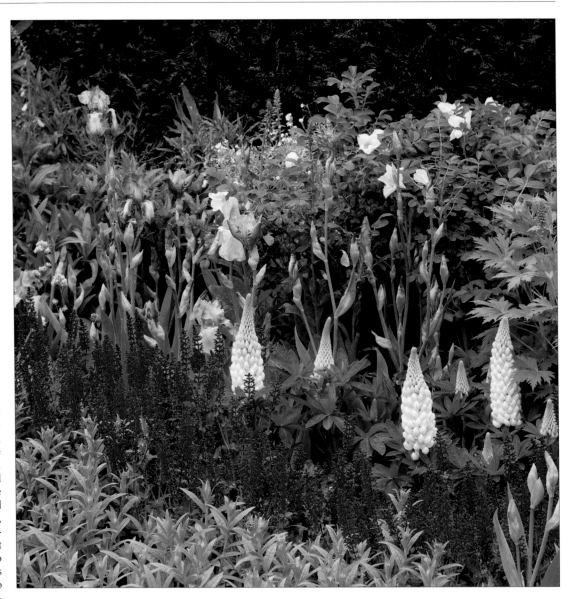

Multi-dimensional planting
This delightful planting combination is a harmonious mix of colours, textures, and forms. Such a scheme demands a sound knowledge of plants, plus the skill to restrict the more boisterous specimens and encourage the less robust.

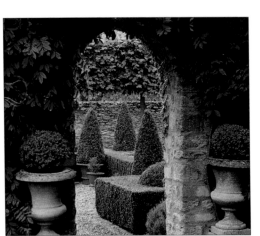

Architectural plants
Clipped evergreens, in the confines of a courtyard, such as this box (Buxus sempervirens), *take on an architectural role. Their structural forms are in perfect sympathy with the shape of the adjacent building.*

taking the owner's wishes and lifestyle into consideration.

A professional designer can, of course, be engaged to execute the entire project but at some considerable cost. However, a single visit, early in the planning process, to offer advice, guidance, and an unbiased opinion can be invaluable and is certainly less expensive, with the option of consultations at a later stage as the project progresses.

Garden types and styles

Categorizing gardens into particular types or styles is fraught with difficulties because every garden is different. Many gardens comprise a series of disparate themes loosely linked together, while others do not fit readily into any single category as they incorporate several styles. All divisions, therefore, are somewhat arbitrary and should be regarded only as very general guidelines.

Developing a style

When starting to make a new garden or reshaping an old one a common theme, even if adapted and personalized, is generally adopted. Plucked from a magazine article, a book, or inspired by a visit to a garden, a particular look can reflect a house interior or evolve from the the style of house and its immediate surroundings. A building and its locality have a great deal to communicate to any receptive garden planner, contributing many simple common-sense details to the scheme.

All gardens should exude a sense of place and of belonging. A garden designed and built in a style that is very alien to the house or landscape

Natural silhouettes
A carefully selected combination of trees and shrubs, centred around this fine Cornus controversa *'Variegata' breaking across the lawn edge, gives an impression of elegance and can be maintained with minimum input. A well-tailored lawn and trimmed evergreens flatter beautifully shaped plants, whereas flowering plants might distract the eye.*

garden. In a prized collection, plants are not purely decorative; they have an integrity, a personality, and a history, particularly where a botanical collection has been established.

Interestingly, both approaches to gardening can lead to an extended social life. The low-maintenance garden is ideal for outdoor entertaining, while for the plant enthusiast there are opportunities to contact and meet up with like-minded collectors.

Enhancing buildings

The garden presents a wonderful opportunity to manipulate the appearance of a house without running into expensive alterations or major reconstruction. Plants can be used to soften an unsympathetic roof line or to disguise the inappropriate use of ugly and incompatible building materials. An unremarkable structure, too, can be greatly improved by the addition of striking, climbing or architectural plants, which will strengthen the appearance of the building and add character. In both cases, the built structure and planted garden can come together and complement each other. With the exception of very few architecturally significant buildings whose façades are better left unadorned, the majority of houses are greatly improved by allowing plants to stand close by or to clamber part-way across a house frontage – by appearing to bring the garden to the house.

may not sit well there, however much it is desired and however great the resources spent on its creation. Developing and refining a design that reflects the sense of place almost invariably gives more harmonious results, especially where relaxation and calm are desired.

Design variations

Within any broad garden style, you can incorporate variations that reflect a personal interest, a lifestyle, or even the age group using the garden. A desire to attract wildlife into the garden or to grow large quantities of culinary herbs will add another dimension to the design. Or you might want to achieve a purely visual effect by introducing a particular flower colour or luxuriant foliage that blends with the house colours or surrounding vegetation.

Personal preferences and the way in which you use your garden at various times of the year all have a bearing on what is required. A garden that looks particularly striking in midsummer, for example, may be wanted if the space is used mainly for outdoor entertaining. A garden for relaxation that requires minimum upkeep but has appeal throughout the year may be an attractive idea, or you may wish to shut out the world and create a secluded haven where you can cultivate specialist plants in peace.

Planting considerations

The choice of plants growing within the framework of the garden will significantly influence its style. Large-leaved, rich-textured foliage gives depth and luxuriance, while a predominance of fine, silver- and grey-

leaved plants will provide a lighter feel. Of equal influence is the degree of maintenance required in a garden. An efficiently maintained garden with a well-defined layout will look surprisingly different from a garden of similar design that has been poorly or erratically maintained.

High and low maintenance

Generally speaking, it is possible to make a distinction between two dif-

ferent styles of garden in terms of their function. A garden may have been designed for visual impact, or the creation of a restful ambience may be a priority. A garden for relaxation should be low maintenance, leaving as much time as possible for enjoying the peaceful setting. In contrast, the pleasure for the plant enthusiast with a specialist collection of plants comes from the hours spent nurturing and maintaining the

The garden room
On this sunny terrace, hard landscaping materials play a strong role, yet are softened by the surrounding planting. In summer, the garden pool will create lively reflections of the surrounding vegetation and buildings.

Formal garden styles

FORMAL gardens are characteristically well proportioned, usually symmetrical and geometrically balanced in layout, and impart a tangible sense of restraint. They usually derive an inherent strength of line from an underlying backbone in the form of walls, paths, or terracing, around which planting is firmly controlled. Formal planting traditionally contains very few different plants, but these are used in quantity to lend a uniformity of texture and colour. The whole emphasis is one of an overriding sense of control.

Ordered layouts
The underlying philosophy of the formal garden is to present a strong, simple statement of a very obvious control of nature. Intricately clipped parterres that form a filigree of crisply shaped evergreens when set against fine gravel, or a flat, closely mown lawn that is framed by neatly trimmed hedges, are good examples of this philosophy in practice.

Historically, the formal style was chosen to convey a sense of power over the wider landscape and, on a large scale, this achieved an intimidating effect that was an intentional expression of wealth and status. A similar impression was conveyed even on a more modest scale, since such layouts required regular, labour-intensive, and costly maintenance.

Ancient inspiration
The grand formal gardens of seventeenth- and eighteenth-century Italy and France, which influenced garden styles throughout Europe, were themselves inspired by the gardens of ancient Greece and Rome. In these, the strongly defined proportions and scale of the buildings were mirrored by the strong, architectural and symmetrical design of the gardens that surrounded them.

These sumptuous but controlled landscapes were frequently laid out as a series of terraces connected by grand flights of steps, and featured water cascades, canals, and fountains amid hedged and tree-lined walkways, ornamented with classical statuary and potted plants.

Classical gardens
Greek and Roman features that still inspire modern formal gardens include neatly mown and edged lawns, tightly clipped hedges and topiary, and planted borders framed by low, trimmed hedges. Straight paths and a network of vistas that terminate in a view or focal point may be lined by *allées* and avenues of identical, regularly spaced specimen plants. Ornamentation is added with restraint and, where several decorative items are used, they are either designed to form a matching set or a single design is replicated to form a sequence of repeated incidents.

Plants for formal gardens
Whether clipped and trained as hedging or topiary, shaped plants are an important element in the formal garden. The striking profiles of evergreen topiary lend height, form, and dramatic sculptural interest to an otherwise two-dimensional layout. Slow-growing evergreens, such as yew (*Taxus baccata*), box (*Buxus sempervirens*), holly (*Ilex aquifolium*), and holm oak (*Quercus ilex*), all withstand the necessary regular trimming over many years. See also TOPIARY, p.76, and HEDGES AND SCREENS, p.84.

Pleached trees and stilt hedges make attractive internal divisions within a formal garden. Their regimented forms and colonnaded trunks provide a sense of rhythm and order when used to flank walkways and *allées*. Limes (*Tilia species*) and hornbeam (*Carpinus betulus*) are the most frequently used species for this type of feature. Such plantings can also be introduced in a highly functional way. Trained and pleached limes, for example, can be used as a garden boundary to create a living wall that gives privacy and an intimate sense of enclosure. See also "Pleached trees", p.75.

Knots and parterres
Knot gardens and parterres are a highly developed type of formal gardening in which control of the planting is absolute. In knot gardens, intricate planting patterns are confined by an edging of dwarf, clipped evergreen shrubs such as box (*Buxus sempervirens*). Traditional knots were inspired by sixteenth-century needlework and decorative plaster ceilings. In parterres, coloured gravels or low plantings fill compartments created by low, trimmed hedging. Both knots and parterres offer year-round structure that is of particular value in winter, especially when located near the house.

Unity and contrast
Elements of naturalistic plantings among otherwise formal layouts create an element of contrast that can sharpen the underlying formality. The lax and free growth of herbs, for example, planted amongst clipped lavender (*Lavandula*), rosemary (*Rosmarinus*), bay laurel (*Laurus nobilis*), or box (*Buxus sempervirens*) can be used to create such contrasts. Similarly, containers on a terrace planted with a set of trimmed Portugal laurel (*Prunus lusitanica*) can bring an element of order and uniformity close to the house that could contrast with less structured planting elsewhere in the garden.

Oriental formality
The gardens of China, which can be traced back over 3,000 years, were created as sublimely peaceful places for contemplation and meditation. They drew inspiration from their dramatic surrounding landscapes, which were replicated in miniature within walled enclosures. Plantings were formal and restrained, often clipped or trained, and usually highly stylized. Each tree or shrub had a symbolic meaning that was intended to stimulate contemplation.

Traditional Japanese gardens borrowed Chinese design ideas more than 1,200 years ago. With a similarly naturalistic inspiration, they used richer, more diverse plantings, symbolically shaped and sited rocks, and raked gravel or sand. Such a garden was based on formal principles of balance, simplicity, and symbolism.

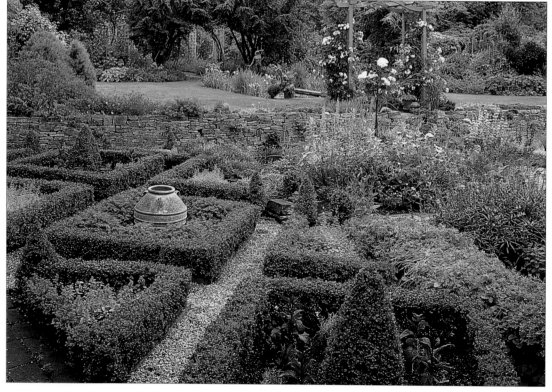

Structured layout
The partitioned squares of this box-edged parterre bring order and year-round structure to an otherwise informal medley of planting. Its strong lines lead the eye to a series of focal points beyond the low wall.

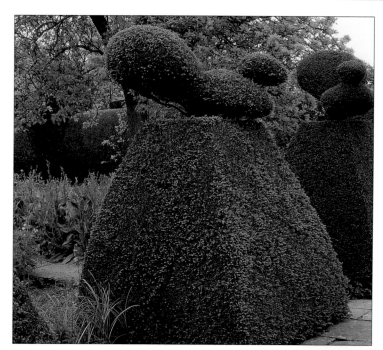

Traditional topiary
Weight and substance are conferred on a design by the imposing forms of mature topiary sculptures, however whimsical the clipped shapes may be. Here, stylized peacocks perch on symmetrically trimmed pediments of yew (Taxus baccata), which flank a broad walkway – the central axis of this formal layout. Their crisp formality is brought into high relief by the informally planted borders around them and the mature trees beyond.

Statuary
Pleasingly proportioned, well-sited and framed ornaments, used with discretion, can often be a great asset to the general garden scene.

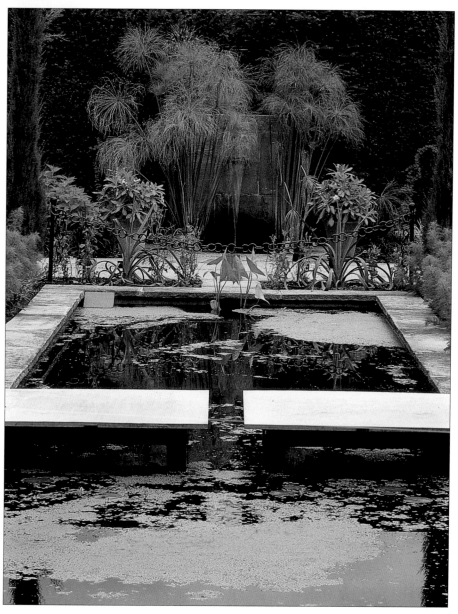

Pleached limes
High-level screening by a stilted hedge of lime (Tilia) encloses yet does not oppress this small knot garden. In winter when the lime leaves fall, the skilful training of the branch framework offers yet more to be admired.

Formal still water
Mirrored reflections double the impact of a symmetrical design. The random drifting of floating plants on the surface of the dark water adds interest and movement to the serenity of this formal garden.

Informal garden styles

INFORMAL gardens, at their best, often look as though nature has played a part in their design. There is an irregularity and a softness in their lines that, although manufactured, could conceivably have occurred naturally. Even though informal gardens may appear slightly out of control, their success depends on strong design and on the firm hand of the gardener to retain a degree of order amongst what might otherwise become chaos.

Elements of informality

A garden with an air of informality offers a relaxed ambience that can provide a sanctuary from the pressures of modern life. In contrast to the hard-edged geometry of the formal style, an informal garden is created with flowing curves and gentle contours. Hard surfaces are softened by plants that spread over their margins, and borders are stocked with billowing mounds of plants that mingle together, apparently at random. Climbing plants scramble freely over walls or through trees and shrubs. While shrubs may be pruned to ensure good health and productivity, they are allowed to assume natural shapes and are rarely clipped in a restrictive way – as they are in strictly formal situations.

Informal elements within a garden can produce a sense of maturity in a relatively short time-scale, for example, when plantings are used to disguise unsightly features with a mantle of growth. Great charm can be given to the most unpromising site if softening growth disguises the hard angles or harsh colours of a building. Even the most uniform, rectangular garden acquires an element of mystery when its stark outlines are masked by layer upon layer of informal planting.

Informal styles

The style and degree of informality of a garden is influenced partly by the nature of the site and partly by individual preference. At one end of the spectrum, it may be possible to augment an existing woodland or meadow area simply by planting more of the natural flora that already grows there. Alternatively, the creation of an informal garden may entail the remodelling of border edges to form curving, sinuous lines, perhaps with a relaxation of the mowing regime and a reduction in border maintenance to permit self-sown plants to thrive. At the other end of the spectrum is a totally new garden, for which there is a range of informal styles from which to choose.

Cottage gardens

The traditional cottage garden was essentially a working garden in which to grow ornamental and edible crops. Fruit, vegetables, herbs, and flowers, such as peonies, delphiniums, and aquilegias, were all combined. The flowers ensured a thriving population of beneficial insects to aid pollination of crop flowers, control harmful insects, and encourage a bird population, all of which helped produce vigorous and healthy crops.

The quaint, homespun appearance of a cottage garden can be created using rustic items such as branchwork arches or woven willow supports for climbers (see WILLOW WALLS, p.87). Brick-patterned or cobbled paths edged with found or reclaimed materials, such as pebbles or tiles, also help define the style.

Wild and woodland gardens

Informal gardens in a more naturalistic style not only provide a beautiful and relaxed type of garden but also offer a lifeline to flora and fauna whose habitats may have become threatened elsewhere.

Areas of turf, for example, where bulbs are naturalized for an early dis-play, can be left uncut so that grasses and meadow flowers can bloom (see MEADOW GARDENING, p.401). An area of water, however small, attracts a range of wildlife into the garden, particularly if edged with waterside plantings to provide safe shelter for birds and amphibians alike. See also "Wildlife ponds", p.284.

Small trees or an area of woodland, especially if underplanted with shrubs and festooned with climbers, provide nesting places for birds and hibernating sites for insects and small mammals. Even in more controlled areas of the garden, seedheads of herbaceous plants, if retained through winter, will provide excellent food for birds when other sources are low.

Controlled chaos

Plants can be ruthlessly competitive and the strongest may smother and eventually kill the weakest. They must be controlled to prevent this. It may be necessary, for example, to divide vigorous herbaceous plants regularly to keep them in check, to thin or reduce over-large shrubs, or to remove colonies of self-sown seedlings. These tasks help to maintain a balance in wild and informal gardens, and will prevent their natural style from degenerating into a wild and unkempt state.

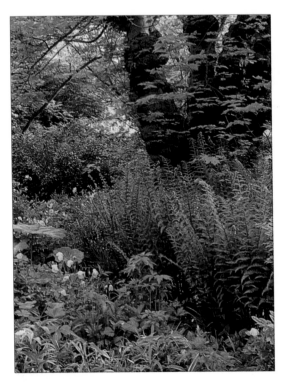

Woodland
In the shade of trees, a woodland flora must be selected to tolerate low light levels and the extremes of dry and excessively damp soil conditions.

Cultivated and self-sown mixture
A shimmering profusion of nectar-rich flowers, in billowing swathes of colour, creates a feature of great beauty and provides an immensely valuable food source in summer for bees, butterflies, and other beneficial insects. Careful management is essential for year-on-year success.

Marginal planting (top)
Even the smallest pond offers the opportunity to blur the distinction between land and water with a range of garden plants. Native wildlife will benefit greatly from the cool, sheltered conditions.

Potager (above left)
Nasturtiums and pot marigolds jostle with herbs and ornamental cabbages in cottage-garden tradition, where not even the smallest space is wasted.

Self-sown (above right)
Melianthus *and Jacob's rod* (Asphodeline), *planted here at the foot of a wall, simulate a self-sown planting. In a mature garden, such combinations may occur naturally – and to great effect.*

Cottage garden style (right)
Roses, delphiniums and climbers are skilfully planted to mingle in the border and spill from supports in a generous, relaxed style.

Hand-crafted gate (above)
Impromptu, rustic materials and a borrowed view accentuate the theme of a country garden.

Mixed maintenance (below)
While fruit trees must be well kept for good yields, the relaxation of the mowing regime here gives this small orchard a charming air of informality.

People-orientated gardens

A GARDEN to be enjoyed by a family almost certainly needs to be a multi-purpose space. To ensure that the design serves the needs of all its potential users, spend some time identifying what these might be. They may include a terrace for dining and entertaining, or areas for children to play safely and experiment with growing their own plants. The garden may have to accommodate herb and vegetable patches to provide kitchen produce, or borders for cut flowers to decorate the home.

As well as fulfilling its functional requirements, a garden such as this can also be highly decorative. A pergola clothed with scented climbers, for example, is not only ornamental but it could also provide shade for a favourite place for midsummer dining. By installing outdoor lighting, its usefulness can be extended to include evening entertaining, perhaps with a barbecue. It may also display

ornaments that are highly individual, perhaps presents from friends, or mementoes of anniversaries or holidays abroad.

The style of planting is very much a matter of personal choice, whether highly traditional or more experimental and innovative. Sources of design inspiration have never been more various, from magazines and television programmes to the wealth of gardens, both private and public, that open to visitors.

Gardens for living

Just as the interior of the home is designed to meet the requirements of those living there, so can the garden be tailored to suit the needs and interests of all the household. This often means extending indoor living to outdoors, using the garden as an extra room. If, for example, dining and entertaining are high on the list of priorities, there should be a flat,

clean, all-weather surface near enough to the kitchen to make outdoor dining convenient.

To make access safe and easy, avoid steps, slopes, or changes of level between the house and eating area. On a very sunny terrace, deciduous (rather than evergreen) climbers trained above head height will provide comfortable shade in midsummer, but little or none in spring and autumn, when warmth and light levels are lower.

Where a suitable sheltered, warm site for an outdoor room does not exist, consider creating one by enclosing an area with hedges or scented-leaved shrubs. They will help trap warm air and provide shelter from cool evening breezes.

To maximize use of the space and to create a pleasant ambience, install subtle lighting for the evenings. Bear in mind that the route to and from the dining area should also be well lit.

Special interests

If the garden as a whole is planned with minimal maintenance in mind, this will allow the development of areas for special-interest activities. A simple lawn, for example, surrounded by robust, low-maintenance plantings can offer a games field and camping site for the children, or an oasis of calm for the adults. Around this, areas of more intense activity can evolve. These might include a small kitchen garden to produce unusual vegetables, fruit, and herbs that are difficult to find in shops. If the area is small, tending it will not be a chore; it will give satisfaction to the gardener and it can even be a learning experience if children are encouraged to participate.

Another special-interest area might be a border for cut flowers, to provide material for floral arrangements in the home throughout the year. It might include shrubs such as forsythias and mahonias for early spring and the bright stems of dogwood (*Cornus alba*) for winter decoration. To allow uninhibited cutting during summer and autumn, set aside a patch for perennials, supplementing them with annuals and biennials to supply flowers for many months.

Special needs

For those in the family who are less mobile or who have limited strength, a garden of raised containers or an entire raised bed removes the strain of bending and should satisfy any latent wish to garden. Permanently sited containers can be set at a suitable

Making room for wildlife

One of the delights of developing a garden is finding that the local wildlife is also happy to visit. Food and shelter are all that is needed to attract birds and insects, and it is easy to include suitable habitats and wildlife-friendly features.

Position bird tables and feeders so that activity may be observed from the house, especially during winter. Nesting boxes may need to be placed on walls or fences with different aspects, according to the preferences of the species you want to attract. A shallow bowl of water provides small mammals and birds with a drink, while a pond will attract a great diversity of wildlife, particularly amphibians and insects such as dragonflies.

Mulches, wood piles, and even your compost heap are also great resources for wildlife, providing nooks and crannies in which to forage, nest, and hibernate. The humble hedge offers shelter and nesting sites, and fruits and seeds from informal mixtures of dense shrubs and climbers like field maple, hawthorn, wild roses, and honeysuckle help keep the natural larder well-stocked. Choose plants that are rich in nectar and pollen (see p.178), and your garden will soon find favour with bees, moths, and hoverflies.

height and regularly reinvigorated with colourful annuals. A row of outdoor tomatoes planted in pots on top of a sunny wall, or a raised herb garden enjoying a sunny aspect and free-draining soil, will give endless pleasure and produce worthwhile quantities of useful crops.

Looking to the futures

With a little foresight, some areas of the garden can be designed to evolve with a family's changing needs. A timber-built playhouse, for example, could in later years become a tool shed or apple store. An irregularly shaped or formal rectangular sandpit, if positioned carefully when the garden is designed, may be transformed into a small pool once the children are old enough to understand the dangers of water. A climbing frame of smooth timber could, later on, become an interesting support over which climbing plants may scramble to create a dramatic effect.

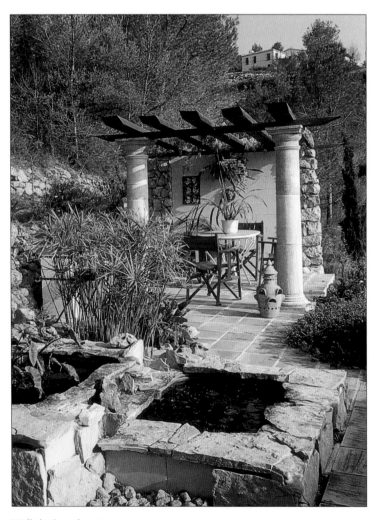

Well-designed terrace
This seating area (above) with its all-weather surface, shelter from wind, and overhead shade provision encourages maximum use of the terrace over a long season.

Gardening interests (right)
A garden mirrors the particular hobbies of its occupants and its design and general layout are unavoidably dictated by these pursuits. A collection of specialist alpines, for example, is best displayed in stone troughs and a greenhouse, here connected to the house by a path with an all-weather surface.

Safe water features (below)
Even the smallest and most shallow of pools can pose a danger to small children. This small fountain, however, has a strong metal grid over its concealed reservoir.

Play area (below right)
A lawn, surrounded by robust, prickle-free plantings, makes an ideal spot for children to enjoy ball and other types of games.

High-level gardening (above)
A raised bed makes gardening comfortable for those with limited mobility. An ideal display setting is created where plant detail can be appreciated at close quarters. The use of pots allows those plants in need of attention (here including some developing topiary shapes) to be brought within very easy reach, and for seasonal changes to be made.

Dual purpose (left)
Here, in late summer, flowers for indoor decoration are grown alongside plants with ripening fruits, to great ornamental effect. This cheerfully haphazard mixture has been planted solely with the needs of the house in mind, yet the result is as decorative as any other type of themed border.

Plant-orientated gardens

IN A PLANT-ORIENTATED garden, the plants take centre stage, rather than being used simply as "soft" design materials. The owner of such a garden can indulge a fascination in collecting and growing a specific range of botanical or exhibition-quality plants. Some plant groups need much more maintenance than others, since they are extremely fussy about their growing conditions. A garden's soil or microclimate might especially suit one specialist group of plants, although more often additional work will be needed to provide the appropriate soil, light, moisture, and shelter.

Pure gardening

The garden that is inspired by plants first and foremost is perhaps the purest form of gardening. There are many and diverse avenues of interest within this type of garden, but all are led by a love and passion for plants.

It is the fascination of collecting, cultivating to perfection, pollination, and propagation that holds the attention and further develops a gardener's interest in horticulture. The search for rare or newly discovered forms can become a life-long occupation. In such a "pure" garden, skill and expertise are obvious at every turn, and demonstrate the gardener's dedication to a wide range of tasks.

Sources for ideas

The site itself may be the inspiration for the plant-orientated garden. Perhaps a dark and damp, north-facing slope will spark an interest in an extensive collection of ferns.

Alternatively, a dry, stony, south-facing bank may encourage the planting of many different Mediterranean natives – such as a collection of *Cistus* species.

Turning what might appear to be a disadvantage into a positive attribute, an area of overgrown woodland may appear lost to cultivation, yet with careful management it can present a wealth of unusual planting possibilities. A collection of shade-loving, woodland-floor natives that is unique to such a site should thrive beneath a deciduous canopy.

Where the conditions provided are substandard, plants will grow poorly, never realizing their full potential. Such poor conditions, however, can often be rectified. Soil conditions can be ameliorated by adding organic matter or improving drainage; shelter can be increased by the use of windbreaks and shelter-belts (see HEDGES AND SCREENS, p.84, and BAMBOOS, p.96); and light levels can be increased by thinning or lifting the canopies of surrounding trees.

Themed collections

An herbaceous border in matching colours, textures, and forms is one way to display a collection that depends solely on good design skills. Many subtly or dramatically different variations are possible. An historical approach may be taken to recreate an early twentieth century border, for example. This would contain tall herbaceous plants that are very dependent on traditional forms of staking with peasticks and hazel wands, for example. Colour-themed

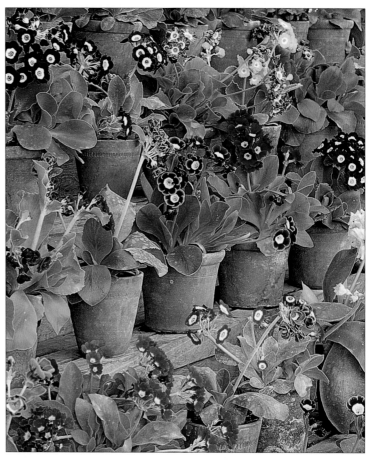

Specialist plants
The display of a very specific plant collection need not be devoid of all aesthetic qualities. Here, many treasured forms of potted auricula primulas are attractively placed on tiered stands.

borders are another possibility for a themed collection (see "Planting for colour and texture", p.48).

A more modern interpretation might be a mixed border, dominated by drifts of shrub roses and self-supporting perennials, self-sown annuals and swathes of ornamental grasses. Alternatively, such a border, particularly in a sheltered situation, might include lush foliage plants and tender bedding perennials in vibrant colours to give a subtropical flavour (see also HARDY PALMS AND THE EXOTIC LOOK, p.60).

Collections with style

The plant-orientated garden may take a very different course from the refinements of the mixed border. A hobby growing plants for exhibition may develop, where perhaps dahlias (see p.234) or pot leeks are grown to perfection, to the exclusion of any aesthetic value their arrangement in the garden might offer. Alternatively, such a well-defined collection could be arranged with every possible

attention paid to aesthetics. A fruit garden, for example, with trees trained in particular forms could provide structural boundaries and internal divisions within the garden as a whole (see GROWING FRUIT, "Trained forms", p.419). Such a display would pay tribute to meticulous, long-term pruning as the trees slowly develop great character, eventually creating an almost timeless ambience.

A collector of trees may be fortunate to have sufficient space to create an arboretum, but this need not be a sterile collection of solitary trees, in serried ranks. Groupings of trees in clumps and copses create a landscape style that is beautiful in its own right (see also ORNAMENTAL TREES, "Trees as design elements", p.54).

To grow a collection of plants indigenous to a particular region may require the controlled conditions of a greenhouse or alpine house. Plants need not be set on gravel-covered, featureless staging. With a little imagination, they can be arranged in a simulation of their native terrain.

Natural plant collections
An extensive specific collection can readily be incorporated into a garden setting. Here a cheerful group of crocuses flourish in an area of the lawn.

Restricted colour (above)
*A white border, tiered in height and with every shade
of green, white, and silver, is a classic, timeless design
theme. The dignified purity of the scheme demands
meticulous staking, dead-heading, and weeding.*

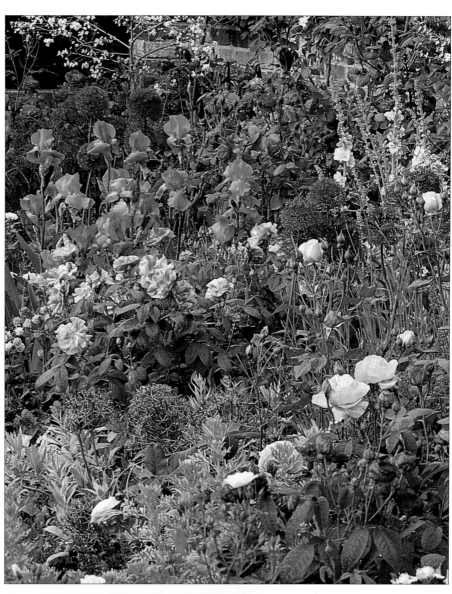

Single-season display (above)
*Some garden designers seek to
exploit every plant type, shape,
form, and colour so that they
perform and peak at the same
time – in this case as a colour-
coordinated collage.*

Tropical style (left)
*A warm, sheltered area
with fertile soil provides an
opportunity to experiment
with tender exotics through
the summer months. Many
will need careful lifting
and storing over winter, but
amply repay such attention.*

Stylized gardens

A HIGHLY stylized garden can be seen as a refined work of art of purely aesthetic value in which plants fulfil a design function of tight and often strictly limited criteria.

Such a garden might serve as a backdrop to a collection of contemporary sculpture, for example, or might form a calm and unobtrusive setting before an architecturally important house. This style of garden demands a high degree of coordination and pre-planning to distil the essence of the style required.

The colours, textures, and finishes of all the materials are of utmost importance. Here, plants are used as a furnishing – their qualities being assessed and employed for their utility rather than for their individual beauty as living plants.

Dominant themes

When a designer's sole aim is to create a very stylized image, the approach is very similar to that of an artist when painting a picture, or a designer contriving a theatrical stage set. The result can be breathtaking, because all attention has been focused towards maximum visual impact, undiluted by sentiment or an interest in individual plants. Selecting plants only for their colour, form, and texture, and arranging them in an almost abstract, pictorial composition, ensures that the finished arrangement forms a cohesive whole of complementary materials.

While this approach is commonly used by landscape architects in large-

Mass bedding
When plants are used as basic building elements to construct an effect, the results can be dramatic. This softly textured landscape has a sculptural quality, which transcends the form of any one individual plant.

scale projects, it might equally well be adapted to smaller, more intimate situations. It avoids the problem of using too many different materials in a confined site, which can prove fussy and distracting. In contrast, minimal materials give an impression of strength and unity. Such essentially sophisticated designs all have at their heart an innate simplicity that is their most telling factor.

Even in gardens of traditional layout, this straightforwardness can underlie the development of an overall concept or theme: for example, a garden based on a restricted colour range, comprising plants only in

shades of green, with black or white flowers. A more radical alternative is a garden that is almost free of plants, consisting only of sweeping grass mounds to be mown in different directions and at varying lengths according to the texture required.

Another alternative that lends style and drama is when a single plant is introduced in great quantity, especially if the plant in question is unusual. Blocks of a hundred or more can be a revelation. A mass planting of peonies, tree poppies (*Romneya coulteri*), or many of the euphorbias can provide a spectacular sight. Less radically, gardens of a

practical nature can be given stylistic treatment. A working kitchen garden can be designed as a decorative potager. While still providing edible crops, there is greater emphasis on an attractive display of colour and texture within the strict confines of its highly structured layout.

Coordinated designs

In domestic situations, one of the greatest challenges is to match a highly stylized garden with the house or locality. One way of doing this is to use plants and materials from the area, but in a very different form. For example, locally abundant trees and shrubs (if they withstand clipping) can be used to create trimmed hedges and feature trees that are then arranged in a tightly regimented scheme within the garden (see ORNAMENTAL TREES, "Pleached trees", p.75, and HEDGES AND SCREENS, p.84). Local stone and gravel could form paving and mulches beneath plantings to create a thoroughly modern reinterpretation of the formal garden.

Small town gardens, especially if framed by boundary walls, are ideal for stylized gardens. Since they are frequently viewed from only one aspect – the house windows – they present unusual possibilities. A truly theatrical, almost two-dimensional garden can be created, with an odd or false sense of perspective achieved by the angles of hard surfaces and by the choice of their colours, shapes, and disposition.

Planting arrangements
With skill, knowledge, and care a series of well-planned "vignettes" may be constructed. Harmonious colours and contrasting leaf forms and shapes can be positioned with all the accuracy and poise of a staged floral design.

Modern style
Even the most familiar plants can be used in a stylized way. Here, their effect is transformed by the use of custom built containers arranged on different levels and painted in vibrant yet sympathetic colours.

Modern design (above)
Squares of mind-your-own-business (Soleirolia soleirolii), forming tight, ground-hugging cushions of growth, alternate with blue glass chips in a contemporary scheme that plays upon geometry and colour blocks.

Japanese raked garden (left)
In this uncompromisingly simple, abstract arrangement of rocks and raked gravel, the eye is drawn only to pure line and the effortless balance of mass and space.

Modern sculpture
A "habitat" created as a setting for a piece of modern water sculpture enables an otherwise alien artefact to appear acceptable within the general garden scene.

Succulents
Strongly architectural plants, such as Agave here, form a dramatic impression in this sunny, dry, terraced bank, where the plants thrive in the hot sun.

Assessing the existing garden

WHETHER you are remodelling your own garden or tackling one inherited from a previous owner, one of the most difficult tasks is to envisage how to transfer your ideas and aspirations onto what is there.

Everything that makes up the existing garden must be scrutinized and assessed in order to determine the components that make a positive contribution to the overall effect, and those that offer least or are farthest removed from your preferred style and taste. No aspect of the garden should escape this scrutiny, for even those factors that might be considered impossible to change can be influenced and ameliorated by skilful design and planting. Nothing can alter the shape and size of a garden, for example, yet there are any number of design solutions that can make narrow gardens appear wider, open sites become more sheltered, and awkward shapes flow more freely.

A time for reflection

The inspiration for your new design may be held entirely in your imagination – or be the result of visiting other gardens or poring over books and magazines. Before beginning to make even the roughest preliminary sketch, however, a period of time spent in the garden doing nothing more than simply mulling over

Water-saving by design

The increasing need to save water is a difficult issue for gardeners, but by building water storage and water-saving tactics into the design, you can balance the need for water conservation with your gardening interests. It is estimated that 24,000 litres (5,280 gallons) of rain could be collected even from a small house annually – enough to fill 150 normal-sized waterbutts – so ensure the house, shed, and greenhouse have gutters and downpipes leading into waterbutts or covered tanks; if space allows, position them in tandem so that two (or more) can be filled after heavy rain. In the greenhouse, plastic or galvanized covered tanks may be sunk in the ground under benches to store water from the roof. And you can also consider channelling water run-off from patios and hard surfaces directly into borders (see p.585).

Deciding on priorities
An existing garden may contain many elements that meet your own requirements, such as a seating area or raised beds, even if the materials or finishes used are not exactly to your taste. Just as plants can be judiciously retained or reshaped to preserve the structure of borders, so much can be done to adapt and personalize hard materials.

possibilities will be well repaid. The earliest planning stage of a garden should be a period of calm, cool observation; critical scrutiny of both what exists and what is desired. If insufficient time is given to important decisions, the result will be poor long-term planning.

The garden's development over an extended period of time needs a vision, seeing beyond the clutter of existing features. It should also at this stage be free of the distractions of budgets, labour, and other practical constraints. Defining a goal for the garden, and the means to that goal, can be the realization of a dream that will bestow a style and a personality – your own personality – on the property as a whole. Even if a master plan has to be tackled piecemeal, having such a plan firmly in mind will enable a greater degree of control over the ongoing development of the garden.

Weighing up the elements

As you appraise the existing garden, you will begin to form a broad idea of the scale of remodelling that a new design will involve. It is worth considering at this stage whether you intend to implement the new design in a single operation, or spread the work and expense over several years.

Carry a notebook with you, in which to enter thoughts and ideas about all of the elements the garden contains, set against what you desire. As the wealth of possibilities is distilled into a concept that could work, many ideas will be dispensed with, refining only those thought appropriate to site and scale, period, and local conditions of soil and weather.

A methodical "audit" of structures, surfaces, features, and plantings, with a view to deciding which you will keep, which you will redesign or relocate, and which are redundant, can be tremendously useful. Examples of the kinds of questions that should be asked and factors that should be considered are detailed in the pages that follow.

Separating materials from their context
Even if you do not like a feature, or its design makes it awkward to garden around, consider whether its materials might be used elsewhere. If not, items such as these old, good-quality slabs and sink could be sold.

USING PHOTOGRAPHS

Difficult decisions can often be simplified and clarified by the use of photographs. A set of pictures portraying the whole garden will help to put all of its features into context, and enable carefully considered conclusions to be drawn. Curiously, a photograph has a focusing and simplifying effect, removing the distractions of a live situation within the garden, and throwing strengths and weaknesses into high relief. The frozen image is easier to analyse, and clearly reveals the underlying composition and workings of the garden. This detachment seems to allow decisions to be made with greater freedom. The dominance of an outsized evergreen shrub, the poorly flowing line of the front of a border, or any weak, muddled plantings are more vividly displayed in static images and these can then be rectified in the new design.

Appraising your own garden

Sentimentality can often play a significantly negative role in a garden long established by its owners. Plants that really have no place in a well-designed and practical layout are preserved and overlooked; geriatric, diseased, or inappropriately sized plants are retained, particularly when they commemorate an event or were a gift, a reminder of a dear friend or relative. With the passing of a garden to new owners, such anomalies tend to be addressed more objectively – the horse chestnut tree planted as a conker years ago, for example, which now excludes all light from a terrace, may be removed without so much as a backward glance.

However, individuality – the life-blood of interesting gardens – often stems from quirks of personal sentiment. Although unconventional, it may be these features that give the garden a unique character, so, again, deep thought before action is essential. The clean sweep or makeover approach may have unexpectedly negative consequences. The removal of a conifer simply because it is "unfashionable", for example, may also mean the loss of useful screening from neighbours, or perhaps a well-placed nesting site, visible from the house, to which birds will no longer return in spring.

Appraising a garden new to you

A new owner will almost certainly wish to make changes to an existing garden. A keen gardener will probably waste little time before introducing personal preferences or old friends in the form of plants or ornaments, but if the garden, or parts of it, is not fundamentally to your taste then a broader view is required.

In many ways, the would-be designer tackling a virgin site – for example, on a new housing development – or a completely neglected, featureless plot has an easier task, with a blank canvas on which to project the new vision. To appreciate fully the complexities of an inherited, well-kept garden requires time and patience. The most valuable advice is not to make any hurried changes; an old garden that has evolved over many years may contain features of great worth, which have stood the test of time. To retain and perhaps reinterpret some existing plants and structures is greatly preferable to clearing the site and beginning from a sterile plot.

These existing elements in a garden, laid out by the previous owners, may summon up a certain atmosphere, which it is important to retain. The over-enthusiastic tidying up of such gardens can suddenly remove any charm or mystery. Such a quality is a rare commodity to be nurtured rather than swept aside. A unique richness may be found within a garden cultivated over several generations, layer upon layer of plantings creating microclimates of mutual benefit, evolving beautifully

Contemplating existing plants
If at all possible, never discard a beautiful, mature, and healthy plant just because it is in a less than perfect setting. This Trachycarpus *is a fine specimen; it would be well worth rejigging plans to accommodate it; indeed, it could suggest the theme of a new planting scheme.*

tiered structures of some complexity. With the passing of time, plants and structures can attain a character that takes them beyond mere furnishings.

Watching the garden unfold

The garden should be monitored during as many seasons as possible (ideally, a full year), during which time observations of factors such as shade cast, prevailing wind, areas of warmth, and seasonal value of plantings can be made. Paths and

terraces can be used in all seasons, the effectiveness of privacy afforded by screening shrubs can be checked – summer and winter – and the maintenance requirement of the entire garden and its plantings gauged.

Letting plants show their worth

Only within specific seasons may the reason for certain plantings be revealed: an old cherry tree with low sweeping branches, which bursts into flower in spring in partnership with drifts of bulbs beneath it, will immediately justify its existence and unconventional stature.

All too easily, mistakes can be made: a hastily removed "laurel", for some reason planted up against the south-facing wall of a house, may be cut to the ground and discarded only to discover later that this was a fine *Magnolia grandiflora* of considerable age. If you find plants difficult to identify, advice may be sought from a local nursery, gardening club, or botanical garden to avoid the unintentional removal of valuable plants.

Once the identities of all important plants are known, again do not be over-hasty in removing any. To retain some items of obvious age and maturity as a permanent or temporary measure will prevent the complete loss of scale within the reworked garden, offer shelter to young, vulnerable plants, and privacy while other plantings are establishing.

Taking inspiration from shapes
This ageing tree cloaked in ivy (far left) may need to be removed, but its overarching low branch creates a pleasing frame for the elements beyond, which might suggest the placement of an arch in its place.

Surfaces, paths, and level changes

Lawns/grassed areas

Assess your garden
- Is the lawn level, composed of good-quality grass, and weed-free?
- Is the lawn in poor condition, shaded by the house or trees, and becoming mossy due to insufficient light or poor drainage?
- Is it large enough to accommodate a tent or to be used for games?
- Are there any trees?
- Would the area be better paved, gravelled, or incorporated into a planted bed?
- Does a close-mown lawn cover an extensive area? Perhaps the far end could be mown less frequently to provide a fringe of meadow grass.
- Is the lawn extensive enough? Without a calming area of green a garden can feel frenetic and look a little over-worked. Even a broad area of gravel or paving will not have the soothing effect of grass.

What to consider
Access There must be adequate access to the lawn not only for pedestrians but for a mower or wheelbarrow, too; consider also that a route will need to be established to dispose of mowings. When a lawn is to replace a hard surface that acts as a thoroughfare through the garden, it is advisable to keep a hard strip to one side for use in bad weather.
Central role Even a relatively small lawn plays a scene-setting role – it provides an open foreground across which to view a scenic background. This role is important enough to justify the removal or reduction of existing planted borders to give an adequate area of grass.

For more information, see:
THE LAWN, pp.384–400

Patios and terraces

Assess your garden
- Is the patio area large enough?
- Is it sunny, or cold and gloomy?
- Does it lie at a junction of paths, making it difficult to position permanent furniture?
- Is it close to the house? A terrace at the far end of the garden might catch the last rays of the setting sun but may not be practical for outdoor eating and entertainment.
- Is the surface in good condition, with a slight fall away from the house to remove standing water?
- What is the patio made of? Gravel is an uncomfortable surface for chairs and tables. More acceptable is a flat surface of paving, or poured concrete with the aggregate exposed to make it non-slip and add texture.

What to consider
Hard surface An area of hard standing within the garden is invaluable both as a working area and for entertaining outdoors.
Aspect and positioning Patios and terraces need separate areas of sun and shade in which to sit at various times of the day and during different seasons. Consider both the view and the aspect.
Surrounding materials Paving often looks best when sympathetic to surrounding building materials. Decide whether the surface should be of one colour and a uniform texture, or highly decorative in design in order to make a statement.
Access Keep a passageway between house and terrace – without steps, if possible. This minimizes accidents when carrying drinks or food.

For more information, see:
"Patios and terraces", p.585

Paths

Assess your garden
- Are paths in good repair and wide enough for walking or pushing a wheelbarrow?
- Are there any broken or uneven surfaces? These can be hazardous and should be repaired or replaced.
- Do the paths follow natural desire lines through the garden, free of temptations to take short cuts?
- Do the paths add both interest and structure to the garden? They should create visual links from one area to another. If any routes appear to be unnecessary, remove them.
- How often are the paths used? Grass paths are attractive yet soft passageways: overuse will result in damage.

What to consider
Routes Paths should follow the most logical and scenic route. Avoid the spaghetti effect of too many paths.
Covering material Gravel paths are cheaper and softer on the eye than paved ones, particularly when curves and sweeps are to be negotiated – straight-edged materials can be difficult to accommodate.
Base material A well-prepared base of compacted hardcore will ensure good drainage and an even surface; the path should retain its good line over time.
Width Paths should be broad enough for two people to walk abreast. If appropriate, the width should be sufficient to take a small garden vehicle and a loaded trailer.

For more information, see:
"Paths and steps", p.593

Steps and slopes

Assess your garden
- Would any sloping sites function better if redesigned to form a series of terraces linked by steps?
- Do existing changes of level divide the garden into workable plots?
- Within the confines of a small garden, would a slight change in level either add importance to an area or provide an opportunity for a change in materials or theme?
- Could a flight of steps physically and visually draw areas together?
- Do retaining walls and planted or grass banks contribute horizontal divisions? Do they have the potential to mark a change in style or detail between levels?

What to consider
Visual impact However cleverly it is interpreted, a flat garden will not possess the liveliness of one that exploits a hillside or the undulation of rolling terrain.
Retaining walls These can be used to exaggerate a slight variation in land heights.
Accentuating features Changes in height can be exploited to display plants and water. A series of pools on different levels, linked by waterfalls, makes a lively composition.
Garden users Steps might not be appropriate for the young or elderly.
Step detail Steps should be well built and even in rise and tread width. If the sides are planted, a central area of sufficient width must be left uncluttered.

For more information, see:
"Paths and steps", p.593

Boundaries and structures

Walls and fences

Assess your garden

- Are existing walls safe? If in doubt, seek expert advice. If work is needed on old garden walls, contact an experienced stonemason or builder familiar with local building techniques so repairs are sympathetic.
- Are the fences in good condition? In particular, inspect the base of fence posts for rots and fungal growth. Individual panels and posts can often be replaced without renewing the entire structure.

- Are walls and fences aesthetic or merely practical? The easiest option for an ugly wall or fence is to disguise it with climbers or shrubs.
- Does the soil at the base need improvement before planting?
- Are mortars or plasters lime-based? If old walls shed detritus containing lime, soil may become inhospitable to acid-lovers like *Camellia*.

What to consider

Cost Traditional brick or stone walls are challenging and expensive to build. A more cost-effective option is a block wall made of plaster. Do not skimp on workmanship if the wall is to be of any height.

Height Restrictions on height usually apply to walls or fences forming the boundary to a neighbouring property.

Materials Use robust fencing for garden boundaries. Lighter strutures such as screens, trellis, or woven willow walls (see p.87) make softer internal garden divisions.

For more information, see:
"Walls", p.596
"Fences", p.600

Hedges

Assess your garden

- Are existing hedges in the right position in the garden? They may filter the wind and provide shelter, but equally may create excessive shade and obscure views.
- Have existing hedges grown too wide or tall for the garden?
- Do you have the right type of hedges for your garden? Evergreen ones sometimes prove oppressive and over-dominant, while deciduous hedges tend to let more light into the garden on dark winter days.

- How long have the hedges been in place? Old hedges can become thin at their base; reducing the height and width of the upper part will encourage regrowth lower down.

What to consider

Shape A hedge need not have the angular rigid lines that are associated with walls and fences, and can trace a sweeping curve to frame an informal border.

Material The hedging material can be varied and mixed in different combinations to offer textures and degrees of formality or informality.

Aesthetics Hedges bearing colourful flowers, fruits, or berries add interest.

Shade from trees Overhanging trees create shade that stifles the growth of hedging plants. Overcome this by planting a mixed hedge using shade-tolerant species beneath trees.

Formal hedges These add structure to a garden design. Clipped hedges act as walls for "rooms" containing different styles. Cut windows and archways to create vistas and passageways between rooms.

For more information, see:
HEDGES AND SCREENS, p.84

Garden buildings

Assess your garden

- Is the building in good repair?
- Does it stand in the best position for its purpose? A garden building – whatever its function – should not dominate the garden. If necessary, consider moving the structure to another site.
- Does the building blend in with its surroundings? One option is to camouflage it using climbers or shrubs. Buildings could be painted a different colour or be refaced with a sympathetic material.

- Would a building be more useful if refitted for a different role? A shed or summerhouse could be used to store garden furniture or apples; a conservatory could double up as a greenhouse for plants.

What to consider

Secondary role Buildings may either form part of the garden scene, adding a modest architectural element, or may be hidden by climbers and shrubs.

Siting Strike a balance between a building's practical use and its aesthetic quality. A summerhouse, conservatory, or greenhouse requires a position with a favourable aspect for its occupants, whether human or plant. A garden shed or store, however, can be sited in a shady corner. All buildings should be readily accessible, ideally from hard standing.

Materials All structures should be constructed from strong materials that are easy to maintain; they must also have adequate foundations.

For more information, see:
CONSERVATORY GARDENING, p.356
GREENHOUSES AND FRAMES, pp.566–83
"Garden sheds", p.605

Pergolas and arches

Assess your garden

- Is the structure structurally sound? It must safely bear both the weight of plants and the overhead structure.
- Is the structure able to withstand the wind resistance created by the plant canopy?
- Are there any weaknesses in existing structures? Check and repair timber and metalwork, if necessary; sound surfaces should be cleaned and treated with preservative or paint. It may be advisable to employ

a structural engineer or qualified builder to look over large structures.
- Are any plantings out of control? They should be drastically cut back to allow light and air into the canopy.
- Are any plants looking tired? Old, twisted and gnarled specimen climbers should be retained for their character, and carefully pruned.

What to consider

Architectural element A pergola or series of arches may define the main axis of a garden, perhaps directing the flow or marking a transition from one section to another.

Materials and design These may be dictated by those already used in the garden or house.

Framework A range of weights can be used for different effects, from a skeletal metalwork frame to a heavy brick and timber beam construction. In winter, deciduous plants will no longer conceal their supports, so structures do need to be elegant.

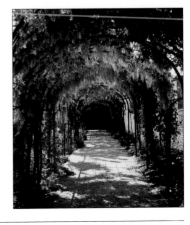

For more information, see:
"Pergolas and rustic work", p.603

Ornamental planting

Trees

Assess your garden

- How mature are the trees? Mature or semi-mature trees are a great asset. Their scale cannot readily be acquired, and the shadows they cast give a special quality to a landscape.
- Do you wish to add a favourite tree? Small trees are ideal in confined spaces. In larger gardens they will, if positioned correctly, enhance the landscape effect provided by larger "specimen" trees.
- Do the existing trees dominate?

Gardens are often planted heavily for immediate results; this may later require the removal of some trees or the reduction of their canopies.

- Do trees encroach on a view or cut out light? They must be checked with appropriate pruning. The same applies if leaves from trees near the house block gutters and downpipes.

What to consider

Function A single tree can fulfil many roles. It may have an elegant form, with flowers, fruit, good autumn colour, and attractive bark, providing almost year-round interest.
Continuity This can be achieved by using lots of one species or cultivar.
Development A mixture of trees can be planted for short- and longer-term effect; part of the enjoyment is watching a tree develop.
Positioning Tree roots, especially those of fast-growing species, can damage drains and foundations. Take care when positioning trees to allow adequate clearance around buildings.

For more information, see:
ORNAMENTAL TREES, pp.52–87

Shrubs

Assess your garden

- Do existing shrubs give decorative value over a long period of time?
- Are they performing well, or are they straggly and undernourished, or perhaps starved of light?
- Are they overgrown, or too large for the position? Not all shrubs respond well to pruning; identify the plants before removing or reducing growth.
- Have grafted shrubs developed suckers from the rootstock? Left in place they may overpower the plant; remove them cleanly at their source.

- Do you require a low-maintenance garden? Shrubs that need regular attention may have to be replaced.
- Have variegated shrubs produced green-leaved stems? Cut these off.

What to consider

Seasonal features For every month there is a shrub that provides colour and scent, even in the dark days of winter. Some are dual-purpose – flowering, then fruiting later. Many shrubs are also suitable for cutting for indoor arrangements.
Shape and form These differ from shrub to shrub, and give the garden a softer edge, reducing the predictably angular lines of the average plot.
Dividing role Where a hedge or fence would create too strong a division across the garden, a block of shrubs can be more sympathetic. They tend to be covered with foliage to ground level, and evergreens will retain their leaves throughout winter.
Wildlife Shrubs can provide habitats for nesting birds or food for over-wintering creatures.

For more information, see:
ORNAMENTAL SHRUBS, pp.88–121
ROSES, pp.146–169

Climbing plants

Assess your garden

- Do existing climbers enhance the garden, allowing plant growth to flow up, over, and around buildings and walls?
- Are plants too vigorous for their supporting structures, whether a tree, wall, arch, or pergola? A plant that outgrows its space will need considerable pruning, which may then reduce flowering and fruiting.
- Are wall-trained shrubs planted too close to buildings? This can damage their foundations. Dense climbers may create damp patches or obscure light from windows.
- Are climbers so overgrown that they are blocking gutters or working their way under roof tiles and weatherboarding? Offending plants must be removed or regularly pruned.

What to consider

Camouflage Used with thought and intelligence, climbing plants can redeem the most mundane or ugly building, disguising it with a thin veil of foliage and softening lines and construction materials.
Use on walls Some climbers cling tightly to the angles of walls while others blur the edges, turning corners into curving, flowing forms.
Maintenance The amount of time you can invest in climbing plants will dictate their appearance. A rampant, trailing climber will, if left unchecked, festoon a building in a few seasons. The same climber, pruned regularly and precisely tied, can offer a neatly tailored, formal layout of well-secured branches.

For more information, see:
"Wall shrubs", p.93
CLIMBING PLANTS, pp.122–45

Herbaceous borders

Assess your garden

- Is the scale, colouring, and content of the border to your liking?
- Will the border look spectacular for one month but depressing for the rest of summer?
- Have vigorous plants swamped other more delicate species and spoiled the design and balance?
- Do any plants need rejuvenating? After lifting and dividing, replant only young vigorous sections .
- Is the border overrun with perennial weeds (see p.670) such as ground elder (*Aegopodium podagraria*) or couch grass (*Elymus repens*)?
- Could borders be reduced in size or the planting simplified for easy maintenance?

What to consider

Colour The primary purpose of herbaceous plantings is to provide uplifting colour.
Positioning Borders that run parallel to a house will be critically observed at close quarters; they may look empty for much of the year. It is better to position borders so you look down their length: the planting will always appear to be full, and gaps will be less noticeable.
Themes A border can adopt a theme, such as a limited colour range, a season, or a genus. Plant foliage could harmonize with the colour or texture of a hedge or material used as an edging, path, or wall.

For more information, see:
PERENNIALS, pp.170–205
ANNUALS AND BIENNIALS, pp.206–23
BULBOUS PLANTS, pp.224–51

Garden features

Kitchen garden

Assess your garden

- Does the current site have the best soil in the garden, a warm, sheltered aspect, and good light? If there is somewhere with more suitable growing conditions, consider relocating the plot to this area.
- Do you intend to keep an existing kitchen garden area? Always assess the condition of the soil before deciding what to grow (see "Soil and its structure", p.616). It may need improvement or deep cultivation.

- Are existing fruit trees and bushes productive, or old and neglected? Old specimens may need pruning to restore them to productivity, or may be better replaced. Consider too your household requirements and any specific likes and dislikes.

What to consider

Priority crops Decide on your main requirement – this might be salad crops, unusual produce that is not available at the greengrocer, or a fresh and cheap fruit and vegetable supply throughout the year.

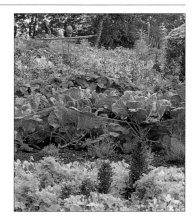

Time available Growing vegetables requires a great deal of time and hard work – keep this in mind when deciding the size of your plot.
Space available Where space is limited and smaller crops are required, vegetables and fruit can be integrated throughout the entire garden. Not only will this benefit the insect population, but it will look attractive, too.

For more information, see:
GROWING FRUIT, pp.416–89
GROWING VEGETABLES, pp.490–548

Herb garden

Assess your garden

- Does an inherited herb garden include plants that are important to you? With such a wide range of plants available, the contents of the herb garden is a personal matter; it may be necessary to discard some of the existing herbs, and replanning and replanting may be required.
- Have fast-spreading herbs, such as mints, come to dominate and smother less vigorous ones? Such plants should be cut back, but this may not be a permanent solution;

consider growing more delicate herbs in the safety of containers, or confining rampant growers to pots.

What to consider

Site and soil To grow well, herbs require a free-draining soil, which need not be particularly rich, and a very sunny site, which receives maximum light and warmth.
Location Ideally a herb garden must be located near the house and within easy reach of the kitchen for use throughout the year. Large quantities of herbs required for culinary or other domestic purposes, such as

making pot-pourri, may be grown in specific areas to be harvested and stored for use out of season.
Planting combinations It is not necessary to group culinary, aromatic, and medicinal plants. The herb garden theme may be extended throughout the cultivated areas of the garden. Flowers, fruit, vegetables, and herbs may be combined, using an extended range of fragrances and colour, as well as flower and leaf shapes and textures.

For more information, see:
GROWING HERBS, pp.402–15

Water features

Assess your garden

- Are the water features in the garden well maintained or in need of repair? Before adopting any existing ponds, pools, or canals, their overall condition should be assessed and any problems addressed.
- Has a pool site become overshadowed by trees, leaving the water too shaded or perhaps full of debris?
- Is the scale of the area of water in relation to that of the garden as a whole inappropriate? Ponds require considerable time and effort to

keep them in good condition. If this commitment cannot be fulfilled, they may be better removed.
- Is the water feature properly protected? Safety must be a primary consideration in family gardens. The smallest pond can pose a threat to children, especially those unfamiliar with the garden.

What to consider

Safety The depth of small pools can be reduced by filling part of them with rounded pebbles while children are small. Ledges around pool sides will help older children scramble out.

Sloping pond margins also allow for escape from deeper water, and may save the lives of pets or small garden mammals.
Scale The smallest amount of water brings movement, sound, and life into a garden, whatever its size. A terrace may host a small spout and basin; a garden may have a modest pond of indigenous plantings; and a landscape a series of interconnected pools and water courses – each one is at an appropriate scale for its setting.

For more information, see:
WATER GARDENING, pp.280–303

Ornaments and pots

Assess your garden

- When moving to a new property, is there a chance of acquiring long-established decorative garden items? If so, seize the opportunity. However, it is rare to inherit statues and large architectural containers with a house and garden. Ornaments are usually removed along with the house contents or sold.
- How well placed are the existing ornaments? A garden that benefits from well-positioned ornaments

will be weakened by their removal or replacement. Conversely, an over-embellished garden will confuse the eye – it must be controlled to restore balance and bring order to the scene.

What to consider

Garden design Well-placed pots and ornaments can be used to enhance existing garden styles. Ornaments should comply with local factors – scale, style, material, and general appropriateness.
Personal taste Statues and pots can be an reflection of personal taste.

The art they introduce to the garden may be traditional or contemporary, representational or abstract. A distinctive individuality can be achieved with the use of commissioned pieces of sculpture or plant containers.
Focal points Ornaments may act as signposts within the garden by encouraging visitors to move through it or to pause to admire a view; they enhance certain points and draw together disconnected areas.

For more information, see:
CONTAINER GARDENING, pp.304–35

Sketching out a plan

BEFORE measuring-up a garden accurately and formulating any new design, a preliminary sketch or sketches will help you assess the overall layout of the existing plot. This will form the basis of a detailed scale plan (see p.36), on which you will be able to mark those features and plants that are to be retained, and the elements to be added (see p.38).

These sketches should comprise rough ground plans on which to note the many practical factors that will affect the final layout and choice of plants. With accompanying notes, they should detail elements particular to the site, such as climate, soil type, views to consider, shade cast, and the orientation of plot and house, as well as the shape and size of the area – factors that cannot be changed. They should also include utilities relating to the house as well as to the garden and its maintenance, such as outside taps and garden sheds. Such items may currently be poorly positioned.

Climate and aspect

The climate of the general locality and that found specifically within the garden are key determining factors, influencing its layout and the choice and placing of plants (see CLIMATE AND THE GARDEN, pp.606–615). Information on the general climatic conditions of the locality, annual rainfall, average temperatures, and quantities of sunlight should be sought and studied. These general conditions will be influenced by the particular terrain within the garden.

Gaining a perspective
An upstairs window may afford a good view when sketching the boundaries and any irregularities in a garden. It is also an ideal vantage point from which to observe and map changing patterns of sun and shade.

A low-lying garden may be sheltered from strong winds but it may also form a frost pocket, whereas a hilltop site may remain several degrees colder than a neighbouring, protected, south-facing slope. A garden near the sea can also be affected by strong winds, possibly salt laden, but the maritime influence will prevent extreme fluctuations in temperature compared to inland regions.

Within the garden, pockets of particular conditions will exist – forming microclimates of warmth or cold, humidity or dryness, each suiting a different range of plants (see "Microclimate", p.611). The orientation of the garden, and of the house within it, will affect the warmth or coldness of the house walls, and where shadows will create deep or partial shade. These factors will affect not only your choice of plants but also decisions on where seating areas should be positioned.

Assessing your soil type

The soil found within a garden is a crucial factor to take into account. The type, texture, and level of acidity or alkalinity (the pH) of the soil are important to recognize (see "Soil and its structure", p.616). Soils vary greatly from region to region, from a heavy clay to a light sandy loam, or a chalky or limestone soil to an acidic peat. Each variation in soil will suit a different plant range. Those happily accommodated will thrive, while those planted in an inappropriate soil type will struggle to survive. Moisture retention and drainage will vary with soil type, as will ease of cultivation, which can be severely hindered by badly drained, heavy soils.

Poor drainage is a factor that may affect more than plant choice. A soft boggy site will be unsuitable for any substantial building work unless the problem can be alleviated by installing drains and soakaways

(see "Improving drainage", p.623). If large areas of rubble or subsoil have been left from building and construction work, it may be simpler to work with them rather than attempt an overhaul. They may be used successfully to form the foundations of a terraced area, or perhaps a gravel garden; this type of site provides ideal conditions for plants that prefer sharply drained soil (see "Gravel beds and paving", p.256).

Utilities and access

Other fixed details occurring within the garden should be noted on the plan, including drives and pathways that service the house, and important yet irritating features to be worked around, such as manhole covers. There may also be meter inspection points and septic tanks to be marked in. An oil tank or coal bunker is often an ugly but essential component of the garden, especially in rural areas; it may be possible to relocate it, but screening is obviously an easier option. A wood pile, however, can look charming in a garden, and is also an attractive wildlife habitat.

Any overhead power or telephone lines need to be entered onto the site plan, because tall-growing trees must not be planted close to overhead cabling. It is also inadvisable to plant twining climbers on a house wall where cabling enters the building, because the plants will use the wires as a climbing frame. Such points on the house wall are often inaccessible, too, and attempts to prune or pull away growth can be hazardous.

Garden topography
An area of water not only increases soil moisture but also the humidity of the surrounding air, to the benefit of many plants. However, water often occupies a low-lying spot, which is very likely to be a frost pocket (see p.607). Plants may need to be selected for their hardiness as well as their suitability for the soil and conditions.

Elements to disguise
Inspection covers must be accessible, but can be hidden by low, spreading plants or by using recessed lids with paving set into them (see p.586).

A rough site plan
Sketch the layout of the garden and the position of the house. Then enter in substantial structural planting such as trees and hedges, the outlines of areas of hard standing and lawns, the route of paths, and any internal garden divisions and buildings such as sheds, screens, and walls. At this point, more generally planted borders and areas may be indicated simply by shading. In this northern hemisphere garden, the diagonal hatching represents shade cast by the sun taking its highest, midsummer route across the sky.

Thinking ahead

While your plans may be at an embryonic stage, ideas for major changes, for example the felling of a tree or construction of a garden building such as a summerhouse, may already be germinating. There are certain legal aspects that will repay investigation right from the start, or you may run the risk of unpleasant surprises thwarting your plans later. These include local building and planning regulations, the possible existence of tree preservation orders, the responsibility for, and delineation between, boundaries separating neighbouring properties, and any statutory environmental protection for your area. Any necessary permissions should be sought as early as possible, even if you eventually do not follow the ideas through, as agreement and clearance, where forthcoming, can take considerable amounts of time.

Other practicalities

There are certain practicalities that few gardens can be without, and a checklist can be compiled to determine whether the existing garden is equipped to suit your needs. Mark the position of outside taps, and consider whether these may need to be moved. To inherit a garden with an established compost heap is a boon, but compost can easily be moved elsewhere, as can other potentially useful structures such as cold frames and incinerators. Draw the current position of these onto the plan, together with sheds and storage bins, and consider whether the capacity these offer is adequate, not only for garden tools but also for general family clutter such as folding chairs, toys, and bicycles.

What lies beyond

Elements quite literally beyond your control should still be noted for consideration on the plan. The immediate surrounds of the garden, where views may be taken advantage of or ugly buildings concealed by carefully positioned trees, will enable an enterprising gardener to exploit the site to the full. Privacy and security at the boundaries of the plot should be examined and noted for their existing effectiveness. Weigh up possible loss of views or sunlight if extra privacy and shelter are required, and ensure that changes will not annoy neighbours in surrounding gardens.

Security can often be improved by opening up the garden, rather than reinforcing enclosure; consider whether driveways and sheds might perhaps be better brought into view.

The impact of a busy road passing the property, perhaps with a junction at which point headlights sweep into the garden, can be reduced or lost if the boundary gaps are filled. Dense, clipped hedges can also act as a useful baffle to noise (see also HEDGES AND SCREENS, p.84).

Views to obscure
An unwelcome reminder of urban life in the form of a distant car park intrudes onto this otherwise charming plot. Planting a narrow, upright tree, or perhaps raising the height of the rear wall slightly with trellis panels on which a climber could be trained, would restore seclusion. Consider the viewpoint of neighbours before implementing changes that could block light.

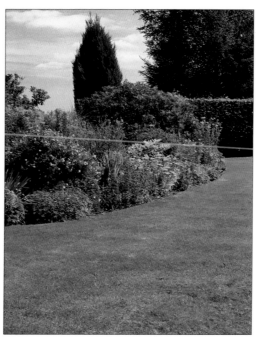

Lengthening a vista
Reshaping this border and introducing more height in the foreground would open up and lengthen a vista towards the conifer, and lead on to views of the countryside beyond. Lowering the hedge would also add distance, but its presence, together with the trees behind it, suggests a shelter belt. Prevailing winds should be investigated, as this site could be very exposed.

Making a scale plan

A FINE, dry day is required for compiling a scale plan, with no limitation on time. The assistance of a second person will greatly ease the task, as will a good-sized sketch pad or a clipboard and paper, two 30m (100ft) tape measures, pencil, rubber, a set of compasses, and an ample supply of stout twine and wire pegs with which to pin the twine in place. With a small garden, a single "field plan" can be made of the entire site. Larger gardens can be broken into separate areas, later to be joined on a final plan put together on a larger surface such as a kitchen table or drawing board.

Making a start

The boundaries of the garden should be measured and entered onto the plan with heights of boundary walls, hedges, or fences marked alongside their lengths. Then the house and other buildings must be plotted and fixed within the boundary. This may be achieved by measuring from two known fixed points on the boundary, such as corners, gate posts, or tree trunks, to a corner or fixed point on the house. If three or four such points are established around the house then an accurate location will be found for the building. Surrounding terraces can be relatively easily measured from the house to their edges, checking that they run parallel to the house and, if not, gauging the discrepancy.

Plotting positions

When plotting outlying features that cannot be related easily to a nearby boundary or house wall, you must create an artificial line from which measurements can be taken. A long tape measure pulled straight out between known and pinpointed features in the garden, such as a central door in the house and a fence post on the far boundary, provides a "datum line". From this, use a second tape to identify the position of features, such as a tree, sundial, or manhole cover, by measuring at a right-angle from the first, datum-line tape. Note the measurement on the first tape where the second crosses it, and the distance from this point to the feature.

Once a datum line has been established, any number of items can be measured using coordinates to the left or right of the line. A number of such datum lines may be necessary to plot all features within a large garden. To pinpoint a single, isolated feature, such as a tree in a lawn, the technique known as triangulation (see p.37) may be used. While

Measuring from a datum line
Except in the tiniest plots, it is almost impossible to position elements such as trees and small buildings on a plan by taking measurements between them and their nearest boundaries. Using a central datum line makes the job much easier. Here, a line in the paving running parallel to the house has provided a useful starting point for a datum line that will run to a fixed, traceable point at far end of the garden.

Measuring the existing layout
Using a datum line, or lines, enables you to build up a plotted plan of the garden by making a series of offset measurements to the right and to the left of the line. The running, or incremental, measurements taken along the datum line are also a valuable way of confirming the site's dimensions.

Tape measure 1 measures down the garden from a fixed point (here, one corner of the house)

House

0m

4m   4.4m

4.8m   7.98m

3m   9.2m

5.8m

8.4m   7.65m   7.35m

8.3m

9.9m   10.2m

11.3m   5.1m

3m   5.1m

15.1m

7.6m

Tape measure 2 is used to make the cross-measurements

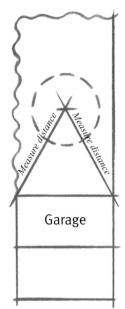

Triangulation

Where a feature such as a tree cannot be directly related to existing straight sight lines, measure against two fixed points to establish its position. To transfer to a plan, scale down the two distances appropriately, and use each as the radius of a circle drawn with compasses around the fixed points – here the two corners of the garage. The point at which the circles intersect will be the location of the feature (here a tree). The compasses can also be used to describe the tree's canopy.

Measure distance   Measure distance

Garage

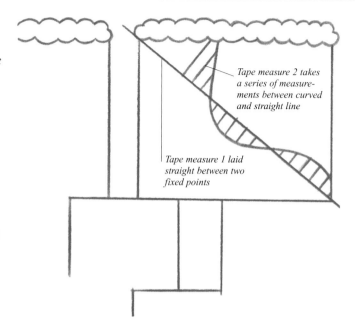

Tape measure 2 takes a series of measurements between curved and straight line

Tape measure 1 laid straight between two fixed points

Establishing an irregular curve

Two tape measures must be used for this: one to lie straight and flat across the curve (or curves) between two given measured and plotted points, the second to be used to measure the curve at regular intervals from the first tape. For example, at 50cm (18in) intervals along the first tape, the second tape is laid across it at right-angles and the distance to the edge of the curve measured and recorded as a series of coordinates.

straight edges are easy to measure and plot, the curved edge of a drive or generous sweep of a border may take more time to replicate precisely on paper (see above, right).

Adding more dimensions

As linear measurements are taken, other useful information can be gathered. Measure and mark the positions of all gates and entrances on the boundary, and all doors and windows of the house. Heights of internal garden divisions such as screens and hedges should be recorded, together with the height and canopy spread of trees, pergolas, or arches.

Changes in level should also be recorded. These are critical factors that may necessitate terracing, retaining walls, steps, and slopes in future plans for the garden where unsatisfactory level changes prevail. Simple slopes and slight changes can be calculated relatively easily, but an undulating site of various levels and cross-falls will be beyond the capabilities of the average gardener. For this a professional surveyor must be engaged. A large-scale garden, which is more difficult to plot and coordinate than a small one, may also be better left to a professional.

Transferring the field plan

With the "fieldwork" statistics accurately gathered, including a number of extra cross-measurements made as a check to the detail and to the overall plan, the information can be committed to paper. A plan created at too small a scale will be difficult to draw and awkward to read. Where practical, as large a scale as possible should be adopted on which every detail can be recorded. Squared or graph paper will enable

TRANSFERRING THE FIELD PLAN TO SQUARED PAPER

Establish the scale of the plan using the largest dimensions possible on a sheet of paper that will accommodate them; if necessary, stick several sheets together. A general garden plan such as this showing basic outlines and features can be drawn at a scale of 1:100. Mark everything on the plan, including features you may not want to keep. This plan, together with your visual memory of what already exists in each area, will help in both imagining and deciding on the scale of new outlines and features (see p.38).

the easy transfer of measurements from field notes to plan, although designs on blank paper using a scale rule, once mastered, will give greater flexibility. A general garden plan detailing all the items and features may be drawn at a scale of 1:100, but a more detailed one of planting within a border (see also p.45) requires a scale of 1:50 or 1:40 for a comfortable depiction of plantings.

When using graph paper, a decision on how many squares are to represent one square metre (square yard) must be made. The biggest scale that the paper can afford should first be calculated by drawing on the greatest measurement, since if this can be accommodated then the entire drawing will fit. Art and design supply stores stock paper in the larger "A" sizes, which may be difficult to find in stationery shops.

Putting pencil to paper

The design novice will almost certainly require several attempts at plotting a scale plan, and even a professional will work only in pencil at this stage. The principal features should be entered onto the plan first, starting with the boundaries and any gateways or openings within them.

From these points, the house with its doorways and windows can be positioned. These openings are important as often a sight line or vista will be revealed from a doorway or window. Once the outer and "inner" perimeters of the garden area are established, small details around the house can be arranged. From here you can draw in paths and driveways, establishing between them areas of lawn, hard standing, and borders. These will facilitate the positioning of more isolated features, such as specimen trees, sheds, and greenhouses.

Omit only those features that will definitely not be retained. At this stage all else must appear on the plan, even elements that may be removed later. The drawing can then be made permanent by inking the lines. A thin line should be used to depict all of the existing detail, to permit the overlay of new ideas and the blocking in or heightening of old features. Thus you will create a new design that includes worthy existing elements enhanced by proposals, suggestions, and experiments new to the site.

Imposing the new design

The original master copy of the plan should remain unmarked. Either take photocopies on which to work, or use tracing-paper overlays laid across the original. With a known scale and an accurate drawing, there are no limits to the possibilities that can be developed on the plan. Different sizes and positions for terraces, drives, court-yards, and ponds can be considered (see STRUCTURES AND SURFACES, pp.584–605, and WATER GARDENING, pp.280–303). Cutting out shapes representing planting, ornaments, pools or buildings from card to place and move around the drawing helps to envisage the impact these features will have on the rest of the site.

This preliminary planning period, although rather abstract and divorced from the physical practicalities of making a garden, is an essential one as all those thoughts, ideas, and dreams of what your personal garden should comprise must be vented, considered, applied, and then adopted or rejected. Many rough drawings should be made to expose all the design possibilities.

Any working drawings that follow the thought process should be kept, as frequently a discarded idea may be resurrected in a different guise. The possibility of two ideas combining and working together when one of the ideas in isolation would be rejected is sufficient reason for retaining every idea and drawing until the project has been completed.

Rounding out the vision

When a scheme has been rigorously scrutinized, experimented with, and passed such tests as practicality, accessibility, and suitability for the site, then the foundations of a new approach to the garden are beginning to be laid. Areas of the plan could be shaded or coloured to give a more powerful representation of the differing elements, aiding final decisions of proportion and scale.

You will also begin to appreciate the proportions of hard landscaping to "soft" – that is, planting – in your design, and adjust them if needed. You may already have ideas about building materials, and the nature of the main planting elements – even the identities of individual structural plants (see also "Principles of plant-ing", pp.42–51). A scrapbook or collage of photographs, or elements of photographs, culled from magazines and catalogues will add colour and texture to your vision, and serve as a reminder of items to order and buy to complete your design.

BUILDING THE NEW DESIGN ON THE EXISTING PLAN

Retain shrubs

Lawn

Retain path base

Garage

Garage

Retain centre of forecourt and remodel sides

Path

House

Retain lawn

Pergola

Rebuild green-house and shed on new site

Terrace

Rebuild compost heaps

Hedge

Seat

Key

——— What you wish to keep from the existing garden

——— What you wish to add to the garden

Having created an accurately plotted field plan (see p.37, and above), use copies of it, or tracing paper, to begin experimenting with your new design. The advantage of using tracing paper is that features and outlines that are to be discarded can simply be left out of the drawing, to produce a much cleaner and clearer picture. In the overlay on the right, elements to be retained from the existing garden – including much of the fine mature hedging, and the most desirable of the trees – have been marked in blue. The driveway has been given a softer profile; more space has been allocated to borders; a potager-style kitchen garden replaces a decrepit orchard; and the main reception room of the house now enjoys a serene vista of terracing with a formal pool.

THE FINISHED DESIGN

This beautifully realized plan has had colour, detail, and texture added, not only in planted areas but also in the choice of hard landscaping materials. An existing garden and house may provide inspiration where materials can be harmoniously linked with those already found on the property. In such a case a seamless flow of materials from the house into the garden will produce a satisfactory design. Even when the identical brick, stone, or concrete cannot be found, a similar colour, texture, and scale of material will be perfectly satisfactory.

A garden devoid of existing materials offers the opportunity to introduce new ones. Local colours and textures should still be respected, yet within the design a particular cobble, sett, brick, or block can be selected. Small-scale, intricately patterned materials are appropriate in small, confined spaces but can look overly complicated and busy on a large scale, whereas bigger units offer a calmer scene.

Timber for pergolas, gates, or fences and gravel for terraces, paths, or a drive must all be chosen for their suitability for the site, aesthetic appeal, and durability. The colour of a fence, whether natural or painted, can alter the appearance of an entire garden, as can the colour and size of gravel and chippings used as loose surfaces.

KEY

1 Evergreen hedge
2 Long grass with bulbs and woodland herbs
3 Gravel drive with timber edging
4 Fine mown lawn
5 Gravel garden with informally placed herbaceous plants
6 Mixed shrub planting
7 Specimen tree
8 Planting with year-round interest
9 Border of shade-loving plants
10 Double garage
11 Potting shed/store

12 Greenhouse
13 Gravel forecourt with enough space for turning
14 Stone-flagged main entrance to house
15 Brick wall with trained fruit
16 Brick paths
17 Vegetables, cut flowers, fruit, and herbs
18 Garden bench
19 Central herb garden
20 Mixed border
21 Stone-flagged terrace
22 Pergola with table and chairs

23 Tree screening neighbouring house
24 Annual colour border
25 Axial vista
26 Sculpture
27 Central mown grass path flanked by meadow grass and bulbs
28 Compost heaps and bonfire site
29 Deciduous hedge
30 Urn ornament
31 Formal canal bridged by stepping stones
32 Sunken garden with steps

Putting the plan into practice

I N the same way that the existing garden has been recorded on paper, you must now translate your new design onto the site. Often it is during this process of measuring and marking out the proposed plan that problems with the design become apparent. You may have been over-ambitious with the available space, for example, or mistaken about the most practical route for a path. Only by standing at proposed vantage points to contemplate imaginary vistas may an unwelcome eyesore be revealed.

Using props

A scheme can be laid out *in situ* using whatever comes to hand to simulate temporarily the key elements of the design. You must work around features that are probably destined to be removed – however inconvenient this may be – as the experimental layout may show that these are valuable elements that are worthy of retention after all.

Canes, tree stakes, hosepipe, string, pots, cardboard boxes, and dustbins can be used to assume roles such as path and border edges, step treads, specimen trees, ponds, or rows of repeating shrubs across the front of an imaginary terrace. The simplest indicators – heavy wooden tree stakes driven into an open lawn – will readily confirm or condemn a suitable location for a broad, spreading tree, where neighbouring plantings, buildings, and views may all be important considerations.

Transferring the design
Formal, symmetrical designs can be as simple to mark out on the proposed site as they are to plot on paper. A grid may be created using string guides that correspond with the scale on the plan, enabling the entire design to be transferred onto the ground with relative ease. It is important that all of the measurements and angles are correctly taken and then carefully checked.

Where possible, props should be left in place for their impact to be experienced over a few days and at different times of day. Where string guides and stakes indicating the edges of borders may be disturbed, a line of sand run from a bottle or spray paint from an aerosol can be used.

Photographs taken of the garden with its props in place may prove invaluable when determining the eventual placement or removal of features. These final decisions should not be hurried; allow enough time to consider and even reconsider. At this point indecision is a strength,

as holding onto an original concept doggedly in the light of subsequent modifications is foolhardy. Opportunities available now will not present themselves again, and matters of construction are more easily resolved on the drawing board than on site with an impatient contractor.

Order of work

A carefully orchestrated schedule of work is needed to coordinate and implement a newly designed scheme. There are many different elements

and skills involved, and each should be undertaken in a logical sequence to provide a smooth running programme and keep disruption to an absolute minimum.

A fundamental decision must be made as to whether the garden improvements are to be undertaken as a single operation or in stages over a number of weeks, months, or years. Try to have all hard landscaping work completed in a single phase, as this eliminates the need for builders to return and create a second period of dust, noise, and inconvenience (see STRUCTURES AND SURFACES, pp.584–605). Timing the operations is important to enable construction work to be completed in favourable weather in summer or autumn, allowing autumn, winter, or spring for planting, sowing, and turfing.

Remodelling in stages

It is often the case, whether through budgetary constraints, available time, or simply the need to retain a useable outdoor area of some sort at all times, that a reworking of the garden can only be implemented piecemeal. A strategy for change must be drawn up. For some period of time the desired garden will overlay the existing layout, which may perhaps look rather curious, with permanently retained features, temporarily kept items, and newly established plantings and features all present. The evolving hybrid will require intricate planning to ensure a smooth transition to the new design.

To assist with a phased series of changes, the first practical measure must be to label the contents of the

Using props
By arranging and rearranging items gleaned from the house and garden, you can simulate the key features of the proposed design. Here cane wigwams indicate the position of obelisks planted with climbers; inverted tubs stand in for shrubs; and the battens and geotextile fabric form a terraced area flanked by massed plantings of lavender. To complete the effect, a specimen tree in the lawn and an undulating border edging of box plants have been added.

garden with written or colour-coded tags indicating plants and materials to stay, to be moved, to remain temporarily, or to be removed at once. Although decisions have been made, a period of final deliberation is useful, during which the labelled plants may be reassessed to avoid any later confusion and irrevocable errors.

Engaging professionals
Once the scale of operations has been identified then the amount of assistance needed to implement the plans can be gauged. It may be possible over a period of time to make all the changes yourself, or some help may be needed to execute, say, construction work or tree felling. Alternatively, a contract landscaping company may be engaged to create the whole garden. Where assistance is being sought, it is important to state accurately what is required and to obtain a detailed price quotation. Good references or, ideally, personal recommendations for the firm are also highly desirable.

Professional advice may also be sought to assess the condition of trees, walls, and garden buildings. With their good condition confirmed or otherwise, the appropriate action can be taken. Even if some elements are unaffected by the current works, examine their condition early on, as to invite tree surgeons or builders back into the finished garden could be disruptive and damaging.

Hard landscaping
Because of the inevitable soil compaction involved, built features should always take priority over new planting. Where only part of the garden is being remodelled, as above, clear an area large enough for you to work comfortably. Conduits laid under paving at the construction stage (right) may be useful in the future to carry utilities such as piping and cabling.

Coping with limited access
A terraced house without direct road access into the garden should ideally have its garden works scheduled to coincide with house refurbishments, as materials must be carried through the house itself, creating possible damage to the interior. Materials can be lifted over adjoining walls, but at some cost. Where skips cannot be brought into the garden, you may have to seek permission to site one at the roadside. Waste cannot be burnt where bonfires are prohibited.

Excavations and spoil
When excavations produce large quantities of soil to be taken off-site, remember to discard subsoil, but keep topsoil. Where levels are being reduced, this will involve taking off and reserving the topsoil, digging out and removing subsoil, and then replacing the topsoil, so that the best soil does not leave the garden. When holes are to be dug, first locate any services – water, electricity, or gas pipes – which may be buried in the garden. Carefully excavate to identify their positions precisely before further work is carried out.

Clearing the area
The first stage of the garden's refurbishment is the removal of all unwanted materials and built structures. With the correct permission, trees can be cut down and taken away. Stumps must also be removed;

leaving them to rot in the soil increases the danger of honey fungus (see p.661). Quality materials in good condition will have a resale value that justifies taking the trouble to find a reputable dealer. Those materials that are eventually to be reused should be cleaned and carefully stacked in a safe place away from site.

In a large garden the area to be worked on should be fenced off, restricting potential damage and spread of materials to one place. Paving and steps to be retained should also be protected by covering with boarding while heavy materials are being manoeuvred. Turf can be stripped and stacked for a short time before re-use or cleared for new turf to take its place.

Plants left in place
Plants to be left *in situ* can be carefully wrapped in sheets and tied for a brief period if, say, surrounding walls are being repaired. Large shrubs, too big for their locations yet too interesting and attractive to remove, could be thinned or reduced, or even cut hard to the ground to encourage regeneration (see "Renovation", p.110). Before cutting them back, some plants can be propagated as an extra safety measure: in the right season, take cuttings of plants such as roses, hebes, or clematis, to ensure the variant survives (see PRINCIPLES OF PROPAGATION, "Cuttings", p.632).

Clumps of many perennials will tolerate being lifted, divided, and potted up if kept well watered in a sheltered, shady corner (see PERENNIALS, "Lifting and dividing", p.193). Taking cuttings or collecting seed (see "Collecting and storing seed", p.629) is another way of preserving such plants to incorporate into the new garden.

Correct timing
Never delay the laying of new turf. The timing of delivery is crucial, as if left rolled (as below) for more than a day or two it will swiftly deteriorate. Nothing gives a new lawn an air of maturity like a scattering of bulbs, such as crocuses (left). Turfing in autumn would allow bulbs to be planted simultaneously, to flower in spring.

Creating the landscape
With unwanted materials out of the way, the cleared site should then have any pernicious weeds eradicated (see "Controlling weeds", p.671). At this stage any adjustments to levels can also be made, as well as any excavations for services such as power for garden lighting, or irrigation systems. Wall footings or path bases can now be excavated, and solid foundations built (see "Paths and steps", p.593, and "Walls", p.596). Construction of walls and built structures can then take place (see STRUCTURES AND SURFACES, pp.584–605, and "Erecting the greenhouse", p.571). To add the finishing touches before planting, fences and timber may be treated or painted, and trellising or support wires put up on walls and fences for climbers.

Ready to plant
Where larger plants are being used in a scheme, it may be necessary to plant them as the hard landscape is being constructed, as at a later stage it may not be possible to manoeuvre them into place. However, the task of reintegrating any preserved plant material into new schemes, and introducing new plants, generally begins once the hard construction is completed and services installed.

Before plants are introduced, however, any soil compaction should be remedied, and the soil improved by the addition of organic matter (see "Improving soil structure", p.621).

Any protection given to shrubs and hard surfaces can now be removed, and surfaces cleaned with a high-pressure hose. With the potentially dirty tasks complete, loose surfaces can have their final layers applied, with clean gravel laid on top. After that, new planting plans (see p.42) can begin to take shape.

Principles of planting

ONCE the general layout of the garden is in place the greatest enjoyment comes with selecting plants. The impact plant choice can make on a garden is extraordinary. Plants give a garden style, charm, character, depth, and warmth – to mention but a few of their qualities. An adjacent street may be enhanced by an overhanging tree, which softens rigid lines and brings seasonal colour and texture to an urban landscape. A sheltered courtyard with high surrounding walls may appear like a prison yard, yet the decorative effect of a climber, such as a wisteria, trained over it will transform the space into a welcoming retreat.

Plants bring calm, clothing severity with flowing form and mellowing tones. As with soft furnishings in a house, they will also help to deaden harsh sounds. It is also increasingly accepted that, allergy sufferers notwithstanding, the presence of plants improves the atmosphere around us, possibly alleviating the effects of pollution, and certainly increasing the oxygen and moisture content of the air as well as adding a pleasing fragrance.

Ensuring plants succeed

Successful plant choice can quite literally make a garden; it might even be said that until plants and flowers are established and growing well a garden does not really exist. The garden's therapeutic powers, which can soothe the mind and alleviate tension, derive mainly from its thriving plants, and perhaps also from the presence of water and the use of sympathetic building materials. The element of quiet combined with charm and style can turn a small plot of planted land into a sanctuary. Even the most elementary of plantings, such as a well-kept lawn that has replaced a hard surface within a built environment, will bring life, colour, and softness to an otherwise harsh and alien site.

Selecting the best plants for success

The wealth of different plants available can be bewildering, but the choice will never be as limitless as it may seem. Within the categories of trees, shrubs, perennials, and so on, many plants can be dismissed immediately as inappropriate on numerous grounds: for example, incompatible soil type, climate, scale, or growth rate. Once the most suitable plants have been identified, personal preference for certain colours and shapes will limit the choice still further.

The manner and frequency of garden use will dictate the range of plants, too: for example, a garden area that is used only in summer will be planted to perform best in that season. Planting immediately around a house and along an entrance drive will also place greater demands on the choice of plant material, because year-round interest of some description will be expected. A carefully selected combination of plants that will provide a display of flowers in each season is needed. Alternatively, group plants together that combine other attributes – mix evergreens with some fruiting trees or shrubs, add plants with attractive stems or bark, and include bulbs and annuals to inject colour and interest at dull times of the year.

Defining a style of planting

In every garden there are so many variables that each one is unique. So, to talk about a particular or specific planting style may appear to impose false categories and divisions. However, there are two extremes between which all plantings fall. These are the formal and informal styles. Deciding on the degree of formality or informality required will greatly assist the initial selection of plants and the diversity of plant material used. A very formal garden, for example, may have an extremely restricted palette of plants compared to a more informal arrangement.

Formal planting

Great strength and order can be given to a garden by using only a small selection of plants but in quantity. The planting, however, does not necessarily need to be arranged in an angular and regimented fashion, or within precisely designated areas. Some formality can be achieved using sweeps of single plants in broad blocks, creating tranquillity in uniformity. Even relatively informal plants grown en masse can assume an orderly role – an expanse of ornamental grasses or bamboos

Contrasting planting styles
The style of planting within a garden or area of it can be broadly categorized as either formal or informal. Some plants lend themselves more to one style than the other. The labour involved in maintaining the formal garden (far right) is evident, but an informal planting, such as the border (right), does not necessarily involve less work: a great deal of skill and care is needed to maintain a balance between the needs and vigour of different plants when growing in close proximity.

"Editing" nature
Careful plant choices, to suit the surroundings and compete successfully with less desirable plants, produce a pleasingly naturalistic woodland scene.

planted to create a solid platform of texture can impose order and structure, for example.

The strongly architectural quality of the conventional formal garden conveys a powerful image – one of symmetry and balance, precision and accuracy. Plants may be interpreted as structural elements, more closely aligned to walls and other built elements. The sheared, trimmed, and pruned formal garden owes as much of its visual impact to the selection of appropriate plants as it does to their subsequent control and maintenance. Formal plantings will impact on a garden, summer or winter. In winter – with all else laid bare – their angular simplicity in clear bright sunshine can be most appealing. See also TOPIARY, p.76.

Formality often requires restraint, which can pose a dilemma for those who would like to design with the widest possible variety of plants. Faced with a spacious driveway approach flanked by mown lawns, for example, some gardeners may find it hard to resist the temptation to choose 20 different species of tree. Yet far greater formal impact would be achieved by repeating a single species, in regular blocks or in a continuous double line, to form a well-designed avenue.

Softening the effect

Strongly formal plantings in a garden can be varied in a number of ways, all with equal effect. Extreme forms of topiary, knot gardens, and parterres, can be planted with or alongside free-flowing informal mixtures of plants to create a marked contrast

of styles. This combination changes with the seasons and will reduce the stark impact of the formal plantings. A garden clearly divided into distinct units can also be planted with an area of marked formality to contrast with an adjacent, informal one.

The juxtaposition of styles presents a lively and stimulating garden of surprises at each turn of house corner, hedge, or shrub. Formality can also blend with informality when formal features are allowed to relax towards the informal. A finely clipped hedge of yew (*Taxus baccata*) can be planted in a serpentine line and clipped to simulate clouds, while *Ceanothus*, planted at regular intervals along the whole length of a broad border, will grow to form large mounds of equally spaced and sized yet irregularly shaped forms. Thus, a degree of formality underpins a broadly informal arrangement.

Informal planting

A planting that appears informal may in fact comprise a wealth of different plants – trees, shrubs, herbaceous perennials, and annuals – their diversity, richness, and profusion all skilfully combined to bring the colour, texture, shape, and form of unrelated plants together with dramatic effect.

As with a formal style, there are as many – if not more – variations on the theme of informality. A cottage-style garden of organized chaos, where garden plants are combined in a seemingly haphazard concoction, can rapidly become truly chaotic – an overgrown wilderness in which many

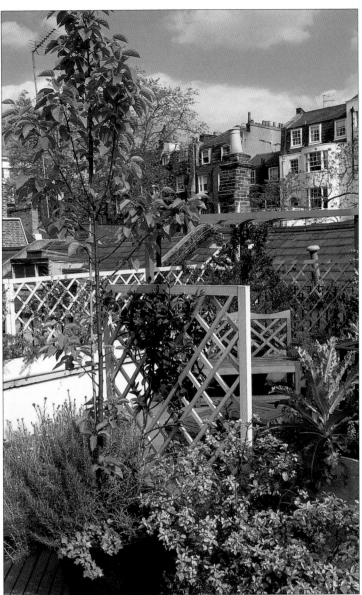

An artificial environment
Select plants suitable for the conditions: a roof may not be a natural growing site, but these sun-loving, wind-resistant plants are thriving here.

plants will not survive the inherent crowding and competition. To preserve and maintain the plant content of such a garden requires expertise and considerable time spent controlling the different plants and keeping their growth in check.

This informality of planting may be taken a few stages further by choosing a combination of plants that will grow together in harmony, whose strengths are well matched and whose climate and soil requirements are met. Herbaceous plants that require little or no support provide a good example. Cultivated garden plants can be combined to create the impression of a wild meadow or indigenous species can be planted to create a "natural" meadow (see MEADOW GARDENING, p.401). Indeed, an entire habitat can

be made up of plants that would naturally occur in the locality. Native plants will also attract wildlife to your garden by providing a welcome source of food and nesting sites.

For many people this may be taking informal gardening too far, but by studying the local environment and taking note of which plants thrive in it, the planting scheme can be adapted to cultivated garden plants. Planting a light tree canopy allows sufficient daylight to penetrate for an understorey of shrubs to be grown. Beneath this, shade-tolerant herbaceous plants will thrive after spring bulbs have faded away. This layered community of plants may appear crowded, yet they will all flourish if the chosen plants are given the appropriate light and conditions at each level of the undergrowth, throughout the season.

How to make planting plans

To plot plant groups, selections, and numbers accurately, first draw a plan to scale, using graph paper if this is helpful. A box drawn to represent 1 sq m (1 sq yd) and another to represent 4 sq m (4 sq yd) is a useful guide to the area covered by a clump of herbaceous plants and the area covered by a shrub or small tree respectively. Always use a scale that is large enough to represent the plants clearly. This may, in fact, require two scales of plan: a large-scale plan to show the general garden area (see pp.36–37) and a smaller one to detail the composition of a border. The simpler the plan the better, both for reading by others and for subsequent alterations. Numbers, symbols, or code initials can be used to indicate individual plants, but, where the scale permits, enter full plant names for instant identification.

Making the most of plants

The majority of gardens benefit from areas of calm, so the temptation to cram them with plants should be resisted. Another common planning mistake is to select as many different plants as possible: using a wide range can weaken the design, whereas the repetition of a few key plants ties the whole plan together.

On the planting plan, shade in any sectors where evergreens are to be planted, and work out how much cover will remain during winter. Also indicate where plants with coloured foliage or strong, bright flowers are to be sited in a border. This helps to assess the proportions of each colour, allowing you to maintain an even distribution, and also to calculate the number of green-leaved plants to balance the display.

Finalizing the plan

After indicating which plants are to be retained, enter key plants onto the plan. These are plants that frame a view, end a view, give height or weight, and in essence anchor the whole scheme. In the early stages such plants need not be specified; an idea of the general height and spread of the plant is all that is necessary. Make a list of suitable plants and have photographs from books, catalogues, and magazines to hand – but aim to be flexible and do not attempt to fix too rigidly on a particular plant. A meticulously planned scheme can lead to an over-designed, predictable garden where heights, colours, and spacings are too accurately determined. A few surprises

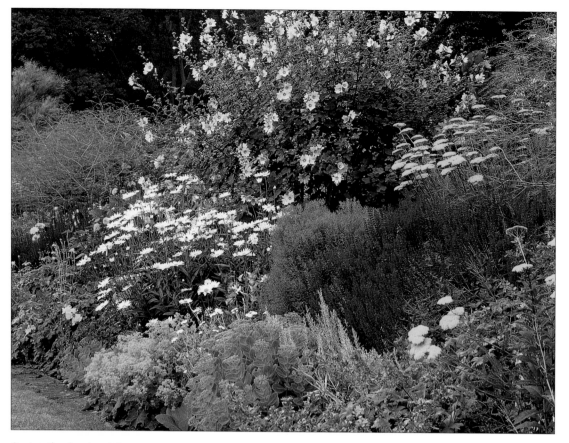

Contrasting border styles
Two borders of similar proportions and background, consisting largely of herbaceous plants in a similarly tiered array of ascending heights, nevertheless look strikingly different owing to the choice of plant material.

The flower border, above, faces onto a mown lawn, with a strip of bricks for easy mowing, where plants spill over the edges; the border, below, planted thickly with grasses is complemented by an informal, gravelled path.

should be "planned" to add spontaneity and liveliness with height occurring at close quarters or a bold colour introduced as a sharp contrast.

Grouping and planting distances

Groupings of odd numbers of plants – generally, threes, fives, sevens, or nines – create satisfactory blocks and can be used to create meandering, shallow drifts. Choosing plants that flower at different times in the drifts will also bring interest to the garden over a long period. Alternatively, a more random planting, repeating single varieties in many small groups of no less than three plants, will produce a lighter, chequerboard effect.

Unlike the interior design of a room, a planting that initially makes little impact can create a spectacular effect in just a few years. When designing and planning a garden, take account of timescale. You will need to decide if you wish to thin out

the planting in the short or long term, and whether temporary fillers are to be inserted between permanent plantings to give a little fullness to an otherwise thinly planted area.

A garden planted with semi-mature plants for an instant effect of fullness and scale can, by its very nature, present problems several years later, when those same plants are outgrowing their positions in the garden. If more space is required, valuable plant material may then need to be sacrificed to save the most treasured specimens.

One solution is to purchase a mixture of a few large but costly specimens, which will give scale, along with quite a few smaller, less expensive plants. A younger plant will frequently grow quicker and eventually overtake one that was more mature when originally planted, if a little patience can be exercised.

To calculate planting distances, you need to know the mature spread

Close spacing

The exceptions to calculating planting distance based on eventual spread are: when using hedging and edging plants; where a dense effect is needed; and when planting out bedding for a display, since bedding plants have a short life span so can tolerate cramped conditions.

of the plant or plants. Consult labels, study reference books, or seek advice from nursery staff to obtain accurate information. The last source may well be the most reliable, especially if the nursery is local, because plant performance varies between different regions. Equally valuable is advice on the time plants

take to reach maturity, since this will help you to decide whether to include either annual or longer-term perennial "filler" plants.

The distance required between two very similar plants is equal to the spread of one of them. To calculate the space needed between two different plants, simply add their spreads together and divide by two.

If possible set out all your plants on the ground, in situ, before planting according to the plan. Minor adjustments may be necessary to accommodate differing sizes of specimens and the ground plan may change if you come across buried pipes, for example, or a manhole cover that must be concealed by evergreens. Once the plants have been satisfactorily placed, they should be carefully planted out and mulched with a weed-suppressing, moisture-retentive organic medium (see TOP DRESSINGS AND MULCHES, "Organic mulches", p.626). Always ensure that the plants are nurtured carefully during their first all-important year, while they are becoming fully established.

Size and scale

In a small area (as right) be careful not to overplant: start with the heights and spreads your plants are likely to achieve when mature, then map out a pattern of overlapping discs that fill, but will not crowd, the available space. With experience, you can estimate how plants will perform in your garden in terms of vigour and size, and, space permitting, begin to sketch in bolder groupings or drifts of plants, as shown in the section of a typically English border (below). To create an annual border requires a slightly different technique: areas are mapped out for sowing, either directly onto the soil (see also p.217) or using a preliminary plan.

Planting for structure, shape, and form

WHEN selecting a plant for a bed or border, its shape, form, and eventual size are often considered of secondary importance to its flowers, fruits, or autumn hues. Yet these colourful qualities are frequently temporary, lasting just a few weeks, unlike the shape of a tree or shrub.

To create an enduring planting scheme that will look good throughout the year, select plants that offer beautiful natural forms. The structure of a plant is best appreciated at first hand, and visiting gardens where plants have matured and developed is an ideal way to appreciate their more subtle qualities.

Architectural plants

Plants with bold foliage or a dramatic form are described as architectural or accent plants; they make ideal specimens, creating considerable impact when used on their own as focal points or to contrast with their neighbours. The divided, toothed leaves of *Melianthus major* or the plume-like flowerheads of *Miscanthus sinensis* are examples of such structural plants, while spreading shrubs, such as *Aralia elata,* and the tiered branches of the tree *Cornus controversa* also offer exceptional architectural qualities.

Altering outlooks

Planting can be used to highlight garden features or disguise eyesores. For example, an ugly box-like building will retain its unsightly silhouette if a clinging creeper, such as *Parthenocissus,* is grown over it, but if a more characterful climber, such as wisteria, is used then the outline will be masked beneath its twisted branches and pendulous flowers.

Similarly, a visual barrier, such as a bank that marks a level change, can be lost when a mound-forming or horizontally tiered subject is grown on the lower level. *Viburnum plicatum* or *Euonymus alatus* would both work well in this situation.

An area of lawn can be enhanced with a specimen tree. When selecting one, the size of lawn and proximity to the house are important factors to consider, as are soil type and local climate. A specimen tree also needs to look appropriate in its setting. One with a rounded canopy will sit well on a lawn, whereas a tall spire-like form can resemble a rocket on its launch pad in such an open area.

Natural strength

Soothing greens and strong structure can help to create a restful scene. A fernery is a classic example of this style, where beautiful shapes and forms provide interest without the distraction of bright colours (see also FERNS, p.194).

Grasses add a graceful, refined structure, and the sound and movement of their rustling leaves makes them indispensable. Even in winter their skeletal forms play an important role in an otherwise bleak landscape. Planted alongside broadleaved *Macleaya cordata*, the elegant grasses *Stipa gigantea* or *Helictotrichon sempervirens* are very eye-catching.

A backdrop of large evergreens will provide colour and form when all deciduous plants have been left bare in winter. Not only do they present foliage interest and strong shapes throughout the year, but they also protect wildlife in bad weather and can be used to create permanent screens and privacy.

Evergreens that grow into naturally neat shapes resemble topiary, giving the garden a sculptural appearance without the need for trimming. Balls of *Hebe topiaria* or *H. buxifolia* make excellent accent plants along the front of a border, while *Choisya ternata* and *Viburnum* x *globosum* 'Jermyns Globe' both grow into large orbs of tight foliage.

Pruning into shapes

A plant's natural structure can be enhanced by pruning. When some willows (*Salix*) and dogwoods (*Cornus*) are pruned to the ground, or coppiced, every two years, they produce an explosion of colourful, straight stems. Limes (*Tilia*) and planes (*Platanus*) may be pollarded: if the branches are pruned back to the same point every year or two, they produce swollen "fists" at the pruning points. Both pruning methods create strong architectural forms that can greatly enhance a garden design. See also "Coppicing and pollarding shrubs", p.107.

Enduring forms
Trees create permanent structure and form in a garden setting. Look for those with interesting leaf shapes, such as Sorbus, *with its divided foliage, and the deeply lobed* leaves of Japanese maples (Acer palmatum). *Both trees have fine autumn tints and beautiful architectural outlines during winter and early spring.*

Plants for focal points
This variegated Yucca *has striking, spiky foliage in contrast to the solid, rounded outline of the giant urn. The* Tulbaghia *in the foreground accentuates the form of the* Yucca.

Topiary-like shrubs (right)
Plants that have a compact shape, such as this golden Choisya ternata SUNDANCE, *blend well with those of a looser habit, such as of the purple* Berberis *behind.*

Drifts of perennials (below)
Perennials and grasses can produce startling shapes when planted in bold drifts. Their loose stems sway in the breeze, creating the impression of rolling sea waves.

Flower forms (bottom left)
The shape and structure of stems and foliage can be matched by bold flowers. The flat flowerheads of this Achillea filipendulina *'Gold Plate' are here set off by pompon blooms of* Verbena bonariensis.

Creating contrasts (bottom centre)
Using a simple colour scheme helps to bring different forms into sharper focus. Here, tall spikes of white lupins are defined by a spreading skirt of Anthemis.

Graceful grasses (above)
A border of mixed ornamental grasses adds structure to the garden throughout the year. Here, fountains of arching flowerheads provide the focal point.

Shapely buildings (below)
Growing a structural climber, such as this wisteria, over a dull shed will give it an attractive covering.

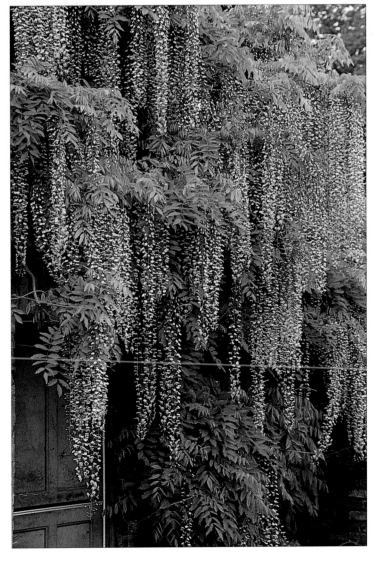

Planting for colour and texture

THE use of plant colours and textures in all their infinite variations is of central importance in successful garden design, even though many flowers – for it is the flowers that dazzle and entice – offer such a brief display. The tree peony (*Paeonia suffruticosa*) is a classic example that may bloom for only a few days, yet its huge, tissue-paper flowers make it worthy of a prominent place within a border.

When using colour in the garden personal taste can be allowed to reign almost unhindered. Yet a totally unlimited palette of colours, where every hue and tone are set against a contrasting shade, may produce an indigestible medley that would challenge even the greatest exponent of colour as a tool of garden design. Restraint should be used to limit the range and quantity of colour. For example, a backdrop of muted greens will quieten a busy foreground of mixed colours and allow the vivid shades to shine.

Colour and distance

Bright, light colours such as lemon-yellows and whites are better reflectors of sunlight than darker hues, which from a distance may be lost or appear muted. Such light colours used in the foreground will visually jump forward from their positions. These shades introduced at a distance will also appear closer, foreshortening the perceived length of a garden, usually detrimentally.

Traditionally, colours with depth, such as blues, mauves, purples, and silvers, are used to create a sense of distance at the farther reaches of a garden, with paler shades of yellow, white, cream, and pink occupying the foreground. Reds, oranges, and deep yellows are best planted in the middle of a bed; at a distance they are lost, while close up they dominate.

The influence of light

Location is an important factor to consider when choosing plant colour schemes. In strong direct sunlight, the more powerful yellows, oranges and reds become almost luminous and can produce a vibrant picture. If, however, you wish to cool down a seating area in a hot, sunny corner, silver and grey foliage and blue flowers will create a more restful setting.

A scheme of pastel colours, such as soft blue, pink, creamy-yellow, and silver will create a beautiful composition under low light conditions. A terrace or patio frequented in the evenings for entertaining and planted

Blocks of colour
Masses of flowers in a single bright colour, such as these vermilion roses, will dominate a planting scheme and arrest the attention of all who pass by.

Cool greens
There are numerous shades of green within the garden and each plays an important role calming, cooling, and harmonizing the design.

with white flowers and pale or white-variegated foliage will, in minimal light, reflect back atmospheric ghostly hues. Equally effective would be a gloomy courtyard enlivened by the use of bright shades.

Combining colours

One of the most challenging areas of garden design is creating effective colour combinations. Blue and white make elegant partners, giving a cool, clean look that is hard to rival, although for sheer purity green and white are unbeatable, especially when on the same flower such as a snowdrop or *Dicentra spectabilis* 'Alba'.

These subtle and refined combinations will be heightened if other plantings display a less restricted palette. Orange and purple, two dominant colours of equal strength, are shockingly brilliant when used together – bright orange calendulas set against the leaden purple foliage

of ornamental cabbages make an eye-catching arrangement. Blue and yellow also create a sharp contrast; the bold intensity of each introduces a lively juxtaposition of colours. When an acid-yellow tulip or *Fritillaria imperialis* 'Maxima Lutea' is mixed with the clear blue of forget-me-nots (*Myosotis*) or ceanothus, the interplay can be truly electric.

Adding texture

Many plants exhibit rich foliage texture, and interesting effects can be achieved when they are planted in broad swathes. A sweep of lavender (*Lavandula*) or rosemary (*Rosmarinus*), clipped annually, will grow into soft mounds of dense aromatic growth, equal in beauty to any herbaceous flower border.

Even plants of little decorative interest individually can be useful in groups. The shrubby honeysuckle, *Lonicera nitida*, or many of the

bamboos provide masses of textural variations, and make excellent hedging (see BAMBOOS, p.96).

A play of different textures creates subtle interest, even within a single plant. A yew (*Taxus*), for example, clipped neatly below but allowed to spread out at the top to form long, loose stems, provides a wonderful textural contrast. A layered look can be achieved with mixed plantings; the feathery fronds of shuttlecock fern (*Matteuccia struthiopteris*) set off by the vast flat leaves of *Gunnera manicata*, in turn backed by white-stemmed birch (*Betula*), for instance.

Tree stems have tactile qualities that should not be overlooked. Old sweet chestnuts (*Castanea sativa*) develop deep, furrowed bark that contrasts well with smooth, horizontal shapes, while shrubs, such as *Hydrangea aspera* subsp. *sargentiana* and *Euonymus phellomanus* also produce eye-catching barks.

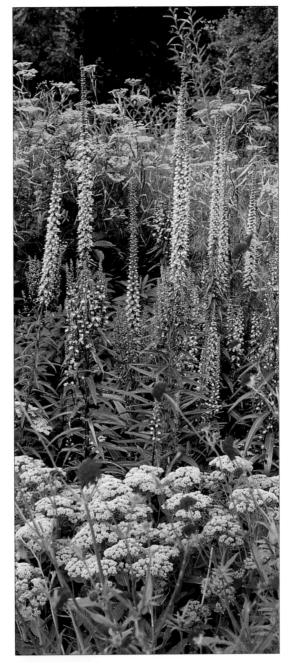

Traditional palette (above)
The classic combination of white, pink, and blue is perfect for this romantically planted garden.

Fiery borders (above right)
Beds of hot reds, oranges, and rich yellows are energizing and best sited where the sun can illuminate the glowing colours.

Spot colour (far right)
Buttons of dark red Knautia macedonica *are thrown into sharp focus when grown against the pale hues of the sedum and foxgloves in the background.*

Simple schemes (right)
Elegant, white daisies and irises edge a tranquil pool, echoing the white window of the house beyond.

Peeling bark (far left)
The beautiful Japanese maple, Acer griseum, *has wonderful chestnut-coloured bark that peels to resemble wood shavings. It is particularly noticeable when used as a specimen tree in a winter garden.*

Pleated leaves (centre left)
The intricately pleated leaves of Veratrum nigrum *provide a strong architectural accent when sited in a sunny or partially shaded spot.*

Textural contrasts (left)
Complementary textures and shapes heighten interest here, where the wispy, hair-like spikelets of Hordeum jubatum *fall gracefully behind* Echinops ritro, *with its stiff upright stems of spiny blue flowers.*

Planting for seasonal and year-round interest

THE art of planting the well-planned garden is for each season to bring new richness and interest. All too often, from late spring to midsummer, a garden builds up week after week to a peak, but then descends rapidly into a flowerless abyss in autumn and winter. With more than half the year remaining and some late fine weather still to come, it is important to plan for these often-forgotten months.

A garden should contain a well-chosen collection of plants to carry interest throughout these seasons of reduced light and growth. A permanent framework of planting, formed by trees, shrubs, and hedges, will create the basic skeleton onto which a series of overlaying levels – climbers, herbaceous plants, bedding plants, and bulbs – can be used to provide beauty and interest throughout each season.

Extended interest
Crocosmia *'Lucifer'* is invaluable for its long-lasting interest. In spring, sword-like, architectural leaves emerge, followed in late summer by sprays of scarlet flowers (right). The seedheads look good, too, when dusted with frost (above).

Spring
Late winter and early spring are not only a time for flowers but also a season for sweet scents. Shrubs, such as Christmas box (*Sarcococca confusa*), the winter honeysuckle (*Lonicera* x *purpusii*), wintersweet (*Chimonanthus praecox*), and the many beautiful species of Daphne fill the air with their powerful perfumes. Bulbs offer early colour, when aconites (*Eranthis hyemalis*) and snowdrops (*Galanthus*) compete to be the first to flower, followed by crocuses, narcissi, and tulips. The bulbs are joined by the earliest flowering perennials, such as hellebores,

and later, as the bulbs die down, other herbaceous plants fill the gaps.

Summer
Early summer heralds an explosion of colour from herbaceous perennials, with every shade, shape, and form working together to create a luxuriance unrivalled throughout the rest of the year. Peonies, delphiniums, campanulas, and lupins give a spectacular display, while roses perform alongside deutzias, mallows (*Lavatera*), and philadelphus in the shrub border. As summer peaks, large-flowered clematis can be used to scramble over spring-flowering

shrubs, such as forsythia. Later on, annuals like *Nicotiana* and *Cosmos* fill gaps between shrubs, and tender or half-hardy perennials, such as penstemons and diascias, brighten bed or border colour schemes.

Autumn
The well-maintained garden, where regular dead-heading and careful interplanting have been carried out, can often reach a peak in this season. As well as the overspill of summer blooms, late-flowering perennials like Japanese anemones, crocosmias, and Michaelmas daisies (*Aster novi-belgii*) perform through the autumn.

As the light pales, clusters of dark pink blooms open on *Clerodendrum bungei*, scenting the cool air with its rich sweet fragrance.

Foliage tints begin to fire up in autumn, with trees such as maples and *Parrotia persica* slowly turning every shade of yellow, orange, purple, and red. The large leaves of *Vitis coignetiae* also provide spectacular colour before they fall. Berries and fruits contribute to the richness of autumn hues, with viburnums and *Euonymus* decorating the garden with their jewelled displays.

Flowering bulbs and corms, such as cyclamen and colchicums, contribute to the autumn display, too.

Winter
The depths of winter are the most testing times in the garden, when colour and interest are most difficult to achieve. It is now that permanent structures take centre stage. The stems of deciduous shrubs and trees, such as silver birch (*Betula*) and colourful dogwoods (*Cornus*), shine out in the weak winter sunlight.

The texture, form, and shape of evergreens furnish the winter garden when all else is bare. A well-trained ceanothus or the rounded clumps of *Euphorbia characias* give substance to otherwise "empty" borders. Meanwhile some evergreen shrubs, such as *Skimmia japonica* and *Viburnum tinus,* put on displays of bead-like flower buds. These are accompanied by the highly scented flowers of *Viburnum* x *bodnantense*, which will break into bloom at the first hint of milder weather.

Seasonal sunlight
Not only planting schemes alter with the seasons; sunlight can also be used throughout the year to highlight evolving shapes and forms. Here, the weak winter sun casts long shadows that stretch over a colourful carpet of Cyclamen coum, *the flowers of which open throughout the winter as light filters through the leafless trees.*

Early to mid-spring

Among the first flowers to bloom in early spring are the bulbs. Here, bold swathes of narcissi have been planted to brighten up the borders with their nodding heads of golden-yellow flowers and strap-like foliage. These are accompanied by spikes of spurge (Euphorbia) and emerging perennials, the foliage of which is now pushing its way through the soil.

Late spring

As spring progresses and light levels increase, borders rapidly fill out with lush foliage and early flowers, which help to camouflage the fading blooms and leaves of early bulbs. Here, blue geraniums and wavy-edged, rounded-leaved lady's mantle (Alchemilla mollis) dominate in the foreground, while similarly tinted flowers thrive towards the end of the garden.

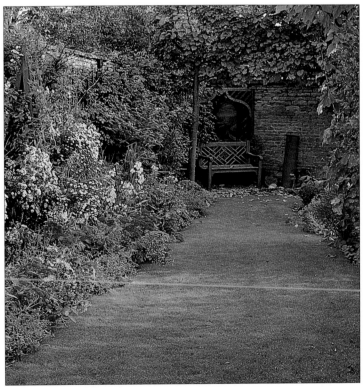

High summer

A profusion of flowers, including the blue geraniums that are still in bloom, heralds the height of summer. Pastel blues, soft yellows, and creamy-whites create a cool border that takes the heat out of the summer sun. These colours also give the illusion of extended perspective, making the border look longer and leading the eye to the seating area at the far end.

Summer into autumn

The pale pastels have given way to splashes of fiery red designed to mirror tree and shrub foliage that will soon be taking on its vibrant autumn tints. This border scheme shows how planting can be used to change the colour and mood, and alter perspectives, in the garden as the seasons progress, building up to a crescendo as summer turns into autumn.

CHAPTER

2

ORNAMENTAL TREES

MORE THAN ANY other plants, trees create a sense of permanence and maturity in a garden. They add height, structure, and sculptural focal points, while their large and distinctive silhouettes form an attractive contrast with the softer lines of other planting. There is an enormous variety of trees, differing in shape and form as well as in the colour and texture of foliage, flowers, and bark. Each has a particular appeal, from the pointed column of a cypress to the blazing autumn colour of a Japanese maple or the patterned trunk of *Eucalyptus*. Trees may be grown in many ways: an informal woodland of hazels and birches, surrounded by bulbs, has naturalistic charm, while an avenue of copper beeches is suitably elegant in a formal setting. Some trees – such as magnolias – are best sited on their own as specimen features.

Trees for the garden

ORNAMENTAL trees are grown for the beauty of their flowers, bark, or decorative fruits, rather than for edible or timber crops. Many fruit trees, however, are graced by beautiful flowers and a few ornamental trees, such as crab apples (*Malus*), bear rich crops of fruits for preserving. The distinction between trees and shrubs is similarly blurred; the former usually, but not always, with a single trunk and the latter, for example lilacs (*Syringa*), multi-stemmed although sometimes reaching tree-like proportions.

Choosing trees

Trees are generally the largest and longest-lived garden plants, and selecting and siting them are major design decisions. The fewer trees a garden can accommodate, the more important careful choice and siting become; in a "one-tree garden" these points are crucial to the success of the design. The general appearance and special features of a tree obviously matter, but its suitability for a garden's soil, climate, and aspect, and its ultimate height, spread, and growth rate, are equally important.

Once a tree is chosen, the design process continues, by deciding where to plant it (see "Choosing a planting site", p.63). Garden centres stock a limited range of the most popular ornamental trees; specialist nurseries, some with a mail-order service, offer a wider choice.

Heights range from about 1m (3ft) for some dwarf conifers to the massive 90m (300ft) of a redwood (*Sequoia*). Growth rates vary from 2.5cm (1in) or less a year for dwarf conifers to 1m (3ft) or more for some poplars (*Populus*). A young tree in a garden centre gives little or no indication of its potential size and some species, particularly conifers, include both miniature and very large cultivars. Select cultivars with care and, if offered substitutes, make sure that they will be equally appropriate for your needs.

Trees as design elements

Trees create a strong visual impact in the same way as do hard landscaping features. They also help to form the permanent framework of a garden, around which the more temporary elements come and go.

Trees may be used as living sculptures (see "Specimen trees", p.55): a simple, contrasting setting is most likely to enhance a tree used in this way. A tree with pale or variegated foliage looks very striking against a hedge of dark green yew (*Taxus baccata*), for example, while

Trees in the large garden
Trees add structure to a garden and form a long-term part of the design framework. A large garden should include several, varying in height and shape. Group several trees together to create a strong impact of colour and form, as in this informal arrangement of maples (Acer) *and other deciduous trees.*

Enclosing space
The arching fronds of palms are used as structural features to enclose and delineate a seating area. They create a lush, cool screen that forms a less rigid division than a wall or fence.

Specimen tree
Trees that are particularly attractive or well shaped are best sited on their own so that they stand out in the scheme. This double pink hawthorn (Crataegus laevigata *'Rosea Flore Pleno'*) *has a fine show of blossom that may be enjoyed from all viewpoints as well as forming a cornerstone in the design.*

the bold winter tracery of bare branches stands out well in front of a white-painted wall.

Used structurally, trees can also define or enclose space. A stately row or an informal clump of trees can mark the boundary of a property, separate one part of the garden from another, or emphasize a path. A pair of trees might act as a verdant frame for a distant view or form an attractive living arch through which the garden is entered.

Shape and form

The shape and form of a tree are as important as its size – in setting the mood and style as well as in practical considerations of space. Some trees, such as many ornamental cherries (*Prunus*), are small and charming, while others, such as cedars (*Cedrus*), are grand and monumental. Most can be formal or informal, according to the setting and treatment. *Rhus typhina* has a striking architectural form, which is ideal for a modern, paved garden, while the arching fronds of many palms bring lushness to a courtyard or conservatory. Rowans (*Sorbus aucuparia*) and hollies (*Ilex*) are typical English cottage garden trees; Japanese maples (*Acer palmatum*) and the large *Salix babylonica* var. *pekinensis* 'Tortuosa' are suitable for Oriental gardens; native species are ideal for wild gardens.

Narrow, upright trees, such as *Malus tschonoskii*, are suitable for small gardens but have a formal, almost artificial appearance. Round-headed or wide-spreading trees seem more informal but cast much more shade and rain shadow, making underplanting difficult, while those with an irregular, open-branch framework have a naturalistic appeal. Cone- or pyramid-shaped trees have a sculptural effect, while weeping trees have a softer silhouette.

Consider how long the tree takes to develop its characteristic shape – in some cases, it can be decades. Prunus 'Kanzan', for example, has a stiff growth habit when young, with awkwardly angled branches; yet after ten years the branches begin to arch and by 30 years the tree has a graceful, rounded crown.

Where space allows, combining contrasting tree shapes can create a dynamic effect, but planting many differently shaped trees may simply appear fussy and uncoordinated.

Specimen trees

A specimen tree is grown on its own to develop and display its full natural beauty without competition from other trees. Depending on the climate, Chinese dogwood (*Cornus kousa* var. *chinensis*), weeping willow (*Salix* x *sepulcralis* var. *chrysocoma*), various ornamental cherries (*Prunus*), and palms such as *Howea* and *Phoenix* are popular specimen trees. A specimen tree can be effective as a focal point in all scales of surroundings, although you should select a tree that is the right size for its setting – tiny specimen trees look lost in vast gardens and outsized ones

---

TREE SHAPES

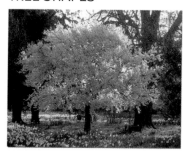

Spreading
Prunus x *yedoensis* (Yoshino cherry)

Pyramidal
Carpinus betulus 'Fastigiata' (Upright common hornbeam)

Conical
Sequoiadendron giganteum (Giant redwood)

Weeping
Salix caprea 'Kilmarnock' (Kilmarnock willow)

Round-headed
Malus 'Magdeburgensis' (Crab apple)

Arching
Archontophoenix alexandrae (King palm)

Columnar
Acer rubrum 'Columnare' (Red maple)

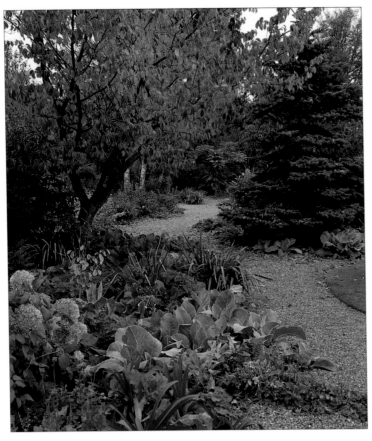

Foliage colour and texture
Here, the autumn foliage of a deciduous tree is offset by the blue-green mass of a conifer, creating a contrasting tableau of colour, texture, and shape.

overbearing in confined spaces. Specimen trees, particularly in formal gardens, are traditionally placed in the centre of a lawn. Siting a specimen tree to one side, however, can add a sense of liveliness and informality to a scheme as well as allowing a view down the garden. Other options include planting a specimen tree next to a gate or

garden entrance, or at the bottom or top of a flight of steps, to mark the transition from one space in the garden to another.

Planting in a swathe of gravel or ground-cover plants such as ivy (*Hedera*) or periwinkle (*Vinca*) provides a complementary foil for a specimen tree. In a mixed border, use a tree as the keystone around which to build the colour and form of the surrounding groups of plants. A specimen tree may be reflected in a garden pond or offset by a statue or white-painted bench beneath it, so that each element enhances the other.

Grouping trees

If space allows, consider planting three or more trees together in informal clumps of the same or different species. A group of trees also creates a more substantial, curtain-like frame than a single tree for one or both sides of a view. Clumps of large trees such as oaks (*Quercus*) or beeches (*Fagus*) make focal points on a grand scale, as exemplified in the landscapes of the great 18th-century English landscape gardener, Capability Brown. In warmer climates, stands of tall, bare-

Colour from flowers
The large blooms of Magnolia campbellii *subsp.* mollicomata *stand out against the bare branches.*

trunked palms can be equally impressive on their own in grass or interplanted with lower-growing or multi-stemmed species.

On a smaller scale, a modest group of deciduous trees with light foliage, such as birches (*Betula pendula*) or maples (*Acer*), can form the backbone of a miniature woodland. The dappled shade and leafy soil are perfect for daffodils, bluebells (*Hyacinthoides non-scripta*), and primroses (*Primula vulgaris*).

Trees in informal groups can be planted closer than the combined potential spread of their crowns. Relatively tall, narrow, or asymmetrical growth may result but the effect can be pleasantly informal, with intermingled branches forming attractive tracery against the sky.

Features of interest

Although trees are most often valued for their architectural qualities, they also provide interest through particular features such as flowers, foliage, berries, and bark. Site a tree so that its attractive characteristics are shown off to advantage (see also "Successional interest", p.57).

Leaves

For sheer mass and duration of display, leaves are by far the most important feature. Their shape, size, and colour offer infinite variation, from the delicate, golden, ferny foliage of *Gleditsia triacanthos* 'Sunburst' to the huge, architectural leaves of palms such as *Phoenix*. Surface texture affects how light is reflected, with glossy leaves adding a

Interest from bark and stems
*The striking, white skeleton of a silver birch (*Betula utilis *var.* jacquemontii*) brings bright relief to the garden in the gloom of winter, while its bold silhouette forms a strong focal point in the planting design all year round.*

bright touch. The density of the canopy ranges from opaque to airy, an important factor if considering underplanting around a tree.

Trees with coloured or variegated foliage, such as the reddish-purple of *Prunus virginiana* 'Schubert' or the yellow-edged leaves of *Ligustrum lucidum* 'Excelsum Superbum', provide a mass of colour that contrasts well with green-leaved trees.

Some leaves, such as those of *Eucalyptus*, are pleasantly aromatic, while others, such as those of an aspen, quiver in the slightest breeze, adding the extra pleasure of sound.

Flowers

Flowers have a fleeting but memorable presence and range from modest to opulent. Autumn, winter, and early spring flowers are especially valuable when there may be less interest from other plants.

Flower colour should complement the larger scheme. Pale flowers stand out against dark leaves, while dark flowers show up best in a pale setting. By training climbers such as clematis or roses up mature trees, you can extend the floral display.

Fragrance is a bonus, ranging from the subtle, winter perfume of *Acacia dealbata* to the heady, summer scent of the Japanese big-leaf magnolia (*Magnolia obovata*) and frangipani (*Plumeria rubra* f. *acutifolia*). For flowers and fragrance, a sheltered situation is best.

Fruits, berries, and pods

These can rival or exceed flowers in beauty, ranging from the bright red, strawberry-like fruits of *Arbutus* and the yellow crab apples of *Malus*

'Golden Hornet' to the sculptural seed pods of magnolias. In warm climates, trees like lemons and figs may be laden with eye-catching fruits.

Certain trees, such as hollies (*Ilex*), need cross-pollination to fruit; others fruit only when mature or when particular climatic conditions are met. Birds find some ornamental berries such as those of rowan (*Sorbus aucuparia*) tempting and may strip them when barely ripe, but you can choose trees with less appealing berries. Other fruiting trees, such as *Crataegus* x *lavallei* 'Carrierei', ripen late and therefore their fruits persist well into spring. Ask garden centre staff for advice.

Bark and branches

Bark can provide colour and textural interest, especially in winter. Options include the mahogany-red, silky sheen of *Prunus serrula*, the ghostly white bark of *Betula utilis* var. *jacquemontii,* and the exotic-looking *Eucalyptus pauciflora* subsp. *niphophila* with its python-like, green, grey, and creamy-white bark.

The scarlet willow (*Salix alba* var. *vitellina* 'Britzensis') bears scarlet-orange young branches, brilliant when lit from behind, and the golden willow (*S. alba* var. *vitellina*) has rich yellow shoots. These fast-growing trees are best pruned regularly to produce new shoots as these have the strongest colour. Some trees bear showy bark only when mature; others colour well when young.

Successional interest

Plants that change character with the seasons give a garden a lively tempo. With careful choice and planning, orchestrate their display as foliage, flowers, fruits, berries, and pods come and go against a permanent framework of branches and bark. By planting trees that flower successively, such as a Judas tree (*Cercis siliquastrum*) for spring, *Catalpa bignonioides* for summer, *Eucryphia* x *nymansensis* for early autumn, and *Prunus subhirtella* 'Autumnalis' for winter, ongoing interest is maintained, with the focal point altering as the seasons change. Some trees provide interest all year round, either from their evergreen foliage, or from their fine shape.

Deciduous trees offer the greatest scope to exploit seasonal changes, especially in spring, when many ornamental cherries (*Prunus*) are covered with beautiful blossom, and in autumn, when many maples (*Acer*) have brilliantly coloured foliage. Evergreen trees, on the other

TREES WITH ORNAMENTAL BARK

Acer capillipes

Eucalyptus dalrympleana

Betula utilis var. *jacquemontii*

Acer griseum

Acer pensylvanicum

Prunus serrula

hand, provide a sense of continuity rather than change. Selecting and planting a mixture of deciduous and evergreen trees provides lasting interest in the garden that changes with the seasons to create a dynamic rather than a static effect.

Spring and summer

In spring, emerging leaves and flower buds bring fresh life to the bare branches of deciduous trees. Some – such as the silver-leaved *Sorbus aria* 'Lutescens' – have particularly fine young foliage. As the trees come fully into leaf, they take on their characteristic outlines while the canopies provide striking blocks of colour and texture as well as shade.

In late spring and summer, flowers, ranging in colour and form from the trailing, yellow chains of *Laburnum* to the upright cream or reddish-pink candles of horse chestnuts (*Aesculus*), add extra colour and interest to lighten the dense effect of the massed leaves.

Autumn and winter

When most herbaceous plants die down in autumn, the colour provided by trees is particularly welcome, whether from leaves turning from green through shades of yellow, orange, and red to brown, or from the bright flecks of colour from fruits or berries. Ornamental members of the Rosaceae, especially those from the genera *Cotoneaster*, *Crataegus*, *Malus*, and *Sorbus*, include many species, cultivars, and hybrids that have a handsome display in autumn; in some cases, the fruits will remain on the tree right through the winter months.

In winter, many trees stand out most effectively with little else in the garden to compete with them. Their skeletons or silhouettes become most noticeable and create greater sculptural impact. The colour and texture provided by coniferous and broad-leaved evergreens may be used to complement and soften the architectural, "hard" look of nearby deciduous trees, while patterned, textured, or peeling bark adds an extra point of interest. A few

conifers, such as forms of Japanese cedar (*Cryptomeria japonica*), have foliage that takes on attractive russet overtones during winter.

Trees for small gardens

For small gardens, trees that do not reach more than about 6m (20ft) in height are the most suitable. There may only be space for just one tree (see "Specimen trees", p.55), so those that provide more than one season of interest are especially valuable. A Japanese crab apple (*Malus floribunda*), for example, produces masses of crimson buds, then pale pink or white flowers, and finally small red or yellow fruits, on arching branches.

A deciduous tree's appearance when leafless is very important in a small garden, since the tree may be bare for six months each year and visible from every window facing the garden. Good choices include *Rhus typhina*, fig (*Ficus carica*), and *Pyrus salicifolia* 'Pendula'. None has showy flowers but all have handsome foliage and winter silhouettes with character.

Heavily thorned or prickly trees such as hawthorns (*Crataegus*) or hollies (*Ilex*) may be unsuitable in a very small garden as they may restrict access on either side, while those such as some limes (*Tilia*) that

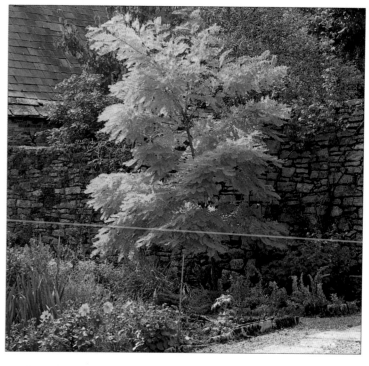

Small-garden tree
The modest stature of this Robinia pseudoacacia *'Frisia' makes it a suitable choice for a small garden. Its airy foliage brightens up the grey stone wall behind and casts only light shade, allowing other plants to grow beneath it.*

drip sticky honeydew should not be sited where they will overhang an area for sitting out. If planning to underplant, choose a light-foliaged, deep-rooted tree, such as *Gleditsia* or *Robinia*, because small plants seldom compete successfully with the shallow, greedy roots of ornamental cherries (*Prunus*), for example.

Trees for avenues

Primarily used in formal settings, avenues rely on the uniformity of trees and spacing for their grand effect. The longer and straighter the avenue, the more impact the rhythm of the trees and their shadows has on the landscape. Trees should be sited so that they lead the eye to an impressive feature or focal point; large trees are often used on either side of a drive to line the route to the house. Long-term, forest trees such as beeches (*Fagus*) and horse chestnuts (*Aesculus*) are traditionally used for avenues, while the strong shapes of conifers may be more striking in a contemporary design. Trees such as whitebeam (*Sorbus aria*) or the evergreen Chinese privet (*Ligustrum lucidum*) are particularly suitable for smaller gardens.

Informal avenues may also be created, perhaps with the young trees bent and tied over each side to form an arch over a walkway. The spacing may be less rigid than for a formal avenue to avoid a regimented look.

Training for effect

Trees may be pleached to create an elegant formality. The side branches are trained to meet in horizontal,

Formal, pleached avenue
In this large, formal garden, rows of pleached limes lead the eye to the two arches framing the view beyond, linking the garden with the landscape.

parallel lines and other growth is cut back or interwoven to form a vertical screen. Beeches, limes (*Tilia*), hornbeams (*Carpinus*), and planes (*Platanus*) are traditional trees for pleaching and, in the fruit garden, espaliered apples and pears provide a variation of this technique.

Pollarding involves regularly lopping back the entire crown to short stumps that produce dense, thin branches and a single, tight ball of foliage. It achieves a formal, if artificial, effect and is useful in urban areas where a natural crown would cast too much shade or impede traffic. Some willows (*Salix*) are often pollarded or coppiced (cut back to ground level) for their colourful young shoots. Coppiced trees look appropriate in a naturalistic or informal setting such as a woodland garden or on the banks of a pond.

Trees for screens and shelter belts

Large-scale tree planting can screen buildings and roads, deaden noise, and provide shelter from wind and frost. A single, straight row of fast-growing Lombardy poplars (*Populus nigra* 'Italica') is often planted to screen eyesores, but their great

height and finger-like shape tend to highlight what they are intended to conceal. Looser, wider stands of mixed deciduous and evergreen trees are usually more natural-looking and effective. Hedges are the most compact and densest form of screening and their size can be controlled (see HEDGES AND SCREENS, pp.84–86).

Trees en masse can filter wind, reducing potential damage more effectively than solid barriers, which often create wind swirl on the leeward side. A shelter belt or group of trees can protect vulnerable plants from frost, especially in spring.

Trees in containers

Growing trees in large pots or tubs greatly extends their design potential. In roof, patio, or courtyard gardens, a collection of containerized trees is the quickest way to create a well-established appearance, adding both height and structure to the design.

Use trees in large pots or tubs to frame a doorway that is surrounded by hard paving or to flank wide steps; these positions are particularly appropriate for topiary (see TOPIARY, pp.76–77). Trees too tender to overwinter outside may be grown in containers, displayed outdoors in summer, and moved to a frost-free place as cold weather approaches. Annuals and tender plants such as petunias, fuchsias, or trailing nasturtiums (*Tropaeolum*) may be included in the container for seasonal colour and interest, or ivy (*Hedera*) for permanent ground cover.

Containerized trees are long-term features, so use containers that are durable and attractive. A wide range of sizes, styles and materials is available, (see CONTAINER GARDENING, "Choosing containers", p.320). Make sure that the containers you choose are frostproof, if they are to be permanent features in an area of the garden that is subject to frost.

Informal walkway
Flowering cherries, arching over a path, bring height and structure to a garden with free, informal planting while complementing the character of the setting. The spring display of the arch draws attention up and away from the borders which will in turn fill out and become the centre of interest as the blossom fades.

Container-planted trees
Small trees grown in containers are valuable for bringing colour, vitality, and sculptural interest to a patio, terrace, or balcony. Here, plain paving acts as a stage on which to display an elegant Japanese maple (Acer palmatum 'Dissectum Atropurpureum') in an ornamental trough.

Planter's guide to trees

TREES FOR SMALL GARDENS

Acer capillipes ♠, *A.* x *conspicuum*
  'Silver Vein' ♠, *A. griseum* ♠,
  A. palmatum, A. palmatum
  'Sango-kaku', *A. pseudoplatanus*
  'Brilliantissimum' ♠
Aesculus californica ♠
Amelanchier lamarckii
Arbutus x *andrachnoides*
Betula albosinensis var.
  septentrionalis ♠, *B. ermanii* ♠,
  B. pendula ♠, *B. pendula*
  'Dalecarlica' ♠, *B. utilis*
  var. *jacquemontii* ♠
Catalpa bignonioides 'Aurea'
Cercidiphyllum japonicum ♠
Cercis siliquastrum
Cinnamomum camphora ❀
Cornus kousa
Crataegus laciniata ♠, *C. laevigata*
  'Paul's Scarlet', *C.* x *lavallei*
  'Carrierei'
Cydonia oblonga
Eucalyptus pauciflora subsp.
  niphophila ♠
Fagus sylvatica 'Dawyck Gold' ♠
Gleditsia triacanthos 'Sunburst' ♠
Grevillea robusta ❀ ♠
Hoheria lyallii
Laburnum x *watereri* 'Vossii'
Maackia amurensis ♠
Magnolia 'Elizabeth',
  M. 'Galaxy' ♠,
  M. x *loebneri* 'Merrill' ♠

Pyrus calleryana
'Chanticleer'

Malus 'Dartmouth',
  M. 'Evereste' ♠,
  M. floribunda,
  M. 'Golden Hornet',
  M. tschonoskii ♠
Melia azedarach
Mespilus germanica ♠
Phoenix dactylifera ❀ ♠
Pinus halepensis ♠
Prunus – many including
  P. 'Okame', *P.* 'Pandora',
  P. 'Spire', *P.* x *subhirtella*,
  P. x *yedoensis*
Pyrus calleryana 'Chanticleer',
  P. salicifolia 'Pendula'
Robinia pseudoacacia 'Frisia' ♠
Sorbus aria (some forms),
  S. aucuparia (some forms),
  S. cashmiriana,
  S. commixta 'Embley',
  S. vilmorinii
Stewartia pseudocamellia
Vitex agnus-castus

WINTER INTEREST

Decorative flowers
Acacia dealbata
Magnolia campbellii 'Charles
  Raffill', *M. sprengeri* (and
  hybrids), *M.* 'Star Wars'
Prunus incisa, P. mume,
  P. x *subhirtella* 'Autumnalis',
  P. x *subhirtella* 'Autumnalis
  Rosea'
Salix daphnoides 'Aglaia'

Golden foliage
Alnus glutinosa 'Aurea'
Chamaecyparis lawsoniana
  'Lanei Aurea', *C. lawsoniana*
  'Stewartii', *C. lawsoniana*
  'Winston Churchill'
x *Cupressocyparis leylandii*
  'Castlewellan', x *C. leylandii*
  'Robinson's Gold'
Cupressus arizonica 'Pyramidalis',
  C. macrocarpa 'Goldcrest',
  C. sempervirens 'Swane's Gold'
Juniperus chinensis 'Aurea'
Pinus sylvestris 'Aurea'
Salix elaeagnos, S. exigua
Sorbus aria 'Lutescens'
Thuja plicata 'Zebrina'
Tsuga mertensiana f. *argentea*

Grey foliage
Cedrus atlantica f. *glauca*
Chamaecyparis lawsoniana
  'Pembury Blue'
Cupressus glabra 'Pyramidalis'
Eucalyptus coccifera ❀,
  E. pauciflora
Tsuga mertensiana 'Glauca'

Decorative bark
Acer capillipes, A. x *conspicuum*
  'Silver Vein', *A. davidii,*
  A. davidii 'Serpentine',
  A. griseum, A. grosseri var. *hersii,*
  A. palmatum 'Sango-kaku',
  A. pensylvanicum (and forms),
Arbutus x *andrachnoides,*
  A. menziesii
Betula albo-sinensis var.
  septentrionalis, B. dahurica,
  B. 'Jermyns', *B. pendula,*
  B. utilis var. *jacquemontii*
Eucalyptus dalrympleana,
  E. pauciflora, E. pauciflora subsp.
  niphophila
Luma apiculata
Pinus bungeana
Prunus maackii 'Amber Beauty',
  P. serrula
Salix acutifolia 'Blue Streak',
  S. alba var. *vitellina* 'Britzensis',
  S. daphnoides,
  S. 'Erythroflexuosa'
Stewartia pseudocamellia
Tilia cordata 'Winter Orange'

TREES FOR CONTAINERS
Acacia baileyana, A. dealbata ❀
Albizia julibrissin ❀
Araucaria heterophylla ❀
Citrus medica ❀
Cordyline australis ❀
Cupressus macrocarpa 'Goldcrest',
  C. sempervirens
Dracaena draco ❀
Eriobotrya japonica ❀
Ficus benjamina ❀
Grevillea robusta ❀
Jacaranda mimosifolia ❀
Juniperus scopulorum 'Skyrocket'
Lagerstroemia indica ❀
Laurus nobilis

Ficus benjamina
'Variegata'

Magnolia grandiflora
  'Galissonnière'
Olea europaea
Prunus 'Amanogawa',
  P. 'Kiku-shidare-zakura'
Salix caprea 'Kilmarnock'
Taxus baccata 'Standishii'
Trachycarpus fortunei

TWO OR MORE SEASONS OF INTEREST

All year round
Acacia dealbata ❀
Acer capillipes, A. palmatum
  'Sango-kaku'
Arbutus x *andrachnoides,*
  A. menziesii
Betula albo-sinensis var.
  septentrionalis, B. ermanii,
  B. 'Jermyns', *B. utilis* var.
  jacquemontii
Cornus kousa var. *chinensis*
Eucalyptus ficifolia ❀
Ilex x *altaclerensis* 'Golden King'
Magnolia grandiflora

Winter/Spring
Acer negundo
Arbutus x *andrachnoides*
Pyrus pashia

Spring/Autumn
Amelanchier lamarckii
Crataegus x *lavallei* 'Carrierei'
Malus 'Evereste', *M.* 'Golden
  Hornet'
Prunus 'Accolade', *P.* 'Okame',
  P. sargentii
Sorbus cashmiriana, S. commixta
  'Embley'

Summer/Autumn
Catalpa bignonioides
Cladrastis lutea
Cornus kousa,
  C. kousa var. *chinensis*
Eucryphia glutinosa
Fagus sylvatica 'Dawyck Gold'
Liriodendron tulipifera
Stewartia pseudocamellia
Tilia 'Petiolaris'

Autumn/Winter
Acer capillipes, A. davidii,
  A. griseum, A. palmatum
  'Sango-kaku', *A. pensylvanicum*
  'Erythrocladum'
Stewartia pseudocamellia

SPECIMEN TREES
Abies magnifica, A. procera
Acer pensylvanicum,
  A. pseudoplatanus, A. rubrum
Aesculus hippocastanum
Alnus cordata
Betula 'Jermyns',
  B. pendula 'Dalecarlica'
Cedrus
Eucalyptus coccifera ❀,
  E. dalrympleana
Fraxinus angustifolia RAYWOOD
  ('Flame')
Liquidambar styraciflua,
  L. styraciflua 'Lane Roberts'
Liriodendron tulipifera
Livistona ❀
Magnolia campbellii,
  M. campbellii 'Charles
  Raffill'

*Liriodendron
tulipifera*

*Metasequoia
  glyptostroboides*
Nothofagus alpina
Nyssa sylvatica
Phoenix ❀
Picea breweriana, P. omorika
Pinus nigra, P. radiata,
  P. sylvestris, P. wallichiana
Platanus x *hispanica*
Roystonea ❀
Salix x *sepulcralis*
  var. *chrysocoma*
Sequoiadendron giganteum
Tilia 'Petiolaris', *T. platyphyllos*
Tsuga heterophylla
Zelkova carpinifolia

Key
❀ Not hardy
♠ May grow to 6m (20ft) or more

Hardy palms and the exotic look

Iₙ the past, in frost-prone regions, many beautiful tropical and sub-tropical plants were grown for their ornamental effect in the protected environment of heated glasshouses. As the costs of maintenance – particularly heating – soared during the twentieth century, the cultivation of these "exotics" declined. Recently, however, a new style of gardening has emerged that recreates the visual impact of tropical and subtropical plants in sheltered, outdoor gardens in temperate regions. This style makes use of hardy, half-hardy, and some tender plants with striking shapes, distinctive textures, handsome, large foliage, and vivid flowers.

In frost-prone climates, most of the plants used should be hardy enough to survive year-round. Planting schemes can then be varied during frost-free months by integrating half-hardy or tender, container-grown exotics into the design (see also p.61). These can be used as focal points, or placed strategically within the overall framework of the planting to create seasonal interest. Such displays require careful planning, of course, as well as the use of a frost-free greenhouse or conservatory in which the plants can be overwintered.

Some half-hardy plants may be planted permanently outside in milder areas, although they will need to be swathed in straw, hessian, or other coverings in severe weather, to protect them from cold winds and frosts that would otherwise desiccate evergreen foliage. Equally important

is to ensure that such plants are grown in free-draining soil, to avoid root decay, particularly during very cold, frosty spells.

Exotic planting schemes of this type are most likely to succeed in coastal or sheltered city gardens in temperate regions, but variations on this theme may be well worth trying in colder areas.

Key framework plants

Exotic-style plants seldom grow as large in temperate climes as in their native regions, although they can still make handsomely sized, vigorous garden plants for outdoor cultivation in the appropriate situation. Plants to use as tree-like, structural elements in the exotic style of gardening can be divided roughly into three groups: palms and palm-like plants, tree ferns, and bananas. Each contains hardy and half-hardy plants with imposing, attractive foliage, and sometimes flowers. These tropical-looking plants can also be blended with more familiar large, hardy foliage plants, such as elegant bamboos (see p.96) and *Gunnera*.

Palms and palm-like plants

Several species of palm are grown successfully outdoors in temperate areas – the most familiar being the Chusan or Chinese windmill palm (*Trachycarpus fortunei*) from the Himalayas. This withstands temperatures of -15°C (5°F) or below, if grown in a reasonably sheltered position. The closely related *T. wagnerianus* has stiffer, more wind-tolerant leaves. Another suitable palm for a garden setting is the Mediterranean dwarf fan palm (*Chamaerops humilis*). Although it originates in hot, dry regions, it will tolerate -10°C (14°F) or below when grown in a sheltered spot. Forms with silvery-blue leaves (*C. humilis* var. *argentea*) are particularly attractive.

Blue hesper palm (*Brahea armata*) from Mexico and California is occasionally grown in very sheltered sites outdoors; in cold areas, it is also an excellent container plant for summer garden displays. The jelly palm (*Butia capitata*), although Brazilian and Uruguayan in origin, is also surprisingly tough and of similar stature and hardiness to *Brahea*.

Known to survive outdoors and develop to about 5m (15ft) in mild temperate areas, the Chilean wine palm (*Jubaea chilensis*), with its delicate feathery foliage, is another

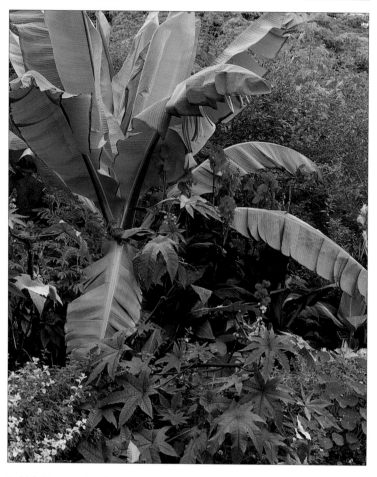

Bold foliage contrast
Huge, paddle-shapsnana leaves here contrast strikingly with the palmate foliage of a castor oil plant (Ricinus), *to provide a strong focal point.*

fine candidate for the exotic style, as is the Canary island date palm (*Phoenix canariensis*). Its delightful dwarf relative, *P. roebelenii*, is better grown in a container in the conservatory, and moved outside in summer.

Unless large specimens are obtained from specialist nurseries, borderline hardy palms should be grown initially in containers until

well established. They can then be planted out in well-drained soil that is reasonably moisture retentive. As the palm stems thicken with age, the plants become more tolerant of lower temperatures, although winter protection is advisable for some years.

Palm-like plants, such as cabbage palm (*Cordyline*) and *Yucca* are also valuable constituents of an exotic

Resistance to cold
Frosted fans of a Chusan palm (Trachycarpus fortunei) *demonstrate the surprising hardiness of this plant.*

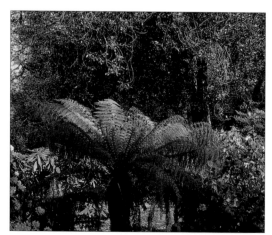

Tree fern
A nearby tree offers shade and shelter for this tree fern (Dicksonia). *It has been carefully planted just beyond the range of the tree's leafy canopy, beneath which the soil would be too dry for it to flourish.*

A RANGE OF EXOTICS

Melianthus major

Brugmansia suaveolens

Hedychium

Tibouchiana urvilleana

Ricinus communis 'Zanzibarensis'

Passiflora caerulea

Canna 'Rosemond Coles'

Hibiscus schizopetalus

Agave americana

Euphorbia mellifera

Exotic gardens
Numerous striking subtropical plants from all corners of the globe are able to flourish in the warmth of sheltered gardens in temperate regions.

garden. The New Zealand cabbage or Torbay palm (*C. australis*) can be grown outdoors in mild temperate areas, where it reaches 6–12m (20–40ft) in height. Green-leaved *C. australis* grows without protection in sheltered gardens but in severe winters may lose some of its foliage, although it often recovers in spring. Variants with coloured leaves are not always tolerant if the temperature drops below freezing for some days.

Species of *Yucca*, such as Adam's needle (*Y. filamentosa*) and Spanish dagger (*Y. gloriosa*), also provide an exotic feel in a garden and can be used as permanent residents within the planting scheme, as both will withstand temperatures down to as low as -15°C (5°F).

Tree ferns

Several species of *Dicksonia* and *Cyathea* are becoming increasingly popular for conservatories and in sheltered gardens. The woolly tree fern (*Dicksonia antarctica*), for example, grows well in humid shade, a habitat that mimics its native temperate rainforests in Australia.

If not already containerized, tree ferns should be planted with the sawn-off "trunk" at least 30cm (1ft) into the ground in a shaded, humid, wind-sheltered site. It is very important, particularly the first year, to keep the plants moist – they must not be allowed to dry out. A trickle, or drip-feed, system (see p.561) to maintain a high level of humidity around the plants will simulate the natural conditions in which they grow. Sometimes it is better to establish tree ferns in containers, placed in a shaded site, as the developing fronds may burn in bright sun.

Although *D. antarctica* will withstand at least -5°C (23°F), its crown and trunk should be insulated where more severe frosts can be expected (see also "Frost protection", p.613). Slightly more tender are the New Zealand species, *D. fibrosa* and *D. squarrosa*. Both are best grown as container plants, which can be given a summer outing. Another tree fern that requires similar cultivation and sheltered conditions is the spectacular sago fern (*Cyathea medullaris*).

Bananas

The two main genera of bananas grown as ornamentals are *Musa* (including *Musella*) and *Ensete* – an impressive giant African genus with enormous architectural foliage. Both should be grown in moist, fertile soil, and mulched with well-rotted manure. Bananas need sun and a sheltered site, to prevent their large, paddle-like leaves from tearing in the wind, as well as plenty of water and frequent applications of fertilizer during the growing season.

A few *Musa* species, including *M. basjoo*, are reasonably frost hardy and will withstand temperatures down to -8°C (18°F). However, even in sheltered gardens, it is always advisable to provide some winter protection. Young plants should have a deep, straw-filled pot – a chimney pot is ideal – fitted over the crown after the foliage has been cut off. A tile across the pot top will prevent rain from rotting the straw. Older plants can be protected with a 15cm (6in) mulch of straw placed around each trunk. The old foliage will die off in winter, and new shoots should appear in mid-spring.

Given suitable over-wintering conditions, *Musa*, *Ensete*, and many other banana genera are among the best of all foliage plants for inclusion in exotic planting schemes.

OTHER PLANTS WITH A TROPICAL LOOK

Acanthus mollis
Aralia elata, A. elata 'Variegata'
Arundo donax ❋
Astelia chathamica
Beschorneria yuccoides
Blechnum chilense
Cycas ❋
Dahlia coccinea ❋,
    D. imperialis ❋
Echium candicans ❋,
    E. pininana ❋
Eryngium agavifolium
Fatsia japonica
Gunnera tinctoria
Impatiens tinctoria
Phormium
Phyllostachys
Rheum palmatum (and cvs)
Solenostemon ❋

Key

❋ *Needs winter protection in frost-prone areas, or use as summer bedding where appropriate*

Dwarf conifers

GREATLY valued for their ease of maintenance, dwarf conifers are particularly suitable for a small, modern garden, whether grown in compact beds or containers. Colours range from rich gold, through brilliant greens to pale blues and silvers, and shapes include globose, pyramidal, and slender, spire-shaped forms. Habits are diverse, with prostrate or mound-forming, erect or weeping types, and the variation in their foliage texture ranges from soft and feathery to dense and spiky. With careful planning, this rich variety of colour, form, and texture can provide interest throughout the year. For details on cultivation, routine care, and propagation, see ORNAMENTAL TREES, pp.63–83.

"dwarf" conifers are simply slower-growing variants of large trees. Conifers can be very difficult to identify when young, since their juvenile foliage often differs widely from that when adult. Check that the plants are correctly named when buying, to avoid introducing plants that will rapidly outgrow their allotted space; if in any doubt seek advice from the retailer.

Selecting the plants

When selecting conifers for a small space, it is important to recognize the true dwarf and slow-growing species and cultivars; sometimes so-called

Designing with dwarf conifers

Dwarf conifers are suitable for a wide range of situations in a garden. They may be planted individually to form a feature, or collectively to create a band of harmonious year-round colour; and they may be used either to complement other plants or to provide effective ground cover. Rock gardens, heather gardens, and ornamental containers are also excellent locations for growing all types of dwarf conifer.

Enhancing conifers
To display dwarf conifers to the best advantage, add heathers to the planting scheme for bright splashes of year-round colour in the garden.

Specimen plants

Some of the slow-growing conifers are suitable for use as specimen plants. Spreading forms, for example, may be used to soften the edges of hard landscaping, while columnar specimens create a focal point.

Group planting

If space allows, a collection of dwarf conifers can make a very attractive feature. The colour spectrum in conifers may also be used to highlight areas at different times of year; blues and silvers, for example, are at their most beautiful in the cool light of winter, while golds and greens appear at their most fresh in spring.

Steep slopes and banks, which often prove difficult to plant effectively, can make striking landscape features when planted with bold drifts of prostrate conifers. Once plants are established, these often problematic areas are easy to maintain and are more or less weed-free.

Plant associations

Dwarf conifers associate well with other groups of plants that are similar in character. They are often used as components of heather gardens to extend the season of interest and provide contrast in colour and form with the foliage and colour variants of *Calluna*, *Daboecia*, and *Erica* cultivars. Other complementary plants for dwarf conifers include *Cytisus*, *Genista*, *Cistus*, and the smaller cotoneaster species and cultivars.

Rock gardens

In the rock garden, dwarf conifers provide the framework for other associated but less permanent plants.

The complete repertoire of colours, textures, and shapes can be used, but take care to select plants that will not become too large or dominant. The smaller species and cultivars, such as *Juniperus communis* 'Compressa', are ideal for the miniature landscapes of compact, raised beds as well as troughs, sink gardens, and other ornamental containers.

Ground cover

Many dwarf conifers make excellent weed-smothering ground cover, either by forming dense mats, as with *Juniperus horizontalis* and its cultivars, or by growing taller and spreading to exclude light beneath their canopy. Some Pfitzer junipers are particularly useful for covering manhole covers or concrete paving. See SHRUBS FOR GROUND COVER, p.101.

Specimen planting
Ideal for a focal point, the golden yew, Taxus baccata 'Aurea', has golden foliage all year round.

A RANGE OF DWARF CONIFERS

Platycladus orientalis
'Aurea Nana'

Pinus sylvestris
'Gold Coin'

Thuja occidentalis
'Caespitosa'

Juniperus squamata
'Blue Star'

Picea pungens
'Montgomery'

Chamaecyparis obtusa
'Nana Aurea'

Juniperus scopulorum
'Skyrocket'

Soil preparation and planting

ONCE PLANTED, a tree may remain in place for decades or even centuries, so it is essential to provide it with the best possible growing conditions. Climate, soil type, and the amount of light and shelter available all affect a tree's growth, so take these factors into account when deciding on a planting position. Careful preparation and planting as well as aftercare are vital in helping a tree to establish quickly and grow well.

Climate considerations

Before selecting a tree, check it will flourish in the temperature range, rainfall, and humidity levels of the site. Special local factors, such as strong winds on exposed hilltop sites, should also influence your choice. Even within a species, different cultivars may be more suited to certain conditions, so one plant may thrive while another may not: various cultivars of *Magnolia grandiflora*, for example, tolerate minimum temperatures ranging from -12°C to 6°C (10–43°F).

In areas subject to spring frosts, choose trees that come into leaf late as frost frequently damages young growth. In cold areas, trees that are not fully hardy may be grown outdoors, but they may need protection from frost during winter (see FROST AND WIND PROTECTION, pp.612–613) and should be planted in a sheltered site. If growing tender or tropical species in temperate areas, keep them under cover or grow them in containers so that they may be brought indoors for the winter.

Trees rarely grow well in regions where the annual rainfall is less than 250mm (10in) and most prefer at least four times this amount. Most trees do not require irrigation, however, except when newly planted, as they obtain enough water from rain and, in some areas, from heavy mists condensing on their foliage.

Choosing a planting site

When planting a tree, try to choose the best position for it within the garden because the microclimate may vary considerably from one part of the plot to another. Make sure that the selected site will provide an appropriate amount of light and shelter: many large-leaved trees, for example, will thrive in a sheltered,

CHOOSING TREES

Container-grown tree

GOOD EXAMPLE

Well-balanced branch framework

GOOD EXAMPLE

Well-established root system

POOR EXAMPLE

Tightly wound, congested roots

Bare-root tree

GOOD EXAMPLE

Fibrous "feeder" roots

Evenly distributed, spreading root system

POOR EXAMPLE

Uneven, "hockey stick" roots

POOR EXAMPLE

Tightly coiled roots

Root-balled tree

GOOD EXAMPLE

x *Cupressocyparis leylandii*

Firm root ball with the covering intact

partially shaded position but may not grow well in an exposed site where the foliage would be subjected to strong winds and high light levels.

In coastal areas, choose a planting site that is sheltered because sea spray and salt-laden winds (even a few miles inland) may scorch foliage and cause damage to the growth buds. Some trees, however, tolerate coastal conditions (see "Trees for exposed or windy sites", p.67), and may be planted as windbreaks to help screen other, more vulnerable, plants from strong winds. Similarly, if trees are being planted on a slope, bear in mind that tender trees are more likely to succeed halfway down where it is usually more sheltered than at either the top or the bottom (see also "Frost pockets and frost damage", p.607).

It is best not to plant trees very close to walls or buildings, otherwise, when young, the trees may suffer from reduced light and moisture as a result of the "rain shadow" effect (see *Rain Shadow*, p.610). Ideally they should be planted half their mature

height away from any structure. In addition, the strong, fibrous roots of some trees, such as poplars (*Populus*) and willows (*Salix*), may damage drains and the foundations of buildings as they develop (see "Tree roots and buildings", p.70). Tender species may be planted near a warm wall; there they will benefit from the wall's retained heat and so may survive in a region where they would fail in more open conditions.

When choosing a site ensure that the trees will not interfere with overhead and underground cables and pipes, which may obstruct trees or be damaged by them.

Selecting a tree

Trees may be bought container-grown, bare-root, or root-balled, although conifers and palms are not usually available bare-root. They may be purchased in a variety of sizes and stages of maturity, from seedlings through to semi-mature trees. Young trees tend to become

Grow your own leaf mould

An additional benefit of choosing deciduous trees and shrubs is that they can provide a rich organic source of humus – leaf mould – from the decaying leaves shed each autumn. Leaf mould has good consistency and moisture-retention, and contains some disease-combating organisms, making it an excellent soil-improver, and a useful ingredient of seed and potting composts. All you have to do is collect the leaves and wait a couple of years for them to decay (see p.628).

Use only leaves from deciduous trees and shrubs, such as beech, oak, or hornbeam; ideally avoid those from trees with prominent, hard-veined foliage, such as sycamores (*Acer pseudoplatanus*), that decay slowly. Evergreen and most conifer foliage takes longer to decompose and is unsuitable for making leaf mould.

established more quickly than older trees, while the latter create a strong and immediate impact in the garden but are more expensive.

Whichever type you choose, check that the tree has healthy, vigorous top-growth and roots with no sign of pests, disease, or damage. Both the branch and root systems should be well developed and evenly balanced around the stem. The top-growth, however, must not be overlarge for the root system, otherwise the roots cannot absorb the nutrients and moisture needed to make new growth, and the tree may fail to establish. The spread of a container-grown tree, for example, should be no more than three or four times the width of its container.

Trees that have been allowed to flower or fruit prematurely, so that they look seemingly impressive to buyers, should also be avoided. Such growth may well have been at the expense of basic root development.

Container-grown trees

These are widely available and may be bought and planted at any time of year, except when the soil is very dry or very wet; container-grown trees are usually more expensive than bare-root or root-balled specimens of a comparable size. This is the best method of buying trees that do not establish easily when transplanted, such as magnolias and *Eucalyptus*, because there is less disturbance to the roots. Such difficult-to-establish trees should also be bought and planted when they are still small. Exotic and less common trees are usually sold in pots.

Before buying a tree, remove it from its container, if possible, so that you can see the roots clearly: do not buy a pot-bound tree with a mass of congested roots or one with thick roots protruding through the drainage holes. Such trees may not establish well. Equally, if the compost does not cling to the root ball when the tree is removed from its container, do not buy it as its root system is not sufficiently established. Make sure that the container is large enough in relation to the tree: as a guide, the container's diameter should be at least one sixth of the tree's height. A tall tree growing in a small container will almost certainly be pot-bound.

The potting medium is also important: trees that are container-ized in soil-based potting composts establish more quickly in open ground than those grown in other types of composts, because they have less of an adjustment to make to the surrounding soil.

Staking

As root systems of newly planted trees need one or more growing seasons to anchor firmly in the soil, staking against strong winds may be necessary. Drive the stake in about 60cm (24in) below soil level so that it is completely stable. After two or three years, the tree should be sufficiently established for the stake to be removed. The method of support chosen depends on the tree, the proposed planting site, and personal preference.

Traditionally, a high, vertical stake has been used, placed on the side of the prevailing wind and long enough to reach to just below the crown. A low stake is now generally preferred, as it allows the tree to move naturally in the wind.

With flexible-stemmed trees, such as crab apples, use a high stake in the first year after planting, cut it down to the lower level in the second year, and remove the stake in the third year.

For container-grown and root-balled trees, a low stake angled into the prevailing wind is preferable as it can be driven in clear of the root ball even after the tree has been planted. Alternatively, space two or three vertical, low stakes evenly around the tree outside the area of the root ball.

In windy sites or for trees more than 4m (12ft) tall, insert two vertical stakes when planting, one on either side of the root ball, to provide support. Large trees are often secured by guy-ropes attached to low stakes. Covering the guys with hosepipe or white tape makes them more visible and so helps prevent the risk of people tripping over them.

High stake
Drive in a single, high stake before planting. Secure the tree to the stake using two padded or buckle-and-spacer ties.

Low stake
A low stake allows the tree's stem some movement; insert it so that only about 50cm (20in) protrudes above ground level.

Angled stake
A low, angled stake may be added after planting. Drive it into the ground at a 45° angle, leaning into the prevailing wind.

Two stakes
Insert two stakes so that they are on opposite sides of the tree, and secure them to the tree with heavy-duty rubber ties.

Bare-root trees

Trees sold bare-root, which are almost always deciduous, are grown in open ground, then lifted with virtually no soil around the roots. As soon as they are exposed to the air, however, the fine feeder roots begin to dry out. A reputable nursery will remove any ragged ends as well as prune away any lopsided, overlong, or damaged roots.

It is essential to buy bare-root trees when they are dormant, preferably in autumn or early spring; they are unlikely to survive transplanting if purchased and planted when in leaf. Ash (*Fraxinus*), poplars (*Populus*), and many rosaceous trees, such as crab apples (*Malus*), are often sold

bare-root from nurseries, while only fruit trees tend to be available bare-root from garden centres.

Make sure that the tree you choose has well-developed roots spreading evenly in all directions. A number of small roots about 2–5mm ($\frac{1}{16}$–$\frac{1}{4}$in) in diameter is a good sign as it indicates that they have been under-cut every year or so, a technique that encourages sturdy growth and vigorous root systems. Examine the roots to check that they are free from damage and disease and that there is no sign of dryness that may have been caused by exposure to wind. Do not buy trees with "hockey stick" roots, where all the growth is on one side; these will not establish well.

Root-balled trees

These trees are also grown in open ground but when lifted the roots and surrounding soil are wrapped in hessian or netting to hold the root ball together and stop the roots drying out. Deciduous trees over 4m (12ft) and many evergreens, especially conifers and palms of more than 1.5m (5ft), are often sold in this way.

Buy and plant root-balled trees when dormant, in autumn or early spring, following the same criteria as for bare-root and container-grown trees. Check that the root ball is firm and its wrapping is intact before purchase: if there is any sign of drying out or root damage, the tree is less likely to establish well and,

Tree ties

Ties must be secure, long-lasting, and able to accommodate the tree's girth as it grows without cutting into the bark. Proprietary ties are available, or you can make them from nylon webbing or rubber tubing. Prevent stakes chafing bark using spacers, or form a padded tie into a figure of eight and nail it to the stake. When using two or three stakes, secure the tree with heavy-duty rubber or plastic strips. If supporting a large tree with guys, use multistrand wire or nylon rope.

Buckle-and-spacer tie
Thread the tie through the spacer, around the tree, and back through the spacer; buckle it so that it is taut but will not damage the bark.

Rubber tie
If using a rubber or plastic tie without a buckle, nail it to the stake to prevent bark damage caused by friction.

because the resulting root system is unstable and not well anchored, the tree will be susceptible to wind-rock, especially when mature.

Seedlings, transplants, and whips

Seedlings up to one year old are available from specialist nurseries. Transplants are seedlings or cuttings transplanted in the nursery and are up to four years old. They make sturdy, bushy plants and are usually 60cm–1.2m (2–4ft) tall. The age and treatment may be given in shorthand: "1+1" denotes a seedling left for one year in the seedbed and then transplanted for a further season; "1 u 1" means that it was undercut (see "Bare-root trees", p.64) after the first year and remained in situ for a further year. Whips are single, whip-like shoots sold by height; they are 1–2m (3–6ft) tall and will have been transplanted at least once.

HEELING IN

If planting is delayed, heel in the tree in a sheltered position. First prepare a trench, then set the tree in it. Angle the tree so that the trunk is supported. Cover the roots and base of the trunk with moist, friable soil and do not allow the roots to dry out.

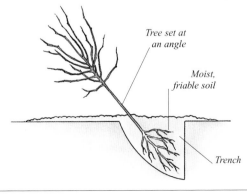

Tree set at an angle

Moist, friable soil

Trench

Feathered trees

These have a single main leader with a spread of lateral branches ("feathers") down to ground level. They will have been transplanted at least once and are usually 2–2.5m (6–8ft) tall.

Standards and large trees

Standards are roughly 3m (10ft) high and pruned to create one single main stem with no lateral branches for about 2m (6ft) above ground level. Central-leader standards are similar to feathered trees but have a clear length of stem at the base; branched-head standards are pruned to have an open centre. Trees of 2.1m (6½ft) in height, with a clear stem of 1.2–1.5m (4–5ft) are known as half-standards; trees of 3.5m (11ft) are selected standards. Larger trees available from specialist nurseries include extra-heavy standards to 5m (15ft) tall and semi-mature trees 5–12m (15–40ft).

Transportation shock

Many trees falter or die of stress and desiccation as a result of being transported on a roof rack, stuck through an opening in a car roof, or exposed on an open truck, where they may be buffeted in the slipstream.

Trees may also experience a setback in their growth rate because their environment has suddenly changed, from one of protected, close planting in the nursery to isolation and exposure to strong winds, hot sun, or hard frosts within the garden.

When to plant

It is best to plant trees as soon as possible after purchase, although container-grown and root-balled trees may be stored in frost-free conditions for a few weeks if kept moist.

Container-grown trees may be planted out at any time of year, except during drought, very wet conditions, or frost; deciduous, bare-root trees should be planted between mid-autumn and mid-spring (avoiding periods of frost and extreme damp). Plant hardy evergreens and hardy, deciduous trees with fleshy roots in mid-autumn or mid- to late spring, and half-hardy trees in mid-spring. Root-balled trees are best planted in early to mid-autumn or mid- to late spring; deciduous trees may be planted out in winter in mild conditions.

Autumn planting allows tree roots to become established before winter sets in. This helps the tree withstand hot, dry spells the following summer. In cold regions, planting in spring may allow trees to establish more successfully. If planting in winter, the ground may be lifted by subsequent spells of frost; if so, the soil should be re-firmed once it has thawed.

Soil preparation

Preparing the site in advance allows the soil to settle and minimizes delay between buying and planting a tree. Choose a well-drained site; one that is poorly drained may need to be improved before planting (see "Improving drainage", p.623). Remove turf and all other plant growth, in an area three or four times the tree's root ball, to eliminate competition for nutrients and water in the soil, then dig the soil, incorporating organic matter in the uppermost part.

Most trees require a soil depth of 50cm–1m (20in–3ft) to grow well. Some may grow on soils only 15cm (6in) deep, although they are then less stable and less drought-tolerant.

TREES FOR ACID SOIL

Abies
Arbutus menziesii
Cercidiphyllum japonicum
Cornus nuttallii
Cryptomeria
Embothrium coccineum
Fagus grandifolia
Magnolia acuminata,
  M. campbellii
  (and cvs)

Magnolia campbellii

Michelia ❀
Oxydendrum arboreum
Picea (most spp.)
Pseudolarix amabilis
Pseudotsuga
Rhodoleia championii ❀
Sciadopitys verticillata
Stewartia
Styrax japonicus
Tsuga heterophylla

TREES FOR VERY ALKALINE SOIL

Acer campestre, A. lobelii,
  A. negundo (and cvs),
  A. platanoides (and cvs)
Aesculus
Carpinus betulus
Cedrus libani
Cercis siliquastrum
Chamaecyparis
  lawsoniana (and cvs)
Crataegus
x *Cupressocyparis*
  leylandii (and cvs)
Cupressus glabra
Fagus sylvatica (and cvs)
Fraxinus excelsior, F. ornus
Juniperus
Malus
Morus nigra
Ostrya carpinifolia
Phillyrea latifolia
Pinus nigra
Populus alba
Prunus avium 'Plena',
  P. sargentii

Prunus sargentii

Pyrus
  (spp. and cvs)
Robinia (spp. and cvs)
Sorbus aria (and cvs)
Taxus baccata (and cvs)
Thuja
Tilia tomentosa

Key
❀ *Not hardy*

Planting trees

Once the site has been prepared, dig the planting hole, between two and four times the width of the tree's root ball, depending on whether the tree is container-grown, bare-root, or root-balled. If doing this in advance, backfill it loosely until ready to plant the tree so that the soil remains warm. Mix the removed soil with well-rotted organic matter and, if planting in spring, about 110g (4oz) of slow-release fertilizer. Fork over the sides and base of the hole to break up the surrounding soil and allow the tree roots to spread into it more easily; this is particularly important in heavy, sticky soils. If you are using a single stake, drive it into the hole just off-centre before planting the tree to ensure that the root ball is not damaged later (see also "Staking", p.64).

Container-grown trees

Thoroughly moisten the compost – if it is very dry, stand the container in water for an hour or two until the compost is moist throughout. Then remove the container, cutting it away if necessary. Gently tease out the roots to encourage them to grow into the surrounding soil; this is essential with a pot-bound plant. Trees with a full but not pot-bound root system could, alternatively, have the outer surface scored with a garden knife, by making two or four shallow vertical cuts, from below, on the root ball before planting. Trim any broken or damaged roots with secateurs.

It is important to check that the planting depth is correct: if a tree is planted too deeply, its roots may not receive enough oxygen and may slow down in growth or even die; if planted too shallowly, the roots may dry out. Place the tree in the hole and

TREES FOR SANDY SOIL

Abies grandis
Acacia dealbata ❀
Acer negundo (and cvs)
Agonis flexuosa ❀
Banksia serrata ❀
Betula pendula (and cvs)
Castanea sativa
Celtis australis
Cercis siliquastrum
Cupressus glabra
Eucalyptus ficifolia ❀
Gleditsia triacanthos
Juniperus
Larix decidua
Melia azedarach
Nothofagus obliqua ❀
Phoenix canariensis ❀
Pinus pinaster, P. radiata
Quercus ilex
Schinus molle ❀
Tabebuia chrysotricha ❀
Thuja occidentalis
    (and cvs)

Tabebuia chrysotricha

TREES FOR CLAY SOIL

Acer platanoides (and cvs)
Castanospermum australe ❀
Crataegus laevigata (and cvs)
Fraxinus
Juglans nigra
Malus
Metasequoia
    glyptostroboides
Populus

Malus
'Cowichan'

Pterocarya
    fraxinifolia
Pyrus calleryana
    'Chanticleer'
Quercus palustris, Q. robur
Salix
Taxodium distichum

Key
❀ *Not hardy*

PLANTING A CONTAINER-GROWN TREE

1 *Soak the root ball of the potted tree in a bucket of water for 1–2 hours. Mark out the area of the hole to be dug – about 3 or 4 times the diameter of the tree's root ball. Lift any turf or weeds, then dig out the hole to about 1½ times the depth of the root ball.*

2 *Scarify the sides of the hole with a fork. Mix the removed soil with rotted organic matter.*

3 *If using one stake, hammer it into the hole, just off-centre and on the windward side. Add up to 20 per cent of the organic matter and soil mixture to the pit.*

4 *Lay the tree on its side and slide it out of the pot. Gently tease out the roots without breaking up the root ball and remove any weeds from the compost.*

5 *Hold the tree next to the stake and spread out the roots. Lay a cane across the hole to check the planting depth. Adjust this by adding or removing some soil.*

6 *Backfill around the tree with more of the topsoil and organic matter. Firm around the tree in stages by treading, then fork over lightly and water well.*

7 *Cut back damaged stems, long sideshoots, and lower feathers. Mulch 5–7cm (2–3in) deep around the tree.*

locate the soil mark – a dark mark near the base of the stem indicating the soil level when the tree was growing in the nursery. Place a cane across the hole alongside the stem and add or remove soil from beneath the root ball, if necessary, so that the soil mark is level with the cane. On free-draining soil, a section of 10cm (4in) diameter perforated drainage pipe can be inserted into the planting hole – the top end should be just above ground level while the lower one should rest among the tree's roots. During subsequent hot weather water can be poured down this pipe, direct to the tree's roots.

Backfill the hole, firming the soil in stages to remove any air pockets; take care not to firm too heavily on clay soils as this may compact the ground and impede drainage. On sandy soils, a shallow moat around the tree helps to channel water to the roots. Conversely, on clay soils, a slight mound around the stem drains water away from the root ball.

Lightly prune the top-growth to balance it with the root system (see "Formative pruning", p.72), then secure the tree to the stake with one or more ties (see "Tree ties", p.65).

PLANTING A ROOT-BALLED TREE

1 *Dig a planting hole 2–3 times the diameter of the tree's root ball. Mix the removed soil with well-rotted organic matter, then place the tree in the hole and untie the wrapping.*

2 *Tilt the tree to one side and roll the material up under the root ball, then tilt the tree the other way and carefully pull out the material. Backfill the hole, firm, mulch, and water well.*

Water thoroughly and apply a thick mulch (see "Mulching", p.68).

Bare-root trees
Prepare the site in the same way as for container-grown trees, ensuring that the planting hole is wide enough for the tree's roots to be spread out fully; trim back any damaged roots to healthy growth. If using a single stake, drive it in just off-centre of the planting hole, and spread the tree's roots around it. Adjust the planting depth if necessary, then partly backfill the hole and gently shake the stem to settle the soil. Firm the backfilled soil in stages, taking care not to damage the roots. Finally, water the tree well; mulch the area around it.

Root-balled trees
The method of planting root-balled trees is very similar to that used for container-grown trees. The planting hole should be twice the width of the root ball, however, or, in heavy, clay soils, three times the width. Place the tree in the hole at the correct depth, then remove the hessian or netting surrounding the root ball. If using an angled stake or two stakes, one on either side of the root ball, drive them in; they should rest firmly against the root ball without piercing it.

In heavy, clay soils, it is possible to improve drainage by planting so that the top of the root ball is slightly above soil level, and covering the exposed part with 5–7cm (2–3in) of friable soil, leaving a gap of 2.5–5cm (1–2in) around the stem. Water thoroughly and mulch.

Aftercare
For the first two or three years after planting, it is important to provide trees with plenty of water, particularly in dry spells. Failure to do this may impede establishment, or the tree may even die. Keep the surrounding area clear of grass and weeds, and feed and mulch regularly (see "Routine care", pp.68–70).

Some trees need extra protection from frost and wind; evergreens in an exposed site should be protected initially from drying winds with windbreaks, for example (see FROST AND WIND PROTECTION, pp.612–613).

Protecting the stem

In many regions, it is necessary to protect young trees from damage caused by rabbits or other animals that strip bark. Either surround the tree with a barrier of chicken wire or wire netting secured in place with several canes or stakes, or place a proprietary tree guard around the tree trunk. There are many types of guard available from garden centres and nurseries, including spiral, wrap-around guards made of flexible plastic, as well as those made from heavy-duty plastic or wire mesh. Degradable, plastic-net tree guards are also available in a range of heights from 60cm (2ft) up to 2m (6ft).

In exposed sites, such as on hillsides, tree shelters may be used to assist young transplants and whips to become well established; these degradable plastic structures are up to 1.2m (4ft) long, and between 8cm (3in) and 15cm (6in) across.

A   B   C   D

Protect the bark of newly planted trees from animal damage with a barrier of wire mesh or plastic netting secured to the ground with canes (A), a rigid, plastic tree shelter (B), a heavy-duty rubber or plastic stem guard (C), or a spiral, wrap-around, plastic guard (D).

TREES FOR EXPOSED OR WINDY SITES
Those marked ✿ are not suitable for coastal sites
Acer pseudoplatanus
Betula pendula ✿,
  B. pubescens ✿
Crataegus x *lavallei*,
  C. monogyna
Eucalyptus gunnii,
  E. pauciflora (and subsp.)
Fraxinus excelsior
Ilex altaclerensis (and cvs)
Picea abies ✿, *P. sitchensis* ✿
Pinus contorta, *P. nigra*,
  P. radiata, *P. sylvestris*
Quercus robur
Salix alba
Sorbus aria, *S. aucuparia*
  (and cvs)

Sorbus aucuparia

TREES THAT TOLERATE POLLUTED AIR
Acer platanoides (and cvs),
  A. pseudoplatanus (and cvs),
  A. saccharinum (and cvs)
Aesculus hippocastanum
Alnus cordata, *A. glutinosa*
Betula pendula
Carpinus betulus (and cvs)
Catalpa bignonioides
Corylus colurna
Crataegus
x *Cupressocyparis leylandii*
Fraxinus
Ginkgo biloba
Gleditsia
Ilex x *altaclerensis*
Liriodendron
Magnolia grandiflora
Malus
Nyssa
Platanus
Populus

Populus x *jackii* 'Aurora'

Pyrus
Quercus x *hispanica* (and cvs),
  Q. ilex, *Q.* x *turneri*
Robinia
Salix
Sophora japonica
Sorbus aria, *S. aucuparia*,
  S. intermedia
Taxus baccata, *T.* x *media*
Tilia x *euchlora*, *T.* x *europaea*,
  T. platyphyllos (and cvs)

Routine care

THE amount of maintenance that a tree needs largely depends on the species, microclimate, soil type, and site. Most trees require watering, feeding, and a clear, weed-free area during the first few years if they are to establish well; container-planted trees should also be regularly top-dressed and occasionally repotted. In addition, other procedures such as removing suckers or controlling pests or diseases are sometimes necessary, while in certain circumstances – for example, if a tree is not thriving – the best solution may be either to fell the tree or to transplant it.

Watering

Most trees need plenty of water to grow well, especially on light, sandy soil or if trees have been planted within the previous two or three years. As a general guide, apply approximately 50–75 litres/sq m (10–15 gallons/sq yd) of water per tree each week in dry weather during the growing season. Once they have become well established, most trees only need to be artificially irrigated during spells of drought.

Fertilizing

All trees will benefit from feeding, particularly on soils that are low in nutrients and during the first few years after planting. However, older trees usually require feeding only occasionally. Trees grown for their flowers and fruit generally require more potash and phosphate than do trees grown for their foliage, which need more nitrogen.

TOP-DRESSING

Trees in pots exhaust supplies of nutrients faster than they do in the open ground because their roots are restricted. You can replenish supplies by top-dressing in spring. Use a trowel or your hands to remove any mulch and the top 5cm (2in) of compost. Replace it with fresh compost mixed with a slow-release fertilizer. Water the compost well, and mulch.

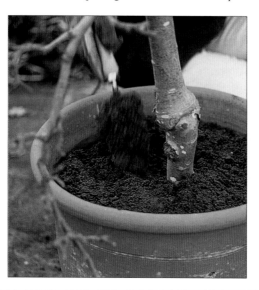

Organic fertilizers such as well-rotted manure or compost are usually applied as a mulch: in autumn, or during any frost-free period in the dormant season, spread the material in a layer 5–8cm (2–3in) deep around the tree, keeping a clear area immediately around the trunk. When feeding a young tree, extend the mulch to the "drip line" – the ground beneath the outer edge of the canopy; an area 3–4m (10–12ft) in diameter is appropriate for a larger tree.

Artificial fertilizers are usually applied in spring. Broadcast the fertilizer around the base of the tree, at a rate of 70g/sq m (2oz/sq yd), or mix it with compost and insert it into small holes dug 2m (6ft) apart around the drip line. Alternatively, apply a proprietary liquid fertilizer around the tree.

Trees planted in grassed areas may need to be fed every year if they are not thriving. The grass between the trunk and the drip line may be removed by hand or with chemicals and a nutrient-rich mulch applied.

Trees in containers

Container-planted trees generally require watering and feeding more frequently than those planted in open ground as the small amount of compost in which they are growing can store only limited reserves of water and nutrients. During hot, dry weather, they may need to be watered at least twice a day. Apply an annual mulch of bark chippings or similar material on top of the compost to help retain moisture. In addition, top-dress the tree each spring before it starts into growth. This involves replacing some of the old compost

with fresh compost enriched with fertilizer. At the same time, prune back any dead, damaged, weak, or straggly stems to rejuvenate the tree and ensure that it produces healthy, vigorous growth.

Every three to five years, repot the tree completely either into the same container or, preferably, into a larger one. To do this, first remove the tree carefully from the container, then tease out the roots, cutting back by up to one third any that are large and coarse. Soak the root system well, if dry, then repot the tree into fresh compost (see "Planting trees in containers", p.334). If using the same container, wash it out before adding fresh compost and repotting.

Mulching

Mulching around a tree keeps weeds under control, reduces the effect of temperature extremes around the roots, and cuts down moisture loss from the soil surface. In general, organic materials such as pulverized bark look most attractive, and they can be used to cover a biodegradable mulch mat. Black plastic is also effective, but do not use clear plastic, because heat is rapidly transferred to the soil and may damage surface roots. Mulches that are rich in nutrients are generally used only if a tree needs feeding.

Mulches are best applied in spring but, provided that the soil is moist,

they may be spread at any time except during frost. Apply mulch over an area 30–45cm (12–18in) larger than the tree's root system. Top up every year or two under young trees.

Weeding

The area beneath a tree's canopy should be kept clear of weeds and grass as this ensures that the fibrous, feeding roots of the tree do not have to compete for a limited supply of water and nutrients. Alternatively, if a tree's growth is too rapid, retaining, or establishing grass around it will help to reduce its vigour by competing for food and water.

Some weedkillers may be used around trees because they do not affect tree roots. Mulching, however, should make weeding largely unnecessary. For treatment of weeds, see WEEDS, pp.669–673.

Suckers and water shoots

Suckers and water shoots will divert nutrients from the main shoots of the tree if they are left to develop unchecked. Remove them as soon as they appear.

Stem and root suckers

A tree may produce both stem and root suckers: a stem sucker is a shoot that appears just beneath the graft

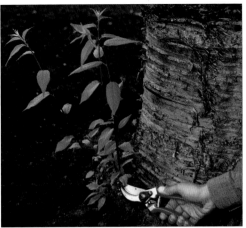

REMOVING SUCKERS

Using secateurs, cut off the suckers as close to the trunk as possible, then pare over the cut surface with a knife; rub out any regrowth as soon as it appears.

union on the rootstock of a grafted tree, a root sucker is one that develops directly from the roots. Suckers of a grafted plant may quickly grow larger than the top-growth or even replace it within a few years so that the root-stock species predominates rather than the grafted cultivar.

Trees that are particularly vigorous or that have roots near the soil surface, such as poplars (*Populus*) and ornamental cherries (*Prunus*), may form root suckers if the root system is damaged. They may be used for propagation, but are a nuisance if they come up in lawns and paths.

Cut or pull off the suckers as close to the base as possible, digging down to where the sucker joins the root, if necessary. For some genera such as *Prunus*, painting the cuts on the roots with ammonium sulphamate usually prevents regrowth and, in small amounts, does not harm the tree.

Water shoots

Epicormic or water shoots may grow directly out of the trunk, often around pruning wounds. Rub them out with your fingers or thumb as soon as they appear, or cut them back to the base and rub them out as they regrow.

Frost and wind

Trees may be damaged by strong winds, and severe frosts may affect young growth, so provide protection such as windbreaks, particularly in exposed sites. Windbreaks may be artificial, such as fencing, or natural, such as hedges (see also "How a windbreak works", p.611).

The soil around newly planted trees may be lifted by frost; if this occurs, refirm it after thawing so that the roots do not dry out (see FROST AND WIND PROTECTION, pp.612–613).

Tree problems

Lack of vigour is a reliable indicator that there is a problem with a tree. As well as checking for pests and diseases, make sure that the tree has not been too deeply planted or that the roots and stems have not been damaged, as these are possible causes of poor growth and dieback.

The commonest pests are aphids and red spider mite (p.646), while honey fungus (p.661) is the most damaging disease, affecting, and often killing, a wide range of trees.

REMOVING WATER SHOOTS

Cut back to the base with secateurs any water shoots that may grow through the bark or sprout at the edges of a wound where a branch has been removed.

Cutting down a small tree

Tree felling may be undertaken at any time of year. It is a skilled and potentially dangerous operation; if the tree is over 5m (15ft), it should be tackled by a tree surgeon. Ensure the tree is not subject to a Tree Preservation Order and, if on a boundary, that it is legally yours.

Make sure there is space for the tree to fall safely and that there is an escape route at right angles to the proposed fall line.

A tree is usually taken down in stages, and you must always wear protective gloves. First remove any large branches in sections (see "Removing a branch", p.71), and then the rest of the trunk.

It is best to remove the stump but if this is impractical it may be treated with chemicals; left to rot it could attract honey fungus (see p.661). Dig out the stump and any large roots with a spade. Sever tough roots with an axe. If you have a large stump, employ a con-tractor to grind it or winch it out.

Alternatively, cut the stump flush with the ground and treat the surface with a proprietary solution of ammonium sulphamate. Wait at least 12 weeks before replanting.

1 *On the side the tree is to fall, make an angled cut just over one-third of the trunk diameter, about 1m (3ft) above ground. Cut out a wedge by sawing horizontally to meet the base of the cut. Remove the wedge to ensure the tree falls in the right direction.*

2 *On the opposite side of the trunk make the final cut just above the base of the wedge cut. Push the tree in the right direction as it starts to fall. If felling a large tree, tie ropes around the trunk to guide its fall.*

3 *Remove the remaining stump by digging a wide trench around it, loosening the roots with a fork or spade, and then winching or digging it out.*

Transplanting a tree

It is best to prepare the tree a year in advance before transplanting as this will greatly increase its chances of re-establishing. Unless the tree is quite young, it may be difficult to transplant and may not adjust well; if taller than 2.5m (8ft), the tree may be difficult to establish in its new position. Large trees may need to be transplanted by specialist arborists.

Preparation

In early autumn the year before the planned move, while the soil is still warm and the tree roots are in active growth, mark out the optimum root-ball diameter for the tree – about one third of the tree's height. Dig a trench about 30cm (12in) wide and 60cm (24in) deep just outside the marked area and mix the removed soil with masses of well-rotted organic matter.

Using a sharp spade, undercut the root ball as far as possible to sever any large, coarse roots. This has the effect of stimulating the growth of fibrous "feeder" roots, which will help the tree to develop and grow successfully after transplanting. Then replace the mixture of soil and organic matter in the trench.

Lifting the tree

Transplant the tree the following autumn (see "When to plant", p.65), first pruning out any thin branches and reducing the tree to a well-balanced framework. Then carefully tie in the remaining branches to the central stem to protect them and to increase the working space around the tree.

Dig a trench just outside the one made the previous year and of similar dimensions, and gradually fork away the excess soil until the root ball is of a manageable size and weight; take care not to damage the fibrous roots. On sandy soil, thoroughly soak the ground before starting to dig, to make the root ball firmer. Then cut with a spade through any roots underneath the root ball to separate it completely from the surrounding soil. To hold the root ball together and stop the roots drying out while the tree is removed from the hole, it should be securely wrapped in some hessian or plastic sheeting. This can be tricky to do, but the easiest way is to tilt the tree first one way and then the other, so that each side of the root ball is raised and the hessian slipped under it. Use rope to secure the

wrapping around the root ball. Then manoeuvre the tree onto a ramp and transport it to its new position.

Replanting

Well before the tree reaches its new site, prepare the planting hole (see *Planting a Root-balled Tree*, p.67). When the tree arrives, lower it into the hole and adjust the planting depth until the dark mark on the tree stem is at soil level. Then undo the root ball ties and, carefully tilting the tree, remove the hessian covering around the root ball. Backfill the hole, working the soil around and over the root ball and firming it in stages, until the soil is level with the dark mark on the tree stem.

It may be necessary to reduce the crown by 25–30 per cent, to minimize water loss and stimulate regrowth the following spring. Until it is well established, support the tree with guy-ropes secured to angled stakes in the ground. Water the tree well, then spread a thick mulch about 10cm (4in) deep on the surrounding soil, to retain moisture and suppress weeds. If it is impossible to replant the tree immediately, give it the same care as you would a newly purchased tree (see *Heeling in*, p.65).

Tree roots and buildings

Many trees, especially large, forest-sized ones in an urban area, grow too large for their surroundings and/or too near buildings, and it is the legal responsibility of the land owner to rectify any damage that their roots or branches may cause.

Tree roots, for example, may crack building foundations, especially if these are less than 0.5m (20in) deep and sited on clay soils. Walls are particularly vulnerable in times of drought, because soil shrinks as the tree roots absorb the moisture needed to survive. Roots may also block drains, which burst and so cause unstable, wet areas underground.

Roots and suckers may disturb paving slabs on paths and pavements, so they become a hazard to pedestrians, and falling branches may damage roofs, guttering, fences, power lines, or even nearby vehicles.

HOW TO MOVE A YOUNG TREE

1 *Prepare the tree for transplanting a year ahead. To transplant, start by tying the branches in to the main stem to protect them from damage while working around the tree. Then, keeping outside the area of the root ball, dig a trench about 30cm (12in) wide and 60cm (24in) deep around the tree.*

2 *Carefully fork away the soil from around the root ball, removing a small amount at a time to avoid damaging the roots.*

3 *Undercut the root ball with a spade and cut back with secateurs any awkward roots protruding from the root ball.*

4 *Roll up a length of hessian (or plastic sheeting) and, tilting the tree to raise one side of the root ball, slide the hessian underneath.*

5 *Carefully tilt the tree back the other way and pull the hessian through underneath; the root ball should now be resting on the centre of the hessian.*

6 *Pull the hessian up around the root ball so that it is completely covered. Tie it securely in place with rope to keep the root ball intact while the tree is being moved.*

7 *Tilt the tree to one side and slide 2 planks underneath it to act as a ramp. Ease the tree up the ramp and then transport it to the new planting site.*

Pruning and training

CORRECT pruning and training helps to maintain a tree's health and vigour, regulate its shape and size, and, in some instances, improve ornamental qualities. It is important to prune young trees correctly to develop a strong framework of evenly spaced branches.

The degree of pruning and training depends on the type of tree and the desired effect: relatively little is required to produce a well-balanced tree whereas creating a pleached avenue with interwoven branches demands considerably more work and expertise.

When to prune

Most deciduous trees are best pruned when dormant in late autumn or winter; they may also be pruned at other times, except in late winter or early spring when many trees "bleed" (exude sap) if cut. Maples (*Acer*), horse chestnuts (*Aesculus*), birches (*Betula*), walnuts (*Juglans*), and cherries (*Prunus*) all bleed extensively, even towards the end of their dormant season; prune these in mid- to late summer after new growth has matured. Evergreens need little or no pruning except the removal of dead or diseased branches in late summer.

The principles of pruning

Always wear strong protective gloves when pruning. The first stage is to remove any dead, diseased, or damaged wood on the tree, and to cut out weak or straggly shoots. Then assess the remaining framework and decide which branches should be pruned back or removed for well-balanced growth. Take care not to impair the natural growth habit of a tree by pruning unless aiming to produce a certain shape or form, such as an espalier. Hard pruning stimulates vigorous growth, whereas light pruning produces only limited growth.

It is important to make pruning cuts accurately to minimize damage to the tree. If cutting back a stem, cut just above a healthy bud, pair of buds, or sideshoot pointing in the required direction of growth. For example, if thinning out congested stems, cut back to a bud or shoot that is growing outwards so it will not rub against another stem as it grows. Cut neither too far from the bud, which leaves a stub that provides an entry point for disease, nor too close, which could damage the bud itself.

When pruning trees with opposite buds, make a straight cut with sharp secateurs directly above a pair of buds; for trees with alternate buds,

WHERE TO CUT

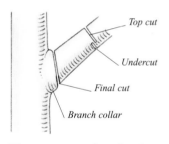

When removing a branch, take care not to damage the branch collar: first remove the bulk of the branch with 2 cuts, then cut off the stub just outside the collar.

Top cut
Undercut
Final cut
Branch collar

CUTTING BACK A STEM

Alternate buds
For trees with alternate buds, make a clean, angled cut just above a healthy, outward-facing bud.

Opposite buds
For trees with opposite buds, make a clean, straight cut directly above a strong pair of buds.

make a sloping cut 3–5mm (⅛–¼in) above a bud so that the base of the cut is just level with the top of the bud, on the opposite side of the stem.

If pruning back a branch completely, cut just outside the branch collar – the slight swelling on the branch where it joins the trunk. This is where the callus is formed that will eventually cover the wound. Never cut flush with the main stem as this damages the tree's natural protective zone, making it more vulnerable to disease. The branch collar on dead branches may extend some way along the branch, but it is still important to make any cut outside it.

Removing a branch

If removing whole branches of less than 2.5cm (1in) diameter, make a single cut with a pruning saw or secateurs. For branches thicker than this, first remove the bulk of the weight: partially undercut the branch at least 30cm (12in) from the trunk, then a little further out saw through from above. If no undercut is made, the branch may break off in mid-cut, ripping the bark back to the trunk so making it vulnerable to infection.

To remove the remaining stub, undercut it just outside the branch collar, then cut through from above. If you find it difficult to locate the branch collar, cut through the stub at a short distance from the trunk, making the cut so that it slopes outwards away from the tree.

If the angle between the branch and the trunk is very acute, it may be easier to cut through the stub from beneath. Do not apply a wound paint or dressing: there is no clear evidence that they speed up the healing process or prevent disease.

CUTTING OFF A BRANCH

1 *Put on protective gloves. Using a pruning saw, undercut the branch 30cm (12in) from the trunk by one quarter of its diameter. This stops the bark tearing.*

2 *Make the second cut about 2.5cm (1in) further away from the trunk, sawing through the branch from above. The undercut will close up, making sawing easier.*

3 *Make the final cut just outside the branch collar, angling the saw slightly away from the trunk. Saw through cleanly until the top cut meets the undercut.*

Formative pruning

Young trees benefit from formative pruning to ensure that they develop a strong, well-balanced framework of evenly spaced branches. At its simplest, this involves the removal of dead, damaged, and diseased wood, as well as any weak or crossing branches.

Formative pruning may also be used to determine the tree's shape as it grows: for example, a young feathered tree may be pruned over several years to form a standard, or trained against a wall as an espalier. The extent of the pruning depends on both the type of tree selected and the required shape when mature. As with all types of pruning, care should be taken not to spoil the tree's natural growth characteristics.

It is particularly important to prune young tropical trees as their growth rate is very rapid and the girth of both main stems and branches develops extremely quickly; provided that they have been pruned correctly during the first few years after planting, they may then be left to grow naturally. Most other evergreens, on the other hand, will develop naturally into well-shaped specimens with little or no attention; pruning is usually restricted to the removal of dead, damaged, or crossing stems, and badly placed laterals.

The formative pruning of ornamental garden trees depends on the type of tree bought or required. Feathered trees have a single, central leader and laterals along the whole length of the stem. Central-leader standards have a clear length of stem at the base, while branched-head standards also have a clear stem but have their central leader removed to encourage the formation of vigorous lateral branches – as commonly seen in many Japanese cherries (*Prunus*).

Feathered trees

Feathered trees may either be simply pruned to enhance their natural shape or more extensively pruned to train them into standards. This process also occurs naturally sometimes. Although many feathered trees retain their lower branches, these die back in some species and the tree ultimately becomes a central-leader standard; other trees may also lose their central-leader dominance and so become branched-head standards.

Early training is straightforward, however, regardless of the eventual habit of the tree. First remove any competing shoots to leave a single main leader. Then take out any small, weak, and poorly placed laterals,

PRUNING AND TRAINING YOUNG TREES

Feathered Tree

Central-leader standard

Cut back laterals by half.

Cut back laterals flush with stem.

Remove congested and crossing shoots, then cut out any laterals that are small, spindly, or badly positioned, to achieve a well-balanced framework of branches.

Year 1
On the lowest third of the tree, cut back laterals to the main stem; on the middle third, cut back laterals by half. Remove any weak or competing leaders.

Years 2 and 3
Continue the pruning process, removing the lowest laterals completely and cutting back by about half those laterals that are on the middle third of the tree.

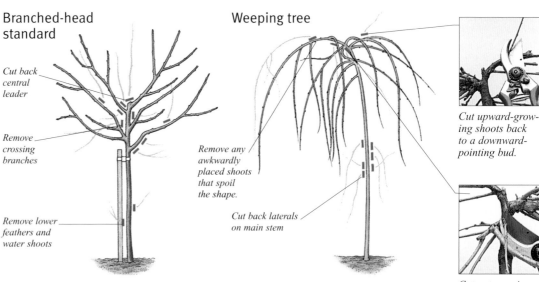

Branched-head standard

Cut back central leader

Remove crossing branches

Remove lower feathers and water shoots

Remove crossing laterals and any growths on the lower third of the tree. Cut back the leader to a healthy bud or shoot.

Weeping tree

Remove any awkwardly placed shoots that spoil the shape.

Cut back laterals on main stem

Cut upward-growing shoots back to a downward-pointing bud.

Cut out crossing, rubbing, or congested growth.

Cut back crossing or vertical branches that spoil the symmetry of the tree. Remove any growths on the main stem.

so that the framework of branches around the main stem is evenly spaced and well balanced.

Central-leader standards

Feathered whips may be pruned over two to three years to form a standard; a technique called "feathering" is often used as it also channels food to the main stem which thickens and becomes sturdier. Initially, prune a feathered whip to remove any competing leaders or weak laterals. Then, on the lowest third of the tree, cut back all the feathers to the main stem; on the middle third, reduce the feathers by about half; leave the top

third unpruned, but remove any vigorous, upright shoots that might form a competing leader.

In late autumn or early winter, cut back the pruned laterals flush with the main stem. Repeat the procedure over the next two or three years to form a tree with approximately 1.8m (6ft) of clear stem.

Branched-head standards

To form a branched-head standard, train the tree initially as a central-leader standard to achieve the desired length of clear stem. Then, in mid- to late autumn, cut back the leader to a strong, healthy bud or

shoot to leave a framework of four or five strong, well-placed lateral branches. At this stage, also remove any crossing or congested laterals and any that spoil the balance of the branch framework.

In subsequent years, prune the tree as much as necessary to keep the crown well balanced and with an open centre; remove any vigorous, vertical shoots that may grow into a new leader; and cut back any feathers to the main stem as soon as possible. Some branched-head standards can be formed by top-working (or top-grafting) as for weeping standards (see p.73).

Weeping standards

A weeping standard is formed by grafting one or two scions of a weeping cultivar onto a stock plant with a clear stem of about 1.8m (6ft). This is known as top-working or top-grafting, a technique that is most commonly used for fruit trees (see "Top-working", p.443) but also for weeping ash (*Fraxinus excelsior* 'Pendula'), the Kilmarnock willow (*Salix caprea* 'Kilmarnock'), and a large number of other weeping ornamental trees. Young, pendulous branches start to develop once the grafts have taken.

Pruning is best restricted to the removal of crossing and vertical branches as well as any that spoil the overall symmetry of the framework. Although upward-growing branches are usually removed, leave some semi-upright stems to develop naturally as they often grow downwards later and produce tiers of weeping branches. If growths appear on the main stem, rub or pinch them out as soon as they appear.

Espalier- and fan-trained trees

The aim of both espalier- and fan-training is to form a symmetrical, attractive network of branches in a single plane by pruning and training a young tree over several years. These techniques are occasionally used for growing ornamental trees against fences or walls, but they are more commonly associated with growing fruit trees.

Pruning times vary according to the selected species: for example, *Magnolia grandiflora*, which flowers from mid- to late summer, should be pruned at the start of growth in spring, while the spring-flowering *Acacia dealbata* should be pruned directly after flowering. For full instructions on the pruning techniques, see GROWING FRUIT, "Espalier", p.442, and "Fan", p.441.

Pruning established deciduous trees

Once a deciduous tree is well established, there is little need for further pruning. Major pruning of a mature tree is best carried out by a tree surgeon or arborist, as the work is both skilled and dangerous, and, if poorly executed, may ruin the tree.

Many branched-head trees become overcrowded in the centre as they mature, restricting the amounts of air and light that reach the central branches. Cut out inward-growing shoots and any branches that spoil the balance of the framework.

If a tree has grown too large for its

REMOVING A COMPETING LEADER

Prune out a competing leader by making a clean cut at the base with secateurs or loppers, taking care not to damage the remaining leader.

situation, do not attempt to restrict its size by heading back all new growth each year; this "haircut" pruning produces an unsightly, congested cluster of shoots each season which spoils the tree's natural appearance and reduces flower and fruit production. The correct treatment is as for the renovation of old trees (see p.74).

As a result of hard pruning or the removal of large branches, a tree may produce a mass of epicormic or water shoots; rub or cut these out immediately (see p.69).

If the central leader is damaged, select a strong shoot close to the top of the main stem and train it vertically as a replacement leader. Tie the selected shoot to a cane or stake secured high on the main stem, and prune out any potential competing shoots. Once the shoot has developed into a strong, dominant growth, the cane may be removed.

If a tree develops two or more competing leaders, remove all but the strongest shoot. The very narrow crotch angle between rival leaders is a source of structural weakness and the tree could split open at this point in a high wind.

Vigorous, upright shoots may develop on young, branched-head trees. If left, these will quickly grow into competing leaders and so it is important to remove them entirely as soon as possible.

Pruning established evergreen trees

Broadleaved evergreens need only minimal pruning. Provided that the trees have an established leader and that any badly placed laterals have been cut out when young, it is only necessary to remove any dead, damaged, or diseased wood.

Conifers require only basic pruning once established, except when they are grown as a hedge (see HEDGES AND SCREENS, pp.84–85).

TRAINING A NEW LEADER

Replace a damaged leader by training in a strong shoot vertically. Attach a cane to the top of the main stem and tie the shoot to the cane. Prune out the old, damaged leader. Remove the cane once the new leader is dominant and growing strongly.

On some pines (*Pinus*), silver firs (*Abies*), and spruces (*Picea*), the terminal bud on the leader may die; if this occurs, train in the best placed lateral as a replacement leader (see above) and cut out any competing, upright shoots. Established palms require no pruning apart from the removal of dead leaves which should be cut back to the main stem.

Root pruning

If an established tree is growing vigorously, but producing very few flowers or fruit, pruning the roots may help to slow down growth and stimulate better overall performance.

In early spring, dig a trench just outside the extent of the tree canopy. Then prune back any thick roots to the inner edge of the trench, using a pruning saw, secateurs, or loppers. Retain any fibrous roots at the inner edge of the trench, backfill the soil, and firm. For further details, see GROWING FRUIT, "Root pruning", p.430. In some instances, it may be necessary to support the tree with stakes or guy-ropes if it seems unstable afterwards (see "Staking", p.64). For root pruning of trees in

HOW TO COPPICE A TREE

Coppicing may be used to restrict a tree's size, enlarge leaves, or enhance stem colour.

Use pruning loppers to cut back all stems to 7cm (3in); do not cut into the swollen, woody base of the tree.

containers, see "Maintaining trees planted in containers", p.68.

Pruning container-planted trees

Container-planted trees should be pruned annually, following the same principles as for other trees, to regulate their shape and size and maintain a strong, balanced framework of evenly spaced branches.

Coppicing and pollarding

Coppicing is the regular pruning of a tree close to the ground to encourage strong, basal shoots to grow. Pollarding is the pruning of a tree back to its main stem or branch framework, stimulating new shoots at this level. Traditionally, both techniques were practised to give a regular supply of firewood or pliable stems for basketwork and fencing. Now they are used in gardens to enhance leaf colour and the size or the colour of ornamental stems, or to restrict tree size.

Coppicing

Trees should be coppiced in late winter or early spring; some willows, when grown for their coloured or glaucous stems, may be left until mid-spring, however, and pruned just before or very shortly after bud break. Cut back all stems to the base, leaving the swollen basal wood unpruned as all new growth occurs here. Less vigorous trees should be coppiced over two years, cutting half the stems one year and the remaining old ones the following year.

Pollarding

To form a pollard, plant a young, branched-head standard (see p.72). When its trunk has reached 2m (6ft), or the desired height, prune back the branches to 2.5–5cm (1–2in) from the main stem in late winter or early spring. This results in a mass of shoots developing from the top of the cut stem. Prune back these shoots annually (or every second year) to stimulate further young shoots to grow from the enlarged head of the stem. Thin them if they become congested. Remove shoots that grow on the trunk as soon as they appear.

To produce a pollard with a main branch framework, allow the tree to develop a well-balanced branch system at the desired height. In late winter or early spring, prune back the branches to about 2m (6ft). Cut back the resulting, secondary shoots every two to five years, depending on the species, until the pollard is established. Thereafter, prune every year

TREES FOR COPPICING AND POLLARDING

Corylus avellana 'Contorta' ⩔
Eucalyptus dalrympleana,
  E. globulus ❋ ⩔,
  E. gunnii ⩔,
  E. pauciflora

  Eucalyptus
  pauciflora

Populus x *canadensis*
  'Aurea', *P.* x *jackii*
  'Aurora'
Salix acutifolia 'Blue Streak',
  S. alba var. *sericea,*
  S. alba var. *vitellina, S. alba*
  var. *vitellina* 'Britzensis',
  S. daphnoides 'Aglaia',
  S. 'Erythroflexuosa',
  S. irrorata ⩔
Tilia platyphyllos (cvs)
Toona sinensis 'Flamingo'

Key

❋ *Not hardy*
⩔ *Coppice only*

PRUNING AN ESTABLISHED, POLLARDED TREE

Prune back the shoots every 1–2 years in late winter or early spring to 1–2cm (¹/₂–³/₄in) from the pollarded head of the main stem. This will stimulate new shoot production the following spring. The new wood of trees such as this Salix alba var. vitellina, *grown for its ornamental stems, is particularly highly coloured.*

Using secateurs or pruning loppers, cut back the old stems to the base, taking care not to damage the enlarged head.

or two, and thin the shoots as required. If too many enlarged heads develop close together, cut out some of them entirely.

Renovating old trees

Trees that have outgrown their situation, or that have been neglected, should be either removed and replaced, or renovated to return them to full health and vigour. Renovation requires considerable care and expertise, and it is advisable to consult an experienced tree surgeon. In some cases, a tree may be too old and potentially dangerous to renovate, so it may be better to replace it. In others, such as with old flowering cherries (and other *Prunus*), renovation is rarely successful because of the risk of silver leaf (see p.647).

Renovation may be undertaken at any time of year except at the start of growth in spring; for most trees, however, and particularly those that produce a lot of sap, such as horse chestnuts (*Aesculus*) and birches (*Betula*), late autumn or early winter is the best time.

The first stage is to remove all dead, diseased, and damaged wood. Then prune out any crossing or congested branches and those that spoil the balance of the framework. It is best to carry out extensive renovation over two or three years to allow gradual recovery since drastic pruning may severely weaken or even kill a tree in poor health. If you need to remove any large branches, do this in sections (see "Removing a branch", p.71).

After renovating the tree, feed it by mulching with well-rotted manure and apply fertilizer to the ground

beneath the tree canopy in spring for two to three years. Hard pruning may stimulate the growth of a mass of sideshoots; if congested, thin some of them out to leave a well-balanced framework. Any suckers and water shoots should be removed as soon as they are noticed (see p.69).

Renovating "haircut" pruned trees

Trees that have had all their new growth trimmed back annually produce a congested cluster of shoots every season on knobbly branches, but without the balanced framework of a true pollard. Such "haircut" pruning is unsightly and reduces flowers and fruit. To correct it, first thin out the knobbly stumps at the ends of the main branches. Cut out most of the young shoots on the remaining stumps to leave just one or two and cut these back by about one third; repeat this procedure in the following three or four seasons to develop a more natural growth habit.

Tree surgeons

For pruning, renovation, or removal of large trees, it is advisable to consult a qualified tree surgeon. The nearest horticultural college or arboricultural association may be able to supply a list of approved consultants and contractors, who comply with required standards of safe working practices and technical competence.

Before inviting contractors to tender, decide exactly what work is required, including the disposal of any debris which may be the most expensive part of tree surgery operations. Quotations are normally provided free, but a fee may be charged if advisory work is involved.

RENOVATING A TREE

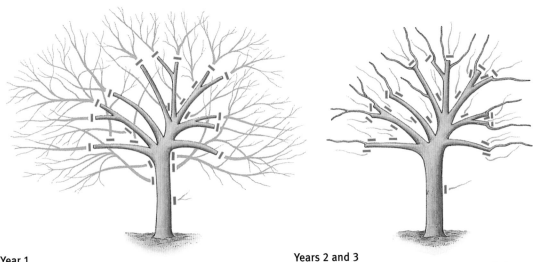

Year 1
Cut out any dead, diseased, and damaged wood, and remove any branches that cross or rub against others and that spoil the balance of the framework.

Years 2 and 3
The following year, thin out the new growth that results from the initial pruning and remove any water shoots. Repeat the next year if necessary.

Pleached trees

Pleached, or plashed, trees are clear-stemmed trees planted in one or more rows with their branches trained horizontally to intertwine, creating a formal, raised "wall" of foliage when in leaf (see "Trees for avenues", p.58). Hornbeams (*Carpinus*) and limes such as *Tilia platyphyllos*, *T. cordata* 'Winter Orange', and *T. x euchlora* make excellent pleached avenues, as they can be clipped precisely and, within four or five years, develop an effective, boxed appearance. It is best to use young trees with pliable stems when pleaching.

Constructing the framework

Until the trees are established, they should be trained in to a framework. First, using one stake for each tree to be planted, set up a row of 2.5–3m (8–10ft) high, stout stakes an equal distance apart. Once driven into the ground to a depth of approximately 60cm–1m (2–3ft), they should be at the required height of the lowest branches – about 2m (6ft) or more if they are to allow people to walk underneath. Attach a secondary framework of wooden battens or wires to these stakes to create the desired, overall height.

Initial training

Plant a young tree next to each stake in late autumn or early winter. Choose trees that are sufficiently tall so that their laterals may be trained in to the framework. After planting, tie in the leader and laterals, pruning out any badly placed ones.

Further training

Throughout the growing season, pinch out all new shoots that cannot be trained sideways. Tie in the leader as it extends, and train along the top batten. Tie in a suitably positioned lateral along the top batten on the other side of the main stem.

In winter, shorten any long laterals back to a strong sub-lateral, and cut sub-laterals back to two or three buds, to stimulate new stems to cover the framework. Continue to develop a boxed effect in subsequent seasons by tying in branches and cutting back the laterals to stimulate new shoots and dense growth.

Once the pleached trees are fully established and the branches have intertwined, the framework may be dismantled. Maintain healthy, dense growth by removing any dead, damaged, or diseased wood, and strongly outward-growing laterals; rub out young shoots on main stems as soon as they are noticed.

ESTABLISHING THE FRAMEWORK

Year 1

Having constructed a strong framework, plant a three- or four-year-old tree in front of each post, aligning as many laterals as possible parallel to the framework. Tie in the leader, adding extra ties during the subsequent growing season as the tree develops.

Remove any laterals that cannot readily be secured to a wire or batten. Tie the remaining laterals along an adjacent wire or batten.

Cut back to the main stem any laterals below the bottom wire or batten.

Year 2

Intertwine and tie in any untrained branches to the framework to fill in spaces. Pinch or rub out any new growth on the clear trunks.

Once the leader is tall enough, bend it over onto the top horizontal of the framework, and tie it in. Train a suitably placed lateral along the top batten on the other side.

In winter, prune back sub-laterals to two or three buds to encourage new growth.

ANNUAL MAINTENANCE

Keep rubbing out shoots on the trunks and remove dead, diseased, or damaged growth. Check old ties and replace where necessary. Feed the trees well in spring.

Cut back to one bud all new shoots that extend beyond the limits of the supporting framework.

Continue to weave and tie in suitably placed stems to the framework. As the gaps between the tiers narrow, shoots from above and below can be drawn and tied together.

Where shoots are growing away from the horizontal surface of the row, that is sticking out at the front or back, shorten to a sideways-facing bud.

Topiary

A FORM of training and pruning trees and shrubs to create attractive, boldly artificial shapes, topiary is a garden art that has been popular since Roman times. Traditionally used to produce strongly architectural and geometric shapes in formal gardens, it has been developed to include birds, animals, and unusual, even whimsical features such as giant chess-pieces and full-size trains.

Designing with topiary

Different styles of topiary may be used to create a variety of effects. Imaginative, living sculptures express personal style and add a humorous or bizarre touch. Using topiary for geometric shapes such as cones, obelisks, and columns provides a strong, structural element in a design. This type of topiary may be valuable both in formal gardens, perhaps to frame a vista or form an avenue, and in informal gardens, as a contrasting foil for less structured planting.

In some gardens, it may be appropriate to treat part of the hedge top as topiary, clipping it into one or more birds, spheres, or cubes, for example. Topiary may also be effective in containers; use a single container plant as a centrepiece, a pair to flank a doorway, or several to line a path. It can also be adopted to create eye-catching stem effects, such as twists and spirals, with one or more stems.

HOW TO CREATE A SIMPLE DESIGN

1 *If using a young plant (here box) to form a geometric shape, first cut the plant to shape by eye.*

2 *The following year, make a cutting guide from canes and wire, place over the plant, and cut the plant to shape.*

3 *When the plant is the desired shape, clip each year with secateurs to retain a crisp outline.*

Plants for topiary

Plants to be used for topiary require dense, pliable growth, small leaves, and the ability to recover quickly from clipping. Evergreens such as common box (*Buxus sempervirens*), privet (*Ligustrum ovalifolium*), yew (*Taxus baccata*), *Lonicera nitida*, and *Osmanthus delavayi* are ideal in a temperate climate. *Cupressus sempervirens* can be trained to suit geometric designs, but only thrives in warmer climates. Bay (*Laurus nobilis*), holly (such as non-spiny clones of *Ilex* x *altaclerensis*), and many other evergreens may be used, but are more difficult to train.

Ivies (such as *Hedera helix* 'Ivalace') are very adaptable and may easily be trained to grow up a frame; alternatively, several cuttings can be taken from an existing plant to grow up a moss-padded structure.

Creating a shape

Most topiary designs are best formed with the aid of a guiding framework, although some simple shapes may also be cut freehand.

Simple designs

Using young plants, select the stem or stems that will form the core of the design. The simplest shape to produce is a cone, which needs only guiding canes. For other shapes, attach a framework made from chicken wire or single wires attached to stakes placed in the ground next to the main group of shoots. Tie in the stems to the wire framework and then pinch back the shoots to encourage them to branch and cover the form.

Train new shoots into the framework to fill in any gaps, until they meet around its perimeter. Growth will vary around the plant, depending on the aspect. Shoots trained downwards always grow slowly.

Complex designs

Frameworks for complex designs are now generally available, although you may decide to make your own basic framework from sturdy materials such as heavy-duty fencing wire. Chicken wire or thin-gauge wire may then be intertwined to form a more precise shape. Garden canes are also useful as a temporary aid in developing and shaping a framework. Tarred twine is good for tying shoots onto a framework, since it eventually decays.

SHAPING A TOPIARY BIRD

1 *In year 1, insert a fan-shaped cane support at an angle to form the bird tail. Select and tie in well-placed shoots to the canes using soft twine. Tip back weaker shoots, to stimulate branching.*

2 *During the growing season, shorten the trained-in shoots by up to one third of their length, cutting just above a node. This will encourage dense, compact growth and a solid mass of foliage.*

3 *In year 2, insert a supporting cane for the bird head and tie three strong shoots to this cane. Trim the tail and tip back shoots on the body. Remove unwanted shoots or wire them to bulk out the tail.*

4 *In year 3, tie down the strongest shoot at the head to form the beak. Continue trimming to shape the body more precisely; keep the tail growth dense. Once the shape is formed, clip regularly.*

Clipped bird
Traditional shapes are still the most popular for topiary. This delightful bird sits on top of its nest surveying the surrounding gardens.

Training stems

Young stems being trained onto a frame grow quickly and considerable work is thus required to tie in new shoots throughout the growing season. Tie in the shoots while they are young and pliable and make sure that previous ties are not broken, rubbing, or in any way restricting the shoots.

If stakes have been used in the framework, make sure that they are still firm and have not cracked, snapped, or bent. If they are defective, replace them with new ones.

Clipping

Topiary involves much more precise clipping than is required for normal hedge cutting. Take time, particularly when initially forming topiary

pieces, to cut the branchlets carefully to the required shape. Do not cut too much in one place as it may spoil the symmetry of a topiary design for a whole season until new replacement growth appears.

Even if you have a good eye for shaping plants, it is sensible to use levels, plumb lines, and any other aids available to check the accuracy of a cut. Always work from the top of the plant downwards and from the centre outwards, cutting both sides together to retain a balanced symmetry.

Rounded topiary pieces are easier to produce and maintain than angular, geometric shapes and may often be cut freehand. To produce a spherical shape, first trim the top of the plant and then cut a channel downwards around the circumference to leave a ring. A further ring at 90° should then be cut, leaving four distinct quarters to be trimmed.

Geometric topiary that has precise, flat surfaces and angled or squared edges is difficult to form and maintain successfully and needs to be tackled with confident, accurate clipping for a well-defined shape. Such geometric designs are best cut using guidelines attached to canes to maintain symmetry.

When to clip

Once a topiary feature is established, it will need frequent routine clipping during the growing season. The time between cuts will depend on the rate of growth. An intricate, geometric design in box may need to be cut at four- to six-week intervals. Trim as soon as any new growth begins to appear uneven.

Architectural designs
Two spiral shapes eye-catchingly enhance the central, cone-shaped topiary along this path as well as complementing the two dome-shaped, side pieces.

If a perfect finish is not required throughout the year, two cuts during the growing season are usually sufficient for a reasonable effect, depending on the plant used. Yew, for example, need be cut only once a year, box (depending on the cultivar) usually needs to be cut twice, and *Lonicera nitida* three times.

Clip plants at the appropriate time of year. Do not clip bushes after early autumn as the young shoots produced after the first clip need to ripen sufficiently to withstand low winter temperatures. In warm climates where growth may be almost continuous, regular trimming will be required throughout the year.

Routine care

Weeding, watering, and mulching is essential in the same way as for free-growing shrubs (see p.100). It is important, however, to apply two or three feeds of a balanced fertilizer at a rate of 60g/sq m (2oz/sq yd) during the growing season.

Winter care

In regions where regular snowfalls occur, netting topiary pieces will help prevent the branches from breaking under the weight of snow. Knock snow off any flat surfaces as it may damage the framework.

Repairs and renovation

If a leader, a section, or a branch of topiary has been damaged or broken, cut it back cleanly with secateurs. Manipulate nearby shoots by tying them in to fill the gap.

If topiary plants have been left unclipped for one or two years, regular clipping should restore the original form within the season. If the topiary has been neglected for years, and the shape has been lost, severe pruning to restore the outline should be carried out the first spring followed by two or three seasons of more precise clipping.

Scorch and die-back

The foliage of some evergreens may be scorched in fierce winters and can die. The damaged foliage will soon be covered by new growth in spring, but cut it back where it is unsightly, taking care to follow the shape of the topiary piece. If shoots do not fill the gap, there may be a root problem, which will need to be treated.

HOW TO MAKE A COMPLEX DESIGN

1 *Make frameworks for large topiary pieces from strong materials as they will be in place for several years. Clip a young plant (here yew) as necessary to keep it within the framework.*

2 *As the plant grows and fills the frame, clip it over once a year, following the outline of the framework and pinching out shoots to encourage bushy growth.*

3 *When mature, the plant will form a dense bush and cover the framework. It needs regular clipping to maintain the precise outline of the design.*

Propagation

TREES may be propagated from cuttings, seed, layering, or grafting. Taking cuttings is probably the most common method of propagation as it is fairly simple and provides new plants relatively quickly, while raising trees from seed or layering is easy but very slow. Grafting is rarely used by amateur gardeners because it requires considerable expertise to grow new plants successfully this way.

Tree species may be propagated from seed but hybrids and cultivars rarely come true to type. Vegetative methods of propagation, such as taking cuttings, layering, and grafting, may be used for hybrids and cultivars as well as species; however, some care in the selection of plant material is required in order to be successful.

Hardwood cuttings

Many deciduous trees may be propagated from hardwood, or dormant, cuttings. In early autumn, prepare the ground for the cuttings while it is still warm. Cuttings can be inserted either outdoors in open ground or, for trees that do not root very easily, in the more stable environment of a cold frame.

Cuttings of trees that root easily, such as willows (*Salix*), may be inserted directly into a trench, while those that are more difficult to root, such as *Metasequoia*, should be inserted in a sand bed, and then transplanted into a trench early the next spring. In either case, make the trench narrow and with one side vertical so that the cuttings are held upright while they root. The depth of the trench will depend on the type of plant required: for multi-stemmed trees, it should be 2.5cm (1in) shallower than the length of the cuttings; for single-stemmed trees, it should be the same depth as the cuttings so that the top bud is barely covered and the lack of light inhibits the growth of all other buds.

For best results, dig the trench in friable, well-drained soil; in heavy, clay soil, add some coarse sand to the base. If preparing a few trenches, space them 30–38cm (12–15in) apart in open ground, or about 10cm (4in) apart in a cold frame.

SLOW-ROOTING HARDWOOD CUTTINGS

1 *For species that do not root easily (here* Metasequoia*), tie cuttings into bundles. Dip the ends in hormone rooting powder.*

2 *Insert the bundles of cuttings in a sand bed and leave in a cold frame over winter. In spring, insert them individually in a trench in a prepared site outside.*

Preparing and inserting the cuttings

Select the cuttings just after leaf fall: choose strong, vigorous shoots of the current season's growth and remove them by cutting just above a bud or pair of buds at the junction between the current and the previous season's growth. Trim down the cuttings as shown and dip the basal cuts in hormone rooting powder to encourage them to root. Place the cuttings against the vertical side of the trench at the correct depth, and backfill with soil. Then firm in gently and water well.

For species that do not root easily, tie the cuttings into bundles of no more than ten and then plunge them in a sand bed (see p.638) in a cold frame for the winter, where they should root before being transplanted.

FAST-ROOTING HARDWOOD CUTTINGS

1 *To prepare the trench, push the spade vertically into the soil, then press it forwards slightly to form a flat-backed trench about 19cm (7in) deep.*

2 *Select strong, straight stems with healthy buds (right); avoid soft, spindly, old, or damaged stems (left). Remove about 30cm (12in) of the stem, cutting just above a bud.*

3 *Remove any leaves. Trim the cuttings to about 20cm (8in): make an angled cut just above the proposed top bud and a horizontal cut below the bottom one.*

4 *Insert the cuttings in the trench 10–15cm (4–6in) apart, and at the correct depth depending on whether a single- or a multi-stemmed tree is required.*

PLANTING DEPTHS

Multi-stemmed trees
For multi-stemmed trees, insert cuttings with the top 2.5–3cm (1–1½in) above the soil surface.

Single-stemmed trees
The top bud of each cutting should be just below the soil surface.

5 *Firm the soil around the cuttings, rake the surface, and label. Space any further rows 30–38cm (12–15in) apart.*

6 *Lift the rooted cuttings the following autumn. Then pot them up individually or transplant them into open ground in their final positions.*

Aftercare

Label the cuttings and leave them until the following autumn. During winter, the ground may be lifted by frost; refirm the soil around the cuttings if this occurs. By autumn, the cuttings should be well rooted and may then be transplanted individually into open ground or into containers, as required. If they have been kept in a cold frame, harden them off in the first spring, then transplant outside; the following spring, pot them up or move them to their final positions in open ground.

Semi-ripe cuttings

Many conifers, as well as certain broadleaved evergreens such as *Magnolia grandiflora* and *Prunus lusitanica*, may be propagated readily from semi-ripe cuttings. These cuttings are taken in late summer or autumn from stems that have virtually ripened, that is, when they have thickened and become harder (see also ORNAMENTAL SHRUBS, "Semi-ripe cuttings", p.112).

Selecting the cuttings

In a closed case, at 21°C (70°F), or in a cold frame, prepare a suitable rooting medium for the cuttings. For example, this might consist of equal parts of grit and peat substitute or peat (see also "Standard cutting compost", p.565). Using a sharp knife, take heel cuttings from healthy sideshoots, including a sliver of hardened wood from the main stem (see ORNAMENTAL SHRUBS, "Heel cuttings", p.113). Alternatively, take 10–15cm (4–6in) long cuttings from leaders or sideshoots and trim immediately below a node.

For cuttings from conifers, choose leaders or sideshoots that are characteristic of the parent plant, as conifer shoots vary considerably in their growth patterns. It is particularly important to select cutting material carefully from slow-growing (dwarf) conifers; some plants may produce reverted or uncharacteristic shoots, but only use shoots that typify what you want to propagate.

Preparing and inserting the cuttings

With both types of cutting, cut off the lower pair of leaves with a sharp knife and reduce the remaining leaves by one third or a half to minimize the loss of moisture; if the cutting tips are soft, pinch them out. To encourage the cuttings to root, use the tip of the knife to make two shallow, vertical wounds, about 2.5cm (1in) long, on opposite sides of each cutting down to the base. Alternatively, make a longer wound along the side of each cutting with a knife, and remove a sliver of bark as well. In either case, dip the basal cut, including the wound, in hormone rooting powder.

Insert the bottom third of each cutting in the rooting medium, taking care to leave enough space between the cuttings so that they do not overlap; this allows air to circulate freely around them. Then firm the compost, water in thoroughly with a solution containing fungicide, and label.

Aftercare

Check the cuttings periodically, watering them only to keep them from drying out. Remove any fallen leaves as soon as they appear since these may rot and spread disease to the cuttings. In frosty conditions, cold frames should be insulated with hessian or a similar covering.

If the cuttings are being kept in a closed case with basal heat they should root by early spring. Cuttings in a cold frame are usually left until the following autumn, although it is preferable to leave them in the frame for a second winter and pot them up the following spring.

During the summer, mist-spray the cuttings frequently to stop them drying out. If the cuttings are in strong, direct sunlight they risk being scorched and it may be necessary to shade them; apply a greenhouse shading paint or place shading material over the frame (see p.576). Once the cuttings root, lift them out carefully with a hand fork and transplant them into individual pots, then harden them off (see p.637) before potting them on further or planting them out in open ground. Rooted cuttings in a cold frame may be hardened off while still in the frame by raising the frame cover for short then longer periods. Once they are sufficiently well rooted, pot them up or transplant them outside. If there may be a delay before potting up, give a liquid feed to the rooted cuttings in the interim.

Softwood cuttings

This method of propagation is suitable for birch (*Betula*), *Metasequoia*, some ornamental cherries (*Prunus*), and a few other tree species, although it is more commonly used for shrubs. Softwood cuttings are taken in spring from the fast-growing tips of new shoots and usually root very easily. They wilt rapidly, however, so it is vital to prepare and insert them as quickly as possible after removing them from the parent plant.

Preparing and inserting the cuttings

In spring, before taking the cuttings, prepare containers by filling them with an appropriate compost and then firming to just below the rim. Take the cuttings by removing the new growth from stem tips, cutting just above a bud or leaf joint with secateurs or a sharp knife. To reduce any moisture loss, immerse the cuttings in water straight away or place them in an opaque, plastic bag and seal it. Even a small loss of water will hinder the development of new roots.

Prepare the cuttings by trimming them with a sharp knife to about 6cm (2½in), cutting just below a leaf joint. Remove the lower leaves. The base of each cutting can be dipped in hormone rooting powder to encourage rooting. Insert the cuttings into the prepared pots of compost, label them, and water them with a dilute solution of fungicide.

To encourage rapid rooting, place the containers in a mist unit or closed case at 21–24°C (70–75°F), preferably with basal heat, and water with a fungicide once a week to protect against rotting and disease. Once they are rooted, the cuttings may be hardened off gradually before they are transplanted carefully into individual pots.

PREPARING A SEMI-RIPE CUTTING

Cut a shoot 10–15cm (4–6in) long from a leader or sideshoot and trim immediately below a node. Strip off the lower leaves (here of Chamaecyparis obtusa *'Nana Aurea') and pinch out the tip if it is soft. Make a shallow wound, about 2.5cm (1in) long, down the side of the cutting and dip it in rooting hormone.*

TREES TO PROPAGATE FROM CUTTINGS

Hardwood
Cordyline ✽
Ficus ✽
Metasequoia glyptostroboides
Morus
Platanus
Populus
Salix

Morus alba 'Laciniata'

Semi-ripe
Austrocedrus ▽
Calocedrus ▽
Chamaecyparis ▽
Cinnamomum ✽, ▽
x *Cupressocyparis* ▽
Cupressus ▽
Drimys winteri
Eucryphia

Eucryphia x *nymansensis* 'Nymansay'

Grevillea ✽
Hoheria
Ilex
Juniperus ▽
Ligustrum lucidum
Magnolia grandiflora ▽
Metrosideros excelsa ✽,
    M. robusta ✽,
    M. umbellata ✽
Michelia ✽, ▽
Nothofagus dombeyi
Podocarpus, some ✽, ▽
Prunus lusitanica
Quercus ilex ▽,
    Q. myrsinifolia ▽,
    Q. semecarpifolia ▽
Schefflera
Taxus
Thuja ▽
Thujopsis ▽
Trochodendron aralioides ▽
Tsuga ▽
Weinmannia ✽

Softwood
Acer cappadocicum
Betula
Catalpa
Celtis occidentalis
Cotinus coggygria
Eucryphia lucida
Ginkgo biloba
Halesia
Koelreuteria paniculata
Lagerstroemia, some ✽
Liquidambar styraciflua
Metasequoia glyptostroboides
Pistacia
Prunus
Ulmus

Key
✽ *Not hardy*
▽ *Take cuttings with a heel*

Raising trees from seed

Tree species may be propagated from seed as their seedlings usually retain the distinctive characteristics of the parent plant; hybrids and cultivars rarely come true to type. Raising a tree from seed is a relatively simple process; it is, however, a slow method if a tree is being grown mainly for its flowers, as the tree will take a number of years to reach flowering size.

Extracting seed

The protective covering of some seeds should be removed first. The method for this varies, depending on the type of seed coat. The coating on winged seed may be removed simply by rubbing it between finger and thumb. Some cones disintegrate naturally and the scales may then be separated. Place pine and spruce cones in a paper bag and keep them in a warm, dry place until the cone scales open and shed the seed into the bag; immerse cedar cones in hot water and leave them to soak until the scales open.

The method of extracting seed from fruits or berries depends on the seed size and type of flesh. Large fruits, such as those of crab apples (*Malus*), may be cut open and the seeds extracted. Soak smaller fruits, such as those of *Sorbus*, in warm water for several days. Viable seed will sink in water; discard any floating seed. Pick the remaining flesh off viable fruits so the seed is clean.

Storing

Once the seed has been extracted, dry it if necessary and place it in a sealed and labelled plastic bag. If planning to sow the seed within a few days, store it at room temperature; for longer-term storage, keep it on the top shelf of a refrigerator so that it is cool but not frozen.

CLEANING FLESHY SEED

1 Remove the fleshy seed with your fingers. Immerse it in warm water, and soak for 1–2 days. Once the fleshy coating has softened and split, drain off the water.

2 Pick off the remaining coating and wipe the seed dry. Sow the seed fresh or store it in a peat/vermiculite mix in a plastic bag in a refrigerator; sow in late winter.

Breaking seed dormancy

Some seeds have a natural period of dormancy to prevent germination in adverse climatic conditions which would threaten the survival of the seedlings; this has to be overcome before the seed will germinate. Several kinds of dormancy occur, sometimes combined, which vary according to the species: most commonly, dormancy is achieved either by a hard, thick seed coat, which prevents water being taken up, or by a chemical inhibitor, which delays germination until there is a significant temperature change. In most cases, dormancy can be broken artificially by wearing away the seed coat or by chilling the seed.

Scarification

Before sowing seeds with an impermeable coating, scarify them to allow germination to occur: large seeds with a particularly hard covering, such as oaks (*Quercus*), may be nicked with a sharp knife, or a section of the seed coat filed away to let in moisture; smaller seeds that are not easily nicked, such as those of pines, may be shaken in a jar that has been lined with sandpaper or partly filled with sharp grit, or they may be filed individually with an emery board. Seed from legumes (for example *Acacia* and *Robinia*) should simply be left to soak in a container of hot water for approximately 24 hours in a ratio of 3 parts hot water to 1 part seed.

Stratification

Dormancy in seed of trees from temperate climates is commonly overcome by chilling or "stratification". Seed may either be sown outside so that it is chilled naturally during winter or, more reliably, stratified artificially by being stored in a refrigerator.

If refrigerating seed, first mix it with moistened vermiculite, peat substitute, or peat. Place it in a clear plastic bag, then seal the bag and put it in a refrigerator. Check the seed regularly through the unopened bag – it should be sown as soon as there are signs of germination.

The length of chilling time required varies considerably: as a guideline, many deciduous species require about six to eight weeks of chilling at 0.5–1°C (33–4°F), while conifers need only about three weeks. Some seeds only germinate after they have been sown and once chilling has ceased. In such cases, sow batches of seed at intervals – for example after four, eight, and twelve weeks of chilling – as this should ensure that at least some seeds germinate.

Sowing seed in containers

This is a simple way of raising a small number of seedlings. Thoroughly clean any work surfaces and containers to be used before sowing the seed to avoid contamination from soil-borne pests and diseases. First fill the pots, pans, or seed trays with seed compost up to the rim.

Large seeds or those that produce seedlings with long tap roots, such as oaks (*Quercus*), should be sown about 8cm (3in) apart in deep single or multi-celled seed trays, or in flexible root trainers. Using a presser board, press the seeds into unfirmed compost, then cover them to their own depth with compost and firm to about 5mm (¼in) below the rim (see p.81).

Sow very large seeds, for example those of horse chestnut (*Aesculus*), singly in 10–15cm (4–6in) pots. Insert the seed in firmed compost, so that just the top of the seed is exposed above the surface.

Small seeds, for example those of *Sorbus*, may be either scattered evenly or, if sufficiently large, individually pressed into prepared pots or trays of firmed compost. They should then be barely covered with sieved compost followed by a layer of fine grit 5mm (¼in) deep.

After sowing, thoroughly water all seeds from above, then label. Place the containers in a cold frame or,

SOWING IN CONTAINERS

1 Sow fine seed (here Sorbus) in containers of firmed seed compost, making sure they are scattered evenly; keep your hand low to stop the seeds bouncing.

2 Hold a sieve containing seed compost over the tray, then tap the side of the sieve until the seeds are just covered to their own depth with sieved compost.

3 Cover the sown seeds with a 5mm (¼in) deep layer of horticultural grit. Label and water the seeds, using a watering can fitted with a fine rose.

4 Once the seedlings are large enough to handle, gently prick them out into individual pots, taking care not to crush the delicate stems or roots.

SOWING LARGE SEED

1 *Press large seeds and those of trees with long tap roots into unfirmed compost in individual pots. Cover with compost.*

2 *Sowing in long Toms – deep pots – allows the tap root (see inset) of each seedling (here* Quercus*) to develop without any restriction.*

Aftercare

Water and label the seedlings, and keep them out of direct sunlight in a temperature similar to that needed for germination until established. Gradually harden them off (see p.637) over a few weeks, feeding them regularly, and spraying them with fungicide. Do not overwater, but make sure that the compost does not dry out. Once hardened off, they may be planted out if there is no danger of frost.

Sowing seed outdoors

If raising a large number of seedlings, seed may be sown in an outdoor seedbed; with this method, the seedlings require less regular attention and their growth is less restricted than if sown in containers, but a special bed must be prepared. If possible, do this a few months before sowing by thoroughly digging the area to a spit deep (see "Single digging", p.619), incorporating organic matter and some coarse grit. Keep the ground clear of weeds.

When ready to sow, rake the soil down to a fine tilth, then broadcast small seeds or station sow larger ones individually. (For depth of sowing, see "Sowing seed in containers", p.80.) Lightly rake over the seeds, cover the bed evenly with a 0.5–1cm (¼–½in) layer of grit, and firm with a presser. If the soil is at all dry, water thoroughly; then label with the plant name and sowing date.

In exposed sites, young seedlings may need to be protected with windbreak netting (see p.613) or with a floating cloche (see p.582). If the seeds are well spaced, disease should not be a problem and the seedlings may be grown on *in situ* for 12 months before being pricked out. Water the seedlings as necessary and check them regularly in case treatment is needed for pests such as greenfly (see "Aphids", p.646) and red spider mite (p.646).

Layering

Layering may be used to propagate hybrids and cultivars as well as species. This method of propagation occurs naturally in some plants, when a low-growing stem roots itself in the ground; once this happens, the stem may be removed from the parent plant and grown on. Air layering, where the shoot remains above ground, may be used for trees without low-growing stems.

The advantage of layering is that the layered stem needs very little attention while the roots become established. It is a slow method, however, because in order to obtain

SIMPLE LAYERING

Cut a 5cm (2in) tongue 30–45cm (12–18in) behind the tip of a vigorous shoot, or remove a narrow ring of bark at this point. Brush the wound with hormone rooting powder and peg the shoot into a shallow hole. Tie the shoot to a supporting cane and backfill the hole.

Vigorous shoot

Friable soil

Peg

Tongue

suitable material the plant must be prepared a year in advance and the layered stem may take a year or more to root.

Simple layering

In this method, a shoot is pegged down into the ground until it has rooted and is then cut off from the parent plant (see also *Propagating a Shrub by Simple Layering*, p.116).

Prepare the parent plant a year before layering is to take place: in late winter or early spring, prune a low branch to stimulate new, young shoots that will root easily. In early spring the following year, select a vigorous shoot and make a small wound 30–45cm (12–18in) from the tip. Brush this with hormone rooting powder to encourage rooting. Add plenty of leaf mould or similar organic matter and sharp grit to the soil where the shoot touches the ground and peg it down into a shallow hole, tying it to a vertical cane.

Backfill the hole and firm the soil well, leaving the shoot tip exposed, then water thoroughly and, if necessary, protect the shoot from rabbits and other animals with wire netting. About 12 months later, check to see whether the shoot has rooted; if it has, sever it from the parent and either plant it in open ground or pot it up; if it has not rooted, leave it in place and check a month later.

Air layering

The principle of air layering is the same as simple layering, except that the layered shoot roots above the ground rather than in it (see also *Air Layering a Shrub*, p.117). In spring, select a strong stem that has ripened in the previous year, and remove any leaves 30–45cm (12–18in) behind the growing tip. Prepare the stem either by cutting a tongue 5cm (2in) long in the bark, 22–30cm (9–12in) behind its tip, or by removing a 6–8mm (¼–⅜in) wide ring of bark from the stem at this point; in either case, brush the wound with hormone rooting powder.

Surround the cut stem with a moist rooting medium and seal it in. To do this, first make a plastic sleeve by cutting off the sealed end of a plastic bag, then slide it along the stem until it surrounds the cut, and secure the lower end with string or tape. Moisten some well-aerated rooting medium (such as sphagnum moss or a mix of equal parts of peat substitute or peat and perlite), then use it to wedge open the tongue; add more medium around the stem inside the sleeve and seal the top.

If the layer has rooted by the next spring, sever the stem from the parent plant, remove the sleeve, and pot on; if not rooted, it should be left in place for another year.

TREE SEED REQUIRING STRATIFICATION

Acer (some)
Betula
Carya
Fagus
Sorbus

TREES TO BE LAYERED

Simple layering
Cercidiphyllum
Chionanthus retusus
Corylus
Davidia
Dipteronia
Eucryphia
Halesia
Hoheria lyallii
Laurus
Magnolia campbellii,
  M. grandiflora,
  M. obovata

Magnolia obovata

Air layering
Ficus ❋
Magnolia grandiflora,
  M. 'Star Wars'

Key
❋ Not hardy

---

within a greenhouse, in a closed propagation case or under a pane of glass. Temperate species are best kept at 12–15°C (54–9°F), and warm-temperate and tropical species at 21°C (70°F) to stimulate germination. Once the seeds have successfully germinated, spray them periodically with a fungicide to discourage damping off (see p.660).

Pricking out

When the seedlings are large enough to be handled by their seed leaves, prick them out so that they have more space to grow. This may be done by knocking the container sides to loosen the compost, and then lifting and transplanting the seedlings into individual pots. Alternatively, remove all the seedlings and compost together from the container so that the seedlings may be separated with minimal root disturbance. After transplanting, firm the compost gently around the seedlings, then level it by gently tapping the pot on the work surface.

Grafting

Grafted plants, unlike cuttings, have the benefit of a developed root system so they establish relatively quickly. Part of a stem (the scion), taken from the plant to be propagated, is joined to a compatible rootstock of another plant, usually of the same genus. In some cases, the rootstock may confer a desirable characteristic, such as a particular growth habit or high resistance to disease, on the resulting plant.

Grafting methods include spliced side, chip-budding, apical-wedge, whip, and whip-and-tongue. For details of whip and whip-and-tongue grafting, see PRINCIPLES OF PROPAGATION, p.636. Check that the rootstocks and scions are compatible.

Spliced side grafting

This is the most common grafting technique used for ornamental trees; a one-year-old stem is used for the scion and grafted onto the side of the prepared rootstock. It is usually carried out just before leaf break, in mid- to late winter, although for maples (*Acer*) summer-grafting is sometimes more successful.

Prepare the rootstocks a year in advance by potting up one- or two-year-old seedlings in autumn and establishing them in an open frame. About three weeks before grafting, bring them into a cool greenhouse to force them gently into growth. Keep the stocks dry, particularly those from trees that "bleed" sap, such as birches (*Betula*) and conifers, as excessive sap may prevent successful union with the scions.

For the scions, collect strong, one-year-old stems from the tree to be propagated; they should have a similar diameter to the rootstock stems if possible. Trim them down to 15–25cm (6–10in), cutting just above a bud or pair of buds, and place them in a plastic bag in a refrigerator until ready to graft. Either cut back the top-growth of the stocks to about 5–7cm (2–3in) or leave some top-growth above the graft and cut this back in stages later (see "Aftercare", p.83).

Prepare the stocks and scions, one pair at a time, with compatible cuts. It is important to unite the rootstock and scion as soon as they have been cut; if they are allowed to dry out even slightly, this is likely to impede successful union. If the scion is narrower than the stock, align one edge to ensure that at least one side of the cambium layer unites. Tie the

TREES TO BE GRAFTED

Chip-budding
Crataegus
Laburnum
Magnolia
Malus
Prunus
Pyrus
Sorbus

Aesculus indica
'Sydney Pearce'

Apical-wedge
Aesculus
Catalpa
Cercis
Fagus

Spliced side
Abies
Acer
Betula
Carpinus
Cedrus
Cupressus
Fagus
Fraxinus
Ginkgo
Gleditsia
Larix
Magnolia
Picea
Pinus
Prunus
Robinia
Sorbus

Robinia pseudoacacia 'Frisia'

Whip-and-tongue
Fraxinus
Gleditsia
Robinia

PROPAGATING TREES BY SPLICED SIDE GRAFTING

1 Trim the scion to a length of 15–25cm (6–10in), cutting just above a bud or pair of buds. Place it in a plastic bag and refrigerate until ready to graft.

2 Using a sharp knife, make a short, downward, inward nick about 2.5cm (1in) from the top of the rootstock.

3 Starting near the top of the stock, make a sloping, slightly inward cut down to meet the inner point of the first cut. Remove the resulting sliver of wood.

4 Make the final cut on the stock by slicing straight up with the knife from the first cut below. This leaves a flat cut on one side of the stock (see inset).

5 Now prepare the scion: make a shallow, sloping cut about 2.5cm (1in) long down to the base; then make a short, angled cut at the base, on the opposite side (see inset).

Growth visible from buds

6 Fit the base of the scion into the cut in the rootstock (see inset). Starting at the top, wrap a length of grafting tape around the union to secure it.

7 Brush grafting wax over the external cut surfaces on both the stock and the scion. In addition, wax the top of the scion if it has been trimmed back.

8 A few weeks later, if the graft has taken, the buds of the scion will show signs of growth. Remove any suckers that may have appeared on the rootstock or they will divert growth away from the scion.

scion in position with clear plastic grafting tape, raffia, or a rubberized strip, then wax over all external cut surfaces to reduce moisture loss. For advice on aftercare, see right.

Chip-budding

Mainly used for fruit trees, this is also a good way to propagate magnolias and plants of the Rosaceae family, for example crab apples (*Malus*). In this method, the scion contains a single bud from which the new growth develops, and the rootstock on which the scion is to be grafted is grown outdoors rather than potted up.

During winter, establish one- or two-year-old seedlings or hardwood cuttings in open ground. These will be used for the rootstocks. In midsummer, remove any lateral branches from the bottom 45cm (18in) of the stem. Select vegetative (non-flowering) shoots as scions (or budsticks) from well-ripened, current season's growth that are of a similar diameter to the rootstock.

The rootstocks and budsticks are then prepared and united (see below). If successful, the graft should unite within a few weeks; the tape or tie may then be removed. For aftercare, see right.

Apical-wedge grafting

This grafting method is similar to spliced side grafting, except that the scion is placed directly on top of the rootstock. In mid-winter, collect some stems of the previous season's growth from the plant to be propagated, and heel them into the ground. In late winter or early spring, lift and wash one-year-old seedlings or vigorous plants for the rootstocks, then cut them back to 5cm (2in) above the roots. Make a vertical cut 2.5–3cm (1–1¼in) down the centre of each rootstock. Cut the base of each scion into a wedge, and insert them into the tops of the stocks; leave the top of the cut on the scion exposed. Bind and pot up the grafted plants, then follow the aftercare guidance given below (see also ORNAMENTAL SHRUBS, "Apical-wedge grafting", p.119).

Aftercare

Deciduous trees should be kept in a greenhouse at 10°C (50°F), while conifers, broadleaved evergreens, and summer-grafted trees should be kept in a closed case in a humid environment at 15°C (59°F). The graft should unite in a few weeks and new growth will be seen on the scion. For even quicker results, place the grafted plants in a hot pipe (see PRINCIPLES OF PROPAGATION, "Hot-air grafts", p.637). Pinch off any suckers below the union as these are growing from the rootstock. After six to ten weeks, harden off the grafted plants. If not cut back at grafting, reduce top-growth of the rootstock to within 10cm (4in) of the union.

Tie the growing bud to the remaining top of the rootstock to ensure that the new shoot grows straight. In mid-summer, cut back the rootstock to just above the union and tie in the new shoot to a supporting cane. Alternatively, the stock may be cut back to just above the union in late spring. Once they are starting to grow vigorously, pot on the grafted trees or transplant them into open ground.

PROPAGATING TREES BY CHIP-BUDDING

1 *Select and cut the budstick (here Malus), choosing a long, vigorous shoot of the current season's ripened wood. It should have well-developed buds and be roughly the thickness of a pencil.*

2 *Cut off the soft wood and strip away any leaves at the tip of the shoot.*

3 *Using a sharp knife, make the first cut 2cm (¾in) below a healthy bud, inserting the blade about 5mm (¼in) deep at an angle of approximately 45°.*

4 *Start making a second cut about 4cm (1½in) above the first. Cut down through the wood to meet the first cut, taking care not to damage the bud.*

5 *Remove the bud chip, holding it by the bud between finger and thumb to keep the cambium layer clean. Place it in a clean plastic bag to prevent it from drying out.*

6 *To prepare the rootstock, cut off all the shoots and leaves from the bottom 30cm (12in) of the stem; it is easiest to do this while standing astride the stock.*

7 *Make two cuts in the rootstock to correspond with those on the bud chip so that the stock can be united with the chip. Remove the resulting sliver of wood, taking care not to touch the stem's cut surface (see inset).*

8 *Place the bud chip into the "lip" of the cut rootstock, so that the cambium layers of the chip and stock match as closely as possible (see inset). Bind the join tightly with grafting tape. If the graft takes, the bud will start to swell and develop; the tape can then be removed.*

9 *Next spring, cut back the stock just above the union; the bud will develop as the leader.*

Hedges and screens

Hedges and screens, both formal and informal, can play an important role in the structure and character of a garden as well as having a variety of practical uses.

Practical uses

Most hedges, whether informal, open hedges or formal, solid, clipped ones, are planted for utilitarian purposes, to delineate boundaries, to provide shelter and shade, and to screen the garden. It is possible, however, to combine use with beauty.

Living barriers

As living barriers, hedges may take some years to establish, but, if properly maintained, they are often preferable to fences because they provide texture, colour, and shape. Most plants used for hedging are long-lived and if correctly maintained will provide effective and sometimes virtually impenetrable barriers for many years.

Shelter

Hedges make excellent windbreaks, filtering fast-moving air and reducing the impact caused by turbulence when wind hits a solid object such as a wall or fence. The porosity of a hedge varies between species and times of year; thus a close-clipped, evergreen yew hedge (*Taxus baccata*) will be considerably less porous than a deciduous beech hedge (*Fagus sylvatica*) during winter. At the ideal of 50 per cent porosity it has been calculated that with a 1.5m (5ft) hedge, wind speed is reduced by 50 per cent at a distance of 7.5m (24ft) from the hedge; by 25 per cent at a distance of 15m (50ft); and by 10 per cent at a distance of 30m (100ft). The shelter provided by hedges is invaluable, particularly in windswept gardens where even hardy plants may suffer damage from gales and strong winds.

Noise barriers

Hedges may contribute to noise reduction by screening out unwelcome sounds. One of the most effective types in this respect is a green "environmental barrier", with a solid core of soil. A horizontal weave of osier (*Salix viminalis*) is threaded through vertical stakes and the core is packed with soil to form a wall. The osier roots into the soil core and the top and side growth is pruned back to the woven wall at intervals.

Ornamental hedges

A wealth of plants of diverse shape, size, texture, and colour can be used for hedges, deciduous or evergreen, formal or informal, or with flowers and fruit. Mixing evergreen and deciduous species selected for flower and foliage creates a living mosaic.

Formal

Yew (*Taxus baccata*) makes an excellent hedge, provided that six to ten years are allowed for establishment, while a hedge of x *Cupressocyparis leylandii* grows extremely rapidly. Low formal hedges are frequently seen in parterres as well as knot gardens and topiary (see TOPIARY, pp.76–77). Various forms of box (*Buxus sempervirens*), especially 'Suffruticosa', are used widely for formal hedges, as are *Santolina* and *Lonicera nitida*. Tapestry or mosaic hedges combine a number of compatible plants within the same hedge line, to provide changing visual effects throughout the year. Species used include *Taxus baccata*, *Ilex aquifolium*, *Carpinus betulus*, and *Fagus sylvatica*.

Mixing evergreen and deciduous species provides an interesting and colourful background throughout the year. Species used must have similar rates of growth if over-vigorous species are not to dominate.

Informal

Informal hedges combine practical and ornamental qualities. Although they are not suitable for creating strictly formal designs, they can still provide effective screening and shelter. Many of the plants used in these informal boundaries produce attractive flowers and fruit, or both, contributing form and colour.

PLANTS FOR INFORMAL HEDGES

Pyracantha 'Golden Charmer'

Fuchsia magellanica

Escallonia 'Langleyensis'

Ilex aquifolium 'Madame Briot'

Rosa 'Roseraie de l'Haÿ'

Garrya elliptica 'James Roof'

FORMAL, CLIPPED HEDGES

Hedging plants	Planting distance	Appropriate height	Clipping times	Responds to renovation
Evergreen				
Buxus sempervirens (box)	30cm (12in)	30–60cm (1–2ft)	Twice/3 times, in growing season	Yes
Chamaecyparis lawsoniana (Lawson cypress) – most cultivars except dwarf types	60cm (24in)	1.2–2.5m (4–8ft), but may be larger	Twice, in spring and early autumn	No
x *Cupressocyparis leylandii* (Leyland cypress)	75cm (30in)	2–4m (6–12ft), but up to 6m (20ft)	Twice/3 times, in growing season	No
Escallonia	45cm (18in)	1.2–2.5m (4–8ft)	Immediately after flowering	Yes
Ilex aquifolium (holly) and cultivars	45cm (18in)	2–4m (6–12ft)	In late summer	Yes
Lavandula (lavender)	30cm (12in)	45–90cm (18–36in)	In spring and after flowering	No
Ligustrum (privet)	30cm (12in)	1.5–3m (5–10ft)	Twice/3 times, in growing season	Yes
Lonicera nitida (honeysuckle)	30cm (12in)	1–1.2m (3–4ft)	Twice/3 times, in growing season	Yes
Taxus baccata (yew)	60cm (24in)	1.2–4m (4–12ft), but up to 6m (20ft)	Twice, in summer and autumn	Yes
Thuja plicata 'Fastigiata'	60cm (24in)	1.5–3m (5–10ft)	In spring and early autumn	No
Deciduous				
Berberis thunbergii	45cm (18in)	60cm–1.2m (2–4ft)	Once, in summer	Yes
Carpinus betulus (hornbeam)	45–60cm (18–24in)	1.5–6m (5–20ft)	Once, in mid- to late summer	Yes
Crataegus monogyna (hawthorn)	30–45cm (12–18in)	1.5–3m (5–10ft)	Twice, in summer and autumn	Yes
Fagus sylvatica (beech)	30–60cm (12–24in)	1.2–6m (4–20ft)	Once, in late summer	Yes

Integrate the different colour backgrounds carefully into the overall design. *Cotoneaster lacteus*, *Berberis darwinii*, or *Forsythia* are often used; hybrid shrub roses and species also make fine informal hedges. Most strong-growing bamboos are suitable for areas where soil moisture is high and a wind filter is needed.

Choosing plants

Before selecting species for hedging consider their eventual height, spread, and speed of development, and ensure that species chosen are hardy within the climatic zone, and suited to the soil type of the garden. Plants for formal hedges must have a dense habit of growth, and be tolerant of close clipping. For informal hedges grown for their flowers or berries, choose plants that need pruning only once a year. The timing of pruning is critical, otherwise the next season's display of flowers or fruit may be spoiled.

The choice of evergreens or deciduous species is partly a matter of taste, but bear in mind that evergreens and conifers provide a dense, wind-proof screen throughout the year, offering protection which may be critical in severe winters.

Soil preparation and planting

Hedges are a permanent feature of a garden. It is therefore important to prepare the site thoroughly before planting, and to top-dress each spring with a well-balanced fertilizer and mulch. Young plants should be planted in a single row in a trench 45–60cm (18–24in) wide, while more mature plants require 60–90cm (24–36in) of prepared ground, depending on the size of the root ball. Double rows, 90cm (3ft) apart, are rarely needed, except possibly for stock-proofing purposes. Young plants are particularly vulnerable to drought, so lay a seep hose along the base of the newly planted hedge and water regularly when the plants are first establishing. Alternatively young hedging plants can be kept moist by planting them through landscape fabric or black plastic sheeting (see "Planting through sheet mulch", p.614). This will also help to discourage competitive weeds.

Aim to prepare the site a month or two before planting to allow the soil to settle. Work well-rotted manure into the bottom of the trench, and mix a general fertilizer with the soil when backfilling the trench.

At planting time, dig a trench rather than individual holes for bundled, bare-root hedging plants, such as mixed native species. For all other hedging plants, soil preparation and planting techniques are the same as for trees and shrubs (see pp.63–67 and pp.97–99).

Spacing for most hedging plants is 30–60cm (12–24in) – see the charts below. If a hedge 90cm (36in) thick or more is required, plant a double, staggered row with spacing of 90cm (36in) within the row, and 45cm (18in) between rows. Plants for dwarf hedges, parterres, and knot gardens should be 10–15cm (4–6in) apart.

Pruning and training

The initial training of a formal hedge is crucial to promote even growth from the base of the hedge to the top. Careful attention to pruning in the first two to three years is essential.

Early pruning and shaping

Most deciduous plants, especially those with a naturally bushy, low-branching habit, need to be cut back by one third on planting, with strong laterals also cut back by one third of their length. In the second winter, cut back again by about one third.

Leyland cypress

The evergreen Leyland cypress (x *Cupressocyparis leylandii*) is an extremely vigorous conifer that, if treated correctly, can make an ideal tall screen or windbreak, often growing 45–60cm (18–24in) in a season. It has, however, gained a bad reputation when planted as a garden hedge, because its rapid growth is frequently allowed to continue unchecked. If not clipped back regularly, Leyland cypress will soon deteriorate and then, because it does not renovate well and remains unsightly when cut back hard, it will need replacing.

In spite of its vigour, Leyland cypress can be maintained very successfully as a garden hedge no more than 2–2.5m (6–8ft) high and 60–100cm (2–3ft) thick. In order to do this, in the first year after planting trim the sideshoots back to within 15–20cm (6–8in) of the main stems. In the following season trim back the sideshoots at least three times during the growing season, and if growth is vigorous probably four times. This treatment will produce very dense compact growth.

When the hedge has reached 30cm (1ft) below the height eventually required, cut back the leader shoots. Then prune back the sides and top of the hedge at least twice a year – in early to mid-summer and again in late summer to early autumn. Taper the sides so they slope towards the top of the hedge.

Year-round colour
x Cupressocyparis leylandii *cultivars produce contrasting shades of foliage in a mixed conifer hedge.*

INFORMAL AND FLOWERING HEDGES

Hedging plant	Ornamental qualities	Planting distance	Appropriate height	When to prune
Evergreen				
Berberis darwinii	Yellow flowers, purple berries	45cm (18in)	1.5–2.5m (5–8ft)	Immediately after flowering
Cotoneaster lacteus	White flowers, red fruits	45–60cm (18–24in)	1.5–2.2m (5–7ft)	After fruiting
Escallonia	White, red, or pink flowers	45cm (18in)	1.2–2.5m (4–8ft)	Immediately after flowering
Garrya elliptica	Grey, green, red, or yellow catkins	45cm (18in)	1.5–2.2m (5–7ft)	Immediately after flowering
Ilex aquifolium	White flowers, berries	45–60cm (18–24in)	2–4m (6–12ft)	In late summer
Lavandula	Purple flowers, grey foliage	30cm (12in)	0.6–1m (2–3ft)	In early to mid-spring
Pyracantha	White flowers, red berries	60cm (24in)	2–3m (6–10ft)	For pruning, see p.109
Deciduous				
Berberis thunbergii	Pale yellow flowers, red fruits, red autumn foliage	30–38cm (12–15in)	1–1.2m (3–4ft)	After flowering, if required to keep in check
Corylus avellana	Yellow catkins	45–60cm (18–24in)	2–5m (6–15ft)	After flowering
Crataegus monogyna	Fragrant white flowers, red berries	45–60cm (18–24in)	3m+ (10ft+)	In winter, remove selected vigorous shoots
Forsythia x *intermedia* 'Spectabilis'	Yellow flowers	45cm (18in)	1.5–2.2m (5–7ft)	After flowering, remove old stems
Fuchsia magellanica	Blue/red flowers, black berries	30–45cm (12–18in)	0.6–1.5m (2–5ft)	In spring, remove old stems
Potentilla fruticosa	Bright yellow flowers	30–45cm (12–18in)	0.6–1.2m (2–4ft)	In spring
Prunus spinosa cultivars	Pale pink or white flowers, red and purple foliage	45–60cm (18–24in)	2.5–4m (8–12ft)	In winter, remove selected vigorous shoots
Ribes sanguineum 'King Edward VII'	Deep pink flowers	30–45cm (12–18in)	1.5–2m (5–6ft)	After flowering, remove selected shoots
Rosa 'Nevada'	Fragrant cream flowers	60cm (24in)	1.5–2m (5–6ft)	In spring, remove thin twigs
Rosa 'Roseraie de l'Haÿ'	Fragrant crimson flowers	45cm (18in)	1.5m (5ft)	In spring, remove thin twigs

FORMATIVE PRUNING

Before pruning
Leaders and laterals have grown unrestricted; the hedge (Lonicera nitida) needs formative pruning.

After pruning
Cut back the laterals by half and prune the leaders to the required height to encourage bushy growth. Water, feed, and mulch if needed.

HOW TO SHAPE A HEDGE

1 *Stretch a taut, level string between two upright posts to act as a guideline for the highest point of the hedge, then cut the top of the hedge along this line.*

2 *Cut a template of the shape required. Place the template on the hedge and cut following the line of the template, moving it along as you proceed, then cut the sides.*

3 *Once you reach the end of the hedge, remove the template, posts, and lines of string. Clip the end of the hedge neatly.*

To shape strong-growing plants and those with an upright habit of growth, such as privet (*Ligustrum*) and hawthorn (*Crataegus*) cut them back to within 15–30cm (6–12in) above ground level in late spring, followed by a further clipping back of laterals in late summer. During the second winter or early spring, cut hard back, removing at least half of the previous season's growth.

Even from this early stage the hedge sides should be cut at a more or less oblique angle (referred to as the batter), with the base as the widest point. A hedge with a flat-topped "A" shape or a gently curved,

pointed top is less vulnerable to snow and strong winds. Snow will quickly fall away down the sides of a tapered hedge; high winds or gales will be deflected by its sloping sides, causing minimal damage to the plants.

A level top is achieved by cutting to a straight edge or garden line stretched between canes. It is important to use a guide when clipping low hedges too, since discrepancies are just as likely to occur when looking down as when viewing from eye level. Once the size and batter have been achieved, clipping to keep the hedge in shape is all that is required in subsequent seasons.

Conifers and many evergreens are used extensively as hedges. In most cases, laterals only are pruned during the early years, particularly in the formative second year, allowing the apical shoot to grow to the desired height before trimming back.

Maintaining a hedge

A formal hedge needs to be clipped regularly to maintain its shape: in most cases the hedge should be

SHAPING HEDGES

Make hedges narrower at the top to deflect strong winds and snow. In heavy snowfall areas, hedges should have pointed tops to prevent snow settling and causing damage.

Hornbeam   Yew

trimmed twice annually, in spring and late summer (see *Formal, Clipped Hedges*, p.84). Most formal hedges are cut with shears or an electric trimmer. Use a straight edge or a garden line as a guide when trimming the hedge to shape.

Informal hedges also need regular pruning to shape. Remove misplaced growths, and cut back within the required bounds. Flowering or fruiting hedges must be pruned only at the appropriate season (see *Informal and Flowering Hedges*, p.85). Informal hedges and those with large evergreen leaves should, where practical, be pruned with secateurs to avoid unsightly damage to the leaves.

Renovation

A number of hedging species, notably hornbeam (*Carpinus*), honeysuckle (*Lonicera*), and yew (*Taxus baccata*), respond well to renovation even where hedges have been neglected and have become overgrown. For best results, deciduous hedges should be renovated in winter, and evergreen ones in mid-spring.

If drastic pruning is required, alternate sides should be cut back in subsequent seasons. If the renovation is to be successful, it is most important to feed and mulch the plants in the season before pruning, and then again after cutting back to encourage healthy new growth.

TRIMMING HEDGES

Trimming with shears
To ensure that the top of the hedge is cut level and flat keep the blades of the shears parallel to the line of the hedge at all times.

Cutting with hedgetrimmers
When using an electrical trimmer, keep the blade parallel to the hedge and use a wide, sweeping action.

HOW TO RENOVATE AN OVERGROWN HEDGE

Cut back growth to the main stems on one side only of a neglected, deciduous hedge, trimming the other side as usual (right). A year later, if growth has been vigorous, cut back growth on the other side to the main stems (far right).

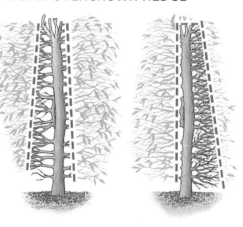

Willow walls

WEAVING with willow (*Salix*) stems has a long and distinguished history. Woven hurdles have been used for fencing since prehistoric times, and, when coated with thick layers of mud, clay, and dung, were a major building material in many parts of the world: wattle and daub.

Living willow, used as sculpture, is a new form of horticultural art. The contrast between the lines of the stems and exuberant, fresh young growth gives even functional items such as seats, screens, arbours, and arches an inherent sculptural quality, which many gardeners are becoming keen to incorporate into their own personal landscapes.

Suitable plants

The species or cultivar of willow must be matched to the size and nature of the proposed living structure. Vigour, physical strength, and aesthetic qualities are the main considerations. Most willows are flexible enough for weaving with the exception of the brittle *Salix fragilis*. Cultivars of *S. alba* are especially suitable, as their brightly coloured stems look spectacular in winter.

Preparation

Planting and weaving should be carried out in winter, when the plants are dormant. Willow can be inserted as normal hardwood cuttings of the current year's growth, about 38cm (15in) long and set 30cm (12in) deep, which are then allowed to grow on site, or as long rods that can be woven together immediately. Rods can establish just as successfully as cuttings provided the ground is well prepared, they are freshly cut, and are kept well watered. Another option is to use multi-stemmed plants, which are easy to develop from nursery-grown stock, hard-pruned to encourage the growth of two or more stems.

Plan the shape and height of the screen; it can follow a straight or curved baseline. Mark out the outline before planting, bearing in mind willows need bright light to thrive.

Work out how many rods of what length will be needed. Rods should be planted at least 15cm (6in) apart, and should be more widely spaced for tall screens using more vigorous cultivars. At 15cm (6in) apart, a 12m (40ft) screen would need 80 rods.

Weaving and tying

Once a row of evenly spaced rods has been planted, weaving can begin so an attractive diamond pattern is created. It is best to try and weave to the desired height in one go to keep the main lines straight. New shoots can be used to continue the structure upwards, but will not follow the

Regular maintenance
Although different willow cultivars vary in vigour, all living willow structures need pruning every winter and new shoots woven in. In summer shoots should be trimmed, but weaving should be avoided, because soft, new shoots are easily broken.

original rods exactly. The weaving itself will hold the stems together to some extent, but crossing points should be tied firmly with tarred twine. For simple screens, tie only every third or fourth crossing point.

The twine will biodegrade over about two years, but grafts may form more quickly than this. Check the tied crossing points regularly, and, if the stems have united, remove the tie.

Where long rods have been planted, remove sideshoots as they appear, so growth is restricted to the stem tips. This will encourage extension growth and the formation of the pressure grafts. Once the stems have united, allow sideshoots to develop and use them to fill in as required, again weaving them over and under the main stems. When structures are established, trim back or weave in new shoots regularly.

Weaving horizontal and vertical stems to form a screen of squares is more difficult. Horizontal living stems cannot be established initially, as they would have to be bent through 90 degrees. Dead stems can be woven in as horizontals until the verticals produce sideshoots which can take their place, but the screen will take longer to establish. Training shoots horizontally also lowers their sap flow and reduces vigour.

More complex structures

The other main weaving technique, which is used to form arches and tunnels, is to bend and twist the stems around each other. The twisted stems need to be tied to hold them together. Extra stability is also provided by planting large rods deeper than 30cm (12in); this does not affect their ability to root successfully.

HOW TO SHAPE A LIVING WILLOW WALL

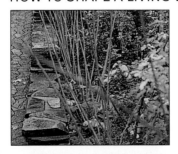

1 *Plant a row of evenly spaced rods. Then weave together by angling them at 45 degrees from the vertical and alternately crisscrossing over and under each rod.*

2 *Tie the crossing points securely with tarred twine. This will force the stems together as they expand and so unite their cambium layers, forming pressure grafts to hold the structure.*

3 *At the top of a screen, join the last row of crossing points with rubber plant ties. These allow the rods to move slightly in the wind and prevent their tops breaking.*

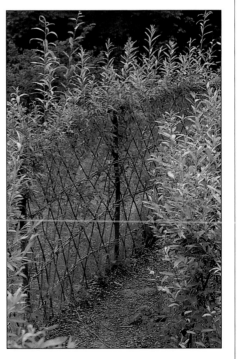

Green trellis
Screens of living willow make excellent garden sculptures. They have even been employed on a scale large enough to shield whole villages from the sights and sounds of heavy traffic.

CHAPTER

3

ORNAMENTAL SHRUBS

VALUED BY GARDENERS for their architectural quality and long-term interest, shrubs play an important role in forming the skeleton of a planting design. In a mixed border, they provide solidity and substance, balancing the softer, more transitory herbaceous plants, while grouping evergreen and deciduous shrubs allows you to create an effective, low maintenance display all year round. As well as a diversity of shapes and forms, shrubs possess a magnificent variety of features: from the shiny, palmate leaves of *Fatsia japonica* or the heavily perfumed plumes of lilacs, to the bead-like berries of pyracanthas or the icy white stems of *Rubus biflorus*. Whatever the size or situation, there is a shrub to suit every garden.

Shrubs for the garden

SHRUBS are woody-stemmed plants that typically produce a framework of branches from the base, unlike the single trunk characteristic of most trees. The division between shrubs and trees is not a rigid one, however, as some shrubs (such as fuchsias) may be trained as standards with a single trunk and a number of trees are multi-stemmed. Similarly, the difference in scale is not a clear demarcation, as some shrubs grow larger than some trees.

Whether the term "shrub" is used very strictly or rather more loosely, it covers an enormous choice of plants suitable for gardens of any size and style. Species have been collected from many parts of the world and these have given rise to numerous cultivars and hybrids of ornamental value.

Choosing shrubs

Shrubs are invaluable in the garden for many reasons; perhaps most important of all, they impart shape, structure, and substance to a design, and provide a framework. They are far from being purely functional keystones, however, for they are also endowed with a variety of ornamental qualities, including fragrant and colourful flowers, evergreen or variegated foliage, attractive fruits, and coloured or shapely stems.

These decorative attributes exert great influence on your choice of plants. There are, however, important practical considerations to be taken into account when deciding which shrubs to grow.

Informal planting

In this garden, an informal grouping of shrubs, including a variegated holly (Ilex aquifolium)*, the fiery* Euonymus alatus*, and a tall* Aesculus parviflora*, provide an effective display of contrasting colours and shapes.*

Compatibility with the given or adapted growing conditions is essential (see "Selecting shrubs for site conditions", p.91), while a shrub's growth rate, habit, and eventual height and spread also determine whether it is suitable for a garden or not and where it is best sited.

Form and size

In size, shrubs range from dwarfs, such as the mat-forming *Cotoneaster salicifolius* 'Gnom' at only 20–30cm (8–12in) tall, which are suitable for the rock garden, to much more substantial plants that are 5–6m (15–20ft) tall, such as some of the handsome, evergreen rhododendrons.

Shrubs have many different forms and habits, including rounded, arching, and vertical. Some – for example *Yucca gloriosa*, with its explosive spray of sword-like leaves and erect panicles of flowers – are worth growing for their form alone. Others, like *Chaenomeles japonica*, have a sprawling habit that often looks better if wall-trained. Most

are invaluable in low-maintenance gardening, especially low-growing shrubs used as ground cover, surrounded by bark or gravel mulches.

Shrubs as design features

When selecting shrubs, consider how they will associate with the other planting as well as any structural elements nearby, such as the house or patio. If they are to form part of the design framework, shrubs with distinctive, sculptural silhouettes are usually most suitable – for example the spreading, wave-like form of *Juniperus squamata* 'Blue Carpet' or the bold, upright mass of *Mahonia* x *media*. Think of them as abstract shapes that may be used singly or in combination to create a balanced scheme of contrasting and complementary forms.

Foundation planting

Shrubs are often used as foundation planting to link the house with the garden, forming a transition between the rigid lines of the building and the softer shapes and textures of border plants and lawn.

This type of planting is effective when used to mark the entrance to the house; symmetrical groups or rows of shrubs could flank the drive or the doorway, for example, or an informal curved bed might border a winding path to the door.

Design the planting so that it complements the style, colour, and scale of the building. Evergreen shrubs are often chosen because of their continuous display but, in an informal setting especially, including deciduous plants as well creates a greater variety of interest while still providing mass and structure.

Selecting shrubs for site conditions

To ensure that shrubs flourish and give pleasure for a long time, it is essential to invest in plants that will thrive in the particular conditions of your garden. Even within a small garden, these growing conditions often vary considerably. Since there are so many shrubs from which to make a selection, there is no need to grow plants that are unsuited to the chosen site.

Soil types
The character of the soil should be the first consideration; in many cases, it may be improved to widen the range of plants that can be grown satisfactorily. It is particularly important to make heavy soils more open and free-draining and light soils more moisture-retentive, as well as to moderate any excessive acidity or alkalinity that may be a problem.

Successful planting must take into account the soil's underlying character, however. Even for relatively

extreme conditions, there is a number of plants from which to choose: dogwoods (*Cornus*) and willows (*Salix*) like moist soils, for example, while broom (*Cytisus/ Genista*), lavender (*Lavandula*), and *Phlomis* thrive on well-drained soils. Rhododendrons and other ericaceous plants generally require acidic conditions; but many shrubs do well on alkaline soils, including *Deutzia*, *Hypericum*, and *Philadelphus*.

If a chosen planting site has only recently been cleared of weeds, plant the shrubs through holes in geotextile or black plastic sheeting, which will keep down competitive weeds until the shrubs are established (see "Planting through sheet mulch", p.614).

Aspect and microclimate
A plant's preference for sun or shade should also be borne in mind. Sun-lovers such as *Cistus* will become straggly if not planted in full sun, but many shrubs tolerate or even prefer some shade. The latter are often ideal for town gardens, where instead of dappled light filtering through the tree canopy there tend to be contrasts between full sun and deep shade cast by nearby buildings.

The hardiness of shrubs is another factor to consider. The temperature range, altitude, degree of shelter,

Growing plants in the right conditions
Light shade from the overhead tree canopy and acid soil are ideal for these impressive banks of rhododendrons lining an informal grass path. Clashing shades have been boldly mixed to create a spectacular avenue of colour.

aspect, and distance from the sea all affect the range that may be grown. The sea moderates temperature, but salt-laden winds can damage many plants in coastal gardens. There are, however, shrubs (such as most *Escallonia* and *Genista*) that benefit from mild conditions and tolerate salt spray. Plants of borderline hardiness for the area that might well succumb in the open garden are more likely to thrive as wall-trained specimens in a sheltered position.

Successional interest
When selecting shrubs, take account of the seasonal interest that they provide and whether it is continuous, as from evergreen foliage, or transitory, as from a burst of summer blooms. A shrub with a brief period of splendour is often best sited near one that reaches its peak shortly afterwards to create a changing but unbroken display.

Spring
As well as new, emerging leaves, shrubs bearing spring flowers are valued for the colour and vitality that they bring. Combine them to provide interest throughout the season – from the early *Salix hastata* 'Wehrhahnii', with its bud-like, silver-grey catkins borne on deep purple stems, to the fragrant, white and pink flower clusters of *Daphne x burkwoodii* 'Somerset' in late spring.

Summer
The choice of summer-flowering shrubs is immense and, again, they are best combined to form a continuous display. Invaluable shrubs

such as *Potentilla* 'Elizabeth' and *Syringa pubescens* subsp. *microphylla* 'Superba' deserve to be more widely grown, since their flowering period often extends from late spring until early autumn.

Autumn
This is the season when many deciduous shrubs really come to the fore, with colourful foliage providing an eye-catching spectacle. Shrubs for autumn interest include *Euonymus alatus*, with its intense red leaves,

Shrubs in a changing climate
While climate change and global warming are regarded as having many drawbacks, gardeners have found that one of the benefits has been to extend the range of shrubs that may be grown in the open garden without protection. Some of these have already been grown successfully in milder areas of the UK, for example in the west of Scotland and the Scilly Isles, although occasionally, during extremely severe winters, they may have suffered damage.

Shrubs now proving their worth outdoors that previously would have been damaged or killed by low temperatures include the attractive wattles, *Acacia baileyana* and *A. pravissima*; *Correa* species, such as *C. backhouseana*, all from Australia; the Mexican *Abelia floribunda*; and South African *Euryops pectinatus*.

RECOMMENDED SHRUBS FOR ACID SOIL

Rhododendron 'Homebush'

Camellia x williamsii 'Donation'

Erica x williamsii 'P.D. Williams'

Eucryphia milliganii

Gaultheria shallon

Vaccinium parvifolium

Rhododendron wardii

Gaultheria mucronata 'Wintertime'

Zenobia pulverulenta

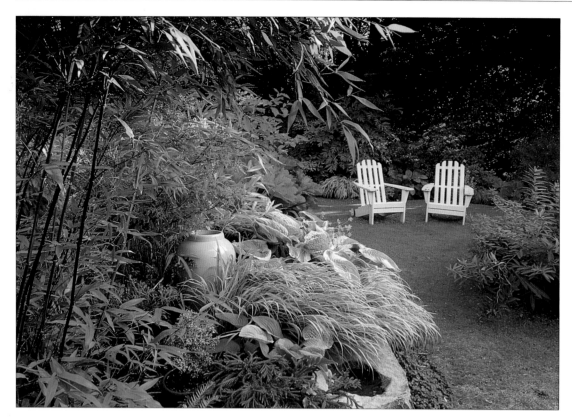

Cooling greens
Bamboos here help to create a soft-textured partition around this quiet sitting "room" in the garden. The wide variety of leaf colour and size of these evergreens provide invaluable sources of plant shape and height, and fit with most types of landscape and climates.

initially, so that in the short term the shrub border might have similar components to a mixed border. Dense planting, including ground cover, may help to keep down weeds although mulching is advisable to reduce weeds and water loss while the plants are becoming established.

Mixed borders

The idea of a mixed border is to combine a framework planting of shrubs with a variety of herbaceous plants to reap the benefits of both. Its main advantage is that the shrubs provide long-term, sometimes year-round, interest and a background to a succession of other plants. As the shrubs provide height and structure, there is less need to grow tall perennials that require staking than in a traditional herbaceous border.

The mixed border may be designed to suit various settings. If situated next to a wall, the planting may include a combination of wall-trained and other shrubs at the back as well as climbers, other plants being introduced in loosely shaped niches between shrubs in the foreground. In an island bed, shrubs are normally used to form an irregular core at the centre, surrounded by other plants in clumps or drifts.

Managing a mixed border is sometimes more complex than caring for a shrub one, because the various plants have diverse needs. It is, however, one of the most effective ways of bringing together the wide-ranging qualities of different plant groups.

Specimen shrubs

Shrubs that are particularly attractive – perhaps because of their fine shape or a characteristic such as exquisite flowers or striking foliage – may be best planted as individual specimens, sited so that they can be seen from a number of viewpoints.

Suitable shrubs

Since a shrub grown in this way clearly stands out in the garden, it is important that its appearance warrants

---

and the various cultivars of *Cotinus coggygria*, with yellow, red, or purple foliage. Colour from berries, such as the yellow clusters of *Pyracantha* 'Golden Dome' or the shiny red fruits of *Cotoneaster* 'Cornubia', is also valuable.

Winter

Shrubs are vital elements in the winter garden, with a rich variety of features. Evergreen foliage probably makes the greatest contribution,

providing bold masses of colour and texture. Flowers also play their part, however, with a choice ranging from the sculptural *Mahonia japonica*, with its spreading, yellow sprays, to the spidery, red flowers borne by *Hamamelis* x *intermedia* 'Diane', while other fragrant shrubs such as *Viburnum* x *bodnantense* may be welcome. Also common are shrubs with ornamental stems, such as *Cornus sericea* 'Flaviramea', which has vivid, lime-green shoots.

Restricted colour border
Here, a restricted colour scheme with a predominance of yellow, gold, and bright green creates a sunny, cheerful effect, with evergreen and deciduous shrubs including elders (Sambucus), *golden conifers, and* Euphorbia.

Shrub borders

One of the most satisfactory ways of using shrubs in the garden is to grow them in a border on their own. From the large range available that will be suitable for the soil, climate, and site, a selection may be made that will give a succession of colour and interest throughout the year. The aim is to create a balanced design, taking into account the shape, form, height, and spread of each shrub, as well as its ornamental qualities and any seasonal changes in appearance.

The planting may rely almost entirely on a blend of foliage textures and colours, but other features may also play a part. Include shrubs with interesting shapes, for example, and others with colourful berries or stems to maintain year-long interest. Resist the temptation to rely on flowers, since their display may be impressive but transitory. By careful selection, however, it is possible to sustain a long succession of flowers.

Some shrubs may be regarded as long-term plants while others tend to mature and fade quickly. When planning a border, space out the long-term shrubs so that they will not need thinning or drastic pruning to keep them in check once mature. Fast-growing shrubs may also be included but they should be thinned as soon as they threaten to crowd out the core planting of shrubs.

Herbaceous perennials, annuals, and other plants may be interplanted its prominent position. Shrubs with shapely silhouettes are especially suitable, such as the dense cone of *Pittosporum* 'Garnettii', although a flowering shrub such as *Camellia* x *williamsii* 'Donation' would also be an impressive focal point.

When selecting a plant to be grown as a specimen, its long-term interest is an important consideration. In a large garden, a relatively short but magnificent display may be sufficient for your needs. A shrub that occupies a prime spot in a small garden, on the other hand, needs to justify its presence by contributing colour and form throughout the year or by having more than one interesting phase – flowers and good autumn foliage, for example.

Siting a specimen shrub

When deciding where to site a specimen shrub, ensure its size will be in keeping with its position in the garden and that it relates well to the overall design. Often the best location is as the focal point of a view from a main window of the house or at the meeting point of two vistas. The background is as important as the shrub itself; usually, a uniform texture and colour, as provided by a dense, evergreen hedge or the green swathe of a lawn, forms the most complementary foil.

There is, however, scope for experimenting with the positioning of specimen shrubs, particularly in combination with other garden features, such as a pool that creates appealing reflections. Before planting, roughly assess the effect of the shrub's scale and position in the design by substituting bamboo canes of the same height and width.

Specimen shrub
In late spring and early summer, the spreading tiers of Viburnum plicatum *'Mariesii' are richly clothed with blooms, but its unusual shape ensures its value as a strong feature throughout the year.*

Wall-trained shrubs
Growing a shrub such as this pyracantha against a wall enhances its display of ornamental, bright orange-red berries.

Wall shrubs

A border at the foot of a warm, sheltered wall is a prime site for many plants; although it frequently tends to be somewhat dry, if the plants are adequately watered, the conditions are suitable for various shrubs that might otherwise be too tender to grow elsewhere in the garden.

Training shrubs against a wall is often the best option for lax shrubs such as *Ribes speciosum* and *Forsythia suspensa* that make tangled growth unless supported. For a number of shrubs, it is the best way of displaying their ornamental features, such as the orange or red berries of pyracanthas. Some hardy shrubs, such as *Chaenomeles*, that may also be grown free-standing, look attractive wall-trained, and complement the unfussy background.

Sometimes no training is needed: shrubs such as myrtle (*Myrtus*) may simply be planted close to the foot of a wall for them to benefit from the warmth and shelter. Other shrubs such as *Buddleja crispa* do need training to flower well.

Dwarf and ground-cover shrubs

Planting low shrubs, such as a number of *Hebe* cultivars or *Daphne* 'Bramdean', within raised beds or containers makes it very easy to appreciate them at close quarters, as well as providing structure and long-term interest in the planting scheme. On a large scale, use low-growing shrubs to balance against contrasting, rounded, or upright forms in beds and borders.

These shrubs are also excellent where interest is needed at ground level; *Helianthemum* cultivars and a vast array of colourful heathers (*Calluna*, *Daboecia*, and *Erica*) brighten up the front of a mixed border or soften the hard edges of a path.

Some spread into an attractive carpet that forms a fine foil for other planting. Those that are relatively fast-growing may be used as ground cover (see p.101). Ground-cover shrubs present one of the best solutions for sites such as steep banks that are difficult to cultivate; even in the unpromising, shady areas directly beneath trees, shrubs such as *Mahonia repens* and cultivars of *Euonymus fortunei* grow well.

Foliage

The substance and the seasonal continuity of a garden depend to a large extent on foliage. Evergreen shrubs, in particular, hold the garden together all through the year. The leaves of deciduous shrubs – from spring growth to autumn leaf – also give a longer period of interest than most flowers.

Colourful ground cover
To create a colourful patchwork effect, use harmonizing and contrasting low-growing shrubs. Here, massed heathers make a fine display.

Colour

Much may be made of foliage colour, which includes not only every shade of green but also silvers and greys, reds and purples, as well as yellow, gold, and variegated forms. The boldest leaf colour effects, such as the yellow of *Choisya ternata* SUNDANCE, the red of the young growth of some *Pieris*, or the white-splashed green of *Euonymus fortunei* 'Silver Queen', may be used in much the same way as flower colour.

Shape and texture

There are many other attributes of shrub foliage that are worth exploiting in an ornamental display. Large or distinctively shaped leaves such as those of *Fatsia japonica* are particularly striking, and changes of texture, from smooth and glossy to matt and felted, also provide satisfying contrasts.

Flowers

Ranging from the tiny, pea-like flowers of many brooms (*Cytisus/ Genista*) to the large, heavy panicles of lilacs (*Syringa*), there is an impressive diversity of shrub flowers.

Colour and form

Shrubs have flowers in every colour, with endless variations of each; for example, shades of pink range from the pale pinkish-white blooms of *Magnolia* 'Pinkie' to the crimson of *Rhododendron* 'Hinode-giri'.

Sometimes it is the sheer mass of flowers that appeals, as with the dense blue clusters of *Ceanothus* or the sprays of star-like, yellow flowers of forsythias, while other shrubs – such as the exquisite but short-lived flowers of *Paeonia suffruticosa* – seduce by the sumptuous beauty of their individual blooms.

In a large garden it does not much matter that a plant's star turn is only brief; in a small garden, this may be

Ornamental stems
An informal group of red-barked dogwoods (Cornus alba) forms a striking blaze of colour rising from a spreading mass of variegated Euonymus fortunei.

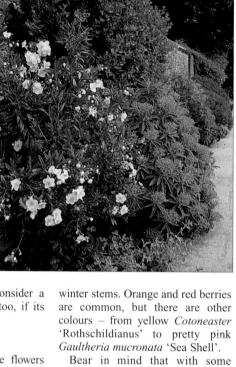

Flowers for scent
Fragrant shrubs such as Euphorbia mellifera *here are often best grown next to a path or patio so that their scent may be easily enjoyed. This white-flowered* Carpenteria californica *also benefits from the warmth and shelter of the wall behind it.*

a serious drawback, so consider a plant's form and foliage, too, if its floral display is very short.

Scent

While the appeal of some flowers lies largely in their colour and form, those that are scented give the garden another dimension. The flowers may be showy and also deliciously fragrant, as are many *Philadelphus*, or, as with the minute flowers of *Sarcococca*, more muted in appearance but casting their fragrance through the garden in midwinter.

Berries

Berrying shrubs are valuable for sustaining colour from late summer into winter, and also for attracting birds. On evergreens such as pyracanthas, bright berries framed by green foliage make an attractive contrast, while those on deciduous shrubs such as *Viburnum opulus* are seen against a changing backdrop of autumn foliage followed by bare

winter stems. Orange and red berries are common, but there are other colours – from yellow *Cotoneaster* 'Rothschildianus' to pretty pink *Gaultheria mucronata* 'Sea Shell'.

Bear in mind that with some species of shrubs male and female flowers are borne on separate plants. Thus, satisfactory fruiting is only achieved when male and female plants are grown in proximity.

Bark and stems

In winter, the silhouettes of bare stems may be very striking. As well as their sculptural simplicity, some, such as dogwoods (*Cornus*), are strongly coloured while others, for example *Salix irrorata*, are overlaid with an attractive, glaucous bloom.

Group a few shrubs of the same type together to reap the benefit of their massed stems, or site a single fine specimen against a simple background. Imagine the brilliant red stems of *Cornus alba* 'Sibirica' offset by a plain, white wall, or the chalk-white skeleton of *Rubus biflorus* by a dark one.

The delicate tracery of fine stems is often overlooked unless it is high-lighted by vivid colouring, but unusual shapes and heavily thorned or contorted shoots provide added interest. The bizarrely twisted stems of *Corylus avellana* 'Contorta' and *Salix* 'Erythroflexuosa' make them interesting curiosities to set against a plain wall or plants of more familiar growth pattern.

Many shrubs grown for their stems require regular pruning, because it is the new wood that is most effective (see "Coppicing and pollarding shrubs", p.107).

Shrubs in containers

Provided that they are watered and fed regularly, many shrubs adapt happily to life in containers: grown in this way, they make versatile as well as ornamental features. Use them as living sculptures to provide strong shapes and a framework to offset other planting. An evergreen shrub or dwarf conifer forms a fine centrepiece in a planter all year round, which may be complemented by bulbs in spring and colourful and trailing annuals in summer.

A container-grown shrub is particularly valuable in a small, paved garden, patio, or balcony. It may be used alone as an isolated specimen or combined with a changing display of other plants in containers. In a larger garden, a single, handsomely potted shrub may make a more striking focal point than a piece of garden statuary, for example. Container-grown shrubs may introduce a formal note simply, as a pair flanking a flight of steps or an archway, or, more elaborately, making a symmetrical framework or an avenue in grander schemes.

Selecting plants

The most suitable shrubs are those with a long season of interest. Good examples for containers include evergreen camellias and rhododen-drons, which remain attractive even after their flowers have faded. For valuable foliage effects, consider the tender *Chamaerops humilis*, which has huge, palm-like, glossy fans, and conifers with their wide range of colours and textures.

Deciduous foliage can change from spring to autumn and, in the case of Japanese maples (*Acer palmatum*), an intricate pattern of delicate stems remains when all the leaves have fallen. Shrubs such as *Spiraea japonica* 'Goldflame', with its strikingly coloured leaves and heads of rose-pink flowers, often look particularly fine grown in an ornamental container.

Practical advantages

An advantage of growing shrubs in containers is that tender plants, such as *Nerium oleander* and palms, may be used to give the garden a Mediterranean or subtropical look in the summer, and then be moved to a protected site for winter. It is also an excellent way of including shrubs that would not otherwise tolerate the soil of the open garden: for example, given lime-free water and ericaceous compost, camellias and rhododen-drons may be grown in pots or other containers even in chalky areas.

Planter's guide to shrubs

EXPOSED SITES

Shrubs that tolerate exposed or windy sites; those marked 🍃 are not suitable for coastal sites
Arctostaphylos uva-ursi
Bupleurum fruticosum
Calluna vulgaris (and cvs)
Cassinia leptophylla subsp. fulvida
Cistus, some ✲
Cordyline ✲
Cotoneaster (dwarf spp.),
    C. horizontalis
Elaeagnus angustifolia
Erica carnea (and cvs)🍃
Escallonia
Euonymus fortunei
    (and cvs)
Fuchsia magellanica
    (and cvs)

*Fuchsia
magellanica*

Gaultheria shallon🍃
Genista, some ✲
Griselinia, some ✲
Halimodendron halodendron
Hebe, some ✲
Hippophäe rhamnoides
Ilex aquifolium
Lavatera
Olearia, some ✲
Ozothamnus, some ✲
Phormium
Prunus spinosa
Pyracantha
Rhamnus alaternus
Rhododendron ponticum🍃
Salix
Senecio, some ✲
Spartium
Spiraea
Tamarix
Ulex
Yucca, some ✲

SHELTERED SITES

Shrubs that prefer sheltered sites
Abelia floribunda ✲
Abutilon, some ✲
Acer palmatum (cvs)
Ardisia ✲
Banksia ✲
Beschorneria ✲
Bouvardia ✲
Brachyglottis ✲
Citrus ✲
Coprosma ✲
Datura ✲
Dendromecon rigida ✲
Euryops pectinatus ✲
Musa basjoo ✲
Nerium ✲
Rhododendron maddenii,
    R. Section Vireya ✲

WALL SHRUBS

Abelia, some ✲
Abutilon, some ✲
Acacia dealbata ✲
Azara, some ✲
Buddleja crispa
Callistemon, some ✲
Camellia, some ✲
Ceanothus, some ✲
Cestrum, some ✲
Chaenomeles
Colquhounia
Daphne bholua
Fremontodendron
Itea ilicifolia
Pyracantha
Solanum crispum 'Glasnevin',
    S. laxum ✲

AIR POLLUTION

Shrubs that tolerate polluted air
Aucuba
Berberis
Buddleja davidii
Camellia japonica (and cvs)
Cornus sericea
Cotoneaster
Elaeagnus
Euonymus japonicus
Fatsia japonica
Fuchsia magellanica (and cvs)
Garrya
Ilex x altaclerensis, I. aquifolium
Leycesteria, some ✲
Ligustrum
Lonicera pileata
Magnolia grandiflora
Mahonia aquifolium
Osmanthus
Philadelphus
Salix
Spiraea
Viburnum

DRY SHADE

Shrubs that tolerate dry shade
Aucuba
Cornus canadensis
Daphne laureola
Euonymus fortunei, E. japonicus
Fatsia japonica
Hedera, some ✲
Ilex aquifolium
Pachysandra

MOIST SHADE

Shrubs that prefer moist shade
Aucuba
Buxus sempervirens
Camellia japonica
Cornus canadensis
Daphne laureola
Euonymus fortunei, E. japonicus
Fatsia japonica

*Sarcococca
hookeriana
var. digyna*

Ilex aquifolium
Lonicera pileata
Mahonia
    aquifolium
Osmanthus, some ✲
Rubus tricolor
Sarcococca
Skimmia
Vinca

TWO OR MORE SEASONS OF INTEREST

All year round
Acacia baileyana ✲
Ardisia japonica ✲
Convolvulus cneorum
Elaeagnus x ebbingei 'Gilt Edge'
Euryops acraeus
Lavandula stoechas
Ozothamnus ledifolius

Winter/Spring
Berberis temolaica
Corylus avellana 'Contorta'
Salix irrorata

Spring/Summer
Calycanthus occidentalis
Pieris 'Forest Flame'

Spring/Autumn
Cornus 'Eddie's White Wonder'

Summer/Autumn
Citrus 'Meyer' ✲
Cornus mas 'Variegata'
Cotinus 'Flame'
Cotoneaster conspicuus
Dipelta yunnanensis
Hydrangea quercifolia
    'Snowflake'
Lonicera korolkowii
Myrtus communis,
    M. communis
    subsp. tarentina

*Myrtus
communis*

Neillia thibetica
Phlomis chrysophylla
Pyracantha
Rosa 'Fru Dagmar Hastrup',
    R. moyesii 'Geranium'

Autumn/Winter
Arbutus unedo
Berberis temolaica
Cornus mas 'Variegata'

FRAGRANT FLOWERS

Abeliophyllum distichum
Buddleja alternifolia
Camellia sasanqua
Chimonanthus praecox 'Luteus'
Choisya 'Aztec Pearl', C. ternata
Clethra alnifolia 'Paniculata'
Colletia hystrix 'Rosea'
Cytisus battandieri
Daphne bholua, D. blagayana,
    D. cneorum, D. odora
Elaeagnus
Erica lusitanica
Hamamelis x intermedia 'Pallida'
Lonicera x purpusii 'Winter
    Beauty', L. standishii
Luculia gratissima
Magnolia sieboldii,
    M. x thompsoniana
Mahonia japonica
Osmanthus delavayi
Philadelphus, many
Pittosporum tobira
Rhododendron auriculatum,
    R. edgeworthii ✲,
    R. 'Fragrantissimum' ✲, R. Ghent
    hybrids, R. Loderi Group,
    R. luteum, R. occidentale (and
    hybrids), R. 'Polar Bear',
    R. Rustica hybrids, R. viscosum
Sarcococca
Viburnum (many)

*Rhododendron
luteum*

AROMATIC FOLIAGE

Caryopteris
Prostanthera ✲
Ruta graveolens
Santolina
Skimmia x confusa

ARCHITECTURAL SHRUBS

Agave ✲
Aralia elata 'Aureovariegata'
Chamaerops ✲
Cocos ✲
Cordyline ✲
Cycas revoluta ✲
Dracaena ✲
Eriobotrya japonica
Howea ✲
Jubaea ✲
Pandanus ✲
Phoenix ✲
Phormium
Sabal ✲
Yucca, some ✲

Key
✲ *Not hardy*

Bamboos

EVERGREEN, woody bamboos are members of the grass family and have delicately handsome foliage and a graceful habit. They store their food in underground stems (rhizomes), from which both woody stems (culms or canes) and roots develop. The culms grow to their full height in one season, but usually take three years to mature fully. Culms produce new leaves each growing season, thus maintaining a fresh look. Most species grow without flowering for 20 years or more. After they have eventually flowered, however, they may be so weakened that they need replacing or cutting back to ground level.

Many bamboos are tropical but a considerable number are hardy in temperate regions. Some will grow 7m (22ft) tall, while others reach less than 50cm (20in). Their great diversity makes them invaluable in the garden: some bamboos make good specimen plants, others useful screens, hedges, or windbreaks; most will grow happily in containers. Some bamboos are reasonably docile and clump-forming, others invasive.

General cultivation

Most bamboos will grow in sun or shade, and prefer humus-rich, moist but well-drained soil. The pH is not important. As bamboos are shallow rooted, their planting hole should be no deeper than 40cm (16in). Dig the site thoroughly and add bone meal and well-rotted manure, before planting the bamboo.

Never let bamboos dry out, especially when young, nor allow their roots to freeze. Container-grown ones should be kept frost-free. Even hardy bamboos may occasionally be slightly frost damaged but they usually recover quickly in spring, provided there is sufficient water.

In spring, give bamboos an annual application of balanced fertilizer, at a rate of 50g/sq m (2oz/sq yd), a mulch of well-rotted manure, and a dressing of calcium silicate.

Restricting bamboo growth

Some of the best-looking bamboos are highly invasive. To keep them in their allotted space, insert a physical barrier into the soil, at least 40cm (16in) deep, around the root ball, and seal well at the join(s); then keep a careful watch and cut off any rhizomes that spread across the top of the barrier. Alternatively, a couple of times a year, insert a sharp spade right around the clump, then pull out any rhizomes that have strayed outside that cut line.

To reduce the vigour of low-growing bamboos, cut them to the ground in early spring. Such pruning will also make the plants look even more attractive as they will display only fresh new culms each summer.

Pests and diseases

Bamboos are particularly vulnerable to the bamboo spider mite – a sap-sucking insect that lives on the underside of leaves covered by a fine web. New plants should be inspected for dots and dashes (like Morse code) of longitudinal, yellow variegations on the leaves. To eradicate bamboo spider mite, remove and burn infected leaves; if necessary, spray with an acaricide that will kill these mites. Whiteflies (p.646) and red spider mite (p.646) will attack bamboo under glass but are not a problem outdoors. Aphids (p.646) are a nuisance on some species, and rabbits (p.666) and squirrels (p.659) may eat the new growth.

Pruning

Dead, damaged, or spindly culms and all those more than five years old should be removed at or very close to the base, in spring. Never partially shorten culms as this ruins their appearance. Loppers or a saw, and stout protective clothing, are often essential when pruning.

If a clump has become too dense and overwhelming for its position, it can be thinned in spring or late summer to let air and light into the centre. Thinning also displays well those species that have coloured stems, or those in which the young culms are the most attractive.

Propagation

Bamboo roots are sensitive to drought so choose a cool, overcast day for propagation to prevent the roots drying out.

Tightly clumped bamboos can be increased by simple division in spring, when new growth is visible (see "Division", p.118). Spray water on divided plants regularly and liberally until they are established.

All bamboos can be propagated in spring by dividing their rhizomes. Lift a clump or part of one, and cut one or more rhizomes into pieces, ensuring that each has at least one growing shoot. Take care not to damage the fine roots. Insert the pieces into individual pots of a free-draining compost and cover the rhizomes to their original depth. Keep them cool and moist, and in good but not strong light until the plants are established.

PROPAGATING BAMBOOS

1 *Dig around the clump to expose the outer rhizomes with new shoots. Separate these from the parent plant.*

2 *Cut the rhizomes, each with at least one shoot, into pieces. Dust the cut surfaces with fungicidal powder (see inset).*

3 *Pot up each piece with the rhizome just below the surface of the compost and the shoots exposed. Firm in and water.*

RESTRICTING THE SPREAD OF BAMBOO

1 *Dig a narrow trench, deeper than the plant's root, all round the clump. Chop through and remove peripheral roots.*

2 *Insert a barrier made of non-perishable material such as slates or rigid plastic. Fill in the trench. Firm the ground well.*

THINNING ESTABLISHED CLUMPS OF BAMBOO

Wearing thick gloves and using loppers, remove weak, dead, and damaged culms, then cut out the oldest ones at the base until the desired effect is achieved. Then, without damaging new shoots, clear away debris at the base to relieve congestion further, let in light and air, and allow young culms to grow unchecked.

Soil preparation and planting

A WIDE RANGE of shrubs can be grown in most gardens, even if the soil falls short of ideal – which is a fertile, well-drained but moisture-retentive loam. Improving the drainage of wet soils and, by the addition of humus, the structure and moisture-holding properties of dry soils greatly increases the range of shrubs that may be grown. The soil acidity or alkalinity, another factor limiting the range of plants that can be grown, may also be modified.

Important though these improvements may be, garden soil will still naturally tend towards being moist or dry, heavy or light, and acidic or alkaline. The best shrubs for your garden are those suitable for the growing conditions available.

Selecting shrubs

Shrubs may be bought direct from garden centres, nurseries, and non-specialist outlets such as supermarkets. Some nurseries also sell shrubs by mail order; plants are normally dispatched during their dormant period. They are sold in containers, root-balled, or bare-root.

Shrubs on sale should be accurately labelled, healthy, undamaged, and free of pests and diseases. When buying direct, inspect the plants thoroughly and select a specimen with evenly distributed branches close to ground level or, with standard shrubs, at the head of a clear stem of the desired height. Shrubs sold in the warm, dry atmosphere of a supermarket have a short shelf life. Reliable suppliers may give a year's guarantee to replace the shrub if it is not true to name or if it dies within the first year, provided that it has been given reasonable care.

Shrubs in containers

Shrubs are most commonly sold as container-grown specimens, the containers ranging from rigid pots to plastic bags. Most shrubs sold in this way have been container-grown throughout their lives. Some are field-grown and potted up (containerized) in the season before sale to prolong their sale life. The two are difficult to distinguish, although container-grown shrubs normally have better-established root systems (often visible through the drainage holes of the pot).

If possible, slide the shrub out of its container; the roots should show healthy, white tips and the root system, if well established, will retain all or most of the compost from the pot. Reject plants with poorly developed root systems and those that are pot-bound (with roots protruding from the container), since these rarely grow well.

A major advantage of container-grown shrubs is that they may be bought and planted out at any time, except when there are extremes of temperature or drought. Containerized shrubs can be safely planted out in winter, but at other times may be slow to establish unless they have a well-developed root system.

Bare-root shrubs

Deciduous shrubs that are easily propagated are sometimes lifted from the open ground during their dormant season and sold with their roots bare of soil. The buying season for these bare-root shrubs is from autumn to spring. To prevent desiccation, they are normally heeled into the ground until they are sold. Before purchasing, check that bare-root shrubs have an evenly developed, fibrous root system.

Root-balled shrubs

These shrubs, usually available in autumn or early spring, have been grown in open ground, then lifted with soil around their root balls; the root balls are wrapped in hessian or netting. Conifers are often sold in this way. Always check that the wrapping is intact, or the roots may have been exposed to drying wind, and that the root ball is firm.

SELECTING A SHRUB

Container-grown shrubs

GOOD EXAMPLE

Vigorous, well-balanced top-growth

POOR EXAMPLE

Twiggy, sparse stems showing little new growth

Pot-bound roots

Prostanthera cuneata

Well-established, fibrous root system

Renovating a poor example

Tease out pot-bound roots and cut back any that are very long or damaged

Root-balled shrub

Wrapping is intact, not split or damaged

Check that the root ball is firm

GOOD EXAMPLE

Well-developed, even branch framework

Viburnum farreri

Healthy, vigorous growth, free from damage and disease

SHRUBS FOR SANDY SOIL

Berberis empetrifolia
Calluna vulgaris (and cvs)
Ceanothus thyrsiflorus
Cistus x *cyprius*
Clethra alnifolia
Cytisus scoparius

Cistus x *cyprius*

Erica arborea,
   E. cinerea
Fuchsia magellanica (and cvs)
Genista tinctoria
Hakea lissosperma
Halimodendron halodendron
Helianthemum
Helichrysum, some ❁
Hippophäe
Lavandula, some ❁
Olearia, some ❁
Ozothamnus, some ❁
Phlomis
Phormium
Spartium junceum
Tamarix
Ulex europaeus
Yucca gloriosa

SHRUBS FOR WELL-DRAINED, CLAY SOIL

Amelanchier
Aralia
Aronia arbutifolia
Aucuba
Berberis

Chaenomeles x *superba* 'Nicoline'

Chaenomeles x
   superba (and cvs)
Cornus alba 'Sibirica'
Cotinus
Cotoneaster
Deutzia
Forsythia
Garrya
Hippophäe
Kalmia latifolia
Lonicera, some ❁
Mahonia x *media*
Philadelphus
Potentilla
Pyracantha
Salix caprea
Sambucus racemosa
Spiraea
Taxus
Viburnum opulus
Weigela

Key
❁ *Not hardy*

When to plant

Autumn to spring is the planting season for bare-root and root-balled shrubs, and the optimum time for container-grown shrubs; however, those of borderline hardiness should be planted out in spring. Autumn planting allows the roots to establish while the ground is still warm, so the shrub should be growing vigorously before dry weather the next summer.

Planting may be carried out during mild weather in winter, but not when the ground is frozen. Roots will not grow away in very cold soil, and there is a risk that they may freeze and be killed.

The major disadvantage of spring planting is that top-growth is likely to develop before the roots establish and, if there is an early spell of dry weather, watering may be required to help the plants survive.

Soil preparation

Many shrubs are potentially long-lived, so the ground needs to be thoroughly prepared before planting. The aim should be to cultivate an area well beyond the planting site for an individual shrub and, preferably, the entire bed.

The best seasons for cultivation are late summer and autumn. Remove or kill all weeds first, taking care to eradicate perennials (see "Weeds", pp.669–673). Double dig (see p.620), incorporating an 8–10cm (3–4in) layer of well-rotted organic matter into the lower trench. If this is impractical, work large quantities of organic matter into the top 30–45cm (12–18in) of soil. Add fertilizer if appropriate (see "Soil nutrients and fertilizers", pp.624–625).

How to plant

The planting hole for a shrub must be wide enough to accommodate the shrub's root ball. For container-grown or root-balled plants, make the hole twice the width of the contained root mass, or as much as three times the width if planting in clay soils. For bare-root shrubs, the hole must be large enough to allow the plant's roots to be spread out fully. The hole must also be sufficiently deep to allow the shrub to be planted at the same level as it was in its container or in the open ground. This is indicated by the soil mark – a dark mark near the base of the stem. A cane laid across the top of the planting hole provides a useful guide to the depth of planting. Treatment of a containerized shrub depends on how developed the root system is when removed from the pot. If the compost falls away, plant as for a bare-root shrub; if it does not, treat as if container-grown. Tease out the root system if at all rootbound. Remove the hessian or netting surrounding a root-balled shrub after it is in the hole. When backfilling the hole, shake a bare-root plant gently to settle the soil. Firm the soil in stages but do not compact clay soils.

PLANTING A WALL SHRUB

1 *Dig a hole at least 22cm (9in) away from the wall. Plant the shrub (here a pyracantha) and tie in the supporting cane to a wire.*

2 *Firm back the soil. Secure lateral bamboo canes to the central cane and to the wires, so that the sideshoots can be supported and tied in (see inset).*

PLANTING A CONTAINER-GROWN SHRUB

1 *Dig a hole about twice the width of the shrub's root ball (here a Viburnum). Mix the removed soil with organic matter. Fork over the base and sides of the hole.*

2 *Placing one hand on top of the compost and around the shrub to support it, carefully ease the plant out of its container. Place the shrub in the prepared hole.*

3 *Lay a cane alongside to check that the soil level is the same as before. Adjust the planting depth, if necessary, by adding or removing topsoil beneath the shrub.*

4 *Backfill around the shrub with the removed soil and organic matter mixture, firming the soil in stages to prevent air pockets from forming.*

5 *Once the hole has been filled with the planting mixture, carefully firm the soil around the shrub with your heel or hands.*

6 *Prune any diseased or damaged wood back to healthy growth and cut back any inward-growing or crossing stems to an outward-growing shoot or bud. You should also remove any very long, weak, or straggly stems, or those that spoil the overall balance of the shrub's framework.*

7 *Water the shrub thoroughly; apply a mulch of well-rotted compost or pulverized bark about 5–7cm (2–3in) deep and 30–45cm (12–18in) wide around the shrub.*

To improve drainage around shrubs to be grown in clay soils, plant the shrub slightly proud of the soil level and mound soil around the exposed section of the root ball up to the level of the soil mark. On sandy soils, plant the shrub in a slight dip to channel water around the plant's roots. Water the shrub and mulch.

Planting wall shrubs

Some shrubs may be trained on wires fixed to a wall or fence. Plant these at least 22cm (9in) from the wall, leaning the plant in towards the wall. Support the main stem and laterals of the shrub with canes, which are then tied into the wires (see also "Wall shrubs", p.108).

Staking

Shrubs do not normally need staking, except for large, root-bound specimens and standards. The former, which ideally should not be selected, will almost certainly need some support in their first year or two at least, until their roots begin to spread out and they become stable.

The best method for any shrub that branches from near ground level is to brace the shrub with guys fixed to three stakes spaced evenly around a circle with a radius of about 1m (3ft) centred on the shrub. To prevent bark damage, cover the guys where they touch the branches with rubber or similar material (see also ORNAMENTAL TREES, "Staking", p.64).

For standards, insert the stake in the planting hole before planting to avoid damaging the root system. The top of the stake should be just below the first branches. Secure the stem to the stake, using a proprietary tie with a spacer or a homemade figure-of-eight tie to prevent chafing.

STAKING A STANDARD SHRUB

1 Drive a stake into the hole just off-centre; the top of the stake should be just below the head of the shrub after planting. Plant the shrub next to the stake.

2 If the depth is correct, backfill and firm in. On free-draining soil, form a dip around the shrub to retain moisture. Secure the stem with a suitable tie (see inset).

Protecting newly planted shrubs

Newly planted shrubs may suffer from desiccation or cold if not protected. Broadleaved evergreens and conifers in exposed positions are particularly vulnerable.

A screen of hessian or mesh significantly reduces the drying force of cold winds. Erect a strong, wooden framework 30cm (12in) away from the windward side of the shrub needing protection. Tack the hessian or the mesh to the frame, which should extend at least 30cm (12in) above and either side of the shrub. More complete protection is given by surrounding individual plants with a four-sided framework to which hessian or mesh is tacked.

Another measure, which may be used either alone or in addition to screening, is to spray the plants with an anti-desiccant product to reduce water loss. Apply a thin film of spray to both sides of the leaves.

A mulch spread around the base of the shrub will help to protect the roots from ground frost. It is best to spread the mulch during periods of mild weather, preferably when the ground is reasonably warm and damp.

In areas of heavy snow, particularly vulnerable, evergreen shrubs may need additional protection. This is best provided by a timber and chicken wire cage. Dislodge any heavy accumulations of snow promptly. More extreme measures may be needed to protect half-hardy and tender shrubs (see FROST AND WIND PROTECTION, pp.612–613).

When removing the insulation in spring, check for pests and diseases that may have benefited from the winter protection.

Planting shrubs in containers

Late summer to autumn is the main period for planting shrubs in containers (see also CONTAINER GARDENING, "Shrubs", p.316). When transplanting a shrub, the new container should be 5cm (2in) larger in depth and diameter than the previous one. If using an old container, scrub its inside surface thoroughly before filling.

Heavy containers should be placed in position before planting. Stand the container on bricks or blocks to allow free drainage. Place broken crocks over the drainage holes and then add a 2.5cm (1in) layer of drainage material, such as coarse gravel.

A loam-based compost, which is nutrient-rich, is preferable to a peat-based one, which contains limited, added nutrients and dries out more rapidly. Shrubs grown in peat-based composts will therefore require frequent feeding. Use an ericaceous compost for rhododendrons and other lime-haters, or to obtain blue flowers on hydrangeas. After placing the plant in the pot, spread its roots out evenly and work compost round them. Ensure that the soil mark is level with the compost surface. Top-dressing the compost with a covering of grit or bark chippings ensures the compost does not form a crust. Such a mulch also looks decorative.

With container planting, ensure that the compost is at least 4cm (1½in) below the rim to allow room for mulching and watering.

SHRUBS FOR ACID SOIL

Andromeda
Arbutus (most spp.)
Arctostaphylos, some ❀ (some spp.)
Calluna
Camellia, some ❀

Camellia x williamsii 'Wilber Foss'

Clethra, some ❀
Cornus canadensis
Corylopsis (most spp.)
Desfontainia spinosa
Enkianthus
Erica (most spp.)
Fothergilla
Gaultheria
Hakea, some ❀
Kalmia
Leucothöe
Menziesia
Philesia magellanica ❀
Pieris
Rhododendron, some ❀ (most spp.)
Styrax officinalis
Telopea speciosissima ❀
Vaccinium
Zenobia pulverulenta

SHRUBS FOR VERY ALKALINE SOIL

Aucuba japonica (and cvs)
Berberis darwinii
Buddleja davidii (and cvs)
Buxus
Chamaerops ❀
Choisya ternata
Cistus, some ❀
Cotoneaster
Cytisus, some ❀
Deutzia
Euonymus
Forsythia
Hebe, some ❀
Hibiscus, some ❀
Hypericum, some ❀
Ligustrum
Lonicera, some ❀
Nerium oleander ❀
Philadelphus
Phlomis fruticosa
Photinia

Philadelphus 'Dame Blanche'

Potentilla (all shrubby spp.)
Rosa rugosa
Rosmarinus
Senecio
Syringa
Viburnum tinus
Vitex agnus-castus
Weigela
Yucca aloifolia ❀

Key
❀ *Not hardy*

Routine care

THE following guidelines for maintenance are generally applicable, although not all shrubs have the same requirements. Newly planted shrubs usually need watering and feeding, while those planted in containers should also be periodically top-dressed or repotted. In addition, dead-heading, removing suckers, weeding, and controlling pests and diseases may all be necessary.

Feeding

Most shrubs benefit from regular applications of organic or inorganic fertilizers, especially if pruned regularly. A wide range of organic-based fertilizers is now available as well as fast-acting and slow-release ones. They are best applied in early spring. Some slow-release fertilizers discharge their nutrients only when temperatures are high enough for plants to use them. A standard rate of application is 60g/sq m (2oz/sq yd) (see also SOILS AND FERTILIZERS, "Types of fertilizer", p.624).

Quick-release powder fertilizers are useful to boost growth as it commences in spring. Liquid fertilizers work even faster than powders – these should be applied once the shrub is in growth.

Fertilizers in granular or powder form should be worked into the soil over an area slightly wider than the spread of the top-growth of the shrub. With surface-rooting shrubs, allow the fertilizer to leach in naturally or water it in to avoid the risk of the roots being injured by forking. The application of fertilizers may affect the soil's pH level; most inorganic, nitrogenous fertilizers, for example, make the soil more acidic (see also SOILS AND FERTILIZERS, "Soil nutrients and fertilizers", pp.624–625).

Watering

Established shrubs require watering only in periods of prolonged drought, but young specimens may need regular watering. Apply the water to the ground around the shrub, soaking the soil. Do not water often and lightly, since this will encourage root growth close to the surface. Shallow roots make shrubs vulnerable in drought conditions. The best time to water is in the evening, when evaporation is minimal.

Mulching

Mulching with well-rotted, bulky manures helps soil conserve moisture and, if nutrient-rich, improves soil fertility. It also moderates extremes of temperature around the roots and inhibits weeds.

Apply the mulch around newly planted shrubs over an area about 45cm (18in) wider in diameter than the plant's root system. The mulch around established shrubs should extend beyond the area of top-growth by 15–30cm (6–12in). A mulch of bark chippings, wood chips, or manure should be 5–10cm (2–4in) deep but kept clear of the stems of the shrub. Do not apply any mulch in cold weather or when the soil is dry.

Weeding

Weeds compete for nutrients and moisture, so it is essential to clear the ground of all weeds before planting. The area around newly planted ground-cover shrubs needs weeding until the plants form dense growth that suppresses competition. For treatment, see "Weeds", pp.669–673.

Removing suckers

Some grafted shrubs, including rhododendrons, are prone to producing growths, or suckers, beneath the graft union, from either stems or roots. Rub out suckers between finger and thumb as soon as they are noticed: if too large to treat in this way, cut them off as close as possible to the stems or roots from which they are growing. Pulling them off helps to remove any dormant growth buds, but take care not to damage the stem or root. Watch for further growth.

Reversion and mutation

Many variegated shrubs are propagated from green-leaved plants that have produced mutated branches, known as sports. From time to time, branches of variegated shrubs revert to the original foliage of the parent plant or mutate to plain cream or yellow leaves. Since these branches are usually more vigorous, they eventually crowd out those showing variegation, and should be cut out.

Dead-heading

Some shrubs, including rhododendrons, lilacs (*Syringa*), and *Kalmia*, benefit if their faded flowerheads are promptly removed, where practical, before seed sets. Removing old flowers diverts energy into growth, improving the flowering potential for the following season, but it is not essential for the health of a shrub.

DEAD-HEADING A RHODODENDRON

Before new buds have fully developed, snap each dead flowerhead off at the base of its stem. Take care not to damage any young growth.

To avoid damage to new buds, dead-head as soon as the flowers fade, using fingers and thumb to pick off each one where it joins the stem. Most flowerheads come away cleanly but trim any snags with secateurs.

Shrubs in containers

Container-grown shrubs need more care than those grown in the ground, since they have less access to moisture and nutrients. Until shrubs reach maturity, repot them every year or two in spring, then top-dress. When mature, just replace the top 5–10cm (2–4in) of potting compost each spring. (See also CONTAINER GARDENING, "Maintaining shrubs and trees in containers", p.334.)

HOW TO REMOVE SUCKERS

Sucker removal
Pull or cut off the sucker (here on a Hamamelis) at the base; if it is pulled off, pare over the wound to leave a clean cut (see inset).

Recognizing suckers
A sucker may usually be distinguished by its leaves: a normal stem from the top-growth, left; a sucker from the root, right.

REMOVING NON-VARIEGATED AND REVERTED SHOOTS

Non-variegated shoot
With variegated shrubs (here Euonymus fortunei 'Emerald 'n' Gold'), cut any plain shoots back to the variegated growth.

Reverted shoot
Cut back reverted shoots (here on E. fortunei 'Emerald Gaiety') to the main stem. If necessary, remove the entire stem.

Shrubs for ground cover

COVERING the ground with a dense carpet of flowering or foliage plants is a planting technique designed primarily to minimize weeding among ornamental plants. Ground cover can also reduce evaporation from exposed, freely draining soils. A dense planting of drought-resistant evergreens, such as *Cistus* x *hybridus* or the pink-flowered *C.* x *skanbergii*, and most cultivars of rosemary (*Rosmarinus*) and lavender (*Lavandula*), will shade the soil and keep it cool, and their slowly decomposing leaf litter also acts as a mulch.

Steep banks, subject to erosion by rain and wind, may be planted with ground-cover shrubs such as *Juniperus squamata* 'Blue Carpet' or *Cotoneaster dammeri*. Their low, spreading habit, evergreen foliage, and vigorous rooted layers combine to form a stable cover that prevents erosion of topsoil.

In a wildlife garden, ground cover can be used to attract bees and butterflies: the low, creeping thymes, such as *Thymus praecox* and its cultivars, for example, are extremely attractive to bees.

Once established, ground-cover plants will smother most weed seedlings that attempt to grow beneath their canopy, by depriving them of light, as well as by competing with them for water and nutrients. In the wild, this is frequently a natural

Textural carpet
A vigorous dwarf juniper, Juniperus squamata *'Blue Carpet', provides a spreading mat of colour and texture up to 3m (10ft) wide.*

process; nature may be imitated in the garden to create attractive, integrated planting schemes that require very little aftercare.

In open gardens, evergreen ground-cover shrubs can act as low boundary markers. They also trap wind-blown rubbish beneath their branches which can be raked out readily and removed.

Selecting plants

Choose attractive, vigorous plants that will quickly cover their allotted space with close, dense growth. Low-growing shrubs with a spreading habit are among the most useful. Evergreens are a good choice for year-round visual interest, especially if, like *Euonymus fortunei* 'Gold Spot' with its golden-variegated, dark green leaves, they will brighten a dark corner.

Plants should be selected to suit the location, for example wet or dry, shady, or hot and sunny situations. They should be easy to care for, routinely requiring either no pruning or perhaps an annual clipping and feed. Choose long-term plants that should remain healthy for five to ten years or more. Finally, look for species, cultivars, and forms that will provide attractive foliage and habit, with flowers and fruits as a bonus.

Combining plants

Massed groupings of a single plant give a unified "carpeting" effect, but plants can be combined provided that they are of similar vigour. Ground-cover plants with various colours, textures, and forms may be mixed to make garden features in their own right, or may provide an attractive linking element in a design. A low carpet of shrubs also makes an excellent, low-maintenance background for naturalized bulbs such as daffodils, and, unlike grass, will not need mowing as the bulb foliage fades.

Some shrubs are particularly useful in providing medium-height cover, or as an under-canopy below trees. *Cotoneaster conspicuus*, with bright scarlet berries, *Prunus laurocerasus* 'Otto Luyken', with glossy, dark green leaves, and also *Fatsia japonica* 'Variegata', with deeply lobed leaves edged with white, cover the ground well and provide interest, even in winter.

General cultivation

Once the ground has been thoroughly prepared, there are several ways of planting ground-cover shrubs to ensure quick cover: plant them at spacings recommended for the species or cultivar concerned and cover the soil with a loose mulch; plant them at recommended spacings through a weed-resistant, black plastic sheet mulch; or plant them more densely than would be usual to provide cover more quickly.

The choice of method will depend on the type and cost of plants used, the climate and soil conditions, and how long you are willing to wait for the final effect. Fast-growing plants in favourable conditions and at recommended spacings will generally fill in within two to three years.

Once established, many shrubby plants benefit from an occasional trim, to keep them compact, as well as the removal of dead or damaged shoots. A few need more intrusive, annual pruning: for example, shrubs such as *Vinca* and *Hypericum calycinum* that, after a few years, become rather straggly, and those such as *Santolina* that tend to open out, revealing their centre.

PRUNING GROUND COVER

Santolina
Some bushy plants need hard pruning. In spring, cut back to just above where new growth is breaking on the main stems.

Hypericum calycinum
In spring, cut the previous season's shoots hard back.

Mulching ground cover

When ground-cover plants have been newly planted at the correct distance, the ground between them will still be bare. Until the plants have begun to spread over the surrounding area, it is advisable to apply a mulch in the gaps around them. This will help to retain moisture in the soil, and will also discourage the growth of weeds. A loose mulch, for example bark chippings, is ideal for the purpose, and should be applied to a depth of about 5cm (2in).

*To preserve moisture between new plants (*here* Erica carnea), apply a loose mulch 5cm (2in) deep. Every spring, renew the mulch around established plants.*

Moving an established shrub

Careful selection and siting of a shrub should make transplanting unnecessary, although sometimes it may be desirable or unavoidable. Before moving evergreens, spray the foliage with an anti-desiccant. With deciduous shrubs, thin out growth by up to one third, to compensate for root disturbance.

When to transplant

Most deciduous young shrubs may be lifted bare-root when dormant. Established shrubs that have large root systems should be lifted with a ball of soil around the roots before being moved. Autumn is the best time to do this. Evergreens should be transplanted in spring, just before new growth occurs, carefully digging up the whole root ball.

Root-balling a shrub

Most often, it is best to root-ball a shrub so that root damage is kept to a minimum. Prepare the new planting position before lifting the shrub.

Dig a trench around the shrub just beyond the spread of its branches. Cut through woody roots but leave fibrous ones intact. If necessary, use a fork to loosen the soil around the root ball and reduce its size. Then under-cut it with a spade; use secateurs to sever any woody tap roots.

Once the root ball is free, work a sheet of hessian or similar material underneath it. Tie the hessian firmly around the ball, lift the shrub from the hole, and transplant it. Remove the hessian before replanting.

Transplanted shrubs require the same treatment as those that have been planted for the first time, although they may take longer to re-establish (see p.99).

Shrub problems

Plants are less likely to succumb to pest attack or disease if they are given good growing conditions and care. Many problems originate from poor drainage, lack of moisture, planting too deeply, compaction of the soil, or exposure to temperature extremes in an unsuitable site.

Physical damage

Wounds caused by a jagged pruning cut, a badly placed cut, or pruning at the wrong time may allow disease fungi to establish. This may also cause die-back. Mechanical wounding, for example by lawnmowers grazing a stem, also provides a convenient entry point for disease.

Pests and diseases

Maintaining good garden hygiene minimizes the chance of pests and diseases establishing a foothold. As shrubs age, however, they lose vigour and become more prone to pests and diseases. Old or diseased shrubs that have lost their vigour are rarely worth saving and should be replaced.

Pests and diseases most likely to affect shrubs are aphids (p.646), red spider mite (p.646), fireblight (p.649), honey fungus (p.661), *Phytophthora* stem rots (see "*Phytophthora* root rots", p.654), and powdery mildew (p.646). Be alert to the signs of a problem, which include streaking and changes of foliage colour, drooping leaves, loss of leaves, distorted growth, and the development of fungi.

Frost and wind

When selecting and siting shrubs it is vital to take account of the general weather pattern of the area as well as the garden's individual microclimate; it is almost impossible, however, to take precautions against freak extremes of temperature or exceptional winds.

There is a wide range of hardy shrubs available and many gardeners choose to rely on these rather than risk the loss of more tender specimens. If growing shrubs that are of borderline hardiness for the area, then it is worth using the appropriate frost and wind protection methods (see pp.612–613).

Container-grown shrubs are more vulnerable to extremes of weather than those grown in the open garden. In areas where temperatures fall only occasionally below freezing, most container-grown hardy shrubs may be overwintered outdoors (except those, such as camellias, that are root-tender). In colder areas, however, move shrubs indoors to where the ambient daytime temperature is about 7–13°C (45–55°F) or higher, according to the species.

TRANSPLANTING A SHRUB

1 *Before moving a large shrub, it may be helpful to thin out growth. This will make handling easier and help it to re-establish. Then, using a spade, mark out a circle around the extent of the shrub's branches (here Ilex aquifolium 'Golden Milkboy'). Tie in any trailing stems or wrap the shrub in hessian, to prevent damage.*

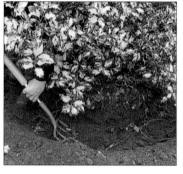

2 *Dig a trench around the circle, then use a fork to loosen the soil around the root ball. Take care not to damage any fibrous roots.*

3 *Continue to carefully fork away soil from around the shrub's root ball to reduce its size and weight.*

4 *Undercut the root ball with a spade, cutting through woody roots if necessary to separate them from the surrounding soil.*

5 *Roll up a length of hessian. Tilt the shrub to one side and unroll the hessian beneath the root ball. Tilt the root ball the other way, and unroll the rest of the hessian.*

6 *Pull the hessian up around the root ball and tie it securely. Remove the shrub from its hole and transport it to its new position.*

7 *Remove the hessian and replant the shrub in the new, prepared hole with the soil mark at the same level as before. Firm, water well, and mulch.*

Pruning and training

Some shrubs, particularly evergreens of naturally compact habit such as *Sarcococca*, make attractive plants with little or no pruning or training. They may require no more than the removal of dead, damaged, and diseased wood. If left untreated, this will be unsightly and, more seriously, may put the health of the shrub in jeopardy. Many shrubs, however, need pruning or a combination of pruning and training to realize their full ornamental potential.

Aims and effects of pruning and training

The most common requirement is for formative pruning that creates a vigorous and well-shaped shrub. Many shrubs also require a regular regime of pruning to maintain or enhance the ornamental quality of their flowers, fruit, foliage, or stems. The timing of this pruning, which may often be critical, varies depending on the growth pattern of the shrub and the effect desired.

Pruning can also be a way of bringing neglected and overgrown plants back to healthy, manageable growth. It is a matter of judgement whether a shrub warrants being rescued. Replacement is often the best course when a shrub requires regular cutting back because it is too large for the space available.

Shrubs grown as topiary or hedges require specialized pruning from

WHERE TO CUT

Opposite shoots
Prune stems with opposite buds to just above a strong pair of buds or shoots, using a clean, straight cut.

Alternate shoots
For shrubs with alternate buds, prune to just above a bud or shoot, using a clean, angled cut.

An angled cut
Angle the cut so that its lowest point is opposite the base of the bud and the top just clears the bud.

their formative stage. For further information see Topiary, pp.76–77, and Hedges and Screens, pp.84–86.

In training, the gardener plays an active role in directing the growth of plants. Most shrubs grown in the open require no training at all. Shrubs grown against supports, however, normally need a combination of pruning and training to form a well-spaced framework of branches.

Principles of pruning and training

Pruning normally stimulates growth. The terminal shoot or growth bud of a stem is often dominant, inhibiting by chemical means the growth of buds or shoots below it. Pruning that removes the ends of stems affects the control mechanism, resulting in more vigorous development of lower shoots or growth buds.

Hard or light pruning

Hard pruning promotes more vigorous growth than light pruning; this needs to be borne in mind when correcting the shape of an unbalanced shrub. Hard cutting back of vigorous growth often encourages even stronger growth. Prune weak growth hard but strong growth only lightly.

How to prune

Pruning wounds, like other injuries that a shrub might suffer, are possible entry points for disease. The risk is reduced by making well-placed, clean cuts with sharp tools.

Stems with alternate or whorled arrangements of growth buds should be cut just above a bud pointing in the desired direction of growth – for example, an outward-facing bud that will not cross another shoot as its

growth develops. Use an angled cut, starting opposite a healthy growth bud, and slant the cut so that it finishes slightly above the bud. If the cut is too close, the bud may die; if too far, the stem itself may die back.

With shrubs that have buds in opposite pairs, cut straight across the shoot just above a pair of healthy buds. Both buds will develop, resulting in a forked branch system.

In the past, gardeners have often been advised to use a wound paint on pruning cuts, but research now suggests that wound paints are not generally an effective way of controlling diseases and in some cases may even encourage them.

Pruning alone will not promote vigorous new growth. Shrubs that are renovated or regularly cut back benefit from feeding and mulching. Apply a general-purpose fertilizer at the beginning of the growing season at a rate of 120g/sq m (4oz/sq yd) and mulch to a depth of 5–10cm (2–4in) with well-rotted organic material in spring, when the ground has warmed up a little.

Cutting back hard for vigour
Promote vigorous growth by hard pruning. Using secateurs, cut back any weak, twiggy, or spindly growth right to the base of the shrub.

Training

The growth of lower buds or shoots on a stem may also be modified by training. When a stem is allowed to grow upright, the lower shoots on the stem usually grow weakly. With stems that are trained more horizontally, however, the lower shoots and buds grow more vigorously. Training branches near the horizontal can substantially increase the amount of flower and fruit that a shrub is able to produce. Wall-trained shrubs should be tied in to supports as growth develops. As stems ripen and turn woody they become far less flexible and are therefore more difficult to train successfully.

Formative pruning

The aim of formative pruning is to ensure that a shrub has a framework of well-spaced branches so that it will develop according to its natural habit. The amount of formative pruning required depends very much on the type of shrub and on the quality of the plants available. When buying shrubs, therefore, you should look for sturdy specimens with a well-balanced branch formation, as well as healthy roots.

Evergreen shrubs generally need little formative pruning. Excessive growth resulting in a lopsided, unbalanced shape should be lightly pruned in mid-spring, after the shrub has been planted.

Deciduous shrubs are much more likely to require formative pruning than evergreen shrubs. This should be carried out in the dormant season, between mid-autumn and mid-spring, at or after planting.

The following guidelines apply to most deciduous shrubs. If a vigorous shoot distorts the framework, cut it back lightly rather than severely, to encourage relatively weak growth. If the shrub does not have a well-spaced, branch framework, cut it back hard to promote strong growth.

In the case of most shrubs, remove completely any spindly and crossing or rubbing branches that clutter the framework. An exception is made for a handful of slow-growing deciduous shrubs, in particular Japanese maples (*Acer japonicum* and *A. palmatum*), which generally need no pruning at all.

Sometimes an apparently good specimen will make too much top-growth in relation to the size of its root system. Reducing the number of stems by up to one third, and then

FORMATIVE PRUNING

*After planting a young shrub (*here* Philadelphus), cut out any dead, damaged, and weak stems, and remove crossing and congested stems to form a well-balanced framework with an open centre.*

Prune back crossing or congested shoots to an outward-facing bud, or right back to the base.

Prune out weak and spindly, or long and straggly stems, cutting them back to the base.

Remove awkward stems that spoil the shape, leaving an evenly branching framework.

shortening those stems that remain, also by one third, will help to create a more stable plant.

Deciduous shrubs

These may be divided into four groups: those requiring minimal pruning; those pruned in spring, that usually flower on the current season's growth; those pruned after flowering in summer, that usually flower on the previous season's wood; and those of suckering habit. Two important factors are the degree to which shrubs produce replacement growths and the age of the flower-bearing wood.

Minimal pruning

Once established, shrubs that do not regularly produce vigorous growths from the base or lower branches need little, or no pruning; simply remove dead, diseased, and damaged wood, and cut out weak or crossing growth. Do this just after flowering. Feed and mulch in spring. Japanese maples and other shrubs prone to heavy bleeding if pruned in spring should be pruned in mid- to late summer, when their sap is least active.

Pruning in spring

Left unpruned, deciduous shrubs that bear flowers on the current season's growth tend to become congested and flower quality deteriorates.

When pruned in spring, these shrubs often produce vigorous shoots that flower in summer or early autumn. Shorten flowered stems in autumn, to minimize the risk of wind-rock.

Some large shrubs, such as deciduous *Ceanothus*, develop a woody framework. In their first spring, lightly prune the main stems of less vigorous shrubs and, in the second spring, reduce the previous season's growth by half. In late winter or early spring of subsequent years, prune hard to leave only one to three pairs of buds of the previous season's growth. Prune framework branches to slightly different heights to encourage flower production at all levels. On mature specimens, cut out some of the oldest wood as part of the annual pruning operation to prevent congestion. For pruning *Buddleja davidii*, see facing page.

Some subshrubs, for example *Perovskia*, may form a woody base that allows them to be pruned hard back to a 15–30cm (6–12in) high framework. Cut back the previous season's growth annually in spring, leaving one or two buds.

A few shrubs, such as *Prunus triloba*, that flower in late winter or early spring on wood produced in the previous season are best pruned hard in spring after flowering, and so may be treated as other shrubs in this group. In the first spring after planting, shorten the main stems

MINIMAL PRUNING OF DECIDUOUS SHRUBS

If pruning is needed, which may not be every year, do it immediately after flowering, taking out any dead wood, weak stems, and congested growth to maintain a balanced, open-centred framework on shrubs such as Hamamelis.

Using secateurs, cut back any crossing or rubbing shoots to clear congested growth, especially from the centre of the shrub.

Cut back any weak, straggly, wayward, or misshapen shoots to the main stems.

SHRUBS THAT ARE PRUNED IN SPRING

*Shrubs (*here* Spiraea japonica) that flower on wood produced in the current season should be pruned in spring to encourage new, flowering stems.*

Prune out stems of the previous year's growth to within 2–4 buds of old wood.

Prune out dead or damaged stems back to healthy growth or cut them right back to the base.

Cut back some of the main stems to the base to retain an open framework.

Pruning *Buddleja davidii*

As it is very vigorous, *Buddleja davidii* needs more drastic formative pruning than most other shrubs that flower on new wood. At the back of a border, where a tall plant is required, prune to leave a woody framework 90–120cm (3–4ft) high. In another position, however, this may be no more than 60cm (2ft) high.

In the first spring after planting, shorten main stems by a half to three quarters, pruning to pairs of shoots or buds. Cut out growths other than main stems. In early to mid-spring of subsequent years, cut back the previous season's growth and shorten new growth from the base. To stop congestion, cut out one or two of the oldest branches as part of the annual pruning.

Using loppers, cut back some of the woody spurs to clear congested growth and produce an open, balanced framework.

Using secateurs, cut back all the main shoots that flowered the previous year to within 1–3 buds of the old wood.

Hydrangeas

For pruning purposes, hydrangeas (excluding climbing species such as *Hydrangea anomala* subsp. *petiolaris*) fall into three groups.

The first group (for example *H. paniculata*) flowers from midsummer on the current season's growth, and these plants should be treated in the same way as other shrubs that require hard pruning in spring (see facing page).

In early spring of the first year after planting, cut out all but two or three strong stems, pruning back to a healthy pair of buds about 45cm (18in) above ground level. If it is in an exposed site, where summer temperatures will not ripen stems sufficiently to withstand very cold winters, prune to just above ground level. Apply a quick-release fertilizer at a rate of about 120g/sq m (4oz/sq yd) and a 10cm (4in) deep mulch in a 60cm (24in) circle around the shrub. In early spring of subsequent years, cut back the previous year's growth to one or two strong pairs of growth buds, feed, and mulch.

The second group, comprising mophead and lacecap hydrangeas (*H. macrophylla*), also flowers from midsummer but on shoots made during the previous growing season. Lightly prune young plants in early spring, cutting out thin, twiggy growth and any old flower-heads. Once the plant is established and about three or four years old, remove some of the oldest wood annually in early spring. Cut out stems that are more than three years old and shorten the other stems that flowered in the previous season, cutting back to a strong pair of buds 15–30cm (6–12in) from the base. Then feed and mulch.

Other species, like *H. aspera*, and related forms constitute a third group and need only minimal pruning in spring.

In spring, prune back all flowered stems, also damaged and weak growth, and cut back some older wood to the base.

Hydrangea macrophylla

Cut back any dead wood to healthy growth or right back to the base, if necessary.

Prune out all flowered stems, making a straight cut above a strong pair of growth buds.

PRUNING DECIDUOUS SHRUBS

Minimal pruning
Amelanchier
Aronia
Buddleja globosa
Caragana
Chimonanthus
Clethra (deciduous spp.)
Cornus alternifolia 'Argentea'

Daphne mezereum

Corokia, some ✿
Corylopsis
Daphne
    (deciduous spp.)
Decaisnea
Disanthus
Enkianthus
Eucryphia
    (deciduous spp.)
Fothergilla
Hoheria (deciduous spp.)
Lindera, some ✿
Magnolia ✿ (deciduous spp.)
Poncirus
Ptelea
Pterostyrax
Rhamnus (deciduous spp.)
Viburnum (deciduous spp.)
Zenobia

Prune in spring
Abutilon, some ✿
Aloysia
Buddleja davidii
Caryopteris x *clandonensis*
Ceanothus x *delileanus* (cvs)
Ceratostigma willmottianum
Colquhounia
Cotinus
Datura ✿
Forsythia (after flowering)
Fuchsia (hardy cvs)
Hibiscus syriacus
Hydrangea
Hypericum, some ✿
Indigofera
Lavatera
Leycesteria, some ✿

Lavatera assurgentiflora

Perovskia
Prunus triloba
    (after flowering)
Sorbaria (some spp.)
Spiraea douglasii,
    S. japonica
Tamarix ramosissima
Zauschneria

Key
✿ *Not hardy*

SHRUBS TO PRUNE IN SUMMER

Buddleja alternifolia
Deutzia
Dipelta
Exochorda
Holodiscus discolor
Jasminum humile
Kolkwitzia
Neillia
Philadelphus
Photinia villosa
Ribes sanguineum
Rubus deliciosus,
  R. 'Tridel'

Neillia thibetica

Spiraea 'Arguta',
  S. prunifolia,
  S. thunbergii
Stephanandra
Syringa
Weigela

Minimal pruning
Calycanthus
Chaenomeles
Cotoneaster (deciduous spp.)
Magnolia x *soulangeana,*
  M. stellata
Rhododendron (deciduous spp.)

by about half to form a basal framework. After flowering in subsequent years, cut back all growth to two to three buds of the framework stems. In areas where annual growth is limited by cool summers, cut back only one third of shoots near to ground level, and the others to 15–30cm (6–12in).

For all shrubs in this group, apply fertilizer just after pruning. In mid-spring, mulch the area matching the spread of the shrub before pruning.

Shrubs pruned in summer after flowering

Many deciduous shrubs that flower in spring or early summer carry their flowers on wood produced in the previous growing season. Sometimes, flowers are formed on last year's wood, as with *Chaenomeles*. Other shrubs bear flowers on short lateral growths produced from last year's wood – for example *Deutzia*, *Philadelphus*, *Syringa*, and *Weigela*.

Without pruning to encourage the development of vigorous, young growths from close to ground level, shrubs in this group tend to become densely twiggy, often top-heavy, and the quantity and quality of flowers deteriorate. The removal of spent flowerheads prevents shrubs expending energy in seed production.

When planting a shrub in this group, cut out all weak or damaged

growth and trim back the main shoots to a healthy bud or pair of buds, to encourage the development of a strong framework. If flowers are produced in the first year, prune again immediately after flowering. Cut back flowered shoots to a strong bud or pair of buds and remove any spindly growth. After pruning, lightly work in fertilizer and apply a mulch around the shrub.

Follow this procedure immediately after flowering in subsequent years. Although it is desirable to cut back flowered wood to the strongest buds, do not adhere to this rigidly since it is also important to maintain a well-balanced shape. Feed and mulch as a matter of course after pruning.

As plants mature, more drastic pruning may be needed to encourage growth. After the third year, up to one fifth of the oldest stems may be cut back annually to within 5–8cm (2–3in) of the ground.

Use discretion when following these guidelines, as harsh pruning of young specimens of some shrubs in this group, like forsythias, may result in an awkward and unnatural shape.

Other shrubs in this group, especially when grown as freestanding rather than as wall shrubs, require very little pruning. *Chaenomeles*, for example, has a naturally twiggy habit, with numerous crossing branches, and mature specimens need little pruning.

Spur pruning will encourage heavier flowering (see GROWING FRUIT, "Winter pruning", p.438); shorten spurs and sideshoots to three to five leaves in midsummer.

Particular care must be taken in pruning shrubs such as lilacs (*Syringa*) that come into growth during flowering. The new shoots that form below the flowers can be easily damaged when the old flowerheads are cut, and this reduces flowering in the next year.

Flowering shrubs of suckering habit

A few shrubs grown for their flowers produce flowers on wood of the previous year but make most of their new growth from ground level. These shrubs spread by suckers and are pruned differently from shrubs that form a permanent woody framework.

After planting, prune suckering shrubs by cutting out weak growth but retain vigorous stems and their sideshoots. The following year, immediately after flowering, remove any weak, dead, or damaged stems, then cut back flowered stems hard to a strong bud or pair of buds.

From the third year, annually cut back a quarter to a half of all flowered stems to 5–8cm (2–3in) above ground level and prune others by about half to vigorous, replacement shoots, then feed and mulch.

PRUNING SHRUBS IN SUMMER

After shrubs such as Weigela *have flowered, cut back flowered shoots and remove dead and spindly stems. Also prune out some old, main stems.*

Using secateurs, cut any dead wood back to healthy growth.

BEFORE

Cut out up to one fifth of the oldest wood to within 5–8 cm (2–3in) of the ground.

Cut out any very weak, twiggy, or straggly stems back to the base just above soil level.

AFTER

Continue cutting out weak or crossing stems to form an open-centred, well-balanced shrub.

PRUNING A DECIDUOUS SUCKERING SHRUB

After flowering, prune back all flowered stems on deciduous suckering shrubs (here Kerria), *most by about half, the remainder almost to the ground. Cut out any weak, dead, or damaged growth.*

Prune flowered stems by about half their length, cutting back to strongly growing, new shoots.

Cut back up to half of the flowered stems to within 5–8cm (2–3in) of the ground. Also cut to the ground any dead or damaged shoots.

Coppicing and pollarding shrubs

A number of deciduous shrubs grown for the ornamental value of their stems or leaves require severe pruning in spring. Most of these shrubs flower on shoots formed the previous season but, when grown for their stems or leaves, their flowers are sacrificed. The method of hard pruning used on these shrubs is essentially an adaptation of traditional methods of managing trees and shrubs to give a constant and renewable supply of wood for canework, firewood, and fencing materials. In coppicing, shrubs and trees are cut back regularly to near ground level. In pollarding, growth is cut back each year to a permanent framework of a single stem or several stems.

Coppicing shrubs such as *Cornus alba* ensures a regular supply of young growths, which are more strikingly coloured than older wood and effective in winter. On shrubs such as *Sambucus racemosa* 'Plumosa Aurea' that are grown for their foliage, hard pruning generally results in larger leaves. Just before growth commences in early to mid-spring, coppice vigorous shrubs such as *Salix alba* subsp. *vitellina* 'Britzensis' (syn. *S. alba* 'Chermesina') by pruning all shoots to within about 5–8cm (2–3in) of ground level. It may be preferable to vary the height to which stems are cut back to avoid a rigid, uniform effect. Weaker shrubs such as *Cornus alba* 'Sibirica' may be cut back less severely by coppicing only about one third to one half of the stems. Then apply a quick-release fertilizer and mulch liberally, covering a circle of 60cm (24in) radius around the shrub.

Shrubs that have been trained so that they have one or more clean, main stems are pruned back – or

POLLARDING A EUCALYPTUS

Establish a framework by cutting back a young shrub to one or more main stems (below). Each subsequent spring, cut the previous year's growth hard back either to within 5–8cm (2–3in) of the framework or to the base, as Eucalyptus can regenerate from ground level (right).

pollarded – to this stem framework each season. The aim of pruning in the first year is to establish the framework; after planting, before growth commences in spring, cut back a young plant to form a standard with a single stem of 30–90cm (1–3ft). Alternatively, leave three, five, or seven stems, depending on the size of plant required and the space available in the garden. Apply a quick-release fertilizer and mulch around the stem (or stems), as for shrubs that are coppiced.

During the plant's first growing season, restrict the number of shoots growing from below the cut to only four or five, rubbing out superfluous shoots, and any that develop low down on the main stem. Continue this process for the next year or two; this allows the main stem to thicken so that it can support heavier top-growth. In spring of the second and subsequent years, reduce the previous season's growths to above a bud within 5–8cm (2–3in) of the framework (see also *Pollarding a Eucalyptus*, above). For a larger specimen, prune only a half or one third of the stems. Feed and mulch.

Evergreen shrubs

The appropriate method for pruning and training evergreens depends on the size they are expected to reach when mature. All evergreen shrubs that show signs of die-back after a hard winter should be treated in the same way, regardless of size.

In mid-spring, prune out all dead wood to where the shrub has started to regenerate and thin out the new shoots if they are over-crowded or crossing. If a shrub shows no sign of life by mid-spring, nick the bark to see if there is any live, green wood beneath. Some shrubs may remain dormant for a whole growing season.

Small shrubs up to 90cm (3ft)

Low-growing evergreens are divided into two groups, requiring different pruning regimes. The first group includes several short-lived shrubs that flower profusely, provided they are trimmed each year and are not over-mature, for instance, cotton lavender (*Santolina chamaecyparissus*), lavender (*Lavandula*), and most heathers (*Calluna, Daboecia*, and *Erica*, but not tree heaths). These shrubs are generally best replaced

COPPICING A SHRUB FOR WINTER STEM EFFECT

With shrubs that have coloured stems (here a Cornus sericea cultivar) cut back hard all the shrub's stems to about 5–8cm (2–3in) from the base before growth begins in spring (see inset). Apply fertilizer around the shrub to promote new growth, and then mulch. Coppicing stimulates the growth of new, vigorous stems whose colour is especially strong.

PRUNING EVERGREEN SHRUBS

After flowering, prune evergreen shrubs (here Prunus lusitanica) *by removing damaged or dead wood and cutting back flowered stems and any awkward or straggly stems that mar the shape.*

Cut back flowered stems to a main stem. Cut out thickly congested and crossing stems.

Cut back awkwardly growing stems to well-placed, healthy, outward-growing shoots.

Cut out any dead or damaged wood back to healthy growth or, if necessary, to the base.

Fan-training ornamental shrubs

A few shrubs, such as ornamental peaches (for example *Prunus persica* 'Klara Meyer'), are suitable for fan-training like fruit trees. In the first spring after planting, cut back the plant 38–45cm (15–18in) above the graft union, retaining three or four strong shoots. Train the shoots on canes tied to horizontal wires. Towards the end of the growing season, remove the central shoot if three strong shoots were retained; if four shoots were kept, space these out to form a fan. In winter, reduce all shoots by half their length.

The following growing season, select two or four new shoots on each stem; attach each of these to a cane tied to the wires. Then, in mid-summer, remove all other shoots. In the third year, immediately after flowering, cut back all framework shoots by a quarter to one third. Tie in two or three new shoots on each framework stem. Remove unwanted shoots in mid-summer. If there are gaps in the fan, prune back adjacent shoots by one third after flowering has finished to encourage new growth. Cut back all other extension growths to 5–8cm (2–3in) to encourage flowering on one-year-old spurs. For full details, see GROWING FRUIT, "Fan", p.453.

Here, Prunus mume *'Beni-chidori' is trained to develop an evenly spaced branch framework, using the same method as fan-trained fruit trees.*

every 5–10 years. Also replace plants that have been unpruned for several years as they become weak and leggy and rarely flower or regenerate well.

In mid-spring, use secateurs or garden shears to cut out weak growth or flowering shoots on newly planted shrubs. This ensures new growth is generated from basal shoots in the centre of the plant. Each subsequent year in mid-spring, remove the old flowerheads, and any dead, diseased, or damaged shoots. Some heathers have attractive winter foliage and these, as well as other evergreens, are sometimes dead-headed in autumn. In very cold areas there is a risk of die-back after autumn dead-heading and for this reason pruning may be delayed until mid-spring. After pruning, apply slow-release fertilizer at a rate of 60g/sq m (2oz/sq yd) and mulch to a depth of 5cm (2in).

The second group comprises slow-growing shrubs – dwarf cotoneasters and hebes. They require less pruning than those in the first group, the main purpose being to remove dead, diseased, or damaged shoots in mid-spring. Deadheading is unnecessary.

Medium-sized, evergreen shrubs up to 3m (10ft) tall

Most intermediate evergreen shrubs, such as *Berberis darwinii*, camellias, *Escallonia*, *Hibiscus rosa-sinensis*, and many rhododendrons, require little pruning once a well-balanced framework has been established.

In mid-spring, just before growth is about to start, remove crossing or weak shoots as well as any that affect the overall symmetry of the shrub. Feed and mulch. Subsequent pruning is normally limited to cutting out straggly growth, restricting size, and shaping the plant to suit its position in the garden. Use secateurs or long-handled loppers to remove all or part of selected branches.

Winter- or spring-flowering shrubs like *Berberis darwinii* and *Viburnum tinus* should be pruned immediately after flowering. Prune others that flower from midsummer, such as *Escallonia*, by removing older wood at the start of growth in mid-spring or by cutting out flowered stems in midsummer. *Hibiscus rosa-sinensis*, with its flowering season from spring to autumn, is best pruned in mid-

spring. Feed and mulch spring-pruned shrubs after pruning. Do not feed or mulch shrubs pruned in late summer until the following spring, to minimize damage from frosts.

Large, evergreen shrubs more than 3m (10ft) tall

Large rhododendrons and other tall evergreens require little pruning but may need shaping when young to create a balanced framework. Prune before young plants start into growth or else wait until flowers have faded.

The aim is to encourage an open-centred bush with well-spaced branches. Cut out all crossing and weak branches, and feed and mulch after pruning. Regular pruning is generally limited to the removal of dead, damaged, and diseased wood. Some large evergreens like laurels (*Prunus laurocerasus*) may also be used for hedging (see pp.84–86).

Palm-like shrubs

The palm-like Cordyline and Yucca need pruning only if they have suffered frost-damage or if a bushy, multi-stemmed specimen is required.

In spring, once new growth has started to appear, cut damaged branches back to just above newly formed shoots. Feed and apply a mulch. To create a multi-branched specimen, remove the growing point before growth commences in spring then feed and mulch. Both genera also respond well to hard pruning and renovation: cut back to suitable sideshoots or basal shoots.

Other palm-like succulents such as *Agave* and *Phormium* require only their dead leaves to be removed or faded flower stems cut out.

Wall shrubs

There are three reasons for growing shrubs against walls. First, some are too tender for the open garden in frost-prone areas, but will thrive if sheltered against a warm wall. Second, training shrubs, including hardy shrubs such as pyracanthas, against a wall makes it possible to accommodate plants for which there might not otherwise be space. Third, some shrubs are natural scramblers (for example *Cestrum elegans*) and therefore need support of some kind.

It is important to train and prune all wall shrubs from an early stage so that they present a compact and "well-tailored" appearance and produce plenty of flowering shoots regularly. When training wall shrubs, provide a framework to which growth can be tied. Trellis, netting, or regularly spaced, horizontal wires as used for wall-trained fruit trees (see p.424) may be used. Plant hardy shrubs in autumn, half-hardy or tender shrubs in spring.

Advice for pruning freestanding shrubs also applies to wall-trained specimens, but more care is needed for formative training and pruning. It is vital to tie in shoots as they grow and cut back sub-laterals growing strongly away from the wall.

Formative training and pruning

During the first growing season, train in the leader and main laterals to form a framework; prune back any outward-growing laterals to encourage short sideshoots to develop close to the framework. Remove completely any laterals growing towards the wall or fence, and any shoots that are growing outwards in the wrong direction. The aim should be to create a neat, vertical "carpet" of foliage to cover the allotted space.

PRUNING CEANOTHUS

Immediately after flowering, cut back new shoots of spring-flowering Ceanothus to 2–3 leaves. Tie in new shoots and trim back outward-growing shoots to keep growth trained close to the wall or fence.

Routine pruning

In the second and following seasons, flowering laterals should form. After flowering, cut back flowered shoots to within 7–10cm (3–4in) of the main framework. This encourages new flowering laterals to develop, providing the next season's display. Continue tying in framework shoots; trim outward-pointing laterals and remove inward-growing and other wrongly aligned shoots. Do not trim wall shrubs after midsummer as this

may reduce the following year's flowering shoots; this is particularly important with *Ceanothus* and many half-hardy evergreen shrubs which might otherwise produce soft growth liable to frost damage. Feed and mulch wall-trained shrubs annually in spring to maintain healthy growth.

Shrubs, such as pyracantha, that are grown both for flowers and fruits or berries need slightly modified pruning. Shoots that have flowered are not cut back, but left to develop fruits. Trim back new laterals to two to three leaves from their base as the fruits swell, so that they are exposed to more light and ripen well. Old fruit trusses may be cut out in spring as young growths develop.

Summer- and autumn-flowering wall shrubs, like some *Ceanothus*, should be trained as described earlier but pruned according to whether they flower on the previous season's wood (see "Shrubs pruned in summer after flowering", p.106), or that of the current season (see "Pruning in spring", p.105). Some half-hardy or tender shrubs – particularly *Ceanothus* – do not break readily from old wood and are difficult to renovate once neglected.

Scrambling shrubs

These also require careful training to contain their flexuous shoots. On some, such as half-hardy *Cestrum*

elegans, that produce flowers in late summer on terminal shoots or short laterals, the flowered shoots may be cut out entirely or cut back to strong, low, lateral growths in spring. Others flower in summer mainly on lateral growths, which should be cut back after flowering to 7–10cm (3–4in) and will often produce further sub-laterals that flower the same season. In spring, these laterals are pruned back again to 7–10cm (3–4in) and will flower in summer.

Training and pruning standard shrubs

Some shrubs, for example, fuchsias and *Buddleja alternifolia*, may be grown as standards. The height of the stem varies according to the vigour of the plant and the effect wanted. For details on training a standard fuchsia, see p.121; for pruning a standard rose, see p.162.

To train a shrub such as *Buddleja alternifolia* as a standard, tie a strong stem to a cane in the first growing season. Pinch all sideshoots back to two or three leaves, leaving a few growing near the stem tip. As the stem grows, continue to pinch out. When the clear stem is at the desired height, stop the terminal shoot to encourage shoots to form the head. In early spring of the following year,

PRUNING AND TRAINING A YOUNG WALL SHRUB

In the first year, prune the shrub (here a pyracantha) to build up a balanced framework, tying in main stems. In subsequent years, tie in new growth in spring; in midsummer, cut back inward- and outward-growing shoots to form a vertical "carpet"; remove entirely dead, damaged, or spindly growth.

Using secateurs, cut back any weak, spindly stems as well as any dead or damaged wood.

Trim back any outward-growing stems to 7–10cm (3–4in) from the framework in midsummer.

Check and replace any broken ties. Use garden twine tied in a figure-of-eight to re-secure the stem to the wire.

PRUNING AN ESTABLISHED WALL SHRUB

Prune mature plants (here, pyracantha) to maintain a well-balanced framework of stems and expose the fruits on berrying shrubs. In late summer, remove outward-growing shoots and, with the exception of shrubs grown for fruits or berries, cut back flowered shoots to promote dense growth. Also check and replace ties where necessary. Tie in new shoots in spring.

Cut back young shoots to 2–3 leaves from their base to expose the ripening berries.

Using secateurs, cut back any damaged or dead wood to healthy growth.

shorten the branches of the head to about 15cm (6in). Retain two or three of the shoots each produces. Feed and mulch. Prune subsequently as for other shrubs pruned in summer after flowering (see p.106).

Some pendulous cultivars are grafted onto a rootstock. Remove any suckers (see p.100) and treat as for roses (see "Suckers and how to deal with them", p.159).

Root pruning

Root pruning is sometimes used to control the top-growth of vigorous shrubs and to make them flower more freely; grafted specimens that are making prolific leaf growth but producing few flowers or fruits usually benefit from root pruning.

In early spring, dig a trench around the shrub to a depth of 30–60cm (12–24in) with a circumference just beyond the spread of the top-growth. Use pruning loppers or a saw to cut back the thick, woody roots; as a guide, shorten them to about half the radius of the trench. Leave fibrous roots unpruned. Control further root spread by inserting a barrier of slates or polycarbonate sheets around the trench (see *Restricting the Spread of Bamboo*, p.96). After backfilling, mulch the area within the trench.

Root pruning is often used to control container-grown shrubs. This is best done when repotting. Shorten up to one fifth of woody roots by a quarter; cut back others so that they fit in the container. Repot, using fresh compost and a slow-release fertilizer and water thoroughly.

Renovation

Old, tangled, or overgrown shrubs may sometimes be renovated by extensive pruning. Shrubs that respond well usually produce young growth from the base. It is not worth trying to salvage a shrub that is badly diseased. Some shrubs do not tolerate drastic pruning; if in any doubt, stagger a programme of heavy pruning over two or three years.

Renovate deciduous shrubs, such as lilacs, after flowering or when dormant; for evergreens, such as *Viburnum tinus*, delay renovation until mid-spring, after flowering.

Renovating old or overgrown shrubs

Cut out all weak and crossing stems and shorten main stems to 30–45cm (12–18in) above the ground, leaving a balanced framework. Apply a slow-release fertilizer at 120g/sq m (4oz/sq yd), and mulch the area around the shrub to a depth of 5–10cm (2–4in). Keep the shrub well watered throughout summer.

In the next growing season, a mass of shoots should emerge from below the cuts on the main stems. Retain only two to four of the strongest on each stem to provide the new branch framework. On deciduous shrubs, cut out superfluous shoots during the dormant season. On evergreen shrubs, do this in mid-spring.

In the following growing season, some secondary growth may occur where shoots have been cut. Rub out these growths.

Staggered renovation

A less drastic method is to spread the pruning over two or three years. Prune deciduous shrubs after flowering, evergreens in mid-spring. Prune half of the oldest stems to 5–8cm (2–3in) from the ground. If possible cut back remaining stems by about half to new, vigorous, replacement shoots. Apply slow-release fertilizer, water well, and mulch. At the same time next year, repeat the process on the remaining old stems. Thereafter, prune the shrub according to its growth and flowering characteristics.

GRADUAL RENOVATION

Renovate deciduous shrubs after flowering and evergreens in mid-spring. Cut back a third to a half of the oldest main stems (here on a Deutzia) *almost to the ground and remove dead, twiggy stems. Over the next year or two cut back remaining old, main stems.*

Cut back about half the stems to within 5–8cm (2–3in) of the base. Cut out the oldest stems and any that spoil the shape.

Cut back older stems by half to new, vigorous shoots, and remove any weak, twiggy growth or dead wood.

Prune back crossing, rubbing, or congested stems to a bud or stem that will not cause more crossing shoots.

DRASTIC RENOVATION

A shrub that produces new growth from the base (here lilac) can be renovated when dormant if it is deciduous or in mid-spring if evergreen. Cut back all main stems to within 30–45cm (12–18in) of the ground. Remove suckers by cutting them off at the base.

Pruning and composting

Most gardeners need to dispose of woody waste material like hedge clippings, tree and shrub prunings, or sometimes large tree branches at least once a year. Rather than burning it, which has an adverse environmental impact, it is better to chop up – or preferably shred – the pruned woody shoots and compost them. Shredded vegetation will rot down faster than chopped clippings or prunings in a compost heap.

If practical, it is best to compost clippings and prunings from deciduous plants separately from those of evergreens – especially those with large, tough leaves like *Prunus laurocerasus* and hollies – because evergreen foliage usually takes longer to break down.

Mixing the shredded material with compost activators like grass mowings or comfrey leaves hastens the composting process. The resulting compost, which takes 3–12 months to mature, may be used as a mulch on established trees and shrubs. See also p.627.

Propagation

THERE are many ways to propagate shrubs to raise new plants, including taking cuttings, sowing seed, layering, division, and grafting.

Taking cuttings is a simple way of propagating many shrubs and, unlike seed, which may produce variable offspring, it may be used for cultivars, hybrids, and sports.

Sowing seed is both simple and inexpensive but it is relatively slow to produce plants of flowering size. Some shrubs may be divided, while others may be layered.

Grafting involves uniting a stem from the plant to be propagated with the rootstock of a compatible plant. It is not commonly used outside commerce, since it requires more expertise and skill than other methods, but it is the most suitable method for some shrubs.

Softwood cuttings

This technique is suitable for raising several, mainly deciduous, shrubs, for example *Fuchsia* and *Perovskia*. Softwood cuttings are taken in spring from fast-growing stem tips when these are about 6–8cm (2½–3in) long. The cuttings have a soft base and a higher capacity to root than cuttings of more mature wood.

Preparing the cuttings

Take the cuttings early in the morning. Select healthy, pliable, single-stemmed shoots and seal them in an opaque, plastic bag. Prepare the cuttings as soon as possible after collection: trim the cuttings just below a node and remove the lower leaves. The soft tip is generally pinched out as it is vulnerable to rotting; its removal also encourages the cutting, once rooted, to form a bushy plant. Use a cutting compost of equal parts peat substitute (or peat) and either perlite or sharp sand. With a dibber, insert them into the compost. Water them in, applying a fungicide to minimize rot, label, and place in a mist unit or propagator.

Aftercare

Softwood cuttings wilt quickly if not kept in a humid atmosphere and aftercare is very important; remove dropped leaves daily, if possible, and apply a fungicidal spray every week. Once rooted, harden off the cuttings and transplant them into individual pots or retain them in the container. If kept in the cutting medium, give a supplementary feed every two weeks during the growing season and pot up the rooted cuttings individually the following spring.

Greenwood cuttings

Almost all the shrubs that may be propagated by softwood cuttings may also be propagated by greenwood cuttings. Take greenwood cuttings, either nodal or heel cuttings (see p.113), from vigorous shoots in late spring or early summer, when these are firm and slightly woody at the base. Follow the method for softwood cuttings.

Remove the soft tips if the cuttings are more than 8–10cm (3–4in) long and trim off the bottom leaves. On a nodal cutting, make a straight cut with a sharp blade directly below the node. Trim off the tail on a heel

TAKING GREENWOOD CUTTINGS

Select and prepare greenwood cuttings (here of Philadelphus) *in late spring when growth has slowed and the new stems are firmer.*

cutting. Dip the cuttings in a rooting hormone and insert them into the compost. Water the cuttings with a fungicidal solution before placing them in a mist unit or propagator. Remove any fallen leaves daily and apply a fungicide once a week.

Once rooted, harden off the cuttings and transplant them or grow them on in the original container.

PROPAGATING BY SOFTWOOD CUTTINGS

1 *In spring, cut off young, non-flowering shoots (here from a hydrangea) with 3–5 pairs of leaves. Seal them in an opaque plastic bag and keep shaded until they can be prepared.*

2 *Reduce each cutting to 8–10cm (3–4in) in length, making a straight cut just below a node (see inset). Trim off the lower leaves and pinch out the growing tip.*

3 *Insert the cuttings into prepared pots of cutting compost, ensuring that the leaves do not touch each other.*

4 *Water the cuttings with a fungicidal solution, then label and place them in a propagator. Maintain a temperature of 18–21°C (64–70°F).*

5 *Once the cuttings have rooted, harden them off, then remove them from the pot and carefully tease them apart.*

6 *Transplant the separated cuttings into individual pots and firm in. Water, label, and keep the cuttings in a shaded position until well established.*

SHRUBS FROM SOFT- OR GREENWOOD CUTTINGS

Abelia, some ✽
Abutilon, some ✽
Aloysia, most ✽ ✽
Calluna
Caryopteris
Ceanothus, some ✽
  (deciduous spp.)
Ceratostigma, some ✽ ✽
Cestrum ✽ ✽
Cotoneaster (deciduous spp.)
Cytisus, some ✽
Daboecia
Daphne x *burkwoodii*
Deutzia (some spp.)
Enkianthus
Erica
Forsythia
Fuchsia, some ✽
Genista, some ✽
Halesia
Hydrangea ✽
Kolkwitzia
Lagerstroemia, some ✽ ✽
Lantana ✽ ✽
Lavatera ✽
Perovskia
Philadelphus
Potentilla
Viburnum (deciduous spp.)
Weigela (some spp.)

Key
✽ *Not hardy*
✽ *Softwood cuttings only*

PROPAGATING BY SEMI-RIPE CUTTINGS

1 *In mid- to late summer, select healthy shoots of the current season's growth for the cuttings. Sever them from the parent plant (here Ilex x altaclerensis 'Golden King') just above a node. They should be semi-ripe: still soft at the top but firm at the base.*

2 *Remove the sideshoots from the main stem. Trim each sideshoot to 10–15cm (4–6in) long, cutting just below a node.*

3 *Trim off the soft tip of each cutting and then remove the lowest pair of leaves, cutting flush with the stem.*

4 *Stimulate rooting by wounding the cutting: carefully cut away a piece of bark about 2.5–4cm (1–1¹/₂in) long from one side of the base.*

5 *Dip the base of each cutting in hormone rooting powder, then insert it into cutting compost in a propagator or in pots in a cold frame.*

6 *Once they are well rooted, carefully lift the cuttings and plant them individually. Gradually harden them off before growing them on in their pots or transplanting them outside.*

If the latter, feed them regularly during the growing season and transplant them the following spring.

Semi-ripe cuttings

Many evergreen as well as some deciduous shrubs may be propagated from semi-ripe cuttings.

Suitable cuttings

The cuttings are normally taken from mid- to late summer and sometimes into the early autumn. Select shoots from the current season's growth that are firm and woody near the base but still soft at the tip. Unlike softwood cuttings, they should offer some resistance when bent. Some shrubs are propagated by variations of this semi-ripe cuttings technique, such as mallet cuttings (see p.113) or leaf-bud cuttings (see p.113).

Preparing the rooting medium

Before collecting the cutting material from the parent shrub, fill sufficient containers of appropriate size, or a propagator (equipped with basal heating) with a suitable rooting medium: use fine-grade pine bark or a mixture of equal parts of peat substitute (or peat) and either grit or perlite.

Preparing the cuttings

Cuttings may be taken with a heel (see p.113) or as nodal cuttings. Heel cuttings should be 5–7cm (2–3in) long, trimmed at the heel; nodal cuttings should be 10–15cm (4–6in) long, taken from leaders or sideshoots, and cut with a sharp knife or secateurs just below a node.

Remove the soft tips of nodal and heel cuttings. In both cases, remove the lowest pair of leaves and with large-leaved plants reduce the size of the remaining leaves by about a half to minimize moisture loss.

An optional step is to prepare the base of the cuttings by making a shallow wound at one side; on plants that are difficult to root, such as *Daphne sericea*, this cut should be made deeper so that a sliver of bark is also removed.

Potting up

Dip the bases of the cuttings, including the entire wound on wounded cuttings, in a rooting hormone before using a dibber to insert them in the prepared compost, either directly in a propagator, or in containers.

Space the cuttings approximately 8–10cm (3–4in) apart, and make certain that their leaves do not overlap, since this may create stagnant conditions in which rot fungi thrive.

Firm the compost mixture around the cuttings. Label each container and water the cuttings thoroughly with a fungicidal solution in order to protect them against damping off diseases (see p.660).

Correct temperature

Overwinter cuttings in containers in a cold frame or greenhouse. Those that have been inserted directly in a propagator should have basal heat maintained at 21°C (70°F).

Aftercare

Inspect the cuttings periodically during the winter period, removing any fallen leaves promptly. Water the containers if the compost mixture shows any signs of drying out. If the cuttings are being overwintered in a cold frame, this may need some form of insulation, such as a hessian cover or a piece of old carpet, to protect the cuttings from damage by frost.

Cuttings kept in a cold frame or unheated greenhouse will almost certainly need a further growing season in their containers before rooting satisfactorily. Keep the frame closed, except on very mild days. The glass should be kept clean and free of any condensation, since the high moisture content of the air inside the frame provides ideal conditions for fungal infection to occur. In late spring and early summer, gradually open the cover for longer and longer periods to harden off the rooted cuttings. If necessary, protect them from strong, direct sunlight by covering the glass with suitable shading material.

Throughout the growing season, apply a liquid feed every two weeks to all semi-ripe cuttings. Check them regularly, and remove any that are weak or showing signs of disease.

Transplanting

Cuttings overwintered in a propagator should have rooted by early spring, since the basal heat helps to speed up root development. Check that there is strong root growth before transplanting the cuttings. Ease them from their containers, separate each cutting carefully, and either pot up individually or plant, clearly labelled, in the open ground. If some cuttings have not rooted but have formed a callus, scrape off some of the callus to stimulate rooting and re-insert the cuttings in the compost mixture.

Cuttings grown in a cold frame may be planted out in autumn, if well developed, or kept in a sheltered position outside or in the cold frame until spring. They are then potted up individually or planted out.

Heel cuttings

Heel cuttings, which may be taken from greenwood, semi-ripe, or hardwood stems, are vigorous sideshoots of the current season's growth. Each cutting is taken with a "heel" of old wood at its base, in which the growth hormones that assist the rooting process are concentrated.

Heel cuttings are particularly suitable for a number of evergreen shrubs such as *Pieris* and some azaleas (*Rhododendron*), deciduous shrubs that have pithy or hollow stems such as *Berberis* and *Sambucus*, and those shrubs that have greenwood stems such as broom (*Cytisus/Genista*).

Select as cuttings healthy sideshoots that are characteristic of the parent plant. Pull the shoot away from the main stem so that a small strip of bark from the parent shoot comes away with it. Avoid tearing too much bark off the main shoot as this may expose it to infection. Trim the heel with a sharp blade and then follow the technique for greenwood (see p.111), semi-ripe (see p.112), or hardwood cuttings (see right), according to the particular stem's maturity.

1 *Pull away healthy sideshoots of the current season's growth (here on* Prunus laurocerasus *'Schipkaensis') with a heel of bark.*

2 *Using a sharp knife, trim off the "tail" at the base of the heel before inserting it in cutting compost.*

Mallet cuttings

A mallet cutting, which is taken from semi-ripe stems, is a ripened shoot of the current season's growth attached to a piece of wood from the previous season, forming a mallet-shaped plug at its base. Mallet cuttings are often used to propagate shrubs with pithy or hollow stems, because rot fungi are less likely to affect older wood. It is particularly suitable for many *Spiraea* and deciduous *Berberis*, which produce short sideshoots on main branches.

In late summer, remove a stem of the last season's growth from the parent and cut it into sections, each containing a vigorous sideshoot of new growth. If the mallet is more than 5mm (¼in) in diameter, slit it lengthwise. Then treat as for semi-ripe cuttings (see p.112).

Leaf-bud cuttings

A leaf-bud cutting is taken from semi-ripe stems and comprises a short piece of stem bearing a leaf and a leaf bud. In comparison with stem cuttings, leaf-bud cuttings make much more economical use of the material from the parent plant. This method of propagation is most commonly used for camellias and mahonia.

In late summer or early autumn, select a vigorous shoot of the current season's growth, bearing healthy leaves and well-developed buds. Using a sharp knife or secateurs, cut the stem just above each leaf, then make a cut about 2cm (¾in) below the petiole so that the shoot is divided into several sections.

Leaf-bud cuttings do not need to be treated with hormone rooting powder before potting up, but may be wounded at the base to hasten rooting. Insert them in containers of cutting compost and treat as for semi-ripe cuttings (see p.112).

To save space in the cold frame or propagator, roll up any large leaves and secure them with elastic bands; a cane inserted down the middle of a rolled-up leaf will help to anchor it firmly in the compost. Trim compound leaves on shrubs such as mahonia by a half.

Hardwood cuttings

An easy way to raise many deciduous and some evergreen shrubs is from hardwood cuttings. Use fully ripe, vigorous growths of the current season, taken from late autumn to midwinter. Take cuttings of deciduous shrubs just after leaf fall, or just before bud burst, in spring.

Preparing the ground

Cuttings are best rooted in a prepared bed or containers kept in

SHRUBS FROM SEMI-RIPE CUTTINGS

Andromeda
Arctostaphylos
Aucuba▽
Azara, some ✿ ▽
Berberis, some ✿ ▽
Boronia ✿ ▽
Brachyglottis ✿
Bupleurum▽
Buxus
Callistemon ✿ ▽
Camellia, some ✿
Cantua ✿ ▽
Carmichaelia, some ✿ ▽
Carpenteria▽
Cassinia▽
Cassiope▽
Ceanothus, some ✿ ▽
Choisya
Colletia▽
Coprosma ✿ ▽
Corokia, some ✿ ▽

Cotoneaster ignescens

Cotoneaster▽
Cytisus, some ✿ ▽
Daphne
Deutzia (some spp.)
Drimys
Elaeagnus▽
Erica
Escallonia▽
Garrya▽
Gordonia ✿ ▽
Grevillea, some ✿ ▽
Griselinia, some ✿ ▽
Hibiscus rosa-sinensis ✿
Ilex, some ✿
Itea ilicifolia▽
Lavandula, some ✿
Leptospermum, some ✿ ▽
Leucothöe▽
Magnolia grandiflora▽
Mahonia
Nerium ✿ ▽
Olearia, some ✿ ▽

Olearia phlogopappa

Philadelphus
Photinia▽
Pieris▽
Pittosporum, some ✿
Prunus (evergreen spp.)▽
Pyracantha
Rhododendron▽
Skimmia▽
Viburnum
Weigela

Key
✿ Not hardy
▽ With a heel

MALLET CUTTINGS

Remove a stem produced the previous year and cut it above each sideshoot and about 2.5cm (1in) below. Reduce it to 10–13cm (4–5in) and trim off lower leaves.

LEAF-BUD CUTTINGS

1 *Select semi-ripe shoots (here of* Camellia japonica*). Make a straight cut 2cm (¾in) below each leaf and a further cut just above.*

2 *Remove a 5mm (¼in) sliver of bark at the base of each cutting (see inset). Insert the cuttings in the compost so that the leaf axils are just visible above the surface.*

SHRUBS FROM HARDWOOD CUTTINGS

Atriplex halimus
Aucuba (some spp.)
Buddleja
Buxus (some spp.)
Cornus alba, C. sericea
Cotoneaster x *watereri*
Deutzia x *elegantissima*
  'Rosealind', *D. longifolia,*
  D. x *rosea, D. scabra*
Forsythia
Hypericum x *moserianum*
Ligustrum ovalifolium
Philadelphus

Deutzia longifolia 'Veitchii'

Ribes
Rosa rugosa
Rubus
Ruta graveolens
Salix
Sambucus
Spiraea
Symphoricarpos
Tamarix
Viburnum (deciduous spp.)
Weigela

a cold frame but they may also be inserted in a bed in open ground.

Prepare the bed in late summer or early autumn, first working the soil until it is friable, and then digging out a flat-backed trench 12–15cm (5–6in) deep. To encourage rooting, put a 2.5–5cm (1–2in) layer of coarse sand in the base of the trench; this is essential on heavy soils. Space the trenches 38cm (15in) apart.

Preparing the cuttings

Take cuttings that are about pencil thickness, cutting at the junction of the current and the previous season's growth.

Trim deciduous cuttings into 15–22cm (6–9in) lengths, cutting at the top just above a bud or pair of buds and, at the bottom, below a bud or pair of buds; make evergreen cuttings 15cm (6in) long, cutting above and below leaves. Take heel cuttings of pithy stems (see p.113). Remove all leaves on the bottom two thirds of evergreen cuttings and cut large leaves in half. Treat the basal cut with a rooting hormone. Removing a sliver of bark near the base may encourage difficult cuttings to root.

Insert the cuttings in containers of cutting compost. Alternatively, place deciduous cuttings against the vertical side of a prepared trench, 15cm (6in) apart in open ground, or

in a cold frame, 10cm (4in) apart. Leave 2.5–5cm (1–2in) of the cuttings above ground. Backfill the trench and firm in the cuttings.

Aftercare

If the ground is lifted by frost, firm it down around the cuttings. Keep the bed weed-free and well watered during the growing season. Cuttings in a cold frame will normally root by the following spring. Harden them off (see p.637) before potting up or planting out. Those in the open ground should be left in place until the following autumn and then transplanted to their permanent position.

Root cuttings

Shrubs that may be propagated from root cuttings include *Aesculus parviflora, Aralia, Clerodendrum, Myrica, Rhus,* and *Xanthorhiza simplicissima*. Lift a young plant prior to regrowth, in mid- to late winter, and tease the soil from its roots. If this is not practical, expose part of the shrub's root system. Cut off young roots – 5mm (¼in) in diameter or more – close to the main stem. Keep them in moist sacking or a plastic bag until they can be prepared.

Preparing the cuttings

First remove and discard fibrous, lateral roots. Then make a straight cut on an undamaged root at the end where it was severed from the plant. At the opposite end of the root, make a slanting cut. Cuttings should be 5–15cm (2–6in) long – thinner cuttings should be longer – and several cuttings may be prepared from the same root. The colder the rooting environment and the thinner the root, the longer the cutting needs to be; cuttings to be rooted outdoors need to be at least 10cm (4in) long. Dust each cutting with fungicide but do not treat with a rooting powder, since this will tend to discourage the production of shoots.

Inserting the cuttings

Aralia and other shrubs that will reproduce readily from root cuttings may be inserted in open ground. For shrubs that root less readily, a controlled environment is preferable. Prepare containers of cuttings compost large enough for several cuttings. Firm the compost lightly and insert each cutting vertically 5cm (2in) apart with the slanted end down. Thinner, longer cuttings can be laid horizontally. Firm the compost so that the flat end of each cutting is just visible. Cover with 3mm (⅛in) of grit (or vermiculite for

those laid horizontally), and water. This watering may be sufficient to last until the shoots develop; excessive moisture may cause rotting.

Aftercare

Cuttings will root in ten weeks outdoors, eight weeks in a cold frame or cool greenhouse. Under glass, cuttings produce shoots in four to six weeks if they are kept at 18–24°C (64–75°F). Cuttings from shrubs that make rapid growth should be repotted as soon as they have rooted. Other root cuttings may be left in their pots for a further 12 months; apply a liquid feed once or twice a month. Then pot up or plant out.

Raising shrubs from seed

Growing shrubs from seed is simple and economical. In genera whose species hybridize readily, only use seed produced by controlled pollination. Garden-raised hybrids, however, can produce interesting new plants when open-pollinated seed is used.

REMOVING SEED FROM BERRIES

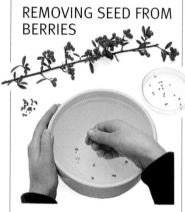

1 *Squash berries (here pyracantha) between finger and thumb, removing most of the outer flesh. Wash seeds by rubbing them in warm water.*

2 *Dry the seeds with tissue and place them in a clear plastic bag with a little coarse sand or moist vermiculite; refrigerate until ready to sow.*

HARDWOOD CUTTINGS

1 *Select strong, healthy, ripened shoots from this year's growth for the cuttings (see inset, left); avoid weak, thin stems (centre) and older wood (right).*

Healthy Weak Old wood

2 *Remove any deciduous leaves and trim off the soft tip. Cut the stem into 15–20cm (6–8in) lengths, dipping the bases into hormone rooting powder.*

3 *Insert the cuttings into prepared pots of cutting compost so that approximately 2.5–5cm (1–2in) of each is visible. Label the pots and place in a cold frame.*

Collecting and cleaning seed
Gather the seed capsules or fruits when ripe. Extract the seed, then clean and dry it before sowing or storing. Soak fleshy fruits in warm water or squash them so that the seed may be picked out more easily. Collect fine seed by gathering whole capsules, preferably when they have already turned brown. Place capsules in a paper bag and keep at room temperature until they split open.

Storing seed
The length of time seed is viable depends on the species and storage conditions. Daphne, *Kalmia*, and rhododendrons, for example, should be sown when fresh. Oily seeds do not store well and should be sown soon after collection. The viability of seed may be prolonged if it is stored at 3–5°C (37–41°F).

Breaking seed dormancy
The seeds of some shrubs have a form of dormancy to stop them germinating in adverse conditions.This dormancy may be broken artificially by scarification or stratification (see PRINCIPLES OF PROPAGATION, "How to overcome dormancy", p.629).

To allow air and moisture to penetrate large seeds with hard coats, such as camellia and peonies (*Paeonia*), scarify them by nicking the seed coat with a knife or filing away a small section before sowing. Hard-coated seeds too small to be nicked may be rubbed with glass-paper. Germination of some seeds may be aided by soaking the seed in either cold water (for example camellia and *Pittosporum*) or hot but not boiling water (for example *Arbutus*, *Caragana*, *Coronilla*, and *Cytisus*) for a few hours. This softens the hard seed coat allowing water to enter and germination to begin.

Seeds that need a period of chilling are stratified – *Acer palmatum*, *Amelanchier*, cotoneaster, *Euonymus*, *Hippophäe*, and viburnum producing seeds that need such treatment. As soon as the seed is gathered, place a layer of crocks in the base of a container that has drainage holes, and scatter the seed between two layers of a sand and peat substitute (or peat) mix. Plunge the container in the open garden or place in a cold frame.

The next spring, by when some of the seed may have germinated, it may be separated out and space sown. Seed of certain hardy shrubs, such as some *Viburnum*, may need further chilling in a refrigerator.

Refrigerating hardy seed may produce more reliable results. Mix the seed with moist vermiculite, peat substitute, or peat, then seal it in a clear plastic bag and refrigerate. The chilling period varies from species to species and it is best to try to sow the seed before it starts germinating in the fridge, that is in mid- to late winter. For safety, keep a few extra seeds in the fridge, checking them each week until germination has started, then remove and sow them.

Sowing seed in containers
Seeds of hardy shrubs are sown in a cold frame in autumn, or placed in a fridge and sown in mid- to late winter, while seeds of temperate and tender shrubs are sown in spring, in pots. Most fine, ericaceous seed is stored in the fridge until mid- to late winter, when it is germinated under mist at a temperature of 15°C (59°F).

Clean all containers, implements, and surfaces. Use a standard seed compost, but for lime-haters use an ericaceous compost. Many large seeds are sown individually into their own module or root trainer. Overfill a pot or tray with compost and gently firm before scraping off the surplus. Firm again with a presser board so that the level is 1cm (½in) below the rim of the pot or tray. Sow the seeds 5cm (2in) apart, then firm them evenly into the compost. Cover with a 5mm (¼in) layer of sieved compost and a 5mm (¼in) layer of clean grit. Label and date each container and water the seeds.

Many medium-sized seeds may also be sown in this way, but the gap between the rim and compost should be 5–8mm (¼–⅜in). Cover seeds with sieved compost and then 5mm (¼in) of clean grit. Place wire netting over the container to protect the seedlings from small animals. When sowing fine seed, firm the compost to within 5mm (¼in) of the container rim. Water and allow the compost to drain before sowing, carefully shaking the seed out over the surface. Do not cover the seed or water it from above.

Aftercare for seedlings in containers
After sowing, place the containers in a propagator, greenhouse, or cold frame. Temperate species need a temperature of 12–15°C (54–59°F); warm-temperate and tropical species prefer 21°C (70°F). For seed sown in spring under glass, a constant temperature of 12–15°C (54–59°F) should be maintained. Inspect containers of seed regularly and water as necessary. Never water fine seed from above; place the container in a shallow water tank for a short time so that water is taken up by capillary action. When the seeds have germinated, spray the container occasionally with fungicide.

SOWING SEED IN CONTAINERS

1 Sow seeds evenly onto a prepared tray of sieved seed compost by tapping them from a folded piece of paper.

2 Cover the seeds with a fine layer of compost, then add a 5mm (¼in) layer of grit. Label and place in a cold frame until the seeds have germinated.

3 When the seedlings are large enough to handle, prick them out, lifting them carefully with a widger and holding them gently by their leaves.

4 Transfer the seedlings into individual pots or insert 3 into a 13cm (5in) pot. After the second pair of leaves has formed, pot them up individually.

Pricking out
Once large enough to handle, prick out the seedlings. Knock the sides of the container gently against, for example, the greenhouse bench to loosen the compost or remove the seedlings and compost together and separate the seedlings, disturbing their roots as little as possible.

Transfer the seedlings into clean pots or seed trays of cutting compost, levelled but not firmed. Make a hole in the compost using a widger and insert the seedling. Level the compost by tapping the top of the container and firm in, then label and water. Until the seedlings are established, place the pots out of direct sunlight in a temperature similar to that needed for germination.

Sowing seed outdoors
Open-ground seedbeds are useful for sowing large batches of seed that do not require daily attention. Such beds are generally 90–100cm (36–39in) wide and raised 15–20cm (6–8in) above the surrounding ground, to improve drainage. Prepare the bed between six months and a year before sowing.

In autumn, rake the soil to a fine tilth. Fine seed is broadcast sown over the area, while medium or large seed is sown up to 10–15cm (4–6in) apart, in rows 45cm (18in) apart. Large seeds may be sown at greater distances apart, if required.

Cover large and medium seeds to a depth of 0.5–1cm (¼–½in) but leave fine seed uncovered. Then place a 0.5–1cm (¼–½in) layer of grit over the seedbed. Firm the grit with a presser board, and label the rows.

Aftercare for seedlings outdoors
Protect seedlings from wind damage by covering them with 50 per cent permeable netting, and from frosts by using firmly secured horticultural fleece. If the seeds are well spaced, they should not be troubled by disease, but greenfly (see "Aphids", p.646), red spider mite (p.646), and mice (p.662) may be a problem.

If the spacing is adequate, the seedlings may be left in the seedbed until the following autumn; they should then be either potted up or transplanted into a separate nursery bed.

SHRUBS SUITABLE FOR SIMPLE LAYERING

Andromeda
Aucuba
Carpenteria
Cassiope
Chaenomeles
Chionanthus
Corylopsis
Daphne blagayana
Disanthus
Elaeagnus commutata
Epigaea
Erica
Fothergilla
Gaultheria, some ✻
Illicium, some ✻
Kalmia
Laurus
Magnolia
Osmanthus,
   some ✻
Rhododendron,
   some ✻
Skimmia
Stachyurus, some ✻
Syringa
Vaccinium corymbosum

Kalmia
latifolia

Key

✻ *Not hardy*

Propagation by layering

Layering is a method of propagating shrubs whereby a stem is encouraged to develop roots before being removed from the parent plant. Dropping and stooling, techniques that are often used commercially, are variations of layering.

Simple layering

Many deciduous and evergreen shrubs may be propagated by this method. In autumn or spring, about 12 months before layering is to take place, prune a low branch on the parent plant to encourage vigorous shoots, which have a greater capacity to root. Between the following late autumn and early spring, prepare the soil around the stem to be layered so that it is friable. Add grit and humus if the ground is heavy.

Retain any leaves at the tip of the selected shoot but strip off others and any sideshoots. Bring the stem down to ground level and mark the ground about 22–30cm (9–12in) behind its tip. Dig a shallow hole or trench at this point for the stem. Wound the stem at the point where it will be pegged into the hole, that is

about 30cm (12in) behind its tip, either with an angled cut or by removing a ring of bark. Dust the cut with a rooting hormone, then peg the stem in the hole with bent wire, turning up the tip and securing it to a cane. Infill the trench and firm the soil, leaving the tip exposed.

Throughout the growing season keep the area around the layer moist. The layer should have rooted by autumn. In the following spring, check that there is a good root system before severing the layer from the parent plant and potting it up or planting it out in the open garden. If it has not rooted or there are only a few roots, keep it attached and in place for another growing season.

Air layering

This technique is particularly suitable for shrubs with branches that are difficult to lower to ground level. It is also good for plants growing in high humidity and rainfall and in warm-temperate situations.

In spring, choose a strong, healthy, one-year-old stem that has ripened. Trim the sideshoots or leaves to leave a clear length of stem behind the tip. Wound the stem with an angled cut and dust the cut surface with a rooting hormone.

Cut off the sealed end of a black or opaque plastic bag, about 22 x 18cm (9 x 7in). Slip it over the stem and secure the end farthest from the growing tip using tape, raffia, or string.

Moisten a well aerated rooting medium of sphagnum moss or equal parts of perlite and peat substitute or peat so that it is wet but not sodden. Pack the moist medium into the bag around the stem's cut surface and seal the top end. Keep the bag in position for a complete season.

The following spring, check that the layer has rooted. If so, sever it immediately below the point of layering. Remove the bag and tease out the roots. Prune back any new growth on the layered stem to a leaf or bud close to the old wood. Pot up using a standard or ericaceous potting compost, as appropriate. Label and place the layer in a cool greenhouse or cold frame until well established. If only a few (or no) roots have developed when the bag is removed, reseal it and leave it in place for several months more. Then follow the process described above.

Tip layering

A few shrubs, mainly species and hybrids of the genus *Rubus*, root readily from the tips of stems and may be propagated in this way. In spring, select a vigorous, one-year-old shoot and pinch out the growing point to promote sideshoots. In late spring, cultivate the soil around the shoot. Work in organic matter and grit, if the soil is heavy.

In midsummer, when the tip growth has firmed slightly, bring the stem down to ground level and mark the position of the tip. At that point, dig a trench about 7–10cm (3–4in) deep, with one side vertical and the other sloping towards the parent plant. Using inverted, "U"-shaped wire staples, peg the growing tip at the bottom of the trench close to the vertical side. Infill the trench, firm lightly, and water.

By late autumn, well-rooted plants should have developed. Sever these at the point where the arched stem enters the trench. Lift the rooted layers and pot on or replant outdoors. (See also *Tip Layering*, p.471.)

Dropping

With this technique a plant is almost buried. It is used to raise dwarf shrubs, such as low-growing rhododendrons and heathers (*Erica, Daboecia, Calluna*), from parent plants that have become straggly.

In the dormant season, thin out branches of plants that have a mass of congested stems, to allow the remaining stems sufficient contact

PROPAGATING A SHRUB BY SIMPLE LAYERING

1 *Select a young, pliable, low-growing stem. Bring it down to the soil and mark its position with a cane about 22–30cm (9–12in) behind the tip.*

2 *At the marked point, dig a hole in the prepared soil about 8cm (3in) deep, with a shallow slope on the side where the stem joins the parent plant.*

3 *Trim off sideshoots and leaves on the selected stem. On the underside of the stem, at a point where it touches the ground, cut a tongue or ring of bark.*

4 *Apply a rooting hormone to the wound on the stem. Peg down the stem with bent wire so that the stem's cut surface is held in contact with the soil.*

5 *Gently bend up the stem's tip vertically and secure it to the cane with a tie. Fill in the hole with more soil. Lightly firm with your fingers and water in.*

6 *Once rooted (see inset), lift the layered stem and cut it off the parent plant, severing it close to the new, young roots. Pot up the layer or plant it out.*

AIR LAYERING A SHRUB

1 *Select a healthy, horizontal stem from the previous year's growth. Trim off any leaves and sideshoots to provide a 22–30cm (9–12in) section of clear stem.*

2 *Slide a plastic sleeve over and along the stem; seal and secure the lower end of the sleeve to the stem with adhesive tape.*

3 *Fold back the plastic. Make a 4cm (1½in) diagonal cut 5mm (¼in) into the stem in the direction of growth, away from the shrub. Apply a rooting hormone.*

4 *Soak about 2 handfuls of sphagnum moss in water, then gently squeeze it out. With the back of the knife, pack the cut with moss, wedging it open.*

5 *Pull back the plastic sleeve over the cut. Carefully pack the sleeve with more moistened moss so that the moss is all around the stem.*

6 *Continue to pack the sleeve until the moss is about 5cm (2in) from the open end. Close the end and secure it firmly in place with adhesive tape.*

7 *The sealed sleeve encourages rooting by retaining moisture. Leave it in place for at least a growing season to allow new roots to develop.*

8 *Once the layer has rooted, remove the sleeve and cut off the layer below the roots. Pot up or plant out the new shrub (here a rhododendron) in the open ground.*

STOOLING

Cover shoots with free-draining soil, adding more as they grow. The shoots will root down and can be separated in autumn and potted on.

with the soil to develop roots once buried. Before growth starts, but after the risk of penetrating frosts has passed, dig a pit large enough to bury the plant with only the branch tips visible. If the soil is heavy, add grit and organic material.

Lift the parent plant with the root ball as complete as possible and "drop" it into the prepared hole. Work the soil around each stem, leaving 2.5–5cm (1–2in) of each tip exposed. Firm the soil and label the plant. In summer, keep the soil moist and, in autumn, carefully tease away the soil around the plant to check for rooting. Sever any rooted shoots from the parent plant, and pot up or plant out, clearly labelled. If rooting has not occurred, replace the soil and leave for a further 12 months.

Stooling

Although primarily used to raise fruit tree rootstocks, stooling may also be used to propagate deciduous ornamental shrubs such as dogwoods (*Cornus*) and lilacs (*Syringa*) from ungrafted plants.

Plant a rooted layer or other young plant in spring, label, and grow on for a season. The next spring, cut back the stem to within 8cm (3in) of the ground and apply a balanced fertilizer at 120g/sq m (4oz/sq yd). When the resulting shoots from this stem (or stool) are 15cm (6in) long, work friable soil enriched with organic matter between the shoots and bury them. Add grit if the ground is heavy. As the shoots grow, continue to mound up soil until about 22cm (9in) of each shoot is buried. Keep the soil moist in dry weather.

In autumn, gently fork away the soil to ground level straight after leaf fall, leaving the rooted shoots exposed. Cut them off and pot them up or plant them out. Provided that the stools are kept fertilized, the process may be repeated annually and the same stool used for propagation in subsequent years.

French layering

This method is a form of stooling and is used to increase the stock of deciduous shrubs such as dogwoods (*Cornus alba, C. sericea*) and *Cotinus coggygria*.

In spring, plant a rooted layer or young plant, label it, and grow it on for a season. Then, in the dormant season, cut back the stool to within 8cm (3in) of the ground. In the following spring, apply a balanced fertilizer at the rate of 60–120g/sq m (2–4oz/sq yd).

The following autumn, cut out all but about the ten best stems; shorten the tips of these so that they are all about the same length. With "U"-shaped wire staples pin each stem to the ground, spreading them evenly around the parent stool. Each bud along the length of the stem should break evenly in spring.

When the new shoots on the pegged-down stems are about 5–8cm (2–3in) long, take out the pegs and cultivate the ground around the parent stool, incorporating a balanced fertilizer at a rate of 60–120g/sq m (2–4oz/sq yd). Space the stems evenly again, dropping each into a 5cm (2in) deep trench. Peg down each stem in the bottom of the trench and cover with soil, leaving the shoot tips exposed. Earth up all but 5–8cm (2–3in) of the new shoots as they develop, until the mound is 15cm (6in) high. Water the area well in dry weather.

After leaf fall, carefully fork away the soil from around the new shoots to expose the stems that were laid horizontally. Cut these flush with the central stool. Then cut the stems to separate the rooted sections. Pot these up or plant them out in the open garden, and label them. The same stool may be used again.

Division

Division is a easy way of increasing shrubs that produce suckers. *Ruscus*, *Kerria*, *Gaultheria*, and *Sarcococca* are all suitable for this. Shrubs must be growing on their own roots not grafted onto another rootstock.

Before growth starts in spring, lift the plant. Break the clump into sections, retaining any with vigorous shoots and well-developed roots. Prune any damaged roots, and cut back the top-growth by one third to a half to reduce water loss. Replant the divisions in the open and water in dry weather. Alternatively, simply lift a suckering root, severing it from the parent plant, and then replant it in the open.

With a few shrubs, including *Rhus*, suckering may be encouraged by digging deeply around the parent plant during summer or autumn. This damages the roots and stimulates adventitious buds to develop suckers in spring. These rooted suckers may then be lifted and potted up or planted out.

Grafting

This technique is used to unite two plants so that they grow together as one. One part, known as the scion, is taken from the plant to be propagated and provides the top-growth of the new plant, while the other part, known as the rootstock or stock, provides the root system. The rootstock and scion must be compatible and they are normally of the same or closely related species.

Grafting is an important way of propagating shrubs that are difficult to root or that are unlikely to come true from seed. By using selected rootstocks, it is possible to improve a plant's vigour, disease-resistance, or tolerance to specific growing conditions, or sometimes to control its basic growth pattern.

Among the many variations of this particular technique, three that are widely used are saddle, spliced side-veneer, and apical-wedge grafting.

In all cases, the stocks and scions should be joined immediately after they have been cut and the cut surfaces of each should be kept clean. All types of graft respond well to hot-pipe callusing, which speeds the formation of the callus (see *Hot-pipe Callusing of Grafts*, p.637).

Saddle grafting

This grafting technique is predominantly used to propagate evergreen rhododendron species and hybrids, with *Rhododendron ponticum* or *R.* 'Cunningham's White' generally serving as the rootstock. About one month before grafting is to commence, in late winter or early spring, bring the rootstock into a greenhouse maintained at a temperature of 10–12°C (50–54°F).

In late winter or very early spring, select the scion material so that it is ready for grafting. The scions selected should be about 5–13cm (2–5in) long, and taken from vigorous, non-flowering, one-year-old shoots on the plant to be propagated. If only shoots with flower buds are available, pinch these out. The scions should be labelled and stored in a plastic bag in a refrigerator.

Select a straight-stemmed rootstock of about pencil thickness and

cut it back to within 5cm (2in) of the base, making a straight cut across the stem with secateurs. Then, using a knife, make two slanting cuts to make an upside-down "V" wound on the top of the stock. Prepare the scion by making two corresponding angled cuts so that its base – the saddle – will fit snugly onto the apex of the rootstock.

Ensure that the two sections of the graft fit well together, and then bind the stock and scion together with a length of clear grafting tape. Cut back any very large leaves by half to reduce moisture loss. Label clearly, and then place the grafted plant in a propagator and shade it from direct sunlight. Check the plant daily for watering and hygiene, and spray it once a week with a fungicide solution. Union normally takes place within four to five weeks.

Once the scion is growing away freely, remove the tape and gradually harden off the grafted plant – opening the propagator for longer periods each day. If the grafted plant is kept in the original pot for a season, give it a liquid feed once a month.

Spliced side-veneer grafting

This grafting technique is used to propagate a variety of both evergreen and deciduous shrubs. Most spliced side-veneer grafting is carried out in midwinter, but deciduous shrubs, such as *Viburnum* x *burkwoodii*, may also be grafted during the summer.

For the appropriate rootstocks, choose one- to three-year-old seed-lings that are compatible with the plant to be propagated. The stems should be of pencil thickness. About three weeks before grafting, bring the rootstock into the greenhouse. Water it sparingly so that the rootstock does not break dormancy too quickly, since vigorous sap movement may prevent successful grafting. If grafting in summer, use two-year-old seedlings for the rootstocks and keep them fairly dry for a month in advance.

For both summer and winter grafting, prepare and unite the stocks and scions in the same way.

Just before grafting takes place, collect vigorous, one-year-old shoots that have some mature wood to be used as scions. They should be of a similar thickness to the rootstocks onto which they will be grafted. If there is any delay, label the scions and place them in a plastic bag in a refrigerator.

When grafting, first trim the scion to a length of 15–20cm (5–8in), or 10–12cm (4–5in) for magnolias. Make a sloping cut at the base of the scion, 2.5–4cm (1–1½in) long then

SUCKERING SHRUBS TO DIVIDE

Amelanchier canadensis
Andromeda
Aronia
Aster albescens
Berberis buxifolia
Buxus sempervirens
Cassiope hypnoides
Ceratostigma plumbaginoides
Clerodendrum bungei
Cornus alba,
   C. canadensis,
   C. sericea

Cornus canadensis

Danäe racemosa
Diervilla lonicera
Erica
Euonymus fortunei
Gaultheria, some ✻
Itea virginica
Kerria
Mahonia repens
Menziesia ciliicalyx
Paxistima
Polygala, some ✻
Rhus, some ✻
Ruscus aculeatus
Sarcococca
Spiraea japonica (cvs)

Key
✻ *Not hardy*

PROPAGATING SUCKERING SHRUBS BY DIVISION

1 *Lift a root with suckers on it, without disturbing the parent plant. Check that there are fibrous roots at the base of the suckers.*

2 *Remove the long, suckering root by cutting it off close to the parent plant. Firm back the soil around the parent plant.*

3 *Cut the main root back to the fibrous roots, then divide the suckers so that each has its own roots. Cut back the top growth by about half.*

4 *Replant the suckers in open ground in prepared planting holes. Firm the soil around the suckers and water in. (The plant used here is* Gaultheria shallon.)

SADDLE GRAFTING

1 Select vigorous, non-flowering shoots of the previous year's growth to be propagated (here a rhododendron) as scions.

2 Prepare a selected rootstock of about the same diameter as the scion by cutting it back to within about 5cm (2in) of the base.

3 Using a sharp knife, cut the stock with two upward-angled cuts so that its apex is shaped like a slightly rounded, upside-down "V".

4 Make compatible, angled cuts on the scion (see inset), trimming its length to about 5–13cm (2–5in).

5 Place the cut scion (see inset) on top of the stock so that they fit together. If the scion is too narrow, place it so one side of the cambium layer meets that of the stock.

6 Bind the scion in place with plastic grafting tape or raffia. Cut back very large leaves by half. Leave the grafted plant in a propagator until union occurs.

turn it over and make a small wedge-shaped cut on the other side.

Reduce the rootstock stem to about 30cm (12in). Make two cuts in the stock, starting 8cm (3in) above soil level, to take out a sliver of wood, leaving a cut that roughly matches that on the scion.

Place the rootstock and scion together so that the cambium layers match as closely as possible, and if necessary on one side only for stocks and scions of differing widths; tie them securely in position with grafting tape. Label the grafted plant and place it in a propagator at an even temperature of 10–15°C (50–59°F). Water the plant regularly and, once a week, spray with a fungicide.

Union should occur in four to five weeks. Harden off the grafted plant over the next four weeks, then remove it from the propagator and grow it on in a cool greenhouse.

As the scion starts to grow, gradually cut back the stem of the stock; by the end of the first growing season, all the stock above the graft union should have been cut back. During the first season, remove the initial tie and, if growth is rapid, replace it with a single, raffia tie.

On plants that have been grafted in summer, cut back the stock to just above the union before growth starts in spring. Replace the old tie with a small one around the union, since there is a tendency for the scion to be pushed off the stock. After repotting, support the leader with a cane.

Apical-wedge grafting

Apical-wedge grafting, or cleft grafting, is a comparatively straight-forward technique and is suitable for the propagation of a number of shrubs, including *Caragana*, *Hibiscus*, and lilac (*Syringa*).

During midwinter, collect vigorous, one-year-old stems for use as scions. Place these in a clearly labelled plastic bag and store them in a refrigerator in order to retard their development.

Also in midwinter, select one-year-old seedlings of compatible shrubs as rootstocks. Stock and scion should both be about the thickness of a pencil. Immediately prior to grafting, lift the rootstock and wash it. Cut its stem horizontally, about 2.5cm (1in) above the roots. With a sharp knife, make a 2.5cm (1in), vertical cut down the centre of the rootstock stem.

Remove the scions from the refrigerator and select one with healthy buds of similar diameter to the rootstock. Trim it down by making a horizontal cut just above a healthy bud or buds and a similar cut 15cm (6in) below. To form the wedge, make a 2.5–4cm (1–1½in) long, sloping cut down towards the middle of the scion base, and a similar cut on the other side.

Push the scion into the prepared cut on the stock. If the scion is narrower than the stock, align one edge of the scion so it is flush with one edge of the stock. Bind them with grafting tape or moist raffia. If raffia is used, coat the union edges with grafting wax to stop moisture loss and to seal the top of the scion.

Either pot up the grafted plants or insert them in potting compost in a seed tray. Label and then, to provide basal heat, place them in a propagator at 10–15°C (50–59°F).

The union of the stock and scion should take place within about five to six weeks. Remove the tape or raffia when there is a firm union. Pot up the plants that are in seed trays and harden them off gradually. Grow the plants on for a further year in a cold frame before planting them out.

APICAL-WEDGE GRAFTING

Make a simple, vertical cut down into the stock. Cut the base of the scion with 2 downward cuts into a "V" and push the base into the stock. Bind them together, pot up, and place in a propagator.

Fuchsias

FUCHSIAS are extremely adaptable plants, cultivated for their very attractive, pendent flowers, which range from modest, slender tubes to fully double, bicoloured blooms with distinctive, swept-back sepals. All the species and cultivars may be used in summer bedding schemes or grown in containers (see CONTAINER GARDENING, "Shrubs", p.316), and many are hardy enough to be used in permanent plantings. Those of upright habit may be trained as standards or as other formal shapes, while lax or trailing cultivars look very attractive when planted in hanging baskets and windowboxes.

Most fuchsias cannot tolerate intense sun or warm greenhouse conditions; in cold areas, many may need frost protection in winter.

Routine care

Water sufficiently to keep the soil moist but not waterlogged – at least once a day for fuchsias growing in hanging baskets, and every few days for those in plastic pots. Never leave containers standing in water.

Fuchsias in hanging baskets benefit from a balanced liquid feed in late summer. Hardy garden fuchsias need a dressing of general fertilizer after pruning in spring and again during summer. Mature plants benefit from an occasional balanced feed in early spring and a high-potash liquid feed when flowering begins.

Vine weevil (p.645), greenfly (see "Aphids", p.646), whiteflies (p.646), red spider mite (p.646), and grey mould (*Botrytis*) (p.646) can be

CUTTINGS

Stem section

Tip cutting

Stem trimmed just above and below one set of leaves

Single-leaf cutting

Stem split vertically to retain only one leaf

Cuttings may be taken at any time of the year from growing tips, when stopping the plant.

troublesome. At the first signs of rusts (p.648) remove infected leaves and spray with a systemic fungicide.

Propagation

Fuchsias grow easily from cuttings, and plants propagated in this way are almost always superior to those raised from seed. Cuttings may be taken at any time of year when plants have suitable, non-flowering shoots. If taken in early spring, they can

HARDY AND TENDER FUCHSIAS

F. 'Celia Smedley'
Upright habit. Suitable for training as a standard. Half hardy.

F. 'Lady Thumb'
Lax habit. Suitable for training as a miniature standard. Frost hardy.

F. 'Thalia'
Upright habit. Suitable for summer bedding schemes. Frost tender.

F. 'Estelle Marie'
Upright habit. Suitable for summer bedding. Half hardy.

F. 'Heidi Weiss'
Upright habit. Suitable for training as a standard. Half hardy.

F. fulgens
Upright habit. Edible but acid fruits. Frost tender.

make exhibition plants by late summer; if taken in late summer, cuttings may be overwintered in a greenhouse for late spring flowering. The tips removed when pinching out, or stopping, will also root. Hardwood cuttings are also successful.

Softwood cuttings

Cut the stem below a node, with the tip and three sets of leaves. Remove the lowest two sets and proceed as for other shrubs (see p.111). To produce several cuttings, cut a young

shoot into sections, each with a group of leaves and approximately 1cm (½in) of stem above and below the leaves. These may be split to form single-leaf cuttings if the bud in the leaf axil is undamaged. Provide bottom heat to accelerate rooting, especially early in the year. Maintain a moist atmosphere, but allow air to circulate freely so that the cuttings do not damp off.

Once rooted, transplant them into 7cm (3in) pots of potting compost, and feed them weekly with a high-nitrogen

HOW TO TRAIN A BUSH FUCHSIA

1 *When the fuchsia cutting has developed 3 sets of leaves, pinch out the growing point. This will stimulate the production of sideshoots lower down the stem.*

2 *A few weeks later, when several sideshoots have developed, pinch out the top set of leaves from each sideshoot to encourage further branching.*

3 *Continue to pinch out the growing points of new sideshoots as they develop.*

4 *Stop pinching out sideshoots when the plant has a symmetrical shape with evenly spaced shoots. Lax plants may need staking.*

HOW TO TRAIN A STANDARD FUCHSIA

1 *When the cutting is about 15cm (6in) high, pinch out any sideshoots as they appear in the leaf axils.*

2 *Continue to do this to produce a long, straight stem. Tie the plant to a cane.*

3 *When the standard reaches the required height, leave it to produce 3 more sets of leaves, then pinch out the growing tip.*

4 *Pinch out the tips of the sideshoots that form at the top of the stem so that they will branch further.*

5 *Once the head has filled out, the leaves on the stem will usually drop off naturally, or they may be carefully removed.*

---

liquid fertilizer. In the early stages, do not use feeds that are high in phosphate and potash.

Pot on into 13cm (5in) pots when the roots reach the outside of the soil ball. Use peat-substitute- or peat-based compost with good drainage. Plant out after the last frost.

Hardwood cuttings

In late autumn, before severe frosts occur, cut the stem just below a node, 22cm (9in) long; remove all the leaves and soft tip. Wound the base of the cutting and dip it into hormone rooting powder or (preferably) liquid. Insert three or four cuttings in a 9cm (3½in) pot of cutting compost, and set in a cold frame. Ensure the compost remains just moist throughout winter. Once the cuttings have rooted, in early spring, pot on or use the young shoots as softwood cuttings.

Training

Fuchsias are most commonly trained into bushes or standards. Fans and espaliers may be created in the same way as fruit trees (see pp.441–442, and "Peaches", p.453).

Bush fuchsias

Begin training bushes as soon as the young plants have developed three sets of leaves. To form a bush, pinch out (stop) the growing tip to stimulate two to four sideshoots to grow. When these have each developed two sets of leaves, stop the shoots until the plant is as bushy as needed.

Pinching out increases the potential number of blooms but delays actual flowering. To time flowering for exhibition purposes, stop for the last time 60 days before the show for single cultivars (four petals), 70 days for semi-doubles (five to seven petals), and 80 days for doubles (eight or more petals).

Standard fuchsias

To train a standard, leave the tip of the young plant to grow and wait until sideshoots appear. Then pinch out all the sideshoots, but do not remove the leaves on the main stem. Tie the stem at intervals to a cane to provide support for the plant.

Continue until the required length of stem has been reached. The recognized stem lengths for a standard are: "mini standard" 15–25cm (6–10in); "quarter standard" 25–45cm (10–18in); "half standard" 45–75cm (18–30in); and "full standard" reaching 75–107cm (30–42in). Now allow a further three sets of leaves to develop, then pinch out the tip. After this, training involves the same stopping procedures as for a bush.

It will take 18 months to achieve a full standard and about six months for a quarter or mini standard.

Growing fuchsias in containers

Fuchsias grow well in pots and hanging baskets and if well cared for will remain in flower from soon after planting until the first frosts. Position them where they will receive some shade for part of the day. For baskets, choose just one cultivar per container, since different cultivars grow at different rates. Mixing fuchsias with other trailing plants makes a very successful basket display. In large patio pots or containers it is possible to use a mixture of fuchsias, such as *F.* 'Checkerboard' or *F.* 'Royal Velvet', with other plants.

Planting

Use three good plants for a 24cm (10in) diameter basket or half basket, a minimum of four for a 30cm (12in) basket, and more for a larger one. For a trailing effect, select young, bushy plants that have been stopped several times.

Use either a standard or a proprietary potting compost, both of which incorporate slow-release fertilizers to reduce the need for regular extra feeding and also water-retaining gels to reduce the frequency of watering.

Overwintering

Some fuchsias are hardier than is thought and often bedded-out plants, such as *F.* 'Mrs Popple', can be left *in situ*, although it is a good idea to take cuttings in early autumn as an insurance against frost damage. Standards should always be brought under cover in winter.

Hardy fuchsias

In areas that are cold in autumn, mulch fuchsias with straw, bracken, or bark over the crowns. Even if the plants are cut back by frost, they will shoot from the crown like an herbaceous plant. Deep planting (see right) is also very useful. Do not prune until regrowth starts in spring, then cut back to ground level.

Non-hardy fuchsias

In late autumn, move frost-tender fuchsias into frost-free conditions. If a minimum temperature of 8°C (46°F) is maintained, they may continue to flower through winter.

If there is no greenhouse available, place tender bedding fuchsias, standards, and other trained fuchsias in frost-free conditions. Lift and pot up plants that have been bedded out. Remove the green tips and leaves. Keep plants dormant through winter – cool and not quite dry. In spring, repot the plants into slightly smaller pots, and prune hard back. Water them and encourage fresh growth by lightly spraying the wood.

OVERWINTERING

Place a frost-hardy fuchsia in a hole 8cm (3in) deeper than the root ball. A combination of such deep planting and a straw mulch protects most borderline fuchsias from cold damage.

CHAPTER

4

CLIMBING PLANTS

WOODY AND HERBACEOUS CLIMBERS make up one of the most versatile plant groups, providing enormous scope for imaginative designs. Whether grown against a house wall or up pillars and over pergolas, climbers bring a strong vertical element to planting schemes. If unsupported, their stems spread luxuriantly, adding colour, texture, and horizontal lines, while some also function as weed-smothering ground cover. When allowed to scramble through other tall plants, climbers can extend the season of interest, and may be used to weave together other colourful and textural elements in the garden. One of their greatest uses is for clothing unsightly garden features, such as fences or walls, tree stumps, sheds, and other garden buildings. Many popular climbers are also fragrant, bearing abundant strongly scented flowers.

Climbing plants in the garden

GARDENS of every size and aspect may be enhanced by climbing plants. Some, such as *Lapageria* and *Passiflora* species, are grown primarily for the exquisite beauty of their flowers; others – *Lonicera periclymenum*, for example – are equally valued for their fragrance. Many are appreciated for their handsome foliage, which can give year-round interest in the case of evergreens, or provide rich and spectacular autumn colour, as with *Parthenocissus* and *Vitis coignetiae*. Even when leafless, their elegant habit and often strong architectural form enhance the stark, winter outlines of hard landscape features. A significant number of climbers bear fruits or berries that are attractive both to the gardener and to wildlife.

In their natural habitats, climbers use various techniques to climb through host plants to gain access to the light. In gardens, natural and purpose-built supports may be exploited to suit the particular mode of growth used by the plant selected.

Climbing methods and supports

Some climbers are self-clinging, attaching themselves to their supports either by aerial roots (adventitious rootlets), as do ivies (*Hedera*), or by adhesive tendril tips, as does Virginia creeper (*Parthenocissus quinquefolia*). These cling to any surface offering sufficient purchase, including walls and tree trunks, and need no additional support except during the early stages, when they require the guidance of a cane, string, or wire until they are able to establish secure contact. Climbers with aerial roots are also particularly well-suited for use as ground cover.

Twining species coil their stems in a spiralling motion around their support – clockwise or anticlockwise depending on their anatomical and morphological characteristics. Both *Lonicera periclymenum* and *Manettia luteorubra*, for instance, twine clockwise, whereas *Ceropegia sandersonii* and *Wisteria sinensis* twine anticlockwise. All twining species need permanent support, usually provided by trellis or wire. They may also be grown up the stems and branches of a sturdy host plant (see also "Growing climbers through other plants", p.126).

A few climbers such as clematis and some nasturtiums (*Tropaeolum*) attach themselves to supports by means of curling leaf stalks. Many others are tendril climbers that twine around their supports by means of contact-sensitive tendrils, which are often modified leaves or leaflets as in *Bignonia capreolata* and sweet peas (*Lathyrus odoratus*); axillary shoots as in *Passiflora*; or terminal shoots as in vines. In *Parthenocissus*, the tendrils develop adhesive discs at the tips once they come into contact with a support.

Scandent, scrambling, and trailing climbers, such as bougainvillea, *Quisqualis indica*, and winter

A floral entrance
Bougainvillea naturally links a series of archways in this elegant courtyard setting. The brilliant spectacle of its showy, pink bracts harmonizes well with the sun-baked supporting wall. In frost-free gardens, it is one of the most vigorous and luxuriant of all climbers.

jasmine (*Jasminum nudiflorum*) produce long, arching stems that attach themselves only loosely, if at all, to their supports. These plants need to be tied in to a wire framework or trellis as they grow. Alternatively, they may be left to spread over walls and banks for a less formal effect. Plants in this group are also sometimes used as ground cover.

Some species, including climbing roses and certain *Rubus* species, are equipped with hooked thorns that help them to scramble

Garden design
Framing a formal piece of statuary during summer, the herbaceous climber Humulus lupulus 'Aureus' helps to reinforce a striking focal point in this garden. Its fresh, lime-green leaves have a distinctive charm of their own.

naturally through host plants. If not grown through other plants, these need to be tied in to sturdy supports.

Site and aspect

To achieve their full potential, a number of climbers prefer a sunny position with their roots in shade, although some need a cooler spot. Others are less demanding and, while they prefer a sunny aspect, they may still tolerate shade – *Parthenocissus* and *Schizophragma* are just two examples.

Tender climbers will require the protection of a south-facing wall in cool climates. There are numerous hardy climbers, however, that will perform perfectly well without any protection at all.

Sunny or sheltered sites

In temperate areas, a sheltered wall provides a suitable microclimate for growing tender or exotic-flowering climbers. *Lapageria rosea* and the common passion flower (*Passiflora caerulea*) both thrive with winter protection in such a position; the heat reflected by the wall helps to ripen the wood so that the plants are better able to withstand cold winter temperatures.

The wall itself also gives protection against several degrees of frost. If frost is likely to occur at flowering time, avoid planting such climbers in positions where the flower buds are exposed to early-morning sun, since the buds will often be damaged as a result of rapid thawing. Sun-loving herbaceous plants and bulbs may be planted near the base of the climbers to help keep their roots cool.

Cool or exposed sites

For shady, north-facing walls and those exposed to cold winds, vigorous, hardy climbers – some honeysuckles and many ivies, in particular – are the most suitable plants. In a heavily shaded site, use green-leaved ivies; those with variegated or yellow leaves prefer more light and may be prone to frost damage.

Climbers on walls, buildings, and fences

Whether they are complementing or camouflaging their support, climbing plants make an immediate visual impact when trained against walls and buildings. Many provide strong colour, while others give a more diffuse and subtle backdrop to the whole garden design. Most buildings may be enhanced by the softening effect of a climber grown against them. In the same way, garden walls and fences become decorative features when clothed with plants bearing blossom and foliage.

Enhancing a building

Before planting, assess the architectural merits of a building and use the plants to emphasize its good points. A well-designed building may be complemented by climbers that have a strong visual impact with, for example, distinctively shaped or coloured foliage or outstanding flowers. *Actinidia kolomikta*, with its pink- or white-tipped leaves and cup-shaped white flowers in summer, is one of the most spectacular climbers for this purpose.

A less visually pleasing building may also be made more attractive by using climbers. Regular panels of plants may be used to break up long stretches of blank wall, and may also serve to exaggerate or mitigate strong vertical or horizontal lines. Narrow panels of foliage that extend upwards can make a building seem taller than it is. On the other hand, wider panels of plants allowed to grow only as high as the first floor will make a tall, narrow building appear broader. The most suitable plants for this purpose include most species of ivy and other self-clinging root climbers, such as *Hydrangea anomala* subsp. *petiolaris* and *Schizophragma integrifolium*; these form rich panels of foliage that may be pruned into the desired shape.

In a more relaxed, informal setting, vigorous climbing plants may be combined to produce a profusion of flowers and fragrance: the dark green year-round foliage and white flowers of *Clematis armandii*, or the strongly fragrant red and yellow flowers of *Lonicera* x *americana*, combine well with many species of climbing rose, perhaps with annual sweet peas (*Lathyrus odoratus*) grown through them. This combination will be effective all year, particularly around a window or doorway, where the flowers and scents may be best appreciated.

Screening with climbers

The more vigorous climbing plants may be used to camouflage an unattractive outhouse, wall, or fence remarkably quickly. Use plants such as *Clematis montana*, for its considerable mass of creamy-white or pink flowers in late spring, or Russian vine (*Fallopia baldschuanica*), which soon produces dense cover combined with panicles of tiny white flowers in late summer. It is known as mile-a-minute vine for a good reason – it is extremely rampant and must therefore be sited with great care, since it will swamp even reasonably vigorous neighbours. It also needs regular and severe pruning to keep it within bounds.

Where all-year cover is required, ivies may be more appropriate; the finely cut, evergreen leaves of *Clematis cirrhosa*, for instance, provide the perfect foil in summer for the soft-pink blooms of the climbing rose 'New Dawn'.

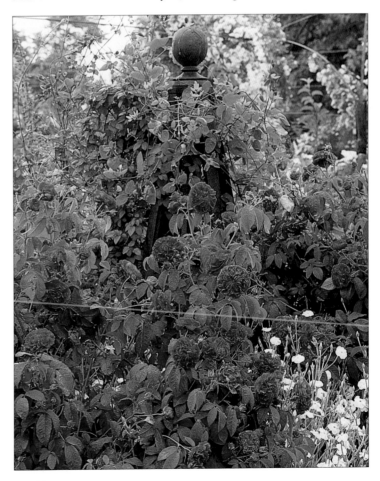

Floral bounty
Climbers such as these roses are displayed at their best when wound around a vertical support, so they are stimulated into producing numerous flowers.

Climbers on pergolas and pillars

Pergolas, pillars, and other purpose-made structures enable climbers to be viewed from all sides and, in addition, contribute strong stylistic elements to the garden design. They may be used to add height to an otherwise flat garden. Depending on materials used, they may be formal and elegant, or informal and rustic. If well designed, they can be at their most attractive when only partially covered with plants. They must, however, be strong enough to bear the often considerable weight of stems and foliage and should also be durable, as the plants will need their support for many years.

Pergolas

Pergolas or arbours festooned with climbers not only provide a cool, shady sitting area in the garden but also bring a sense of seclusion and privacy to an otherwise open site.

Introducing a fedge

A fairly new feature used in some gardens, particularly those of bird- and wildlife-enthusiasts, is the "fedge". This is a composite word derived from "fence" and "hedge", and usually applies to planting climbers along fences, wattle hurdles, and wires, or a metal framework, and including some shrubs to thicken the structure.

Fedges are often found naturally at field margins, or in gardens where an old farm hedge forms a boundary. Plants often occurring in such natural fedges include holly, ivy, hawthorn, elm suckers, guelder rose, blackthorn, and dogwood, as well as dog roses, blackberries, wild honeysuckle, and old man's beard. This tangle of species provides protection from predators and ideal habitats for birds, voles, hedgehogs, field mice, and many insects in the leaf litter at the base.

In the garden it is easy to create similar fedges, using both native plants and more exotic species with attractive flowers and fruits that encourage wildlife. They are also easy to maintain, as no formal clipping, pruning or feeding is required; just keep plants within bounds by cutting back wayward shoots and, if necessary, removing or restraining a vigorous species that becomes too dominant.

Growing on pergolas (right)
Wisteria sinensis 'Alba' is the ideal choice for a pergola over a walkway. It produces a mass of fragrant white blooms in early summer that hang down in garlands, releasing their welcome scent at just the right height to be appreciated.

Natural support (far right)
The scarlet flowers of Tropaeolum speciosum *are made yet more intense by the rich, deep-green backcloth provided by a hedge of yew* (Taxus baccata).

The most suitable plants to choose are those that put on their best display at the time of day or during the particular season when the structure is most often used.

If an arbour is to be used often on summer evenings, suitable plants might include common jasmine (*Jasminum officinale*), *Lonicera periclymenum* 'Graham Thomas', or the climbing rose 'Madame Alfred Carrière', all with beautifully frag-rant blooms in pale colours that show up well in the fading light. For summer shade, use large-leaved climbers such as *Vitis coignetiae* (which also gives splendid autumn colour) or *V. vinifera* 'Purpurea', whose claret-coloured young leaves turn dusky purple as they mature. Alternatively, use the massed floral display of *Wisteria sinensis* 'Alba' as a summer canopy. The flowers of this plant look very effective if it is grown up a pergola flanking a walk-way. Ensure that the crossbeams are high enough, however, so there is no need to stoop to avoid the flowers.

For winter interest, plant ever-greens, such as ivy or, in mild areas, tender *Lardizabala biternata*. Alternatively, use deciduous plants such as *Celastrus* or wisteria, whose bare stems take on beautiful sculptural qualities in winter.

Pillars

To add a strong vertical element to a mixed or herbaceous border, climbers such as clematis or *Passiflora* may be grown up and around pillars. Also consider using pillars to mark an axis or focal point, perhaps at the corner of a border or at a point where the garden level changes. A series of pillars at the back

of a flower bed or along a path may also be linked by rope or chain swags, and climbers trained along them.

For an evergreen climber, or as a temporary feature, a stout post with mesh panels wrapped around it will provide adequate support. If growing a deciduous plant, which means that the pillar will be visible in winter, buy a ready-made trellis obelisk or column, which will be attractive when it is bare of flowers.

Growing climbers through other plants

In the wild, many climbers grow naturally through other plants, which is a habit that may be copied

to great advantage in the garden – although the climbers should not be too vigorous for the hosts. Always plan colour combinations carefully before planting, taking flowers, foliage, and fruit into consideration; the climber may either complement or contrast with its host when the latter is putting on its best display, or extend the season of interest.

Climbers that are suitable for growing through shrubs include *Clematis viticella* hybrids and those large-flowered clematis that are pruned close to the base each year. It is also a useful method of growing most annual climbing plants and *Tropaeolum speciosum*, with its fiery red flowers and stems that are best supported by another plant.

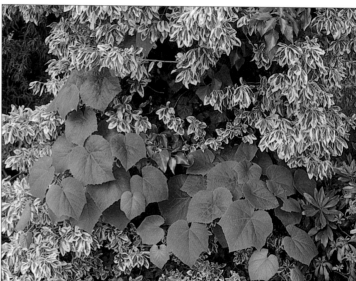

Plant association
The heart-shaped leaves of Vitis coignetiae *make a striking contrast in shape and texture with those of* Euonymus fortunei *'Silver Queen'.*

For growing through trees, vigorous species, such as *Ampelopsis brevipedunculata* var. *maximowiczii* or *Schizophragma hydrangeoides*, produce beautiful combinations of foliage, fruit, and flower. Alternatively, try mingling the cascading blooms of *Rosa filipes* 'Kiftsgate' with the white or pink sprays of *Clematis montana*. Both produce strong, twining stems that quickly scramble into the branches of a tree.

Climbers as ground cover

Some climbers, particularly those with aerial roots or with a scandent, trailing, or scrambling habit, may be grown without support to produce swathes of ground cover. They are particularly effective when allowed to spread over a sloping bank or when trailing over a wall, where they will often root into the soil beneath.

Climbers that attach themselves by adhesive tendrils, like *Parthenocissus*, and those that are self-layering, are effective in suppressing weeds when grown as ground cover. Take care when siting these plants, because if there is any other plant nearby that could serve as a support, it may be swamped. To reduce the risk of this, choose less vigorous climbing species or relocate other plants to allow the climber to spread.

Twining climbers may also be used as ground cover if the shoots are spread evenly across the ground; wire hooks may be used to keep the shoots in place. The large, deeply coloured flowers of *Clematis* 'Ernest Markham' and *C.* 'Jackmanii' are effective at ground level, as are the blue-green leaves and scarlet flowers of *Tropaeolum speciosum*.

Colourful climbers

Colour effects vary according to light levels in different parts of the garden. In a sunny spot, bright or deep colours, which absorb light, show up more strongly than paler colours. The latter will successfully illuminate a dull space and may be used to great effect in areas that are most often viewed in the evening.

Before planting climbers, consider the colour of the garden's permanent features. If the wall or support is already bright, use plants with more subtle colouring – unless you wish to create a particularly vibrant effect.

Colour combinations
Growing different climbers together or in combination with other plants

Ground cover
Clematis 'Abundance' *and* C. 'Etoile Violette' *make a carpet of colour, using winter-flowering heathers* (Erica) *as host plants.*

adds another dimension to colour schemes. Climbers can be useful for interweaving the different colour components of a planting scheme, creating brilliant effects with complementary colours or more subtle harmonies with closely related tones.

Flowers for colour
The flowers of climbers occur in colours across the spectrum, from the deep violet of *Clematis* 'Etoile Violette' through the brilliant scarlet of *Campsis radicans* to the soft, creamy-white of *Araujia sericifera*. Many of the most vividly coloured climbers are tropical in origin, and not always hardy in temperate zones.

Climbers with strongly coloured flowers have a bold and exuberant appearance, but need thoughtful placement if they are not to be overwhelming. Those with softer colours, such as pink *Clematis montana* var. *rubens* 'Elizabeth', are more suitable for subtle-hued planting schemes.

Foliage and fruits for colour
Use the leaves of climbers as well as their flowers: the skilful use of foliage can produce beautiful effects, the leaf tone providing soothing contrasts and balancing vivid flower colour. *Humulus lupulus* 'Aureus' has yellow leaves that appear almost gold if placed against a dark background. Even more striking is *Actinidia kolomikta*, which has leaves splashed with creamy-white and pink. The variegated ivies are almost as showy and, as they are evergreen, give a year-long display.

Other climbers bear fruits that are at least as colourful as their flowers: outstanding among these are the fruits of *Akebia quinata* (purplish), the slightly frost-tender *Billardiera longiflora* (purple-blue, red-pink, or white), and *Celastrus orbiculatus* (green, then black, splitting to show yellow insides with red seeds).

Interest through the seasons

For continuity of interest throughout the year, devise a planting scheme in which different climbers succeed each other as the seasons progress. This technique may be applied to climbers that are being grown together or to those in separate parts of the garden.

Spring and summer
Numerous climbers put on their best show during the spring and summer months. Early-flowering *Clematis macropetala* with *Lonicera periclymenum* 'Serotina', which reaches its flowering peak in mid-summer, make an extremely effective combination. The blooms of the clematis also leave behind silvery-grey, fluffy seedheads to augment the beauty of the honeysuckle's scented tubular flowers, and often continue their eye-catching display throughout the autumn months and sometimes even into early winter. See also ANNUALS AND BIENNIALS, "Climbers and trailers", p.211.

Autumn colour
Some climbers provide glorious autumn leaf colour: the deeply cut, sometimes crinkled, leaves of *Parthenocissus tricuspidata* are perhaps the most spectacular of all,

Complementary colours
An old stone wall provides a natural setting for climbing plants. This one has an unobtrusive wire framework attached, with clematis and the golden-leaved hop, Humulus lupulus 'Aureus', *twining around it.*

Foliage effects (left)
Actinidia kolomikta *is a deciduous climber with highly unusual and decorative foliage; many of the leaves are tipped with bold splashes of pink or white. Small, cup-shaped, scented white flowers also appear in the summer.*

Climbing annuals (right)
Lablab purpureus *is often grown as an annual for quick cover in summer. This huge and gnarled old tree trunk lends its support to the twining stems and pea-like, pink and purple flowers.*

turning scarlet, crimson, and deepest burgundy before they fall.

Winter interest

Climbers that flower in winter are few and are not generally hardy; one rare exception is winter jasmine (*Jasminum nudiflorum*), which produces delicate yellow blooms even on a north-facing wall. The slightly tender *J. polyanthum* produces a profusion of flowers in a sheltered situation, and *Clematis cirrhosa* flowers in all areas in frost-free weather.

Evergreens with unusual foliage provide interest in winter, too. Ivies are the most versatile, since most are

Autumn foliage
This striking display of autumn colour is produced by the crimson leaves of Parthenocissus tricuspidata *with the reddening foliage of* Vitis coignetiae.

hardy. Some are boldly variegated too: the colourful *Hedera helix* 'Buttercup' and 'Goldheart' are good examples. Others are grown for their leaf shape – the bird's-foot ivy (*H. h.* 'Pedata'), with leaves shaped like a bird's foot, and 'Parsley Crested', with crinkly edged leaves, are two foliage plants of merit.

Scented climbers

Perfumed climbers, such as the tropical *Beaumontia grandiflora* and the sweet pea (*Lathyrus odoratus*), have special appeal. To appreciate

the fragrance to the full, plant sweet peas near doorways or windows. If planted in a border, place them close to the outer edge.

Some release their fragrance at a particular time of day; jasmines (*Jasminum*) are often more heavily scented at night, so are well placed over an arbour or near a terrace or patio that is used in the evening.

Annual climbers

Annual climbers and those that are treated as annuals in cool-temperate climates, such as *Eccremocarpus scaber* and *Pueraria lobata*, are particularly useful for short-term effects. Annuals provide an excellent way of introducing variety into planting schemes, since they can be changed every year, if desired. They may also be used to fill gaps and introduce a vertical element when trained up bamboo wigwams, for example, in the border until more permanent plants become well established (see "Annuals and biennials as fillers", p.211).

Climbers in containers

Climbers in containers may be trained over walls and pillars in the same way as those grown in the open ground; if the support is fixed to the container, the plant may be moved around as desired. Some lower-growing climbers, such as *Clematis macropetala*, may also be grown without support – plant these in tall containers, so that their stems

Climbers for wildlife

A number of vigorous climbing plants are routinely recommended for screening unsightly buildings or other features, and to provide privacy from overlooking properties. While this may be their primary purpose, they often also become havens for wildlife, as most form tangles of vegetation that provide very suitable accommodation for nesting birds, and help them to escape the attention of predators.

As they are likely to be part of long-term plantings in a garden, they should also be chosen for the attractiveness of their flowers, foliage, and fruit, which will also be appreciated by birds in search of food and by pollinating insects.

Apart from their aesthetic and wildlife value, many of these climbers require little attention once established other than the occasional cutting back of long, wayward growths intent on conquering nearby trees or fences, and the removal of dead or damaged branches.

Suitable climbers for these purposes include the mile-a-minute vine (*Fallopia baldschuanica*), although this may prove too rampant for many gardens; vigorous roses like *Rosa brunonii* and *R. filipes* 'Kiftsgate'; *Clematis montana* and its cultivars; the large-leaved evergreen *Hedera colchica* and *H. canariensis* and other ivies; and *Vitis coignetiae*, valued for the brilliance of its autumn colour.

trail gracefully to the ground. Ivies are very suitable for growing in this way but need regular pruning once established.

In gardens where space is limited, it is still possible to grow more rampant climbers, such as bougainvillea and wisteria, in containers. Their growth will be checked but severe pruning will also be required. Regular repotting and feeding will be needed to keep them healthy.

Containers are especially suitable for less hardy climbing species that may need winter protection, such as *Hardenbergia comptoniana* and *Senecio macroglossus* 'Variegatus'. Simply take the containers indoors or into a heated greenhouse at the onset of autumn frosts, putting them outside again the following spring.

Planter's guide to climbers

NORTH-FACING WALLS

Climbers that may be grown against north-facing walls

Agapetes ✤ (some spp.)
Akebia quinata
Allamanda cathartica ✤
Aristolochia littoralis ✤
Berberidopsis corallina
Cissus ✤
Clematis, some ✤
Clerodendrum thomsoniae ✤
Clytostoma calystegioides ✤
Codonopsis convolvulacea
Dioscorea discolor ✤
Epipremnum ✤
Hardenbergia ✤
Hedera, some ✤
Hoya ✤
Humulus lupulus
Hydrangea anomala subsp.
   petiolaris
Kadsura japonica
Lapageria rosea ✤
Lathyrus latifolius
Lonicera x americana,
   L. x brownii, L. x heckrottii,
   L. sempervirens,
   L. x tellmanniana
Mitraria coccinea ✤
Monstera deliciosa ✤
Parthenocissus, some ✤
Philodendron ✤
Pileostegia viburnoides
Stigmaphyllon ciliatum ✤
Syngonium podophyllum ✤
Tetrastigma voinierianum ✤
Tropaeolum speciosum
Vitis coignetiae

AIR POLLUTION

Climbers that tolerate polluted air

Campsis radicans
Clematis, some ✤
Fallopia

Clematis
'Elsa Späth'

Hedera, some ✤
Hydrangea anomala
   subsp. petiolaris
Parthenocissus, some ✤
Vitis, some ✤

SHADE

Climbers that tolerate shade

Asteranthera ovata
Euonymus fortunei and variants
Fallopia
Humulus lupulus
Parthenocissus tricuspidata
Strongylodon macrobotrys ✤

FRAGRANT FLOWERS

Anredera cordifolia ✤
Beaumontia grandiflora ✤
Clematis armandii, C. montana
Hoya australis ✤ , H. carnosa ✤
Jasminum officinale,
   J. polyanthum
Lathyrus odoratus
Lonicera spp. (not L. sempervirens
   or L. x tellmanniana), some ✤
Quisqualis indica ✤
Solandra maxima ✤

Stephanotis
floribunda

Stephanotis floribunda ✤
Trachelospermum
Wisteria

CLIMBERS FOR CONTAINERS

Bougainvillea ✤ (prune very hard)
Cissus ✤ (some spp.)
Clematis alpina, C. macropetala
Dioscorea discolor ✤
Epipremnum ✤
Gynura aurantiaca ✤
Hardenbergia ✤
Hedera helix
Jasminum officinale,
   J. polyanthum
Lapageria rosea ✤
Lophospermum erubescens ✤
Monstera deliciosa ✤
Philodendron ✤ (some spp.)
Senecio macroglossus
   'Variegatus' ✤
Stephanotis floribunda ✤
Streptosolen jamesonii ✤
Syngonium ✤ (some spp.)
Tetrastigma voinierianum ✤
Thunbergia alata ✤
Wisteria (prune very hard)

EVERGREEN CLIMBERS

Allamanda ✤
Anemopaegma ✤
Anredera ✤
Araujia ✤
Argyreia ✤
Asteranthera
Beaumontia ✤
Berberidopsis
Calceolaria pavonii ✤
Calochone ✤
Cissus ✤
Clerodendrum splendens ✤ ,
   C. thomsoniae ✤
Clytostoma ✤
Combretum grandiflorum ✤
Decumaria sinensis ✤
Dioscorea discolor ✤

Distictis ✤
Dregea sinensis
Epipremnum ✤
Gynura ✤
Hardenbergia ✤
Hedera, some ✤
Hibbertia scandens ✤
Holboellia ✤
Hoya ✤
Jacquemontia ✤
Kennedia ✤
Lapageria ✤
Lardizabala ✤
Macfadyena ✤
Mandevilla ✤
Merremia ✤
Monstera ✤
Mussaenda ✤
Mutisia, some ✤
Pandorea ✤
Pileostegia
Podranea ✤
Pyrostegia ✤
Rhoicissus ✤
Semele ✤
Senecio confusus ✤ ,
   S. macroglossus ✤ ,
   S. mikanioides ✤ S. tamoides ✤
Solandra ✤
Stauntonia
Stephanotis ✤
Stigmaphyllon ✤
Strongylodon ✤
Syngonium ✤
Tecomanthe ✤
Tecomaria ✤
Tetrastigma ✤
Trachelospermum

CLIMBERS TO GROW THROUGH OR OVER OTHER PLANTS

Bomarea
caldasii

Bomarea
   caldasii ✤
Bougainvillea ✤
Celastrus
Clematis, some ✤
Codonopsis convolvulacea
Humulus lupulus
Lonicera, some ✤
Mutisia, some ✤
Tropaeolum peregrinum ✤ ,
   T. speciosum
Vitis coignetiae
Wisteria sinensis

FAST-GROWING CLIMBERS

Allamanda cathartica ✤
Ampelopsis

Anredera cordifolia ✤
Antigonon leptopus ✤
Aristolochia littoralis ✤
Clematis, some ✤
Clytostoma callistegioides ✤
Cobaea scandens ✤

Cobaea
scandens
f. alba

Epipremnum aureum ✤
Fallopia
Humulus lupulus
Kennedia rubicunda ✤
Macfadyena unguis-cati ✤
Passiflora caerulea ✤ ,
   P. manicata ✤
Periploca
Philodendron hederaceum ✤
Plumbago auriculata ✤
Pyrostegia venusta ✤
Quisqualis indica ✤
Stigmaphyllon ciliatum ✤
Strongylodon macrobotrys ✤
Thladiantha dubia
Vitis vinifera

ANNUAL CLIMBERS

Convolvulus tricolor
Eccremocarpus scaber ✤
Ipomoea ✤ (some spp.)
Lablab purpureus ✤
Lathyrus odoratus
Lophospermum erubescens ✤
Quisqualis indica ✤
Thunbergia alata ✤
Tropaeolum peregrinum ✤

HERBACEOUS CLIMBERS

Bomarea caldasii ✤
Canarina canariensis ✤
Codonopsis convolvulacea
Humulus lupulus
Lathyrus grandiflorus,
   L. latifolius
Thladiantha dubia
Tropaeolum speciosum,
   T. tricolor ✤ , T. tuberosum ✤

CLIMBERS FOR GROUND COVER

Asteranthera
Clematis, some ✤
Hedera, some ✤
Kennedia ✤
Parthenocissus
Pileostegia
Plumbago auriculata ✤
Tecomaria ✤
Trachelospermum

Key
✤ Not hardy

Soil preparation and planting

Given ideal growing conditions, climbing plants bring enduring rewards, so always ensure that they are well suited to the type of soil in which they are planted. Climbers seldom thrive in excessively damp or dry conditions. A few, such as *Agapetes* and *Mitraria*, do not tolerate alkaline conditions; others, such as clematis, thrive on alkaline soils but also grow well on all but the most acid soils. Many climbers are vigorous and require ample nutrients so dig and fertilize the soil well before planting (see also "Soil nutrients and fertilizers", pp.624–625).

When planting climbers, it is important to use the correct support. Choose one that will easily accommodate the eventual height, spread, and vigour of the plant.

Types of support

The three main types of support used are wooden or plastic trellis panels, wire or plastic mesh, and wires (usually plastic-covered) stretched between vine eyes or rust-proof nails. Horticultural string or reinforcing wire may be adequate for annuals or for herbaceous climbers if the supports are replaced each

CLIMBERS WITH A VIGOROUS HABIT

Actinidia deliciosa
Akebia quinata
Beaumontia grandiflora ❀
Bougainvillea ❀
Cissus ❀
Clematis montana
Distictis buccinatoria ❀

Distictis buccinatoria

Fallopia baldschuanica
Ipomoea horsfalliae ❀
Mandevilla ❀
Parthenocissus quinquefolia,
 P. tricuspidata
Passiflora, most ❀
Petrea volubilis ❀
Solandra maxima ❀
Solanum wendlandii ❀
Tetrastigma voinierianum ❀
Vitis coignetiae
Wisteria sinensis

Key
❀ *Not hardy*

year. Make sure that all supports are fixed securely in the correct position before planting. Do not use "U"-shaped metal staples to attach the stems of any plant to its support: plants rapidly outgrow these staples and the stems may become constricted and die back.

Choose a support that will match the size and strength of the climber. One that is not sufficiently sturdy for a vigorous climber may quickly become engulfed and will eventually collapse. Trellis is the most reliable support for all twining climbers, and may also be used for scramblers if they are tied in. Wires or mesh are appropriate supports for tendril climbers.

If the support is not to be a permanent structure, use climbers that are either herbaceous (*Lathyrus grandiflorus* and *L. latifolius*, for example) or cut to ground level each year (late-flowering *Clematis viticella* hybrids and cultivars), or annual climbers such as *Ipomoea hederacea*. When growing plants against a flat, free-standing trellis or over a pillar, bear in mind that climbers grow towards the light, and produce their flowers on one side of the support only, so position plants to provide their display where it will be most prominent.

Trellis and mesh

To allow air to circulate freely, fix a trellis panel or mesh so that it is held slightly away from the wall or fence and make sure that the base of the framework is approximately 30cm (12in) above soil level.

Walls are likely to need maintenance (repointing, painting, or rendering) at some time: wherever possible attach trellis and mesh with hooks at the top and hinges at the base, or hooks top and bottom. Climbers with flexible stems may then be lowered from the wall or, if hooks only are used, taken down and laid flat on the ground while the wall is repaired. Alternatively, use climbers that withstand drastic cutting back. Never try to lower rigid-stemmed climbers or shrubs, such as climbing roses or pyracantha.

Wires

Wires may be stretched horizontally or vertically between vine eyes or rust-proof nails. As with trellis panels, the wires should be held 5cm (2in) from the surface of the wall or fence, and must be kept taut to prevent sagging; either tighten the vine eyes with pliers or attach

Climbing methods

Climbers attach themselves to supports by various means. Many climbers have aerial roots that readily attach to vertical surfaces without support. Other methods, all of which require some support, include twining stems and leaf stalks, and coiling tendrils. Scandent and scrambling climbers, such as bougainvillea, produce long stems that need to be tied in at regular intervals.

Aerial roots
Ivy (Hedera) *is a self-clinging plant.*

Leaf stalks
Clematis climbs using its leaf stalks.

Coiling tendrils
Passiflora attaches itself with tendrils.

Twining stems
Akebia weaves its stems in a spiral around the support.

Fixing a trellis panel to a wall

To mount a trellis support, first securely attach vertical wooden battens at least 5cm (2in) thick to the wall and trellis. This allows the trellis to be suspended away from the wall and enables air to circulate freely. The trellis may then be permanently fixed to the battens with screws (right); this restricts access to the wall, however. Using hooks and hinges (below) allows the plant and support to be lowered, if required. Hooking the trellis to the battens at both top and bottom allows it to be removed from the wall altogether.

Using battens
Screw the trellis to thick wooden battens.

Trellis fixed at top with hook and vine eye

Hinge fitting at base

Using hooks and hinges
To allow access to the wall for maintenance, attach battens to both the wall and the trellis. Fix hinges along the bottom of the panel with hooks at the top to hold it in place.

HOW TO SELECT CLIMBERS

GOOD EXAMPLE

GOOD EXAMPLE

Label

Vigorous, sturdy stems

Healthy buds

Honeysuckle (*Lonicera*)

Roots are visible and healthy but not coiled

POOR EXAMPLE

POOR EXAMPLE

Spindly, weak growth with damaged buds

Roots coiled tightly around the root ball

Natural support
Plant one or two seeds or plug plants, here sweet peas (Lathyrus odoratus) at the base of each obelisk leg so that the young plants can conveniently clamber up the structure as they develop.

tensioners at approximately 2m (6ft) intervals. Space the wires 30–45cm (12–18in) apart, with the lowest horizontal wire (or the base of vertical wires) 30cm (12in) above soil level.

Buying climbers

Climbing plants are usually sold container-grown, although a few (including climbing roses) may be sold with bare roots. Choose a healthy plant with a well-balanced framework of strong shoots, and reject any that show signs of pest infestation or disease. Bare-root plants should have plenty of healthy, well-developed, fibrous roots that are in proportion to the amount of top-growth. For pot-grown plants, turn the pot over and check that the tips of the young roots are just showing; if so, the plant is well-rooted. Reject pot-bound plants – those that have tightly coiled roots around the root ball or a mass of roots protruding through the drainage holes in the pot – as they seldom grow on satisfactorily.

Planting outdoors

Climbers that are not fully hardy (such as *Solanum crispum* and *S. laxum*) should be planted in spring, so that they are well established before their first winter. Evergreen and herbaceous climbers are more quickly established if planted in spring when the soil is warming up, but they may also be planted in autumn in a protected situation or if the weather is mild. All other container-grown climbers may be planted in spring, autumn, or any other time of year as long as the ground is not frozen or waterlogged. Planting during dry spells in summer is not recommended, but if this is unavoidable, make sure that the plant is watered daily while dry conditions persist.

Positioning the plant

Walls and solid fences create their own rain shadow, so plants that are to be trained against them should be planted at least 45cm (18in) from the foot of the support. In this way, they normally receive sufficient rain to be grown without additional water once established. A pillar or free-standing trellis does not produce the same density of rain shadow and so the planting distance need be only 20–30cm (8–12in).

When grown through another plant the climber will compete with the host plant for food and moisture; to

CLIMBERS FOR SANDY SOIL

Adlumia fungosa ❋
Anredera cordifolia ❋
Bomarea andimarcana ❋
Ceropegia ❋ (spp. only)
Clianthus puniceus ❋
Ercilla volubilis
Gloriosa superba ❋
Ipomoea ❋
Kennedia rubicunda ❋
Lophospermum ❋
Maurandya

Kennedia rubicunda

Merremia tuberosa ❋
Mutisia oligodon
Parthenocissus, some ❋
Passiflora, most ❋ (some spp.)
Periploca graeca
Petrea volubilis ❋
Solanum wendlandii ❋
Streptosolen jamesonii ❋

CLIMBERS FOR CLAY SOIL

Aristolochia macrophylla
Campsis
Celastrus scandens
Clematis, some ❋ (most)
Distictis ❋
Euonymus fortunei 'Silver Queen'
Hedera, some ❋
Humulus lupulus 'Aureus'
Hydrangea anomala subsp. *petiolaris*
Lathyrus latifolius
Lonicera, some ❋ (some spp.)
Parthenocissus, some ❋

Parthenocissus tricuspidata 'Lowii'

Passiflora, most ❋
Vitis coignetiae
Wisteria

CLIMBERS FOR ACID SOIL

Agapetes ❋ (several spp.)
Asteranthera ovata ❋
Beaumontia grandiflora ❋
Berberidopsis corallina
Billardiera ❋ (spp. only)
Kennedia ❋
Lapageria rosea ❋
Lardizabala biternata ❋
Mitraria coccinea ❋
Mutisia, some ❋ (some spp.)

Key
❋ *Not hardy*

minimize this, plant the climber so that its roots stay as far away as possible from those of its host. If the host plant has deep roots, and a sufficient depth of soil is available, plant the climber fairly close to the host's main stem. If the host plant has a mass of rhizomatous or shallow roots, however, plant the climber about 45cm (18in) from the main root spread. A cane tied to the host plant, inserted just behind the climber's main stems, may be used to train the climber towards it at an angle.

Preparing the soil

Eradicate all weeds from the planting area (see "Weeds", pp.669–673), then dig in bulky organic matter. This will improve the water retentiveness and fertility of sandy soils, and lighten the texture of heavy clay soils. Carefully fork in a dressing of slow-release fertilizer, at a rate of 50–85 g/sq m (2–3oz/sq yd).

The planting hole should be at least twice the diameter of the container in which the climber was grown in order to allow the roots ample room to spread in the prepared soil. This may not be possible,

CLIMBERS FOR VERY ALKALINE SOIL

Actinidia kolomikta
Akebia quinata
Ampelopsis brevipedunculata
  var. *maximowiczii*
Campsis x *tagliabuana*
  'Madame Galen'
Celastrus scandens
Clematis, some ✵ (cvs)
Eccremocarpus scaber ✵
Fallopia baldschuanica
Hedera, some ✵
Hydrangea anomala
  subsp. *petiolaris*
Jasminum officinale,
  J. polyanthum ✵

Lathyrus grandiflorus

Lathyrus grandiflorus,
  L. latifolius
Lonicera, some ✵ (some spp.)
Maurandella antirrhiniflora
Parthenocissus tricuspidata
Passiflora caerulea ✵
Schizophragma integrifolium
Solanum crispum
Trachelospermum jasminoides
Vitis, some ✵
Wisteria sinensis

Key
✵ *Not hardy*

however, if the climber is to be encouraged to grow through a tree or shrub, in which case dig a hole large enough to accommodate the root ball and leave plenty of room for the roots to spread.

How to plant

Before removing the plant from its pot, make sure that the compost is moist – water the plant well so that the root ball is thoroughly wet and then leave it to drain for at least an hour. Remove the surface layer of compost to eliminate weed seeds, and then invert the pot, taking care to support the plant as it slides out. If the roots have begun to curl around inside the pot, gently tease them out. Any dead, damaged, or protruding roots should be cut back to the perimeter of the root ball.

Position the plant so that the top of the root ball is just level with the surrounding soil. It is advisable to plant clematis more deeply, however (see *Planting a Clematis*, p.139). Climbers that have been grafted (as is the case with most wisterias) should be planted with the graft union 6cm (2½in) below soil level. This encourages the scion itself to root, and reduces the incidence of sucker growths from the stock. For information on planting bare-root climbers, see "Planting a bush rose", p.157. When planting in a container, select a deep pot, and, if the climber is to remain outdoors in winter, it should be frostproof. The potting medium should be moisture-retentive but free-draining; use loam-based potting compost or a mixture of 2 parts peat substitute or peat to 1 part sharp sand, supplemented with a slow-release fertilizer. Bed any supporting trellis into the compost before planting (see CONTAINER GARDENING, "Planting a climber in a container", p.325).

Fill the planting hole with soil, then firm the plant in and water well. Insert canes at the base of the plant and secure them to the support. Fan out the main shoots and tie them individually to the canes and to the support itself (if they will reach) to train them in. Do not damage the stems by attaching them too tightly. Remove dead or damaged growth and cut back wayward shoots.

Tendril climbers readily attach themselves to a support, but the shoots may require gentle guidance and some tying in until they become firmly established. Twining climbers soon fasten their shoots to a support in their natural direction of growth (clockwise or anticlockwise) but may also need initial tying in. Scramblers that do not support

themselves should have their shoots fastened to the support at regular intervals with appropriate ties. For further information, see "Training established climbers", p.136.

Watering and mulching

Water the newly planted climber thoroughly, then cover the surface of the soil surrounding the plant with a 5–7cm (2–3in) layer of mulch to a radius of about 60cm (2ft). This is beneficial to the roots because it retains moisture throughout the area, giving the roots a chance to establish themselves. In addition, the mulch discourages the germination of weeds that would otherwise compete with the newly planted climber for nutrients and moisture.

PLANTING A CLIMBER AGAINST A WALL

1 *Fix a support 30cm (12in) above the soil and 5cm (2in) from the wall. Dig a hole 45cm (18in) from the wall. Loosen the soil at the base and add compost.*

2 *Soak the climber's root ball well. Position it in the hole at a 45° angle, placing a cane across to check the planting level. Spread the roots away from the wall.*

3 *Fill in around the plant and firm and level the soil, ensuring that no air pockets remain between the roots and that the plant is fully supported.*

4 *Untie the stems from the central stake and select 4 or 5 strong shoots. Insert a stake for each shoot and attach it to the lowest wire. Tie in the shoots.*

5 *Trim back any weak, damaged, or wayward shoots to the central stem using secateurs. This establishes the initial framework for the climber.*

6 *Water the plant thoroughly (here* Jasminum mesnyi*). Cover the surrounding soil with a deep mulch to retain moisture and discourage weeds.*

Routine care

CLIMBERS need feeding annually to maintain healthy growth, and the soil around their base should be kept moist. Climbers grown in containers need top-dressing or repotting regularly, and adequate watering is essential. Regular dead-heading helps to prolong flowering. Plants also need protection from pests, diseases, and, if tender, frost.

Feeding

Feed climbers in spring during their first two seasons with a dressing of 50–85g (2–3oz) of a balanced fertilizer. Thereafter, apply a slow-release fertilizer annually at the manufacturer's recommended rate.

Watering

During dry periods, water climbers weekly. Soak thoroughly around the base of the plant; apply a 5–7cm (2–3in) mulch over the whole root area to prevent the soil drying out.

Dead-heading and tying in

Where practical, dead-head climbers as the flowers fade. This enables the plant to concentrate its energies on producing further flowers, rather than fruits or seedheads. If fruits or seedheads are needed for ornamental purposes, dead-head only a quarter to one third of the flowered shoots. This will be enough to encourage a continuing display of flowers.

Tie in new shoots as they develop, while still flexible, and cut back overgrown plants as needed (see "Pruning and training", pp.134–137).

Pests and diseases

Check carefully for signs of pests and diseases and treat any affected plants as recommended in PLANT PROBLEMS, pp.639–673.

Protecting tender climbers

In winter, and particularly in cold periods or when frost is likely, wrap up the top-growth and base of tender climbers grown outside in protective covering (see FROST AND WIND PROTECTION, pp.612–613).

CUTTING BACK CLIMBERS

Where a climber (here Hedera colchica *'Sulphur Heart') has outgrown its allotted space, cut it back with secateurs. Trim the stems irregularly for a natural effect.*

Maintaining container-grown climbers

Container-grown climbers may need to be watered once or twice a day in dry weather. When frost is likely, they may be moved indoors or plunged in the ground in a sheltered part of the garden. During the year, a climber grown in a container uses up most of the nutrients in the potting medium. The top-dressing (i.e. the top layer of the compost and any mulch) should therefore be renewed annually. When the plant is watered, the fresh nutrients will gradually permeate and replenish the compost below. All but the most slow-growing climbers need to be moved into a larger container, using fresh compost, every three to four years. Spring-flowering plants should be repotted in autumn, others in autumn or spring.

RENEWING THE TOP-DRESSING OF A CONTAINER-GROWN CLIMBER

1 *In spring or early summer, scrape away and discard the top 2.5–5cm (1–2in) of compost in the container. Take care not to disturb any surface roots of the climber and the companion planting.*

2 *Replace the discarded compost with a layer of fresh compost mixed with a little slow-release fertilizer. Firm gently to eliminate air pockets. Make sure that the compost level is the same as before. Water well.*

3 *To aid moisture retention during the summer months, cover the compost in the container with a light, decorative mulch such as cocoa shells or bark chippings.*

REPOTTING A CONTAINER-GROWN CLIMBER

1 *Every 3 or 4 years repot container-grown climbers (such as this honeysuckle) to prevent them from becoming pot-bound. Soak the compost well, then carefully slide the root ball out of the container.*

2 *Tease out the roots and trim back the thicker roots by about one third. Leave fibrous roots intact and retain as much compost as possible around them.*

3 *Prune the top-growth by a third and remove dead or damaged stems. Repot the plant in fresh, moist compost mixed with slow-release fertilizer.*

4 *Ensure that the final planting level is the same as before. Using figure-of-eight knots, tie the main shoots securely but not too tightly to the supports.*

Pruning and training

Duringthe early years, pruning is carried out in order to build a strong framework for a plant, to promote vigorous growth of healthy, productive wood, and to facilitate training over the support. Training should be aimed at guiding a selected number of strong, major stems over and across a support while they are flexible to create a pleasing shape.

Some climbers, such as Russian vine (*Fallopia baldschuanica*), send out a mass of small shoots in addition to main stems, and these need to be regularly tied in during initial training in order to retain the required shape. Frequently, however, vigorous climbers are difficult to train after the first year and are best left to grow freely; restrict them only when they grow beyond their allotted space in the garden.

Basic principles

Routine pruning is essential for the successful cultivation of almost all established climbers. Without this control the plants may fail to flower well, and, equally importantly, some of the more vigorous climbers may swamp nearby plants or damage roofs, gutters, and masonry. Training may be combined with pruning to achieve the most desirable structure and appearance for the plant.

Where to cut

The stems should be cut 2–3mm ($\frac{1}{16}$–$\frac{1}{8}$in) above a plump bud. Select an appropriately placed bud that faces the direction in which a new shoot is required. Then, as the shoot develops, it can be tied in to fill the framework or to replace an old shoot.

Make each pruning cut cleanly with sharp secateurs, at an angle slanting slightly away from the bud. This ensures that rainwater does not gather around the bud and encourage possible disease infection. The position of the cut is important: a cut that is made too close to the bud may damage it, while one made too far away from the bud will leave a stub that dies back and may provide an entry point for disease.

Using the correct tools

A pair of sharp secateurs is the best tool for most types of pruning. Long-handled loppers may also be useful, especially for thicker stems, and shears may be used where a great deal of dead or weak growth needs to be removed (see "How to prune honeysuckle", p.137).

Formative pruning and training

At planting time, and as the plant starts to grow, training consists of tying in the strongest shoots to the support to achieve a balanced framework – plants naturally grow upwards towards the light, rather than sideways. During the growing season, a little guidance and tying will be needed to ensure that the soft, twining stems or tendrils attach themselves to their support while they are still pliable and before the wood becomes too mature, because hardened stems cannot be bent into the required position within the support without damaging them.

Provided that the climber is not one that is cut down every year, carefully reposition any stems that are growing in undesirable directions, such as across one another or away from the support. Do this in late winter or early spring following initial planting, once all danger of severe frost has passed. You should also tie the stems in while they are young and supple. Sometimes a young stem may break when being trained, so do not cut away any surplus growths until all selected stems have been tied in. Where growth is sparse or overlong, stems can be shortened to stimulate branching. Continue guiding and tying stems as they grow to develop a well-spaced framework on the climber.

MAINTENANCE PRUNING, DORMANT SEASON

Climbers that flower on the current season's shoots, such as Solanum crispum *shown here, should be pruned in late winter or early spring.*

FORMATIVE PRUNING AND TRAINING

In order to establish a healthy, strong framework for a climbing plant, begin pruning and training as soon as possible after planting, in late winter or early spring. The plant here is Jasminum mesnyi.

Where leading shoots grow vigorously without developing sideshoots, cut them back in order to stimulate branching further down the stem.

Cut out all congested growth, removing crossing shoots and the weakest of any shoots that are competing.

Remove dead or frost-damaged shoots and stems, cutting back to live, healthy wood.

To encourage flowering, cut back sideshoots to 5 or 6 strong, healthy buds, making an angled cut just above a bud.

Pruning established climbers

The time of year to prune established climbers depends on their flowering habit. Some flower on the current season's shoots or, occasionally, on shoots that are produced late in the growing season of the previous year. These are usually pruned while dormant, in late winter or early spring, before new buds begin to develop, and will flower later in the same season on new shoots.

Other climbers flower on the previous year's ripened shoots, or on even older shoots. These should be pruned immediately after flowering, to allow new shoots time to grow and ripen before the winter: these are the shoots that will bear next season's flowers. Some early-flowering climbers will produce a second crop of flowers later in the season, if pruned early enough.

Distinguishing between first- and second-year shoots is not normally difficult: first-year shoots are still pliable and usually green, while second-year ones are usually grey or brown. Shoots more than two years old have a distinct, usually dark bark, and are tough and woody.

When pruning, always remove all dead or damaged wood and any congested, twiggy growth. Cut back stems that have grown beyond the plant's allotted space, both to maintain the shape of the climber and to control excessive growth.

For methods of pruning clematis, see pp.139–140.

MAINTENANCE PRUNING AFTER FLOWERING

Climbers that flower on the previous year's ripened shoots, such as Jasminum beesianum, should be pruned immediately after flowering to allow new shoots to develop before the onset of winter.

Cut back shoots that have flowered, pruning to a vigorous shoot lower down.

Remove all dead or damaged wood, cutting cleanly close to a healthy shoot or stem.

Where there is congested growth, weak shoots should be removed.

For methods of pruning clematis, see pp.139–140.

FLOWERING HABITS

Climbers that flower on current season's growth
Anredera cordifolia ✸
Antigonon leptopus ✸
Bignonia
Billardiera longiflora ✸
Campsis
Clematis, some ✸
  (large-flowered cvs)
Clerodendrum thomsoniae ✸
Clianthus ✸
Clytostoma ✸
Distictis ✸
Eccremocarpus scaber ✸
Fallopia baldschuanica
Ipomoea ✸
Lapageria ✸
Lonicera, some ✸
Mandevilla ✸
Mikania ✸
Mutisia decurrens
Parthenocissus, some ✸
Pileostegia viburnoides
Plumbago ✸
Podranea ✸
Pyrostegia venusta ✸

Solanum crispum

Solanum crispum,
  S. laxum ✸
Stephanotis ✸
Streptosolen ✸
Thladiantha, some ✸
Thunbergia gregorii ✸
Vigna caracalla ✸
Vitis, some ✸

Climbers that flower on previous season's growth
Actinidia, some ✸
Allamanda cathartica ✸
Aristolochia, some ✸
Beaumontia ✸
Bougainvillea ✸

Bougainvillea 'Miss Manila'

Clematis montana
Decumaria sinensis ✸
Hoya ✸
Hydrangea
Jasminum, some ✸
Pandorea jasminoides ✸
Passiflora, most ✸
Pileostegia
Schizophragma
Solandra maxima ✸
Streptosolen jamesonii ✸
Strongylodon ✸
Wisteria

Key
✸ *Not hardy*

Pruning wisteria

Wisteria may be reluctant to flower unless the vigorous, leafy summer shoots are severely curtailed, and the plant's energies diverted into producing flower buds. Flowering is also improved if the main stems are trained horizontally rather than vertically. The flower buds are produced on short spurs, and the aim of pruning is to encourage these spurs to develop along the framework branches of an established plant. The simplest method is to carry out a two-stage pruning regime. In late summer, cut back long growths and shorter, lateral growths. Leave stems unpruned only if they are needed to extend the framework, and train them in. In midwinter cut back summer-pruned spur shoots to two or three buds. At the same time, reduce to 15cm (6in) any long growths that developed after summer pruning.

1 *In late summer, restrict the growth of vigorous, leafy shoots to encourage more new buds to grow next year.*

2 *Cut back long shoots to about 15cm (6in), leaving 4–6 leaves. Make the cut well clear of the last bud, as the buds are easily damaged.*

Winter
Prune again shoots shortened in summer. Reduce them to 8–10cm (3–4in), leaving only 2–3 buds.

EARLY WINTER PRUNING

When pruning deciduous climbers in early winter it is easy to assess the framework of the plant and train in any new growth. The climber shown here is Schisandra glaucescens.

Thin out overcrowded stems, removing weak and crossing shoots.

Remove dead wood, pruning to the base of the stem if this is necessary.

Tie in new shoots, spacing them to produce a balanced framework.

To promote flowering, prune all sideshoots to about 5 buds.

Evergreen climbers

Prune evergreen climbers in summer, after they have had their main flush of growth and when the pruning marks will soon be disguised by further growth. Evergreen climbers that are grown for their flowers, as well as their foliage, produce flowers on the previous season's wood, so delay pruning these until after flowering. In both cases, remove dead or damaged wood and trim stray shoots to shape.

Early winter pruning

Climbers that have already had at least one pruning during the previous growing season may be pruned again in winter to tidy up their appearance (see illustrations above). This is particularly useful for deciduous plants, as the frameworks may be assessed more easily when the branches are bare. Do not remove ripened wood, which will carry the next season's flowers. If in mild spells winter-pruned plants are stimulated into new growth, the new young shoots may later be damaged by frost. Prune these back in spring.

Ornamental vines (*Vitis*) should be pruned in early winter, when the plants are dormant and pruning cuts may be made without the risk of "bleeding", or loss of sap, occurring.

If the stems are cut in spring when the sap is rising, they will "bleed" profusely; this is difficult to stop and weakens the plants. (For pruning of grape vines, see pp.462–465.)

Training established climbers

Climbers that attach themselves by means of aerial roots need very little training, except in the first few years until enough aerial roots have formed to support the plant. All other climbing plants need their new shoots trained in each year to establish the desired shape.

Each year during the growing season, select the strongest new stems, before they become hard and woody, and train them in to continue the basic framework. Follow the shape of the allocated space and allow the leading stem to extend in a straight line until it has reached the required height. Tie all stems securely to the support at regular intervals

Pruning bougainvillea

Bougainvillea is rampant and flowers reliably whether pruned or not. Prune between midwinter and early spring to keep the plant in check. Shorten sideshoots to within a few centimetres of the main stems, but leave any needed to extend the main framework.

1 *Trim wayward sideshoots to within 2.5–5cm (1–2in) of the main framework stems.*

2 *Cut cleanly, close to a healthy bud. The buds will soon produce new growth.*

Training climbers on pergolas and pillars

To produce an even distribution of growth over a pergola or pillar, tie in the main stems throughout the growing season, spreading them out as required to fill any gaps. To promote flowering lower down a plant's stem, regularly train sideshoots of twining species around their support, making sure that the shoots are following their natural direction of growth: clockwise or anticlockwise.

After the flowering season, remove any dead or diseased shoots and prune the main stem and any leaders. This will encourage strong lateral growth to be produced in the following year.

1 *Guide stray sideshoots onto the support in their natural direction of growth and tie in.*

2 *In late summer, cut back all the leading stems by one third to promote lateral growth.*

using plastic twist-ties or vine ties. Make sure that the ties are tight enough to prevent the stems from being blown about in strong winds and rubbing against the support; they should not restrict development of the plant's stems, however. The ties will need to be loosened periodically as the stems thicken with age.

Renovating an old or neglected climber

Unpruned climbers – or those that have not been trained – often become a mass of tangled, woody stems, and produce a poor display of flowers. Such plants may be pruned hard to rejuvenate them. Most climbers withstand pruning close to the base or to main framework stems, but a plant in poor health may not survive this treatment. In this case, it is preferable to reduce the size of the plant gradually over a period of two or three years, in conjunction with annual feeding.

For a plant that is to be pruned to the base, cut down all existing growth in early spring to within 30–60cm (1–2ft) of the ground. To promote rapid new growth, apply a dressing of quick-acting, balanced fertilizer at a rate of 50–85g/sq m

How to prune honeysuckle

Climbing honeysuckles (*Lonicera*) require little pruning to flower profusely but tend, if neglected, to develop into a mass of thin, tangled stems that bear foliage and flowers only at the top of the shoots. To renovate a honeysuckle in this condition, prune it severely in late winter or early spring, at the beginning of the growing season. New shoots will soon begin to develop and these should be trained in to provide an evenly balanced framework.

If such severe pruning is not required, it is still possible to renovate the plant by removing dead or damaged shoots and stems from beneath new, young growth. Use a pair of shears, rather than secateurs, for speed.

Renovation pruning
If the plant is badly overgrown, cut back all the stems with long-handled loppers to within 30–60cm (1–2ft) of ground level.

Alternative method
If it is undesirable or unnecessary to prune so severely, cut away all dead material from underneath the new, fresh growth.

(2–3oz/sq yd). Soak the root area with water, and then apply a mulch. Train in all new growth as for newly planted climbers.

Renovation over a two- to three-year period (see below) is more difficult, as the stems frequently become entangled. In late winter or early spring, remove as much of the congested growth as possible, then cut to the base one in every two (or three) main stems. Gently unravel the top-growth of the severed stems. If any shoots are damaged, cut them out once the pruned main stems and their top-growth have been removed. Cut out any weak, spindly shoots, since these will not flower satisfactorily, and remove any dead wood. Feed, water, and mulch, as when pruning a climber to the base, to encourage healthy new growth. Train in fresh basal shoots to fill gaps, making sure they do not become entangled with old shoots. The following spring, repeat the process and feed, water, and mulch the plant.

RENOVATING A NEGLECTED CLIMBER

A neglected climber (here Celastrus orbiculatus*) may be renovated gradually over two or three seasons by pruning hard each late winter or early spring.*

Remove as much congested growth as possible.

Remove weak, twiggy, or damaged shoots so that only strong shoots remain.

Using long-handled loppers, cut back to the base one third to one half of the old stems, retaining the more vigorous ones.

All dead or diseased wood should also be removed. Prune to a healthy bud, using sharp secateurs.

CLIMBERS THAT MAY BE CUT TO THE BASE

Allamanda cathartica ❈
Anredera cordifolia ❈
Antigonon leptopus ❈
Aristolochia, some ❈
Campsis x *tagliabuana*
Clematis, some ❈ (most spp.)
Clerodendrum thomsoniae ❈
Clytostoma calystegioides ❈
Distictis buccinatoria ❈
Fallopia baldschuanica
Lonicera, some ❈ (most spp.)
Macfadyena unguis-cati ❈

Passiflora x *caponii*
'John Innes'

Manettia
  cordifolia ❈,
    M. luteorubra ❈
Passiflora, most ❈
Petrea volubilis ❈
Pyrostegia venusta ❈
Quisqualis indica ❈
Solandra maxima ❈
Solanum, some ❈
Stigmaphyllon ciliatum ❈
Strongylodon macrobotrys ❈
Thunbergia ❈

Key
❈ *Not hardy*

Clematis

CLEMATIS are suitable to grow in any aspect and climate. Of all climbers, they offer the longest flowering period with species or hybrids that bloom in almost every month of the year, many with the additional interest of silvery seedheads appearing after flowering has occurred. They are diverse in habit, varying from herbaceous plants, such as *C. integrifolia* and the clump-forming *C. recta*, to spreading subshrubs such as *C.* x *jouiniana*, as well as the better-known climbers.

Clematis also present a huge range of flower colour and flower forms, ranging from the attractive sprays of delicate, ivory-coloured bells in *C. rehderiana*, and exotic-looking, fleshy, golden lanterns in *C. tangutica*, to the simple but richly coloured blooms of *C. viticella* and its many hybrids, or the more complex forms of large-flowered double clematis such as *C.* 'Proteus' and *C.* 'Vyvyan Pennell'.

Where to grow clematis

Clematis can be chosen for almost any garden situation. The vigorous, spring-flowering species and cultivars are ideal for clothing and camouflaging unsightly buildings, fences, and walls, or for scrambling over old trees, tree stumps, and arbours, adding colour and interest to otherwise dull features.

Less rampant types may be wall-trained on trellis and pergolas or allowed to cascade over terraces; at ground level more delicate species will spread horizontally where their blooms can be best appreciated.

Some clematis are suitable for container cultivation, on patios, or, for tender species, under glass. Others have great potential for being grown through host plants – trees, climbers, and sturdy shrubs, for example – to provide an extended season of interest, a splash of colour, or to create unusual and enchanting plant associations.

Clematis groups

Clematis may be divided into three main groups, based on their flowering time and habit.

Group 1 is made up of the early-flowering species and their cultivars, and the Alpina, Macropetala, and Montana groups, which flower directly from the previous season's ripened stems. In Group 2 are the early, large-flowered cultivars, blooming on short, current season's stems, which arise from the previous season's ripe wood. Groups 1 and 2 are sometimes known as "old wood"-flowering clematis. Group 3 includes the late-flowering species, late, large-flowered cultivars, and herbaceous types, which flower on the current season's growth.

Early-flowering species and cultivars

The slightly tender, early-flowering evergreen species and their forms originate from regions with warm climates and are best grown, therefore, with protection in areas with hard frosts. Among the hardiest evergreens are the vigorous *C. armandii* and smaller *C. cirrhosa*. Both grow best in a south- or south-west-facing site and are effective when growing through other wall-trained plants.

The Alpina and Macropetala groups withstand very low winter temperatures and are ideal for growing through wall-trained trees and shrubs on any aspect. Do not grow them through climbing roses or other shrubs that need annual pruning, since these clematis need little or no cutting back. They are suitable for exposed sites such as north-east corners of buildings but also are superb container plants for the patio and can be trained on any support.

The members of the Montana group are fully hardy and vigorous, climbing 7–12m (22–40ft). These plants will cover walls and arbours and are effective growing through conifers or old fruit trees that are past their productive best, but may damage the foliage of evergreens with their rampant, dense growth.

Early, large-flowered cultivars

These are fully frost hardy, growing to 2.5–4m (8–12ft). The more compact cultivars such as *C.* 'Edith', which are normally the first to flower, are ideal for containers. The double and semi-double cultivars and the midsummer flowering types with very large flowers are best grown through the branches of other wall-trained trees or shrubs, where their flowers are protected from severe wind or heavy rain. Paler-flowered cultivars with mauve-striped or pink flowers will bleach in full sun and so are best planted in partial shade, where their flowers may be used to lighten a dark wall. The deep reds and purples are more suitable for sunny situations because they develop better colour in warmth.

Late-flowering species and cultivars

This group of clematis includes the late, large-flowered cultivars such as *C.* 'Jackmanii', small-flowered *C. viticella* and its hybrids, and a whole range of species and their forms, including the herbaceous clematis. The Jackmanii types are superb when grown through climbing roses, shrub roses, or through most medium-sized shrubs, both evergreen and deciduous, whether free-standing or wall-trained. The *C. viticella* hybrids in particular are excellent for growing through ground-cover plants, especially the summer- or winter-flowering heathers (*Calluna*, *Daboecia*, and *Erica*).

Of the other members in this group, *C.* x *jouiniana* makes ideal ground cover and the miniature, tulip-like flowers of *C. texensis* and its hybrids look well against a background of low-growing evergreens. The vigorous *C. orientalis* and *C. tangutica* need a large wall or tree where they can grow unconfined and display their many flowers and their fluffy seedheads. *C. heracleifolia* var. *davidiana* and other herbaceous species do not climb and should be grown in mixed or herbaceous borders; *C. integrifolia*, for example, associates very well with Floribunda bush roses.

Soil preparation and planting

When using vigorous clematis to clothe trellis or pergolas, ensure that the support structure is strong and sound before planting. Similarly, when growing clematis through old trees, the branches must be robust enough to bear the often

CLEMATIS

Group 1

C. montana var. *rubens*

C. 'Frances Rivis'

C. 'Markham's Pink'

Group 2

C. 'The President'

C. 'Henryi'

C. 'Nelly Moser'

Group 3

C. 'Ernest Markham'

C. 'Jackmanii'

C. 'Madame Julia Correvon'

considerable weight. For clematis grown through other host plants, it is essential to match the vigour of the clematis with that of its host, if the host is not to be swamped. Also ensure that the pruning requirements of host and clematis are compatible.

Most climbing species can be sited in part shade or in sun, provided that the roots are cool and shaded. Either underplant them with low shrubs or plant on the shaded side of the host tree or wall. The herbaceous species thrive in a sunny situation. To grow clematis on a patio, use a container with dimensions of 45cm diameter x 45cm deep (18 x 18in).

Most clematis will thrive in any rich, fertile, and well-drained soil, especially if it is neutral or slightly alkaline. The evergreens and species such as *C. tangutica* and *C. orientalis* should not be grown in soil that lies wet during the winter months as they have fine, fibrous root systems, which quickly rot. Planting details are the same as for other climbers (see "Soil preparation and planting", pp.130–132), except that clematis should be planted about 5cm (2in) deeper than normal to encourage basal buds to develop below soil level. If the stems are damaged the plant may then grow again from below soil level.

Routine care

Keep newly planted specimens well watered until established and mulch climbing and herbaceous species annually in spring with garden compost or well-rotted manure.

Fresh young growth is very susceptible to slug damage (p.644) in early spring. Clematis are prone to attack from aphids (p.646), and the later-flowering, large-flowered

Colour contrast
Clematis are excellent as companion plants and can be grown through a variety of host plants to create an unusual display. Here, the bright petals of C. 'Venosa Violacea' present an attractive contrast to the green of Juniperus sabina 'Tamariscifolia' over which it is scrambling.

PLANTING A CLEMATIS

Plant clematis 5cm (2in) deeper than the nursery planting level. This helps buds to develop below soil level and overcome clematis wilt.

cultivars may be affected by powdery mildew (p.646). Clematis wilt, a condition caused by a fungus, can attack newly planted, large-flowered clematis (see p.665).

Pruning and training

Pruning requirements vary for each group, so always check before cutting back. If pruned incorrectly, the flowering wood may be cut out.

Initial pruning and training for all groups

Clematis climb by means of leaf-stalk tendrils that attach themselves to their support. They need to be trained to reach their support and new growth will need tying in during spring and summer. Tie just below a node (or leaf axil bud), and space stems evenly on the support, leaving enough room for further growth to develop.

Clematis require special care in initial training and pruning. If they are left untrained, plants frequently produce one or two stems that are 15–18m (50–60ft) long, and then a top-heavy tangle of growth leaving a bare base. To avoid this, all newly planted clematis should be pruned hard the first spring after planting.

Unless the plant already has three or four stems growing from the base, cut back all the stems just above a strong, healthy pair of leaf buds about 30cm (12in) above soil level. If this hard pruning does not produce three or four extra stems in early spring, any new stems should be pruned again to about 15cm (6in), just above a strong pair of leaf buds.

Group 1
Many of these vigorous clematis require little, if any, regular pruning, especially if cut back hard when first planted. If restricting the size or tidying tangled growth is necessary, pruning should be done after flowering. Any dead, weak, or damaged stems can also be removed at this time. New growth will ripen during late summer and autumn and pro-vide flowers the following spring. Any excess growth may be reduced during the autumn, and tied into its support, but bear in mind that this will reduce the flowering display. *C. armandii*, which produces a mass of flowers on trailing stems, may be thinned annually to avoid congestion; cut back to well-placed, young shoots immediately after flowering.

PRUNING GROUP 1 CLEMATIS

Ripened stems of Group 1 clematis produce flower stems for the next season, so prune after flowering only if the plant has become overgrown.

GROUP 1 – EARLY-FLOWERING SPECIES

C. alpina and cvs
C. armandii and cvs
C. cirrhosa

Clematis armandii

C. macropetala and cvs
C. montana and cvs
C. montana var. *grandiflora*
C. montana var. *rubens*

Flower stem growing directly from last season's ripened stem

Cut back to a healthy pair of buds or to the main stem any shoots that are damaged.

Thin or remove stems that are growing densely or that have outgrown the available space, cutting them back to their point of origin.

Group 2

The solitary, large flowers are produced on stems of lengths varying from 15cm to 60cm (6–24in) which arise from the previous season's ripened stems. Prune these plants in early spring before the new growth commences.

Remove any dead, weak, or damaged stems and cut back healthy stems on the framework to just above a strong pair of leaf buds. These buds will produce the first crop of flowers. This group may also produce a second, but smaller, flush of blooms on new shoots in late summer.

Flowers on current season's stems developed from previous season's axillary buds

Previous season's flower stem

Position of previous season's leaves

Dormant axillary buds

PRUNING GROUP 2 CLEMATIS

Group 2 clematis flower on current season's stems, so prune in early spring before growth starts.

Cut back old stems to a strong pair of buds. Growth from these will produce this season's flowers.

Before new growth starts, cut out any damaged stems to their point of origin or to ground level.

Group 3

Flowers produced by this group are on stems of the current season's growth. Prune in early spring before new growth commences. Remove all the previous season's stems down to a strong pair of leaf buds just above the base of the previous season's growth, i.e. 15–30cm (6–12in) above soil level. As new growth appears, tie it to its support or host. Take care with the soft and

often brittle, new stems. Space them evenly and tie in at regular intervals.

Clematis growing over host or ground-cover plants, such as heathers, should also be pruned. In late autumn remove excessive growth to keep the plant and host tidy and less prone to wind damage. When clematis are grown over winter-flowering heathers, all clematis top-growth should be removed down to 30cm (12in) in late autumn, before the heathers come into flower.

Propagation

Clematis species can be propagated by seed sown in autumn and over-wintered in a cold greenhouse or frame (cultivars do not come true from seed). Cultivars are usually increased by softwood or semi-ripe cuttings (see p.632) or layering (see p.631); division (see p.378) or basal cuttings (see p.202) are used for herbaceous types.

Internodal cuttings of softwood and semi-ripe wood are usually preferred to nodal cuttings, but both methods may be used successfully. Take them in spring just above a node and trim the stem to 2.5–5cm (1–2in) below the node. Remove one of the pair of leaves 1cm (¼in) away from the node. Reduce the remaining leaf area by half and cut the stem above the node back to approximately 1cm (¼in). Treat the base with hormone rooting powder. Root in a closed propagating case with bottom heat. Harden off the new plants gradually (see p.637) before planting out the young clematis in spring.

PRUNING GROUP 3 CLEMATIS

Group 3 clematis produce flowers on the current season's growth, so prune in early spring before new growth begins.

Flowering stems on current season's new growth

Cut just above the lowest pair of strong buds on each stem – this will be 15–30cm (6–12in) above soil level. Make a straight cut with sharp secateurs, ensuring that the buds are not damaged.

INTERNODAL CUTTINGS

Node

Leaf removed

Make cuttings 5cm (2in) long by trimming just above a node and 3.5cm (1½in) below the node. Remove one leaf from each cutting.

GROUP 2 – EARLY, LARGE-FLOWERED CULTIVARS

C. ANNA LOUISE ('Evithree')
C. ARCTIC QUEEN ('Evitwo')
C. 'Barbara Jackman'

Clematis 'Vyvyan Pennell'

C. 'Carnaby'
C. 'Daniel Deronda'
C. 'Duchess of Edinburgh'
C. 'Elsa Späth'
C. 'Général Sikorski'
C. 'Lasurstern'
C. 'Lincoln Star'
C. 'Marie Boisselot'
C. 'Mrs N. Thompson'
C. 'Niobe'
C. 'Vyvyan Pennell'

GROUP 3 – LATE-FLOWERING SPECIES AND CULTIVARS

C. 'Comtesse de Bouchaud'
C. 'Duchess of Albany'
C. 'Etoile Violette'
C. *florida* and cvs
C. 'Gipsy Queen'

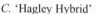

Clematis 'Perle d'Azur'

C. 'Hagley Hybrid'
C. 'Huldine'
C. 'Lady Betty Balfour'
C. 'Perle d'Azur'
C. PETIT FAUCON ('Evisix')
C. 'Star of India'
C. *tangutica* and cvs
C. 'Ville de Lyon'
C. *viticella* and cvs

Propagation

CLIMBING plants may be propagated from seed, from stem or root cuttings, or by layering. Wisteria is also often propagated by grafting (for further information on this technique, see ORNAMENTAL TREES, "Grafting", p.82).

Propagation from seed is the most cost-effective way of producing large quantities of plants; it is also the only practical method for increasing annuals and the easiest method for propagating herbaceous climbers. Hybrids and cultivars, however, seldom reproduce true from seed, and it is therefore advisable to propagate these by vegetative methods, such as cuttings. Also, woody plants may take several years to reach flowering size if they are raised from seed.

Propagation from stem cuttings that are taken from soft or semi-ripe wood may be carried out success-fully for almost all climbers and is the best method for selected cultivars. Propagation from hardwood cuttings is normally applied only to vines (*Vitis*); root cuttings may be used for a small number of

plants, such as *Celastrus*. Some climbers produce new plants naturally by self layering. If only a few plants are required, simple and serpentine layering are both straightforward methods of propagating climbers that are difficult to raise successfully from cuttings.

Propagating climbers from seed

Most species produce viable seed without any difficulty. In the case of plants that are not fully hardy, however, a long, hot summer is necessary for the seed to ripen fully. To obtain seed from unisexual plants, such as *Actinidia deliciosa* and *Celastrus*, plants of both sexes must be grown reasonably close together to ensure that they pollinate each other.

The sex of any seedling is unknown until the time that it reaches flowering size. Named, vegetatively propagated male and female clones are, however, available for some plants, such as *Actinidia*

deliciosa. For sowing and planting annual climbers, see ANNUALS AND BIENNIALS, pp.216–221.

Preparing the seed
For certain climbers it may be necessary to soak the seeds in water before sowing them: *Hardenbergia* seeds should be left in the water for 24 hours, and *Lapageria* seeds for 48 hours. Seeds with a hard outer coating may need to have their dormancy broken by a period of cold, which is best achieved by putting them in a refrigerator for six to eight weeks (for further information, see PRINCIPLES OF PROPAGATION, "Cold stratification", p.630.)

Sowing
If sowing seed in a clay pot, first cover the drainage holes with crocks (this is not necessary when plastic pots, seed trays, or pans are used), then fill the pot, pan, or tray with seed compost, firming with a presser board to ensure that there are no air spaces or hollows. Large seeds should be evenly spaced; press them gently into the compost and then

cover to their own depth with a layer of sifted compost that has been mixed with a small amount of fine, horticultural grit. Mix tiny seeds with a little fine, dry sand so that they may be sown evenly and thinly; no extra covering of compost is needed.

Label the pot and water the compost with a fine spray. Then add a thin layer of fine grit or place clear plastic film or glass over the pot to prevent the compost from drying out.

The seeds of certain climbers such as *Mutisia* and *Thladiantha* require artificial heat to germinate when grown in a cool climate and so should be placed in a propagator at 13–16°C (55–61°F). *Cobaea*, if grown as an annual, should be sown in late winter with heat so that the young plants are well developed by the time they are planted outside. Most other seeds should be kept in a warm place out of direct sun. Hardy climbers such as most clematis, however, germinate best after being subjected to cold conditions: plunge the containers in a cold frame outdoors.

Pricking out
As soon as the seedlings emerge, remove the glass or plastic film, if used. When the first pair of true leaves has formed (the seedling's first leaves may differ significantly from the leaves of the adult plant) prick out the seedlings singly into small pots. If they are very small, however, it is best to use a tray, pricking out in rows separated by the space of about one leaf's width.

Inspect the base of the pots or tray at frequent intervals; as soon as the roots are visible through the drainage holes, pot on the seedlings. Seedlings that were germinated in a cold environment should be grown on initially in warmer conditions under cover.

Planting out
Plant out the seedlings when they are well established. Fast-growing climbers, both annual and perennial, may be planted where they are to flower. If frosts are likely and the climbers are not fully hardy, either plant them under a cloche for protection or delay planting out until all danger of frost has passed.

Slow-growing climbers should be potted on each time the roots begin to appear through the base of the pot. In their first season, grow them on in a sheltered position or in a nursery bed. Provide canes to support the plants in all cases and keep the compost of pot-grown plants moist.

SOWING SEED

1 Harvest seed (here clematis) from the plant when ripe – it should pull away from the seedhead easily. There is no need to remove the fluffy "tails".

2 Sow thinly in a prepared pan or other container of firmed, moist, gritty seed compost.

3 Cover the seeds with a thin layer of gritty compost, add a shallow layer of fine grit, and label. Plunge in a sand bed or frame outdoors.

4 After germination, prick out the seedlings: loosen a clump with a widger, then lift and replant the seedlings singly, holding each gently by the leaves.

5 When the seedlings have developed their first pair of true leaves, pot them on individually in moist potting compost. Label, and place in a cold frame.

6 Grow on the seedlings until well established. They are then ready for planting out in their permanent positions.

CLIMBERS FROM SOFTWOOD CUTTINGS

Allamanda ❀
Anemopaegma ❀
Anredera cordifolia ❀
Antigonon ❀
Asarina ❀
Bignonia
Ceropegia ❀
Clematis,
　some ❀

*Allamanda
cathartica*
'Hendersonii'

Clerodendrum, some ❀
Clitoria ❀
Codonopsis
Convolvulus, some ❀
Cryptostegia ❀
Distictis ❀
Hedera, some ❀
Hibbertia ❀
Hydrangea
Ipomoea ❀
Lonicera, some ❀
Manettia ❀
Mikania ❀
Parthenocissus, some ❀
Periploca
Schisandra
Schizophragma

*Senecio
macroglossus*
'Variegatus'

Senecio, some ❀
Solanum, some ❀
Sollya ❀
Streptosolen ❀
Thladiantha, some ❀
Thunbergia ❀
Tropaeolum, some ❀
Wisteria

CLIMBERS FROM SEMI-RIPE CUTTINGS

Actinidia, some ❀
Agapetes ❀
Akebia
Ampelopsis
Anemopaegma ❀
Araujia ❀
Aristolochia, some ❀
Asteranthera
Beaumontia ❀
Berberidopsis
Berchemia
Billardiera ❀
Bougainvillea ❀
Campsis
Celastrus
Cissus ❀

Key
❀ *Not hardy*

Propagation from softwood cuttings

Softwood is the youngest, greenest part of a stem and is produced continuously at the tip. Take softwood cuttings in late spring or early summer, shortly after new growth has started, and before the stems have begun to harden. Prepare a pot, pan, or tray by filling it almost to the brim with moist cutting compost, and firm.

Taking the cuttings

Cut lengths of stem approximately 15cm (6in) long, making cuts above leaf joints or nodes on the parent plant. Then trim the base of each cutting immediately below a node. (Clematis is an exception to this rule: cuttings can be internodal, with a small piece of stem below the node – see "Propagation", p.140.)

Softwood cuttings are particularly vulnerable to water loss, so place them immediately in a clear plastic bag to retain moisture.

Preparing and inserting the cuttings

Remove the leaves from the bottom third of the stems with a sharp knife. The base of each cutting can be dipped into a fungicide powder, to prevent them from rotting, or else you should water the compost well with proprietary fungicidal solution after the cuttings have been inserted. Make holes with a dibber, then insert each cutting into the compost.

Label and water the cuttings. Place them in a propagator, cover trays with sheets of glass, or affix clear plastic bags over pots with an elastic band. Keep the cuttings in good light and check them daily to make sure that they do not dry out.

Potting up

The cuttings generally take four to eight weeks to root, although honey-suckles (*Lonicera*) may take longer. Pot them up in standard, loam-based compost. Alternatively, use a mixture of two parts peat substitute or peat to one part sand; as this contains no nutrients, apply a liquid or foliar feed every two weeks.

Cuttings taken in early spring should be ready to plant out during autumn; any taken later should be overwintered under cover and planted out the following spring once there is no danger of frost. In cold areas, all tender cuttings should be overwintered in a frost-free place, gradually hardened off the following spring, and then planted out when all danger of frost has passed.

Propagation from semi-ripe cuttings

From midsummer to early autumn, take semi-ripe cuttings from healthy shoots. Prepare a pot or pan of moist cutting compost, as for softwood cuttings. Select 6–15cm (2½–6in) stems that have not fully hardened, making the cuts above leaf joints or nodes. Then trim the bases to just below a node.

PROPAGATION FROM SOFTWOOD CUTTINGS

1 *Fill a 13cm (5in) pot with moist, standard cutting compost. Strike off any surplus with a straight edge to level the surface and firm lightly.*

2 *Select 15cm (6in) lengths from the soft growing tips of healthy shoots (here Solanum crispum). Place the cutting material in a clear plastic bag to prevent drying out.*

3 *Trim each cutting to 5–10cm (2–4in), depending on species, straight across just below a leaf joint. Remove the lower leaves, cutting flush with the stems.*

4 *Insert two or three cuttings to a pot, with the lowest leaves just above the compost. The cuttings must not touch each other, to prevent spread of disease.*

5 *Water the cuttings, label, and place the pot or pots in a propagator or in clear plastic bags (filled with air so that the sides do not touch the cuttings).*

6 *After they have rooted, pot on the cuttings into individual pots. Keep the cuttings moist by spraying lightly with a mist spray.*

PROPAGATION FROM SEMI-RIPE CUTTINGS

GOOD EXAMPLE

POOR EXAMPLES

Honeysuckle (*Lonicera*)

Trimmed "heel"

Semi-ripe wood

Trimmed below node

Soft, weak growth

Wood too ripe

Select 6–15cm (2½–6in) lengths from healthy new wood and trim just below a node. Some cuttings are taken with a small heel of bark at the base (see inset). These should be trimmed before use.

Alternatively, make a clean cut where the selected shoot is attached to the parent plant. Some cuttings root more readily if taken with a "heel"; by gently tugging a shoot away from the parent plant, the shoot peels away with a small triangular section of bark, or heel, at its base. Trim the heel of each cutting, then wound the stem by carefully cutting away a piece of bark 1–2cm (½–¾in) long from the base of the cutting. Dip the entire wound into hormone rooting powder, before inserting the cutting into the compost and labelling. Place the pot or pan in a propagator or cold frame. Semi-ripe cuttings generally take eight to twelve weeks, or longer, to root.

When the cuttings have rooted, pot them on, using a standard potting compost and grow on in a cold frame once re-established. The rooted cuttings should be hardened off and planted out the following spring.

Propagation from hardwood cuttings

Take hardwood cuttings from autumn to midwinter from healthy shoots that have become woody during the growing season. Using secateurs, remove a length of stem, cutting just above a bud. Trim off any sideshoots, then divide the stem into pieces 12–20cm (5–8in) long, using a sloping cut above a bud at the top and a straight cut at the bottom. Alternatively, longer cuttings may be taken with two or more buds. To encourage rooting, wound each cutting at the base by removing a thin

PROPAGATION FROM HARDWOOD CUTTINGS

Soft, under-ripe wood

Overripe wood

Healthy, woody shoot

1 *Remove a healthy stem from the current year's growth, cutting just above a bud. Do not use overripe and soft, new growth.*

2 *Trim off tendrils and sideshoots. Cut the stem into pieces, with an angled cut above a bud and a straight cut at the base.*

3 *Pare away the outer wood of each cutting, making a clean, downward cut, to reveal the cambium layer (see inset).*

4 *Insert the cuttings into gritty compost so that the top buds just show above the surface. Label, water, and place in a cold frame.*

5 *When the cuttings are well rooted, pot up each one individually. Stake, as required, and grow on before planting out.*

sliver of wood with a sharp knife. An application of hormone rooting powder to the wounded section may speed up rooting for climbers that are difficult to root, but is not always needed if suitable stems are taken at the appropriate season.

Inserting the cuttings

Prepare a pot or pan of free-draining cutting compost (add a little extra sand or grit to the compost), filling the pot almost to the brim, and moisten the compost well. Insert the cuttings around the edge of the pot, approximately 5cm (2in) apart. Gently insert the cuttings by two thirds to three quarters of their length, so that just the top buds are visible. Firm the compost, then water

the cuttings, label the pot, and place it in a cold frame to overwinter. Alternatively, insert the cuttings directly into a cold frame, or in a trench in a sheltered part of the garden (see ORNAMENTAL TREES, "Hardwood cuttings", p.78). Hardwood cuttings of plants that are not fully hardy should be overwintered in a frost-free place.

Hardwood cuttings may take several months to root, but most should be ready for potting up or transplanting by mid-spring of the following year. Either pot them into a standard potting compost, or grow them on in a sheltered place before planting them out in their permanent positions the following autumn.

CLIMBERS FROM SEMI-RIPE CUTTINGS (CONT.)

Clematis, some ❀
Clianthus ❀
Clytostoma ❀
Decumaria ❀
Dioscorea ❀
Distictis ❀
Dregea
Ercilla
Euonymus
Fallopia
Hardenbergia ❀
Hedera, some ❀
Hoya ❀
Jacquemontia ❀
Jasminum, some ❀
Kennedia ❀
Lonicera, some ❀

Mandevilla x amabilis

Macfadyena ❀
Mandevilla ❀
Manettia ❀
Mitraria ❀
Mutisia, some ❀
Paederia
Pandorea ❀
Passiflora, most ❀
Petrea ❀
Pileostegia
Plumbago ❀
Podranea ❀
Pyrostegia ❀
Quisqualis ❀
Sarmienta ❀
Schisandra
Schizophragma
Senecio, some ❀
Solandra ❀
Solanum, some ❀
Stauntonia
Stephanotis ❀
Stigmaphyllon ❀
Strongylodon ❀
Tecoma ❀
Tecomanthe ❀
Tecomaria ❀
Thunbergia ❀
Trachelospermum
Tripterygium

CLIMBERS FROM HARDWOOD CUTTINGS

Actinidia kolomikta ❀
Bougainvillea ❀
Lonicera, some ❀
Parthenocissus, some ❀
Vitis, some ❀

Actinidia kolomikta

Key
❀ *Not hardy*

Root cuttings

A few climbers, notably *Celastrus* and *Solanum*, may be propagated from root cuttings, taken from late winter to early spring.

Taking the cuttings

Dig a hole 45–60cm (18–24in) away from the base of the plant to expose roots that are about 1cm (½in) thick; these provide the best cutting material. Remove sections of root up to 20–30cm (8–12in) long, depending on how many cuttings are required. Cut straight across the top of the root (nearest the plant) and cut the base of the root at an angle. Place the cutting material in a clear plastic bag to prevent it from drying out.

Preparing and inserting the cuttings

Wash the sections of root to remove any soil, then cut them into smaller pieces and remove the fibrous laterals. Make a horizontal cut at the top and a slanted cut at the base. Insert the cuttings, slanted cut downwards, in a pot filled with a rooting medium of equal parts peat substitute or peat and sand. Space them approximately 7cm (3in) apart, with the tips protruding slightly. Cover with a 1cm (½in) layer of sand. Moisten the compost thoroughly, label the pot, and place it in a cold frame or propagator. Keep the compost moist.

Hardening off and potting on

Buds will appear near the top of the cuttings in spring. Pot up the cuttings individually during early summer, and harden them off gradually, occasionally applying a liquid or foliar feed. Stake the cuttings as they develop. The new plants may be planted in their permanent positions the following autumn.

PROPAGATION FROM ROOT CUTTINGS

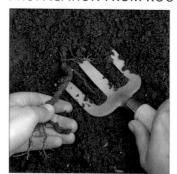

1 *Dig a hole well away from the base of the plant to expose some of the roots.*

2 *Cut off sections of root with secateurs. The pieces should be about 1cm (½in) thick and at least 10cm (4in) long.*

3 *Wash the roots and divide into pieces 4–5cm (1½–2in) long, cutting horizontally at the top and obliquely at the base (see inset).*

4 *Insert each cutting vertically into a pot of compost, so that the tips are just protruding above the surface of the compost.*

5 *Cover with a 1cm (½in) layer of sand. Water, label, and place in a cold frame.*

6 *Pot on into individual pots once the cuttings are well rooted and young shoots are 2.5–5cm (1–2in) high.*

Self-layering climbers

Many climbers have trailing shoots that root naturally. A shoot that has self layered may be lifted and from the parent plant in autumn, but, if not strongly rooted, wait until spring. Choose a healthy, well-rooted layer that has fresh new growth. Lift it carefully and cut it off. Trim back the layered shoot, retaining only the piece or pieces of stem that have produced new roots and that have new buds forming. Strip off any leaves growing near the roots. Pot up the rooted layers individually into standard cutting compost consisting of half peat substitute or peat and half sand, and water them in well. If the layer is severed and potted in autumn, leave it (particularly if evergreen) in a cold frame to establish and then plant out the following spring. Plant out other layers once they have strong roots and shoots.

PROPAGATION OF SELF-LAYERING PLANTS

1 *Select a low-growing shoot that has rooted into the ground and lift the rooted section with a hand fork.*

2 *Carefully sever the shoot from the parent plant (here ivy), cutting between nodes, using a pair of sharp secateurs.*

3 *Cut the shoot into sections, each with a healthy root system and vigorous new growth. Remove the lower leaves.*

4 *Replant each section of rooted shoot either into a pot of cutting compost or in its permanent position.*

Simple layering

The long, trailing shoots produced by climbers may often be propagated by simple layering if they do not root naturally. A shoot is wounded and pegged down into the surrounding soil; this induces it to root at a node to provide a young plant.

Layers of many climbers that have been pegged down between autumn and early spring will develop strong roots by the following autumn, at which time they may be separated from the parent plant. *Akebia*, *Campsis*, and *Vitis* should be layered in late winter, because, if the stems are wounded in spring, the layers "bleed" sap and are less likely to root.

Soil preparation

If the surrounding soil is poor, fork in some organic compost at least a month before layering takes place. Alternatively, fill a pot with potting compost and plunge it into the ground at the place where the layer is to be pegged down.

Making the layer

Choose a healthy, vigorous, non-flowering shoot or stem that is long enough to trail along the ground. Trim the leaves and any sideshoots from the section of stem to be layered to provide a clear length of stem for about 30cm (12in) behind the tip of the shoot.

Gently bend the stem down to the ground and, to encourage root formation, wound the underside of the stem close to a node, making an angled cut halfway through with a sharp knife. For most climbers apply hormone rooting powder to the wound; vigorous climbers such as wisteria, however, do not require it.

Peg the stem firmly to the ground with one or more "U"-shaped pieces of wire, and cover with not more than 8cm (3in) of soil. Attach the tip of the layered stem to a stake so that it stays upright.

Separating the rooted layer

In autumn, when new shoots and roots have grown from the buried part of the stem, the rooted layer may be severed from the parent plant and potted up or planted out. Trim back the old stem before replanting, and stake the new plant. If the layer is planted in a container, it should be overwintered in a cold frame. Apply a foliar or liquid feed at regular intervals during spring and summer. Pot on, as necessary, before gradually hardening off and planting out the layer into its permanent position the following autumn.

PROPAGATION BY SIMPLE LAYERING

1 *Select a young, low-growing shoot (here* Akebia quinata*). Trim off the leaves to provide a clear length of stem behind the tip.*

2 *Make an angled cut on the underside of the shoot to form a "tongue" in the centre of the trimmed length of stem.*

3 *Using a clean brush, dust the incision with fresh hormone rooting powder (see inset) and gently shake off any surplus.*

4 *Peg down the shoot firmly in the prepared area, using wire staples. Cover with up to 8cm (3in) of earth.*

5 *The following autumn, sever the layered shoot close to the parent plant. Lift with a hand fork and trim back the old stem.*

6 *Plant the layer in a 13cm (5in) pot of standard potting compost or into its permanent position. Then water and label.*

Propagation by serpentine layering

Carefully bend a trailing shoot down to the prepared soil and trim off leaves and sideshoots. Make several wounds close to nodes, leaving at least one bud between each incision. Apply hormone rooting powder and peg down the wounded sections, as for simple layering. Separate plantlets in autumn, when roots will have formed from each of the wounds. Trim the old stem from the new plants before replanting and staking.

Several new plants may be produced by serpentine layering. Peg down layers with wire staples (see inset).

CLIMBERS TO LAYER

Self layering
Asteranthera
Celastrus
Ficus pumila ✣
Hedera, some ✣

Hedera helix
'Atropurpurea'

Hoya ✣
Hydrangea
Mitraria ✣
Monstera deliciosa ✣
Parthenocissus, some ✣
Periploca
Philodendron ✣
Scindapsus ✣
Tecomaria ✣
Trachelospermum
Tripterygium
Vigna ✣

Simple layering
Actinidia, some ✣
Akebia
Beaumontia ✣
Cissus ✣
Ercilla
Humulus
Lapageria ✣
Lonicera, some ✣

Lonicera
x *americana*

Mandevilla
Monstera ✣
Mucuna
Mutisia, some ✣
Passiflora, most ✣
Pileostegia
Podranea ✣
Schizophragma
Solanum, some ✣
Strongylodon ✣
Tecomanthe ✣
Thunbergia ✣
Vitis amurensis, *V. coignetiae*
Wisteria

Serpentine layering
Ampelopsis
Campsis
Celastrus
Clematis, some ✣
Fallopia
Holboellia ✣
Kennedia ✣

Parthenocissus
tricuspidata

Parthenocissus,
some ✣
Sarmienta ✣
Schisandra

Key
✣ *Not hardy*

CHAPT

5

ROSES

GARDENERS AND POETS since before Roman times have revered the rose as the queen of flowering plants for the extraordinary beauty of its blooms. The rose family offers an enormous range of flower colour, shape, and scent, from the simple purity of the wild rose to the pastel charm of an old garden rose, or the jewel-like brilliance of a modern hybrid.

Few plants are so varied as the rose in its growth habit, height, foliage, and form; it is possible to clothe the whole garden in rose blooms, from the delicacy of a tiny pot rose to the foaming mass of a huge rambler. Whether grown alone in the splendour of a formal garden or used to heighten a mixed planting, roses epitomize the glory of a summer's day.

Roses in the garden

WHETHER you choose to grow old garden roses for their grace of habit, foliage, and scent, or modern roses for their long flowering season and showy blooms, the diversity of roses (*Rosa*) makes it possible to find a plant for almost every part of the garden, and to create any style or mood of planting, whether restrained classicism or luxuriant informality.

Roses are adaptable plants that grow happily in almost all parts of the world. They are most vigorous in warm, temperate regions, although some adapt well to subtropical or cold regions. In hot climates, they may flower virtually continuously throughout the year.

Choosing roses

The number of rose cultivars available is bewildering, with many new ones each year. Before choosing, it is well worth visiting some established gardens to observe as many different roses as possible growing in garden conditions. Do this over a period of time to assess the plants' habit, eventual height, health, vigour, fragrance, fastness of flower colour in strong sun, and all the other desirable features of a good rose. Note, too, whether a rose produces a single flush of blooms or if it is a remontant rose, which, being a repeat- or perpetual flowering plant, will have a greatly extended flowering period.

Most national rose associations publish listings that give details of where species roses and cultivars stocked by member nurseries may be purchased; these are often invaluable in locating suppliers of more unusual roses. In addition to their selling name, many roses now have coded cultivar names – for example the rose sold as CASINO has the coded cultivar name 'Macca' – so you can be sure that you are buying the correct plant (see also "Plant names", p.677).

Flower shapes

The genus *Rosa* comprises many flower forms, from the simple, single flowers of species roses to the elegantly furled blooms of the modern rose and the cabbage-like complexity of many old rose flowers.

The main flower shapes shown right give a general indication of the flower shape when in its perfect state (which in some cases may be before it has fully opened). The flowers may be single (4–7 petals), semi-double (8–14 petals), double (15–20 petals), or fully double (over 30 petals).

Fragrance

Roses have long been prized for their scent; most old garden species and some modern roses possess enchanting and diverse perfumes with hints of clove, musk, honey, lemon, spice, and even tea, as well as the "true rose" fragrance. It is not easy to be specific about rose scent as its character and intensity may vary greatly with the time of day, the air humidity, the age of the bloom, and the "nose" of individual gardeners; some will find a particular cultivar fragrant, while others will not.

Old-World charm
The open blooms and sprawling habit of shrub roses, including 'Constance Spry', 'Céleste', and 'Cerise Bouquet', blend with perennials in a subtle colour theme to create a mood of informal and restful abundance. The proximity of the beds and the grass walk provides a secluded setting in which to enjoy the heady rose scents.

FLOWER SHAPES

Flat *Open, usually single or semi-double, with petals that are almost flat, shown above in R. moyesii 'Geranium'.*

Cupped *Open, single (as in this R. rugosa 'Rosea') to fully double, with petals curving out from the centre.*

High-centred *Semi-double to fully double Hybrid Tea type, with high, tight centres, such as R. 'Silver Jubilee'.*

Urn-shaped *Classic, curved, and flat-topped, semi- to fully double, Hybrid Tea type. R. SIMBA ('Korbelma') is a fine example.*

Rounded *Double or fully double, with even-sized, overlapping petals in a bowl-shaped outline (here, R. 'Alpine Sunset').*

Rosette *Flattish, double or fully double, with slightly overlapping unevenly-shaped petals (here, R. 'Tour de Malakoff').*

Quartered-rosette *Flattish, double or fully double (as in this R. 'Gloire de Dijon'), with petals in a quartered pattern.*

Pompon *Small, rounded, double or fully double, usually in clusters, with many small petals, such as R. PINK BELLS ('Poulbells').*

The different rose types

More than a hundred wild (or species) roses exist, and all 13,000 cultivated roses now commercially available descend from them. The ancestry of almost all of them is so mixed, after centuries of casual and indiscriminate breeding before cross-pollination was understood and proper records of parentage kept, that it is impossible to classify them precisely. For example the hybridizing of miniature roses with Floribunda roses has led to dwarf Floribunda bush roses, intermediate in stature between the parents.

Roses are continually evolving, so categories (or classes) that rose lovers devise are subject to change and should be regarded as signposts for guidance, not inflexible definitions. The following is based on recommendations of The World Federation of Rose Societies and The Royal National Rose Society.

Species roses

Species, or wild, roses and species hybrids (which share most characteristics of both parent species) are generally large, arching shrubs or climbers bearing one flush of single, five-petalled flowers during spring or midsummer and then decorative hips in autumn.

Old garden roses

This large category is split into two groups, based mainly on ancestry.

GROUP A

Mostly of European origin, freely bearing clusters of fragrant blooms in summer on matt-foliaged, shrubby plants. Alba, Damask, and Gallica were originally grown for their scent. Two Damasks and one Scots rose flower in autumn.

Alba ("white") Large shrubs with plentiful, greyish-green foliage and white, cream, or blush, scented flowers. Ancient.

Centifolia ("hundred-petalled") Also called Provence roses. Dense, leafy, prickly, rather lax shrubs, including pink, white, and purplish forms, usually well scented. 1450s onwards.

Damask (possibly "from Damascus") A varied group of leafy, often lax shrubs. Most are pink flowered (some are white) and fragrant. Ancient.

Gallica ("French") Generally dense and leafy, with a compact, shrubby, suckering habit. There are pink, maroon, purple and striped forms, many with good fragrance. Ancient.

Moss These shrubs bear unusual, "moss-like" growth on stems and calyx, otherwise generally similar to Centifolia. 1720s onwards.

Scots (or Scotch) Prickly, usually low-growing shrubs bearing white, pink, purple, yellow, or striped flowers. Selections or hybrids of *R. pimpinellifolia*. 1790s onwards.

Sweet Briar Hybrids from *R. rubiginosa* (syn. *R. eglanteria*), noted for its apple-scented leaves. Large, twiggy, prickly shrubs in pink, fawn-yellow, or purple. 1890s onwards.

GROUP B

Hybrids between Oriental and European roses. Almost all produce flowers in autumn as well as summer.

Bourbon (from an island group) Leafy shrubs and climbers of rather lax, open habit. Flowers, often fragrant, include pink, white, purplish, and striped forms. 1817 onwards.

Boursault Generally smooth-stemmed, dark-wooded shrubs with early flowers; may need protection from disease. 1820s onwards.

China Hybrids with *R. chinensis* in their parentage. Shrub, bush, and climbing roses, with shiny, pointed leaflets and twiggy, sometimes sparse growth. Diverse flower forms and colours include pink, white, red, buff, and yellow. Minimal scent. 1750s onwards.

Hybrid Musk Vigorous, remontant shrubs with abundant foliage and often fragrant, mainly double blooms borne in trusses. 1910 onwards.

Hybrid Perpetual Vigorous shrub, bush, and climbing roses of upright, leafy habit, with large, full-petalled, often fragrant flowers in red, pink, white, or purple. 1830s onwards.

Noisette (named after a French grower) Silky-petalled, cream, yellow, or buff flowers in clusters on vigorous shrubs or climbers with shiny leaves. Spicy scent. Developed from *R. moschata*, Chinas and Teas. 1805 onwards.

Portland (also known as Damask Portland) Leafy, stiff-growing shrubs bearing sizeable, fragrant flowers in white, pink, purple, or carmine, raised from earlier roses interbred with Chinas. Autumn flowering not dependable. 1780s onwards.

Sempervirens ("evergreen") White or pink, cluster-flowered, summer-blooming climbers, with shiny leaves. 1820s onwards.

Tea (possibly from the delicate "tea" aroma) Bushes and climbing roses noted for the elegance and beauty of their silky-petalled, spicy-scented flowers, most of which are coloured yellow, buff, pink, white, or carmine. 1810 onwards.

Modern garden roses

Most modern roses produce excellent repeat flowers throughout summer and autumn and have glossy foliage, both characteristics showing the influence of Oriental roses.

Climber Vigorous, stiff-stemmed climbing roses of varied character and available in many colours, suitable for training on solid supports. 1870s onwards.

Climbing Miniature Remontant climbers with small leaves and flowers, some fragrant, in many colours. 1990s onwards.

Floribunda Cluster-flowered bushes, providing excellent continuity of blooms, some fragrant, in many colours. Garnette roses do well under glass, for the cut flower market. 1909 onwards.

Ground cover Shrub roses with a markedly creeping or spreading habit, in many colours. Some are fragrant. 1919 onwards.

Hybrid Tea Bush roses with large, high-centred flowers in many colours, usually full-petalled, often fragrant, borne singly or in threes. 1860s onwards.

Miniature Tiny counterparts of Hybrid Tea and Floribunda roses, rarely fragrant. 1920s onwards.

Patio (dwarf cluster-flowered bush) Resembling Floribunda, shrub, or ground-cover roses but with smaller, neater appearance, giving a scaled-down effect. Little scent. 1980s onwards.

Polyantha ("many flowers") Bush, shrub, and climbing roses bearing big clusters of small blooms, mostly in white, pink, or red. Slight scent. Derived from *R. multiflora*. 1870s onwards.

Rambler Vigorous climbing roses in many colours, having lax growth and long, flexible shoots, easy to train on supports. Some are fragrant and most bear clusters of small flowers freely but in summer only. 1890s onwards.

Rugosa ("wrinkled") Vigorous, hardy shrubs related to *R. rugosa*, many recognizable by their wrinkled leaves and showy hips, with scented flowers mostly in white, pink, or purple. 1790s onwards.

Shrub Roses of ampler and leafier growth than bush roses, very varied in character, colour range, blooming period, and fragrance. 1890s onwards.

DESIGN FOR A FORMAL ROSE GARDEN

Here, all is symmetry and order, with clean lines and colour laid out in patterns of geometric simplicity. This design creates a restrained setting in which to enjoy the classic beauty of roses. Formal yew hedges enclose beds of massed bush roses in pale and deep golds and white, which in turn focus on a graceful, trailing rose in the centre. Red standard roses lift the planting with a bold contrast of colour and form.

1 *Yew* (Taxus baccata)
2 *Rosa* 'Golden Showers'
3 *R.* SUFFOLK ('Kormixal')
4 *R.* 'Korresia'
5 *R.* AMBER QUEEN ('Harroony')
6 *R.* 'Hakuun'
7 *R.* MARGARET MERRIL ('Harkuly')
8 *R.* SWANY ('Meiburenac')

With most roses one must be quite close to smell them; they are best enjoyed by planting them near a door or a window where their scent may drift into the house on summer evenings, around the patio or along a path, or in a sheltered position in the garden. Other roses, particularly many of the tree-climbing ramblers, are so freely scented that they can perfume the whole garden.

Flower colour

Modern roses embrace virtually every colour of the spectrum, from pale pastels to bold, bright reds and yellows. The blue rose remains the stuff of legend, despite the use of the word "blue" in such cultivars as 'Blue Parfum', which is actually mauve. The old garden roses range in hue from white, through the palest of blush pinks, deep pink, crimson, and violet, to purple; many are striped pink and white or purple and white. Most roses look good together and with other plants, but combining too many brilliant colours, for example bright vermilion with cerise pink, may create a discordant effect. Plant white roses or those with softer, pastel hues between groups of strongly toned roses to cool them down and prevent them from clashing.

Foliage colour

As well as producing a fine flowering display, some groups of roses provide colour in other ways to extend the season of interest. The Alba roses and many of the species roses have pleasing foliage, from a soft grey-green to a deep, glossy blue-green, making them attractive even when the bush is not in flower. The bright-green foliage of Rugosa roses has an interesting wrinkled (or rugose) texture and, if the roses are planted as a hedge, it makes a good background for other plantings. The leaves of some species are a dusky plum-purple, as in *R. glauca*, while the foliage of some, such as *R. virginiana*, turns in colour to vivid sunset tints in autumn.

Ornamental hips or thorns

Rugosa roses with single or semi-double flowers also develop bright red, decorative rosehips at the end of the flowering season. Some of the species roses too, such as *R. moyesii* and its hybrids, produce ornamental and sometimes showy hips in autumn that range in colour from yellow and orange, through all the shades of red, to a blackish-purple.

R. sericea subsp. *omeiensis* f. *pteracantha* has huge, flat thorns which, when young, glow ruby red if the sun is behind them.

The garden setting

One of the best settings for the beds of a rose garden is a smooth, green lawn, but the subtle grey and honey tones of stone paving can be just as attractive. A mellow brick path may complement a rose planting alongside it, especially one of soft, pale tones. Whatever the material, avoid multi-coloured patterns that may compete with the roses. Gravel, although pleasant in appearance and texture, can be troublesome to look after as weeds soon appear and the stones may gradually spread or disappear into the soil.

Edging plants may be used to frame a rosebed. A traditional box hedge makes a formal boundary but many other plants may be used more informally, particularly those that possess grey-green or silver-grey foliage. *Anaphalis nepalensis* var. *monocephala*, with woolly, lance-shaped leaves, or the more dwarf forms of lavender are suitable, as is catmint (*Nepeta*) if there is room for it to sprawl over the path.

Many of the more restrained hardy geraniums, in particular those with blue flowers, are similarly appealing, and even miniature roses, in contrasting or complementary colours, may be grown on the sunny side of a bed.

Formal rose gardens

The most popular way to grow roses is in a formal rose garden, devoted to displaying the glories of the rose in beds shaped to reflect the plant's classic elegance. Generally, Hybrid Tea or Floribunda bushes and standards are used as permanent bedding plants, grouped in blocks of colour. The rather stiff and upright growth of many such bushes lends itself to the formality of bedding and tends not to blend so well with other plants, although roses may be attractively underplanted (see p.151).

Rosebeds may be designed in any shape or size – square, oblong, triangular, or round; at the edges of paths or drives they may be narrow and ribbon-like. Before creating new rosebeds, draw a plan on paper and experiment with different shapes and layouts of beds in order to decide which is the best design for the site that has been chosen. Do not make the beds so wide that access to the roses for spraying, mulching, and pruning becomes difficult.

If mixing rose cultivars in the same bed, plant no fewer than five or six plants of the same cultivar together in a regular formation for substantial clumps of colour; not all cultivars reach their peak of flowering at exactly the same time. A garden planted with variations on a colour theme, for instance pale and deep pinks with a touch of white, creates a harmonious effect that is more pleasing than mixed, bright colours.

When planting, bear in mind the variations in eventual height of different cultivars. For a bed in an open area, choose cultivars of a more or less uniform height. A rosebed that is backed by a wall or hedge is more attractive if the roses at the front are shorter than those behind.

Standard roses may be used to give height to any bedding scheme. Placing a single standard in the centre of a round bed that echoes the shape of the rose creates a graceful symmetry, while several standards placed at intervals of about 1.5m (5ft) along the middle of a long bed help to break up its uniformity.

Informal plantings

The charm of roses may be exploited in a wide range of informal planting schemes, particularly with herbaceous plants or other shrubs. Roses suitable for virtually any site in the garden may be chosen from the multitude of shrub, miniature, climbing, and ground-cover roses of varied stature and habit now available.

Roses combine happily with other plantings; for example miniature roses give both summer colour and height to a planting of rock plants that are mainly spring-flowering, and a ground-cover rose may clothe a bank with fragrant flowers.

The belief that roses do not mix with other plants probably dates from the days when many commonly used cultivars were large and ungainly and did not suit the Edwardian and Victorian bedding schemes. They were grown in separate walled gardens simply to provide cut blooms for the house. It has, however, long been recognized that roses need not be grown in isolation.

Roses with herbaceous plants

Growing roses in beds or borders with herbaceous plants both highlights the beauties of the rose in flower and provides interest when the rose itself is dormant. The growth habit of many shrub roses, such as the light and airy China roses or the lax and open Damasks, perfectly suits the casual profusion of an informal planting.

Muted drifts of flower or foliage, for example the haze of tiny, white

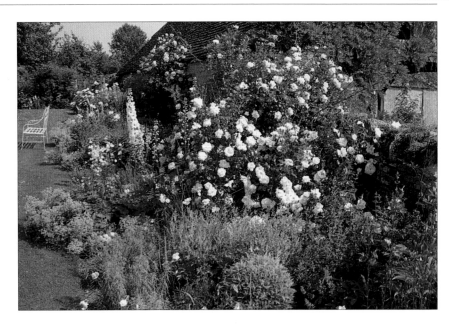

Informal style
Large roses, including 'Penelope' in the foreground, clothe the background walls with a fragrant mass of summer colour and provide a magnificent foil for the tall spikes of plants such as campanulas and delphiniums and the low mounds of the other perennial plants in an informal mixed border of cool blues and whites.

Crambe cordifolia flowers, best complement the showy flowers of roses in the summer. At other times of the year, use more flamboyant flowering plants or some with evergreen foliage to extend the season and conceal the bare rose stems.

Many plants may enhance a planting dominated by roses. The tall spikes of purple foxgloves (*Digitalis purpurea*), white *Lilium regale*, or other white and pink lilies pushing up through a planting of lush, old garden roses, for example, make for a striking contrast, both in habit of growth and flower form.

Roses with other shrubs

Both shrub and species roses combine well with other shrubs, as long as they receive enough sunlight.

They provide abundant, beautiful, often fragrant flowers to set against the foliage of other spring-flowering shrubs, sometimes right through the summer. Many such roses have almost evergreen foliage and coloured hips in the autumn (see "Ornamental hips or thorns", p.150). Smaller shrub roses as well as the Gallicas, most of the Damasks, the Portland roses, and many modern cultivars of similar stature make an excellent ornamental foreground to any planting of shrubs.

Roses that have long, questing branches, such as the freely flowering 'Scharlachglut' or 'Complicata' with its deep pink blooms, may scramble through and enliven a dull, evergreen shrub. Ramblers may adorn a tree's foliage with their blooms or transform a dead tree.

The soft colours of old roses are particularly attractive when planted with subshrubs that combine grey-green leaves with blue flowers, such as the free-flowering *Caryopteris* x *clandonensis*, the ethereal fronds of *Perovskia atriplicifolia*, certain hebes, and most lavenders.

Underplanting a rosebed

The display in a rosebed may be enhanced and extended beyond the rose flowering season by growing low, shallow-rooted plants between the roses. A wide range of plants may clothe the ground and provide the roses with a background of contrasting colour, texture, and form. Violets (*Viola*) are a favourite choice: the white, soft blue, and mauve cultivars complement roses well. All such ground-cover plants make mulching difficult, however.

Take care not to tread on the ground-cover planting when spraying the roses in a particularly wide bed.

When planting between roses, take account of the eventual heights of the various companion plants, and place them so that they will not obscure each other or the roses when they are mature.

The yellow-green of *Alchemilla mollis*, pink and white heads of *Armeria maritima*, and spreading, hardy geraniums also make a fine display under roses.

Spring bulbs brighten up bare rosebeds early in the year: try planting blue or white *Chionodoxa*, daffodils, snowdrops (*Galanthus*), and white, starry *Tulipa turkestanica* to create a gay patchwork of colour. Their only drawback is their dying foliage, which looks untidy until it is removed and may make it difficult to maintain the bed for the roses.

Autumn tints
The brilliant scarlet hips of this species rose contrast vividly with its yellowing foliage.

Flowers and foliage
Richly coloured rose blooms are set like jewels against an underplanting of herbs with elegant, grey-green foliage, and the golden tones of gravel.

Many fragrant, evergreen herbs are good companions for roses: use cotton lavender (*Santolina chamaecyparissus*), various thymes (*Thymus*), or sages (*Salvia*) – either the culinary kind or any that have attractive, variegated leaves. Roses always look well when they are contrasted with the silver foliage of perennial plants such as the fern-leaved *Artemisia ludoviciana* and *A. frigida*, or the grey, woolly-leaved, mat-forming *Stachys byzantina*.

Terraces

On a steep hillside, terraces may be used to transform a difficult site into a striking showcase for roses. They provide areas sufficiently level for planting and retain moisture which the roses need while creating eye-catching graduations of height and perspective. The terrace walls look best if made of weathered brick or mellow stone. Bush roses may be grown in the terrace beds, and ramblers or ground-cover roses planted to tumble over the retaining walls, creating curtains of bloom.

Smaller terraced beds are ideal, too, for growing miniature roses. It is much easier to savour the beauty and scent of their tiny, individual flowers if they are raised some way above ground level. Each bed for miniature roses should be approxi-

Summer retreat
A mature rambler rose in full, glorious bloom transforms this trelliswork arbour into an eye-catching feature that is at once intimate and airy. The floral canopy fills the air within the arbour with its delicious perfume, and provides a cool, leafy shelter from which to enjoy the views of the surrounding garden.

mately 45–60cm (1½–2ft) wide. Place miniature standards along the top bed of the terrace to draw the eye and use some of the smaller and more dainty ground-cover roses to tumble over the walls. This kind of terracing also makes an excellent surround for a sunken rose garden.

Specimen planting

A large shrub rose on its own makes a handsome specimen plant, perhaps in a lawn or to mark a focal point in a garden, as long as it is an outstanding rose of its type; any defects in a specimen are immediately obvious. Used in this way, weeping standard roses can be especially striking. These are formed by grafting rambler cultivars onto a 1.5m or 2m (5ft or 6ft) stem, so that their long, flexible shoots, laden with blossom in summer, hang down all round, right to the ground. They usually flower for a limited period, unless a standard grafted from a remontant, ground-cover rose is chosen.

Climbing roses grown as standards may provide a profusion of blooms throughout the entire summer, but their stiff growth does not produce the same, dramatic waterfall effect as weeping standards.

Many of the larger shrub roses, with their graceful, arching habit, almost evergreen foliage, and abundant flowers, are natural choices for planting as specimens in larger gardens. 'Nevada', for example, which can reach 2 x 2m (6 x 6ft) or even more, is smothered with large, cream blooms in early summer, and again in late summer. Other roses, particularly species roses and their hybrids, such as 'Frühlingsgold', have no second blooming.

For a small garden where space for flowering plants is limited, use remontant roses that earn their space in the garden by blooming all summer and well into the autumn, such as the strongly scented 'Roseraie de l'Haÿ'. Smaller shrub roses, such as 'Chinatown' which has masses of gold blooms tinged with pink, and 'Sally Holmes' with large, white flowers clustered above the foliage, are not quite large enough to justify being planted on their own, but are very handsome if planted in specimen groups of three.

Walls, arbours, and pergolas

Most ramblers and climbing species roses are very vigorous, and produce an exuberance of bloom in mid-summer. They may clothe structures such as arbours, walls, and fences, disguise unsightly features, or give height to the summer display in the garden. Be sure to choose a rose with an eventual height that will cover the intended area well without outgrowing it.

Ramblers and climbing roses may be trained on a range of plastic-coated metal bowers, tunnels, arches, and tripod pillars now on the market. Although metal supports may not look so attractive initially as ones made from rustic poles, they have a much longer life and are soon concealed once the roses trained on them become well established. Rustic arches, even if treated, eventually rot at soil level.

Other climbing plants, such as clematis, or wall shrubs may be planted to grow through the rose, to complement the rose blooms as well as to extend the flowering season; climbers with blue flowers are particularly effective. Some of the more vigorous shrub roses, particularly Bourbons, also make excellent short climbers for a pillar or small wall.

Ramblers

Ramblers have more flexible shoots than climbers and are easier to train along complex structures such as pergolas, arches, and trellises. When grown against walls, however, their mass of shoots may become mildewed as a result of the poor air circulation.

Singular splendour
A standard rose, 'White Pet', provides a handsome focal point.

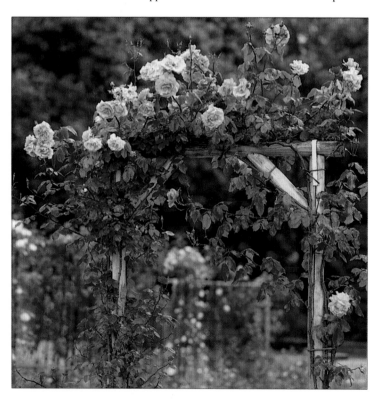

An ornamental arch
The old-fashioned, rich pink flowers of Rosa *'Bantry Bay' festoon this rustic arch to form an enticing and decorative frame to the view beyond.*

Decorative hedging
Rosa gallica
'Versicolor', also
known as 'Rosa
Mundi' is one of the
oldest roses available
and has unusually
striped petals. It forms
an attractive informal
hedge that bursts into
a riot of flower in the
summer to create an
enchanting ribbon of
colour. Here, the line
of the rose hedge
provides a pleasing
contrast of height and
perspective with the
tall spikes of
hollyhocks (Alcea).
The deep pink flowers
in the rose hedge show
reversion to its parent,
R. gallica var.
officinalis.

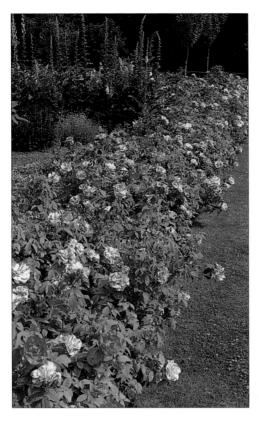

To cover a long pergola, use one of the vigorous, small-flowered, white ramblers such as 'Bobbie James', but remember that they can grow to 10m (30ft) or more and will overwhelm a small structure.

For a picturesque effect, try training roses along chains or ropes that are suspended between uprights to create great swags of bloom.

Climbers

The stiffer shoots of climbing roses are easier to prune than those of ramblers and happily grace walls and fences. Many of the less robust modern climbers may be grown on pillars or as freestanding shrubs with great effect. Pink 'Aloha' is beautifully scented but is too stiff and upright in habit for an arch, although it would be suitable for the pillar supports of a tall pergola.

The Bourbon rose 'Zéphirine Drouhin', which has pink flowers and repeats well, is an old favourite for growing on arches and pergolas, as it is the only currently available climber that is both thornless and fragrant. It is, however, prone to mildew.

Rose hedges and screens

Roses may, if they are carefully chosen, provide some of the most colourful and attractive plants for an informal hedge or screen. A few, for example *R. rugosa* and its hybrids,

may be shaped to some extent by gentle clipping in winter to make dense hedges while maintaining the natural outline of the shrub. No rose is fully evergreen, so few provide a screen that gives complete privacy all year, although the thorns make the hedge virtually impenetrable. For further details, see HEDGES AND SCREENS, pp.84–86.

The Hybrid Musk roses, such as the apricot 'Buff Beauty', grow into a thick, thorny screen up to 2m (6ft) in height covered in fragrant flowers all summer long – if their natural

unpredictability of growth is curbed by training on horizontal wires or chain-link fencing. If a rose hedge is to line a path, use upright cultivars since those of unpredictable growth may impede the pathway.

For a small garden, a hedge of tall, Floribunda roses is preferable. These are generally upright plants with little spread and, if planted in two staggered rows (see *Planting Distances for a Rose Hedge*, p.157), cultivars such as the apricot-yellow ANNE HARKNESS ('Harkaramel') rapidly form a pretty screen about 1.2m (4ft) tall. Some shorter-growing old garden roses, such as 'Charles de Mills', have attractive foliage and form hedges of similar height but flower only at midsummer. Their vulnerability to mildew is, however, increased by close planting.

A delightful way of dividing one part of a garden from another is to train climbing roses or ramblers on decorative screens formed by constructing open, wooden frameworks of the desired height. Ready-made wooden and plastic trellis is available but make sure that it is sturdy, since it has to support a considerable weight and to last for years.

Ground-cover roses

Some low-growing roses readily spread along the ground to form a dense and floriferous carpet. These may be used to continue the theme of a rosebed, or as a prettily spreading edging to a cottage border, as well as to disguise an unsightly feature such as a manhole cover, or scramble down a steep bank that is otherwise difficult to plant.

A carpet of bloom
This ground-cover rose, SURREY, *attractively masks an expanse of bare earth with a succession of double flowers from summer to autumn.*

Some more recently introduced cultivars, such as NIPPER ('Hareco'), cover the soil very well although, at 1–1.2m (3–4ft), they grow too tall for true ground cover. Other roses that are suitable for a small space are 'Flower Carpet' or those named after English counties.

Ramblers such as PHEASANT ('Kordapt') and GROUSE ('Korimro'), which both have small, pink flowers and glossy foliage, make marvellous ground-cover roses, but their vigour makes them unsuitable for a small garden. They grow naturally along the ground, rooting as they go and covering it very closely, but need strict control to stop them from spreading too far.

If you have a sunken rose garden with fairly low walls, roses such as AVON ('Poulmulti') or SUMA ('Harsuma') have the right kind of low, spreading growth, if planted along the top, to form waterfalls of flowers over the walls.

Much attention has been given to developing ground-cover roses, but some cultivars that are sold as such are simply low-growing but fairly wide-spreading bushes. They are seldom dense enough in growth to be very effective weed-smotherers, and in winter they shed their leaves, so allowing in air and light which enable weeds to germinate.

Roses in containers

Roses are invaluable for their summer colour and fragrance in patio gardens where the surface is mostly paved and there are few or no beds. Containers of many sorts, including hanging baskets, are suitable as long as they are in a position that receives sun for at least half the day (see also CONTAINER GARDENING, pp.304–335). Select bushy and compact modern cultivars (see CONTAINER GARDENING, p.317), as leggy roses with bare stems at the base look unsightly. If grouping roses in a container, ensure that it is large enough for the plants to be spaced out to allow for future growth.

Even quite vigorous climbers may, given the support of a wall, be grown in tubs or half-barrels. They should be planted and trained as other climbing roses but as the nutrients in the containers will be quickly exhausted (and the roses difficult to repot), they will require regular feeding.

Roses grown in containers do not have to be confined to a patio garden. They may bring colour to other paved areas, such as the centre of a herb garden, the surrounds of a pool, or even a roof garden.

Roses for display and exhibition

Entering roses in a local flower show and, with experience, in a town or county horticultural show, can be very rewarding. Higher levels of competition than this require much more dedication and time than the average gardener can give.

Rules for exhibiting roses vary from country to country, depending on the requirements of national, and local, rose associations. It is as important for serious exhibitors as it is for judges to be familiar with the details of such rules, so always study the schedule before entering a show.

Cultivating roses for exhibition

Grow several bushes of the same cultivar to ensure a wide choice of blooms. Ordinary garden bush roses can be used for exhibition purposes, provided that they are well looked after in the garden and the foliage is kept free from disease. Prune cultivars severely to produce a

DISBUDDING ROSES

Terminal bud left to develop

Pinch out sidebuds

Hybrid Tea roses
As soon as they are large enough to handle easily, pinch out all the sidebuds, leaving the main, central bud to grow on.

Pinch out terminal bud

Sidebuds left to develop

Floribunda roses
Pinch out the young, central bud of each smaller spray in the truss for uniform flowering.

CHINESE HATS

To protect a show bloom from rain damage, insert a stake or cane with a "Chinese hat" by the rose stem and tie the stem in to the stake.

limited number of strong shoots with only eight or nine blooms a season from which to choose exhibition blooms. Maintain vigorous growth with extra fertilizer. Roses are often disbudded to produce exhibition quality blooms. Remove the newly formed sidebuds from Hybrid Tea roses so that the main bud develops strongly. Disbudding the central bloom of Floribunda roses ensures that all the other buds open at roughly the same time.

Some blooms are easily damaged by rain, and showing rules permit the use of individual bloom protectors, or "Chinese hats", in the form of plastic cones fixed to canes. They are by no means essential, however, and are not easy to use on the large trusses of Floribunda bushes.

Selecting blooms

Timing is crucial in exhibiting. A Hybrid Tea bloom should, at the moment of judging, be only three quarters open, and a Floribunda truss should have the maximum number of blooms open, although the stamens should not yet have blackened. Blooms should be of average size for the cultivar. Good, healthy foliage is also important.

Preparing for a show

It is better for the novice exhibitor to restrict entries in any one show to a maximum of three classes at first, until they have gained experience. They should cut about double the number of roses to be entered, with stems at least 30cm (12in) long,

on the evening before the show. Remove the lower leaves and thorns from the cut stems; plunge the stems into buckets of cold water, right up to the necks of the flowers. Keep the containers overnight in a cool place.

Do not be put off if your blooms suffer weather damage. Others are in the same position. If the blooms must be transported any distance, keep each bloom or truss separated, using tissue paper, so that they are not bruised or otherwise damaged.

Staging the blooms

Once at the show, collect your class entry cards from the show secretary and carry your roses straight to the staging table. Use vases or bowls that are as plain as possible. Staging the blooms always takes longer than expected, but greater speed and skill will come with experience.

Arrange the roses symmetrically, placing any larger bloom in the front so it is less noticeable. The blooms should be close, but not touching; a good blend of colours may win an extra point. Cut out faded Floribunda blooms if this does not leave obvious cut stems or gaps. Use a water-colour brush to remove insects or dust specks and sponge off any traces of insecticide deposit with cotton wool. If needed, "dress" Hybrid Tea blooms by gently teasing any petals that are slightly out of place into the correct position. Do not reposition the petals too much, since over-dressed blooms may lose points.

When arranging the blooms, check that they conform to the schedule,

EXHIBITION STANDARD BLOOMS

A Hybrid Tea rose
'Dream Time'

High, conical centre

Circular outine

Firm, unblemished petals

Bloom ¾ open

Clean, undamaged leaves of good size

Outer petals evenly reflexed

A Floribunda rose
HANNAH GORDON ('Korweiso')

Firm, unblemished petals

Pleasing outline

Blooms fully open

Unfaded stamens

Clean, undamaged leaves of good size

Good, fresh colour

for example "One bloom each of three cultivars of a Hybrid Tea rose in a vase"; if there is any deviation, the arrangement will be judged as N.A.S. (Not According to Schedule). Place the class card, and one listing the cultivars, in front of the vase. Tidy away the debris and top up the vases with water.

EQUIPMENT FOR EXHIBITING ROSES

Plain vase

Block of oasis to arrange the roses

Knife to cut oasis

Ruler to measure stems

Cotton wool for cleaning leaves

Schedule of shows

Entry card

Soft wool tie to prevent blooms opening in transit

Soft brush to clean petals

Scissors to snip out faded blooms

Variety card

Planter's guide to roses

MOST FRAGRANT FLOWERS

Reliable, with excellent scent
Rosa ALEC'S RED ('Cored')
Rosa 'Arthur Bell'
Rosa x *centifolia* cultivars
Rosa 'Climbing Etoile de Hollande'
Rosa 'Compassion'
Rosa DOUBLE DELIGHT ('Andeli')
Rosa FRAGRANT CLOUD ('Tanellis')
Rosa GERTRUDE JEKYLL ('Ausbord')
Rosa 'Korresia'

Rosa FRAGRANT CLOUD

Rosa L'AIMANT ('Harzola')
Rosa 'Madame Hardy'
Rosa 'Madame Isaac Pereire'
Rosa MARGARET MERRIL ('Harkuly')
Rosa NEW ZEALAND ('Macgenev')
Rosa PERCEPTION ('Harzippee')
Rosa 'Prima Ballerina'
Rosa 'Rose de Resht'
Rosa ROSEMARY HARKNESS
  ('Harrowbond')
Rosa 'Roseraie de l'Haÿ'
Rosa SCEPTER'D ISLE ('Ausland')
Rosa 'Wendy Cussons'

DECORATIVE HIPS

Rosa 'Fru Dagmar Hastrup'
Rosa 'Geranium'
Rosa glauca
Rosa rugosa 'Alba', *R. rugosa* 'Rubra'
Rosa 'Scabrosa'
Rosa 'Sealing Wax'

HEALTHIER ROSES

Roses with good disease resistance
Rosa ALEXANDER ('Harlex')
Rosa ANNE HARKNESS ('Harkaramel')
Rosa ARMADA ('Haruseful')
Rosa 'Arthur Bell'
Rosa 'Ballerina'
Rosa CHATSWORTH ('Tanotax')
Rosa 'Dortmund'
Rosa ELINA ('Dicjana')
Rosa ESCAPADE ('Harpade')
Rosa FELLOWSHIP ('Harwelcome')
Rosa GORDON'S COLLEGE
  ('Cocjabby')
Rosa HERTFORDSHIRE ('Kortenay')
Rosa LOVELY LADY ('Dicjubell')
Rosa MARJORIE FAIR ('Harhero')
Rosa MISTRESS QUICKLY ('Ausky')
Rosa OPEN ARMS ('Chewpixcel')

Rosa PINK FLOWER CARPET
  ('Noatraum')
Rosa QUEEN MOTHER ('Korquemu')
Rosa ROSE GAUJARD ('Gaumo')
Rosa rugosa hybrids
Rosa SAVOY HOTEL ('Harvintage')
Rosa SURREY ('Korlanum')
Rosa 'The Fairy'
Rosa WINE AND DINE ('Dicuncle')

MIXED FLOWER BORDERS

Front of border
Rosa AVON ('Poulmulti')
Rosa BABY LOVE ('Scrivluv')
Rosa BERKSHIRE ('Korpinka')
Rosa HERTFORDSHIRE ('Kortenay')
Rosa KENT ('Poulcov')
Rosa 'Mevrouw Nathalie Nypels'
Rosa PRINCESS OF WALES
  ('Hardinkum')
Rosa 'The Fairy'
Rosa THE TIMES ROSE ('Korpeahn')
Rosa VALENTINE HEART ('Dicogle')

Middle ground
Rosa ANNA LIVIA ('Kormetter')
Rosa ARMADA ('Haruseful')
Rosa 'Ballerina'
Rosa BETTY HARKNESS ('Harette')
Rosa BONICA ('Meidomonac')
Rosa 'Buff Beauty'
Rosa ESCAPADE ('Harpade')
Rosa FRIEND FOR LIFE ('Cocnanne')
Rosa 'Fru Dagmar Hastrup'
Rosa gallica 'Versicolor'
Rosa HERITAGE ('Ausblush')
Rosa ICEBERG ('Korbin')
Rosa JACQUELINE DU PRÉ
  ('Harwanna')
Rosa MARJORIE FAIR ('Harhero')
Rosa 'Penelope'
Rosa ROSY CUSHION ('Interall')

Middle to rear
Rosa 'Cornelia'
Rosa 'Fantin-Latour'

Rosa GERTRUDE JEKYLL

Rosa 'Felicia'
Rosa GERTRUDE JEKYLL ('Ausbord')
Rosa 'Golden Wings'
Rosa GRAHAM THOMAS ('Ausmas')
Rosa 'Marguerite Hilling'
Rosa 'Nevada'
Rosa 'Roseraie de l'Haÿ'
Rosa 'Sally Holmes'
Rosa WESTERLAND ('Korwest')

SOUTH- AND WEST-FACING WALLS

Rosa ALTISSIMO ('Delmur')
Rosa ANTIQUE ('Kordalen')
Rosa BREATH OF LIFE ('Harquanne')
Rosa CLAIR MATIN ('Meimont')
Rosa 'Compassion'
Rosa CRIMSON CASCADE
  ('Fryclimbdown')
Rosa 'Danse du Feu'
Rosa 'Dreaming Spires'
Rosa DUBLIN BAY ('Macdub')
Rosa GOOD AS GOLD
  ('Chewsunbeam')
Rosa HIGH HOPES ('Haryup')
Rosa 'Madame Alfred Carrière'
Rosa 'New Dawn'
Rosa PENNY LANE ('Hardwell')
Rosa SUMMER WINE ('Korizont')
Rosa 'White Cockade'

NORTH- AND EAST-FACING WALLS

For structures over 2m (6ft)
Rosa 'Albéric Barbier'
Rosa 'Compassion'
Rosa 'Dortmund'
Rosa 'Morning Jewel'
Rosa 'New Dawn'

For areas up to 2m (6ft)
Rosa ARMADA ('Haruseful')
Rosa 'Chinatown'
Rosa 'Cornelia'
Rosa 'Penelope'
Rosa 'Prosperity'

ATTRACTIVE FOLIAGE

Rosa fedtschenkoana
Rosa glauca
Rosa gymnocarpa var.
  willmottiae
Rosa nitida
Rosa primula
Rosa sericea subsp. *omeiensis*
  f. *pteracantha*
Rosa virginiana

GROUND-COVER ROSES

Rosa AVON ('Poulmulti')
Rosa BERKSHIRE ('Korpinka')
Rosa HERTFORDSHIRE ('Kortenay')
Rosa RED BLANKET ('Intercell')
Rosa ROSY CUSHION ('Interall')
Rosa SURREY ('Korlanum')
Rosa SWANY ('Meiburenac')

SPECIMEN SHRUB ROSES

Rosa 'Cerise Bouquet'
Rosa 'Complicata'
Rosa 'Felicia'
Rosa 'Fritz Nobis'
Rosa 'Marguerite Hilling'
Rosa 'Nevada'

Rosa 'Scabrosa'
Rosa xanthina 'Canary Bird'

ARCHES AND PILLARS

Rosa 'Aloha'
Rosa ALTISSIMO ('Delmur')
Rosa 'Bantry Bay'
Rosa BRIDGE OF SIGHS
  ('Harglowing')
Rosa CITY GIRL ('Harzorba')
Rosa 'Compassion'
Rosa 'Dortmund'
Rosa 'Dreaming Spires'
Rosa DUBLIN BAY ('Macdub')
Rosa 'Golden Showers'
Rosa 'Goldfinch'
Rosa LAURA FORD ('Chewarvel')
Rosa 'Leverkusen'

Rosa CITY GIRL

Rosa 'New Dawn'
Rosa 'Phyllis Bide'
Rosa ROSALIE CORAL ('Chewallop')
Rosa 'Veilchenblau'
Rosa WARM WELCOME ('Chewizz')

PERGOLAS

Rosa 'Albéric Barbier'
Rosa 'Albertine'
Rosa 'Alister Stella Gray'
Rosa 'Climbing Cécile Brünner'
Rosa 'Easlea's Golden Rambler'
Rosa 'Emily Gray'
Rosa 'Félicité Perpétue'
Rosa 'François Juranville'
Rosa HIGH HOPES ('Haryup')
Rosa 'Madame Alfred Carrière'
Rosa 'Madame Grégoire Staechelin'
Rosa 'Maigold'
Rosa 'Sander's White Rambler'
Rosa 'Sympathie'

ROSES TO GROW UP TREES

Rosa 'Bobbie James'
Rosa 'Blush Rambler'
Rosa 'Emily Gray'
Rosa filipes 'Kiftsgate'
Rosa mulliganii
Rosa 'Paul's Himalayan Musk'
Rosa 'Rambling Rector'
Rosa 'Seagull'
Rosa soulieana
Rosa 'Treasure Trove'

Soil preparation and planting

GROWING roses in the garden is not difficult if their basic needs are satisfied. They are relatively long-lived flowering plants, so it is worth investing time and effort in choosing a suitable site, properly preparing the soil, selecting cultivars appropriate to the conditions, and planting the roses correctly.

Site and aspect

All roses need a site that is open to the sun and sheltered from strong winds, with good air circulation and a fertile soil. They do not thrive in deep shade, under trees, if crowded by other plants, or in "rose-sick" (see right) or waterlogged soil. Most sites may be improved to meet these needs, for example by erecting windbreaks or by draining heavy, wet soils (see SOILS AND FERTILIZERS, "Improving drainage", p.623). Planting roses in an appropriate compost in raised beds or containers may solve the problem of unsuitable soil.

Evaluate the planting site carefully before choosing a cultivar: the enormous variety of the rose family provides plants that tolerate a range of conditions. Most modern roses do not flourish on chalk, but almost all the old garden roses grow well in alkaline conditions if given large quantities of organic material when being planted and mulched. *Rosa rugosa* and *R. pimpinellifolia* groups do well on sandy soil. These are generalizations since even among modern roses there may be great differences between cultivars: for example, on poor soils 'Just Joey' and FULTON MACKAY ('Cocdana') suffer but SAVOY HOTEL ('Harvintage'), THE TIMES ROSE ('Korpeahn'), and others thrive if given extra food and moisture. Certain rootstocks may help in some circumstances: for example *R. canina* tolerates and often grows well in heavy, cold soils.

Soil quality

Roses grow in most types of soil, but prefer slightly acid conditions, about pH 6.5. A water-retentive yet well-drained soil is best of all. Always clear weeds when preparing the soil to avoid the young roses having to compete with them for light, moisture, and nutrients.

Improving the soil

The drainage of clay soils, water-retentiveness of light, sandy soils, and pH level of alkaline soils may be improved by incorporating plenty of organic matter. If, on chalk, the topsoil is very shallow, excavate it to about 60cm (24in) when planting, and replace some of the chalk with extra organic matter. For further information on how to influence the soil acidity, and on general soil preparation, see "Soil cultivation", pp.618–621. If possible, prepare the soil approximately three months before planting to allow it to settle.

Rose-sick soil

New roses do not thrive if planted in a rosebed where roses have been grown for two years or more, as they will almost always succumb to "rose sickness" (see "Replant disease/soil sickness", p.665): it seems that the fine feeding roots of new roses are more prone to attack than are the older, tougher roots of roses that are already growing in the bed.

If replacing only one or two roses in an established bed, dig a hole at least 45cm (18in) deep by 60cm (24in) across and exchange the soil with some from a part of the garden where roses have not grown for several years. As this is a daunting task to carry out for an entire rosebed, either locate the bed on a different site, or have the soil chemically sterilized by a qualified contractor.

Choosing roses

Where and how you buy roses will depend to some extent on the particular cultivars that you wish to buy. Many old roses are obtainable only from specialist nurseries, by mail-order if they are not situated locally. Bear in mind that catalogue photographs may not always accurately represent the colour of the flower, nor is it possible to assess the quality of the plant before it arrives, although with a reputable nursery this should not be a problem. Beware of special "bargains", often advertised in the press, that offer bedding or hedging roses cheaply as the plants may be of poor quality.

Nurseries in the UK now generally use *R.* 'Laxa' as a stock, since it is comparatively sucker-free and does well on most soils. Rootstocks may be purchased by those wishing to bud their own roses (see also "Hybridizing", pp.168–169).

Bare-root roses

Mail-order suppliers, stores, and supermarkets sell roses with bare roots, sometimes packaged in plastic. The bare-root roses are in a semi-dormant or dormant state and their roots are virtually clean of soil. Provided that they have not dried out in transit and are planted as soon as possible after arrival, they should establish perfectly satisfactorily.

When buying a bare-root rose in a store, examine it carefully. If the environment in which the rose has been kept is too warm, the rose either dries out or starts growing prematurely, producing blanched, thin shoots that usually die after planting. Do not purchase any roses that display such symptoms.

Container-grown roses

Roses grown in containers may be planted at any time, except during periods of prolonged drought or when the ground is frozen. Many garden centres and suppliers trim the roots of unsold bare-root roses and pot them into containers for convenience of sale; before buying a rose in a container, check that it has not been recently potted up by holding the plant by its main shoot and gently shaking it. If the rose is not firmly rooted and moves about in the compost, it probably has not been grown in its container.

Suppliers whose priority is quick, convenient production tend to select roses that fit into standard-sized containers rather than picking the largest and best plants. These roses are acceptable provided that they are in general good health and do not have spindly, weak growth. Treat them as bare-root roses where

SELECTING HEALTHY ROSES

A bare-root bush rose
GOOD EXAMPLE

Strong bud union

Good network of fibrous roots

BAD EXAMPLE

Spindly, damaged shoots

Stunted root system

A container-grown rose
GOOD EXAMPLE

Vigorous foliage of a good colour

Healthy root system

BAD EXAMPLE

Spindly shoots

Black spot

Dead or dying leaves

Weeds

A standard rose
GOOD EXAMPLE

Strong, healthy shoots, evenly distributed

Sturdy, well-balanced top-growth

Moist compost

Stem has been securely staked by grower

Straight stem

BAD EXAMPLE

Dead wood

Unbalanced, one-sided head

PLANTING DISTANCES FOR A ROSE HEDGE

Tall hedging roses
Plant the roses in a line 1–1.2m (3–4ft) apart, so that, when mature, the branches intermingle to form an effective screen.

Modern bush roses
For a denser hedge, plant roses in a staggered formation in 2 rows, 45–60cm (18–24in) apart.

storage and planting are concerned. If any roots are growing through the drainage holes in the container, knock the plant out of its pot and check that its roots are not thickly coiled around the root ball – a sign that the rose is pot-bound and has been in the container for too long.

Selecting a healthy rose

Whether bare-root or container-grown, the plant should have at least two or three strong, firm shoots and a healthy network of roots in good proportion to the top-growth. Any foliage on container-grown roses should be vigorous. If buying a climbing rose, check that the shoots are healthy and at least 30cm (12in) long. Choose a standard rose with a balanced head since it is likely to be viewed from all sides; a straight stem is best, although a slightly crooked stem is acceptable.

Preparing to plant

Following a few simple principles at the planting stage, such as observing correct planting distances and depths, handling the roots carefully, and providing proper support where necessary, avoids problems with routine care later on. Delay planting for a few days if the ground is too wet, frozen, or too dry for roots to adjust easily to the soil.

When to plant bare-root roses

Bare-root roses are best planted just before or at the beginning of their dormant period, in late autumn or early winter, to lessen the shock of transplanting. Early spring may be better in areas that suffer from bad winters. Plant the roses as soon as possible after purchase. If there is any delay, perhaps because of unsuitable weather, it is best to heel them into a spare piece of ground,

with the roots buried in a shallow trench (see ORNAMENTAL TREES, *Heeling in*, p.65). Alternatively, store the roses in a cool and frost-free place, and keep the roots moist.

When to plant container-grown roses

These may be planted at any time of the year in suitable weather conditions. Container-grown roses, unlike bare-root roses, may be left outdoors in their containers for three weeks or more while awaiting planting, as long as they are kept properly watered. Even though they are frost hardy, do not risk exposing them to prolonged frost as the roots in the containers may suffer some damage in very cold conditions.

Spacing bedding roses

The growth habit determines the planting distances between bedding roses. Over-close planting makes mulching, spraying, and pruning more difficult and may create stagnant air conditions which allow rapid spread of mildew and black spot. A narrow, upright cultivar needs less space for healthy growth than a lax, spreading one and so tolerates closer planting. Plant the bushes 45–60cm (18–24in) apart and about 30cm (12in) from the edge of the rosebed.

If underplanting modern roses or very large species roses, allow more space, about 75–120cm (2½–4ft), depending on their ultimate size and growth habit. Space miniature roses roughly 30cm (12in) apart, according to the varying spread and final height of the plants.

Spacing roses for a hedge

The size and growth habit of the chosen cultivar governs the position of roses in forming a hedge. To gain uniformly dense growth, plant tall, hedging roses such as 'Penelope' and 'Golden Wings', which reach

1.2m (4ft) or more across, in a single line, and modern bush roses such as ALEXANDER ('Harlex') in two rows in a staggered formation.

Planting a bush rose

The first stage in planting a rose is to prepare the plant. If the roots of a bare-root rose look dry, soak the plant in a bucket of water for an hour or two until thoroughly moist. Place a container-grown rose in a bucket of water until the compost surface appears moist. If the root ball is wrapped in plastic or hessian, cut away the wrapping carefully. Remove any loose compost, gently tease out the roots, and prune any damaged or diseased roots or shoots; on bare-root roses, remove any buds or hips and most remaining leaves.

Make a planting hole that is wide enough to accommodate the roots or root ball, and deep enough so that, when planted, the bud union of the rose is about 2.5cm (1in) below

ground level or 1cm (½in) for miniature roses. The bud union is easily recognizable as a bulge at the base of the shoots where the cultivar has been grafted onto the rootstock.

Add a planting mixture of garden compost, soil, and a little general fertilizer to the base of the planting hole. Position the rose in the centre of the hole and check that the planting depth is correct. If the roots of a bare-root rose all point in one direction, place the rose close to one side of the hole and fan the roots out as widely as possible. Then fill the rest of the hole with the soil that was removed from it, shaking the rose a little to allow the soil to settle around the roots or root ball.

Tread the rose in firmly, but not too hard. Use the toe rather than the heel to apply the right amount of pressure, especially on heavy soil that might easily become compacted. Take care not to damage the shoots. Label and water well, but do not mulch until the following spring (see "Mulching roses", p.159).

HOW TO PLANT A BARE-ROOT BUSH ROSE

1 *Remove diseased or damaged growth. Cut out any crossing shoots and thin or straggly stems at the base to produce a balanced shape. Trim any thick roots by about one third.*

2 *Dig the planting hole in a prepared bed and fork half a bucketful of organic compost, mixed with a small handful of general fertilizer, into the bottom of the hole.*

3 *Place the rose in the centre of the hole and spread out the roots evenly. Lay a cane across the hole to check that the bud union will be 2.5cm (1in) below soil level when the rose is planted.*

4 *Fill in the hole with soil, firming with your hands in stages to ensure that there are no air pockets among the roots. Lightly tread down the surrounding soil. Rake over the soil and water well.*

HOW TO PLANT A CLIMBING ROSE

1 *Place the rose in the planting hole, leaning it towards the wall at an angle of about 45° so that the shoots reach the lowest support wire. Place a cane across the hole to check the planting depth.*

2 *Use canes to guide the shorter shoots towards the wires. Tie all the shoots to the canes or wires with plastic straps (see inset).*

Planting a climbing rose or a rambler

Train climbers grown against a wall or fence along horizontal wires that are about 45cm (18in) apart and held in place by tapered vine eyes or strong nails driven into the surface. If the brickwork or masonry of a wall is very hard, drill holes for the vine eyes with a 4.7mm (³⁄₁₆in) bit. Keep the wires 7cm (3in) away from the wall to allow air circulation and discourage diseases.

The ground next to a wall is likely to be dry, since it is in a rain shadow and the masonry absorbs moisture from the soil. Plant about 45cm (18in) from the wall where the soil is less dry and water from any eaves will not constantly drip on the rose.

Prepare the soil and planting hole, and trim the rose as for bush roses. Position the plant, leaning it towards the wall at 45°, and fan out its roots towards moist ground. If necessary, train the shoots along canes pushed into the ground, but keep each cane far enough from the roots to avoid damaging them.

After filling in and firming, as for a bush rose, attach the shoots to the support wires with the small, ready-made, plastic straps that are designed for tying in roses. Take care not to tighten the straps too much around the rose's stems as room must be left for the shoots to grow.

Do not prune the main shoots of a climber at this stage: wait until the beginning of the next growing season before lightly pruning, and be prepared to wait a year or two before the rose begins to climb. In the first year, keep the roots thoroughly watered and uncrowded by other plants to help them establish.

Planting a rambler by a tree

It is essential to match the vigour of the rose to that of the tree in which it is to grow, as the considerable weight of some ramblers is quite capable of pulling over a small or weak tree.

Plant a rose that is to scramble up a tree on the windward side of the tree so that the rose's young, flexible shoots blow towards and around the tree, rather than away from it. Dig a planting hole at least 1m (3ft) away from the trunk to increase the amount of rain that reaches the roots of the rose. Train all the new shoots towards the tree along sloping canes, carefully but securely tied at their upper ends to the trunk, the other ends inserted just behind the rose. If planting in this way on a boundary, bear in mind that the blooms grow towards, and are visible from, the direction of the strongest sunlight.

Planting a standard rose

Most nurseries bud their standard roses on *Rosa rugosa* stocks which have a tendency to sucker, although a few nurseries are experimenting with other rootstocks. To keep suckering to a minimum, plant the rose no deeper than the soil mark: deeper planting will increase sucker growths. If necessary, trim off the top layer of roots so that the bottom layer does not sit too deeply in the soil.

A standard rose needs a stake, placed on the side of the prevailing wind, to support it. Paint the whole stake with a preservative that is not toxic to plants and allow it to dry. Insert the stake very firmly near the centre of the planting hole before positioning the rose, so as to avoid damaging the roots and thereby encouraging suckers. Position the rose next to the stake and check that it just reaches the base of the lowest branches; if necessary, adjust the height of the stake. Use a cane or rake handle to make sure the soil mark and soil surface are level.

Fill in and firm the soil as for a bush rose. Secure the stem to the stake with two rose ties – these should incorporate a buffer to prevent the stake from rubbing the stem – but do not tighten them fully until the rose has settled in the soil. The ties will need to be loosened at least once during the growing season as the diameter of the stem increases.

Planting roses in containers

The container should be at least 30–45cm (12–18in) deep for bush roses or 23–35cm (9–14in) deep for miniatures to allow for root growth. Place a layer of crocks over the drainage holes and fill the container with a standard, loam-based potting compost. Plant in the same way, and at the correct depth, as for bush roses (see p.157). See also "Planting large and long-term plants", pp.324–326.

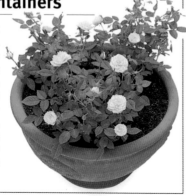

HOW TO PLANT A STANDARD ROSE

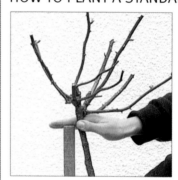

1 *Position the stake in the hole so that the rose stem will be in the centre. Drive the stake into the ground and check that the top is just below the head of the rose.*

2 *Place a cane across the hole to check the planting depth. Use the old soil mark on the stem as a guide and plant at the same depth. Fill in the hole and firm.*

3 *Use a rose tie (see inset) just below the head of the rose and another halfway up the stem to attach the rose to the stake. Cut out weak or crossing shoots.*

Routine care

Roses need regular care to produce healthy, vigorous plants that are resistant to pests and diseases. Attention paid to fertilizing, watering, mulching, weeding, and maintenance will be rewarded with a fine display throughout the season.

Fertilizing

Roses are gross feeders and quickly exhaust even a well-prepared rose-bed rich in nutrients. Many essential mineral salts rapidly leach out in the rain, especially from light soils. To flourish, roses require regular feeds in a balanced formulation of essential nutrients (nitrogen, phosphates, and potassium) and trace elements. Many suitable proprietary compound rose fertilizers are available. For information on how to deal with particular nutrient deficiencies, see Plant Problems, pp.639–673.

After pruning in the spring, and when the soil is moist, sprinkle a small handful or 25–50g (1–2oz) of fertilizer around each rose. Hoe or rake it in lightly and evenly, keeping it clear of the stems. Repeat the application about a month after midsummer, when the roses are developing a second flush of bloom. Do not apply a general feed later in the year, because this encourages soft autumn growth that may suffer frost damage. A dressing of sulphate of potash, however, applied at a rate of 60g/sq m (2oz/sq yd) in early autumn, protects late shoots by helping them to ripen.

Foliar feeding (spraying a liquid feed on the leaves and bypassing the roots) is usually only needed to obtain extra-large blooms and leaves on exhibition roses. It may help, however, in a prolonged drought or on chalky soils: in both instances, roses may have difficulty in taking in nourishment through the roots.

Roses in containers soon use up the compost nutrients. Compensate for this loss by top-dressing annually with a balanced fertilizer and foliar feeding once or twice in the growing season to maintain vigorous growth.

Watering

Roses need plenty of water for healthy growth, especially if newly planted. Watering too little and too often can be counter-productive as it encourages roots to grow towards the surface and compete for water and light; instead, give the roses a good bucketful of water to soak the soil thoroughly around their roots.

Roses are deep-rooted plants and can flourish in long, dry summers and near-drought conditions, particularly if they are well established. In such conditions, the flowers may be smaller than usual and may open very quickly. The petals may also be vulnerable to scorching by the sun. During the flowering season, do not water roses in strong light as the blooms may spoil. Water roses in containers every other day, or daily in exceptionally hot and dry weather.

Mulching roses

An 8cm (3in) layer of mulch applied in early spring after pruning and feeding helps to smother any weed seeds, and maintain high moisture levels and even temperatures in the

Suckers and how to deal with them

Suckers are shoots that grow below the bud union, directly from the rootstock onto which a cultivar has been grafted. They are usually narrower and a much lighter green than those of the cultivar, often with thorns of a different shape or colour, and paler green leaves may have seven or more leaflets.

Remove suckering shoots as soon as they appear, to prevent the rootstock from wasting energy on the sucker's growth at the expense of the cultivar. Some rootstocks produce suckers more readily than others, especially if they have been planted at the wrong depth. Root damage, caused by severe frosts or accidental nicks from hoes, other implements, or a stake, may also stimulate the production of suckers.

Pull the sucker to detach it from the rootstock: this removes any dormant buds that may be present at the point where it joins the roots. Do not cut it, as this is the equivalent of pruning it and only encourages more vigorous sucker growth. However, it may sometimes be necessary to cut a sucker if it originates from beneath the rose and if pulling it off would mean damaging or lifting the rose.

Shoots on stems of standard roses are also suckers, as the stem is part of the rootstock. They normally have the dull, dark green leaves typical of *Rosa rugosa*. Snap them off or pare them from the stem with a knife.

On standards, pull away any suckers growing from the stem, taking care not to rip the bark.

REMOVING A SUCKER FROM A BUSH ROSE

1 *Carefully scrape away soil to expose the top of the rootstock. Check the suspect shoot arises from below the bud union.*

2 *Using a glove to protect your hand, pull the sucker away from the rootstock. Refill the hole and gently firm the soil.*

HOW SUCKERS GROW

Sucker

The sucker (right) grows directly from the rootstock. If only cut back at ground level it will shoot again and divert further energy from the rose.

Growing roses the organic way

Organically grown roses need the same soil preparation and treatment before planting as those grown non-organically, but ensure manures, compost, and other materials are from organic sources. Mulch in spring with mature, friable compost to a depth of 8–10cm (3–4in); this improves soil structure and helps increase beneficial soil organisms, particularly mycorrhizal fungi, that assist in water and nutrient uptake.

When planting rosebeds, leave an adequate distance between plants to ensure good air circulation; spacing varies depending on the vigour and size of mature species and cultivars. This helps prevent the spread of diseases, such as black spot, rose rust, and powdery mildew. Applications of sulphur dust may help to discourage these diseases, but it is vital to prune out and destroy infected shoots, and dispose of all infected fallen leaves. A few roses are reasonably disease-resistant, including 'Charles de Mills', 'Buff Beauty', 'Maigold', 'Fritz Nobis', and *R. filipes* 'Kiftsgate'.

Pests such as greenfly may be controlled partially using insecticidal soaps or pyrethrum. Encouraging their natural predators, like ladybirds and lacewings, by providing over-wintering sites is likely to reduce pest populations.

soil. Well-rotted stable manure is an ideal mulch, providing many of the nutrients that roses need, but if this proves difficult to obtain, bark chips or cocoa shells are both satisfactory alternatives. For further details, see also SOILS AND FERTILIZERS, "Top-dressings and mulches", p.626.

Dead-heading

Removing faded flowers stimulates the earliest possible development of new, young shoots and more blooms during the flowering season. Once a rose flower has been fertilized, it soon fades, and, if left on the plant, may delay the production of new shoots below the old flower cluster.

In some roses, a seed pod or hip forms, and this diverts energy from further flower production; remove the dead flowers regularly unless you require the hips for ornamental purposes. In autumn, even if some roses continue to bloom, stop dead-heading to avoid encouraging new, soft growth which would be damaged by the first frosts.

Moving roses

A rose may be moved at almost any age, but the older it is the greater is the risk that it may resettle badly. The roots of older roses are thick and spread deeply, and also have fewer of the fine feeding roots that are essential for re-establishing the plant. It is not difficult to move roses that are up to three or four years old, but do not

Blind shoots

These are shoots that develop without a terminal flower bud. They divert the plant's energy in the same way as a sucker (see "Suckers and how to deal with them", p.159), so prune any out as soon as they appear.

Cut the blind shoot by about a half to an outward-facing bud to encourage it to grow away and flower. If no bud is visible, cut back to the main stem.

HOW TO DEAD-HEAD ROSES

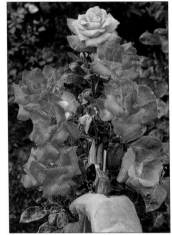

1 **Floribunda roses** *The central bloom of a truss will fade first and should be cut out to maintain the display.*

2 *When all the flowers have faded, remove the whole truss by cutting back to an emerging bud or fully formed shoot.*

Hybrid Tea roses *Cut back stems with faded flowers to an outward-facing bud (see inset) or fully formed shoot.*

risk planting in old rosebeds (see "Rose-sick soil", p.156).

If circumstances allow, move a rose only when it is dormant and always into a well-prepared bed. First loosen the soil by cutting down on all sides with a spade at least 25cm (10in) out from the root ball. Insert a fork well away from the centre of the plant and lift it, taking a good ball of soil with it and disturbing the roots as little as possible; on light soils, use a spade as the soil is likely to fall away from the roots. Trim off any coarse roots and wrap the root ball in plastic or hessian to prevent the roots from drying out; water immediately after replanting and regularly until the rose is established.

Autumn cut-back

Strong winds may loosen the roots, making roses vulnerable to frost damage. In heavy soils, compacted earth may form into a small funnel around the base of the stem and fill up with water that later freezes. The expansion of the water as it freezes may damage the bud union – the most vulnerable part of the rose. To prevent this, shorten tall Hybrid Tea or Floribunda bushes in autumn.

Winter protection

In temperate climates, roses need protection only in a very bad winter. In very extreme climates, severe winters can kill roses outright if they are not protected; any plants that do

survive have to make completely new growth each year and will have a very short flowering season.

Hybrid Tea and Floribunda roses tolerate temperatures as low as -10 to -12°C (10–14°F) for a week or so if soil is mounded over the crown. Pack the crowns of standards with straw or bracken. In colder conditions provide more protection, or choose roses that tolerate extreme cold. Roses hardy between -20 and -23°C (-4 to -10°F) include Bourbon, Centifolia, and China roses, *Rosa californica*, and *R. wichurana*. Grow Alba, Damask, and Gallica roses, and some species roses, like *R. foetida* and *R. palustris*, if temperatures fall to -30°C (-22°F).

A few roses, such as *R. virginiana, R. blanda, R. canina, R. glauca,* and *R. rugosa*, survive cold as severe as -37°C (-35°F). For full instructions on protecting roses, see FROST AND WIND PROTECTION, pp.612–613.

Pests and diseases

Aphids (p.646), powdery mildew (p.646), rose die-back (p.665), black spot (see "Bacterial leaf spots and blotches", p.648), and rusts (pp.648 and 653) are common problems; spray as a precaution if necessary. Inspect roses regularly, and act as soon as symptoms become apparent.

CUTTING BACK IN THE AUTUMN

Before (*left*) *In mid- to late autumn, cut back Hybrid Tea and Floribunda roses that are over 75cm (2½ft) in height (left) to avoid the effects of wind-rock.*

After (*below*) *Reduce the entire bush by a half to one third of its height, cutting all shoots above a bud.*

Pruning and training

T HE purpose of pruning is to speed up the natural process of new, vigorous, disease-free shoots developing to replace the old, weakened ones, and so produce an attractive shape and the optimum display of blooms. Training a plant on supports stimulates the production of flowering sideshoots and directs new growth into the given space. The severity of pruning depends on the rose type; certain principles of pruning, however, apply to all roses.

Basic principles of pruning roses

A pair of sharp, high-quality secateurs is essential; long-handled pruners and a fine-toothed pruning saw are also useful for removing gnarled, woody stumps and thicker shoots. Wear strong, protective gloves for all pruning tasks.

How to prune

Always make a clean, angled cut above a bud that faces in the direction in which the resultant new shoot should develop. This is usually an outward-facing bud, but it may face inwards on a lax, spreading rose if the centre of the bush needs filling out. Cut to the appropriate height if a dormant bud is not visible, and cut out any stubs that develop later.

Remove dead and dying shoots, cutting back to disease-free, white pith, even if this means pruning almost to ground level; also cut out crossing growths that might prevent the free circulation of light and air into the centre of the plants.

Opinions differ as to whether to prune bush roses further. The Royal National Rose Society has been conducting pruning trials to assess the merits of different pruning methods. Whereas the traditional practice is to remove all thin, twiggy growths that seem incapable of producing flowering shoots, the trial results indicate that it may, in fact, be beneficial to leave them on the plant, because they tend to come into leaf early, and thus provide a valuable source of energy to the rose at the beginning of the growing season.

When to prune

Prune roses when they are dormant or semi-dormant, that is between autumn leaf-fall and when the buds are just beginning to break in the spring. Pruning a rose in active growth is sometimes necessary but severely checks growth. Do not prune in frosty conditions as the growth bud below the cut may be damaged and the shoot may die back. Following a very severe winter, cut back frost-damaged shoots in spring to a healthy bud; if the winters are always severe, prune roses in spring, immediately after removing any winter protection material. Conversely, in a climate so warm that the roses flower almost continuously, prune them in the cooler months to induce dormancy and give them an artificial period of rest.

MAKING A PRUNING CUT

Position the thin blade of the secateurs just above the bud. Take care not to make the cut too far from the bud, or leave a snag, because disease may enter the stem and cause die-back. If this happens, cut back the shoot as far as is necessary to reach good, healthy wood.

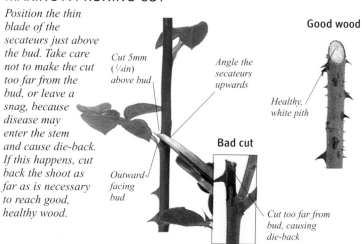

Cut 5mm (¼in) above bud

Angle the secateurs upwards

Good wood

Healthy, white pith

Bad cut

Outward-facing bud

Cut too far from bud, causing die-back

HOW TO PRUNE A HYBRID TEA ROSE

Prune the rose fairly hard, in autumn or spring, by trimming off any unproductive growth and then reducing the main shoots to form a strong, balanced framework.

Cut out crossing and congested stems, to create an open-centred plant.

Remove dead wood and any that shows signs of damage or disease.

Prune main shoots to within about 20–25cm (8–10in) of ground level.

Pruning roses after planting

Almost all newly planted roses should be pruned hard to encourage the development of vigorous shoot and root systems. Climbing roses are the exception to this rule – give them only a light, cosmetic pruning in the first year to remove any weak, dead, or damaged shoots. Remove any weak, dead, or crossing growth from standard roses. Less severe pruning and regular fertilizing are preferable for roses grown in soils that are deficient in nutrients.

PRUNING A NEWLY PLANTED BUSH ROSE

Prune a newly planted bush rose to about 8cm (3in) above ground level. Cut back to outward-facing buds and remove any frost-damaged growth.

Modern garden bush roses

Modern roses flower on new or the current season's growth, so they are pruned fairly severely to stimulate vigorous, new shoots and to produce a good display of blooms.

Hybrid Tea roses

Remove dead, damaged, and diseased shoots, cutting back to healthy growth. Twiggy shoots may be left on the plant, if desired (see "How to prune", left). Use long-handled pruners or loppers to cut away any stumps from previous prunings that, although healthy, have not subsequently produced any worthwhile new growth.

Thin out any weak or crossing shoots from the centre of the bush to leave a well-balanced framework and allow free air circulation. It is not as important to produce a balanced framework with bedding roses planted close together as with one that is grown as a specimen, and is seen from all sides.

In temperate climates, the main shoots should then be pruned back to between 20–25cm (8–10in) for general display purposes, but in extremely mild areas, the shoots may be cut down less severely to about 45–60cm (18–24in). To achieve blooms that are of exhibition quality, cut the main shoots hard back to leave only two or three buds.

Floribunda and Polyantha roses

When pruning these types of rose, cut out any unproductive wood as for Hybrid Tea roses (see p.161). Reduce any sideshoots by about one third on smaller cultivars and by two thirds on taller-growing cultivars, such as 'Sally Holmes'. Cut back the main shoots to 30–38cm (12–15in), but reduce the shoots of taller cultivars by about one third of their length. Do not prune them any harder, unless growing the roses for exhibition, since this reduces the number of blooms that will be produced in the following season.

Patio roses

These are smaller versions of the Floribunda roses, and should be pruned in autumn or spring following the same principles.

Miniature roses

There are two distinct methods of pruning miniature roses. The simpler of the two is to give them only the minimum of attention: remove shoots that have died back, thin out occasionally the shoots of those cultivars that produce a dense tangle of twiggy growth, and shorten any over-vigorous shoots that may throw the whole plant out of balance.

The second method is to treat the plants as if they were miniature Hybrid Tea or Floribunda roses. Cut back all growth except the strongest shoots, and then shorten these by about one third. This method is used satisfactorily for cultivars introduced from the USA to the UK that do not adapt easily to their new conditions. Such plants benefit from the extra stimulus of a severe pruning and produce strong, new growth. It can also improve poor shape (see below).

HOW TO PRUNE A FLORIBUNDA OR POLYANTHA ROSE

In autumn or spring, cut out unproductive growth and prune the sideshoots. Reduce the main shoots by a proportion suitable to the height of the cultivar.

Remove crossing or congested wood back to the main stem.

Prune out all dead, damaged, or diseased wood to a healthy bud.

Prune main shoots to 30–38cm (12–15in) from ground level.

Reduce sideshoots by one to two thirds, cutting to a bud.

Standard roses

Most standards are formed from Hybrid Tea or Floribunda bush cultivars or from small shrub roses that are budded onto a straight, unbranched stem, usually 1.1–1.2m (3½–4ft) high. Prune as for the bush or shrub rose equivalents, cutting back shoots by about one third, so that they are roughly equal in length. It is especially important with a standard rose to achieve a balanced head that looks pleasing from all sides. If the head is unbalanced, prune the shoots on the thicker side less hard so that they do not produce as much new growth as those on the thinner side.

Weeping standards

These roses are usually formed from cultivars of small-flowered ramblers grafted onto especially tall standard stems of about 1.5m (5ft). The flexible shoots are pendent and require only limited pruning: remove the old, flowered wood when the blooms have faded, leaving growth from the current season intact.

Shrub, species, and old garden roses

Although these vary enormously in their growth habit, most modern and old garden shrub roses, and all the species roses, flower on wood that is two or more years old. They should be pruned fairly lightly to leave the flowering wood intact. Many flower freely for years without any formal pruning if allowed to develop naturally. It is necessary only to cut out any dead, damaged, diseased, or weak wood to keep the roses really healthy. Despite this, some pruning may help to increase the number and quality of the blooms.

Give mature, remontant shrub roses, including Hybrid Musk and Tea roses, a light renewal pruning each winter by cutting down some of the older, main growths to the base. This encourages the production of vigorous, new basal shoots that will flower the following summer. Over a four-year period of renewal pruning, all the shoots are replaced and, with regular fertilizing, the bushes will remain free-flowering and healthy for many years. Treat non-remontant roses similarly but prune them immediately after flowering.

Rugosa and China roses may be given similar, annual, renewal pruning to keep them in good health.

HOW TO RESHAPE A MINIATURE ROSE

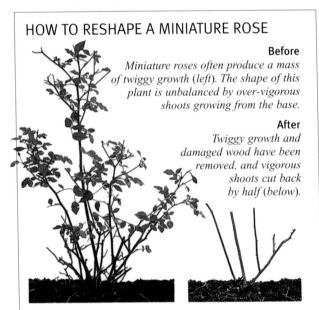

Before
Miniature roses often produce a mass of twiggy growth (left). The shape of this plant is unbalanced by over-vigorous shoots growing from the base.

After
Twiggy growth and damaged wood have been removed, and vigorous shoots cut back by half (below).

HOW TO PRUNE A STANDARD ROSE

Before
In the spring, prune a standard rose to prevent the plant from becoming too top-heavy and to retain an evenly shaped, floriferous head.

After
All dead and damaged wood, and any crossing stems, have been removed to leave healthy shoots. The main shoots have been reduced to 20–25cm (8–10in) and the sideshoots by about one third.

PRUNING A GALLICA ROSE

Throughout the flowering season, thin out the rose to keep it healthy. The annual pruning after flowering involves cutting back sideshoots, unproductive wood, and some older shoots to encourage new growth.

Thin out twiggy growth regularly, and remove spent blooms by cutting back to the main shoot.

Every 3–4 years, cut out up to one quarter of old main shoots at the base.

Shorten sideshoots, but not the main shoots, by about two thirds. Cut out any dead, diseased, or weak wood.

PRUNING ALBA, CENTIFOLIA, DAMASK, MOSS, AND PORTLAND ROSES

Prune after flowering, cutting back both main shoots and sideshoots. If necessary, prune again in late summer to remove any overlong shoots that have developed.

Reduce main shoots that are old and woody by one quarter to one third.

LATE SUMMER

Cut back any overlong, whippy shoots by about one third.

Prune sideshoots to about two thirds of their length.

Gallica roses

Many of these produce a twiggy tangle of shoots that should be regularly thinned out. After flowering, shorten the sideshoots only and remove any dead or diseased wood. Gently clip over Gallica roses used for hedging to maintain a tidy shape. Do not attempt to shape them into a formal hedge as this would remove many of the sideshoots on which flowers are borne the following year.

Species, Noisette, Scots, Sempervirens, and Sweet Briar roses

Much of the charm of these roses lies in their arching shoots which, in the second and subsequent years, carry flowers all along their length, often on short sideshoots. Formative pruning is needed to establish a balanced framework of strong, new growth. Thereafter these roses need only the removal of dead and diseased wood, unless they become too dense or produce few flowers, in which case renewal prune them in the same way as non-remontant shrub roses.

Severe pruning encourages strong vegetative growth but produces few, if any, flowers until the second year. If the bush becomes lopsided, reshape it after flowering and trim back all the overlong shoots.

Alba, Centifolia, Damask, Moss, and Portland roses

After flowering, reduce both main shoots and sideshoots. At the end of the summer, cut back any vigorous,

Ground-cover roses

The majority are low-growing, spreading, modern shrub roses, so renewal-prune them as for shrub roses. Some, mostly related to *Rosa wichurana* (a rambler), creep over the ground. Prune these only to stop them spreading beyond the space available (see also below).

Prune shoots to well within the intended area of spread, cutting to an upward-facing bud.

overlong shoots that might whip about in the wind and cause wind-rock damage to the roots.

Bourbon and Hybrid Perpetual roses

These are usually remontant, so prune them, and all hybrids derived from *Rosa rugosa*, in early spring as for Hybrid Tea roses (see p.161), but much more lightly.

Pegging down roses

This technique is an effective, although time-consuming, way of increasing flower production on Bourbon and Hybrid Perpetual roses that tend to send up long, ungainly shoots with flowers only at the tips. Instead of pruning the shoots in late summer or autumn, bend them over gently, taking great care not to snap them. Peg the shoots firmly into the ground. Alternatively, tie the tips to pegs in the ground, to wires strung between pegs, or to a low wire frame placed around the plant. Prune sideshoots on the pegged shoot to 10–15cm (4–6in).

This has much the same effect as horizontally training the shoots of climbing and rambler roses (see p.164) and produces an arching mound covered with a large number of flowering sideshoots in the following season.

Select long, non-flowering shoots and prune the soft tips. Gently bend each shoot over and fasten it to the soil with sturdy wire hoops (see inset).

Climbing roses and ramblers

These roses require minor pruning but regular annual training. Neither climbing nor rambler roses are self-supporting and, if trained incorrectly, may not flower freely and may become bare at their base. Some bush roses that send out large shoots at awkward angles, such as some Hybrid Musks, may also be trained against walls or other supports.

Climbing roses

In their first year, and in their second unless they have made exceptional growth, do not prune climbing roses except to remove any dead, diseased, or weak growth. Never prune climbing sports of bush roses (roses with the word "climbing" before the cultivar name, such as 'Climbing Shot Silk') in the first two years, since they may revert to the bush form if cut back hard too soon. Prune climbing miniature and Boursault roses in the same way as climbing roses.

Begin training as soon as the new shoots reach the supports; train them sideways along horizontal supports to encourage flowering. Where this is not possible, such as on a narrow area between a door and a window, choose a cultivar that is halfway between a tall shrub and a climbing rose. Many of these flower well from the plant base without special training: examples are 'Golden Showers', 'Joseph's Coat', and some more vigorous Bourbon roses.

Many climbing roses flower well for years with little pruning, except the removal of dead, diseased, or

HOW TO PRUNE AND TRAIN A CLIMBING ROSE

In the first two years after planting, restrict pruning to cutting out unproductive growth. From the third year, prune in autumn after flowering.

Reduce the sideshoots by about two thirds or about 15cm (6in), cutting above an outward-facing bud.

Tie all new shoots into horizontal wires 15–20cm (6–8in) apart: the shoots should not cross each other.

Remove any diseased, dead, or twiggy growth, cutting back to healthy wood or the main shoot.

twiggy growth. Prune them in the autumn, after flowering. Leave unpruned the strong main shoots unless they are exceeding their allotted space, in which case shorten them as appropriate. Otherwise simply shorten the sideshoots. Train in all the new season's growth to the supports while it is still flexible.

Occasional renewal pruning may be necessary if the base of a climbing rose becomes very bare. Cut back one or two of the older, main shoots to within 30cm (12in) or so above ground level to encourage vigorous new shoots to develop and replace the older growths. Repeat this as required in subsequent years.

Rambler roses

Like climbing roses, ramblers flower satisfactorily for a good many years without any formal pruning. They produce much more growth from the base than most climbers and, if not carefully trained, grow into a tangle of unmanageable shoots. This results in poor air circulation, which encourages the incidence of disease, and makes it extremely difficult to spray the plants thoroughly.

Prune ramblers in late summer. In the first two years, restrict pruning to cutting back all the sideshoots by about 7.5cm (3in) to a vigorous shoot; also remove dead or diseased wood. In later years, prune the rose

more heavily to maintain its framework. Untie all the shoots from their supports and, if possible, lay them on the ground. Cut no more than a quarter to one third of the oldest, spent shoots to ground level, leaving the new shoots and some older, but still vigorous, shoots for tying in to form a well-balanced framework.

Remove any unripe wood from the tips of the main shoots and cut back any sideshoots. Cut back any wayward shoots that are outgrowing the available space or spoiling the overall shape of the rose. Train in the shoots, as close to the horizontal as possible, to encourage flowering on new, short sideshoots that will develop all along the main shoots.

Training on arches, pergolas, pillars, and trees

Climbing roses or ramblers may be trained up pillars, arches, or pergolas. Twist the main shoots around the uprights to encourage flowering shoots to form low down. Carefully train the shoots in the direction of their natural growth before they have matured and hardened. This is vital for climbers that have stiff, semi-rigid shoots. Tie them in using twine or plastic rose ties; these are easy to undo when pruning or to loosen as the shoots develop. Once the main shoots reach the top of the support, regularly prune them to keep the rose within bounds.

An excess of overlong sideshoots may spoil the appearance of a pillar rose but a little additional pruning soon remedies this. Cut sideshoots back to three or four buds or by about 15cm (6in) in the spring.

HOW TO PRUNE AND TRAIN A MATURE RAMBLER ROSE

After the first two years, prune in late summer as soon as flowering is over, cutting out any dead, diseased, or weak wood. Then train in the new shoots.

Cut sideshoots down to leave between 2 and 4 healthy buds or shoots.

Cut back any old, spent shoots to ground level, using loppers.

Tie all shoots into the wires as close to the horizontal as possible. Secure any loose wires.

Propagation

Roses may be propagated in three main ways: by taking cuttings, by budding onto a rootstock, or from seed. Taking cuttings is the easiest method but it involves the longest wait: it takes about three years, except for miniature roses, for the new plant to become established. Budding needs rootstocks that have grown on in advance, but usually produces stronger and more vigorous plants. Many species roses (*Rosa glauca*, for example) readily breed true from seed. Cross hybrid roses with other hybrids, or sometimes with species, to produce new cultivars.

Hardwood cuttings

Most roses may be propagated from hardwood cuttings, in particular some cultivars that are related quite closely to wild species, such as rambler roses. Cuttings taken from miniature roses root so easily and develop so quickly that they are propagated in this way commercially. Hybrid Tea roses of complex parentage do not root so readily and may not be of sufficient size to sell commercially for two or three years, so they are seldom available on their own roots.

One advantage of roses grown from cuttings is that they do not have a different rootstock and so do not produce suckers. The disadvantages include a loss of vigour with some cultivars (although this may be useful with miniatures), and a tendency towards vigorous but non-flowering growth in the first few years, particularly with species roses. In many climates, roses from hardwood cuttings are the most reliable, but success in rooting them is variable; it is therefore sensible to take a good number of cuttings to allow for possible failures.

Preparing the cuttings

In early autumn, select material for cuttings from the current season's growth. Trim any old flowerheads from the chosen shoots and put the shoots into a transparent plastic bag to stop them from drying out. Prepare the cuttings by trimming off their leaves and shortening them to 23cm (9in). Breaking off the thorns will make the cuttings easier to handle. Moisten the base of each cutting, dip it into hormone rooting powder, and shake off the surplus.

Take shorter lengths of stem for miniature rose cuttings, which need be only 5–10cm (2–4in) long.

Preparing the cutting bed

Choose an open site for the cutting bed, preferably one that is sheltered from the midday sun. Single dig the area required, firm, and rake it to produce an even surface.

Inserting the cuttings

Make a series of planting holes, 15cm (6in) deep, with a cane or dibber, and trickle a little coarse sand into the bottom of each one to improve the drainage. Alternatively, dig a narrow, slit-like trench to the same depth and trickle sand along the base. On light, sandy soil, it is sufficient to push a spade vertically into the earth along a centre line, working it backwards and forwards to widen the slit.

Insert the cuttings vertically into the holes or trench, leaving about one third of their length above ground. They should be inserted far enough apart so that, once rooted, they may be lifted individually without disturbing adjacent cuttings. Firm and water the soil around the cuttings. In any dry spells that follow, water them again; after frost, which may loosen the roots in the ground, refirm the soil.

Another option is to root hardwood cuttings in deep pots of light, sandy soil. Plunge the pots in soil or sand in a shady outdoor site, and water them as needed. Growing bags or pots in a cold frame or cool greenhouse may be more convenient for miniature rose cuttings.

Development of the cuttings

During the autumn a callus should develop at the base of each cutting, from which the roots will be produced in spring. Once rooted, the young plants should develop strongly, but if flower buds form during the summer, remove them so that the plants can concentrate their energy on the production of new, strong, vegetative growth. The following autumn, if they are large enough, that is about 23–30cm (9–12in), transplant the young roses to their permanent positions; if they are not yet large enough, leave them to grow on for another year.

Semi-ripe cuttings

Semi-ripe cuttings may be more successful than hardwood cuttings in areas that are subject to severe winters. In the late summer after flowering, select mature sideshoots that are still green. Take 15cm (6in) lengths, cutting above a bud where the shoot is beginning to turn woody, and trim off the soft tips. Prepare cuttings about 10cm (4in) long, following the same procedure as for hardwood cuttings.

Insert them into deep pots of sandy compost (equal parts peat substitute, or peat, and sand). Cover the pots with plastic bags, or put them in a propagator, to prevent the cuttings from losing moisture, in a cool, frost-free place. In spring, plant out the rooted cuttings in a nursery bed.

HOW TO PROPAGATE ROSES FROM HARDWOOD CUTTINGS

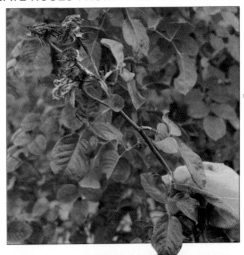

1 *Select a healthy, well-ripened shoot of roughly pencil thickness (here 'Dreaming Spires'), that has flowered in the summer and is about 30–60cm (12–24in) long. Remove it, cutting at an angle, just above an outward-facing bud. Prepare the cuttings by removing the leaves and soft tip wood.*

2 *Cut into 23cm (9in) lengths, making an angled cut above the top bud and a straight cut below the bottom bud. Dust the base with hormone rooting powder.*

3 *Make a row of planting holes 15cm (6in) deep and the same distance apart. In heavy soil, put a little coarse sand to a depth of about 2.5cm (1in) in each hole.*

4 *Insert a cutting into each hole: make sure that it reaches the bottom and that about 15cm (6in) of the cutting is buried. Firm the soil, water, and label the cuttings.*

5 *A year later, lift each rooted cutting with a hand fork, taking care not to damage the roots. Plant them in a bed or put them in a cold frame to grow on.*

HOW TO BUD-GRAFT A ROSE

1 Select a flowered shoot about 30cm (12in) long, with 3–4 growth buds. Remove it, making an angled cut above an outward-facing bud on the parent plant.

2 Hold the budwood so that the buds point downwards. Insert the knife 5mm (¼in) from a bud. With a scooping action, remove the bud with a 2.5cm (1in) long "tail".

3 Holding the scion by the tail, peel away the coarse wood from the green bark. Discard the wood. Trim off the tail, to leave a scion about 1cm (½in) long.

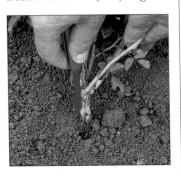

4 Clean the bark on the stem of the rootstock, by gently using a soft, dry cloth. This will remove any soil or grit, which could blunt the blade of the budding knife.

5 Make a 5mm (¼in) horizontal cut into the rootstock bark, 5–10cm (2–4in) above ground level. Then make a vertical cut upwards, to join the horizontal cut.

6 Using the reverse blade of the knife, gently prise open the flaps of bark created by the two cuts. The thin, green cambium will be revealed underneath.

7 Hold the scion by the leaf stalk and slip the tapered end under the bark flaps in the rootstock. Sit the bud neatly under the flaps: if needed, trim the scion across the top so it fits the T-cut.

8 To ensure close contact between scion and rootstock, secure a rubber grafting patch around the graft, pinning it on the side opposite the bud. The rubber patch will gradually rot away.

The following spring
In early spring, cut off the top of the rootstock, just above a dormant bud. For a multi-stemmed plant, cut back to 8cm (3in) the shoot emerging from the bud, in late spring.

T-BUDDING ONTO A STANDARD ROOTSTOCK

To create a standard rose with a well-balanced head, graft 2 or 3 buds, 8cm (3in) apart and staggered vertically, around the rootstock stem at the desired height – generally 1.1–1.2m (3½–4ft) above ground level. Secure each bud with a rubber grafting patch (right). In spring, cut back the stock just above the new shoots that are developing from the grafted buds (far right).

Bud-grafting

The budding process involves uniting plant material taken from two different roses in order to combine the virtues of both. A dormant bud (the scion) from the top-growth of one plant, usually chosen for its display, is inserted under the bark and just above the roots of a rootstock, normally a rose species or a specific clone that is selected for its vigour and hardiness. Different rootstocks may be used to suit the soil conditions or climate or to promote the vigorous growth of the scion.

Choosing a suitable rootstock

Many stocks are used to suit varying conditions: the hardy and vigorous *Rosa multiflora* is widely used as a rootstock, particularly where the winters are cold; it is also suitable for use on poor soils although plants budded onto this stock are not long-lived. *R. canina* produces hardy plants and is popular where winters are severe or on heavy soils, but it suckers freely; the crimson climber 'Dr Huey' (at one time known as 'Shafter' when used as a stock) is more often used where the dormancy period is shorter. The selected clone 'Laxa' has now largely replaced most other commercial stocks, as it performs reliably in most soils and climatic conditions, is almost thornless, easy to use for budding, and rarely produces suckers. Any commercial supplier of rootstocks, or a local nursery, should be able to provide information on the best stock to use for local growing conditions.

Stocks may be obtained from wild hedgerow roses, but their quality is unreliable and it is better to use stocks with more uniform growth characteristics.

Planting the rootstocks

Plant the rootstocks in autumn in a nursery bed, about 30cm (12in) apart and with 75cm (30in) between the rows. For bush roses, the scions are inserted at the point where the shoots and roots join (the "neck"), so for ease of budding, plant the rootstocks at an angle of 45°, with the top of the root just at soil level. Mound soil up to the base of the shoots to keep the bark moist and supple at the point where the scion is to be inserted. Standard rootstocks must be grown on to about 2–2.2m (6–7ft), and any buds rubbed off before they develop to create a straight, bare stem.

When to bud-graft

Budding should be carried out from mid- to late summer, preferably in

PROPAGATION **167**

cool, showery conditions. If the weather is very dry in the months that precede budding, water the rootstocks regularly and thoroughly. This ensures a free flow of sap that prevents the wood from drying out, so that it is possible to lift the bark from the wood without bruising the wood underneath. Speed is also important to prevent the wood of both bud and rootstock from drying out before they have been grafted together.

A budding knife, with a single, specially formed blade and a sharp, tapered end (see "Garden knives", p.555) may be used but an ordinary horticultural knife is also suitable. Any knife used for budding must be kept scrupulously clean and sharp.

Selecting the budwood
Prepare scions from well-ripened shoots that have fat, dormant growth buds in their leaf axils. These shoots are known as the budwood. Cut off the leaves and leaf stalks; alternatively, leave the stalks as "handles" for inserting the buds later. Place the budwood in a plastic bag to prevent it from drying out before it is used.

Preparing the scion
Hold a piece of budwood upside down and, from just above the base of a bud, use the budding knife to scoop out the bud together with a thin tail. This shield-like piece of bark, about 2.5cm (1in) long, within which the growth bud is contained, is known as the scion. Remove the woody material behind the bud, and shorten the tail so the scion is about 1cm (½in) long. If retained, the wood will prevent the bud from uniting with the rootstock or "taking". The base of the bud should then be visible as a small, circular growth. It is difficult to do this without damaging the bud if the shield has been cut too deeply from the shoot.

Preparing the rootstock
For a bush rose, clear the soil from the rootstock neck, take off the thorns, and wipe the neck clean. Using the blade of the budding knife, make a "T"-shaped cut in the neck, penetrating the bark without cutting into the wood, as this causes damage.

Grafting the bud onto the rootstock
Carefully peel back the cut bark of the rootstock with the blunt side of the knife blade, taking care not to tear the bark or the wood beneath. Gently push the scion into position in the "T" so that the bud faces upwards. Trim off any of the tail that may still be visible and, if necessary, the leaf stalk. Use a rubber grafting

patch to hold the bud securely in place and keep the flaps of bark tightly closed to avoid moisture loss. The patch is easily pinned in place and does not inhibit the growth of the bud as it soon rots away. Inserting two scions, opposite one another on the rootstock, is sometimes recommended to produce balanced shoot growth more rapidly but is seldom practised commercially except on standard roses.

Cutting back the rootstock
If the scion takes successfully, the bud will quickly swell and will then produce a shoot, generally by the following spring. Once the shoot develops, cut off the growth of the rootstock above the scion. If the shoot needs support, tie it to a cane, but this is not usually necessary.

Bud-grafting a standard rose
Budding onto a standard rootstock is performed near the top of the stem at the desired height, usually about 1.1–1.2m (3½–4ft); weeping standards are usually budded a little higher, at about 1.5m (5ft). Insert two or three buds around the stem to achieve an evenly balanced head. If using *Rosa canina* rootstocks, insert the buds into equally spaced lateral growths, close to the main stem. It is more usual to place three buds around the main stem of *R. rugosa* stock, staggered vertically.

Layering roses

Any rose which possesses shoots that are long and flexible enough to be bent over and pegged into the ground may be successfully propagated by simple layering.

In late summer after flowering, choose a shoot of healthy, mature wood and trim some of the leaves to create a clear length of stem. Work some peat substitute or peat into the ground where the shoot is to be layered and peg the shoot down into the prepared ground to encourage it to root. The next spring, separate the rooted layer from the parent by cutting the shoot just behind the roots, and plant it out into its destined position to grow on.

Ramblers and climbing roses are ideal for layering, although if they are planted in narrow beds along the base of a wall there may not be a large enough area of exposed soil to peg down the shoots, particularly if other plants are growing around the base of the rose. Many shrub roses, such as Damask, Centifolia, Bourbon, and most Alba and species roses, are suitable for layering as

HOW TO LAYER ROSES

1 Make a 2.5cm (1in) slit on the lower side of a long, ripe, but flexible shoot. Dust the cut with hormone rooting powder and then wedge it open with a match (see inset).

2 Position the shoot in a small depression in prepared soil and peg it down firmly with a wire hoop. Cover it with soil, firm, and tie in the tip of the layered shoot to a short cane.

they have a lax growth habit and are likely to have more exposed soil around the base into which the selected shoots may be inserted.

Modern shrub roses such as 'Chinatown', which are in fact very tall-growing Floribunda roses, have fairly stiff shoots, so train these shoots horizontally while they are still young and flexible to prepare for layering. Cultivars of ground-cover roses lend themselves to this method of propagation. The shoots of some, such as PHEASANT ('Kordapt') or GROUSE ('Korimro'), root naturally into the soil; simply separate them from the parent and plant them out.

The modern Hybrid Tea and Floribunda roses found in the majority of gardens are mostly too stiff and upright in their habit of growth for successful layering and should be increased by taking cuttings. Only a few which are lax, wide-spreading growers, such as QUEEN MOTHER ('Korquemu'), are easily increased by layering.

Propagation by division

If a rose is growing on its own roots, taking rooted suckers and planting them out is an easy method of propagation. Most roses from nurseries are grafted onto rootstocks, however, so suckers will be from the stock and the plant is therefore not suitable for propagation by division.

Some species grown from seed and other roses grown from cuttings sucker naturally. In the dormant period, detach the rooted suckers or shoots from the parent and plant them out, either in a nursery bed or into permanent positions. Deep planting of budded shrub roses sometimes stimulates the cultivar shoots to produce roots. Treat such rooted shoots as rooted suckers.

Roses that sucker freely such as the cultivars of *Rosa pimpinellifolia*, *R. rugosa* and some Gallica roses are readily propagated in this way.

PROPAGATING ROSES BY DIVISION

1 In late autumn or early spring, select a well-developed sucker. Scrape away the soil to expose its base. Sever it from the rootstock, with as many roots as possible.

2 Prepare a hole, wide and deep enough for the roots. Plant the sucker immediately and water and firm the soil (see inset). Trim shoots to 23–30cm (9–12in).

RAISING ROSES FROM SEED

1 *Slit open a ripe hip (see inset), taken from the parent plant, with a clean, sharp knife. Take out individual seeds carefully with the back of the knife blade.*

2 *Place the seed in a plastic bag of moist peat substitute or peat and keep it for 2–3 days at room temperature. Then put it in a refrigerator for 3–4 weeks.*

3 *Sow the seeds singly onto the surface of a sandy compost (1 part sand:1 part peat substitute). Cover with grit, label, and put in a cold frame.*

4 *When the seedlings have their first pairs of true leaves, prick them out singly into 5cm (2in) pots filled with loam-based potting compost.*

Propagating roses from seed

Species roses, unlike cultivars, are self-fertile and may be raised from seed in the same way as other shrubs. Although seeds are not generally available from commercial sources, it is easy to extract them from mature roses in the garden. Hybrid roses do not breed true to type from seed so they are usually propagated by bud-grafting (see p.166).

Extracting and sowing seed

In the autumn, when the rose hips are swollen and ripe, extract the seeds and stratify them in a refrigerator before sowing (see "How to overcome dormancy", p.629). Stratification – the simulation of natural temperature changes – is necessary for all seed of species roses.

Sow the rose seed into seed trays, packs, or into individual pots, which should be at least 6cm (2½in) deep. If using a seed tray, place the seeds on the compost about 5cm (2in) apart, and cover them to their own depth with sand or grit. Then leave the tray or pack in a cold frame to protect it from mice and other animals. The seed may take up to a year to germinate. Prick out the seedlings into individual containers as soon as the first true rose leaves have formed; the first pair, the seed leaves, are oval, unlike typical rose leaves. Care is needed in handling the seedlings as they are very fragile at this stage in their development.

Grow on the young seedlings in the cold frame until they have become established in their pots. Then harden them off by moving them out of the cold frame during the day. Once acclimatized, the seedlings may be kept in the open, and potted on as necessary until they are large enough to be planted out.

Hybridizing

New rose cultivars are created by hybridizing, a process by which one cultivar or species is cross-pollinated with another and the new seed sown and grown on. The aim is to create a new rose that inherits the best characteristics of both parents.

Selecting the parents

Most roses are of mixed ancestry, so it is impossible to predict the results of hybridization, and the chances of producing a quality cultivar, with distinct characteristics, are small. Knowledge of the parent roses' genetic characteristics, in particular their chromosomal number and structure, is important in breeding.

The chromosomes are the parts of plant cells that control the inheritance of characteristics through the genes. Roses may have different chromosome numbers, although the total number per cell in each case is always a multiple of seven. Most of the species roses have 14 (diploid), 28 (tetraploid), 42 (hexaploid), or 56 (octoploid) chromosome numbers. When two roses have been cross-pollinated, equivalent chromosomes from the parents arrange themselves in pairs, which then fuse and count as one in the chromosome number of the new cultivar. Most garden roses are tetraploids and two tetraploids brought together in this fusion

HOW TO HYBRIDIZE ROSES
Preparing the seed parent

1 *Select an unblemished bloom (here PRINCESS MICHAEL OF KENT) that has not fully unfolded its petals and should therefore not yet have been pollinated.*

2 *Remove the petals, taking off the outer ones first. Work gradually towards the centre, taking care not to damage the stigmas as they become exposed.*

3 *Using tweezers or a small pair of scissors, remove the stamens around the stigmas and all fragments of stamens or petals.*

4 *Use a magnifying glass to inspect the rose and make sure that no fragments remain. If left they may decay and allow rot fungi to enter the rosehip.*

5 *Make a paper cone, twisting its point firmly closed (see inset). Holding back the sepals, cover the flower with the cone, and tie securely around the stem.*

Alternative step
Place a clean, dry, plastic bag over the flower and secure it with a firm tie. The flower is thus protected from pollinating insects.

produce another tetraploid rose. A diploid (14) crossed with a tetraploid (28), however, results in 7 + 14 chromosomes, or a total of 21 (triploid) in the new rose. As this is not an even number there are seven chromosomes left without comparable chromosomes with which to pair. Triploids are often sterile and of little or no use in breeding.

Where the chromosome count is known, it is given in the most recent edition of *Modern Roses* (American Rose Society for the International Registration Authority for Roses). This publication also details the pedigree of large numbers of roses.

Heredity is not the only factor influencing the selection of parent plants. Some hybrid roses make good pollen (male) parents, but poor seed (female) parents, and vice versa. Some are completely infertile and others almost so, and in a rose with a very large number of petals, such as a Centifolia, a proportion of these may have taken the place of the stamens, so that little pollen is available for hybridizing. Crossing a non-remontant rose with a remontant one may be a problem if remontancy is one of the desired characteristics, as the first generation from such a cross is always non-remontant. At least one more cross is needed before remontancy reappears in the offspring.

This is a simplification of a very complex subject and there is a good deal of chance involved in rose breeding. However scientific an approach is taken, the result is still largely unpredictable. As a general principle, choose the healthiest cultivars available as parents, and start with what is perhaps the easiest cross of all, that between two different cultivars of Floribunda roses.

Controlling the growing environment

Except in a frost-free climate, use pot-grown roses in a greenhouse, as this allows greater control of temperature, humidity, insect pests, and diseases, and gives the hips a better chance of ripening properly. Precise record-keeping is essential: after crosses have been made, carefully identify all the flower stems with a dated label on which is written the names of both parent plants, giving the seed parent first, for example ANNE HARKNESS ('Harkaramel') x MEMENTO ('Dicbar').

Preparing the seed parent

First select a bloom of the rose you have chosen for the seed parent, at the stage where it is starting to unfold but before insects could have reached the stamens in the centre and contaminated them with alien pollen. Carefully remove the petals and the stamens (emasculation), and make sure that no tissue is remaining that could later lead to rot in the hip. Tie a paper cone or plastic bag over the emasculated flower and leave it for one to two days to allow the stigmas to fully mature.

Preparing the pollen parent

Cut the flower that is to be the pollen parent, which should be at about the same stage as the seed parent. Stand the pollen parent in a vase of water and protect it from insects until the anthers release the tiny, orange pollen grains, usually on the day after being cut. The stigmas of the seed parent should begin to exude a sticky secretion, indicating that they are ready to receive the pollen. Pull off the petals from the pollen parent, leaving the anthers intact.

Pollinating the seed parent

Remove the protective covers and brush the stamens of the pollen parent against the stigmas of the seed parent; their sticky secretion helps the pollen adhere to the stigmas. Replace the cover on the pollinated flower and label the stem.

An alternative method is to cut off the pollen parent's anthers, place them in a small, clean container, such as a plastic pill-box, labelled with the name of the rose, and store it in cool, dry conditions until the released pollen grains are visible in the box. Using a fine brush, dust pollen from the box onto the stigmas of the seed parent. If carrying out more than one cross with different roses, make sure that the brush has been thoroughly cleaned between each operation, preferably with methylated or surgical spirit.

If the cross has not taken successfully, the newly forming hip will shrivel quickly. If it has been successful, the sepals will begin to lift and the hip to swell; once this is evident, remove the protective cone or bag to allow the hip to grow.

The hip will continue to swell; it normally takes about two and a half months to ripen, according to the climate. As it ripens, the hip changes its colour from green to red, to yellow, or possibly maroon, depending on the individual rose.

Harvesting and sowing

Remove the ripened hip from the plant and carefully extract the seeds. Sow and raise the seed (see "Extracting and sowing seed", p.168). Seed resulting from hybridization, however, may be sown fresh without a stratification period.

Selection

The seedlings are likely to flower in the first year – often within a few weeks of germination in a greenhouse – but it is only in the second year that the blooms will be more or less typical of the new hybrid and it is possible to judge whether it should be kept and developed or discarded.

Promising new seedlings can be budded onto rootstocks (see "Budgrafting", p.166) when they have stems of sufficient thickness, that is about 5mm (¼in). Even experienced hybridists, however, find judging the potential challenging, as it is not easy to detect faults until a selection has been grown in trials for a few years.

Preparing the pollen parent

6 *Select an unblemished bloom that is not yet fully open (here* ELINA*). Cut the stem of the flower at an angle just above a bud.*

7 *Place the chosen flower in water and keep it indoors, free from insects, until it opens fully (usually overnight).*

8 *When the flower is open and the anthers split, revealing the pollen, gently remove all the petals.*

9 *The exposed anthers are now ready to release their tiny pollen grains.*

Pollinating the seed parent

10 *Uncover the seed parent and brush the anthers of the pollinator across its stigmas. The pollen grains will adhere to the sticky stigmas of the seed parent.*

11 *Replace the protective cone over the seed parent and tie securely. Label the rose with the names of the seed parent and pollen parent, and leave it to ripen.*

CHAPTER

6

PERENNIALS

WITH FLOWERS IN every colour of the rainbow, a breathtaking range of shapes and textures, and often fine scents, perennials richly deserve their popularity. Their diversity makes them suitable for most gardens, while their reliability makes them a lasting source of pleasure. For many people, a traditional herbaceous border is the epitome of garden beauty, but perennials can be equally effective in mixed borders, interplanted with shrubs, annuals, bulbs, and vegetables, or grown in containers or as ground cover. Foliage ranges from lacy fern fronds to the strap-like leaves of crocosmias; and there are flowers to suit all tastes, from delicate *Gypsophila* to sumptuous peonies. Some, like many sedums, are followed by pretty seedheads. Against a more static background of woody plants, perennials provide an almost unlimited, changing planting palette.

Perennials for the garden

ALTHOUGH botanically speaking these plants should be referred to as herbaceous perennials, they are usually known as just "perennials". "Herbaceous" explains the fact that the part above ground dies down each year, while "perennial" refers to the fact that the root system lives for three or more years. A few perennials, such as *Helleborus foetidus*, are evergreen, and so have a valuable winter presence.

Most perennials will flower, set seed, and then die back to ground level by autumn, going dormant for the winter season. Some retain a woody base, such as *Achillea filipendulina*, or fleshy shoots, such as *Sedum telephium*, while others disappear completely underground. Some perennials, such as *Doronicum orientale*, go completely dormant during the heat of summer, instead of in the cold of winter. Most perennials flower during summer, though some, such as *Liriope muscari* and *Iris unguicularis*, enliven the garden in autumn and winter, while *Helleborus orientalis* and *Pulmonaria* welcome in early spring.

Choosing perennials

More than any other group of plants, perennials have an immense variety of shape, form, colour, texture, and scent. Mostly valued for their flowers, many also have attractive foliage – from ribbed, unfurling hosta leaves, or sword-like straps of iris, to transparent tracery of fennel (*Foeniculum vulgare*). Particularly in a small garden, some perennials should have ornamental leaves, to extend the season of interest – the foliage usually outlasting the flowers.

Perennials range in height from the *Acaena* at just 5cm (2in) tall to the statuesque *Helianthus salicifolius*, whose feathered stems reach 2.5m (8ft) or more. Low-growing perennials are ideal for the front of borders or in between shrubs, while tall plants belong at the back of a border to give height and structure to the planting design. Perennials with an attractive structure, such as the African lily (*Agapanthus*) or some grasses such as *Chionochloa rubra* and *Carex comans* 'Frosted Curls', are good specimen plants in a border or container.

Some perennials, such as many carnations and pinks (*Dianthus*) and highly perfumed lily-of-the-valley (*Convallaria majalis*), are worth growing for their fragrance alone. Carnations and pinks are ideal for raised beds or windowboxes, while ground-covering lily-of-the-valley thrives in shady shrubberies. Other perennials, such as *Sedum spectabile* and many of the daisy and umbel family, such as asters and *Angelica*, bear flowers that attract beneficial insects such as bees and butterflies.

It is also possible to prolong the season of interest into autumn and winter by selecting plants with interesting seedheads and winter silhouettes. Fennels, *Iris sibirica*, and *Achillea* are a few examples of flowers that will surprise you at a

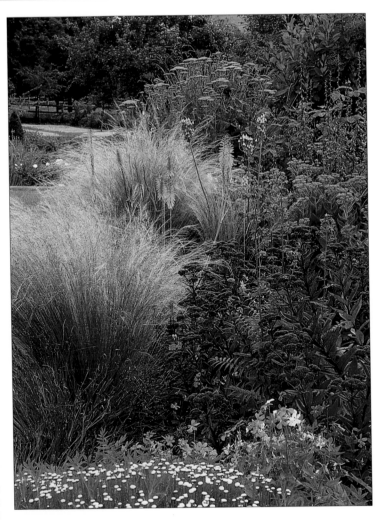

Perennial border
The addition of the elegant ornamental grasses and Achillea *'Terracotta' gives this scheme a contemporary feel that fits well with the traditional, hot-coloured flowers, such as* Crocosmia *and the poker-headed* Kniphofia.

Formal borders
In this formal garden, a traditional grass path divides a pair of wide, straight borders. The plants are arranged by height, with low plants such as Sedum spectabile *at the front so that all can be clearly seen. While the planting in each border is not a rigid mirror-image of the other, a number of plants are repeated on both sides to provide a balanced, harmonious effect.*

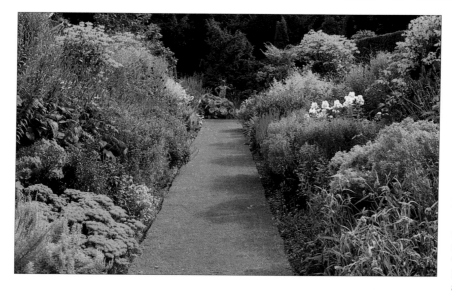

time of year when you least expect it. Birds will gain twofold from these seedheads: they enjoy eating the seeds, and benefit from the insects that overwinter in the cavities created by hollow stems and seedheads.

As with all plants, when choosing perennials for a planting scheme, make sure that they are appropriate for the growing conditions, such as soil, micro-climate, and aspect of the bed or border. Given the correct environment, plants are much more likely to flourish, and require less maintenance than those struggling in an unsuitable position (see also "Site and aspect", p.183).

Herbaceous and mixed borders

Perennials are traditionally used in borders: these are long, rectangular beds, fronted by lawn or a path and backed by a hedge or wall, either as a single border or as double, facing borders. Popularized in the late 19th century, herbaceous borders were planted only with perennials, in groups or drifts, the shortest plants at the front, grading up with lupins, phlox, and the like, to the taller ones such as delphiniums at the rear. Their season of interest was restricted to the summer months, as in many gardens the borders were but one of many areas of interest, each with a different seasonal highlight. As gardens reduced in size during the 20th century, and space became more restricted, the flowering season and plant range of borders were forced to extend. As a result, mixed borders have become increasingly popular; they now contain a variety of plants including bedding plants, shrubs, climbers, and even small flowering trees, as well as perennials. The advantage of a mixed border is that it

can be less labour-intensive than an herbaceous one, because larger areas may be filled with less-demanding woody plants (see "Designing beds and borders", p.174).

A successful border requires regular maintenance. Careful staking is needed, as the perennials may grow long and lanky as they compete for the somewhat reduced light levels caused by the close planting, and the presence of a wall or hedge in the background. Water and nutrient levels also need monitoring regularly in any such dense planting scheme.

Additional chores generated by a

mixed border involve bedding out early bulbs and wallflowers, followed by dahlias, cannas, and other tender plants, to extend the length of interest into early spring and autumn. Plants also need to be dead-headed regularly and kept tidy over the longer flowering period.

Island beds

Surrounded by lawn or paving, island beds can be seen and accessed from all sides, so the planting design should be effective from all viewpoints. As

with borders, beds that are dedicated solely to herbaceous plants are at their most impressive in summer. For a more enduring display, interplant the perennials with a variety of bulbs and perhaps one or two shrubs.

Because access to the centre of the bed may be difficult, plants should be sturdy, dwarf, or compact, which should reduce the need for staking; generally, though, there will be less requirement for support as higher light levels and better air circulation promote sturdier plant growth than within borders.

Geometrical, round, square, or rectangular island beds suit a formal setting; in an informal garden or one with gently undulating ground, loosely curved island beds are more appropriate. Avoid intricate shapes and tight curves, since they are awkward to maintain and may detract from the planting itself. To gain space, small gardens can be filled with island beds.

Raised island beds can provide improved growing conditions for demanding perennials, tougher alpines, and Mediterranean plants in gardens where the soil is poor or tends to become waterlogged. The increased bed height also enables plants to be tended with minimal stooping – which is often an important factor for gardeners who are less able or elderly.

Island bed
This bed is shaped to reflect the surrounding contours. Most of the tallest plants should be sited in the middle; the lowest ones at the edge. Here, height is provided by Astilbe, Lobelia, *and* Filipendula, *which are planted with variegated Solomon's seal (*Polygonatum*),* Blechnum, *and hellebores, among other perennials.*

Mixed borders
Colourful tulips provide spring interest, while shrubs such as a golden-leaved Spiraea japonica *'Goldflame' and the sculptural mass of* Euphorbia characias *subsp.* wulfenii *add colour and form from spring through to autumn, extending the period of interest beyond the summer burst of colour offered by the hardy* Geranium *species and other perennials.*

Contrasting shapes
The pointed swords of red Crocosmia *here create a strong vertical accent behind the rounded* Ligularia *leaves in this large border.*

Designing beds and borders

When designing a planting scheme, the principles are broadly similar whether planning an herbaceous or mixed border or an island bed. Considerations of height, mass, scale, texture, sequential interest, form, and colour are all variable factors that influence the design. Planting is a very individual issue.

Everybody has favourite plants and colours as well as set ideas as to which plants look good together.

Imagination and personal taste will inevitably influence your planting schemes, but there are a few basic guidelines to follow.

General principles

Herbaceous borders may be designed and planted in various styles so that they set or strengthen the character and tone of the garden. Crisply edged, straight-lined borders backed by well-trimmed hedges create a dominant structure, which will be attractive in winter, but which can be softened by planting during summer. Irregularly shaped island beds, weaving their way through the garden, are much more relaxed, but will do little for the garden during winter. Self-contained, stately plants such as lupins, delphiniums, and veronicas, arranged according to a restricted colour scheme and planted in a rhythmical pattern look somewhat formal. For a more relaxed approach, introduce plants with a loose, less ordered habit, such as baby's breath (*Gypsophila*) and lady's mantle (*Alchemilla mollis*), and then add key feature plants such as *Sedum* 'Herbstfreude' at random rather than at strict intervals.

Before starting a planting plan, prepare a comprehensive list of plants you want to use. This should contain any existing plants you would like to retain, as well as a thoroughly researched list of others that will cover all seasons, and are well suited to your garden. It may be easier to compile this list with the help of a good local nursery catalogue, as you will know where to obtain the plants.

Allow sufficient room for the plants to spread as they mature, taking account of the different rates at which they develop. Slow-growing plants can be surrounded by shade-tolerant ground cover (see PERENNIALS FOR GROUND COVER, p.180) to fill the area while waiting for the main plant to achieve its desired size. Start by placing the key plants, such as shrubs, roses, and any imposing perennials and grasses, as well as the important feature plants, which you may wish to repeat at regular intervals to create a symmetric rhythm to the border. Position the smaller plants last. Set out the plants according to your planting plan and make any adjustments to the scheme at this stage, before planting them. However carefully the scheme has

Massed form and colour
Large drifts of perennials and grasses create a generous sense of space within a garden. The vertical spires distract the eye from the horizontal bands of colour created by the wide-scale plantings. Even after flowering is over, such a display will look effective until the flowerheads are cut off in late winter.

Harmonizing textures

A mixture of moisture-loving plants with airy and feathery flowers, such as Astilbe, Lythrum virgatum, Filipendula palmata, *and tall, yellow* Ligularia stenocephala *forms a satisfying pattern of textures. The fluffy outline of the* Filipendula *flowerheads successfully breaks up the general mass of vertical heads on the other plants.*

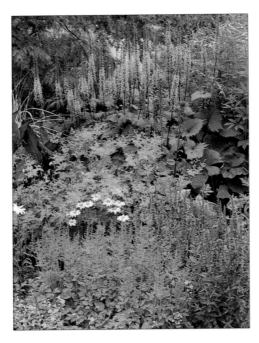

been planned, minor adjustments are inevitable, as no two gardens are alike, and plants react differently, however well you know them.

Scale of planting

Although the size of beds and borders is usually dictated by the surrounding space, the scale of planting should take account of the scale of the garden and adjacent buildings.

The extent of a border or bed will vary but, as a rough guide, the larger the garden setting, the more generous the border or bed can be. Two large beds are better than three or four little ones; they will enhance the feeling of space, and prevent the garden from looking too bitty.

A border should be no less than 1.5m (5ft) deep, and preferably 3–5m (10ft–15ft), depending on a path's length and width. This will give a good planting width and will create a layered, well-balanced effect.

Large borders, seen from a great distance, and flanked by a wide path, should be planted with bold groups of plants, to create sufficient visual impact. The smaller the viewing distance, the smaller the planting scale should be, so that the border remains interesting as you stroll along it (see also "Planting in groups", right).

Varying plant height

Traditionally, tall plants are placed at the back of a front-facing border, grading down the heights as they approach the front, to create a tiered effect in which no flowering plant is hidden behind another. In an island bed, the tallest plants are placed in the centre, with the smallest round the outer edge. This planting rule will create quite a formal, rigid

scheme. Mystery and contrast can be added by introducing the occasional taller but translucent plant near the front; this will give a stronger undulation to the overall scheme. Particularly slim plants such as *Verbena bonariensis* or many grasses such as *Stipa gigantea* provide extra height, while allowing the eye to wander past them. Plant textural perennials, such as *Molinia caerulea* subsp. *arundinacea* 'Transparent' with its soft flower panicles, so that they are close enough to touch from the edge of the bed.

As a rule, later-flowering perennials tend to be the tallest, as they have the longest growing period. This can result in late summer flowers towering over the dead flower stalks of earlier plants. To hide gaps where earlier flowerers such as Oriental poppies have vanished, plant some of the lower late flowers such as *Aster* x *pringlei* 'Monte Cassino' near to the front of the bed.

Generally, the wider the bed or border, the taller the plants may be; very tall plants in narrow borders may look awkward and the angle from the tallest to the shortest, uncomfortably steep.

Planting in groups

Several plants of the same cultivar can successfully be massed together to create larger groups. Particularly towards the rear of a border, or the centre of a bed, large clumps of one plant will create a good impact, whereas near the front smaller clumps will increase variety and interest. Depending on the scale of the scheme, always aim to plant in groups of three or more, up to a dozen or so. For a fluid, informal

style, plant in odd numbers – even numbers creating a formal rigidity to a bed or border.

Groups of varying sizes should also be introduced. If in doubt, create an "outline" of the plants – using bamboo canes, brooms, or other more bulky props – to see what would fit the space.

Small-leaved perennials are more impressive when planted in large groups: small-leaved London pride (*Saxifraga* x *urbium*), for example, is best planted in groups of seven or more, while large-leaved *Bergenia* species and hybrids look effective in threes. The huge *Gunnera manicata*, however, is striking enough to be planted singly (see "Specimen planting", p.179).

Plants that have strong outlines, such as *Kniphofia caulescens* with its upright, pokerhead flowers, are more dramatic when planted in smaller groups than those of less distinct forms such as the loose-flowered *Geranium phaeum*.

Forms and outlines

Perennials have widely differing forms and silhouettes, including upright, rounded, or arching, as well as horizontally spreading outlines. Juxtapose groups of plants with contrasting forms to create a series of vignettes, which build up within a bed or border. The slim flower spikes of delphiniums or *Eremurus*, for example, act like giant, colourful exclamation marks, when viewed against the foaming, cloud-like cushions of *Gypsophila paniculata* or *Crambe cordifolia*. Contrast is introduced when the strong vertical lines of irises and other strap-leaved plants are set against the

horizontal planes of the flowerheads of *Achillea* 'Moonshine' or *Sedum telephium* 'Matrona'.

Some plants are two tiered, and have their own contrasting form: a fine example is *Rheum palmatum* 'Atrosanguineum', which makes a lower layer of reddish-purple leaves 1m (3ft) tall, over which tower smoky-pink plumes of tiny flowers.

Understanding plant textures

Although flowers, and to a lesser extent stems, contribute to the overall texture of a planting scheme, it is foliage that provides the strongest impact, because it is present for a much longer period of time during the year. Even when seen from a distance, it can create striking contrasts and subtle harmonies. The dainty leaves of *Coreopsis verticillata* or the filigree fronds of fennel (*Foeniculum vulgare*) are very delicate, whereas large, individual leaves such as those of *Hosta sieboldiana* var. *elegans* create a bold, textural effect.

Grasses, particularly, can add a wide range of textural variety to a garden. The narrow flowering stems and strap-shaped leaves tend to be very supple, yet strong, waving in the wind, bringing flowing movement into a garden, as well as a gentle rustling sound of the foliage. Many, such as *Miscanthus sinensis* 'Malepartus' or *Calamagrostis* x *acutiflora* 'Karl Foerster', are so strong that their dried flower stems will remain standing well into autumn, or even throughout winter.

Texture is also affected by a leaf's surface, whether it is the matt, waxy foliage of *Sedum spectabile*, the glossy, leathery leaves of *Bergenia*

Contrasting forms

This grouping of foliage plants gives prominence to differences in form and texture. The impressive, jagged foliage of Rheum palmatum *at the rear contrasts with the heart-shaped leaves of* Ligularia dentata *and the softly arching straps of an ornamental grass. The* Rodgersia *adds a distinct colour and texture accent with its large, ribbed, dark red foliage.*

purpurascens, or the woolly texture of *Lychnis coronaria*. It is important to understand how a leaf's texture will affect your planting scheme: glossy surfaces, for example, reflect light, adding sparkle on a sunny day, while matt ones absorb light, creating a more sombre effect.

As with form, juxtaposing groups of plants with contrasting textures increases interest; for example, the downy, pleated leaves of lady's mantle (*Alchemilla mollis*) contrast well with the spiny stems and jagged foliage of sea holly (*Eryngium*). Ground-cover perennials such as hardy *Geranium* species and cultivars and *Ajuga reptans* are especially useful to grow as a low foil for other plants, and to fill a gap in a planting scheme, and so complete the textural tapestry (see also PERENNIALS FOR GROUND COVER, p.180).

Colour blends and contrasts

Choosing colours is a very personal affair. Everyone has preferences as well as dislikes. It is important to select hues that you feel comfortable with, regardless of their current fashion status, or your best friend's opinion. A restricted colour palette can be wonderful, but may be hard to adhere to in a small garden.

For the widest plant choice, opt for an extensive range of colours that will either appear at the same time or follow on in a seasonal succession. If you are concerned about creating too dramatic clashes, try using all but one of the colours. The most awkward ones to combine are oranges and pinks. Using one or other with yellows, violets, blues, and reds can look very attractive. Alternatively you could opt for complementary colours – those opposite each other in the colour wheel – such as oranges and blues, yellows and violets, or greens and reds. Another possibility is to use adjacent hues in the wheel, combining all the hot colours such as yellows, oranges, and reds, or the

cool pinks, blues, purples, and mauves. Such combinations were frequently used by the doyenne of colour schemes, Gertrude Jekyll.

In a monochrome planting design, foliage plays as important a role as flowers. Such a one-colour scheme, however, not only restricts the plant range but can also prove visually boring unless there is considerable contrast and variety within the design. When creating a white garden, for example, it is important to include different types of white, such as cream, pinkish white, and blueish white, as well as shades of green. Introducing contrasting leaf tones, shapes, and textures helps to bring tension to a scheme. Thus, in a white garden, use silver, grey, and glaucous leaves as well as light, mid-, and dark green ones.

Unusually tinted foliage plants will emphasize a colour scheme, particularly in a mixed border, where golden-, silver-, or red-leaved shrubs can help to enhance flowers. They should be used as small accents, and not become the main features.

Colour intensities can also play an important part in garden design. Light colours such as white, pale pink, and pale yellow reflect higher levels of light than do darker shades – blue, red, and violet – and will be seen from further away. They also start shimmering at dusk when light levels have dropped – causing some flowers seemingly to disappear, while others develop an almost luminous character. The latter can be used near an area where you are likely to sit in the evenings. Light colours also help to enliven dark corners, or can be employed to draw attention to a focal point. Dark colours, on the other hand, are better used in the foreground, nearest to the viewpoint.

Seasonal interest

Although, in a mixed border, it is possible to plan a succession of colour schemes that change with the course of the seasons, to do so

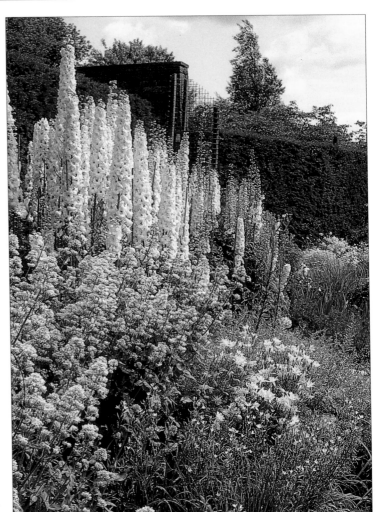

A "white" garden
Contrasting flowers and leaves in white, silver, and green here help to build up the tension in this monochrome planting of delphiniums, valerian (Centranthus ruber *'Albus'*), Anthericum liliago, *aquilegias, and artemisia.*

involves coordinating the timing of each plant's display, so that one feature smoothly follows another and fading flowers pass unnoticed, eclipsed by nearby plants coming into bloom. A scheme that manages to maintain a succession of interest requires forethought, yet mistakes are easily corrected by re-siting the offenders the following autumn.

The spring season may be announced as early as midwinter, when the first snowdrops (*Galanthus*) and winter aconites (*Eranthis hyemalis*) reveal their petals, soon followed by hellebores. Some winter-flowering shrubs and climbers, such as wintersweet (*Chimonanthus praecox*) and honeysuckle (*Lonicera x purpusii*) at the rear of mixed borders will help to increase the early show. Later in the season such woody plants can support not-too-vigorous herbaceous climbers such as the flame creeper (*Tropaeolum speciosum*) or *Clematis viticella* hybrids. In late winter and early

spring, yellow is predominant, from primroses (*Primula vulgaris*), daffodils, and *Doronicum*, and pale blue, from irises and *Pulmonaria*, interspersed with grape hyacinths (*Muscari*). With tulips, spring comes to an end.

By early summer, most of the bulbs have finished their performance, and the real season for perennials starts. There are showstoppers such as Oriental poppies, with their short-lived but showy flowers, and the wonderfully baroque peonies as well as dainty, long-spurred *Aquilegia chrysantha* and the numerous hardy geraniums. Once there is little risk of frost, the remainder of the tender plants will gradually vie for attention, including dahlias, argyranthemums, osteospermums, and cannas. These all flower over a long period, and are invaluable for providing colour until the first frosts arrive in autumn. There are hundreds of plants to choose from, including lupins, old-fashioned scabious, fluffy meadow

Long-lasting display
The rich brown seedheads of Sedum spectabile *may be left uncut to provide interest in late autumn and winter long after the succulent leaves have died back.*

rue (*Thalictrum*), strongly scented phlox, red hot pokers (*Kniphofia*), and numerous daisy family members such as fleabanes (*Erigeron*), *Helenium*, coneflowers (*Echinacea purpurea*), sunflowers (*Helianthus*), *Rudbeckia*, chrysanthemums, and asters – the last two being vital for autumn flowers.

It is sometimes possible to extend the effect of a particular plant or group by growing next to it a plant that creates a similar impression. The deep blue flower spikes of *Delphinium* 'Blue Nile', for example, could be followed by those of *Aconitum carmichaelii*, and, if the latter is planted in front, the yellowing delphinium foliage will be hidden from view. Plant perennials such as lupins (*Lupinus*) that die back early in front of plants such as *Physostegia* that develop later in the season, in order to hide any awkward gaps or fading leaves.

In mixed borders, bulbs are particularly useful for providing colour in late winter and spring when perennials are starting into growth. Similarly, the new growth of the latter masks the fading foliage of the bulbs once their flowers have finished. For example, the black-purple leaves of the evergreen *Ophiopogon planiscapus* 'Nigrescens', the soft grey-blue foliage of *Acaena saccaticupula* 'Blue Haze', or the copper variants of *A. microphylla* make excellent foils for snowdrops (*Galanthus*) and continue to provide interest after the snowdrops are past their best. Daffodils and tulips, planted towards the rear of a border, will have finished flowering by the time perennials come into growth, and so hide the dying foliage.

Particularly in small gardens, shrubs are invaluable to maintain the shape and structure of the design in late autumn and winter, as well as contributing colour and texture. The inclusion of deciduous shrubs with attractive autumn foliage (such as *Cotinus coggygria* 'Royal Purple') and those with bright fruits (such as many shrub roses) will also help to distract attention from perennials with dying foliage.

Naturalistic planting styles

Particularly in a large area, sizeable drifts of perennials look good when planted in naturalistic settings. Plants should be chosen to match the given habitat – such as woodland plants for woodland conditions, and waterside plants for boggy margins – and the planting pattern should reflect each plant's natural regeneration

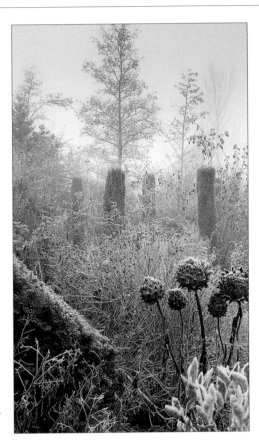

Rimed in frost
By retaining attractive seedheads, such as those of Cynara *and* roses *(here) and other eye-catching perennials, the season of interest in the garden can be extended well into winter. After a heavy frost, this border, with its columnar conifers and yew hedge in the foreground, is transformed into a glimmering wonderland.*

habits. Such planting schemes should be allowed to evolve gradually. Plants that increase by self-seeding in the immediate vicinity should be dotted about singly, while those with spreading rootstocks, such as asters, are best planted in drifts. All soil should be covered, either by plants or with a mulch.

In creating a matrix of vegetation, a much more natural and relaxed effect is obtained, one in which plants can evolve and change. Looking after such a scheme becomes more an issue of vegetation management than gardening in the conventional way, as you need to control vegetation groups, occasionally reducing a

species or cultivar if it is getting out of hand. Ideally such a scheme is looked after by somebody who understands its aims and who knows which seedlings to leave and which ones are likely to become a threat. Maintenance is minimal, as there is little or no need for staking or dead-heading, because plants are usually selected with their autumn and winter appearance in mind and are allowed to retain their seedheads. Grasses play an important part in naturalistic plantings. They bring movement and are likely to remain looking good into autumn and winter, especially on a frosty morning.

Cottage gardens

Traditional cottage gardens are a glorious mixture of herbs, roses, climbers, annuals, vegetables, and fruits, as well as perennials. They are noted for their simplicity in form, maximizing the space for production, with little money invested in elaborate structures. Planting areas are intersected by narrow paths and adorned with simple structures such as arches supporting climbers. In the past, cottagers bred plants themselves and produced enchanting perennials such as pansies (*Viola* x *wittrockiana*), auriculas (*Primula auricula*), and scented pinks (*Dianthus*). Plants were exchanged or passed on to other gardeners, as there were few plant nurseries until the late 19th century. Many of these

Naturalistic planting
The bronze inflorescences of reed grass Calamagrostis x acutiflora *'Karl Foerster' provide vertical interest behind a sizeable, horizontal drift of* Helenium *'Moerheim Beauty' and* Hordeum jubatum. *The dark evergreen background brings the ornamental grasses and other perennials further into focus.*

old cultivars have now been lost, or have been superseded by stronger or more reliable ones.

Other typical cottage plants are peonies (*Paeonia*), lupins (*Lupinus*), Madonna lilies (*Lilium candidum*), Oriental poppies, delphiniums, and phlox, while wild flowers with fragrant, double, extra-large, or unusually coloured blooms, such as primulas and daisies (*Bellis perennis*), are also very appropriate.

Perennials in woodland gardens

Deciduous woodland provides conditions of shelter, light shade, and humus-rich soil suitable for many perennials. A small grove of birches (*Betula*) and other light-foliaged, deciduous trees may provide a suitable setting for a number of shade-loving plants; site the perennials where they will not face too much competition from tree roots. If such roots are unavoidable, make sure the planting area is generously mulched with a medium- to low-fertility mulch, such as leaf mould, each year, to give the shallow-rooted perennials a moist rooting zone.

Woodland gardens are normally rather informal, imitating nature in their layout, structure, and planting. Therefore straight lines and sharply defined planting groups should be avoided by intermingling plant communities at the edges and scattering individual plants such as foxgloves through the area. Many ferns thrive in the low light levels of a woodland setting and add architectural interest to a scheme, whether they are planted in bold swathes or scattered through other planting.

Moist woodland
Where there is a permanent source of water from a pond or stream, a wide range of moisture-loving perennials such as candelabra primulas and skunk cabbage (Lysichiton) *can be grown for a prolonged, spring and early summer display. The fresh green fronds on the ferns here add a luxuriant touch to this wooded setting.*

Some of the most enchanting perennials are the small woodland plants that usher in spring. In order to grow, they make use of the light and rain that penetrate through to the woodland floor during autumn, winter, and spring, and then lie dormant, having adapted to the low light levels and dry conditions that prevail in summer. For colour and interest in spring, while the overhead canopy is still leafless, plant perennials such as cyclamen, snowdrops (*Galanthus*), primroses (*Primula vulgaris*), wood anemones (*Anemone nemorosa*), and dog's-tooth violet (*Erythronium*). Combine them with woodland bulbs and shade-loving shrubs. In cool, dry woodland shade, grow ground-cover perennials such as lily-of-the-valley (*Convallaria majalis*), Solomon's seal (*Polygonatum*) with its pearly-white flowers, and *Pulmonaria*, some of which have attractive foliage.

Insect-friendly perennials

Colourful perennial flowers are often rich in pollen and nectar – and irresistible food sources for insects like bees, butterflies, and moths. In return they inadvertently ensure the next generation of seed is produced by transferring pollen from one plant to another. Perennials also attract predators, such as lacewings and hoverflies, whose larvae feed on aphids.

By including certain perennials in your plantings, you can entice beneficial insects into the garden throughout the growing season, from the opening of the first hellebore flowers in spring, until the asters and anemones fade in autumn.

Spring insect magnets whose attractions continue into summer include geums, polemoniums, oriental poppies, *Anchusa azurea*, and *Liatris spicata*. Campanulas, *Gypsophila paniculata*, *Sidalcea*, and *Veronica longifolia* work their charm in summer, while salvias, heleniums, rudbeckias, geraniums and *Verbena bonariensis* provide temptations lasting into autumn.

Spring show
Most woodland perennials, such as aquilegias and peonies here, flower early in the growing season, while light levels are still relatively high. Many become dormant once the trees burst into foliage, and remain so until leaf fall. In summer in a woodland garden, attention switches to foliage shape and colours such as on Bowles' golden grass (Milium effusum 'Aureum') *here.*

Among the few shade-tolerant, summer-flowering perennials are *Kirengeshoma palmata*, with its waxy, soft yellow, tubular bells, and *Aster divaricatus*, which bears white, starry flowers on lax, wiry stems.

Specimen planting

In large areas of lawn or gravel, stately perennials with an architectural form or sculptural foliage, such as *Acanthus spinosus*, may be sited on their own as specimen plants to create a striking effect. In smaller gardens, a specimen perennial, surrounded by low ground cover, could be used to provide a focal point where a border projects onto a lawn or hard paving, or in a corner of a garden where two borders meet. The jutting, sword-shaped leaves and arching, fiery-red flower stems of *Crocosmia* 'Lucifer', for example, look spectacular rising above the frothy, lime-green mass of lady's mantle (*Alchemilla mollis*) or a neatly cropped blanket of *Acaena microphylla* 'Kupferteppich'.

For year-round interest, evergreen perennials such as *Phormium tenax* and *Euphorbia characias* subsp. *wulfenii* are excellent. In sheltered areas, try *Melianthus major* with its neatly serrated, grey-green foliage. Many of the grasses will provide a long show. Especially well behaved and elegant are *Molinia caerulea* subsp. *arundinacea* 'Karl Foerster', with its slender flower spikes that arch elegantly in the rain, the tall, light panicles of *Stipa gigantea*, and the airy, silky plumes of *Miscanthus sinensis* 'Grosse Fontäne', which will be especially eye-catching through autumn and well into winter, if left uncut.

Other perennials that provide a briefer display may also make spectacular accent plants because of their form, flowers, or foliage. These range from the towering, felty stems of *Verbascum olympicum* to the massive leaves of the moisture-loving *Gunnera manicata* or the glorious, pink blooms of *Paeonia lactiflora* 'Sarah Bernhardt'. As these are all plants that die down in winter, it may be desirable to place another

Perennials in containers
A clump of one type of perennial in a large pot can perform the role of a specimen plant in a paved area. Those with fine flowers or foliage, for example Chionochloa rubra, *left, are particularly attractive in appropriate containers and may be left for years to increase in size.*

feature, such as a pot-grown plant, nearby, as this will create interest during their dormant period.

Specimen plants are best offset by a plain backdrop, such as a hedge, wall, or stretch of lawn, so that nothing detracts from their impact.

Growing perennials in containers

Perennials are as welcome in containers on a paved patio, courtyard, balcony, or roof garden as they are in open beds and borders (see also CONTAINER GARDENING, p.315). Growing them in this way also makes it possible to include plants that must be brought under cover during the winter months, as well as those that require a different soil type or moisture levels from the garden soil, such as the ornamental rhubarb *Rheum palmatum* 'Atrosanguineum', which does best when it has its feet moist. Pots are also ideal for plants that might otherwise invade a garden, for example variegated ground elder (*Aegopodium podagraria* 'Variegatum') or *Houttuynia cordata* 'Chameleon'.

Container-grown evergreen perennials such as *Bergenia purpurascens* and *Liriope muscari* can provide a fine display all year round, while herbaceous perennials may be better planted with an evergreen shrub or winter-flowering bulbs such as winter aconites (*Eranthis hyemalis*), to extend the season of interest.

In general, containers look better when grouped together rather than scattered around the garden, and the plants also benefit from the favourable microclimate created by each other's company.

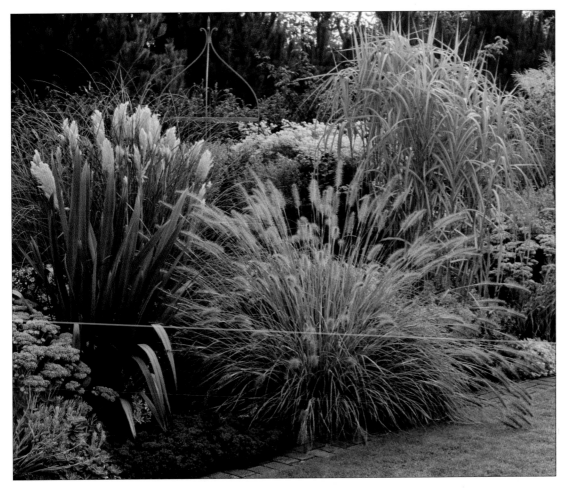

Year-round interest
This strikingly lush herbaceous border contains few flowers but provides a long season of interest. Feathery Pennisetum alopecuroides *and strap-leaved* Phormium, Sedum *'Autumn Joy' are placed to the fore, while plumes of* Cortaderia selloana *'Pumila' form part of the backdrop. Left uncut, this display will last into winter.*

Perennials for ground cover

GROUND-COVER planting is particularly suitable for areas of minimal maintenance, such as woodlands and shrubberies, or on embankments, which need stabilizing with plants. It is also important in areas that would otherwise have bare soil, as ground cover not only prevents topsoil erosion and nutrients leaching out but also reduces evaporation and weed growth.

Many ground-cover perennials will cope with shady conditions, as their natural habitat is the understorey in woodlands. They are therefore ideal when planted among taller perennials, shrub roses, or other shrubs, especially when such plants are young and will take several years to bulk out. The ground can be covered with shade-tolerant, early-flowering perennials such as *Viola odorata*, *Pulmonaria* 'Sissinghurst White', or *Doronicum orientale*. These can be removed and planted elsewhere when the shade becomes too dense for healthy growth.

Plants to use

A variety of perennials can be used as ground cover. Some, such as the day lily (*Hemerocallis*) or the mouse-tail plant (*Arisarum proboscideum*), develop through underground tuberous growths, which gradually form large, dense clumps. Some of these die back quite early, so are suitable under spreading, late perennials or deciduous shrubs and trees.

Carpeting plants produce surface runners that root where they touch the soil. Alpine strawberries, the purple-leaved *Ajuga reptans* 'Catlins Giant', or the silver-variegated *Lamium maculatum* 'Beacon Silver' are good colonizers, often covering large areas within a few years.

The most effective type of ground-cover plants produce underground roots, which send up new shoots. Good examples of these are the stately *Acanthus mollis*, goose-necked *Lysimachia clethroides*, or *Euphorbia cyparissias* 'Fens Ruby' with its fine, needle-like, glaucous foliage and dark red buds in spring. Such persistent spreaders can become problematic if they are too invasive.

Some ground-cover perennials are better weed suppressants than others. The most valuable establish quickly, have dense foliage that blocks out light to prevent weed germination, and retain their leaves during the dormant season. Good examples are *Bergenia cordifolia* and *B.* 'Abendglut', with its red foliage in winter, *Epimedium*, and some of the geraniums, particularly *Geranium* 'Tiny Monster' and *G. macrorrhizum* cultivars, which flower over a long period, have scented foliage,

Leafy carpet
To the rear, Hosta fortunei *'Albomarginata' gives the planting a structural element. In front,* Viola sororia *surrounds* Epimedium x youngianum *'Niveum'.*

and provide some autumn colour. Clump-forming plants that bear low, spreading stems, such as *Euphorbia myrsinites*, also quickly and extensively cover the surrounding soil.

Mixing plants

To create a more naturalistic effect and extend the season of interest, drifts of one plant can be interspersed with key specimens of another species, flowering at a different time. Ground cover that flowers later in summer can be interplanted with bulbs: medium-height perennials can be mixed with daffodils and bluebells, while low-growing ones look good interspersed with crocus and snowdrops. Low-growing, early-flowering species that are not too rampant can be planted with summer- and autumn-flowering, sturdy perennials, such as *Persicaria polymorpha* or *Kirengeshoma palmata*, as well as a wide variety of ferns.

General cultivation

Particularly in areas where established trees and shrubs create competition for light and moisture, it is important to plant in early autumn, soon after leaf fall, giving the ground cover plenty of time to become established before the trees produce new growth and leaves.

Plant ground-cover perennials in well-prepared soil and water them well, especially in areas where there is considerable competition from tree roots. Additional mulching will help to keep the area weed-free, increase fertility, and retain moisture.

Most ground-cover perennials need only little routine care (see pp.191–193). *Epimedium* foliage, however, should be cut back in late winter, enabling flowering stems to come up before the new leaves.

ORNAMENTAL GROUND-COVER PLANTS

***Anaphalis triplinervis*
'Sommerschnee'**
Plant 50cm
(20in) apart.

***Sedum spurium*
'Schorbuser Blut'**
Plant 15cm
(6in) apart.

***Symphytum*
'Goldsmith'**
Plant 50cm
(20in) apart.

***Pulmonaria angusti-
folia* subsp. *azurea***
Plant 30cm
(12in) apart.

Tiarella cordifolia
Plant 30cm (12in)
apart.

***Ajuga reptans*
'Braunherz'**
Plant 15cm
(6in) apart.

MORE PERENNIALS FOR GROUND COVER

Ajuga reptans
Anaphalis triplinervis
Asarum europaeum
Cornus canadensis
Epilobium angustifolium var.
  album
Epimedium
Euphorbia cyparissias,
  E. griffithii
Fragaria vesca
Geranium
Heuchera
Luzula sylvatica
Lysimachia clethroides
Persicaria
Prunella
Pulmonaria
Sedum cauticola, S. spathuli-
  folium, S. spurium
Stachys
Symphytum
Tellima
Tiarella
Viola odorata, V. riviniana
  'Purpurea'

Planter's guide to perennials

EXPOSED SITES

Perennials that tolerate exposed or windy sites
Achillea
Anaphalis
Armeria maritima
Artemisia absinthium
Calamagrostis x acutiflora
   'Karl Foerster'
Centaurea dealbata, C. hypoleuca
Centranthus ruber
Crambe maritima
Eryngium variifolium
Euphorbia characias
Festuca glauca
Lavatera maritima, L. thuringiaca
Limonium platyphyllum
Nepeta
Phlomis russeliana
Sedum spectabile, S. telephium
Stachys byzantina
Yucca filamentosa, Y. flaccida

MOIST SHADE

Perennials that prefer moist shade
Ajuga reptans
Astilbe
   simplicifolia

Hemerocallis
'Marion Vaughn'

Astrantia major
Brunnera macrophylla
Carex (except
   C. buchananii and C. comans)
Convallaria majalis
Darmera peltata
Geranium sylvaticum
Hemerocallis
Hosta
Kirengeshoma palmata
Ligularia przewalskii
Milium effusum 'Aureum'
Molinia
Myrrhis odorata
Persicaria bistorta 'Superba'
Primula bulleyana, P. florindae,
   P. japonica, P. pulverulenta
Rodgersia aesculifolia, R. pinnata
Thalictrum
Trillium grandiflorum, T. sessile

DRY SHADE

Perennials that tolerate dry shade
Acanthus mollis
Aconitum carmichaelii, A. napellus
Adiantum pedatum
Anemone hupehensis, A. x hybrida
Aquilegia vulgaris
Asarum europaeum
Asplenium
Campanula trachelium
Dicentra
Digitalis grandiflora, D. lutea

Epimedium
Geranium
Helleborus foetidus, H. orientalis
Iris foetidissima
Lathyrus vernus
Luzula sylvatica 'Marginata'
Matteuccia
Ophiopogon
Saxifraga umbrosa, S. x urbium
Symphytum grandiflorum
Tellima grandiflora Rubra Group
Vinca minor
Viola odorata, V. riviniana

WINTER AND EARLY SPRING INTEREST

Decorative flowers
Bergenia 'Ballawley', B. cordifolia
Doronicum
Epimedium
Euphorbia amygdaloides
   var. robbiae, E. characias
Helleborus
Iris lazica, I. unguicularis
Lathyrus vernus
Pulmonaria

Decorative leaves
Arum italicum 'Marmoratum'
Carex comans bronze
Festuca glauca
Heuchera 'Chocolate Ruffles',
   H. 'Pewter Moon'
Iris foetidissima 'Variegata'
Lamium maculatum 'Beacon
   Silver', L. maculatum GOLDEN
   ANNIVERSARY ('Dellam'),
   L. maculatum 'White Nancy'
Liriope muscari 'Variegata'
Ophiopogon planiscapus 'Nigrescens'
Phormium (cvs)
Stachys byzantina 'Silver Carpet'
Tiarella polyphylla
Vinca (variegated cvs)

FRAGRANT FLOWERS

Convallaria majalis
Cosmos atrosanguineus ✿
Dianthus, many
Dictamnus albus
Filipendula ulmaria
Galium odoratum
Hemerocallis
Hesperis matronalis
Hosta plantaginea var. grandiflora
Iris graminea
Oenothera odorata
Paeonia lactiflora
Phlox paniculata
Viola cornuta, V. odorata

FLOWERS FOR CUTTING

Alchemilla mollis
Allium
Alstroemeria

Aquilegia
Aster
Astrantia
Centaurea
Cephalaria
Crocosmia
Dahlia ✿
Delphinium, some ✿
Dianthus
Dicentra
Doronicum
Erigeron
Gypsophila
Helenium
Kniphofia, some ✿
Monarda
Paeonia
Phlomis tuberosa 'Amazone'
Phlox
Rudbeckia
Scabiosa
Sedum spectabile, S. telephium
Solidago
Veronica

FLOWERS FOR DRYING

Achillea
Alchemilla mollis
Anaphalis
Aruncus dioicus
Astilbe
Catananche
Centaurea
Cynara ✿
Echinops bannaticus,
   E. ritro
Gypsophila
Limonium, some ✿
Persicaria
   amplexicaulis
   'Firetail'
Rodgersia
Sedum spectabile,
   S. telephium
Solidago

Cynara
cardunculus

ARCHITECTURAL PLANTS

Acanthus hungaricus, A. mollis
Angelica archangelica, A. gigas
Arundo donax 'Variegata' ✿
Cortaderia selloana
Crambe cordifolia
Cynara ✿
Eupatorium purpureum subsp.
   maculatum 'Atropurpureum'
Foeniculum vulgare
Gunnera manicata ✿
Helianthus salicifolius
Helleborus argutifolius
Hosta sieboldiana var. elegans
Inula magnifica
Ligularia dentata 'Othello'
Lysichiton americanus
Macleaya
Melianthus major ✿
Miscanthus sinensis

Persicaria polymorpha
Rheum palmatum 'Atrosanguineum'
Rodgersia
Sedum telephium 'Matrona'
Stipa gigantea
Verbascum olympicum

DECORATIVE SEEDHEADS

Acanthus
Achillea
Eryngium
Foeniculum vulgare
Hosta
Inula magnifica
Iris
Lunaria rediviva
Miscanthus
Molinia
Papaver orientale
Physalis alkekengi
Sedum

ATTRACTIVE TO INSECTS

Aster
Digitalis
Echinacea purpurea
Foeniculum vulgare
Helenium
Inula
Nepeta
Oenothera
Salvia
Sedum
Verbascum

FAST-GROWING PERENNIALS

Achillea filipendulina 'Gold Plate',
   A. grandifolia
Artemisia lactiflora
   Guizhou Group
Arundo donax 'Macrophylla' ✿
Centaurea macrocephala
Cephalaria gigantea
Crambe cordifolia
Eupatorium purpureum subsp.
   maculatum 'Atropurpureum'
Ferula communis
Gunnera manicata ✿
Macleaya cordata
Malva alcea var. fastigiata
Persicaria polymorpha
Phormium tenax ✿
Rheum palmatum 'Atrosanguineum'
Romneya coulteri
Rudbeckia laciniata 'Goldquelle'
Salvia uliginosa ✿
Solidago canadensis
Stipa gigantea
Thalictrum rochebruneanum
Vernonia crinita
Veronicastrum virginicum

Key
✿ Not hardy

Irises

THE genus *Iris* includes some of the loveliest of flowering plants. Their intricate blooms offer a rich spectrum of colours as well as satin or velvet textures. Species can be selected for diverse situations, ranging from woodland and rock garden, waterside and bog, to herbaceous borders. Botanically, *Iris* is divided into Subgenera, Sections, and Series; these divisions vary in their cultural needs and form a convenient horticultural classification.

Routine care and propagation

Species may be propagated in the autumn or spring by division of offsets or rhizomes, or by seed in autumn (named cultivars by division only). For further information, see PERENNIALS, "Routine care", pp.191–193; BULBOUS PLANTS, "Routine care", pp.242–244, and also "Propagation", pp.245–250.

Rhizomatous irises

Irises in this group have rhizomes as rootstocks, with sword-shaped leaves arranged in a basal fan. Botanically, they are divided into several Subgenera and Series but for horticultural purposes the main groups are bearded, crested, and beardless irises.

Bearded irises

Characterized by a "beard" of numerous hairs along the centre of the falls, this group includes the common irises that are grown in gardens, with many cultivars and hybrids, most flowering in early

summer. Suitable for herbaceous and mixed borders, they are easy to grow in rich, well-drained, alkaline soil in sun; many also tolerate poorer soils and partial shade.

Oncocyclus irises are natives of areas with little summer rainfall and need the protection of an alpine house or frame in climates that are subject to summer rains. They have large, beautiful, and sometimes bizarre blooms but are exacting in their requirements and are not easy to grow. They need a fertile, sharply drained soil and full sun, with a dry, dormant period after flowering. If they are grown in pots, the compost must be nutrient-rich, well drained, and preferably alkaline.

Repot before growth begins in early spring, if required. When the foliage dies down after flowering, stop watering, and keep the rhizomes dry while they are dormant. Resume watering in spring.

Regelia irises, with their bearded standards and falls, are related to the Oncocyclus irises and have similar cultural requirements although they are easier to grow. Some species, such as *I. hoogiana*, may be grown outside, given good drainage and a hot, dry site in the summer. The Regeliocyclus group (Regelia x Oncocyclus hybrids) is more easily grown in the open.

Crested irises

These have ridges, or cockscomblike crests, instead of beards.
Evansia irises are usually found in damp woodland. Larger species, such as *I. confusa* and *I. japonica*, are not fully hardy and need a sheltered position in humus-rich

Informal elegance
The colourful blooms of Siberian irises (blue and white) and I. pseudacorus *(yellow) provide a focal point by a garden pond.*

RHIZOMATOUS AND BULBOUS IRISES

I. 'Bold Print'
(bearded)

I. 'Carnaby'
(bearded)

I. innominata
(Pacific Coast)

I. 'Caprician Butterfly' (Japanese)

I. bucharica
(Juno)

I. 'Joyce'
(Reticulata)

soils, with some shade provided in warm climates. Smaller species, such as *I. cristata* and *I. gracilipes*, are ideal for planting in peaty pockets in a shaded rock garden.

Beardless irises

Irises in this group do not have bearded falls, but usually have crests. Most have similar cultural requirements to bearded irises, but some prefer heavier soil.

Pacific Coast irises, a group that includes *I. innominata* and *I. tenax*, are useful for cutting. Many good, free-flowering hybrids have been produced which are excellent for humus-rich, acid soils, in sun in cool regions or in shade in warmer climates. Others from groups that need similar conditions include: *I. missouriensis*, which is more tolerant of alkaline soils; *I. verna* and *I. prismatica*; and *I. setosa*, which is more tolerant of sun.

Water irises are a group of elegant, moisture-loving plants that thrive in pond margins, bog gardens, or rich, permanently damp soils. They include *I. laevigata, I. pseudacorus, I. ensata* (syn. *I. kaempferi*), *I. fulva, I. versicolor*, and *I. x fulvala*. All need similar damp conditions but can be difficult to establish.

Siberian irises have slender leaves and beautifully formed, delicately marked flowers. This group includes *I. chrysographes, I. clarkei, I. forrestii*, and *I. sibirica*. They are easily grown in borders in rich soil that does not dry out, and are particularly

suited to very moist, waterside soil. The flowers last well when cut.
Spuria irises have narrow, reedlike foliage and elegant blooms. Spurias – *I. orientalis, I. graminea*, and *I. spuria* – are suited to sunny herbaceous borders, in well-drained soil; they tolerate drier conditions than the Siberian irises.

Bulbous irises

The storage organs of these irises are bulbs, sometimes with thick, fleshy roots. Subgenera include Reticulata, Juno, and Xiphium irises.

Reticulata irises

Dwarf, hardy bulbs, which flower early. They prefer a sunny position in well-drained, acid or alkaline soil, or may be grown in pots in the bulb frame.

Juno irises

Junos need similar conditions to the Oncocyclus irises and are also difficult to grow. Vigorous species, such as *I. bucharica* and *I. magnifica*, grow well in warm, outdoor sites.

Xiphium irises

These include the brightly coloured Dutch, English, and Spanish irises, often grown for cut flowers. Any alkaline, well-drained soil in full sun is suitable. In cold areas, lift the bulbs in autumn to overwinter in a frost-free place. Replant in spring.

Soil preparation and planting

Herbaceous perennials originate from many regions, which have widely varying climatic and soil conditions, so whether the proposed site is sheltered or exposed, fertile or stony, there is always a number of plants that will thrive. It is better to select plants that will flourish in the given growing conditions rather than struggle against nature.

Site and aspect

When deciding which plants to grow, take into account climate, aspect, and soil type, as well as the amount of sun, shade, and shelter the site receives at different times of day and from season to season. For example, the shade cast by deciduous trees is most dense in late spring and summer when the trees are in leaf.

Different areas of the garden may provide varying growing conditions: for example, a south-facing border would be ideal for plants that thrive in sun, such as sedums, while a north-facing site or a position beneath a tree would be better for shade-loving species, such as hostas, provided that they can be kept moist.

The ground next to a wall, fence, or hedge is usually fairly dry due to the effect of rain shadow, but since it also tends to be warm and sheltered, it may be a good position for plants that are not fully hardy.

Altering conditions

In small gardens especially, it may be necessary to adapt some elements to create growing conditions that suit a wide range of plants. Heavy, water-logged soils may be drained or the plants grown in raised beds or containers, while lighter soils may benefit from the addition of organic matter. Shade from trees may be reduced by judicious pruning, and shelter provided by shrubs, hedges, or windbreaks (see also Frost and Wind Protection, pp.612–613, and Hedges and Screens, pp.84–86).

Soil preparation

The ideal soil for the majority of perennial plants is a fertile loam that is well drained but retains adequate moisture. Use a proprietary soil-testing kit to find out the degree of acidity or alkalinity of the soil, because this partly determines which plants will thrive there.

It is also important to check soil drainage; if much of the ground remains waterlogged in wet weather, then it will be necessary to install soakaways or drains (see "Improving drainage", p.623).

Clearing the site

All weeds should be cleared from the site prior to planting because, once other plants are established, perennial weeds, in particular, are difficult to eradicate. If the ground is infested with weeds, treat the whole area with an appropriate weedkiller during the season before planting. If there are few perennial weeds, however, they may be forked out when preparing the soil in winter.

During the first growing season, any remaining perennial weeds should be carefully removed with a hand fork as soon as they are noticed, or spot-treated with a systemic weed-killer, taking care not to harm the newly planted perennials. Annual weeds may be either sprayed or forked out before the site is planted.

Improving the soil

All soils may be enhanced by the addition of humus or well-rotted organic matter or by proprietary soil improvers (see Soils and Fertilizers, "Soil nutrients and fertilizers", pp.624–625); this increases the water retention of light, free-draining soils and helps to open up heavy, clay soils. It also improves soil fertility. Before planting (preferably a few weeks in advance), apply a 5–10cm (2–4in) layer of well-rotted organic matter, then fork or dig it into the top spit of the soil. Allow the soil to settle. If the soil is sufficiently fertile and rich in humus, it may be unnecessary to use fertilizer, although they may require feeding in subsequent seasons (see "Fertilizing", p.191).

CHOOSING PERENNIALS
GOOD EXAMPLE
POOR EXAMPLES

Lupin

Strong, healthy top-growth

Moist compost

Established, vigorous roots

Weak, woody top-growth

Under-developed root system

Dry compost

Moss and weeds growing on the compost

Pot-bound roots

Selecting plants

Most perennials are sold container-grown, but bare-root plants are also sometimes available from autumn to early spring, when they are dormant. When selecting plants, look for healthy, vigorous specimens with no sign of dieback or abnormally coloured leaves that may indicate a lack of nutrients. If you are buying herbaceous plants at the beginning of the growing season, check that there are strong, emerging shoots: plants that have a few fat, healthy looking buds are better than those that have a large number of weaker ones.

One or two annual weeds growing in the compost may be removed easily enough, but do not buy any container-grown plants with perennial weeds, moss, or liverworts. These often indicate that the plant has been in its container for too long and may be starved of nutrients or that the compost is poorly drained, in which case the plant's roots may have rotted or died back.

When possible, remove the plant from its container and inspect the roots: do not choose a plant with a mass of tightly coiling roots or one that has large roots pushing through the drainage holes. The roots should, however, be sufficiently established to retain most of the compost when the plant is removed from its pot. For plants growing in plastic bags, check that there is good root growth by feeling them through the bag.

If buying bare-root plants, ensure that the root systems are strong and have not dried out, and that the young shoots are not wilting. Plant them as soon as possible after purchase, protecting them against moisture loss by wrapping them in plastic or wet newspaper until ready to plant.

Dividing large plants

When buying fibrous-rooted plants, choose large examples with healthy shoots that may be divided before planting, rather than a few smaller, cheaper specimens. Divide the plant by prising it apart with your hands or two hand forks used back-to-back, taking care that each division has its own root system and retains as much soil around the roots as possible (see also "Dividing perennials", p.200).

Preparing the ground for naturalistic plantings

To create naturalistic displays or a meadow garden (see p.401) you may need to reduce the fertility of your soil. Developing this type of feature is easier in gardens with sandy soil, or close to chalk downland, where soil fertility is usually low. On richer soils you can reduce fertility in a number of ways:
■ Do not add fertilizers or manures.
■ Ensure the site is well drained.
■ To create conditions for dryland species, spread a deep 10cm (4in) layer of gritty sand over the area.
■ If the site is already under grass, mow at regular intervals, removing and composting all grass cuttings.
■ On rich grassland remove the top layer of turf; stack it to provide loam for potting compost.
Where grassland is well established, you can reduce its vigour by scattering seed of yellow-rattle (*Rhinanthus minor*) over the area. This is a semi-parasitic native that partially obtains its nutrition from different grass species and, as a result, inhibits growth. Alternatively, apply growth retardants prior to sowing or planting other species. If necessary, apply again in winter, when other species are dormant.

PERENNIALS FOR SANDY SOIL

Acanthus spinosus
Achillea
Alchemilla
Armeria
Asphodeline lutea
Centranthus ruber
Dianthus, some ❋

Echinops ritro
'Veitch's Blue'

Echinops
Eryngium x *tripartitum*
Gaillardia x *grandiflora* (cvs)
Globularia
Limonium platyphyllum
Nepeta x *faassenii*
Origanum vulgare 'Aureum'
Papaver orientale
Romneya coulteri
Sedum, some ❋
Sempervivum
Sisyrinchium, some ❋

PERENNIALS FOR CLAY SOIL

Aruncus dioicus
Astilbe
Butomus ◆
Caltha ◆
Cardamine pratensis
Darmera peltatum
Dodecatheon
Eomecon
Filipendula ulmaria 'Aurea'
Gunnera manicata ◆
Hemerocallis
Hosta
Houttuynia
Lobelia cardinalis ❋
Lysichiton ◆
Lysimachia, some ❋
Lythrum
Mimulus guttatus ◆
Myosotis scorpioides ◆
Persicaria
Phormium
Pontederia ◆

Primula bulleyana

Primula bulleyana,
  P. florindae, P. rosea
Ranunculus ficaria cultivars,
  R. flammula ◆
Rheum
Rodgersia
Sagittaria, some ❋
Scrophularia auriculata
Trollius

Key
❋ *Not hardy*
◆ *Tolerates waterlogged soil*

When to plant

Perennials grown in containers may be planted out at any time of year when the soil is workable, but the best seasons are spring and autumn. Planting in autumn helps the plants to establish quickly before the onset of winter since the soil is still warm enough to promote root growth yet is unlikely to dry out. Spring planting is preferable for late-flowering perennials, and in cold areas is also better for perennials that are not entirely hardy or that dislike wet conditions, like *Kniphofia, Schizostylis, Lobelia cardinalis*, and *Scabiosa caucasica*. It should ensure that they are fully established before their first winter.

Bare-root specimens should generally be planted in spring or autumn, although a few, such as hostas, may be transplanted successfully during the growing season.

Planting perennials

Plant perennials in prepared ground, taking care to position them at the right depth (see below): for example, those prone to rotting at the base are best planted proud of the soil so that excess water may drain away.

Container-grown plants
Water the plant thoroughly, preferably the night before it is to be planted. Then dig a planting hole, then remove

HOW TO PLANT A CONTAINER-GROWN PERENNIAL

1 *In a prepared bed, dig a hole 1½ times wider and deeper than the plant's root ball.*

2 *Soak the compost in the pot before sliding the plant out (here an* Aster*).*

3 *Gently scrape off the top 3cm (1½in) of compost to remove weeds and weed seeds. Carefully tease out the roots around the sides and base of the root ball.*

4 *Check that the plant crown is at the correct depth when planted and fill in around the root ball. Firm in around the plant and water thoroughly.*

Planting depths

Aster

Sisyrinchium striatum 'Aunt May'

While most perennials are best planted out at the same soil level as they were in their pots, a number grow better if planted higher or deeper, depending on their individual requirements. Some prefer a raised, well-drained site while others thrive in deeper, moist conditions.

Hosta

Polygonatum

Ground-level planting
The majority of perennials should be planted so that the crown of the plant is level with the surrounding soil.

Raised planting
Set plants that are prone to rot at the base, and variegated plants that tend to revert, with their crowns slightly above the ground.

Shallow planting
Plant perennials that require a moist environment with their crowns about 2.5cm (1in) below ground level.

Deep planting
Plant perennials with rhizomatous root systems so that the crowns are about 10cm (4in) below the soil surface.

the plant from its container, taking care not to damage the roots. To help the plant establish quickly, carefully loosen the sides and base of the root ball, particularly if root-bound, by teasing out the roots with your fingers or a hand fork. Place the plant at the appropriate depth in the prepared hole, backfill with soil, and firm. Loosen the surface of the soil with a hand fork and water in thoroughly.

Bare-root plants

To prevent dehydration, plant bare-root perennials as soon as possible after purchase. Prepare a hole as for container-grown plants, spread out the roots evenly, work in soil between the roots, then water well.

Transplanting self-sown seedlings

A number of perennials, for example *Aquilegia* and foxgloves (*Digitalis*), regularly produce self-sown seedlings that may be moved to another position in the garden or nursery bed.

Before lifting the seedlings, prepare suitable planting holes, spacing them to allow room for the plants to develop. Then gently lift each seedling with a trowel, taking care to retain as much soil around the roots as possible, and replant it immediately. Firm it in well and water it thoroughly. Shade the plants in sunny weather, and water them regularly until they are established.

Raised beds

These beds are often used for growing acid-loving plants in a garden with alkaline soil or for providing a free-draining bed on heavy, clay soil. Plants that will only thrive in acid soil are best planted in a raised bed filled with an ericaceous compost (see also THE ROCK GARDEN, "Raised beds", p.257, and "Ericaceous plants", p.257).

Raised beds may be constructed from a variety of materials including wood, bricks, stone, and logs (see also STRUCTURES AND SURFACES, "Raised beds", p.599). Include a deep layer of coarse drainage material (such as broken bricks) in the base – about one third of the depth of the bed is ideal. Cover this with a layer of fibrous material and fill in with topsoil before planting.

Containers

As well as being a highly attractive way of displaying a number of plants, growing perennials in containers provides an opportunity to include plants that would not flourish in the open garden, either because they are too tender, or because the soil type is not suitable. If growing different plants together in one container, take care to choose those that thrive in similar conditions.

When choosing a container, make sure that it is sufficiently deep and wide to allow room for the plants' roots to develop properly. Consider how the selected plants will look when in full growth in relation to the container to achieve a pleasing balance between them. Tall plants in deep, narrow containers and small plants in large, wide ones may seem out of proportion.

TRANSPLANTING SEEDLINGS

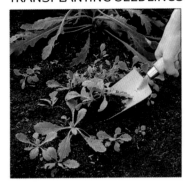

Lift seedlings with soil around their roots so as not to break up the root ball. Plant out and water well.

Planting in containers

If using a heavy container such as a stone urn, lead trough, wooden half-barrel, or large terracotta pot, place it in position before filling and planting since it will be very cumbersome to move afterwards; plastic containers are, of course, considerably lighter, but they are less stable and may be blown over in strong winds. Set the container on a support of blocks or bricks to allow free drainage.

Make sure that the container has drainage holes in the base or low on the sides to prevent water-logging. Cover the holes with 5–8cm (2–3in) of broken crocks or stones and add a layer of fibrous material, for example upside-down turves or coir fibre; this allows water to filter through freely yet prevents compost from being washed down into the base and blocking the drainage holes.

Most potting composts are suitable, although acid-loving plants must be planted in an ericaceous compost. A prepared, general compost with a slow-release fertilizer added (see p.323) suits most plants; those that need extra drainage (such as *Sedum* or *Achillea*) prefer a compost containing extra grit or sharp sand.

Before planting, arrange the plants on the compost to ensure that they have enough room to develop freely. Plant as for perennials in open ground and keep well watered until established.

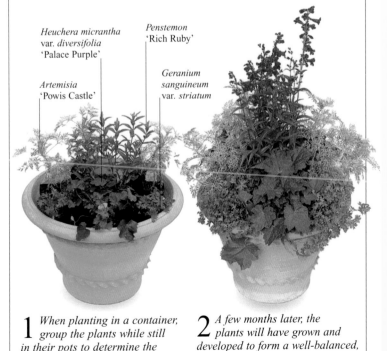

Heuchera micrantha var. *diversifolia* 'Palace Purple'

Penstemon 'Rich Ruby'

Artemisia 'Powis Castle'

Geranium sanguineum var. *striatum*

1 *When planting in a container, group the plants while still in their pots to determine the spacing and arrangement. Then plant, firm in, and water well.*

2 *A few months later, the plants will have grown and developed to form a well-balanced, attractive display.*

PERENNIALS FOR ACID SOIL

Anigozanthos manglesii ✳
Cypripedium reginae
Darlingtonia

Anigozanthos manglesii

Drosera, some ✳
Nepenthes ✳
Pinguicula, some ✳
Sarracenia flava ✳
Trillium
Uvularia

PERENNIALS FOR ALKALINE SOIL

Acanthus spinosus
Achillea filipendulina 'Gold Plate'
Aconitum
Anchusa
Anemone hupehensis, *A.* x *hybrida*
Anthyllis
Bergenia
Berkheya, some ✳
Brunnera
Campanula lactiflora
Catananche
Centranthus
Clematis heracleifolia, *C. recta*
Coronilla varia
Corydalis lutea
Dianthus
Doronicum
Eremurus
Eryngium, some ✳
Galega
Geranium pratense
Gypsophila paniculata
Helenium
Helleborus, some ✳
Heuchera
Kniphofia, some ✳
Linaria purpurea
Linum narbonense
Lychnis chalcedonica
Paeonia
Salvia nemorosa
Saponaria
Scabiosa

Scabiosa caucasica 'Clive Greaves'

Sidalcea
Stachys, some ✳
Verbascum
Veronica spicata

Key
✳ *Not hardy*

Hostas

GROWN primarily for their bold, sculptural foliage, many hosta species and cultivars also produce attractive white, lilac, or purple flowers. Being easy to maintain and long-lived, hostas make a valuable addition to any garden.

Although there are more than 2,000 registered cultivars, there is no agreed formal classification system for hostas. Many nurseries, however, follow the American Hosta Society sizing, which is based on the foliage height of the clump when mature: dwarf hostas are less than 10cm (4in) tall; miniatures are 10–15cm (4–6in) tall; small 15–25cm (6–10in) tall; medium 25–45cm (10–18in) tall; large 45–70cm (18–28in) tall; and extra large taller than 70cm (28in).

Using hostas in the garden

Hostas are highly sought after as foliage plants for light to moderately shaded areas, and make eye-catching displays in pots or beside ponds. The range of colours, textures, and shapes of their foliage is stunning: modern hybrids may have leaves patterned in shades of green, white, and gold, or edged in a contrasting colour. Their texture may be rich and glossy or soft and velvety. Leaves may be narrow and ribbon-like, heart-shaped or almost circular.

There are hostas suitable for most degrees of shade, from light or dappled, to moderate. In general, the blue-leaved hostas flourish in light shade all day, while yellow-leaved cultivars prefer some sun.

Hostas for shady places

Hostas make excellent companion plants for other shade-loving perennials. They act as a foil for bright flowers such as those of *Astilbe*, while their large leaves make a counterpoint to the finer foliage of other plants including Japanese painted fern (*Athyrium niponicum* var. *pictum*) and sedges (*Carex*). For shady places in the rock garden, choose miniature hostas such as *H. venusta* and *H. 'Shining Tot'*.

Consider planting a hosta to enliven a shady entrance. To make an impact, choose a variety that has striking foliage, such as the plate-like *H. 'Blue Angel'* or the white-margined *H. 'Patriot'*, both of which have showy flowers in midsummer. Fragrant hostas ideal for planting close to the house include *H. 'Sugar and Cream'*, *H. 'So Sweet'*, and *H. plantaginea*, which is one of the last to flower.

On a shaded patio, grow hostas in containers to contrast with more flamboyant annuals. Golden-yellow *H. 'Richland Gold'* or the yellow-centred *H. 'June'* are excellent plants for pots or other containers.

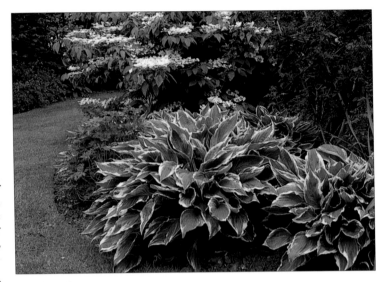

Mixed border
Hostas blend well with other shade plants, acting as a foil for summer flowers, and providing interest after the flowers have finished.

Ground cover

Hostas make particularly striking ground cover when planted as a mass. Choose cultivars carefully for continuous interest from both foliage and flowers. For example, a combination of *H. 'Green Piecrust'*, *H. 'Krossa Regal'*, *H. 'Honeybells'*, and *H. plantaginea* makes an exotic planting that will flower for several months in succession. A more subtle effect is achieved by restricting the design to a few hostas within a limited spectrum of leaf colours. For a fast-growing, low ground cover, choose cultivars such as *H. 'Pearl Lake'* and *H. 'Ground Master'*.

Hostas in other positions

Several hostas planted together may be used as a low summer hedge that needs no clipping. The lance-leaved hosta (*H. lancifolia*) is ideal for this and will take full sun in all but the hottest regions; it gives a display of slender purple bells in late

HOSTAS FOR DIFFERENT SITUATIONS

H. tokudama f. aureonebulosa
Medium-size, for medium shade

H. decorata
Medium-size, for light to moderate shade

H. 'Gold Standard'
Medium-size, prefers light shade

H. 'Halcyon'
Medium-size, for light shade

H. plantaginea
Large, likes full sun and a little light shade. Scented flowers

H. ventricosa var. aureomaculata
Large, prefers light to medium shade

H. montana 'Aureomarginata'
Extra-large hosta, for light to medium shade

H. lancifolia
Medium-size, tolerating full sun

H. 'August Moon'
Large hosta; colours well in some direct sun

H. sieboldiana var. elegans
Extra-large; light shade

H. ventricosa
Large, for light to moderate shade

summer. Most hostas will grow well in sites that are close to water; *H.* 'Sum and Substance', *H. undulata* var. *erromena*, and *H. undulata* var. *albomarginata* are especially good in soils that are moist.

Cultivation

Hostas tolerate a wide range of soils, except for unimproved heavy clay or pure sand. They grow best in good, moist loam, rich in organic matter, with a pH from 6.5 to 7.3. Prepare the soil well before planting, particularly if it is lacking in nutrients (see "Soil preparation", p.183).

Planting hostas

Bare-root hostas can be planted in spring or autumn. Container-grown hostas can be planted at any time, but do not disturb the roots if planting while they are in active growth (see "Planting perennials", p.184). In spring or autumn, however, unless the container is full of roots, it is better to shake off much of the compost and treat as a bare-root hosta.

Plant with the crown at ground level (see "Planting depths", p.184). Do not allow any manure to come into contact with the roots at planting, as it may cause discoloured foliage in the first year. Leave a slight depression around the plant at first so that, when you water, the moisture soaks directly down to the roots of the plant.

Routine care

Hostas take about five years to reach maturity and can then be left undisturbed for many years. Hostas do best if the soil is moist at all times.

To produce lush foliage of a good colour, top-dress hostas with compost or well-rotted manure; these increase the soil humus and nutrient content. In spring, apply a well-balanced fertilizer to hostas in poor soil.

Mulching

Apply a spring mulch while the soil is moist. Use only well-rotted materials in order to discourage slugs. In regions with very cold winters, apply a mulch of straw or leaves around each hosta before the ground has frozen; take care not to cover the crown of the plant. On new, shallow-rooted plants the mulch prevents them from lifting after a severe frost, while on established plants it often reduces crown rot. If very coarse material is used as a mulch, it should be removed in the spring.

Pests and diseases

Slugs and snails (p.644) may devastate hostas, sometimes reducing leaves to tatters by the end of the season; earwigs (p.644) will also chew holes in the foliage. Crown rot (p.665) may cause problems, especially on heavy soils or in climates that are relatively humid.

Propagation

Hostas are easily increased by division (see "Dividing hostas", p.200) or cutting a slice out of a crown with a sharp spade. Although the offspring only rarely come true to type, hostas may be raised from seed collected when the capsules turn brown. Sow in autumn or winter (see p.198).

Division by "topping"

A practical method of propagating hostas is to "top" them: small cuts are made in the rootstock in spring to stimulate new buds and roots. This method is useful for hostas that are slow to increase.

By autumn, the cuts will have callused and developed new roots and dormant buds. The entire plant can then be lifted in autumn or the following spring and divided into pieces, each with its own bud. After transplanting, the new plants should be allowed to grow on for at least a year before this process is repeated.

PROPAGATING HOSTAS BY "TOPPING"

1 *In spring when the buds have started to grow, carefully scrape away the soil from around the base of a young plant to expose the crown.*

2 *Carefully wipe the surface of the rootstock clean with a soft, moistened cloth, taking care not to disturb the roots.*

3 *With a sharp knife, make a vertical cut through the crown. Unless the plant is very small, make a second cut at right angles to the first.*

4 *Dust each cut with hormone rooting powder and insert a toothpick to hold the cut open.*

5 *Pack the surrounding soil back around the crown of the plant, firm it well, and water thoroughly. By autumn, dormant buds will develop.*

6 *Lift and divide the clump the following spring when new shoots emerge. Alternatively, divide the previous autumn.*

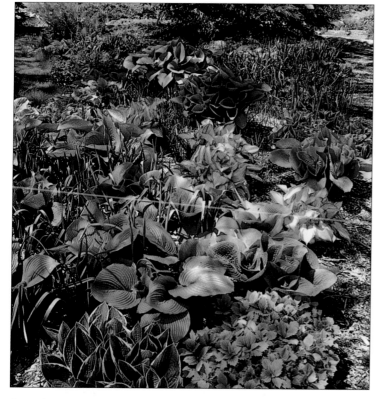

Ground cover
In a border with dappled shade, hostas make ideal ground cover. Select leaf colours to go with the varying degrees of shade.

Chrysanthemums

THE rich colours and luxuriant shapes of their long-lasting flowerheads make the florists' chrysanthemum popular for providing displays in the garden, cutting for the house, and for exhibiting.

Classifying chrysanthemums

The florists' chrysanthemum is derived from a number of species from eastern Asia and is of complex hybrid origin. A varied range of different flower types has been developed – these are grouped both according to the shape and arrangement of their petals and the florets within the flowerheads, and by their season of flowering.

Chrysanthemums naturally form a number of flowerheads on the same stem; these are known as "sprays". "Disbudded" chrysanthemums are formed by removing the lateral buds of spray types at an early stage; this leaves a single, terminal bud that will then produce a much larger flowerhead.

Early-flowering chrysanthemums bloom from late summer to early autumn, and are grown outdoors. Late-flowering ones are grown in pots outdoors in summer and brought into a greenhouse, where they flower from autumn until late winter. Cultivation is similar for early- and late-flowering types, but plants for exhibition need more time and attention. Early charms (dwarf chrysanthemums) flower from late summer to mid-autumn and are grown outdoors.

Early-flowering chrysanthemums

Early-flowering cultivars may be ordered from a specialist for delivery in spring. To be sure of selecting the desired colours, it is best to see the plants at flowering time, or to choose them from an illustrated catalogue.

Once established in the garden, plants that are growing vigorously and that are producing good, healthy blooms should be marked so that they can be used for propagating new plants from cuttings.

Disbudded chrysanthemums
These (here C. 'George Griffiths') are formed by removing all but one of the flower buds on each lateral, producing large, individual blooms.

Soil preparation and planting

Fully hardy in most areas, early-flowering chrysanthemums require a fairly sunny but sheltered site. They generally prefer a well-drained, slightly acid soil that has a pH value of 6.5. For most soils, the ground should be prepared in late autumn or early winter, incorporating plenty of well-rotted organic matter. Light soils will not need to be prepared until the early spring, with the organic matter applied as a mulch in early summer.

Prior to planting out in late spring, insert 1.2m (4ft) canes about 45cm (18in) apart (a split cane may be tied to the top to support a tall cultivar, if this proves necessary). Plant each chrysanthemum next to a cane, with the root ball just covered with soil. Tie the stem of each plant securely to the supporting cane.

TYPES OF CHRYSANTHEMUM FLOWERHEAD

Incurved
C. 'Yellow John Hughes'
Fully double flowerheads with incurved petals closing tightly over the crown.

Fully reflexed
C. 'Primrose West Bromwich'
Fully double flowerheads with curved petals reflexing back to touch the stem.

Reflexed
C. 'Brietner'
Fully double flowerheads with partly reflexed petals and a spiky outline.

Intermediate
C. 'Beacon'
Fully double flowerheads with loosely incurving petals and a regular shape.

Spider
C. 'Muxton Plume'
Fully double flowerheads with pendent, long, fine florets with hooked or coiled tips.

Quill
C. 'Honeycomb'
Fully double flowerheads with straight, tubular florets that open at the tips to form spoon shapes.

Anemone-centred
C. 'Pennine Oriel'
Single flowerheads each with a dome-shaped disc and flat, or occasionally spoon-shaped, petals.

Pompon
C. 'Salmon Fairie'
Fully double, dense flowerheads bearing tubular florets with flat, rounded petals.

Single
C. 'Golden Woolman's Glory'
Flowerheads with prominent central discs and 5 rows of flat-petalled florets.

Spoon
C. 'Pennine Alfie'
Single flowerheads with straight, tubular florets. Petals open at the tips to form a spoon shape.

Stopping

Soon after planting (refer to a growers' catalogue or specialist publication for precise timing), the plants need to be "stopped". This consists of pinching out the growing tips to encourage flower-bearing laterals.

When the laterals are about 8cm (3in) long, reduce them to the number required: four laterals to each main stem should be sufficient for a general display on cultivars grown as sprays, whereas four to six are needed for disbudded plants and two or three for those grown for exhibition.

About one month after stopping, hoe and water in a balanced fertilizer, at a rate of 70g/sq m (2oz/sq yd). Repeat this feed about one month later, to encourage strong growth. Remove any sideshoots that develop from the laterals as soon as possible so that all the plant's energy is concentrated on the laterals.

Disbudding

Seven or eight weeks after stopping, a main, or apical, bud, surrounded by

STOPPING AND REMOVING LATERALS

Stopping
When the cutting is 15–20cm (6–8in) high, pinch out 1cm (½in) at the tip to encourage laterals.

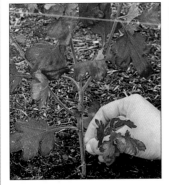

Removing excess laterals
About 2 months later, select 3 or 4 healthy, evenly spaced laterals and remove any others.

DISBUDDING

For disbuds, once the side buds around each apical bud have tiny stalks, pinch them out so that only the central bud develops.

sideshoots, should be visible at the end of each lateral.

If only one flower per stem is required, snap off all the sideshoots from each lateral. The apical buds can then develop unhindered and each lateral will bear a single bloom (the "disbud"). To produce a spray of small, even-sized flowerheads, pinch out the apical bud only; this allows all the sideshoots to develop and produce a spray of flowers.

Routine care

Water plants regularly, and apply a balanced liquid feed at weekly or 10-day intervals while the buds are developing. Feeding must be discontinued just before the buds show colour, so the blooms do not become soft and prone to damage.

Overwintering

Early-flowering chrysanthemums may be overwintered in the ground in mild climates that are frost-free, and their stems cut down only in spring. In temperate climates, however, plants are best lifted and stored. After flowering and before the first frosts, cut the stems to about 22cm (9in) and remove all shoots. Keep the plants labelled while in store to identify them the following year.

Lift the plants, wash the roots, and store the stools (rootstocks) in batches of six or eight in a shallow box of loam-based potting compost. Make sure that the compost is slightly moist and that the stocks are not buried too deeply. Do not water them in: keep them almost dry to minimize the risk of rot. Place the containers in a frost-free cold frame or cold greenhouse for two months.

Bring the boxed stools into a greenhouse in mid-winter, water them, and keep them at a temperature

OVERWINTERING

1 *After flowering, cut back the stems, lift the plant (here a young plant is used), and wash the roots. Trim any straggly roots to leave the root ball about the size of a tennis ball.*

2 *Line a 10cm (4in) deep box with paper and place the plants with stems upright on a 2.5cm (1in) layer of damp compost. Fill around them with more compost and firm; store the box in a cool, light place.*

of about 7°C (45°F). They will soon produce young shoots.

Taking cuttings

Take cuttings four to six weeks after new shoots have appeared and discard the parent plant. Select close-jointed shoots near the base of the stem, with soft but firm growth, and remove them with a knife or snap them off. Trim them to about 4cm (1½in), cutting just under a leaf node. Dip the base of each cutting in a rooting hormone, insert them in standard cutting compost, and then place the pots in a propagator, preferably with gentle bottom heat at 10°C (50°F). Rooting occurs in two to three weeks (see also *How to Propagate by Basal Stem Cuttings*, p.202).

Aftercare

Once rooted, move the cuttings from the propagator to slightly cooler conditions for about a week, then plant them in batches of six to eight to a pot or box, filled with moist loam-based or loamless potting compost. If there are just a few cuttings, pot them up individually. Keep them slightly dry for a few weeks, in frost-free conditions. Check regularly for pests and diseases, and treat them accordingly (see PLANT PROBLEMS, pp.639–668). After a month or so, transfer the plants to a cold frame and gradually harden them off; protect from severe frost and provide ample ventilation.

Late-flowering chrysanthemums

Indoor or "late" chrysanthemums are grown in containers and are brought into a house or a temperate or

warm greenhouse to flower. Their cultivation requirements are similar to early-flowering chrysanthemums.

Planting

Plants may be potted up using moist loam-based or loamless potting compost in late spring and staked as for early-flowering cultivars. The stakes may be tied between support wires to hold them upright in windy weather. Stand the pots outdoors throughout the summer, in a sunny, sheltered position. Water when necessary, never allowing the compost to dry out completely.

Late-flowering spray
Allow indoor spray chrysanthemums (here C. 'Pin Nu Rosemary') grown without daylength regulation to bear 6–7 flowerheads per stem.

Stopping and disbudding

Stop the plants in midsummer; they will produce their flower buds 10–12 weeks later. Disbud and remove sideshoots in the same way as for early-flowering chrysanthemums.

Routine care

In early autumn, move the pots to a cool greenhouse with the temperature kept to about 10°C (50°F). The greenhouse should be shaded, if necessary, to keep the temperature low. Continue to feed with a balanced liquid fertilizer until the flower colour just begins to show. Bring them into a warmer place to flower.

Overwintering

Cut back the plants after flowering to about 22cm (9in). It is not necessary to lift the stools; keep them in their pots in a cool greenhouse or frame at about 5°C (41°F) and in good light for about a month. Then bring them into growth at about 7°C (45°F) to produce shoots for cuttings in late winter, about four to six weeks later.

Taking cuttings

Take cuttings and root them in a propagator, as for early-flowering chrysanthemums. Cuttings of late-flowering spray cultivars do not need to be rooted until early or midsummer.

Once rooted, treat the cuttings as for early-flowering cultivars. In late spring, when the plants' roots have filled their pots, pot them on into their final containers. Use 24cm (9in) or 25cm (10in) pots, depending on root vigour. Use a moist loam-based potting compost, with additional slow-release fertilizer. Stake tall cultivars, as well as those with large flowerheads, before final potting.

Early charms

Sometimes known as garden 'mums or cushion 'mums, these dwarf chrysanthemums have become very popular. They are planted direct in garden beds or borders or in pots or tubs on the patio.

Their cultivation requirements are similar to early-flowering chrysanthemums when grown outside and to late-flowering ones when container-grown, except that charms should not be disbudded.

Plant out in late spring, setting the plants 30–38cm (12–15in) apart in a bed, or insert three plants in a 30cm (12in) pot. Stop the growing points

Charm chrysanthemums
These are dwarf plants, bearing a mass of single flowers, each with a diameter of about 2.5cm (1in). The star-shaped blooms (here of C. 'Morning Star') densely cover each plant to form a rounded head.

immediately, and again when lateral shoots reach 5cm (2in) long. Continue to stop container-grown early charms, to encourage a large, well-shaped plant. Early charms are self-supporting, so do not need to be staked. Apply a balanced fertilizer regularly (see p.191).

Early charms can be grown in open ground year-round in mild climates that are frost-free. Elsewhere, in mid-autumn dig up the plants, place them in a loam-based potting compost in a box, and store dry in a frost-free greenhouse over the winter months. At the same time, bring container-grown plants into the greenhouse for winter.

Taking cuttings

In late winter or early spring take cuttings for container-grown early charms and root them in a propagator. Take cuttings in mid-spring for charms to be planted in a garden bed. Once rooted, harden off the cuttings and pot on or plant out.

Growing blooms for exhibition

Blooms grown outdoors for exhibition require protection from the elements. White and yellow blooms may be covered satisfactorily with special greaseproof bags of various sizes. Spray or dust the buds to remove any pests before covering them. The developed blooms are heavy, and care must be taken to support the stems so that the heads do not snap off in high winds.

Blooms of other colours, and any particularly large reflexes, sprays, and plants grown in rows, are better protected by a specially prepared structure, like a small greenhouse with unglazed sides.

It is possible to advance or retard the flowering time of indoor cultivars by regulating the periods of light and darkness. Bud-forming (which usually requires 10 hours of continuous darkness) can be advanced by excluding daylight or, conversely, delayed by extending the period of daylight with artificial light.

Late-flowering spray chrysanthemums intended for exhibition may be subjected to extended hours of darkness for a period of three weeks to encourage bud initiation on the required date. This is achieved by completely blacking out the greenhouse for at least 14 hours a night, or, if only a small number of plants is being grown, by placing black plastic bags over individual plants.

Preparing for exhibition

Blooms for exhibition are cut when fully or virtually fully open; the stems are then plunged immediately in deep water for 24 hours.

Exhibition classes will usually be for sprays with one, three, or five blooms in a vase. A single bloom is staged in the centre and at the top of the vase and held upright with paper. A group of three is staged with either two blooms at the back and the third slightly lower in front, or one at the back and two slightly lower in front. Five blooms are always staged with three flowerheads in an arc at the back and two slightly lower in front.

All the blooms in a vase should match as closely as possible in size and form. If there is any variation between the blooms, stage those with the best outline at the back, and place those with the best developed centres at the front.

There is also a class for charms (dwarf plants that produce hundreds of star-shaped flowers), which are shown in a 30cm (12in) pot, or larger.

PROTECTING BLOOMS FOR EXHIBITION

1 *When the blooms are just beginning to open, enclose each one in a 15 x 15cm (6 x 6in) grease-proof bag fastened with a twist-tie. Leave this on for 7–10 days.*

2 *The bud should then be at the "paintbrush" stage with the colour just showing. Remove the bag and replace it with a 30 x 33cm (12 x 13in) bag.*

PROTECTING A ROW OF BLOOMS

Construct a temporary "greenhouse" of wooden supports with a clear plastic roof (do not enclose the sides). The structure should be 2.2m (7ft) at the ridge and 2m (6ft) at the eaves. The slope allows rain to run off, so it is important to keep the soil around the plants moist.

Routine care

Although most perennials will thrive with little maintenance, certain routine tasks help to keep them looking attractive and healthy. Occasional watering and feeding is necessary and the surrounding ground should be kept clear of weeds. In addition to this, many perennials produce further growth and flowers if dead-headed or cut back, while dividing the plants renews vigour. Tall, fragile perennials, or those with top-heavy flowerheads, may also require staking, particularly in exposed gardens.

Watering

The amount of water that plants require depends on the site, climate, and the individual species; provided that they are grown in appropriate conditions, established perennials often need little or no additional irrigation. If there are prolonged dry spells during the growing season, give extra water to the plants. If they wilt or die back from lack of water they will normally recover fully after heavy rainfall or will become dormant until the following season. The most efficient way to provide extra water is using drip or trickle irrigation, rather than an overhead spray (see also TOOLS AND EQUIPMENT, "Watering aids", pp.560–561).

Young plants need sufficient water to become established but they should not be watered once they are growing satisfactorily, except in very dry weather. Irrigation, if necessary, is best applied in the evening, when water evaporates less quickly from the soil surface.

Fertilizing

In soil that has been thoroughly prepared before planting, few perennials require more than an annual top-dressing of bone meal or a balanced slow-release fertilizer, preferably applied in early spring after rain.

If conditions are dry, first water the soil thoroughly, then work the fertilizer into the soil surface with a hand fork. Do not let the fertilizer touch the leaves since it may scorch them. Plants grown primarily for their ornamental foliage, for example *Rheum* and hostas, benefit from an occasional liquid feed during the growing season.

If a plant is not growing well, in spite of being in a suitable site, look carefully to see if it has been attacked by pests or disease and treat accordingly. Foliage that is yellowing prematurely may indicate problems with soil drainage or a lack of certain nutrients. If appropriate drainage or feeding does not seem to improve the condition of the plant, sending a soil sample for analysis by a laboratory will determine which elements are lacking (see also "Soil nutrients and fertilizers", pp.624–625).

Mulching

An annual mulch of organic matter, such as proprietary mulch or bark chippings, helps to suppress weed growth, reduce soil moisture loss, and improve the structure of the soil. Apply mulch when the ground is moist during spring or autumn by spreading a 5–10cm (2–4in) deep layer around the crowns of the plants (see also SOILS AND FERTILIZERS, "Mulches", p.626).

Weeding

Keep beds and borders free from weeds at all times, if practical, as they compete with the ornamental plants for moisture and nutrients in the soil. Underplanting with suitable ground-cover plants (see p.180) or mulching in spring helps to reduce problems with annual weeds. Any weed seedlings that do appear from wind-blown seed or seeds that have been dormant in the soil should be removed by hand before they become established.

If perennial weeds appear in the ground after initial cultivation, carefully dig them out with a hand fork. It is usually impractical to apply systemic weedkillers at this time because, to be effective, they must be applied when the weeds are in full growth, usually as they reach the flowering stage. At this point it is virtually impossible to avoid spraying the ornamental plants accidentally at the same time.

If the roots of a perennial weed have grown into those of a border plant, dig up the plant in early spring, wash the roots, and carefully pull out the weed. Then replant the border plant, ensuring that no part of the weed is left in the original site. Do not hoe around perennials since this may cause damage to any surface roots and emerging shoots. For further information on controlling weed growth, see PLANT PROBLEMS, "Weeds", pp.669–673.

APPLYING MULCH

Clear any weeds, and apply a 5–10cm (2–4in) layer of mulch to moist soil; do not damage the young shoots of the plant (here a peony).

Improving flowering

Certain perennial plants may be cut back during growth in one of two ways to improve the number or size of their flowers or to extend the flowering season.

Thinning

Although most herbaceous plants produce numerous vigorous shoots in spring, some of these may be spindly and thin; if these weak shoots are removed at an early stage of growth, the plant then goes on to develop fewer, sturdier shoots that usually produce larger flowers. When the plant is about a quarter to a third of its eventual height, pinch out or cut back the weakest shoots. This thinning technique may be used successfully with, for example, delphiniums, phlox, and Michaelmas daisies (*Aster*).

Stopping

It is possible to increase the number of flowers on perennial plants that readily produce sideshoots, such as *Helenium* and *Rudbeckia* species and cultivars, by removing or "stopping" the growing tip of each stem; this also produces sturdier growth and prevents the plant from becoming too tall and straggly. Stopping should generally be carried out when the plant is about one third of its ultimate height, and in this case 2.5–5cm (1–2in) of each shoot is pinched off with the fingers or cut back with secateurs just above a node. This encourages the buds in the uppermost leaf axils of the shoot to develop.

Individual plants in a group may be stopped a few days apart; this has the added effect of producing a longer flowering season overall. For further information on how to produce fewer but larger blooms, see DAHLIAS, "Stopping and disbudding", p.235.

Dead-heading

Unless decorative seedheads are required or the seed is to be collected to raise further plants, remove the

HOW TO THIN AND STOP PERENNIALS

Thinning
Thin young shoots (here of a phlox) when no more than a third of their final height. Remove about 1 shoot in 3 by cutting or pinching out weaker shoots at the base.

Stopping
When the shoots (here of an Aster) are one third of their final height, "stop" them by pinching out the top 2.5–5cm (1–2in) to promote bushier growth.

CUTTING BACK TO EXTEND FLOWERING

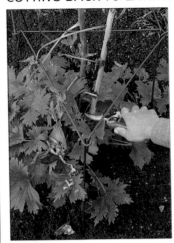

Delphinium
After flowering, when new basal shoots are visible, cut back old stems to ground level.

Phlox
Cut back the central part of the flowerhead as the blooms fade to encourage the sideshoots to flower.

flowers as they begin to fade. Further flowering sideshoots may then develop on the plant and extend the flowering season.

With a number of perennials, for example delphiniums and lupins (*Lupinus*), cutting back the old stems to their base when the first flowers have faded may encourage new shoots to develop that will produce a second display of flowers later in the season.

Cutting back

Woody-based perennials, such as penstemons, should be pruned back annually in early spring. Cut the overwintering stems with secateurs close to the base, where young shoots will develop; or shorten the stems by about half to three quarters, removing twiggy, weak, or unproductive growth. This will encourage vigorous shoots to develop, which will produce flowers throughout summer and autumn.

Autumn clearance

Once perennial plants have finished flowering in autumn, cut down the shoots to the base and remove all dead or faded stems and leaves, as well as any weed growth, so that the beds or borders are tidy. The top-growth of plants that are not fully hardy, however, may be left over winter to provide the crown with some protection from frost; the dead top-growth is then removed in spring. Some perennial plants, such as *Sedum spectabile* and many grasses, have foliage or flowerheads that

remain attractive even when brown, and these may be left on the plant to provide winter decoration if required until early spring.

Transplanting established perennials

Most perennials may be transplanted easily if you wish to change the planting scheme in the garden. If possible, move them when dormant in late autumn, or when just coming into growth in spring. Plants that dislike cold, wet conditions, such as *Kniphofia*, and those that are not fully hardy should be moved in spring once the soil has warmed up enough to encourage rapid growth. A few long-lived plants, notably

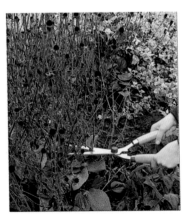

Cutting down in the autumn
In autumn or early winter, cut dead stems (here of Rudbeckia) to ground level, or to just above new growth.

Staking

Tall and fragile perennials may need stakes to support them, particularly in windy situations. Insert stakes early in the season, since staking is harder to do and more likely to damage the plant when growth is more developed. Push the stakes deep into the ground so that they can be raised in stages as the plant grows.

For delphiniums and other tall, single-stemmed perennials, use sturdy canes that are two-thirds of the stem's eventual height: push a cane firmly into the ground near the base of each shoot, taking care not to damage the roots. Secure the stem to the cane with figure-of-eight twine ties as it grows.

To support plants with many stems, it may be easier to use a number of canes placed at intervals in a circle around the plant.

Loop twine around the canes at about one-third and two-thirds of the plant's height. Clump-forming plants, such as peonies (*Paeonia*), may be supported with proprietary devices such as ring stakes and link stakes, or similar homemade supports constructed from large-gauge wire mesh fixed to stakes. Stems grow through the support and eventually hide it.

There are two fairly unobtrusive methods of staking. Push several twiggy hazel stems, or peasticks, into the soil next to the young shoots and bend them inwards at right-angles to form an effective "cage" that is soon covered by the plant as it grows. Alternatively, insert one stout stake in the centre of a small group of plants or stems and radiate ties out to each stem.

Ring stake
Stake low, clump-forming plants (here peony) early in the season. Raise the stake as the plant grows.

Link stakes
For taller plants such as this Aster, push link stakes deep into the soil, then raise them as the plant grows.

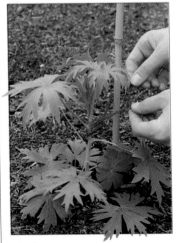

Single cane
Stake single-stemmed plants (here delphinium) when 20–25cm (8–10in) high. Tie in the stem loosely.

Ring of canes
Encircle weak-stemmed plants (here Centaurea) with twine, looped around split canes to secure it.

Storing plants

Perennials may be lifted and stored over winter if necessary or if replanting is to be delayed – if transplanting when moving house, for example.

Lift the plants in winter when they are dormant and place them in a box half-filled with moist bark or compost. Cover the roots with more bark or compost to keep them from drying out. Store in a cool, frost-free place.

peonies (*Paeonia*) and hellebores (*Helleborus*), resent disturbance and take two or more years to establish after transplanting. They should be lifted only if it is necessary to propagate them.

Prepare the new site as for planting, and dig a hole of suitable size. Lift the plant, keeping as much soil around the root ball as possible. It is best to divide the plant at this stage (see "Lifting and dividing", below). Remove any weeds from the clump by hand, then replant the divisions as for container-grown perennials (p.184), firming in and watering well.

Moving plants during the growing season

Occasionally, it may be necessary to move a plant while in full growth; mature plants may not transplant successfully, however, and should be treated carefully if transplanting is essential at this time. To minimize the stress caused to the plant, soak it in a bucket of water for several hours after lifting it. Then cut back the top-growth to within 8–12cm (3–5in) of the base and pot up the plant into a good potting compost. Keep the plant in a cool, shaded position, spraying daily but lightly until there are signs of healthy, fresh growth, then replant it in its new, prepared position.

Lifting and dividing

Where it is practical, perennials in a bed or border should be lifted, then divided, and replanted every three to five years. Fast-growing, vigorous

species, particularly those that have a mat-forming habit, such as *Ajuga* and *Stachys*, may need to be divided every other year. Plants that have become woody, with signs of dieback at the centre, or that look congested and flower less freely than in previous years, are in need of being divided.

Lifting plants makes it possible to clear the site of any weeds, and dig over and incorporate well-rotted organic matter or fertilizer as required. Dividing a plant rejuvenates it, keeps it healthy, and checks over-vigorous growth.

In late autumn or early spring, lift the plant, taking care not to damage its roots, and divide it into several portions by gently pulling them away from the main plant. Use a spade or fork to split larger clumps (see below). Discard the old, woody centre; each division should contain a number of healthy, young shoots and its own root system (see also "Dividing perennials", p.200). Then dig over and fertilize the original site as necessary and replant the divisions, leaving enough space between each for the plants to develop. Alternatively, replant the divisions in well prepared ground in a new position, as required.

Perennials in containers

Perennials planted in containers require more care than those in open ground as they have limited reserves of food and water. Ensure that the compost does not dry out during the growing season: daily watering may be necessary in hot, dry weather. Plant roots should always remain moist but not wet. Water-retaining

Maintaining naturalistic planting schemes

Perennials have a reputation for high maintenance: grown in beds or borders they are lifted, divided, mulched, staked, dead-headed, and cut back, and of course, weeding is an ongoing task. In a naturalistic scheme the workload is significantly lower, with two main periods of activity in spring and autumn.

Naturalistic schemes require a different style of management. The aim is to maintain the range of colours and textures, to prevent native weeds from dominating, and to promote self-seeding. Mulching and dead-heading are not required, as both discourage or suppress successful self-seeding. Staking is also unnecessary in a feature that favours a wild and untamed look.

The management regime is very simple. In spring, hand-weeding is essential: remove completely any aggressive species – native grasses, dandelions (*Taraxacum officinale*), foxgloves (*Digitalis*), and creeping buttercups (*Ranunculus repens*) – to prevent them taking over. Other weeds, such as campion, and plants that self-seed prolifically can be tolerated, but thin them out to ensure they do not dominate. The remaining plants may be left to their own devices – regardless of how congested they appear to be – until the whole display is cut down after seeding in late summer or autumn, when you should take the opportunity to repeat the spring weeding process.

granules can be added to compost (see CONTAINER GARDENING, p.323) to help conserve soil moisture.

Mulching helps to reduce soil water evaporation as well as suppressing weeds; if using an organic mulch, replace it periodically.

Every year or two in spring or autumn, divide the plants and replant the most vigorous portions using fresh compost, otherwise they soon exhaust the available nutrients and become too large for the container. If using the same container, wash the inside well before replanting, or pot up into a larger container (see "Repotting woody plants", p.334). Cut back the roots of shrubby perennials by a quarter before repotting.

In cold areas, bring in half-hardy and tender plants in the autumn, and

protect them until all danger of frost has passed (see FROST AND WIND PROTECTION, pp.612–613).

Pests and diseases

Perennial plants, if grown in fertile soil, are not usually seriously troubled by fungal diseases, insects, or other pests. Damage by slugs and snails (p.644), attack by vine weevil (p.645), aphids (p.646), and thrips (p.647) and, with certain plants (such as *Aster novi-belgii* cultivars), infestations of powdery and downy mildew (p.646) do occur but seldom cause concern. In the growing season, check plants regularly for signs of attack, and treat with an appropriate fungicide as necessary.

DIVIDING HERBACEOUS PERENNIALS

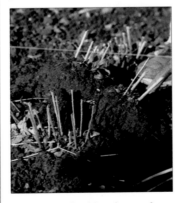

1 *Select a healthy plant and water it well to ensure roots are moist. Cut down old stems so the crown is clearly visible. Dig around the clump and lever it out.*

2 *Shake off surplus soil. If you cannot tease the clump apart by hand, insert two forks back to back and use them to split it. Repeat until you have enough segments.*

3 *Replant each section in fresh, well-prepared ground before the roots dry out. Check the plants are at the same depth as before, firm in and water well.*

Ferns

AMONG the most popular of the foliage plants, ferns add texture and atmosphere to the house or garden, where they are particularly effective in settings by streams or in damp, shady corners.

Cultivation

Hardy ferns are suitable for growing in the open garden, whereas tender tropical ferns are best cultivated indoors in a greenhouse or conservatory, or as house plants.

Hardy ferns

Most hardy ferns are easily grown and are suitable for shaded, moist conditions. Being very tough, they require the minimum of cultivation and upkeep once they have become established. With the exception of *Thelypteris* and all the *Blechnum* and *Cryptogramma* species, which require acid soil, ferns prefer neutral to alkaline conditions. Well-dug garden soil, with added humus, will suit most species.

Planting may be carried out at any time if container-grown plants are used. In dry weather water them regularly until established. Always plant in full or dappled shade; some genera, such as *Dryopteris*, will tolerate dry conditions if they are well shaded, but almost all require damp conditions to thrive.

Many ferns, such as *Athyrium*, *Cryptogramma*, and *Osmunda*, die down at the first touch of frost, but some of the *Dryopteris* retain their fronds well into winter. Leaving the old fronds on the plant until early spring protects the crowns, but these should be removed as the young ones start to uncurl. All species and cultivars of *Asplenium*, *Cyrtomium*, *Polystichum*, and *Polypodium* make good plants for the cold greenhouse, flourishing in the coldest weather under glass without the need for any artificial heat.

Tender tropical ferns

Ferns that will not withstand frost make excellent greenhouse or conservatory foliage plants, grown in pots or hanging baskets. Some also make good house plants. Most require a winter minimum temperature of 10–15°C (50–59°F) but do not like hot, dry conditions and should be shaded from direct sunlight; a north-facing position on a bed of gravel that can be damped down in hot weather is ideal.

Tender ferns are usually sold in very small pots and should then be potted up into 13cm (5in) or 15cm (6in) pots using a soil-less potting compost. For this, use 3 parts peat-substitute- or peat-based potting mixture to 2 parts coarse sand or medium-grade perlite. Add a cupful

Water setting
Matteuccia thrives in damp conditions by a stream and provides a striking contrast of form and texture with the Rodgersia *in the foreground.*

of charcoal granules to every litre (1¾ pints) of mixture and, following the pack instructions, a balanced granular or powdered fertilizer.

The root ball should not dry out completely; keep the plant in its pot inside a watertight outer container with about 2.5cm (1in) of sand or gravel permanently kept damp at its base. Ferns, particularly *Adiantum* species, do not like to be sprayed or overwatered, and *Nephrolepis*, which are probably the easiest to keep as house plants, should be nearly dry before watering. Feed the ferns occasionally with a house plant liquid fertilizer.

Propagation

Ferns are mainly raised from spores, but may be propagated by division or, in some species, by bulbils.

Rock crevice
The lance-shaped fronds of the semi-evergreen Ceterach officinarum *contrast well with the rock behind that provides shade and shelter.*

PROPAGATION BY BULBILS

1 *Select a frond that is drooping under the weight of bulbils. The bulbils may have tiny green fronds emerging from them. Cut off the parent frond close to the base. The plant shown here is* Asplenium bulbiferum.

2 *Peg down the frond onto prepared compost. Make sure the frond's ribs are flat.*

3 *Water thoroughly, label the tray, and put it in a plastic bag. Seal the bag and leave the tray in a warm, light place until the bulbils have rooted.*

4 *Remove the wire pegs and lift each rooted bulbil with a widger or knife; if necessary, cut it away from the parent frond.*

5 *Put each rooted bulbil into a 7cm (3in) pot of moist, soil-less compost. Keep moist in a warm, light place until the plants are large enough to replant.*

Bulbils

Asplenium bulbiferum and some of the hardy *Polystichum* species produce bulbils or small plantlets along the fronds. These may be used for propagation by pegging down that part of the frond with bulbils onto a tray of seed or cutting compost. The bulbils soon produce rooted plantlets which can then be separated and potted up. During the dormant season, it may take up to six months before the new plants are ready for planting out or potting on.

Spores

Ferns produce neither flowers nor seeds, and have a unique way of reproducing. Fronds carry on their undersurfaces very small capsules (sporangia), which release large numbers of powdery spores, which, when sown on damp compost, produce small growths (prothalli). Each prothallus carries both the male and female organs: the male organ (antheridium) produces spermatozoids which swim across the surface moisture of the prothallus to fertilize the "egg cell" lying within the female organ (archegonium). After fertilization, a zygote is formed which eventually develops into a tiny new fern. In this way the normal cycle of growth is continued.

Growing ferns from spores may take 18 to 24 months from sowing the spores to planting out the mature ferns. Collect the spores by removing from the parent plant fronds that are almost ready to shed their spores. Ripe sporangia are plump and vary in colour between species; many are dark brown, some blue-grey, others orange. Immature sporangia are flat and green or pale yellow. If the sporangia are dark brown and rough,

they will probably already have shed their spores. Lay the fronds on a sheet of clean paper and leave them in a warm room. In a day or so the spores will be shed onto the paper, looking like brown dust. Transfer them to a labelled seed envelope.

Fill a 7cm (3in) pot with standard seed compost; firm and smooth the surface. Sterilize the compost by carefully pouring boiling water through a piece of paper towel laid on the surface until water comes through the drainage holes. When the compost has cooled, remove the paper towel and sow spores thinly over the surface. Cover the pot, or put it in a propagator, and leave it in a warm, light place out of direct sunlight. To keep the surface constantly moist, mist-spray it regularly with previously boiled, lukewarm water. Remove the cover when the top of the pot is covered with a green, velvet-like "moss"; if the compost seems dry, moisten it by standing the pot in a saucer of water for a short period.

Depending on the species, it takes from six to twelve weeks for the young prothalli to cover the compost surface. Prick them out by lifting small pieces of the "moss". Space them evenly, green side up, on the surface of other pots of sterilized seed compost, press them down, and spray with lukewarm water that has been boiled. Cover the pots with clingfilm or return them to the propagator. As the prothalli develop, spray them daily with lukewarm water until tiny plantlets appear. When they are large enough to handle, transplant them separately into pots of soilless compost and grow them on, potting up as necessary, until they are large enough to plant out.

Formal plantings
The clean, horizontal line of the golden box (foreground) provides a perfect foundation for the striking, shuttlecock shapes of Matteuccia struthiopteris.

PROPAGATION BY SPORES

1 *Examine the undersides of the fronds to find one with sporangia that are ready to release their spores. Cut off the selected frond with a clean, sharp knife and place it carefully on clean, white paper to collect the spores. The plant shown here is* Adiantum raddianum *'Fritz Lüthi'.*

Not ready **Ready** **Too late**

2 *Sow a few of the collected spores onto a pot of prepared sterile compost by tapping them from a piece of folded paper. Cover with some clingfilm or place the pot in a propagator.*

3 *Mist-spray twice a week until the surface is covered with a bumpy green "moss". Lift small clumps with a widger or a knife.*

4 *Divide the clumps into small pieces and gently firm them down onto sterile compost. Spray with water and then return them to the propagator.*

5 *When leaf-like plantlets appear, lift them carefully. Firm into packs or small pots of moist compost. Pot on when they have developed small fronds.*

Carnations and pinks

CARNATIONS and pinks belong to the genus *Dianthus*. They have attractive, usually fragrant flowers and grey-green, evergreen foliage. They are grouped according to their growth habit, flower characteristics, and hardiness: the upright, bushy border carnations and low, spreading pinks are both hardy and prolific.

Modern pinks are repeat-flowering and more vigorous than the old-fashioned cultivars. (For dwarf pinks see ROCK, SCREE, AND GRAVEL GARDENING, "Choosing plants", p.255.) Border carnations and pinks will provide an increasing supply of flowers over three or four years. Perpetual-flowering carnations and spray carnations grow much taller than border carnations, are not frost hardy, and can flower throughout the year. The old-fashioned Malmaison carnations have large, double, very fragrant blooms and should be grown in a conservatory or cool greenhouse. They flower sporadically throughout the year. Annual and biennial carnations and pinks (*Dianthus chinensis* and its hybrids as well as *D. barbatus*, sweet William) are treated as other hardy or half-hardy annuals (see ANNUALS AND BIENNIALS, "Sowing and planting", pp.216–221).

Carnation flowers may be in one colour ("self"), in two or more colours ("fancy"), or edged in a contrasting colour ("picotee"). Pinks flowers may be in one colour ("self"), with a central zone or eye of a second colour ("bicolour"), in two or more colours ("fancy"), or marked with a different colour just inside the edge of every petal, and usually with a central eye of the same colour ("laced"). All carnations and pinks provide long-lasting cut flowers.

General cultivation

Border carnations and pinks prefer a sunny, open site and a free-draining soil with a pH of 6.5–8. Perpetual-flowering carnations should be grown in a greenhouse, and will bloom in minimum temperatures of 10–12°C (50–54°F); at 5°C (41°F), only a few flowers are borne in winter.

In winter, clear away any dead leaves or other debris from around the plants, and firm any young plants growing outdoors that have been lifted by frost.

Border carnations

For best results, obtain these from specialist growers as rooted layers in autumn or pot-grown plants in spring.

To prepare the bed for planting, single dig in autumn, incorporating humus-forming material, and the following spring fork in a balanced fertilizer at the manufacturer's suggested rate. Water the young plants before planting them out 38–45cm (15–18in) apart in moist soil. Firm them, ensuring that the lowest leaves are clear of the soil surface. Water only if dry conditions persist during the first month after planting; once established, the plants need watering only in very dry weather. Stake plants with twigs or canes.

Border carnations are bushy, so they do not need pinching out. If grown for garden display, it is not necessary to disbud one-year-old plants. To produce larger blooms on two-year-old plants, remove surplus buds. Hold the brittle main stem by the node at the base of the bud stalk, and sharply pull the stalk sideways to remove it, leaving two or three buds per stem. Leave the crown bud only on three- and four-year-old plants.

Pinks

Buy pinks as rooted cuttings in autumn or as pot-grown plants in spring. Plant them as for border carnations, but space them 22–30cm (9–12in) apart. When growing modern, repeat-flowering pinks from cuttings, pinch out the growing tips of the young plants to leave five or six pairs of leaves. Old-fashioned pinks do not usually need pinching out.

Perpetual-flowering carnations

These are best obtained as rooted cuttings or pot plants in spring and early summer. If growing rooted cuttings, break off their growing tips a week or two after potting them up to induce axillary growths (breaks); the plant is then described as "stopped and broken". Such plants with three to five sideshoots may be purchased in spring and are ready for potting on into 14cm (5½in) pots of standard potting compost. Water thoroughly, and support with 1.2m (4ft) canes.

A month or so after repotting, stop a few sideshoots a second time, to extend the flowering season. (Do not "second-stop" spray carnations.) Disbud plants gradually over several days so that the calyx (the green petal casing) does not split. Leave only the crown bud and place a calyx band over the bud. With spray carnations, remove only the crown bud. Pick flower stems with seven nodes on their stems to induce strong sideshoots to develop lower down.

Water the plants only when the compost begins to dry out, preferably early in the day. Feed with a balanced liquid fertilizer, at first fortnightly, then weekly by midsummer for a good flowering display. In late autumn, change to a monthly, high-potash feed for sturdy foliage, and continue with it throughout winter.

During spring, repot one-year-old plants into 21cm (8in) pots. Then sprinkle one level teaspoonful of ground limestone on the surface to prevent the compost becoming sour through constant watering. A month later, resume feeding the plants as usual for the growing season. Discard plants at the end of the second year, replacing with young stock.

DISBUDDING

To produce one large bloom on each flower stem of perpetual-flowering carnations, support the stem with one hand and pinch off each bud except the crown bud (left). For spray cultivars, pinch off the crown bud of each flower stem as the colour begins to show (right).

TYPES OF CARNATION AND PINK

Perpetual
D. 'Clara'
Repeat flowers usually unscented; half hardy.

Border carnation
D. 'Bookham Fancy'
Flowers often scented; frost hardy.

Old-fashioned pink
D. 'Musgrave's Pink'
Scented; frost hardy.

Modern pink
D. 'Doris'
Scented flowers in 2 or 3 flushes; frost hardy.

Spray
D. 'Cartouche'
Five or more flowers per stem; half hardy.

Malmaison
D. 'Souvenir de la Malmaison' Fragrant flowers; half hardy.

STOPPING AND BREAKING

When a rooted cutting of a perpetual-flowering carnation has 8 or 9 pairs of leaves, snap or pinch out the top 3 or 4 pairs. A month or so later again remove the tops of a few sideshoots, leaving 5 or 6 nodes on each sideshoot.

Pests and diseases

Carnations and pinks may be attacked by aphids (p.646), caterpillars (p.645), thrips (p.647), fungal leaf spots (p.648), and rusts (p.648). Greenhouse-grown carnations are most prone to infestation by red spider mite (p.646). In hot, dry summer conditions, frequent spraying with clear water acts as a deterrent. In winter, use insecticidal and fungicidal smokes and dusts, not sprays, to discourage fungal diseases.

Propagation

All carnations and pinks can be raised from cuttings, but for best results border carnations are layered. All *Dianthus* may be grown from seed (see ANNUALS AND BIENNIALS, "Sowing", p.216, and PERENNIALS, "Seed", p.198). Most perennial *Dianthus* do not breed true, and most do not flower in the first year.

Exhibition plants are normally discarded after one year. With successful plants, take cuttings or propagate by layering (as appropriate), before throwing them away.

Cuttings

Take cuttings from pinks in the summer. Choose healthy shoots with four or five pairs of leaves and break them off cleanly. Trim off the bottom pair of leaves just below a joint. Insert the cuttings about 4cm (1½in) apart into trays or pots of clean, sharp sand, or a mixture of standard cuttings compost and sand in equal parts; keep the leaves clear of the rooting medium. Cover them with a plastic bag or put in a propagator or mist unit and treat as for stem tip

PREPARING CUTTINGS

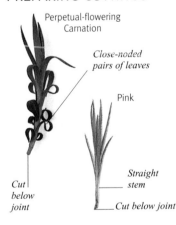

Perpetual-flowering Carnation

Close-noded pairs of leaves

Pink

Cut below joint

Straight stem

Cut below joint

Select non-flowering, closely jointed shoots. Remove the bottom pairs of leaves to create small stems and trim them. Any hook on a stem should be cut out, below a joint.

LAYERING BORDER CARNATIONS

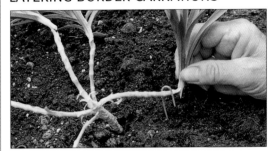

1 *Slit the stems of non-flowering sideshoots to encourage new roots to form; then pin the shoots into the soil surrounding the plants. Gently push the tongue of each shoot into the soil, and pin it down securely with a layering pin.*

2 *Ensure the layered shoot is held almost vertical, with the slit kept fully open in the soil. Stake the leafy tip, if necessary. Spray the rooting area lightly to keep it moist. After 5 or 6 weeks, separate and lift the rooted layers. Pot them on or plant them out.*

cuttings (see p.202). The cuttings should root after two to three weeks; pot them singly in 7cm (3in) pots of standard potting compost to grow on in a cold frame or greenhouse.

Perpetual-flowering and spray carnation cuttings may be taken at any season, if bottom heat of 20°C (68°F) is provided. Choose strong, axillary shoots that have developed after the flowers have been picked, and prepare them as for pinks. Dip the base of each cutting into water and then into hormone rooting powder, after which they should be treated in the same way as pinks.

Layering

Propagate border carnations after they have flowered by layering the one-year-old plants. Dig in equal parts of sharp sand and either damp cuttings compost, sieved garden compost, or peat substitute, to a depth of 7cm (3in) around the parent plant, and firm. Select a few well-spaced, non-flowering sideshoots and remove all but the top four or five pairs of leaves on each shoot. Just below the node with the lowest leaves, cut downwards through the next node, forming a tongue. Pin the shoot so the tongue is held in the prepared soil. When the layered shoots have rooted, detach them from the parent and plant them out to flower the following year.

To propagate exhibition plants in their pots, remove a ring of compost about 2.5cm (1in) wide and 7cm (3in) deep from the surface around the plant. Replace it with equal parts of standard cuttings compost and sharp sand, then layer the plants around the pot rim. In six weeks, when the layers have rooted, pot them singly into 7cm (3in) pots of standard potting compost.

When the roots reach the edge of the compost, pot them on into 15cm

(6in) pots with the top of the root ball flush with the compost surface. Firm the compost to about 2.5cm (1in) below the pot rim. Alternatively, insert two plants in a 21cm (8in) pot. Stake them with 1m (3ft) canes and water thoroughly; then water only when the compost is drying out.

Exhibiting blooms

Carnations and pinks have been grown as exhibition plants for centuries. Pinks and perpetual-flowering carnations are grown as in "General cultivation" (see opposite), but border carnations are usually grown in a light, airy greenhouse to protect the blooms. In summer, the greenhouse must be well ventilated, lightly shaded, and mist-sprayed frequently.

Preparing for a show

When the buds on pinks or carnations begin to form, feed at 10-day intervals with a balanced, liquid fertilizer until they show colour, then give just one high-potash feed. As soon as their buds are large enough to handle, carnations should be disbudded; do this over several days. Slip calyx

bands over the remaining buds to prevent their calyces from splitting. Pinks, on the other hand, are never disbudded, although exhibitors may remove any spent blooms.

Select blooms for exhibition from well-watered plants either early in the morning or during late evening, if possible 48 hours before a show. Trim the stems with a sloping cut just above a node and place them up to their necks in water in a cool, dark place, free from draughts, until needed.

CALYX BANDS

Calyx band

Split calyx

When a bud shows colour, put a soft wire ring or a rubber band around it (left) to stop it splitting and forming an untidy bloom (right).

BLOOMS FOR EXHIBITION

A good show bloom displays all the characteristics of its class, and reveals no evidence of pests or disease. Calyx bands left on the bloom or a burst calyx invite disqualification.

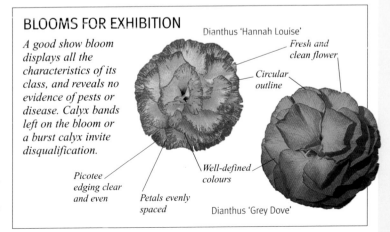

Dianthus 'Hannah Louise'

Fresh and clean flower

Circular outline

Picotee edging clear and even

Petals evenly spaced

Well-defined colours

Dianthus 'Grey Dove'

Propagation

PERENNIAL SEED NEEDING SPECIAL TREATMENT

Stratification
Aconitum
Adonis amurensis
Campanula, some ✿
Meconopsis
Primula, some ✿

Scarification
Anthyllis
Baptisia
Galega
Lathyrus
Lupinus

Lupinus
'The Chatelaine'

Sowing when fresh
Helleborus
Meconopsis
Primula, some ✿

Soaking
Arum, some ✿
Baptisia
Euphorbia, some ✿

PERENNIALS THAT FLOWER FROM SEED WITHIN TWO YEARS

Alchemilla
Anemone
Aquilegia
Aster, some ✿
Astrantia
Campanula, some ✿
Catananche
Centaurea
Cuphea ✿
Delphinium
Gaura
Gazania ✿
Linaria
Lobelia, some ✿
Lychnis
Malva

Meconopsis grandis

Meconopsis
Osteospermum, some ✿
Papaver
Polemonium
Primula, some ✿
Salvia, some ✿ (not shrubby spp.)
Scabiosa
Sidalcea
Silene, some ✿
Verbascum

Key
✿ *Not hardy*

THERE are several ways of propagating herbaceous perennials. Growing them from seed is ideal where a large number of new plants is required. Little experience or expertise is needed to raise seedlings successfully, but this method is generally only suitable for propagating species rather than cultivars.

For many perennials, the simplest and commonest propagation method is to lift them and divide clumps into separate plants, but others are better raised from seed or by vegetative means, such as cuttings or, more rarely, grafting. Vegetative methods should be used for propagating almost all named cultivars.

Seed

Raising plants from seed is a simple and inexpensive way to propagate many perennials but, apart from a few named cultivars (for example, *Lathyrus latifolius* 'Blushing Bride'), most cultivars do not come true from seed. Most species also show some variation in habit and flower colour so, if collecting seed yourself, always gather it from plants with the best flower and growth characteristics.

Seed of early-flowering perennials, which ripens on the plant in early to mid-summer, usually germinates quickly if sown as soon as it is ripe, producing young plants that may be overwintered successfully in open ground or in a cold frame. For most perennials, however, sow the seed immediately after it has been gathered in autumn so that it germinates early the following spring. If stored in cool, dry conditions, most seed also germinates well when sown in spring.

Seed of some herbaceous plants, however, such as peonies (*Paeonia*) and hellebores (*Helleborus*) usually remains dormant for a considerable period – peonies for up to 18 months – unless suitable conditions are provided or occur naturally to break dormancy and induce germination. Some require a period of exposure to cold or light, while others have hard seed coats that should be weakened by scarification or softened by soaking before sowing (see also PRINCIPLES OF PROPAGATION, "How to overcome dormancy", p.629).

Pre-germination treatment of seeds

Seeds that need to be subjected to a cold period to break dormancy may either be sown outside in autumn or winter (see also *Sowing Seed that Requires Chilling*, p.199) or chilled in a refrigerator for a few weeks before sowing in spring. This method of breaking dormancy is suitable for many genera, including *Aconitum, Adonis, Campanula*, and *Primula*. Seeds of a few plants, such as those of *Gentiana asclepiadea*, require a period of exposure to light for successful germination.

Scarifying and soaking

A number of perennials, particularly those of the pea family Leguminosae, have seeds with hard coats that impede rapid and even germination. Just before sowing the seeds, scarify them either by rubbing them with an emery board or sandpaper or by chipping them slightly with a sharp blade to allow water to be taken up and then germination to occur.

Alternatively, many seeds may have their hard coats softened by being soaked in hot, but not boiling, water for 12–24 hours; this allows the seed to absorb water and germination to take place. Soaking is suitable for a number of perennials, for example *Arum, Baptisia*, and *Euphorbia*. Once soaked, the seed should be sown immediately.

Double dormancy

Peony and *Trillium* seeds usually require two periods of cold to trigger germination of both roots and shoots. Root development from the germinating seed occurs during the first season but the shoots do not normally start to appear until the seeds have received a second period of cold, usually during the following winter. Sow the seeds in containers in autumn in the normal way.

Sowing seed in containers

Unless a very large number of plants is required, it is usually easiest to sow seed in containers. A plastic half-tray will accommodate as many as two or three hundred seeds, while even a large square pot will be adequate for sowing up to 50 seeds, depending on their size. Square pots fit closely together in rows and provide a greater area of compost than round pots of the same width.

Fill the pot or tray with an appropriate seed compost. Loam-based composts are often preferred to peat-based ones if the young seedlings are to be kept in them for more than a short period after germination. Gently press the compost around the edges of the pot or tray, then roughly level the surface and firm it with a presser board or the base of another pot, so that the soil is about 1cm (½in) below the container rim.

Sowing

The seeds should always be sown thinly – about 0.5cm (¼in) apart; sowing too densely may result in thin, spindly plants that are prone to damping off (see p.664). Fine seeds, and those that require light to germinate, for example some gentians (*Gentiana*), may be

---

Collecting seed

Collect the seed as it ripens: shake it from the pods or tie the seedheads into small bunches, enclosed in paper bags, and hang them upside-down so that the seeds fall into the bags. Make sure that the seed is completely dry before storing it in clean paper bags or envelopes labelled with the plant name and harvesting date.

Collect ripened seed pods (here of Meconopsis) *when they have turned brown. Shake the seeds out of each pod onto a piece of paper and store in a cool, dry place until ready to sow.*

left uncovered or sprinkled with a shallow layer of fine, sieved compost, perlite, or vermiculite and then gently firmed with a presser board. Larger seeds, such as those of peonies, should be covered with a 0.5cm (¼in) layer of sieved compost.

Aftercare

Label the containers with the seed name and sowing date, then water them using a can with a fine rose, taking care not to dislodge the seeds. Alternatively, if small seeds are being sown, stand the containers in a bowl or tray of water for a short time until they have absorbed enough to moisten the compost throughout; this method prevents the seeds from being washed away. Minimize evaporation by covering the containers with glass, a plastic sheet, or plastic film, and place them in a cold frame or greenhouse. In sunny weather, provide some shade with newspaper or shade netting. Once the seeds have started to germinate, remove the cover and reduce any shading.

Plunging the containers in an outdoor bed

If the containers are to be placed outside unprotected from the weather during autumn and winter to break seed dormancy, add a covering of grit over the sown seeds. This prevents them from being washed out of the containers by heavy rain and, to some extent, deters mosses and liverworts from growing on the surface of the compost. Cover the containers with fine-mesh chicken wire to protect the seed if rodents or birds are likely to be a problem.

Plunge the pots in an open sand bed as this provides stable, even conditions for germination. Once the seed has germinated and the seedlings are visible, place the containers in a cold frame and care for the seedlings as for those raised under cover.

Pricking out

Once the seedlings are large enough to handle, that is when the first or second pair of true leaves has formed, they may be pricked out. Either space them evenly in seed trays with about 30–40 in each tray or prick them out into individual containers. The latter is advisable for seedlings that do not tolerate much root disturbance. Alternatively, prick out the seedlings into modules (compartmentalized trays). In all cases, a good, loam-based potting compost should be used.

Water the seedlings thoroughly, label them, and then place them in a cold frame or cool greenhouse until they are established. They may then

RAISING PLANTS FROM SEED

1 *Fill a 13cm (5in) pot with moist seed compost. Firm the compost to about 1cm (½in) below the rim of the container.*

2 *Using a clean, folded piece of paper, scatter the seeds (here* Chrysanthemum x superbum) *sparingly over the compost.*

3 *Cover the seeds with a shallow layer of fine, sieved compost. Label and then water without displacing the seeds.*

4 *Cover with a clear plastic sheet or clear film to retain moisture. Place the pot in a cold frame until the seedlings develop 2 pairs of leaves.*

5 *Prick out the seedlings into pots; degradable pots (inset) allow planting out direct. Handle the seedlings by the leaves since the stems are easily damaged.*

6 *When the seedlings have developed into small plants with a good root system, plant them out or pot them up, as appropriate.*

SOWING SEED THAT REQUIRES CHILLING

1 *In autumn, sow the seed thinly in pots of compost, then cover with a thin layer of fine compost and top-dress with fine grit.*

2 *Label the pots with the seed name and date of sowing, and water thoroughly. Then plunge the pots in an open sand bed outside to encourage the seeds to germinate.*

be potted on individually or planted out in their permanent site in open ground when they are large enough.

Sowing outside in open ground

If large numbers of plants are needed, it may be more convenient to sow seed outside. Prepare an area in fertile, well-drained soil by clearing any weeds and cultivating the soil to a fine tilth. Using a line or a straight-edged board as a guide, make a seed drill using a draw hoe, onion hoe, or the point of a large label.

The depth of the drill depends on the size of the seed to be sown: about 0.5cm (¼in) deep is adequate for small seeds, while large seeds require a drill at least 1cm (½in) deep. If the seedlings are to be transplanted when young, set the drills 10–15cm (4–6in) apart; if, however, they are to be grown on in rows, allow

about 15–22cm (6–9in) between them. Sow small seeds thinly so that they are about 0.5cm (¼in) apart, large seeds such as peonies at intervals of 2.5cm (1in) or more.

After sowing, cover the drills by raking soil lightly over them, then label each drill with the name of the seed sown and the date. Water the drills carefully, trying not to wash away the soil. For further details, see ANNUALS AND BIENNIALS, *Sowing in Drills*, p.217.

Dividing perennials

This method is suitable for propagating many perennials that have a spreading rootstock and produce plenty of shoots from the base. As well as being a way of increasing stocks, in many cases division rejuvenates the plants and keeps them vigorous, because old or unproductive parts may be discarded (see also "Lifting and dividing", p.193).

Some perennial plants can be divided simply by pulling sections apart by hand, or by using two forks back-to-back; other plants that have fleshy roots are best split apart by using a spade or knife.

When to divide

Most plants should be divided when they are dormant, between late autumn and early spring, but not in extremely cold, wet, or dry weather since these conditions may make it difficult for the divided plants to re-establish successfully.

Fleshy-rooted perennials are usually best left until the end of their dormant season, in spring, before being divided. At this time their buds will be starting to shoot, which will indicate the most vigorous areas of growth, and therefore the best way of dividing up the plant.

Preparation

First lift the plant to be divided by loosening the surrounding soil, taking care not to damage the roots, then levering it up gently with a fork. Shake off as much loose soil from the roots as possible and remove any dead leaves and stems to make it easier to see the best points for division. This also enables you to see which are the healthy parts of the plant to be retained and which are the old, unproductive parts that can be discarded.

Wash most of the soil off the roots and crowns of fleshy-rooted plants, so that all the buds are clearly visible and therefore do not become damaged inadvertently when you are dividing the plant.

Fibrous-rooted plants

Insert two border or hand forks back-to-back near the centre of each plant so the tines are close together and the handles apart; then push the handles gently backwards and forwards so that the prongs gradually tease the plant apart and separate the clumps into two smaller portions. Repeat this process with each portion to divide the plant into more sections, each with some new shoots.

Plants that tend to form woody clumps or that have thick, solid roots should be cut into portions with a spade or sharp knife; make sure that there are at least two growth buds or shoots on each piece. Discard the old, weak, and often woody growth from the centre of the plant; the sections containing vigorous, young shoots and healthy roots tend to grow at the perimeter of the plant.

Perennial plants that have loose, spreading crowns and numerous shoots, for example Michaelmas daisies (*Aster*), are easy to pull apart by hand or with two hand forks. Simply separate off single stems growing at the edges of the crown so that each has its own root system.

Fleshy-rooted plants

Plants that have bulky, almost solid, fleshy roots, such as *Rheum*, may need to be divided with a spade as it would be difficult to separate the crowns using back-to-back forks. After cleaning the plant so that the developing buds are clearly visible, slice through between them with a spade, taking care to leave two or more buds on each piece. Then trim each division neatly with a knife, discarding any old, woody material and any damaged or rotting roots.

Plants with numerous, intertwined crowns, such as *Arthropodium* and tufted ornamental grasses, may also be divided with two forks.

Replanting and aftercare

After dividing a plant, dust any cut surfaces with an appropriate fungicide (see PRINCIPLES OF PROPAGATION, "How roots form", p.632). Replant the divisions as soon as possible.

Dividing hostas

Large hostas with tough rootstocks should be divided using a spade. Include several buds on each division and trim any damaged parts with a knife. Hostas that have looser, fleshy rootstocks may be separated by hand or with back-to-back forks; each division should have at least one "eye" or shoot.

Tough, fibrous roots
Divide the crown with a spade; each section should include several developing buds.

Loose, fleshy roots
Divide small plants and those with a loose rootstock by pulling the clump apart by hand.

HOW TO PROPAGATE PERENNIALS BY DIVISION

1 *Lift the plant to be divided, taking care to insert the fork far enough away from the plant so that the roots are not damaged. Shake off surplus soil. The plant shown here is a Helianthus.*

2 *Separate plants with a woody centre by chopping through the crown with a spade.*

3 *Divide the plant into smaller pieces by hand, retaining only healthy, vigorous sections, each with several new shoots.*

4 *Cut back the old top-growth and replant the divided sections to the same depth as before. Firm in and water thoroughly.*

ALTERNATIVE METHOD

Divide fibrous-rooted, herbaceous plants (here Hemerocallis) using 2 forks back-to-back.

It is important that they do not dry out, so if replanting is unavoidably delayed for a couple of hours, dip the plants briefly in water and keep them in a sealed plastic bag in a cool, shady place until you are ready to replant them.

Large divisions, if replanted immediately, may still provide a good show of flowers in the same season although the stems are often slightly shorter than those of more established plants. Very small divisions, however, are best grown on for a season in a nursery bed or in pots in order to become established. In general, the divisions should be replanted at the same depth as the original plant, but those that are prone to rotting at the base are best set slightly proud of the surrounding soil level to keep the crowns of the plants free of excess water (see also "Planting depths", p.184).

When replanting, ensure that the roots are well spread out in the planting hole and the plant firmed in. Water newly planted divisions thoroughly; take care not to expose the roots by washing away any soil.

Division of rhizomatous plants

Divide plants with thick rhizomes, such as *Bergenia* and rhizomatous irises, by splitting the clump into pieces by hand, then cutting the rhizomes into sections, each with one or more buds (see right). Bamboos have tough rootstocks that either form dense clumps with short rhizomes or have long, spreading rhizomes; divide the former with a spade or use two back-to-back forks; use secateurs to cut the latter into sections, each of which should have three nodes or joints (see also BAMBOOS, p.96).

1 Lift the plant to be divided (here an iris), inserting the fork well away from the rhizomes to avoid damaging them.

2 Shake the clump to remove any loose soil. Using your hands or a hand fork, split the clump into manageable pieces.

3 Discard any old rhizomes, then detach the new, young rhizomes from the clump and neatly trim off their ends.

4 Dust the cut areas with fungicide. Trim long roots by one third. For irises, shorten the leaves to about 15cm (6in) long, to prevent wind rock.

5 Plant the rhizomes about 12cm (5in) apart. The rhizomes should be half buried, with their leaves and buds upright. Firm in well and water.

Dividing peonies

Peonies should be divided with particular care as they dislike being transplanted and tend to re-establish slowly. For best results, lift and divide the plants towards the end of the dormant season in early spring, when the swelling, red growth buds are clearly visible. Cut the crown into sections, each with a few buds, taking care not to damage the thick, fleshy roots.

1 Lift the plant in early spring, when healthy growth buds are visible on the crown. Cut it into sections, each one with several buds.

2 Dust all the cut surfaces of the divided sections with fungicide to discourage infection and rot.

3 Plant out the divided sections approximately 20cm (8in) apart. The buds should just be visible at the surface. Firm the soil well.

PERENNIALS TO DIVIDE

Achillea
Aconitum
Adenophora
Anemone hupehensis
Arum, some ✼
Aster, some ✼
Astilbe
Astrantia
Bergenia
Buphthalmum

Aster novae-angliae 'Harrington's Pink'

Campanula, some ✼
Carex
Centaurea dealbata
Clematis (herbaceous)
Coreopsis verticillata
Crambe cordifolia
Doronicum
Epilobium
Galega
Geranium, some ✼
Helenium
Helianthus
Helleborus orientalis

Helleborus orientalis

Hemerocallis
Heuchera
Hosta
Iris (rhizomatous)
Kniphofia, some ✼
Liatris
Lobelia cardinalis ✼
Lychnis
Lysimachia
Lythrum
Miscanthus
Nepeta
Oenothera fruticosa
Ophiopogon, some ✼
Paeonia
Phormium
Physostegia
Polemonium
Pulmonaria
Rheum
Rudbeckia
Salvia nemorosa, S. pratensis
Saponaria
Scabiosa caucasica
Schizostylis
Sedum spectabile
Sidalcea
Smilacina
Solidago
Stachys byzantina
Symphytum
Tanacetum coccineum
Thalictrum
Tradescantia Andersoniana Group
Trollius
Veronica

Key
✼ *Not hardy*

PROPAGATING PERENNIALS BY STEM TIP CUTTINGS

1 *Select short lengths of soft wood about 7–12cm (3–5in) long from the tips of strong, healthy shoots. The plant shown here is a Penstemon cultivar.*

2 *Trim the lower end of each cutting just below a node, with a straight cut, reducing the length to 5–7cm (2–3in). Remove the lower pairs of leaves.*

3 *Insert the cuttings around the edge of a 15cm (6in) pot of cuttings compost and water in. Cover with a plastic bag, held away from the cuttings by canes.*

4 *When the cuttings have rooted, gently lift them and pot them up individually into 10cm (4in) pots.*

PERENNIALS FROM STEM CUTTINGS

Tip
Arctotis ❋
Argyranthemum ❋
Calceolaria integrifolia ❋
Cuphea ❋
Dianthus, some ❋
Diascia
Erysimum
Felicia, some ❋
Lobelia cardinalis
Lotus berthelotii ❋
Oenothera macrocarpa
Osteospermum, some ❋
Parahebe
Penstemon, some ❋
Salvia, some ❋
Scrophularia auriculata
Sphaeralcea ❋
Tradescantia, some ❋
Trifolium pratense
Verbena ❋

Osteospermum
'Buttermilk'

Viola, some ❋
Zauschneria californicum
  subsp. *cana*

Basal
Anthemis tinctoria
Aster, some ❋
Chrysanthemum, some ❋
Delphinium, some ❋
Lupinus
Monarda
Phlox paniculata (variegated
  cvs only)
Physostegia
Sedum, some ❋

*Anthemis
tinctoria
'E.C. Buxton'*

Key
❋ *Not hardy*

Stem tip cuttings

This method of propagation is used most commonly for herbaceous perennials that are difficult to divide successfully and for cultivars that do not come true from seed. Cuttings may be taken at any time during the growing season provided that suitable shoots are available.

Select strong growing tips without flower buds, rejecting any that are thin, weak and leggy, or damaged. If there is likely to be any delay before inserting the cuttings, place them in a sealed plastic bag to protect them from dehydration.

Preparing and inserting the cuttings

Take cuttings with secateurs or a sharp knife, cutting across the stem immediately above a node. Remove the leaves from the lowest third of each cutting, then trim the cuttings to just below a node or to 5cm (2in) long. Dip each base into hormone rooting powder or gel. Then insert the cuttings into prepared pots or trays of an appropriate cuttings compost and firm in with your fingers. Leave sufficient space between the cuttings so that the leaves do not touch each other and air can circulate freely. This inhibits the spread of damping off diseases (see p.664).

Aftercare

Water the cuttings using a watering can with a fine rose and treat them with a fungicide to reduce the risk of infection and rot. It is important that the cuttings are maintained at a high humidity level otherwise they will wilt, so, if possible, keep them in a mist unit or propagator. Alternatively, cover the cuttings with a plastic tent or bag; this should be supported on canes or hooped wires to prevent the plastic from touching the leaves since any condensation forming on the foliage could encourage fungal infection. When the weather is hot, shade the cuttings with newspaper, proprietary shade netting, or other semi-translucent material to prevent the leaves from scorching or wilting. The shading should be removed as soon as possible to ensure the cuttings get plenty of light.

Inspect the plants daily, removing any fallen and dead leaves and any material that is infected. Water the compost as necessary to keep it moist but not wet. After about two to three weeks, the cuttings should produce roots and may be potted on into individual pots. Any healthy cuttings that have not developed roots by this stage should be re-inserted and cared for as before until they have rooted.

Basal stem cuttings

This type of cutting is suitable for a number of herbaceous plants that produce clusters of new shoots at the base in spring. Short, basal cuttings of plants with hollow or pithy stems,

HOW TO PROPAGATE BY BASAL STEM CUTTINGS

1 *Take cuttings when the shoots (here of* Chrysanthemum*) are 7–10cm (3–4in) high, slicing at the junction with the woody tissue.*

2 *Remove the basal leaves from each cutting. Make a straight cut just below a node, if visible, or so the cuttings are 5cm (2in) long.*

3 *Dip the cuttings in hormone rooting powder or gel, then insert into a prepared pot of moist cuttings compost. Place the pots in a propagator or plastic bag.*

4 *When the cuttings have rooted, separate them, retaining as much compost as possible around the roots. Pot up the cuttings individually.*

such as lupins (*Lupinus*) and delphiniums, as well as those that have soft tissues, may be rooted successfully from sturdy shoots that are taken from plants in mid-spring.

If required, the plants to be propagated may be lifted and grown in pots or trays in a warm greenhouse to encourage the production of basal shoots earlier than if the plants were growing in the open ground. The cuttings should then be rooted, and young plants established, earlier in the season. The plants from which cuttings have been taken may then be replanted in the garden.

Preparing and inserting the cuttings

Select strong, sturdy shoots whose first leaves have just unfolded and, using a sharp knife, remove them as close to the base as possible; include part of the woody, basal tissue in the cutting. Do not use any shoots that are hollow or damaged.

Trim off the lower leaves of the cuttings, dip them in hormone rooting powder, and insert them in cuttings compost, either individually or several to a pot, or in trays. Firm in the cuttings, water thoroughly, and place in a cold frame or propagator. Alternatively, cover each container with a clear, plastic bag supported on wire hoops firmly inserted into the compost. Shade the cuttings from direct sunlight to prevent the leaves from scorching or wilting.

Aftercare

Check the cuttings every few days, removing any dead or decaying foliage as soon as possible to prevent the spread of rot. Ensure that the compost is moist, but not wet, at all times, and wipe away excess water and condensation from the glass or plastic covers. The cuttings should normally be well rooted within a month and they may then be potted on into individual pots filled with equal parts of loam, sand, and peat substitute or peat.

Root cuttings

This is a useful method of propagating perennials that have fairly thick, fleshy roots, such as *Verbascum* and *Papaver orientale* cultivars. It is also the only way of raising new, healthy plants from border phlox cultivars that are affected by eelworm. As the eelworms occur in the top-growth of affected phlox, but not in the roots, taking root cuttings makes it possible to produce healthy, eelworm-free plants. However, this method cannot be used for those phlox cultivars with variegated foliage, because the resulting plants produce only plain green leaves.

Take care to minimize damage to the parent plant when cutting its roots, and replant it straight after taking the cuttings. Root cuttings are most successful when they are taken during the plant's dormant period, usually in winter.

Preparation

Lift a strong, healthy plant and wash off the soil so that all the roots can be clearly seen. Select roots that are young, vigorous, and relatively thick, as these are more likely to provide successful new plants than those that are weak and thin or old, gnarled, and woody. Cut off the young roots close to the crown and replant the parent plant.

When propagating plants with thick roots, for example *Acanthus, Anchusa, Romneya,* and *Verbascum,* choose roots that are about the thickness of a pencil and cut them into sections 5–10cm (2–4in) long. With thin-rooted perennials, cut the roots into 7–13cm (3–5in) lengths so there is sufficient food-storage for the developing cuttings.

Cut each section so that the top end (that nearest the plant's stem) is cut straight across and the bottom end (nearest the root tip) is cut at an angle; this makes it easy to insert the cuttings the correct way up. Shoots will develop from the top end of the cutting and roots from the lower end. Trim off any fibrous roots before inserting the cuttings.

Inserting the cuttings

After preparing the cuttings, dust them with fungicide to protect against rot. Then insert them vertically, straight ends at the top, in prepared pots or trays of cuttings compost about one and a half times their depth; the tops of the cuttings should be level with the surface. Cover the pots with a thin layer of fine sand or grit, label, and place them in a propagator or cold frame. Do not water the cuttings until they begin to root. Once young shoots have developed, pot them up singly into an appropriate compost.

Plants with thinner roots, such as *Anemone hupehensis, A. x hybrida, Campanula,* phlox, and *Primula denticulata,* are often treated slightly differently as their roots may be too fine to insert vertically. Lay the root cuttings flat on the surface of pots or trays of firmed compost, then cover with more compost. Then treat as for standard root cuttings.

HOW TO PROPAGATE PERENNIALS BY ROOT CUTTINGS

1 *Lift the plant (here* Acanthus*) when dormant and wash the roots. Select roots of pencil thickness and cut them off with a knife, cutting close to the crown.*

2 *Trim the roots and cut each into lengths of 5–10cm (2–4in). Make a straight cut at the upper end of each cutting and an angled cut at the lower end (see inset).*

3 *Insert the cuttings into holes made in pots of moist cuttings compost, and firm. The top end of each cutting should be flush with the compost surface.*

4 *Top-dress the pots of cuttings with coarse grit, label them, and place them in a cold frame until the cuttings root.*

5 *When the cuttings have developed young shoots, pot them up into individual pots filled with loam-based potting compost. Water and label the pots (see inset).*

ALTERNATIVE METHOD FOR THIN ROOTS

Place the trimmed cuttings horizontally on moist, firmed compost. Cover with compost and firm lightly.

PERENNIALS FROM ROOT CUTTINGS

Acanthus
Anchusa azurea
Anemone hupehensis,
  A. x *hybrida*
Arnebia
Campanula, some ❀
Catananche caerulea
Echinops

Catananche caerulea 'Major'

Erodium,
  some ❀
Eryngium,
  some ❀
Gaillardia
Geranium, some ❀
Gypsophila
Limonium platyphyllum
Mertensia
Morisia
Papaver orientale
Phlox paniculata, P. subulata
Primula denticulata
Pulsatilla vulgaris
Romneya
Trollius
Verbascum

Key
❀ *Not hardy*

Pelargoniums

PELARGONIUMS are almost all tender, evergreen, perennial plants of South African origin. When introduced to Britain, they were given the common name geranium because of their botanical similarity to the hardy, herbaceous species of the genus *Geranium*, which was commonly cultivated in Europe at that time. This common name still remains in widespread use today, although almost all the plants usually referred to as geraniums belong to the genus *Pelargonium*.

Types of pelargonium

Pelargoniums may broadly be divided into five groups, according to the main characteristics of the plants. The groups are: zonal, dwarf and miniature zonal, regal, ivy-leaved, and scented-leaved.

Zonal

These pelargoniums have rounded leaves, usually marked with a distinct, dark zone, and single, semi-double, or double flowers. Some cultivars, however, do not have a zone and others have gold- or silver-variegated, or tricoloured leaves.

In temperate climates, they grow well in the open garden and are ideal for summer bedding as they bloom continuously from early summer until late autumn. They also thrive in windowboxes, hanging baskets, and containers. Zonals will happily adapt to the growing conditions in a greenhouse or conservatory.

TYPES OF PELARGONIUM

Zonal
P. 'Dolly Varden'
Rounded leaves, with a darker zone, and single to double flowers.

Regal
P. 'Purple Emperor'
Deeply serrated leaves and broadly trumpet-shaped flowers.

Ivy-leaved
P. AMETHYST ('Fisdel')
Trailing plants with lobed leaves and single to double flowers.

Scented-leaved
P. 'Royal Oak'
Plants with small, often irregularly star-shaped flowers, grown for their fragrant leaves.

Dwarf zonal
P. 'Timothy Clifford'
Bushy, free-flowering plants, similar to zonals, 13–20cm (5–8in) tall.

Dwarf and miniature zonal

Dwarf zonal pelargoniums should be 13–20cm (5–8in) tall, measured from soil level to the top of the plant, not including stem length and flower. They make excellent windowbox plants and pot plants for displaying in greenhouses and conservatories. Miniature zonals should be 7–13cm (3–5in) tall, as measured in the same way as dwarfs. These very floriferous plants bear double and single blooms in a wide range of colours, and have green to greenish-black leaves.

In recent years, F1 and F2 hybrid zonal pelargoniums have been developed. These are grown from seed and are used mainly for bedding. They are single-flowered and are available in the same range of colours as the cultivars that have been propagated vegetatively.

Regal

These pelargoniums are small shrubby plants with rounded, deeply serrated leaves and wide, trumpet-shaped flowers, often in exotic colours.

They may be grown in the open garden but, in temperate countries, they are much more extensively used as greenhouse, conservatory, and house plants, since the flowers are quickly spoilt by rain. In warmer climates, where they may be planted out permanently, they make splendid flowering shrubs, almost continuously in bloom year round.

Ivy-leaved

These trailing pelargoniums have rounded, lobed, ivy-like leaves, and flowers similar to those of zonals, available in a rich assortment of colours. They are used mainly in hanging baskets and other containers, where their flowers on trailing stems can be displayed to best advantage. They may also be planted so that they spill over the edge of a raised bed or a wall.

Scented-leaved

Scented-leaved pelargoniums have small, delicate flowers with five petals, and fragrant foliage for which they are chiefly grown. They make excellent house and greenhouse plants, and in temperate climates may be grown outside during the summer and autumn, in containers or as bedding plants.

General cultivation

Pelargoniums may be grown in all types of well-drained compost – loam-based, peat substitute, or peat – provided it is fresh and has been stored away from direct sunlight. Take care with watering, however, as some composts drain more freely than others and pelargoniums must be kept on the dry side until well established. They then may need plenty of water in the growing season.

Give pelargoniums a weekly application of a high-potash feed such as tomato fertilizer. Start these feeds three weeks from potting up and use throughout the summer. This helps the plants to continue producing a mass of good-quality blooms without becoming too leafy.

Overwintering

Pelargoniums must be kept frost-free, except for *P. endlicherianum*, a hardy species from Turkey, which survives in a raised outdoor bed. In temperate climates, plants grown outside may be saved for the next season by moving them under cover before the first frost is expected. Remove the plants from the ground or container, and shake as much compost from the roots as possible. Then trim the stems by half and remove any remaining leaves. Using fresh potting compost, repot the prepared plants into a box or small pots, to make the best use of storage space. (Old or badly stored compost may be a reason for losses during winter.) Then water the compost well and leave the box or pots in an airy position for two to three days, while

P. 'Dolly Varden'
P. 'Frank Headley'
P. 'Mrs Quilter'
P. 'Lady Plymouth'

Pelargoniums in containers
Planting a combination of zonal and scented-leaved types provides attractive foliage as well as a long-lasting display of decorative blooms.

Contrasting habits
Use trailing, ivy-leaved pelargoniums to spill over the edge of a container. These will make an attractive contrast with upright forms in the centre.

the cut stems seal to prevent blackleg disease (see p.664). Then store in good light in a frost-free place.

Shoots will soon appear. Water only on a fine day, when the foliage will dry more quickly, and feed every six weeks over the course of winter with a well-balanced fertilizer. During very cold weather, keep the plants dry and add extra protection, such as horticultural fleece, which lets through light.

By spring the shoots will be large enough to use as cuttings. Alternatively, the stools may be potted up separately and grown on for planting out in early summer.

Propagation from cuttings

Pelargoniums are easily propagated from cuttings, and the method used is the same for all types. Taking cuttings is an inexpensive way of producing new plants and allows the old plant to remain flowering outside in the garden until the first frosts, thus prolonging the display.

Selecting the cuttings

Although it is possible to take cuttings from spring onwards, the best time is in late summer, when light conditions are good and the weather is still warm. Select strong, healthy shoots (non-flowering ones if from a regal or scented-leaved pelargonium), cutting just above the third joint below the growing tip. Trim each cutting just below the lowest joint and carefully remove the lower leaves.

Inserting the cuttings

Choose the pot size according to the number of cuttings: a 13cm (5in) pot will take up to five cuttings. Fill the pot with standard seed or cutting compost, press down firmly, and place the pot in a container of water until the compost surface becomes moist. Remove the pot and allow it to drain. Insert the cuttings, pressing them down gently to eliminate any air pockets beneath the bases of the cuttings. Do not water them yet.

Aftercare

Place the pot in a light, warm position, but not in full sun. One week after insertion, water the cuttings from below (as above). Water again a week or 10 days later, by which time the cuttings should be rooting. If watered from above, the cuttings may suffer from grey mould/*Botrytis* or other damping off diseases. Do not use propagators or cover them with plastic sheeting, for the same reason. Always allow free circulation of air around them. As soon as the cuttings have rooted (when fresh leaves appear), pot them up singly into 7cm (3in) pots.

Growing F1 and F2 hybrids from seed

Seed-sown F1 and F2 hybrids are difficult for the amateur to produce as they require a specialized environment. In hot countries they will flower from seed in six months, but in colder countries it can take 15 months. To shorten this time, commercial nurseries grow on seedlings at high temperatures in artificial light for 14 hours a day over five winter months. They also treat the plants with dwarfing compounds in order to maintain a compact habit and to achieve early flowering.

Sowing the seed

Sow seed in early summer (see ANNUALS AND BIENNIALS, "Sowing in pots or trays", p.218). When the seedlings are 15cm (6in) high, pinch out the growing tips to encourage bushy growth. Grow on as cool greenhouse plants throughout the winter and spring, to flower the following summer.

TAKING CUTTINGS

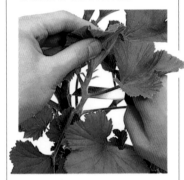

1 *Choose a healthy shoot and cut straight across the stem just above the third joint below the growing tip.*

2 *Using a sharp knife, remove leaves from each cutting, leaving two at the top. Pinch out any flowers or buds.*

3 *Carefully trim the base of each cutting to just below the lowest joint with a straight cut.*

4 *Make holes 2.5cm (1in) deep in pots of moist, firmed seed or cuttings compost. Insert the cuttings and firm.*

OVERWINTERING

1 *Lift the plants before the first frosts and shake off any loose soil. Cut down the stems to about 10cm (4in) and remove the leaves.*

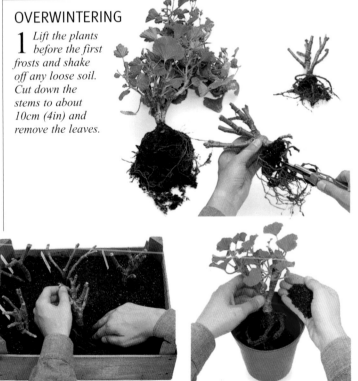

2 *Half-fill a box at least 15cm (6in) deep with fresh compost. Put in the plants so that they do not touch each other. Infill with compost; then water and drain.*

3 *Store in a well-lit, frost-free place. In spring pot up the plants, or use the new shoots to take cuttings from, as necessary, when they are sufficiently large.*

CHAPTER

7

ANNUALS AND BIENNIALS

ANNUALS AND BIENNIALS are traditionally regarded as a quick and inexpensive means of achieving colour in the garden. To restrict their use in this way, however, is to overlook the vast range of foliage, fragrance, texture, and stature they have to offer. Their uses are as varied as their attributes: in just a few months they can enliven a garden or, as cut or dried flowers, add a splash of colour indoors. Although short-lived, a large number of these plants flower freely over many weeks and even months. The gardener can use this profusion of colour to create infinite patterns of bedding with plants that are planned to flower in succession. While annuals and biennials are most often used to fill beds and containers, some varieties with a trailing or climbing habit are particularly striking grown up a support or when allowed to sprawl luxuriantly over a bank.

Annuals and biennials for the garden

THE term "annual" describes a plant whose entire life cycle, going from germination to seed production through to death, takes place within the space of one year. Those that are able to withstand frost are known as hardy annuals; those that are not are known as half hardy and must be raised under glass and planted out in the spring only after all danger of frost has passed.

"Biennials", however, require two growing seasons. In their first season after sowing they produce leaf and root growth; they then overwinter and flower in the following year.

Many plants used for annual bedding are in fact shrubby in their natural habitats, for example pelargoniums, snapdragons (*Antirrhinum majus*), or even the castor oil plant (*Ricinus communis*). In temperate climates they prove more vigorous and free-flowering if grown from seed as annuals. They are then discarded at the end of the growing season, although many can be overwintered under glass or as cuttings, protected from frost.

Annual borders

Whole borders or beds devoted to annuals produce colourful effects. Ideal in a new garden where they quickly provide a vibrant show, annuals may also be used as features in established gardens. The plants may be changed several times in a season to create different displays.

Colour effects

The most effective annual borders are often those that exploit a limited range of colours – dazzling oranges and reds, muted pinks and purples, soft blues and mauves. Plan the planting with a broad sweep of colour, selecting tones that, when adjacent, blend together harmoniously. Greys, greens, and whites are particularly useful for providing a respite from the more vibrant reds and blues. Many annuals, such as antirrhinums, pansies and violas (*Viola* x *wittrockiana*), and petunias, are available in a very wide range of colours, making it possible to select a particular plant whatever the colour range required. A bed devoted to pure white flowers looks fresh and crisp, but plain green-foliaged plants prevent the planting looking cold. Creams should not be substituted for the cleaner whites or mixed with them.

Form and texture

Border compositions are often enhanced by the leaf texture or the overall plant shape as much as by colour alone. Place plants with contrasting textures of either leaf or flower in adjacent groupings. Their differing characteristics will then be

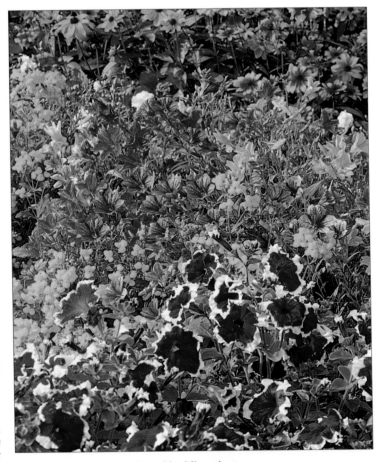

Summer-flowering annuals and bedding plants
Frost-tender perennials grown as annuals bring exotic colour to gardens in temperate climate zones. Although they only last a season, high-impact schemes like these can be designed and implemented in a matter of weeks.

A tapestry of summer colour
These beautiful drifts of half-hardy and hardy annuals are attractively offset by the mellow tones of the mature wall in the background.

better appreciated. Form and texture of annuals are often overlooked but they add greatly to the character of a planting, whether it be with the wispy foliage of *Nigella*, the bold spikes of *Salvia splendens*, or the spreading informality of the poached-egg flower (*Limnanthes douglasii*) to provide contrast. Consider adding annual vegetables with attractive foliage to provide boldness and solidity to annual flower plantings; purple-leaved cabbage and Brussels sprouts, and various kales are especially suitable.

Including a variety of shapes and sizes adds interest to the scheme. Select from, for example, the daisy-like shapes of *Gaillardia*, the golden discs of sunflowers (*Helianthus annuus*), the large bells of petunias, the feathery plumes of *Celosia cristata* 'Childsii' (*C. plumosa*), the cylindrical spikes of *C. cristata*, or the tiny pompons of double daisies (*Bellis perennis*) or double-flowered fever-few (*Tanacetum parthenium* 'Virgo').

Grouping the plants

Most annuals look their best when planted in large groups of one cultivar to give a bold block of colour. Single plants can otherwise easily become isolated and weaken the structure of the planting. Sow in irregular patches so that the effect as the plants mature is similar to the interlocking drifts of flowers made by perennials in a traditional herbaceous border. The shapes and sizes of the groups should be varied to create a natural, free-flowing look.

When a border is to be viewed mainly from one direction, perhaps from a path or lawn, or is backed by a fence or hedge, graduate plants

according to height. Plant the tallest plants, such as hollyhocks (*Alcea*), the taller *Amaranthus*, and tall sunflowers, at the back, and naturally low-growing species such as *Ageratum*, sweet alyssum (*Lobularia maritima*), and *Phlox drummondii* to clothe the front of the border. For those that are intermediate in height, juxtapose groups of slightly different heights to achieve variation. This creates a billowing, undulating informality.

Combine plants that flourish in similar conditions. For instance, species or cultivars of *Nicotiana*, which have loose clusters of scented tubular flowers on tall stems, combine well with the low-growing, flower-covered, compact shapes of busy Lizzie (*Impatiens* cvs), since both generally prefer cool and shady sites.

Foliage plants

There are several annuals grown chiefly for their foliage to harmonize or contrast with bright flower colour, and to add to the range of textures in a bed or border.

Senecio cineraria with its silver-grey leaves is easily cultivated from seed. Although frequently treated as a half-hardy annual, it is in fact a

perennial, and may be kept for years if it is protected from frost. Similar in its requirements, but much more upright in its habit, *Tanacetum ptarmiciflorum* has upright, flat sprays of silvery dark grey foliage. A clump of castor oil plants (*Ricinus communis*), an evergreen shrub that flourishes in cooler climates when treated as a half-hardy annual, provides an eye-catching feature, with its green or purplish-bronze leaves. The bushy, bright green, cypress-like columns of the annual *Bassia* (syn. *Kochia*) *scoparia* f. *trichophylla* contrast well with colourful planting schemes, while selected cultivars of coleus (*Solenostemon*) and *Amaranthus* provide a range of foliage colour: reds and purples, yellows and greens, and two or three colours often combined in one leaf. The foliage of golden feverfew (*Tanacetum parthenium* cvs) remains sunny all summer, while some fibrous-rooted begonias are well worth growing for their attractive bronze leaves.

Some ornamental vegetables also make excellent foliage plants to use with annuals. Cultivars of *Beta vulgaris* such as 'Ruby Chard', with

its vivid red, upright stalks, 'Bright Yellow', with its dazzling, buttercup-yellow stems, or the mixed 'Bright Lights', which contains six different colours, are especially vivid. The ornamental cabbages and kales (*Brassica oleracea* forms) provide low-growing, muted foliage in purples, pinks, greens, and white late in the season and some edible curly kales such as the purple-leaved 'Redbor' are also very effective together with red cabbage and purple-leaved Brussels sprouts.

Annual grasses

One of the most impressive foliage plants is a grass – the variegated maize, or Indian corn (*Zea mays* 'Quadricolor'), which has broad, strap-like, green leaves striped white, cream, and pink. For a lighter, more delicate touch, other annual grasses make delightful additions to the summer border. Hare's tail (*Lagurus ovatus*) produces soft grey-green heads on wiry, upright stems and also dries exceptionally well. The rustling, heart-shaped flowers of quaking grass (*Briza maxima*) open green then turn straw-coloured and will usually self-sow; this is very

An annual border
A complete border may be devoted to annuals, biennials, and other short-lived plants. In this design, good use has been made of the different heights and growth habits of a *wide variety of plants. Newer cultivars of sunflower* (Helianthus), *of medium height and with robust, self-supporting stems, lend valuable stature and focus.*

suitable for Mediterranean-style plantings on dry soil. Taller and more imposing in stature, foxtails (*Setaria italica*) produce fat green heads like hairy caterpillars.

Seasonal display

Plan the planting so that the flowering periods of the annuals coincide as much as possible as this should avoid gaps appearing in the scheme. To provide interest over a long period, use annuals that bloom in succession; for specific colour combinations, make sure that the chosen plants bloom at the same time.

For a spring display choose wallflowers (*Erysimum*), forget-me-nots (*Myosotis*), daisies (*Bellis*), pansies and violas (*Viola* x *wittrockiana*), primroses (*Primula vulgaris*), and polyanthus. For summer and early autumn, the range of flowering plants is much greater, and the combinations are seemingly limitless.

Petunias have been diversified so greatly that elaborate colour schemes may be created using them alone. Choose from the boldly contrasting, striped blooms, the bright, single colours, or the subtly shaded ones, using them either singly or in combination. Where possible, select hybrids that are not spoiled by rain.

Tagetes also offer a wide range of colours, from cream to deep orange to mahogany-red, and the flowerheads vary from the single daisies of *Tagetes tenuifolia* to the great globes of the African cultivars. Easy-to-grow French marigolds, derived from *Tagetes patula*, with single and double flowerheads, display colouring in the full range from lemon, through gold and orange to chestnut and mahogany. Their bushy growth may be used to provide an effective display of colourful ground cover.

Formal bedding schemes

The wide variation of colour, shape, and size, as well as the uniformity of growth obtainable in many modern cultivars of annuals, provides opportunities to create long-lasting displays from spring to autumn. One of the glories of annuals is the intensity of colour achieved when a single cultivar of one of the low-growing, floriferous kinds is massed in a bed so that individual plants merge together. A scarlet carpet of pelargoniums or of *Salvia splendens*, for example, makes a vivid display when set into a fresh, green lawn. Patterned designs, using annuals of different colours, may produce similarly bold effects.

The dense growth habit and continuous flowering of many annuals make them ideal candidates for these complex, formal patterns. There is a wide range of dwarf and intermediate cultivars available. Plants may be used to add colour to designs that have been delineated with bricks, gravel, or other architectural materials.

Annuals are excellent for knots and parterres, where small evergreen plants, such as box (*Buxus*), thyme (*Thymus*), or lavender (*Lavandula*), are clipped to create permanent outlines. Vary colour schemes with the seasons: a winter planting of pansies that continues into spring may be followed by a summer one of dwarf zinnias, for example.

Alternatively, annuals, biennials, and other temporary plants can be used alone to create designs that are expressed in the use of contrasting colours and form. An outline of low, mound-forming plants in a single colour will help to define a pattern and contain the infilling plants. White always makes a crisp, clear

A mixed border
Annuals and biennials create a rich tapestry effect when planted among perennials. Tall, yellow spires of biennial Verbascum, *golden sunflowers, and marigolds are interwoven with blue cornflowers and pink* Cosmos.

edging – double daisies (*Bellis perennis*) in spring, sweet alyssum (*Lobularia maritima*) or white *Lobelia erinus* cultivars in summer. The fillers may be flowers with a looser, more irregular shape, such as antirrhinums.

Mixed borders

A mixed border, containing shrubs, perennials, bulbs, and annuals, is one of the delights of the garden. With such a diversity of plants, it offers the greatest possible variety in terms of colour, texture, season of interest, and design. Annuals and biennials warrant a place in any permanent planting scheme, in which they can be sown each year or left to self-seed. If allowed to self-sow, they will produce a random effect and a profusion of flowers reminiscent of the traditional cottage garden, where all manner of plants, including salad and vegetable crops, happily jostle for space in the same informal plot.

Used as colour highlights among perennials and shrubs, annuals and biennials bring life to established borders. Possible effects range from cheerful mixtures of *Clarkia* (syn. *Godetia*), *Cosmos*, *Eschscholzia*, and corn poppies (*Papaver rhoeas*) to carefully co-ordinated toning schemes. For example, flowering annuals such as crimson *Amaranthus caudatus* and white *Nicotiana* x *sanderae*, or scarlet begonias, pelargoniums, and *Verbena* cultivars will add highlights to a "red" border

with a framework of purplish foliage.

Self-sown annuals and biennials may soon become a permanent feature in a mixed border, helping to unify the planting and introducing a pleasing unpredictability. In early summer *Nigella damascena* makes a hazy web of colour, filling gaps and weaving together neighbouring blooms and the young leaves of later-flowering plants. The spire-like stems of certain biennials such as *Verbascum* and foxgloves (*Digitalis*) add an invaluable vertical accent to plants growing lower down.

Architectural plants

Handsome leaves, eye-catching flower shapes, and striking habits of growth make certain plants stand out from their companions. Annuals or biennials with such architectural qualities can be key features in a mixed bed or border, enhancing the composition. These plants create the greatest impact when they complement – rather than dominate – the other plants in the vicinity. The large, spiny, grey leaves and tall, widely branched flower stems of the Scotch thistle (*Onopordum acanthium*), for instance, make a statuesque centrepiece in a border that features other types of silver-foliaged plants. The flower spikes of the Excelsior Series foxgloves and Imperial Series and Sublime Series larkspur (*Consolida*) rise gracefully above all the neighbouring plants. Shapely blooms, such as those of the spider flower (*Cleome*) and floss flower (*Ageratum*), will also command attention.

Semi-permanent bedding scheme
Perfect for colouring in a pre-existing pattern of box (Buxus), *lavender, and* Santolina, *here forget-me-nots* (Myosotis) *make vivid monochrome panels.*

Architectural plant
The toothed, glossy leaves of Ricinus communis *(castor oil plant) vary from mid-green to reddish purple to bronze-red and add structural interest to any border. This cultivar, 'Impala', has striking reddish purple foliage and a fairly compact habit. The female flowers have a noticeable red stigma and young shoots and leaves are carmine-red.*

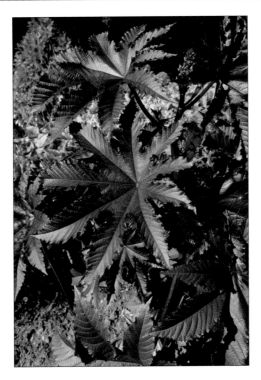

Trailing treasure
With its tumbling form, shapely leaves, and long-lasting, attractive double flowers, this scarlet nasturtium, Tropaeolum 'Hermine Grashoff', *needs no companion plants to make a vivid and striking focal point in a decorative terracotta container. Although a short-lived perennial, this nasturtium is raised from cuttings each year.*

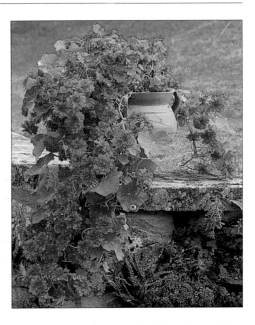

Plants grown primarily for their foliage also play an architectural role. In large borders the green or purple leaves of *Ricinus communis* add a strong textural quality, as do the bold leaves of the ornamental cabbages (*Brassica oleracea* forms).

Annuals and biennials as fillers

As they grow rapidly and are relatively cheap to raise, use annuals and biennials to fill gaps that occur, either through failure of a plant or between immature perennials and recently planted shrubs in a new border. Sow seed where the plants are to flower, choosing cultivars in a height and colour range to suit the permanent planting scheme.

At the end of the season, plant wallflowers (*Erysimum*) in the same gaps for their winter foliage and spring flowers. Multi-coloured carpets of winter-flowering pansies and violas (*Viola* x *wittrockiana*), primroses (*Primula vulgaris*), or polyanthus may be interplanted with spring-flowering bulbs, such as daffodils, hyacinths, or late-flowering tulips.

Until alpines become established, gaps in the rock garden may be filled by sun-loving annuals that enjoy the same conditions. To avoid overwhelming their delicate colours and modest stature, however, choose annuals that are on a similar scale, such as *Viola tricolor*, *Lobelia erinus*, and *Portulaca*.

Annuals and biennials for ground cover

Some annuals and biennials may be used as temporary ground cover, creating pools of colour within an otherwise bare space. There are annuals to suit shade as well as sun, poor soil as well as rich. Single-colour cultivars of sweet alyssum (*Lobularia maritima*) or annual candytufts (*Iberis*) may be used to provide dense cover in a sunny spot or busy Lizzies (*Impatiens* cvs) in shade, where their spreading growth and colourful, continuous blooms will quickly cover the ground. For a more textured quality as well as lively colour, sow corn poppies (*Papaver rhoeas*) or *Eschscholzia*; both spread quickly. Attractive ground cover is also swiftly created by using cultivars of *Convolvulus tricolor* in blue, purple, or rose, or the bushier nasturtiums in red, orange, and yellow, some with variegated leaves.

Climbers and trailers

Vigorous annuals and biennials that climb and trail quickly may transform an expanse of wall or fence with a colourful curtain of foliage and flower, weaving a screen to provide privacy, or embellishing an existing structure such as an arch. A number of annuals have attractive leaves as well as beautiful flowers, and a few, for example sweet peas

Annuals and biennials in a changing climate

If, as predicted, global warming brings earlier springs, and hotter summers and autumns with lower rainfall and frequent periods of drought, gardeners may need to choose many more plants that are adapted to such conditions. In some Mediterranean countries and parts of South Africa, Chile, Mexico, and Australia, spectacular displays of annuals occur in semi-arid, almost desert conditions, and more of these species could be tried in our gardens, alongside old favourites like Californian poppies and poached-egg plants.

Among the attractive annuals that thrive in dry summers are Iceland poppies, love-in-a-mist (*Nigella*), spider flower (*Cleome*), *Cosmos*, purple *Phacelia* and *Gilia capitata*. Colourful succulent annuals ideal for parched soils include mesembryanthemums *Dorotheanthus*, sun plants, *Portulaca grandiflora* and their *Calandrinia* relatives. For more height, sunflowers, Blessed Mary's thistle, *Silybum marianum*, purple *Verbena bonariensis*, and long-blooming *Salvia farinacea* are all good options for dry conditions.

Ground-cover annuals
Busy Lizzies (Impatiens cvs) *in contrasting tones form a carpet of intense colour in the cool shade under trees or shrubs.*

(*Lathyrus odoratus*), offer the additional pleasure of scent (see Sweet Peas, pp.214–215).

Plants with a climbing or trailing habit are particularly valuable in restricted spaces such as patios and balconies, where they make use of the vertical space as well as the ground area. Moreover, many annual climbers can be grown in pots, and are ideal for furnishing new gardens, softening surfaces, and disguising or distracting from an unsightly view.

In addition to favourites such as sweet peas and morning glory (*Ipomoea*), an increasing range of half-hardy and tender climbers is now more widely available as seeds or young plants. Exuberant plants such as the climbing cultivars of nasturtium or *Thunbergia alata* (black-eyed Susan) may be used to provide an abundance of summer flowers along with more permanent

perennial climbers. Particularly striking and effective, if slower to grow away initially, are *Cobaea scandens* with its large bell-shaped flowers in purple or greenish-white, and *Rhodochiton atrosanguineus*, an intriguing plant with curious, deep purple, tubular flowers in dusky maroon calyces.

Climbing annuals can also be very effective when they are grown through host plants, such as ivy (*Hedera*) or conifers. Use the climbing annual canary creeper (*Tropaeolum peregrinum*), which has pale green, dissected leaves and bright yellow, fringed flowers. Another good choice is the half-hardy climber *Eccremocarpus scaber*, the fiery Chilean glory flower, which climbs by means of tendrils and has a long flowering season, with clusters of tubular flowers that glow yellow, orange, or red among small, tooth-

Windowbox compositions
This restrained cream, blue, and green colouring mixes begonias and pansies with trailing Lobelia, *ivy, and* Lysimachia nummularia.

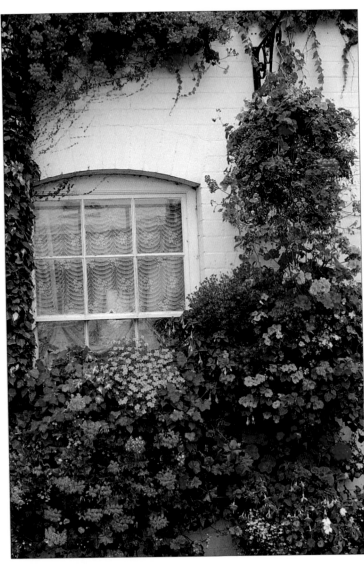

Planting in the vertical plane
Hanging baskets and windowboxes transform a bare wall. Trailing plants such as ivy-leaved pelargoniums reach down to meet upright, bushy annuals, making a continuous curtain of colour.

shaped, pinnate leaves. For a dense, leafy screen, plant scarlet runner beans (*Phaseolus coccineus*), which have delicate, scarlet flowers, and the bonus of edible pods. For a more exotic look, try the purple lablab bean (*Lablab purpureus* 'Ruby Moon') with purplish-green foliage, bright purple flowers, and deep shining purple pods.

Annuals for cutting and drying

Many annuals can provide excellent cut flowers for the house. If space is available in your garden, it is worth growing flowers especially for cutting. They may be either integrated into borders or sown in a separate area. Taller cultivars may be particularly suitable; choose from a range including antirrhinums, cornflowers (*Centaurea cyanus*), stocks (*Matthiola*), and *Gypsophila*. Sweet peas (*Lathyrus odoratus*) are particularly good as cut flowers and fill the house with their heady fragrance; if the flowers are cut regularly the plants will continue to produce blooms for many weeks. Larkspur (*Consolida*) is also useful for cutting and is equally attractive whether fresh or dried.

Many annuals may be dried as "everlasting" flowers to be used for decoration indoors; they include *Xerochrysum*, *Amaranthus caudatus*, and *Limonium*. Others such as honesty (*Lunaria*) and *Nigella* are often grown for their decorative seed-heads. Annual grasses, such as *Aira elegantissima* and *Pennisetum setaceum*, are also worth cultivating for their dried seedheads.

Annuals in containers

Whether it is a pot, tub, or window-box, any container is a potential focal point in the garden, and the plants grown in it can make an eye-catching feature. F1 and F2 hybrid annuals, with their even growth habit and consistent flower colours, are specifically bred to provide uniform, long-lasting displays. Most annuals, however, may be used in containers, either on their own or to complement other plants (see also CONTAINER GARDENING, p.315).

Annuals are available for a year-round display. In spring and early summer, winter-flowering pansies and violas, primroses, dwarf wallflowers, and polyanthus cultivars will continue to thrive in sheltered spots. Protected but sunny sites on patios are also ideal for petunias, calibrachoas, gazanias, zinnias, and busy Lizzies (*Impatiens* cvs), which maintain their colour throughout summer.

Hanging baskets and windowboxes

Plants with a trailing habit are ideal for growing in windowboxes and hanging baskets, and effective displays may be created by a mass of foliage and flower. Reliable performers include sprawling petunias, trailing *Lobelia erinus*, such as the Cascade and Regatta Series, and some *Verbena* x *hybrida* cultivars, which are available in a wide range of colours, including pure reds and scarlets as well as deep purples, crimsons, and whites. Trailing violas and trailing F1 pelargoniums, renewed annually from seed, are also good value (see also PELARGONIUMS, pp.204–205).

Planter's guide to annuals and biennials

EXPOSED SITES

Annuals and biennials that tolerate exposed or windy sites (may require support)
Borago officinalis
Calendula
Centaurea cyanus
Cerinthe
Clarkia
Dianthus barbatus, D. chinensis
Echium vulgare
Erysimum
Eschscholzia
Glaucium flavum

Glaucium flavum

Iberis amara,
    I. umbellata
Lavatera trimestris
Limnanthes
Linum grandiflorum
Lobularia maritima
Lunaria
Malcolmia
Malope trifida
Oenothera biennis
Papaver rhoeas, P. somniferum
Petunia ✽
Rudbeckia hirta (hybrids)
Salvia viridis
Tagetes tenuifolia ✽
Vaccaria hispanica
Xanthophthalmum carinatum,
    X. coronarium, X. segetum

DRY SHADE

Annuals and biennials that tolerate dry shade
Digitalis purpurea
Matthiola longipetala
    subsp. *bicornis*

MOIST SHADE

Annuals and biennials that enjoy moist shade
Impatiens walleriana ✽
Matthiola longipetala
    subsp. *bicornis*
Mimulus x *hybridus* 'Calypso' ✽,
    M. x *hybridus* Magic Series ✽,
    M. Malibu Series ✽
Oenothera biennis
Primula Polyanthus Group,
    P. vulgaris
Viola x *wittrockiana*

FRAGRANT FLOWERS

Amberboa moschata
Calomeria amaranthoides ✽
Centaurea moschata
Dianthus Giant Chabaud Series

Exacum affine ✽
Heliotropium, some ✽
Lathyrus odoratus
Lobularia maritima
Matthiola Brompton Series,
    M. East Lothian Series,
    M. incana Ten Week Mixed
Nicotiana alata ✽, *N.* x *sanderae* ✽
    (some cvs)
Primula, some ✽
Reseda odorata
Viola x *wittrockiana*

TRAILING PLANTS FOR CONTAINERS

Arctotis venusta ✽
Asarina
Begonia Panorama Series ✽
Bidens ferulifolia ✽
Brachyscome iberidifolia
Calibrachoa (Million Bells)
Convolvulus tricolor
Heliotropium, some ✽
Impatiens walleriana ✽
Lobelia erinus Cascade Series ✽,
    L. erinus Fountain Series ✽,
    L. erinus Regatta Series ✽
Lobularia maritima Trailing Series,
    L. maritima 'Wandering Star'
Pelargonium Multibloom Series ✽,
    P. 'Summer Showers' ✽ (and
    suitable other F1 and F2 Series)
Petunia ✽, especially Surfinia Series
Sanvitalia procumbens
Scaevola
Tropaeolum majus semi-trailing cvs
    including *T. majus* 'Empress of
    India', *T. majus* Gleam Series,
    T. majus Whirlybird Series
Verbena x *hybrida* ✽ (trailing types)
Viola x *wittrockiana* Splendid Series

FLOWERS FOR DRYING

Ageratum ✽
Amaranthus ✽
Ammobium alatum
Avena sterilis
Briza maxima, B. minor
Calendula
Celosia ✽
Centaurea cyanus
Clarkia
Consolida ambigua
Gomphrena globosa ✽
Helipterum ✽
Hordeum jubatum
Lagurus ovatus
Limonium sinuatum ✽
Lonas
Moluccella laevis ✽
Nigella
Panicum miliaceum 'Violaceum'
Pennisetum villosum
Salvia viridis
Setaria glauca ✽
Stipa pennata

ANNUAL CLIMBERS

See list on p.129.

ARCHITECTURAL PLANTS

Alcea rosea
Amaranthus caudatus ✽,
    A. tricolor ✽
Bassia scoparia f. *trichophylla* ✽
Brassica oleracea Osaka Series,
    B. oleracea 'Tokyo'
Campanula medium (tall cvs)
Canna
Cleome hassleriana ✽
Consolida
Digitalis purpurea Excelsior Group
Helianthus annuus
Onopordum acanthium,
    O. nervosum
Ricinus communis ✽

Ricinus communis

Salvia sclarea
    var. *sclarea*
Silybum marianum
Tagetes erecta (tall cvs)
Verbascum bombyciferum,
    V. densiflorum
Zea mays 'Quadricolor' ✽

POT PLANTS

Annuals suitable for growing from seed as (greenhouse) pot plants
Antirrhinum, some ✽
Begonia semperflorens ✽
Calomeria amaranthoides ✽
Campanula pyramidalis ✽
Capsicum ✽ (ornamental fruit cvs)
Centaurea moschata
Datura (dwarf cvs)
Exacum affine ✽
Impatiens walleriana ✽ (tall cvs)
Isotoma
Osteospermum ✽
Pelargonium ✽ (F1 and F2 hybrids)
Pericallis x *hybrida* ✽ (cvs)
Petunia ✽
Primula malacoides ✽,
    P. obconica ✽,
    P. sinensis ✽
Psylliostachys suworowii ✽
Salpiglossis ✽
Schizanthus ✽
Solenostemon ✽
Thunbergia alata ✽
Torenia fournieri ✽
Trachelium caeruleum ✽
Trachymene coerulea ✽

PERENNIALS THAT MAY BE GROWN AS ANNUALS

Achillea Summer Pastels Group
Agastache aurantiaca
Alcea 'Majorette', *A.* Summer
    Carnival Group
Coreopsis grandiflora 'Early Sunrise'
Delphinium Centurion Series
Dianthus 'Champion', *D.* 'Floristan'
Diascia
Leucanthemum x *superbum*
    'Snow Lady'
Linaria purpurea cvs
Lobelia x *speciosa* Fan Series,
    L. x *speciosa* Compliment Series
Nemesia
Penstemon Tubular Bells Series
Prunella 'Pagoda'
Veronica 'Sightseeing'

FLOWERS FOR CUTTING

Agrostemma githago 'Milas'
Antirrhinum ✽ (tall cvs)
Calendula
Callistephus ✽ (tall cvs)
Centaurea cyanus
Consolida ambigua
Coreopsis grandiflora
    'Early Sunrise'
Cosmos ✽

Cosmos

Dianthus barbatus,
    D. Giant Chabaud Series,
    D. Knight Series
Erysimum cheiri
Gaillardia pulchella
Gilia capitata
Gomphrena globosa ✽
Gypsophila elegans
Helianthus annuus,
    H. Colour Fashion Series
Helipterum ✽
Lathyrus odoratus
Limonium sinuatum ✽
Lunaria annua
Matthiola Brompton Series, *M.* East
    Lothian Series, *M. incana, M.
    incana* Ten Week Mixed
Moluccella laevis ✽
Nigella damascena
Papaver croceum, P. croceum
    'Summer Breeze'
Psylliostachys suworowii ✽
Rudbeckia hirta (hybrids)
Salvia viridis
Xanthophthalmum carinatum,
    X. coronarium, X. segetum
Xeranthemum annuum ✽
Zinnia ✽

Key
✽ *Not hardy*

Sweet peas

SWEET peas (*Lathyrus odoratus*) have been dubbed "the queen of annuals" for their beautiful flowers, marvellous scent, and long flowering period. Trained up wigwams, pillars, or canes, they provide long and colourful displays. Grow them among perennials or shrubs or as a decorative contribution to the vegetable garden or potager.

Types of sweet pea

Most familiar are the Spencer and Grandiflora cultivars, which climb a supporting framework by means of leaf tendrils. The large-flowered Spencer cultivars may grow 2–3m (6–10ft) high depending on growing conditions; Grandiflora cultivars have smaller, "old-fashioned" flowers but they are more highly scented.

Old fashioned sweet peas
Old-fashioned sweet peas are closer to the species than most of the modern cultivars. They have delicately coloured, small, highly scented flowers.

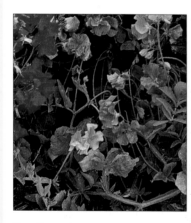

Dwarf sweet peas
Dwarf sweet peas grow to about 45cm (18in) high and need little or no support. They grow well when planted in tubs, windowboxes, and hanging baskets.

Intermediate sweet peas, such as Knee-hi Group and Snoopea Group, reach about 1m (3ft) tall if supported but Snoopea especially will make good ground cover if not supported. Dwarf types include 'Pink Cupid', Bijou Group, and Patio Mixed.

Growing sweet peas from seed

Seeds may be sown in mid-autumn in fairly mild districts, or in late winter or early spring where winters are colder. The process is identical in both cases. Protect seedlings and plants from being eaten by mice.

Sowing

Sweet pea seeds vary in colour from pale buff to black. To help them germinate, nick the darker seeds with a sharp penknife, removing a small piece of seed coat opposite the eye. Sweet pea seeds may be soaked to achieve fast germination, although there may be a problem with rotting.

Sow in seed trays, root trainers, pots (one, two, or three seeds per pot), or in special sweet pea tubes, 5cm (2in) in diameter and 15cm (6in) deep. Use a loamless potting compost with 20 per cent grit added or a standard seed compost.

Dark seeds germinate well in fairly damp compost, but pale ones require a compost that is only just moist. Cover the containers with glass and keep them at about 15°C (59°F). When the seedlings appear, transfer them to a cold frame.

Potting on

Prick out seedlings from trays and then pot them on individually when plants are about 3.5cm (1½in) high. Fill 6cm (3in) pots, or sweet pea tubes, with a similar compost to that used for sowing. Pinch out the root tips and then repot.

Only pinch out autumn-sown sweet peas (Spencers) if they have failed to produce sideshoots by mid-winter. Stop spring-sown seedlings at the second pair of leaves.

Overwintering seedlings

Keep the cold frame open as much as possible during slight frosts, as this will help to harden off the plants. In frosts below -2°C (28°F) close and insulate the frame. In heavy rain, prop open the lights on the frame, for ventilation. Control aphids (p.646) and give a dilute liquid feed in late winter.

BUSH SWEET PEAS

Peastick supports
Peasticks are the traditional means of supporting sweet peas. Insert the peasticks when the seedlings are planted out, leaning the sticks in towards the centre of the clump for extra stability.

Wire rings
Bush sweet peas may be grown up wire rings anchored with several bamboo canes. The plants will grow through the wire, hiding their supports.

Wigwam
A wigwam of canes secured near the top also provides a sturdy support. One seedling beside each cane is usually enough to provide a dense mass of flowers.

Hardening off spring-sown plants

This demands more care as the plants are smaller and growth is softer than on autumn-sown plants. Keep the cold frame well ventilated, but close the lights if frost threatens and protect well with polystyrene sheets or fleece during any very hard frosts.

Planting

Sweet peas thrive in sunny, open sites and well-drained, humus-rich soil (see "Soil structure and water content", p.620). Three weeks prior to planting, carefully rake in a balanced fertilizer at a rate of 85g/sq m (3oz/sq yd). For the best results, trench or double dig the ground in autumn (see "Double digging", p.620). Add well-rotted manure to the lower spit.

Plant out autumn-sown sweet peas in mid-spring, spring-sown ones in late spring. Set plants 23cm (9in) apart just behind and to one side of their support, with the bottom shoot level with the soil. Water during dry spells and when flower buds appear. Apply liquid feed two or three times at fortnightly intervals from mid-summer onwards. Dead-head plants to encourage continuous flowering.

INITIAL TRAINING OF CORDONS

1 *After fixing the wires and posts, insert 2.5m (8ft) tall canes 23cm (9in) apart at a slight angle along the row and attach them to the wires using "V" clips.*

2 *About 2 weeks after planting the young sweet peas, select the strongest shoot of each plant and attach it to the cane with a wire ring loosely fastened beneath a leaf node.*

3 *At the same time, pinch or cut out all the other sideshoots to concentrate the vigour into the main shoot.*

4 *Keep pinching out any sideshoots or tendrils that form and any flower stems carrying fewer than 4 buds.*

LAYERING CORDONS

1 *In early summer, when the sweet peas have reached a height of 1.2m (4ft), they are ready to be layered. This will give them more space to continue growing and flowering.*

2 *Carefully untie the plants from their canes and lay them on the ground to their full length. If the plants are in double rows, do this for one row at a time.*

3 *Attach the shoot tip to a new cane further along the row, so that it reaches 30cm (1ft) up the cane. Work along the row until all the plants are fixed to new canes.*

4 *Repeat for the second row of plants, if required. Flowers will then continue to be produced on the new growth stimulated by the layering method. Sweet peas can be layered again later in the season, provided the plants remain healthy and disease-free. Once they reach the top wire, untie each stem and attach the tip to a new cane further up the row.*

Bush sweet peas

Sweet peas are usually allowed to develop naturally into bushes. Support the plants with peasticks, trellis, canes, or rigid plastic netting. Canes and sticks may be grouped in circles, wigwam-style, or arranged in rows. A double row of peasticks and canes must be well supported, preferably with a post at each end and a strainer wire. Tie young plants to their supports with plastic ties; thereafter they need little tying in. Sideshoots are left to develop, producing more flowers on short stems.

Cordon sweet peas

Sweet peas trained into cordons produce top-quality flowers so are usually grown like this by exhibitors.

Providing supports

At each end of a row, drive in a post with a 45cm (18in) cross-piece near the top, set at 2m (6ft) above ground level. Stretch two parallel wires between the cross-pieces. Place 2.5m (8ft) canes, spaced 23cm (9in) apart, at a slight angle against the wires and secure them with "V" clips. Rows should run north to south to expose plants evenly to sunlight.

Initial training

Leave plants to establish for two weeks. Then pinch out the weaker shoots to leave the strongest shoot on each plant as well as the shoot immediately below the growing point in case the main leader is damaged by, for example, birds. Train the shoots up the cane, tying them with raffia, tape, or rings at each node. Remove sideshoots and tendrils as they grow. When flower stems form, remove any with fewer than four buds.

Layering

When plants are 1.2m (4ft) tall, they should be untied and trained up a new cane further along the row (see *Layering Cordons*). Do this on a warm day when plants are not too sappy. They will then continue to grow and flower for several weeks.

Sowing and planting

ANNUALS AND BIENNIALS FOR SANDY SOIL

Anchusa capensis
Argemone mexicana ❋
Brachyscome iberidifolia
Calendula officinalis
Camissonia cheiranthifolia
Centaurea cyanus
Clarkia amoena
Coreopsis tinctoria
Dianthus
Eschscholzia californica
Glaucium flavum
Lavatera trimestris
Limnanthes douglasii
Limonium sinuatum ❋
Linaria maroccana
Lobularia maritima
Mentzelia lindleyi
Oenothera biennis

Papaver rhoeas
Shirley Series

Papaver rhoeas,
P. somniferum
Platystemon californicus
Portulaca grandiflora ❋
Rudbeckia hirta
Schizanthus ❋
Tagetes ❋
Verbascum bombyciferum
Xerochrysum bracteatum ❋

ANNUALS AND BIENNIALS FOR VERY ALKALINE SOIL

Ageratum houstonianum ❋
Antirrhinum majus ❋
Calendula officinalis
Callistephus chinensis ❋
Calomeria amaranthoides ❋
Cosmos
Dianthus, some ❋
Erysimum cheiri
Gomphrena globosa ❋
Lavatera trimestris
Limonium sinuatum ❋

Lobularia maritima
Matthiola Brompton Series, *M. incana*
Primula
Salvia viridis
Tagetes ❋
Tropaeolum, some ❋
Ursinia anthemoides ❋
Xeranthemum annuum ❋
Zinnia ❋

Lavatera trimestris 'Silver Cup'

Key
❋ Not hardy

Aᴺᴺᵁᴬᴸˢ and biennials are among the easiest of plants to raise from seed. They may also be obtained as seedlings or young plants from nurseries or garden centres, and will provide an instant display of colour in a garden border or container placed indoors or outside.

Buying seeds

Always buy fresh seeds that have been stored in cool conditions. The viability of seeds of different species varies greatly; while some, such as peas and beans, may remain viable for a few years if kept cool and dry, most start to deteriorate after a year, especially if they are stored in damp, warm conditions. Seeds in sealed foil packets last for several years; once the packets are opened, however, the seed viability deteriorates.

F1 and F2 hybrid seeds are available for many annuals and for some biennials; these produce plants that are vigorous and true to type with even growth and flower characteristics. These seeds are ideal for the gardener seeking uniformity, but for most ordinary garden purposes well-produced, open-pollinated seeds are equally satisfactory.

Pelleted and primed seeds

Seeds may be individually coated with a paste, or pelleted, to form a smooth ball. This enables them to be handled separately, so that they may be more easily spaced in containers or the open ground. If pelleted seeds are space-sown at the correct distance for the cultivar concerned they need not be thinned so, although they cost more, fewer are required. The seeds should be watered thoroughly after sowing to ensure that the moisture needed for germination to occur penetrates the seed coat as quickly as possible. Pelleted seeds are normally available in a number of hybrids and species, especially where the seed is small, as well as in some open-pollinated genera, such as *Lobelia* and *Alyssum*.

Primed seeds have been treated so that they are ready to germinate as soon as they are sown. They are particularly useful for species and cultivars that do not germinate easily.

Seed tapes and gels

Seed tapes are tissue-like, soluble strips with evenly spaced seeds embedded within them. The tapes are laid at the base of a drill, then covered with a thin layer of soil. Gel kits may

be purchased for fluid sowing – seeds are added to a paste so that they are suspended and therefore evenly spaced throughout. The mixture is then squeezed along a pre-prepared drill. It is important not to allow the mixture to dry out. Both these methods distribute the seeds evenly so that less thinning is required than for hand-sown seeds.

Buying seedlings

Seeds of some plants that germinate less readily are available from some seed firms at the chitting stage – when the seed coat has burst open and roots and seed leaves are starting to emerge. The seeds are usually sown on agar jelly and despatched in a sealed plastic container. Healthy seedlings should have fresh, moist roots and seed leaves; reject any that have pale green leaves or are overcrowded. The jelly contains enough food and moisture to sustain them for a few days but the seeds should be transferred to the required growing conditions as soon as possible so the seedlings have sufficient light to develop.

Seedlings of selected cultivars may be purchased as plug plants, when they have developed at least one pair of true leaves and are ready for pricking out (see p.219). This is useful for plants with very small seeds, such as begonias, which are

MAIL-ORDER PLUG PLANTS

A rigid moulded plastic container separates and protects the tiny plants when these are sent by post.

Hardy and half-hardy annuals and biennials

Annuals complete their life cycle in a year, while biennials require two years. Horticulturally, annuals and biennials are termed hardy or half hardy. Hardy annuals are resistant to frosts and so may be sown early in open ground and will be established before more frost-prone annuals. Half-hardy annuals withstand only a limited amount of cold and are killed or badly damaged at freezing tem-peratures; they need to be maintained in frost-free conditions of 13–21°C (55–70°F) in order to germinate and establish.

Hardy biennials should be sown by midsummer to allow the plants to become well established by the winter. Overwinter half-hardy biennials in a cool greenhouse or insulated cold frame.

difficult for many gardeners to germinate successfully. The plugs are sent out in a rigid transparent plastic container to keep them as fresh as possible. If pricked out within 24 hours of arrival and kept within a protected environment they will usually grow as well as plants from home-germinated seeds.

Small seedlings already well established in wedges or plugs of compost are also readily available. Depending on size, they can be grown on in their module trays or be potted up individually in small pots or hanging baskets. They should be grown on in a greenhouse or cold frame, or on a sunny windowsill, until they are ready to be hardened off and planted out. They are much cheaper than bedding plants.

Sowing

When and where to sow annuals and biennials depends on when they are required to flower and the tempera-ture they need for germination.

Hardy annuals

Sow hardy annuals where they are to flower when the soil has warmed up to at least 7°C (45°F) in the spring. If sown in successive batches until midsummer, hardy annuals provide a long summer display.

Some hardy annuals, if sown *in situ* in the autumn, germinate to produce small plants that overwinter satisfactorily outdoors and flower in late spring or early summer the following year. Love-in-a-mist (*Nigella*), cornflower (*Centaurea cyanus*), and poppies (*Papaver*) are some examples.

Seeds of hardy annuals may also be sown in pots or seed trays and either planted out in their final flowering positions in late autumn or overwintered in a cold frame to be planted out in spring. This is a useful

ANNUALS THAT ARE BEST SOWN IN SITU

Agrostemma
Anchusa capensis
Borago officinalis
Centaurea cyanus, C. moschata
Clarkia
Collinsia bicolor
Consolida ambigua
Cynoglossum amabile
Eschscholzia californica

Eschscholzia californica

Gilia capitata
Gypsophila elegans
Limnanthes douglasii
Linaria maroccana
Linum grandiflorum
Malcolmia maritima
Malope trifida
Mentzelia lindleyi
Papaver rhoeas, P. somniferum
Phacelia campanularia
Scabiosa atropurpurea
Silene coeli-rosa

practice in gardens with clay soil that is slow to warm up in spring.

Hardy biennials

Most hardy biennials may be sown outdoors from late spring until midsummer. The optimum time varies according to what is being grown: forget-me-nots (*Myosotis*) grow rapidly so should not be sown until midsummer, while Canterbury bells (*Campanula medium*) need longer to develop and should be sown in late spring or early summer.

The young plants may be transplanted to their final flowering position in autumn or, if they are not crowded, the following spring. Premature flowering reduces the spring display, so pinch out any buds that form in the first season.

Half-hardy annuals and biennials

In warm climates, sow seed directly outside once the soil temperature reaches the optimum for germination. In colder regions, sow half-hardy annuals in containers in spring at 13–21°C (55–70°F), according to the particular genus. Half-hardy biennials may be sown under the same conditions in midsummer. Frost-tender perennials, such as busy Lizzies (*Impatiens* cvs), gazanias, and some *Lobelia* species, may be raised from seed in the same way as half-hardy annuals.

Many tender perennials (including *Argyranthemum* and *Osteospermum*) may be propagated by cuttings taken in autumn (see PERENNIALS, "Stem tip cuttings", p.202) and be overwintered in frost-free conditions for planting out in late spring.

Sowing in open ground

There are two main methods of sowing outdoors *in situ*: broadcast and in drills. For both, a seedbed in a sunny place should be prepared. Dig over the soil to one spade's depth, then rake and firm it by treading gently on the surface. Do not sow in soil that is too rich, as this will encourage leaf rather than flower production. In soils lacking nutrients, however, a dressing of 70g/sq m (2oz/sq yd) of a balanced fertilizer may be added before sowing (see "Soil nutrients and fertilizers", pp.624–625) to boost production.

Before sowing a border, prepare a plan showing the position of each cultivar, using any areas likely to be shaded to grow those that are shade-tolerant. Mark the area for each cultivar with grit or a cane so that it is easy to check the balance of colours, heights, and habits of the different plants before sowing the seed.

MARKING OUT ANNUAL BORDERS

1 *Sprinkle grit or sand on the soil or score the soil with a stick to mark out interlocking areas for sowing seeds.*

2 *The seedlings may appear too sparse at first but will blend together as they grow.*

Open ground sowing is particularly suitable for annuals that produce deep tap roots such as *Clarkia*, *Gypsophila*, and poppies (*Papaver*), because they are best sown where they are to flower since they do not transplant readily.

Sowing broadcast

Sprinkle seeds thinly and evenly on the surface of the prepared seedbed and rake them in lightly. Label, then

water the area with a watering can fitted with a fine rose.

Sowing in drills

Seeds sown in drills produce seedlings growing in straight rows at regular intervals so they are readily distinguished from weed seedlings, which are randomly distributed. The seedlings initially look regimented but, once thinned, will form a dense and informal planting, and the rows

SOWING IN DRILLS

1 *Using a line of string as a guide, make a furrow about 2.5cm (1in) deep with a hoe.*

2 *Holding the seeds in one hand, pick up several at a time and scatter them evenly along the drill.*

ALTERNATIVE STEP

If the seeds are pelleted, place them individually in the base of the drill.

3 *Rake the soil back over the drill without dislodging the seeds. After labelling the row, water the soil using a fine rose.*

SOWING SEED BROADCAST

1 *Prepare the soil by raking to produce a fine tilth. Scatter the seeds thinly over the prepared area by hand or from the packet.*

2 *Rake over the area lightly at right angles to cover the seeds so that they are disturbed as little as possible.*

SELF-SEEDING ANNUALS AND BIENNIALS

Annuals and biennials that self seed either true to type or with minor variations if closely related cultivars are not growing nearby

Agrostemma
Borago officinalis
Calendula officinalis
Centaurea cyanus
Clarkia amoena
Collinsia bicolor
Digitalis purpurea
Eschscholzia californica
Hesperis matronalis
Limnanthes douglasii
Linaria maroccana
Lobularia maritima
Lunaria annua
Malcolmia
Myosotis
Nicotiana langsdorffii
Nigella damascena
Oenothera biennis
Omphalodes linifolia
Onopordum acanthium,
   O. nervosum
Papaver rhoeas, P. somniferum
Platystemon californicus
Silene armeria
Silybum marianum
Tanacetum
   parthenium

Tanacetum parthenium

Tropaeolum majus
Vaccaria hispanica
Verbascum
Viola (many spp.)
Xanthophthalmum segetum

THINNING SEEDLINGS

Individual seedlings
Press on either side of the seedling to be retained (here larkspur, Consolida ambigua) *while pulling out the unwanted ones around it. Refirm and water.*

Seedling groups
Lift groups of seedlings (here sweet William, Dianthus barbatus) *with plenty of soil around the roots if they are to be replanted. Firm in and water the remaining seedlings.*

in adjoining areas can be arranged at different angles.

Using either a trowel tip or the corner of a hoe, mark out shallow drills 8–15cm (3–6in) apart depending on the ultimate size of the plants. Sow seeds thinly and evenly by sprinkling or placing them along each drill at the appropriate depth for the annuals being sown, then carefully draw back the displaced soil with a rake or hoe to cover them. Label each row and water well with a watering can fitted with a fine rose.

Thinning

To prevent overcrowding, the seedlings usually need to be thinned. Do this when the soil is moist and the weather mild, taking care to retain the sturdier seedlings where possible

and achieve an even spacing. To minimize disturbance to a seedling being retained, press the soil around it with your fingers as the surplus seedlings are extracted.

If seedlings are very dense, dig them up in clumps, retaining plenty of soil around the roots; disturb as little as possible the other seedlings in the ground. Some biennials such as forget-me-nots (*Myosotis*) and honesty (*Lunaria*) germinate readily and if sown where they are to flower should be thinned appropriately – forget-me-nots to 15cm (6in) and honesty to 30cm (12in), for example.

The thinnings may be used to fill sparse areas caused by uneven sowing or irregular germination, or may be transplanted for use elsewhere in the garden. For

transplanting, select the strongest and healthiest of the thinned seedlings, then replant them where needed at the appropriate spacings and water them lightly to settle their roots.

Many annuals and biennials scatter their seeds freely, often producing dense clumps of seedlings; these need to be thinned carefully to the appropriate distances apart, so that the young plants retained may develop without competition.

Sowing in pots or trays

Half-hardy annuals are usually sown in containers so that they may develop under cover and be planted out as young plants when conditions are favourable. Hardy annuals may also be sown in containers left outside, and the seedlings transplanted to their flowering positions when there is sufficient room.

Pots, seed pans, seed trays, and module trays are all suitable containers, depending on the number of seeds to be sown and the space they require. Degradable pots are also useful for seedlings that do not transplant well, because the whole pot may be planted out without disturbing the roots.

Sowing the seeds

Fill the chosen container to its rim with standard seed compost and press in lightly around the edges with the fingertips to make sure that there are no air pockets. To settle the compost, tap the container against a hard surface and then gently firm the compost level so that the top of the compost is just below the rim of the container. Water with a fine rose and leave for an hour or so to drain.

Sow the seeds thinly on the surface of the compost, tapping them from the seed packet or from V-shaped paper to achieve an even spread. Large or pelleted seeds may be sown individually in compartmented packs or spaced out in trays or pans. Very small seeds are easier to sow if they are mixed first with the same bulk of fine sand; this produces a more even distribution.

Cover the seeds to about their own depth with sieved compost, perlite, or vermiculite; then water lightly, so as not to disturb the seeds or the surface of the compost. Dust-like seeds, such as those of begonia, should be left uncovered and watered from below: place each container within 2.5cm (1in) of its rim in water until the surface of the compost is moist. Do not leave them soaking for too long since waterlogging may

Protecting and supporting seedlings

Support is required for slender-stemmed or tall annuals. Carefully insert peasticks or thin twigs into the soil around young plants; the supports should be slightly shorter than the ultimate height of the plants so that they will be concealed when the plants reach their mature size. These supports may also help to protect the seedlings from possible rodent and bird damage.

Alternatively, stretch wire netting, with a mesh no greater than 2.5cm (1in), over the seedbed, bending it down at the edges so it does not touch the seedlings. Secure firmly in the soil, using sticks or wire pins. The plants grow up through the mesh and cover the netting when fully grown.

Supporting with twigs
Peasticks or thin twigs may be pushed into the soil among the seedlings. Tall annuals (here larkspur, Consolida ambigua) *grow to hide the support.*

Wire protection and support
Protect seedlings (here Eschscholzia) *with mesh wire netting bent to form a cage. The netting will support the seedlings as they grow through.*

SOWING IN A TRAY

1 Fill the seed tray with a standard seed compost and level with a presser board to 1cm (½in) below the rim.

2 Using a V-shaped piece of paper, sprinkle the seeds thinly over the compost surface, to achieve an even covering.

3 Cover the seeds with a layer of sieved moist compost, perlite, or vermiculite to about the same thickness as the seeds themselves. Water the seeds in lightly.

4 Place a piece of glass or clear plastic sheeting over the tray to maintain even humidity.

5 Shade the tray with netting if the tray is in direct sunlight. Remove both glass and netting as soon as germination starts.

Seeds with special requirements

A few seeds need special conditions to germinate successfully. Coleus (*Solenostemon*), begonia, and busy Lizzie (*Impatiens*) seeds require light and prefer a constant temperature of 21°C (70°F). Primulas prefer light, but need temperatures of no more than 20°C (68°F). Some seeds including *Phacelia*, pansies (*Viola* x *wittrockiana*), and other *Viola* should be germinated in the dark. Seeds of *Thunbergia alata* and pelargoniums require scarifying, sowing, and 21–24°C (70–75°F) to germinate. Seeds of *Moluccella* should be stratified: the seed pan is set in a refrigerator for a couple of weeks before bringing it into a temperature of 18–21°C (64–70°F) for a further two or three weeks.

---

cause rotting before germination or encourage seedling diseases (see "Damping off", p.660).

To maintain even humidity place a piece of glass or clear plastic sheeting over the container; do not let it touch the compost surface as this may disturb the seeds. Place the container on a heated mat (see GREENHOUSES AND FRAMES, "Propagation aids", p.580), in a propagator or on a greenhouse bench, and shade with fine netting or newspaper if it receives direct sunlight. As soon as the first seedlings germinate, the cover should be removed. Keep them in good light and the compost moist until they are ready for pricking out.

Pricking out

Seedlings raised in trays or shallow pans need to be transplanted into larger containers before they become overcrowded, as they will quickly become weak and spindly when deprived of sufficient space or light. This is known as pricking off or pricking out seedlings. The process enables the seedlings to continue to develop until they are ready for planting out in the garden.

Fill the new containers with potting compost and firm gently. Small pots, no more than 7cm (3in) in diameter, or module trays, are ideal for individual seedlings; larger pots, pans, or trays may be used for several seedlings.

To prick out, first knock the container of seedlings against a table top or bench to loosen the compost slightly and remove it intact from the container. Then hold each plant gently by the small seed leaves to avoid bruising the stems or growing tips and loosen it with a widger or other small implement. Then carefully lift each plant from the soil, retaining some of the moist seed compost around the roots to ensure that there will be little or no check to growth when the seedlings are replanted.

Use a dibber to make holes in the compost and insert a seedling into each hole. Make sure that all the roots are covered with compost, then gently firm in each seedling using fingers or a dibber, and level the compost. As each container is filled, water it from a can fitted with a fine rose to settle the compost around the roots. Cover the containers with clear plastic for a few days while the seedlings re-establish, but make sure that the plastic does not touch the leaves because this may encourage rotting. Then return the seedlings to their previous growing conditions to develop further.

If seedlings are ready for planting out, but this is delayed because of a late frost, pot them on into a larger container and give a liquid feed, to ensure that growth is not checked.

Seeds that have been sown singly in packs or space-sown will not need pricking out and may be hardened off before planting out.

Hardening off

All half-hardy annuals that have been raised either under glass or in any other controlled environment before being planted outdoors need to be acclimatized gradually to the natural conditions outdoors. The aim

PRICKING OUT INTO MODULES

1 When the seedlings (here Tagetes) are large enough to handle, tap the tray on a hard surface to loosen the compost.

2 Carefully separate the seedlings, handling them by their seed leaves. Keep plenty of compost around the roots.

3 Transplant each seedling into a separate cell of a module tray. Firm the soil around each one with fingers or a dibber, and water.

Annuals in pots

Many annuals make excellent pot plants. Prick out young seedlings into divided trays or individual pots and, when the roots have just filled the container, transfer each seedling to a larger pot prepared with loam-based potting compost. The pot size will vary according to the species or cultivar and time of sowing. Put plants sown in late summer into 9cm (3½in) pots over the winter when growth is slow, and transfer them later to their final pots – either 13cm (5in), or 19cm (7in), or much larger pots for groups of three or five plants per container. Transplant spring-sown annuals directly into their final pots or containers.

Many annuals (here Schizanthus) *are very useful for providing an early, colourful display in a cool greenhouse in spring.*

is to harden the plants, reducing their dependence on artificial heat and protection without exposing them to sudden environmental changes that might cause damage.

Hardening off is most easily done using a greenhouse and a cold frame. Six or seven weeks before planting the seedlings outdoors, move them to a cooler part of the greenhouse for about a week. Then transfer them to a closed cold frame; increase the ventilation little by little, eventually dispensing with the frame light (the lid) entirely for the last few days unless frost is forecast.

Keep a close watch on the plants for any indication that the change in temperature is too great or too swift: there may be a check in growth, for example, or the leaves may yellow.

Other equipment that is ideal for hardening off includes glazed frames, the covers of which may be removed completely when conditions are favourable, and cloches, which may be lifted off and replaced as

necessary. Alternatively, the young plants may be placed outdoors in sheltered positions and protected (normally only necessary at night) with horticultural fleece, plastic, or other coverings on temporary wood or bamboo frames. Unless weather conditions are poor, the covers should be removed during the day to ensure that the plants always receive sufficient light and ventilation.

Planting out

Plant out half-hardy seedlings once all danger of frost has passed. This is particularly important in the case of the more tender plants, such as begonias and *Salvia splendens*. Provided they have been hardened off, some half-hardy annuals will, however, tolerate cool, but not frosty, conditions for short periods.

Before planting out, prepare the bed (see "Sowing in open ground", p.217), water the young plants thoroughly, and then leave them to drain for an hour or so. To remove a

plant from its pot, invert it, supporting the stem with a finger on either side. Then tap the rim against a hard surface to loosen the root ball from the pot. Break apart packs or divided trays to remove each seedling with its root ball undisturbed.

If plants are in trays without divisions, hold the tray firmly with both hands, and tap one side sharply on the ground to loosen the compost. Then gently slide out the contents in one piece. Separate individual plants carefully with the fingers, keeping as much soil as possible around the roots. Alternatively, remove each plant gently using a widger or other small tool, taking care not to damage the young roots.

Make a hole sufficiently large to accommodate the root ball readily. Space the plants so that the leaves will just touch when the plants are fully developed. Normal planting distances range from 15 to 45cm (6 to 18in) depending on the habit of the species or cultivar being grown.

Check that the plants are at the same depth as in the container, then firm the soil around the base of the stem, without compacting the soil too much. After planting, gently break up the soil surface between the plants with a hand fork. To settle them in, water the plants thoroughly using a watering can fitted with a fine rose so that the soil is not washed off the roots.

Stopping or pinching out

As young annuals develop, some may require stopping or pinching out in order to encourage the plants to produce sideshoots and develop a bushy habit.

Stopping is done by nipping the growing tip off a young plant. Even with annuals that branch naturally it may be necessary when a few plants in a bed produce stronger shoots than others. If an even growth habit

of plants is required, stop tall plants when they have reached five or six joints by removing the tip of each long shoot back to the required height.

Stopping delays flower production and so should not be carried out if an early display is preferred. Nor should it be done on plants such as antirrhinums or stocks (*Matthiola*) that have strong terminal shoots, as these develop the main flower spikes and will also produce lateral growths naturally during the summer to continue the flowering display.

PLANTING OUT INTO OPEN GROUND

1 *Break the pack apart and carefully remove each seedling (here* Tagetes) *with its root ball intact.*

2 *Place each plant in a hole large enough to take its root ball, ensuring that the plant is at the same level as it was in its container.*

3 *Return the soil around the roots and gently firm so that there are no air pockets. Water the area.*

HARDENING OFF

Tunnel cloche
Place half-hardy annuals (here Tagetes) *in a tunnel cloche. Lift the sides for ventilation.*

Cold frame
Seedlings may also be placed in a cold frame left open for progressively longer intervals.

FIRST-YEAR GROWTH

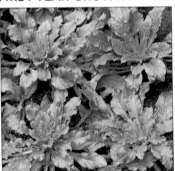

*Biennials such as Canterbury bells make only vegetative (*leafy*) growth in their first year. Flowers develop the following summer.*

HOW TO BUY PLANTS

Bedding plants

GOOD EXAMPLE

Compact, vigorous growth

POOR EXAMPLE

Healthy, green foliage

Petunias

Leggy, bare stems

Dead leaves

Pot-grown annuals

GOOD EXAMPLE

Bushy, sturdy growth

Healthy buds developing

POOR EXAMPLE

Moist compost

Busy Lizzie (Impatiens cv)

Yellowing, discoloured leaves

Bedding plants

Buying more mature annuals and biennials to plant out directly into beds, borders, or containers can save time and may be necessary if no greenhouse is available to grow half-hardy annuals from seed. In addition, whereas seeds of many annuals may be bought only as mixtures, commercial growers are usually able to obtain colours separately, providing gardeners with a much wider range of plant materials with which to plan their bedding schemes.

Judging the quality of bedding plants

Sturdy young plants with evenly balanced, short-noded shoots and healthy foliage are most likely to establish well and give the best results. The plants should have well-developed root systems but must not be pot-bound. Do not purchase plants in dry compost or with yellowing or diseased foliage because they do not always establish well and often produce few flowers.

Half-hardy bedding plants are sold at various stages from seedling to flowering plant, frequently well ahead of the date at which it is safe to plant them outdoors. Make sure that you have appropriate conditions under cover to grow them on properly if necessary. Check also that they have been hardened off if they are for immediate planting outside. Acclimatize the seedlings slowly until the danger of frost is past; sudden exposure to frost or even cold wind may kill them since they may have been produced in heated greenhouses. They may then be planted outdoors.

Annual climbers

Climbing annuals should be planted where they are able to grow naturally through a shrub or tree or be trained against a fence, wall, or some other support. If a twining annual is to climb through a shrub, position the plant on the side where it will receive the most sunlight. Where the climber is intended to be grown up a wall or fence, provide a support that will suit its habit of growth (see CLIMBING PLANTS, "Types of support", p.130); then plant it 30cm (12in) from the base of the wall or fence.

Planting bedding plants to a design

Before planting up a bed or border, assemble all the bedding plants to be used and check them off against the plan. Place the plants, still in their containers, roughly in position on top of the prepared soil to ensure that the bed will be neither too crowded nor too sparsely planted. Now is the time to make any final adjustments to plant positioning – it will be too late once they are in the ground. Keep a few plants in reserve to replace any that may die.

1 *Mark out the design of the whole bed before starting to plant. Work from the centre outwards, or from the back of the bed to the front. Use a plank or kneeler for kneeling on so that the soil does not become compacted, making it difficult to work and inhibiting drainage.*

2 *Plant the seedlings carefully, handling the plants as little as possible. Firm the soil around each. Complete one section of planting before moving on to the next.*

3 *As each section of planting is completed, trim off any damaged, uneven, or straggly shoots to make the patches of plants more compact. Water thoroughly section by section so that the seedlings planted first do not dry out while the others are being planted.*

Routine care

SINCE they have a relatively short life, annuals generally require little maintenance unless they are grown in a container (see CONTAINER GARDENING, "Routine care", p.332). They do need to be watered regularly during drought, however, especially if they are grown in containers, and dead-headed to prolong flowering. Continue to pinch out the growing tips (see p.220). Tall annuals may require staking when or soon after planting to prevent them from blowing over or toppling under their own weight. When the foliage starts to die down after flowering or at the end of the season, the plants should be cleared away.

Watering, feeding, and weeding

Young annuals and biennials that are planted in open ground should be watered on a regular basis with a sprinkler or watering can, soaking the bed thoroughly. Once the plants have become established, water only during prolonged dry weather. Those planted against a wall or fence may need extra attention when watering, because they may naturally receive less water (see *Rain Shadow*, p.610).

Annuals rarely need extra feeding if the soil has been well prepared. A liquid fertilizer may be applied on very poor soils as flower buds develop. Biennials may benefit from a little food, but only those grown for show purposes need regular feeding. Over-rich conditions produce vigorous vegetative growth at the expense of flowers. Container plants may benefit from the addition of slow-release fertilizers and the application of foliar feeds (see CONTAINER GARDENING, "Fertilizing", p.332).

Keep annuals and biennials free from weeds as these compete for light, water, and soil nutrients. Pull out any weeds by hand while they are still small and remove self-sown seedlings in the same way if they are not required or are too numerous.

Providing supports

Many annuals and biennials have rather slender stems, which benefit from some support. Use small, bushy branches, or peasticks, for plants

Pot-grown annuals
Push canes into the compost, and tie string around them, to support tall annuals like Salpiglossis.

with a mature height of up to 1m (3ft). When the plants are only a few centimetres high, insert the sticks in the soil around them so that they can grow up through the sticks, which will quickly be covered and hidden. Take particular care not to damage the plants, especially their young roots, when pushing in the sticks.

Taller annuals will flourish and flower more freely if artificially supported by a wigwam, tripod, obelisk, pergola, trellis, fence, wall, or strong tree or shrub, or on wires or trellis between pillars. Supports should be positioned before the annuals are planted. Tall annuals in containers may be supported by inserting a few canes around the edge of the pot and tying soft string around the canes – the supports are hidden by the plants as they develop.

Very tall plants, like hollyhocks (*Alcea*) or sunflowers (*Helianthus*), may need to be individually staked. Push the cane into the soil where it will be least visible and, as the plant develops, tie in the stem as required.

Many twining annuals and those that have tendrils, such as sweet peas, reach 2–3m (6–10ft) during their short life, and these are best guided to their support with plastic ties or soft twine until they take hold. The twine should be tied loosely around the leading shoot and support using a figure-of-eight knot, to prevent chafing against any hard surfaces and to allow for stem expansion.

Controlling annual and biennial "volunteers"

Discovering self-sown seedlings (often called "volunteers") is one of the great pleasures of gardening – especially if they are growing in the right place. Annuals and biennials such as marigolds, honesty, and foxgloves are particularly keen self-sowers, but a range of other plants also oblige. With meadow gardening and naturalistic styles on the increase, gardeners can exploit this volunteer force to produce colourful, long-lasting, informal displays in sunny, open areas, particularly on sandy soils.

To achieve similar results on heavier but well-drained soils, cover the area with a layer of gritty sand, 4in (10cm) deep, and sow seed (or use plugs) of suitable annuals and biennials that will flower, self-seed, and continue the display in the following and subsequent years. Once established, many should self-seed naturally, although there will always be some that fade away.

Such schemes are not entirely self-sufficient as inevitably species of some genera, like *Eschscholzia*,

Limnanthes, and *Myosotis*, can become dominant and may need thinning out in spring if too dense. Others may fail and leave gaps that need seeding with different species to provide further variety.

The aim is not to exactly replicate a natural feature like the South African veld in spring, but to create a kaleidoscopic mix of plants from a number of countries with similar habitats. Try blending common annual cornflowers, poppies, forget-me-nots, and campions with Californian natives like *Collinsia*, *Ipomopsis*, *Gilia*, and *Leptosiphon* species, as well as *Osteospermum*, *Gazania*, *Heliophila*, and *Nemesia* species from South Africa. Various attractive annual grasses like Hare's tail grass (*Lagurus ovatus*) and quaking grass (*Briza* species) might also be included.

By their nature, such plantings are experimental and need amending as some species die out and local weeds creep in; when successful they provide great satisfaction throughout summer and autumn.

Annuals as dried or cut flowers

Dried or fresh flowers of many annuals and biennials are decorative indoors. Harvest "everlasting" flowers, such as *Xeranthemum*, *Helipterum*, and *Limonium*, when they are about half open, then hang them upside-down in a warm, well-ventilated area. Cut *Helichrysum* flowerheads before they show colour to help keep their shape when dried. Cut fresh flowers as the buds show colour. Dip Iceland poppy (*Papaver nudicaule*) stems into boiling water for a few seconds, to seal them and avoid air locks that prevent water uptake.

1 *Cut flowers for drying (here statice,* Limonium sinuatum*) as the heads start to open. The best time of day to do this is when the weather is cool, in early morning or in the evening.*

2 *Many everlasting flowers may be dried upside-down in bunches fastened with soft string or raffia. Once they have dried, any excess stem may be cut off to suit the flower arrangement.*

DEAD-HEADING

To prolong the flowering period, remove flowerheads as they fade, cutting near the base of the stalk. The plants (here pansies) will produce new blooms for some time.

Some scrambling annuals that do not twine or have tendrils will also need to be tied in to their support.

Dead-heading

In many cases, the flowering season of plants may be extended and their appearance improved by promptly removing any flowerheads that are fading or dead; this prevents a plant from setting seed, and its energy is used to produce additional flowers. Snap off any faded flowers between the fingers and thumb, breaking the stems cleanly; use a pair of sharp scissors or secateurs for tougher stems or where there is a danger of disturbing the plant as the dead flowerheads are removed.

Do not dead-head if the seeds or fruits form part of the ornamental characteristic of the plant – as they do with honesty (*Lunaria*), *Hibiscus trionum*, and ornamental maize (*Zea mays*). Nor should plants be dead-headed if their seeds are required for growing the plant again during the following season.

A few annuals and biennials, such as poppies (*Papaver*), do not produce any more flowers after dead-heading.

Saving seeds

Seeds are easy to collect from many annuals for sowing the following year. It is often worth saving seeds only from annuals and biennials that stay true to type, such as *Nigella* or honesty, as seeds saved from most garden-grown cultivars and all F1 hybrids will not produce plants that possess flower or habit characteristics similar to those of their parents.

Dead-head plants with poor flowers so seeds are not formed and later collected for sowing the next year. Such seeds are unlikely to produce plants with good-quality flowers.

Self-sown seedlings are likely to vary to some extent in character and quality but may nevertheless produce quite acceptable plants. Distinct cultivars of *Eschscholzia*, Excelsior Series foxgloves (*Digitalis*), sweet alyssum (*Lobularia maritima*), marigolds (*Calendula*), forget-me-nots (*Myosotis*), and many other annuals and biennials usually vary in flower colour and other characteristics from the original plant.

When seed capsules turn brown and begin to split, cut them off and spread them on paper-lined trays in a warm, sunny place until they are fully dry. Extract the seeds and clean away any debris. Packet, label, and store them in dry, cool conditions until they are required for sowing.

Clearing the bed

In autumn, once the flower display is over, lift and compost all dying plants after any seeds required have been gathered. Burn diseased plants so that they do not spread infection

AUTUMN CLEARANCE

When annuals have finished flowering, carefully loosen the soil around their roots with a fork, then rake up and compost the old plants.

elsewhere in the garden. Perennials grown as annuals or biennials, such as pansies (*Viola* x *wittrockiana*) and polyanthus, may be lifted and replanted elsewhere, where they may grow and flower satisfactorily for several years. Others, such as wallflowers (*Erysimum*) and antirrhinums, seldom grow as well after their first year, so are generally not worth retaining for future use.

Tender perennials like begonias and busy Lizzies (*Impatiens* cvs) may be lifted and potted up in late summer to continue flowering in the house, conservatory, or greenhouse. Hollyhocks (*Alcea*) and other short-lived perennials may be cut down in autumn and retained since they sometimes survive for several seasons, although the quality and vigour of the plants will deteriorate. Retain a few plants of the new F1 and F2 strains of pelargonium in a frost-proof greenhouse or conservatory since they will usually survive, if kept quite dry, and flower again the following year. *Eccremocarpus scaber*, too, will survive for years in protected positions outside.

Pests and diseases

The pests most likely to be troublesome to annuals and biennials when they are seedlings, as well as when they are more mature, are slugs and snails (p.644), aphids (p.646), and caterpillars (p.645); plants may also be attacked by rusts (pp.648 and 653) and other fungal problems (see "Fungal leaf spots", p.648). Fungicides may prevent or check these diseases but often little can be done beyond pulling out and burning badly affected plants. Young seedlings growing under cover may suffer from damping off (p.664) – a group of soil-borne diseases that causes the plants to rot and collapse.

CUTTING DOWN SHORT-LIVED PERENNIALS

1 *Not all seedheads ripen at the same time. To prevent self-seeding, remove flowered stems before any seedheads ripen fully.*

2 *Short-lived perennials such as hollyhocks may flower for several seasons if cut down immediately after flowering.*

3 *Carefully cut each stem at its base, ensuring that the new growth that has been produced during the growing season is not damaged in the process.*

SAVING SEEDS

1 *Seeds may be collected when the capsules or seedheads (here* Nigella*) have been dried on blotting paper or newspaper and release their seeds.*

2 *Once the seedhead has dried, shake seeds out, and separate from any other debris. Store in a labelled envelope in a dry place at a constant, cool temperature.*

CHAPTER

8

BULBOUS PLANTS

FROM THE CHEERFUL, golden daffodil trumpeting the arrival of spring to the cyclamen, herald of autumn, bulbous plants ring the seasonal changes throughout the year with glorious flower displays. Some possess handsome foliage, and others are valued for their fragrance, but it is their blooms that make bulbs essential. They offer a wide variety of colour and form, from bright, primary shades to delicate, pastel hues, and the tall grandeur of gladiolus spikes to the dainty bells of tiny fritillaries. Whether they form bold patterns in a formal bed, fill in the detail in a mixed border, provide a splash of colour in containers, or create highlights beneath trees or in grass, bulbs bring vitality to the permanent plantings of the garden.

Bulbs for the garden

GROWING bulbs is an easy way of brightening up the garden with decorative, often flamboyant, and sometimes fragrant displays. The bulbs that are grown in the garden are dominated by hardy favourites, for example crocuses, cyclamen, daffodils, hyacinths, and tulips, of which there is an immense variety of both species and cultivars. Many tender bulbs also deserve a place in the garden, including the starry *Ixia*, *Sparaxis* with its loose, gaudy spikes, and the fiery *Tigridia*.

The key characteristic of bulbs is that they provide visual interest for only one season, remaining dormant and unnoticed for the remainder of the year. This can be an asset with careful planning, making bulbs in-valuable as border plants as well as ideal for naturalizing in grass or growing in containers.

In many gardens, bulbs may be left to increase naturally from year to year while their dying foliage is hidden by the developing growth of herbaceous plants or shrubs that provide a succession of interest. Many bulbs, including the popular crocuses, daffodils (*Narcissus*), and snowdrops (*Galanthus*), increase very rapidly in most sites. Bulbs may also be lifted after flowering and replanted each year to provide room for other seasonal plants, making them especially convenient for small gardens or restricted areas.

Seasons of interest
The main bulb season is from early spring to early summer, but many other bulbs flower outdoors or under cover at other times of the year. For colour in winter when most of

Effective use of bulbs in a mixed border
The arching green spikes and vibrant red flowers of Crocosmia *'Lucifer', planted in large clumps at* *intervals, give this mixed summer border a hot and fiery look, while foliage fills every last gap.*

the garden is dormant, early bulbs such as the pink *Cyclamen coum*, the tiny, deep blue *Iris histrioides* 'Major', and snowdrops may be grown outdoors, and other bulbs forced indoors. Bulbs that flower in summer or autumn are often larger, and of more exotic shapes and hues, than spring bulbs.

Where to grow bulbs
If given the well-drained soil that they need to grow and flower well, bulbs are among the easiest of all garden plants to cultivate. There are numerous cultivars and species now available that thrive in all aspects except deep shade.

Many bulbs in cultivation come from areas with a Mediterranean climate, so need to be grown in sunny sites and prefer hot, dry summers – although a huge range of bulbs flourishes in the open garden in regions with summer rainfall.

Bulbs that would normally grow in woodland thrive in moist, light shade. Many others, including some bulbs described as "sun-loving", are happy in light shade cast by nearby shrubs, walls, or trellises. Even dry shade is tolerated by most hardy cyclamen. Bulbs with white or pale flowers appear almost luminous in dusky light, so look very effective when planted in a shaded site.

Whatever the setting, bulbs look best planted in groups of the same species or cultivar, whether jostling shoulders with other plants or forming a single, swaying sea of colour in a formal bed or in grass.

The different types of bulbous plant

Bulb (*Hyacinthoides* x *massartiana*)

Corm (*Gladiolus callianthus*)

In this book, the term "bulb" refers to all bulbous plants, including corms, tubers, and rhizomes as well as true bulbs. The terms "corm", "tuber", and "rhizome" are used only in their specific sense throughout. With all bulbous plants, a portion of the plant is swollen into a food storage organ that enables the plant to survive when dormant or when conditions are unsuitable for growth.

Bulbs

True bulbs are formed from fleshy leaves or leaf bases, and frequently consist of concentric rings of scales attached to a basal plate. The outer scales often form a dry, protective skin or tunic, as found in daffodils, Reticulata irises, and tulips. With some lilies (*Lilium*) and *Fritillaria* species, the scales are separate and no tunic is formed. Juno irises are unusual in having swollen storage roots beneath the bulbs.

Corms

Corms are formed from the swollen bases of stems and are replaced by new corms every year. They are common in the family Iridaceae,

Tuber (*Dahlia* 'Monk Marc')

Rhizome (*Iris* 'White City')

which includes crocuses, gladioli, *Romulea*, and *Watsonia*; usually they have a tunic that has been formed from the previous year's leaf bases. In the Liliaceae and related families, they are found in such genera as *Brodiaea* and *Colchicum*.

Tubers

Tuberous is a term applied to many plants with swollen, often irregularly shaped stems or roots used for food storage. It is often misapplied, for example to the tuber-like roots – actually rhizomes – of *Anemone blanda* and the long, thin rhizomes of *A. nemorosa* (for convenience, both are included here as "bulbous plants"). True tubers of various kinds are found in *Dahlia*, *Corydalis*, some orchids, such as *Dactylorhiza*, cyclamen species (although these are often called "corms"), and in plants such as *Ranunculus asiaticus* where they are lobed or clustered together.

Rhizomes

Rhizomes are swollen, usually more or less horizontal, underground stems, found in the Iridaceae, notably in irises, and in Liliaceae.

Formal beds

Bulbs make a valuable contribution to formal bedding displays. Spring-flowering bulbs are excellent for planting en masse in a bed that is to be occupied by bedding annuals at a later point in summer, since they may be lifted and stored during their dormant season. Classic bedding

A pageant of colour
Serried ranks of tulips parade along these formal beds in bold, bright blocks of contrasting colour, creating an energetic counterpoint to the quiet orderliness of the formal garden. White tulips intersperse those of stronger hue to prevent the colour combinations from appearing too strident.

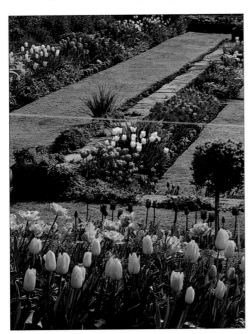

bulbs are hyacinths and tulips because of their strong, sculptural forms; in general, the larger, showy flowers of hybrid bulbs are best grown in a formal position in the garden. Plant in blocks of colour, each block one type of bulb, or in mixed groups that flower at different times throughout the season in order to provide a prolonged display of

colour during the spring. Bulbs may either completely fill the bed, or could be combined with companion plants with flowers in complementary or contrasting colours, such as deep blue forget-me-nots (*Myosotis*) or fiery wallflowers (*Erysimum*).

There is also scope for effective formal planting with summer- or autumn-flowering bulbs: *Galtonia*, with its elegant, white or green spikes, or the more compact cultivars of gladioli, especially the Primulinus or Butterfly groups, look impressive when planted in large blocks bordered by purple-blue violas, or any similar, low-growing ground cover. *Agapanthus* Headbourne Hybrids, with their large, rounded flower-heads of blue or white, combine well with the graceful, pink blooms of *Nerine bowdenii*.

Mixed herbaceous and shrub borders

Bulbs fill in the permanent planting of a border with a lively variety of seasonal colour. Loose drifts may blend in with the general scheme or draw the eye with splashes of colour. Architectural bulbs, such as *Crinum* x *powellii*, with its huge, pink or white trumpets, punctuate the flow of

a border with an arresting contrast of height and form. Grow some bulbs through low ground-cover plants so that their blooms appear to float above the mat of foliage. For a more informal cottage border, choose species bulbs since florid hybrids may sometimes look out of place.

Mixed plantings for spring flowering

Planting bulbs in a mixed border extends the flowering season, and provides an array of fresh, bright colour from late winter through to early summer. Before the herbaceous perennials and deciduous shrubs in the border begin to grow and spread, bring the front of the border to life with the smaller daffodil species, pale or dark blue Reticulata irises, snowdrops, and the golden cups of winter aconites (*Eranthis hyemalis*).

Plant starry carpets of pink and blue *Anemone blanda*, *Chionodoxa*, and *Scilla bifolia*, or pale yellow drifts of the more freely increasing dwarf daffodil species and hybrids beneath such early-flowering shrubs as *Corylopsis*, forsythia, and witch hazel (*Hamamelis*) to complement their display.

For later in spring, a much wider range of bulbs is available and larger plants, such as the tall daffodils, *Fritillaria* species (for example the purple-black *F. persica* and the regal *F. imperialis*) or tulips, may be used in casual groups to give height among the shrubs and perennials.

Mixed plantings for summer and autumn flowering

A number of bulbs add greatly to the beauty of the garden in summer. Although they are often regarded as only of secondary importance, in fact many summer- and autumn-flowering bulbs are tall and robust enough to hold their own among the surrounding flowering perennials and they offer a dazzling range of colours and flower forms.

Early in the season, try *Camassia leichtlinii* with its creamy-white flower plumes, vivid gladioli, *Triteleia laxa* (syn. *Brodiaea laxa*) for its loose, purple-blue clusters of bloom, and the bold, scarlet goblets of *Tulipa sprengeri*.

Follow them in mid- to late summer with the huge, purple globes of *Allium aflatunense*, arching sprays of blazing red or yellow *Crocosmia*, sun-loving lilies (*Lilium*) and, later, slim pink, red, or white spires of *Schizostylis*. In warmer gardens, greenish-white *Eucomis* with its pineapple-like flowerheads brings an exotic touch to the border planting.

In autumn, continue the display with the fragrant, pink trumpets of *Amaryllis belladonna*, the brilliant yellow funnels of *Sternbergia lutea* or *S. sicula*, and blue to white forms of autumn-flowering crocuses.

Naturalizing bulbs

When left undisturbed, many bulbs will readily increase to form flowing drifts of colour. Allowing them to

Woodland charm
Hardy Cyclamen coum *and crocuses in deep and pale shades of pink, lilac, and violet colonize a woodland, clustering prettily around the feet of the trees to provide a show of colour when the trees are bare.*

naturalize in this way gives interest to areas of the garden that otherwise might not be given over to flowering plants. Species, which are more delicate in hue and form than the majority of cultivars, create a natural effect when planted in large, informal groups.

Planting bulbs with specimen trees

Bulbs make perfect partners for specimen trees that have deep roots and light, deciduous canopies. Select bulbs that will flower predominantly in spring or autumn to form a decorative ground cover when the tree has few leaves to deepen the shade. In spring, the soil beneath the tree tends to be moist and sunlit, creating an ideal environment for anemones, crocuses, daffodils, or *Scilla*. Hardy, autumn-flowering cyclamen, with mottled, silvery foliage and softly folded petals, tolerate the dry summer conditions, and enjoy partial shade.

The flowers of bulbs can effectively complement a tree's habit. White-flowered bulbs, for example, mirror the white blossom of ornamental cherries (*Prunus*), the crisp shape of crocuses echo the chalice form of magnolia blooms, and bulbs with pendent flowers imitate the habit of a weeping tree.

Use dwarf cultivars to naturalize the area around a newly planted tree or shrub, since rapidly increasing bulbs such as daffodils reduce the available food.

Woodland settings

Bulbs are invaluable when planted in large, informal pools of colour, as they enhance the natural beauty of deciduous woodland and any mossy ground cover. Many bulbs relish these woodland conditions, and will blend well with other woodland plants, such as ferns, hellebores (*Helleborus*), and primulas.

Plant bulbs for a succession of flowers, as well as contrast of form and height; subtle variations on a colour theme will reflect the tranquil mood of woodland. Snowdrops (*Galanthus*) and cyclamen species in pinks and purples make a striking combination, while drifts of *Scilla* and *Chionodoxa* add shades of blue. Spanish bluebells (*Hyacinthoides* x

massartiana, syn. *H. hispanica* of gardens) or many of the more rampant grape hyacinths (*Muscari*) provide swathes of blue, pink, and white, together with tiny, white sprays of lily-of-the-valley (*Convallaria majalis*). These can all colonize considerable areas once established. English bluebells (*Hyacinthoides non-scripta*) should only be planted on their own because they will rapidly invade other plantings.

Planting in grass

Bulbs can transform grass, whether they are planted on a bank, a section of a lawn, or an entire meadow; they will create a gay carpet of spring or autumn colour that spreads more thickly year after year. The bulbs must be robust species that will be able to withstand competition from grass roots. Many of the larger bulbs look best in grass in which their fading foliage is less obtrusive once they have finished flowering.

Plant earlier-flowering bulbs in grass that is to be mown from spring onwards so that their leaves have sufficient time to die down before the grass is cut. Later-flowering bulbs, such as terrestrial orchids (*Dactylorhiza*), may be grown with grass and wild flowers in "meadows" that are not cut until mid- or late summer. Bulbs that bloom in autumn start into growth and flower before the end of the usual mowing season so the grass must be left unmown after late summer. Alternatively, plant bulbs in irregular but defined areas so that it is possible to mow around them.

Daffodils are the classic choice for grass and a remarkable range – especially the more robust species and hybrids – may be grown in this way. In addition to this, many crocuses will grow well in grass. Alternatively, a more delicate effect may be achieved by coupling the pendent bells of the summer snowflake (*Leucojum aestivum*) with the snake's-head fritillary (*Fritillaria meleagris*) which will shiver softly in the breeze.

Where the grass is less vigorous, particularly in partly shaded areas, some of the dwarf bulbs do well: the purple flowered *Crocus tommasinianus*, *Chionodoxa*, some daffodils (for example, *Narcissus cyclamineus*), *Scilla*, and snowdrops all flourish in these conditions.

An area on the outskirts of a garden that is naturalized with bulbs provides a harmonious transition between the flowerbeds of a formal garden and the grassy fields of the surrounding countryside by combining elements of both.

Spring spectacle
Naturalized crocuses in bloom cover this lawn with vivid pinks, purples, and yellows. The bulbs are planted in great swathes of a single hue, that merge with each other to create a sea of colour. Snowdrops (Galanthus) planted among the crocuses provide highlights of white.

Bulbs with alpines

Using bulbs in the rock garden, trough, or raised bed prolongs the season as most alpines flower in late spring. The erect habit, upright flowers, and spear-like leaves of bulbs contrast well with the low, mounded, or spreading habit of most alpine plants, as well as introducing a greater variety of form. Choose dwarf bulbs with dainty blooms to complement the character of the alpines, and plant some bulbs to grow through and lift the alpine planting. Avoid mat-forming alpines that exhaust the soil around the bulbs and so deprive them of food.

In the rock garden

Many smaller bulbs, especially the more temperamental species for which sharp drainage is essential,

An alpine setting
The strange beauty of the bell-like flowers of Fritillaria acmopetala *is best shown off in the small-scale planting of an alpine garden.*

thrive in rock gardens, in sun or partial shade. Dwarf bulbs look attractive when planted in pockets of rock or offset against the grit top-dressing of the bed, which also stops their delicate flowers from being muddied during wet weather. If planting very small alpines in the bed, do not use the taller bulb species, which would appear out of proportion to their neighbours.

Bulbs in troughs

Old stone troughs make an attractive setting for a collection of dwarf bulbs and smaller alpine plants where their tiny charms may be appreciated at close hand. The bulbs benefit from the gritty, well-drained soil, and may easily be given the careful watering that they need.

To keep the display in proportion, grow the smallest species and their less robust hybrids; rapidly increasing bulbs may swamp neighbouring alpines. Grow the smaller *Fritillaria* species for their intriguing flowers, whether the purplish-brown and yellow *F. michailovskyi* or the chequered green *F. whittallii*.

Rhodohypoxis are excellent for growing in troughs, producing pink, red, or white starry flowers throughout most of the summer. Keep the bulbs moist during the growing season, and give them an occasional liquid feed. The genus *Cyclamen* includes species that are suitable for troughs in spring and autumn, and they range in hue from pure white to deepest purple-pink.

Planting bulbs in a leafmould bed

A shady raised bed filled with leaf mould and well-rotted garden compost provides a perfect environment for

the dwarfer "woodland" bulbs, whether they are planted on their own or along with ericaceous shrubs or alpines. Try erythroniums, with their dainty, reflexed flowers in shades of pink, white, or yellow, which you can then view from underneath, or plant any of the trilliums in a leaf mould bed.

Bulbs to associate with water gardens

A few bulbs flourish in damp, poorly drained conditions and provide some of the most striking flowering plants to grow around water. Their strong shapes and colours create pleasing reflections; plant them in clumps to contrast with the flat, open surface of the water. Several handsome rhizomatous irises as well as the arum lily (*Zantedeschia aethiopica*), with large, white spathes above broad, arrow-shaped leaves, thrive in pond margins. Both the snake's-head fritillary and summer snowflake (*Leucojum aestivum*) grow naturally in water meadows, and therefore will enjoy a moist site or damp beds around ponds.

Other bulbs that will enhance water gardens include the magnificent, purple-red *Iris ensata* (syn. *I. kaempferi*), the white-flowered *I.* 'Geisha Gown', with its deep pinkish-purple veins, and *Dierama pendulum*, with its wand-like flower sprays. However, all of these prefer a soil that is not only moist but is well drained, too.

Bulbs in pots
In the absence of a flowerbed, a large, fat-bellied pot will provide an ideal location for a simple but very effective spring-bulb display. Containers can be moved into a more prominent position as the plants reach their peak. In this arrangement, the rich purple hyacinth flowers nestle amongst the nodding heads of yellow daffodils, providing a colourful show that heralds the arrival of spring.

Growing bulbs in containers

Growing bulbs in ornamental pots, windowboxes, and other containers provides a varied and spectacular display, which can be extended throughout the season by moving containers into view as they come into flower (see also "Changes in focus", p.306). Careful choice of bulbs may lengthen the season to include late winter as well as spring and summer. Plant a single species or cultivar in each container to provide a uniform, even effect and then group the containers together for a mass of colour.

Place pots of bulbs with fragrant flowers (for example hyacinths or Tazetta daffodils) close to the entrance of the house where they may be fully appreciated. Pots used for spring bulbs may be used for summer-flowering plants later: when the bulbs die down, lift and replant them in the garden (or store them) and replace them with annuals or tender perennials.

Some larger bulbs are sufficiently striking to be planted on their own in containers. Tall lilies (*Lilium*) or *Crinum* x *powellii*, in pink or white forms, are particularly effective. Any *Agapanthus* species or hybrid will provide a long season of showy flowers. Alternatively, group several types of bulb of varying heights and colours in a large container such as a half-barrel to provide a feature on a patio.

Windowboxes

When planting in windowboxes, choose smaller bulbs that are in proportion to the size of the container. They are excellent for planting in layers below other plants to make best use of limited space; the bulbs thrust through the surface planting to create a pleasing contrast of height and form. Blending the plants with winter-flowering pansies (*Viola* x *wittrockiana*) and ivy (*Hedera*), followed by trailing tender perennials and annuals, gives a prolonged display of colour.

Bulbs under cover

Growing bulbs under cover extends the range that may be cultivated to include many rare species that need particular care. In temperate or cold regions, tender bulbs may be grown that would not survive unprotected in the garden. In regions with summer rainfall, it is the most practical way of growing many of the species bulbs currently in cultivation because they need a dry, summer resting period in order to flourish and flower well. Bulbs may be planted in pots or in a greenhouse bed or bulb frame. This allows easier control of the local environment to accommodate the individual needs of a wide range of bulbs, be it a summer drying-off period or protection from excessive winter wet, cold, or frost.

Bulbs in pots

Growing bulbs in pots allows each plant to be grown in conditions that best suit its individual requirements, especially when cultivating small stocks of uncommon bulbs. The pots are easily transferred from outdoors to the shelter of frames or greenhouses when required, or from the greenhouse to the conservatory to enjoy them when in full flower.

Pot cultivation in an unheated greenhouse enables many bulb species that are otherwise of border-line hardiness in temperate climates to be grown. Many are South African and South American bulbs with an exciting diversity of richly coloured blooms, such as *Watsonia* with its dense spikes of deep pink, white, and red. To enjoy tender bulbs, such as *Gloriosa*, and winter-flowering *Veltheimia*, the shelter of a frost-free greenhouse is needed. Overwinter other tender species or cultivars of such genera as begonias, *Canna*, or *Crinum* in a cool greenhouse and bring them out when in bloom to enhance the summer display in the open garden.

If desired, bulbs may be grown in shade and the compost adjusted accordingly in order to grow small "woodland" bulbs, including *Trillium rivale*, which has finely spotted petals in pink or white, or tender, terrestrial orchids such as the free-flowering *Calanthe* species.

Gardeners with an alpine house may add a little height and splashes of colour to the display by inter-spersing the plants with pots of dwarf spring bulbs. The alpine house environment is especially suitable for rare or tender bulbs (for example, ice-white *Narcissus cantabricus* or bright blue *Tecophilaea cyanocrocus*).

Greenhouse beds

Tender bulbs may be planted out directly in prepared greenhouse beds, rather than in pots, for a more natural and vigorous display. The bulbs may be combined in a mixed bed with other plants that flower in summer when the bulbs are dormant. Choose companion plants that tolerate a dry period coinciding with that needed by the bulbs, or that can be plunged in plastic pots and watered without the moisture reaching the bulbs around them.

Spreading, heat-loving plants, such as *Osteospermum* or gazanias, and many silver-foliaged plants could be used in this way, and then removed or cut back hard at the end of summer when the bulbs start into growth. Late-flowering *Brodiaea*, *Calochortus*, and *Triteleia* prolong the flowering season still further: group them together and water them separately. Summer-growing bulbs, such as *Eucomis*, some *Gladiolus* species, and the tender *Nerine* species do not need interplanting.

Bulb frames and raised beds

The term "bulb frame" usually refers to a raised bed devoted solely to bulbs; it is covered with a cold frame or Dutch lights during the natural resting period of the bulbs in summer, and also in winter to protect them from excessive rainfall which could cause them to rot. Alternatively, a frame may simply cover bulbs in pots plunged in a sand bed. Such frames may be made more attractive by using stone for the sides.

Bulb frames are the best alternative to the alpine house as a place to grow tender or demanding bulb species without the root restriction of pots, and are used mainly by enthusiasts or collectors. This method of cultivation is suitable for most bulbs, other than those used to some summer rainfall, such as "woodland" and high mountain species. Some crocus,

Bulbs for cut flowers

Many bulbs have flowers that can be cut for the house since their shapely, often solitary, flowers on long stems make them especially suitable for floral arrangements. A few have powerful scents that can fill a room and most are long-lasting if they are picked before the blooms reach maturity. Some, such as daffodils, are so vigorous and prolific that they may be cut without leaving a gap in the garden display. Alternatively, set aside a separate area to grow bulbs especially for cutting.

Gladioli make fine cut flowers and are often used in this way, since the taller cultivars are difficult to place satisfactorily in an open border.

The pretty, wonderfully fragrant freesias are the only tender or half-hardy bulbs that are commonly grown under cover to provide cut flowers. They have a long flowering season during the winter but make somewhat straggly pot plants that need staking, so they are best cut for display indoors where they will last well.

Schizostylis coccinea 'Sunrise'

Crocosmia 'Lucifer'

Narcissus 'Cheerfulness'

Dahlia 'Zorro'

Freesia 'Everett'

Gladiolus 'Tesoro'

Zantedeschia aethiopica 'Crowborough'

Nerine bowdenii

Alstroemeria Ligtu Hybrids

Tulipa 'Clara Butt'

Allium giganteum

Lilium 'Enchantment'

daffodil, *Fritillaria*, and tulip species, Juno and Reticulata irises, and the more difficult *Brodiaea* and *Zigadenus* species tend to be less successful in temperate climates as open garden plants; they may not survive unless they are protected from excess moisture in bulb frames or seasonally covered raised beds throughout the dormant season.

Forcing bulbs

A good way of bringing colour and fragrance indoors during the winter and early spring is to force bulbs in pots. The bulbs are kept in a cool, dark place for a few months before bringing them into the light to encourage them to flower earlier than they do naturally. *Hippeastrum* with its giant, exotic blooms, scented hyacinths, and daffodils, especially *Narcissus papyraceus*, or the 'Paper White' narcissi, are all suitable and are often offered for sale as "prepared" bulbs. These have been given an artificial cold period in imitation of winter cold to speed up the natural flowering cycle. Many hardy spring bulbs, such as tulips, can be forced for early flowers, but some, such as crocuses, may abort their flowers if forced too quickly. A gentler method is to grow bulbs under cover in pots and bring them indoors when the flowers begin to show colour, a week or two before they would normally bloom in the open garden, so that the warmth stimulates them into bloom.

Planter's guide to bulbous plants

EXPOSED SITES

Bulbs that tolerate exposed or windy sites

Anemone
Chionodoxa
Colchicum
Crocus
Cyclamen, some ✽
Fritillaria (dwarf spp.)
Galanthus
Ipheion
Iris reticulata (cvs)
Muscari, some ✽
Narcissus (dwarf spp. and cvs)
Ornithogalum, some ✽
Oxalis, some ✽

*Oxalis
depressa*

Scilla, some ✽
Sternbergia lutea
Triteleia
Tulipa (dwarf spp.)

WALL PROTECTION

Bulbs that prefer the protection of a wall

Agapanthus, some ✽ (most spp.)
Alstroemeria (except Ligtu
    Hybrids)
Amaryllis belladonna
Anomatheca laxa
Belamcanda chinensis
Bloomeria crocea
Eucomis
Fritillaria persica
Gladiolus ✽ (tender spp.)
Gynandriris sisyrinchium
Habranthus, some ✽ (some spp.)
Ixia ✽
Lycoris squamigera
Moraea spathulata
Nerine bowdenii
Rhodophiala advena
Scilla peruviana
Sparaxis ✽
Sternbergia lutea, S. sicula
Tulbaghia, some ✽
Watsonia ✽
Zephyranthes candida

DRY SHADE

Bulbs that tolerate dry shade

Anemone nemorosa
Arum italicum 'Marmoratum'
*Cyclamen coum,
    C. hederifolium, C. repandum*
Galanthus nivalis (forms)
Hyacinthoides non-scripta
Ranunculus ficaria (cvs)

MOIST SHADE

Bulbs that prefer moist shade

*Anemone apennina, A. blanda,
    A. ranunculoides*
Arisaema, some ✽ (most spp.)
Arum italicum
Cardiocrinum
Corydalis (some spp.)
Eranthis
Erythronium
*Fritillaria camschatcensis,
    F. cirrhosa*
Galanthus
Ipheion uniflorum
Leucojum aestivum, L. vernum
Lilium (some spp.)

*Lilium
hansonii*

*Narcissus cyclamineus,
    N. triandrus*
Nomocharis
Notholirion
Scilla bifolia
Trillium
Tulipa sylvestris

FLOWERS FOR CUTTING

Agapanthus, some ✽
Allium (some spp.)
Alstroemeria (taller spp. and cvs)
Amaryllis belladonna
Anemone coronaria St Bridgid
    Group, *A.* De Caen Series
Camassia
Clivia ✽
Crinum, some ✽
Crocosmia

Dierama, some ✽
Freesia ✽
Galtonia
Gladiolus, some ✽
Iris Dutch Hybrids,
    I. latifolia, I. xiphium
Ixia ✽
Lilium
Narcissus
Nerine, some ✽
Ornithogalum, some ✽
    (tall spp.)
Ranunculus asiaticus ✽ (forms)
Sparaxis ✽
Tulipa
Watsonia ✽
Zantedeschia, some ✽

ARCHITECTURAL PLANTS

Allium cristophii, A. giganteum
Canna ✽
Cardiocrinum giganteum
Crinum x *powellii*
Fritillaria imperialis
Lilium (most spp. and cvs)

ROCK GARDENS

Bulbs suitable for planting in rock gardens

Albuca humilis ✽
Allium (dwarf spp.)
Anemone (some spp.)
Bellevalia (some spp.)
Brodiaea (smallest spp.)
Bulbocodium vernum
Colchicum (small spp.)
Corydalis (some spp.)
Crocus
Cyclamen (hardy spp.)
Fritillaria (many spp.)
Gagea, some ✽ (some spp.)
Galanthus
Ipheion
Iris (dwarf spp.)
Leucojum (some spp.)
Merendera
Muscari, some ✽
    (non-invasive spp.)
Narcissus (dwarf spp. and hybrids)
Ornithogalum, some ✽ (dwarf spp.)
Oxalis, some ✽ (some spp.)
Puschkinia
Rhodohypoxis

Romulea, some ✽ (some spp.)
Scilla, some ✽
Sternbergia lutea, S. sicula
Tulipa (dwarf spp.)
Zephyranthes candida
Zigadenus

BULBS FOR ALPINE HOUSES

Albuca ✽
Anemone (some spp.)
Anomatheca
Arum, some ✽ (some spp.)
Babiana ✽
Bellevalia
Biarum
Bongardia chrysogonum
Bulbocodium vernum
Calochortus
Colchicum (small spp.)
Crocus
Cyclamen, some ✽
Fritillaria (most spp.)
Gagea, some ✽
Galanthus
Habranthus, some ✽
Hippeastrum, some ✽ (dwarf spp.)

Moraea huttonii

Iris (dwarf spp.)
Leontice
Leucocoryne ✽
Leucojum (some spp.)
Merendera
Moraea, some ✽ (some spp.)
Muscari, some ✽ (some spp.)
Narcissus (dwarf spp.)
Ornithogalum, some ✽ (dwarf spp.)
Oxalis, some ✽ (some spp.)
Pancratium, some ✽
Pinellia
Rhodohypoxis
Romulea, some ✽
Scilla, some ✽
Sternbergia
Tecophilaea
Tulipa (dwarf spp.)
Zephyranthes, some ✽
Zigadenus

Key
✽ *Not hardy*

Tulips and daffodils

TULIPS (*Tulipa*) and daffodils (*Narcissus*) are highly valued for the bold splashes of colour they bring in spring. Grow them together to extend the flowering season in a mixed border: some daffodils bloom very early in the year, while many tulips last into late spring. Tulips are excellent for beds or borders, while many daffodils are especially suitable for naturalizing in grass. Dwarf forms are ideal for rock gardens, alpine houses, or containers, where they may be seen at close range.

Tulips

This diverse, versatile genus is horticulturally classified in 15 divisions based on flower form, but may conveniently be grouped by flowering season and garden use.

Early tulips

Single, early tulips have classic, goblet-shaped blooms, some with striped, flushed, or margined petals. Early doubles have long-lasting, open bowl-shaped flowers, often flecked or margined in toning colours. Traditionally used for cutting, in formal bedding, or as border edgings, many can also be grown in pots indoors. In informal schemes their elegant outlines contrast well with spreading or prostrate plants.

Mid-season tulips

This grouping includes Triumph tulips, with their simple, conical blooms, and the Darwin hybrids, with rich and intensely coloured flowers, often with a satiny, basal blotch and dark, velvety anthers. Both types are sturdy, robust, and noted for their weather resistance.

Late tulips

Some of the most vibrant colours and intricate forms are seen in late-flowering tulips. They include the graceful lily-flowered types, vivid and extravagant Parrot tulips, green-tinged Viridifloras, as well as exuberantly striped and feathered Rembrandts. Peony-flowered forms are suited to informal cottage gardens. All are effective used informally with dark green or grey ground cover or in formal bedding schemes.

Dwarf species and hybrids

The compact Kaufmanniana hybrids produce their brightly coloured blooms very early in the spring while the slightly taller Fosteriana and Greigii tulips usually flower a little later. Many have very attractively marked foliage. The dwarf species are ideal for containers, raised beds, or rock gardens. *Tulipa sprengeri* and *T. sylvestris* tolerate light shade and will naturalize in fine grass.

Cultivation and propagation

Most tulips thrive in fertile, well-drained, humus-rich soils, in sun and with shelter, and in ideal conditions some robust cultivars persist from year to year. Many, however, are best regarded as annual bedding plants, being lifted after flowering and either discarded (if diseased) or replanted until they have died down. The bulbs seldom flower well in the

Tulips in a spring border
The strong, vertical stems and neat flower-cups of tulips provide height and structure, as well as vivid colour, in an informal spring border.

Growing in containers
The lily-flowered tulip 'West Point' here displays its ornate blooms.

Types of tulip

Tulips include an impressive range of flower forms, from the simple, upright goblets of single-flowered tulips to the frilled and twisted petals of Parrot tulips and the open, double blooms of peony-flowered forms. They are available in most colours, except blue, from the purest white to the deepest purple, with many glorious shades of yellow, red, and crimson in between. Many of the dwarf tulips also have attractively marked leaves.

SINGLE

Tulipa 'Dawnglow'
Darwin hybrid

T. 'Queen of Night'
Single, late

T. 'Spring Green'
Viridiflora

DOUBLE AND PARROT

T. 'Peach Blossom'
Double, early

T. 'Estella Rijnveld'
Parrot

DWARF SPECIES AND HYBRIDS

T. tarda
Dwarf species

T. 'Dreamboat'
Greigii hybrid

T. 'Giuseppe Verdi'
Kaufmanniana hybrid

T. 'Greuze'
Single, late

Extending the flowering season
Growing tulips and daffodils together provides a continuous display of colour from early spring until well into summer.

second year but if replanted in autumn may reach flowering size again within two years.

Dwarf tulips generally prefer open, gritty soils, and full sun; lift and replant them only when overcrowded. Propagate by offsets (see p.245) or, for species, by seed (see p.246). Tulips are prone to tulip fire (see p.649) and other bulb problems (see p.244).

Daffodils

Grown for their cheerful spring blooms, daffodils (*Narcissus*) are among the easiest and most rewarding of bulbs to grow. They are horticulturally divided into 13 groups, based on the form of the flowers.

Daffodils in containers

Most daffodils can be grown in pots, if they are deep enough to allow the bulbs to be covered to 1½ times their own depth. Tazettas, with clusters of up to 12 scented blooms, are often grown under glass or as pot plants to bloom from late autumn to spring. The richly fragrant jonquil hybrids are also useful as container plants for house decoration. Small species, such as *N. cantabricus* and *N. romieuxii*, produce blooms early in the year in the alpine house; they may also then be brought indoors.

Daffodils in the garden

Valuable for formal spring bedding and to give early interest in the mixed border, daffodils are among the most reliable of bulbs for naturalizing: they rarely need lifting in borders or grass. Even tiny species, such as *N. cyclamineus* and *N. minor*, will thrive in fine turf. Dwarf daffodils are ideal for rock gardens and raised beds, some, such as *N. romieuxii*, *N.* 'Tête-à-tête', and *N. asturiensis*, flowering early in the year.

Cultivation and propagation

Daffodils will grow in almost any soil type, but prefer well-drained, moist, slightly alkaline conditions.

Naturalizing daffodils in grass
In an informal or wild garden, daffodils may be grown in grass, bringing welcome colour to a dark corner or the ground beneath a tree.

They thrive in sun or light, dappled shade. Plant the bulbs 12–15cm (5–6in) deep in late summer or early autumn. When bulbs are naturalized in grass, do not cut the old foliage until at least six weeks after they have flowered. Bulbs in containers must be grown in cool conditions, with plenty of fresh air. Temperatures above 7–10°C (45–50°F) usually cause flowers to abort. Place the pots in a cold frame after planting, and

bring them into a cold greenhouse about 12–16 weeks later. Once flower buds have formed, blooming can be advanced by raising the temperature gently although not exceeding 13°C (55°F).

Propagate by offsets (see p.245), or by chipping (see p.249); new hybrids and species may also be raised from seed (see p.246). Daffodils may be affected by both narcissus eelworm (p.663) and bulb flies (p.663).

Types of daffodil

Daffodils provide a wide variety of shapes and forms, ranging from the tiny, exquisite Cyclamineus hybrids, with their swept-back petals, to the tall, trumpet daffodils and the showy double forms. Modern developments include the split corona and collarette types. In addition to the characteristic bright yellow flowers, cultivars include those with pale butter-yellow blooms or brilliant white petals and fiery orange cups.

DWARF SPECIES AND HYBRIDS

Narcissus triandrus
Dwarf species

N. romieuxii
Dwarf species

N. 'Jumblie'
Cyclamineus hybrid

N. 'Pride of Cornwall'
Tazetta

SINGLE

N. 'Passionale'
Large-cupped

N. 'Fortune'
Large-cupped

N. 'Ambergate'
Large-cupped

DOUBLE

N. 'Irene Copeland'
Double

N. 'Tahiti'
Double

Dahlias

Dahlias flower from the middle of summer through to the first frosts in autumn, providing bright colour in the garden for several months. All are frost tender. They can be grown in various soil types, providing that they are fertile and well drained. Dahlias make an excellent border plant as well as being ideal plants for summer display in containers (see also CONTAINER GARDENING, "Bulbs", p.316).

If grown for exhibition or for cut flowers, they are best planted in rows in specially prepared beds. Dwarf bedding dahlias are grown in two ways: either by vegetative propagation, that is by cutting or division of tubers of named cultivars, or by growing annually from seed (see Annuals and Biennials, "Sowing in pots or trays", p.218). These dwarf dahlias are suitable for planting in containers. Dahlia flowerheads have a diversity of petal forms in a wide colour range, from white to rich yellow through pinks and reds to purples.

Dahlias are divided into ten groups: single-flowered; anemone-flowered; collerette; waterlily; decorative; ball; pompon; cactus; semi-cactus; and miscellaneous. Four of these groups have been subdivided by the size of their blooms. For waterlily dahlias, there are miniature, usually under 102mm (4in) in diameter; small-flowered, usually 102–152mm (4–6in) in diameter; and medium-flowered ones, usually 152–203mm (6–8in) in diameter. Decorative, cactus, and semi-cactus dahlias have two additional subdivisions: large-flowered, usually 203–254mm (8–10in) in diameter; and giant-flowered ones, usually over 254mm (10in) in diameter. Ball dahlias are subdivided into: miniature ball, usually with flowers 52–102mm (2–4in) in diameter; and small ball, usually 102–152mm (4–6in) in diameter. Pompon dahlia flowers should be under 52mm (2in).

DAHLIA FLOWER GROUPS

(1) Single
D. 'Yellow Hammer'
Flowerheads with 8–10 broad florets surrounding an open, central disc.

(2) Anemone
D. 'Comet'
Fully double flowerheads with one or more rings of flattened ray florets surrounding a group of shorter, tubular florets.

(3) Collerette
D. 'Easter Sunday'
A single yellow disc of stamens in the centre, with a collar of small florets lying between the stamens and the large, outer florets.

(4) Waterlily
D. 'Pearl of Heemstede'
As their name implies, these flowerheads look like water lilies, and have broad, flat florets.

(5) Decorative
D. 'Frank Hornsey'
Fully double. Florets have broad petals rounded at the ends, usually curling gently inwards along their length, flat, and slightly twisted.

(6) Ball
D. 'Wootton Cupid'
Rounded flowerheads that have spirally arranged florets. The petals are rolled for over half their length.

(7) Pompon
D. 'Small World'
Similar to ball dahlias but smaller, to a maximum diameter of 52mm (2in), and more globular; the petals are rolled for their length.

(8) Cactus
D. 'Shirley Alliance'
Fully double, with narrow, pointed petals curled backwards or quilled, which are either straight or incurving.

(9) Semi-cactus
D. 'So Dainty'
Fully double. The ray florets have pointed, straight or incurving, broad-based petals that curve backwards.

Cultivation

Dahlias thrive in well-drained, fertile soils of about pH7. Prepare the soil early in the year. They are gross feeders, so dig in a heavy dressing of manure or garden compost; then add bone meal at 125g/sq m (4oz/sq yd), leaving the bed roughly dug so that frost can break up the soil.

Where and when to plant

Dahlias may be planted as pot-grown plants, as dormant tubers, or as rooted cuttings taken from tubers. Plants in leaf may be preferable to tubers, as they are often more vigorous. Dormant tubers, however, may be planted directly, about six weeks before the last frosts, whereas plants in leaf should not be planted until all danger of frost has passed.

Choose an open, sheltered site that is not overshadowed. Immediately before planting, top-dress with a blood, fish and bone at 125g/sq m (4oz/sq yd) worked well into the soil. Tie young plants into their stakes to support them as they develop.

Planting pot-grown dahlias

When planting pot-grown dahlias, canes should be positioned at the appropriate spacings. Plants that are 120–50cm (4–5ft) tall are planted 60–90cm (2–3ft) apart, and those that are 75cm–1.1m (2½–3½ ft) tall

PLANTING TUBERS

Insert a 1m (3ft) stake in a planting hole. Place soil around the tuber so that the base of the new shoots is 2.5–5cm (1–2in) below soil level.

60cm (2ft) apart. Bedding dahlias growing less than 60cm (2ft) tall are planted 45cm (18in) apart. Water the plants in their pots and leave to drain. Plant with care, to avoid disturbing the root ball, and firm gently, leaving a slight depression at the stem base. Water thoroughly. The plants will make a tuber by late autumn; this may be lifted and stored for replanting in spring.

Planting tubers

Dormant tubers may be planted directly in the border about six weeks before the last frosts are expected. The ground is prepared as for pot-grown plants. Prepare a planting hole about 22cm (9in) across and about 15cm (6in) deep, place the tuber in the hole, and cover over. Mark the position of the tuber with a labelled split cane placed just to the side; this will indicate the exact position of the tuber when inserting its support stake. The tuber takes about six weeks to develop a shoot above ground. If the shoot emerges above ground level while there is still a risk of frost, cover the shoot for protection.

Planting rooted cuttings

Established tubers may be grown on in the cold frame or greenhouse, to provide cuttings (see "Propagation", facing page). Plant out rooted cuttings after all danger of frost has passed. As growth develops, water the plants moderately; to retain moisture, mulch when the plants reach 30–38cm (12–15in) tall with well-rotted compost or manure. Do not place the mulch close to the base of the plants since this may encourage stem rot. If composted grass cuttings are used, ensure that they are not treated with selective weedkiller.

STOPPING

1 *When the plant is about 38cm (15in) high, pinch out the central shoot to encourage the development of sideshoots.*

2 *When the plant has 6–8 sideshoots, pinch out the top pair of buds. Tie in the stems to stakes.*

Stopping and disbudding

When the dahlias have grown to about 38cm (15in), stop the plants by removing each growing point to encourage sideshoots. Insert two more canes and tie the shoots in.

The number of shoots allowed to develop should depend on the size of the blooms required. For giant or large blooms, restrict each plant to 4–6 shoots; for medium and small blooms, allow 7–10 shoots. To produce high-quality blooms, disbud some from each shoot (see below).

DISBUDDING

To encourage show-quality flowers, pinch out the side (wing) bud and 1 or 2 pairs of sideshoots below the terminal bud.

Summer feeding

Four to six weeks after planting, feed with a high nitrogen and potash fertilizer, either in granular form, or by weekly applications of liquid fertilizer as a root or foliar feed. As flower buds develop, extra potash in the liquid fertilizer gives strong stems and good flower colour, especially in pinks and lilacs; this is important when growing for exhibition.

The tuber's development during late summer and early autumn is stimulated by the shortening day length. During this period, apply a split application of sulphate of potash and superphosphates at the manufacturer's recommended rate. Avoid contact with leaves or stems as this may cause scorch.

Pests and diseases

Dahlias are affected particularly by aphids (p.646), thrips (p.647), red spider mite (p.646), and earwigs (p.644). These may be controlled by spraying regularly. Lift and burn any plants infected with viruses (p.649).

Lifting and storing tubers

When the foliage has been blackened by the first frosts in autumn, trim back the stems to about 15cm (6in). Carefully lift and clean the soil from the tubers, trim off any fine roots, and treat the tubers with fungicide. Place them upside down for a few weeks to ensure that no moisture remains in the stems and leaves.

Label the tubers and pack them in wooden boxes in vermiculite, coir, or a similar medium. Store in a dry, cool, frost-proof place. Inspect the tubers regularly in winter; if any mildew or rot has developed, cut it out with a clean, sharp knife and dust the cut surfaces with sulphur.

LIFTING AND STORING

1 *Cut the stems to about 15cm (6in) above ground level. Loosen the soil and ease the tubers out. Remove excess soil.*

2 *Store the tubers upside down for about 3 weeks in a frost-free place so that the stems dry out thoroughly.*

3 *When the stems have dried out, place the tubers in a wooden box and cover them with coir, vermiculite, or a similar medium. Set the box in a cool, frost-free place. Keep the tubers and stems dry until spring.*

Propagation

Divide established tubers in spring. First bring them into growth in a cold frame or greenhouse. Press the tubers gently onto the top of a tray of compost, spray with water, and keep warm and damp. As shoots develop, divide the tuber into sections with a sharp knife, ensuring that each piece has at least one growing shoot. Pot up each section separately using a general-purpose compost.

Alternatively, in late winter, force tubers at 15–18°C (59–64°F). When shoots each have a growing point and two or three pairs of leaves, take basal cuttings, trim at a node, and root in a propagating case with bottom heat. Grow on under glass and harden off before planting out.

Showing dahlias

Cut blooms with a sharp knife in the morning or evening, making sure that the stem length is in proportion to the bloom. When exhibiting, blooms should always be well developed with undamaged petals. Read the schedule and present the correct number of stems staged in the vase, with the blooms facing the front.

HOW TO PROPAGATE BY BASAL CUTTINGS

1 *In late winter, force the tubers in a greenhouse. Take cuttings when the young shoots are 7.5cm (3in) long.*

2 *Cut each shoot with a growing point and 2–3 pairs of leaves from the parent tuber. Trim at a node. Remove bottom pair of leaves.*

3 *Insert the cuttings in a pot of moist compost. Place in a propagator or plastic bag to root. Then pot up singly to grow on.*

Soil preparation and planting

Most bulbous plants have long, dormant periods underground after flowering and require relatively little attention for much of the year. The initial stages of selecting good stock, preparing the soil, and planting bulbs correctly do, however, contribute significantly to long-term success in cultivating bulbs.

Buying bulbs

There is considerable variation in the quality and size of bulbs that are available commercially, so examine any bulbs carefully before buying them. Different types of bulb are sold at various times of the year; always buy them when they are as fresh as possible. Select bulbs that are appropriate to the planting site: most enjoy sun, some prefer shade, and others will naturalize in grass.

Conservation

Conservation of bulbs in the wild is of the utmost importance and there are strict rules governing their importation. Wherever possible, check that the bulb stocks on sale at nurseries and garden centres have been obtained from sources of cultivated bulbs, rather than from stocks that have been collected in the wild.

Dry bulbs

Most bulbs are sold in a dry state during their dormant period. Buy these as early as possible before they start into growth; most daffodils, for example, normally start producing roots in late summer, and most other spring-flowering bulbs will begin to grow by early autumn. Autumn-flowering crocuses and *Colchicum* species and hybrids in particular benefit from early planting: specialist nurseries sell them in midsummer.

All autumn-flowering bulbs are best bought and planted by late summer. Bulbs tend to deteriorate if kept dry too long; they will have a shorter growing period and will take some time to recover and flower satisfactorily, so buy and plant them as soon as they are available. Some dry bulbs, usually those that have a summer growing season, such as *Galtonia*, gladioli, and *Tigridia*, are available for purchase in spring.

When buying bulbs, make sure that they are healthy and firm with strong growing points, and no soft or diseased areas or any signs of insect damage. Bulbs that are much smaller than average for their type, and bulb offsets, will not produce flowers in their first season.

Juno irises are unusual in having permanent storage roots beneath the bulb; if these have broken off, do not buy the bulb since it will not develop satisfactorily. Tulips should have intact skins, or tunics, otherwise they will be vulnerable to disease.

Moist bulbs

Although most bulbs may be stored dry, a few are better kept in slightly moist bark, peat substitute, or some similar material. This particularly applies to some of the shade-loving bulb species, such as *Erythronium*, *Anemone nemorosa*, and *Trillium*, that are normally found growing in damp woodland.

When buying cyclamen tubers, look for those with fibrous roots that are stored in moist bark or that are in root growth in pots. Cyclamen that have healthy roots establish much more effectively than dry tubers and so, although more expensive, are a much better buy.

Pot-grown bulbs

Pots of bulbs in active growth, and frequently in flower, are often sold in nurseries and garden centres. These are usually bulbs that were not sold when dormant and have been potted up. They grow satisfactorily and may be planted at once, without disturbing the roots. Alternatively, they may be kept in pots until they have flowered and planted as dry bulbs after they have died down. They are more expensive, however, than dry bulbs.

The influence of different soil types

Bulbs grow in a range of soil types, habitats, and climates throughout the world; the conditions in which they occur naturally indicate their needs in cultivation. Most hardy bulbs are from Mediterranean-type climates and thrive in a warm, sunny site, in freely draining soils that warm up

HOW TO SELECT BULBS

GOOD EXAMPLES

Tulip

Hyacinth

Daffodil (Single-nosed)

Daffodil (Twin-nosed)

POOR EXAMPLES

Split tunic

Signs of disease

Diseased tissue

Damaged outer scales

No tunic

Deterioration of bulb tissue

Soft nose

Offset too small to flower

CHOOSING CORMS, TUBERS, AND OTHER BULBOUS PLANTS

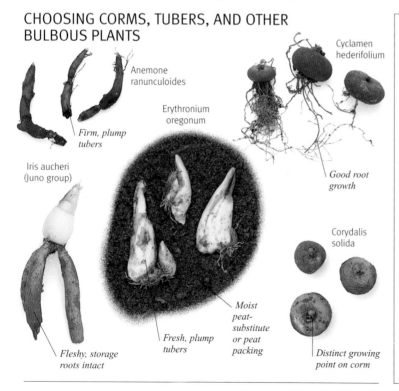

Anemone ranunculoides

Firm, plump tubers

Iris aucheri (Juno group)

Erythronium oregonum

Cyclamen hederifolium

Good root growth

Corydalis solida

Moist peat-substitute or peat packing

Fresh, plump tubers

Distinct growing point on corm

Fleshy, storage roots intact

Transplanting or buying snowdrops

Dry snowdrop (*Galanthus*) bulbs often fail to establish so some gardeners transplant or buy snowdrops "in the green", ie after flowering but still in leaf.

As leaves and roots remain active for some time after the flowers fade, transplanting at this stage causes nutrient loss. It is therefore advisable to delay transplanting until the foliage starts to turn yellow at the tips. This allows the bulbs to develop fully and avoids loss of bulb weight that occurs if snowdrops are dug up in full growth.

Snowdrop bulbs should never be allowed to dry out. If there has to be a delay in planting, put the bulbs in a slightly damp loam-based compost and keep in cool conditions until needed.

quickly in spring, and become dry in summer. Some species tolerate heavy soils that are moist during the growing season, as long as they are baked dry in summer. If the soil is moderately fertile and humus-rich, many bulbs increase steadily from year to year by seed or vegetative means. Most prefer a near-neutral or slightly alkaline soil.

Good drainage is vital because most bulbs are prone to rot while dormant if the soil is wet and poorly aerated. A few occur in the wild in riverside or swampland habitats; these thrive in moist (or even permanently wet) soils that do not dry out even in summer.

Light soils

Sandy or light soils usually warm up rapidly in spring and provide the good drainage that most bulbs need, although they are often deficient in humus and nutrients. Dig in plenty of well-rotted garden compost or manure before planting and, in early spring, top-dress with a balanced fertilizer applied at the manufacturer's recommended rate. Always incorporate manure below the level at which the bulbs are planted to avoid the risk of disease or chemical damage. If using fresh manure, dig it in at least three months before planting. More fertile, sandy soils and loams benefit from extra organic matter, but fertilizer dressing is unnecessary in the first year. In rock gardens, dig in coarse grit to make up at least one third of the top 30cm (12in) of soil for the extra drainage that most dwarf bulbs need.

Heavy soils

Heavy clay soils often need a lot of work to improve their drainage; on very poorly drained soils, a drainage

system must first be installed to grow bulbs successfully. Coarse sand or grit at a rate of at least 1½–2 buckets/sq m (sq yd) dug into the whole planting area will be required to make a significant difference. Heavy applications of well-rotted organic matter also improve the soil structure and therefore the drainage. For further information, see "Soil structure and water content", p.620.

Shady areas

Shade-loving bulbs most often occur naturally in woodland habitats, but grow well in any shady situation, as long as the soil is properly prepared: it should be rich in nutrients and humus and also retain moisture. Incorporate plenty of leaf mould or some other organic matter, such as well-rotted manure or garden compost, before planting. Acid-loving "woodland" bulbs thrive in the peat garden where at least half the soil is leaf mould, peat substitute, or peat.

Planting time

Dry bulbs should be planted as soon as possible after purchase. If the bulbs have been stored over winter (see "Lifting, drying, and storing", p.243), plant them at the end of their dormant period before they start growing. Pot-grown bulbs may be planted after purchase throughout the season, or kept in their pots until after they die down and treated as dry bulbs. Plant summer-flowering bulbs, including those that bloom in late summer under cover, and bulbs in the green, in early to mid-spring.

Planting in the open

Bulbs are usually best planted several to a large hole dug out with a spade. Alternatively, they may be planted singly. Do not make the outline of the planting area or the spacing of the bulbs symmetrical as this will look unnatural and if one or two bulbs fail they leave unsightly gaps.

In a rock garden, remove any top-dressing before planting bulbs and replace it afterwards.

Planting depths and spacing

Plant bulbs with two to three times their own depth of soil above them (deeper in light than in heavy soils) and two to three bulb widths apart. Remove soil to the correct depth, fork some bone meal into the bottom of the hole, and insert the bulbs.

Occasionally it is difficult to identify the "top" of a bulb, especially with rootless cyclamen tubers. The

CORRECT PLANTING DEPTHS

The planting depth depends on the size of the bulb. Use the length of the bulb as a rough guide and plant the bulb 2–3 times deeper than that length.

PLANTING BULBS IN THE OPEN

1 *Dig out a large hole in well-prepared ground and plant the bulbs (here tulips), with growing points uppermost, at least twice their own depth and width apart.*

2 *For a natural effect, space the bulbs randomly. Once they are in position, gently draw the soil over them with your hand to avoid displacing or damaging them.*

3 *Tamp down the soil over the planted area with the back of a rake. Avoid treading on the soil surface, as this might damage the growing points.*

PLANTING BULBS SINGLY

Plant each bulb in a separate hole at the appropriate depth. Draw back the prepared soil with a trowel and firm it down gently afterwards.

upper surface is usually flatter than the lower, or sometimes concave. *Corydalis* tubers can be almost globular, but there is usually some sign of shoot growth on the top. If it is impossible to be sure, plant the bulb on its side.

Replace the soil, breaking down any clods. Firm gently so that there are no air spaces around the bulbs.

Bulbs in the green

It may be necessary to plant bulbs in the green if transferring them from another garden, if space is restricted and bulbs are lifted each year (see right) to make way for other plants, or if planting snowdrops that have been sold in this state.

Use a trowel or a widger to create randomly spaced holes sufficiently wide to spread out the roots, and plant each bulb individually, at the same level as it was planted before. This is indicated by the colour change between the green top-growth and the chlorotic, yellow-green leaf bases that were underground. Water thoroughly after planting.

Pot-grown bulbs

Bulbs that have been purchased as pot-grown plants may be planted as dry bulbs after they have died down. When planting them, make a hole large enough to accommodate the whole pot, so that the contents may be planted without disturbance.

LIFTING BULBS

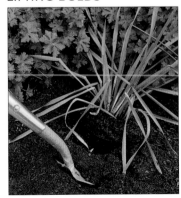

These bulbs (here planted in a lattice pot for convenience) have been left until the leaf tips start to turn yellow before being dug up and replanted elsewhere in the garden.

PLANTING CYCLAMEN IN ROOT GROWTH

1 *Select a planting site where the soil is rich in leaf mould or humus, or prepare the soil as necessary, working in organic matter well below the depth of the planting hole to encourage the roots to grow into the soil after planting. Leave it to settle for a day or two, then make a hole that is deep enough to plant the tuber with its roots spread out below it.*

2 *Plant the tuber so that it will lie with its upper surface just visible at soil level. Fill in around the roots with soil, taking care not to damage the roots.*

3 *Gently firm the soil around the tuber with your fingers, leaving the growing point just exposed. Lightly cover it with a loose mulch.*

If bulbs become pot-bound, gently tease out the roots at the base before planting to encourage them to grow out into the soil. If they are growing in a peat-based compost, keep the bulbs under cover in winter. Otherwise the peat acts as a sponge and the dormant bulbs rot in the waterlogged compost.

Planting tubers and corms in root growth

A number of "woodland" species, such as cyclamen, are best planted when they are in root growth, rather than as dry bulbs, as they will then become established more quickly.

They are also more likely to flower in their first season after planting; dry corms or tubers are much less reliable in this respect. Planting in root growth also eliminates any problems in distinguishing between the bottoms and tops of tubers or corms. Work plenty of leaf mould or well-rotted, organic matter into the

soil before planting to create the moist, humus-rich conditions that "woodland" bulbs require, otherwise the bulbs will not thrive.

Planting depth and spacing

Calculate the spacing and planting depth for corms and tubers in the same way as for dry bulbs (see "Planting in the open" and *Correct Planting Depths*, p.237), but allow additional space for the roots.

Cyclamen are unusual in that they grow near the soil surface in the wild, so do not plant the tubers too deeply or they may not flower. Make sure that their tips are at about the same level as the surrounding soil. They may be planted more closely than other bulbs, but they should be spaced at least their own width apart.

Planting

Plant the corms or tubers singly or as a group. It is important for the planting hole to be sufficiently deep and wide to accommodate the roots properly. Spread them out in the hole as this helps the plants to establish more quickly. Fill in the hole and firm it well to remove any air spaces.

The tips of cyclamen tubers may be left exposed or, if preferred, lightly covered with a loose mulch. Use leaf mould or, if the bed already has a top-dressing, coarse grit.

PLANTING LARGE BULBS IN GRASS

1 *Clean the bulbs (here daffodils), removing any loose, outer coatings and old roots. Scatter the bulbs randomly over the planting area, then make sure that they are at least their own width apart.*

2 *Make a hole for each bulb, using a long- or short-handled bulb planter to remove a core of turf and soil to a depth of about 10–15cm (4–6in).*

3 *Place a balanced fertilizer, mixed with a little of the soil from the core, into each hole and put in a bulb, making sure that the growing point is uppermost.*

4 *Break up the underside of the core over the bulb, so that it is completely covered with loose soil. Then replace the remains of the core on top of it.*

5 *Replace the lid of turf, and firm it in gently, taking care not to damage the growing point of the bulb. Fill in any gaps in the turf with more soil.*

Naturalizing in grass

When planting bulbs for naturalizing in grass, first cut the grass as short as possible. Random rather than regimented planting achieves a more natural effect; scatter the bulbs by hand over the chosen area and plant them where they have fallen,

PLANTING SMALL BULBS IN GRASS

1 *Using a half-moon edger (or spade), cut an "H" shape in the turf. Cut to the full depth of the half-moon blade to make sure that it penetrates the soil below.*

2 *Undercut the turf and fold back the two flaps to expose the area of bare soil that is underneath. Be careful not to crack or tear the turf unduly.*

3 *Using a hand fork, loosen the soil beneath to a depth of at least 7cm (3in), mixing in a little bone meal at a rate of about 15g/sq m (½oz/sq yd).*

4 *Press the bulbs (here crocuses) gently into the soil, taking care not to damage the growing points. Space the bulbs randomly but at least 2.5cm (1in) apart.*

5 *Score the underneath of the turf with a hand fork in order to loosen the soil, so that the bulbs will be able to penetrate the turf easily.*

6 *Roll the turf flaps back into position, taking care not to dislodge the bulbs or damage the turf. Firm down the turf, particularly along the joins.*

USING A FORK TO PLANT SMALL BULBS

1 *Push a garden fork into the grass to the appropriate depth and rock it back and forth. Repeat at random over the rest of the planting area.*

2 *Thoroughly mix a little fertilizer with some garden soil. Trickle a small amount of this mix into the bottom of each hole, using a widger or a small spoon.*

3 *Place a single bulb in each hole, growing point uppermost, ensuring that it is buried at twice its own depth. Then cover all the planted bulbs with soil.*

BULBS TO NATURALIZE

Allium moly
Anemone apennina,
  A. blanda (and cvs),
  A. pavonina
Camassia
Chionodoxa forbesii
Colchicum autumnale,
  C. speciosum

Crocus pulchellus

Crocus biflorus,
  C. chrysanthus,
  C. Dutch Hybrids,
  C. flavus, C. nudiflorus,
  C. ochroleucus,
  C. pulchellus, C. speciosus,
  C. tommasinianus
Dactylorhiza fuchsii,
  D. maculata
Eranthis hyemalis
Erythronium californicum
'White Beauty',
  E. dens-canis, E. revolutum
Fritillaria meleagris,
  F. pyrenaica
Galanthus elwesii,
  G. nivalis, G. plicatus
Gladiolus communis subsp.
  byzantinus
Hyacinthoides
  x massartiana
Leucojum aestivum,
  L. vernum
Muscari, some ❋

Narcissus 'Fortune'

Narcissus (some
  dwarf and most large spp.),
  N. bulbocodium,
  N. cyclamineus, N. minor,
  N. obvallaris, N. poeticus,
  N. pseudonarcissus,
  N. pumilus, N. triandrus
Ornithogalum nutans
Puschkinia scilloides
Scilla bifolia, S. siberica
Tulipa sprengeri

Key
❋ *Not hardy*

---

making sure that they are at least one bulb's width apart. Dig planting holes with a trowel or use a bulb planter; this useful implement cuts out neat plugs of turf and soil to a depth of about 10–15cm (4–6in) and is most suitable for larger bulbs.

Check that all the holes are at the correct depth and that the bulbs are the right way up, before inserting them and replacing the turf.

Planting large groups of small bulbs in grass

It is easier and less time-consuming to plant large numbers of very small bulbs, such as crocuses, by lifting a section of turf and planting a whole group of bulbs in the soil beneath rather than planting each bulb individually. Loosen the soil beneath the turf since it may be compacted; fork in a little balanced fertilizer or

some bone meal. Position the bulbs randomly, at least their own width apart. Replace the turf over the bulbs and firm it by hand or by tamping it down gently with the back of a rake.

Alternatively, use a broad-tined garden fork or a spade to make holes in the turf, and rock the tool back and forth in the ground to enlarge the holes slightly so that they easily accommodate the bulbs. The tines

should be inserted to three times the depth of the bulb, for example 7cm (3in) for crocuses. Repeat this at random for the entire planting area, so that the final arrangement of holes, in straight but criss-crossing lines, gives a natural effect. Mix a little bone meal with soil and place some in each hole before planting the bulbs singly, then top-dress the whole area with more prepared soil.

BULBS TO KEEP DRY DURING DORMANCY

Anemone biflora,
*   A. tschernjaewii*
Bellevalia (some spp.)
Bongardia
Calochortus

Calochortus
luteus

Colchicum (most spp.)
Corydalis (some spp.)
Crocus (some spp.)
Cyclamen, some ❀ (some spp.)
Gladiolus, some ❀
Iris, Oncocyclus Group
Leontice
Leucocoryne ❀
Merendera (most spp.)
Moraea ❀ (winter-growing spp.)
Narcissus atlanticus,
*   N. cantabricus, N. romieuxii,*
*   N. rupicola, N. rupicola* subsp.
*   marvieri, N. rupicola* subsp.
*   watieri*
Pancratium, some ❀
Ranunculus
*   asiaticus* ❀

Narcissus rupicola
subsp. *watieri*

Romulea, some ❀
*   (some spp.)*
Tecophilaea cyanocrocus
Tigridia ❀

Key
❀ *Not hardy*

HOW TO PLANT BULBS IN POTS

Growing tip
uppermost

1 *Plant the bulbs (here daffodils) at twice their own depth, and one bulb's width apart.*

2 *Cover the bulbs with compost to 1cm (½in) below the rim. Top-dress with grit (see inset), and label.*

PREPARING CLAY POTS

Before planting bulbs in a clay pot, place a single crock – or several, according to the drainage requirements of the plant – over the drainage hole in the base before adding compost.

Composts for bulbs under cover

A good compost mixture with the required humus content and drainage for use in bulb frames and greenhouse beds may be prepared as follows: mix together 2 parts peat substitute or peat, 3 parts coarse grit, and 4 parts loam; then add a base fertilizer or some bone meal at a rate of 25g/5 litres (1oz/1 gallon) and (except for lime-hating plants) garden lime at a rate of 25g/18 litres (1oz/4 gallons).

Make up sufficient compost to prepare a bulb bed that is at least 30cm (12in) in depth, with a layer, 5cm (2in) deep, of well-rotted garden compost or manure beneath it.

A similar compost is suitable for most bulbs, whether in pots or other containers. If using a proprietary potting compost, mix in some grit or coarse sand – at least one third, by bulk – because these composts are often not sufficiently well-drained for use with bulbs.

"Woodland" bulbs grown in pots or containers require a well-drained compost with additional organic matter that is rich in nutrients, for example a mixture of 3 parts leaf mould, 2 parts loam, and 2 parts grit.

Planting in pots and under cover

It is easy to grow most bulbs under cover in pots because the growing conditions can be precisely tailored to the particular needs of the plant. Suitable composts may be used for different types of bulb, and plants can be given the correct seasonal care, such as a summer drying-off period, restricted winter watering, or plunging in a bed.

Similar control is possible when cultivating bulbs that are planted directly into a greenhouse bed or bulb frame; the planting method is the same under cover as for bulbs grown in the open (see "Planting in the open", p.237).

Choosing clay or plastic pots

Bulbs may be planted in either clay or plastic pots. Clay pots are not so readily available but they are more suitable for bulbs that are unable to tolerate excessive moisture, because the compost dries out more quickly after watering than in plastic pots. Plastic pots are now extensively used and are perfectly satisfactory as long as they are filled with a freely draining compost; water the compost less frequently than with clay pots. For plants that need moist conditions, such as "woodland" bulbs, the greater water retentiveness of plastic pots is particularly valuable.

If using clay pots, place one or more crocks over the drainage hole; no "crocking" is necessary for plastic pots as long as the compost itself is well drained. A piece of perforated zinc placed over the drainage hole prevents worms entering the pot.

Planting bulbs in pots

Bulbs should be planted in pots at the same depths as bulbs grown outdoors (see "Planting depths and spacing", p.237). This may not be possible with larger bulbs, in which case make sure that each bulb has at least 2.5cm (1in) of moist compost beneath it in the pot. Plant bulbs of flowering size at a distance of one bulb's width apart. If planting a mixture of larger bulbs with smaller offsets, space the flowering-sized bulbs a little more widely, and scatter the small offsets between them.

Cover the bulbs with some moist compost, leaving sufficient room below the pot rim for a top-dressing, and firm it well. Top-dress the pot with a generous layer of horticultural grit, which helps to retain moisture and improves the appearance of the pot. Label with the plant name, the date of planting, and source. Watering is not necessary until the compost is almost dry. When the roots start into growth, it is time to start watering again.

Lattice pots

Bulbs grown in beds under cover are often planted in pots with open-meshed, or latticed, sides, which allow different types of bulb to be closely planted without mixing them up or restricting their roots. Plant the bulbs in the pots, label them, and plunge them in a bulb bed containing the same compost as the pots. The pots may be lifted from the bed without disturbing their neighbours later. Alternatively, but less conveniently, groups of bulbs in beds may be separated by tiles or pieces of slate sunk into the bed between them.

Planting in lattice pots

Plant up the lattice pots with bulbs in the usual way. Sink the labelled pots up to their rims in a bulb bed so that the compost just covers them. Stagger the rows for economical use of space.

BULBS IN A PLUNGE BED

Plunge the labelled pots up to their rims in a sand bed or cold frame. Check the pots regularly to ensure that the compost does not dry out.

Plunging the pots

After planting, keep the pots in a cold frame or cold greenhouse. Bulbs in pots are more susceptible to frost damage than those in the garden; in severe winters, pots in an unheated greenhouse may freeze solid. Protect them by sinking the pots in a plunge bed of coarse sand or grit, mixed with enough peat substitute to stop the grit collapsing into the hole when pots are taken out. Alternatively, provide minimal heating in very cold periods. Summer plunging is important for bulbs in clay pots which dry out quickly, but is also advisable for plastic pots to prevent overheating.

Planting in ornamental containers

Bulbs may be planted in tubs, troughs, patio pots, or any ornamental container that is clean and has sufficient drainage holes in the base to allow water to drain away quickly.

Place a layer of crocks or another drainage material at least 3cm (1in) deep in the bottom of the container. Raise it off the ground with bricks or special "pot feet". This stops water accumulating in the base and, if the pot is made of ceramic or terracotta, helps guard it against frost damage.

Vary the compost, whether it be loam-based, rich in leaf mould, or very gritty, to suit the requirements of different types of bulb. The compost must be free-draining or it may become waterlogged and the bulbs may rot. Insert them at the same depths and spacing in the compost as for standard pots (see p.240). Do not press the bulbs into the compost too firmly as this may compress the soil just beneath the roots of the bulbs and impede their growth.

Bulbs for forcing

Some bulbs can be planted in bowls and kept in the dark to encourage them to flower early. The best way to force most other bulbs for the house is to plant them in ornamental bowls in the same way as for pots (see p.240) and then to bring them indoors just as they begin to flower. The pots of bulbs are best displayed in a cool room with temperatures only slightly higher than that of the greenhouse or frame in which they were grown. In hotter conditions, the flower stems grow very quickly and tend to look out of character, and the flowers do not last as long as in cool conditions. Return the bulbs to the greenhouse or bulb frame as soon as the flowers fade.

Hyacinths

The most popular of all bulbs for forcing is the fragrant hyacinth. Specially prepared bulbs may be

Growing hyacinths in water

Hyacinth bulbs may be forced in water, in special glasses designed to hold one bulb with its base just at water level. Place a bulb in its glass in a cool room away from sunlight and keep the water level topped up to just below the base of the bulb. It rapidly produces roots which grow down into the water.

Wait until the flower buds begin to show colour before moving the rooted hyacinth into a warm, brightly lit room. The flowering shoots then develop and produce blooms. After flowering, discard the exhausted bulb since it is unlikely to provide a good display the following year.

Fill the glass with water up to the "neck" and place the bulb in the top so it sits just above the water. Leave in a cool place. As the roots grow, keep the water topped up.

BULBS FOR SUCCESSIONAL INTEREST

Crocuses — Tulips

To provide a display of flowers over a prolonged period, choose two or more types of bulb that come into flower at different times during the season, and plant them together in the same container. Position the early- and late-flowering bulbs in layers, each at approximately twice its own depth. Arrange the bulbs in a random pattern rather than in rows to achieve an informal effect.

purchased and, if they are given suitable treatment, will come into flower by the middle of winter.

Buy the prepared hyacinth bulbs in early autumn and plant them in bowls filled with bulb fibre that has been well moistened beforehand. Plant the bulbs close together, so they are not quite touching one another, with their growing tips protruding just above the top of the compost. Put the newly planted bulbs in a cool, dark place: a closed cupboard in a cool room is suitable. This encourages the flowering stems to develop before the leaves and allows the root systems to become well established. Keep the bulb fibre just moist by carefully watering between the bulbs if it starts to become dry.

Leave the bowls in the dark for about eight weeks, or until the new shoots are about 4–5cm (1½–2in) high; the emerging flower buds that are visible between the tips of the yellow-green leaves should be just starting to show signs of colour.

Once they have reached this stage, bring the bulbs into the daylight, but not into bright sunlight. Do not remove the bowls of bulbs from the dark earlier than this, otherwise the leaves will grow very rapidly and obscure the flowers – a major cause of disappointment with forced bulbs. Once exposed to the light, the leaves will gradually acquire their natural green colour as the plants grow on and begin to flower.

Daffodils

Many daffodils, such as *Narcissus* 'Paper White', may be grown in bulb fibre in the same way as hyacinths. They do require more light, however, and should be placed on a sunny windowsill as soon as the shoots appear above the compost. If the light is inadequate, daffodils may become drawn and excessively tall, and will require staking.

Hippeastrum

The large-flowered *Hippeastrum* hybrids are very popular as indoor flowering plants. Garden centres and stores often supply them complete with a suitable bulb compost, ready to be planted in pots and grown in a warm, light room until flowering is over. *Hippeastrum* hybrids are more easily kept from year to year if they are grown for most of the year in a greenhouse and only brought into the house while they are in flower.

FORCING HYACINTHS IN A CONTAINER

1 *Place some moist bulb fibre in the bottom of a container. Position the bulbs and fill in with more fibre, leaving the bulb crowns just visible at the surface. Leave them in a cool, dark place.*

2 *When the flower spikes are visible between the pale leaves, bring the container into bright, indirect light.*

Routine care

Bulbs do not require a great deal of maintenance if the correct environment is provided. If they flower poorly, the most likely cause is overcrowding: this is easily remedied by dividing them and replanting them in a fresh site. For pest and disease problems that will require control, see PLANT PROBLEMS, "Bulb, corm, and rhizome problems", p.663.

Bulbs in grass

Bulbs left to naturalize in grass do not need as much attention as those planted in other sites in the garden, but correct timing in mowing is very important. Dead-heading regularly and feeding occasionally helps the bulbs to remain healthy.

Fertilizing

Do not feed bulbs in grass regularly, especially with nitrogenous fertilizer because it increases the vigour of the grass at the bulbs' expense. If a feed is needed (eg for daffodils that fail to flower freely), use a high-potash fertilizer to aid flower production.

Dead-heading

Regular removal of faded blooms extends the season and improves the vigour of bulbs by stopping them wasting energy on unwanted seed production. After flowering, pinch through the stems below the seed pods. If the seed capsules are to be harvested later or left to seed naturally, leave a number to ripen on the plant and then cut the stems to the ground after harvesting the seed.

When to mow

If cultivating early-flowering bulbs such as daffodils, do not cut the grass until at least six weeks after they have flowered, or until the foliage is turning yellow. If growing bulbs that increase by self-seeding, do not mow the grass until the seed capsules have been able to shed all their seed – usually about three weeks after the leaves begin to die down.

Autumn-flowering bulbs such as *Colchicum* start into growth before the end of the lawnmowing season. When the first leaves or tips of the flowering shoots appear, mow with the blades set high enough to avoid them; stop mowing when the shoots are too tall to escape the blades.

In wild-flower meadows that include flowering bulbs like hardy orchids, delay mowing until mid- to late summer, when all foliage has died down.

Bulbs in borders and woodland

The maintenance required for bulbs in herbaceous or mixed borders, or in woodland, depends on whether they are permanent displays, or temporary "fillers". Permanent plantings need little maintenance until bulbs get overcrowded, when they should be lifted and divided (see p.243).

If the ground is well prepared, no feeding is necessary during the first year, but an application once or twice in a season of a low-nitrogen, high-potash fertilizer, which promotes flowering rather than leafy growth (see Soils and Fertilizers, "Types of fertilizer", p.624) will encourage a fine display in subsequent years.

Bulbs need adequate moisture in the growing season, especially in woodland, and may need watering if there is an early drought. Dead-head at regular intervals in the same way as for bulbs in grass.

Care of temporary plantings is the same as for the first-year care of bulbs that are permanently planted. Lift the bulbs for storing at the end of the growing season (see p.243).

Removing dead leaves

After bulbs in borders have finished flowering, allow their leaves to die down completely before removing them. Do not "tidy" foliage by tying leaves together while still green; this

see p.243).

Leave the leaves: bulbs and photosynthesis

When your bulbs have finished flowering, it is important to allow their leaves to develop fully and die down naturally, as they would in the wild. Removing the leaves too early prevents photosynthesis (the process by which the foliage manufactures food) from taking place, weakening the bulb and reducing flowering the next year.

If bulbs are naturalized in grass, resist the temptation to mow as soon as flowers fade. Trials with daffodils (*Narcissus*) at Wisley showed a reduction in vigour and in flowering the following season when foliage was cut down less than six weeks after flowering.

Continue watering bulbs in pots after flowering; a liquid feed helps to maintain the foliage in good condition, and allows next year's flowers to start developing.

Staking

A few tall bulbs with slender stems need staking. Stake these plants as soon as they are tall enough for a tie to be put around them; tie in the stems again when the plants are near their full height and are about to flower. Where the bulbs are planted in groups, place bamboo canes on the inward-facing side of the stems so that they are concealed by the growing plants. Insert the stakes well away from the base of the stems so that the bulbs are not damaged.

1 Support a tall, single-stemmed plant such as a gladiolus with a bamboo cane when the plant is 15cm (6in) tall. Attach the stem to the cane with string or raffia.

2 When the flower buds are forming, tie in the stem to the cane just below the buds to prevent the stem from breaking when the buds open.

STAKING BULBS IN GROUPS

For plants such as lilies that grow in clumps, place one or more canes in the centre of the clump. Tie in surrounding stems to each cane with a figure-of-eight loop so that the stems do not rub against the canes.

DEAD-HEADING

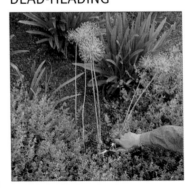

Unless the seed is to be used for propagation, cut down all dead flower stems of bulbs in the border (here Allium) with secateurs to ground level.

WHEN TO HARVEST SEED

If seed is required, do not dead-head until the seed capsule (here Fritillaria) is brown and begins to split. The ripe seed is then ready to harvest for sowing or storing.

reduces their capacity to photo-synthesize and store energy in the bulb for the next growing season, so the bulb loses vigour. It also makes them die down prematurely.

Overcrowded bulbs

If mature bulbs flower less freely than in previous years, the deterioration is usually due to overcrowding. This may not be obvious unless the bulbs are visible near the soil surface, as is often the case with *Nerine*.

Lift crowded clumps during the dormant season, before root growth starts. Separate into individual bulbs and replant them in irregular groups. Insert each one at two to three times its own depth and two to three bulb widths apart. Plant small offsets or bulblets between bulbs of flowering size, or plant in pots or a "nursery bed", in a frame or in the garden, as for two-year-old seedlings (see "Care of seedlings", p.246).

If, on lifting, the bulbs are found not to be overcrowded, but are deteriorating or no longer thriving, inspect them for pests and diseases (see p.244). If there is no obvious explanation for their failure, replant them in a different site that is well drained and has sufficient light and nutrients. Alternatively, grow the bulbs in pots in a cold frame or greenhouse until they recover.

Lifting, drying, and storing

Bulbs planted temporarily in beds or borders should be left *in situ* until the foliage has begun to yellow. Then lift and clean them, lay them out on a tray to dry, and store them in paper (not plastic) bags in a dry place until the next planting season. If there is any sign of fungal disease, dust them with fungicide. Alternatively, lift them in full growth soon after flowering or as the foliage dies down and replant them immediately in another part of the garden so that they may die down naturally.

Dwarf bulbs in raised beds or rock gardens

The principles of routine care of bulbs in borders also apply to dwarf species in raised beds or in the rock garden. Many rarer bulbs are slow to increase, and do not become overcrowded for several years. Keep them reasonably moist in the growing season, particularly during drought conditions, and feed regularly with a high-potash, low-nitrogen fertilizer.

If seed is required, harvest the seed capsules when ripe, then clear away dead leaves to tidy the bed and reduce the likelihood of disease.

HOW TO DIVIDE AN OVERCROWDED CLUMP

1 *When bulbs planted in the open become overcrowded, use a garden fork to lift the whole clump as the leaves die down. Take care not to damage them.*

2 *Divide the clump of bulbs (here Nerine) by hand, separating it first into smaller clumps and then into individual bulbs. Remove any dead or diseased material.*

3 *Discard any unhealthy bulbs. Clean the good bulbs with care, removing the loose tunics, in preparation for replanting them singly in freshly prepared soil.*

Bulbs in containers outdoors

Bulbs in containers should not be allowed to dry out when in growth and should be fed regularly with a high-potash fertilizer to boost the production of flowers. Wait until the foliage of spring-flowering bulbs has died back naturally, then lift and clean them, and store them in a cool, dry place during summer. Replant the bulbs in a container of fresh compost in early autumn for a display in the following spring. Alternatively, if the container is needed before the foliage has died down, transfer the bulbs while still in the green to a spare bed, and allow them to die back before lifting, cleaning, and drying them in the normal way.

Spring-flowering species such as crocuses, daffodils, and hyacinths may also be transplanted directly into the garden for naturalizing. Store summer-flowering bulbs in a cool, dry place over winter and replant them in spring.

Some bulbs, such as lilies (*Lilium*), do not grow well if allowed to dry out completely after flowering. Keep them moist by plunging them in their pots in a shaded place or in a cold frame to rest. Repot the lilies every year in the spring.

Bulbs in frames and covered raised beds

Bulbs that are grown in frames or under cover need similar treatment after planting to those in borders (see p.242) but require special care with watering and feeding.

Remove the covers to the raised beds or frames during the growing season, but replace them temporarily during excessively cold or wet weather. Keep the bulbs watered in dry periods. When most of the bulbs are beginning to die down, replace the covers until the start of the next growing season.

HOW TO LIFT, DRY, AND STORE BULBS

1 *When the leaves are turning yellow, about a month after flowering, gently lift the bulbs (here tulips) with a fork. Put them in labelled containers to avoid confusing different plants.*

2 *Clean the soil off the bulbs and rub off any loose, flaking tunic tissue. Cut or carefully pull off the dying foliage. Discard any bulbs that show signs of damage or of disease.*

3 *Place the bulbs on a wire tray, spaced so that they do not touch, and leave them to dry overnight. Then dust them with fungicide and store them in clean, clearly labelled, paper bags.*

Improve the vigour of the bulbs by feeding them once the nutrients in the original compost are exhausted. Use a granular fertilizer sprinkled on the compost surface as the bulbs come into growth, or apply a liquid feed every two or three weeks. In the latter part of the season, use a high-potash, low-nitrogen feed to produce a good display of blooms.

Bulbs in pots under cover

Bulbs that need a warm, dry summer, and a winter and spring growing period, grow well in an unheated or cool greenhouse, where the bulbs' feeding, watering, and drying off may be controlled to satisfy their needs. Keep such bulbs dry from the time their leaves die down until their natural growing period starts in late summer or early autumn.

During the growing season, give the pots a good soaking when they are nearly dry, but take care not to overwater them, especially in winter. Give them extra water in the growing season up to flowering time, after which gradually reduce watering until the leaves die down. Do not allow some hardy bulbs, such as crocuses from mountainous areas and "woodland" bulbs, to dry out completely; keep the compost slightly moist during the summer.

Bulbs such as *Galtonia* from areas with summer rainfall, for example parts of South Africa and South America, must be watered regularly so that they keep growing during the summer; they should then be allowed to dry out during their natural dormancy in winter.

Renewing compost

Changing the top layer of compost in a pot of bulbs supplies them with enough nutrients for a further year. Before they start to grow, gently scrape away the old compost to expose the tops of the bulbs. If they are healthy and not overcrowded, cover them with fresh, moist compost of the same type that is in the pot. Separate and repot over-crowded bulbs or, if they are hardy, plant them out.

Repotting

Bulbs may sometimes be kept in the same pot for several years but they eventually become overcrowded and need repotting – usually indicated by a failure to flower well and by under-sized or unhealthy foliage. At the end of dormancy, repot the bulbs to encourage them to start into growth. Pot up larger bulbs singly, as for the

initial potting up, and in a similar compost (see "Planting in pots and under cover", p.240). Plant small bulbs or bulblets between the adult ones or pot them up separately (see "Care of seedlings", p.246).

In early spring, repot tender bulbs that are dormant in winter when the new growth is about to begin.

Fertilizing

If the bulbs are kept in the same pot for several years, feed them regularly throughout the growing season at alternate waterings with a liquid feed containing a high-potash, low-nitrogen fertilizer. Extra feeding is unnecessary if the bulbs are repotted, or the top layer of compost in the pot is replaced each year.

Care of forced bulbs

When they are ready to be brought into the light, place forced bulbs (see p.241), according to their needs, on a shady windowsill or in a cool, bright room. The bulbs tolerate slightly warmer conditions when their flower buds are well formed. Rotate the bowl periodically if the shoots turn to the light and keep the compost

moist. Forced bulbs are generally in a poor condition after flowering. Discard them or plant them out in the garden where they will eventually, perhaps after two years or more, flower again in their normal season.

Hippeastrum hybrids that have been forced may be kept in a good condition each year by replanting them after flowering in a humus-rich, well-drained compost in the same pot. Do not water them from early autumn until midwinter, and repot them if they are overcrowded.

Bulb problems

Bulbs occasionally fail to flower, and are then known as "blind" bulbs. Within a long-established clump, this problem is often due to overcrowding, so bulbs should be lifted and replanted separately in fresh soil (see "Overcrowded bulbs", p.243). Shortage of water during the growing season is another possible cause of "blind" bulbs.

Newly planted bulbs that are blind may not have been stored correctly, or they may not yet be fully mature.

Iris danfordiae, *Fritillaria* species such as *F. recurva* and *F. thunbergii*, and some other bulbs do not flower regularly even in nature and so are described as "shy-flowering". Do not dig up such bulbs unless they look unhealthy or seem crowded since they may eventually flower if left undisturbed. It may be helpful to plant the bulbs especially deeply because this discourages them from dividing into bulblets.

Pests and diseases

During the growing season, keep a careful watch for the symptoms of pests and diseases and control any problems as soon as they arise. When planting, repotting, or propagating dormant bulbs, inspect them and destroy any badly afflicted bulbs.

Bulbs may suffer especially from rot or fungal diseases, including ink spot (p.663) which severely affects Reticulata irises. Daffodils may fall prey to narcissus bulb fly (see "Bulb flies", p.663). Aphids (p.646) sometimes infest bulbs and can cause the spread of viruses (p.649). Red spider mite (p.646) occasionally affects bulbs grown under cover.

REPOTTING OVERCROWDED BULBS

1 *Remove some compost from the pot to inspect the bulbs (here daffodils). If they have become overcrowded in the pot, they should be repotted.*

2 *Carefully tip out the contents of the pot, and remove the bulbs from the compost. Discard any dead material or any bulbs that show signs of pests or diseases.*

3 *Separate any pairs or clumps of bulbs with large offsets into individual bulbs by gently pulling them apart.*

4 *Select only healthy bulbs and clean them, rubbing with finger and thumb to remove any loose, outer tunics. Dust the bulbs with fungicidal powder.*

5 *Replant the bulbs in a pot of fresh, moist, bulb compost. Insert them at twice their own depth, and space them at least their own width apart.*

Propagation

MANY bulbs increase naturally by forming offsets or bulblets around the bulb, and may be propagated by separating these from the parent bulbs. Those that do not divide freely may be increased by cutting them into sections and treating these as new bulbs. Some are propagated by other vegetative means, such as scaling or scooping. Seed propagation yields larger stocks but most bulbs take several years to flower.

Dividing bulbs

During the growing season, many bulbs increase by forming offset from the main, parent bulb, usually within the bulb tunic. Separate them every year or two and plant them out or pot them up individually. If left, they may become too overcrowded and take longer to develop to flowering size. The offsets may be small and numerous as with some *Allium* species or larger and fewer as with daffodils and tulips.

Other bulbs may form bulbils in the leaf axils, as with lilies (*Lilium*) and some *Calochortus* species, or bulblets around the base of the bulb; both may be used for propagation. Some lilies, such as a few American species and hybrid lilies, are rhizomatous and produce small "offset" rhizomes. Pot these up, placing them horizontally, to grow on for one or two years before planting out.

Propagation from offsets

Some bulbs, for example *Crinum*, may be increased by lifting and dividing a clump. Pull the offsets gently from the parent plant or cut the basal plate at the point at which they are attached to the larger bulb. Clean off any loose material or soil, and dust cut surfaces with fungicide.

Replant the larger bulbs in the garden in a well-spaced group. Pot up smaller offsets separately, or insert several in a larger pot or deep tray. Keep them for one or two seasons in a cold greenhouse to grow on; then plant them out in the open.

Propagation from bulblets and bulbils

Bulbs raised from bulblets will generally flower a year or two earlier than those grown from seed. When repotting bulbs, remove the bulblets from around the base of the parent bulb and insert them in rows in trays. Use well-drained cutting compost with a little slow-release fertilizer added. Space the bulblets in a tray as

for seed (see "Sowing the seed", p.246) and cover them with a 2.5cm (1in) layer of compost. Label, and grow them on in a shaded part of the garden. Keep the compost moist; if using clay pots, plunge them in beds to keep them damp. Treat the bulblets thereafter as for seed (see p.246).

Bulbils may be removed and treated similarly (see LILIES, *Propagating from Stem Bulbils*, p.251).

Gladiolus cormels

Gladioli often form small cormels at the base of the corm. Remove these from the parent corm and

treat them as bulblets. Alternatively, plant them in rows in fertile, well-drained soil, either in a bulb frame in cold areas or in a nursery bed. They may be left until they flower two to three years later, and then may be lifted and planted in their permanent positions.

HOW TO PROPAGATE BULBS FROM OFFSETS

1 *In the spring, before active growth begins, lift a clump of bulbs (here* Crinum*) with a garden fork. Shake excess soil from the roots and pull the clump apart.*

2 *Select a large bulb with several well-developed offsets. Clean the soil from the offsets and pull them away from the parent bulb, taking care to preserve any roots.*

3 *Prepare 15cm (6in) pots with a moist, sandy compost. Insert a single offset into each pot, and cover it with about 2.5cm (1in) of compost. Label, and water.*

HOW TO PROPAGATE GLADIOLUS BY CORMELS

1 *When the plant has finished flowering and the foliage is dying back, use a hand fork to lift the corm. Cormels should have developed all around the basal plate of the corm. Store all the corms over winter in a cool, dry place.*

2 *In late winter or early spring, pull off cormels; they should readily come away from the parent corm. The cormels may vary in size but all may be used.*

3 *Half-fill a tray with moist, gritty compost. Insert cormels, growing points upwards, in rows 2.5cm (1in) apart. Fill the tray with more compost; level, firm, and label it.*

BULBOUS PLANTS TO DIVIDE

Offsets
Allium (some spp.)
Alstroemeria (vigorous hybrids)
Arum, some ✽
Cardiocrinum
Crinum, some ✽
Crocus
Galanthus
Iris Juno Group
Leucojum
Lilium
Narcissus
Nerine, some ✽
Ornithogalum, some ✽
Oxalis
Sternbergia
Tulipa

Gladiolus 'Deliverance'

Bulblets
Allium (some spp.)
*Fritillaria acmopetala,
F. crassifolia, F. pudica,
F. recurva, F. thunbergii*
Iris Reticulata Group (some spp.)
Muscari, some ✽ (some spp.)

Cormels
Gladiolus (spp. and hybrids)

Key
✽ Not hardy

Bulbs from seed

This method of propagation may initially be slow to give results but eventually it produces a large number of bulbs that are free from any viruses (except those specifically transmitted by seed), unlike division which passes on any disease present in the parent bulb to the young plants. It is a method that is particularly suitable for bulbous "woodland" species, such as *Erythronium*, which resent root disturbance.

Most bulbs take from three to five years to reach mature flowering size from seed. In *Cardiocrinum* the bulb that has flowered dies, leaving a clump of smaller bulbs that may be divided (see p.245) or their seed may be collected and sown regularly every year to ensure a steady succession of healthy plants that will mature and provide flowers in each growing season.

Collecting seed

The seed capsules of most bulbs are carried on the old flowering stems, but some plants, mainly crocuses and Reticulata irises, have capsules formed at or just above ground level which are difficult to see.

Watch the ripening capsules carefully for signs of splitting, because the seed may be shed very quickly. Remove the capsules as they begin to turn brown and start to split. Extract the seed as soon as possible. Allow the seed to dry without any artificial heat, and store it until sown in labelled, paper packets in a cool, dry, and airy place. Do not use plastic bags as they seal in the moisture and the seed may rot. A few bulbs, such as *Corydalis*, shed seed when the capsules are still green and this seed should be sown immediately; cut off and store the capsules in paper bags until the seed is shed.

When to sow seed

The following method is suitable for most spring-flowering, hardy bulbs, for example, *Fritillaria*, daffodils, and tulips. The best time to sow is early autumn, but if seed is available earlier, sow immediately. Germination should follow in early spring.

Seed compost for bulbs

Use a proprietary, loam-based seed compost, with a quarter-part coarse sand added if the mixture does not have a sandy appearance. A suitable loam-based compost may be made from 2 parts sterile loam, 1 part peat substitute, and 1½ parts very coarse sand or seed-grade perlite with superphosphate added at a rate of 25g/18 litres (1oz/4 gallons) and lime at a rate of 25g/18 litres (1oz/4 gallons). Proprietary composts containing a peat substitute may also be used, but they contain only enough nutrients for a year.

Sowing the seed

Clay or plastic pots may be used but it is easier to maintain adequate moisture levels in plastic pots. If using a clay pot, place some crocks at the bottom for drainage. Fill the pot with compost and firm it before sowing the seed thinly on the surface. Space large, flat seed of bulbs such as *Fritillaria* or tulips one seed's width apart, and smaller, rounded seed about 5mm (¼in) apart. Sieve a light covering of the compost over the seed so that it is no longer visible, and then cover it with a generous layer of flint grit or aquarium gravel. Label the pots with the plant name, source, and date. Stand them in a shady place in the open garden, or plunge them in a sand frame, and keep them moist.

Care of seedlings

When the seedlings have germinated bring the pots into full light in a cold frame or greenhouse. Keep them moist until they show definite signs of dying down, and then stop watering them. Seedlings of bulbs that are not naturally dry in summer even in their dormant period, such as certain *Crocus* species from mountainous areas, should be kept slightly moist. Start watering again in early autumn, or as soon as there is new growth, and keep the pots watered until the growth dies down.

Leave most bulbs for two growing seasons before repotting, unless they grow very vigorously. It is not essential to feed seedlings in the first growing season, but larger bulbs form if they are fed regularly in the second. Use a proprietary liquid feed as used for tomatoes, but at half the manufacturer's recommended strength.

Removing seedlings from pots

After the seedling bulbs have completed two seasons of growth, or one in the case of very vigorous bulbs, pot them up into the compost recommended for mature bulbs (see "Composts for bulbs under cover", p.240). After the foliage has completely died back towards the end of the dormant period, empty out the contents of the pot. Separate out the young bulbs, clean them, and repot them in fresh, moist compost to start them into growth. It is better to grow them in pots for two or three years until they are large enough to establish successfully outdoors.

Keeping seedlings in pots

Seedling bulbs may be grown on in pots and planted out together with the compost to avoid handling the bulbs and disturbing their root growth. Pot on a complete potful of one-year-old seedlings into a slightly larger pot and feed them regularly while they are in growth in the second year. If they are large enough by the end of the season, plant the entire potful of young bulbs in the open garden when they are dormant or just starting into growth. Give them an extra feed after planting to avoid any delay in flowering. If they are too small, keep them in the pot, and feed them regularly for another year.

"Woodland" species

Many shade-loving bulbs grow best in a compost that contains some leaf mould. For seed sowing, use a compost of 1 part sterilized leaf mould, 1 part peat substitute or peat, and 1 part sterilized loam, with a further 1½ parts of coarse, horticultural sand or seed-grade perlite.

The growth of many of these bulbs, for example *Erythronium* and *Trillium*, is slow. Planting the whole panful of seedlings after two or three years' growth into a well-prepared shady bed is better than regular repotting over several years which will repeatedly disturb the roots.

HOW TO PROPAGATE BULBS FROM SEED

1 *Prepare the pot: fill it to within 2cm (¾in) of the brim with proprietary seed compost mixed with a quarter part coarse sand. Firm it well with a tamper.*

2 *Sow the seed evenly over the compost by tapping the open packet, holding it near the surface so that the seed (here* Fritillaria meleagris) *does not bounce out.*

3 *Use a sieve to scatter a thin layer of fine compost evenly over the seed. There should be just sufficient compost to conceal the seed.*

4 *Top-dress the pot with about 1cm (½in) of coarse grit, adding it carefully to avoid disturbing the compost or seeds.*

5 *Label the pot. Place it in a shady situation in the open. Plunge the pot in damp sand and water, as required, to keep the compost moist.*

POTTING UP SEEDLINGS

1 *Carefully knock out the entire pot contents; some of the bulbs (here* Fritillaria raddeana) *will be visible among the compost. Remove all the bulbs carefully.*

2 *Replant the young bulbs in a pot of fresh, gritty bulb compost, placing them at twice their own depth and spaced their own width apart.*

Cyclamen

Seed of hardy cyclamen germinates most readily if it is sown as soon as it is ripe, usually in midsummer. If using dry seed, soak it for about 24 hours before sowing to aid germination. To sow, see facing page.

The seedlings generally grow strongly in their first year and the young tubers may then be repotted in seedling compost (see above),

TWO-YEAR-OLD BULB SEEDLINGS

After two years, seedling bulbs (here Calochortus tolmiei) *may vary noticeably in size but all should develop satisfactorily.*

preferably while they are still in growth. Add 1 part leaf mould to 3 parts of the compost to encourage vigorous growth. The tubers usually develop well if planted several to a pan, rather than singly. Insert them with their roots spaced out and cover the tops with surface grit.

Place the pans in a shaded cold frame to grow on for a second year. In spring of the third year, repot the tubers singly using the same compost mix and leave them until they are approaching flowering size. Plant them out in the garden in late summer.

Growing lilies from seed

Sow the seed in pots about 10cm (5in) deep filled with peat substitute, peat, or seed compost based on loam or peat, preferably as soon as they are ripe (in late summer or early autumn). Sow the seed thinly to avoid the need for pricking out, cover it with fine grit, and place the pots in a cold frame or cold greenhouse.

In certain lilies, the seedlings germinate two to six weeks after sowing. Others may take several months to germinate. Lily seeds differ in the way they germinate. With hypogeal lilies, root formation occurs initially; a cold period is then needed to stimulate leaf production. Seed of epigeal lilies usually – but not always – germinates fairly rapidly with both root and shoot development occurring almost together (see also PRINCIPLES OF PROPAGATION, *How a Seed Germinates*, p.630).

Overwinter the containers in a cold frame or sheltered place outdoors, then bring them into a cold greenhouse in spring. Do not feel discouraged if no seedlings appear after the first year; germination can take up to two or occasionally more years, depending on the species.

Leave the germinated seedlings in their containers for their first growing season and give them liquid

EXTRACTING CYCLAMEN SEED

Harvest the seed capsules in early summer when they are beginning to split. Shake out the seeds and soak them in a bowl of tepid water overnight to assist germination.

PLANTING OUT "WOODLAND" BULBS

1 *Plant out "woodland" species without separating the young bulbs. Invert a pot of two-year-old bulbs (here* Erythronium). *Slide out the mass of bulbs and compost.*

2 *Plant the entire potful of compost and bulbs, so that the top of the bulb mass is at least 2.5cm (1in) below the surface. Firm, label, and water lightly.*

fertilizer regularly. Alternatively, prick them out when they have two true leaves into a loam-based potting compost. Repot them regularly or transfer them to nursery beds until they are large enough to be planted out in the garden. This process takes from one to three years, depending on the species.

Tender bulbs

Sow the seed of tender bulbs as described for lilies, but keep the pots at a temperature above freezing point during the winter, plunged in bulb frames or beds under cover. Seed of many tender species, for example *Hippeastrum*, germinates more quickly if bottom heat is used (this is generally supplied by soil-warming cables; see GREENHOUSES AND FRAMES, "Soil-warming devices", p.580) and a temperature of 21°C (70°F) is maintained.

If the germination characteristics of a particular plant are uncertain and there is plenty of seed available, sow half with bottom heat and half in normal greenhouse temperatures. If germination has not taken place within six to eight weeks in heat, move the pots to a cooler place. Some genera, notably *Alstroemeria*, germinate rapidly when a warm period is followed by a cool period.

Sow fleshy seeds of bulbs such as *Amaryllis* fresh, directly from the seed capsule while it is still green. If left in the capsule, the seed may germinate *in situ*, and it should then be removed and sown in the normal way. Grow on the seedlings (see "Care of seedlings", p.246). Seedlings of some genera, such as some *Hippeastrum* species, remain in active growth for more than one season; if so, keep them moist, and they may grow until they flower without going dormant.

Large flat seeds of such tender genera as Hippeastrum can also be germinated easily by floating the seed on water in a container, placed in a warm (21°C/70°F) greenhouse or on a windowsill. Germination takes three to six weeks, after which the seedling can be potted up in seed compost in a 7cm (3in) pot.

Seeds with erratic germination

Seed of certain bulbs, for example Juno irises, germinates very erratically, sometimes over several years. If, after two seasons, only a few seedlings have appeared, repot the entire potful without disturbing the compost; late-germinating seedlings often appear a year or so later.

Germination in plastic bags

Seed of some genera may be germinated in plastic bags rather than pots; this is most frequently done with lilies (*Lilium*) but is applicable to most bulbs with large seeds, for example *Fritillaria*, tulips, and tender genera such as *Hippeastrum*.

Mix the seed with three or four times its bulk of moist peat substitute, peat, vermiculite, or perlite. The medium used should not exude water when squeezed. Add a little fungicide, place the mixture in small, plastic bags, then seal and label them.

For seed that benefits from an initial warm period, such as that of the smaller *Hippeastrum* species, keep the bags at about 21°C (70°F) – in an airing cupboard or near a central heating boiler. When the seed has germinated, prick out the seedlings into pots or trays of well-drained cutting compost and keep them in a cool place. If germination has not occurred after six to eight weeks, transfer the bags to a cold frame or cool greenhouse until it does.

HOW TO SCALE LILIES

1 Clean the lily bulb; remove and discard any damaged, outer scales. Gently snap off about 6 good scales, as close as possible to the base of the bulb.

2 Place some fungicidal powder in a plastic bag and add the scales. Shake the bag gently so that all the scales are thoroughly coated with the fungicide.

3 Remove any surplus fungicide from the bag. Place the coated scales into a second bag containing a 50:50 mix of peat substitute, or peat, and perlite.

4 Blow up the bag, then seal and label it. Store at 21°C (70°F) in a warm, dark place for 3 months. Then transfer to a refrigerator for 6–8 weeks.

5 When small bulblets have developed on the scales, remove the scales if they are soft. If they are fleshy and firm, leave them attached to the bulblets.

6 Plant the groups of bulblets either singly in small pots or several in a pan. Top-dress the pots with grit, label them, and leave them in a warm, light place.

7 The following spring, harden off the young bulbs by placing the pots in a cold frame.

8 In the autumn, when the bulbs have grown on, remove them from the pots and separate them. Pot them up individually or plant them in their permanent positions.

Scaling

Scaling is an important method of propagating lilies (*Lilium*) but it may also be used for other genera that have bulbs consisting of scales, for example some species of *Fritillaria*. The bulbs of most lilies are composed of concentric rings of scales attached at their lower ends to a basal plate. If these scales are detached from the parent bulb close to the base, so that they retain a small piece of basal tissue, they may develop bulblets, often near the base.

Remove lily scales for propagation in late summer or early autumn before root growth starts. Lift the dormant bulbs, then remove a few of the scales. Usually only a few are needed and the parent bulb may be replanted to flower the following season. If many new plants are required, scale the whole bulb. Alternatively, without lifting the parent bulbs, remove the soil from around them and snap off a few scales.

Select only disease-free, plump, unblemished scales. If using only a few scales for propagation, coat them with fungicide, then mix them together with damp peat substitute and perlite or vermiculite in a plastic bag. Seal the bag and place it in a warm, dark place at about 21°C (70°F) for three months. Then place the bag in a cold place, such as a refrigerator (but not a deep-freeze), for six to eight weeks to encourage bulblets to develop. When these form, fill some pots with a free-draining potting compost. Insert one or more scales, with their small bulblets attached, so that the tops of the scales are just below the compost surface.

Keep the pots in a shaded cold frame or cool greenhouse in hot weather. During the summer, plunge the pots of hardy bulbs in a frame or in a sheltered position in the open garden. At the end of the first growing season, separate the bulblets and repot them individually in a freely draining compost suitable for mature bulbs (see "Composts for bulbs under cover", p.240). Grow them on in a cold frame or a cool greenhouse until the following spring when they may be repotted into a container or planted in their flowering position in the garden.

HOW TO PROPAGATE BULBS BY TWIN-SCALING

1 Remove the brown, outer scales of a bulb (here a daffodil). With a sharp knife, trim off the roots without damaging the basal plate, and slice off the nose.

2 Place the bulb upside down on its cut end. Cut downwards through the basal plate to divide it into small sections, each piece having a section of basal plate.

3 Divide the sections into pairs of scales by peeling back the layers. Use a scalpel to cut each pair away with a piece of the basal plate attached (see inset).

Alternatively, after dusting with fungicide, insert the scales in trays filled with 2 parts damp vermiculite, perlite, or peat substitute mixed with 1 part coarse sand. Keep them moist and shaded, preferably in a warm greenhouse at about 21°C (70°F), for two months. In spring, move them to a cool place to promote good leaf growth; the bulblets may then be repotted singly and grown on for a year before being planted out.

Twin-scaling

This technique (see facing page) is used to build up stocks of genera such as daffodils, hyacinths, and snowdrops (*Galanthus*). Be sure to keep your hands, the knife, and the cutting surface scrupulously clean. Remove any old, outer scales from healthy, dormant bulbs. Cut each bulb into sections and then slice into pairs of scales, with each pair retaining a small section of the bulb's basal plate. After dusting the twin-scales with fungicide, place the twin-scales in a clear plastic bag filled with a mixture of equal parts perlite and moist peat substitute or peat. Inflate the bag, then seal, and label it. Store the bag at 21°C (70°F) in a dark place. When bulblets have formed, generally by spring, remove the twin-scales from the bag and pot them on, in the same way as for single scales (see p.248).

Cutting bulbs into sections

Sectioning bulbs is not widely used by amateur growers but it is useful for plants that do not divide freely or set seed. Bulbs may be sectioned near the end of the dormant period: parts of the basal plate may be cut through, or the entire bulb may be cut into pieces.

HOW TO PROPAGATE BULBS BY CHIPPING

1 *When the foliage has died down, lift the dormant bulbs and select a healthy, undamaged specimen (here* Hippeastrum*). Trim off the growing tip and roots without cutting into the basal plate.*

2 *Place the bulb on a clean cutting surface, with its basal plate uppermost. With a clean, sharp knife, carefully cut down into the bulb, dividing it into halves.*

3 *Cut each half of the bulb again in the same way, making sure that the basal plate is divided equally between the individual segments.*

4 *Repeat until the bulb has been cut into about 16 chips. Soak them in fungicide for 10–15 minutes, occasionally agitating the container. Drain off any excess moisture.*

5 *Half-fill some plastic bags with 11 parts vermiculite, moistened with 1 part water. Put several chips in each bag. Seal the bags with rubber bands or plastic twist-ties. Store in a warm, dark, airy place.*

6 *When bulblets appear around the basal plate of the chips, plant the chips individually into 6cm (3in) pots filled with a well-drained potting compost. Place in a sheltered position to grow on.*

Chipping

Many bulbs may be propagated at the end of the dormant period, for example in the early autumn, by cutting them into several segments or "chips". Chipping allows more rapid propagation of bulbs that do not increase rapidly by offsets. Large bulbs, such as daffodils or *Hippeastrum*, may be cut into as many as 16 chips; smaller daffodil bulbs and others, such as snowdrop bulbs, are usually chipped into four or eight.

Good hygiene is essential to avoid disease infecting the chips. Wear gloves if you are allergic to the sap that the bulbs release when cut. Clean and sterilize the bulbs with methylated spirit. Use a knife or scalpel that has been sterilized in methylated spirit to cut the bulbs on a clean, disinfected surface. Soak the chips in a fungicide such as benlate after cutting. Alternatively, dust the cut surfaces with flowers of sulphur.

Store the chips in the dark for 12 weeks in plastic bags of vermiculite that contain plenty of air. A temperature of 20–25°C (68–77°F) gives good results for most genera. Separate the young bulblets that develop on the chips, and pot them on into pans of freely draining potting compost. They tend to reach flowering size in two or three years.

Cutting up bulbs that have growing points

Some cyclamen species, particularly *C. hederifolium* and *C. rohlfsianum*, form multiple growing points on the

BULBS TO PROPAGATE BY CHIPPING

Erythronium
Fritillaria
Galanthus
Hippeastrum,
  some ❁ (spp.
  and hybrids)
Hyacinthus
Iris
Narcissus
Nerine, some ❁
Scilla, some ❁
Sternbergia

Hippeastrum 'Striped'

Key
❁ *Not hardy*

surface of the tubers. The corms of several genera, such as *Crocosmia* and *Gladiolus*, do the same. Such tubers and corms may be propagated by cutting them up, as long as each section has a growing point.

Prepare 5–6cm (2–3in) pots with several holes in the bottom for good drainage and almost fill them with well-drained potting compost.

CUTTING UP BULBS FOR PROPAGATION

1 *Take a large, healthy bulb (here* Cyclamen hederifolium*) and cut it into 2 or 3 pieces with a clean knife. Each piece must have at least one growing point. Dust the cut surfaces with fungicide.*

2 *Leave the pieces on a wire tray in a warm, dry place for 48 hours, until the cut surfaces form a callus (see inset). Pot them up individually into pots containing sharply drained compost.*

Dust the pieces with fungicide, and insert them singly, growing points uppermost, in the compost. Cover the tubers with more compost. Top-dress the pots with grit, label, and leave in a cold greenhouse until they begin to grow. Keep the compost moist enough to sustain the sections until growth starts.

Grow them on in well-lit conditions in a cold frame, and shade them from the hot summer sun. Water with care; do not let the young plants dry out when in growth. Plant them out the next autumn.

Simple cutting

Make cuts 0.5cm (¼in) deep with a sharp knife through a bulb's basal plate; the number of cuts depends on the bulb's size. Dust the cuts with fungicide. Keep the bulb in a plastic bag of damp perlite or vermiculite, and some fungicide, in a warm place.

The damage to the basal plate induces bulblets to form along the cuts. When these have formed, insert the bulb upside-down in a gritty compost made of 1 part peat substitute to 1 part perlite or coarse sand. Bulblets will develop above the old bulb. A year later, carefully separate the bulblets, and plant them in trays in a cool greenhouse to grow on.

HOW TO PROPAGATE HYACINTHS BY SCOOPING

1 Use a clean, sharpened teaspoon, or a knife, to scoop out the inner part of the bulb's basal plate, leaving the outer rim intact. Discard the basal plate.

2 Dip the cut surfaces in fungicide, then lay the bulbs, with their scooped areas uppermost, on a tray of sand. Place the tray in an airing cupboard.

3 Water the sand lightly as needed to keep it moist. When bulblets form around the edge of the scooped base, separate them from the parent and pot them up.

Scooping hyacinths

Scooping is a technique used for the commercial propagation of hyacinths. The centre of the basal plate of the bulb is scooped out and discarded, the exposed surface dusted with fungicide, and the bulb kept upside-down in warm, dark conditions. Numerous small bulblets eventually form on and around the cut surface. They may then be separated from the parent bulb and grown on in the same way as bulblets (see "Propagation from bulblets and bulbils", p.245) in individual pots.

Basal cuttings

The sprouting tubers of a few bulbs may be used in late winter for basal cuttings – young shoots that retain a piece of the parent tuber from which new roots develop. The cuttings are placed in a pan of moist compost until they root and are then potted up. For details of the technique, see DAHLIAS, How to Propagate by Basal Cuttings, p.235. Grow on rooted cuttings in a warm greenhouse until danger of frost is past. Harden them off in a cold frame and plant out in early summer. Propagate tuberous begonias and gloxinias (Sinningia speciosa) in this way in spring.

Scooping and scoring trilliums

Various cutting techniques may be used to propagate Trillium rhizomes in late summer, after the leaves have died down.

One method that avoids lifting the parent plant is to remove sufficient soil to expose the tops of the rhizomes and to score lightly a shallow cut around the growing point of each rhizome. Dust the cuts with a fungicide and cover the rhizomes with a top-dressing of peat substitute and coarse sand in equal parts, or cover them with soil if it is light and well draining. Small rhizomes should form along the cut surfaces and in time become large enough to propagate.

Alternatively, lift the rhizomes and scoop out their growing points. Make concave "scoops", rather than cutting across the base of the growing points, to ensure that no soft tissue remains that could rot. Dust the cut surfaces with fungicide and replant the rhizomes. Small rhizomes should then form around the excised growing tip.

One year later, expose the rhizomes, remove the young ones, and grow them on in pots as described for young seedlings (see "Care of seedlings", p.246).

HOW TO PROPAGATE TRILLIUMS BY SCORING

1 Carefully scrape away the topsoil to expose the rhizome. Score a shallow incision around it with a sharp, clean knife, just below the growing point (see inset).

2 Use a clean, soft brush to dust the cut surface of the rhizome with fungicidal powder.

3 Carefully cover the scored rhizome with a mix of peat substitute and coarse sand in equal parts to the same level as before. Gently firm it with your fingers.

4 A year later, remove the topsoil to expose the rhizomes and remove any young ones that have formed. Pot them up individually and grow them on.

CUTTING OUT GROWING POINTS

1 Remove the growing point of the rhizome entirely by making a cut in the form of a concave "scoop" with the tip of a clean, sharp knife.

2 Dust the cut surfaces of the parent rhizomes with fungicide. Cover them up again with soil and firm the soil down lightly.

Lilies

LILIES (*Lilium*) are among the most graceful of summer-flowering plants – their tall, slim stems bear flowers with an enormous variety of dazzling colours and exotic shapes. There are a great many to choose from – more than 80 species of lilies and thousands of hybrids, which are more tolerant of different conditions and so are often easier to grow.

Lily classification

Lilies are classified into nine divisions based on their origin, parentage, and flowers. It is now possible to cross lilies between different Divisions, using embryo-culture.

Div.I Hybrids of Asiatic species such as *L. cernuum* and *L. davidii*.
Div.II Hybrids of *L. martagon* and *L. hansonii*.
Div.III Hybrids of *L. candidum* and *L. chalcedonicum*.
Div.IV Hybrids of American species lilies such as *L. parryi*.
Div.V Hybrids of *L. longiflorum* and *L. formosanum*.
Div.VI (Aurelian hybrids): Trumpet lilies and *L. henryi* crosses.
Div.VII (Oriental hybrids): From Far Eastern species.
Div.VIII All other hybrids.
Div.IX All species and cultivars.

Where to grow lilies

Lilies need a well-drained position, and are excellent woodland plants and superb companions for roses. They often do not survive the competition experienced in herbaceous borders but can be grown in pots and placed where needed when in flower. Div.V lilies are not fully hardy, but make excellent pot plants for the cold greenhouse and conservatory.

Planting and care

Always buy fresh bulbs and plant them immediately. Do not buy any shrivelled bulbs. Most lilies grow well in a range of soils, but if grown in pots need slow-release fertilizer. Div.III lilies prefer alkaline soils and full sun; Div.VII hybrids must be grown in lime-free soil or ericaceous compost in containers; Div.IV hybrids are best suited to damp, woodland conditions. Plant lilies in autumn at two and a half times the depth of the bulb in well-prepared, free-draining soil; *L. candidum* needs only 2.5cm (1in) of soil above the bulb and should be planted in late summer. The routine care of lilies is similar to that of most bulbs (see pp.242–244); stake the plants well so that their flowering stems do not snap.

Propagation

Lilies may be propagated easily by stem bulbils, scaling, seed, or by simple division for *L. pardalinum* and Div.IV hybrids. Always propagate from healthy stock.

Bulbils and bulblets

Species such as *L. lancifolium* (syn. *L. tigrinum*), *L. bulbiferum*, and their hybrids produce stem bulbils in the leaf axils and bulblets at the base of the old flowering stem. Remove these and pot them up to grow on. The following autumn, plant them out together, or pot up individually.

Seed, scaling, and division

Seed sowing produces vigorous, virus-free bulbs (see "Growing lilies from seed", p.247), but is slow; Div.V lilies are easy to propagate in this way. For details of division and scaling, see pp.245 and 248.

LILY FLOWERS

Lilium martagon (long-lived and useful for shady areas)

***L.* Oriental Hybrids** (very scented; need acid soil)

***L.* 'Bright Star'** (an Aurelian hybrid; likes lime)

***L.* 'Connecticut King'** (an old Div.I hybrid; now in pink, red, and white forms)

L. regale (fragrant trumpets; easy to grow)

***L.* 'Scheherazade'** (hybrid cross Aurelian x Oriental)

Pests and diseases

Lilies are particularly vulnerable to several viruses (p.649) transmitted by aphids. *L. lancifolium* and some of its hybrids are carriers but show no symptoms; keep them away from other lilies to minimize infection. Grey mould (*Botrytis*) (p.646) may cause problems in damp, windless conditions, and poorly drained positions may encourage basal rot. Red lily beetle (p.644) destroys the foliage and flowers.

PROPAGATING FROM STEM BULBILS

1 *Throughout late summer, as soon as the bulbils loosen and are ripe, collect them from the leaf axils of the lily stems by carefully picking them off.*

2 *Insert the bulbils in pans of moist, loam-based potting compost, pressing them gently into the surface. Cover with grit, and label (see inset). Place in a cold frame until young bulbs develop.*

RAISING LILIES FROM BULBLETS

1 *After flowering, lift the bulb and dead stem, pick off the bulblets, and replant the main bulb. Alternatively, leave the bulb in the ground, cutting the stem above it to remove the bulblets.*

2 *Plant the bulblets, at twice their own depth, into 13cm (5in) pots of moist, loam-based potting compost. Cover with a layer of grit, label, and place in a cold frame until the spring.*

CHAPTER

9

Rock, Scree, and Gravel Gardening

Climate change and a growing interest in hard landscaping are inspiring many gardeners to create planting environments with rock and stone products – features that mimic high alpine habitats, or the sun-baked, stony soil of Mediterranean and desert environments. With this has come a growing appreciation of the often diminutive beauty and resilience of plants adapted to grow in such regions. Whether a traditional rock garden, or a simple gravelled bed or paved area studded with aromatic creeping plants and succulents, such features bring many rewards to the plant enthusiast.

Rock and rock plants in the garden

Alpines are plants that grow at high altitudes above the tree line, although the term is often loosely used to include a vast range of low-growing rock garden plants, including many bulbs, that may be grown successfully at relatively low altitudes. Their diminutive form and graceful habit make them suitable for grouping together in fascinating, brilliantly coloured collections.

True alpines

Alpines may be deciduous or evergreen woody plants, or they may be herbaceous, or grow from bulbs, corms, or tubers; few are annuals. They are characteristically hardy, adapted to survive in extremes of climate, and compact, with few over 15cm (6in) tall. In their native mountains, the dwarf or creeping habit of alpines reduces their wind resistance, and helps them resist the crushing weight of heavy snow in winter.

Plants in alpine regions experience very high sunshine and fresh, constantly moving air. Their cushion- or mat-forming habit and their small, fleshy, hairy, or leathery leaves protect them from water loss in high winds and hot sun. For example, edelweiss (*Leontopodium alpinum*) has its entire surface covered in woolly hairs, which help to conserve moisture, while the leaves of houseleeks (*Sempervivum*) have fleshy, water-retaining tissue.

Alpines are adapted to extremes of temperature, but few withstand constant wetness at the roots in winter or warm, humid, summer conditions. In their native habitats, they often grow in thin, poor soil that lacks nutrients and has a low organic content but allows rapid drainage. Most develop extensive, spreading root systems to seek out nutrients and moisture.

Rock garden plants

Rock plants are simply slow-growing plants of relatively small stature that are suitable in scale for growing in rock gardens. They include dwarf trees and shrubs, which are useful for framework (background) plantings, architectural plants, which give focus to a planting scheme, and many other plants that are not necessarily from alpine regions. Some, like *Armeria maritima*, occur in coastal habitats, while many miniature bulbs are native to sunny, Mediterranean hillsides. In common with true alpines, they share the need for free-draining soil and so are suitable for planting among alpines. Small perennials and dwarf drought-tolerant plants can be used to set the framework in a rock garden; they are also useful in a low-maintenance, gravel or scree garden.

Since many true alpines bloom in the spring and early summer, rock garden plants are especially valuable if they are late blooming, as they may extend the season of interest.

A well-furnished rock garden
This gently sloping rock garden is studded with a diverse range of alpine plants, from low-growing Dianthus *and saxifrages in the foreground to the dwarf shrubs* Genista lydia, Helianthemum, *and* Potentilla *at the rear.*

Alpines and rock plants in the garden

The restricted size of alpine and rock garden plants fits particularly well into the confines of the small, modern garden. Few other types of plant are so characteristically neat and compact and this allows a substantial collection of species and hybrids to be grown in a relatively small space.

Easily grown alpines

Many alpine species, and their more showy cultivars, are undemanding in their cultural requirements and easy to grow in the open garden. They present a wealth of habit and form, from tiny, cushion-forming plants to spreading mound- and mat-formers; some of the easier alpines bloom well into summer, almost invariably producing a profusion of flowers. The low-growing cultivars of *Aubrieta*, *Dianthus*, *Phlox*, and *Veronica* form mats of clear, bright colour, and may be used to edge beds, their informal, spreading habit gently softening straight lines.

Specialist alpines

Other alpine genera, like the Aretian *Androsace* and the tight cushion-forming saxifrages, have special requirements, in particular a need for very free-draining soil and protection

Planting in the open garden
Daphne x burkwoodii 'Somerset' bears a profusion of scented pink flowers that spill over the edge of a border and drift into the plants on either side.

from excessive winter wet. Most also require plenty of sun but their roots must be cool; lower-altitude, woodland species often prefer dappled shade and may need moist, acid soil.

The rich and varied colours and diverse forms of many specialist plants may still be enjoyed, however, as long as they have well-drained conditions and a suitable aspect. The best way to fulfil these requirements is to raise the plants above the underlying soil, planting them in specially

constructed or carefully controlled environments and using prepared, gritty, free-draining soil or composts.

Some alpine plants need a cool root run and shelter; rock gardens and pockets within stone or brick walls are ideal for such plants and display them to their best advantage in natural-looking surroundings. In more formal settings or if space is limited, raised beds or troughs and sinks are attractive alternatives, especially when they are constructed

from materials that complement any existing hard landscape features. Free-standing troughs and sinks also allow colour to be introduced at a variety of heights and on hard surfaces such as patios and paths.

The rock garden

A sunny, south- or south-west-facing slope makes an ideal site for the stony outcrops of a rock garden. Well-constructed gardens emulate natural rock formations and make striking features. They replicate, as nearly as possible, the natural habitat of alpine plants, creating the conditions in which they thrive – the soil beneath the rocks provides the cool, moist, but freely draining root run that they particularly enjoy.

Planning a rock garden

For the greatest visual impact, a rock garden should be constructed on as generous a scale as the site allows. Where possible, choose a naturally sloping, open site that provides good drainage. A series of rocky outcrops with gullies running in between is highly effective, especially if streams and pools are included in the design.

A sunny aspect will suit most rock plants, although those that prefer shade may be grown in cooler, shady pockets on the north side of large rocks. Careful placing of the rocks at the construction stage (see p.263) will provide a wide range of planting areas and rock niches to meet the needs of many different alpines.

Choosing plants

Several alpine species, such as *Gentiana verna*, with its flowers of intense blue in spring, prefer deep pockets of well-drained, gritty soil, while the mat-forming *Persicaria affinis* 'Donald Lowndes', for example, thrives in broader terraces between rock strata. Both *Lewisia* Cotyledon Hybrids and *Saxifraga* 'Tumbling Waters', which have cascades of white flowers over rosettes of lime-encrusted foliage, are most at home in the narrow crevices between vertical stone faces. Alpine or dwarf pinks such as *Dianthus alpinus* and *D.* 'Mars' provide evergreen, grey or green mats or cushions of neat foliage and masses of often clove-scented, single to double, red, pink, or white blooms throughout the summer and into autumn; they are at home in any well-drained site.

Plan the planting scheme to include as much seasonal variation as possible. Alpine bulbs such as *Crocus laevigatus* and *Iris histrioides* 'Major' help bring the garden

A blaze of summer colour
The brilliant red flowers of Sedum spurium *and* Helianthemum *cascading down the rocky outcrop make a striking contrast with the grey-green stems and leaves* of both Dianthus *and* Hebe pinguifolia *'Pagei' just behind them. The fresh green foliage of the surrounding plants provides a bright but cool counterpoint.*

Scree rock garden
Many rock plants retain the charm of wild flowers but selected forms and hybrids often display greater numbers of attractive, sometimes larger flowers in a range of clear colours. Some need a specialized environment, such as this scree bed, but many more are amenable plants that grow in any well-prepared site.

to life in winter or early spring, and *Cyclamen hederifolium* and *Sternbergia lutea* add interest in autumn. For year-round colour, include a few evergreens, such as the dwarf *Chamaecyparis obtusa* 'Nana Pyramidalis' and *Juniperus communis* 'Compressa', and dwarf shrubs such as *Hebe buchananii* 'Minor'.

Add texture and structure to the planting by using species with unusual leaves or stems and variation in height and form. Contrasting leaf texture can be particularly striking: bold, fleshy, rosette-forming plants may be used to offset the delicate, feathery leaves and flowers of *Pulsatilla* species, for instance, and a combination of spreading, cushion-forming, and trailing alpines with several dwarf shrubs or trees provides great visual interest. The sword-shaped, silver leaves of *Celmisia coriacea* contrast well with mat-forming plants such as *Polygala calcarea* 'Bulley's Form', with deep blue flowers in late spring and early summer, and *Campanula cochleariifolia*, with clusters of pale blue or white bells in summer.

Scree formations

On mountains, natural weathering produces a mass of small, broken rocks and stones. These loose stony slopes, known as screes, are home to plants that need plenty of moisture at their roots during the growing season, but grow best through an apparently dry 15cm (6in) surface layer of stones. Scree dwellers are among the most beautiful and jewel-like of alpine plants and well worth the extra care needed to grow them.

The scree bed

Scree beds attempt to re-create the specialized habitat of natural scree dwellers. Screes are deep, preferably gently sloping beds of loose rock fragments of varying size, into which is mixed a suitable compost (see p.262). Screes may be constructed on flat sites, raised from ground level to assist drainage, becoming, in effect, a form of raised bed (see p.257).

Scree dwellers usually form low mats or cushions of dense foliage, and many bear small brilliant blooms in such profusion that flowers almost completely obscure the leaves. The neutral background of small stones offers an ideal foil for rich textures and colours of this type of planting.

Specialist plants such as *Vitaliana primuliflora*, *Anchusa cespitosa*, and *Myosotis alpestris*, thrive in screes. Other rock garden plants which are easier to grow also appreciate these conditions. Some, such as *Achillea clavennae* and *Artemisia glacialis*, are grown primarily for their silver foliage, which provides a cool contrast for stronger colours. A number of species, including pink *Androsace carnea* subsp. *laggeri*, naturally self seed. Tiny, blue, bell-shaped flowers of *Campanula cochleariifolia* can also spring up around the garden but may become a nuisance if they begin to compete with less robust species.

Integrating the scree bed

If space is available, scree beds may be integrated with a rock garden to form a bold, unified design and provide a range of habitats. A backing of large rocks skirted by scree beds is particularly effective. Alternatively, add pockets of scree mixture to a rock garden to accommodate scree dwellers needing good drainage around their necks. *Dianthus haematocalyx,* for example, is a tightly tufted pink that benefits from a soil surface of loose, dry stones.

The visual effect of a scree bed is enhanced by incorporating just a few larger rocks. Plants may then be allowed to skirt their base or to grow over them to soften their outlines.

Gravel beds and paving

Areas of gravel or shingle and paving are alternatives to traditional, labour-intensive and water-hungry features such as herbaceous borders and lawns. Conservation concerns about the sourcing of hard materials have been partially allayed by the increasing range of manufactured stone products, many utilizing by-products of the quarrying industry. In appearance these are far more naturalistic than previous offerings, and hence much more attractive and easy to blend in to the garden.

Rock gardens and climate change

Rock, scree, and gravel gardens are sometimes considered to be labour-intensive, but in a changing climate where prolonged drought and hot summers are likely to become more frequent, their popularity may well increase. It is both a satisfying and enjoyable method of growing a wide range of attractive plants in a relatively small area, and an ecologically sensible way to garden.

Many of the plants used in these features are drought resistant, often with long taproots that delve deep into the soil to obtain water. The roots keep cool under the rocks, scree, or gravel as rainwater passes easily to the soil beneath, while evaporation from the surface of these materials is minimal.

Many alpine plants and small shrubs flourish in these conditions, and successional interest may be achieved by including small early- and late-flowering bulbous plants to complement the numerous colourful alpines available. Provided regular removal of weeds that arise from wind-blown seeds is carried out, these are all low-maintenance ways of creating attractive and colourful garden areas.

These hard landscaping features must be planted if they are not to appear harsh and sterile. However, in order to use successfully the rock garden and drought-tolerant plants that complement such materials, it is esssential that the underlying soil has the free drainage that they need. It may be necessary to improve the drainage by adding grit to the soil or even installing a rubble sub-base to act as a soakaway for excess water (see p.623). Incorporating a slope will also assist drainage. A gently sloping site facing the sun, with free-draining soil top-dressed with gravel or pebbles, is an ideal environment for a Mediterranean-style mixed planting. Coastal plants such as sea pinks (*Armeria*), sea lavender (*Limonium*), and horned poppies (*Glaucium flavum*) will also thrive. Instead of dwarf conifers as accent plants, try small grey-leaved shrubs such as *Convolvulus cneorum* and spiky perennials such as *Phormium*.

On a sunny patio, crevices and planting spaces between pavers filled with free-draining soil provide ideal conditions for low-growing, sun-loving plants. Patios also make attractive settings for containers of rock plants (see also "Troughs, sinks, and other containers", p.258).

Ericaceous plants

Alpine plants that require an acid soil or a woodland environment are not always easily accommodated in a rock garden. Acid-loving plants such as *Arctostaphylos*, *Cassiope*, gentians, and most *Vaccinium* species will only thrive in soil with a low pH, and woodland plants prefer moist, shady conditions and leafy, humus-rich soil. Specially constructed beds containing ericaceous compost provide a moist, acidic growing medium and, when sited in dappled shade, closely imitate woodland conditions.

Site and materials

Such acidic-humus beds may be constructed either as individual garden features or as extensions to a rock garden. The shady, north-facing side of a rock garden provides ideal conditions. Do not place an acidic-humus bed directly beneath trees since the drip from the leaves after rain may damage plants. For best results, the site should be in sun for part of the day.

Traditionally, such beds were filled with moss peat, which has a naturally low pH, good aeration, and excellent water retention. In view of current anxieties about conserving existing peat reserves, alternative composts based on leaf mould, bark, or coconut fibre, which have similar characteristics, should be used. Bark and coconut fibre often have large amounts of nitrogen added, mostly in the form of urea. These are suitable for fast-growing plants but too over-powering both for ericaceous ones and most rock garden plants.

A low raised bed
Here, a raised alpine bed flanks one side of a narrow stone path. The plants draw the eye along the path and entice the visitor to the open lawn beyond.

Raised beds

In small gardens, raised beds make highly economical use of limited space. In larger gardens, narrow raised beds may make a useful and attractive boundary feature. The formal appearance of raised beds blends in well with the design and layout of many modern gardens and, in areas where suitable rock is not easily available, or is prohibitively expensive, a raised bed provides a good substitute for a rock garden.

As drainage is independent of the underlying soil, raised beds are especially useful in gardens with poorly drained soils (such as wet, heavy clay) that are otherwise unsuitable for the cultivation of alpines. In addition, the dimensions of a raised bed may be planned so that the bed will easily accommodate a frame light to allow cultivation of choice species that require protection from too much winter wet, without restricting airflow around the plants.

Various materials may be used for constructing a raised bed, including traditional bricks or dry stones and wooden railway sleepers. For further information, see STRUCTURES AND SURFACES, "Raised beds", p.599.

Planting in raised beds

Large raised beds may be divided into separate areas or compartments, and different composts used in each to suit the specific requirements of different plant groups. Rocks may be added to the surface of the compost and bedded in to provide textural contrast and vertical niches and crevices for plants that demand them.

Rectangular raised beds present several aspects so that plants with different requirements may be planted in niches on their sunny or shady side. In addition to growing plants in

A tapestry of colour
A vivid display in which the rich colours and varied forms of the alpines blend with the evergreen shrubs and dwarf conifers, which form the framework of this attractive rock garden.

the bed itself, the walls may be designed to incorporate planting niches, in the same way as walls that are used for trailing species.

Choose plants that will give successional interest as the seasons progress. Dense, evergreen rosettes of *Haberlea rhodopensis* send up sprays of funnel-shaped flowers in spring, and may be succeeded in summer by *Aquilegia flabellata*, a clump-forming alpine that produces bell-shaped, soft blue flowers, each with fluted petals and a short spur. Both these plants prefer semi-shade and are small enough to be planted in a raised bed without overcrowding it.

For a sunnier aspect, choose compact species of *Dianthus*, such as *D. alpinus* and *D.* 'Bombardier', with *Erinus alpinus* 'Dr Hähnle' trailing from the retaining wall.

Walls

Garden walls may be modified to provide excellent sites for alpines and rock garden plants. The walls of raised beds and those used to retain banks of earth on a terraced slope may be modified in the same way. If possible leave spaces, crevices, or cracks between the stones or brickwork during the construction of such walls so that these may be planted up when building is complete.

Choosing plants

Mat-forming plants are most suitable, like *Acantholimon glumaceum*, which forms evergreen cushions that are clothed in pink flowers during summer, or *Dianthus deltoides* and other alpine pinks. Plants prone to rotting at the collar, such as *Lewisia* and *Ramonda* species, are well suited to being grown in walls, since the roots enjoy the cool conditions and extra drainage provided by the crevices. Trailing, semi-evergreen *Asarina procumbens*, with creamy-white, snapdragon-like flowers, and shrubby *Penstemon newberryi* f. *humilior*, with a profusion of flowers on arching branches, are also ideal.

Dry-stone walls

These provide ample room for the root systems of many rock garden plants to penetrate, and also allow sharp drainage. Free-standing, single or double dry-stone walls with carefully chosen plants make extremely attractive features. The well-drained tops provide an ideal home for mat-forming plants, such as *Gypsophila repens* or *Saponaria ocymoides*; both will cascade attractively over the edge of the wall. The neat, spreading rosettes of lime-encrusted saxifrages

An alpine trough collection
A collection of troughs makes an appealing feature. Large troughs accommodate dwarf trees and shrubs as well as smaller alpine plants.

and houseleeks (*Sempervivum*) may be dotted at intervals across the surface, and using both vertical faces of a wall will allow both sun and shade-loving plants to be grown.

Troughs, sinks, and other containers

Containers provide an opportunity to grow alpines in a small garden, and may also be used to flank pathways or steps. Old stone sinks and troughs make handsome containers for rock plants, although both are scarce and expensive. However, troughs made of reconstituted stone or hypertufa, and glazed sinks coated with this material (see p.266) are inexpensive alternatives. Troughs and sinks can be used as features for patios and courtyards, or on terraces and gravelled areas in larger gardens (see also CONTAINER GARDENING, "Using containers", pp.306–318).

Planting in troughs

The smallest alpine species are often the most intricate. *Antennaria dioica* 'Minima' and other compact alpines and rock plants should be used for such displays. By careful selection, a plant community of dwarf and slow-growing species may be planted to make up a rock garden in miniature.

Try to introduce some variation in height. Use small conifers, such as *Chamaecyparis obtusa* 'Nana Pyramidalis' or *Juniperus communis* 'Compressa', and dwarf trees such as *Ulmus parvifolia* 'Geisha' as framework plants, choosing others such as *Campanula zoysii*, *Dianthus alpinus*, or *D. microlepis* for the middle and foreground. Miniature shrubs may be added to provide contrasting form and colour throughout the year.

Other containers

If an appropriate compost is used and the plants are well maintained, almost any container may be used to good effect, provided that it has adequate drainage. Large flower pots and tubs are suitable for small collections of the tiniest alpines, especially those that trail over edges, such as *Silene schafta*. Small containers suit compact, slow-growing alpines such as *Androsace chamaejasme* and *Sempervivum arachnoideum*. Old chimney pots make very attractive features planted with *Sedum* or *Sempervivum* species.

The alpine house

In the wild, many alpines spend their winter dormancy insulated by a deep snow blanket that shields them from

An unusual container
Many different types of container may be used for rock plants and alpine species. Here, part of a hollowed-out tree trunk has been planted with Sedum spathulifolium *'Cape Blanco', valued for its small clusters of tiny, yellow flowers above the rosettes of silvery-green leaves.*

excess water, cold drying winds, and severe frosts; temperatures under the snow cover hover at, or just below, freezing point. In gardens at lower altitudes, where conditions are very different, the more exacting alpines need the protection of glass.

A simple, open cloche may be sufficient protection for some plants but a specially designed greenhouse, or alpine house (see GREENHOUSES AND FRAMES, "Alpine house", p.569), greatly extends the range that may be grown, and allows the enthusiastic gardener to try growing some of the most challenging plants. Containers are especially suitable for cultivating miniature species, and allow plants such as the tiny *Primula scotica*, with its golden-eyed purple flowers, to be appreciated and grown in a situation where they will not be swamped by larger and more vigorous neighbours. Ranging several containers together provides a good opportunity to build up collections devoted to plants of one genus that flourish under similar environmental conditions.

Using an alpine house

An alpine house will accommodate a huge range of the choicest alpines in carefully controlled conditions. The season of interest in the alpine house may be maintained throughout the early winter months, when colour in the open garden is scarce. Interest increases rapidly in early spring, when the majority of true alpines flower. Where dwarf shrubs, bulbs, conifers, and ferns are also included in the collection, there will be something to attract attention throughout the year (see also ALPINE HOUSES AND FRAMES, pp.277–279).

Planter's guide to rock plants

EXPOSED SITES

Rock plants that tolerate exposed or windy sites

Antennaria dioica
Campanula portenschlagiana
Carlina acaulis
Chiastophyllum oppositifolium
Crepis incana
Dryas octopetala
Erigeron karvinskianus
Eryngium, some ✽, ◣
Euphorbia myrsinites
Hebe, some ✽, ◣
Helianthemum
Limonium bellidifolium
Pterocephalus perennis
Sedum, some ✽, ◣
Sempervivum
Silene uniflora
Veronica spicata

AIR POLLUTION

Rock plants that tolerate polluted air

Aubrieta
Aurinia saxatilis
Campanula garganica,
    C. poscharskyana
Erinus alpinus
Euphorbia, some ✽, ◣
Sedum, some ✽, ◣
Sempervivum

DRY SHADE

Rock plants that tolerate dry shade

Ajuga pyramidalis, A. reptans
Dianthus carthusianorum,
    D. deltoides
Diascia barberae 'Fisher's Flora',
    D. barberae 'Ruby Field'
Erodium guttatum
Genista sagittalis
Gypsophila repens
Helleborus, some ✽
Lamium maculatum
Saponaria ocymoides
Waldsteinia
    ternata

*Waldsteinia
ternata*

MOIST SHADE

Rock plants that prefer moist shade

Adonis amurensis
Cassiope
Cyclamen hederifolium,
    C. purpurascens
Daphne blagayana

Galax urceolata
Hepatica nobilis,
    H. transsilvanica
Hylomecon japonica
Iris cristata
Meconopsis cambrica
Primula, some ✽ (many spp.
    and cvs)
Sanguinaria canadensis
Shortia uniflora
Stylophorum diphyllum
Trillium

SCREE GARDENS

Acantholimon glumaceum
Aethionema grandiflorum,
    A. 'Warley Rose'

*Androsace
lanuginosa*

Alyssum montanum
Androsace lanuginosa,
    A. sarmentosa,
    A. sempervivoides
Dianthus alpinus, D. anatolicus,
    D. erinaceus
Erinus alpinus
Gypsophila aretioides
Linaria alpina
Papaver burseri,
    P. fauriei,
    P. rhaeticum
Pritzelago alpina
Sempervivum
Silene acaulis
Viola cornuta 'Minor', V. jooi

CREVICES AND PAVING

Aubrieta deltoidea (many cvs)
Aurinia saxatilis
Campanula cochleariifolia,
    C. portenschlagiana
Erinus alpinus
Erodium reichardii
Geranium sanguineum var. striatum
Globularia cordifolia
Mentha requienii
Onosma alborosea, O. echioides
Pratia pedunculata
Scabiosa graminifolia
Thymus, some ✽

WALL CREVICES

Antirrhinum hispanicum, A. molle
Aurinia saxatilis 'Citrina'
Campanula portenschlagiana
Erinus alpinus
Globularia cordifolia

Haberlea rhodopensis (shade)
Lewisia Cotyledon Hybrids
Onosma taurica
Polemonium pulcherrimum
Ramonda myconi (shade)
Saxifraga callosa, S. cochlearis,
    S. longifolia, S. paniculata
Silene uniflora 'Robin Whitebreast'

PLANTING IN TROUGHS

Anchusa cespitosa
Androsace (small spp. and cvs)
Antennaria dioica 'Minima'
Arenaria purpurascens
Asperula suberosa
Daphne (some)
Dianthus alpinus, D. freynii,
Dryas octopetala 'Minor'
Edraianthus pumilio
Gentiana saxosa, G. verna
    subsp. angulosa
Helianthemum oelandicum
Linum suffruticosum subsp.
    salsoloides 'Nanum'
Myosotis alpestris
Omphalodes luciliae ✽
Oxalis enneaphylla
Paraquilegia anemonoides
Petrophytum hendersonii
Phlox subulata
Primula farinosa,
    P. marginata

*Saxifraga
sancta*

Saxifraga, some ✽ (many spp.
    and cvs)
Sedum cauticola
Soldanella alpina, S. montana
Thymus serpyllum 'Minus'
Vitaliana primuliflora

PLANTING IN TUFA

Androsace (small spp. and cvs)
Campanula piperi, C. zoysii
Draba mollissima, D. polytricha
Edraianthus pumilio
Paraquilegia anemonoides
Physoplexis comosa
Potentilla nitida
Saxifraga, some ✽ (many types,
    especially the Kabschias)
Viola cazorlensis, V. delphinantha

RAISED BEDS

Aethionema 'Warley Rose'
Androsace
Antirrhinum molle, A. sempervirens
Aquilegia discolor, A. flabellata
Armeria juniperifolia

Bolax gummifera
Callianthemum anemonoides
Campanula raineri, C. zoysii
Daphne arbuscula, D. cneorum,
    D. petraea 'Grandiflora',
    D. x susannae 'Cheriton'
    D. x whiteorum 'Beauworth'
Dianthus, some ✽
Draba rigida var. bryoides
Edraianthus dinaricus,
    E. graminifolius
Erinacea anthyllis
Gentiana acaulis,
    G. verna subsp. angulosa
Globularia meridionalis, G. repens
Haberlea rhodopensis
Leontopodium alpinum,
    L. alpinum subsp. nivale
Lewisia (some spp. and hybrids)
Origanum (some spp. and hybrids)
Oxalis adenophylla,
    O. enneaphylla, O. 'Ione Hecker'
Papaver burseri, P. fauriei
Paraquilegia anemonoides
Primula auricula, P. marginata
Ramonda myconi
Saxifraga cotyledon, S. longifolia,
    S. 'Tumbling Waters'
Sempervivum
Silene acaulis
Verbascum 'Letitia'

DWARF SHRUBS

Berberis x stenophylla 'Corallina
    Compacta'
Betula nana
Chamaecyparis obtusa 'Intermedia'
Cryptomeria japonica 'Vilmoriniana'
Daphne cneorum, D. retusa,
    D. sericea
Erinacea anthyllis
Euryops acraeus
Genista delphinensis
Hebe buchananii
    'Minor'
Ilex crenata 'Mariesii'
Juniperus communis
    'Compressa'

*Ozothamnus
coralloides*

Lotus hirsutus
Ozothamnus coralloides.
Picea abies 'Clanbrassiliana',
    P. abies 'Gregoryana', P. glauca
    var. albertiana 'Conica'
Potentilla fruticosa 'Nana Argentea'
Salix x boydii
Sorbus reducta

Key

✽ *Not hardy*
◣ *Rock garden species only*

Construction, soil preparation, and planting

Various methods may be used to grow alpine plants in gardens. Planting them in a rock garden is perhaps the best-known method, although this can take up a great deal of space. For a smaller display, screes, raised and peat beds, and the crevices of walls can make very attractive features. Where space is more limited, troughs, sinks, and other containers may also be used for a fine alpine display.

ROCK PLANTS FOR ACID SOIL

Arctostaphylos alpina
Cassiope
Corydalis cashmeriana,
   C. flexuosa
Cyananthus
Epigaea gaultherioides,
   E. repens
Galax urceolata
Gaultheria
Gentiana sino-ornata
Glaucidium palmatum
Haberlea rhodopensis
Kalmia angustifolia,
   K. microphylla
Leiophyllum buxifolium
Leucopogon fraseri
Leucothöe keiskei
Linnaea borealis
Lithodora diffusa
Menziesia ciliicalyx
Mitchella repens
Ourisia caespitosa,
   O. coccinea, O. 'Loch Ewe'

Phyllodoce
caerulea

Paris polyphylla
Phyllodoce caerulea,
   P. nipponica
Pieris nana
Polygala chamaebuxus,
   P. vayredae
Primula boothii alba,
   P. gracilipes,
   P. nana,
   P. sonchifolia
Pyrola rotundifolia
Rhododendron (dwarf spp.)
Sanguinaria canadensis
   f. *multiplex*
Shortia soldanelloides
Soldanella villosa
Tanakaea radicans
Vaccinium delavayi,
   V. myrtillus, V. uliginosum

Buying plants

The rock garden should be regarded as a feature that will provide, with careful choice of plants, interest all year round.

Before buying any plants, refer to standard texts to find out the likely range of plants that is suitable for a particular type of locality in terms of climate, soil, and general situation. Visit established rock gardens in parks and botanic gardens, as well as specialist nurseries, to assess the relative merits of various plants for your own requirements. The shape, form, and colour of foliage, fruits, stems, and the overall growth habit are often as important as flowers.

Where to buy plants

Plants are available from a wide range of sources, including garden centres and specialist nurseries. Non-specialist outlets often sell a limited range of colourful cultivars and easily grown species; these may form large, spreading clumps that quickly overwhelm more delicate plants in the rock garden.

The experienced nurseryman is able to advise on the most suitable choice of plants for a particular situation, and often has display beds of mature plants. These give a good indication of the ultimate size, spread, and habit of different plants, and are invaluable at the planning stage. Such specialist outlets may also be consulted for information on composts and suppliers of rock.

A much wider range of plants will be offered by the specialist grower, who is also able to provide detailed advice on cultivation – this is particularly useful for the beginner. Demand for rare or unfamiliar plants sometimes means that general suppliers may carry stocks of plants that are best left to the specialist, since they are often unsuitable for the average rock garden. Such plants may be attractive but are often expensive and may be difficult to cultivate. They offer a rewarding challenge, but only purchase them after obtaining advice on growing them.

Selecting alpine plants

Choose plants that have healthy, compact foliage, and no sign of pests and diseases or water deprivation. Do not buy plants with yellowing or weak growth, since this indicates that they have been kept in poor light. Labels should bear the name of the plant as well as details of flowering times and brief cultivation

HOW TO SELECT ALPINE PLANTS

GOOD EXAMPLE

Saxifraga

Healthy looking, compact growth

Weed-free compost

POOR EXAMPLES

Unbalanced, weak growth

Weeds in compost

Roots curled around inside of pot

requirements. Plants should not be pot-bound and the roots should either not be visible, or only just, through the hole in the base of the pot. Do not purchase any plants that have rooted into the material on the surface of the display area, since these are almost certain to be pot-bound.

The top-growth of a plant may remain healthy for some time after the root system has been damaged or has actually died, so check that the plant has a healthy root system by sliding it out of its pot and inspecting the root ball carefully.

Large specimens are sometimes available but unless they are grown on correctly, with careful attention to watering, they may take much longer to become established than smaller, vigorous ones.

Select plants that are as weed-free as possible. Before planting, gently scrape off the grit or surface compost so that any weed seeds are removed. Introducing weeds such as pearlwort (*Sagina procumbens*) and hairy

bittercress (*Cardamine hirsuta*), causes problems as, once established, they are difficult to eradicate.

A number of plants that are sold for growing in the rock garden, such as some of the ornamental onions (*Allium*), are over-prolific seeders. Choose plants carefully to avoid introducing such problem plants.

Siting a rock garden or scree bed

Good siting is critical for a rock garden or scree bed, because alpine plants require good light and well-drained conditions in order to thrive. The rock garden or scree should also blend in well with the rest of the garden. Before beginning construction, sketch out a rough plan on paper showing the rock garden or scree bed in relation to other garden features. A scree may be integrated into a rock garden or, alternatively, built as a separate feature.

SITING A ROCK GARDEN

Sloping ground

Limit of afternoon shade from nearby plants

Limit of morning shade from hedge

Build a rock garden on sloping ground, if possible, to ensure sharp drainage. Choose an open site that receives full sun, away from the roots and overhanging branches of trees and large shrubs.

Choosing the site

Choose an open, sunny site away from overhanging trees; trees drip water onto plants beneath, and leaves shed in autumn may also smother plants or create a damp atmosphere that rots them. Tree roots may also compete with the plants for moisture and nutrients. Do not site a rock garden or scree in a frost pocket or on a site exposed to cold, drying winds. A sloping site is ideal for a rock garden; it will have excellent drainage, and artificial outcrops of rock may be made to look more natural, and provide different pockets and aspects to suit a variety of plants. Scree beds (see p.264) or raised beds (see p.269) are usually better for level sites.

A rock garden or scree is best sited where it will blend into an informally planted area of the garden, on a slope, by a terrace, or as a natural-looking outcrop from an area of shrubs. Plan any water features, such as a pond or stream, into the scheme from an early stage. If the rock garden or scree is to be next to a lawn, ensure that it does not interfere with cutting and edging. It is unlikely to look natural next to herbaceous borders, bedding displays, or any other formally planted areas, such as the vegetable or fruit garden. If the main garden is formal, it may be better to grow alpines in a rectangular raised bed (see p.269) rather than trying to integrate the informality of a rock garden into the design.

Choosing stone

Buy salvaged or second-hand natural stone for rock garden construction wherever possible; otherwise try local quarries to inspect the rock and

Natural strata

Sedimentary rock, such as chalk and limestone, occurs naturally in distinct layers, or stratum lines, that are clearly visible to the eye. Rocks of this type may easily be split along the stratum lines for use in rock gardens.

Sedimentary rocks that occur in nature always have stratum lines following the same direction; it is important to place the stones in a rock garden to simulate the same kind of effect, otherwise they will look too obviously artificial.

Natural stratum lines

choose suitable pieces that are not too large to handle after being delivered. Choose stone in a range of different sizes to construct a natural-looking outcrop. Garden centres may offer a range of stone, although there is sometimes a limited choice of size and shape. Reconstituted stone products may also be available.

Natural stone

Some types of rock, especially water-washed limestones, are now under great threat in their native surroundings and, for conservation reasons, should not be used. Occasionally, long-quarried, weathered limestone is available second-hand, but do not purchase freshly quarried limestone or rock that has been collected from its natural surroundings or removed from stone walls.

Do not use soft, quick-weathering rock, such as shales and chalk, or hard, featureless, igneous rocks without strata, such as granite and basalt. Hard stone with no clear strata may be inexpensive but is difficult to

use, takes several years to acquire a weathered appearance, and seldom looks natural. Other materials, such as slate, are also used but are sometimes difficult to blend in.

The most suitable rocks are the various sandstones, in which the natural strata or layers are clearly visible. One great advantage of using rocks with stratum lines is that they may easily be split. Alternatively, you may be lucky enough to find a source of tufa, also known as "old horse bone" – a porous, limy rock filled with numerous air pockets. Its light weight makes it easy to transport and handle. Cavities for plants may be dug or drilled out of its relatively soft surface. It provides ideal conditions for many plants that require free drainage.

Artificial rocks

Reconstituted rocks made from quarry waste and even fibreglass "rocks" can also be obtained; they may be more or less convincing in appearance and need careful blending in with suitable top-dressings (see pp.264–265) and planting to appear natural. It is possible to produce artificial rocks on a garden scale from a mix of 2 parts sharp sand, 2 parts coir, and 1 part Portland cement, to which colouring powders may be added. The mix is worked into moulds formed from polythene-lined holes excavated in the soil.

Soils and soil mixes

In nature, many alpines and rock garden plants grow in "soil" that is largely made up of rock fragments and gravel, usually with some accumulations of humus-rich detritus, which retains moisture. Such a growing medium is extremely well drained and it is important to simulate this as closely as possible in a rock garden or scree bed. Ordinary

Types of stone

Tufa is an excellent choice for the rock garden because its soft, porous nature means that plants may be grown in cavities on its surface as well as in crevices between the stones. Natural-looking, weather-worn sandstone is also a good choice, as is limestone (if available second-hand).

Tufa

Sandstone

Limestone (Kentish Rag)

ROCK PLANTS FOR SANDY SOIL

Acaena caesiiglauca,
  A. microphylla
Achillea x *kellereri*
Aethionema 'Warley Rose'
Arabis procurrens
  'Variegata'
Arenaria montana
Armeria juniperifolia
Artemisia schmidtiana 'Nana'
Ballota pseudodictamnus
Cytisus x *beanii*
Dianthus carthusianorum,
  D. deltoides
Erodium guttatum
Gypsophila repens
Helianthemum
Iberis saxatilis

Lewisia
Cotyledon
Hybrids

Lewisia Cotyledon
  Hybrids
Linum suffruticosum
Onosma echioides, O. taurica
Phlox bifida
Saponaria ocymoides
Sedum, some ❋
Sempervivum

ROCK PLANTS FOR VERY ALKALINE SOIL

Aethionema
Alyssum
Anemone multifida
Aubrieta
Campanula, some ❋
Dianthus, some ❋
Draba
Erysimum helveticum
Geranium farreri
Gypsophila repens
Helianthemum
Leontopodium alpinum
Linaria alpina
Origanum

Origanum
'Kent Beauty'

Papaver burseri,
  P. fauriei
Pulsatilla
Rhodanthemum
  hosmariense
Saponaria ocymoides
Saxifraga, some ❋
Sedum, some ❋ (spp. only)
Sempervivum (spp. only)
Silene schafta
Thymus caespititius

Key
❋ *Not hardy*

garden soils may be adapted, to some extent, for cultivating most rock garden plants and alpines by adding peat substitute (or peat) and/or grit, but large quantities of grit are required to provide the rapid drainage needed for the more moisture-sensitive species, such as those grown in scree beds.

Standard mix

A mix of 1 part sterilized garden soil, 1 part peat substitute (or peat), and 1 part sharp sand or coarse grit is suitable for most rock garden plants.

The humus-rich materials ensure moisture retention, while the sand or grit maintains good drainage.

Scree mixture

Scree plants will require a very free-draining compost. Make up a soil mixture using the same ingredients as for the standard mix, but in different proportions: 3 parts coarse grit or stone chippings (not sand) instead of 1 part. In order to produce an even freer-draining compost, increase the proportion of stony material included

in the mix. In dry areas, this proportion of stone chippings may have to be reduced to 2 parts; alternatively, use a more water-retentive mix consisting of 2 parts loam, 2 parts leaf mould, 1 part sharp sand, and 4 parts stone chippings.

Special mixes

Some choice alpines, such as the tiny, cushion-forming *Androsace* species and saxifrages, need very free-draining compost. These plants usually come from high altitudes

where soil nutrient levels are low. Use a mix of 2 or 3 parts chippings or gravel, to 1 part loam or leaf mould (or peat substitute or peat).

For acid-lovers use a mix of 4 parts lime-free leaf mould, peat substitute (or peat), composted bark, or bracken litter with 1 part coarse sand. On an alkaline soil, however, growing plants in pockets of acid mixture is only effective in the short term, due to the inevitable percolation of lime, which soon kills them. A better solution is to grow these plants in ericaceous beds (see p.269).

Constructing a rock garden

Never attempt to construct rock gardens when the soil is wet, since heavy rocks may compact the soil and severely damage its structure; this interferes with drainage and causes problems with the establishment and growth of the plants. If the site is grassed, cut the turf carefully and remove it for later use when constructing the rock garden.

Clearing weeds

Remove all perennial weeds from the site and, if siting the rock garden near trees or shrubs, remove any suckers that these may have produced. Perennial weeds are very difficult to eradicate from an established rock garden, so it is essential to dig them out or kill them (see PLANT PROBLEMS, "Weeds", pp.669–673).

Drainage

Make sure that the site, particularly if level, is well drained, and if necessary install a soakaway or other drainage system (see SOILS AND FERTILIZERS, "Improving drainage", p.623). This is important on heavy clay soils. Do not simply dig deep holes – these act as sumps in which the water remains, unless they are connected to a drainage ditch. Raising the rock garden above the level of the surrounding ground helps to improve drainage. On naturally sloping sites drainage is not usually a problem, although a drainage ditch may be needed at the lowest point.

If the underlying drainage is good, just dig the soil over and remove any perennial weeds. Then consolidate the soil by treading gently to avoid subsequent sinking; fork over the surface of the soil to maintain good soil structure.

Building the base

Put down a 15cm (6in) layer of coarse rubble, broken bricks, stones, ballast, angular gravel, or pea shingle.

PLANTING AND TOP-DRESSING

1 *Before starting to plant, water all the plants and allow them to drain. To check the planting arrangement, set out the pots on the surface of the bed, taking account of the eventual height and spread of the plants.*

2 *Carefully remove each plant from its pot and loosen the root ball a little to encourage the roots to spread. Remove any moss and weeds before planting.*

3 *Using a trowel, dig a hole large enough to accommodate the root ball. Ease the plant into the hole, and label.*

4 *Fill in around the plant with compost and firm gently, making sure that there are no air pockets between the root ball and the compost.*

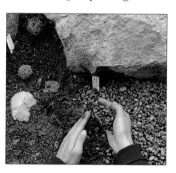

5 *Top-dress the compost with a layer of grit or gravel, easing a little around the collars of the plants.*

6 *Continue to plant in the same way until the rock garden is complete. Check that the whole area is properly top-dressed and water in the plants well.*

The finished rock garden
The plants will soon grow away to produce an attractive and mature-looking rock garden.

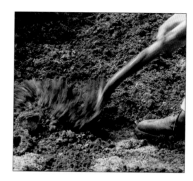

Drainage
Unless a site is very well-drained, the drainage can be improved by digging over the soil and mixing it thoroughly with plenty of sharp sand or gravel. Firm well after digging and let it settle before planting.

Spread over this a layer of inverted turves, if available; these prevent compost from the rock garden clogging the free-draining layer at the base, without inhibiting normal drainage. If turves are not available, use a polypropylene sheet, with holes punctured at regular intervals to allow water to drain through.

Purchase topsoil or bring in good soil from elsewhere in the garden, ensuring that it is as weed-free as possible; use this for the top layer of the rock garden. Specially prepared, sharply drained compost (see p.262) should be used for filling in between stones where plants are to be grown.

Placing the stone

Rock is heavy and rough on the hands, so wear gloves and protective footwear. Use rollers to move large rocks, and arrange for the consignment to be delivered as close to the site of the rock garden as possible. To manoeuvre large rocks into their final positions, it may be necessary to use a block and tackle, with a steel crowbar as a lever for final adjustments. Mark the approximate positions of larger rocks first, to avoid unnecessary labour.

Select first the large stones that will act as "keystones". These are the dominant rocks from which each outcrop is developed. Position the largest of the keystones first, and then arrange the remaining ones so that the strata flow naturally from them to form outcrops. Further large stones acting as subsidiary keystones may then be used to extend the outcrops. Use enough rock to make the outcrops realistic, while leaving sufficient room for planting. Check progress visually as construction proceeds. If the rocks being used have stratum lines, ensure that these all run in the same direction and at the same angle.

The rocks should be placed to provide the widest range of opportunities for planting. For example, butting rocks together serves to create the narrow crevices in which a variety of plants may thrive. Where space allows, a carefully planned, tiered rock garden may produce a number of useful, broad planting pockets between the rocks.

Bury the rocks to a third of their volume and tip them backwards slightly. This ensures stability and allows water to drain back off the rock into the soil of the bed rather than onto the plants beneath. Stand on the rocks to make sure that they are completely stable.

As rocks are positioned, infill planting spaces with prepared compost and firm it in. Any obvious unconformities in the rocks may then be masked by careful planting.

To provide a cool, well-drained cavity for alpines and rock plants, plant them between two layers of stone as the rock garden is constructed. Position the plants in the soil close to a stone that has already been firmed in and add a little compost around the roots, firming gently. Use small rocks to protect the plants as the next stone is positioned against the first to form a planting pocket. The small rocks can then be removed and the second stone firmed in place. Add more compost around the plants and infill with soil between the stones before top-dressing.

Planting a rock garden

Alpines and rock garden plants are almost always purchased as pot plants and may be planted at any time of the year, although it is better not to plant them when the ground is either wet or frozen, or during very warm or dry periods.

Water all the plants thoroughly before planting and allow them to drain. Set the plants out in the planned positions while still in their pots to give an idea of the finished planting. Make any rearrangements at this stage and adjust planting distances, allowing for the vigorous and rapid growth of some types. Slide each plant carefully out of its pot and remove any weeds from the compost. Inspect the roots and top-growth for pests and diseases and treat, as necessary, before planting (see PLANT PROBLEMS, pp.639–673).

Make a planting hole with a trowel or hand fork, ensuring that the hole is big enough to accommodate the roots. Loosen the root ball gently, position the plant in the hole, and

Crevice gardening

Creating special crevice gardens, either as part of a rock garden or as a separate feature, has become popular as a method of growing a large number of alpines and rock plants in a relatively limited area. Crevices are ideal for growing alpines that enjoy cool, well-drained sites which allow their extensive root systems to spread widely into the soil below.

Plants in crevices may be hard to establish and need extra care when planting. To avoid the risk of a rock slipping when planting horizontal crevices, support the upper rock with small stones and plant between them. When planting in vertical crevices, small stones can also be used to retain the compost (see "Planting in vertical crevices", p.268). If planting in the crevices of an established rock garden, use a small tool, such as a widger, to make a planting hole.

Use young, rooted cuttings with vigorous root systems. If only pot-grown plants are available, trim the root balls and top-growth to the appropriate size. Put a small stone in the crevice, place a little compost on top, then ease in the roots with a widger so that the plant faces outwards. Add more compost and firm in, placing a small stone on top of the root ball for extra support.

Crevice garden construction
Layers of narrow rocks or slates may be placed almost vertically to mimic rock strata; fill between rocks with a free-draining soil mixture: 2 parts loam, 2 parts leaf mould, 1 part sharp sand, and 4 parts stone chippings.

Using colour and texture
This crevice garden is dominated by its rocks and punctuated by plants. Here, contrast is achieved and interest is added by using a seam of broken slate among the larger, more structurally important rocks. The red foliage of the Sempervivum *complements both types of rock.*

firm in the compost. The plant should sit with the collar slightly above the surface of the compost to leave room for a top-dressing of gravel or chippings.

When all the plants are in place, water them in thoroughly. Keep them moist, watering at intervals until they are established and starting to make new growth. If planting is followed by a dry period, water the plants at approximately weekly intervals until the roots have penetrated the surrounding compost. Thereafter, there should be no need to water except during a drought.

Aftercare

Use netting or other deterrents to protect newly planted alpines from birds. Periodically refirm any plants that may have worked loose, adding new compost if necessary. Label the plants or maintain a planting plan to record their names at the time of planting; update planting plans and labelling as plants are added, replaced, or relocated.

Wildlife in the rock garden

Although rock gardens are not garden features that are obviously likely to benefit wildlife, there are many rock garden species and cultivars that bees and butterflies, as well as other beneficial insects, visit to obtain nectar and pollen.

Among rock-garden plants that will attract insects are *Aubrieta*, *Arabis*, and *Iberis* species and cultivars, as well as dwarf marjorams, like *Origanum amanum* and *O.* 'Kent Beauty', sedums, pinks, campanulas and some *Crocus* and *Muscari* species.

Similarly, dwarf shrubs like *Daphne cneorum*, *D. collina*, and *D.* x *hendersonii* cultivars, rock roses (*Helianthemum* species and cultivars), and lavenders, which are all rich in nectar or pollen, provide food for a multitude of butterflies, moths, beetles, bees, and many other insects.

Constructing a scree bed

Prepare the site in a similar way to a rock garden, installing artificial drainage, if necessary (see SOILS AND FERTILIZERS, "Improving drainage", p.623). Sloping sites have naturally good drainage but on flat ground screes are best raised slightly above the ground to assist drainage, and retained within low walls, logs, or old railway sleepers in the same way as raised beds (see p.269).

Scree beds should be 30–40cm (12–16in) deep; about half the depth should be composed of coarse rubble, as for rock gardens, and the upper layer of scree mixture (see p.262). Mark out the site with a rope or hosepipe and on previously grassed areas remove the turf. Lay the rubble foundation and line with thinly cut, inverted turves or a poly-propylene sheet, pierced at regular intervals for good drainage.

Finish off the bed with a 15–20cm (6–8in) layer of scree mixture, and firm by gently treading over the whole area. Water the bed and allow it to settle, then top up with scree mixture any areas that may have sunk before pricking over the surface with a hand fork.

Planting in a scree bed

It may be more difficult to establish plants in a scree bed than in a rock garden, since the freely draining compost tends to dry out before the plants are established. Care during planting and conscientious watering are the keys to success. The well-developed root systems of pot-grown alpines do not readily penetrate the gritty scree compost, so gently shake off most of the compost (especially if peat-based) from the roots. Keep the bare roots moist. Place the plant in a planting hole with its roots spread out, and infill carefully with scree mixture. Top-dress around the plant with rock chippings and water immediately and thoroughly.

Scree mixes are fast-draining, so water young plants regularly until they are established. Try to minimize wetting the foliage. In their natural habitats, scree dwellers have deep and extensive root systems to seek out water and nutrients, so when established they will survive for long periods without watering.

Top-dressings, gravels, and pebbles

After planting is completed, a rock garden or scree bed may then be top-dressed with stone chippings, grit, or gravel. This material should match as closely as possible the rock used at the construction stage.

Top-dressing has a number of advantages: it provides an attractive and natural setting for the plants and blends in better with the rocks than bare soil, creates especially good drainage around the collars of the plants, inhibits weed growth, con-serves moisture, and protects the soil surface from compaction during heavy rain or watering. The layer of top-dressing on a rock garden should

MEDITERRANEAN-STYLE PLANTING ON AN INCLINE

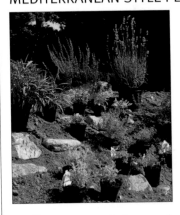

1 *If necessary, work sharp sand or grit into the soil to improve drainage. Dig and firm in larger stones. Arrange the plants in their pots (here a selection of herbs).*

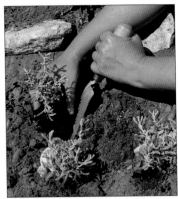

2 *Plant the large and then the small plants at the same depth as they were in their containers, and water well. Let the soil surface dry a little before top-dressing.*

3 *Add smaller stones and then a thick layer of stone chippings or shingle. Use a trowel or your hands to spread it carefully between and around the plants.*

The finished "Mediterranean" bank
Such a drought-tolerant garden provides an attractive low-maintenance area that should need little watering once the plants are established. The surface layer of chippings or shingle will help to conserve moisture in the soil, reflect heat onto the sun-loving plants, and keep down weeds. Remove any weeds that do appear by hand as soon as you spot them.

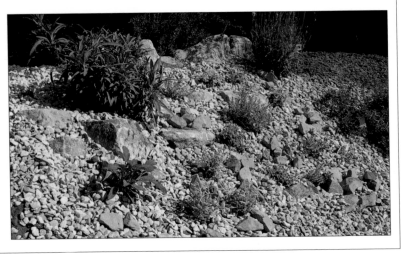

PLANTING UP A GRAVEL GARDEN

1 Cut weed-suppressing membrane to fit the bed or border. For a large area, cut several pieces, leaving a generous overlap, and pin securely in place.

2 Place the plants on top of the membrane, moving them around until you are happy with the overall arrangement. Keep in mind their eventual height and spread.

3 Cut a cross in the fabric directly under each plant and fold back the flaps. Ensure there is a large enough space to dig a good-sized planting hole.

4 Using a trowel, dig a planting hole a little larger than the plant's rootball. Remove the plant from its pot, placing it into the hole at the same level as in its pot.

5 Fill around the rootball with soil and firm in. Tuck the flaps back around the plant stem, pinning the membrane in place if there are any gaps. Water well.

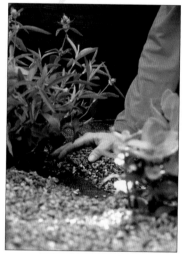

6 Spread a thick layer of gravel or another top-dressing over the membrane. Be generous to prevent the membrane showing through. Level with a rake.

The finished gravel garden
Water regularly until the plants are established, using a watering can fitted with a fine rose or a hose set to a fine spray to avoid dislodging the gravel. If necessary gently level the gravel at intervals, and pull out any weeds that may appear.

be at least 2.5cm (1in) deep; on a scree bed it may be 2–15cm (¾–6in) deep, depending on the plants grown; for most screes, a 2–3cm (¾–1¼in) layer is sufficient.

On gravel beds and gardens, a water-permeable geotextile fabric may be used beneath the layer of gravel to further assist in weed suppression and to extend the life of the top-dressing by preventing it gradually working into the soil. These fabrics also help to retain more moisture in the soil than a surface layer of gravel or shingle alone. They are ideal where a very low-maintenance feature is required, although because they largely prevent ornamental plants from self-seeding, they do prevent plants from spreading in a natural fashion.

Stone chippings and gravels with which to dress areas of planting in gravel are offered by garden centres and builders' merchants in a variety of grades and colours. If the surface is to be walked upon regularly, or used as a patio area on which to set garden furniture and containers, a fine grade of gravel, often referred to as "pea shingle", is recommended as it provides a smooth, more easily negotiable surface. Small pavers may be set unobtrusively in the gravel layer to provide strategic support points where stability is important – for example, beneath table legs.

Choose a colour for the top-dressing that blends in with local stone for the most natural look. Striking, modernistic effects may be created by using contrasting tones – for example, "rivers" of dark slate chippings flowing between outcrops of paler rock – although such features need considerable skill in their design and planting to avoid a clumsy impression.

Cobbles and pebbles

Never collect any quantity of cobbles or pebbles from beaches, where they may form important defences against erosion by the sea; in areas that have statutory environmental protection or where man-made sea-defences exist, it may actually be against the law to remove pebbles.

Good garden centres should offer responsibly sourced, washed pebbles. You may also be able to find them in aquatic departments now that they have become popular decorative items with which to dress small fountain features.

Troughs, sinks, and other containers

Alpines and rock plants look particularly attractive grown in troughs and sinks, although most frost-proof containers with good drainage are suitable. Choose the correct site at the outset as, once filled, they are difficult to move. Rocks may be placed in the containers to create the effect of a miniature rock garden; do this before planting up the container.

Types of container

Old, stone animal troughs and sinks, traditionally used to grow alpines, are now scarce and expensive. Glazed sinks coated in hypertufa, or troughs made entirely of hypertufa or reconstituted stone are now often used, as are large pottery and terracotta pots and tubs. All should have drainage holes to ensure that there is a free flow of water through the compost. If extra drainage holes are needed, they should be at least 2.5cm (1in) in diameter; if the base of the container is not flat, make the drainage holes at the lowest point. Plants in glazed sinks do not need nearly as much water as those in stone or hypertufa troughs, so, to prevent waterlogging in all but dry areas, an extra drainage layer should be added under the compost.

Covering glazed sinks

Deep, glazed, flat-bottomed sinks may easily be made to resemble stone containers by coating them with hypertufa. Ensure that the sink is clean and dry then score the surface with a tile- or glass-cutter to help the hypertufa adhere to the sink. To aid adhesion further, paint the surface with a bonding agent before applying the hypertufa.

Make hypertufa from 1–2 parts sifted peat substitute (or sphagnum peat), 1 part coarse sand or fine grit, and 1 part cement. Add sufficient water to form a thick paste. Apply this to the outside of the sink and also inside, down to well below the final level of the compost. Put the hypertufa on by hand (wear gloves); it should be 1–2cm (½–¾in) thick. Roughen the surface so that it resem-

GLAZED SINK WITH HYPERTUFA COATING

Glazed sinks covered with hypertufa make fine containers for alpines.

bles stone. When the hypertufa is fully dry, after about a week, scrub the surface with a wire brush and coat with a weak solution – about 3tsp to a litre (2tsp to a pint) of water – of permanganate of potash or liquid manure to discourage algae and encourage moss and lichen.

Hypertufa troughs

Troughs may be made entirely from hypertufa, if required. Prepare the mixture as for coating but increase the proportion of sand and grit to three parts to make a stiffer mix.

Use two wooden boxes that fit inside one another, with a cavity of 5–7cm (2–3in) between them. Stand the larger box on blocks so that it may be lifted once finished; pour two thin layers of the hypertufa mix into the base, with strong wire netting between the layers and parallel to the vertical sides. Press thick dowels or pegs through the hypertufa to make drainage holes. Fit the smaller box inside the larger, with netting between the two, and fill the space with the mix, tamping it down to remove air pockets.

When the cavity is full, cover the trough with a sheet of plastic for at least a week while the mix sets and protect the trough from frost, if necessary. When the mix has set hard, remove the boxes and dowels. If the boxes do not slide off easily, ease them off carefully with a fine chisel and a small hammer. Roughen the surface of the trough with a wire brush and paint on a coat of liquid manure or permanganate of potash to encourage growth.

HOW TO MAKE A HYPERTUFA TROUGH

1 *You will need two boxes to make the trough, one slightly larger than the other. Coat the surfaces of the boxes with oil to prevent the hypertufa sticking.*

2 *Place a 2.5cm (1in) layer of hypertufa mix in the base of the larger box and put wire netting on top of this layer and around the sides to reinforce the trough. Then add another layer of hypertufa.*

3 *Press several thick, wooden dowels into the wire and hypertufa base to make the drainage holes for the bottom of the trough.*

4 *Put the smaller box centrally on top of the hypertufa base, making sure the vertical netting is between the two boxes. Fill the cavity with the hypertufa mix, tamping down well as you fill.*

5 *Cover the top of the hypertufa with plastic sheeting until the mix has set (which usually takes about a week). Secure the sheeting in place with a weight and protect the trough from frost.*

6 *When the hypertufa has set, remove the wooden shuttering from the outside of the trough. If the hypertufa has stuck to the box, carefully dismantle the box with a hammer and chisel.*

7 *The surface of the hypertufa will be smooth and straight; for a more natural-looking appearance, scrub the outside of the trough with a wire brush or coarse-grained sandpaper to roughen the surface.*

8 *Remove the smaller box, using a hammer and chisel if necessary. To encourage moss and lichen growth, paint the outside surface of the trough with liquid manure.*

Siting containers

An open position, with sun for at least part of the day, is ideal for most plants. Do not place containers in windy sites, unless tough plants are being grown, or on lawns, since it is difficult to maintain the surrounding grass. Avoid slopes, which cause instability, and put containers as close as possible to a tap or hosepipe.

Raise troughs and sinks off the ground, up to a height of about 45cm (18in); the plants may then be viewed comfortably and water will drain away readily. Stone or brick pillars at the corners of a container provide sturdy, stable supports. These must bear the weight of the container without danger of tipping, and should not block the drainage holes. Sinks with single drainage holes should be tilted so that excess water drains off.

Placing rocks and tufa

Virtually any type of rock may be used in troughs and sinks. Rocks give height, and allow a greater depth of compost. A few large rocks are better than many small ones. Niches and crevices in the rocks may also be used to support plants, especially if hard tufa is used. Tufa's light weight and the ease with which planting holes can be excavated in it make it ideal. Roots spread into the porous rock, which is well aerated but also retains water.

Whatever type of rock is used, bury from one third to one half of each stone in the compost to ensure that it is firmly seated.

Filling the container

Rock garden plants need a loam-based potting compost, with some additional drainage material, in order to extract the nutrients they need to thrive. Add about one third by volume of perlite or 6–9mm (¼–⅜in) stone chippings, and mix in some slow-release fertilizer to the compost. Acid-loving plants need a lime-free compost, with added granite or sandstone chippings.

Cover the drainage holes with broken crocks or wire gauze and fill the bottom quarter to one third of the container with coarse aggregate, gravel, or stone chippings. Fill up with slightly moist compost, and firm it gently.

Position pieces of rock or tufa on the compost, and bed them in as the container is filled. Place rocks to form crevices and niches, providing both shaded and sunny faces to suit different plants, and add randomly placed smaller pieces of stone to simulate a small-scale rock garden. Water thoroughly and leave to drain completely before planting.

Planting

Choose slow-growing plants that will not swamp their neighbours and quickly exhaust the available nutrients. Do not overplant the container, and replant as soon as it becomes overcrowded (see "Replanting an alpine trough", p.271).

Position container-grown plants, still in their pots, on the compost or make a plan on paper of the planting scheme. Make planting holes, carefully slide the plants out of their pots, and loosen the root balls. Place the plants in the holes, fill in with compost, and firm. When complete, water thoroughly. Then add a top-dressing of chippings or gravel to help ensure sharp drainage.

Planting in tufa

If plants are to be grown in tufa rock, use a drill or a hammer and chisel, and make holes 10–12cm (4–5in) apart. They should be about 2.5cm (1in) in diameter and 5–7cm (2–3in) deep, angled at 30–45° on vertical or sloping surfaces, or straight down on horizontal planes. Soak the tufa, then put a little sharp sand in each hole, and add some compost. Use young, rooted cuttings or small plants, since they establish easily. Wash the roots before planting; ease them into the holes with a small dibber or a pencil and sprinkle in compost until the hole is full. Ensure that the neck of the plant is bedded in and not standing proud of the hole. Firm the compost and wedge small pieces of tufa around the plants to hold them in place. Water thoroughly and keep the tufa moist until the plants are established. In hot, dry weather, soak the tufa regularly.

HOW TO PLANT UP AN ALPINE TROUGH

1 *If planting in tufa, first drill holes in it about 2.5cm (1in) wide, 7cm (3in) deep, and no less than 10cm (4in) apart. Immerse the tufa in water overnight.*

2 *Lay fine-mesh netting over the trough base or cover the holes with crocks, and add 7–10cm (3–4in) of coarse grit.*

3 *Partly fill the trough with a gritty, moist compost, firming it in stages. Set the tufa in place so that at least ⅓–½ of it is buried to keep it stable.*

4 *Continue to fill with compost and firm well to allow about 5cm (2in) for top-dressing and watering. Insert a little compost into the tufa holes for planting.*

5 *Wash the roots of the plants to go in the tufa, and ease them into the planting holes. Dribble compost into the holes, firm, and put small rock pieces around the plants.*

6 *Set the plants, still in their pots, on the compost to check that the arrangement and spacing are satisfactory, then plant and firm them in.*

7 *Water the compost thoroughly, then top-dress the trough with a 2.5–5cm (1–2in) deep layer of coarse gravel or stone chippings.*

The finished trough

Helianthemum oelandicum subsp. alpestre

Androsace pubescens

Sisyrinchium 'E.K. Balls'

Penstemon pinifolius

Sempervivum arachnoideum

Saxifraga cotyledon

Draba aizoides

Oxalis 'Ione Hecker'

Talinum okanoganense

Saxifraga cochlearis 'Minor'

Phlox douglasii cv.

Saxifraga paniculata

Oxalis enneaphylla 'Minutifolia'

Rhodohypoxis baurii

Dianthus 'La Bourboule'

Walls

Alpines and rock garden plants may be grown in the crevices of dry-stone walls, including the retaining walls of raised beds and sloping banks. Trailing plants are especially effective when grown in this way. For details on constructing a wall, see "Dry-stone walls", p.598.

If possible, plan for any planting in walls before construction work starts. The most practical approach is to leave planting niches at intervals in the wall and plant them up when the building work is finished.

It is also possible to position the plants as construction proceeds. This produces excellent results, since the plants may be placed at the desired level, and ensures good contact between the roots of the plants and any soil behind the wall. Planting during construction also makes it easier to eliminate air pockets in the compost and firm around the roots.

Planting in existing walls is another option but some of the soil will need to be removed first with a widger or teaspoon before planting. Use young plants or rooted cuttings, since these fit easily in the crevices.

HOW TO BUILD A DRY-STONE RETAINING WALL

Making the footings
Dig a trench 38cm (15in) deep; fill it with 25cm (10in) of rubble with a large, sturdy stone on top.

Placing the stones
Slope the stones backwards and downwards for stability and so that water is carried into the compost.

Filling between stones
As you build, fill crevices between the stones with a compost of loam, leaf mould, and sand or grit.

Planting

Use the following compost mix for filling the planting crevices in walls: 3 parts loam (or good sterilized garden soil), 2 parts coarse peat substitute (or peat), and 1–2 parts sharp sand or grit. Use extra grit, sand, or stone chippings for plants that are to be grown in the wall itself, since this will help to ensure good drainage. Choose plants that grow well in the aspect and conditions available in the wall. Carefully remove old compost from the roots and ease them into the hole, using a widger, small dibber, or pencil. Do not try to cram roots into too small a space as this damages the plants. Holding the plant in position with one hand, trickle in fresh, moist compost, then firm it with the widger to remove any air pockets. It may also be helpful to wedge small stones around the collars of the plants to hold them in place and prevent the compost from becoming dislodged.

Water thoroughly from the top of the wall and spray the plants regularly until established. After several days, top up any sunken areas with spare compost. Periodically check the plants and firm any that have worked loose.

HOW TO PLANT IN A DRY-STONE WALL

1 *If planting in an existing wall, check that there is an adequate amount of compost in the crevices to support the plants.*

2 *Use seedlings or small rooted cuttings. Place them on the flat of a stone and, using a widger, ease the roots into the crevices. The plant shown here is a Sempervivum.*

3 *Bed the plants down into the compost and pack more compost into the crevices to hold the plants in position. Firm the plants in with your fingers.*

4 *For larger plants, scoop out some compost from the crevices. Ease the roots into the holes and add more compost while holding plants in position.*

5 *When all the plants are in position, water them from the top of the wall or with a mist spray. Keep the plants moist until established and refirm any that work loose. Planted with the Sempervivum are two saxifrages.*

PLANTING IN VERTICAL CREVICES

1 *Fill the crevice with a gritty compost. Carefully ease in the roots of the plant (here Campanula).*

2 *Cover the roots with compost, then wedge in a small stone, sloping it down the rock-face. Firm further compost into the crevice.*

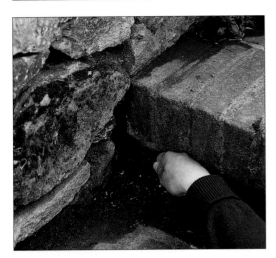

Softening surfaces
Soften the edges of steps, retaining walls and paving by inserting low, spreading plants in gaps and crevices. Fill in any gaps around them with gritty compost. Take care that growth does not obscure steps and render them hazardous.

Raised beds

A wide range of alpine plants may be grown in raised beds, both in the beds themselves and in crevices in the supporting walls. The bed's design should harmonize with the house and garden. Depending on the needs of the chosen plants, a raised bed may be positioned in either sun or shade. Fill the bed with well-drained compost to suit the plants (see "Soil for raised beds", below). If necessary, plants may be protected in winter with glass or plastic covers placed over the bed.

Siting

For most alpines and rock garden plants, raised beds should be sited in an open, sunny position away from the shade cast by overhanging trees or nearby buildings and fences. Place a raised bed in shade only if woodland or other plants requiring cooler, shadier conditions are to be grown.

To aid mowing, a raised bed that is positioned on a lawn should have a surround of paving slabs or bricks set just below the level of the grass. Raised beds that are constructed for elderly or disabled gardeners may need to be built with wheelchair access, and the beds should be of a height and width to allow plants to be tended easily from a seated position. On sites where the construction of a ground-based scree bed is not possible because of poor drainage, a scree may be placed on the surface of a raised bed instead (see p.264).

Materials and design

Raised beds may be made from stone, brick, old wooden railway sleepers, or any other suitable and attractive material. Stone is the dearest; new or second-hand bricks and sleepers are cheaper and easier to use.

The bed may be almost any shape but it should harmonize with the general design of the garden. Rect-angular beds are the most common. The ideal height for a raised bed is 60–75cm (24–30in), although a tiered bed is also attractive and may be more appropriate where space is limited. The width of the bed should be no more than 1.5m (5ft) to allow comfortable access – the centre of the bed should be within arm's reach to allow weeding from all sides.

Large beds may need an irrigation system; install water pipes and inlets before filling the beds with compost.

Construction

Retaining brick walls for raised beds should be vertical; the thickness of one brick is usually adequate. They are built in the same way as a conventional wall and may be mortared but small gaps should be left between bricks at intervals for plants to be inserted. There should also be gaps at the base for drainage. For further information, see STRUCTURES AND SURFACES, "Raised beds", p.599.

Raised beds may also have stone retaining walls. If they are built without mortar they need a slight inward slope for stability (see "Dry-stone walls", p.598). Dry-stone walls are time-consuming to build, since each stone needs to be chosen and positioned carefully. Large crevices may be left between the stones to be planted up with alpines. If wooden sleepers are used, crevice-planting is not possible.

Soil for raised beds

Use a mix of 3 parts loam (or good sterilized garden soil), 2 parts coarse fibrous peat substitute (such as acidic leaf mould or garden compost) or peat, and 1–2 parts grit or sharp sand. For plants that need acid conditions, use lime-free loam and grit. To grow plants that need different soil types in a large bed, divide it into sections with plastic sheeting to keep the sections apart, and fill each with appropriate compost (see p.322).

Preparing the raised bed

Fill the bottom third of the bed with coarse gravel, stones, or rubble, then place a layer of inverted turves or fibrous peat substitute (or peat) over the top to prevent the drainage material from becoming clogged. Fill the bed with prepared compost, which should be well worked into all the corners and firmed as filling proceeds. Incorporate a slow-release fertilizer. Some settling always occurs, so water the bed thoroughly and leave it for two or three weeks. Top up any sunken areas with spare compost before planting.

Adding rocks gives the effect of a rock garden in miniature and enhances the appearance of raised beds. Set pieces of rock of varying sizes into the compost to provide suitable sites for a range of different plants. Several large pieces of rock arranged together as outcrops are more effective than scattered rocks.

Planting and top-dressing

Make a planting plan or set out the plants on the surface of the bed to see how they will look. Dwarf conifers and small shrubs, tufted and cushion-forming alpines, trailing alpines at the edges of the bed, and smaller bulbs are ideal. Select plants for year-round interest. Plant as for rock gardens (see p.263); crevices in the retaining walls may also be planted up as for dry-stone walls (see p.268).

After planting, top-dress the bed with stone chippings or coarse grit, to match any rocks. Work a 1cm (½in) deep layer of the top-dressing carefully around the plants and beneath their collars. This looks attractive, suppresses weeds, and reduces evaporation. Water the bed regularly until the plants are established.

Winter protection

Many alpines dislike excessive winter moisture, even in the well-drained conditions of a raised bed. The alpine beds can be protected with cloches or sheets of glass or plastic, supported with bricks or a wire frame. Fasten down the covering, so that it does not blow away. Such protection should be put in place in late autumn and removed the following spring. If the whole bed needs protection, build a wooden framework for a glass or plastic roof. Plenty of air must circulate around the plants to ensure that they remain as dry as possible, so do not cover the sides of the protective frame.

Beds for ericaceous plants

Acidic-humus or peat beds provide ideal conditions for a wide range of acid-loving and woodland plants. In gardens with alkaline soils, such beds should always be isolated from the ground with a plastic or butyl rubber liner so that lime cannot enter. Surround each bed with logs or old railway sleepers.

Consider the needs of the plants when deciding where to place an acidic-humus bed, and construct the bed so that it blends in well with the rest of the garden. It is not necessary to use pure peat in the bed, since acidic peat substitutes are widely available. A wide range of acid-loving plants may be grown both in the bed and in wall crevices to produce an attractive display.

Siting

Choose a site that receives sun and dappled shade, ideally facing away from direct sun. An area next to a rock garden, on a slope, or by the side of a building is appropriate. Acidic-humus beds on exposed sites in full sun lose moisture rapidly, and need frequent watering. Dense shade of trees is unsuitable, and the tree roots nearby soon exhaust the moisture and nutrients. Waterlogged sites and frost pockets are not suitable either.

A finished bed
Plant up acidic-humus beds with acid-loving rock garden plants for a fine display. Water often to keep the soil moist, especially in the first year. Top-dress the bed with bark chippings to conserve moisture and suppress weeds. Feed the plants regularly with a balanced fertilizer.

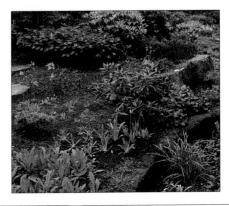

Routine care of rock plants

EVEN when alpines and rock plants are established in the garden, it is essential to care for them regularly. Beds, troughs, and sinks must be kept clean and free of weeds. Although the plants do not usually need nutrient-rich soil, they should be fed at intervals and watered whenever the soil becomes dry. Top-dressings, which improve drainage around the collars of the plants, suppress weed growth, and reduce evaporation of water from the soil, should be replenished occasionally.

Alpines and rock garden plants benefit from periodic removal of dead wood, leaves and flowers, and should be kept trimmed. Troughs, sinks, and other containers should be replanted as soon as they become overcrowded. Check plants routinely for signs of pest infestation and disease, and treat them as necessary. In cold or wet weather, some plants may need winter protection.

Weeding

The use of sterilized compost when planting should minimize problems with weeds, at least for the first years. Always try to remove all weeds as soon as they appear, certainly before they flower and set seed. If perennial weeds do become established and are difficult to remove, paint the foliage carefully with a translocated weed-killer, which is transmitted to the roots and kills them. For further information, see PLANT PROBLEMS, "Controlling weeds", p.669.

When weeding, use a three-pronged hand cultivator to loosen and aerate compacted soil around young plants, if necessary, taking care not to disturb the plant roots.

Feeding

Newly planted areas should not normally need feeding for some years if the original compost has been correctly prepared and includes slow-release fertilizer. After some time, however, the growth of the plants may begin to slow down and flowering become sparser. This may be remedied by applying a dressing of slow-release fertilizer around the plants each spring.

Alternatively, carefully remove any top-dressing and a layer of about 1cm (½in) of compost from the surface of the bed and replace it with fresh compost and a further top-dressing of grit.

Top-dressing

The type of top-dressing used for alpines and rock garden plants depends on the plants that are grown, although it should match any of the rocks and stones that feature in beds and rock gardens as closely as possible. Top-dressings used in troughs, sinks, or raised beds should also harmonize with the pot or retaining walls.

Coarse grit or stone chippings are suitable for most situations, but limestone chippings should never be used around lime-hating plants. For plants grown in peat beds, a top-dressing of bark chippings will complement the plantings.

Renewing top-dressings

Top-dressings may need to be renewed from time to time, since grit or stone chippings gradually wash away, especially on slopes, and bark tends to decompose and mix in with the underlying compost. Watch for bare patches throughout the season and top up as necessary. Pay close attention to top-dressings in the autumn, to ensure good soil coverage in winter and avoid compaction by heavy rain. Check again in spring and top up, as necessary. A slow-release fertilizer may be applied at the same time.

Watering

Established plants growing in rock gardens and screes root deeply into the soil and do not usually need more water than is supplied by rainfall. In droughts, however, the area should be thoroughly soaked. Do not water in very frosty conditions

WEEDING

Weed around young plants with a 3-pronged cultivator, which also loosens and aerates the soil. Remove any top-dressing first and replace it after weeding.

1 *Remove the old top-dressing and some compost (see inset). Fill in around the plants with fresh compost (see p.262).*

2 *Top-dress the bed with a fresh layer of coarse grit or gravel, adding some around and beneath the collars of the plants.*

or during the heat of the day – early mornings or late evenings are the best times; soak occasionally rather than giving small amounts of water frequently. If the compost is dry at a depth of 3–5cm (1¼–2in), water thoroughly until the water has penetrated to the full depth of the roots. During an average summer this should only be needed two or three times but in very dry summers may be required more frequently.

Watering in containers, raised beds, and under cover

Alpines and rock garden plants that are grown in raised beds, sinks and troughs, under frames, and in the alpine house will need more regular watering, since the soil dries out more quickly than in rock gardens and scree beds.

It is preferable to hand-water troughs and sinks if specialist collections of plants are being grown, so that each plant may be provided with the correct amount of water. This is time-consuming, however, particularly where there are several containers to be watered.

Plants grown in pots in alpine houses and frames should be watered individually. If the pots are plunged in gravel or stone chippings, water both the pots and the surrounding material. Some alpine plants have water-sensitive foliage and therefore dislike overhead watering; if this is the case, regularly soaking only the plunge material should provide sufficient moisture.

Trimming and pruning

Alpines and rock garden plants need to be cut back periodically to maintain a natural, compact shape and healthy growth, and to restrict them within their allotted space.

Pruning woody plants

To keep rock garden shrubs and woody perennials healthy, any dead, diseased, or damaged wood should be removed. Check the plants on a regular basis and prune them as cleanly as possible, using secateurs or sharp scissors.

Severe pruning is unnecessary because most dwarf shrubs are slow-growing and do not outgrow their positions for many years. When

REMOVING DEAD GROWTH

In spring, after all danger of frost has passed, cut out any dieback from plants, trimming carefully to healthy growth with sharp scissors or secateurs.

REMOVING DEAD ROSETTES

1 *To remove dead rosettes from plants such as saxifrages, cut out the rosettes with a sharp knife without disturbing the rest of the plant.*

2 *Top-dress the exposed soil to prevent weeds growing through the gaps until the plant produces fresh growth.*

CUTTING BACK AFTER FLOWERING

1 *After flowering, cut back stems (here* Helianthemum) *to half their length to encourage healthy, new growth.*

2 *The plants will remain compact and produce a good crop of flowers the following year.*

RENOVATING AN ALPINE BED

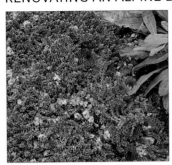

1 *Plants that spread rapidly (here* Paronychia chionaea) *may eventually smother less vigorous plants nearby. Cut them back in spring.*

2 *Dig up or pull out clumps of encroaching plants. Straggly plants should be cut back severely. Make sure that plants nearby have plenty of room to grow.*

3 *Add a dressing of balanced fertilizer to the bed, before placing a fresh layer of top-dressing on the surface of the compost around the plants.*

pruning, aim to maintain the natural shape of the plant, especially in the case of dwarf conifers.

Removing dead flowers and foliage

Regularly remove all dead flowers and leaves, and any unwanted seedheads, with a sharp knife, secateurs, or scissors. Pick over small alpine plants by hand, using tweezers, if necessary, to remove dead leaves and flowers. Carefully cut out dead rosettes from plants such as saxifrages; do not pull them off by hand, as this may loosen healthy rosettes.

Helianthemum species and cultivars, in particular, need clipping with shears annually after flowering, cutting back the stems by about half their length to encourage growth for flowering the following year. Genera such as *Arabis*, *Aubrieta*, and *Aurinia* also benefit from hard annual pruning (after flowering), which helps to keep them compact and free-flowering. Plants may produce a second flush of flowers if cut back before they set seed.

Encroaching plants

Over-vigorous plants as well as old, straggly plants that are beginning to encroach on their neighbours should be cut back in early spring. Mat-forming plants may simply be pulled out by hand, others may need to be lifted with a hand fork. Support nearby plants and refirm any that are accidentally lifted. Remove or cut back plants to allow a clear area of bed around all the remaining plants so that they can grow unimpeded. Hard-pruned plants should be top-dressed with a balanced fertilizer in order to promote strong, new growth.

Winter protection

Plants in troughs, sinks, or raised beds, and some alpine bulbs, may need protection from winter wet. Use a single, propped pane of glass, an open cloche, or, for large areas, a frame light, which will give overhead protection without inhibiting air circulation. Ensure that covers are firmly secured. Some protection from severe cold may be provided by placing a layer of evergreen branches or pine boughs over the plants.

Controlling pests and diseases

Few serious problems affect alpines and rock garden plants, but some of the more common pests and diseases may need to be controlled. Regular, basic garden hygiene is often sufficient to control most problems encountered. Aphids (p.646) are likely to be troublesome if alpines are grown in too rich a soil, which induces soft, lank growth.

Coarse top-dressings around plants tend to deter slugs and snails but some control is still necessary, particularly for choice alpines, such as *Campanula zoysii*, which are susceptible to attack from these pests. Control insects such as ants (p.666), which will excavate under cushion-forming plants. Prevent birds from disturbing newly planted specimens by covering them with wigwams of sticks or wire pushed into the soil.

Fungal diseases may quickly become established in alpine houses and frames (see pp.277–279).

Replanting an alpine trough

Plants in containers eventually need replanting when nutrients in the compost are exhausted. Water thoroughly before carefully removing the plants. Discard the compost and replace it with a fresh, suitable mix (see p.262), containing a slow-release fertilizer. Trim roots and top-growth before returning plants to the container; allow for their eventual spread and top-dress with gravel.

Helianthemum sp.

Iris cristata

Ramonda myconi

Helianthemum sp.

Propagation

MANY alpines and rock garden plants may be propagated from seed, although some plants are sterile and do not produce seed. In addition, cultivars seldom come true from seed and must be increased in other ways. Alternative methods include cuttings (of various types) and division.

Seed

Propagation from seed is the best way to produce large numbers of plants. Since many alpines flower in early spring, ripe seed is often available from midsummer, and may be sown straight away. Germination will usually occur rapidly and strong seedlings will be produced before winter. Autumn-sown seeds may remain dormant until spring; if germination occurs, overwinter the seedlings in frames. It may sometimes be better to store seed over winter and sow in early spring, although short-lived seed should be sown as soon as it is ripe.

Seed collection and storage

Collect seed as the seedheads become ripe. Remove them while still attached to the stems and place them in paper (not plastic) bags to dry out. Enclose in envelopes any that might split open on drying. Store seeds in a cool, dry, well-ventilated place. Most alpines have seed capsules from which seed may be extracted by rubbing between the fingers. Fleshy fruits may need to be squashed and left on paper to dry.

Separate the seed from the debris by sieving or hand-picking when dry. Put it in sealed, labelled envelopes, and place these in an airtight container in a cool place.

Pre-sowing treatment

Seeds with hard coats need special treatment to allow them to absorb water. Scarify by chipping the seed coat with a sharp knife or rubbing with a file or fine abrasive paper. In some cases, soaking the seed for 12–24 hours will accelerate the take-up of water.

Hard-cased seeds of woody rock garden plants do not respond to scarification alone; they also need exposure to cold (stratification). Store the seeds in boxes of moist sand outdoors for two or three months during winter, and sow in spring; alternatively, sow the seed in pots of seed compost and keep these in the freezer or refrigerator, sealed in plastic bags, for several weeks before plunging the pots in the ground outside until the seed germinates. Some seeds, such as *Trillium* and peonies (*Paeonia*), need alternating periods of cold and warmth to germinate successfully.

Sowing the seed

Use clean clay or plastic pots, and place broken crocks over the drainage holes. A compost of equal parts sieved peat substitute (or peat) and perlite is suitable, or use loam-based seed compost, mixed with an equal amount of perlite or sharp sand. Fill the pots and firm the compost. Tap out small seeds thinly and evenly and space large seeds by hand, covering them with their own depth of compost. Mix fine seeds with fine, dry, silver sand before sowing but do not cover with more compost.

After sowing, cover all but fine seeds with a 5–10mm (¼–½in) layer of 5mm (¼in) diameter grit or pea shingle, to deter mosses and liverworts and protect the seed from heavy rain or watering. Label the pots and stand them in water to half their depth, removing them when the compost surface becomes moist. Keep the compost moist at all times.

Germination

Speed of germination depends on the type and age of the seed, and when it is sown. Some seed takes months or even years to germinate.

A cool, sheltered site outdoors is ideal for the seeds of most alpines. Plunge pots in moist sand to maintain an even temperature and reduce the need for watering. When seedlings appear, move the pots to a cold frame. Germination may be speeded up by placing the pots in gentle heat in early spring, but do not expose the seeds to high temperatures.

Pricking out and potting up

Prick out seedlings when they are 5–10mm (¼–½in) tall and when two true leaves have formed. Knock out the compost and separate the seedlings. Handle only by the leaves or cotyledons to avoid damage to stems and roots. Pot up seedlings individually in small clay pots or plastic pots, or in module packs using low-fertility loam-based potting compost mixed with an equal amount of grit. Fill the container, settle the compost, and make a hole for the roots. Put the seedling in the hole, fill with compost, and firm lightly.

Top-dress seedlings in individual pots with a 5–10mm (¼–½in) layer of grit. Water them thoroughly with a fine-rosed watering can and place the containers in a lightly shaded position, until the seedlings are established. Water as required. When the roots are visible through the drainage holes, pot them on.

Seeds that are slow to germinate often do so erratically, and if only a few seedlings appear prick them out as soon as they are large enough to handle. Disturb the rest of the compost as little as possible, and cover it with fresh top-dressing. Put the pot back into the frame in case more seeds germinate.

ROCK PLANT SEED TO SOW FRESH

Anemone
Codonopsis
Corydalis
Cyclamen (alpine spp.)
Dodecatheon
Hepatica
Meconopsis
Primula
Pulsatilla
Ranunculus

SOWING SEED

1 *Prepare a pot by filling it with equal parts of seed compost and horticultural sand. Firm the compost gently to level the surface and eliminate air pockets.*

2 *Small seed (here Lewisia) should be tapped out evenly over the surface of the compost. Space larger seed by hand.*

3 *Cover the seeds with a fine layer of compost, then top-dress with grit to protect the seeds and prevent the growth of mosses. Water in and label.*

4 *Prick out seedlings when they have 2 true leaves (see inset). Lift the seedlings carefully, handling them by the leaves only.*

5 *Fill pots with equal parts of loam-based potting compost and grit. Pot up the seedlings singly, firming with a dibber.*

6 *Top-dress with grit, water, and place the seedlings in light shade. Pot on the seedlings when the roots fill the pot.*

ROCK PLANTS FROM CUTTINGS

Softwood
Adenophora
Anthemis
Asyneuma
Aubrieta (spp. and cvs)
Campanula, some ❋ (spp.
    and cvs)
Cassiope

Aubrieta x cultorum
'Argenteovariegata'

Daphne jasminea
Dianthus, some ❋
Dionysia
Draba
Eriogonum ovalifolium
Eriophyllum lanatum
Gypsophila aretioides,
    G. repens
Penstemon, some ❋
Phlox, some ❋ (spp. and cvs)
Polygala, some ❋
Primula (alpine spp.)
Silene acaulis
Viola, some ❋ (spp. and cvs)

Viola
'Jackanapes'

Greenwood
Anchusa cespitosa
Aubrieta (spp. and cvs)
Aurinia
Cassiope
Erodium, some ❋
Geranium, some ❋

Semi-ripe
Cassiope
Claytonia
Clematis alpina,
    C. x *cartmanii* 'Joe'
Convolvulus boissieri,
    C. sabatius
Daphne
Diascia
Erica, some ❋
Erinacea anthyllis
Hebe, some ❋ (spp.
    and cvs)
Helianthemum

Helianthemum
'Fire Dragon'

Key
❋ *Not hardy*

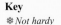

Softwood and greenwood cuttings

Softwood cuttings are taken from the non-flowering, leafy shoots of a plant during periods of active growth, usually in spring.

Greenwood cuttings are taken in early summer when growth has slowed down; although slightly riper than softwood cuttings, they require the same treatment.

Taking the cuttings

Take the cuttings early in the morning, when the shoots are fully turgid. For softwood cuttings select strong, young shoots that are soft and pliable, with no trace of woodiness or hardening; greenwood cuttings may be just beginning to harden at the base. Cuttings should be about 2.5–7cm (1–3in) long and taken with a sharp knife. Place them immediately in a plastic bag to conserve moisture and prevent them from wilting.

Inserting the cuttings

Trim the base of each cutting cleanly with a sharp knife just below a node (leaf joint) and remove the lower leaves. Pinch off any shoot tips that are soft, particularly if these are showing signs of wilting.

Fill pots with standard cutting compost and make holes for the cuttings with a small dibber. Insert each cutting into the compost by up to half its length so that the lowest leaf is just above the surface.

Label the cuttings and water with a fungicide solution, then place them in a closed propagator with gentle bottom heat, or in a mist propagation unit. Alternatively, seal the pots in plastic bags. Keep the cuttings in good light but out of direct sun, as otherwise the air and soil temperature may become too hot and the cuttings wilt.

Remove with tweezers dead and diseased cuttings, since these may infect their healthy neighbours. Watering is seldom required until after rooting. Look for signs of new growth, and check for rooting by gently pulling at the cuttings. Once they are well rooted, pot them up.

Potting up

Water the rooted cuttings well, and gently slide them out of the pot. Carefully separate them before potting them up individually, using equal parts of potting compost and grit.

Top-dress with a 1cm (½in) layer of sharp grit. Water the cuttings thoroughly and return them to the propagator, keeping them out of direct sun. Keep the cuttings well watered. Once fresh growth appears, place the cuttings in a cold frame and harden them off carefully before planting them out.

Semi-ripe and ripewood cuttings

Semi-ripe cuttings are taken in mid-to late summer from non-flowering shoots of the current season's growth; the shoots offer distinct resistance to pressure when bent gently and should be beginning to harden at the base. Ripewood cuttings are taken from evergreen plants during late summer and autumn when the wood has fully ripened.

Taking the cuttings

The cuttings will vary in length with the plant concerned from 1 to 4cm (½ to 1½in) or more. Cut them from the parent plant using a sharp knife or secateurs. Make a clean cut below a node and remove soft tissue at the tips. Trim off the lower leaves and dip the ends of the cuttings into hormone rooting powder. Alternatively, take cuttings with a "heel" and trim the heel with a sharp knife to remove any snags.

Potting up

Small cuttings root best in pots of cutting compost, topped with a 1cm (½in) layer of fine sand. Make holes in the sand and insert the cuttings by one third to one half of their length. Label, water with a fungicide, and place in a propagator in a cool greenhouse. Check regularly for disease. Water sparingly and, as growth begins, apply a dilute liquid feed.

If a large number of cuttings is taken, they may be inserted into a cold frame with drainage at the base. Fork over the soil in the frame and then add a mixture of 1 part peat substitute (or peat) and 1 part grit; top with a 2.5cm (1in) layer of sand. After inserting the cuttings, water them and close the frame. Open the frame in mild weather. If there is a danger of frost, insulate the frame.

The following spring, when the cuttings have rooted, repot or pot up those in frames in equal parts potting compost and grit, or plant out in a nursery bed but only after danger of frost is passed. Water well.

Grow on, keeping the rooted cuttings moist and sheltered from direct sun. Give a liquid feed in the growing season. Transplant into their permanent positions in autumn.

SOFTWOOD CUTTINGS

1 *In spring, choose young, non-flowering shoots (here, from* Gypsophila repens) *and take cuttings 2.5–7cm (1–3in) long. Put the cuttings in a plastic bag.*

2 *Trim off the base of the cuttings, and the lower leaves and soft tips (see inset). Fill a pot with moist compost, inserting the cuttings by up to half their length.*

3 *Water and label the cuttings. Place the pot in a sealed plastic bag, keeping it in good light but out of direct sun.*

4 *When rooted, pot up the cuttings singly, holding them by the leaves only. Top-dress the pots, water well, and label.*

Leaf cuttings

This method is suitable for plants with fleshy leaves, such as *Haberlea*, *Ramonda*, and *Sedum*.

Using a sharp knife, cut healthy, strong, and relatively young leaves from the stem at their base. Prepare pots with a mixture of equal parts of standard cutting compost and sand; insert each cutting at a 45° angle, so that it is just held in place by the compost. Enclose each pot in a plastic bag and, when the plantlets appear, pot them up individually.

Basal cuttings

Some plants, such as *Primula marginata* and its cultivars, may be propagated from basal cuttings. These are taken from young shoots at the base of the plant at, or just above, soil level. Basal cuttings are usually taken in spring, but may also be taken in summer or autumn.

Use a well-drained, proprietary cutting compost, or a mix of equal parts of loam and peat substitute (or peat) with 2 parts grit. Fill pots with compost, and firm.

Trim the base of each cutting cleanly just below a node. Make sure that the cutting is not hollow at the base. Remove the lower leaves and dip the base in hormone powder.

Insert one third to one half of each stem into the compost, keeping the leaves clear of the soil. Water well and place the pots in a shaded, closed propagator or cold frame. Rooting takes three to six weeks, after which the cuttings may be potted up individually or lined out in nursery beds or a cold frame to grow on.

BASAL CUTTINGS

Primula marginata

In spring, take cuttings 5–7cm (2–3in) long with new leaves and a short stem. Trim the base and remove the lower leaves, inserting the cuttings to the depth indicated.

ROCK PLANTS FROM CUTTINGS (CONT.)

Semi-ripe (cont.)
Lepidium nanum
Lewisia
Linum arboreum
Lithodora diffusa

Polygala chamaebuxus

Origanum amanum,
  O. rotundifolium
Ozothamnus selago
Parahebe catarractae
Phlox 'Chattahoochee',
  P. subulata (and cvs)
Polygala
Rhododendron (spp. and cvs)
Veronica

Dryas octopetala

Ripewood
Dryas
Juniperus communis
  'Compressa'
Rosa
Salix

Rosette
Androsace
Armeria juniperifolia
Azorella trifurcata
Bolax gummifera
Draba
Helichrysum milfordiae
Jovibarba
Saxifraga, some ❋ (spp. and cvs)
Sempervivum (spp. and cvs)

Sempervivum tectorum

Leaf
Haberlea
Jancaea (spp. and hybrids)
Primula gracilipes
Ramonda
Sedum, some ❋

Key
❋ *Not hardy*

Selecting cutting material

For all types of cutting, always choose strong, healthy stems or leaves that show no sign of pests or diseases. Non-flowering shoots that are in active growth should be used. Except for basal cuttings, do not take the cuttings from the base of any plant because this part may be weaker than elsewhere. Do not take all the cuttings from the same area on the parent plant since this may make it look lop-sided.

After taking the cuttings, immediately place them in a clean, plastic bag to prevent any moisture loss. Many cuttings will root readily if they are inserted into pots of cutting compost with added grit. Alternatively, simply use horticultural sand. Insert the cuttings at the depths indicated.

Semi-ripe
(Phlox)
In mid- to late summer, select shoots that are just hardening but not woody. Remove 3cm (1¼in) lengths, trimming to about 1cm (½in).

Greenwood
(Erodium)
Take cuttings from the soft tips of new shoots in early summer. Remove 2.5–7cm (1–3in) lengths and trim them to about 1cm (½in).

Rosette
(Saxifraga)
In early to mid-summer, select new rosettes. Cut the rosettes about 1cm (½in) below the leaves. Trim each cleanly across the base.

Ripewood
(Dryas)
In late summer and autumn, select new shoots and take cuttings about 2.5cm (1in) long. Trim to about 1cm (½in) below the base of the leaves.

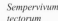

Leaf
(Sedum)
Throughout the growing season, select mature leaves that are undamaged, cutting off selected leaves. Trim each cleanly across the base.

Division

Many alpines and rock garden plants may be successfully propagated by division, and in some cases division is the only practicable method of increasing the stock if seed is rarely produced or the plant is sterile.

Plants that are particularly suitable for division include mat-forming species, which produce a mass of fibrous roots, and clump-forming plants that produce clusters of shoots that are readily separated.

ROCK PLANTS FROM "IRISHMAN'S" CUTTINGS

Achillea ageratifolia
Arenaria montana,
   A. purpurascens
Gentiana acaulis, G. verna
Primula auricula (and cvs),
   P. marginata (and cvs)
Silene
Veronica peduncularis
Viola cornuta (and cvs)

ROCK PLANTS TO DIVIDE

Achillea ageratifolia
Alchemilla alpina,
   A. ellenbeckii
Allium sikkimense
Antennaria dioica
Arenaria montana
Artemisia schmidtiana 'Nana'
Campanula carpatica,
   C. cochleariifolia
Chiastophyllum oppositifolium
Gentiana acaulis,
   G. sino-ornata
Primula allionii

Gentiana
sino-ornata

Sagina subulata 'Aurea'
Viola cornuta

ROCK PLANTS FROM ROOT CUTTINGS

Anacyclus pyrethrum
   var. *depressus*
Carduncellus rhaponticoides
Centaurea pindicola
Gentiana lutea
Meconopsis delavayi
Morisia monanthos
Papaver lateritium
Phlox nana subsp. *ensifolia*
Primula denticulata
Pulsatilla
Roscoea cautleyoides
Weldenia candida ❋

Key
❋ *Not hardy*

A number of clump-forming plants have a tendency to die out at the centre. These may be divided to rejuvenate them by replanting only the youngest, most vigorous pieces.

When to divide

Most plants are best divided in early spring, when new growth is just beginning; do not divide plants in cold and frosty weather, or when the ground is frozen or waterlogged.

Plants may also be divided in early autumn, which allows new roots to be made while the soil is still warm. Where hard winters are expected, spring division may be safer, since this allows a full growing season for establishment. Some plants, for example primulas and *Meconopsis*, should be divided immediately after flowering, when they enter a period of strong, vegetative growth. They must be well watered after replanting until they are fully re-established.

How to divide

Lift plants and shake off the soil. For large clumps, insert the tines of two garden forks back-to-back into the centre of the clump; lever the plant into two halves. Tease these smaller clumps apart by hand or cut them

"IRISHMAN'S" CUTTINGS

1 *Lift the rooted shoots close to the base of the plant (here* Veronica) *and remove them with a sharp knife. Trim off sideshoots and straggly roots (see inset).*

2 *Pot up the cuttings individually. Place a little gritty compost in a pot, insert the cutting, then add more compost. Firm gently, water, and top-dress.*

with a sharp knife to produce a number of small pieces with healthy roots and growth buds. The older, woody, central part of the plant should be discarded.

If not replanting or potting up the divisions immediately, wrap them in plastic bags or moist sacking and store them out of direct sun. Divisions of most hardy plants may

HOW TO PROPAGATE BY DIVISION

1 *Plants with fibrous roots (here* Gentiana acaulis) *may be divided and replanted to provide new plants. Lift a clump of the parent plant and shake off the soil.*

2 *Using hand forks back-to-back, loosen the root mass and divide the clump into pieces. If necessary, cut away sections from the clump with a knife.*

3 *The plants should have a good root system. Replant them outdoors into their permanent positions, firming around the roots. Add top-dressing around the plants and water thoroughly with a fine-rosed watering can.*

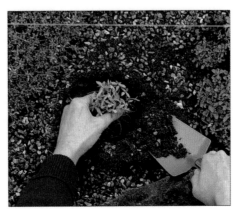

be replanted immediately into their permanent positions. If, however, plants are particularly precious, or the divisions are quite small, it may be safer to pot them up and place them in a cold frame until they are established before planting them out. Use 1 part low-fertility, loam-based potting compost and 1 part grit or a lime-free mix for acid-lovers. If replanting in the open ground, make holes large enough to allow the roots to be spread out fully. Firm in and water well. Keep the soil moist until the plants are established.

"Irishman's" cuttings

These are essentially sideshoots that have already rooted. Thymes and other creeping rock plants produce this sort of cutting. The technique is particularly useful for plants with woody rootstocks that are not easily divided, or for those that naturally produce offsets or runners.

Before taking the cuttings, brush away surface soil from the base of the parent plant. Cut rooted pieces from the plant with a sharp knife and pot them up in equal parts of low-fertility, loam-based potting compost and grit. Alternatively, plant them out in a cool, sheltered spot in the garden until well established.

Root cuttings

A limited number of alpines and rock garden plants, such as *Morisia monanthos* and *Primula denticulata*, may be propagated from root cuttings. Take root cuttings from the healthiest-looking roots in either late autumn or winter, when the plants are dormant.

Selecting material

Choose a strong, healthy plant and lift it from the soil. Select young, vigorous roots and cut them from the parent plant. The cuttings should be about 5cm (2in) long. Cut the roots straight across at the top end (nearest the plant's stem) and use sloping cuts at the lower end (nearest the root tips). Wash the cuttings in tepid water and replant the parent stock immediately or, if old and straggly and no longer required, discard it.

Inserting the cuttings

Use pots at least 10cm (4in) deep. Put broken crocks over the drainage holes and place over these a 2.5cm (1in) layer of low-fertility loam-based potting compost. Fill the pots with washed sand, then firm. Make several planting holes in each pot around the edges.

Insert the cuttings into the holes, with the straight ends uppermost and the tops level with the surface of the sand. Cuttings of plants with thin, wiry roots may be laid flat on the surface of the compost. Top-dress with fine grit. Label the pots, water thoroughly, and place them in a cold frame on a layer of grit or gravel or in a propagator. Close the frames in cold weather; otherwise they should be ventilated freely.

Water the pots when new growth appears. When the new shoots are growing strongly, check that the cuttings have rooted before potting them up: gently knock them out of their pots to inspect their roots.

Potting up rooted cuttings

Slide the cuttings out of their pots and separate them carefully. Pot them up singly, using low-fertility, loam-based potting compost mixed with an equal amount of sand. Instead of sand, a mix of peat substitute (or peat) and sand may be used.

HOW TO PROPAGATE BY ROOT CUTTINGS

1 *In late autumn or winter, using a hand fork, carefully lift a healthy plant (here* Primula denticulata*) with a well-developed root system.*

2 *Wash the roots clean of earth, then select thick, healthy roots for the cuttings. Using a sharp knife, cut off selected roots close to the crown of the plant.*

3 *Prepare 5cm (2in) lengths of root, cutting each one straight at the thicker end (closest to the parent plant) and angled at the lower end.*

4 *Place a layer of compost in the base of a pot, then fill almost to the brim with sharp sand. Insert the cuttings so that straight ends are just level with the sand surface.*

5 *Cover the sand with a 1cm (½in) layer of grit. Water and label the cuttings, then place the pot in a propagator or on the greenhouse bench.*

Top-dress the pots with 1cm (½in) of sharp sand or grit. Water and then place outside, out of direct sun. Leave until the new plants are established, watering as required.

Scooping rosettes

Plants that grow quickly or form rosettes, for example *Primula denticulata*, may be propagated *in situ* in midwinter from root cuttings by scooping out the rosettes with a sharp knife, to expose the top of the rootstock. Select strong-growing rosettes and brush the tops of the roots with fungicidal powder to prevent grey mould/*Botrytis* (see p.646); cover the pots with a thin layer of horticultural sharp sand.

Shoots should soon appear on each root apex. When the shoots are about 2.5–5cm (1–2in) tall, they are ready to be lifted. Separate the clumps into individual, small plants that have healthy-looking, vigorous shoots and roots, pulling them apart by hand or dividing them with a sharp knife.

Pot up the young plants to grow on, using equal parts of potting compost and horticultural sand. Water thoroughly, and place outside in a shady site. Keep moist and plant out the young plants when their roots have filled the pots.

HOW TO SCOOP ROSETTES

1 *Scoop out the live crowns of rosette-forming plants (here* Primula denticulata*) with a sharp knife, so that the tops of the roots are visible (see inset).*

2 *Dust the exposed roots with fungicidal powder (see inset) to protect them from moulds and fungi. Lightly cover with sharp, horticultural sand.*

3 *When new shoots appear from the roots, lift the whole clump, using a hand fork or trowel. Take care not to damage the new roots.*

4 *Divide the clump into individual plants, each with one shoot and well-developed roots. Pot them up using equal parts potting compost and sand.*

Alpine houses and frames

Although some high-altitude alpines grow well in the open garden in temperate climates, provided that their specific requirements of situation and soil are satisfied, most will perform considerably better if they are grown under cover. Many alpines bloom in late winter and very early spring when, if left in the open, their delicate flowers may be damaged by inclement weather, eaten by slugs or snails, or pecked by birds.

In an alpine house, plants are protected from winter wet, cold, drying winds, and sudden sharp frosts, as well as from the attentions of most pests. This enables a far wider range of alpines and rock plants to be grown, either in pots or in ground-level or raised beds, to provide an eye-catching and lasting display.

Using an alpine house
Part of the house may be used to grow on young plants (foreground) in beds supported by brick pillars.

Using an alpine house

An alpine house is an unheated greenhouse, usually with raised benches, designed for growing and displaying alpines and rock plants under controlled conditions. Often, half of the house is used for growing the plants, and the other half for displaying them. Alternatively, the plants may be grown in cold frames (either attached to or sited very near the alpine house) and brought temporarily into the house for display when they are at their best.

Displaying the plants

Displays may be of plants in pots simply standing on the staging or, more commonly, plunged up to their rims in a layer of sand. Plunging keeps roots cool and moist and reduces temperature fluctuations, while allowing easy irrigation of plants that dislike overhead watering. Specially built display beds are an attractive option. Create miniature rock gardens in the alpine house, either waist-high where staging is strong enough to support the weight, or at ground level. These may have some permanent planting as well as areas of sand or sandy compost into which different plants may be plunged, according to season. Lightweight tufa rocks may be incorporated and planted up to enhance this type of display.

Siting the alpine house

Choose a firm, level site away from the shade of trees, fences, walls, and tall buildings if possible. Siting the alpine house on a north–south axis is ideal but any open, sunny

An alpine house display
A wide range of rock plants may be grown in pots and attractively displayed in raised sand beds in an alpine house.

position is acceptable. Always avoid hollows where cold air forms frost pockets and do not site it in exposed, windy situations. Try to position the alpine house where it will harmonize with other garden features, perhaps even using it as a focal point. For further information on greenhouses, ventilation, shading, and staging, see Greenhouses and Frames, pp.575, 576, and 579.

Using frames

Frames should be sited near the alpine house, where they may be used to protect a range of choice plants from climatic extremes, as an "overspill" area, or for storage when plants are not in flower. They are

very useful for bulbs which need to be kept dry when dormant, or for plants that will not tolerate the very hot conditions that may arise in summer. Frames incorporate a top light that must be opened as required to provide good ventilation; a standard Dutch light frame is suitable but other types are available. The lights may be removed in summer if required, but they should be kept on if the frame contains dormant bulbs. Those plants that do not tolerate direct summer sun can be protected by covering the frame with mesh shading (see Greenhouses and Frames, "Meshes and fabrics", p.576). Pots in a frame are usually plunged in a material such as washed builder's sand over a layer of rubble to give them good drainage.

CARE OF ALPINES AND DWARF BULBS AFTER FLOWERING

Alpines indoors
After flowering, pots of alpines needing a careful watering regime (here Dionysia *spp.) should be plunged in sand under cover.*

Alpines outdoors
Alpines that tolerate variable summer weather conditions, such as saxifrages, may be plunged in open cold frames after flowering.

Bulbs indoors
Pots of dwarf bulbs (here irises) that have finished flowering may be kept dry by plunging in sand or gravel under staging.

Protecting flowering alpines
Alpines coming into flower may be grown in outdoor frames before bringing them into the alpine house for display.

Alpines in pots

Growing alpines in pots ensures that special watering, compost, or feeding requirements can be provided for individual plants.

Plastic and clay pots

Although plastic pots are suitable for growing alpines and retain moisture well, clay pots are more attractive – important if the plants are to be exhibited. The compost in plastic pots dries out more slowly than in clay pots so take care not to over-water the plants. Clean and sterilize all pots before use: sterilants based on dilute solutions of sodium hyperchlorite are suitable, but do not use tar-based disinfectants.

Composts

All alpines need a freely draining compost and benefit from a layer of broken crocks in the bottom of clay pots, or grit in plastic pots, since even moisture-loving plants will not tolerate stagnant conditions.

Most species grow well in loam-based potting compost, mixed with an equal amount of grit. Those from high, alpine habitats of scree and rock-face crevices, such as the Aretian *Androsace* species and other cushion-forming plants, need a less fertile and more freely draining mix if they are to retain their neat, natural habit. In rich composts, they quickly become soft and lush and are then more prone to attack by pests and diseases. For these plants use a mix of up to 3 parts grit to 1 part loam-based compost. Introduce plants to these "lean mixes" when they are young, since they may not adapt easily if they have been potted on from a more fertile medium.

A number of species, usually ones from woodland habitats, or those which occur in humus-rich pockets in rocky habitats, such as *Haberlea* and *Ramonda*, prefer well-drained composts that are rich in organic matter. For these, a mix of 1 part each of loam-based compost and grit, with 2 parts leaf mould, peat substitute, or peat will be suitable. Take care to check on the individual needs of each plant before selecting an appropriate compost, and ensure that for lime-hating plants all ingredients are lime-free.

Top-dressings

After planting up the pots (see right), top-dress them with a layer of grit or stone chippings to enhance the plant's appearance, to keep the neck of the plant well drained, and to prevent the growth of mosses and liverworts. Use a top-dressing that is appropriate to the pH requirements of the plant, for example limestone chippings for lime-loving species or granitic grit for lime-hating plants.

Some small, cushion-forming alpines are very sensitive to the presence of water around their necks, so, as well as top-dressing with grit, prop small wedges of rock beneath their cushions in order to keep them clear of the surface.

Repotting

When a plant has outgrown its pot, transfer it carefully into a slightly larger pot, disturbing the root ball as little as possible. Pot on herbaceous and shrubby plants in spring and summer, when they are growing strongly; bulbs should be potted on when they are dormant. Plant to the same level as in the previous pot, firm in fresh compost, and then add a new layer of top-dressing.

Water well after potting by standing the pot in at least 2.5–5cm (1–2in) of water until the top of the compost becomes moist. Then remove the pot to avoid the risk of root rot.

Planting in beds

The beds may be at ground level or raised some 1m (3ft) high. A raised bed allows plants to be tended and

REPOTTING A SAXIFRAGE

1 *The roots of this saxifrage can be seen growing through the drainage hole at the bottom of the pot. The plant is pot-bound and should be repotted.*

2 *Choose a pot that is one size bigger than the one that the plant is growing in. Use crocks and gravel to provide drainage at the base of the pot.*

3 *Arrange the crocks carefully over the drainage hole. The crocks should then be covered with a layer of gravel.*

4 *Remove the plant from its pot by tapping gently on the base to loosen the root ball; tease out the roots to encourage fresh roots to penetrate the new compost.*

5 *Cover the crocks in the larger pot with a little compost; position the plant so that the neck is at the same level as in the original pot, and fill in with compost.*

6 *Spread the gravel top-dressing over the surface of the compost, taking care to tuck it under the collar of the plant to keep it sharply drained.*

7 *Place the pot in a bowl of water and leave it until the surface of the compost and gravel appears damp.*

8 *Then remove the pot and place it on a layer of sand in a cold frame, where any excess moisture can easily drain off. This will prevent any risk of root rot.*

9 *The repotted plant may then be plunged in sand in a cold frame or bed to grow on.*

REMOVING DEAD LEAVES

Tweezers should be used regularly to remove any brown or withered leaves from alpine plants such as this Campanula chamissonis.

viewed more easily and is especially useful for elderly or disabled gardeners. The staging must drain well and be solidly constructed to bear the weight of the bed (see also GREENHOUSES AND FRAMES, "Raised beds", p.578).

Use a compost of 3 parts loam (or good sterilized garden soil), 2 parts coarse fibrous peat substitute (or peat), and 2 parts sharp sand or grit. Add rocks to the bed to create a miniature rock garden. Tufa is particularly useful because it is light-weight, very moisture-retentive, and as plants can be grown in the rock itself. Plant out alpines in the bed, avoiding species that are invasive and free-seeding, but leave some gaps for plunging a succession of seasonal, pot-grown specimens. Grow ferns and other shade-loving species under a raised bed.

Routine maintenance

As alpines have quite specialized growing requirements, they need considerable attention through the growing season. Plants that are regularly repotted rarely need additional feeding, but where fertilizers are used be sure that they are low in nitrogen – high-nitrogen feed will lead to soft, lush growth that is uncharacteristic of alpines and more prone to pests and diseases.

Ventilation

Ventilating surfaces must occupy at least 25 per cent of the glass area, as the aim is to provide the maximum possible air circulation at all times. In spring and summer, the vents and the greenhouse door can remain open permanently, unless there is strong wind or heavy rain. Use a screen of small-diameter mesh over vents and doors to keep out cats and birds. During heavy rain and windy weather, close the vents on the receiving side to avoid drip on the foliage and reduce strong draughts that may damage foliage and flowers. In severe winds, it is safest to close all vents and doors.

In winter, open the vents fully (unless it is windy, raining, or snowing) but close them before nightfall to retain any residual warmth. In very cold weather, allow temperatures in the alpine house to rise gradually before ventilating; on bright, sunny days, however, open the vents as soon as possible to prevent the temperature from rising too rapidly. In damp, foggy weather, especially in areas with high levels of atmospheric pollution, close down the house completely to keep out cold, damp air, and use a cool air fan to maintain air circulation.

Temperature

Shading will be necessary during sunny weather, from late spring to autumn, to avoid scorching tender, new growth, and to help reduce temperatures. Do not use heavy shading as this might cause etiolation or lop-sided "drawing" of plants towards the available light source. In very hot weather, damp down the house floor to reduce temperatures and maintain atmospheric humidity; plants may be gently misted over with cool water in the evenings.

Heating should be used to stop the pots freezing in severe weather, and a method of heating that does not produce excessive fumes or moisture is best (see GREENHOUSES AND FRAMES, "Heating", p.574).

Hygiene

Remove dead foliage and faded flowers regularly to reduce the risk of fungal attack. Check the plants for pests and diseases and treat any outbreaks promptly (see PLANT PROBLEMS, pp.639–673). Always keep the floor of the house clean to minimize the risk of diseases, and make sure that the glass is clean so that plants receive maximum light.

Watering

Water regularly throughout the season, especially on sunny spring and summer days, when water loss is rapid. If plants are allowed to dry out between waterings, growth may be severely checked, and flower buds may shrivel. For pots standing on staging, water from above but avoid splashing the foliage. Plunged pots derive moisture from the surrounding material but may need additional watering in warm periods. For plants that are sensitive to moisture on their foliage, water the plunge medium around the pots. As autumn approaches, reduce watering as plants prepare for dormancy. During winter, alpines need to be kept dry but not dust dry (for plunged pots, the plunge medium should be just damp to the touch).

Winter maintenance

A spell of clear, dry weather during late winter is a good time to store the plants in a frame and clean the alpine house (see GREENHOUSES AND FRAMES, "Routine maintenance", p.583). Clean and top up the sand or grit on beds and renew labels. Then transfer pots back from the frame.

Exhibiting

Alpines for showing should be in the best possible condition on exhibition day. No matter how perfect the plant, it will lose marks if poorly presented in a less than scrupulously clean pot, or if top-dressings are thin or show evidence of algal growth. Remove all evidence of weeds, pests, and

TRANSPORTING PLANTS

When transporting fragile plants (here Fritillaria uva-vulpis), *make a tripod from split canes bound at the top with twine, and tie in stems.*

diseases. Check plants for dead, discoloured, or misshapen leaves and faded flowers, and remove these carefully with tweezers.

Clay pots should be scrubbed clean with a wire brush or scourer. Alternatively they may be double-potted: insert the specimen in its pot into a larger, new pot, covering the inner rim with top-dressing. Renew all top-dressings with materials appropriate to the plant's natural habitat, then relabel. Support tall, fragile plants during transport with tripods of split canes. Water plants thoroughly the day before the show and allow to drain before packing for transportation. Carry spare top-dressing to renew any lost in transit.

PREPARING PLANTS FOR EXHIBITION

1 *Use fine sand together with a wire brush or scouring pad to clean the outside of clay pots. This will remove any algae or limescale that may be present.*

2 *Replenish the top-dressing. For this* Dionysia aretioides *the medium is coarse gravel; but stone chippings, grit, or pine needles may be used, depending on the plant.*

3 *Add new, clearly written labels. Pack the pots carefully in a tray using newspaper to hold them steady, and carry extra top-dressing for last-minute renewal.*

CHAPTER
10

WATER GARDENING

A WATER FEATURE is an irresistible attraction in any garden. Whether it is a formal pool graced by water lilies and the bright gleam of goldfish, a trickling stream bordered by ferns, or a simple pond reflecting the sculptural silhouette of a clump of irises, there is a style suitable for every setting. Creating a water garden provides habitats for a specific range of plants as well as attracting a host of wildlife, including newts, frogs, toads, dragonflies, and perhaps even water birds. Water may be either restful or exciting: still water is valued for its properties of reflection and tranquillity, while moving water – whether a classical fountain or a rushing waterfall – adds a delightful sound and a dynamic vitality to the garden.

Water features in the garden

UNLIKE any other element in the garden, water brings an ever-changing pattern of reflections, sound, and movement that is particularly appealing. Even when frozen, its surface provides contrasts of colour and texture. A pond is a popular form of water feature but there are others: a waterfall, fountain, or watercourse, for instance.

A garden water feature allows you to grow many plants that do not thrive in any other conditions, from the floating frogbit (*Hydrocharis morsus-ranae*) and water hyacinth (*Eichhornia crassipes*) to the bog garden candelabra primulas.

When deciding which type of water feature to create, bear in mind the size and style of the garden. If large and informal, a meandering watercourse may be effective, while in an enclosed town garden, a raised formal pool might be appropriate. Water may even be included in a garden for children in the form of an attractive "bubble fountain" – in which the water splashes over stones and is recirculated without forming an area of any depth.

A naturalistic water garden
In an informal or semi-wild garden, a gently meandering stream provides a lush, cool area by which to sit and relax. Clouds of pink rhododendrons add both height and colour to the scheme, while marginal plantings of bright yellow Iris pseudacorus, *ferns, and rushes form a transition between the stream and the garden.*

Siting a pond

Exploit the reflective quality of water by siting a pond where it mirrors an eye-catching feature – a specimen plant or statue, perhaps. It may help to lay a reflective sheet on the proposed site to give an idea of reflections to be seen during the day and evening; check it from major viewpoints such as the house and patio.

An open, sunny position, away from overhanging trees, provides the best conditions in which to grow most water plants.

If planning to create a pond on wet land that is prone to flooding, check that there is no danger of fertilizer or pesticide residues leaching into the water from an adjacent vegetable garden or farmland. These substances invariably affect pond life adversely. Direct potential overflows to a suitable drainage system. Land with a high water table may cause problems because, in very wet periods, water pressure from below may push a pond liner out of shape.

Do not site a pond in a frost pocket or in a very exposed position, since this restricts the range of plants that may be grown and protection may have to be provided in winter.

Informal ponds

In an informal garden, a natural, sunken pond may look most effective. Usually, this is in an irregular, curved shape, bordered with natural materials such as turf or stones to link it with the garden. The water surface is, however, only part of the total scheme: the inclusion of marginal and moisture-loving plants

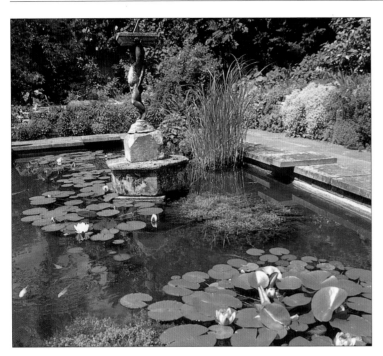

A formal pool
Water lilies (Nymphaea) *bring elegance and colour to a rectangular pond. A sundial links the informality of the plants to the pool's formal margins.*

around the pond, to soften or hide its outline completely, helps to create a lush and refreshing effect.

As when planting in a border or bed, consider how the plants will combine to create complementary and contrasting associations of colour, texture, and form.

Formal ponds

In contrast to the natural effect of an informal pond, a formal pool makes a much bolder feature. It may be raised or sunken and is usually of a regular, geometric design. As a rule, less space is devoted to planting than in an informal pond, although plants with floating leaves and flowers (eg water lilies) are often included; sculptural plants such as certain ferns, grown next to the pool, provide attractive reflections. A fountain or water spout to complement the style of the pond can be an ornamental and dramatic addition.

Far from being disguised, the edge of the pond may form an important feature, perhaps made of attractive paving or, if the pool is raised, wide enough to form a seat; this type of design is particularly suitable for elderly or disabled people.

In many cases formal ponds are sited so that they form a striking focal point in the garden, at the main axis of paths, for example, or where they may be conveniently viewed and enjoyed from the windows or terrace of the house.

Fountains

The style and size of a fountain should be considered in the context of the surrounding pool and the overall design of the garden. Often used in a formal garden as a focal point, a fountain is also invaluable for adding height to a design, and for its dynamic contribution of sound and movement and the scattering of light. In addition, a fountain is particularly effective if lit at night.

A cobble or bubble fountain, in which water bubbles over stones into a small underground reservoir, looks more informal than a standard fountain and is ideal in a garden that is used by children.

As well as being ornamental, fountains also provide a practical function: the splashing action introduces oxygen into the water and this is beneficial to any fish. Most water plants do not flourish in disturbed water, however, so they should not be grown close to a fountain.

Water spouts

While a fountain or waterfall might be too large in an average garden, a water spout provides all the pleasure of running water scaled down for the smallest garden or even a conservatory. There are many styles, from the classical lion's head or gargoyle above a pool to the simplicity of an oriental bamboo pipe trickling water over stones. A water spout is

usually fixed to a wall, with a pump and pipe similar to those used for a watercourse; the pump moves water from a pool or reservoir to the rear of the spout and out of the "mouth".

Streams, waterfalls and watercourses

Few gardens have a natural stream or waterfall, but it is possible to create a circulating watercourse spilling out into a pool or underground reservoir. Making a watercourse or waterfall is an attractive way of exploiting a change of level in the garden. It may be used to link parts of the garden as well as providing points of interest between levels.

In an informal garden, a watercourse may be made to look more natural by being edged with rocks or stones and moisture-loving plants such as ferns and irises. Ornamentals that have large leaves, for example *Rheum palmatum*, are particularly valuable for watercourses made from liners or preformed units since they help to disguise the edges.

Bog and wildlife areas

In an informal or naturalistic design, a bog garden makes an attractive and unconventional feature. Usually most appropriate next to ponds, bog gardens provide a gradual and natural transition from aquatic to moisture-loving plants and ideal conditions for wildlife.

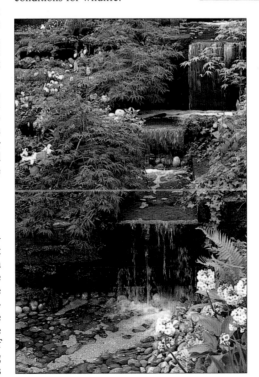

Water conservation versus water features

As changes in weather patterns become more frequent and global warming increases, it is important to take into account the adverse environmental impact of using the mains water supply in a garden. This is particularly the case when water features need topping up.

During periods of hot, dry weather when evaporation from the surface is high, it is important to raise water levels to maintain the pond's ecological balance. As the water level drops, the water quality in the pond deteriorates as the oxygen level decreases and the water temperature rises. This adversely affects the health of water plants, fish and other wildlife in the pond. It is possible to alleviate this, to some extent, by adding to the number of oxygenating plants in the pond and spraying the water surface from a hose, which increases the oxygen content of the water, but these measures are only palliative. Topping up the pond with mains water is the easy solution but, in times of severe drought and water shortages, there is inevitably an environmental cost. It is better to plan ahead and collect rainwater in water butts for this purpose. Never be tempted to use "grey" water (see p.615) in ponds.

An informal watercourse
A terrace of weirs formed from thick slabs of stone creates cascades of water that spill into a shallow, cobble-lined pool. Overhanging plants such as ivies (Hedera), *Japanese maple* (Acer palmatum), *and primulas help to break up the rigid line of the stone, while the meandering path of the watercourse gives the scheme an appealing informality and charm.*

Bog gardens

Creating a bog garden is a far better way of using waterlogged land than struggling against nature by trying to drain it. Although the ground next to a man-made pool is unlikely to be wet enough to provide suitable conditions for growing bog plants, using a liner under the soil will retain sufficient moisture.

Bog gardens bring a freshness of growth in late summer when many other plants are showing the effects of drought; most bog plants, however, die back naturally after frost, so they do not provide great interest in winter months.

Wildlife ponds

Simply adding a water feature will increase diversity in the wildlife garden, as such features provide habitats for waterfowl, frogs, newts, and an enormous range of insects. Limiting the planting to native species only will attract more wildlife, although many native plants can prove invasive; the inclusion of some exotic ornamentals creates a greater opportunity to make the pond a highly decorative feature as well. Informal ponds with muddy bottoms and shallowly sloping edges interspersed with large, flat stones are particularly suitable, providing ideal conditions for amphibians.

Water in small gardens

In a small garden or patio, or where major construction work is imprac-tical, it is still possible to have a water feature. The most suitable one might be a small quantity of water being continually recirculated by a small pump, which fills a basin or other container, or a "bubble" fountain, which conceals a reservoir. Such "covered" features are particularly suitable in family gardens, where safety is a concern.

Wall fountains are available in many styles, both formal and informal, in a range of materials such as stonework, pottery, or metal. A miniature pool could also be introduced by using an appropriate ornamental container, such as a sealed and lined half-barrel or terracotta pot (see also WATER GARDENS IN CONTAINERS, p.331). Larger containers could also include a simple fountain or Japanese water feature.

Plants are generally incidental within a small feature, but if it includes any moving water, it is important that the surrounding plants are able to tolerate the high humidity caused by the fine spray.

Fluid attraction
Reservoir features such as this textured fibreglass millstone fountain create a source of movement and sound. Simple child-safe water features work well in a small garden, but may also provide a surprise element in a larger one.

Water garden plants

In any water garden, plants are vital to the scheme. Lush foliage and flowers enhance the pool and link it with the rest of the garden, while certain plants help to maintain clear water and, in the case of oxygenators, good conditions for fish.

Plants suitable for a water garden range from those that thrive in deep water to those requiring moist soil only around their root tips. They are usually grouped into six categories: oxygenators, deep-water plants, surface floaters, marginals, bog plants, and moisture-loving plants.

Oxygenators

Lagarosiphon major (syn. *Elodea crispa*) and *Myriophyllum* are typical oxygenators: submerged, rapidly growing plants that help to clean and oxygenate the water. During sunny weather, submerged algae may turn a new pond completely green within a week or two; oxygenators compete for the dissolved mineral salts on which algae thrive and starve them out so the water eventually becomes clear once more. Oxygenators are essential if fish are kept in the pool.

Deep-water plants

These flourish in a depth range of 30–90cm (12–36in). This category includes plants such as *Aponogeton* and *Orontium*, with water lilies (*Nymphaea*) forming the largest group (see pp.286–287). Apart from their ornamental value, their floating leaves also help to reduce algae by cutting down the amount of light allowed to reach the water.

Surface floaters

Floating plants, such as *Trapa natans* and *Azolla filiculoides*, perform a similar function to deep-water plants, especially in the establishment phase. It is vital not to let them cover too much water as oxygenators suffer if there is not enough light.

Marginals

Marginal plants grow in shallow water usually about 7–15cm (3–6in) deep. Many of these plants are extremely attractive, such as *Iris laevigata* 'Variegata' with fans of green- and cream-striped leaves and lavender-blue flowers, and they are valuable in an informal pond for breaking up the outline. In a wildlife pool, marginal plants provide cover for wildfowl and other small creatures. Some species such as *Mentha aquatica* and *Veronica beccabunga* also help to oxygenate the water.

Bog plants

Bog-loving plants such as *Lysichiton* or some *Caltha* species thrive in waterlogged soil and can withstand occasional flooding. Under a bog-plant heading, nursery catalogues may include plants that grow in moist or even wet soil but do not tolerate a waterlogged soil; when ordering, ensure that any plants chosen tolerate high water levels around the roots.

Moisture-loving plants

These thrive in soils that contain extra moisture without being water-logged. Moisture-lovers include many herbaceous perennials, such as *Astilbe*, *Ligularia*, and *Primula florindae*. They all associate well with marginal plants in the areas surrounding natural, informal pools where growing conditions are ideal.

Planting associations

Create a varied and attractive display by mixing plants with different heights and growth habits around the pool. Similar design principles should be applied as for planting in the rest of the garden to develop a successful scheme with a diversity of shapes and forms (see also "Principles of planting", pp.42–51). Site *Gunnera manicata*, for example, so that its immense, platter-like leaves tower over the jutting swords of *Acorus calamus*. Use plants at the edge of the pond to act as a foil for floating plants or deep marginals – an island of water lilies such as *Nymphaea alba* with its pure white blooms would be beautifully offset by a drift of ostrich-feather ferns (*Matteuccia struthiopteris*).

Bog garden
The boggy ground next to a pond is ideal for plants such as Primula bulleyana *and* Iris laevigata, *which thrive in such an environment.*

Plants with contrasting colours and textures also provide some spectacular combinations. For example, the upright, scarlet flower spikes of *Lobelia cardinalis* would form a fine contrast with the heart-shaped, blue-grey leaves of *Hosta sieboldiana*.

Plan the planting to supply interest throughout the seasons. Including evergreen foliage plants such as *Bergenia* at the pool edges provides continuity of form and colour, while other types of plant – ranging from the golden flowers of the marsh marigold (*Caltha palustris*) in spring to the summer-long display of the water forget-me-not (*Myosotis scorpioides*) with its delicate, blue flowers – may be used to create a changing, seasonal display.

Fish

While most ornamental fish live in harmony with aquatic plant life and will be happy in all but the smallest ponds, the inclusion of larger specimen fish necessitates certain precautions in pond design. Pools for koi carp, for example, should be large and at least 1m (3ft) deep, with vertical sides projecting above the surface so that the carp cannot leap out. Goldfish and orfe are easier to manage, the latter being ideal decorative fish that enjoy shallow water and feed on any insect larvae present. In the wildlife garden, native species such as tench may be suitable and less damaging to tadpole populations inhabiting the pond.

Planter's guide to water plants

SHALLOW MARGINALS

(6in/15cm depth of water)
Acorus gramineus,
 A. gramineus
 'Variegatus'

*Calla
palustris*

*Alisma
 plantago-aquatica*
 var. *parviflorum*
Calla palustris
Caltha leptosepala,
 C. palustris, C. palustris var.
 alba, C. palustris 'Flore Pleno'
Carex elata 'Aurea',
 C. pendula, C. riparia
Colocasia esculenta ❀
Cotula coronopifolia
Cyperus involucratus ❀ ,
 C. longus, C. papyrus 'Nanus'
Decodon verticillatus
Eriophorum angustifolium,
 E. latifolium

*Hydrocleys
nymphoides*

Houttuynia cordata,
 H. cordata 'Chameleon',
 H. cordata
 'Flore Pleno'
Hydrocleys nymphoides ❀
Iris laevigata, I. versicolor
Juncus effusus, J. effusus f. *spiralis,*
 J. effusus 'Vittatus', *J. ensifolius*
Lobelia paludosa
Lysichiton americanus,
 L. camtschatcensis
Mentha aquatica
Mimulus cardinalis,
 M. cupreus, M. guttatus,
 M. ringens
Myosotis scorpioides,
 M. scorpioides 'Mermaid'
Peltandra sagittifolia
Persicaria amphibia

Sagittaria latifolia, S. sagittifolia,
 S. sagittifolia 'Flore Pleno'
Sparganium natans
Typha minima
Zizania aquatica ❀

DEEP MARGINALS

(12in/30cm depth of water)
Acorus calamus,
 A. calamus 'Variegatus'
Alisma lanceolatum,
 A. plantago-aquatica
Butomus umbellatus
Cyperus papyrus ❀
Glyceria maxima 'Variegata'
Hottonia palustris
Iris pseudacorus
Nelumbo lutea ❀ , *N. nucifera* 'Alba
 Grandiflora' ❀ , *N. nucifera* 'Alba
 Striata' ❀ , *N. nucifera* 'Rosea
 Plena' ❀
Phragmites australis,
 P. australis 'Variegatus'
Pontederia cordata, P. cordata
 var. *lancifolia*
Ranunculus lingua 'Grandiflora'
Saururus cernuus
Schoenoplectus lacustris,
 S. lacustris subsp.
 tabernaemontani 'Albescens',
 S. lacustris subsp.
 tabernaemontani 'Zebrinus'
Sparganium erectum
Thalia dealbata ❀ , *T. geniculata* ❀
Typha angustifolia, T. latifolia
 'Variegata', *T. laxmannii*
Zantedeschia aethiopica
 'Crowborough'

DEEP WATER PLANTS

Aponogeton distachyos
Euryale ferox ❀
Nuphar advena, N. lutea
Nymphaea, some ❀ (most spp.)
Nymphoides indica, N. peltata
Orontium aquaticum
Victoria amazonica

SUBMERGED OXYGENATORS

Callitriche hermaphroditica
Ceratophyllum demersum

Ceratopteris thalictroides ❀
Crassula helmsii
Egeria densa ❀
Fontinalis antipyretica
Hydrocleys parviflora ❀
Lagarosiphon major
Mentha cervina
Myriophyllum aquaticum ❀
Potamogeton crispus

FLOATING AQUATICS

Azolla filiculoides
Ceratopteris pteridioides ❀
Eichhornia azurea, E. crassipes ❀

*Pistia
stratiotes*

Hydrocharis morsus-ranae
Lemna trisulca
Limnanthemum lacunosum
Limnobium spongia,
 L. stoloniferum
Nymphaea
Pistia stratiotes ❀
Riccia fluitans
Salvinia auriculata ❀ ,
 S. natans ❀
Stratiotes aloides
Trapa natans
Utricularia minor, U. vulgaris
Wolffia arrhiza ❀

BOG AND MOISTURE-LOVING PLANTS

Alnus glutinosa, A. incana
Anemone rivularis
Aruncus dioicus 'Kneiffii'
Arundo donax 'Variegata'
Astilbe x *arendsii, A. chinensis,*
 A. simplicifolia
Astilboides tabularis
Cardamine pratensis
Carex elata 'Aurea', *C. pendula*
Cimicifuga americana,
 C. racemosa

Cornus alba
Darmera peltata
Eupatorium purpureum
Euphorbia palustris
Filipendula rubra, F. ulmaria
Gunnera manicata, G. tinctoria
Hemerocallis (most spp.)
Hosta (most spp.)
Iris ensata, I. sibirica
Leucojum aestivum
Ligularia dentata,
 L. przewalskii
Lobelia cardinalis
Lythrum salicaria
Mimulus cardinalis, M. luteus
Osmunda regalis
Parnassia palustris
Persicaria amplexicaulis,
 P. bistorta, P. campanulata
Phalaris arundinacea
Phragmites australis

*Trollius
europaeus*

Primula alpicola, P. denticulata,
 P. florindae, P. japonica,
 P. prolifera, P. pulverulenta,
 P. rosea, P. secundiflora,
 P. sikkimensis
Rheum alexandrae,
 R. palmatum,
 R. palmatum 'Atrosanguineum'
Rodgersia aesculifolia, R. pinnata,
 R. podophylla
Salix alba, S. babylonica,
 S. babylonica var. *pekinensis*
 'Tortuosa', *S. daphnoides*
Scrophularia auriculata
 'Variegata'
Senecio smithii
Taxodium distichum
Trollius chinensis,
 T. x *cultorum,*
 T. europaeus

Key
❀ *Not hardy*

Water lilies

THE elegant, mainly floating cups and lush foliage of water lilies such as *Nymphaea* are a graceful addition to any water garden, whether it is in a natural, rural setting or a formal, city courtyard. The flower forms vary from open and star-like to goblet-shaped, peony blooms, with colours ranging from the simple purity of white or cream to striking shades of red, yellow, or even blue. Some are offset by dark purplish-green leaves, while others have foliage that is attractively mottled. Certain species have richly perfumed flowers; these are best grown in a raised pool where their scent may be easily enjoyed.

While most water lilies bloom in the daytime, some tropical cultivars such as 'Missouri' and 'Red Flare' open at dusk – these are best enhanced by complementary lighting to create a bold display after dark. Native to tropical and subtropical zones, these lilies may be grown in temperate regions in a conservatory pool or outdoors in hot summers. Water lilies usually grow more quickly than those that are hardy and require high light intensity, an ample food supply, and warm water at a minimum of 20°C (68°F).

Water lilies need several hours of full sun each day, otherwise they develop a mass of leaves but few blooms, so they should be grown in an open, sunny part of the pool. They also prefer calm water; if there is a fountain or waterfall, grow the lilies well away from it so that they are not disturbed by the movement. Tropical species usually grow more quickly than those that are hardy and require high light intensity, an ample food supply, and warm water at a minimum of 20°C (68°F).

As well as being decorative, water lilies help to keep the water clear because their large, spreading leaves create shade, thereby helping to control the growth of algae.

HARDY AND TROPICAL WATER LILIES

Nymphaea 'Attraction'

N. tetragona 'Helvola'

N. 'Fire Crest'

N. 'Chromatella'

N. 'American Star'

N. 'Blue Beauty'

N. 'Escarboucle'

N. 'Virginia'

N. 'Carnea'

Care and cultivation

Most water lilies have thick tubers which grow roughly vertically, with fibrous roots beneath; cultivars of *N. odorata* and *N. tuberosa* have longer, fleshy rhizomes which grow horizontally near the soil surface.

Planting

Plant between late spring and late summer so that the plants will be well established before winter; do not plant out tropical water lilies until the risk of frost has passed.

For planting, use containers that are 30–35cm (12–14in) across and 15–19cm (6–7½in) deep, depending on the size and vigour of the cultivar. Alternatively, plant in submerged beds 30–45cm (12–18in) deep and 45–60cm (18–24in) square.

Prepare the plant by trimming back long roots and cutting off old or damaged leaves and flower buds. The older leaves make the plant more buoyant and difficult to anchor under water and they produce little food for the plant. New leaves will quickly replace them. When planting tropical water lilies, insert a sachet of slow-release fertilizer.

If the planted container is not too heavy, water well before placing it in the pond so that any soil shrinkage can be rectified. Lower the basket into place with strings as for planting deep water plants (see p.299).

In a new pool, the containers may be positioned on the bottom before the pool is filled. Cover them with only 8–15cm (3–6in) of water initially; raise the containers on blocks if necessary so that they have the correct depth of water above them. As the plants grow, gradually lower the containers in stages until they finally rest on the bottom. Tropical water lilies may be planted at their permanent depth immediately, however, as they grow quickly and prefer shallower water than most hardy cultivars.

Feeding

Water lilies usually benefit from limited additional feeding; insert a proprietary sachet of slow-release fertilizer into the soil or compost approximately every six weeks during the growing season. This gradually releases small quantities of plant food without discolouring the water or encouraging algae.

PLANTING A TUBEROUS WATER LILY

1 *Using secateurs or a sharp knife, trim back to within 5cm (2in) of the tuber any roots that are damaged or excessively long.*

2 *Cut off any dead or damaged leaves, or those with broken stalks. Retain new, young leaves and flower buds.*

3 *Line the basket and partly fill it with dampened soil. Position the tuber so that the crown is within 4cm (1½in) of the rim.*

4 *Pack soil firmly around the tuber, ensuring that the crown remains 4cm (1½in) above the level of the soil.*

A floating garden
The strong, straight lines of a wooden deck bridge offset the plate-like leaves and colourful blooms of an island of water lilies.

Other maintenance tasks

Water lily flowers last only 3–4 days and should be removed before they sink and rot, as should the leaves. These can go yellow or brown quite quickly, depending on prevailing conditions; regularly cut their stems below the water line, and discard.

During hot weather, spray leaf surfaces forcibly with water to dislodge insects such as leafhoppers and aphids. In areas subject to winter frosts, take in tropical water lilies and store the tubers at 5–7°C (41–45°F) in moist sand, and protect them from rodents.

Division

To maintain healthy growth, divide water lilies when the foliage is crowding the water surface, or when the roots have outgrown the container. Cut off pieces from the crown, each

with a young, strong shoot and about 15cm (6in) of attached tuber, and replant these in fresh soil. The old crown may be discarded.

Propagation

Most tuberous water lilies may be propagated by means of bud cuttings; rhizomatous types may have their rootstocks divided (see p.302). Some water lilies may be raised from seed, or by separating plantlets.

Bud cuttings

Some tuberous water lilies produce sideshoots or "eyes" that may be used to propagate new plants. Cut the eyes from the roots and dust them with charcoal or sulphur. Press each cutting into a prepared pot, top-dress, and immerse in water; leave the pots

in a greenhouse or cold frame at 15–18°C (59–64°F). As the plants develop, pot them on and gradually increase the water depth until they are ready to plant in the pool the following spring.

Seed

With the exception of *N. odorata* and *N. tetragona*, hardy water lilies do not readily set seed but tender or tropical water lilies set large quantities. Before collecting seed,

enclose the ripening capsules in muslin bags to prevent them from floating away. Sow hardy seed at once before it dries out; tropical water lily seed should be washed and allowed to dry, then stored in bags at room temperature. Tropical water lily seed is best sown in spring.

Sow the seed evenly, still attached to its jelly-like bladders, in pans of seed compost. Sprinkle with compost, water, then place the pans in a container and cover with 2.5–5cm (1–2in) of water. Hardy water lily seed requires a minimum temperature of 13°C (55°F) to germinate, tropical seed 23–27°C (73–81°F).

When the seedlings are large enough to handle, carefully lift, rinse, and plant them in pans submerged in 5–7.5cm (2–3in) of water. Pot on later into 6cm (2½in) pots in 8–10cm (3–4in) of water.

After overwintering, the tubers produce young plants that may be detached and potted on.

Plantlets

Certain day-blooming, tropical water lilies produce plantlets that may form and bloom while still attached to the parent leaf. Alternatively, they may be transplanted into shallow pans in water and then grown on at a temperature of 15–18°C (59–64°C); gradually increase the water level, then pot them up into aquatic containers.

PROPAGATION BY BUD CUTTINGS

1 *Remove the plant from its container and wash it. Using a sharp knife, remove strong-growing buds from the root by cutting flush with the tuber.*

2 *Fill 10cm (4in) pots with soil or aquatic compost, firm, and press a single cutting into the surface. Top-dress with grit.*

3 *Immerse the pots in water and keep them in a greenhouse or cold frame, partially shaded; plant out the following spring.*

PROPAGATION BY DIVISION

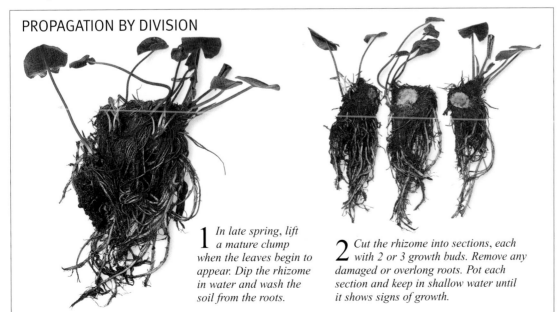

1 *In late spring, lift a mature clump when the leaves begin to appear. Dip the rhizome in water and wash the soil from the roots.*

2 *Cut the rhizome into sections, each with 2 or 3 growth buds. Remove any damaged or overlong roots. Pot each section and keep in shallow water until it shows signs of growth.*

Constructing ponds

For many years, man-made ponds were generally constructed from heavy materials such as stone, concrete, or brick. Since the advent of plastics and fibreglass, however, it has become easier to install your own pond and also to create a more naturalistic design, if desired.

The best shape, size, and material for the pond depends to a large extent on the size and style of your garden, the preferred method of construction, and cost. Flexible liners allow you maximum freedom of shape and size, and are ideal where a natural look is required since the edge may be easily concealed and the lining material itself is relatively unobtrusive; they are the best choice for large ponds. Rigid, preformed ponds are easier to install, but there is only a limited range of shapes and sizes. While they are excellent for small ponds, larger units are difficult to manoeuvre and very large sizes are not available. Hard materials such as concrete provide the strongest and most long-lasting ponds but these are also the most difficult and slowest to construct.

Ponds built by any method can accommodate a simple fountain, or a pump that drives a recirculating water feature (see p.292). Pumps may be powered by a suitable, safe, external electricity supply; solar-powered pumps are also available.

Flexible liners

Most new garden ponds are constructed using a flexible lining sheet of synthetic rubber or plastic, which provides a waterproof barrier between the soil and the water. These flexible liners are available in a wide range of sizes and can be cut to fit any shape of pond. Before buying a liner, decide on the site and size of the pond: marking out the desired shape with sand or string and pegs makes it easier to check the effect.

Butyl rubber is one of the most expensive pond lining materials. It is much stronger than either polythene or PVC, with a life expectancy of about 40–50 years, but it is also more expensive. Butyl is very pliable, and is tough enough to resist tearing or deterioration caused by ultra-violet light, bacterial growth, and temperature extremes. For a sizeable informal pond, particularly if part of the material may be exposed to sunlight, it is best to use a top-quality butyl liner that is 7mm (¼in) thick.

PVC liners are reasonably strong and tear-resistant, and some are guaranteed for ten years. They are resistant to both frost and fungal attack, but after several years of exposure to sunlight they may harden and crack.

Polythene is the cheapest of all the lining materials; it is easily torn and cracks after constant exposure to sunlight. If it can be protected from light or from accidental damage, it is an economical material to use. It is particularly suitable as a lining for bog gardens, where it is covered by a layer of earth. Low-density polyethylene (LDPE) is an improved form of polythene, which is more flexible and can be repaired. The material, which is guaranteed, is comparable to PVC in longevity.

Measuring for the liner

To calculate the size of the liner required, first determine the maximum length, width, and depth of the pond. The liner should measure the maximum width of the pond plus twice its depth, by the maximum length plus twice its depth. Add 15cm (6in) on both width and length measurements to allow for a flap at the edge of the pond, to prevent leakage. A pond measuring 2 x 2.5m (6 x 8ft) and 60cm (2ft) deep would require a 3.5 x 4m (11 x 13ft) liner.

Installation

First spread out the liner away from the site, in the sun if possible as the warmth will make it more flexible

MAKING A POND WITH FLEXIBLE LINER

1 Mark out the proposed shape of the pond using sand or string. Then position marker pegs at equal intervals around it, setting the first peg at the ideal level for the pond edge.

2 Use a straight edge and spirit level to align the remaining pegs with the first one. Then excavate the hole until it is 23cm (9in) deep all round. Slope the sides slightly outwards.

3 Rake the base of the hole so that it is flat. If a marginal planting shelf is desired, make a line, 23–30cm (9–12in) wide, with sand all around the hole, for the shelf.

4 Dig within the marked central area to a further 50–60cm (20–24in) deep. Remove any roots and sharp stones, then rake over the base until it is level.

5 Press a layer of sand or sifted soil, 2.5cm (1in) deep, over the base and sides of the hole. If using underlay fabric, drape it over the hole's contours and press it down.

6 Carefully unroll the flexible liner over the sand or underlay until it is draped over the entire hole and there is generous overlap at the sides. Fold in the creases evenly.

7 Fill the pond with water, using bricks to hold the liner in position. Move the bricks as the liner settles. Trim its edges, leaving a 15cm (6in) overlap.

and easier to handle. Mark the required shape of the pond on the site with sand or string, then position a line of datum marker pegs just outside the outline. Check that the rim of the pond is level all round by using a straight edge and spirit level across both the length and the width of the hole. This is extremely important, as if the pond is not level water may spill over the edge.

Dig to a depth of about 23cm (9in), making the pond sides slope outwards at an angle of 20° from the vertical; this slope prevents the sides from caving in, makes it easier to install the liner, and ensures that if the pond freezes the ice can expand upwards without causing damage. Reserve the spoil, as such topsoil could prove invaluable elsewhere in the garden.

If planning to grow marginal plants, mark a shelf about 23–30cm (9–12in) wide to provide adequate planting positions, and then continue digging at a slight angle until the desired depth – normally 50–60cm (20–24in) – is reached. If including edging stones, remove 5cm (2in) depth of soil to a width of 30cm (12in) all around the pond, so that the stones can be firmly bedded in later.

Once the hole is excavated, remove any roots and sharp stones that could puncture the liner, and tamp the soil firmly. To protect and cushion the liner, spread a 2.5cm (1in) layer of damp sand in the hole. If your soil is relatively stone-free, proprietary pond underlay fabric, consisting of a polyester matting, may be substituted; on stony soil, use underlay fabric over the sand layer to give the flexible liner extra protection.

Drape the liner over the hole, so that the centre touches the base, leaving an overlap on all sides. Anchor it with bricks all the way round before starting to fill the pond slowly with water. Weighed down by the water, the liner will sink to mould itself into the contours of the pond. To prevent stretching, gradually move the bricks anchoring the liner to allow it to settle naturally into the excavation, and tug at the edges to minimize creasing.

When the pond is filled, remove the remaining bricks and check again that the rim is level all round; add or take away soil if necessary until it is level. Cut off any excess liner, leaving a 15cm (6in) flap all around the edge; this surplus may be hidden beneath soil, rocks, turf, or paving stones bedded on mortar (see also "Edging a pond", p.291). Take care not to let any mortar slip into the water; if this happens you should empty the pond and refill it.

PREFORMED MOULDS

Preformed fibreglass or plastic ponds are available in a wide range of sizes and shapes. Most designs include planting shelves for marginal plants.

Preformed ponds

The simplest ponds to install are those preformed from fibreglass or plastic. These are available in a variety of shapes and are often contoured to provide ledges on which to grow marginal plants. Fibreglass ponds are more expensive than those made of plastic, but they are tough and weather resistant, with a life expectancy of at least ten years.

Installation

Level the site as much as possible and clear away any debris. If the mould is symmetrical in shape, invert it and mark out its outline using pegs and string. For asymmetrical shapes, stand the mould the right way up, supporting it on bricks to prevent it from flexing and cracking; mark out the contours with long canes, pushed vertically into the ground, and string or rope around their base.

To dig a hole that matches the mould, first remove soil down to the level of the marginal shelf. The topsoil may be reserved for use in the garden, while the subsoil should be set aside for backfilling around the pond later. Place the pond in the prepared hole, and press it down firmly onto the earth to leave a clear impression of the shape of the base. Lift out the mould, then dig out the central, deeper area that has been marked out by the pond base, allowing approximately 5cm (2in) extra depth all over the entire hole for the cushioning material.

Clear the hole of any sharp stones, tree roots, or debris, tamp the soil firmly, and line the excavation with pond underlay or a 5cm (2in) layer of damp sand. Put the mould in place and check that it is level all the way round, otherwise the water will run to one end when the pond is filled.

Ensure that the pond sits firmly on the bedding layer, then add about 10cm (4in) of water. With sand or sifted soil, backfill around the sides to the same depth as the water, ramming the soil firmly under the shelf; ensure that there are no gaps and that the pond remains absolutely level. Continue this process of adding water, backfilling, and checking the level until the pond is full. Finally, firm the earth around the pond and mask the lip with turves or with paving stones bedded on mortar (see also "Edging a pond", p.291).

INSTALLING A PREFORMED POND

1 *Firmly support the fibreglass or plastic mould with bricks to keep it level and upright, and then mark out its shape by pushing a series of canes into the ground all around the edges. Lay a length of rope around the canes to mark out the precise outline that will need to be excavated.*

2 *Excavate the hole 5cm (2in) deeper than the mould, following its profile of shelves and base as accurately as possible.*

3 *Use a plank of wood, laid across the width of the pond, and a tape measure to check that the depth of the hole is correct, and use a spirit level to check that the base is flat.*

4 *Remove any tree roots and sharp stones, and then line the hole with a 5cm (2in) layer of sand. Lower the mould into place and check with a spirit level and plank that the mould is set level.*

5 *Fill with water (here pond water) to a depth of 10cm (4in). Backfill around it to the same depth with sifted soil or sand. Tamp firmly. Continue to add water, backfill, and tamp.*

MAKING A CONCRETE POND

1 *Excavate a hole to the desired size. Dig a trench, 20cm (8in) wide, around the perimeter of the base. Presoak the trench, pour in concrete, tamp, and level with the hole base. Leave to dry.*

2 *Add a layer of sand to the soil base and firm it level with the concrete foundation trench. Skim the sand with a 1cm (½in) layer of fibre-reinforced cement, over-lapping the concrete by 5cm (2in).*

3 *After 24 hours, build walling block walls onto the foundations. Fill the voids with a fairly stiff concrete mix. Once dry, fill the gap between the block and soil walls with the same mix.*

4 *To achieve a smooth, level top to the walls, mortar one or two courses of house bricks onto the walling blocks. Scoop up any excess mortar carefully, so that a smooth finish is achieved.*

5 *After 48 hours, first dampen then render the walls with a 1cm (½in) layer of fibre-reinforced cement. Make a chamfer between the wall sides and the rendered pond base.*

6 *Mortar coping stones (such as the engineering bricks used here) onto the wall sides so there is a 5cm (2in) overlap on the inside of the pond.*

7 *After 48 hours, brush the interior walls of the pond to remove any debris. Then paint the whole inner surface with a proprietary waterproof sealant.*

Concrete ponds

The rigidity of concrete is an advantage when creating formal ponds or pools, with their straight edges and vertical sides, and particularly on light sandy soils where the sides of an excavation would otherwise be likely to collapse. Concrete is durable and suitable for ponds of almost any size, and especially where vertical walls are desired – for example, in a koi carp pool. Construction does, however, require more skill and expertise than is needed for installing a liner or preformed pond.

Construction

The most common way to build a concrete pond is to use concrete walling blocks for the sides. These are skimmed with cement mixed with sharp sand and a fibrous reinforcing material. This proprietary material, similar to glass fibre, may be obtained from builders' merchants or aquatic specialists. The fibres give the cement rendering a degree of flexibility, preventing hairline cracks caused by slight earth movements and hence reducing the risk of leaks.

When digging the hole for the pond, allow an extra 20cm (8in) in length and width for the side walls and their foundations. Make the sides of the hole as near vertical as possible. Dig out a foundation trench 20cm (8in) wide and 10cm (4in) deep around the base, fill with concrete and allow to dry. Prepare the soil base by raking level and adding a well-compacted layer of sand to the level of the foundations. Skim the base with a 1cm (½in) layer of fibre-reinforced cement.

Allow 24 hours for the cement to dry, then build the walls onto the line of the foundations. Fill any voids in the centre of the walling blocks with cement, as well as any gaps between the walls and the surrounding soil. One or two courses of house bricks can be mortared above the walling blocks. After a further 48 hours, dampen the walls of the pond and render them with a 1cm (½in) layer of fibre-reinforced cement. Mortar the final surround to the pond edge onto the top of the walls, allowing a 5cm (2in) overlap on the inside edge. Leave the cement to dry for 48 hours, and then paint the whole of the inside with waterproof sealant to prevent lime in the concrete and cement mixes from leaching out into the water and harming plants and fish.

Where the proposed pond's outline is irregular or there is difficulty in obtaining concrete walling blocks, a shell can be created by pouring wet concrete into a mould made of timber shuttering. This was once the standard method of making a concrete pond but has been largely superseded by the use of walling blocks with fibre-reinforced cement rendering. The concrete in shuttered ponds is prone to deterioration through cracking and should be strengthened with reinforcing mesh (see *Constructing a Concrete Pond with Shuttering*, p.291).

Wait a few days before filling any concrete pond, then check the alkalinity of the water with a pH test kit. If close to neutral (pH7) it is safe to introduce plants, and, after a further two weeks, fish. If alkaline, this may be due to hard mains water or ineffective sealant. In either case, delay planting water lilies and marginals for a few weeks as the pH will gradually become more neutral. Oxygenators and surface-floaters generally tolerate alkaline water, and may therefore be introduced sooner.

Raised ponds

The walls of raised ponds must be strong enough to resist the pressure of the water; if necessary, seek professional help. They are more vulnerable to frost damage than sunken ponds, and a minimum depth of 60cm (24in) is needed for fish.

Construction

The best way to construct a raised pond is with double walls, similar to house cavity walls. The exterior wall

Raised pool
Wide slabs have been used for this contemporary raised pool so that the edge also forms a seat. The adjacent patio is also made from the same slabs in order to create a harmonious design.

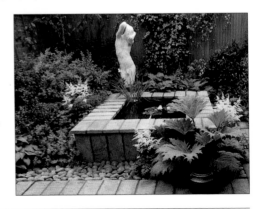

CONSTRUCTING A CONCRETE POND WITH SHUTTERING

Making the pond
Line the pond area with plastic sheeting. Build the pond in stages, allowing the concrete to set at each stage. Lay the base first, using reinforcing wire mesh between 2 layers of concrete. Once set, install vertical shuttering braced at the corners, insert mesh between the pond wall and shuttering, and pour in concrete. Repeat the process for a marginal shelf.

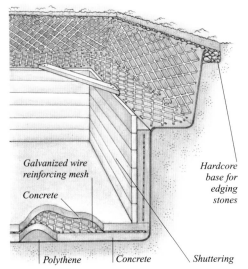

Galvanized wire reinforcing mesh

Concrete

Polythene   Concrete   Shuttering

Hardcore base for edging stones

Making a walled marginal shelf
A walled marginal shelf allows direct planting. Proceed as before, making the vertical shuttering higher to retain at least 23cm (9in) of soil (left). Once set, concrete the base of the shelf as before and then the outer shelf wall. After the concrete has set, lay the edging stones so that they will overlap the water by about 5cm (2in). Apply sealant and fill the marginal shelf with soil. Plant up and then fill the pond with water (right).

---

can be made from walling stones or bricks. The interior wall, which will be hidden, can be constructed with a cheaper brick or walling stone. The walls need to be close enough together to be linked with proprietary, wire wall ties. The entire pond must finally be lined.

Mark out the shape with string and pegs, then construct concrete foundations for the walls (see *Making a Concrete Pond*, p.290), 10–15cm (4–6in) deep and 38cm (15in) wide. Rake over the base, remove sharp stones, and cover with a layer of sand or polyester matting. Then construct the double side walls, incorporating wire ties at intervals to link the walls.

Lining a raised pond

A raised pond can be skimmed with fibre-reinforced cement, as for sunken ponds, or lined with flexible liner, which may be fitted so that an attractive stone or brick surface is exposed above the water on the inner wall. Extra liner will be needed (about 1m/1yd in width and length). Before laying the final brick or stone courses of the walls, which will be visible, spread a 2.5cm (1in) layer of damp sand over the base, followed by underlay and liner, draping them over the inner wall and into the cavity of the double wall. The top courses of the walls should then be mortared in place, securing the liner; the surplus liner is then taken up behind the top courses and tucked back under the coping. This prevents leaks while ensuring no liner will be visible at the water's edge, and therefore no white "tide lines" appear on black liners if the water level drops in summer. Trim any surplus liner and mortar coping stones on top of the walls.

Making planting beds

It may be desirable to plant vigorous water plants in permanent beds or containers such as concrete pipes or half-dustbins rather than in planting baskets. These larger beds allow a greater root run and tall plants are less likely to be displaced by wind. Beds may be sited on the marginal shelves or on the pond base for growing deep-water aquatics.

Retaining walls of mortared bricks or building blocks may be built on top of a pond liner before the pond is filled, first protecting the liner with a cushioning strip of surplus liner offcuts. You should allow a minimum depth and width of compost of 23cm (9in). Apply pond sealant to the bed before planting. With a concrete pond, planting beds may be incorporated during construction.

Edging a pond

While informal ponds can be edged in a naturalistic fashion with soil, turf, or rocks and pebbles, paving may be desired to enhance the clean lines of a formal pool, or to create a small "viewing area" at one side of a pond. Safety must be the paramount consideration; slabs must be securely mortared down, on solid foundations if your soil is light, or if they are to overlap the water.

The choice of materials is also important for safety around water. Traditional, natural stone surfaces, such as old, reclaimed, sandstone paving, are likely to be extremely slippery in wet weather. By contrast, many precast concrete paving slabs have roughened or riven surfaces, making them more resistant to algae growth and less slippery.

Styles of pond edging

Formal pools require a crisp outline so straight- or curved-edged, precast concrete paving is ideal. For circular ponds, small units such as waterproof bricks and granite or sandstone setts are also suitable, as they will not need cutting. Similarly, irregularly shaped, random or crazy paving can be used, with the shortest edges laid along the pond side to create the curve. Timber decking is appropriate to both formal and informal ponds as it can easily be cut to shape. For an informal pond, stone products such as washed cobbles and small boulders make a gradual transition to planted surrounds, and are easy to lay.

Simple and easy edging
Conceal a flexible liner with rocks and stones that gradually decrease in size as they get closer to the water, creating a beach-like effect.

Informal but mortared
Align irregularly shaped slabs so that one side follows around the shape of the pond's rim. Always secure them with cement for safety.

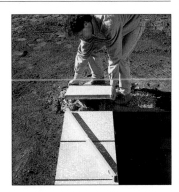

Geometric formality
Manufactured paving blocks give a uniform and clean appearance to the edge of a pond. They must be mortared into position.

Constructing moving-water features

THE principle behind all features in which water travels along any type of watercourse is that the water moves naturally from a higher to a lower point, where a powered pump drives it back through a delivery pipe to the top, or "head", of the feature. The gradient may only need to be very slight – in, for example, a formal canal – to achieve the desired effect. Steeper gradients may be used to create faster-moving stream-like features, perhaps with intermediate pools and waterfalls.

Pumps and filtration

Two types of pump are available for garden use: surface-mounted and submersible models. The power of pump required will depend on the volume of water to be moved and the gradient of the feature. A submersible pump is quite adequate for most small water features. Larger installations may need a surface-mounted pump housed in a separate, ventilated chamber.

If using a submersible pump, place it in the base or reservoir pool, raised on bricks or blocks to help prevent debris from being sucked into the inlet strainer. Link the reservoir and header pools with flexible pipe attached to the pump. The pipe may be pushed well down

into the header pool to hide it; in this case, a non-return valve should be fitted. Alternatively, keep the end of the pipe above the water surface and disguise it at the pool edge with an overlapping stone or slab. Sink the pipe in a trench alongside the watercourse to conceal it.

Seek the advice of a qualified electrician, if necessary, to install a safe external power supply. Only use approved waterproof connectors with pumps and other electrical fitments. Protect outdoor cables with armoured sleeving and always include a residual current device.

Most pumps incorporate a filter. Filter kits that fit onto the pump's suction inlet are also available. Usually there should be no need for a separate filtration system. However, if there are large numbers of fish or if it is difficult to maintain submerged plants, an independent physical or biological filtration system may be needed.

Using flexible liner

Flexible liners (see also p.288) are ideal for informal and meandering watercourses. They can be used to give a natural appearance, and the

material easily enables changes of direction and width. The edges can also readily be disguised.

If the water movement is powered by a pump, the outlet for the proposed watercourse, usually a header pool, must contain enough water not to show major variations in level when the pump is turned on and off. One unobtrusive way of creating an outlet is with an underground header pool lined with a flexible liner. Cover the pool with a sturdy mesh and place a layer of rocks and cobbles on top of it; the water pours out between the rocks into the watercourse. As well as the flexible liner, non-porous

rocks are needed to disguise the watercourse edges and to create waterfalls, while small pebbles or cobbles make an attractive addition to the base of the watercourse.

Calculating liner size

The route, dimensions, and changes of level in the watercourse are the factors that determine how much lining material will be required.

If the route is fairly straight, one piece of liner may be used. This should be the maximum width plus twice the depth by the length of the watercourse, allowing for any changes in height between the top and

CIRCULATING STREAM WITH WATERFALLS

Moving from the reservoir to the header pool, each pool should be raised higher to allow water to fall naturally, but must be deep enough to allow some water to be retained should the pump be switched off.

Non-return valve

Water pump

Header pool

Delivery pipe concealed under soil to the side of the stream

Base or reservoir pool

MAKING A WATERCOURSE WITH FLEXIBLE LINER

1 *Build a soil bank to the required height, if necessary, and mark out the watercourse, with the position and depth of any height changes. Working from the bottom, shape the steps and header pool.*

2 *When complete, compact the soil with the back of a spade. Remove sharp stones and line the course with a cushioning underlay of sand or polyester matting, cut to fit.*

3 *Lay the liner in place, ensuring that the bottom edge generously overlaps the base pool. Cut to fit, leaving 30cm (12in) on each side. Smooth the liner into the contours of the channel.*

4 *Starting at the base, set rocks in place to form the steps. Tuck the edges of the liner behind the rocks. Work upwards, arranging and mortaring rocks and pebbles so the water spills in the desired way (see right).*

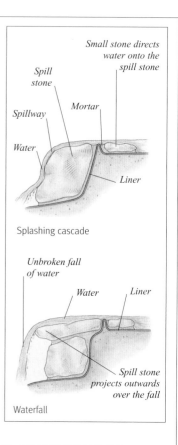

Small stone directs water onto the spill stone

Spill stone

Spillway

Mortar

Water

Liner

Splashing cascade

Unbroken fall of water

Water

Liner

Spill stone projects outwards over the fall

Waterfall

MAKING A WATERCOURSE WITH RIGID UNITS

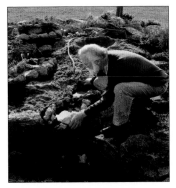

1 *Mark out the watercourse. Working from the bottom up, dig a shallow trench with a slight backward slope. Bed the first unit on soft sand, its lip slightly overlapping the edge of the pond.*

2 *Repeat the process up to and including the header pool. The lip of each unit should overhang the unit below it. Hide the delivery pipe in a 15cm (6in) trench alongside the stream.*

bottom, plus at least 30cm (12in) so that it can overlap into the base pools. A twisting watercourse is best made from a succession of liner pieces, each overlapping the one below it by at least 15cm (6in) to prevent leaks and avoid unwieldy folds. Allow for these overlaps when calculating the amount of liner needed.

Construction

If necessary, make a bank of soil slightly larger than the dimensions of the watercourse. Then mark the outline on the soil. Starting from the lowest point, cut steps into the bank to form the falls and cascades; the flatter sections – the "treads" of the steps – should be made with a slight backward gradient to the water flow so that they retain some water when the pump is turned

off. For the header pool, dig a hole at the uppermost point at least 60cm (24in) square and 40cm (16in) deep. Rake the base and remove any sharp stones, then compact the soil with the back of a spade. Spread a layer of polyester matting underlay or firmed sand over the course. The flexible liner may then be fitted into the channel, allowing approximately 30cm (12in) of liner on either side, which will later form the side walls.

If using more than one piece of liner to form the length of the watercourse, overlap the pieces by 15cm (6in). Place the higher piece so that it overlaps the lower one where there is a fall or downwards slope so that water flows away from the join. Dig a channel next to the watercourse for the pipe that will circulate water from the base to the header pool.

Set rocks in place to form the steps and sides of the watercourse, arranging them until the grouping is satisfactory. Use a hose or watering can to check that water spills over falls in the desired way. Then lift the liner at the sides behind the rocks and pack soil in to just above the waterline. For stability, mortar rocks into position with waterproof cement.

Using rigid units

Preformed modular units may be combined in several ways and installed to incorporate falls of different heights. Such units usually take the form of saucer-like pools (see above left) in various sizes, materials (such as fibreglass or PVC), and finishes (such as textured rock or grit). Plants and natural rocks and pebbles are used to blend the units into their surroundings.

Mark out the proposed area with string and dig out the watercourse to accommodate the units. Allow extra depth for a level layer of sand, 5cm (2in) deep, beneath them. Work from the bottom upwards, positioning the lowest unit so that the lip overlaps the base pool. Install the unit, making any final adjustments by backfilling or removing excess sand so that it is level. Once the first unit is level, a small amount of water may be added to increase stability.

The following units, and the final header pool, are then installed in the same way. Once each is positioned and the levels checked, partially fill it with water and backfill with sand around the outside edges as before. Install the pump, and conceal and soften the edges of the watercourse with rocks and plants.

Canals and formal rills

Canals and rills are ideal in formal gardens for linking features such as raised pools or fountains or for adding emphasis to sculptures and urns. Keep the canal width in scale with the garden, erring on the narrow side rather than the wide. Even a canal only 12in (30cm) wide will have a dramatic impact. Because garden canals need a crisp outline, and are shallow, they are best made of concrete. Bricks or glazed tiles used along the edge in a contrasting colour to the surrounding paving will add emphasis. When planning construction, remember that pipes and cables may need to run beneath any surrounding paving, and install conduit pipes accordingly.

After marking out the canal's width and length on a level site, excavate the area to a depth of 20cm (8in) and add a layer of sand, 5cm (2in) deep. Check that the sides are level then drape a polythene sheet into the excavation and pour in concrete. Tamp it with a flat-sided piece of wood. Once the concrete has hardened, after 48 hours, construct the side walls using bricks mortared onto the base. If decorative brick paviours or tiles are to form the surrounding edges, mortar these at right angles to the wall bricks with a slight overlap on the inside edge of the canal. Once the mortar has hardened, use a plasterer's float to skim the inside of the canal with a fibre-reinforced cement mix 1cm (½in) thick (see *Making a Concrete Pond*, p.290). Finally, when the skim is dry, paint the inside surfaces of the canal with a proprietary water sealant.

MAKING A CANAL OR FORMAL RILL WITH CONCRETE

1 *Excavate the canal site to a depth of 20cm (8in). Cover the base and sides with soft sand, 5cm (2in) deep. Check the site is level, then line the canal with heavy-duty polythene sheet.*

2 *Pour a 5cm (2in) layer of concrete onto the polythene sheet, then tamp down and level it with a thin, straight plank. Check that the sides of the canal are at exactly the same height.*

3 *After 48 hours, mortar a course of bricks onto the foundations to make the canal walls. Mortar decorative paviours at right angles on top of the bricks, overlapping the inside edge of the canal by 5cm (2in).*

4 *After 48 hours, dampen then skim the floor and insides of the canal walls with a 1cm (½in) layer of fibre-reinforced cement. When dry, paint on a coat of proprietary water sealant.*

Small water features

To look at their best, water features should be in scale with their surroundings. Fortunately, for small gardens, there are suitably diminutive features, including ones that re-circulate water, which will fit into a variety of nooks and crannies. They can be used to provide an endless trickle of water over a brimming pot, a gurgling bubble fountain over pebbles, or a stylish fountain fitted to a wall. Such moving-water features bring small spaces to life by introducing a mixture of sound and movement, adding an element of surprise, and providing a theme for interesting plant selections in the vicinity.

Small water features are much safer for small children than an open pond as there is little or no exposed water. They are also generally quick and easy to construct and there are no large volumes of soil to be disposed of. Those features that do not include aquatic plants, like the pebble fountain here, can also be sited in shade, whereas a planted pond could not. Maintenance is much easier, too, the main job being regular replenishment of water to compensate for losses by evaporation.

Wall fountains

Small, enclosed town gardens, court-yards, patios, and conservatories, where there is often insufficient space for a freestanding feature, make ideal situations for a wall fountain. These range from antique stone masks (or less costly plaster or fibreglass copies) to modern metal designs. Wall trellis can be used to hide the water delivery pipe between the reservoir pool and the fountain's spout. The reservoir must have enough capacity for prolonged running of the submersible pump: a minimum of 22–27 litres (5–6 gallons) is required for even a small wall fountain. The reservoir can be open and attractively planted (see below), or concealed below ground.

Cobblestone fountains

Another successful and popular small water feature is the cobblestone fountain, which has several variations on a theme – all basically relying on water being pumped up through cobblestones or pebbles, which are supported on a piece of galvanized-steel mesh, and falling back into a reservoir pool below ground.

Cobble fountains are available in kit form and provide a cheap, simple, and creative opportunity to enjoy moving water within the garden. One of their greatest fascinations can be the top of the water spout, which can be adjusted either to gush or bubble gently. The source of the water spout need be no more than a rigid tube from the pump – the wider the pipe, the more restful the fountain becomes. The sound of the fountain changes as the height of the spout increases above the reservoir. A further refinement is possible by altering the water level: if the reservoir is full, splashing dominates the sound; if only half full the sound takes on an echoing dimension, emphasizing the cascading rivulets of water falling down beneath the cobbles.

MOUNTING A SIMPLE WALL FOUNTAIN

1 Screw a trellis panel to battens on the wall. Thread the delivery pipe up behind the struts and connect to the mask's mouth. Screw the mask in place.

2 Connect the delivery pipe to the pump outlet. Stand the pump on a brick in the reservoir. Fill the reservoir with water, turn on the pump, and adjust the flow.

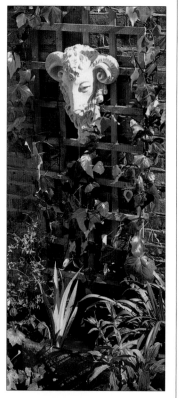

Finished feature
Planting in and around the reservoir conceals the pump, while climbers hide the trellis and vertical delivery pipe.

INSTALLING A KIT-STYLE COBBLESTONE FOUNTAIN

1 Dig a hole that is wider and slightly deeper than the tub reservoir. Insert the tub, using a spirit level to ensure that it is level. Backfill around the sides, and firm the soil with a stick.

2 Lay polythene sheet over the tub; cut out a circle 5cm (2in) smaller than the tub width. Connect the delivery pipe to the pump outlet. Put the pump on a brick at the bottom of the tub.

3 Centre the galvanized-steel mesh over the hole in the polythene. Make a small hole in the mesh and feed the delivery pipe through it. Fill the bin with water to 15cm (6in) from the top.

4 Arrange a few cobblestones around the pipe and cut it to length. Then turn on the pump. Lift the mesh and experiment with the pump's flow adjuster until you achieve the desired fountain effect.

5 Add more cobblestones as required. Once the area onto which the water falls is established, trim the surplus polythene sheet, burying the edges, 10cm (4in) wide, under the soil. Alternatively, to allow for possible future enlargement, fold or roll up the surplus before burying it.

Natural and wildlife ponds

Most garden ponds attract some wildlife, but the more informal and natural they are, the more inviting they become to a wide range of creatures. You could be lucky and have a natural pond in your garden, but if not it is possible to construct one that will have a naturalistic look and great appeal to wildlife.

A wildlife pond should be positioned where it can be viewed from a house window, yet not so close that shy creatures might be deterred from visiting. Ideally some vegetation should be planted on the far side of the pond, to give cover. A wildlife pond should also have a shallow beach at one edge, and a layer of soil over the bottom. The beach allows easy access for drinking birds, amphibians, and other animals, and the mud layer provides a home for myriad small creatures in summer and a hibernation spot in winter.

Lining a natural pond

Traditionally, natural ponds were lined with compacted or "puddled" clay to make them watertight, but the cost of importing clay has made this practice prohibitively expensive in all but heavy clay areas.

A more economical way to clay-line ponds is to use sodium bentonite. This powdered mineral clay swells to ten to fifteen times its volume when mixed with water, forming a waterproof gel. It is also available sandwiched in a tough, woven geotextile mat (see right), which, for ponds of more than 50 sq m (60 sq yd), can be moved only with the use of heavy-lifting equipment.

Flexible, low-density polythene or PVC liners can be used, too. As such liners will be covered by a generous layer of soil, they need not be resistant to ultra-violet deterioration.

Bog gardens make ideal companions for ponds and should be made independently with a separate lining, pierced in a number of places on the bottom to allow slow drainage.

Planting the pond

To encourage the maximum variety of wildlife, the planting in a natural pond should contain a high proportion of native species. As many of these are rampant and quickly smother smaller species, it is a good idea to create pockets of different sizes and depths for different species (see also below).

The soil layer will encourage plants to spread. Tempting though it is to plant thickly for a natural effect, avoid really rampant growers in small ponds. Many of these have vicious root systems that can penetrate flexible liners. Eventually, even deeper zones may become choked by native marginals forming rafts with their thick, spongy roots, and periodic cutting back will be required. Some native submerged species such as water fringe (*Nymphoides peltata*) also tend to spread uncontrollably to cover the water surface, excluding sunlight, if not thinned. It may take some experimentation before a stable balance of planting is achieved.

Quick to establish
Native plants will rapidly cover a pond surface and must be chosen carefully if a clear area of water is required. Similarly, vigorous marginals will soon surround the pond, but keep open a small area for access.

Woven geotextile matting

For convenience when lining a pond, bentonite is available as an impregnated, geotextile quilt, known as Bentomat, which can be draped over the pond excavation in overlapping strips. The matting is sufficiently thick that it is not vulnerable to tunnelling animals or most plant roots. It should be covered with a soil layer, 30cm (12in) thick, to prevent chemicals leaching from its clay-derived ingredient.

Waterproofing
Line the hole with textile matting, and then conceal it with topsoil.

CREATING A VARIETY OF HABITATS

A great advantage of using flexible liner in a water garden is the wide range of planting opportunities and levels you can provide, increasing the feature's attraction and usefulness to aquatic wildlife and other garden creatures. Varied environments maximize the range of sheltering, feeding, and breeding sites on offer.

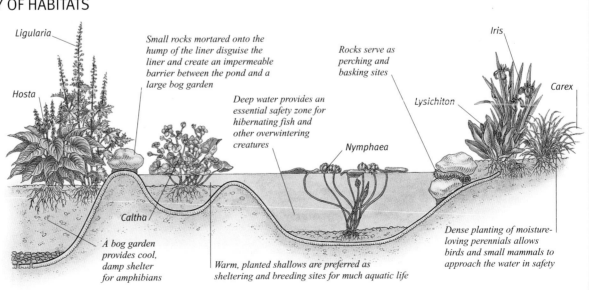

Ligularia

Hosta

Small rocks mortared onto the hump of the liner disguise the liner and create an impermeable barrier between the pond and a large bog garden

Deep water provides an essential safety zone for hibernating fish and other overwintering creatures

Rocks serve as perching and basking sites

Iris

Carex

Lysichiton

Nymphaea

Caltha

A bog garden provides cool, damp shelter for amphibians

Warm, planted shallows are preferred as sheltering and breeding sites for much aquatic life

Dense planting of moisture-loving perennials allows birds and small mammals to approach the water in safety

Waterside decking

TIMBER decking is an ideal material for edging water where there is also a need for an outdoor living area. It can be extended over the water, providing the illusion that water is running underneath, or more simply form a waterside seating area. Often the void underneath the decking makes an ideal place to house equipment such as clarifiers, pumps, cable switches, and transformers.

Where possible use decking tiles (see also p.592) or grooved decking planks made of long-lasting hardwood; if softwood is used, ensure that it has been pressure-treated. Planks sold for decking are usually 15–20cm (6–8in) wide, in 3–4m (10–13ft) lengths, and come in various thicknesses – use a minimum of 2.5cm (1in) thickness to reduce the risk of warping.

The decking planks or tiles should be secured to supporting joists, which are normally made of 8 x 5cm (3 x 2in) treated timber and placed 75cm (30in) apart, at right angles to the line of planks. The planks or tiles are then screwed onto the joists, leaving 6mm (¼in) gaps between them to allow for expansion.

The joists must be supported on perpendicular timber "bearers", firmly bedded on sand or hardcore. On soft ground, trench foundations beneath the bearers are advisable. Alternatively precast concrete decking pads can be used. These are 45cm (18in) square and 10cm (4in) thick and are placed 1.2m (4ft) apart. Over water, concrete footings and posts with metal shoes must be used (see below and right).

Wooden decking tiles set with the diagonal treads at right angles to each other. This reduces the chances of slipping

Bricks inserted under bearers keep the decking supported and level

Joist

Bearer

Last joist positioned just 40cm (16in) from the middle joist to ensure that the decking tiles overhang the edge of the jetty

Bearer extends under jetty joists

Decorative fascia board

Metal shoes under timber uprights prevent the wood from rotting

Brick piers to which metal post shoes are bolted raise a jetty area above the water

Concrete and hardcore footings support the decking where the ground slopes away

DIFFERENT TYPES OF FOUNDATIONS

Bearers and joists on sand
This simple foundation comprises a grid of wooden joists laid at right angles over bearers resting on 5cm (2in) of sand. This is suitable only for small decks.

Hardcore footings
For an extra strong foundation, bed the bearers in excavated trenches containing hardcore covered with 5cm (2in) of sand. Use bricks for stability and to adjust the bearer height.

Steel supports
On wet ground or under water, use timber uprights slotted into steel "shoes", which are bolted into concrete. These will prevent the uprights rotting in the water.

USING FLEXIBLE LINER

Where decking borders the water, flexible liner should be brought up and behind the joists to prevent leaks. Where the underlay and flexible liner have to fit around a sharp corner, they should be carefully pulled and pleated before being secured with battens. Then conceal the liners from side-view by nailing fascia boards to the outer edge of the liner-covered outer joists.

Bearer   *Joist*   *Fascia board*

Decking tile screwed onto joists

Flexible liner and underlay

Planting and stocking

W HILE most plants are grown for their ornamental features, some also help to maintain the quality and appearance of water by keeping down algae (see "Water garden plants", p.284). There is a wide range of planting containers available, allowing flexibility when planting and making routine maintenance relatively simple.

Selecting water plants

When selecting plants, look for clean, fresh-looking, and vigorous specimens, growing in tanks that are free from algae and duckweed (*Lemna*). Check that the undersides of the leaves are free from jelly-like deposits of snail or whelk eggs, and that there are no strands of blanket-weed in the foliage. Vacuum-packed plants should appear plump and green; if they look weak and limp they are unlikely to grow well.

A good nursery or other supplier will be able to advise on the quantities of plants to buy, so that you obtain the required delicate balance between submerged, oxygenating plants (such as *Ceratophyllum demersum*) and floating-leaved plants (such as water lilies). The latter should cover one third to half of the water surface to provide some shelter from the sun. If buying plants by mail order, use a specialist supplier. It is worth paying a slightly higher price since the plants are more likely to be disease-free, and to have been propagated in the nursery. Reputable suppliers should also pack the plants with care, and dispatch them on the same day they are lifted.

When buying oxygenators for a new pool, you should allow at least five bunches for every square metre or yard of water surface. They are

SELECTING PLANTS FOR THE WATER GARDEN

Marginal plant
GOOD EXAMPLE

Well-developed plant

Healthy leaves

POOR EXAMPLE

Caltha palustris

Weak growth

Weeds indicate that plant may be pot-bound

Oxygenator
GOOD EXAMPLE

Potamogeton crispus

Healthy, vigorous growth

POOR EXAMPLE

Limp, tired stems

Surface-floater
GOOD EXAMPLE

Young, fresh growth

POOR EXAMPLE

Stratiotes aloides

Damaged growth

Old, rotting foliage

generally sold individually as small, weighted, fibre plugs, which can be thrown on the water, or as bunches of unrooted cuttings, about 23cm (9in) long. The lead clasp used to hold the bunches together will pull the plants down to the bottom of the pool, where they will root.

Since oxygenators are extremely susceptible to drying out, they should be kept moistened in a plastic bag or submerged in water until they are ready for planting in the pond.

Containers and planting beds

The most convenient way of growing aquatics is in purpose-made baskets or crates. This makes it easy to lift and divide or replace the plants when necessary, and it is also a relatively simple matter to alter the planting arrangement when desired.

PLANTING BASKETS

Planting baskets are available in various sizes to suit different plants. All except those with a very close-weave mesh should be lined.

Standard mesh   Close-weave mesh

Proprietary containers
Aquatic containers have wide, flat bases to provide stability in the water, which is important for tall marginals on narrow shelves. Containers have open lattice walls, allowing water and gases to circulate through the soil. Most should be lined with close-weave polypropylene sheeting or hessian to prevent the soil from seeping out, although very fine-mesh containers that eliminate the need for a liner are also available.

Crates and containers range in size from 40 x 40cm (16 x 16in) square with a 30 litre (6½ gallon) capacity, suitable for medium-sized water lilies, down to 4cm (1½in) in diameter with a 50ml (2fl oz) capacity, for aquarium planting. Larger, circular tubs without lattice walls are also available for vigorous water lilies.

Planting directly in soil beds
In wildlife ponds, aquatics may be planted directly into soil on the bottom of the pool and on marginal shelves. In most pools, however, this is inadvisable since the vigorous species spread rapidly, swamping their slower-growing neighbours. In addition, subsequent removal or thinning of plants can be very difficult.

Permanent beds
A good compromise is to build permanent planting beds on the pool base and around the edges during construction, which are easily planted up before the pool is filled (see also "Making planting beds", p.291). This maintains a natural appearance while controlling the plants' spread.

Planting

The pool should be filled with water a few days before planting to allow the water temperature to reach that of the surrounding air, and to "mature". During this period the water in the pool may become populated with micro-organisms that disperse impurities in the water and create an environment beneficial to plants, fish, and other pond life.

Unlike the majority of terrestrial plants, aquatics should be planted while in active growth, preferably between late spring and midsummer. If planted in late summer and early autumn, the plants have little time to become established before they die down. Water lilies must have time to build up food reserves before winter if they are to survive and grow satisfactorily the following season.

The planting medium
Aquatic plants grow quite happily in good garden soil, preferably a heavy loam; if possible, use soil that has not been fertilized or manured recently. Sieve out any loose organic matter as this will rot or float when the planting crate is submerged. Old turves that have rotted down thoroughly for several months make ideal aquatic compost. If the suitability of the garden soil is in any doubt, buy aquatic compost from a specialist supplier.

Proprietary composts made for terrestrial plants should not be used for aquatics; as well as peat, which tends to float, they contain added fertilizers, which will encourage the growth of algae (see p.300).

Planting depths

The ideal planting depth varies, depending on the type of plant, and can differ even within a given group of plants. Planting depths should be measured from the top of the soil in the crate or planting pocket to the water surface (see right).

It is important not to plant too deeply: without adequate sunlight for photosynthesis, plants will die. When planting young specimens, it may be necessary to stand the containers on bricks or blocks at first so that the plants are not completely submerged. As the plants grow, gradually lower the crates until they reach the appropriate depth.

Bog and moisture-loving plants

The area bordering a natural pool is ideal for bog and moisture-loving plants, but correct growing condi-

tions can be supplied next to a man-made pond by creating special beds.

Mark out the planting beds, then dig out at least 45cm (18in) depth of soil, removing any roots of perennial weeds such as couch grass. Form sloping sides at the edges. Drape a flexible liner (thick-gauge plastic sheeting is suitable for this purpose) into the hole, ensuring that the top edge of the liner finishes just below the existing soil level.

Although a number of vigorous, moisture-loving plants tolerate saturated soil, most of them will grow better if the liner is pierced to allow some slow seepage of water from the bed. This slight movement of water through the soil also helps to prevent stagnant conditions from developing. Cover the drainage holes with gravel so that they do not become clogged up with soil.

Simplify watering in summer by sinking a perforated, rigid pipe into the bed. The pipe should be blocked at the far end and covered with a layer of gravel or stones to prevent the holes from becoming blocked with soil. Fit the end of the pipe to a hose connector, which should remain above the soil surface.

Refill the bed with soil, and then mulch with a deep layer of coarsely sieved organic matter to help prevent moisture loss. Do not incorporate bulky additives throughout the whole bed as sufficient moisture is retained by the liner.

Planting, which is best done in spring, is carried out in the same way

PLANTING DEPTHS

Place plants at the appropriate depth for the species, measured from the top of the soil to the water's surface. When planting young water lilies (Nymphaea), raise the crates on bricks. Lower the crates as the plants grow.

as in ordinary soil, although the whole bed should be thoroughly soaked afterwards. Plants should be placed in the hole at the same depth as they were in the container. Plants that enjoy moist conditions will grow vigorously, so very invasive species are best confined to sunken containers to prevent them from crowding out other plants.

Marginal plants

Primarily included for their ornamental flowers or foliage, marginal plants are grown at the pool edges with their roots in shallow water. Ornamental pools usually include a shelf to accommodate marginal plants, which may either be grown in baskets or in pockets built directly onto the shelf (see also "Making planting beds", p.291).

Most marginals require approximately 8–15cm (3–6in) of water

above their crowns; it may be necessary to raise the planting baskets to ensure that the plants are at the correct depth until they are established. The more vigorous species, known as deep marginals, should be planted in 30cm (12in) or more of water, either on a deeper shelf or on the bottom, away from the margin.

When planting marginals, take into account their height, spread, and vigour. Plant rampant growers singly in containers to stop them smothering slower-growing plants. If planting in containers, always make sure that there is sufficient room for root development; for most marginals, a container at least 23cm (9in) in diameter is necessary. Plant marginals in prepared containers or planting beds of loam and top-dress with pea shingle; if using containers, place them on the marginal shelf or the bottom of the pond, as appropriate, so that the plants are at the correct depth.

Creating a balanced ecosystem

A successful pond requires a healthy ecosystem. Considering these important factors will help you to achieve the right balance:

- Position the pond in an open site away from trees to prevent autumn leaves falling into the water and decomposing; this reduces oxygen levels.
- Make the pond at least 45–60cm (18–24in) deep to keep the water temperature reasonably constant and ensure it does not fluctuate too much.
- Maintain a neutral pH. Too acid or alkaline conditions, caused by topping up with rainwater or tap water, reduces water quality and adversely affects plants and fish.
- Use water lilies and floating plants to cover and shade about half the surface, but ensure they do not become too dominant.
- Use submerged oxygenating plants to release oxygen into the water and absorb carbon dioxide produced by fish and aquatic animals (i.e. newts, frogs, insects, and water snails).
- Remove excess floating plants and fish as they reduce oxygen levels and encourage unwanted algae to spread rapidly.
- Do not use nitrogenous or other fertilizers to improve plant growth, or overfeed fish, as these will pollute the water and encourage unwanted algae.

Choosing oxygenating plants with care

Surface-floating plants can discourage algae growth when planting a pond in temperate regions. Many plants sold for this purpose are from tropical areas, so must be used with caution anywhere other than very small ponds and aquaria.

The floating species to avoid are water hyacinth (*Eichhornia crassipes*), water lettuce (*Pistia stratiotes*), water clover (*Marsilea quadrifolia*), water chestnut (*Trapa natans*), butterfly fern (*Salvinia auriculata*), and fairy moss (*Azolla filiculoides*). Although many of these would be killed by frost in temperate ponds and waterways, there is a greater risk of some surviving as global temperatures rise. These gradually choke waterways – as has already occurred in some warmer regions.

Take great care not to introduce certain species, sometimes sold as oxygenators, that spread fast and are difficult to eradicate. Foremost

of these is *Myriophyllum aquaticum* (*M. proserpinacoides*), which is now considered noxious in warm climates due to its rapid spread and invasive habit. While not all *Myriophyllum* species are rampant, *M. spicatum* and *M. verticillatum* are best avoided as they also spread freely and rapidly.

Curly water thyme (Lagarosiphon major) *is a submerged oxygenator from Africa. Cut back regularly to keep in check; remove dead stems to stop them decomposing in the water.*

Water crowfoot (Ranunculus aquatilis) *is from temperate parts but still spreads fast. Its stems are submerged, but the floating leaves and flowers will give some shade.*

Planting oxygenators

Incorporating oxygenating plants is one of the first priorities when planting in a new pool. This is because their cleaning and oxygenating properties are vital to the health of the fish population and the oxygen content of the water.

Keep the plants wet after purchasing them and until they are ready to plant. Even during the planting process, they should not be left exposed to the air longer than is absolutely necessary.

Species vary in the effectiveness with which they oxygenate the water, depending on the time of year and the pH of the water, so plant a selection of four or five species to ensure that enough plants thrive to maintain correct oxygen levels throughout the year. Keep only a single species in each container to prevent stronger-growing plants from crowding out less vigorous species.

Prepare a planting crate and make planting holes in the soil, then insert bunches of cuttings into the holes and firm them in. Cover the soil with grit or 1–2.5cm (½–1in) pea shingle, water thoroughly, and place the crate on the bottom of the prepared pond at a depth of 45–60cm (18–24in).

Almost fill a lined crate with damp compost. Plant bunches of cuttings (here Lagarosiphon major). *Trim off excess liner, then top-dress the soil.*

Deep-water plants

As with marginals, these plants are usually grown in aquatic containers or planting beds. Most of them are best planted fairly shallowly at first so that their leaves are able to float and photosynthesize in the sun.

Whether planting in beds or free-standing containers, settle the plants firmly in the soil as they are very buoyant and may be dislodged. Always plant in moist soil, and soak containers well before immersing them in the pool. A top-dressing of small gravel or pea shingle to a depth of 2.5cm (1in) prevents soil from floating out and clouding the water and discourages fish from disturbing the plant roots.

When submerging the containers in deep water, thread string through the sides to form handles; this makes it much easier to position the crate, as it may then be gradually lowered onto the bottom.

Stocking with fish

Like water plants, fish are best introduced to the pool during the warmer months. In cooler temperatures, fish become semi-dormant and are more prone to stress when moved. Allow at least two weeks after planting before stocking with fish to allow plant roots to establish.

Unless there is supplementary filtration, overstocking with fish may encourage algae which feed on excess waste. As a guide, calculate a maximum of 50cm (20in) of fish body length (when fully grown) per square metre or yard of water surface or 5cm (2in) per 1,000sq cm (1sq ft). It is advisable to stock the pool in two stages, introducing half the fish eight to ten weeks before the rest. This allows the bacteria that feed on the fish waste products to multiply to a sufficient level to deal with the waste. If too many are introduced at once, the water may become polluted and the fish starved of oxygen. Leaving a fountain or waterfall on overnight to agitate the water will provide temporary relief.

Fish are usually supplied in a large, clear plastic bag containing a small amount of water and inflated with oxygen. On arrival, do not release the fish straight into the pond: they are very sensitive to sudden changes in temperature, and the water in the pond is likely to be colder than that in the bag. Float the bag unopened on the water until the water temperature in the bag is the same as in the pool. In hot, sunny weather, shade the bag with a cloth. A small amount of pool water may be gradually introduced into the bag before the fish are released. Do not lift the bag to examine the fish closely as this causes them extreme stress.

Other water creatures

As well as fish, a number of other aquatic life forms may be introduced to the pond as scavengers. Ramshorn snails are often sold specifically for this purpose. Ordinary pond snails are likely to be a nuisance, because they eat water lily leaves.

Mussels, and in particular the swan mussel, are excellent scavengers, cleaning up where ornamental fish have been overfed. Mussels require deep water that remains cool even in the height of summer.

DEEP-WATER AND MARGINAL PLANTS

1 *Choose a planting crate to accommodate the plant roots and line it with hessian or close-weave polypropylene.*

2 *Fill the crate with heavy, moist loam to a depth of at least 5cm (2in). Set the plant (here* Aponogeton distachyos) *in the centre of the crate.*

3 *Fill with more loam to within 1cm (½in) of the rim of the crate, firming the plant in well to give it good anchorage.*

4 *Top-dress the container with washed gravel or pea shingle to a depth of 2.5cm (1in).*

5 *Trim away any surplus liner with scissors. Tie string "handles" to the rim of the crate on opposite sides.*

6 *Hold the crate by the string handles and gently lower it onto blocks or the marginal shelf. Release the handles.*

ADDING FISH TO A POND

Float the unopened bag until the water temperature in the bag matches that of the pond. Slowly introduce some pond water to the bag before gently releasing the fish.

Routine care

Good construction and siting and ensuring the right balance of water, plants, and fish should help to keep a pond relatively trouble-free, but occasionally structural repairs may be necessary, if the pool is damaged or leaks, for example. Algae and weeds must also be kept in check, while many plants will benefit from periodic division.

Structural repairs

Any sudden or persistent loss of water is likely to indicate a leak. If a pool is leaking, it will be necessary to drain and inspect it. Accommodate the fish and plants in a suitable container, such as a paddling pool.

Most ponds may be drained either with an electric pump or by siphoning off the water. Check first that the pond's edges are level; water may be overflowing at the lowest point. With a watercourse, switch off the pump and check the level in the base pool: if constant, the leak is in the watercourse.

REPAIRING A FLEXIBLE POND LINER

1 *Dry the area of damaged liner and then clean it carefully with methylated spirits and a soft cloth.*

2 *Apply special double-sided adhesive sealing tape over the tear and allow it to become "tacky".*

3 *Cut out a patch from spare liner and press it firmly onto the adhesive, ensuring that the edges are stuck down flat.*

Flexible liners

If the water level in a lined pool drops or the flow of water in a watercourse decreases, check that no part of the edge of the liner has slipped below water level. Leaks may also be caused by punctures. The simplest way to repair a butyl liner is with double-sided adhesive tape obtainable from water garden suppliers. This is used to secure a patch of butyl liner over the hole. The pool may be refilled after one hour.

Preformed pools and units

If a pool or watercourse unit is inadequately supported or the ground underneath it is not properly consolidated, it may eventually crack under the weight of the water. Repair cracks with a fibreglass repair kit as used for car bodies and boat hulls. Position any patch on the underside of the unit so that it is hidden from view in clear water. Allow the compound to harden thoroughly as it may be toxic when fluid. Before refilling with water, ensure that the base is firmly bedded down and that soil is compacted around the sides to support the water pressure.

Concrete pools

The most common cause of leaking is through cracks created by frost damage or subsidence. Inspect the pool carefully as water can escape through even a hairline crack. If the crack is very fine it is usually necessary to widen it slightly and brush clean any loose debris before sealing it with mortar. Leave the mortar to dry, then paint it with sealant.

Water quality

Once a good balance of plants and animal life is established, the water should remain clear without needing further attention. If there are marked changes in the numbers of fish or plants, or if there is a sudden introduction of mains or flood water, however, the water balance may be upset and a surge of unsightly, algal growth may result.

Algae

Algae depend on sunlight, carbon dioxide, and dissolved mineral salts for their survival. Reduce the amount of light that they receive by growing sufficient plants (water lilies, deep-water aquatics, and floaters) so that their floating leaves cover between 50 and 70 per cent of the water surface. The introduction of oxygenating plants, which absorb minerals and carbon dioxide, helps starve the algae. In addition, regularly remove dead and decaying leaves and flowers.

Green water due to algal growth may occur in a newly planted pool, or one that has recently been cleaned. Normally this problem clears itself. If it does not, control the algae by anchoring a fine-net bag filled with barley straw under the water or by using a proprietary pad of barley straw. You should replace these every four to six months.

If the water is persistently cloudy, it may be necessary to check it with a simple pond test kit. If this shows the water to be very acid or alkaline, there are proprietary pH adjusters in simple-to-use, granular form, which should be applied according to the manufacturer's instructions.

Blanketweed

A filamentous form of algae called blanketweed (*Spirogyra*) is sometimes found in pools with otherwise clear water; if left unchecked, it chokes the plants and restricts the free movement of fish. Remove periodically by winding it onto a stick or lifting it out with a garden rake; in severe cases use an algicide. Clear out the dead material quickly, since decaying matter will reduce the water's oxygen content.

REMOVING BLANKETWEED

Insert a stick into the mass of blanketweed (Spirogyra) and twist it. The weed wraps around the stick and may then be pulled free.

REPAIRING A CRACK IN A CONCRETE POND

1 *If a crack is very fine, use a club hammer and chisel to widen it slightly.*

2 *Clean off any algae and debris from the surrounding area with a wire brush.*

3 *With a trowel, fill the crack with mortar or a proprietary sealing compound. Allow it to dry.*

4 *Brush with a pool sealing compound to prevent any toxins leaching out into the water.*

THINNING OUT AN OVERGROWN OXYGENATOR

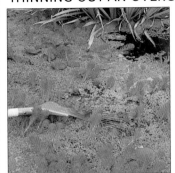

1 In spring or autumn, thin out overgrown submerged plants, either by "combing" them off the water's surface with a rake, or by lifting out the basket and trimming back with a sharp knife.

2 Thinning out oxygenating plants prevents them from becoming congested. Do not remove too much growth, however, since this may leave the pond's surface area too exposed to sunlight, and allow algae to proliferate. Oxygenators are best thinned little and often.

FLOATING BALL

In winter, float a ball on the water. When ice forms, pour boiling water over the ball and remove it, then cover the hole with a sack. In a thaw, remove the sack and replace the ball.

Pond cleaning

If the water is kept clear of fallen leaves and the plants are regularly trimmed, it should only be necessary to clean the pond every few years to remove decaying organic matter from the base (see also *Weed-infested Ponds*, p.673). After cleaning, the water chemistry must again be carefully balanced.

Plant care and control

Water plants do not require much attention, but periodic division and repotting helps to keep them healthy and attractive. Their overall vigour normally makes it necessary for them to be kept in check rather than encouraged, although certain water lily cultivars will require some feeding (see p.286).

Thinning out and division

In late spring or early autumn thin out or divide plants that are overgrown or crowding their neighbours. Lift container-grown plants and check whether they have become root-bound. If so, remove the plants from their containers and divide them with back-to-back forks or by hand. Tight and thick roots may need to be split with a spade or a knife. Replant the divided clumps singly.

After the first growing season, submerged oxygenating plants may become overgrown and entangled with weeds. In small pools, the oxygenators are easily thinned by pulling out a few handfuls; in larger ponds, use a garden rake to comb out excess growth.

Alternatively, lift the container from the pool and cut back the plants by one third to a half. Do not thin out all the plants drastically at any one time since this causes a sudden change in the water balance and encourages algal growth.

Autumn maintenance

The most important task in autumn is to keep the water free from decaying vegetation. When the waterside plants begin to die down, remove dead and dying foliage regularly and prune back the excess growth of submerged plants. If there are deciduous trees and shrubs nearby, cover the surface of the pool with a fine-mesh plastic net to catch fallen leaves, and keep it in place until the trees are bare of foliage.

In cold areas, protect tender plants by removing them from the pool and placing them in a bucket of water in a frost-free place to overwinter. Cut off the ripe seed pods of invasive plants to prevent them from setting seed. Before they go into hibernation for the winter, feed the fish with floating wheatgerm pellets, which can be digested easily in the cool autumn water.

If a pump is fitted, remove it from the pool and clean it thoroughly. Replace any parts that may be worn, and store it in a dry place until spring.

Winter care

In winter, ice may form, trapping methane gas released by submerged, decaying vegetation, with potentially lethal effects on the fish. Ice also exerts pressure on the sides of concrete pools as it expands and may cause them to crack. Ensuring that a small area of the pool remains ice-free prevents this and allows methane to escape into the air. Either float a ball on the surface or use a floating electric pool heater. This gives out just enough heat to maintain a small area of open water.

Pests and diseases

Pests are less of a problem in a pool stocked with fish, since the fish eat the insect larvae. Any infestations can be cleared by hand or washed off plants with a hosepipe; insecticide sprays are unsuitable for water gardens and are highly toxic to fish. In late summer, aphids (p.646) often attack the aerial parts of water lilies and other aquatics, causing discoloration and decay. Dislodge them with a jet of water or submerge the leaves for 24 hours, weighting down affected parts with sacking.

Diseases affecting aquatic plants are relatively few, and mostly concern water lilies. Fungal disease is indicated by the premature yellowing or spotting of the leaves. If the symptoms persist, treat the plant with copper fungicide in a separate tank.

REPOTTING A MARGINAL

1 Plants that are growing in containers will eventually become root-bound and need thinning out. Roots protruding through the container wall indicate that a plant should be divided and repotted. The plant shown here is Iris pseudacorus.

2 Remove the plant from its container and divide it into smaller clumps, teasing the roots out by hand. Very tightly packed roots may be prised apart with hand forks used back-to-back.

3 Repot each clump in a separate container filled with damp soil. Water well and top-dress with grit or pea shingle before placing in the pool. Trim off surplus hessian with scissors.

Propagation

Most water plants, especially marginals, may be propagated by division. Other methods are also used, depending on the type of plant: many submerged oxygenators and some creeping marginals, for example, are propagated by cuttings, while a number of floating plants naturally produce runners, plantlets, or turions, which grow into new plants. Moisture-loving species that grow around the pool edge, as well as some aquatics, may be raised from seed or increased by division.

Cuttings are best taken and plants divided in spring or early summer, when high temperatures and long daylight hours provide excellent conditions for new plant growth.

WATER PLANTS FROM CUTTINGS

Bacopa monnieri
Cabomba caroliniana ❋
Callitriche hermaphroditica
Ceratophyllum demersum
Crassula helmsii
Decodon verticillatus
Egeria densa ❋
Hydrilla verticillata
Hydrocleys parviflora ❋
Hygrophila polysperma ❋
Lagarosiphon major
Limnophila heterophylla
Ludwigia arcuata
Myriophyllum papillosum ❋
Potamogeton crispus
Trapa natans

WATER PLANTS TO DIVIDE

Tubers
Aponogeton distachyos
Colocasia esculenta ❋
Nelumbo nucifera ❋
Zantedeschia, some ❋

Rootstock
Acorus calamus
Butomus umbellatus
Calla palustris
Caltha palustris

Caltha palustris
'Flore Pleno'

Cryptocoryne
beckettii
var. ciliata ❋
Damasonium alisma
Darmera peltata
Decodon verticillatus

Key
❋ *Not hardy*

Division

A large number of marginal plants may be readily propagated by division. The exact technique that should be used depends on both the plant's root system and its pattern of growth. For further information, see "Dividing perennials", p.200.

Plants with fibrous or creeping roots

Plants that have extensive fibrous or creeping roots, such as *Typha latifolia*, may be divided by levering apart the rootstocks. Simply pull the rootstocks apart with your hands; if the roots are tightly compacted, use two garden forks positioned back-to-back and lever apart.

Each divided portion should include a growing point (a horizontally placed, terminal shoot). Cut off the old, brown roots and remove any dead leaves. Trim the new roots before replanting the divided portions in individual containers. Level the soil with the base of the shoots. Firm them in, then top-dress lightly with a layer of gravel. Cover the container with approximately 5–8cm (2–3in) of water.

Butomus umbellatus may be divided but may also be propagated from bulbils that form in the axils of the leaves. These are separated and then grown on individually (see LILIES, *Propagating from Stem Bulbils*, p.251).

Rhizomatous plants

For plants with strong, rhizomatous roots, such as irises, pull apart the root mass and divide it into sections with a sharp knife, each containing at least one bud and preferably some young roots. Cut off any long roots

and trim back the foliage, if needed. Do not trim the foliage back to below the water line since the newly cut surface tissue may begin to rot.

Plant the division in a suitable container, firming the soil around the roots but leaving the rhizome itself almost exposed. Cover the soil with a layer of gravel and immerse

the crate in the pool so that the roots are covered by about 5–8cm (2–3in) of water. Rhizomatous plants with creeping, surface stems, such as *Calla palustris*, may be lifted and divided into sections, each containing a bud. Replant the sections individually in the same way as other rhizomatous plants.

PROPAGATING BY CUTTINGS

1 *In spring and summer, cut off healthy young shoots. Tie with wire into small bunches of three to six cuttings 10–15cm (4–6in) long.*

2 *Using a dibber, make holes in damp soil in a prepared planting crate lined with hessian. Insert the bunches of cuttings to a depth of about 5cm (2in).*

DIVIDING FIBROUS ROOTSTOCKS

Remove the plant from the container or lift it from the soil with a fork. Insert two forks, placed back-to-back, into the root mass and lever them apart, dividing the plant. Repeat to divide further, then trim and replant the divisions. The plant shown here is Acorus calamus.

DIVIDING RHIZOMATOUS PLANTS

1 *Lift the plant (here* Acorus calamus). *Split the root mass into sections with your hands. Each part should have a good root system and several healthy shoots.*

2 *Use a sharp knife to trim back long roots and foliage by approximately one third to a half of their original length.*

3 *Line a container with hessian and part-fill with damp soil. Plant each division so that the rhizome is just covered with a thin layer of soil.*

Cuttings

Most submerged oxygenating plants may be quite easily propagated by softwood cuttings taken in spring or summer; this process also helps to keep plants in check. Fast-growing oxygenators, for example *Elodea canadensis* and *Potamogeton crispus*, should be regularly replaced by young stock.

Prepare the cuttings by pinching or cutting off healthy, young shoots, inserting them into pots or trays of loam, and submerging them. The cuttings may be inserted individually or tied into small bunches of six. Cuttings of some creeping marginal plants, for example *Mentha aquatica* and water forget-me-nots (*Myosotis scorpioides*), should be inserted singly rather than in bunches. The cuttings establish quickly and may be potted up and planted in position after two to three weeks.

Some tuberous water lilies may also be propagated by cuttings, although a different method is used (see "Bud cuttings", p.287).

Runners and plantlets

Many of the floating plants that are invasive in tropical lakes and rivers propagate themselves by means of runners or plantlets produced on long, adventitious shoots. The water hyacinth (*Eichhornia crassipes*) and *Pistia stratiotes* can populate vast areas of warm water in this way. In shallow water, the young plantlets quickly root into the rich mud at the bottom, drawing up fresh nutrients and sending out yet more runners. The plantlets may simply be snapped off and replaced on the water surface to grow separately.

A dwarf form of the Egyptian paper reed, *Cyperus papyrus* 'Nanus' (syn. *C. papyrus* 'Viviparus'), forms young plantlets in the flowerhead. If the head is bent over and immersed in a container of soil and water the plantlets root and develop; these can be divided and potted up separately.

Turions

Some water plants, for example *Hydrocharis morsus-ranae*, produce swollen buds known as turions that become detached from the parent and survive the winter at the bottom of the pool. In spring these turions rise to the surface of the water again and develop into new plants.

The turions of *Hottonia palustris* develop from the mud in spring without floating to the surface. Since

PROPAGATION OF RUNNERS OR PLANTLETS

1 *Some floating plants (here water hyacinths,* Eichhornia crassipes) *form offsets. In spring, remove an offset from the parent by snapping the connecting stem.*

2 *Place the offset directly on the water surface, supporting it gently with your hand until it floats upright.*

these are difficult to collect, wait for them to develop into young plants before lifting and replanting them in their new positions.

The turions may also be collected in autumn and stored in loam in a submerged seed tray covered with 15cm (6in) of water throughout the winter. In spring, when the emerging buds float to the surface, they may be collected and potted up into prepared containers of loam.

Seed

Most moisture-loving plants, and certain of the aquatics, including *Aponogeton distachyos*, *Euryale ferox*, *Orontium aquaticum*, *Trapa natans*, and tropical water lilies (see *Hardy and Tropical Water Lilies*, p.286) may be grown from ripe seed collected in summer or autumn.

Keep the seeds cool and moist until ready to sow. If using dried seeds, germination will be delayed or the seeds may lose viability. Aquatic plant seeds should be grown in submerged or partially submerged conditions, similar to their natural habitat. When sowing seed, first prepare containers such as seed trays or pans by filling them with an appropriate aquatic compost or garden loam passed through a 7mm (¼in) sieve. The growing medium should not contain any fertilizers, since they encourage algae, which could smother germinating seedlings.

Sow the seeds on the surface of the growing medium, and then cover them with a shallow layer of fine grit before placing the tray in a large watertight container, such as a plastic bowl or an aquarium. Fill the container with water until the pan is just covered, and leave it on a greenhouse bench in partial shade, or on a well-lit windowsill, at a minimum temperature of 18°C (64°F). The following spring, the seeds should start to germinate.

When the first pair of true leaves appears, carefully prick out the seedlings into individual pots and leave them immersed in water in the greenhouse for another year. Transfer the plants to the pool when the water warms up in spring.

WATER PLANTS TO DIVIDE (CONT.)

Rootstock (cont.)
Eriophorum angustifolium
Lysichiton
Mentha aquatica
Menyanthes trifoliata
Myosotis scorpioides
Nuphar lutea
Pontederia cordata
Ranunculus lingua
Sagittaria sagittifolia
Saururus cernuus
Thalia dealbata ❉
Typha latifolia

Lysichiton camtschatcensis

Offsets
Eichhornia crassipes ❉
Hydrocharis morsus-ranae
Limnanthemum lacunosum
Limnobium stoloniferum
Marsilea quadrifolia
Pistia stratiotes ❉
Sagittaria graminea,
   S. sagittifolia 'Flore Pleno'
Salvinia auriculata ❉,
   S. natans ❉
Stratiotes aloides

Salvinia auriculata

Plantlets
Aponogeton undulatus ❉
Azolla filiculoides ❉
Baldellia ranunculoides
Ceratopteris cornuta ❉
Eichhornia crassipes ❉
Hottonia palustris
Nuphar advena
Nymphaea, some ❉
Utricularia gibba ❉

Key
❉ *Not hardy*

SOWING SEED

1 *Sow the seeds evenly by tapping them from paper onto a pan of firmed aquatic compost or sieved garden loam.*

2 *Cover the seeds with a shallow layer of fine grit. Then place the pan in a large plastic bowl.*

3 *Gradually add water to the bowl so that the pan is just covered. Place in a well-lit position at about 18°C (64°F) until germinated.*

CHAPTER

11

CONTAINER GARDENING

GROWING PLANTS IN containers is an exceptionally versatile way of gardening. An enormous range of plants adapt well to these essentially artificial conditions, whether they be short-lived bedding plants, which make colourful summer displays in pots, hanging baskets, or windowboxes, or relatively large shrubs and trees, which can live for many years in large containers. With such a diversity of plants to choose from, container gardens can be created almost anywhere, from spaces as confined as a patio, roof garden, balcony, or windowbox to areas in the larger garden.

Using containers

GROWING plants in containers is one of the most flexible of gardening techniques. For many modern gardeners, who are aiming to create a pleasing environment in a limited space, container gardening is practical and appealing. For centuries plants have been grown in containers to allow them to be sited where there is no garden soil, for example in a paved courtyard, on a balcony (see p.312), or under cover in the home (see INDOOR GARDENING, pp.352–383), greenhouse, or conservatory (see CONSERVATORY GARDENING, p.356). Plants are also pot-grown to give them prominence in a display – their unique qualities being easier to appreciate when they are placed in an inconspicuous pot – or to enhance them in a container that is attractive in its own right.

Growing plants in containers also allows the cultivation of genera that may not thrive in a particular garden's soil, by using tailored formulations of growing mixes. These include lime-free (ericaceous) mixes for lime-hating plants, such as rhododendrons and azaleas, or very gritty mixes for alpine plants or succulents, which need sharp drainage.

Changes in focus
In a conventional garden, plants are grown in the open ground and displays are relatively static because the components cannot easily be moved about. In such gardens, containers can play a role as focal points, for specimen planting, and for filling gaps in beds and borders. In the container garden, pot-grown plants are easily regrouped: with subtractions and additions, a planting scheme can be quickly rejuvenated or even completely transformed. Container gardening, therefore, is ideal for the experimental gardener wishing to create stimulating arrangements that can be changed when they have outlived their initial appeal.

Formal and informal styles
These two broad approaches to garden design are as relevant to container gardening as they are to gardening in open ground. The formal style is based on geometric order, with a division of space into balanced, often symmetrical units, and the repetition of elements at regular intervals. The informal approach has little or no geometry and the elements are arranged without obvious symmetry. At their most effective, informal arrangements take their cue from the irregularity of natural landscapes, although there is usually a carefully thought out, underlying balance of mass, form, and space.

Many popular manufactured containers are of a regular outline that is perfectly suitable for formal arrangements. Most plants, however, naturally grow in an informal way and so can be used to obscure the lines of the container. When arranging container-grown plants, it is just as easy to create an informal style – with soft, "freestyle" planting – as it is to ensure formality by planting to emphasize and echo the regularity of the container's shape.

An alternative approach to the informal style is to use "found" or reclaimed containers, such as chimney pots, old sinks, or drinking troughs, whose original purpose was quite other than for growing plants.

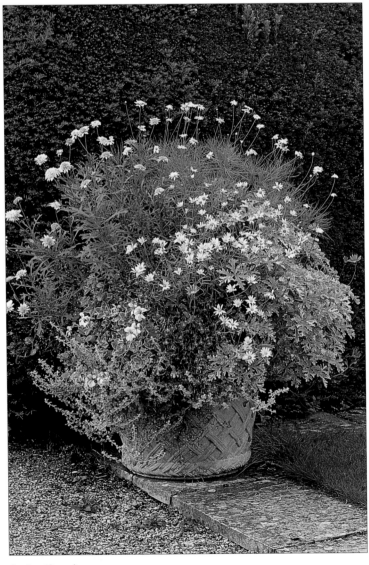

Contrasting shapes
The strong lines of this formal terracotta pot are softened and enhanced by an exuberant and informal planting of mound-formers and trailers.

Selecting a container

The choice of container is a matter of personal taste and aesthetics. Whether the container is manufactured or improvised, however, it must satisfy key practical requirements to make it suitable for the cultivation of plants. The most fundamental elements are that a container holds sufficient growing mix to sustain the plants and has provision for excess water to drain away.

The materials of which containers are made will also affect the final choice. These include unglazed and glazed terracotta, natural or reconstituted stone, concrete, metal, wood, fibreglass, and plastic. No material has a longer history of use than unglazed terracotta and its warm, earthy colour and matt-textured surface provide one of the most sympathetic foils for foliage and flowers. Terracotta lends itself to decoration with incised or relief patterns that are pleasing, but not distracting. It also blends in well with most architectural features, whether they are of stone, wood, or metal.

More opulent effects can be achieved with containers of marble, or more austere ones in other types of stone. The severity of concrete containers, or the strong lines of light-reflecting, galvanized zinc ones, lend themselves particularly well to an ultra-modern style, while wooden ones can be used to create more rustic atmosphere. Containers in fibreglass and plastic can look inconspicuous, but both materials have practical virtues, in terms of moisture retention, for example; and

Coordinated container

A large earthenware tub is an ideal container for an elegant bamboo; its subtle, earth-toned glaze echoes the bamboo fence behind, the whole lending a distinctly appropriate and stylish note to an Oriental-style garden.

the best successfully imitate much more expensive materials.

Plants and their containers should complement rather than compete with each other, and the texture, colour, and surface finish of a container are considerations as important as the

material itself. To a large extent, this is a matter of individual preference, but it is worth bearing in mind that containers of an assertive colour, a bold, high-gloss finish, or with conspicuous decoration will demand an equally strong planting scheme.

Size, shape, and scale

The size and shape of a container are governed by practical considerations as well those of visual appeal. The container must be large enough to accommodate the plant or plants to be grown. It is equally important to match the size of the pot to the visual mass of the planting it will hold. A small stone trough, for example, would be in scale with diminutive alpines; an Ali Baba jar would suit a vigorous trailing specimen, and a Versailles tub is ideal in both style and capacity for a topiary specimen. For a packed and colourful display of upright and trailing summer plants, a generously proportioned copper vessel (as once used for boiling or washing) might be appropriate.

As a general rule, the larger the pot the better, and larger pots need less frequent watering. One advantage of smaller pots, however, is that they can be dropped into arrangements as plants reach their prime, and removed when past their best. This technique

works best in conjunction with a holding area, such as a cold frame, in which plants are brought to near perfection, and to which they are returned to recover when their display is over.

Single specimens in containers

Growing single plants in individual containers is very practical: the growing mix, watering, and feeding regime can be geared to the plant, which is also freed of competition for moisture and nutrients. It can also work well in design terms, particularly if the plant has a strong architectural shape. The spiky New Zealand cabbage palm (*Cordyline australis*) and yuccas make fine specimens, as do plants of softer, weeping form, such as cultivars of the Japanese maple (*Acer palmatum*). Arching and mound-forming grasses, such as the green-and-gold variegated *Hakonechloa macra* 'Aureola', also look good alone in containers, as do species that are formally trained, such as a frame-grown common ivy (*Hedera helix*) or a clipped topiary specimen, such as box (*Buxus sempervirens*). Clematis and other moderately vigorous climbers can be allowed to trail from tall containers, or be trained upwards

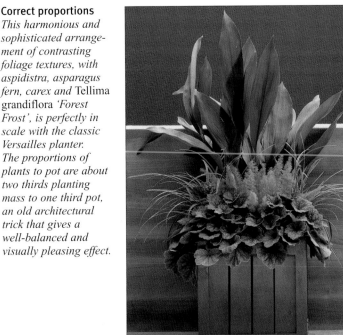

Correct proportions

This harmonious and sophisticated arrangement of contrasting foliage textures, with aspidistra, asparagus fern, carex and Tellima grandiflora 'Forest Frost', is perfectly in scale with the classic Versailles planter. The proportions of plants to pot are about two thirds planting mass to one third pot, an old architectural trick that gives a well-balanced and visually pleasing effect.

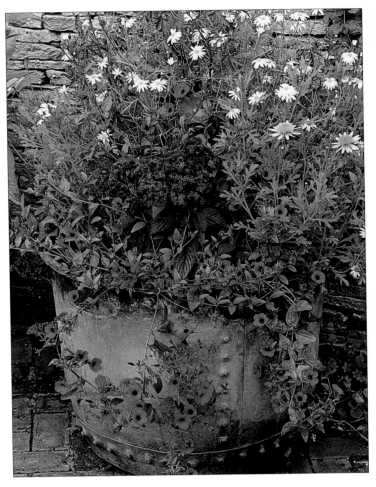

Mixed planting
Magenta petunias form a harmonious fringe beneath rich violet heliotropes, their intensity offset by copper and soft pinks and white highlights.

on a simple obelisk. Lax shrubs, such as groundcover roses, look perfect when trailing their stems over the container's edge, and many other quite modest plants – heathers, primulas, and violas – radiate a special charm when given the luxury of their own pot.

Mixed planting

Individual plants in their own containers can be grouped to give the impression of a mixed planting. But a greater challenge is to bring together a number of plants that complement each other and give a sustained display for several weeks or even months. The keys to success are to select plants that share the same or similar cultural needs, and to create arrangements of compatible colours and contrasting forms and textures in foliage and flowers. Mixed displays are most effective with a strong structure, for example where a vertical or domed centrepiece is surrounded by lesser "uprights", with trailing plants breaking over the edge of the container to form an irregular "skirt".

A spring mixture, for example, might contrast upright dwarf irises and crocuses with a mat of small-leaved thyme (*Thymus serpyllum*); richly coloured polyanthus among mounds of sky-blue forget-me-nots (*Myosotis sylvatica*); or daisies (*Bellis perennis*) with tulips as strong verticals. In summer, the choice is almost endless – by selecting long-flowering bedding and foliage plants, it is possible to assemble rich arrangements to provide many months of colour.

Colour themes

When packing several plants close together, colour clashes become much more conspicuous than in the less condensed conditions of the open garden. In containers, it is perhaps more important to devise combinations of plants based on colour harmonies or contrasts. The harmonies of closely related colours can be quiet and subtle, as in a warm scheme based on cream, soft yellow, and pale apricot, while more heavily saturated colours – rich purples with violets and blues – create more vibrant harmonies. Contrasts are based on complementary colours: red with green, blue with orange,

or yellow with violet. The eye is comfortable with these opposites, which tone well with one another.

Alternatively, more shocking combinations can be tried, for example orange with magenta-pink. Colour clashes can be stimulating, but, in a small space, it is often helpful to ease the tension by using pale flower colours – creams or near-whites – or foliage as a buffer. Grey-leaved plants, such as *Helichrysum petiolare*, are invaluable in this respect, as are white- or cream-variegated plants, such as small-leaved cultivars of common ivy (*Hedera helix*).

Siting containers

Planted containers can be used simply as isolated features, but are often most effective in the garden when used as an integral part of a wider design. In the formal garden, for example, containers can provide accents that reinforce a sense of geometry. Similarly, looser arrangements can underline the more subtle rhythms of a more naturalistic theme.

The position of containers should be based on practical as well as aesthetic considerations. Container-grown plants need frequent watering in summer, so easy access to a water supply is vital, especially in sunny sites where plants may need attention at least once daily during spells of hot, dry weather.

It is worth bearing in mind, too, that thieves target gardens as well as houses, and a valuable urn or antique jar is safer placed in full view of the house, rather than in a more secluded position, and may even be best fixed or bolted to the ground.

Avenue design
A broad walk flanked by an avenue of citrus trees in terracotta pots achieves formality through repetition of simple elements. Such a design demands discipline, but the elegant effect becomes its own reward.

Defining accents

Placing containers to create a succession of accents is a useful technique for delineating areas of the garden, or marking boundaries. At its simplest, a row of containers may mark a boundary, perhaps in conjunction with a wall or fence. Try lining pots along the base of a fence or along the top of a wall, provided they are secure and will not topple, or even suspend them from it. The effect can be achieved at little cost – perhaps with brightly painted, recycled tins planted with long-flowering and colourful pelargoniums. Containers can also be used to define compartments within a garden, for example when set singly or in clusters at the corners of a rectangular paved area.

Container accents are invaluable for enhancing other features. A squared arrangement around a circular pool, for example, forms a very effective contrast; alternatively place pots in the curved quadrants to emphasize the line of the pool's edge. Accents such as this can fulfil a dual role: they can define a shape while also softening a hard outline. This is especially useful in integrating the severe geometry of a rectangular pool into the wider garden: containers arranged around the pool echo its shape, yet, if filled with loose arrangements of plants, they soften the effect. It is best to set containers back from the water's edge so that they are not a hazard, and to reduce the risk of dead leaves and flowers fouling the water.

Containers as focal points

The main lines of a small, modern garden in a formal style rarely terminate in a natural view of a landscape or an architectural landmark,

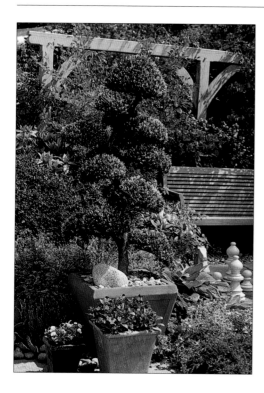

Focal points
A unusually clipped shrub planted in an angular terracotta pot draws the eye in this intimate and stylish patio garden. Standing out vividly against the softer lines and textures of the surrounding plants, its bold sculptural shapes echo the distinctive contours of the outdoor chess set.

but, even on a small scale, a vista that does not lead to a natural conclusion can seem unsatisfying. Features that are traditionally introduced to terminate vistas include trees and statuary, but on a smaller scale an urn, or large pot or tub, can fulfil the role equally well. Such focal points give an almost instant effect and, in comparison with statuary, are generally much less costly. Even an empty container can make an effective eye-catcher, provided that the scale is right; but when planted with an upright plant or group of plants, surrounded by a fringe of trailers, the design is far more handsome.

There is no simple rule of thumb for ensuring the correct scale; it is often most satisfactory to do it "by eye". Make a preliminary test by positioning a cane where the container is to stand, and then check its position from various points along the vista. In some cases, it may be necessary to raise the container on a plinth to achieve the desired effect. This can be a ready-made, architectural plinth or can be improvised, for example, with a stack of unmortared bricks, or wooden blocks, depending on the desired style.

In garden compartments, a central focal point is usually a good idea. A planted container is often a much simpler and cheaper option than a statue, sundial, or fountain. A formal herb garden divided into quarters, for example, may include a central paved or gravelled area – an ideal spot for a large pot planted with an architectural specimen, such as angelica (*Angelica archangelica*).

Alternatively, to maximize the growing area, the container could stand on a plinth in the middle of the bed, but ensure that access for watering and maintenance is provided for, perhaps by means of stepping stones.

Containers may also be used as focal points to direct the eye through the garden, for example by placing a large pot at a turning point on a path, or to act as a distant feature that leads the observer on to another view or vista. In gardens where one mass of planting deliberately masks another, the unexpected has special value. A carefully placed container can introduce such an element of surprise, and an empty container of architectural quality – erect or on its side – can be just as dramatic as one full of plants.

Emphatic arrangements

Containers, especially if arranged in pairs, are an ideal way of marking a transition in the garden. This can be as simple and low-key as a one-step change of level, for example by using clipped balls of box (*Buxus sempervirens*) in terracotta pots to flank the step, emphasize the change, and warn people against tripping. Grander flights of steps can be treated in a more lavish way, with paired containers at top and base and others at different landings, to create a dramatic setting. But when using containers on steps in this way, they must be carefully placed so as not to present a hazard.

Paired containers can also play a supporting role to another feature, such as a garden bench, that may not have sufficient impact to terminate

a vista by itself. Setting matched containers on either side strengthens the central feature, which assumes greater visual weight. For strictly formal, long-term designs, pots could be planted with a topiary or, to ring the seasonal changes, a spring display of tulips could be followed with summer bedding plants that will bloom continuously for several months.

Paired containers can lend particular emphasis when positioned to form an "avenue". This formal pattern can work well on a relatively small scale: even in confined spaces, the effect can be monumental, for example when citrus trees in large terracotta pots or urns are placed in bays along a broad walk. On a more modest scale, pots of evergreens or seasonal flowers can be introduced to mark the main axis of a tiny garden.

Containers in borders

Containerized plants, when rising above plantings in open ground, can be used to create contrast or to reinforce a colour theme in beds and borders: for example, violet-purple flowers like heliotrope (*Heliotropium*

arborescens) or petunias could oppose a border theme of oranges, creams, and yellows. Alternatively, subtle harmonies can be created, like the pale pink of the double tulip 'Angélique' in pots beside beds of wallflowers, such as *Erysimum cheiri* Fair Lady Series, in shades of pink, yellow, and cream.

Container-grown plants are particularly valuable when the garden is relatively empty. Winter-flowering pansies, such as *Viola* x *wittrockiana* Universal Series, brighten dull days for many weeks in winter and early spring and can gradually be supplemented with a succession of bulbs, such as daffodils and tulips. In the autumn garden, container-grown shrubby plants such as *Argyranthemum*, fuchsias, and *Phygelius* will perform well until the first frosts.

Another approach is to boost beds and borders with pot-grown plants plunged into the ground. This is a particularly useful way to fill gaps in a border when the foliage of summer perennials, such as the Oriental poppies (*Papaver orientale cultivars*), has died back. It can also be used to

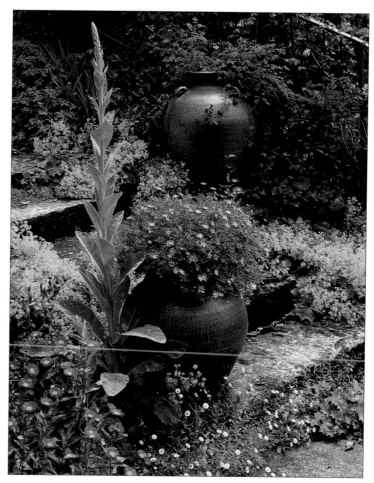

Transitional arrangements
Simple urns mark changes of level, with a cleverly placed verbascum that lends emphasis with its strong vertical line; the whole scheme is enhanced by a marriage of complementary colours – yellows and mauves.

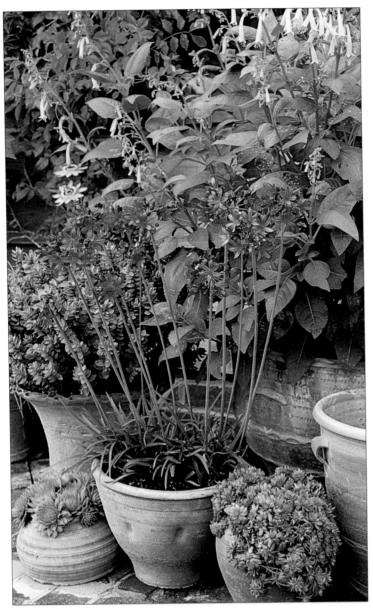

Unity and diversity
A variety of unglazed terracotta pots creates a sense of unity within a group and forms a warm but neutral foil for this colourful and attractive arrangement.

lemon verbena (*Aloysia triphylla*) or myrtle (*Myrtus communis*), often succeed here when they may not thrive in a more open garden. In some cases, the proximity of buildings and walls means that a paved garden receives little or no direct sun for all or part of the day. While painting walls white helps to make such shady areas brighter, the plants that really thrive in these conditions are committed shade lovers, such as hostas and ferns. These plants grow more lush and look beautiful for much longer periods in cool shade, providing the possibilities of sumptuous arrangements of foliage colour and texture.

Where direct light penetrates for several hours a day, many more plants will thrive, especially those that occur naturally in the dappled shade of a woodland setting, such as camellias and rhododendrons. When light levels are low, try moving the plants around from time to time, so that they have more exposure to sunlight; it helps promote balanced growth and encourages them to flower more freely.

Two other features of a paved environment affect the choice of plants: the weight of a pot and the watering regime. Solid walls often create turbulence as they deflect wind, and unstable pots may be toppled by sudden downdraughts; the growing mix also dries more rapidly in windy conditions. Containers close to walls may also stand in a rain shadow, where natural rainfall does not penetrate (see *Rain Shadow*, p.610). Even after heavy rain, plants may not receive sufficient water, so provision must be made for adequate watering.

Choosing containers

There are no hard-and-fast aesthetic rules when choosing containers for paved areas. They can be matched closely in texture and material to architecture and hard surfaces – terracotta pots are ideal against brick, for example. An equally valid approach is to use containers that stand out in a paved setting. Glazed jars, painted wooden tubs, and galvanized metal cubes and containers are just some of the choices that can help to define a distinctive style.

Arranging containers

Any arrangement of containers must take account of practicalities. For example, it is important to leave some clear space for access and to allow enough room for the unrestricted use of furniture. But from autumn to spring, when many paved areas are less heavily used, containers can be rearranged to provide displays that are visible from indoors. Stacked arrangements of pots loaded with

Cornerpiece
Billowing foliage and a restricted colour scheme create a beautiful cornerpiece; the red blooms pick up and echo a warm-toned brick wall.

bulbs, evergreens, or winter-flowering pansies (*Viola* x *wittrockiana* cultivars), placed in view of French windows, allow the display to be enjoyed in warmth and comfort.

The most difficult aspect of managing changing displays is finding a place for plants before and after their most decorative season – only a limited number of those past their best can be hidden among plants in their prime. In the absence of a holding area, one solution is to rely heavily on annuals and biennials that are discarded when their season is over, leaving containers available for a succession of seasonal displays. Another option is to use containers that are ornamental in their own right; if carefully selected, they can be attractive even when empty. And if more permanent plantings of bulbs, perennials, and shrubs should outlive their usefulness, they are often gratefully received by friends with more space in their gardens.

Formal arrangements

The most usual formal arrangements in paved areas are paired containers flanking doors, benches, or other furniture set against walls. Where there is room, the symmetry can be expanded to include matching clusters of containers, with additions and subtractions as the seasons advance. At times of the year when the paved area is much used, arrangements – formal or otherwise – are best kept to the perimeter, but this does not preclude using them as a focal point, perhaps where they can be viewed from a door or window.

supplement the display when newly planted perennials and shrubs have yet to attain their full size in a bed.

Containers in paved gardens

The pleasures of gardening, and the contribution that plants make in enhancing the living environment, are being appreciated by more and more people. At the same time, gardens are increasingly being thought of as outdoor rooms, to be used for relaxing and entertaining, dining, and cooking. In the summer months, an outdoor room may even be much busier than living rooms indoors.

For many people, particularly in urban areas, the garden is a small

paved space bounded by walls or fences: a courtyard, patio, or terrace. There are also other areas of hard landscaping in gardens, such as paths and forecourts, and while the range of surfaces includes a huge variety of stone, tile, gravel, or concrete, or even wooden decking, open soil is often at a premium. The only way to include plants in such sites, where soil and space are so limited, is to grow them in containers.

Plants for paved areas

A large number of plants is suitable for containers in paved areas. In enclosed gardens, especially near sunny walls, there is often a very favourable, warm, and sheltered microclimate (see p.611). Tender plants, such as the fragrant-leaved

Although space may be limited, there is no need to restrict containers to small pots with flowers just above ground level. Such arrangements can appear mean in scale; fewer but larger plants will have much more impact. If there is no room for loose, rounded shapes, such as those of *Fatsia japonica* or the mophead *Hydrangea macrophylla* cultivars, consider naturally narrow, upright plants, such as a slow-growing conifer like *Juniperus communis* 'Sentinel', or plants such as yew (*Taxus baccata*) and box (*Buxus sempervirens*), which can be clipped to form a narrow cone or column.

To bring colour to the scheme, use flowering plants, such as clematis and miniature climbing roses, or variegated foliage plants, such as cultivars of common ivy (*Hedera helix*), and train them onto upright obelisks or narrow, willow-wand pyramids.

Many urban gardens have a paved path between a wall or fence and the house. Without plants, these passage-ways can appear bleak, but there is seldom enough room at ground level for pots or tubs. One solution is to place deep, narrow troughs at the foot of the wall. They can be filled with free-standing arrangements, or even with climbing plants that will cover the wall if given support. Another option is to fix containers securely to the wall top, so that plants can cascade down the wall's face. There is also a wide range of flat-backed, half-round containers available that are specifically designed

Formal entrance
An elegant facade is enhanced by tightly clipped lollipop trees (here privet); pink pelargoniums bring this quietly understated colour scheme to life.

to be mounted on the vertical surface of a wall or stout fence.

Stands for containers

A plant stand with shelves at different heights provides a support for a neat and attractive display of container-grown plants and has the advantage that a diverse display can be created within a relatively small area. The most suitable and durable are usually made of aluminium and are of simple design with stepped and slatted shelves. The slats allow water to

drain away freely and the "rake" of the shelves means that plants on the top shelf do not overshadow those lower down. Most stands can be fixed against a wall or placed in a more open position, but some are specifically designed to fill corners, and these make good use of a potentially awkward space. An alternative to proprietary stands are those made from stacked bricks, clay drainpipes, or upturned flower-pots as uprights, and plain wooden planks as a standing surface. Such improvised structures have the advantage of being easily dismantled and reassembled as the need arises.

The position of a stand is frequently a matter of compromise, especially in the summer when the area is most heavily used. A good position for viewing from the house is against a wall opposite a door or window over-looking a courtyard or patio. In winter, when the patio is less often used, a staged display can be placed more centrally. Wherever the stand is put, the best results are usually achieved with a balanced combination of flowering and foliage plants.

Informal clusters

Stray containers, unless carefully placed, can be both a nuisance and a hazard in paved gardens, but informal clusters can be an effective way of displaying plants and their pots. An interesting range of plants in containers of different heights and sizes can, to some extent, mimic the layered effect of plants in the open garden. This can be enhanced by standing some containers on bricks to give additional prominence and by varying the height of their contents.

Any irregularly shaped cluster is a useful way of filling a corner, and informally planted containers along the borders of a patio or terrace can help mitigate the formal severity of paving. Very pleasing, unifying effects can be achieved by using differently shaped containers in the same material – unglazed terracotta pots, for example, are available in a wide range of shapes and sizes.

Keep it clean

The main disadvantage of clustered containers is that, inevitably, dust, dead leaves, and other detritus accumulate around their bases, which can be difficult to sweep away. A power hose is useful for keeping the surfaces clean, but it is also worth considering investing in wheeled bases for pots. These not only make it easier to sweep detritus away but are also an invaluable aid when moving heavy pots to re-create displays as plants fade at the end of their season.

Tiered container display
A banked mass of brilliant colour is achieved here by using pots of various sizes, with additional height gained by means of upturned empty pots – an inexpensive alternative to staging. *The range of bronze-tinted greens found in the pelargonium leaves forms a linking element and is a complementary foil for the brilliant reds.*

Balconies and roof gardens

BALCONIES and areas of flat roof can be converted to architecturally pleasing spaces in which container-grown plants can be used with extraordinary effect to create gardens in the air. Large-scale roof gardens can incorporate many of the features of a garden at ground level, including seating for relaxing and entertaining, barbecues, ornamental pools, and trees and climbers on supports. But even the smallest balcony can be transformed into a green and flower-filled outdoor room – a valuable extension of the living space indoors and a beautiful frame for the world beyond.

Special challenges

Almost any balcony or flat roof area has garden potential, but such spaces do present special challenges and safety is a major consideration. Plants, moist growing mix, containers, and all the other features that make up a garden constitute a considerable load, which must be within the structure's load-bearing capacity. In addition, flooring must be waterproof and adequately drained. It is always advisable to consult an architect or structural engineer before planning a roof or balcony garden, and a check that local by-laws permit such structures to be made. Expert advice should include suggestions for fortifying structural support, or on how to site heavy elements to use the existing load-bearing capacity of walls or cross-beams. With careful choice of materials, the accumulated weight of garden components can be minimized. For example, consider wooden decking rather than tiling as a flooring material. Select plastic or fibreglass containers rather than those made of very heavy materials, such as stone and concrete; and use loamless

rather than loam-based growing mix to reduce the load further.

Balconies and roof gardens need barriers to protect those using the space: consult relevant building regulations governing minimum standards and heights for railings and walls. Balconies and roof gardens are much more likely to be affected by turbulence and strong winds than gardens at ground level, so all containers must be firmly secured. It is important, too, that none of the contents of a balcony or roof garden falls off, so putting at risk people and property below. Even within a roof garden or balcony, falling pots and large plants can cause damage, for instance, to windows. To prevent them being blown over, lightweight containers may need ballast or fixing in position. Bear in mind that tall,

narrow-based pots are much less stable than squat, broad-based ones.

The blustery winds that are a typical feature of balconies and roof gardens may damage fragile growth and wither tender foliage on plants such as Japanese maples (*Acer palmatum* cultivars). Drying winds combined with full sun create testing growing conditions. The most successful plants are tough and drought-tolerant; however, a wide range of plants will grow well provided they receive an adequate and regular water supply. On a large roof garden, an automated irrigation system can be the most efficient way to maintain satisfactory moisture levels, provided that provision is made for dealing with excess water. It is important that the structure incorporates drainage channels so that water does not form pools,

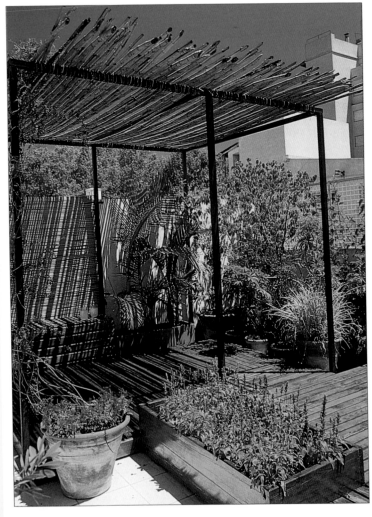

Shade in summer
This lightweight bamboo screening provides invaluable shade from fierce overhead summer sun on a roof or balcony garden.

Well-managed space
On this wood-decked, first-floor terrace, container-grown plants are carefully grouped so that they do not impede access to the steps.

Planting for an exposed position
Flowers and foliage plants, including grey-leaved Senecio cineraria *and spreading* Scaevola *with fan-shaped flowers, make a wind-tolerant mixture.*

for example, after a storm. Wooden decking can be laid to disguise any drainage systems required.

Planting on balconies

Plants for balconies can be grown in pots and troughs that stand on the balcony floor, in wall-mounted containers, or in those that are securely fixed to railings. When a balcony forms a garden extension to a room, the appearance of the containers and plants is most often judged from inside. Use planting to frame rather than obscure a good view, perhaps by grouping containers at either side of a clear central area. If, on the other hand, the view is dull or mediocre, use container-grown plants to block it out. In a similar way, trailing plants, spilling from pots or troughs mounted at the top of railings, can ensure privacy by screening the room within from view.

Balcony plantings can be just as attractive from within as from outside a building. Balconies, like window-boxes, may be planted to complement the architecture, perhaps with schemes that coordinate with plantings at ground level and on the floors above. Good trailing plants for sunny balconies include ivy-leaved pelargoniums; these are reasonably drought-tolerant and flower freely through summer and into autumn. Many bushy and upright plants also adapt well to life on sunny balconies, including aromatic herbs, such as hyssop (*Hyssopus officinalis*) and long-flowering annuals, such as the kingfisher daisy (*Felicia bergeriana*). While the choice for shady balconies is more limited, elegant schemes can be created using cultivars of common

ivy (*Hedera helix*) and evergreens, such as box (*Buxus sempervirens*), which provide year-round interest. Add extra colour with compact, shade-tolerant annuals and biennials, such as winter- and summer-flowering pansies (*Viola* x *wittrockiana*) or busy Lizzies (*Impatiens walleriana*), which bloom for several months during summer.

Planting in roof gardens

Large balconies and roof gardens often provide viewing platforms for dramatic cityscapes. If this is the case, capitalize on the view and use planting to frame it. Whether the

design is formal or informal, try to group containers so that the revelation of a view is gradual. Alternatively, create frames for a series of different vistas, which will ensure that the grandest one of all does not lose its novelty.

Carefully placed containers
These colourful hanging baskets of petunias, placed near pillars so as not to obscure the lush garden beyond, provide a jewel-like contrast to the predominantly green foliage. The surrounding plants have been encouraged to grow through the terrace railings to soften the lines, creating a relaxed and exotic effect.

Minimalist formality
Strip decking, squared-up layout, and rounded topiary all contribute to the formality of a roof garden that includes planted and empty containers.

Perhaps more common than a beautiful prospect is a dreary view from a draughty and overlooked space. In this case, the best option is to create a more inward-looking garden. A climbing plant, barrier, or trellis not only helps to block out ugly views but also establishes an intimate atmosphere and helps reduce wind turbulence. Within the defined space, the design could be strictly formal, using relatively few shrubs trimmed to simple geometric shapes, or you could assemble plants to suggest the medley of a traditional cottage garden. For colourful, long-lasting displays, massed bedding plants are a good option, but there is also scope to experiment with vegetables and herbs, or subtropical and tropical plants. By creating compartments with screens, or even a pergola, variety is increased and intimacy enhanced.

Whatever the chosen style, arrange containers so as not to clutter areas used for seating or entertaining. For the most wind-resistant results, choose bushy and compact plants; they are less likely to be damaged or desiccated by strong winds. Compact cultivars of most popular bedding plants are readily available and there are many bushy shrubs to choose in preference to those that are tall and top-heavy.

Hanging containers

A variety of manufactured and improvised containers can be suspended or mounted to create a planted environment above ground level. They are particularly useful where space is limited, but even in conventional gardens there are many opportunities to use aerial displays of plants. They are invaluable for softening architectural environments; helping to lift the eye above other planting; and can be integrated into ambitious schemes in which plants are arranged on several levels.

Hanging baskets

The traditional hanging basket is a simple suspended container consisting of a wire frame in which a liner holds sufficient growing mix to sustain one or, more usually, several plants. A number of other suspended containers – either ready-made or improvised – serve the same purpose and are planted and displayed in a similar way to hanging baskets.

Wire-framed baskets and other suspended containers are best planted so that the container itself is concealed by full and trailing growth. This may be achieved with a single vigorous trailer, such as *Tradescantia zebrina*, a popular house or conservatory plant that can also be moved outdoors in summer.

In general, however, it is easier to create a floating cloud of foliage and flowers with a mixture of several different, less tender plants. The aim is to achieve a loosely rounded shape, using plants of different habit, so that growth hides the container. One approach is to use upright and rounded plants to form a crown above an irregular, hanging fringe of trailing or spreading plants. This could be achieved by including erect cultivars of pelargoniums and *Verbena* x *hybrida*, flanked by trailing fuchsias, lobelias, and petunias. Another option is to use containers that are in themselves ornamental, so that, even when the display is at its peak, some of the container is visible.

Hanging baskets are often hung as isolated features, perhaps to take advantage of an existing support. This might be an arch or the cross-piece of a pergola, for example. Another approach is to fit specially made supports for single or multiple hanging baskets. Brackets can be simple and inconspicuous, or ornamental and in a style that suits the surroundings. A hanging basket can make a dramatic focal point to enliven a blank wall, especially if it can be seen from a window or door. They can also be eye-catching when

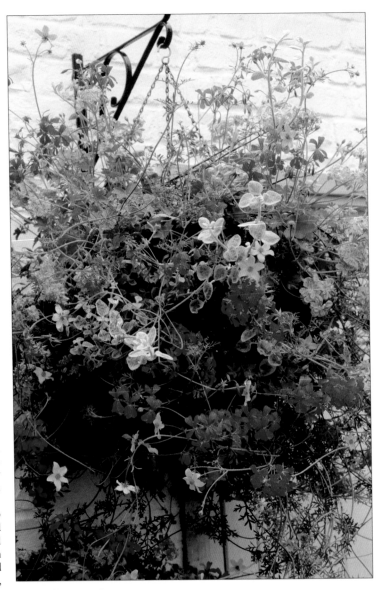

Elevated eye-catcher
This vibrant combination of trailing plants ensures a long season of colour; they mask the basket, but the ornamental bracket can still be seen.

suspended from the corner of a building, but for safety they must be well above the height of passers-by.

The most obvious of the multiple arrangements are pairs of baskets, mounted, for example, either side of a door or combined with other containers. A handsome design can be created by using a large container, such as an urn, at ground level against a wall, with hanging baskets mounted above it and on either side. The plants in the hanging baskets may match or contrast with those in the large container. For a more ambitious scheme, hanging baskets can be hung in rows, for example, on a series of arches, or on brackets along a wall. Carefully coordinated or contrasting plantings can be dramatically staged by using a cast of smaller baskets either side of a large one, or by introducing variations in

the height at which the containers are suspended. Using the cross-pieces of a pergola, a sequence of paired hanging baskets either side of a path makes an impressive avenue, although it is worth bearing in mind that such features will be time-consuming to water.

Windowboxes

These containers are available in a wide range of materials, including wood, terracotta, concrete, and plastic. They are sometimes designed to be ornamental on their own account, with painted or relief decoration. Plain wooden windowboxes can be painted to match other architectural details, but for more adventurous effects consider painting windowboxes on the front of a building in a bold colour to make them stand out. The planting style and content of a

windowbox depends to some extent on the position from which it is viewed. For some apartment-dwellers, for example, their whole garden may amount to one or two windowboxes, so the view from inside matters more than that from ground level. The greatest pleasure may be had from choosing plants of refined beauty, good scent, or aromatic foliage. If windowboxes form an integral part of the decoration of a house front, on the other hand, the view from outside is what really counts. The most valuable plants in this sort of display will be those that perform reliably over a long season, and might include evergreens such as box (*Buxus sempervirens*) or hebes.

If windowboxes are in windy, exposed positions, they may not be suitable for tall plants, which will be battered by wind; they may also block out the light. But to avoid a dull, uniformly low display, position compact but rounded plants, such as pelargoniums, in the centre, with lower plants on either side and trailing plants cascading from the front. There are many variations to play on this theme, using a wide range of plants, including evergreens for winter or year-round effect.

Wall-mounted containers

The types of containers that can be wall-mounted include semi-circular wire or strip-metal baskets, metal-frame mangers, and plastic or terracotta half-pots. Brackets can also be fixed to walls to hold standard pots of small or medium size, and more solid brackets can be used to support troughs – but be sure that they are fixed securely. Wall-mounted containers filled with plants are invaluable in breaking up the blankness of bare walls, whether used on their own or in conjunction with other planting. They are also useful where windows open outwards or lack a sill. The best alternative to a windowbox can be a trough mounted on brackets below the window. Wall-mounted containers are perhaps of greatest value in narrow spaces, or where a courtyard or passage is partly shaded. In a raised position, plants have greater access to light, and will often thrive better when elevated than they would at ground level.

In general, stone or brick walls make a beautiful backdrop to plantings, but, to take full advantage of their possibilities, it is important to choose containers that tone or contrast with the background colour. Full planting and generous use of trailing plants is generally the best option but, if the container itself is decorative, it should obviously be

All-round display
*The shocking
– but stunning –
combination
of scarlet
pelargoniums and
mauve petunias
in this cascading
windowbox
arrangement will
give just as much
pleasure to the
occupants within
as it does to the
viewers in the
street below.*

programmes, many plants are available of more compact habit, with single, semi-double, or double flowers in many colours or shades, sometimes with even more dramatic differences of flower or petal form. It is now possible to put together an extremely varied mixture, even with a limited number of plants.

Although the range is much smaller, another important group is that comprising annuals and biennials that flower in winter and early spring. The winter-flowering pansies (*Viola* x *wittrockiana*) create colourful displays before the main bulb season and then often carry on for many weeks more. Other plants that help to give continuity through spring are daisies (*Bellis perennis*), primulas of the Primrose and Polyanthus groups, and wallflowers (*Erysimum cheiri*).

Most annuals and biennials are relatively easy to raise from seed; the F1 and F2 hybrids, although more expensive, provide more vigorous and uniform plants. If space does not permit raising plants from seed, there is usually a good selection of very young plants at garden centres in late spring and early summer, and these can be a convenient way of acquiring a good range of plants in small numbers. Plant up pots just before annuals come into flower, so the container garden is almost instantaneously colourful and remains so for months.

visible. The siting of wall-mounted containers is also important. Too many, indiscriminately arranged, will create messy and rather fussy effects. A few large containers create more impact than many small ones, and in addition will be easier to maintain, especially when watering. Nevertheless, with careful placement, either in a symmetrical or asymmetrical pattern, pretty displays can be made with individual pots of flowers. For winter and spring colour, try double primroses, such as the rich violet *Primula vulgaris* 'Miss Indigo' or soft yellow 'Double Sulphur', or daisies, such as *Bellis perennis* Pomponette Series. For summer, there is a huge range of vibrant pelargoniums that flower for several months, and often into autumn.

Plants for container gardening

All categories of plants – annuals, biennials, perennials, shrubs, and trees – are available for the container gardener. The traditional approach focuses on compact, long-flowering summer annuals, which are undeniably valuable for creating colourful displays; but container gardening becomes much more interesting and challenging if the repertoire of plants is extended. Using all types of plants allows for arrangements of different scale and exploits the range of habits. Foliage, for example, is often neglected in favour of flowers, yet it has special value in the container garden. Evergreens

provide year-round pleasure, and even deciduous foliage is longer lasting than most floral displays. It can create rich but calming textures that are a welcome alternative to hectically colourful flowers. Good foliage plants, such as ferns and hostas, are often the best choice for sombre or shady corners. Suitability for the light levels available is often the key issue when choosing plants for particular positions. Other growing conditions, such as the growing mix, can be tailored to the plants' requirements.

Annuals and biennials
Summer-flowering annuals, including a number of tender perennials that are usually grown as annuals, are justly popular plants for container gardening. As a result of breeding

Perennials
The perennials that are traditionally used in container gardening are tender ones that are raised annually from seed, or overwintered under glass. Pelargoniums are tender, shrubby perennials that make excellent container specimens. Some are

Massed annual planting
Soft mauve petunias – a plant so often used in riotous combinations – can look unexpectedly eye-catching when planted alone in a large clump.

Unusual arrangement
A surprisingly successful mixture of hardy astilbes and tender begonias shows that, at times, the experimental breaking of rules is most rewarding.

Stone trough
This deep stone trough displays tulips to perfection; it is totally in scale with the planting and the bulbs grow tall and straight in this sheltered niche.

F1 or F2 hybrids raised annually from seed, while others can be over-wintered to provide material for cuttings that are brought on for the new season; the parent plant can then be discarded. The zonal and trailing ivy-leaved pelargoniums flower prolifically over a long season and are the most widely used in outdoor container gardening – the trailing ivy-leaved kinds being particularly useful in hanging baskets and windowboxes or on balconies.

Scented-leaved pelargoniums are an interesting and underused group. The silver-margined, eucalyptus-scented leaves of *Pelargonium* 'Lady Plymouth', for example, are excellent for breaking up large blocks of flower colour and the leaves release their evocative fragrance when handled. The flowers tend to be small, but the spice-scented *P.* 'Copthorne' is one of several with large, attractively marked blooms.

Border perennials are not widely used in container gardening, but there is no reason not to experiment. Those with evergreen foliage help to fill the gap between autumn and spring; many bergenias, for example, have large spoon-shaped leaves that take on rich copper-red tones in cold weather, and the sprays of pink, magenta, or white flowers in spring are long-lasting. *Heuchera* is another useful genus: *Heuchera micrantha* var. *diversifolia* 'Palace Purple' has large, glossy, jagged leaves that are deep bronze-red, topped in summer by showers of tiny white flowers and pink seedheads.

The length of their flowering season makes some hardy herbaceous perennials potentially useful plants for containers. Although individual flowers are short-lived, the low-growing day lilies bloom over many weeks in mid- to late summer – those of *Hemerocallis* 'Stella de Oro' being pale orange – and many produce sheaves of attractive foliage. Other herbaceous perennials with distinguished foliage include hostas, in an enormous range of sizes, colours, and textures. A clump of the blue-grey, corrugated leaves of *Hosta sieboldiana* var. *elegans* fully justifies a container for itself.

Bulbs

In this context, the term "bulbs" also includes plants with corms, tubers, and rhizomes. It is a group that is very important in container gardening; their value lies in their remarkably reliable flowering, even though few have foliage of any great ornamental value and individual plants rarely flower for more than a few weeks. By planting a range of spring bulbs, however, a succession of colourful explosions can be enjoyed from late winter through to the following autumn.

This long season begins with snowdrops, dwarf irises, and early crocuses, overlaps with the earliest daffodils, which are followed by the later daffodil varieties, hyacinths, and tulips. There are many other small bulbs, such as *Scilla*, *Muscari*, and *Puschkinia*, that fit into this flowering programme. The most useful summer and autumn bulbs include lilies and dahlias, with their huge variety in flower colour and shape as well as in height.

Match bulbs and containers for size and take account of the position the containers will occupy. Tall-growing tulips, for example, are likely to suffer wind damage when planted in windowboxes. There are excellent dwarf tulips, as well as other low-growing bulbs that are better for exposed positions.

The flowers of bulbs generally last longer if the containers are in light or partial shade, but the flowers of some, including crocuses and tulips, open fully only in sun. For densely packed containers, two or even three layers of bulbs can be planted at different depths (see p.327).

With bulbs, there is inevitably a gap between planting and flowering. One way to overcome this is to keep containers in a cold frame until bulbs begin to flower. The containers can then be brought into view and be removed once flowering is over. Another option is to plant bulbs of different kinds in the same container to give a successional display, or to create mixed plantings. Many dwarf bulbs combine well with winter-flowering pansies (*Viola* x *wittrockiana*) and low evergreens, such as thymes (*Thymus*) or small-leaved cultivars of common ivy (*Hedera helix*). Bulbs can also be used as an underplanting to spring flowering shrubs such as *Skimmia*.

Although some containerized bulbs flower well for several years if the growing mix is renewed annually, the performance of most bulbs deteriorates after the first season. For high-quality displays, it is best to plant new stock each year. Otherwise, allow bulbs to die down in their containers, then lift and store for replanting later in the growing season, or replant directly in the garden for reduced displays in subsequent years.

Trees

Many evergreen and deciduous trees can adapt to life in containers and, if well cared for, will flourish for many years, although they seldom reach the size they would attain in the open garden. Those that feature foliage, flowers, and fruits among their ornamental virtues include small rowans, such as *Sorbus cashmiriana*, and flowering crab apples, for example *Malus* 'Red Jade'; both have spring flowers and long-lasting fruits, borne amid a blaze of autumn foliage colour. The height and architectural presence of container-grown trees, such as hornbeam (*Carpinus betulus*) or coloured-barked birches, such as *Betula albosinensis* var. *septentrionalis*, lend a strong structural element to a design. They are particularly useful for screening and help create privacy and areas of cool shade.

When choosing trees for patios, courtyards, and roof gardens, scale is important. Compact conifers, like conical *Chamaecyparis lawsoniana* 'Ellwoodii', are among the most useful. Deciduous small trees include the Kilmarnock willow (*Salix caprea* 'Kilmarnock') with pendulous branches loaded with white then yellow catkins in spring. Trees that respond well to clipping are of particular value where space is limited. One of the most useful ever-greens for container gardening is the sweet bay (*Laurus nobilis*), which can be trimmed in a variety of shapes.

Shrubs

Shrubs, which are much more widely used in container gardening than trees, span a range from large spreading specimens, which require heavy, broad-based containers, to

Monochrome display
The simplicity of this windowbox arrangement of box (Buxus sempervirens) and ivy (Hedera helix) is a perfect match for its elegant architectural setting.

A movable feast
For those gardeners who feel that no garden is complete without roses – the most romantic flowers – modern rose breeders have made possible their introduction into even the most confined of spaces. Most patio roses, the diminutive counterparts of Floribunda bushes, such as this Rosa SURREY, *bloom almost continuously throughout summer. The upright, bushy mound of growth is carefully balanced here by a wide terracotta pot.*

Container supports
Wigwams and obelisks, whether bought or simply improvised, are ideal supports for climbers in pots and, here, elevate a simple, cool-coloured arrangement to a well-balanced focal point.

dwarf bushes, for example *Hebe cupressoides* 'Boughton Dome', which are suitable for windowboxes. When choosing a shrub, consider its scale within the setting, the plant's shape, and the qualities of foliage, flowers, and fruits that will keep the plants interesting over a long period.

Compact evergreens with good foliage and pleasing shape include a large number of dwarf conifers. Some broad-leaved evergreens, such as box (*Buxus sempervirens*) or *Osmanthus* x *burkwoodii*, that tolerate clipping, can be trimmed to formal or more whimsical shapes.

In some cases, it is foliage colour that gives a plant a special value, as with variegated plants, such as *Euonymus fortunei* 'Emerald Gaiety'. Many low-growing cultivars of heather (*Calluna vulgaris*) provide coloured winter foliage as well as flowers. With camellias, dark, glossy foliage is matched by single to fully double flowers of great beauty. Some rhododendrons also combine highly ornamental foliage and exquisite flowers; *R. yakushimanum* hybrids have a pleasingly dense habit and densely furry undersides to the new leaves that follow the flowers.

For delicate summer foliage textures and brilliant autumn colours, the Japanese maples (*Acer palmatum* cultivars) are hard to beat. Other deciduous shrubs grown mainly for their flowers include *Hydrangea macrophylla* cultivars, with flower-heads that last for months, often with pleasing colour changes as they age. Fuchsias produce new flowers without interruption throughout summer

until checked by frosts. The trailing kinds are useful for spilling over the rim of hanging baskets and tall containers, while some of the erect ones, such as *F.* 'Lady Thumb', make compact bushes that are ideal centre-pieces in any container.

Roses
The most suitable roses for container gardening are miniature roses, patio roses, and some of the ground-cover roses. Miniatures, such as POUR TOI ('Para Ti') and LITTLE BO-PEEP ('Poullen'), are small twiggy bushes, to 30cm (1ft) high, with a myriad of tiny leaflets; they are perfect for windowboxes, needing only 20–25cm (8–10in) depth of soil. Patio roses are slightly larger bushes covered with clustered flowers from summer to autumn; reliable performers include the brilliant orange TOP MARKS ('Fryministar'), the soft apricot-peach SWEET DREAM ('Fryminicot'), and the pale pink PRETTY POLLY ('Meitonje'). They look especially good in a stone trough or an unglazed terracotta pot.

Ground-cover roses are more lax in growth and are ideal for hanging baskets and tall pots, where the sinuous stems can trail over the pot rim or basket's edge. Try PINK BELLS ('Poulbells') with its bright pink, pompon blooms, or MAGIC CARPET ('Jaclover') with its semi-double, magenta flowers.

Climbers
The versatility of climbers in containers can hardly be overstated. They can be as effective trained

upwards on obelisks or other frames as they can be when used in less conventional ways. Some can simply be allowed to trail. A small-flowered clematis, such as *C.* 'Frances Rivis', looks particularly elegant when spilling from tall pots or jars. Some of the more compact, large-flowered clematis, like the white-flowered *C.* 'Miss Bateman', are also successful if grown this way. Other more unusual, trailing plants include the tender perennial *Rhodochiton atrosanguineus* with its pendent, red-purple, tubular flowers.

Cultivars of common ivy (*Hedera helix*) can look just as good as trailers or climbers. The small-leaved kinds are among the best trailing evergreens for hanging baskets, and for softening the hard edges of

windowboxes and other containers. These adaptable plants also lend themselves to more elaborate training. Try growing them on wire frames – they can make a very effective imitation of clipped topiary (see TOPIARY, p.76).

Strict training is usually the best way to manage vigorous climbers, including wisterias and vines (*Vitis*). With rigorous summer and winter pruning, they can be grown as standards. But among the easiest are annuals, such as the sweetly scented sweet peas (*Lathyrus odoratus*) or those like *Ipomoea tricolor*, that are treated as annuals. Grow them on wig-wams of bamboo canes laced together with string, on rustic pyramids made of brushwood branches, or on custom-made trellis panels.

Specialized container gardens

Container gardening is a versatile technique that, with a little imagination, can be adapted to suit a wide range of styles and types of gardening. Pools and herb or vegetable plots, for example, more often associated with larger gardens, can be scaled down to suit smaller plots by using containers. It is equally possible to provide a touch of subtropical splendour in cool-temperate zones.

Fruit, vegetables, and herbs

An interesting selection of fruits and vegetables can be grown outdoors in containers such as tubs, large pots, and growing bags. Some are highly ornamental, as well as yielding reasonable crops when grown on a small scale. Crop plants grown in containers, however, generally require more attention to feeding and watering than they do in the open garden.

Strawberries are a good choice among fruits as they generally crop well. At the other end of the scale are tree-fruits, such as apples, grown on a dwarfing rootstock; single-stemmed Ballerina apple trees are ideal, but must be fed and watered conscientiously. Figs need root restriction to crop satisfactorily and so are well suited to container cultivation. They do, however, need to be moved under glass in winter in cool regions.

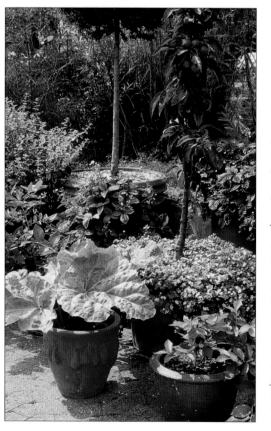

Vegetable garden
Many edible plants can be successfully cultivated in pots and other containers provided they are watered and fed regularly. Here herbs such as bay, fennel, and variegated lemon balm are grown alongside a Ballerina apple tree, strawberries, and rhubarb. In temperate areas, tender plants such as citrus (in the foreground) must be moved under cover during the winter months.

Among vegetables the best choices are those that are compact, quick-growing, and highly productive. Radishes and lettuces, some of which are very ornamental, mature quickly; climbing peas and beans (on wigwams) and courgettes crop well if adequately fed and watered. Fruiting vegetables such as tomatoes, aubergines, and peppers are particularly attractive and, since they need sun and warmth to grow well, are ideal for containers in sheltered courtyards or roof gardens.

For many gardeners, the challenge is part of the pleasure of growing fruits and vegetables, but herbs are, on the whole, an easier proposition. A good range, including shrubby ones such as rosemary (*Rosmarinus officinalis*) and thyme (*Thymus vulgaris*), and annuals or biennials, such as chervil (*Anthriscus cerefolium*) and parsley (*Petroselinum crispum*), can be grown in a small space, providing leaves for culinary use from aromatic plants that are good to look at and handle.

Water gardens

A pool can make an attractive water feature in a small garden. Glazed jars are among the most suitable containers for this purpose where there is no risk of frost. If they are to be used in areas prone to hard frost, they cannot be left outdoors year-round. Other suitable containers include wooden tubs and half-barrels, glazed sinks, and large metal pots or cauldrons. The wood of tubs and barrels is often impregnated with chemicals that are harmful to plants and they are best lined with butyl rubber or PVC. It is also a wise precaution to seal the inside of metal containers with a rubber sealant to prevent any contamination of the water. Fish in raised containers may not survive freezing conditions and should be brought indoors in winter.

The plants that can be accommodated in a small water garden are a narrow but select group. Several water lilies, such as the yellow, free-flowering *Nymphaea* 'Pygmaea Helvola', can be grown in water that is only 20–45cm (8–18in) deep, and shallow water also suits the mauve-flowered water hyacinth (*Eichhornia crassipes*) and the sculptural, floating *Pistia stratiotes*. Marginal plants of suitable scale include *Juncus effusus* 'Spiralis' and *Typha minima*. Always plant an oxygenator, such as *Myriophyllum verticillatum*, to help keep the water fresh. Lift plants at the end of summer, and overwinter in frost-free conditions. See also WATER GARDENING, pp.280–303.

Subtropical container gardens

Even in cool-temperate regions, the choice of plants for containers on patios or terraces and in courtyards can help to create the impression of a warmer climate. One way to achieve this is to use plants that are natives of hotter regions of the world, and give them protection from frost in a greenhouse or conservatory during the cold months, moving them outdoors for the frost-free summer

Tropical effects
Spiky plants, such as Cordyline *and* Agave, *are strongly architectural and lend an effective suggestion of the subtropics; their relatively sombre colours are enlivened here by the hot scarlets of the most easily grown of annuals – nasturtiums* (Tropaeolum majus).

months. Plants that instantly create a tropical effect include angels' trumpets (*Brugmansia*) and *Abutilon* hybrids. The display can be enhanced – and management made easier – by adding hardy or frost-hardy plants of subtropical appearance, including the lush, large-leaved Japanese banana (*Musa basjoo*) or palms such as the Chusan palm (*Trachycarpus fortunei*). To reinforce the design, include evergreen shrubs, such as the frost-hardy *Fatsia japonica*, with large, glossy leaves, and New Zealand flax (*Phormium*) with evergreen, sword-like leaves. Many hardy bamboos, such as *Sasa veitchii* and *Fargesia murielae*, also have a graceful, subtropical appearance. To these can be added the frost-tender castor oil plant (*Ricinus communis*), which is raised annually from seed.

To create desert effects, cacti and other succulents are ideal. As many have low moisture and nutrient needs, they are perfect for low-maintenance containers. Some, such as *Sempervivum*, are hardy, too. The tender succulent *Agave americana* and its variegated cultivars, with magnificent, sword-like leaves, are fairly tolerant of summer rainfall, as are yuccas, which make good companions.

Plants that evoke a Mediterranean climate include olive trees (*Olea europaea*), lemon trees (*Citrus limon*), bougainvilleas, and oleanders (*Nerium oleander*), all of which look beautiful in terracotta pots. They must be moved under cover in winter, but hardier plants, such as lavenders and rosemary, also suit this style. Although the last two tolerate frost, it is best to insulate their containers in winter to protect roots.

Planter's guide to container plants

TREES AND SHRUBS

See also p.37 for larger trees. For dwarf conifers, see p.38

Abutilon ✲
Acer japonicum, A. palmatum
Anisodontea capensis ✲
Argyranthemum ✲ (subshrub)
Brugmansia ✲
Buxus balearica ✲, *B. microphylla,*
    B. sempervirens
Calluna vulgaris
Camellia
x *Citrofortunella microcarpa* ✲
Codiaeum variegatum var. *pictum* ✲
Cuphea ✲

Rhododendron yakushimanum

Dracaena, some ✲
Erica
Euonymus fortunei
x *Fatshedera lizei* ✲
Fatsia japonica
Fuchsia, some ✲
Gardenia ✲
Hebe, some ✲
Hibiscus rosa-sinensis ✲
Hydrangea macrophylla (and cvs),
    H. paniculata, H. quercifolia
    'Snowflake'
Lantana ✲
Lavandula, some ✲
Nerium oleander ✲
Prunus laurocerasus
Rhododendron
Rosa (Ground Cover, Miniature,
    and Patio hybrids)
Santolina ✲
Senecio cineraria ✲ (as an annual)
Skimmia japonica
Solanum rantonnetii ✲
Tibouchina ✲
Viburnum davidii, V. tinus
Yucca, some ✲

PALMS AND CYCADS

Chamaedorea ✲
Chamaerops ✲
Cocos ✲
Cycas revoluta ✲
Howea ✲
Jubaea ✲
Phoenix ✲
Rhapis ✲
Sabal ✲
Trachycarpus fortunei
Washingtonia

BAMBOOS, GRASSES, AND GRASS-LIKE PLANTS

Carex, some ✲
Deschampsia cespitosa (cvs)
Fargesia murielae, F. nitida
Hakonechloa macra (cvs)
Himalayacalamus falconeri ✲
Imperata cylindrica 'Rubra' ✲
Indocalamus tessellatus
Pennisetum alopecuroides ✲
Phalaris arundinacea var. *picta*
Phyllostachys aurea, P. flexuosa,
    P. nigra
Pleioblastus variegatus,
    P. viridistriatus
Shibataea kumasasa

PERENNIALS

See also Planter's guide to rock plants, Planting in troughs, p.195

Achimenes ✲
Agapanthus, some ✲
Alchemilla
Astilbe
Begonia Rex Group ✲
Bergenia
Calceolaria integrifolia ✲ (cvs)
Campanula (dwarf), some ✲
Canna ✲
Catharanthus roseus ✲
Chrysanthemum, some ✲
Convolvulus
    sabatius ✲

Agapanthus

Dianthus
Diascia
Ensete ventricosum ✲
Fittonia ✲
Glechoma hederacea
    'Variegata' ✲
Heuchera
Hosta
Houttuynia cordata 'Chameleon'
Lamium maculatum
Lysimachia nummularia 'Aurea'
Musa basjoo ✲
Nepeta
Osteospermum ✲
Pelargonium ✲
Peperomia ✲
Phlox (dwarf)
Phormium, some ✲
Plectranthus ✲
Primula Polyanthus Group
Salvia discolor ✲, *S. uliginosa*
Tiarella
Tolmiea menziesii
Tradescantia fluminensis ✲ (cvs),
    T. zebrina ✲

CLIMBERS

☆ **Annual, or commonly grown as one**

Bougainvillea ✲
Clematis, many
Clerodendrum thomsoniae ✲
Cobaea scandens ✲ ☆
Eccremocarpus scaber ✲ ☆
Hedera helix
Jasminum ✲
Lathyrus odoratus ☆
Passiflora ✲
Rhodochiton atrosanguineus ✲ ☆
Stephanotis ✲
Thunbergia alata ✲ ☆
Trachelospermum ✲

CACTI AND SUCCULENTS

See p.342

FERNS

Adiantum, some ✲
Asplenium scolopendrium
Athyrium
Blechnum, some ✲
Davallia ✲
Dicksonia antarctica ✲
Nephrolepis ✲
Platycerium ✲
Polypodium, some ✲
Polystichum

BULBS

Amaryllis belladonna ✲
Anemone blanda, A. coronaria
    (cvs), *A.* x *fulgens*
Begonia ✲ (tuberous)
Chionodoxa
Clivia ✲
Crocus
Cyclamen, some ✲
Dahlia ✲
Freesia ✲
Hippeastrum ✲
Hyacinthus (cvs)
Iris (bulbous)
Ixia ✲
Lachenalia ✲
Lilium, some ✲
Muscari
Narcissus, some ✲
Nerine, some ✲
Scilla (some spp.)
Tulipa

ANNUALS AND BIENNIALS

§ Perennial or subshrub commonly grown as an annual or biennial

Ageratum ✲
Antirrhinum ✲ (dwarf cvs)
Bellis perennis (cvs)
Bidens ✲ §
Brachyscome ✲
Brassica oleracea (ornamental cvs)
Calendula officinalis

Celosia ✲ §
Dianthus barbatus, D. chinensis §
    (cvs)
Erysimum
Exacum affine ✲ §
Gazania ✲ §
Helichrysum petiolare ✲ §
Heliotropium ✲ §

Viola x *wittrockiana*
Princess Series

Impatiens ✲ §
Iresine ✲ §
Lobelia erinus ✲ § (cvs)
Lotus berthelotii ✲ §,
    L. maculatus ✲ §
Matthiola Brompton Series, *M.* East
    Lothian Series
Mimulus hybrids ✲ §
Nicotiana ✲ §
Pericallis ✲ §
Petunia ✲ §
Primula Polyanthus Group §
Ricinus communis ✲ § (cvs)
Salvia coccinea ✲ §, *S. farinacea* ✲ §,
    S. patens ✲ §, *S. splendens* ✲ §,
    S. viridis
Scaevola ✲ §
Schizanthus pinnatus ✲ (cvs)
Solanum capsicastrum ✲ §,
    S. pseudocapsicum ✲ §
Solenostemon ✲ §
Tagetes ✲
Tropaeolum majus ✲ (cvs and
    hybrids)
Verbena hybrids ✲ §
Viola x *wittrockiana* §
Zinnia ✲

FRUIT

Apples (on dwarfing
    rootstocks)
Blueberries
Citrus ✲
    (most)

Lemons

Figs
Grapes
Peaches (dwarf)
Strawberries

HERBS

**Most herbs described on pp.407–410
can be grown in containers**

Key

✲ *Not hardy*

Choosing containers

A SUITABLE container in which to grow plants must satisfy many criteria. It should hold sufficient compost to give plants adequate space for root development and to supply the moisture and nutrients necessary for growth. A container must also allow excess water to drain away, usually by means of one or more drainage holes in the base. Stability is also important; if a container is easily knocked or blown over, it may create a safety hazard and both the container and the plants in it may suffer damage.

Many commercially available containers satisfy these requirements and, being mass-produced, are relatively inexpensive. Other, more expensive ones are made individually or in small quantities, but these, along with home-made or improvised containers, often have more character and make an eye-catching statement of individual taste.

Assorted containers
Plants can be successfully grown in a wide variety of purpose-made and improvised containers – in many shapes and sizes – provided they have at least one drainage hole.

Materials and finishes

Containers are available in a range of materials and finishes, each having practical and aesthetic advantages that should be taken into account before making a choice. Bear in mind where a container is to stand; its weight, for example, can be an important factor. Decide whether the style of container is to complement that of the garden or whether the container will play a functional but subordinate role to the plants it contains. Consider also matching accessories, such as trays or saucers, which are useful for watering from

Change of use
A galvanized tub makes an eye-catching container for a clump of mixed tulips and grape hyacinths (Muscari). With adequate capacity for compost, and holes drilled in the base for drainage, this old-fashioned bath tub has been cleverly transformed into an unusual and attractive container for plants.

below and help to keep the surfaces the pots stand on free of stains. Detached clay pot feet are particularly useful for lifting flat-bottomed containers above smooth surfaces so that excess water can drain freely.

Clay
Traditional unglazed pots of fired clay (terracotta) have been valued for centuries for their beauty as plant containers – large jars and urns can be very handsome features in a garden, even when left unplanted. Clay is

readily moulded to many sizes and shapes, and can be either plain or have a moulded decoration. Small to medium-sized plain pots are generally inexpensive, although costs rise as sizes increase. The most expensive are frost-resistant ones, which will not flake or crack if exposed to low temperatures during winter. Before the winter cold sets in, clay containers that are not frostproof should be protected with an insulating material, such as bubble plastic, or be moved under cover. All clay pots must be handled carefully; any kind of shock is likely to cause chipping, cracking, or breakage.

Clay is a porous material, so a pot should be soaked in clean water before being filled with potting compost. Evaporation from planted clay pots helps keep plant roots cooler in summer than in non-porous ones and, while more frequent watering is necessary, there is less risk of water-logging. This makes clay ideal for alpines and other plants that demand good drainage. The porosity also gives acceptable results with capillary watering systems (see p.577).

In most circumstances, the weight of terracotta pots filled with moist compost is an advantage because it produces stability. Once planted, however, they are hard to move and the weight can be a serious drawback if they are to be placed on balconies

and roof gardens (see pp.312–313).

Clay's warm, earthy colour, in shades of orange- or red-brown, can at first seem rather brash but, once weathered with algae, terracotta blends unobtrusively into many settings and complements a wide range of plants. If necessary, algal growth can be scrubbed off between plantings, using warm soapy water and a stiff-bristled brush.

Glazed ceramics
Whether glossy or matt, the variously coloured, shaped, and textured finishes on glazed pots can make them distinctive ornamental features in the garden. In addition to brightly coloured and vividly patterned glazes, those imitating the subdued green of celadon ware may also be worth considering for a more subdued design. Unless specifically labelled as frost resistant, glazed containers should not be left outdoors during winter. Since their surface is not porous, there is less water loss than from unglazed pots and they are also easier to wipe clean.

Plastic
Plastics are versatile materials that can be moulded into many different shapes and are now widely used in the manufacture of inexpensive containers. The most durable pots are made of a polythene and polypropylene mix,

Container accessories
A saucer will protect a surface from staining, but it must not store excess water. Raise flat-bottomed pots up on pot feet, so they drain freely.

which does not become brittle in low temperatures – unlike polypropylene when used on its own.

Plastic containers are made in almost any colour; they can be plain, textured, or with a relief design, and can be glossy or matt. Plastic is often used to simulate other materials and perhaps this is why it is sometimes viewed as second-rate, but it does have many virtues. It is lightweight, for example, and, therefore, useful on indoor shelves, balconies, and roof gardens that are not strong enough for heavier materials. Plastic is not porous, so water is not lost through the sides of containers, and frequency of watering is less than with clay pots. Plastic pots are also more

effective with capillary watering systems than clay ones (see p.577).

Growing bags are specialized plastic containers made from flexible sheet plastic and filled with a lightweight loamless compost. The compost will sustain a main crop such as tomatoes and usually also a secondary crop, after which the compost can be spread in the garden and the container disposed of. Growing bags are functional containers that make few concessions to good looks, but they can be masked by plants in full growth if necessary.

Wood
Wood is a particularly useful material for made-to-measure containers such as windowboxes. It is also the material of first choice for a number of other traditional containers, including Versailles tubs and half-barrels, in which the timbers are held together by metal bands. Hardwoods, which should come from a renewable source, last longer than softwoods, but are more expensive. Preservative treatments will extend the life of softwoods but check before using that the preservative is labelled as being harmless to plants.

Stone and concrete
Natural stone, available in many different textures and colours, is a prestige container material that is expensive and heavy. Marble, which is often used in classical urns, can be

Size and proportion
When planning the scale and proportion of a display, it is important to consider the growth habit of the species you have chosen. Here plants have been carefully selected to complement the size of container.

Adapting containers

Plants can be grown in almost any container that holds compost and permits free drainage of water. Drill drainage holes in the base of galvanized metal containers, old buckets, and tins to transform them. Potential containers that are already pierced, such as kitchen colanders, should be lined so that the compost does not fall out. Use dark-coloured, flexible plastic sheeting or a plastic bag of an appropriate size. Prick the bottom of the liner so that excess water can drain away freely.

Colander basket
To convert a colander into a hanging container, fit chains and line it with pierced sheeting.

Drilling drainage holes
Masking tape placed over the position of the drainage hole gives the drill bit a secure grip.

intricately carved and given a high polish, while sandstone containers are frequently left with a rough finish. Various kinds of reconstituted stone are also used in the manufacture of containers. These too are heavy and expensive, but generally cheaper than natural stone. Concrete containers may be cheaper still.

All heavy containers should be placed in their final position in the garden or conservatory before being filled with potting compost. The algal growth that develops on such materials helps to soften the initial raw appearance. Concrete and rough stone are difficult to clean.

Metal
Lead is a traditional material for cisterns, garden ornaments, and containers, and can be introduced to reinforce a period style in a garden. Whether antique or modern, lead containers are expensive, heavy, and easily dented or distorted, because of the softness of this metal.

Cast iron was in vogue in the nineteenth century and the numerous vase and urn shapes popular then are available again now. Cast iron, however, is expensive and will rust unless powder-coated or painted.

Galvanized metal containers are both lightweight and available in a wide range of attractive shapes and sizes. Now often used to lend a

modern flavour, especially in urban gardens, most are sufficiently inexpensive to discard as tastes and fashions change.

Many hanging baskets and brackets are made of wire, which is usually covered with plastic to provide a suitable background colour to plants and to prolong the life of the container.

Fibreglass
Fibreglass is a lightweight material that is easily moulded into many different shapes. It is frostproof, strong, and long-lasting; although rather brittle, it can be repaired. Because of its relative cheapness and versatility, it is often used to simulate other materials, including stone, metal, and wood.

Unusual container materials
A number of domestic, agricultural, architectural, and industrial items can be transformed into highly individual containers (see "Adapting containers", above). Salvaged and recycled items, such as chimney pots or old paint tins, can also make unorthodox plant containers.

Most such containers can be decorated with paints, stains, or other materials, which are available for use on an extensive variety of surfaces and container types.

Composts for containers

THE growing medium used in containers should give plants the best chance of maximizing their ornamental or productive potential. It must be well aerated and moisture retentive, with a resilient structure that can withstand heavy watering. Ordinary garden soil should not be used; its structure, chemical balance, and nutrient levels are variable, and it will almost certainly contain weed seeds, pests, and disease organisms. The best results are achieved with precisely formulated potting composts that are produced commercially or prepared or modified at home.

Potting composts

There are two main types of potting compost: loam-based ones, which should have sterilized, high-quality soil, or loam, as their main ingredient; and loamless composts, which contain no soil and are usually based on a peat substitute or peat.

Loam-based composts

These potting mixes are free draining and have good aeration and structure,

Composts for plants with special needs
Azaleas and other rhododendrons are intolerant of alkaline soils. In a container they are best grown in an ericaceous compost, which is loam based but lime free.

which encourages root development. They provide a steady supply of nutrients to sustain the long-term growth of plants and are less prone to waterlogging than loamless composts. They also dry out more slowly, making them easier to manage in containers. Being heavier than loamless composts, loam-based ones are especially useful in counter-balancing top-growth. Plants that are cultivated in loam-based compost and then transplanted into garden soil are likely to become established quickly and develop well. The structure and nutrient content of loam-based composts do, however, deteriorate in storage. Buy a recognized brand name from a reputable supplier and use the compost as soon as possible.

The loam used in these composts should have a high organic content. Good-quality loam is prepared commercially by stacking turf for at least six months. It is then sterilized by heat or chemical treatment to kill pests, diseases, and weed seeds.

Loam-based composts are widely available in three standard formulations drawn up by the John Innes Horticultural Institute. All contain 7 parts (by volume) sterilized loam, 3 parts peat substitute or peat, and 1 part sand. To this mixture is added in specified quantities ground limestone and John Innes Base fertilizer, which consists of 2 parts hoof and horn, 2 parts superphosphate of lime, and 1 part potassium sulphate.

The JI No.1 formulation has relatively little fertilizer and so is suitable mainly for growing on seedlings and sowing large seed. It can also be used for slow-growing ornamentals that do not require high nutrient levels, such as alpines. To make JI No.1, mix 36 litres (8 gallons) of loam, peat substitute or peat, and sand in the proportions specified above, then add 110g (4oz) John Innes Base and 20g (¾oz) ground limestone.

JI No.2 contains double the fertilizer and limestone content of JI No.1 and is suitable for a wide range of plants needing average nutrient levels.

JI No.3, with three times the fertilizer and limestone content of JI No.1, is for vigorous plants and those such as trees and shrubs that will remain in their container for more than one growing season.

Ericaceous potting composts

Although the John Innes formulations cover the needs of large numbers of plants, none is suitable for camellias, rhododendrons, and other plants that

thrive only on neutral to acid soils. These require special loam-based composts that are similar to the John Innes formulations but without the ground limestone. Such low-pH composts are usually labelled "ericaceous", a reference to the Ericaceae, a family of plants that is generally intolerant of lime.

Loamless potting composts

Loamless, or soilless, composts are widely used in container gardening. They are usually based on 3 parts (by volume) of peat substitute or peat and 1 part sand. The fertilizer content varies. Some also contain perlite or vermiculite to aid aeration and drainage.

All loamless potting composts are relatively clean to use as well as lightweight, and are generally less expensive than loam-based ones. Where peat has been used rather than a substitute material, however, the price advantage has to be

set against the environmental consequences of irreplaceable peat extraction from endangered bog and wetland habitats. Suitable peat substitutes for use in potting composts are fine bark, coir (coconut fibre and bark), and leaf mould.

Many composts based on peat substitutes need careful watering; although the surface may be dry, the layers beneath are often adequately moist. Peat combines moisture retentiveness with good aeration, but it does dry out rapidly and, once dry, is difficult to re-wet. Conversely, if overwatered, it is prone to waterlogging. In pots, loamless composts based on peat should be kept evenly moist at all times.

Most loamless composts, including peat-based ones, break down rapidly so that the compost shrinks and loses structure. In general, they do not provide such a firm roothold as loam-based composts. Also, plants moved from them to the open garden frequently adapt poorly to garden soil.

COMMON INGREDIENTS FOR POTTING COMPOSTS

Loam
Sterilized garden soil, with good nutrient supply, drainage, aeration, and moisture retention.

Grit
Various grades of grit are added to compost to improve drainage and aeration.

Peat
Well-aerated and moisture-retentive but low in nutrients. Hard to re-wet.

Vermiculite
Expanded, air-blown mica acts like perlite, but holds more water and less air.

Fine bark
Used as a peat substitute, especially in composts formulated for acid-loving plants.

Perlite
Expanded, volcanic rock granules retain moisture but drain freely. Aids aeration.

Coir
This peat substitute dries less rapidly than peat but needs more frequent feeding.

Sand
Coarse and fine (silver) sands aid the creation of more open-textured composts.

Leaf mould
Used as a peat substitute and compost additive, especially for woodland plants.

MODIFYING COMPOSTS

Most alpines need few nutrients and good drainage, so plant them over a layer of broken crocks in a 50:50 mix of JI No.1 compost and grit.

Loamless composts are suitable for short-term use, such as growing seedlings and annuals and sowing large seeds. Although they provide a suitable medium for many plants in containers, hanging baskets, and on balconies and roof gardens, the shortcomings of loamless composts mean that they are not suitable for long-term plantings, such as of trees and shrubs.

Peat substitutes and peat are naturally low in nutrients, which tend to leach quickly. Regular use of soluble fertilizers can overcome this, but their effect does not last. A more efficient way of maintaining a steady nutrient supply is to incorporate slow-release inorganic fertilizers into the potting mix. These are complete formulations, some slowly degrading in the soil, others absorbing water until they burst open, spreading their fertilizer. Many discharge their nutrients over several months. The expense of slow-release fertilizers is offset by the convenience and the time that is saved in not having to make frequent applications of soluble fertilizers. Yet the nutrient-release pattern of slow-release

GOOD DRAINAGE

To ensure good drainage, place terracotta pot shards in the bottom of a container; large pebbles and chunks of polystyrene are also effective as drainage material.

fertilizers, especially that of long-term formulas, can be very difficult to predict as it is affected by the pH level, moisture content, and temperature of the compost.

To maintain a reservoir of moisture in a container without waterlogging the compost, incorporate water-retaining granules or crystals into the growing mix. When wetted, the granules swell to make a fragmented gel. They may not be effective over very long periods, but the reduction of water loss is particularly useful in loamless composts and in exposed containers such as hanging baskets, which dry out rapidly.

Special composts
As well as ericaceous composts, there are other specialized composts produced commercially to suit the requirements of particular groups of plants. Orchid composts are free-

draining and often contain charcoal and fine bark for good aeration. Cactus composts are even more free-draining, containing a high proportion of grit, and are usually low in nutrients. Aquatic composts, which are heavy for better anchorage, are particularly variable as the major constituent – soil – is not of a consistent standard. Bulb fibre compost is made from undecomposed sphagnum moss, which has an open structure and so is suitable for growing bulbs in containers that do not have drainage holes.

Modifying composts
Both commercially produced and home-made composts can be easily adapted for particular plants or groups of plants. Perlite and vermiculite are commonly put in home-made composts to improve both drainage and aeration. The addition of various grades of grit and sharp sand make composts drain more freely. Grit, for example, is often mixed in equal parts by volume to JI No.1 to make a free-draining compost for alpine plants. Leaf mould, which is an excellent peat substitute in home-made composts, can also be added to ready-made composts to produce a moisture-retentive growing mix suitable for woodland plants.

Mulches
Mulches are materials used to cover soils or composts to slow down water loss, to even out soil temperature fluctuations, and to discourage the growth of weeds. The most useful and neatest mulch for most containerized plants is grit spread evenly over the compost to a depth of approximately 1cm (½in). A mulch of limestone chippings is suitable for

Environmentally-friendly growing media

For gardeners preferring to grow plants in containers according to organic principles, it is important to choose a compost suitable for the type of plant to be grown in the pot. Long-term container plants such as shrubs need a loam- or soil-based nutrient-rich compost that is also water-retentive. Use a mix of 1 part loam, 1 part general leaf mould and 1 part garden compost or well-rotted manure by volume, adding a further part of 2mm grit if the plants require sharp drainage. Comfrey leaf mould (see p.625), which is nutrient-rich, may be substituted for general leaf mould, if available.

Short-term, quick-growing container plants as well as hanging basket plants – usually annuals or perennials grown as annuals – are best grown in a loamless or soilless compost consisting of 3 parts peat substitute or well-rotted leaf mould to 1 part comfrey leaf mould by volume. To improve water retention, an organic moisture retainer based on coarse seaweed meal may be added to the compost.

In both cases, worm compost may be used in place of comfrey leaf mould as it is both water retentive and nutrient rich, a bonus for many of the quick-growing plants used.

alpines that prefer alkaline soils, while granite chippings can be used for lime haters. Coarse gravel used as a top-dressing for trees and shrubs can also help to stabilize containers. Organic mulches generally include granulated bark and cocoa shell; some of these tend to be blown about unless they are damp. Composted pine needles can be used for acid-loving or ericaceous plants.

Mixing compost

The principal difficulty for amateur gardeners preparing their own loam-based compost is sterilizing the loam. Special soil-sterilizing units used for large-scale heat treatment are expensive, but smaller scale units are available from specialist suppliers. To treat small quantities, put the soil through a 5mm (¼in) sieve to remove stones and lumps. Then spread it 8cm (3in) deep on a baking tray and bake for 30 minutes at 200°C (400°F) in a domestic oven. Alternatively put the soil in a roasting bag and heat in a microwave on full power for ten minutes.

Assemble the ingredients on a clean, flat surface. (For exact quantities, see "Loam-based composts", p.322.) Mix the sterilized loam and peat substitute or peat (well moistened if it is dry). Combine the ground limestone and John Innes Base with some of the sand to ensure even distribution and incorporate this thoroughly into the remaining sand, loam, and peat substitute or peat.

COMPOST ADDITIVES

Water-retaining granules
When wetted, these granules expand, providing a reservoir of moisture on which plants can draw.

Slow-release fertilizers
These discharge nutrients over an extended period, eliminating the need for frequent liquid feeds.

Planting large and long-term plants

Although many gardeners concentrate on planting annuals to create colourful container displays for late winter, spring, and summer, there are many longer-lived plants that do well in pots. They lend an appearance of maturity and provide a valuable core to a container garden, which can then be supplemented seasonally as other plants reach their peak. Large container-grown, frost-tender plants, such as brugmansias, can be stood outdoors for the summer and moved back under glass between autumn and spring.

Plants and materials

For plants to do well for several years in containers, they must have the potential for long life and be given optimum growing conditions to ensure sustained good health.

Selecting plants

Whether buying plants or making a choice from stock raised at home, the best results are achieved by using container-grown, young but well-developed and vigorous plants that are free of pests and diseases. Look for good leaf colour and examine the undersides as well as the tops of leaves for signs of disease or pest infestation. Reject any plants with any signs of disease or damage. Slide the plant out of its container and check that the roots are well developed. If the roots are tightly congested, the plant has probably been too long in its container and may not establish quickly or well. Other signs that indicate that a plant has been overlong in its container include missing or illegible labels, containers covered with algal growth, or compost encrusted with liverworts or moss. If buying a bare-root tree, check that the root system is well developed and has plenty of fibrous roots. Root-balled trees and shrubs should have a firm ball of soil and roots encased in an undamaged plastic mesh or hessian cover and should show no signs of having dried out. Before purchasing, also make a visual check from all angles to ensure that growth is evenly balanced.

Choosing containers

Containers of many different materials are suitable for growing large and long-lived plants, provided that they have adequate drainage. For plants with extensive top-growth, it is important that the container should lend weight and stability; the most suitable include broad-bottomed containers such as Versailles tubs and terracotta urns (see p.320).

Select a container that is in proportion with both the aerial parts of the plant and its root ball. It must be big enough to permit good root development and to hold sufficient compost to supply adequate moisture and nutrients. As a rough guide, a container should be about 5cm (2in) wider and deeper than that from which the plant is being moved. Trees, however, need more room to develop; allow a depth of at least one and a half times that of the root ball and a diameter between a sixth and a quarter of the tree's current height.

SELECTING A SHRUB

Good example

Many shrubs are sold container-grown. Choose a plant with a balanced framework of shoots and reject specimens showing signs of any pests or disease.

Healthy leaves and vigorous well-balanced growth

Label in good condition indicating that plant is fresh stock

Clean container and weed-free compost

Suitable potting composts

Plants that are to remain in their containers for several years need a growing mix that will provide a steady and continuous supply of nutrients. The most suitable potting composts are loam-based with slow-release fertilizer incorporated. The nutrients in composts based on peat substitute or peat are leached relatively quickly, so plants grown in them need feeding at frequent intervals throughout their life. Although a potential disadvantage on balconies and rooftops, the weight of loam-based composts provides stabilizing ballast and a more secure roothold for plants than loamless composts. The majority of long-term plants thrive in the standard JI No.3 compost (see p.322). Use a lime-free ericaceous compost for lime haters.

Planting a container

Before planting, assemble the container, drainage crocks, compost, and any supports, as well as any pot feet, bricks, or blocks on which the container is to stand. Scrub the inside and outside of containers that are being re-used, to remove any disease-

---

PLANTING A SHRUB

1 *Place a layer of clean crocks in the base of a container with drainage holes. Fill the pot with a suitable potting compost, breaking it up if it contains lumps.*

2 *Place the shrub in its container in the centre of the pot and fill around it, firming in the compost. Lift out, leaving the hole intact. Water the plant before planting.*

3 *Remove the shrub from its original container and gently tease out the roots. Lower the shrub into the hole, firm in the compost all around, and water in well.*

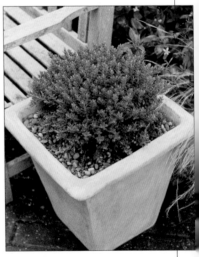

The finished planting

causing organisms. Soak new terracotta pots in clean water. Place the container in its display position before planting; it will be heavy and difficult to move once it has been filled with compost.

Place a layer of crocks over the drainage holes to prevent the growing mix being washed out. If pots are to stand directly on the soil, use a sheet of zinc gauze over the drainage holes and beneath the crocks to prevent invasion by earthworms or other creatures. Cover the crocks with a layer of gravel for extra drainage, then add potting compost to a depth of 5–10cm (2–4in). If a support is required, place it in position.

Tap the container of the selected plant to loosen the root ball and carefully ease the plant out. It is important to position the plant in the new container at the same depth as it had been growing previously. This level can be detected by the soil mark, indicated by a change of colour on the stem. Place the plant in the partially filled container, adjusting its height by adding compost if necessary. Top up with more compost, firming gently at intervals, until the finished surface is 5cm (2in) below the container's rim, which will leave room for water. Top-dress with an organic or grit mulch 2.5–4cm (1–1½in) deep.

Water thoroughly, using rainwater for lime-hating plants.

Stakes and other supports

Many large container-grown plants need some form of permanent support. The most common support is a single stake, inserted at planting before the compost is added. This allows roots to spread around the stake and avoids the risk of root damage, which may occur if the stake is pushed in after planting. The stake should reach to just below the head of a standard tree or shrub. To hold the stem firm, use an adjustable tie with a spacer to prevent bark rubbing and adjust it regularly as the stem girth increases.

Other kinds of supports include wooden, metal, and wire frames. Metal frames are available in various shapes, including an umbrella-like support for weeping standards like wisteria. Wire frames are particularly useful for evergreen climbers, such as short-jointed cultivars of common ivy (*Hedera helix*), which can be trained to form topiary-like shapes (see also TOPIARY, pp.76–77).

Container-grown climbers can be trained on to trellis fans (see below). Rustic supports consisting of a wigwam of bamboo canes are effective for slender climbers such as

Staking plants
Tall container-grown plants should be staked from an early age so that they develop a straight stem and even growth all round.

Rhodochiton atrosanguineus. Wickerwork hoops – a traditional support for pinks (*Dianthus*) – can be adapted for use with shrubby perennials such as pineapple sage (*Salvia elegans* 'Scarlet Pineapple').

PLANTS WITH SPECIAL SOIL REQUIREMENTS

Ericaceous compost
Agapetes ✽
Andromeda
Arctostaphylos
Asteranthera ovata ✽
Beaumontia grandiflora ✽
Berberidopsis corallina ✽
Billardiera ✽
Calluna vulgaris (and cvs)
Camellia

Rhododendron 'Vuyk's Scarlet'

Daboecia
Erica
Gardenia ✽
Gaultheria
Hakea
Kennedia ✽
Lapageria rosea ✽
Lilium (some spp.)
Lithodora
Mitraria coccinea ✽
Mutisia ✽
Pieris
Rhododendron
Vaccinium

Moist, humus-rich compost
Acer
Camellia
Clematis
Hibiscus, some ✽
Hosta
Rhododendron
Rosa
Viola

Free-draining compost
Agave ✽
Armeria
Artemisia
Bougainvillea ✽
Calendula
Convolvulus
Dianthus
Dorotheanthus, most ✽
Erysimum
Eschscholzia
Helianthemum
Juniperus
Lavandula
Rosmarinus
Salvia
Santolina
Sempervivum
Thymus
Yucca, some ✽

Lavandula stoechas

Key
✽ *Not fully hardy*

Planting a climber in a container

Trellis panels, often with "legs" at the base, are specially made for containers and are available in wood or plastic-covered wire. Before using, treat wooden ones with a preservative that is harmless to plants. Match the size of both the container and the trellis panel to the vigour of the selected climber. A heavy container in concrete, stone, or terracotta provides the most stable base.

Place the container in position before planting. This should be beside a wall or fence so that the trellis can be fixed to it for increased stability – a planted trellis presenting a large surface area to the elements. Fill the pot with a loam-based compost such as JI No.2 or 3. To avoid damaging the plant's roots, bed the support firmly into the compost along one side of the container; then plant the climber. After planting, secure the trellis top.

1 *Put crocks in the base of the pot. Place the support to one side of the pot and bed it in by working compost around it.*

2 *Plant the climber at the same level as in the original pot, firming the compost so that the surface is 5cm (2in) below the rim.*

3 *Tie the main shoots to the support, and water the plant to settle the roots. Fix the trellis to a wall or fence for stability.*

Pruning and training

As with the pruning of trees, shrubs, and climbers in the open garden, the aim of pruning plants in containers is to maintain good health and maximize the ornamental display. In the early stages, pruning aims to encourage the development of a well-balanced plant with evenly spaced stems. Many deciduous and evergreen plants need little pruning beyond this. To keep plants healthy, cut out out all dead, damaged, and diseased wood and, on variegated plants, remove shoots with leaves that have reverted to plain green. Such tasks can be done at almost any time of the year, although in spring you should check all plants thoroughly and deal with any problems.

Several plant groups, such as hydrangeas, roses and clematis, however, do need annual pruning. For further information, see pruning and training ORNAMENTAL SHRUBS (pp.88–121); ROSES (pp.146–169), CLIMBING PLANTS (pp.122–145), and CLEMATIS (pp.138–139). Topiary specimens require strict formative training and subsequent regular clipping (see TOPIARY, pp.76–77).

Standard specimens

Many trees, shrubs, and climbers can be grown as standards. However standards have a relatively high centre of gravity, so choose a container that is heavy and broad-based. Most container-grown trees are best trained as standards; the simple outline occupies little ground space and allows light to reach plants grown beneath them. Shrubs or subshrubs that respond well to this treatment include fuchsias (see p.121) and argyranthemums. With strict pruning, even vigorous climbers, including ornamental or fruiting vines and wisterias, can be grown as standards.

During formative training, the stem must be staked until it is sturdy enough to support the head itself, although many standards will require a permanent stake. Ties must be firm; adjust them regularly to avoid constricting the stem as it expands. With trees, retain the lower branches in the initial stages to encourage stem thickening and remove them gradually over two or three years.

With shrubs, shorten the laterals on the main stem, which should also be supported, with a cane. Retain laterals for a year to build stem strength, then remove them completely. For fuchsias, pinch out the laterals (see PINCH PRUNING, p.377). On all shrubs, allow the main stem to grow at least 20cm (8in) beyond the desired head height, then cut it back to a bud or pair of buds to encourage the growth of laterals to form the head. Subsequently, tip prune the laterals to encourage further branching and form a dense crown of foliage.

Standard shrub
When grown as a standard, shrubs such as this Syringa meyeri '*Palibin*' *develop a "bouquet-like" head, which needs a heavy container to maintain stability.*

PLANTS TO GROW AS STANDARDS

Shrubs and sub-shrubs
Argyranthemum
Brugmansia
Buxus sempervirens
Camellia
Caragana arborescens
x *Citrofortunella microcarpa* ❋
Ficus carica
Fuchsia, many ❋
Gardenia jasminoides ❋
Heliotropium ❋
Hibiscus rosa-sinensis ❋
Lagerstroemia indica ❋
Laurus nobilis
Leptospermum scoparium ❋
Ligustrum (some spp.)
Nerium oleander ❋
Pelargonium, many ❋
Rosa (many spp.)
Rosmarinus officinalis
Salix caprea 'Kilmarnock'
Solenostemon, some ❋
Viburnum tinus

Climbers
Bougainvillea ❋
Lonicera (some spp.)
Rosa (some spp.)
Vitis (some spp.)
Wisteria

Key
❋ *Not hardy*

TRAINING A STANDARD WOODY-STEMMED CLIMBER

Stages of development
In the early stages of training (here a vine), aim to develop a vigorous main vertical stem. Let sideshoots grow during the growing season so that their leaves may "feed" the stem, then remove them in the dormant season. Form the head by developing well-spaced laterals at an appropriate height and by pruning annually to maintain a supply of flowering spurs.

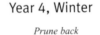

Year 4, Winter

Prune back each well-spaced lateral to 2 strong buds

Year 5 and onwards

Shorten fruiting shoots, when they reach 30–45cm (12–18in) long, in summer

Year 1, Winter

Year 2, Winter

Year 3, Winter

Shorten the previous season's growth by at least a half, to where it is brown and ripened

In this and the subsequent year, prune back into brown, ripened wood, cutting to a bud

After planting, cut hard back to a bud

Remove any laterals below the cut on the main stem. In subsequent years remove laterals below the head

Prune flowered shoots back to two strong buds in winter

Thin spur systems as they build up and become congested

Planting seasonal displays

For many gardeners the essential plants for container gardens are the large number of annuals that provide colourful displays over a long period in summer. Other plants to be planted each year include biennials for winter, spring, and summer, and bulbs for spring, summer, and autumn. In general, fresh bulbs planted annually give better results than those used for several years.

Annuals and biennials

A wide selection of annuals and biennials is available as young stock from garden centres as early as mid-spring. Many are also easily raised from seed in a greenhouse or an enclosed porch. If potting up early under glass, harden plants off by moving containers outdoors in the day but returning them under cover at night until there is little risk of frost.

Before potting up, always water the chosen plants thoroughly. Then assemble the essential components, such as a clean container, drainage crocks, loam-based or loamless compost, slow-release fertilizer, water-retaining granules, and the selected plants. Place the drainage crocks concave side down over the drainage hole and three quarters-fill the container with potting compost mixed with slow-release fertilizer and water-retaining granules, if desired.

With the plants still in their pots, experiment with arrangements that will balance their trailing, bushy, and upright habits. Once the design is satisfactory, begin planting in a systematic way, for example, by working from the centre outwards or from one side of the container to the other.

CONTAINERS THROUGH THE SEASONS

Spring
A shallow terracotta pot planted with spring miniatures, including narcissi, muscari and bellis, provides a welcome splash of colour.

Winter
A harmonious mix of hellebores, hyacinths and polyanthus in subtle shades of pink make a charming late-winter feature.

Autumn
A blend of deep purple foliage, shimmering grasses and ruby red dahlias creates a wonderfully dramatic late-season display.

To loosen each plant, tap the container, remove the plant and place it in its new pot. Add or subtract compost as necessary so that each plant is at the same depth as in its original container, there are no air pockets within the compost, and the final level is about 5cm (2in) below the rim. Water to settle the plants in.

Annuals and biennials for winter and early spring flowering should be potted up in autumn. Garden centres and nurseries, however, sometimes delay making available for sale plants that flower in late winter and

early spring. These can be planted during winter provided the compost is not frozen.

Bulbs

Most spring-flowering bulbs are best planted in early autumn, as soon as they become available. Tulip bulbs, however, are best planted in late autumn or early winter, when they are less susceptible to the fungal disease tulip fire (*Botrytis tulipae*) (see pp.649 and 656). Although bulbs can be mixed satisfactorily in a single container, it is generally better to

plant different bulbs in separate containers because of the difficulties of synchronizing flowering times.

To extend the flowering display of the same type of bulb, plant more than one layer of bulbs in the container, provided it is deep enough to take several layers as well as compost below and above each bulb. For most bulbs, allow a minimum planting depth equal to six times the height of the bulb. To plant two layers of daffodils or tulips, for example, place drainage material in the base of a clean container and then

PLANTING A MIXED SUMMER CONTAINER

1 *To work out an attractive design, arrange your selected plants, still in their pots, to get an idea of how they will fit together in the display. Mix bushy or upright plants with tumblers and trailers.*

2 *Establish your central feature plant and then work outwards. It is possible to position plants closer together in the pot than in the open garden, but there must still be adequate room for growth.*

3 *Tilt some plants on their side so that they face out towards the rim of the pot. Some of the root ball may be left exposed on the soil surface – if you ensure that it is kept moist the plant will thrive.*

4 *Once you are satisfied with the overall arrangement, add more potting compost to fill the container to about 2.5cm (1in) below the rim. Water thoroughly to settle the plants in.*

PLANTING A WINDOWBOX

1 *While the plants are still in their pots, decide how they are to be displayed in the new container, before beginning to plant them up. Begonias, lobelia, and busy Lizzies (Impatiens cvs) are to be used in this arrangement.*

2 *Cover the base of the windowbox with crocks or gravel, then add potting compost until the box is half to three quarters full. Slide each plant out of its pot, supporting the root ball with your fingers. Gently tease out the plant roots.*

3 *Scoop back the compost. Firm the plant in position so that it is at the same soil level as in its old pot and about 1cm (½in) below the rim of the windowbox.*

4 *Pot up the remaining plants, then add more potting compost, pressing it especially into the sides and corners, so that there are no air pockets. Add more compost if necessary so the surface is 5cm (2in) below the rim and level. Then water thoroughly.*

---

cover with a layer of loam-based, loamless, or bulb compost not less than 5cm (2in) deep. Place in the first layer of bulbs so that they are 2.5–10cm (1–4in) apart depending on type. Cover with compost so that just the tips are visible. Arrange a second layer of bulbs in the spaces between the first. Top up the container with compost until it is within 5cm (2in) of the container rim.

Lilies are among the most important bulbs for summer displays (see LILIES, p.251). They can be planted singly, or in groups of three or more in large containers. In general, lilies look better on their own rather than mixed with other plants in the same container. The best time to plant is in autumn, when bulbs are newly lifted. Select lily bulbs with plump, fleshy scales that are free of disease.

Lilies thrive in a well-drained growing medium, such as 4 parts loam-based compost (JI No.2) mixed with 1 part grit and 1 part leaf mould, to which slow-release fertilizer has been added. Stand the container on pot feet, then fill with the compost mix. Plant with the tip of the bulb 10–15cm (4–6in) below the compost surface (about two or three times the height of the bulb) and three times the bulb's diameter apart. Stem-rooting lilies, which produce roots on the stem above the bulb as well as from the bulb itself, should be planted more deeply, at about three to four times the height of the bulb.

Bulbs with bedding plants

Mixtures of spring bulbs and annuals or biennials make very effective displays in a single container. Try planting tulips with forget-me-nots (*Myosotis*) or wallflowers (*Erysimum*), and small bulbs, such as scillas, with winter-flowering pansies (*Viola* x *wittrockiana*). Plant bulbs in autumn under a good covering of compost and add the annuals or biennials so that, when they are watered in, the surface of the compost is about 5cm (2in) below the container's rim.

Fruit, vegetables, and herbs

Although the yield is less when compared with crops grown in open ground, leafy salad crops and other vegetables, such as courgettes and beans, can be successfully cultivated in loamless compost if watered and fed regularly. Strawberries generally prefer a loam-based potting compost, but tolerate a loamless one, and they must be kept moist at all times. Use specially made strawberry planters or adapt a wooden barrel by cutting planting holes, 5cm (2in) wide and 25cm (10in) apart at different levels in the sides. Alpine strawberries, such as *Fragaria* 'Baron Solemacher', are a good choice for a partially shaded site.

Herbs are among the most useful culinary plants for containers. Many are easily grown in pots of loamless compost with added grit (one fifth by volume) to ensure good drainage. Most need little extra feeding.

Securing windowboxes

A fully planted windowbox may appear to be stable, but when placed at a height on a wall or against a building it is often subject to wind turbulence. If dislodged, such a heavy container poses a serious threat to the safety of people passing beneath and may cause considerable damage. All window-boxes must therefore be secured firmly with heavy-duty metal brackets or wedges. The latter are ideal for sloping windowsills with a depth of at least 20cm (8in); they can be further secured in position by using mirror plates and hooks.

Mirror plates
These plates are fixed to the back of the windowbox, then hooked securely to the window frame.

INSERTING WEDGES ON A SLOPING SILL

1 *Place a spirit level across a windowsill, then measure the gap between it and the sill to find the height of the wedge needed. Mark this dimension on a wooden offcut that is 30mm (1¼in) shorter than the sill depth.*

2 *Mark a diagonal line to the opposite corner of the offcut. Then with another offcut, mark out an identical wedge. Cut out both wedges and treat with preservative. Tack with panel pins to the bottom of the windowbox.*

Planting hanging baskets and mangers

Hanging baskets and wall-mounted containers provide great opportunities to create colourful and imaginative plant displays. Nearly all of them are of open construction and are used with a liner that holds in the compost and retains moisture while allowing excess water to drain away. Hanging containers must be fixed to a secure overhead support or attached firmly to a wall well out of the way of passers-by.

A variety of styles

The standard hanging basket is of lightweight construction in wire, usually plastic-coated, suspended by means of chains. Half-baskets of similar construction are designed to be wall-mounted. More solid baskets and containers, such as hayracks or mangers, are usually made of enamelled or plastic-coated strip metal. Alternatives to openwork containers are suspended or wall-mounted pots with solid sides. Many such pots have the advantage of being self-watering, incorporating a reservoir that keeps the compost moist.

Types of liner

Many different liners are available, some of which are made to fit specific sizes of baskets, while others are cut to size. Most are patterned or coloured so that they are camouflaged within the containers. All can be pierced to allow planting in the sides, although such holes are easier to make with some materials than others (see *Planting a hanging basket*, p.330).

Sheet plastic is among the most versatile of basket liners. It can be easily cut to size and slashed to provide drainage or planting holes. Dark-coloured plastic is relatively inconspicuous, particularly as growth develops. If desired, it can, however, readily be disguised with straw or less bulky hessian, for example (see *Planting a hayrack*, below). In addition to plastic, hanging baskets can be lined with coir, foam, recycled paper, or wool (see right).

Composts and additives

The most suitable composts for the majority of seasonal displays are loamless formulations, which are light and easy to handle. For longer-lasting displays, for example, of ground-cover roses, loam-based potting composts are preferable (see "Composts for containers", p.322).

Fertilizers can be added as slow-release inorganic fertilizers or as liquid feeds. The addition of water-retaining granules helps to reduce fluctuations in moisture levels.

Planting seasonal displays

Use trailing plants in tiers to envelop the sides of a hanging basket in flowers and foliage. Position lax plants round the rim and bushy or upright plants in the centre to form a crown. If the basket can be kept frost free, plant a summer basket in mid-spring. Harden off gradually by moving the basket outdoors by day and move to its final display position only when risk of frost has passed.

Use the same planting technique for spring, autumn and winter displays. Hardy plants do not need hardening off, but should be kept in a sheltered place until well established.

LINING MATERIALS FOR BASKETS

Coir
Natural look; tricky to cut for side planting.

Foam
Absorbent, easily cut; can be conspicuous.

Recycled paper
Cheap, available with push-out planting holes.

Wool
Hard to cut, but good insulation for plant roots.

Securing baskets and mangers

When filled, hanging baskets and other wall-mounted containers can be heavy so they must be securely fastened to strong wall-mounted brackets or overhead supports, such as the cross-beams of a pergola. Wall-mounted containers, which must be hung plumb and level, are usually supplied with brackets; if fixing to masonry, insert wall plugs into the holes before screwing into position.

Bracket for a hanging basket
Holding the bracket plumb and level, mark the position of back plate holes. Insert wall plugs and secure with galvanized screws.

Hayrack fixtures
Mark and drill holes for a hooked bracket. Use a wall plug and galvanized screw when fixing.

PLANTING A HAYRACK

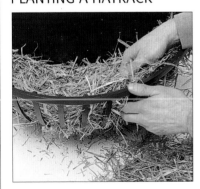

1 *Openwork manger-style baskets must be lined. To camouflage the liner, work in straw against the inner face of the curved front of a hayrack so that, when compressed, it forms a layer 2.5cm (1in) thick.*

2 *Cut a piece of sheet plastic to make a slightly over-sized liner, and fit it inside the hayrack. Fold the excess towards the straw and tuck in all round, to make a neat edge. Cut slits in the liner, at the bottom for drainage and at the front, if desired, for planting holes. Fill the hayrack to one third of its depth with potting compost.*

3 *Remove plants from their pots, tease out the root balls, and insert the plants in the compost. Adjust the compost until the plants are at their original planting depth. Top up and firm the compost to within 2.5cm (1in) of the rim. Fix the hayrack in position. Water well.*

PLANTING A HANGING BASKET

1 Place the basket on a bucket or large flower pot, so that it is centred and level. Adjust the liner (here, of coir) to fit the basket snugly, making several radial cuts. (With a pre-cut liner, simply overlap the segments.)

2 Press the liner down firmly against the bottom and sides of the basket, moulding it to the basket wires. Use scissors to trim off any liner that extends above the rim of the basket, making a neat, level top edge.

3 Using sharp scissors or a craft knife, make a series of slits 5cm (2in) long in the side of the liner for planting in tiers, so that trailing plants, inserted in the slits at one or two levels below the basket rim, will fill out and mask the wire frame.

4 Add potting compost mixed with slow-release fertilizer and water-retaining granules until it is level with the first tier of slits in the side of the liner. Gently firm the potting compost.

5 To protect the soft growth of plants that are to be inserted through the slits in the liner, wrap each plant in an offcut of polythene sheet, to form a cone over the stems and leaves.

6 Guide each plant cone through a slit in the liner, from the inside. When the plant is in position with the root ball on the inside and the stems outside, gently remove its polythene cover.

7 Continue planting through the sides, using the same method. Gently tease out the root balls and add compost, working it around the roots, until the basket is filled within 5cm (2in) of the rim.

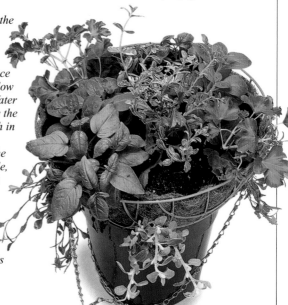

8 Plant lax plants, here fuchsias, pelargoniums, and petunias, around the rim, spaced so that they are not immediately above the plants below.

9 Add more compost, working it in round the roots. Leave a gap for a bushy plant; Felicia amelloides 'Variegata' with blue, daisy-like flowers is the centrepiece here.

10 Complete the planting and top off with compost so that the finished surface is 2.5cm (1in) below the basket rim. Water thoroughly. Allow the plants to establish in a sheltered place before hanging the basket. Meanwhile, keep the compost evenly moist, but do not overwater. In frost-prone areas, keep baskets under glass until there is little risk of frost.

Water gardens in containers

SEVERAL factors determine the success of a container water garden. The plants must be carefully selected and then placed in their appropriate light conditions if they are to achieve their potential. The pot should blend with its surroundings and provide an adequate depth and surface area of water to suit the chosen plants. Vigorous plants can quickly take over if the the gardener fails to exercise proper control. The surface should also be partly covered with foliage, so the water does not become fouled by algal growth.

Choosing plants

There are one or two plants, notably the deep marginal lotus (*Nelumbo*), that are very effective used on their own in a small water garden. However, the more usual approach is to scale down the planting of a conventional pond, using a mixture of marginals, deep water plants, submerged oxygenators, and floating aquatics (see WATER GARDENING, "Planting and stocking", p.297).

The number that can be accommodated depends largely on the volume and surface area of the water. In a standard half-barrel, which holds 50 litres (12 gallons), there is room for one dwarf or pygmy water lily, three or four shallow marginals, one or two plants of a non-invasive oxygenator, and a floating aquatic.

Siting the container

Ensure the container is correctly positioned before being filled, as once it holds water and plants it will be heavy and difficult to manoeuvre. It must be on a firm, level surface and near to a water supply so that it can be topped up as necessary. The ideal site is sheltered, but well away from trees, and in sun but shaded during the hottest parts of the day.

Planting

Cover the base of the container with 5cm (2in) of washed gravel, then two thirds fill with water. Plant aquatics individually in ordinary garden soil in plastic-mesh baskets lined with hessian to prevent the soil washing out. Place the plants deeply in the baskets, work the soil round the roots, and firm in gently so that the finished surface is 2.5cm (1in) below the rim. Top-dress with washed gravel. Stand containers of marginals on bricks so that the plants reach the water's surface (see *Planting depths*, p.298). Finish filling the pool slowly to within 5cm (2in) of the rim to avoid disturbing the compost in the planting baskets. If including floating aquatics in the planting design, add them when the container has been filled.

Miniature pond
Floating aquatics, including the tender water lettuce (Pistia stratiotes) and compact shallow marginals, such as a variegated Japanese rush (Acorus gramineus), crowd the surface of this pond made from a half-barrel. Marginals are planted in purpose-made plastic baskets and placed on bricks so that they stand just above the water surface.

WATER PLANTS FOR CONTAINERS

Shallow marginals
(15cm/6in depth of water)
Acorus gramineus 'Ogon',
 A. gramineus 'Variegatus'
Juncus effusus f. *spiralis*
Myosotis scorpioides
Typha minima

Deep marginals
(30cm/12in depth of water)
Cyperus papyrus 'Nanus' ✸
Nelumbo 'Pygmaea Alba' ✸

Deep water plants
Nuphar pumila
Nymphaea 'Aurora',
 N. candida, *N.* 'Ellisiana',
 N. 'Laydekeri Liliacea',
 N. 'Laydekeri Purpurata',
 N. 'Laydekeri Rosea
 Prolifera', *N. odorata* var.
 minor, *N.* 'Pygmaea
 Helvola', *N. tetragona*

Submerged oxygenators
Eleocharis acicularis
Fontinalis antipyretica
Myriophyllum aquaticum

Floating aquatics
Azolla filiculoides ✸
Eichhornia crassipes ✸
Pistia stratiotes ✸
Wolffia arrhiza ✸

Key
✸ *Not hardy*

PLANTING A CONTAINERIZED WATER GARDEN

1 *Pre-soak the barrel to swell the wood and make it watertight and set it on a level base. Cover the bottom with gravel. Fill two thirds full with water.*

2 *Line a plastic-mesh basket with hessian, fill with garden soil, and plant up (here Myriophyllum aquaticum). Top-dress with gravel or coarse grit.*

3 *Lower oxygenators, water lilies, and other deep water plants carefully onto the bottom of the barrel so as not to disturb the soil in each basket.*

4 *Place bricks or half-bricks on the bottom of the barrel to raise the height of any container holding marginal plants.*

5 *Adjust the bricks until the plant is slightly exposed above the water's surface. Top up the barrel to within 5cm (2in) of the barrel's rim, if needed.*

Routine care

THROUGHOUT the growing season, container-grown plants need regular checking. The compost must be kept moist, so frequent watering is essential, as is feeding during the growing season to maintain healthy growth and productivity. Dead-heading helps to prolong flowering. Plants also require protection from pests and diseases, and, if tender, from frost. Long-term plants need special attention with regard to repotting and top-dressing.

Watering

Plants in containers have access to very limited reserves of water when compared with those in open ground and so are dependent to a greater extent on the gardener for their water supply. Even after rainy weather, extra watering may be needed, as the pot plant's foliage may shed the rainwater outside the container. In addition, containers, especially windowboxes and those fixed against walls, are often in a rain shadow, where the rainfall they receive is much reduced (see *Rain Shadow*, p.610). In hot, dry, or windy weather, plants may need watering two or even three times a day.

The simplest way to know when a plant should be watered is to push a finger into the compost to check if it is moist below the surface. Such a probe is especially useful for plants grown in composts based on peat substitutes; these composts often appear dry on the surface, when they are adequately moist beneath. Do not water if the compost is moist; plants are as likely to be killed by over-watering as they are from lack of it.

Watering methods

The most popular method of watering is by hand, using a watering can or a hose. Always water thoroughly with the tip of the spout or hose directed at the compost surface rather than the foliage. Maintain the flow until water runs out of the drainage holes. Superficial watering on a regular basis can lead to a build-up of salts in the compost that impede drainage and lead to stunted growth or rotting. Tap water is satisfactory for most plants, but if it is hard it will not suit lime-hating plants such as rhododendrons. Rainwater from a water butt can be used for these (see "Collecting water", p.614).

Automated or drip-feed irrigation systems (see TOOLS AND EQUIPMENT, "Watering aids", p.560) can be adapted for use in containers. These

WATERING HANGING BASKETS

Watering high-level containers
A lance attachment with a trigger-action is a useful extension to a hose. Alternatively, fit a cane to the hose to gain the necessary rigidity and height when watering.

Adjustable container heights
A rise-and-fall pulley attachment allows a hanging basket to be raised, lowered, and held in a locked position. This simplifies watering and grooming of the plants in the basket.

systems are excellent, labour-saving ways of watering containers, including windowboxes and growing bags. They do, however, need regular maintenance to ensure that lines and drip heads flow freely.

Containers above head height, such as hanging baskets and windowboxes, are difficult to reach with conventional hoses and watering cans. A rigid hose lance attachment is invaluable for this, and simple to use. Alternatively, invest in a compression sprayer with a rigid extension and nozzle. Hanging baskets can also be suspended on a locking pulley system. They can be lowered for watering and raised to the required height for display.

Fertilizing

Plants growing in loam-based potting composts containing slow-release fertilizers will be fed sufficient nutrients over many seasons, until they are renewed when repotted or top-dressed (see p.334). Nutrient levels in loamless composts, however, decline quickly, partly because they are easily leached out by watering. They therefore need boosting with liquid fertilizers. These are quick acting and contain a balanced supply of nitrogen, phosphorus and potassium, the major elements needed for plant growth, along with trace elements.

Apply liquid fertilizers to moist compost two or three times between the start of growth, in early spring, and midsummer, depending on the manufacturer's instructions regarding the strength and frequency of application.

Foliar feeding – the application of dilute liquid fertilizers as a foliar spray – can usefully supplement other kinds of feeding. Although its effect is not long lasting, it too is a

fast-acting treatment for plants that are growing slowly or showing signs of stress. Apply foliar feeds in dull, overcast conditions, never when plants have sunlight on them.

Grooming

The general appearance of a container garden is greatly improved by regular maintenance. By paying close attention

Organic and "home-grown" liquid feeds

A number of organic liquid feeds are now available in garden centres, to maintain plants grown in containers and hanging baskets. These commercial preparations are mainly derived from organic cow, poultry, and other animal manures. Seaweed extracts are also readily available and are particularly valuable as a source of trace elements as well as other nutrients. All may be used as dressings around the plants or as foliar feeds on established plants in containers and hanging baskets to help lengthen the flowering season.

Additionally, organic liquid feeds may be home-made using the

foliage of comfrey (*Symphytum officinale*) or nettles (*Urtica dioica*), both of which are rich in plant foods – and very easy to grow. It is also easy to make: well-developed fresh leaves may be pressed down into a container of water and steeped (soaked) for about a month before draining off the resulting rather strong-smelling liquid and using it either undiluted or diluted with water (see p.625).

Comfrey feed is rich in potash and is best used undiluted for greedy container-grown tomatoes when in fruit; nettle-based mixtures provide a good general liquid feed if used diluted with 5–10 parts of water.

TRIMMING SHOOTS

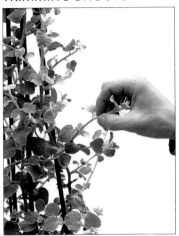

Vigorous plants, such as this trailing Helichrysum petiolare, *should be trimmed or pinched back to curb excess growth and encourage good, bushy cover.*

to the plants, early infestations of pests and diseases are often identified. These can then be treated in their early stages before they do serious damage to the plants.

In spring, overwintered plants frequently need to be tidied. Prune out any frost-damaged growth and remove dead and blemished leaves; all are potential sources of infection by fungal diseases. Shorten any weak or straggling stems, for example of trailing ivies, cutting back to strong buds to encourage new shoots. Pinching back overlong shoots in spring is also beneficial to most plants, because it will encourage bushy new growth.

During summer, vigorous plants may need to be curbed, to prevent overcrowding. Tie in climbers to their supports on a regular basis and check that existing ties are not restricting the stems. When grown on upright supports, the stems of vigorous trailing plants, such as *Helichrysum petiolare,* should be tied in frequently, too. The stem tips and sideshoots may also need pinching back to ensure the desired dense coverage of their supports.

Dead-heading

The removal of dead and fading flowers prevents the formation of fruit and seed, which diverts a plant's energy from the creation of more flowers. Dead-heading is a task that many gardeners find enjoyable and is the most effective way of prolonging the flowering season of a wide range of annuals that are the mainstay of the container garden in summer. Dead-heading can be done by pinching between finger and thumb on many

DEAD-HEADING

Pinch out dead blooms between thumb and forefinger. Such dead-heading encourages flowering and removes a potential source of infection by grey mould (Botrytis).

soft-stemmed annuals, or by using scissors or secateurs for firmer flower stems, such as those of roses.

Renewing spent plants

The usual pattern of seasonal designs is to plant up for two or three main displays in a year. But sometimes, part of a display fades prematurely, leaving a conspicuous gap. Rather than starting again with a completely fresh planting, it is often possible to remove faded plants and insert replacements in the gap. This is not invariably successful, especially if pests or diseases have caused early failure of plants, and small new plants can find it difficult to compete with those that are well established.

For the best chance of success, take out as much of the old compost as possible, without disturbing the

roots of those that remain. Part-fill the holes with fresh, moist compost of the same type that is already in the container. Then plant the replacement plants, adding more compost and working it in firmly around the root balls. Finally, top up the compost to its previous level and water in thoroughly.

Pests and diseases

The range of pests and diseases that attack container-grown plants are much the same as those that are troublesome in the open garden (see PLANT PROBLEMS, pp.639–673). Because of the condensed nature of the container garden, however, damaged plants are more conspicuous. Even if they can be nursed back to health, diseased and damaged plants detract from the overall effect and may form a source of infection for neighbouring plants. In many cases, the best policy is to discard plants that are sickly or badly damaged. If replanting whole containers, dispose of the old compost, clean the container thoroughly, and begin again with fresh compost.

Many problems can be avoided or contained by good hygiene and sound cultivation. Healthy plants show greater resistance to disease and recover more rapidly from pest infestations. Always use sterilized potting compost, clean all containers thoroughly before use, and check new plants to ensure that they are not carriers of pests and diseases.

Prevalent pests

There are several particularly troublesome pests in the container garden. Aphids (see p.646) and other sap-sucking pests cause distorted and

RENEWING A CONTAINER DISPLAY

1 *Dead-head flowers regularly in order to keep the display attractive. When plants have finished flowering, remove them, taking care not to damage the roots of remaining plants in the pot.*

2 *Add fresh, moist compost and fill the gaps with new plants or bulbs that will continue the floral display. Firm in gently and water thoroughly to help the new plants to establish.*

GOOD HYGIENE

Inspect plants regularly for signs of pests or diseases, and remove unsightly yellow or decaying leaves promptly to prevent rot.

stunted growth, and unsightly black sooty mould may infest the honeydew that they excrete. In addition, they often spread virus diseases.

Adult vine weevils (see p.645) cause largely cosmetic damage to leaves by cutting irregular holes in leaf margins between spring and autumn, but their curved, creamy-white larvae cause far greater damage (see p.660). They feed on plant roots, frequently remaining undetected until the plant wilts. Check the roots of all new plants for signs of infestation before planting.

Slugs and snails (see p.644) eat young growth, frequently causing fatal damage before their silvery slime trails are noted. They may hide beneath pots or their rims, so check such places regularly and dispose of them promptly.

Various fungal diseases, including grey mould (*Botrytis*) (see p.646), attack a wide range of plants, but by far the most serious diseases in the container garden are viral. Viruses (see p.649), which are spread by sap-sucking insects, seriously weaken plants and cause stunted, distorted, and often mottled growth. There is no effective way of treating them, and the only practical course is to destroy affected plants.

It is largely a matter of personal choice whether or not to rely on chemical pest and disease control. Frequent checks made on the state of the plant's health allow infestations or infections to be dealt with promptly before they present serious problems (see PLANT PROBLEMS, "Integrated control", p.640). It is preferable to try an organic or biological control initially, then to resort to chemicals should these fail.

TOP-DRESSING

1 To top-dress a container-grown plant (here a rhododendron), remove the top 5–10cm (2–4in) of the old compost, taking care not to damage the plant roots.

2 Replace with fresh compost of a similar type and to the same level as before. Water well. Apply a mulch of bark chippings or grit if required.

Maintaining shrubs and trees in containers

Container-grown shrubs and trees require more care and attention than those in the open ground, since they have less access to moisture and nutrients. Repotting or top-dressing once a year will ensure continued growth and good health.

Repotting woody plants

If grown indefinitely in containers trees, shrubs, and many long-term shrubby perennials will become pot-bound and will exhaust the nutrients in the potting compost. A vigorous young tree or shrub is likely to outgrow its pot every one or two years. The roots of mature trees and shrubs, in which growth will naturally have slowed down, will take longer to become congested. As a general guide, mature trees and shrubs need repotting every three or four years. Check the state of the roots by laying the container on its side and easing the plant out. Often, however, the plant itself will indicate it needs repotting by exhibiting a lack of vigour and poor colour in the leaves. Growth may also appear uneven or unbalanced. If the plant is top-heavy, it will almost certainly benefit from being repotted.

Repotting is best done in early to mid-spring, as or just before growth begins for the new season. Mature plants can be returned to their original pots, but vigorous young plants generally need to be moved to pots that are one-and-half times the size of the old one. Expect to continue replanting them in ever larger containers until they reach maturity and growth slows.

When the tree or shrub has been eased out of its container, remove the surface compost and any weeds or moss, and discard all of this material as well as any loose compost. The roots are delicate and should not be handled unnecessarily, although this is a good opportunity to tease out tangled roots and shorten by up to two thirds a proportion of non-fibrous roots. If there is any delay between removal and repotting, keep the root ball covered with a sheet of plastic or damp hessian to prevent it being desiccated by the drying effects of sun or wind.

Use an appropriate loam-based compost to which slow-release fertilizer has been added, and repot so that the surface of the plant's root ball is at the same level as before when firmed in and watered.

Top-dressing long-term plants

In years when shrubs and trees are not being repotted, their compost should be refreshed in spring. Having removed any mulch, the top 5–10cm (2–4in) of compost should be loosened and discarded, taking care not to damage the shallow roots of plants such as camellias and rhododendrons. The replacement compost must not only be fresh but also of the same type as the potting compost still in the container. It should also contain a slow-release fertilizer. Use an ericaceous compost and soft water or rainwater when top-dressing lime-hating plants.

Surface-rooting plants can be top-dressed in a different way, because their fibrous feeding roots are easily damaged when the top layers of compost are removed. For surface rooters, discard the compost from the bottom of the root ball, and replace it with a smaller quantity of enriched compost. The shrub will then sit lower in its pot than previously, leaving room for a smaller top-dressing.

Holiday care

The most essential requirement in the gardener's absence is regular watering. An automated irrigation system (see TOOLS AND EQUIPMENT, "Hose timers", p.561) is an ideal but expensive solution. Failing this, the best option is to ask a friend or neighbour to come in to water on a regular basis. To make the task easier, it is worth grouping the containers together. This massing of the plants together also has the advantage of slowing the rate of water evaporation from each; it will do so to such an extent as to be an adequate solution in itself for an absence of a few days. Place containers in a shaded and sheltered place and water thoroughly just before going away.

Reduce evaporation even further by packing a number of containers in a crate, tray, or similar container with drainage holes, which which is filled with damp sharp sand, compost, or peat substitute. For short-term absences, and with relatively small plants, a more fiddly method is to enclose small potted plants in sealed and inflated plastic bags. If the bagged plants are kept in cool shade, the rate of water loss will be negligible. This is, however, only a short-term fix; fungal diseases

---

REPOTTING A CONTAINER-GROWN SHRUB

1 Carefully lay the shrub on its side; support the main stems with one hand and ease it out of its pot. If necessary, slide a long-bladed knife between compost and pot to loosen the root ball.

2 If the roots have become very congested, gently tease them out. Remove the surface compost and any moss or weeds. Prune back about a quarter of the non-fibrous roots by up to two thirds.

3 Place crocks over the pot's drainage holes, then add the potting compost. Position the plant centrally and vertically in the pot, spreading its roots out evenly within the container.

4 Add more compost around the roots, gently firming until it is at the same level on the plant as it was in its previous pot. Prune out any dead or damaged growth and water in well.

The more the merrier
When containers are closely grouped, air movement between them and the plants they contain is reduced, so less water is lost to evaporation.

proliferate in such conditions and the bags must be removed promptly when the gardener returns.

Capillary matting can be used to supply water to containers (see INDOOR GARDENING, "Care of indoor plants before going away", p.374). Another way of exploiting capillary action is to use a filled bucket as a water reservoir and strips of capillary matting as a "wick". The bucket must be raised above the container it is to serve and the wick must be tucked into the compost. Proprietary wicking systems are also available and these are specially designed for holiday care.

Emergency measures

If plants have wilted when you return from holiday, do not despair immediately. Even when compost has become so dry that it has shrunk away from the sides of the pot, plants can sometimes be salvaged by deep immersion. Partially fill a bucket with water, place it in a shady site, and plunge the plant in its container so that the top of the container is just below the surface of the water. Hold the container down until the flow of air bubbles that arises from the compost has ceased, then leave the plant to soak for a further 30 minutes. When the compost is thoroughly wet, remove the container from the bucket and allow to drain well. If woody plants do not revive within two or three hours, there is little point in keeping them. However, it is worth cutting back perennials; they may produce new growth from the base.

Winter protection

In frost-prone areas, container-grown plants that need protection from severe cold include those that are known to be tender, those that are marginally hardy, and a number of plants that are reasonably hardy such as rosemary (*Rosmarinus officinalis* cultivars) and lavender (*Lavandula* cultivars) that may suffer frost damage to the roots if the compost in the containers becomes frozen.

The most straightforward way of avoiding frost damage is to move plants under glass in autumn. Depending on the local climate, even an unheated greenhouse, conservatory, or glassed-in porch can give adequate protection to most plants, especially if they are kept almost dry during the coldest, darkest months.

In some cases, the overwintered plant can be used to provide cuttings in spring and may itself then be discarded. Where space is a problem, it can be much less space-consuming to overwinter plants as cuttings. Overwintered rooted cuttings of plants that make rapid annual growth, such as *Helichrysum petiolare*, will develop in time to use in displays for the following summer. It is always worth overwintering under glass cuttings of marginally hardy plants left outdoors, as an insurance against winter losses. *Pelargonium*, a major genus for container gardening, warrants special attention (see *Overwintering*, p.204).

If vulnerable plants are too large to be moved indoors, another way to protect them is to wrap them in insulating material. The plant itself can be protected with horticultural fleece or bubble plastic. It is important also to insulate the container. A layer of straw or hessian tied snugly around the container can provide effective insulation for the plant roots and will also help to preserve the pot itself from frost damage. During winter, keep plants in a sheltered site, avoiding frost pockets. The weight of snow can break branches and stems of plants, so do not allow heavy accumulations to build up.

Spring is often a more difficult season than winter. There may be periods without frost and unseasonably warm days in which plants begin to make growth, but the risk of frost remains and its effect on unprotected, soft new growth can be devastating. The same is true of cold, dry spring winds. During a hardening-off period of several weeks, plants that have been overwintered under glass can be gradually acclimatized to outdoor conditions. It is essential, however, to remain vigilant and provide protection at night, when there is greatest risk of temperatures falling below freezing. Keep a sheet of horticultural fleece handy to cover any vulnerable plant if the forecast is for a cold night.

Security

Although it is far from being a universal problem, gardens are sometimes targeted by thieves, and container-grown plants and the containers themselves are particularly vulnerable. It is difficult to take measures to put off the determined thief, without compromising the relaxed atmosphere of the garden and the quality of its display. There are, however, some sensible precautions that you can take.

Valuable containers in exposed positions close to public access excite interest, so reposition these or chain them to the ground, although it is difficult to do this inconspicuously, and the very fact that the container is chained can, in itself, highlight its value. In front gardens, it is generally advisable to use plain but serviceable containers. Plants of great rarity are unlikely to be recognized as such, but they may be difficult to replace, so it is better to grow them in places away from public view.

Lights that are activated automatically by movement provide some measure of security, as do well-maintained walls, gates, and fences. Although these are not impregnable, they do provide the strongest barriers to both thieves and vandals.

FROST PROTECTION

Wrap top-growth loosely but securely in horticultural fleece. A double layer of hessian tied firmly around the pot will protect roots from freezing during the winter months.

CHAPTER

12

CACTI AND OTHER SUCCULENTS

WITH A UNIQUE variety of sizes and shapes, and a wealth of colour and texture, cacti and other succulents can make spectacular displays. Their forms range from the symmetrical rosettes of *Echeveria* to the squat, globular *Echinocactus* and the fluted columns and candelabra of some desert cacti. Many bloom only briefly and bear large, brightly coloured flowers, while others flower for longer periods, producing a profusion of exquisite blooms. In cool-temperate climates, most cacti and succulents are grown in the greenhouse or as house plants, but hardier species also make beautiful garden specimens. In warmer climates, they offer scope to create an outdoor desert garden. Whether grown as focal plants or grouped for contrast of form and texture, cacti and other succulents are ideal for containers, both indoors and out.

Using cacti and other succulents

MANY cacti are native to the desert regions of the southern USA, Mexico, and South America, where rainfall is low and intermittent, and there are great extremes of temperature. In contrast, some of the most floriferous cacti originate in the warm, humid rainforests of Central and South America. These plants are usually epiphytic, which means that they grow on other plants, either weaving through host trees or lodging in niches in their branches.

Other succulent plants occur in a far greater range of habitats than cacti, and, since they are found in at least 20 different plant families, show a wide diversity of characteristics. Their natural habitats include the semi-arid regions of Central America, Africa, and Australasia, as well as the more temperate and cold climates of Asia, and northern parts of Europe and America.

Characteristics of succulents

Cacti and other succulents exhibit a few adaptations such as reduced leaf size and loss of leaves in very dry weather, designed to conserve water by reducing transpiration. The one distinguishing feature that is common to all, however, is the presence of water-storing, fleshy tissue in the stems, leaves, or roots. It is this tissue that allows succulent plants to withstand long periods of drought.

Cacti are easily distinguished from other succulents by structures called areoles – the cushion-like growths on their stems from which the spines, hairs, flowers, and shoots develop.

Succulent plants may be loosely divided into three groups, depending on which part of the plant contains the moisture-retaining tissue. Some genera, for example *Euphorbia*, may be represented in more than one group. Most cacti are stem succulents, as are some succulent plants from the Asclepiadaceae and Euphorbiaceae families. Others, including *Aloe, Echeveria, Lithops,* and *Sedum*, are leafy succulents. Plants in the third group are known as caudiciform succulents and have the water-storing tissue in a swollen rootstock (the caudex), although this often extends into the stem, as in *Adenium obesum*. Plants that belong to this group are mostly found within the families Apocynaceae, Cucurbitaceae, and Convolvulaceae.

Form and habit

The diverse forms and growth habits of cacti and succulent plants may be used to create a range of effects. Tall columns of *Cleistocactus strausii*, for example, make strong, vertical lines that contrast with foreground

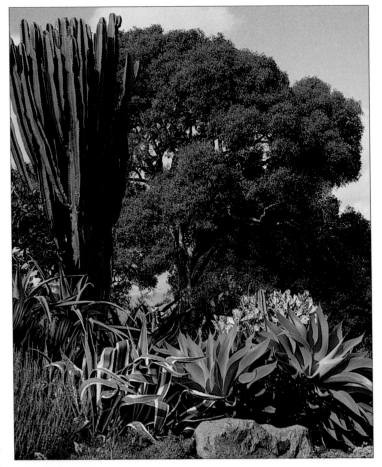

A natural grouping
Collections of succulent plants make an impressive sight. Here Euphorbia canariensis *towers above* Agave americana *'Marginata' and* A. attenuata.

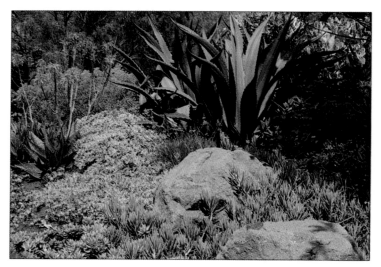

Variety of form
The strong, architectural leaves of Agave americana (*centre*) *make a fine contrast with the orange flower spikes of the* Aloe (*left*) *and the prostrate, blue-grey leaves of a* Senecio *cultivar in the foreground.*

FLOWERING CACTI AND SUCCULENTS

Thelocactus setispinus

Oroya peruviana

Parodia chrysacanthion

Strombocactus disciformis

Lithops pseudotruncatella var. dendritica

Rebutia fiebrigii

plantings of smaller, spherical forms, such as *Echinocactus grusonii*, or the flattened segments of some *Opuntia*.

Several species have a creeping habit that adds a horizontal element to the garden design. *Carpobrotus edulis*, *Lampranthus*, and *Ruschia*, make dense carpets of growth that provide excellent ground cover.

Trailing succulents like *Ceropegia linearis* subsp. *woodii*, *Rhipsalis*, and *Schlumbergera* produce cascades of slender stems or leaves that are seen to best effect in hanging baskets. Several are scrambling climbers: *Selenicereus* and *Aloe ciliaris* add height to mixed plantings if given the support of trellis or the branch of a tree. In warm, frost-free climates, the jointed, climbing stems of *Hylocereus* are most effective when allowed to spread over walls.

Flowering cacti and other succulents

Cacti and succulents often produce exquisite blooms and flower regularly once they have reached maturity, but this may take between 1 and

40 years. Most are day-blooming, with individual blossoms sometimes lasting several days. Some epiphytic cacti are winter-flowering and have blooms carried in succession over extensive periods.

Others bloom only briefly, the flowers sometimes appearing soon after sunset and fading as evening advances. Many of the large, columnar cacti produce buds that gradually unfold during the evening and then fade in the early morning hours.

The flowers, often of delicate appearance and silken texture, are usually extremely large in comparison with the size of the plant, and their colour range is mainly at the warm end of the spectrum with a profusion of rich yellows, hot scarlets, and vivid carmines. A few genera, often those of the family Mesembryanthemaceae, and some of the epiphytes, have sweetly scented blooms. Some species, especially members of Agavaceae, are monocarpic, and die after they flower and set seed. A number of small, non-flowering offsets often form around the flowering rosette; when mature, they flower in subsequent years.

Outdoor display

With careful selection and skilful arrangement, collections of cacti and succulents may be grown outdoors even in relatively cool conditions. But few succulents tolerate excess moisture; even hardy species require good drainage – these grow well in raised beds where water drains away freely. Among the hardiest are *Opuntia humifusa*, *Sedum*, and houseleeks (*Sempervivum*), along with some *Crassula* and *Umbilicus*.

With sharp drainage and a good baking in summer, several desert plants, particularly some *Opuntia*, and *Echinocereus* withstand surprisingly low temperatures – although not the combination of cold and wet.

In mild areas with few frosts, the range of plants extends to include the spectacular rosettes of *Agave americana* and its cultivars, *A. filifera*, and *Beschorneria yuccoides*. Half-hardy species need a freely draining site with the shelter of a warm, sunny wall for additional protection. Where

temperatures are unlikely to fall much below 7–10°C (45–50°F), as in the southern and south-western USA and southerly parts of Europe, there are few restrictions outdoors.

Mixed plantings

When growing non-succulent and succulent plants together, it is important to choose plants that have similar needs for light, soil type, and

Cacti and succulents in a changing climate

With climate change causing milder winters, warmer summers and autumns, and higher mean annual temperatures, many cacti and succulents once grown only in greenhouses or as houseplants, are now successful outside with no, or minimal, winter protection.

Clearly there will be regional differences and while snow and frost may become rare events over the next 50 or more years, it is forecast that a larger percentage of our annual rainfall will occur in winter than at present. This may limit the cultivation of cacti and succulents that require dry winters; they would need to be grown in very well-drained sites.

Some species of *Agave*, *Aloe*, *Echeveria*, succulent *Euphorbia*, and other genera thrive unprotected in the Scilly Isles already, and are now being tried outside elsewhere in the UK.

HARDY AND HALF-HARDY CACTI AND SUCCULENTS

Opuntia ficus-indica (hardy)

Maihuenia poeppigii (hardy)

Beschorneria yuccoides (half hardy)

Agave filifera (half hardy)

watering regime. In frost-free gardens, compatible non-succulents include *Fuchsia*, *Nerium*, *Gazania*, and *Rehmannia*, all of which provide additional colour and variety. Bulbous plants such as *Clivia*, *Cyrtanthus*, and *Sprekelia* are also good choices in mixed plantings in the appropriate climates.

In cooler regions, slow-growing and compact annual species as well as plants that are grown as annuals, such as *Lampranthus* and *Portulaca grandiflora*, are suitable for planting outdoors among groups of perennial cacti and succulents.

Desert gardens

In arid climates where temperatures seldom fall below 10°C (50°F), the complete range of cacti and other succulents may be grown in a desert garden to create a fine landscape feature. In places where the subsoil is particularly heavy, collections of plants may be grown in raised beds to ensure the excellent drainage that these plants require.

Use smaller species at the front of the bed, so that their delicate beauty is not obscured by taller plants. Allow clump-forming plants, such as *Echeveria*, *Haworthia*, and *Mammillaria*, sufficient space to develop fully. These low-growing, cluster-forming species flower at different periods from spring to autumn, to give colour during the warmer months.

For background planting, erect, columnar cacti and other succulents are ideal. Choose plants such as the tall, single-stemmed *Cephalocereus senilis*, the branching *Cleistocactus strausii*, or the towering, tree-like form of *Euphorbia candelabrum*.

A desert garden
The branching arms of Euphorbia candelabrum *balance the surrounding globular and columnar cacti to complete this striking collection.*

Containers outdoors

Most cacti and succulents have shallow roots and respond well to being grown in containers. Select containers that enhance the shape and form of the plants – a wide, shallow bowl, for example, is the natural choice for displaying low-growing and creeping species, whereas those with stronger form, such as *Agave attenuata*, are much more suitable for large pots or urns.

Troughs are particularly useful for creating imaginative combinations of plants of quite different sizes and habits, and hanging baskets are suitable for displaying trailing and pendent species.

Choosing and siting plants

In cool regions, but where temperatures seldom fall below freezing, many species will thrive outdoors in troughs and pots, provided that these are raised above the ground to allow water to drain away freely. A warm, sheltered position such as a corner of a covered patio or balcony, where the plants can more easily be protected from rain, will provide the ideal environment.

The foliage shapes of *Sedum* and neat rosettes of *Sempervivum* may be used to form a contrast with the leafy forms and brilliant blooms of *Lewisia* species and cultivars, or with the green-flowered *Echinocereus viridiflorus* and the scarlet, early

summer blooms of *Echinopsis chamaecereus*. Other species, such as *Agave parryi*, with symmetrical rosettes of plump, grey-green leaves, or *Opuntia polyacantha*, which puts on a brilliant display of yellow flowers, may make striking focal points if they are planted on their own in large bowls.

In warmer climates, there is much greater scope for growing cacti and other succulents outdoors in containers. In large pots, group plants that flower at different periods and have striking foliage forms: the purple-leaved *Aeonium* 'Zwartkop', *Aloe vera*, which has yellow flowers, and red-flowered *Crassula perfoliata* var. *minor* provide structural interest all year, and give a succession of attractive blooms through the warmer months.

Where temperatures do not consistently fall below 13°C (55°F), many dwarf cacti, such as *Gymnocalycium*, *Mammillaria*, and *Rebutia*, make fascinating displays of form and texture in outdoor bowls and troughs in the garden. These dwarf, cluster-forming species also give a magnificent display of vibrant colour that lasts for many weeks in summer.

Indoor display

The protected environment of the greenhouse or conservatory, which allows almost complete control of light, temperature, humidity, and water, provides ideal conditions for an extensive range of succulents and cacti – most plants recommended for outdoor cultivation in warm climates will thrive under cover in cooler regions. The adaptations these plants

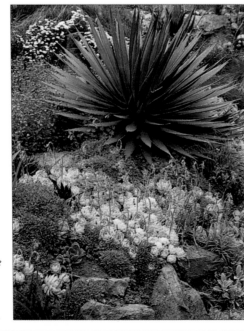

Mixed planting
The neat rosettes and delicate, nodding flowerheads of Echeveria *provide a dainty contrast with the strap-like leaves of* Agave filifera *(centre), the focal point of this attractive arrangement.*

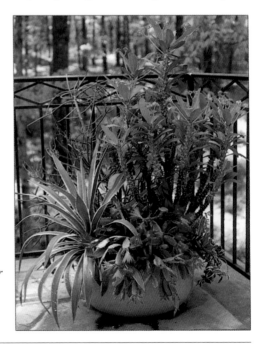

An outdoor container
This varied collection of tall, spreading, and pendent cacti and other succulents creates a highly decorative and unusual feature on a balcony outdoors.

An indoor bed
The bright foliage of Agave americana *'Mediopicta', offset by the rosettes of* Orostachys chanetii, *is a fine centrepiece in this greenhouse bed.*

A hanging basket
The graceful stems and flowers of Kalanchoe manginii *cascade like a waterfall against the house wall.*

have made to help them to survive in harsh, arid environments in the wild also make them very suitable for the warm, dry conditions of a centrally heated home, where many other plants may fail to thrive.

The variation in shape and habit, and their beautiful flowers, ensure that these plants provide interest throughout the year, and, since different species are adapted to a variety of environmental conditions, they may be selected for a number of situations in the home.

Providing the right conditions

Most cacti and succulents need high light levels, warmth, and good ventilation to thrive, although some, the leafy succulents in particular, may need protection from direct sun in summer to avoid leaf scorch.

There is an important group that requires shady conditions, or at least filtered light: the epiphytes, mainly from humid and shaded rainforests of Central and South America.

Epiphytic plants are among the most floriferous of cacti and other succulents, and they can be used to great effect to add bold splashes of colour and interest to shady corners of the home or garden. The best known of this group are the Christmas cactus (*Schlumbergera* x *buckleyi*), *Hatiora gaertneri*, and *H. rosea*. Some of the loveliest are the magnificent hybrids created by crossing *Epiphyllum* with species or hybrids of *Echinopsis*, *Heliocereus*, *Hylocereus*, and *Nopalxochia*. These hybrids produce extraordinarily beautiful, and sometimes fragrant, flowers in spring and summer, in colours ranging from pure white, through cream, yellow, and orange to red and deepest purple.

Plants for the greenhouse and conservatory

Plants in a greenhouse or conservatory may be grown in pots or open beds, either at floor level or raised on benches. Planting in open beds offers potential for growing larger species and even for creating a miniature desert garden.

When in growth, many species from warm habitats need bright light, a fairly dry atmosphere, and a temperature of 18°C (64°F) if they are to develop to their full potential and bear flowers. These conditions are more easily provided under glass than in a home environment, and many cacti grow and flower most successfully in a greenhouse.

Some, notably *Rhipsalis*, require relatively high levels of humidity (80 per cent) to thrive, and will nearly always perform best in the humid atmosphere of a conservatory. Other groups that are very suitable for the conservatory and greenhouse are those that need space to flower well.

Greenhouse display
The rich colour and diverse forms of, among others, Crassula, Echeveria, Echinocactus, *and* Mammillaria *provide a sumptuous collection of plants for the greenhouse bench.*

Among them are the clambering *Selenicereus* (the most outstanding species being Queen-of-the-night, *S. grandiflorus*) and several species of *Hylocereus*, which all prefer a site in filtered light.

When drawing up planting plans for a greenhouse or conservatory, combine groups of cacti and other succulents that have similar cultural needs, to make maintenance easier.

Container-growing indoors

If provided with warm, bright, and draught-free conditions, many cacti and other succulents will thrive in indoor containers. Use small pots for displaying individual plants, or large bowls for planting a variety of compatible species together.

Make sure that you wear thick, leather gloves when handling spiny plants including *Agave*, *Aloe*, and *Opuntia*, because their sharp spines may easily become embedded in your fingers if you brush against them, causing a painful injury.

Bowl gardens

If planted with different species that have the same cultural requirements, bowl gardens are a particularly effective way to grow succulent plants indoors. One or two plants with an erect habit, for example young specimens of *Cephalocereus*, *Cleistocactus*, or other columnar genera, may provide the focal point of the bowl. Alternatively, use a leafy succulent such as *Crassula ovata* as the main plant. Fill the rest of the bowl with smaller plants, such as *Echeveria* and *Haworthia*. Free-flowering cacti such as *Mammillaria*, *Parodia*, and other globular cacti are also good choices for planting in a bowl garden indoors.

Hanging baskets

Cacti and succulents in hanging baskets make colourful displays in the home or conservatory. Pendent cacti such as *Aporocactus flagelliformis*, and trailing succulent plants such as *Kalanchoe*, *Hatiora gaertneri*, and *Schlumbergera* are the most suitable plants to choose, since they will trail attractively over the edge of the basket. *Sedum morganianum* and other semi-trailing species are also very effective in hanging baskets (see also "Planter's guide to cacti and other succulents", p.342).

Plant hanging baskets with just one specimen, or use several species for a harmonious but varied arrangement. In general, non-epiphytic plantings require bright light, but epiphytes need partly shaded conditions or bright but filtered light, so position the baskets accordingly.

Planter's guide to cacti and other succulents

DAMP CONDITIONS

Succulents that tolerate damp conditions
Crithmum maritimum
Salicornia europaea
Suaeda maritima, S. vera
Umbilicus horizontalis var.
  intermedius, U. rupestris

SHADE

Succulents that tolerate light shade
Lewisia Cotyledon Hybrids,
  L. leeana
Orostachys chanetii ❋, *O. spinosa* ❋
Rhodiola wallichiana
Sedum dasyphyllum, S. sediforme,
  S. spectabile, S. ternatum,
  S. villosum
Sempervivum arachnoideum,
  S. ruthenicum

BOWLS AND TROUGHS

Sun
Adenium obesum ❋
Aeonium arboreum ❋,
  A. nobile ❋
Agave filifera ❋, *A. stricta* ❋,
  A. victoriae-reginae ❋
Aloe humilis ❋, *A. longistyla* ❋,
  A. rauhii ❋
Astrophytum myriostigma ❋,
  A. ornatum ❋
Cephalocereus senilis ❋
Cereus uruguayanus ❋, *C. validus* ❋
Cleistocactus strausii ❋
Cotyledon campanulata ❋,
  C. orbiculata var. *orbiculata* ❋
Crassula ovata ❋,
  C. perfoliata var. *minor* ❋,
  C. rupestris ❋, *C. socialis* ❋
Echeveria agavoides ❋,
  E. derenbergii ❋, *E. pilosa* ❋
Echinocactus grusonii ❋
Echinocereus berlandieri ❋,
  E. pentalophus ❋

*Echinocereus
pentalophus*

Echinopsis atacamensis subsp.
  pasacana ❋, *E. chamaecereus* ❋,
  E. eyriesii ❋, *E. haematantha* ❋,
  E. marsoneri ❋, *E. oxygona* ❋,
  E. pachanoi ❋, *E. pentlandii* ❋,
  E. spachiana ❋
Espostoa lanata ❋
Euphorbia flanaganii, E. milii ❋,
  E. obesa ❋
Faucaria felina ❋
Ferocactus cylindraceus ❋,
  F. latispinus ❋

Gasteria batesiana ❋,
  G. bicolor var. *liliputana* ❋
Glottiphyllum linguiforme ❋
Gymnocalycium baldianum ❋,
  G. gibbosum ❋, *G. mihanovichii* ❋
Haworthia cooperi ❋,
  H. limifolia ❋, *H. reinwardtii* ❋
Jatropha podagrica
Kalanchoe blossfeldiana ❋
Lithops dorotheae ❋,
  L. karasmontana subsp. *bella* ❋
Mammillaria bocasana ❋,
  M. compressa ❋, *M. gracilis* ❋,
  M. hahniana ❋, *M. mystax* ❋,
  M. rhodantha ❋,
  M. spinosissima ❋,
  M. zeilmanniana ❋
Opuntia microdasys ❋
Orbea variegata ❋
Pachypodium geayi ❋, *P. lamerei* ❋
Parodia leninghausii ❋,
  P. mutabilis ❋
Rebutia albiflora ❋, *R. arenacea* ❋,
  R. aureiflora ❋, *R. heliosa* ❋,
  R. marsoneri ❋, *R. minuscula* ❋,
  R. senilis ❋, *R. steinbachii* subsp.
  steinbachii ❋
Sansevieria trifasciata 'Hahnii' ❋,
  S. trifasciata
  'Laurentii' ❋

*Thelocactus
bicolor*

*Thelocactus
bicolor* ❋,
  T. rinconensis ❋

Partial shade
Epiphyllum oxypetalum ❋
  (and hybrids)
Hatiora gaertneri ❋, *H. rosea* ❋
Hoya australis ❋, *H. carnosa* ❋
Schlumbergera x *buckleyi* ❋,
  S. truncata ❋ (and hybrids)

HANGING BASKETS

Aporocactus flagelliformis ❋
Ceropegia haygarthii ❋, *C. linearis*
  subsp. *woodii* ❋
Disocactus ❋
Epiphyllum oxypetalum ❋
  (and hybrids)
Hatiora gaertneri ❋, *H. rosea* ❋,
  H. salicornioides ❋
Heliocereus ❋ (most spp.)
Hoya lanceolata subsp. *bella* ❋,
  H. linearis ❋, *H. polyneura* ❋
Kalanchoe jongsmanii ❋,
  K. manginii ❋, *K. pumila* ❋
Rhipsalis cereuscula ❋,
  R. mesembryanthemoides ❋,
  R. pachyptera ❋
Schlumbergera x *buckleyi* ❋,
  S. truncata ❋ (and hybrids)
Sedum morganianum ❋
Selenicereus ❋

LOWER TEMPERATURES

Succulents that tolerate temperatures down to 0°C (32°F)
Agave americana ❋, *A. lophantha* ❋,
  A. parryi ❋, *A. utahensis* ❋
Echinocereus viridiflorus ❋
Echinopsis chamaecereus ❋
Opuntia erinacea ❋, *O. ficus-indica* ❋
Sedum anglicum, S. cyaneum ❋,
  S. dasyphyllum, S. formosanum ❋,
  S. hispanicum, S. lanceolatum,
  S. rupestre, S. spectabile
Sempervivum (most spp.)
Umbilicus (spp. only)

Succulents that tolerate temperatures down to 7°C (45°F)
Agave attenuata ❋, *A. parviflora* ❋
Aloe arborescens ❋, *A. aristata* ❋,
  A. brevifolia ❋, *A. distans* ❋,
  A. variegata ❋, *A. vera* ❋
Austrocylindropuntia subulata ❋
Bulbine frutescens ❋, *B. latifolia* ❋,
  B. mesembryanthemoides ❋
Caralluma europaea ❋
Carpobrotus acinaciformis ❋,
  C. edulis ❋
Cereus aethiops ❋, *C. jamacaru* ❋
  (and other columnar spp.)
Crassula sarcocaulis ❋,
  C. sarmentosa ❋
Delosperma ❋ (most spp.)
Echeveria coccinea ❋,
  E. cuspidata ❋, *E. elegans* ❋,
  E. gibbiflora ❋
Echinocereus enneacanthus ❋,
  E. pentalophus ❋
Echinopsis chamaecereus ❋,
  E. viridiflorus subsp. *chloranthus* ❋
Gasteria carinata ❋,
  G. carinata var. *verrucosa* ❋,
  G. disticha ❋
Gibbaeum album ❋

*Kalanchoe
delagoensis*

*Kalanchoe
  delagoensis* ❋, *K. marmorata* ❋
Lampranthus falcatus ❋,
  L. roseus ❋
Lewisia Cotyledon Hybrids
Maihuenia poeppigii ❋
Opuntia fragilis ❋,
  O. polyacantha ❋, *O. robusta* ❋,
  O. subulata ❋
Orostachys chanetii ❋,
  O. spinosa ❋
Pelargonium acetosum ❋,
  P. echinatum ❋,
  P. tetragonum ❋
Senecio haworthii ❋,
  S. macroglossus ❋

FLOWERING CACTI

Day-flowering
Aporocactus flagelliformis ❋
Astrophytum myriostigma ❋

*Astrophytum
myriostigma*

Bergerocactus emoryi ❋
Cleistocactus strausii ❋
Echinocereus engelmannii ❋,
  E. triglochidiatus ❋
Echinopsis aurea ❋,
  E. famatimensis ❋,
  E. mamillosa ❋, *E. oxygona* ❋
Epiphyllum anguliger ❋,
  E. crenatum ❋
Gymnocalycium bruchii ❋
Hatiora gaertneri ❋, *H. rosea* ❋,
  H. salicornioides ❋
Heliocereus speciosus
  var. *superbus* ❋
Mammillaria blossfeldiana ❋,
  M. bocasana ❋, *M. grahamii* ❋,
  M. hahniana ❋,
  M. spinosissima ❋,
  M. zeilmanniana ❋
Matucana aureiflora ❋
Nopalxochia phyllanthoides ❋
Opuntia lanceolata ❋,
  O. paraguayensis ❋
Parodia brevihamata ❋,
  P. graessneri ❋, *P. haselbergii* ❋,
  P. leninghausii ❋,
  P. mammulosa ❋, *P. mutabilis* ❋
Rebutia arenacea ❋,
  R. aureiflora ❋, *R. marsoneri* ❋,
  R. neocumingii ❋, *R. senilis* ❋
Schlumbergera x *buckleyi* ❋,
  S. truncata ❋
Thelocactus bicolor ❋

Night-flowering
Cephalocereus senilis ❋
Echinopsis deserticola ❋,
  E. mirabilis ❋, *E. spachiana* ❋,
  E. terscheckii ❋
Epiphyllum cartagense ❋
Espostoa lanata ❋, *E. melanostele* ❋
Haageocereus acranthus ❋,
  H. pseudomelanostele ❋,
  H. versicolor ❋
Harrisia gracilis ❋, *H. pomanensis* ❋
Hylocereus ocamponis ❋
Pachycereus pringlei ❋
Selenicereus anthonyanus ❋,
  S. grandiflorus ❋,
  S. macdonaldiae ❋
Stenocereus ❋ (most spp.)

Key
❋ *Not hardy*

Soil preparation and planting

MANY cacti and other succulents grow naturally only in desert or jungle conditions, but they also make striking displays out of doors in cooler climates. Whether they are grown indoors or outside, specially prepared, well-drained soil or compost is essential. A sunny site with adequate protection from frost is also required for most species.

Buying cacti and other succulents

When buying cacti and other succulents, choose only healthy, unblemished plants that show new growth or have flower buds forming. Do not buy damaged or slightly shrivelled specimens, or any with dull, dry, or flaccid segments. Also reject plants that have outgrown their pots.

Planting in a raised bed or desert garden

Cacti and other succulents require well-drained conditions, so they benefit from being planted in a bed

RAISED BED CONSTRUCTION

Top-dressing *Compost* *Drainage material*

A raised bed has a deep gravel base and free-draining compost.

SELECTING CACTI AND SUCCULENTS

GOOD EXAMPLE

New buds forming

POOR EXAMPLE

Healthy growth

Rebutia

Damaged growth

GOOD EXAMPLE

Plump, fleshy leaves

Healthy, new growth

POOR EXAMPLE

Crassula ovata

Shrivelled leaves

Handling cacti

Most cacti have sharp spines. When moving or planting them, either wear leather gloves or take other protective measures.

When handling spiny cacti, such as this Ferocactus, *wrap a loop of folded paper around the plant.*

that is raised at least 25cm (10in) above ground level. To ensure good drainage make the bed slightly sloping and provide a thick base of gravel or crocks that is at least one third of the total height of the bed.

Never construct the bed on a concrete or other impermeable base as this impedes drainage. Choose a bright, sunny site with a minimum temperature of 5°C (41°F). In cooler areas, provide adequate protection for tender species (see FROST AND WIND PROTECTION, pp.612–613).

Preparing the soil and compost mix

Cacti and other succulents do not usually thrive in ordinary garden soil, because it is not sufficiently

well drained; it needs to be replaced by, or supplemented with, a carefully prepared growing medium. Good garden loam that has a pH level of 4–5.5 may be used as the basis of a homemade compost. It must be sterilized first, however, to kill pests or weed seeds that might be present, and to eliminate diseases.

To prepare the compost, mix 2 parts sterilized garden loam with 1 part peat substitute or fine shredded sphagnum or sedge peat, 1 part sharp sand or washed grit, and a little slow-release fertilizer.

If the garden loam is alkaline, use a loam-based proprietary compost mixed with sharp sand or grit in a ratio of 1 part sand or grit to 3 parts compost.

Placing the plant in the bed

Remove the plant from its pot. Carefully tease out the roots, checking them for disease or pest infestation (see also p.345), and treat any infections before planting.

Dig a hole of appropriate size and place the plant so that its base is at the same level in the soil as it was in its container. Fill in around the roots with compost, and firm, making sure that the stems and leaves are above soil level. Top-dress with grit, to protect the plants from excess moisture and reduce soil water evaporation. Allow the plants to settle, then water, lightly at first, gradually increasing the amount until the plants are well established and producing new growth.

PLANTING IN A BED OUTDOORS

Harden off indoor plants for a few days in the shade prior to planting out. Select a planting position in a prepared, well-drained bed, allowing space for the development of the plant and those around it. Clear the top-dressing from the planting area, then dig a hole large enough to accommodate the root ball.

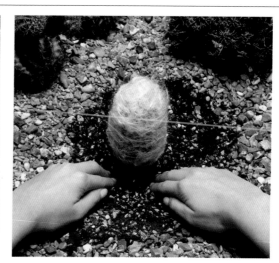

1 *Remove the cactus from its pot, wearing gloves if need be. Gently tease out the roots and place the cactus in the hole at the same depth as it was in the pot.*

2 *Spread out the roots, then fill in and firm the compost. Replace the top-dressing. Water after 3–4 days when the plant has settled.*

Succulents in containers

A collection of cacti and other succulents grown in pots, bowls, or troughs provides an attractive focal point on a patio or windowsill.

Preparing the potting compost

The compost used should be well-drained and preferably slightly acid with a pH of 5.5–6.5. Use 1 part sand or grit to either 3 parts loam-based compost or 2 parts loamless compost.

A slightly more acid potting compost may be needed for epiphytic succulents, such as certain *Hoya*, and cacti – *Rhipsalis* and *Schlumbergera* in particular – native to forest areas. Mix 1 part humus (such as peat substitute, sphagnum peat, or leaf mould) with 2 parts standard potting compost; add sufficient sand or grit to ensure adequate drainage.

Choosing the container

Both clay and plastic containers are suitable for growing cacti and other succulents. Potting compost in plastic pots retains moisture longer than that in clay ones, which means that the plants need less frequent watering, but clay pots provide better aeration around the roots. Choose containers that have one or more holes in the base to ensure that water drains away quickly. The size of pot or container should always be proportionate to the size of the plant but never less than 10cm (4in) deep; for tuberous-rooted species such as *Echinocereus*, a pot with a depth of at least 15cm (6in) is preferable.

Planting in containers

Always wash all containers thoroughly before use to remove possible sources of infection. Place a layer of drainage material (washed gravel or broken crocks) in the base, to approximately one third of the depth of the container; large troughs as well as deep bell- or urn-shaped pots need at least an 8cm (3in) base of gravel or crocks to ensure sufficiently sharp drainage. Fill the container with compost to within 1cm (½in) of the rim.

Carefully remove the plant from its pot, discarding any top-dressing and loosening the root ball. Insert it into the new container so that the plant is at the same level in the compost as it was in the original pot. Firm it into the compost, and top-dress with coarse gravel or with grit.

When planting several cacti or other succulents in one container, space the plants so that there is room for them to develop. To create a more natural effect, decorative pieces of rock or pebbles may be added to the composition.

Allow the plants to settle for a few days before watering; water routinely (see p.345) only when the plants are well established.

Hanging baskets

To create an attractive and slightly unusual feature, plant trailing succulent species in a hanging basket. Make sure that the basket is completely clean. Wire baskets should be lined with a proprietary liner or a layer of sphagnum moss. Do not line the basket with plastic sheeting, because this will restrict drainage. If using a plastic basket that has a fixed drainage tray, place a layer of small pebbles or gravel in the base instead of sphagnum moss.

Fill the basket with an appropriate potting compost, without disturbing the moss or pebbles, then insert the plants in the same way as for other containers. Do not overcrowd the basket, as most suitable species have a naturally spreading or pendent habit; one plant is often sufficient to fill an average-sized basket. Top-dress with gravel or grit if extra drainage is required; allow to settle for a few days before watering. Once the plant is established and showing new growth, routine watering may be applied (see p.345).

PLANTING IN A BOWL

Crassula ovata • Cereus uruguayanus • Mammillaria muehlenpfordtii • Aloe 'Black Gem' • Mammillaria polythele

1 Select a group of plants that have similar cultivation requirements. Arrange the group by positioning the pots in the container, placing the taller plants at the back or in the centre of the planting.

2 Prepare the container, placing a shallow layer of drainage material – gravel or crocks – in the base and covering this with a layer of compost (1 part sharp sand, 3 parts loam-based potting compost).

3 Remove the plants from their pots, place them in the container, and infill with compost.

4 Top-dress the planted container with a 5mm (¼in) layer of 3mm (⅛in) gravel.

PLANTING IN A HANGING BASKET

1 Line a wire hanging basket with a layer of moist sphagnum moss. The layer should be 3cm (1¼in) thick when compressed.

2 Fill the basket almost to the brim with a mix of 1 part sharp sand to 3 parts loam-based potting compost. Prepare a hole for the plant in the centre of the basket.

3 Insert the plant (here a Schlumbergera), spreading out the roots. Infill with compost so that there are no air pockets around the roots.

4 Wait for 2–3 days after planting before watering the finished basket.

Routine care

Cacti and other succulents need little maintenance in order to thrive, but they must have adequate light, warmth, and ventilation. Feed and water as appropriate for the particular species, and check regularly for signs of diseases or pests. Repot plants in containers as soon as they outgrow them, to prevent them from becoming pot-bound.

The right environment

Place cacti and other succulents in a position that is appropriate to their cultural needs. Most species need to be in full sun, although some prefer to be situated in dappled shade. The maximum daytime temperature in spring and summer should be 27–30°C (81–6°F), and the night-time temperature 13–19°C (55–66°F). During the dormant season, most plants should be kept at a temperature of at least 7–10°C (45–50°F), although species originating from the tropics and equatorial regions may require a warmer environment, with a minimum temperature range of 13–19°C (55–66°F).

Ventilation

Although good ventilation is essential, cacti and other succulents should not be exposed to draughts. For plants grown in a greenhouse it may become necessary to use blinds or to apply proprietary shading paint to the outside of the glass, if ventilation is insufficient to keep the temperature below 27–30°C (81–6°F) (see "Shading", p.576). If the weather is exceptionally hot, watering the greenhouse floor will help to reduce the temperature. Occasionally, plants grown in the open may need some shade to protect them in conditions of extreme heat.

Watering and feeding

Water only when the plants are in active growth (not during their resting period). For most cacti and other succulents this is in summer, but epiphytes and succulents from forested areas bloom principally between late autumn and early spring. In the dormant season, do not water unless temperatures remain high, and then only enough to prevent complete dehydration.

Watering

During the growing season, moisten the soil or potting compost thoroughly with water, allowing it almost to dry out before watering again. Provided that the plants are grown in a free-draining medium, surplus moisture will drain away quickly.

Water early in the day or in the late evening, as the plants may scorch if they are covered in water droplets in bright sunshine. Alternatively, plants that are grown in pots may be watered by placing the container in a shallow pan of water, so that the water permeates the compost but does not touch the stems or leaves. Remove the container from the water to drain as soon as the surface of the compost appears moist; the plants will rot if left standing in water.

Epiphytic plants and those that need shaded conditions should be kept moist but not wet: an occasional, light mist-spray maintains a reasonable level of humidity.

Feeding

During the growing season, feed cacti and other succulents to help maintain healthy, vigorous growth and to encourage flowering. Several proprietary fertilizers are available but a standard, well-balanced liquid fertilizer containing all the major nutrients is satisfactory. Apply every two to three weeks during the growing season. Never apply fertilizer when a plant is dormant or the soil is dry, because this may damage the stems and foliage.

Hygiene

Cacti and other succulents may need occasional cleaning, as dust sometimes accumulates on the leaves or between the spines. During the growing season, house plants may be sprayed lightly with water; succulents in the greenhouse or garden may be hosed down carefully, provided that they are not in direct sun.

Pests and diseases

Check cacti and other succulents routinely for pests and diseases. The most prevalent pests are mealybugs (p.646), scale insects (p.648), red spider mite (p.646), root mealybugs (see "Mealybugs", p.646), and sciarid flies (see "Fungus gnats or sciarid flies", p.666).

Diseases of cacti and succulents are rare, although poor cultural conditions or excess nitrogen in the soil may encourage the development of black rot, which principally affects epiphytic cacti and *Stapelia*. The plants become disfigured and may die. There is no treatment, so, if it appears that a plant is likely to die as a result of infection, take healthy shoots or sections as cuttings and grow them on to replace the diseased plant.

Repotting

Cacti and other succulents should be repotted as soon as the roots reach the sides of their pot – usually every two to three years for fast-growing species. Repot slower-growing plants every three to four years, even if they have not yet outgrown their pot.

Carefully remove the plant from its original container. Inspect the roots, looking for signs of pests or disease, and treat if appropriate. Cut out any roots that are dehydrated or dead, and dust the remainder with fungicide. Choose a new container one size larger than the original, and repot in fresh compost, ensuring the planting depth is the same.

REPOTTING SUCCULENTS

1 *When a succulent (here Aloe arborescens) has outgrown its container, repot it, selecting a container that is at least one size larger than the current one. Carefully slide the plant out of its pot.*

2 *Gently tease out any roots that have become coiled or compressed.*

3 *Place some crocks and a little compost in the new pot. Position the plant at the same depth as it was in the previous container.*

4 *Carefully infill around the root ball with more compost. As you add the compost, firm it in stages to eliminate any air pockets between the roots. Wait until the plant is settled in the new pot before watering.*

Propagation

CACTI and other succulents may be propagated from seed, from leaf or stem cuttings, by division, or by grafting. Division and cuttings are the easiest methods. Raising plants from seed is slower and more difficult but provides the opportunity to obtain selected variants from within species, and to raise new hybrids by hand pollination. Grafting is useful for rare species and hybrids, and for slow-growing succulents that are difficult to propagate by other methods.

Propagating plants from seed

Seeds of cacti and other succulents vary widely in shape and size, and some have special requirements. Some fine seeds are slow to germinate, while some of the larger ones have a thick coating (eg those of several *Opuntia* species) and seldom germinate unless they have been stratified – they should be placed in a refrigerator for 48 hours.

Sowing

Sow seed under cover between late winter and late spring. Place a layer of coarse gravel, combined with a sprinkling of charcoal chippings, in the base of a seed tray or pot. Fill to the top with seed compost, then level and firm lightly.

Sprinkle fine seeds evenly over the surface, barely cover with sterilized, sharp sand or a sand and grit mix, then water lightly from above. Larger seeds should be pressed into the compost, allowing ample space between them, and covered with coarse sand or grit. Stand pots or trays of larger seeds in tepid water and leave them until the upper surface of the soil is moist, then remove the containers and let the surplus moisture drain.

Place the containers in a propagator, maintaining a temperature of 21°C (70°F). Alternatively, seeds in pots may be sealed in a clear plastic bag. Keep the seeds in partial shade until they have germinated.

Care of seedlings

When the seedlings appear, remove the pots from the plastic bags or the propagator and provide additional ventilation. Spray the seedlings with fungicide to discourage damping off (see p.664). Maintain a temperature of 21°C (70°F), giving further light and air as the seedlings develop.

Pricking out

After six to twelve months (depending on the species), when the seedlings are at least thumbnail-sized, prick them out into a seed tray or, if substantial (as below), singly into small pots. Prepare the pot with a layer of crocks and fill almost to the brim with compost, then firm gently.

PROPAGATION FROM SEED

1 *Cover the base of the pot with crocks, then add at least 1cm (¹/₂in) of coarse gravel mixed with a little charcoal.*

2 *Fill the container to the brim with fresh seed compost, then level with a suitably shaped presser board to 1cm (¹/₂in) below the rim.*

3 *Sprinkle fine seeds evenly over the surface of the potting compost, tapping the seed packet side with a finger.*

4 *Cover the seeds with a top-dressing of sterilized, fine gritty sand – only a very thin layer is required. Water lightly.*

5 *Label and place the pot in a plastic bag. Keep in partial shade, at a minimum temperature of 21°C (70°F).*

SOWING LARGE SEED

Press each seed into the compost, sowing at twice the seed's own depth. Space seeds about 1cm (¹/₂in) apart, so that they have room to develop.

PRICKING OUT SEEDLINGS INTO INDIVIDUAL POTS

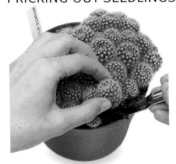

1 *When the seedlings are thumbnail-sized or larger, lift a clump from the pot, taking care not to damage the roots.*

2 *Divide the clump into individual small plants, retaining as much compost as possible around the roots (see inset).*

3 *Insert each seedling into a tray or pot containing 3 parts cactus compost to 1 part gritty sand. Keep the top-growth clear of the compost.*

4 *Top-dress with a 5mm (¹/₄in) layer of 3mm (¹/₈in) gravel, and label. Do not water the seedlings for 3 or 4 days.*

Remove a group of seedlings and separate them out carefully. Plant out the seedlings singly, top-dress them with a thin layer of gravel, and then label each pot. Keep the young plants at a minimum temperature of 15°C (59°F). After a few days, water them, sparingly at first, but then gradually increasing the amount until, after three weeks, the normal watering routine may be followed (see p.345).

Leaf cuttings

Some succulent plants, for example many species of *Crassula* and *Echeveria*, may be propagated from leaf cuttings. These should be taken from the parent plant in spring or early summer when there is plenty of new growth.

Choose firm, fleshy leaves and remove them carefully from the parent plant. Sever them with a sharp knife or pull them gently downwards, ensuring that a small piece of stem remains attached to the base of each. Put the severed cuttings on a clean piece of paper and place them in partial shade at a minimum temperature of 10°C (50°F). Leave them for a day or two until each one has formed a noticeable callus.

PROPAGATION FROM LEAF CUTTINGS

1 *Remove a healthy leaf by carefully pulling it away from the parent plant. It should break off at the base, with a small piece of stem attached.*

2 *Allow 24–48 hours for the wound to callus (see inset). Fill a pot with equal parts fine peat substitute (or peat) and sand. Insert the cutting so that the base is just held in the compost.*

3 *Top-dress with gravel or grit, and label. When new growth has been developing for about two weeks (see inset), the rooted cutting is ready to pot up into loam-based potting compost.*

Fill pots almost to the brim with equal parts of fine peat substitute (or peat) and sharp grit or sand. Each cutting should be inserted in an upright position in a pot so that the stem of the leaf is just held in place in the top of the compost. Firm the compost around the cuttings with your fingers.

Cover the surface with a light top-dressing of gravel or grit to help keep the cuttings in position. Label the pot, and place it in dappled shade, making sure that you maintain a regular temperature of 21°C (70°F). Keep the young cuttings moist by watering them every day with tepid water. Use a fine mist-spray to cause least disturbance to the cuttings.

Rooting does not take long, and normally occurs within a few days. Approximately two weeks after new growth appears, pot up the rooted cuttings into suitably sized pots, filling them with standard, loam-based potting compost.

Producing hybrids

When growing cacti and other succulents in a mixed collection, cross-pollination may occur, i.e. pollen from the flowers of one species or cultivar may pollinate those of another to produce hybrid offspring. Sometimes these hybrids are improvements on other types raised and may be worth propagating. More frequently, however, they are not worth keeping.

To be sure of raising plants with the desired characteristics, it is necessary to control the pollination process. Controlled pollination may be used to produce further plants of the same species, which retain the parental characteristics, or purposely to produce hybrid offspring from different species (which combine the characteristics of the parent plants).

To produce a new hybrid, choose the parent plants (usually species of the same genus) in an attempt to combine the best characteristics (eg leaf shape or flower colour) of both parents. To prevent open pollination by insects occurring, just before the stigma appears receptive or the anthers are ready to dehisce, tie a small paper bag loosely over the flowers that are to be used. Transfer the pollen from the anthers of one parent flower to the stigma of the second parent by hand, using a soft, fine brush. Then re-cover the hand-pollinated flower with a paper bag.

Many cacti and other succulents are not self-fertile, and it is essential to cross-pollinate in order to obtain seed. If a species is self-fertile, however, cover the flowers with a bag, as above, to prevent cross-pollination by insects. A gentle tap on the bag is usually sufficient to spread pollen onto the stigmas within the flower and effect self-pollination.

As the fruits ripen they become soft and fleshy and may release seed. If not, slice the fruits open and leave them for two or three days in a partially shaded but warm position so that the pulp dries out. Then wash the seed to remove the pulp and dry it on blotting paper before sowing.

To produce a batch of hybrid seed (here from a Schlumbergera), *dust pollen from the anthers of one of the selected parent flowers onto the stigmas of the other parent, using a fine-haired brush.*

CACTI AND SUCCULENTS FROM LEAF CUTTINGS

Adromischus cooperi ✿
Aeonium arboreum ✿
Begonia peltata ✿,
   B. venosa ✿
Cotyledon ladismithensis ✿,
   C. orbiculata var. *oblonga* ✿
Crassula, many including
   C. arborescens ✿,
   C. ovata ✿, *C. perfoliata* ✿,
   C. socialis ✿
Dudleya, most ✿
Echeveria, many including
   E. agavoides ✿,
   E. elegans ✿
Gasteria batesiana ✿
Graptopetalum ✿
Kalanchoe, many including
   K. beharensis ✿,
   K. daigremontiana ✿,
   K. tomentosa ✿
Lenophyllum pusillum ✿,
   L. texanum ✿

*Pachyphytum
oviferum*

Orostachys chanetii
Othonna dentata
Pachyphytum ✿
Peperomia dolabriformis ✿
Sedum, many including
   S. hintonii,
   S. sempervivoides ✿
Streptocarpus saxorum ✿
Thompsonella platyphylla ✿
Umbilicus chloranthus ✿

Key
✿ *Not hardy*

CACTI AND SUCCULENTS FROM STEM CUTTINGS OR SECTIONS

Adromischus ✤
Aeonium ✤
Aporocactus ✤
Bergerocactus ✤
Caralluma ✤
Cephalocereus ✤
Cereus ✤
Ceropegia ✤
Cleistocactus ✤
Cotyledon ✤
Crassula ✤
Disocactus ✤
Echeveria ✤
Epiphyllum ✤
Euphorbia, some ✤
Greenovia ✤
Heliocereus ✤
Huernia ✤
Kalanchoe ✤
Lampranthus ✤
Nopalxochia ✤
Opuntia, some ✤
Oreocereus ✤
Oscularia ✤
    (some spp.)
Pachycereus ✤
Pachyphytum ✤
Pedilanthus ✤
Pelargonium ✤ (some spp.)
Pereskia ✤
Rhipsalis ✤
Ruschia ✤
Sarcocaulon ✤
Schlumbergera ✤
Sedum, some ✤ (some spp.)
Selenicereus ✤
Senecio, some ✤
Stapelia ✤

Kalanchoe 'Wendy'

Key
✤ *Not hardy*

Stem cuttings and stem sections

Stem cuttings may be used to propagate many species of succulent, including *Euphorbia*, *Stapelia*, and most columnar cacti.

Take stem cuttings or sections in early to mid-spring. The amount and type of stem material that is removed depends on the plant. Some cacti, such as *Opuntia*, consist of a series of rounded pads or sections that may be severed with a sharp knife at the joint or base for propagation. For plants that have flattened, leaf-like stems, for example *Epiphyllum*, make a cut across a stem to produce a section 15–22cm (6–9in) long. To avoid disfiguring the plant, remove a complete "leaf" at the point where it joins the main stem, and treat this as the cutting or cut it into several sections (see below). Most columnar cacti, and some *Euphorbia* species, may have sections of stem removed to provide cuttings (see below).

All *Euphorbia* species and some asclepiads produce a milky latex when cut; to stop the flow, dip the cutting into tepid water for a few seconds. Seal the cut on the parent plant by holding a damp cloth against the wound. Avoid getting the sap on your skin, because it can cause irritation.

Leave stem cuttings in a warm, dry place for anything from two days to two months to allow a callus to form, before potting them up in suitable compost.

Inserting the cuttings

Insert one stem cutting centrally into a prepared pot, or place several small ones around the edge of the container. The cuttings should be inserted just deep enough to stay upright but not too deeply, as otherwise the base of the cuttings may rot before they have rooted. Stem cuttings from succulents that bear true leaves, such as *Pereskia*, need to have the lower leaves removed before they are inserted, in the same way as non-succulent plants. Apply a mist-spray of tepid water occasionally, but do not overwater, as this may cause the cuttings to rot. Rooting normally takes place after approximately two weeks, although cuttings from some genera such as *Selenicereus* may take a month or more.

STEM CUTTINGS

2 *Trim the stem (see inset) below a node. Remove the lowest pair of leaves, if necessary.*

1 *Choose a healthy, vigorous stem (here from* Kalanchoe *'Wendy'). Make a straight cut, severing the stem as close to the base as possible.*

3 *Insert each cutting into a compost of equal parts fine peat substitute (or peat) and sharp grit or sand. The leaves should be just clear of the compost surface.*

PAD SECTIONS

1 *Sever a pad, making a straight cut across the joint, and leave it in a warm, dry place for about 48 hours to allow the wound to callus (see inset).*

2 *Insert the cutting into a pot containing equal parts fine peat substitute (or peat) and sharp grit or sand, and label. Once rooted, pot on into standard potting compost.*

Propagation from stem sections

Many cacti and other succulents may be propagated from a small section of stem rather than using a complete one. Use lengths of about 15–22cm (6–9in), depending on the species. For columnar cacti, remove a section of stem (below), cutting it off at the appropriate point; for cacti with flattened, leaf-like stems, cut the stem laterally into pieces (right). Then treat each section as a stem cutting.

Columnar stem section
Sections of stem taken from some columnar cacti may be treated as cuttings.

Leaf-like stem section
Stems (here of Epiphyllum *'Oakwood') are cut into sections and inserted with the end nearest the parent stem in the compost.*

Division of offsets

A large number of clump-forming cacti and other succulents, such as *Conophytum*, *Mammillaria*, and *Sedum*, may be propagated from offsets early in the growing season.

Clump-forming offsets

Scrape away the top layer of soil from around the parent plant to reveal the base of the offsets, and carefully detach one or more from the parent plant, as required, with a sharp knife. Treat any wounds on the offsets with fungicide, leaving them to dry for two to three days to allow a callus to form. Pot up undamaged offsets immediately.

Rootless offsets should be inserted into compost made up of equal parts fine peat substitute (or peat) and sand. If the offsets have already developed roots, use a standard potting compost. Use appropriately sized containers with a layer of crocks at the bottom. Pot up offsets separately and water them in lightly.

Keep the potted offsets in semi-shade for about two weeks at a minimum temperature of 15°C (59°F), and water them again after the first week. Once new growth appears, the plants should be potted on into a standard potting compost and the normal watering routine applied (see p.345).

Offset tubers

Some tuberous-rooted succulents, such as *Ceropegia*, produce small, offset tubers around the main tuber of the parent plant. These may be treated as divisions and grown on to produce new plants. During the dormant season, remove some compost to reveal the offsets and separate them from the parent plant using a clean, sharp knife. Treat the cut surfaces of rootless offsets with

fungicide and allow a callus to form. Insert each offset tuber in a clean pot that contains a mix of equal parts peat substitute (or peat) and coarse sand.

If the offsets have roots, place them directly into a standard potting compost. Top-dress with a thin layer of washed, sharp grit, and label. Place the pots in semi-shade and maintain a temperature of 18°C (64°F).

Allow the tubers to settle for three or four days and then water them regularly with a fine mist-spray. As soon as growth starts and some young shoots begin to appear, follow the normal watering routine (see p.345). Pot on into a standard potting compost as soon as the young plants have several shoots and have become well established.

DIVISION OF CLUMP-FORMING OFFSETS

1 Gently scrape away the top surface of compost around an offset. Cut straight across the joint and allow the wound to callus (see inset).

2 Using a compost mix of equal parts coarse sand and peat substitute (or peat), insert the offset just below the surface of the compost.

3 Top-dress with 5mm (¼in) of grit, label, and place in semi-shade. Water after 3–4 days.

4 When new growth appears pot on into standard potting compost, top-dressing as before.

DIVISION OF OFFSET TUBERS

1 Scrape away some compost from around the main tuber and carefully detach offset tubers. Lift them without damaging the roots, if present (see inset).

2 Treat wounds with fungicide, and allow to callus. If roots are present, insert into potting compost, otherwise use equal parts of fine peat substitute (or peat) and sand.

3 Top-dress with a 5mm (¼in) layer of 3mm (⅛in) sharp grit. Label the pot but do not water for several days.

CACTI AND SUCCULENTS FROM DIVISION OF OFFSETS

Agave, some ✿
Aloe ✿
Aloinopsis ✿
Begonia natalensis ✿,
   B. sheperdii ✿
Carruanthus ✿
Conophytum ✿
Copiapoa ✿
Coryphantha ✿
Crassula, many including
   C. perforata ✿,
   C. socialis ✿
Dactylopsis ✿
Delosperma ✿
Dinteranthus ✿
Dracophilus ✿
Duvalia ✿
Ebracteola ✿
Echeveria, many including
   E. agavoides ✿,
   E. derenbergii ✿,
   E. elegans ✿,
   E. setosa ✿
Echidnopsis ✿
Echinocereus ✿
Echinopsis ✿
Epithelantha ✿
Erepsia ✿
Escobaria ✿

Lithops karasmontana

Faucaria ✿
Gasteria ✿ (most spp.)
Glottiphyllum ✿
Greenovia ✿
Gymnocalycium ✿
Haworthia ✿ (most spp.)
Huernia ✿
Juttadinteria ✿
Lithops ✿
Mammillaria ✿
Meyerophytum ✿
Opuntia ✿
Orostachys ✿
Parodia ✿
Pleiospilos ✿
Pterocactus ✿
Rebutia ✿
Rhombophyllum ✿
Sedum, some ✿
Sempervivum
Stapelia ✿
Stomatium ✿
Thelocactus ✿
   (a few spp.)

Parodia erinacea

Key
✿ Not hardy

CACTI AND SUCCULENTS FROM DIVISION OF ROOTSTOCK

Agave, some ❊
Aloe ❊
Argyroderma ❊
Caralluma ❊

Aloe variegata

Carpobrotus ❊
Delosperma ❊
Duvalia ❊
Faucaria ❊
Fenestraria ❊
Frithia ❊
Glottiphyllum ❊
Gymnocalycium ❊
Huernia ❊
Mammillaria ❊
Rebutia ❊
Ruschia ❊
Sansevieria ❊
Stapelia ❊
Titanopsis ❊

Key
❊ *Not hardy*

Division of rootstock

Many species of Aizoaceae such as *Delosperma* and *Frithia*, some clump-forming cacti, and genera such as *Aloe* are readily propagated by division. For some cultivars of *Sansevieria*, division is the most reliable method of retaining the variegation, as leaf cuttings may produce plants that revert. Divide clump-forming cacti and other succulents in the early stages of the growing season.

Lift the whole plant from its pot, and carefully pull apart or cut the rootstock into a number of smaller pieces, each with a healthy bud or shoot and well-formed roots. Treat all cut areas with fungicide and pot up each section separately into standard potting compost. Label, water, and place in a semi-shaded position until well established.

Alternatively, cut away a piece of the rootstock without lifting the plant, and ease a section out of the soil with a hand fork. Dust the cut surfaces with fungicide and pot up as for offset tubers (see p.349). Fill any gaps that are left around the parent plant, using a standard compost, and water lightly.

DIVISION OF ROOTSTOCK

1 *Lift the plant (*here* Sansevieria trifasciata). Divide it into sections by cutting straight through the rootstock.*

2 *Discard old, woody material and any soft or damaged roots before replanting each new section.*

Grafting

Some cacti and other succulents, notably certain members of the Asclepiadaceae, such as *Edithcolea* and *Pseudolithos*, are slow to mature and flower when grown on their own roots. By grafting them onto established specimens of related species that are quicker to mature, they can be induced to flower much faster. During the growing season the top-growth, or scion, of the required plant is grafted onto the rootstock of one of

APICAL-WEDGE GRAFTING

1 *Prepare the rootstock by trimming off the tip, making a straight cut through the stem with a clean, sharp knife.*

2 *Make a slender "V"-shaped cleft (see inset) in the stock, to a depth of about 2cm (³⁄₄in).*

3 *Select the scion material and remove from the parent plant (*here* a* Schlumbergera*), cutting straight through at a node with a sharp knife.*

4 *Trim the lower end of the scion to a narrow wedge shape to match the "V"-shaped cleft in the stock plant.*

5 *Insert the scion wedge into the cleft in the stock plant (see inset), making sure that they are in close contact.*

6 *To secure the scion in place in the clefted stock, insert a cactus spine through the grafted area.*

Alternative method
Bind the graft firmly, but not tightly, with raffia or a weak clothes peg.

the more vigorous species. Three grafting methods may be used: apical-wedge grafting, flat grafting, and side grafting.

Apical-wedge grafting

Epiphytic cacti are often propagated by apical-wedge grafting in order to create an erect "standard" or tree-like plant. Use *Pereskiopsis* or *Selenicereus*, which are sturdy but of slender growth, as the rootstock.

To produce the rootstock, take a stem cutting (see p.348) of the selected plant. When this has rooted and shows evidence of new growth, it is ready to be used for grafting. Slice off the tip and then make two slanted, downward cuts into the top of the rootstock stem to produce a narrow, vertical, "V"-shaped slit approximately 2cm (¾in) long.

Select a healthy shoot from the scion plant and prepare it by trimming the lower end into a wedge shape to match the cleft in the stock. Insert the prepared scion "wedge" into the cleft so that the cut surfaces match as closely as possible. Secure the stock and scion firmly in position either by pushing a cactus spine horizontally through the graft or,

alternatively, by binding with raffia or a weak clothes peg.

Place the grafted plant in partial shade at a temperature of 21°C (70°F). The stock and scion should unite within a few days; once this has happened, remove the spine or raffia, dusting any holes made by the spine with fungicide. When fresh growth appears, water and feed as for established plants (see p.345).

Flat grafting

This method is used to propagate crested variants (succulents with atyp-ical, often contorted, growth), certain other succulents with tufts of hair, and *Gymnocalycium mihanovichii* and *Echinopsis chamaecereus* as their seedlings may be lacking in chloro-phyll. Genera that can be used as rootstocks include *Echinopsis*, *Harrisia*, and *Hylocereus*.

Make a straight, horizontal cut through the stem of the rootstock at the required height. Then remove the rib margins with a sharp knife to form a bevelled edge, and trim off any spines near the cut.

Prepare the scion in a similar way, and position its base on the cut surface of the stock plant. Place elastic bands

over the top of the scion and under the base of the pot to keep the scion securely in place; make sure that the bands are not too tight.

Leave the grafted plant in a well-lit position, but not in full sun. Keep the compost barely moist until the scion and the stock have united (normally in one to two weeks), when the elastic bands may be removed. Thereafter, water and feed as for established plants.

When grafting asclepiads, the fleshy tubers of *Ceropegia* or the robust stems of *Stapelia* may be used as rootstocks. The former, in particular, make excellent stock plants for some of the Madagascan and Arabian asclepiads, which may otherwise be difficult to propagate.

Side grafting

This method is useful if the scion is too slender to be grafted onto the top of the stock. It is very similar to spliced side grafting, used for woody plants. Prepare the stock by slicing off the top at an oblique angle, then trim the base of the scion to match the stock as closely as possible. Secure them together with a spine or raffia and treat as for flat grafting.

FLAT GRAFTING

1 *Slice off the top of the rootstock with a sharp knife, to produce a flat surface.*

2 *Trim the cut surface to produce a slightly bevelled edge; hold the stem without touching the wounded area.*

3 *Cut the scion material, slicing through at the base. Bevel the edge of the scion (inset) so that it will fit closely onto the stock.*

4 *Place the scion on the stock and secure firmly, but not tightly, with elastic bands. Label with the name of the scion plant.*

5 *Place the pot in good light at a minimum temperature of 16°C (61°F). Remove the elastic bands when new growth appears.*

SIDE GRAFTING

If the scion plant is slender it may be grafted onto the side of the stock. Make a slanted cut in both stock and scion, place the cut surfaces together, and fasten with a cactus spine and raffia. Leave in good light at 16°C (61°F) until new growth appears.

CACTI AND SUCCULENTS TO GRAFT

Flat grafting
Alluaudiopsis ✽
Astrophytum ✽
Austrocactus ✽
Aztekium ✽
Blossfeldia ✽
Coleocephalocereus ✽
Discocactus ✽
Duvalia ✽
Echinopsis ✽
Edithcolea ✽
Epithelantha ✽
Frailea ✽
Gymnocalycium mihanovichii (and cvs) ✽
Hoodia ✽

Gymnocalycium mihanovichii 'Red Head'

x *Hoodiapelia* ✽
Lophophora ✽
Maihuenia ✽
Mammillaria ✽
Mila ✽
Neolloydia ✽
Nopalxochia ✽
Orbea ✽
Parodia ✽
Pediocactus ✽
Pelecyphora ✽
Pseudolithos ✽
Pygmaeocereus ✽
Rebutia ✽
Tavaresia ✽
Trichocaulon ✽
Uebelmannia ✽

Disocactus flagelliformis

Side grafting
Disocactus flagelliformis ✽
Disocactus ✽
Echinocereus ✽
Haageocereus ✽
Hatiora ✽
Lepismium ✽ (flat-stemmed spp.)
Rhipsalis ✽ (spp. with rounded or angled stems)
Selenicereus ✽
Weberocereus ✽ (spp. with rounded stems)

Apical-wedge grafting
Disocactus ✽
Hatiora ✽
Schlumbergera ✽
Selenicereus ✽

Schlumbergera 'Gold Charm'

Key
✽ Not hardy

CHAPTER

13

INDOOR GARDENING

THE GARDEN MAY be enjoyed in comfort, whatever the season, by bringing it indoors, with tender plants offering leaf and flower colours and forms as rich as those of outdoor varieties. Gardening under cover also opens up opportunities for creating different effects, from ornamental table displays of flowering pot plants, to leafy terrariums or bottle gardens. In regions subject to frost, a conservatory can be transformed into a small-scale jungle with the lush foliage and exotic flowers of tropical plants, guaranteed to brighten up even the dullest of winter days. Indoor plants are also highly versatile, and some require little maintenance when bought as design accessories that are displayed, enjoyed, and then discarded. Alternatively, the enthusiast may choose to grow collections of rare plants that demand more regular care and attention.

Displaying plants indoors

THE range of plants that may be grown in a home and a greenhouse offers a wealth of form, colour, and texture. Plants may be chosen for their handsome foliage or the beauty of their blooms, from the exuberant hues of bougainvillea to the cool elegance of *Zantedeschia aethiopica*. Others, such as *Solanum pseudocapsicum*, are valued for their brightly coloured fruits.

The choice of plants depends on whether the display is to be permanent, when plants with interesting form and foliage are the best choice for a year-round display, or temporary, when the seasonal interest of plants such as *Cyclamen persicum* may be used to give spots of colour.

Plants may reinforce or contrast with the style of the indoor setting, whether it is a rustic cottage kitchen or a formal and sophisticated urban living room. The plants may dominate the scene and give a room its essential character, create pockets of interest, or simply add to the detail. Whatever effect is desired, select plants that will both thrive in and enhance their intended position.

Foliage and form

Plants that have attractive foliage are invaluable for long-term indoor display. They may have huge leaves, as does *Fatsia japonica*, or a mass of dainty ones, such as those of *Soleirolia soleirolii*, syn. *Helxine soleirolii*. Leaves may have subtle or striking patterns and colours, as do *Calathea* species, or interesting shapes, for example the Swiss-cheese plant (*Monstera deliciosa*).

Foliage also has different textures, from the high gloss of the rubber plant (*Ficus elastica*) to the corrugated surfaces of *Pilea involucrata*, and the soft velvet of *Gynura aurantiaca*. Some plants are chosen for their strong forms, whether they are spiky bromeliads, graceful palms and ferns, or pebble-like *Lithops*.

Grouping plants

When planning an arrangement, choose plants with strongly coloured flowers or patterned leaves carefully, so that they do not detract from each other. Experiment with contrasts by placing plants together in shops, nurseries, and garden centres before making a purchase.

Architectural plants such as palms make very fine specimen plants or striking focal points in a group. Smaller plants have impact when arranged together on a tiered stand, but may be used singly as a dainty finishing touch. A tight group of identical plants, for example a bowl of white hyacinths, makes a strong yet simple statement.

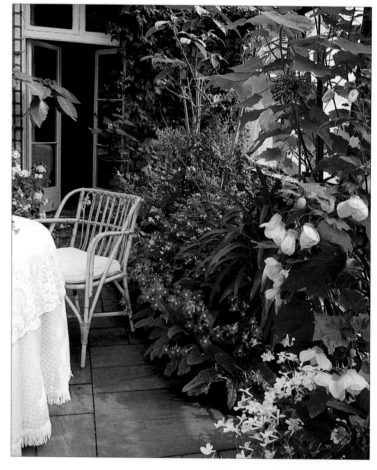

A garden room
Yellow Abutilon, *blue* Agapanthus, *purple and white* Streptocarpus, *and lush foliage create a garden-like setting in which to relax.*

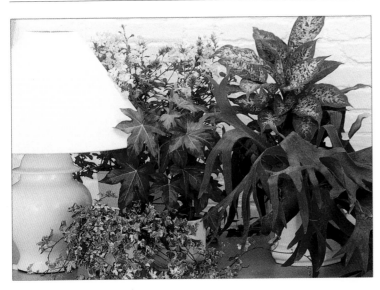

A contrast of strong shapes
Variegated ivy (Hedera), Dieffenbachia, Fatsia japonica, *and the sculptural fronds of* Platycerium bifurcatum *complement the very pale blue* Plumbago.

The indoor environment

The specific temperature and light requirements of plants are the most important factors in deciding where to position them indoors (see "Planter's guide to indoor plants", p.361). If the conditions are incompatible with the plants' needs, they will soon become stressed and unhealthy. Newly purchased plants that have just come from controlled conditions are especially vulnerable.

Temperature

Although most modern houses are kept warm during the day in winter, the temperature is often allowed to drop markedly at night – a problem for many house plants of tropical origin. Place these plants where they are protected from draughts and are not subject to wide fluctuations in temperature. Do not leave tender plants on windowsills at night, especially if the drawn curtains close off residual warmth from the room, or place plants directly above radiators or heaters that are in use. To flower, indoor plants need warmth, but if the temperature is too high for the individual species, the blooms quickly fade and die.

Light

Most plants thrive in bright, filtered sunlight or in a well-lit position that is not in direct sun. Plants that have variegated leaves need more light than those with plain, green leaves, but over-strong sunlight will damage the foliage. Flowering plants such as *Hippeastrum* need good light if they are to flower well, but excessive light can shorten the life of the blooms. Indeed, few indoor plants can tolerate direct sunlight.

Insufficient light results in plants with pale, stunted new leaves, and drawn-out, or etiolated, growth with long, thin, weak stems. Some variegated plants may begin to produce plain leaves. In time, the mature leaves will turn yellow and fall. A plant thus weakened is especially vulnerable to pests and diseases.

The amount of natural light in a room depends on the number, size, height, and aspect of the windows. Light levels fall quickly as the distance from the window increases. In winter, there is far less natural light than in summer, and some plants may need to be moved in response to the seasonal light variation – a plant trolley is ideal for this purpose.

If plants start to grow lopsidedly towards a source of light, turn them slightly when watering them. If light levels are too low for healthy growth (most plants need 12–14 hours of daylight per day) supplementary growing lamps are effective (see *A Growing Lamp*, p.577). These are particularly valuable when growing African violets (*Saintpaulia*), which need a long daylength if they are to flower continuously.

Positioning plants

With a little forethought and planning, it is possible to find handsome house plants that flourish in almost every site indoors, from a brilliantly lit room to a dim passage or alcove.

The indoor setting

Give careful consideration to the impact of plants within a room. Are they in proportion to the room? A tiny pot plant is lost in a large space. Is the background suitable? Plain, pale walls show flowering plants to advantage. Does the flower or foliage colour blend with the decor?

High-level hanging baskets and shelves suit trailing plants, while eye-level positions are best for plants with delicate flowers or foliage. Train climbers, such as *Philodendron hederaceum*, *Cissus antarctica*, and ivy (*Hedera*), on a trellis or other support to create a screen.

Use plants to enliven empty corners or space, such as an unused fireplace, which provides an instant frame for a display. Large plants or groups may play an architectural role as room dividers or as a link between the house and the garden.

Plants and light levels

Bright, sunny conditions suit succulent plants as well as plants with woolly, waxy, or grey leaves. *Hoya carnosa*, pelargoniums, and *Ananas comosus* var. *variegatus* will also appreciate direct sunlight. In places with indirect or filtered light, grow foliage begonias such as *Begonia rex*, epiphytic orchids, such as *Phalaenopsis*, and *Spathiphyllum* with their striking, white spathes.

For corners that are remote from a window, choose ferns and tough-leaved plants such as *Chamaedorea*, *Fatsia japonica*, and ivy. Expose the plants to slightly brighter light occasionally, if only for a few days.

Kitchens and bathrooms

Temperatures and humidity in kitchens and bathrooms, especially small ones, can fluctuate, so choose plants that can tolerate extremes. Smooth, hard bathroom surfaces contrast well with the soft, feathery forms of ferns and grasses, and some *Cyperus* species. Bathrooms often have low levels of light, ideal for *Episcia*, *Nephrolepis*, or *Pilea*. Fill high-level bathroom space with trailing plants such as *Philodendron hederaceum*. Do not put trailing plants on top of kitchen cabinets since they may interfere with the cupboard doors; also the light levels high up are likely to be extremely low, so plants will become thin and straggly. In brightly lit positions, use hanging baskets to grow a selection of herbs or tiny tomato cultivars. Herbs are also ideal for growing on a sunny kitchen windowsill.

Tolerant plants

Attractive foliage plants that tolerate a wide range of conditions include *Aspidistra*, *Chlorophytum*, *Cissus antarctica*, and *Sansevieria*. Flowering plants are more exacting, but chrysanthemums (see pp.188–190) or forced bulbs (see p.231) may give short-term floral colour.

HAZARDS OF A WINDOWSILL

Too much sunlight, excessive heat from radiators, and draughts through the frame can weaken or kill house plants that are placed on a windowsill.

VARIATION OF LIGHT LEVELS WITHIN A ROOM

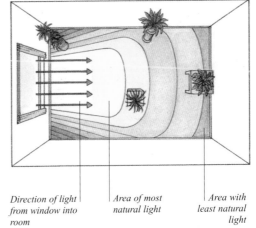

Direction of light from window into room | Area of most natural light | Area with least natural light

The farther away from a window a plant is sited, the less natural light it will receive. If the plant is 2m (6ft) away, the light level may be as little as 20 per cent of that by the window. Plants that are placed close to a window but to one side of it derive little benefit from the position, especially if the windowsills are very deep.

Conservatory gardening

A CONSERVATORY is often treated solely as an additional interior living room, comfortably furnished and usually ornamented with potted plants. However, plant enthusiasts may instead want their conservatory to be an enclosed extension to the garden; a protected environment that will meet the needs of more unusual plants. Incompatibilities exist between the two approaches – for example, the warm, humid conditions required by subtropical plants will quickly rot soft furnishings, books, and magazines – and many keen gardeners opt for a greenhouse (see GREENHOUSES AND FRAMES, pp.566–583) which can be tailored more exactly to meet the needs of plants. But there is no doubt that a conservatory is often preferred, and when a new conservatory is intended primarily as a place in which plants will thrive, it is worth spending time at the design stage to ensure that the end result is practical and successful in its aim.

Siting and orientation

With a greenhouse, the orientation and site can usually be chosen for maximum light and best growing conditions, but with a conservatory the priorities are usually where it looks best attached to the house, while at the same time conveniently connecting with a kitchen, passageway, or other living area. A conservatory in full sun all day needs generous through-ventilation; large roof ventilators, windows that open

A place for plants
The keen gardener will find that plants and potting activity soon come to dominate space in the conservatory. Make sure flooring and furniture are practical and resilient – popular conservatory materials such as wicker, rattan, and natural fibre matting of seagrass are particularly unforgiving of compost spills.

and doors that can be folded back in summer, coupled with effective roof shading. One oriented to receive only morning or evening sun, in shade during the hottest parts of the day, will suit plants tolerant of a wide range of conditions. If the best site is relatively sunless, this should not automatically be considered a disadvantage. The shade will encourage foliage growth and the conservatory will have a relatively even temperature, ideal for shade-tolerant plants.

Basic materials

Most conservatories have brick or timber base walls supporting a glazed timber or metal framework and a ridged roof. Shelves or staging may be needed to raise small plants to the light. Wide interior window-sills can be useful for pots. Unlike most greenhouses, conservatories are normally double-glazed, to retain heat from within the house. Because of its more robust structure, a conservatory will never allow in as much light as does a greenhouse, which should be borne in mind when selecting plants, especially if the conservatory receives little sun – tomatoes may crop better in a greenhouse, for example, or an oleander be more likely to flower on a south-facing terrace.

The most practical flooring materials are slatted and oiled hardwood, tiles, or stone, which are easy to keep clean yet tolerate the humid atmosphere generated by plants, and also water when damping down.

Ventilation

Ample roof ventilation is essential for successful conservatory cultivation. There are no precise formulae for calculating the amount of ventilation required, as it depends on aspect and the design of the building.

Roof ventilators allow upward convection of warm air into the roof to escape, and through ventilation works best when at least one-third of the glazed area can be opened. Greenhouse ventilators, hinged from the roof ridge, modified to take the weight of double-glazing, and water-tight when closed, are effective if

Ensuring a through draft
If the building is in full sun, double doors that open out and can be hooked back will considerably aid ventilation. As many windows as possible should be openable.

Roof and side blinds
The traditional fabric, pinoleum, is made from woven pine "reeds" and provides 70–75 per cent shading. Satisfactory alternatives are stiffened cotton, foil-backed plastic to reflect the sun, and fibreglass mesh.

large enough. Electric or mechanical screw-jack openers should be used to operate the ventilators unless the roof is unusually low, in which case wax-operated greenhouse openers are suitable. See also GREENHOUSES AND FRAMES, "Ventilation", p.575.

Shading

Unless the conservatory receives no direct sunlight, shading will be needed to protect plants from scorching. Roller or concertina blinds are the most usual solution, fitted from the roof and supported by fine taut wires to prevent sagging. Internal roof blinds can be problematic if climbers are being grown, but while external blinds, as used on greenhouses, are practical they may not look appropriate. Side blinds fitted to windows and doors are used more for privacy than shading. See also GREENHOUSES AND FRAMES, "Shading", p.576.

Heating

Because a conservatory is adjacent to the house, it is relatively easy to keep warm and can often be connected to the domestic central heating. It should ideally have separate pipework and controls to maintain minimum nocturnal temperatures for plants, which may be greater than that desired in the house. If a domestic connection is not feasible, use a thermostatic convector heater. All types of heater are best positioned in a corner on the external, colder sides of the room, as are thermostats.

Underfloor heating, of which there are two types, is another possibility. The first uses electric cable or a small hot-water pipe snaking back and forth over insulation, beneath the floor screed. These heat up the floor slab to provide even, continuous heating and are best used in a north-facing conservatory where there will be little direct sunshine. The second type of underfloor heating is trench heating, which consists of central heating pipes, usually finned to give greater output, set in a channel 30cm (12in) wide, placed around the perimeter of the conservatory and covered with a grille of plain or decorative cast-metal. Trench heating is more expensive to install than electric cables, but is more quickly adjusted; it is also easier to raise humidity simply by pouring water through the grille to create steam.

Humidity

Conservatories can become very dry, which will not suit many plants and will also encourage pests and diseases. Grouping plants together will help, as transpiration from their leaves will produce a miniature, moist climate. Trays of gravel or shallow dishes kept filled with water will increase humidity. On hot days, damping down – splashing water on the floor – will be necessary, especially as doors and windows will need to be open simultaneously to provide ventilation. Another reliable source of humidity is a wall fountain or, if there is sufficient space, an indoor pool. See also GREENHOUSES AND FRAMES, "Humidity", p.576.

Watering

Irrigation systems, although effective, are often difficult to disguise in a conservatory. Most gardeners rely on hand watering. The water used should be at the same temperature as the plants and their compost. Traditional conservatories often had storage tanks inside, set in the floor. Water drawn from the mains or from an outdoor butt or tank should be left in watering cans or buckets for a couple of hours before use.

In a hard water area, watering will leave deposits of scale and gradually increase the alkalinity of the soil, which for many conservatory plants such as citrus, camellias, and gardenias will cause chlorosis and poor growth. This can be overcome by installing a water softener or by using rainwater collected from the conservatory's guttering into a water butt (see also p.614). Ideally a pipe should be fitted just above its base leading to a tap in the conservatory, and the butt raised high enough for the tap to be fed by gravity, or use an electric pressure-release pump.

Displaying plants

Some plants are better grown in soil beds than in pots. Beds in the floor are rarely practical as they will interfere with damp courses, are difficult to keep clean (especially if pets have access to the room), and are permanent, making it inconvenient to alter the layout. Raised brick or block beds are preferable, and make gardening particularly convenient for the elderly or less able. Raised beds should be as deep as practical to allow ample root growth and have a waterproof lining, with a gravel base layer for drainage (see also "Raised beds", p.269).

Climbers can be grown on wall trellis or wires fixed to the wall and roof. Container-grown plants may be also trained on freestanding supports such as tapering wire frames (see also CONTAINER GARDENING, p.325). In a timber roof, fit long-stemmed screw eyes to keep training wires 15cm (6in) or more away from the glass. With a metal or plastic roof, self-tapping screws and specially made brackets are generally available. Make sure that climbers are kept well clear of light fittings.

Plant health

Conservatories have the same range of problems as a greenhouse (see p.375), but, because of the proximity to the house and the fact that a conservatory is used for people, the methods of control will vary. Biological control is effective for many pests if used at the right time (see PLANT PROBLEMS, "Biological control", p.642). Routine fumigation will be out of the question in most cases, as will the regular use of sprays. If these are needed, it is best to take the plants outside on a mild day, cleaning them thoroughly before treating. Allow the spray to dry before bringing plants indoors again.

Purpose-built beds
This raised planting bed sits on a watertight, edged gravel base which can be topped up with water, increasing the humidity levels for plants such as bromeliads (here Neoregelia) that enjoy such conditions.

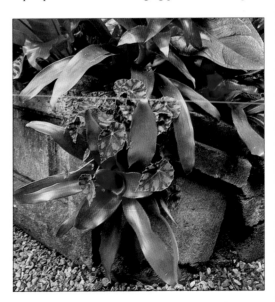

Growing fresh air

House plants are grown mainly for their aesthetic value, but there are additional benefits. The process of transpiration, in which leaf pores (stomata) emit water vapour, means house plants can increase humidity. This is beneficial in centrally-heated homes and offices where a dry atmosphere may cause individuals to suffer symptoms associated with "sick building syndrome".

Some plants are believed to help remove harmful gaseous pollutants – like ammonia, ethyl alcohol, acetone, and various bio-effluents – from the air. Popular house plants shown to absorb such pollutants include the Areca, dwarf date, lady, and bamboo palms (*Dypsis lutescens*, *Phoenix roebelenii*, *Rhapis excelsa*, and *Chamaedorea seifrizii*); the weeping fig and India rubber tree (*Ficus benjamina* and *F. elastica* 'Robusta'); peacock plant (*Calathea makoyana*); Boston fern (*Nephrolepis exaltata* 'Bostoniensis'); Queensland umbrella tree (*Schefflera actinophylla*); *Dieffenbachia seguine* 'Exotica'; *Dracaena fragrans* Deremensis Group; *Philodendron erubescens*, and peace lily (*Spathiphyllum* hybrids), as well as chrysanthemums, ivies (*Hedera helix*), and Indian azaleas (*Rhododendron simsii* cultivars).

Containers

Choose a container whose material, colour, and shape blends with the decor and shows the individual plant or group to its best advantage. The choice is enormous, both in style and materials, allowing a range of effects from rustic to ultramodern. The most unlikely household objects – coal scuttles, birdcages, cooking utensils, kettles, urns – can be used to provide unusual and striking plant holders.

Hanging baskets

Hanging baskets are popular features on porches, balconies, patios, and terraces, but are also attractive ways to grow indoor plants. Hang them in stairwells, from rafters, by windows, or from free-standing supports for an economical and colourful use of space (see CONTAINER GARDENING, "Hanging baskets", p.314).

Arching fern fronds, the rosettes of epiphytes, and cascading habit of many foliage plants lend themselves perfectly to hanging baskets. Vary the planting during the year to make seasonal displays. Christmas cactus (*Schlumbergera buckleyi*) provides a mass of bright colour for winter, as do fuchsias in summer. Temporary arrangements may be created by planting up a basket with pot plants, but they will need replanting each year. Permanently planted baskets are easier to manage, especially if devoted to a single, large plant.

Choosing hanging containers

Hanging baskets are available in various materials and designs. When choosing and positioning them, take into account the fact that most plants require frequent watering. Plastic-coated wire hanging baskets are practical indoors only in rooms that have water-resistant floors; some rigid, plastic baskets have in-built drip saucers which provide a practical solution. Also available are attractive, although heavy, pottery and terra-cotta hanging pots, and wrought iron, wooden, or wicker baskets.

A planted basket is heavy, especially when just watered, so it must be supported by strong rope or chain from a hook or bracket fixed securely to a ceiling joist or a solid wall.

Terrariums and bottle gardens

Terrariums are enclosed glass containers, often decorative in their own right, used to display small plants in the home. They were popular in the 19th century as a way of providing a suitable microclimate for ferns, but any slow-growing ornamental plants that need a humid atmosphere thrive in a terrarium. A selection of plants with contrasting leaf textures and colours is the most effective – avoid flowering plants because the dead blooms rot in the moist conditions. Terrariums may be built permanently into a window to house a lush arrangement of larger plants.

Bottles may also be used to create a diminutive landscape of foliage plants. As long as the neck is sufficiently wide to allow the insertion of the plants and routine aftercare, any shape or colour of bottle may be used, but bear in mind that tinted glass cuts out some of the light.

Indoor lighting

Flood- and spotlights may enhance displays; up- or downlighting make dramatic contrasts of light and shade. Do not place plants too close to light sources, as heat may damage them. Ordinary incandescent bulbs do not significantly improve growth or food production (photosynthesis).

Plants for the office

Introducing plants into an office not only brightens it up, but deadens noise, refreshes the air, and creates a less stressful ambience. In a modern, open-plan office that is fully glazed and air-conditioned, temperatures are constant, air pollution is minimized, and light is plentiful: ideal growing conditions. Old buildings with small windows and little climatic control present more of a challenge.

Use self-watering pots, especially if they are near electric equipment, or plunge several plants into a large container. Ensure responsibility for care is clearly assigned.

Suitable plants

Evergreen, shiny-leaved plants are as tough and tolerant in an office as they are at home. The popular genus *Ficus* includes plants of every shape and size, from lustrous, huge-leaved *F. lyrata* (give it solitary splendour in a large space) to *F. deltoidea* with its small, leathery-textured leaves.

Philodendron is another large and impressive genus, including climbers and trailers, with handsome leaves. The tenacious, long-lived Swiss-cheese plant (*Monstera deliciosa*) climbs slowly but eventually reaches several metres in height and spread.

Sun rooms and conservatories

The garden may be brought indoors, either into a sun room, a living space furnished with container plants, or a conservatory, often devoted to plants. In temperate climates, both may be used to give winter shelter to pot-grown plants that spend the summer months outdoors; a conservatory may also provide the warm, humid environment needed by tropical and subtropical plants (see also CONSERVATORY GARDENING, pp.356–357).

High light levels in conservatories encourage coloured leaves to assume intense hues, and plants flower well. Fragrant plants such as *Jasminum polyanthum* are welcome in confined spaces where scent lingers in the air.

Seasonal colour

In this room, a white poinsettia (Euphorbia pulcherrima)*, carmine azalea* (Rhododendron)*, and Calamondin orange* (x Citrofortunella microcarpa) *add winter interest to a permanent framework of evergreen foliage plants.*

COOL CONSERVATORY

The foliage and flowering plants shown here are among the many that thrive in the cool, but frost-free, conditions of a lean-to conservatory to create a fine display.

1 *Plumbago auriculata* (syn. *P. capensis*)
2 *Chlorophytum comosum*
   (syn. *C. capense* of gardens)
3 *Campanula isophylla*
4 *Saxifraga stolonifera* 'Tricolor'
   (syn. *S. stolonifera* 'Magic Carpet')
5 *Pelargonium* Mini Cascade
6 *Camellia japonica*
7 *Sedum morganianum*
8 *Streptocarpus* 'Heidi'
9 *Ceropegia linearis* subsp. *woodii*
10 *Callistemon citrinus* 'Splendens'
11 *Correa pulchella*
12 *Calceolaria* 'Sunshine'
13 *Nierembergia scoparia* 'Purple Robe'
14 *Prostanthera rotundifolia*
15 *Polygala* x *dalmaisiana*
   (syn. *P. myrtifolia* 'Grandiflora')
16 *Rehmannia elata*
17 x *Citrofortunella microcarpa*
   (syn. *Citrus mitis*)

Select plants to suit the conservatory aspect and temperature. Bear in mind glass structures can be costly to heat in winter and very hot in summer.

Create a profusion of planting by making full use of the space: grow plants at different levels in raised and ground-level soil beds, in pots on the floor, on windowsills, shelves, and in hanging baskets. Large tropical or subtropical plants and free-standing climbers may be trained on trellis or wires fixed to the walls and roof. Use plants that complement those in the open garden; this visually links the two, and creates a sense of space.

Indoor water features

A sunken or raised pool or a half-barrel may accommodate tropical water lilies or other tender aquatic and marginal plants. A simple and elegant water spout will provide the restful murmur of falling water and help to maintain humidity (see also WATER GARDENING, pp.280–303).

Growing plants in a greenhouse

The control of light, temperature, and humidity in a greenhouse will allow a much more extensive range of plants to be grown than in a garden that is subject to frost. Using a greenhouse also extends the season of display and cropping from early spring until late autumn, or even all year round if desired.

Multi-level display
Staging, shelves, and floor space are used to maximum advantage in this cool greenhouse. Busy Lizzie (Impatiens cultivars), Plumbago, and Streptocarpus flowers are complemented by a variety of foliage plants, including ivy (Hedera), scented-leaved pelargoniums, Hypoestes, Pellaea, and Tolmiea.

Uses for greenhouses

Greenhouses are useful in cool temperate climates, where there is frost, strong winds, or excessive rain: they may be used for propagation; raising and growing tender plants or flowers for cutting; or for crops like salads, early vegetables, or even fruit. Many plants grow faster under cover and fruit or flower more profusely than they do outdoors. Half-hardy plants may be grown in containers outdoors and transferred to temporary shelter in the greenhouse when needed.

Some gardeners use greenhouses to grow specific plants like auriculas or fuchsias (see pp.120–121); others may house collections of carnivorous plants, alpines (see pp.277–79), orchids (see pp.368–69), cacti (see pp.338–51), or ferns (see pp.194–5).

The greenhouse layout

The traditional, free-standing greenhouse interior comprises a central path with waist-high staging at the sides and far end; wider greenhouses may also have staging in the centre. Staging (see also p.579) is essential; even if it is removed in summer for border crops, it may be used at other times of year for raising seedlings, propagating cuttings, and displaying pot plants. Slatted or meshed staging is best for pot plants to avoid pools of standing water and ensure air circulates freely, especially in winter.

For extra display space, use tiered staging, bench beds, or soil borders. If the glass begins at ground level, ferns and other shade-loving plants,

and dormant plants, may be grown or rested under the staging. Raised beds are useful for displaying small plants, such as alpines and cacti, that are planted directly in the beds or in pots plunged into gravel or sand.

The ornamental greenhouse

Although a greenhouse is often used more for practical purposes than a conservatory, part or all of it may be devoted to ornamental displays. Groups are usually more attractive than widely spaced plants. Feature a single genus such as *Streptocarpus*, or mixed plants displayed in random patterns or as a miniature landscape. Try to include contrasts of leaf form, size, and texture and control the use of colour from flowers and foliage to create a harmonious arrangement.

A lean-to greenhouse against the house wall may double as a conservatory. Make the most of the back wall by growing climbers, which need only a 30cm (12in) wide bed or pot. Paint the wall white to help to reflect light and provide a contrasting background for the plants.

The greenhouse environment

Essential requirements for success are adequate ventilation and heat, as well as shading in summer; piped water and electricity are also useful.

The temperature of a greenhouse depends on its purpose, but there

An interior garden
Where space allows, a naturalistic landscape may be created within a greenhouse. Here, foliage plants, including Cordyline, Eucomis, Justicia, *and* Phormium, *provide a lush framework that is offset by the colourful blooms of flowering plants such as blue* Agapanthus, *pink fuchsias, and white and salmon pelargoniums.*

are four basic conditions: cold or unheated, cool or frost-free, temperate, and warm. For further information, see GREENHOUSES AND FRAMES, "Creating the right environment", pp.573–577; see also "Planter's guide to indoor plants", p.361.

The cold greenhouse

An unheated greenhouse protects against extremes of wind and rain and is significantly warmer, even in summer, than outdoors. It extends the growing season by providing the plants with an artificially early spring and late autumn.

Most hardy annuals, biennials, and shrubs may be overwintered in an unheated greenhouse, and half-hardy annuals, bulbous plants, and shrubs grown on to plant out in summer, when the garden soil has warmed up and danger of frost is past. A cold greenhouse is also useful for raising seed and enabling an early start to be made with fruit or vegetables. As an alpine house, it may be used to provide the specialized conditions needed for growing alpines and rock plants in pots (see ALPINE HOUSES AND FRAMES, pp.277–279).

An unheated greenhouse does not exclude frost for more than an hour or two, so it is not suitable for overwintering plants that are not frost hardy. Sunlight, or even bright light, raises the temperature during the day,

but night temperatures can drop almost as low as those in the open garden. In temperate climates, most greenhouses built against a warm house wall give conditions similar to those in a cool greenhouse (see below), but this will not prevent tender plants from being killed by a few days of really sharp frosts.

The cool greenhouse

Freedom from frost increases the range of plants that may be grown. A frost-free greenhouse is also easier to manage, since protective measures are unnecessary. Day temperatures of 5–10°C (41–50°F) and a night-time minimum of 2°C (36°F) allow ornamentals to be enjoyed all year.

In a cool greenhouse, hardy bulbous plants, particularly those with delicate blooms that are not noticed in an open garden, flower earlier, providing colour in late winter and early spring. Here tender patio plants may be raised and overwintered; house plants may be revived and propagated in warmer months; and winter-flowering plants such as the aromatic *Prostanthera* may be grown in bench beds or in pots. Grown under cover, chrysanthemums and perpetual-flowering carnations (*Dianthus*) provide a good supply of cut flowers, while hardy annuals raised from seed sown in late summer sowings give early flowers.

The cool greenhouse should be heated enough to exclude frost and maintain a minimum temperature in all weathers (see GREENHOUSES AND FRAMES, "Heating", p.574). Even if the entire greenhouse is not heated, an electrically heated propagator, or a propagating bench, will enable an early start to be made on raising new plants in the spring.

An ornamental collection
A warm greenhouse may be devoted to displaying a collection of plants from a particular group, such as orchids or cacti. Tropical plants such as these forest cacti thrive in the heat and high humidity provided by the greenhouse. A luxuriant show is provided by the richly hued flowers and cool, fleshy foliage of x Aporophyllum, Epiphyllum, Heliocereus, *and other forest cacti at the height of their glory during summer.*

The temperate greenhouse

Raising the temperature to 10–13°C (50–55°F), with a night-time minimum of 7°C (45°F), widens the scope still further. If they are kept in a temperate greenhouse, plants associated with the essentially frost-free climates of California, the Mediterranean, South Africa, and parts of Australia and South America may be enjoyed in harsher climates than they could normally bear. These include genera such as *Brunfelsia*, *Jacaranda*, and *Strelitzia*, and orchids such as *Cymbidium* species and hybrids. If zonal pelargoniums are kept at 9°C (48°F) they will flower all the year round.

The warm greenhouse

A minimum temperature of 13°C (55°F) to 18°C (64°F) in a warm greenhouse allows cultivation of subtropical and tropical plants, as well as year-round propagation or flower displays. Tender plants, for example many bromeliads (see pp.362–363) and a number of orchids (see pp.368–370), may be grown to bring indoors when at their best.

The warm greenhouse needs controllable heating throughout the year, even in summer in cooler climates. This incurs considerable heating costs in temperate zones. Equipment such as thermostats, double glazing, fans, and automatic ventilation, an automated watering and damping-down system, and shading help to control conditions and facilitate routine care. A warm section in a cool greenhouse is a useful, cheaper option; a warm conservatory, or plant room, is another possibility.

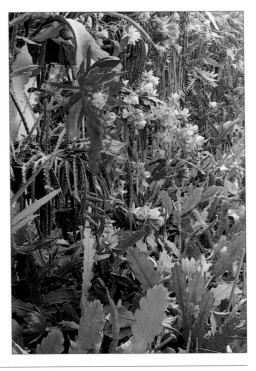

Planter's guide to indoor plants

WARM GREENHOUSE

(Minimum 13–18°C/55–64°F)

Flowering plants
Aeschynanthus ✻ ☺
Anthurium ✻ ☺
Aphelandra ✻ ☺
Brunfelsia ✻ ☺
Columnea ✻ ☺
Euphorbia fulgens ✻,
  E. pulcherrima ✻
Hibiscus rosa-sinensis ✻
Hoya lanceolata ✻
Justicia ✻
Kohleria ✻ ☺
Medinilla ✻ ☺
Pachystachys ✻
Ruellia ✻ ☺
Saintpaulia ✻ ☺

Sinningia
'Red Flicker'

Sinningia ✻ ☺
Smithiantha ✻ ☺
Spathiphyllum ✻ ☺

Foliage plants
Aechmea ✻ ☺ (and most bromeliads)
Aglaonema ✻ ☺
Begonia rex ✻ ☺ (and other spp.)
Calathea ✻ ☺
Chamaedorea ✻ ☺ (and most palms)
Codiaeum ✻ ☺
Dieffenbachia ✻ ☺
Dracaena ✻ ☺
Ficus, some ✻
Fittonia ✻ ☺
Maranta ✻ ☺
Peperomia ✻ ☺
Philodendron ✻ ☺
Tradescantia, some ✻, ☺

TEMPERATE GREENHOUSE

(Daytime 10–13°C/50–55°F; night minimum 7°C/45°F)

Flowering plants
Achimenes ✻
Begonia ✻ ☺
Catharanthus ✻
Cyclamen, some ✻, ☺
Exacum ✻ ☺
Haemanthus ✻
Impatiens, some ✻, ☺

Impatiens, Novette
Series *'Red Star'*

Schlumbergera ✻ ☺
Strelitzia ✻ ☺
Streptocarpus ✻ ☺

Foliage plants
Asparagus, some ✻
Jacaranda ✻
Solenostemon ✻ ☺

COOL GREENHOUSE

(Daytime 5–10°C/41–50°F; night minimum 2°C/36°F)

Flowering plants
Abutilon, some ✻
Bougainvillea ✻
Browallia ✻
Brugmansia, some ✻
Calceolaria, some ✻, ☺
Callistemon, some ✻
Cestrum, some ✻
Chrysanthemum, some ✻, ☺
x Citrofortunella ✻
Cuphea ✻
Freesia ✻
Fuchsia, some ✻
Gerbera ✻
Hippeastrum, some ✻
Hoya ✻
Jasminum, some ✻
Lachenalia ✻
Lantana ✻
Lapageria ✻
Nerium ✻
Passiflora ✻
Pelargonium ✻
Plumbago, some ✻
Primula, some ✻
Schizanthus ✻
Senecio, some ✻

Senecio articulatus
'Variegatus'

Sprekelia ✻
Streptosolen ✻
Tibouchina ✻ ☺
Veltheimia ✻
Zantedeschia, some ✻
Zephyranthes, some ✻

Foliage plants
Aspidistra ✻
Chlorophytum ✻
Cissus rhombifolia ✻
Rhoicissus ✻
Ricinus ✻

COLD GREENHOUSE

Flowering plants
Agapanthus (hardy spp.)
Anemone
Antirrhinum (hardy spp.)
Camellia (hardy spp.)
Crocus
Cyclamen
  (hardy miniature spp.)
Dicentra
Erica
Erysimum (hardy spp.)
Hyacinthus
Jasminum (hardy spp.)
Narcissus
Rhododendron (hardy azaleas in
  shady greenhouse)

Foliage plants
Adiantum ☺ (hardy spp.)
Euonymus
Fatsia ☺
Hedera ☺ (hardy spp.)
Laurus nobilis
Phormium
Tolmiea

DIRECT LIGHT INDOORS

Plants for a warm room (18°C/64°F and over)
Ananas ✻ ☺
Bougainvillea ✻
Euphorbia pulcherrima ✻
Hibiscus rosa-sinensis ✻
Hippeastrum, some ✻
Justicia ✻
Opuntia, some ✻
Senecio, some ✻
Solanum capsicastrum ✻ ☺

Plants for a cool room (5–18°C/40–64°F)
Billbergia ✻
Browallia ✻
Campanula isophylla ✻ ☺
Capsicum ✻ ☺
Chlorophytum ✻
Clivia ✻
Crassula, some ✻
Cyclamen, some ✻, ☺
Cyrtanthus ✻
Echeveria ✻
Gerbera ✻
Hyacinthus ✻
Jasminum, some ✻
Kalanchoe ✻
Nerine, some ✻

Pelargonium
'Caligula'

Pelargonium ✻
Solenostemon ✻ ☺
Streptocarpus ✻ ☺
Veltheimia ✻

INDIRECT LIGHT INDOORS

Plants for a warm room – medium light (18°C/64°F and over)
Adiantum, some ✻, ☺
Aechmea ✻ ☺
  (and all bromeliads)
Caladium ✻
Codiaeum ✻ ☺
Cryptanthus ✻ ☺
Dieffenbachia ✻ ☺
Exacum ✻ ☺
Howea ✻
Hypoestes ✻
Kohleria ✻ ☺
Mandevilla ✻ ☺
Maranta ✻ ☺
Neoregelia ✻ ☺

Peperomia ✻ ☺
Pilea ✻ ☺
Saintpaulia ✻ ☺
  (needs direct light
  in winter)
Sansevieria ✻
Schefflera ✻
Sinningia ✻ ☺
Spathiphyllum ✻ ☺
Stephanotis ✻ ☺
Streptocarpus ✻ ☺
Syngonium ✻ ☺
Thunbergia ✻
Tradescantia, some ✻, ☺

Pilea
cadierei

Plants for a warm room – poor light (18°C/64°F and over)
Asplenium, some ✻
Calathea ✻ ☺
Chamaedorea ✻ ☺
Cissus ✻
Dracaena ✻ ☺
Episcia ✻ ☺
Fittonia ✻ ☺
Philodendron ✻

Plants for a cool room – medium light (5–18°C/41–64°F)
Epiphyllum ✻ ☺
Epipremnum ✻
Fatsia ☺
Grevillea ✻ ☺
Monstera ✻
Platycerium ✻ ☺
Primula malacoides ✻, P. obconica ✻
Schefflera ✻ ☺
Sparrmannia ✻ ☺

Plants for a cool room – poor light (5–18°C/41–64°F)
Aspidistra ✻
x Fatshedera ☺
Hedera, some ✻, ☺
Pteris ✻ ☺
Rhoicissus ✻

HYDROCULTURE

Anthurium ✻
Chamaedorea ✻ ☺
Cissus ✻
Codiaeum ✻ ☺
Dieffenbachia ✻ ☺
Dracaena ✻ ☺
Euphorbia milii ✻
Ficus benjamina ✻
Hedera, some ✻, ☺
Monstera ✻
Nephrolepis ✻ ☺
Saintpaulia ✻ ☺
Schefflera ✻
Spathiphyllum ✻ ☺
Streptocarpus ✻ ☺

Key
✻ *Not hardy*
☺ *Requires high humidity*

Bromeliads

BROMELIADS, the 2,000 or so members of one of the most diverse and exotic families, the Bromeliaceae, are a fascinating group of plants that can make curiously beautiful specimens for the home, the warm greenhouse, or conservatory. Most are tropical epiphytes growing naturally on tree branches and rock faces, clinging by means of anchorage roots. These plants obtain moisture and nutrients via their leaves directly from the atmosphere, often from mists and low, moisture-laden cloud. Others are terrestrial, growing in the earth.

Almost all bromeliads are rosette-forming, frequently with strikingly coloured or variegated foliage, and many produce flamboyant blooms. Their forms range from the long and graceful, silvery strands of Spanish moss (*Tillandsia usneoides*) to the imposing *Puya alpestris*, which holds its massive spike of tubular, metallic-blue flowers above a rosette of arching, spiny foliage.

WRAPPING WITH MOSS

Position moistened sphagnum moss around the roots of a plant (here a cultivar of Tillandsia latifolia) *and attach them to the mount by binding the root ball to it with wire, string, or raffia. The moss must be kept moist at all times.*

Displaying epiphytes

Most epiphytes are displayed to their best advantage if attached to a section of tree or branch, simulating the way that they grow in nature. This method also avoids the risk of root and basal rot, which may occur if plants are grown in compost. Old, branched sections of trees cut to size are ideal. Attractive pieces of driftwood can also be used.

When attaching the plant to its display mount, it is usually easiest to start working from the bottom of the root ball. Move upwards, gradually firming moss around the roots and keeping it in position with wire, string, or raffia.

Bromeliad trees

If using an upright branch, secure it firmly in a deep container with cement or, if small, a strong adhesive. Alternatively, an artificial tree or branch may be constructed from a metal or wire framework covered in bark. There is a wide range of epiphytes suitable for displaying in this way, including many species from the genera *Aechmea, Cryptanthus, Guzmania, Neoregelia, Nidularium, Tillandsia,* and *Vriesea.* Use young plants if possible because they are easier to mount and tend to become established more quickly.

Prepare the plants by removing any loose compost from around the roots, then wrap the roots in moistened sphagnum moss and bind them to the support. Soon the plants will root onto their support and the binding may be removed. Some small plants may be lodged securely in crevices without being bound, as described for *Tillandsia,* below.

Displaying *Tillandsia*

Tillandsia species may be mounted individually or in groups on pieces of driftwood or cork bark, on rocks, or even on natural crystal. Lodge the plant in a crevice or press it onto the mount and secure with twine. Such airplants should never be glued.

Epiphytes as pot plants

A number of naturally epiphytic genera, particularly those with coloured foliage and the usually epiphytic species and cultivars of *Aechmea, Billbergia, Neoregelia, Nidularium,* and *Vriesea,* may also be grown as pot plants, provided that an appropriate compost is used. It must be an extremely open, porous mixture, high in humus and almost lime-free. For this, use half coarse sand or perlite, and half peat substitute (or peat). To ensure that any extra moisture drains away swiftly, add pieces of partly composted tree bark to the potting medium.

Growing terrestrials

There are several hundred terrestrial bromeliads belonging to the genera *Ananas, Deuterocohnia, Dyckia, Hechtia, Portea,* and *Puya,* but one of the best known is pineapple (*Ananas comosus*). In warm regions where temperatures never fall below 7–10°C (45–50°F), a wide variety of terrestrials may be grown outdoors. *Fascicularia bicolor* may even be grown without protection in temperatures as low as 0°C (32°F).

Terrestrial bromeliads often have stiff, spiny leaves and a spreading habit. While they may be grown in pots as house plants, they perform much better if given more space in a greenhouse or conservatory border or, where conditions permit, out of doors. With their eye-catching foliage and strong outlines, they make a

BROMELIADS SUITABLE FOR GROWING INDOORS

Ananas bracteatus 'Tricolor'

Tillandsia stricta

Tillandsia caput-medusae

Neoregelia carolinae f. *tricolor*

Bromelia balansae

Vriesea splendens

Aechmea fasciata

Cryptanthus bivittatus

Nidularium regelioides

Guzmania lingulata var. *minor*

distinctive addition to the garden, particularly if combined in schemes either with cacti and other succulents or with subtropical plants.

Bright filtered light is preferred by epiphytic bromeliads during the summer, while bright light with several hours of direct sunlight will keep leaf colour high and encourage flowering in winter and spring. Terrestrials prefer bright light throughout the year. Low levels of light and short day-lengths will usually induce a period of rest.

Routine care

As most bromeliads originate from tropical rainforests, they need warm, humid conditions in order to thrive; most need a minimum temperature of 10°C (50°F). In the right conditions they require little maintenance but, indoors, attention is needed to maintain the necessary humidity.

Watering

As epiphytes draw moisture from the air, they should be mist-sprayed once every day rather than watered conventionally; use soft water or rainwater when possible, particularly for genera that do not tolerate lime, such as *Aechmea*, *Neoregelia*, *Nidularium*, *Tillandsia*, and *Vriesea*. In spring and summer, add a dilute quarter-strength liquid feed of an orchid fertilizer to the spray every four to five weeks to keep the plants healthy and vigorous (see ORCHIDS, "Feeding", p.370). Provided they have adequate humidity, plants grown in cool temperatures can be encouraged to take a winter rest by reducing the frequency of watering.

Where plants are growing with sphagnum moss around their roots, the moss must be kept constantly moist by regularly spraying it with tepid water and also mist-spraying the foliage occasionally.

Bromeliads whose rosettes form a natural well or "urn" in the centre should be kept filled with water, particularly in hot, dry conditions. Change the water and apply a dilute foliar feed to the leaves occasionally Stop watering the "urn" as soon as a developing flower spike becomes obvious; this prevents detritus in the "urn" possibly causing blemishes to the flowerhead.

Propagation

Bromeliads may be propagated by vegetative methods or by seed. Most epiphytic plants produce offsets that may be removed and grown

DIVIDING ROOTSTOCKS

Gently tease or cut the offset away from the parent plant (here Billbergia nutans) so that the root system remains undamaged.

on separately, while stoloniferous terrestrial kinds may be divided at the start of the growing season.

Offsets of epiphytes

Many epiphytic bromeliads are monocarpic, meaning that the rosettes flower only once and then die. Before they flower, however, they form offsets around the base of the mature rosette. The offsets should be left in place until they are about one third the size of the parent plant. (If they are removed earlier than this, the offsets will take longer to become established on their own.) In many cases, the offsets may be removed by hand, but some will have to be cut off with a sharp knife, as close to the parent plant as possible. If the offsets have already developed any roots, these should be carefully retained. Replant the parent plant, so that it can produce more offsets.

Once removed, the offsets should be transferred immediately into prepared pots of free-draining compost, comprising equal parts peat, well-rotted leaf mould, and sharp, gritty sand, with their bases just held firm in the compost (see "Epiphytes as pot plants", p.362). Keep the young plants slightly shaded at about 21°C (70°F), and lightly mist-spray them with tepid water daily.

Offsets of the non-monocarpic species may be detached from the parent plant and attached to mounts in the same way as for adult plants. The offsets may have no roots, but these will soon develop if the plants are regularly mist-sprayed and if a few strands of moist sphagnum moss are fixed at the base of the rosettes to retain moisture.

Offsets of terrestrials

Some terrestrial bromeliads, for example some *Ananas* and *Hechtia*, have stoloniferous rootstocks that also produce offsets. At the start of the growing season, lift the parent plant from the ground, or remove it from its container, so that the offsets may be cut off without injuring the parent plant. Very often the offsets will have some roots growing from them and as many of these as possible should be retained as possible. Replant the parent and pot up the young offsets in a compost of 1 part shredded peat substitute (or peat), 1 part leaf mould, and 3 parts coarse sand.

Raising plants from seed

Most bromeliad seeds are sown like other seeds, although it is important to sow them when they are fresh because, with a few exceptions, they do not remain viable for long.

A less conventional method is used for *Tillandsia* seeds, which are

generally "winged" for easy dispersal – much like dandelion "clocks". Sow the seeds on bundles of conifer twigs, such as *Thuja*, that are packed with well-moistened sphagnum moss and then bound together. Hang the bundles in a slightly shaded position, mist-spray them regularly, and ensure that there is free air circulation but no draughts. If kept in a temperature of about 27°C (81°F), seeds will germinate in around three to four weeks. Young plants may then be transferred to branches or other types of support and grown on.

PROPAGATING TILLANDSIA BY SEED

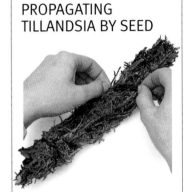

1 *Make a bundle of* Thuja *twigs interspersed with moist sphagnum moss, binding it with string, raffia, or wire.*

2 *Sprinkle the seed evenly over the prepared bundle; it will adhere readily to the moist moss.*

3 *Water the seeds with a light mist-spray and then hang up the bundle in position (see inset). Continue to mist-spray on a regular basis.*

PROPAGATING BY DIVISION OF OFFSETS

1 *When the offsets are about one third of the size of the parent plant (here* Aechmea*), sever them at the base with a knife. Retain any roots that they may have.*

2 *Pot each offset into a mix of equal parts shredded peat, decomposed leaf mould, and sharp, gritty sand, inserting it so that the base stays on the surface.*

Soil preparation and planting

STRONG, healthy plants, suitable for an indoor environment, are vital for success. Since pot plants grow in a limited amount of soil, it is important to use appropriate composts and to maintain nutrient levels in the compost with correct feeding.

Choosing plants

Most indoor plants are container-grown. If possible, check their date of delivery at the point of sale and buy those that have recently arrived. Each plant should be labelled with its full name and cultivation details.

Look for sturdy plants with strong stems, healthy foliage, and vigorous growing points; reject any that have weak growth, dieback, or discoloured, wilting, or brown-edged leaves. Choose younger plants, which should adapt more easily than larger specimens to new conditions. Do not buy pot-bound plants or those with dry, weedy, or moss-covered compost – they have been starved of nutrients and seldom recover fully. Make sure that the growing tips and leaves are free of pests and diseases.

Flowering plants should have plenty of buds that are just starting to colour. Climbing plants should be correctly pruned and trained. Do not

SELECTING A HOUSE PLANT

GOOD EXAMPLE

Vigorous, healthy top-growth

Strong stems

Leaves of good colour

Moist, weed-free compost

Solenostemon (Coleus)

Label

POOR EXAMPLE

Spindly, unbalanced top-growth

Pallid leaves

Dry or weed-infested compost

buy tropical plants in winter, since sudden fluctuations in temperature may have damaged them. If transporting plants in cold weather, wrap them in plastic for insulation.

Positioning a plant

Place each plant in a room that provides the levels of temperature, humidity, and light that it requires.

Flowering house plants that are of subtropical or tropical origin flower poorly or not at all if kept too cool or in poor light, whereas many foliage plants tolerate cool and shady areas. Cacti and other dry-atmosphere plants need light, airy, and dry conditions; plants such as *Begonia rex* require more humidity. If conditions in your home are not ideal for a particular plant, a different cultivar of the same genus may be more suitable.

Potting mixtures

Always use good-quality, prepared potting composts for indoor plants. Loam-based composts are generally most suitable, because they contain and retain more nutrients, dry out less quickly, and are easier to re-wet than peat-substitute- or peat-based mixes. They are also heavier, providing stability for big pot plants.

Composts based on peat substitute or peat are often used for short-lived plants, for example *Primula malacoides*. They have little inherent fertility compared with loam-based mixes, and plants grown in them require careful, regular feeding. These composts tend to lose their structure in time, causing poor aeration and watering difficulties.

Lime-haters such as camellias need special lime-free or ericaceous composts. Other groups of plants such as orchids (see pp.368–370) need special composts. For further information, see "Composts for containers", pp.322–323.

Grouping plants

For ease of management, group together plants with similar needs for water, humidity, temperature, and

---

Plant supports

Various supports are available for house plants. Choose one that is suitable for the growth habit of the plant, taking into account its speed of growth and eventual size.

Plants with aerial roots grow well up a moss pillar; tie in the shoots until the roots penetrate it; keep the pillar damp by misting. Trailing or climbing plants with several stems may be trained onto wire hoops. Use a single hoop or several, depending on the plant's vigour. A balloon shape of up to eight wires is attractive, allowing good air circulation and access to light for plants with many stems.

Many climbers support themselves by means of twining stems, leaf stalks, or tendrils, and grow readily up bamboo tripods; they may need tying in at first. Single-stemmed plants need only a bamboo cane for support; insert the cane before planting to avoid damaging the roots. For details of support aids, see TOOLS AND EQUIPMENT, "Ties and supports", p.564.

Philodendron hederaceum

Natural direction of growth

Moist moss

Shoot pinned to moss pillar

Moss pillar
Twine stems with aerial roots round a pillar, tying them in so that they are in contact with the moss.

Jasminum officinale

Wire hoops tied together at the top

Wire hoop
Train trailing plants around wire hoops inserted into the potting compost. Tie them in regularly as they grow, adding extra hoops if necessary.

Ficus benjamina 'Variegata'

Cane

Plastic twist-tie

Stake
Insert a cane into the compost before plant-ing. Tie in the stem of the young plant.

Trachelospermum jasminoides

Tripod formed by tying 3 canes together with twine

Bamboo tripod
Encourage stems or tendrils of climbing plants to twine around the canes by tying them in.

light. If planting into the same container, ensure the potting compost is suitable for all the plants. In permanent arrangements, use plants with similar growth rates, otherwise vigorous specimens may swamp their more delicate neighbours.

To increase the humidity level in a dry, centrally heated building, group individually potted plants on wet gravel in shallow bowls or trays. Alternatively, place plants on up-turned pots in a tray of water, with their roots above water level.

Plunging pot plants

Plants arranged in large containers may be plunged in their individual pots in water-retentive material, such as clay pellets, to reduce water loss and improve the local humidity. Clay can absorb up to 40 per cent of its own weight in water, so use a watertight outer container. Any plant that is past its best or too big may then be easily removed. Alternatively, divide (see "Propagation by division", p.378) and replant it.

Coconut fibre, bark, and peat are used as plunge materials, but plants may root into the medium, making them difficult to remove. Overwatering peat may result in waterlogging, which can rot the roots. Moisture indicators are useful in gauging when the plants need water.

GROUPING PLANTS

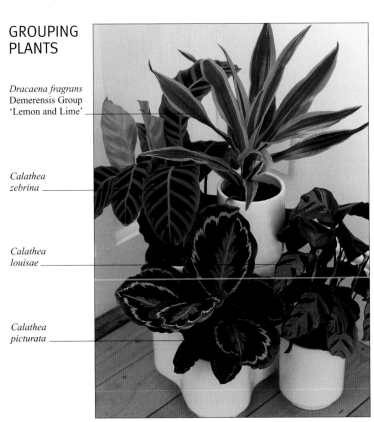

Dracaena fragrans Demerensis Group 'Lemon and Lime'

Calathea zebrina

Calathea louisae

Calathea picturata

This arrangement of complementary foliage plants is easy to manage as they require similar levels of light, temperature, and water. The grouped plants work together to create the slightly higher humidity calatheas prefer.

Planting a hanging basket or box

Conventional wire baskets, with a 5cm (2in) mesh, make versatile hanging containers for a balcony, conservatory, or greenhouse (see CONTAINER GARDENING, "Hanging containers", p.314). A traditional, slatted, wooden orchid box is an attractive alternative; this can be purchased or easily built (see right). Where dripping water would cause damage, use solid or plastic-lined baskets or boxes, with integral drip trays or an outer container that has no drainage holes. Water these with care to avoid waterlogging.

While planting a hanging container, place it on a bucket or large pot to keep it stable and clear of the ground. Line an open-sided container with green florist's foam or plastic sheeting, to reduce moisture loss. Alternatively, use sphagnum moss; a plant saucer placed between the moss and the compost forms a small reservoir of moisture. Multi-purpose composts based on loam, peat substitute, or peat are suitable, although loam-based composts are easier to re-wet.

Plant the container in stages from the base. If necessary, cut the plastic to insert plants through the sides of the hanging basket or box.

HOW TO MAKE A SLATTED WOODEN BOX

1 *Measure and mark 20 x 20mm (¾ x ¾in) timber into 14 side pieces, each 25cm (10in) long. To ensure a straight edge use a panel saw and mitre box to cut the lengths. Place one of the side pieces over an offcut of wood and secure to the workbench.*

2 *Mark drilling holes on one face of the side piece, centred on the width and 1.5cm (½in) in from each end. Drill the holes using a 3mm (⅛in) wood bit. Mark and drill similarly placed holes on the other side pieces, always drilling with the offcut underneath.*

3 *Cut out a 25cm (10in) square of plywood board. Mark and drill holes 1.5cm (½in) in from each side at the corners of the square, using the 3mm (⅛in) wood bit. Mark and drill 7–9 evenly spaced holes for drainage, using a 8mm (⅜in) wood bit.*

4 *Use pliers to cut 2 lengths of strong, plastic-coated wire, at least 30cm (12in) long. Working from the same side, thread each length of wire through 2 corner holes in the plywood board, then pull flush with the board.*

5 *Make sure that there are 4 equal lengths of wire above the board, then build up the sides of the box. After threading the final side piece, twist each wire end around a pencil to make a secure loop. Cut off excess wire. Finish with a non-toxic paint.*

Creeping fig (Ficus pumila 'Variegata')

Blechnum chilense

RECOMMENDED PLANTS FOR TERRARIUMS

Acorus gramineus var. *pusillus*
Adiantum raddianum ❋
Asparagus densiflorus
　'Sprengeri' ❋
Asplenium nidus ❋
Begonia 'Tiger Paws' ❋
Callisia ❋
Ctenanthe amabilis ❋
Chamaedorea elegans ❋
Cissus discolor ❋
Codiaeum ❋
Cryptanthus acaulis ❋,
　C. bivittatus ❋,
　C. bromelioides ❋, *C. zonatus* ❋
Dracaena sanderiana ❋
Elatostema repens ❋
Episcia ❋
Ficus pumila ❋
Fittonia albivenis
　Verschaffeltii Group ❋
Hedera (miniatures) ❋
Hypoestes phyllostachya ❋
Nertera granadensis

Pellaea rotundifolia ❋
Peperomia caperata ❋
Pilea cadierei ❋
Plectranthus oertendahlii ❋
Pteris cretica ❋
Saintpaulia (miniatures) ❋
Sansevieria trifasciata 'Hahnii' ❋
Schefflera elegantissima
　(seedlings) ❋
Selaginella ❋
Soleirolia soleirolii

Fittonia albivenis
Verschaffeltii Group

Strobilanthes dyeriana ❋
Syngonium hoffmannii ❋
Tradescantia cerinthoides ❋,
　T. fluminensis ❋, *T. spathacea* ❋

Planted hanging baskets and boxes are heavy, so ensure that supporting chains and fixings are sound. A universal hook fixing allows the container to be rotated to receive an even amount of light.

Planting in a terrarium

Before planting, clean the terrarium thoroughly to avoid contamination with algae and fungal diseases which thrive in enclosed and humid environments. Choose a mixture of tall, upright plants and smaller, creeping ones and decide how to arrange them before starting to plant.

Since a terrarium is self-contained, it must have a layer of drainage material, such as clay pellets, gravel, or pebbles, as well as some horticultural charcoal, which absorbs any gaseous by-products and helps keep the compost fresh. A lightweight, free-draining, but moisture-retentive potting compost is the most suitable planting medium. Extra peat substitute or peat may be added to keep the soil well aerated.

Use young plants with root systems that are sufficiently small to establish easily in shallow compost. Soak them thoroughly before planting, and remove dead foliage. Insert the plants into the compost, allowing space for them to spread. If the terrarium is too small to accommodate a hand easily, attach a split cane to a widger to assist planting, and a cork or cotton reel to another cane to make a firming implement. Cover bare areas with moss or pebbles to stop the compost drying out, and water lightly before replacing the lid.

Once established, terrariums require very little or even no watering (see "Maintaining terrariums and bottle gardens", p.373). If excess condensation appears on the glass, ventilate it a little until only a slight misting of the glass is discernible in the morning.

PLANTING A TERRARIUM

1 *Plan the arrangement with taller plants either at the back (as here) or in the centre, depending on whether the terrarium will be viewed from the front only or from all sides. The plants used here are:*

Asparagus densiflorus 'Sprengeri'
Ctenanthe amabilis
Ficus pumila 'Variegata'
Selaginella martensii
Soleirolia soleirolii
Selaginella kraussiana 'Aurea'

2 *Cover the terrarium base with a 2.5–5cm (1–2in) deep layer of pebbles and a few pieces of horticultural charcoal. Add 2.5cm (1in) of moist potting compost.*

3 *Remove each plant from its pot and shake off any loose compost. Gently tease out the roots, reducing the size of the root ball, to help the plant establish.*

4 *Use a widger or other small implement to make hollows for the plants, and insert them carefully, allowing space between them for further growth.*

5 *Fill in around the plants with more moist compost and firm the surface. A cork fixed to the end of a split cane provides a tamper of suitable size.*

6 *Using tweezers, place a layer of moss (or pebbles) over any bare areas of compost between the plants. This will prevent the compost from drying out.*

7 *Spray the plants and the moss lightly with a fine mist of water and replace the lid. The terrarium is now ready for display.*

GROWING PLANTS IN A SOIL BENCH

Zonal pelargonium

Ficus benjamina

Streptocarpus

Fittonia albivenis Argyroneura Group (syn. F. argyroneura)

Surface level with greenhouse window

Loam-based potting compost, about 30cm (12in) deep

38cm (15in) deep bench

7cm (3in) layer of coarse gravel for drainage

Strengthened timber frame

Drainage holes

Prepare the soil bench for planting by placing a layer of drainage material in the bottom and then filling the bench with loam-based potting compost. Plant a selection of ornamentals for a fine display in the greenhouse.

Soil preparation and planting under cover

Conservatories and greenhouses allow control of the environment, and extend the range of plants that can be grown in temperate or cool climates.

Soil beds and bed benches

Although conservatory and greenhouse ornamentals may be grown in pots, a large number, particularly climbers and woody shrubs, may be planted permanently in soil borders. For a new conservatory, consider at the planning stage if soil borders are needed. Raised and well-drained soil beds provide a good method of display. Prepare soil beds well, since ornamentals will be in place for some years. Make the beds about four weeks before planting to allow the soil to settle, and at least 30–45cm (12–18in) deep, with 7–15cm (3–6in) of drainage material at the base.

A bench bed is useful for propagating and raising different plants, and for specialized plant collections. Bench beds are shallow raised beds, usually at waist height, on supporting frames or pillars. They are ideal for small plants and for use with soil-warming cables (see p.580), mist units (see p.580), and automated watering systems (see p.577). Site the bench to make maximum use of available light.

Bench beds are usually built from aluminium or wood, lined with wire mesh or perforated plastic. They should be at least 15–22cm (6–9in)

deep and no more than 1m (3ft) wide for easy access. A 7cm (3in) layer of drainage material is sufficient.

Composts under cover

For soil beds, use a well-drained, loam-based compost enriched with organic matter at a rate of about 10 litres/sq m (2¼ gallons/10 sq ft). Do not use unsterilized garden soil as it can harbour pests, diseases, and weeds. No safe chemical soil sterilization methods are readily available to amateurs, and heat-sterilizing units, although effective, are expensive.

In general, use loam-based composts under cover. They contain their own nutrients and trace elements that do not leach out as readily as in less rich peat-substitute- or peat-based composts; loam-based composts are also easier to re-wet.

It is important to select the appropriate compost for specific purposes and for groups of plants with special needs. Most container-grown plants require a good-quality, loam-based compost that is free-draining and of approximately neutral pH. Tropical plants prefer more humus-rich, leafy soils, so incorporate additional leaf mould in the compost before filling containers or soil beds. Most ferns, heathers, and many lilies (*Lilium*) need an ericaceous compost, as do hydrangeas in order to produce blue flowers rather than pink ones.

Ornamental plants grown in borders need a dressing every year of 50–85g/sq m (2–3oz/sq yd) of a balanced fertilizer with a mulch of well-rotted compost in spring. If the

Planting a bottle garden

Bottle gardens provide an attractive way of growing very small, slow-growing plants in an enclosed microclimate. Many of the smaller plants grown in terrariums are suitable (see *Recommended Plants for Terrariums*, p.366).

Use any clean, plain, or slightly coloured, glass bottle, as long as the neck is wide enough to allow plants to be inserted easily. If the neck is too narrow to take a hand, make special tools, from split canes, loops of wire, and common household utensils such as a dessert fork and teaspoon, to help with planting and routine care.

With the aid of a wide funnel or cardboard tube, pour clay pellets into the bottle to provide a 3cm (1¼in) layer of drainage material and add a handful of horticultural charcoal to keep the compost sweet. Cover it with a 5–7cm (2–3in) layer of dampened, peat-substitute-based potting compost.

If the bottle is to be viewed from the front, use a widger to bank up the compost at the back. Level the compost if the bottle is to be viewed from all sides.

Begin planting at the sides of the bottle and work in towards the centre. Remove the plants from their pots, and shake off any excess compost. Carefully lower each plant into a planting hole, using tweezers, tongs, or a length of wire twisted into a noose. Space the plants at least 3cm (1¼in) apart to allow room for growth. Cover the roots with compost, and use a cork tamper to firm it gently.

Trickle a cupful of water down the sides of the bottle interior to dampen the compost, and cover bare areas with sphagnum moss to keep it moist. Clean the inside of the glass with a sponge fixed to a length of cane or stiff wire. If the bottle garden is not sealed after planting, water occasionally.

Hypoestes phyllostachya 'Purpuriana'

Asplenium nidus

Dracaena sanderiana

Saintpaulia cv

Hedera helix 'Eva'

Selaginella kraussiana

Hypoestes phyllostachya 'Splash'

Sphagnum moss

planting needs renewal after several years, remove and dispose of the plants, having propagated them first. Then dig in some well-rotted compost or manure and incorporate a slow-release fertilizer or base dressing prior to replanting.

In beds of ornamental plants, there is seldom such a build-up of pests and diseases that it is necessary to change or sterilize the soil. With crop plants grown in borders where pests and diseases may increase rapidly, the soil usually has to be replaced annually or sterilized if a suitable method is available. Crop plants are better cultivated in growing bags or containers, where the compost can be disposed of if problems occur. Always ensure that the bases of

containers with drainage holes do not come into contact with the border soil. This avoids cross-contamination by pests and diseases.

Planting

Always select plants that grow well in the range of temperatures provided (see "Planter's guide to indoor plants", p.361). Make sure that ornamentals or crop plants are planted at spacings that allow free air circulation and so inhibit the spread of pests and diseases. Position the plants to receive optimum light and ventilation for their growing requirements. Make full use of temperature, light intensity, humidity, and air-circulation controls that are provided in a well-built and fitted-out greenhouse.

Orchids

INCLUDED in the orchid family are some 750 genera, nearly 25,000 species, and more than 100,000 hybrids. Their exotic blooms and intriguing habit make them very desirable ornamental plants, mostly for indoor display, although some terrestrial species are hardy.

Terrestrial orchids

As the name suggests, these orchids grow in the ground, in widely varying habitats. Most of those that inhabit temperate to cold regions die down after flowering and exist in a resting state as tubers or similar underground storage organs during the winter. These hardy and near-hardy terrestrials often have flowers that, although individually small, are borne in dense spikes. Many are attractive plants for the rock garden or alpine house (see pp.277–279).

Some terrestrials, such as the slipper orchids (*Paphiopedilum*), come from warmer regions, where they inhabit sheltered sites, such as the forest floor. These remain evergreen throughout the year, but – because they are delicate – they need to be cultivated in a greenhouse.

Epiphytic orchids

Epiphytic orchids, which form a very large proportion of those grown by enthusiasts, are fundamentally different in their structure and habit of growth. As implied by their name (derived from the Greek *epi*, upon, and *phyton*, plant), they make their homes in the branches of trees.

They are not parasites (as they do not feed off the tree) but "lodgers": they take their nourishment from substances dissolved in the rain-water and from debris accumulated around their roots. A few orchids known as lithophytes live in a similar manner on rocks. In temperate climates, epiphytes need to be grown under glass.

Sympodial and monopodial

Epiphytes have two methods of growth: sympodial and monopodial. Sympodial orchids, such as *Cattleya* and *Odontoglossum* species and hybrids, have creeping rhizomes. Each season new growths arise from growing points on the rhizomes, and these develop into swollen stem structures known botanically as pseudobulbs. Flowers of the different

sympodial species vary greatly, and may appear from the top, base, or side of the pseudobulbs.

Monopodial orchids grow in an indeterminate manner. The stem elongates indefinitely, growing taller as new leaves are produced at the apex. Monopodials include many of the most spectacular orchid genera, such as *Dendrobium* and *Vanda*. These occur wild in warmer regions of the world, climbing towards the light through dense, jungle foliage. Most monopodials bear their flowers in branched, often gracefully arching, sprays from axillary points along their stems, from which aerial roots are also often produced.

Where to grow orchids

Some orchids demand fairly rigorous growing conditions, but many hybrids are bred for ease of cultivation, and can be successfully grown in the home. Before choosing which to grow from the vast range of types available, consider the conditions and care that you are able to provide. Many indoor plants need a slightly humid environment out of a draught.

While the hardy terrestrials (notably *Cypripedium*) do well in a rock garden or alpine house, others (usually described as half hardy) may also be grown in unheated conditions in mild areas. They include the cool-growing genera *Pleione* and *Bletilla*, which need only enough heat to ensure frost-free conditions.

A cool greenhouse, with a minimum night temperature in winter of 10°C (50°F), is suitable for a large number of different orchids,

including some *Brassia*, *Coelogyne*, *Cymbidium*, *Dendrobium*, *Laelia*, *Odontoglossum*, *Oncidium*, and *Paphiopedilum* species and hybrids.

An intermediate house, with a minimum winter night temperature of 13–15°C (55–59°F) will greatly extend the range of possibilities, to include species and hybrids of *Cattleya* and its relatives, and a wider selection of the *Odontoglossum* group and of *Paphiopedilum* species and hybrids.

A warm house, with a minimum night temperature of at least 18°C (64°F), provides the necessary conditions for species and hybrids of *Phalaenopsis* and *Vanda* and their many relatives, as well as the

heat-loving species and hybrids of *Dendrobium*, and many orchids from the hot and humid lowlands of the tropics and subtropics.

Choosing plants

It is best to obtain plants from a specialist orchid nursery, which can also provide valuable advice on suitable species for the conditions you have at home. Hybrid orchids are generally the easiest to grow, being themselves bred partly for vigour and ease of care. The species thrive best in environments similar to those in which they grow naturally, which are not always easy to re-create.

Owing to commercial techniques of mass production, orchids are no longer prohibitively expensive. For a modest price, plants that are attractive but have not yet won an award may be bought when you visit specialist nurseries and see them in flower. Least expensive of all are the unflowered seedlings that may take several years to come into bloom; the result is uncertain, but there is always the exciting possibility that one of the seedlings may be a future award-winner.

Cultivation

The unusual structure and growth habit of epiphytic orchids give them a reputation for being delicate and

---

RECOMMENDED ORCHIDS

Dendrobium nobile

***Cymbidium* Strath Kanaid**

***Vanda* Rothschildiana**

Paphiopedilum callosum

Cattleya bowringiana

Miltonia candida

COMPOST FOR EPIPHYTIC ORCHIDS

Fibrous peat

Crushed charcoal

Coarse grit

Medium bark

Orchid compost

The different components combine to provide the perfect growing medium: bark and peat substitute or peat retain moisture, grit aids drainage, and charcoal prevents the compost from becoming too acid.

difficult to grow. With a little knowledge, however, most of the difficulties are easily remedied or avoided.

Compost

Although most epiphytes can be grown in pots, their roots are specially adapted to open conditions on trees or rocks (lithophytes), so they cannot endure the close-textured composts suitable for most other plants. Orchid composts must drain very freely after watering; if they remain wet for long the roots are likely to rot. Chopped pine or fir bark makes an excellent potting medium, with some additions to keep the mixture open and prevent it from becoming sour. A suitable compost mix is as follows: 3 parts medium-grade bark (dust-free), 1 part coarse grit or perlite, 1 part charcoal pieces, and 1 part broken dry leaves or fibrous peat substitute or peat. A popular inorganic alternative to bark is rock-wool, which is made from molten mineral rock fibres. Its porous structure provides the precise water:air ratio needed for healthy orchid growth. Specialist mixes can usually be obtained from orchid nurseries.

Terrestrial orchids also require a much more free-draining potting mixture than most plants. A suitable compost can be made up of 3 parts fibrous peat substitute or peat, 3 parts coarse grit, and 1 part perlite, with the addition of 1 part charcoal.

Potting

When a plant has filled its container, it should be transferred to a new pot a size or two larger to provide space for further growth. Choose a pot that will accommodate the roots and allow for one or two years' growth but no more; a pot that is too large for the root system is likely to lead to stagnant conditions in the compost. To assist drainage, many growers fill the bottom quarter of the pot with broken crocks, pieces of polystyrene, or large grit. This also adds extra weight to plastic pots, making them less likely to be knocked over.

Hold the plant with one hand so that the crown is just below the rim of the pot and place the compost around the roots, tapping the pot sharply in order to settle the compost. Use relatively dry compost, which should be thoroughly watered after repotting. The plant, especially the roots, should be disturbed as little as possible.

Some epiphytes do well in containers that allow more air to reach the roots, such as hanging baskets made of wire or wooden slats. Such containers are essential for species of *Stanhopea*, because their flowers grow down through the compost to emerge on the underside.

When potting on sympodials, old pseudobulbs of two to three seasons' growth that have lost their leaves (usually called "back-bulbs") may be removed and used for propagating (see p.371). Place the rear of the plant against one side of the pot, leaving space on the opposite side for the new growth to develop.

Support

Many flower spikes are sturdy enough not to need support. Others, however, require careful staking to look their best, particularly long flowering stems that carry many heavy blooms. Use upright canes or stout wires, to which the stems may be tied as unobtrusively as possible. Do this as the stems are growing and before the flower buds open. Avoid changing the position of the plants or the effect will be spoilt because the flowers will face in different directions.

Growing on bark

Some orchids that do not grow successfully in containers will thrive if mounted on pieces of either bark or tree-fern with moss at their roots, although they do then require a constantly humid atmosphere. Initially they must be tied firmly to the slab; nylon thread is ideal for this purpose. New roots will gradually appear, which will adhere to the slab and thus secure the plant.

Routine care

For successful cultivation, it is vital to provide orchids with their particular care requirements.

Watering and humidity

These are perhaps the most important factors in orchid cultivation. Watering should be frequent enough to avoid drying, but not so frequent that the compost becomes soggy – once or twice a week for most of the year is usually sufficient. In the summer months, plants may need watering every day, while during the period of short winter days this task may require doing only once every two or three weeks.

Rainwater is usually recommended, but drinkable tapwater is quite safe. Water plants in the early morning. Do not let water remain too long on

DISPLAYING EPIPHYTIC ORCHIDS

Most epiphytes may be grown in pots, although they may also be successfully cultivated in a hanging basket or on bark. Keep the plants in a constantly humid atmosphere until established.

Growing on bark
Tie moistened moss to a piece of bark then attach the roots of the orchid (here Dendrobium Happiness) with nylon thread.

Pot-grown
Choose a pot that will allow for no more than 2 years' growth, place crocks or grit in the base, and fill with standard orchid compost. Plant the orchid (here Zygopetalum mackaii) and firm in.

Hanging basket
Plant the orchid in standard orchid compost in a hanging basket lined with sphagnum moss. The flower stems of some orchids (here Stanhopea tigrina) grow through the compost to emerge below.

the foliage, or it may cause leaf scorch if the plants are exposed to hot sun. Overwatering must be avoided, but water thoroughly, so that the compost is evenly moist. Allow the compost to become nearly – but not quite – dry before watering again; if in doubt, delay watering.

During the growing season, orchids need a high level of humidity. This may be achieved by damping down the orchid house by spraying water over the paths and earth and on the staging between plants. Do this early in the morning; as the day progresses, the water will be drawn up as vapour. This daily damping down may be discontinued when natural conditions are cold and damp. Be careful, however, because in extremely cold weather the heating system may make the air very dry, and the greenhouse may need to be damped down more often.

Orchids grown in the home as windowsill plants must be chosen from those that do not demand very high humidity. Even these may benefit from additional local humidity by standing them on a layer of moist gravel or expanded clay aggregate in a tray or deep saucer.

Feeding

Since modern orchid composts contain little nourishment, orchids will need feeding during their growing period. Liquid fertilizers are the most convenient and these can be added during watering. Any proprietary, general-purpose brands sold for pot plants may be used. Orchids are not heavy feeders, so it will be necessary to dilute the fertilizer to half the strength recommended for other pot plants. Feed the orchids once every three weeks from spring to autumn, and only every six weeks (if at all) during the winter.

Ventilation

Most orchids, especially the popular cool-greenhouse kinds, require free-moving air conditions. They dislike cold draughts, however, which can cause flower buds to drop and slow down growth. Ventilators should be only partially opened in spring, when sunny days may be accompanied by chill winds, and closed well before the temperature starts to drop in the late afternoon. As days become warm, ventilators may be opened wider and for a longer time. Remember, however, that water vapour is quickly lost through open ventilators and humidity is reduced, so that extra damping down is needed. A small electric fan, inexpensive both to buy and run, will keep the air moving without letting out humidity or letting in draughts.

Shading

Although different orchids may have different light requirements, from the shade-loving *Paphiopedilum* orchids to the sun-loving *Laelia* species and hybrids, some form of shading is needed to protect new growth from being scorched by the sun and to prevent the greenhouse from over-heating. The cheapest method is to use a greenhouse shading compound. White is more efficient than green in reflecting back the sun's rays, and it becomes almost transparent in rain, letting in more light on dull days. More effective, but more expensive, are manual or automatic roller blinds, made either of wood slats or plastic mesh.

Resting

An important and integral part of an orchid's lifecycle is the resting period, when growth is halted. During this time, which in the case of some orchids may last only a few

weeks and in others several months, they need very little water, if any, in order to survive.

Although plants' requirements vary, the general rule is that those orchids that lose their leaves when resting should not be watered until new growth begins. Water sparingly at first, then normally (taking care not to overwater). Plants that keep their leaves will need to be given only a little water during the resting period to avoid dehydration.

Propagation

Vegetative propagation methods are the easiest for the amateur to learn. They also have the advantage

---

PROPAGATING BY ADVENTITIOUS GROWTHS

1 *When a new plantlet with aerial roots has formed from a leaf node, cut it away carefully from the parent plant with a sharp knife.*

2 *The selected cutting should have healthy leaves and an evenly developed root system.*

3 *Holding the plantlet by its stem at planting level, pot up the young plant in a 7cm (3in) pot with the roots just below the compost surface.*

PROPAGATING BY STEM CUTTINGS

1 *Cut off a section of stem at least 25cm (10in) long, just above a leaf node or at the base of the plant (here Dendrobium).*

2 *Divide this into lengths of about 7cm (3in), cutting midway between leaf nodes. Each cutting should have at least 1 node.*

3 *Lay the cuttings in a tray on a layer of moist sphagnum moss and store in a humid place out of direct sunlight.*

4 *After several weeks, the dormant buds will have developed into plantlets, which will then be ready to pot up.*

of producing offspring which are identical to the parent plant, so that the results are predictable.

Adventitious growths

The simplest cuttings, which are known as "keikis", are small plantlets that appear adventitiously (that is, atypically) from the nodes on stems of monopodial orchids, such as some *Dendrobium* and reed-type *Epidendrum*, also *Phalaenopsis* occasionally. As soon as these plantlets have developed a few vigorous roots, they should be severed from the parent plant with a sharp knife, and then potted into a standard orchid compost. Water them sparingly at first, but remember to spray the leaves with a fine mist until the roots have established and the plants have had a chance to become accustomed to their new environment.

Stem cuttings

Cuttings may also be made from the stems (often called canes) of many *Dendrobium* orchids. With a sharp knife, cut off sections up to 30cm (12in) in length. Divide these into cuttings 7–10cm (3–4in) long, each with at least one dormant bud. Lay the cuttings on damp sphagnum moss or a similar moist material, and keep them in a humid, shaded place. When the buds have produced plantlets, detach these and pot them up separately.

Division

The usual method of propagating sympodial orchids such as *Cattleya*, *Cymbidium*, and *Odontoglossum* is by division. Simply cut through the rhizome between pseudobulbs and pot up the pieces separately. Each piece should have at least three healthy pseudobulbs and a healthy dormant bud to produce new growth.

Back-bulbs offer another way of propagating sympodials such as *Cymbidium*. Remove a back-bulb, preferably one with roots, by pulling or cutting the rhizome just beyond it. Insert the back-bulb at one side of a pot of grit, sharp sand, or standard orchid compost. Position the cut surface of the bulb nearest the edge as the bulb will shoot from the other side. Place in a cool, shady spot, and keep moist. Shoots should appear in two or three months. When the bulbs have developed roots, pot them on.

Commercial techniques

Growing orchids from seed is difficult and requires specialized knowledge and skills. Orchids raised commercially from seed are germinated in flasks of nutrient jelly in a controlled laboratory environment. They are sometimes also propagated by meristem culture: microscopic pieces of plant tissue are grown on under laboratory conditions to mass-produce replicas of the original plant. As a result, first-class cultivars may be purchased at a reasonable price. Both are, however, highly specialized techniques seldom practised by the amateur gardener.

PROPAGATING BY DIVISION

1 When the orchid has grown too large for its pot and has several leafless bulbs, it may be divided. The plant shown here is a Cymbidium.

2 Remove the orchid from its pot, then divide the plant by separating or cutting it into 2 sections; each section should have at least 3 healthy pseudobulbs.

3 When dividing the orchid, any leafless back-bulbs may be pulled away. Discard shrivelled ones, and retain those that are firm for potting up separately.

4 Trim each section of the divided plant by removing surplus compost and cutting off any dead roots with secateurs.

5 To replant each section, hold the plant with the oldest pseudobulbs at the back of the pot and at planting level, and place the compost around it. New growth will develop in front of the plant.

PROPAGATING WITH BACK-BULBS

1 Plant selected back-bulbs singly in 7cm (3in) pots. Insert each bulb with the cut side nearest the edge of the pot.

2 Within 2 or 3 months the old back-bulb will produce a healthy new shoot.

PROPAGATING IN FLASKS

Meristem culture takes place under sterile conditions. Microscopic pieces of plant tissue are placed in a flask on a special nutrient medium such as agar-agar jelly; they then develop into young orchid plants.

Routine care

U NLIKE plants grown outdoors, indoor plants are not subject to the extremes of the seasonal cycle so need relatively little attention. They require only watering and fertilizing, and an annual potting on, to perform at their best.

Watering and humidity

A common problem in the care of indoor plants is overwatering. In general, water when the compost is nearly dry. Take special care with coconut fibre composts, because the surface is inclined to dry out while the rest stays moist.

Water plants frequently while they are in active growth, less in winter when they are dormant – twice a month or even less may be enough. Wet the compost thoroughly, but do not leave the pot standing in water. Some plants, such as cyclamen, are susceptible to root rot; to water them, stand the pots in a little water until the compost is dark and damp. If tap water is hard, use distilled water or rainwater for lime-hating plants.

Buildings are often poorly ventilated and the atmosphere dry and unsuitable for many indoor plants. Maintain humidity by grouping pot plants on wet gravel in trays or in containers (see "Grouping plants", p.364), or on capillary matting (see "Care of house plants before going away", p.374).

Electric and ceramic humidifiers are readily available; bowls containing water placed in a room so that the water evaporates are also effective. Plants that need high humidity benefit from being mist sprayed with soft water. Use sprays sparingly on plants with hairy leaves, and avoid sunlight, since spots of water on the leaves can cause scorch.

Cleanliness

Always remove dead leaves and flowers promptly since they may harbour diseases or pests. Do not allow dust or grime to build up and block the leaf pores; dust the foliage with a soft brush. Thoroughly spray the plants occasionally to keep them clean and fresh, but do not spray cacti or plants with hairy leaves unless it is warm enough for any excess moisture to evaporate rapidly, or the leaves may rot. Only use leaf shine on glossy-leaved plants and check that it is compatible with individual species.

Fertilizing

Pot plants grow in relatively small volumes of compost and soon use up the available nutrients. Frequent watering also leaches out nutrients and the plants could starve without regular feeding throughout the growing season.

Balanced fertilizers are available in various forms: water-soluble or liquid (most convenient for indoor plants), granular, and solid. Always be careful to follow the manufacturers' instructions and never apply fertilizer to dry compost because it will not soak through evenly and may damage the roots.

Stopping

The appearance of many pot plants, especially trailing plants, may be improved by pinching out growing tips on young plants to encourage production of more sideshoots. This keeps the foliage bushy and increases the number of flower buds. Only stop plants that are in active growth.

MAINTAINING PLANT HYGIENE

Cleaning smooth-leaved plants
Gently wipe each leaf (here variegated Ficus elastica) *with a clean, moist, soft, and lint-free cloth.*

Removing dead leaves
Pinch out dead leaves and stems at the base of the plant (here Nephrolepis exaltata) *or cut them out.*

Neglected plants

With the exception of orchids and palms, most plants that have weak, leggy, or damaged growth produce new, vigorous growth if cut hard back to a healthy bud or joint in early spring. Cut back a neglected fern to the crown; keep the root ball moist and in medium light to induce growth. Plants that root readily are best renewed from cuttings, while some plants are rejuvenated by air layering (see p.383). Revive exhausted plants by repotting or by resting in a shaded greenhouse. To rescue over-watered plants, remove sodden compost from the root ball, trim off rotting foliage and roots, and repot in fresh compost. Refresh an under-watered plant by immersing the pot in water until the bubbles stop, and allow to drain.

Caring for house plants the organic way

House plants often spend years in pots, so it is important to grow them in a fertile medium, such as one containing equal amounts of loam, manure, and leaf mould, which is nutrient- and humus-rich.

Plants in the same pot for more than a year will need feeding: liquid feeds based on seaweed extracts are ideal; homemade comfrey or nettle feeds are also suitable (see p.332). Top-dressing with worm or garden compost is another way to provide nutrients (see pp.627–628).

Regular hygiene is vital for good health: remove dead or damaged foliage, and keep ahead of pests and diseases using biological controls. If possible, water with filtered or "grey" water that is not contaminated with detergents, soap, or grease. Remove dust, grime, and watermarks from glossy-leaved plants like *Ficus elastica* by sponging or spraying the foliage with filtered water. Avoid using leaf-shines that are not organically approved.

RENEWING TOP-DRESSING

Hippeastrum

1 *Use a widger to remove the top 2½–5cm (1–2in) of the old compost, taking care not to damage the plant's roots.*

2 *Replace it with fresh, moist compost including a small amount of fertilizer. Firm in around the crown and water.*

PRESERVING HUMIDITY AROUND POT PLANTS

Create suitably humid conditions for indoor plants by providing them with their own microclimate. Loosely pack a shallow tray with clay pellets or gravel and fill it with water. Group several pot plants on the tray. Keep the water topped up so that the gravel or pellets remain wet.

Pila cadierei

African violet (Saintpaulia)

Begonia

Streptocarpus

Potting on and top-dressing

Indoor plants also need periodic potting on to accommodate their growth and to replenish the compost. A pot-bound plant has retarded growth, fails to thrive, and water rinses clean through its pot. Pot on before this stage so that the plant's development is unimpeded. A few plants, such as *Hippeastrum*, enjoy confined roots, so do not pot them on; instead they should be top-dressed.

The best time to pot on is at the start of the growing season, although fast-growing plants may need potting on several times in one season. The process may delay flowering because the plant initially concentrates its energy on new root growth. Never pot on a dormant plant.

Potting on

Ensure that the root ball is completely moist so that it comes easily out of its pot without damaging the roots. Turn the pot upside down and slide the plant out into your hand. If the pot is too big to lift easily, run a knife around the inside; then lay the pot on its side. Support the plant with one hand and rotate the pot, gently tapping the sides with a wood block to loosen the compost fully before removing the plant.

Put fresh potting compost in the new pot until the plant is positioned at the same depth as before, with space allowed for watering. Check that the roots are spread out and the plant centred, fill in with more compost, and firm gently. Water, but do not feed the plant for four to six weeks so that it will send out new roots into the compost in search of food. Keep the plant out of direct sun for a few days to recover.

Repotting

If a plant is in the largest available container, has grown to its full size, or is very slow-growing, repot it into the same size pot to renew the compost. Take the plant out of its pot, removing as much of the old compost as possible. Prune out damaged or diseased roots before repotting the plant in fresh compost.

Top-dressing

With plants that react badly to root disturbance, or enjoy confined roots, do not repot, but at the start of each growing season replace the old, surface compost with fresh compost of the same type and enrich it with balanced fertilizer.

POTTING ON AN INDOOR PLANT

1 *Before potting on a plant (here* Dracaena fragrans *'Warneckei'), make sure that its root ball is moist by watering it thoroughly an hour beforehand. Select a pot that is one or two sizes larger than the old one. Make sure the pot is clean (whether washed, disinfected, or new) to avoid spreading diseases. The fresh potting compost should be of the same type as that in the old pot.*

2 *Remove the plant by inverting the pot and sharply tapping the rim on a hard surface to loosen the root ball. Support the plant as it slides out of the pot.*

3 *Gently tease out the root ball with a hand fork or fingers. Put some moist potting compost in the base of the new pot.*

4 *Insert the plant so that its soil mark is level with the rim base. Fill in with compost to within 1.5cm (½in) of the rim, firm, water, and place in position (right).*

Keeping plants from year to year

When all danger of frost is past, flowering plants grown for winter colour should be plunged in outdoor beds in their pots to "rest" during the warmer months. Choose a cool place, with indirect light, and keep them watered with soft (lime-free) water. At the end of summer, repot or top-dress them, bring them indoors, and feed them regularly once flower buds appear. To keep a cyclamen after flowering, do not water it until new growth starts, then remove old roots, and repot in loam-based potting compost so that the corm is level with the surface. Put it in a cool, well-lit place, and water regularly.

Winter-flowering pot plants
*In late spring, transfer the plants, here azaleas (*Rhododendron*), to a plunge bed in semi-shade outdoors. Sink each pot up to its rim in weed-free soil or another suitable plunge material, allowing space for the plants to grow. Bring them in before frost threatens, and keep them cool until the buds open.*

Cyclamen
Let the leaves die down naturally after flowering. Place the plant on its side, in its pot, under a greenhouse bench or in a cold frame.

REPLANTING A TERRARIUM

Asparagus densiflorus 'Sprengeri'

Ficus pumila 'Variegata'

Hypoestes phyllostachya 'Splash'

Dracaena

1 *When a terrarium becomes overgrown, carefully remove any plants that have grown too large. Divide them or select new, small plants. Try to leave the surrounding compost undisturbed.*

2 *If needed, trim the remaining plants with scissors. Thin out the surface moss where necessary by removing some with tweezers, keeping adjacent plants firmly in place with a cork and cane tamper.*

3 *Divide low-growing plants that have outgrown their allotted space. Use a widger to replant the divisions and the new plants (see inset). Firm with a little fresh compost, using the tamper.*

Selaginella kraussiana 'Aurea' *Fittonia albivenis* Verschaffeltii Group *Selaginella martensii*

4 *Trickle water down the inside of the glass until the compost is just damp. Then replace the lid.*

Hanging baskets

Hanging baskets need regular care. Never allow the compost in a basket to dry out. Water it thoroughly; in very warm weather, this will need to be done both morning and evening. If the plants wilt, soak the basket in a bowl filled with water.

Feed plants in a basket regularly with a balanced liquid feed, and control any pests. Dead-head flowering plants, clip back over-long trailers, and thin untidy or tangled growth. Remove and replace dead plants.

Terrariums and bottle gardens

A closed container rarely needs water; but if required use a long-necked watering can to trickle water against the glass inside to avoid disturbing the compost. Use just enough water to clean the glass and moisten the surface. If the glass is continuously obscured by mist, the compost is too wet – remove the cover or cork until it clears. To get rid of condensation or algae inside the glass, use a small sponge attached to a length of cane. Keep the container out of direct sunlight and move it occasionally, especially if it is in a shaded place in winter. Remove dead leaves and control pests and diseases.

Trim the plants from time to time so that each has enough light and space. A razor blade inserted into the end of a cane is useful for pruning plants in small-necked bottle gar-

dens. If any plants encroach upon others, either replace them with smaller plants or replant the entire container (see above).

Greenhouse plants

These need regular, sometimes daily, attention, even if the greenhouse is equipped with automatic systems. Watering, ventilation, misting, and feeding are especially important in

summer, as is heating in winter and proper hygiene at all times. Routine care of pot plants, including feeding and potting (see pp.372–373), is similar to that of indoor plants.

Watering

In the enclosed greenhouse environment, correct watering is crucial. The amount needed varies with the season and the weather. In summer, water more on sunny than on cloudy days. Use a hose in a big greenhouse,

with a low water pressure to avoid washing surface compost away from the roots. A watering can is best in a small or mixed greenhouse, where plants have differing water needs: some pot plants may need watering several times on a hot day. Stand the can in the greenhouse until the water temperature is the same as that of the plants. Do not overwater, especially in winter, since wet soil leads to rotting. For full instructions on watering (eg by capillary matting, drip feeds,

Care of indoor plants before going away

When going away, it is possible to ensure that indoor plants do not dry out. To keep water loss to a minimum, move plants into the shade and use one of the following watering methods. To use a capillary mat, group pot plants on an upturned tray, draining board, or shelf. Let the mat trail into another tray, the sink, or bath that is filled with water to supply the plants. Holes in plastic pots allow water through,

and clay pots are as good if saturated beforehand. Stand large or single pots on wick waterers, which draw water into the compost from a reservoir by means of a wick. Alternatively, water

the plant thoroughly, allow it to drain, and place it in a sealed, plastic bag to avoid moisture loss. Check for and control any pests or diseases before going away.

Guzmania lingulata

Syngonium podophyllum 'Albolineatum'

Aglaonema

Capillary matting
Place pot plants on one end of a piece of wet matting. Leave the other end submerged in a water reservoir. The plants must be above the water so that they can draw it up as they need it.

Adiantum capillus-veneris

Ficus pumila 'Variegata'

Plastic bag
Hold a clear, plastic bag away from the foliage with split canes. Seal with a plastic twist-tie or fold the neck of the bag under the pot.

or trickle systems), see p.577. Self-watering pots are also useful; an outer pot holds water that is borne by capillary action along a wick to the compost in an inner pot.

Humidity

Plants need moist, but not stagnant, air. In hot, sunny weather, damp down by splashing the floor, particularly hard surfaces, with water each morning and evening, or more often in very hot weather. This keeps the greenhouse humid and temporarily cools the air. Soil floors hold most moisture, while tiled or concrete floors dry most quickly. If the air is too humid, water vapour cannot transpire from the leaves to keep them cool, and they may overheat and wilt, so ventilate the greenhouse to dry out the air. In very hot climates or for plants with particular needs, automated damping down systems and special humidifiers may be necessary (see GREENHOUSES AND FRAMES, "Humidity", p.576).

Dank, cold air encourages fungal diseases to attack plants. In winter, keep the air dry by ventilating when weather permits or install a fan or a de-humidifier.

Temperature regulation

Use ventilation to control temperatures in the greenhouse and avoid severe fluctuations that can harm plants. Too much ventilation slows growth, and too little leads to high temperatures. On windy days, ventilate the greenhouse on the leeward side to avoid harmful draughts. For more information, see GREENHOUSES AND FRAMES, "Ventilation" (p.575) and "Shading" (p.576).

Hygiene

Keep the greenhouse clear of all debris that may harbour pests, and remove dead leaves and flowers before they rot. Wash or renew the aggregates on benches if they are infested with tiny snails or clogged with soil. Each autumn, take the plants outside and clean the greenhouse. Choose a still, warm day when the change in their environment is least likely to affect the plants. A thorough scrub-down is preferable, otherwise give the greenhouse a good sweeping and hosing down (see GREENHOUSES AND FRAMES, "Routine maintenance", p.583).

Frost protection

In unheated greenhouses, stop plant roots freezing in cold weather by keeping them nearly dry. Cover plants with a layer of plastic sheeting, fibre fleece, or newspaper, and beds with bracken or straw. Lag the base of shrubs and climbers with insulating material, secured with netting or twine. Plunge small pots in sand.

Pests and diseases

Regularly check buds, growing points, and the backs of leaves, and take early remedial action. Destroy badly infested plants, and isolate less

Hydroculture

This system has developed from hydroponics, a method of growing plants in water with additional nutrients. In hydroculture, "water roots", which differ from roots growing in soil, are supported by inert growing media, with water and nutrients added as required. Plant roots need oxygen to thrive and this method allows more air to the roots than potting composts.

Hydroculture has advantages: it is easy to provide precise amounts of water and nutrients; the growing medium is clean, well drained, not too acid, odourless, and free from clogging, discouraging diseases, pests, and weeds; growth is often faster and stronger than in soil. Bulbs, cacti, bonsai, orchids, and many popular office plants flourish under hydroculture.

The porous clay granules used as the growing medium absorb more than their own weight in water and nutrients; these are taken up by the plant as required, which means watering is less frequent. Unlike ordinary compost, the terracotta pellets do not shrink or compact, and are clean, easy to use, and attractive. Water indicators change colour when the root ball is dry, and suitable nutrients are added at every watering, so plants are kept well nourished. Different types of liquid food have been formulated for foliage and flowering plants.

Other methods of hydroculture require a two-part container – an aggregate one and a watertight one – but the clay medium is suitable for any pot. Another advantage is that, when transplanting, it is not necessary to wash the old potting compost off the plant roots.

Setting up the system

Choose a watertight container at least twice the size of the current plant pot. Measure and note how much water it holds: future waterings need a quarter of that volume to avoid waterlogging. Fill about a third of the pot with granules. If the plant was previously in potting compost, gently wash soil or debris off the roots. Carefully place the root ball on the granules and infill with more. Push the tip of the watering indicator gently into the centre of the root ball, ensuring the gauge window is visible. Pour a measured amount of water (quarter of the pot capacity) containing a suitable liquid feed over the granules. The gauge window will turn from red (dry) to blue (wet). Set the plant in a suitably lit position.

Routine maintenance

Wait until the gauge turns completely red before watering with the same volume of water and liquid feed, and replace water indicator once a year.

House plants need watering and feeding all year. Plants in active growth use more water than those resting (semi-dormant) so the red-window signal appears more often.

In active growth, feed succulents, cacti, and orchids at half strength. During winter dormancy, keep cacti and succulents in a brightly lit place; do not feed succulents but water at half the normal volume. Cacti should be drier – water sparingly to prevent dehydration but do not add fertilizer. Give orchids a quarter-strength feed every 4–6 weeks if growth or flower spikes appear in a rest period.

A TABLE-TOP DISPLAY

Chamaedorea elegans

Euphorbia milii

Syngonium podophyllum

Aucuba japonica 'Variegata'

Pilea 'Norfolk'

Repot plants into larger containers as required. Clay granules can be re-used: wash them thoroughly, break up any lumps, and dry.

Propagation from cuttings

Due to good aeration, cuttings root quickly in moist granules. Prepare as normal (see p.380), and insert cuttings to a third of their length in a watertight pot filled with granules. Treat as for rooted plants, but feed at half the usual rate. Free-draining pots can be used in greenhouses, but increase humidity by covering with a plastic bottle or bag to prevent excessive water loss and drying out. Keep cuttings in bright, indirect light until rooted. Remove covers when new growth appears. Repot the plants and start normal watering and feeding.

Seeds will germinate and grow on in clay granules in watertight or free-draining pots. After sowing, add one-quarter water measure and half-strength feed, then cover with plastic film or a bag. Place in a shaded position until new growth appears; take off the cover and move the pot into bright, indirect light. If the pot is watertight, start normal watering and feeding, but let granules in free-draining pots dry out between applications.

affected specimens until they are clear of trouble. Isolate newly purchased plants for two weeks and control pests and diseases before placing them with other plants. Particular problems may be caused by vine weevil grubs (p.666) and red spider mite (p.646), especially in dry, centrally heated air in winter.

In warm, moist, greenhouse conditions, pests and diseases, such as grey mould/*Botrytis* (p.646) and powdery mildew (p.646), aphids (p.646) and hence viruses (p.649), and whiteflies (p.646), can spread rapidly. During the annual clean-up, (see "Routine maintenance", p.583) remove plants likely to be harmed by chemicals; fumigate the greenhouse and control any pests or diseases before replacing the plants. See also PLANT PROBLEMS (pp.639–673).

Training and pruning plants grown under cover

Tʜᴇ basic principles of training and pruning under cover are much the same as for outdoors, although it may be necessary to adapt these to accommodate extended flowering periods and limited space. Climbing plants that are too tender to be grown in the open may be readily cultivated under cover. If properly trained and pruned, they make efficient use of confined space and provide shade for other plants.

Plant supports

Plants that need support when grown under cover include ornamental climbers, some shrubs, annuals, fruiting vegetables, fruit trees, and vines (*Vitis*). True climbers find their own way up supports (see "Climbing methods and supports", p.124), while shrubs grown as climbers against a wall need tying in.

Some climbers need a permanent, rigid support securely attached to the framework of a wooden greenhouse or to the glazing bars of an alloy-framed one. Wires, stretched horizontally along the walls of the greenhouse, are useful for training all climbers. In lean-to greenhouses,

CLIMBING PLANTS TO GROW UNDER COVER

Prune after flowering
Allamanda cathartica
   'Hendersonii' ❋ ◉
Bougainvillea ❋
Clerodendrum thomsoniae ❋ ◉
Distictis buccinatoria ❋
Jasminum, some ❋
Kennedia rubicunda ❋
Mandevilla splendens ❋ ◉

Mandevilla splendens

Pandorea
   jasminoides ❋
Passiflora, most ❋
Senecio, some ❋
Solanum wendlandii ❋ ◉
Stephanotis floribunda ❋ ◉
Thunbergia ❋

Prune as required
Agapetes macrantha ❋
Cissus ❋
Cobaea scandens ❋
Gynura aurantiaca ❋ ◉
Hoya ❋
Ipomoea horsfalliae ❋
Lophospermum erubescens ❋

Key
❋ *Not hardy*
◉ *Requires high humidity*

ESTABLISHING THE SUPPORT FRAMEWORK

Stretch wires tightly between vine eyes (see inset). Tie in the stronger shoots and prune them to downward-growing buds to encourage horizontal growth.

stretch the wires between vine eyes attached to the rear wall to avoid cutting out light. Alternatively, attach the wire to drilled and bolted, vertical wall battens. Keep the wires taut by using a straining bolt at the end of each wire. Space the wires at equal intervals: vines require a 25cm (10in) spacing; fruit trees 38–45cm (15–18in). Tie in the stems of climbers with soft string to horizontal or vertical support wires.

Netting may be attached to the framework of the greenhouse and used to support plants. Plastic netting perishes and needs replacing after one or two seasons, so it is not suitable for perennials. Instead, use plastic-coated wire netting.

There are also some useful purpose-made, wire-mesh frameworks and various forms of wooden trellis available: fix them securely to battens attached to the greenhouse wall. Train the plants gently along netting or mesh as they grow, and tie them in with soft string.

Annual ornamental climbers, or fruiting vegetables such as tomatoes, may be tied with soft string to bamboo canes placed vertically at 15–30cm (6–12in) intervals. Alternatively, drop lengths of strong string from secure fixings in the roof to the base of the plants. Tie the string loosely below the plant's first true leaf, then wind it around the stems and run it back to the frame. Never let the string become too tight around the stem of the plant. For details of the treatment you should give to particular plants, see the pruning and training sections in the relevant chapters.

Pruning plants grown indoors

Like plants that are grown outdoors, many indoor plants require regular pruning to maintain their vigour and encourage flowering. Others simply become too big for the available space, or need cutting back to main-

tain an attractive and balanced framework. With pruning, cutting back, or pinching out, most plants may be trained and shaped. Drastic pruning is required only to remove old, weakened sections or to renovate a neglected plant.

Pinching out

To improve the shape and increase the number of flowering shoots that are produced on young, scandent, or trained shrubs, pinch out the tips of new shoots during the growing season. Shrubs that respond well include fuchsias, *Abutilon, Brunfelsia, Centradenia, Hibiscus, Reinwardtia,* and *Tibouchina.* Repeated "pinch pruning" (see p.377) can also be used to form certain plants into novel shapes for display.

When and what to prune

The best time for pruning depends on the flowering season of the plant and on the age of wood on which plants bloom. Some plants flower only on the new season's growth, and on these the old growth may be safely cut back in the spring without harming production of the next season's flowers. Others flower on older wood, so should be cut back only after flowering. See pruning guides

CUTTING BACK AFTER FLOWERING

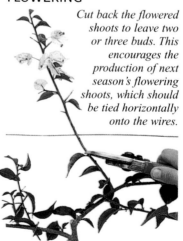

Cut back the flowered shoots to leave two or three buds. This encourages the production of next season's flowering shoots, which should be tied horizontally onto the wires.

for shrubs (pp.103–110), climbers (pp.134–137), and on pruning to produce fruit on vines (pp.461–466) and tree fruits (pp.435–460).

Pruning to restrict growth

Under glass, space for shrubs and climbers is always limited. Although major problems may be avoided by choosing the most suitable plant for the size of the greenhouse, it may be necessary to restrict growth to stop plants blocking the light. Climbers growing in the ground have a freer root run and so have to be rigorously controlled when they have filled their allotted space since they may overwhelm other plants.

Few shrubs and ornamental climbers grown under glass flower on old wood (but do check first), so pruning back fairly hard after flowering is generally advisable and safe. Cut back over-long stems in autumn; remove unwanted shoots whenever they appear.

Some plants flower for much of the year under glass, yet must be pruned to control them. In early spring, cut out the previous season's growth on mature *Abutilon* hybrids, and cut back *Coronilla* and *Hibiscus.* The flowers of *Hoya* are produced on short, woody spurs on both new and old growth; retain as many of these spurs as possible. Each can produce flowers over several years. *Agapetes* also flowers on old wood, but may need cutting back to induce bushiness.

The stems of some plants – particularly figs, like the rubber plant (*Ficus elastica*), and euphorbias, such as poinsettia (*Euphorbia pulcherrima*) – exude sap profusely when cut. The flow can be staunched by wetting the wound.

AUTUMN PRUNING TO RESTRICT GROWTH

In the autumn, cut out the weaker shoots and reduce dense growth; this allows plenty of light to penetrate the foliage and encourages the development of strong shoots to form a sturdy framework.

Pinch pruning

Also known as "finger-and-thumb pruning", the technique of repeated pinch pruning as a plant develops can be used to produce decorative shapes in a range of tender subshrubby plants, such as coleus (*Solenostemon*), fuchsias, *Helichrysum*, and *Pelargonium*. Simple shapes such as fans and cones are well within the grasp of a novice gardener; with experience, all manner of forms are possible – favourites being a ball, pillar, and pinch-pruned standard. Pinching, though in itself a simple technique, must be repeated at frequent, regular intervals during the growing season. No tools are generally required.

Shaping the plant

Plants must be healthy in order to respond well to this technique. Site plants growing under glass in a well-lit, well-ventilated position. Always pinch prune young plants right from the start, encouraging them to form bushy mounds before beginning to form a more specific shape.

With finger and thumb, pinch out the tip of the shoot just above an opened leaf. Remove only the very tip to stimulate the maximum number of buds into producing sideshoots. Side buds will then break and develop into shoots. When these have developed two to four leaves (or two pairs), repeat the process.

Pot young plants on regularly, while they are maturing. For some shapes, such as a fan, two or more specimens should be planted in the same pot. Do not pinch prune a week or so before or after potting to enable root systems to re-establish well. After that, start pinching the growing tips out of young plants regularly once again, to encourage dense growth and a compact form.

Finished coleus fan

Training frames and supports

Once plants are in their final pot, a supporting framework may be erected around them to assist training to the desired shape. Bamboo canes, wire and wire netting, both large- and small-gauge, can be used to create a variety of interesting forms, such as cones, pillars, and fans. If a large framework is needed, ensure that the pot is also sufficiently large to give the trained plant stability. The head of a pinch-pruned standard needs no frame, but is formed entirely by bushy growth, pinch pruned to create and maintain an even shape (see also *How to Train a Standard Fuchsia*, p.121). However, no subshrub can, in one season, produce a stem sturdy enough to support the head, so staking with a cane is required initially.

Routine care

Pick off discoloured leaves as soon as you see them. Feed young plants with a fertilizer high in nitrogen in order to stimulate growth, then, when pinching stops, switch to a high-potash feed to stimulate flower development or, in coleus, to allow the leaf colour to develop fully.

With flowering plants, such as fuchsias, once the shape is formed to your satisfaction, stop pinching about two months before flowers are desired, to give the terminal flower bud time to develop. Flowering should be simultaneous – and dramatic. With foliage plants, where flowers are not wanted (such as coleus and *Helichrysum*), continued pinching will prevent the formation of flower buds.

In cool climates, plants can be moved out of doors after the danger of frost has passed, either onto a patio or planted out as summer bedding, then if desired brought back under glass to overwinter. In spring, trimming and pinching are resumed as new growth begins.

Do not feed flowering plants while they are overwintering.

PINCH-PRUNING A COLEUS FAN

1 *Pinch out all shoots as they develop until the plants are 25cm (10in) tall. Then pinch only on two opposite sides, developing a flattened shape to the plants.*

Supporting framework
When the plants are 50cm (20in) tall (see left), they will need the support of a framework, made from canes arranged and tied as a fan.

2 *Carefully insert the canes that form the fan's ribs into the pot, along the flattened outline of the plants, and tie in cross-bars to brace them.*

3 *Using figure-of-eight knots and soft twine, tie in stems to the canes wherever possible, gently drawing some growth down to the horizontal.*

4 *Allow all shoots that extends towards the perimeter of the fan to grow on, tying them in at regular intervals to the cane framework. Continue pinching all shoots on the flat faces of the fan.*

Side view of fan
Once the frame is covered, the fan shape can be maintained by pinching all growth. This will also stimulate fresh, bright young leaves.

Propagation

PROPAGATING indoor plants is an economical way to increase your stock and to replace old plants with younger, more vigorous specimens. Successful propagation requires clean conditions, warmth, light, and sufficient humidity.

The easiest method of propagation is by division, which produces only a few plants at one time. The majority of new plants for growing indoors or under cover are grown from seed or cuttings, however, since these methods usually yield a greater number of new plants. Some plants may be increased by layering.

Propagation by division

Division is a quick and easy way of propagating plants. Many plants produce plantlets, runners, offsets, or bulbils, which root themselves and may be severed from the parent and potted up.

Dividing the rootstock

Before dividing a pot plant, water the root ball thoroughly and allow it to drain. Herbaceous and clump-forming plants may be gently pulled apart or cut into separate pieces, each with its own root system, and repotted. Use a sharp knife to separate the fleshy roots of rhizomatous plants; retain vigorous sections with young growth and fibrous, feeding roots. Prune any long, thick roots, and any that are damaged. Dust the wounds with fungicide. Replant each division in a clean pot using a similar compost to that used for the parent plant. Water the plants and keep them in good light, but out of direct sun, until they are established. See also "Potting on and top-dressing", p.372.

Dividing plantlets

Plantlets are small versions of the parent plant that grow on its leaves, stolons, stems, or inflorescences. Once they are large enough to handle, detach them with about 3cm (1¼in) of the leaf stalk or stolon, where appropriate. Insert the plantlet stalk in a pot of peat-substitute- or peat-based potting compost so that the plantlet rests on the surface. Water the pot and cover it with a plastic bag to preserve the humidity. Roots should form in about three weeks. After this, the plantlet takes up to five weeks to resume growth, at which point it is ready to pot on.

Dividing rooting runners

Some plants, such as *Saxifraga stolonifera* (syn. *S. sarmentosa*) and *Episcia*, spread by runners. If these are rooted individually in pots of compost, they may then be severed from the parent to make new plants.

Dividing offsets and bulbils

Offsets are small plants that develop around the base of plants. Choose a well-developed one with some roots; cut or break it off cleanly from the main stem and insert it in a pot of

INDOOR PLANTS TO DIVIDE

Plantlets/runners
Chlorophytum ✸
Cryptanthus ✸ ☺
Haworthia ✸
Saxifraga stolonifera ✸ ☺
Maranta leuconeura var. *kerchoviana*

Rootstock
Adiantum ✸ ☺
Anthurium ✸
Aspidistra ✸
Calathea ✸ ☺
Cyperus ✸
Maranta leuconeura ✸ ☺
Microlepia strigosa ✸
Phlebodium aureum ✸ ☺
Pteris cretica ✸ ☺
Sansevieria ✸
Stromanthe ✸ ☺

Key
✸ *Not hardy*
☺ *Requires high humidity*

PROPAGATING POT PLANTS BY DIVISION

1 *Thoroughly water the plant (here Calathea) an hour before dividing it. Support the plant, then invert the pot and tap its rim on a hard surface. Slide out the plant.*

2 *Remove surplus compost, either by gently shaking the plant or by teasing some of the compost away with your fingers, so that the roots are accessible.*

3 *Use hands or a hand fork to prise the root ball into sections, each with a portion of roots. Take care not to damage the stems or fibrous roots.*

4 *Using a clean, sharp knife, trim back any thick roots so that the divisions will fit into their new pots, but take care to leave the delicate, fibrous roots intact.*

5 *Select sections with healthy, young shoots (see inset) for replanting. Insert each section in a pot of moist, loam-based potting compost. Gently firm the compost and water well to encourage the roots to establish. Label the pot.*

PROPAGATING BY ROOTING RUNNERS

1 *Peg down runners (here Saxifraga stolonifera) in individual 7cm (3in) pots of moist, standard cutting compost. Keep them well watered.*

2 *After a few weeks, separate each rooted plantlet, in its pot, from the parent by cutting the runner close to the young plant. Label the pot.*

moist potting compost. Cover the pot with a plastic bag until new growth is produced.

Some plants produce bulbils on the fronds or in the leaf axils. Detach these and root them in moist, loam-based potting compost. For further information, see LILIES, *Propagating from Stem Bulbils*, p.251.

Growing indoor plants from seed

The seed of pure species breeds true, but that of many hybrid indoor plants does not. Uniform results may be obtained, however, from selections, or first generation (F1) hybrids, of biennials, annuals, and a small number of perennials, such as cyclamen and pelargoniums.

Seed composts and containers

Use a compost prepared specifically for seed (see TOOLS AND EQUIPMENT, "Standard seed compost", p.565). It should be a free-draining and open-textured mix, which holds moisture without becoming sodden or forming a hard crust on the top. A variety of containers may be used, such as half-

pots, pans, and half or quarter seed trays. Always use a size of container that is appropriate to the number of plants required. Special cellular trays that allow each seed to grow in its own individual plug of soil are also readily available.

When to sow

Most seeds are spring-sown, but seeds of early spring-flowering species are usually sown in autumn. Annuals may be sown in several batches from spring to early summer for a succession of blooms. Seeds of many exotic species are spring-sown but often germinate freely if sown as soon as they are ripe. It may be difficult, however, to keep the young seedlings alive in winter.

Preparing the seed

Some seeds need special treatment to help them germinate. Seeds with hard coats often need pre-sowing treatment, such as soaking in warm water; the time required varies from about 10 minutes for *Cordyline australis* to about 72 hours for banana seed. Other hard-coated seeds, such as *Caesalpinia pulcherrima*, will not germinate unless the seed coat is chipped with a knife or file. If the seed is too

small to handle, gently abrade it between two sheets of fine sandpaper. Follow the supplier's instructions on the seed packet to ensure success.

Sowing the seed

Overfill the container with standard seed compost and tap it on the bench; scrape off the surplus so that the compost is level with the container rim. Firm the compost to within 1cm (½in) of the rim.

Water the compost before sowing the seed, and allow the container to drain well. Watering with a watering can after sowing may "bunch" the seed or wash it together, leading to problems with overcrowding and damping off later.

Sow all seed thinly and evenly. Tiny seed is easier to sow if it is first mixed with horticultural sand. Place large seeds far enough apart to allow the seedlings to grow without being thinned later on. Alternatively, sow the seeds singly into small pots, cellular trays, or soil blocks.

As a general rule, cover seeds with compost to the depth of their smallest diameter. Very tiny seeds, however, or seeds that require light to germinate, should be left uncovered on the surface of the compost. Then cover

the container with a sheet of glass, a plastic bag, or a propagator lid to maintain humidity and stop the compost drying out. Place the container in the correct temperature, in good light but out of direct sunlight, and leave the seed to germinate.

Germination temperatures

Seeds usually germinate at 5°C (10°F) higher than the minimum needed by the same plant in growth. As a general rule, a temperature of 15–18°C (59–64°F) is suitable. The correct temperature varies for different seed, so follow the instructions given on the seed packets. Plants that are raised under cover for growing outside germinate at 10°C (50°F) or less. Many tropical or subtropical plants need 24–26°C (75–79°F) to germinate. If it is hard to maintain such temperatures indoors, consider using a heated propagating case. Although there are many different types and sizes, most have thermostats that allow a specific temperature to be maintained.

Aftercare of sown seed

Wipe off any condensation on covers to discourage fungal diseases. After seven to ten days, check the containers daily for signs of germination and remove the covers as soon as the seedlings appear. Germination times vary greatly, however, so some larger seeds may take several months to germinate. Keep the compost moist; use either a watering can or, for very delicate seedlings, a mist-sprayer.

Feeding should not be necessary if seed was sown in compost containing a small amount of nutrient, although seedlings that are to stay in their container for some time may benefit from a liquid feed as they grow. If the seedlings start to bend towards light, turn them daily and shade with cardboard or shade netting if there is danger of sun scorch.

Pricking out the seedlings

When the seedlings are 1cm (½in) high, they may be pricked out into larger pots or packs. Water them first, allow them to drain for an hour, then loosen them by tapping the side of the container. Lift the seedlings out of the container using a small, flat implement. If the seedlings are clumped together, use a dibber or pencil to tease them apart. Handle the seedlings carefully by the leaves since the stems are easily damaged.

Use a dibber to make holes in some fresh compost in a container. Lower each seedling into place so that it is at the same depth as before. Place more compost around the roots and lightly firm in each seedling.

INDOOR FLOWERING PLANTS FROM SEED

Alonsoa ❋
Begonia (fibrous-rooted and tuberous kinds) ❋ ◎
Browallia ❋
Caesalpinia pulcherrima ❋
Campanula ❋ ◎
Clitoria ❋
Cobaea ❋
Cuphea ❋
Cyclamen, some ❋ ◎
Exacum affine ❋ ◎
Impatiens ❋ ◎
Jacaranda mimosifolia ❋
Pelargonium (modern multi-bloom hybrids) ❋
Pericallis x *hybrida* ❋
Primula kewensis ❋ ◎,
   P. malacoides ❋ ◎,
   P. obconica ❋ ◎,
   P. sinensis ❋ ◎

Primula malacoides

Salpiglossis ❋
Schizanthus ❋
Sinningia ❋ ◎
Thunbergia ❋
Torenia ❋

Key
❋ *Not hardy*
◎ *Requires high humidity*

RAISING INDOOR PLANTS FROM SEED

1 *Mix very fine, dust-like seed (here Campanula) with dry, fine sand in a bag; this makes it possible to sow the seed more evenly. Sow larger seed by hand.*

2 *Sow the mixture thinly onto a pot of moist, seed compost, using a small funnel of paper held close to the compost surface. Label, and place in a propagator.*

3 *When the seedlings are large enough to handle by their leaves, use a dibber to prick them out into a container of moist potting compost.*

4 *Once the seedlings have become established, pot them on singly into individual pots or modules to grow on. Water, and label each pot.*

Small seedlings should be set about 2.5cm (1in) apart, and larger ones about 5cm (2in). Water the seedlings with a fine-rosed watering can. For seedlings sown individually in a cellular tray, lift the seedling with its plug of compost, and pot it up.

Potting on

Once the roots of plants have filled the containers, they need potting on (see p.372). The new pot should be large enough to allow for a 2.5cm (1in) gap all around the root ball. Insert the plant so that the base of its stem is level with the surface of the compost. Settle the compost by tapping the pot on a bench, firm it lightly, and water it using a fine rose.

Once potted on in normal compost, the new plants can be treated as mature specimens. Ensure that the correct conditions are maintained; different indoor plants have widely varying requirements.

Propagation from cuttings

Most tender, indoor plants may be readily propagated from softwood (tip) cuttings (rooted in compost or in water), leaf-bud or leaf cuttings. Semi-ripe or woody cuttings may be taken from indoor shrubs. The chief factors for success are timing, hygiene, warmth, and humidity.

Semi-ripe cuttings

Take cuttings of semi-ripe wood from the current season's growth, in summer after the main flush of fast, spring growth but before the wood is fully ripe; suitable material is firm, but flexible, and offers some resistance if bent. Plants grown under cover may reach maturity before midsummer, so check any new shoots carefully from early summer onwards. For details of the technique, see ORNAMENTAL SHRUBS, "Semi-ripe cuttings", p.112.

Leaf-bud cuttings

Genera such as *Ficus* and *Hoya* may be increased by leaf-bud cuttings, a type of semi-ripe cutting. Cut stems into 2.5–5cm (1–2in) lengths, each with a single leaf and leaf axil bud. Then insert them into pots of cutting compost and place the pots in a propagator at a temperature of 15–18°C (59–64°F). For further details, see ORNAMENTAL SHRUBS, "Leaf-bud cuttings", p.113.

Softwood cuttings

These are taken in early spring. Select new, short-noded sideshoots and remove them with a clean, sharp knife. When preparing cuttings, make clean, precise cuts so that no snags are left on the stems. Dip the base of each stem in hormone rooting powder, and, using a dibber or pencil, insert several cuttings into a pot of standard cutting compost. The cuttings may be close together in a pot or placed around the edges as long as their leaves do not touch.

Place the pot in a propagator or cover it with a plastic bag to reduce water loss – make sure that the bag does not touch the cuttings, however. Leave the pot in a warm, light position but out of direct sunlight. Check the cuttings each day or two and, if necessary, clear any condensation by opening the propagator or bag for a while.

It should take about four to six weeks for new roots to form. At this stage, when young growth may be seen, transfer the cuttings to individual pots of peat-substitute- or loam-based compost to grow on. Keep the young plants in a warm, lightly shaded place until they are well established.

PROPAGATING FROM SOFTWOOD CUTTINGS

1 *Fill a 13cm (5in) pot with moist cutting compost and tamp it down until it is level.*

2 *Using secateurs or a clean, sharp knife, cut off, just above a node, some new, short-noded shoots 10–15cm (4–6in) long. The plant shown here is* Gynura aurantiaca.

3 *Trim each cutting just below a node, removing the lower leaves to create a length of clean stem at the base (see inset). Do not leave snags, which might rot.*

4 *Dip the base of the cuttings into hormone rooting powder. Insert them in the pot so that the leaves are just above the compost.*

5 *Water and label the cuttings. Place the pot in a propagator in a warm, light place and maintain a soil temperature of 18–21°C (64–70°F) until the cuttings are rooted and ready to pot on.*

Rooting softwood cuttings in water

The simplest method of rooting soft-wood cuttings is to place them in a glass or jar of water in a light, warm position. Prepare each cutting as for a normal softwood cutting, ensuring that the lower leaves are cleanly removed. Support the cutting on netting placed over the glass so that the stem is suspended in the water. When the roots develop and there is fresh growth, pot up the cuttings. Prepare pots with drainage material and 2.5cm (1in) of compost. Hold each cutting in a pot with its roots spread and fill in with compost until the roots are covered. Then firm and water the cuttings thoroughly.

Propagating from leaves

Some plants may be propagated easily from whole leaves or leaf sections. In some cases, the leaves are inserted in compost (or water), while in others they are scored or cut up before being inserted in or secured flat onto the compost. Each leaf should produce a number of small plantlets where the leaf veins have been cut.

Whole leaves

Certain plants, often those with fleshy leaves growing in rosettes such as African violets (*Saintpaulia*) and gloxinias (*Sinningia speciosa*), as well as Rex and rhizomatous begonias, and some succulents (see p.347) may be increased from leaf cuttings.

For the cuttings, choose healthy, undamaged, fully grown leaves and cut them off close to the base of the leaf stalks. Trim each stalk with a straight cut 3cm (1¼in) below the leaf blade; insert the cuttings individually into prepared pots of cutting compost (1 part sand and 1 part peat

PROPAGATING SOFTWOOD CUTTINGS IN WATER

1 Using a sharp, clean knife, remove healthy, short-noded cuttings, 10–15cm (4–6in) long, from a healthy, vigorous plant (here Solenostemon). Cut each stem carefully just above a node.

2 Trim each cutting below a node and remove the lower leaves to create a length of clean stem at the base (see inset).

3 Insert the stems through a piece of wire netting over the top of a jar of water. Ensure that the stems are in the water.

4 Keep the water topped up so that the lower end of each cutting is always below the surface. A network of roots should develop.

5 When the cuttings are well rooted, carefully plant each one into a 7cm (3in) pot of sandy potting compost.

substitute or peat), label, and water. Place the pots in a propagator or cover each one with a clear plastic bag or improvised cloche (see below). As soon as each cutting produces plantlets, remove its cover. Grow on the cuttings until the plantlets are large enough to be teased apart and potted on individually. Alternatively,

leaves with long stalks (especially African violets) may be rooted in water, although rooting tends to take longer than in compost.

Scored or cut leaves

The leaves of plants with prominent veins, such as Rex begonias and various members of the family

HALF-LEAF SECTIONS

1 Divide the leaf by cutting out the midrib and exposing the veins (here, Streptocarpus).

2 Insert the sections, cut edges down, in shallow trenches. Gently firm them in.

PROPAGATING INDOOR PLANTS FROM LEAF CUTTINGS

1 Cut healthy leaves from the parent plant (here Saintpaulia). Insert each stalk in a small pot of cutting compost so that the leaf blade is just clear of the compost.

2 Water, label, and cover the pots. Small cloches made from the bases of plastic drinks bottles are suitable. Leave them in a warm, light place out of direct sunlight.

3 Each leaf should produce several plantlets. When these develop, remove the covers, and grow them on until they are large enough to pot up individually.

Gesneriaceae, for example *Streptocarpus*, will produce small plantlets if they are scored or cut up and the cut veins are then kept in contact with moist compost; the leaves may be divided either in half or into small sections, or they may be scored through.

Whichever method is used, keep the container in a propagator or in a clear plastic bag in a light place but out of direct sunlight; inflate the bag so that it does not touch the leaf sections, and seal it. The leaves being propagated should be kept at 18–24°C (64–75°F).

When clumps of plantlets develop from the cut veins, carefully lift and separate them, retaining a little compost around the roots of each plantlet, and pot them up individually into 7cm (3in) pots containing cutting compost.

Some succulent plants, including *Sansevieria* and those that have flattened, leaf-like stems such as *Epiphyllum*, may also be propagated from "leaf" sections although these are treated slightly differently. For details, see CACTI AND OTHER SUCCULENTS, "Propagation from stem sections", p.348.

PROPAGATING FROM CUT LEAVES

1 *Select a young, healthy leaf (here* Begonia rex*) and make a 1cm (½in) long incision with a sharp knife straight across each of the strongest veins on the underside of the leaf (see inset).*

2 *Place the leaf, cut side downwards, on a tray of cutting compost. Pin its veins to the compost. Label, and place the tray in a propagator or a plastic bag.*

3 *Leave the tray in a warm place out of direct sunlight. When the plantlets have developed, carefully separate them from the leaf (see inset) and pot them on singly.*

LEAF SQUARES

1 *Cut 4 or 5 square sections the size of a postage stamp from a healthy leaf. Each piece should include a strong vein.*

2 *Place the sections, veins downwards, on moist compost. Pin with wire hoops, then treat as other leaf sections.*

Propagation of tuberous begonias

When begonia tubers die back naturally in autumn, store them in their pots at 5–10°C (41–50°F) in a dry place over winter. Alternatively, lift and clean the tubers, dust their crowns with fungicide, and store them in boxes of dry sand, peat substitute, or peat.

At the beginning of the growing season, place the tubers in a tray of moist, sandy compost (1 part sharp sand, 1 part peat-substitute- or peat-based compost). Store them at a minimum temperature of 13–16°C (55–61°F). When new buds are visible, cut the tubers into sections, making sure that each has at least one bud and some roots. Dust the sections with fungicide and leave them to dry for a few hours in a warm place. When the cut surfaces have formed calluses, pot up the sections in loam-based compost. Do not firm the compost heavily or water it, since this encourages fungal attack.

Alternatively, allow new shoots to develop on the tubers, and use these as basal cuttings. Take the cuttings so that each retains an eye. Dip the base of each cutting in hormone rooting powder and insert them, 2cm (¾in) deep, around the edge of a pot or pan of loam-based potting compost.

1 *In autumn, lift the dormant tubers and clean them. Dust the crowns with fungicide and overwinter them in a dry place.*

2 *In spring, place the tubers, concave side upwards, 5cm (2in) apart and 2.5cm (1in) deep, in a tray of moist, sandy compost.*

3 *When shoots appear, cut tubers into sections, each with a bud and some roots. Dust cut surfaces with fungicide and allow to dry.*

4 *Pot up the sections singly in 13cm (5in) pots, with the top of each level with the compost surface. Label each container.*

5 *Keep the pots in a propagator in a warm, frost-free place until the sections are established, then pot them on singly.*

BASAL CUTTINGS

Remove 5cm (2in) shoots from the tuber, each with a eye of the tuber at the base. Pot them up and treat as divided tubers.

Propagation by layering

Layering involves wounding the stem of a plant, inducing it to produce roots, and then separating the rooted stem. This method has a high success rate since the layered stem receives nutrients from the parent plant while it is developing.

Some indoor plants may be propagated by layering – either in air or in the soil. Air layering produces a fairly large, new plant from an older specimen but it may take some considerable time. Simple layering in soil provides new stock quite quickly.

Air layering

This is an excellent method for replacing old or damaged house plants, for example the rubber plant (*Ficus elastica*) and its relatives. The top of the plant, or tip of a branch, may be encouraged to form new roots, and is then severed from the parent.

Choose a section of stem of new growth that is straight, about 10cm (4in) long, and of at least pencil thickness. Cut the bottom off a clear, plastic bag to create a transparent sleeve and slip it over the stem or, if the leaves are too large to permit this, fold a clear, plastic sheet around the stem and tape up the seam. Secure the sleeve below the selected area of the stem.

Using a sharp knife, make a shallow, upward-slanting cut in the side of the stem, then wedge this tongue open with moist sphagnum moss. Alternatively, on woody plants, score two rings 1–2cm (½–¾in) apart below a healthy leaf joint on the selected area of the stem; the scores should be just deep enough to penetrate the bark without harming the wood. Peel off the bark between the rings, leaving the cambium undisturbed.

In both cases, dust the cut area with rooting powder. Pack the sleeve with damp moss, and seal it so that the area is tightly enclosed to prevent it from drying out. If the stem is heavy, provide cane support.

It may be many months before the roots show. If the moss begins to dry out, open up the plastic, add a little water, and reseal. When roots appear, sever the layered stem from the parent and pot it up into a loam-based potting compost. Water the young plant sparingly until it is established.

Simple layering

Climbing or trailing shoots may be layered into soil while they are still attached to the parent plant.

Choose a long, vigorous shoot and peg it down into a small pot of moist cutting compost. After three to four weeks, roots should start to grow into the compost and new shoots begin to form; the rooted layer may then be detached from the parent plant. If required, several shoots may be layered at the same time, each in its own pot.

When severing the new plants, always take care not to spoil the shape of the parent plant. For further information, see CLIMBING PLANTS, p.145.

SIMPLE LAYERING

Select a long, healthy shoot and peg down the young growth into a small pot filled with moist cutting compost. Leave it until roots have formed before detaching it from the parent plant.

Parent plant

Long, vigorous stem

Leaf node

Wire staple

Moist cutting compost

Philodendron hederaceum

PROPAGATING BY AIR LAYERING

1 *Trim the leaves (here Ficus elastica) from a straight length of stem (see inset). Slide a plastic sleeve over the stem and fix the lower end with adhesive tape.*

2 *Fold down the sleeve. Hold the stem firmly and cut a "tongue" in it, making a slanted, upwards incision 5mm (¼in) deep and 2.5cm (1in) long.*

3 *Apply hormone rooting powder to the wound and push moist sphagnum moss into the incision, using a split stake or the back of a knife blade.*

4 *Roll the sleeve back into position around the packed incision. Fill the sleeve with more moist sphagnum moss.*

5 *When the sleeve is tightly packed with moss, secure the upper end to the stem with adhesive tape.*

6 *When the new roots are visible through the sleeve, cut through the stem just below the root ball with secateurs. Remove the plastic sleeve.*

7 *Gently loosen the moss ball and tease out the roots. Pot the rooted layer into a container that allows a 5cm (2in) space around the root ball. Fill this with loam-based potting compost and firm it very gently, making sure that the new roots are not damaged. Water, label, and place the pot in a shaded position until the young plant is established.*

CHAPTER

14

THE LAWN

FROM THE STRIPED green sward in a formal garden to the closely mown turf of a sports area or rough grassland under a grove of trees, there is a lawn to suit all situations. Whether it is a showpiece in its own right, a foil for colourful borders, a playing surface for children, or simply a relaxing haven, the lawn can be both functional and a design feature. Frequently undervalued as merely a flat surface underfoot, the lawn can make a much more important contribution to the garden, softening hard surfaces, helping to define distinctive features, and unifying the garden as a whole. For centuries, grass has been used to create lawns because it is visually appealing, tolerates wear, and may be cut very low without being damaged, although chamomile and other low–growing herbs make wonderful scented alternatives for ornamental use.

Creating lawns

A HEALTHY, well-maintained lawn is an attractive feature that also provides a clear area in which to walk, play, and relax. In addition to such ornamental and utility lawns, grass may be used to cover the ground in other areas such as sports or games lawns, in orchards and wild gardens, for wide paths and gently sloping banks.

Some broadleaved plants, for example chamomile (*Chamaemelum nobile*), may also be used to form lawns; they should, however, be considered primarily as ornamental, to be admired rather than extensively used, because they are less tolerant of wear than grass (see "Non-grass lawns", p.389).

When deciding on the type and shape of the lawn as well as where to site it, consider how it will link to the rest of the garden – to other plants, features, and the overall layout – so that it forms a congruous, unifying part of the design.

Grass

Grass is most commonly chosen for a lawn because it is hard-wearing and usually attractive all year. It may also be repeatedly cut low without damage as the growing points are at the base of the plants.

Mown lawns

Mown areas of grass include high-quality lawns, utility lawns, and sports lawns. A primarily ornamental, high-quality lawn is suitable where a perfect, even appearance is paramount; it stands some wear but requires a considerable amount of maintenance to keep it in pristine condition. If the grass is likely to be subject to heavier wear – by being used as a play area, for example – opt for a utility lawn; this should also be attractive but may contain minor imperfections and requires less maintenance.

Sports areas, such as for lawn tennis or bowls, demand a particularly hard-wearing surface that can be cut very low. To stop unnecessary additional wear, they are best sited separately from the main lawn.

Long grass and grassland

As part of a wild garden or orchard, unmown grass or flower-rich grassland is attractive, but as the grass is relatively long, it is not practical for a utility lawn. It needs very little maintenance, however, so may be suitable for an area such as a slope or a stream bank where mowing is difficult. Flower-rich grasslands often thrive on impoverished soils, so this may be a good way of using a part of the garden where little else grows.

Mixing long and short grass

Using different grasses in various parts of the garden, or varying the height of cut, helps define separate areas and adds textural contrast. A closely mown path running through long, flower-rich grassland provides an eye-catching shift in height, colour, and texture, and also encourages people to walk only on the path.

A formal lawn
Here, the close-clipped, pristine expanse of a high-quality, formal lawn provides a uniform, fine-textured foil for an elegant planting of white Agapanthus, *silver-grey* Senecio, *and other complementary plants, and a platform to offset an ornamental garden seat and pots of marguerites* (Argyranthemum frutescens).

Lawns and biodiversity

The traditional "bowling green" lawn supports relatively little biodiversity as it is essentially a monoculture, a mix of only two or three grass species, blended to provide a dense green sward in which other plant species are discouraged. It is possible to produce a fine lawn following organic principles, but it requires a great deal of care and attention to prevent an influx of unwanted species from wind-blown seed.

If a perfect lawn is not essential, you could adopt a less rigid regime and improve the lawn's biodiversity. This involves mowing less frequently using a higher cut to create a longer sward 8–10cm (3–4in) tall, allowing a number of low-growing plants like clover, daisies, and self-heal (*Prunella*) to establish, which help to support insects and other wildlife. Should broad-leaved species increase too rapidly, control them by mowing slightly more often, setting the blades lower to decapitate flowers and reduce self-seeding. Leaving grass clippings on the lawn is sometimes recommended, but it is usually better to compost them.

In large gardens, consider having a low-cut lawn sited near the house where its fine appearance may be easily enjoyed; a path or steps could then lead to a utility lawn farther away; while an area of long grass and wild flowers could lie at the far end of the garden. Mixing grass height in this way provides contrasting but complementary ornamental, wildlife, and play areas; mowing time is also reduced as part of the area requires cutting only infrequently.

Position and form

The lawn may well be the largest single area in the garden, so plan its position and shape carefully within the context of the overall design. Take into account practical and aesthetic considerations so that the lawn will be pleasurable to use, convenient to maintain, and an enhancing, integral part of the garden plan.

Siting a lawn

A lawn is best positioned in an open sunny area, as grass requires good light, well-drained, nutrient-rich soil, and regular moisture to thrive. A partially shaded spot can be used, provided it is laid with shade-tolerant turf or sown with a seed mixture that is suitable for shade (see "Choosing the right mixtures", p.389). Alternatively it might be better to introduce a non-grass lawn of shade-tolerant plants that tolerate some wear (see "Non-grass lawns", p.389). A chamomile or other herb lawn may also suit a garden where there is no space in which to store a mower, as these plants do not need mowing to keep them tidy.

If the proposed lawn is to surround a tree, an area the width of the tree's canopy should preferably be left ungrassed around it, because the grass cannot compete with the tree for nutrients and moisture. Alternatively plant difficult areas with shade-tolerant grass (see "Problem areas", p.389) or other ground cover.

Shape

The shape of the lawn may harmonize with the garden style or be used to dictate it. A symmetrical layout of geometrically shaped lawns bordered by paths would be appropriate in a highly stylized, formal garden. In a small garden, a simple shape such as a circle could be visually striking and might be echoed imaginatively by the introduction of a circular pool or patio and containers packed with ornamental plants.

A curved, irregular design lends the garden fluidity, linking the different elements with a sweeping plane of even colour. Broad, flowing

Informal lawn
The bold, curving sweep of an informal lawn is echoed by a winding, gravel path beyond and a ribbon of gold-leaved plants in an adjacent border.

curves can be created to set off the planting in a border, and to lead the eye to a focal point. Steer clear of fussy, scalloped edges or awkward angles, however, as they may detract from the impact of any planting and make mowing difficult.

Space permitting, it may be more effective to have more than one lawn; perhaps two or more similar or complementary shapes linked by paths or archways. The farther lawn could be partially screened to provide a half-glimpsed reflection of the nearer one.

Design functions

As well as being attractive in its own right, the lawn may fulfil different design criteria for both plants and hard features. Uniform areas of grass create a natural bond between otherwise disparate elements, leading the eye from one part of the garden to another. A statue or specimen tree sited in a lawn has maximum impact since the surrounding sea of plain colour separates it from other, more distracting elements. In a large lawn, one or two flower beds or trees may be effective if they are positioned so that they break up the green expanse, but do not dot the entire lawn: as well as making maintenance more time-consuming, the overall effect may be cluttered and disjointed.

The uniform texture and colour of grass form a neutral background that enhances other planting particularly well. The level surface acts as a foil for more sculptural plants – the strong silhouette of a columnar tree, the jutting spread of a prostrate shrub – as well as the variety of shapes, colours, and textures found in a mixed or herbaceous border.

Paths and access

Narrow areas of grass are usually subject to heavy wear and are difficult to mow; for these reasons, paths narrower than about 1m (3ft) may be impractical. For a frequently used route across a lawn, a hard path or stepping stones helps to prevent uneven wear.

If possible, leave at least one side of the lawn open for access; if there are only one or two narrow openings, the grass may become damaged at these points and need constant repair.

Edging

Edging the lawn with paving stones or bricks helps to define its shape and that of the borders, and also has practical advantages. It makes it easier to cut the lawn right to its edge

Grass paths
Including a closely mown grass path through the garden allows a clear view of adjacent plants; here, a broad, straight path contrasts with the informal planting of daffodils and shrubs and indicates where people are to walk.

while avoiding the risk of damaging other plants. Trailing plants may be allowed to overhang the edge, breaking up any effect of rigidity, but without depriving the grass beneath of light. In addition, ornamental containers may be set on the hard edging as focal points or to provide an interesting change of level. Alternatively, a narrow "mowing strip" of bare earth may be left at the edge of a lawn; this is particularly useful if the lawn is adjacent to a wall or fence.

Climatic considerations

Turf grasses are often divided into two main groups depending on their temperature tolerance. Cool-season grasses that grow mainly in a temperate climate prefer temperatures of 15–24°C (59–75°F); those that grow best in subtropical or tropical climates, thriving in temperatures of 26–35°C (79–95°F), are known as warm-season grasses.

In large countries that cover a number of climatic zones, local advice can be sought on the best grass species to use. In temperate regions, warm-season grasses are not normally used for lawns because they turn brown during winter as they become dormant, although some can be grown satisfactorily.

Cool-season grasses

Temperate or cool-season grasses are widely used for lawns throughout the UK, Northern Europe, North America, and other regions with similar climates (see "Climate zones", p.606). The grasses that are most commonly found in cool-season lawns are bents (*Agrostis*), fescues (*Festuca*), meadow grasses (*Poa*, also known as blue grasses), and perennial ryegrass (*Lolium perenne*).

Bents are low-growing and the most tolerant of close mowing. Fescues are fine-leaved and may be cut low; they are quite hard-wearing and some species tolerate poor soils. Meadow grasses are more resistant to wear but do not withstand low mowing, and some have quite coarse leaves. Ryegrass is very hard-wearing and tolerates most soils, including heavy clay, but is coarse-textured and should not be closely mown. Annual meadow grass (*Poa annua*) is also found in many lawns, but is often considered a weed grass as it quickly runs to seed and forms coarse patches of grass.

Cool-season grasses are usually sown as mixtures of more than one species, although in some areas of temperate North America, smooth-stalked meadow grass, which is also known as Kentucky blue grass (*Poa pratensis*), is grown on its own. If sowing a single species lawn, however, it is common to mix several cultivars together as this improves the lawn's disease resistance and the overall colour (see also "Choosing the right mixtures", p.389).

Warm-season grasses

These occur naturally in tropical and subtropical regions of South America, Africa, and Asia, especially southern China; they are therefore adapted to growing successfully in a wide range of warm climatic zones.

The major warm-season grasses that are planted in lawns and other areas of intensive use are the various species and cultivars of Bermuda grasses (*Cynodon*), St Augustine grass (*Stenotaphrum secundatum*), and zoysia grasses (*Zoysia*).

The Bermuda grasses include common Bermuda grass (*Cynodon dactylon*), African Bermuda grass (*C. transvaalensis*), Bradley Bermuda grass (*C. incompletus* var. *hirsutus*), and Magennis Bermuda grass (*C. x magennisii*).

Three species of zoysia grasses are appropriate for use as lawns: Japanese lawn grass (*Zoysia japonica*), Manila grass or Japanese carpet grass (*Z. matrella*), and also Mascarene grass (*Z. tenuifolia*). Zoysia grasses grow particularly well in areas that have very warm summers combined with cool winters.

Warm-season grasses are usually grown as a single species turf as they have a strong, creeping habit and do not mix well together. If other grasses are included, they tend to form unsightly, distinct patches of differing colour and texture. Warm-season species become dormant and lose their colour at temperatures below 10°C (50°F), which can be problematic where conditions are ideal only during summer. In these areas, cool-season grasses, such as ryegrasses and fescues, may be over-sown in autumn to improve the colour of the lawn in winter.

Selecting the right grass

Before selecting seed or turf, assess the relative importance of the lawn's appearance, wearability, and maintenance needs. Of the many different grass mixtures available, some are particularly good for areas of heavy use while others may give attractive colour and texture. The grass seed should also be suitable for the growing conditions such as the soil type and drainage, and the degree of shade.

High-quality lawns

To create formal, high-quality lawns, where a perfect appearance is the prime consideration and very heavy wear is not anticipated, select mixtures of grass species that create an attractive, uniform texture and colour.
Cool season For the highest quality lawns, a grass mixture of fine-leaved bents and fescues is used. Browntop and highland bent (*Agrostis tenuis* and *A. castellana*) are mixed with Chewing's fescue and slender, creeping red fescue (*Festuca rubra* var. *commutata* and *F. rubra* var. *rubra*).
Warm season Cultivars of the common Bermuda grass are excellent for high-quality lawns. There are several

Play areas
If the lawn is to include an area for games or play, as in this garden, use a particularly hard-wearing grass mixture in order to prevent the lawn from becoming patchy.

improved cultivars that tolerate heat, drought, and heavy wear. Zoysia grasses also form a high-quality, slow-growing turf.

Utility lawns

Lawns that are primarily functional, perhaps providing a play area for children or a space for outdoor entertaining, need to be relatively hard-wearing but they must still provide an attractive, even surface; grasses for this purpose do not usually create the perfect texture and colour of a high-quality lawn, as this is inevitably of secondary importance.
Cool season For hard-wearing lawns, the major grass is perennial ryegrass; it is usually mixed with red fescue (*Festuca rubra* var. *rubra*), smooth-stalked meadow grass (*Poa pratensis*), and browntop or highland bent (*Agrostis tenuis*, *A. castellana*). Lawns of only smooth-stalked meadow grass are quite widely planted in temperate regions of North America.
Warm season The Bermuda grasses (see "High-quality lawns", left) are tough enough for most utility lawns but need frequent mowing. St Augustine grass has a less fine texture but is also suitable, particularly for shady areas. For a low-maintenance lawn, choose bahia grass (*Paspalum notatum*), carpet grass (*Axonopus*), or centipede grass (*Eremochloa ophiuroides*). These require less frequent mowing, but have coarse-textured leaves. They do not provide a fine finish.

Games and sports areas

Areas of grass used for ball games or sports need particularly wear-tolerant species and selected cultivars. In addition, some sports lawns must be able to tolerate a very low cut in order to minimize the effect of the grass on the run of the ball.

Cool season A mixture of bents and fescues as for high-quality lawns (see p.388) is suitable for areas such as croquet lawns, bowling greens, and golf putting greens; very heavy use, however, soon damages the grasses. If a more hard-wearing surface is needed, such as for lawn tennis, it is better to opt for a mixture containing perennial ryegrass (see "Utility lawns", p.388).

Warm season The Bermuda grasses (see "High-quality lawns", p.388) should provide a reasonably hard-wearing, attractive surface. Some cultivars are more tolerant of wear than others, so take care to select those recommended as suitable for games areas.

Flower-rich grassland

For flower-rich areas, whenever possible use grass species that are native to the area: as well as being more likely to flourish, they do not look incongruous or artificial (see also MEADOW GARDENING, p.401). Usually a flower-rich seed mixture consists of slow-growing grasses and various native, broad-leaved flowering species. As well as climate, soil type, soil moisture, and aspect may affect the choice of species sown; some prefer extremely dry, well-drained conditions, while others grow well on marshy ground.

Cool season Bents and fescues are usually included, while a short-lived grass, such as Italian ryegrass (*Lolium multiflorum*), may be added for initial, fast ground cover. If mown, Italian ryegrass will die out within two years, leaving behind the fine-leaved grasses and broadleaved flowering plants. Some species need a cold period before they will germinate, and so may not appear in the first year after sowing.

Warm season In areas where warm-season grasses are grown, it is rare for flower-rich grassland to be cultivated: as warm-season grasses grow vigorously they tend to smother the flowering plants.

Problem areas

For lawns in difficult sites, such as shady, wet, or dry areas, choose a grass mixture that is specially designed for such conditions. In extreme cases, it may be better to grow ground-cover shrubs or perennials instead (see pp.101 and 180).

Cool season In wet, shady areas, grass does not readily grow into a dense, vigorous sward, and regular mowing will compact the soil and reduce grass growth. Some species, however, are more tolerant than others: wood meadow grass (*Poa nemoralis*) is often sown with rough-stalked meadow grass (*P. trivialis*), although neither survives close mowing or heavy wear. Fescues may also be included; they grow reasonably well in these conditions and take a lower height of cut when mowing. Turf timothy (*Phleum pratense* subsp. *bertolonii*) is sometimes used in place of perennial ryegrass in moist, not too shady areas.

In very dry regions, use grasses native to such areas, such as western wheatgrass (*Elymus smithii*) which grows naturally on the great plains of North America, or fairway crested wheatgrass (*Agropyron cristatum*) which is native to the dry, cold plains of Russia and Siberia. The wheat-grasses generally produce medium- to low-quality lawns; couch grass or quackgrass (*Elymus repens*) may become a weed in lawns that are left to grow over 2.5cm (1in).

Warm season For shady areas, St Augustine grass is a good choice; it is also salt-tolerant and so is valuable for coastal gardens. It is coarser than the various forms of either Bermuda grasses or zoysia grasses, however, so is generally only used where finer species do not thrive.

Choosing the right mixtures

Many modern grass mixtures have been specially produced to provide qualities particularly valued in lawns, such as even colour, disease resistance, wear and shade tolerance, and compact growth. Shade-tolerant mixtures, for example, may include fescues and bents such as Chewing's fescues, hard fescues, and browntop bent. When selecting grass seed or the type of turf best suited to your site, make sure that the mixture includes not only the correct species (such as *Festuca rubra* var. *commutata*) but also a modern cultivar of that species. For further details on lawn seed mixtures and single species grasses see *Sowing Rates*, p.394, and for the range of turf types see "Turfing", p.392.

The grass mixture should not contain agricultural cultivars; these are bred to produce vigorous, vertical leaf growth for grazing and need frequent mowing. They also tend to spread less, and so do not always produce a dense, uniform cover.

Non-grass lawns

Although lawns are usually established with grasses, other evergreen species are sometimes used. These include chamomile (*Chamaemelum*

Flowers in grass
The grass in this informal orchard is dotted with bright yellow buttercups (Ranunculus) *and the vivid red, white, and purple cups of naturalized tulips.*

nobile), *Cotula*, *Dichondra micrantha*, and even various species of moss. Unlike grasses, these ground-cover plants do not stand up to heavy, continual wear, so they are rarely the best choice for a main lawn; they may, however, be used for primarily ornamental areas. Grow them in a patio or courtyard garden to provide a welcome patch of green; as a living surround at the base of a fountain, raised pond, pedestal urn, or statue; or next to a patio or path to creep over the edges and relieve the rigidity of the hard surface.

Chamomile leaves release a sweet, apple-like fragrance when crushed underfoot but they do not tolerate heavy wear; the non-flowering clone, 'Treneague', is naturally low-growing and especially suitable for lawns. *Cotula*, which has fern-like leaves, is considerably more hard-wearing as it forms a thick carpet of creeping stems; it also flourishes in moist conditions. *Dichondra* grows most successfully in warm areas and does not survive temperatures lower than -4°C (25°F).

Another option is to create a "tapestry lawn" with a patchwork effect by growing a number of low, mat-forming plants together. It is best to use plants that grow at a similar rate, like the various creeping thymes (such as *Thymus caespititius*, *T.* Coccineus Group, *T.* 'Doone Valley', and *Thymus polytrichus* subsp. *britannicus*), otherwise one species may gradually predominate and so upset the balance of the original design. As for other non-grass lawns, tapestry lawns should not be heavily used.

Chamomile lawn
The soft, spreading cushion of a chamomile lawn provides a central focal point in a herb garden or a patio, and softens the hard effect of the gravel edging and formal sundial.

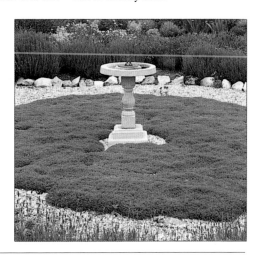

Soil and site preparation

THOROUGH site preparation is the key to establishing a successful new lawn. Although this may be time-consuming and expensive, in the long run it is easier and cheaper to prepare the site properly at the outset than to try to alleviate problems later. The general principles of preparation apply to all sites, but decisions on drainage, soil improvement, and irrigation should depend on the individual site and the climate.

Clearing the site

It is important to clear the site completely, removing any large stones and rubble, and all plant growth, including any tree stumps or roots. If the site is already partially turfed but in too poor a condition to be worth renovating, then remove all the turf (see also "Renovating a neglected lawn", p.399).

Eradicating weeds

Take particular care to eliminate any perennial weeds with underground rhizomes or deep tap roots, such as couch grass or quackgrass (*Elymus repens*), dandelion (*Taraxacum officinale*), docks (*Rumex*), and the perennial stinging nettle (*Urtica dioica*), because they regenerate rapidly from small pieces of root or rhizome (see PLANT PROBLEMS, "Perennial Weeds", pp.670–673). Once the lawn grass is established, broadleaved weeds may still be controlled using selective weed-killers, but weed grasses will be more difficult to eliminate, so it is sensible to use a weedkiller to clear the ground initially.

Annual weeds, for example fat-hen (*Chenopodium album*) and shepherd's purse (*Capsella bursa-pastoris*), may be controlled by mowing after the grass has germinated. It is preferable, however, to remove annual weeds before sowing as part of the site preparation.

Preparing the soil

The ideal topsoil for a lawn is a well-drained, sandy loam at least 20cm (8in) and preferably 30cm (12in) in depth, overlying a well-structured and free-draining subsoil. In these conditions the grass becomes deep-rooted and obtains ample water and nutrients from the soil. If the soil depth varies, during dry weather brown patches will rapidly appear where the soil is shallow.

Other soils may also be suitable, but if the soil does not drain freely and the lawn is likely to be heavily used, especially in wet conditions, the drainage should be improved. If the topsoil is very shallow or poor, it may be necessary to add new top-soil; this may be moved from other parts of the garden or bought, although for large areas the latter is very expensive.

If the soil has a naturally high sand content, and is, therefore, too free-draining, incorporate some well-rotted, organic matter to help retain nutrients and water (see "Soil structure and water content", p.620). Be careful, however, not to add too much because organic matter quickly rots down, and this may result in soil sinkage and an uneven surface.

After clearing the site, plough, cultivate, or dig over the whole area, removing any large stones that are brought to the surface, then rake the ground to produce a fine tilth. Breaking up the soil in this way makes subsequent levelling easier, as well as relieving compaction and improving the soil structure. On heavy, clay soils, however, rotavating or ploughing may create a compacted layer below the soil surface which could impede drainage: if necessary, break it up using a subsoiling machine or by double digging. For further information, see "Soil cultivation", pp.618–621.

Drainage

Lawns on free-draining soils, and those in regions with low rainfall, are unlikely to require draining. In heavy, clay soils, drainage may be improved by incorporating up to two parts of sand to every one part of soil by double digging, but this is expensive and laborious. In any soil that is not free-draining, it is preferable to install a drainage system during the preparation stage to avoid continual and expensive attempts to alleviate the problem after the lawn has been established.

The best type of drain for lawns consists of a row of pipes laid in a trench, which is backfilled with gravel. The ideal depth of the drain, and the distance between drains, will vary from site to site depending on the type of soil and the rainfall. For most loamy soils receiving moderate rain-fall, one drain every 5–8m (15–25ft) is needed. Heavier, clay soils or sites in areas with a high rainfall will need drains laid at closer intervals (see also SOILS AND FERTILIZERS, "Improving drainage", p.623).

Adjusting the soil pH

For new lawns, the pH is unlikely to need adjusting, unless previous use has left the site in extremely poor condition. Most grasses grow satisfactorily at pH levels of 5.5–7. Fine fescues and bents grow best at pH 5.5–6.5, while perennial ryegrass, the meadow grasses, and many warm-season grasses grow better at pH 6–7. Soil-testing kits for measuring pH are available from most garden centres.

If the soil is very acidic (below pH 5), dig or cultivate lime into the soil, the exact amount depending on the degree of acidity (see "Liming", p.625). Then leave the site for about a month before applying fertilizer. Lime may be added once the lawn is established but, as large amounts spread on grass may encourage certain diseases, only use a small quantity and repeat the following year if necessary. If uncertain about what to do, seek advice from an agricultural or horticultural college, or an agricultural advisory service.

Levelling the site

In gardens that have only minor undulations and deep topsoil, the site may be roughly levelled by raking soil from the high spots to fill the hollows, firming at intervals to consolidate the ground. Although it is not essential for the ground to be precisely level, awkward bumps and

---

HOW TO LEVEL THE GROUND

1 *Firm the site well, especially at the edges, by tamping with the back of a rake or by treading. Mark some pegs at the same distance from the top of each. Insert a row of pegs at the site edge. If next to paving, the marks should be level with its surface.*

2 *Add a second, parallel row of pegs about 1m (3ft) from the first row. Place a spirit level on top of these to check that they are level with the previous row. Adjust the pegs as necessary.*

3 *Repeat the process to create a grid of pegs all at the same level. Rake up the soil to the top of the marks on the pegs, adding topsoil to fill any hollows. Once the ground is level, the pegs may be removed.*

ACCURATE LEVELLING

To level the ground, first create a grid of pre-marked pegs and knock them into the soil at the same depth. Add or remove soil until it is level with the marks on the pegs.

hollows may cause problems when mowing. In some instances – for example, for a paddock or an area of rough grass – levelling by eye is sufficient. But if a perfectly level surface is required, such as for a formal lawn, a more accurate method should be used.

Achieving an accurate level

After levelling the ground roughly, an exact level may be achieved by knocking pegs into the ground all at the same depth to form a grid.

Start from a straight edge such as a path or patio, or create a taut line with string. Then take a number of identical pegs and make a mark on each one at the same distance from the top. Starting from the straight edge, knock the pegs into the ground at equal intervals so that the marks are at the required level of the lawn or approximately 2cm (¾in) below this if turfing. Add a second row of pegs and then further rows until the site is covered by a grid of pegs.

Use a spirit level – placed on a straight plank of wood if necessary to span across the rows – to check

that the pegs within the rows are all at the same height. Then adjust the level of the soil so that it is aligned with the mark on each peg.

Substantial levelling

If the site needs more substantial levelling or the topsoil is very shallow, the subsoil must be levelled first. To do this, remove the topsoil, rotavate or dig over the subsoil, then rake, level, and firm it roughly before replacing the topsoil in an even layer at least 20–30cm (8–12in) deep. To prevent the filled areas from sinking later, firm them thoroughly at intervals, adding more topsoil if necessary, and allow the site to settle before preparing the surface.

Creating a slope

Making the lawn slope gently away from the house or patio improves drainage and ensures that water does not drain into the foundations. A method similar to levelling is used, but each successive row of pegs is marked farther up or down to form a sloping grid. For example, to create a gradient of 1:100, make the marks

on each row of pegs successively lower by 2cm (¾in) and space pegs 2m (6ft) apart. A lawn angled towards a house must have its drain or soakaway sloping in the opposite direction, that is away from the house, to prevent water from reaching the building.

Final site preparations

Once the soil has been drained and levelled, the final surface may be prepared so that the site is ready for establishing a lawn.

Firming and raking

Tread the soil evenly all over to firm it and to ensure there are no soft spots which might later sink, making the turf vulnerable to being scalped during mowing. It may be necessary to tread the area about three times before the soil is sufficiently consolidated, but take care not to compress the soil too much, and do not firm wet soil as it will become compacted. Even after firming, the soil may settle further over the course of a year or two, leaving small hollows. These should be levelled by applying a sieved, sandy top-dressing (see p.398).

After firming, thoroughly rake the surface to produce a fine tilth and a level surface. If sowing seed, remove any stones larger than about 1cm (½in) across during raking; if turfing, it is only necessary to remove stones over 2.5cm (1in).

Leave the prepared site for about three to four weeks to allow any weed seeds to germinate; any emerging weeds should then be either hoed off carefully or treated with a contact weedkiller and gently raked off two or three days later once they have died, taking care not to disrupt the levelled soil unduly.

Fertilizing

A few days before establishing the lawn, and once the surface has been prepared, apply fertilizer to the site. This should contain the three major nutrients to ensure good growth: nitrogen (N), phosphorus (P), and potassium (K). Sites that have not been fertilized for many years may be deficient in all three. Phosphorus is especially important during the early stages of growth. Use a balanced organic fertilizer, such as pelleted chicken manure, or a compound granular or micro-granular fertilizer that contains all three of the nutrients; apply it according to the manufacturer's instructions at a rate of 150–200g/sq m (4–6oz/sq yd).

CREATING A SLOPE

Decide how many rows of pegs will be used and mark the pegs for each row at different heights in order to achieve the desired gradient (see above). Using a spirit level, create a grid of pegs as for levelling, and rake soil up to the marks.

INSTALLING A DRAIN

Drains at the base of a sloping lawn must be angled away from the house walls. Dig a trench at the lowest point, lay pipes in the base, and cover with hardcore. Add topsoil then turf or seed.

Soil built up to slope away from house walls

Topsoil

Drain at lowest level

Hardcore / Gravel

Pipe

PREPARING THE SOIL SURFACE

1 *Firm the surface by treading it evenly, or by tamping it with the back of a rake. Repeat, if necessary, until the entire site is well firmed.*

2 *Rake the soil to a fine tilth and leave it to allow any weeds to germinate. When they appear, apply a contact weedkiller and, after about 2–3 days, rake off the weeds.*

3 *Apply a base dressing of a compound granular organic fertilizer and lightly rake it into the surface. Leave the site for a few days before turfing or seeding.*

Establishing a lawn

THERE are various methods of establishing a lawn. For cool-season grasses in temperate areas, the gardener may choose between seeding or turfing; for warm-season grasses in subtropical and tropical regions, vegetative propagation methods may also be used.

Seeding a lawn is usually the cheapest method, but it takes up to a year before the lawn can be subjected to heavy wear. Establishing a lawn by vegetative means takes longer and is more costly than seeding. Turfing, although more expensive, gives an immediate visual effect, and the lawn may be used within two to three months; it is advisable to use turf if you have pets that may disturb grass seedlings before they are established.

Turfing

There is a range of turf types available, including purpose- and custom-grown turf, meadow and treated meadow turf, and sea-marsh turf; the type chosen largely depends on considerations of site and expense. Always buy turf from a reputable garden centre or turf farm.

If possible, inspect the turf before buying it to make sure that it is in good condition, of the right quality (see "Selecting the right grass", p.388), and that the soil is a free-draining loam rather than a heavy clay. Check that there are no weeds, pests, or diseases, nor an excessive amount of thatch (the organic matter consisting of decaying grass, stolons, and rhizomes that accumulates on the soil surface); there should, however, be enough organic matter to hold the turf together.

Purpose-grown turf

Purpose-grown turf is widely available and contains different grasses for various uses. It is raised from the newest grass cultivars and treated to make it free from weeds and disease. Turf that is guaranteed free of annual meadow grass (*Poa annua*) is also available from the top producers, although at a high price. If you need a very large quantity of special turf, and are prepared to wait 18 months for it to be grown and harvested, it may also be grown to order, but this is expensive.

Meadow turf

This is usually grown for agricultural purposes and therefore is less fine in texture; it may have been either

HOW TO ESTABLISH A LAWN USING TURF

1 *Lay the first row of turf alongside a straight edge such as a patio or path. Place each new piece or roll exactly flush with its neighbour.*

2 *Place a plank on the first row of turf. Use this to kneel on. Then lay the next row with the turf joints staggered, as in a brick wall. Proceed in exactly the same way for the rest of the lawn.*

3 *Tamp down each turf with the back of a rake to make sure that there are no air pockets. Alternatively, roll the lawn with a light roller.*

4 *Apply a light top-dressing of sieved, sandy loam and brush this in well, filling any gaps between the turves.*

5 *If no rain is forecast, water the turves well. Take care to keep them moist until they have rooted into the topsoil or they may shrink and gaps will appear.*

sown recently or grown in a long-established field. It is usually the cheapest turf, as it may contain coarse, vigorous, agricultural grasses and broadleaved weeds such as daisies (*Bellis perennis*). The quality varies greatly, however, so it is especially important to buy meadow turf from a reputable supplier to ensure that it is of reasonable quality. If the weeds are eliminated by the use of selective weedkillers, the improved turf is described as treated meadow turf. Lawns established with meadow turf may have a coarse appearance and need more frequent mowing, but are perfectly adequate for utility or family use.

Sea-marsh turf

Once considered the finest turf available, sea-marsh turf contains fine fescues and bents. As it frequently grows in river estuaries where there are silt and clay deposits, however, it may contain a silty layer, which restricts drainage, thus reducing its wear-tolerance. Purpose-grown turf, containing new cultivars of fine

fescues and bents, is often preferred, since it is usually grown on better soil and is readily available.

Turf sizes

Turf is available in a range of sizes and shapes. High-quality turf is often sold in rolls 40cm (16in) wide and up to 2.2m (7ft) long, while lower quality turf comes in shorter lengths. Major producers also usually supply turf of all qualities in units of 1sq m (1sq yd).

STORING TURF

Lay the turves as soon as possible; if it is essential to store them, spread them out flat – grass side up – so that they receive enough light, and keep them watered.

Storing turf

Turf is best lifted and relaid in its new position within the same day. If there is an unavoidable, long delay, lay the turf flat on paving or plastic sheeting, preferably in a slightly shaded area, and keep it watered; in hot weather, it may dry out very quickly, so check it regularly. If turf is left rolled up, it will not receive enough light, so the grass will turn yellow and eventually die.

Laying turf

Turf may be laid at almost any time of the year except during prolonged spells of extreme temperatures. If possible, choose a time when rain is expected in the next day or two. Turf should be laid on moist, but not wet, soil to encourage rapid rooting. Provided the site is correctly prepared, turf is comparatively easy to lay. Expert contractors will, however, do the job for you, if required.

Starting at the edge of the site, lay the first row of turf in a straight line. Standing on planks placed on the turf, rake over the soil on which the next row is to be laid. Lay this next row so that the end of each turf piece or roll is staggered with adjacent pieces or rolls.

Do not finish a row with a small segment of turf beside the edge, as it will be vulnerable to damage and drying out. If necessary, lay the last complete piece of turf at the edge, and fill the gap behind with the trimmed segment. Lay further rows until the site is covered.

When all the turf has been laid, cut the edges to shape. For a curved edge,

TRIMMING THE LAWN EDGE

Curved edge
Lay a hose or rope to the required shape and secure with wire hoops. Standing on a board, cut just inside the hose.

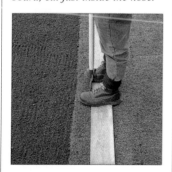

Straight edge
Stretch a taut string along the required line and align a plank with this. Then, standing on the plank, cut along its edge.

lay a hose or rope along the curve required, and cut just inside it. For a straight edge, mark the proposed lawn edge with taut string. Align a plank with this guideline and cut along it using a half-moon or powered edger. Move the plank along the guideline and repeat the procedure until the entire edge has been cut.

Aftercare

Either tamp down the turves with the back of a rake or roll the lawn with a light roller to ensure that there are no air pockets. In wet conditions, however, do not roll until the turves have rooted and knitted together. Brush or lute a light top-dressing (see p.398) between the turves to encourage the roots to spread.

Do not allow the turf to dry out before the grass has rooted through. It is essential to water the turf thoroughly so that it reaches the soil below, otherwise the turves may shrink in dry or hot weather.

Moving turf

Sometimes it may be necessary to lift and relay an area of turf. It should be cut and lifted in uniformly sized pieces so that they fit together easily when they are relaid.

Cutting

First, divide the turf to be lifted into lengths 30cm (12in) wide by cutting along the edge of a plank with a half-moon edger. Move the plank 30cm (12in) in from the previous cut to form each new length. Then cut each length at right angles to form pieces about 45cm (18in) long. Alternatively, a mechanical turf lifter may be hired; this cuts the turf to the size and depth required and also lifts it.

LIFTING TURF FOR RELAYING

1 *Cut the turf to be lifted into strips: insert 2 short canes a little way apart, 30cm (12in) in from the turf edge, and lay a plank flush against them. Stand on the plank and cut along its edge.*

2 *Cut each strip into turves about 45cm (18in) long, then undercut the turves to a depth of at least 2.5cm (1in). To stack them, lay grass to grass, soil to soil, on a path or piece of plastic sheeting.*

3 *Trim the lifted turves so that they are all the same depth: place each turf upside down in a prepared box and slice off any soil above the correct level. Relay the turves as required.*

Lifting

Once cut, lift the turves with a flat spade or turf float, carefully severing them from the underlying soil and roots. Remove a wedge of turf next to the first piece to be lifted, then insert the spade under the turf without damaging the edge. Undercut each turf to a depth of at least 2.5cm (1in). Stack the lifted turf grass to grass, soil to soil, on a hard surface such as paving.

Trimming

After the turves have been lifted, trim them all to the same depth using a specially constructed shallow box the same size as the cut turves. Leave one of the shorter sides open and, if possible, cover the remaining top edges with a smooth metal strip. Place each turf upside down in the box and, using a sharp blade, remove the excess soil by slicing along the top of the box.

Establishing a non-grass lawn

To create a new lawn from broad-leaved species, such as chamomile (*Chamaemelum nobile*), prepare the site as for a grass lawn, including a dressing of fertilizer on the base. Plant pot-grown specimens, rooted cuttings, divisions, or seedlings at 15–30cm (6–12in) intervals. They may be planted closer together or farther apart – the closer they are, the faster they will form a lawn and, of course, the greater the expense. Keep the site well watered during dry periods. Once the plants have covered the site, trim the lawn with a rotary mower, nylon-line trimmer, or hand shears when necessary. If growing chamomile, it is bestto use the non-flowering cultivar 'Treneague' which is naturally very low-growing. Flowering forms may be grown from seed but they require more frequent trimming and the dead flowerheads may be unsightly.

1 *Plant rooted cuttings or divisions (here chamomile) 15–30cm (6–12in) apart in prepared ground. Keep the area well watered and free from weeds.*

2 *After several weeks, when the plants have grown together to form a lawn, lightly trim them with a nylon-line trimmer or garden shears.*

Seeding

Grass seed is best sown in warm, moist conditions so that it will germinate and establish quickly: early autumn is usually best. Spring-sown grass is also successful but the soil is colder than in autumn and there is more competition from weeds. Seed may be sown in summer if irrigation is available, but in hot conditions young grass seedlings suffer heat stress and may wilt or even die.

Sowing rates

Grass sowing rates vary, depending on the mixture or species (see chart, below). Although there is some leeway to allow for factors such as depletion caused by birds eating the seeds, it is important not to sow seed in much greater or smaller quantities than the recommended rate. Sowing too little seed may allow weed seedlings space to compete with the grass, and the lawn will take slightly longer to establish. Sowing too much seed may cause more problems by producing humid conditions among the seedlings. This encourages damping off (see p.664), which can damage the young lawn in a very short time, particularly in warm, humid weather (see also "Lawn problems", pp.667–668).

Sowing seed

Seed may be sown either by hand or, faster and more evenly, by a machine. First calculate the amount of seed needed by multiplying the size of the area to be sown (in square metres or yards) by the recommended sowing rate (the amount of seed per square metre or yard). Before sowing the seed, shake the container to mix the seeds thoroughly and ensure that small seeds do not settle to the bottom and thus give an uneven distribution of grass types.

Sowing by machine

This is the best way to sow grass seed over a large area. Measure out the correct amount of seed for the lawn and divide it in half. For even coverage, sow half of the seed in one direction and half at right angles to this. A well-defined lawn edge may be achieved by laying plastic sheeting or hessian at the site edge and running the machine just over it; this also prevents the uneven distribution that may occur when stopping the machine at the end of a strip.

Sowing by hand

If sowing by hand, first divide the area into small, equal-sized sections, using string and canes or pegs; this makes it easier to sow the seed evenly. Then measure out the correct amount of seed for one section and accurately divide the batch of seed in half. Transfer one half-batch into a measure, such as a small cup, to make it easier and faster to measure out each subsequent amount. Work on one section at a time, scattering half the seed of a batch in one direction, then sowing the other half at right angles to this before moving on to the next section.

Aftercare

After sowing, lightly rake over the surface. Unless rain is forecast, water the site with a sprinkler. Germination will occur in one to two weeks, depending on grass species, soil and air temperature, and moisture. Protect the site from birds by covering it with netting or brushwood until the seedlings have established.

Water the site regularly in dry weather since young grasses are very susceptible to drought. Once the seedlings have emerged, the surface may be gently firmed with a light-weight roller (100kg/220lb), although this is not essential.

Cutting

When the grass has reached approximately 5cm (2in), cut it to a height of 2.5cm (1in). For the first two or three cuts, use a rotary mower, because a cylinder mower with a roller may tear the vulnerable young leaves. Then carefully rake up and remove all excess clippings. If the lawn was sown in late summer or early autumn, continue to mow when necessary through late autumn in order to maintain it at about 2.5cm (1in) high. During the following spring, gradually lower the height of the cut until the desired height is reached, depending on the type of grass used (see also "Frequency and height of cut", p.395). Young grasses are particularly vulnerable to damage by wear, so try to use the lawn as little as possible during its first full growing season.

ESTABLISHING A LAWN BY SOWING SEED

1 *If using a machine, sow half the seed in one direction and half at right angles to this. For a defined edge, lay down plastic sheeting and push the machine just over it at the end of each row.*

Alternative step
If sowing by hand, mark the site into equal areas. Weigh out enough seed for a single area, then scatter it evenly, half in one direction and half at right angles to this.

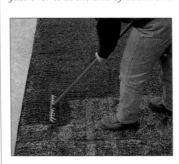

2 *After sowing, lightly rake over the surface. In dry conditions, water the site regularly to encourage the seeds to germinate.*

3 *The grass seedlings should take 7–14 days to emerge. Once the grass is about 5cm (2in) high, cut it to a height of 2.5cm (1in) with a rotary mower.*

Vegetative propagation

Lawns grown from warm-season grasses, or the cool-season creeping bentgrass (*Agrostis stolonifera*), which produce vigorous stolons and rhizomes, may also be established by vegetative means such as stolonizing, sprigging, or plugging. The best time of year for creating a lawn by one of these methods is late spring or early summer, on a site prepared as for sowing grass seed. It will take about two months for the material to root and spread over the soil. As for grass seedlings, regular irrigation is essential.

To establish a lawn by stolonizing, spread stolons evenly over the soil at the supplier's recommended rate, top-dress with a light, sandy soil, roll, and water. Alternatively, for sprigging, stolons and rhizomes are planted in holes or furrows 2.5–5cm (1–2in) deep and 8–15cm (3–6in) apart, then firmed in and watered. For plugging, small pieces of turf, or plugs, are planted at intervals of 25–45cm (10–18in).

SOWING RATES

Mixtures	g/sq m	oz/sq yd
Fescues and bents	25–30	3/4–7/8
Perennial ryegrass and other species	35–40	1–1 1/8
Flower-rich mixtures (depending on mixture)	2.5–5	1/16–1/8
Single species		
Bents (*Agrostis*)	8–10	1/4–5/16
Carpet grass (*Axonopus*)	8–12	1/4–3/8
Common Bermuda grass (*Cynodon dactylon*)	5–8	1/8–1/4
Centipede grass (*Eremochloa ophiuroides*)	1.5–2.5	1/24–1/16
Red fescue (*Festuca rubra* var. *rubra*)	15–25	1/2–3/4
Perennial ryegrass (*Lolium perenne*)	20–40	5/8–1 1/8
Bahia grass (*Paspalum notatum*)	30–40	7/8–1 1/8
Smooth-stalked meadow grass/Kentucky blue grass (*Poa pratensis*)	10–15	5/16–1/2

Routine care

ONCE the lawn is well established, regular maintenance is needed to ensure its health and attractive appearance. The attention required depends on the lawn's size and type as well as the site and climate. In general, the most frequent tasks are mowing and watering, but annual maintenance may include fertilizing, top-dressing, aerating, and, where necessary, controlling moss, weeds, pests, and diseases. For large lawns, using mechanical or powered tools, which may be hired, often makes maintenance tasks faster and easier (see "Lawncare tools", pp.558–559).

Mowing

In addition to making the lawn a pleasure to walk on, regularly cutting the grass helps to create a dense, healthy sward with an even, attractive finish. Mowing is needed most frequently in the warm, moist conditions of early and late summer; during drought conditions, however, it is best either not to mow at all or to set the mower to a higher cut. Delay mowing during very wet or frosty weather: wet grass can clog the mower or the mower may slip, and mowing in frost damages the grass. If mowing a fine lawn, brushing with a besom beforehand raises the grass and so achieves a better cut. Brushing the lawn in the morning also helps to remove dew and dries the grass surface, making it considerably easier to mow.

Mowers

For most lawns, a cylinder or reel mower, or a rotary (including the hover type) mower is suitable. A mower with a roller provides the finest finish for a lawn and creates

BRUSHING AWAY DEW

To remove excess moisture and raise the grass before mowing, brush away the dew with a besom; for large areas, drag a piece of hessian over the lawn.

stripes, but a mower with no roller gives a perfectly acceptable surface for a utility lawn. A mulching mower leaves clippings on the lawn to nourish the grass – ideal in an organically managed garden. The type of mower selected should depend on the size of the lawn and the finish required (see also "Lawnmowers", p.557).

Frequency and height of cut

The frequency of mowing and the height of cut depends on a number of factors, including the type of grasses grown, how the lawn is used, and the time of year, but little and often is a good general rule to follow. Try to remove no more than a third of the leaf growth at any one time. If the grass is cut sporadically and drastically, it will struggle to recover after each mowing and there will be a noticeable decline in the lawn's quality. Frequent mowing is necessary in summer when the grass grows quickly; during spring and autumn, the rate should be reduced and, in winter, occasional "topping" – removing just the grass tips – may be all that is needed.

High-quality lawns may be cut even as low as 0.5cm (¼in) but they should be mown frequently – every two or three days in summer – to maintain their appearance. Utility lawns should be left to grow longer than this, because the grasses do not tolerate such a low cut; this also helps to protect the surface against heavy wear and tear.

It is not necessary to mow all areas to the same height. Try two or three heights of cut for different grass areas to add texture and interest to the garden. For practical reasons, cut the main area to be used for walking or playing to a height of about 1–2.5cm (½–1in). Keeping the grass at this length protects the surface against wear. Mow the areas under trees less frequently – every one or two weeks in summer – to a height of 5–10cm (2–4in). Leave any areas of flower-rich grassland at 10cm

MOWING STRIPES

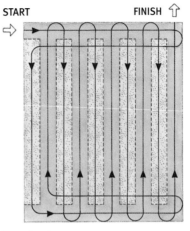

Regular shape
First mow a wide strip at each end of the lawn for turning space, then mow up and down the lawn in slightly overlapping runs.

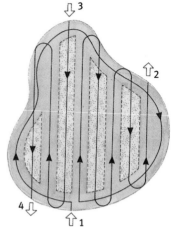

Irregular shape
Mow a strip around the lawn edge, then mow a straight strip up the centre. Mow up and down one half of the lawn, then the other half.

(4in) or more; they will need no more than three cuts per year and should not be cut until the flowering species have shed their seed in mid-summer (see MEADOW GARDENING, p.401). Since they are mown infrequently, these areas produce much more growth and debris which should be raked up and removed after mowing.

Mowing stripes

Use a mower fitted with a roller to achieve a classic, striped finish to the lawn. If the lawn is square or rectangular, first mow a wide strip at either end of the lawn. Then mow up and down in straight strips, slightly overlapping the previous run to make sure that all the grass is mown.

If the lawn is of an irregular shape first mow all around its edge. Then, starting at the centre of one end, mow a straight line down the middle by picking out an object or tree beyond the end of the lawn and then pointing the mower directly towards it. Mow straight strips up and down

one half of the lawn, then return to the centre and mow the other half in a similar fashion.

Mowing sports lawns

On areas to be used for ball games, such as croquet, bowls, or putting, vary the direction each time you mow to prevent a "grain" from developing. Grain is produced by grass growing in one direction and affects the run of the ball.

Grass clippings

On fine lawns where a high-quality finish is required, use a mower that collects grass clippings as it cuts or rake them up afterwards and add them in layers to the compost heap. Do not compost them, however, for the first few cuts after application of weedkiller. Removing grass clippings tends to discourage earthworms and lessens the spread of annual meadow grass and weeds such as speedwell. It may also help to prevent a build-up of thatch and thus maintain a finer finish to the lawn.

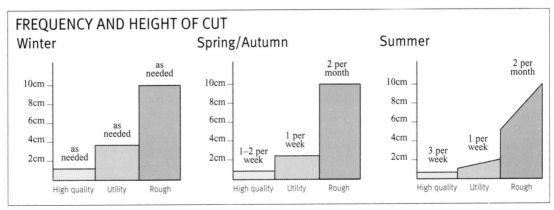

FREQUENCY AND HEIGHT OF CUT

Utility lawns containing earthworms may benefit from a light layer of clippings left on the lawn as they will be recycled by the worms, thereby returning plant nutrients to the soil. The majority of the clippings should be raked up, however, as excessive amounts may cause damage to the turf beneath as they rot down. In general, it is better to remove grass clippings and replace the lost nutrients by feeding.

Removing fallen leaves

In autumn and winter, clear away any fallen leaves from the lawn by brushing or raking them up and removing them; a layer of leaves left on the lawn reduces evaporation, and the resulting humidity can encourage turf diseases.

Trimming edges

After mowing, create a neat finish by trimming the lawn edges with long-handled edging shears, a mechanical edging machine, or a nylon-line trimmer with an adjustable head for edging (see "Lawncare tools", pp.558–559). If the lawn edges become irregular, recut them once or twice a year with a half-moon edger, cutting against a plank for a straight line; for very large lawns, it is faster and less laborious to use a powered edging machine for this task.

CLEARING LEAVES

Remove any fallen leaves and debris by brushing the lawn briskly with a besom or a spring-tined rake. For large lawns, use a leaf-sweeper or blower to speed up the task.

Fertilizing

As with all plants, grasses require nutrients to grow; regular applications of fertilizer help ensure a vigorous, healthy lawn. Most of the nutrients that are essential for growth are plentiful within the soil, but four – nitrogen (N), phosphorus (P), potassium (K), and iron (Fe) – are often applied as a supplement. Nitrogen is the nutrient most commonly added, especially when grass clippings have been removed: it is essential for producing further

growth that is stimulated by mowing. Nitrogen-deficient grass is generally yellow-green in appearance and lacking in vigour.

Fertilizers are the easiest way to apply nutrients to a lawn; both organic and artificial products are available (see also "Soil nutrients and fertilizers", pp.624–625). The exact amount of fertilizer that is required depends on how quickly water drains from the soil, how much rainfall or irrigation is received by the lawn, whether or not the grass clippings are removed, and on the type of grasses being grown. On heavy, clay soils that are rich in nutrients, and where rainfall or irrigation rates are low, only light fertilizing is necessary. Light, sandy soils that are well watered, however, need greater amounts of fertilizing because they lose nutrients quickly by leaching.

Types and constituents of fertilizer

For most lawns, two applications of fertilizer a year are sufficient (see chart, opposite). Apply a spring/summer fertilizer at the beginning of summer, and an autumn/winter one after routine maintenance in early autumn. Both contain nitrogen, phosphorus, and potassium, but in differing proportions, because nitrogen, applied too late in the year,

may stimulate soft, lush growth and encourage diseases such as snow mould/*Fusarium* patch (see p.667). Select a fertilizer containing a mixture of both slow- and fast-release nitrogen; this helps the lawn to "green up" within two to three days and stay green for several weeks.

Soluble lawn tonics are high in fast-release nitrogen, and are applied to the grass by watering can or hose. Such summer feeds have a quick but short-lived, greening effect.

Iron (Fe), although not generally used on its own, is a constituent of lawn sand, which is used to control moss. Some complete fertilizers also contain iron. "Weed and feed" compounds are available to control moss and broadleaved weeds and to fertilize the lawn all in one operation. Iron darkens the grass, making it appear greener without stimulating growth. It is especially useful in autumn when the grass may lose some of its colour but excessive growth is undesirable.

How to apply fertilizer

It is essential to apply fertilizer evenly to avoid variations in growth and the risk of damaging or even killing the grass. Any variation in the rate of application will generally be more than obvious within a week, and excessive doses may leave a bare

CUTTING THE EDGE OF THE LAWN

Edging by machine
Periodically recut the lawn edge to retain the lawn's shape and create a well-defined finish. For large lawns, use a powered edger: align the cutting blade along the required new edge and guide the machine forward.

Trimming the edge
After mowing, trim the grass overhanging the lawn edge with long-handled edging shears; or use a nylon-line trimmer adapted to work vertically.

Edging by hand
If recutting the edge manually, use a sharp half-moon edger, cutting along the line of a plank for a straight edge.

Lawns and watering

As a consequence of changing climatic conditions, and the hotter summers and autumns of recent years, acute water shortages and periods of drought are now commonplace in the UK. While gardeners value the aesthetic effect of high-quality lawns in their gardens, it is important to use little or no water during drought periods simply to maintain green lawns.

During prolonged dry spells, grass will turn brown and appear to be dead. Most lawn grasses, however, simply become dormant under such conditions and experience in recent years has shown that once the rains come in late autumn they quickly recover and become green again.

Thorough initial preparation of the lawn pays off during drought, as it establishes strong-growing, deeply rooted turf. Annual maintenance is equally important: the grasses will withstand water shortages better than those on untended lawns.

It is, however, essential to water newly made lawns thoroughly in dry periods to maintain growth and

colour – provided there are no hosepipe restrictions in force. Start to water as soon as you notice that the grass does not spring back up after the lawn has been walked on – a state known as "footprinting".

The best time to water is either early morning or in the evening, to minimize evaporation. It is vital to give the lawn enough water; the soil should be moistened to a depth of 10–15cm (4–6in). Shallow watering encourages plant roots to remain near the surface, making the lawn more susceptible to drought. Dig a small hole to check the soil is damp to the required depth, and note how long it took to water sufficiently. Alternatively, use a battery-powered moisture meter to register soil moisture levels.

On heavy soils where drainage is restricted, do not apply too much water, as this inhibits oxygen and mineral intake by the grass roots. If pools remain on the lawn for some time after heavy rain or watering, it may need additional drainage (see "Improving drainage", p.623).

HOW TO APPLY FERTILIZER

Weigh out the correct amount of fertilizer for the area and divide it in half. Apply the first half in one direction, working up and down the lawn in adjoining but not overlapping runs. Apply the second half at right angles to this. Close off the supply when you turn the machine at the end of each run.

patch behind. Although fertilizer may be spread manually, it is both easier and more accurate to apply it by machine.

Probably the simplest method of spreading fertilizer is to use a continuous belt or drop spreader. This is pushed up and down the lawn, as if mowing, but so that each pass abuts the previous one, without overlapping it. To ensure coverage is even, it is best to divide the fertilizer into two batches and apply half in one direction; the rest is distributed at right angles to it.

Alternatively, a spinning disc or broadcast spreader may be used to apply the fertilizer over a larger area; the spread may be uneven, however. To reduce the risk of fertilizer being distributed unevenly, set the machine to half the application rate and make adjacent runs at half the distance apart of the machine's spread. For example, if the extent of spread is 2m (6ft), make the runs 1m (3ft) apart. After using either type of machine, be certain to wash it out thoroughly because fertilizers are corrosive and may, therefore, damage any metal parts.

Before applying fertilizer, calibrate the spreader to obtain the correct distribution rate. To calibrate a

UNEVEN DISTRIBUTION

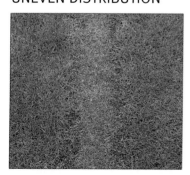

Take care to apply fertilizer evenly as uneven distribution may make the lawn patchy; it may damage or even kill areas of grass.

spreader, first find a dry, flat area of concrete or asphalt, and chalk out a measured area of 4sq m (4sq yd), for example. Set the spreader to medium and fill it a quarter full. Using the machine, spread the fertilizer as evenly as possible over the marked area, as if over the lawn, then brush up all the fertilizer within the area and weigh it. Divide this weight by the area, in this case 4sq m (4sq yd), to give the application rate in grams per square metre (ounces per square yard). Adjust the machine setting accordingly, and then check the application rate again over the same measured area. Continue this process until the rate is correct.

Annual maintenance

In addition to routine tasks such as mowing and watering, regular maintenance is required to keep a lawn healthy and to reduce the risk of serious pest or disease problems (see chart, below). A maintenance programme should involve aeration (including thatch removal, or scarifying), fertilizing, and the control of weeds, moss, pests, and diseases (see "Lawn weeds", p.400, and "Pests and diseases", p.400).

It is also important for the continued good health of the lawn to top-dress the grass as well as to rake or brush it regularly to clear away leaves and other debris (see "Removing fallen leaves", p.396). Tasks that may be necessary at least once a year include recutting any edges that have become uneven or jagged and repairing any damaged or worn patches of grass by returfing or reseeding (see "Repairing lawn damage", p.399).

Winter, when the lawn is no longer in need of quite such regular attention, is the most convenient time to check all equipment carefully. Sharpen all cutting edges, oil tools where necessary, and send the mower for servicing, so that it will be in peak condition for the first cut of the new season.

Aerating the turf

Aeration is vital since it allows deep root growth and so helps the turf to become established as well as reducing soil compaction. It is also important to reduce excessive thatch, the organic matter consisting of decaying blades of grass, rhizomes, and stolons that accumulates on the soil surface. A certain amount of thatch – up to about 1cm (½in) deep – is beneficial as it reduces evaporation and helps to protect the lawn from wear. In excess, however, it prevents water from reaching the soil beneath and may itself become saturated, interfering with drainage. The removal of thatch also encourages new grass growth and so promotes a healthy, vigorous sward.

There are several ways to aerate the soil and remove thatch. These include scarifying, slitting, hollow tining (also known as coring), and spiking. It is preferable not to undertake these tasks in dry conditions, however, because they make the lawn more vulnerable to drought in the short term. Autumn is often the best time since the warm, moist conditions allow the grass to recover quickly from these renovation procedures. Whichever the aeration technique, first mow the lawn to its normal summer height. After maintenance work, apply a low nitrogen feed and

ANNUAL MAINTENANCE PROGRAMME

Maintenance procedure	Early/mid spring	Mid/late spring	Early/mid summer	Mid/late summer	Early/mid autumn	Mid/late autumn	Winter
Mowing	Roll before mowing if turf is lifted by frost	Mow weekly. Adjust mower to summer cut height	Mow 1–3 times a week as required	Mow 1–3 times a week (set mower higher in dry periods)	Raise height of cut as growth rate slows	Set mower to winter cut height	Lightly mow if there is new growth
Watering		May be needed in dry regions	Water as necessary	Water well in dry periods	Occasionally water if dry		
Fertilizing		Apply spring fertilizer	Summer fertilizer		Apply autumn fertilizer		
Aerating and scarifying		Lightly scarify		Spike or slit areas subject to heavy wear	Scarify and aerate lawn, or hollow tine to remove thatch	Aerate lawn if not done in early autumn	
Weed and moss control		Apply lawn sand in place of spring feed if moss present	Apply weedkiller	Apply weedkiller if not applied in early summer	Apply weedkiller; treat moss with lawn sand		
Pest and disease control					Apply pesticide/fungicide as necessary		
Other procedures	Recut edges if required. Carry out any restoration work	Brush away any worm casts on the lawn			Top-dress after autumn renovation	Remove fallen leaves	Remove leaves. Service tools

SCARIFYING

By machine
For large areas of lawn, use a mechanical or powered scarifier. Work the machine back and forth across the lawn as if mowing.

By hand
Pull a spring-tined rake vigorously across the lawn to remove thatch and dead moss. Ensure that the tines of the rake reach well down into the soil surface.

avoid using the lawn for one to two weeks to encourage recovery.

Scarifying

This technique helps to remove thatch and permits air to enter the surface of the lawn. These processes are important because the soil organisms that naturally break down thatch require air to live. For small areas, scarifying may be done manually by vigorously raking the lawn with a wire or spring-tined rake. This is hard work, however, so it may be worth hiring a mechanical or powered scarifier instead. To remove the maximum amount of thatch, scarify the lawn in two directions, one at 90° to the other. Any moss should be killed prior to scarifying so that it will not spread to other parts of the lawn (see "Moss", p.400).

Slitting

For slitting, a special machine is used that penetrates the soil with flat, knife-like blades to a depth of 8–10cm (3–4in). The blades cut slits through the thatch which allow air into the soil thereby encouraging a dense, healthy sward.

Hollow tining or coring

This removes thatch, aerates the soil, and relieves soil compaction, all in one operation. A mechanical or hand tiner removes a core of grass, thatch, and soil, making a series of holes across the lawn, about 10cm (4in) apart. Remove the cores, then fill the holes with a sandy top-dressing (see below) to prevent them from closing and to allow air and water into the lawn. Hollow tining may take longer to do than spiking and slitting because soil is removed rather than simply pushed sideways.

Spiking

This allows air into the soil, thereby encouraging root growth; it can also relieve soil compaction. Use a mechanical or hand spiker, or, for small areas, a garden fork. Angle the spikes back slightly to raise the turf gently without breaking it up. This encourages deep root growth by creating fissures in the soil.

Top-dressing

Immediately after carrying out any autumn maintenance work, apply a top-dressing, on a dry day if possible.

AERATING

Aerating by machine
For large lawns, use a mechanical or powered aerator; work the machine in slightly overlapping runs.

Slitting
Slitting, which must be done with a special machine, allows air into the soil; push the machine back and forth across the lawn.

Hollow tining
Use a purpose-designed tool, working methodically across the lawn to lift out cores of grass and soil 0.5–2cm ($^1/_4$–$^3/_4$in) wide.

Spiking
For small lawns, spiking using a garden fork is adequate; insert the fork straight, then lean it back slightly to let in more air.

This helps reduce thatch by keeping the lawn open and aerated, fills core holes, and helps to level the surface. For most lawns, a sandy mixture of six parts medium-fine sand, three parts sieved soil, and one part peat substitute, peat, or leaf mould is suitable. After scarifying, apply the mixture of top-dressing at a rate of 1kg/sq m (2lb/sq yd), but if the lawn has been both scarified and hollow tined, apply the dressing at the rate of 3kg/sq m (6½lb/sq yd).

Ensure that the top-dressing does not smother the grass by luting or brushing it into the surface and any core holes. Luting also helps level any slight surface irregularities.

Rolling

Rolling is not essential, but if done in spring it may help to resettle the

TOP-DRESSING

Medium-fine sand

Sieved soil

Peat substitute

1 *Prepare the top-dressing by mixing medium-fine sand with topsoil and peat substitute, peat, or leaf mould. Pass the mixture through a 5mm ($^1/_4$in) mesh sieve.*

2 *Weigh out the correct amount of top-dressing for the lawn area and apply it on a dry day. For a large lawn, it is best to use a machine.*

Alternative step
For small areas, the top-dressing may be applied by hand; spread it evenly over the lawn with a shovel or spade.

3 *Use a lute or besom to work in the dressing, keeping a steady pressure to distribute it evenly, and water thoroughly.*

surface after any maintenance work carried out the previous autumn and any possible upheaval caused by frost. A roller or, alternatively, a cylinder mower may be used; if using the latter, raise the blades to prevent damaging the lawn. The traditional practice of rolling lawns frequently is unnecessary and could cause problems of compaction, particularly on heavy soils.

Renovating a neglected lawn

In some cases, a neglected, patchy lawn may be improved by renovation; if, however, it is dominated by weeds and moss, it may be preferable to remove the old turf and establish a new lawn instead. The best time to start renovation work is in spring because the grass will grow well during spring and summer and should therefore be well established by the end of the season.

A renovation programme involves a series of procedures that restore the lawn to a good condition. First, in early spring, cut the grass to about 5cm (2in) using a rotary mower, and remove any clippings. After one week, mow again, preferably with a cylinder mower set at its highest cut. Over the next couple of weeks gradually reduce the height of cut until it reaches the correct level. At this stage, feed the lawn with a liquid or granular fertilizer and, two weeks later, apply a weedkiller. If there are any bare or uneven patches, they may be reseeded after one or two weeks. At the beginning of autumn, aerate the lawn, top-dress, and apply an autumn feed. A regular maintenance programme should then be followed so that the lawn is kept in tiptop condition (see *Annual maintenance programme*, p.397).

Repairing lawn damage

If an area of the lawn becomes damaged or patchy, perhaps because of uneven wear, it may usually be repaired by removing the affected part, then turfing or seeding. It is important to use turf or seed that is the same type as the rest of the lawn so that it blends in well; if this is unknown, use a piece of turf from a less prominent part of the lawn to replace the damaged area. If the problem of lawn damage occurs repeatedly, it may be necessary to consider introducing a completely different and more hard-wearing

surface, such as gravel or paving (see STRUCTURES AND SURFACES, pp.584–605).

Repairing a damaged edge

Edges that have been damaged in only one or two small areas may be repaired quite simply. Using a half-moon edger and a straight edge, such as a short plank of wood, mark out a small section of turf containing the damaged part. Slice under the section of turf with a turf float or spade and push it towards the lawn

edge until the poor area is outside the lawn. Then trim off the damaged part to align the turf with the existing lawn edge. This leaves a gap within the lawn, which should be gently forked over and a granular or liquid fertilizer added. Then returf or add a little soil and reseed with an appropriate grass mixture. Ensure that the repair will be flush with the rest of the lawn.

Alternatively, lift the turf, then turn it around and replace it so that the damaged area is within the lawn.

Repair the damage by turfing or seeding, taking care to ensure that any new turf is laid level with the surrounding lawn.

Repairing a damaged patch

If there is a damaged patch within the lawn, first carefully cut out and lift a piece of turf containing the damaged area. Fork over the soil underneath then fertilize it, if required, and lightly firm the soil. Lay a new piece of turf to fit the exposed space, raising or lowering

---

HOW TO REPAIR A DAMAGED EDGE

1 *Using canes and string, mark out a small, straight-sided section of turf containing the damaged part; cut out the area with a half-moon edger.*

2 *Carefully undercut the turf with a spade, then slide it forward until the damaged part is beyond the lawn edge.*

3 *Align a plank with the lawn edge, then cut along it to trim off the damaged section so that the turf is level with the rest of the lawn edge.*

4 *Cut a new piece of turf to fit the resulting gap and ease it into the hole; if it is too large, trim it so that it forms an exact fit.*

5 *Adjust the soil level beneath the new turf, if necessary, by adding or removing soil until the new piece sits level with the rest of the lawn.*

ALTERNATIVE METHOD

1 *Cut out a section containing the damaged part. Turn it so that the damaged piece faces the lawn and firm it into place.*

6 *Once the level is correct, tamp the new piece firmly into place with the back of a rake or a medium-weight roller.*

7 *Sprinkle some sandy top-dressing over the repaired area, particularly into the joins, and water thoroughly.*

2 *Add a little sandy loam, if necessary, so that the damaged part is level with the rest of the lawn, then sow grass seed over the damaged section, and water well.*

HOW TO REPAIR A DAMAGED PATCH

1 *Using a half-moon edger and the edge of a plank, cut around the damaged area, then undercut the turf with a spade and remove it.*

2 *Lightly fork or rake over the area of exposed soil to loosen it, and then apply a liquid or granular fertilizer if required.*

3 *Carefully tread over the soil to consolidate it and firm the surface before returfing.*

the soil level beneath, if necessary, so that the new turf is level with the rest of the lawn, and tamp it down in position with the back of a rake or your hands. Top-dress and water the repaired surface well.

Levelling a hump or hollow

Small humps or hollows within the lawn may be levelled easily. First cut a cross through the turf that is growing over the affected area and peel back the cut turf. To level a hollow, fork over the soil beneath and fill in with topsoil, then lightly firm the ground. For a hump, gradually remove the excess soil until the ground is level, and firm. Fold back the cut turf and tamp it down with the back of a rake before top-dressing and watering.

On larger uneven areas, it may be necessary to remove complete sections of turf entirely, level the soil beneath (see "Levelling the site", pp.390–391), and then carefully relay the turf over the original but newly levelled area.

4 *Place a new piece of turf in the hole, cutting it to fit with a half-moon edger.*

5 *Check that the new turf is level with the rest of the lawn; if necessary adjust the soil level beneath the turf. Then firm in the turf and water well.*

Lawn weeds

Although some weeds, such as slender speedwell (*Veronica filiformis*) and daisies (*Bellis perennis*), may look attractive in utility lawns, they are generally considered undesirable in high-quality, closely mown lawns. Many broadleaved weeds can survive in grass that is mown, but excessive

numbers may make the grass suffer so, even in a utility lawn, control may be needed. Unless the lawn clippings are collected, mowing may even spread weeds that can root from small pieces of stem. On small lawns, daisies and plantains (*Plantago*) may be cut out singly by hand, but for a large lawn, the simplest method is to use a "weed and feed" mixture. This

may be applied with a fertilizer spreader or by hand, according to the instructions given.

Moss

Almost always undesirable, moss may be found in lawns for many reasons, including soil compaction, poor drainage, low fertility, insufficient light, mowing too closely, and extremes of soil pH. If the lawn is occasionally affected by moss, treat it with a chemical moss killer or lawn sand, then remove it by scarification (see p.398). If the problem continually recurs, attempt to identify and correct the possible causes; this may involve improving soil aeration, drainage, and fertility and, on light soils, top-dressing to assist water retention. Adopting an annual maintenance programme should help to control the problem. For further details see PLANT PROBLEMS, "Lawn weeds", pp.672–673.

Pests and diseases

Several turf diseases, including brown patch (see "Drought", p.667), dollar spot, fairy rings, snow mould/ *Fusarium* patch, and red thread attack lawns, particularly in hot, humid countries; *Fusarium* patch is a problem in cold regions too and may even occur under snow. Preventive sprays may be necessary, but in cooler temperate and maritime climates it is usual to spray only in serious cases. For treatment of pests and diseases, see "Lawn problems", pp.667–668.

Earthworm casts should be tolerated because of the good these creatures do in the garden environment. The casts, however, provide ideal sites for the germination of weed seeds so they should be regularly dispersed with a besom, particularly before mowing the lawn.

LEVELLING A HOLLOW OR HUMP

1 *Cut a cross right through the hump or hollow in the turf, using a half-moon edger; the cross should reach just beyond the affected area.*

2 *Fold back the cut sections of turf, taking care not to pull them too harshly or they may crack.*

3 *For a hollow, fill in the ground beneath with a good, sandy topsoil; for a hump, remove some of the soil until the entire surface is level.*

4 *Replace the folded back turf and lightly firm to check that the level is correct. Adjust the soil level beneath, if necessary, firm, top-dress, and water well.*

Meadow gardening

A WILD-FLOWER meadow is an attractive and colourful feature that brings a breath of the countryside into the city or suburbs. It can be the ideal way of using a part of the garden that is difficult to cultivate conventionally, perhaps because it is too dry, slopes steeply, or has poor soil, and can play a small part in the conservation of species that are threatened by the destruction of their natural habitats. A meadow also attracts seed-eating birds, small mammals, and insects into the garden – many butterflies and beneficial insects rely on long grasses as food for their larval stages.

Types of meadow

Grassland plants occur in habitats ranging from cornfields and dry downlands to wetlands and woodland margins. When planning a meadow, consider soil type, moisture levels, and the degree of sun and shade – the growing conditions determine the plants that will both thrive and look natural. An open, sunny site with well-drained soil is ideal for ox-eye daisies (*Leucanthemum vulgare*), field scabious (*Knautia arvensis*), and lady's bedstraw (*Galium verum*). It also suits a cornfield area with annual poppies (*Papaver rhoeas*) and cornflowers (*Centaurea cyanus*), for which the soil must be well cultivated each spring if they are to persist. In damp ground, plants such as meadow-sweet (*Filipendula ulmaria*), ragged robin (*Lychnis flos-cuculi*), and common spotted orchid (*Dactylorhiza fuchsii*) will flourish. Shady areas beneath trees are perfect for dog's-tooth violets (*Erythronium dens-canis*) and snowdrops (*Galanthus nivalis*). A look at the local wild flora will indicate which species to grow, but never take plants or seeds from the wild. A huge range of wild flowers is now offered by specialist nurseries as plugs and young plants.

Extending the season

Meadows generally peak in summer, but can be given a longer span of interest. Try introducing spring bulbs, such as crocus (especially *C. tommasinianus*, *C. vernus*, and *C. chrysanthus* cultivars), wild daffodils (*Narcissus pseudonarcissus* and *N. poeticus*), snake's head fritillaries (*Fritillaria meleagris*), and tulips. Early summer bulbs include starry-flowered quamash (*Camassia quamash* and *C. leichtlinii*) and for autumn there are *Colchicum autumnale* and *Crocus speciosus* cultivars (see "Naturalizing bulbs", p.228).

Establishing meadows

Meadow flowers are perfectly adapted to soils of low fertility and thrive best among fine turf grasses, such as bents (*Agrostis*) and fescues (*Festuca*),

The wild-flower meadow
Many wild species bloom more profusely in the garden than in the wild, providing a rich food source for bees, butterflies, and their larvae.

that will not swamp them. Many ordinary grass seed mixes contain vigorous, hard-wearing rye grass (*Lolium perenne*) that out-competes the wild flowers, so choose a mix that does not include it. Various meadow mixes are available that are appropriate for different sites and soils. The simplest way to reduce soil fertility is to avoid using fertilizers and to mow regularly and remove the clippings. Stripping existing turf helps, but it is not advisable to remove topsoil unless it is very deep and fertile, since this may damage soil structure.

Sowing and planting

Sow a meadow in early autumn, or in spring in cold areas or on wet soils. Eliminate all perennial weeds with weedkiller or a black plastic sheet mulch. Cultivate the soil to a fine tilth and water. Allow a flush of annual weeds to germinate and hoe them off, then firm the soil by treading or rolling. Sow seed at the recommended rate and rake in lightly.

If establishing a meadow in existing grassland, such as an orchard, reduce fertility over one or two years by mowing and removing the clippings weekly. Introduce pot- or plug-grown wild flowers in spring or autumn.

Maintenance

Spot treat vigorous perennial weeds with weedkiller or dig them out. Reduce the sward to 8cm (3in) with a scythe or nylon-line trimmer. For a spring-flowering meadow, do not mow the meadow between early spring and midsummer; and cut the sward from midsummer onwards. Leave the mowings to dry and shed their seed before raking up and removing. For later summer flowers, cut the sward from early autumn onwards and again as grass growth begins in spring. Gather the spring mowings immediately.

Aiding natural distribution
After cutting, allow clippings to dry and then shake out the seeds. It is worth collecting some to grow on as pot or plug plants for next year.

FLOWERING PLANTS FOR MEADOW HABITATS

Leucanthemum vulgare
(ox-eye daisy)

Geranium pratense
(meadow cranesbill)

Primula veris
(cowslip)

Campanula glomerata
(clustered bellflower)

Galanthus nivalis
'Flore Pleno'
(snowdrop)

Erythronium dens-canis
(dog's-tooth violet)

CHAPTER

15

GROWING HERBS

WHETHER GROWN ON their own as an ornamental feature, with other plants in a border, or among the ordered ranks of a vegetable plot, herbs are an invaluable addition to any garden. They have always been prized for their culinary, cosmetic, or curative uses, but they also make decorative garden plants. Although few have spectacular flowers, many are graced by attractive foliage and almost all are worth growing for their scent alone – ranging from the citrus tang of lemon balm to the aniseed aroma of fennel and the sweet apple perfume of chamomile. Their fragrance is hard to resist and their nectar-filled flowers tempt bees and butterflies, so adding the drowsy hum of insects to complete the restfulness of a herb garden.

Designing with herbs

HERB growing combines the delights of the flower garden with the productivity of the vegetable plot. The results are decorative, excellent in aroma and flavour, and inexpensive to produce. By definition, a herb is any plant that has culinary or curative uses, so the range is surprisingly wide. Herbs include annuals, perennials, shrubs, and trees, not just herbaceous plants.

Historically, herbs have been used for flavouring and preserving food, as well as for making medicines and toiletries. Their aesthetic appeal has always been important, too, and their ornamental qualities, as well as their practical uses, are of equal value today.

Herbs in the home

Although fresh and dried herbs are widely available, they rarely have as fine an aroma or flavour as those harvested from your own garden. Enjoy their scents indoors as well as outside by using them fresh in flower arrangements or dried to make pot-pourri or to fill herb pillows. All over the world, herbs are considered invaluable in cooking to enhance and enliven other foods, elevating even the simplest meal to the level of *haute cuisine*. The curative and cosmetic properties of herbs are also renowned: for thousands of years, they have been used in many medicines and beauty products.

Culinary uses

Freshly harvested herbs are an important ingredient in many classic combinations, such as tomato and basil salad, potato mayonnaise with chives, and Pimm's with borage. In some cases, the flowers may be used as an edible decoration: borage, chives, elder, and marigold are all easy to grow and produce attractive flowers. Stalks, such as angelica for crystallizing, or branches of rosemary for barbecues, are also easily grown but are rarely available otherwise. Aromatic seeds, or spices, are easier to obtain but again are mostly cheap and easy to produce.

Certain herbs, such as lemon balm and peppermint, may be infused in boiling water to make herb teas, which are good alternatives to ordinary tea and coffee since they do not contain tannin or caffeine. Most are made from dried leaves, flowers, or seeds, although they may also be made from fresh herbs.

Medicinal herbs

In many parts of the world herbal medicine is commonplace and the herb garden is a source of home-grown treatments for all sorts of ailments; mint, for example, is a mild local anaesthetic, a powerful antiseptic, and a remedy for digestive problems. The essential oils of many herbs are also used by trained aromatherapists when massaging different parts of the human body. In general, it is inadvisable to use herbs for medicinal purposes without specialist knowledge or advice.

Cosmetic and scented preparations

A number of herbs have beneficial effects on the condition of skin or hair, and are included in beauty products: rosemary, chamomile, and mint are used in shampoos and conditioners, thyme as an antiseptic for mouthwashes, and marigold and elderflower in skin lotions.

Aromatic herbs may be enjoyed all year round if they are made into scented household articles such as pomanders and linen sachets.

Structured informality
A profusion of herbs brings a wealth of fine scents and contrasting textures. Clipped dwarf hedges add structure, while bold blocks of golden marjoram contrast with casual plantings of feathery fennel and alpine strawberries.

Herbs in the garden

The majority of herbs grown today are still the wild species, but many cultivars are also now available, differing in habit or in the colour of their foliage or flowers. This diversity makes them more valuable as decorative garden plants, while their scent and other properties are usually similar to if not identical with that of the species.

The appeal of herbs lies largely in their fragrance which, in contrast to other plants, usually derives from the foliage, not the flowers. Essential oils are released when the leaves are warmed or crushed: on a sunny day, the scent of a herb garden fills the air.

Some herbs have brightly coloured flowers which may be used to great effect: the orange of marigolds (*Calendula officinalis*) offset by bronze fennel (*Foeniculum vulgare*

'Purpureum'), or the brilliant blue of borage (*Borago officinalis*) with silver-grey wormwood (*Artemisia absinthium*), for example.

Certain herbs are reputed to benefit other plants: some pungent plants such as southernwood (*Artemisia abrotanum*) repel insects if crushed or infused, while growing chamomile (*Chamaemelum nobile*) in the garden reputedly increases the health and vigour of other plants nearby.

Where to grow herbs

As for other plants, herbs should be grown in conditions that are similar to their natural habitat to ensure that they are healthy and vigorous. Many herbs are Mediterranean in origin, and these usually prefer plenty of sunshine and a free-draining soil.

However, some herbs tolerate a damp, partially shaded site, provided they are not waterlogged or in dense or permanent shade. Most variegated and golden cultivars thrive in light shade. Pineapple mint (*Mentha suaveolens* 'Variegata') and golden forms of lemon balm (*Melissa officinalis*) and feverfew (*Tanacetum parthenium*) retain their colour best when they are lit by morning or evening sun but shaded at midday.

Herbs may be grown in a variety of situations, the choice largely depending on personal preference and convenience. A separate herb garden in an attractive design provides an appealing feature and need not take up much space, but it may be preferable to have a culinary herb patch, or herbs in containers, within easy reach of the kitchen.

HERBS THAT TOLERATE MOIST SHADE

Angelica (*Angelica archangelica*)
Chervil (*Anthriscus cerefolium*)
Chives (*Allium schoenoprasum*)
Elder (*Sambucus nigra,*
  S. nigra 'Aurea',
  S. nigra 'Marginata')
Feverfew (*Tanacetum parthenium,*
  T. parthenium 'Aureum')
Lemon balm (*Melissa officinalis,*
  M. officinalis 'All Gold',
  M. officinalis 'Aurea')
Lovage (*Levisticum officinale*)
Mint (*Mentha*)
Parsley (*Petroselinum crispum*)
Sorrel (*Rumex acetosa*)
Sweet cicely (*Myrrhis odorata*)
Tansy (*Tanacetum vulgare*)
Woodruff (*Galium odoratum*)

Some herbs are decorative enough to be grown with other plants in a bed or border, while others may be better sited in the vegetable garden. Herbs intended for culinary or medicinal use should always be sited away from possible contamination by pets or roadside pollution.

Herb gardens

If there is space, it is worth creating a separate herb garden and growing many different herbs together for a strong impact and to enjoy their combined scents in one place. Making a special feature of the plants provides the opportunity to create an interesting pattern or design using blocks of complementary or contrasting colours. As well as being an ornamental way of displaying the herbs, it makes harvesting easier. Traditionally, herb gardens have been bordered by low, clipped hedges of box (*Buxus sempervirens*), but a less formal edging of hyssop (*Hyssopus officinalis*) or lavender (*Lavandula*) would also be suitable.

Beds and borders

Herbs may also be grown with other ornamental garden plants. This is useful where there is no space for a separate herb garden, or for herbs that are border plants in their own right, such as bergamot (*Monarda didyma*) and rue (*Ruta graveolens*). Grey-leaved species are especially fine in a silver border or as a contrast to plants with blue, purple, or pink colouring, such as purple sage (*Salvia officinalis* 'Purpurascens').

Stately, architectural plants are valuable as focal points on their own or at the back of a border. Fill gaps in borders with colourful annuals, such as poppies (*Papaver*), blue borage, and dark opal basil (*Ocimum basilicum* var. *purpurascens*).

Planting aromatic herbs next to doorways, paths, and seats makes it easy to enjoy their scents to the full. Low, spreading herbs, such as wild thyme (*Thymus serpyllum*), lawn chamomile (*Chamaemelum nobile* 'Treneague'), and creeping savory (*Satureja spicigera*), are suitable for rock gardens or en masse to form a fragrant carpet. These and other, more upright, herbs such as chives (*Allium schoenoprasum*) make an attractive edging to a border or path.

Herbs in vegetable gardens

For culinary herbs that are used in large quantities, such as parsley (*Petroselinum crispum*), the vegetable plot may be the best site. This may also be the most convenient place for fast-growing herbs, such as chervil (*Anthriscus cerefolium*) and dill

(*Anethum graveolens*), that are sown in succession and do not transplant successfully. The herbs may be grown in straight rows among the vegetables or as an ornamental border around the edge of the vegetable garden.

Growing herbs in containers

Many herbs thrive in containers. From a hanging basket to a chimney pot, almost any container is suitable, provided that it has drainage holes and that a layer of porous material is added before planting in it.

In small gardens or on balconies, the entire herb garden may consist of containers, imaginatively positioned on walls, steps, shelves, and windowsills, as well as at ground level. If space is at a premium, using a strawberry planter (a pot with planting pockets) offers an attractive and functional way of growing a number of different plants together. Even if you have a separate area for herbs, it is often convenient to have one or two pots of commonly used herbs near the door.

Some of the best herbs to grow in containers are chervil, parsley, chives, compact marjoram (*Origanum vulgare* 'Compactum'), rock hyssop (*Hyssopus officinalis* subsp. *aristatus*), and thymes (*Thymus*). Large plants, such as rosemary (*Rosmarinus officinalis*) and bay (*Laurus nobilis*), often look good grown as single specimens in pots or tubs. Growing slightly tender herbs, such as myrtle (*Myrtus communis*), lemon verbena (*Aloysia triphylla*), and rose-scented geranium (*Pelargonium graveolens*), in containers is convenient because they may simply be brought inside during winter; they also make good conservatory plants.

Paving and patios

Planting herbs in the gaps between paving stones is an attractive option for those herbs that prefer well-drained conditions, such as thymes

Cartwheel bed
A cartwheel design provides a decorative and practical way of growing a small range of herbs.

Container gardening
Even in the smallest garden, there is room to grow a variety of aromatic herbs in a group of pots.

and creeping savory; allow the plants to spread onto the paving so that an occasional light tread may release their fragrance.

Patios are often ideal for displaying a variety of tender or Mediterranean herbs that enjoy warmth and shelter, while an exotic touch may be added by including tender plants such as lemon trees (*Citrus limon*), cardamom (*Elettaria cardamomum*), or ginger (*Zingiber officinale*) grown in ornamental containers.

Raised beds

Growing herbs in raised beds makes it easier to enjoy their fragrance at close quarters as well as being practical for the disabled or elderly, providing easy access for planting, maintenance, and harvesting. Raised

A herbal remedy?

With climate change bringing us milder, wetter winters and periods of drought in hotter summers and autumns, we are likely to increase the range and quantity of herbs grown in our gardens. Many herbs are naturally adapted to life in a Mediterranean climate (including areas like California, South Africa, and parts of Australia), but woodlanders like rhododendrons, and many other plants that enjoy the variable climatic conditions of the UK, are unlikely to thrive without the humidity and cool, moist climate they require. Such changes are likely to take place over a long period, but the pattern of gardening will almost certainly be changed as a result.

beds must have strong retaining walls and should be no more than approximately 75cm (30in) wide and at a comfortable height for working (see also "Raised beds", p.599).

Raised beds are also a good option on paved areas against a wall (but not above the damp course in a house wall) and in any site where the soil is not free-draining. Choose small, compact herbs for raised beds, and control their spread by regular pruning and dividing.

Herb garden design

Whether informal or formal, a herb garden should be designed so that it is congruous with the style of the rest of the garden and the house. Take into account maintenance resources when planning: in general, informal herb gardens need less initial structural work than formal ones, and routine care may be less time-consuming, depending on the plants used and the size and complexity of the design. It is also possible to combine elements of both formal and informal designs; for example, a well-defined, symmetrical pattern of paths could form a framework for a free planting of herbs of different heights, habits, and colours.

Informal designs

An informal design largely depends upon the complementary habits and colours of the herbs for its success. Variegated and coloured-leaved forms, such as golden marjoram (*Origanum vulgare* 'Aureum') and purple sage, are especially effective in such a scheme. Try green- and gold-leaved plants together, for example, or those that have purple and silver foliage.

There is greater freedom to use plants of different heights and habits

Formal herb garden
This well-planned layout is divided by brick paths, which provide a formal framework for a number of geometric herb beds.

than in a formal scheme: tall ones may be introduced to create a striking effect without upsetting the balance and impact of the design, and the overall impression of colourful harmony and rich abundance allows greater flexibility for experimenting with bold combinations.

Formal designs

These designs are usually based on geometric patterns and framed by low hedges or paths. Each small bed created by the pattern is then planted with one kind of herb, giving bold blocks of colour and texture. At its simplest, the design may take the form of a cartwheel bedded into the soil with a different herb planted in each segment. These designs often look particularly impressive when viewed from above, so consider siting the herb garden where it may be overlooked from an upper window

or a slope. When choosing plants, do not include tall, invasive, or sprawling herbs that may spoil the rest of the design when fully grown. Tall herbs should be positioned around the bed edges, where they will not swamp neighbouring plants.

A formal garden with paths is labour-intensive at first but soon looks mature and needs little structural maintenance. One that includes a framework of dwarf hedges that require regular clipping may be

considerably more demanding. The hedging may outline the design or take on the complex shapes of a knot garden (see also "Formal Gardens", p.18). Suitable plants for dwarf hedges include box, hyssop, lavenders, (*Teucrium* x *lucidrys*), germander, and winter savory (*Satureja montana*) planted 22–30cm (9–12in) apart.

Making a plan

To draw up a plan, first measure the site and surrounding features accurately, taking account of any changes in level. Also note where shadows fall at different seasons as well as at different times of day.

Whether the garden is to be formal or informal in style, remember that herbs should be within arm's reach for convenient harvesting; for beds or borders in open ground, provide access by paths or stepping stones so that the soil is not walked on as this could lead to compaction.

Transfer the measurements to squared paper, working to scale; in order to compare a number of different designs, draw each scheme on a sheet of tracing paper laid over the master plan.

Finally, decide which herbs to grow, taking into account their cultivation requirements, habit, colour, height and spread, and the amounts that will be required for harvesting, then mark them on the plan. Herbs in containers may also be included to provide focal points in the garden.

Herbs in a patio garden
Enliven a patio or courtyard, and soften the effect of the hard materials, by planting herbs directly into the gaps between paving or in gravel.

PLANNING A FORMAL HERB GARDEN

There are many possible formal designs, although imagination should be restrained by considerations of balance and proportion. Cartwheel and chessboard schemes are popular but unusual geometric patterns also provide plenty of opportunity to create an eye-catching feature.

Directory of common herbs

Chives
(Allium schoenoprasum)

Hardy, herbaceous, clump-forming perennial needing sun or semi-shade and moist but well-drained, rich soil. Good as a low edging for borders. May be forced for winter use (see p.411). Use the leaves, which have a mild onion flavour, as a garnish and flavouring in salads, dips, soft cheeses, and soups; the edible flowers make a decorative addition to salads.
Harvesting and storing Cut leaves and flowers as available to use fresh. For freezing and drying, cut leaves before flowering occurs and chop finely.
Propagation By seed sown in spring (see p.198) or by division in autumn or spring (p.200).
Related species and variants Variations in height, flower colour, and flavour are available; Chinese or garlic chives (*A. tuberosum*) have a mild garlic flavour and white flowers.

Lemon verbena
(Aloysia triphylla)

Half-hardy, upright, deciduous shrub requiring a sunny, well-drained soil. Plants may be cut back by frost but usually grow again. The leaves have a strong, clean, lemon scent and are used in herb teas, desserts, and, dried, in pot-pourri and teas.
Harvesting and storing Pick leaves during the growing season for using fresh or for drying.
Propagation By softwood or green-wood cuttings (see p.111).

Dill (Anethum graveolens)

Hardy, upright annual with feathery, blue-green leaves. Grow in sunny, well-drained, rich soil but not near fennel, since cross-pollination may result in the loss of its distinctive flavour. Runs to seed quickly. Use the leaves or, for a stronger flavour, the aromatic seeds in soups, sauces, potato salad, pickles, and fish dishes.
Harvesting and storing Pick leaves in spring and summer before flowering occurs. Cut seedheads as they ripen in summer.
Propagation By seed sown in spring and early summer (see p.216); may not transplant well.

Angelica
(Angelica archangelica)

Hardy biennial with large, divided leaves and large flowerheads. Grow this bold, architectural plant in sun or shade and moist, rich soil. Unless seeds are required, remove seedheads before ripening to prevent unwanted seedlings. The young stalks may be candied; the leaves are used in cooking, especially in fruit desserts and fish dishes.
Harvesting and storing Gather fresh leaves in spring and summer. Cut young stalks for crystallizing either in spring or early summer. Cut seedheads as they ripen in summer.
Propagation By seed sown in autumn or spring (see p.216).

Chervil (Anthriscus cerefolium)

Hardy annual needing semi-shade and moist, rich soil. Runs to seed quickly in hot, dry conditions. The leaves have a fine, subtle flavour that is reminiscent of parsley and anise. Use the leaves in egg dishes, salads, soups, and sauces.
Harvesting and storing Gather leaves before flowering occurs. Freeze or dry them gently to preserve their delicate flavour.
Propagation By seed sown at monthly intervals from spring to early autumn (see p.216); do not transplant. May also be sown in trays under glass in early autumn for winter use.

Horseradish
(Armoracia rusticana)

Hardy perennial with persistent, stout, white-fleshed roots, which have a pungent flavour and are grated into coleslaw, dips, and sauces, especially in horseradish sauce. Young leaves are used in salads or sandwiches. Needs sun and moist but well-drained, rich soil.
Harvesting and storing Pick the young leaves in spring. Harvest the roots in autumn when the flavour is best, or as required.
Propagation By 15cm (6in) root cuttings in winter (see p.203) or by seed sown in spring (p.198).

Southernwood
(Artemisia abrotanum)

Hardy, semi-evergreen subshrub with finely divided, grey-green foliage. May be used to form a low hedge or in mixed borders. Grow in sunny, well-drained, rich, neutral to slightly alkaline soil. Use the aromatic leaves in pot-pourri and as an insect repellent.
Harvesting and storing During summer, pick leaves as required for using fresh or for drying.
Propagation By semi-ripe heel cuttings in late summer (see p.113).

Wormwood
(Artemisia absinthium)

Hardy, deciduous subshrub with deeply divided, greyish-green leaves. Good as a border plant or informal hedge. Requires sun and well-drained, neutral to alkaline, rich soil. Prune to within 15cm (6in) of the ground in spring. The aromatic leaves are intensely bitter; they were formerly used to flavour alcoholic drinks but are now regarded as toxic. The foliage is attractive in herbal decorations and posies.
Harvesting and storing Pick foliage in the summer for use fresh or dried in decorative arrangements.
Propagation By semi-ripe heel cuttings in late summer (see p.113).
Variants 'Lambrook Silver' is a cultivar with deeply divided, silver-grey foliage.

French tarragon
(Artemisia dracunculus)

Half-hardy, subshrubby perennial with upright stems and glossy, narrow leaves. Grow in sun and well-drained, neutral to alkaline, rich soil. In cold areas, may need winter protection, but may be forced for winter use. The leaves are commonly used in *sauce béarnaise*, tartare sauce, *fines herbes*, in egg and chicken dishes, and to flavour vinegar.
Harvesting and storing Cut sprigs of foliage throughout the growing season, leaving two thirds of the stem to regrow. The leaves are best frozen but may also be dried satisfactorily.
Propagation By division of rhizomes in autumn or spring (see p.201). Seed is not available: that sold as tarragon is the Russian subspecies.
Related species Russian tarragon (*A. dracunculus* subsp. *dracunculoides*) is hardier but it has an inferior flavour.

Borage
(Borago officinalis)

Hardy, upright annual that needs sunny, reasonably drained soil. Add the cucumber-flavoured leaves, and the flowers, to cold drinks (such as Pimm's) and salads. Flowers can be crystallized for use in cake decoration.
Harvesting and storing Pick young leaves and use fresh. Gather the flowers (without calyces) during summer to use fresh, freeze in ice cubes, or crystallize.
Propagation By seed sown in spring (see p.216). Self-sows in light soils.
Variants There is also a form with white flowers, *B. officinalis* 'Alba'.

Marigold (*Calendula officinalis*)

Bushy, hardy annual with bright orange flowers. Grows in sun and well-drained, even poor soil. Dead-head to prolong flowering. Use the petals to flavour and colour rice, soft cheese, and soups, and to garnish salads. Chop the young leaves into salads. Dried petals may be used to add colour to pot-pourri.

Harvesting and storing Pick open flowers in summer and remove petals for drying. Gather leaves when young.

Propagation By seed sown in autumn or spring (see p.216). Self-sows freely.

Variants Double-flowered forms in cream, yellow, orange, and bronze are widely available.

Caraway (*Carum carvi*)

Hardy biennial needing sunny, well-drained, rich soil. Aromatic seeds are used in baking, cheeses, confectionery, and meat stews like goulash. Add the leaves to soups and salads.

Harvesting and storing Gather leaves when young. Collect the ripe seedheads in summer.

Propagation By seed sown in spring, late summer, or early autumn (see p.216).

Chamomile (*Chamaemelum nobile*)

Hardy, dense, creeping, evergreen perennial needing sunny, light, well-drained, sandy soil. Good at the edge of paths and borders, or between paving stones. May be planted as an ornamental lawn (see p.393). Use the apple-scented leaves in pot-pourri; the aromatic flowers are used in pot-pourri and herb teas.

Harvesting and storing Pick leaves at any time as required. Gather flowers when fully open in summer and dry whole.

Propagation By seed sown in spring or autumn (see p.198) or by division in spring (p.200).

Variants 'Treneague' is a dwarf, non-flowering form that is particularly suitable for lawns and gaps in paving. *C. nobile* 'Flore Pleno' has attractive double flowers.

Coriander (*Coriandrum sativum*)

Hardy annual with divided foliage and small, white or pale mauve flowers. Grow in sun or semi-shade and well-drained, rich soil The plants have an unpleasant smell and should not be grown indoors. The lobed, lower leaves are used in curries, chutneys, sauces, and salads. The seeds, which have a sweet, spicy flavour, are used in curry powder, baking, chutneys, and sausages.

Harvesting and storing Pick young leaves for using fresh or for freezing. Gather seedheads as they ripen and use whole or ground.

Propagation By seed sown in spring (see p.216).

Cumin (*Cuminum cyminum*)

Tender annual with white or pale pink flowers. Needs sunny, well-drained, rich soil, and heat for the seeds to ripen. The aromatic seeds are used in curries, pickles, yoghurt, and Middle Eastern dishes.

Harvesting and storing Gather seedheads as they ripen.

Propagation By seed sown in early spring in a warm situation or under cover (see p.217).

Fennel (*Foeniculum vulgare*)

Hardy perennial with fine, filigree leaves and clusters of yellow flowers. Grow in sun and well-drained, rich soil. Use the leaves and leaf sheaths for their aniseed flavour in salads, and meat and fish dishes. Seeds are used in baking, fish dishes, and herb teas.

Harvesting and storing Cut leaves and leaf sheaths when still young. Gather seedheads as they ripen.

Propagation By seed sown in autumn or spring (see p.198) or by division in spring (p.200).

Variants 'Purpureum' is an attractive bronze cultivar; Florence fennel (*F. vulgare* var. *dulce*) is grown as an annual for use as a vegetable (see p.540).

Woodruff (*Galium odoratum*)

Hardy, creeping perennial that has star-shaped, white flowers above whorls of narrow leaves in spring and early summer. An excellent ground-cover plant in damp shade. The dried leaves are used in pot-pourri and herb tea.

Harvesting and storing Gather the leaves for drying just before the flowers open in spring.

Propagation By division in autumn or spring (see p.200) or by seed sown in early autumn (p.198).

Hyssop (*Hyssopus officinalis*)

Hardy, semi-evergreen subshrub with spikes of small, dark purple-blue flowers. Needs sunny, well-drained to dry, neutral to alkaline soil. The aromatic leaves are used in soups, bean dishes, stews, game, and pâté.

Harvesting and storing Gather leaves any time for fresh use; pick young leaves in early summer to dry.

Propagation By seed sown in autumn or spring (see p.114) or by softwood cuttings in summer (p.111).

Orris (*Iris germanica* 'Florentina')

Hardy perennial with off-white flowers and sword-shaped leaves that needs sunny, well-drained soil. Plant so that the rhizomes are partially exposed. The thick rhizome develops a violet scent after drying and prolonged storage. It is ground for using as a perfume fixative in pot-pourri and linen sachets.

Harvesting and storing In autumn, dig up rhizomes at least three years old. Peel, split, and dry, leaving for up to two years before grinding.

Propagation By division or offsets in late summer (see p.201).

Bay (*Laurus nobilis*)

Hardy, evergreen tree or shrub needing sun or semi-shade and moist but well-drained soil. In cold areas, it may need protection from frost and wind. May be clipped for topiary or pruned hard to restrict size. Use the leaves in *bouquet garni*, and for flavouring stock, marinades, sauces, milk desserts, and meat and fish dishes.

Harvesting and storing Pick leaves any time for using fresh. Dry mature leaves in summer.

Propagation By seed in autumn (p.114) or by semi-ripe cuttings (p.79).

Variants 'Aurea' has yellow-flushed leaves.

Lavender (*Lavandula angustifolia*)

Hardy, evergreen, bushy shrub with upright, mauve flower spikes. Grow in sunny, well-drained soil. Good for low hedging. The flowers are used in pot-pourri, linen sachets, herb pillows, and tea. They may also be crystallized or used to flavour oil or vinegar.

Harvesting and storing Gather flowering stems in summer, and air-dry.

Propagation By seed in spring (see p.114) or by semi-ripe cuttings in summer (p.112).

Related species There are several other species and many cultivars, varying in habit, foliage, flowering time, and flower colour. They include dwarf cultivars, such as 'Hidcote', and white-flowered forms, for example 'Nana Alba'; French lavender (*L. stoechas*), which is borderline hardy, has dark purple flowers crowned by conspicuous purple bracts.

Lovage (*Levisticum officinale*)

Hardy perennial needing sun or semi-shade and deep, moist but well-drained soil. A tall plant, suitable for the back of a border. The leaves have a strong flavour, resembling celery and yeast, and are used in soups, stocks, and stews; add the fresh, young leaves to salads. The aromatic seeds are used in baking and vegetable dishes, and the young stalks may be crystallized. Blanch plants under pots in spring for use as a vegetable.

Harvesting and storing Pick young leaves in spring and freeze or dry. In spring, gather young stalks for crystallizing. Cut stalks after two to three weeks of blanching in spring, leaving central shoots to grow.

Propagation By seed sown as soon as ripe in late summer or autumn (see p.198) or by division in spring (p.200).

Lemon balm (*Melissa officinalis*)

Hardy, clump-forming perennial that needs sunny, moist but well-drained, poor soil. Add the lemon-scented leaves to cold drinks, sweet and savoury dishes, or infuse them.

Harvesting and storing Pick leaves before flowering for using fresh or for drying.

Propagation By seed sown in spring (see p.198) or division in spring or autumn (p.200). Self-seeds.

Variants Yellow-variegated cultivars, such as 'Aurea', are available; grow them in partial shade to avoid leaf scorch.

Mint (*Mentha spicata*)

Hardy, herbaceous perennial that may be invasive (see p.411). Grow in sun and poor, moist soil. Use the leaves to make mint sauce, in salads, drinks, and with potatoes or peas.

Harvesting and storing Pick leaves before flowering and dry or freeze, or chop and infuse in vinegar.

Propagation By stem tip cuttings in spring or summer (see p.202), by division in spring or autumn (p.200), or by seed sown in spring (p.198).

Related species There are numerous species and cultivars with slightly differing foliage and scents. Some, such as pineapple mint (*M. suaveolens* 'Variegata'), have variegated leaves. Peppermint (*M. x piperita*) has purplish-green leaves used in peppermint tea and in syrups and desserts, while eau-de-cologne mint (*M. x piperita* f. *citrata*) has a fine perfume. Bowles' mint (*M. x villosa* var. *alopecuroides*) has rounded leaves with a fresh, spearmint aroma and purplish-pink flowers.

Bergamot (*Monarda didyma*)

Hardy, herbaceous perennial with heads of red, claw-shaped florets in summer. An excellent border plant for sunny, rich, moist soil. Infuse the aromatic leaves in tea for an "Earl Grey" flavour, and add them to summer drinks, salads, pork dishes, or pot-pourri. Use the attractive florets to add colour to salads and pot-pourri.

Harvesting and storing Pick leaves in spring or just before flowering occurs in summer for using fresh or drying. Gather flowers in summer, to dry.

Propagation By seed in autumn or spring (see p.198), by stem tip cuttings in spring (p.202), or by division in spring (p.200).

Related species and variants Hybrids with red, pink, white, or purple flowers are available. *M. fistulosa* has lavender flowers and tolerates drier soil.

Sweet cicely (*Myrrhis odorata*)

Hardy, herbaceous perennial needing semi-shade and moist, rich soil. The fern-like leaves, which have an aniseed flavour, are used in fruit dishes or are added to salads. The thick tap root can be eaten raw or cooked as a vegetable. The large seeds are added to fruit dishes.

Harvesting and storing Pick leaves in spring and early summer for drying. Collect unripe seeds in summer and dry or pickle them. Dig up roots in autumn for using fresh.

Propagation By seed sown outdoors in autumn (see p.199) or by division in spring or autumn (p.200). Self-sows readily.

Basil (*Ocimum basilicum*)

Half-hardy annual with toothed, pointed oval leaves. In cold regions, basil must be grown under cover or in a sheltered, sunny position in light, well-drained to dry, rich soil. Grows well in pots on a sunny windowsill. The highly aromatic leaves are used in salads, vinegars, pesto, and tomato pasta dishes.

Harvesting and storing Pick leaves when young in summer and freeze, dry, or use to flavour herb oil or vinegar; or pack leaves in jars of oil.

Propagation By seed sown in spring (see p.217).

Related species and variants Var. *purpurascens* is an attractive, purple-leaved variety with pink flowers. The compact bush basil (*O. minimum*) is hardier but has less flavour. *O. basilicum* 'Green Ruffles' has crinkled, toothed, pale green foliage.

Marjoram (*Origanum vulgare*)

Hardy, herbaceous perennial that has tiny, white, pink, or mauve flowers in summer. Needs full sun and well-drained, preferably alkaline soil. The aromatic leaves are used widely in cooking, especially in pizzas and pasta sauces.

Harvesting and storing Pick leaves during the growing season; for drying or freezing, pick just before flowers open.

Propagation By seed in spring or autumn (see p.198), by division in spring or autumn (p.200), or by stem tip cuttings in spring (p.202).

Variants There are various species and hybrids, differing in hardiness, flavour, and flower and foliage colour, for example golden marjoram (*O. vulgare* 'Aureum'). The low-growing 'Compactum' is ideal for containers and edging.

Parsley (*Petroselinum crispum*)

Hardy biennial with bright green, crinkled leaves. Grow in sun or semi-shade and well-drained, rich soil. Good for growing in pots. Use the leaves whole or chopped as a garnish and in *bouquet garni*, sauces, and egg and fish dishes.

Harvesting and storing Pick leaves from plants in their first year and use fresh or freeze.

Propagation By seed sown at intervals from early spring to autumn (see p.216).

Variants Italian parsley (*P. crispum* var. *neapolitanum*) is flat leaved, with a stronger flavour.

Aniseed (*Pimpinella anisum*)

Half-hardy annual with deeply divided leaves and, in late summer, heads of tiny, white flowers. In cold regions, it must have a sunny, sheltered position in well-drained, sandy soil for the seed to ripen. Add the leaves to fruit salads. The aromatic seeds are used in baking, confectionery, and both sweet and savoury dishes.

Harvesting and storing Pick lower leaves in spring for immediate use. Collect seedheads as they ripen in autumn.

Propagation By seed sown in spring in its final position, because it is difficult to transplant successfully (see p.217).

Rosemary (*Rosmarinus officinalis*)

Hardy to frost hardy, evergreen shrub with dense, needle-like leaves and pale blue flowers in spring and summer or, in mild regions, all year round. Grow in sunny, well-drained, poor to moderately fertile soil. May be grown

as an informal hedge. The leaves, which have a strong, resinous aroma, are used in meat dishes, especially with lamb, and to make pot-pourri and hair rinses. The flowers may be added to salads.
Harvesting and storing Pick leaves and flowers as required for immediate use. Gather sprigs for drying during the growing season.
Propagation By seed sown in spring (see p.114) or by semi-ripe cuttings in summer (p.112).
Variants Cultivars with flowers in various shades of blue, pink, and white are available. The vigorous, erect cultivar 'Miss Jessopp's Upright' is suitable for hedging; 'Severn Sea' has bright blue flowers and a dwarf, arching habit that is ideal for containers.

Sorrel (*Rumex acetosa*)

Hardy, upright perennial that needs sun or semi-shade and moist soil. Prolong leaf production by removing flower spikes. Protect with cloches for a winter supply. The sour-tasting, young leaves are used in salads, soups, and sauces.
Harvesting and storing Pick young leaves before flowering occurs, for using fresh or freezing. May be frozen.
Propagation By division in either spring or autumn (see p.200), or by seed sown in spring (p.198).
Related species The low-growing species, French, shield, or buckler-leaf sorrel (*R. scutatus*), has small, fine-flavoured leaves.

Rue (*Ruta graveolens*)

Hardy, evergreen subshrub with divided, grey-green foliage and greenish-yellow flowers in summer. Thrives in a hot dry position. An excellent plant for borders or low hedges. Handling rue on sunny days may cause a skin rash. Use the pungent leaves with discretion in salads, sauces, and to flavour cream cheese.
Harvesting and storing Pick leaves as required for immediate use, protecting hands with rubber gloves on sunny days.
Propagation By seed sown in spring (see p.114), or by semi-ripe cuttings in summer (p.112).
Variants Some cultivars have cream-variegated and blue leaves, for example, 'Variegata' and the compact 'Jackman's Blue'.

Sage (*Salvia officinalis*)

Hardy, evergreen subshrub with grey-green foliage. Grow in sunny, well-drained, rich soil. An excellent plant for shrub borders and rose gardens. The aromatic leaves are used in stuffings, meat dishes, to flavour cheese, and in herb teas.
Harvesting and storing Pick leaves as needed to use fresh. Gather leaves before the flowers open for drying.
Propagation By seed sown in spring (see p.114), softwood cuttings in spring and summer (p.111), or semi-ripe cuttings in early autumn (p.112).
Variants Cultivars include purple sage (*S. officinalis* 'Purpurascens') with strongly flavoured, purple leaves, and the less hardy 'Tricolor', with white-margined, pink-flushed leaves.

Cotton lavender (*Santolina chamaecyparissus*)

Hardy, evergreen subshrub with silver-grey leaves and, in summer, masses of yellow, button flower-heads. Grow in sun and well-drained, poor to moderately fertile soil. Good as a low hedge, it also provides a contrasting colour in knot gardens (see "Formal garden styles", p.18). Add the scented leaves to pot-pourri, and dry the flowers for decorative purposes.
Harvesting and storing Pick leaves for drying in spring and summer. In summer, gather flowers as they open for drying.
Propagation By cuttings of semi-ripe sideshoots in late summer (see p.112).

Winter savory (*Satureja montana*)

Hardy, evergreen subshrub with tiny, white to pink flowers in summer. Grow in sunny, well-drained soil. Use the aromatic leaves in bean and cheese dishes.
Harvesting and storing Pick any time for using fresh. Gather leaves to dry or freeze as flower buds form.
Propagation By seed sown in spring (see p.114), by division in spring or autumn (p.118), by softwood cuttings in summer (p.111), or by layering in spring (p.116).
Related species Creeping savory (*S. spicigera*) is a low species ideal for containers, edging, and rock gardens. The annual summer savory (*S. hortensis*) has lilac flowers and a fine flavour.

Alecost (*Tanacetum balsamita*)

Hardy perennial which requires semi-shade and well-drained soil. The leaves have a citrus-mint fragrance; they should be used sparingly in cooking, and may be added to pot-pourri.
Harvesting and storing Gather fresh leaves in spring and summer for using fresh or for drying.
Propagation By division (see p.200), seed (p.198), or basal cuttings (p.202) in spring.
Variants Subsp. *balsametoides* is camphoraceous.

Feverfew (*Tanacetum parthenium*)

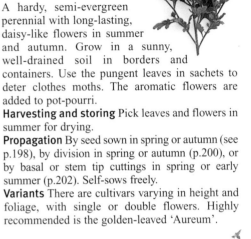

A hardy, semi-evergreen perennial with long-lasting, daisy-like flowers in summer and autumn. Grow in a sunny, well-drained soil in borders and containers. Use the pungent leaves in sachets to deter clothes moths. The aromatic flowers are added to pot-pourri.
Harvesting and storing Pick leaves and flowers in summer for drying.
Propagation By seed sown in spring or autumn (see p.198), by division in spring or autumn (p.200), or by basal or stem tip cuttings in spring or early summer (p.202). Self-sows freely.
Variants There are cultivars varying in height and foliage, with single or double flowers. Highly recommended is the golden-leaved 'Aureum'.

Thyme (*Thymus vulgaris*)

Hardy, evergreen, low-growing subshrub with tiny leaves and, in summer, pale lilac flowers. Grow in sunny, well-drained soil. May be grown as an edging for borders, between paving stones, and in containers. Add the aromatic leaves to *bouquet garni*, stuffings, sauces, soups, stocks, and meat dishes.
Harvesting and storing Pick leaves at any time to use fresh. Gather flowering tops for drying, stripping leaves and flowers from the stalks when quite dry. Fresh sprigs may also be infused in oil or vinegar.
Propagation By seed (see p.114) or division (p.118) in spring, by layering in spring or autumn (p.116), or by softwood or semi-ripe cuttings in summer (p.112).
Related species and variants There are many species and cultivars, varying in height, foliage, and flower colour. Wild thyme (*T. serpyllum*) is a low, mat-forming plant with mauve flowers; *T. serpyllum* 'Snowdrift' and *T.* Coccineus Group have, respectively, white and magenta flowers; and *T.* 'Doone Valley' has scented foliage with gold markings. *T.* x *citriodorus* has lemon-scented leaves and lilac flowers; *T. vulgaris* 'Silver Posie' produces silver-margined leaves.

Ginger (*Zingiber officinale*)

Tender, deciduous perennial needing sun or semi-shade and well-drained soil. The thick, tuberous rhizome is highly aromatic and is used in baking, preserves, confectionery, chutneys, sauces, and many Oriental dishes.
Harvesting and storing Dig up young rhizomes and peel them for using fresh or preserving in syrup. For drying, dig up the rhizomes as the leaves turn yellow.
Propagation By division of rhizomes as they start to sprout (see p.201).

Soil preparation and planting

THE ideal site for a herb garden is sunny, open but sheltered, with neutral to alkaline soil, and good drainage. These conditions suit the majority of common herbs such as lavender (*Lavandula angustifolia*), winter savory (*Satureja montana*), sage (*Salvia officinalis*), marjoram (*Origanum vulgare*), rosemary (*Rosmarinus officinalis*), and thyme (*Thymus vulgaris*), most of which are Mediterranean in origin.

Preparing the site

If possible, prepare the ground well in advance, preferably in autumn. First, remove all weeds, taking care to eliminate any persistent, perennial weeds such as couch grass (see PLANT PROBLEMS, "Perennial weeds", p.670). Then dig over the soil, leaving it in a rough state, to be broken down by frost.

In early spring, remove any weeds that have appeared subsequently, fork in well-rotted organic matter (such as garden or mushroom compost), and rake the soil to a fine, level tilth. The aim is to provide a free-draining and reasonably fertile soil. Feeding with manure or artificial fertilizers is not recommended, especially for Mediterranean herbs, since it produces soft growth with little aroma or resistance to frost.

On heavy, clay soil, you may need to improve the drainage (see SOILS AND FERTILIZERS, "Improving drainage", p.623); alternatively, grow the herbs in raised beds or in containers. Most herbs tolerate a slightly acid soil; if the pH is below 6.5, however, add a dressing of lime when preparing the soil (see SOILS AND FERTILIZERS, "Liming", p.625).

Planting invasive herbs

If planting invasive herbs, such as mint (*Mentha*), tansy (*Tanacetum vulgare*), or woodruff (*Galium odoratum*, syn. *Asperula odorata*) in open ground, restrict their spread by growing them in sunken containers. Old buckets, large pots, or even heavy-duty plastic bags are suitable, although you must make drainage holes at the base. For best results, lift and divide the plants each spring and replant young, vigorous pieces in the containers using fresh compost; if not replenished, nutrients are quickly depleted and the herbs may deteriorate and become more prone to disease, such as rusts (see p.648).

1 *Dig a hole large enough to accommodate a large pot or old bucket. Make drainage holes in the pot base, then place it in the hole and fill with a loam and compost mixture.*

2 *Plant the herb (here mint), firming in well; add enough compost to conceal the pot's rim, and water thoroughly. Each spring, replant and replace the compost in the pot.*

Herbs in winter

Although herbs are harvested mainly during spring and summer, the availability of many can be extended almost all year round.

Sown in late summer or early autumn, a number of herbs such as chervil (*Anthriscus cerefolium*), coriander (*Coriandrum sativum*), and parsley (*Petroselinum crispum*) continue to grow throughout the winter if they are protected from frost by a cold frame or cloches. They also grow well in pots placed on a sunny windowsill.

Herbaceous perennials that die down in winter, such as chives (*Allium schoenoprasum*), French tarragon (*Artemisia dracunculus*), and mint, may be forced for winter use. In early autumn, dig up mature plants, divide them, and replant in containers of loam-based potting compost. If kept in a light place that is free from frost and draughts, they produce fresh shoots throughout the winter that may be harvested regularly. Discard forced plants in spring or plant them out; if planted out, do not pick their leaves for at least a season to allow them time to recover vigour.

Evergreen herbs, such as winter savory, thyme, and rosemary, may be gathered throughout the year, but limit winter harvesting as there is no new growth at this time.

Planting container-grown herbs

Container-grown herbs may be planted throughout the year, but the best time is in spring when they establish rapidly. If they have been kept in a heated greenhouse during the winter, gradually harden them off (see p.220) in a cold frame before planting them out.

Soak well before planting, as dry root balls are difficult to wet once below ground. To avoid trampling and compacting the soil in a bed when planting out, it is best to stand on a plank in order to reach the planting positions. Set out the herbs, while still in their pots, according to your planting plan and check that each has sufficient room to develop, depending on its growth rate and spread.

Whatever the weather, water thoroughly after planting in order to settle the soil around the plants and provide even moisture for new root growth. After planting, pinch out the tips of clump-forming herbs and trim back shrubby herbs to encourage new sideshoots and to develop a bushy habit.

HOW TO GROW HERBS FOR FRESH WINTER USE

1 *Choose a dry day in early autumn to lift a clump of herbs (here chives) from the garden using a fork.*

2 *Divide the clump into smaller pieces with your hands or a hand fork. Shake loose as much of the soil from the roots as possible.*

3 *Plant up the divided pieces into pots or trays of potting compost; water well and cut back the top-growth.*

4 *Place the plants in a light, frost-free place. Once they are about 10cm (4in) high, harvest the leaves regularly to maintain a supply of new growth.*

Planting a herb garden to a design

Whether creating an intricate, formal design or a simple, informal one, careful planning, both on paper and on site, is essential for success. Make plans well in advance: start in the winter for planting in the spring, or as early as the preceding summer if you are raising the plants yourself.

As for all planting, thoroughly prepare the ground, clearing any weeds and raking the surface of the soil to a fine tilth (see "Preparing the site", p.411).

Once you have determined the design and the planting scheme on paper, mark the basic outline of the herb garden, including any paths, on the prepared site. Make any adjustments to the layout at this stage if required. It is most convenient to use container-grown herbs, since they can easily be set out according to the plan and the arrangement checked before actual planting begins.

If using turf or heavy materials such as paving, bricks, or stone, lay them before planting, while paths made of lighter, loose materials, such as grit, gravel, or bark chippings, may be laid before or after planting. When making paths of grit or gravel, provide retaining battens or edging tiles to prevent the material from spreading onto the plants in the beds.

1 *First prepare the soil for planting. Then, using string and canes, or grit, mark out the planned design for the herb garden, including any paths or paved areas, on the site.*

2 *Lay out the plants, still in their pots, to check the overall effect and spacing. If using grit or gravel for the paths, sink battens at the edges to keep the material in place.*

3 *Once the design is finalized, plant the herbs and water them; you may prefer to plant them densely to achieve the desired effect quickly.*

4 *Lay the paths, adding grit or gravel evenly in between the battens; level the surface.*

5 *Keep the herb garden watered and weeded. Pinch out growing tips to promote bushy growth and prune as necessary.*

DESIGN FOR A HERB GARDEN

1 Chives (*Allium schoenoprasum*)
2 Compact marjoram (*Origanum vulgare* 'Compactum')
3 Bergamot (*Monarda didyma*)
4 Wormwood (*Artemisia absinthium*)
5 Hyssop (*Hyssopus officinalis*)
6 Wild thyme (*Thymus serpyllum*)
7 Silver-variegated thyme (*Thymus vulgaris* 'Silver Posie')
8 Marjoram (*Origanum vulgare*)
9 Pineapple mint (*Mentha suaveolens* 'Variegata')
10 Chamomile (*Chamaemelum nobile*)
11 Buckler-leaf sorrel (*Rumex scutatus*)
12 French tarragon (*Artemisia dracunculus*)
13 Variegated sage (*Salvia officinalis* 'Icterina')
14 Parsley (*Petroselinum crispum*)

15 Sweet cicely (*Myrrhis odorata*)
16 Cotton lavender (*Santolina chamaecyparissus*)
17 Creeping savory (*Satureja spicigera*)
18 Golden lemon balm (*Melissa officinalis* 'Aurea')
19 Chinese chives (*Allium tuberosum*)
20 Orris (*Iris germanica* 'Florentina')
21 Borage (*Borago officinalis*)
22 Pink hyssop (*Hyssopus officinalis* f. *roseus*)
23 Purple sage (*Salvia officinalis* 'Purpurascens')
24 Pink lavender (*Lavandula angustifolia* 'Loddon Pink')
25 Common thyme (*Thymus vulgaris*)
26 Purple basil (*Ocimum basilicum* var. *purpurascens*)
27 Rosemary (*Rosmarinus officinalis*)
28 Summer savory (*Satureja hortensis*)
29 Southernwood (*Artemisia abrotanum*)
30 Sweet marjoram (*Origanum majorana*)
31 Alecost (*Tanacetum balsamita*)
32 Golden feverfew (*Tanacetum parthenium* 'Aureum')
33 Chervil (*Anthriscus cerefolium*)
34 Marigold (*Calendula officinalis*)
35 Bronze fennel (*Foeniculum vulgare* 'Purpureum')
36 Woodruff (*Galium odoratum*)
37 Cotton lavender (*Santolina chamaecyparissus* 'Lemon Queen')
38 Sorrel (*Rumex acetosa*)
39 Lemon thyme (*Thymus* x *citriodorus*)

This small garden includes a wide range of aromatic and culinary herbs; they have been grouped in beds of restricted colour and divided by symmetrical paths for a traditional, formal effect, softened by the informal plant groupings within the beds.

Routine care

Most herbs flourish and require little attention once they are established. Maintenance largely consists of cutting back plants in spring and summer to encourage healthy growth, and tidying up dormant plants in winter. Herbs in containers usually need routine watering and feeding during the growing season, while periodic repotting or top-dressing is also necessary. Growing herbs in the right conditions should minimize any pest or disease problems; take action as necessary (see PLANT PROBLEMS, pp.639–673) but you must wait one or two weeks after any chemical treatment before using the herbs.

Cutting back

Herbs that are valued for their fresh, young foliage may be cut back to produce a regular supply of leaves. Remove the flowering stems of sorrel (*Rumex acetosa*) as they appear; chives (*Allium schoenoprasum*) and marjoram (*Origanum vulgare*) may

be left until after flowering as the flowers are useful as flavourings; variegated forms of marjoram, mint (*Mentha*), and lemon balm (*Melissa officinalis*) produce bright new foliage if the plant is cut back shortly before flowering as its colours fade.

The growth of invasive herbs should be checked regularly: even when planted in sunken containers, they produce surface runners which must be removed before they spread too far. Remove any reverted, plain shoots from variegated herbs as soon as they appear.

Dead-heading and pruning

Unless planning to save the seed, remove the dead flowerheads from most herbs so that energy is channelled into growth. Dead-heading annuals such as borage (*Borago officinalis*) lengthens the flowering season. Certain herbs such as angelica (*Angelica archangelica*) self-sow prolifically; these may become a nuisance if they are left to set seed.

Dead-head and prune shrubby herbs, such as lavender (*Lavandula*) and thyme (*Thymus*), by trimming lightly with shears after flowering. Hard pruning in spring encourages sideshoots and new growth from the base; thyme, however, is best pruned little and often during the growing season.

Mulching

Mulch only established herbs that thrive in moist soil, such as mint and bergamot (*Monarda didyma*). In summer, mulch after rain to retain moisture and to improve the soil as it breaks down. Use an inorganic mulch such as grit around Mediterranean or grey-leaved plants in heavy soil to reduce the risk of rotting.

Autumn clearance

The extent to which herbs are cut back in autumn partly depends on personal preference. In cold areas, leaving the dead foliage of herbaceous perennials until spring helps to protect them against frost and wind. Remove any dead leaves that have fallen on thyme and other low-growing, evergreen herbs as they may encourage fungal attack.

Winter protection

In cold weather, tender herbs should either be brought under cover or otherwise protected (see FROST AND WIND PROTECTION, pp.612–613). In

spring, cut them back and plant them out again, or propagate new plants from cuttings. The hardiness of a number of herbs, such as sage (*Salvia officinalis*) and lavender, depends on the variety; check this when buying.

Herbs in containers

Most herbs are easy to grow within containers and need little maintenance (see also CONTAINER GARDENING, p.318). In hot weather, check soil moisture daily and water thoroughly when dry. During the growing season, feed the herbs every two weeks with a weak liquid fertilizer.

In cold periods, bring herbs in containers under cover in good light. Frost-proof pots may be left outdoors, but insulate them with sacking to protect the herbs' roots.

Repotting

Inspect herbs periodically to check that they are not becoming pot-bound. Also look out for such signs as rapid drying out, pale foliage, and weak new growth. Repot in the growing season to encourage new root growth.

If repotting is impractical, renew the top 2.5–5cm (1–2in) of compost, incorporating well-rotted organic matter or a slow-release fertilizer. It will then be unnecessary to feed the herbs for about a month.

PRUNING LAVENDER

1 *In late summer or early autumn, cut off all the dry flower stalks with secateurs and lightly clip the shrubs to maintain a neat finish.*

2 *Early the following spring, cut back shoots by 2.5cm (1in) or more of the previous year's growth, making sure that some green growth remains.*

REPLANTING A STRAWBERRY PLANTER

1 *Each spring, replace or divide and replant the herbs in a strawberry planter if they have outgrown the pot or need rejuvenating.*

2 *First lift the plants from the top, then dig out the compost, carefully removing the plants from the pockets. Tip out any remaining compost. Replace the drainage material.*

3 *Add fresh compost up to the level of the lowest pockets. Divide or replace the old plants. Place each plant at the inside of a pocket, then gently pull the foliage through the hole.*

4 *Pack compost around the roots and up to the next level, firming well after each addition. Water the compost thoroughly.*

Propagation

Herbs may be propagated by a wide variety of methods, depending on the type of plant and the quantity of new plants required. Sowing seed is a simple, inexpensive way to raise a large number of plants and is necessary for annuals and biennials, although it may also be used for other plant groups. Cuttings may be used to propagate various perennials as well as shrubs and trees, while division is suitable for a number of perennials and layering is a good method for some shrubby herbs. For further information on propagating individual species and cultivars, see "Directory of common herbs", pp.407–410.

Raising new plants from seed

It is easy to collect seed from most herbs and to grow them from your own seed (see PRINCIPLES OF PROPAGATION, "Seeds", p.629); they may be sown in containers or, where large quantities are required, in drills in the open ground. Seed may also be sown direct into the cracks between paving stones where it would be difficult to insert plants. Prepare a fine seedbed for any seedlings that you intend to transplant outside from containers. Spring is generally the best time for sowing seed, although some annual herbs may also be sown in early autumn.

Annuals and biennials

Hardy annuals such as borage (*Borago officinalis*) and marigolds (*Calendula officinalis*) may be sown in the spring or – to provide flowers late in the next spring – in autumn. Sow biennial herbs, for example caraway (*Carum carvi*) and angelica (*Angelica archangelica*), outdoors in late summer or early autumn for flowering the following summer. Thin out the seedlings twice: once after germination so that two or three remain at each position, and again after a few weeks so that only the strongest is left in place.

Short-lived, hardy herbs that are used regularly in large quantities, such as parsley (*Petroselinum crispum*), coriander (*Coriandrum sativum*), and chervil (*Anthriscus cerefolium*), may be sown at intervals of three to four weeks from early spring to early autumn. This provides a succession of foliage for harvesting throughout the year, although in some areas it may be necessary to provide protection from frost with cloches. Annual herbs of the Umbelliferae family – chervil and dill (*Anethum graveolens*) for example – are difficult to transplant successfully and are best sown directly in their ultimate positions.

Basil (*Ocimum basilicum*) is one of the more difficult herbs to grow from seed in cold areas. Sow basil seed very thinly in late spring, and keep it at a minimum temperature of 13°C (55°F). Prick out the seedlings once they are large enough to handle and keep them in a sunny, well-ventilated place. In cold, damp conditions, basil seedlings are prone to damping off (p.664) and grey mould (*Botrytis*) (p.653). Plant out the seedlings once all danger of frost is past or, in poor summers, grow them in containers under cover. In warm climates, basil may be sown directly into an outdoor seedbed (see ANNUALS AND BIENNIALS, "Sowing in open ground", p.217).

Perennials

If raising perennial herbs from seed, sow the seed in warmth in spring and grow on the seedlings in pots until they are large enough to be hardened off and planted out. Plant and care for them as for container-grown herbs (see p.411).

Most cultivars of perennial herbs do not come true from seed and must be propagated by cuttings or layering; an exception to this is variegated rue (*Ruta graveolens* 'Variegata'). Non-flowering forms, such as lawn chamomile (*Chamaemelum nobile* 'Treneague'), cannot be raised from seed; propagate by cuttings or division to obtain new plants.

Mound layering

This method is particularly suitable for propagating shrubs such as sage (*Salvia officinalis*), rosemary (*Rosmarinus officinalis*), lavender (*Lavandula*), and thyme (*Thymus*) that tend to become woody at the base or centre with little or no new growth. In spring, mound free-draining soil over the base of the plant, leaving just the top exposed. This stimulates new shoots to develop roots in a manner similar to stooling (see ORNAMENTAL SHRUBS, p.117). Leave the soil in place, replenishing it if it is washed away, until new roots have grown in late summer or autumn. Then cut the shoots off from the parent plant and treat them as rooted cuttings.

SOWING PARSLEY SEED IN CONTAINERS

1 Soak the seed in warm water for several hours, then dry it. Tap seeds from a piece of paper onto firmed seed compost. Just cover with sieved compost.

2 Once the seedlings are large enough to handle, carefully lift them with a widger, holding them by the leaves not the stems.

3 Prick out the seedlings individually into prepared modules or pans of firmed compost. When they are approximately 5–6cm (2–2½in) high, transplant them outside into prepared ground.

MOUND LAYERING SHRUBBY HERBS

1 To stimulate rooting, mound 7–12cm (3–5in) of sandy loam over the crown of the plant (here thyme) so that just the tips of the shoots are visible.

2 Once the layered stems have established new roots, remove them with a knife or secateurs. Pot up the rooted layers individually or plant them out.

HERBS TO PROPAGATE BY MOUND LAYERING

Cotton lavender (*Santolina chamaecyparissus*, *S. pinnata*, *S. rosmarinifolia*)
Hyssop (*Hyssopus officinalis*)
Lavender (*Lavandula angustifolia*, *L. stoechas*)
Rosemary (*Rosmarinus officinalis* 'Prostratus')
Sage (*Salvia lavandulifolia*, *S. officinalis*)

Salvia officinalis

Southernwood (*Artemisia abrotanum*)
Thyme (*Thymus cilicicus*, *T. x citriodorus* and cvs, *T. vulgaris* and woody cvs)
Winter savory (*Satureja montana*)
Wormwood (*Artemisia absinthium*)

Harvesting and preserving

THE flavour of herbs may vary according to the growing conditions, the season, and the time of day. As the level of essential oils fluctuates with light and temperature, it is important to harvest herbs at the right time to ensure that the oil levels are at their peak. There are various methods of preserving herbs so that their scents and flavours may be enjoyed all year round. For advice on specific herbs, see the "Directory of common herbs", pp.407–410.

Harvesting

Herbs should be harvested on a fine, dry day after the dew has dried but before the plants are exposed to hot sunshine, which evaporates the essential oils. Always try to harvest herbs in a way that helps to maintain the plant's shape and vigour: choose straggly or invasive shoots, and with clump-forming herbs, such as chives (*Allium schoenoprasum*) and parsley (*Petroselinum crispum*), pick the outer leaves to encourage new growth in the centre. Only use foliage free from damage and insects.

Leaves and shoots may be picked at any time during the growing season but are at their best before the herb develops flowers. Evergreen herbs may be harvested lightly in winter. Always handle aromatic leaves gently as bruising releases the essential oils. Use or preserve herbs as soon as possible after harvesting.

Collecting flowers, seed, and roots

When harvesting flowers, pick them on a warm, dry day, when they are fully opened. Collect seed by cutting off whole seedheads in summer or early autumn as they turn brown but before they are completely ripe and starting to shed. Roots may be lifted at any time of year, but the flavour is best in autumn.

Preserving

The main methods of preserving herbs are drying and freezing. In addition, a number are suitable for flavouring vinegars, oils, or jellies, while a few may be crystallized (candied) for decorating cakes and desserts. Store dried herbs in dark glass or ceramic containers, as exposure to light will speed the deterioration of their aromas.

Air-drying

Do not wash herbs as this may encourage moulds to develop. Dry herbs by hanging them upside-down in a warm, dry place such as an airing cupboard. Alternatively, place leaves, flowerheads, or petals in a single layer on a rack covered with muslin, netting, or kitchen paper. Leave them in a warm, dark, and well-ventilated place until crisp.

Microwave drying

Wash the herbs and pat them dry, then place sprigs or leaves in a single layer on kitchen paper. Microwave them for two to three minutes, checking them every 30 seconds and rearranging them if necessary to ensure even drying. Cool, then crumble and store as for air-dried herbs.

Drying seedheads

Cut seedheads in summer or early autumn as they turn brown, then place them in a paper bag or hang them upside-down and cover them with muslin to hold the seeds as they fall. Keep them in a warm, dry place to ripen; when dry, remove the seeds and store them. Seed for sowing should be kept in a cool, dry, frost-free place.

Drying roots

Most roots are best used fresh, but some may be dried and ground. First wash the roots thoroughly, then peel, chop, or slice them, before spreading them out on absorbent paper. Dry them in a cool oven or a warm airing cupboard at 50–60°C (122–40°F) until brittle, then crush or grind them before storing.

Freeze-drying

Many soft-leaved herbs, such as parsley and basil, retain their colour and flavour better when frozen than when dried. Simply pack whole sprigs into labelled plastic bags, and freeze them; they crumble easily for use once frozen. For long-term storage, blanch them before freezing by dipping them first in boiling water, then in iced water. Pat dry and freeze.

Freezing in ice

Herbs may be frozen in water to form ice cubes; this is a good way of preserving borage flowers and mint leaves to use as a decorative addition to drinks, and the ice also protects the herbs from damage during storage. Herbs for cooking should be chopped before freezing since this is difficult to do once they have thawed. Place the ice cubes in a sieve and drain the water before use.

Making herb vinegars

Many herbs, such as thyme, French tarragon, oregano, and lavender, may have their flavours preserved by being steeped in vinegar.

To make flavoured herb vinegars, lightly crush some fresh herbs and then loosely fill a clear glass jar with the crushed herbs. (Do not use metal-lidded containers to make the herb vinegar, because the acid vinegar will corrode the lid and so taint the contents.) Warm either wine or cider vinegar and pour it over the herbs, and seal the jar. Leave the jar in a sunny spot for two weeks, shaking or stirring daily. Strain and bottle, adding a fresh sprig of the herb for identification. For a stronger flavour, replace the herbs and leave the herb vinegar for a further two weeks.

Basil leaves may be preserved by being packed in jars of oil; the leaves themselves may then be used in pasta sauces and other cooked dishes. Never be tempted to make your own herb-flavoured oils, because there is a risk of botulism.

FREEZING HERBS IN ICE CUBES

Freeze borage flowers and mint leaves singly in ice-cube trays for adding to drinks. Chop fresh herbs such as parsley or chives and place in ice cube trays, adding about 1tbsp of water to each 1tbsp of herb.

DRYING SEEDHEADS

Cover the seedheads with muslin or a paper bag, secured in place with string or an elastic band, then hang them upside-down in a warm place until dry.

CHAPTER

16

GROWING FRUIT

THE SATISFACTION OF growing, harvesting, and tasting your own fresh fruits is one of the great pleasures of gardening. A fruit garden may be highly decorative as well as productive: some plants have attractive, fragrant blossom or fine foliage while, in many cases, the fruits themselves are as ornamental as they are edible. In most areas, a wide range of fruits may be grown, while in cool regions growing under cover makes it possible to cultivate an even greater variety. In a large garden, there may be room to devote an area exclusively to fruit – whether in a formal layout with neat rows of trees, bushes, and canes, bordered by trained fans or cordons, or in an informal orchard. If space is limited, incorporate fruits into the rest of the garden, perhaps edging a bed with alpine strawberries or growing a grape vine over a pergola. Even in a small patio garden, there should be space for one or two citrus trees in pots or wall-trained apples or pears.

Planning the fruit garden

FRUITS have traditionally held a prominent place in the garden, and today, with a wide range of cultivars and many dwarf fruit trees available ideal for the average garden, fruit growing is increasing in popularity. There are always some fruits that will thrive in the given climatic and growing conditions, although the majority prefer a good loam and a sunny situation. In warm climates, a wide range of fruits may be cultivated outdoors although some fruits that require periods of cold dormancy before flowering will not usually be successful.

Where only a few fruit plants are required, the gardener may prefer to grow them within the ornamental garden rather than in a specialized fruit garden; many fruit trees are suitable for growing as specimens in a lawn. Alternatively, if space is very limited, most fruits may be cultivated in containers, either free-standing or trained against a support such as a garden fence, or grown on a "family" tree (see p.420).

If planning to grow plants in large numbers, however, it is best to create a separate fruit area within the garden; this makes it possible to grow fruits with similar requirements together, and to protect them against birds and frost damage. This is possible even in a small garden, as long as suitable rootstocks are chosen and trees are carefully trained. If grown as espaliers, fans, or cordons around the borders of a garden, fruit trees may be both ornamental and a source of fresh crops.

Another consideration may well be the type of blossom you wish your trees to bear: some apple cultivars such as 'Arthur Turner', 'Ashmead's Kernel', and 'Bramley's Seedling' produce flowers in particularly impressive colours and/or sizes.

Thoughtful planning as well as careful selection of cultivars and methods of training make it possible to provide fresh fruit supplies over several months, and if there is some storage and freezing space available, the produce from a fruit garden may be enjoyed all year round.

In cool areas, the range of fruits that may be grown is even wider if some protection under cover is available. Reliable crops of peaches, nectarines, figs, grapes, or more tender fruits may be obtained by growing plants in a greenhouse, although ample room is needed for even a single tree. Protection and shelter is required by many of these fruits if they are grown outdoors.

The range of fruits

The different groups of fruit plants may be categorized according to their stature, their growth and fruiting habit, and their frost-hardiness.

Wall-trained peach tree
A sunny, south-facing garden wall is ideal for accommodating a fan-trained peach tree, providing warm and sheltered ripening conditions and a high yield of fruits from a limited space.

TREE FORMS

When selecting a tree form, there are three main factors to consider: growth habit, space, and maintenance. An espalier, for example, is ideal for growing against a wall, particularly for apples, which develop naturally on short spur shoots. Several cordons will occupy the same space as a fan, and so might be better in a small garden. Multiple cordons may be grafted with more than one cultivar, giving you the opportunity to have one "arm" as a pollinator for the main cultivar. Free-growing forms, like bush or spindle, need pruning only once a year; more elaborate shapes, such as cordons and espaliers, require training and pruning more often.

Bush

Half-standard

Standard

Spindlebush

Pyramid

Dwarf pyramid

Cordon

Multiple cordon

Espalier

Fan

Palmette

Stepover

Tree fruits (top fruits) include apples, peaches, and figs. The term embraces both pome fruits (those containing a core with pips, such as apples, pears, and medlars) and stone fruits (those containing stones, such as cherries, peaches, and plums), as well as a few other fruits, including mulberries and persimmons. The term "vine" may also be used to describe woody, fruiting climbers, such as kiwi and passion fruits, in addition to its more normal usage for *Vitis vinifera*, the grape vine.

The category soft fruits includes bush fruits, cane fruits, and straw-berries, which are almost herbaceous. Bush fruits are naturally shrubby, forming a compact, bush shape, although they may also be trained into other forms. Blackcurrants, redcurrants, whitecurrants, goose-berries, and blueberries are the most commonly grown bush fruits. Plants described as cane fruits produce long, cane-like shoots that bear the fruits; raspberries, blackberries, and hybrid berries, such as loganberries, are in this group. Most cane fruits develop their canes in one season, and bear fruit on these the next, while producing new canes that will fruit in the following year.

Certain fruit-bearing plants cannot withstand frost and require warm,

subtropical temperatures in which to develop and ripen fully; these may be categorized as tender fruits. Tender fruits include pomegranates, pineapples, tamarillos, prickly pears, and all kinds of citrus. Some of these are also tree fruits, but have been grouped here with tender fruits because of their need for consistently warm temperatures.

Nuts include all plants that produce fruits with a hard outer shell around an edible kernel, for example cobnuts, almonds, and pecans.

Unrestricted and trained forms

Many fruits, particularly tree fruits, and to a lesser extent vines and some soft fruits, may be trained into a wide variety of forms. When deciding which forms to grow, bear in mind the space available for the mature tree or bush, the relative ease of harvesting, and the degree of pruning and training needed to produce a plant that crops well. The choice of rootstock for fruit trees also determines their ultimate size (see "Rootstocks and tree size", p.423).

With the correct technique, trees and bush fruits may be trained almost as desired. The principle is to

train young shoots into the required shape while they are still pliable; the branches then retain this form with regular, basic pruning.

Unrestricted tree forms

These forms develop, with limited pruning, in much the same way as a natural tree; they include the bush tree, standard, half-standard, and spindlebush. The bush and spindle-bush are more compact than the standard and half-standard, and are suitable for small gardens.

A bush tree has a trunk up to 90cm (3ft) tall, with branches radiating out from the top third. It has an open centre, thus allowing the branches maximum light and space. Bush trees are small to medium sized, that is 1.5–4m (5–12ft).

The half-standard is similar to the bush but the trunk measures 1–1.5m (3–5ft) and the overall height is 4–5m (12–15ft). The standard is similar in form, but with a trunk measuring 1.5–2.2m (5–7ft) and an overall height of 5m (15ft) or more.

The spindlebush is a small tree growing up to 2.2m (7ft) tall with branches that are trained to radiate out from the central leader at a wide angle. It has fewer branches than other lightly pruned forms, but each branch is pruned to be as productive

as possible. The lowest branch is usually about 45cm (18in) from ground level.

Trained forms

Some fruit trees and bushes are suitable for growing in trained (or restricted) forms. These include cordons, fans, and espaliers. They need careful training initially, and are then maintained by regular summer pruning, to restrict vegetative growth, with a minimum of winter pruning. Most require support wires, either secured to free-standing posts or against a wall or fence. Wall-trained forms are often favoured in temperate climates for fruits such as peaches because the fruits receive maximum sun and also benefit from the reflected heat of the wall. All the trained tree forms are ideal for small gardens as they make it possible to cultivate a variety of fruits in a restricted space. Maiden trees that have been grafted onto dwarfing rootstocks are usually used for training restricted forms.

A cordon is restricted to a single stem, 1.5–2m (5–6ft) long, clothed with fruiting spurs to produce a high yield in a small area. It is usually grown against a wall, or on posts and wires, and is planted at an angle of about 45°. It may also be grown

Family trees
In small gardens, a convenient way to grow a variety of fruits is to plant a family tree, in which two or more cultivars are grafted onto the same rootstock so the tree bears different fruits on different branches.

Fruit for frost-free areas
Oranges grow well in warm, virtually frost-free regions such as Mediterranean countries, South Africa, and California. They often produce two crops a year and may bear flowers at the same time as an earlier crop is maturing.

vertically or horizontally. Most commonly used for apples and pears, it is useful for red- and whitecurrants and gooseberries, too. Double (sometimes known as "U"), triple, or multiple cordons may be formed by pruning a maiden plant so that it forms two or more parallel stems. Cordons that have more than a single stem are usually trained vertically, while stepover cordons, with the main stem trained horizontally, are increasing in popularity. They are usually free-standing, supported on strong wires, and can be used to create an attractive, low edging to a bed.

A fan is trained with the main branches radiating in a fan shape from a short 24cm (10in) trunk and is suitable for tree fruits that are grown against walls and fences.

An espalier is trained with pairs of horizontal branches extending at regular intervals from a central stem. Each branch is clothed with short, fruiting spurs. The number of pairs of branches depends on space and tree vigour. This method is particularly suitable for apples and pears grown against walls or fences. It is not suitable for stone fruits. A less rigid variation on the espalier is the palmette form, in which staggered tiers of branches are angled slightly

upwards rather than horizontally.

Unlike the other trained forms, the pyramid is free-standing; its branches radiate from a central trunk, with an overall pyramidal form that is maintained by regular summer pruning to produce small to medium-sized trees. Dwarf pyramids are grown on a more dwarfing rootstock.

Apple and pear trees can be trained into complicated forms such as arcure and goblet. These shapes, among others such as espalier, are of French origin. For the arcure, leading shoots are trained left then right in alternate years, curving downwards in an arc. The goblet has shoots trained horizontally from a predetermined height on the trunk. From these, further shoots are trained upwards, to form the goblet. For all such shapes, wires and bamboo canes are used to train the shoots into the desired form. All surplus shoots should be removed in summer, once those needed are in place (see p.438).

"Family" trees

"Family" trees carry several cultivars – usually three – of the same fruit on a single tree. Such trees provide for a succession of fruit and are a very

useful space-saving measure. Used originally by the Greeks and Romans, they were reintroduced during the 1950s and have remained a popular way in which to grow apples and pears.

When young, a tree is grafted with two other cultivars suitable for cross-pollination and of similar vigour. Good apple combinations include: 'Egremont Russet' with 'James Grieve' and 'Sunset'; 'Bramley's Seedling' with 'Red Pippin (Fiesta)' and 'Falstaff'; and 'Charles Ross' with 'Discovery' and 'James Grieve'. For pears, try 'Beth' with 'Concorde' and 'Conference'; and 'Williams' Bon Chrétien' with 'Conference' and 'Doyenné du Comice'.

All such trees are available on a variety of rootstocks, and it is important to select one that will suit your soil and grow to the tree size required (see pp.435 and 444). 'MM106' is used for medium-sized apple trees, and 'Quince A' for pears. Apple 'M9' and pear 'Quince C' are for smaller "family" trees. Smallest of all is 'M27', which is best for pot-grown "family" apple trees. 'Quince C' rootstock is generally reserved for a few of the most vigorous cultivars such as 'Doyenné du Comice'.

Trees grown on 'M9', 'M27', and 'Quince A' must be permanently staked, because of their small, brittle root system.

Integrating fruits into the garden plan

Fruits may be grown either in a separate area on their own or intermingled with other, ornamental

plants; the choice depends on space, personal preference, and the range of fruits to be included. In either case, assess the impact that the fully grown fruit plants will have on the adjacent or surrounding plants. Planning and siting are particularly important because most fruits are long-term plants that require consistently good conditions to flourish and crop well over many years; in addition, with the exception of a few fruits such as strawberries, it is seldom practical or worthwhile transplanting them to other positions.

The planned fruit garden
Where a range of different fruits is required, it is well worth growing the

Trained cordons
Apple cordons provide good coverage of a fence, while alpine strawberries edge the border.

plants together in a single area. When planning a fruit garden, take into account the preferred growing conditions of each type of plant and recommended planting distances; for example, site tall fruit trees where they will cast least shade on smaller bushes nearby. Also make sure that the space allocated for each plant is sufficient for it to develop naturally to its mature size.

Plants that have similar cultivation requirements may be grouped together in order to simplify practical operations such as applying fertilizer: for example, redcurrants and goose-berries need more potassium than other fruits. Grouping plants also makes it easier to protect them from birds (with a fruit cage) or wind damage (with a windbreak).

For an eye-catching border, edge the fruit garden with a row of trained trees; cordons (especially stepover ones) or dwarf pyramids are particularly suitable because they need a minimum of support and occupy comparatively little space.

In planning the position of fruit trees (particularly apples, pears, sweet cherries, and some plums), remember that a self-sterile cultivar

should be sited near a cultivar with which it will cross-pollinate (see "Pollination requirements", p.424), or it will produce few if any fruits.

For many fruits there is a wide choice of cultivars that ripen at different times; this makes it possible to plan for a succession of fruits that may be regularly harvested rather than a single glut. Some fruits, late-ripening apples and pears for example, may be stored for long periods, so if a steady supply is required, more space should be devoted to growing these than to earlier-ripening cultivars.

Fruit in the small garden

There are various ways to make the most of a limited area for fruit growing so that it provides a high yield and is an attractive feature. Whenever possible, choose trees that have been grafted on dwarfing rootstocks (see p.423) and use training methods that make the best use of the available space. For example, plant "family" trees (see p.420) or Ballerina cultivars (see p.435). Train trees and soft fruits such as redcurrants and gooseberries as cordons against the house or garden wall, rather than

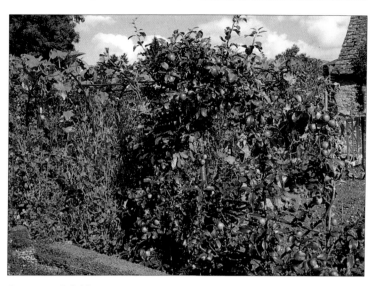

Ornamental divider
Trained apples form an attractive screen providing a fine display of spring blossom followed by handsome fruits in autumn.

as bushes, since cordons require less room for a comparable fruit yield than fans or espaliers. Grow grape vines over a sturdy pergola or ornamental arch as part of the garden design. Cane fruits may also be trained in a variety of ways depending

on the space available. Strawberries may be grown in vertical growing bags attached to a stake, fence, or other similar structure.

If there is room for only a single tree then it is essential to choose a self-fertile cultivar (see "Pollination

PLAN FOR A LARGE FRUIT GARDEN

A large plot, 11 x 17m (35 x 56ft), provides space for a range of fruit. Here, the chosen apple and pear cultivars will crop over a long period, and the soft fruit has been grouped for easier maintenance. The more tender peaches and grapes thrive in a lean-to greenhouse.

1 Apple 'Discovery' (on 'M26'/'MM106')
2 Apple 'Epicure' (on 'M26'/'MM106')
3 Apple 'St Edmund's Pippin' (on 'M26'/'MM106')
4 Apple 'Sunset' (on 'M26'/'MM106')
5 Apple 'Cox's Orange Pippin' (on 'M26'/'MM106')
6 Apple 'Ashmead's Kernel' (on 'M26'/'MM106')
7 Plum 'Czar' (on 'Pixy')
8 Plum 'Victoria' (on 'Pixy')
9 Damson 'Prune' (on 'Pixy')
10 Pear 'Onward' (on 'Quince A')
11 Pear 'Concorde' (on 'Quince A')
12 Pear 'Doyenné du Comice' (on 'Quince C')
13 Pear 'Joséphine de Malines' (on 'Quince A')
14 Blackcurrant 'Boskoop Giant'
15 Blackcurrant 'Ben Lomond'
16 Blackcurrant 'Ben Sarek'
17 Redcurrant 'Red Lake'
18 Gooseberry 'Careless'
19 Gooseberry 'Leveller'
20 Raspberry 'Autumn Bliss'
21 Acid cherry 'Morello'
22 Raspberry 'Malling Jewel'
23 Loganberry (thornless)
24 Tayberry
25 Blackberry 'Merton Early'
26 Grape 'Black Hamburgh'
27 Peach 'Peregrine' (on 'St Julien A')
28 Strawberry 'Elsanta'
29 Sweet cherry 'Stella' (on 'Colt')
30 Fig 'Brown Turkey'

Growing fruit the organic way

Cultivation techniques for growing organic and non-organic fruit do not differ greatly. For best results:

- Choose plants that come from certified organic, disease-free stock: this should be indicated by an "organic" symbol on the label .
- Make sure that any bulky manures that are needed for ground preparation are derived from either non-intensive or organic sources.
- Ensure soil is free of perennial weeds before planting, as they are difficult to eradicate or control once fruit trees and bushes are established.
- Obtain hay or straw mulches from organic sources.
- Avoid using chemical sprays; control pests and diseases with biological or organic methods.

SMALL FRUIT GARDEN

This small, fenced area supports no fewer than 17 fruit cultivars, providing abundant crops from early summer to autumn. The plot measures 4 x 9m (12 x 28ft) with a 2m (6ft) fence surrounding it; careful choice of cultivars and rootstocks coupled with correct training of the trees allows a wide range of fruits to be accommodated.

1 Sweet cherry 'Stella' (on 'Gisela 5')
2 Pear 'Beth' (on 'Quince C')
3 Pear 'Concorde' (on 'Quince C')
4 Pear 'Doyenné du Comice' (on 'Quince C')
5 Raspberry 'Tulameen' (summer-fruiting)
6 Plum 'Victoria' (on 'Pixy')
7 Raspberry 'Autumn Bliss' (autumn-fruiting)
8 Peach 'Rochester' (on 'St Julien A')
9 Gooseberry 'Invicta'
10 Gooseberry 'Leveller'
11 Whitecurrant 'White Grape'
12 Redcurrant 'Red Lake'
13 Apple 'Epicure' (on 'M9')
14 Apple 'Lord Lambourne' (on 'M9')
15 Apple 'Sunset' (on 'M9')
16 Blackcurrant 'Ben Sarek'
17 Acid cherry 'Morello' (on 'Colt')

compatibility", p.423). It is also worth selecting plants with a prolonged cropping season, unless there is ample storage and freezer space.

Mixed planting

In a garden that is largely ornamental or where there is insufficient space for a dedicated fruit garden, fruits may be planted among other plants. One or more fruit trees may make attractive specimens in the lawn, or grown in containers on a sunny terrace or patio. Fruit cordons or dwarf pyramids look effective when used as an ornamental divider, providing an unusual and productive screen, with attractive blossom in spring and ripening fruits from late summer to autumn. Trained forms of

bushes or trees may be grown on almost any type of garden structure such as a pergola, fence, or shed, provided that the aspect is suitable.

When fruits are planted along with ornamentals, make sure that all the plants' needs are compatible. If, for example, the fruits need protection from birds with netting, this may impede the growth of surrounding plants and look out of place. Particular care is also needed to ensure that any fruit tree sprays that are used do not adversely affect any nearby ornamental plants.

Strawberries are often grown among other plants either in the vegetable garden or – a popular use for alpine strawberries – along the edge of a border or raised bed.

Choosing a site

A sunny, sheltered position, where the plants will produce fruits of good quality and flavour, is ideal. Sites with some light shade are also acceptable but provide fewer ripening hours, so are best used for soft fruits or early-ripening cultivars of apples, pears, and plums. Plants on a south-facing slope may produce crops earlier than elsewhere but, as they also flower earlier, they are more likely to suffer frost damage.

Growing against supports

Walls, fences, pergolas, and arches all provide an ideal site for growing trained trees, especially if they are exposed to maximum sun. These structures make good use of space in the garden and allow the fruits to develop and ripen well; fruits trained on supports are also easier to protect from birds and frost than fruits in the open garden.

The wall or fence must be high enough to accommodate the chosen fruits: 1.2m (4ft) would be enough for soft fruits, or apples or pears trained as cordons or espaliers, but a height and spread of 2m (6ft) or more are required for a fan-trained apple, pear, cherry, plum, or peach. Pergolas and arches are likely to provide sufficient height, but ensure that there is enough space for the plants to spread as they mature. The structure must be sufficiently sturdy to be able to support heavy crops, even in strong winds.

Frost and wind

Avoid planting in frost-prone sites because flowers, unopened buds, and fruitlets are all susceptible to frost damage. The coldest air collects where the ground is lowest, and a frost pocket will form in a valley floor or at the foot of a sloping garden, behind walls, hedges, or buildings.

Exposure to wind discourages pollinating insects and therefore greatly reduces the regularity of cropping. Strong winds also cause considerable crop damage. Draughty sites, such as between two buildings, are not recommended, but a suitable, well-placed windbreak may be very effective in diverting or filtering wind to improve the conditions. Trees or large shrubs are preferable to solid barriers as they filter wind that would otherwise swirl over the barrier and damage plants on the other side (see also CLIMATE AND THE GARDEN, "How a windbreak works", p.611).

Growing fruits under cover

Crops native to warm climates, such as peaches, nectarines, and grapes, are ideal for greenhouse cultivation in cooler climates, but skill and attention to detail are required to maintain them in good condition and to obtain satisfactory crops. Greenhouse or frame protection can also be a very satisfactory means of growing temperate fruits, such as strawberries, because, with careful

Fruit in a border

The compact, rounded shape of a lemon tree laden with fruit punctuates an informal planting, providing a pleasant contrast to the colourful display of roses and double daisies.

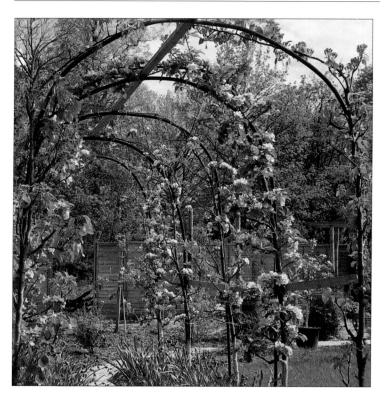

A cordon arch
Fruit trees trained as vertical cordons over a series of arches provide an attractive, architectural feature as well as abundant crops of fruit. The structure must be sufficiently strong to support the weight of trees heavily laden with fruit in autumn.

selection of early-fruiting cultivars, the season can be lengthened by several weeks in early summer. In areas with a short growing season that experience early autumn frosts, it also improves cropping of perpetual or late-fruiting cultivars.

If fruits are to be grown with other plants in the same greenhouse, ensure that their temperature, humidity, and ventilation requirements are compatible. It is important that the greenhouse has the maximum possible number of bottom and top vents to provide a free flow of air. As for planting in open ground, the soil needs to be fertile and well-drained for the plants to thrive.

A number of tender fruits such as tamarillos (tree tomatoes) and pomegranates and even olives may be grown successfully under cover; in temperate climates, they are often grown as ornamentals as they seldom crop heavily, even under glass.

Trained fruits

Compatible tree and soft fruits that are suitable for training may also be grown in a greenhouse. Check that there is sufficient space for the chosen cultivar to develop and grow to its mature size, and ensure that suitable fittings for training the plant in the chosen form are in position before it is planted.

Fruits in pots

Strawberry plants that are grown in individual pots in a greenhouse or under a cloche will produce ripe fruits earlier than those in the open, thereby prolonging the fruiting season if both cultivation methods are used. Tender fruit trees such as citrus may be grown in pots that are placed outdoors during summer and returned under cover for winter.

Growing fruits in containers

Container-growing is useful for cultivating fruits where space is limited. The pots should be placed in sunny, sheltered sites and may be used on paved areas such as patios to provide ornamental features as well as crops of fruits. It is also a way of controlling the root growth, and therefore the vigour, of plants such as figs that (particularly in temperate climates) may make excessive vegetative growth at the expense of the crop. Container-grown fruit trees can also be moved in and out of cover to avoid frost or to give the plant a higher or lower temperature, according to its seasonal needs. Early-flowering trees such as peaches and nectarines in particular benefit from such flexible growing conditions.

Most fruits may be grown successfully in a large pot, half barrel, or similar container with a diameter of 30cm (12in) or more. Strawberries may be grown singly in 10cm (4in) pots, in strawberry planters (containers with side planting pockets), in growing bags, troughs, and even hanging baskets. Fruits need more regular care in containers than in the open ground, particularly with watering and feeding, because the roots are confined and easily dry out.

Deciding which plants to grow

Whether planning an entire fruit garden or choosing just two or three trees, it is vital to select plants that will thrive in the given soil and climatic conditions without growing too large for their allotted space.

It also makes sense to choose well-flavoured, less commercial cultivars that are seldom readily available in the shops. More unusual fruits, such as red- or whitecurrants, are also worth considering, because they are often expensive to buy. If freezing soft fruits, such as strawberries or raspberries, is a priority, seek out cultivars that are suitable for the purpose.

Check the compatibility of different cultivars for pollination purposes before deciding which to grow (see "Pollination requirements", p.424). The final choice should also depend on the size of the crop required and the harvesting time.

Rootstocks and tree size

Tree size is determined largely by the rootstock onto which the tree has been grafted. Choose rootstocks that are of appropriate vigour for the planting area or training space available. Apple trees grown on dwarfing rootstocks such as 'M27' or 'M9', for example, are likely to suit most gardens; their relatively small size makes picking, pruning, and spraying easier. If a large tree is required, select one that is grown on a more vigorous rootstock. For further details, see pp.424 and 435.

Pollination compatibility

Most cultivars of apples, pears, sweet cherries, and some plums are not satisfactorily self-fertile, and therefore need to be planted close to one or more suitable cultivars of the same fruit that are in flower at about the same time, so that insects are able to cross-pollinate all the trees. For example, the apple cultivars 'Cox's Orange Pippin', 'Bramley's Seedling', and 'Lord Lambourne' need to be planted together for all to be

successfully cross-pollinated. (See under individual fruits for further details.) When planning a fruit garden, take account of the minimum number of trees required for pollination to occur and position compatible cultivars adjacent to each other to ensure satisfactory cropping.

Crop size and timing

Within the limits of space available, the amount of fruits that are required will determine the number of plants that should be obtained, bearing in mind that crop levels inevitably vary from year to year. The amount of storage or freezer space available may govern the size of crop that can be handled. Try to balance the numbers of early-, mid-, and late-ripening cultivars of each fruit grown in order to provide a consistent supply of fruits over a long period rather than a brief glut.

Early-ripening apples and pears do not keep well for more than a day or two, so do not grow more than can be consumed quickly: one or two cordons yielding 2–5kg (5–11lb) per tree should suffice. If you have plenty of storage space, plant a high proportion of late-ripening cultivars, the fruits of which can be stored for several months. Plums are also liable to produce gluts and the fruits must be used quickly unless they are frozen or otherwise preserved.

When deciding whether to plant early- or late-ripening cultivars, remember to take climatic factors into account: for example, late-ripening apples or pears are not a good choice for a region with a short summer or if the proposed site is shady, because there will not be enough time or sun for the fruit to ripen fully.

Grape canopy
When grape vines are grown under cover, take care to prevent ripening fruit being scorched by the sun.

Site, soil preparation, and planting

Aʟʟ fruits require soil that is well-structured, adequately drained, and fertile to thrive. Before planting fruits, therefore, choose and prepare a suitable site so that it provides the necessary conditions.

Preparing the site

Prepare the site at least two months before planting. Remove all weeds, especially perennial ones, before any soil preparation takes place (see PLANT PROBLEMS, "Weeds", pp.669–673).

Soil types

A loam soil is ideal and produces high yields of good-quality fruits. Clay soils may produce very good crops if drainage is good but are slow to warm up in spring; growth and therefore cropping may be later. On sandy soils, plants come into growth earlier since the soil warms up quickly in spring. Heat is lost equally rapidly, however, which creates a greater risk from frost; sandy soil is also prone to drought. Sandy soils are usually less fertile than others, so the quality and flavour of fruits that are grown on these may be inferior to those produced on more fertile soil.

On chalk soils, lime-induced chlorosis caused by manganese and iron deficiencies (see p.651) may be severe, causing the leaves of plants to turn yellow and adversely affecting the quality and yield of fruit. In extreme cases, it will prove impossible to grow certain fruits satisfactorily; pears and raspberries, in particular, suffer badly. The use of sequestered iron alleviates the problem, but regular treatment may be necessary and is expensive. Annual mulches of farmyard manure and compost help by providing some of the trace elements required.

Improving the soil

For soft fruits, dig in generous amounts of well-rotted manure or garden compost and fertilizer to improve water retention and fertility. In preparation for planting tree fruits, fertilizers should not be used unless the soil is very poor and infertile, since it may produce excessive, soft growth rather than fruiting wood.

Drainage problems

Although poor drainage is more likely on heavy, clay soils, it may occur in many types of soil. Improve the soil structure where possible (see SOILS AND FERTILIZERS, "Soil structure and water content", p.620), and install a drainage system if necessary (see "Installing drains", p.623). Where drains cannot be installed, plant fruits in raised beds (see STRUCTURES AND SURFACES, "Raised beds", p.599).

Adjusting the pH level

Soil with a pH level of 6–6.5 is ideal for all fruits except blueberries, which need an acid soil of pH4–5.5. Soils below about pH5.8 will need liming (see p.625). If planting in soil with a pH level over 7, top-dress regularly with sulphate of ammonia and mulch with acid compost to reduce the pH in the short term.

Preparing the support for a trained fruit tree or bush

If a fruit tree or bush is to be trained against a solid support such as a wall or fence, fix horizontal, parallel wires to the support with vine eyes and a tightener to keep the wires taut as the fruits develop. The vine eyes should hold the wires 10–15cm (4–6in) from the support to allow air to circulate around the branches and leaves of the plant. The spacing of the wires will vary, depending on the type of fruits grown. If using a free-standing post-and-wire support, secure the wires firmly to the posts. Just before planting, attach bamboo canes to the wires at the appropriate angles, and tie in the young plants to begin the training process.

Buying plants

Always choose fruits that will thrive in the conditions in your garden. Check that the ultimate size of the plant or tree will fit the available space and that there is room to train it into the desired form. Pollination needs also must be considered before deciding which cultivars to buy.

Specialist fruit nurseries are often the best and most reliable source of supply. They offer a wide range of old and new cultivars and will also advise about suitable rootstocks. Wherever possible, buy fruits that are certified free from disease.

It is best to buy young plants, since these become established quickly and may be shaped and trained to your own requirements. Plants are available bare-root or in containers. Container-grown plants are available all year round, but bare-root plants only in late autumn and winter when the plants are dormant and may safely be lifted. Reject plants

BUYING FRUIT TREES

Bare-root tree

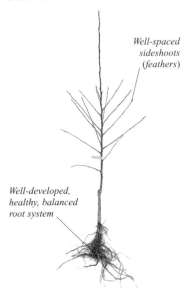

Well-spaced sideshoots (feathers)

Well-developed, healthy, balanced root system

Container-grown tree

Moist, weed-free compost

Vigorous, healthy roots that have not become congested and pot-bound

with a pot-bound root system, since they seldom develop well. When buying bare-root plants, make sure the roots have not dried out and select plants with balanced main and fibrous roots.

Choose fruit trees that are healthy with sturdy growth and, if two or three years old, with well-spaced laterals. Inspect plants carefully and do not buy any with signs of pest infestation, damage, disease, or those that are lacking in vigour.

Pollination requirements

Most soft fruits and some tree fruits are self-fertile, that is they produce a crop without needing a pollinating cultivar nearby, and may therefore be grown singly. Apples, pears, many sweet cherries, and some plums are not reliably self-fertile, however. To produce a successful crop, self-sterile cultivars need to be cross-pollinated by another cultivar of the

ROOTSTOCK

A graft union between rootstock and scion is identifiable by a noticeable kink in the stem 10–30cm (4–12in) above the soil mark, especially on young fruit trees that have only recently been propagated. When planting, make sure that the graft union is not below soil level.

same fruit. Usually, one pollinating cultivar is sufficient but some apples and pears must be grown close to two other cultivars for all trees to produce good crops.

For cross-pollination to occur, the flowering periods of the different cultivars must overlap. Cultivars are therefore divided into flowering groups, from early to late, which are indicated by numbers under the individual fruit entries. Cultivars for cross-pollination should be in the same, preceding, or following group. A cultivar in group 3, for example, is compatible with others in groups 2, 3, and 4.

Certain cultivars of some fruits, however, will not cross-pollinate, although they may flower at the same time. For sweet cherries and pears, these are classified in incompatiblity groups, which are indicated in the lists. Seek advice, if in doubt. A few sweet cherry cultivars will pollinate all other cultivars in flower at the same time; these are known as universal pollinators.

Selecting rootstocks

Many tree fruit cultivars offered for sale will have been grafted onto a compatible rootstock, since cultivars do not breed true from seed, and cannot be raised consistently from cuttings. The rootstock controls the growth rate and size of the mature tree, while the scion determines the fruits produced. Some rootstocks have a dwarfing effect (useful for a small garden) and induce early fruiting. A few rootstocks are resistant to certain pests and diseases.

Selecting fruit trees

Young fruit trees may be purchased at several stages of growth – choose the one most appropriate for the form that the tree is to take. Maiden whip trees (with no sideshoots) take at least one year longer than other forms to train and fruit. One-year-old feathered maidens are popular with experienced growers since their sideshoots enable the earliest possible training. Two-year-old trees fruit more quickly, and good specimens are easily trained. Three-year-old, trained trees are more expensive and can be harder to re-establish.

Planting in open ground

Container-grown plants may be planted at any time of year except when the ground is frozen or waterlogged, or during drought. Try to plant bare-root plants from late autumn to early spring, while they are dormant; soak the roots well before planting. In frosty periods, heel them in temporarily in moist, frost-free soil until conditions are suitable for planting.

Planting fruit trees

If planting a number of trees, measure the site and mark out the planting positions with canes. Dig a hole for each tree at least one third wider than the tree's root system; firm the base of the hole and slightly mound it.

Insert a stake into the hole about 7cm (3in) away from the centre to allow for the tree's growth in girth as it matures. The height of the stake depends on the form into which the tree is to be trained (for details, see under individual fruits). Fruit trees on dwarfing rootstocks need permanent staking; remove the stake of those on other rootstocks after three years.

Place the tree in the hole, making sure that the soil mark on the stem is at ground level, and spread out the roots. Do not cover the union between rootstock and scion, since this encourages scion-rooting and the rootstock's influence will be lost.

Backfill in stages with soil, while another person holds the tree upright, shaking it gently from time to time so that the soil settles in between the roots. Firm the soil; when the hole is nearly full, break up the soil around the edges to obtain a uniform soil firmness over a greater area. Firm and level the area, and attach the tree to the stake using a soft, pliable, plastic tie with a firm cushion between tree and stake to prevent chafing. Protect the tree from rabbits and other animals with a wire netting surround.

Fruit trees to be planted against a wall or fence should be positioned 15–22cm (6–9in) away from the support, with the branches sloping gently inwards. This ensures that the roots are in good soil and allows for future expansion of the trunk.

Planting soft fruits and vines

Bush and cane fruits are planted as for fruit trees, but no staking is needed. Plant only up to the soil mark: planting too deeply will inhibit the plants' growth. For vines, make the planting holes or trench wide enough for the roots to be fully extended, and train the vines against a support.

Planting in containers

Water the young plant thoroughly before planting. Use a moist, soil-based potting compost, leaving 2.5cm (1in) between the compost surface and the rim of the pot for watering. Water again after planting and keep the compost moist until growth begins, then water regularly.

PLANTING CORDONS

In the open ground
Space trees 75cm (2½ft) apart (top). Attach a cane at an angle of 45° to horizontal wires (bottom left) stretched between sturdy posts. Tie each tree securely to a cane (bottom right).

Against a fence
Fix wires 10–15cm (4–6in) away from the fence to allow for the growth of the trees and to promote good air circulation. Plant the trees 15–22cm (6–9in) from the fence.

PLANTING A FRUIT BUSH

1 *Dig a hole large enough to accommodate the roots of the bush when spread out. Place a cane across the hole to check that the level of the surrounding soil is the same as the soil mark on the main stem.*

2 *Backfill the hole with soil; tread in the soil gently to ensure that no air pockets remain between the roots. Rake over the soil lightly to level the surface.*

PLANTING A FRUIT TREE

1 *Dig a hole one third wider than the tree's root system. Drive in a stake to a depth of 45cm (18in) about 7cm (3in) from the centre of the hole.*

2 *Slightly mound the soil at the base of the hole and place the tree in the centre. Use a cane to check that the soil mark on the stem is level with the soil surface.*

3 *Spread out the tree's roots, then gradually fill the hole with soil. Firm to ensure that the tree is well anchored and that there are no air pockets between the roots.*

4 *Attach a buckle-and-spacer to the top of the stake and then to the tree so that the cushion is between the stem and the stake (see inset). Adjust as necessary.*

Routine care

Most fruit plants need regular maintenance to ensure that they are healthy and produce high-quality crops. Routine operations vary, depending on the type of fruit, growing conditions, and season.

Fruit thinning

Fruit thinning is necessary for a number of tree fruits, particularly apples, pears, and plums, to provide good-sized, high-quality fruits. It also prevents branch breakages by ensuring balanced crop distribution. In addition, thinning helps to prevent biennial bearing (to which some fruit cultivars are prone), that is, bearing heavy crops one year and little or none the next.

Thin by hand or with scissors, leaving the fruits room to develop fully and receive enough sun and air to ripen. Details of how and when to thin are given under each fruit.

Fertilizing, mulching, and watering

Apply manures and fertilizers when needed, observing crop performance and checking for leaf discoloration that may denote nutrient deficiencies. In hot, dry summers, watering will usually be necessary; a seep hose (see p.561) uses water most efficiently, and a soil auger is invaluable for ascertaining visually the level of soil moisture at depth.

Care of tree fruits
In early spring, mulch newly planted trees and any that are not thriving with manure or compost. At the same time check that any problem is not

FERTILIZING FRUIT TREES
Using string and a peg, mark a circular area around the tree, slightly beyond the spread of the branches. This indicates where fertilizer should be applied – over the whole span of the tree's root system.

HOW TO THIN FRUIT

1 *Thinning of some fruits is required to obtain fruit of a good size and quality; if it is left unthinned, the fruit is usually small and of poor flavour.*

2 *Remove unhealthy or disfigured fruits first, then reduce the remainder to at least 5–8cm (2–3in) apart, depending on the type of fruit.*

caused by a pest or disease; if it is, treat as recommended in PLANT PROBLEMS, pp.639–673. Once the trees reach flowering size, apply a balanced fertilizer at a rate of 105–140g/sq m (3–4oz/sq yd) in early spring. Do not overfeed, particularly with nitrogen, as this may produce soft, disease-prone growth.

If a particular nutrient is needed, use specific fertilizers: potassium sulphate for potassium deficiency; ammonium nitrate to supply nitrogen; superphosphate to provide phosphorus. Apply these in spring at a rate

Organic fertilizers for fruit trees

Tree fruits that are in good health and fruiting freely seldom need additional fertilizers. If growth is weak, apply top-dressings of well-rotted organic manure or garden compost in spring. However, if these top-dressings are not available, a number of organic fertilizers may be applied in spring or early summer.
- Blood, fish, and bone is a good general fertilizer that will encourage growth.
- Hoof and horn provides slow-release nitrogen.
- Seaweed meal – applied as a base dressing when planting –

and dilute seaweed extract, which is applied as a foliar spray, are both good sources of nitrogen.
- Pelleted chicken manure also has a high NPK content and is a useful base dressing on poor soils.
- Organic garden wood ash will provide fruits with potassium (potash), which is important for fruit production.

Other useful fertilizers for fruit trees include:
- Bonemeal and rock phosphate as base fertilizers before planting.
- Ground or dolomitic limestone to raise soil pH if required.

of 35g/sq m (1oz/sq yd), except superphosphate, which is normally applied at three times this rate every three or four years. Correct magnesium deficiency (p.651) by spraying the foliage, after flowering, with a solution of Epsom salts. In severe cases, repeat the treatment after three weeks. Other deficiencies, especially of manganese/iron (p.651), may also arise. If, more rarely, deficiencies of zinc, copper, or other elements are suspected, seek specialist advice.

Apply fertilizers evenly over an area just beyond the branch spread. Where trees are grown in grass, mow regularly and leave the mowings *in situ*; they rot down and return nutrients to the soil, helping particularly to avert potassium deficiency.

Care of soft fruits
Mulch soft fruits regularly in spring with well-rotted manure. Use fertilizers as indicated for tree fruits; nitrogen and potassium are the most essential nutrients. Apply fertilizer over the whole area; in the case of raspberries, spread the dressing at least 60cm (2ft) either side of the row, avoiding the foliage. With strawberries, dig manure into the soil prior to planting.

Fruit in containers
Although soil-based potting composts contain nutrients, plants should be fed in the growing season in order to replace the nutrients as they are used; nitrogen and potassium in particular are often needed. Fruit plants in containers require watering more frequently than those planted in open ground. Check the compost

regularly – at least once a day in hot, dry weather – and keep it moist.

Each winter, fruit trees and bushes in pots should be top-dressed or repotted. To top-dress, replace the top 2.5cm (1in) of compost with fresh compost. In alternate winters, where possible, repot the plant. Remove the plant from its container, and gently comb away some of the old compost from the root ball, using a hand fork or wooden stick. Cut out any coarse roots, taking care not to damage the fibrous roots, and repot into a larger, clean container (see also "Planting in containers", p.425).

Stakes and ties

The stakes and ties of both free-standing and trained fruits should be checked regularly. When the cushioning or ties are weak or worn out, the tree may rub against the stake, and *Nectria* canker (p.664) on apples, or bacterial canker (p.665) on stone fruits may develop. Check the base of the stake: this may rot and then topple with the tree in high winds, particularly just before a heavy crop is to be gathered. On trained trees, ensure that branches are not tied too tightly to canes or wires since this will restrict growth. Loosen any ties if necessary.

Supporting branches
Tree fruits grown in unrestricted forms may need to have their branches supported when the tree is heavily laden with fruit, even if the fruits have been correctly thinned. If only one or two branches are affected, support them on forked stakes or

rope them to stronger branches. If several branches are overloaded, secure a sturdy stake either to the trunk or to the main stake and tie a rope to each branch and to the top of the stake; this technique is known as "maypoling".

Protecting plants

Fruit trees and bushes may need to be protected from bad weather or frost with windbreaks or fleece. Protection against birds and animals may also be required.

Wind protection

Maintain windbreaks (see p.611) properly so that they remain effective, and prune natural barriers such as trees or shrubs if they become thin to encourage bushier growth. Check that posts supporting windbreak netting or fences are secure and repair them as necessary.

Frost protection

Most frost damage is caused by spring frosts that kill or injure buds, flowers, or fruitlets overnight. Severe winter frosts may cause bark splitting and dieback, but in areas where low temperatures are common, select cultivars that are bred to withstand the conditions. In subtropical regions, there should be few problems; if necessary, cover small trees and bushes with polyester fabric or spun polypropylene sheets.

A very slight frost seldom causes any serious damage: -2°C (28°F) is frequently the danger point. The duration of the frost is usually more important than the temperature alone: -3°C (27°F) for a quarter of an hour would cause little or no damage whereas, sustained over three hours, it could cause substantial losses.

If frost is forecast, protect straw-berries, bushes, and even small trees by using fleece, hessian, or layers of newspaper to cover the plant completely and trap warm air around it. Remove the covers each day once the temperature has risen above freezing point, and replace when frost is again forecast. For further information, see FROST AND WIND PROTECTION, pp.612–613.

Protection from birds

In winter, bullfinches and tits damage fruit buds by feeding on the nutritious centre of the buds and discarding the outer bud scales. This damage is much more serious than the loss of ripe fruit because it denudes whole branches permanently, making it necessary to prune them back to obtain new, young shoots, which will not fruit for two or more seasons. The best protection from bird damage is to place nets over the trees or bushes. If snow is forecast, support the net or remove it temporarily because the weight of the snow on the net may damage branches underneath.

Ripening fruit should also be protected against birds; small areas may be temporarily covered with netting but for large areas it is preferable to erect a fruit cage instead. It is impractical to protect large fruit trees, although those trained against supports may be enclosed by attaching netting to the support. The mesh of any net used must be small enough to exclude tiny birds. Protect strawberries in a patch with a low, temporary cage.

Pest, disease, and weed control

It is advisable to check plants once a week for signs of pest and disease problems; they may then be treated at an early stage before extensive damage has been caused (see PLANT PROBLEMS, pp.639–673). If virus diseases (pp.649 and 659) are suspected, seek professional advice to ensure that this is the problem; strawberries, raspberries, loganberries, blackberries, and blackcurrants are especially vulnerable. The only practical solution is to dig up infected specimens with their roots and burn them, otherwise the virus may spread to adjacent plants.

Weed control is also essential to produce the best fruit yields. Remove seedling weeds and mulch to inhibit germination of weed seeds. Perennial weeds should be dug out or spot-treated as soon as they are noticed. For further details, see "Weeds", pp.669–673.

Plants under cover

In cool-temperate climates, some fruits may need to be grown under cover. These include all the tender fruits, and a number of other fruits which either have flowers that are vulnerable to damage by spring frosts or require a long ripening period, for example peaches and many late-ripening grapes.

In subtropical climates, fruit trees are rarely grown under cover, since the only climatic problems encountered are exceptionally cool periods and heavy rainfall, which most are able to tolerate.

Plants that need to be under cover all year are best grown in greenhouses; walk-in polytunnels are of limited use because temperature levels and adequate ventilation are hard to maintain (see also GREENHOUSES AND FRAMES, "Choosing a greenhouse", pp.568–571).

Particular care is needed in order to maintain free air circulation around plants grown in greenhouses to discourage diseases that may be caused by the increased heat and humidity. Support wires for trained fruits should be secured at least 30cm (12in) away from the glass or plastic of the greenhouse. Control any pests and diseases and apply fertilizer as recommended under individual tree fruit entries. For details of pruning fruits grown in a greenhouse, see "Pruning under cover", p.430.

Growing tender fruits (for example citrus, guava, pomegranate, and olive) in containers makes it possible to bring them under cover when necessary. In cool areas, place tender plants grown in pots outside in a sunny position in spring and bring them under cover again in autumn. Overwinter the plants in the greenhouse at a temperature of at least 10–15°C (50–59°F).

PROTECTING AGAINST BIRD AND ANIMAL DAMAGE

Bud-stripping
Birds stripping buds from branches over winter cause permanent damage, leading to unproductive, bare wood.

Netting strawberries
Protect fruit by erecting a frame 1.2m (4ft) high and draping and tying 2cm (³/₄in) mesh netting over it. Secure the base so that birds and squirrels cannot get underneath.

Fruit cage
Fruit bushes or small fruit trees may be protected by a cage constructed from metal supports covered with wire or plastic netting.

Protecting trained trees
Fruit trees trained against supporting wires may be protected with a 2cm (³/₄in) mesh net fixed at the top and secured firmly to the support.

Pruning and training

FRUIT trees and bushes need correct, regular pruning and, in many cases, training to yield a good crop. The degree and method required depend on the desired shape and the fruiting time and habit as well as on the individual type of fruit. Relatively limited pruning is needed to produce an open-centre bush tree, for example, while extensive, formative pruning and training are required for a fan or espalier to produce a symmetrical network of well-trained branches.

Aims of pruning and training

Initially, young trees and bushes should receive formative pruning and training to produce the desired shape (such as a bush) and to develop a strong, balanced framework. With established plants, the aim of subsequent pruning is to maintain the health and shape of the plant and ensure a good yield of fruit.

Pruning

This is the cutting out of unwanted shoots and branches, either because they spoil the plant's framework or because they are unproductive. Correct pruning maintains an open, uncrowded structure to allow the maximum amount of sun to reach the ripening fruits and to simplify spraying and harvesting. It also includes the removal of dead, diseased, damaged, or old, unfruitful wood.

On young plants, pruning may be combined with training to form a particular shape; unwanted shoots are removed completely, while those retained may be cut back to stimulate the growth of sideshoots. The established, cropping tree, bush, or plant is pruned to encourage optimum growth and fruit production.

Training

The selection and, in many cases, the tying in of shoots to create a specific shape is known as training. Forms close to the natural shape, such as the bush, require much less training than, for example, a fan, which is produced by precise selection, spacing, and tying in of individual shoots onto a supporting framework.

Over- and underpruning

Take care not to over- or underprune as this restricts fruitfulness and may encourage disease. Repeated, severe pruning results in increased, vigorous, vegetative growth, and little or no fruit, since few fruit buds are able to develop. This is especially damaging on a plant that is already vigorous. Underpruning leads to overcrowded branches that will receive less sun, which is essential to ripen the fruit; the branches may also rub together, exposing the tree to the risk of diseases such as *Nectria* canker (p.664). Pruning a young tree too lightly may also cause early overcropping that could stunt the tree and even break branches by overloading them.

When to prune

The time of pruning depends both on the specific treatment and on the kind of fruit. In the pruning procedures described here and under the individual fruits, "year one" refers to the first twelve months after planting, "year two" to the following twelve months, and so on.

Winter pruning is standard practice on all untrained apple, pear, quince, and medlar trees, on vines, and on black-, red-, and white-currants, gooseberries, and blueberries. Pruning of untrained trees of stone fruits (plum, cherry, peach, nectarine, and apricot) must be delayed until spring for young trees or summer for established ones, in order to minimize the risk of silver leaf infection (p.647). Summer pruning is essential on trained forms of tree fruits, grape vines, currants, and gooseberries. This reduces their vigour and contains them within the restricted space that they occupy; it also concentrates the plants' energies on fruit production. Many of the tender fruits need to be pruned directly after fruiting.

How to prune

When deciding on the extent of pruning apple and pear trees, always take into account the vigour both of the individual shoot and of the whole tree. Vigorous growth should be pruned lightly; this usually involves thinning out a percentage of shoots completely and leaving the remainder unpruned. Prune weak growth more severely, but check first that no disease, such as canker, is causing the weakness.

Where to cut

It is important always to prune to just above a healthy bud and to make a clean cut; cutting midway between buds or leaving a ragged end may cause dieback and increase the shoot's vulnerability to disease. If removing a shoot or branch completely, cut it back to the point of origin but leave the bark ridge and branch collar intact rather than cutting flush with the parent stem.

WHERE TO MAKE A PRUNING CUT

Cutting to a bud
Cut just above a bud at a 45° angle, sloping the cut away from the bud. Do not cut too close or the bud may be damaged, nor too far away, or the stem may die back.

Cutting to a replacement shoot
As when cutting to a bud, make an angled cut sloping away from the replacement shoot.

Cutting back to a main branch
Make a clean cut, leaving the branch collar intact (inset, top). The tree is then less susceptible to disease and the wound heals faster (inset, bottom).

INCORRECT PRUNING

Underpruning
A tree that is pruned irregularly or very lightly will develop overcrowded shoots that will not receive sufficient light to ripen the fruits, which may be small. The branches may also rub together, increasing the risk of certain diseases.

Overpruning
If a fruit tree is pruned excessively, this will stimulate a mass of vigorous, vegetative shoots. These shoots will produce few, if any, fruit buds, so the crop will be poor.

REMOVING A BRANCH

1 *Using a pruning saw, make the first cut approximately 30cm (12in) away from the trunk. Saw at right angles to the branch from underneath, to about one quarter of the way through.*

2 *Start the second cut at the top of the branch, slightly further out than the first cut. Saw right through the branch; if it breaks away, the bark will tear only as far as the first cut.*

3 *When making the final cut, take care not to damage the bark ridge at the top of the branch or the collar at the base. If necessary, start the cut from below and cut down from above to meet it.*

4 *Pare away rough edges with a sharp knife. The exposed area will seal itself more quickly with the bark ridge and collar left intact. This also reduces the risk of disease entering the wound. Do not apply wound paint, as it might seal in an existing infection.*

To prevent the branch or bark from tearing before cutting is completed, undercut first before finishing the cut from above. Cut back to the point of origin or to a well-placed, healthy branch as a suitable replacement. Do not leave a stub or the cut end will die instead of healing. Pare away any rough edges with a sharp knife.

Fruiting habits

How a plant is pruned depends on its fruiting habit. For example, sweet cherries form fruit mainly on spurs of two-year-old and older wood, so many of the older shoots must be retained. Acid cherries, however, fruit on one-year-old shoots; when pruning, leave most of the young shoots but remove some of the old, unproductive wood.

Training for shape

A young tree is usually bought as a "feathered maiden" (a one-year-old tree with sideshoots). Initial pruning consists of selecting shoots to be retained, shortening them as required, and removing unwanted shoots. If a young tree is bought as a maiden whip (a one-year-old tree without sideshoots), it should be cut down to a bud after planting, the height depending on how the tree is to be trained. This encourages the growth of sideshoots. When these develop, the tree, now two years old, is equivalent to a feathered maiden. Formative pruning continues for the first two or three years until the desired shape has been obtained.

Training for fruitfulness

The vigour and fruitfulness of shoots may be adjusted by raising or lowering selected laterals or, with oblique cordons, the whole tree. Horizontal growths are more fruitful than vertical ones, so tying a lateral closer to the horizontal makes it produce more fruit. If one lateral is less vigorous than another and more sideshoots are needed, raising it will stimulate vegetative growth. For an established, cropping tree or bush, pruning is more important than training; even on an untrained tree, less fruitful or unbalanced shoots may be tied down in summer to increase their yield.

PRUNING A MAIDEN WHIP TO FORM A FEATHERED TREE

Winter, Year 1
To produce vigorous "feathers" (sideshoots) on a maiden whip tree, cut it back with an angled cut just above a bud at the required height.

Winter, Year 2
By the following winter, a number of new sideshoots should have been produced below the pruning cut.

TRAINING ON CANES

1 *The vigour of laterals of trained trees may be altered by adjusting the angle at which they are trained. This technique corrects uneven growth on either side of the same tree.*

2 *Lower a young, strong-growing lateral, with its cane, at the start of or during the summer to reduce its vigour; raise a lateral to encourage it to grow more quickly. Retie the canes to the wires.*

3 *By the end of the summer, the branches may be returned to their original positions; they should be more even in length.*

Curbing excessive vigour

Extremely vigorous trees that produce rapid vegetative growth at the expense of cropping may benefit from root pruning. On apples and pears only, bark-ringing (see p.437) may also be used as a last resort to curb vigour; it should not be used on stone fruits as it may kill them. Both methods will induce the formation of fruit buds, so the beneficial effects will be seen in increased blossom and fruiting one or possibly two years later.

Root pruning

Trees may be root pruned at any age, but only when they are dormant. When pruning the roots of a young tree, first lift it by digging around it, then remove soil carefully from around the fibrous roots, taking care not to damage them. Cut back a few of the thick roots in the process. Then replant the tree firmly and stake it.

Larger trees need to be root pruned *in situ*, pruning one side of the root system one winter, and completing the other side a year or two later. To do this effectively, make a trench 45cm–1.2m (18in–4ft) wide, de-pending on the size of the tree, to expose the main roots. These should be severed and a section of each root removed. Then fill in the trench, firm, and mulch; in some cases, staking may be required to provide support until the tree is fully stable.

Pruning under cover

Prune back branches and shoots of plants grown in a greenhouse so that they do not touch the glass or plastic surfaces, as otherwise they may suffer sun scorch and growth will be constricted or damaged. Regular pruning also allows more light to reach the developing fruits and helps them to ripen.

Renovation

If a tree is too old to crop well, and has rotten or severely diseased branches or trunk, it should be grubbed out and burnt. If the trunk and the main branches are sound, however, and the tree is merely overcrowded, it can be rejuvenated by means of renovative pruning followed by correct, routine care.

Renovation work should be carried out in spring or summer on stone fruits and in winter on apples, pears, and other pome fruits. Cut out any branches that are dead, damaged, or diseased, or so low that they may trail on the ground when laden with fruit. Also remove crowded or crossing branches, because these will shade the developing fruits, and, if they rub together, may become prone to diseases such as canker. On a vigorous tree, it is advisable to stagger this pruning over more than one year; pruning too severely on a single occasion may only induce more vigorous, vegetative growth.

Once this initial thinning has been achieved, more precise pruning, such as spur thinning, may be carried out (as described for routine pruning under individual fruit entries). Chemical inhibitors are available to curb the regrowth of water shoots around the cuts, but wound paints are not recommended because they may seal in any infection.

ROOT PRUNING TO IMPROVE FRUITING

1 *Mark out the position for a trench around the tree using string and a peg. The trench should be at the same distance from the tree all the way round, just below the outermost spread of the branches.*

2 *Dig out a trench around the tree at the marked line; it should be at least 45cm (18in) wide and approximately 60cm (24in) deep.*

3 *At the base of the trench, use a fork to remove soil from around the thick roots without damaging the fibrous roots.*

4 *Sever each woody root on either side of the trench with a pruning saw, discarding the central section. Leave the fibrous roots unpruned.*

5 *Backfill the trench with soil, firm well, then cover the area with an organic mulch to retain moisture and help the tree re-establish. Stake if necessary.*

RENOVATING A NEGLECTED TREE

1 *Remove overcrowded, rubbing, or crossing branches to let in light and air by cutting them back to their point of origin, or to a vigorous sub-lateral facing the required direction.*

2 *Any branches that are damaged or affected by a disease such as canker (shown above) should be removed completely, or cut back to a healthy shoot.*

Harvesting and storing

Many home-grown fruits may be enjoyed long after their normal harvesting time if correctly harvested and stored. While most are at their best eaten fresh, some keep their flavour well even after prolonged storage. For details on harvesting and storing specific fruits, see the individual fruit entries.

Harvesting

Most fruits are best picked when fully ripe for using fresh. Fruits for storing are usually harvested slightly earlier, however, when they are mature but not yet completely ripe and still firm. Since not all the fruits on a single plant ripen at the same time, it is usually necessary to harvest over a period and this provides a succession of fresh supplies.

For tree fruits such as apples and pears, test for ripeness by holding a fruit in the palm of the hand, then gently lift and twist. If ripe, the fruit will come away easily complete with its stalk, otherwise it should be left for a day or two.

When harvesting, discard any damaged, diseased, or bruised fruits as they will quickly become infected with rot, which then spreads rapidly to adjacent fruits when in storage.

Soft fruits must be picked completely dry otherwise many may be affected by rot unless the fruits are used immediately. Regular picking, at least every other day, is advisable for strawberries, raspberries, blackberries, and hybrid berries.

Always take care not to damage the plant when harvesting – by pulling fruit off sharply, for example. Some types of fruit, such as cherries, grapes, and mangos, should be cut off the plant to avoid the risk of accidental damage.

Storing

There are various ways of keeping fruits for later use, including cool storage, freezing, and preserving; the most suitable method depends on the type of fruit. Some fruits, especially those such as apples, apricots, and figs that have a high acid and sugar content, may also be oven-dried at 120–140°F (49–60°C) but this is difficult to do successfully at home.

FREEZING SOFT FRUITS

Spread out soft fruits, such as raspberries, on trays so that they are not in contact with each other, then freeze them. Once they are frozen, they may be packed into suitable containers and kept in the freezer until they are required for use.

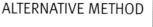

When preparing fruits for storage, handle them carefully to avoid bruising. Always store different cultivars in separate containers that are free from any residues or aromas that may taint the fruits.

Cool storage

Apples and pears in particular may be kept for several weeks, or even months in the right conditions – consistently cool, dark, and slightly damp. Various other tree fruits, such as lemons, may also be stored this way although they do not usually keep for such a long period, while most nuts keep well for up to a few months. Soft fruits cannot be stored in this way. The required temperature and degree of humidity vary for different fruits, but most should be stored in slatted trays and boxes to allow free air circulation. Some apple and pear cultivars, however, tend to shrivel and are better kept in clear plastic bags. Check unwrapped fruits regularly and remove any that show signs of disease or rotting.

Freezing

This is ideal for most soft fruits, except strawberries, and for a number of tree fruits. Small fruits such as raspberries are usually frozen whole, while large fruits such as apples are best chopped or sliced beforehand to ensure even and thorough freezing. Remove any stalks (and "strigs" of currants) then open-freeze whole fruits spread out on trays. Once they are frozen – after two to four hours – transfer the fruits to plastic boxes or bags, excluding as much air as possible, and keep them frozen until needed. Strawberries and some soft-fleshed tree fruits such as plums are often puréed before being frozen.

Preserving and bottling

All soft fruits and a number of tree fruits such as apricots and damsons may be made into preserves. In most cases, the entire fruit is used, while some such as grapes and blackberries are better strained and only the juice used to make a sweet jelly.

Citrus fruits, pineapples, and most stone fruits such as cherries may be bottled in sugar syrup with alcohol (such as rum, brandy, or *eau de vie*) if desired to preserve them. Citrus peel may also be candied or dried for use in baking.

STORING APPLES

1 *Wrap each fruit individually in greaseproof paper to prevent rot and keep it in good condition.*

2 *Carefully fold the greaseproof paper around the fruit, holding it lightly so that you do not bruise it.*

3 *Place each wrapped fruit on its folded end in a wooden slatted box, or other well-ventilated container, and store in a cool place.*

ALTERNATIVE METHOD

Store fruits of cultivars that tend to shrivel quickly in a plastic bag. Make several holes in the bag before filling it with no more than 3kg (6lb 8oz) of fruit. Seal the bag loosely.

FRUITS THAT FREEZE WELL

Apples **P**
Apricots **P**
Blackberries and all hybrid berries **Sk**
Blackcurrants **Sk**
Blueberries **Sk**
Cherries (acid) **Sk**
Cherries (sweet) **Sk**
Damsons **Sk** (with or without stones)
Gages **Sk**
Gooseberries **Sk**
Grapes **Sk**
Nectarines **P**
Peaches **P**
Plums **Sk**
Raspberries **Sk**
Redcurrants **Sk**
Whitecurrants **Sk**

Key
P *Remove cores or stones and slice and peel if required*
Sk *Remove stalks (and stones where applicable)*

Propagation

Tree fruits (except figs) are usually propagated by grafting; figs, vines, and many soft fruits by cuttings, although if *Phylloxera* (see p.461) is a problem, grape vines should be grafted. Some fruits produce runners, layers, or suckers, all of which may be used to produce new plants. Several tender fruits and some nuts may be grown from seed but hardy fruits seldom come true.

Bud-grafting

Both chip-budding and T-budding are used to increase the stock of fruit trees. They are economical methods of propagation, since a new tree is produced from a single bud. Grafting should be carried out in mid-summer, using as the rootstock an established plant with a stem that is at least 1cm (½in) thick. A bud from the scion plant is cut from a ripe shoot (the budstick) of the current season's growth, and grafted onto an incision in the rootstock.

Propagating by chip-budding

Select a healthy budstick and carefully remove a bud (the bud chip), taking care not to damage the cambium layer. Remove a sliver of rind from the rootstock and place the bud chip onto the exposed wood of the rootstock so that the cambium layers are in close contact. Bind the bud chip tightly onto the rootstock to hold it in place. When the bud and rootstock have united the bud will start to swell and the binding may be removed. The following winter, trim the rootstock just above the grafted bud to encourage a strong shoot to develop from the graft in spring.

CHIP-BUDDING

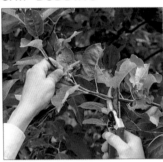

1 *Choose a vigorous shoot of the current season's ripened wood as the budstick. The shoot should be approximately pencil thick and have well-developed buds.*

2 *Hold the budstick firmly and, using a clean, sharp knife, slice off the soft tip and remove all the leaves to produce a clear length of stem.*

3 *To remove a bud chip, first slice into the budstick about 2cm (³/₄in) below a bud. Cut down to a depth of about 5mm (¹/₄in), slanting the blade at an angle of 45°.*

4 *Make another incision about 4cm (1¹/₂in) above the first. Slice downwards behind the bud towards the first incision, taking care not to damage the bud.*

5 *Remove the bud chip, holding it by the bud to keep the cambium layer clean. Place the bud chip in a plastic bag to stop it drying out.*

6 *To prepare the rootstock, stand astride the plant and, using a sharp knife, remove all the shoots and leaves from the bottom 30cm (12in) of stem.*

7 *Make a shallow cut in the stock. Remove a sliver of rind to reveal the cambium layer (see inset), leaving a "lip" at the base. Do not touch the exposed wood.*

Bud chip in position on rootstock

8 *Place the bud chip onto the prepared lip of rind, offset if necessary, so that the exposed cambium layers of bud chip and rootstock match and touch.*

9 *Bind the bud chip to the rootstock with plastic tape. Carefully remove the tape after a few weeks when the bud chip has united with the rootstock.*

10 *The following late winter, remove the top of the rootstock. Cut cleanly with secateurs just above the grafted bud, using an angled cut.*

11 *During the summer, a shoot from the grafted bud will develop. The new tree is then at the maiden whip stage (see "Selecting fruit trees", p.425).*

Propagating by T-budding

In this technique the rootstock and scion bud are prepared in a similar way to chip-budding, except that two slits are made in the rootstock, to form the shape of a "T". This allows the bark of the rootstock to be lifted slightly so that the scion bud may be tucked behind it. Removing the scion bud with a leaf stalk attached makes it easier to handle; the stalk is removed before the bud is bound to the rootstock. The rootstock should be cut back the next winter.

For this technique to be successful, the bark of the rootstock must lift smoothly: in dry weather, rootstocks need to be watered for up to two weeks before T-budding takes place.

Whip-and-tongue grafting

This is a common method of grafting for tree fruits. It may be used as an alternative to budding but it is usually more successful with pome than with stone fruits. Use well-established rootstocks that have been planted either the previous winter or, preferably, two winters before grafting takes place.

The scion material should have at least three buds and should be taken in mid-winter from a healthy shoot of the previous season's growth. Heel it in until ready for grafting. In late winter or early spring, prepare the stock by cutting off the top of the stem and removing any sideshoots. Using a sloping cut, slice off a small piece of bark from the top of the remaining stem; make a further shallow incision in the exposed cambium layer, to create a tongue.

Trim the scion to a length of three or four buds then, using a sloping cut, slice off a small piece of bark close to a bud but on the opposite side to it. Make a further, shallow incision, to match that in the stock, and carefully hook the resulting tongue onto the one on the rootstock. Make sure that the cambium layers of both stock and scion are in

---

T-BUDDING

1 *Select a ripened shoot as the scion from the current season's growth and remove the leaves. Remove a bud by slicing underneath it (see inset).*

2 *Make a "T"-shaped cut in the stock about 22cm (9in) above ground level and prise open the flaps of bark.*

3 *Place the bud behind the flaps of bark, trimming the top level with the horizontal cut on the stock. Bind the bud as for chip-budding.*

WHIP-AND-TONGUE GRAFTING

1 *In mid-winter, remove healthy, vigorous hardwood shoots from the scion tree. Cut lengths of about 22cm (9in), cutting obliquely just above a bud.*

2 *Make bundles of 5 or 6 scions. Choose a well-drained, sheltered site and heel them in to keep them moist but dormant, leaving 5–8cm (2–3in) above the soil surface.*

3 *In late winter or early spring, prepare the rootstocks just before bud break. Cut off the top of each rootstock about 20–25cm (8–10in) from ground level.*

4 *Trim off any shoots from the rootstock with a sharp knife, then make a 3.5cm (1½in) upward-sloping cut on one side to receive the scion.*

5 *Make a slit 1cm (½in) deep about one third of the way down the exposed cambium layer, to form a tongue into which the scion may be inserted (see inset).*

6 *Lift the scions, cut off any soft growth at the tips, and trim to 3 or 4 buds. For each, cut off a piece of bark behind a bud that is about 5cm (2in) from the base.*

7 *Without touching the cut surface with your hand, cut the cambium layer (see inset) to match the tongue in the rootstock.*

8 *Place the scion into the tongue on the stock (inset, top). Use the arches of the cambium layers as a guide (inset, bottom) to ensure the exposed surfaces fit together well.*

9 *Bind together stock and scion with clear plastic tape. When the cut surfaces start to callus, remove the tape by carefully scoring it downwards.*

close contact, then bind the graft firmly. Remove the binding carefully when a callus has formed around the graft union. By spring, buds on the scion will have started to grow. Select the best shoot that develops (keeping others pinched back) to form a maiden whip tree (see "Selecting fruit trees", p.425).

Cuttings

Hardwood, softwood, and leaf-bud cuttings may be used to propagate certain fruits. Cutting material should always be selected from a healthy parent plant that crops regularly.

Hardwood cuttings

Figs, vines, currants (white, red, and black), and gooseberries may be propagated from hardwood cuttings, usually taken in autumn.

Select a well-ripened shoot of the current season's growth and trim off the leaves and soft tip. Remove some or most of the buds, depending on the fruit being propagated, and trim off the top and base. The exact preparation and length of the cuttings vary slightly; details are given under individual fruit entries.

If the soil is well cultivated and not too heavy, the cuttings may be inserted into a narrow trench in the open ground. If the soil is heavy, however, place the cuttings in a pot of moist, sandy compost. The cuttings should be ready for transplanting one or two years later.

Softwood cuttings

Guavas, pomegranates, tree tomatoes, and blueberries are propagated from softwood cuttings (where the climate is warm enough for the wood to ripen sufficiently, blueberries may also be propagated from hardwood cuttings). Take the cuttings in midsummer and place them in pots of cutting compost (see p.478). Harden off the young plants before they are transplanted to their permanent positions.

Leaf-bud cuttings

Stocks of blackberries and hybrid berries may be increased quickly by leaf-bud cuttings (see p.472). Take the cuttings in late summer: remove short lengths of stem, each with a bud and leaf attached; insert them in compost with the buds just above the surface. Once rooted, the cuttings may be potted up or planted out.

Runners, layers, and suckers

Some fruits send out runners, layers, or suckers, which root naturally at stem nodes while still attached to the parent plant. This process may be exploited to increase fruit stocks.

Runners

Strawberries (but not all alpine strawberries) produce creeping horizontal stems, or runners, which root where they come into contact with the ground and may be used for propagation. As the runners are produced, spread them out evenly. Allow them to root, and then lift and sever them (see p.470).

Layers

Blackberries and hybrid berries may be propagated by layering, although some hybrids are slow to root. The tip of a shoot is induced to root by carefully pegging it down in the soil or in a pot of moist compost (see "Tip layering", p.471). A year later, when the tip has rooted and produced new growth, it may be severed from the parent plant and transplanted to its permanent position.

Suckers

Established cane fruits such as raspberries naturally produce suckers that are usually hoed off. If retained, rooted suckers may be lifted and severed in autumn, when the plants are dormant but the soil is still warm. Transplant the rooted suckers directly to their permanent positions (see *Propagating by Suckers*, p.474). Figs, cobnuts, and filberts also produce suckers: if the suckers have good root systems, sever them with a spade and replant in the same way.

Seed

Propagation from seed is the usual method of increasing stock of many tender fruits, including avocado (see p.486), guava, and papaya.

The alpine strawberry is one of the few hardy fruits that may be raised successfully from seed (see p.470). Cobnuts, filberts, walnuts, and sweet chestnuts may also be raised from seed with a reasonable chance of success, although cultivars selected for the quality of their fruit need to be propagated vegetatively. For details, see ORNAMENTAL TREES, "Raising trees from seed", p.80.

HARDWOOD CUTTINGS

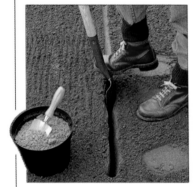

1 Dig a narrow trench 15cm (6in) deep. If the soil has a high clay content, sprinkle a little sand into the base of the trench to improve drainage.

2 Choose a ripened stem from the current season's growth (here, from a fig tree). Remove lengths of at least 30cm (12in), cutting flush with the main stem.

3 Cut off all the leaves and the soft growth at the tip of each cutting, then trim to about 23cm (9in): make an angled cut above the top bud and a straight cut at the base.

4 Place the cuttings in the prepared trench, spacing them 10–15cm (4–6in) apart and burying two thirds of the stems. Firm the soil, and label.

5 The cuttings will take several months to root. Towards the end of the following growing season, they should have developed sturdy new growth.

6 After leaf-fall in autumn, carefully lift the rooted cuttings, wrapping the roots in plastic to stop them drying out. Transplant the cuttings to their permanent positions to grow on.

Tree fruits

Pears

Apples

Apples

Quinces

THE fruits in this group, known also as "top fruits", are the largest-growing forms in the fruit garden. They may be divided into two main categories: "pome fruits", such as apples and pears, have a pip-containing core; "stone fruits", such as cherries and apricots, have a hard, central stone. There are also certain other fruits within this group that fit into neither of the above categories, such as figs, mulberries, and persimmons.

Cultivating tree fruits is a long-term undertaking that requires careful planning. The size and shape or form of the trees are important considerations. Left to grow naturally, many fruit trees would become impracticably large for the average-sized garden. Smaller forms grown on dwarfing rootstocks have been developed, however; fruit trees may also be trained and pruned as fans, espaliers, or cordons and grown flat against walls or fences, making it

feasible to grow them successfully in even the smallest of spaces.

Another factor to consider is the number of trees required. Many fruit trees are self-sterile and, to produce crops, need at least one other suitable cultivar of the same fruit to act as a pollinator. Even self-fertile trees crop more heavily if pollinators are present.

Some tree fruits such as figs prefer a long, hot growing season and are

difficult to cultivate in cooler climates; growing them under cover provides protection and improves fruit and crop size, as well as flavour.

Once a tree fruit has been selected and planted, it is important to follow the correct pruning methods. Good pruning not only builds a strong framework of branches, but also encourages and maintains maximum cropping for many years.

Strategic defences

The young shoots of many fruit trees can provide a tasty meal for rabbits, hares, and deer. All three of these unwelcome visitors are liable to vandalise tree bark by rubbing it off, or gnawing it away. Rabbits are particularly partial to bark at the base of young apple trees; if bark is lost from most, or all, of the trunk's circumference, the tree will die.

The most environmentally friendly solution is to banish them from the garden with wire fencing. To exclude rabbits this should be 90cm (3ft) tall and extend 30cm (12in) below ground, angling out at the base to prevent tunnelling beneath. A deer-proof fence should be a minimum of 2m (6ft) tall. Alternatively, you can protect individual plants with tree guards and netting (see pp.67 and 427).

Apples (*Malus domestica*)

Apples are one of the most widely grown, hardy fruits and both dessert and culinary cultivars offer a great variety of flavours and textures. Tree size may also be varied – dwarfing rootstocks and "family" trees (see p.420) allowing a number of different apples to be grown in a small garden on a single tree. Apple trees may readily be trained into almost any shape. Cordon-, espalier-, and fan-shaped forms are particularly useful for growing against walls and fences. Ballerina trees are dwarf, single-stemmed, compact apple trees with short fruiting spurs. Several cultivars are now available in this form.

The extensive choice of cultivars covers a period of ripening from mid-summer to late winter, and fruit may be stored until mid-spring, given suitable conditions. There are cultivars and rootstocks suitable for most climates, including those with severe winter temperatures. For flowering to occur, the trees must be subjected to at least 900 hours below 7°C (45°F): the chilling requirement. Apples are not grown successfully in tropical or subtropical regions.

Site and planting

When planting, ensure that each tree has sufficient space to develop to its full size. Select the most appropriate size of tree (largely determined by

the rootstock) for your garden. In most cases, more than one apple tree will be required for pollination.

Site
A sunny, sheltered site is essential for consistently good crops. Walls for trained fruit should preferably be in full sun. For shaded areas or those in a region with short summers and cool temperatures, choose cultivars that ripen early. Where late frosts occur, select late-flowering cultivars so that the blossom will not be damaged.

Apples will grow in most well-drained soils, if it is given adequate preparation (see p.424). The more dwarfing the rootstock, however, the more fertile the soil should be.

Rootstocks
Choice of rootstock depends on the tree size required and the soil type. Apple rootstocks are prefixed by M or MM, which stand for Malling and Malling Merton respectively, the research stations where the rootstocks were developed. A wide range of rootstocks is available, from the very dwarfing 'M27' to the extremely

vigorous 'M25'. For normal garden purposes, 'M9' is recommended for dwarf trees, 'M26' for larger ones, and 'MM106' for medium-sized trees (see *Planting Distances*, p.436). Cultivars on 'M27' bear fruit within three years of being grafted but need good growing conditions to maintain high yields. Where the soil is poor, use a more vigorous rootstock to compensate: for example, for a dwarf tree use 'MM106' instead of 'M9' or 'M26'. The vigour of the chosen cultivar also determines the size of the mature tree. Triploid cultivars grow larger than diploids (see below); use a more dwarfing rootstock for a triploid than for a diploid cultivar to attain a tree of similar size.

Pollination
No apples are reliably and consistently self-fertile: diploids must be planted near a second, compatible cultivar; triploid apples, which will not pollinate other cultivars, require two compatible cultivars nearby to pollinate them. Cultivars are divided into flowering groups according to their time of flowering; a cultivar from

one group may be cross-pollinated by another from the same group or one in the group before or after it if flowering times overlap (see also *Dessert Apples to Try*, p.436, and *Culinary Apples to Try*, p.437). Some cultivars are incompatible: of those listed on pp.436 and 437, 'Cox's Orange Pippin' will not pollinate 'Kidd's Orange Red' or 'Suntan' and vice versa. If in doubt about compatibility, ask a fruit nursery for advice.

Planting
Bare-root trees are best planted when dormant, preferably during autumn when the soil is still warm; they may be planted until late winter (except when it is frosty) but keep them moist in spring so that they establish well. Container-grown trees may be planted at any time, unless the ground is frozen or very wet; water before planting so that the roots are moist. Using the soil mark as a guide, plant each tree at its original planting depth (see also *Planting a Fruit Tree*, p.425).

If the tree is to be trained, fit the supports and wires before planting (see under individual tree forms). For untrained trees, staking at planting is vital and should be permanent for those on dwarfing rootstocks.

Planting distances (see p.436) depend upon how the trees are to be trained, as well as on the vigour of the chosen rootstocks and cultivars.

ROOTSTOCKS

4m (12ft)
3m (9ft)
2m (6ft)
1m (3ft)

'M27' 'M9' 'M26' 'MM106' 'MM111'

DESSERT APPLES TO TRY

'George Cave'

Early
'Discovery' **Fg3, Rs, Tb**
'Epicure' **Fg3, Sb,☆**
'George Cave' **Fg2, Sb**
'Irish Peach' **Fg2, Tb,☆**
'Katy' **Fg3, Sb**
'Tydeman's Early Worcester' **Fg3, Tb**

Mid-season
'Alkmene' **Fg2, Sb**
'Charles Ross' **Fg3, Sb**
'Cox's Orange Pippin' **Cs, Fg3, Sb, Ss,☆**
'Delbarestivale''B, Fg2, Sb, Ss, ☆**
'Egremont Russet' **Bp, Fg2, Sb,☆**
'Ellison's Orange' **Cs, Fg4, Rs, Sb**
'Fortune' **B, Cs, Fg3, Rs, Sb,☆**
'Golden Delicious' **Fg4, Sb, Ss**
'Greensleeves' **Fg3, Sb**
'James Grieve' **Cs, Fg3, Sb, Ss**
'Jester' **Fg4, Sb**
'King of the Pippins' **Fg5, Sb**
'Lord Lambourne' **Fg2, Tb**
'Mother' **Fg5, Sb,☆**
'Ribston Pippin' **Fg2, Sb, Ss, T,☆**
'St Edmund's Pippin' **Fg2, Tb,☆**
'Spartan' **Cs, Fg3, Sb**
'Sunset' **Fg3, Sb,☆**
'Worcester Pearmain' **Fg3, Ss, Tb**

'Worcester Pearmain'

Late
'Ashmead's Kernel' **Bp, Fg4, Sb,☆**
'Cornish Gillyflower' **Fg4, Tb,☆**
'D'Arcy Spice' **Fg4, Sb,☆**
'Falstaff' **Fg3, Sb**
'Fiesta' **Fg3, Sb**
'Jonagold' **Fg4, Sb, T, Vg**
'Jupiter' **Fg3, Sb, T, Vg**
'Kidd's Orange Red' **Fg3, Sb, ☆**
'Orleans Reinette' **Fg4, Sb, Ss,☆**
'Pixie' **Fg4, Sb,☆**
'Rosemary Russet' **Fg3, Sb**
'Saturn' **Fg3, Rs, Sb**
'Sturmer Pippin' **Fg3, Sb**
'Suntan' **Bp, Fg5, Sb, T, Vg, ☆**
'Winston' **Fg4, Sb**
'Winter Gem' **Fg4, Sb, Vg, ☆**

Key
B *Biennial bearing*
Bp *Bitter pit susceptible*
Cs *Canker susceptible*
Fg *Flowering group (numbers indicate period of flowering)*
Rs *Some resistance to scab*
Sb *Spur bearer*
Ss *Scab susceptible*
T *Triploid (unsuitable as pollinator)*
Tb *Tip bearer or partial tip bearer*
Vg *Vigorous growth*
☆ *Excellent flavour*

Routine care

Establish a regular maintenance programme to ensure that trees stay healthy and crop well. Feed and mulch periodically as required. Pruning and fruit thinning are annual tasks that are required to ensure satisfactory cropping. Check trees regularly for signs of pests and diseases and damage from rubbing stakes and ties.

Blossom thinning and biennial bearing

Certain apple cultivars, such as 'Laxton's Superb', tend to produce heavy crops in alternate years, and bear little or no blossom or fruit in intervening years. This is known as biennial bearing.

Blossom thinning can largely correct this; it involves removing nine of every ten blossom clusters by pinching them out, leaving the rosette of young leaves around each intact. The tree then produces a moderate, rather than heavy, crop and its resources are channelled into producing fruit buds for the following year, which would otherwise have been fruit-less. On large trees, where it would be impractical to thin blossom over the entire tree, biennial bearing can be corrected by blossom-thinning a few branches.

If trees that normally crop regularly start to crop biennially, this may be due to the loss of blossom from frost and hence the crop; this may then induce a tree to overcrop the following year. The tree may not have sufficient resources to develop adequate fruit buds for the third year and a biennial tendency is set in motion. Disease or pest infestation causing a setback in one year may produce a similar effect.

Fruit thinning

Thinning is essential where heavy crops have set, to improve fruit size, quality, and flavour, and to help prevent branches from breaking. On young trees, over-heavy cropping strains the tree's resources and slows the growth of new buds. Some thinning is useful on the young fruitlets, but it is simpler to carry out the main task in early summer, after the "June drop", when the tree naturally sheds imperfect and infertile fruits.

Use scissors to remove the centre (or "King") fruit of each cluster, which is sometimes abnormally shaped; then cut out any fruits that are damaged. In about mid-summer, thin the clusters again so that there is one good fruit per cluster. Fruit of dessert cultivars should be spaced 10–15cm (4–6in) apart, and that of

culinary cultivars 15–22cm (6–9in) apart; these distances may vary according to the individual cultivar and the size of fruit required.

Fertilizing, watering, and mulching

Water trees in spells of hot, dry weather, apply fertilizer annually, and mulch as necessary (see "Care of tree fruits", p.426). If growth is poor, apply ammonium sulphate in spring at a rate of 35g/sq m (1oz/sq yd).

Stakes and ties

Inspect stakes and ties regularly to check that they are not rubbing against the bark of trees and that

ties are effective; adjust them as necessary. Trees grown on dwarfing rootstocks such as 'M9' and 'M26' produce few tap roots and therefore need permanent staking to provide support and compensate for their lack of anchorage.

Pests and diseases

Common pests that may be troublesome include birds (p.657), wasps (p.659), codling moth (p.659), and aphids (p.646). The most common diseases that can affect apples include scab (p.658), powdery mildew (p.658), brown rot (p.658), bitter pit (see "Calcium deficiency", p.658), and *Nectria* canker (p.664).

PLANTING DISTANCES

Tree form	Rootstock	Distance between trees	Distance between rows
Bush	'M27'	1.2–2m (4–6ft)	2m (6ft)
	'M9'	2.5–3m (8–10ft)	3m (10ft)
	'M26'	3–4.25m (10–14ft)	5m (15ft)
	'MM106'	3.5–5.5m (11–18ft)	5.5m (18ft)
Half-standard	'MM111'	7.5–9m (24–28ft)	7.5–9m (24–28ft)
Standard	'MM111', 'M25' (or seedling crab)	7.5–10.5m (24–32ft)	7.5–10.5m (24–32ft)
Spindlebush	'M9' or 'M26' (and triploids on 'M27')	2–2.2m (6–7ft)	2.5–3m (8–10ft)
	'MM106'	2–2.2m (6–7ft)	4m (12ft)
Cordon	as bush	75cm (30in)	2m (6ft)
Fan/espalier	'M9'	3m (10ft)	
	'MM106'	4.25m (14ft)	
	'MM111'	5.5m (18ft)	
Dwarf pyramid	'M27'	1.2m (4ft)	2m (6ft)
	'M9' or 'M26'	1.5m (5ft)	2–2.2m (6–7ft)
	'MM106'	2m (6ft)	2.2m (7ft)

APPLE THINNING

1 *Thinning is essential if the tree is carrying a heavy crop. After the "June drop", which is a normal occurrence, the remaining fruits will need further thinning if the crop is still heavy.*

2 *Remove sufficient small fruitlets (especially any that are malformed or very small) to leave about 10–15cm (4–6in) between each and only one fruitlet per cluster.*

Pruning and training techniques

Apple trees produce flowers and fruit mainly on shoots that are two years old and older, and on short spurs that are produced on the older wood. Two-year-old shoots carry both large fruit buds and smaller, pointed growth buds. Fruit buds produce flower clusters and then fruit, while growth buds form into fruit buds for the following year or into sideshoots or fruiting spurs. One-year-old shoots may also carry fruit buds but these flower later than those that occur on older wood. Tip-bearing cultivars produce markedly fewer spurs (see below).

Once their branch framework is established, trained apple trees need to be pruned (mainly during the summer) in order to maintain the desired shape, curb vegetative growth, and stimulate the production of fruit buds. Untrained trees require moderate pruning during the winter to stimulate growth for the next season's fruit and to maintain an open and well-balanced structure so that they crop well and the fruit is of good quality.

FRUIT BUDS AND GROWTH BUDS

Fruit bud

Growth bud

Large fruit buds develop on 2-year-old and older wood. The smaller buds are growth buds, and are found mainly on one-year-old wood.

NICKING AND NOTCHING

Nicking
To weaken bud growth, make a nick in the bark just below the bud and into the cambium layer.

Notching
To stimulate bud growth, make a notch through the bark into the cambium layer just above the bud.

Tip bearers and spur bearers

Cultivars differ in the way they bear most of their fruit. Tip bearers carry much of the crop at, or near, the shoot tips, whereas spur bearers carry it along the whole shoot on short-jointed spurs from which further growth develops each year.

Tip bearers are not easily trained as cordons, espaliers, fans, or pyramids, because on each shoot there is bare, unproductive wood that limits the cropping capacity of the tree. They are best grown as standard, half-standard, or bush forms; once they are established, they need renewal pruning only (see p.438).

Nicking and notching

Sometimes it may be necessary to correct the balance of the branch framework of a trained tree; this may be achieved by nicking, which weakens the growth of a particular bud, or notching, which strengthens it. Notching may also be used to stimulate the production of side-shoots on bare lengths of stem.

Nicking and notching are most effective in spring when the sap is rising. Make a nick or a small incision with a sharp knife just below a bud to inhibit its growth; make a notch just above it to increase its vigour and stimulate new growth.

Bark-ringing

On excessively vigorous apple and pear trees (but not on stone fruits) that produce unsatisfactory crops, bark-ringing may be used as a last resort to curb vegetative growth and induce a greater fruit set. In late spring, remove a narrow band of bark from around the trunk through to the cambium layer at a height of about 1m (3ft). This reduces the flow of nutrients and hormones back to the roots, so that they are concentrated in the upper part of the tree.

Bark-ringing must be carried out carefully or the tree may die. First measure out the width of the band, which must be only 3mm (⅛in) on a small tree, graduating to no more than 1cm (½in) on a very large tree, then score the band with a knife. Cut through the bark and the cambium layer and remove the bark within the band down to the hardwood all the way round. Seal the wound at once with several layers of water-proof adhesive tape; it must cover the wound without touching the cambium layer.

BARK-RINGING

1 *Stick tape around the trunk as a guide for 2 parallel cuts. The ring may be 3mm–1cm (⅛–½in) wide, depending on the age and size of the tree.*

2 *The parallel cuts should be made through both the bark and the cambium layer. Carefully remove the ring of bark with the blunt side of the knife blade.*

3 *Wind water-proof tape around the ring so that it covers the wound without touching the cambium layer. Remove the tape when the wound has healed.*

The wound should heal over by the autumn, when the waterproof tape may be removed. The following year, the tree should produce much more blossom and, consequently, a much heavier crop of fruit because the reaction of any wounded plant is to reproduce.

Winter pruning

There are three main techniques for winter pruning, all of which stimulate new growth. Spur pruning and thinning should be carried out only on cultivars that produce plenty of spurs, not on tip bearers. Renewal pruning is appropriate for spindle-bushes and all tip bearers, as well as for vigorous cultivars that would be overstimulated by hard pruning. Regulated pruning is suited to cultivars that are naturally very vigorous, particularly triploids such as 'Bramley's Seedling', 'Blenheim Orange', and 'Jonagold'.

It may be necessary to vary the degree and type of pruning from year to year depending on the extent of growth, the quantity of fruit produced, and the age of the tree.
Spur pruning involves cutting back branch leaders and young laterals to stimulate the growth of sub-laterals and fruiting spurs. The extent of pruning required depends on the tree's vigour – the greater the vigour, the lighter the pruning, since pruning stimulates growth.

Shorten branch leaders on vigorous trees by no more than a few buds but on weaker ones by up to one third to stimulate new sub-laterals to form. Shorten young laterals to three or six buds where growth is good but to three or four buds on weaker trees so that spurs form. On a stronger tree, shoots up to 15cm (6in) long may be left unpruned.
Spur thinning is necessary as a tree ages to prevent fruits from becoming overcrowded. If left unthinned, the spurs become entangled and carry inferior fruit. When spur systems become congested, remove the older wood in favour of the younger. In time, it may be necessary to saw off whole spur systems.
Renewal pruning involves the annual cutting back of a proportion of older, fruited shoots to their base to stimulate the growth of new, young wood. Keep the centre of a bush tree open by pruning out any vigorous growth that is crossing or shading other laterals so that all the branches are well spaced. Remove a little, if any, of the tip from branch leaders and none at all on vigorous trees.
Regulated pruning consists of removing shoots and sometimes long sections of large branches that are crowded or crossing, particularly in the centre of the tree, to keep the branch framework open. Remove old wood to make room for young shoots. Do not tip prune the branch leaders.

Summer pruning

This is carried out to keep trained trees within their allotted space. It involves removing a large proportion of the new growth each summer to slow down vegetative growth.
The Modified Lorette System is the standard method of summer pruning in temperate climates with cool, un-predictable summers. It is carried out once the young shoots have become woody at the base. Maiden (new) laterals more than 22cm (9in) long that grow directly from the main stem or a main branch should be reduced to three leaves above the basal cluster. Prune back sideshoots arising from spurs and existing laterals to one leaf above the basal cluster. Continue to prune in this way as shoots mature. To help prevent

WINTER PRUNING
Spur pruning

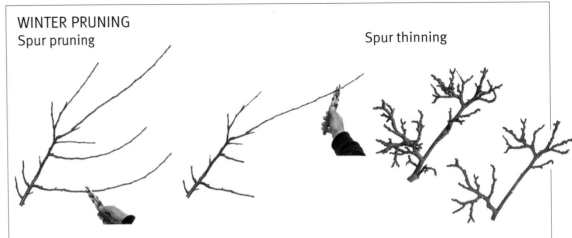

1 *Cut back young laterals to between 3 and 6 buds of the current growth, depending on the vigour of the shoot.*

2 *Prune back the current season's growth on branch leaders by one quarter to one third of their length.*

Spur thinning

On older trees, spur systems may become too dense. Thin these out by removing weak spurs and any on the undersides of the branches.

Renewal pruning

Prune out a good proportion of the older shoots that have already borne fruit (left). This will encourage new shoots to develop (right).

Regulated pruning

On this tree there is congested growth; correct this by removing any branches that are crossing or touching each other, and thinning out any sub-laterals or laterals that are overcrowded.

SUMMER PRUNING (MODIFIED LORETTE SYSTEM)

Prune trees when the lowest third of all new growth has become woody.

Cut back laterals on the main stems to 3 leaves above the basal cluster.

Basal cluster

Trim any side-shoots to 1 leaf.

Before pruning

After pruning

sideshoots, or secondary growths, from developing behind the pruning cut, leave a small number of the longer shoots unpruned; tie these shoots securely to other branches so that they are roughly horizontal and draw the sap down. Do not shorten any of them until after fruiting. Then, in mid-autumn, cut back any secondary growth shoots to one bud.

The Full Lorette System should be used in warmer climates. Prune back new laterals to about 5cm (2in), repeating at intervals through the summer. Shorten the laterals to 2cm (¾in) once they are woody at the base. Prune any secondary growths in late summer in the same way.

Bush

The open-centre or goblet-shaped bush is comparatively simple to maintain; it is ideal for larger gardens where there is plenty of space.

Formative pruning

Start with a well-feathered maiden tree; the laterals will form the first branches. After planting, while the tree is dormant, cut back the leader to a strong lateral 60–75cm (24–30in) above ground level, leaving at least two or three well-spaced laterals below it radiating out like the spokes of a wheel. These form the basis of the branch system; shorten them by two thirds, cutting to an upward-pointing bud. Remove all other laterals.

If a maiden whip is used, or a feathered maiden tree that has few or no suitable laterals, cut back the leader in winter to a strong bud 60–75cm (24–30in) from the base, then make a small nick under the top two buds; this depresses their growth and encourages shoots from the lower buds to grow at wider angles. Remove any unwanted laterals completely.

By the end of the following summer, three or four strong, healthy laterals should have developed to produce a plant equivalent to a pruned, feathered maiden.

Strong growth should develop the following summer. If one lateral grows faster than the others, tie it down nearly horizontally to slow its growth. Remove weak, inward-, and downward-growing shoots.

In the second winter, select several well-spaced growths arising from the original laterals to build up the branch framework, and shorten them by half, cutting to outward-facing buds. If any are not needed for the framework, shorten them to four or five buds, and remove altogether any shoots crossing the open centre. As growth continues in the second

APPLE BUSH
Year 1, Winter pruning

Prune back the leader to a selected lateral, leaving 2 or 3 strong laterals below it.

Cut back each of these laterals by two thirds to an upward-facing bud. Remove all other laterals.

Year 2, Winter pruning

Sub-laterals that are not needed for secondary branches should be pruned back to 4 or 5 buds.

Prune back branch leaders and well-placed sub-laterals by half to outward-facing buds.

Established bush, spur pruning in winter

Prune weak branch leaders, leaving half the previous season's growth. Strong branch leaders should be cut back by one quarter or less. Leave very vigorous leaders completely unpruned.

Cut back to 5 or 6 buds any young sideshoots growing from permanent branches to form spurs.

summer, remove any vigorous, upright shoots that unbalance the shape of the tree. By the third winter, the final branch formation should be established, with eight to ten main branches as well as several subsidiary ones.

Routine pruning

Only winter pruning (see p.438) is necessary for bushes once the framework is established; the pruning required will depend on the amount of growth made by the tree and on whether it is a tip or spur bearer. A tip bearer requires renewal pruning, while spur bearers require spur pruning and thinning.

Standard and half-standard

Few gardens are large enough to accommodate a standard or half-standard tree, but they make fine specimen trees where there is space.

Two or three years' training and pruning is needed to produce a clear stem of 1.2–1.3m (4–4½ft) for a half-standard, or 2–2.1m (6–6½ft)

Established bush, renewal pruning in winter

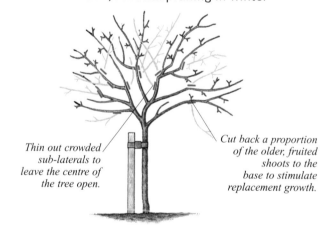

Thin out crowded sub-laterals to leave the centre of the tree open.

Cut back a proportion of the older, fruited shoots to the base to stimulate replacement growth.

for a standard. After planting a feathered maiden or maiden whip, tie in the leading shoot to a cane and cut any laterals hard back to 2.5cm (1in) in winter. In spring and summer, periodically pinch or cut back any feathers to a few leaves; this helps to thicken the main stem. Repeat this procedure in the second year.

In the following winter, remove most of the laterals and cut back the leader to the desired height, either

for a half-standard or standard; if the tree is not of the required height, grow it on for a third year. Several laterals should then develop below the cut; select and retain three or four well-spaced laterals to form the basic branch framework. Then train as for an open-centre bush (above).

Subsequent pruning of the tree is also as for a bush, but growth will be much stronger because the tree is grafted on a vigorous or extremely vigorous rootstock. Carry out regulated pruning on the established tree; it is only necessary to prune hard if the tree is not growing satisfactorily.

Spindlebush

A spindlebush is trained into the shape of a pyramid or cone, to a height of 2.2m (7ft); once it is established, only renewal pruning and pruning to keep the shape are required.

A number of variations of the spindlebush have been developed but the basic aim is to keep the three or four lowest branches dominant by removing shoots that would otherwise develop in the centre of the tree. Any shoots that do develop higher in the tree are allowed to fruit and are then pruned hard back, to be replaced by fresh growth.

Formative pruning

Plant a strong feathered maiden of a spur-bearing cultivar (see *Dessert Apples to Try*, p.436), supporting it with a 2m (6ft) stake. Cut back the leader in the winter to about 1m (3ft), or to just above the top-most lateral if this is higher. Select three or four vigorous and evenly spaced laterals that are about 60–90cm (2–3ft) from the base. Prune back each lateral by half to a downward-pointing, healthy bud and remove all other laterals.

If growth is strong, tie down any upright laterals towards the end of the first summer, in order to suppress growth and encourage the tree to fruit. If growth is weak, the upright laterals do not need to be tied down until the next summer.

Tie down the laterals with strong string secured to wooden or hooked metal pegs driven into the ground at an angle around the tree. If using wooden pegs, hammer a large "U" staple into the top of each one so that a string may be secured to it. Tie each string loosely so that it pulls down the branch to a 30° angle. Long branches may need to be tied in two places.

Remove any excessively vigorous shoots growing upwards from the main stem or laterals; do not attempt to tie them down since they may break. Train the central stem vertically by tying it to the stake.

The second winter after planting, shorten the central leader by one third of the new growth, cutting to a bud on the opposite side of the pruning cut made the previous winter. This helps to maintain a straight stem. Make sure that the strings are not constricting the tied-down shoots; once the growths have hardened and will remain in a more

or less horizontal position, remove the strings. The following summer, tie down some of the vertical shoots and remove completely any that are exceptionally vigorous or too close to the main stem, or that unbalance the branch framework.

By the third winter, laterals higher in the tree should have developed and been tied down to form further tiers of branches. They should be nearly horizontal, as this encourages early fruiting, and should not overshadow the lower framework branches if this can be avoided.

In the third summer, when the tree should produce fruit for the first time, tie down selected new side-shoots in late summer and remove any excessively strong shoots.

Routine pruning

From the fourth or fifth year onwards, renewal pruning (see p.438) is necessary in winter: shorten some of the old, fruited wood. Some of the shoots, particularly those that are higher in the tree, should be pruned hard back close to the trunk to encourage the development of replacement growths.

If the central leader is too vigorous, it may be cut back a little to a weaker lateral that will replace it. This concentrates vigour in the lower branches and helps to retain the pyramid shape, allowing maximum light to reach the fruits. In summer, continue cutting out completely any excessively vigorous and strongly upright-growing shoots.

Cordon

A spur-bearing feathered maiden may be trained as an oblique cordon on wires that are secured to posts or to a wall or fence. Tip bearers are not suitable as cordons (see "Tip bearers and spur bearers", p.437). Space three horizontal wires about 60cm (24in) apart; the lowest wire should be 75cm (30in) from the ground. Fix the wires about 10–15cm (4–6in) clear of the supporting wall or fence to allow free air circulation and so prevent the build-up of pests and diseases. Attach a cane to the wires at an angle of 45°, then plant a feathered maiden by it (see p.425) and tie in the main stem to the cane, using a figure-of-eight knot.

APPLE SPINDLEBUSH
Year 1, Winter pruning

Prune the leader by making an angled cut just above a suitable bud about 1m (3ft) from the ground.

Cut back 3 or 4 strong laterals by half to downward-facing buds. Remove other laterals.

Year 1, Summer pruning

Tie down each of the 3 or 4 main laterals to pegs in the ground so that the branches are at a 30° angle.

Cut to the base any vigorous upward-pointing laterals or sub-laterals.

Year 2, Summer pruning

Repeat summer pruning as for Year 1, concentrating on removing any upright growths.

Established spindlebush, Winter pruning

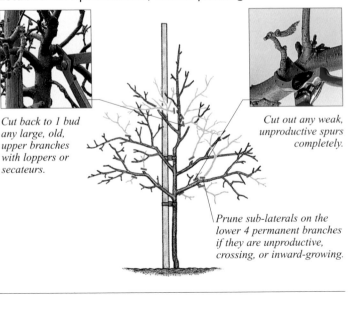

Cut back to 1 bud any large, old, upper branches with loppers or secateurs.

Cut out any weak, unproductive spurs completely.

Prune sub-laterals on the lower 4 permanent branches if they are unproductive, crossing, or inward-growing.

Formative pruning

In the winter immediately after planting, shorten to three or four buds all lateral shoots that are over 10cm (4in) in length. For tip-bearing cultivars, shorten the leader by about one third; do not attempt to prune the cordon further.

From the first summer onwards, prune the new shoots in mid- to late summer, once they have become woody at the base. Not all shoots ripen together, so pruning should continue over several weeks. Use the Modified or Full Lorette System (see "Summer pruning", pp.438–439).

Routine pruning

Winter pruning is essential to prevent congestion: reduce overgrown spur systems and remove completely those that are overcrowded. If the cordon is not producing enough well-spaced laterals, shorten the leader by about one quarter of its length to encourage strong growth.

Once a cordon has extended beyond the top wire, lower its angle of growth slightly to provide space for the leader to extend. When it reaches the top wire, trim it back to one leaf of new growth in late spring. Alternatively, if the leader is vigorous, cut it back in late spring to a sideshoot near the top wire.

Continue pruning on the Modified or Full Lorette System; on an established cordon, this largely involves cutting sideshoots to one leaf.

Double cordon

A double cordon is usually grown vertically. Feathered maidens and maiden whips may be trained as double cordons. The process is similar in each case, except that maiden whips must be pruned to stimulate low sideshoots before training can begin (see "Forming a double cordon", right). Alternatively, cut back a feathered maiden to two suitable and oppositely placed laterals. Tie them at about 30° to support canes and shorten by half. In summer, once a spacing of 45cm (18in) between the young leaders is attainable, turn and tie them to an upright position.

Fan

A wall or fence is an ideal support against which to grow a fan-trained apple tree; select a spur-bearing cultivar on a dwarfing rootstock so it may be comfortably accommodated in the available space. Tip bearers are not suitable to grow as fans (see "Tip bearers and spur bearers", p.437). Fix horizontal support wires about 15cm (6in) apart, starting at 38cm

APPLE CORDON
Year 1, Winter pruning

Cut back laterals that are over 10cm (4in) to 3 or 4 buds. Do not prune laterals that are shorter than this.

Year 1, Summer pruning

Once the bases of the shoots have become woody, prune all new laterals to 3 leaves.

Trim back any sideshoots to 1 leaf.

Established cordon, winter pruning

Thin spurs as they become congested on older cordons.

Established cordon, summer pruning

When the bases of the laterals have become woody, cut back the new growth to 1 leaf.

Trim any maiden laterals to 3 leaves.

Forming a double cordon from a maiden whip

To train a maiden whip as a double cordon, cut back the newly planted tree to about 24cm (10in) from soil level during the first winter, leaving a strong bud on either side below the cut. The following summer, when new shoots have been produced, tie the two uppermost shoots to canes at an angle of 45°, lowering them to 30° later in the season. When the tips of these shoots are more than 45cm (18in) apart, train them upwards by tying them to vertical canes.

Once the basic "U"-shape of the double cordon has been formed, the two vertical arms should each be pruned in the same way as a single cordon.

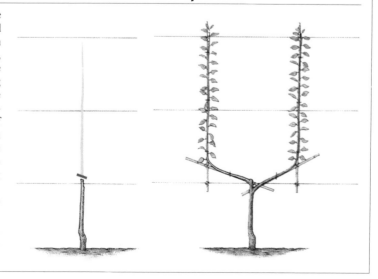

(15in) from soil level. The initial development of the framework is as for peaches (see p.453); once established, it should be pruned on the Modified Lorette System (see p.438) with each rib being treated like a single cordon.

Espalier

For this tree form, one or more pairs of opposite shoots are trained at right angles to the main stem onto support wires 38cm (15in) apart. An espalier usually has two or three tiers but more are possible with trees of sufficient vigour. If a maiden whip is used, the first tier may then be trained more readily at the required height. Only spur bearers are suitable to grow as espaliers (see "Tip bearers and spur bearers", p.437).

Formative pruning

After planting a maiden whip, prune back the leader to a bud just above the lowest wire. The following summer, train the uppermost shoot vertically to form a new leader; as the two strongest laterals below this develop, tie each to a cane at an angle of 45° to form the first branch tier. Cut or pinch back all other, lower shoots to two or three leaves. Tie down the laterals of the first tier into their horizontal position towards the end of the first growing season. If the two main arms develop unevenly, lower the more vigorous shoot to check growth and raise the weaker shoot to induce vigour. Once the two are balanced, tie them into their horizontal positions (see also *Training on Canes*, p.429).

The following winter, remove completely any laterals that have developed other than the main arms. To create the second tier, first look for two strong buds about 38cm (15in) above the first tier, then cut back the central leader to the bud above these. Shorten each first tier arm by one third to a downward-facing bud; where growth is very vigorous, leave the arm unpruned.

The bud to which each arm is cut back will produce a shoot that should be trained horizontally during the second summer after planting. Cut back other sub-laterals according to the Modified Lorette System (see p.438). The second pair of arms will form and these should be trained in the same way as the first pair. Repeat this process as necessary to obtain the required number of tiers.

Routine pruning

Once the arms of the top-most tier are well established, prune back the central leader in winter to just above

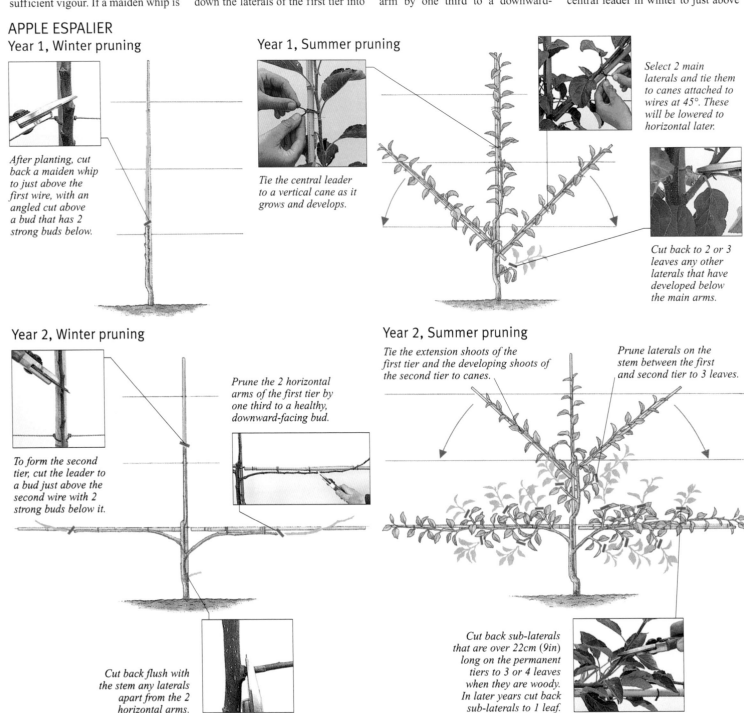

APPLE ESPALIER
Year 1, Winter pruning
After planting, cut back a maiden whip to just above the first wire, with an angled cut above a bud that has 2 strong buds below.

Year 1, Summer pruning
Tie the central leader to a vertical cane as it grows and develops.

Select 2 main laterals and tie them to canes attached to wires at 45°. These will be lowered to horizontal later.

Cut back to 2 or 3 leaves any other laterals that have developed below the main arms.

Year 2, Winter pruning
To form the second tier, cut the leader to a bud just above the second wire with 2 strong buds below it.

Prune the 2 horizontal arms of the first tier by one third to a healthy, downward-facing bud.

Cut back flush with the stem any laterals apart from the 2 horizontal arms.

Year 2, Summer pruning
Tie the extension shoots of the first tier and the developing shoots of the second tier to canes.

Prune laterals on the stem between the first and second tier to 3 leaves.

Cut back sub-laterals that are over 22cm (9in) long on the permanent tiers to 3 or 4 leaves when they are woody. In later years cut back sub-laterals to 1 leaf.

PICKING

Support the apple in the palm of the hand and twist it slightly. If the apple comes away easily from the spur, it is ready for picking.

this tier. The espalier should thereafter be pruned in summer following the Full or Modified Lorette System (see pp.438–439).

Dwarf pyramid

The dwarf pyramid is a compact tree form that is suitable for a small garden or container. Such a shape is suitable for spur-bearing cultivars (see "Tip bearers and spur bearers", p.437). It needs permanent staking if grown on an 'M27' or 'M9' rootstock; cultivars on other rootstocks need staking for four or five years. For pruning, see "Pear: Dwarf pyramid", p.445.

Secondary growth often develops after summer pruning. These unwanted shoots inhibit the formation of fruit buds, so prune two or three weeks later than usual to help retard their growth if this is a problem. If secondary growth continues to appear, leave one or two shoots unpruned to act as sap-drawers (see "Summer pruning", p.438).

Harvesting and storing

Early-ripening apples should be gathered just before they are fully ripe or they soon become mealy. Late-maturing cultivars must not be picked too soon, however, or the fruits will shrivel in store.

Wrap fruits individually in greaseproof paper and store them in slatted boxes or crates in a cool place (see p.431). Fruits from young or overvigorous trees store less well than those from more mature trees and should therefore be used first. For further information on harvesting and storing, see p.431.

Propagation

Apple trees may be propagated by chip-budding or T-budding in summer (see pp.432 and 433) or whip-and-tongue grafting in early spring (see p.433). If possible, use certified scions and rootstocks.

Grafting over

Grafting over is a technique used to graft scions of a selected cultivar onto an established apple or pear tree to replace the original cultivar or to create a "family" tree (see p.420). This is usually done to introduce a new pollinator for adjacent trees or to try a new cultivar; as the roots and main branch system are already established, the new cultivar should bear fruit quickly. There are two methods: top-working and frame-working.

Top-working

Initially, this entails heading (cutting) back most of the main branches to within 60–75cm (24–30in) of the main branch fork in spring. Leave one or two smaller branches unpruned to act as sap-drawers to reduce the number of new shoots that may form around the pruning cuts. Trim the cuts where branches have been sawn off. Two or three scions are used per branch but only the most vigorous one is grown on; the presence of the others may initially help to stop canker developing. These may be either rind- or cleft-grafted (the latter is rarely used by amateurs).

For rind grafting, take dormant scions from the previous season's growth of the desired cultivar and prepare them with angled top cuts and tapering basal cuts. Cut away a sliver of bark on the other side of the tapering cut to prevent the bark from being damaged when inserted into the branch. When rind grafting branches of about 2.5cm (1in) in diameter, place two scions opposite each other. Larger branches can accommodate three, evenly spaced scions. Make a vertical cut for each scion in the bark of the prepared branch. Carefully lift the bark and slide the scion into position underneath. Bind the graft firmly into position and seal the cut surfaces with grafting wax. Scion growth is rapid and ties must be released.

Retain the most vigorous scion and remove the others. Frequently, more than one shoot will develop from the selected scion; allow the best one to grow unchecked as the basis for the new branch. Shorten any others if they are less vigorous than the retained shoot but remove them completely if they are of equal vigour. After three or four years the new cultivar should start to crop regularly. Subsequently prune the new branch, according to the individual tree form.

Frame-working

In this method, most of the branch framework is retained and many scions are grafted onto different parts of the tree. Frame-working is preferred by commercial growers as trees crop more quickly than if top-worked.

HOW TO RIND GRAFT

1 *In early spring, cut off most of the main branches to within 60–75cm (24–30in) of the trunk. Leave 1 or 2 branches uncut to draw the sap.*

2 *Make a vertical cut 2.5cm (1in) long through the bark of one of the trimmed branches. If it is 2.5cm (1in) in diameter, make 2 evenly spaced cuts; if larger, make 3 cuts.*

3 *Use the blunt side of the knife blade to ease the bark away from the cambium layer.*

4 *Prepare scions 3 buds long, each with an angled cut at the top and a 2.5cm (1in) tapering cut at the base. Insert them with the tapering cut facing inwards.*

5 *When 2 or 3 scions have been inserted, bind the grafts tightly with strong string or grafting tape, winding it round the whole branch to hold the scions in place.*

6 *Apply grafting wax to the exposed areas. When the scions have united with the branch, retain the most vigorous and remove the others.*

Pears (*Pyrus communis* var. *sativa*)

Pears need more consistently warm conditions than apples to crop reliably. Late-ripening cultivars require dry and warm conditions throughout late summer and early autumn. They have a winter chilling requirement of 600–900 hours below 7°C (45°F).

Pears may be trained in a similar way to apples; bush, dwarf pyramid, cordon, and espalier forms are the most suitable for small gardens. They are usually grown on quince, rather than pear, rootstocks. Some new rootstocks are under trial (see also "Family trees", p.420).

DESSERT PEARS TO TRY

'Beth'

Early
'Beth' **Fg4, Sb,**☆
'Beurré d'Amanlis' **Fg2, Sb, T**
'Clapp's Favourite' **Fg4, Sb**
'Dr Jules Guyot' **Fg3, Sb**
'Doyenné d'Eté' **Fg2, Sb**
'Jargonelle' **Fg3, Rs, T, Tb**
'Williams' Bon Chrétien' **Fg3, Ig1, Sb, Ss**

Mid-season
'Abbé Fetel' **B, Fg3, Sb**
'Belle Guérandaise' **Fg2, Sb**
'Belle Julie' **Fg3, Sb**
'Beurré Hardy' **Fg3, Sb**
'Beurré Superfin' **Fg3, Sb,**☆
'Bristol Cross' **Fg4, Sb**
'Calebasse Bosc' **Fg4, Sb**
'Comte de Lamy' **Fg4, Sb**
'Concorde' **Fg4, Sb**
'Conference' **Fg3, Sb**
'Cosica' **Fg3, Tb**
'Doyenné du Comice' **Fg4, Ig2, Sb, Ss,**☆

'Conference'

'Fertility' **Fg3, Sb**
'Fondante d'Automne' **Fg3, Ig1, Sb,**☆
'Louise Bonne of Jersey' **Fg2, Ig1, Sb**
'Marie Louise' **Fg4, Sb**
'Merton Pride' **Fg3, Sb, T**
'Onward' **Fg4, Ig2, Sb,**☆

Key
B *Biennial bearing*
Fg *Flowering group (numbers indicate period of flowering)*
Ig *Incompatibility group (pears within each group will not pollinate each other)*
Rs *Some resistance to scab*
Sb *Spur bearer*
Ss *Scab susceptible*
T *Triploid (unsuitable as pollinator)*
Tb *Tip bearer or partial tip bearer*
☆ *Excellent flavour*

Site and planting

Pears flower earlier than apples, in mid- to late spring, and may be damaged by frosts. Pears are not fully self-fertile; cross-pollination is needed for a good crop.

Site

Pears require a warm, sheltered, and sunny site. The soil should retain moisture – particularly for trees on quince rootstocks (see below) – but must also be well drained; pears tolerate wetter conditions than apples. Trees on poor or sandy soils produce fruits of inferior flavour, while those on shallow soils overlying chalk may suffer from lime-induced chlorosis, a nutritional problem caused by deficiencies of manganese/iron (see p.651). Such sites may be improved by regularly mulching with large amounts of organic matter and occasionally applying chelated iron and manganese.

Rootstocks

As well as producing relatively small trees, growing pears on quince rootstocks induces early fruiting. 'Quince A' is moderately dwarfing (similar to 'M26' in apple); 'Quince C' is more dwarfing (similar to 'M9' in apple). A few cultivars, however, do not make a good union with quince rootstocks and may need double-working (see p.446).

Pollination

Provision for cross-pollination should always be made by planting two compatible cultivars. Some cultivars are triploid, and a very few are male sterile: these require two pollinators nearby. Incompatible cultivars are indicated in the lists *Dessert Pears to Try*, left and p.445, and *Culinary Pears to Try*, p.445.

Planting

Plant pears in autumn when the soil is still warm or by mid-winter at the latest. This allows trees to establish

ROOTSTOCKS

4m (12ft)
3m (9ft)
2m (6ft)
1m (3ft)

'Quince C'   'Quince A'

before coming into growth, which may occur very early in a mild spring. Planting distances (see below) depend on the choice of rootstock and the form in which the trees are grown (see "Pruning and training", right).

Routine care

Regular maintenance including fruit thinning, feeding and watering, and checking for pest and disease problems, is similar to that required for apples (see p.436). For general information, see pp.426–427.

Fruit thinning

After the natural shedding of fruitlets at or soon after mid-summer, thin out to leave one fruit per cluster if the crop is heavy, but two if cropping is lighter.

Feeding, watering, and mulching

Water and fertilize trees as needed (see p.426). It is particularly important to give pears adequate nitrogen: in spring, apply light dressings of up to 35g/sq m (1oz/sq yd) of ammonium sulphate to maintain levels during the growing season. Mulch around newly planted trees in spring.

Pests and diseases

Pears may be affected by birds (p.657), rabbits and hares (p.666), wasps (p.659), aphids (p.646), winter moth caterpillars (p.645), fireblight (p.649), pear midge (p.658), scab (p.649), and brown rot (p.658). Pear leaf blister mites produce pustules in the leaves, and gall mites (p.652) cause blackish-brown leaf blotches

and stunted leaves. Some pears, especially 'Conference', may develop parthenocarpic fruits. These have a cylindrical shape and may be produced when partial fertilization has occurred; the fruit grows but is misshapen. Treat by providing a suitable pollinator and giving shelter to encourage more pollinating insects.

Pruning and training

Pruning requirements and techniques are similar to those for apples, but pears tolerate harder pruning once they have started to crop. Fruiting occurs predominantly on two-year-old and older wood. On pears, spur production is usually more prolific than on apples, and spurs should be thinned regularly on established trees. Very few pear cultivars are tip bearers.

Training and pruning to develop a cordon or an espalier are as for apples. Both are pruned by the Modified Lorette System in temperate areas or, in warmer climates, by the Full Lorette System (see "Apples: Summer pruning", pp.438–439). A fan is formed in the same way as for peaches (see p.453) but, once established, prune as for an apple fan (see p.441). Pears should be pruned two or three weeks earlier than apples, once shoots mature at the base.

Where excessive vigour occurs at the expense of cropping, root pruning (see p.430) where practicable or, as a last resort, bark-ringing (see p.437) may be carried out.

Bush

Initial training and pruning of a bush are as for apples (see p.439). Several pear cultivars (for example 'Doyenné du Comice') have an upright growth habit; when pruning branch leaders of these cultivars, cut to an outward-pointing bud. Shoots that are upright should be tied down before they ripen fully at the base, as part of the initial training process, to encourage a wider angle of growth. Pruning on very vigorous trees should be much lighter after the second year. Where vigour is lacking, shorten new laterals to five or six buds or fewer.

The few tip bearers (for example, 'Jargonelle' and 'Joséphine de Malines') need to be renewal pruned as described for tip-bearing apples (see p.437). Established spur-bearing trees need considerable spur shortening and thinning, and occasional branch thinning, in winter.

PLANTING DISTANCES

Tree form	Rootstock	Distance between trees	Distance between rows
Bush	'Quince C'	3.5m (11ft)	5.5m (18ft)
	'Quince A'	4.75m (14ft)	5.5m (18ft)
Cordon	'Quince A' or 'C'	75cm (30in)	2m (6ft)
Espalier	'Quince C'	3.5m (11ft)	
	'Quince A'	4.75m (14ft)	
Fan	As espalier	As espalier	
Dwarf pyramid	'Quince C'	1.2m (4ft)	2m (6ft)
	'Quince A'	1.5m (5ft)	2m (6ft)

Dwarf pyramid

Prune back the leading shoot of a feathered maiden after planting to 50–75cm (20–30in) from the ground, and reduce any laterals to 15cm (6in); remove weak or low laterals. In the first summer, prune extension growth on the laterals, and any new laterals, to five or six leaves to downward-facing buds. This encourages horizontal growth and induces early fruiting. Cut back sub-laterals to three leaves. The following winter, prune the leading shoot to leave 25cm (10in) of the new growth, cutting to a bud on the opposite side to that of the previous year's pruning. In each subsequent year, prune the leader to buds on alternate sides. When the leader reaches the required height, prune back in late spring to leave one bud of the new growth.

Once the initial framework has been formed, nearly all pruning is carried out in mid- to late summer, depending on season and location. It

PEAR, DWARF PYRAMID
Year 1, Winter pruning

Cut back the leader with an angled cut just above a bud, 50–75cm (20–30in) from the ground.

Prune back each lateral to a downward-facing bud about 15cm (6in) from the main stem.

Cut back entirely any low laterals on the main stem.

Year 1, Summer pruning

Cut back new growth at the tips of the main laterals to 5 or 6 leaves on the extension growth.

Prune new laterals growing directly from the main stem to 5 or 6 leaves.

Cut back any sub-laterals growing from the main laterals to 3 leaves. These will start to form spurs for the following summer.

Year 2, Winter pruning

Prune the previous season's growth on the leader to about 25cm (10in).

Year 2 and routine summer pruning

Trim sub-laterals from existing laterals or spurs to 1 leaf beyond the basal cluster.

Cut back new growth at the ends of the permanent branches to 5 or 6 leaves.

Cut back laterals growing from the main branches to 3 leaves.

Established dwarf pyramid, winter pruning

When the leader reaches the required height, prune it to 1 bud of the previous season's growth.

Before
The spurs on the darker wood at the base of this shoot are congested and require thinning.

After
Thin by removing any unproductive or overlapping spurs. Trim out excess fruit buds to leave 2 or 3 evenly spaced buds per spur.

DESSERT PEARS TO TRY (CONT.)

Mid-season (cont.)
'Packham's Triumph' **Fg2, Sb**
'Pitmaston Duchess' **Fg4, Sb, T**
'Santa Claus' **Fg4, Sb**
'Seckle' **Fg2, Ig1, Sb,☆**
'Thompson's' **Fg3, Sb**

Late
'Bergamotte Esperen' **Fg3, Sb**
'Beurré d'Anjou' **Fg2, Sb**
'Easter Beurré' **Fg2, Sb**
'Glou Morceau' **Fg4, Sb**
'Joséphine de Malines' **Fg3, Tb**
'Olivier de Serres' **Fg3, Sb**
'Passe Crasanne' **Fg2, Sb**
'Winter Nelis' **Fg4, Sb,☆**

CULINARY PEARS TO TRY

Mid-season
'Beurré Clairgeau' **Fg2, Sb**

Late
'Bellissime d'Hiver' **Fg2, Sb**
'Black Worcester' **Fg3, Sb**
'Catillac' **Fg4, Sb, T**
'Double de Guerre' **Fg4, Sb**
'Uvedale's St Germain' **Fg2, Sb, T**
'Vicar of Winkfield' **Fg2, Sb, T**

'Joséphine de Malines'

'Catillac'

Key
Fg *Flowering group (numbers indicate period of flowering)*
Ig *Incompatibility group (pears within each group will not pollinate each other)*
Sb *Spur bearer*
T *Triploid (unsuitable as pollinator)*
Tb *Tip bearer or partial tip bearer*
☆ *Excellent flavour*

is important that shoots have grown woody at their base before they are pruned; the operation is therefore spread over three or four weeks and a few shoots may not be ready to prune until early autumn. Do not shorten shoots that are 15cm (6in) or less in length. Cut back branch leaders to six leaves of new growth and prune any sub-laterals to one leaf above the basal cluster. Any shoots arising directly from the main branches should be shortened to three leaves. If secondary growth develops, leave a few shoots unpruned as for apples (see "Summer pruning", p.438) to draw the sap.

The only major operation for winter pruning is the shortening of the central leader already described plus, in later years, some spur thinning and shortening. If the spur systems are allowed to become congested, the tree loses vigour and small, overcrowded fruits are produced.

Harvesting and storing

Time of picking is most important, especially for cultivars that ripen in late summer and early autumn. If left on the tree too long, the fruits will have turned "sleepy" and brown at the centre. Gather them at the first sign of a change of ground colour on the skin from dark to slightly lighter green. If in doubt, gently lift and twist

a fruit: if it comes away easily, it is almost ripe and will be at peak flavour in a few days. If the stalk breaks, wait for some days longer. Several harvests need to be made because all fruits do not ripen simultaneously. Fruits of late-ripening cultivars and those grown in cool climates must be left on the tree until mature to develop their full flavour.

Store pears in cool conditions, laying them in slatted boxes; do not wrap otherwise the flesh discolours. The fruits of later-ripening cultivars should be conditioned before eating: keep them at room temperature for a day or two and eat when the flesh gives under gentle pressure by the thumb near to the stalk. The flavour should then be at its fullest.

Propagation

For most pear cultivars, whip-and-tongue grafting or chip- or T-budding (see "Propagation", p.432) onto a 'Quince A' or 'Quince C' rootstock is usually successful. Grafting over may also be used to change the cultivar of an existing tree to another, preferable cultivar (see p.443).

Double-working pear cultivars

The few pear cultivars that are incompatible with quince rootstocks need to be double-worked: a cultivar that is compatible with both the quince rootstock and the selected scion cultivar is used as an "interstock" between the two. The cultivar 'Beurré Hardy' is the most widely used interstock; 'Vicar of Winkfield', 'Pitmaston Duchess', and 'Beurré d'Amalis' may also be used for all pear cultivars that require double-working. These include 'Dr Jules Guyot', 'Souvenir de Congrès', 'Marguerite Marillat', 'Williams' Bon Chrétien', 'Marie Louise', 'Packham's Triumph', and 'Thompson's'. Two methods of double-working may be used: double chip-budding and double grafting.

Double chip-budding entails carrying out chip-budding two years in succession: in the first

Double budding
Insert the bud chip 5cm (2in) above the first graft and on the opposite side, so that the resulting stem will grow out straighter when the bud develops. Cut off the interstock above the new bud once the scion shoot has developed. Remove any shoots on the interstock.

year, a scion of the interstock is budded onto a quince rootstock; in the second year, a scion of the selected cultivar is budded onto the interstock on the opposite side. The method is as for chip-budding (see p.432).

For double grafting the same principle is followed. Graft the interstock onto the quince rootstock in early spring using the whip-and-

Double grafting
This follows the same principle as double budding: cut back the interstock a year after it is grafted, once the sap starts to rise, and graft on the required scion. Leave 5cm (2in) between grafts; position the scion graft on the opposite side from the previous one.

tongue method (see p.433). In late winter or early spring, cut back the grafted interstock and graft the incompatible cultivar scion onto the interstock. Alternatively, it may be budded onto the interstock in summer, following the grafting of the interstock in spring. Remove shoots from the interstock but retain those from the cultivar scion.

Quinces (*Cydonia oblonga*)

Quinces are fruits grown mainly in temperate regions. As bushes, they reach 3.4–5m (10–15ft); they may also be trained as fans. The apple- or pear-shaped fruits are covered with greyish-white down. The most widely grown cultivars are 'Meech's Prolific' and 'Vranja', and there are also some promising, newly introduced cultivars. Quinces have a chilling requirement of 100–450 hours below 7°C (45°F) in order to flower.

Site and planting

Quinces require a reasonably sunny, sheltered site. The protection provided by a wall may be beneficial in cold areas. Moisture-retentive, slightly acidic soils are preferred; marked alkalinity usually causes lime-induced chlorosis.

'Quince A' is normally used as a rootstock. Where trees are grown on their own roots, suckering may be difficult to control. Quinces are generally self-fertile but the provision of pollinators is claimed

to improve cropping levels. Plant quinces in autumn or winter if bare-root, or throughout the year if container-grown, spacing them about 4–4.5m (12–15ft) apart.

Routine care

Cultivation requirements are as described under "Care of tree fruits", p.426. Once established, quinces need little attention. Occasional feeding at the standard rate may be necessary, particularly on poor soils, while watering and mulching may also be required. Quinces are comparatively easy to grow but fungal leaf spots (p.648) may be troublesome.

Pruning and training

Quinces fruit on spurs and on the tips of the previous summer's growth. Bushes may be left to grow into multi-stemmed trees or pruned in the early stages as for apple bushes (see p.439) with an open-centred, well-spaced branch framework. Pruning of established trees is minimal, with

occasional thinning in winter of old, overcrowded growth. Not every lateral should be pruned, however, since this removes too many fruit buds.

Harvesting and storing

Pick the fruits when the skins have turned from green to gold, usually in late autumn. Store in boxes in a cool, well-ventilated, dark place. Do not wrap the fruits: quinces stored in plastic bags will discolour internally.

Quince tree
Leave a generous grass-free area around young quinces, so that all the nutrients are absorbed by the trees and not shared with the grass.

Because quinces have a strong aroma, they should be stored separately, so that they do not contaminate other fruits. They are often used in preserves.

Propagation

Quince trees may be propagated either by chip-budding onto 'Quince A' rootstocks in summer (see p.432) or by taking hardwood cuttings in autumn (see p.434).

Medlars (*Mespilus germanica*)

Medlars are decorative, spreading trees with golden autumn colour and large, white or pinkish-white flowers in mid- to late spring. They are most commonly grown as bushes, or as half-standards. Recommended cultivars are 'Dutch', 'Large Russian', and 'Nottingham'. Medlars are self-fertile and have a chilling requirement of 100–450 hours below 7°C (45°F). The fruits are apple-shaped and somewhat flattened with prominent, horny calyces. The fruits are used for preserves.

Ripening medlars
The small, brown fruits ripen in autumn and measure 2.5–5cm (1–2in) across.

Site and planting
A sunny, sheltered site is preferable, although medlars tolerate partial shade. They may be grown in a wide range of soils, with the exception of those that are very chalky or badly drained. Adequate moisture is essential to obtain strong growth and a good crop of fruits.

Trees grown for the quality of their fruits are usually grafted on 'Quince A' rootstocks, although half-standards are sometimes available on seedling pear rootstocks.

Medlar trees are best planted in late autumn to winter. Half-standards should be spaced at a distance of 8m (25ft), and bushes at 4.25m (14ft).

Routine care
Cultivation requirements are generally as for apples (see p.436). Medlars may sometimes be affected by leaf-eating caterpillars (p.645) and fungal leaf spots (p.648).

Pruning and training
Train a bush tree as for apples (see p.439). For half-standards, pruning is initially as for apples. Once the main framework is established, occasionally thin branches in winter to maintain an open framework, removing overcrowded, diseased, or dead growth.

Harvesting and storing
Leave fruits on the tree for as long as possible so that they develop their full flavour. Pick them in late autumn

Medlars

when the stalk parts easily from the tree, preferably in dry weather. The fruits are unpalatable immediately after picking, and must be stored before use. Dip the stalks in a strong salt solution to prevent rotting, then store the fruits, calyces downwards, on slatted trays, so that the fruits do not touch. Use when the flesh has become soft and brown.

Propagation
Propagate by chip- or T-budding (see pp.432 and 433), or whip-and-tongue grafting (see p.433).

Plums, gages, damsons, and bullaces (*Prunus* x *domestica*)

Various kinds of plum are grown for their fine fruits. These include: European plums (selections of *Prunus* x *domestica*); damsons, Mirabelles, and bullaces (*P. insititia*); gages (*P.* x *domestica* and *P. insititia*); cherry plums (*P. cerasifera*); and the Japanese or Salicine plums (*P. salicina*).

Regions with cool-temperate climates are ideal for European plums, damsons, and bullaces; in warmer areas with earlier springs, Japanese plums and Mirabelles are more widely grown. All types of plum prefer areas that have plenty of sun and relatively low rainfall. Cherry plums, or myrobalan, are rarely grown for their fruit, but are often used as vigorous rootstocks for a number of fruiting plums, and for some ornamental trees.

There is a wide range of cultivars adapted to different climates and, with more dwarfing rootstocks now available, plums are ideal for even small gardens; damsons usually make smaller trees than plums. The compact pyramid tree and dwarf bush forms are particularly suitable for small gardens; for the choicest fruit in cool climates, grow fan-trained trees on warm, sunny walls. European plums and damsons have a chilling requirement of 700–1,000 hours below 7°C (45°F), and the Japanese plum one of 500–900 hours.

Site and planting
Plums need a warm, sheltered site to ensure that the flowers are pollinated successfully. Their pollination requirements are complex – some cultivars are self-fertile while others require suitable pollinators planted nearby. Make sure that there is enough room on the proposed site for the required number of trees, allowing for their mature height.

Site
All plums flower early in spring, Japanese plums markedly so and cherry plums earlier still, so that spring frosts are always a hazard. They are, therefore, best planted in a relatively frost-free site. Plums need to be sheltered from wind to avoid damage to the trees and also to encourage pollinating insects.

Most soils are suitable, but avoid those that are very chalky and poorly drained. Plums on poor, sandy soils need extra feeding and watering to maintain good growth and cropping, and to improve flavour (see "Feeding, watering, and mulching", p.448).

Rootstocks
'Pixy' (semi-dwarfing) and 'St Julien A' (moderately vigorous) are best for small to medium-sized plum trees, 2.2–4m (7–12ft). For trees up to

ROOTSTOCKS

4m (12ft)			
3m (9ft)			
2m (6ft)			
1m (3ft)			
'Pixy'	'St Julien A'	'Brompton'	'Myrobalan B'

4.25m (14ft), choose 'Myrobalan B' (incompatible with some cultivars) or 'Brompton' (universally compatible). 'Marianna' is excellent for Japanese plums, but is incompatible with some European plums. Plums tend to produce suckers, but this is less common with modern rootstocks.

Pollination
European plums and damsons may be self-fertile, partially self-fertile, or self-sterile. Fortunately, some very popular cultivars, such as 'Victoria', are self-fertile, but planting suitable pollinators nearby will ensure more consistent cropping. Cultivars that are

not self-fertile must always be planted with compatible pollinators nearby. Cherry plums are self-fertile. Some Japanese plums are self-fertile, but most give better results when planted near a suitable pollinator. Plum cultivars that will not pollinate certain others are indicated in the lists of recommended cultivars on pp.448 and 449, which also give details of flowering times. Seek advice about pollination of individual trees when buying.

Planting
This should be completed as early as possible in late autumn or early

PLANTING DISTANCES

Tree form	Rootstock	Distance between trees	Distance between rows
Bush	'St Julien A'	4–5m (12–15ft)	5.5m (18ft)
Half-standard	'Brompton' or 'Myrobalan B'	5.5–7m (18–22ft)	7m (22ft) minimum
Fan	'St Julien A'	5–5.5m (15–18ft)	
Pyramid	'St Julien A' or 'Pixy'	2.5–4m (8–12ft)	4–6m (12–20ft)

DESSERT PLUMS AND GAGES TO TRY

Early
'Blue Rock' **Fg1, I, Psf**
'Early Laxton' **Fg3, Psf**
'Edda' **Cu, Fg3, Ss**
'Opal' **Fg3, Sf**
'Sanctus
   Hubertus'
   Fg3, Sf

'Opal'

Mid-season
'Avalon' **Fg2, Ss**
'Blue Tit' **Fg5, Sf**
'Cambridge Gage'
   Fg4, I, Psf,☆
'Count Althann's Gage'
   Fg4, Ss,☆
'Early Transparent Gage'
   Fg4, Sf,☆
'Excalibur' **Fg3, Ss**   'Cambridge
'Goldfinch' **Fg3, Psf**   Gage'
'Imperial Gage' **Fg2, Sf**
'Jefferson' **Fg1, I, Ss,☆**
'Kirke's' **Fg4, Ss,☆**
'Laxton's Gage' **Fg3, Sf**
'Merton Gem' **Fg3, Psf**
'Ontario' **Fg4, Sf**
'Oullins Gage' **Fg4, Sf**
'Reine Claude Vraie' **Fg5, I, Ss,☆**
'Royale de Vilvoorde' **Fg5, Ss, ☆**
'Utility' **Fg1, Psf**
'Victoria' **Cu, Fg3, Sf, Sls**

Late
'Angelina Burdett'
   Fg1, Psf,☆
'Anna Späth'
   Fg3, Psf
'Ariel' **Fg2, Psf**
'Bryanston Gage'
   Fg3, Ss
'Coe's Golden Drop'
   Fg2, Ss,☆   'Victoria'
'Golden Transparent'
   Fg3, I, Sf,☆
'Late Muscatelle' **Fg3, Ss, ☆**
'Late Transparent' **Fg5, Ss,☆**
'Laxton's Delight' **Fg3, Psf,☆**
'Reine Claude de Bavay'
   Fg2, Sf,☆
'Reine Claude Violette', syn.
   'Purple Gage' **Fg3, Psf,☆**
'Severn Cross' **Fg3, Sf**
'Washington' **Fg3, Ss,☆**

Key
Cu *Also for culinary
        use*
Fg *Flowering group
        (numbers indicate
        period of flowering)*
I   *Cultivars in this
        group may be*
        incompatible   'Coe's
J   *Japanese*   Golden
Psf *Partly self-fertile*   Drop'
Sf *Self-fertile*
Sls *Silver leaf susceptible*
Ss *Self-sterile*
☆   *Excellent flavour*

winter as growth starts early in spring. All trees are best staked for two years; stake those on 'Pixy' rootstocks permanently. Planting distances (see p.447) are determined by the chosen tree form and by the vigour of the rootstock.

Routine care

Feed and water trees regularly, and check for pests and diseases. Thin fruit as necessary. If spring frosts are likely, protect wall-trained trees in bloom with a cover (see FROST AND WIND PROTECTION, pp.612–613).

Fruit thinning
Thinning gives larger, better-flavoured fruits and reduces the risk of branches breaking from the weight of too many fruits. Fruitlets may be thinned early if the set is heavy. After the stones have formed and natural fruit drop has occurred, thin the remaining fruit to about 5–8cm (2–3in) apart for small fruits and 8–10cm (3–4in) for larger cultivars (such as 'Victoria'). Scissors are best for this job since they are quicker to use than secateurs.

Feeding, watering, and mulching
Plums need plenty of nitrogen; apply a spring dressing at the rate recommended under "Care of tree fruits", p.426. Mulch annually with well-rotted manure or compost, and water as required, particularly in prolonged hot weather. Plums planted against walls or fences will need more regular watering than those in the open.

Pests and diseases
Plums may be attacked by rabbits and hares (p.666), wasps (p.659), aphids (p.646), and winter moth caterpillars (p.645). Diseases that may affect plums include silver leaf (p.647), bacterial canker (p.665), and brown rot (p.658). Any trees that are badly

infected with silver leaf, bacterial canker, or (less commonly) with viruses (p.649) should be dug up and burnt without delay. Plum pox (sharka) is a particularly serious virus that reduces yields and can be seen as blotches on fruits and leaves.

All stone fruit trees may be affected by the physiological disorder known as gumming. Trees that have this problem exude a translucent, amber-coloured, gum-like substance from the trunk and branches, while plums may also form gum around the stone within the fruit. The gum is produced by the trees as a result of stress that is caused by disease, adverse soil conditions, or physical damage caused by, for example, strong winds or a heavy crop. If gumming is noticed, try to identify the cause and alleviate the problem if possible.

Birds may also be troublesome; if they attack the fruit buds, it may be necessary to place fine mesh nets over the trees during the winter to prevent damage (see also p.657).

PLUM BUSH
Year 1, Early spring pruning

Prune back 3 or 4 laterals by about two thirds to a half, cutting to outward-facing buds.

Cut off any laterals below those selected flush with the main stem.

Prune out the leader above the top-most selected lateral, using an angled cut.

Pruning and training

Plum trees produce fruit at the base of one-year-old shoots, as well as on two-year-old wood and spurs. Once initially trained, they require less pruning on unrestricted forms than apples or pears. In cool-temperate climates it is essential to prune in summer (after training) to minimize the risk of silver leaf (p.647). Trained trees require routine summer pruning to maintain their restricted shape. Remove any damaged or diseased branches immediately, cutting back to healthy wood.

Bush
In early spring when the buds are breaking, start training a newly planted feathered maiden. Select three or four strong, evenly spaced laterals, the highest at about 90cm (3ft) from ground level, and prune them by about two thirds or a half, to healthy, outward-facing buds. These laterals will form the basic framework

Year 2, Early spring pruning

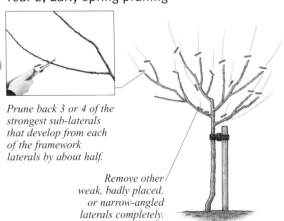

Prune back 3 or 4 of the strongest sub-laterals that develop from each of the framework laterals by about half.

Remove other weak, badly placed, or narrow-angled laterals completely.

Fruiting habit

Plum trees develop fruit at the base of one-year-old shoots and then along the stems on two-year-old wood and spurs.

of branches. Then prune out the leader, making an angled cut above the highest of the selected laterals. Cut back to the main stem unwanted laterals below those selected.

The following early spring, choose three or four of the strongest sub-laterals that have developed on each of the pruned laterals and shorten them by half. To achieve a balanced framework, trim off weak or badly placed laterals and pinch out any shoots growing from the main stem. Subsequently, restrict pruning of young trees to the removal in summer of excessively vigorous or awkwardly placed growths. With older trees, thin some branches in summer to avoid overcrowding, and seal wounds with bituminous paint.

If using a maiden whip, prune it to about 90cm (3ft). The following spring, laterals should have developed, and it may then be trained as a feathered maiden.

Half-standard
Choose three or four well-spaced laterals on a feathered maiden; cut back the leader just above the uppermost lateral at 1.3m (4½ft), then prune each of the chosen laterals by one third to a half. Remove any lower laterals. Subsequent pruning of the sub-laterals and training to form an open-centre head is the same as for a bush. Half-standard trees are less easy to manage than pyramid or bush plums when mature because of their greater size.

Spindlebush
Similar in shape to a plum pyramid (see p.450), the spindlebush requires a little more space but does not need the same annual summer pruning. Pruning and training are as for apple spindlebushes (see p.440) but prune in early spring when the buds break.

Tie down upright shoots and keep the top of the tree in check by removing the more vigorous shoots and retaining the less vigorous ones to produce fruit. In this way the conical shape is maintained.

Fan
Train a plum fan initially as for a peach fan (see p.453) to produce main branches or ribs to train against horizontal support wires. When

CULINARY PLUMS TO TRY

Early
'Czar' **Fg3, Sf, Sls**
'Rivers's Early Prolific' **Fg3, I, Psf**
'Pershore' **Fg3, Sf**
'Sanctus Hubertus' **Fg3, Psf**

Mid-season
'Belle de Louvain' **Fg5, Sf**
'Cox's Emperor' **Fg3, Psf**
'Purple Pershore' **Fg3, Sf**

'Marjorie's Seedling'

Late
'Giant Prune' **Fg4, Sf**
'Marjorie's Seedling' **Fg5, Sf**
'Warwickshire Drooper' **Fg2, Sf**

DAMSONS TO TRY

Early
'Merryweather' **Fg3, Sf**

Mid-season
'Bradley's King' **Fg4, Sf**
'Farleigh' **Fg4, Psf**
'Prune'

Late
'Fogmore Damson' **Fg5, Psf**
'Prune' **Fg5, Sf, ☆**

Key
Fg *Flowering group (numbers indicate period of flowering)*
I *Cultivars in this group may be incompatible*
Psf *Partly self-fertile*
Sf *Self-fertile*
Sls *Silver leaf susceptible*
☆ *Excellent flavour*

ESTABLISHED PLUM FAN
Spring pruning

Thin new sideshoots to about 10cm (4in) apart.

Cut out any sideshoots that are growing towards the centre of the fan or are badly placed.

Summer pruning

Tie in any ribs needed to extend the framework or replace older wood.

Cut back sideshoots that are not needed for the permanent rib framework to 5 or 6 leaves.

Cut back wrong-pointing or awkward shoots to shoots facing in the required direction or flush with the rib.

AFTER FRUITING

In the autumn, after the fruit has been harvested, prune back to 3 leaves all the sideshoots that were shortened to 5 or 6 leaves earlier in the summer.

training the young fan, retain some sideshoots to fill in gaps and pinch back others to one bud. Remove any very vigorous sideshoots or those growing at an awkward angle.

On an established fan, in spring or as soon as they appear, remove sideshoots growing inwards towards the wall or fence, or the centre of the fan. Thin the remainder to 10cm (4in) apart and pinch or cut them back to six leaves during the summer unless they are required to fill spaces in the fan framework. After the crop has been picked, shorten these shoots to three leaves.

Pyramid

Plant a feathered maiden against a strong stake and, in early spring, cut back the central leader to a healthy bud at a height of about 1.5m (5ft). Remove any laterals growing below 45cm (18in) from the ground. Shorten the remaining laterals over 22cm (9in) long by half their length. When the bases of the young shoots are turning woody later in the summer, cut back extension growth on the main branches and new (maiden) laterals, to about 20cm (8in); at the same time, reduce sub-laterals to about 15cm (6in). To start forming the pyramid shape, cut main branches and sub-laterals back to downward-facing buds so that growth is more or less horizontal. Remove any laterals that are very vigorous or upward-pointing. Tie in the central leader to the stake, but do not prune it until the following spring, then shorten it by two-thirds of its new growth. Once the tree has reached a height of about 2m (6ft) on 'Pixy' or 2.5m (8ft) on 'St Julien A', cut back the central leader. This should be delayed until late spring, however, since this reduces its subsequent growth; cut it back to a bud about 2.5cm (1in) from the old wood. Continue annual summer pruning as previously described, cutting branch leaders to downward-pointing buds and removing any excessively vigorous, upright shoots, especially those growing in the upper parts of the tree, to maintain the pyramid shape.

On mature pyramids, overcrowding will develop; in summer, trim off any badly placed, old wood as necessary. Maintain the pyramid shape by keeping any vigorous or dominant upper branches in check.

Harvesting and storing

For the best flavour, allow fruits to ripen fully; for freezing or preserving, pick them when ripe but still firm. In wet weather, gather the ripening crop before brown rot or wasps spoil it. Split skins may occur with some cultivars in moist conditions. Keep the fresh fruits in a cool, dark place and use within a few days.

Propagation

Chip- or T-budding is most usual (see pp.432 and 433); whip-and-tongue grafting (see p.433) is less reliable for plums than for apples and pears.

PLUM PYRAMID
Year 1, Early spring pruning

Cut back the leader with an angled cut above a strong bud about 1.5m (5ft) from soil level.

Prune the remaining laterals by half to downward-facing buds.

Remove completely any laterals less than 45cm (18in) from soil level.

Year 1, Summer pruning

Any new laterals forming too narrow an angle with the main stem should be removed. Do not prune the central leader.

Cut back any sub-laterals to 15cm (6in) with an angled cut just above a leaf.

Cut back new growth at the tips of the main branches to about 20cm (8in) and to a downward-pointing bud.

Year 2, Early spring pruning

Just before bud burst, shorten the central leader by two thirds of its new growth.

Established pyramid, summer pruning

Remove any sub-laterals that are crossing or overcrowded.

Repeat the routine summer pruning of main branches and sub-laterals.

Cut back any dead or unproductive wood to a healthy shoot or to the point of origin.

Peaches and nectarines (*Prunus persica* and *P. persica* var. *nectarina*)

Peaches and nectarines are grown in many temperate regions. They have a chilling requirement of 600–900 hours below 7°C (45°F). Sunny, reasonably dry summers are essential to produce good crops; in cooler climates, peaches may be grown under cover. A range of cultivars is available for different climates (see *Peaches to Try*, right, and *Nectarines to Try*, p.452); they are yellow-, pink-, or white-fleshed. On cling peaches the flesh tends to cling to the stone; other peaches are known as freestone. The nectarine is a smooth-skinned form of the peach and requires very similar treatment, although it prefers slightly warmer growing conditions.

Peaches and nectarines are usually grown in bush form, but fans are popular in temperate climates since they allow the fruits to receive maximum sunlight for ripening. Some naturally compact (genetic dwarf) cultivars are ideal for growing in pots.

Site and planting

Peaches flower early in the year and so should be protected from frost; a south-facing wall is an ideal site.

Site

Maximum sun is necessary, in a sheltered site that is not susceptible to spring frosts. In cooler climates, a sunny wall or a greenhouse is needed. Peach trees in areas with high rainfall may be badly affected by peach leaf curl (p.651) unless given some protection (see "Routine care", right).

Deep, fertile, slightly acid soils (pH6.5–7) are ideal for growing peaches. If grown on sandy soils they need extra feeding and watering; shallow, chalky soils often give rise to lime-induced chlorosis.

Rootstocks

The plum rootstock 'St Julien A' is used to provide a moderately vigorous tree, while 'Brompton' is used if more vigour is required. In some areas, peach seedling rootstocks are preferred, using vigorous selections resistant to root-knot eelworms.

HAND-POLLINATION

Peaches may be hand-pollinated once the blossom is fully out. On a warm, dry day, use a small, soft brush to transfer the pollen from the anthers of one flower to the stigmas of another.

Pollination

All recommended cultivars are self-fertile, so a crop can be obtained from a single tree. In areas with wet or uncertain weather, pollination may be erratic but can be improved by hand-pollination using a soft brush or rabbit's tail.

Planting

Plant peach trees by midwinter if possible, as growth starts very early. Stake bush trees for the first two years. Planting distances vary depending on the tree form and choice of rootstock (see chart, below).

Routine care

For details of cultivation, see "Care of tree fruits", p.426. Lime-induced chlorosis may lead to manganese/iron deficiency (p.651), which must be treated as soon as possible. Protect the developing foliage of fan-trained

PROTECTING PEACH FANS

In the autumn, at leaf fall, cover the tree with a polythene shelter open at both ends for ventilation. This keeps the leaf buds dry and inhibits peach leaf curl spores from germinating.

peaches against peach leaf curl, and frost to some extent, with a polythene lean-to in winter and early spring.

Fruit thinning

To produce large fruits, thinning will be needed. When the fruitlets are the size of hazelnuts, thin them to one fruit per cluster. Later, when they are walnut-sized and some fruitlets have been shed naturally, thin to a spacing of 15–22cm (6–9in); in warm climates closer spacing may be used.

Feeding, watering, and mulching

In dry areas, watering is needed to support growth and fruiting. Mulching in spring once the soil has warmed up helps the soil to retain its moisture.

PEACHES TO TRY

Early
'Amsden June' **Wh**
'Duke of York'
　Wh,☆
'Hales Early' **Y**
'Kestrel' **Y,☆**
'Saturn' **P**

Mid-season
'Bonanza' **Gd, Y**
'Garden Lady' **Gd, Y**
'Peregrine' **Wh,☆**
'Redhaven' **Y**
'Rochester' **Y**
'Terrace Amber' **Gd, Y**

Late
'Bellegarde' **Y,☆**
'Dymond' **Y,☆**
'Royal George' **Y,☆**

Key
Gd *Genetic dwarf*
　　(good for pot culture)
P *Pink flesh*
Wh *White flesh*
Y *Yellow flesh*
☆ *Excellent flavour*

ROOTSTOCKS

4m (12ft)
3m (9ft)
2m (6ft)
1m (3ft)

'St Julien A'　　'Brompton'

PLANTING DISTANCES

Tree Form	Rootstock	Distance between trees	Distance between rows
Bush	'St Julien A'	5–5.5m (15–18ft)	5.5m (18ft)
	'Brompton' or seedling peach	5.5–7.5m (18–24ft)	7.5m (24ft)
Fan	'St Julien A'	3.5–5m (11–15ft)	

THINNING

1 *As they form, thin peaches to one fruit per cluster, removing first any fruits growing towards the wall or fence.*

2 *These remaining fruits will need thinning again later, in order to leave one fruit every 15–22cm (6–9in).*

NECTARINES TO TRY

Early
'Early Rivers' ☆
'John Rivers' ☆

Mid-season
'Elruge' ☆
'Humboldt' ☆
'Lord Napier' ☆

'Elruge'

Late
'Nectarella' C
'Pineapple' ☆

Key
C   *Compact growth*
☆   *Excellent flavour*

Adequate nitrogen is essential to promote new growth for cropping and potassium is needed to enhance hardiness and fruit quality.

Pests and diseases

Peaches may be attacked by aphids (p.646), birds (p.657), red spider mite (p.646), earwigs (p.644), and root-knot eelworms (p.660); common diseases include peach leaf curl (p.651), bacterial canker (p.665), grey mould (*Botrytis*) (p.646), and gumming (see "Plums: Pests and diseases", p.448).

Growing under cover

Peach trees under cover are best fan-trained so that the fruits receive maximum sun. The greenhouse must be able to accommodate a minimum span of 2.75m (9ft). Fertile, moisture-retentive soil is essential.

A trained tree should be grown against suitable support wires spaced at 15cm (6in) intervals, starting at 38cm (15in) from the ground. Secure the wires so that they are held about 22cm (9in) away from the glass. Full ventilation is essential in winter to allow adequate chilling.

In early spring, but not too early if no heat is available, reduce ventilation to start the tree into growth. Keep the temperature at 8–10°C (46–50°F) for up to two weeks and then raise it to 20°C (68°F).

Trees under cover grow rapidly; always feed and water them well. Occasional, copious watering is preferable to frequent, light applications. Syringe the foliage with a mist of tepid water and damp down the greenhouse floor on bright days.

Pollinate the trees by hand when in bloom (see *Hand-pollination*, p.451). Do not syringe or damp down during the flowering season as this

may prevent pollination, but start again once the flowers have dropped in order to help control red spider mites and mildew; stop syringing and damping down when the fruits begin to ripen.

Fruit thinning is essential to ensure that the fruits develop to their full size (see p.451).

Pruning and training

Peach and nectarine trees bear fruit only on shoots produced the previous year. The first fruits usually develop the third year after planting. Pruning is aimed at encouraging new growth and replacement shoots to maintain a well-balanced, open branch framework. There are three different kinds of bud: plump fruit buds; small, pointed growth buds; and triple buds that have a plump, central fruit bud with growth buds

PEACH BUSH
Year 1, Early spring pruning

Select 3 or 4 strong laterals. Cut back each by two thirds to an outward-facing bud.

Trim back to the stem any unwanted laterals.

Prune back the leader to the topmost lateral.

Year 1, Summer pruning

Cut back flush with the stem any sideshoots below the main laterals.

Remove any shoots that are growing inwards or downwards.

Year 2, Early spring pruning

Prune weak sub-laterals to about 10cm (4in).

Before bud-break, cut back the strongest laterals and sub-laterals by a half to form the main branches.

Established bush, early summer pruning

Cut back to a healthy bud or shoot up to one quarter of shoots that have fruited.

Remove old, unproductive wood, as well as any crowded and crossing branches.

on either side. On branches where extension growth is required, prune back to a growth bud, or, failing this, to a triple bud.

Bush

Plant a feathered maiden between late autumn and late winter. In early spring select three or four strong, well-spaced laterals with the top-most one about 75–90cm (2½–3ft) from the ground; prune back the leader to just above the top lateral. Prune back each of the selected laterals by two thirds and remove all other unwanted laterals. During summer, remove any badly placed or low shoots that have developed.

The following early spring, before bud-burst, select strong laterals and sub-laterals to form the basic frame-work. Cut these back by about half to a bud; prune any other sub-laterals to about 10cm (4in).

Once the tree is well established, keep the centre open by removing some of the older, fruited shoots each summer; occasionally, unproductive branches may need to be cut out.

Fan

Partially trained fans are sometimes available; if buying one of these, make sure that it has been correctly trained (as shown below). A fan should be developed from two laterals trained out approximately 30cm (12in) above the ground at 40°. The central leader immediately above them should have been removed to channel vigour equally to both sides of the tree. A fan that retains its long, central leader and has laterals radiating out at an angle along its length will produce excessive growth at the top of the fan, leaving the base bare.

Formative pruning

Set up support wires as for an apple fan (see p.441). After planting a feathered maiden, choose two laterals about 30cm (12in) above the ground and remove the leader above them. Prune the selected laterals to about 38cm (15in) to form the first two "arms" and tie them to canes at 40°. Prune back all other laterals to one bud as a reserve until the two arms have developed.

In summer, tie in the leader and arms to canes as they develop, to start forming the framework "ribs". Select and train in two equally spaced shoots on the upper side of each arm and one underneath. Pinch back any other shoots on the stem to one leaf, and remove any shoots on the ribs that are badly placed. Before bud-burst in the second spring, cut back the extension growth on the ribs by one third to a strong, healthy bud, in order to promote growth and the fan's development.

In early summer, continue tying in the selected developing ribs. Pinch back weak shoots and remove any that are very vigorous or pointing in the wrong direction.

The following early spring, shorten the ribs by one quarter of last year's growth. During the third summer, select further shoots to complete the main ribs of the fan. Any space in the centre of the tree will soon be filled in by sideshoots. Thin sideshoots produced from the ribs early in the season to 10–15cm (4–6in) apart; retain those that lie naturally along the plane of the fan but remove any that are awkwardly placed and growing

straight outwards or inwards towards the wall or fence. Tie in the retained shoots; they should produce fruit the following year. Pinch back any shoots that are overlapping, to four to six leaves.

Routine pruning

The aim of pruning in spring is to ensure a constant supply of well-placed, young shoots each year. At the base of each flowered shoot that will carry fruit in the forthcoming summer, there are usually two buds or young shoots; pinch out (disbud) one of these to prevent growth from becoming congested. The remaining one will carry fruit the following year. A second bud about halfway up the shoot may also be retained as a reserve in case the other one becomes damaged. After harvesting, remove the fruited wood, and tie in a replacement shoot at the base of each shoot that is cut out.

Continue this process annually; retain two replacement shoots if there is space in the framework. Without rigorous pruning, a peach tree soon becomes congested with old wood that bears no fruit.

PEACH FAN
Year 1, Early spring pruning

Choose 2 laterals, one on either side, 30cm (12in) from the ground to form the main arms. Cut out the leader just above the higher lateral.

Prune back each arm to about 38cm (15in) to a strong bud to encourage shoots, or "ribs", to form.

Cut back other, lower laterals to 1 bud.

Tie each main arm to a bamboo cane attached to the wires at 40°.

Year 1, Summer pruning

Choose 2 ribs on the top of each arm and 1 underneath and tie them to well-spaced canes attached to the wires. Pinch back other shoots to 1 leaf.

Year 2, Early spring pruning

In early spring, cut back the extension growth on the ribs by one third to strong, healthy buds facing in the required direction.

Year 2, Early summer pruning

Train in developing ribs by tying them to canes to extend the permanent framework.

Cut back any wrong-pointing sideshoots to the point of origin, and remove any shoots emerging below the two main arms.

Year 3, Early spring pruning

Cut back each of the main ribs by one quarter to stimulate further growth and extend the framework.

Year 3, Early summer pruning

Thin young sideshoots to 10–15cm (4–6in) apart by pinching out unwanted shoots. Pinch out any shoots that are growing towards the wall or fence or in the wrong direction.

Year 3, Summer pruning

Pinch back any shoots that overlap the ribs to 4–6 leaves as they develop.

As the remaining sideshoots develop, tie them to canes to fill in the framework. These shoots should fruit the following year.

Established fan, pruning after fruiting

Cut back each fruited shoot to a suitable replacement near its base.

Tie in the replacement shoot to fill the gap. These shoots should be evenly distributed over the whole fan.

Harvesting and storing

Harvest the fruits when they are fully ripe. Rest them in the palm of the hand and apply gentle pressure with your thumb on the part of the fruit nearest to the stalk. If the flesh "gives" slightly, the fruit is ready for picking. For the finest flavour, peaches and nectarines are best eaten as soon as possible after picking. If necessary, they can be stored for a few days by placing the fruits in a container lined with soft material and keeping it in a cool place.

Propagation

Peaches and nectarines are usually propagated by chip- or T-budding (see pp.432 and 433) in summer. Seedling peaches are variable in quality, but are often vigorous and may produce excellent crops.

Apricots (*Prunus armeniaca*)

Apricots are more difficult to grow than many other fruits. Not all cultivars thrive in certain areas, so always seek advice when selecting trees. The chilling requirement for apricots is 350–900 hours below 7°C (45°F), most cultivars being at the lower end of this range. They flower extremely early in the year.

Although dry, sunny summers are needed for successful cropping, drought conditions may cause serious bud drop late in the season.

In cool climates, apricots may be grown under cover or fan-trained against a warm wall. In warm areas, the bush form is popular.

Site and planting

Apricot trees should be planted in a sunny, sheltered, and frost-free site to produce good crops of fruit. In cool areas, it is essential to grow them against a sunny wall or in a greenhouse to protect the flowers from frost and low temperatures in late winter and early spring.

A deep, slightly alkaline loam is the most suitable soil. Apricots are least likely to thrive on sandy and chalky soils. It is also best to avoid planting them on heavy soils, particularly in areas that have cool, wet winters, since this may make them prone to die-back.

For rootstocks, both seedling apricots and peaches are widely used.

A seedling peach tolerates wetter conditions than a seedling apricot and produces a smaller tree. The plum rootstock 'St Julien A' is also often used, and a new plum rootstock, 'Torinel' is becoming popular; both are moderately vigorous. Apricots are self-fertile; in cool areas, however, flowers should be pollinated by hand.

Plant in late autumn or very early winter (see *Planting Distances*, p.455) before bud-break. Stake bush trees securely for the first two years.

PLANTING DISTANCES

Tree Form	Rootstock	Distance between trees	Distance between rows
Bush	'St Julien A'/'Torinel'	4.5–5.5m (15–18ft)	5.5m (18ft)
	Seedling peach or apricot	5.5–7m (18–22ft)	7m (22ft)
Fan	'St Julien A'/'Torinel'	4.5–5.5m (15–18ft)	

Routine care

In general, maintenance and cultivation requirements are as for other tree fruits (see "Care of tree fruits", p.426).

In warm regions where heavy cropping is common, blossom may need thinning to counteract biennial bearing (see p.436). Remove badly placed fruitlets and carry out the main thinning after any fruits have dropped naturally and the stones have started forming. Thin so that there is a single fruit on each truss, to leave about 7cm (3in) between fruits.

In cool areas, branch die-back occurs quite frequently; cut back affected branches to clean wood as soon as possible. Birds (p.657), earwigs (p.644), bacterial canker (p.665), brown rot (p.658), and gumming (see "Plums: Pests and diseases", p.448) may be troublesome.

Pruning and training

Fruits are borne both on one-year-old shoots and on older spurs. Pruning is aimed at maintaining the shape of the tree and removing old, unproductive wood. If young trees are too vigorous, they may be root-pruned (see p.430). Prune and train an apricot bush as for plums (see p.448).

The initial training of a fan is as for peaches (see p.453). On an established fan, thin young shoots to 10–15cm (4–6in) apart as they develop in the spring, and remove any shoots that are pointing downwards, towards the centre of the fan, or inwards to the wall. Retain growths that are needed to fill gaps in the framework. Pinch back sub-laterals to six leaves if they are not needed to fill gaps and any sideshoots to one leaf later in the season. After fruiting, prune sub-laterals to three leaves.

Harvesting

Pick the fruit when it is fully ripe and comes away easily from its stalk. Use immediately because fresh apricots do not store well; alternatively they may be frozen, used in preserves, or dried (see p.431).

Propagation

Apricots may be propagated by chip- or T-budding (see pp.432 and 433), using seedling peach or 'St Julien A' rootstocks.

APRICOTS TO TRY

Early
'Early Moorpark'
'Hemskerk' ☆
'New Large Early'
'Tomcot'

'Hemskerk'

Mid-season
'Alfred'
'Breda'
'Delicot'
'Farmingdale'
'Flavercot'

Late
'Moorpark'
'Shipley's'

Key
☆ Excellent flavour

ESTABLISHED APRICOT FAN, EARLY SUMMER PRUNING

To fill gaps in the framework, tie in young sideshoots once they have hardened at the base.

Cut or pinch out altogether any shoots pointing downwards or towards the wall or fence.

Cut or pinch back to 5 or 6 leaves any sub-laterals not needed as replacement shoots.

THINNING

Thin out the young shoots to leave them 10–15cm (4–6in) apart. Tie them in to the wires as they develop.

AFTER FRUITING

Using secateurs, cut back to 3 leaves the shoots that were reduced to 6 leaves earlier in the summer.

Sweet cherries (*Prunus avium*)

Sweet cherry trees may grow to a height and spread of 7.5m (25ft) and, as many cultivars are self-sterile, two trees are often needed to produce a crop. Choose a self-fertile cultivar where just one tree is required or space is limited. New dwarfing rootstocks (see p.456) allow sweet cherries to be grown in an average garden in bush form. Fan-training a sweet cherry on a wall or fence also restricts its growth and makes it easier to protect the tree from attack by birds and from rain just before picking, which may cause the fruits to split. Sweet cherries have a chilling requirement of 800–1,200 hours below 7°C (45°F).

Duke cherries are thought to be hybrids between the sweet cherry and the acid cherry. They are not very widely grown but where chosen require similar treatment and spacing to sweet cherries. Some Duke cherry cultivars are self-fertile and combinations of acid cherries and Duke cherries are compatible.

Site and planting

Sweet cherries need a warm, sheltered site to produce a good crop. It is important to choose cultivars carefully to make sure that they will pollinate each other; this should be checked before buying trees (see "Pollination requirements", p.424).

ROOTSTOCKS

5m (15ft)
4m (12ft)
3m (9ft)
2m (6ft)
1m (3ft)

'Gisela 5'   'Malling F12/1'

SWEET CHERRIES TO TRY

Early
'Early Rivers' **Fg1, Ig1, Ss,**☆

Mid-season
'Hertford' **Fg4, Ss**
'Merton Glory' **Fg2, Ss, Up,**☆
'Sunburst' **Fg4, Sf**
'Summer Sun' **Fg3, Ss**

Late
'Lapins' **Fg4, Sf**
'Napoleon Bigarreau' **Fg4, Ig3**
'Noir de Guben' **Fg1, Ss, Up,**☆
'Penny' **Fg4, Ss**
'Regina' **Fg4, Ss**
'Stella' **Fg4, Sf,**☆
'Sweetheart' **Fg5, Sf**

Key   'Stella'
Fg *Flowering
group (numbers
indicate the
period of
flowering)*
Up *Universal pollinator*
Ig *Incompatibility group
(cherries within each
group will not pollinate each other)*
Sf *Self-fertile*
Ss *Self-sterile*
☆ *Excellent flavour*

Site

Choose an open, sunny, and sheltered site. If the cherry is to be grown as a fan, the support must be at least 2.5m (8ft) high and 5m (15ft) wide for 'Colt' or 1.8m (6ft) high and 4m (12ft) wide for 'Gisela 5', with a reasonably sunny aspect; a tree on a cold wall will produce fruit of poor quality and flavour. A good, deep, well-drained soil is essential, as trees grown on shallow, poor soils produce small fruits and are less long-lived.

Rootstocks

'Gisela 5' is a useful dwarfing rootstock for fans and bushes, and produces fairly heavy crops quite early in the life of the tree. 'Colt', a semi-dwarfing rootstock, is suitable for bush or fan-trained trees in small gardens. The very vigorous 'Malling F12/1' is used where there is space.

Pollination

The pollination needs of sweet cherries are complex. The majority are self-sterile and they fall into distinct groups within which any combination is incompatible. Unless a self-fertile cultivar is obtained, it is vital to choose a pair of trees that are from different groups and that flower at the same time. A few sweet cherries are universal pollinators, that is they will pollinate any cherries that flower at about the same time (see *Sweet Cherries to Try*, left).

Planting

Sweet cherries should be planted in late autumn or winter if bare-root, or at any time if container-grown.

Construct the necessary supports and wires before planting fan-trained plants. Allow about 5–5.5m (15–18ft) between trees that are to be fan-trained and between half-standards.

Routine care

Fruit thinning is unnecessary. Little or no feeding should be needed, apart from mulching as described under "Care of tree fruits", p.426. If growth is poor, apply ammonium sulphate at the standard rate of 35g/sq m (1oz/sq yd). Sweet cherries need thorough watering in dry conditions, but sudden watering on dry soils may cause the fruits to split.

As the fruits begin to colour, protect them from birds by draping netting over fan-trained trees. Bush and half-standard trees are difficult to net, however, so pick fruits as soon as they ripen.

The most likely pests and diseases to afflict sweet cherries are birds (p.657), cherry blackfly (see "Aphids", p.646), winter moth caterpillars (p.645), brown rot (p.658), silver leaf (p.647), and bacterial canker (p.665); cut out any branches with signs of silver leaf or bacterial canker as soon as they are noticed.

Pruning and training

Sweet cherries fruit on spurs on two-year-old and older wood. Mature trees should be pruned in summer to restrict vegetative growth and induce the formation of fruit buds. Train and

prune half-standards and bushes as for plums (see p.448).

Fan

Sweet cherry fans are established as for peaches (see p.453). If there are conveniently placed laterals on a feathered maiden, however, it may be possible to select four rather than two arms to speed up the development of the fan. Tie these arms to canes (attached to wires), which radiate out at 35–45° from the stem. In the spring following planting, prune back the arms to 45–60cm (18–24in) and remove all other laterals that have developed.

During the summer, select two or three well-placed shoots, or "ribs", from each arm and tie them in to fill the available space; remove the remainder. All ribs on the young tree may be tip pruned at bud-burst (but never earlier) to reduce the risk of silver leaf and bacterial canker.

On older fans, spurs may be thinned or shortened in spring (see "Winter pruning", p.438) and ribs pruned to shorter replacement shoots to reduce height. In summer, pinch back all shoots not needed for the framework to six leaves, then to three after fruiting. Upright or very vigorous growths should be removed or tied horizontally to prevent the fan from becoming unbalanced.

Harvesting and storing

Pick fruits when fully ripe, complete with stalks, and eat or cook them immediately. If the fruits are to be frozen (see p.431), pick when firm.

Propagation

Chip- or T-budding are the usual methods of propagation (see pp.432 and 433). 'Colt' rootstocks are compatible with all cultivars, as is the more vigorous 'Malling F12/1' rootstock.

ESTABLISHED SWEET CHERRY FAN, SUMMER PRUNING

Tie in shoots that are needed to replace old ribs or fill bare spaces.

Cut back to 5 or 6 leaves any new growth not needed to extend the fan framework.

AFTER FRUITING

After the crop has been harvested, cut back all the sideshoots that were pruned to 6 leaves in early summer to 3 leaves.

Acid cherries (*Prunus cerasus*)

Acid or sour cherry trees are much smaller than sweet cherries and most cultivars are self-fertile so they are more suitable for the average garden. The fruiting habit also differs in that the crop is mostly borne on one-year-old shoots produced the previous summer. The fruit is not usually eaten raw but is prized for preserves and other culinary uses. Acid cherries have a chilling requirement of 800–1,200 hours below 7°C (45°F).

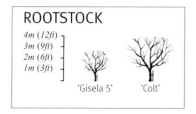

ROOTSTOCK

4m (12ft)
3m (9ft)
2m (6ft)
1m (3ft)

'Gisela 5'   'Colt'

Site and planting

Site and soil requirements are generally as for sweet cherries (see p.455) except that acid cherries may also be grown successfully against a north- or east-facing wall or fence.

The recommended rootstocks, as for sweet and Duke cherries, are 'Colt' and 'Gisela 5'. It is best to obtain cultivars such as 'Morello' (the most popular) from a specialist fruit supplier to avoid inferior, less fertile selections. Plant trees to be trained as bushes and fans 4–5m (12–15ft) apart and for fans provide a minimum support height of 2.1m (6½ft).

Routine care

Acid cherries have the same cultivation requirements as sweet cherries (see p.455). Greater attention to feeding, particularly with nitrogen, may be necessary to encourage young, replacement shoots, but do not overfeed. Irrigation is important in dry areas. Netting is essential to protect the fruits from birds (see p.427); since acid cherries may be trained into small tree forms, such as the bush or dwarf pyramid, they may be grown in a fruit cage. Acid cherries are affected by the same pests and diseases as sweet cherries (see "Routine care", p.456).

Pruning and training

Acid cherries are pruned on a renewal system to produce a constant supply of one-year-old wood on which fruit is produced. A proportion of the older wood should be removed each year. Prune trees in spring and summer since this reduces the risk of silver leaf (p.647).

Fan

This is trained as for a peach fan (see p.453). Renewal pruning to encourage young growth once cropping starts is important because of the restricted space. In spring, on an established fan, pinch out badly placed or overcrowded new shoots and thin the rest to leave them 10cm (4in) apart. Tie these into support wires as they develop. Retain one or, where space permits, two developing shoots low down on each fruiting shoot. Tie in one of these to replace each fruiting shoot that is cut out after harvesting. The second shoot may be used as a reserve in case the first is damaged, or to fill a gap in the fan. To rejuvenate older fans, prune back to young shoots on older wood in spring and autumn.

ACID CHERRIES TO TRY

Late
'Montmorency' **Fg5, Sf**
'Morello' **Fg6, Sf**   'Morello'
'Nabella' **Fg4, Sf**

Key
Fg *Flowering group (numbers indicate the period of flowering)*
Sf *Self-fertile*

ESTABLISHED ACID CHERRY FAN
Spring pruning

Remove any wrong-pointing, young shoots, cutting them back flush with the stem.

Thin the young, developing shoots to about 10cm (4in) apart, if necessary.

Summer pruning, after fruiting

Cut back each fruited shoot to a suitable replacement near its base.

Tie in the replacement shoots to maintain even spacing. These should fruit the following year.

Remove any wrong-pointing shoots that have developed and were not removed in the spring, cutting them back flush with the stem.

ESTABLISHED ACID CHERRY BUSH, PRUNING AFTER FRUITING

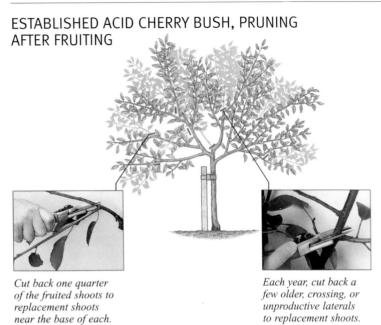

Cut back one quarter of the fruited shoots to replacement shoots near the base of each.

Each year, cut back a few older, crossing, or unproductive laterals to replacement shoots.

Bush

The bush is built up as for peach (see p.453). After the third or fourth year, once the bush is established, renewal pruning is essential. In early autumn, after fruiting, cut out one quarter of the fruited shoots, preferably to replacement shoots, to maintain even spacing and leave room for the young growth that will carry the next year's crop. Remove old or unproductive wood at the same time. If pruning is neglected, fruiting will decrease and be restricted to the tree's outer edge.

Harvesting

Cut the stalks with scissors as hand picking may injure the shoots and encourage infection. Cook, freeze, or preserve soon after picking (see "Harvesting and storing", p.431).

Propagation

The usual methods are chip- or T-budding (see pp.432 and 433). 'Colt' rootstock is compatible with all cultivars; 'Gisela 5' is widely compatible.

HARVESTING ACID CHERRIES

Harvest by cutting each stalk close to the lateral, not by pulling as this may damage the bark and increase the risk of bacterial canker.

Persimmons (*Diospyros kaki*)

Persimmons are deciduous, slow-growing trees that will eventually reach a height of 10–15m (30–50ft) and a spread of about 10m (30ft). The fruits are usually globular, and they may be yellow, orange, or red when fully ripe; some cultivars produce seedless fruits.

Outdoor cultivation in subtropical areas with a minimum temperature of 10°C (50°F) is possible, but a range of 16–22°C (61–72°F) during autumn is preferable. Most cultivars have a low chilling requirement of 100–200 hours below 7°C (45°F); in addition, during the active growing season they need at least 1,400 hours of sunshine to fruit successfully.

Site and planting

A sheltered and sunny site is best; provide protection with windbreaks, if necessary. A well-drained and fertile soil is essential, with a pH of 6–7; mature trees are relatively drought-resistant, but they require irrigation if there is inadequate rain in the growing season.

Persimmon

Vigorous seedlings of *Diospyros kaki* are suitable as rootstocks, but *D. virginiana* is most frequently used for this purpose.

Although some persimmon cultivars have both male and female flowers on the same tree, a number have only one or the other. The most widely grown cultivars have only female flowers; these will produce fruit without pollination although the fruits are small and astringent. A pollinator cultivar, with male flowers, must therefore be grown nearby. A ratio of one pollinator plant to eight or ten female-flowering plants is usually adequate.

In well-manured ground, prepare planting holes; add organic material and general-purpose fertilizer. Trees should be spaced at about 5m (15ft).

Routine care

Apply fertilizer around the trees every three to four months, using a general-purpose mixture with medium nitrogen levels. Conserve moisture in the soil by mulching with organic matter, and water regularly in the dry season. Keep the ground around the trees weed-free.

The major pests that affect persimmons grown in the open are thrips (p.647), mealybugs (p.646), scale insects (p.648), and fruit flies. Common diseases that may cause problems include crown gall (p.655), anthracnose (p.666), and other fungal leaf spots (p.648).

If cultivating persimmons under cover, pests such as red spider mite (p.646) and whiteflies (p.646) may also be troublesome.

Growing under cover

If you are growing persimmons in a greenhouse, plant them in prepared beds or in large containers with a minimum diameter of 35cm (14in); use a very fertile compost incorporating a general-purpose fertilizer with medium nitrogen levels. Maintain a temperature of at least 16°C (61°F) and a humidity of 60–70 per cent. Water regularly during the growing season and apply a general-purpose fertilizer every three to four weeks.

It is necessary to pollinate the flowers by hand for a successful fruit set (see *Hand-pollination*, p.451). During the summer, move plants in containers into the open; leave them until the autumn until their chilling requirement has been met.

Pruning and training

Cultivars vary greatly in vigour. Dwarf and semi-dwarf cultivars are usually trained in a similar way to an apple spindlebush (see p.440). Prune trees for the first three years during the dormant season to form a framework. Subsequent pruning should be relatively light: restrict it to the removal of crowded, crossing, or unproductive branches, and to cutting back branch leaders annually by about one third of their new growth.

Harvesting and storing

Pick fruits when they are fully ripe. Cut fruits from the tree, leaving the calyx and a short fruit stalk attached. Seal the fruits in clear plastic bags and store them at 0°C (32°F); they should remain in good condition for up to two months.

PERSIMMONS TO TRY

'Fuyu'
'Gailey' (pollinator)
'Hachiya'

'Hanafuyu'

'Hanafuyu'
'Hayakume'
'Jiro'
'Tamopan'
'Zenjimaru' (pollinator)

Propagation

Persimmon trees may be propagated by seed, by grafting, from cuttings, or from rooted suckers.

Sow seed taken from mature fruits immediately in containers; kept at 28°C (82°F), it usually germinates in two to three weeks. In 12 months, the seedlings provide stocks suitable for grafting. Handle seedlings carefully when transplanting.

Cultivars may be propagated by chip- or T-budding (see pp.432 and 433), or by whip-and-tongue grafting (see p.433). Softwood cuttings (see p.79) taken in summer and treated with hormone rooting powder should root in a mist unit with basal heat.

Rooted suckers may be detached from the base of the parent tree (if it has not been budded or grafted). Establish them in containers before planting in their final positions.

Figs (*Ficus carica*)

Figs are among the oldest fruits in cultivation, and belong to the family Moraceae. They have a low chilling requirement of 100–300 hours below 7°C (45°F) and thrive in regions with a long, hot growing season.

Site and planting

Figs require a sunny position and in cool areas need a wall or fence for more warmth and protection from frost; this should be at least 3–3.5m (10–11ft) wide by 2.2m (7ft) high.

Figs prefer slightly alkaline, deep, rich, moisture-retentive soils, and a warm, dry climate. Cooler, wetter conditions induce too much growth, with poorer crops. When the pH is less than 6, lime the soil (see p.625).

Where space is limited, a concrete or brick "pit", or box, may be built below soil level to restrict the root system and produce a smaller tree. The pit should be 60cm (2ft) square and have a base that is not solid but filled with broken bricks or stones to a depth of 25–30cm (10–12in); this will provide drainage and restrict root growth downwards.

In cool climates, figs may also be grown in pots placed in a sunny, sheltered site and transferred to cold but frost-free conditions in winter. Use a container 30–38cm (12–15in) in diameter, with several large drainage holes, and filled with a loam-based potting compost.

No rootstocks have been introduced, and trees are grown on their own roots. Modern cultivars are parthenocarpic, producing seedless fruits.

Select two-year-old, pot-grown specimens and plant these in winter, teasing the roots gently loose from the soil ball before planting. Unrestricted trees need to be spaced 6–8m (20–25ft) apart; those planted in a pit need only half this spacing.

Routine care

To protect branches carrying the embryo figs from frost, tie a dense layer of bracken or straw around

FRUIT PLACEMENT

Ripening fruits

Embryo fruits

them (see also FROST AND WIND PROTECTION, *Hessian and Straw Cover*, p.612). At the same time, remove any unripe figs from the previous summer. It may be necessary to protect the ripening fruits against birds and wasps.

Feeding, watering, and mulching

A spring mulch of well-rotted manure is all that is normally required, but trees with restricted roots need extra nutrients. This may be in the form of a balanced fertilizer applied at a rate of 70g/sq m (2oz/sq yd), and supplemented during the summer with occasional liquid feeds. Avoid overfeeding fig trees.

Watering is essential in hot, dry weather, especially where the roots are restricted. Pot-grown figs need regular watering throughout the growing season. Repot and root-prune them every two years.

Pests and diseases

Figs in the open are usually problem-free, but wasps (p.659) and birds (p.657) may attack fruits. Under cover, red spider mite (p.646), mealybugs (p.646), whiteflies (p.646), wasps, (p.659), mice (p.662), and *Nectria* canker (p.664) may be troublesome.

Growing under cover

In cool areas, fan-trained figs may be grown under glass and will crop more regularly than in the open. The roots must be contained to restrict growth. Once growth starts, water regularly but reduce watering as the fruits ripen to prevent the skins splitting. Prune as for figs grown outdoors but leave a more open tree to allow as much light as possible to reach the leaves and fruit.

Pruning and training

In warm climates, figs need only light pruning and are usually grown in bush form. Two crops per season are normally produced, an early one from embryo figs (about the size of small peas) formed late in the previous season, followed by the main crop which is both formed and ripened during the same summer. Meanwhile, further embryo fruits develop to repeat the process.

In cool climates, figs are trained either as open bushes or fans. Only the first crop from embryo figs will have time to ripen. Remove those

ESTABLISHED FIG BUSH
Spring pruning

Cut back frost-damaged shoots to healthy wood and thin out wrong-pointing shoots and any that are overcrowded.

Cut out some of the remaining shoots or, on older trees, branches to 1 bud to promote new growth.

Summer pruning

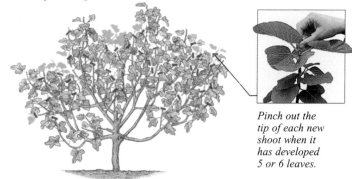

Pinch out the tip of each new shoot when it has developed 5 or 6 leaves.

that do not ripen to concentrate the tree's energies into producing new embryo fruits.

Bush

Purchase a tree with three or four branches arising about 60cm (2ft) above ground. Prune these back by half their length in the first winter to encourage further branches to form and establish a basic framework. Pot-grown trees should branch at 38cm (15in) from the base so that they are compact and not top-heavy.

Pruning of established trees differs with the climate. In warm climates in spring, shorten spreading branches to more vertical shoots and leave some growth in the tree's centre to protect the bark from sun scorch. In cooler climates, remove crowded, crossing, or frost-damaged branches; keep the centre open by taking out all upright shoots and pruning to buds on the lower sides of branches.

Lengths of bare wood should be cut back to one bud to promote new growth. In the summer, pinch out new shoots or sideshoots to five or six leaves to encourage fruit to form.

Fan

Plant a two-year-old tree with two or three strong shoots. Tie down the two best-placed as for peach fans (see

FIGS TO TRY

Early
'Black Ischia' ☆
'St Johns' ☆
'White Marseilles' ☆

'Brown Turkey'

Mid-season
'Brown Turkey'
'Brunswick'
'Negro Largo' ☆

Late
'Bourjasotte Grise'

Key

☆ *Excellent flavour*

p.453) and tip prune lightly. Prune back trees without suitable side-shoots to about 40cm (16in) to encourage lateral growth. The fan is then developed as for peaches but with greater space between branches to allow for the fig's larger foliage.

Prune the established fan in early spring to remove old, fruited wood and any that is frost-damaged or badly placed, and leave the younger wood. Also prune back a proportion of younger shoots to one bud to induce fresh growths close to the main branches. Wherever possible, tie in the unpruned shoots to fill any spaces and remove all others. Pinch out the tips of new growths to five leaves in midsummer. The resulting new shoots should then develop embryo fruits for overwintering.

Harvesting and storing

Pick the fruits when fully ripe. Ripe fruits tend to hang down, are very soft to the touch, and may have slight splits in the skin. Figs are best eaten fresh, but may also be dried.

Propagation

Seed-raised plants vary in fruit quality. Hardwood cuttings of one-year-old wood from selected cultivars should be used. Take cuttings (see p.434) 30cm (12in) long and insert them in well-prepared, well-drained ground. Protect them from frost with cloches. Figs may also be propagated by rooted suckers, severed from the parent tree and transplanted.

ESTABLISHED FIG FAN
Spring pruning

Once all risk of frost has passed, cut all frost-damaged shoots back to their point of origin.

Cut back a proportion of young shoots to 1 bud to encourage replacement growth that will produce embryo fruits.

Tie in the shoots so that they are evenly spaced over the fan.

Cut off wrong-pointing shoots to the point of origin or to a well-placed sub-lateral.

Cut back a proportion of old, bare wood to 1 bud or node to promote new growth.

Summer pruning

Pinch back new shoots to 5 leaves to encourage embryo fruits to form in the leaf axils.

Mulberries (*Morus nigra*)

Mulberries belong to the Moraceae family. Black mulberries reach a height of 6–10m (20–30ft), and are grown for their fruit. White mulberries (*M. alba*) are not usually grown for their fruit. They grow up to 6m (20ft) tall. The chilling requirement is high and the trees begin growth late in the season.

Site and planting
Moist, slightly acid soils are preferable. Mulberries are usually grown on their own roots, and are self-fertile. Plant in late autumn to winter, 8–10m (25–30ft) apart; in cold areas, plant in spring.

Routine care
Cultivation requirements are similar to those of apples (see p.436). Mulch and water as needed in dry weather. Mulberries are mainly untroubled by pests and diseases.

Pruning and training
Mulberries are grown as either half-standards or standards. Prune them only to establish a strong framework of four to five branches, and thereafter only remove branches if they are badly placed or crowded. The trees should be pruned when fully dormant in winter since shoots and roots bleed profusely if they are cut

or otherwise damaged between early spring and autumn.

Harvesting and storing
Pick the fruit when it is fully ripe in late summer, or allow it to drop onto a suitable temporary surface (such as a sheet of plastic) to keep it clean. Eat mulberries fresh, or freeze them (see p.431).

Propagation
Mulberries may be propagated by simple or air layering (see p.116) or by hardwood cuttings about 18cm (7in) long, taken with a heel (see p.113), known as "truncheons".

Black mulberry

Vines

Vines require warm, sheltered positions for successful fertilization, and to ripen their fruits. Grapes, kiwi fruits, and passion fruits all belong to this group. In cool areas, they should be given a sheltered environment or they may be grown under glass. Vines fruit on long, flexible stems of one-year-old wood and need to be pruned after fruiting each year to encourage them to produce a supply of new shoots; these grow rapidly and need to be carefully trained into their supports so that they receive the maximum amount of light and air.

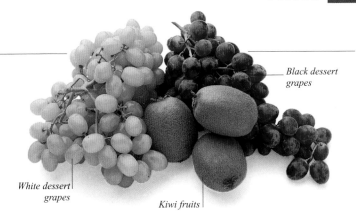

Black dessert grapes

White dessert grapes

Kiwi fruits

Grapes (*Vitis vinifera*)

Through the ages grapes have traditionally been one of the choicest fruits for eating or for wine-making. The European grape (*Vitis vinifera*) and its cultivars are generally considered to be of the highest quality. The American grape (*V. labrusca*) tolerates colder climates and has been hybridized with *V. vinifera* to widen the choice in cooler climates of cultivars for dessert and wine grapes. Many cultivars are suitable for both dessert and wine use.

The fruits need a hot, dry summer to ripen. Warm-temperate regions suit a wide range of cultivars; many may be grown successfully in cooler climates, however, in protected sites or in greenhouses. Decorative pergolas, arches, or other suitable structures may support vines. Pruning methods vary: vines grown for dessert grapes are pruned to produce fewer, higher-quality fruits; vines grown for wine grapes are pruned to obtain the greatest quantity of fruits.

Dessert grapes

It is comparatively easy to produce high-quality dessert grapes in warm areas. In cooler climates, they may be grown against a sunny, warm wall or, preferably, in a greenhouse. Dessert grapes are usually divided into sweetwater, muscat, and vinous groups. Sweetwater are sweet grapes, ripening earliest; muscats have the finest flavour and are second to mature; vinous grapes tend to have less flavour, but are strong-growing and crop late. Vines are usually self-fertile and wind-pollinated, but hand-pollination is advised when growing them under glass (see right).

Site

A warm, sheltered, sunny site free from frosts at flowering time is ideal. Vines need a reasonably fertile, well-drained soil, with a pH of 6–7.5. Avoid planting them on very rich soil as this encourages excess growth at the expense of fruits. Sharp drainage is essential as grapes will not tolerate wet soils; improve the soil or install a drainage system if necessary (for details, see SOILS AND FERTILIZERS, "Improving drainage", p.623).

In cool climates, vines grown on a warm, sunny wall give reasonably good results but will not match the quality of vines grown under glass. Early-ripening cultivars should be used for wall cultivation to obtain dessert fruits by late summer. Support vines with horizontal wires, held in place by vine eyes, 2.5–5cm (1–2in) from the wall.

Vines are usually grown on their own roots, except in areas where *Phylloxera* is a hazard (see "Pests and diseases", right); in this case, seek local advice on which rootstock to use. The use of a rootstock may have other advantages, too, such as greater tolerance of a high pH or wet soil conditions, and control of overvigorous growth.

Planting

Cultivate the soil thoroughly before planting. In poor or sandy soils, incorporate upturned turves at the foot of the planting trench, adding ample, well-rotted manure or compost, then firm the area and water well. Plant bare-root vines in winter but containerized specimens may be planted at any season. Space single cordons at least 1.2m (4ft) apart, double or "U" cordons at twice that spacing; the arms of multiple cordons should be 60cm (24in) apart.

Routine care

Water thoroughly during the growing season whenever conditions are dry, reducing watering as the fruit ripens. Particular care is needed with grapes grown on a wall, since they may be in a rain shadow. Mulch to retain moisture. Once vigorous young shoots develop, feed with a high-potash fertilizer every two or three weeks; if growth is poor, give high nitrogen instead. Stop feeding as soon as the fruits start to ripen.

If using the cordon system, retain no more than one bunch per 30cm (12in) of vertical stem, or rod, for best-quality grapes; remove intermediate bunches at an early stage. Thin the fruits to obtain both well-shaped bunches and large, evenly sized grapes (and to discourage mildew). Do not touch the fruits themselves since this may spoil their bloom. Some cultivars need a second thinning as the fruits develop further.

Pests and diseases

Vines are affected by problems such as scale insects (p.648), vine weevil (p.645), wasps (p.659), downy mildew (p.646), and grey mould (*Botrytis*) (p.658). Under cover, red spider mite (p.646), whiteflies (p.646), mealybugs (p.646), and powdery mildew (p.658) may also be troublesome.

Vine *Phylloxera* is a serious pest in warmer climates, where this aphid-like insect attacks the roots of European vines; galls may also form on the leaves. The attack causes severe stunting and is often fatal. Little treatment is available, although the use of resistant rootstocks and resistant hybrids of American grape cultivars has greatly reduced its incidence. Net vines to protect them against birds (see "Protection from birds", p.427).

Growing under cover

In cool climates, grow vines in a greenhouse, preferably with heating. Other crops with compatible temperature and humidity requirements may also be grown in the greenhouse. In a lean-to greenhouse, the warmth from the back wall is particularly beneficial, especially if there is little or no direct heating. Greenhouses with both top- and side-ventilation give the best results.

The soil must be fairly fertile, weed-free, and well drained, with a pH of 6–7.5. Any drainage must be 75cm (2½ft) deep as vines are deep-rooted. Plant as for vines in the open.

Either train vines directly onto the back wall or plant them at the foot of the glass wall, training them on support wires that are 22cm (9in) or more from the glass. In freestanding houses, plant vines at one end, then train up and along the roof on wires. For details of cultivation, see "Routine care", above. A soil auger may be used to gauge levels of moisture in the soil; use tepid water for the first waterings of the season.

Control ventilation carefully; keep it at a maximum in winter to ensure adequate winter chilling of the vines.

THINNING GRAPES

1 *Once the bunches have been thinned to 30cm (12in) apart, the fruits will need thinning as they swell to increase the size of individual grapes and allow air circulation between them.*

2 *Use a forked cane and vine scissors to expose portions of the bunch and snip off unwanted grapes. The thinned bunch should be wide at the top and tapering towards the base.*

DESSERT GRAPES TO TRY

Early
'Black Frontignan' (black) **Mu**
'Cardinal' (black) **Sw**
'Chasselas Rose' (white) **Sw**
'Chasselas Vibert' (white) **Sw**
'Ciotat' (white) **Sw**
'Foster's Seedling' (white) **Sw**

'Foster's
Seedling'

'Gagarin Blue' (black) **Vi**
'Gamay Hatif' (black) **Sw**
'Himrod Seedless' (golden) **Sw**
'King's Ruby' (black) **Sw**
'Lady Hastings' (black) **Mu**
'Madeline Royale' (white) **Sw**
'Madresfield Court' (black) **Mu**
'Perle de Czaba' (white) **Mu**
'Primavis Frontignan' (white) **Mu**
'Roem van Boskoop' (black) **Sw**
'Royal Muscadine' (white) **Mu**
'St Laurent' (white) **Mu**
'Thompson's Seedless' (white) **Sw**

Mid-season
'Black Monukka' (black) **Mu**
'Canon Hall Muscat' (white) **Mu**
'Muscat Bleu' (black) **Mu**
'Muscat Hamburgh' (black) **Mu**
'New York Muscat' (white) **Mu**
'Oliver Irsay' (white) **Mu**
'Reine Olga' (black) **Sw**

Late
**Late-ripening cultivars ripen
outside only in areas with
reliably warm summers.**
'Alicante' (black) **Vi**

'Alicante'

'Appley Towers' (black) **Vi**
'Mrs Pince's Black Muscat'
   (black) **Mu**
'Muscat of Alexandria'
   (white) **Mu**
'Trebbiano' (white) **Vi**

'Muscat of
Alexandria'

Key
Mu *Muscat*
Sw *Sweetwater*
Vi *Vinous*

Reduce to a minimum in late winter to induce growth. Vary the amount according to the weather to maintain even temperatures. Slight ventilation is always advisable and adequate warmth is needed at flowering to aid pollination. Pollination requires extra attention under glass. With many cultivars, a shake of the rod around midday, or sharp tap with a stick, is usually sufficient to ensure pollination. Muscat grapes need more positive treatment. This entails running cupped hands down and over the blossom trusses to allow adequate pollen distribution. After fruit set, good air circulation is needed to control grey mould (*Botrytis*) and mildew.

Damping down and mist-spraying help control red spider mite. Do not damp down on dull days, or during flowering or ripening periods.

Fork over the bed carefully in late winter, avoiding the root area; remove 1cm (½in) of soil from the surface and replace it with loam-based compost. After the first watering, mulch with well-rotted manure or compost around the base of the vines.

Once the fruits ripen, they need a "finishing period" during which they remain on the vine to attain maximum colour and flavour: allow two to three weeks for early cultivars, and longer for late-ripening ones. Provide good ventilation, netting ventilators to exclude birds if these are a problem.

Pruning and training

The usual method for dessert grapes is to develop single or double ("U") cordons or rods on which permanent fruiting spurs are formed. These produce high-quality fruits.

Vines fruit on the current season's growth. Spring and summer pruning, therefore, is aimed at restricting new growth from the rods so that one bunch of grapes develops from each spur. It also restricts the growth of foliage sufficiently to expose the developing fruit to sun, particularly in cool climates. In hot climates, take particular care that sun scorch does not occur on the vine. Carry out winter pruning before midwinter to restrict sap-bleeding.

Single cordon After planting, while the vine is dormant, shorten the stem to a strong bud a few centimetres above the ground. In summer, train one leading shoot onto a vertical bamboo cane and pinch or cut back any laterals to five or six leaves. Shorten all the sub-laterals (shoots that are growing from the laterals)

GRAPE, SINGLE CORDON

Year 1, Winter pruning

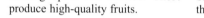

At planting, cut back the main stem by two thirds to a strong bud not far from ground level.

Year 1, Summer pruning

As the main leader develops, tie it in to the vertical cane.

Pinch back to 1 leaf any sub-laterals that form from the laterals.

Cut back each of the main laterals to 5 or 6 leaves.

Year 2, Winter pruning

Cut back the leader by about two thirds of the new growth.

Prune back the laterals that have formed to 1 strong bud.

Year 2, Summer pruning

Pinch out any flower trusses that form on the laterals.

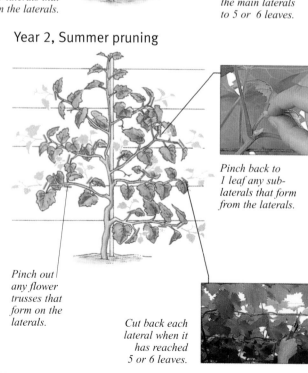

Pinch back to 1 leaf any sub-laterals that form from the laterals.

Cut back each lateral when it has reached 5 or 6 leaves.

back to one leaf. Remove any shoots that develop from the base.

During the second winter, reduce the leader by two thirds of the new growth to well-ripened wood and prune laterals back to one bud. In the second summer, tie in the leading shoot as it extends. Pinch or cut sideshoots back to five or six leaves and sub-laterals to one leaf, for the first summer. Remove any flower trusses; do not allow the vine to fruit until the third year.

In the third winter, shorten the leading shoot by two thirds of its new growth and cut back all the laterals to one strong bud to create spurs that will bear fruiting shoots.

Routine pruning Carry out routine pruning from the third year onwards. In spring, let two shoots grow at each spur and pinch out others. Retain the stronger of the two for fruiting, and pinch back the weaker to two leaves, keeping it as a replacement in case the fruiting shoot breaks. In summer, as flower trusses develop, retain the best, pruning out the others to leave one per lateral. Stop laterals at two leaves beyond the chosen flower trusses. Pinch out laterals not carrying flowers at about five leaves and any sub-laterals at one leaf.

Each winter continue to remove two thirds of the new growth from the leader, but when it has reached the top of its support cut it back annually to two buds. Cut laterals to one strong bud. If spur systems become congested in later years, either remove part of the system with a pruning saw or, if there are too many spurs on the rod, remove some of them completely. The spurs should be 22–30cm (9–12in) apart. The rod should be untied from its wires to about halfway down its length and bent over until nearly horizontal for a few weeks during winter to encourage the even development of shoots the following spring; then retie the rod vertically.

Double cordon This may be formed by training in two shoots horizontally in the first summer. Prune each back to 60cm (2ft) the following winter. The next year, train the extension growths vertically. These form two vertical arms; prune each arm as a single cordon.

Multiple cordon Train in two shoots in the first summer and in winter prune each back to 60cm (2ft). Train the extension growths horizontally, and choose a strong shoot every 60cm (2ft) to train vertically in order

HARVESTING DESSERT GRAPES

Avoid touching the fruits and spoiling the bloom. Cut each bunch complete with a "handle" consisting of 5cm (2in) of woody stem from either side of the bunch.

Year 3, Winter pruning

Cut back the leader, removing about two thirds of the new growth.

Spring pruning

When shoots form at each spur, thin to 2 shoots, one to form the main lateral, the other as an insurance shoot.

Cut back laterals to 1 strong bud.

Established single cordon, summer pruning

If any lateral is not fruiting, cut back the tip to 5 or 6 leaves.

Cut all fruiting laterals back to 2 leaves beyond the flower truss.

Pinch back any sub-laterals that form on the laterals to 1 leaf.

Pinch out any weak flower trusses to leave no more than 1 per lateral.

Established single cordon, winter pruning

When the leader reaches the top of the support, cut the new growth back to 2 buds.

Cut the vine loose, and tie the upper half in a near horizontal position.

Cut back all lateral shoots to the first strong bud.

If spurs become congested, saw off any surplus wood with a pruning saw.

MULTIPLE CORDON

A multiple cordon may be trained with as many vertical rods as space allows. Once established, each arm is pruned in the same way as a single cordon.

WINE GRAPES TO TRY

Early
'Dunkelfelder' (black)
'Huxelrebe' (white)
'Madeleine Angevine 7972'
    (white) **Du**
'Madeleine Sylvaner' (white) **Du**
'Ortega' (white) **Du**
'Précoce de Malingre' (white)
'Reichensteiner' (white)
'Siegerrebe' (golden) **Du**

'Siegerrebe'

Mid-season
'Bacchus' (white)
'Dornfelder' (black) **Du**
'Kernling' (white)
'Léon Millot' (black) **Du**
'Müller Thurgau' (white) **Du**

'Müller
Thurgau'

'Orion' (white)
'Phönix' (white) **Du**
'Pinot Noir' (black)
'Regent' (black)
'Rondo' (black)
'Schönburger' (white)
'Seibel 13053' (black)
'Seyval Blanc' (white)
'Triomphe D'Alsace' (black) **Du**

Late
**Late-ripening cultivars ripen
outside only in areas with
reliably warm
summers.**

'Black
Hamburgh'

'Black Hamburgh' (black) **Du**
'Chardonnay' (white)
'Chenin Blanc' (white)
'Gewürztraminer' (white)
'Pinot Gris' (white)
'Riesling' (white)
'Sauvignon Blanc' (white)
'Scheurebe' (white)
'Schuyler' (black) **Du**

Key
Du *Also for dessert use*

to form the number of arms required.
Once established, prune each arm as
a single cordon.

Alternative pruning methods Some
cultivars will not produce adequate
fruit-bearing shoots from the basal
buds left by spur pruning. In such
cases, longer lengths of ripened
wood, or canes, are retained when
winter pruning the buds from
which fruit-bearing shoots will be
produced. Other canes are cut back
to three or four buds to produce
strong new growths to replace the old
fruiting canes the following winter.
This process is repeated annually.
Many other renewal systems may
also be used to train dessert grapes
(for details on the double Guyot
system, see "Pruning and training:
Guyot system", p.465).

GRAPE, DOUBLE GUYOT
Year 1, Winter pruning

*After planting in
winter, cut back the
vine to about 15cm
(6in) from the soil
level, leaving at
least 2 strong buds.*

Year 2, Winter pruning

*Prune the leader
back to about 38cm
(15in) from soil
level, just below the
bottom wire, to
leave 3 good buds.*

Harvesting and storing
Tie back or remove some of the
foliage to allow more sun to reach
the ripening fruits. Cut ripe bunches
from the vine with a short piece of
woody stem – the "handle" – and
place in a container with soft lining
so that the fruits are not damaged and
their bloom is not spoiled.

Bunches may be stored for a week
or two at room temperature by
cutting a longer handle and placing
this in a narrow-necked container of
water, with the fruit hanging down
on the outside of the container.

Propagation
Vines may be propagated by hardwood cuttings or grafting (for details,
see "Wine grapes: Propagation",
p.466, and "Bud-grafting", p.432).

Year 1, Summer pruning

*Prune any laterals
that develop back
to 5 leaves.*

*As it develops, tie
in the leader to a
vertical stake with
a loose figure-of-
eight knot.*

*Remove any
competing shoots
developing below
the main leader.*

Year 2, Summer pruning

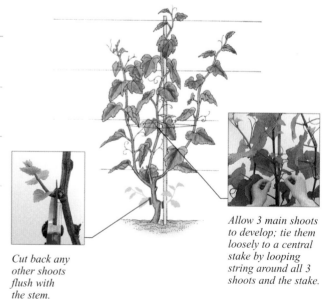

*Cut back any
other shoots
flush with
the stem.*

*Allow 3 main shoots
to develop; tie them
loosely to a central
stake by looping
string around all 3
shoots and the stake.*

Wine grapes

Grapes may be grown for wine in
areas with long, dry, sunny summers
and adequate soil moisture. In cooler
climates, early- and mid-season
cultivars grown on warm walls or
under cover give good results.

Site and planting
Most well-drained soils with a pH
of 6–7.5 are suitable. Clear weeds
before planting. Rootstocks are as
for dessert grapes (see "Dessert
grapes: Site", p.461). The flowers are
usually self-fertile, and are wind-
pollinated. Before planting, erect a
row of support posts. Fix a single
wire 38cm (15in) above the ground
and double wires at 75cm and 1.2m
(30in and 4ft). Each of the double

wires is looped round the posts to form a figure of eight. Plant one- or two-year-old vines in winter, 1.5–2m (5–6ft) apart, in rows 2m (6ft) apart.

Routine care

Remove any weeds, and water to establish young vines in dry conditions; water cropping vines only in drought conditions since too much water reduces grape quality. Give a light, annual, early spring application of a balanced fertilizer, and apply sulphate of potash in alternate years. Use a foliar spray of magnesium sulphate to correct deficiencies of magnesium (see p.651). Mulch every other year with plenty of well-rotted compost, or annually if the soil quality is poor. Fruit size is not important for wine quality so thinning is only necessary in cold areas, to improve sugar levels.

Pruning and training

Some cultivars need spur pruning (see "Dessert grapes: Pruning and training", p.462); many, however, require annual replacement of old canes to fruit regularly.

Guyot system This is widely used for wine grapes, since it produces a prolific crop in a limited space. It involves annual training of horizontal rods from which fruiting shoots are trained vertically. In the double

Year 3, Winter pruning

Prune these shoots back to 8–12 buds, to leave 60cm (2ft) of strong growth.

Gently bend down the 2 strongest sideshoots and tie them to the bottom wire, one on either side. As shoots develop from these, train them vertically.

Prune the third, central shoot back, leaving at least 3 or 4 good buds to encourage the formation of new shoots during the following season.

Year 3, Summer pruning

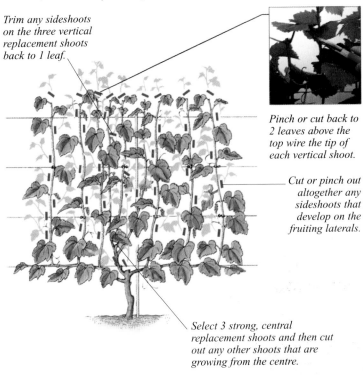

Trim any sideshoots on the three vertical replacement shoots back to 1 leaf.

Pinch or cut back to 2 leaves above the top wire the tip of each vertical shoot.

Cut or pinch out altogether any sideshoots that develop on the fruiting laterals.

Select 3 strong, central replacement shoots and then cut out any other shoots that are growing from the centre.

Established double Guyot, winter pruning

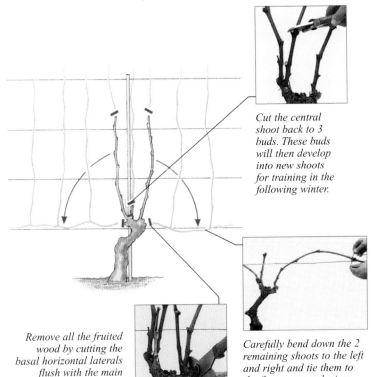

Cut the central shoot back to 3 buds. These buds will then develop into new shoots for training in the following winter.

Remove all the fruited wood by cutting the basal horizontal laterals flush with the main stem, leaving the 3 replacement shoots.

Carefully bend down the 2 remaining shoots to the left and right and tie them to the first or second wires. Tip prune to 8–12 buds.

Established double Guyot, summer pruning

Pinch out the tips of the vertical fruiting shoots, 2 leaves above the top wire.

Pinch or cut back to 1 leaf any sideshoots that have been produced on the 3 vertical replacement shoots.

Cut out overcrowded shoots that are either likely to obscure the developing fruits or are surplus to requirements.

Pinch out completely any sideshoots on fruiting shoots.

Guyot two rods on each plant are trained in this way, in the single Guyot system only one.

To train a vine by the double Guyot system, cut it back during the first winter to two strong buds above ground level. In the first summer, let one shoot develop and tie it to a vertical cane or wires. Remove other

REMOVING FOLIAGE

When the grapes are developing, cut off any leaves that shade the ripening fruit directly. Do not remove too many as this may cause scorch from excess sunlight.

HARVESTING WINE GRAPES

Bunches of wine grapes may be harvested simply by cutting the stalk with secateurs.

low shoots and cut any laterals to five leaves. In the second winter, cut back to just under the lowest wire, making sure that there are at least three strong buds remaining.

The next summer, let three strong shoots develop and tie them in vertically. Remove low shoots. In the third winter, tie down two of the shoots to the bottom wire, one on either side. Tip prune these to eight to twelve buds; they will produce fruiting shoots the following summer. Cut the third shoot back to three or four buds to produce replacement shoots, so that the whole process may be repeated. (For the single Guyot system allow two shoots to develop; tie down one and cut back the other.)

During the third summer, select three of the best central shoots growing from the rod and tie loosely to a central post or cane; cut out other, weaker, central shoots. Pinch back to one leaf any sideshoots that form on the three replacements. Train the shoots from the two arms vertically through the parallel wires. If growth is strong, allow a few bunches of grapes to develop on them. Pinch or cut out shoot tips at two leaves above the top wire; remove any sideshoots on the fruiting shoots.

Routine pruning For winter pruning, cut out all old, fruited wood leaving only three replacement shoots. Tie two of these down, one on either side, and tip prune as for the third winter. Prune the third shoot to three strong buds. Routine summer pruning and training of replacement shoots is as for the third summer. Cut out any overcrowded shoots obscuring the fruits. Remove any leaves shading the grapes six weeks before they are expected to ripen.

Harvesting

Cut the bunches from the vines with secateurs; the grapes should be fully ripe and completely dry.

Propagation

Propagate from hardwood cuttings prepared in winter when pruning, using wood from the hardened base of one-year-old shoots. To plant in the open, take sections about 20cm (8in) long, trimming above and below a bud, and insert the cuttings 15cm (6in) deep in sandy soil.

Under cover it is possible to use shorter one- or two-bud cuttings. Grow these singly in 9cm (3½in) pots or insert five cuttings in a 21cm (8in) pot. Place the pots in a cold frame. Pot on each young rooted plant the following summer.

HARDWOOD CUTTINGS

Trim the stems into lengths of about 20cm (8in), making an angled cut above a bud at the top and a flat cut below a bud at the base. Insert the cuttings to two thirds their length into a trench in sandy soil.

TWO-BUD CUTTINGS

1 *While pruning at leaf fall, trim off a long section of ripened wood from the current season's growth. Then remove any leaves or tendrils remaining.*

2 *Divide the stem into cuttings with 2 buds, with an angled cut above the top bud and a horizontal cut between 2 nodes below the lower bud. Remove a 1cm (½in) length of rind above the lower cut.*

3 *Insert cuttings in a compost of 2 parts peat, 1 part loam, and 1 part sand, the lower bud just below the surface. Label, water, and place in a greenhouse.*

4 *When the cuttings have rooted, they should be potted on individually into 10cm (4in) pots to grow on.*

Kiwi fruits (*Actinidia deliciosa*)

Deciduous trailing climbers, kiwi fruits were originally known as Chinese gooseberries. The vines will grow up to 9m (28ft) in length. The berries have a hairy, brown skin and green pulp, with small, black seeds.

Warm, moist conditions are preferable during the growing season, the optimum temperature range being 5–25°C (41–77°F). Dormant plants will, however, tolerate several degrees of frost and require chilling for a period of at least 400 hours below 7°C (45°F) to encourage good flower production.

Site and planting

Kiwi fruits can only be grown in the open in sunny, sheltered areas, since plants in growth are sensitive to adverse weather conditions. The soil should be well-aerated, deep, and rich in organic matter, with a pH of 6–7. Incorporate a general-purpose fertilizer into the site at a rate of 50–110g (2–4oz) per plant.

Kiwi fruits are mostly dioecious, with plants bearing either male or female flowers. One male is needed for every eight or nine female plants to ensure adequate fertilization.

Erect a post and wire support, with wires at 30cm (12in) intervals. Plant either rooted cuttings or grafted plants 4–5m (12–15ft) apart in rows 4–6m (12–18ft) apart, staking the vines until they are tall enough to reach the supporting wires.

Routine care

Mulch the plants heavily and apply a general-purpose fertilizer rich in phosphate and potassium. Water regularly, particularly in prolonged dry periods. Keep rows weed-free. Fruit thinning is rarely necessary.

KIWI FRUITS TO TRY

'Abbot' **F**
'Allison' **F**
'Bruno' **F**
'Hayward' **F**
'Jenny' **Sf**
'Montgomery' **F**
'Tomuri' **M**

'Bruno'

Key
F *Female*
M *Male*
Sf *Self-fertile*

HOW TO SUPPORT KIWI FRUIT

A common method is to train the plants as espaliers on horizontal wires with two main laterals per plant arising from the main stem, with fruiting laterals (see inset) at intervals of about 50cm (20in).

Plants grown in the open may be liable to root rot (see *Phytophthora* root rots, p.661). Under cover they may be infested with thrips (p.647), scale insects (p.648), and root-knot eelworms (p.660). Fruit rots may also occur as a result of infection of the petals. Infection spreads to the fruits, which then drop early. The spread of the disease is promoted by high humidity. Spraying flowers at petal fall with thiram or a similar fungicide gives reasonable control.

Growing under cover

This is rarely practicable due to the long, trailing growth of the plants; in exposed conditions, however, plants grown in the open may be protected from excessive wind and hail by a light plastic screening material.

Kiwi fruits may be grown in walk-in polytunnels if the appropriate environmental conditions can be provided. Soil preparation and cultivation details are the same as for plants grown in the open.

Pruning and training

Commercial crops are often grown on a "T" bar or overhead pergola structure. Another commonly used system is to train plants as espaliers on horizontal wires: each plant then has two main laterals arising from the main stem, and fruiting branches at intervals of 50cm (20in). For details, see "Apple: Espalier", p.442.

The fruits are produced on one-year-old wood only, so all fruited sideshoots should be cut back to two to four buds in the dormant season.

Harvesting and storing

Kiwi fruits start to bear fruit three to four years after planting. Harvest them as they soften. Snap or cut them from the branch, with the calyx attached; keep them cool. If wrapped in plastic film, fruits store for several months at 0°C (32°F).

Propagation

Both soft- and hardwood cuttings may be rooted successfully. Softwood cuttings should be taken in spring; trim to 10–15cm (4–6in) and insert in cutting compost (see p.434). Hardwood cuttings are taken in late summer; these should be 20–30cm (8–12in) long and inserted in sandy compost (see p.434).

Selected cultivars may also be grafted onto vigorous seedling stocks; the most common methods are T-budding and whip-and-tongue grafting (see p.433).

Passion fruits (*Passiflora* spp.)

Passion fruits are climbing plants, with individual stems reaching many metres in length. The globular fruits are either purple or yellow when ripe, and may be up to 7cm (3in) in diameter. The two species most commonly grown for their fruits are the yellow-fruited *P. edulis* f. *flavicarpa* and the purple *P. edulis*.

The optimum temperature range for the purple passion fruit is about 20–28°C (68–82°F). The yellow passion fruit prefers temperatures over 24°C (75°F) and does not tolerate frost; purple types may withstand frost for short periods. Moderate to high humidity is required for satisfactory growth.

Site and planting

Select a sunny site, protected by windbreaks, if necessary. Soils may vary in type but must be well drained, with a pH of about 6.

Cross-pollination by insects, normally bees, is usual, but hand-pollination may be necessary in wet weather; hand-pollination has been found to increase the yield of plants that are grown in the open.

Passion fruits require support, in the form of a wire trellis. Before planting, insert stout uprights, 3m (10ft) long, at intervals of 4m (12ft) each way. Link adjoining uprights in rows by tying with one or two strands of wire.

Take care to prepare the planting holes thoroughly, adding both organic material and a general-purpose fertilizer with medium to high levels of nitrogen. Establish the plants at about 3–4m (10–12ft) apart each way, or less if only a few plants are grown. The yellow form is usually planted 3m (10ft) apart each way.

Routine care

Apply a general-purpose fertilizer that has a medium to high nitrogen content at a rate of 0.5–1kg (1–2lb) per plant per year, preferably in equal dressings at intervals of three to four months. Apply an organic mulch in spring, and weed and water regularly during the dry season.

Pests affecting plants in the open as well as under cover include fruit flies, aphids (p.646), red spider mite (p.646), and various scale insects (p.648). Root-knot eelworms (p.660) and *Fusarium* wilt (p.654) may also be serious in some subtropical areas.

"Woodiness" is caused by cucumber mosaic virus (see "Viruses", p.659), which is transmitted by aphids. As passion fruit vines are susceptible to eelworms and various wilt diseases, replace the plants every five or six years with healthy seedlings, or rooted cuttings, or grafted plants.

Growing under cover

This is possible in temperate areas, but fruits may not be produced unless the optimum temperatures and conditions are provided; hand-pollination is generally necessary. Provide wire supports as for outdoor plants. Grow plants either in prepared beds or in large containers at least 35cm (14in) in diameter. Use a well-drained, fertile compost with

Passion fruits

a high organic content, incorporating a general-purpose fertilizer into the compost before planting. Maintain a minimum temperature of 20°C (68°F) and humidity of 60–70 per cent. Apply a liquid feed or a general-purpose fertilizer at monthly intervals, and water regularly.

Pruning and training

Train two main growing stems along the wires to form a permanent framework. If these have not produced laterals by the time they are 60–90cm (2–3ft) long, pinch out their tips. Allow the lateral shoots, on which the fruits will be produced, to hang down as they develop each spring. Prune these laterals so that they are never less than 15cm (6in) from the soil. Once the plant is established, each winter cut back the current season's fruited shoots as these will not bear fruit again.

Harvesting and storing

Pick fruits when they begin to change colour, from green to either purple or yellow. The fruits should be ripe 8–12 weeks after fruit set depending on the cultivar. Fruits may be stored for up to 21 days if maintained at an even temperature of at least 6–7°C (43–45°F) and at a constant humidity level of 85–90 per cent.

Propagation

This is usually by sowing seed or raising cuttings; passion fruits may also be propagated by bud-grafting.

Seed may be extracted from the fully ripe fruits, and should be fermented for three to four days, then washed and dried. Sow the seed under cover in trays or 7–9cm (3–3½in) pots of seed compost, and keep at a temperature of at least 20°C (68°F). When the germinated seedlings are 20–35cm (8–14in) tall, transplant them to open ground, after hardening off, or grow them on under cover.

Cuttings 15–20cm (6–8in) long should be prepared and inserted into a tray or pot filled with cutting compost. Apply bottom heat and mist-spray to encourage rooting.

For details of bud-grafting, see p.432. Healthy bud-grafted plants should be transplanted into their permanent positions to grow on when approximately 15cm (6in) tall.

If eelworms or wilt diseases are a serious problem, the purple cultivars may be grafted onto resistant rootstocks. Vigorous seedlings of the yellow-fruited type are normally used for this purpose.

Soft fruits

ALL the usually cultivated soft fruits are bush or cane fruits, except for strawberries, which are herbaceous perennials. Bush fruits include blueberries, gooseberries, and black-, red-, and whitecurrants. Cane fruits include blackberries, hybrid berries, and raspberries. All produce succulent fruits that are eaten fresh, or preserved, bottled, or frozen. Most soft fruits grow best in cool climates. They prefer a well-drained, moisture-retentive, and fertile soil. A sunny site is best and gives fine-quality fruit, but in most cases a little shade is tolerated. Almost all cultivars are self-fertile. Pruning methods depend on whether fruit is produced on one-year-old wood, on older wood and spurs, or on both.

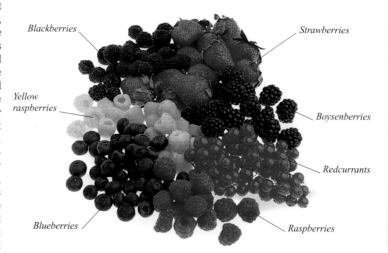

Blackberries

Strawberries

Yellow raspberries

Boysenberries

Redcurrants

Blueberries

Raspberries

Protective measures

Birds can be a headache in the fruit garden: not only are they attracted by ripening fruits, but when food is scarce in winter, tits and bullfinches in particular may strip branches of nutritious buds, causing permanent damage to the plants and ruining the crop.

If practical, the best defence is a physical barrier such as netting, secured at the base to prevent a ground assault (see p.427).

Improvised bird-scarers are also worth a try, such as sight or sound deterrents like reflective CDs, or windmills. Keep them effective by moving them around the garden, and vary the "threat" to prevent birds becoming used to them.

Strawberries (*Fragaria* x *ananassa*)

Strawberries are low-growing, herbaceous plants that may be grown in most gardens, either in the open ground or in containers. There are three distinct types of strawberry plant: summer-fruiting, perpetual-fruiting, and alpine.

Summer-fruiting strawberries produce nearly all their fruit in an intensive two- to three-week period in midsummer. Some cultivars also give a smaller, autumn crop.

Perpetual-fruiting (ever-bearing) strawberries crop briefly in summer, cease for about two months, and then produce a succession of fruits in autumn. They grow best in regions that have mild, frost-free autumn weather.

Alpine strawberries, which are raised from seed, produce small, delicately flavoured fruits.

Variations in daylength (see GROWING VEGETABLES, p.495) affect the formation of flowers in some cultivars. It is therefore important to choose those appropriate for the latitude of the particular garden: nearer the tropics, for example, the cooler temperatures that are essential for growth and cropping may be found only at high altitudes.

Site and planting

Strawberries are best grown where new plantings may be made regularly on fresh ground, since cropping, fruit size, and plant health deteriorate if the same ground and plants are used after the third year. If you have room, grow one-, two-, and three-year-old plants in succession, discarding the oldest plants and planting new runners in fresh ground each year.

Site

Sunny, warm sites give the best-flavoured fruit. Sandy soils produce the earliest crops, loams and well-drained clays the heaviest and most finely flavoured; chalky soils do not produce good results. Slightly acid conditions with a pH of 6–6.5 are ideal. Good drainage is vital to avoid soil-borne diseases. Planting strawberries after potatoes can be risky, since the ground may be infected with *Verticillium* wilt (p.653).

To prolong the fruiting season, plantings may be split – choose a warm, sheltered position for the earliest crops, sunny, open ground for the main crop, and a less sunny site for late-ripening fruits.

Pollination

Most cultivars are self-fertile. However, 'Pandora' is a self-sterile cultivar; to

ensure that it fruits, several plants of a different cultivar that flowers at the same time (late) need to be grown nearby.

Planting

The planting time for strawberries depends on geographical location. Seek expert advice if in doubt. In cool-temperate regions, late summer to early autumn planting is best and ensures the heaviest crops during the following summer. For later plantings, remove flowers in spring in order to allow the plants to become well established before they begin to bear fruit.

Use plants of certified stock, if possible, and plant them in fresh ground, where strawberries have not been grown for at least three years. Replace plants every two or three years and grub out and burn any old

PLANTING STRAWBERRIES UNDER A PLASTIC MULCH

1 *In moist soil, mark out a 90cm (3ft) wide bed with string. Mound the soil in the centre, and cover the bed with a length of black plastic 1.2m (4ft) wide.*

2 *Dig a narrow trench on either side of the bed and, using a spade, anchor the edges of the plastic sheet firmly in the trenches to stop it blowing away.*

3 *Make cross-shaped cuts in the plastic (see inset) at 45cm (18in) intervals. Plant the strawberries through the slits and firm the soil around their crowns.*

4 *Tuck in the cut plastic around the crowns of the plants. The finished row of strawberries should be slightly raised so that rain drains away from the plants.*

plants that remain nearby to prevent the spread of virus diseases. Clear all weeds and apply generous amounts of well-rotted farmyard manure over the area, unless plenty remains in the soil from the preceding crop. On hungrier sandy or chalky soils, rake in a dressing of a balanced fertilizer as well, at a rate of 105g/sq m (3oz/sq yd), just before planting. Space strawberries at 45cm (18in) intervals in slightly raised rows, 75cm (2½ft) apart, so that rainwater runs off. Plant with the base of the central crown at soil level, firm in the plants, and water well. On wet sites, plant in raised beds (see STRUCTURES AND SURFACES, "Raised beds", p.599).

Strawberries may also be planted through sheets of black plastic, which smother weeds, retain soil moisture, and encourage early cropping by warming the soil. Anchor the plastic firmly before planting, then make planting slits by cutting the plastic at the required intervals.

HOW TO KEEP STRAWBERRIES CLEAN

When the strawberries are in flower or the fruits are forming, put a thick layer of straw underneath and between the plants to prevent the ripening fruits from touching the soil.

ALTERNATIVE METHOD

Alternatively, strawberry mats may be laid carefully around the crowns to protect the developing fruits.

REMOVING RUNNERS

Remove excess runners as they develop. Pinch them out close to the parent plant, taking care not to damage any other foliage.

Routine care

Strawberries need regular watering. Ripening fruits should be netted against pests, and kept off the soil to keep them clean. Remove surplus runners, weed, and regularly check for pests and diseases. Flowers may need protection from frost in spring: fleece or double-thickness sheets of newspaper are very effective.

Before the fruit trusses develop fully, lay clean, dry straw or proprietary mats beneath them to prevent soil splash; this is not needed for plants grown through plastic. Protect the fruits from birds before they redden, using fruit nets (see p.427).

Pinch out runners as they appear, unless they are needed to help form matted rows (see "Growing under cover", below).

Watering and weeding

Water when newly planted, then regularly in the growing season, especially after flowering to promote the development of quality fruits. Water plants under plastic only in very dry weather, watering through the planting slits. Keep beds free of weeds.

Pests and diseases

Strawberries may be eaten by birds (p.657), grey squirrel (p.659), and slugs (p.644), and are vulnerable to aphids (p.646), vine weevils (p.645), viruses (see p.659), grey mould (*Botrytis*) (p.658), fungal leaf spots (p.648), and red spider mite (p.646). Dig up and burn diseased or stunted plants. Red core and strawberry beetles are not widespread, but are serious where they occur. Red core is a soil-borne disease, more prevalent in heavy soils, causing the foliage to collapse and die. The only remedy is to change the site. Strawberry beetles take seeds from the outside of the fruits, encouraging rotting. They feed on weed seeds, so weed beds well.

PICKING FRUITS

Pick dessert strawberries by the stalk to avoid bruising the fruit. Strawberries for jam may be picked without the stalk.

Growing under cover

Strawberries grown in a heated greenhouse fruit up to one month earlier than those grown outdoors, but have less flavour. Establish runners in 6cm (2½in) pots of seed compost as early as possible (see p.470). Before the roots fill the pots, transplant into 15cm (6in) pots of potting compost; keep the plants outside until midwinter, protected from heavy rain, then place them in the greenhouse in a position of maximum light. When new leaves form, maintain minimum temperatures of 7°C (45°F) at night and 10°C (50°F) during the day.

Adjust the ventilation to maintain these temperatures. Water and damp down frequently to keep a moist atmosphere and reduce the risk of red spider mite infestation. Increase the temperature by about 3°C (5°F) when flower trusses start to develop; during flowering, raise the temperature again by the same amount and stop damping down. Pollinate flowers by hand with a soft brush; do this around midday on a bright day. Remove late-forming flowers to improve the size of the ripening fruits. To enhance their flavour, lower the temperature as they begin to ripen.

For plants grown in the open, cloches placed over plants in late winter advance ripening by about three weeks (see p.582), and polytunnels by one to two weeks. Both should be well ventilated on warm days. Under cloches or plastic tunnels, strawberries may be grown in "matted rows", in which the planting distance is halved to give maximum yield. Runners may be retained to increase the density of the planting. Revert to the usual spacing after the first year by removing every other plant, otherwise fruit quality will deteriorate and routine care will become difficult.

STRAWBERRIES TO TRY

Summer-fruiting

Early
'Cambridge Vigour' **R**,☆
'Elvira'
'Honeoye' ☆
'Mae'
'Rosie'

Mid-season
'Cambridge Favourite'
'Cambridge Late Pine' ☆
'Elsanta'
'Eros'

'Elsanta'

'Hapil' ☆
'Pegasus' ☆
'Red Gauntlet'
'Royal Sovereign' ☆
'Symphony' ☆
'Tamella' ☆

Late
'Alice' ☆
'Florence'
'Rhapsody'
'Sophie'

Perpetual-fruiting

'Aromel' ☆
'Bolero'
'Calypso'
'Challenger'
'Mara des Bois' ☆

Alpine

'Alexandra'
'Alpine Yellow'
'Baron Solemacher'

Key

R *Ripens mid-season when two years and older*
☆ *Excellent flavour*

Harvesting and storing

Harvest dessert strawberries when fully ripe, complete with stalks, and use them at once for the best flavour. Pick strawberries for jam when ripe but still firm. Pick the fruit every other day and remove and burn diseased or damaged fruit. Strawberries may also be bottled or preserved. If frozen, the fruits, except those of the cultivar 'Totem', lose their firmness.

After harvesting, clear surplus runners, weeds, and straw from the site. Cut off the old foliage from plants, taking care not to damage the young leaves. Apply a balanced fertilizer and water it in if the soil is dry. Where plants are growing through a plastic mulch, make a fresh planting unless they are thriving.

Propagation

Each year plant one or two certified virus-free young plants well away from established fruiting beds. Control aphids and remove all flowers as they develop. The plants will produce a healthy supply of runners for transplanting for up to two years; then start afresh with new, certified stock. Some perpetual-fruiting cultivars produce few runners.

CLEARING THE FOLIAGE AFTER HARVESTING

As soon as the crop has been picked, remove the old foliage to leave 10cm (4in) of stem above the young leaves and crown. Clear away and burn straw, foliage, and other debris from around the plants to minimize the risk of pests and diseases.

HOW TO PROPAGATE BY RUNNERS

1 *Plant certified virus-free plants especially to produce runners. As they form, spread them out evenly around the parent plant.*

2 *Once a runner has rooted and is making vigorous new growth, lift it carefully, using a hand fork, without damaging the roots.*

3 *Sever the rooted runner from the parent plant. Transplant it to well-prepared soil or pot it up singly for planting out later.*

Alpine strawberries

Alpine strawberries (*Fragaria vesca* 'Semperflorens') have small, fragrant, sweetly flavoured fruits and make a neat and attractive edging for flower borders or vegetable plots. They tolerate cooler conditions than most other strawberries and prefer partial shade in the summer in warm areas. Their fruiting season lasts from midsummer through to late autumn.

Plants deteriorate after about two years, so should be propagated regularly from either runners or seed.

To separate seed from the fruits, leave the strawberries to dry and squash them between finger and thumb. Sow the seed in pots of standard seed compost and maintain them at 18–24°C (64–75°F). Prick out seedlings when they have two true leaves. Plant out young strawberries in early summer.

Alpine strawberry

HOW TO PROPAGATE FROM SEED

1 *Use dried fruits, squashing them gently between finger and thumb so that the seeds fall off. Hold the fruits over a clean container to collect the seeds.*

2 *Fill a 6cm (3in) pot with seed compost. Sprinkle the seeds thinly on the surface, then cover them with a thin layer of compost and a layer of fine grit.*

Blackberries and hybrid berries (*Rubus fruticosus* and *Rubus hybrids*)

The fruits of cultivated blackberries and hybrid berries such as loganberries and boysenberries are borne on canes in late summer. The hybrids have arisen from crosses between different *Rubus* species or cultivars.

Site

Before planting, the ground should be well prepared and fertilized, as for raspberries (see p.472). Buy blackberries and hybrid berries from specialist nurseries and, if possible, choose plants that are included in a certification scheme to ensure healthy, virus-free stock. Thornless cultivars are usually less vigorous than prickly ones. Blackberries and

hybrid berries are all self-fertile and consequently may be grown singly.

Blackberries and hybrid berries need a sunny or partially shaded position. Do not plant them in exposed sites.

Provide support for the canes: walls and fences, with horizontal wires set up at 30cm (12in) intervals, are ideal.

A post 3m (10ft) long sunk 60cm (2ft) into the ground may also be used as a basic support, but for vigorous cultivars erect a post-and-wire fence. Position the posts at 4–5m (12–15ft) intervals with four horizontal wires running between them, the lowest at 90cm (3ft) from the ground, the highest at 2m (6ft). On light, sandy

soils, you should provide extra support for the end posts by bracing them with diagonal wooden props. This will help to prevent the wires from sagging under the weight of the canes.

Planting

Plant during winter; if the weather is severe, delay until late winter or early spring. Some hybrids may be killed in very cold areas so seek local advice. Plant shallowly, spreading out the roots well and firming the soil at the base of the plants. Space more vigorous cultivars 4–5m (12–15ft) apart, less vigorous ones 2.5–3m (8–10ft) apart. After planting, shorten the canes to 22cm (9in).

BUYING HEALTHY BLACKBERRY PLANTS

Well-developed, fibrous roots

Strong, healthy cane

METHODS OF TRAINING

Alternate bay
*Train new canes to one side of the plant,
while the older ones fruit on the other side.*

Rope
*Train fruiting canes in groups along wires,
leaving new canes to grow centrally.*

Fan
*Fan-train fruiting canes individually to the left
and right, and train new canes centrally.*

Weaving
*Weave fruiting canes through the lower wires.
Train new canes centrally and along the top wire.*

BLACKBERRIES TO TRY

Early
'Bedford Giant' **Rg**
'Himalaya Giant' **Rg**
'Merton Thornless'
'Sylvan'

'Bedford Giant'

Late
'Ashton Cross'
'Fantasia'
'Helen'
'Loch Ness'
'Oregon Thornless'
'Thornfree'
'Waldo'

HYBRID BERRIES TO TRY

Boysenberry
Loganberry
Tayberry
Thornless
    Loganberry

Key
Rg *Rampant growth*   Tayberry

ESTABLISHED BLACKBERRIES AND HYBRID BERRIES
Pruning after fruiting

*Cut down all the fruited
canes to ground level near
the base of the stem.*

*Tie the new canes
securely to the
horizontal wires
according to the
training system used.*

Tip pruning frost-damaged stems

*Inspect the canes for
signs of frost damage
in early spring and, if
necessary, cut back the
tips of affected canes to
healthy wood.*

Routine care
Maintenance requirements are as for raspberries (see p.473).

Pests and diseases
Problems may be caused by raspberry beetle (p.658), birds (p.657), grey mould (*Botrytis*) (p.658), and viruses (p.659), although resistance varies from one hybrid to another.

Pruning and training
The plants fruit on one-year-old wood, so training needs to separate fruiting canes from newly developing ones. For small gardens, the rope and fan methods (see above) are best. The alternate bay and weaving systems use much more space, but weaving is the best method for vigorous plants.

After cropping, cut out the fruited canes at ground level. Retain and tie in those canes that have grown during the current season but remove any that are weak or damaged. In early spring, cut back the tip of each cane if it shows any signs of die-back resulting from frost.

Harvesting and storing
Pick the fruits regularly; unlike raspberries, the central plug stays within the picked fruit. For exhibiting, pick fruits complete with their stalks. They may be stored by bottling, preserving, or freezing.

Propagation
To provide a few new plants, use tip layering (see below). In summer,

TIP LAYERING

1 *Bend over the tip of a healthy, vigorous shoot and place it in a hole 10cm (4in) deep. Fill the hole with soil and firm down well.*

2 *Once the tip has rooted in late autumn or winter, cut the old stem close to the young, rooted plant to sever it from the parent. Pot it up, if required, or transplant in spring.*

bend a shoot to ground level and place the tip in a hole dug in the soil. Cover it with earth and firm. Once the tip has rooted in late autumn or winter, sever it from the parent plant. Transfer the young plant to its final growing position in spring.

To produce a larger number of young plants, remove shoots, 30cm (12in) long, of the current season's growth in late summer; take leaf-bud cuttings from them, with a leaf and a piece of stem. Place several cuttings in one 14cm (5½in) pot in a moist atmosphere or cold frame; they should root in six to eight weeks. Harden them off and plant them out in late autumn or, where winters are harsh, in early spring. Transplant the young canes to their final positions a year later.

HOW TO PROPAGATE BY LEAF-BUD CUTTINGS

1 *Select a strong, healthy shoot from the current season's growth, taking at least 30cm (12in) of stem with plenty of well-developed leaf buds.*

2 *Make a cut 1cm (½in) above a bud: slice downwards to remove the bud and a portion of stem about 2.5cm (1in) long, with a leaf attached.*

3 *Place 3 cuttings in a 14cm (5½in) pot, with the stem portions at an angle and growth buds just above the soil. Water, label, and place in a cold frame.*

Raspberries *(Rubus idaeus)*

A number of raspberry cultivars have been produced by crossing the European wild red raspberry (*Rubus idaeus*) with the American raspberry (*R. idaeus* var. *strigosus*) and the North American black raspberry (*R. occidentalis*).

Raspberries are a cool-season crop, growing best where there is plenty of moisture. Fruits vary in colour from dark red through to yellow. There are two main types of raspberry: summer-fruiting, which has a short season of heavy cropping in high summer, and autumn-fruiting, which has a protracted cropping period beginning in late summer and continuing until the start of winter frosts.

Site and planting

The site needs thorough preparation before planting, since raspberries do not crop well on poor soils, particularly if in competition with weeds. Raspberries are self-fertile.

Site

Raspberries should be planted in a sheltered, sunny position. They tolerate partial shade, and in hotter regions some shade may be a positive advantage.

The soil should not only be rich in humus and moisture-retentive but also well drained, as raspberries do not tolerate poor drainage. Sandy, chalky, and poor, stony soils need an annual, heavy dressing with humus-rich material, and regular watering. In addition, if raspberries are grown on lime-rich soil they may suffer from chlorosis (see "Manganese/iron deficiency", p.651).

Preparation

Clear all perennial weeds before planting as they are extremely difficult to deal with later. Prepare an area at least 90cm (3ft) wide and dig in plenty of well-rotted manure.

Construct permanent supports. For a post-and-wire support, set a single row of stout posts 3m (10ft) apart. Run three lengths of wire or nylon string between the posts setting them at heights of 75cm (30in), 1.1m (3½ft), and 1.5m (5ft). Keep the wires or strings taut and tie in the canes with twine by "continuous lacing" (weaving between the canes and wires) to prevent the canes from being blown along the row.

The parallel wires method requires two rows of posts, with posts at the above spacing and rows 75cm (30in) apart. Run two pairs of parallel wires along the posts, one pair at 75cm (30in), the other at 1.5m (5ft), then criss-cross between them with wire or strong string. The canes are supported by the cross-wires and do not need to be tied in.

For the Scandinavian system, erect two rows of posts, as above, but with 90cm (3ft) between rows, then run a single wire along each row at a height of 90cm (3ft). Twist fruiting canes along the wires, allowing new canes to grow in the open, central space.

Obtain certified virus-free canes; otherwise use suckers taken from established plants of known good health and cropping performance.

Planting

Plant dormant canes in well-manured ground at 38–45cm (15–18in) intervals, in rows 2m (6ft) apart. Plant in autumn or early winter, as

SUPPORTING AND TRAINING METHODS

The post-and-wire method is useful if space is limited. The parallel wires method gives the canes more room, but is not suitable in windy conditions. The Scandinavian system bends young canes around each other and the wire; the canes are not tied in or tip pruned. This method needs more space than the others.

Scandinavian system

Post and wires

Parallel wires

HOW TO PLANT RASPBERRIES

1 *Prepare a trench 5–8cm (2–3in) deep in well-manured ground. Plant the canes 38–45cm (15–18in) apart. Spread out the roots carefully and backfill the trench with soil.*

2 *Firm the soil around the bases of the canes, ensuring that they remain vertical. Prune canes back to a bud, about 25cm (10in) from the ground. Rake over the soil lightly.*

this encourages the canes to establish quickly. Spread out the roots evenly at a depth of 5–8cm (2–3in), and gently firm them in. Prune the canes to 25cm (10in) from the ground.

Routine care

In spring, mulch with well-rotted manure. Apply this on either side of the row, taking care not to bury the canes. If manure is unavailable, apply regular dressings of a balanced fertilizer (see "Care of soft fruits", p.426) and mulch with compost or leaf mould to conserve moisture.

Flowers usually appear too late to be damaged by frost so do not need protection. Remove weeds and water the plants regularly and thoroughly. Remove any suckers more than 22cm (9in) from the main row.

Pests and diseases

Raspberry beetle (p.658) and birds (p.657) are the main pests. Grey mould (*Botrytis*) (p.658), spur blight/cane blight (p.653), and viruses (p.659) may also be a problem.

Pruning and training

As soon as new canes are established, by about midsummer, cut out any of the canes that were shortened at planting time.

Summer-fruiting raspberries should have all fruited canes removed at ground level after cropping. Tie in the new canes (see *Supporting and Training Methods*, p.472), spacing them evenly 8–10cm (3–4in) apart. Cut out damaged and weak canes so that those remaining receive as

much light and air as possible. Loop over and tie in tall canes to prevent wind damage. The following spring, trim canes to 15cm (6in) above the topmost wire, cutting back any tips with frost damage. Remove dead, diseased, or crowded canes or any more than 22cm (9in) from the row.

Autumn-fruiting raspberries (see p.474) should have all canes cut to ground level in late winter. The new canes grow, then fruit in the autumn.

Harvesting and storing

Pick the fruit when it is firm to ripe for preserves and freezing, and when it is fully ripe for eating fresh, harvesting every other day, if possible. Detach

HOW TO REMOVE UNWANTED SUCKERS

If suckers become overcrowded or are growing too far outside the row, as here, lift them and sever from the parent plant.

PRUNING AT THE END OF THE FIRST SEASON

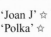

1 *By about midsummer, cut down to ground level the old canes that were shortened when planting was carried out.*

2 *Tie the current season's strongest canes to the support wires (see inset) when they reach about 90cm (3ft). Remove weak shoots and those growing more than 22cm (9in) from the row.*

SUMMER-FRUITING RASPBERRIES TO TRY

Early
'Glen Ample'
'Glen Clova' **Pv**
'Glen Lyon'
'Glen Moy' ☆
'Southland'
'Sumner'
'Valentina' (yellow) ☆

Mid-season
'Glen Prosen' ☆

'Malling Jewel'

'Malling Jewel' ☆
'Tulameen'

Late
'Glen Magna'
'Leo'
'Malling Admiral'
'Octavia'

AUTUMN-FRUITING RASPBERRIES TO TRY

'All Gold' (yellow)
'Autumn Bliss'

'Autumn Bliss'

'Joan J' ☆
'Polka' ☆

Key
Pv *Partially virus-susceptible (must not be planted alongside 'Malling Jewel')*
☆ *Excellent flavour*

ESTABLISHED RASPBERRIES, PRUNING AFTER FRUITING

1 *When all the fruit has been picked, cut back all the fruited canes to ground level.*

2 *Tie the current season's strongest canes to the support wires when about 90cm (3ft) tall, spacing them 10cm (4in) apart: here the continuous lacing method is used.*

3 *At the end of the growing season, loop any tall canes over the top wire and tie them in.*

SPRING PRUNING

Before the growing season begins, tip prune all the canes to a healthy bud. Wherever possible, the cut should be made about 15cm (6in) above the top supporting wire.

the fruit from the central plug and the stalk; fruits for exhibiting should be picked complete with stalk, however. Remove and burn diseased or damaged fruits promptly to prevent the spread of infection to healthy fruits.

Propagation

In late autumn, select strong suckers that are growing away from the main fruiting row, and lift and replant them while they are dormant. Ensure that they are from plants that are known to be healthy and free-cropping; where doubt exists, use certified virus-free canes from specialist nurseries instead.

PROPAGATING BY SUCKERS

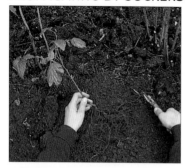

Lift suckers carefully in autumn and sever them from the parent plant. Remove any remaining foliage. Ensure that the suckers are healthy and replant where new stock is required. Water in thoroughly.

Autumn-fruiting raspberries

These should be sited in a sunny, sheltered position where the plants will quickly become established and the fruits should ripen in as short a time as possible. The fruits are borne freely on the upper part of the current season's canes. Planting and cultivation requirements are as for summer-fruiting raspberries.

Pruning of autumn-fruiting raspberries is carried out in late winter before growth starts; the fruited canes are all cut down to the ground to stimulate new canes, which will fruit in the autumn.

Late winter pruning
Before new growth starts, cut down all the canes to ground level. Fruit will be produced in autumn on the new season's canes.

Blackcurrants (*Ribes nigrum*)

Blackcurrants thrive only in cool-temperate regions. The bushes flower early, so are prone to frost damage on exposed sites. They fruit in midsummer. In parts of the USA their cultivation is prohibited because they are hosts for a rust disease on white pine. Jostaberries, a hybrid between blackcurrants and gooseberries, are cultivated in the same way.

Site and planting

The ground should be well prepared before planting to provide the best conditions for the continual production of new fruiting shoots. Remove all weeds from the site before planting and dig in plenty of manure.

Site

Choose a sunny, sheltered site; some shade is tolerated. Protect from spring frosts if necessary (see FROST AND WIND PROTECTION, pp.612–613). Blackcurrants grow in a range of soils but deep, moisture-retentive soil is most suitable; avoid wet, poorly drained ground. A pH of 6.5–7 is preferable; lime very acid soils (see p.625). Blackcurrants are self-fertile.

Planting

Plant disease-free bushes from certified stock. Bushes that are sold under certification schemes are normally two years old, but one-year-old plants from disease-free stock are also ideal. Planting in late autumn is preferable but blackcurrants may be planted throughout the winter. Handle the plants carefully to avoid damaging the basal buds. Space the bushes 1.2–1.5m (4–5ft) apart, with the same distance between the rows.

After planting, cut down all the shoots to one bud to encourage strong, new growth.

Routine care

In winter, apply sulphate of potash at a rate of 35g/sq m (1oz/sq yd) and a nitrogenous fertilizer at the same rate in spring. Mulch well in spring all round the bushes, with well-rotted manure, compost, or leaf mould, to conserve soil moisture.

Water in dry weather, but not as the fruits ripen, since this may cause the skins to split. Net bushes to protect ripening fruits from birds.

Pests and diseases

Aphids (p.646), birds (p.657), winter moth caterpillars (p.645), grey mould (*Botrytis*) (p.658), powdery mildew (p.658), and fungal leaf spots (p.648) may affect blackcurrants. Big bud mites (p.655) destroy the buds and carry reversion virus. Affected plants will need to be removed.

BLACKCURRANT BUSH
Year 1, Winter pruning

Pruning and training

Blackcurrants are grown with as many young shoots as possible originating at or near ground level. Most of the fruits are borne on shoots produced the previous season, and regular pruning is essential to maintain high yields. Pruning, together with adequate feeding, encourages strong, new shoots to develop.

Cut all stems to one bud above ground level straight after planting. The following year, remove any very weak, downward-pointing, or horizontal shoots. Thereafter, prune established bushes as buds begin to burst, before late winter, by cutting to the base one quarter to one third of two-year-old wood, and any older, weak wood. No tip pruning is required. New shoots are a pale tea colour, two-year-old wood is grey, and older wood black.

If a bush needs rejuvenating cut out a greater proportion of the old wood, retaining only those branches from which strong, young shoots have

NEW AND FRUITED SHOOTS

Pale, new shoot

Dark, fruited wood

developed. If few shoots develop yet the bush is healthy, cut down the whole plant to just above ground level in winter. Most bushes then rejuvenate well if fed and mulched, but one year's crop is sacrificed. The new shoots that develop may need thinning, retaining the strongest. After ten years or so it is better to replace a bush than to try to rejuvenate it.

Immediately after planting, cut back all stems to 1 bud above soil level.

Year 2, Winter pruning

The bush should develop 7 or 8 strong, new shoots. Cut back any weak or low-growing shoots to about 2.5cm (1in) above soil level, to encourage new growth from the base.

Established bush, pruning after fruiting

Cut out the old wood and one quarter to one third of two-year-old stems to stimulate new growth.

Remove any weak, damaged, or low-growing shoots, cutting close to the main stem.

BLACKCURRANTS TO TRY

Early
'Ben Gairn' **Rr**
'Big Ben'
'Boskoop Giant'

Mid-season
'Ben Connan'

'Ben Lomond'

'Ben Hope' **Rb**
'Ben Lomond'
'Ben Nevis'
'Wellington XXX'

Late
'Baldwin'
'Ben Alder'
'Ben More'
'Ben Sarek'
'Ben Tirran'

'Ben Sarek'

Key

Rb *Resistant to big bud mite*
Rr *Resistant to reversion virus*

Harvesting and storing

Blackcurrants are borne on "strigs" in bunches. Harvest the fruits when dry and ripe but still firm. Remove the whole bunch, not the individual fruits, which may otherwise be damaged. Early-ripening cultivars soon shed their fruits but late-ripening cultivars retain their fruits much longer. Fruits may either be eaten fresh or stored by bottling, preserving, or freezing.

Propagation

Blackcurrants are propagated from hardwood cuttings (see p.434) taken from healthy bushes in autumn. Retain all buds on the cuttings to encourage basal shoots to grow.

HARDWOOD CUTTINGS

Insert 20–25cm (8–10in) cuttings in a trench, leaving two buds exposed.

Red- and whitecurrants (*Ribes silvestre*)

Red- and whitecurrants require a cool climate. Whitecurrants are simply a colour variant of redcurrants; both fruit in midsummer and need the same growing conditions.

Site and planting

Red- and whitecurrants need a sunny site but tolerate some shade; in hot climates some shade may be necessary. Protect plants from winds to prevent their stems breaking, and in high temperatures to prevent scorching.

Prepare the soil well before planting, as for blackcurrants (see p.474). Heavier, moisture-retentive, but well-drained soils are preferable. Potassium deficiency may occur on very sandy soil. All cultivars are self-fertile.

When buying young bushes, ensure that the plants are from healthy stock that crops well. There is no certification scheme, however. Plant in autumn or winter: space bushes 1.2–1.5m (4–5ft) apart, cordons at 30cm (12in), and fans at 1.8m (6ft).

Routine care

For details of maintenance, see blackcurrants (p.474). Maintain high potash levels by applying potassium sulphate if necessary (muriate of potash may scorch the foliage).

Pests and diseases
Keep the plants covered with netting throughout the winter to prevent birds from damaging the buds. If the buds are damaged, delay winter pruning until just before bud-burst and then prune to healthy buds. Aphids (p.646), sawfly larvae (p.645), grey mould (*Botrytis*) (p.658), and coral spot (p.665) may affect plants.

Pruning and training

Red- and whitecurrants are normally grown as open-centre bushes but may be trained on supporting wires as cordons, double cordons, or fans. Fruits develop on spurs produced by pruning back the sideshoots.

Bush
A one-year-old bush should have two or three strong, young shoots; shorten these by half in late winter. Remove any that are less than 10cm (4in) from the ground to produce a short leg.

The following winter, shorten new growth by half to form the main branches, pruning to an outward-pointing bud. Prune sideshoots

REDCURRANT BUSH
Year 1, Winter pruning

Remove any side-shoots growing within 10cm (4in) of soil level by cutting flush with the stem. This will form a short leg at the base.

Prune each stem to an outward-facing bud (or to an upright shoot) about half-way along its length.

Year 2, Winter pruning

To form the permanent branches, shorten leaders and sideshoots by half of the new growth, cutting to outward-facing buds.

Cut back to 1 bud any sideshoots crowding the centre or growing downwards.

Established bush, winter pruning

Prune sideshoots to 1 bud.

Cut 5–7cm (2–3in) from the tips of the leaders to stimulate new growth the following season.

growing in- or downwards to one bud. Prune established bushes by cutting back sideshoots to one bud and tip pruning main branches.

Cordon

Single cordons are usually trained vertically. Set up wires at 60cm (24in) and 1.2m (4ft) from the ground. Select a main shoot on a one-year-old plant and train it against a cane;

prune back the shoot by half, then cut back all other shoots to one bud.

In summer, prune sideshoots to five leaves of new growth. Shorten these sideshoots to one or two buds in winter, and prune the leader by one quarter of the new growth. When the leader reaches the top of its support, trim it to one bud. A double cordon is developed by training two shoots at about 30° to the ground as for apples

(see "Forming a double cordon", p.441); they are subsequently trained vertically when 30cm (12in) apart. Each branch is then pruned as for a single cordon.

Fan

Fan-trained red- and whitecurrants are established as for a peach fan (see p.453). Each branch should then be pruned as a cordon.

Harvesting and storing

Harvest red- and whitecurrants as for blackcurrants. The plants tend to retain their ripe fruits a little longer than most blackcurrants. They may be bottled, preserved, or frozen.

Propagation

Take hardwood cuttings in early autumn. Use young shoots 30–38cm (12–15in) long, and remove all but the top three or four buds, to produce a plant with a short stem.

Insert the cuttings in moist, fertile soil, burying them by about half their length, and firm well. Once rooted, transplant to their final positions.

RED- AND WHITECURRANTS TO TRY

Early
'Jonkheer van Tets' (red)
'Laxton's No.1' (red)

'Jonkheer van Tets'

Mid-season
'Red Lake' (red)
'Stanza' (red)
'White Dutch' (white)
'White Grape' (white)

Late
'Blanka' (white)
'Redpoll' (red)
'Redstart' (red)
'Rondom' (red)

'White Grape'

HARDWOOD CUTTINGS

Cuttings should be 30cm (12in) long. Retain only the top few buds.

REDCURRANT CORDON
Year 1, Winter pruning

Cut back the leader by half of its new growth to stimulate new sideshoots.

If there are any sideshoots at planting, cut them back to 1 bud.

Year 1, Summer pruning

Prune back the current season's sideshoots to 5 leaves.

Established cordon, winter pruning

If the leader has reached the top wire, prune to 1 bud, or prune it back by one quarter of the summer's growth.

Trim back to the point of origin any shoots growing less than 10cm (4in) from the ground.

Cut back all the sideshoots to 1 or 2 buds to encourage the development of new spurs near the main stem.

Gooseberries (*Ribes uva-crispa*)

Gooseberry fruits ripen yellow, red, white, or green, depending on the cultivar. The Worcesterberry (*Ribes divaricatum*) resembles an over-vigorous, very thorny gooseberry bush, with small, red-purple fruits that make excellent jam, and has similar needs to a gooseberry bush.

Site and planting

Gooseberries are easy to grow. Like currants (*Ribes*), they need cool conditions and, if summer temperatures are high, adequate shade. Growing conditions and planting distances are as for redcurrants (see p.475). All cultivars are self-fertile.

Routine care

General maintenance is largely as for blackcurrants (see p.474). Gooseberries require high potassium levels and regular mulching, ideally with well-rotted manure. New shoots on young bushes are vulnerable to breakage and need protection from

strong winds. If the crop is heavy, thin the fruits in late spring.

Pests and diseases

Birds (p.657) may cause severe bud loss, so cover plants with netting. If the buds have been attacked, delay winter pruning until bud-burst, then prune to live buds. Gooseberry plants may be affected by powdery mildew (p.658), sawfly larvae (p.645), and bacterial or fungal leaf spots (p.648).

Pruning and training

Young plants may be trained as bushes, cordons, or fans as for redcurrants. A number of gooseberry cultivars, such as 'Leveller', have a natural drooping habit, however; to prevent stems from trailing to the ground, prune to upward-pointing buds, particularly when training young bushes.

Bush For initial pruning, see redcurrants (p.475); aim to create an open-centre bush on a stem 10–15cm (4–6in) long. Established bushes may be pruned by regulated or spur pruning in winter, to give large fruits.

Regulated pruning is the simpler method: remove low, crowded, and crossing shoots to maintain well-spaced growth at the centre of the bush; also remove any old, unproductive branches and select new, young shoots to replace them.

Spur pruning is more labour-intensive: all sideshoots are shortened to a suitable bud 8cm (3in) from the

Gooseberry standard

main branches. The branch leaders also need to be tip pruned.

Standard Cultivars to be trained as standards are grafted onto *Ribes odoratum* or *R. divaricatum* stock. Select one shoot of the rootstock and train it vertically, keeping any sideshoots short. It will take about three years to grow to a suitable height. When the stem has thickened and reached about 1.1–1.2m (3½–4ft), trim off the sideshoots and graft on the selected cultivar using whip-and-tongue grafting (see p.433). Use a strong stake to support the stem. The scion will develop and branch naturally the following summer. The next winter establish the framework as for a bush and then prune and train in the same way.

Cordon and fan These are trained as for redcurrants (see p.476). Once established, prune in summer, reducing new sideshoots to five leaves. In winter, shorten shoots to 8cm (3in) and tip prune leaders.

Harvesting and storing

Fruits should ripen by midsummer. Gooseberries for cooking should be picked while still green, but allow dessert-quality cultivars to ripen fully on the bush for the best flavour, ensuring that they are protected from

GOOSEBERRIES TO TRY

Early
'Golden Drop' (yellow)
'May Duke' (red)
'Rokula' (red) **Rm**

'Invicta'

Mid-season
'Careless' (white)
'Greenfinch' (green) **Rm**
'Invicta' (green) **Rm**
'Keepsake' (green)
'Lancashire Lad' (red) **Rm**
'Langley Gage' (white)
'Leveller' (yellow)
'Pax' (red) **Th, Rm**
'Whinham's Industry' (red)
'Whitesmith' (white)

'Whinham's Industry'

Late
'Captivator' (red) **Th**
'Hinonmäki Röd' (red)
'Lancer' (green)
'London' (red)
'White Lion' (white)

Key

Rm *Some resistance to mildew*
Th *Nearly thornless*

birds. Yellow-, white-, and red-berried cultivars should be left to ripen to their full colour before they are picked. Gooseberries freeze well.

Propagation

Take hardwood cuttings in early autumn. Gooseberry hardwood cuttings may be difficult to root; retaining all the buds often improves the success rate. Remove all low buds and sideshoots when the rooted cutting is lifted. If this is not done, troublesome suckers will develop.

GOOSEBERRY BUSH
Year 1, Winter pruning

Prune back all the shoots by a half to three quarters to an outward-facing bud.

Established bush, regulated pruning, winter

Cut out older branches to prevent overcrowding and to maintain an open centre.

The bush should have mainly young shoots, evenly spaced, pointing up- or outwards.

Established bush, spur pruning, winter

Prune all new sideshoots to a bud about 8cm (3in) from their base.

Tip prune the branch leaders to 3 or 4 buds of the new growth. This encourages the formation of spurs.

HARDWOOD CUTTINGS

1 *In early autumn, trim young shoots to 30–38cm (12–15in), with an angled cut above a bud at the top and a straight cut at the base. Dip in rooting hormone and insert in a trench to half their length.*

2 *The following autumn, carefully lift the rooted cuttings. Remove basal buds or shoots less than 10cm (4in) from the base (see inset), before transplanting the young plants.*

Blueberries (*Vaccinium corymbosum*)

Highbush blueberries are derived from the American wild blueberry. They produce clusters of fruits that are a dark, hazy purple-blue with a grey bloom; their flavour is enriched by cooking or preserving. They require a cool, moist climate, needing 700–1,200 hours below 7°C (45°F) and very acid soil (pH 4–5.5). Highbush blueberries grow to a height of 1.3–2m (4½–6ft) and are deciduous, with white flowers in spring, and striking gold and scarlet autumn colour.

Rabbit-eye blueberries (*Vaccinium ashei*) are grown in the same way as the highbush group, but tolerate less acid soils and drier conditions; they are cultivated mainly in Australia and the USA. The fruits are smaller and more gritty than highbush blueberries.

Cropping, in mid- to late summer, is light at first but after five or six years yields of 2.25kg (5lb) of fruit per bush may be obtained, and on older bushes considerably more. Blueberries are self-fertile, but crop better when two or more cultivars are planted close together.

Site and planting

Blueberries need a sunny location, although they tolerate some shade. The soil must be well drained. Clear all perennial weeds from the site before planting and, if the soil is alkaline, correct this by mixing a 15cm (6in) layer of acidic compost with the existing soil to a depth of at least 60cm (2ft). Alternatively, apply flowers of sulphur at a rate of 50–120g/sq m (2–4oz/sq yd).

Blueberries may also be grown in large pots or tubs with a diameter of 30–38cm (12–15in), filled with ericaceous compost.

Highbush blueberry bush

Plant from late autumn to late winter, spacing bushes 1.5m (5ft) apart. Cover the roots with 2.5–5cm (1–2in) of soil, and mulch with acid compost or leaf mould. Growing a mixture of cultivars results in better fertilization and heavier crops.

Routine care

To promote growth and cropping and to maintain acidity, apply a dressing each spring of sulphate of ammonia at 35g/sq m (1oz/sq yd) and sulphate of potash at 35g/sq m (1oz/sq yd).

Keep plants mulched with acid compost, and water as needed with rainwater. Avoid root disturbance when weeding.

Pests and diseases

The fruits may be eaten by birds, so provide protection by netting the bushes (see "Protection from birds", p.427). Other pests and diseases rarely cause any trouble.

ESTABLISHED BLUEBERRY BUSH, WINTER PRUNING

Cut weak or unproductive shoots back to where a strong new shoot can take over.

Cut to ground level older, non-fruiting branches to stimulate new basal shoots.

Cut back any low or downward-pointing branches to their point of origin or to a branch growing in the required direction.

Pruning and training

Blueberries fruit on two- or three-year-old wood. New bushes need little pruning for two or three years, but cut out weak shoots to provide a strong basic framework.

Thereafter, prune to ensure regular production of new shoots from the base, as for blackcurrants (see pp.474–475), by cutting out some of the oldest wood each year.

Harvesting and storing

The fruits ripen over a period of several weeks. Pick over the bushes carefully, harvesting only the ripe fruits, which should part easily from the cluster. Blueberries may be successfully stored for later use by preserving, bottling, or freezing.

Propagation

Take 10–15cm (4–6in) softwood cuttings in midsummer, dip them in hormone rooting powder, and then insert them in an acidic, peat/sand rooting medium. Place the cuttings in a propagator until rooted, then transplant to a larger pot. Harden off before planting out.

HIGHBUSH BLUEBERRIES TO TRY

Early
'Bluecrop'
'Bluetta'

Mid-season
'Berkeley'
'Chandler'
'Herbert'
'Ivanhoe'

Late
'Coville'
'Grover'
'Jersey'

'Bluetta'

BLUEBERRY SOFTWOOD CUTTINGS

1 Select suitable softwood material and take cuttings at least 10cm (4in) long. Cut just above a leaf joint.

2 Trim the base of each cutting just below a node with a sharp knife, and remove the leaves from the lower third of the cuttings. Dip the ends of the cuttings in hormone rooting powder.

3 Prepare a pot of acid cutting compost. Make holes with a dibber and insert each cutting so that the basal leaves are just above the compost. Water, label, and place the pot in a propagator.

Tender fruits

Most tender fruits originate from tropical and subtropical regions, where they thrive in the warm, dry conditions. Apart from olives, many may be eaten straight from the tree, or stored for a short period of time in suitable conditions. Members of the citrus family that are too acid for eating, such as lemons and limes, are grown either for their juice or for use in preserves and marmalades. Since tender fruits are generally grown in hot climates, where the soil may be lacking in nutrients, it is important to prepare the site adequately when planting: an extra 110–180g (4–6oz) of slow-release fertilizer forked into the base of the planting hole will help the plants to establish quickly.

In cool-temperate climates, some tender fruits may still be grown, in containers or under cover, as long as the correct temperature and humidity levels are provided (see CONTAINER GARDENING, "Subtropical container gardens", p.318). Although many do not consistently ripen their fruits under cover, they nevertheless make attractive ornamentals.

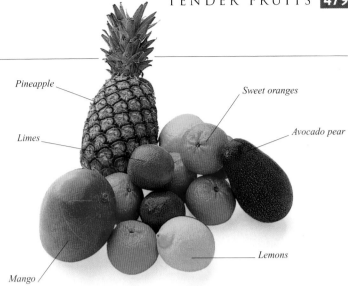

Pineapple
Limes
Sweet oranges
Avocado pear
Lemons
Mango

Pineapples (*Ananas comosus*)

Pineapples are tropical perennials producing terminal fruits, each composed of up to 200 seedless fruitlets. For best results they need full sun and temperatures of 18–30°C (64–86°F) with humidity of 70–80 per cent. Cultivar groups include the Cayenne Group, the Queen Group, and the Spanish Group, of which the Spanish has the sweetest flavour.

Site and planting

Select a sunny site that is sheltered from strong winds. Pineapples tolerate a wide range of soils, but prefer a sandy, medium loam with a pH of 4.5–5.5. Plant "slips" or suckers about 30cm (12in) apart, with 60cm (24in) between rows, or at a spacing of 50cm (20in) each way.

Routine care

Use a general-purpose fertilizer with medium potassium and high nitrogen levels at intervals of two to three months, at a rate of 50g (2oz) per plant. Correct any iron and zinc deficiencies by spraying with a 2 per cent solution of ferrous or zinc sulphate. Water pineapples regularly in dry weather and apply an organic mulch to conserve soil moisture.

Pests and diseases

Pests that may affect pineapples include mealybugs (p.646), root-knot eelworms (p.660), scale insects (p.648), red spider mite (p.646), and thrips (p.647).

The most serious disease affecting pineapple plants in the open is heart rot, caused by *Phytophthora cinnamoni* and *P. parasitica*, fungi that often affect pineapples grown in wet conditions. Since this is difficult to treat, it is advisable to guard against infection by planting resistant cultivars where these are available; all suckers that are required for propagation should be dipped in a fungicide, since the fungus enters through wounds.

Growing under cover

Plant rooted pineapple "slips" or cuttings in well-prepared beds with good drainage, or use pots at least 30cm (12in) in diameter. Use compost with a high organic content and apply a liquid feed every three to four weeks. Maintain a temperature of at least 20°C (68°F) and humidity of about 70 per cent. Water regularly and thoroughly, particularly while young plants are establishing.

Harvesting and storing

Harvest the fruits when they begin to turn yellow by cutting the stem 2.5–5cm (1–2in) below each fruit. Pineapples may be stored for up to three weeks at 8°C (46°F) and at 90 per cent humidity.

Propagation

The terminal crown shoot may be used as a cutting; remove it with about 1cm (½in) of the fruit attached. Pineapples may also be propagated

PROPAGATING PINE-APPLES FROM SUCKERS

Sever basal slips or suckers and leave to dry before inserting in a sandy cutting compost (see inset).

by "slips" or suckers that develop from below the fruit or suckers produced in the leaf axils; these may be detached with a sharp knife. Dip the cut surfaces of slips or suckers in a fungicide, then leave them to dry for several days. Remove the lower leaves and insert the cuttings in pots of sandy compost. Pot them on into 15cm (6in) pots when rooted.

PINEAPPLES TO TRY

Cayenne Group
'Baronne de Rothschild'
'Cayenne Lissa'
'Smooth Cayenne'

Queen Group
'Natal Queen'
'Ripley Queen'

Spanish Group
'Red Spanish'
'Singapore Spanish'

PROPAGATING PINEAPPLES FROM THE CROWN SHOOT

1 *Scoop out the crown shoot of a ripe pineapple with a sharp knife, ensuring that you do not cut through the base of the shoot. Dip the wound in fungicide and leave for several days to dry.*

2 *Insert the prepared cutting into a pot of cuttings compost and maintain at a temperature of at least 18°C (64°F). The cutting should be rooted and ready to pot on within a few weeks.*

Pineapple

Papayas (*Carica papaya*)

Papayas (or paw-paws) are slender, generally single-stemmed, tropical trees, growing up to 4–5m (12–15ft) with a spread of 1–2m (3–6ft) at the crown. The fruits may be up to 20cm (8in) long when mature. A temperature range of 22–28°C (72–82°F) with humidity of 60–70 per cent is normally required; some cultivars will withstand temperatures as low as 15°C (59°F), although flowering and fruiting may then be poor.

Site and planting

Choose a warm, sunny site with protection from strong winds. Papayas require fertile, well-drained soil, with a pH of 6–7; good drainage is essential, since the trees are sensitive to waterlogging.

Many cultivars of papaya are dioecious, with male and female flowers produced on separate plants, but hermaphrodite cultivars are sometimes available. One male tree is usually sufficient to pollinate five or six female trees. Pollination is normally by insects and wind. Plant at a spacing of 2.5–3m (8–10ft).

Routine care

Apply a general-purpose, balanced fertilizer, 1–1.5kg (2–3½lb) per tree per year, in two or three separate dressings during the growing season. Water regularly in dry conditions and conserve moisture by using an organic mulch (see SOILS AND FERTILIZERS, "Organic mulches", p.626). Papayas may be affected by viruses and eelworms after three or four years; if this happens, they should be replaced with either young plants of named cultivars or seedlings.

Pests and diseases

Common pests in the open are root-knot eelworms (p.660); papaya diseases include anthracnose (p.666), powdery mildew (p.646), and damping off of seedlings (p.664). Papaya trees grown under cover may also be attacked by aphids (p.646), thrips (p.647), whiteflies (p.646), and mealybugs (p.646).

PAPAYAS TO TRY

'Graeme' **D**
'Guinea Gold' **H**
'Higgins' **H**
'Honey Gold' **D**
'Hortus Gold' **D**

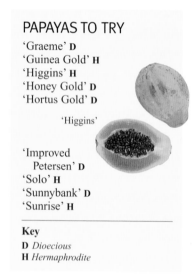
'Higgins'

'Improved
   Petersen' **D**
'Solo' **H**
'Sunnybank' **D**
'Sunrise' **H**

Key
D *Dioecious*
H *Hermaphrodite*

Growing under cover

In temperate areas, papayas may be grown successfully under cover, if adequate light and temperature levels are provided. Raise seedlings or cuttings as described under "Propagation", below. Transplant them when they are 20–25cm (8–10in) tall into prepared beds, or pots with a minimum diameter of 35cm (14in). Use a fertile compost, to which a slow-release fertilizer has been added. Maintain a temperature of at least 22°C (72°F) and humidity of 60–70 per cent. Apply a liquid feed or light dressings of fertilizer with medium to high nitrogen content every three to four weeks. The plants should be watered regularly.

Pruning and training

Remove any lateral branches, since these are unproductive. After fruiting, prune to 30cm (12in) from the ground; of the new shoots that arise, select the strongest as the new leader and cut back the others.

Harvesting and storing

Harvest the fruits when they are orange to red. They may be stored at 10–13°C (50–55°F) with 70 per cent humidity for up to 14 days.

Propagation

Seed is the usual method of propagation. Sow the seed under cover in trays or, preferably, in bottomless pots

Papaya tree

6–9cm (2½–3½in) in diameter. Handle the seedlings carefully, since papayas are sensitive to root disturbance. Harden them off, then plant them out when they are 30–45cm (12–18in) tall. To obtain adequate numbers of female plants when dioecious cultivars are used, plant seedlings in clumps of three or four, thinning to one female plant after flowering begins. Hermaphrodite seedlings may be planted singly.

Cuttings are usually obtained by pruning mature trees to 30–40cm (12–16in) from the ground and using the new shoots as cuttings. Dip their bases in hormone rooting powder and grow them on under cover.

Citrus (*Citrus* spp.)

The genus *Citrus* includes oranges, lemons, and a number of other edible species (see p.481). Citrus form small, widely branching trees on trunks of 50–60cm (20–24in) in circumference. The trees will reach a height of 3–10m (10–30ft) and a spread of 5–8m (15–25ft). Limes are the most compact, grapefruits the largest and most vigorous. Lemon trees have a more upright habit than the other species. Also discussed here is the kumquat, which was formerly included within the genus *Citrus* but is now classified as *Fortunella*. Its cultivation requirements are similar to those of *Citrus*.

Citrus is a subtropical genus. All species and hybrids are evergreen and have aromatic leaves. For optimum growth, they require a temperature of 15–30°C (59–86°F), although most species will survive short periods at 0°C (32°F). They thrive at altitudes of 100m (320ft) or above, with humidity levels of 60–70 per cent, unless otherwise stated. Flowering is not seasonal but occurs during warm periods with regular rainfall; flowers and fruits may coincide. Many species of citrus make excellent plants for growing in containers under cover in temperate areas.

Site and planting

Citrus prefer a sunny aspect and should be protected by windbreaks in exposed areas. They tolerate a wide range of soils but do best in fertile, well-drained, slightly acid soils (pH 6–6.5). Young citrus respond well to a high soil fertility.

Rootstocks

Sweet orange may be used, since it is compatible with all widely grown citrus species and cultivars. Rough lemon rootstocks produce early-bearing, vigorous trees tolerant of tristeza (quick decline) viruses, but their fruits may have thick rinds and a low acid and sugar content. Sour orange is also a good universal rootstock, but it is susceptible to tristeza viruses.

Trifoliate orange is a dwarfing rootstock that is suitable for cooler areas. It has some resistance to eelworms but is not compatible with certain cultivars of lemon. Cleopatra mandarin and Troyer citrange are also used as rootstocks. Seedling rootstocks may also be raised – for details, see "Propagation", p.481.

Pollination

Most citrus, including sweet orange, are self-fertile, so a pollinator is not normally required; many, for instance the 'Washington' sweet orange, also produce seedless fruits.

Planting

Planting distances vary between 5m (15ft) and 10m (30ft) each way, depending on the vigour of the species or cultivar chosen. Citrus are sensitive to waterlogging, so on a site

Sweet orange tree

where the soil is not sufficiently well drained, plant each tree on a slight mound, 5–7cm (2–3in) high. For pot-grown citrus see CONTAINER GARDENING, "Planting large and long-term plants", p.324.

Routine care

During the first few years, feed citrus trees with a balanced fertilizer that has a high nitrogen and medium potassium level at a rate of 1kg (2lb 4oz) per tree per year. The fertilizer should be given in two or three doses, applied at regular intervals around the base of each tree, when the trees are in active growth. Double the quantity of fertilizer after five years. A mulch helps to retain moisture.

Remove all weeds around the bases of the trees, and water thoroughly in dry weather, particularly when the flowers or fruits are developing. The non-seasonal habit of fruiting makes fruit thinning unnecessary. Remove any suckers.

Pests and diseases

Various mealybugs (p.646), scale insects (p.648), thrips (p.647), red spider mite (p.646), aphids (p.646), root and crown rots (see *"Phytophthora* root rots", p.654), anthracnose (p.666), blue mould (p.658), and scab (p.649) may affect citrus grown in the open ground as well as under cover. Root-knot eelworms (p.660) may be serious pests on some soils. In the tropics and subtropics, fruit flies may be a problem.

Many citrus species and cultivars may be infected with tristeza virus, which is spread by aphids and causes stem pitting on grapefruits, limes, and citrons. Infected trees will lose vigour and produce small fruits. The virus is most likely to affect cultivars that are budded onto sour orange rootstocks. Spray against aphids, or use alternative rootstocks.

Growing under cover

In temperate areas, several cultivars of sweet orange, tangerine, lemon, and lime, as well as the Seville orange and kumquat, may be grown under cover, although they may not be relied on to bear fruit. Prepare the beds well, or use large containers, at least 60cm (2ft) in diameter, filled with a nutrient-rich compost. Maintain a minimum temperature of 20°C (68°F) with at least 75 per cent humidity, and water the plants regularly. Apply a liquid fertilizer each month once the young trees are well established.

Pruning and training

Shorten the main branches of newly planted trees by one third in the first year. This encourages lateral growth and produces a rounded overall shape. After fruiting, prune citrus trees only to remove dead, diseased, or crossing branches and any that touch the soil. Citrus may also be trained as standards or half-standards (see p.439), particularly if they are grown as ornamentals.

Harvesting and storing

Citrus fruits may take from six to eight months, or even longer, from fruit set to ripen, depending on the climate (the lower the temperature, the longer the period required). In areas of low sunshine, mature citrus fruits may remain green.

Harvest the fruits when they have ripened by cutting them at the fruit stalk with secateurs or a sharp knife or by pulling the fruit stalk from the tree with a slight twist. Undamaged fruits may be stored for several weeks at 4–6°C (39–43°F).

Propagation

Some citrus may be raised from seed. Most citrus seeds are polyembryonic and therefore "clonal", reproducing characteristics of the parent tree. The quality of fruits from non-polyembryonic cultivars is variable. For named cultivars the usual means of propagation is by budding.

To raise citrus trees from seed, use fresh seed, sowing it in trays or pots of seed compost at a depth of 3–5cm (1¼–2in). Water the seeds frequently and maintain a temperature of 25–32°C (77–90°F). When the seedlings are large enough to handle, prick them out into 10 or 12cm (4 or 5in) pots. When they are 20–30cm (8–12in) high, transplant them into 21–30cm (8–12in) pots, or plant them out, after hardening them off. Alternatively, repot them into 25–38cm (10–15in) pots and plant in the open when they are 60–90cm (2–3ft) tall.

T-budding (see p.433) is the usual method of propagating citrus vegetatively. Use seedling citrus stocks with stems 1cm (½in) in diameter. After three to four weeks, remove the budding tape and cut the stock growth above the budded area half-way across. When the bud shoot is 2.5cm (1in) long, the stock growth above the budded shoot may be removed entirely.

Ripe sweet oranges

Species of citrus

Limes (*Citrus aurantiifolia*)

There are two main groups of lime. One has an acidic taste, the other is fairly sweet and is often used as a rootstock. One of the acidic cultivars grown most commonly is 'West Indian'. Its fruits are round, small, and thin-skinned, with few seeds; the skin and pulp are green.

Most limes are grown as seedlings but may also be reproduced by bud-grafting onto rough lemon rootstock.

Sour, Seville, or bitter oranges (*Citrus aurantium*)

The sour, or bitter, orange is an upright-growing tree, which is relatively cold-hardy. The fruits, used for making marmalade, are about 7cm (3in) in diameter, rounded, with thick peel. They are fairly acidic, but some forms bear fruits that have a lower citric acid content.

Lemons (*Citrus limon*)

Most lemon cultivars produce seeded fruits that may remain green, rather than turning yellow, even when fully mature. To grow successfully in the open, they prefer an altitude of 300–500m (1,000–1,600ft), with little variation in temperature, and need a minimum temperature of 20°C (68°F). As with other citrus, fruits may take 9–11 months to mature, and they often appear on a tree at the same time as its flowers.

Citrons (*Citrus medica*)

The fruits of the citron are ovoid and yellow, with a thick rind and a rough surface, and may be up to 15cm (6in) long; the pulp contains little juice.

Two main groups of citron cultivars have been recorded: acid cultivars such as 'Diamante' and 'Ethrog', and non-acid cultivars such as 'Corsican'. Citrons are grown mainly for their peel, which is usually candied for

CITRUS TO TRY

Limes
'Persian' (sweet)
'West Indian' (acid)

'Persian'

Sour oranges
'Bouquet de Fleurs'
'Chinotto'

Lemons
'Garey's Eureka'
'Genoa'
'Lisbon'
'Meyer's Lemon'
'Villa Franca'

Grapefruits
'Foster' (pink flesh)
'Marsh Seedless' (white flesh)

'Red Blush'

'Red Blush',
(pink flesh)
'Star Ruby' (red flesh)

Mandarins
'Clementine'
'Encore'
'King'
'Miyagowa'

'Clementine'

Tangelos
'Minneola'
'Ugli'

Sweet oranges
'Jaffa' (Common)
'Malta Blood' (Blood)
'Moro Blood' (Blood)
'Ruby' (Blood)
'Sanguinelli' (Blood)
'Shamouti' (Common)

'Jaffa'

'Trovita' (Common)
'Valencia' (Common)
'Washington' (Navel)

use in the confectionery trade. Citrons make very attractive ornamentals, however; in temperate areas they may be grown under cover (see p.481).

Grapefruits (*Citrus x paradisi*)
The fruits of the grapefruit are large, rounded, up to 10–15cm (4–6in) in diameter, and yellow. Most cultivars are well adapted to growing at or just above sea level, provided the temperature exceeds 25°C (77°F). There are two principal groups of grapefruit in cultivation, one with white pulp, the other with pink; seeded and seedless cultivars are available in both groups.

Mandarins or tangerines (*Citrus reticulata*)
Mandarins, or tangerines, generally require temperatures above 18°C (64°F), but very high temperatures may result in loss of fruit quality.

Cross-pollination between trees frequently occurs; this gives rise to fruits with many seeds.

The Satsuma Group is the one most frequently cultivated; the fruits of cultivars in this group are mainly slightly flattened and seedless, with a well-developed orange colour and sweet flavour. Some cultivars have a "navel", a miniature fruit that develops at the end of the fruit. The other three groups are the Cleopatra Group, which is widely used as a rootstock but has unpalatable fruits itself, the King Group, and the Common Mandarin Group (which includes the cultivar 'Clementine').

Tangelos or ugli fruits (*Citrus x tangelo*)
This hybrid between the grapefruit and the mandarin inherits some characteristics from each of its parents; the orange fruits are larger than those of the mandarin but have a

relatively thin, easily peeled skin. They may be grown under cover in temperate areas, where they may occasionally bear fruit.

Sweet oranges (*Citrus sinensis*)
Sweet orange cultivars are usually classified into three groups: Valencia, navel, and blood oranges. Most sweet oranges, including the widely grown 'Jaffa' orange, belong to the Valencia (or Common) Group. The fruits are medium to large and spherical to ovoid, with few or no seeds. Oranges in this group may have a slightly acid taste but have an excellent flavour.

Navel oranges have a small secondary fruit at the main fruit apex and are usually seedless. They grow well in slightly cooler climates, peel and separate easily, and have excellent flavour. Blood oranges are similar but their pulp, juice, and rind are red (except when they are grown at high temperatures).

Sweet oranges are usually grown from seed, but a few specific cultivars are propagated vegetatively by bud-grafting (see p.432). Seedlings are also widely used as rootstocks for grafting with other species. Two sweet orange crops at different stages of development may be borne on a tree at the same time.

Kumquats (*Fortunella japonica, F. margarita*)
Originating in China, kumquats are hardier than the citrus fruits described above: they can withstand temperatures down to -5°C (23°F) for short periods. The fruits, which may be eaten unpeeled, are small and yellow. Those of *Fortunella japonica* are rounded in shape, while those of *F. margarita* are ovoid.

The calamondin (x *Citrofortunella microcarpa*) is a mandarin-kumquat hybrid; it is grown as an ornamental in temperate regions.

Tamarillos (*Cyphomandra betacea*)

Also known as tree tomatoes, tamarillos are subtropical trees growing to 3–5m (10–15ft), with a spread of 1.5–2.5m (5–8ft). They are most productive at 20–28°C (68–82°F) with 70 per cent humidity. The red, orange, or yellow fruits are ovoid and may be 7.5cm (3in) long.

Ripe tamarillos

Site and planting
Tamarillos need a sunny position and protection from the wind in exposed sites, since the stems are quite brittle. Fertile, loam soils produce the best results. Allow a planting distance of about 3m (10ft) each way.

Routine care
A general-purpose fertilizer with medium to high nitrogen should be applied every two to three months at a rate of 110g (4oz) for each tree. Water well during dry periods, and use an organic mulch around the base of the plants to prevent loss of moisture from the soil.

Pests and diseases
Tamarillos in the open may be affected by aphids (p.646). They are susceptible to cucumber mosaic virus and potato virus "Y" (see "Viruses", pp.649 and 659); *Phytophthora palmivora* and *P. infestans* (see "Tomato/potato blight", p.649) may also cause problems. Under cover, plants may

sometimes be attacked by thrips, (p.647), whiteflies (p.646), red spider mite (p.646), and powdery mildew (p.658).

Growing under cover
Tamarillos may be grown in containers with a diameter of at least 35cm (14in) or in well-prepared beds. Use compost mixed with a general-purpose fertilizer. Maintain the correct temperatures and humidity, water regularly, and apply a liquid feed every three to four weeks.

Pruning and training
When plants reach a height of 1m (3ft), remove the growing point to encourage branching. Little pruning is needed apart from removing crowded and crossing branches, and diseased or dead wood.

Harvesting and storing
Tamarillos usually fruit one to two years after planting. Detach the fruits using a sharp knife when they start to

Tamarillos

change colour. They may be stored for up to two weeks at a temperature of 4–6°C (39–43°F).

Propagation
Sow seed under cover; pot seedlings individually into 10cm (4in) pots when they are 3–5cm (1¼–2in) tall. When they reach 15–25cm (6–10in), harden them off and plant them out in the open. Propagation is also easy from virus-free softwood cuttings: select shoots 10–15cm (4–6in) long and use a sandy (but not acid) compost. Follow the procedure as for blueberries (see p.478).

Loquats (*Eriobotrya japonica*)

A member of the family Rosaceae, the loquat is an attractive, evergreen tree growing to 7m (22ft) or more tall, with a spread of about 5m (15ft). Loquats are best suited to a subtropical environment and need a minimum temperature of 15°C (59°F) to flower and fruit regularly. They are widely grown in the Mediterranean region. In

cooler climates loquats may be successfully grown under cover, since they are able to withstand relatively low temperatures for short periods. Some cultivars have a low chilling requirement.

Loquats bear clusters of fragrant, cream-coloured flowers, followed by bunches of round, yellow fruits

3–8cm (1¼–3in) long with tough skins. The pulp is soft and sweet.

Suitable rootstocks for loquats include quince (*Cydonia oblonga*), medlar (*Mespilus* spp.), and vigorous loquat seedlings. Most loquat cultivars are self-pollinated, but cross-pollination by insects may also occur.

Site and planting
Select a warm, sunny situation. Windbreaks should be erected to reduce wind damage and moisture evaporation. Loquats tolerate a wide range of soils, but prefer a well-drained, fertile, slightly acid loam. The trees should be planted at a distance of 4–5m (12–15ft) each way.

Routine care

Apply a top-dressing of general-purpose fertilizer at a rate of about 450g (16oz) per tree every three to four months. Loquats must be regularly watered to keep the roots moist during dry periods; regular applications of organic mulch help to reduce water loss. Keep the surrounding area free of weeds.

To ensure the production of large fruits, thin the bunches at an early stage of their development. Remove any that are weak or damaged, leaving healthy, evenly spaced fruitlets.

Pests and diseases

Plants in the open have few problems. Under cover, however, loquats may be attacked by thrips (p.647), mealybugs (p.646), red spider mite (p.646), whiteflies (p.646), and powdery mildew (p.658).

Growing under cover

Young, seed-raised plants may be grown in containers or planted out in well-prepared beds when they are about 45cm (18in) tall. Use a loam-based compost, with a slow-release fertilizer incorporated, and maintain a temperature of at least 18°C (64°F) during the summer. Water them regularly, and apply a liquid feed every month.

Pruning and training

Minimal pruning is required for loquats other than tip pruning all over-vigorous shoots and removing wayward branches; any crossing, damaged, dead, or diseased branches should also be removed.

Harvesting and storing

Harvest when the fruits soften and begin to turn rich yellow or orange. Short-term storage is possible at temperatures of 5–10°C (41–50°F).

Propagation

Loquats may be propagated by seed, sown 2–3cm (¾–1¼in) deep in pots of sandy seed compost, and maintained

Ripe loquats

Loquat tree

at not less than 18°C (64°F). Transplant seedlings to their final positions when they are 7–10cm (3–4in) high. Other techniques that may be used for propagating loquat cultivars include T-budding (see p.433), air layering (see INDOOR GARDENING, p.383), and spliced side grafting (see *Propagating Trees by Spliced Side Grafting*, p.82).

Mangos (*Mangifera indica*)

Mangos are tropical, evergreen trees that often reach 30m (100ft) when grown from vigorous seedlings. If dwarfing rootstocks and compact-growing clones are used, the trees' height may be restricted to 7–10m (22–30ft). The spread is about 8m (25ft) for dwarf types.

Mango fruits vary from 5 to 30cm (2 to 12in) in length and may weigh from 100g (3½oz) up to about 2kg (4lb 6oz). They have a leathery skin and may be orange, yellow, green, or red, depending on the cultivar. The single seed may comprise 25 per cent of the total volume of the fruit. Cultivars are available that are adapted to growing in subtropical areas with a temperature range of

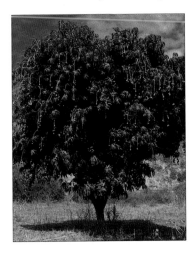

Mango tree

21–25°C (70–77°F) with humidity above 60 per cent; the higher temperature is regarded as the optimum for most cultivars. For successful flowering and fruit set, mangos require a high light intensity and a dry period.

Site and planting

Select a warm, sunny aspect. If necessary, provide protection from strong winds, since high moisture loss may seriously affect the growth of the trees; very low humidity may worsen the situation, and lead to leaf scorch, seed abortion, and fruit drop.

Soil type is less important for mangos than it is for most other tree crops, and both sandy loams and medium clays are suitable, provided they are well drained. Mangos need a pH of between 5.5 and 7.5.

Dwarfing rootstocks are rapidly becoming available; these are often more suitable, particularly for small gardens, than non-selected local cultivars. If dwarfing rootstocks are not available, polyembryonic seedlings produced from parent trees selected for their high quality of fruit and yield are to be preferred.

Pollination is only successful in relatively dry weather, since high humidity and heavy rainfall limit fertilization (flowering usually begins after a period of cool or dry weather). A solution of potassium nitrate, applied as a spray, may promote flowering. Pollination is mainly by insects, although some mango cultivars are self-fertile.

Space compact and dwarf cultivars 8m (25ft) apart each way; more vigorous cultivars require a spacing of 10–12m (30–40ft).

Routine care

Feed with a general-purpose fertilizer with medium potassium and high nitrogen levels, at a rate of 1–1.5kg (2–3½lb) per tree, per year. This should be applied in three or four doses during the growing season; after the fourth year of growth, double the amount.

Water mangos well during dry periods, particularly in the first three years of growth, since plenty of moisture is essential for root development. An organic mulch retains moisture and suppresses weed (see "Organic mulches", p.626). Fruit thinning is rarely necessary.

Pests and diseases

In the tropics, mangos are liable to attack by fruit flies and mealybugs (p.646); various types of scale insect (p.648) may also be a problem. Diseases that may affect trees in the open include anthracnose (p.666) and powdery mildew (p.646).

Mangos grown under cover may also be subject to damage by aphids (p.646), whiteflies (p.646), thrips (p.647), red spider mite (p.646), and certain forms of powdery and downy mildew (p.646).

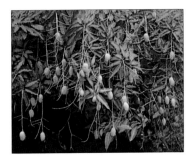

Mangos

Growing under cover

Mangos grown from seed are likely to be too vigorous for growing under cover unless they have been grafted onto a dwarfing rootstock, when they will form attractive, ornamental trees. They may be grown in large containers or well-prepared beds. In temperate regions, flowering will generally occur under cover only towards the end of the growing season, and only if the optimum growing conditions have been provided. However, fruiting cannot be guaranteed, and is dependent on successful pollination.

Transplant young plants when they are about 1m (3ft) tall. They will require a compost containing a slow-release fertilizer with a medium potassium and high nitrogen content. Ensure that a minimum temperature of 21–25°C (70–77°F) and humidity of about 75 per cent are maintained. Mangos grown under cover should

MANGOS TO TRY

'Alphonso'
'Haden'   'Tommy
'Keith'   Atkins'
'Kensington'
'Kent'
'Palmer'
'Tommy
    Atkins'
'Zill'

be watered regularly and given a liquid feed every month. Supplement this with sprays of a nitrogenous fertilizer if the leaves turn yellow due to lack of nitrogen.

Pruning and training

Restrict pruning to tip pruning the leading shoot when it is about 1m (3ft) long to encourage lateral branching. Remove overcrowded or very vigorous growth during the early years to ensure an evenly spaced, rounded tree canopy. Once the tree is established, pruning is limited to the removal of diseased, dead, or crossing branches, or those that are congested.

Harvesting and storing

Mangos fruit three to four years after planting. The fruits should be picked when they begin to change colour. Handle them carefully to avoid any damage by bruising.

Any mangos that are slightly immature may be stored at 10°C (50°F) for two to four weeks, maintaining humidity of 90–95 per cent; they should ripen during this time.

Propagation

Propagation from seed is possible for polyembryonic cultivars, or various methods of grafting may be used instead. For seed propagation, remove the pulp of ripe fruits; to hasten germination, soak the seed in water for 48 hours and carefully remove the seed coat. Sow immediately in beds or containers, using well-prepared compost, and with the convex side of the seeds uppermost, lightly covering them with compost, and water.

The resulting seedlings may be polyembryonic and similar to the parent tree, but they are also likely to be very vigorous and take five to eight years to bear fruits that may prove variable in quality. A mango seed usually produces at least one such vigorous seedling resulting from self- or cross-pollination; any such seedlings should be discarded. The remaining seedlings are ready for transplanting to containers at least 15cm (6in) in diameter within six to eight weeks and may be used for rootstocks. Alternatively, they may be grown on as fruiting trees.

Mangos may also be propagated vegetatively, although stem cuttings often fail to root successfully. "Approach" grafting is a recommended alternative. Take a container-grown rootstock that is about one year old. Place the container near the scion branch still growing on the parent tree. Using a sharp knife, take a shallow, vertical slice 5–6cm (2–2½in) long from the side of the rootstock and scion, thus exposing the cambium layers. Place the matching cut surfaces together and bind them firmly. After two or three months the two should have united; cut the top off the rootstock, and sever the scion from the parent plant.

Other successful methods of propagating mangos are by T-budding (see p.433) and air layering (see INDOOR GARDENING, p.383).

Olives (*Olea europaea*)

Olives are evergreen trees, growing 9–12m (28–40ft) tall, with a spread of 7–9m (22–28ft). The fruits may be gathered while they are still green, or when they are fully ripe and have turned black. They may measure up to 4cm (1½in) long.

Olives grow well in subtropical areas with an optimum temperature range of 5–25°C (41–77°F). They need long, hot summers for the fruits to ripen fully, followed by winter temperatures that are low enough to meet the chilling requirement of the specific cultivar, so seek specialist advice on which cultivars grow best in your area. Very low winter temperatures may result in frost damage. Hot, dry winds and cool, wet weather in the flowering period reduce fruit set. In temperate areas olives are occasionally grown as ornamental trees (but seldom flower or fruit) or else in containers (see "Subtropical container gardens", p.318). Given suitable growing conditions, an olive tree may attain a great age.

OLIVES TO TRY

European cultivars
'Aglandau'
'Bouteillan'
'El Greco'
'Manzanillo'

Subtropical cultivars
'Allegra'
'Oblonga'

Black table
olives

Site and planting

A wide range of soils is suitable, although low to medium fertility is preferable, since soils that are very fertile are likely to result in excessive vegetative growth. The site must be well drained. Olives grow well on alkaline soils, including those with a high level of salts, provided that the pH level does not exceed 8.5. In exposed areas, grow by a wall or use a windbreak for protection.

Most cultivars are self-fertile but pollinators may be necessary to increase fruit yield in cooler climates. Olives are mainly pollinated by wind but also by insects; high humidity levels inhibit pollination.

The usual planting distance varies from 5m (15ft) to 7m (22ft) each way, depending on the habit of the cultivar; all olives should be staked to avoid wind damage. Closely planted trees may be thinned by removing alternate trees when the canopies begin to overlap.

Routine care

Top-dress with a general-purpose fertilizer with medium to high levels of nitrogen at a yearly rate of about 0.5–1kg (1–2lb) per tree, applied in two or three doses when the trees are in active growth. Applications of potassium and, possibly, boron supplements may be necessary on some soils. Water olives regularly during dry periods, particularly for the first two to three years after planting. Mulching with organic material is also beneficial. Keep the planting area free of weeds.

Olive tree

Fruit thinning may be necessary, if the trees show signs of biennial bearing (see "Apples: Blossom thinning and biennial bearing", p.436). Thinning is generally done by hand, although professionals use a spray containing α-naphthalene acetic acid after flowering.

Pests and diseases

Olives grown in the open may be affected by various types of scale insect (p.648) and root-knot eelworms (p.660). Olive diseases include *Verticillium* wilt (p.653). Trees grown under cover may be affected by whiteflies (p.646), thrips (p.647), and red spider mite (p.646).

Growing under cover

Rooted cuttings or budded plants should be grown either in prepared beds, or in containers no smaller than 30–35cm (12–14in) in diameter; use a fertile compost that incorporates a slow-release fertilizer with medium levels of

Olives

potassium and nitrogen. Apply a liquid feed every three to four weeks and water the trees regularly.

Maintain a high temperature – above 21°C (70°F) – in summer and as low a temperature as possible in winter. Olives grown in containers may be placed in the open during the summer months.

Pruning and training

Prune newly planted olives by removing the leading shoot when it is about 1.5m (5ft) tall; select three to four strong laterals to provide the basic branch framework of the tree. Subsequent pruning consists of removing older branches to encourage the growth of new shoots, because fruits are produced on one-year-old wood mostly at the edges of the tree canopy.

Harvesting and storing

Olive trees grown in the open are likely to flower and fruit in three to four years from planting; yields generally increase until the tree is 15 years old, after which they remain fairly constant.

Olives are processed to remove their bitterness by immersion in a brine (5–6 per cent sodium chloride) solution. Fruits used for this treatment should be harvested when they are fully ripe but still green. Olives for eating may be harvested when black and firm, then packed in dry salt. When thoroughly dehydrated, the olives are stored in oil. Fruits for oil production should be left on the tree until they are fully ripe. They are harvested by shaking the tree so that the olives fall onto a cloth or fine netting placed on the ground below the tree canopy.

Propagation

Olives are usually propagated by stem cuttings, but selected cultivars may also be increased by bud-grafting.

Cuttings may be hardwood (from one- or two-year-old wood), leafy, semi-ripe cuttings from the current season's growth, or softwood ones.

Hardwood cuttings, which are taken during winter, should be about 30cm (12in) in length. Remove the leaves from the lower half of each cutting, and soak its base for 24 hours in hormone rooting solution. Insert the cuttings to half their length in cutting compost, leaving them for about 30 days to root while maintaining a temperature of 13–21°C (55–70°F). Transplant the rooted cuttings singly into pots, and raise them in greenhouse conditions.

Alternatively, take softwood or semi-ripe cuttings 10–15cm (4–6in) long (see ORNAMENTAL TREES, p.79). Named olive cultivars may be propagated by T-budding (see p.433), always budding onto vigorous, olive seedling rootstocks.

Prickly pears (*Opuntia ficus-indica*)

This member of the cactus family is grown mainly in the subtropics. Although many of its forms are relatively low-growing and spreading in habit, some may eventually attain a height of 2m (6ft).

Most prickly pears will tolerate semi-arid conditions, with an optimum temperature range of 18–25°C (64–77°F); they will survive at lower temperatures, with a minimum of 10°C (50°F). Full sunlight is essential for satisfactory growth.

The stems of prickly pears consist of flattened, elliptic sections, 30–50cm (12–20in) long, which

Prickly pear

are almost spineless in many of the cultivated forms but very spiny on wild and naturalized plants.

Prickly pear fruits, which are produced from the upper part of the sections, are purple or red when ripe, and about 5–10cm (2–4in) long. They contain a soft, juicy pulp with many seeds. Prickly pears are pollinated by insects.

Site and planting

Prickly pears thrive in subtropical regions, where they are able to tolerate lengthy periods of drought. They are sensitive to poor drainage and saline conditions, however, and prefer sandy, well-aerated soils, with an ideal pH of 5.5–7.

Rooted sections are usually established 2–2.4m (6–7½ft) apart, with a spacing of 2–3m (6–10ft) between each row.

Routine care

Fertilizers are not normally required, unless the soil is particularly poor. Keep the planting site weed-free. Pests are rarely serious. Some forms of *Pythium* spp. (see "Damping off" p.660), however, may affect prickly pears in humid conditions.

Growing under cover

Use a sandy compost to which a slow-release fertilizer has been added. Maintain the temperature at

PROPAGATING PRICKLY PEARS FROM STEM SECTIONS

1 Using a sharp knife, cut a whole section away from the parent plant. It is advisable to wear gloves, since the spines irritate the skin.

2 After allowing the section to dry out for a few days, place it in a sandy compost, and firm it in. The section should have rooted in 2–3 months.

18–25°C (64–77°F) with humidity of 60 per cent or below. Little watering is required once the plants have become established.

Harvesting and storing

Prickly pears produce fruits three to four years after planting. Detach them carefully from the stem sections using a sharp knife. They are best eaten within a few days after they have been harvested, but may be stored for short periods in cool conditions, if necessary.

Propagation

Detach whole stem sections from the parent plant; if these are very large, cut them horizontally into two or three pieces. Allow them to callus in a sunny, sheltered place for several days before inserting them into a sandy compost. The sections should take two to three months to root; they may then be potted on into 15–20cm (6–8in) pots, or transplanted to their final positions. Water the new plants regularly until they are established.

Avocado pears (*Persea americana*)

The avocado pear is a subtropical, evergreen tree that may grow to a height of 10–15m (30–45ft), with a similar spread. Its fruits are pear-shaped, with a large, central, rounded seed. Fruit size and skin texture vary with the cultivar and colours range from green to russet. The three main types of avocado are Guatemalan, Mexican, and West Indian.

The optimum temperature range for growth and fruit development is 20–28°C (68–82°F) with humidity of over 60 per cent; some Mexican and Guatemalan cultivars and hybrid forms are able to withstand temperatures as low as 10–15°C (50–59°F), but they do not usually produce flowers at such low temperatures.

Site and planting

Avocado trees may be grown in the open in subtropical areas, provided the temperature is within the range given above. Their branches are brittle, so it is necessary to provide wind-breaks in exposed areas to prevent them from being seriously damaged by the wind.

Select a site with maximum exposure to sun if possible. Avocados need a well-drained soil, since their roots are extremely sensitive to waterlogging. Medium loam soils with a pH of 5.5–6.5 are preferable, but sandy or clay loams may

AVOCADO PEARS TO TRY

'Ettinger' (Mexican x Guat.)
'Fuerte' (Mexican x Guat.)
'Hass' (Guatemalan)
'Lula' (Guatemalan)
'Nabal' (Guat.)
'Pollock' (West Indian)
'Zutano' (Mexican x Guat.)

'Lula'

Avocado tree

also be suitable, if the drainage is good, or has been improved (see also "Preparing the site", p.424).

If grafted plants are to be used, those on rootstocks that are known to be both vigorous and resistant to avocado root rot (*Phytophthora cinnamoni*) are preferable. Avocados may be self-pollinated, but the best crops are produced if at least two cultivars are planted near to each other. Choose cultivars whose flowering periods coincide or overlap. When planting, allow 6m (20ft) each way between the trees.

Routine care

Apply a general-purpose fertilizer with a medium potassium and nitrogen content, when the trees are in active growth. The recommended rate is 1.5–2kg (3½–4½lb) per tree every year, preferably in two or three doses. Use an organic mulch around the base of each tree, leaving 25cm (10in) clear around the stems.

Water avocado trees during dry periods, particularly during the first three years when they are becoming established. Keep the area around the base of the trees free from all weeds.

It is not normally necessary to thin the fruits on avocado trees.

Pests and diseases

Avocados may be affected by avocado root rot (see "*Phytophthora* root rots" p.654), anthracnose (p.666), and *Cercospora* spot or blotch (see "Fungal leaf spots", p.648); also by such pests as whiteflies (p.646), thrips (p.647), red spider mite (p.646), and mealybugs (p.646).

Growing under cover

Establish young plants either in well-prepared beds or in containers with a minimum diameter of 21cm (8in). Maintain temperatures of 20–28°C (68–82°F) and humidity of 70 per cent. For container-grown plants, pot on into containers at least 30cm (12in) in diameter, taking care not to disturb the plants' root systems.

Water containerized avocados regularly, and apply either a general-purpose fertilizer with a medium level of both potassium and nitrogen at intervals of two to three weeks, or a liquid feed. In temperate climates, flowering and fruiting are rare under cover, due to the trees' daylength and light intensity demands.

Pruning and training

Avocado trees need little pruning beyond shaping the tree during its early growth to ensure that an evenly spaced, rounded canopy develops. Once the tree is established, remove any diseased, damaged, or crossing branches after fruiting.

Harvesting and storing

Seed-raised trees start to bear fruit when they are between five and seven years old; budded or grafted plants are productive at three to five years after planting. The fruits may remain on the tree for up to 18 months without maturing, but they usually ripen rapidly after harvesting.

Cut the fruits from the tree using secateurs. Handle them carefully to avoid bruising. Store them at temperatures above 10°C (50°F) and at 60 per cent humidity. Any damaged fruits should be discarded.

Propagation

Avocado trees are easily grown from seed and reproduce virtually true to type. Select healthy, undamaged seeds and soak them in hot water for 30 minutes at 40–52°C (104–125°F) to inhibit infection from avocado root

Ripe avocados

rot. Cut a thin slice from the pointed end, then dip the wound in a fungicide. Sow the seed in sandy compost with the cut end slightly above the soil surface; germination usually takes about four weeks. The seedlings may be grown on in containers until they are about 30–40cm (12–16in) tall. They should then be ready for transferring to their final positions.

To propagate named cultivars onto disease-resistant rootstocks, side-wedge grafting (see PRINCIPLES OF PROPAGATION, p.636) or saddle grafting (see ORNAMENTAL SHRUBS, p.118) may be used.

GROWING AVOCADOS FROM SEED

1 Soak the seed in hot water and then prepare it by cutting about 1cm (½in) off the pointed end with a sharp knife. Dip the wound in fungicide.

2 Place the seed in a 15cm (6in) pot of moist seed compost so that the cut top of the seed is just above the soil surface.

3 Several weeks later the seed will have germinated to produce a shoot and roots.

Guavas (*Psidium guajava*)

Guava trees grow to a height of up to about 8m (25ft) and have a spread of 7m (22ft). They are widely grown in both tropical and subtropical regions and thrive in temperatures ranging from 22–28°C (72–82°F). The preferred humidity level is 70 per cent or less: a higher level may affect the quality of the fruits produced.

Guava fruits are 2.5–10cm (1–4in) in diameter, with either white or pink flesh. The flowers are normally pollinated by insects, particularly bees.

Site and planting

A sheltered site is preferable, protected by windbreaks if necessary. Guavas will tolerate a wide range of soils, but a well-drained loam is ideal. The pH may range from 5 to 7, but a pH of approximately 6 is most desirable.

When planting, allow a spacing of 5m (15ft) in each direction between the trees. The young trees should be securely staked in areas that are exposed to strong winds.

Routine care

Guavas respond well to applications of a general-purpose fertilizer with a medium potassium and nitrogen content. Use this at a rate of 1–2kg (2–4½lb) of fertilizer for each tree per year, divided into two or three top-dressings during the growing season. Weed the area around the bases of the trees, keep them well watered, and apply a mulch of organic matter, which will help to retain soil moisture.

Guavas

Guava tree

using a fairly rich potting compost mixed with a slow-release fertilizer. Maintain a minimum temperature of 22°C (72°F) with humidity of 70 per cent. Water plants regularly, and apply a liquid feed every three to four weeks. To improve the chances of fruiting, cross-pollination by hand may be necessary. A relatively dry atmosphere should be maintained during the flowering period.

Pests and diseases

Pests are rarely a serious problem, but in the open, aphids (p.646), fruit flies, and root-knot eelworms (p.660) may require control. Anthracnose (p.666) occurs in many areas. Plants under cover may also be infested by whiteflies (p.646), and thrips (p.647). Guava seedlings are sensitive to damping off (p.660).

Pruning and training

When the young trees are about 1m (3ft) tall, cut back the leading shoot by about two thirds, to encourage branching. Subsequent pruning can be limited to the removal of any dead, crossing, or diseased branches, and any low branches that droop down and touch the soil.

Growing under cover

Guavas may be grown in well-prepared beds or containers at least 30–35cm (12–14in) in diameter,

Harvesting and storing

Guavas cultivated in the open generally fruit after one to three years, depending on cultivar and environmental conditions. The fruits ripen about five months after fertilization and may be picked when they begin to turn yellow. Handle them carefully, since they bruise easily.

They may be stored for up to three or four weeks at a temperature of 7–10°C (45–50°F), with relative humidity of 75 per cent.

Propagation

Guavas are usually propagated from seed; for the increase of specific cultivars, air layering, cuttings, or grafting may be used.

Sow seed in a fertile, sterile compost in trays or 7cm (3in) containers; germination normally occurs in two to three weeks. The seedlings may vary in quality: pot the strongest ones on into 15cm (6in) pots when they are 20cm (8in) tall. Harden the young plants off and transplant them when they are 30cm (12in) tall.

Selected guava cultivars may be side-wedge grafted (see p.636) onto vigorous seedling guava rootstocks, the stems of which should have a diameter of at least 5mm (¼in). No specific rootstocks are recommended; select only strong, healthy plants, preferably self-pollinated, as parents for rootstock seeds.

Guavas may also be increased by softwood cuttings 12–16cm (5–6in) long (see p.632). Plants produced by

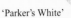
these graftings or cuttings may be planted out when they are about 30cm (12in) tall. In the open, guavas may be increased by simple layering (see ORNAMENTAL TREES, p.81) or by air layering (see INDOOR GARDENING, p.383). With the latter, hormone rooting powder applied to the girdled sections increases the success rate.

Pomegranates (*Punica granatum*)

Pomegranates form small, ornamental trees or bushes 2–3m (6–10ft) tall with a spread of 1–1.5m (3–5ft). They are evergreen in the subtropics but deciduous in cooler climates. The globular fruits are up to 10cm (4in) in diameter with leathery, yellow or red skins. The optimum temperature range is 18–25°C (64–77°F), but temperatures just below freezing are tolerated for short periods. Dry weather and a high temperature, ideally 35°C (96°F), are required for fruiting. In temperate climates, therefore, pomegranates are usually grown for their orange-red summer flowers and autumn colour; a dwarf variant of the species, *Punica granatum* var. *nana*, fruits freely under cover in temperate areas.

Pomegranate flower and fruit

Site and planting

Select a sunny aspect, sheltered by windbreaks in exposed conditions. Heavy loam soils with a pH level of about 7 are generally suitable, if they are well drained. Most cultivars are self-fertile. Plant seedlings, rooted cuttings, or suckers 4–6m (12–20ft) apart each way.

Routine care

Once plants are established, apply a general-purpose fertilizer every two to three months at a rate of 110g (4oz) for each tree per year. Mulch the site and keep it free of weeds; water the trees regularly during dry weather. Cut out all suckers.

Pests and diseases

Pomegranates grown in the open are generally trouble-free; under cover, they may be affected by whiteflies (p.646), aphids (p.646), red spider mite (p.646), and thrips (p.647).

Growing under cover

Plant pomegranates in well-prepared beds or containers with a minimum diameter of 35cm (14in), using potting compost with slow-release fertilizer added. Maintain a temperature range of 18–25°C (64–77°F) and humidity of 60–70 per cent. Apply a liquid fertilizer every three

to four weeks, and water the plants regularly. Plants in containers may be moved into the open in summer.

Pruning and training

Select three or four main branches to form a framework and remove any crowded, crossing, or diseased branches. Cut out any suckers not required for propagation.

Harvesting and storing

Fruiting should start about two to three years after planting. Harvest the pomegranates when they turn yellow or red; they may then be stored for several weeks at 4–6°C (39–43°F).

Propagation

Pomegranates are usually propagated from cuttings or root suckers. Insert hardwood cuttings (see p.434) in sandy compost, and give bottom heat until they have rooted. Softwood cuttings (see *Blueberry Softwood Cuttings*, p.478) require bottom heat and mist (use compost with neutral pH). Pot on both types into 10–15cm (4–6in) pots when they have rooted. Root suckers may be carefully separated from the parent plant and replanted. Alternatively, dry off the seed; sow it in pots or trays of seed compost, maintaining a temperature of 22°C (72°F).

Pomegranate tree

Nuts

Pecan nuts

Walnuts

Cobnuts

Sweet chestnuts

Almonds

SEVERAL nut-bearing trees and bushes are suitable for gardens; they prefer a sunny, open situation. Some, such as sweet chestnuts, walnuts, and pecans, eventually form large trees and make handsome specimens. In small gardens, an almond tree may make a fine feature, although it may produce nuts only in warm climates. Cobnuts and filberts may be pruned as compact bushes in a fruit garden or planted in informal groups in a wild garden. Most nuts (but not almonds) are monoecious, having separate male and female flowers on the same plant.

Pecan nuts (*Carya illinoinensis*)

Pecans are deciduous trees that may grow to 30m (100ft) high with a spread of 15–20m (50–70ft), so they are suitable only for large gardens. They grow best in warm-temperate climates: temperatures over 38°C (100°F) may lead to bark damage and the production of low-quality nuts; flowers may be damaged if the temperature drops below 1°C (34°F). Pecans have a chilling requirement of 150–250 hours below 7°C (45°F) in order for flowering to occur.

Pecans are monoecious but the male flowers are often open before the females on the same tree, so it is best to grow two or more cultivars near to each other to ensure that fertilization takes place. Since pecans are wind-pollinated, heavy rainfall when the trees are flowering may adversely affect pollination; after such conditions, crops may be poor. The nuts are ovoid, 2–2.5cm (¾–1in) long, and have a relatively thin shell.

Site and planting

Choose selected cultivars that have been grafted onto pecan seedling stock as trees raised from seed may not produce fruit of good quality. Pecans quickly develop a long tap root, so plant young trees: older, pot-grown plants with congested roots are seldom successful. Pecans need a site that is sheltered from strong winds and thrive on deep, fertile soils with a pH of 6–6.5.

Plant the trees when they are dormant (see *Planting a Fruit Tree*, p.425), spacing them 8m (25ft) apart.

PECANS TO TRY

'Desirable'
'Elisabeth'
'Elliot'
'Mohawk'
'Moore'
'Moreland'

Pecans

Routine care

Apply a top-dressing of a balanced fertilizer at a rate of 70–140g/sq m (2–4oz/sq yd) annually. Keep the planting site weed-free, and water the trees during dry periods until they are established. Pecans are moderately resistant to drought but require plenty of water during the summer months.

Pecan trees are seldom affected by pests and diseases; *Phytophthora* root rots (p.661) and aphids (p.646) may sometimes be a problem.

Pruning and training

Train pecans with a central leader initially (see "Central-leader standards", p.72). Once the trees are established, pruning is restricted to removing crossing and congested branches and any dead wood.

Harvesting and storing

The first crop may be produced after five years; full production is reached after 15–20 years. The nuts are usually harvested by hand. They may be stored, in cool, dry, airy conditions, for several months.

Propagation

Whip-and-tongue grafting of selected cultivars onto vigorous pecan seedling rootstocks is the most usual method of propagation (see p.433). The seedlings to be used as stock plants should be raised in deep pots or plastic sleeves, since their long tap roots are sensitive to damage during transplanting.

Sweet chestnuts (*Castanea sativa*)

Sweet or Spanish chestnuts are deciduous, summer-flowering trees up to 30m (100ft) tall with a spread of 15m (50ft). They are monoecious and wind-pollinated. Some cultivars may need a pollinator. The shiny, rich brown nuts thrive in areas with cold winters and warm summers. Two or three kernels are usual, but some cultivars, such as 'Marron de Lyon' and 'Paragon', have a single kernel.

Site, planting, and routine care

A fertile, moisture-retentive soil with a pH of 6 is preferred; allow 10–12m (30–40ft) between trees (see *Planting a Fruit Tree*, p.425). Water young trees and keep the site weed-free. On well-prepared sites, applications of fertilizer are unnecessary. Trees may be affected by honey fungus (p.665).

Pruning and training

Train as central-leader standards (see p.72). On established trees, remove congested, crossing, or dead branches.

Sweet chestnuts

Harvesting and storing

Nuts are borne after about four years. Harvest them in the autumn. Hull the nuts, soak them for 48 hours, discarding any that darken, then dry and store them in a cool, airy place.

Propagation

Propagate from selected cultivars by bud-grafting or whip-and-tongue grafting onto seedling stock of sweet chestnut (see pp.432 and 433).

Cobnuts and filberts
(*Corylus avellana* and *C. maxima*)

Cobnuts (or hazels) and filberts are valued for their winter catkins and their nuts. Unpruned, they reach a height and spread of 4–5m (12–15ft). They are deciduous and monoecious, and crop best in cool, moist summers. The chilling requirement is 800–1,200 hours below 7°C (45°F). Winter temperatures below -10°C (14°F) may damage the male flowers (catkins), although the female flowers are usually less vulnerable. The outer husk or calyx of the cobnut does not completely envelop the nut. The filbert has a husk that is longer than the nut and often completely encloses it; a sub-group of filberts has frilled husks and is known as frizzled filberts. Cobnuts and filberts are wind-pollinated; many are self-

Cobnuts

Filberts

fertile. For cobnuts, recommended self-fertile cultivars include 'Cosford' and 'Nottingham'; recommended filberts are 'Kentish Cob', 'Butler', 'Ennis', and 'Gunslebert'. The nuts of cobnuts and filberts are brown and egg-shaped.

Site and planting

A partially shaded, sheltered position is preferable. A soil pH of 6 is best; very rich soil may cause excessive soft growth at the expense of cropping. Adequate moisture with good drainage is important. Plant in autumn or early winter, 5m (15ft) apart (see *Planting a Fruit Tree*, p.425).

Routine care

Weed and mulch regularly; water in dry spells. On poor soils apply a balanced fertilizer in spring at a rate of 100g/sq m (3oz/sq yd). The fruits may be attacked by hazelnut weevil, for which there is no chemical control for amateur gardeners. Squirrels (p.659) can strip the tree of nuts.

Pruning and training

Cobnuts and filberts are usually grown as open-centre bushes, each with a 45cm (18in) stem and eight to twelve main branches. On young plants, prune the leaders in winter to 55cm (22in); good laterals should then develop. Remove any shoots growing low down on the main stem and all but the best-placed, strongest shoots needed to develop the framework. Shorten these by one third in winter. The following winter remove any excessively strong, upright growth and, if necessary, tip prune sideshoots to form a well-balanced framework.

BRUTTING COBNUTS

In the late summer, strong shoots of the current season's growth that are about 30cm (12in) long are broken and left hanging. This helps the formation of flower buds.

Established bushes bear heavier crops if pruned in late summer using a method known as "brutting". Break the longer sideshoots halfway along their length, and let them hang. This opens up the bush and encourages more female flowers to form. In winter, when the catkins release pollen, shorten the brutted shoots to three or four buds; remove old or overcrowded shoots.

Harvesting and storing

Nuts are borne after three or four years. Gather them when the husks begin to yellow. Dry, then store.

Propagation

Suckers produced from tree roots may be used for propagation. In winter, remove them, each with a root ball, and grow on in a nursery bed or plant directly in their final positions. Trees may also be propagated by simple layering (see p.116) in autumn.

Walnuts (*Juglans regia*)

English walnuts (strictly speaking Persian) are deciduous trees that may reach a height of 18m (60ft) with a similar spread; they are suitable only for large gardens. Named cultivars should always be planted for fruit, since seedlings may produce poor-quality nuts. Walnuts are monoecious and wind-pollinated. Most are self-fertile but some cultivars produce male catkins and pollen before the female flowers are receptive. To overcome this problem, plant nearby a reliable pollinator such as the old French cultivar 'Franquette'. Walnuts have a chilling requirement of 500–1,000 hours below 7°C (45°F). The gnarled nuts develop within a pitted shell.

Site, planting, and routine care

A well-drained, moisture-retentive soil is best. Walnuts prefer a pH of

WALNUTS TO TRY

All cultivars listed are self-fertile.
'Broadview'
'Buccaneer'
'Franquette'
'Lara'
'Mayette'
'Parisienne'

6.5–7 but tolerate some alkalinity. Since flowers and young shoots are susceptible to frost damage, avoid cold sites. Walnuts have a long tap root, so select young plants rather than older, pot-grown ones whose roots may be congested. Plant in late autumn or winter (see *Planting a Fruit Tree*, p.425), with 12–18m (40–60ft) between trees.

Walnuts may be slow to establish, but after two or three years, once the root system is well developed, stronger growth occurs. Bacterial leaf blotch and blight may be a problem (see "Bacterial leaf spots and blotches", p.648).

Pruning and training

Walnuts should be trained as central-leader standards (see p.72). Prune in midwinter since the trees do not bleed when they are dormant. Remove any strong shoots that make a narrow angle with the stem, to leave a well-balanced framework of evenly spaced branches. Thereafter, little pruning is required apart from cutting out overcrowded, crossing, or congested branches in winter and removing dead wood as required.

Harvesting and storing

Walnut trees may need many years before they start bearing. Walnuts for pickling should be picked in summer before the hulls and shells harden. In early autumn, the hull or casing cracks to release the nut, still in its shell.

Walnuts

Gather the crop before the shells become discoloured. Clean, then gently dry the nuts. Store them in cool, airy, slightly humid conditions.

Propagation

The usual methods are whip-and-tongue grafting (see p.433) or chip-budding (see p.432) cultivars onto seedlings of the American black walnut (*Juglans nigra*). In cool climates keep a grafted tree under glass until the graft has taken, then move the container to a protected site in the open. Plant young trees in their final positions in autumn or winter.

Almonds (*Prunus dulcis*)

Unpruned, sweet almonds grow about 5–6m (15–20ft) tall, with a similar spread. They crop regularly only in areas with warm, dry summers and frost-free winters. The chilling requirement is 300–500 hours below 7°C (45°F). In cool areas they are often grown as ornamentals. Almonds are insect-pollinated. Most cultivars are partly self-fertile, but crops will be better if a pollinator is planted nearby. The nuts are flattened and pointed, with a pitted shell.

Site, planting, and routine care

Almonds require a sheltered, frost-free site and a well-drained soil, preferably with a pH of 6.5. Plant them 6–7m (20–22ft) apart (see *Planting a Fruit Tree*, p.425).

Cultivation of almonds is as for peaches (see p.451). Peach leaf curl (p.651) and bacterial canker (p.665) may affect almond trees.

Pruning and training

Almonds are usually pruned and trained as bushes, as for peaches (see p.452). Nuts are borne on one-year-old wood. In summer, on established trees, remove one quarter of the old shoots that have previously cropped to encourage fresh growth.

Harvesting and storing

The nuts are borne after three to four years. Gather them as their hulls start

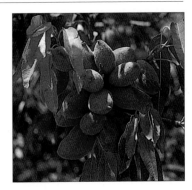

Almonds

to crack. Clean and dry the almonds before storing them.

Propagation

Almonds are usually propagated by chip-budding (see p.432). Root stocks vary according to soil type: almond seedlings are often used in dry regions while peach seedlings are more suitable for heavier soils.

ALMONDS TO TRY

'Balatoni'
'Ferragnes'
'Ingrid'
'Macrocarpa'
'Titan'

CHAPTER

17

GROWING VEGETABLES

MORE AND MORE gardeners are discovering the deep satisfaction of growing their own vegetables. They do so for many reasons: for the majority it is the joy of savouring a freshness and flavour that is so often missing from shop-bought produce, while some relish the chance to grow unusual cultivars. Organic gardeners want to harvest crops that are untainted by chemical residues. Then again, there are those who find a well-tended vegetable patch every bit as beautiful as a herbaceous border. Modern science and methods of cultivation, coupled with the outstanding vigour and disease-resistance of many of today's vegetable cultivars, enable even newcomers to vegetable growing to experience the satisfaction of bringing to the table fine vegetables that they have sown, tended, and harvested in their own gardens.

Designing a vegetable garden

A HEALTHY, productive area for growing vegetables may be created in a garden of any size, from a large, sunny area to a few containers on a patio. The vegetables may be grown in a separate vegetable plot or integrated with flower beds.

Good growing conditions are essential if vegetables of quality are to be produced. However, virtually any site can be made suitable, perhaps by erecting windbreaks if it is exposed, or taking the necessary steps to improve soil fertility and drainage. This cannot be done overnight, but within a year or two very satisfactory results may be obtained.

Choosing the site

Most vegetables lead short but pampered lives so the ideal situation for a vegetable garden provides warmth, sunlight, shelter, and fertile, well-drained, loamy soil with an adequate water supply. The chosen site should be open but not exposed, and not overshadowed: trees shade and drip on plants and remove nutrients and moisture from the soil, while buildings may create shade and funnel damaging winds across the plot.

Shelter from wind

Providing shelter from wind is one of the most important factors in vegetable growing. Wherever possible, avoid

A well-designed garden
This thriving vegetable garden is both well designed and effectively maintained, with an open, but not exposed, aspect. The beds all contain different crops, and a network of paths allows easy access to each bed.

windy sites: even light winds may decrease vegetable yields by 20–30 per cent, while strong winds are often devastating. Vegetables in coastal gardens may be damaged by desiccating wind-borne, salt spray.

Windbreaks

In gardens exposed to wind, windbreaks should be erected; they should be about 50 per cent permeable, allowing the wind to filter through, rather than solid structures which force the wind over them, creating an area of turbulence the other side (see also FROST AND WIND PROTECTION, pp.612–613, and CLIMATE AND THE GARDEN, "Wind", p.610).

An effective windbreak may be a living barrier, such as a hedge, or a structure like a slatted fence or a screen of windbreak netting. Hedges are attractive but take time to become established, require maintenance, take up considerable space, and compete for soil, water, and plant nutrients; they are therefore only appropriate in quite large gardens. For further information, see HEDGES AND SCREENS, pp.84–85. A windbreak of trees could be used at the boundaries of a very large garden. In smaller sites, fences, hurdles, or windbreak netting battened to posts or stakes are more practical.

A windbreak provides maximum shelter over a distance roughly five times its height. A very exposed garden may need a windbreak at least 2m (6ft) high. In this case, nets and posts must be strong, as they will be subjected to great strain in high winds. Alternatively, erect lower, short-term windbreaks between rows of plants or beds; netting windbreaks

no more than 45cm (18in) high and 3–4m (10–12ft) apart, attached to canes, are very effective for this.

If gaps in buildings or trees create a wind funnel across the garden, erect a barrier extending 1m (3ft) across the gap in each direction. Deciduous shrubs or a hedge may be planted in the gap, with an artificial windbreak to shelter the plants until they are established.

Slopes

A sloping site is less easy to work than a flat one and soil erosion after heavy rain may be a problem on steep slopes; setting the beds across the slope may help. A site on a south-facing slope is an advantage in cool-temperate climates because it warms up rapidly in spring. In hot climates, site beds on a north-facing slope because this position will give them relief from intense sun.

Positioning

The orientation of vegetable beds often makes little difference to open-ground crops, but greenhouses and frames should be oriented so that their sloping surfaces face the sun to maximize efficiency. Position tall crops, such as climbing beans, carefully: in temperate climates, place them where they will not shade dwarf-sized plants from the sun, but in hotter climates use them to provide such shade.

Sites below garden walls

In temperate and northern climates, the ground at the foot of a south-facing garden wall is a warm, sheltered place that is useful for growing early spring and late autumn

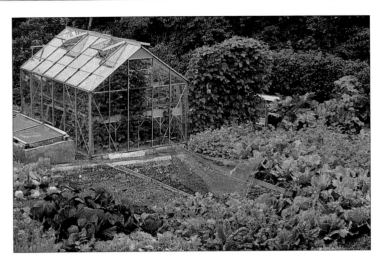

Allocating space
Each element in this garden has been sited to produce optimum growing conditions for the crops. The greenhouse and frame are positioned to receive maximum light, the hedge filters the prevailing wind, and tall plants, such as the runner beans, do not overshadow the smaller vegetables.

crops and, in summer, tender, sun-loving crops such as tomatoes and peppers. Keep the beds well watered so that the soil does not dry out. North-facing walls can provide some shade for plants such as lettuces and peas that suffer in high temperatures.

Maintaining soil fertility

A friable loam is ideal for growing vegetables: it is rich in plant nutrients, and supports a population of earthworms and micro-organisms to break down organic matter. It has a good structure, and remains workable even in adverse conditions: it does not become sticky in wet

weather or dusty in dry periods, but always retains a crumbly texture, so that the soil is well aerated; this is important both for the living organisms in the soil and the roots of the vegetables. An ideal soil to encourage most vegetables to flourish, and to need little extra feeding, is both well drained and moisture-retentive with an optimum of pH 6.8.

Soil types

Vegetables may be grown successfully on a range of different soil types. At one extreme are porous, sandy soils, which warm up quickly in spring and are ideal for early crops. They are easy to cultivate year-round, but lose nutrients rapidly to leaching, so that crop feeding and irrigation are especially important. At the other extreme are heavy clays, which hold nutrients well, but are relatively slow to warm, sticky, and prone to waterlogging; they are best cultivated in autumn and winter.

In practice, many soils are a mixture of types. The key to success is timely cultivation and, above all, the incorporation of well-rotted organic matter to improve nutrient and water-holding capacity. An adequate lime content is critical in soil fertility and sites should be tested for pH levels frequently. For further information, see "Soil and its structure", pp.616–617.

Using organic matter

Crops continuously remove nutrients from the soil and from naturally decomposing organic matter. In almost all soils, fertility must be maintained by replenishing organic matter regularly. The main forms available to gardeners are animal

Alternating rows
Provided that the fertility of the soil is maintained, rows of vegetables may be arranged to maximize yields by alternating rows of fast- and slow-growing crops (here different types of lettuce and a range of brassicas). The fast-growing lettuces will have been harvested by the time the brassicas have reached maturity.

manures (preferably with a high straw content but little sawdust or woodshavings), seaweed, or homemade garden compost.

A layer of organic matter 8–10cm (3–4in) deep, applied over most of the ground each year, will maintain structure and fertility. It may be spread on the surface or dug into the soil. If organic matter is spread on the soil surface in the autumn, earthworms will work it in. This is particularly beneficial on light soils where heavy winter rainfall can cause leaching of nutrients. Any organic matter remaining on the surface in spring should be forked in. Dig organic matter into heavy soils in autumn, spreading it evenly throughout the soil as deeply as possible; dig light soils at the end of November to avoid weed growth and to allow frost tilth. Well-rotted organic matter is a useful mulch and can be used at any point in the growing season (see also "Mulching", p.502).

Green manuring

This is the practice of growing crops specifically to dig into the soil to improve its fertility. In the vegetable garden green manures may be grown and then dug in between crops, or grown over winter in order to augment soil nutrients and avoid leaving the soil bare (see SOILS AND FERTILIZERS, "Green manures", p.625). Avoid using brassicas because of their susceptibility to clubroot.

Drainage

Good drainage is absolutely essential; where there is a serious problem, it may be necessary to lay land

Intercropping
Lettuces and sweet corn planted together mature at varying rates. The fast-growing lettuces are ready to harvest before the sweet corn is fully grown.

drains (see SOILS AND FERTILIZERS, "Improving drainage", p.623).

In most cases, working in copious quantities of organic matter improves drainage markedly, since this will encourage earthworm activity, which improves the soil structure by creating an extensive network of small drainage channels.

Preserving soil structure

Good soil structure is easily destroyed by physically damaging it, for example, by walking on it or cultivating it when it is either very wet or very dry, or from heavy rain beating down on the surface. Laying out the garden in narrow beds (see THE BED SYSTEM, p.496) to minimize the need to tread

on the soil, and keeping the surface mulched (see "Mulching", p.502) will help to preserve the structure.

Planning the vegetable garden

The layout of a vegetable garden is determined by the size, shape, and nature of the garden and the demands of the household. It is important to plan for crop rotation (see CROP ROTATION, p.498) so that the four main vegetable groups – legumes, brassicas, roots, and crops of the onion family – can be grown on different sites in successive years to minimize the build-up of pests and diseases. Gardeners with space for a kitchen garden usually opt either for traditional, allotment-style rows, or for permanent beds in which different crops are grown each year (see THE BED SYSTEM, pp.495–496), but there are alternatives for those with limited space. It is also important to plan for perennial vegetables and herbs.

A place for perennials

The majority of vegetables are grown as annuals on a different piece of ground each year. The few perennial vegetables, such as globe artichokes, rhubarb, and asparagus, should be grouped in a permanent bed at one side or end of the garden, separated from the annual vegetables. These should be mulched regularly to retain moisture, prevent compaction, and control weeds.

Vegetables in containers

Gardeners who are limited to patios, terraces, concreted yards, roofs, or balconies often grow vegetables in

containers to provide a productive display that can also, especially with imaginative cultivar choices, be very attractive (see CONTAINER GARDENING, p.318). Although vegetables are more difficult than flowers to grow successfully in containers, they are worth the effort involved. Suitable containers range from terracotta pots and tubs to proprietary growing bags filled with compost. Plant them up with dwarf and the more decorative cultivars, and use modular plants instead of seeds for maximum year-round production.

Maximizing space

To maximize yields in a given area, crops may be combined in a single bed. Seeds of a fast-growing crop, such as radishes, can be intersown simultaneously and in the same row as slower growing parsnips. Garlic, shallots, onion sets, and bunching onions are also suitable for inter-cropping. Likewise, a rapidly maturing "catch crop" such as lettuce, can be grown among slow-maturing brassicas. A chequerboard pattern will give maximum efficiency, but alternate rows also work well. Alternatively, catch crops can be sown before or between rows of slower crops, for example, spinach with tomatoes or winter brassicas. The fast-growers make immediate use of the available space, but mature before the slower-growing crops need the room. Ensure that the short-term crop is not shaded by the slower-growing one. Careful timing is essential and, in dry summers, lack of water can be a problem.

Vegetables in flower beds

As many gardens are too small to allow a complete area to be devoted entirely to vegetables, there has been a move in recent years towards integrating them into flower beds, or planting them in groups of beds to create an attractive pattern. Wherever possible, vegetable cultivars are selected for their decorative qualities, and then are grouped in order to display them to maximum effect. This approach is known as "potager gardening" in Europe and "edible landscaping" in the USA. There is enormous scope to develop individual ideas. The only requirement for growing vegetables within flower beds is to ensure that soil fertility is maintained at the level necessary for the chosen vegetables.

Climatic factors

Most vegetables grow only when the average daytime temperature rises above about 6°C (43°F) between

Growing vegetables the organic way

You can grow your own organic vegetables simply by following the basic principles that generally apply to organic gardening.

- Maintain a fertile soil that is free draining and humus-rich. This is perhaps the single most important factor.
- Ensure only organic soil-improvers and mulches are used.
- Where possible, choose pest- and disease-resistant cultivars.
- Practise good hygiene: remove decaying foliage and debris regularly to help maintain a good airflow around the plants and lessen the likelihood of disease spreading through the crop.
- Use organically-approved sprays – which do not harm beneficial

predators – only if you need to treat a very severe pest or disease problem.

Crop rotation – the practice of growing related types of vegetables in different sections of the vegetable garden in consecutive years – is essential to avoid a build-up of pests and diseases in the soil. For example, if brassicas, which are susceptible to attacks from cabbage root fly and clubroot, are planted year after year in the same site, the plants may become stunted and deformed by these and other pests and diseases, and the crop yield will be very poor. Avoid growing the same type of crop on the site for at least 3–4 years to minimize these problems.

spring and autumn. The number of "growing days" with suitable daytime temperatures that occur between these seasons is governed by factors such as latitude, altitude, and degree of exposure, and largely determines sowing dates and the type of crops that may be grown outdoors in any given locality.

Temperature requirements

Vegetables are sometimes classified as warm- or cool-season crops, depending on their physiological needs, particularly those relating to temperature. Most brassicas and several bulb and stem vegetables cannot withstand intense heat, whereas more tender vegetables, such as tomatoes, are damaged or killed by freezing temperatures. Cultivars of some vegetables have been bred to resist cold, and the growing season of many vegetables may be extended at either end of the season by growing them under cover (see p.505). Refer to detailed information on individual vegetables for their specific temperature requirements, pp.507–548.

Daylength

The number of daylight hours, or daylength, differs according to the latitude and season, and vegetable cultivars have a varying response to daylength at different stages of their growth. Short-day plants grow and seed only if the daylength is less than 12 hours; long-day plants only if it is more than 12 hours.

This affects the sowing time, particularly of crops that are grown for their seeds, such as beans; others must be harvested before flowering. Onions, for example, are naturally long-day plants: when the daylength is 16 hours or more, onions stop making leafy growth and start to develop a bulb. The more leafy growth that has been made up to this point, the larger the bulb that forms; onion seeds should therefore be sown early in the year so that the plant will develop as much leafy growth as possible before the daylength increases.

Cultivars are available that have been specially bred and adapted to long or short days, or that are daylength neutral. Examples are

A productive display
This example of potager planting groups marrows climbing a supporting arch with a profusion of yellow and red nasturtiums beneath. All thrive in warm, sunny conditions.

mentioned throughout the chapter; the safest course is to choose cultivars recommended for your area, and to check sowing and harvesting instructions on the seed packet.

Rainfall

The average annual rainfall of a district has a significant influence on the growth of vegetables. In areas of low precipitation, there is a risk of drought at the important stages of crop development, such as the swelling of peas and beans, or leaf growth in lettuces. In low-rainfall areas, watering and surface mulching to conserve moisture become critical considerations.

In high-rainfall areas, it is essential to maintain or create free soil drainage and more vigilance is called for to recognize and deal with the effects of slugs, snails, and fungal leaf diseases, all of which proliferate in damp conditions. With high rainfall, nutrients are also more likely to be leached from the soil and supplementary feeding may be necessary.

Aspect

Although the climatic factors of a locality cannot be altered, their worst effects can be alleviated by good soil management and by taking steps to improve the microclimate (the environmental conditions within a garden). Consequently, it is important to develop and take advantage of the physical aspects of your chosen vegetable plot.

Providing wind shelter through the use of fences, screens, or hedges reduces water loss from vegetables and soil and promotes higher average soil temperatures, which in turn aids growth. Walls or fences facing the sun form warm niches that are particularly beneficial to crops such as tomatoes, peppers, and sweet corn, which do best at higher temperatures. Ground that slopes towards the sun warms soonest in spring and is therefore ideal for early vegetables. Conversely, be alert to the disadvantages of tall walls in producing shade from sun and rain, and avoid planting in frost pockets.

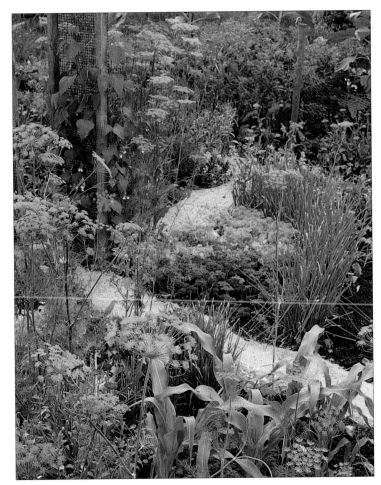

Combining vegetables and herbs
This informal garden has vegetables intermingled with herbs. Runner beans climb up an arch, parsley and chives ring red and green "Salad Bowl" lettuces at the edge of the centre bed, and sweet corn develops among feathery dill.

Vegetables in a windowbox
Vegetables can thrive in small containers, such as this windowbox. Here shallow-rooted lettuces, young cabbages, tomatoes, and strawberries have been chosen not only for their culinary uses, but also for their decorative qualities.

The bed system

Fʀᴜɪᴛ and vegetables are best grown in open ground, either on the flat or in raised beds. In these situations the soil benefits from rainfall and weathering, and the plants have a free root run. In the traditional garden, it is usual to set aside a particular garden area specifically for fruit and vegetables. This area can be a wide, open plot, but an excellent, more modern alternative is to set out the vegetable garden as a series of narrow beds divided by pathways.

The vegetable patch

In the traditional kitchen garden, long rows of vegetables usually run across the plot. This is a perfectly good way to grow produce; it allows large areas of ground to be cultivated and used with maximum flexibility.

Growing crops, however, requires constant access for sowing, thinning, planting out, watering, top-dressing, pest and disease control, weeding, harvesting, and clearing. Each task involves treading on the ground, which compresses the soil. This reduces the air in the soil, impedes drainage, and results in poor growth. Compaction can be reduced by taking care not to tread on wet soil and by walking on planks to spread the weight, but narrow beds totally avoid the need to walk on cropped areas.

Using beds

In a bed system, the cropping area is divided into semi-permanent or fixed beds. Beds should be narrow enough to bring their central areas within arm's reach, so that cultivation tasks can be carried out from the dividing

Close cropping
The high soil fertility in this raised bed permits close and equidistant plant spacing in staggered rows. Narrow beds like these are also particularly convenient when using a standard width of horticultural fleece to protect crops.

pathways, without stepping onto the soil. This avoids soil compaction and has the additional advantage that harvesting and other tasks can be done soon after rain without the usual risk of damaging soil structure. There is also less need to dig beds once they are established and fertile, and what cultivation is necessary is greatly reduced because of the smaller cropped area. Since the regular addition of bulky organic manures is concentrated on a smaller area, it is easier to build up high levels of

fertility, and to improve soil aeration and drainage, which in turn leads to stronger root growth.

The concentration of cropping areas into relatively confined spaces makes the bed system an ideal solution for worthwhile vegetable production in small gardens. The increase in soil fertility and lack of need for access along crop rows allows plants to be grown at closer spacings. Cos or cabbage lettuces, for example, may be grown 20cm (8in) apart each way in staggered rows, as

opposed to rows 30cm (12in) apart in more traditional layouts. Each plant gains the maximum root space in the smallest possible area, making the best use of the soil available and increasing the total yield.

The close spacing of plants has further indirect benefits. Irrigation using low-level distribution systems such as seep hoses (see p.561) becomes more manageable, since smaller areas are served; water can also be used less wastefully using more conventional watering techniques.

MAKING A RAISED BED

1 *Measure and mark out beds. Edge with 15 x 2.5cm (6 x 1in) boards, sunk into a 5cm (2in) slit trench and supported by timber pegs driven into the ground every 1–1.2m (3–4ft).*

2 *Fill the bed with good-quality topsoil that has been enriched with organic matter such as well-rotted manure or garden compost. Take care to avoid creating air pockets at the edges and corners.*

3 *Spread out the soil evenly using a rake. Break up any lumps, aiming to achieve an even, firm texture. Make the finished soil surface roughly level with the top of the boards, topping up as necessary.*

4 *Level the soil with the back of the rake to leave a smooth finish. Top up with more soil as necessary in later weeks when the filled bed settles and the level of the soil falls.*

PLANTING IN A BED

The bed should be no more than 1.5m (5ft) wide, so that the centre is within easy arm's reach from either side. All work can then be carried out from the surrounding paths without any need to tread on the soil, thus avoiding damage to the soil structure.

Close spacing results in more effective smothering of annual weed growth, so weeding is also reduced.

Using a bed system can make crop rotation (see p.498) much easier, as each crop group can be allocated to a bed and moved on to a different one the following year according to the rotation requirements.

Planning bed layouts

Beds may be rectangular, square, or even curved; the prime consideration is that they must allow the whole bed to be cultivated from the paths.

The ideal width is 1.2m (4ft); this can be increased to 1.5m (5ft) if it makes better use of available space, or reduced to 1m (3ft) for areas that are to be protected with glass or plastic cloches. Narrow strips are particularly suitable for strawberries, for ease of mulching and harvesting.

The bed length can be adjusted to suit the site; while their orientation is not of vital importance, running them from north to south generally ensures the most even distribution of sunlight.

The width of the paths between beds needs to be at least 45cm (18in) to allow for easy access, both on foot and with wheelbarrows.

Types of beds

Many terms are used to describe beds: they include flat or semi-flat beds, deep beds, and raised beds. A flat or semi-flat bed is simply marked out from the surrounding garden and cultivated. With yearly additions of bulky organic dressings, soil depth is increased as the bed surface is gradually raised above path level.

Deep beds

Organic growers often aim to minimize soil cultivation to preserve its natural structure and fertility and reduce the growth of weeds. Deep beds are an ideal way of achieving this. In deep beds, soil is improved to the required depth with one thorough cultivation that incorporates large amounts of organic matter (see *Double digging*, p.620). After this, further digging is avoided so that a natural soil structure develops, encouraged by the organic matter and a high worm population. Further organic matter is added only as mulches and top-dressings. The only disturbance to the soil surface occurs when planting, so weed seeds below germination level remain dormant and only weed seedlings from wind-blown seeds need to be removed.

Raised beds

Raised beds are constructed by marking out beds and building the sides up to 30cm (12in) high, using timber, such as railway sleepers, bricks, or cement blocks. Walls can be dispensed with, but in that case, the base of the bed should be about 30cm (12in) wider than the finished top to ensure stability.

Raised beds bring all the advantages of flat beds, but have improved drainage and warm up faster in spring. Making a raised bed higher along one side than the other, so that the sloping surface faces the sun, warms the bed even more effectively and promotes early plant growth.

Raised beds provide a means of gardening successfully on the most unpromising ground, such as where a site is naturally very badly drained or perhaps even concreted over.

Higher beds can also extend the pleasure of gardening to people of limited mobility. Walls can be built up to 60–90cm (24–36in) and the base filled with rubble (for good drainage). The bed is then topped with 30–45cm (12–18in) of fertile soil.

Making paths

Paths between beds can be maintained as soil areas from which weed growth is regularly skimmed off. A mulched path requires more initial effort, but reduces maintenance in the long term, especially if it is laid over a weed-suppressing landscape fabric. When topped with bark or gravel, this creates a firm, hard-wearing surface.

Grass pathways are most successful when a durable edging, such as rigid plastic or concrete blocks, is laid around the beds; the grass surface must stand proud of the edging to allow for unobstructed mowing.

The "no-dig" system

Paradoxically, cultivating the soil creates conditions in which weeds flourish; it exposes weed seeds to the light needed for germination. It may also cause a natural soil structure to deteriorate as air incorporated by digging causes rapid breakdown of organic matter. The "no-dig" system is a method of cultivation used by organic gardeners to preserve soil structure and reduce loss of nutrients. It exploits minimal soil disturbance and regular surface applications of organic matter (applied well in advance of cropping so earthworms can incorporate it) will help to suppress weeds, conserve moisture, and maintain soil fertility and structure. The success of the technique demands thorough initial weed clearance, especially of perennial weeds, by means of sheet mulches (or chemicals for non-organic gardeners). The no-dig technique is well suited to bed systems, and can be useful in reducing the labour of trenching and earthing up potatoes.

NO-DIG POTATOES

1 *To grow potatoes, lay the tubers on the soil surface, then cover with a 15–20cm (6–8in) layer of mulch.*

2 *Cover the mounded mulch with black plastic, fixing it down securely. Make slits for potato shoots to grow through.*

MAKING A PATH BETWEEN BEDS

1 *Mark out, level, and firm the path. Cut a 2.5cm (1in) slit along each edge. Cut landscape fabric to length, and 20cm (8in) wider than the path.*

2 *Fold the fabric edge into the slit on one side. Secure with 10 x 2.5cm (4 x 1in) wood edging and hammer level. Pull fabric taut and repeat on opposite side.*

3 *Cut crosses in opposite pairs in the fabric close to each plank, 2m (6ft) apart. Knock a wooden peg through each cross, to 2.5cm (1in) below the plank top.*

4 *Apply the mulch (here of bark chips). Rake and tamp down, so that the mulch is level with the plank tops and the support pegs are concealed.*

Crop rotation

Crop rotation is a system by which vegetable crops are grown on different areas of the plot in succession in consecutive years.

Advantages of rotation

The principal reason for rotating crops is to prevent a build-up of soil-borne pests and diseases specific to one group of crops. If the same type of "host" crop is grown every year in the same soil, its pests and diseases increase rapidly in number and often become a serious problem, whereas in the absence of their host they gradually die out. Various types of potato and tomato eelworm (nematodes), clubroot which attacks almost all brassicas, onion white rot, sclerotinia, blights, mildew, and rusts are some of the common garden problems that may be alleviated by rotation.

Other benefits stem from rotating vegetables. Some crops, for example potatoes, blanket the soil so well that they smother most weeds, so it is useful to follow them with crops that are difficult to weed, such as onions. In addition, most root vegetables, and especially potatoes, help break up the ground and keep the soil structure open and well aerated.

Most vegetables in the legume family, including peas and beans, fix nitrogen in the soil by means of nodules on their roots and make it available for the next crop. Therefore nitrogen-hungry crops, such as leafy brassicas, potatoes, or spinach, should follow legumes. Conversely, root crops, which have a relatively low nitrogen requirement, can follow on from brassicas. So, methodical rotation ensures that the best balance of nutrients is maintained.

Several vegetables, including perennial types and many salad plants, do not fall into a principal rotation group. Salad plants stay in the ground for a short time and are therefore useful for intercropping or to fill temporary gaps in vegetable beds. As with the other vegetables, they should not be grown in the same patch year after year. Perennial vegetables are best grown in a permanent bed of their own and so are not rotated. For the most important vegetable groups, see *Rotation of Vegetable Crops*, above right.

Drawbacks of rotation

A weak point in the rotation theory is that to be completely effective rotation should take place over a much longer timescale than the usual three or four years: clubroot and white rot infections can stay in the soil for up to 20 years or more. Rotations on

that scale are out of the question in small gardens. Another shortcoming is that, in practice, the distance between beds is often so small that soil-borne pests and diseases can easily spread from one to the next.

Crops in the general groups are likely to be needed in different quantities, so plot size will vary. Some crops, such as parsnips and brassicas, will be very long-season crops that stand in the ground for progressive harvest. Each of these considerations makes strict rotation difficult to carry out in the garden. Some gardeners maintain that, in very small areas, there is merit in not following a rotation, preferring to crop repeatedly on the same ground, then avoiding it selectively when a pest or disease infestation builds up, but this is a risky policy.

It is, however, better to regard rotation as an aid to the suppression of pests and diseases, rather than as a means of total prevention or cure. On balance, the best advice is to move crops around the vegetable garden, endeavouring to have a break between growing crops in the rotation groups outlined.

Planning for rotation

Despite the disadvantages, rotation is a sensible practice, and gardeners should try to build it into their garden plans. The most crucial aspect is to have at least one but preferably two complete cropping seasons without repeating a vegetable group in a given site if at all possible.

Draw up a list of the main vegetables that you want to grow, including a rough indication of the quantities required. Growing vegetables that are unsuited to the local climate is usually unsatisfactory, particularly in small gardens. Neither is it sensible to grow crops that are likely to be cheap to buy when your own crop is ready.

List the various beds in the vegetable garden. Group the selected vegetables in their rotation groups (for example all legumes and pod crops, or all brassicas), with a miscellaneous category for vegetables not in the main groups (see above). Members of the miscellaneous group may be placed in one main group or another, depending on available space and quantities required.

Month-by-month planning

Make a chart with a column for each month of the year; for every vegetable on your list fill in the months during which it will be in the ground. Remember that this period may be shortened by raising plants in containers (see "Sowing indoors",

ROTATION OF VEGETABLE CROPS

Legumes and pod crops
Okra
Dolichos beans
Scarlet runner beans
Lima beans
French beans
Peas
Broad beans

Alliums
Bulb onions
Pickling onions
Spring onions
Shallots
European Welsh onions
Oriental bunching onions
Leeks
Garlic

Brassicas
Kales
Cauliflowers
Cabbages
Brussels sprouts
Purple sprouting broccoli
Calabrese
Oriental mustards
Chinese broccoli
Pak choi
Mizuna greens
Chinese cabbages
Komatsuna
Kohl rabi
Swedes
Turnips
Radishes

Solanaceous, root, and tuberous crops
Sweet peppers
Tomatoes
Wonderberries
Aubergines
Celery
Celeriac
Beetroot
Cocoyams
Carrots
Sweet potatoes
Parsnips
Scorzonera
Salsify
Potatoes

p.501) for transplanting later, and lengthened by the use of some form of cover early and late in the season (see "Growing under cover", p.505). Some crops are sown once a year (parsnips and winter cabbages, for example), but with others, such as lettuces and radishes, repeat sowings may be made to provide a continuous supply throughout the year.

Planning a layout

Allocate each bed (or several beds if needed) to a different rotation group of vegetables, and write in the most important crop that each bed will grow. Refer to your month-by-month chart, and indicate a suitable crop to precede or follow it. For example, if Brussels sprouts are cleared from the ground in mid-spring, they may be followed by carrots, lettuces, or peas. Assume that most pieces of ground will bear only two crops a year. Use this plan in subsequent years and move the crops to different beds.

It is best to look on the overall plan as a rough guide only. Many factors – not least the unpredictability of the

weather and seasons – have a bearing on the success and failure of crops. The real key to success lies as much in the flexibility of the basic plan as in strict adherence to it.

Keeping records

Keeping a record of operations in the vegetable garden is always time well spent and a diary of each year's planting is especially valuable in planning rotations. It is also helpful to make notes on weather conditions, most importantly the dates of the first and last frosts. Such records can provide an invaluable guide to improving performance in future seasons.

Detailed records of cultivars grown, sowing and planting dates, quantities harvested – and those particularly enjoyed – form a valuable reference for subsequent years. They can help identify gluts and shortcomings, so as to avoid them in following years. It is also useful to record problems encountered and treatment given, whether they be pests and diseases or cultural disorders: to be forewarned is to be forearmed.

Sowing and planting

THE most common method of raising vegetables is from seed. There are several methods for sowing outdoors or under cover; use the most suitable for the chosen cultivar and the space available. Care in the early stages ensures healthier, more productive crops. Thin or transplant seedlings to their final position in a bed, greenhouse, or container before they become overcrowded.

Choosing seed

In the past, seed was sold only as ordinary, "naked" seed, but it is now also available prepared in a variety of ways to make both sowing and germination easier. Seed can also be purchased pre-germinated.

Purchasing seed

Always buy good-quality seed, preferably vacuum-packed to preserve viability, such as those supplied by reputable mail order companies. Many of the best cultivars are F1 hybrids, bred by crossing two selected parents. Although expensive, they are very vigorous and productive. Vegetable seeds differ widely in their viability: to be safe, use seed under three years old, or test a sample before sowing. Store seed in cool and dry conditions; lettuce seeds are best kept in a refrigerator.

Prepared seed

Pelleted seeds are individually coated with clay to form tiny balls and are easier to sow evenly than naked seed. This is particularly useful for handling small seeds such as those of carrots. Pelleted seeds should be carefully placed in a drill one by one, which saves transplanting later. They are sown in the normal way, but it is important that the clay coating is kept moist until after germination.

Seed is also available embedded, evenly spaced, in paper sheets or tapes, which disintegrate in the soil after sowing. The tapes are laid in a drill and covered with soil, as for ordinary seed. The backing gives protection in the early stages of germination and reduces thinning later.

Sometimes seeds are marketed in a gel in small tubs. They grow to the seedling stage in the tub, and may then be pricked out into a pot or directly into the ground. This saves an initial thinning after sowing.

Pre-germinated seed

Chitted or pre-germinated seed is purchased and sown just after germination, when the first root is emerging. Chitted seed is dispatched in small plastic containers; each seed is then sown carefully into a pot or a seed tray. This is a good method for seed that needs temperatures that are difficult to maintain without an electric propagator or for those in which germination is unreliable.

To start ordinary seed early, it may be pre-germinated at home. This is useful for seed that germinates slowly in cold soil and may rot before germination. Space seeds on damp, paper towelling and put them in a warm place. Keep them moist until germination, then sow them carefully in containers or in open ground. This method may also be used to test a sample of old seed for viability before sowing.

Sowing outdoors

Vegetables are either sown *in situ*, where they grow to maturity, or in a seedbed from where they are transplanted to their permanent position. *In situ* sowing is used for crops that are harvested young, such as spring onions and radishes, or vegetables that do not transplant well, such as carrots and parsnips. Brassicas may be sown in a seedbed or grown in modules together with a wide range of other crops.

Successful sowing outdoors requires warm and well-prepared soil. Germination occurs for most vegetables once temperatures are over 7°C (45°F), so do not sow seed in cold soil. In several cases, such as lettuces, germination is poor at high temperatures. Particular temperature requirements for germination are given in individual vegetable entries. Soil temperature may be measured with a soil thermometer but most gardeners use their own knowledge of the soil to assess if it is warm enough for germination to occur.

Preparing the ground

Before sowing, dig the soil, then rake the surface until it has a fine texture or tilth, removing stones and large clods of earth. Rake when it is neither very wet and heavy nor very dry. If soil sticks to your shoes, delay until it has dried out a little, but not so much that it is dusty.

If sowing in wet soil, standing on a board avoids damaging the structure of adjacent soil. This is not necessary with the bed system (see p.496) since the seed may be sown from the surrounding path.

SOWING IN A DRILL

1 *Mark out the drill using pegs and string. Use the corner of a hoe or a trowel to make the drill, ensuring that it is the depth required for the seed.*

2 *Stand on a plank placed parallel to the drill to prevent compaction of the soil. Sprinkle the seeds thinly and evenly along the drill, then cover and firm with care.*

ALTERNATIVE METHODS

Wet conditions
If the soil drains slowly or is very heavy, sprinkle a layer of sand at the base of the drill, sow the seed, then cover it.

Dry conditions
When the soil is very dry, water the base of the drill, then sow the seeds and lightly press them in before covering with dry soil.

Guidelines for sowing

Seeds are sown at different depths according to their size. Unless otherwise directed, sow small seed, such as onions, about 1cm (½in) deep, brassicas 2cm (¾in) deep, peas and sweet corn about 2.5cm (1in) deep, and beans up to 5cm (2in) deep. The most important requirement is to sow thinly so that seedlings are not crowded in the early stages. Various methods of sowing are described below; whichever is used, it is vital to conserve surface moisture. In dry weather, cover the soil after sowing with horticultural fleece. Remove any covering when the seedlings appear.

Sowing in a drill

This is the most common method of sowing vegetables. Mark a row with a string line and make a small, even channel (a "drill") in the soil to the required depth. There are several methods of sowing: sprinkle a pinch of seed from between thumb and fingers, or gently tap seed out from your palm or the packet. Small hand-held devices are available, designed to gradually release differently sized seeds; or station sow in groups of up to three seeds at the final planting distance, then thin to one seedling per station. If seed is sown directly into a drill, place each seed at half the required distance between the mature plants, for example at 2.5cm (1in) intervals to thin to 5cm (2in). After sowing, cover the seed with soil, drawing it back lightly with a rake, firm the area gently, and water with a can fitted with a fine rose to avoid capping.

If sowing in unavoidably wet conditions, line the drill before sowing with dry, sharp sand or vermiculite. If conditions are dry, water the drill before lightly pressing each seed into the soil; then cover them with dry soil.

SOWING IN A WIDE DRILL

1 Use a draw hoe to mark out parallel drills 15–23cm (6–9in) wide and flat at the base.

2 Sow seeds the required distance apart in the drill.

3 Cover the seeds with soil using the hoe. Take care not to dislodge them.

4 Protect them from birds or animals by pegging wire netting over the drill.

This slows down the evaporation rate and helps to keep seeds moist until germination.

Wide drills

Use wide, flat drills for plants that are grown closely together, such as peas, early carrots, and crops grown for harvesting at the seedling stage (see "Successional crops", right). Make each drill up to 23cm (9in) wide and to the required depth. Space the seeds evenly in the drill, and cover carefully with soil.

Large seed

The seed of beans may be sown individually. Place a seed in a hole made by a dibber or a finger, ensuring that each seed is at the base of the hole and in contact with the soil. Cover sowings of tender plants, such as pumpkins and marrows, with glass jars or cut-off plastic bottles and remove once the seedlings emerge.

Broadcasting seed

In this method, the soil is first raked to produce a fine tilth; the seed is then scattered as evenly as possible either by hand or from a packet. Rake the soil lightly again afterwards to cover the seed.

etables. This is a very productive way to make use of a small area, and such crops are ideal for sowing under or between other, slower-maturing vegetables. To obtain seedling crops, sow seed in wide drills and cover with fleece. Seedlings do not need thinning and will be ready for the first cut in a few weeks.

Using fleece for protection

Fleece tucked into the soil or held down with bricks, helps to warm the soil before sowing. After sowing, it encourages early establishment and keeps off birds, rabbits, cats, and some insect pests. Remove it before the seedlings' growth is restricted.

Thinning

Young seedlings must be thinned to prevent overcrowding. Thin to the final spacing in stages, to allow for losses from pests and diseases; at each stage, aim to leave a seedling just clear of its neighbours. If the seeds have been sown in situ, continue to thin until they are at the spacing required for mature plants. Clear thinnings away as their scent may attract pests. Seedlings of plants such as lettuces, cabbages, and onions may be lifted for transplanting when conditions are suitably moist, and the soil refirmed around the remaining seedlings; lettuces are liable to bolt if it is too warm.

Planting

Plant or transplant vegetables into their final position when they are as young as possible so they can grow without further check. Exceptions to this are plants that have been raised in containers or modules (see p.501). Do not transplant root vegetables

Successional crops

Vegetables that grow fast, but rapidly pass their prime or run to seed, such as lettuces, should be sown little and often. To avoid gluts or gaps in cropping, wait until one sowing emerges before making the next.

Many leafy or salad vegetables may be sown for harvesting at the seedling stage and, once cut, often regrow to produce successional flushes of cut-and-come-again veg-

BROADCASTING

1 Prepare the area to be sown by raking carefully in one direction to produce a fine tilth. Sprinkle the seed thinly and evenly over the surface.

2 Rake lightly at right angles to the original direction to cover the seed, then water thoroughly with a can fitted with a fine rose.

THINNING SEEDLINGS

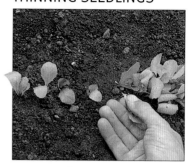

To thin small seedlings, nip them out at ground level so that the roots of the remaining seedlings are not disturbed.

once the tap root has started to form as this may distort its shape.

Before taking plants from a seedbed, water around their roots; if the ground into which they are being planted is dry, water the drill. Pick up a plant by a leaf rather than the stem or roots, which are easily damaged. Make a hole slightly bigger than the roots and position the plant in this hole, replacing the soil so that the

TRANSPLANTING SEEDLINGS

Lift seedlings gently, keeping as much soil around the roots as possible. Before replanting, place the seedlings in a clear plastic bag to retain moisture.

PLANTING DEPTH

Plant vegetable seedlings so that their lowest leaves are just above soil level. Planting too high exposes the stalk, which may not support the weight of the mature vegetable.

lower leaves are just above soil level. Firm around the stem to anchor the plant. In hot weather, water seedlings, and then shade them with horticultural fleece until they are established. Keep the soil moist for a few days after planting (see "Critical watering periods", p.502).

Spacing

Different vegetables have individual spacing requirements, which sometimes determine their final size. Traditionally, vegetables are grown in rows with a recommended spacing between the plants, and between the rows. Alternatively they may be grown with equidistant spacing between the plants – the average of the recommended spacing between plants and rows; so plants 15cm (6in) apart, in rows 30cm (12in) apart, may alternatively be grown 23cm (9in) apart each way. This method gives good results: plants have an equal share of light, air, moisture, and nutrients, and as they mature they form a canopy over the soil that suppresses weeds (see also THE BED SYSTEM, p.496). Vegetables may also be grown close together within widely spaced rows.

Sowing indoors

Vegetable seed may be sown indoors, in a cool greenhouse, or on a windowsill. This is helpful in climates with cool or short summers for tender vegetables, and for those needing a long growing season. It also helps to produce healthy seedlings and overcomes germination problems, since temperature is more easily controlled. After germination, keep most seedlings at a lower temperature in a spacious, light, protected environment until they are planted out. Where this is impossible, it may be practical to buy more mature plants.

Sowing in containers

Modules are individual units in which seeds are sown and plants grown on for planting out directly. This produces high-quality plants that grow on well: seedlings have no competition and develop a healthy root ball that is hardly disturbed when planted out in their final position. They do, however, need more space and compost in the early stages than those planted in trays.

Many types of module are available, the cheapest being plastic or polystyrene cellular trays. Small containers include clay or plastic pots, degradable pots, and soil blocks made of compressed compost. The compost may be enclosed in netting, which roots can penetrate.

SOWING AND TRANSPLANTING

1 *Fill the module with seed compost and make a hole 5mm (¼in) deep in each section. Sow one or two seeds per section. Cover with compost, then water.*

2 *Remove each plant from the module. Make a hole to take its root ball. Place the plant in the hole with its lower leaves just above the surface; firm and water.*

Sow into modules of 24 or 40 cells – these fit neatly into a standard seed tray. Sow two or three seeds per unit; then thin the seedlings to leave the strongest. In some cases, such as leeks, onions, turnips and beet, several seeds are sown together, planted out as a unit at a wider spacing than usual, and grown on to maturity.

Alternatively, sow seed in a small pan or seed tray, in standard seed compost (see "Sowing in pots or trays", p.218). When the seedlings have two or three small leaves, prick them out into a seed tray of potting compost, spaced 2.5–5cm (1–2in) apart, or into

---

modules. Seedlings usually need to be kept slightly warm. Put them in a well-lit, draught-free place to grow strongly and evenly. Transfer plants to individual pots before planting out.

Hardening off

Plants raised indoors need to be acclimatized to lower temperatures and wind before being planted in the open. Harden them off in cloches or cold frames over 10–14 days. Increase ventilation gradually during the day and then at night, until the seedlings can be left out all the time; partly cover with fleece after planting.

Vegetative propagation

A few vegetables are usually raised vegetatively, from offsets, tubers, corms, bulbs, or cuttings. This may be because they rarely set seed or, if raised from seed, are variable, or because vegetative propagation is faster. Details are given under individual vegetables (pp.507–548).

Growing vegetables in containers

Containers are useful for growing vegetables where space is limited, or to extend the vegetable garden into a paved area. They are also used in the greenhouse, especially if soil is infected with soil-borne diseases and it is impractical to sterilize or replace it. Vegetables need a richer growing medium and a more consistent and thorough watering than flowers and so are hard to grow well in containers unless carefully maintained (see also CONTAINER GARDENING, p.328).

Choosing the vegetables

The best vegetables for containers are compact, quick-maturing plants, such as lettuces, radishes, and beetroot, or robust, undemanding, leafy vegetables such as spinach beet; fruiting vegetables, such as peppers, aubergines, and tomatoes, also flourish. Fast-maturing, seedling crops also grow well. Dwarf cultivars are excellent since they do not need support. Do not use vegetables that are deep-rooting, slow to mature, very tall or large, or gross feeders, such as brassicas, parsnips, or celery. Raise plants for containers in modules; sow cut-and-come-again seedling crops directly in the container.

Preparing the container

The larger the container, and the greater its volume of compost or

soil, the better. Large vegetables and gross feeders, such as potatoes and tomatoes, generally need a container that measures at least 25cm (10in) deep and wide. It should also be strong and stable.

Good drainage is essential. If there are no drainage holes, make several of at least 1cm (½in) diameter in the base; cover them with crocks to prevent blockage. For growing bags, holes are best cut at the base along each side; the soil will not stagnate and infection is unable to enter if the bags are laid on diseased soil.

The soil or compost must be light and well aerated, since frequent watering will compact it. Lighten garden soil with well-rotted compost mixed with coarse sand and peat substitute or peat.

In hot and windy weather containers dry out rapidly by evaporation through the top and, if not made of plastic, the sides. To minimize this do not put them in exposed sites or at the foot of a hot wall. Line non-plastic containers with plastic sheeting perforated with drainage holes.

Dwarf broad beans

Fast-maturing, compact lettuces

Stable plastic container to retain moisture

Peas supported by peasticks

Routine cultivation

THE best vegetables are produced when plants are maintained in the optimum conditions for growth. Keep free from weeds and water thoroughly as required. Mulches may be used to retain moisture and to suppress weeds. The level of nutrients must be maintained as crops grow.

Watering

Most crops need fairly moist soil, but vary in the amount of water required, and in when they need it most (see "Critical watering periods", below). Overwatering may lead to loss of flavour in tomatoes and carrots, and, in root crops, to the development of leaves at the expense of root.

How to water

It is more effective to water heavily and occasionally rather than frequently and lightly; very young plants, however, should be watered lightly and frequently so that they never dry out. Light watering evaporates rapidly without reaching the plants' roots, and encourages shallow surface rooting rather than the deep rooting that enables plants to withstand drought. Direct the water at the base of each plant. Water in the evening when less moisture will evaporate, and allow time for the plants to dry before nightfall.

Watering equipment

Use a can fitted with a fine rose to water young plants. For general watering in small gardens, a can may be adequate; in larger gardens, use a hand-held hose, regulating the flow with a fixture attached to the end.

A practical choice in vegetable gardens is either a seep hose or a porous hose laid among the plants (see also TOOLS AND EQUIPMENT, "Seep hoses", p.561). Water seeps through the holes or pores, usually watering a strip about 30cm (12in) wide. The tube is easily moved from crop to crop, and some porous types may be buried shallowly in the soil.

Critical watering periods

There are periods in the growing cycle of vegetables when water is particularly beneficial; these vary according to the individual vegetable. In prolonged, dry weather confine watering to these periods.

Germinating seeds, seedlings, and newly transplanted plants should never be allowed to dry out, so water frequently and lightly and ensure that water reaches the roots.

Leafy and salad vegetables, such as spinach, chard, most brassicas, and lettuces, require a thorough watering once a week to help them crop heavily. The most critical period is between ten days and three weeks before maturity; during this period, but only in very dry conditions, apply a single, heavy watering of 22 litres/sq m (5 gallons/sq yd). Outside this period, give half this amount weekly during dry weather.

The critical point for fruiting crops like tomatoes, peppers, courgettes, beans, cucumbers, and peas is when flowers form and fruits or pods develop. If it is dry at this time, water weekly at the rate for leafy crops (above). Do not water heavily before the critical period; this produces leafy growth at the expense of fruit.

Root crops like carrots, radishes, and beetroot need moderate watering in the growing period. In the early stages, water at a rate of 5 litres/sq m (1 gallon/sq yd) if the soil is dry. Increase this rate four-fold when the roots start to swell, watering every two weeks if dry conditions persist.

Minimizing the need to water

To conserve soil moisture, particularly in dry areas, dig the soil deeply, working in plenty of organic matter to improve soil structure and moisture retention and to encourage deep rooting. Keep the soil surface mulched (see "Mulching", right), and keep down weeds, which compete for moisture. Do not hoe in dry weather since this encourages moisture to evaporate from the soil. However, a dust mulch, produced by very shallow hoeing once a week, helps retain moisture in the root area and also limits run-off after rain. Erect windbreaks to protect from desiccating winds (see "Shelter from wind", p.492). In areas prone to drought, adopt slightly wider spacing so that the roots can spread further to take moisture from a larger area.

Controlling weeds

A vegetable garden should be free of weeds. They compete for water, nutrients, and light, may physically suffocate plants, and may harbour pests and diseases (see PLANT PROBLEMS, "Weeds", pp.669–671).

Minimizing weed growth

During the growing season weed growth may be reduced by mulching (see below) and by planting crops at equidistant spacing (see "Spacing",

WATERING VEGETABLES WITH A SEEP HOSE

A seep hose laid between rows of vegetables ensures that the water reaches the roots of the plants and penetrates deeply into the soil.

p.501). Once they have reached a reasonable size, most form a weed-suppressing canopy over the ground.

Stale seedbeds

Spring sowings or plantings are the most vulnerable to annual weeds. If soil has not been cultivated recently and may be full of weed seeds, prepare in advance; allow the first flush of weeds to germinate, and hoe them off before sowing or planting (see also SOILS AND FERTILIZERS, "The stale seedbed technique", p.620).

Mulching

A mulch is a layer of organic or inorganic material laid on the soil around plants. Where the surface is

Organic weed control

Clear perennial weeds from the vegetable garden before planting crops. Dig out deeply rooted and spreading perennials; take care not to leave behind small pieces of root that will sprout again. If the problem is very serious, smother weeds with a light-proof mulch, such as old carpet or heavy, black, plastic sheeting. All but the most persistent weeds die if covered for 6–12 months. While crops are growing, take care to prevent or control perennial weeds.

Annual weeds germinate and grow very rapidly, and become a nuisance if they are allowed to seed freely in the vegetable patch. Pay attention to weeding in the first three weeks after crops germinate, when they are most affected by competition. Pull up weeds by hand, or hoe shallowly to avoid bringing deeper weed seeds to the surface. Remove them to prevent re-rooting.

kept mulched, the need to cultivate is lessened or even eliminated.

Organic mulches

Bulky organic mulches add nutrients to the soil and improve the structure. They may be well-rotted animal manures, garden compost, spent mushroom compost, dried lawn clippings, seaweed or strulch (composted straw). Do not use any materials derived from wood, such as sawdust and shredded bark, unless they are at least two years old because they use up soil nitrogen during decomposition.

CONSERVING SOIL MOISTURE

Vegetables such as runner beans drop their flowers if the soil around their roots dries out. Water the crops well, then apply a mulch by forking it onto the border. A mulch prevents soil-moisture evaporation, and also insulates the soil, suppresses weeds, protects the surface from heavy rain and erosion, and reduces damage to soil when it is trodden on.

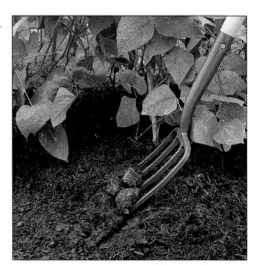

Organic mulches are best applied to growing crops in spring and early summer when the soil is moist. They maintain the temperature and moisture levels of the soil once they are applied so, if possible, mulch after the soil has warmed up in spring but before it starts to dry out. Never mulch cold, wet, or very dry soil. In areas with high rainfall and on heavy soil, however, an organic mulch is best spread on the ground in autumn to allow the worms to work it in.

In practice it is often easiest to apply organic mulches when planting, watering plants first if necessary. Alternatively, mulch young seedlings that are already planted and growing strongly and are at least 5cm (2in) high. A mulch may be 2.5–7cm (1–3in) deep or more; aim for a deep mulch if the purpose is to keep down weeds.

Plastic film mulches

These are sheets of plastic that may be black, white, or transparent. Depending on which kind is used, they raise soil temperatures to bring on crops early, suppress weeds, reflect heat up to ripening fruit, and keep fruiting vegetables clean and free from soil splash. Shiny film mulches help deter flying pests.

Black films are mainly used to suppress weeds, although they also raise the soil temperature. Early potatoes may be grown under black films instead of being earthed up (see "Potatoes", p.547).

White films are mainly used to reflect light and warmth onto ripening fruit such as tomatoes and melons. Some films are made with the lower side black to suppress weeds, and the upper side white to reflect light. These films raise soil temperatures about 7°C (12°F) more than black films. Transparent films are used mainly to warm up the soil in spring, or to prevent soil splash.

It is simpler to lay films before planting or sowing crops. If desired, lay seep or porous hoses in position first, then lay the film on the ground or over the bed to be covered. Make slits 7–10cm (3–4in) deep in the soil around the bed, and anchor the mulch by tucking the edges into the soil, using a spade (see *Anchoring Plastic Sheeting*, p.626). This is easier on slightly mounded beds. To plant, cut cross-shaped slits in the film with a knife, make a hole in the soil beneath, then carefully ease the plants through into the soil, and firm. Sow large seeds such as sweet corn by making holes in the plastic and pushing the seeds through. When seedlings appear, guide them through the holes so that they are not trapped.

PLANTING THROUGH A BLACK-AND-WHITE PLASTIC MULCH

1 *Dig a trench around the area to be planted, lay down the mulch with the white side upwards, and secure its edges firmly into the earth.*

2 *Make cross-shaped slits in the plastic the required distance apart and dig a hole in the soil large enough to take the plant's root ball.*

3 *Remove the plant (here a tomato) from its pot, and place it in the hole. Firm the soil around the root ball and water. Stake if necessary.*

When necessary, water carefully through the planting holes. Slugs may be attracted to films: lift the film edges carefully and remove them or use a proprietary slug killer.

Alternatives to plastic mulches are Permealay fabric (permeable black material) or biodegradable paper.

Feeding

In fertile garden soils, into which plenty of organic matter is regularly worked, most crops grow satisfactorily without additional fertilizers. As it takes a few years to build up soil fertility, however, supplementary feeding will be necessary on poor soils or to correct deficiencies and, in some cases, to obtain higher yields.

Soil nutrients

Plants need a range of nutrients; the three most important for vegetables, and those most often in short supply, are nitrogen (N), phosphorus (P), and potassium or potash (K). For further information, see "Soil nutrients and fertilizers", pp.624–625.

Maintain adequate levels of phosphorus and potassium with annual applications of garden compost at 2–5kg/sq m (5–11lb/sq yd), or manure at 5.5kg/sq m (12lb/sq yd). Alternatively, use artificial fertilizers such as superphosphate or triple superphosphate (for P) and sulphate of potash (for K) at levels that are recommended by the manufacturer, or apply them in compound fertilizers containing N, P, and K.

Potassium is washed out of the soil only slowly, so reserves last into the following season. Phosphorus is not lost through leaching, but may be "locked up" in insoluble forms and

not available to plants; reserves may need replenishing if soil analysis indicates that they are low. Nitrogen is constantly leached out and reserves need to be replenished continually, by adding either organic matter (which releases nitrogen as it breaks down) or artificial fertilizers.

Vegetables vary in their need for nitrogen. For further information, see *Nitrogen Requirements*, p.504. This indicates the broad requirements of different groups using a fertilizer with 21 per cent nitrogen content. Rates therefore vary according to the fertilizer used; nitrogenous fertilizers include sulphate of ammonia, ammonium nitrate, and nitrate of potash.

Applying fertilizers

Fertilizers are sold in dry forms (dusts, granules, and pellets) and as concentrated liquids (see "Types of fertilizer", p.624). They can be applied either as a base-dressing before sowing or planting, or as a top-dressing to give a boost during growth (see "Applying fertilizers", p.625).

Apply nitrogenous fertilizers as close to sowing as possible to avoid leaching; additional applications may be made later in the growing season. Never apply nitrogen in the autumn or it will be washed out of the soil before most vegetables are planted, and autumn-planted crops will be too soft to survive the winter. Phosphate and potassium fertilizers are applied at any time, often in the autumn, or, where compound fertilizers are used, at the same time as nitrogen, in spring.

Feeding in organic systems

If extra feeding is necessary, use slower-acting organic fertilizers. These include fish, blood, and bone

meal, a general fertilizer applied as a base- or top-dressing, and dried blood (relatively fast-acting) and hoof and horn (slower-acting), both of which provide a source of nitrogen.

Various proprietary and general-purpose liquid feeds are available, some based on animal manures and others on seaweed extracts. The latter are particularly rich in trace elements as well as plant hormones that appear to be beneficial to growth, even though their nutrient levels are not very high. They are either watered in or applied as a foliar feed.

Container-grown vegetables

The compost in containers can dry out very rapidly in hot weather. To conserve moisture, keep the upper surface mulched with up to 5cm (2in) of organic material, stones, or a sheet mulch. Be prepared to water containers thoroughly twice a day and, in very hot weather, water growing bags three times a day.

Regular weekly feeding may be necessary; use an organic or artificial fertilizer at diluted strengths, according to the manufacturer's instructions. Top-dress the compost in the container in spring, and change the compost every two or three years when it becomes compacted and less productive – small containers may become root-bound and grow only one crop.

Pests and diseases

Healthy plants can resist most pest and disease attacks. Therefore good basic care of plants will keep problems caused by pests and diseases to a minimum. Learn to recognize the most common pests and diseases in your garden, and take the appropriate preventive measures wherever feasible. Avoid using chemicals in the vegetable garden as far as possible. Apart from their inherent danger and the risk of residues in the soil as well as on the plants, they may kill the natural enemies of many pests and diseases. If using chemical controls seems unavoidable, try to use organically approved products at least. In a few cases, biological control – the introduction of a pest's natural enemy – may be used. For general information and details about specific pests and diseases, see PLANT PROBLEMS, pp.639–673.

Common pests

Animals and birds that may attack vegetables include deer, rabbits, mice, moles, and pigeon. In cases of persistent attack, erect wire fences or nets around the garden or over crops, use humane animal traps, and deter large birds with humming wire and small ones with strands of black cotton. In damp climates slugs and snails may be the most serious pests. They are mainly night-feeders; collect them after dark by torchlight and destroy them. When chemical controls are used, handle them with care.

Soil pests, such as slugs and cutworms, commonly attack young plants, sometimes biting through the stems of plants at ground level. They tend to be worse in newly cultivated ground. Thorough digging exposes them to the birds. Many soil pests are night-feeders and may be easily caught by torchlight.

Healthy practices

To reduce pests and diseases, keep soil fertile and well drained, work in organic matter, and rotate crops (see p.498). Grow crops that suit the climate, and if possible choose pest- or disease-resistant cultivars. Raise plants to a good size in modules to reduce damage from slugs and snails when planting out; harden off plants raised indoors. For plants grown under cover, use clean seed trays and pots and sterilized potting compost. To avoid problems like mildew, give plants enough space to ensure good air circulation.

Microscopic soil pests – eelworms or nematodes – attack certain plant groups, including potatoes. Rotate crops to prevent pests becoming established, and grow resistant cultivars where they are available.

Sucking insects, including species of aphid, carrot fly, cabbage root fly, and thrips or thunderflies, damage a range of plants by sucking the sap, and may spread virus diseases in the process. Knowledge of pest habits may help prevent attacks – by earlier or later sowings, for example. Use sticky yellow traps to catch aphids, collars (see *Collaring Seedlings*, p.507) to deter cabbage root fly, and film barriers against carrot fly (see p.544). Chemical or organic sprays may control outbreaks.

Various caterpillars attack a range of plants. Pick them off by hand or

CREATING HEALTHY GROWING CONDITIONS

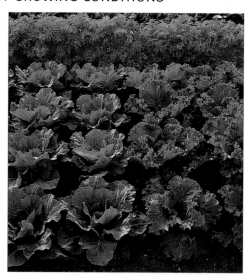

Keep vegetable beds (here of ornamental cabbages and carrots) and paths free of weeds and debris; remove and burn diseased plant material. Water and feed carefully – excess can be as damaging as insufficiency. Thin seedlings early to avoid overcrowding, and remove the thinnings. Encourage rapid germination of home-grown plants by sowing indoors if conditions are adverse outside.

use the biological control *Bacillus thuringiensis*, or organic or chemical sprays. Place fine nets over vegetables to prevent adult butterflies or moths laying eggs on the plants. Small beetles, such as flea beetles, nibble seedling leaves of brassicas. They may be controlled with sprays, and plants may be protected with fine nets of fleece. Large beetles such as the Colorado beetle pose serious problems in some countries.

Pests may multiply rapidly in high temperatures under glass. The most serious are glasshouse whitefly and red spider mite; both attack a wide range of crops, and are now resistant to most standard chemical sprays. Discourage them with maximum ventilation and by damping down to increase humidity. As soon as these pests are noticed, introduce a form of

biological control to restrict numbers (see "Biological control", p.642).

Common diseases

Diseases are caused mainly by fungi, bacteria, and viruses. Infected plants develop a range of symptoms which in some cases merely disfigure plants, but in others will kill them. Damping off diseases, for example, infect and usually kill young seedlings; dig up and burn affected plants.

Diseases spread very rapidly in conditions that are favourable to their development and once established are difficult to control. Preventive measures and good garden hygiene are vitally important to prevent diseases spreading and becoming established. A few sprays may be used in anticipation of an attack. Choose disease-resistant cultivars.

Clubroot, a soil infection, is a serious problem affecting members of the cabbage family. Raise soil pH by applying lime (see "Liming", p.625), and grow crops in modules in sterile soil, making them vigorous and helping control it. Formulations of calcium cyanamide can also be used as a dressing to help cut down infections.

Physiological disorders

Some problems with vegetables are due to incorrect cultural conditions. Most common is premature bolting (flowering and setting seed), caused by sudden low or high temperatures, drought, or sowing at the wrong time. Fruits failing to set may be due to lack of pollination, erratic watering, drought, high night temperatures and windy, cold conditions. If there are mineral deficiencies in the soil, cauliflower curds may fail to grow. For more details, and advice on how to create healthy growing conditions, see individual crops, pp.507–548.

NITROGEN REQUIREMENTS (USING FERTILIZER WITH 21 PER CENT N CONTENT)

Very low 12g/sq m (½oz/sq yd)	Low 25–35g/sq m (1–1½oz/sq yd)	Medium 45–55g/sq m (1½–2oz/sq yd)	High 70–100g/sq m (2½–3½oz/sq yd)	Very high 110g/sq m (4oz/sq yd)
Carrots Garlic Radishes	Asparagus Beans (all) Celeriac Chicory (all) Courgettes Cucumbers Endive Florence fennel Gherkins Globe artichokes Kohl rabi Marrows New Zealand spinach Okra Onions (all) Parsnips Peanuts Salsify Scorzonera Swedes Tomatoes Turnips (and turnip tops)	Amaranths Aubergines Broccoli raab Cabbages (for storage) Calabrese Cauliflowers Cocoyams Hot peppers Jerusalem artichokes Kales Lettuces Potatoes (early) Pumpkins Rhubarb (young) Spinach Sprouting broccoli Sweet corn Sweet/chilli peppers Sweet potatoes Watermelons Wonderberries	Beetroot Brussels sprouts Celery Ceylon spinach Leeks Potatoes (maincrop) Spinach beet Sweet melons Swiss chard	Cabbages (spring, summer, winter) Chinese broccoli Chinese cabbages Komatsuna Oriental mustards Mizuna greens Pak choi Rhubarb (cutting years)
(Peas do not require any extra nitrogen)				

Growing under cover

THE productivity of a vegetable garden may be increased greatly in climates with a short growing season by growing plants under cover in a protected environment for some or all of their life cycle. The shorter the growing season, the more effective the cover will be.

Under cover, air and soil temperatures are increased, and crops are sheltered from chill winds. This lengthens the growing season by up to two months. The quality and yields of many crops are improved by higher temperatures and shelter.

Cover may be used to start crops early in spring for planting outside when temperatures rise. Half-hardy summer vegetables that would not mature outdoors during the growing season may ripen under cover; in cool climates, okra and aubergines, for example, only ripen fully under cover. The winter cropping period of many vegetables may be extended; for example, lettuces, Oriental brassicas, peas, and spinach all stop growing in the open but continue under cover.

Make the most of cover by ensuring that the soil underneath is fertile and weed-free. Vegetables require extra watering under cover – mulch them where practical to cut down watering. Plants started under cover may be set back if abruptly exposed to the elements. Harden them off gradually where appropriate.

Greenhouses and frames

Cover may be provided by anything from a greenhouse to a cold frame or a plastic tunnel cloche. For full details, see GREENHOUSES AND FRAMES, pp.566–583.

Greenhouses

A permanent, glazed greenhouse provides an excellent growing environment. It is easily ventilated and retains heat at night better than plastic film. Diseases may build up in soil if crops such as tomatoes are grown for several consecutive years, and the soil must then be changed or sterilized, or crops grown in containers. Supports may be required for tender, climbing vegetables.

Walk-in polytunnels

These are made of heavy-duty, clear plastic sheeting on metal supports. They are cheaper and easier to erect than greenhouses, and may be moved to a different site if required. Ventilation is hard to control, however, increasing the risk of pests and diseases if temperatures rise rapidly; holes may be cut in the film in summer and taped over in winter. The film needs to be renewed every three to five years.

Tunnel cloches

These are cheap, mobile, and flexible; the lightweight plastic film may be rolled back for ventilation and watering. They provide shelter from wind and are useful in most gardens, especially for the final stages of hardening off seedlings and protecting vegetables in unsettled spring and autumn weather. However, low polytunnels are limited by their height and flimsiness, and give little protection from low temperatures. They also need to be well anchored in windy situations.

Garden frames

Being relatively small, frames are most beneficial in gardens lacking the space for a greenhouse or polytunnel. Some types are portable. They are easily ventilated, and may be heated by electric soil-warming cables. They are useful for raising and hardening off seedlings; their low height limits the range of crops grown, although the lids may be

Plastic bottle cloches
Simple cloches made from plastic bottles will protect individual young plants; in exposed conditions, traditional glass cloches offer better protection against frost and wind.

removed to allow semi-hardy crops to mature. Garden frames may be blacked out for forcing crops such as Witloof chicory and endive.

Cloches

Although individual cloches only cover a small area, when placed end to end they can be used to cover an entire row. To make maximum use of cloches, move them from one crop to another during a season; for example protect overwintering salads, start tender early potatoes or dwarf beans in spring, then ripen melons in midsummer.

Floating mulches

These are various types of film, including fine netting film, and non-woven fleecy film. Perforated plastic film is sometimes recommended but it overheats in hot weather and offers minimal frost protection. All may be laid over low tunnel cloche hoops or directly over crops after sowing or planting, and anchored shallowly in the soil or weighted down. The mulches are lifted by the crops as they grow.

Floating mulches promote earlier crops and higher yields by raising temperatures and protecting plants from wind as well as, in certain cases, insect pests. All types give better ventilation than unperforated plastic films.

Weed beds carefully before laying floating mulches, since they are awkward to lift for weeding later.

Netting films

Fine netting films are strong and last for several seasons. They are well ventilated so may usually be kept on until plants mature. They have little effect on temperature, but protect against wind and therefore tend to produce larger, and sometimes more leggy, plants. Provided that they are well anchored at the edges, they protect against many insect pests.

Fleecy or fibrous films

These light, soft, non-woven films usually last one season only; they are more permeable to light and air than plastics. Depending on the film's weight, it may protect against frost and flying insect pests; be careful with cucurbits, however, as they need to be uncovered to allow bees to pollinate the flowers. Many vegetables may be grown under fleecy film until they are mature, especially if using one of the thinner textured films.

USING FLOATING MULCHES

Floating mulches are spread over a bed of seedlings and earthed in at the edges so that they are loose enough to allow for growth. Netting film protects plants against insect pests and wind damage, while fleecy film is effective against frost, as well as deterring insect pests.

Netting film

Fleecy film

TUNNEL CLOCHE

Use wire hoops pushed into the ground 90cm (3ft) apart to support plastic film, which is tied at each end to a stake. Tie strings over the plastic and secure them at the base of each hoop.

Harvesting and storing

How and when vegetables are harvested, and whether they are used fresh, stored, or both, depends on the nature of the vegetable and the climate. The shorter the growing season and the more severe the winter, the greater the incentive to store vegetables, either naturally or by freezing. For details, see individual vegetables (pp.507–548) and *Vegetables that Freeze Well*, below.

Harvesting

Follow the guidelines under individual vegetables for how to harvest. Most vegetables are harvested at

VEGETABLES THAT FREEZE WELL

Asparagus 1
Aubergines 1 2
Beetroot 1 3
Broad beans 1
Broccoli raab 1
Brussels sprouts 1
Cabbages 1 2
Calabrese 1
Carrots 1 3
Cauliflowers 1 2
Celery 2
Chinese broccoli 1
Chinese cabbages 1 2
Courgettes 1
Dolichos beans 1
French beans 1
Hot peppers 1 2
Kales 1
Kohl rabi 1 2
Lima beans 1
Marrows 1 2
New Zealand spinach 1
Okra 1
Parsnips 1 3
Peas 1
Potatoes (small and new
    potatoes only) 1
Pumpkins 2
Rhubarb 2
Scarlet runner beans 1
Spinach 1
Spinach beet 1
Spring onions 2
Sprouting broccoli 1
Swedes 1 2
Sweet corn 1
Sweet peppers 1
Swiss chard 1
Tomatoes 1
Turnips 1 2 3
Wonderberries 1

Key

1 Blanch
2 Dice, slice, purée, or shred
3 Freeze only when young

maturity, but some, notably leafy plants and brassicas, may be cut at various stages, and will often resprout for a second and third crop.

Cut-and-come-again harvesting

This method of harvesting is suited to vegetables that resprout after an initial cut has been made, enabling them to be used fresh over a fairly long period. Crops may be harvested at the seedling stage, or later when they are semi-mature or mature.

Harvest seedling crops when they are 5–10cm (2–4in) high, cutting about 2cm (¾in) above soil level. Some, for example salad rocket, salad rape, and cress, may be cut and left to resprout several times in succession. See also "Successional crops", p.500.

Some semi-mature or mature crops, if harvested by cutting 2.5–5cm (1–2in) above soil level, will resprout and after a few weeks produce more leaves and, in some cases, edible flowering shoots (see "Cultivating Oriental brassicas", p.513).

The technique is suited to certain types of lettuce, endive, sugar loaf chicory, Oriental greens, and Swiss chard. It is useful in cool climates in autumn and early winter as plants treated this way survive lower temperatures than they would otherwise and may be very productive, especially under cover.

Storing

The length of time that vegetables may be stored depends on the storage conditions and on the vegetable or cultivar. For details, see individual vegetables. The main cause of deterioration after harvesting is water loss, so aim to keep this to a minimum. Do not store damaged or diseased specimens since they may rot.

Vegetables often freeze well; almost all need to be blanched either in steam or boiling water and cooled quickly before freezing. The only exception to this is sweet peppers, which may be frozen without any initial preparation.

Leafy vegetables and brassicas

Leafy vegetables and various types of brassica, such as calabrese and cauliflower, have such a high water content that few of them store well. An exception is the winter storing cabbage, which may be stored either hanging in nets or on a bed of straw, in a frost-free shed or cold frame.

Storing strings of onions
Plait together the dried onion leaves to form strings of bulbs. These may be hung outside in warm weather to dry further, and then brought indoors to be stored in frost-free conditions.

Several brassicas freeze well: some cultivars are bred for the purpose. Freeze only top-quality produce.

Fruiting vegetables

Vegetables such as aubergines, tomatoes, and cucumbers usually have an optimum time for harvesting, although fruits may also be harvested immature. If they are to be stored for winter use, they are best made into preserves or deep frozen.

Sweet peppers keep in good condition for many months if whole plants are pulled up and hung in a dry, frost-free place. Some cultivars of marrow and squash may be stored for several months. Leave the fruit to mature on the plant, then pick and "cure" it in the sun to harden the skin, forming an effective barrier to water loss, and store it in a dry, frost-free environment (see also "Pumpkins and winter squashes", p.525).

Bulbs

Certain cultivars of onion, shallot, and garlic will keep for many months. Lift the crop when mature or nearing maturity, and dry it in the sun (or under cover in wet climates), until the outer skins are papery. Handle the bulbs carefully to avoid bruising. Hang them as plaited strings, in nets, or spaced out on trays, in well-ventilated, frost-free conditions (see also *Storing Onions in a Box*, p.535).

Root vegetables

Some root vegetables, such as carrots and potatoes, may be either harvested young and eaten immature or left to mature and lifted and stored at the end of the season. A few, such as parsnips, are extremely hardy and,

except in severe winters, may be left in the ground until required.

Prepare vegetables carefully for storing, removing any foliage since this will rot. Store only healthy, unbruised specimens. Potatoes are susceptible to frost; store them packed in light-proof sacks in a frost-free place.

Root vegetables such as beetroot and carrots easily lose moisture, so store them in layers in boxes of moist sand, peat substitute, or peat in a cool shed or cellar (see *Storing Carrots*, p.544). They may also be stored in outdoor clamps: pile them on straw and cover with more straw, and, in cold areas, a layer of soil to give protection against frost (see *Making a Swede Clamp*, p.543).

STORING RED CABBAGES

Lay the cabbages on slats covered with straw in a cool, well-ventilated, frost-free place. Leave gaps between them to allow free air circulation and discourage rotting.

Western brassicas

WESTERN brassicas include kales, cauliflowers, cabbages, Brussels sprouts, broccoli, sprouting broccoli, calabrese, turnip tops, kohl rabi, swedes, and turnips. For information on kohl rabi, swedes, and turnips, see pp.540, 542, and 543 respectively.

Western brassicas are naturally biennial but are cultivated as annuals for their leaves and roots, and as biennials for flowerheads and shoots. Each type displays considerable variation, and there is often a range of cultivars for different seasons. They are usually cooked, but some are used raw. Western brassicas are cool-season crops with varying degrees of frost tolerance; most

perform poorly at high temperatures, so in warm climates grow them in winter. In temperate climates, they may provide crops for much of the year.

COLLARING SEEDLINGS

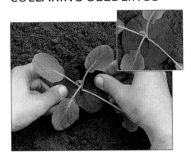

Where cabbage root fly is a problem, place a collar around the stem of each seedling. Make sure that it is flat on the ground to prevent the adult fly from laying its eggs at the base of the stem.

Siting Western brassicas

An open situation with fertile, well-drained, moisture-retentive soil is required. Rotate brassicas (see p.498) to avoid a build-up of clubroot. If this is a problem, lime the soil (see p.625) to bring the pH to 6.5–7 and discourage the disease. Most Western brassicas need high levels of nitrogen (see p.504), but they should not be planted on freshly manured ground since this causes overlush, leafy growth that is prone to pests. A base-dressing may be applied to the area before planting (see "Applying fertilizers", p.503).

Sowing and planting

Western brassicas prefer firm soil; they may be planted after a previous vegetable crop without forking the soil. Brussels sprouts and purple sprouting broccoli are best sown in a seedbed to produce taproots for better anchorage when planted. Crops like calabrese should be sown *in situ* because they do not transplant well. If sowing indoors, sow in pans and prick out into modules, transferring to 9cm (3½in) pots if clubroot is a problem, then transplant so that the plants have a healthy start and are more likely to mature without infection. Tall, top-

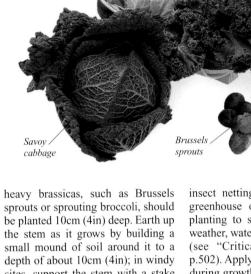

Winter cabbage

Calabrese

Cauliflower

Curly kale

Savoy cabbage

Brussels sprouts

heavy brassicas, such as Brussels sprouts or sprouting broccoli, should be planted 10cm (4in) deep. Earth up the stem as it grows by building a small mound of soil around it to a depth of about 10cm (4in); in windy sites, support the stem with a stake 1m (3ft) high. Plant brassicas firmly, with the lower leaves just above soil level. In some cases, spacing may be varied to determine the size of the brassica. If plants are widely spaced, they may be intercropped with salad seedlings or radishes.

Cultivation

It is important to protect seedlings from sowing to planting with fine

insect netting, even if grown in a greenhouse or frame. Mulch after planting to suppress weeds. In dry weather, water as for leafy vegetables (see "Critical watering periods", p.502). Apply a nitrogenous fertilizer during growth.

Pests and diseases

Flea beetles (p.644), slugs and snails (p.644), damping off (p.660), cabbage root fly (p.660), white blister (p.646), whiptail (p.652), and cutworms (p.660) all affect young plants. Caterpillars (p.645), cabbage whitefly (p.646), mealy aphids (see "Aphids", p.646), clubroot (p.649), and birds (p.657) attack plants at all stages.

Kales (*Brassica oleracea* Acephala Group)

Grown as annuals or biennials depending on the type, dwarf kales are 30–40cm (12–16in) tall, with a 30cm (12in) spread; tall types grow to 90cm (36in) and spread up to 60cm (24in). Some American kales are known as collards. Most kales produce leaves from a central stem;

Curly kale

the leaves may be plain or curly (see below) or curly-broad hybrids. Good cultivars include 'Afro', 'Black Tuscany', 'Redbor', 'Red Russian', and 'Reflex'. The leaves of all kales, and the spring-flowering shoots and young leaves of broadleaved types, are used cooked or raw. Kales are the hardiest brassicas, some surviving at -15°C (5°F); many also tolerate high temperatures. All prefer fertile, well-drained soils that will not become waterlogged, and require medium nitrogen levels (see p.504).

Sowing, planting, and routine cultivation

Sow seed in early spring for summer crops, and in late spring for autumn and winter crops. Sow *in situ* or in seedbeds or seed trays for transplanting; dwarf forms should be spaced 30–45cm (12–18in) apart, tall forms 75cm (30in) apart. Give overwintering types a nitrogenous

top-dressing in spring to encourage growth. In severe winters, grow dwarf cultivars under cloches or low polytunnels. Kales are usually unaffected by pests and diseases.

Growing under cover

For very early, tender kales, sow seed in early spring in rows 15cm (6in) apart, or in wide drills. Either harvest them as large seedlings, or thin the seedlings to 7cm (3in) apart and cut when they form plants 15cm (6in) tall, leaving the stumps to resprout for a second harvest.

Harvesting and storing

Some cultivars mature seven weeks after sowing, but plants can stand a long time in the ground. Snap off the leaves as required in autumn and winter to encourage new growth. Pick the shoots in spring when they are about 10cm (4in) long, before the flowers open. Kales freeze well.

Ornamental kales
Ornamental kales are grown mainly for winter decoration in the garden or for garnishing salads. Leaves are variegated green, red, white, or purple.

Cauliflowers (*Brassica oleracea* Botrytis Group)

Grown as annuals or biennials, cauliflowers form a head (or curd) of about 20cm (8in) in diameter; plants are 45–60cm (18–24in) tall, with a spread of up to 90cm (36in). They are classified by the main season of use, usually winter (with a distinction between those for frosty and frost-free areas), summer, and autumn, although these groups overlap (see *Cauliflower Types*, below). Most types of cauliflower have creamy or white curds, but there are attractive, distinctively flavoured types with green or purple curds. The curds, and in some cases the young green leaves surrounding them, are cooked or used raw in salads. Smaller curds, or mini-cauliflowers, about 5cm (2in) in diameter, may be specially grown from early summer cultivars.

Cauliflowers are a cool-season crop and do not usually grow well in areas with high summer temperatures. Several cultivars are frost hardy, but cauliflowers may only be harvested all year round in areas with frost-free winters. For details on soil and site see "Siting Western brassicas", p.507; overwintering cauliflowers need a sheltered situation outside, and are not usually grown to maturity

under cover. All cauliflowers need a moisture-retentive soil, with medium nitrogen levels (see p.504), and a pH of 6.5–7.5.

Sowing and planting

Success with cauliflowers depends on sowing the correct cultivar at the appropriate time, and allowing plants to develop with as few checks to growth (from transplanting or dry soil, for example) as possible. Where drought is likely in summer, grow spring-heading types, which will benefit from autumn rainfall, or fast-maturing mini-cauliflowers.

The main sowing times and spacings are given in the chart below. Cauliflowers are usually sown in seed trays, modules, or a seedbed for transplanting, but may be sown *in situ* and thinned to the correct spacing. Generally, the later the planting, the larger the cauliflower will grow and the wider the spacing required. Seed germinates best at a temperature of about 21°C (70°F).

For a very early summer supply, sow seed in autumn, in modules or seed trays, then pot up seedlings. Put the pots into a well-ventilated frame or under cloches for the winter. Alternatively, sow *in situ* in frames or under cloches, thinning to 5cm (2in) apart. Harden off seedlings before planting them out in spring. For a later crop, sow indoors in gentle heat in early spring, and prick out into small pots or modules. For summer/autumn and winter groups, sow the first batch

indoors in seed trays or modules, or *in situ* in frames or under cloches. Successive sowings may be made in a seedbed outdoors, or in modules for transplanting later on.

To obtain mini-cauliflowers, select an early summer cultivar to be sown in spring or early summer; sow several seeds per station, 15cm (6in) apart, thinning to one seedling after germination. Alternatively, raise plants in modules and plant them out 15cm (6in) apart. For a continuous supply, make successive sowings.

Routine cultivation

Cauliflowers need regular water throughout the growing period. In dry conditions, water at a rate of 22 litres/sq m (5 gallons/sq yd) every two weeks. Overwintering types require low nitrogen levels when planted or they will be too soft to survive the colder conditions, so do not apply too much base fertilizer. However, a nitrogenous fertilizer or organic liquid feed must be applied in spring about 6–8 weeks before the expected harvest or poor-sized cauliflowers will be produced.

To prevent white curds discolouring in the sun, tie the leaves over the curds. This may also be done in winter to protect curds of overwintering types from the elements; most modern cultivars, however, have leaves that naturally tend to cover the curds.

PROTECTING CAULIFLOWER CURDS

1 *In winter and early spring, protect mature curds of over-wintering types from severe frost.*

2 *Wrap the leaves up around the central curd, securing them with soft string.*

Pests and diseases

For cauliflower pests and diseases, see "Cultivating Western brassicas", p.507. Cauliflowers are also attacked by pollen beetles (p.657).

Harvesting and storing

The time from sowing to maturity varies from approximately 16 weeks for summer/autumn cauliflowers to about 40 weeks for winter ones. Cut the curds while they are still firm and tight, especially when maturing in frosty weather. Mini-cauliflowers mature about 15 weeks after sowing and should be picked immediately since they deteriorate quickly. All cauliflowers, and in particular the mini-cauliflowers, freeze well.

CAULIFLOWERS TO TRY

Winter
'Galleon'
'Patriot'
'Penduick'
'Prestige'
'Vilna'
'Walcheren Winter 3-Armado

Summer
'Beauty' F1
'Gypsy'
'Idol'
'Nautilus'

Autumn
'Autumn Glory'
'Aviso'
'Kestel'
'Moby Dick'
'Pavilion'
'Plana' F1
'White Excel'

Green cultivars
'Alverda'
'Minaret'
'Romanesco Veronica'

Purple cultivars
'Graffiti'
'Purple Cape'
'Violet Queen'

Mini-cauliflowers

Purple-headed cauliflower

CAULIFLOWER TYPES

Group	When to sow	When to plant	Spacing in rows	When to harvest
Winter (frost-free areas)	Late spring	Summer	70cm (28in)	Winter/very early spring
Winter	Late spring	Summer	70cm (28in)	Early spring
Summer	Autumn/early spring (sow under glass)	Spring	60cm (24in)	Early to midsummer
Autumn	Mid- to late spring	Early summer	60cm (24in)	Late summer to late autumn

Cabbages (*Brassica oleracea* Capitata Group)

Most cabbages are grown as annuals. Plants are generally 20–25cm (8–10in) tall, with a spread of up to 70cm (28in). The average head is about 15cm (6in) in diameter.

They are grouped according to their season of maturity, although there is some overlap between the groups. Leaves are dark or light green, blue-green, white, or red, and smooth or crinkled (savoy). Cabbage heads are pointed or round, and vary in their density. Spring greens are either loose-leaved cultivars or standard spring cabbages harvested before the head forms. Cabbage leaves are eaten either cooked or raw and sliced in salads. They may also be pickled. If they are tender enough, stems and stalks may be sliced finely and cooked. Some types of winter cabbage may be stored.

Cabbages grow best at 15–20°C (59–68°F). Do not plant in temperatures over 25°C (77°F) or they are liable to run to seed. The hardiest cultivars may survive temperatures as low as -10°C (14°F) for short periods. Cabbages are not usually grown under cover.

To grow well, cabbages need soil that is fertile, moisture-retentive, and humus-rich with a pH level above 6. Spring, summer, and fresh winter cabbages require very high nitrogen levels, and winter storage cabbages

Mature spring cabbages

medium nitrogen (see p.504). Do not give spring cabbages a nitrogenous base-dressing at planting, since the nitrogen will probably be washed from the soil over the winter or produce soft growth that is liable to frosting; top-dress in spring instead.

Sowing and planting
Sow the chosen cultivars at the correct time for their group (see below). Sow seeds in seedbeds or modules and transplant seedlings to their final position about five weeks later. Appropriate spacing varies according

to type (see chart below) and it may be modified to vary the size of the head; adopt closer spacing for smaller heads, and wide spacing to produce larger heads. A collar may be placed around each seedling stem when transplanting to protect against cabbage root fly (see *Collaring Seedlings*, p.507). Ensure that young seedlings have sufficient moisture to become well established.

For spring greens either grow a greens cultivar, spacing the plants approximately 25cm (10in) apart, or use a heading spring cultivar and space plants 10–15cm (4–6in) apart.

Autumn cabbage

Red summer cabbage

Savoy cabbage

CABBAGES TO TRY

Spring
'Advantage' F1
'Duncan' F1
'Durham Early'
'First Early Market 218'
'Greensleeves' (greens only)
'Myatt's Offenham Compacta'
'Pixie'
'Pyramid' F1

Early summer
'Charmant' F1
'Elisa' F1
'Hispi' F1

Summer
'Castello'
'Derby Day'
'Greyhound'
'Minicole' F1
'Shelta' F1

Autumn
'Autoro' F1
'Quickstep'
'Sherwood' F1
'Winnigstadt'

Winter (for storage)
'Hidena' F1
'Marathon' F1

Winter (to use fresh)
'Celtic' F1
'January King Hardy
   Late Stock 3'
'Marabel' F1
'Protovoy' F1
'Tarvoy' F1

Red cabbage
'Rodeo'
'Ruby Ball'

CABBAGE TYPES

Group (time of maturity)	Description	Main sowing period	Average spacing
Spring	Small, pointed or round heads	End of summer	30cm (12in)
	Loose-leaf greens	End of summer	25cm (10in)
Early summer	Large, mainly round heads	Very early spring (sow under glass)	38cm (15in)
Summer	Large, round heads	Early spring	45cm (18in)
Autumn	Large, round heads	Late spring	45cm (18in)
Winter (for storage)	Smooth, white-leaved, winter white types	Spring	45cm (18in)
Winter (to use fresh)	Blue, green, and savoy leaf types	Late spring	45cm (18in)

HARVESTING SPRING GREENS

Plant spring cabbages 15cm (6in) apart. When they have grown on, but before they start to form a compact heart, harvest alternate plants, cutting them at the base. Use these as spring greens.

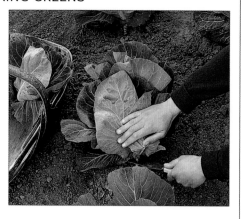

HOW TO OBTAIN A SECOND CROP

1 *To produce a second crop of greens, make a cross-shaped cut in the stalk after harvesting the cabbage head.*

2 *A few weeks later, several miniature heads should have sprouted, ready for a second harvest.*

Cut them young as loose greens; every second or third plant may be left to heart up if a heading cultivar is used.

Routine cultivation

To increase their stability, earth up winter cabbages as they grow. Protect spring cabbages under cloches or floating mulches, and apply a liquid feed or a nitrogenous top-dressing in spring; feed others in the growing season. Keep cabbages moist throughout their growth (see "Critical watering periods", p.502).

Pests and diseases

For pests and diseases that may affect cabbages, see "Cultivating Western brassicas", p.507. Seedling blight (p.654) may also occur.

Harvesting and storing

Spring and summer cultivars vary in their ability to stand in good condition once the head has matured; modern cultivars often stand longer than traditional ones. Normally the plant is dug up once the head has been cut, but spring and early summer cultivars may produce a second crop if the head is cut to leave a 10cm (4in) stalk in the ground. Using a sharp knife, make a shallow cross in the top of the stem to encourage new growth. Provided that the soil is fertile and moist, three or four more heads may develop together on the stalk.

Storage cabbages (winter white cultivars and appropriate red cabbages) should be lifted before heavy

PREPARING CABBAGES FOR STORING

Before storing cabbages, carefully remove any loose or discoloured, outer leaves without damaging the head (see inset). Inspect the cabbages regularly while they are in store and remove leaves that are rotting.

frost. Dig them up and carefully remove any loose, outer leaves. Place them on slatted supports or straw on the floor of a shed, or suspend them in nets. Store the heads at just above freezing point, with relatively high

humidity. They may also be stored in a cold frame, provided that it is ventilated on warm days to discourage rotting (see also *Storing Red Cabbages*, p.506). Cabbages may keep for four or five months.

Brussels sprouts (*Brassica oleracea* Gemmifera Group)

These are biennials grown as annuals, and vary in height from about 35cm (14in) for the dwarf forms to 75cm (30in) for the tall forms, with a spread of up to 50cm (20in) in both cases. Brussels sprouts are loosely divided by their time of maturity into early, mid-season, and late groups. The earlier types tend to be dwarfer and less hardy. The modern F1

Dwarf Brussels sprout plant

cultivars are an improvement over older, open-pollinated ones; they perform better on fertile soils, are less prone to lean (as they have a stronger root system), and have more compact, even sprouts. The tight sprouts that develop on the stem are cooked but may also be shredded raw into salads. The mature leaves at the top of the plants may also be eaten. There is a well-flavoured, but less productive, red cultivar, 'Rubine'.

Brussels sprouts are typical cool-season brassicas; the hardiest cultivars survive temperatures of -10°C (14°F). If sown in succession, Brussels sprouts provide a constant crop from early autumn to late spring. A general base-dressing may be applied shortly before planting; high nitrogen levels are needed (see p.504). Avoid using freshly manured ground as this encourages blown and loose, rather than firm, sprouts. For soil and site requirements, see "Siting Western brassicas", p.507.

EARTHING UP BRUSSELS SPROUTS

About a month after planting out, earth up Brussels sprouts by drawing the soil around the base of the stem to increase stability; this is usually difficult to do using collars. At this stage they may also be staked if they are in an exposed site.

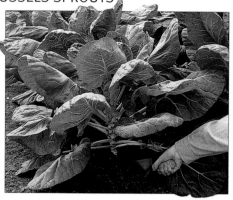

Sowing and planting

Sow in succession from early to mid-spring starting with the early-maturing cultivars. For a very early crop, sow in gentle heat under cover in early spring. Sow 5cm (2in) apart either in seed trays or in a seedbed to produce

good sturdy plants for transplanting; they will produce taproots and, when planted in firm soil, these give good anchorage. Cover with insect netting (environmesh) supported on hoops to allow erect plants. Most Brussels sprouts do not grow well in modules.

Thin out or transplant to the required spacing in early summer, generally four to five weeks after sowing. Plant dwarf cultivars about 45cm (18in) apart, and tall cultivars about 60cm (24in) apart. Use closer spacing to produce smaller sprouts of a more uniform size, and wider spacing for large sprouts that mature in succession and so may be picked over a longer period. Wide spacing also encourages good air circulation, which keeps plants healthy and disease-free. Plant tall cultivars

REMOVING LEAVES

Snap off any yellowing or diseased leaves that develop as these may carry fungal diseases that could spread to the whole crop. This also improves air circulation.

deeply and earth up the stems as they grow to provide extra stability. Keep young plants moist until they are well established. Brussels sprouts, with their slow rate of growth, may be intercropped in the first few months with fast-maturing vegetables.

Routine cultivation

Keep beds weed-free. Since plants are widely spaced, extra watering is required only in very dry conditions, when they should be watered at the rate for leafy crops (see "Critical watering periods", p.502). A top-dressing of a nitrogenous fertilizer or an organic liquid feed may be applied in late summer if the plants are not growing vigorously.

If sprouts are wanted for freezing, grow an early cultivar that matures in autumn, and nip off the sprout top or growing point in late summer, when the lower sprouts are roughly 1cm (½in) in diameter. All the sprouts will then mature for picking together, rather than in succession.

Pests and diseases

Mealy aphid can colonize individual sprouts; to control, treat with insecticidal soap, pyrethrum, rotenone, or bifenthrin. Downy mildew is also a problem (p.646). For other diseases likely to affect Brussels sprouts, see "Cultivating Western brassicas", p.507.

Harvesting and storing

Brussels sprouts are ready to harvest about 20 weeks after sowing. Their

F1 AND OPEN-POLLINATED SPROUTS

Modern F1 hybrids produce sprouts that are compact, evenly spaced, and of uniform size. Traditional, open-pollinated cultivars are more likely to produce blown sprouts widely varying in size.

F1 hybrid

Traditional cultivar

flavour is improved after exposure to frost. Pick the lowest sprouts first by snapping them off at the base; the upper sprouts will continue to develop. If sprouts are intended for freezing, pick them before the outer leaves are damaged by winter weather; freeze only top-quality sprouts. Sprout tops may be harvested by cutting them off at the end of the season.

After harvesting, dig up the plants and break up the stems with a hammer. This deters the build-up and spread of brassica diseases, and enables the stems to rot down more quickly when composted.

Where winters are very severe, uproot the whole plants before the ground freezes and hang them in a cool, frost-free place; the sprouts will remain fresh for several weeks.

BRUSSELS SPROUTS TO TRY

Early
'Diablo' F1
'Nelson' F1
'Oliver' F1
'Peer Gynt' F1

Mid-season
'Bosworth' F1
'Cromwell' F1
'Romulus' F1

Late
'Cascade' F1
'Montgomery' F1
'Wellington' F1

Sprouting broccoli (*Brassica oleracea* Italica Group)

These large, biennial plants may reach a height of 60–90cm (2–3ft) and a spread of 60cm (2ft). There are purple and white forms; the purple is more prolific and hardier. The flowering shoots that develop in spring are eaten cooked. Sprouting

broccoli is grown mainly in the British Isles, where it is considered one of the hardiest winter vegetables, surviving temperatures of about -12°C (10°F). Because it is a slow-maturing vegetable that occupies the ground for up to a year, broccoli

requires a fertile soil and medium nitrogen levels (see p.504). Avoid shallow and sandy soils and sites exposed to strong, winter winds.

Sowing, planting, and routine cultivation

Sow from spring to midsummer, either in a seedbed or in modules. Transplant from early to mid-summer, spacing plants at least 60cm (2ft) apart, and planting them deeply for stability.

Plants may need staking in the autumn. If wood pigeon (p.645) eat leaves, cover the plants with netting for the winter. For further cultivation requirements, see "Cultivating Western brassicas", p.507.

Pests and diseases

Sprouting broccoli is prone to the common brassica pests (see "Cultivating Western brassicas", p.507); in mild years it may be host to whiteflies. Pigeons can be attracted in winter.

SPROUTING BROCCOLI TO TRY

'Claret' F1
'Red Arrow'
'Redhead'

'Rudolph'
'White Sprouting'

Harvesting and storing

Depending on the cultivar, pick shoots from early spring to late summer, when they are about 15cm (6in) long, while the flowers are in bud. Pick regularly to encourage more shoots; plants may crop for up to two months. Sprouting broccoli freezes well.

Purple sprouting broccoli

Calabrese (*Brassica oleracea* Italica Group)

Also known as American or Italian broccoli, calabrese is grown as an annual or biennial, and produces compact plants about 45cm (18in) tall, with a spread rarely over 38cm (15in). Cultivars are classified as early, mid-season, and late, with the earliest maturing the fastest. F1 hybrids are more productive than the original cultivars. The compact, terminal head and the young sideshoots are eaten lightly cooked.

Calabrese is a cool-season crop and should not be grown in areas where the average mean temperature is above 15°C (59°F). Young plants tolerate some frost, but it may damage embryonic and young heads once they start to develop. Calabrese needs an open site in moisture-retentive, fairly fertile soil with medium nitrogen levels (see p.504).

Sowing and planting

Sow in succession from spring to early summer for a crop during summer and autumn. Calabrese seedlings do not transplant well, so either sow two or three seeds per station *in situ*, or sow in modules and transplant seedlings to moist ground, disturbing the roots as little as possible. For an early crop, make the first sowings indoors; these are, however, especially prone to bolting when transplanted.

HARVESTING CALABRESE

1 *Just before the flower buds open, harvest the first central head by cutting through the stalk.*

2 *This encourages sideshoots to develop; these can also be harvested and more sideshoots will be produced.*

Calabrese plants grow well at various spacings. For the highest overall yield, space plants 22cm (9in) apart each way, or 30cm (12in) apart in rows spaced at 45cm (18in). Closer spacing produces smaller terminal shoots, which mature together and are suitable for freezing.

Routine cultivation

Keep the bed weed-free. Calabrese plants need plenty of water to crop well – 11 litres/sq m (2 gallons/sq yd)

every two weeks. In very dry conditions, water as for leafy crops (see "Critical watering periods", p.502). A nitrogenous top-dressing or an organic liquid feed may be applied once the terminal heads have been cut in order to encourage additional sideshoots to develop.

Pests and diseases

For pests and diseases that may affect calabrese, see "Cultivating Western brassicas", p.507. Problems

CALABRESE TO TRY
Early
'Arcadia' F1

'Green Comet' F1
'Hydra' F1
'Marathon' F1

Mid-season
'Belstar' F1
'Decathlon'
'Fiesta' F1
'Kabuki' F1

Late
'Corvet' F1

may also be caused by pollen beetles (p.657) and downy mildew (p.646).

Harvesting and storing

Calabrese is a fast-maturing brassica, ready 11–14 weeks after sowing. The main head should be cut when it is 7–10cm (3–4in) in diameter, while still firm and before the flower buds open. Sideshoots will subsequently develop; cut these when they are about 10cm (4in) long. Calabrese freezes well.

Turnip tops and broccoli raab (*Brassica rapa*)

Over the centuries different brassicas have been grown for cutting in the immature stages for use as quick-maturing greens. The two types commonly used for this purpose today are turnip tops (*Brassica rapa* Rapifera Group) and broccoli raab (*Brassica rapa* Utilis Group), which

is also known as turnip rape and by a number of Italian names such as *cime di rapa*, *rapini*, and *broccoletti*.

They are grown as annuals or biennials, generally with single stems that reach a maximum height of about 30cm (12in). The leaves, young stems, and sweetly flavoured

young flowerheads are eaten cooked as spring greens, or raw in salads.

Turnip tops and broccoli raab are cool-season brassicas. Grow them in spring and autumn in hot climates, or all year where summers are cool. All turnip cultivars are suitable; broccoli raab has no named cultivars. Both grow best in fertile, moisture-retentive soil and require low to medium nitrogen levels (see p.504).

Sowing, planting, and routine cultivation

Sow thinly broadcast or in rows about 10cm (4in) apart. For larger plants only, thin to 15cm (6in). For an early crop in cold areas, make the first sowing indoors in early spring. Plants need little attention subsequently.

Harvesting and storing

Harvest plants within seven to eight weeks of sowing. Make the first cut when they are leafy and 10cm (4in) tall, or wait until the immature flowering shoots appear and the plant

Turnip tops

is 20–25cm (8–10in) tall. Cut about 2.5cm (1in) above ground level. In cool weather, the plants resprout to give two or three further cuttings over a period of four or five weeks. Cut as long as the stems are tender. Use turnip tops and broccoli raab fresh as they do not store well.

Broccoli raab

Oriental brassicas

Loose-leaved Chinese cabbage

Tight-headed Chinese cabbage

Pak choi

Pak choi

SEVERAL Oriental brassicas are now being introduced to the West. They have many features in common with Western brassicas but tend to be faster growing and have a wider range of uses than Western brassicas. If they are given the right conditions they are highly productive. They are grown as annuals or biennials.

Oriental brassicas are cultivated mainly for the leaves and leafy stems, but also for the young, sweetly flavoured flowering shoots. Leaf shape and colour vary from the glossy, white-ribbed leaves of some pak choi cultivars, and the feathery green leaves of mizuna greens, to the purplish-green of Oriental mustards. Oriental brassicas are nutritious, succulent, and crisp, and are mild to peppery in flavour. Cook them, preferably by stir-frying or steaming, or use young leaves and shoots raw in salads.

Oriental brassicas are best suited to climates with cool summers and mild winters, although many cultivars are available that are adapted for hotter climates. The majority will withstand light frost, especially if harvested when they are semi-mature as a cut-and-come-again crop (see p.506). A few Oriental brassicas, such as komatsuna and some of the mustards, are extremely hardy.

In temperate climates, Oriental brassicas grow best in late summer and autumn. Where winter temperatures fall several degrees below freezing, they may be grown as a winter crop under cover in unheated structures; if planted late in the summer, they may crop from autumn to spring, although they will stop growing at low temperatures.

Oriental brassicas require similar conditions to Western brassicas (see "Siting Western brassicas", p.507) but, being fast-growing, hungry, and thirsty plants, the soil must be rich in organic matter, moisture-retentive, and fertile. They never develop well in poor, dry soil. Most of them have very high nitrogen requirements (see p.504).

Sowing and planting Oriental brassicas

All standard methods of sowing may be used; where there is a risk of plants going to seed prematurely (bolting), sow seed in modules or *in situ*. Many have a tendency to bolt when days are lengthening, particularly when this is combined with low spring temperatures. In these cases, in northern latitudes, delay sowing until midsummer, unless plants are started off in heat or cultivars with bolting resistance are used. If bolting continues to be a problem, grow Oriental brassicas as seedling crops, and harvest the leaves before the plants start to bolt.

Their rapid rate of growth makes Oriental brassicas ideal for inter-cropping among slower-maturing vegetables, especially for cutting as a cut-and-come-again seedling crop, when their flavour is superb.

Cultivating Oriental brassicas

Oriental brassicas are generally shallow-rooting and so need regular watering. In very dry conditions, water at the rate for leafy crops (see "Critical watering periods", p.502). They should also be kept mulched.

Oriental brassicas are susceptible to the same pests and diseases as Western brassicas (see "Cultivating Western brassicas", p.507). Those with tender leaves are very prone to slugs and snails (p.644), caterpillars (p.645), and flea beetles (p.644). They may be grown under fine nets to provide some protection.

Harvesting and storing Oriental brassicas

Most Oriental brassicas mature within two to three months after being sown. They may be harvested at four different stages from seedling to mature plant.

At the seedling stage they may be harvested using cut-and-come-again techniques (see "Cut-and-come-again harvesting", p.506), or left a few weeks longer and cut as semi-mature plants. When the plants are fully mature they may be either harvested all at once or alternatively cut about 2.5cm (1in) above ground level so that they sprout again for a second crop. The flowering shoots that develop naturally from mature plants may also be harvested before the flowers open.

In the West, Oriental brassicas are mainly used fresh, although most will keep for a few days if refrigerated. In the Orient, leaves are pickled or dried, and Chinese cabbages are stored for off-season supplies.

Oriental mustards (*Brassica juncea*)

The mustards are a varied group of annuals and biennials, forming large, often coarse-leaved plants. Leaf texture may be smooth, blistered, or deeply curled (for example 'Art Green'). Some cultivars are purple-leaved. The mustards are naturally very robust and less prone to pests and diseases than most Oriental brassicas. Several, including the purplish-green 'Giant Red' and 'Osaka Purple' survive at least -10°C (14°F). The distinctive flavour may be piquant in certain cultivars, becoming stronger as they run to seed. The leaves are used cooked but may also be eaten raw in salads when young or if sliced.

Sow from mid- to late summer in temperate climates, and until early autumn in warm climates, for harvesting from autumn to spring. The seed is small and is sown in shallow soil *in situ* or in modules. Thin or plant out seedlings 15cm (6in) apart for harvesting young, and 35cm (14in) apart for larger plants. If they are planted under cover in autumn, plants are more tender, but will run to seed earlier the following spring.

Oriental mustards mature in 6–13 weeks, depending on the cultivar. Cut single leaves as required.

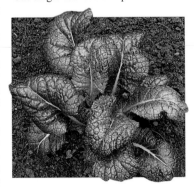

Purple-leaved Oriental mustard

Chinese broccoli (*Brassica rapa* var. *alboglabra*)

These annuals, also known as Chinese kale, form stout plants with thick, blue-green leaves, growing up to 45cm (18in) tall. The succulent, fine-flavoured, chunky flower stems, which may be 2cm (¾in) thick, are generally cooked.

Chinese broccoli tolerates higher summer temperatures than many other brassicas, and withstands light frost. In warm and temperate climates, sow from late spring to late summer. For a very early crop, make the first sowings under cover in spring to transplant outside. For a protected early winter crop, plant under cover in autumn. In cool climates, delay sowing until midsummer since sowings earlier than this may bolt.

Sow seed *in situ* or in modules. For small plants, to be harvested whole

Chinese broccoli

as soon as the flowering shoots appear, grow plants 12cm (5in) apart with 10cm (4in) between rows. For large plants, to be cropped over a longer period, space plants 30cm (12in) apart each way. Cut the main shoot first, as for calabrese (see p.512); further sideshoots will continue to develop for harvesting later. Large plants take nine to ten weeks to mature.

Pak choi (*Brassica rapa* var. *alboglabra*)

Pak choi is a biennial usually grown as an annual, forming a loose head of fairly stiff leaves with wide midribs that broaden out markedly and overlap at the base. There are many types, the most common being white-ribbed or green-ribbed, available as F1 cultivars 'Joi Choi' (white) and 'Canton Dwarf' (green). They vary in size from squat forms about 10cm (4in) tall to large plants about 45cm (18in) tall. Pak choi is succulent and mild in flavour, and may be eaten either cooked or raw.

Pak choi grows best at cool temperatures of 15–20°C (59–68°F). Most cultivars will tolerate some frost in the open but survive lower temperatures under cover grown as winter cut-and-come-again crops. A few are suited to hotter climates.

In temperate climates, sow seed throughout the growing season. There is some risk of premature bolting with spring sowings, so confine these to cut-and-come-again seedling crops. Sow seed *in situ* or in modules. Spacing depends on the cultivar and size of plant required, ranging from 10cm (4in) apart for small cultivars to about 45cm (18in) apart for the largest ones. In late summer, transplant pak choi under cover for an autumn crop.

Pak choi may be harvested at any stage from seedlings to the young flower shoots of mature plants.

Pak choi

HARVESTING SEEDLINGS

Pak choi may be harvested at the seedling stage. If they are cut about 2.5cm (1in) from the ground, new leaves will sprout.

Seedling leaves will be ready for harvesting in three weeks. They may be cut 2.5cm (1in) above ground level and will resprout. Mature plants may be cut higher and will also re-sprout for a second harvest.

Mizuna greens (*Brassica rapa* var. *nipposinica*)

Annuals or biennials, depending on climatic conditions, mizuna greens have dark green, glossy, deeply serrated, almost feathery leaves and slender, white, juicy stems forming a rosette up to 45cm (18in) in diameter and about 23cm (9in) tall. They are highly decorative, especially when grown as an edging or in blocks. Mizuna greens are eaten cooked, or raw when leaves are harvested young and tender.

They are very adaptable, capable of tolerating both high summer temperatures (provided that they are in moisture-retentive soil) and winter temperatures down to -10°C (14°F).

They may be sown throughout the growing season. Bolting resistance is good and seed may therefore be sown in seed trays or modules, in a seedbed for transplanting, or *in situ*. For an extra, tender, winter crop, sow in late summer to transplant under cover. Space plants 10cm (4in) apart for small plants harvested young, up to 45cm (18in) apart to obtain large plants. Mizuna greens are useful for intercropping if cut at the seedling stage.

Mizuna greens mature eight to ten weeks after sowing and may be harvested at all stages; seedling leaves may be ready within two or three weeks (see "Harvesting and storing Oriental brassicas", p.513). The plants are vigorous, and are capable of resprouting several times after they have been cut initially.

Mizuna greens

Chinese cabbages (*Brassica rapa* var. *pekinensis*)

These are annuals or biennials usually grown as annuals. Chinese cabbages have dense, upright heads. The leaves are marked by prominent white veins, the broadened midribs overlapping at the base rather like pak choi. The barrel type forms a stout head about 25cm (10in) high, the cylindrical type a longer, less compact head up to 45cm (18in) high. Leaf colour ranges from dark green to almost creamy white, especially in the centre. There are also some very attractive, loose-headed types. Mild-flavoured with a crisp texture, Chinese cabbages are excellent in salads and lightly cooked.

For preferred climatic conditions, see "Pak choi" (left). Most headed types are likely to bolt if they are sown in spring, unless a temperature of 20–25°C (68–77°F) is maintained during the first three weeks of growth. It is safer to delay sowing until early summer. Some loose-headed types may be sown in spring. If they start to bolt, treat them as cut-and-come-again crops, although the leaves of some cultivars may be rough-textured and hairy when young. Sow seed in modules or *in situ*; thin or transplant seedlings to 30cm (12in) apart. Plenty of moisture throughout growth is vital. Chinese cabbages have soft leaves which are susceptible to pests (see "Cultivating Oriental brassicas", p.513).

Chinese cabbages mature eight to ten weeks after sowing, and can be harvested at any stage since they respond well to cut-and-come-again treatment both after the main heads have been cut, and during growth, as semi-mature plants.

CHINESE CABBAGES TO TRY

'Early Jade Pagoda' (cylindrical)
'One Kilo S.B.' F1 (barrel)
'Yuki' (barrel)

HARVESTING CHINESE CABBAGES

1 *Harvest Chinese cabbage (here a loose-leaved cultivar) by cutting about 2.5cm (1in) above soil level.*

2 *After a few weeks, new leaves will have formed and may be cut. Stumps may resprout several times.*

Komatsuna (*Brassica rapa* var. *perviridis*)

The komatsuna group, also known as spinach mustard, is extremely diverse; its members form large, productive, robust, healthy plants, often with glossy leaves that may be up to 30cm (12in) long and 18cm (7in) wide. The flavour of the leaves resembles cabbage, with a touch of spinach, and they are eaten cooked, or raw, finely sliced in salads.

Komatsuna plants tolerate a wide range of temperatures and will survive -12°C (10°F). Some cultivars are suitable for tropical climates.

Plants are less likely to bolt from early spring sowings than most Oriental brassicas and are more drought-tolerant. For sowing and spacing, see "Mizuna greens" (left). Komatsuna makes a useful and successful winter crop under cover.

Komatsuna

Leaves may be harvested at all stages (see "Harvesting and storing Oriental brassicas", p.513). Mature plants are usually ready to be harvested eight weeks after sowing.

Leafy and salad vegetables

THIS group of vegetables is grown for the great variety of leaves that it produces, which may be eaten raw in salads, or cooked. The freshly picked leaves are delicious and highly nutritious. The range of leaf colour also gives them decorative value. Careful choice of cultivar and the right growing conditions ensure a year-round supply. If seeds are sown in succession, gluts of crops maturing together may be avoided. Due to the high moisture content of the leaves, many store for only two or three days; a few are suitable for freezing, however.

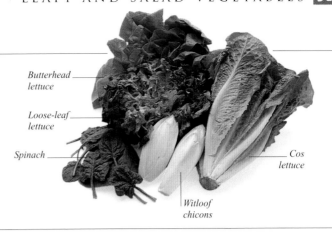

Butterhead lettuce

Loose-leaf lettuce

Spinach

Witloof chicons

Cos lettuce

Amaranths (*Amaranthus* spp.)

These rapidly growing annuals reach a height of about 60cm (24in) and a spread of 30–38cm (12–15in). *Amaranthus cruentus*, the most commonly grown as an edible crop, has oval, light green leaves; amaranth cultivars are mostly local – they include 'Fotete', 'Green Spinach', and 'Stubby'. *A. tricolor*, or Chinese spinach, has red, yellow, or green leaves and greenish-white flowers; cultivars include 'Lal Sag Rouge', 'Tampala', 'Banerjee's Giant', and 'Crystal'. *A. caudatus* has pale green leaves and is often grown as an ornamental plant for its vivid red, tassellike flowers. Amaranth species are also known as African or Indian spinach. The leaves of the plants and immature flower buds are cooked and eaten in the same way as spinach.

Amaranths are tropical and subtropical plants that require temperatures of 22–30°C (72–86°F) with a humidity of above 70 per cent to crop well. They may also be grown in temperate climates in greenhouses or outdoors in a sunny, sheltered site. Moderately deep, well-drained, fertile soil with a pH of 5.5–7 and medium to high nitrogen levels are required (see p.504).

Amaranthus cruentus

Sowing and planting
Sow outdoors in spring, once the temperature is high enough, in rows 20–30cm (8–12in) apart. Thin seedlings to 10–15cm (4–6in) apart when they are about 5–7cm (2–3in) high. Protect with plastic covers or under cloches until the young plants have become established.

In cool areas, or for an earlier crop, seed may be sown in trays in a greenhouse; prick out seedlings into 6 or 9cm (3 or 3½in) pots when they are large enough to handle. Transplant them outdoors when they are 7–9cm (3–3½in) tall, spacing them 10–15cm (4–6in) apart.

Routine cultivation
Keep amaranth beds weed-free, and water regularly. Apply a balanced fertilizer or organic liquid feed every two to three weeks. Give additional dressings of nitrogen and potassium every three weeks on less fertile soils. Apply an organic mulch around the base of the plants to retain moisture and warmth. When the plants are 20cm (8in) tall, pinch out the growing point to encourage lateral shoots and to produce a heavier crop.

Pests and diseases
Downy mildew (p.646), powdery mildew (p.646), caterpillars (p.645), and aphids (p.646) may affect amaranths outside, and thrips (p.647) and damping off (p.664) under cover.

Growing under cover
When seedlings are 7–9cm (3–3½in) tall, transplant them to 21cm (8in) pots, growing bags, or beds, spacing them 38–50cm (15–20in) apart each way. Keep them at a minimum temperature of 22°C (72°F). Water, and maintain 70 per cent humidity by damping down in hot weather.

Harvesting and storing
Amaranths are ready to harvest eight to ten weeks after sowing. Using a sharp knife, cut young shoots up to 10cm (4in) long when the plants are about 25cm (10in) tall; they will produce further shoots over several months. Continue picking them as required. Amaranths are best eaten fresh; alternatively, they may be stored for up to one week at 0°C (32°F) and 95 per cent humidity.

Amaranthus tricolor

Ceylon spinach (*Basella alba*)

Also known as Indian or vine spinach, these short-lived, twining perennials may grow to 4m (12ft) tall if supported. Var. *alba* has dark green leaves; var. *rubra* has red leaves and stems. The oval or round leaves are eaten cooked; the purple berries are not normally eaten.

Ceylon spinach is a tropical and subtropical plant that requires a temperature of 25–30°C (77–86°F). Lower temperatures reduce the growth rate, resulting in smaller leaves. Larger leaves are, however, produced in light shade. Well-drained and highly fertile soil with a pH of 6–7.5 and high nitrogen levels (see p.504) are required for good growth.

Sowing and planting
Sow in seed trays or 6 or 9cm (3 or 3½in) pots, maintaining the required temperature range. When seedlings are 10–15cm (4–6in) tall, transplant them to well-prepared beds, spacing the plants 40–50cm (16–20in) apart each way.

Routine cultivation
Support plants by staking or by tying in stems to a vertical or horizontal trellis. Keep plants weed-free and water as necessary. Mulch with organic material. Apply a balanced fertilizer or liquid feed every two to three weeks during the growing period. When the seedlings reach a

SUPPORTING CEYLON SPINACH

Ceylon spinach may be supported on a trellis parallel to the ground, raised about 30cm (12in) above soil level. The stems should be evenly spaced on the trellis so that they do not become overcrowded.

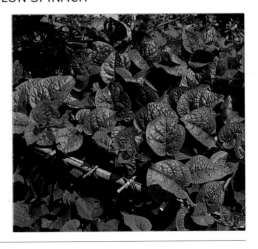

height of about 45cm (18in), remove the growing point to encourage branching. Remove flowering shoots to encourage leaf production.

Propagate plants by taking cuttings 10–15cm (4–6in) long; insert these in small pots until rooted and then transplant as described for seedlings.

Pests and diseases

Ceylon spinach is generally free of pests and diseases. Root-knot eelworms (p.660) may, however, affect plants, and, under cover, aphids (p.646), whiteflies (p.646), and glasshouse red spider mite (p.646) may also be troublesome.

Growing under cover

Transplant seedlings to growing bags or to 20–25cm (8–10in) pots. Remove the growing tips when the seedlings are about 30cm (12in) tall to encourage branching, and damp down regularly to maintain high humidity. Tie in developing shoots.

Harvesting and storing

Harvest 10–12 weeks after transplanting by cutting young terminal shoots that are 15–20cm (6–8in) long; this encourages further shoots to develop over several months. Eat leaves within two days of picking, or refrigerate them for a few days.

Swiss chard and spinach beet (*Beta vulgaris* subsp. *cicla* var. *flavescens*)

These spinach-like biennials belong to the beet family. Swiss chard, also known as seakale beet, forms large, glossy-leaved plants. Individual leaves may be up to 45cm (18in) long and 15cm (6in) wide. The midribs widen into broad leaf stalks up to 5cm (2in) in diameter that may be white, red, creamy-yellow, or pink. Leaf colour varies with the cultivar, from deep green ('Fordhook Giant') to greenish-yellow ('Lucullus') and reddish-green ('Rhubarb Chard'). 'Bright Lights' is a very colourful cultivar. The leaves and midribs are normally cooked; the latter require

White-stemmed Swiss chard

longer cooking and are often treated separately. Spinach beet, or perpetual spinach, forms smaller-leaved plants, with narrow, green leaf stalks. It is eaten lightly cooked or raw.

Although chard and spinach beet are essentially cool-season crops, growing best at 16–18°C (61–64°F), they tolerate higher summer temperatures than spinach (see p.519) without bolting, and survive winter temperatures of -14°C (7°F). They may be grown in a wide range of soils other than acid ones, provided that the soil is moisture-retentive and fertile, containing plenty of organic matter. Plants may remain in the ground for up to 12 months, and so need high nitrogen levels (see p.504).

Sowing and planting

For a continuous supply, sow seed in spring (plants may crop until late spring the following year), and again in mid- to late summer (for plants cropping until the following summer). Sow *in situ* in rows 38cm (15in) apart for spinach beet or, for Swiss chard, 45cm (18in) apart; thin seedlings early to 30cm (12in) apart. Plants may be grown closer together

Red-stemmed Swiss chard

in more widely spaced rows, but avoid overcrowding.

Alternatively, seed may be sown in seed trays or modules for transplanting. Germination is usually rapid. Spinach beet may be sown closely for use as a cut-and-come-again seedling crop (see "Successional crops", p.500).

Routine cultivation

The chards and spinach beet are naturally healthy and vigorous and usually require little attention. Give an organic mulch to keep down weeds and preserve moisture; apply

a nitrogenous fertilizer or organic liquid feed during the growing season if plants are not developing well.

Pests and diseases

Birds (p.657) may attack seedlings. Fungal leaf spots (p.648) and downy mildew (p.646) may also be problems.

Growing under cover

In cool climates, the chards and spinach beet are excellent winter crops under cover. Sow seed in modules during late summer and transplant under cover in early autumn, or broadcast spinach beet for cut-and-come-again seedling crops. They often crop throughout winter and early spring.

Harvesting and storing

Leaves are ready to be harvested 8–12 weeks after sowing. Cut the outer leaves first and continue picking as required; alternatively, harvest the whole plant by cutting the leaves about 2.5cm (1in) above ground level. Further leaves are then produced from the base over many months. Both Swiss chard and spinach beet may be frozen.

Endive (*Cichorium endivia*)

Endive is an annual or biennial plant that forms a flat or semi-upright rosette of leaves 20–38cm (8–15in) in diameter. The two most distinct types of endive are the serrated- or curled-leaved endive, and the broad-leaved escarole, but there are also intermediate types. Outer leaves are dark to light green and the more tender, inner leaves creamy-yellow. Endive is slightly bitter and is blanched to make it sweeter. Used mainly in salads, it is shredded to reduce bitterness, or may be cooked.

Endive is a cool-season crop that grows best at 10–20°C (50–68°F), but withstands light frost in the open; the hardier cultivars survive -9°C (16°F). Bitterness generally increases at high temperatures. Some curled types are quite heat-tolerant, while escarole types tend to

withstand greater cold. There is a risk of premature bolting from spring sowings if temperatures fall below 5°C (41°F) for an extended period. Endive performs much better than lettuce in the low light levels of northern winters and therefore makes a useful winter greenhouse crop.

For soil and site requirements, see "Lettuces", p.518. Summer crops may be grown in light shade; always grow autumn crops on well-drained soil to avoid the risk of rotting. Endive has a low nitrogen requirement (see p.504).

Sowing and planting

Choose appropriate cultivars for each season. Sow in late spring for a summer crop or in summer for an autumn crop, either *in situ* or in modules or seed trays. Thin or plant out the

seedlings 25–38cm (10–15in) apart, using the wider spacing for spreading cultivars. Curled types may be sown as cut-and-come-again crops (see "Successional crops", p.500), most usefully in late spring and late summer.

Routine cultivation

To blanch leaves, choose nearly mature plants with dry leaves and blanch a few at a time since they deteriorate rapidly after blanching.

For complete blanching *in situ*, cover each plant with a bucket. For partial blanching, lay a large plate or piece of cardboard over the centre. With escarole types bunch up the leaves and tie them together. Protect the plants against slugs until they are ready for harvesting, which is after about ten days. In autumn, plants for blanching should be lifted before

BLANCHING ENDIVE

1 *Ensure that the endive is dry, then lay a plate over the centre to blanch the leaves partially.*

2 *The centre should have turned white and be ready for harvesting after about 10 days.*

severe weather disfigures them; transplant them into a darkened frame or dark area under greenhouse staging, then blanch as for Witloof chicory (see below).

Pests and diseases

Slugs (p.644) and aphids (p.646) are the most common problems. For other pests and diseases that affect endive, see "Lettuces", p.518.

Growing under cover

Protecting plants under cover provides a year-round supply. For use in winter and early spring, transplant seedlings in early autumn from seed trays or modules under cover. Sow as a cut-and-come-again seedling crop under cover in spring for harvesting early, and in early autumn for a late crop.

Harvesting and storing

Harvest endive between 7 and 13 weeks after sowing, depending on the cultivar and season. Pick individual leaves as needed, or cut across the crown, leaving the plant to resprout. Mature plants respond well to cut-and-come-again treatment (see "Cut-and-come-again harvesting", p.506). Endive leaves do not store well, so should be eaten fresh.

Chicory (*Cichorium intybus*)

There are many types of chicory, all with a distinctive, slightly bitter taste. Nearly all are hardy and are useful crops in the winter months. Their diverse colours make them attractive in salads, and some types may also be cooked. All types have low nitrogen requirements (see p.504).

Witloof or Belgian chicory

Similar in appearance to dandelions, these biennials have pointed leaves about 20cm (8in) long, with a spread of about 15cm (6in). Their "chicons" (the whitened, compact, leafy shoots obtained from lifting the roots and forcing and blanching them to make them sweeter) are eaten raw or cooked. The green leaves may also be used, but taste more bitter.

CHICORY TO TRY

Witloof
'Zoom' F1

Red chicory
'Indigo' F1
'Palla Rossa'
'Rossa di Treviso'
'Rossa di Verona'

Sugar loaf
'Bianca di Milano'
'Biondissimo di Trieste'
'Pain de Sucre'

Witloof chicory grows best at 15–19°C (59–66°F). It is generally forced for winter use. Grow plants in an open site in reasonably fertile – but not freshly manured – soil.

The plants require a fairly long growing season. Sow seed outdoors *in situ* in spring or early summer, in rows 30cm (12in) apart. Thin the seedlings to about 20cm (8in) apart. Keep plants weed-free. Water the plants whenever necessary to prevent the soil from drying out.

Witloof chicory may be forced *in situ* in light soils and areas with mild winters. In early winter, cut the green leaves about 2.5cm (1in) above ground level. Cover the stumps with soil, making a ridge about 15cm (6in) high; the chicons will grow and force their way through.

Force indoors if the garden soil is heavy or winters are severe, or if an earlier crop is required. Dig up the plants in late autumn or early winter. Cut the leaves to 2.5cm (1in) and trim the roots to about 20cm (8in); reject any that are very thin. The roots may be forced immediately or stored for forcing a few at a time in succession during the winter and early spring. To store the roots, lay them flat in boxes with moist sand between each of the layers and keep them in a frost-free shed or cellar until they are required.

To force indoors, plant several of the prepared roots in a large pot or box filled with compost or garden soil, and cover with an inverted pot or box of the same size. Block any drainage holes to keep out light. Keep the soil moist, and maintain a temperature of 10–18°C (50–64°F). Roots may also be planted under greenhouse staging, or in a garden frame. Make a light-proof area by stretching black plastic sheeting over wire hoops or attaching it to a

wooden support. Do not use plastic sheeting in spring if temperatures soar, since aphid damage and rotting may occur. Witloof chicory is normally free of pests and diseases.

Harvest chicons forced outside after 8–12 weeks when about 10cm (4in) high by moving the soil and

cutting the heads 2.5cm (1in) above the neck. Plants forced indoors should be ready after three to four weeks. Stumps may resprout to give a second crop of smaller chicons. Keep chicons wrapped or refrigerated after cutting since they become green and bitter on exposure to light.

FORCING AND BLANCHING CHICORY

1 *In late autumn or early winter, lift the mature plant carefully. The central leaves may be tender enough to eat.*

2 *Using a sharp knife, trim the leaves to 2.5cm (1in) from the crown and slice off the base of the root and any side roots, leaving a 20cm (8in) length.*

3 *Put a layer of moist potting compost or garden soil into a 24cm (9in) pot. Place three trimmed roots in the mixture and firm so that they stand upright, then fill the pot to within 2.5cm (1in) of the rim and firm, leaving the crowns exposed.*

4 *Line another pot with cooking foil or black plastic to cover the drainage holes and place it over the roots to block the light. Keep at 10–18°C (50–64°F). Harvest the chicons 3–4 weeks later by cutting just above soil level.*

Red chicory

This is a varied group of perennials usually grown as annuals. The typical red chicory, also known as radicchio, is a low-growing plant with bitter, reddish-green outer leaves and a compact heart. It is eaten raw in salads, shredded to reduce bitterness, or may be cooked.

Red chicory tolerates a wide range of temperatures and soil conditions, but is mainly grown for use in the cooler months. Cultivars vary in their frost tolerance. 'Treviso' is exceptionally hardy; it may be forced in the same way as Witloof chicory (see p.517). The new F1 hybrids produce more solid heads than traditional cultivars. Sow in early and midsummer, *in situ* or in seed trays for transplanting. Plant 24–35cm (10–14in) apart depending on the cultivar. Transplant summer-sown crops under cover in autumn.

Eight to ten weeks after sowing, pick single leaves or harvest the whole head. Chicory stands a long time after maturing; in cold climates, protect with low tunnels in late autumn so that the plants develop more solid heads.

Sugar loaf chicory

Sugar loaf chicory is green-leaved, forming a conical head not unlike cos lettuce in both shape and size. Its inner leaves are naturally blanched and slightly sweetened. For use, and for climate, soil, and cultivation requirements, see "Red chicory" (left).

Sugar loaf chicory may be sown in spring as a cut-and-come-again seedling crop (see p.500); harvest the seedlings before temperatures rise, causing leaves to coarsen. For mature plants, thin seedlings to 25cm (10in) apart, and harvest during late summer or autumn. The plants tolerate light frost, and provide winter crops if grown under cover.

Harvest leaves as needed, or cut the heads when mature. The heads keep for a few weeks in cool, dry, frost-free conditions. They may also be piled up, turned inwards and covered with straw to form clamps (see *Making a Swede Clamp*, p.543).

Sugar loaf chicory

Lettuces (*Lactuca sativa*)

Lettuces are annual, low-growing plants; they usually have green leaves, although some cultivars have red or reddish-green leaves.

There are several distinct types. Cos (romaine) lettuces have long, substantial, well-flavoured leaves with fairly loose hearts; semi-cos are shorter with very sweet, crunchy leaves. Butterhead lettuces have smooth, soft leaves, forming a rounded, compact heart; crispheads (known as icebergs when marketed with the outer leaves removed) have crispy leaves forming a heart. Loose-leaf lettuces, typified by the "Salad Bowl" types, do not form hearts so are slow to bolt and may be cut over a long period; their leaves are often indented and are very decorative. They are the most nutritious form of lettuce and may also be used for cut-and-come-again seedling crops (see p.500).

Lettuces vary from 10cm (4in) to over 30cm (12in) in spread. The cos types are about 25cm (10in) tall, others about 15cm (6in) high. Lettuces are primarily used as salad vegetables, but outer and older leaves may also be cooked or used in soups.

Lettuces are cool-season crops, growing best at 10–20°C (50–68°F). Cool nights are essential for good results. Some cultivars are tolerant of heat or frost. Germination is poor above 25°C (77°F); at these temperatures, plants tend to bolt rapidly and may become bitter, although loose-leaf lettuces are slower to bolt than other types.

Grow in an open site, or in light shade in very hot weather. Lettuces need fertile, moisture-retentive soil and, although they fall into none of the rotation groups, should not be grown in the same patch of soil for two years in a row to prevent the build-up of fungus disease. They require medium nitrogen (see p.504).

Loose-leaf lettuces ('Lollo Rossa')

Sowing and planting

Cultivars appropriate for the season must be sown. For a year-round supply in cool climates, sow from early spring to late summer at two- to three-week intervals. At the end of summer or in early autumn, sow hardy cultivars that overwinter outdoors or under cover for a spring crop. In warm climates, only heat-tolerant cultivars should be sown during the summer.

In cool climates, sow seed *in situ*, in a seedbed, or in trays or modules for transplanting. Sowings in summer are best made *in situ*, since seedlings wilt when transplanted unless they have been raised in modules. Seed may become dormant in high temperatures; this is most likely to occur several hours after sowing and may be overcome by watering after sowing to cool the soil, by putting seed trays or modules in a cool place to germinate, or by sowing seed in the afternoon so that the critical period occurs at night when temperatures are lower.

HARVESTING LOOSE-LEAF LETTUCES

Loose-leaf lettuces may be harvested by cutting across the leaves 2.5cm (1in) above ground level. Leave the stump to resprout.

LETTUCES TO TRY

Cos
'Corsair'
'Lobjoits Green Cos'
'Nymans'
'Pinokkio'
'Winter Density'

Semi-cos
'Jewel'
'Little Gem'
'Little Gem Pearl'
'Little Leprechaun'
'Rusty'

Butterhead
'Cassandra'
'Clarion'
'Diana'
'Sunny'
'Valdor' **Ow**

Loose-leaf
'Cocarde'
'Green Salad Bowl'
'Lollo Rossa'
'Red Salad Bowl'

Crisphead
'Dickinson'
'Lakeland'
'Minigreen'
'Robinson'
'Saladin'

Key
Ow *Overwinters under cover*

Transplant lettuces in moist conditions when they have five or six leaves, with the base of the leaves positioned just above soil level. In hot weather, shade young plants until they are established. Space small cultivars 15cm (6in) apart, and larger ones about 30cm (12in) apart.

Sow hardy cultivars for over-wintering outdoors *in situ* or under cloches or in frames; thin to about 7cm (3in) apart in autumn and to the full distance apart in spring. Floating mulches or cloches put over the plants in spring improve their quality, and help them to mature earlier.

Most types of lettuce may be grown as cut-and-come-again seedling crops, especially the loose-leaf lettuces, including the traditional European "cutting" cultivars, and some cos varieties (see "Successional crops", p.500).

Routine cultivation

Keep lettuce beds weed-free. Apply a nitrogenous fertilizer or organic liquid feed if growth is slow. In dry conditions, water the plants at a rate of 22 litres/sq m (5 gallons/sq yd) per week. The most critical watering period is about seven to ten days before maturity (see also p.502). In late autumn or early winter, protect lettuces with cloches to improve the quality of the crop.

Pests and diseases

Problems include greenfly and root aphid (see "Aphids", p.646), cut-worms (p.655), leatherjackets (p.660), slugs (p.644), mosaic virus (see "Viruses", p.649), downy mildew (p.646), boron deficiency (p.654), and grey mould (*Botrytis*) (p.653); birds may attack seedlings (p.657). Some cultivars show aphid resistance

PROTECTING SEEDLINGS

Protecting seedlings with fleece helps them mature more quickly early in the season.

and others show some tolerance to mosaic virus and downy mildew.

Growing under cover

In cool climates, earlier lettuce crops may be obtained by sowing or planting in early spring in an unheated greenhouse, beneath cloches or perforated fleecy films, or in cold frames. Some cultivars may also be grown under cover in winter for early spring cropping; for midwinter crops, gentle heat is usually required.

Harvesting and storing

Loose-leaf lettuces should be ready about seven weeks after sowing, butterheads after 10 or 11 weeks, and cos and crispheads after 11 or 12 weeks. Cut cos, butterhead, and crisphead types soon after maturing to prevent bolting. They may be stored for a few days in a refrigerator. Pick the leaves of loose-leaf types a few at a time, as required, since they do not store well, or cut across the plants 2.5cm (1in) above soil level, leaving the stumps to resprout within a few weeks.

Spinach (*Spinacia oleracea*)

Spinach is a fast-growing annual that reaches a height of 15–20cm (6–8in), with a spread of about 15cm (6in). The highly nutritious leaves are smooth or crinkled, and round or pointed, depending on the cultivar. They are eaten lightly cooked or, when young, raw in salads.

A cool-season plant, spinach grows best at 16–18°C (61–64°F), although will grow well at lower temperatures. Small plants and seedlings may survive -9°C (16°F). Grow cultivars recommended for the area; for example, many are prone to bolt in long days (see "Daylength", p.495), especially after a cold period or in hot, dry conditions. Recommended spinach cultivars include 'Atlanta', 'Monnopa', 'Palco', and 'Medania'. Spinach plants tolerate light shade

during summer, and need a soil with medium nitrogen levels (see *Nitrogen Requirements*, p.504). For other soil requirements, see "Swiss chard and spinach beet", p.516.

Sowing and planting

Sow in cool seasons as spinach will not germinate in temperatures above 30°C (86°F). Sow *in situ*, placing individual seeds about 2.5cm (1in) apart in rows spaced about 30cm (12in) apart. For a continuous crop, sow in succession, after seedlings of the previous sowings have appeared. Thin early as for Swiss chard (see p.516), to about 7cm (3in) for young plants, or to 15cm (6in) apart for large plants.

Spinach may also be grown as a cut-and-come-again seedling crop

for use in salads (see p.500). For this, sow in early spring and early autumn under cover, and also in late summer for an overwintering crop in the open. For routine cultivation, pests and diseases, and growing under cover, see "Swiss chard and spinach beet", p.516.

Harvesting and storing

Cut leaves between five and ten weeks after sowing at any stage once the plants are about 5cm (2in) tall. Either cut individual leaves, or cut the heads about 2.5cm (1in) above the ground and leave them to resprout; alternatively, pull up whole plants. In warm areas, harvest plants young, before they start to run to seed. Use the leaves fresh soon after picking, or store by freezing.

Spinach

New Zealand spinach (*Tetragonia tetragonioides*, syn. *T. expansa*)

A half-hardy, creeping perennial, New Zealand spinach is also grown as an annual. The plants have thick, triangular leaves about 5cm (2in) long with a spread of 90–120cm (3–4ft). The leaves are used in the same way as spinach (see above).

New Zealand spinach tolerates high, even tropical, temperatures, and drought, but cannot withstand frost. It grows best in an open site on reasonably fertile and moisture-retentive soil, and needs low nitrogen (see p.504). It is generally less prone to bolting than spinach.

Seeds may be slow to germinate, so to aid germination soak them in

water for 24 hours before sowing. In cool climates, sow seed indoors and plant out at 45cm (18in) each way after all risk of frost has passed. Otherwise sow seed *in situ* outdoors after the last frost, thinning in stages to the final spacing. Keep seedlings weed-free (mature plants cover the soil, suppressing weeds). Pest or disease problems are rare.

Start picking the young leaves and the tips of the stems six or seven weeks after sowing. Pick frequently to encourage further young growth for three or four months. New Zealand spinach should be used fresh immediately after cutting, or frozen.

PICKING NEW ZEALAND SPINACH

Pick the young leaves and tips of stems of New Zealand spinach before seedheads start to form. Plants will continue to make new growth that may be harvested until the first frosts.

Minor salad vegetables

THERE are many lesser-known vegetables worth cultivating to use raw in salads, either on their own or mixed with other vegetables. They are suitable for growing in small gardens and containers. The leaves are distinctly flavoured and nutritious, especially if used young. Apart from summer purslane and iceplants, all tolerate a few degrees of frost, or even lower temperatures on well-drained soil with wind protection. In cool climates, most may be grown under cover in winter for higher yields. Most salad plants are fast-maturing but make lusher growth in nitrogen-rich soil. Many are best sown as cut-and-come-again crops (see p.500). They are usually free of pests and diseases.

Land cress (*Barbarea verna*)

This biennial, low-growing plant has a spread of 15–20cm (6–8in); land cress is also known as upland cress. The glossy, deep green leaves have a strong flavour similar to watercress, and are used as a watercress substitute, either raw or cooked. Land cress is very hardy, remaining green in winter. It grows best in the shade; in heat it runs to seed rapidly, becoming coarse and very hot-tasting. It may be intercropped between taller vegetables or used to make a neat edging for beds.

Grow land cress in fertile and moisture-retentive soils. Sow seed in spring for an early summer crop, or in late summer for an autumn and overwintering crop. It may be grown in unheated greenhouses in winter. Sow *in situ*, thinning to 15cm (6in) apart, or in seed trays to transplant. Pick leaves seven weeks after sowing when they are 7–10cm (3–4in) long.

Land cress

If a few plants are left to run to seed in spring they seed freely, and the seedlings may be transplanted where they are needed. Flea beetles (p.644) may affect young plants.

Mustard (*Sinapis alba*)

Mustard is similar to cress in its habit and is often partnered with it. It is grown for the sharply flavoured seedling leaves which may be used raw in salads. It is a cool-season crop that runs to seed very rapidly in hot weather; its leaves tend to become coarse if it is grown in areas with heavy rainfall.

In temperate climates, outdoor sowings are most successful in spring and autumn *in situ*, using any of the methods suggested for cut-and-come-again seedlings (see p.500).

Mustard, like cress, is a useful crop for growing under cover from autumn to spring. It may be sown without soil either on moist paper towelling in a saucer placed on a windowsill, or in a sprouter; alternatively it may be sown in a seed tray of potting compost or soil. These methods may be used all year round. Mustard germinates faster than cress, so if the two are required together, sow the mustard two or

Mustard

three days later than the cress. A sowing every seven to ten days ensures a continuous supply.

Harvest mustard by cutting as required when the seedlings are about 3.5–5cm (1½–2in) tall. It runs to seed much more rapidly than cress, and will normally provide no more than two or three cuts.

Salad rape (*Brassica napus*)

This annual plant has light green, mild-flavoured leaves and is often used as a substitute for mustard in mustard and cress packs. It is fast-growing but slower to run to seed than mustard or cress. The leaves are used raw as seedlings, while larger leaves may be cooked as greens.

Salad rape survives temperatures of -10°C (14°F), and tolerates moderate heat. The plants grow in a wide range of soils. In temperate climates, sow under cover in early spring and late autumn; sow in succession outdoors until early autumn. Indoors, grow on a windowsill as for mustard (below, left). Outdoors, sow broadcast, or in rows or wide drills. Make the first cut after ten days; when plants reach 60cm (24in), harvest small leaves over several months.

Cut leaves of salad rape at any stage from seedling to 7cm (3in) long. In good conditions, three cuts of seedling leaves may be possible.

Salad rocket (*Eruca vesicaria* subsp. *sativa*)

This hardy, spicy-leaved Mediter-ranean plant is used in salads; older plants may be cooked. Salad rocket is also known as rucola, erugala, Mediterranean rocket, or roquette. It grows best in cool weather in moisture-retentive soil; in cool climates, it is excellent under cover in winter, and as a cut-and-come-again crop. Sow broadcast or in rows to cut as seedlings, or thin to 15cm (6in) to cut when larger. Seedlings are ready in three weeks. Flea beetles (p.644) may attack salad rocket.

Salad rocket

Cress (*Lepidium sativum*)

This fast-growing plant is grown for its seedling leaves, which are used raw. Cress is also known as garden cress, curly cress, or peppercress. There is a fine-leaved and a broad-leaved form. It is a moderately hardy, cool-season crop, running to seed rapidly in hot weather, unless sown in light shade. In cool climates, cress grows well under cover in the winter months. It may stop growing at very low temperatures, but starts again when temperatures rise. It is useful for inter- and undercropping.

Except in very cool areas, cress is best sown in spring and late summer or early autumn; avoid sowing in hot weather. Either sow on moist paper in a saucer and place on a windowsill or sow in a sprouter; this will give one cut. To obtain several consecutive cuts, sow in a seed tray of light soil, or in the ground,

Broad-leaved cress

broadcast, in single rows, or in wide drills. Cut ten days after sowing when seedlings are up to 5cm (2in) high. If sown in the ground, up to four successive cuts may be made.

Iceplants (*Mesembryanthemum crystallinum*)

Grown as perennials in warm climates and as tender annuals elsewhere, iceplants have a sprawling habit, succulent stems, and thick, fleshy leaves, covered with sparkling bladders. The leaves and young stems taste refreshing and slightly salty. They are used raw in salads or cooked like spinach.

Iceplants need a sunny position in light, well-drained soil. In warm climates, sow *in situ* outdoors; in cool climates, sow indoors in the spring, transplanting to 30cm (12in) apart after all risk of frost has passed. Slugs (p.644) may attack seedlings. Plants may be propagated by means of cuttings (see PERENNIALS, "Stem tip cuttings", p.202). The first picking of the young leaves and tender pieces of stem may be made

Iceplants

about four weeks after planting. Harvest plants regularly to encourage further growth, and remove any flowers that appear. Leaves and stems keep fresh for several days.

Winter purslane (*Montia perfoliata*)

This is a hardy annual with heart-shaped leaves and dainty flowering shoots. The mildly flavoured, slightly succulent leaves, stems, and flowering shoots are used raw in salads. Also known as miner's lettuce or claytonia, it thrives in cool weather. It prefers well-drained conditions but grows well even in poor, light soil. Once established, it self-seeds rapidly; invasive seedlings are shallow-rooted and easily pulled up.

Make the main sowing in late summer for an autumn to early winter crop outdoors. Sow in spring for a summer crop. Grow either broadcast as a cut-and-come-again seedling crop, or in rows, or 10cm (4in) wide drills; seed may be sown *in situ* or

Winter purslane

in seed trays. Transplant or thin seedlings to 15–23cm (6–9in) apart. Start cutting 12 weeks after sowing, leaving the plants to resprout.

Summer purslane (*Portulaca oleracea*)

This half-hardy, low-growing plant has slightly succulent leaves and stems that are used raw or cooked. There are green- and yellow-leaved forms: the green type has thinner leaves, is more vigorous, and possibly better flavoured, but the yellow or golden form is attractive in salads. The plants need a warm, sheltered site with light, well-drained soil.

Grow summer purslane either as a cut-and-come-again seedling crop or as single plants. In cool climates, sow in a seed tray in late spring, planting out 15cm (6in) apart, after all risk of frost. Make earlier and late summer sowings under cover as a cut-and-come-again seedling crop. In warm climates, sow *in situ* outside throughout the summer. Cut the seedlings, or young shoots of single

Golden summer purslane

plants, from about four to eight weeks after sowing. Cut regularly, always leaving two basal leaves, and remove any flowers that develop. Slugs (p.644) may attack plants.

Watercress (*Rorippa nasturtium-aquaticum*)

A hardy aquatic perennial, water-cress (also known as *Nasturtium officinale*) has nutritious, sharply flavoured leaves, used in salads and soups. Its natural habitat is fresh running streams, with slightly alkaline water at about 10°C (50°F).

Root cuttings by placing stems in fresh water; they will soon root and may be planted at the edge of a stream in spring, spaced 15cm (6in) apart. Watercress may be grown in moist garden soil, but it is easier to grow in 15–21cm (6–8in) pots. Put a layer of gravel or moss in each pot, fill with rich soil, and stand it in a dish of cool, clean water. Plant three

Watercress grown in a pot

or four rooted cuttings per pot, and stand it in a sheltered position in good light. Change the water at least daily in hot weather. Cut leaves as needed.

Dandelions (*Taraxacum officinale*)

Hardy, perennial weeds, dandelions spread up to 30cm (12in). Wild and cultivated forms are grown for the young leaves, which are used raw. The cultivated forms are larger and slower to run to seed. Dandelion leaves are slightly bitter but blanching sweetens them. The flowers and roots are also edible. Dandelions tolerate a range of well-drained soils.

Sow in spring, in seed trays for transplanting, or *in situ*, spacing 35cm (14in) apart. Blanch in succession from late summer, covering dry plants with a large, light-proof bucket. Harvest the leaves when they are elongated and creamy-yellow. Dandelions die back in winter, but reappear in spring; the plants will continue to grow for several years.

BLANCHING DANDELION

When the plant has several leaves, cover it with a bucket 30cm (12in) tall. Harvest the creamy-yellow, elongated leaves after several weeks.

Corn salad (*Valerianella locusta*)

Grown for autumn and winter salads in cool climates, these hardy annuals form small, mild-flavoured plants. Corn salad is also known as lamb's lettuce or mache. There are two types: the floppy, large-leaved type, and the smaller, upright type with darker green leaves, which is reputedly the hardier. They tolerate a wide range of soils. In cold climates, grow them under cover in winter to obtain more prolific and tender-leaved plants. Corn salad is a useful crop for inter- or undercropping vegetables such as winter brassicas.

Corn salad may be grown as a cut-and-come-again seedling crop, or as individual plants. Sow from mid-summer onwards *in situ*, broadcast, in rows, or in wide drills. Keep the seeds moist until they have germinated. Thin seedlings to 10cm (4in) apart. Corn salad is slow-growing

Large-leaved corn salad

and may take 12 weeks to mature. Harvest leaves individually or cut across the plants, leaving them to resprout for a second cut.

Fruiting and flowering vegetables

Sᴏᴍᴇ of the most exotic and succulent vegetables fall into the fruiting and flowering group of vegetables. Many – tomatoes, peppers, aubergines, and melons, for example – are tropical or subtropical in origin; in cooler areas these may need to be grown under cover or in a warm situation. In temperate climates, others such as marrows, sweet corn, and pumpkins need to be germinated indoors but may be planted outdoors to grow to maturity. All need a warm, sheltered situation to ripen their fruits and for pollination to be successful.

Honeydew melon · Aubergines · Marrow · Sweet peppers · Courgettes · Cherry tomatoes · Musk melon · Plum tomatoes · Greenhouse cucumber · Sweet peppers · Sweet corn

Sweet peppers (*Capsicum annuum* Grossum Group)

Also called capsicums, or bell peppers, these annuals have a bushy habit and may grow up to 75cm (30in) tall with a spread of 45–60cm (18–24in). The fruits are usually oblong, ranging in size from 3–15cm (1¼–6in) long and 3–7cm (1¼–3in) in diameter, and may be green, cream, yellow, orange, red, or dark purple. The mature fruits are eaten cooked or raw, whole or sliced.

Sweet peppers are tropical and subtropical plants needing a minimum temperature of 21°C (70°F) with a humidity of 70–75 per cent. Temperatures over 30°C (86°F) may reduce fruit set and cause buds and flowers to drop. In temperate climates, plants may be grown under cover or outside in a sunny, sheltered site. Moderately deep, fertile, well-drained soil with medium nitrogen levels (see p.504) is required.

Sowing and planting
Sow seed in spring in the greenhouse in trays of compost with a pH of 5.5–7. Prick out the seedlings

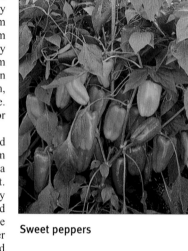

Sweet peppers

into 6–9cm (3–3½in) pots and plant out 10–12 weeks after sowing in well-prepared beds, spacing the plants 45–50cm (18–20in) apart each way. In temperate climates, pot on seedlings and do not plant out until all risk of frost has passed.

Routine cultivation
Pinch out the terminal growing point of established plants to encourage a bushy habit and stake cultivars over 60cm (24in) tall. Water regularly to prevent leaf and bud drop, and mulch with organic material. Apply a balanced fertilizer or liquid feed every two weeks during the growing season, then stop feeding to encourage ripening. Protect plants outdoors with plastic covers, if necessary.

Pests and diseases
Plants may be attacked by aphids (p.646); under cover they may also be affected by glasshouse red spider mite (p.646), whiteflies (p.646), thrips (p.647), and blossom end rot (see "Calcium deficiency", p.658).

Growing under cover
Sow as above in early spring. When seedlings are 8–10cm (3–4in) tall, pot them into 21cm (8in) pots or trans-plant into growing bags or prepared greenhouse beds. Space plants 50cm

RIPENING SWEET PEPPERS
As they ripen, the fruits change colour from green to red, yellow, or dark purple, and the flavour becomes sweeter.

(20in) apart and stake taller cultivars. Maintain the recommended temperature and a humidity of 70–75 per cent by regularly damping down.

Harvesting and storing
Harvest the peppers 12–14 weeks after transplanting and before the first frost if the plants are growing outside. Some cultivars are best used when the fruits are green, but others may be left on the plants for two to three weeks until they change colour to red or creamy-yellow. Cut off individual peppers; they may be stored in cool, humid conditions for up to 14 days at 12–15°C (54–59°F). Entire plants may also be stored (see "Fruiting vegetables", p.506).

HARVESTING PEPPERS

Some peppers are best harvested when green; others may be left to turn red or yellow. Cut the stalk about 2.5cm (1in) from the fruit.

SWEET PEPPERS TO TRY
'Ace' F1 (red)
'Ariane' F1 (orange)
'Bell Boy' F1 (red)
'Bendigo' F1 (red)
'Gypsy' F1 (red)

'Luteus' (yellow)
'Mavras' F1 (black)
'Redskin' (red)
'Unicorn' F1 (red)

Dwarf
'Gourmet' (orange)
'Mohawk' (red)
'Topgirl' (red)

Chilli peppers (*Capsicum annuum* Longum Group)

This form of *Capsicum annuum* has pointed fruits up to 9cm (3½in) long. Popular chilli pepper culti-vars include 'Apache', 'Fiesta', 'Jalapeno', and 'Thai Dragon'; they are becoming increasingly popular as ornamental plants.

Cultivated in the same way as sweet peppers, chilli peppers are slightly more tolerant of high temperatures. Pick them for use at any stage when the colour is green to red. If growing outside, harvest before the first frost is expected.

The hot flavour increases with the chilli's maturity and comes from the white pith and seeds inside. If it is too hot, the pith and seeds may be removed and discarded.

Ripening chilli peppers

Red chilli peppers

Hot peppers (*Capsicum frutescens*)

These plants, also known as cayenne peppers, are branching perennials that grow up to 1.5m (5ft) tall and bear small, narrow, orange, yellow, or red fruits which may hang from the branches or be carried upright, depending on the cultivar. They are highly pungent and are used in sauces and as a general flavouring.

Hot peppers are tropical and sub-tropical plants and therefore cannot tolerate frost. Plants should be spaced 60cm (24in) apart in each direction, and cultivated in the same way as sweet peppers (see p.522), although they generally require more water. Staking is not normally necessary.

Hot peppers need a long growing period, and the first fruits are usually produced about 15–18 weeks after planting. They should be allowed to ripen fully before being picked. They may be frozen or dried and stored for several months.

Hot peppers

HOT PEPPERS TO TRY

'Filius Blue'
'Fuego'
'Habanero'
'Hungarian Hot Wax'
'Prairie Fire'
'Red Cayenne'
'Red Cherry'
'Super Chilli'
'Tabasco'
'Yellow Cayenne'

Watermelons (*Citrullus lanatus*)

Watermelons are annual, tropical or subtropical plants with spreading stems that grow to 3–4m (10–12ft). Their fruits are rounded or oblong, green or cream, striped or mottled, and may grow to 60cm (24in) in length; they are eaten raw. Plants need a temperature of 25–30°C (77–86°F) and may be grown outdoors only in sunny, sheltered areas, but may also be grown under cover. Well-drained, sandy loam soils with medium levels of nitrogen (see p.504) and a pH of 5.5–7 are needed. Incorporate well-rotted manure and a general-purpose fertilizer into the soil before planting.

Watermelon

Sowing and planting
Sow in early spring under cover, in trays or 6–9cm (3–3½in) pots, at a temperature of at least 22–25°C (72–77°F). When the seedlings are 10–15cm (4–6in) tall, harden them off. Plant them out after all risk of frost has passed, spaced at least 1m (3ft) apart. Protect from wind and cold weather with plastic screens.

Routine cultivation
Mulch to retain moisture and apply a balanced fertilizer or liquid feed every two weeks until the fruits begin to develop. Pinch out the growing points of the main shoots when they are 2m (6ft) long and train sideshoots between other plants in the row. To assist formation of fruits, hand-pollinate the flowers (see "Marrows and courgettes", p.526). Reduce sub-lateral growths from the sideshoots to two or three leaves after fruits start to develop, and place a pad of dried grass or a block of wood beneath each fruit to protect it from soil-borne pests and diseases.

Pests and diseases
Humidity levels over 75 per cent encourage leaf diseases, particularly powdery mildew (p.646) and mosaic virus (see "Viruses", p.649). Other common pests include aphids (p.646), root-knot eelworms (p.660), and fruit flies (p.659).

Growing under cover
Watermelons are extremely vigorous and are not normally grown in a greenhouse. They may be grown under plastic covers, spaced 1m (3ft) apart; remove covers at flowering time to reduce humidity and to encourage insect-pollination.

Harvesting and storing
Harvest 11–14 weeks after sowing; mature fruits give a hollow sound when tapped. They may be stored for 14–20 days at 10–12°C (50–54°F).

WATERMELONS TO TRY

'Charleston Grey'
'Crimson Sweet'
'Moon and Stars'
'Sugar Baby'
'Yellow Baby'

Sweet melons (*Cucumis melo*)

These climbing annuals, normally trained as cordons, reach a height of about 2m (6ft) with laterals extending to 60cm (24in). The three major types are cantaloupe, winter or casaba, and musk (including honeydew) melons. Cantaloupe melons have grey-green, thick, rough skins with deep grooves; individual fruits weigh up to 750g (1lb 11oz). Winter mel-ons have smooth, yellow, or yellow and green striped skin, and weigh up to 1kg (2lb 2oz). Musk melons vary in size but are usually smaller than cantaloupe and winter melons and often have fine reticulated markings on smooth skins. Winter melons and some cultivars of cantaloupe melons are suitable for growing in a greenhouse.

Sweet melons are tropical plants requiring a minimum temperature of 18°C (64°F) for germination, rising to 25°C (77°F) during the growing period. In very sunny, sheltered sites, growing in the open is possible but in temperate climates plants are grown in cold frames or in a greenhouse. They need a well-drained, fertile soil with a pH of 6.5–7, a high humus content, and high nitrogen levels (see p.504). Add a general-purpose fertilizer and well-rotted compost or manure.

Sowing and planting
Sow seed under cover in early spring in trays or in 6–9cm (3–3½in) pots (two seeds per pot), removing the weaker one if both germinate. After about six weeks, and when risk of frost is passed, harden off and plant out the seedlings, spaced 1m (3ft) apart with 1–1.5m (3–5ft) between rows. Plant each seedling on a slight mound and protect young plants until they are established from wind and cold weather with plastic tunnels.

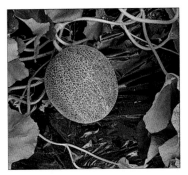

Musk melon

SWEET MELONS TO TRY

'Blenheim Orange'
'Castella'
'Durandal' F1

'Edonis' F1
'Galia' F1
'Minnesota Midget'

'Ogen'
'Sweetheart'

STOPPING SWEET MELONS

Allow one flower per lateral to set, and then pinch or cut out the growing tip of each lateral at 2–3 leaves beyond the developing fruit.

Routine cultivation

After five leaves have developed, pinch out each growing point to encourage further shoots. When these are well developed, reduce them to about four of the most vigorous shoots. Train two shoots on either side, between adjacent plants in the row. Remove any protective covering when the plants begin to flower to encourage insect-pollination. Hand-pollinate if required (see "Marrows and courgettes", p.526).

Thin to one fruit per shoot when the fruits are 2.5cm (1in) in diameter, and stop all sub-laterals at two to three leaves beyond the developing fruits. Pinch out the main shoots when they are 1–1.2m (3–4ft) long and remove any further sub-laterals that form. Place a pad of dried grass, a tile, or a piece of wood beneath each developing fruit to protect it from soil-borne diseases.

Water regularly and feed every 10–14 days with a liquid feed as the fruits begin to develop; reduce watering and feeding as fruits ripen.

Pests and diseases

Aphids (p.646) and powdery mildew (p.646) may be troublesome. Under cover, the plants may be affected by glasshouse red spider mite (p.646), the fungal disease powdery mildew (p.646), whiteflies (p.646), and *Verticillium* wilt (p.653).

Growing under cover

To raise sweet melons in a cold frame, plant seedlings singly in the centre of the frame. Train the four laterals to grow towards the corners. As the plants develop, increase ventilation and gradually reduce humidity. Once fruits start forming, remove the lights, replacing them at night only in cold weather. In hot weather, shade lightly.

Sweet melons may be grown in a greenhouse if the distance from the base of the side walls to the ridge is at least 2m (6ft). Plant seedlings onto well-prepared mounds (see "Cucumbers and gherkins", below). Grow as single or double cordons, training on canes tied to horizontal wires up to the ridge. Space plants 38cm (15in) apart for single cordons, 60cm (24in) for double cordons. They may also be grown in growing bags or 24–25cm (9–10in) pots placed on greenhouse staging.

For a single cordon, pinch out the growing point when the main shoot is 2m (6ft) long to encourage lateral growth. Stop laterals at five leaves and sub-laterals at two leaves beyond the flowers. For a double cordon, pinch out the main shoot and let two shoots develop vertically; train as above. Support developing fruits in 5cm (2in) mesh slings or nets fixed to the ridge. To aid pollination do not damp down during flowering. Maintain a temperature of 24°C (75°F) at night and 30°C (86°F) in the day.

Harvesting and storing

Harvest 12–20 weeks after sowing. Cantaloupe and musk melons are sweet-smelling when mature, and the fruit stalks crack. Separate the fruits gently from the stalks. Store for 14–50 days at 10–15°C (50–59°F), depending on the cultivar.

Cucumbers and gherkins (*Cucumis sativus*)

Most are annual, trailing vines that grow to 1–3m (3–10ft); there are a few compact bush cultivars. The immature fruits are eaten raw, pickled, or cooked in soup.

Outdoor or ridge cucumbers are rough-skinned, spiny, and 10–15cm (4–6in) long. Modern cultivars, many of Japanese origin, are smoother and up to 30cm (12in) long, with improved cold tolerance and disease resistance. They are mainly grown outdoors or in frames and are insect-pollinated. Gherkins are ridge cucumbers with short, often stumpy fruits up to 7cm (3in) long, harvested young, and used mainly for pickling. Apple and lemon cucumbers are round, yellow-skinned, ridge cucumbers that grow up to 6cm (2½in) in diameter. European or greenhouse fruits are smooth and over 30cm (12in) long. They do not require pollination to set fruit and, if pollinated, may produce bitter fruits; use the modern all-female cultivars to remove the risk of accidental pollination.

Cucumbers are warm-season vegetables, growing best at a mean temperature of 18–30°C (64–86°F). They have no frost tolerance and most are damaged at temperatures below 10°C (50°F). In northern latitudes, ridge types may produce male flowers alone early in the season; female flowers, then fruits, occur later. Grow cucumbers in a sheltered site in fertile, humus-rich soil that is well drained but moisture-retentive: the roots must not be allowed to dry out. Lime very acid soils. The young plants need low nitrogen levels (see p.504) but, after planting, may require higher nitrogen levels. Rotate indoor crops.

Greenhouse types must be grown with minimum night temperatures of 20°C (68°F) and in high humidity; shade glass or grow under polycarbonate to avoid scorching. Never grow ridge types in the same greenhouse as all-female cultivars since cross-pollination will occur.

Sowing and planting

Cucumbers transplant badly, so seed for outdoor varieties should be sown *in situ* after all risk of frost has passed, or in small pots or modules. If sowing outside, prepare holes 30cm (12in) wide and deep, working in plenty of well-rotted compost as you backfill. Cover with about 15cm (6in) of manured soil made into a small mound to ensure sharp drainage. Place seeds on their side about 2cm (¾in) deep, sowing two to three per pot or site.

Seed germinates at a minimum soil temperature of 20°C (68°F). Thin to one seedling after germination. Seed sown in pots needs a minimum temperature at night of 16°C (61°F) until the seedlings are planted out, about four weeks after sowing. Space

Gherkin

climbing types 45cm (18in) apart; bush types, and climbing types if trailing over the ground, should be spaced about 75cm (30in) apart. In cool climates, protect plants with cloches or fleecy film after planting.

Routine cultivation

Grow trailing types up supporting fences, nets, or canes, or allow them to twine up strings. Nip out the growing point after five or six leaves have appeared, and train the resulting stronger growths up the support, tying them in if necessary. When these shoots reach the top of the support, nip them out two leaves beyond a flower; laterals will develop on which more fruits will form. As fruiting continues, feed plants every two weeks with a high-potash fertilizer or equivalent organic liquid feed. Regular watering is essential during the growing period,

SOWING AND PLANTING OUT

1 *Fill a 5cm (2in) pot with seed compost to within 2.5cm (1in) of the rim. Place 2 or 3 seeds on their sides in the compost, then cover them to a depth of about 2cm (¾in). Water well and label.*

2 *Prepare a hole 30cm (12in) wide and 30cm (12in) deep, and fill with well-rotted compost. Pile the soil on top to make a mound about 15cm (6in) high. Plant the cucumber on top of this mound. Firm in and water.*

Bush cucumbers

particularly after transplanting and during flowering and fruiting (see "Critical watering periods", p.502).

Pests and diseases

Cucumbers may be affected by snails (p.644), aphids (p.646), powdery mildew (p.646), cutworms (p.655), glasshouse red spider mite (p.646), whiteflies (p.646), cucumber mosaic virus (see "Viruses", p.649), and foot and root rots (p.654).

Growing under cover

Grow as in the open using suitable cultivars; the all-female selections are recommended. To grow as cordons, remove all side shoots to the top of the support and take off cucumbers up to 45cm (18in) from the ground to avoid overloading. Tie in the main shoot to the top wire and allow side shoots to develop; pinch to two leaves and let subsequent shoots hang down to crop. Damp down greenhouses to control pests.

Harvesting and storing

Harvest cucumbers regularly from about 12 weeks after sowing when the sides of the fruits are parallel and they are about 15–20cm (6–8in) long. Harvest gherkins when they are 2.5–7cm (1–3in) long or when they have reached pickling size.

Climbing cucumbers

CUCUMBERS AND GHERKINS TO TRY

Ridge cucumbers
'Burpless Tasty Green' F1
'Bush Champion' F1
'Marketmore'

Smooth cucumbers
'Carmen' F1
'Flamingo' F1
'Petita'
'Zeine' F1 (mini cucumber)

Japanese cucumbers
'Tokyo Slicer' F1

Gherkins
'Diamant' F1
'Venlo Pickling'

Pumpkins and winter squashes (*Cucurbita maxima, C. moschata, C. pepo*)

This is a diverse group of annuals, also known as winter squashes, with fruits ranging from 450g (1lb) to over 30kg (66lb). The skin may be smooth, warted, or ridged, and green, cream, blue-green, yellow, orange, red, or striped – the colour often changing with maturity. Their shapes vary considerably and may be round, long, squat, onion-shaped, or a two-layered, "turban" shape. Most form very large trailing plants with huge leaves; some are compact and bushy. Both young and mature fruits may be eaten cooked, either fresh or after storage. Shoots and young leaves may be cooked and flowers may be eaten raw or cooked. Some cultivars have edible seeds.

Pumpkins on a tripod

For climate, site, and soil preparation requirements, see "Cucumbers and gherkins", p.524. Pumpkins require medium to high nitrogen levels (see p.504).

Sowing and planting

Seed may be soaked overnight before sowing to hasten germination. Sow as for cucumbers (see p.524). Space plants 2–3m (6–10ft) apart, depending on the cultivar. For large cultivars, prepare holes up to 45cm (18in) deep and 60cm (24in) wide. Insert a marker cane when planting so that the centre of the plant can be found if watering is necessary. Protect and mulch after planting.

Routine cultivation

A top-dressing of a general fertilizer may be applied soon after planting. Shoots may be trained in circles on the ground using bent wire to hold down the stems, or grown on supports, such as tripods, which for vigorous cultivars must be very strong. Where only a few large fruits are needed, remove all but two or three of the other fruits while still young.

Hand-pollinate as for marrows (see p.526), if necessary. Pumpkins are deep-rooting so watering should only be needed in very dry weather.

Pests and diseases

The most serious pests and diseases are slugs (p.644) in the early stages and cucumber mosaic virus (see "Viruses", p.649).

Harvesting and storing

Cut away any foliage shading the fruits to encourage them to ripen. Harvest pumpkins 12–20 weeks after planting. Leave fruits for storing on the plant to mature as long as possible: the stem starts to crack and the skin hardens when the fruit is ripe. Pick before the first frosts, cutting each fruit with a long stalk.

After harvesting, most storage types must be exposed to the sun for ten days to "cure" or further harden the skin so that it forms a barrier, slowing the rate of water loss. Cover the fruits at night if frost threatens, or cure indoors at 27–32°C (81–90°F) for four days. Store pumpkins in a well-ventilated place at about 10°C (50°F) with a humidity of 95 per cent. They may be kept from four to six months or even longer, depending on the conditions and the cultivar grown. Store white varieties such as 'Ghost' F1 in the dark to keep them white.

VARIETIES TO TRY

'Baby Bear' p
'Butternut' s
'Crown Prince' s
'Dills Atlantic Giant' p
'Gem' s
'Ghost' F1 p
'Harrier' F1 s
   (early sweeter)
'Hooligan' p
'Kabocha' s
'Mars' p
'Queensland Blue' s
'Rouge Vif D'Etamp' p
'Small Sugar' p
'Table Ace' s (acorn type)
'Triple Treat' p (edible seeds)
'Turk's Turban' s
'Uchiki Kuri' s
   (onion type)

Key
p *pumpkin*   s *squash*

CURING PUMPKINS

When ripe, cut the pumpkin off the plant with as long a stalk as possible using secateurs or loppers; take care not to pull, as damage may cause rotting. Leave in the sun for about 10 days so that the skin hardens. 'Acorn' may be stored without curing.

Marrows and courgettes (*Cucurbita pepo*)

Also known as vegetable marrows or summer squashes, marrows are annuals that trail for several metres or form compact plants of 90cm (3ft) spread. They commonly have cylindrical fruits about 30cm (12in) long and 13cm (5in) in diameter. Courgettes are marrows harvested young; only tender-skinned cultivars are suitable. Marrows are usually trailing, while courgettes are bushy. The skin of marrows may be green, yellow, white, or striped. Custard marrows have flattish, fluted-edged fruits; crookneck squashes have swollen fruits with a bent neck. There are also round-fruited cultivars. Spaghetti marrows are marrow-like in shape, but with hard skins; their flesh resembles spaghetti when cooked. All the fruits are generally cooked. Young leaves and shoot tips may also be cooked, and flowers eaten raw or cooked.

Marrows and courgettes are warm-season crops, needing temperatures of 18–27°C (64–81°F). Frost tolerance, soil, and soil preparation are as for cucumbers (see p.524). They need low nitrogen levels (see p.504).

Sowing and planting
Sow as for cucumbers (see p.524) when the soil temperature is at least

Bush marrow

Hand-pollinating

Marrows and courgettes are generally insect-pollinated but in cold seasons, if fruits are not setting, it may be necessary to hand-pollinate. The female flower has a tiny bump (the embryonic fruit) behind the petals which the male flower lacks (see below); this makes it easy to distinguish between them.

Male flower

Female flower

Embryonic fruit

To hand-pollinate, take a male flower, remove all the petals and press it against the female flower. Alternatively, use a fine paintbrush to transfer the pollen from the stamens of the male flower to the stigma of the female.

15°C (59°F). Place each seed about 2.5cm (1in) deep or a little deeper in light soils. Sow seed *in situ* once all risk of frost has passed, or germinate in pots indoors. Space bush types 90cm (3ft) apart, and trailing types 1.2–2m (4–6ft) apart. In cool areas, protect young plants with cloches or floating mulches. In hot areas, floating mulches will protect young plants against insects. Mulch after planting.

Routine cultivation
Trailing types may be grown up strong supports. The shoots may also be trained in circles, using bent wire to peg down the stems. Towards the end of the season, nip off the ends of the shoots. Feed and water as for cucumbers (see pp.524–525).

Pests and diseases
Slugs (p.644) may attack in the early stages of growth; cucumber mosaic virus (see "Viruses", p.649) may also be a problem.

Growing under cover
This is only appropriate in cool climates when a very early crop is required. Use bush cultivars.

Harvesting and storing
Harvest marrows seven to eight weeks after planting. Some types may be stored for a few weeks if they are kept well ventilated at about 10°C (50°F) with a humidity of 95 per cent. Spaghetti marrows may be stored for several months. Pick courgettes when they are about 10cm (4in) long, preferably with the flower attached as this indicates freshness. Harvest shoots from the top 15cm (6in) of stem; new growth is soon made. If harvesting flowers, pick male ones after the females have set.

HARVESTING COURGETTES

Cut courgettes when they are 10cm (4in) long, with a short stalk. Handle the fruits carefully to avoid bruising them. Regular harvesting will encourage more fruits.

Globe artichokes (*Cynara scolymus*)

These perennial plants have blue-grey leaves and thistle-like flowers. Globe artichokes may grow up to 1.2–1.5m (4–5ft) tall with a 90cm (3ft) spread. They are grown for the green and purple flower buds, which have edible, fleshy pads (the "hearts") at the base of the outer

scales and the top of the flower stem; the hearts are cooked or pickled. A reliable cultivar is 'Vert de Laon'.

Globe artichokes grow best in cool climates at 13–18°C (55–64°F) and tolerate light to medium frosts. They need an open but not exposed site, with fertile, well-drained soil into

which plenty of compost or well-rotted manure has been dug, and low levels of nitrogen (see p.504).

Sowing and planting
Globe artichokes are normally increased by division. Using a sharp knife, two hand forks, or a spade,

divide healthy, established plants in the spring; each division should have at least two shoots with a tuft of leaves and a good root system. Plant these divisions 60–75cm (24–30in) apart and trim the tips of the leaves to 13cm (5in). Globe artichokes may be raised from seed either indoors or

DIVIDING ARTICHOKES

In spring, lift an established plant and divide it using two hand forks, a spade, or a knife. Each division should have at least two shoots, and strong roots.

outdoors in spring, but the results are variable; thin or plant out seedlings at the correct spacing. In future years, divide the most productive plants to build up a good stock. Named cultivars can only be raised from divided offsets. Plants should be replaced every three years to maintain vigour and cropping levels.

Routine cultivation

Keep the planting area free of weeds and well mulched to conserve soil moisture. Do not allow the roots of globe artichokes to dry out in summer or become waterlogged in winter. If heavy frosts are expected, earth up the base of each plant, covering with a thick layer of straw; remove the covering in spring.

Pests and diseases

Root aphids (see "Aphids", p.646) may cause problems.

Harvesting and storing

In favourable conditions, some heads may be cut in the late summer of the first season. More flowering stems will be produced in the second season. Pick before the scales open, when the buds feel plump. Remove the hairy choke and stalk before freezing; the hearts may be pickled.

Globe artichoke

Tomatoes (*Lycopersicon esculentum*)

These are annual plants in temperate areas and short-lived perennials in the tropics. The main trailing stem of the indeterminate (mid-size, non-bushy) types grows to over 2.5m (8ft) long in warm climates, with vigorous sideshoots. The shorter (semi-determinate) types and the bush (determinate) types stop growing earlier than the indeterminates, with the stems ending in a fruit truss. Compact dwarf types may grow up to 23cm (9in) across and as tall.

Ripe tomato fruits are red, yellow, orange, pink, or white, and round, flat, plum- or pear-shaped. The tiny currant tomatoes (*Lycopersicon pimpinellifolium*) are 1cm (½in) in diameter, cherry types 2.5cm (1in), the ribbed Marmande and giant beefsteak types up to 10cm (4in). All are eaten raw or cooked.

Tomatoes grow best at 21–24°C (70–75°F), but do not grow well below 16°C (61°F) or above 27°C (81°F) and do not tolerate frost. They need high light intensity. In cool climates, grow them in a sheltered site outdoors or under cover; they are often grown in containers. Tomatoes tolerate a wide range of fertile and well-drained soils, with a pH of 5.5–7; lime very acid soils (see "Liming", p.625). Crops need to be rotated (see p.498).

Prepare the ground by working in plenty of well-rotted manure or compost at least 30cm (12in) deep, since tomatoes are deep-rooted and gross feeders. Apply a basic fertilizer before planting: tomatoes need high levels of phosphorus (see "Soil nutrients", p.503) but low levels of nitrogen (see p.504).

Sowing and planting

In warm climates, sow seed *in situ* in spring and thin seedlings to the correct spacing. In cool climates, six

Bush tomatoes

to eight weeks before the last frost, sow seed 2cm (¾in) deep, at about 15°C (59°F), in seed trays or modules. Transplant into 5–6cm (2–3in) pots at the two- or three-leaf stage; give the seedlings ample ventilation, space, and light. They can stand short periods of low temperatures if day temperatures rise to compensate. Harden off before planting out when night temperatures are over 7°C (45°F) or soil temperatures at least 10°C (50°F) and the risk of frost is over. Plant when the flowers on the lower truss are visible.

Cordons Train indeterminate and semi-determinate types as cordons with 38–45cm (15–18in) between plants in single rows 45cm (18in) apart, or in double rows with 90cm (3ft) between the pairs of rows.

Bush and dwarf types Bush types sprawl on the ground; space them 30–90cm (12–36in) apart, depending on the cultivar. Dwarf types may be more closely spaced than this. Cover with cloches or floating mulches in the early stages. Bush types grow well when mulched with plastic film (see "Mulching", p.502).

Routine cultivation

All types of tomato should be watered and mulched heavily once the soil is warm. In dry conditions, water tomatoes weekly at a rate of 11 litres (2 gallons) per plant. Plants in containers need more frequent watering and supplementary feeding with a tomato fertilizer. Take care not to overwater or overfeed as this may reduce flavour.

Cordons Tie in cordons to the support canes or wires as they grow, and remove all sideshoots when they are about 2.5cm (1in) long. In late summer, remove the terminal shoot two leaves above a truss to allow the remaining fruits to develop and ripen before the first frost. In cool climates, remove supports at the end of the season, bend over the plants *in situ* on straw, and cover with cloches to encourage ripening (see p.528).

TRAINING CORDON TOMATOES

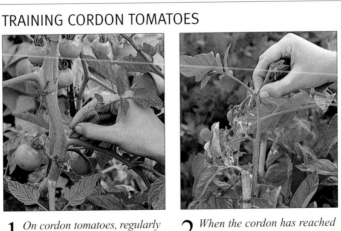

1 *On cordon tomatoes, regularly pinch out sideshoots as they develop to concentrate the plant's energies into swelling the fruits.*

2 *When the cordon has reached the required height in late summer, nip out the tip of the main shoot 2 leaves above the top flower truss.*

TOMATOES TO TRY

Baskets/containers
'Balconi Red'
'Balconi Yellow'
'Tumbler'

Cordon, standard
'Alicante'
'Crystal' F1
'Golden Sunrise'
 (yellow)
'Shirley'
'Tigerella'

Cherry, cordon
'Gardener's Delight'
'Ruby' F1
'Sun Baby' F1 (yellow)
'Sungold' F1

Beefsteak, cordon
'Legend'
 (blight resistant)
'Marmande'

Plum, cordon
'Ildi' (yellow)
'Olivade' F1
'Roma' VF

TOMATOES RIPENING UNDER A CLOCHE

In cool climates, tomatoes will continue to ripen at the end of the season if they are cut down from their supports, leaned over horizontally on a bed of clean, dry straw, and covered with cloches. The roots stay in the ground.

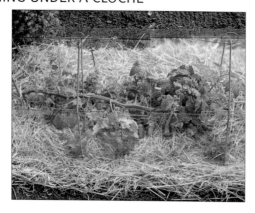

Pests and diseases

Outdoor tomato plants are affected by damping off in seedlings (p.660), leafhoppers (p.647), potato cyst eelworms (p.666), and tomato blight (p.658). Tomatoes under cover are affected by whiteflies (p.646), potato mosaic virus (see "Viruses", p.649), tomato leaf mould (p.648), grey mould (*Botrytis*) (p.658), magnesium deficiency (p.651), boron deficiency (p.654), seedling blight (p.654), foot and root rots (p.661), and blossom end rot (see "Calcium deficiency", p.658). Use disease-resistant cultivars where possible. Interplanting with French marigolds may help to deter whiteflies.

Growing under cover

In cool climates, tomatoes may be grown in greenhouses or polytunnels. Polytunnels, which can be moved to a fresh site, are better than greenhouses, where soil-borne diseases may develop unless the soil is replaced every three years. Alternatively crops may be grown in containers or by ring culture (plants are grown in "rings" or bottomless pots filled with compost, resting on shingle or gravel). Cultivars may also be grafted onto disease-resistant rootstocks. After the first truss has set feed weekly with a high-potash fertilizer or an organic liquid feed.

Harvesting and storing

Pick fruits as they ripen. Harvest the earliest bush types seven to eight weeks after planting; before the first frosts, these may be pulled up by the roots and hung upside-down indoors to ripen. Harvest cordon types after 10–12 weeks. Tomatoes freeze well.

GROWING BAGS

Tomatoes may be planted in growing bags outdoors or in greenhouses. Growing in bags prevents the plants from being infected by soil-borne diseases.

Wonderberries (*Solanum* x *burbankii*)

These annual plants grow to about 75cm–1m (30in–3ft) tall with a spread of 60cm (24in). Several cultivated forms of the wonderberry, or sunberry, are grown; all have oval, light green leaves as well as round, purple berries up to 1cm (½in) in diameter. The leaves and young shoots are used like spinach. The unripe fruits contain a poisonous alkaloid, so pick only ripe berries and cook them thoroughly.

Wonderberries are tropical and sub-tropical plants needing temperatures of 18–25°C (64–77°F) with a humidity of at least 70 per cent. They may be grown in the open in sites that are both sunny and sheltered, but in temperate areas, greenhouse cultivation is recommended. A fertile, well-drained soil that has a pH of 5.5–7 is preferable; medium nitrogen levels are required (see p.504).

Sowing and planting

Sow seed in spring in trays in the greenhouse. Prick out the seedlings when they are large enough to handle, into 6–9cm (3–3½in) pots. When they are 8–10cm (3–4in) tall, harden them off and transplant them; space plants 40–50cm (16–20in) apart, with about 60cm (24in) between rows.

Routine cultivation

Wonderberries need high levels of soil moisture; mulch well and water regularly. Apply a general-purpose fertilizer or an organic liquid feed every 10–14 days during the growing period. Pinch out the growing point when plants are 30cm (12in) tall to encourage lateral branching, and stake plants that grow higher than 60cm (24in). Keep the ground around plants free from weeds.

Pests and diseases

Aphids (p.646) are the major pest. Under cover, glasshouse red spider mite (p.646) and thrips (p.647) may also attack plants.

Growing under cover

When seedlings are about 10–15cm (4–6in) tall, transplant into 21cm (8in) pots or growing bags, leaving at least 50cm (20in) between plants, or transplant into well-prepared greenhouse beds, spacing plants 50–60cm (20–24in) apart each way. Reduce the level of humidity during flowering to promote pollination.

Harvesting and storing

Harvest shoots 9–11 weeks after transplanting; continue removing shoots 10–15cm (4–6in) long to encourage lateral growths. To produce berries, do not remove

Wonderberries

shoots but allow the plants to become bushy and to flower. Harvest the fruit about 14–17 weeks after sowing, removing bunches with a sharp knife. Ripe berries may be stored for 10–14 days at 10–15°C (50–59°F).

Aubergines (*Solanum melongena*)

Short-lived perennials normally cultivated as annuals, aubergines form small bushes about 60–70cm (24–28in) tall with a spread of about 60cm (24in). Also known as eggplants or garden eggs, cultivars differ mainly in the shape, size, and colour of the fruits, which may be oval, pear-shaped, or round, dark purple, yellowish-green, or white, and weigh 200–500g (7–18oz). The fruits are usually sliced and cooked.

Aubergines are tropical and sub-tropical plants requiring temperatures of 25–30°C (77–86°F), with a minimum humidity of 75 per cent. Below 20°C (68°F) growth may be checked, although many cultivars may be grown in temperate areas in greenhouses or outdoors in a sunny, sheltered site, with protection.

Aubergines require a deep, fertile, well-drained soil and medium nitrogen levels (see p.504).

Sowing and planting

In spring, sow seed under cover in trays using a light, slightly acid (pH 6–6.5) compost: soak the seed in warm water for 24 hours first to aid germination. Prick out into 6–9cm (3–3½in) pots. In warm climates, plant out the seedlings into well-prepared beds when they are 8–10cm (3–4in) tall, spacing them about 60–75cm (24–30in) apart each way. Pinch out their terminal growing

AUBERGINES TO TRY

'Black Beauty' F1
'Black Enorma'
'Bonica' F1
'Ghost Buster' F1 (white)
'Mohican' F1 (white)
'Moneymaker' F1
'Rosanna' F1

points to promote a bushy habit. In temperate climates, pot up singly into 15cm (6in) pots; plant out after risk of frost has passed. Protect from heavy rain, wind, and low temperatures.

Routine cultivation

Stake cultivars over 60cm (24in) tall. Keep plants well watered, or the leaves and buds are liable to drop, and mulch to preserve moisture. Apply a balanced fertilizer or liquid feed every two weeks during the growing season. Prune back mature plants in order to stimulate growth. To produce large fruits, restrict the number per plant to five or six.

Pests and diseases

Aubergines may be attacked by aphids (p.646). Under cover, red spider mite (p.646), mealybugs

(p.646), caterpillars (p.645), thrips (p.647), and powdery and downy mildew (p.646) may be troublesome.

Growing under cover

Sow seed in early spring at 20–30°C (68–86°F). When the seedlings are 8–10cm (3–4in) tall, transfer them to 20cm (8in) pots or growing bags, and pinch out the tips. Maintain the temperature above the minimum required during the growing period. Damp down greenhouses to help discourage red spider mite.

Harvesting and storing

Harvest 16–24 weeks after sowing, when fruits reach full colour and are unwrinkled. Cut the fruit stalks close to the stem. Aubergines may be stored for up to two weeks in humid conditions at 12–15°C (54–59°F).

HARVESTING AUBERGINES

Cut aubergines while their skin is still purple and shiny; once it loses its shine, the flesh will taste bitter. Cut the stalk at least 2.5cm (1in) from the fruit.

Aubergines

Sweet corn (*Zea mays*)

Sweet corn is an annual that grows to at least 75cm–1.7m (2½–5½ft) and has an average spread of 45cm (18in). Male tassels and female ears (cobs) are borne on the same plant. The cobs are golden, white, or bicoloured white and yellow, and cooked or eaten raw when young. New, "supersweet" (sugar-enhanced) cultivars are available.

Sweet corn needs a long growing season of 70–110 frost-free days after planting. It needs temperatures of 16–35°C (61–95°F), but pollination is poor in hot, dry conditions; in warm climates, grow in an open site. In cool climates, grow early-maturing cultivars in a frost-free, sheltered site. Sweet corn is shallow-rooting and grows on a wide range of fertile, well-drained soils with medium nitrogen (see p.504).

SWEET CORN PLANTED IN A BLOCK

Male and female flowers are carried on the same plant. The male flowers (inset, top), which release pollen, are produced in tassels up to 40cm (16in) in length at the tip of the plant. The female flowers (inset, bottom) are silky strands under which each cob forms. The strands are sticky to collect pollen. The female flowers are wind-pollinated so plant in a block rather than a row to ensure good pollination.

SWEET CORN TO TRY

'Golden Bantam'
'Sundance' F1

Supersweet
'Earlibird' F1
'Northern Extra Sweet'
'Ovation'

Extra tender sweet
'Lark' F1
'Swallow' F1
'Swift' F1

Sowing and planting

Seed does not germinate at soil temperatures below 10°C (50°F). In warm climates, sow seed in spring *in situ*, 2.5cm (1in) deep and 7cm (3in) apart, thinning to the correct spacing after germination. Seed may be sown through plastic mulches. In cool climates sow indoors in modules and plant out seedlings when the soil temperature reaches 13°C (55°F), or sow *in situ* after all risk of frost has passed; cover with fleece to keep warm and protect from birds and frit fly. In wet soils, use treated seed that will not rot.

To ensure good pollination and full cobs, plant corn in blocks of at least four plants each way. The average spacing is 30cm (12in) apart; short cultivars may be closer, tall ones further apart. In cool climates, cover

with floating mulches or cloches after sowing or planting, removing them at the five-leaf stage. Fine-net floating mulches will protect the plants against frit flies. Supersweet types need higher temperatures to germinate and grow and should not be planted with other types as the sweetness will be lost if they are cross-pollinated. Mini-corn is obtained by planting early cultivars about 15cm (6in) apart and harvesting them when the cobs are about 7cm (3in) long.

Routine cultivation

Hoe shallowly when weeding to avoid damaging the roots. In exposed areas, earth up the stems to 13cm (5in) to increase stability. Watering is not necessary, except

in very dry conditions, until flowering starts and again later when the grains are swelling. Water at a rate of 22 litres/sq m (5 gallons/sq yd).

Pests and diseases

Mice (p.662), slugs (p.644), and birds are the most serious pests. The maggots of frit flies may attack the bases of seedlings, causing the growing points to wilt and die. Raise seedlings in pots, or under fine nets, until past the five- or six-leaf stage.

Harvesting and storing

Plants normally produce one or two cobs. Pick just before required, as the sweetness soon deteriorates; supersweet types retain their flavour for about a week. Sweet corn freezes well.

TESTING SWEET CORN FOR RIPENESS

Once the silks have turned brown, peel back the sheath and press into a kernel with a fingernail. If the liquid that appears is milky, the cob is ripe; if watery, it is underripe, and if doughy, overripe.

Podded vegetables

French beans
Scarlet runner beans
Dried French beans
Peas
Mangetout peas
Haricots
Broad beans
French beans
Sugar peas
Peanuts
Shelled peanuts

Vegetables in this group all produce seed pods. Some are grown for these pods, which may be cooked and eaten whole, while others are grown for the seeds, which are extracted and cooked or eaten raw. The seeds of some may be dried; most may be frozen. Several of the plants are decorative as well as functional and may be used for screening, or trained over arches. Podded vegetables often need sheltered conditions at specific temperatures for pollination; they generally require a rich soil to which organic matter has been added before planting.

Okra (*Abelmoschus esculentus*)

These tender, annual plants are also known as ladies' fingers. The fast-maturing cultivars may grow to 1m (3ft) with a spread of 30–40cm (12–16in); the slow-maturing ones (mainly grown in tropical areas)

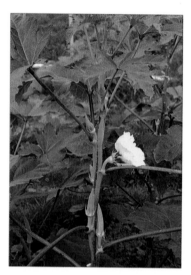

Okra

are up to 2m (6ft) tall. The pods are 10–25cm (4–10in) long and white, green, or red. Recommended cultivars include 'Clemson Spineless', 'Pure Luck', and 'Penta Green'. Immature pods are eaten as a cooked vegetable; mature pods may also be dried and powdered for use as a flavouring.

In warm-temperate and subtropical areas, plants may be grown in the open only in very favourable, sunny conditions. Seeds germinate only at soil temperatures of at least 16°C (61°F); after germination a stable temperature in the range 20–30°C (68–86°F) is needed for optimum growth. Most modern cultivars are daylength-neutral (see "Daylength", p.495). Plant in well-drained soil, adding plenty of organic material. Okra plants need low to medium nitrogen levels (see p.504).

Sowing and planting

Soak seed for 24 hours before sowing to aid germination. When soil temperatures reach 16–18°C (61–64°F), sow seed *in situ* in rows 60–70cm (24–28in) apart, leaving 20–30cm (8–12in) between plants. In warm-temperate areas, sow in spring under cover at 20°C (68°F) or above, in trays or 6–9cm (3–3½in) pots. When seedlings are 10–15cm (4–6in) tall, harden off and transplant to well-prepared beds, spacing as above.

Routine cultivation

Stake tall plants and protect from strong winds with plastic covers or screens, if necessary. Remove all weeds, water regularly, and apply an organic mulch to retain soil moisture. Pinch out the growing points when seedlings are about 60cm (24in) tall to promote branching. Apply a general-purpose fertilizer or liquid feed at two-week intervals to encourage rapid growth. Do not overfeed with nitrogen since this delays flowering.

Pests and diseases

Plants are likely to be damaged by aphids (p.646), caterpillars (p.645), and powdery mildew (p.646); white-flies (p.646), glasshouse red spider mite (p.646), thrips (p.647), and fungal leaf spots (p.648) may also be troublesome under cover.

Growing under cover

Seedlings may be transplanted into well-prepared beds in the green-house or in growing bags, spacing the young plants at least 40cm (16in) apart. Maintain a temperature above 20°C (68°F) and a humidity of over 70 per cent. Spray the plants as necessary to control pests and diseases, and apply an organic liquid feed or a general-purpose fertilizer.

Harvesting and storing

Four to six pods per plant are produced. They may be harvested approximately 8–11 weeks after sowing, depending on the cultivar. Sever the pods from the plant with a sharp knife when they are bright green; overmature pods may become fibrous. Pods may be stored in perforated bags at 7–10°C (45–50°F) for up to ten days.

Peanuts (*Arachis hypogaea*)

These tender, annual plants, also known as groundnuts and monkey-nuts, originate from South America. Plants grow to a height of 60cm (24in) with a spread of 30cm (12in) for the more upright Spanish-Valencia types, or up to 1m (3ft) for the less common, prostrate, Virginia types. The Spanish-Valencia types are often divided into Spanish, with two seeds per pod and light brown seed coats, and Valencia, with up to four seeds per pod and dark red seed coats. The stems of the Valencia types are usually thicker than those of the Spanish. The Virginia forms have two seeds per pod, with dark brown seed coats.

The fertilized flowers produce shoot-like structures that penetrate the soil where the immature fruits develop into peanuts. Removed from their pods, the nuts are eaten fresh or roasted, or used in cooking.

Peanuts are tropical plants that need average temperatures of about 20–30°C (68–86°F) and a relative humidity of 80 per cent, although some forms will grow well in the warmer subtropics. A frost-free site is essential. Rainfall at flowering time may adversely affect pollination.

Peanut cultivars are generally daylength-neutral (see "Daylength", p.495). Sandy, well-drained loams with a pH of 5.5–6.5 containing calcium, potassium, and phosphorus are preferable. The plants also need low nitrogen levels (see p.504).

Sowing and planting

Sow seeds *in situ*, removed from their shells, in spring or when soil temperatures exceed 16°C (61°F). In temperate climates, sow under cover in trays or 9cm (3½in) pots, keeping temperatures over 20°C (68°F).

When the seedlings are 10–15cm (4–6in) tall, harden them off and transplant them to well-prepared beds. Whether directly sown or transplanted, the plants should be spaced 15–30cm (6–12in) apart with about 60–70cm (24–28in) between the rows. Protect them with cloches or polytunnels where necessary.

Routine cultivation

Earth up around the roots when the plants are 15cm (6in) tall, and hoe regularly to encourage the fertilized flowers to penetrate the soil. Remove all weeds, and water well in dry periods. Do not water plants during the flowering period, however, as this may lead to poor pollination.

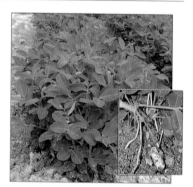

Spanish-Valencia peanut plant

Pests and diseases

Plants may be affected by aphids (p.646), thrips (p.647), and caterpillars (p.645); under cover, glasshouse red spider mite (p.646) and whiteflies (p.646) may be a problem. Fungal leaf spots (p.648), root and stem rots (see "Seedling blight", p.654), and rosette virus (see "Viruses", p.649) may also be troublesome.

Growing under cover
Sow seed as described above. Transplant the seedlings when they are 10–15cm (4–6in) tall into growing bags, or well-prepared greenhouse beds. Maintain a temperature over 20°C (68°F), reducing humidity at flowering time to aid pollination.

Harvesting and storing
Harvest the pods 16–20 weeks after sowing for the upright types, and three to four weeks after this for the prostrate types. Virginia types, which produce two seeds per pod, may require up to 25 weeks from sowing to harvesting. Assess the stage of maturity by uprooting one or two pods; they keep for several months. Dry the pods in the sun, then remove the peanuts for storing in cool, dry conditions.

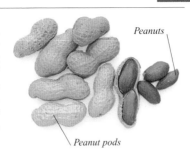
Peanuts

Peanut pods

Dolichos beans (*Lablab purpureus*)

These dwarf or climbing, short-lived, tender perennials are also known as hyacinth beans and lablab beans. Both long- and short-podded cultivars occur. Climbing forms may grow to 4–6m (12–20ft), while dwarf forms reach 1m (3ft) with a spread of about 60cm (2ft). The pods range in colour from green to purple. Young pods and mature seeds are eaten cooked; the latter should be cooked thoroughly. Young seedlings, raised in the dark, may be used as bean sprouts.

Dolichos beans may be grown in subtropical and warm-temperate regions in very favoured, sunny sites with protection. The plants require a temperature of 18–30°C (64–86°F) with a minimum humidity of 70 per cent; cool weather may adversely affect pollination as it discourages pollinating insects. Daylength-neutral cultivars are available (see "Daylength", p.495).

Most soils are suitable for dolichos beans, particularly those containing plenty of organic matter; good drainage is essential. Some cultivars respond well to applications of superphosphate. Dolichos beans need low nitrogen levels (see p.504).

Dolichos beans

Sowing and planting
Sow *in situ*, in spring or at other times of the year if temperatures are high enough. In temperate areas, sow seeds under cover, in trays, or in 6–9cm (3–3½in) pots at a depth of 2.5cm (1in). When the seedlings are 10–15cm (4–6in) tall, harden them off and transplant into well-prepared beds. Space climbing cultivars 30–45cm (12–18in) apart, allowing 75–100cm (30–36in) between rows; space dwarf cultivars 30–40cm (12–16in) apart with a distance of 45–60cm (18–24in) between rows.

Routine cultivation
Climbing cultivars should be supported by stakes, at least 2m (6ft) high. Water the plants regularly, and mulch to conserve moisture. Protect as necessary with plastic screens or covers and remove all weeds. Apply a general-purpose fertilizer or liquid feed every 10–14 days until flowering. Pinch out the growing points of dwarf cultivars to encourage them to develop a bushy habit; the shoots of climbing cultivars should be trained or tied in to the stakes.

Pests and diseases
Aphids (p.646), thrips (p.647), caterpillars (p.645), root-knot eelworms (p.660), powdery mildew (p.646), fungal leaf spots (p.648), and some viruses (p.649) may be troublesome; under cover, whiteflies (p.646) and glasshouse red spider mite (p.646) may also affect plants.

Growing under cover
Transplant seedlings to growing bags or well-prepared beds in the greenhouse, spacing the plants at least 50–60cm (20–24in) apart. Alternatively, seedlings may be grown on in 21–25cm (8–10in) pots (two plants may be grown in the larger pots). Maintain a temperature of at least 20°C (68°F) and reduce humidity by providing adequate ventilation at flowering time to improve pollination. Dolichos beans may also be propagated from softwood cuttings (see PRINCIPLES OF PROPAGATION, "Stem cuttings", p.632), taken early in the growing season, which root readily in high humidity.

Harvesting and storing
Harvest the young pods six to nine weeks after sowing, when they are fully grown but before the seeds develop; the mature pods containing seeds may be harvested after 10–14 weeks before they become fibrous. If the plants remain healthy after the first crop, cut back the main stems to about half their length to encourage a second crop. Dolichos beans freeze well.

Scarlet runner beans (*Phaseolus coccineus*)

Scarlet runner beans

These perennial climbers are grown as annuals in temperate and cool climates. Plants grow to over 3m (10ft) tall, with a spread of about 30cm (12in); some naturally dwarf cultivars form bushes about 38cm (15in) tall. They have pink, red, white, or bicoloured flowers.

The flat pods, over 25cm (10in) long and up to 2cm (¾in) wide, are eaten cooked; immature seeds and mature, dried seeds may also be cooked. With some cultivars, it may be necessary to remove the "strings" along the pods.

Scarlet runner beans are a temperate or cool-season crop that does not withstand frost. Plants need a growing season of about 100 frost-free days and they grow best at 14–29°C (57–84°F). At higher temperatures, especially if combined with high humidity, the pods may not set unless the plants are in light shade. In cool climates, choose a sheltered situation to encourage pollinating insects. Plants are deep-rooting and need fertile, moisture-retentive soil. Prepare the soil by digging a trench one spade deep and 60cm (24in) wide, working in well-rotted straw or compost. Runner bean crops should be rotated (see p.498), and need low nitrogen levels (see p.504).

Sowing and planting
Before planting climbing types, erect a strong support system of poles or canes over 2.5m (8ft) long, tied to a horizontal pole or to each other to form a "wigwam". Commercial supports or towers are available.

SCARLET RUNNER BEANS TO TRY

Standard
'Celebration'
'Enorma'
'Liberty'
'White Emergo'
'Wisley Magic'

Dwarf
'Gulliver'
'Pickwick'

Stringless
'Lady Di'
'Polestar'
'Red Rum'
'White Lady'

Plants may also be twisted up nylon netting, strings, or wires pegged to the ground; do not use plastic-coated netting since the plants do not cling onto it. Sow seed *in situ* 5cm (2in) deep, after all risk of frost has passed bearing in mind that a minimum soil temperature of 12°C (54°F) is needed for germination. In cool areas, sow seed indoors in seed trays and harden off seedlings before transplanting outside. Grow climbers in double rows 60cm (2ft) apart or in circular "wigwams", spacing the plants 15cm (6in) apart. Bush forms may be grown in groups at the same spacing. Mulch well to retain moisture after germination or planting out.

BEAN SUPPORTS

There are various ways to support climbing beans, depending on the space available. Mature plants will obscure the support structure beneath.

Crossed cane row

Two rows of 2.5m (8ft) canes, crossed and secured to a horizontal bar

Wigwam

2.5m (8ft) canes tied near the top

Netting support

10cm (4in) square nylon net fixed to a pole frame

Runner beans on a wigwam

Routine cultivation
Protect seedlings with cloches or floating mulches. To convert climbing forms into bushes, nip out the growing shoots when plants are 23cm (9in) high. Such plants crop earlier but have lower yields.

Watering is especially important when the flower buds appear and pods are setting (see "Critical watering periods", p.502). At these times water at a rate of 5–11 litres/sq m (1–2 gallons/sq yd) twice a week.

Pests and diseases
Slugs (p.644) in the early stages, pollen beetles (p.657), bean seed fly (p.666), anthracnose (p.666), foot and root rots (p.654), halo blight (see "Bacterial leaf spots and blotches", p.648), seedling blight (p.654), and viruses (p.649) may be troublesome.

Harvesting and storing
Harvest after 13–17 weeks. Pick pods when they are at least 17cm (7in) long and tender; continue picking at frequent intervals to prolong the cropping period. Runner beans freeze well.

Lima beans (*Phaseolus lunatus*)

Dwarf Lima beans

Also known as butter beans, lima beans are tender annuals and short-lived perennials. Some forms of lima bean climb while others are dwarf and branching. Climbing cultivars may grow to a height of 3–4m (9–12ft), dwarf cultivars to 90cm (3ft), spreading to 40–45cm (16–18in). The young pods and mature seeds are eaten cooked; the seeds may also be dried or germinated in the dark for use as bean sprouts.

The lima bean is a tropical plant that needs a minimum temperature of 18°C (64°F) for germination. Temperatures above 30°C (86°F) may adversely affect pollen formation. In subtropical and warm-temperate areas, growing in the open is possible only in full sun, using plastic screens or covers for protection until the plants are fully established.

Small-seeded cultivars flower only in short daylengths of about 12 hours but the large-seeded cultivars are normally daylength-neutral (see "Daylength", p.495). Most cultivars thrive in a wide range of soil types, but a sandy, well-drained loam with a pH of 6–7 is preferable. Lima beans require low to medium nitrogen levels (see p.504). The procedures for sowing, planting, routine cultivation, and growing under cover are as described for dolichos beans (p.531).

Pests and diseases
Aphids (p.646), thrips (p.647), caterpillars (p.645), whiteflies (p.646), and glasshouse red spider mite (p.646) may be troublesome. Diseases include powdery mildew (p.646), fungal leaf spots (p.648), and some viruses (p.649).

LIMA BEANS TO TRY

Climbing
'Christmas Pole'
'King of Garden Pole'

Dwarf
'Fordhook 242'
'Henderson' (bush)

Harvesting and storing
Harvest whole pods young, mature seeds about 12–16 weeks after sowing. Store both above 4°C (39°F) at 90 per cent humidity for up to two weeks. Lima beans may be frozen.

French beans (*Phaseolus vulgaris*)

These tender annuals have climbing, dwarf, and intermediate forms. They are also known as kidney, snap, or string beans. Height and spread are as for scarlet runner beans (see p.531). The pods are 7–20cm (3–8in) long. They may be round, flat, or curved in shape; diameter ranges from pencil-thickness (for the filet types) to about 2cm (¾in); they may be green, yellow, purple, red, or green flecked with purple. The yellow, waxpod types have a waxy texture and excellent flavour. Types vary in the stringiness of the pods; stringless cultivars are available. Never eat the pods raw as the seeds inside contain toxins that must first be destroyed by cooking. Use the immature pods, the half-ripe, shelled bean seeds (flageolets), or the dried, mature bean seeds (haricots). Special cultivars are grown for drying.

French beans grow in similar conditions to scarlet runner beans (see p.531) but seeds will only germinate at a minimum temperature of 12°C (54°F). The optimum growing temperature is 16–30°C (61–86°F); seedlings do not tolerate temperatures below 10°C (50°F). The plants are self-pollinated, and grow best in rich, light soil. Good drainage is essential to prevent root rot. Work plenty of well-rotted compost or manure into the soil before planting, and always rotate crops (see p.498). Seed may be dressed with the appropriate rhizome inoculant, or rhizobium granules may be applied to the soil at planting; this treatment increases current and subsequent yields by encouraging the formation of nitrogen-fixing root nodules. French beans usually need low nitrogen levels (see p.504).

PRE-GERMINATING FRENCH BEANS

1 *Spread the beans out on moist tissue paper in a tray without drainage holes. Keep damp, at a minimum of 12°C (54°F).*

2 *When the delicate shoots begin to appear and before they turn green, carefully pot up the beans or sow them directly in their final position outside.*

Sowing and planting
Seed may be pre-germinated before sowing. Sow seed or pre-germinated seeds 4cm (1½in) deep *in situ* or indoors as for scarlet runner beans (see p.531), and make successive sowings throughout the summer. If necessary, warm the soil beforehand with cloches or an inorganic sheet mulch. Space climbing forms as for scarlet runner beans. Dwarf types may be grown at an equidistant spacing of 22cm (9in) in staggered rows for the highest yields. In cold climates, protect after planting with cloches or floating mulches.

Routine cultivation
Support climbing types as for scarlet runner beans; use twigs to support intermediate types. Stems may also be earthed up to keep plants upright. Mulch and do not allow plants to dry out completely; extra watering at a rate of 22 litres/sq m (5 gallons/sq yd) may be necessary in dry conditions at flowering time.

Pests and diseases
Slugs (p.644), bean seed fly (p.666), root aphids and black bean aphid (see "Aphids", p.646), anthracnose (p.666), foot and root rots (p.654), halo blight (see "Bacterial leaf spots and blotches", p.648), and viruses (p.649) may affect French beans.

Growing under cover
In cold climates, dwarf French beans may be grown to maturity in a greenhouse or polytunnel, or under cloches. Space plants as in the open.

EARTHING UP

Plant out the beans 15cm (6in) apart, and once they have formed several pairs of leaves earth them up to support them.

Harvesting and storing
Harvest after 7–13 weeks. Pick young beans regularly to use fresh or freeze. For shelled beans, see below; store in an airtight jar.

DRYING FRENCH BEANS

In damp climates, pull up plants and hang them by the roots in a dry, frost-free place. Once dried, remove the pods and extract the beans.

FRENCH BEANS TO TRY
Dwarf
'Cantare'
'Cropper Teepee' (green roundpod)
'Delinel' (filet)
'Goldukat' (wax podded)
'Purple Queen' (purple podded)
'Purple Teepee' (purple podded)
'Safari'
'Sonesta' F1 (wax podded)
'Sprite'
'Tendergreen' (stringless)

For drying
'Barletta Lingua-di-Fuoco'
'Canadian Wonder'
'Dutch Brown'

Climbing
'Cobra' (round)
'Eva' (round)
'Hunter' (flat)
'Kingston Gold'
'Sultana'

Peas (*Pisum sativum*)

Peas are annuals that grow from 45cm (18in) to over 2m (6ft) tall, with an average spread of 23cm (9in). Plants cling to supports with tendrils; modern semi-leafless types are almost self-supporting. Peas are grouped according to the time taken to mature. The early groups are shorter and lower yielding than later types. Pods are usually green but there are purple-podded cultivars.

Shelling-pea types are grown for the fresh peas in the pods; some may be dried. Petit pois are small, fine-flavoured peas. Wrinkle-seeded cultivars are usually sweeter but less hardy than the smooth-seeded types. Edible-podded types (mangetout, sugar peas) are eaten before the peas mature. Mangetout types are flat-podded and eaten young, while the round-podded sugar types are used when semi-mature. Peas and pods are usually cooked, but may be eaten raw.

Semi-leafless peas

Peas are a cool-season crop, growing best at 13–18°C (55–64°F). The flowers and pods cannot withstand frost. Grow peas in an open site, in reasonably fertile, moisture-retentive, well-drained soil; they will not tolerate cold, wet soil, or drought. Work plenty of well-rotted compost or manure into the soil before planting. Peas should be rotated (see p.498). The plants have nitrogen-fixing nodules on their roots, and do not require any extra nitrogen during growth.

Sowing and planting
Make the first outdoor sowings as soon as the soil is about 10°C (50°F). Germination is much slower at lower temperatures. The first sowings may be made under cloches or floating mulches using dwarf cultivars. For successive crops, either sow seeds at 14-day intervals or sow cultivars from different groups at the same time so that they mature in succession. Avoid midsummer sowings in warm areas, as high temperatures also affect germination. If sowing an early type late, allow about ten weeks before frost is expected for the pods to ripen. Where winters are mild,

sow hardy, early-maturing cultivars in late autumn to overwinter. There is a high risk of loss to mice, but surviving plants crop very early.

Sow the seed 3cm (1¼in) deep in patches so that plants can support each other, spacing individual seeds 5–7cm (2–3in) apart. Alternatively, make a flat-bottomed drill up to 23cm (9in) wide, spacing seeds 5cm (2in) apart each way (see "Wide drills", p.500). The drills should be 60–90cm (24–36in) apart, using wider spacing for tall cultivars. Seed may also be sown in double rows 23cm (9in) apart, spacing seeds 1cm (½in) apart.

Routine cultivation
Protect seedlings against birds with horizontal netting as pea guards. Once tendrils have developed, remove the pea guards and erect supports: use wire netting, pea nets, or brushwood on either side of a drill. Semi-leafless

and dwarf types need less support. When the peas have several leaves, mulch them to keep the roots cool.

Once plants are flowering and forming pods, water every week (unless rainfall is high) at a rate of 22 litres/sq m (5 gallons/sq yd).

Pests and diseases
Jays (p.659), wood pigeon (p.645), pea moth (p.659), and pea thrips (p.659) are the most common pests; mice (p.662) may also be troublesome since they eat seeds. Damping off (p.660), foot and root rots (p.654), seedling blight (p.654), and *Fusarium* wilt (p.654) are occasional problems.

Growing under cover
Early spring and late autumn sowings may be made under cover; grow dwarf peas to maturity under cloches for early or overwintering crops.

Harvesting and storing
Harvest early types 11–12 weeks after sowing, and maincrop peas after 13–14 weeks. Pick edible-podded

SUPPORTING PEAS

When seedlings have developed tendrils, push peasticks into the ground, as upright as possible, all around the outside of the patch (above). As the peas grow, the tendrils wrap around the peasticks and the peas grow up them (right).

types when the immature peas are just forming inside the pods, shelling peas and sugar snap types when the pods have swollen. Edible-podded

types may be left to mature and shelled normally. All may be frozen. For storing pods on plants, see *Drying French Beans*, p.533.

PEAS TO TRY

Early
'Douce Provence'
'Early Onward'
'Feltham First'
'Kelvedon Wonder'
'Misty'

Maincrop
'Ambassador'
'Cavalier'
'Hurst Greenshaft'
'Onward'
'Rondo'
'Show Perfection'

Sugar and mangetout peas
'Delikata' m
'Delikett' s
'Norli' m
'Sugar Ann' s
'Sugar Lord' s

Key
m *mangetout*
s *sugarsnap*

Broad beans (*Vicia faba*)

These annual plants are also known as fava beans. They range in height from 30cm (12in) for dwarf cultivars to about 1.5m (5ft), with an average spread of 45cm (18in). Broad beans are grouped according to the time they take to mature. The broad pods are up to 2.5cm (1in) wide and 7–15cm (3–6in) long, with green, white, or pinkish-red seeds 2–2.5cm (¾–1in) long. The immature bean seeds, as well as the young pods and leafy shoot tips, may be cooked. The shelled beans freeze well.

Broad beans are a cool-season crop, growing satisfactorily only at temperatures below about 15°C (59°F). Some cultivars are very hardy, the immature plants surviving -10°C (14°F) on well-drained soil. Some that are adapted to higher temperatures have recently been bred. Grow spring and early summer sowings in an open site, and autumn sowings for overwintering in a sheltered site, in reasonably fertile, well-manured soil. Rotate broad bean crops (see p.498). The plants need low nitrogen levels (see p.504) because their root nodules fix atmospheric nitrogen.

Sowing and planting
Sow seed *in situ* in spring and early summer as soon as the ground is workable. Seed germinates at fairly low temperatures. For an early crop, sow seed in late autumn to early

Dwarf broad beans

winter of the previous year – the plants need only be 2.5cm (1in) high before winter. In very cold areas seed may be sown indoors in winter and transplanted outside in spring after the risk of frost has passed.

Sow seed about 4cm (1½in) deep, spaced about 23cm (9in) apart each way. Grow either in double rows, with 90cm (3ft) between the pairs of rows, or evenly spaced in blocks across a bed. The taller cultivars may be supported with strands of wire attached to strong canes or poles placed around the rows or blocks of plants. If necessary, dwarf cultivars may be supported with twigs to keep their pods clear of the ground. Over-wintering crops and those sown

in early spring may be protected with cloches or floating mulches in the early stages of growth.

Routine cultivation
Do not allow the plants to dry out; water as for French beans (see pp.532–533). Once flowering starts, pinch out the growing tips in order to encourage pods to form and to combat blackfly. Earth up overwintering plants to protect them.

Pests and diseases
Mice (p.662), jays (p.659), wood pigeon (p.645), tropical root rots

PINCHING OUT

When the beans are in full flower, pinch out the growing tip of each plant. This will remove any blackfly and concentrate the plant's energy into producing beans.

(p.661), blackfly (see "Aphids", p.646), chocolate spot (p.649), and foot and root rots (p.654) may affect broad beans.

Harvesting and storing
Harvest broad beans that were sown in spring after 12–16 weeks, and those sown in autumn after 28–35 weeks. Pick them while the pods are plump with the swelling beans and before they become leathery. The beans may be frozen, or dried at the end of the season for use during the winter months as for French beans (see pp.532–533).

BROAD BEANS TO TRY

Dwarf
'The Sutton'

Early
'Aquadulce
  Claudia'
  (autumn sowing)
'Express'
'Witkiem Manita'

Late
'Imperial Green
  Longpod'
'Jubilee Hysor'
'Masterpiece
  Green
  Longpod'
'Medes'

Bulb and stem vegetables

V EGETABLES grown for their bulbs or stems include members of the onion family as well as a varied group of other plants that, with the exception of Florence fennel, are mostly hardy and slow-maturing. Celeriac, kohl rabi, and Florence fennel form swollen stems just above ground level, rather than true bulbs. The onion family should be rotated as one group; for rotation groups for the other vegetables, see p.498. Both asparagus and rhubarb are perennial vegetables that should be planted in permanent beds that have been specially prepared for them.

Garlic
Leeks
Spring onions
Bulb onions
Celery
Florence fennel
Red bulb onions
Asparagus
Pickling onions

Bulb onions (*Allium cepa*)

These are grown as annuals. The bulbs may be rounded, flattened, or have a long, torpedo shape. They normally have brown or yellow skins with white flesh, although some have red skin and pinkish-white flesh; the leaves grow 15–45cm (6–18in) long. Immature and mature bulbs are eaten either raw or cooked. Some cultivars are suitable for storage. The green-leaved thinnings may be used as spring onions (see p.536).

Bulb onions are a cool-season, frost-tolerant crop, growing best at 13–24°C (55–75°F). Cool temperatures are required in the early stages of growth. Cultivars need different daylengths in order for the bulbs to swell; long-day types should be chosen for northerly latitudes, and short-day types for southerly latitudes (see also "Daylength", p.495).

Grow them in an open site, on fertile, medium to light soil that is well drained. Prepare the soil by digging in a good deal of well-rotted manure, preferably the autumn before planting. Do not plant on newly manured ground. A general feed may be worked into the seedbed before sowing. They have low nitrogen requirements (see p.504).

Sowing and planting

Onions may be raised from seed or sets (small bulbs specially grown and harvested immature the previous year). Seed is cheaper but slower to develop; sets are easier to grow but usually only available for certain cultivars. Bulb onions require a long growing season, particularly if large bulbs are required or if they are to be stored.

Sow in spring when the soil is workable, on a firm seedbed, sow-ing seed very thinly 1cm (½in) deep, in rows 23–30cm (9–12in) apart. Thin out the seedlings in stages. For the highest yield of medium-sized onions, space 4cm (1½in) apart; for larger onions, thin seedlings to 5–10cm (2–4in) apart.

To extend the growing season in northern latitudes, start under cover in seed trays or modules at temperatures of 10–15°C (50–59°F) from late winter to early spring. Harden off seedlings at the two-leaf stage and plant out at the appropriate spacing. Modules may also be multi-sown with five seeds per section and each section planted out as a unit, with 25cm (10in) between units (see also *Transplanting Leeks*, p.537).

Certain cultivars may be sown in summer or autumn to overwinter for earlier crops the following year. This is inadvisable where winters are very severe or very wet since seeds may rot before germination. Traditional, summer-sown cultivars are reasonably hardy and may be sown *in situ* in late summer, thinning to 2.5cm (1in) apart in autumn and in stages to the final spacing in spring. Japanese overwintering onions are also suitable for sowing at this time; they are hardier than other bulb onions, but are unsuitable for storage. The precise sowing date for these is critical. Sow during the summer at the recommended date for the area, spacing and thinning as above.

Most sets are planted in the early spring. If using heat-treated sets, consult the suppliers for planting times. Plant at the above spacing in shallow furrows so that the tips protrude just above the soil. Recently introduced sets for planting during autumn may be available.

Routine cultivation

Keep the site weed-free, especially when the onions are young and susceptible to competition from weeds. Onions are fairly shallow-rooted and need little water once established, except in very dry conditions. Over-wintering onions may be given a nitrogenous fertilizer or organic liquid feed if necessary in spring.

Pests and diseases

Onion fly (p.663), bean seed fly (p.666), onion white rot (p.663), downy mildew (p.646), and, in storage, onion neck rot (p.663) are common problems that affect onions.

Harvesting and storing

Spring-sown bulb onions will take 12–18 weeks to mature; summer-sown onions up to 42 weeks. Pull or lift them as needed to use fresh.

For storage, wait until the leaves have died back naturally (do not bend them over by hand), and then carefully uproot all the onions. In

BULB ONIONS TO TRY

Onions for autumn harvesting
'Giant Fen Globe'
'Golden Bear'
'Hi Keeper' F1
'Rijnsburger Robusta'

Red onions (use fresh or store)
'Long Red Florence'
'Mammoth'
'Red Pearl'

Pickling
'Brown Pickling' SY300

Traditional and Japanese overwintering onions
'Express Yellow'
'Reliance'
'Sonic'

Sets for autumn planting
'Centurion' F1
'Sturon'

Exhibition cultivars
'Kelsae'
'Tasco'

sunny conditions, leave them in the sun to dry for about 10 days, either hung in nets or supported off the ground on an upturned seed tray to allow maximum ventilation. In wet conditions, hang them in a greenhouse. The outer skins and leaves must all be thoroughly dry before the bulbs are put into storage.

Handle the bulbs gently since any bruises may encourage storage rots. Do not store onions that are bull-necked; these should always be used first. Store onions either hanging in nets or plaits (see *Storing Strings of Onions*, p.506) or packed carefully in layers in boxes. They must be kept at 0–7°C (32–45°F) and in low humidity (ie below 40 per cent). Average storage life is three to six months, depending on the cultivar.

STORING ONIONS IN A BOX

Prepare onions carefully for storing. Bull-necked onions (those with thick necks above the bulbs, see far right) should be rejected. Be careful not to damage any onions for storing as this encourages rot. Place them in layers in a box and store them in a place that is well ventilated and frost-free.

Spring onions

Traditional European spring onions, or bunching onions, are cultivars of bulb onions suitable for using young when leaves are 15cm (6in) tall, with a whitened shank and tiny bulb. 'White Lisbon' is a widely grown cultivar, but 'Feast' and 'Guardsman' are more mildew-resistant. For climate, soil requirements, and pests and diseases, see "Bulb onions", p.535. Lime acid soil (see p.625).

In spring, sow thinly *in situ*, in rows 10cm (4in) apart, or bands 7cm (3in) wide and 15cm (6in) apart. For continuous crops, sow every three weeks in summer. Overwintering cultivars (eg 'Ramrod' and 'White Lisbon Winter Hardy') may be sown in late summer for an early spring crop; protect in winter with cloches. Water the onions in dry conditions.

THINNING SPRING ONIONS

If densely sown, harvest seedling spring onions to leave the others spaced 2.5cm (1in) apart. Those remaining will continue to grow and may be harvested when required.

Pickling onions

These bulb onion cultivars produce small, white bulbs (also known as mini-onions) in northerly latitudes, and larger bulbs in southerly latitudes. They may be used when they reach about thumb-nail size, either fresh or for pickling. Cultivars include 'Barletta' and 'Paris Silver Skin'. They prefer fertile soil, but tolerate fairly poor soil. For climate, cultivation, and pests and diseases, see "Bulb onions", p.535.

In spring sow seed *in situ*, either broadcast or in bands about 10cm (4in) wide, spacing seeds 1cm (½in) apart. Thin them only if larger onions are required. Harvest them after about eight weeks when the foliage has died back; use them fresh, or dry and store as for bulb onions (see p.535) until required for pickling.

Pickling onions

Shallots (*Allium cepa* Aggregatum Group)

These distinctly flavoured onion-shaped bulbs form clumps of about a dozen bulbs. There are yellow- and red-skinned forms; all may be eaten raw or cooked, and used fresh or after storing. The leaves of young shallots may be used as spring onions. Suitable cultivars are 'Golden Gourmet', 'Jermor', 'Pikant' and 'Santé'.

Climate and soil requirements, routine cultivation, and pests and diseases are as for bulb onions (see p.535). Buy virus-free sets that are ideally about 2cm (¾in) in diameter. Plant in early spring or during winter

in mild areas. Plant as for bulb onion sets (see p.535), spacing the sets about 18cm (7in) apart each way. Each set will develop into a clump, maturing in early summer. For an early crop of green leaves, plant small sets in autumn, spacing them in the ground, or in seed trays under cover about 2.5cm (1in) apart.

Harvest green leaves as needed. For good-sized bulbs, do not pick the leaves; lift the bulbs once the foliage has died down. To store them, dry as for bulb onions (see p.535); good stocks store for up to a year.

PLANTING SHALLOTS

Make a drill 1cm (½in) deep. Push the sets into the drill about 18cm (7in) apart so that the tips show above the soil.

Shallots

European Welsh onions (*Allium fistulosum*)

These onions are very hardy perennials. They have hollow leaves up to 45cm (18in) tall and 1cm (½in) in diameter, growing in clumps of 23cm (9in) diameter on average; the bases of the leaves are thickened at and below ground level. The leaves remain green all year, even at temperatures as low as -10°C (14°F), so they are a useful winter vegetable. The leaves and tiny bulbs may be eaten either raw or cooked.

Climate and soil requirements, cultivation, and pests and diseases are as for bulb onions (see p.535). Sow seed *in situ* in spring or summer in rows about 30cm (12in) apart. Thin the seedlings in stages until they are about 23cm (9in) apart, or propagate by dividing established clumps and carefully replanting the younger, outer sections of the clumps to the above spacing. Leaves may be

Welsh onions

harvested from 24 weeks after sowing; cut individual leaves as required, or pull up part or all of the clump. Established clumps can become very thick and should be divided every two or three years. Welsh onions do not store well.

Oriental bunching onions

These have been developed from European Welsh onions. They are perennials usually grown as annuals or biennials for harvesting at any stage from seedlings to large plants. Mature plants have thickened, white shafts 2.5cm (1in) in diameter and 15cm (6in) high. All parts are edible. There are cultivars for planting and harvesting year-round, and for a wide range of climatic conditions.

For soil requirements, see "Bulb onions" (p.535). Sow seed *in situ* in spring and summer, in rows 30cm (12in) apart. Thin out in stages up to 15cm (6in) apart, depending on the size required. Seed may also be sown in trays and planted out. Sow the hardiest cultivars, such as 'White

Evergreen' or 'Ishikura', in autumn and overwinter to use in early spring. Some cultivars, such as 'Ishikura', may be earthed up several times during growth to obtain long, white shafts. Young leaves may be picked four weeks after sowing.

Oriental bunching onions

Leeks (*Allium porrum*)

These are biennials grown as annuals, reaching 45cm (18in) tall and 15cm (6in) across. The edible part is the sweetly flavoured, thick, white shank that forms below long, blue-green leaves. This may be blanched by earthing it up or by deep planting. Leeks with short, thick shanks are called pot leeks. All types are used cooked, as a vegetable or in soups.

Leeks are a cool-season crop, and grow best below 24°C (75°F), but will tolerate higher temperatures if kept moist. Cultivars range from early and moderately hardy to late and very hardy. Grow in open sites on fertile, moisture-retentive soil, working in plenty of manure or compost and a nitrogenous fertilizer if the soil is low in nitrogen (high levels are needed; see p.504). Do not plant on compacted soils. Leeks must be rotated (see p.498).

Sowing and planting

Leeks need a long growing season; start them as early in the year as possible, sowing in succession. Sow 1cm (½in) deep in an outdoor seedbed for transplanting when 20cm (8in) tall. Alternatively sow *in situ* in rows 30cm (12in) apart. Thin

Leek plants

SOWING IN A MODULE

Fill a module with seed compost to within 1cm (½in) of the top. Sow 4 leek seeds in each module on the surface of the compost. Cover with a thin layer of compost, and water.

or transplant seedlings at the three-leaf stage to 15cm (6in) apart. Use closer spacing if smaller leeks are preferred. For well-blanched stems, make holes 15–20cm (6–8in) deep with a dibber and drop a seedling in each, making sure that the roots reach the soil at the base. Water gently, then allow soil to fall in around the plants as they grow. Leeks may also be planted on the flat and blanched by hoeing up soil around the stems, 5cm (2in) at a time, as they grow.

To extend the growing season, sow under cover as for bulb onions (see p.535). Leeks respond well to being multi-sown in modules with up to four seeds per cell. Plant out the groups of seedlings at an even spacing of 23cm (9in).

Routine cultivation

Water thoroughly until the leeks are well established, and thereafter only in exceptionally dry conditions. Keep beds weed-free. Mulch to retain soil moisture if necessary.

Pests and diseases

Stem and bulb eelworms (see "Eelworms", p.652), onion fly (p.663), rusts (p.648), and onion white rot (p.663) may be troublesome.

TRANSPLANTING LEEKS

Each section of a module may be planted out as a whole; plant the clumps 23cm (9in) apart.

SINGLE SEEDLINGS

Leeks sown outdoors may be transplanted to their final position in holes 15–20cm (6–8in) deep and 10–15cm (4–6in) apart.

Harvesting and storing

Leeks may be harvested 16–20 weeks after sowing but can stand for many months. Lift them as required from summer onwards; the hardy cultivars may be lifted throughout

HEELING IN LEEKS

To store outdoors, lift the leeks and lean them against one side of a "V"-shaped trench. Cover the roots and white stems with soil and firm lightly. Lift and use as required.

winter into spring, except in very severe climates. Leeks do not store well out of the ground. If the site they occupy is required, prolong the season by digging them up and heeling them in elsewhere.

LEEKS TO TRY

'Autumn Mammoth – Argenta' l
'Autumn Mammoth – Goliath' e, m, l
'Jolant' e
'Kayak' l
'Longbow' m, l
'Mammoth Blanch' e, m
'Oarsman' F1 l
'Porvite' e
'Swiss Giant – Pancho' e
'Toledo' m
'Welsh Seedling' (for exhibition)

Key
e *early*
m *mid-season*
l *late*

Garlic (*Allium sativum*)

Biennials grown as annuals, garlic plants grow up to 60cm (2ft) tall with a spread of about 15cm (6in). Each produces an underground bulb up to 5cm (2in) in diameter. There are pink- and white-skinned forms and many selections are available that are adapted to different climatic zones. Suitable garlic cultivars include 'Germidour', 'Purple Wight', 'Solent White', 'Wight Cristo' and 'Elephant' (not true garlic). The strongly

flavoured cloves, used for seasoning, may be eaten both cooked and raw, and are either used fresh or may be stored for a year-round supply.

Garlic tolerates a wide range of climates, but needs a period of one to two months at about 0–10°C (32–50°F) in winter. Use those recommended for your area. Garlic grows best in an open, sunny position on light soil that does not have to be very fertile, so do not grow

it on freshly manured ground. Good drainage is vital. Garlic needs very low levels of nitrogen (see p.504).

Sowing and planting

For planting, split off individual cloves at least 1cm (½in) in diameter from a mature bulb. Always use healthy, virus-free stock. To produce large bulbs, garlic needs a long growing season, so wherever possible plant cloves in the autumn.

In very cold areas and on heavy soils, delay planting until the early spring, or plant the cloves in modules in winter, one per section. Then place the modules in a sheltered position outdoors to provide them with the necessary cold period. Plant them out in the ground after they have started to sprout in spring.

Plant the cloves upright with the flat base-plates downwards, at about twice their own depth. Space them

PLANTING GARLIC CLOVES IN MODULES

Plant one clove 2.5cm (1in) deep in each section of a module. Cover the cloves with more compost.

about 18cm (7in) apart each way or 10cm (4in) apart in rows 30cm (12in) apart. The bulbs tend to push themselves upwards as they grow.

Routine cultivation

Little attention is required during growth other than keeping the beds free of weeds. For pests and diseases that may affect garlic, see "Bulb onions", p.535.

Harvesting and storing

Garlic takes between 16 and 36 weeks to mature, depending on the variant and when it has been planted.

Uproot the plants as soon as the leaves have started to fade so that the bulbs do not resprout; if they are allowed to resprout they are much more likely to rot when stored.

Dry them thoroughly after lifting as for bulb onions (see p.535). Handle the bulbs very carefully when preparing them for storage to avoid bruising. Store the bulbs hanging in bunches or plaits made with the dried leaves or place them loose on trays kept in dry conditions at 5–10°C (41–50°F). Garlic may be stored for up to 10 months, depending on the variant and storage conditions.

STORING GARLIC

After harvesting the garlic, tie the leaves loosely together with raffia or plait them. Then hang each bunch in a cool, dry place.

Celery (*Apium graveolens*)

A biennial plant, celery grows to 30–60cm (12–24in) tall, with a spread of 30cm (12in). Traditional trench celery has large, white, pink, or red stems that are blanched before use. Self-blanching types have creamy-yellow stems that may be partially blanched. There are green-stemmed types, and intermediates are also available. Celery stalks are eaten raw or cooked and the leaves used as a seasoning or garnish.

As a temperate-climate crop, celery grows best at 15–21°C (59–70°F). Depending on the cultivar and conditions, it tolerates light or moderate frost; trench cultivars with red stems are hardiest. Some have improved resistance to bolting. Grow celery in an open site in fertile, moisture-retentive, but well-drained soil; lime acid soil (see p.625). Rotate celery (see p.498), but do not plant it near parsnips since both are susceptible to celery fly. Dig plenty of well-rotted organic matter into the soil before planting. For trench

Celery seedlings in a block

celery, prepare a trench 38cm (15in) wide and 30cm (12in) deep in autumn before planting; work in manure or compost, and replace the soil to ground level. Celery needs high nitrogen levels (see p.504).

Sowing and planting

Sow in spring *in situ* after all risk of frost is past, or indoors in seed trays or modules at 15°C (59°F) no more than 10 weeks before the last expected frost. Use seed treated with a

fungicide to avoid celery leaf spot. Sprinkle it onto the compost or cover it shallowly as light is needed for germination. Do not sow too early; plants may bolt if the temperature falls below 10°C (50°F).

Thin out seedlings with four to six true leaves; plant out indoor-sown seedlings after all risk of frost is past. Reject any with blistered leaves. Plant self-blanching types 23cm (9in) apart in blocks to increase natural blanching. Young plants may be covered with cloches or floating films which should be removed after a month. Plant trench celery seedlings 38cm (15in) apart in single rows. They may be planted in trenches, or on the flat.

Routine cultivation

Celery requires steady growth, with no checks from water shortage or sudden drops in temperature. Apply a nitrogenous fertilizer or organic liquid feed about one month after planting. Once the plants are established, water them weekly at a rate of 22 litres/sq m (5 gallons/sq yd).

To sweeten self-blanching types, tuck a thick layer of loose straw around the plants when they are 20cm (8in) tall. To blanch celery in a trench, tie the stems loosely together with soft string and fill in the trench gradually, earthing up the stems as they grow. If planted on the flat, wrap purpose-made collars or 23cm (9in) strips of heavy, light-proof paper around the stems when the plants are 30cm (12in) tall. To extend the blanched area, add a second collar three weeks later. In winter, cover trench celery with straw or bracken to protect against frost.

Pests and diseases

Slugs (p.644), celery fly (see "Leaf miners", p.647), carrot fly (p.660), boron deficiency (p.654), fungal leaf

CELERY TO TRY

Self-blanching
'Galaxy'
'Golden'
'Loretta'
'Victoria' F1

Trench
'Giant Pink'
'Ideal'

Green
'Hopkins Fenlander'
'Tango' F1

LIFTING CELERY

Lift self-blanching celery plants before the first frosts. Clear the straw from around the stem and use a fork to uproot the whole plant.

spots (p.648), and violet root rot (p.661) are the most common pests and diseases.

Harvesting and storing

Harvest self-blanching and green celery 11–16 weeks after planting and trench celery in late autumn. Cut the stalks before they become pithy. Before frost threatens, lift and store the remaining plants in high humidity in a cool, frost-free place. They will keep for several weeks.

BLANCHING CELERY

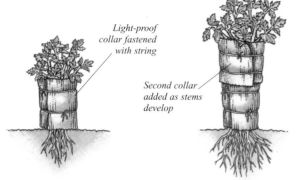

Light-proof collar fastened with string

Second collar added as stems develop

1 *When the celery is about 30cm (12in) tall, wrap the stems loosely with light-proof paper so that the leaves are still exposed to the light.*

2 *As the stems continue to grow, a second collar may be added to blanch the new growth.*

Celeriac (*Apium graveolens* var. *rapaceum*)

This is a biennial plant that grows about 30cm (12in) high with a spread of 38cm (15in). The swollen "bulb" at the stem base is cooked and also grated raw in salads. The leaves are used for seasoning and garnishing.

Celeriac is a cool-temperate crop, withstanding temperatures of -10°C (14°F) if the crowns are protected with straw. Plants tolerate light shade

PLANTING OUT CELERIAC FROM A MODULE

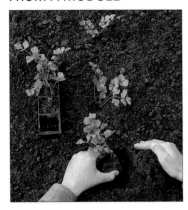

Plant out celeriac from a module when it is 8–10cm (3–4in) high with 6 or 7 leaves. Space the young plants 30–38cm (12–15in) apart; take care not to bury the crowns.

if the soil is moist. For soil requirements, see "Celery", p.538; celeriac needs low nitrogen levels (see p.504).

Sowing and planting
Celeriac needs a six-month growing season for the bulb to develop. Germination may be erratic. Sow seed indoors in early spring, preferably in modules. If using trays, prick out the seedlings to 5–7cm (2–3in) apart or pot them singly into small pots or modules. Harden off the young plants before planting out when they are about 7cm (3in) tall. Space them 30–38cm (12–15in) apart with their crowns at soil level, not buried.

Routine cultivation
Mulch after planting, and water well, especially in dry conditions. Plants may be fed during the growing season (see "Celery", p.538). Towards the end of the summer, remove some of the coarse, outer leaves to expose the crowns; this encourages the bulbs to develop. To protect from frost, tuck a loose layer of straw 10–15cm (4–6in) thick around the crowns.

Pests and diseases
Celeriac may be affected by the same pests and diseases as celery (see p.538), but is normally healthy.

CULTIVATING AND PROTECTING CELERIAC

1 *Towards the end of the summer, as the swollen stem bases develop, remove a few of the outer leaves to expose the crowns.*

2 *Before the first frosts, mulch around the base of the plants with a 15cm (6in) layer of straw to protect the crowns.*

Harvesting and storing
Celeriac may be harvested from late summer until the following spring. The bulbs are ready for use when they are 7–13cm (3–5in) in diameter.

The flavour is best and the bulbs will keep longer if the roots are left in the ground over winter. Where winters are very severe, dig up the plants in early winter without damaging the bulbs; trim off the outer leaves, leaving a central tuft, and store the plants in boxes of damp soil in a cool, frost-free place.

CELERIAC TO TRY
'Balder'
'Diamant'
'Ibis'
'Monarch'
'Prinz'

Asparagus (*Asparagus officinalis*)

Asparagus is perennial and may be productive for up to 20 years. Its light, fern-like foliage grows over 90cm (3ft) tall, with a spread of about 45cm (18in). It is cultivated for the delicious young shoots or spears that push through the ground in spring. Male and female plants are available; the females produce berries. Male plants are higher yielding; choose all-male, F1 hybrid cultivars for the best yield

and results. Asparagus is normally eaten cooked.

Asparagus is a cool-season crop, growing best at 16–24°C (61–75°F) in regions with cool winters that provide the necessary dormant period. Choose an open site, avoiding exposed situations and frost pockets. Asparagus tolerates a wide range of moderately fertile soils although acid soils should be limed (see p.625).

Good drainage is essential. Do not make a new asparagus bed where asparagus has been grown before, since soil-borne diseases may persist. Remove all perennial weeds from the site and prepare the ground by digging it over and working in manure or compost. Asparagus may also be grown in raised beds to improve drainage. It has low nitrogen requirements (see p.504).

Sowing and planting
Asparagus is traditionally grown by planting one-year-old purchased plants or "crowns" in spring. The crowns are fleshy and must never be allowed to dry out before planting.

Grow them about 38cm (15in) apart, either in single or double rows, with the rows spaced 30cm (12in) apart. Plant the crowns about 10cm (4in) deep by first making a small trench with a central, mounded ridge along the flat base. Spread out the roots evenly over the ridge and cover them with soil to the level of the crowns. Fill in the rest of the trench with soil gradually as the stems

ASPARAGUS TO TRY
Traditional
'Connover's Colossal'

All-male cultivars
'Backlim'
'Cito'
'Dariana' F1
'Franklim' F1
'Gijnlim'
'Grolim'
'Jersey Knight' improved F1
'Lucullus'
'Pacific' F1

grow, always leaving 8–10cm (3–4in) of the stems exposed.

Raising asparagus from seed is cheaper, but the results are more variable. Sow seed 2.5cm (1in) deep *in situ* in spring, and thin out to about 7cm (3in) apart. Plant out the largest the following spring;

PLANTING ASPARAGUS CROWNS

Dig a trench about 30cm (12in) wide and 20cm (8in) deep with a central, mounded ridge that is 10cm (4in) high. Place the asparagus crowns on the ridge about 38cm (15in) apart. Spread the roots out evenly and cover them with about 5cm (2in) of soil to the level of the crowns.

CUTTING BACK ASPARAGUS STEMS

Using secateurs, cut back the stems in autumn to within about 2.5cm (1in) of ground level.

alternatively, sow indoors in modules in early spring at 13–16°C (55–61°F). The seedlings grow rapidly, and may be planted out in permanent positions in early summer.

Routine cultivation

Asparagus requires little attention other than keeping the beds weed-free. Hoe shallowly to avoid damaging the roots. When the foliage turns yellow in autumn, cut the stems back to about 2.5cm (1in) above the soil.

Pests and diseases

Slugs (p.644) at an early stage and asparagus beetle (p.644) on more mature plants are the most serious pests. The soil-borne fungal disease violet root rot (p.661) may destroy plants in long-established beds.

Harvesting and storing

Asparagus must be allowed to build into a strong plant before it is harvested in mid-spring. Good, modern cultivars may be cut lightly in the second season. The following year, limit cutting to a six-week period; subsequently, cutting may continue over eight weeks if the plants are growing well. Harvest the spears when they are about 15cm (6in) high and fairly thick. Cut each one at an angle, taking care not to damage nearby spears. Remaining spears will continue to grow. Asparagus freezes well.

HARVESTING ASPARAGUS

When the spears are 12–15cm (5–6in) high, cut each stalk 2.5–5cm (1–2in) below soil level.

Kohl rabi (*Brassica oleracea* Gongylodes Group)

These annual plants from the brassica family are grown for the white-fleshed, turnip-like, swollen stem or "bulb" that forms just above the ground. Kohl rabi reaches 30cm (12in) high and has an average spread of 30cm (12in). The outer skin is green (sometimes described as "white") or purple. The bulbs are nutritious, well flavoured, and used cooked or raw.

Kohl rabi is a cool-season crop, growing best at 18–25°C (64–77°F). Young plants tend to bolt prematurely in temperatures below about 10°C (50°F). For soil requirements, see "Siting Western brassicas", p.507. Kohl rabi grows well in light soils and withstands drought better than most brassicas. It has low nitrogen requirements (see p.504).

Sowing and planting

In mild climates, sow seed outdoors in succession from spring through to late summer, using the hardier purple

Green kohl rabi

forms for late sowings. In hot climates, sow in spring and autumn. Sow *in situ* either in rows about 30cm (12in) apart, thinning seedlings to about 18cm (7in) apart, or space the seeds about 25cm (10in) apart in

each direction. Under cover, sow earlier in gentle heat in trays or modules. Plant out seedlings when they are no more than 5cm (2in) high. Protect early outdoor crops with cloches or floating mulches.

Routine cultivation

Kohl rabi is fast-maturing; little attention is required during growth other than keeping beds weed-free.

Pests and diseases

Flea beetles (p.644), cabbage root fly (p.660), and clubroot (p.660) may affect kohl rabi. See also "Cultivating Western brassicas", p.507.

Harvesting and storing

Depending on the cultivar and season, kohl rabi may be ready for cutting between five and nine weeks after sowing. Traditional cultivars should be eaten when they are no larger than tennis balls or they will

KOHL RABI TO TRY

'Green Vienna'
'Kolibri' F1 (purple)
'Korist' F1 (green)
'Lanro' F1 (green)

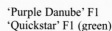

'Purple Danube' F1
'Quickstar' F1 (green)

become woody; improved, modern cultivars are still tender at a diameter of about 10cm (4in).

Leave later crops in the earth until heavy frost threatens, as the flavour deteriorates once lifted. In cold areas, lift in autumn. Leave a central tuft of leaves on each bulb to help keep them fresh; store them for up to two months in boxes of moist sand.

Florence fennel (*Foeniculum vulgare* var. *dulce*)

Grown as an annual, Florence, or sweet, fennel is distinct from the perennial herb fennel. The plants grow up to about 60cm (2ft) high and have a spread of about 45cm (18in). The anise-flavoured, flattened "bulb" of overlapping scales that develops at the base of the leaf stalks is eaten cooked or raw. The highly decorative fern-like foliage may be used as a flavouring or garnish.

Florence fennel tolerates a wide range of climates, from temperate to subtropical. It thrives at a warm, even temperature, but mature plants can withstand a light frost. Grow it in an open situation, in very fertile,

moisture-retentive, but well-drained soil into which plenty of humus has been worked. Florence fennel grows well in light soils but must not be allowed to dry out. It has low nitrogen requirements (see p.504).

Sowing and planting

In cool, northern latitudes, sow seed from early to midsummer; traditional cultivars are likely to bolt if sown in spring, so use modern, bolt-resistant cultivars for earlier sowings. In warmer climates, sow in spring for a summer crop and again in late summer for an autumn crop. Florence fennel does not trans-

plant well and may bolt prematurely if checked, so either sow seed *in situ* or in modules for transplanting when the seedlings have no more than four leaves. Space the young seedlings about 30cm (12in) apart each way. Early and late crops may be protected from the frost by covering with cloches or floating mulches.

Routine cultivation

Little attention is required; keep beds weed-free. Florence fennel needs to be kept moist, so water thoroughly and mulch. When bulbs start to swell, earth them up to half their height to make them whiter and sweeter.

Florence fennel

HARVESTING FLORENCE FENNEL

1 *Cut the fennel bulb about 2.5cm (1in) above soil level. Leave the base in position.*

2 *Feathery leaves will usually sprout from the base of the stem within a few weeks.*

Pests and diseases
Florence fennel rarely suffers from any pests or diseases. Most problems stem from lack of water, fluctuating temperatures, or from transplanting, all of which may cause bolting.

Harvesting and storing
Harvest the bulbs when they are well rounded, about 15 weeks after sowing or two to three weeks after earthing up. Pull them up whole, or cut across the bulbs about 2.5cm (1in) above ground level. The stump will normally resprout to produce small sprigs of ferny foliage that may be used for flavouring or as a garnish. Florence fennel does not store well; eat it as fresh as possible.

FLORENCE FENNEL TO TRY
'Amigo'
'Pronto'
'Romanesco' **Br**
'Rudy' F1
'Selma'
'Victoria' F1
'Zefa Fino' **Br**

Key
Br *Bolt-resistant*

Rhubarb (*Rheum* x *cultorum*)

This perennial lasts over 20 years in good conditions. Rhubarb grows about 60cm (24in) or more high and up to 2m (6ft) across. The leaves may be 45cm (18in) wide. The pale-green or pinkish-red leaf stalks, which may be 60cm (2ft) long, are harvested young and used cooked.

Rhubarb is a temperate-climate crop and does not thrive in heat; the roots survive at least -15°C (5°F). Recommended cultivars include 'Early Victoria', 'German Wine', 'Grandad's Favourite', 'Stein's Champagne', 'Strawberry Surprise', 'Timperley Early', and 'Victoria'. It grows on a range of soils, as long as they are rich and well drained. Before planting, dig in plenty of manure or compost. Rhubarb needs medium nitrogen levels when young and very high levels once mature (see p.504).

Sowing and planting
Rhubarb is normally propagated by planting "sets", each consisting of a fleshy rootstock with at least one bud. Sets are about 10cm (4in) in diameter. Plant in the dormant season from autumn to spring, preferably autumn. Buy virus-free sets, or separate a set from a healthy, two- or three-year-old plant, once leaves have died back, by lifting the plant and slicing through the crown; then replant the parent. On light soils, plant so that 2.5cm (1in) of soil covers the buds; on heavy or wet soils, plant with buds just above ground level. Space 90cm (3ft) apart.

Rhubarb may also be raised from seed, although the results are variable. Sow seed in spring, 2.5cm (1in) deep in rows 30cm (12in) apart, in a seedbed outdoors. Thin the seedlings to 15cm (6in) apart, and plant out the strongest ones in their permanent positions in autumn, or in spring the following year.

Routine cultivation
Mulch the plants heavily, and water them in dry weather. Apply a heavy dressing of manure or compost every

DIVIDING RHUBARB

1 *Lift or expose the crown. Cut through it carefully using a spade, ensuring there is at least 1 main bud on each section. Prepare the soil by digging in manure.*

2 *Replant the sections (sets) 75–90cm (2½–3ft) apart. Fill in around each root so that the bud is just above the surface. Firm, and rake around the bud.*

autumn or spring and a nitrogenous dressing or organic liquid feed in spring. Remove any flowering stems.

Rhubarb may be forced in the dark to obtain very tender sticks. Cover the dormant crowns in late winter with a 10cm (4in) layer of straw or leaves, then a forcing pot, or a large bucket, at least 45cm (18in) high; leave this on for about four weeks until stems are large enough.

Pests and diseases
Honey fungus (p.661), crown rot (p.665), and viruses (p.649) may attack established plants. Blackfly may also be a problem.

Harvesting and storing
Harvest in spring and early summer. Start pulling set-raised plants lightly the year after planting; with seed-raised plants, wait until the second year. In subsequent years, pull heavily until quality starts to deteriorate. Forced stems are ready about three weeks earlier than unforced ones.

HARVESTING RHUBARB

When the rhubarb stems are ready, they may be harvested by gripping each stem at the base and twisting it while pulling it upwards and outwards.

FORCING RHUBARB

For an earlier, tender crop, cover the dormant buds (see upper inset) in winter with straw or leaves inside a forcing pot or any large container that excludes the light. The plant will produce tender, pink stems a few weeks later (see lower inset).

Root and tuberous vegetables

Root vegetables are the mainstay of the kitchen garden. As the name suggests, most are grown for their swollen roots or tubers. A few, such as turnips, beetroot, and coco-yams, are also used for their young, leafy growth; some radish cultivars also produce edible seed pods.

A variety of root vegetables may be grown and harvested in succession for a steady supply; many store quite easily, sometimes still in the ground, for use throughout the winter. Salsify and scorzonera may both be over-wintered for their flowering shoots, produced in the spring.

Sweet potato · Carrots · Swede · Sweet potato · Turnips · Potatoes · Jerusalem artichokes · Parsnips

Beetroot (*Beta vulgaris* subsp. *vulgaris*)

Beetroot is a biennial plant grown as an annual. It grows to about 15cm (6in) tall and about 12cm (5in) across. The swollen root forms at ground level and may be round, flat, or cylindrical. It is on average 5cm (2in) in diameter, and about 10cm (4in) or more deep in the long forms. The flesh is normally red but may be yellow, white, or even have concentric pink and white rings. The skin is similarly red, yellow, or off-white. The sweetly flavoured roots are mainly used cooked, either fresh or stored, but may also be pickled. The fresh, young leaves (tops) may be used as greens.

Beetroot grows best and develops the deepest colours in cool, even temperatures, ideally of 16°C (61°F). Grow it in an open site on rich, light soil with high nitrogen levels (see p.504). Apply half the nitrogen before sowing. Lime very acid soils.

THINNING SEEDLINGS

When the beetroot seedlings have produced 3 or 4 leaves, thin clumps growing close together to the required spacing by nipping off the top green leaves at soil level without disturbing the remaining seedlings.

Sowing and planting
Beetroot "seeds" each contain a cluster of two or three seeds, the seedlings of which must be thinned out early. Some cultivars, such as 'Cheltenham Mono' and 'Monopoly', have been bred to produce single, or monogerm, seed, which needs little or no thinning.

Soak seed in warm water for 30 minutes before sowing to overcome slow germination. Some cultivars may bolt if sown early or in unfavourable conditions so choose bolt-resistant cultivars for early sowings.

In spring, sow seed *in situ* out-doors when the soil is workable and has warmed up to at least 7°C (45°F). Sow seed 1–2cm (½–¾in) deep, with the spacing determined by the type of beetroot and the size required. Grow maincrop beetroot in rows 30cm (12in) apart, thinning to 7–10cm (3–4in) apart. For pickling beetroot about 2.5cm (1in) in diameter, space rows 7cm (3in) apart, thinning seedlings to 6cm (2½in).

For earlier crops, sow in early spring under cloches, in frames, or indoors in seed trays or modules, transplanting outside when seedlings are 5cm (2in) tall. Sow three monogerm or ordinary seeds per module (see "Sowing in containers", p.501), thinning as necessary. Early beetroot needs plenty of space, so plant indoor-sown seedlings in rows 23cm (9in) apart, then thin them to 9cm (3½in) apart. For continuous supplies of young beetroot, sow seed at intervals of two to three weeks throughout summer. Sow cultivars

HARVESTING BEETROOT

Grip the stems and pull the beetroot from the soil; it should lift easily since it is shallow-rooted. Avoid damaging the roots, which will bleed if they are cut.

intended for storage in late summer, at least ten weeks before the first heavy frost is expected.

Routine cultivation
Water only to prevent the soil from drying out, at a rate of 11 litres/sq m (2 gallons/sq yd) every two weeks. Apply the remaining nitrogenous fertilizer during active growth.

Pests and diseases
Beetroot may be affected by sparrows (see "Birds", p.657), cutworms (p.655), aphids (p.646), damping off (p.660), fungal leaf spots (p.648), and boron deficiency (p.662).

BEETROOT TO TRY
'Albina Vereduna'
'Alto' F1 (long)
'Boltardy' **Br**
'Bull's Blood'

'Burpee's Golden'
  (stores well) **Br**
'Cheltenham Green Top'
'Chioggia'
'Forono' (stores well)
'Pablo' F1
'Pronto'
'Red Ace' F1
'Regala' **Br**
'Solo' F1 (long)
'Wodan' F1

Key
Br *Bolt resistant*

Harvesting and storing
Harvest beetroot at any stage from small, immature roots 2.5cm (1in) in diameter to fully mature roots; this will be from 7 to 13 weeks after sowing, depending on the cultivar, the season, and the size required. In mild areas, beetroot may be left in well-drained soil in winter, protected with a layer of straw up to 15cm (6in) deep, but they eventually become rather woody. Otherwise lift them before severe frost. Twist off the leaves (cutting causes "bleeding") and store the roots in moist sand in a frost-free place. Beetroot normally keeps until mid-spring.

Swedes (*Brassica napus* Napobrassica Group)

Biennials from the brassica family, swedes are grown as annuals and reach a height of 25cm (10in) with a spread of 38cm (15in). The root flesh is usually yellow, but sometimes white, and the skin generally purple, buff, or a combination of both. The large, often irregularly shaped,

underground roots, which may be 10cm (4in) in diameter and as long, are sweetly flavoured and used cooked. This hardy, cool-season crop grows best on light, fertile soil with low nitrogen levels (see p.504). For climate and soil requirements, see "Siting Western brassicas", p.507.

Sowing and planting
Swedes need a growing season of up to 26 weeks to mature fully. Sow seed from early to late spring *in situ*, 2cm (¾in) deep in rows 38cm (15in) apart, thinning early and in stages until the seedlings are about 23cm (9in) apart.

SWEDES TO TRY
'Brora'
'Magres'
'Marian'
'Ruby'

Routine cultivation

Keep beds weed-free; if conditions are very dry, water at a rate of 11 litres/sq m (2 gallons/sq yd).

Pests and diseases

Downy mildew (p.646), powdery mildew (p.646), boron deficiency (p.662), and violet root rot (p.661) may affect swedes. Some cultivars are resistant to mildew. For other pests and diseases, see "Cultivating Western brassicas", p.507.

Harvesting and storing

Swedes generally mature in autumn and, being hardy, may be left in the soil until the end of the year, when they should be lifted carefully to prevent them from becoming woody; except in very cold climates, covering with a thick layer of straw provides sufficient protection until the swedes are lifted. Store swedes in clamps outdoors or in wooden boxes under cover (see *Storing Carrots*, p.544) for up to four months.

MAKING A SWEDE CLAMP

Choose a sheltered, well-drained site and stack the roots on a 20cm (8in) layer of straw in a pyramid, with their necks facing outwards. Cover with a layer of longer straw. In very cold climates, protect further with a 10cm (4in) layer of soil.

Turnips (*Brassica rapa* Rapifera Group)

These are biennials from the brassica family grown as annuals. The plants are about 23cm (9in) high with a spread of about 25cm (10in). The underground roots swell to 2.5–7cm (1–3in) in diameter and are round, fairly flat, or long. The flesh may be either white or yellow and the skin white, pink, red, or yellow. The young leaves, known as turnip tops, may be eaten as greens (see "Turnip tops and broccoli raab", p.512). Turnip roots are used either fresh or stored and are normally cooked.

Turnips are a temperate-climate crop, growing best at about 20°C (68°F). They are reasonably hardy, tolerating light frost. For general climate and soil requirements, see "Siting Western brassicas", p.507. Grow turnips in moist soil as they bolt prematurely in dry conditions. Early types, many of which are small and white, are fast-growing and excellent for early spring and summer crops; hardier types are used fresh during summer and winter and for storage. They require low to medium nitrogen levels (see p.504).

Sowing and planting

Start sowing seed of early turnips in spring as soon as the ground is workable, or sow under cover. Make

HARVESTING TURNIPS

Harvest turnips by pulling them from the soil by their leaves. Do not leave them in the ground too long or they may become woody.

successive sowings at three-week intervals until early summer. Sow maincrop types from mid- to late summer *in situ*, 2cm (¾in) deep. Space early types in rows that are 23cm (9in) apart, thinning seedlings to 10cm (4in); space maincrop types in rows 30cm (12in) apart, thinning to 15cm (6in).

Routine cultivation

Keep beds free from weeds. During dry conditions water at a rate of 11 litres/sq m (2 gallons/sq yd).

Pests and diseases

Flea beetles (p.644) may affect seedlings; other problems include violet root rot (p.661) and boron deficiency (p.662). Turnip gall weevil causes hollow swellings on the roots that may be mistaken for clubroot but are rarely serious; discard all affected plants. For other pests and diseases, see "Cultivating Western brassicas", p.507.

Harvesting and storing

Harvest early turnips after about five weeks, maincrop types after six to ten weeks. Pull them before they become woody. Lift turnips for storage before the first frost, then store them for up to three or four months in outdoor clamps covered with straw.

TURNIPS TO TRY

'Atlantic'
'Golden Ball'
'Green Top Stone'
'Ivory'
'Market Express' F1
'Oasis'
'Purple Top Milan'
'Tokyo Cross' F1

Cocoyams (*Colocasia esculenta*)

These herbaceous, frost-tender perennials grow to about 1m (3ft) tall, with a spread of 60–70cm (24–28in). The plants have large, long-stalked leaves, which may either be green or greenish-purple. Cocoyams, sometimes known as taro, are grown for their large, swollen tubers, which

Cocoyam plant

are eaten cooked. The young leaves and shoots are also edible, and may be cooked and used as greens.

Cocoyams are tropical and subtropical plants requiring temperatures of 21–27°C (70–81°F), with humidity levels over 75 per cent. In temperate areas they need a very sheltered, sunny site, or they may be grown under cover. Cocoyams are adapted to short daylengths of about 12 hours (see "Daylength", p.495); they rarely produce flowers. Some forms are tolerant of light shade. Moisture-retentive soil is essential because many forms of cocoyam are sensitive to dry soil conditions.

Fertile soil that has a high organic content and a slightly acid pH level of 5.5–6.5 is recommended. Cocoyams require medium to high levels of nitrogen (see p.504).

Sowing and planting

Seeds are rarely available, therefore propagation is usually from existing tubers. Plant mature tubers or portions of tubers with dormant buds *in situ* in well-prepared beds. Space the tubers about 45cm (18in) apart with 90cm (3ft) between rows.

Cocoyams may also be propagated by cuttings. Sever the tops of tubers with a horizontal cut; each cutting should consist of several leaves 10–12cm (4–5in) long, a central growing point, and a small portion of the tuber. Plant the cuttings in their final positions at the above spacing; if the temperature is below the optimum 21°C (70°F), plant them in 21–25cm (8–10in) pots of standard compost to grow on under cover until the temperature is high enough for transplanting outside.

Routine cultivation

Cocoyams need a constant supply of water for the highest yields, so water regularly. Apply an organic mulch to conserve moisture, and feed with a general-purpose fertilizer at two- to three-week intervals. Keep beds free of weeds. The plants should be earthed up around the stems once they are established to encourage the tubers to develop.

Pests and diseases

These are rarely serious for cocoyams that are grown in the open, but aphids (p.646), thrips (p.647), red spider mite (p.646), and fungal leaf spots (p.648) may reduce tuber yields. Under cover, cocoyams are liable to the same pests and diseases as those grown outside; whiteflies (p.646) may also be troublesome.

Growing under cover

Propagate from tubers (see p.543). When these have rooted, transfer them to well-prepared greenhouse beds, 21–30cm (8–12in) pots, or growing bags, ensuring that the roots are disturbed as little as possible.

Water and feed the plants regularly, maintaining a temperature of 21–27°C (70–81°F) and a humidity of more than 75 per cent by damping down. Tubers that are cultivated under cover tend to be smaller than those grown outdoors.

Harvesting and storing

Cocoyams are slow to develop and reach maturity. Harvest the tubers 16–24 weeks after planting when the leaves start to turn yellow and plants die down. Lift cocoyams grown in the open carefully using a fork; plants under cover may be lifted gently out of their pots or growing bags. Try not to damage the tubers since this encourages rotting.

Healthy tubers may be stored for about eight to twelve weeks at a temperature of 11–13°C (52–55°F), with humidity of 85–90 per cent.

Cocoyam tuber

Carrots (*Daucus carota*)

These are biennials grown as annuals. Their swollen, orange tap roots may be up to 5cm (2in) in diameter at the neck and up to about 20cm (8in) in length. The feathery, green foliage grows to about 23cm (9in), with a 15cm (6in) spread. Carrots are normally long and tapered but may be rounded. There are many types: early ones are usually small and slender and used young; maincrop types are larger and used fresh or stored. All are eaten either cooked or raw.

Carrots are a cool-season crop, and tolerate the same temperatures as beetroot (see p.542). Grow in an open site on light, fertile soil. Deep-rooted types require reasonably deep, stone-free soil. Work in plenty of organic matter, preferably in the autumn before sowing. The fertile, loose soil of established raised beds is particularly suitable for growing carrots. Rake the soil into a fine tilth before sowing. Carrots should be rotated (see p.498). They need very low nitrogen levels (see p.504).

Sowing and planting

Sow early types in spring *in situ* as soon as the soil is workable and has warmed up to 7°C (45°F). Earlier sowings may be made under cloches, in frames, or under floating mulches; remove these after a few weeks. Sow maincrop types from late spring until early summer. A second sowing of early types may be made in late summer and protected with cloches.

Sow seed sparingly about 1–2cm (½–¾in) deep, either broadcast or in rows 15cm (6in) apart. Thin early carrots to 7cm (3in) apart; maincrop carrots should be thinned to 4cm (1½in) to obtain medium-sized carrots or farther apart if large carrots are needed. Carrots do not transplant well unless sown in modules: sow seed of deep-rooted cultivars singly, those of round-rooted ones, several together. Round-rooted carrots sown in modules do not need thinning and should be planted out as a group at slightly wider spacing than for maincrop carrots.

Routine cultivation

Remove weeds regularly once the carrots have germinated and until the foliage hinders further weed growth. Water at a rate of 16–22 litres/sq m (3–5 gallons/sq yd) every two or three weeks.

Pests and diseases

Carrot fly (p.660) may be a serious problem; surround with a low barrier where possible. The egg-laying, adult fly is attracted by the smell of carrot foliage; thin in the evening, nipping off the seedlings at ground level and removing the tops from the site. Root and leaf aphids (see "Aphids", p.646), carrot motley dwarf virus (see "Viruses", p.649), violet root rot (p.661), and boron deficiency (p.662) may be troublesome.

Harvesting and storing

Harvest early cultivars about seven to nine weeks after sowing, maincrop cultivars after 10–11 weeks. Pull them by hand or fork them out. On well-drained soils in areas with mild winters, carrots may be left in the soil in winter (see *Protecting Parsnips*, p.546). Otherwise lift them before heavy frost, cut or twist off the foliage, and store healthy roots in boxes in a cool, dry place for up to five months.

CARROTS TO TRY

Early
'Adelaide' F1
'Amsterdam Forcing 2 – Sweetheart'

'Nairobi' F1
'Nandor' F1
'Newmarket' F1
'Sytan'

Maincrop
'Autumn King – Vita Longa'
'Autumn King 2'
'Berlicum – Berjo'
'Camberley'
'Chantenay Red Cored 2'
'Flyaway' F1
'Kingston' F1
'Maestro'

'New Red Intermediate' (exhibition cultivar)
'Parabell'
'Parmex' (round-rooted)
'Sugarsnax'
'Yellow Stone'

PROTECTION AGAINST CARROT FLY

Surround the patch of young carrots with a protective barrier 60–90cm (2–3ft) high. The barrier may be made of fine mesh netting or stiff, clear plastic, both of which also help to warm the soil inside – to be sure, also cover the top with fleece or mesh using pegs for easy removal.

THIN SOWING

Sow carrot seeds about 2.5cm (1in) apart so that the seedlings will need little thinning later. The seed should be 1–2cm (½–¾in) deep.

HARVESTING YOUNG

Early cultivars may be harvested when they are very young. Pull them up in a bunch when they are 8–10cm (3–4in) long.

STORING CARROTS

Twist the foliage off the carrots; place them on a layer of sand in a box. Cover them with more sand and continue in layers.

Jerusalem artichokes (*Helianthus tuberosus*)

These are perennial plants, also known as sunchokes or girasoles. The distinctively flavoured tubers are 5–10cm (2–4in) long, about 4cm (1½in) in diameter and, in most cultivars, very knobbly. 'Fuseau', however, produces smooth tubers. The plants may grow up to 3m (10ft) tall. The tubers are normally cooked but may be eaten raw. Jerusalem artichokes grow best in temperate climates and are very hardy. They

Smooth 'Fuseau' tubers

Knobbly Jerusalem artichoke tubers

tolerate a wide range of soils and require medium nitrogen levels (see p.504). They may be planted as a windbreak screen.

Sowing and planting

Plant tubers as soon as the ground is workable in spring. Those the size of a hen's egg may be planted whole; cut large ones into pieces, each with several buds. Make a drill, planting about 12.5cm (5in) deep and 30cm (12in) apart. Cover with soil.

Routine cultivation

When the plants are about 30cm (12in) tall, earth up the stems to half their height for stability. In late summer, cut the stems back to 1.5m (5ft), removing any flowerheads at the same time. In very exposed sites, stake or support the stems. Water in very dry conditions. When the leaves start to yellow, cut the stems back to just above ground level.

PLANTING

Make a drill 10–15cm (4–6in) deep. Place the tubers in the drill 30cm (12in) apart with the main bud facing upwards. Cover carefully so the tubers are not dislodged.

Harvesting and storing

Harvest the tubers 16–20 weeks after planting. Lift them only when re-quired, since they keep best in the ground, and take care not to damage the roots. Save a few tubers to replant or leave some in the soil for the

CUTTING DOWN

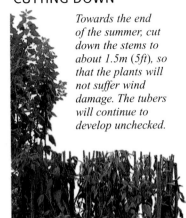

Towards the end of the summer, cut down the stems to about 1.5m (5ft), so that the plants will not suffer wind damage. The tubers will continue to develop unchecked.

following year. Otherwise, remove even small tubers since they rapidly become invasive. In severe climates or on heavy ground, lift in early winter and store in a cellar or in clamps outdoors (see *Making a Swede Clamp*, p.543) for up to five months.

Sweet potatoes (*Ipomoea batatas*)

These tender perennials are grown as annuals. They have trailing stems that grow to 3m (10ft) or more if unpruned. Cultivars vary considerably in leaf shape and tuber size, shape, and colour. Tubers are eaten cooked; the leaves may be used in the same way as spinach (see p.519).

Sweet potatoes are tropical and subtropical plants that need a temperature of 24–26°C (75–79°F). In warm climates, they need a sunny aspect; in temperate climates, they should be grown under cover, but tuber yields are smaller. Most cultivars are short-day plants (see "Daylength", p.495).

Highly fertile, well-drained, sandy loams with a pH of 5.5–6.5 and medium to high nitrogen levels (see p.504) are required.

Sowing and planting

In the tropics and subtropics, plant sweet potatoes at the start of the rainy season. In warm and temperate climates, plant in spring. Make raised ridges about 75cm (30in) apart, then plant the tubers 5–7cm (2–3in) deep in the ridge, spacing them 25–30cm (10–12in) apart. Alternatively, take 20–25cm (8–10in) long stem cuttings from mature plants and insert them to half their length just below the apex of the ridge.

Cultivars raised from seed will provide reasonable crops. Sow indoors in trays or 21–25cm (8–10in) pots at a temperature of at least 24°C

(75°F). When seedlings are 10–15cm (4–6in) high, harden them off and transplant outside.

Routine cultivation

Water and weed regularly, and mulch to conserve moisture. Train shoots to spread around the plant. Apply a general-purpose fertilizer at two- to three-week intervals until the tubers have formed. Protect from winds.

Pests and diseases

Aphids (p.646), caterpillars (p.645), root-knot eelworms (p.660), fungal leaf spots (p.648), *Fusarium* wilt (p.661), seedling blight (p.654), and various viruses (p.649) affect sweet potatoes growing outdoors. Under cover, whiteflies (p.646), thrips (p.647), and glasshouse red spider mite (p.646) may be troublesome.

Growing under cover

Sow seed, as described below left, transplanting seedlings to growing bags or prepared beds. Alternatively, take cuttings and insert three or four into 15cm (6in) pots. Maintain a minimum temperature of 25°C (77°F) and a humidity of over 70 per cent by damping down regularly. When roots develop, transfer plants to greenhouse beds or growing bags. Water regularly and remove the growing points of shoots longer than 60cm (2ft) to encourage lateral shoots. Keep the temperature below 28°C (82°F), and the growing area well ventilated.

Harvesting and storing

Harvest 12–16 weeks after planting, when the stems and leaves turn yellow. Crops from seed are ready three or four weeks later. Lift the tubers, using

Sweet potato plant

a fork, without damaging them and, for better flavour, leave in the sun to cure. In order to store sweet potatoes they must first be cured for four to seven days at temperatures of 28–30°C (82–86°F) and humidity of 85–90 per cent (see "Pumpkins and winter squashes", p.525). They may be stored in shallow trays at 10–15°C (50–59°F) for several months.

STEM CUTTINGS FOR GROWING UNDER COVER

1 *Select healthy, vigorous shoots and cut them off the parent plant with secateurs.*

2 *Remove the lower leaves and trim each shoot below a node to 20–25cm (8–10in). Insert in pots and grow on under cover.*

SWEET POTATOES TO TRY

'Beauregard' ✳ (orange-fleshed)
'Bunch Porto Rico' (bush/ red flesh)
'Gold-rush' (orange-fleshed)
'New Jewel' (deep orange flesh)
'Vardaman' (bush/deep orange flesh)
'White Delight' (white flesh)

Key
✳ *Resistant to root-knot eelworm*

Parsnips (*Pastinaca sativa*)

Parsnips are biennials grown as annuals. The tap root grows to 5cm (2in) across at the neck and about 10cm (4in) long in short forms and up to 23cm (9in) in long types. The leaves are about 38cm (15in) long and 30cm (12in) wide. The roots are eaten cooked.

Parsnips are a hardy, cool-season crop, and prefer light, deeply cultivated, stone-free soils. On shallow soils, grow the shorter forms. Lime very acid soils and rotate crops (see p.498). Parsnips have low nitrogen requirements (see p.504).

PARSNIPS TO TRY

'Countess' F1
'Dagger' F1
'Gladiator' F1 (long)
'Javelin' (long)
'Tender and True' (long)

Sowing and planting

Always sow fresh seed. Parsnips need a long growing season and so should be sown as soon as the soil is workable in spring, but not in cold or wet soil. Sow seed *in situ* 2cm (¾in) deep in rows 30cm (12in) apart. Thin the seedlings to 10cm (4in) apart to produce large roots, or 7cm (3in) for smaller roots. A faster-germinating crop such as radishes may be inter-sown; to allow for this, station sow several parsnip seeds at intervals of 10cm (4in), and thin to one seedling per station. To start parsnips earlier, sow seed in modules with gentle heat under cover and transplant seedlings before the tap roots develop.

Routine cultivation

Always keep beds free of weeds. In very dry conditions water the plants as for carrots (see p.544).

Pests and diseases

Parsnips may be attacked by celery fly (see "Leaf miners", p.647), root aphids (see "Aphids", p.646), and carrot fly (p.660). Use cultivars that are resistant to parsnip canker

(p.661) whenever possible; of those recommended, all but 'Tender and True' are resistant. Boron deficiency (p.662) and violet root rot (p.661) may occasionally be troublesome.

Harvesting and storing

Parsnips mature in about 16 weeks. Their flavour is improved by frost and, except in very severe climates,

INTERSOWING

In a prepared drill, sow 3 parsnip seeds every 10cm (4in) and then sow radish seeds between them, about 2.5cm (1in) apart.

they may be left in the soil during winter and lifted as required. The leaves die back in winter, so mark the ends of the rows with canes so that the plants are easily found to harvest. Where winters are very severe, cover the rows with 15cm (6in) of straw to keep the soil from freezing and to make lifting easier. Young parsnips may be lifted and frozen.

PROTECTING PARSNIPS

In severe climates, cover the plants with layers of straw or bracken, to a depth of 15cm (6in). Hold in place with wire hoops and mark each row.

Radishes (*Raphanus sativus* and *Raphanus sativus* Longipinnatus Group)

There are several types of radish, some biennial and others annual; all are grown for the swollen roots. Small, round types have roots up to 2.5cm (1in) in diameter; small, long types up to 7cm (3in) long. The leaves of both may grow to about 13cm (5in) high. Large forms include oriental radishes (Longipinnatus Group), known as mooli or daikon, and the large, overwintering, winter radishes. Roots of large, round cultivars may be over 23cm (9in) in diameter, those of large, long cultivars up to 60cm (24in) long, while the plants grow 60cm (24in) tall with a spread of 45cm (18in).

Radish skin colour is red, pink, white, purple, black, yellow, or green; the flesh is normally white. Small roots are used raw when fresh, and large roots are used raw or cooked, fresh or stored. Immature seed pods from cultivars such as 'Münchner Bier' and young seedling leaves from most cultivars are edible raw.

Radishes are mainly a cool-season crop, but there are cultivars suited to a wide range of growing conditions. Some mooli and all overwintering types are frost-tolerant. Grow radishes in an open site, although mid-summer crops tolerate light shade.

Radishes prefer light, rich, well-drained soil, preferably manured for the previous crop, and very low nitrogen levels (see p.504). Radishes should be rotated (see p.498).

Sowing and planting

Once the soil is workable, sow standard, small types outdoors throughout the growing season. Sow at 15-day intervals for a continuous crop. Very early and late sowings may be made under cover, using small-leaved cultivars bred for growing under cover. Delay sowing most oriental mooli until summer to prevent bolting. Some bolt-resistant cultivars may be sown earlier. Sow overwintering radishes in summer.

Radishes are normally sown *in situ*. Small types grow very fast and may be used for intercropping (see "Parsnips", above). Broadcast seed very thinly, or sow 1cm (½in) deep in drills 15cm (6in) apart. Thin the seedlings to at least 2.5cm (1in) apart, never allowing them to become overcrowded. Alternatively, seeds may be spaced 2.5cm (1in) apart so that no thinning is needed. Sow large types about 2cm (¾in) deep, in rows about 23cm (9in) apart, thinning to 15–23cm (6–9in), depending on

the cultivar. Small types may be used for cut-and-come-again seedling radish leaves (see "Successional crops", p.500).

Routine cultivation

Radishes should never be allowed to dry out. In periods of dry weather, water the crop every week at a rate

HARVESTING

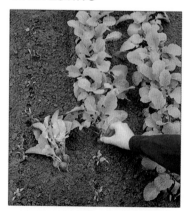

Radishes are ready to harvest 3–4 weeks after sowing. If the radishes are being used for intercropping, pull them up carefully without disturbing the roots of the other seedlings in the row.

RADISHES TO TRY

Small
'Cherry Belle'
'Flamboyant Sabina'

'French Breakfast 3'
'Rougette'
'Rudi'
'Scarlet Globe'
'Sparkler'

To sow under cover or outside
'Marabelle'
'Mirabeau'
'Rudi'
'Saxa'

Mooli
'April Cross' F1
   (slow bolting)
'Minowase Summer
   Cross' F1

Overwintering
'Black Spanish Round'
'Mantang Hong' F1

of 11 litres/sq m (2 gallons/sq yd). Overwatering, however, encourages leaf rather than root development.

Pests and diseases
Radishes may be attacked by flea beetles (p.644), cabbage root fly (p.660), and slugs (p.644).

Harvesting and storing
Small radishes mature three to four weeks after sowing, most large types after eight to ten weeks. Pull small types soon after they mature, since most will become woody if they remain in the ground for long. Large types, however, may be left in the ground for several weeks with no risk of deterioration. Overwintering radishes may be left in the soil for lifting when required, except in severe winter weather or if they have been grown in heavy soil. In these cases, lift the roots and store them in boxes of moist sand in a frost-free place, or outside in clamps for three or four months (see *Making a Swede Clamp*, p.543). Where radish seed is required for propagation, leave a few plants to produce seed. Harvest the pods while they are still young and green, then dry them, and collect the seeds.

Scorzonera (*Scorzonera hispanica*)

This hardy perennial is normally grown as an annual. Plants grow to about 90cm (3ft) tall and have yel-low flowerheads. The black-skinned, white-fleshed roots are 20cm (8in) or more long, and about 4cm (1½in) across at the neck. They have an unusual flavour and are eaten cooked. The young leaves and shoots (chards) of overwintered plants are edible, and the young flower buds and their flower stalks are also delicious cooked. For soil, climate,

and manuring requirements, see "Carrots", p.544. A fertile, deep, light soil is essential for good roots to develop. Scorzonera has low nitrogen requirements (see p.504).

Sowing and planting
Sow fresh seed *in situ* in spring about 1cm (½in) deep, in rows about 20cm (8in) apart, thinning out seedlings to 10cm (4in) apart. Water at a rate of 16–22 litres/sq m (3–5 gallons/sq yd) in dry spells. For routine cultivation, see "Carrots", p.544. Pests and diseases rarely affect scorzonera.

Harvesting and storing
The roots need at least four months to develop. They may be left in the soil throughout the winter (see *Protecting Parsnips*, p.546), or lifted and stored in boxes in cool conditions. Start lifting the roots for use in the autumn and continue into spring. If they are only pencil-thin, leave the remaining plant roots to thicken for harvesting the following autumn.

For chards, cover the plants with about 13cm (5in) of straw or leaves in early spring. The young, blanched leaves will push through this layer. Cut them when about 10cm (4in) tall.

For flower buds, leave a few roots in the soil during winter with no covering; these will flower the following spring or early summer. Pick the unopened buds with about 8cm (3in) of stem.

Scorzonera roots

Scorzonera plants

Salsify roots

Salsify (*Tragopogon porrifolius*)

A hardy biennial with purple flowers, salsify is known as vegetable oyster or oyster plant, due to its taste. Similar to scorzonera in appearance and use, it has the same climate, soil, cultivation, harvesting, and storage requirements. Salsify roots need to be eaten in their first winter.

If the roots are overwintered, the flower buds may be eaten the following spring. Pick the buds with short stalks, preferably in the morning before they open.

Potatoes (*Solanum tuberosum*)

Potatoes are tender perennials that grow to an average height of 60cm (2ft), with a similar spread. There are numerous potato cultivars, displaying enormous variation in their underground tubers.

A typical mature tuber is about 7cm (3in) long and 4cm (1½in) wide with white or pinkish-red skin and white flesh, but there are yellow- and blue-fleshed cultivars, often used in salads. Potatoes are eaten cooked, fresh or after storing.

Potatoes are a cool-season crop, growing best at 16–18°C (61–64°F). Neither plants nor tubers tolerate frost. Depending on the cultivar, they require a growing season of 90–140 frost-free days. They are divided into early, second early, and maincrop groups, depending on the number

of days required to mature. The earlies grow fastest but are generally lower-yielding. Potatoes need at least 500mm (20in) of rainfall or irrigation during the season.

Grow potatoes in an open, frost-free site; they need well-drained, fertile soil at least 60cm (2ft) deep that is rich in organic matter. Although tolerant of a wide range of soils, acid soils (pH5–6) are preferred.

Potatoes are subject to several soil-borne pests and diseases, and so crops must always be rotated (see p.498). Prepare the ground well by digging in plenty of organic matter. A general fertilizer may be worked in just before planting. Early potatoes need medium nitrogen; high nitrogen is required for maincrop potatoes (see p.504).

Planting
Grow cultivars recommended for the area. Plant small tubers (known as "seed potatoes") that have been specially raised and are certified disease-free. In northern latitudes with a short growing season, potatoes (especially the earlies) are sprouted, or chitted, indoors to start them into growth about six weeks before planting. Place the tubers in a shallow tray, with the eyes or buds uppermost, in even light in a cool but frost-free room. Planting is easiest when the sprouts are about 2cm (¾in) long, but they may be planted with sprouts of any length. For large, early potatoes, leave only three sprouts per plant, rubbing off the others. Otherwise, the more sprouts per tuber, the higher the yield.

SPROUTING SEED POTATOES FOR PLANTING

To sprout seed potatoes, place them in a box or tray in a single layer with the end of the potato containing the most "eyes" uppermost. Store in a light, frost-free, but well-ventilated place until the sprouts have grown to about 2cm (¾in) in length.

Plant outside when there is no longer risk of heavy frost and once the soil temperature has reached 7°C (45°F). Make drills 7–15cm (3–6in) deep or make individual holes, and place tubers upright with the eyes or sprouts at the top, covering them with at least a 2.5cm (1in) layer of soil. Plant early potatoes 35cm (14in) apart in rows 43cm (17in) apart, second early and maincrop potatoes 38cm (15in) apart in rows 68cm (27in) and 75cm (30in) apart respectively.

In cool areas, cover early potatoes with cloches, clear plastic sheeting, or floating film mulches (see p.505). When shoots emerge, cut holes in the film and ease the foliage through. Remove floating films about a month later, cutting them down the centre first to acclimatize the potatoes to cooler conditions for a few days.

POTATOES TO TRY

Early
'Accent'
'Arran Pilot'
'Concorde'
'Foremost'
'Maris Bard'
'Pentland Javelin'
'Red Duke of York'
'Winston'

Second early
'Estima'
'Kestrel'
'Kondor'
'Lady Christl'
'Nadine'
'Picasso'
'Roseval'
'Wilja'

Maincrop
'Cara'
'Desirée'
'Maris Piper'
'Maxine'
'Navan'
'Nicola'
'Pentland Crown'
'Romano'
'Sante'

For salads
'Anya'
'Charlotte'
'Mimi'
'Pink Fir Apple'
'Ratte'

Early potatoes may also be planted under black plastic sheeting, which excludes light and makes earthing up unnecessary; this is not recommended for maincrop potatoes since watering is difficult. Lay the plastic on the ground, anchor the edges in the soil, and plant the potatoes through cross-shaped slits in the plastic. Alternatively, plant the potatoes, cover them with plastic, make slits, and pull the stems through when the plants start to push up the plastic.

Potatoes are sometimes grown from seedlings, plantlets, or eyes. These are planted in seed trays and transferred outside, after hardening off, once all risk of frost has passed.

Routine cultivation

If frost threatens after the leaves have appeared, cover them at night with a light layer of straw or newspaper. Plants normally recover from light frost damage. Unless grown under black plastic, potatoes need to be earthed up to prevent tubers near the surface from becoming green and unpalatable and sometimes toxic. When the plants are about 23cm (9in) tall, hoe up soil around the stems to a depth of about 13cm (5in). This may be done in stages.

In dry conditions, water early potatoes every 12 days at a rate of 16 litres/sq m (3 gallons/sq yd). Delay watering maincrop potatoes until the young potatoes are the size of marbles (check the size of the tubers by scraping back the soil beneath one plant) then give one watering of at least 22 litres/sq m (5 gallons/sq yd). Potatoes may be given an organic liquid feed or a nitrogenous top-dressing during growth.

Pests and diseases

Cutworms (p.660), slugs (p.644), potato cyst eelworms (p.666), millipedes (p.644), blackleg on potatoes (p.664), and violet root rot (p.661) may be troublesome. For full details of potato blight (including resistant cultivars) and other pests and diseases affecting potatoes, see "Potato tuber problems", p.662.

Harvesting and storing

Harvest early potatoes when, or just before, the flowers open. Potatoes under black plastic may be harvested by lifting the sheeting – they should be on the surface. Leave healthy maincrop potatoes in the soil for as long as possible; in autumn, cut the haulm (the stems) of each plant to about 5cm (2in) above ground level, and leave the potatoes for another

two weeks, to harden the skins, before lifting. In areas with warm, wet summers where potato blight is prevalent, cut the haulm in late summer and burn the foliage; lift the potatoes two weeks later.

Lift potatoes for storage on a dry, sunny day and leave them in the sun for two hours, then store them in the dark in paper sacks in a cool, frost-proof place. Give extra protection if frost threatens. Potatoes may also be stored for up to six months outdoors in well-insulated clamps (see p.543) or in a cellar. Young or new potatoes may be frozen. For new potatoes to be eaten during winter, plant a few tubers in the middle of summer and cover with cloches in autumn.

PLANTING POTATOES

1 *Make a drill 7–15cm (3–6in) deep, using a draw hoe. If planting maincrop potatoes, place them in the drill 38cm (15in) apart with the sprouts upwards. Cover carefully once planted.*

2 *Draw up the soil around the stems when the foliage is about 23cm (9in) high. Earthing up prevents tubers that form near the surface from turning green and being unfit to eat.*

ALTERNATIVE METHOD

1 *To plant under black plastic, unroll the plastic and anchor it by burying the edges. Make a cross-shaped cut where each potato is to be planted. Place each potato 10–12cm (4–5in) deep in the soil under each cut.*

2 *Once the haulm has been cut, the plastic can be pulled back and the crop of potatoes will be lying on the soil surface, ready to harvest.*

HARVESTING POTATOES

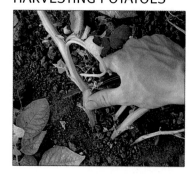

In autumn, cut the haulm (stems) cleanly with a knife just above ground level. Leave the potatoes in the ground for another 2 weeks before lifting.

Salsify (*Tragopogon porrifolius*), see Scorzonera, p.547

PART TWO

MAINTAINING THE GARDEN

PRACTICAL ADVICE ON TOOLS AND EQUIPMENT, GREENHOUSES, AND BUILDING
MATERIALS AND TECHNIQUES; UNDERSTANDING SOIL TYPE AND CLIMATE, HOW
PLANTS GROW AND REPRODUCE, AND HOW BEST TO DEAL WITH PROBLEMS

1
TOOLS AND EQUIPMENT

KEEPING A GARDEN looking its best throughout the year involves a certain amount of maintenance, from routine tasks such as mowing the lawn to occasional procedures such as deep-soil cultivation. While it is unnecessary and expensive to invest in an entire catalogue's worth of garden equipment, having the correct tool for the job makes the work easier and produces a more professional result. Besides basic tools that will be in almost constant use, for example a spade, fork, or pair of secateurs, there will be other items that you cannot do without – perhaps a wheelbarrow for moving garden refuse, or a sprinkler system for watering. Assessing the type of work you do in the garden makes it easier to decide which tools you need; choosing them with care ensures that they will be comfortable to use as well as durable and functional.

Buying and using tools

The majority of modern gardening tools are based on traditional designs, although some may be improvements or variations on old concepts. A few completely new tools, however, have been successfully introduced. For example, until the 1980s, shredders and nylon-line trimmers were hardly known; yet they are now firmly established because they fulfil a demand not met by traditional tools.

Before buying a tool, the most important point to bear in mind is its function – it must perform correctly the task it is meant to do. Consider exactly what you need a particular tool for and how frequently you will use it. A simple, inexpensive pair of secateurs, for example, will be adequate if wanted only for pruning a few rose bushes once a year; if required for intensive use, however, it is much better to invest in a high-quality pair. Before purchasing a tool, wherever possible always try to check that it is:
■ the best type of tool for the task;
■ the right size and model to suit your needs;
■ comfortable to use.
In large gardens, or for laborious or time-consuming tasks, consider using powered tools; however, since they are expensive and require careful handling and safety precautions, be sure that they are really needed.

To ensure that tools perform well and last a long time, it is important that they are properly maintained. Immediately after use, always clean off any soil, grass clippings, or other plant material and wipe metal parts with an oily rag; all pruning and cutting tools will also need regular sharpening. Tools that are not needed over the winter months should be cleaned and well oiled and then stored in a dry place.

In addition, factors such as expense and storage space must be taken into account: if a tool is needed only infrequently, hiring may be a more sensible option, especially for relatively expensive, bulky tools.

Hiring tools

If you decide to hire, book equipment in advance, especially tools likely to be in seasonal demand, such as powered lawn rakes and cultivators, and check whether the hire firm will deliver and collect the tools.

The condition of hired tools varies considerably. Some, especially powered tools, may even be potentially dangerous to operate. For this reason, you should always:
■ Check for missing or loose parts. These may not be obvious, but if in doubt do not accept the tool.
■ Look for loose bolts and fittings on tools such as powered cultivators that are subject to vibration.
■ Ask for powered tools to be started, and check carefully for excessive vibration and noise.
■ On electrical tools, check that the voltage is correct or that a suitable transformer is supplied if relevant. Look for frayed, cut, or exposed wires. Do not assume that the wiring is fine just because the tool works.
■ On four-stroke engines, check the oil in the engine and transmission.
■ Ask either for a demonstration or instructions if you have never operated the tool before. This is particularly important with powered tools such as chainsaws, which can be dangerous to use.
■ Buy or hire any recommended protective clothing (for example goggles, gloves, and ear protectors).
■ Before signing the delivery note, comment on the contract or delivery note if you have noticed any faults.

Safe use of tools

If you are not sure how to use a tool, ask for advice when buying or hiring, or contact the manufacturer. Correct use gives good results and helps prevent accidents. Make sure that the weight and length of the tool are suitable: a tool that is too heavy will be difficult to handle; one that is too short may cause back strain. Keep all powered tools in good repair and follow any safety recommendations. To minimize risks, make sure that a mains electric tool is fitted with a residual current device – sometimes called an earth leakage circuit breaker – which severs the supply in microseconds if the circuit leaks power (see also "Electrical safety", p.556).

Digging correctly
Keeping your back straight, not curved, when digging, hoeing, or raking helps to prevent backache.

Using powered tools
Take particular care when using powered tools, and always wear appropriate protective clothing.

Cultivation tools

The type of cultivation tools required depends on the nature of your garden. If you grow mainly vegetables or are cultivating a new garden, tools for digging will be a priority. If, however, the garden is well established, with lawns and perennial borders, surface cultivation tools such as hoes will be more important.

Spades

A spade is an essential tool, excellent for general cultivation, lifting soil, and digging holes for planting. There are two major types: standard digging spades, and the smaller and lighter border (also called ladies') spades. Some manufacturers also produce an intermediate-sized or medium spade that is suitable for general digging but lighter than a standard spade.

Some spades have a tread, which makes it easier to push the blade into the soil and less likely to damage footwear; these spades are, however, heavier and more expensive. For extensive digging, a larger spade (known as a "heavy"), which has a 30 x 20cm (12 x 8in) blade, may prove quicker to use.

If you find digging difficult or have a large area to dig, it may be worth buying an automatic spade to make the task less of a strain.

Forks

Garden forks are used for general cultivation, lifting rootcrops (which are more likely to be damaged with a spade), and shifting bulky material such as manure and garden compost. They are also ideal for relieving soil compaction, and for lightly forking in top-dressings of organic matter. Two forks back-to-back can be used to divide congested clumps of perennials with little effort.

Most garden forks have four square metal prongs, and are generally available in two sizes: standard and border (or ladies'). Less common are medium, or youth, forks, an intermediate size between standard and border forks. Other variations are also sometimes found. For example, a potato fork has broad, flat prongs and, generally, a larger head than a standard fork; it may be easier to use than a spade when digging heavy ground.

The head and neck of a fork should be forged in a single piece, the shaft fitting into a long socket in the neck.

Standard digging spade
This is useful for shifting large amounts of soil, but it is heavy and therefore may be unsuitable or uncomfortable for some gardeners. It has a rectangular blade of about 28 x 19cm (11 x 7in).

"D"-type moulded hilt gives a good grip

Plastic hilt is comfortable even in cold weather

Tread makes digging easier

Coated blade may be easily cleaned

Stainless steel blade
This is useful for a spade as it makes light work of digging and never rusts.

Automatic spade
Operating on a spring-and-lever system, the spade throws the soil forward without the need to bend. It may be worthwhile for the disabled or for those with back trouble or with a large area to dig.

Border spade
With a blade only 23 x 13cm (9 x 5in), this is designed for digging in confined spaces, for example a planting hole in a border, but it is also good for any general light work.

Standard fork
This fork is useful for cultivating heavy soil, lifting vegetables, and shifting large loads, but some people may find it heavy to manoeuvre. Its head is about 30 x 20cm (12 x 8in).

Wooden shaft fitting into long socket in neck

Neck and head formed from one piece of metal for strength

Head

Potato fork
Primarily for lifting potatoes, this flat-tined fork may also be used for digging, and moving compost or garden refuse.

Border fork
This is best for light work in borders and similar restricted areas. The size of the head – 23 x 14cm (9 x 5½in) – makes it suitable for anyone needing a small, lightweight fork.

Which metal?

Carbon steel is used for most garden tools. If cleaned and oiled after use, it should not rust, and it can be sharpened. Although stainless steel is more expensive and cannot be sharpened, it does make digging easier since the soil falls away from the blade more readily. Tools that have a "non-stick" coating may make working the soil and cleaning easier but the coating may wear off after long use.

Handles and hilts

A spade or fork shaft should be the correct length for the user's height to minimize back strain. The standard shaft length is 70–73cm (28–29in); a longer shaft, available up to 98cm (39in) long, will almost certainly be more comfortable for people over 1.7m (5ft 6in) tall.

Shafts are made from wood or metal, the latter sometimes covered with plastic or nylon. Both are generally strong, but even metal shafts may break if put under too much stress, and, unlike wooden ones, they cannot be replaced. Metal shafts, even plastic-coated, are colder than wood to hold in winter. Handle the tool, as if using it, to assess which type feels best.

"D"-type hilts
These are the most common type, but they may be uncomfortable for those with large hands, particularly when wearing gloves.

"Y"-type hilts
Similar to "D"-type hilts, but they may be weaker as they are formed by splitting the shaft wood.

"T"-type hilts
These have a cross-piece joined to the shaft end. Some gardeners find them comfortable, but they are not commonly available and may have to be ordered.

Hoes

Hoes are used for weeding and aerating soil; some types may be used to form seed drills. The Dutch hoe is probably the most versatile and is ideal for weeding between rows of plants and for creating drills. Apart from draw, digging, and onion hoes, there are proprietary hoes available for specific uses.

Using a Dutch hoe
Hold the hoe so that the blade is parallel to the soil surface.

Dutch hoe
This traditional hoe is excellent for weeding around plants. It cuts through surface weeds without damaging the plant roots.

Combination hoe
This is suitable for chopping off weeds, drawing drills, and earthing up. Use the prongs to break up soil and draw seed drills.

Triangular hoe
Use the point for drawing a "V"-shaped drill; the flat side is for weeding narrow spaces in between plants.

Digging hoe
This has one or two chisel-like blades. It is used with a swinging motion to break up small areas of hard ground.

Short-handled hoe for use in confined areas

Moulded handle ensures a secure grip

Onion hoe
This small hoe (above), also called a hand, or rock garden, hoe, is for weeding between onions and other closely grown plants where a normal hoe might cause damage. It is like a short-handled version of a draw hoe, and is used while squatting or kneeling.

Draw hoe
This hoe (right) is good for chopping weeds, drawing up earth around plants, making flat-bottomed seed drills, and, with the blade corner, making "V"-shaped drills.

Curved neck makes the hoe easier to use in between plants without damaging them

Rakes

Rakes are excellent for levelling and breaking up the soil surface before planting and for gathering garden debris. There are two main types: general garden rakes and lawn rakes (see "Rakes and aerators", p.559).

A one-piece rake head is stronger than a bolstered (riveted) one, and the wider the head, the faster an area is covered; 12 teeth are adequate, 16 or more are preferable for large areas. A 1m (3ft) wide wooden rake is useful in a large garden.

Garden rake
This has short, wide, rounded teeth and is valuable for levelling soil, clearing the ground, and general garden tidying.

Bolstered rake
This cheaper garden rake has nail-like, riveted teeth.

Heads and shafts

Most rake and hoe heads are made from solid carbon steel; stainless steel ones are more expensive and do not work any better, although they are easier to clean and do not rust. Some rakes have a "non-stick" coating.

Shafts may be made from wood, aluminium, or plastic-covered metal. Shaft length is important: you should be able to stand upright while hoeing or raking to reduce strain on the back. Most people find a 1.5m (5ft) shaft comfortable, but a longer handle may be preferred.

Trowels and hand forks

A trowel is useful for digging holes for small plants and bulbs, and for working in containers and raised beds. A hand, or weed, fork may be used for weeding, lifting small plants, and for planting.

Most trowel blades and hand fork prongs are made from stainless steel, coated steel (eg chrome-plated), or ordinary carbon steel. Unlike carbon steel, stainless steel does not rust and is easy to keep clean but it is expensive. Coatings gradually tend to wear off in time. Some trowels have extra-long handles – up to 30cm (12in) – for more leverage. Hand forks with handles 1.2m (4ft) long reduce the need to bend when weeding the back of a border. Wooden, plastic, and plastic-coated handles are all generally comfortable to hold; metal ones tend to be cold.

Hand fork
Often used for lifting small plants or loosening the soil when weeding. Unlike a trowel, it does not compact the soil, so it may be preferable to use when planting in heavy soil.

Narrow-bladed trowel
Sometimes known as a rock garden or transplanting trowel, this is ideal for working in very confined areas such as rock gardens as well as for general transplanting tasks.

Wide-bladed trowel
This is useful for planting bulbs and bedding or other small plants, especially in confined areas such as containers and windowboxes.

Hand-weeding tools

For weeding between paving, bricks, or rocks, a patio weeder, which has a narrow, hooked blade, is ideal. A daisy grubber has a pronged blade suitable for levering up lawn weeds.

Specialized weeders
A patio, or paving stone, weeder (right) can be used in narrow crevices. A daisy grubber (far right) may be used to lift lawn weeds without damaging the turf.

Manual cultivators

A hand, or pronged, cultivator is used to break up the surface of compacted soil or to loosen weeds. It has a three- or five-pronged, metal head on a long shaft and is pulled through the soil, generally from a standing position. Some adjustable models have removable, central prongs.

Specialized hand cultivators may be useful for certain regular tasks. A star-wheeled cultivator, or miller, for example, forms a fine tilth when pushed to and fro through the soil, so is good when preparing a seedbed.

Adjustable models
Cultivators with removable central prongs are suitable for tasks such as cultivating each side of a row of seedlings. Some models have a detachable handle which may be fitted to other types of compatible tool head, for example a rake or hoe.

Star-wheeled cultivator
This creates a fine tilth for a seedbed.

A single detachable handle may be combined with a variety of tool heads

Removable prongs
When working in very confined areas, it may be useful to remove some prongs to make the head smaller.

Powered cultivators

A powered cultivator is used for tackling laborious tasks like turning over the soil in neglected ground. It breaks up compacted soil and reduces it to a tilth fine enough for planting. It is impractical for use in heavily planted areas, however, and does not eliminate the need for hand digging. Petrol-powered cultivators are powerful and generally have a wide range of attachments but need more maintenance than electric ones. Electric cultivators are excellent for small jobs. They are easier to manoeuvre, less noisy, and cheaper than petrol-engined types but trailing cables may be a problem.

On most cultivators the handle height is adjustable. Some also have handles that pivot and lock sideways, allowing you to walk alongside the machine without trampling the ground already cultivated.

Cultivators come in three main types: front-, mid-, and rear-engined. **Front-engined cultivators** have rotors behind the driving wheels. They are easy to steer, but, because of the way the weight is distributed, are best for shallow cultivation.

Mid-engined cultivators are propelled by rotors rather than wheels. This may make control difficult, but the engine weight over the rotors makes deep cultivation easier than with a front-engined type.

Rear-engined cultivators are best for manoeuvring in difficult places and for forming deep holes. The rotors, on a boom at the front, are swept from side to side as the cultivator is propelled along. The machines may be tiring to control.

Potato lifter
This attachment lifts potatoes out onto the soil surface for easy collection.

Five-tine cultivator attachment
This is used to weed between rows and for general cultivation. The tines can be adjusted for depth and width.

Powered cultivator
This front-engined petrol model is stable and easy to control. It is expensive, but makes an excellent job of straightforward cultivation over a large area.

Deadman's handle (cuts power if grip relaxed)

Blade engagement

Accelerator

Clutch

Horizontal handle adjuster

Vertical hand height adjuster

Choke

Lever adjusts depth of cultivation

Fold-away stand ensures stability when machine is not in use

Rotors should be well away from operator's feet

Rear rotors produce a fine finish for a seedbed

Transporter wheel aids steering

Pruning and cutting tools

When pruning, it is important to use the appropriate tool for the task and to make sure that it is sharp so that it cuts cleanly, easily, and safely. Using a blunt blade can leave a plant with a ragged wound that is prone to infection or that can cause die-back. Take particular care when working with powered tools, such as hedge-trimmers or brushwood cutters (see "Electrical safety", p.556).

Secateurs

Secateurs are used for pruning woody stems up to about 1cm (⅓in) thick and soft shoots of any thickness; they may also be used for taking cuttings for propagation. They can be used single-handed and are more controllable and easier to handle safely than a knife, particularly by inexperienced gardeners.

There are three main types of secateur: by-pass, parrot-beak, and anvil. By-pass and parrot-beak secateurs have a scissor-like action; anvil secateurs have a sharp, straight-edged upper blade that cuts against a square-edged lower anvil. In some designs (swing anvils), the blade is pivoted in such a way that it remains parallel to the anvil as it cuts, slicing rather than crushing the stem.

For cutting soft-stemmed plants, a light, comparatively cheap pair is perfectly adequate. For pruning fruit trees and shrubs with woody shoots up to 1cm (⅓in) thick, a pair of heavy-duty secateurs is well worth the additional expense as the mechanism will not become strained.

If possible, try out the secateurs to check that they are comfortable and easy to operate; the handle material and shape, how wide they open, and the pressure of the spring keeping

By-pass secateurs
These use a scissor-like action. They have a sharp, convex, steel upper blade that cuts against a concave or square, steel lower blade to make a clean cut.

Brightly coloured handles are easy to spot

Moulded grip is comfortable in use

Sharp, steel blade makes a clean, precise cut

Safety catch may be moved with the thumb

Flower gatherers
These are designed to grip the flower stem after cutting.

Safety catch
This catch clips the handles together.

Ratchet system
This makes cutting tough stems easier.

Anvil secateurs
These must be kept sharp, otherwise the blade crushes the stem against the anvil instead of cutting it.

Parrot-beak secateurs
These give a clean cut, but may be damaged if used to cut wood more than 1cm (⅓in) thick.

them open all vary considerably. Metal handles may be very cold to hold, but most handles are now plastic or plastic-covered metal. All secateurs are fitted with a safety catch that locks the blades in the shut position. Check that it is easy to operate with one hand and that it cannot be flicked off accidentally.

Secateur blades may be made from stainless steel, carbon steel, or coated steel. Coated blades are easy to wipe clean, but are unlikely to last as long as high-quality stainless or carbon steel blades, which keep their

sharpness and cut cleanly and easily. When buying high-quality secateurs, ensure that they can be dismantled for sharpening without special tools and that new blades are available.

Some models have a ratchet system for cutting through a stem in stages. These require less effort and so are suitable for those who find conventional models a strain.

Flower gatherers, or flower pickers, hold the flower stem after cutting. They are invaluable for cutting flowers on a regular basis, otherwise secateurs or scissors will suffice.

Maintenance

Clean the blades of cutting tools after each use with an oily rag or wire wool to remove any sap that has dried on; then lightly oil them. Periodically tighten the blade tension of garden shears; this makes them cut more efficiently and produces a better finish.

Most pruning tools are easy to sharpen. Remove blades that are badly blunted or damaged, and regrind or replace them.

Long-handled pruners or loppers

A pair of long-handled pruners, or loppers, is useful for removing woody stems or branches 1–2.5cm (½–1in) thick, where secateurs might be damaged, and for thinner branches that are difficult to reach.

The long handles give additional leverage, making it easier to cut through thick stems. They are usually wood or plastic-covered tubular steel or aluminium. Blades are made of stainless steel, carbon steel, or coated steel, as for secateurs.

The weight and balance of long-handled pruners are important as you may have to hold them at full

stretch or above your head. Make sure that you will be able to operate them easily and without strain.

Most long-handled pruners have a by-pass blade motion, others an anvil action. Both are satisfactory designs, and the choice is a matter of personal preference. Designs with a ratchet are sometimes available and are particularly useful for cutting through thick or tough branches and to reduce the strength needed for cutting.

All long-handled pruners require regular maintenance to keep them in peak working condition.

Long-handled by-pass pruners
Using long-handled pruners makes it possible to prune stems that are high up or that are too tough or thick for secateurs.

Buffers prevent jarring when operating pruners

Anvil pruners
The blades open wide for cutting thick stems.

Tree pruners

A tree pruner is suitable for cutting branches up to 2.5cm (1in) thick that would otherwise be out of reach. The cutting device is positioned at the end of a pole that is usually 2–3m (6–10ft) long, although some extend to 5m (15ft). The carbon steel blade is operated by a lever system or a cord; both are efficient, although the lever system is more popular. Some cord models have telescopic poles so that the length may be adjusted; they are also more convenient to store. Tree pruners may have saw or fruit-picker attachments.

Hooked end is lowered over the branch to be cut

Tree pruner

Pruning saws

Use a pruning saw for severing branches more than about 2.5cm (1in) thick. Because sawing in a confined space between other branches, and often at an awkward angle, may be difficult, various types of pruning saw have been developed. Those most commonly available are: general-purpose pruning, Grecian or rigid-handle curved, double-edged or two-edged, folding, and bow saws. If pruning is a major task in the garden, it may be necessary to have more than one saw for different types of

work. A Grecian saw is one of the most useful pruning saws for an amateur gardener.

All pruning saws should have hardpoint, heat-treated teeth, which are harder and stay sharper for longer than ordinary saw teeth. They must be professionally sharpened. Saw handles are plastic or wood; choose whichever feels more comfortable and has a secure grip. Score a groove in the branch in which to insert the saw blade in order to reduce the risk of its slipping during use.

General-purpose pruning saw
Invaluable for most pruning jobs, this saw has a small blade, generally not more than 45cm (18in) long, so that it can be easily used in confined areas and at awkward angles.

Folding saw
The saw blade folds into the handle, like a knife. It is suitable only for small branches, as it is designed to fit into a pocket and is not particularly strong.

Grecian saw
This is excellent for confined spaces as it has a curved blade and cuts only on the pull stroke. In restricted areas, it is easier to use pressure on a pull, rather than a push, stroke.

Double-edged pruning saw
This is very flexible as it has both coarse and fine teeth but may be difficult to operate in confined spaces without the top teeth damaging a nearby branch.

Bow saw
This is used to cut through thick branches quickly, but is too large to operate in a confined area.

Garden knives

A garden knife may be used for light pruning tasks instead of secateurs, and is more versatile. It is also convenient for taking cuttings, harvesting certain vegetables, preparing material for grafting, and cutting string.

There are various types of garden knife available, including general-purpose, grafting, budding, and pruning or peach pruners. Most knives have a carbon steel blade which is either fixed or folds into

the handle. If choosing the folding type, check that it is easy to open, and that the spring holding the blade in position is neither too strong nor too slack. Always dry knife blades after use, and wipe them over with an oily rag. Sharpen knives regularly, to the same angle as when new.

A Stanley-type knife with disposable blades is a good alternative to a garden knife, or use disposable craft knives and scalpels for taking cuttings.

General-purpose garden knife
This is useful for all cutting tasks except heavy pruning.

Multi-purpose knife
There are various models available. This one has a large blade for general use and pruning, a small one for grafting, and an attachment for budding.

Grafting
This straight-bladed knife is suitable for general tasks, and for making accurate cuts when grafting.

Budding
The blade projection is used for prising open the rootstock incision when propagating by bud-grafting.

Pruning
The large blade curves downwards for a controlled cut when pruning.

Garden shears

Shears are used mainly for trimming hedges, but are also invaluable for cutting small or awkward areas of long grass (see also "Lawncare tools", pp.558–559), clipping topiary, and cutting back herbaceous plants.

For soft-stemmed hedges, a light pair is adequate but for large hedges with tough, woody stems a heavy-duty pair will be needed.

Weight and balance are both important; before buying, check that the shears are centrally balanced and the blades are not too heavy, or they will then be tiring to operate.

Most shears have straight blades although a few have wavy edged blades: these cut through mature wood easily and help to trap the shoots so that they are not pushed out with the scissor-action of the blades. They are difficult to sharpen (see also "Maintenance", p.554).

Standard shears
Shears usually have one notched blade to hold a thick shoot during cutting.

Single-handed shears
These have a spring mechanism similar to secateurs that allows them to be operated with one hand. Some types have blades that swivel – useful for cutting at an angle or vertically (as for edging a lawn). They are only suitable for cutting grass or very soft stems.

Hedgetrimmers

For gardeners with large hedges to cut, a powered hedgetrimmer may be worthwhile as it takes much less time and effort to use than ordinary manually operated shears.

The longer the blade, the faster the hedge can be cut and the easier it is to reach a tall hedge or across the top of a wide one. Hedgetrimmers with very long blades are heavy and often poorly balanced, however. A 40cm (16in) blade is adequate for normal garden use, but if cutting extensive hedges a 60cm (24in) blade saves considerable time. Blades may be either single- or double-sided; the latter speed up the cutting time but are not as easy to control as single-sided blades, so hedge-shaping may be more difficult.

The ease of handling is also affected by the blade action. Models with reciprocating- or double-action blades, which move against each other, are generally preferable for the majority of gardeners. Single-action models, in which one moving blade cuts against a second, stationary blade, cause vibration and can therefore be tiring to operate.

The finish of the cut is largely controlled by the spacing of the teeth along the blade. Narrowly spaced teeth produce a smooth, even finish

Protective clothing
When operating powered tools, wear protective clothing such as goggles, ear protectors, and thick gardening gloves (see also p.563).

Powered hedgetrimmer
This makes hedgetrimming faster and easier than it is when using garden shears. Electric models are light and easy to manoeuvre, while petrol versions are powerful and unhampered by trailing cables.

on a hedge that is regularly trimmed, while more widely spaced teeth usually cope better with thicker twigs but leave a rougher cut.

Petrol or electricity?

Hedgetrimmers may be powered by petrol or electricity, either from the mains or batteries. Petrol hedgetrimmers may be operated anywhere and are generally powerful and relatively free from vibration. They are, however, noisier, heavier, and more expensive than electric ones and usually require more maintenance.

Electric hedgetrimmers are more commonly used by amateurs and are better for small jobs. Being lighter, they are easier to handle than petrol trimmers; they are also cleaner to use and cheaper to buy.

Mains electric hedgetrimmers are the most convenient for hedges within 30m (100ft) of a power supply. As with other electric tools, the trailing cable can be inconvenient and even hazardous, and the machine must not be used in wet conditions. Safety features are very important when handling such a potentially

dangerous tool: for example, they should always be operated with a residual current device, or earth leakage circuit breaker (see also "Electrical safety", below).

Battery-powered hedgetrimmers are good for hedges in a distant part of a large garden or where there is no convenient power supply. They are usually run from a spare car battery. When fully charged, they are reasonably powerful but maintaining a charged battery and moving it around the garden can be time-consuming and laborious. They are more expensive than mains electric models.

Rechargeable hedgetrimmers

Hedgetrimmers powered by a rechargeable battery are cordless, easy to manoeuvre, and comparatively cheap. They are excellent for small, regularly trimmed hedges, but they lack the power to cut thick shoots and long hedges satisfactorily. As there are no trailing cables, rechargeable machines present fewer safety hazards than other types of electric trimmer. They can be recharged from a special mains unit.

Brushwood cutters

A brushwood cutter is excellent for slashing through tough weeds, undergrowth, and very long grass. The rotating head has a metal slasher or fine-toothed blade. This makes it suitable for far heavier tasks than those that can be tackled with a nylon-line trimmer (see "Lawncare tools", pp.558–559), but it is more tiring to operate. Some models take

plastic blades, but these are not as tough or durable. In addition to their cutting blade, some may be fitted with a nylon line for trimming grass.

As they need powerful engines to work effectively, most brushwood cutters are petrol-driven. Electric models are usually lighter, less noisy, and require less maintenance, but are less efficient for heavy work.

Electrical safety

- Keep leads only just as long as is necessary. Trailing cables are inconvenient and potentially hazardous, as they may be cut by moving blades.
- Have outside sockets installed by a qualified electrician at suitable points in the garden to keep leads short and safe.
- If extension leads are needed, ensure that they have the same number of wires as the tool: if the tool is earthed, the extension cable should be too.
- If the circuit is not already protected, attach a plug fitted with a residual current device (RCD) to the tool, or buy an adaptor RCD to insert between the plug and socket.
- Do not use an electric tool during or just after rain as this may cause electrical faults.
- Always disconnect the power supply before adjusting, inspecting, or cleaning a tool.
- Never touch a severed or damaged cable before disconnecting it from the mains.

Chainsaws

Chainsaws are suitable for sawing logs or large branches and for extensive tree surgery and felling. As they cut with a powered, toothed chain revolving at high speed, they can be extremely dangerous; it is essential to be trained in their use and never to work alone, in case of accidents. As with all electrical equipment, you must always wear appropriate safety equipment and follow strict rules for the safe use of electricity (see right).

Electric chainsaws are useful for small jobs and are cheaper than petrol types, which are more powerful, noisy, heavy, often difficult to start, and create fumes.

Electric chainsaw
An electric chainsaw is suitable for most sawing tasks; it is lighter and easier to handle than a petrol-powered version and generally requires less maintenance.

Side handle to help balance saw

On-off switch

Chain brake

Revolving, toothed chain cuts through the wood

Reservoir containing oil, to lubricate the chain

Electrical lead

Lawnmowers

When choosing a lawnmower, take into account the size of your lawn and the type of cut required. If only a small area needs mowing, a manual lawnmower may suffice, but for a larger lawn, buy a powered one. There are cylinder, rotary, and hover mowers available: cylinder models usually provide the finest cut, while rotary types are better for long, over-grown grass; hover mowers are best for irregular lawns.

Grass should be mown more closely in summer than in winter, so check that the height of cut is easily adjustable (see also THE LAWN, "Frequency and height of cut", p.395). A mulching mower chops grass finely and discharges the clippings close to the soil surface, for rapid decomposition and soil nourishment. If you need a fine finish without loose grass, choose a lawnmower with a grass collector. Such models are more usually cylinder mowers than hover ones (see also "Grass clippings", p.395).

Manual lawnmowers

Manual mowers are relatively cheap, quiet, have no awkward cables, and need very little maintenance. There are two types: those driven by wheels at the side and those operated by a chain drive from a heavy rear roller. A side-wheel mower is easy to push but awkward at the edge of a lawn.

Powered lawnmowers

There are two basic types of powered lawnmower: cylinder, and rotary or hover (hover mowers work on the same principle as rotary ones). Most run on petrol, mains electricity, or rechargeable battery. Powered mowers are potentially dangerous on steep slopes as they are designed for flat surfaces. Ride-on or tractor-hauled models are convenient for large areas. **Cylinder mowers** are self-propelled or have a powered blade; the latter type may be heavy and tiring to operate. Most have a rear roller, essential if you want a lawn with a striped pattern; the heavier the roller, the more pronounced the stripe.

Petrol-driven cylinder mowers often have broader cutting widths than electric ones. This reduces the cutting time but makes them more difficult to manoeuvre.

Rotary and hover mowers have replaceable metal or plastic blades that cut the grass with a scissor-like

SELECTING A LAWNMOWER

Manual, rear-roller mower
With this kind of mower it is easy to mow up to and over a lawn edge, as the cylinder is supported by a back roller.

Powered, cylinder mower
A mower of this type provides a fine, close-cut finish and is probably the best choice for a high-quality lawn. It may have an interchangeable lawn-rake blade. The blade cylinder is driven by a rear roller.

Plastic blade
Cheap to replace, the blade rotates horizontally to cut the grass.

Cylinder blades
The blades are set along a cylinder that rotates forward and cuts against a fixed blade.

Deadman's handle (cuts power if grip relaxed)

Electric hover mower
A hover mower is ideal for cutting grass on small lawns and in awkward places such as beneath low, overhanging plants and next to paving. It is easy to manoeuvre on flat surfaces and shallow slopes but may overbalance and cut out on a steep slope. Some hover mowers have grass collectors.

Petrol-driven rotary mower
A ride-on mower is useful for extensive grassed areas, including rough and long grass, as it has a powerful engine. The replaceable metal blade cuts horizontally.

motion, as they rotate horizontally. Rotary mowers have wheels while hover mowers ride on a cushion of air. Some rotary mowers are fitted with rollers, and these are best for fine lawns. Both types work better than cylinder mowers for sites that are slightly uneven or have long grass, but most models cannot cut the grass very low. Rotary blades can become unbalanced so regular service checks are advisable.

Which power source?

Batteries and electricity are more convenient and cleaner than petrol, but not suitable for powerful engines. For cordless mowers, a handy power outlet is needed for recharging – batteries cannot always be removed from the mower. For an electric mower, access to a power supply is also essential, but the trailing flex may be a hazard. Electric mowers should not be used on wet grass.

Petrol lawnmowers are also not hampered by cables but are more expensive to buy and maintain. They may not start readily unless they are fitted with an electric ignition.

Safety

■ Blades must be well protected so that they do not come into contact with the operator's feet, especially when using on slopes. The operator should always wear strong shoes.
■ The blade brake must stop the blades rotating within five seconds of being turned off.
■ The mower should have a lock-off switch, which requires two operations to turn on an engine. This reduces the risk of a child accidentally switching it on.
■ A deadman's handle should be fitted. Held when mowing, this turns off the engine when released.

Maintenance

A few simple precautions keep a mower working efficiently.
■ After use, disconnect power, then clean engine and blades.
■ Check that the blades are sharp and replace blunt ones.
■ Oil and lubricate regularly.
■ Service the mower yearly.
■ Periodically check that spark plugs are clean and adjusted.
■ Clean filters and air intakes of petrol mowers regularly.
■ Periodically check the oil level on four-stroke engines.
■ Before you store a petrol-powered model, drain the tank.

Lawncare tools

As well as a lawnmower, a number of other tools are useful for maintaining a healthy and attractive lawn. Manual tools are usually adequate for most lawns but, for large areas, powered tools are faster and less tiring to use.

Edging tools

A neat, well-defined edge provides the perfect finishing touch to a well-mown lawn and emphasizes the lawn's shape and outline (see also *Cutting the Edge of the Lawn*, p.396). There are two main lawn edging tools: half-moon edgers and long-handled shears, although powered edging machines and certain nylon-line trimmers may be used.

Shafts for long-handled shears are wooden, steel, or plastic-coated steel; all are strong and the choice is really a matter of personal preference.

Long-handled edging shears
These are useful for trimming overhanging grass around the lawn edge. The handles should be sufficiently long so that there is no need to stoop. If either too short or too heavy, the shears may be tiring to operate.

Half-moon edger
Also known as an edging iron or lawn edger, this is used with a rocking motion to cut away worn or uneven lawn edges and to remove small areas of turf for repair. It has a sharp, curved, metal blade attached to a long, wooden or metal handle.

Tang of blade is well secured to shaft neck

Lawn edging materials

In order to prevent a lawn from gradually decreasing in size when turf is removed with tools such as a half-moon edger, outline the lawn with bricks, paving slabs, terracotta edging tiles, or some metal or plastic edging strips. This helps to ensure an even edge to the lawn and inhibits grass from spreading onto paths and borders. A brick or paving-slab edge also enables hover and side-wheel mowers to be driven right to the lawn edge. Plastic strips, which are usually coloured green, are less likely than metal edging strips to damage mower blades, and are also cheaper.

Nylon-line trimmers

A nylon-line trimmer is useful for trimming grass in awkward areas that cannot easily be reached by a mower. It may also be used for slashing ground-cover plants or soft-stemmed weeds, although a more powerful brushwood cutter may be needed for tough undergrowth (see p.556). As the nylon cutting line is flexible and easily replaced, it is possible to work right up to a wall or paving without damaging the tool. It is also safer than a fixed blade if there is an accident. Always wear goggles, as flying stones may be hazardous.

Nylon-line trimmers may be driven by mains-powered electricity, rechargeable battery, or petrol, and similar considerations of safety, convenience, and weight apply. Mains-powered electric models are light and easy to operate, but their area of use is restricted by the cable length. For safety, they should have a deadman's handle and be connected to a residual current device. Cordless nylon-line trimmers with rechargeable batteries are suitable for small to medium areas, especially where there is no external power supply. They too are lightweight, quiet, and easy to use. Under no circumstances must electric-powered trimmers be used while grass is wet (see also "Electrical safety", p.556).

Petrol-driven trimmers are ideal for larger gardens, but they are heavier, more expensive, and need more maintenance than other trimmers. For safety, they should have a quick, easy way to stop the engine.

Trimmer
This has a flexible, nylon, cutting line which rotates at high speed to cut through grass and other soft-stemmed plants or weeds. Some models have an adjustable head that may be tilted vertically for trimming lawn edges.

A shaft-handle makes the tool easy to manoeuvre

Shield protects user from whirling cutting line

Cutting guide
This keeps the nylon line just off the ground to stop it cutting too low and to produce an even trim.

Garden rollers

A garden roller, which may be made of metal or water-filled, hollow plastic, is used to level the surface during initial ground preparation before sowing grass seed or laying turf. It also settles the soil around young grass seedlings. Rolling established lawns regularly is no longer recommended, however; on heavy soils particularly, it tends to compact the turf and therefore impede drainage, which may cause problems such as moss and poor grass growth.

Long-handled lawn shears

Long-handled lawn shears are helpful for trimming grass in awkward places, such as beneath overhanging plants or around trees, paving, or walls, and for tidying any stalks missed during mowing. The blades, set at right angles to the handles, are positioned parallel to the ground, not vertically as in edging shears.

While lawn shears are useful for very small areas, they have now largely been superseded by powered, nylon-line trimmers, which are faster and more versatile. Trimmers are heavier to hold and manoeuvre than shears, however, and less energy-efficient than hand tools.

Long-handled lawn shears
These may be useful for cutting grass in small areas that would be difficult to cut with a mower.

Rakes and aerators

Tools for clearing up fallen leaves and garden debris and for reducing thatch (a layer of decaying organic matter) and soil compaction help to keep a lawn in good condition.

Lawn rakes are primarily used to gather up fallen leaves. Some types may be helpful in removing thatch and dead moss. There are three types of lawn rake: spring-tined, flat-tined, and scarifying, or aerator, rakes (see also "Rakes", p.552). In addition, powered lawn rakes are available, which are suitable for large lawns.

Aerators help to reduce thatch and let air into the soil, encouraging good root growth. On very small areas, aerating may be done with a garden fork, but for most lawns a purpose-built machine such as a hollow-tined aerator or a slitter is better.

Spring-tined lawn rake
This is used for clearing out dead grass and moss, removing small stones and debris, and lightly aerating a lawn. Its light head has long, flexible, rounded wire tines.

Flat-tined lawn rake
Excellent for gathering up leaves and loose material, this has long, flexible, flat tines of plastic or metal, and a light head to minimize damage to new growth.

Scarifying rake
This cuts deeply into thatch and even into the turf itself. Its rigid, metal tines are usually flat, with sharp points. As it may be heavy and tiring to use, a model with wheels either side of the rake head may be preferable.

Powered lawn rake
Easier to use than an ordinary rake, its plastic or metal tines effectively scarify turf, while its collecting box removes debris.

Star-wheeled slitter
This aerates the turf faster than a hollow-tined aerator but, if the ground is hard, it may not penetrate enough to be effective.

Hollow-tined aerator
This powered, hollow-tined aerator penetrates deeply through the turf into the soil. The tines remove cores of soil, opening up compacted turf.

Sweepers and blowers

At its simplest, a leaf sweeper may be an ordinary besom brush or stiff broom used to sweep away small debris; this kind of basic sweeper is ideal for clearing pathways and small areas of the garden.

For large lawns, however, using a purpose-designed leaf sweeper saves both labour and time. The leaves are lifted from the surface of the grass by rotating brushes and they are then thrown into a large collecting bag, from which they can be readily emptied and composted.

Electric- or petrol-powered vacuum leaf collectors and blowers may prove worthwhile in very large gardens, but they are expensive to buy and they may be noisy to operate.

Some powered models have flexible attachments designed for use among flower beds and other areas of the garden that are particularly hard to reach.

Besom
This is an inexpensive brush suitable for sweeping up leaves and light debris.

Leaf sweeper
This gathers up garden leaves, using rotating brushes, and collects them in a large bag. It is light, easy to push, and quiet in operation.

Backpack leaf blower
This blower is carried on the operator's back while it blows, rather than sweeps, garden leaves into a pile for collection. It is useful for small, tight, or irregularly shaped areas, but is bulky to store and noisy, so always wear ear protection when operating such a machine.

Control handle and starter

Fertilizer spreaders

A fertilizer spreader is suitable for the accurate distribution of fertilizer, grass seed, and granular weedkillers. It comprises a hopper on wheels with a long handle. Check that the application rate is adjustable and that the flow may be switched off when turning at the lawn edge. After setting the application rate always check that it is correct by fertilizing a test area first (see "Applying fertilizers", p.625). A hose attachment used for applying a fertilizer with water is useful for feeding a lawn (see "Sprayers", p.560).

Fertilizer spreader
A spreader applies fertilizer evenly, so avoiding scorching the grass.

Watering aids

Irrigation makes it possible to grow plants that require more water than is provided by rainfall, and to grow plants both indoors and in the greenhouse. Equipment such as hoses and sprinklers help make routine watering easier and faster.

Watering cans

A watering can is practical in the house, greenhouse, or for small areas outside. Choose a lightweight can that will not be too heavy to carry when full. The opening of the watering can should be wide enough to make filling easy, and the can itself should feel comfortable and well balanced. A can that has a strainer at the base of the spout helps to prevent the rose from becoming clogged by debris in the water.

Water butts

A water butt collects rainwater from the house or greenhouse roof, which is invaluable during dry periods and for acid-loving plants. The butt should have a tap, and a lid to keep out debris, which pollutes the water and might block the tap. If necessary, raise the butt on blocks so a watering can will fit under the tap. Some butts divert water back to the drain when they are full. See WATER CONSERVATION AND RECYCLING, pp.614–615.

Garden watering cans
These should have a generous capacity to reduce the need for repeated refilling. For general-purpose use, a 9 litre (2 gallon) can, which holds 8kg (18lb) of water, is a convenient size.

Plastic or metal?
Most watering cans are now made from plastic, but traditional galvanized metal ones, which are heavier and more expensive, are still available; both types are sturdy and durable.

Greenhouse watering can
This has a long spout, so that it is easy to reach plants at the back of a bench, and a reversible rose for both fine and coarse sprays for watering seedlings and mature plants.

Indoor watering can
This should have a long spout to reach into plant pots and windowboxes, and to help control the flow.

Which rose?

Coarse-spray rose

Fine-spray brass rose

Fine-spray, brass-faced, plastic rose

A fine rose is best for seeds and seedlings because the resulting spray does not damage them or wash the compost or soil away from them. For more established plants, a coarse-spray rose, which delivers the water faster, is preferable.

Roses are manufactured in a choice of materials: brass, brass-faced plastic, and all-plastic. Plastic is less durable and cheaper than brass but is still satisfactory for most uses. In general, metal roses give a finer spray.

Using a dribble bar, which is attached to a watering can, makes it more accurate than a rose for applying weedkiller. It also reduces spray drift which can be a problem with a rose.

Caution with weedkiller

Do not use the same watering can or sprayer for watering the garden and for dispensing liquid weedkillers. Keep a dedicated one, clearly marked, for applying chemicals.

Hosepipes

A hosepipe is invaluable for irrigating distant parts of the garden and for areas that require copious watering. Most hosepipes are made from PVC; they vary in the way they are finished or reinforced, which affects their durability, flexibility, and resistance to kinking. Any kinks interrupt water flow and eventually weaken the hose wall. Double-walled and reinforced hoses are resistant to kinking but relatively expensive. Some hosepipes are available on a wall-mounted, retractable reel, for tidy storage, while others are on wheels or retract into a plastic box with a carrying handle. These allow waterflow through the hose even when partially wound, so the hose can always be tidy yet ready for immediate use.

All types of hose are made in various fixed lengths with connectors and nozzles pre-fitted or as accessories. Some hoses can be lengthened with one or more extensions. Wherever

an external, cold-water supply is connected to a garden hose, it is advisable to fit the tap or outlet with a double-check, or non-return, valve, to prevent back siphonage of potentially contaminated water into other parts of the system. Check with your local water authority if this is a legal requirement in your area.

Hose reel
A reel with a handle or wheels is easy to move around the garden. Some reels allow waterflow through the hose even when partially wound.

Sprayers

Use sprayers to apply pesticides, herbicides, and fertilizers, and to water or mist-spray plants. Compression types, pumped up before use, are suitable for general use; small trigger-pump sprayers are for misting house plants or applying pesticides to a few plants. In countries where regulations permit, hose attachments that incorporate reservoirs are available for dispensing fertilizers and weedkillers.

Trigger-action hose attachment

Nozzle allows spray to be adjusted to jet or mist

Trigger

Fertilizer pulse hose attachment

Central chamber for fertilizer

Compression sprayer
This sprayer is pumped up with the handle and is suitable for treating large areas.

Hose-end attachments
Most attachments simply allow the intensity and range of the water spray to be adjusted. Some have a trigger-action nozzle.

Responsible watering

Numerous watering aids are now available, but it is important to accept that it will not be possible to use them in prolonged periods of drought when water use is severely restricted. Watering by hose or using sprinklers will not be legally acceptable, and while watering with cans is possible, it would be impractical in many gardens, except for short periods.

The practical solution is to store as much rainwater as possible in covered waterbutts or other strong plastic containers designed to fit under downpipes. A water pump in the container connected to a hose can then distribute water as required. It is preferable to use a trickle system or a seep-hose so that as little water as possible is lost by evaporation.

Ensure that all watering and spraying equipment, including connectors, is in good condition to avoid losing water through leaks or evaporation.

Seep hoses

Seep hoses are useful for lawns or rows of plants. They are plastic or rubber hoses with small perforations along their entire length. With the holes facing upwards, it produces a fine spray over a rectangular area. With the holes placed towards or under the soil, water is directed to the base of plants – ideal for vegetables and other plants grown in rows.

Porous hoses are similar, and particularly suitable for newly planted beds, borders, and vegetable gardens. They allow water to seep slowly into the soil and can be attached to a hose timer. They may be buried up to

TYPES OF SPRINKLER

Static sprinkler
Primarily for lawns. Most have a spike to push into the ground. They usually spray in a circle, but a few water in a semi-circular, fan, or rectangular, shape. Liable to form puddles, so move about for even distribution of water.

Rotating sprinkler
Good for beds, borders, and lawns. Cover large circular areas and apply water evenly. Spray is delivered from nozzles on the arms attached to a spinning pivot, driven by the force of the water. Long-stemmed types are best for beds or borders.

Pulse-jet sprinkler
Invaluable for large, circular areas of lawn, beds, or borders. A single jet on a central pivot rotates in a series of pulses, ejecting spurts of water. Except on lawns, the delivery head is set on a tall stem for increased coverage.

Oscillating sprinkler
This is best used at ground level; it is not suitable for positions where surrounding foliage will interfere with the range of the spray. Water is sprayed through a series of brass jets in the oscillating arm. This sprinkler delivers water fairly evenly over a rectangular area, the size of which may be easily adjusted.

30cm (12in) below the surface as a permanent system, but a shallow covering is usually sufficient. Porous hoses can be laid on the soil surface, but cover with a mulch. The water is released directly into the area of the plant's roots, so it is distributed very economically with no run-off and little evaporation. The low humidity levels reduce the incidence of fungal diseases as well as the spread of pests and diseases often triggered by water splash. Weed germination is also discouraged by the dry soil surface.

Porous hoses are easily cut into flexible lengths and laid in any shape or pattern provided there is no kink. They work effectively on a slope, laid along rather than down the incline. Pipes may be left outside all year, even when on the soil surface, but connections can be varied, and the system moved around as needed.

Garden sprinklers

A garden sprinkler delivers a fine spray of water over a specific area. It works while unattended, saving time

and effort. However, in hot, sunny weather, much water is lost by evaporation, so sprinklers are less efficient than seep or porous hoses.

A sprinkler is attached to a garden hose or a static water-pipe. There are various types for different needs: some are best for lawns, while others are preferable for irrigating a flower bed or vegetable patch. The simplest form is a static sprinkler. Other types, such as rotating, pulse-jet, and oscillating ones, use water pressure to rotate the sprinkler heads, providing better and more even coverage.

A travelling sprinkler (also called a walking sprinkler) is useful for large, level areas like big lawns; it is convenient but expensive. It delivers spray over a rectangular area while it is propelled along a track (usually a hosepipe) by the force of the water.

Underground sprinklers

These are permanent systems, ideal for lawns and rock gardens. They are unobtrusive and simple to operate, and are best installed when the area needing irrigation is first constructed, preferably by a professional. PVC

pipes and connecting joints are laid in the form of a grid so that they supply various watering heads, to which hoses or sprinklers are attached. The sprinkler from each head delivers an even supply of water to a circular area. Always continue watering until the ground is thoroughly wet, as this helps to even out the distribution to any overlapping areas. This type of watering system requires non-return valves to meet water authority standards, and possibly a water meter.

Hose timers

Hose timers may be used with ordinary garden sprinklers or more elaborate watering systems. They fit between a tap and the hose or irrigation pipe. Most such timers turn off the water after a predetermined time. The more sophisticated ones will turn on and off several times a day and can be pre-programmed as well as linked to a moisture detector that prevents watering if the ground is sufficiently wet.

Computerized timer
This allows you to programme watering times and duration in advance, to irrigate plants while you are busy or on holiday.

Water timer
This can be set to turn off the water after a pre-set period, from about 5 minutes to 2 hours.

Trickle, or drip feed, systems

These are used for plants that benefit from individual watering, like plants requiring more water than others growing around them. Water drips or is sprayed gently beside the plant – a variety of nozzles being available. A trickle system works well in a shrub border, along a hedge, or for rows of vegetables; it is also ideal for plants in containers, growing bags, and windowboxes. Unless fitted with a timer, trickle systems tend to waste water, and need regular cleaning to prevent tubes and drip heads getting blocked with algae and debris.

Trickle watering system
The delivery hose is connected to a unit that filters the water and reduces the pressure. The water then flows along a network of tubes supported by spikes stuck into the ground. Systems of this kind can be extended by buying additional drip heads and lengths of tube.

Filter removable for cleaning

Connector for tube

Hose connection

Central unit reduces water pressure

Drip heads

Cleaning tool

Spike

General garden equipment

As well as tools for cultivating and maintaining the garden, a wide range of other accessories, such as carrying equipment and planting aids, may be useful, depending on your own individual requirements.

Wheelbarrows

Wheelbarrows are useful for transporting plants, soil, and materials such as compost and garden debris. They may be made of metal or plastic, the former being more durable. Painted metal soon rusts if the paint is chipped; even galvanized metal bins rust eventually. Plastic bins, although lighter, may split.

A ball-wheeled wheelbarrow is more stable than a standard model, making it easier to use over recently dug ground. Most suitable for very heavy work is a builder's barrow, which has an inflatable tyre to cushion the load. Barrows with two wheels and a pram-type handle (sometimes called garden carts) are stable and easy to load and unload, but are less manoeuvrable than standard barrows on uneven ground.

Sheets and bags

A carrying sheet or bag is suitable for transporting light but bulky garden waste such as hedge clippings; when not in use, it takes up very little space. It should be lightweight, with

Carrying bag

Carrying sheet

Trug

strong handles, and made of a tough, tear-proof material, such as woven plastic. Carrying bags have a larger capacity than sheets. Trugs and baskets are good for light tasks such as carrying flowers or fruit.

TYPES OF WHEELBARROW

Traditional wheelbarrow
Most barrows have a single, solid wheel and a shallow bin, although some models may be fitted with an extension to increase their capacity.

Ball-wheeled wheelbarrow
If you are transporting very heavy loads, or using a barrow on rough ground, a model with a ball wheel or inflatable tyre is easier to push than a solid-wheeled one, but the wheel may become punctured.

Plastic bags

Clear plastic bags are excellent for a number of purposes: preventing cuttings material from drying out after collecting it, for example, and for covering cuttings in pots to raise humidity around them. Most food and freezer bags are suitable provided that they are made of polythene and are not too thin – other materials being less effective at retaining moisture.

Kneelers and knee pads

A cushioned-pad kneeler, covered with a waterproof material, is simply knelt on for extra comfort, when weeding, for example, whereas knee pads are strapped to the knees and often sold in only one size, so check that they fit before buying. Kneeling

stools support the knees on a slightly raised platform and have hand rests to give support when kneeling and standing. They may also be turned upside-down for use as a small stool for working at raised beds or greenhouse benches.

Kneelers
A kneeling stool (top) can be inverted for use as a stool and is light to carry. A cushioned pad (bottom) keeps knees clear of damp, hard ground.

Compost bins

A compost bin should have a lid to keep warmth in, easy access to the compost by slats or panels, and a capacity of at least 1 cu m (1 cu yd) to generate sufficient heat to accelerate the rotting process. Avoid wire mesh bins or those with large gaps between the slats, because they allow the heat gen-erated to escape.

Traditional, wooden compost bins are available pre-cut for easy self-assembly. Plastic compost bins are generally more effective than metal or wooden ones because they conserve moisture and reduce the need to water. There are plastic bins available that may be rotated to turn the compost, but this does not necessarily make good compost more quickly than a well-designed, traditional bin. See also SOILS AND FERTILIZERS, *Making a Compost Bin*, p.627.

Incinerators

Incinerators burn rubbish more quickly and cleanly than bonfires, but many gardeners now recycle garden waste by shredding and composting it. Open-mesh incinerators, some of which fold up after use, are good for burning dry material such as twigs and leaves; galvanized steel, dustbin incinerators are good for slowly burning damp, woody material. Both must be well ventilated.

Shredders

A compost shredder chops woody or tough garden waste, such as old Brussels sprout stems and prunings, until it is fine enough to break down quickly on a compost heap. Shredders are usually electrically powered and should not be left outdoors when not in use. Most machines operate by a fast-spinning blade but some have a crushing–cutting action and these are both much quieter and much easier to use.

Small shredders accept only thin, woody stems and need constant, time-consuming feeding. It may therefore be better occasionally to hire a bigger machine that will chew up relatively large branches, too.

Power should cut out if inlet funnel is removed

Three sturdy legs ensure shredder is stable in use

Using a shredder
The inlet funnel should not allow direct access to the blades. Wear goggles and gloves to protect against flying debris and thorny stems.

Planting and sowing aids

General garden tools or household items are often used for planting and sowing; for example a stick or pencil, instead of a dibber, will make a planting hole. Specialized tools, however, do make some tedious and repetitive jobs simpler and quicker.

Seed sowers and planters

These facilitate accurate and even sowing of seed. There are four main types: shakers, plungers, wheeled sowers, and seed-tray sowers.
Shakers are hand-held devices that may be used for sowing seed in prepared drills. Skill is required to ensure even seed distribution.
Plungers insert each seed individually to a predetermined depth.
Wheeled seed sowers are good for distributing seeds evenly. With a long handle, they can be worked from a standing position.
Seed-tray sowers are thin, plastic or wooden boards with moulded protrusions on one side. When pressed onto the seed compost they firm the surface and make evenly spaced holes for sowing seed.

Bulb planters

A bulb planter is useful if planting a number of bulbs individually; for planting groups of small bulbs, a trowel or hand fork is better. A bulb planter is usually pushed into the soil with your foot. It removes a plug of soil or turf, which is then replaced on top of the bulb after planting; those with a claw-like action release the plug by pressure on the handle.

Gardening gloves

There is a range of gardening gloves for various purposes: some keep hands clean when working with soil or compost, while others also provide protection against thorns.

Leather and fabric gloves are useful for tasks such as pruning roses to guard against thorns. When buying leather ones, check that the leather extends far enough to protect all of the palm. All-leather or suede gloves give very good protection, but may be uncomfortably hot in warm weather. Gauntlet types cover the wrists and lower forearms.

Many gloves are made of fabric and vinyl. Some are impregnated with vinyl, others just have a vinyl grip on the palms. They are good for most jobs and keep hands cleaner than fabric alone. Vinyl-coated gloves are useful for messy jobs, such as mixing concrete, but are too thick for jobs needing a sensitive touch.

Fabric with vinyl grip

Suede gauntlets

Suede and fabric

Cotton fabric

Dibbers and widgers

A dibber is a pencil-shaped tool used for making planting holes. Use a small dibber to transplant seedlings or insert cuttings, a large one for transplanting vegetables such as leeks that require a wide hole to allow space for growth, and for planting through a plastic mulch. A widger, which is like a narrow spatula, is good for lifting seedlings and rooted cuttings with the minimum of root disturbance.

Garden lines

A garden line is mainly used in vegetable plots as a guide for forming straight rows, but is also invaluable for other tasks, such as marking out areas when planning or designing, or forming a straight edge when planting up a hedge or constructing a wall or patio.

Garden line
Most garden lines have a pointed stake at either end for inserting into the ground. Grooves allow you to stretch a level line between the stakes.

Sieves

Garden sieves generally have a mesh of 3–12mm (⅛–½in) and are used to separate out coarse material from soil or potting compost. Choose a sieve with a large mesh to remove twigs and stones from soil before sowing or planting; use one with a smaller mesh when covering fine seeds after sowing. Those with a wire-mesh tend to be more effective and durable than plastic ones.

Wire-mesh sieve

Sieve with fine, plastic mesh

Thermometers

The best type of thermometer for garden and greenhouse use is a minimum-maximum thermometer, because this records both the lowest and highest temperatures reached. A greenhouse thermometer together with a hygrometer, which measures air humidity, are useful to monitor conditions under glass. A soil thermometer outdoors is helpful in deciding when to sow seed.

Minimum-maximum thermometer

Greenhouse thermometer

Rain gauges

A rain gauge is used for measuring amounts of rainfall or irrigation; it is helpful for identifying areas of the garden that are affected by rain shadow. It should have clear markings and a smooth inside surface for easy cleaning. Many gauges have a short spike for inserting into the ground.

Measurements are clear so that water level is easy to read

Spike for stability

Plastic rain gauge

PLANTING AND SOWING TOOLS

Small dibber

Wooden garden dibber for outdoor use

Bulb planter

Widger

Wheeled seed sower

Metal garden dibber

Ties and supports

Ties are used for various purposes in the garden but in particular to secure a climbing, scrambling, or fragile plant; supports are needed to protect some plants from wind or rain. Ties must be secure without constricting the stem, and must be checked annually; use a light material such as twine or raffia on soft-stemmed plants.

General ties

Garden string or twine in 3-ply is adequate for most tying jobs. Raffia, which is good for binding joins after grafting and as a lightweight tie, and soft strings, such as jute fillis, may disintegrate after a year or so. Clear plastic tape is excellent for use in grafting; special rubber ties are also available. Tar-impregnated string or polypropylene twine is a reliable, weather-resistant tie.

Plastic-coated tying wire is strong and lasts for several years. It is good for fixing labels to training wires or trellis and for joining canes. It may come on a reel with a built-in cutter, which is convenient to use.

Plant rings

These are split rings of wire; plastic-covered rings are also available. Plant rings are designed to be opened and closed easily around a plant stem and its support. They are suitable for light jobs, such as attaching a house plant to a cane.

Labels and markers

Labels for garden use should be durable, weather-resistant, and large enough to contain all the information you want to note. Plastic labels are cheap and may be reused; if written on with pencil, they should remain legible for a season. Most plastic labels discolour gradually with age and become brittle, but they are ideal for labelling trays of seeds and cuttings. Looped labels and those with ties may be secured around the stem of a plant and are useful if labels at eye level are required.

For more permanent, water-resistant markers, use those coated with a black material; these are written on by scratching through to the white plastic beneath, but they cannot be marked with a new name. Aluminium labels, which are more expensive, will last almost indefinitely, but the lettering may have to be renewed every few years.

Tree ties

Rubber tree ties are strong, durable, and good for securing a young tree to a stake. They should be easily adjustable so that an expanding stem is not constricted. Select one with a buffer so that the stake does not chafe the stem, or use a padded tie in a figure-of-eight form (see also "Tree ties", p.65). Nail ties to the stakes.

Wall fixings

Purpose-designed plant stickers may be used for tasks such as securing the stem of a climber direct to a wall or other support. Lead-headed nails are stronger; they have a soft spur that may be bent over to fix stems and small branches to a wall.

Vine eyes hold stretched wires to which wall plants are then secured. On wall masonry, use flat vine eyes; for timber and wall plugs, screw in eyelet vine eyes.

Canes and stakes

Bamboo canes are excellent for supporting single-stemmed plants, but they eventually split and rot. More permanent and expensive are PVC stakes and plastic-covered steel rods. Support clumps of border plants with metal link or ring stakes (see PERENNIALS, "Staking", p.192). Trees and standard roses should be supported with sturdy, wooden stakes.

Netting

Netting is available in various materials and mesh sizes for a range of uses, such as supporting plants, protecting fruit from birds, and shading greenhouse plants (see "Shading", p.576). For plant support, choose a mesh of 5cm (2in) or more; it may be hard to disentangle plants from a smaller mesh. For plants such as sweet peas, thin, flexible plastic netting is adequate; heavier plants need semi-rigid plastic nets.

For fruit protection, use purpose-designed, plastic netting with a mesh of 1–2cm (½–¾in). Protect seedlings and winter vegetables from birds with 2.5cm (1in) mesh netting, or, if you are worried about bird safety, with cellulose-thread webbing, which repels not traps birds, and is biodegradable. Wire netting may be

placed around plants to provide protection from animals such as rabbits. It is also useful for reinforcing concrete when constructing a pond or trough. For general pest and weather protection, cover plants with a finely woven mesh sheet that is reusable.

Use windbreak netting to protect vulnerable plants in exposed sites (see *Windbreaks*, p.611). Knitted plastic netting may deteriorate in about four years, whereas moulded plastic should last at least twice as long. Windbreak webbing is even more long-lasting but very obtrusive.

NETTING

Plastic netting

Shade netting

Plant support netting

Wire netting

Chicken wire

Pig wire

WALL FIXINGS

Flat vine eye

Eyelet vine eye

Lead-headed nail with spur

PLANT SUPPORTS AND TIES

Stakes and supports

Bamboo cane

Rose stake

Green bamboo cane

Moss pillar

Split cane

Tree stake

Tree tie

Rose tie

Plastic ties

Plant rings

Garden twine

Twist ties

Ring stake

Link stakes

Pots, trays, and growing media

Pots are available in a wide range of sizes but there are two basic shapes: round and square. Although round pots are traditional, square pots hold more compost for the same diameter; to save space use square pots, which pack neatly together. Round pots are classified by the inside diameter at the rim; square ones by the length of the rim along one side. Most pots have slightly sloping sides so that a plant and its root ball may be easily removed intact for repotting or planting out.

Pots are usually made of clay (terracotta) or plastic. Clay is traditional; plastic, however, is more common. Most plastic pots are manufactured from polypropylene, which deteriorates in cold weather. Pots made of a polypropylene and polythene mix do not become brittle in cold weather.

Standard pots are as deep as they are broad; they are the most common type of pot. Pans or seed pans are one third the depth of a standard pot of the same diameter. They are useful for germinating seeds. Half-pots are half to two thirds the depth of a standard pot of the same diameter. They are often used commercially for plants with relatively small root balls, such as evergreen azaleas. For very deep-rooted seedlings, sweet pea tubes or – for plants that will remain in the pot for some time – long Toms are used. Whalehide ring pots are designed to be used for the ring culture of tomatoes (see p.528).

Single and multi-celled seed trays
These are used for sowing seeds, inserting cuttings, or growing on young plants. Use a rigid, outer tray to hold flimsy, single-use modules containing plastic cells. Cells are useful for pricking out seedlings and sowing seeds singly.

Pots and pans
Pots and pans are used for cultivating plants both indoors and outside. The smaller pots, pans, and half-pots are suitable for propagating and growing on young plants.

Ornamental terracotta pots

Standard pots

Large standard pot

Half-pot

Seed pan

Seed, seedling, and cutting pots

Pans

in greenhouses. Other containers designed for specific uses include lattice pots with mesh sides, which can be used for aquatic plants.

Degradable pots and pellets
These are good for plants that resent root disturbance, because they can be planted out into the bed. The plants' roots grow through the sides and base of the pots into the surrounding ground. They are generally made from compressed peat and various other fibres (often sphagnum moss and wood fibre, sometimes impregnated with plant food).

Peat pellets are good for seeds and for rooting cuttings and must be expanded with water before being

used. Many gardeners create their own degradable pots from cones made from double-thickness newspaper.

Seed trays
Traditional, wooden seed trays have largely been replaced by plastic ones, which are easier to clean but often more fragile. Very thin plastic trays are cheap and flexible but are unlikely to last more than a season. Strong plastics are more rigid and expensive; they may become brittle and split with age but, if stored out of sunlight when not in use, they should last for several years.

Module trays
Multi-celled, or module, seed trays are particularly good for seedlings such as peas and broad beans that hate being pricked out. The tapered sides to each cell allow young plants to be transplanted with only minimal damage to their fragile roots, so they establish quickly in their new surroundings. Module trays are available in plastic, polystyrene, and biodegradable paper, and in a wide range of cell sizes and numbers, from four to several hundred.

Growing media
When sowing seed and rooting cuttings, a higher success rate is achieved using propagation composts.

Standard seed compost
Fine seed needs good contact with the compost to germinate and should be sown in purpose-made seed compost, which is fine-textured, moisture-retentive, and low in nutrients, as salts may damage seedlings.

Standard seed compost (based on the John Innes formula) is made using 2 parts (by volume) sterilized loam, 1 part peat substitute (or peat), and 1 part sand. To each cubic metre is added 1.2kg superphosphate of lime and 600g ground limestone (2lb and 1lb respectively for a cubic yard).

Standard cuttings compost
Compost mixes for rooting cuttings are free-draining and intended for use in high-humidity environments. They may be based on bark, perlite, or mixes containing a high percentage of coarse sand. Cuttings composts are low in nutrients, so cuttings need feeding once rooted.

A standard cuttings compost typically contains 50:50 sand and peat substitute (or peat). To each cubic metre (yard) is added 4.4kg (7½lb) dolomitic lime; 1.5kg (2½lb) each of hoof and horn or dried blood, superphosphate of lime, and calcium carbonate; and 150g (4oz) each of potassium nitrate and potassium sulphate. A specialist micro-nutrient fertilizer should also be added.

Inert growing media
Sterile inert growing materials do not harbour the potential pest and disease problems associated with soil-based or loamless potting composts. Some of the most popular are rockwool, perlite, vermiculite, and clay granules (see also "Hydroculture", p.375).

Long Tom
This pot suits deep-rooted plants that would be restricted by a standard pot.

Whalehide ring pot
This bottomless pot for ring culture holds the potting compost over the aggregate.

Sweet pea tubes
These are excellent for seedlings that quickly develop long root systems.

Bulb basket
Such a basket protects bulbs from animals and is also easy to lift after flowering.

Biodegradable pots
Use for propagating plants that resent root disturbance when transplanted.

Lattice pot
This pot for aquatics lets in water, but should be lined with hessian to retain soil.

2
GREENHOUSES AND FRAMES

MANY PEOPLE RESIST the idea of installing a greenhouse in the mistaken belief that it is expensive or requires detailed gardening knowledge to maintain and use properly. This is not the case. The rewards of gardening under cover more than compensate for the initial cost and effort and open up a whole new world of gardening pleasures. As well as being an all–weather space for tasks that crop up throughout the year, a greenhouse can be a cost-effective investment, allowing you to propagate plants for the garden at little cost. Even if you have a small plot you will be able to find a compact model to suit; or you could consider installing a cold frame – smaller in scale but a great boon to practical gardening.

Gardening under cover

Greenhouses, cold frames, and cloches are useful additions to any garden and are available in an extensive range of sizes to fit whatever space is available. Each type of structure has a distinctive function but they are usually used in conjunction with each other. The most productive gardens use all three.

Unheated structures

Unheated greenhouses are used primarily to advance or extend the growing season of hardy and half-hardy plants. Cold frames fulfil a similar function, although they are also often used for hardening off plants that have been propagated in a greenhouse and for storing "resting plants". Cloches are used *in situ* over plants in the garden itself.

Heated structures

A heated greenhouse is far more versatile than either an unheated greenhouse or a cold frame, and allows a much greater range of plants to be grown. These include many frost-tender species that do not grow satisfactorily in temperate or cold climates without protection. In addition, a heated greenhouse provides a suitable environment in which to propagate plants.

Siting the greenhouse

An amateur greenhouse is best positioned so that it blends in with the overall garden design. It should also be positioned in a sheltered site but where enough light is available for the plants to grow and thrive: too much shade will limit the range of plants that may be grown easily, whereas an exposed site will make the greenhouse expensive to heat or may mean that the plants are not adequately protected on cold nights.

Early planning

It is always worth spending the time to make sure that you have chosen the right spot before buying a greenhouse. If possible, make detailed notes in winter or spring of where shadows are cast in the garden by houses and any neighbouring garages, trees, or other large, nearby features, so that you do not site a greenhouse where it will be in shade for more than a few hours each day. Orienting the greenhouse north–south by its longer axis makes the best use of light in summer. For raising plants in spring, or over-wintering tender specimens, an east–west orientation will provide good light for much of the day.

If there is a possibility that you will want to extend the greenhouse

Greenhouse style
This traditional greenhouse is an integral part of the garden. Hedges and trees provide shelter but are not close enough to significantly reduce light. Maintenance is minimal: treat the timber with wood preservative regularly.

Elegant design
Greenhouses with plastic-covered frames can be extremely attractive, as well as functional. This one is a decorative garden feature in its own right.

later, or build a second, smaller one, allow enough space on the site.

Free-standing greenhouse
The best place to site a free-standing greenhouse is in a sheltered, light area away from buildings and large trees. If the site is high or exposed, choose a position that is sheltered by a hedge that acts as a windbreak, or build a fence or other screen.

Windbreaks should not cast too much shade onto the greenhouse itself; however, they need not be tall – a 2.5m (8ft) hedge provides shelter for a distance of 12m (40ft) or more.

Do not position a free-standing greenhouse near or between buildings, since this could create a wind funnel effect that may damage the greenhouse and the plants inside. Positions at the bottom of a slope or near walls,

POSITIONING THE GREENHOUSE

If the greenhouse is used mostly in the summer, its longer axis should run north to south. If good light in spring is a priority, however – when the sun is lower in the sky – orient the greenhouse east to west to make the best use of available light.

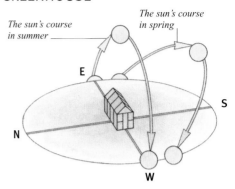

The sun's course in summer

The sun's course in spring

hedges, or fences on the side of a slope should not be used to site a greenhouse because cold air may become trapped there (see CLIMATE AND THE GARDEN, "Frost pockets and frost damage", p.607).

Lean-to greenhouse
Place a lean-to greenhouse against a wall that receives a mixture of sun and shade. Do not site it where there is sun for most of the day, otherwise the greenhouse may overheat in summer, even with shading and a good ventilation system.

Access
Bear in mind the need for easy access. A site that is reasonably close to the house is preferable to one at a distance. Also make sure that there is a

clear area in front of the greenhouse door for loading and unloading. Any paths leading to the greenhouse need to be level. Preferably, they should have a hard, resilient surface and be wide enough to accommodate a wheelbarrow.

Mains services
Choose a site that will be convenient for mains water and electricity connection, if these services are needed. Although electricity is not essential for heating, it is useful for lighting as well as for some thermostatic controls and timing switches. A mains water connection makes watering plants more convenient, especially if an automatic system is used, and reduces the need to trail lengths of hose around the garden.

CHOOSING THE SITE

An open but sheltered site is best for a greenhouse – it should not be positioned in the path of a wind funnel. If there is no natural protection from the wind, construct a windbreak.

This greenhouse is in an open position, away from the shade cast by buildings and trees

A line of trees provides shelter from the prevailing wind.

GOOD POSITION

POOR POSITIONS

This greenhouse lies in the shade cast by the nearby tree and will also be affected by falling leaves in autumn if the tree is deciduous.

This greenhouse lies directly in the path of a possible wind funnel. It is also too close to the hedge, which may make maintenance difficult.

Shade cast in summer

Shade cast in winter

A wind funnel may be created between 2 adjacent buildings.

Greenhouses, guttering, and water storage
Using water sparingly is as important in greenhouses and frames as in the open garden, and it is essential to store water for use during very dry periods to maintain glasshouse plants and propagate material effectively. Capillary systems, seep hoses, and trickle systems can be regulated to deliver water to plants in need of moisture growing in greenhouses or frames, but the structures themselves can provide a valuable source of rainwater if guttering, downpipes and storage tanks are installed. Not all greenhouses are equipped with guttering, so check it is included before you buy.

More storage can be provided by sinking galvanized or plastic tanks under greenhouse benches. Fill them with roof water by diverting a downpipe inside the greenhouse above the container.

Check taps, joints, and containers regularly to ensure water is not lost from leaks.

Choosing a greenhouse

Before purchasing a greenhouse, consider carefully how it will be used to select the most suitable style, size, and materials – a greenhouse that is used as a garden room, for example, will differ significantly from one that is purely functional. If growing tropical and subtropical plants, an attractively shaped greenhouse, perhaps with room for central staging, might enhance the floral display.

Many different styles of greenhouse are available. Some make best use of space or provide optimum ventilation; others conserve heat well or allow better light penetration. When priorities have been decided, the final choice of style will depend on personal preference.

Conventional greenhouses

The more conventional types of greenhouse are suitable for a wide range of plants and include traditional span, Dutch light, three-quarter span, lean-to, and Mansard (or curvilinear) greenhouses. All of

TRADITIONAL SPAN

DUTCH LIGHT

these may have an aluminium or timber framework, and either all-glass or part-solid walls (except Dutch light greenhouses). Conventional greenhouses also have a wide range of compatible accessories, including staging and shelves.

Traditional span
The vertical sides and even span roof of a traditional span greenhouse are extremely practical in terms of

growing space and headroom. For raising seedlings and growing border crops, a traditional span greenhouse is likely to provide the best use of space for the least cost.

Dutch light
The sloping sides of Dutch light greenhouses are designed to allow in maximum light, so these greenhouses are suitable for border crops, especially low-growing ones such

as lettuces. The large sheets of glass are expensive to replace because of the size – the traditional dimensions are 145 x 77cm (59 x 30¼in). The glass panes slide into the frame and are secured using cleats fixed with galvanized nails.

The panes of glass on the roof overlap slightly to keep out rain and increase rigidity. This may cause loss of heat, however, if the panes overlap too loosely.

THREE-QUARTER SPAN

LEAN-TO

MANSARD

Three-quarter span
A three-quarter span greenhouse is positioned with one of its sides against a wall. Light is a little more restricted than in a free-standing model, so this type of greenhouse is best positioned beside a sunny wall, although this may mean that extra shading is required in summer. The wall provides extra warmth and insulation in the greenhouse, especially if it is a house wall (see also "Lean-to", right).

Lean-to
Where there is insufficient space for a free-standing structure, a lean-to greenhouse is an invaluable choice, particularly if a mainly decorative show-house is favoured.

Many are similar in appearance to conservatories, and may be used as garden rooms. Installing electricity, mains gas, or a water supply in a lean-to that is adjacent to a house wall is cheaper and generally involves less work than laying cables

or pipes to a greenhouse that is some distance from the house. In addition, the warmth of the house wall may reduce the level of heating required; brick walls store heat, from both the sun (especially if the wall is south-facing) and the domestic heating system, which is then released into the greenhouse.

The brick wall also provides good insulation, so that less heat escapes from a lean-to than from many other types of greenhouse.

Mansard
The Mansard (curvilinear) greenhouse has slanting sides and roof panels, designed to allow maximum entry of available light. The full benefit is gained only in an open position with no shade from surrounding buildings or trees. A Mansard greenhouse is suitable for plants that need maximum light during the winter, when daylight hours are short and light levels are also frequently low.

DOME-SHAPED

POLYGONAL

ALPINE HOUSE

Specialist greenhouses

There are many specialist types of greenhouse, including dome-shaped, polygonal, alpine house, conservation, mini, and "polytunnel", all of which differ markedly in appearance from the more conventional types. Some are designed as highly decorative garden features in their own right, while others may offer particularly good value for money or be used for specific types of plant.

Dome-shaped

This is an elegant design that is particularly useful in exposed positions as it is stable and offers less wind resistance than traditional greenhouses. Light transmission is excellent because the multi-angled glass panes and aluminium frame allow maximum light transmission. Dome-shaped structures may have limited headroom around the edge, and plants may also be difficult to reach. Extensions are not generally available and fittings may be limited to those produced by the manufacturer.

Polygonal

Octagonal and other polygonal greenhouses are frequently chosen where appearance is important, and may provide a focal point within the garden. They are generally more expensive than traditional greenhouses of similar size and, because they are not very common, there may be a limited choice of accessories. The irregular shape may also restrict growing space. Fitting replacement panes of glass in a polygonal greenhouse is more difficult than in a conventional structure.

Alpine house

This type of greenhouse is traditionally timber-framed with louvre vents extending all along the sides for the most effective ventilation. Usually, alpine houses are not heated and are closed only in the coldest winter weather, so insulation is not required. Unsuitable for tender plants, they are used for plants that thrive in bright, well-ventilated conditions, yet which require some overhead protection from dampness and rain. The shape is similar to that of a traditional span greenhouse.

CONSERVATION

MINI

POLYTUNNEL

Conservation greenhouse

This type of greenhouse has many special features that are designed to save as much energy as possible. It is therefore usually more expensive than other types of greenhouse of similar size. The roof panels are angled to allow optimum light penetration, and mirrored surfaces are also used to reflect light within the greenhouse itself. Plastic double glazing and purpose-made insulation are fitted as standard.

Mini-greenhouse

These useful, low-cost greenhouses are good for a limited space, as they are available in various heights, widths, and depths. There are also free-standing and wheeled versions. A mini-greenhouse is the best choice if only a small number of plants will be grown. It is covered with glass or plastic and is usually aluminium framed. It should preferably face south–east or south–west so that maximum light penetrates. The staging is available in a range of depths and movable heights. Access may be a problem – all work has to be done from the outside. Rapid temperature changes often occur, so fit a louvre vent if available. Shading in summer is also essential if plants are not to scorch.

Plastic "polytunnel" greenhouse

Where visual appearance is not important and low-cost protection is required – such as in the vegetable plot – a "polytunnel" greenhouse has many benefits. It comprises a large, tunnel-shaped frame covered with heavy-duty transparent plastic sheets and is widely used for crops that require some protection but not the warm conditions of a traditional greenhouse. Polytunnels keep out the worst of the winter cold and provide useful wind protection throughout the year. Since they are light and relatively easy to move, they are often used in plots where crop rotation is carried out.

For a very large growing area, commercial polytunnels are a cost-effective investment, but for a small garden a more traditional shape may be a better choice. A few polytunnels include some staging, although most are intended primarily for growing crops at ground level, planted either directly into the soil, in pots, or in growing bags.

Ventilation may be a problem: the door offers a reasonably efficient method of ventilation – especially in large tunnels with openings at each end – and some have sides that roll up. The plastic sheeting may need to be replaced every few years – it will gradually become opaque, restricting light penetration.

Choosing the size

A greenhouse will almost inevitably seem too small once it is filled with plants so, if possible, buy one that may be extended. Although a large greenhouse costs more to heat than a small one, it is possible to partition off a section in winter, and leave the remainder unheated (see "Thermal screens", p.574).

Space considerations

A greenhouse that is used primarily for ornamentals should have plenty of room inside for staging, which may be tiered, and possibly a central or end display. To provide space for propagation and growing on, it may be necessary to divide up the space with a partition. Alternatively, use a cold frame for propagation.

Length, width, and height

A length of 2.5m (8ft) and a width of 2m (6ft) are the minimum, practical dimensions for a general-purpose, traditional greenhouse. A smaller greenhouse than this limits the range of plants that may be grown, and may make it difficult to control the environment – draughts and rapid heat build-up in summer tend to be more of a problem in small greenhouses, and may lead to sudden fluctuations in temperature. In greenhouses that are more than 2m (6ft) wide, it may also be difficult to reach pots and ventilation towards the back of the staging. Staging to a width of 60cm (2ft) on either side allows a path of the same width down the middle.

If border crops are to be grown, choose a greenhouse that is 2.5m (8ft) wide with borders to a width of 1m (3ft). A width of 2.5m (8ft) is also suitable if a wider path is required for a wheelchair or to enable a wheelbarrow to be used easily.

Many small greenhouses have low eaves and comparatively low ridges, which make it tiring to work over the border or staging for long periods. To gain more height, build the greenhouse on a brick base or dig out a sunken path.

Choosing the materials

Greenhouses are made in a range of materials. The most important considerations when choosing both the framework and glazing for the greenhouse are practicality, expense, and the amount of maintenance required. The appearance of the materials may also be important; metal is sturdy but traditional wood is often preferred.

BUYING A GREENHOUSE

Before buying a greenhouse, use the following as a checklist; it may save disappointment later.

Ridge height should be at least 2.1m (6½ft); remember to allow for roof ventilator openings protruding.

Roof ventilators are usually inadequate as supplied – the total ventilation area should equal one sixth of the floor area. Extra ventilators may be needed.

Glass should be easy to replace; use panes of a standard size – 60cm (24in) square or 60 x 45cm (24 x 18in). The large panes of Dutch light greenhouses are expensive to replace. Consider double-glazing if high temperatures are to be maintained, although this adds considerably to the cost.

Cross bracing on aluminium alloy greenhouses must be strong enough to make the structure rigid.

Eaves height affects the headroom – it should be at least 1.3m (4½ft) for ease of working.

Doors may be hinged or sliding. They must be wide enough: 60cm (24in) is the minimum practical width. For wheelchair or wheelbarrow access they should be wider and without a "lip". Sliding doors are easily adjusted for ventilation and are less likely to slam in wind than hinged doors. Check that doors are a good fit when closed, otherwise they may let in draughts.

Use ground anchors if the structure is not secured to a brick base.

Gutters and downpipes reduce the risk of water cascading from the roof and damaging the plants nearby.

A base may be an optional extra – bear this in mind when comparing prices since most timber-framed greenhouses need one. Some have a step that makes wheelchair access and use of a wheelbarrow difficult.

Use base cladding to reduce heat loss in the winter, unless border crops are to be grown.

A kick panel at the foot of the door minimizes the risk of breaking the glass panel.

Side ventilators allow free circulation of air. Louvre windows must close tightly to minimize heat loss in cold weather.

The framework

Timber frameworks have been the traditional choice and are generally considered to be the most attractive. They tend to be expensive, however, and are also heavy to construct. If possible, choose a durable wood. Always look for a manufacturer that offers hardwood frames made from renewable sources. A quality greenhouse will be rot-resistant, will not warp easily, and, if treated every year or two with special wood preparation, will retain its colour well.

Greenhouses constructed with redwood and deal are cheaper than those described as "cedar". Before being assembled, they should be pressure-treated with preservative; they also require regular painting to prevent rotting (see also "Timber framework", p.583).

Greenhouses with aluminium alloy frames are almost completely

CONSTRUCTION MATERIALS

Timber
A timber frame is the traditional choice for garden greenhouses. Hardwoods are low maintenance.

Aluminium
Aluminium alloy frames are light but extremely sturdy and need only minimum maintenance.

Steel
Plastic-coated, steel frames are very strong but must be treated regularly to prevent rust.

maintenance-free. They do not retain heat quite as well as timber frames but the difference is minimal.

Galvanized steel is also often used for greenhouse frames. Steel frames are light and easy to construct but extremely strong. They are cheaper than timber or aluminium frames but must be painted regularly (see "Metal framework", p.583).

Aluminium and steel frames are narrower than timber ones and allow larger panes of glass to be used, resulting in better light penetration.

Glass panes

Horticultural glass is the most satisfactory glazing material for a greenhouse: it allows excellent light penetration but is thinner and less expensive than ordinary glass. It is easy to clean, does not discolour, and retains considerably more heat than plastic glazing materials. Glass is not as robust as plastic glazing, however, so breakages and cracks may be a problem, since the panes must be replaced quickly.

Plastic glazing

Plastics are generally more expensive and less durable than glass; they discolour more readily and also tend to become scratched over time, which is both unsightly and, more importantly, may cut down on the amount of light that is transmitted if the discoloring is severe.

Acrylic sheets are used to glaze the curved eaves of many greenhouses because the acrylic may be shaped easily to give an elegant outline to the structure. Condensation occurs more readily on its surface than on a conventional glass pane. Rigid polycarbonate sheets are also often used to glaze greenhouses. They are easy to handle, lightweight, virtually unbreakable, and have good insulating properties. They are relatively easily scratched, however, and they tend to discolour.

Twin-walled polycarbonate has particularly good insulating qualities, but its opacity may be a major problem in a greenhouse.

Sizing

Most local glass merchants will cut glass panes to size for little cost. It is important to make sure that any measurements you give are accurate; calculate them carefully, ensuring that there will be sufficient clearance for the glass to engage with the mounting system that is to be used.

GLAZING MATERIAL

Rigid plastic glazing material is light and easy to fit. This is twin-walled polycarbonate, which provides good insulation.

If plastic glazing material is used it will be supplied in sheets and is not usually difficult to cut to size at home using a sharp craft knife and straight edge.

Erecting the greenhouse

A greenhouse requires far less maintenance and lasts much longer if it is properly erected in the first place. The information listed below is necessarily of a general nature, because it applies to many different greenhouse types and designs: always follow the manufacturer's instructions for particular advice. If in doubt on any point, check the details with either the supplier or the greenhouse manufacturer.

Some manufacturers that supply by mail order also erect greenhouses, if required, but usually expect the ground to be levelled beforehand and any brick base (see below) to be prepared in advance.

Preparing the site

Always erect a greenhouse on firm, level ground, otherwise the frame may warp and become twisted and cause the glass to crack. The chosen site must first be cleared of weeds, since persistent weeds are very difficult to eradicate when the greenhouse is erected and in position. If the site selected for the greenhouse has been recently dug over, allow the soil to settle for a few weeks, and then consolidate it with a heavy roller.

Foundations

Aluminium greenhouses that are smaller than 2m wide and 2.5m long (6 x 8ft) do not usually require a thick concrete base. Simply dig a hole at each corner approximately 25–45cm (10–18in) deep, then wedge in the ground anchors (see p.572) with rubble and pour in a concrete mix to fix them securely.

If a more substantial foundation is required, dig a trench approximately 25cm (10in) deep, filling it with 15cm (6in) of consolidated hardcore. Fix the anchoring bolts in place and finish off with poured concrete or paving slabs, making sure that the ground is level.

Brick bases

A brick base must be constructed to the precise measurements provided by the greenhouse manufacturer, on solid concrete footings approximately 13cm (5in) deep (see *How to Make a Concrete Footing*, p.596). The finished level of the footings should be at or below soil level.

Wooden greenhouses

The sections of a wooden greenhouse are usually supplied complete and should only need to be bolted together and then fixed to the base.

Base

Interlocking concrete blocks may be used for the base, otherwise a solid concrete foundation or brick base should be built (see "Foundations" and "Brick bases", above).

Sides, gable ends, and roof

Before the greenhouse is delivered, check what kind of bolts or fixings are required and whether they will be supplied. First bolt the sides and gable ends together to form the main framework. Follow the manufacturer's advice for the exact method of fixing this to the base or foundations, as designs vary. The foot of the frame may contain integral anchorage points for securely bolting it down. Bolt any internal partitions to the frame, then add the roof sections and bolt them in place.

Some wooden greenhouses are supplied as sections with unglazed frames, with the glass or plastic glazing supplied separately. Others have pre-glazed frames but these are heavy to move – two or more people may be required to support them.

If the timber has not been treated and is not rot-resistant, it is important to paint all the woodwork with a preservative at this stage, before the greenhouse is glazed.

Glazing

If putty is to be used for glazing it is usually supplied with the greenhouse. Apply it to the glazing bars, and bed-in the glass carefully. The glass panes are usually secured in place with galvanized steel or brass sprigs; if these are not supplied, they may be purchased from any hardware shop.

If a dry glazing system (that is, one that does not require putty) is to be used, simply follow the supplier's instructions.

Whichever method is used, glaze the sides and gable ends first, overlapping the panes by 1cm (½in). Use soft metal overlap clips to hold the glass panes firmly together.

BUILDING A BRICK BASE

If using a brick base for the greenhouse, build it in advance, and lay proper foundations first. Check with the greenhouse manufacturer before building the base to make sure that the dimensions are correct.

CONCRETE FOUNDATIONS

For solid greenhouse foundations, dig a trench to match the dimensions of the greenhouse, filling it with hardcore and a layer of concrete.

Ground level

10cm (4in) layer of concrete

15cm (6in) layer of hardcore

GLAZING BARS AND CLIPS FOR METAL GREENHOUSES

Glazing bars
These form the framework of the greenhouse.

"W"-shaped wire clip
Use this type of clip to hold glass and plastic panes firmly in place.

Sprung band clips
An alternative clip, these fix onto the frame.

Ventilators and door

Ventilators are supplied as an integral part of the pre-assembled sections, so the number you ordered should be in place. Screw on hinged doors and simply insert sliding doors into the runners.

Metal greenhouses

Greenhouses with metal frames are delivered in home-assembly kit form, and the frame is supplied in sections – the base, sides, gable ends, and roof. The sections are in turn divided into separate component pieces that need to be bolted together.

Base

Assemble the base first, ensuring that it is perfectly level and square to prevent any warping and twisting of the frame; measure from each corner to the one diagonally opposite – the measurements must be the same. The base must be securely anchored; this is particularly important in windy or exposed areas.

If fixing ground anchors to a concrete foundation, use the anchoring

A GROUND ANCHOR

Rubble and concrete

Ground anchor

Small greenhouses may be secured using ground anchors. Wedge them in place with rubble first before pouring in a concrete mix.

bolts provided, otherwise simply set the ground anchors in rubble and concrete at each corner of the base.

Sides, gable ends, and roof

Assemble the sides, gable ends, and roof sections in the sequence recommended by the manufacturer in the instruction sheet. The sides are usually put together first.

First make sure that everything has been included, as listed by the kit contents list, then before assembly lay out on the ground all the pieces for each section, in their correct relative positions. Bolt the pieces for each section (sides and gable ends) together. Decide at this point where the vents are to be positioned and leave suitable gaps for them, as necessary. Do not fully tighten the nuts until all the sections are assembled and have been loosely put together.

Bolt the sections together one to another, and then to the base, then bolt on the roof bars and ridge bar.

Ventilators

Ventilator frames are assembled separately, then bolted onto the roof and sides as required, before glazing. This gives greater flexibility than with wooden greenhouses when choosing both the number and position of ventilators. The hinges of roof ventilators usually slide in a groove in the moulding.

Glazing

Glazing strips are usually used for metal greenhouses. Cut the strips to the appropriate length and then press them into the grooves in the glazing bars – shaped pieces of metal that form the framework to hold the glass securely in position.

Glaze the sides of the greenhouse first, placing the glass squarely between the glazing bars, leaving about 3mm (⅛in) clearance on each

side of the glass panes for the glazing clips to be attached. The upper panes of glass should overlap the lower ones by about 1cm (½in). Secure them with overlap glazing clips – pieces of metal bent into "S" shapes that hook over the lower pane and hold the upper one firmly in position.

Once each pane is in position, use glazing clips, pressing them into place between the glazing bars and panes to hold the glass. A little pressure will be required to overcome the natural spring in the metal.

Glaze the gable ends of the greenhouse and then the roof, using the same technique.

Fitting the door

Metal greenhouses usually have sliding doors. These should be bolted together and slid into the runners

provided in the end frame. A stop is supplied for bolting on afterwards to prevent the door from coming off the runners if it is opened too quickly. The door should be glazed when it has been fixed in position.

Fitting the staging

The staging supplied by the manufacturer is designed to be bolted or screwed to the framework. This is best done at the same time as the greenhouse is erected, if possible, especially for octagonal and dome-shaped greenhouses, which have staging specially designed to fit. If solid staging is used, leave a gap several inches wide between the inside of the greenhouse and the staging, to allow free air circulation.

Installing electricity, gas, and water

Installing an outdoor power supply is not a job for the amateur. The installation of electricity in a greenhouse must be carried out by a qualified electrician, although considerable savings may be made by excavating the trench for the cable yourself and then refilling it later when the job is completed. Alternatively, the cable may be run overhead if your greenhouse is close to the house and it will not be unsightly; your electrician will be able to advise you on whether or not this is a practical option. Armoured cable and waterproof fittings should always be used for safety.

Electricity has many practical uses in the greenhouse: it provides power for heating, propagators, lighting, timers, soil-warming cables, and electrically powered garden tools of various types.

Mains gas is useful for heating the greenhouse, although mains gas heaters are less widely available than bottled gas heaters. Consult an approved fitter to discuss the feasibility and cost of laying on mains gas. Again, you can save money by offering to do the spadework yourself.

If you already have an outdoor water tap, you may be able to take a spur from this and run it to the greenhouse. The pipe must be buried below frost level – at least 30cm (12in) deep – and the above-ground parts should be very well lagged. In the UK, it is essential that an anti-siphoning device is incorporated in order to meet legal requirements.

FITTING A PANE IN A METAL GREENHOUSE

Attach overlap glazing clips to the base pane. Wearing gloves, lift the pane into place, gently pressing the top edge into position before hooking the bottom edge onto the lower pane. Secure the pane with glazing clips (see inset), pressing them gently until they slot into position.

Creating the right environment

Creating the right balance of conditions in a greenhouse to suit the plants grown there is the essence of successful greenhouse gardening.

For tender plants, the temperature maintained is vital. In a heated greenhouse, be sure to choose an efficient, reliable, and economic heater. In any greenhouse, good insulation that will retain heat and keep out draughts must be balanced with the need for thorough ventilation. Shading is essential in the majority of greenhouses during the summer to help prevent the plants from overheating; see PRINCIPLES OF PROPAGATION, *Shading Greenhouses* (*Temperate climates*), p.636.

Atmospheric humidity should be kept at a level that suits the plants inside. Automatic methods of watering tend to increase humidity so, for most plants, special humidifiers may not be essential. Special lighting is often useful to increase the growth potential of plants.

Greenhouse temperature

The choice of plants to be grown in a greenhouse is determined largely by the temperature at which it is maintained (see "The greenhouse environment", p.359). There are four categories of greenhouse: cold, cool, temperate, and warm. The environment is controlled slightly differently in each type.

Cold

A cold greenhouse is not heated at all. Insulation (see p.574) is needed to keep out the worst of the winter cold and some form of shading (see p.576) is needed in summer. Thorough ventilation (see p.575) is important all year round.

A cold greenhouse may be used to grow summer crops, to overwinter slightly tender plants, or to propagate cuttings (although a propagator will increase the success rate, see p.580). An unheated greenhouse may also permit an early display of hardy plants and many types of spring bulb.

An unheated greenhouse is suitable for alpines – some are specifically designed to provide maximum ventilation for this type of plant (see "Alpine house", p.569), although any greenhouse with louvre ventilators along the sides is adequate.

Cool/frost-free

A cool greenhouse is one that is heated just enough to keep out frost. This means that a minimum daytime temperature range between 5°C (41°F) and 10°C (50°F), and a night-time temperature of no less than 2°C (36°F), is needed.

To ensure that these temperatures are maintained, a heater capable of a large temperature lift is a necessity in winter, in case the outside temperature falls many degrees below freezing. An electric heater with a thermostat (see p.574) is most likely to do this efficiently.

Insulation, thorough ventilation, and shading control are necessary, as with cold greenhouses.

A frost-free greenhouse may be used to grow all the types of plant mentioned for cold greenhouses. In addition, frost-tender plants may be overwintered, and summer crops or flowering pot plants grown. A propagator will be needed for germinating seeds. Young seedlings will benefit from the extra light provided by a growing lamp (see p.577).

Temperate

A slightly warmer greenhouse with a minimum daytime temperature range between 10°C (50°F) and 13°C (55°F), and with a minimum night-time temperature of 7°C (45°F), is suitable for growing a good selection of hardy, half-hardy, and tender pot plants, as well as vegetables.

Additional warmth is necessary in spring for propagation, supplied by a propagator or by boosting the ordinary heating for the required period. Supplementary lighting provided by a growing lamp is useful. Shading and good ventilation are required, especially in summer.

Warm

A warm greenhouse has a daytime temperature range between 13°C (55°C) and 18°C (64°F), with a minimum night-time temperature of 13°C (55°F). Such high temperatures enable an amateur gardener to grow a large range of plants, including

HOW A GREENHOUSE WORKS

Short waves

Long waves

Light passes through glass as short-wave radiation, warming everything inside, including floor, staging, soil, and plants. Heat then re-radiates from these as long waves, which cannot pass through the glass, leading to a build-up of heat inside the greenhouse.

tropical and subtropical ornamentals, fruits, and vegetables. A warm greenhouse may also be used to propagate plants and raise seedlings without the aid of propagation equipment, although a growing lamp would also be useful.

In hot weather very good ventilation, preferably automatic, an efficient method of shading, and high humidity (see p.576) are essential.

HOW TO BALANCE THE ENVIRONMENT OF A GREENHOUSE

	Heating (see p.574)	Insulation (see p.574)	Ventilation (see p.575)	Shading (see p.576)	Humidity (see p.576)	Watering (see p.577)	Lighting (see p.577)
Cold No minimum temperature	None.	Insulate against severely cold draughts and damp, foggy weather in winter.	Through ventilation is essential to prevent damp, stagnant conditions in winter.	Shade vulnerable plants in summer with a shading wash, blinds, meshes or fabric, or rigid sheets.	Unlikely to be a problem in summer. Maintain a "dry" atmosphere in winter by ventilating.	Water by hand in winter. Use a capillary system, seep hose, or trickle system in summer.	Growing lamps are unlikely to be needed for the type of plants grown.
Cool Minimum temperature 2°C (36°F)	A thermostatically controlled electric heater is preferable but gas or paraffin heaters may also be used. A frost alarm is useful if tender plants are grown.	In winter, as for a cold greenhouse. In spring, good insulation is extremely important if frost-tender plants are grown.	Ventilate freely, especially if a gas or paraffin heater is used, to disperse water vapour and toxic fumes.	Shade to control the temperature in summer – shading washes or blinds do this most efficiently. Fit automatic blinds, if possible.	"Damping down" is beneficial to increase humidity in summer.	As for a cold greenhouse, except that an overhead system may also be used in summer.	Growing lamps may be useful, especially in spring when natural light is poor, for plants at an early stage of development.
Temperate Minimum temperature 7°C (45°F)	A heater (preferably electric) fitted with a thermostat is required. A frost alarm is also essential.	As for cold and cool greenhouses. Thermal screens are useful in spring for propagation.	As for a cool greenhouse. Automatic vent openers are extremely useful in summer.	As for a cool greenhouse.	Maintain high humidity in spring and summer, especially around cuttings and seedlings.	An automatic watering system is useful throughout the year.	Growing lamps are useful in winter and spring for extending daylength.
Warm Minimum temperature 13°C (55°F)	As for a temperate greenhouse.	Good insulation is essential throughout the year to minimize heating costs.	Automatic vent openers fitted to several vents simplify temperature control enormously.	Automatic blinds are desirable in summer.	High humidity is required throughout the year.	As for a temperate greenhouse.	As for a temperate greenhouse.

Heating

It is important to maintain the correct temperature in the greenhouse for the range of plants you have chosen to grow. Select a heater that is powerful enough to maintain the required minimum temperature efficiently. Other factors to consider when choosing a greenhouse heater include convenience, the cost of installation, and running costs.

Electric heaters

These are the most reliable, efficient, and convenient to use in the greenhouse, although an electricity supply will be needed to run them (see "Installing electricity, gas, and water", p.572). They are usually thermostatically controlled, which means that no heat is wasted, and they do not require regular refuelling or maintenance. In addition, electric heaters do not produce fumes or water vapour.

A number of different types of electric heater is available. These include fan heaters and water-proof tubular heaters, both of which heat the greenhouse effectively. Convector heaters are also used but these do not distribute heat as efficiently. Tubular heaters need to be fitted to the sides of the greenhouse, just above floor level. Other heaters may be moved around as desired.

Electric fan heaters are particularly useful because they promote good air circulation, which helps to maintain an even temperature and minimizes the spread of disease. They may also be used to cool the greenhouse in warm weather if the heating element is switched off.

Gas heaters

Gas heating systems may be run off the mains supplies (see "Installing electricity, gas, and water", p.572) or from bottled gas. They are not as convenient to use as electric heaters: although they may have thermostats, these are not usually calibrated in degrees so you will need to experiment to find the correct setting.

If bottled gas is used, the cylinders need to be regularly replaced: always have two bottles connected by an automatic switch-over valve in case one runs out. Propane gas releases fumes and water vapour as it burns, so ventilation is important. Keep gas cylinders in a safe place and have them checked regularly by an authorized dealer.

Paraffin heaters

These are not as efficient as electric or gas heaters in their use of fuel because they are not controlled by a thermostat. Paraffin heaters may therefore be expensive to run if a high temperature needs to be maintained, since some energy may be wasted, although they are inexpensive to buy in the first place and there is no installation cost.

When using paraffin heaters, thorough ventilation is required because some plant-toxic fumes and water vapour are produced as a byproduct of combustion – a humid, stagnant atmosphere may encourage disease if ventilation is poor. Other drawbacks include the need to transport and store fuel, and to check the fuel level and wick every day to ensure that it is burning cleanly.

Circulated hot water

Solid fuel hot water systems are now rarely used in greenhouses. Oil- and gas-fired circulated hot water systems are still sometimes used, but seldom on the small scale of the amateur greenhouse.

Although the distribution of heat through hot water pipes provides good heat transfer, often only about 50 per cent of the energy released is used – the rest is lost through the glass walls. The need for regular stoking and clearing out of the fire also makes solid fuel inconvenient.

Thermometer and frost alarm

If the heater in a greenhouse is not thermostatically controlled, use a maximum/minimum thermometer to check that the correct overnight temperatures are being maintained for the plants grown.

In regions that suffer extremely low temperatures, a frost alarm is a useful safeguard if the greenhouse contains tender plants. If the air temperature unexpectedly drops to near freezing, for example through a power failure or heater breakdown, an alarm bell will sound remotely (this will usually be somewhere in the home), allowing you time to protect the plants.

A FROST ALARM

Install a frost alarm if growing tender plants that may be damaged or killed if the temperature falls.

INSULATION MATERIAL

Bubble plastic is useful for insulating a greenhouse and reduces heat loss considerably. Cut it to size and attach it securely to the framework.

Insulation

Insulation in the greenhouse may reduce heating costs considerably; if a minimum temperature of 7°C (45°F) is required, for example, the cost of insulation may be recovered within just a few seasons – and even in a single winter period in particularly cold areas. The higher the temperature to be maintained, and the colder the region, the more cost-effective insulation is likely to be. Care in choosing the right material is needed, however, since some insulation materials may reduce the amount of light reaching the plants.

Double-glazing

The most efficient method of insulating the entire greenhouse is to fit double-glazing. This is best done at the time of construction, if at all possible. Double-glazing is expensive, of course, but the benefits could be enormous.

Flexible plastic insulation

Bubble plastic, which consists of double or triple skins of transparent plastic with air cells in between, is a very efficient method of insulation. A single layer of plastic sheeting is not as efficient as bubble plastic at reducing heat loss but is less expensive and does not cut out so much light. Plastic sheets may be used in winter as a form of double-glazing. To attach the insulation material, use suction-pad fasteners or clips that fit into the greenhouse frame.

Thermal screens

These consist of sheets of clear plastic or translucent material, such as a cross-laminated fabric, that are attached to wires between the eaves and drawn horizontally across the width of the greenhouse in the evening. They are useful for conserving heat at night because they restrict the amount of heat that rises above the eaves, trapping the warmth lower down around the plants.

Vertical screens may also be used to partition off a heated section at one end of the greenhouse with plastic sheeting, leaving the remainder of the area unheated. Plants may be overwintered and early seedlings raised in the heated section.

Special kits for making thermal screens are available, or plastic sheeting and the necessary fixings may be obtained separately.

Base cladding

Base cladding on the floor of glass-to-ground greenhouses reduces heat loss significantly. In winter, place polystyrene panels along the foot of the glass panes to provide extra insulation, removing them before summer border crops are planted.

THERMAL SCREENS

Horizontal screen between the eaves

Vertical screen that acts as a partition

Thermal screens may be drawn horizontally between the eaves. They may also be drawn vertically to partition off a section of the greenhouse that needs to be heated to a high temperature.

Ventilation

Good ventilation is essential in a greenhouse, even in winter, to avoid a build-up of stuffy or damp, stale air, and to control temperature. It is important that the area covered by ventilators should be equal to at least one sixth of the floor area.

Extra ventilation

Few greenhouses are supplied with enough ventilators as standard, so order additional air vents, hinged and louvre windows, or extractor fans when buying a greenhouse. This is an especially important consideration with timber greenhouses, since it is usually difficult to add them later.

Extra ventilation is particularly important if paraffin or bottled gas heating systems are used, to prevent water vapour and fumes from building up to an unacceptable level.

Wind ventilation system

Air exchange in a greenhouse occurs when external movements of air, caused by gusts of wind, replace interior warm, humid air with fresh air. If ventilators are placed on the sides and roof of the greenhouse, and are also staggered, this will ensure that air circulates throughout the entire area – if vents are placed directly opposite one another, air will simply blow straight through the greenhouse.

Doors may also be kept open in summer to increase ventilation; it is worth fixing a sheet of netting across the doorway, however, to keep out birds and pets.

Chimney ventilation system

Chimney effect ventilation depends on warm, humid air rising out of roof vents and being replaced by fresh air that is drawn in as a result through lower ventilators, which are usually positioned along the sides of the greenhouse either above or below the staging.

Fan ventilation system

Fan ventilation is a mechanically driven system that works by extracting air from the greenhouse at head height, or slightly higher, and drawing in fresh air through vents lower down and usually at the opposite end of the greenhouse.

Hinged ventilators

These may be fitted to the sides or roof of the greenhouse and should open wide, to an angle of about 45°. This will allow maximum airflow while at the same time preventing direct gusts of wind from entering

THE PRINCIPLES OF GREENHOUSE VENTILATION

Wind effect
Fresh air blows into the greenhouse, circulates, and then escapes through an open vent on the opposite side.

Chimney effect
Warm air rises and escapes through open vents in the roof, drawing fresh, cooler air in lower down.

Fan ventilation
Air is drawn out by a fan at the top of the greenhouse and drawn in through open vents lower down.

the greenhouse and possibly causing damage to the plants or even to the structure itself.

Louvre ventilators

Usually positioned below the height of the staging, louvre window ventilators are particularly useful for controlling the flow of air throughout the greenhouse in winter, when roof ventilators may allow too much heat to escape. The louvre vents must close tightly, however, so that they exclude all draughts.

Automatic vent openers

Autovent openers simplify temperature control significantly in the greenhouse, since they are designed to open automatically whenever the temperature inside rises above a predetermined level. These devices are essential if a heating system that has no thermostat has been installed in the greenhouse.

With any type of greenhouse, automatic vent openers should be fitted to at least some of the hinged or louvre ventilators; this is easily done by closely following the manufacturer's instructions.

They may be set to open at a range of temperatures, but make sure you choose an automatic system that will function within the temperature range required in your greenhouse. It is best to set this to operate at a temperature that is just below the

optimum for the plants. In this way, the vents will open and the greenhouse will be well ventilated before the temperature inside rises to an unsuitable level for the plants.

Many different designs of autovent are available. Some models work by the expansion and contraction of a plug of wax that is contained in a metal or plastic cylinder; the movement of the wax works a piston that opens and closes the ventilator. Other models make use of metal rods that alter their shape as the temperature rises and falls, activating the ventilation mechanism.

Extractor fans

The type of extractor fan that is designed primarily for use in kitchens and bathrooms is also ideally suited for use in the greenhouse. An additional bonus with using these extractor fans is that most of them are fitted with a thermostatic control, which is an essential requirement for the greenhouse.

Choose a fan that is powerful enough for the particular size of your greenhouse – the extraction rate is usually quoted in cubic metres or cubic feet per hour. As a general guide, a 2 x 2.5m (6 x 8ft) greenhouse requires a fan with a capacity of 300cu m (10,000cu ft) per hour, but a smaller one may be perfectly adequate if other types of ventilation are also used.

A louvre window – positioned at the opposite end of the greenhouse to the extractor fan and set lower down – is essential to provide a flow of fresh air to replace the stale air that is drawn out by the fan.

Buy a fan that is fitted with louvre flaps that close when the fan is not actually working so that draughts are excluded. To extend the working life of the fan, the motor should not be set to run at maximum capacity; it is much better to choose a model that is slightly more powerful than is strictly necessary for the greenhouse.

LOUVRE VENTS

These are fitted on the side of the greenhouse above ground level to improve the flow of air through the interior. The opening mechanism has a lever and is simple to operate (see insets).

HINGED VENTS

Vents that open by a hinge mechanism are normally fitted to the roof of the greenhouse. Make sure that they open wide and that they are securely fixed when open.

AUTOVENT OPENER

This autovent works by the expansion and contraction of wax in a cylinder as the greenhouse temperature rises and falls.

Shading

This will help to control the temperature of the greenhouse if the ventilation system is insufficient. It also protects vulnerable plants from too much direct sunlight, reducing the risk of leaf scorch, and preventing flower colours from fading in strong sunlight. Shading applied primarily to control heat should be on the outside of the greenhouse; internal shading is unlikely to reduce the temperature significantly.

The amount of shade required in a greenhouse depends on the season and the plants being grown. In the months of strongest sunlight, shading that reduces the light by 40–50 per cent is suitable for a typical mixed greenhouse. Ferns generally prefer approximately 75 per cent filtering of light, while most cacti and other succulents require very little or no shading at all.

Shading washes

These are often the most effective and cheapest method of reducing heat from the sun, while still allowing enough light to penetrate for good plant growth. Paint or spray the wash onto the outside of the glass at the beginning of the sunny season and remove it in late summer by rubbing or washing it off, using a cleaning solution if necessary.

Shading washes are inexpensive but they may be messy to apply and remove, and their appearance is sometimes unattractive in a small garden where the greenhouse is a major feature. Some washes become more transparent when wet, so that on rainy days or when the weather is dull they allow more light penetration.

Blinds

These are used mainly on the outside of the greenhouse and control temperature effectively. They are more versatile than shading washes,

since they may be rolled up or down, depending on the intensity of light required. They may be used where only a section of the greenhouse needs to be shaded. Manually operated blinds need constant attention, however. Automatic blinds, which come into operation as soon as the temperature rises to a predetermined level, are more convenient to use, but they are expensive.

Meshes and fabrics

Flexible mesh shading materials are suitable for either interior or exterior use. They are less adaptable than blinds because they are generally fixed in position for the entire season, and they are less satisfactory than shading washes in helping to control plant growth.

Woven and knitted fabrics are also suitable for both interior and exterior greenhouse use. The amount of light reduction varies considerably, depending on the type of fabric fitted, but the quality of light allowed through to the plants is usually perfectly adequate for good growth, although the temperature is not significantly reduced.

FLEXIBLE MESH

Plastic mesh netting may be cut to length and used either internally or externally for shading plants in a greenhouse.

SHADING THE GREENHOUSE

Shading washes are applied to the outside of a greenhouse to prevent the temperature inside from rising too high, without greatly reducing light. The washes may be left on throughout the season.

ROLLER BLINDS

Blinds are a versatile method of shading the greenhouse. They should be hard wearing, since they will be in place for long periods.

Cross-laminated fabric and some plastic meshes are recommended for internal shading only.

Tinted bubble plastic may also be used for shading. It cuts down the light by almost 50 per cent, but it reduces temperature only slightly.

Rigid sheets

Rigid polycarbonate sheets (usually tinted) are sometimes used for shading in greenhouses. The sheets may be fixed either inside or outside, as recommended by the greenhouse manufacturer. They cut down the light effectively, but unless they are white in colour the quality of light transmitted may not be sufficient for good plant growth.

Humidity

Humidity is a measure of the quantity of water vapour in the air. The humidity of the air affects the rate at which plants transpire; this is their mechanism for drawing water (along with nutrients) from roots to leaves, where the water then evaporates from leaf pores into the air. As water evaporates, the plant is cooled down.

Establish the preferred humidity levels of the plants in your greenhouse, then control the amount of moisture in the atmosphere to suit them. Humidity may be increased using various techniques (see "Humidifiers", below) and reduced by ventilation (see p.575).

Plant requirements

A very humid atmosphere reduces the rate of transpiration and evaporation to a level that may be harmful to some plants and they may suffer

damage from overheating unless cooler, drier air is brought in by ventilation. Many tropical plants from humid climates, however, require high levels of humidity for healthy growth, and will not survive in a dry atmosphere.

If the air is dry and the humidity level low, plants transpire more rapidly, often losing a great deal of moisture. Plants that are not adapted to cope with low humidity will wilt as a result, unless additional water is supplied at the roots. Dry-climate plants often have specific anatomical features that reduce the transpiration rate in drought conditions (see WATER CONSERVATION AND RECYCLING, pp.614–615).

Measuring humidity

The level of humidity in a greenhouse depends to an extent on the temperature of the air – warm air is capable of holding more moisture than cold air before it becomes saturated. Relative humidity is a measure of the amount of water vapour in the air expressed as a percentage of saturation point at the same temperature. A "humid" atmosphere is defined as having a relative humidity of about 75 per cent; a "dry" atmosphere has a relative humidity of about 35 per cent.

Wet and dry bulb thermometers, used in conjunction with hygrometric tables, may be used to measure the relative humidity of the atmosphere. Hygrometers, which have a dial that gives readings for both the temperature and the humidity, are also available. As a general guide, a relative humidity below 75 per cent, but above 40 per cent, is beneficial for most greenhouse plants during the growing season – at levels above 80 per cent, diseases such as grey mould (*Botrytis*) and mildew may become a problem.

In winter, humidity should be maintained at a lower level, but the exact level required will depend on the types of plant grown and the temperature of the greenhouse.

Humidifiers

Greenhouses may be "damped down" during the summer by splashing water – predominantly on the floor and on any staging – from a watering can or hose. This has the effect of increasing the level of atmospheric humidity. An automatic spray system simplifies humidity control, especially for plants that require very high humidity. In a small greenhouse, mist-spraying by hand or providing a tray filled with water that slowly evaporates into the air is usually adequate.

Watering

A traditional watering can is still the best, if perhaps time-consuming, method of watering a mixed collection of plants in a small greenhouse. Because you can readily monitor the flow, it ensures that all the plants are watered according to their individual requirements.

An automatic watering system is a useful addition to a greenhouse in summer, however; if the greenhouse is left unattended on a regular basis, an automatic system becomes essential, since some pot plants may need to be watered several times a day in very hot weather.

Capillary systems

Watering systems that rely on capillary action to draw up water are often used in a greenhouse.

Plant pots may be placed on a 2–5cm (¾–2in) layer of clean sand (which retains moisture well) that is placed on the greenhouse staging and kept permanently wet. Moist sand adds considerable weight to the staging, however, so make sure that it is sturdy enough to take the extra load. In addition, protect wooden staging from the wet sand by lining it with sheets of heavy-duty plastic, otherwise it will rot. Alternatively, the sand may be placed in aluminium or plastic trays.

Add a length of plastic gutter to the edge of the bench and keep it filled·with water. This may be done by hand or automatically from an overhead tank connected to the mains, in which case the system should be controlled by a ballcock.

Capillary matting, which is widely available in rolls and is simply cut to the required size, is far lighter, easier to keep clean, and just as effective as sand. To keep the capillary matting continuously moist, trail the edge into a water trough or other reservoir of water. The water may be topped up by hand or supplied automatically from the mains, as above.

For a capillary system to be effective, there must be sufficient contact between the compost in the pots and the source of moisture so that water is continuously supplied to the plants' root systems. Plastic plant pots usually allow good contact between the compost and the moist sand or matting. Clay pots, however, may each require a wick. This is cut out of a piece of spare capillary matting and placed in the drainage hole of the pot to bridge any gaps between the compost and the mat.

During the winter months, do not use capillary watering systems in the greenhouse, since most plants are dormant, or growing only slowly, and therefore require a reduced intake of water. The perpetually damp mat or sand may also increase humidity in the greenhouse to unsatisfactory levels for the plants (see "Humidity", p.576).

Overhead systems

A system of overhead pipes, with nozzles from which water is sprayed onto the plants below, is widely used in commercial greenhouses. This is an ideal system for watering a large number of plants that are all at a similar stage of growth. It is not suitable for the small, amateur greenhouse, however, that contains a wide variety of plants. Overhead watering systems are also expensive to install and create too humid an atmosphere if used in the winter.

Seep hoses

These are widely used in the garden, and inside the greenhouse to water border crops or to keep capillary matting moist. In very hot weather, however, seep hoses may not supply a sufficient flow of water to the plants (see also p.561).

Trickle irrigation systems

This type of irrigation system consists of a series of small-bore tubes, each with an adjustable nozzle. The tubes are placed in the individual pots or growing bags, or near plants growing in the greenhouse border.

Most trickle irrigation systems are fed with water from a reservoir that is filled in turn from a hose connected to the mains water supply. It is possible, however, to use water supplied direct from the mains.

The rate of water delivery must be monitored very carefully and adjusted according to the needs of the plants; these needs vary depending on time of year and the vagaries of the weather (see also p.561).

Lighting

If an electric power supply is already installed in the greenhouse (see "Installing electricity, gas, and water", p.572), lighting units are not expensive to add at any time, and running costs are also low. In addition, the lights produce a little extra heat for the plants. Ordinary fluorescent lamps provide enough illumination to work by comfortably.

Growing lamps

The special quality of lighting produced by growing lamps is required to increase light intensity and daylength (see THE VEGETABLE GARDEN, "Daylength", p.495) for specific purposes during spring and winter when light levels are low.

Fluorescent tubes that produce good light to improve plant growth may be obtained from specialist aquarium suppliers and garden centres. They do not produce much heat, and so may be placed close to the plants. The lights are fitted with reflectors that cast the light downwards, where it will do the most good. For greatest effectiveness, the tubes should be mounted 25–30cm (10–12in) above the foliage. Mercury fluorescent lamps and mercury vapour lamps also provide a suitable quality of light to encourage good plant growth.

Metal halide lamps are the best, if most expensive, form of growing lamp, emitting light that is close to the spectrum of natural light. They illuminate a large area but cast their light in a circular pattern, which may be inconvenient in a small greenhouse, since the corners may not be strongly lit.

Most growing lamps that are suitable for use in the greenhouse need special fittings because of the moist, humid atmosphere. If in any doubt, always ask the advice of a qualified electrician.

WATERING SYSTEMS

Overhead reservoir

Tubes supply each plant with water

Gutter filled with water

Capillary matting

Capillary watering
An overhead reservoir feeds water to a gutter fixed to the staging. The matting soaks up water, which is absorbed by compost in the trays.

Trickle irrigation
Trickle systems supply water directly to each pot by means of tubes, which are fed from an overhead reservoir.

Light meters

Where lighting is a very important factor, special plant light meters may be useful in the greenhouse, because they measure light levels much more accurately than can be judged by eye.

Light meters are usually supplied with information about the light levels that are preferred by a wide range of commonly cultivated plants, so follow the instructions for the particular plants grown.

A GROWING LAMP

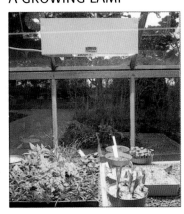

This provides additional light to improve plant growth. Secure it directly above the plants, if possible.

Using the space

To make best use of the limited space in a greenhouse, plan the layout carefully. Cultivation in raised beds, borders, growing bags, or containers placed on the ground, staging, or shelves are all suitable methods; often, a combination is best.

Raised beds

These are used mainly in alpine houses, where sharp drainage is required. Raised beds may be expensive to construct using new bricks, but old bricks are satisfactory. Leave a large gap between a raised bed and the wall of a greenhouse so that air

can circulate and moisture from the compost does not penetrate the wall. For details see STRUCTURES AND SURFACES, "Raised beds", p.599.

Beds that are raised to normal bench height are suitable only for lean-to greenhouses or for those with a tall brick base. For small plants that do not require a great depth of soil, a stone trough placed on brick pillars or "legs" may be used. Alternatively, construct a raised container by fixing rigid metal sheets or paving slabs on top of brick pillars, making the walls by laying several brick courses around the top, and lining with a sheet of butyl rubber. The butyl sheet should have several holes pierced

in it to ensure that the bed will be adequately drained.

Raised beds for taller plants need not be so high and so do not need to stand on brick pillars. They are usually built up from ground level with basal seep holes for drainage and simply filled with compost.

Borders and growing bags

A glass-to-ground greenhouse is required to grow plants directly in the border, to ensure that plants receive enough light. Borders with a width of 1m (3ft) are acceptable in

a greenhouse that is 2.5m (8ft) wide but make the beds wider if staging is placed over the borders, so that the staging does not prevent you from reaching the far side easily. Plants in containers may also be placed on top of the border rather than on staging, if required.

The soil in greenhouse borders may become infected with disease if the same plants are grown repeatedly over many years. If this is the case, or if the greenhouse floor is concreted over, growing bags may be used. Growing bags provide a convenient method of cultivation, since they retain moisture well and remove the need to dig and fertilize the soil

INSIDE THE GREENHOUSE

Organize the elements within the greenhouse sensibly to make the best possible use of the limited space. Here is a well-planned layout for a lean-to greenhouse.

DISPLAYING THE PLANTS

Shelving and staging enable attractive tiered displays of plants of varying heights to be made. If the greenhouse is heated, a wide variety of plants may be grown throughout the year to maintain the display of flowers and foliage. Place dormant or "resting" plants beneath the staging to make more room for other plants in season.

FIXED STAGING

Most greenhouse manufacturers supply permanent, purpose-built staging that is made from the same materials as the greenhouse. It is best fitted at the same time as the greenhouse is constructed.

before planting. All the nutrients in the compost contained in the growing bags are used up during the season, so fresh growing bags should be used each year.

Staging

Staging is important for any ornamental or mixed greenhouse – by bringing plants to waist height, watering and care are made easier. Even if removed for summer crops, staging is necessary for propagating and growing on young plants.

Positioning the staging

The most satisfactory arrangement for a small or mixed greenhouse is to have a central path with staging along the sides, and possibly across one end, removing half of it for border crops when necessary and retaining the permanent staging to display ornamentals. The permanent staging should be positioned on the side where it will cast the least shade on the border crops.

Central staging

Larger ornamental greenhouses that are designed primarily as show houses may have staging placed in the centre, with a path around the edge. Two staging benches may be placed back-to-back, preferably with tiered staging in the centre to enhance the display of plants.

The right size and height

Most staging benches are 45–60cm (18–24in) wide. Wider benches are useful in a large greenhouse but they may be difficult to reach across. All staging needs to be of sturdy

construction to support the considerable weight of plants, containers, and compost. Always leave a generous gap between the back of any staging and the sides of the greenhouse to allow air to circulate.

Most amateur greenhouses also have to serve as a potting shed. A convenient height for staging that is also used as a work surface is approximately 75–90cm (30–36in); it should be lower if a sitting working position is required.

Free-standing staging

It is sometimes useful to have staging that can be dismantled and stored away, bringing it into the greenhouse for short periods, for instance when raising seedlings in spring. Free-standing staging may not fit the

FREE-STANDING STAGING

Movable benches allow great flexibility, since they may be moved around to accommodate the plants, or removed altogether.

greenhouse quite so well as staging that is built-in and may not look as attractive but is more flexible in use. It must be easy to assemble and sturdy since it will be in use for many years. If border crops are grown for most of the year, open-mesh staging which folds back neatly against the side of the greenhouse is convenient for short periods.

Free-standing modular staging systems can be built up in tiers and provide an attractive way of displaying plants. Slatted, mesh, or solid modular systems are available.

Permanent staging

Built-in staging and shelves may put a strain on the framework of a greenhouse, especially light, aluminium alloy structures. Gravel or sand, if used, adds extra weight to the staging, particularly when it is wet. Buy staging that is purpose-built, if possible; if in doubt, check with the greenhouse manufacturer before fitting any permanent staging.

Slatted and mesh staging

If you are growing alpines or cacti and succulents in pots, it is preferable to use slatted or mesh benches, which allow a freer flow of air than solid staging. However, slatted and mesh staging are not suitable for capillary watering systems.

SLATTED STAGING

Wooden-slatted staging is an attractive choice. The slats allow better air circulation around the plants than solid-surface staging does, but slats are not suitable for a capillary watering system, unless pots are placed in trays on the bench.

For a timber greenhouse, use wooden slatted benches; for an aluminium alloy or galvanized steel greenhouse, metal or plastic-mesh benches are more appropriate.

Solid surface staging

Solid staging allows more pots to be accommodated than slatted staging (it is difficult to keep pots upright between the slats), but may require more ventilation.

If using a capillary watering system, choose solid aluminium staging that has a level surface for the matting or sand. Some types of staging have reversible sections that produce raised flat surfaces for mats if placed one way, and dish-like sections for sand or gravel if reversed.

Shelves

Shelves in the greenhouse may be used for both storage and display. Permanent shelves often cast shade on the plants below so it is preferable to install fold-away shelves, which may be used in spring when space is short and then put away for the rest of the year.

In a small greenhouse, shelves can be used to display trailing plants where there is not enough head-room for hanging baskets.

Propagation aids

The propagation of many plants requires higher temperatures than may realistically be maintained in the greenhouse. To save on fuel bills, therefore, propagation aids are often used to provide the extra heat required. They may also increase the success rate when sowing seed or rooting leafy cuttings. Choose a propagator for the greenhouse that is large enough to hold at least three standard seed trays.

An electric power supply in the greenhouse is essential if heated propagators, mist units, or soil-warming cables are to be used. Mist units require a mains water supply as well as a power supply.

Unheated propagators are of limited use in the greenhouse but usually provide sufficient humidity for rooting tip, softwood, or semi-ripe cuttings in summer. On a small scale, a similar effect is created by enclosing a pot of cuttings in a clear plastic bag.

Heated propagators

A heated propagator should have a heating element that is capable of providing a minimum compost temperature of 15°C (59°F) in winter and early spring, when temperatures outside may fall below freezing.

If tropical plants are to be propagated, the unit must have a more powerful heating element that can maintain a temperature of 24°C (75°F). The propagator should preferably be fitted with an adjustable thermostat, which allows greater flexibility of temperature.

Use rigid plastic lids, since these are more likely to retain the heat than thin plastic covers. Adjustable ventilators are useful because they allow moisture to escape and prevent the atmosphere inside the propagator from becoming too humid.

Domestic propagators

Some small heated propagators are designed for windowsill use. Usually holding just two seed trays, they are generally too small to be of practical use in the greenhouse and often do not have a thermostat. They may not generate enough heat in a cold or cool greenhouse, since the heating element is intended to operate in a room indoors.

Heated bases

These are designed to be used with unheated propagators or ordinary seed trays, either of which may be placed on the heated base. A plastic hood must be placed over seed trays to maintain warmth and humidity. Heated bases do not raise the temperature as efficiently as heated tray propagators (see below).

Heated tray propagators

These have a self-contained heating element in the base, and are best when fitted with an adjustable thermostat.

Mist units

Cuttings may often be rooted more rapidly and in greater numbers in a mist unit than by using other more conventional means. Mist units, which are normally used mainly by specialist horticulturists, automatically maintain a high humidity around cuttings and are useful for difficult plants.

The easiest and most convenient mist units to use are self-contained, enclosed ones that include a heating element, thermostat, sensor, transparent cover, and a misting head. The constantly humid atmosphere created by the misting head provides a suitable environment in which to root cuttings quickly – by maintaining a constant film of water on the propagating material. Heat loss by evaporation is also reduced, and there is also less risk of the cuttings being affected by fungal diseases because, when the misting head is in operation, most disease spores are washed out of the air and from the leaves before they can infect plant tissues.

For large numbers of plants, a mist propagation unit is more practical. Some units are designed for use without a cover on an open greenhouse propagating bench; they are used in conjunction with soil-warming cables and also require a specially constructed greenhouse bench. If sited

in a greenhouse where a mixed collection of plants is grown, however, the high humidity created by an open mist unit may prove unsuitable for some types of plant. In this situation, it would be preferable to install a closed mist unit.

Soil-warming devices

An electric horticultural blanket or a heated tray filled with moisture-retentive matting or sand will also create the basal heat and high humidity needed for successful propagation. More expensive still are soil-warming cables intended primarily for heating the substrate in a conventional propagator or on a mist bench in the greenhouse. Such soil-warming cables may also be used to heat the air in an enclosed space, such as a

cold frame or home-made propagator. The safest system to use is a cable with a wired-in thermostat that is connected to an insulated, fused socket. Buy a screened cable, as it is much less dangerous if the cable is accidentally cut.

Soil-warming cables are sold in lengths that are designed to heat a given area. A 75-watt cable, for example, measures 6m (20ft) and provides enough heat for a bench area of 0.7sq m (7sq ft) in a greenhouse that has some form of heating. A cable with a higher wattage would of course be needed for use in a similar area in an unheated greenhouse or in a cold frame that is outside the greenhouse.

The cable should be laid at a depth of 5–8cm (2–3in) in a series of "S" bends (ensuring that the loops do not touch) in a bed of moist sand.

PROPAGATING BLANKET

This specialized horticultural blanket is made of electric wires encased in aluminium foil to provide an even spread of heat. When not in use, it can be rolled up and stored.

Thermostat can be set to required temperature

Propagator

Probe monitors temperature at surface

Capillary matting

Plastic sheet protects blanket

Electric blanket

Polystyrene insulation pad

Greenhouse bench

USING SOIL-WARMING CABLES

In this propagating case, cables are used to heat the sand base and the air. Each set of cables has a thermostat, which ensures that the temperature never falls below a pre-set level.

Thermostat regulates air temperature

Cables also heat the air

Control box

Thermostat controls soil temperature

Soil-warming cable

Sand bed

Drainage holes

Layers of sand

A WINDOWSILL PROPAGATOR

Portable propagators should be used indoors, where they will retain the high humidity needed to germinate seeds or root cuttings.

Cold frames and cloches

Cold frames and cloches relieve pressure on greenhouse space, but they are also extremely useful in their own right. They are likely to be used most intensively in spring to harden off plants raised in a greenhouse, but they may also be used throughout the year to grow a wide range of crops. In the colder months, they are useful for protecting winter flowers, overwintering the seeds of hardy annuals sown in autumn, and sheltering vulnerable alpines from the worst of the wet weather.

Cold frames

The most popular type of cold frame has glass (or clear plastic) sides as well as glass "lights" (frame tops which contain the panes of glass), although sometimes timber and brick are used for the construction. Glass-to-ground models usually have a metal framework.

Frame lights

Choose a frame that has removable or sliding "lights" for easy access; some also have sliding front panels, which may be useful for extra ventilation. Hinged "lights" that are wedged open still provide protection from heavy rain but sliding "lights"

are often removed entirely during the day, leaving the plants completely vulnerable to heavy rain. Lightweight aluminium frames with their "lights" wedged open may be at risk in strong winds, however, so choose a model which has a hinged top and adjustable casement stays to secure the "lights" safely.

Wooden frames

Traditional timber frames are now difficult to obtain and are usually expensive, but may be made cheaply at home from second-hand timber. The wooden sides retain heat well. It is not very difficult to fix soil-warming cables (see p.580) to the inside of the frame to provide extra warmth. Paint or stain the wood to preserve it.

Aluminium alloy frames

These are widely available and relatively inexpensive. They vary considerably in design but are usually sold packed flat for easy transportation, and assembled on site. Aluminium alloy frames let in more light than either wooden or brick frames, but they do not have such good insulating qualities and may not be as strong or robust. It may be necessary to use ground anchors for lightweight frames.

VENTILATION METHODS OF COLD FRAMES

Hinged lights
Hinged tops may be wedged open on warm days to prevent the plants from overheating.

Sliding lights
Sliding tops are less vulnerable to gusts of wind but plants are not protected from heavy rain.

Brick frames

These are rarely used nowadays but they may still be built at home if a cheap supply of old bricks is available and if the "lights" can be made. Brick frames are generally warm and draught-proof.

Suitable sizes

The minimum practical size for a cold frame is 1.2m x 60cm (4 x 2ft). Often, however, the frame has to fit into whatever space is available (as near the greenhouse as possible), so choose the largest affordable frame that fits the space.

Height is important if the frame is to be used for plants in pots or for tall vegetable crops. In order to increase the height of a frame temporarily, raise it on loose bricks.

Insulation

The range of plants that may be successfully overwintered in a frame is increased if the frame is well insulated. The frame needs to be draught-proof; there should be no gaps around the glass or framework, and the top and any sliding front panels must fit well.

Glass-to-ground and plastic-sided frames may need insulating in cold weather with sheets of expanded polystyrene or bubble plastic (see "Flexible plastic insulation", p.574). Cut the sheets to size, and place them against the inside of the frame.

On cold nights, particularly when a sharp frost is predicted, frames may require additional outer protection: use layers of hessian or old carpet to cover the tops, tied down firmly or held in position with pieces of heavy timber. This protective covering should always be removed during the day, otherwise plants may suffer from lack of light. Alternatively, use

several layers of thick, clear plastic sheeting or bubble plastic for extra protection – this may be left in place during the day since it does not reduce the light to the same degree.

Ventilation

Good ventilation is essential in warm weather. Most frames have "lights" that may be wedged open to allow fresh air inside; often, the "lights" also slide along to allow more ventilation, and are eventually removed completely when young plants need to be hardened off.

Light

Aluminium frames (but not brick or wooden frames) may be moved around the garden to take advantage of the best light at various times of the year. If a frame is permanently sited, it should be positioned where it will receive the maximum amount of light in winter and spring, provided that the site is not too exposed.

Frames need shading in summer but, for year-round use, one that lets in as much light as possible is best.

Glazing materials

Horticultural glass is the best glazing material for cold frames; it transmits light well, allows the frame to warm up quickly, and retains heat better than most plastic materials. Broken or cracked panes should be replaced at once, so a frame that allows the individual panes to be replaced should be chosen. Some are glazed using glazing clips or glass panels that slide into the framework; this makes glass replacement fairly simple.

Where glass may be a potential danger for children or animals, or where the cost of the frame is the main consideration, use plastic glazing material.

HOW TO USE COLD FRAMES

Planting in the frame
Plants may be grown directly in the cold frame, if required. Always prepare the base with a thick layer of drainage material, such as broken crocks or coarse gravel, before adding a 15cm (6in) layer of good garden soil or compost.

Protecting crops
Here, the cold frame has been placed directly onto the soil in the vegetable plot. Vegetables are growing through slits in a plastic mulch (see "Plastic film mulches", p.503) laid on the surface of the soil.

Cloches

A wide range of cloche designs and materials is available – choose a cloche that suits the types of plant to be grown. Cloches tend to be used mainly in the vegetable garden but they are equally useful for protecting ornamental plants and seedlings that need a little extra warmth during winter or early in the season (see also "Frost protection", p.613).

Materials

Glass is the best choice of material if cloches are to be used extensively and moved from crop to crop. It has good light transmission and allows the frame to warm up quickly in sunlight. For safety, select toughened, 4mm (⅛in) float glass, which breaks into little pieces rather than large shards. Clear plastic material (of various thicknesses) is an alternative; plastic cloches are generally less expensive than those made of glass but do not allow such good light penetration, nor do they retain as much heat or last as long.

Single thickness plastic is the least satisfactory material for retaining heat, but is cheap and useful where high temperatures are not necessary. Plastic cloches last longer if they have been treated with an ultraviolet inhibitor and are stored out of direct sunlight when not in use.

The minimum thickness that is suitable for cloches is 150 gauge, but 300, 600, or 800 gauge provides much greater protection. PVC is thicker and more rigid, and has similar qualities to polypropylene (see below). Moulded PVC and PVC sheeting should last for five years or more if treated with an ultraviolet inhibitor.

Cloches made from twin-walled polycarbonate offer good insulation and should last for 10 years or more. Polypropylene is used in some injection-moulded cloches and in corrugated sheets; it retains heat better than plastic, but not as well as

Tent cloche

Barn cloche

glass or twin-walled polycarbonate. It lasts for five years or more if treated with an ultraviolet inhibitor.

End pieces

These are an important part of most cloches – without them a cloche may become a wind tunnel, damaging the plants inside. The end pieces should fit well to preclude draughts but they should be easy to remove to provide ventilation when required.

Tent cloche

A tent cloche is inexpensive and simple to construct: two sheets of glass are held together by wire or plastic clips, to form a tent shape. It is suitable for germinating seeds, for protecting young seedlings in spring, and for low-growing plants.

Tunnel cloche

A tunnel cloche may be made from either rigid or flexible plastic. Generally, flexible plastic, continuous tunnel cloches are used for crops such as strawberries and early carrots. The plastic must be supported by wire hoops (positioned over the row of vegetables) and tensioned with wires. Use heavy-duty plastic that has been treated with an ultra-violet inhibitor.

Rigid models are generally more attractive but more expensive than tunnel cloches that are made of flexible plastic. They are also easier to

Tunnel cloche

move around, since they do not need to be dismantled first. Some tunnel cloches have self-watering features.

Barn cloche

This has almost vertical sides that support a sloping, tent-shaped top. Its extra height makes it useful for relatively tall plants but extra materials and complicated fittings make it more expensive than a tent cloche.

Some glass and rigid plastic barn cloches have lifting or removable tops to provide ventilation in warm weather, while still offering wind protection. This makes weeding, watering, and harvesting easier.

Flexible PVC is sometimes used for barn cloches, but these tend to be lower and therefore less versatile than those using other types of material, unless the top is removable or can be wedged open.

Wall-of-water cloche

This unusual design of cloche is useful for single plants and consists of a circle of clear plastic tubes, into which water is poured. The tubes form the wall of the cloche, which alters in shape depending on the water level. The water protects the plant from several degrees of frost.

Self-watering cloche

Watering plants beneath cloches is difficult and time-consuming if the cloches have to be lifted or moved.

Self-watering cloche

A self-watering cloche is designed to allow rainwater to trickle through gradually to the plants below. Alternatively, it may have a tubular system that is connected to a hosepipe.

Floating cloche

A "floating" cloche (also known as a floating mulch) consists of a sheet of perforated plastic sheeting or polypropylene fibre fleece, which is placed over the ground where crops have been sown.

Floating cloches are permeable, allowing rainwater to penetrate to the soil below. This is a great advantage, since it reduces the need to water. The perforations in plastic floating

cloches enable the sheet to stretch a little as the crop grows beneath it. Fibre fleece is sufficiently light-weight to rise with the growing crop. Both perforated plastic and fibre floating cloches allow air to pass freely through the material and also have useful insulating properties; fibre fleece also protects plants from one or two degrees of frost. For further information, see GROWING VEGETABLES, p.505.

The sheets or fleeces should be anchored firmly into the soil at the edges of the beds with soil, stones, or pegs. Whole beds may be covered with a floating cloche, if desired, or pieces may be cut to fit smaller areas or even individual plants.

Individual cloche

These are usually used to protect individual plants in the early stages of growth but they may also be placed over any vulnerable, small plants during severe winter weather, such as frost, deep snow, heavy rain, and high winds.

Individual cloche

Home-made individual cloches, such as waxed-paper protectors and cut-off plastic bottles, are easy to make and are much less expensive than purpose-made models but may not be so attractive as ready-made, rigid plastic or glass, bell or dome-shaped cloches. These have curved walls, from which condensation trickles to the ground rather than falling on the plants, and so possibly causing disease or scorching.

Individual bell cloche

Routine maintenance

Regular maintenance is necessary to preserve greenhouses, and to keep frames and cloches clean. Autumn is usually a convenient time to attend to maintenance: cleaning and disinfecting the structure and equipment at this time of year minimizes numbers of overwintering pests and diseases.

It is important to do this work on a mild day before very cold weather begins. Tender plants can then be put outside while you prepare for winter.

Exterior maintenance

Choose a dry, still day for routine work on the outside of the greenhouse. Before making a start, gather together all necessary materials for cleaning, repairing, and repainting.

Cleaning glazing panels

Glass may be cleaned with water only, using a hose and long-handled brush, but if it is very dirty, better results are achieved by brushing with a solution of kettle descaler. Protect skin and eyes by wearing gloves and goggles, and rinse off the solution thoroughly with running water.

A proprietary window cleaning solution may be used but it will not remove ingrained dirt. Shading washes are best removed by rubbing them off with a cloth.

Repairing glass

Slightly cracked panes of glass and plastic may be temporarily repaired with transparent glazing tape. Broken and badly cracked panes, however, should be replaced as soon as possible to prevent harm to plants.

To replace a pane in an aluminium alloy greenhouse, remove the spring glazing clips and adjoining pane, and reglaze with the old clips (see p.572).

If the panes are bedded on linseed putty, remove the glazing tacks and panes of glass carefully. Chip away the putty with a chisel to leave a smooth surface. Clean glazing bars with abrasive paper before reglazing.

Apply priming paint to unpainted or untreated wood on glazing bars. Pay attention to knots in wood where moisture might enter. When paint is dry, replace panes by setting them on a bed of putty or glazing mastic, using glazing tacks to hold them.

Gutters and downpipes

Keep gutters and downpipes in good repair. Use a hosepipe to clear blockages. Small leaks in gutters may be sealed with mastic or other sealant, but badly leaking sections of gutter will need to be replaced completely.

Structural framework

Aluminium greenhouses require only minimal structural attention.

CLEANING BETWEEN PANES

To remove dirt or algae from gaps between overlapping panes in the greenhouse, use a thin, rigid strip of plastic to loosen any deposits before spraying or hosing down with water.

Although they lose their bright colour, the greyish patina that forms protects the metal from the weather.

Check steel frames and fittings for rust and, if necessary, treat with rust remover. Repaint every few years.

Cut out rotting wood and replace it; apply woodworm killer, and renew rusty hinges as necessary. Softwood greenhouses need regular painting: strip off flaking paint, wash down, then apply primer and exterior paint. Hardwood greenhouses are more rot-resistant, only requiring a coat of wood preservative every year or two, which also restores the colour.

Ventilators

Check windows and ventilator fans for ease of operation, oil working parts, and clean glass or plastic.

Interior care

Before cleaning and disinfecting the interior, turn off electric power at the mains, cover sockets and fittings with plastic, and remove the plants.

Cleaning and disinfecting

Glass and plastic glazing should be cleaned as described above. Scrub glazing bars with disinfectant – fine wire wool may be used (but not on anodized "coloured" aluminium).

Scrub brickwork and paths with a garden disinfectant and rinse with clean water. Disinfectant may be used, diluted according to the manufacturer's instructions, to sterilize staging and surfaces. Apply with a paintbrush, or spray, wearing protective gloves, face mask and goggles.

Fumigation

Return plants to the greenhouse. If necessary, fumigate using fungicidal and insecticidal smoke. Follow the instructions supplied. Ensure vents are closed before lighting the fumigant. Do not inhale smoke, and lock the door until it is safe to re-enter.

MAINTAINING THE GREENHOUSE

An annual check in autumn will be enough to keep your greenhouse in good working order.

Check all ventilators, ensuring they are watertight.

Repair broken ventilator fittings.

Clear leaves etc. from gutters.

Cover electric power points with plastic before cleaning inside the greenhouse.

Remove weeds from inside the greenhouse.

Check for dirt between overlapping panes. Clean as necessary.

Check for rusty hinges and treat with rust remover or replace.

Give panes a thorough clean, inside and out.

Strip areas of flaky paint and repaint or treat with preservative.

Replace cracked panes.

Remove rotten wood and replace it.

Clean and disinfect all inside surfaces.

3
STRUCTURES
AND SURFACES

THE STRUCTURES AND hard surfaces of a garden act as the framework around which plants can grow and mature. Pergolas, fences, or trellis add vital height, as well as offering privacy and shelter, while paths lead visitors on a tour around the garden's splendours. A terrace adjoining the house can, depending on aspect, make the perfect setting for breakfast, or an ideal spot to relax in the evening sun. As well as being functional, structures and surfaces can be attractive design features, providing year-round architectural interest. They can also be used as foils for planting: a circular patio makes a striking contrast with spreading plants, while a large rustic arch will form a complementary support for rambling roses.

Designing with structures and surfaces

Hard landscape elements are vital in helping to form the framework of a garden design and may be as ornamental as they are functional. In a new garden, features such as a terrace or a pergola are valuable for providing interest while the plants are growing and becoming established. In a more mature garden, sympathetically designed structures complement softer elements such as a lawn or the planting in a border and give the garden solidity and substance all year round.

When planning and designing structures, consider them in the context of their setting and in relation to each other. Materials, style, size, and shape should all be congruous both with the house and the overall design of the garden. A terrace or wall adjacent to the house often looks most effective if built of the same materials, forming a cohesive link between house and garden. Local materials are often preferable because they tend to look appropriate in the setting. The degree of formality is another important consideration to be made; in a formal garden, for example, a mellow brick wall boundary would be ideal, while in an informal, cottage garden a picket fence or woven wattle hurdles would be more suitable.

Structures may be used to link, define, or separate different elements or parts of the garden. A gently

Designing with hard landscape
Here, hard materials have been used to form the main framework of the design, creating interest while the planting is becoming established and providing a foil for the softer shapes of the plants. The curving path adds a sense of movement, while the innovative use of mixed materials provides satisfying textural contrasts.

curving path leads the eye along the garden, providing a unifying line, while a wide, straight path separates the features on either side. Steps create an interesting change of level and demarcate separate areas as well as joining them visually and providing access from one part to another. If the steps adjoin a patio, they may look best if constructed from the same materials and in a similar style – curved steps would look attractive linked to a circular patio, for example.

The order in which you undertake construction work largely depends on your individual priorities and the requirements of the site. It might be, for example, necessary to erect a flanking wall first because it will help to retain the soil of a raised bed; in another garden, laying a path might be the first priority to allow easy access with wheelbarrows to the rear of a site where work is in progress.

This chapter covers most straightforward structural projects that may be undertaken by an amateur, from hard surfaces such as patios, terraces, and paths, to boundaries and divisions, for example walls and fences, as well as other structures such as raised beds and pergolas. Certain hard landscape elements are covered in full in other chapters: see WATER GARDENING, pp.280–303, for details on constructing ponds and watercourses, and ROCK, SCREE, AND GRAVEL GARDENING, pp.252–279, for rock gardens and alpine troughs.

Patios and terraces

A patio is an ornamental feature as well as a functional one, providing an area for meals and relaxation, with plants in beds or containers, and perhaps a raised pool. An open paved area, with a balustrade or low wall, is more accurately described as a terrace. Patios and terraces are usually paved, although timber decking (see pp.591–592) is a popular alternative.

Choosing a site

Patios and terraces are usually sited close to the house, often with French windows allowing direct access. This provides a convenient power source for lights and other equipment, but if the site is not warm and sheltered, it may be better to find an alternative position. Designing the patio at an angle of 45° to the house, perhaps at a corner, may ensure that it receives sun for most of the day. A patio may also be built away from the house to exploit a fine view across the garden.

Two or more small patios may be more useful than one large one. One may be sited in an open, sunny spot, the other in a cooler place to provide a shady retreat on a summer's day.

Shelter and privacy

A warm, sheltered patio can be enjoyed for a longer period than one subject to strong winds. If the site is overlooked or exposed, create shelter and seclusion with screens or trellis with climbing plants. A pergola (see pp.603–604) roofed with trellis will screen the patio from above and provide shade. Avoid siting a patio near large trees: these will cast too much shade and drip long after rain has stopped, their roots may dislodge the paving, insects could be troublesome, and falling leaves and bird droppings may be a nuisance.

A suitable size

Size is less important for a terrace that links house and garden than for a patio that is to serve as an "outdoor

DRAINAGE SLOPE

Mark a number of pegs at the same distance from the top of each, then knock them in, in rows 2m (6ft) apart – the first at the top of the slope. Put a 2.5cm (1in) offcut on a peg in the second row. Make the two rows of pegs level, remove the offcut, and repeat.

room". Keep it in proportion to the garden: too small and it may look trivial; if too large, it may be overpowering. As a guide, allow 3.3sq m (4sq yd) for each person likely to use it. For a family of four, a patio about 13sq m (16sq yd) is a practical size.

Choosing a surface

Simplicity is the key to good design. If the patio is to have furniture, climbers, and containers, paving should be unobtrusive. Bear in mind that coloured paving may look fussy and often weathers to dreary shades. Variety is best achieved by mixing textures: small areas of brick or gravel among paving slabs, railway sleepers intersecting bricks or clay pavers, or cobbles with stone slabs.

Also consider whether you need a hard-wearing surface, or one that is not slippery when wet: choose from concrete (p.586), paving slabs (p.587), natural stone (p.588), tiles (p.588), bricks and pavers (p.589), or granite setts and cobbles (p.591).

Foundations

Patios, paths, and drives (see p.593) need firm foundations to ensure the paved surface remains stable once in use. The load-bearing requirements must also be considered: few patios have to support very heavy loads, but drives need more substantial foundations because they may be used by heavy vehicles. Climate is another factor: in areas with prolonged dry periods, for example, concrete foundations may crack if not sufficiently deep; seek local advice if necessary.

Before undertaking any excavation work, check the location of all the service pipes and cables on your property with the local authority or supplier to avoid damaging them.

Water run-off

To drain off water, the surface of a patio should slope slightly; a fall of

2.5cm for every 2m (1in for every 6ft) is usually sufficient. Calculate the combined depth of the sub-base and surface material and mark this as a line at the same distance from the top of each of a number of levelling pegs. Insert one row at the top of the slope so that the mark is at soil level, the top of the peg indicating the desired level of the finished paving. Insert a second row of pegs 2m (6ft) down the slope. On each peg in this row in turn, place a small, 2.5cm (1in) thick offcut of wood, a "shim", and lay a spirit level on a plank between this peg and one in the first row. Adjust the height of the lower peg until the top of the shim and the upper peg are level. Remove the shim and repeat the process down the slope. Then rake the soil so that it is level with the mark on each peg. The base and surface of the finished construction should be parallel.

Basic procedure

Remove any plant growth from the area, including tree roots, then dig out loose topsoil until firm subsoil is reached. Consolidate this using a plate compactor. For most patios and paths, but not those that might bear heavy loads (see p.586), firm subsoil or a 10cm (4in) layer of

---

PREPARING THE SUB-BASE FOR PATIOS AND PATHS

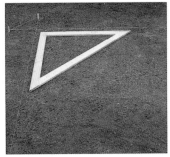

1 *Mark out the area with pegs and string, setting the string at the ultimate level of the path or patio. Use a builder's square to check that the corners are set at right angles.*

2 *Dig down to firm subsoil and tamp down with a plate compactor. Allow for a 10cm (4in) depth of hardcore, a 5cm (2in) layer of sand, if required, plus the thickness of the surface layer.*

3 *Drive in a grid of levelling pegs every 2m (6ft). For a patio, incorporate a slight slope so surface water drains away. Use a spirit level and plank to ensure that pegs are level with strings.*

4 *Spread a 10cm (4in) layer of hardcore over the entire site, and then compact it so that it is level, using the pegs as a guide. Add sand, if necessary, and compact the area again.*

Directing water run-off

In the never-ending battle to conserve water, it is worth knowing that rainwater running off a sloping patio does not need to go to waste. If you install a concrete gutter at the edge of the patio, you can channel the water towards a flower bed, onto the lawn, or perhaps into a pond or water feature. If you have room for one, you could even divert the flow towards a storage tank to be used for gardening purposes; this will allow you to selectively irrigate the garden when and where water is really needed.

HOW TO LAY CONCRETE

1 *After marking out the site, dig it out to a depth of 20cm (8in). Drive levelling pegs into the ground 1m (3ft) apart along the string lines. Set them horizontal using a plank and a spirit level.*

2 *Remove the string lines and nail wooden planks to the inner faces of the pegs, butted end-to-face at the corners. This formwork holds the concrete in place until it sets hard.*

3 *Divide large sites into sections no more than 4m (12ft) long using formwork. Spread hardcore 10cm (4in) deep and tamp it down with a roller or stout timber.*

4 *Starting with the first section, tip in the concrete and spread it level so that it is just proud of the formwork. Work the concrete well into the edges.*

5 *Using a wooden beam that spans the width of the formwork, compact the concrete with a downward chopping motion. Then slide the beam from side to side to level the surface.*

6 *Fill any hollows that appear after levelling using fresh concrete, and level it again.*

7 *Lay a protective, water-proof covering such as plastic sheeting over the concrete until it dries. Remove the formwork when the concrete has set hard.*

hardcore, covered with 5cm (2in) sand, is an adequate foundation. Use more hardcore to bring the surface of the sub-base up to the required level.

On unstable soils like peat or heavy clay (which may shrink in dry weather and damage the paving), lay 15cm (6in) of compacted hardcore as a sub-base. Top this up with sand or ballast to produce a level surface.

Load-bearing surfaces

For areas that will support heavy weight, lay a sub-base of at least 10cm (4in) of compacted hardcore or rubble, with 10cm (4in) of concrete on top. This concrete may be the top surface or a base for material like asphalt or pavers bedded in mortar. On clay or unstable soils, or if the surface is to be used by heavy vehicles, lay 15cm (6in) of concrete on top of the hardcore. If mixing your own concrete for the foundations, see below. When laying large areas, it is essential to leave expansion gaps (see "Expansion joints", p.594).

Concrete

Concrete is quick and easy to lay and is a hard-wearing, durable surface. It may be made more attractive by adding a textured finish (see p.594).

If you intend to lay a large area of concrete and there is access for large vehicles, having ready-mixed concrete delivered will make the job easier and quicker. Give the supplier the site measurements and information about the intended use of the surface to ensure the correct amount and mix is delivered or use a supplier who will mix it for you on site. This saves time and effort, but requires preparation and usually some helpers, since you have to tackle the job straightaway.

Concrete and mortar mixes

The following proportions for concrete and mortar mixes are suitable for most projects. For an explanation of terms, see p.591.

Wall footings, drive foundations, and bases for pre-cast paving
1 part cement
2½ parts sharp sand
3½ parts 20mm (¾in) aggregate
(or 5 parts combined aggregate to 1 part cement, omitting the sand)

***In situ* (poured) concrete paving**
1 part cement
1½ parts sharp sand
2½ parts 20mm (¾in) aggregate
(or 3½ parts combined aggregate to 1 part cement, omitting the sand)

Bedding mortar (for bedding paving, and jointing paving bricks)
1 part cement
5 parts sharp sand

Masonry mortar (for garden brickwork)
1 part masonry cement
3 parts soft sand
All these proportions are measured by volume and not by weight. The consistency of the mix required for different jobs varies. When mixing concrete or mortar, start by adding about half a part of water to one part cement. This makes a very stiff mix. Continue adding water gradually until you reach the right consistency.

In hot climates, setting retardants may sometimes be necessary in mortar and concrete mixes, while in cold climates, antifreeze products may have to be incorporated: seek local advice. Ideally, avoid laying concrete and mortar when the weather is close to freezing or above 32°C (90°F).

Laying concrete

Mark out the area to be concreted using string and dig down about 20cm (8in) until firm subsoil is reached. Drive wooden levelling pegs into the ground at intervals of 1m (3ft) around the edge, using the string as a guide. Nail planks to the inside faces of the levelling pegs to make a formwork at least 20cm (8in) deep, which will confine the concrete until it sets.

Divide large sites up into small sections that are no more than 4m (12ft) long using more planks. On top of the subsoil, spread a 10cm (4in) layer of compacted hardcore. Taking one section at a time, pour freshly mixed concrete inside the formwork to a depth of 10cm (4in) and work it into the edges. Use a wooden beam spanning the width of the formwork to compact the mix, then level the concrete by drawing the beam back and forth across the top of the formwork.

Inspection covers

Inspection covers for access to mains services must always be unobstructed: do not pave over them. Proprietary metal trays are available in which to bed paving slabs, clay pavers, or other materials. These minimize the unsightly impact of an inspection cover in a paved area and may be lifted out as required. If it is important to maintain the same pattern of laying as the surrounding area, you may need to cut the slabs or pavers that fit within the tray. The trays may also be filled with turf, or used for planting.

Paving slabs

Concrete paving slabs are popular for patios, paths, and drives. They are available in a range of sizes, textures, and colours, and are easy to lay once the base has been prepared. Many garden centres and builders' merchants stock a range of pre-cast concrete slabs. Some designs may be available only in one area. Large suppliers usually produce catalogues and deliver direct.

Sizes and shapes

Most slabs are either 450 x 450mm (18 x 18in) or 450 x 600mm (18 x 24in), with smaller slabs designed to integrate with them. Not all slabs have a shaped edge designed to butt join; a half slab may be slightly less than half the size of a full one, to allow for mortar between the joints.

Circular slabs are suitable only for stepping stones and small areas of paving with an infill of a loose material, such as gravel. Hexagonal slabs are useful if you prefer a pattern without regular, parallel lines; half slabs are available for a straight edge. Some slabs are made with a "bite" out of one corner, so that four slabs together form a planting hole.

Quantities

If laying a pattern with slabs of different sizes or colours, draw a plan on graph paper to calculate the number of each required, and allow up to five per cent extra for breakages (especially if many have to be cut, see p.588). Try to work to dimensions that minimize the need to cut slabs.

Laying paving slabs

If laying a patio, establish a line that you can use as a straight edge and ensure that there is a slight slope for drainage; always slope the patio away from a building. A house wall is a practical base line to work from, but you may want to leave a small gap between the wall and paving for planting. The top of the paving must be a minimum of 15cm (6in) below the damp-proof course. Mark out the area to be paved with pegs and string. Make it a size that requires as few slabs as possible to be cut. If the slabs are not to be butted, allow about 0.5–1cm (¼–½in) for mortar joints; metric slabs are usually designed to be laid with narrower joints than imperial slabs; if in doubt, seek advice from the supplier.

Preparing the site

Clear the site and prepare a sub-base of hardcore (see p.585). You will need wooden spacers about 1cm (½ in) thick to place between the paving slabs to allow for mortar.

Positioning the slabs

Work from one corner, placing a row of slabs in each direction with spacers between to make sure that the dimensions are correct. Adjustments are easy to make at this stage. Using a bricklayer's trowel, lay a strip of bedding mortar along each edge where the slab is to be laid, to form an area slightly smaller than the slab. If the slab is 45cm (18in) or more across, lay a cross of mortar within the box. The mortar ridges should be about 3–5cm (1¼–2in) high. This "box and cross" method combines strength with easy adjustment. Lay the slab in position and tamp it down with the handle of a club hammer or mallet. Use a spirit level to check that it is firm and straight. Repeat with successive slabs, using spacers between each one. Check the levels in each direction after every three or four slabs. Remove the spacers while you can still reach them without

HOW TO LAY PAVING SLABS

1 *Mark out the area and prepare the sub-base (see p.585). Lay strips of mortar to form a square just smaller than the slab. Include a cross strip for large slabs.*

2 *Position the slab and tamp down. Use a spirit level to check it is level. Repeat, using spacers for 1cm (½in) mortar gaps between the slabs.*

3 *Remove the spacers before the mortar sets. After two days, fill the joints with a stiff mortar. Scrape away so they are recessed about 2mm (⅟₁₆in). Brush slabs clean.*

Using a jigger
This device has a central slit. After aligning the slit and joint, the gap can be filled without spilling mortar on the slabs.

walking on the paving, and before the mortar sets. If you have to walk on the paving before the mortar has dried, stand on planks in order to spread your weight.

Finishing off

After a couple of days, fill the joints with a very stiff mortar mix (it should almost be "crumbly" to avoid staining the surface of the paving). Rub a

HOW TO CUT SLABS

1 *Place the slab on a firm, flat surface and, using the corner of a bolster and a straight edge, score a groove on both faces and edges to mark the cutting line.*

2 *Using a bolster and club hammer, carefully work along the scored line to deepen the groove on the faces and edges of the paving slab.*

3 *Raise the slab onto a length of timber. Align the groove with the edge of the timber and tap the slab sharply with a hammer handle until it splits.*

dowel or a rounded piece of wood over the pointing for a crisp finish, leaving it about 2mm (1/16in) below the paving surface. Alternatively, brush a dry mortar of 1 part cement to 3 parts sand into the joints. Brush any surplus off the surface. Spray the joints with a fine mist from a compression sprayer or a watering can fitted with a fine rose. Sponge excess mortar from the surface immediately, before it stains the slabs.

Cutting paving slabs

If you have many slabs to cut, it is best to hire a block splitter or angle grinder. For only a few, use a bolster (a broad-edged cold chisel) and club hammer. Always wear goggles when cutting paving blocks. Score the line where you need to cut with a corner of the bolster all around the slab, then chisel a groove about 3mm (1/8in) deep along this line; you may have to work around the slab several times, using the bolster to define and deepen the groove. If the slab has to fit into a tight space, cut it about 6mm (1/4in) smaller than needed to allow room for any rough edges that may be left when the slab splits.

Place the slab on a firm surface and raise the smaller part of the slab to be cut on a length of timber. Tap it sharply with the handle of a club hammer until a split forms along the line of the groove. Trim any rough pieces carefully with the bolster.

Crazy paving

Crazy paving has an informal appearance. It can be laid on sand, which will allow plants to be grown

between the joints, or on mortar for a firmer finish; if using the latter, fill in the joints with bedding mortar.

Defining the edges

Use string lines to mark out the area to be paved and prepare a sub-base for the paving (see p.585). Allow a slight slope for drainage (see "Water run-off", p.585) if necessary. Define the edges by laying a few metres (yards) of edging material first, working from one corner if laying a patio, the two edges if laying a path. This may simply be large pieces of crazy paving, with at least one straight edge, which can be laid to form the sides of the patio or path, or it could be wood, brick, or concrete. If using paving slabs, mortar these into position, even if bedding the remaining slabs on sand.

Laying the crazy paving

Loose lay an area about 1m (3ft) square without mortar, fitting the pieces together like a jigsaw. Keep the gaps small. It may be necessary to trim some pieces to size. Introduce a large piece occasionally, and infill with smaller ones.

Bed the pieces on sand or mortar, using a spirit level on a straight edge to ensure that they are level. Use a mallet or a block of wood and a hammer to bed each piece firmly in position. Lift pieces and add or remove sand or mortar as necessary until they are level.

Filling the joints

If bedding crazy paving on sand, finish off by brushing dry sand into the joints. If using mortar, mix a stiff, crumbly, almost dry mortar and use a pointing trowel to fill the joints (see "Finishing off", above). If using a dark-coloured stone, such

as slate, use a concrete dye (a powder you mix with the sand and cement) to make the joints less conspicuous. The colour will look different when dry, so test the dye on a small area and leave it to dry before deciding on the amount of colour to add.

Natural stone

Natural stone looks good, but is expensive and difficult to lay. Some types, such as sandstone, may be available cut into regular sizes and with an even edge. "Dressed" stone looks more natural; it is trimmed to a regular shape and has an attractive, uneven finish.

Lay sawn or dressed stone in the same way as paving slabs, adding or removing mortar to produce a level surface. Random stone is irregular in outline and thickness, and has no straight edges. This stone is suitable for laying as crazy paving, and it looks much more appealing than broken concrete paving slabs.

Tile surfaces

Quarry tiles, which are made of clay fired to a very high temperature, are useful for linking outdoor and indoor areas – perhaps where the paving inside a conservatory links with that outside. Glazed ceramic tiles may be more ornamental, giving an enclosed patio the impression of a Mediterranean courtyard for example, but many are not frost-proof. When selecting tiles, always check that they are suitable for using outdoors in your area before buying them. Tiles are difficult to cut,

HOW TO LAY CRAZY PAVING

1 *Using string lines and pegs to mark the height of the edges, prepare a sub-base (see p.585). Lay the edging pieces first, placing their straight edges outermost.*

2 *Fill in the centre with large slabs, infilled with smaller ones. Check that central slabs are level with the edging pieces and bed them on sand or mortar. Use a block of timber and a club hammer.*

3 *Fill the joints with almost dry mortar, or brush in sand. With a mortar finish, use a trowel to bevel the mortar so that any surface water drains away from the slabs.*

especially if they are not rectangular, so where possible design the area to make use of full tiles.

Laying tiles

Since tiles are thin and sometimes brittle, they need to be laid on a concrete sub-base (see "Load-bearing surfaces", p.586). Quarry tiles may be laid on bedding mortar (see p.591). Soak the tiles for a couple of hours before use so that they do not absorb too much moisture from the mortar.

Glazed ceramic tiles are best glued to a level concrete base using outdoor tile adhesive (obtainable from a builders' merchant). Spread this on the back of the tiles, following the manufacturer's instructions, then press the tiles into position on the prepared concrete base.

Finish off an area of glazed tiles with a grout (available from builders' merchants) to fill the gaps, perhaps coloured to match or contrast with the tiles.

Bricks and pavers

Bricks and clay or concrete pavers are most effective when laid in small areas; a large expanse is best broken up with other materials, for example, gravel or railway sleepers, otherwise the effect may well prove to be overwhelming.

For a patio situated next to a house built of brick, using bricks or pavers is an excellent way of linking the house and garden visually. Bricks and pavers also offer greater de-sign flexibility than large, stone

HOW TO LAY BRICK PAVING

1 *First, prepare the sub-base (see p.585), allowing space for the edging bricks. Use string lines and pegs to set the edging bricks at the desired height.*

2 *Mortar in the edging bricks, and bed the others in the required pattern, tamping them level. At intervals, check levels in all directions.*

3 *Spread a thin layer of dry mortar over the surface and brush it between the joints. Sprinkle with water to set the mortar, and clean the surface.*

or concrete slabs, as they can be laid in a variety of patterns.

Choosing bricks

The range of bricks available is sufficiently extensive for it to be possible to find a type that suits a patio or terrace designed and constructed in any style.

For a large volume of bricks, contact a brick company to see if they will deliver. Builders' merchants supply bricks in any quantities. Be sure to choose bricks that are appropriate for outdoor paving and resistant to wetting and freezing.

Choosing pavers

Clay pavers are as attractive as bricks and are usually produced in shades of red. They have a thinner profile

than concrete pavers or bricks. Concrete pavers may lack the warm colours of bricks but they will make a practical surface. They are generally found in grey, blue-grey, or buff shades and are produced in a range of shapes.

Laying bricks

First make a suitable sub-base (see p.585). Bricks should ideally be bedded on mortar. First lay edging strips (or edging bricks), bedded on a concrete footing and then fixed with mortar between the joints. Prepare the bedding mortar (see p.586) and lay it to a depth of 2.5cm (1in). Bed the bricks onto this, spacing them evenly to leave joints for mortar; use

thin strips of hardboard or wood as spacers between bricks if desired. Once an area is complete, brush a dry mortar over the bricks. To remove air pockets, press this into the gaps with a narrow piece of wood. In damp weather, moisture from the ground and air will set the pointing; in dry weather, speed up setting by spraying with water.

Patterns in brick

Bricks may be laid in several different ways to create attractive patterns; three examples are shown below.

Basket-weave

Interlocking boxes

Herringbone

Types of brick

Bricks are available in a wide range of styles, textures, and colours, providing an attractive and practical building material; take care to choose the most appropriate type so that they are suitable for the proposed purpose and that they coordinate well with the house, patio, or other hard landscape features.

Engineering bricks
Engineering bricks are very hard-wearing. If used for paving, make sure they have good wet-weather grip. They may cost more than ordinary bricks.

Cored bricks
Cored bricks have holes. They may be used on edge for paving with a narrower profile, but are not economical for large areas.

Facing or stock bricks
These are used to "face" buildings, providing an attractive finish. They are available in a variety of colours, and may be rough or smooth in texture. They may be unsuitable for paving as they may not be able to withstand severe weather conditions.

Bricks with "frogs"
A frog is an indentation in one side of a brick. Frogged bricks may be used for paving, if they are laid on edge or the frogs face downwards.

Cutting bricks and pavers

Bricks and thick pavers may be difficult to cut. If cutting is necessary, the easiest option is to use a hydraulic block splitter. These are often available from hire shops and are operated by applying pressure on a lever. Using this method, the bricks and pavers are cut quickly and neatly.

Alternatively, bricks and pavers may be cut to the desired shape with a bolster and club hammer (see "Cutting paving slabs", p.588).

Laying pavers

Pavers are bedded onto sand using a plate compactor; they nest together with small gaps between. Since the pavers can be lifted and relaid, this type of paving is sometimes called "flexible paving". Blocks 60–65mm (2½–2¼in) thick are adequate for garden projects.

Preparing the site and laying edge restraints

First, prepare a sub-base of 8cm (3in) compacted hardcore on firm soil (see p.585). Where there are no existing firm edges (such as walls), lay permanent edging strips. By far the simplest way to do this is to use specially made edge restraints or edging pieces, which are available from paving manufacturers. These must be concreted into position. Alternatively, use 100 x 35mm (4 x 1½in) treated or creosoted timber held in place with strong pegs at least 50mm (2in) square.

Large areas should be broken up into manageable sizes, such as 1m (3ft) squares, using temporary timber rails. Spread a layer of sharp

Pavers, tiles, setts, and cobbles

Pavers (also called paviors) vary greatly in size, colour, and thickness. They are also finished in many different ways, so that their texture and final shape, either formal and geometric or more informal and natural, contribute greatly to the style of the garden. More distinctive effects may be possible using terracotta tiles, granite setts, Belgian blocks, or rounded cobbles.

Clay pavers
These red pavers may be laid either as "stretchers", that is longitudinally, or as "headers", placed end on.

Wire-cut clay pavers
Wire-cut clay pavers have a dragged finish and a roughened surface on all sides, which serves to provide extra grip in the finished paving.

Interlocking pavers
These clay or concrete pavers can be used to create unusual patterns. Pressed pavers in blocks (far right) are produced in a range of colours.

Terracotta tiles
Like bricks, terracotta tiles are made of clay but allowed to dry in the sun. They are porous and may crack if used in areas prone to frost.

Granite setts
Cut from hard granite, this form of paving is extremely durable. Like cobbles, the roughened surface of the setts creates a natural effect.

"Belgian" blocks

Cobbles
Cobbles (below) are large, rounded stones formed by the action of the sea or glaciers. To protect the environment, buy glacially formed cobbles that have been quarried commercially rather than coastal ones that may have been taken from a beach. Cobbles may be embedded separately in the ground or be edged and set in bedding mortar to form an interestingly textured finish.

Imitation granite setts
These reconstituted stone pavers are lighter and cheaper than granite. "Belgian" blocks have a more weathered look.

HOW TO LAY FLEXIBLE PAVING

1 *After preparing the sub-base (see p.585), set edging strips of concrete or timber in position around the edges of the site. Use a spirit level and a club hammer to tap the edges level.*

2 *Divide large areas into bays 1m (3ft) square with battens. Add 5cm (2in) of sand. Level the sand to the tops of the battens with a length of wood. Remove the battens and fill the vacated spaces with sand.*

3 *Lay the pavers to the required pattern, working from one corner of the site. Lay only whole blocks at this stage, leaving until last any cut ones required to fill the gaps in the design.*

4 *Vibrate the pavers into the sand or tamp down with a club hammer and length of timber. Brush dry sand over the surface and make 2 or 3 passes with a plate compactor.*

sand evenly to a depth of about 5cm (2in). The top surface of the sand should be about 4.5cm (1¾in) below the desired level of the finished paving when using 60mm (2⅜in) pavers, or about 5cm (2in) below when using 65mm (2½in) blocks.

Positioning and bedding the pavers

Do not walk on the sand while laying the pavers, and keep it dry. Working from one corner of the site, lay the pavers. When some are laid, place a kneeling board over the pavers to continue working. Lay as many whole blocks as possible, then fill in with cut pavers around obstacles such as inspection covers as necessary (see p.586).

When about 5sq m (6sq yd) of paving has been laid, bed the pavers into the sand. The easiest way to do this is with a plate compactor, but do not go too near the incompleted edge. If only laying a small area of paving, the blocks may be tamped down with a heavy club hammer over a block of wood that is large enough to span several pavers at once. Continue to lay pavers and bed or tamp them down.

When the whole area is finished, brush dry sand into the joints and settle in position with the plate compactor. Use a mowing edge of bricks, pavers, or concrete slabs where it is difficult to mow right to the lawn edge. Bed the paving material on mortar, with the top just below the grass level, so that the mower is not damaged.

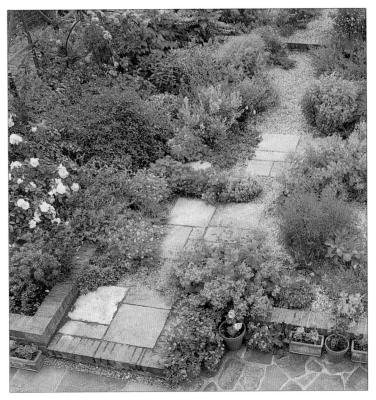

A combination of paving effects
A mixture of different paving materials, including square stone slabs, crazy paving, and brick edging, blends well with informal planting.

Setts and cobbles

Bed granite or imitation setts on 5cm (2in) of bedding mortar (see p.586) and brush stiff mortar into the joints (see "Finishing off", p.588). Spray the surface with water to clean it and set the mortar mix.

Cobbles may also be set in mortar. They are uncomfortable to walk on, so use them for small areas or with other materials. When laying, form firm edges with bricks or lengths of concrete edging. Lay 3.5cm (1½in) of bedding mortar over 8cm (3in) of compacted hardcore.

Terms explained

Aggregate is crushed stone or gravel used in making concrete. Graded 20mm (¾in) aggregate is suitable for most concreting jobs. Combined aggregate contains sand as well as stone.
Ballast is combined aggregate.
Bedding mortar is used for laying paving stones. It is made with sharp sand.
Cement is a grey powder containing limestone, the setting agent of concrete and mortar.
Concrete is a hard-setting building material made of a mixture of cement, aggregate, sand, and water.
Dry mortar is a stiff mix of sand and cement often used to fill the joints in paving.
Hardcore is rubble such as broken bricks used as a sub-base under concrete foundations.
Masonry cement has additives that make it unsuitable for concrete. Use only for mortars.
Mortar is a mixture of cement, sand, and water used principally for bricklaying.
Portland cement is not a brand name, but a type of cement. Use ordinary Portland cement for most concreting jobs. It can also be used for mortars.
Sand is graded by particle size. Sharp (concreting) sand is coarse; soft (builders') sand is more evenly graded for masonry mortar.

Decks

Timber decking is popular as a hard surface in warm, dry climates. Decks may be used anywhere, however, provided that timber pressure-treated with preservative is used.

It is best to build the deck on a level or gently sloping site. For a raised deck on a steep, sloping site and for decking that extends over water (see WATERSIDE DECKING, p.296), it is advisable to seek specialist assistance, since it would need to be well designed and constructed.

In some countries, building regulations state that all exterior areas of decking must be able to support a stipulated minimum weight. It may also be necessary to obtain a building permit and have the work inspected. If in doubt, check with your local authority building department. Simple parquet decking (see p.592) laid on gravel and sand should not require permission.

Timber decking
A wooden patio or verandah overlooking the garden makes a very imposing feature, especially when crowned with a pergola to provide summer shade. Timber decking, however, needs to be very well constructed, and it is usually best to have the job done by experts. Features such as rails, steps, and timber supports require regular maintenance (see p.592).

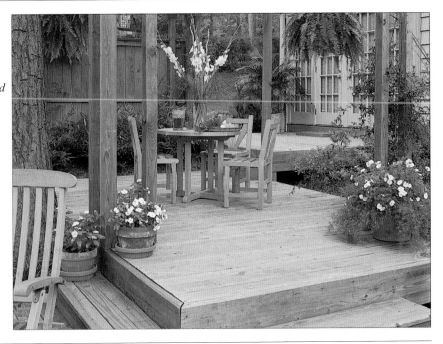

Timber for decking

Western red cedar is a good choice because of its natural rot resistance, although regularly treating it with a preservative ensures a longer life. Other timbers are suitable but must be pressure-treated with a preservative. Timber merchants will be able to advise on the most suitable timber and grade to use. Short lengths of timber can be made up into decking panels to produce a variety of attractive patterns.

Chequerboard   Herringbone   Parallel slats   Angled chequerboard   Parallel jointed

Slatted decking

This type of decking is suitable for level or gently sloping ground. It is simple to construct.

For an area beside a house, construct a concrete foundation (see *How to Lay Concrete*, p.586) with a gentle fall away from the house for water drainage. Onto the concrete base, mortar a row of bricks spaced about one brick apart at right angles to the intended direction of the decking. Add further rows of bricks at intervals of 40cm (16in). Check constantly that all the bricks are level, because they will support the joists.

Lay joists 75 x 50mm (3 x 2in) over the bricks, inserting a sheet of plastic or other damp-proof material between the bricks and the joists. If joining lengths of timber, make sure there is a brick beneath the point where the joists abut and screw a plain bracket across the join. Check levels between joists accurately with a spirit level and a straight edge. Lay 250 x 25mm (10 x 1in) planks at

Decking stepping stones

Decking can be used to create an unusual "stepping-stone" path across a pond. When positioned and angled for aesthetic effect, the squares add a stylish, geometric element to informal planting and the soft play of light on the pond surface. Here, parallel slats are laid in alternate directions to add a dynamic sense of movement to the overall design.

right angles to the joists. Allow 10mm (½ in) gaps for free drainage and a little movement in the timber. Ensure that joints in the decking are staggered from row to row and that the planks are butt-joined over a supporting joist. Secure the planks with brass or other rust-proof screws, countersunk beneath the surface. Fill the holes with wood filler that matches the colour of the wood.

Finish the deck neatly with a low brick or block edging, cutting the decking so that it overlaps the edging by 5cm (2in). Alternatively, a length of facing timber can be screwed or nailed along the cut edges.

Parquet decking

It is possible to buy small, parquet-type, timber squares intended primarily for paths, which can also be used for decking. Alternatively they can be easily made. About 1m (3ft) square is a practical size. Buy 100 x 50mm (4 x 2in) treated timber,

cut into 1m (3ft) lengths, and sand the ends smooth. Two lengths form the supports at opposite sides of the square, while the others are laid across them as slats. Use spacers to ensure that the slats fill the area evenly and fix the slats with two nails at either end. Prepare a base on firmed ground or subsoil with 8cm (3in) of compacted gravel topped with 8cm (3in) of sand. Level and tamp before laying the squares in alternate directions. Nail them together if necessary to stop them moving, driving the nails in at an angle.

Applying stains

Western red cedar turns a very obvious red colour when wet. It may, however, be stained any colour to suit the surroundings. It is best to use microporous stains, which allow any moisture in the wood to escape; if trapped beneath an impermeable layer, it would eventually cause the surface colour to lift. All wooden surfaces for staining should be dry and free from dirt. Follow instructions regarding stirring or thinning and apply the stain with a good-quality

paint brush, brushing in the direction of the grain. Do not overload the brush, since this will lead to uneven coverage, but work the stain well into the wood. Several applications will be needed, but wait until each coat is completely dry before applying more. See also "Wood preservatives", p.602.

Maintenance

All wooden surfaces need regular maintenance. Once a year, check all surface areas for splits or cracks. Damaged timbers will need to be replaced. Check, too, that no bolts, screws, brackets, or nails have rusted. If galvanized fittings are abraded, their protective coating may be damaged and rust will appear. Brass fittings, which do not rust, are pref-erable in timber decking. If the stain wears thin in areas of heavy foot traffic, clean the surface and re-apply the stain (see above). Fungus growths are likely to appear at some stage. Fungicides are available, but it is better to remove growths by brushing with a stiff broom or use a scrubbing brush and a mild solution of bleach.

SUPPORT FOR TIMBER DECKING

Planks butt-joined over a joist

Joists butt-joined over a supporting brick

Damp-proof membrane

When joining two lengths of timber to form a joist, make sure that the join lies over one of the supporting bricks. Lay the planks at right angles to the joists, positioning all butt-joints directly over a supporting joist.

Paths and steps

Paths and steps play a valuable part in good garden design. They help form the framework of the garden, link its various elements, and may lead the eye to a focal point. Consider setting a path at an angle, off-centre, or following an indirect route. Steps provide interesting changes of level and create very different effects, depending on whether they are straight or curved, wide or narrow, and shallow or steep.

Practical considerations

Paths to the garden shed or the greenhouse need to be wide enough to take a wheelbarrow and should also provide a dry and solid surface. Those to the front door or for strolling through the garden should be sufficiently wide for two to walk abreast: about 1–1.2m (3–4ft).

Materials and design

The choice of materials and the laying pattern may be used to set or enhance the garden style. Combining materials, for example paving stones with cobbles, bricks with gravel, or concrete paving slabs with bricks or clay pavers, often makes a very effective design for a path.

"Stepping-stone" paths may be laid in many parts of the garden. They are a good choice, for example, when you do not want to spoil the line of a lawn, but they can become muddy in wet weather. Place the paving stones on the surface first to check the spacing; they should be spaced at a natural pace. On lawns, set them into the grass so that their surface is safely below mowing level.

Where winters are relatively dry, paths may be made of timber, either in the form of log sections used as stepping stones or to make a series of square, slatted units as described in "Parquet decking", opposite.

On sloping sites, steps may be an essential part of a path. They may also be valuable as a design feature even on a relatively flat site. Steps should harmonize with their setting: for example, in a woodland garden, shallow log risers and gravel treads would be suitable, while in a modern setting, brick risers and concrete slab treads would be more appropriate.

Drives

A drive can have a considerable impact on a design, especially in a small garden. There may be little choice where to position a drive, unless a new garage is to be built at the same time; it is possible to make a drive look attractive, however, by choosing a suitable surface and positioning ornamental plants nearby.

Asphalt

Asphalt is best used for drives and paths that need not be attractive – the path to the shed, for example. It can also be used to cover a damaged concrete path. As well as black, asphalt is available in red and green. Stone chippings may be rolled into the surface to add texture. Asphalt is best laid in warm weather. Unless well laid, asphalt may break up after a few years; for heavily used areas such as a main drive it is worth having it laid by a qualified contractor.

Preparations

Asphalt can be laid on any firm surface, such as concrete or gravel. Never lay it on bare earth or hardcore

Brick pathways
A brick path can become a design feature in its own right, adding texture and colour to a garden entrance. Here, the soft pink of the brick harmonizes with the surrounding plants and leads the eye to the rose-covered arch and the informal grass area beyond.

since it will be difficult to obtain a firm and level surface that will last. If necessary, make a stable base by spreading a mixture of gravel and sand 5–8cm (2–3in) thick over firm ground or compacted hardcore. If an old path or drive is the base, first paint inside any holes or cracks with bitumen emulsion (tar paint) and leave for about 20 minutes before filling them with macadam. To ensure good water drainage, lay a drive on a slight slope.

The edges of an asphalt path often weaken and crumble, so use concrete edging blocks (from builders' yards), bricks, or lengths of creosoted timber to provide a firm edging.

Application

Apply a layer of bitumen emulsion to bind the surface. Stir it first, then pour it from the container and spread it with a stiff brush. (Wash the brush in hot, soapy water afterwards.) When the emulsion has turned black, apply the macadam and rake it to an even depth of about 2cm (¾in).

Firm the surface by tamping it with the back of a rake to remove large air pockets, then make several passes with a heavy garden roller. Keep the surface of the roller damp to prevent the macadam sticking to it. Top up any visible depressions, and roll the surface again. If using stone chippings, sprinkle evenly and roll again to bed them in.

Bricks and pavers

The sympathetic colouring of bricks and clay pavers makes them excellent materials for paths within the garden. Because the individual units are small, it is relatively easy to adjust to changes of level and even to lay a path to a curve. A variety of effects can be created depending on the laying pattern used (see "Patterns in brick", p.589).

Construction

Mark out the proposed line of the path with pegs and string, calculating where cut bricks or pavers may be needed to create a sharp curve. If the path will be subjected to heavy wear, prepare a concrete foundation (see "Load-bearing surfaces", p.586). For one that will receive lighter use, an 8cm (3in) sub-base of firmed hardcore levelled with ballast should be sufficient.

First lay a suitable edging (see p.594) along one side of the path, then lay the path itself in sections about 1m (3ft) long. Pavers should be bedded in a 5cm (2in) layer of dry sand (see "Laying pavers", p.590), while bricks will require a 2.5cm (1in) bed of mortar (see "Laying bricks", p.589). As you complete each section, tamp the bricks or pavers into place, checking that they are level with a straight edge and spirit level. Then lay the edging on the other side of the path to complete this section. Repeat the process until the path has been laid.

To finish off a path made of pavers, brush dry sand into the joints. For a brick path, brush a dry mortar mix in between the joints (see "Finishing off", p.588), making sure that there are no large air pockets. If necessary, compact the mortar using a piece of wood slightly thinner than the joints. Finally, sprinkle with water from a watering can fitted with a fine rose, or use a compression sprayer to moisten the mortar and clean the bricks if necessary.

Subtlety with stone
Here, the mottled texture of the embedded stones is complemented by Alchemilla mollis *and defined by seams of moss.*

Log sections
Logs sawn into sections make a harmonious series of stepping stones through an area of woodland, blending perfectly with the setting.

Concrete

Concrete cast *in situ* is an economical and hard-wearing surface material that is especially suitable for wide paths and drives. Its appearance can be made more attractive by adding texture (see below). Concrete can also be coloured using special dyes added to the mix. Since the colour often looks different once the concrete has dried, use dyes with caution. Colour a small, test piece first and let it dry rather than judge the effect by the wet mix.

Break up a wide concrete path with rows of bricks or lengths of broad timber that will become part of the finished design. These will avoid the need for laying expansion joints during construction.

Preparing a base

Prepare a suitable foundation (see "Basic procedure", p.585). Next, make the formwork to hold the concrete in place until it sets. Use lengths of timber 2.5cm (1in) thick, and at least the depth of the concrete. Use 5 x 5cm (2 x 2in) pegs, not more than 1m (3ft) apart to hold the formwork in place. Lengths of timber may be satisfactorily joined by nailing a block of wood to the outside of the two pieces to bridge them together.

Making curves

To make gentle curves, mark out the shape that you want to create, and hammer pegs into the ground set closely together. Soak lengths of softwood in water to make them pliable and then bend and nail them to the pegs. Sharp curves can be made in a similar way, with the addition of a series of saw cuts on the inside of the curve. The saw cuts should reach about half-way through the timber to increase its flexibility. Alternatively, use several thicknesses of thin hardboard, which is easy to bend and shape.

Expansion joints

Concrete will crack if not laid with breaks to allow for expansion and a degree of movement. Divide the area into sections no more than 4m (12ft) long, using fixed pieces of timber as temporary divisions. If using ready-mixed concrete, where the load has to be used all at once, use hardboard cut into sections and leave these in position until the concrete has set.

Laying concrete

Make up the concrete (see p.586) and pour it into the formwork. If mixing in small batches, fill alternate "bays", then remove the dividers once the concrete has set and pour concrete into the remaining bays. Use a length of wood to tamp the concrete level, working from the centre towards the joints. If the path or drive is wide, a tamping board used with a helper will make the job easier. Tamping leaves a slightly ridged surface. If you require a smooth finish, use a wood float in gentle, sweeping motions. A steel float will produce an even smoother surface.

Concrete paving slabs

Paving slabs are available in a wide range of colours, shapes, and finishes. They are easier to lay than *in situ* concrete, but are more difficult to lay to a curve than bricks or pavers. They combine well with other materials, for instance with cobbles set along the edge, or with small strips of gravel between each slab. This is a useful technique for creating curved paths since it makes the uneven joints less obtrusive. For details on laying paving slabs, see p.587.

Grass

Grass paths are useful for linking a series of lawns, or for broad walks between beds. They should be as wide as possible or they will not stand up to concentrated wear. Put down turf for a grass path in the same way as for a lawn – for full instructions, see THE LAWN, "Laying turf", p.393.

HOW TO LAY A GRAVEL PATH

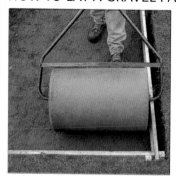

1 *Dig out the base of the path to a depth of 18cm (7in) and set the edges. Compact the base. Drive in pegs at 1m (3ft) intervals to anchor the edge restraints.*

2 *If the path borders a lawn, excavate an extra 2.5cm (1in) so that the path is below turf level (inset). Put down successive layers of hardcore, sand and coarse gravel, and pea gravel. Rake level.*

Gravel

Gravel is easy to lay, presents no problems when creating curves, and is not expensive. However, unless well bedded and used with retaining edges, loose gravel can get onto adjoining surfaces, it can be uncomfortable and noisy to walk on, and it is not an easy surface on which to push a wheelbarrow or a pushchair. See also ROCK, SCREE, AND GRAVEL GARDENING, "Gravel beds and paving", p.256.

Construct a firm base by excavating the ground to take about 10cm (4in) of compacted hardcore, 5cm (2in) of a sand and coarse gravel mix, and 2.5cm (1in) of gravel. For a fine finish choose pea gravel. Gravel can also be laid over geotextile fabric (see p.256).

Apply the gravel in several stages, raking and rolling it to produce a slight camber for drainage and watering it to help compaction.

In a formal setting with mainly straight edges, concrete edging strips can be used; in other settings bricks or treated timber may be more appropriate. If using timber, anchor it with pegs about 1m (3ft) apart.

Edging paths

Plastic edge restraints, easily cut to size, are available to hold a path of bricks or pavers in place invisibly. Lengths of treated timber may also be used, held in place with wooden pegs. It is also possible to use timbers temporarily while building the path, then remove them and fill in the gaps with concrete. For a brick edging, lay the bricks on edge or angled at 45°, and secure with a little mortar.

Adding texture

An *in situ* concrete path can be made more attractive by adding texture. Use these techniques on a few sections only, or alternate patterns between sections, to create an interesting overall effect.

Exposed aggregate gives a pleasant, non-slip finish. Spread gravel or crushed stone evenly over the concrete before it sets, then tamp it gently into the surface. When the concrete is nearly hard, brush the surface to expose more of the aggregate, then spray it with water to wash away fine particles.

Brushed finishes are extremely easy to create. After tamping the concrete gently, push the bristles of a soft broom all over the surface to produce a fairly smooth finish; for a ridged effect, use a stiff broom once the concrete has begun to set. You can also brush in a series of swirls, or straight or wavy lines, as desired.

Stamped patterns can be made with special tools, but ordinary objects found in the home or garden may also be used imaginatively, for example pastry cutters and sea shells. This technique is best kept to very small areas. To create attractive leaf impressions, use large leaves, such as sycamore or horse chestnut. Press the leaves into the surface with a trowel and then brush them out once the concrete has hardened.

Coarse texture

Medium-coarse texture

Fine texture

Building steps

To calculate the number of steps you need to build, divide the height of the slope by the height of one riser (including the depth of the paving slab and mortar). It may be necessary to adjust the height of the steps to fit the slope. Mark the position of the risers with wooden pegs and then excavate the soil to form a series of earth steps.

Make a concrete footing (see p.596) for the base riser and leave it to set. Then construct the riser using bricks or blocks set in masonry mortar (see p.586). Check that they are level using a straight edge and spirit level, and backfill behind the riser with compacted hardcore or sand and gravel.

Prepare a bed of mortar on top of the riser and lay the first tread; it should slope forward slightly to shed water, and overlap the riser at the front by 2.5–5cm (1–2in). Mark the position of the next riser on the tread and mortar it into position.

Tread to riser ratio

For ease of use, it is important that the width of the tread and the height of the riser are in the correct proportion to each other. As a general rule, the width of the tread and double the height of the riser should total about 65cm (26in). First, choose the height of the riser, double it and deduct it from 65cm (26in) to give the width of the tread. You may wish to add 2.5–5cm (1–2in) for an overhang.

For the steps to be safe, the treads should measure at least 30cm (12in) from front to back. The height of the risers is normally between 10cm (4in) and 18cm (7in).

Paving stone treads
Brick risers
Gravel infill

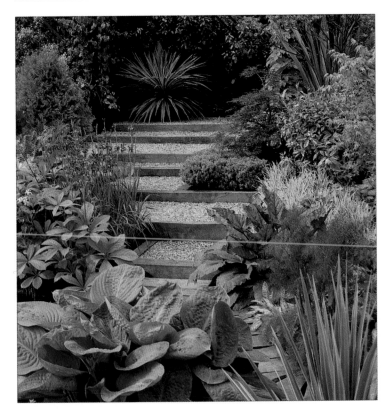

Timber and gravel steps
Here railway sleepers are infilled with gravel to create a curving flight of gently rising steps, with flanking plants softening the edges.

HOW TO BUILD STEPS INTO A BANK

1 *Measure the height of the bank to work out how many steps are needed (see left). To do this, drive a peg into the top of the slope and a post at the bottom. Tie string horizontally between the two, then measure the distance between ground level and the string.*

2 *Use string and pegs to mark the sides, then run strings to mark the fronts of the treads. Dig out the steps and compact the earth at each tread position.*

3 *Construct a footing for the riser, 15cm (6in) deep and twice the width of the bricks. Fill with concrete over a 7cm (3in) hardcore base.*

4 *When the concrete has set, lay the first riser on the footing. Use a string line stretched between the pegs to ensure the bricks are straight and level.*

5 *Backfill with hardcore to the height of the bricks and tamp down. Set the paving slabs on 1cm (½in) of mortar, with a small gap between them.*

6 *The slabs should have an overhang of 2.5–5cm (1–2in) at the front and a slight, forward slope for drainage. Mark the position of the second riser on the slabs and mortar the bricks in place. Fill in and set the treads as before. Continue for the remaining steps. Lastly, mortar the joints between the slabs.*

Walls

Boundary walls have been a feature of gardens since the early days of enclosures. In the nineteenth century, walled gardens were a common feature on large estates, providing security, privacy, and ornament. Nowadays, however, large boundary walls are uncommon, having given way to cheaper fences or hedges.

Garden walls are often decorative as well as practical. Low walls are very suitable for dividing off parts of the garden. Because they require less substantial foundations and few or no supporting piers, low walls are also easy and cheap to construct (see opposite). If they have a planting cavity, low walls can look particularly attractive in the garden.

Materials

Boundary walls may be constructed from various materials including brick, and, for low walls, concrete walling blocks that are purpose-made for outdoor use. When buying bricks, always check with the supplier that they are suitable for garden walls: they should be frost-proof and able to withstand moisture penetration from both sides.

Walls may also be constructed from a combination of materials, for example brick with facing panels of local stone such as flint. Large, plain walls may be painted with a masonry paint (in pale or bright colours) on the garden side. This reflects the light and contrasts well with wall shrubs or other plants.

How high to build?

There may be restrictions placed on the height of walls in the deeds of the property, or in local authority or highway regulations. Check this before building. A low, decorative wall is a straightforward DIY job, but brick and concrete block walls higher than about 1m (3ft) require advice from a builder or structural engineer. Any wall higher than 1m (3ft) should have a strengthening pier every 2.5m (8ft).

Combined materials
Brick and flint are juxtaposed here to create a striking garden divider. The mixture of straight and curved lines reinforces the blend of styles. When combined in this way, diverse materials can effectively enhance each other.

Concrete footings for walls

The width of the footing for all walls should be two to three times the width of the wall. For walls lower than 1m (3ft), deep and substantial foundations are not necessary.

For a half-brick wall (i.e. the width of a single brick), dig a trench the length of the wall and 38cm (15in) deep. Place 13cm (5in) of hardcore in the bottom and tamp it down. Then pour in 10cm (4in) of concrete. Allow this to harden completely for a few days before laying the bricks or concrete blocks.

Walling materials

Bricks are the most popular choice of walling material, although concrete blocks manufactured to imitate natural clay bricks may also be used. If you want to build a wall to match the brickwork of existing buildings, used bricks are available in many colours and styles.

Smooth-textured bricks
These are most suitable for facing the front of a wall. They come in a range of colours.

Mottled engineering bricks
These contribute a rough-hewn appearance; they are also the hardest of all the bricks.

Pre-cast concrete blocks
These contain medium-textured aggregate.

Rock-faced concrete blocks
The brick-red colour imitates the look of clay bricks. They are also available coloured to look like sandstone.

Smooth blocks
Concrete blocks are suitable for a modern design.

HOW TO MAKE A CONCRETE FOOTING

1 *Mark out the site of the foundations with string lines stretched between wooden pegs.*

2 *Dig a trench of the required depth. Check that the base is level and the sides vertical. Drive in pegs to the level for the concrete. Align with a spirit level and a length of wood spanning the pegs.*

3 *Soak the trench with water and allow it to drain. Then add 13cm (5in) of hardcore and tamp it down. Pour in concrete, slicing into the mix with a spade to work it in and dispel air bubbles.*

4 *Compact the concrete by tamping it down firmly with a length of timber. Level it to the tops of the pegs. Leave the surface rough as a key for the mortar for the first course of bricks.*

HOW TO BUILD A SIMPLE LOW WALL

1 *Once the concrete footing has dried fully – at least 2 days – set out the position of the wall with 2 string guides, 2 bricks' width plus 10mm (½in) apart. Dry-position the lowest course, 10mm (½in) between bricks.*

2 *Chalk the brick positions on the footing. Throw a mortar bed 10mm (½in) thick along all the first course. As you set each brick on it, check that it is level both from end to end and front to back.*

3 *Before laying, butter an end face of each brick with 10mm (½in) of mortar. Fill the central gap.*

4 *Throw a mortar bed on top of the first course of length-ways bricks (the stretcher) and lay the next course (the header) at right angles to the first. Check constantly and adjust all levels.*

5 *Raise up both ends of the wall by 4 courses, alternating stretchers and headers. Scrape off excess mortar as you bed each brick. Neaten joints with a pointing tool. Then complete each course.*

6 *On the fourth row, insert a half brick after the first header, to maintain staggered joints and avoid having a weak joint running down the wall. As you build, regularly check the levels, as before.*

7 *Complete the wall with a header course, laying the bricks on edge. To help deflect rainwater, point the mortar joints by running a pointing tool against the vertical, then horizontal joints.*

For a full-brick wall, which is two bricks wide, or for a double wall with a space for planting cavities, dig the trench 5cm (2in) deeper and add 5cm (2in) extra concrete. For a brick or concrete block wall, the top of the footing need only be 15cm (6in) below ground level.

For screen block walling, the top of the footing may be just below ground level, provided reinforcing rods are used. On heavy clay or in cold areas, increase the depth of the footing so that it is below the frost line. For higher walls, specialist advice should be sought.

leave "weep" holes (un-mortared gaps between bricks) for drainage in the first course that is completely above ground level.

Before the mortar dries, use a pointing trowel to give the joints a neat, bevelled finish. Vertical joints should all be bevelled in the same direction, horizontal ones should slope slightly downwards to aid water run-off.

Combination bricks

"Combination blocks" that give the appearance of being several individual bricks may look crude close up, but once in a garden setting, and especially when weathered, they are far less noticeable, and make simple garden wall construction very much quicker and easier. Some are regularly shaped while others interlock, like a jigsaw, for greater stability.

Combination coping block

Bricklaying

To ensure that the first course is straight, stretch two parallel strings along the footing, the space between them equal to the width of the wall plus 10mm (½in). Lay a 10mm (½in) bed of masonry mortar (p.586) along the footing. The first brick of a course is laid un-mortared, then the second is "buttered" on one end and laid up against it. As you lay, check frequently with a spirit level that the bricks are level and horizontal. If too high, tap them down gently with the trowel handle. Insert more mortar under any that are too low. Check also that the mortar joints are all 10mm (½in) thick.

Repeat the process for each subsequent course and reset the builder's line for a position guide. For walls with planting cavities,

Brick bonding

There are many brick bonding patterns. If you are a beginner at bricklaying, keep to one that is easy to lay and does not require many cut bricks. The simplest of all is a running, or stretcher, bond, in which all the bricks are laid lengthways.

Screen block walling

In parts of the garden where a brick wall would form too solid a barrier, a screen wall of purpose-made, pierced concrete blocks may be more appropriate. Such walls are supported by hollow pilaster blocks, normally reinforced with iron rods set in the footing and filled with mortar or concrete, yet they are not strong.

Popular bonds

Running bond is used for walls one brick thick; Flemish and English bonds combine stretchers and headers (bricks laid respectively lengthwise and widthwise) in a full-brick wall.

Running bond

Flemish bond

English bond

TYPES OF COPING

A decorative finish
Upright stones have been set in mortar as a coping for a dry limestone wall.

A full-brick wall
This Flemish-bonded wall is topped by a course of "headers" – bricks laid across the full width of the wall.

Stone coping
Large, stone slabs form a solid coping that complements a wall of flints mortared in courses.

Softening the wall
The hard line of the wall's edge is softened by a colourful display of trailing flowering plants to create a curtain effect. The crevices between the dry stones provide ideal spaces for shallow-rooting rock garden plants.

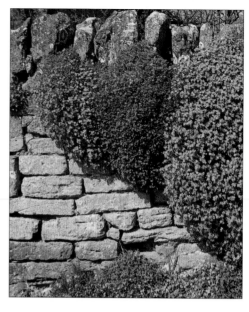

Coping

Coping, which forms the top course of a wall, prevents frost damage by shedding rainwater so that it does not seep into the joints. It also gives the wall a "finished" appearance.

Specially made, curved coping bricks are available, but these are often only the width of the wall and are strictly cappings, as they do not throw the drips clear of the wall. Wider concrete slabs are used for copings on brick as well as concrete block walls. If an ordinary brick finish is required, lay a double course of flat roof tiles before the final row. Coping is especially important for pierced screen block walls, because it helps to bond the blocks.

Dry-stone walls

Dry-stone walls may be laid on a concrete footing (see p.596) or a foundation of rubble. They may be planted with alpines (see p.268), and look particularly attractive if a cavity is left in the top for trailing plants.

Dig a trench and make a firm base of compacted hardcore or rubble. The base of the wall should be one or two courses below ground level. Use a taut line to maintain a level construction, and build up the wall with broad tie-stones and smaller random stones to bond the wall together. The wall should be wider at the bottom than at the top. To achieve a consistent slope or "batter", make a batter board, a wooden frame in the shape of the desired cross-section of the wall. An inward slope of about 2.5cm for every 60cm (1in for every 24in) is usually sufficient. Use a spirit level to keep the batter board perpendicular. Finish off with

large, flat stones or a row of vertical stones laid on edge (and mortared if desired) as a decorative coping.

Retaining walls

Retaining walls may be used to terrace a garden or contain the soil in a raised bed (see facing page). Dry stones, concrete walling blocks, or bricks may be used. Seek professional advice for any retaining wall more than 75cm (30in) high or one on a steep slope, because it may be necessary to reinforce it to withstand the pressure of soil and water. Rather than building one large retaining wall, terracing the garden in a series of shallow steps may be easier. In some countries, permission is required to build a high retaining wall, and regulations may demand that contractors be hired to construct it from poured concrete.

Insert a drain (see "Installing drains", p.623) running horizontally along the back of the wall, and backfill the lower half of the wall with gravel or rubble. If using bricks or concrete blocks, build the wall on a concrete footing (see p.596) set below the lower soil level, and leave "weep" holes for drainage between every second or third brick in the lower courses of the wall.

Dry-stone walling is a good choice for a low retaining wall, since alpines can be grown in the exposed face. Place large stones on a firm foundation of concrete or compacted hardcore, and lay subsequent courses of stone with an inward slope (a batter) of 2.5–5cm for every 30cm (1–2in for every 12in) of height. The wall should be perpendicular on the retaining side (see *How to Build a Dry-stone Retaining Wall*, p.268). If it is not to be planted with crevice plants, the wall may be mortared to make it stronger (see "Bricklaying", p.597); otherwise pack garden soil between the stones for additional stability.

Constructing retaining walls

Coping

Gravel infill

Weep hole

Mowing edge

Construction
On the left is a section of a brick wall with a vertical, unmortared joint acting as a weep hole. On the right is a wall built of hollow concrete blocks (see below). Hollows may be filled with wet concrete, or with soil for plants.

Recessed mowing edge

Concrete block filled with soil

Any retaining wall used to hold back soil on a slope must be extremely strong. Bear in mind that the higher the wall, the stronger it will need to be. Remember, too, that wet earth is heavier than dry earth, and water must be allowed to drain out through weep holes left at the base of the wall. If the units of construction are large, the retaining wall will be even stronger than if small bricks or blocks are used.

Reinforcing rods
The strength of a wall built with hollow concrete blocks will be greatly increased if hooked rods are set in the concrete foundation. Further reinforcing rods may be added passing up through the blocks.

Mortar

Reinforcing rods

Base of vertical rod set in concrete

Hooked rods reinforcing concrete foundation

Raised beds

Raised beds may provide a strong design element in a garden, perhaps surrounding a sunken garden or providing changes of level. Small groups of raised beds, or a series of linked beds, are ideal for an area that is mainly paved, while a single, distinctive raised bed makes a good home for an attractive specimen plant.

Where the soil in a garden is poor, or unsuitable for growing certain plants, raised beds can be extremely useful: they enable acid conditions to be created in a garden with alkaline soil, for instance. Moreover, plants in raised beds have more room to develop and require less attention than those in tubs and other containers, in which the soil dries out quickly.

Raised beds have the great advantage that they can be reached without stooping. Recessed or "knee-hole" beds, also known as tabletop beds, make access particularly convenient for wheelchair users. A well-planned series of raised beds makes gardening a practicable possibility for elderly, disabled, or infirm gardeners. The bed height will need to be tailored to the requirements of the individual gardener and narrow enough for the whole bed to be within easy reach. The beds should be linked by easily negotiated, wide garden paths (see pp.593–594).

Materials

Raised beds may be built from a wide range of materials: mortared bricks (see "Types of brick", p.589), concrete walling blocks (see "Walling materials", p.596), unmortared natural stone (see "Dry-stone walls", p.598), railway sleepers, or sawn logs. If using bricks or concrete blocks, you may wish to finish off the bed with a coping (see p.598) wide enough to sit on.

Brick beds

A large, rectangular, brick bed is easy to construct, but may appear rather unimaginative. A number of smaller, linked beds at different heights will create a more visually stimulating feature, as will a circular raised bed. Always choose frost-proof bricks. A half-brick wall is usually strong enough.

Rectangular beds

Prepare a footing (see *How to Make a Concrete Footing*, p.596) at a depth that allows the first course of bricks to lie below ground level. When the footing has set, use a masonry mortar mix (see p.586) to lay the courses of bricks (see "Bricklaying", p.597). Lay whole bricks at right angles to form the corners.

Circular beds

For a circular bed, the bricks should ideally be cut to give a smooth curve but it is possible to use full bricks. First lay the bricks loosely with a circumference large enough to ensure that there are no wide gaps at the edge. Prepare the footing, and, when this has set, lay the bricks so that they almost touch on the inside edge of the wall. Use wedges of mortar to fill the gaps on the outer face. Stagger the courses as with a conventional bond and use half bricks for the final course to give a better curve.

Ericaceous plants

If plants that require acid soil are to be grown in a raised bed, line the inside of the walls, when completed, with a butyl rubber liner or several coats of a waterproof, bitumen-based paint. This stops lime in the mortar from leaching into the bed.

Concrete block beds

Concrete walling blocks are a good choice for raised beds if matching materials have been used for other garden structures and surfaces. The blocks may be too large for circular beds, but are ideal for rectangular ones. The beds are constructed in a similar way to brick beds.

Natural stone

Raised beds may be built using natural stone laid dry. Use the technique for dry-stone retaining walls (see "Dry-stone walls" and "Retaining walls", p.598), but keep the beds low and small.

For a bed higher than about 60cm (24in), it is best to mortar the stones securely in place. Even with a low bed, it may be necessary to mortar the corners for stability.

Sleepers

Railway sleepers, which blend unobtrusively with most plants and garden surfaces, are ideal for large, low, raised beds, but they are heavy and difficult to handle: do not make the walls more than three sleepers high. Use a chainsaw to cut the sleepers to length, but build the walls

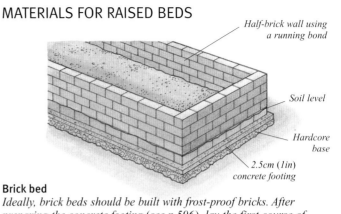

Brick bed
Ideally, brick beds should be built with frost-proof bricks. After preparing the concrete footing (see p.596), lay the first course of bricks below soil level. Stagger the courses to strengthen the walls.

Half-brick wall using a running bond

Soil level

Hardcore base

2.5cm (1in) concrete footing

Sleepers laid like bricks in a running bond

Rammed gravel base

Sleepers
Railway sleepers are particularly good for low raised beds, but beds must be lined if the sleepers have been treated with toxic preservative. No footing is needed because the sleepers are themselves very stable.

MATERIALS FOR RAISED BEDS

in multiples of full or half sleeper lengths. This will reduce the amount of sawing involved.

It is not necessary to provide a footing, since the length and weight of the sleepers make them extremely stable. Create a level surface to lay them on, using rammed gravel, then bond the sleepers like bricks, and, if more than two courses high, use metal rods driven into the ground to secure them in place: either drill holes for the rods in the sleepers, or position the rods on the outside of the raised bed as a brace.

Sleepers may already be impregnated with bitumen or a wood preservative that is toxic to plants, in which case the bed sides must be lined with a geotextile fabric, PVC, or butyl.

Sawn logs

Logs make attractive edgings for woodland-style beds, and for very low, informal beds in a natural setting. For higher raised beds, logs of a uniform size and thickness should be used. These may not be readily available, however, and the corner joints are difficult to construct. If this type of raised bed is to be built, it may be better to buy it in easily assembled kit form.

Raised beds and watering needs

The growing medium in a raised bed drains more rapidly than the soil in ordinary garden borders, so it is important to water plants more often. In particular, soil in contact with the retaining walls tends to dry out and shrink. In extreme conditions, this could expose the fibrous feeding roots of plants growing around the edges of the bed, making them vulnerable to frost, heat, or drought. Depending on the plants grown, it may also be necessary to add more humus to the soil to help retain moisture (see p.621).

Fences

Fences are commonly used as property boundary markers, but they may also act as windbreaks or as a decorative feature within the garden. They may be erected more quickly and cheaply than brick- or block-built walls, and they have the additional advantage of providing almost instant privacy. In general they do, however, require more maintenance than a wall. To make a fence into a decorative element, it may be clothed with climbers or have trellis panelling fixed to the top or sides.

The first step before erecting any fence is to mark out the line of fencing with a string line. If it is to be on a boundary between two properties, all the fencing and fence posts must be on your side of the boundary. For other legal requirements regarding fences, see "Laws on fences", p.602.

Panel fences

One of the simplest forms of fencing is a panel fence. It may be constructed using wooden or concrete posts. With concrete posts, the panels are simply slotted into grooves on either side of the post. For details, see *How to Erect a Panel Fence*, facing page. Another advantage of concrete is that it does not rot.

If you prefer timber posts, the panels have to be screwed or nailed into position. Protect the bases of timber fence posts by using either metal post supports or concrete spurs (see facing page). The latter are short posts that are embedded in a firm concrete foundation. They are bought ready made with two holes through which the timber posts are bolted to the spur just above ground level.

To build a fence with timber posts, dig a hole for the first post, then stretch a string line along the run of the fence to ensure that it is straight. For a panel 2m (6ft) high, you will need 2.75m (9ft) lengths of timber for the posts and the post holes should be 75cm (30in) deep. Fill the bottom with a 15cm (6in) base of hardcore, then stand the post in the hole and pack it round with more hardcore to

Fence types

Basket-weave fencing is usually sold as prefabricated panels, generally in a range of heights. Thin, interwoven slats of pine or larch are fixed in a light, softwood frame. It provides good privacy, but is not very strong.

Closeboard fencing consists of overlapping, vertical, feather-edged boards, usually of softwood, nailed to a pair of horizontal arris rails. The thick edges of the boards are nailed over the thin edges. It may be constructed *in situ*, but is also available (as shown here) in the form of panels. Closeboard is one of the strongest forms of fencing, offering good security and privacy.

Waney-edged fencing, made of overlapping, horizontal planks, is one of the most commonly used forms of panel fencing (see also p.605). It provides adequate levels of security.

Shingle fences consist of overlapping cedar shingles (wooden "tiles"), nailed to a timber framework to produce a strong, solid fence. They offer good security and privacy, depending on their height.

Wattle hurdles are panels of interwoven woody stems and give a rustic effect. Two examples are shown here. They may be made *in situ* or bought as ready-made panels. They are held in place by stout stakes and are particularly useful when a new hedge is becoming established in a garden, offering interim privacy as well as good protection against both small and large animals. Within a relatively short period of time, however, they can begin to look ragged and unattractive, and they are also troublesome to maintain and repair.

Lattice fences are made either from sawn timber or rustic wood. They resemble large partitions of diamond-shaped trellis. They can be used as an informal boundary marker, but offer very little privacy.

Picket fences have vertical wooden "pales" spaced about 5cm (2in) apart, fixed to horizontal rails, and are more decorative than functional. Plastic picket fences are available that require far less maintenance than traditional wooden ones. Neither kind offers much security or privacy.

Ranch-style fencing uses thin, planed planks attached horizontally to stout posts. The timber is either painted or simply treated with preservative. There are plastic versions of this style of fencing available, which need less maintenance, but neither is secure.

Cleft chestnut paling consists of split vertical stakes about 8cm (3in) apart, linked by strands of galvanized wire. It is suitable only as a temporary fence.

Post-and-rail fences have two or more horizontal poles or rough sawn timber rails fixed between adjacent posts. They form an inexpensive boundary marker.

Interference fencing has horizontal boards fixed on both sides of the posts, the planks on one side facing the gaps on the other. It makes a better windbreak than a solid fence, and it provides acceptable if not total privacy.

Chain link consists of a wire mesh, which is usually attached to concrete, timber, or iron posts. Galvanized wire mesh lasts for 10 years, plastic-coated wire mesh longer. It is a good choice where an animal-proof boundary is required.

Welded wire consists of an open, wire mesh stapled to wooden posts and rails. It is used primarily as a barrier to fence off larger animals where appearance is unimportant.

Post-and-chain fences may have chains made of metal or plastic which are attached to wooden, concrete, or plastic posts. They are used to mark boundaries where more substantial fences are not allowed.

Concrete fences are made of concrete panels, usually pierced, slotted into concrete posts. They offer the security and permanence of a masonry wall and require much less maintenance than a timber fence.

hold it in position. Check that it is upright with a spirit level. Using the panel as a width guide, dig a hole for the second post, making sure that it is aligned with the string line. Level the ground between the post and the hole and lay a gravel board – a length of wood (or concrete) fixed between fence posts at ground level to prevent panels from coming into contact with the soil and rotting. A wooden gravel board should be secured to the first post with galvanized nails. Attach a fence panel to the post using 75mm (3in) galvanized nails driven through pre-drilled holes, or screw them together with metal fixing brackets. Place the second post into its hole, ensuring that it is vertical and fits closely against the fence panel; fix the gravel board and panel as before. Repeat with the remaining posts, gravel boards, and panels.

Lodge the posts firmly in position with wedges of scrap timber and hardcore, checking that they are vertical with a spirit level. Pack a stiff concrete mix (see p.586) around the base of each post, and use a trowel to create a slope away from each side as a run-off for water.

Saw the tops of the posts to an equal height above the panels if necessary. Treat any sawn surfaces with wood preservative and finish each post with an overhanging wooden cap that deflects rainwater.

Metal post supports

Instead of digging holes for fence posts, metal post supports may be sunk into the ground instead, and wooden posts inserted into them. This reduces the length of the timbers needed for fence posts and keeps them out of contact with the soil, thus prolonging the life of the wood. Use 60cm (24in) supports for fences that are up to 1.2m (4ft) high and 75cm (30in) supports for fences up to 2m (6ft).

Before driving the support into the ground, fit an offcut of wood from a post into the socket. This protects the support from damage. Most manufacturers also provide a special attachment that fits over the offcut of wood while the support is hammered into place.

Check continually that the spike is entering the ground vertically. Hold a spirit level against each of the four sides of the socket in turn. To secure the post, tighten the clamping bolts in the socket, or if these are not provided, fix it with screws or nails through the slatted holes. For added strength, metal post supports may also be set in a foundation of hardcore and concrete.

HOW TO ERECT A PANEL FENCE

1 Dig a hole 75cm (30in) deep and pack a 15cm (6in) layer of hardcore in the base. Insert the first concrete post and check the height of the post against the fence panel.

2 Pack hardcore around the post and pour in concrete. Tamp it down. Add more concrete and tamp again. Keep checking that the post is vertical.

3 Lay a fence panel on the ground to position the next hole accurately. Use a string line as a guide, then dig the next hole.

4 Fit a gravel board between the post holes. Level the ground until the board lies horizontally. Check with a spirit level.

CONCRETE SPURS

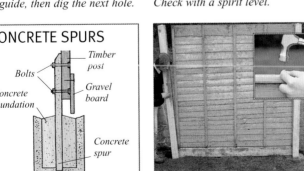

Timber post

Bolts

Concrete foundation

Gravel board

Concrete spur

To avoid damage through contact with damp soil, bolt timber fence posts to a concrete spur set in a concrete foundation.

5 Slot the panel into the groove in the first post. Insert the next post and pack into position with hardcore. Secure moulded wooden coping to the top of the panel.

ERECTING A FENCE USING METAL POST SUPPORTS

1 Place an offcut of wood and the fixing accessory in the socket of the post support. Use a sledgehammer to drive the support directly into the ground.

2 Keep checking that the support is being driven in vertically. Hold the spirit level against all four sides in turn.

3 Insert the fence post into the socket at the top of the support and secure it by nailing through the slatted holes. Some sockets are fitted with clamping bolts.

4 Using a string guide, hammer in further post supports. Nail fencing (here a panel of picket fence supported on bricks to keep the rails horizontal) to the posts.

USING ARRIS RAILS

The ends of the rails are chiselled to fit into mortise slots cut in the support posts. Vertical, feather-edged boards are nailed to the back of the rails.

Closeboard fencing

The overlapping vertical boards of a traditional closeboard fence are nailed to two horizontal rails, triangular in section, which are known as arris rails. Fence posts are available with mortise slots cut into the sides to hold the rails, but it is possible to chisel out the slots yourself. The usual heights for the rails are 30cm (12in) below the top of the fence and 30cm (12in) above the ground. Shape the ends of the arris rails so that they fit into the mortise slots and treat the cut ends with preservative.

Set up the fence posts as for panel fences (see p.600). Insert the arris rails into the mortise slots as you go. Wedge the first post firmly in place with hardcore, then prop the next post loosely in position. Insert the first pair of arris rails in the slots, pulling the second post into position. Attach the arris rails so that the flat backs face the correct side for the panels. Check with a spirit level that the second post is vertical and that the rails are horizontal. You may need to raise or lower the post a little. When satisfied, ram hardcore around the base to secure it.

Assemble the remaining posts and rails in the same way and nail them together for added strength. Cement round the bases of the posts to make permanent foundations. As a base support, lay gravel boards along the bottom of the fence (see "Panel fences", p.600). Nail small blocks of wood to the bottom of the fence posts as brackets for the boards, or nail the boards to pegs driven into the ground.

To fix the first feather-edged board, rest it on the gravel board and attach it to the back of the arris rails by nailing through the thicker edge. Then lay the thicker edge of the next board over the thin edge of the first, overlapping it by about 1cm (½in) and hammer nails through the boards

into the rails. Cut a spacer from a piece of scrap wood to ensure that the overlap for all the boards is uniform.

Sloping ground

There are two ways to erect a fence on sloping ground: the fence may be constructed as a series of stepped horizontal sections or may slope with the ground. The method you should employ is largely dictated by the type of fencing you want to use.

A stepped fence

Panel fences, which cannot be satisfactorily cut, should be stepped. The upright posts need to be longer than they would be on level ground, the extra height depending on the width of the fence panels and the gradient. The triangular gap beneath each panel may be filled by building a low brick wall, stepped so that the panels sit on it. Alternatively, cut angled gravel boards and fix them in the gaps.

SLOPING GROUND

Stepped fence
The panel fence is erected as it would be on level ground, except that the posts must be longer by the height of the supporting brick wall.

Sloped fence
The line of the fence runs parallel to the slope, while the posts and the fencing boards are the same height they would be on level ground.

A sloped fence

To build a fence that slopes with the ground, set a temporary post at the top of the slope and stretch a string line between this and the bottom post. Use a fencing system that consists of individual planks nailed to rails (such as a closeboard or a picket fence). Instead of running horizontally between the posts, the rails run parallel to the slope. Cut the base of each plank at an angle to match the slope. Fix the planks to the rails vertically, resting them on a gravel board.

Wood preservatives

If possible, buy timber that has been factory-impregnated with preservative in a special vacuum press, since home treatments, usually applied only with a brush, are much less effective in penetrating the wood. When constructing a fence with pre-treated timber, any cut ends should be soaked in preservative for 24 hours before use. Keep all preservatives away from plants, and always wear gloves and old clothes.

Unless fences are made of a natural rot-resisting timber, such as oak or cedar, treat them regularly with a wood preservative. Preservative should be applied only to dry timber.

Creosote is a widely used and effective treatment for preserving fencing. It has a very powerful smell, however, which many people find unpleasant. Wear protective clothing when applying this substance, since it is poisonous if swallowed, inhaled, or absorbed through the skin. Creosote is not recommended for fences used to support plants. It is also harmful to wildlife. Alternatives favoured by organic gardeners are based on natural plant oils and resins.

Water-based preservatives are less unpleasant to use, and less toxic to plants. They improve the appearance of the timber and prevent the growth of surface moulds. They are, however, generally less effective at controlling rot. Many now come in a range of colours, either as stains or

paints. Wood stains darken and/or colour the timber and are translucent, allowing the natural beauty of the wood to show through, whereas paint is opaque and several layers – of primer, undercoat, and top coat – may be required to provide full protection to the wood.

Maintenance

Broken timber support posts are one of the most common problems. If the damage is at soil level, the most effective method of repair is to use a concrete spur (see p.601). This is a short post sunk into the ground alongside the existing one and bolted to it to give support.

Dig a hole 45–60cm (18–24in) deep around the damaged post and saw off the rotten part. Paint the cut end of the timber post with a wood preservative. Place the concrete spur in the hole, resting it against the post, and pack hardcore around the base to support it. Push bolts through the holes in the spur and hammer hard enough to leave an impression on the wooden post. Remove the bolts and spur, then drill holes through the post for the bolts. Bolt the concrete spur onto the post, tightening the nuts from the spur side so that the wooden post is not damaged.

Make sure that the post and spur are vertical, if necessary bracing them in position temporarily with stakes driven into the ground. Then fill the hole with a fairly stiff concrete mix (see "Concrete and mortar mixes", p.586), ramming it down firmly to remove any air pockets. After about a week, once the concrete has set, remove the supporting stakes and saw off any surplus length from the protruding bolts.

Broken arris rails are easily repaired with specially angled metal brackets. Some of these brackets are designed to brace a broken rail in the middle, others to support a rail that has rotted where the end fits into the post. Both types are simply screwed into place.

Laws on fences

It is always prudent to consult your neighbours before you construct any fencing. On certain sites, you may also need to consult your local authority's Building Control Department for permission according to the planning rules: these govern the size and appearance of constructions and their effect on, for example, neighbouring gardens and adjoining paths.

Structures that front a boundary on a road must conform to building regulations, especially with regard to safety. Planning permission may need to be granted. Bear in mind the following points about gates, walls, and fences: they should not be more than 2m (6ft) high, and should be no more than 1m (3ft) high if they adjoin a public thoroughfare.

Trellises

Trellises, which are usually made of wood, are both a practical and a decorative feature in a garden. They may be secured to the tops of fences or walls or fixed against them. Alternatively they may be used on their own as partitions or screens. Curved and more intricately designed trellis panels are available for creating garden arbours. Panels are available in a range of shapes and patterns, most consisting of standard diamonds or squares; herringbone trellis is particularly effective for screening.

Trellises are most frequently used to support climbing plants. For a free-standing screen, heavy duty trellis is essential, particularly if it is to support vigorous climbers; the timber frame should be at least 2.5cm (1in) in section. If the trellis is to be used to extend the height of a wall or a fence, a lighter weight may be acceptable. When buying trellis, make sure it has been pressure-treated, and treat any sawn ends with a wood preservative (see

p.602). Trellis primarily intended for supporting climbers is also available in wire and plastic.

Erecting trellis

For a free-standing trellis, panels may be fixed to fence posts in the same way as ordinary fence panels (see "Panel fences", p.600). To attach panels to a fence with timber posts, use metal post extenders. Remove the post cap and slide the metal extender over the top of the post. Insert the required length of extension post and replace the original cap on top of the extension. To fix a lightweight trellis above a masonry wall, attach long battens of 5 x 2cm (2 x ¾in) timber to the sides of the trellis and screw them to the wall. If the trellis is to be fixed against a wall, allow at least 2.5cm (1in) between the wall and the trellis for good air circulation. Hinged fixings allow access for maintenance (see CLIMBING PLANTS, "Fixing a trellis panel to a wall", p.130).

TRELLISES

Trellises can complement the architectural detailing of the structure to which they are attached as well as providing support for climbing plants. They are available in planed hardwood or less expensive sawn softwood. Jointed trellis is much sturdier than concertina-style trellis held together by small tacks.

Lattice panel

Diamond-shaped lattice panel

Large-squared trellis

Pergolas and rustic work

The term pergola originally meant a covered walkway formed by plants grown up trellis. Today the term describes any structure consisting of uprights supporting horizontal beams, over which plants are grown.

Traditionally pergolas were made of rustic poles, but sawn timber is often a better choice, especially where the pergola is combined with timber decking, or where the house forms one of the supports. Sawn timber may be used in combination with brick columns or with painted scaffold poles serving as uprights. Hardwoods such as oak are often used for sawn timber pergolas, but softwoods are perfectly adequate, provided they have been pressure-treated with a preservative.

Pergola construction

Draw your design on graph paper to work out the quantities of materials required, but buy a little more than you think you will need, as you may wish to modify the design slightly during construction. The height of the pergola should be at least 2.5m (8ft) if plants are to be grown over it so as to allow room to walk beneath. If the pergola spans a path, the uprights should be positioned far enough apart to allow for the growth of plants on either side.

Supports

Set wooden support posts in hard-core and concrete in holes at least 60cm (2ft) deep (see "Panel fences", p.600), or use metal post supports (see p.601). If you are building a pergola over a patio, special metal shoes designed to be fixed in a concrete base are available. To avoid breaking up an existing concrete or paved surface,

Timber pergola on a brick patio

The materials used to construct this pergola are few and simple, yet the design is most effective. A large square trellis has been fixed behind the square brick pillars that support the cross-beams.

build a brick shoe and fit the post into it (see *Joints and Supports*, p.604).

Sawn timber support posts should be 100 x 100mm (4 x 4in) in section. Scaffold poles may be used instead of timber uprights but must be set in concrete because of their greater weight. Alternatively, if the weight that is to be carried is substantial, build brick or concrete block

columns on substantial footings (see "Bricklaying", p.597).

Cross-beams

For cross-beams (roof beams), use either the same timber as for the uprights or planks 50 x 150mm (2 x 6in) in section. These are sometimes sold ready-shaped and notched to fit over the tops of the uprights. Lighter

JOINTS AND SUPPORTS

Wooden pergola
The basic unit of construction of most pergolas is a simple arch.

Brick shoe
A metal-lined shoe is used on top of a solid flat surface such as concrete.

Brick and wood pergola
Brick columns support a wooden cross-beam.

Dowel joint
To anchor a wooden beam on top of a brick column, use a wooden dowel mortared into the brick.

Single-sided pergola
The timber cross-beam is supported on one side by a scaffold pole and on the other by a joist shoe fitted into the wall.

Notched joint
A wooden cross-beam fits neatly over an upright support.

Half-lap joint
Intersecting, horizontal beams may be joined almost invisibly.

Bird's mouth joint
This joint fixes a horizontal strut into an upright rustic pole.

Concrete casing
If using metal uprights, sink them in a concrete casing.

Joist shoe
A joist shoe gives adequate support for a lightweight beam. Heavy beams may require a timber wallplate.

timber may be used for decorative rafters laid between the cross-beams.

Joints for beams and uprights

It is possible to assemble all the overhead timberwork by means of galvanized brackets and screws, but the structure will be stronger, and more attractive, if you use carpentry joints (see above). To fix an overhead beam to an upright, use a simple notched joint. This kind of joint is especially useful if the cross-beams are to project beyond the uprights – to serve as supports for hanging containers, for example.

Treat the cut surfaces of the joint with wood preservative (see p.602) before nailing them together. Avoid driving the nails in at right angles; skew-nailed joints hold together better when the structure flexes in the wind. If extra strength is needed, screw a "T"-bracket where the upright meets the horizontal.

If you are using scaffold poles to support timber cross-beams, effective joints may be created by drilling circular holes of the same diameter as the scaffold into the beams. The depth of the holes should be half the thickness of the timber.

Timber pergolas are often supported by a wall of the house. To attach a wooden cross-beam to the wall you will need to use a metal joist shoe mortared into the brickwork. When the supports are brick columns, the wooden horizontals are fixed with

dowels, which are mortared into the brick (see above).

You may wish to roof over the pergola with a network of intersecting rafters. Where two beams of equal thickness meet, a half-lap joint gives a strong, neat finish.

Many designs also incorporate corner braces between the uprights and the cross-beams to give the pergola greater rigidity. The timber for the braces should measure about 50 x 50mm (2 x 2in) and should fit as closely as possible into notches cut in the beams.

Cut the braces to the required length, then hold them up to the framework to mark the position and shape of the notches. Use a drill and chisel to cut the notches. When all the necessary adjustments have been made, treat all the cut surfaces with preservative before nailing the braces into the notches.

Rustic work

Rustic work comprises all kinds of garden structures made from poles (usually of larch or fir), rather than sawn timber. A popular material for arches and screens as well as pergolas, the poles may either be dressed, that is with the bark stripped off, or be left with the bark on as an attractive finish. If you use poles with bark, bear in mind that the bark is likely to become a refuge for wildlife including garden pests.

The vertical poles that support the structure should be about 10cm (4in) in diameter. They may be bedded in concrete (see "Panel fences", p.600) or set in the open ground. In the latter case, sink them to 45–60cm (18–24in) of their length to ensure stability. If the bark is to be left on, strip it from the bases of the poles up to a point that extends 2.5cm (1in) above soil level when they are in position. Whether the bark is left on the poles or stripped off, soak the ends in wood preservative overnight. Set the uprights in their positions. The cross-beams and corner braces needed to complete the structure may be fixed later, once the concrete around the supports (if this is used) has set.

The poles used for the main cross-beams and corner braces should have a diameter of about 8cm (3in), but thinner poles may be used for the decorative latticework.

It is possible to pre-assemble some sections of the structure by laying them out on the ground according to the design, then cutting some of the poles to length and making the necessary joints. Saw all the cross-pieces only as you need them to ensure that they fit exactly.

There are many joints that may be used in the construction of a rustic pergola or arch. Half-lap joints (see above), similar to those used for sawn timber, are useful where the poles intersect. To attach a horizontal cross-beam to an upright, use a bird's mouth joint (see above). All cut ends

should be painted with preservative before you assemble the structure.

As with sawn timber, it is always best to nail the joints together at an angle to give them extra rigidity.

Other plant supports

It is possible to provide support for climbers without erecting a trellis or pergola. Striking effects can be achieved with interwoven willow wands and other relatively simple structures (see also WILLOW WALLS, p.87, and CLIMBING PLANTS, "Climbing methods and supports", p.124).

Tripods

Rustic tripods are an excellent way of integrating climbers into a mixed or herbaceous border. Dressed rustic poles are better than those with bark for this purpose, as they are less likely to attract pests. For large plants, use poles of about 15cm (6in) diameter. If the tripod is in a bed, sink the poles in holes filled with gravel.

Pillars

For a more formal effect along the back of a border or to flank a path, erect a row of single pillars made of brick or reconstituted stone. The bases of the pillars should be set firmly in concrete. To help climbers grow up the pillars, use plastic-covered large-mesh netting. Secure the net around the pillars by tying it together with plastic-covered wire.

Garden sheds

Sheds are valuable outbuildings for storing garden tools and equipment. They may house a miscellany of domestic items from bric-à-brac to bicycles, and sometimes double as a workshop, too. A simple tool store will keep hand tools dry and clean, but a larger shed with space to set up a workbench along one of the walls is a better investment.

Designs

Different designs of shed are available. Some have an apex roof (like an inverted "V"), while others have a pent roof (sloping in one direction only) or a flat roof.

An apex-roof shed has more headroom in the centre than a pent-roof shed, an advantage if a workbench is to be placed along one side.

A pent-roof shed usually has its door and window on the higher side.

A sensible arrangement is to place a workbench beneath the window and to store tools on the lower side.

As a rule, flat roofs are found only on sheds made of concrete.

Materials

Garden sheds may be constructed from a variety of materials – wood, concrete, steel, aluminium, or glass-fibre. The choice of material depends on the intended life and uses of the shed as well as on expense and maintenance requirements.

Wood

The most widely used material for a garden shed is wood; it blends in sympathetically with plants, especially after the new timber has weathered with age. Durable woods such as cedar are preferable, since they are naturally resistant to rot.

Most sheds, however, are made of softwood, which is much cheaper than cedar. Try to find a shed made of pressure-treated timber rather than of wood that has simply been dipped or painted. Treat with a preservative when new, and maintain regularly. Wooden sheds should be lined with water-proof building paper (from a builder's merchant) to reduce the risk of moisture penetration and to protect tools from rusting.

Concrete

Sheds made from concrete are robust and long-lasting but not particularly attractive, so are best sited alongside the house rather than in a conspicuous part of the garden. Generally constructed of pre-cast concrete sections, the roof is usually flat; many have plastic sections in the roof to admit light. A concrete shed must be erected on a firm, concrete base (see p.586).

The concrete walls may have a finish of exposed aggregate or imitation brick. When painted, these may make an excellent background for climbers and wall shrubs.

Metal

Steel sheds are very durable if they have been treated during manufacture to resist rust. They are usually green, but may be painted and usually do not include windows.

Sheds made of interlocking sheets of aluminium are also available. Most have a sliding door, and some an acrylic sheet window. Often small, these sheds are intended primarily as tool stores and are virtually maintenance-free.

Glass-fibre

Small glass-fibre sheds are available that are easy to assemble, and require no maintenance. They are just large enough to store tools.

CHOOSING A TIMBER SHED

The life of a wooden shed depends on the quality of the construction and of the timber. Whenever possible, compare erected sheds – most major suppliers will have a good selection to choose from. Pay close attention to the features indicated below.

Roofing felt
Choose a thick felt with a stone-chip finish. Poor felt will let in moisture that will damage the wood after three or four years.

Roof
It must be strong, and should not sag or flex if you push the centre of one of the roof panels.

Gutters
Help extend the life of the shed by keeping cladding dry, diverting rainwater into a bed or storage tank. They are not standard fittings, but are easy to fix yourself.

Windows
These must fit well and should have rust-proof fittings. If hinged from the top, water is less likely to enter if they are left open in the rain. Check that there is a sloping sill and a drip groove underneath to prevent water from damaging the cladding.

Eaves
These should overhang the sides and ends by at least 5cm (2in).

Headroom
Make sure that you can stand comfortably; bear in mind that cross-braces are found in some designs.

Door
This should be solid with good cross-bracing. Check for strong hinges and a good lock. Metal fittings should be rust-resistant – galvanized metal or aluminium.

Floor
It should be firm – test it by jumping up and down on it.

Cladding
Inspect the shed from the inside to make sure that no daylight is visible through the boards. See right for different types of cladding.

Bearers
If the shed is not erected on a concrete base, pressure-impregnated bearers help to keep the shed timber dry. If not using bearers, lay the shed on a damp-proof material.

TYPES OF CLADDING

Tongue-and-groove
This cladding usually offers good weather protection.

Feather-edged, overlapping weatherboard
This may warp or buckle unless it is thick.

Rebated weatherboard
This gives a closer fit than feather-edged weatherboard.

Rebate ship-lap
This is durable, and has an attractive finish.

Waney-edged weatherboard
This rough-edged board (also called rustic cladding) may be less weather-proof.

4
CLIMATE AND THE GARDEN

CLIMATE HAS A major influence on plant growth, and much of the satisfaction in gardening lies in meeting the challenges of the weather, often by exploiting its effects to the gardener's advantage. Choosing plants that thrive in the prevailing climate is fundamental to success, although many will adapt to weather conditions alien to their natural habitat.

The effects of climate on plants are complex, and responses to the weather are shaped by many factors, including a plant's location within the garden, stage of maturity, and the length and intensity of exposure to inclement conditions. Through an understanding of the effects of climate, a gardener will be better able to grow healthy, productive, and attractive plants.

Climate zones

World climate may be divided into four broad but clearly defined zones; these are tropical, desert, temperate, and polar.

Tropical climates are characterized by high temperatures and heavy, sometimes seasonal, rainfall, and support luxuriant, evergreen vegetation. Deserts have average daytime temperatures in excess of 38°C (100°F) but often very cold nights, with annual rainfall of less than 25cm (10in); only adapted plants, such as cacti, survive in these conditions. Temperate regions have changeable daily patterns but rainfall is usually evenly spread throughout the year and temperatures are less extreme than in the tropics or deserts; deciduous plants are more common than evergreens, as they are better adapted to these conditions. Polar regions experience extreme cold, strong winds, and low rainfall, so little plant growth is possible.

In addition to these four broad zones, intermediate zones, including subtropical and Mediterranean, are also recognized.

Regional climate

Conditions within climate zones are determined by geographical factors such as latitude, altitude, and proximity to the sea, all of which affect both rainfall and temperature.

The European continent
The extremes of summer and winter temperatures in north-eastern and central parts of Europe are influenced by latitude and the continental land mass. The Atlantic ocean and Mediterranean sea are too far away to have any moderating influence on temperatures in winter – the cold land mass of Asia is more influential at this time of year. Further south, however, the combined influences of the sea and relative proximity to the equator mean that the Mediterranean climate consists of mild winters with limited rainfall and hot, dry summers.

The British Isles
The maritime climate of the British Isles is influenced by warm air currents and rain from the surrounding oceans. Westerly parts, in particular, benefit from the tempering influence of warm air currents from the Gulf Stream, so winters there are milder and prolonged frosts rare.

The North American continent
North America has much regional variation. For example, the average minimum temperature in the region from Saskatchewan to Labrador in the north of the continent is between -50°C (-58°F) and -35°C (-31°F), whereas that in the area between Arizona and Virginia in the south is between 5°C (41°F) and 10°C (50°F).

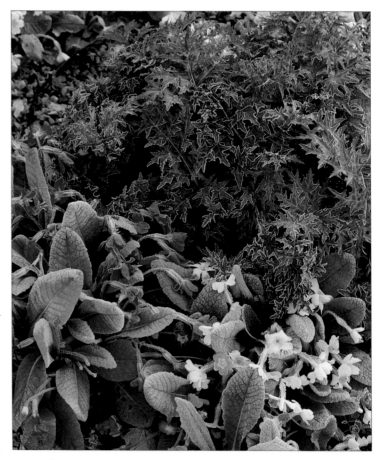

Spring frost
The play of light on the frost-tinged foliage and flowers of hardy plants brings an ethereal quality to the garden. Selecting plants to fit your local weather patterns should help produce satisfying results throughout the year.

Elements of climate

The elements of climate that directly affect plants and the techniques used to grow them are temperature, frost, snow, rain, humidity, sun, and wind. Of these, temperature is regarded as the most important: it determines the choice of plants to be grown, and the length of the growing season.

Temperature

Vital processes like photosynthesis, transpiration, respiration, and growth are significantly affected by temperature. Each species has a minimum and a maximum temperature beyond which these processes will not take place. The maximum temperature is about 35°C (96°F) for most plants; the minimum is highly variable. Where extremely low temperatures occur, plant tissue may be physically destroyed (see "Freezing and thawing", below).

Air and soil temperatures are the most important climatic factors influencing the onset and breaking of plant dormancy, largely determining the length of the growing season.

Air temperature

Sunshine produces radiant energy that raises the ambient or air temperature. In temperate and cooler climates, a sheltered site that benefits from the warming effect of full sun may be used for plants from warmer areas that might not otherwise thrive.

Altitude has an important effect on air temperature: given the same latitude, highland sites are cooler than lowland ones – for every 300m (1,000ft) increase in altitude, the temperature drops by 0.5°C (1°F). High-altitude sites thus have a shorter growing season, which together with the cooler temperatures affects the range of plants that may be grown.

Soil temperature

The temperature of soil is important for healthy root growth and affects the rate at which plants absorb water and nutrients from the soil. Successful seed germination and shoot development also depend on suitable soil temperatures (see PRINCIPLES OF PROPAGATION, "Requirements for germination", p.630).

The speed at which soil warms up and the temperature maintained during the year depend on soil type and the aspect of the site. Sandy soils warm up faster than clay, and well-drained, fertile soils stay warm longer than those that are compacted or infertile (see also SOILS AND FERTILIZERS,"Soil types", p.616).

Sites with a natural, gentle incline towards the south warm up quickly in spring because they gain more benefit from the sun than level or north-facing ground. They are ideal for early vegetable crops. North-facing slopes stay relatively cool and may be used to grow plants that thrive in cooler conditions.

Dormancy

Plants become dormant to limit their exposure to winter weather; most have at least a short period of full dormancy. Many woody plants shed leaves in autumn to avoid excessive transpiration, while herbaceous and bulbous plants die down in winter and remain dormant below ground.

The temperature of the soil and air are the most important factors involved in the onset and breaking of dormancy. It is possible to exploit this knowledge by, for example, keeping plants in a dormant state through cold storage: dormant scions for grafting may be stored until sap rises in the rootstock, and shrubs may be stored in the same way until the soil is warm enough for planting.

However, bulbs in pots and winter-flowering azaleas, for example, may be awakened from dormancy and brought into early flowering if they are placed in a warm greenhouse.

FROST POCKETS

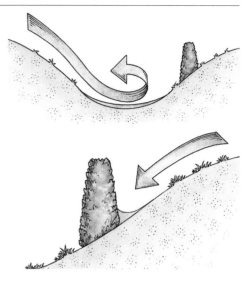

As relatively warm air rises, cold air sinks to the lowest point it can reach, and a "frost pocket" may occur. Valleys and ground hollows are ideal for frost pockets, and any plants in the vicinity will suffer as a result. Frost also collects behind closely planted hedges and other solid obstructions such as walls and fences, with the same effect.

Frost

Frost is a great hazard in gardening and considered more crucial than the average minimum temperature for the area. An unexpected severe frost has serious implications; even hardy plants are vulnerable to unusually low temperatures, particularly if they have produced new growth in spring.

Frost occurs when the temperature is consistently below freezing, and takes several forms. In hoar frost, ice crystals form from water condensed from a humid atmosphere. Black frost is likely in a dry atmosphere, and blackens the leaves and stems of plants. Ground frost results when the soil temperature falls below freezing point; the penetration depth depends on its intensity and duration. Still, clear nights when cold air collects at a level just above the ground are particularly dangerous. Most at risk are those trees, shrubs, and climbers whose woody tissue has not ripened (hardened) well, usually due to a lack of sun and warmth during autumn.

The risk of spring frost in any area determines the date after which it is safe to sow or plant out tender plants, like chrysanthemums, runner beans, tomatoes, dahlias, and half-hardy bedding plants; the onset of autumn frost signals the end of their growing season. To be kept from year to year, tender plants should be taken indoors or given protection (see FROST AND WIND PROTECTION, pp.612–613).

Frost pockets and damage

Where dense, cold air flows downwards, pools of frost may collect; any valley or hollow is a potential frost pocket. Cold air accumulates in the depression, increasing the area of potential damage as it backs up the sloping sides of the valley.

Thick barriers of established trees or hedges along hillsides may obstruct the passage of cold air down a slope, but frost pockets will form in front of them. Avoid this by thinning or removing the trees or hedges to allow cold air to flow through.

When the ground is frozen, water is no longer available to plant roots. Deep-rooted trees are not affected by heavy frosts, as their roots penetrate well below the frost-line, but plants with shallow roots, such as small evergreen shrubs, may not be able to replace the moisture lost by continual transpiration. Severe ground frost often causes newly planted, young, or shallow-rooted plants to rise or "lift" out of the soil; these should be gently refirmed when the thaw begins.

The risk of frost damage to plants kept outside may be reduced by various means. See FROST AND WIND PROTECTION, pp.612–613.

Freezing and thawing

Frost itself does not always cause great damage to plants, and alternate freezing and thawing may be more devastating. Cell sap expands on freezing and can destroy plant cell walls, frequently killing tender plants. The flowers, shoots, buds, and leaves of hardier plants may also

Gardeners and global warming

Climate change will inevitably affect gardeners. We will need to plan ahead to take advantage of growing a wider range of plants over a longer season – and to cope with drought and changing patterns of pests and diseases. Predictions include:

- Higher mean temperatures, with earlier springs and warmer, later autumns increasing the length of many plants' growing seasons.
- Hotter – and drier – summers and autumns; more drought, and rapid evaporation of water from the soil.
- A reduction in annual rainfall with most rain falling in winter, leading to waterlogging in some soils.
- Higher carbon dioxide levels will cause temperature increases; both contribute to more plant growth.
- An upsurge of pests like aphids, as they are able to complete more life cycles in a single season.
- An increase in disease: warmer, wetter winters will favour the spread of *Phytophthora* and other water-transmitted diseases.
- Weeds may increase more freely as conditions favour germination and growth over longer periods.

THE CLIMATE OF EUROPE

N

0   300   Kilometres

0   200   Miles

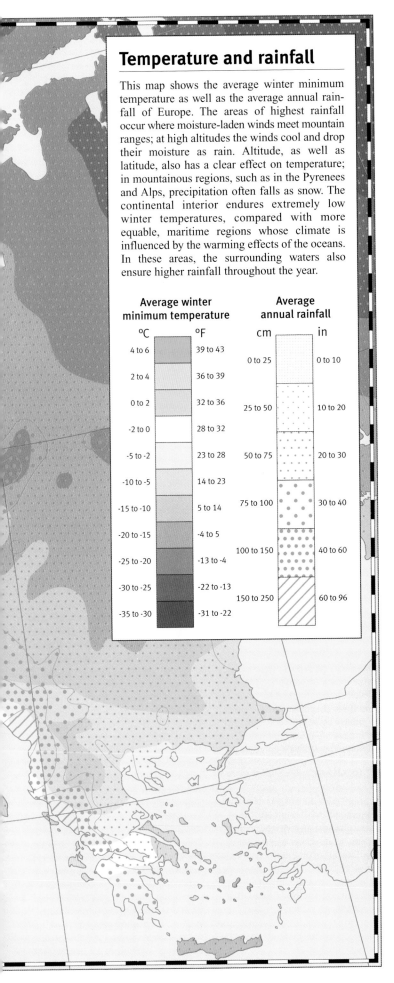

Temperature and rainfall

This map shows the average winter minimum temperature as well as the average annual rainfall of Europe. The areas of highest rainfall occur where moisture-laden winds meet mountain ranges; at high altitudes the winds cool and drop their moisture as rain. Altitude, as well as latitude, also has a clear effect on temperature; in mountainous regions, such as in the Pyrenees and Alps, precipitation often falls as snow. The continental interior endures extremely low winter temperatures, compared with more equable, maritime regions whose climate is influenced by the warming effects of the oceans. In these areas, the surrounding waters also ensure higher rainfall throughout the year.

Average winter minimum temperature

°C	°F
4 to 6	39 to 43
2 to 4	36 to 39
0 to 2	32 to 36
-2 to 0	28 to 32
-5 to -2	23 to 28
-10 to -5	14 to 23
-15 to -10	5 to 14
-20 to -15	-4 to 5
-25 to -20	-13 to -4
-30 to -25	-22 to -13
-35 to -30	-31 to -22

Average annual rainfall

cm	in
0 to 25	0 to 10
25 to 50	10 to 20
50 to 75	20 to 30
75 to 100	30 to 40
100 to 150	40 to 60
150 to 250	60 to 96

THE EFFECTS OF SNOW

Snow damage
The considerable weight of thick snow may force apart hedges or evergreen shrubs and trees if it is allowed to settle for too long. Always clear snow from such plants as soon as possible.

Arched hedge
Shape a hedge to prevent snow collecting on it.

Snow protection
A snow blanket protects high-altitude plants from freezing temperatures.

show damage when the thaw begins, and sometimes the roots are harmed. In cases of severe frost, the bark of some woody plants may split open.

Repeated hard freezes followed by rapid thaws and subsequent soil waterlogging causes most damage to roots. Late spring frosts particularly damage new top-growth, causing blackening of the leaves and injury to new buds and flowers.

Duration of frosts
The duration of frost is also relevant to the amount of damage caused: for example, a temperature of -3°C (27°F) for fifteen minutes might cause no damage, but the same temperature sustained over three hours could cause substantial losses.

Frost and cultivation
Despite the danger to plants, frost can aid cultivation. Soil water expands when it freezes, shattering clods into smaller soil particles; this is particularly useful on clay soils, in encouraging the development of tilth. Low soil temperatures also reduce numbers of some soil-inhabiting pests.

Snow

When atmospheric temperature falls close to (but not below) freezing, water droplets freeze in clouds or rain and may fall as snow.

Snow provides a useful supply of water on thawing and often gives plants valuable insulation; a blanket of snow prevents the soil beneath from falling below 0°C (32°F) even though the temperature of the air may drop below this point. However, heavy snow followed by severe frost may damage shoots and branches. Where possible, remove thick layers of snow from vulnerable plants.

Rainfall

Water is the main constituent of cell sap and is vital for photosynthesis, the complex means by which carbon dioxide and water are converted into living plant tissue. Photosynthesis is also fundamental to the process of transpiration, whereby a plant is kept turgid and nutrients are transported through it. Respiration, germination of seeds, and development of roots, shoots, leaves, flowers, and fruit are dependent upon good water supplies.

Rainfall is the principal source of water for plants in the open. Much rain is lost through evaporation and run-off but moisture that soaks into the soil is absorbed by soil particles or held as a thin film around them. Water and essential nutrients, which are absorbed in solution, are then extracted from soil by plant root hairs.

For optimum growth, plants need a steady supply of water. In practice, rainfall is variable, however, in both regularity and quantity.

Waterlogging
In badly drained soil, a build-up of water leads to waterlogging. Most plants can survive an occasional heavy downpour, but where water-logging is prolonged, roots may die through asphyxiation, except in the case of specially adapted plants, such as marginal aquatics, swamp cypress (*Taxodium distichum*), and willows (*Salix*). On permanently waterlogged sites, most plants fail to establish unless drainage is improved (see SOILS AND FERTILIZERS, p.623).

Drought
Plant development is more often restricted by too little available water rather than by too much. Drought during summer, when temperature and sunlight are at maximum levels, is a common problem. Wilting is the first outward sign of drought; plant functions slow down until more water is available, and water loss by transpiration is reduced by partial closure of stomata in the leaves. See

RAIN SHADOW

Ground in the lee of a wall or solid fence (see shaded area above) receives less rainfall than ground on the windward side, since the wall or fence creates an area of rain shadow.

Basic Botany, "Leaves", p.675.

Plants from regions of low rainfall often have special adaptations, like hairy, sticky, glossy, spiny, narrow, or fleshy leaves, that help reduce water loss through transpiration. Cacti and succulents have water-storing tissue in their leaves, stems, or roots, and can survive long periods of drought.

The soil

In areas of low rainfall, various techniques may be used to increase the amount of water available to plants from soil, such as removing weeds (see pp.669–673), mulching, and increasing humus content by digging in organic matter (see Soils and Fertilizers, "Mulches", p.626, and "Using soil additives", p.621). Plants derive more benefit from rainfall if grown in open positions away from buildings, fences, and trees, which often produce rain shadows.

Torrential rain may damage soil structure but the worst effects can be avoided by gardening on well-drained sites. If this is not possible, drainage may be improved by deep digging or by installing artificial drainage aids (see Soils and Fertilizers, "Double digging", p.620, and "Installing drains", p.623).

SUNSHINE AND SHADE

Shade cast in summer

Shade cast in winter

The shade cast on a garden by buildings and fences, as well as trees and large shrubs, changes according to the angles of sunlight, which differ according to season.

Humidity

Humidity levels are determined by the quantity or proportion of water vapour in the atmosphere and the moisture content of the soil.

The point at which air becomes saturated varies according to sunlight, temperature, and wind. Atmospheric humidity is referred to as "relative" humidity – the amount of water vapour in air expressed as a percentage of saturation point.

The effects of humidity

In areas of heavy rainfall, atmospheric humidity is high. Certain plants, like ferns and mosses, thrive in exceptionally humid conditions. Humidity may be increased by damping down around plants (see Greenhouses and Frames, "Humidifiers", p.576). This is also of value when propagating plants to reduce water lost by transpiration.

High relative humidity may have unfavourable effects: fungal diseases like grey mould flourish in the moist conditions created by high humidity.

Sunlight

Sunlight provides radiant energy to raise the temperature and humidity of soil and air, and plays a major role in stimulating plant growth.

For most plants, sunshine and the consequent high temperatures encourage maximum new growth, flowering, and fruiting. A sunny summer also results in greatly enhanced food storage in plants and helps to firm protective tissue, which means that better propagating material is produced.

Daylength

The duration of daylight in a given 24-hour period (daylength) is determined by latitude and season, and affects flowering and fruiting in some plants, such as strawberries,

Kalanchoe, and chrysanthemums. "Short" days have less than 12 hours of daylight, while "long" days have more than 12 hours. By using artificial lighting or blacking out the natural light, the flowering times of plants that are daylength-sensitive may be manipulated to advantage. Germination of seeds and seedling development may be advanced by the same method (see Greenhouses and Frames, "Growing lamps", p.577).

Plants and sunlight

Plants always grow towards the direction of sunlight: a shrub positioned close to a wall, for example, will develop more shoots and foliage on the side farthest from the wall. In the same way, plants that are subjected to a poor or localized light source become drawn or etiolated as they try to reach more light. The intensity of sunlight dictates flower opening in some plants: for example *Ornithogalum umbellatum* only opens its flowers in good light conditions.

Sun or shade

Most leafy plants require the maximum amount of light to achieve optimum growth. Some garden plants thrive in direct, strong sunshine, while others will not tolerate it. Half-hardy plants, most fruits and vegetables, roses, and plants of Mediterranean origin all thrive best in full sun. On the other hand, many rhododendrons prefer to have some shade, whereas ivies (*Hedera*) and periwinkles (*Vinca*) tend to do best in heavily shaded areas.

WIND TURBULENCE

Exposed areas on rising ground may suffer severe wind damage. Gusts of air meeting resistance from the land are diverted around the sides and over the top of hills, gathering in intensity at the same time.

WIND FUNNELLING

A wind funnel created between buildings and trees may cause a great deal of damage to plants in its path, since air is forced through the narrow channel at great speed. If gardening in such an area is unavoidable, construct a windbreak to protect your plants.

Excessive sunshine

Strong sunlight may scorch the flowers and leaves of plants, especially if they have been recently watered. It occasionally causes splitting of fruits or bark. To prevent such problems, always choose an appropriate site when planting, and for vulnerable plants provide artificial shade in summer, especially in greenhouses and frames (see Greenhouses and Frames, "Shading", p.576).

Wind

Wind often damages plants and adversely affects their environment but it also has some benefits: it plays an important part in pollen and seed dispersal and may also be useful in cooling plants down, provided that they have enough water to prevent desiccation. In addition, gentle winds prevent the development of a stagnant atmosphere, and deter plant diseases that might otherwise thrive.

On the other hand, wind may discourage beneficial insects and make it difficult to control pests, diseases, and weeds: spraying is likely to be less effective in windy conditions or damaging to non-target plants due to spray drift. Many more serious problems are caused by the wind, however, although there are various ways of protecting plants.

Wind damage

If woody plants are exposed to strong winds continuously, their top-growth becomes unbalanced, giving the plants a one-sided appearance. The exposed shoot tips are also likely to be damaged or "scorched". Trees that grow on hill tops and on exposed, coastal sites are examples.

Strong winds and gales

The greater the velocity of wind, the more damage it causes. In high winds, shoots and stems of plants may be broken and, in gale force conditions, trees may be uprooted or their root systems seriously weakened. Strong winds may also damage fences, greenhouses, and other garden structures. On sandy or peat soil, the wind may cause soil erosion.

Wind scorch

Strong winds in high temperature increase the rate at which water is lost from plants, leading to desiccation of leaves and shoots. Even moderate winds have a detrimental effect, and may prevent plants from reaching their full growth potential. Similar wind damage occurs if temperatures are very low; plants cannot replace lost moisture if soil water is frozen (see p.607).

Effects of topography

The severity of the wind depends to a large extent on topography. Coastal sites often have no natural protection from salt-laden wind coming in from the sea. Hill-top sites may be equally exposed, because the wind gusts around and over the hill.

Wind funnels are created by the channelling of air between hillsides and along valleys, through corridors of established trees, or between adjacent buildings. This intensifies wind speed and strength, so avoid planting in these areas. Windbreaks are an effective means of providing shelter from wind. They may be fences, screens, or hedges (see HEDGES AND SCREENS, pp.84–86).

How a windbreak works

Whatever the type of windbreak, it should be 50 per cent permeable. Solid barriers deflect wind upwards, producing an area of low pressure directly behind them, which draws air downwards to fill the vacuum, causing further turbulence.

Fences or screens need to be up to 4m (12ft) high for maximum

WINDBREAKS

Place windbreaks at a distance of 10 times their height.

A series of windbreaks
Across a large area of flat ground, construct several semi-permeable fences or screens to break the force of the wind.

Reducing wind speed
A windbreak should be semi-permeable. Gusts of air still pass through, but at reduced speed.

Non-permeable windbreak
A solid windbreak is ineffective. Air is forced upwards, then pulled down to create a downdraught.

protection as a garden boundary, but may be as low as 50cm (20in) for low-growing plants like vegetables and strawberries. For the greatest benefit across a large area, place windbreaks at regular intervals roughly equal to ten times their height.

Microclimate

Differences in topography frequently mean that local microclimates show variations from the more generalized pattern within a specific climatic region. A site in a natural dip or hollow may be relatively warm if it is protected from the wind; on the other hand, if the hollow is shaded from sunshine it will be quite cool and may form a frost pocket in winter (see p.607). Rainfall may be significantly less in gardens in the lee of high ground than in others in the same locality but on the windward side.

The garden and its plants further modify local climate and introduce features that give rise to a microclimate specific to the garden; this may differ markedly from that of the surrounding area. To alter the microclimate of a garden, a gardener can readily adapt certain features to provide specific conditions.

Orientation

The soil in raised or sloping beds that face the sun will warm up quickly in spring, producing ideal conditions for growing early crops or flowers. If the soil is free-draining, the same area may be used for plants that prefer dry conditions.

South-facing fences and walls are excellent places to grow tender climbers, wall shrubs, and trained fruit trees, since they are in sun for

much of the day, which improves flowering and fruiting. Walls also absorb a great deal of heat that is then released overnight; this can confer a few degrees extra frost protection during winter.

Wind shelter

A row of trees or a fence provides a sheltered area for plants that might otherwise suffer wind damage. The growing conditions on each side of such a windbreak will be different: the ground close to a hedge or

fence on the leeward side will rarely receive rain and may also be sheltered from the warming effect of the sun.

Shaded areas

Areas of shade in the garden beneath tree canopies, hedges, or large shrubs receive the same sort of light as in natural woodland and may be suitable for plants that enjoy such an environment. If a greater degree of shade is required, plants may be grown against north-facing walls, although these sites will be colder.

A bog garden

The edges of a pond or stream, or a low-lying part of the garden, may be used to create the bog-like conditions in which moisture-loving plants thrive.

Greenhouses and frames

Using greenhouses, frames, and cloches gives complete control over the elements, enabling a gardener to provide a variety of microclimates in a small space (see GREENHOUSES AND FRAMES, pp.566–583).

THE MICROCLIMATE OF A GARDEN

The potential for several different growing environments exists in even the smallest gardens. Naturally occurring features create their own areas of microclimate and garden features may be either exploited or manipulated, as necessary, to provide the conditions that plants from many different regions enjoy.

Avoid planting in areas of wind turbulence.

Raised beds provide well-drained conditions.

Trees provide a natural windbreak.

A sunny terrace is suitable for tender and sun-loving plants.

The edges of a pool may be planted with bog plants.

A greenhouse provides a suitable environment for tender plants.

Water plants thrive in a pool.

Frost and wind protection

SELECT PLANTS that will thrive in a given climate zone before altering the growing conditions. Trying to grow very tender plants in a cold climate will almost always end in disappointment. For species that normally do well in a site but may suffer in harsh winters, providing protection against frost and wind is a sensible precaution. Efficient wind protection enables gardeners to grow a wide range of plants and is particularly useful for large plants, for those in open ground that cannot easily be brought under cover, and for early-flowering plants and trees that are more susceptible to frost than later-flowering species. Protection is also needed from strong winds, which can cause broken stems and browning of foliage. In regions that regularly experience extremes of low temperatures, plants such as roses may need to be trenched before winter.

Preventive measures

Gardeners can take precautions to avoid the worst effects of frost: do not plant in frost pockets and choose sheltered sites (such as in front of a warm wall or on a sunny bank) for susceptible plants. Tender climbers,

---

PROTECTING SMALL TREES AND SHRUBS

Bracken or straw insulation
Tie in the branches, then surround the tree with wire netting secured to 3 canes in a partial circle 30cm (12in) from the tree. Pack bracken into the gap, then secure the netting to a fourth stake. Cover the top with more straw. Attach a sheet of plastic to the netting.

Straw barrier
Pack a thick layer of straw between 2 layers of wire netting. Surround the plant, filling any gaps with extra straw, and tie in place.

Hessian strips
Tie in the branches or leaves of the crown, then wrap the tree in strips of hessian, winding it round and tying it in place at intervals with string or twine. Protect the base of the trunk with straw or bracken.

Hessian and straw cover
Pack straw around the shrub's branches, working from the bottom up. Loosely wrap hessian around, and tie with string.

Netting over a framework
When wall-trained fruit trees blossom, protect them from frost at night with woven nylon netting, rolled down to cover the tree but held away from the blossom by canes.

Straw and netting for wall-trained plants
Protect a tree or shrub against a fence or wall by packing straw or bracken behind the branches. Fix netting at the top and bottom of the fence. Pack more straw between netting and plant, until it is covered.

TRENCHING ROSES (EXTREME WINTER-COLD REGIONS ONLY)

Mounding up earth
Protect the graft union of bush roses from extreme cold by mounding up earth around the crown, to a depth of 12cm (5in).

1 *Loosen the root ball then dig a trench long enough to take the height of the bush when laid on its side and about 30cm (12in) deeper than the width of the bush.*

2 *Line the trench with a 10cm (4in) layer of straw and lay the bush down. Pack straw around and above the shoots.*

3 *Insert stakes and tie strings between them to hold the bush down. Infill with soil, mounding it up to cover the bush to a depth of 30cm (12in).*

for example, may be grown against a house wall (which will be warmer than a garden wall) or in containers that can easily be moved to a sheltered position. Seedlings, summer bulbs, and tubers should only be planted out when all danger of spring frost has passed, and roses and other shrubs should not be fed late in the season, since this encourages new, soft growth that may then be damaged by autumn frost. Allowing herbaceous plants to die down naturally means that the foliage and stems will protect the crowns in winter, while a deep mulch of slowly decomposing organic matter provides useful protection for the roots of all plants. Check plants regularly in winter, firming any that have been lifted out of the ground by frost.

Frost protection

The aim of frost protection is to insulate the plants from the extremes of freeze and thaw conditions by maintaining a constant temperature.

Insulation
Wrapping plants in hessian, carpet, or double thicknesses of newspaper is effective in protecting the top-growth from damage. Any warm air escaping from the soil is trapped beneath the cover and acts as an insulating layer. Hessian helps to slow the warming process caused by a thaw and keeps the plant dormant through any mid-winter mild spells. Bracken or straw packed around the plant beneath the hessian provides additional insulation and is suitable for wall-trained trees and shrubs, climbers, potatoes, strawberries, and small fruit trees and bushes. Once

temperatures rise above freezing this cover can be removed. Wall-trained plants need to be detached from their support if possible and the stems gathered together before wrapping.

Small shrubs and trees growing in areas below their usual winter hardiness level can be protected by building a loose wire-netting cage around them and then packing this with dry leaves or straw. Plastic sheeting tied or stapled over the top of the cage will keep the insulating layer dry. Alternatively, pack the straw in between and behind the stems before covering over.

Mounding with mulches or soil
For perennial plants that die down to a resting crown, place a mulch or a few forkfuls of leaves over the crown and keep it in place with bracken or prunings from evergreens. Roses and other woody plants can be protected by mounding earth around the base or laying them in a trench. In very cold regions, the earth mound should be covered with a layer of straw. Root vegetables can be protected from frost damage in the same way and can then be harvested even during frosty spells.

Cloches
If only a few individual plants need protection, the best solution is to use a cloche, which acts like a miniature greenhouse, warming the soil and maintaining an even temperature. Emerging shoots of frost-sensitive plants, such as asparagus, can be protected with almost any household container: an old bucket, a large plant pot, or a tough cardboard box will all do the job quite adequately. Specially designed, clear plastic cloches are commercially available. More permanent cloche protection

can be provided by glass cloches, polythene panels, polytunnels, or cold frames (see GREENHOUSES AND FRAMES, pp.566–583).

Wind protection

Wind protection aims to reduce the wind speed before it reaches any plants, thereby reducing physical damage to branches and stems and preventing further water loss. Many tender plants have greatly improved chances of survival if they are planted in the lee of a good hedge. A 1.5m (5ft) hedge will reduce the wind

speed by 50 per cent for plants within 7.5m (23ft) of the hedge (see HEDGES AND SCREENS, pp.84–86).

Tree and shrub species vary widely in their ability to withstand wind. The most tolerant are those with small, thick, spiny, or waxy leaves, such as *Thuja plicata*, *Escallonia*, and hollies (*Ilex*). Of deciduous trees, alders (*Alnus*), rowan (*Sorbus aucuparia*), willows (*Salix*), common elder (*Sambucus nigra*), and hawthorn (*Crataegus monogyna*) are particularly wind hardy. Windbreaks made from canes and netting, or proprietary products, will aid a hedge while it is becoming established.

WINDBREAKS

Double netting
Protect plants with fragile stems from wind by using flexible double netting supported by canes pushed into the soil.

Proprietary windbreaks
Protect plants with proprietary windbreaks fixed to stout stakes.

Woven hurdles
Place woven hurdles at intervals between the plants, setting them at an angle into the prevailing wind, to deflect any strong gusts.

COVERS FOR FROST AND SNOW PROTECTION

Cloche
Use a cloche to protect seedlings, tender herbaceous plants, or young shrubs. Cover the open ends with glass or plastic to stop wind blowing straight through.

Tunnel cloche
Protect low-growing plants such as strawberries with a tunnel cloche stretched over wire hoops. The polythene may be raised at either side for ventilation during the day.

Newspaper
Protect the new growth of potatoes and other tender crops against frost at night by covering them with sheets of newspaper, earthed in on either side to keep them in place.

Horticultural fleece
This lightweight woven fabric warms the soil and gives frost protection while at the same time allowing light and water to pass through to the plants below.

Water conservation and recycling

WATER conservation in the garden begins with choosing the right plants for the soil and climatic conditions. In dry areas, where the need for water conservation is at its greatest, select species that have fleshy or waxy-surfaced leaves and grasses, which are well adapted to withstand drought, as are a great many plants native to Mediterranean climates. The appropriate plants must then be planted in well-prepared soil (see SOILS AND FERTILIZERS, "Soil cultivation", p.618). Improving the soil by incorporating organic matter (see "Soil structure and water content", p.620) and the use of mulches (see "Top-dressings and mulches", p.626) can largely eliminate the need for supplementary watering. It will, however, be necessary to water plants in containers, which are unable to develop extensive root systems and receive little benefit from natural rainfall. They are also much more susceptible to drying out in windy situations. Where extra watering is needed (see "Reducing high water dependency", right), apply it as efficiently as possible, using the following guidelines.

To reduce transpiration, water plants early in the morning or in the evening, and avoid watering in direct sunlight. Water thoroughly when required, ensuring moisture reaches the plant roots. Do not simply wet the soil surface by indiscriminate hosing or by giving a little water at frequent intervals (see SOILS AND FERTILIZERS, "Watering techniques", p.622). Inadequate amounts of water encourage surface rooting, which in the long term makes the plant more vulnerable. When symptoms of

Planting through sheet mulch
Cut a slit in a sheet mulch such as geotextile fabric and plant through the hole. The mulch will reduce evaporation and suppress weeds.

Enhancing water retention in soil
Water absorption can be a problem on poorly structured light or neglected soil (left). Such soils should be improved by the addition of bulky organic matter such as well-rotted farmyard manure or garden compost (right).

water stress first occur, apply no more than 24 litres of water per sq m (4.5 gallons per sq yd); give this every 7–10 days to maintain plant growth if necessary. Avoid the use of a sprinkler, which indiscriminately and wastefully discharges high volumes of water over a wide area.

Collecting water

In many temperate areas, the water collected from rain falling on the roof of an average house could and should be used to supplement water from the mains supply, which should be used as efficiently as possible. As a rough

guide to the amount of water that could be saved from a roof, multiply its surface area by the annual rainfall in the vicinity (all in metres). To convert to litres, multiply the resulting figure by 1,000. For example, with an annual rainfall of 0.6m (2ft), runoff from a garden shed roof measuring 2.5 x 3.5m (8 x 11ft) would be more than 5,000 litres (1,100 gallons). A house roof measuring 17 x 7m (56 x 22ft) would shed nearly 72,000 litres (16,000 gallons).

Rainwater is readily stored by connecting a water butt or tank to a downpipe. If the butt or tank has a lid and is free from algae, the water will remain oxygenated for about 6 months. (Anaerobic water should not be used on plants.) Such water reservoirs should stand on a firm base and, to facilitate filling a watering can from the bottom tap, they should be raised on a plinth of bricks or walling blocks.

As rainfall occurs at irregular intervals, often in heavy bursts, a rainwater butt will frequently overflow. The amount stored can easily be increased by using several butts joined to one another by short pipes inserted into the overflow

Reducing high water dependency

Although some garden features and crops do require supplementary watering, their needs can be reduced in the following ways.

New plantings
- Create a saucer-shaped dip around each plant stem to hold water and avoid runoff.
- Lay trickle, or drip feed, irrigation, which targets water to the roots of each plant (see p.561).
- Ensure that the growing mix of container-grown plants is saturated by immersing the plants in a bucket before planting; this ensures that the air is completely expelled. Water again thoroughly immediately after planting.
- Destroy competitive weeds by hoeing the soil shallowly.

Containers and hanging baskets
- Incorporate water-retaining granules in the growing mix.
- Level the growing mix to within 2.5–5cm (1–2in) of the container rim so there is space for sufficient water to soak the growing mix thoroughly at each watering.

- Place plants in a sheltered spot that is shaded for part of the day. Keep away from drying winds.
- Group containers together rather than placing them individually.

Food crops
- Select crops carefully, especially in dry areas. Several vegetables will fail to develop adequately if short of water at critical periods in their development. Examples are potatoes, which need plenty of water as their tubers are ripening, and tomatoes, courgettes, and runner beans when flowering and fruit is swelling.
- Irrigate with seep or trickle hoses so that supplementary watering is targeted where it is most needed.

Lawns
- Reduce the size of the lawn and create gravel beds or surfaces.
- Select a mixture of lawn grass species that are relatively resistant to drought conditions.
- Raise the mower blade height at which the grass is cut, from eg 1cm (½in) to 2.5cm (1in).
- Apply an appropriate fertilizer

during autumn to encourage drought resistance in the sward.

Patios
- Create partial shade with timber structures, to reduce the considerable glare from the sun on some patio surfaces. The reflection may affect adjacent plants, increasing their moisture loss. Although trees will provide shade, dry zones occur around the roots, and these can nullify the advantage of shade.
- Angle any slope on a patio so water runs off onto the garden and is not lost in adjacent drains.
- Use decking, which allows water to percolate through the gaps, rather than concrete or stone slabs.

Water features
- Convert moving water to still water features. The former inevitably has a higher evaporation rate, particularly when placed in a sunny, exposed position.
- Plant water lilies to minimize evaporation from ponds and similar uncovered surfaces.
- Top up any water loss with stored rainwater rather than mains water.

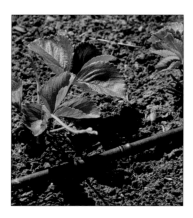

Seep hoses
Hoses with small perforations along their entire length are an excellent way to irrigate strawberries (here) and other plants grown in a row.

Targeted water outlets
Trickle, or drip feed, systems deliver water through individual drippers that are placed permanently near the roots of each plant.

Recycling grey water
Water from showers or baths can be diverted from dedicated downpipes to an adjacent water butt, for immediate distribution and reuse around garden plants. The water butt must be covered with a lid not only for safety but also to prevent the accumulation of debris and algae.

sockets. Larger water tanks are also available. Any recycled ones must be thoroughly cleaned of residues from previously stored fluids.

By adjusting the downpipes from rainwater gutters, water butts can be placed against a wall, which should not be in full sun. If the butt or a series of butts are obtrusive, the rainwater downpipe can be fitted with a small device that diverts the rainwater through a pipe to a more distant receptacle – for example, one sited behind a garden shed or trellis.

Where there is an insufficient slope for the water to run naturally into these storage tanks, a sump pump should be installed in a small butt or receptacle at the base of the downpipe. Very large storage tanks,

Rainwater butt
Collect rainwater off greenhouse, shed, and house roofs by attaching pipes between each gutter and water butt. Always buy as large a butt as you can afford and position it sufficiently high for a watering can to fit conveniently under its tap.

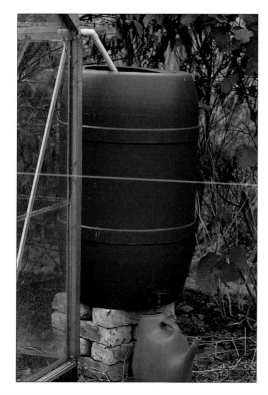

even if they are placed low enough to be gravity-fed from the house, will need a pump to redistribute the water around the garden. Sump pumps that have an on/off, cut-out float on the intake are ideal because they prevent damage to the pump if the tank runs dry and the pump has been left on accidentally. The system can be constructed so the pump drives water through a series of small diameter pipes to the areas of the garden requiring irrigation.

Rainwater diverters fitted on the downpipe or the overflow socket on a rainwater butt can also channel the excess water to a garden pond. Ponds used for this purpose should be free of blanketweed and should preferably contain oxygenating

plants. In a large informal garden, a saucer-shaped, heavily planted pond can be created with a pebbled edging, for a beach-like effect (see WATER GARDENING, "Styles of pond edging", p.291). This will conceal any large variance in water level from summer to winter. As with other water reservoirs, any pond is likely to require an electric submersible pump to redistribute the water to the rest of the garden.

Grey water

Grey water is the term used for domestic waste water other than sewage (which is referred to as black water). As large volumes of water are available from this source – the average bath using 120 litres (26 gallons) – in extreme drought conditions it can be a valuable source of water provided it is not too heavily contaminated with soaps, detergents, fats, or grease. Buckets of grey water can be taken direct from a bath (or sink) to the garden, or the water could be siphoned from the bath to the garden using a garden hose. Siphoning aids are available from good hardware merchants. Pipe diverters used in the same way as rainwater diverters can be fitted to the waste-water drain from the bathroom and fed into a dedicated grey-water butt or reservoir, for use soon after it has cooled.

Some types of domestic waste water are better than others. In order of preference they are shower, bath, bathroom sink, and utility sink, provided bleaches or strong detergents have not been used. Water from dishwashers and washing machines is generally unsuitable for garden use, as it contains too much detergent.

Grey water should never be used on newly propagated or container-grown plants or those grown in a conservatory or greenhouse.

How to use grey water

- Store in a dedicated container and don't mix with other water.
- Use grey water as soon as it has cooled and never keep longer than a few hours. Storing it on summer days can quickly produce a bacterial soup, which can smell unpleasant and breed disease pathogens.
- Apply grey water on soil or compost adjacent to a plant; never water directly on foliage.
- Never use grey water on fruit, vegetables, or herbs or on acid-loving plants as the detergents in the water will be alkaline.
- Never apply grey water with a sprinkler to the lawn or to any area where the water might form puddles, as such water is unhygienic. Insects (such as mosquitos) may breed in the water; children may be attracted to play in the puddles, and animals may drink from them.
- Avoid using grey water with "dripper" or fine nozzle irrigation systems, because these will quickly clog up.
- Try to rotate the types of water applied to the garden and avoid the persistent use of grey water in one particular area. Harmful sodium levels may build up if grey water is overused. This can be detected by a soil test. If the pH level is over 7.5, plant growth may be adversely affected. Over-high levels can be remedied with gypsum; apply at a rate of 1kg per 10 sq m (1lb per 50 sq ft) until the pH level reaches 7 or below.

5
SOILS AND FERTILIZERS

SOILS ARE HIGHLY complex and dynamic materials that are made up of minute particles of weathered rock and organic matter, known as humus, as well as plant and animal life. Healthy soil is essential to successful plant growth: it physically supports plants and supplies them with water, air, and mineral nutrients. If the soil in your garden does not at first appear to be ideal, there are many solutions and most soils can be improved with a little time and effort. For

example, waterlogged soil can be drained and its structure improved, and the water-holding capacity of light soils can be increased by digging in organic matter, such as compost or well-rotted manure. Fertilizers increase nutrients, and lime can be applied to make acidic soils more alkaline, while mulches prevent weed seeds from germinating and reduce water loss from the soil. Finally, nutrients from organic waste can be returned to the soil by making garden compost.

Soil and its structure

Most soil is classified according to its clay, silt, and sand content. The size and proportion of these mineral particles affects the chemical and physical behaviour of the soil. Particles of clay are less than 0.002mm (1/16,000in) in diameter; silt particles are up to 25 times larger than the largest clay particles; and sand particles may be 1,000 times larger – up to 2mm (1/16in) in diameter.

Soil types

Loam soils have the ideal balance of mineral particle sizes, with between 8 and 25 per cent clay, which results in good drainage and water retention, combined with high fertility.

Clay soils are heavy, slow draining, and slow to warm up in spring, but are often highly fertile. They are easily compacted, however, and may bake hard in summer.

Both sandy and silt soils have a low proportion of clay particles, making them much less water-retentive than clay. Sandy soils are particularly light and free-draining and need frequent irrigation and feeding; however, they warm up quickly in spring and are easily improved with organic matter. Silts are more retentive and fertile than sandy soils but tend to compact more easily.

Soil characteristics

Clay soils have more than 25 per cent clay particles and are char-acteristically wet and sticky. Soils containing less than 8 per cent clay are classified as either silt or sandy soil, depending on whether silt or sand particles predominate. Peat is formed where wet, acid conditions prevent full decomposition of organic matter, which therefore remains on or near the soil surface. Chalky soil, however, is alkaline and free-draining, and allows organic matter to decompose rapidly.

Sandy soil
A dry, light, free-draining soil, easy to work but relatively infertile.

Peat
Rich in organic matter, peat is dark and moisture-retentive.

Clay
A heavy, slow-draining soil, usually with a high nutrient value.

Chalk
Pale, shallow, and stony, chalk is free-draining and moderately fertile.

Silt
Silt is reasonably moisture-retentive and fertile but compacts easily.

Organic or peat soils are wet and acidic; they support excellent plant growth, however, if drained, fertilized, and limed.

Chalk or limestone soils are shallow, free-draining, and alkaline, and have moderate fertility.

The profile of the soil

Soils may be divided into three layers, or horizons: topsoil, subsoil, and a layer derived from the parent rock. Topsoil contains most soil organisms and many of the nutrients. It is generally dark, because it contains organic matter that is added artificially or naturally by leaf fall. Subsoil is usually lighter in colour; if it is white, the parent rock is probably chalk or limestone. If there is little or no colour change between topsoil and subsoil, the topsoil may be deficient in organic matter.

Weeds and wild plants help to indicate the type of soil in a garden and any characteristics that it may have, although their presence is only a guide. Birch (*Betula*), heathers (*Calluna, Daboecia, Erica*), foxgloves (*Digitalis*), and gorse (*Ulex europaeus*) are all signs of acid soil, as are many garden plants such as rhododendrons. Beech (*Fagus*) and ash (*Fraxinus*)

SOIL PROFILES

Topsoil contains organic matter and is usually dark

Subsoil is lighter and less fertile than the topsoil

Soil is usually made up of layers of topsoil and subsoil, and a lower layer derived from underlying rock. The depth of each layer can vary.

Identifying your soil

Rub a small amount of moist soil between your fingers. A sandy soil feels quite gritty and will not stick together or form a ball, although a sandy loam is slightly more cohesive. A silt soil feels silky or soapy to the touch. A silty loam may show imprints when pressed with a finger. A loamy clay soil holds together well and may be rolled into a cylindrical shape. Heavy clay soil may be rolled even more thinly, and develops a shiny streak when smoothed. All clay soils feel sticky and slightly heavy.

Sandy soil
Sandy soil feels gritty when rubbed between finger and thumb. The grains do not stick together.

Clay soil
Clay soil feels sticky when wet and may be rolled into a ball that changes shape when pressed.

---

indicate that the soil is likely to be alkaline. Wild plants may also reveal the chemical profile of the soil: nettle and dock, for example, suggest a rich, fertile soil that is high in phosphorus, while clover indicates a soil that is low in nitrogen.

Acidity and alkalinity

Soil pH is a measurement of acidity or alkalinity – the scale ranges from 1–14. A pH below 7 indicates an acid soil, while a pH higher than 7 indicates an alkaline soil. Neutral soil has a pH of 7.

The pH of soil is usually controlled by its calcium level. Calcium is an alkaline element that almost all soils tend to lose through leaching (meaning that it is washed through the soil by water). Soils over chalk or limestone, which are rich in calcium, are more or less unaffected; other soils, especially sands, gradually turn more acidic.

Alkalinity may be increased, if necessary, by liming (see p.625), or introducing lime-rich material such as mushroom compost.

TESTING PH LEVEL

Soil test kits use a chemical solution that changes colour when mixed with soil in a small test tube. The colour is then matched against a chart that indicates the pH level of the soil sample.

A yellow or orange colour indicates acid soil

Bright green indicates neutral soil

Dark green indicates alkaline soil

Electronic pH meters and soil test kits may be used to measure soil pH. Make several tests in different parts of the garden, as the pH often varies, even within a small area; readings are particularly unreliable after the soil has been limed.

The effect of pH

Above all, pH affects the solubility of soil minerals and hence their availability to plants. Acid soils tend to be deficient in phosphorus. Alkaline soils tend to lack manganese, boron, and phosphorus.

Soil pH also affects the number and type of beneficial soil organisms, as well as pests and diseases. For example, worms dislike acid soils, but clubroot, leatherjackets, and wireworms are common in acid conditions. On alkaline soils, potato scab occurs more frequently.

Optimum pH

The pH range for good plant growth is between 5.5 and 7.5. A pH of 6.5 is usually optimum, depending on the plants to be grown. Peaty soils have an optimum pH of 5.8, however. The highest vegetable yields are

---

generally obtained from neutral soils but most ornamentals tolerate a wide pH range. Some are more sensitive; calcicoles (lime lovers) and calcifuges (lime haters) are adapted to extreme pH ranges and their growth suffers if they are planted in soil with the wrong pH level.

Soil organisms

Certain soil organisms are essential to maintain soil fertility. Beneficial bacteria and fungi prefer well-aerated soil and generally tolerate a wide pH, although most fungi prefer acidic soil conditions. Some fungi (mycorrhizae) live in association with plant roots, and improve the take-up of nutrients from the soil.

Small soil animals, such as mites, play a vital part in the breakdown of organic matter. Microscopic worms and nematodes (eelworms) help to control pests – although some are themselves pests.

Larger soil animals, particularly earthworms, improve soil structure when feeding and burrowing; the passage of soil through an earthworm's body binds soil particles into crumbs, increasing aeration and improving drainage.

BENEFICIAL ORGANISMS

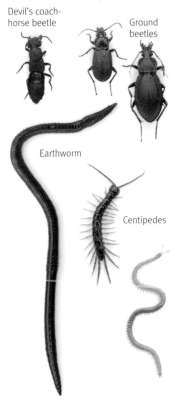

Devil's coach-horse beetle

Ground beetles

Earthworm

Centipedes

Healthy soil contains a teeming community of earthworms and other organisms, which help to aerate the soil and break down organic matter.

Soil cultivation

Correct methods of soil cultivation, including weeding, digging, and adding soil improvers, are vital to successful long-term plant growth.

Weeds compete with cultivated plants for space, light, nutrients, and water – in fact, all the essentials. They may also harbour diseases of many types, which makes their eradication or control vital.

Several digging techniques are used to cultivate the soil in different ways, depending on the condition of the soil and the plants that are to be grown. If the condition of the soil is poor, it may be improved by the addition of organic material, usually at the same time as digging.

Clearing an overgrown garden

Badly neglected, overgrown plots may be cleared using either tools or chemicals: use whichever method is convenient (see also PLANT PROBLEMS, "Controlling weeds", p.669).

Mechanical clearance

Slash as much top-growth as possible using a nylon-line trimmer, brushwood cutter, or scythe, and clear it away from the area. Then, with a rotary mower, cut any remaining growth as low as possible before digging out and removing all the vegetation that is left on the site.

Alternatively, use a rotavator to churn up the soil and chop up the weeds. Make several passes with the rotavator to break up the matted vegetation, then rake it up and remove it from the surface. The chopping action of the tines, however, will cut the roots or rhizomes of

perennial weeds into pieces that regenerate rapidly. After rotavating, therefore, it is essential to rake over the plot and remove by hand all remaining weed fragments. Repeat treatments will be necessary.

Chemical clearance

Following the manufacturer's instructions carefully, spray with a translocated weedkiller, leave it to take effect, and then cut down the top-growth. If necessary, respray any vegetation that escaped the first application of weedkiller.

Remove the dead vegetation or incorporate it into the soil. Most gardeners prefer to prepare the whole site for planting, but trees, shrubs, and other vigorous ornamentals may be planted directly into holes prepared in the dead vegetation.

On sandy soil, many weedkillers are rapidly leached out, so use only weedkillers that break down when in contact with soil. In organic gardens, where it is not desirable to use chemicals, or if the layout of a garden makes it difficult to apply weedkiller evenly, use mechanical or other methods of weed control, such as mulching (see p.626) and organic practices, including the deep-bed system (see p.496).

Weed control

In practically all gardens the soil is full of weed seeds and fragments of perennial weed roots. Weed seeds are brought into the garden from neighbouring land by the wind and in the soil or compost around bought plants. Cultivation, by its very nature, disturbs the soil, and often brings weed seeds to the surface,

CLEARING A SITE OF WEEDS

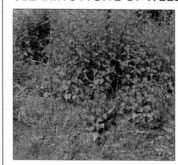

Using weedkiller
A neglected or weed-infested site must be thoroughly cleared before planting takes place. Treat coarse weeds with a chemical weedkiller.

Forking out weeds
Fork up the roots of large weeds and pull them out, holding the main stem close to the soil so that the whole root system is removed.

where they are able to germinate (see "The stale seedbed technique", p.620). Soil cultivation also allows small pieces of perennial weed roots to regenerate and start a new growth cycle over again.

It is virtually impossible to clean a soil completely of weeds, but regular weeding, rather than sporadic attempts that are then followed by periods of neglect, is the best method of control. Although tedious, hand-weeding, using a hand fork, is one of the most effective methods of controlling weeds, since you can ensure that the whole plant is removed from the bed. It also causes the least disturbance to existing plants.

Hoeing

Hoes are used to remove annual weeds and also help to aerate the soil (see also p.552). Unless used carefully, however, they may damage

the surface roots and top-growth of nearby cultivated plants. Hoeing mainly affects the surface soil and seldom goes deep enough to destroy the roots of perennial weeds; dig these out or destroy them with a translocated weedkiller (see PLANT PROBLEMS, "Foliage-acting weedkillers", p.671).

Sterilizing the soil

Some soil pests and diseases, for example honey fungus (*Armillaria*) and nematodes, are so aggressive and persistent that soil sterilization may be the only effective treatment to eliminate them.

Soil sterilants should only be used as a last resort, since they are indiscriminate and kill all organisms, beneficial as well as harmful. This may lead to long-term problems in the garden, because harmful pests

ROTAVATING THE SOIL

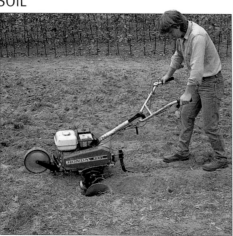

1 *For cultivating large areas of soil, it is worth hiring a motorized rotavator. Adjust the handlebars to a comfortable position and press down on the handlebars so that the tiller blades penetrate the soil to their full depth.*

2 *After rotavating, rake up and remove any pieces of perennial weeds from the surface of the soil, otherwise they will re-establish and grow again.*

SOIL STERILIZATION

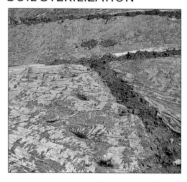

Soil sterilization may be the only method of eradicating some pests or diseases. Cover the sterilized soil with plastic weighted down (any soil used for this should be discarded).

are likely to re-invade and thrive unhindered, since there will be no natural predators to control them.

Chemical soil sterilants are highly poisonous and should be applied only by a trained operator. The sterilant is applied as a drench that percolates and vaporizes through the pores of the soil. The soil surface is then covered with plastic to prevent the gases from escaping. After a soil sterilant has been applied, it will be several weeks before it is safe to plant in the treated soil.

Digging and forking

Cultivating the soil by digging and forking helps to provide suitable conditions for good plant growth by aerating the soil and breaking up any surface crust (cap). Organic matter and fertilizers may be added at the same time, if required. On heavily compacted ground, digging helps to improve soil structure and drainage.

The most common method of cultivation is digging with a spade; single and double digging are in general the most effective and labour-efficient digging methods. Some garden beds, however, may not be suited to such a methodical approach to soil cultivation, especially where there are already many established plants. In these circumstances, forking and simple digging may be useful alternatives.

Disadvantages of digging

Digging increases the rate of breakdown of organic matter, particularly in sandy soils, which in the long term reduces soil fertility. Also, digging heavy, wet soils can cause compaction and make conditions worse. If these soils have a good existing structure, digging can be avoided, particularly for tree and shrub beds.

FORKING

Fork over the soil when it is moist but not waterlogged. Work methodically, inserting the fork then turning it over (see inset) to break up the soil and aerate it.

The "no-dig" and deep-bed techniques, popular with organic gardeners in particular, are cultivation methods that minimize soil disturbance, even in the vegetable garden (see The Bed System, p.496). In most cases, initial deep cultivation of the soil, incorporating organic matter to improve its structure, is necessary before these methods can be successfully adopted.

When to dig

It is preferable to dig in autumn, if possible. The soil is then exposed to winter frosts and snow, which help to break down large clods of soil and improve soil structure, especially on heavy ground.

From mid-winter until early spring, the ground is often wet or frozen and impossible to work. Heavy soil must never be dug when it is wet.

Using a fork

Much digging work involves lifting and turning the soil. Forks, which are shaped to penetrate the soil easily, are excellent for opening up and loosening soil – but not for lifting it. Forking is less harmful to the soil structure than using a spade, because it tends to break the clods along existing, natural, fracture lines rather than along artificially sliced ones.

Forking is suitable for rough digging and for turning the soil but not for creating fine tilths (see "Forming a tilth", p.620). It is also useful for clearing weeds from the soil, particularly perennial weeds such as couch grass (*Elymus repens*), without leaving behind small pieces that will regenerate.

Simple digging

When digging, some gardeners prefer simply to lift out a spadeful of soil, invert it, drop it back in its original position, and chop it up. This method is known as simple digging. It is a quick and relatively easy form of cultivation and is suitable for cleaning the soil surface of any debris and non-persistent weeds, incorporating small amounts of manure and fertilizers, or creating a surface tilth. Simple digging is often the best option when working in irregularly shaped beds or around existing plants.

Single digging

Single digging is the term applied to a methodical and labour-efficient approach to cultivation that ensures an area has been completely dug, to a uniform standard, and to the depth of a spade (known as a "spit").

Mark out with lines the area to be cultivated; then, beginning at one end

SIMPLE DIGGING

Most spades have a blade 25cm (10in) long. This is the depth of trench required when digging one "spit" deep.

1 *Drive the spade into the soil to its full depth, keeping the blade upright. Press down firmly on the blade with the ball of your foot.*

2 *Pull back on the handle and lever soil onto the blade. Bend knees and elbows to lift the spade; do not try to lift too much, especially where the soil is heavy.*

3 *Twist the spade to turn the soil over. This introduces air into the soil and encourages the breakdown of organic matter.*

SINGLE DIGGING

Mark out the bed, then dig a series of trenches, working backwards so that you do not compact the soil. Turn the soil from each trench into the one in front, using soil from the first trench to fill the last.

1 *Dig out a trench 1 spit deep and about 30cm (12in) wide. Insert the spade vertically and lift the soil onto the ground in front.*

2 *Dig a second trench, turning the soil into the trench in front. Invert the soil to bury annual weeds and weed seeds.*

of the plot, dig out trenches to a spade's depth and about 30cm (12in) wide. Place the soil from the first trench in a pile on the ground in front. Work backwards along the plot, turning the soil from each subsequent trench into the one in front.

Adopt this method on regularly shaped plots and in situations where soil uniformity is important – in vegetable gardens and allotments, for example. Single digging is also useful where large quantities of organic matter need to be dug in.

Take the opportunity to incorporate lime (if needed) and fertilizers, such as bonemeal, into the bottom of each trench before replacing the soil. Weeds, especially deep-rooting perennial ones, should be removed as a matter of course.

Double digging

Double or trench digging, in which the soil is worked to a depth of two spits rather than one, should be carried out if the ground has not been previously cultivated or if drainage needs to be improved. Lime and fertilizers should be incorporated, if required, and perennial weeds removed, as in single digging.

On sites where the topsoil is less than two spits deep, standard double digging should be used, since this method ensures that the soil from the upper and lower spits are kept separate. The lower spit containing subsoil should not be brought to the surface – it may be forked or dug over *in situ*, although if more thorough cultivation is required it is also turned.

First mark out the area with lines, as for single digging, then remove the soil from the upper and lower spits of the first trench and from the upper spit of the second, laying it aside on the ground in three separate,

DOUBLE DIGGING

Standard double digging

Dig out trenches 2 spits deep and turn soil from each trench into the ones in front; do not mix soil from the upper and lower spits.

Double digging for deep topsoils

Where the topsoil is at least 2 spits deep, soil from the upper and lower spits may be mixed or transferred. Dig out 2 spits from the first trench, setting the soil aside to fill the final trench, then transfer soil from the upper spit of the second trench to the bottom of the first. Soil from the lower spit of the second trench should be transferred to the top of the first, and so on.

clearly marked, piles. Soil may then be transferred from the lower spit of the second trench to the base of the first trench, and from the upper spit of the third trench to the top of the first. In this way, topsoil and subsoil remain completely separate. Continue digging further trenches in the same way and, at the end of the bed, use soil saved from the first two trenches to fill the appropriate spits of the final two.

If the topsoil is more than two spits deep, there is no need to keep

soil from the upper and lower spits separate, and all the soil from one trench may simply be transferred to the trench in front (see above).

Forming a tilth

A "tilth" is a fine surface soil that is suitable for seed germination. It consists largely of small, even soil particles, and is moisture retentive and level. A surface tilth ensures good contact between seed and soil,

IMPROVING STRUCTURE

To improve soil structure, dig in organic material such as well-rotted manure or compost, according to the needs of the soil.

so that moisture is absorbed easily.

Prepare seedbeds about one month before sowing by digging the soil and then leaving it to weather. Just before sowing, break up any remaining clods of soil with a rake, level the ground by treading gently, and then rake the surface to provide the fine tilth required for seeds.

Soil structure and water content

For plants to grow and flourish over a period of many years, the soil needs to have a good, inherent structure. On medium and heavy soils, in particular, plant growth depends on good soil structure.

In a well-structured soil, the particles form crumbs that exist as part of an interconnecting network of pores, through which water, nutrients, and air circulate. The structure of the soil therefore affects its ability to hold water, the rate at which it drains, and soil fertility. A poorly structured soil may become too freely drained or waterlogged, and nutrients will be lost by leaching.

SURFACE TILTH

A crumbly, even-textured soil with fine particles makes a good tilth for seed germination. It retains water and nutrients, while providing free drainage needed for good growth.

The stale seedbed technique

This method of cultivation involves disturbing the soil by shallow digging to bring weed seeds to the surface. Any existing weeds are removed at the same time. The weed seeds are then allowed to germinate and grow, and the seedlings killed with a contact weedkiller or by shallow hoeing – this time disturbing the soil as little as possible. Seed may then be safely sown in the weed-free ground, as required. Further weed seeds inevitably germinate during the season, but since the main weed flush has been destroyed, subsequent weed control will be relatively simple.

1 *As an experiment, the soil on the right of this plot has been dug over, while the soil on the left has been left undisturbed.*

2 *After a few weeks, weed seeds have germinated on the cultivated ground. The undisturbed soil has relatively few weeds.*

Poorly structured soil

A poorly structured soil tends to be too wet in winter and too dry in summer. Water frequently runs off the surface rather than percolating deep down, yet once the soil is wet it drains slowly. A soil such as this is difficult to work, and in summer it may become hard and concrete-like. As a result, plant roots have great difficulty penetrating the soil and plant growth is adversely affected.

Cultivating heavy soil during wet weather may make it compacted. When soil particles are compressed, the amount of air in the soil is reduced and so drainage is hindered.

Walking on the soil in wet conditions damages the structure of the surface layer – the soil crumbs break down and fine particles at the surface form a crust, which then effectively prevents air and oxygen from reaching the plants' roots and also prevents seeds from germinating. This is known as "capping" and may occur on some soils, particularly silts, following heavy rain or if the soil is watered too heavily.

Improving soil structure

To improve poor structure, cultivate the soil to as great a depth as possible by double digging (without mixing subsoil with topsoil), incorporating organic or inorganic additives to help bind the soil particles into crumbs. This will do much to improve both aeration and water retention. On severely waterlogged sites, a suitable drainage system may need to be installed (see p.623).

Using soil additives

The choice of additives to use is dependent on the type of soil. Most may either be applied to the surface or incorporated into the soil. Organic material such as animal manure and garden compost improves the structure of any type of soil and also provides valuable nutrients. In addition, animal manure encourages earthworms, which will further benefit soil structure (see "Soil organisms", p.617).

A light, sandy soil may be improved with small amounts of clay (a process known as marling), but enormous quantities of grit or sand would be needed to lighten a very heavy soil.

On compacted soil and clay soil, add manure, compost, and/or lime (but not for acid-loving plants) to improve its structure by encouraging crumb formation.

On silt, add small amounts of clay to improve soil structure, and use manure and compost to encourage crumb formation.

The amount of additive required depends on the soil condition, but a good rule of thumb is to apply about a 5–10cm (2–4in) layer of bulky additives. Some materials, particularly inorganic compounds and water-retaining gels, should be added in much smaller quantities, so it is important to follow the manufacturer's instructions.

Subsidiary benefits of soil additives

Additives also maintain a good balance of air and water in soil. Sand, gravel, and coarse organic matter may be used to improve drainage in silty, compacted, and heavy clay soils. Sand or gravel should be used along channels in the soil, keeping a path open for water, rather than being worked in. Some additives, such as peat substitute, peat, well-rotted manure, and water-holding gels (which hold many times their weight in water) act as "sponges" and may be used to improve water retention in free-draining, sandy soil. On compacted soil, water-holding gels are useful for improving water retention without reducing aeration.

Additions of clay will improve the fertility of impoverished soil. Clay, peat substitutes (or peat), and, to some extent, bark help to retain nutrients that might otherwise be lost by leaching.

Problems with additives

Some additives should not be used in certain soil conditions. Fine sand, for example, added in small amounts to heavy soil may make poor drainage worse by blocking the soil pores. Use a more open material, such as gravel or coarse sand, instead.

Fresh manure gives off ammonia and sometimes other substances that may be toxic to plants. If it is not possible to compost the manure or mature it until it is well rotted, apply it to the soil surface in the autumn and leave the soil uncultivated over winter. The manure will gradually rot down and be incorporated into the soil by earthworms.

Fresh straw, leaves, and bark use up nitrogen during their decomposition process, contributing to a possible nitrogen deficiency in the soil unless some additional nitrogen fertilizer is applied to the soil at the same time.

For garden compost (see p.627), never use plant remains that are infected with viruses or any material that contains perennial weeds – both are difficult to control or eradicate. This material should be burned.

SOIL ADDITIVES

Adding composts, well-rotted manure, or peat substitutes such as coconut fibre improves the soil structure and helps to hold moisture in the soil. Mushroom compost is alkaline in nature and therefore should not be used with plants requiring acid conditions. Lime binds clay soil particles together into crumbs by a process known as flocculation.

Mushroom compost   Manure
Lime   Coconut fibre

COMPARING SOILS

Good soil
A well-structured soil has a crumbly, moist texture, with a network of pores that holds both air and water. The soil crumbs bind together but do not form a hard "cap".

Poor soil
This topsoil is hard and compacted, making it almost impossible to cultivate. Drainage will be poor. Cracks appear where the soil has dried out.

SOIL PROBLEMS

Compaction
In compacted soil, the pores between the soil particles have been badly compressed. This results in slow drainage and poor aeration.

Blue mottling
Blue mottling on the soil surface indicates stagnant, waterlogged soil that needs to be drained. The soil may also have an unpleasant smell.

Hardpan
This is an almost impermeable layer of severely compacted soil. Water will not drain through until the hardpan is broken up and drains are installed.

Capping
A crust or "cap" forms on the soil when soil crumbs on the surface are damaged by heavy rain or watering, or by walking on the soil when it is wet.

Water

Adequate water is crucial for good plant growth; the amount available depends to some extent on the plant itself but also on soil type and structure, and the method of watering. Water is often in short supply and should not be wasted, so it is important to use good watering and water-conserving techniques. It is also useful to know which plants are susceptible to drought (and when) and which are drought resistant.

An excess of water in the soil (waterlogging) can be as damaging to plants as a lack of soil water. Cultivating the soil and adding organic matter and grit will do much to improve drainage in saturated soil but on severely waterlogged sites an effective drainage system should be installed.

Soil water

In a well-structured soil, water is held in fine capillary pores, which are usually less than 0.1mm ($\frac{1}{160}$in) in diameter, with air in the larger pores; it is therefore possible for soil to be described as "both moist and well drained".

Water is most readily available to plants from pores of the largest diameter. As the pores become smaller, it becomes increasingly difficult for the plants to extract moisture, which means that some soil water always remains unavailable.

Clay soils

Clay soils hold the greatest amount of water but they have a high percentage of fine capillary pores, so plants are not always able to extract enough water for their needs.

HOW NOT TO WATER

Do not water plants at a rate that causes puddling on the soil surface, since this leads to run-off and erodes the soil.

METHODS OF WATERING

Basin watering
Scoop out soil from around the base of the plant, and fill the resulting basin with water.

Pot watering
Bury a large pot that has a drainage hole close to the plant and fill the pot slowly with water.

Sandy soils

Sandy soils contain coarse pores; the water held within them is more readily available than in clay. Sandy soils, however, drain quickly, and there is relatively little capillary movement of water sideways and upwards.

Loams

Loams usually contain a balanced mix of coarse and relatively fine pores – the coarse pores allow rapid drainage while the finer ones retain water, much of which may be extracted by plants in dry conditions.

The water table

Moisture rises towards the soil surface by capillary action from the water table below. Heavy clay soils may be saturated to 2m (6ft) above the water table, with some moisture available to plant roots as much as 3.5m (11ft) above it. Silt and most clay soils are saturated to 1.5m (5ft), with moisture available to roots 2.5m (8ft) above the water table. The figures for fine sand are 1.5m (5ft) and 2.4m (7½ft) respectively, and for coarser sand 30cm (1ft) and 1m (3ft). On gravel, there is no water rise at all. In many gardens the water table is too low to have any influence.

Watering techniques

The aim of watering is to recharge the soil so that reserves will be sufficient to last until the next watering or rainfall. Always water thoroughly so that water is available deep in the soil. Frequently applying a little water is of limited value, because much of it simply evaporates off the soil surface before it has a chance to penetrate down to the roots of plants.

Moisture take-up

The water supply to a plant is limited by the size of its root system. When planted in soil where the drainage has been improved (see p.623) and any compaction rectified by double digging (see p.620), plants are able to develop deeper root systems, with a comparative increase in growth.

Yet the main limitation when watering is the rate at which the soil takes up moisture. On average, soil absorbs about 8mm (⅜in) depth of water per hour. Water applied to the soil faster than it is absorbed (for example, by a hand-held hose or watering can with a rose) collects in a pool on the surface until the area covered is sufficient to take it all in. After watering in dry conditions, it is worth testing the soil with an auger – it may be surprising just how little the water has penetrated. If the soil around the plant roots is still dry, give the area several further applications once the water from the first application has soaked in.

To reduce run-off, the ground may be modified by terracing or "dishing" to create a hollow trough around each plant (see above), which ensures that water reaches the roots. Pot watering (see above), sprinklers (see p.561), and trickle or drip feed systems (see p.561) are efficient methods of watering, since water is supplied to the roots over several hours.

Water-conserving techniques

Mulching the surface of the soil (see p.626) improves rain penetration and minimizes evaporation. By controlling weeds effectively (see p.618), you will ensure that no soil water is wasted on unwanted plants. See also WATER CONSERVATION AND RECYCLING, p.614.

Water deficiency

Once a plant begins to wilt, its growth rate has already begun to slow down. In many areas, water use will exceed water supply during summer, so the soil suffers a net loss of moisture. Digging additives such as manure into the soil improves structure (see p.621) and water retention, which helps to prevent a water deficit from occurring, but unless an existing deficit is made up by irrigation, the soil becomes progressively drier. Regular watering is therefore essential.

The local meteorological office will have figures for the typical monthly water loss from the soil and through leaves by transpiration (known as potential evapotranspiration), and also for the average monthly rainfall. These figures are useful when calculating how often to water but, for greater accuracy, it is better to take your own rainfall measurements each month rather than using the average figures.

Seasonal and establishment needs

The point at which a water deficit begins to affect plant growth depends on the plants themselves. High-yield plants usually need plenty of water, so the soil should be kept moist. Some plants have critical periods of growth, during which time water supplies are vital: the first half of summer, for example, is much more important than the second for young ornamental trees. Fruit trees need ample water as the fruits swell, as do potato tubers.

Watering is especially important for newly planted or transplanted plants, and those in shallow soils and in containers. Seedlings, too, have low drought resistance, and a reliable water supply is essential. Standard trees are likely to require watering throughout their first season, since their top-growth is frequently out of proportion to their roots.

Drought conditions

Even well-established garden plants suffer during prolonged drought, although no perceptible damage may be seen for some time. Moderate drought may, however, improve the flavour of some fruits and vegetables, especially tomatoes.

In areas of low rainfall, there is increasing interest in using plants that are adapted to droughts (xerophytes): lavenders (*Lavandula*), and *Phlomis*, as well as many grey- and silver-leaved plants, are good examples.

Grass tolerates prolonged, dry weather well. Lawns may become brown, but they quickly recover once rain falls. Watering in summer is not essential, therefore, unless you want to keep your lawn looking green.

Waterlogged soil

Waterlogging occurs when the water entering the soil exceeds the amount draining out. Particularly vulnerable are areas where the water table is high (see p.622) or where the soil is compacted and poorly structured.

Roots (except those of bog plants) are unable to function effectively in waterlogged soil and may eventually die if drainage is not improved. Wet soil is often low in certain nutrients (notably nitrogen) and, as a result, mineral deficiencies may prove a problem. Since wet soil tends to be cold, plant growth may be slow in spring. Diseases such as clubroot (see p.649) also flourish in waterlogged soil. Rushes, sedges, and mosses

growing on the ground suggest that the soil may be waterlogged, and a sharp division between peaty topsoil and subsoil also indicates poor drainage. On waterlogged clay, the soil may have a stagnant smell and a yellow or blue-grey colour, which is known as gleying.

Poor drainage may be confirmed by pouring water into a hole 30–60cm (12–24in) deep. If the water remains for hours or even days, then the soil needs draining. If digging deeper or trying to push a metal rod into the soil meets with resistance, this indicates that there is a layer of hardpan (see *Soil Problems*, p.621).

Improving drainage

Where waterlogging is not severe and there is excess surface water only, this may be diverted from the site by shaping garden surfaces so that the water flows into drainage ditches. To improve drainage where there is a high water table, install

an underground drainage system, preferably using a specialist contractor to carry out the work. If drains already exist, check for blockages in the drainage ditches, or for damaged pipes. Underground drains will not help if there are drainage barriers, such as a hard pan, above them.

Ditches and French drains

A system of open ditches is the best method of carrying away any excess water from the surface. These should be 1–1.2m (3–4ft) deep, with sloping sides. Just as effective but less obtrusive are French drains, which are gravel-filled drainage ditches topped with upturned turf and topsoil.

Drainage systems and soakaways

A soakaway is a rubble-filled pit into which excess water runs via underground drains or drainage ditches (see below). This method of drainage is effective on sites where there is surface compaction, since it breaks

through any layer of hardpan. To construct a soakaway, dig a hole approximately 1m (3ft) wide and at least 2m (6ft) deep. Fill it with broken bricks or stones completely surrounded by geotextile fabric. Install perforated plastic pipes or tile drains at least 60cm (24in) below ground level (see below) to lead from the surrounding land to the soakaway.

Water storage areas

Alternatively, create a water storage area where water collects in a pond or large container, or gradually soaks away. A pond is beneficial to wildlife, but its success depends on the degree of sediment in the drainage water – too much will make the pond rich in nutrients, therefore becoming prone to silting up and excessive algal growth.

Water collected in containers may be recycled for use in the garden. Collecting water that is allowed gradually to soak away helps to replenish groundwater reserves and reduces silt pollution of rivers.

HOW TO BUILD A SOAKAWAY

Turf

Topsoil

Geotextile fabric liner prevents silt blocking the gaps between the rubble

Broken bricks or stones

Hardpan

2m (6ft)

1m (3ft)

1 *In a waterlogged part of the garden, dig a hole 2m (6ft) deep with 1 x 1m (3 x 3ft) sides. Line the sides and bottom with a geotextile fabric. Then fill the lined soakaway hole with rubble, such as broken bricks or stones, to a depth of 1m (3ft).*

Topsoil

Flexible, corrugated plastic drainage pipe slopes towards soakaway

Geotextile fabric liner ensures free flow of water

Soakaway filled with broken bricks or stones

minimum 60cm (2ft) below ground level

2 *Fold the liner over the rubble. Then place the end of a perforated plastic pipe on top of the liner, so that it is ideally 60cm (2ft) below ground level. Fill in the hole with topsoil, and turf the top.*

Installing drains

A system of perforated corrugated plastic pipes laid in a herringbone pattern underground provides an effective method of drainage into a rubble-filled ditch or soakaway. Lay the pipes well below ground level, so they do not interfere with future cultivations. Water from the surrounding site can seep into the pipes, which must be angled so they carry

the water to the soakaway. Compared with tile drains (see below), plastic pipes are flexible, easily cut, and absorb the natural movements within the soil. To join two pipes, cut a hole in one pipe to match the diameter of the other pipe; then push it in. Install drains before plants are in place, if possible, as the work causes great upheaval.

A TILE DRAINAGE SYSTEM

In an old-fashioned tile drain system, the rigid pipes are covered by large- and small-gauge gravels and inverted turves to prevent them becoming blocked by soil particles.

High ground

Arrows show the direction of water flow

Two grades of gravel, under upturned turves, surround tile drain

Trenches for tile drains, about 60cm (24in) deep

Gravel-filled drainage ditch or soakaway

Lowest level

Soil nutrients and fertilizers

The nutrients utilized by plants are composed of mineral ions, absorbed in solution from the soil through the roots and used with carbon dioxide and water to make food. Macronutrients, required in relatively large amounts, include nitrogen (N), phosphorus (P), potassium (K), magnesium (Mg), calcium (Ca), and sulphur (S). Micronutrients, or trace elements, are equally important but required only in small amounts; they include iron (Fe), manganese (Mn), copper (Cu), zinc (Zn), boron (Bo), molybdenum (Mb), and chlorine (Cl).

To ensure healthy plant growth, fertilizers containing nutrients may be added to the soil, but this is only necessary if the soil is unable to provide the nutrients required. On most soils, only nitrogen, which promotes vigorous growth, phosphorus (phosphates), for assisting strong root growth, and potassium (potash), which improves flowering and fruiting, need adding regularly. Nitrogen deficiency (see p.650) causes reduced growth, while potassium deficiency (see p.650) causes leaf discoloration. Phosphate deficiency (see p.650) is less common but is most likely to occur in young plants with poor root systems. Manganese/iron deficiency (see p.651) causes browning of leaves, and may be a problem if acid-loving plants are grown in alkaline soil or watered with hard water.

Types of fertilizer

Deciding the amount and which type of fertilizer to apply can be complex. Understanding how each type works will make gardening more productive and perhaps more environmentally friendly. Note that in this context, the term "organic" may simply mean "of living origin", while "inorganic" refers to artificial,

chemical formulations. Gardeners practising organic growing, in the environmentally conscious sense, should carefully check the labelling and provenance of any fertilizer to ensure that it meets their concerns.

Bulky organic fertilizers

Weight for weight, bulky organic fertilizers supply fewer nutrients than inorganic fertilizers. One tonne/ton of manure typically contains 6kg (13.2lb) of nitrogen, 1kg (2.2lb) of phosphorus and 4kg (8.8lb) of potassium; the equivalent amount of nutrients in a chemical form is provided by 30kg (66lb) of inorganic fertilizer.

Manures are, however, integral to organic growing because the organic matter that makes them so bulky provides greater benefits than a simple nutrient analysis suggests. Manures have high levels of micronutrients, and are a long-term source of nitrogen. They also provide conditions in which worms thrive. Adding manure improves the structure and water content of most soils (see p.620); and since this encourages root growth, it increases plant uptake of nutrients.

Concentrated organic fertilizers

Traditional concentrated organic fertilizers include dried blood, fish and bone meals, and hoof and horn. Seaweed meal and pelleted chicken manure are popular with gardeners using organic methods. Compared with bulky organic materials, they are easy to handle and contain fairly consistent proportions of nutrients but are relatively expensive for each unit of nutrient. Their characteristic slow release of nutrients is partly dependent on breakdown by soil organisms, so they may not be effective when these organisms are inactive, as in cold weather.

Despite some concerns, there are no documented health risks from

processed animal-protein fertilizers, such as bone meal, manufactured for domestic gardens; indeed some argue they are an environmentally sound way of using waste. However, wearing gloves and a dust mask when applying such products, and hand-washing produce (or indeed substituting garden compost where edible crops are being grown) will provide peace of mind. If you prefer not to use animal-derived products at all, seaweed meal is often a perfectly adequate source of plant nutrition.

Soluble inorganic fertilizers

Concentrated inorganic fertilizers contain high percentages of a given nutrient, weight for weight, and most are easy to transport, handle, and apply, although a few are unpleasant

to handle; wearing gloves and a dust-excluding mask is always advisable. They are usually the cheapest source per unit of nutrient. They give a quick-acting boost to plants deficient in nutrients, and permit precise control over the timing of nutrient release. However, a large proportion of soluble fertilizer may be wasted on sandy soils because of leaching.

When using soluble inorganic fertilizers, be selective about which mineral ions are applied to the soil, since some may damage particular plants. Redcurrants, for example, are sensitive to chloride salts such as potassium chloride; sulphates should be used instead. Large applications of some inorganic salts make the soil more saline and may harm beneficial soil organisms. Apply soluble

NUTRIENT CONTENT OF FERTILIZERS

	% Nitrogen (N)	% Phosphate (P_2O_5)	% Potash (K_2O)
Organic			
Animal manure	0.6	0.1	0.5
Blood, fish, and bone			
Bone meal	3.5	20	–
Cocoa shells	3	1	3.2
Garden compost	0.5	0.3	0.8
Hoof and horn	13	–	–
Mushroom compost	0.7	0.3	0.3
Pelleted chicken manure	4	2	1
Rock phosphate	–	26	12
Seaweed meal	2.8	0.2	2.5
Wood ash	0.1	0.3	1
Inorganic			
Ammonium sulphate	21	–	–
Growmore	7	7	7
Potassium sulphate	–	–	49
Single superphosphate	–	18	–
Slow-release fertilizer	14	13	13

COMPARING FERTILIZERS

Garden compost

Mushroom compost

Cocoa shells

Blood, fish, and bone

Soluble inorganic fertilizer

These comparisons show the relative amounts of different types of fertilizer required to supply roughly the same quantity of nutrients.

SLOW-RELEASE FERTILIZERS

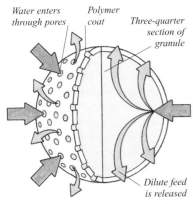

Water enters through pores · Polymer coat · Three-quarter section of granule · Dilute feed is released

Water enters the fertilizer granules through pores in the polymer coat, which builds up pressure inside, splitting the granules open.

inorganic fertilizers in split applications, sparingly but fairly frequently, rather than in a single, large dose.

Slow-release fertilizers

These are complex fertilizer formulations that are designed to release nutrients gradually, over many months or even years in some cases. Some slowly degrade in the soil, while others absorb water until they swell and burst open. Many have membranes of varying thickness that gradually release nutrients from an internal store. These fertilizers are expensive and are not generally economical to use in the wider garden, but they are especially valuable in the care of container plants (see p.323).

Green manures

These are plants grown purely to be dug back into the soil to improve fertility and add to the organic content. They are used on land that would otherwise be left fallow and can help to prevent nutrients from being washed away, since fallow land is more prone to leaching. Do not use invasive plants as green manures.

Making comfrey fertilizers

Comfrey (*Symphytum*) is a coarse, invasive herb, but it is an extremely useful green manure, especially *S.* x *uplandicum* 'Bocking 14'. The foliage is also an excellent base for organic liquid feed and leaf mould.

Comfrey liquid feed contains good levels of nitrogen and phosphates, and high levels of potassium. A typical recipe is to steep (soak) 3kg (7lb) of cut leaves in 45 litres (10 gallons) of water in a covered container for 4–5 weeks. Strain off the pungent liquid and use undiluted as a liquid feed.

For high-nutrient leaf mould, fill a plastic container, or dustbin, with a mixture of chopped comfrey leaves and damp, two-year-old leaf mould in alternating layers, 10cm (4in) thick. As the comfrey decomposes, its nutrients are absorbed by the leaf mould. After 3–5 months, the enriched leaf mould is ready for use in potting mixtures, as a mulch, or as a soil conditioner.

Borage (*Borago officinalis*), ryegrass (*Lolium perenne*), and comfrey (*Symphytum officinale*) are excellent perennial green manures. Mixtures of fast-germinating annuals can also be used. Legumes such as annual lupins have nitrogen-fixing bacteria in root nodules, which enable them to obtain nitrogen from air in the soil. The organic matter these plants provide may contribute as much nitrogen to the soil as would be added in a standard fertilizing regime; it has a low carbon to nitrogen ratio and so breaks down rapidly, providing easily available nitrogen.

Applying fertilizers

Concentrated fertilizers may be scattered over the surface of the soil or placed around individual plants. Some fertilizers are also available in liquid form for application to the soil surface or as foliar feeds directly onto leaves. All products, organic or inorganic, should be handled with care. Always wear protective clothing where advised. Do not apply on windy days and spread granular or powdered products carefully on the soil – never touching plant stems. Use only the recommended quantities; too much can damage plants.

Broadcast fertilization

Scattering fertilizer over the whole soil surface benefits the greatest area of soil and minimizes the risk of plant injury from overfeeding. In dry weather, uptake of some nutrients, particularly immobile nutrients like phosphates, may be poor; whenever possible, dig phosphates into the soil.

Fertilizer placement

Fertilizing around the base of a plant is an economical and efficient feeding method, as plant roots quickly spread through the fertilized area.

Liquid fertilizers

An efficient way to apply nutrients, especially if soil is dry, is to dissolve fertilizer in water before application. Do not use liquid feeds when rain is forecast, as they may be washed away. Liquid fertilizers sprayed onto leaf surfaces (foliar feeds) can help correct mineral deficiencies caused by some soil conditions, such as high pH. For deep-rooted plants, like fruit trees, foliar feeds may also be used to correct deficiencies in nutrients that are relatively insoluble.

Liming

Liming or adding lime-rich material like mushroom compost increases soil alkalinity. This may be necessary to improve yields on vegetable plots but rarely worthwhile for ornamental plants – it is better to choose plants adapted to the existing conditions.

Ordinary lime (calcium carbonate) is bulky but easy to handle and safe to use. Quicklime (calcium oxide) is more efficient at raising pH but is caustic and may scorch plants; there is also a risk of over-liming. Slaked or hydrated lime (calcium hydroxide), made by treating quicklime with water, is slightly less efficient than quicklime, but less caustic.

Applying lime

Lime may be spread on the soil at any time, but apply as far in advance of planting as possible, and ideally dig in thoroughly. Choose a still day and wear goggles. Do not lime every year – overliming contributes to nutrient deficiencies – and take pH readings in different parts of the plot first, as uneven rates of breakdown cause temporary localized problems. The table below shows average amounts of lime required for soils to achieve pH 6.5 (see also "Optimum pH", p.617). To raise soil pH quickly, add lime during digging. For established plantings, apply it as a top-dressing and water in. Do not apply lime at the same time as manure; they will react and release nitrogen in the form of ammonia. This may damage plants and wastes nitrogen; apply lime and manure in alternate years.

Starting pH	Sand (g/sq m)	Loam (g/sq m)	Clay (g/sq m)
4.5	190g	285g	400g
5.0	155g	235g	330g
5.5	130g	190g	260g
6.0	118g	155g	215g

GREEN MANURING

Sow seed for green manures on fallow ground. Cut the plants to the ground when about 20cm (8in) tall, digging them in after a day or two.

HOW TO APPLY FERTILIZER

Broadcasting
To apply fertilizer in accurate amounts over large areas, mark out the plot into square metres or yards, using string or canes. Fill a pot or bowl with the recommended quantity of fertilizer and sprinkle it evenly over each section of the plot.

Placement
Sprinkle the fertilizer around the base of the plant, making sure that none touches the leaves or stem.

Top-dressings and mulches

Top-dressings and mulches are materials that are applied to the surface of the soil. They are used to improve plant growth in some way, either by adding nutrients to the soil, by increasing the organic content, or by reducing water loss from the soil. Alternatively they may be used in a decorative manner.

Top-dressings

The term "top-dressing" is used in two ways. First, it describes surface applications of soluble fertilizers around plants. Second, it refers to additives that are applied to the soil surface or to lawns. For example, a lawn may be top-dressed with sand or fine organic material, which will eventually be washed in by rain.

Gravel or grit is sometimes used as a top-dressing for plants in beds and containers to provide quick drainage away from the "collars" of plants that are sensitive to excess moisture. They also act as a mulch and discourage growth of mosses or lichens on the soil surface.

Plants may also be top-dressed with gravel or stone chippings simply to achieve a decorative effect.

Mulches

Mulches are available in organic and inorganic forms and improve plant growth in several ways: they regulate soil temperature, keeping plant roots

MATERIALS USED AS TOP-DRESSINGS

Top-dressings as additives
Some top-dressings, such as well-rotted manures and compost, are added to the soil around plants to provide humus and a steady supply of nutrients. Sand, mixed with loam and peat or coir, is used as a top-dressing on lawns to improve aeration.

Sand

Decorative top-dressings
Materials such as gravel and grit are added to the compost surface in containers or to the soil surface in a border or bed, particularly around low-growing plants such as alpines. These materials improve surface drainage as well as setting off the plants.

Gravel

Compost

Leaf mould

Coarse grit

Cornish grit

warm in winter and cool in summer; they reduce water loss from the soil surface; and they help to stop weed seeds germinating by preventing light from reaching them.

Always remove all perennial weeds before mulching, otherwise they benefit from the effects of the mulch, to the detriment of your plants. A mulch should not be applied when the soil is cold or frozen, since the insulation effect will be counter-productive, and the soil remain cold – instead, wait until the soil has warmed up in spring.

Organic mulches

To be effective, an organic mulch should be long-lasting and not easily dislodged by rain. It should also have a loose structure that allows water to pass through it quickly.

Coarse bark is one of the most useful organic mulches because it inhibits weed seeds in the soil from germinating, and weeds that do appear are easily removed. Garden compost, leaf mould, and peat substitutes such as coir are not quite as effective because they provide an ideal medium for the germination of weed seeds and are quickly mixed into the soil, although they do improve the soil's texture as a result.

Inorganic mulches

Inorganic mulches made of bio-degradable horticultural paper or thin sheets of woven or bonded, water-permeable fabrics (known variously as sheet mulches, landscape fabric, or geotextile) are widely available and simple to lay and secure

with metal pegs. They are easy to plant through, and provide good weed suppression while allowing water to penetrate to plant roots.

A disadvantage of sheet mulches is that, once they are in place, organic matter cannot be incorporated into the soil. However, because they form such a barrier, they are useful laid beneath a layer of loose mulch to extend its life.

Mulches made from impermeable plastic sheet are particularly useful when laid temporarily to warm soil before sowing early crops, or longer-term for perennial weed suppression. However, once in place, almost no water evaporates from the soil; do not, therefore, lay plastic sheet mulches over waterlogged soil.

"Floating" mulches are sheets of light perforated plastic or fibre fleece used like cloches – as the crop grows, the floating mulch is raised by the plants. Their main purpose is to increase temperature; they may also act as a barrier against pests.

LOOSE MULCHES

Applying the mulch
A loose mulch regulates soil temperature, retains moisture, and discourages weeds. It should preferably be about 10–15cm (4–6in) deep.

Area to mulch
For small to medium-sized plants, spread a mulch to the full extent of the foliage canopy.

ANCHORING PLASTIC SHEETING

A plastic sheet mulch controls weeds effectively over a large area and raises soil temperature slightly. Using a spade, anchor the sheet by sinking the edges into 5cm (2in) slits dug into the soil.

Composts and leaf mould

There are two distinct forms of compost: garden compost is decayed organic matter and is a soil additive; potting and propagation composts are made from precise combinations of (mainly) organic materials, and are used for growing plants in containers (see CONTAINER GARDENING, "Composts for containers", p.322) and for propagation (see PRINCIPLES OF PROPAGATION, "Requirements for germination", p.630).

Garden compost

The contribution of garden compost to the productivity of the garden can be enormous. As well as supplying nutrients directly, the high levels of humus it contains increase the soil's nutrient-holding capacity and help improve soil drainage and aeration. It also contributes a healthy population of beneficial soil micro-organisms. It should be added to the soil when the rate of breakdown of the organic matter has levelled off; by this stage, it should be dark, crumbly, and smell sweet and earthy.

Making garden compost

To make a compost heap, build up a mixture of nitrogen-rich material (such as grass clippings) and carbon-rich material (such as bark and scrunched up newspaper), preferably in a ratio of 1:2. Almost any vegetable matter, including seaweed, may be composted, but protein and cooked vegetable waste should not be used, as these attract vermin.

Do not put grass clippings on the heap for the first few mowings after the application of a weedkiller, and never add thick layers of grass clippings, as they inhibit air movement. In fact no vegetation that has been treated with herbicide should be used, as the chemicals may persist, making the compost unsuitable for food crops; it may also damage plants mulched with contaminated compost. There is a health risk, too, especially to children, if cat or dog waste is included, which may contain eggs of the *Toxocara* parasite.

Pruning clippings may be added to a compost heap, although any woody stems should be shredded first. Avoid composting any material that is diseased or infested with pests, as they may survive life in the heap and be spread around the garden in the finished compost. Use only young weeds; those with seed, or about to set seed, should be put in a dustbin, as should all pernicious, perennial weeds. It is especially important to avoid those with creeping root systems, such as couch grass (*Elymus repens*) and ground elder (*Aegopodium podagraria*).

Compost additives

Many materials will compost satisfactorily, but additional nitrogen will speed up the process. The nitrogen may be provided as an artificial fertilizer, proprietary, high-quality, nutrient-rich, starter compost, or as manure, which has the advantage of containing high levels of beneficial micro-organisms. Add this to the compost heap as required, so that there are alternate layers of organic material and manure.

If the material in the compost heap is too acidic, micro-organisms will not work efficiently – adding lime will make it more alkaline.

The composting process

The process by which organic matter is broken down in a compost heap relies on the activity of a number of beneficial, aerobic bacteria and micro-fungi. To proliferate and work efficiently, these micro-organisms need air, nitrogen, moisture, and some warmth.

To ensure adequate airflow, first make the base of the compost heap from a thick, open layer of twiggy material. To maintain good aeration, it is essential that compost materials are never allowed to become either compacted or too wet. Mix fine- and coarse-textured matter when building the heap, if necessary putting fine

MAKING A COMPOST BIN

1 *To make the first side, lay 2 timber battens (to act as the uprights) on the ground at least 1m (3ft) apart. Nail planks across them, butting the joints together. Leave an 8cm (3in) gap at top and bottom.*

2 *Make the second side; nail scraps of wood across the top to hold the sides in place temporarily. Nail on the back planks.*

3 *Nail 2 battens inside each upright (inset) for the front planks to slide between. Fix a piece of wood at the base as a "stop".*

4 *Nail planks across the top and bottom of the front panel, to stabilize the bin when the front planks are removed.*

5 *Check that the front planks slide easily between the battens. If necessary, saw a little off the ends.*

Using the bin
Place a thick layer of twiggy material at the base; build up the heap in 15cm (6in) layers, sprinkling each layer with a little manure.

Manure

Garden and kitchen waste

Twin compost bin system
Fill the first bin (left) with alternating layers of organic matter. When it is full, turn the contents into the second bin (right) to continue rotting, and start refilling the first bin. Keep both bins well covered at all times.

What not to compost

Recycling kitchen and garden waste in the compost heap can provide gardeners with an excellent source of humus to improve soil structure and to mulch beds and borders.

However, take care to leave out waste materials that may not break down and decay or are otherwise unsuitable – tins, glass, plastics, synthetic fibres, and coke or coal ash (wood ash may be added, as it is a good source of potash).

Additionally, it is often considered better to avoid composting leaves infected by blackspot, mildew and other diseases, such as clubroot and rusts, as well as material that may be infected with honey fungus, eelworms, or the overwintering eggs or pupae of harmful insects. The heat produced in the composting process may, in many instances, kill disease spores, but generally it is safer to burn suspect material rather than risk re-infection when the compost is used.

Organic materials that should not be added to the compost heap are:

- Dairy products, oil, fat, fish and meat waste, which attract rats.
- Used cat litter, dog faeces, or disposable nappies as there may be health implications.
- Laminated cardboard cartons, such as milk and juice cartons, which may contain plastic.
- Glossy magazines, or very densely packed paper, like telephone directories, which rot too slowly.

Cardboard and crumpled-up newspaper, however, are suitable for inclusion in the compost heap, particularly for mixing with quick-rotting vegetable matter.

materials to one side until there is an opportunity to mix it with coarser grades. Turn the compost regularly to avoid compaction and speed up the composting process.

During composting the heap should be damp, but not wet, so water it in dry weather, if necessary. Cover with sacking, plastic sheeting, or carpet.

The process of bacterial decomposition itself generates a high temperature, which speeds the natural breakdown of organic matter and also helps to kill weed seeds and some pests and diseases. To heat up sufficiently, a compost heap should be at least 1 cubic metre (1 cubic yard) in size but 2 cubic metres (2 cubic yards) is preferable. Compost reaches its maximum temperature in two or three weeks and matures in about 3–12 months.

An ammonia odour indicates that the compost is too rich in nitrogen; add in more carbon-rich material, such as cardboard egg boxes or kitchen paper rolls. A smell of rotten eggs means that the heap lacks air; turn the heap and incorporate coarse, bulky materials.

Slow composting

Composting may be undertaken in a non-intensive way. Heaps of pruning clippings, for example, eventually rot down, even if they are not in a bin. No starter material is added, and the heap is not turned. There will, however, be some material that does not break down fully – this will need to be composted again.

Municipal composting

A number of local authorities operate community recycling centres that produce garden compost from "green" waste. This is derived from municipal parks and gardens and from separated domestic collection by their waste-management divisions. The product is often offered for resale to the home gardener and makes a good mulch material.

Worm compost

Worm-worked compost is highly fertile and is formed when worms consume and digest organic matter, expelling the end-product as fine-textured wormcasts. By far the most productive are small, red brandling worms and striped tiger worms. Wormeries are ideal for recycling kitchen waste, and can be purchased in kit form, or as a worm "culture" for making a homemade worm bin.

To give the culture a good start, introduce the worms into a 5cm (2in) layer of garden compost or manure over a layer of damp straw or shredded newspaper. Add layers of kitchen waste – to a maximum depth of 15cm (6in) – and allow the worms to work most of it before adding more.

The worms work only at temperatures above 15°C (59°F), so store the wormery under cover during winter. Do not allow excess liquid to build up in the bin. When the bin is full, remove the worms from the compost by sieving and use them to start the next culture.

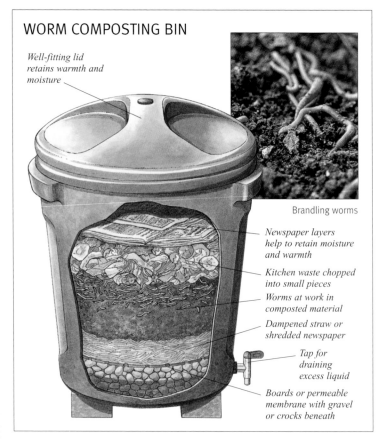

WORM COMPOSTING BIN

Well-fitting lid retains warmth and moisture

Brandling worms

Newspaper layers help to retain moisture and warmth

Kitchen waste chopped into small pieces

Worms at work in composted material

Dampened straw or shredded newspaper

Tap for draining excess liquid

Boards or permeable membrane with gravel or crocks beneath

Leaf mould

Although leaves can be included on the compost heap, they are best composted separately as they are slow to break down. They rely more heavily on micro-fungi than on bacteria, and need less air and warmth. Stack leaves, as they are collected in autumn, in a wire netting cage or bin, treading them down firmly each time the bin is filled. Except for watering in dry weather, they need little further attention while they decompose. Two bins are useful as leaves take so long to break down. Alternatively, use black plastic bags; pack the leaves down firmly, and leave them.

Using the bin

Leaf mould is an excellent soil conditioner and mulching material. It can also be used as a compost additive in homemade potting. It should not be removed from the bin until it has decomposed completely, which is likely to take a year or more. Use one bin while the other is rotting down.

6
PRINCIPLES
OF PROPAGATION

PLANT PROPAGATION is not difficult once the basic principles are understood, and it is the best and cheapest way to increase plant stocks. In addition, it provides many opportunities for gardeners to exchange plants, thereby increasing the varieties available in cultivation. Techniques range from the simple division of overcrowded perennials to more advanced methods, such as hybridizing in order to create plants with new characteristics, such as novel flower colours. For many people, the transition from a seed into a healthy plant, or the development of a cutting into a new tree or shrub, is fascinating. Successful propagation is well within the reach of any gardener once they grasp the techniques in this chapter.

Seeds

Seed is much the commonest way by which flowering plants reproduce in nature. It is normally a sexual method and, as such, always presents the possibility of a variety of genetic combinations, so that the resulting seedlings are variable. Such variation provides the basis by which plants adapt to their environment, and enables the breeding and selection of cultivars with new combinations of desirable characteristics. Seeds may more or less breed true but often vary greatly within a species. In horticulture, variation is disadvantageous if the plants raised are to retain particular characteristics, but advantageous when new, improved characteristics are being sought.

REPRODUCTIVE PARTS OF A ROSE FLOWER

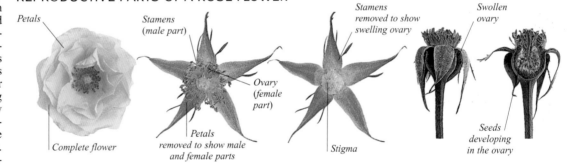

Petals
Stamens (male part)
Ovary (female part)
Complete flower
Petals removed to show male and female parts
Stamens removed to show swelling ovary
Stigma
Swollen ovary
Seeds developing in the ovary

The parts of a flower needed for reproduction are the stamens – the male part, which bears the pollen – and the pistils – the female part, which comprises one or more stigmas, style, and ovary. The petals attract pollinators.

How the seed develops

Most plants are hermaphrodite – that is, each flower bears male and female parts. As the flower matures, pollen is transferred onto one or more stigmas of the same flower (self-pollination) or of a flower on another plant of the same species (cross-pollination) by insects, birds, water, or wind. The pollen grains then produce pollen tubes, which grow down the style towards the ovules in the ovary, and fertilization occurs when the male and female nuclei fuse. From these develop the embryos, which, nourished by adjacent storage tissue in a seed, are capable of forming complete new plants.

Collecting and storing seed

In general, seed should be collected as soon as it is ripe and then stored in a cool, dry, dark, airy place such as a domestic refrigerator until it is used. Certain seeds, however, have special needs. Some are viable for only short periods and should be sown as soon as possible. Others may be stored for very long periods at low temperatures without losing viability. Fleshy fruits should be soaked and softened in water, the seeds removed from the flesh, and then air-dried at 10–20°C (50–68°F). Before they are sown, however, seeds of most stone fruits (eg cherry) and that of some berried shrubs (eg *Berberis* and *Cotoneaster*) need stratifying (see p.630).

As soon as a seed capsule splits, harvest it together with other capsules that are nearing maturity. Dry them in clean paper bags before separating out the seeds. When mature, wind-distributed seed will start dispersing, so quickly cover the seed-bearing branches with fine muslin or paper bags; alternatively, cut one or two seed-bearing branches and place them in water indoors to mature.

How to overcome dormancy

The seeds of some plants have in-built mechanisms to assist in controlling the time of germination; for example, many seeds do not germinate in late autumn, when conditions are unfavourable for seedling growth, but remain dormant until the temperature and other factors are more suitable. This dormancy is achieved by a variety of means including the presence of chemical inhibitors in the seed, by hardened seed coats that must rot or be breached before the seed can germinate, or by the need for the seed to experience alternating cold and warm periods. Several methods have been developed horticulturally to overcome this natural dormancy so the seeds will germinate more quickly and are therefore less likely to fail.

Scarification

The aim is to break down the hardened seed coat and allow water to enter, thereby speeding up germination. Large, hard-coated seeds, such as those of the legume family, may be nicked

SCARIFICATION

Before planting, carefully nick the hard coat on seeds such as Paeonia delaveyi *var.* delaveyi *f.* lutea *with a clean, sharp knife so the seed can absorb moisture.*

with a knife. Smaller seeds may be shaken in a jar lined with abrasive paper or one containing sharp gravel.

Warm stratification

This is used for hard-coated seeds of many woody species (see *Tree Seed Requiring Stratification*, p.81). Place the seeds in a plastic bag in moist (but not wet) standard seed compost, and store for 4–12 weeks at 20–30°C (68–86°F). This is usually followed by a period of cold stratification before sowing. See also "Breaking seed dormancy", p.115.

Cold stratification

Soak the seeds for a period of up to 24 hours, then add them to moist (but not wet) vermiculite in a plastic bag or place them in an open dish on moist filter paper. Refrigerate the seeds at 1–5°C (34–41°F) for 4–12 weeks. If germination has occurred, sow the seeds immediately.

Alternatively for large seeds, place the seeds in a pot containing 1 part seed to 3 parts moist sand. Cover with mesh and leave in a cold frame for one or two winters until they germinate; then sow the seed at once.

Requirements for germination

In order to germinate, a seed needs water, air, warmth, and, for a few

POST-SCARIFICATION SOAK

Before / *After*

After scarification, soak seeds such as lupin in water for 24 hours, so they swell slightly, then sow them.

species, light. The growing medium needs to be a fine compost capable of drawing water up to seeds placed near its surface. To aid this capillary rise, the compost is firmed lightly. Without this firming, air pockets occur, and the water columns essential for capillary rise are broken. The compost, however, must not be compacted or so damp that air cannot penetrate; seeds will almost certainly fail in such anaerobic compost as they cannot obtain the oxygen vital for growth. For most successful results, the temperature for germination of most seeds should be 15–25°C (59–77°F); heated propagators are useful for maintaining a steady temperature (see "Heated propagators", p.637). Some large seeds such as those of *Hippeastrum* germinate easily if floated on water rather than laid on soil (see BULBOUS PLANTS, "Tender bulbs", p.247).

Light requirements vary during germination: a few seeds need light (eg *Alyssum, Begonia, Calceolaria,* and *Genista*), but others are inhibited by it (eg *Allium, Delphinium, Nigella,* and *Phlox*). There is no way of distinguishing seeds requiring dark conditions from those needing light by physical examination: if the dark/light requirement is unknown, initially sow the seed in the dark; if it fails to germinate after a period of some weeks, place it in the light.

Sowing and aftercare

After sowing the seed in containers or in open ground, do not allow the compost to dry out or become too waterlogged. Cover the containers with 5mm (¼in) of coarse sand or fine (5mm) grit for autumn-sown seeds; for spring sowings, replace the grit with a 1cm (½in) layer of vermiculite: fine grade for small or medium-sized seeds, and medium grade for large seeds. Place the containers in a suitable environment (see "The propagation environment", p.636). The first sign of germination is the emergence

HOW A SEED GERMINATES

In hypogeal germination (right), the cotyledons, or seed leaves, stay below soil level, whereas in epigeal germination (far right), they appear above ground.

Soil level

True leaves

Radicle

Cotyledon

True leaves

Cotyledon

Radicle

SEEDLING GROWTH

Evenly coloured, rich green foliage

Long, thin stems

Healthy seedlings

Sturdy, well-spaced nasturtium (Tropaeolum) *seedlings flourishing under glass and ready to be pricked out.*

Unhealthy seedlings

If not pricked out early enough, the seedlings will become pale, crowded, and etiolated – and may die.

of the radicle, or primary root, followed, in epigeal germination, by the cotyledons, or seed leaves, which provide the initial food reserves. The true foliage leaves appear later and generally differ from the cotyledons.

When the seedlings are large enough to handle, they should be "pricked out" (see ANNUALS AND BIENNIALS, "Pricking out", p.219). Failure to do so results in weak growth, because the crowded seedlings compete for light and nutrients and readily succumb to fungal infection. Once transplanted, return the seedlings to the warm

TRUE LEAVES

True leaf

Cotyledons

As the cotyledons, or seed leaves, wither, the true leaves gradually take over the process of photosynthesis.

germination environment in order to re-establish; then gradually harden them off by placing the containers in cooler conditions (see "Hardening off", p.637). A cold frame, closed at first, then opened in stages, provides a suitable environment for hardening off seedlings.

Producing hybrids

When hybridizing plants, it is important to prevent self-pollination. For controlled cross-pollination, petals, sepals, and stamens are removed from the flowers on the proposed female parent and the denuded flowers protected from insects by paper or plastic bags until the stigmas on the female plant are sticky and receptive. Pollen, previously collected from air-dried stamens, is then transferred to the stigmas and the flowers are protected from insects once again until fertilization has occurred. Hybrid seed will develop in the ovaries and should be collected when ripe and according to its requirements (see also ROSES, "Hybridizing", p.168).

F1 and F2 hybrids

For the gardener seeking uniformity and near-perfection, F1 and F2 hybrid seed is available for a limited range of plants, mostly annuals. Such seed needs a complex plant breeding technique and is therefore more expensive.

The first generation derived from crossing two carefully maintained, genetically inbred plants of the same species is termed "first filial generation", or F1, hybrid. F1 hybrids are usually more vigorous than their parents and give uniformity in flower characteristics such as colour and form that seldom occurs with open-pollinated seed. Sometimes two controlled crosses from four selected lines are used to produce a "second filial generation", or F2, hybrid – retaining some of the vigour and uniformity of the F1 parents but often with other favoured characteristics less evident in the F1s.

Layering

Layering is a natural form of propagation: roots are induced to develop by covering a stem with soil while it is still attached to the parent plant. The rooted portion of stem is then separated from the parent plant and grown on.

The stem to be layered is often cut, ring-barked, or twisted. This partially interrupts the flow of hormones and carbohydrates, which, as they accumulate there, help to promote root growth. The tissues beyond the constriction are slightly water-stressed, and this, too, favours root formation. Another important root stimulus is the exclusion of light from the stem: light-starved cells then become thin-walled and roots form more readily. In order to stimulate rooting further, use a rooting hormone at the point of layering.

Methods of layering

Layering methods are classified in three groups: those in which a stem is brought down to the soil (simple, serpentine, natural, and tip layering); those in which soil is mounded over a stem (stooling, trench layering, and French layering); and air layering, where the "soil" is brought up to the plant stem. The word "soil" is used loosely here to mean any growing medium such as peat, sand, sawdust, or sphagnum moss.

Simple layering

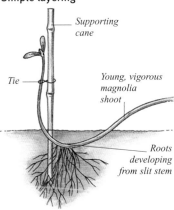

Supporting cane

Tie

Young, vigorous magnolia shoot

Roots developing from slit stem

Simple layering

This is best carried out between autumn and spring. The parent plant must be young and pruned the season before to produce vigorous, flexible stems, which can be brought down to soil level and will root readily. A slanting cut is made on the underside of the stem to be layered, which is secured at this point into the soil. The shoot tip is tied to a cane in the soil. If the layer is well rooted the next autumn, it can be cut from the parent plant (see also ORNAMENTAL SHRUBS, "Simple layering", p.116, and CLIMBING PLANTS, "Simple layering", p.145).

Serpentine layering

Parent plant

Soil level

Peg holding clematis stem under mounded soil

Roots appearing between nodes

Serpentine layering

This modified form of simple layering is used for plants with pliable stems, such as clematis. Long, young stems are mounded with soil, leaving buds exposed to produce aerial shoots (see also CLIMBING PLANTS, "Propagation by serpentine layering", p.145).

Natural layering

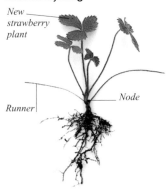

New strawberry plant

Runner

Node

Natural layering

Some plants, such as strawberries, reproduce naturally by sending out a series of runners. These then root at a node, forming a new plant. Once the new plant is fully established, sever it from the parent and grow on (see also "Strawberries: Propagation", p.470).

Tip layering

Growth bud on new plant

Young, vigorous blackberry shoot

Roots emerging on new plant

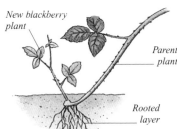

New blackberry plant

Parent plant

Rooted layer

Tip layering

This method is for shrubs and climbers that produce roots from their shoot tips; the blackberry is a common example. In summer, a young, vigorous shoot tip is buried in soil in a hole 7–10cm (3–4in) deep. A new shoot,

growing from the tip, appears a few weeks later; the young plant may then be separated from its parent. Grow on the rooted layer *in situ*; transplant it the following spring, if required (see also *Tip Layering*, p.471).

Stooling

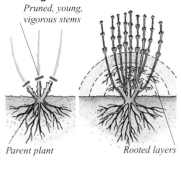

Pruned, young, vigorous stems

Parent plant

Rooted layers

Stooling

Although used by amateurs for only a few woody plants, stooling, or mound layering, is important for the commercial production of rootstocks. Stems of a young parent plant are cut back in late winter or early spring to within 8cm (3in) of the ground. Once new shoots are about 15–20cm (6–8in) long, mound soil up over their bases, then twice more until summer. On plants that root easily, such as thyme and sage, stems do not need cutting back before mounding. By autumn, the stems will have rooted; they are then separated from the parent plant and transplanted (see also GROWING HERBS, "Mound layering", p.414).

Trench layering

Trench, or etiolation, layering is mainly for fruit rootstocks, especially those that do not root well. The parent plant is planted at an angle, allowing the shoots to be pegged down in shallow trenches and covered with soil. The rooted shoots can be detached from the parent to form new plants.

Trench layering

Parent planted at 30–40° angle

Soil level

5cm (2in) deep trench

Young, vigorous shoots pinned in position

French layering

Soil mounded over shoot

Stem pegged down

Rooted layer

French layering

French, or continuous, layering is a modified form of stooling. In late winter, peg young shoots from the parent stem to the ground. Any new growths are gradually earthed up to a depth of 15cm (6in). These new shoots should have rooted by autumn and after leaf fall may be separated and grown on (see also ORNAMENTAL SHRUBS, "French layering", p.117).

Air layering

Diagonal slit in stem to form a tongue

Sealed, plastic sleeve packed with moist sphagnum moss

Air layering

Use air, or Chinese, layering (also known as marcottage) on some trees, shrubs, climbers, and house plants, such as rhododendrons, magnolias, and rubber plants (*Ficus elastica*). In spring or summer, choose a strong-growing, healthy shoot of one- to two-years old, as these root most readily. Trim off sideshoots and leaves for 30cm (12in) back from the tip. Make a slit in the stem and apply hormone rooting compound to it. Keep the wound open by packing it with moist sphagnum moss. Then cover the wounded area with more sphagnum moss and seal with plastic, preferably black, until roots develop (see *Air Layering a Shrub*, p.117, and INDOOR GARDENING, "Air layering", p.383). Rooting may take up to two years.

Cuttings

Propagation from cuttings is the commonest vegetative method. There are three main types: stem, leaf, and root. Stem cuttings produce roots directly from the stem itself or from the mass of thin-walled, wound-healing tissue (callus) that develops at its base. These roots are called adventitious, which means added, or artificial. Some large leaves can be used as cutting material and will develop adventitious roots from near their veins. Vigorous, young roots may also be used for cuttings – propagation by root cuttings is a simple and economical method neglected by most gardeners. Suitable species will produce both adventitious stem buds and roots on the root cutting.

How roots form

Adventitious roots most often develop from young cells produced by the cambium – a layer of cells that generates tissues involved in the thickening of stems. They are usually located close to food- and water-conducting tissues, which provide nourishment as they develop.

Adventitious root growth is also helped by natural hormones called auxins, which accumulate in the base of a cutting. Natural auxins can be supplemented by synthetic auxins, which are available as talc-based powders or as solutions. These aid rooting when applied to the bases of cuttings and are recommended for all plants except those that root very easily. Use only a little hormone, however, as too much could harm immature tissue.

Rooting hormones can be bought with low concentrations of active ingredients for soft cuttings and higher concentrations for hardwood material; some contain a fungicide, which helps to prevent infections entering the cuttings through the wounded tissues.

CALLUS PADS

Adventitious roots developing from the callus pad

Protective callus pad

Some plants (here Choisya ternata) *form a protective callus pad of wound-healing tissue at the base of a stem cutting, where they have been severed from the parent plant.*

SOFTWOOD CUTTINGS

Prepared cutting trimmed below the node

Rooted cutting

The soft, green stem on a softwood cutting (here Hydrangea macrophylla) *usually turns brown as it matures and develops its root system.*

Stem cuttings

Stem cuttings are often classified by the maturity of the stem tissue into softwood, greenwood, semi-ripe, and hardwood (or ripewood). The distinction is useful, though imprecise, because tissues develop continuously throughout the growing season.

Softwood cuttings

These are taken in spring and are generally made from the tips of shoots (tip cuttings) on the parent plant, but the new, young basal shoots (basal cuttings) of herbaceous perennials are also used (see PERENNIALS, "Basal stem cuttings", p.282). Since young material roots most readily, softwood cuttings often provide the best chance of rooting species that are difficult to propagate. Retain the soft tip where possible, as this is where the rooting auxins are produced. Softwood cuttings need a supportive environment, because they lose water and wilt quickly (see "The propagation environment", p.636).

Greenwood cuttings

These are taken from early to mid-summer, from slightly more mature wood, when growth begins to slow. They root slightly less readily but survive better than softwood cuttings, although they still require a supportive environment in which to develop.

Semi-ripe cuttings

Taken in late summer, semi-ripe cuttings are less prone to wilting since the stem tissues are firmer and woody (see ORNAMENTAL SHRUBS, "Semi-ripe cuttings", p.112). Some species with large leaves, for example *Ficus* and

camellia, may be propagated more economically by taking a short section from a semi-ripe stem just above and below a leaf bud, retaining a single leaf (see ORNAMENTAL SHRUBS, "Leaf-bud cuttings", p.113).

Hardwood cuttings

Fully mature, hardwood (or ripewood) cuttings are taken at the end of the growing season from autumn through to spring, when the tissues are fully ripened. They are the easiest to maintain in a healthy condition but are often slow to root. Hardwood cuttings fall into two categories: leafless deciduous cuttings and broadleaved evergreen cuttings. Growth of many glossy-leaved evergreens, such as holly (*Ilex*) and rhododendron, wilts readily when young early in the season since their protective leaf waxes develop slowly; they are therefore best propagated by semi-ripe or hardwood cuttings (see also ORNAMENTAL TREES, "Hardwood cuttings", p.78; CLIMBING PLANTS, "Propagation from hardwood cuttings", p.143; and ROSES, "Hardwood cuttings", p.165).

SEMI-RIPE CUTTINGS

Stem with opposite buds cut below a node

New growth has developed from each node

The green stem (here Weigela) *has a darker and woodier base.*

LEAF-BUD CUTTINGS

Healthy, green leaf

Leaf bud from which new shoot will develop

A short piece of semi-ripe stem (here camellia) *provides sufficient food reserves for a leaf-bud cutting, since it produces some food through its leaf.*

HARDWOOD CUTTINGS

Leafless, woody stem

Fibrous roots

Fleshy roots

Hardwood cuttings (here Salix alba) *are the longest type of stem cutting since they need large food reserves while their roots slowly develop.*

When to take stem cuttings

There are no hard and fast rules about when to take stem cuttings of a particular species, so if cuttings taken in spring fail to root, further cuttings can be taken later in the season and treated according to the relative maturity of the shoots.

Plants that are difficult to root are best propagated early so that the new plants have time to mature before winter. As the action of root-producing hormones is suppressed by flower-initiating ones, use cuttings without flower buds wherever possible; if cuttings with flower buds have to be used, remove the flower buds.

Preparing stem cuttings

Stem cuttings are usually prepared by trimming just beneath a node, or leaf joint, where the cambium (the layer of cells involved in stem thickening) is most active. Many easy-rooting

NODAL CUTTING

Sharp, clean blade reduces the chances of infecting the cutting

Node

Most cuttings (here Hydrangea paniculata) *root most satisfactorily at their nodes and so should be trimmed just below a node.*

INTERNODAL CUTTINGS

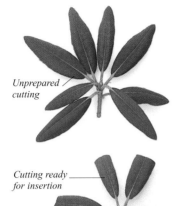

Internodal cuttings (here Clematis montana) *maximize propagating material in an economical way.*

cuttings, for example willows (*Salix*), have pre-formed roots at the nodes, and these start to develop when the stem is cut from the parent plant. For these and for cuttings with densely crowded leaves on each stem, cut between nodes (internodal cutting).

The cutting length depends on the species but is commonly 5–12cm (2–5in) or about five or six nodes in length. The lower leaves are stripped to give a clean stem for insertion. To help the cuttings root, semi-ripe and hardwood cuttings are often "wounded" by removing a sliver of bark from the lowest 2.5cm (1in) of the cutting. This exposes a larger area of cambium, stimulating roots to form. Some cuttings, especially semi-ripe ones, may be taken by pulling a sideshoot away from the main shoot with a small "heel" of bark still attached (see ORNAMENTAL SHRUBS, "Heel cuttings", p.113). A heel may provide a cutting with added protection until it has produced roots, although there is no satisfactory scientific explanation for this response.

With the exception of leafless, hardwood stem cuttings, which contain food reserves from the previous

WOUNDING

Bark

Green, pithy centre to stem

Cambium layer exposed after wounding base of stem

*Use a very sharp, clean knife to make a shallow, angled, downward cut at the base of semi-ripe and hardwood cuttings such as vine (*Vitis*).*

PREPARING CUTTINGS

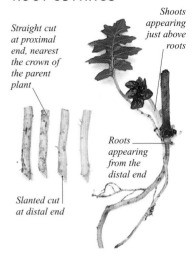

Unprepared cutting

Cutting ready for insertion

To reduce stress from water loss on leafy cuttings (here rhododendron), remove some leaves, halve others.

growing season, few cuttings are able to produce roots and shoots without supplementing their food reserves through photosynthesis. However, active leaves lose water through their pores, which is not easily replaced, and excessive water loss will cause failure. To achieve a balance between retaining photosynthetic tissue and reducing water loss, trim away all but four full-sized leaves, leaving any immature leaves. If the remaining leaves are large, as on many broad-leaved trees and large shrubs, reduce each by half to minimize water loss.

Leaf cuttings

For some plants, whole leaves (with or without leaf stalks) or sections of leaves may be taken as cuttings and inserted or secured onto the compost. With whole leaves laid flat, the veins should be nicked at intervals as new plantlets form at the cut surfaces of large leaf veins. Propagate plants such as *Sinningia* and *Streptocarpus* from cut sections of fully expanded, undamaged leaves. African violets

LARGE LEAVES

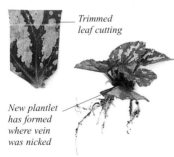

Trimmed leaf cutting

New plantlet has formed where vein was nicked

Large leaves of plants such as begonia may be divided into small pieces, each of which will form callus at a nicked vein and then adventitious roots.

(*Saintpaulia*) and *Peperomia* may be propagated from entire leaves with their stalks (see INDOOR GARDENING, "Propagating from leaves", p.381).

Root cuttings

Root cuttings are taken in the dormant season from young, vigorous roots of about pencil thickness for most trees and shrubs, but the roots may be somewhat thinner for some herbaceous plants such as phlox.

The length of the cutting

This is dependent on the environment in which the root cutting is to develop: the warmer the environment (within reason), the faster new shoots will appear and, therefore, shorter cuttings with smaller food reserves may be used successfully although these should not be less than 2.5cm (1in) in length. Root cuttings are preferably grown on in a greenhouse. A cold frame is also suitable, but the cuttings may be slower to develop shoots. For *Ailanthus* and lilac (*Syringa*), which can be propagated in open ground, 10–15cm (4–6in) long root cuttings should be used.

Inserting root cuttings

It is important to insert root cuttings the correct way up since the new roots always form at the distal end (that is, the end that was farthest from the crown of the parent plant). Cuttings should be inserted vertically so that their other (proximal) ends are flush with the soil surface; herbaceous root cuttings, however, are frequently inserted horizontally (see also PERENNIALS, "Root cuttings", p.203).

The rooting medium

Cuttings need air (to obtain oxygen) and water in their rooting medium, but if the medium is too wet, the cuttings rot. Standard cutting compost must, therefore, have a more open structure than loam-based potting compost. The rooting medium should

SMALL LEAVES

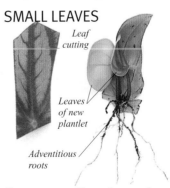

Leaf cutting

Leaves of new plantlet

Adventitious roots

To encourage callus to form, and rooting to occur, small leaves such as Peperomia may be trimmed at the edges.

ROOT CUTTINGS

Shoots appearing just above roots

Straight cut at proximal end, nearest the crown of the parent plant

Roots appearing from the distal end

Slanted cut at distal end

To help distinguish the two ends when taking root cuttings (here Acanthus mollis), make differently angled cuts.

PROTECTIVE ENVIRONMENT

Leafy cuttings grow best in a humid environment, such as within a plastic bag secured over a container; keep the plastic away from the leaf surfaces.

also be warm in order to speed up development of the roots: 18–25°C (64–77°F) is ideal for cool temperate species, and up to 32°C (90°F) for those from warm climates. If necessary, use bottom heat (see p.636).

Caring for the cuttings

After insertion, keep leafy cuttings turgid in the humid atmosphere of a closed case, mist unit, propagator, or other similar environment. Leafless cuttings that have been planted outdoors, either direct in the soil or in a container, should be protected by a clear plastic tunnel or a cold frame.

Every ten days or so, water the rooting medium lightly if required, and spray with a fungicide to help prevent disease; at the same time, lift the lights or remove the plastic over enclosed cuttings, to enable air to circulate, for a 5–10-minute period.

Once rooted, cuttings should be potted up individually and those growing under cover gradually hardened off (see p.637).

Storage organs

Storage organs have diverse structures, and include bulbs, corms, rhizomes, root and stem tubers, and turions. Most plants with storage organs increase naturally by producing offsets; lift and divide these to avoid overcrowding. Offsets flower faster than seed-raised plants and are identical to the parent, while seed-raised plants may be variable in character. The main propagation methods apart from division are to cut the storage organs into sections and to stimulate them to produce offsets by wounding; these sections or offsets form complete plants if put in a warm, dark place. Dust cut surfaces with a fungicide as they are prone to fungal attack.

Bulbs

Bulbs may be propagated by chipping; division of offsets, bulbils, or bulblets; scaling or twin-scaling;

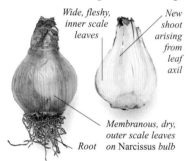

Wide, fleshy, inner scale leaves

New shoot arising from leaf axil

Membranous, dry, outer scale leaves on Narcissus bulb

Root

Non-scaly, or tunicate, bulb

New shoot

Narrower, fleshy scale leaves of lily bulb

Root

Scaly bulb

and scooping or scoring. The gardener can tell only from experience which is best for which bulb, but for lists of plants appropriate to each method, see BULBOUS PLANTS, "Propagation", pp.245–250.

Chipping

Non-scaly, or tunicate, bulbs such as snowdrops (*Galanthus*) that do not naturally increase quickly may be multiplied rapidly by chipping. This method involves cutting each bulb into up to 20 pieces, depending on its size. Each piece, which generally comprises three or more scale leaves and a section of basal plate, is then soaked

CHIPPING

Scale leaf

Bulblet

Bulblets develop between the scale leaves on a chipped bulb such as snowdrop (Galanthus) in air temperatures that do not exceed 25°C (77°F).

in or dusted with a fungicide. The chips may be incubated (see "Chipping", p.249) or placed in vermiculite in a container in a frost-free greenhouse and left undisturbed. New bulbs form usually within 12 weeks, but a few may take almost two years. Separate the bulblets and repot or replant.

Division of offsets

Bulbs have wide, fleshy scale leaves, which act as food storage organs. At their base are axillary buds, which may enlarge naturally to form offsets. When the bulbs are lifted at the end of the growing season, these may be separated and planted out individually (see "Dividing bulbs", p.245).

DIVISION OF OFFSETS

Carefully remove each offset from a bulb (here Narcissus) by cutting or pulling.

Offset

Parent bulb

Bulbils or bulblets

Bulbils are produced on flowerheads or stems; bulblets develop on the bulb itself or on stem roots. Both may be detached and planted up to develop into new bulbs (see also LILIES, "Bulbils and bulblets", p.251).

Scaling

Scaling involves the removal of bulb scales, which are then induced to form bulblets. It is used for bulbs such as

BULBLETS AND BULBILS

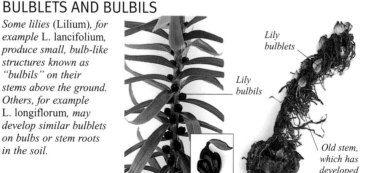

Some lilies (Lilium), for example L. lancifolium, produce small, bulb-like structures known as "bulbils" on their stems above the ground. Others, for example L. longiflorum, may develop similar bulblets on bulbs or stem roots in the soil.

Lily bulblets

Lily bulbils

Old stem, which has developed roots

SCALING

Scale leaf

New top-growth

Rooted bulblet

Bulblets appear at the base of individual scale leaves of loose-scaled bulbs, here lily (Lilium).

TWIN-SCALING

Two leaf scales and a section of basal plate are used for non-scaly bulbs (here Narcissus).

Fleshy scale leaves

Bulblet

Basal plate

fritillaries (*Fritillaria*) and lilies (*Lilium*) that are made up of fairly loose scales. Individual scale leaves are pulled away from the basal plate of a mature bulb and then left in a plastic bag containing moist vermiculite or a peat:grit mix, in a warm, dark place. Bulblets appear at the scale bases, usually after two months. Grow on the scales in a container until the bulblets are large enough to be separated (see also "Scaling", p.248).

Twin-scaling

Non-scaly, or tunicate, bulbs such as daffodils and snowdrops may be twin-scaled. In this, the bulb is cut vertically into eight to ten sections and each of these is divided into pairs of bud scales with a small section of basal plate. These are then incubated and grown on in the same way as in scaling above. (See also "Twin-scaling", p.249.)

Scooping and scoring

Some bulbs, such as hyacinths, can be propagated by either scooping or scoring the bulb. This causes callus tissue to develop, which encourages bulblets to form. For scooping, the basal plate of a mature bulb is scooped out at the centre, leaving just the outer

SCORING

Callus tissue

Bulblets developing inside cut

Basal plate

Shallowly cutting the basal plate of some bulbs (here hyacinth) stimulates the growth of bulblets.

edge of the basal plate intact; for scoring, two shallow cuts at right angles are made into the basal plate. The bulb is then stored basal plate uppermost, in a warm, dark place, until bulblets have formed; these are then detached and grown on (see also "Simple cutting", p.250; "Scooping hyacinths", p.250; and "Scooping and scoring trilliums", p.250).

Corms

Corms are reduced, compact, underground stems with a solid internal

Gladiolus corm

Food storage tissue

Thickened stem base

structure. Most corms produce several buds near the apex; each bud naturally forms a new corm. Miniature corms, or cormels, are produced as offsets

RAISING CORMELS

New corm

Old corm

Cormels

Separate the new corm and cormels from the old corm when dormant, and grow on.

DEVELOPMENT OF A CORMEL

Cormels may take up to three years to reach flowering size. The sequence below shows their development in the first year.

between the old and new corms in the growing season (see also BULBOUS PLANTS, "Gladiolus cormels", p.245). Larger corms may be increased artificially just before the growing season, by cutting them into pieces, each with a growing bud, and dusting with fungicide. Place in a pot or the open ground and lightly cover with soil, while new corms develop.

Rhizomes

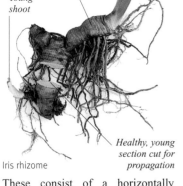

Growing shoot on parent plant

Fleshy storage organ

Young shoot

Healthy, young section cut for propagation

Iris rhizome

These consist of a horizontally growing shoot, usually below but sometimes on the soil surface. They are propagated by cutting the rhizome into young, healthy sections, each with

one or more growth buds, which are planted up individually (see also PERENNIALS, "Division of rhizomatous plants", p.201; BULBOUS PLANTS, "Scooping and scoring trilliums", p.250; and ORCHIDS, "Division", p.371).

Root tubers

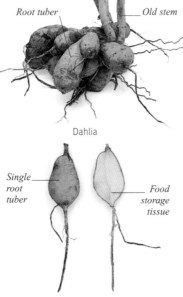

Root tuber — *Old stem*

Dahlia

Single root tuber

Food storage tissue

A root tuber is a portion of root at the stem base that swells during summer and is modified into a storage organ, or tuber, as in dahlias. Such plants may be propagated in spring by

dividing a cluster of tubers into healthy pieces, each with a developing shoot (see also *Cutting up Bulbs for Propagation*, p.249). Root tubers may also be propagated by basal cuttings of the young, emerging shoots in spring (see DAHLIAS, *How to Propagate by Basal Cuttings*, p.235).

Stem tubers

The stems of some plants (eg potatoes) are modified to produce tubers, which act as storage organs. Tuberous begonias, for example, form perennial tubers at the bases of their stems. In spring, these can be cut into pieces, each with a growth bud and then dusted with fungicide. Each piece will produce basal shoots, which can be used as basal cuttings (see DAHLIAS, *How to Propagate by Basal Cuttings*, p.235) or grown on to form a new tuber (see "Propagation of tuberous begonias", p.382).

Jerusalem artichoke

Old stem

Stem tuber

Bud

Food storage tissue

Other types of storage organ

Plants such as *Saxifraga granulata* and some *Kalanchoe* and *Asparagus* species develop round, bulb-like buds in their shoot axils. These buds can be separated and grown on individually in the same way as bulblets or cormels (see p.634).

In some water plants, such as *Hydrocharis* and *Myriophyllum*, these relatively large bud structures are known as "turions". When mature, they drop off the parent plant, sink to the bottom, and become new plants.

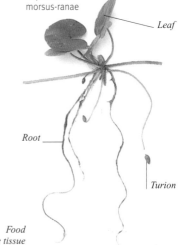

Hydrocharis morsus-ranae

Leaf

Root

Turion

Grafting and budding

In a wide range of woody plants and a few herbaceous ones, a budded stem, or scion, is grafted onto a rootstock, or stock, of another species or cultivar, to achieve a composite plant with more desirable characteristics. Most apple, pear, and stone fruit trees are propagated in this way. The stock may be more resistant than the scion to root disease or more suited to a particular environment. Often (especially with fruit trees), the stock is selected because it controls the growth of the scion to produce a dwarfed or a particularly vigorous plant. Sometimes, a scion cultivar that is difficult to increase from cuttings is grafted onto easily rooted stock. The rootstock also influences the age at which the tree bears fruit and its size and skin quality – dwarfing rootstocks generally conferring earlier fruit-bearing. Conversely, the rootstock's growing cycle may be affected by the scion cultivar, which in its turn influences cold hardiness. Reactions to soil acidity can also be affected by interactions between rootstock and scion cultivars.

The scion may take the form of a single bud on a short portion of stem (usually known as budding) or it may be a multi-budded length of stem.

When to graft

Field (outdoor) grafting is normally undertaken from late winter to early spring, when the cambium is particularly active, and mild conditions also favour the growth of callus cells. Hot weather later in the season may dry out the thin-walled, cambial cells. Bench grafting, generally done in the greenhouse or potting shed, is undertaken in winter and summer.

T-budding, on the other hand, is most often done in mid- to late summer, when well-developed scion buds are available and young stock material is of suitable diameter. For success, the stock plant needs to be growing actively, so that the bark can be lifted from the wood to allow the bud to be inserted. Chip-budding, however, may be undertaken over an extended season because the chip is positioned beside the stock rather than slipped under its bark.

How to graft

Because grafting cuts inevitably damage plant cells, and the thin-walled cells at the graft union are

vulnerable to fungi and bacteria, it is essential that knives are sterile and sharp, so that a single cut is sufficient. The propagation environment, prepared plant material, and ties must also be scrupulously clean.

Once stock and scion material have been selected and cut to shape, according to the type of graft, position the two pieces carefully so that there is maximum cambial contact. If the grafting materials are of different widths,

CAMBIUM LAYER

Node — *Bark*

Cambium

Pithy centre

For successful grafting, the scion cambium must be matched as closely as possible to that of the stock.

ensure the cambium on at least one side of the graft is in contact. Central to the grafting process is the activity of the cambium – a continuous, narrow band of thin-walled cells between the bark and the wood – which produces new cells that allow stem thickening. Within days of grafting, the region between the stock and scion should fill with thin-walled callus cells. The cambial cells on the stock and scion next to the young callus then link to neighbouring cells, so that a complete cambial bridge forms between the two parts. Further divisions of this new cambium produce water- and food-conducting tissue, which functionally joins the scion and stock.

Grafts should be bound with clear plastic tape, which seals the join well. Waxing is not necessary in hot-pipe callusing (see p.637). Pot-grown stocks once grafted should be kept in a suitable protective environment (see "Greenhouses", p.636, and "Cold frames", p.637).

Regularly examine the graft, and remove the tape once the graft appears to have taken. The following growing season, cut back the stock plant just above the new shoot that has developed from the grafted scion.

Chip-budding

A "chip" of ripe wood is removed from the rootstock and replaced with a matching "chip" of similar size from the scion, or budstick, containing a bud (see "Propagating by chip-budding", p.432).

T-budding

In this technique, just the scion bud is grafted onto the rootstock by cutting a "T" in the stock bark and inserting the bud beneath (see ROSES, "Bud-grafting", p.166).

Spliced side grafting

A short, downward cut through the cambium layer of the stock is followed by a sloping cut down towards the base of the first cut. The chip is removed and then replaced by the scion, which is shaped to match the stock (see ORNAMENTAL TREES, "Spliced side grafting", p.82, and ORNAMENTAL SHRUBS, "Spliced side-veneer grafting", p.118).

Side-wedge (or inlay) grafting

A downward, slightly inward cut is made into the side of the stock. The scion is then prepared by making two oblique cuts at the base. The scion's wedge-shaped base is inserted into the rootstock cut so that the cambium aligns and is bound in position.

Apical-wedge grafting

A 2–3cm (¾–1¼in) vertical cut is made centrally into the stock; the wedge-shaped scion is inserted into this (see ORNAMENTAL SHRUBS, "Apical-wedge grafting", p.119).

Saddle grafting

The top of the stock is saddle-shaped, with upward-sloping sides. The scion is then shaped so that it fits closely over the top of the rootstock (see ORNAMENTAL SHRUBS, "Saddle grafting", p.118).

Whip grafting

Cut back the stock at an oblique angle to 5–8cm (2–3in). Then prepare the scion to match. If the scion is thinner than the stock, first cut the stock horizontally, then obliquely to match.

Flat grafting

Both the stock top and scion base are cut horizontally (see CACTI AND OTHER SUCCULENTS, "Flat grafting", p.357).

Whip-and-tongue grafting

Make matching sloping cuts on the rootstock and scion, then cut shallow tongues along the sloping cuts, so that the scion interlocks securely with the stock (see GROWING FRUIT, "Whip-and-tongue grafting", p.433).

Whip-and-tongue graft
The rootstock and scion gradually unite to function as one plant.

The propagation environment

During propagation, plants are at their most vulnerable and their environment is, therefore, vitally important. The choice of environment depends on which propagation method is chosen and on the relative maturity of the plant material itself. Propagation from leafy cuttings, for example, requires a more closely regulated environment than for leafless cuttings.

Greenhouses

It is essential that a greenhouse has adequate ventilation and, in the growing season, appropriate shading (see "Creating the right environment", p.573). From spring to early autumn, apply a shading wash to the outside of the glass so that plants are not stressed unnecessarily by extreme weather conditions (see "Shading washes", p.576). Additional protective shading can be provided

by mounting shade cloth on wire runners across or along the length of the bench or greenhouse. The curtain can be withdrawn during dull weather.

Protecting leafy cuttings

Because leafy cuttings, initially, have no roots and cannot easily take up water to replace that lost from the leaves, they must have further protection within the greenhouse.

Clear plastic sheeting or a plastic bag placed over a tray of cuttings and tucked under is perfectly satisfactory if appropriate shading is provided. Water vapour condensing on the inside of the plastic helps to protect the cuttings against desiccation. Soft cuttings may succumb to disease if the plastic touches them; insert a framework of split canes or wire in the compost to keep the plastic off the cuttings. In such closed systems, however, excessive air temperatures may build up in very hot conditions and the containers

RIGID-TOPPED PROPAGATOR

When the vents are closed, moisture is retained within the unit. Cuttings therefore remain turgid, and so are more likely to root quickly and healthily.

of cuttings should be kept in a shaded but light place out of the sun.

Rigid plastic propagators need similar shading to plastic sheeting. Initially the vents should be kept closed, to maintain a moist atmosphere. Once rooting has taken place and the cuttings are ready to be hardened off, the vents should be opened.

A mist unit provides the best system for summer propagation, but for winter and early- and late-season propagation it should be combined with bottom heat. Ideally, the mist unit should maintain a constant water film on the leaf surfaces; some water will still be lost from the leaves by transpiration but this is amply replaced by "applied" water from the misting process. Since the mist is applied in bursts, the greenhouse humidity fluctuates and so, inevitably, the water film on each leaf is imperfect, and some water loss occurs. Complete mist systems comprise supply pipes, water filter, nozzles, and a solenoid

and sensor to regulate the misting frequency (see "Mist units", p.580).

For softwood cuttings, which wilt readily, the best system is to arrange a low, clear plastic tent just above the misting nozzles. This ensures a higher ambient humidity between mist bursts than does open mist. It is important to shade such a closed mist system in bright weather.

Bottom heat

Most biological processes are speeded up when temperatures are higher, and so raising compost temperature tends to increase the rapidity with which seeds germinate and cuttings root.

Cables or heating mats are most convenient for small greenhouses (see "Propagation aids", p.580). The temperature is controlled by a rod thermostat or electronic controller. If they are used in closed mist systems, excessive air temperatures may build up in bright conditions, during which the heating must be switched off.

SHADING GREENHOUSES (TEMPERATE CLIMATES)

To prevent the greenhouse from overheating when propagating, add one or more layers of shading, depending on the weather conditions and season. Greenhouses in open, sunny sites are particularly vulnerable to overheating.

		Spring	Summer	Autumn	Winter
Dull days	Whitewash	▬▬▬▬▬▬▬▬▬▬			
Bright days	Layer of shade cloth	▬▬▬▬▬▬▬			
	Additional shade cloth		▬▬▬▬▬		
	Whitewash	▬▬▬▬▬▬▬▬			

HOT-PIPE CALLUSING OF GRAFTS

1 *Cut 2.5cm (1in) wide slots in the pipe. Place each plant with its sealed and bound grafted area vertically inside a slot.*

2 *Cover any roots with moist soil. Lay some capillary matting over the slots and secure with cut-out pieces of pipe or insulating tape.*

Hot-air grafts

Hot-pipe callusing applies thermostatically controlled hot air to a grafted plant to speed the formation of callus tissue, which is the first sign of a successful graft union. A soil-warming cable is threaded twice through a length of plastic drainpipe, 8cm (3in) across, in which slots have been cut – 2.5cm (1in) wide for bare-rooted stock; 8cm (3in) wide for container-grown ones. The pipe is then positioned just above ground level. Each scion and graft is sealed with melted wax, so it is less likely to dry out, and then taped and placed in a slot within the plastic pipe. Any bare roots are covered with soil, to keep them cool but moist, and then the whole pipe is wrapped with insulating material. If the temperature within the pipe is set to 20–25°C (68–77°F), callusing should occur within a few weeks.

Heated propagators

These self-contained units are very useful for extending the propagation season (see "Heated propagators", p.580). Since the units have heat loadings well in excess of the 160 watts/sq m (15 watts/sq ft) recommended for mist systems, they must be fitted with effective thermostats, otherwise high temperatures may damage cuttings in sunny weather.

Cold frames

Cold frames provide a valuable gain in soil and air temperatures while maintaining high humidity and providing adequate light for young plants. They can be used to raise seedlings early in the season, protect grafts, and propagate leafless and leafy cuttings. They may also, if required, be fitted with bottom heat (see p.636).

Because such low structures have no great volume, they will easily overheat in sunny conditions unless ventilated and shaded well (see "Cold frames", p.581). Conversely, when temperatures fall below -5°C (23°F), it is important to insulate frames with thick layers of hessian, coconut matting, polystyrene tiles, or bubble plastic.

Cloches and polytunnels

Glass and clear plastic cloches and tunnels are most often used to give seedlings an early start in the season in the vegetable garden. A wide range of easily rooted cuttings also do well in such an environment (see "Cloches", p.582). Additional shading, such as shade netting, is required in bright, sunny weather.

Growing the propagated plant

To propagate plants effectively, a gardener needs not only to prepare the material properly but also to care for and grow on the young plants in a suitable environment until they have developed sufficiently to thrive in the garden. At key stages in propagation, practical inexperience or carelessness may kill well-rooted plants.

Caring for the plants

Since most forms of propagation involve cutting various parts of the plants being increased, plant tissues are exposed to possible disease infection; it is therefore important to maintain hygienic conditions in the propagating area. Tools and benches should be regularly and thoroughly cleaned (using a mild disinfectant if necessary), and dead and damaged plant material removed. Potting composts must always be fresh and sterile.Fungicidal solutions may also be applied to protect seedlings (eg Cheshunt compound) and leafy cuttings (eg captan), following the manufacturer's instructions.

When preparing pots or trays of compost for sowing seed, lightly firm the compost using a presser board, especially around the edges of the container. Water is drawn up through the compost by capillary action and, without this firming, air pockets occur and the water columns essential for capillary rise are broken. However, do not firm loam-based composts: a medium filled with roots must

FIRMING THE COMPOST

Ensure that seeds are germinated in evenly pressed, level compost so that capillary action and therefore seedling growth are not hindered by air pockets in the compost.

Continuous capillary action

Air holes

Broken capillary action

be well aerated and have an open structure for optimum plant growth.

The composts in which propagated plants are growing should be moist, but not wet, at all times. Too wet a medium will reduce the oxygen available and the roots may die or succumb to disease. It is also important to maintain the correct environment until the young plants are sturdy enough to be hardened off (see "The propagation environment", p.636). Prick out seedlings to avoid their becoming overcrowded, as unless air is allowed to circulate freely around the young plants stagnant conditions may arise and cause damping off (p.660). Remove fallen leaves and dead matter immediately.

Most organic potting mixes are acid, that is, with a pH value of less than 7, and the ideal range for an organic mix is pH 5–5.5. Simple test kits are available to measure the pH. A very alkaline soil or compost reduces the amount of phosphorus, iron, manganese, and boron available to the plant, whereas too acidic a soil means that calcium and magnesium may be in short supply. For feeding the plants, apply a proprietary liquid fertilizer strictly in accordance with the manufacturer's instructions.

DAMPING OFF

Seedlings are more likely to damp off if they are overcrowded, especially if grown in damp, poorly ventilated conditions, or if they are allowed to suffer frost damage.

Hardening off

Hardening off the propagated plants, by which process the young plants are acclimatized to the outside air temperature, must not be rushed, because, over a period of days, the natural waxes coating the leaves need to undergo changes in form and thickness to reduce water loss. The stomatal pores on the leaf also need to adapt to less supportive conditions.

First, turn off the heat, if appropriate, in the propagator or mist unit. Then, during the daytime, raise the covers for increasingly long periods. Finally, the covers may be removed for both day and night. If the plant has been in the protective environment of a greenhouse and eventually needs to be planted outdoors, move it next into a cold frame. This, too, should be closed at first, then opened in stages. Alternatively place in the shelter of a wall, fence, or hedge and cover with horticultural fleece, gradually lifting it first during the day, and then at night. The hardening off process may take two to three weeks.

Outdoor nursery beds

Large numbers of new plants and seedlings in containers can be grown on in an outdoor nursery bed, once they have been hardened off. At its simplest, this can be an area of cleared and levelled ground covered with water-permeable woven fabric, black polypropylene, or weed matting,

NURSERY BED WITH RAISED EDGES

Edging boards can be used to enclose a nursery bed. Woven fabric is placed directly onto well-drained soil.

Optional edging board 8cm (3in) above soil level

Woven fabric

Two-way flow of water through the soil

Well-drained soil bed

SAND BED

With this type of nursery bed, woven fabric can be placed over an enclosed bed of coarse sand.

Edging board 8cm (3in) above soil level

Sand bed

Two-way flow of water through the sand

Soil bed

Plastic sheeting cut 2.5cm (1in) below the top of the edging boards

which will suppress weeds, provide a clean growing environment, and help to isolate plants placed on its surface from soil-borne diseases. The plants are placed on the fabric and gain access to soil water through capillary action. Edging boards can be added (as above) to "corral" the plants neatly and reduce the effect of drying winds, making watering

more effective. The fabric should be sterilized regularly to maintain a clean growing environment.

The nursery bed may be of any size, but it is essential that it is on free-draining soil. If your soil is a heavy clay, it is worth raising the nursery bed by first laying down plastic sheeting, and then adding a layer of coarse, lime-free sand, 8cm

(3in) deep. The entire sand bed will need to be enclosed by edging boards (see above right). The boards and plastic sheeting will retain moisture and ensure that watering is effective, while the drainage afforded by the sand will prevent a waterlogged environment. A covering layer of water-permeable woven fabric can be added to prevent erosion of the sand

by wind, and also disturbance by domestic animals, keeping the sand cleaner and more hygienic.

A sand bed has the advantage over a basic nursery bed of reducing the amount of watering necessary, minimizing the risk of potting composts drying out. More complex sand-bed designs incorporate drainage pipes and automatic watering systems.

Advanced techniques

Since the mid-20th century, new propagation methods have been introduced commercially. Some are confined to "laboratory nurseries" using advanced technologies, but others affect several branches of horticulture and have direct or indirect relevance to gardening. (See also INDOOR GARDENING, "Hydroculture", p.375.)

Micropropagation

Micropropagation uses explants, tiny pieces of young plant material. Each is grown on in a medium containing organic nutrients, mineral salts, hormones, and other elements needed for growth, and kept in a controlled environment. The explant multiplies to form numerous shoots or complete plantlets, which are rooted as "microcuttings" or, if already rooted, weaned to greenhouse conditions.

MICROPROPAGATION

A microscopic portion of plant tissue is extracted from a plant under sterile conditions. This portion, or explant, is then divided (right) and grown on in test-tube conditions (far right). Once sufficiently large, these embryo plants may be further divided or grown on to form plantlets.

Embryo plant

Sterile, test-tube conditions

Sterile conditions are vital, and transferring plant material from the culture to a greenhouse is difficult.

Micropropagation is used for high-value plants, for example to rapidly introduce new cultivars; plants difficult to propagate by other means; and to produce disease-free stock.

Advances in seed propagation

New methods have been developed to improve the speed and uniformity of seed germination. Seeds are soaked in salt solutions, like sodium chloride or potassium nitrate, or in polyethylene glycol solutions. They are thus primed for germination but are dried before the radicle emerges and are then packaged for sale. The seeds can be sown conventionally as required.

Fluid drilling and pelleted seed have been developed to make uniform seed sowing easier. In fluid drilling, seed primed for germination is contained within a gel base, for example in a fungicide-free wallpaper paste, which can then be squeezed along the seed drill. In pelleted seed, primed seed is coated in an inert material that may contain fungicides, nutrients, and/or a fluorescent dye. Such readily handled seeds can be sown very evenly.

Artificially produced seeds

Some flower tissues, when introduced into a special liquid culture, develop numerous embryos, each similar to an embryo in a seed. If these are given a synthetic coating (a process called somatic embryogenesis), numerous genetically uniform, artificial "seeds" may be produced.

Genetically modified plants

Genetic modification (GM) uses DNA technology to identify and extract genes from plant cells and introduce them into other cells, not necessarily of the same species or genus. This makes it possible to recombine genes of fundamentally changed parents in the breeding process, resulting in completely new plants. Potentially, GM techniques may extend the range of flower colours and scents; enhance fruit flavours; increase tolerance of drought and low temperatures; and produce medicinal compounds. GM methods also engender resistance to pests and diseases, such as cucumber mosaic virus in lettuces, tomatoes, and peppers, or herbicide resistance in tobacco plants.

Fundamental interference with the natural order by manipulating genes raises public concern. Questions are asked about potential risks to the environment. Could progeny arising through GM introduce genes into natural plant populations through normal cross-pollination, with deleterious consequences? Might GM plants show undesirable traits such as invasiveness and produce "superweeds"? Are there potential hazards to human health through consumption of GM food crops? Ethical issues also arise including freedom of choice, dominance of commercial influence, and the non-reversibility of the basic procedures.

As opportunities and challenges presented by genetic modification unfold, gardeners should be aware of the facts. Statutory regulations govern the development of the technique and mechanisms are in place to evaluate both the benefits and the potential risks.

7
PLANT PROBLEMS

Even the most experienced gardener may suffer problems caused by plant diseases and disorders, the ravages of pests, and the choking of plants by weeds. By following the principles of good cultivation and garden management, however, it should be possible to keep these problems to a minimum.

When problems do occur, it is important first to diagnose them correctly, before deciding upon the appropriate course of action required to remedy the situation. For some problems, treatments include a wide variety of organic and biological methods in addition to the use of chemicals.

Pests, diseases, and physiological disorders

Most plant problem symptoms are easy to see. A tree, shrub, or plant may wilt or become discoloured, or it may fail to come into leaf or to bloom at all. Pests, which may be the cause of the plant's poor health, may be seen on part or all of the plant. Sometimes an infestation or disease in the roots may be noticed first through symptoms in the leaves. This chapter gives detailed information on how to prevent and control the pests, diseases, and physiological disorders that can cause such problems.

What is a pest?

Pests are animals that cause damage to cultivated plants. Some, such as slugs, snails, and rabbits, are well known; most, however, are small invertebrates such as mites, eelworms, woodlice, and millipedes, which are less evidently plant pests. The largest group by far in this category are the insects. Pests may damage or destroy any part of a plant or, in some cases, even the whole plant. They feed in various ways – by sap sucking, leaf mining, defoliating, or tunnelling through stems, roots, or fruits. Sometimes they cause abnormal growths known as galls. Some pests also indirectly damage plants by spreading viral or fungal diseases, while others coat plants with a sugary excrement that encourages the growth of sooty moulds.

What is a disease?

A plant disease is any pathological condition caused by other organisms, such as bacteria, fungi, or viruses. Fungal diseases are commonest; bacterial diseases relatively rare. The symptoms that these organisms produce vary considerably in appearance and severity, but the growth or health of the plant is almost always affected and, in severe attacks, the plant may even be killed. The rate of infection is affected by factors such as weather and growing conditions. In some cases, the disease-causing organism (pathogen) is spread by a carrier, such as an aphid. The pathogen is sometimes visible as a discoloration on the plant, as with rusts. Symptoms such as discoloration, distortion, or wilting are typical signs of disease infection.

HOW TO DIAGNOSE PLANT SYMPTOMS

In a case where it is obvious that the leaves have been eaten away by some kind of pest, turn to the section on "Eaten leaves" to identify the cause.

When a plant shows several symptoms, look either in the section on the whole plant or in the part that deals with the worst aspect, here discoloured leaves.

What is a disorder?

Plant disorders usually result from nutritional deficiencies or from unsuitable growing or storage conditions. An inappropriate temperature range, inadequate or erratic water or food supply, poor light, or unsatisfactory atmospheric conditions may all lead to physiological disorders. Problems may also be caused by deficiencies of the mineral salts that are essential for healthy plant growth.

Weather, cultural, or soil conditions may lead to a range of plants being affected. The problems become apparent through symptoms such as discoloured leaves or stem wilt. A plant that lacks water, food, or the right environmental conditions will not only appear unhealthy but will also be less able to resist attack from insect pests or diseases caused by fungi, viruses, or bacteria. Unless problems are correctly diagnosed and treated, in extreme circumstances affected plants may die.

How to use this chapter

This chapter is organized according to the site of symptoms (such as distorted flowers or discoloured leaves), in sections covering leaves, stems, flowers, fruit, roots and tubers, bulbs, whole plant, and lawns. Within these, symptoms are grouped by type; for example, all yellow leaf spots will be found together.

To identify a problem, look in the appropriate section. If you cannot find it there, turn to the cross-references at the end of that section. Each entry lists the plants affected, the symptoms, the cause of the problem, and how to control it. Some notes on the controls currently approved appear on p.668; however these are subject to change. Always check labelling for specific uses, as not all brands of any one chemical are recommended for the same problems or the same plants.

Integrated control

The phrase "integrated control" is used to describe what is widely agreed to be best practice in the limitation and management of pest and disease problems. It aims firstly to do everything possible to prevent problems occurring, but then, should this be inadequate, to consider all the options for dealing with a problem – for example, using organic or biological controls – before resorting to chemicals. Gardeners practising integrated control combine the best aspects of organic and inorganic methods, always opting for the organic one first. They choose resistant plants and maintain high standards of garden hygiene, ensuring plants are healthy and thus have the best chance of resisting attack; they practise crop rotation. They seek to prevent pests from landing on plants, by the use of traps, barriers, and repellents. Plants are inspected regularly to spot problems early, and care is taken to ensure an accurate diagnosis. Chemicals are used sensibly and correctly, and only when warranted by serious pest or disease attack.

PREVENTING BUILD-UP OF DISEASE

Practising crop rotation stops specific soil-borne problems building up in the same plot of ground, for example clubroot of brassicas – here, plants are being removed after cropping.

Prevention of problems

Always buy strong, vigorous plants that look healthy. Do not purchase plants that are showing dieback or discoloured stems, that have leaves that are an abnormal colour for the time of year, or that are wilted or distorted. Do not buy plants showing significant pest infestations or disease. Check the root ball of container-grown trees and shrubs: do not buy them if they are either pot-bound or showing poor root development.

Check that the plant is suitable for its intended position, taking into account the type, texture, and pH of the soil, the aspect of the site, and whether the plant is prone to frost damage. Plant carefully, making sure that the ground is well prepared and that the roots are properly spread out. Follow the individual plant's requirements for watering, feeding, and, where appropriate, pruning.

Garden hygiene

Maintaining a tidy and well-managed garden is one of the most important ways to reduce the risk of pest and disease attack. Examine plants regularly to identify any new problem as soon as possible, since a well-established infection or infestation is always far more difficult to deal with than one that is identified and treated early.

The regular removal and disposal of diseased parts of plants, and some pests such as cabbage white caterpillars, may be laborious but certainly helps to control problems. Debris from infested or diseased plants should in many cases be burned; otherwise the pest or pathogen may survive, over-winter, and re-infect plants in spring.

If a plant is badly diseased or infested by pests, it may be impossible to revive it; such plants should be removed, especially if there is a risk that the trouble might spread to healthy plants nearby.

Crop rotation and replant problems

Rotating vegetable crops, usually on a three- or four-year basis, helps prevent soil-borne pests and diseases from building up to a damaging level. For further details on planning a crop rotation system, see GROWING VEGETABLES, "Crop rotation", p.498. Although a strict rotation plan is generally used for vegetables, it is also worth rotating annuals and bulbs where feasible, as this reduces the

build-up of diseases like foot and root rots and tulip fire. Growing a particular kind of plant in the same ground for a number of years may also lead to problems (see, for example, "Rose-sick soil", p.156). If a disease such as foot or root rot becomes evident, remove all the plants and grow other botanically unrelated plants that are not susceptible on the site.

Resistant plants

Some plants are resistant to attack by pests or diseases. Plant breeders have been able to profit from this and have produced cultivars with a higher-than-average resistance to some pests or diseases. Cultivated plants resistant to pests include some butterhead lettuces, which are seldom affected by the lettuce root aphid. Plants resistant to disease include some tomato cultivars, which resist tomato leaf mould, and the climbing rose 'Maigold', which shows some resistance to diseases such as powdery mildew, rusts, and black spot.

In some cases, the resistance appears to be total, but even a resistant plant may succumb to a given disease if its growing conditions are poor, for example, or if other factors, such as the weather, weaken the plant. Before buying plants, check if there are disease- or pest-resistant cultivars readily available. The range of resistant plants varies from year to year, so check catalogues annually for this type of information.

Correcting cultural disorders and deficiencies

Unsatisfactory growing conditions may result not only in poor general growth, but also in some very specific symptoms that closely resemble those caused by pests and diseases. When problems manifest themselves and an obvious cause – such as pest infestation – is not immediately apparent, it is worth considering the plant's growing environment as a whole – recent weather conditions, for example, or the health of your soil, or indeed whether some aspect of plant care was not provided. At best, the plant may be restored to complete health by some simple measure – the addition of a mineral supplement, for example, or less frequent watering. At worst, you may have to accept plant

SYMPTOMS OF CULTURAL DISORDER

Bitter pit in apples, caused by a lack of calcium, may be triggered by dry conditions in soils that in fact do contain sufficient calcium levels.

FRIENDS AND FOES

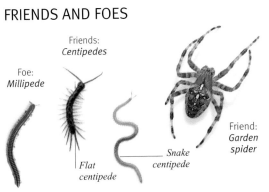

Foe:
Millipede

Friends:
Centipedes

Flat centipede

Snake centipede

Friend:
Garden spider

Friend:
Hedgehog

Companion planting
French marigolds (Tagetes patula) *attract hoverflies, which feed on aphids that may attack nearby plants.*

losses caused by freak extremes of weather – or learn that certain plants simply are not suited to the conditions you are able to provide.

It is also worth remembering that the risk of certain pest and disease problems can be minimized by altering growing conditions. Liming in the vegetable garden (see p.625) is a classic example; by increasing the alkalinity of the soil, it reduces the risk of clubroot affecting brassica crops.

Organic controls

Organic control uses natural methods to help plants both resist and recover from attack by pests and diseases. Such methods have long played their part in gardening, but in recent years they have attracted an increasing level of interest, especially as some harmful organisms have become immune to chemicals that once controlled them. Gardeners have become increasingly aware of the damage that irresponsible use of chemicals can do to the environment, and especially to creatures that are the gardener's natural allies – those that are predators or parasites of plant pests.

Attracting pest predators

Insects and other creatures found in gardens are by no means all destructive. Many are not only useful to the plant but actually essential for its survival; for example, a large number of fruits, vegetables, and flowers rely on pollinating insects, such as honey bees, to carry pollen from one flower to another to enable fertilization to take place. In other cases, some species of natural predator can help to control certain types of pest and should therefore be encouraged to visit the garden. A natural balance between pests and predators may take a few years to accomplish but, once established, such a garden will be much healthier than one that relies on chemical remedies alone.

Areas of undisturbed land will attract beneficial animals, especially if planted with a wide range of native species. Flat stones placed in the bed or border will be used by thrushes as anvils on which to smash snail shells. Predators such as hoverflies and ladybirds can also be encouraged by the introduction of colourful flowers, especially if flat or open-centred in form, and so they, too, will help keep pests to a minimum.

Recognizing beneficial garden animals

Hedgehogs, shrews, frogs and toads feed on many ground-dwelling plant pests such as slugs and snails. Birds may be the cause of some damage in the garden, but this disadvantage is usually far outweighed by the enormous quantities of insect pests

that many devour. Some invertebrates, for example centipedes, prey on soil-dwelling pests. It is possible to distinguish centipedes from the somewhat similar millipedes (which are often harmful) by the number of legs that are carried on each segment of their bodies: centipedes have only one pair per body segment, whereas millipedes have two pairs (see also *Friends and Foes*, above).

Spiders are also useful allies as their webs trap countless insects. Certain insects, however, may be invaluable in the garden. Ladybird beetles are a familiar example in many countries, and both the larvae and the adult beetles feed on destructive pests such as aphids. Lacewing larvae, too, have a voracious appetite for aphids, and they can be encouraged by planting flowers, such as pot marigolds (*Calendula*), and the provision of a nesting box in which they can overwinter. Ants and wasps, whose activities might damage some plants, may still help the gardener by preying on other insect pests. Ground beetles are voracious consumers of numerous pest species.

Companion planting

Certain companion plants grown in association with a crop may help to reduce pest attack. For example, some strong-smelling herbs such as mint and garlic may repel pests that are attracted to plants by smell, thereby keeping them away from nearby plants. Deliberate planting of host plants may deflect pests away from other plants or attract predators to feed on the pests: nasturtiums (*Tropaeolum*), for example, are susceptible to aphids, so plant French marigolds (*Tagetes patula*)

nearby as these attract hoverflies, which have larvae that feed on the aphids.

Traps, barriers, and repellents

These work by stopping pests getting near plants. Many can be constructed from everyday items. Earwigs may be trapped in inverted flower pots, and wireworms in old potatoes or carrots spitted on a stick and buried. In the greenhouse, saucers of water under bench legs will foil ants and woodlice – not in themselves pests of established plants, but partial to delicate seedlings. Glasshouse whiteflies, being attracted to the colour yellow, may be caught on strips of yellow plastic covered in non-dry glue. Place these near the top of plants and move them up as the plants grow. Consider introducing biological controls (see p.642) if the infestation is increasing.

Pheromone traps can be purchased from some garden centres and by mail order. They release the chemicals used by specific insects, such as the codling moth, to attract a mate. The trap captures the males by luring them onto a sticky sheet, thereby also reducing the mating success of the remaining females. Such a trap also allows the gardener to monitor infestation levels, and determine whether and when further control methods are needed.

ORGANIC EARWIG TRAP

An inverted flower pot filled with dried grass and placed over a cane attracts earwigs (see p.644). Examine the pot and remove any earwigs daily.

CODLING MOTH TRAP

Hang a pheromone trap in apple and pear trees in late spring. It will catch male codling moths and so reduce mating opportunities.

Controlling slugs and snails

Gardeners who prefer not to use slug pellets can try various alternative methods of control. Do not underestimate the value of picking the pests off individually, especially when several pairs of hands are available to help. Slugs and snails are most active at night, and can be readily spotted by torchlight, especially on a damp evening. Gather up the pests and kill them by dropping in a strong salt solution.

- Use biological control with a nematode that infects soil-dwelling slugs with a fatal bacterial disease. Apply to moist soil in spring to autumn.
- Lure slugs and snails into a hollowed-out grapefruit or orange half that is set, open side downwards, on stones just above the ground. Slugs and snails attracted by the citrus scent will move under the fruit skin and are likely to remain there, until morning at least. They can then be drowned in a strong salt solution.
- Part-fill a jar with beer or milk and almost sink it in the ground. The rim should be about 1cm (½in) above the surface to prevent useful predators such as ground beetles from toppling in. The smell of the beer or milk will attract slugs and snails, which should fall in and drown. Specially designed slug "traps" are available by mail order.
- Create a wide, physical barrier of a coarse material such as sand, grit, wood ash, soot, pine needles, or broken eggshells around special plants. These should be either too dry or too scratchy for slugs and snails to be attracted to cross.
- Cover or surround vulnerable seedlings and small plants using plastic bottles that have had their tops and bottoms cut off (see picture opposite). Press the bottles into the soil so that they encircle individual plants.
- Place a proprietary porous mineral product as a barrier around plants that need protection. However, such barriers are less effective in wet conditions, when pests are most active.

Traps and barriers can be used to great effect against slugs and snails (see "Controlling slugs and snails"). Larger barriers, from horticultural fleece to fruit cages, can be erected around and over plants to deter winged insects such as carrot fly and cabbage root fly, as well as birds, rabbits, and deer. Grease bands bar the way to pests climbing up trees and pots, and proprietary brassica collars, or ones cut from carpet or underlay, will prevent female cabbage root fly from laying their eggs around young brassica plants (see p.660).

Repellents, such as ultrasonic devices or humming tapes, are sometimes used to protect plants against moles, cats, and birds, which may be encouraged to move elsewhere. However, individuals differ in sensitivity to sound and, while bird-scaring devices and pet repellents may work initially, they often require changing frequently as the creatures become familiar with them.

Acceptable organic treatments

A few chemical preparations originate from natural sources; pyrethrum, for example, is derived from the pyrethrum daisy. Other organic treatments are rotenone, soft soap, plant oils, and sulphur dust, and these may be obtained as ready-made powders or liquid sprays. They have short persistence, however, and act only on contact with the pest or disease, which necessitates regular and thorough applications. Organically "acceptable" insecticides are, like synthetic pesticides, non-selective and may kill non-target insects as well as pests. Their short persistence does, however, make them more environmentally friendly.

Biological control

Some of the most troublesome pests, especially red spider mite, whiteflies, and vine weevil grubs, can be dealt with very effectively using biological controls. The term biological control describes the limiting of pest damage by the deliberate introduction of natural enemies, such as predators, parasites, or diseases. Biological controls are living organisms, usually nematodes or small predator insects or mites, which have no detrimental effects on non-target species. They are bred and supplied under controlled conditions, and as they are alive, they must be introduced onto your plants or into the soil

Individual cloche
Cut-down plastic bottles protect tender stems from voracious pests at ground level.

as soon as they have been obtained. These tiny creatures may prey on their host or target pest during a specific stage of its development, or they may spread disease among them. For example, the microscopic pathogenic nematode *Steinernema kraussei* is watered into potting compost or soil containing vine weevil grubs, which it infects with a fatal disease, while the predatory mite *Phytoseiulus persimilis* feeds on the eggs, nymphs, and mature forms of red spider mite. Not all pests and diseases, however, can be countered by appropriate biological controls; other controls may be introduced as more research is carried out on pest and disease ecology.

Most of the biological controls require daytime temperatures of at least 21°C (70°F) and good light intensity in order to breed faster than the pests. They can therefore be introduced into a heated greenhouse earlier than an unheated one or the open ground. Another key to successful use is to

USING BIOLOGICAL CONTROLS

Biological control at work
Minute Encarsia formosa *wasps attack and parasitize whitefly larvae, causing them to blacken and eventually die.*

Yellow sticky trap
A useful adjunct to biological controls, these can detect light infestations and alert the gardener if populations start to increase.

Pest	Biological Control
Aphids	Fly larva predators (*Aphidoletes aphidimyza*)
Leather-jackets	Pathogenic nematode (*Steinernema feltiae*)
Chafer grubs	Pathogenic nematode (*Heterorhabditis megidis*)
Fungus gnats larvae	Predatory mites (*Hypoaspis miles*)
Mealybugs	Ladybirds (*Cryptolaemus montrouzieri*)
Red spider mites	Predatory mites (*Phytoseiulus persimilis*)
Soft scale insects	Parasitic wasp *Metaphycus helvolus*
Thrips	Predatory mites (*Amblyseius* spp.)
Underground slugs	Pathogenic nematode (*Phasmarhabditis hermaphrodita*)
Vine weevil grubs	Pathogenic nematode (*Steinernema kraussei*)
Whitefly	Parasitic wasp *Encarsia formosa*

ensure that the pest has been correctly identified and therefore the appropriate specific control measures adopted. If you are not sure what pests you have, see pp.644–668.

Biological controls may be obtained from mail-order specialist suppliers. These generally advertise in the gardening press and on the internet. Good garden centres will also be able to provide advice on suitable controls and where to buy them.

Greenhouse controls

Some biological controls are suitable for use only in the greenhouse or conservatory. Introduce the control before plants are heavily infested, as it may be a number of weeks before it becomes effective. Restrict the use of pesticides, since most are harmful to biological controls; the least harmful are fatty acids and plant oils, which control a range of small insects and mites.

Open-garden biological controls

Use of biological controls is less practicable in the relatively uncontrolled conditions of the open garden, especially where pesticides are used, since they may kill the controls as well as the pests. Of the controls listed in the table (facing page), only those for chafer grubs, leatherjackets, vine weevil, and underground slugs are suitable for use in the open ground, provided the soil temperature is suitably high.

Chemical control

Chemical control is the term used to describe the action of destroying plant pests and diseases by applying synthetic compounds to plants or soil. Although the emphasis on organic control is presently becoming stronger, the responsible and sparing use of chemicals still has a valuable role to play in pest and disease control. A sensible combination of the most suitable aspects of both methods may provide the best solution to difficult and often recurrent problems.

Pesticides and fungicides

Most pesticides (which are used to kill insects, mites, and other pests) and fungicides (which are used to control diseases caused by fungi) either work by being brought into contact with the pest or disease organisms, or are systemic.

Contact pesticides kill pests when they crawl over a treated surface or when they are directly hit by the chemical (when sprayed, for example). Contact fungicides may kill germinating fungal spores and prevent further infection, but they have little effect on established fungal growths.

Systemic chemicals are absorbed into the plant tissues and are sometimes transported by the sap stream throughout the entire plant. Fungicides of this type, for example myclobutanil, kill fungi in the plant tissues. Systemic pesticides, such as imidacloprid and thiacloprid, are predominantly used against certain sap-sucking pests but will also control some pests that have chewing mouthparts, such as vine weevil grubs and some beetles and caterpillars. Thorough spraying of affected plants, especially on the undersides of leaves, is essential if these pesticides are to work.

Pesticide-resistant strains can occur, particularly with persistent greenhouse pests such as whitefly and red spider mite. Fungi that are frequently treated

APPLYING CHEMICALS WITH CARE

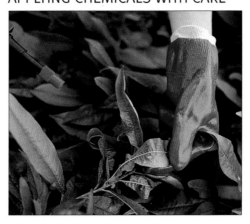

Thorough application
To avoid a wasted application, spray well into the centre of plants and beneath foliage, especially with products that have a contact action.

Separate equipment
Keep watering cans, sprayers and nozzles specifically for use with herbicides; residues in equipment can harm non-targeted garden plants.

with systemic fungicides may also develop resistant strains. This problem can sometimes be overcome by using a different type of compound, but with greenhouse pests the use of biological control (where possible) is often a better alternative (see p.642).

Formulation of chemical preparations

The active ingredient of a chemical preparation kills the organism, and the way in which a preparation has been formulated determines its efficacy and use. Pesticides and fungicides are available as concentrated liquids, dusts, powders (with which a wetter may be incorporated to ensure thorough penetration of the active ingredient), smokes, baits, and ready-to-use dilute liquids. These are formulated for maximum effectiveness and safety, for gardeners and for the environment.

Phytotoxicity

A few plants suffer adverse reactions to fungicides and insecticides. This is known as phytotoxicity. The manufacturer's instructions often list those species that should not be treated. However, such lists cannot be complete, since the reaction of many ornamental plants to certain chemicals may be unknown. If in doubt about whether a certain chemical is suitable, first test the fungicide or pesticide on a small area of the plant before undertaking treatment of the whole plant. Alternatively, where several plants of the same type are grown together, test the chemical on only one of them.

Various other factors, including the stage of growth and the environmental conditions surrounding the plant, can increase the likelihood of a plant being damaged by chemical treatments. For example, young seedlings, cuttings, and flower petals are much more sensitive than mature foliage to variations in the growing conditions, and may therefore be adversely affected by the application of some chemical treatments. Similarly, plants that are suffering any stress should never be treated with chemicals.

In order to avoid problems with side-effects on plants, never spray them when they are in bright sunlight, or when they are either dry at the roots or have been exposed to unusually high or low temperatures.

Using chemicals safely

If you follow the instructions precisely – that is, only in the way and for the purpose that the manufacturer describes – chemicals should be effective with little risk to the user or the environment. It is now illegal in the UK and other countries for gardeners to use chemicals other than in accordance with the instructions. Always take the following precautions:

- think before you spray: is it really necessary, or could you use organic remedies or biological controls instead?
- choose the chemical carefully – make sure it is the right one for the job;
- apply the preparation at the rate and frequency stated on the label;
- never use any type of chemical on plants in ponds;
- never mix different chemicals unless the manufacturer recommends this;
- always observe any suggested precautions;
- always spray when the wind is still, or almost still, to avoid damaging adjacent plants;
- always spray in the evening, when there are few bees and hoverflies around;
- do not spray on hot, sunny days, as such weather increases the risk of scorching plants;
- avoid contact with the skin and eyes by wearing goggles, rubber gloves, and long-sleeved clothing;
- do not inhale dusts, smokes, or sprays;
- make sure that the chemical does not drift into other people's gardens;
- keep pets and children away during treatment;
- never eat, drink, or smoke when applying a chemical;
- dispose of any excess carefully and wash out any apparatus thoroughly;
- do not use apparatus for anything other than chemicals;
- store chemicals out of reach of children and animals;
- store chemicals in their original containers, with their original labels, and keep any explanatory leaflets with them.

Leaf problems
Eaten leaves

Slugs and snails

Plants affected Non-woody plants, especially young ones (see also "Slugs", p.662).
Symptoms Holes appear in the foliage and stems may be stripped; silvery trails may be left on the leaves or the soil surface. Small holes on the outside of potato tubers lead to large cavities inside.
Cause Slugs (eg *Milax*, *Arion*, and *Deroceras* spp.) and snails (eg *Helix aspersa*), slimy-bodied

Slugs under leaves

Holes in leaves

Silvery slime trails

Stems stripped

molluscs that feed mainly at night or after rain.
Control Cultivate regularly to expose eggs. Use traps or barriers (see p.641), or handpick. 'Kestrel' and 'Sante' potatoes are slug-resistant. Biologically control underground slugs with the pathogenic nematode *Phasmorhabditis hermaphrodita*. Scatter ferric phosphate or metaldehyde slug pellets, spray plants and soil surface with liquid metaldehyde, or use an aluminium sulphate-based product.

Earwigs

Plants affected Shrubs, perennials, and annuals, commonly dahlias, clematis, and chrysanthemums. Also apricots and peaches.
Symptoms Young leaves are eaten in summer. See p.657 for other symptoms.
Cause Earwigs (*Forficula auricularia*) – yellowish-brown insects up to 18mm (¾in) long with a pair of curved pincers. Earwigs hide during the day and feed at night.
Control Place inverted pots, that have been loosely stuffed with hay or straw, on canes among susceptible plants; ear-

Adult earwigs

Leaves eaten away

wigs use these as daytime shelters from which they can be removed and destroyed. Alternatively, spray at dusk with bifenthrin.

Woodlice

Plants affected Seedlings and other soft growth, including strawberry fruits.
Symptoms Holes may appear in seedlings and in leaves near shoot tips but woodlice are not generally pests; they mainly eat decaying plant

material and are often found on plants that have already been damaged by other pests and diseases.
Cause Woodlice (eg *Oniscus, Porcellio*, and *Armadillidium* spp.), also known as slaters or pill bugs. They are grey or brownish-grey, sometimes with white or yellow markings, and up to 1cm (½in) long with hard, segmented bodies. They feed at night and hide away out of sight in dark shelters during the day.
Control Clear away plant debris and keep greenhouses tidy to reduce shelter. Water seedlings to help them through this vulnerable period.

Millipedes

Plants affected Seedlings and other soft growth, strawberry fruits, and potato tubers.
Symptoms Seedlings and soft growth are eaten; slug damage on bulbs and potato tubers is enlarged. Damage is rarely serious.
Cause Millipedes (eg *Blaniulus, Brachydesmus*, and *Cylindroiulus* spp.),

Common millipedes

black, grey, brown, or creamy-white animals that feed below or at soil level. They have hard, segmented bodies with two pairs of legs per segment (centipedes, which are beneficial predators, have only one pair per segment). The spotted snake millipede (*Blaniulus guttulatus*) is the most damaging species. Its slender, creamy-white body is up to 2cm (¾in) long with a row of red dots along each side. Millipedes are encouraged by soils that have a high organic content.
Control Cultivate the soil thoroughly and maintain good hygiene. Use inorganic rather than organic fertilizers in areas where millipedes are a problem, especially where potatoes are being grown. Millipedes are difficult to control but are rarely a problem in their own right; slug control helps to avoid millipede problems.

Flea beetles

Plants affected The seedlings of brassicas, turnips, swedes, radishes, wallflowers (*Erysimum*), and stocks (*Matthiola*).
Symptoms Small holes and pits are scalloped from the upper leaf surface; seedlings may die.

Cause Small, black or metallic-blue beetles (eg *Phyllotreta* spp.), sometimes with a yellow stripe running down each wing case. They are usually 2mm (¹⁄₁₆in) long, with enlarged hind legs that enable them to leap off plant surfaces when disturbed. They overwinter in plant debris.
Control Clear plant debris, particularly in autumn. Sow seed under fleece or fine mesh and water seedlings regularly to help rapid growth through the vulnerable stages. Dust seedlings with rotenone or pyrethrum if damage occurs.

Asparagus beetle

Plants affected Asparagus.
Symptoms Leaves are eaten; the epidermis is removed from stems, causing the upper growth to dry and turn brown. Damage occurs between late spring and early autumn.
Cause Both the adult and larval asparagus beetle (*Crioceris asparagi*). The adult beetles are 7mm

Adults　*Larvae*

(¼in) long, with yellow and black wing cases and a reddish thorax. The larvae are greyish-yellow.
Control Pick off light infestations by hand. If serious, spray with pyrethrum or rotenone; when plants are in flower, spray at dusk to protect bees.

Viburnum beetle

Plants affected *Viburnum*.
Symptoms Holes are eaten in the leaves; this begins during early summer, when the foliage may be reduced to just veins, with further damage occurring in late summer.
Cause The viburnum

beetle (*Pyrrhalta viburni*). The first period of damage in early summer is caused by the creamy-white larvae of the viburnum beetle, which are up to 7mm (¼in) in length and have black markings. The second phase of damage, occurring in late summer, is caused by the adult beetles, which are greyish-brown in colour.
Control Spray with bifenthrin, imidacloprid or pyrethrum when the larvae first appear.

Red lily beetle

Plants affected Bulbous lilies (*Lilium*) and also fritillaries (*Fritillaria*).
Symptoms Leaves and flowers eaten from early spring to mid-autumn.
Cause The adult and larval red lily beetle (*Lilioceris lilii*). Adults

are 8mm (⅜in) long and bright red. Larvae are reddish-brown with black heads, and covered in black excrement.
Control A long egg-laying and emergence period (mid-spring to midsummer) makes control difficult. Pick off by hand; otherwise spray with bifenthrin or imidacloprid.

Vine weevil

Adult vine weevil

Plants affected Shrubs, mainly rhododendrons, hydrangeas, *Euonymus*, and camellias; also strawberries, grape vines (*Vitis vinifera*), and many herbaceous plants.
Symptoms Notches in leaf margins, often near the ground, from mid-spring to mid-autumn.
Cause Adult vine weevil (*Otiorhynchus sulcatus*), a greyish-black beetle 9mm (⅜in) long, with a short snout and a pair of elbowed antennae. It feeds at night and hides by day.

Irregular holes in leaf margins

Control Damage occurs over an extended period, and control is difficult, although good hygiene and the removal of plant debris reduce the number of hiding places. Use a biological treatment to control the grub stage, watering the nematode *Steinernema kraussei* onto the compost in late summer. Once established, plants can tolerate damage to their leaves.
See also "Vine weevil grubs", p.666.

Capsid bugs

Plants affected Shrubs and perennials (especially chrysanthemums, fuchsias, hydrangeas, *Caryopteris*, and dahlias), annuals, some vegetables (rarely), and fruits.
Symptoms The leaves at shoot tips are distorted with numerous small holes. Damage occurs in summer. See p.657 for other symptoms.
Cause Capsid bugs (eg *Lygus rugulipennis* and *Lygocoris pabulinus*), green or brown insects 6mm (¼in) long that suck sap from shoot tips. Their toxic saliva kills plant tissues, causing leaves to tear.
Control In winter, clear up plant debris. Spray at first sign of damage using bifenthrin.

Leaf-cutting bees

Plants affected Roses mainly but also trees and other shrubs.
Symptoms Lozenge-shaped or circular pieces of uniform size are removed from the margins of the leaf.
Cause Leaf-cutting bees (*Megachile* spp.), which use the leaf pieces to build their nests. They are up to 1cm (½in) long, and have ginger hairs on the underside of their abdomen.
Control Leaf-cutting bees are of some benefit as pollinators and, unless plants are heavily damaged, control is not necessary. If they are a persistent nuisance, swat them as they return to the leaf.

Sawfly larvae

Plants affected Trees, shrubs, herbaceous perennials, and fruits. Particularly affected are conifers, willows (*Salix*), *Aruncus dioicus, Geum, Aquilegia,* Solomon's seal (*Polygonatum*), roses, gooseberries, and currants.
Symptoms Plants may be defoliated.

Sawfly larvae eating

Cause The larvae of various sawfly species (eg *Diprion, Nematus,* and *Pristiphora* spp.); caterpillar-like larvae up to 3cm (1¼in) long and generally green, sometimes with black spots. Larvae of Solomon's seal sawfly (*Phymatocera aterrima*) are greyish-white in colour. Most larvae grip the leaf edge

Leaves eaten away

and wave their bodies in an "S" shape when they are disturbed, but this does not occur with those on *Geum* or Solomon's seal.
Control Where possible, remove by hand. Spray serious infestations with pyrethrum, bifenthrin, thiacloprid or rotenone.

Winter moth caterpillars

Plants affected Many deciduous trees, fruit trees, and roses.
Symptoms Leaves are eaten between bud burst and late spring. Blossom and fruitlets may also be severely damaged.
Cause Pale green caterpillars, 2.5cm (1in) long, of the winter moth (*Operophtera brumata*).
Control Place sticky grease bands at least 15cm (6in) wide around tree trunks in mid-autumn, to prevent the wingless female moths from climbing up to lay eggs on the branches. Spray after bud burst with rotenone, pyrethrum, or bifenthrin.

Cabbage caterpillars

Plants affected Mainly brassicas, including cabbages, cauliflowers, and Brussels sprouts. Some perennial and annual ornamentals, eg nasturtiums (*Tropaeolum*).
Symptoms Holes appear in the foliage between

late spring and early autumn, and caterpillars may be found in the hearts of brassicas and on leaves.
Cause Caterpillars of the large cabbage white butterfly (*Pieris brassicae*), which are yellow and black with distinct hairs; those of the small cabbage white (*P. rapae*), pale green with velvety hairs; and those of the cabbage moth (*Mamestra brassicae*), yellowish-green or brown, with few hairs.
Control Pick off the young caterpillars by hand. For serious infestations, spray the foliage with rotenone, pyrethrum, or bifenthrin.

Wood pigeon

Plants affected Brassicas and bush fruits, especially blackcurrants, and the seeds of peas, beans, and other vegetable crops.
Symptoms Leaves of brassicas are eaten, especially in cold weather, and young plants are uprooted; blackcurrants are stripped of buds, leaves, and fruits; seeds are eaten.
Cause The wood pigeon (*Columba palumbus*).
Control Netting is the only effective way to prevent damage to crops. Scaring devices, such as humming tapes, scarecrows, or aluminium foil strips, work only initially; they lose their deterrent effect as birds become used to them. Repellent sprays must be used frequently to remain fully effective.

Caterpillars

Plants affected Many garden plants.
Symptoms Leaves, and possibly flowers, are eaten.
Cause Caterpillars of various species of butterfly and moth, which feed on plant material. The most common in gardens are winter moth and cabbage caterpillars (see left), webber moth caterpillars (see p.647), and tortrix moth caterpillars (see p.648).
Control Pick off caterpillars by hand, if practical, and cover crops with horticultural fleece. For serious infestations, spray the foliage with rotenone, pyrethrum, or bifenthrin.

Rabbits and hares

Plants affected Low-growing plants, young trees.
Symptoms Low-growing leaves are eaten, and the bark of young trees is gnawed away, especially during spells of cold weather.
Cause and control See p.666 for details.

Deer

Plants affected Most garden plants, especially trees, shrubs (including roses), and herbaceous plants.
Symptoms Shoots and leaves are eaten; tree bark is rubbed and frayed, and stripped in winter.
Cause and control See p.666 for details.

See also "Webber moth caterpillars", p.647; "Tortrix moth caterpillars", p.648; "Bacterial leaf spots and blotches", p.648; "Shothole", p.648; "Cutworms", p.655; and "Birds", p.657.

Discoloured and wilted leaves

Aphids

Plants affected Most plants.
Symptoms Leaves are often sticky with honey-dew (aphid excrement), blistered, or blackened by sooty moulds; stems and buds may also be covered. See also p.651.

Blackfly on stem

Cause Aphids (including those known as green-fly, blackfly, or plant lice) that cluster on stems and the undersides of leaves, sucking the sap; some attack roots. They are up to 5mm (¼in) long, and green, yellow, brown, pink, grey, or black; some, such as the woolly beech aphid, are covered in a fluffy, white wax. Aphids may transmit viruses (see p.649).

Blistered leaf

Control Apply a plant oil wash in winter against aphid eggs on deciduous fruit trees and bushes. Encourage ladybirds and lacewings. In greenhouses, introduce biological-control *Aphidoletes aphidomyza* and *Aphidius* spp. Spray plants, before heavy infestations develop, with bifenthrin, plant oils, fatty acids, pyrethrum, or rotenone, or use a systemic insecticide, such as imidacloprid or thiacloprid.

Whiteflies

Plants affected Indoor and greenhouse plants, some vegetables and fruits.
Symptoms Leaves are covered with sticky honeydew (whitefly excrement) and sooty mould. Small, white-winged insects fly off the plants when disturbed.

Adult whiteflies

Cause Whiteflies, active, white-winged insects about 2mm (⅟₁₆in) long; the immature, scale-like nymphs, which are immobile, whitish-green (or black if parasitized), flat, and oval are also found. Several species occur, the most wide-spread of which is the

Whitefly nymphs

glasshouse whitefly (*Trialeurodes vaporariorum*). In the open, brassicas are attacked by the cabbage whitefly (*Aleyrodes proletella*).
Control The parasitic wasp *Encarsia formosa* provides effective biological control in the greenhouse between mid-spring and mid-autumn, provided it is introduced early. Greenhouse and garden whiteflies may be sprayed with imidacloprid, bifenthrin, pyrethrum, fatty acids, or plant oils, but pesticide-resistant strains of greenhouse whitefly do occur.

Mealybugs

Plants affected Indoor and greenhouse plants, cacti and other succulents, vines (*Vitis*), some tender fruits, *Citrus*.
Symptoms A fluffy, white substance appears in leaf and stem axils. Plants may be sticky with honeydew (excrement) and black-

ened with sooty moulds. Roots can also be affected.
Cause Various mealybugs (eg *Pseudococcus* and *Planococcus* spp.); soft-bodied, greyish-white, wingless insects up to 5mm (¼in) long, often with white, waxy filaments trailing from their bodies. Root damage is caused by root mealybugs (*Rhizoecus* spp.).
Control In warmer months introduce the ladybird *Cryptolaemus montrouzieri* for biological control. If this fails, spray with imidacloprid, plant oils, or fatty acids several times at intervals of two weeks.

White blister

Plants affected The Cruciferae family, commonly brassicas, honesty (*Lunaria*), *Arabis*, and *Alyssum*.
Symptoms White, glisten-ing, fungal spore clusters, often grouped in concentric circles, develop on lower leaf surfaces. Severely affected foliage, and the heads of

brassicas, may also be distorted by this condition.
Cause The fungus *Albugo candida*, which is most troublesome on closely spaced plants.
Control Remove and burn affected leaves. Rotate plantings, and increase spacing. Cultivars such as Brussels sprout 'Bridge F1' resist white blister well.

Powdery mildew

Plants affected Most outdoor and many indoor plants.
Symptoms A fungal growth, usually white and powdery, appears on the leaves; on rhododendrons it is buff-coloured and felty. Usually found on the upper surface, it may either appear on the

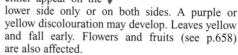

lower side only or on both sides. A purple or yellow discolouration may develop. Leaves yellow and fall early. Flowers and fruits (see p.658) are also affected.
Cause Various fungi, including species of *Sphaerotheca*, *Erysiphe*, *Oidium*, and *Uncinula*, which thrive on plants growing in dry soil. Some have restricted host ranges; others attack widely. Spores are spread by wind and rain splash, and the fungus may overwinter on host-plant surfaces.
Control Avoid growing susceptible plants on dry sites, and water and mulch as necessary. Remove affected areas immediately. If the problem persists, spray with sulphur, myclobutanil, or penconazole; avoid wetting foliage.

Downy mildew

Plants affected Annuals, perennials, bulbous plants, vegetables, and some fruits, including brassicas, stocks (*Matthiola*), lettuces, and *Nicotiana*.

Symptoms A fluffy or mealy, white fungal growth develops on the lower surface of the foliage, while the upper surface is blotched either yellow or brown; the older leaves are usually the most seriously affected. Growth is stunted and the plant is prone to secondary infections such as grey mould (*Botrytis*) (see below).
Cause Species of *Peronospora* and *Bremia* fungi, which are encouraged by humid conditions.
Control Sow seeds thinly and do not overcrowd plants. Improve ventilation, air circulation, and drainage; avoid overhead watering. Remove affected leaves.

Grey mould (*Botrytis*)

Plants affected Trees, shrubs, perennials, annu-als, bulbous plants, vegetables, fruits, and most indoor plants. Soft-leaved plants are particularly vulnerable to this condition.
Symptoms A fuzzy, grey fungal growth appears on the foliage, causing it to discolour and rapidly deteriorate; the infection may then spread into the main body of the plant. See pp.653, 656, and 658 for other symptoms.
Cause and control See p.653 for details.

Red spider mite

Plants affected Trees, shrubs, perennials, bulbs, annuals, cacti, succulents, vegetables, and fruits. Beans, cucumbers, mel-ons, apples and plums are particularly susceptible.
Symptoms The leaves become dull and yellowed as a fine, pale mottling

develops on their upper surface. They fall prema-turely, and a fine silk webbing may cover the plant.
Cause Red spider mites, eight-legged animals less than 1mm (⅟₁₆in) long. They are yellowish-green with black markings, but may be orange-red in autumn. There are several species, the most common of which is the two-spotted, or glasshouse, red spider mite (*Tetranychus urticae*); this affects both garden and indoor plants in summer.
Control The rapid reproduction of the mites and the existence of pesticide-resistant strains makes control difficult. To discourage those in greenhouses spray water under leaves, maintain high humidity and shade greenhouse to avoid high temperatures; the predatory mite *Phytoseiulus persimilis* provides an effective biological control of *T. urticae* if it is introduced before heavy infestations develop. Non-resistant red spider mites may be controlled with sprays of bifenthrin, plant oils, or fatty acids on three or four occasions at five-day intervals.

Thrips

Plants affected Shrubs, perennials, annuals, bulbous plants, vegetables, fruits, and indoor and greenhouse plants.
Symptoms A silver-white discolouration with tiny black dots appears on the upper leaf surface. See p.656 for other symptoms.
Cause Various species of thrips or thunderfly (eg *Thrips simplex, T. tabaci, Frankliniella occidentalis,* and *Kakothrips pisivorus*), which are brownish-black insects with narrow bodies up to 2mm (1⁄16in) long, sometimes crossed with pale bands. The immature nymphs are pale yellow-orange but otherwise resemble the adults. Both adults and nymphs feed on the upper surface of the leaf. They thrive in hot, dry conditions.
Control Water plants regularly and reduce the temperature in greenhouses with shading and ventilation. Before heavy infestations arise, use biological-control *Amblyseius degenerans* against western flower thrips (*Frankliniella occidentalis*). Spray all thrips with pyrethrum, thiacloprid or bifenthrin as soon as damage is seen.

Silver leaf

Plants affected Broad-leaved trees and shrubs, especially those in the Rosaceae family; plums and cherries are most often attacked.
Symptoms A silver-grey discolouration appears on the foliage, often starting on a single branch and spreading throughout the crown. The branches subsequently die back; infected limbs have a central dark stain lower down.
Cause The fungus *Chondrostereum purpureum,* which is also commonly found on felled logs and dead branches. The spores are produced from small, leathery brackets attached to the bark. The upper surface of the bracket is pale grey and slightly hairy, the lower surface purple and smooth. Spores may infect fresh wounds (less than a month old). There is no risk of infection from the silvered foliage.
Control Avoid injury to plants. Prune susceptible trees in summer, when infection is less likely to occur. Remove affected limbs to 15cm (6in) past the stained wood.

Leafhoppers

Plants affected Trees, shrubs, perennials, annuals, vegetables, and fruits. Rhododendrons, pelargoniums, primulas, roses, and tomatoes are usually most vulnerable.
Symptoms A coarse, pale spotting appears on the upper leaf surface, except on rhododendrons where damage is restricted to the spreading of rhododendron bud blast (see p.656).
Cause Leafhoppers, such as the rose leafhopper (*Edwardsiana rosae*) and glasshouse leafhopper

Spots on leaves

Adult leafhoppers

(*Hauptidia maroccana*), green or yellow insects 2–3mm (1⁄16–1⁄8in) long that leap from the plant when disturbed. Their bodies are widest just behind the head and taper back. The rhododendron leafhopper (*Graphocephala fennahi*) is turquoise-green and orange, and 6mm (1⁄4in) in length. The creamy-white, immature nymphs are less active.
Control Spray beneath the leaves with bifenthrin or pyrethrum when leafhopper activity is seen – adults readily jumping off leaves when disturbed.

Pear and cherry slugworm

Plants affected Pear and plum trees; also fruiting and ornamental cherries (*Prunus*), *Chaenomeles,* hawthorns (*Crataegus*).
Symptoms The leaves develop whitish-brown patches where the larvae graze away the surface.

Cause Pear and cherry slugworm (*Caliroa cerasi*) – the larval stage of a small black-bodied sawfly. The larvae are up to 10mm (1⁄2in) long and are broadest at the head end. They are covered by a black slimy substance and consequently resemble slugs. They feed mainly on the upper leaf surface. Two or three generations occur between early summer and early autumn.
Control Spray with pyrethrum, rotenone or bifenthrin as soon as the larvae are first seen.

Suckers (psyllids)

Plants affected Bay (*Laurus nobilis*), box (*Buxus*), and pears.
Symptoms Bay leaf margins are yellowed, thickened, and curled; box leaves are stunted; pear leaves are sticky with honeydew (excrement) and blackened with sooty mould. Damage occurs during summer. See pp.651 and 656 for other symptoms.
Cause Suckers (eg bay sucker, *Trioza alacris,* the box sucker, *Psylla buxi,* and the pear sucker, *Psylla pyricola*), the flattened and immature nymphs of small, aphid-like, winged insects. The nymphs are 2mm (1⁄16in) long, and generally grey or green in colouring.
Control Prune out and burn affected shoots immediately. Spray the plant thoroughly with pyrethrum or bifenthrin, either in spring or when the damage is first seen.

Leaf and bud eelworms

Plants affected Annuals and many herbaceous perennials. Most often attacked are penstemons, chrysanthemums, and *Anemone x hybrida.*
Symptoms Brownish-black patches appear on leaves as islands or wedges between the larger veins.

Dark patches

Cause Microscopic nematodes (*Aphelenchoides* spp.) that feed in large numbers inside infested leaves.
Control Burn all affected leaves or destroy the whole plant as soon as the infestation is noticed. For chrysanthemums, dip the dormant stools in clean water held at 46°C (115°F) for five minutes to obtain clean cuttings. There is no effective pesticide available to amateur gardeners.

Wedges between veins

Leaf miners

Plants affected Trees, shrubs, perennials, and vegetables, such as lilacs (*Syringa*), hollies (*Ilex*), apples, cherries, celery, and chrysanthemums.
Symptoms White or brown areas within the leaf, often of characteristic shape for the particular leaf miner, eg linear, circular, or irregular.

Linear blotching

Cause Larvae of various flies, eg celery leaf miner (*Euleia heraclei*), and chrysanthemum leaf miner (*Chromatomyia syngenesiae*); moths, eg apple leaf-mining moth (*Lyonetia clerkella*); beetles, such as the beech leaf mining weevil

Irregular discolouration

(*Rhynchaenus fagi*); and sawflies, eg the birch leaf-mining sawfly (*Fenusa pusilla*).
Control Remove and destroy affected leaves if the plant is lightly infested. None of the pesticides currently available to amateur gardeners is likely to control leaf miners.

Webber moth caterpillars

Plants affected Many trees, shrubs, perennials, and annuals, particularly fruit trees, *Euonymus,* willows (*Salix*), junipers (*Juniperus*), hawthorns (*Crataegus*), and cotoneasters.
Symptoms Shoots of the affected plant are defoliated, and the feeding area is completely covered with a dense, greyish-white, silk webbing.
Cause The caterpillars of various moths, such as the brown tail moth (*Euproctis chrysorrhoea*), the lackey moth (*Malacosoma neustria*), small ermine moths (*Yponomeuta* spp.), the hawthorn webber moth (*Scythropia crataegella*), and the juniper webber moth (*Dichomeris marginella*). The caterpillars of the last two species are no more than 2cm (3⁄4in) long; the other caterpillars are up to 5cm (2in) long and often have hairy bodies.
Control Remove small infestations by careful pruning. If the problem is very serious, spray the plants with pyrethrum or bifenthrin.

Tortrix moth caterpillars

Plants affected Trees (ornamental and fruit), shrubs, perennials, annuals, and bulbous plants.
Symptoms Two leaves may be bound together with fine, silky threads, or one leaf may be either similarly attached to a fruit or folded over on itself. Brown, dry, skeletal patches appear on the leaves.
Cause The caterpillars of tortrix moths, such as *Cacoecimorpha pronubana*, which graze away the inner surfaces of leaves. They are up to 2cm (¾in) long, and are generally dark green with brown heads. The caterpillars wriggle backwards rapidly when they are disturbed.
Control Squeeze bound-up leaves to crush the caterpillars or pupae. Pheromone traps are available for use against *C. pronubana*; these trap the males and reduce the likelihood of the females mating successfully. If the problem is serious, spray the affected plants very thoroughly with bifenthrin or pyrethrum.

Scale insects

Soft scale

Egg deposits

Plants affected Trees, shrubs, cacti and other succulents, fruits, indoor and greenhouse plants.
Symptoms Foliage may be sticky with honeydew (excrement) and blackened with sooty moulds. Plant growth may be slow. White deposits containing eggs may also appear. See also p.653.
Cause Scale insects, including brown scale (*Parthenolecanium corni*), soft scale (*Coccus hesperidum*), mussel scale (*Lepidosaphes ulmi*), and horse chestnut scale (*Pulvinaria regalis*). They are yellow, brown, dark grey, or white, up to 6mm (¼in) long, flat or raised, and circular, pear-shaped, or oval. They are found on lower leaf surfaces and stems.
Control Spray deciduous fruit trees with a plant oil wash in winter. Use biological-control *Metaphycus helvolus* on soft scale insects in greenhouses. Spray other plants with imidacloprid, plant oils, or fatty acids when the newly hatched scale nymphs are present – throughout the year on greenhouse plants, early to midsummer outside.

Bacterial leaf spots and blotches

Plants affected Trees, shrubs, roses, perennials, annuals, bulbous plants, vegetables, fruits, and indoor plants.
Symptoms Various spots or patches develop. They may appear water-soaked, and are often angular with a yellow edge or halo ("halo blight"). Black spots appear on delphinium leaves. See also "Shothole" and "Fungal leaf spots", right.
Cause *Pseudomonas* bacteria, spread by insects, rain splash, or wind-borne seeds.
Control Avoid wetting the foliage. Remove leaves affected by black spot. Spray plums and cherries (not other plants) with copper oxychloride or Bordeaux mixture.

Black spot on delphinium

Rusts

Plants affected Trees, shrubs, perennials, annuals, bulbous plants, vegetables, fruits, and indoor plants.
Symptoms Small, bright orange or brown patches of spores develop on the lower leaf surface, each corresponding to a yellow discoloration on the upper surface. Spores may appear in concentric rings or pustules, sometimes pale beige, eg those of chrysanthemum white rust. Winter spores, dark brown or black, are sometimes also produced. The leaves may also fall early. See p.653 for other symptoms.

Small, brown pustules

Pale discolouration

Cause Fungi, most often species of *Puccinia*, which are encouraged by high humidity. The spores are spread by rain splash and air currents. A few rusts are systemic.
Control Remove all affected areas. Improve air circulation by increasing ventilation and plant spacing where possible, and try to discourage the development of lush growth. Affected plants should be thoroughly sprayed with a fungicide containing penconazole or myclobutanil.

Rust on bluebell leaf

Corky scab

Plants affected Cacti and other succulents, especially *Opuntia* and *Epiphyllum*.
Symptoms Corky or brown, irregularly shaped spots appear. These areas later become sunken.
Cause Either extremely high humidity or excessively high light levels.

Control Take measures to improve the growing conditions of the plant. In extreme cases, however, the plant must be discarded, after having been used for propagation purposes, if desired.

Shothole

Plants affected Edible and ornamental cherries (*Prunus*), peaches, gages nectarines, plums, and *Prunus laurocerasus*; also other trees, shrubs, and woody perennials.
Symptoms Discoloured (usually brown) spots develop on the foliage; the dead leaf tissue then falls away, leaving holes. In severe cases large areas of leaf are lost.
Cause The bacteria *Pseudomonas syringae* pv. *morsprunorum* and *P. syringae* pv. *syringae* cause shothole in *Prunus* species, and *P. syringae* pv. *syringae* also causes the problem in other hosts. The fungus *Clasterosporium carpophilum* causes similar symptoms in *Prunus* spp.
Control Try to improve the general growing conditions and the overall health of the affected plant. In the case of plums and cherries, spray with a copper-based fungicide.

Fungal leaf spots

Plants affected Trees, shrubs, perennials, annuals, bulbous plants, vegetables, and fruits, as well as many indoor plants.
Symptoms Discrete, concentrically zoned spots appear on the leaves; close inspection may reveal pinprick-sized, fungal, fruiting bodies. Spots are often brown or slate grey. In severe cases they coalesce. Early leaf fall may occur – for example, rose black spot – but in some instances there is little damage or effect on overall plant vigour.
Cause A wide range of fungi.
Control Remove all affected parts of the plant, and rake up and burn any leaves that have already fallen. Spray roses with myclobutanil, penconazole, or mancozeb. The first two may give control of other spots, but there are no efficacy data.

Tomato leaf mould

Plants affected Almost exclusively greenhouse tomatoes.
Symptoms Purplish-grey, fuzzy, fungal patches develop on the lower leaf surface, each corresponding to a yellow discolouration on the upper surface. Leaves turn brown, wither, and die but do not fall. The lower leaves are affected first.
Cause The fungus *Fulvia fulva* (syn. *Cladosporium fulvum*), which thrives in warm, humid environments. The spores are spread by insects, tools, and handling, or on air currents. They overwinter on plant debris and on greenhouse structures.
Control Remove affected leaves, and improve ventilation and air circulation. Consider growing cultivars bred for resistance to the disease, eg 'Shirley' and 'Grenadier'.

Chocolate spot

Plants affected Broad beans.

Symptoms Chocolate-coloured spots or streaks appear on both the leaves and the stems, sometimes coalescing to cover a whole leaf. In extreme cases the plant is killed.

Cause *Botrytis fabae*, a fungus that thrives in wet spring weather. Plants growing in very acid soils are susceptible, as are those with soft, lush growth. Winter-sown crops are most severely affected by this condition.

Control Sow seed thinly, first dressing the soil with sulphate of potash, and avoid excessive use of nitrogen fertilizers. Remove and burn affected plants at the end of the harvest.

Scab

Plants affected Pears, *Citrus*, loquats, pyracanthas, and *Malus*, including both ornamental and fruiting species.

Symptoms Dark and greenish-brown patches, scabby and sometimes blistered, develop on the foliage; any affected leaves may fall early. See p.658 for other symptoms.

Brown patches

Cause The fungi *Venturia inaequalis*, *V. pirina*, *Spilocaea pyracanthae*, and *S. eriobotryae*, which thrive in damp weather. They may overwinter on infected leaves or shoots. Citrus scab is caused by *Elsinoe fawcettii*.

Control Keep the plant open-centred, and prune out any infected shoots and fruits. Rake up and

Dark blotches

burn all the fallen leaves. Spray plants with a suitable fungicide, such as mancozeb, myclobutanil, or penconazole. Do not store any affected fruits.

Lily disease

Plants affected Lilies (*Lilium*), especially *L. candidum* and *L. x testaceum*.

Symptoms Dark green, water-soaked blotches develop on the leaves, later turning a pale brown; the foliage then withers but remains on the stem. Where the pathogen

enters a leaf axil the stem may rot. Black sclerotia (fungal resting bodies) may form on dead tissues.

Cause The fungus *Botrytis elliptica*, which is encouraged by wet weather. Spores produced on the leaf lesions (or, in spring, from the sclerotia) are spread by rain splash and wind.

Control Grow on a well-drained site; clear away affected debris. There is no chemical treatment available for lily disease.

Viruses

Plants affected All plants.

Symptoms Leaves are undersized, distorted, or grouped in rosettes. Patterns of yellow discolouration (mosaics, ringspots, mottles) are common. See pp.656 and 659 for other symptoms.

Cause A large number of viruses, some with many hosts. Submicroscopic virus particles in the sap of infected plants may be transmitted to healthy tissues by sap-feeding pests like aphids (p.646), by soil-dwelling nematodes, through handling, or on pruning or propagating tools; some are seed-borne.

Yellowish streaks

Ringspots

Control Buy certified (virus-free) plants where possible. Keep potential carriers, eg aphids (see p.646), under control, and make sure that the site is free of weeds as these may harbour viruses. Remove and burn affected plants as soon as possible; always handle suspect plants after those which appear healthy, and do not propagate from them. Always use a new site for any replacement plants.

Tulip fire

Plants affected Tulips.

Symptoms The leaves are covered with pale brown, spore-producing blotches. Both leaves and shoots are deformed and stunted, and later become covered in dense, grey, spore-bearing, fungal growths, and black

sclerotia (fungal resting bodies). The bulbs develop sunken, brown lesions and small, black sclerotia. Plants may fail to mature or flower buds fail to open. See p.656 for other symptoms.

Cause The fungus *Botrytis tulipae*, which flourishes particularly in wet seasons; the spores are spread by wind and rain. The sclerotia persist on infected bulbs or in the soil, later germinating when tulips are planted again in the same area.

Control Remove and burn affected leaves and shoots (or preferably the entire plant) immediately. Plant from early winter onwards. Lift and dry bulbs at the end of the season, discarding any with sclerotia, and dust the remaining bulbs with sulphur. Wait at least two years before replanting the site with tulips; alternatively, change the soil.

Clubroot

Plants affected The family Cruciferae, especially brassicas (eg cabbages, swedes, and Brussels sprouts), and radishes. Also some ornamentals, like stocks (*Matthiola*), candytufts (*Iberis*), and wallflowers (*Erysimum*).

Symptoms Plants are stunted and discoloured; foliage wilts in hot weather. See also p.660.

Cause Slime mould *Plasmodiophora brassicae*, which thrives in poorly drained, acid soils, and on manure and plant debris. It is easily spread on boots and tools, and the spores may remain viable for 20 years or more. Susceptible weeds (for example, charlock and shepherd's purse) may be a source of infection.

Control Remove and burn affected plants. Keep the area free of weeds, where feasible improve drainage, and lime the soil. Choose resistant cultivars where available, such as calabrese 'Trixie', kale 'Tall Green Curled', swede 'Marian', and Chinese cabbage 'Harmony'. Raise new plants in pots of soil-based compost so that their roots are well developed when planted out.

Tomato/potato blight

Plants affected Tomatoes (in the open and occasionally under cover), potatoes.

Symptoms Brown discolouration develops on the leaf tips and edges; in damp conditions these may be ringed with a white, fungal growth. The

leaf tissue is killed, and where the patches coalesce the whole of the affected leaflet may eventually die. See pp.658 and 662 for other symptoms.

Cause The fungus *Phytophthora infestans*, which thrives in warm, moist conditions. Spores produced on tomato and potato foliage, and on potato haulms, are carried by wind and rain; they may be washed into the soil to infect potato tubers.

Control Avoid overhead watering. Grow tomatoes under glass rather than in the open. Earth up potatoes deeply to provide a barrier for the tubers against falling spores, and choose resistant cultivars, eg 'Kondor', 'Romano', 'Cara', and 'Wilja'. Protect both tomatoes and potatoes by spraying thoroughly with mancozeb, Bordeaux mixture, or a suitable copper-based fungicide. In wet seasons spray plants before the blight appears; spray tomatoes as soon as they have been stopped.

Fireblight

Plants affected Members of the family Rosaceae that bear pome fruits, eg pears, apples, some *Sorbus*, cotoneasters, and hawthorns (*Crataegus*).

Symptoms The leaves generally turn blackish-brown, shrivel and die, and they remain clinging to the stem. The leaves of some *Sorbus* and hawthorns may turn yellow and fall. Oozing cankers appear on the branches, and it is possible that the whole tree could eventually die.

Cause The bacterium *Erwinia amylovora*, which is produced from the cankers, attacks via the blossom. It is carried from plant to plant by wind, rain splash, insects, and pollen.

Control Remove the affected plants or prune out affected areas to at least 60cm (24in) past the damaged area; remember to dip the saw in disinfectant before using it on another tree. Fireblight is no longer a notifiable disease.

Climate change and gardening

Scientists broadly agree that human activities, which release greenhouse gases like carbon dioxide into the atmosphere, are responsible for accelerating the rate of climate change. These gases absorb the reflected heat energy of the sun, causing a warming effect. For gardeners in the UK, climate change is likely to result in hotter, drier summers; warmer, wetter winters; greater likelihood of extreme events such as gales; and a further lengthening of the growing season. Gardeners may have to adapt to increased risks of frost damage as plants come into leaf earlier in spring, then suffer drought stress in summer, and possibly waterlogging in winter. Climate change may also affect pests and diseases (see p.659).

Primula brown core

Plants affected Primulas.
Symptoms Leaves yellow, wilt, and die, and the plant becomes loose in the ground as the roots rot back from the tips.
Cause and control See p.661.

Insecticide/fungicide damage

Plants affected Some indoor and garden plants.
Symptoms Discrete spots or patches, often bleached or scorched, appear on leaves, which may fall; the plant usually survives.
Cause Often chemicals used at the wrong rate or interval, or applied during hot, sunny weather. Some plants are damaged by fungicides or insecticides applied correctly and susceptible species may be noted on the packaging; check carefully before using.
Control Use proprietary chemicals for specific uses and plants indicated on the product label. Always follow the manufacturers' instructions.

Contact weedkiller damage

Plants affected All plants.
Symptoms Pale, bleached spots appear on the foliage, sometimes turning brown, and small bumps on stems. Bulbs exposed to contact weedkillers before the foliage dies down show a very pale, almost white, leaf colour in the next year. In severe cases, vigour is reduced and the plant may die. Usually plants grow out of the symptoms.
Cause Spray drift due to windy conditions, or to careless application. Poorly cleaned sprayers and watering cans may also lead to contamination.
Control Follow the manufacturers' instructions. Use a dribble bar applicator or watering can in preference to a sprayer, and keep separate equipment for use with weedkillers only.

Drought

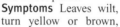

Plants affected All plants, especially those that are young and container-grown, or in light, sandy soils.
Symptoms Autumn colour develops early and defoliation may occur, sometimes followed by die-back. Plants wilt and growth is stunted. See pp.657 and 664 for other symptoms.
Cause Prolonged or repeated water shortage caused by dry soil, excessive water loss from leaves of plants on exposed sites, injured or restricted roots, or soil compaction. Plants in small containers are vulnerable in hot weather, since peat-based composts allowed to dehydrate are hard to re-wet.
Control Water plants regularly, especially those in hot positions. Mulch when soil is thoroughly moist, to improve moisture retention. It is easier to prevent drought than to treat it; plants, however, are less likely to be damaged by short, sudden droughts than prolonged ones.

High temperatures and scorch

Plants affected In particular plants with fleshy leaves or flowers, those near glass, and seedlings; also trees, shrubs, perennials, annuals, bulbous plants, vegetables, fruits, and indoor plants.
Symptoms Leaves wilt, turn yellow or brown, become dry and crisp, and may die; the tips and margins are often affected first. In extreme cases the stems die back. Scorching produces brown patches on the upper or exposed parts of the plant; foliage close to glass is very susceptible. Affected leaves may shrivel completely. Scorched petals turn brown and become dry and crisp. Roses may fail to open as the outer petals dry up and restrict the bud. Fruits are also affected (see p.658).
Cause Very high or fluctuating temperatures in a closed environment (eg a greenhouse); scorching is caused by bright, but not necessarily hot, sunlight. Scorch problems are increased by moisture on the leaves and fruit, and by faults in the glass near plants, both of which magnify the sun's rays. Apple fruits may discolour if picked too early or stored with insufficient ventilation.
Control Where possible shade greenhouses, provide adequate ventilation to keep temperatures down, and move plants away from any faults there may be in the glass. Avoid overhead watering and spraying in sunny weather. Harvest only ripe apples and store them under suitable conditions.

Low temperatures

Plants affected Trees, shrubs, perennials, annuals, bulbous plants, fruits, vegetables, indoor plants; seedlings and young plants are most vulnerable.
Symptoms Leaves, especially those of seedlings, are sometimes bleached, and brown, dry patches develop; evergreen foliage may turn brown. Frost injury results in puckered, withered, or discoloured (often blackened) leaves, and a lifting of the lower leaf surface, giving foliage a silvered appearance. Rotten patches, brown and dry or dark and soft, develop on petals, especially on exposed flowerheads. Frost injury may leave petals withered or discoloured and kill the whole flower. See p.653 for other symptoms.
Cause Low temperatures or occasionally great fluctuations in temperature. Plants in exposed positions or frost pockets are likely to be affected.
Control Check the plant's suitability for the site. Provide winter protection for young, tender and exposed plants. Harden off plants raised under protection and/or cover with fleece.

Nitrogen deficiency

Plants affected Most outdoor and indoor plants.
Symptoms Pale green leaves are borne, and these sometimes develop either yellow or pink tints. Overall growth is reduced and the whole plant may eventually become slightly spindly.
Cause Growing plants either in poor, light soils or in restricted surroundings such as hanging baskets, windowboxes, or other types of container.
Control Use green manures on affected areas, or apply a high-nitrogen fertilizer, eg sulphate of ammonia, nitrochalk, or manure.

Potassium deficiency

Plants affected Edible and ornamental fruiting plants, mainly currants, apples, and pears.
Symptoms Foliage turns blue, yellow, or purple, with a brown discolouration either in blotches or on the leaf tips or margins. Some leaves may roll inwards; they are fairly soft and therefore prone to attack by pathogens. Flowering, fruiting, and general growth of the whole plant may be reduced.
Cause Growing plants in soils either with a light texture or with a high chalk or peat content.
Control Improve the soil texture. Dress with sulphate of potash or a high-potash fertilizer.

Phosphate deficiency

Plants affected Potentially all plants; but this deficiency is unlikely to occur in most gardens.
Symptoms Plant growth is slow and the young foliage may appear dull or yellowed.
Cause The leaching out of phosphates in acid soils and areas of high rainfall. Plants growing in either heavy clay soils or deep peat soils, or those overlying iron pans, are most likely to be at risk.
Control Apply superphosphate. Bone meal is also useful although slower acting.

Manganese/iron deficiency

Plants affected Trees, shrubs, perennials, annuals, bulbous plants, vegetables, fruits, and indoor plants. Acid-loving plants growing in alkaline soils are often affected.
Symptoms A yellowing or browning starts at the leaf margins and extends between the veins. The overall leaf colour may also be rather yellow.
Cause The cultivation of plants in unsuitable soils or composts; acid-loving plants, in particular, are unable to absorb adequate trace elements from alkaline soils. Regular watering with very hard water, buried debris (e.g builders' rubble), and rain run-off from mortar in walls are all possible causes of a locally raised soil pH.
Control Choose plants compatible with the soil type and clear the area of any builders' debris. Use rainwater, not tap water, for susceptible plants. Acidify the soil before or after planting, and apply acid mulches. Apply a chelated iron or fritted form of trace elements and manganese sulphate.

Magnesium deficiency

Plants affected Trees, shrubs, bulbs, perennials, annuals, vegetables, and fruits; also many indoor plants. Tomatoes, chrysanthemums, and roses are most often affected.

Symptoms Distinct areas of discolouration, usually yellow but occasionally red or brown, develop between the leaf veins (interveinal chlorosis), and affected leaves may fall early.
Cause Acid soils; heavy watering or rainfall, both of which leach out magnesium; or high potash levels, which make it unavailable. Plants fed on high-potash fertilizers to encourage flowering or fruiting (eg tomatoes) are susceptible.
Control Treat plants and/or soil with Epsom salts in autumn; either add them neat to the soil at a rate of 25g/sq m (1oz/10sq ft), or apply a foliar spray of 210g Epsom salts in 10 litres of water (7½oz in 2¼ gallons), adding a wetting agent like soft soap.

Waterlogging

Plants affected Potentially all plants.
Symptoms Leaves turn yellow and the plants wilt.
Cause Too much water in the growing medium, due to poor structure or drainage, or overwatering.
Control Improve soil structure and drainage.
See also pp.660 and 664.

See also "Irregular water supply", "Oedema", "Peach leaf curl", "Hormone weedkiller damage", "Phytoplasmas", all below; "Azalea gall", p.652; "Smuts", p.652; "*Verticillium* wilt", p.653; "*Fusarium* wilt", p.654; "*Phytophthora* root rots", p.654; "Foot and root rots", p.654; "Etiolation", p.655; "Blossom wilt", p.656; "Carrot fly", p.660; "Narcissus eelworm", p.663; "Iris rhizome rot", p.663; "Onion fly", p.663; "Blackleg on potatoes", p.664; "*Seiridium* canker", p.664; "Clematis wilt", p.665; and "Anthracnose", p.666.

Distorted leaves

Irregular water supply

Plants affected Potentially all garden plants, especially those grown in containers.
Symptoms Leaves and flowers become puckered and distorted or are undersized. See pp.653 and 659 for other symptoms.
Cause An irregular supply of water, leading to irregular patterns of growth and consequent distortion in the upper parts of the plant.
Control Provide a regular and adequate supply of water for plants, especially in hot or windy weather, and pay particular attention to any plants that are growing in containers. Apply a regular mulch around the plants, where appropriate, since this will do most to conserve the moisture in the soil and prevent problems from occurring.

Oedema

Plants affected Potentially all plants, but particularly pelargoniums, camellias, *Eucalyptus*, and succulents.
Symptoms Raised, warty patches appear on the foliage. These are initially of a similar colour to that of the rest of the leaf but later turn brown.
Cause Excessively high moisture levels in either the air or the growing medium, which give the plant cells an unusually high water content. As a result of this, small groups of cells swell, forming the outgrowths, and later burst, leaving brown patches on the leaves.
Control Improve air circulation around the plants by increasing ventilation, and by attending carefully to plant spacing. Decrease the amount of watering and wherever possible try to improve drainage. Leaves affected with this condition should not be picked off at any time.

Peach leaf curl

Plants affected Peaches, nectarines, almonds, and closely related ornamental species (*Prunus*).
Symptoms Leaves become distorted, blistered, and sometimes swollen, later turning a deep red; a white, fungal growth then develops on the leaf surfaces. The foliage falls, but a second flush of healthy leaves will be produced afterwards.
Cause The fungus *Taphrina deformans*, which is encouraged by cool, wet conditions. Spores are carried by wind or rain to shoots, bud scales, and cracks in the bark, where they overwinter.
Control Pick off affected leaves. Shelter plants so that spores cannot land; an open-sided, wooden frame covered with heavy-duty plastic is ideal. To prevent infection, spray leaves with Bordeaux mixture or a suitable copper-based fungicide in mid- to late winter, repeating the application 14 days later.

Hormone weedkiller damage

Plants affected Broadleaved plants, mainly roses, grapes tomatoes, and conifers.
Symptoms Leaves are small, narrow, often thickened, and with prominent veins. They may be cup-shaped and extremely distorted. The petioles become twisted. Small bumps may appear on stems. See p.659 for other symptoms.
Cause Contamination by a growth regulator or hormone-type weedkiller, often from a considerable distance; minute quantities may cause extensive damage. Common sources of trouble are spray drift, contaminated sprayers or watering cans, and water from polluted butts.

Distorted leaves

Stunted leaf buds

Control Always apply weedkillers according to manufacturers' instructions, placing protective barriers around adjacent garden plants to prevent spray drift. Keep one sprayer or watering can for use with weedkillers only. Store weedkillers away from compost, fertilizers, and plants. Affected plants usually grow out of the symptoms.
See also "Selective weedkillers". p.671.

Aphids

Plants affected Trees, shrubs, climbing plants, perennials, annuals, bulbous plants, fruits, and vegetables.
Symptoms Leaves are stunted and distorted.
Cause and control See p.646 for details.

Suckers (psyllids)

Plants affected Bay (*Laurus nobilis*), box (*Buxus*), and pears.
Symptoms The leaf margins of bay are yellowed, thickened, and curled; box has stunted stems and cupped, slightly distorted leaves. Damage occurs to box in spring, and to bay throughout the summer. See p.647 for symptoms on pears.
Cause and control See p.647 for details.

Phytoplasmas

Plants affected Trees, shrubs, perennials, annuals, bulbous plants, vegetables, fruits (especially strawberries), and indoor plants.
Symptoms Leaves may be undersized, distorted, and covered with patterns of discolouration. This condition on strawberry plants causes green petals on the flowers and produces young leaves that are small, irregularly shaped, and yellowed; in addition, the older foliage turns a distinctly red colour when flowering has ceased. See p.656 for other symptoms of phytoplasmas.

Cause Phytoplasmas, which are believed to be related to bacteria. Phytoplasmas are spread from plant to plant by leafhoppers (see p.647), which commonly pick up the infection from clover plants that are suffering from a condition known as phyllody disease.
Control Discard all affected plants, buy only certified fruit stock, and control pests that are potential carriers (leafhoppers), and weeds, which may harbour the disease.

Gall mites

Plants affected Trees and shrubs, including plums, pears, walnuts, vines (*Vitis*), maples (*Acer*), limes (*Tilia*), elms (*Ulmus*), hawthorns (*Crataegus*), rowan (*Sorbus aucuparia*), broom (*Cytisus*), beeches (*Fagus*), and blackcurrants.

Pale leaf blotches

Symptoms These vary according to the species of mite, and include: whitish-green or red pimples or spikes on foliage (maples, elms, limes, and plums); creamy-white or pink hairs on lower leaf surfaces (maples, limes, and beeches); raised, blistered areas on upper leaf surfaces, with pale hairs underneath (walnuts and vines); thick, curling leaf margins (beeches and hawthorns); pale leaf blotches, later turning brownish-black (rowans and pears); and stunted leaves (broom). Plant vigour is not affected.

Stunted leaves

Cause Microscopic gall mites, or eriophyid mites, secreting chemicals that induce abnormal growth. The adults are tiny, creamy white mites with tubular bodies and two pairs of legs.
Control Remove affected leaves and shoots if desired. There is no effective chemical control.

Gall midges

Plants affected Many garden plants especially violets (*Viola*), *Gleditsia*, and blackcurrants.
Symptoms Violet leaves thicken and fail to unfurl. *Gleditsia* leaflets swell and fold over to form pod-like galls. Blackcurrant shoot-tip leaves fail to expand normally and the shoot tips may be killed.
Cause Whitish-orange maggots up to 2mm (⅛in) long that feed within the galled tissues; three or four generations may occur in a summer. These are the larvae of three species of midge: the violet gall midge (*Dasineura affinis*), the gleditsia gall midge (*D. gleditchiae*), and the blackcurrant gall midge (*D. tetensi*).
Control Remove and destroy affected leaves. The larvae are well protected inside the galls, so there is little prospect of being able to control them with the use of pesticides.

Gall wasps/cynipid wasps

Plants affected Oaks (*Quercus*) and roses.
Symptoms Symptoms on oaks include: flat discs on the lower surface of leaves in autumn; benign, spherical, woody growths (marble galls) or pithy oak apples on shoots in spring; yellowish-green

or red bunches of currant galls on the catkins; and yellowish-green, sticky "knopper" galls on acorns. Species rose stems and hybrid rose suckers develop swellings covered in yellowish-pink, moss-like leaves ("bedeguar" galls or "Robin's pincushions") in late summer. Damage to these plants is minimal.
Cause The larvae of gall wasps, or cynipid wasps; they secrete chemicals that induce galls as they feed.
Control No treatment is necessary.

Azalea gall

Plants affected Rhododendrons and azaleas, especially Indian azalea (*Rhododendron simsii*) grown as an indoor plant.
Symptoms Fleshy, pale green swellings (galls) develop on the foliage or flowers, later turning white.

Cause The fungus *Exobasidium vaccinii* var. *japonicum*, which is encouraged by high humidity. The spores are insect- or air-borne.
Control Remove and destroy the galls as soon as they are seen, before the fungus produces spores.

Whiptail (molybdenum deficiency)

Plants affected All brassicas, especially cauliflowers and sprouting broccoli.
Symptoms The leaves develop abnormally and appear narrow and ribbon-like; the heads of cauliflowers and sprouting broccoli are extremely small or, more commonly, do not develop at all.

Cause A deficiency of the trace element molybdenum, most often occurring in acid soils.
Control Increase the alkalinity of the soil by liming. Treat the soil with molybdenum before sowing or planting out susceptible crops.

Bulb scale mite

Plants affected Daffodils and *Hippeastrum*, especially those grown indoors.
Symptoms Growth is stunted, leaves become curved, and saw-toothed scarring appears along the leaf margins and flower stems.

Cause The microscopic, white bulb scale mite (*Steneotarsonemus laticeps*), which feeds in the neck region of the bulb.
Control Discard infested bulbs. Buy only those of good quality from reputable suppliers. There is no chemical control available to amateur gardeners.

Rose leaf-rolling sawfly

Plants affected Roses.
Symptoms Rose leaflets roll downwards at the edges to form tight tubes during late spring and early summer.
Cause Rose leaf-rolling sawfly (*Blennocampa phyllocolpa*). Females lay their eggs in the leaflets, secreting chemicals that cause the

rolling. Pale green, caterpillar-like larvae then feed inside the rolled leaflets. The adults are black, 3–4mm (⅛in) long, and have transparent wings.
Control Pick off and burn rolled leaves. Alternatively, spray with bifenthrin against adult sawflies.

Smuts

Plants affected *Trollius*, *Anemone*, violets (*Viola*), winter aconites (*Eranthis hyemalis*) and maize.
Symptoms Round or elliptical swellings, often pale green or dirty white, develop on the leaves. They rupture, releasing powdery, black

masses of spores; severely affected leaves wither and die. Leaf stalks may show similar symptoms.
Cause Various fungi, eg *Urocystis* and *Ustilago*; spores are spread by rain splash and air currents.
Control Burn affected plants; infection may recur even if the problem appears to have been controlled.

Eelworms

Plants affected Phlox and onion.
Symptoms Phlox are stunted, with narrow shoot-tip leaves and swollen stems; onion leaves and stems are swollen and soft. Plants may be killed by a heavy attack.
Cause Microscopic eelworms or nematodes (*Ditylenchus dipsaci*) feeding in the plant tissues.
Control Burn affected plants. Where infested onions have been growing, plant non-susceptible vegetables (lettuce and brassicas) for the next two years. Eelworm-free phlox can be obtained from root cuttings. There is no chemical control available for garden use.

See also "Powdery mildew", p.646; "Leaf and bud eelworms", p.647; "Scab", p.649; "Viruses", p.649; "Leafy gall", p.655; "Narcissus eelworm", p.663; "Anthracnose", p.666.

Stem, branch, and leaf-bud problems
Stems discoloured or with pests visible

Low temperatures

Plants affected Trees, shrubs, perennials, annuals, bulbous plants, vegetables, fruits, and indoor plants. Soft-stemmed and young plants are most vulnerable.
Symptoms Brown, dry patches develop on the stems – especially those of *Acer*. Stems may blacken, wither, and crack or split, giving access to various organisms that cause die-back. The cracks become enlarged if moisture accumulates within them and then freezes, and this may lead to the death of the whole plant. See p.650 for other symptoms.
Cause Low temperatures or occasionally great fluctuations in temperature. Plants that are growing in exposed positions are the most likely to be affected by this problem.
Control Provide winter protection from frost and wind for young or tender plants, as well as for those growing in exposed positions (see p.612).

Verticillium wilt

Plants affected Many garden and greenhouse plants.
Symptoms Staining of the vascular system of stems and roots, creating longitudinal brown stripes (revealed by removal of bark or outer stem). Woody plants deteriorate over several years, and may die.
Cause Several species of the fungus *Verticillium*, which may be present in the soil or in plant remains, or are introduced in new stock.
Control Remove any affected plants and soil in the vicinity of the roots. Clean pruning tools thoroughly after use on diseased or suspect plants (see p.554). Keep weeds under strict control and do not grow susceptible plants on the affected area.

Slime flux/wet wood

Plants affected Trees, shrubs, and woody perennials; clematis is particularly affected.
Symptoms The stem dies back and a pink, yellow, or off-white slime oozes from its base. This is often thick and may have an unpleasant smell.
Cause Injury to the stem (often through frost or wounding) when sap pressure is high, just before the leaves break. The sap released from the wound has a high sugar content and is colonized by various micro-organisms (in particular yeasts, bacteria, and fungi), which cause the thickening and discolouration.
Control Avoid injury to stems, particularly those of susceptible plants. Remove the affected stems immediately, cutting well back into healthy growth, below ground level if necessary. Given adequate food and moisture, the plant should subsequently produce more shoots.

Spur blight/cane blight

Plants affected Raspberries. Spur blight may also attack loganberries.
Symptoms With spur blight (shown here), purple areas develop around the nodes in late summer; these increase in size and turn a silvery-grey. Numerous tiny, black, spore-producing structures develop in the centre of each blotch. Buds may die, or may produce shoots that die. With cane blight, deterioration starts just above soil level as the fungus enters through points of injury and causes the base of the cane to develop dark discolouration and to become brittle. The foliage withers. Weakened plants are much more likely to be affected by this problem than well-maintained, strong specimens.
Cause The fungi *Didymella applanata* (spur blight) and *Leptosphaeria coniothyrium* (cane blight).
Control Maintain plants well. At the first sign of disease, cut out affected canes, going to below soil level for cane blight. Spray with copper fungicide.

Scale insects

Hemispherical scale (above)
and mussel scale (right)

Plants affected Indoor and greenhouse plants, trees, shrubs, fruits, and cacti and other succulents.
Symptoms The stems are sometimes sticky with honeydew (excrement) and blackened with sooty moulds. Heavily infested plants may also show slow growth. White, waxy deposits containing eggs also occasionally appear on the stems.
Cause and control See p.648 for details.

Rusts

Plants affected Trees, shrubs, annuals, perennials, bulbous plants, vegetables, fruits, and indoor plants; mints (*Mentha*), roses, raspberries, and blackberries are commonly affected.
Symptoms Pustules containing bright orange or dark brown spores develop either on, or apparently bursting from within, the stem. Some plants, eg junipers, develop gelatinous growths. In severe cases stems become extensively distorted and ruptured. Die-back may follow. See also p.648.
Cause A range of fungi encouraged by high humidity. Spores are spread by rain splash and air currents, and may overwinter on plant debris.
Control Remove affected areas and improve air circulation, increasing ventilation and plant spacing. Spray with a suitable fungicide, eg myclobutanil or penconazole.

Grey mould (*Botrytis*)

Plants affected Trees, shrubs, perennials, annuals, bulbous plants, vegetables, fruits, and indoor plants. Soft-leaved plants are vulnerable.
Symptoms Dead and discoloured patches develop on the stems and leaves. Rapid deterioration may occur, causing the upper parts of the stem to die. Fungal spores develop on decaying plant material. See pp.656 and 658 for other symptoms.
Cause The fungi *Botrytis cinerea* and, on snowdrops (*Galanthus*), *B. galanthina*, which thrive in damp conditions and where air circulation is poor. Fungal spores are spread on air currents or by rain splash; infection is most likely where plants are damaged. Fruits may also become infected by contact with those already diseased. Hard, black, resilient sclerotia (fungal resting bodies), produced on plant remains, fall to the ground and may cause later infections.
Control Avoid injury to plants, clear up dead and dying plant material, and provide good air circulation, ensuring at all times that plants are adequately spaced and those under cover are well ventilated. Remove and burn any affected areas (and in the case of snowdrops the entire clump) immediately.

Irregular water supply

Plants affected Potentially all plants, especially those in containers.
Symptoms The outer stem layer or bark of the stem or trunk may split or crack. See pp.651 and 659 for other symptoms.
Cause An irregular supply of water, leading to irregular growth. Sudden availability of water after a drought caused by climatic conditions or a prolonged dry period due to erratic watering brings rapid swelling, which causes the stem to rupture and crack.
Control Provide a regular and adequate supply of water, especially during hot or windy weather. Do not suddenly overwater plants after drought conditions in an attempt to make up for a severe lack of moisture. Mulch, where appropriate, to conserve as much moisture in the soil as possible.

Dutch elm disease

Plants affected Elms (*Ulmus*) and *Zelkova*.
Symptoms Notching appears in twig crotches, and young twigs may be crook-shaped. Longitudinal, dark brown streaks develop under the bark. Leaves in the crown wilt, yellow, and die. The tree

Crook-shaped twigs

may die within two years.
Cause *Ophiostoma novo-ulmi*, a fungus spread by elm bark beetles as they feed on the bark. Infected trees may pass the disease to healthy ones via common root systems.
Control Remove all suckers in gardens.

Longitudinal streaks

Woolly aphid

Plants affected Apples, cotoneasters, pyracanthas.
Symptoms A fluffy, white, mould-like substance appears on the bark in spring. Starting on the larger branches around old pruning cuts and in bark cracks, it later spreads to the new shoots where soft

swellings may develop. Aphids may be visible.
Cause The woolly aphid (*Eriosoma lanigerum*), which is a small, greyish-black insect that sucks sap from the bark and secretes white, waxy threads.
Control Spray plants with bifenthrin, imidacloprid or thiacloprid when the pest is seen.

Froghoppers (cuckoo spit)

Plants affected Trees, shrubs, perennials, annuals.
Symptoms Globules of white froth containing a small insect appear on stems and leaves in early summer. Where the pest feeds on shoot tips growth may be distorted but damage is minimal.

Cause Froghopper nymphs, or spittlebugs (eg *Philaenus spumarius*), cream-coloured sap-suckers that secrete a protective froth over themselves. The adults are darker in colour, up to 4mm (⅛in) long, and live openly on the plant.
Control If treatment is necessary, remove nymphs by hand, blast with a jet of water, or spray with imidacloprid (not edible plants) or bifenthrin.

Adelgids

Plants affected Conifers, particularly *Abies*, pines (*Pinus*), spruces (*Picea*), *Pseudotsuga menziesii*, and larches (*Larix*).
Symptoms A fluffy, white, mould-like substance appears on the leaves and stems. Knobbly swellings

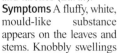

develop on *Abies*, and swollen stem tips (pineapple galls) appear on the young shoots of spruce.
Cause Adelgids, or conifer woolly aphids (for example *Adelges* spp.), are small, greyish-black, aphid-like insects that suck sap from the bark or the leaves. The bark- and leaf-feeders secrete white, waxy threads.
Control Established trees can tolerate the damage, but spray small trees with bifenthrin on a mild, dry day in mid- to late winter or early summer.

Fusarium wilt

Plants affected Perennials, annuals, vegetables, and fruits; most commonly affected are China asters (*Callistephus*), carnations (*Dianthus*), sweet peas (*Lathyrus odoratus*), beans, and peas.
Symptoms Black patches develop on stems and foliage; these patches are sometimes covered with a white or pale pink fungal growth. Roots turn black and die. Plants wilt, often suddenly.
Cause Various forms of the microscopic fungus *Fusarium oxysporum*, which are present in the soil or on plant debris, or are sometimes seed-borne; they may also be introduced on new stock. They will build up in the soil when the same type of plant is grown in the same site year after year.
Control There is no cure for affected plants. Remove them and the soil in their vicinity, and destroy the plants. Avoid growing susceptible plants in the area. Propagate only from healthy stock; if possible, grow resistant cultivars.

Phytophthora root rots

Plants affected Trees, shrubs, and woody perennials; maples (*Acer*), Lawson cypress (*Chamaecyparis lawsoniana*), apples, yew (*Taxus baccata*), rhododendrons, raspberries, and heathers are most commonly attacked.
Symptoms Patches of dead tissue may appear on the base of the stem or the trunk, with bluish-

black stains in the tissue beneath; the foliage is sparse and chlorotic. Die-back may follow, and plants may even be killed. See p.661 for other symptoms.
Cause Various species of the fungus *Phytophthora*, which is frequently found in wet or waterlogged soil. Roots are attacked by swimming spores that build up in the soil and in infected plant remains.
Control Always avoid heavy watering, and wherever possible improve soil drainage in the area. Dig up and burn all affected plants. Buy only good-quality plants from reputable sources, and choose those that are tolerant or resistant to *Phytophthora*, such as *Tsuga heterophylla* and x *Cupressocyparis leylandii*. There is no effective chemical control available to amateur gardeners.

Foot and root rots

Plants affected A wide range, especially petunias, *Viola* spp. and other bedding plants, tomatoes, cucumbers, peas, beans, and young, container-grown plants.
Symptoms The stem bases discolour, and rot or shrink inwards. This causes the upper parts of the plant to wilt and collapse; the lower leaves will usually show the symptoms first. The roots turn black and break or rot.
Cause A range of soil- and water-borne fungi that flourish where growing conditions are not adequately hygienic. They are often introduced through the use of unsterilized compost and non-mains water, and build up in the soil, especially if susceptible plants are repeatedly grown on the same site.
Control Rotate susceptible plants. Maintain strict hygiene and only use fresh, sterilized compost, and mains water. Remove affected plants and the soil in the vicinity of their roots.

Seedling blight

Plants affected Many vegetable crops grown in warm climates (not present in UK), including beans, peas, cabbages, sweet potatoes, and tomatoes.
Symptoms Seedlings show symptoms of damping off (see p.660). The collar or stem of older plants rots at soil level, and shoots yellow, wilt, and die.
Cause Invasion via the base of the plant by the fungus *Athelia rolfsii* (syn. *Corticium rolfsii*); nematode and insect wounds promote infection. Plants in light, sandy soils, well supplied with moisture, are most at risk.
Control Maintain crops well, remove diseased plants and debris, and avoid growing plants in contaminated areas; burn infected residues or bury them deeply.

Boron deficiency

Plants affected Carnations (*Dianthus*), lettuces, celery, and tomatoes; also all fruits (most commonly pears, plums, and strawberries). The condition is fairly rare.
Symptoms The growing tips die, causing the plants to become stunted and bushy. Celery stems

start to develop transverse cracks and the exposed tissues turn brown; lettuces fail to heart up. Pears become distorted and dimpled with brown, flecked flesh (very similar symptoms to those of the virus disease called stony pit). Plums are misshapen and may show gumming (see "Pests and diseases", p.448). Strawberries are small and poorly coloured. See p.662 for other symptoms.
Cause and control See p.662 for details.

See also "Mealybugs", p.646; "Powdery mildew", p.646; "Chocolate spot", p.649; "Fireblight", p.649; "Lily disease", p.649; "Contact weedkiller damage", p.650; "Smuts", p.652; "Etiolation", p.655; "Fungal brackets", p.655; "Lightning", p.655; "Chafer grubs", p.660; "Leatherjackets", p.660; "Damping off", p.664; "Blackleg on cuttings", p.664; "Blackleg on potatoes", p.664; "Coral spot", p.665; "Honey fungus", p.665; "Crown rot", p.665; "Replant disease/soil sickness", p.665; "Rose die-back", p.665; "Peony wilt", p.665; and "Vine weevil grubs", p.666.

New *Phytophthora* species

Discovered in coastal California and northern Europe in the 1990s, *Phytophthora ramorum* causes fatal bark infections in native trees such as American oaks – hence the popular name Sudden Oak Death. In Europe, hosts include rhododendron, viburnum, camellia, and pieris. If the pathogen builds up in the understorey, it can cause fatal bark infections in trees, especially beech. It was detected in the UK in 2002, and during surveys, another species – *P. kernoviae*, also affecting rhododendrons and beech – was found; this is currently only known in the UK and New Zealand. Both are notifiable (see p.665 and www.defra.gov.uk/planth/pramorum.htm).

Stem distortion and abnormal growth

Etiolation

Plants affected Seedlings of all garden plants, and soft-stemmed plants.
Symptoms Stems are elongated and often pale, and the plant may grow towards the available light source, developing a lop-sided habit. The leaves are chlorotic and flowering is often reduced.
Cause Insufficient light, often due to poor siting of the plant or shading from adjacent plants, buildings, and similar structures. Overcrowded plants are susceptible to the condition.
Control Choose and site plants carefully. Ensure that adequate light is provided for seedlings as soon as germination has occurred. Plants only slightly affected should recover if conditions are improved.

Cutworms

Plants affected Low-growing perennials, annuals, root vegetables, and lettuces.
Symptoms Stem bases and leaves of low-growing plants are visibly gnawed and roots may also be affected. Plants grow slowly, wilt, and may ultimately die.
Cause Caterpillars of various moths (eg *Noctua* and *Agrotis* spp.), usually creamy-brown in colour and 4.5cm (1¾in) long. At night they feed above soil level.
Control Where damage is seen, search for and destroy the cutworms. Spray vulnerable plants at dusk with bifenthrin, if leaf damage is occurring.

Hormone weedkiller damage

Plants affected Broadleaved plants (mainly roses, tomatoes, and grapes) and conifers.
Symptoms Small bumps may appear on stems. Leaves are distorted and petioles twisted or spiralled. See also pp.651 and 659.
Cause Contamination by a growth regulator or hormone-type weedkiller, often from a considerable distance; even minute quantities may cause extensive damage. Sources of trouble are spray drift and the use of contaminated sprayers or watering cans. Plants that have been affected usually grow out of the symptoms.
Control Apply weedkillers according to the manufacturers' instructions, placing protective barriers around adjacent plants. Keep one sprayer or watering can for use with weedkillers only, or preferably use dribble bars. Store weedkillers away from compost, fertilizers, and plants.

Leafy gall

Plants affected Shrubs, perennials, and annuals, especially dahlias, chrysanthemums, and pelargoniums.
Symptoms Tiny, distorted shoots and leaves develop on the stem at or near ground level.
Cause *Rhodococcus fascians*, a soil-borne bacterium that enters host plants through small wounds. It is easily spread on tools or through propagating from infected plants.

Control Destroy affected plants and remove the soil in their immediate vicinity, and wash after handling them. Maintain strict hygiene, sterilizing tools, containers, and the greenhouse regularly. Do not propagate from infected plants.

Crown gall

Plants affected Trees, shrubs (most commonly cane fruits and roses), woody and some herbaceous perennials.
Symptoms Irregular, rounded, often woody swellings occur on or burst from the stem, but plant vigour is not seriously affected. See p.661 for other symptoms.

Cause *Agrobacterium tumefaciens* bacteria, prevalent in wet soils, which enter through surface wounds.
Control Avoid plant damage and improve soil drainage. Cut out and destroy all the affected stems.

Forsythia gall

Plants affected Forsythias.
Symptoms Rough, woody rounded galls form on the stems of this shrub. They persist from year to year but rarely have adverse effects.
Cause Unknown; possibly bacterial infection.
Control No action is strictly necessary but the unsightly galled stems may be removed.

Fungal brackets

Plants affected Trees, shrubs, woody perennials.
Symptoms Fungal fruiting bodies, often bracket-shaped, appear commonly on the lower trunk, but also on the upper section or on the crown, sometimes near branch stubs or other wounds. Either short-lived or perennial, they vary in appearance, often according to weather conditions. General growth is slow, and the tree may develop an excess of dead wood and a thin crown.
Cause and control See p.661 for details.

Witches' brooms

Plants affected Trees, mainly birches (*Betula*) and hornbeams (*Carpinus*); shrubs; woody perennials.
Symptoms Dense clusters of small shoots appear on otherwise normal branches. Leaves discolour early and remain small but vigour is unaffected.
Cause Fungi (especially *Taphrina*) and mites (for example *Eriophyes*), which cause the proliferation.
Control Cut branches back below the affected area.

Big bud mites

Plants affected Commonly hazels (*Corylus*), yew (*Taxus baccata*), brooms (*Cytisus*), and blackcurrants.
Symptoms The buds are abnormally enlarged and fail to break.
Cause Microscopic gall mites feeding inside the buds. Hazels are attacked by *Phytoptus avellanae*, brooms by *Aceria genistae*, yew by *Cecidophyopsis psilaspis*, and blackcurrants by *C. ribis*. Blackcurrant big bud mites can spread the virus-like disease known as reversion (see also "Viruses", p.659).
Control Remove and burn affected buds during the winter. Yew and hazels are fairly tolerant but heavily infested blackcurrants and brooms should be dug up and destroyed as soon as symptoms are noticed. The blackcurrant cultivar 'Ben Hope' is resistant to big bud mite.

Lightning

Plants affected Tall trees.
Symptoms Bark may be stripped, and a deep furrow may appear on one side, often following the spiral grain. The heartwood may be shattered, leaving the tree susceptible to disease. Dead wood increases in the crown and the upper crown dies.
Cause Lightning.
Control Lightning conductors may be fitted to valuable tall trees but this is unlikely to be feasible.

Mechanical wounding

Plants affected Potentially all plants.
Symptoms A neat-edged wound is visible on the stem or bark. Sap from the injured area may ferment into a slime flux (see "Slime flux/wet wood", p.653), and pathogens entering the wound cause die-back or even death. A healed wound may leave a raised area.
Cause Careless use of garden machinery and tools.
Control Remove severely damaged shoots or stems. Wounds on woody plants should be left alone.

Voles

Plants affected Shrubs and young trees.
Symptoms Bark is gnawed from stems and roots.
Cause Voles.
Control Mouse traps are the most effective solution. See also "Mice, rats, and voles", p.662.

See also "Asparagus beetle", p.644; "Vine weevil", p.645; "Eelworms", p.652; "Rusts", p.653; "Irregular water supply", p.653; "Fasciation", p.657; "Grey squirrel", p.659; "Nectria canker", p.664; "*Seiridium* canker", p.664; "Honey fungus", p.665; "Replant disease/soil sickness", p.665; "Anthracnose", p.666; "Rabbits and hares", p.666; and "Deer", p.666.

Flower problems
Discoloured flowers

Grey mould (*Botrytis*)

Plants affected Trees, shrubs, perennials, annuals, bulbous plants, vegetables, fruits, and indoor plants.
Symptoms A fuzzy, grey, fungal growth appears on the flowers in patches, leading to total deterioration. This may later spread to the stems and body of the plant. See also pp.653 and 658.
Cause The fungi *Botrytis cinerea* or *B. galanthina*.
Control Avoid injury to plants, clear up dead material, and provide good ventilation. Remove affected areas as soon as noticed. No fungicides are currently available.

Fungal patches

Total deterioration

Viruses

Plants affected Most plants, particularly those that are vegetatively propagated.
Symptoms Flowers are small and distorted, patterned with streaking or colour-breaking. See also pp.649 and 659.
Cause A large number of viruses. Submicroscopic virus particles in the sap of infected plants may be transmitted to healthy tissues by aphids, nematodes, and certain other pests, through handling, or on garden tools; some are seed-borne.
Control Buy certified (virus-free) plants, if available. Control potential carriers, eg aphids, and keep down weeds. Remove and burn affected plants; handle suspect plants after healthy ones, and do not propagate from them. Use a new site for any replacement plants. There is no chemical control.

Thrips

Plants affected Perennials, often *Achimenes*, *Primula obconica*, *Sinningia*, *Streptocarpus*, African violets (*Saintpaulia*), chrysanthemums, cyclamen, roses, gladioli, pelargoniums.
Symptoms White flecks appear on the petals, and loss of pigmentation can be severe. Heavy attacks prevent the buds opening. Leaves develop a silver-white discolouration.
Cause Various species of thrips, eg gladiolus thrips (*Thrips simplex*) and rose thrips (*T. fuscipennis*) in gardens, and western flower thrips (*Frankliniella occidentalis*) in greenhouses. They are sap-suckers that may enter and damage unopened flower buds. The adults are narrow-bodied, up to 2mm (⅟₁₆in) long, and brown or black; the immature nymphs are creamy yellow. They thrive in hot, dry conditions.

Control Water plants regularly and, in greenhouses, maintain a cool, humid atmosphere. Use biological control with the predatory mite *Amblyseius*, or spray with pyrethrum, imidacloprid, or bifenthrin.

Blossom wilt

Plants affected Ornamental and fruit apples, pears, and *Prunus* spp.
Symptoms The flowers turn brown and wither, but remain tightly clinging to the stem. The adjacent leaves then turn brown and die, and in severe cases the spur may be extensively damaged. Many tiny, buff-coloured spore masses appear on the affected areas, and in winter pustules form on the bark.
Cause *Monilinia* spp., which flourish in damp conditions and also cause brown rot in fruits (see p.658). The spores are carried on air currents and infect the plant via the flowers.
Control Remove and burn all infected parts. Do not leave brown-rotted fruit on the trees.

Tulip fire

Plants affected Tulips.
Symptoms Bleached, and often elongated, spots ap-pear on the petals; severely affected flowers may wither. Some buds remain tightly closed and become covered in a dense, grey, fungal growth. See p.649 for symptoms affecting the leaves.
Cause The fungus *Botrytis tulipae*, which flourishes in wet seasons, because the spores are spread by wind and rain. The sclerotia (fungal resting bodies) persist in the soil, and will later germinate when tulips are planted in the area again.
Control Remove and burn affected leaves and shoots immediately. Lift and dry off bulbs at the end of the season, discarding any with sclerotia, and dust with sulphur. Wait two years before replanting the site with tulips, or change the soil. Plant deeply from early winter onwards.

Phytoplasmas

Plants affected Trees, shrubs, perennials, annuals, bulbous plants, vegetables, fruits (especially strawberries), and indoor plants.
Symptoms Flowers are green, undersized, and sometimes distorted. They do not revert to their usual colour and subsequent flushes are also green. Symptoms on clematis are similar to those caused by frost injury, but "frost-damaged" flowers will be replaced by normal-coloured blooms later in the season. On strawberries,

the condition causes green petals on the flowers and produces discoloured, misshapen leaves. See also p.651.
Cause Phytoplasmas, which are believed to be related to bacteria. They are spread by leafhoppers (see p.647), which commonly pick up the infection from clover plants suffering from phyllody disease.
Control Discard affected plants, buy certified fruit stock, and control both pests (potential vectors) and weeds (which may harbour the disease).

Rhododendron bud blast

Plants affected Rhododendrons and azaleas.
Symptoms The buds form but do not open. They turn brown and dry, sometimes developing a silver-grey sheen, and during spring become covered in black, fungal bristles. The affected buds are not shed.
Cause The fungus *Pycnostysanus azaleae*, which infects through wounds made by the rhododendron leafhopper (*Graphocephala fennahi*).
Control If practical, remove and destroy all affected buds before midsummer, when the leafhoppers become prevalent; also spray against them in late summer and early autumn (see p.647).

Potassium deficiency

Plants affected Both edible and ornamental fruiting plants, but mainly currants, apples, and pears.
Symptoms Flowering, subsequent fruiting, and general growth may be reduced. See p.650 for details of other symptoms.
Cause Growing plants in soils with either a light texture or with a high chalk or peat content.
Control Improve the soil texture. Dress with sulphate of potash or a high potash fertilizer.

Apple sucker

Plants affected Apples.
Symptoms The blossom browns as though it is frost-damaged; small, green insects appear on the flower stalks.
Cause Apple sucker (*Psylla mali*) nymphs, which are flattened, pale green insects, up to 2mm (⅟₁₆in) in length, that suck sap. Heavy attacks will kill the blossom and prevent fruit set.
Control Apply a plant oil wash in winter. Alternatively, spray with pyrethrum or bifenthrin at the green cluster stage of bud development, before the petals show colour.

See also "Powdery mildew", p.646; "High temperatures and scorch", p.650; "Low temperatures", p.650; "Azalea gall", p.652; "Chrysanthemum petal blight", p.657; "Michaelmas daisy mite", p.657; and "Fireblight", p.649.

Distorted and eaten flowers

Drought

Plants affected All plants, especially those in light, sandy soils or containers.
Symptoms The buds fail to develop fully, and the flowers are small and sparse. See also pp.650 and 664.
Cause Chronic (prolonged) or repeated drought. Plants in small containers are particularly vulnerable during hot weather, and peat-based composts that are allowed to dry out too much are extremely difficult to re-wet. Dry, brown buds on certain plants, eg camellias and rhododendrons, are the result of a water shortage the previous year during the period of bud initiation.
Control Water plants regularly, and frequently check those in hot or sunny positions. Mulch, where appropriate, to improve moisture retention. Try to prevent drought rather than treat it: plants exposed to a chronic water shortage are far less likely to recover than those suffering a sudden shortage.

Capsid bugs

Plants affected Shrubs, perennials, and annuals, mainly dahlias, fuchsias, hydrangeas, chrysanthemums, and *Caryopteris*.
Symptoms Flowers develop unevenly with undersized ray petals. Fuchsia flowers abort completely.
Cause and control See p.645 for details.

Earwigs

Plants affected Shrubs, perennials, and annuals, commonly chrysanthemums, dahlias, and clematis. Also apricot and peach trees.
Symptoms Petals are eaten in summer. See p.644 for other symptoms.
Cause The earwig (*Forficula auricularia*), which is a yellowish-brown insect 2cm (¾in) long.
Control Place inverted pots, stuffed with hay or straw, on canes among plants; earwigs hide in these, and can be destroyed. Alternatively, spray at dusk with bifenthrin.

Fasciation

Plants affected All plants, most commonly delphiniums, forsythias, *Daphne*, and *Prunus subhirtella* 'Autumnalis'.
Symptoms Peculiar, broad, flattened flower stems develop. The main stems are also broad and flattened.
Cause In many cases, early damage to the growing point caused by insect, slug or frost attack, or handling; it may also be due to bacterial infection or genetic malfunction.
Control Fasciation does no harm; affected areas may either be left on the plant or pruned out.

Proliferation

Plants affected Mainly roses, especially the older varieties, but occasionally other ornamentals and fruiting plants.
Symptoms The flower stem grows through the centre of the existing flower, and a new flower may form above the first. In some cases several flower buds form together, surrounded by one set of petals.
Cause Early damage to the growing point of the bud, often through frost or insect attack. Where the problem recurs, a virus (see p.656) may be the cause.
Control Severely and repeatedly affected plants, which may be virus-infected, should be destroyed. In all other cases treatment is unnecessary.

Chrysanthemum petal blight

Plants affected Chrysanthemums and other members of the Compositae family and *Anemone*. The disease is rare.
Symptoms The outer florets develop brown or water-soaked oval spots; if the whole flowerhead becomes affected, it withers and dies. *Botrytis cinerea* may colonize the affected bloom (see "Grey mould/ *Botrytis*", p.656), masking the original symptoms.
Cause The fungus *Itersonilia perplexans*, which attacks susceptible plants, usually those under glass.
Control Remove and destroy affected blooms.

Michaelmas daisy mite

Plants affected Michaelmas daisies (*Aster*), especially *A. novi-belgii*.
Symptoms Plants flower poorly; some flowers may be converted into rosettes of small leaves. Greyish-brown scars appear on stunted stems.
Cause The Michaelmas daisy mite (*Phytonemus pallidus*), a microscopic mite that feeds in flower buds and shoot tips.

Distorted and healthy (inset) flowers

Control Discard infested plants, replacing them with less susceptible perennial asters, eg *Aster novae-angliae* or *A. amellus*. There is no effective chemical control available to amateur gardeners.

Hemerocallis gall midge

Plants affected Daylily (*Hemerocallis*).
Symptoms Flower buds become abnormally swollen and fail to open. The problem occurs between late spring and midsummer.
Cause The Hemerocallis gall midge (*Contarinia quinque-*

notata), a tiny fly that lays its eggs in the developing buds. Affected buds contain white maggots, up to 2mm (⅟₁₆in) long, feeding between the petals.
Control Pick off and burn galled buds. The late-flowering cultivars escape damage.

Pollen beetles

Plants affected Roses, sweet peas (*Lathyrus odoratus*), daffodils, marrows, runner beans, and other garden flowers.
Symptoms Small, black beetles are found in the flowers in spring and mid- to late summer.
Cause Pollen beetles (*Meligethes* spp.), which are 2mm (⅟₁₆in) long and black. They eat some pollen but otherwise cause little direct damage to the blooms.
Control Pollen beetles cannot be controlled, because vast numbers fly into gardens from oil seed rape fields, where they breed. It is not advisable to use insecticides: they can cause damage to the petals and harm useful pollinators, eg bees. Cut flowers can be freed of the beetles by placing them during the day in a shed or garage with one light source (eg an open door) towards which the beetles fly.

Birds

Bullfinch damage

House sparrow damage

Plants affected Trees (ornamental and fruit), most fruits, and shrubs, especially forsythias, gooseberries, cherries (*Prunus*), pears, almonds, and *Amelanchier*, crocuses, primrose (*Primula vulgaris*), and polyanthus (*Primula*).
Symptoms Flower buds are pecked from trees and shrubs; outer bud scales are left scattered on the ground. Crocus and primrose flowers are shredded. Vegetables, especially peas and beans, fruits, seeds, and seedlings are pecked or eaten.
Cause Birds, including bullfinches (trees, shrubs, and fruits) and house sparrows (crocuses and primroses). Vegetables, fruits, and seedlings may be pecked or eaten by many birds including wood pigeons (p.645), blackbirds and starlings (p.659), and jays (p.659).
Control Netting or very fine mesh is the only certain way of preventing damage. Scaring devices, eg humming tapes, scarecrows, or aluminium foil strips, are effective only initially; birds soon lose their fear. Repellent sprays, usually based on aluminium ammonium sulphate, must be used frequently to maintain their effectiveness.

See also "Caterpillars", p.645; "Low temperatures", p.650; "Irregular water supply", p.651; "Azalea gall", p.652; "Etiolation", p.655; "Viruses", p.656; "Thrips", p.656; and "Phytoplasmas", p.656.

Fruit, berry, and seed problems

High temperatures and scorch

Plants affected Soft fruits, tree fruits, tomatoes, and apples, especially green-skinned cultivars.
Symptoms Discoloured patches develop on the skin, particularly on the upper-most surfaces of fruits, or on the ones that are more highly exposed.
Cause and control See p.650 for details.

Grey mould (*Botrytis*)

Plants affected Fruiting trees, shrubs, perennials, annuals, and indoor plants. Soft, thin-skinned fruits, eg strawberries, raspberries, grapes, and tomatoes, are vulnerable.
Symptoms Normally, a grey, fuzzy, fungal growth

develops on a soft, brown rot. The damage spreads rapidly and the whole fruit may collapse. Unripe tomatoes may develop "ghost spot", where a pale green ring appears on the skin but the rest of the fruit colours normally and does not rot (the unaffected parts may be eaten). See also pp.653 and 656.
Cause and control See p.653 for details.

Powdery mildew

Plants affected Most fruits, commonly grapes, peaches, and gooseberries.
Symptoms Whitish-grey, fungal patches appear on the skin, often turning brown as they mature. The berries of grapes become hard and extensively cracked, and

may fail to swell fully; secondary fungi may then invade. Cracking of gooseberries is uncommon and fungal growth can be rubbed off.
Cause and control See p.646. Grow gooseberries showing some resistance, for example 'Invicta' and 'Greenfinch'. Spray with myclobutanil.

Brown rot

Plants affected Culti-vated fruits, especially apples, plums, peaches, nectarines, and pears.
Symptoms Soft, brown areas develop on the skin, and penetrate throughout the flesh. Concentric rings of creamy-white pustules then start to appear on the

surface. Affected fruits either fall or may become dry and wizened and remain on the tree.
Cause The fungus *Monilinia* (*M. fructigena* and *M. laxa*). The pustules produce spores, and these are then carried by wind or insects to other fruits;

infection occurs through wounds or blemishes on the surface of the fruit.
Control Prevent injury to fruits (eg that caused by pests), and pick off and burn those affected.

Tomato blight

Plants affected Tomatoes, mainly in the open but also in greenhouses.
Symptoms The fruits first develop a brown discolouration and then start to shrink and rot. Even fruits that may have seemed healthy when picked may begin to deteriorate rapidly within a few days.
Cause and control See p.649 for details.

Raspberry beetle

Plants affected Mainly raspberries, but also blackberries and hybrid cane fruits.
Symptoms Ripe fruits are dried up and brown at the stalk end; an insect larva may be found inside the fruit.
Cause The raspberry beetle (*Byturus tomentosus*). The females lay eggs on the flowers in early to midsummer. Brownish-white larvae up to 6mm (¼in) long hatch two weeks later. They feed initially at the stalk end of the fruit but then move to the inner plug.
Control Only chemical sprays provide an effective control. Apply rotenone to raspberries when the first pink fruit appears; to loganberries when 80 per cent of the petals have fallen; to blackberries when the first flower opens. A second application may be required for raspberries and loganberries two weeks after the first. Spray at dusk to avoid harming bees.

Scab

Plants affected Pears, pyracanthas, *Citrus*, *Malus*, and loquats.
Symptoms Blackish-brown, scabby patches develop on the skin, and a severe attack will leave fruits small and distorted. In some cases cracks may develop, which will make the fruit vulnerable to secondary infections.
Cause and control See p.649 for details.

Calcium deficiency

Plants affected Apples (the condition is known as bitter pit), container-grown tomatoes, and sweet peppers (blossom end rot).
Symptoms The flesh of apples is brown-flecked and tastes bitter; the skin

Bitter pit

is sometimes pitted. Bitter pit may affect fruits on the tree or in store. Tomato and pepper fruits develop a sunken, blackish-brown discolouration at the flower end.

Blossom end rot

Cause A lack of calcium, possibly combined with other nutritional imbalances, resulting from an irregular or poor supply of moisture to the roots, preventing adequate calcium uptake. Groups of cells deprived of calcium collapse and discolour.
Control Avoid very acid growing media. Water regularly and, where feasible, mulch plants. Apples may be sprayed with calcium nitrate every ten days from early summer until harvesting.

Pear midge

Plants affected Pears.
Symptoms The fruitlets turn black, starting at the eye end, and fall from the tree. Small maggots are found inside fruitlets.
Cause The pear midge (*Contarinia pyrivora*). The adults lay eggs on the unopened flower buds; these hatch into orange-white maggots 2mm (⅟₁₆in) long that feed in the fruitlets, leaving them black and rotten.
Control Collect and burn damaged fruitlets before the maggots fall into the soil to pupate. Pear midge is difficult to control on large trees.

Shanking of vines

Plants affected Grape vines (*Vitis vinifera*).
Symptoms Berry stalks wither. Berries have a watery or sour taste; black varieties turn red, and white ones remain translucent. They remain on the bunch but shrivel up and are vulnerable to disease, eg grey mould (*Botrytis*) (see above).
Cause Heavy cropping, either over- or under-watering, or stagnant soil conditions.
Control Cut out withered berries and regularly apply a foliar feed. Decrease the crop for a few years and try to improve general soil conditions.

Wasps

Plants affected Tree fruits, such as plums, pears, apples, and figs, as well as grapes.
Symptoms Large cavities are eaten in ripe fruits in late summer; wasps may be seen feeding.
Cause Wasps (*Vespula* spp.), which are attracted to fruits initially damaged by birds.
Control Protect fruits by placing bags made of muslin or nylon tights over the trusses before damage begins. Make a wasp trap using beer in a jar; cover it with a paper lid in which a wasp-sized hole has been pierced. Locate and destroy wasp nests.

Irregular water supply

Plants affected Potentially all fruiting plants.
Symptoms Fruits are mis-shapen and undersized, and a sudden availability of water may cause their skin and flesh to crack, leaving them vulnerable to the diseases that cause rotting. See pp.651 and 653 for other symptoms.
Cause and control See p.651 for details.

Viruses

Plants affected Pears, cucumbers, melons, pumpkins, tomatoes, strawberries, and raspberries.
Symptoms Fruits may be undersized, distorted, dis-coloured, and grouped in rosettes. Cucumber mosaic virus produces warty, dis-torted cucumber, melon, and pumpkin fruits, blotched dark green and yellow; pear stony pit virus produces distorted and pitted pear fruits with patches of dead, stony cells. See also pp.649 and 656.
Cause and control See p.649 for details.

Hormone weedkiller damage

Plants affected All fruits, but commonly only tomatoes.
Symptoms Plum-shaped tom-atoes form. Although they ripen normally and are safe to eat, they may taste unpleasant and be hollow. Fruits that form before contamination occurs are not usually affected. See p.651 for other symptoms.
Cause and control See p.651 for details.
See also "Selective weedkillers", p.671.

Climate change, pests and diseases

The predicted changes in climate are likely to have two main effects on garden pests and diseases: changes to the severity of problems already present, and the establishment of new pests and diseases for which the climate was formerly unsuitable. Hotter, drier summers may lead to more problems with powdery mildews – favoured by conditions of water stress – but fewer problems with downy mildews and potato blight, which require wet conditions. Pests like red spider mite may become more troublesome. Warmer wetter winters will favour *Phytophthora* root diseases. Overall warmer conditions may also allow new pests to spread, for example the rosemary beetle, a Mediterranean species recently established in the UK. However, climate change will not be responsible for all new pests: the horse chestnut leaf miner arrived in the UK in 2002 after spreading across Europe and its establishment is the result of natural dispersal.

Blackbirds and starlings

Plants affected Tree and soft fruits.
Symptoms Peck marks appear on ripe tree fruits, leaving them susceptible to brown rot (see p.658); soft fruits are eaten whole.
Cause Blackbirds, starlings, and other birds (see p.657).
Control Either net the plants at fruiting time or grow them in a permanent bird-proof cage.

Codling moth

Plants affected Apples and pears.
Symptoms Holes are tun-nelled in ripe fruits.
Cause The caterpillars of the codling moth (*Cydia pomonella*), which feed in the core of the fruit; when they are mature, each caterpillar makes a frass-filled tunnel to the outside of the fruit.
Control Hang pheromone traps in the trees from late spring to mid-summer to catch the male moths, reducing egg fertilization. Use of traps will also indicate when females are flying, so sprays can be timed more accurately to control caterpillars as they hatch. If needed, spray with bifenthrin in early summer and again three weeks later.

Plum moth

Plants affected Plums.
Symptoms The fruits ripen prematurely and then drop. A pink cater-pillar and its excrement may be found inside the fruit.
Cause The plum moth (*Cydia funebrana*), which lays its eggs on the fruitlets during early summer. These hatch into caterpillars known as red plum maggots, which grow up to 1cm (½in) long.
Control Pheromone traps may reduce the mating success of the females, and consequently result in fewer maggoty fruits, if they are hung in the tree in late spring to catch the male plum moths. There are no effective insecticides available for garden use against the plum moth.

Apple sawfly

Plants affected Apples.
Symptoms Fruitlets are tunnelled and drop off during early to mid-summer. The damaged fruits will sometimes remain on the tree and become mature, but they are misshapen and have a long, ribbon-like scar on the skin.
Cause The larvae of the apple sawfly (*Hoplocampa testudinea*), white caterpillar-like insects up to 1cm (½in) long with brown heads. They are less widespread than codling moth (see above).
Control If sawfly have been a problem in previous years, spray with bifenthrin within seven days of petal fall; spray at dusk to avoid harming bees.

Pea thrips

Plants affected Peas.
Symptoms The pods turn silver-brown and they may remain flat apart from a few seeds at the stalk end.
Cause The pea thrips (*Kakothrips pisivorus*), which is a narrow-bodied, blackish-brown, sap-feeding insect up to 2mm (¹⁄₁₆in) long. The immature nymphs have a similar appearance but are orange-yellow. Both the adults and the nymphs feed on the plants; they thrive in hot, dry conditions.
Control Water plants regularly where the damage occurs, and spray the plants with pyrethrum or bifenthrin.

Pea moth

Plants affected Peas.
Symptoms Peas in pods are eaten by caterpillars.
Cause The pea moth (*Cydia nigricana*), which lays eggs on pea plants in flower in early to mid-summer. The caterpillars are creamy-white with brown heads, and are up to 1cm (½in) long.
Control Use pheromone traps to catch the males, reducing the chances of the females mating successfully; or spray plants with bifenthrin, 7–10 days after flowering begins. Early- or late-sown peas should not need spraying.

Jays and pigeons

Plants affected Peas and broad beans.
Symptoms Developing pods are pecked and the seeds are eaten.
Cause Jays and pigeons.
Control Netting is the only effective protection. Scaring devices are only effective initially as birds soon lose their fear. Repellent sprays must be used frequently if their effectiveness is to be maintained.

Grey squirrel

Plants affected Young trees, flower buds, fruits, and nuts.
Symptoms Bark is gnawed away. Flower buds, ripening fruits, and nuts are eaten.
Cause Grey squirrel.
Control Traps work only if used over a wide area.

See also "Woodlice", p.644; "Millipedes", p.644; "Winter moth caterpillars", p.645; "Wood pigeon", p.645; "Potassium deficiency", p.656; "Birds",p.657; "Boron deficiency", p.662; and "Drought", p.664.

Root and tuber problems

Waterlogging

Plants affected All plants.
Symptoms Some roots may rot off completely. Those remaining are frequently blackened with a peeling outer surface. The first visible symptom is usually wilting leaves.
Cause High water levels in the growing medium, owing to factors such as poor soil structure, compaction, impeded drainage, or overwatering.
Control Where feasible, improve the structure and drainage of the soil and build raised beds; if necessary, choose plants that are likely to survive in wet conditions. Check that drainage holes for container-grown plants are adequate, and that flow through them is not impeded; repot plants every two years. Regular application of a foliar feed during the growing season may help to stimulate growth, allowing damaged roots to be replaced.

Damping off

Plants affected The seedlings of all plants.
Symptoms Affected roots darken and rot off, causing the seedling to collapse and die. The disease often starts at one end of the seed tray, spreading rapidly to the other. A fluffy, fungal growth may appear on the compost as well as on dead seedlings.
Cause Various fungi – in particular *Pythium ultimum* and some *Phytophthora* – which are soil- or water-borne and attack seedlings via either the roots or the base of the stem. They flourish in moist and unhygienic conditions.
Control There is no effective control once the disease is established. To prevent it, sow seed thinly, improve ventilation, maintain strict hygiene, and avoid overwatering. Use only sterilized compost, mains water, and clean trays and pots. Water occasionally with a suitable copper-based fungicide.

Root-knot eelworms

Plants affected Many garden plants, including fruit trees, vegetables, and ornamentals in warm climates. Plants in greenhouses are also susceptible.
Symptoms Galls or swellings appear on the roots or tubers. Overall growth is stunted, and the plant may wilt, yellow, and sometimes even be killed.
Cause Root-knot nematodes (*Meloidogyne* spp.), which are thin, transparent, and only 0.5mm (½in) long. The larvae penetrate the roots.
Control Burn all affected plants. Rotate vegetable crops; choose resistant plants. There is no chemical control available to amateur gardeners.

Vine weevil grubs

Plants affected Many shrubs, perennials, bulbous plants, and those that are grown indoors; most commonly affected are begonias, cyclamen, fuchsias, *Impatiens*, primulas (including the Polyanthus Group), *Sedum*, and strawberries. Container-grown plants are particularly vulnerable.
Symptoms The outer tissues of woody seedlings and cuttings are gnawed from the stem bases and roots below ground level. Plants grow slowly, have a tendency to wilt, and finally collapse and die.
Cause and control See p.666 for details.
See also p.666; and p.645 for information on damage caused to leaves by adult vine weevils.

Chafer grubs

Plants affected Young annuals, bulbous plants, lawns, and vegetables.
Symptoms Large cavities appear in root vegetables. Stem bases are eaten, and small plants wilt and may eventually die.
Cause The root-feeding, creamy-white larvae of beetles such as cock chafers (*Melolontha melolontha*) and garden chafers (*Phyllopertha horticola*). They are plump, "C"-shaped, and up to 5cm (2in) long, with brown heads and three pairs of legs.
Control Search for and destroy the larvae, or water in biological-control pathogenic nematodes (*Heterorhabditis megidis*) when the soil is moist and warm (at least 12°C/54°F) from midsummer.
See also p.667 for problems caused on lawns.

Cutworms

Plants affected Low-growing perennials, annuals, root vegetables, and lettuces.
Symptoms Cavities appear in root crops, and tap roots may be severed, causing plants to wilt and die. See p.655 for other symptoms.
Cause The caterpillars of various moths (eg *Noctua* and *Agrotis* spp.), usually creamy-brown in colour and up to 4.5cm (1¾in) in length. They eat roots and the outer tissues of stem bases.
Control Search for and destroy the cutworms near plants showing signs of damage.

Leatherjackets

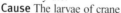

Plants affected Young annuals, bulbous plants, lawns, and vegetables.
Symptoms The roots are eaten, the stems are severed at ground level, and plants turn yellow, wilt, and may eventually die.
Cause The larvae of crane flies, also known as daddy-long-legs (eg *Tipula* spp.), which feed on roots and stems. Leatherjackets are up to 3.5cm (1½in) long; they have tubular, greyish-brown bodies with no legs.
Control Where damage is seen on the plants, search for and destroy the leatherjackets, or in late summer apply biological-control pathogenic nematodes (*Steinernema feltiae*) to moist, warm (12–20°C/54–68°F) soil. Leatherjacket damage can occur on land that has recently been brought into cultivation, and so the problem should diminish there within a few years.
See also p.667 for problems caused on lawns.

Carrot fly

Plants affected Mainly carrots, parsnips, parsley (*Petroselinum crispum*), and celery.
Symptoms Rusty brown tunnels are bored under the outer skin of mature roots. Small plants develop discoloured foliage and may die.
Cause Creamy-yellow maggots, larvae of the carrot fly (*Psila rosae*), which feed in the surface tissues of the larger roots; in autumn they may bore deeper. They are slender, legless, and up to 1cm (½in) long.
Control Enclose susceptible plants within a clear polythene fence at least 60cm (24in) high, or grow under horticultural fleece, to exclude the low-flying female flies. Some cultivars, eg 'Flyaway' and 'Resistafly', are less vulnerable to attack. Lift carrots for storage in autumn to limit damage.

Cabbage root fly

Plants affected Brassicas (including cabbages, cauliflowers, Brussels sprouts, turnips, swedes), radishes.
Symptoms Plants grow slowly and wilt; seedlings and transplants die; tunnels appear in root crops.
Cause Root-feeding larvae of the fly *Delia radicum*, white, legless maggots up to 9mm (⅜in) long. Several generations occur between mid-spring and mid-autumn, causing damage mainly to young plants.
Control Place proprietary collars, or those made from underlay or cardboard, about 12cm (5in) in diameter, around the base of transplanted brassicas to prevent the female flies from laying eggs in the soil, or lay landscape fabric over the whole planting area and insert the young brassicas through planting holes in the fabric. Alternatively, grow under horticultural fleece or insect-proof mesh. There are no pesticides approved for garden use.

Clubroot

Plants affected The family Cruciferae, especially certain brassicas (for example cabbages, Brussels sprouts, and swedes) and radishes, and some ornamentals, including candytufts (*Iberis*), wallflowers (*Erysimum*), and stocks (*Matthiola*).
Symptoms Swollen and distorted roots; stunted and often discoloured plants; wilting in hot weather. See p.649 for other symptoms.
Cause The slime mould *Plasmodiophora brassicae*, which thrives in poorly drained, acid soils and is also found on manure and plant debris. It is easily spread on boots and tools, and the spores remain viable for 20 years or more, even in the absence of a host plant. Weeds susceptible to this disease (eg shepherd's purse and charlock) may be a source of infection. In dry summers it may not occur, as moist conditions are needed for spores to germinate.
Control Remove and burn affected plants at the first sign of disease. Clear weeds, improve drainage, and lime the soil. Raise new plants in soil-based compost to encourage a strong and healthy root system.

Violet root rot

Plants affected Vegetables, mainly carrots, parsnips, asparagus, swedes, turnips, potatoes, celery.
Symptoms Roots, tubers, and any other parts below ground level are covered in a dense, matted, purple fungal growth to which soil particles become attached. The upper parts of the plant become stunted and discoloured. There may be secondary rotting.
Cause The fungus *Helicobasidium brebissonii*, which is harboured by some weeds. It thrives in both acid and waterlogged soils.
Control Burn infected plants immediately. Avoid growing susceptible plants on the affected site for at least four years; keep the area free of weeds.

Root aphids

Plants affected Lettuce, beans, carrots, parsnips, Jerusalem artichokes, auriculas, roses, *Dianthus*.
Symptoms Slow growth and tendency to wilt in sunny weather in mid- and late summer. A white waxy powder may appear on roots and nearby soil.
Cause Aphids, up to 3mm (⅛in) long and generally creamy-brown, which feed on roots and stem bases. Different species of root aphid attack specific plants, for example *Pemphigus bursarius* on lettuce and *Thecabius auriculae* on auriculas.
Control Rotate vegetable crops and grow root-aphid-resistant lettuce cultivars. Root aphids are difficult to treat with insecticides, but lettuce and beans can be watered with diluted bifenthrin; treat pot-grown ornamental plants with imidacloprid.

Foot and root rots

Plants affected A wide range, especially petunias and other bedding plants, tomatoes, cucumbers, peas, beans, and young, container-grown plants.
Symptoms The roots turn black and break or rot. See p.654 for details of other symptoms.
Cause and control See p.654 for details.

Phytophthora root rots

Plants affected Trees, shrubs, and woody perennials; commonly maples (*Acer*), yew (*Taxus baccata*), Lawson cypress (*Chamaecyparis lawsoniana*), apples, rhododendrons, raspberries, and heathers.
Symptoms The larger roots die back from the stem or trunk, although the fine roots may appear perfectly healthy; affected roots usually turn black. See p.654 for other symptoms.
Cause and control See p.654 for details.

Tropical root rots

Plants affected Annual and perennial crops, temperate and tropical, including broad beans, French beans, cucumbers, melons, pumpkins, peanuts.
Symptoms Annual plants show a mid-season wilting, with rotting of the base of the stem and upper portion of the root; the infected tissues develop lesions and often turn red before decaying. The leaves become chlorotic as their water supply is restricted, and young seedlings may show signs of damping off (see p.660). Groundnut shells become blackened and rapidly decay. The infected tissues of perennial crops turn purple and the plants wilt.
Cause Various forms of the soil-borne fungi *Fusarium solani*, *Thielaviopsis basicola*, *Thanatephorus cucumis*, *Phytophthora* spp., and *Pythium* spp. among others. The disease is carried in the soil and infected debris; crops grown in poorly drained, acid soils are particularly at risk. High soil temperatures will encourage the development of pea root rot (*Aphanomyces euteiches*).
Control Rotate crops on a long cycle. Use heat- or fungicide-treated seed, if feasible. Where possible, improve soil drainage.

Crown gall

Plants affected Trees, shrubs (most commonly cane fruits and roses), and woody perennials.
Symptoms Irregular, rounded swellings develop on the roots; occasionally the whole root system is distorted into a single, large swelling. See p.655 for symptoms.
Cause The bacterium *Agrobacterium tumefaciens*, prevalent in wet soils. The bacteria enter the plant through wounds made on the surface and cause cells to proliferate.
Control Avoid damaging plants and improve soil drainage. Cut out and destroy any affected stems in order to prevent secondary infection.

Honey fungus

Plants affected Trees, shrubs, climbers, and some woody perennials; most commonly affected are privets (*Ligustrum*), rhododendrons, and *Wisteria*.
Symptoms In autumn, fruiting bodies sometimes develop in clusters on underground roots, at the base of the trunk, and occasionally at some height from the ground; they die back after the first frost. The plant deteriorates and eventually dies. See p.665 for other symptoms.
Cause The fungus *Armillaria* (principally *A. mellea*) spread either by rhizomorph movement from an infected plant or stump, or through root contact.
Control Dig out and burn affected plants, stumps, and as much of the root system as possible; if necessary, have the stump chipped or ground out by a contractor. Avoid the more susceptible plants, choosing those showing some resistance, eg yew (*Taxus baccata*), *Cornus*, beech (*Fagus*), and *Hebe*.

Fungal brackets

Plants affected Mainly trees, and especially mature or overmature specimens, but also shrubs and woody perennials.
Symptoms Fungal fruiting bodies, often bracket-shaped, may appear above ground, following the line of the roots; they are attached to the roots by tiny fungal threads. They vary in appearance, often according to weather conditions. The roots may become hollow and eventually die, making the tree extremely unstable in the ground. Stems are also affected (see p.655).
Cause Various fungi, eg *Meripilus* or *Ganoderma*.
Control Seek professional advice, particularly if the tree poses a potential hazard. Removal of fruiting bodies will not prevent further decay, and does little to reduce the chances of spread to other trees.

Parsnip canker

Plants affected Parsnips.
Symptoms The shoulders of affected parsnips discolour and rot; the crown, shank, and roots of the plant may also rot, and the foliage may show some spotting. This condition occurs mainly in autumn and winter.
Cause Various species of fungus, primarily *Itersonilia pastinacae*. Some are soil-inhabiting and others produce spores that are washed into the soil from leaf lesions.
Control Rotate crops. Prevent injury to parsnip roots, particularly the type of injury caused by carrot fly larvae (see p.660). Sow late and closely in order to produce parsnips with small roots, which are less prone to disease, and earth up the rows to provide a barrier against spores washed down from the leaf lesions. Remove all affected plants immediately. Grow parsnips in a deep loam soil with a high pH, and choose a resistant cultivar, eg 'Avonresister' or 'Gladiator'.

Verticillium wilt

Plants affected A large number of garden and greenhouse plants.
Symptoms The roots deteriorate and die, and if cut longitudinally in the early stages of degeneration they may show a central, vascular column of brown discolouration.
Cause and control See p.653 for details.

Fusarium wilt

Plants affected Perennials, annuals, vegetables, and fruits; most commonly affected are China asters (*Callistephus*), carnations (*Dianthus*), sweet peas (*Lathyrus odoratus*), beans, and peas.
Symptoms The roots of affected plants turn black and eventually die.
Cause and control See p.654 for details.

Primula brown core

Plants affected Primulas.
Symptoms The roots rot and, if split longitudinally, show a distinct brown core; many are killed and plants become loose in the ground. Leaves yellow, wilt, and die. Flowers wilt.
Cause The fungus species *Phytophthora primulae*, which can remain viable in the soil for many years.
Control Dig up and burn all the affected plants. Grow any new primulas on an entirely fresh site.

Mice, rats, and voles

Plants affected Shrubs, young trees, crocus corms, seedlings of peas and beans, seeds, vegetables, and fruits kept in storage.
Symptoms The outer layer of stems and roots is gnawed. Seeds, seedlings, corms, vegetables, and fruits are eaten.
Cause Mice, rats, and voles.
Control Mouse or rat traps provide the best solution; difenacoum, brodifacoum, bromadiolone or coumatetralyl poisoned baits can be used.

Boron deficiency

Plants affected Roots of carrots, parsnips, swedes, turnips, and beetroots. The condition is fairly rare.
Symptoms The roots are of a poor shape and texture, and are rather grey. They may split longitudinally and sometimes contain cavities. A brown discolouration – known as brown heart – may occur in the lowermost sections, often in concentric rings; it is found mainly in turnips and swedes, and leaves them poor-tasting and fibrous. Beetroot shows internal discolouration and may develop cankers. See p.654 for other symptoms.
Cause A lack of boron in the soil, or an inability of the plant to take up the trace element owing to unsuitable growing conditions. Most common on very chalky or heavily limed soils, those that have been very dry, and those where the boron has been leached out. It rarely affects greenhouse plants.
Control Maintain correct soil moisture levels and avoid excessive liming. Before introducing a susceptible plant to a problem site, apply borax at 35g/20sq m (1oz/20sq yd), mixing with horticultural sand for easy and accurate application. Use fritted trace elements.

See also "Aphids", p.646; "Mealybugs", p.646; "Slugs", "Wireworms", below; "Onion fly", p.663; "Fungus gnats or sciarid flies", p.666; and "Bean seed fly", p.666.

Potato tuber problems

Slugs

Plants affected Potatoes.
Symptoms Circular holes are bored in the outside of potato tubers, and extensive cavities appear in the interior during late summer.
Cause Slugs.
Control Use biological control with pathogenic nematode *Phasmarhabditis hermaphrodita*, or scatter metaldehyde pellets. Grow less susceptible cultivars; harvest tubers as soon as mature.
See also "Slugs and snails", p.644, for leaf problems.

Wireworms

Plants affected Potatoes and other root crops, seedlings, perennials, annuals, and bulbous plants.
Symptoms Tunnels up to 3mm (⅛in) in diameter, superficially similar to those made by slugs, are bored through root crops. Underground parts of other plants are damaged. Small plants wilt and die.
Cause The slender, stiff-bodied, yellowish-orange larvae of click beetles (eg *Agriotes* spp.), which feed on roots and stem bases. They are up to 2.5cm (1in) long, with three pairs of short legs at the head end and a peg-like protuberance beneath the rear end. The problem mainly occurs when grassland is brought into cultivation.
Control Where damage is seen, search for and destroy the wireworms. Lift root crops as soon as they are mature. The pest is less numerous once the ground has been cultivated for two to three years.

Potato blight

Plants affected Potatoes.
Symptoms Dark and sunken patches begin to develop on the skin, and there are reddish-brown stains in the flesh beneath. The tubers start to develop a dry rot and they may also be affected by secondary, soft-rotting bacteria. See p.649 for symptoms that affect the foliage.
Cause The fungus *Phytophthora infestans*, which thrives in warm, moist conditions. Spores produced on the foliage and on potato haulms are carried from plant to plant by wind and rain, and may be washed down into the soil to infect potato tubers. The same fungus may also attack tomatoes.
Control Avoid overhead watering. Earth up potatoes deeply to protect against falling spores, and choose resistant cultivars, eg 'Cara', 'Kondor', 'Romano', 'Wilja', or the new Sarpo cultivars, such as 'Mira'. Spray with mancozeb or a copper-based fungicide; in wet seasons spray before blight appears.

Common potato scab

Plants affected Potatoes.
Symptoms Raised, scabby patches develop on the skin, and these sometimes rupture. Damage may be superficial, but in some cases the tuber becomes extensively cracked and disfigured. The flesh is not generally damaged.
Cause *Streptomyces scabies*, a bacterium-like but mycelium-producing organism, common in soils that are sandy and light with a high lime content, and those only recently cultivated. Disease development is most common during hot, dry summers, and when soil moisture levels are low.
Control Improve soil texture and avoid liming; water regularly. Do not plant potatoes on soil that has recently been used for brassicas. Grow resistant cultivars, eg 'King Edward'; very susceptible cultivars include 'Maris Piper' and 'Desiree'.

Bacterial rotting

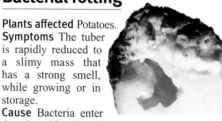

Plants affected Potatoes.
Symptoms The tuber is rapidly reduced to a slimy mass that has a strong smell, while growing or in storage.
Cause Bacteria enter the tuber either through wounds or through damage caused by infections.
Control Maintain good growing conditions, and harvest potatoes carefully in order to avoid injury. Remove all affected tubers immediately.

Internal rust spot

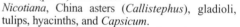

Plants affected Potatoes.
Symptoms Rust-brown flecks develop throughout the flesh.
Cause Cultivation either in sandy, acid soils that are low in organic matter, or in soils that are generally low in nutrients, in particular potash and phosphorus.
Control Incorporate humus into the soil before planting and apply a general fertilizer in spring. Water regularly. Grow resistant cultivars, eg 'King Edward'. Water on calcium nitrate in June.

Potato spraing

Plants affected Potatoes.
Symptoms A brown, arc-shaped discolouration, sometimes with a corky texture develops inside the often misshapen tuber. Potatoes alone show these symptoms, but the viruses (p.649) can infect *Nicotiana*, China asters (*Callistephus*), gladioli, tulips, hyacinths, and *Capsicum*.
Cause A number of viruses, including tobacco rattle virus, and, less often, potato mop-top virus; these are transmitted by free-living nematodes in the soil.
Control Avoid growing other host plants on the affected site, and grow all potatoes on a fresh site. Use seed certified free of virus.

Brown rot and Ring rot

Plants affected Potatoes and some solanaceous weeds (brown rot); potatoes (ring rot).
Symptoms Similar for both diseases – plants may wilt but symptoms are mainly seen in the tubers. Initially, a brown ring just beneath the skin when the tubers are cut in half. Later decay sets in.
Cause Bacterias *Ralstonia solanacearum* (BR) and *Clavibacter michiganensis* subsp. *sepedonicus* (RR).
Control Use only certified disease-free seed. Both diseases occur in mainland Europe. Recent outbreaks in the UK have been eradicated.

See also "Millipedes", p.644; "Blackleg on potatoes", p.664; and "Potato cyst eelworms", p.666.

Bulb, corm, and rhizome problems

Storage rot

Plants affected Bulbs and corms, especially if damaged or poorly stored.
Symptoms Discoloured, sometimes sunken patches develop on the surface of the bulb, or beneath the outer scales or skin. A fungal growth may appear on the patches, spreading through bulb tissues.
Cause A range of fungi and bacteria. Fungal rots are generally hard and dry and eventually the bulb becomes mummified, but if bacteria are also present the rot may be soft and foul-smelling. Infection is often restricted to a very few, closely related bulbs or corms, and may affect both those in the ground and those in store. Temperatures that are too low or too high and over-damp conditions encourage the disease.
Control Store and plant only healthy bulbs, and avoid injury to them. Store in suitable conditions, and ensure that bulbs do not touch to prevent spread of storage diseases by contact; immediately remove any that show signs of deterioration. Dusting them with sulphur may prevent attack.

Bulb flies

Plants affected Daffodils, *Hippeastrum*, snowdrops (*Galanthus*), bluebells (*Hyacinthoides non-scripta*), *Cyrtanthus purpureus*, and *Sprekelia*.
Symptoms Bulbs fail to grow or produce only a few grass-like leaves. Maggots may be found in the bulbs.
Cause The large narcissus bulb fly (*Merodon equestris*), which resembles a small bumblebee, has larvae that usually feed singly inside healthy bulbs. The females lay eggs on the bulbs at soil level in early summer. The plump brownish white larvae are up to 18mm (¾in) long and they fill the centre of the bulbs with muddy excrement during summer to spring. Small bulb flies (*Eumerus* spp.) are black with white crescent markings on their abdomens. Their larvae are up to 8mm (⅜in) long and feed in bulbs already damaged by other pests, diseases or physical injury. There are often several small bulb fly larvae in the same bulb.
Control Avoid planting in warm, sheltered places, which attract adult flies. Discourage egg-laying by firming the soil around the necks of bulbs as they die down, or cover with fine-meshed screens or horticultural fleece in early summer.

Narcissus basal rot

Plants affected Daffodils.
Symptoms After about one month in store, the basal plate of the bulb becomes soft and brown, and rots. The deterioration spreads to the inner scales, which turn dark brown, and a pale pink, fluffy, fungal growth may then appear between the scales and on the basal plate. The bulb gradually dries out and becomes mummified. Bulbs which become infected in the ground may, if not lifted, rot away in the soil. In some cases, foliage symptoms of yellowing and wilting occur first.
Cause The soil-borne fungus *Fusarium oxysporum* f. *narcissi*, which infects bulbs through the basal plate; the fungus is encouraged by high soil temperatures. If the infected bulb is not lifted, it may infect adjacent bulbs. Stored bulbs that are infected but do not show symptoms also act as a source of infection when planted.
Control Lift bulbs early in the season, before soil temperatures rise, and dip them in a solution of carbendazim. Check bulbs thoroughly for signs of disease before storing.

Narcissus eelworm

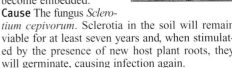

Plants affected Daffodils, bluebells (*Hyacinthoides non-scripta*), and snowdrops (*Galanthus*).
Symptoms Bulbs cut transversely reveal brown concentric rings. Plant growth is stunted and distorted, and infested bulbs invariably rot.
Cause The narcissus eelworm (*Ditylenchus dipsaci*), which is a microscopic nematode that feeds within bulbs and foliage. Where bulbs have been naturalized, the area of infestation will increase each year as the pest spreads through the soil. Weeds may also harbour narcissus eelworm.
Control Dig up and burn both the infested plants and any others within 1m (1yd) of them. Immersing dormant daffodil bulbs in water at 44°C (112°F) for three hours kills the eelworms without causing bulb damage, but the constant temperature is difficult to maintain without special equipment. Avoid replanting affected areas with susceptible plants for at least two years, and keep weeds under control. No chemical treatment is available.

Iris rhizome rot

Plants affected Irises.
Symptoms The base of outer leaves decays and the rot then spreads into the rhizome, attacking the youngest parts first. The infected area is reduced to a foul-smelling mass.
Cause The bacterium *Erwinia carotovora* var. *carotovora*, which thrives in waterlogged soil. The bacteria enter the rhizomes through wounds or other damaged areas.
Control Check all rhizomes for any kind of damage before planting, and be extra careful to avoid injuring them. Plant the rhizomes shallowly, and always in good, well-drained soil. Take steps to ensure that slugs (see p.662), which may be the cause of injury to rhizomes, are kept under control. The prompt removal of any rotting tissue may help to check the problem temporarily, but in the long term the whole rhizome is best discarded.

Onion white rot

Plants affected Onions, shallots, leeks, garlic.
Symptoms The base of the bulb and the roots are covered in a fluffy, white, fungal growth in which hard, black sclerotia (fungal resting bodies) become embedded.
Cause The fungus *Sclerotium cepivorum*. Sclerotia in the soil will remain viable for at least seven years and, when stimulated by the presence of new host plant roots, they will germinate, causing infection again.
Control Dig up and burn affected plants as soon as possible. Do not grow susceptible crops on the affected site for at least eight years.

Onion neck rot

Plants affected Onions and shallots.
Symptoms The scales at the neck become soft and discoloured; a dense, fuzzy, grey, fungal growth develops on the affected area; and hard, black sclerotia (fungal resting bodies) may form. In some severe cases the bulb eventually becomes mummified. The symptoms frequently do not appear until the bulbs are being kept in storage.
Cause The fungus *Botrytis allii*, spread mainly by seed-borne fungal spores and the sclerotia present on plant debris.
Control Obtain sets and seed from a reputable source. Encourage the growth of hard, well-ripened onions; do not feed after midsummer, avoid high nitrogen fertilizers, and water regularly. After harvesting, allow the tops of onions to dry off as rapidly as possible. Store under cool, dry conditions with good air circulation, discarding damaged bulbs. Avoid the more susceptible white-bulbed onions.

Onion fly

Plants affected Mainly onions, sometimes shallots, garlic and leeks.
Symptoms Growth is poor, the outer leaves turn yellow, and maggots may be found in the bulb.
Cause The root- and bulb-feeding larvae of the onion fly (*Delia antiqua*), white maggots up to 9mm (⅜in) long.
Control Carefully lift and burn infested plants. Egg-laying females can be excluded by growing onions under horticultural fleece. There are currently no pesticides available to amateur gardeners.

See also "Slugs and snails", p.644; "Millipedes", p.644; "Red lily beetle", p.644; "Tulip fire", p.649; "Bulb scale mite", p.652; "Grey squirrel", p.659; and "Mice, rats, and voles", p.662.

Whole-plant problems

Drought

Plants affected All plants, especially those that are newly planted, container-grown, or in light, sandy soils.
Symptoms Autumn coloration develops early and defoliation, followed by die-back, may occur. Plants wilt and growth is stunted. Flowering and fruit set may decrease markedly. Fruits may be small, sometimes distorted, and of a poor texture. See pp.650 and 657 for other symptoms.
Cause Chronic (prolonged) or repeated drought due to inadequate or unavailable soil moisture; excessive water loss from the leaves of plants on exposed sites; injured or restricted roots; or soil compaction. Plants in small containers are vulnerable during hot weather, and peat-based composts that dry out too much are extremely difficult to re-wet. Dry, brown buds on certain plants, such as camellias and rhododendrons, are the result of a water shortage the previous year during the period of bud initiation.
Control Water plants regularly, and frequently check those in hot or sunny positions. Plants raised from seed resist drought better than transplanted ones; puddling-in reduces planting stress. Mulch, where appropriate, to improve moisture retention.

Low temperatures

Plants affected Trees, shrubs, perennials, annuals, bulbous plants, vegetables, fruits, indoor plants; seedlings, young plants and container-grown plants are especially vulnerable.
Symptoms The leaves are sometimes bleached, and brown, dry patches develop; evergreen foliage may turn brown. Rotted patches develop on petals, especially on exposed flowerheads. Frost injury causes leaves to pucker and petals to wither or discolour. In some cases, whole flowers may be killed. See also pp.650 and 653.
Cause and control See p.650 for details.

Waterlogging

Plants affected All plants.
Symptoms Leaves may turn yellow, and plants tend to wilt. Bark peels off branches. Roots may rot off completely. Those remaining often begin to blacken and their outer surface peels away very easily.
Cause Excessive water levels in the growing medium, owing to poor soil structure, compaction, impeded drainage, or overwatering.
Control Where feasible, improve the structure and drainage of the soil and build raised beds; if necessary, choose plants that are most likely to survive in wet conditions. Check that drainage holes for container-grown plants are adequate, and that flow through them is not impeded; re-pot plants every two years. The regular application of a foliar feed during the growing season may help to stimulate growth, allowing waterlogged roots to be replaced.

Damping off

Plants affected The seed-lings of all plants.
Symptoms The seedlings collapse and die as their roots darken and rot off; the disease often attacks seedlings at one end of a seed tray, rapidly spreading to the other. A fluffy, fungal growth may appear both on the compost and on any dead seedlings.
Cause Various fungi (most particularly *Pythium ultimum* and some *Phytophthora*), which are soil- or water-borne and attack the seedlings via the roots or stem bases. These fungi flourish in moist and unhygienic conditions.
Control There is no control once the disease is established, so it must be prevented. Sow seed thinly, improve ventilation around seedlings, maintain strict hygiene, and avoid overwatering. Always use sterilized compost, mains water, and clean trays and pots. Water seedlings occasionally with a suitable copper-based fungicide.

Blackleg on cuttings

Plants affected Cuttings, most particularly those of pelargoniums.
Symptoms Stems become blackened, shrunken, soft, and rotten, usually at the base; the plant discolours and eventually dies.
Cause A variety of micro-organisms, eg *Pythium* and *Rhizoctonia*, which are often spread by propagating in unhygienic conditions. Un-sterilized compost, dirty pots, trays, and tools, and the use of non-mains water are commonly to blame. The disease is also transmitted by soil moisture.
Control Use clean equipment, sterilized compost, and mains water. Dip cuttings in rooting powder before potting up. Remove affected cuttings immediately.

Blackleg on potatoes

Plants affected Potatoes.
Symptoms The stems collapse, blacken and rot at the base, and the foliage discolours. The disease usually occurs at the start of the season, but any tubers that have formed may also rot. Most of the crop remains healthy; only a few plants show symptoms.
Cause The bacterium *Erwinia carotovora* var. *atroseptica*, which is usually introduced on slightly infected seed tubers that do not show any symptoms at all when they are being planted.
Control Remove affected plants immediately. Inspect tubers on lifting and do not store any that are suspect. The bacteria are unlikely to build up to dangerous levels in the soil, and potatoes can be planted on the site again under a rotation scheme.

Bad pruning

Plants affected Woody perennials, shrubs, and trees.
Symptoms The plant has a poor, unnatural, or uneven shape. Vigour may be reduced and flowering is limited. Snags or whole limbs may die back.
Cause The removal of limbs too close to, or far from, the main limb or trunk. A flush cut, where no snag is left, leaves a large wound and, more importantly, no branch collar – the area that most rapidly produces callusing wood to heal the wound. Conversely, too long a snag encourages die-back. Carelessly removed branches may damage adjacent bark.
Control When pruning a tree or shrub always be careful to follow the correct method at the appropriate time of year, checking the extent of pruning necessary. Use sharp pruning tools and do not leave any snags or flush cuts. If necessary, employ a reputable tree surgeon.

Nectria canker

Plants affected Woody perennials, shrubs, trees, especially apples, flowering crab apples (*Malus*), beeches (*Fagus*), poplars (*Populus*), *Sorbus*, mulberries (*Morus*), and hawthorns (*Crataegus*).
Symptoms Small areas of bark, often close to a bud or wound, darken and sink inwards; the bark cracks, forming loose, flaky, concentric rings. Enlarged cankers restrict nutrient and water flow, and lead to stem and leaf deterioration. In extreme cases the whole shoot becomes ringed and dies back. White pustules appear in summer, red pustules in winter.
Cause Spores of the fungus *Nectria galligena* infect wounds caused by pruning, leaf fall, irregular growth, frost, and woolly aphids (see p.654).
Control Prune affected branches or, on larger limbs, remove the entire cankered area. Spray the affected tree with Bordeaux mixture, on a still day. Avoid susceptible cultivars, eg the apples 'Cox's Orange Pippin', 'Worcester Pearmain', and 'James Grieve'.

Seiridium canker

Plants affected Conifers, mainly cypresses (*Cupressus*) especially *C. macrocarpa* and *C. sempervirens*, and x *Cupressocyparis leylandii*.
Symptoms Some scattered branches develop dull foliage, which later yellows, dies, turns brown, and is eventually shed. Affected branches develop cankers, which produce copious amounts of resin and are covered with pinhead-sized, black, blister-like, fruiting bodies. When cankers girdle a branch or main stem it dies.

Cause Air-borne spores released from the fruiting bodies of the fungus *Seiridium cardinale* invade trees through the ends of cut branches, fine cracks in the bark, leaf scales, and twig crotches. Infection occurs most readily during the dormant season.
Control Cut out all affected branches or, if severely damaged, remove the whole tree. There is no available chemical control.

Bacterial canker

Plants affected *Prunus*, in particular cherries and plums.
Symptoms Flat or sunken, elongated cankers develop on the stems; droplets of golden or amber-coloured gum ooze from the affected area. The stem starts to deteriorate, and the foliage and flowers may wither and die, or the buds do not break. Foliage may show symptoms of shothole (see p.648).
Cause The bacteria *Pseudomonas syringae* pv. *syringae* and *P. syringae* pv. *morsprunorum*.
Control Remove cankered branches back to healthy wood. Spray the foliage with Bordeaux mixture or other suitable copper fungicide in late summer and early autumn.

Coral spot

Plants affected Broadleaved trees and shrubs, especially *Elaeagnus*, elms (*Ulmus*), beeches (*Fagus*), maples (*Acer*), magnolias, and currants.
Symptoms Affected shoots die back, and the dead bark becomes covered in orange-pink pustules about 1mm (1/16in) in diameter. Until recent years, the

disease was most commonly found on dead branches and woody debris, but it has become more aggressive and now affects living shoots as well as dead.
Cause The fungus *Nectria cinnabarina*. Spores that have been released from the orange pustules are spread by rain splash and on pruning tools. They enter the wood through damaged or dying areas and wounds and infect the plant.
Control Clear away all woody debris. Cut back affected branches to a point well below the obviously infected area.

Honey fungus

Plants affected Trees, shrubs, climbers, and some woody perennials; especially *Wisteria*, rhododendrons, and privets (*Ligustrum*).
Symptoms A creamy-white mycelium develops under the bark at the base of the trunk or the stem, sometimes it also extends upwards; tough, black rhizomorphs (ie fungal strands) appear. In autumn fruiting bodies grow in clusters and die back after the first frost. Gum or resin exudes from cracks in the bark of conifers. Plants deteriorate and finally

Mycelium under bark

Fruiting bodies

die; prolific flowering or fruiting may occur shortly before death. Roots are also affected (see p.661).
Cause The fungus *Armillaria* (principally *A. mellea*) spread either by rhizomorph movement from an infected plant or stump, or through root contact.
Control Dig out and burn affected plants, stumps, and root systems; if necessary, have stumps chipped or ground out by a contractor. Avoid susceptible plants; choose those with some resistance, eg yew (*Taxus baccata*), *Cornus*, beech (*Fagus*), and *Hebe*.

Crown rot

Plants affected Mainly perennials and indoor plants; also trees, shrubs, annuals, bulbous plants, vegetables, and fruits.
Symptoms The base of the plant rots and may smell unpleasant. Plants may wilt, wither, and die.
Cause Bacterial and fun-

gal organisms entering the stem through surface wounds; over-deep planting also leads to infection.
Control Avoid injury to the stem base and keep the crown free of debris; do not mulch right up to the plant. Ensure that planting depths are correct. Complete removal of the affected area may prevent disease spread, but frequently the whole plant is killed and should be dug up and destroyed.

Replant disease/soil sickness

Plants affected Mainly roses, commonly those on *R. canina* rootstocks, and fruit trees.
Symptoms Vigour is reduced; growth and roots are stunted.
Cause Several factors may be involved, including soil-dwelling nematodes and the viruses they transmit, soil-borne fungi, and nutrient depletion.
Control Do not grow replacement plants in a site previously occupied by the same or a closely related species. Change the soil to a depth of at least 45cm (18in) and a width several centimetres greater than the spread of the roots. There is no suitable chemical sterilant available for amateurs, but the ground can be treated by a contractor.

Rose die-back

Plants affected Roses.
Symptoms The plants die back, and may discolour. A fungal growth may develop. Deterioration is extensive in some cases.
Cause Poor planting, poor maintenance, or a poor environment. Severe or repeated attacks of frost, leaf disease, or fungi may also be responsible.
Control Plant roses correctly. Feed and water them regularly. Prune them, and keep diseases and pests under control. Remove all dead or diseased tissue back to healthy wood.

Notifiable pests and diseases

The UK is always under threat from pests and diseases not currently present in the country. If a new pest or disease is deemed a sufficiently serious threat to crops or the environment, it may be made compulsorily notifiable. Current examples are the potato pest Colorado Beetle, and *Phytophthora ramorum* and *P. kernoviae* (see p.654). When a problem is notifiable, the Plant Health and Seeds Inspectorate (PHSI) must be informed of outbreaks. This government agency has specific powers to destroy affected plants, if appropriate, in order to eradicate the problem, as is currently the case for *P. ramorum*. This can be very effective, as with potato wart disease, which has been controlled by a combination of compulsory notification and resistant varieties. Sometimes the best efforts to eradicate fail and notifiable status will be lifted. An example is fireblight disease of pome fruits, notifiable when it arrived in the UK in the 1950s, but now accepted as established.

Clematis wilt

Plants affected Clematis, mainly large-flowered cultivars, eg 'Jackmanii'.
Symptoms The terminal shoots wilt, starting with the youngest foliage, and the petioles begin to darken where they join the leaf blade. A small spot of discolouration

may develop under the lowest pair of wilting leaves. Whole sections of the plant may start to die back.
Cause The fungus *Phoma clematidina*, which produces spore-releasing, fruiting bodies on the older stems. Other, non-pathogenic causes of wilt (eg drought, poor drainage, and graft failure) may be mistaken for this disease.
Control Cut back any affected stems to healthy tissue, below ground level if necessary. *Clematis* spp. are regarded as resistant to clematis wilt, for which there is no effective treatment.

Peony wilt

Plants affected Peonies (*Paeonia*).
Symptoms Affected shoots wilt, wither, and turn brown at the stem base. The infection generally starts at the stem base, which may become covered in a grey, fuzzy, fungal growth resembling grey mould. Small, hard, black, sclerotia (fungal resting bodies) form both on and within the affected stems.
Cause The fungus *Botrytis paeoniae*. The sclerotia drop into the soil and remain until conditions are favourable (wet years in particular); they then cause new infections.
Control Cut out the affected shoots of herbaceous peonies to below ground level, as soon as any signs of disease appear; thin out dense plants.

Anthracnose

Plants affected Willows (*Salix* – mainly *S. x sepulcralis* var. *chrysocoma*); dogwood (*Cornus florida, C. kousa, C. nuttallii*); *Antirrhinum*.

Symptoms Dark, elliptical, rough cankers, about 6mm (¼in) long, on the stems; small, dark brown leaf spots turn yellow, curl, and fall early. The disease is rarely fatal.
Cause The fungus *Marssonina salicicola* on willow, *Discula destructiva* on dogwood, and one or more species of *Colletotrichum* on *Antirrhinum*. They are usually encouraged by mild, damp weather. Spores produced from the cankers and foliage lesions are spread by rain splash.
Control Prune out and burn the cankered shoots, where possible. Rake up and burn affected leaves.

Potato cyst eelworms

Plants affected Potatoes and tomatoes.
Symptoms Plants yellow and die, starting with the lower leaves, and potato tubers remain small. Roots of lifted plants show numerous white, yellow, or brown cysts up to 1mm (¹⁄₁₆in) in diameter.

Cysts on roots

Cause Root-dwelling eelworms, or nematodes, that disrupt water and nutrient uptake. Mature females swell and their bodies (known as cysts) burst through the root walls. Cysts contain up to 600 eggs; these remain viable for many years. Cysts of the golden cyst eelworm (*Globodera rostochiensis*)

Yellowed leaves

change from white through yellow to brown as they mature; those of the white cyst eelworm (*G. pallida*) change directly from white to brown.
Control Crop rotation discourages the build-up of infestation. Some potatoes are resistant to the golden cyst eelworm, eg 'Accent', 'Pentland Javelin', 'Rocket', and 'Swift' (earlies), and 'Cara', 'Maris Piper', 'Picasso' and 'Stemster' (maincrop); others, eg 'Maxine', 'Sante' and 'Valor' are also tolerant of the white cyst eelworm. There is no chemical control available for amateur use.

Vine weevil grubs

Plants affected Shrubs, perennials, bulbous plants, and indoor plants; fuchsias, begonias, cyclamen, *Impatiens, Sedum*, primulas (including the Polyanthus Group), and strawberries are commonly affected. Container-grown plants are particularly vulnerable.

Symptoms Plants grow slowly, wilt, collapse, and die. Roots are eaten and the outer tissues of woody

plants are gnawed from the stems below ground.
Cause The plump, white larvae of the beetle *Otiorhynchus sulcatus*, which are up to 1cm (½in) long and slightly curved, with brown heads and no legs. The adults lay eggs in spring and summer, and damage occurs from autumn to spring.
Control Maintain good hygiene to avoid providing shelters for the adults. Biological-control treatments using nematodes (*Steinernema kraussei*) are available; watered onto the potting compost in late summer, these treatments kill the larvae; a moist, well-drained compost with a temperature of 5–21°C (41–70°F) is required. Alternatively, treat susceptible pot plants with a drench of thiacloprid in late summer, or grow ornamental seedlings and cuttings in a compost premixed with imidacloprid, to kill small larvae.
See also "Vine weevil", p.645.

Fungus gnats or sciarid flies

Plants affected Plants grown under cover. Seedlings and cuttings are more susceptible than established plants.
Symptoms Both seedlings and cuttings fail to grow; greyish-brown flies run over the compost surface or fly among the plants. Larvae may be visible.

Cause The larvae of fungus gnats or sciarid flies (for example *Bradysia* spp.), which feed mainly on dead roots and leaves but may also attack young roots. They are slender, white-bodied maggots up to 6mm (¼in) long with black heads. The adult flies are of a similar length. They do not cause any problems on healthy, established plants.
Control Keep greenhouses tidy, and remove dead leaves and flowers from the soil surface to avoid providing shelters. Use sticky yellow traps suspended above plants to trap the adult flies. Introduce predatory mite *Hypoaspis miles* to feed on the flies' larvae. If necessary, use compost premixed with imidacloprid to control the larvae.

Bean seed fly

Plants affected French and runner beans, courgettes.
Symptoms Seeds either fail to germinate or emerge blind. Seedlings are eaten.
Cause The larvae of the fly *Delia platura*, which are white, legless maggots up to 9mm (⅜in) long that eat the germinating seeds and seedlings.
Control Avoid sowing when the soil is cold and wet (to encourage rapid germination), or pre-germinate seeds before sowing. If the problem is recurrent, sow seeds in pots or trays in a greenhouse and transplant once the seedlings have emerged.

Ants

Plants affected Many annuals and low-growing perennials.
Symptoms Plants grow slowly and have a tendency to wilt. Heaps of soil may also appear, sometimes burying some low-growing plants.
Cause Various species of black, yellow, or reddish-brown ants (eg *Lasius* and *Formica* spp.), which

disturb the roots as they construct their nests. They do not usually feed on the plants, however, and cause relatively little damage.
Control Ants are often abundant and impossible to eliminate; as far as possible their presence should be tolerated. If the problem is severe, dust the soil with bendiocarb.
See also p.668 for problems caused on lawns.

Rabbits and hares

Plants affected Young trees; low-growing plants.
Symptoms Tree bark is gnawed away, especially during cold weather. Low-growing plants are eaten, sometimes grazed down to ground level.

Cause Rabbits and hares.
Control Exclude the animals from gardens with wire netting at least 1m (3ft) high and sunk another 30cm (12in) below ground level. Alternatively, place less elaborate fencing around individual susceptible plants. Protect the base of trees with wire netting or spiral tree-guard collars. Repellent substances, based on aluminium ammonium sulphate, give only limited protection and need frequent application, especially during wet weather or periods of rapid plant growth.

Deer

Plants affected Most plants, especially trees, shrubs (including roses), and herbaceous plants.
Symptoms Shoots and leaves are eaten; tree bark is rubbed and frayed. In winter, bark may be eaten.
Cause Mainly roe and muntjac deer, which feed on shoots, leaves, and bark. Bark is frayed when males mark trees with their scent glands or rub the velvet from their new antlers.

Eaten rose shoots

Control Protect gardens with wire mesh fences at least 2m (6ft) high, or place wire netting around stems and trunks. Repellent sprays or scaring devices, such as hanging tin cans,

Branch damage

provide only short-term protection from deer.

See also "Clubroot", p.649; "Irregular water supply", p.651; "*Verticillium* wilt", p.653; "Slime flux/wet wood", p.653; "Spur blight/ cane blight", p.653; "Grey mould (*Botrytis*)", p.653; "Dutch elm disease", p.653; "*Fusarium* wilt", p.654; "*Phytophthora* root rots", p.654; "Foot and root rots", p.654; "Cutworms", p.655; "Crown gall", p.655; "Fungal brackets", p.655; "Lightning", p.655; "Mechanical wounding", p.655; "Blossom wilt", p.656; "Root-knot eelworms", p.660; "Chafer grubs", p.660; "Leatherjackets", p.660; "Carrot fly", p.660; "Cabbage root fly", p.660; and "Wireworms", p.662.

Lawn problems

Drought

Plants affected Lawns and other grassed areas.
Symptoms Yellowish-brown, straw-like patches of variable size develop on the lawn; in extreme cases the whole area may become discoloured. Damage usually occurs in late spring or summer.
Cause Dry weather and inadequate watering. Free-draining, sandy soils are most at risk.
Control To improve drought resistance, water in the evening, feed regularly, leave cut grass on the lawn if drought conditions are forecast, and spike and top-dress in the autumn. Allow the grass to grow fairly long before cutting, and avoid mowing too closely. Lawns will recover when rains return, so watering can be omitted during water shortages.
See also pp.650, 657, and 664 for problems caused to other plants.

Cats and dogs

Plants affected Lawns, seedlings, garden plants.
Symptoms Gardens, especially lawns and other grassed areas, are fouled with droppings; grass and foliage are scorched with urine; and newly sown areas are scratched up.
Cause Cats and dogs. Cats prefer dry soil and newly cultivated areas.
Control When cats and dogs are seen urinating on plants, wash it off immediately with water, to avoid scorching. Repellent substances based on pepper dust or aluminium ammonium sulphate are available, but these often give only temporary protection. Ultrasonic devices may encourage cats and dogs to go elsewhere.

Dollar spot

Plants affected Lawns and other grassed areas, particularly those containing fine-leaved bents and creeping fescues.
Symptoms Small, pale, straw-coloured patches develop in early autumn. At first they are 2.5–7cm (1–3in) in diameter, but coalesce to form larger areas, and darken as they age.
Cause The fungus *Sclerotinia homeocarpa*, encouraged by heavy or compacted soils and by a high pH; alkaline soils or those treated with lime are likely to produce symptoms. The disease appears mainly in mild, damp weather.
Control Improve soil aeration and remove thatch in the lawn, using a spring-tined lawn rake.

Starvation

Plants affected Lawns and other grassed areas.
Symptoms The grass is thin, patchy, and often rather pale; it may be invaded by moss and weeds or attacked by pathogens. Growth is likely to be slow.
Cause Inadequate feeding or unsuitable fertilizers.

Control Feed the lawn in spring and preferably also in summer and autumn, choosing feeds appropriate to the time of year. Encourage root growth by spiking and scarifying in autumn.

Snow mould/*Fusarium* patch

Plants affected Lawns, particularly those that contain a high proportion of annual meadow grass (*Poa annua*).
Symptoms Patches of grass become yellow and die, often coalescing to form large areas. In damp weather a white, fungal growth appears, causing the grass blades to stick together. It is most prevalent in late autumn and winter, especially on areas of grass that have been walked on while snow-covered.
Cause Principally the fungus *Monographella nivalis* (syn. *Fusarium nivale*), which is encouraged by poor aeration and excessive nitrogen fertilizers.
Control Improve maintenance in susceptible areas, regularly aerating and scarifying the turf. Avoid using high-nitrogen fertilizers in late summer to early autumn.

Slime moulds

Plants affected Common grasses, and occasionally some other plants.
Symptoms Clusters of beige, orange, or white fruiting bodies smother individual blades of grass, and spores are then released, giving the slime mould a grey appearance; the grass looks unsightly but is not harmed. The condition is particularly common in late spring and again in early autumn.
Cause Slime moulds. They tend to thrive during periods of heavy rain.
Control Hose down the affected area. Encourage root growth by spiking and scarifying in autumn.

Red thread

Plants affected Lawns, especially of finer grasses such as the fescues.
Symptoms Tiny, pale pink to red, gelatinous, branching threads of a fungus develop on small patches, about 8cm (3in) in diameter, of grass, which later become bleached. The lawn is very rarely killed completely but it is weakened and its general appearance is somewhat spoiled.
Cause The fungus *Laetisaria fuciformis*, which is common after heavy rain. It is also troublesome when the soil is nitrogen deficient or poorly aerated.
Control Improve turf maintenance and drainage, aerating, scarifying, and feeding as necessary.

Dog lichens

Plants affected Lawns and other grassed areas, particularly those that are in poor condition.
Symptoms Groups of greenish-black, curled, or leafy growths with a pale creamy-white lower surface appear in the lawn.
Cause *Peltigera canina*, which is most troublesome on grassed areas that are badly drained, poorly aerated, compacted, or shaded.
Control Rake out lichens and treat with a moss killer containing ferrous sulphate, which will give some control. Improve lawn aeration and drainage, and remember to feed and top-dress regularly.

Algae and gelatinous lichens

Gelatinous patch

Plants affected Lawns and other grassed areas.
Symptoms Slippery patches of green or greenish-black form on the surface.
Cause Gelatinous lichens and algae, which are particularly commonly found on any poorly drained, poorly aerated, or compacted sites.
Control Try to improve the drainage, and also aerate the lawn. Prune back any trees or shrubs that noticeably overhang the area, creating densely shaded, damp sections. Apply any proprietary lawncare products that contain ferrous sulphate.

Green, algal slime

Leatherjackets

Plants affected Lawns and other grassed areas.
Symptoms Brown patches in the lawn in spring and summer, and maggots are sometimes visible.
Cause Leatherjackets, the larvae of crane flies, or daddy-long-legs (eg *Tipula* spp.), which feed on the roots. They are greyish-brown, tubular, legless maggots up to 3.5cm (1½in) long (see p.660).
Control Soak affected areas of the lawn with water, and cover with sacking or black plastic sheeting for a day to bring the leatherjackets to the surface; they can then be removed and killed. Alternatively apply biological-control pathogenic nematodes (*Steinernema feltiae*) or treat with imidacloprid in early autumn. Problems are worse after wet autumns.
See also p.660 for problems caused to other plants.

Chafer grubs

Plants affected Lawns and other grassed areas.
Symptoms Patches of the lawn are ripped up by birds, foxes, or badgers as they feed on chafer larvae. Damage occurs in autumn, sometimes continuing through a mild winter, and is found mainly on sandy soils where grass growth is already poor.

Cause The root-feeding grubs of certain beetles, in particular the garden chafer (*Phyllopertha horticola*), and the Welsh chafer (*Hoplia philanthus*). The grubs are plump, "C"-shaped, and can be up to 2cm (¾in) long. They have white bodies, brown heads, and three pairs of legs.
Control Feed and water the lawn as necessary, to encourage good growth. If damage is severe, repair lawns by sowing or turfing in the spring. Water in biological-control pathogenic nematodes (*Heterorhabditis megidis*) in midsummer or treat with imidacloprid.
See also p.660 for problems caused to other plants.

Toadstools

Plants affected Lawns and other grassed areas.
Symptoms Fungal, fruiting bodies develop, sometimes in distinct circles ("fairy rings"), and often on buried, woody material. Most cause little damage, but fairy rings are both harmful and disfiguring.
Two circles of very lush, green grass form, one within the other, sometimes several metres in diameter, and the grass in between them dies off; toadstools then emerge on the outer part of this middle zone. A white, fungal growth permeates the soil in the area of the ring.
Cause Various fungi, including *Coprinus*, *Mycena*, and the fairy-ring-producing *Marasmius oreades*. They all have underground mycelia and are spread to new sites by wind-borne spores.
Control Brush off *Coprinus* and *Mycena* when they first appear, before spores are produced. If the fungi are on buried wood, remove it. There is no chemical control available. Feed lawns to mask green ring.

Ants

Plants affected Lawns and other grassed areas.
Symptoms Small heaps of fine soil are deposited on the surface of the lawn, mainly in summer.
Cause Ants (eg *Lasius flavus*), usually yellow-brown, which carry soil up to the surface as they remove it to extend their underground nests.
Control When the soil dries, remove the heaps with a brush. Dust the nest site with bendiocarb, permethrin, or pyrethrum.
See also p.666 for problems caused to other plants.

Earthworms

Plants affected Lawns.
Symptoms Small, muddy deposits or worm casts are left on the lawn surface in spring and autumn.
Cause Earthworms, mainly surface-casting types, especially *Allolobophora* spp.
Control Disperse dry casts by brushing. There are no effective treatments currently available to amateur gardeners. Acidification treatments do not make the soil sufficiently acidic to deter worms.

Moles

Plants affected Lawns, seedlings, young plants.
Symptoms Heaps of soil (molehills) appear on the lawn and cultivated areas. Roots of young plants and seedlings are disturbed.
Cause Burrowing moles.
Control Moles are most efficiently controlled by trapping, although they may sometimes be driven away, at least temporarily, by ultrasonic devices.

Controls currently approved

Organic insecticides

Fatty acids/insecticidal soaps A modern version of the traditional soft soap spray for use against small insects, including aphids, whiteflies, red spider mite, thrips, scale insects, and mealybugs.

Ferric phosphate Pelleted bait for controlling slugs and snails.

Plant oils Extracted from plants, including oil seed rape. Available as sprays for use against a similar range of pests as fatty acids.

Pyrethrum Extracted from the flowers of *Pyrethrum cinerariifolium*. Available as sprays and dusts for controlling aphids, whiteflies, thrips, leafhoppers, ants, small caterpillars, and other small insects.

Rotenone or Derris Extracted from the roots of *Derris* and *Lonchocarpus* species. Available as sprays and dusts for controlling aphids, thrips, red spider mite, raspberry beetle, flea beetles, sawfly larvae, and other small caterpillars.

Synthetic insecticides

Aluminium sulphate Applied to soil as crystals for the control of slugs and snails.

Bendiocarb A dust for controlling ants, woodlice, and wasp nests.

Bifenthrin A synthetic compound related to pyrethrum. Available as sprays for controlling aphids, whiteflies, thrips, leafhoppers, small caterpillars, beetles, and red spider mite.

Imidacloprid A systemic insecticide absorbed into plants through the roots and foliage. Controls vine weevil grubs, leatherjackets, chafer grubs, fungus gnat larvae, whiteflies, and aphids. Spray formulations additionally control red lily beetle, scale insects, and mealybugs.

Metaldehyde Pelleted baits or a liquid drench for controlling slugs and snails.

Plant oil winter wash Spray for dormant fruit trees and bushes to control overwintering eggs of aphids, apple sucker, mussel scale, and other pests.

Thiacloprid A systemic for controlling vine weevil grubs on container-grown ornamental plants. Also controls aphids, whitefly and some beetle pests.

Organic fungicides

Bordeaux mixture A mixture of copper sulphate and calcium hydroxide approved under some organic regimes. Labelled in UK for control of potato and tomato blight, celery leaf spot, apple and pear canker, bacterial canker of *Prunus*, peach leaf curl, and some soft fruit rusts.

Sulphur Available in UK as dust, or as a liquid suspension with fatty acids.

The dust may be used for control of a wide range of powdery mildews, and storage rots of bulbs, corms, etc. The liquid formulation is used for powdery mildew and pest control on roses and other ornamentals. Sulphur as chips or powder (not the fungicide form) can also be used in gardens to acidify soil that is excessively alkaline, although use of the fungicide form at rates recommended for disease control is not likely to have much effect.

Synthetic fungicides

Cheshunt compound A copper-ammonium complex for control of damping-off problems in seedlings.

Copper oxychloride Protects against similar diseases to Bordeaux mixture.

Mancozeb A protectant fungicide labelled in UK for control of lettuce downy mildew, potato and tomato blight, apple and pear scab, peach leaf curl, blackcurrant leaf spot, and some rusts.

Myclobutanil A systemic fungicide available in UK in several formulations for control of rose black spot, rusts, and powdery mildew on ornamentals, apple and pear scab, and some soft fruit powdery mildews.

Penconazole A systemic fungicide for control of powdery mildew on ornamentals and rose black spot; also provides some control of rusts on ornamentals. Some plants, for example fuchsias, may be sensitive to this product.

Pesticide regulation and approval process

The European Union requires all pesticide active ingredients (AIs) sold within the EU to be listed. For a place on the EU list, manufacturers must submit safety data, and they will decide whether or not to compile this on economic grounds. Once listed, products containing those AIs may be marketed.

Approval to market is regulated by national governments (in the UK, the Pesticides Safety Directorate), which require further safety data on the product. Again, the decision to seek approval will be made on economic grounds and will reflect the likely demand, which will vary from country to country.

Due to health and safety laws, which cannot be enforced on the general public, most pesticides are only available to qualified professionals. A very restricted range of products deemed safe to use without protective clothing is available to amateur gardeners.

Weeds

WEEDS are, quite simply, plants that grow where they are not wanted. They have important features in common: they are usually fast-growing and invasive, competing with cultivated plants for food and water; they are able to grow in almost any soil or site; and they often show a marked resistance to control. Weeds may occur in almost any part of the garden.

Cultivated plants may be placed in the weed category in certain circumstances, depending on their habit. If they prove too invasive for their site and overwhelm their neighbours, or if they self-seed freely throughout the garden, they may properly be classified as "weeds".

Categorizing weeds

Annual weeds complete their entire lifecycle within one year. They set seed which germinates freely; occasionally, as in the case of groundsel (*Senecio vulgaris*), they may even produce several generations in one season. It is important, therefore, to remove annuals at the seedling stage, before they are able to produce seed.

Perennial weeds, by contrast, survive from year to year. Some grow readily from seed, like annuals, but more usually persist by means of various storage organs, such as rhizomes, bulbs, bulbils, tubers, and thick tap roots. Many perennials are able to proliferate because of poor cultivation techniques that leave small pieces of rhizome or root in the soil when digging over or rotavating.

Controlling weeds

Weeds may be controlled in two main ways: they may either be discouraged from growing by the use of good, basic gardening techniques; or they may be removed by manual, mechanical, or chemical means.

The choice of how to remove different weeds depends on various factors: the habit of the plants themselves, the preference of the gardener, and the location of the weeds – whether in borders, lawns, paths, or neglected sites.

CULTIVATED PLANTS AS WEEDS

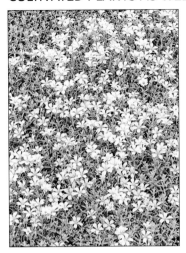

Snow-in-summer
Any plant may become a weed if it dominates other garden plants. The dense growth and rapid spread of Cerastium tomentosum *may cause problems in a rock garden.*

Russian vine
Although often planted to cover unsightly features rapidly, the Russian vine (Fallopia baldschuanica) *is an invasive climber that can soon swamp more delicate plants in the vicinity.*

Annual weeds

In common with other annual plants, annual weeds grow, flower, set seed, and die within one year. They occur most frequently in regularly cultivated areas, such as vegetable plots or annual borders, where frequent digging deters perennial kinds. Their rapid growth makes them troublesome among crops raised from seed *in situ* as they smother slower-growing plants and reduce yields of others by competing for moisture, nutrients, and light.

The need for control

It is important to destroy annual weeds before they produce seeds, since many seeds are small, light, readily wind-borne, and quick to germinate. Quick-maturing species like shepherd's purse (*Capsella bursa-pastoris*) may produce several generations in a single season. Common chickweed (*Stellaria media*) smothers nearby plants and is another weed that should be controlled at the seedling stage. Its seeds start to germinate in the autumn and continue growing in a mild winter to form dense mats.

Many seeds may be buried once they are shed, and lie dormant for many years until they are brought to the surface during site or crop cultivation. The weeds then germinate and grow rapidly. If a site is heavily infested, it should be cultivated regularly when it is crop-free in order to kill germinating seedlings.

Annual weeds may be controlled by hand, mechanical, or chemical means (see "Preventing weeds", p.670).

COMMON ANNUAL WEEDS

Shepherd's purse
(*Capsella bursa-pastoris*)

Annual meadow grass
(*Poa annua*)

Hairy bittercress
(*Cardamine hirsuta*)

Common chickweed (*Stellaria media*)

Groundsel
(*Senecio vulgaris*)

Annual nettle (*Urtica urens*)

Perennial weeds

Perennial weeds persist from year to year, surviving and resting through winter cold and summer heat by storing food reserves in fleshy roots, bulbs, rhizomes, or tubers.

They may be divided into two groups: herbaceous kinds and woody-stemmed kinds. Herbaceous perennials die back to ground level in the autumn. They survive the winter by storing food in their roots and then reappear in spring. Examples are the perennial stinging nettle (*Urtica dioica*), broadleaved dock (*Rumex obtusifolius*), and field bindweed (*Convolvulus arvensis*). Also included in this group are the stemless herbaceous perennials that have leaves arising directly from their roots or rhizomes, for example, dandelion (*Taraxacum officinale*) and ground elder (*Aegopodium podagraria*).

Woody-stemmed perennials, such as common elder (*Sambucus nigra*) and bramble (*Rubus fruticosus*), survive the winter by storing food in stems and branches. The woody-stemmed, evergreen, common ivy (*Hedera helix*) can also be an invasive weed.

The need for control

Perennial weeds have underground fleshy roots, rhizomes, and other storage organs that are not easily controlled. Hoeing and digging, along with machine cultivation, tend to break the roots and rhizomes into sections without killing them; many survive to grow and increase the infestation. With most perennial weeds, use of weedkillers is the most practical and effective approach.

Preventing weeds

Both annual and perennial weeds may be prevented from establishing in various ways. These will do much to avoid the need for tedious weeding later on, especially if you adopt methods that rely on the principle of depriving light from the soil surface. Without light, plants cannot grow.

Working the soil

Before planting, it is extremely important to clear the site completely of all weeds, either manually or with chemicals. Weeds are often difficult to eradicate from among established plants, which may need to be lifted and the weeds extracted from the washed root system.

Conditioning very acid soils with lime will deter some lawn weeds, such as field woodrush (*Luzula campestris*), that thrive where the soil is acid.

Cultivating healthy plants

Vigorous, healthy plants are able to compete more effectively with weeds than are poor, weak specimens. Plants with spreading foliage provide a dark cover over the soil that discourages weed germination under the canopy.

Some vegetable crops, for example potatoes, compete well with annual weeds and may be grown to help maintain clean ground for a subsequent crop (see GROWING VEGETABLES, "Crop rotation", p.498).

Plastic mulch materials

Covering the soil with plastic mulch sheeting after planting prevents annual weeds from establishing. Such materials can also be effective in suppressing most perennial weeds if undisturbed for at least two years. Plastic mulch sheeting is generally permeable, allowing water and nutrients to pass through to the roots. Cover the sheeting with a bark mulch to improve its appearance. Black plastic sheeting is particularly useful in fruit and vegetable gardens; make slits in it through which the crops can grow.

Organic mulching

In early spring, apply a mulch 5–8cm (2–3in) thick of weed-free, organic material such as leaf mould, peat substitute, or processed bark to help prevent weed seeds germinating and smother weed seedlings. Do not use garden compost or insufficiently rotted manure as they often contain weed seeds.

Established perennial weeds may grow through the mulch but, as they tend to root into the loose material, they are easy to remove.

Ground-cover plants

Some plants grow in dense carpets that suppress the germination of weed seeds. They are useful for areas where, because of shade, or very wet or dry soil, weeds thrive. Choose ground-cover plants carefully as some are invasive (see PERENNIALS FOR GROUND COVER, p.180).

Grassing down borders

Some persistent perennial weeds, such as horsetail (*Equisetum arvense*) and oxalis (*Oxalis corymbosa* and *O. latifolia*), may resist repeated attempts to eradicate them with weedkiller or to dig them out. An alternative approach is to grass down any badly infested borders and maintain them as close-mown turf for several years. Given time, this treatment will generally eliminate most of the infestation of persistent perennial weeds.

PERENNIAL WEEDS
Weeds with rhizomes and stolons

Ground elder
(*Aegopodium podagraria*)

Hedge bindweed
(*Calystegia sepium*)

Creeping thistle
(*Cirsium arvense*)

Field bindweed (*Convolvulus arvensis*)

Couch grass
(*Elymus repens*)

Coltsfoot
(*Tussilago farfara*)

Willow herb
(*Epilobium* sp.)

Horsetail
(*Equisetum arvense*)

Creeping yellow cress
(*Rorippa sylvestris*)

Controlling weeds

Once weeds are present, they may be eradicated in one of three ways: hand-weeding, mechanical control, and chemical control. There are three different types of weedkiller: those that act on the leaves, those that act on the soil, and those that act on specific types of plant.

Hand-weeding and hoeing

Hand-weeding, hoeing, and forking are often the only practical ways of removing weeds in flower beds, the vegetable garden, and small patches of ground where weedkillers cannot be used safely without risk of harming nearby garden or crop plants.

Hand-weed or hoe in dry weather, if possible, so that the weeds shrivel and die rapidly. In wet weather, remove uprooted weeds from the site to prevent them from rooting back into the soil. Hoe only lightly around cultivated plants to prevent their surface roots from being damaged.

Removing weeds mechanically

Market gardeners often use rotary cultivators (rotavators) with hoeing or cultivating attachments for annual weed control between rows of vegetables, but they may be unsuitable for perennials. They simply cut the rhi-zomes of weeds such as couch grass and ground elder into many pieces that will continue to grow as new plants. Wherever possible, use weedkillers to kill persistent perennial weeds before digging or cultivating.

Foliage-acting weedkillers

Leaf-acting products enter the weeds through leaves or green stems and are applied with a sprayer or watering can and fine rose or dribble-bar. There are two different types: systemic and contact. The first acts by translocation, moving from the leaves to the roots, and so destroys both annual and perennial weeds. For maximum effect the weeds should be in vigorous growth. The second type works by killing only by direct touch. They destroy annual weeds and the green leaves and stems of perennial weeds, although not the roots of perennials, which will usually regrow strongly. Some weedkillers act through both leaves and roots.

Soil-acting weedkillers

These are applied to the soil and are absorbed into the roots of growing weeds. From there they move to the parts above ground, killing the weeds by interfering with their metabolism. They remain active in the soil, sometimes for months, killing weeds as the seeds germinate. They kill established annual weeds and may also kill or suppress many established perennial weeds. When planning to use areas that have been treated with soil-acting weedkillers, check the manufacturer's literature for details of residual activity and do not sow or plant until the recommended period has elapsed.

Selective weedkillers

These weedkillers kill broadleaved weeds but not narrow-leaved grasses.

Range of chemicals

From time to time the range of weedkillers available to gardeners changes – a new product is introduced or an existing one withdrawn. When buying weedkillers, always check within the range currently available that the products can be used safely and effectively in the situations where weeds are troublesome. A weedkiller may include one of these chemicals.

Glufosinate ammonium (contact action) and **diquat** (contact action) are both quick-acting and will kill annual weeds but only check the growth of perennial weeds. They are useful for killing overwintering annual weeds before spring sowing or planting and are inactivated in soil.

Glyphosate (translocated, foliage-acting) is one of the most useful weedkillers for controlling perennial weeds. It is a foliage-acting weedkiller that moves down to the roots, killing or strongly checking even the most difficult weeds. It is not selective and should be kept well away from all garden plants, but especially raspberries, roses, and other suckering woody plants. With most weeds, it is most effective when growth is well advanced, usually from midsummer onwards, but check the manufacturer's recommendations. As it does not remain active in the soil it is safe to cultivate as soon as weeds are dead.

Dichlobenil (soil-acting, granular) is a weedkiller that may be applied, before growth begins, to the soil around some well-established ornamental shrubs, including roses, to control or suppress some perennial weeds, such as ground elder, and to control germinating weed seeds. It is residual and continues to act for several months.

Amitrole (foliage-acting, translocated) is usually combined with contact and soil-acting herbicides to control weeds that have become established in cracks and crevices in paved areas, paths, and drives.

Organic weedkillers

Some weedkillers based on natural products, such as vinegar (acetic acid) and pelargonic acid, are now offered to control weeds. As they are based on natural materials these controls are more acceptable to some gardeners than man-made chemicals. They work by contact action.

Weeds with tubers and fleshy roots

Bryony (*Bryonia dioica*)

Oxalis (*Oxalis corymbosa* and *O. latifolia*)

Lesser celandine (*Ranunculus ficaria*)

Weeds with deep roots

Japanese knotweed (*Fallopia japonica*)

Dock (*Rumex* sp.)

Bramble (*Rubus fruticosus*)

Perennial stinging nettle (*Urtica dioica*)

Using weedkillers safely

Care must always be taken when applying weedkillers:
- wear protective clothing, for example rubber gloves and old clothes, when mixing and applying weedkillers;
- do not apply weedkillers in windy conditions when there is a risk of spray being blown across to nearby plants, which may suffer serious damage;
- use only for appropriate purposes as recommended on the product label, for example do not use a path weedkiller to keep down weeds in a rose bed;
- always dilute soluble weedkillers according to the manufacturer's instructions;
- always apply weedkillers at the recommended rates on the labels;
- always keep in original containers and make sure that the labels are well secured to the containers so that contents are known and no errors in usage occur;
- never store diluted weedkillers for future use;
- store away out of reach of children and animals, preferably in a securely locked cupboard in a workshop or shed.

Lawn weeds

Various perennial weeds can be troublesome in lawns. Their common survival factor is their ability to grow and thrive in the adverse conditions of short, regularly mown grass. They usually originate from seeds carried by the wind or by birds. Once lawn weeds have germinated, most are then rapidly spread by the action of mowing and early treatment is necessary if they are to be eradicated.

Among the most troublesome lawn weeds are: slender speedwell (*Veronica filiformis*), field woodrush (*Luzula campestris*), annual meadow grass (*Poa annua*), and mind-your-own-business (*Soleirolia soleirolii*, syn. *Helxine soleirolii*). These persistent weeds do not respond to treatment by lawn weedkillers, and need other forms of treatment.

In lawns where the grass is too sparse to offer adequate competition, moss may also become a problem.

Preventing weeds and moss

Good lawn care is an effective preventive measure. The presence of numerous weeds in a lawn usually indicates that the grass is not growing sufficiently vigorously to prevent weeds from establishing. Lack of regular feeding and drought are among the most common reasons for poor growth. Soil compaction and mowing the grass too closely and too regularly may also lead to the spread of moss. For further details on lawn care, see THE LAWN, "Routine care", pp.395–400. Coarser weed grasses (for example, *Holcus lanatus*) may remain a problem, and clumps or affected areas of turf may need to be removed and the cleared patch returfed or re-seeded.

Raking before mowing and lifting creeping stems may help to check the spread of creeping weeds, such as trefoils (*Trifolium* spp.), slender speedwell (*Veronica filiformis*), and sorrels (*Rumex* spp.), if the grass is mown straight afterwards and the clippings picked up by the mower.

Removing weeds

There are two main ways of treating lawn weeds, depending on the severity of the problem. They may be removed by hand or treated with an appropriate weedkiller.

Weeding by hand

Hand-weeding is an effective method of removing a few, scattered rosetted weeds such as daisy (*Bellis perennis*), dandelion (*Taraxacum officinale*), and plantains (*Plantago* spp.). Use a daisy grubber or hand fork to lift the weeds, then firm back displaced turf.

Dealing with moss

Moss may be killed with moss preparations or lawn sand. This is only a short-term solution, however: unless the original conditions that encouraged moss are identified and corrected, the problem usually recurs.

Removing weeds with chemicals

Weedkillers intended specifically for use on lawns work by translocation – moving within the plant from the leaves to the roots – and the weeds begin to distort and shrivel within a few days of application. The chemicals are selective and do not harm lawn grasses at normal dilution rates, but do not use them on seedling grasses within six months of germination.

You should also avoid using lawn weedkillers on newly laid turf, until one growing season has passed after laying or planting.

LAWN WEEDS

Yarrow (*Achillea millefolium*)

Common mouse-ear chickweed (*Cerastium fontanum*, syn. *C. vulgatum*)

Mouse-ear hawkweed (*Pilosella officinarum*)

Field woodrush (*Luzula campestris*)

Broadleaved plantain (*Plantago major*)

Self-heal (*Prunella vulgaris*)

Creeping buttercup (*Ranunculus repens*)

Sheep's sorrel (*Rumex acetosella*)

Pearlwort (*Sagina procumbens*)

Lesser yellow trefoil (*Trifolium dubium*)

Common white clover (*Trifolium repens*)

Slender speedwell (*Veronica filiformis*)

The range of chemicals

Proprietary lawn weedkillers normally combine two or more active ingredients in order to control a wider range of weeds. These include:
2,4–D, a selective weedkiller that is particularly effective against broad-leaved, rosetted weeds, such as plantains and daisies. This chemical is usually combined with mecoprop–p.
Mecoprop–p, which kills various difficult, small-leaved, and creeping weeds, such as trefoils (*Trifolium* spp. and *Lotus corniculatus*). It is usually combined with 2,4–D.
Ferrous sulphate, the active ingredient in lawn sands; it is used to eradicate moss.
MCPA, a selective herbicide used in both problem-weed mixtures and lawn weedkillers to control weeds that

have resistance to other chemicals.
Dicamba, usually combined with 2,4–D or MCPA to control a wider range of weeds.
Lime, which may be applied on very acid soils in winter in the form of ground chalk or limestone at 50g/sq m (2oz/sq yd) to deter sorrels and field woodrush. Sorrels can be partially controlled by repeat treatment with 2,4–D preparations; field woodrush is resistant to lawn weedkillers.

Buying weedkillers

Lawn weedkillers are usually sold as a concentrated liquid and therefore need to be suitably diluted. They may also be obtained in the form of soluble powder, ready-to-use spray, aerosol, or in combination with liquid or granular lawn fertilizers.

Applying weedkillers

Feed the lawn at the start of the growing season, applying weedkiller two to three weeks later when grass and weeds are growing strongly. In the spring, creeping lawn grasses soon colonize any bare patches left as weeds shrivel and die. Great care should be taken when applying weedkillers (see the recommendations on p.671).

Wheeled sprayers can be used for large areas; a watering can with a fine rose or dribble-bar attachment is better for small lawns. Divide the lawn into strips using two garden lines to ensure that the grass has been given complete and uniform coverage.

If possible, wait for two or three days after mowing before applying the weedkiller, so that the weeds have time to develop new leaf surfaces to absorb the chemicals. Do not mow the

grass for two or three days after spraying to allow time for the weedkiller to work its way down towards the roots. Also, do not put the grass clippings on the compost heap for the first few cuts after the application of weedkiller.

How often to apply

Some lawn weeds, such as daisies and plantains, are killed by one or two applications of weedkiller; others, for example the trefoils, may need two or three applications, at four- to six-week intervals.

Where a weed shows no response to repeated applications of various weedkillers, the only solution is to remove it by hand. This will either mean removing and replacing infested areas of turf or, alternatively, feeding, scarifying, and aerating the turf to strengthen it and weaken the weed.

Neglected sites

Different treatments need to be adopted according to how long the area has been neglected and how great a hold the weeds have obtained. Sites that have been neglected for some time may take a season, or even longer, to clear for vegetable growing.

Short-term neglect

On sites that have been neglected for up to a year, most of the weeds are likely to be annuals. Kill these with one or two applications of glyphosate in spring or summer.

It is often easy to deal with short-term neglect without chemicals. A covering of opaque plastic sheeting can suppress weeds within a few months. For speedier results a medium power rotovator prepares the soil satisfactorily in dry spells with two to three cultivations at fortnightly intervals. Alternatively, planting a smothering crop of mustard, potatoes or pumpkins can suppress weeds and clear the ground.

Winter clearance

If the site is being cleared during the winter, remove any overwintering top-growth of annual weeds with a rotary mower. Then dig out any perennial weeds by hand, if possible, before cultivating the area. Clear neglected vegetable plots and allotments progressively, beginning at the warmer, sunnier end, where the earliest sowings of crops are to be made and the seedbeds are to be sited.

Longer-term neglect

After a second year of neglect, perennial weeds will become well established, competing vigorously

with annual weeds. If the site remains neglected for a further year, by the end of the third growing season the weed population will usually be largely, or entirely, strong-growing perennial weeds. Badly infested sites are difficult to clear by hand or by use of a rotavator (the latter may do no more than turn the weeds back into the soil again). It is more practical to use translocated and soil-acting weedkillers, allowing a full growing season for treatment to take effect.

Cutting down weeds

If beginning clearance in spring, cut down weeds with woody stems, for example brambles or elder, to within 30–45cm (12–18in) from the ground, then spray the whole weed-infested area with glyphosate.

To remove weeds from a neglected area without weedkillers, cover the site with opaque plastic sheeting and leave for at least six months. After this, cultivation will be easy, but woody stumps may need to be grubbed out. Deep digging is the traditional means

of clearing neglected ground, but is laborious for all but small areas. For speedier results, a high power rotovator makes the soil workable in dry spells in summer, and repeated rotovation can eliminate many weeds. However, follow-up action, either by cultivation or covering with opaque sheets, may be necessary the next year.

Summer spraying

Another method is to cut the weeds back in spring and then allow them to grow unchecked until midsummer; then spray the site with glyphosate, which acts more effectively on the vigorous young growth stimulated by the spring cut. It is a translocated weedkiller and it usually takes three to four weeks to show any effect; it leaves no active residues in the soil and as soon as weeds are dead the site can be cultivated and planted. Very persistent weeds, such as horsetail and bindweed, may need subsequent spot-treatment, again with glyphosate, possibly for a further two or three growing seasons, to control them fully.

Uncultivated ground

Where previously cultivated land is to be left uncultivated, and is free from perennial weeds, it can be kept clear by regular light cultivations, at intervals throughout the year, with a hoe or with a mechanical tool, such as a rotary cultivator. Alternatively, at intervals, developing weed seedlings can be killed by application of glyphosate.

If perennial weeds are infesting the site, let them grow until midsummer, then spray with glyphosate.

Weeds in cracks and crevices

Weeds in the cracks in paths and brickwork are hard to remove by hand, so chemical control is usually required.

Path weedkillers

In early spring, apply a proprietary path weedkiller. Such weedkillers are mixtures of contact and soil-acting chemicals, the latter usually remaining active in the soil for several months. They may also include a foliage-acting, translocated herbicide, such as amitrole, to deal with any established perennial weeds not usually controlled by the low-strength, soil acting chemicals in these mixtures.

Spot treatment

Perennial weeds growing in paths may be spot-treated or sprayed with glyphosate when regrowth is vigorous. Dichlobenil granules carefully sprinkled or brushed into the spaces between paving stones will control weeds but should not be applied if crevice plants are being cultivated.

WEED-INFESTED PONDS

In the absence of herbicides, control weeds such as azolla and duckweed by dragging, raking, or netting. Algae is a special case. Bags of barley or lavender straw submerged in early spring and replaced every month may give good control. Proprietary algae remedies, ultraviolet light and filtration can also be effective.

8
BASIC BOTANY

FAMILIARITY WITH THE BASICS of botany (the study of plants) helps the gardener to understand how to keep plants healthy as well as many horticultural techniques, such as propagation. The study of the internal arrangement of plant structures (anatomy) and their external construction (morphology), for example, provides an explanation of how to graft or make pruning cuts that heal quickly. Physiology – the study of a plant's metabolism – offers insight into a plant's need for water and light, the processes of photosynthesis, transpiration, and respiration, and the role of nutrients. The identification and classification of plants (taxonomy) shows close relationships between genera or species that have similar cultivation needs.

Plant diversity

There are more than 250,000 species of seed-bearing plant. They include annuals, which flower, seed, and die in a year or less; biennials, which grow from seed in their first year and then flower, seed, and die in the second season; and perennials, which live for several to many years, and include woody plants. Commonly, the term perennials is applied to herbaceous or border plants, while trees and shrubs are referred to as woody plants. The roots, stems, leaves, and flowers of plants may become modified for particular purposes and environments.

Roots

These anchor the plant in the soil and absorb water and mineral salts from which the plant manufactures its food. Fleshy tap roots penetrate vertically downwards, forming sparse lateral roots that are, in turn, finely branched. Fibrous roots comprise a network of fine, thread-like roots that emerge from the base of the stem or from tap roots in some plants. The root tips bear fragile root hairs, which are in intimate contact with soil particles from which water and mineral salts are absorbed. Roots are sometimes modified to form storage organs, as is the case in many terrestrial orchids or swollen tap roots such as carrots, or in some tubers such as dahlias.

Stems

Plant stems provide the above-ground framework of the plant, supporting the leaves, flowers, and fruits. Some stem cells are specialized to provide a strong framework; some conduct water and mineral salts (the xylem), or

BASIC PARTS OF A PLANT

Flowers for seed production

Leaves for photosynthesis and transpiration

Leaves and flowers arising from a very short basal stem

Roots for water and nutrient intake

Polyanthus (Primula)

ROOT SYSTEMS

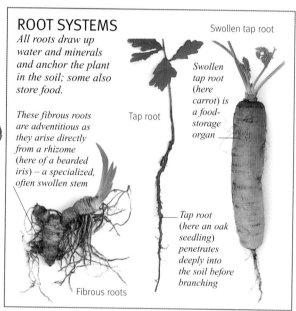

All roots draw up water and minerals and anchor the plant in the soil; some also store food.

These fibrous roots are adventitious as they arise directly from a rhizome (here of a bearded iris) – a specialized, often swollen stem

Tap root

Swollen tap root

Swollen tap root (here carrot) is a food-storage organ

Tap root (here an oak seedling) penetrates deeply into the soil before branching

Fibrous roots

TYPES OF STEM

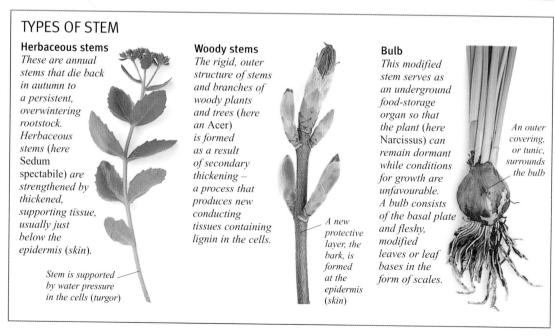

Herbaceous stems
These are annual stems that die back in autumn to a persistent, overwintering rootstock. Herbaceous stems (here Sedum spectabile) are strengthened by thickened, supporting tissue, usually just below the epidermis (skin).

Stem is supported by water pressure in the cells (turgor)

Woody stems
The rigid, outer structure of stems and branches of woody plants and trees (here an Acer) is formed as a result of secondary thickening – a process that produces new conducting tissues containing lignin in the cells.

A new protective layer, the bark, is formed at the epidermis (skin)

Bulb
This modified stem serves as an underground food-storage organ so that the plant (here Narcissus) can remain dormant while conditions for growth are unfavourable. A bulb consists of the basal plate and fleshy, modified leaves or leaf bases in the form of scales.

An outer covering, or tunic, surrounds the bulb

LEAF FORMS

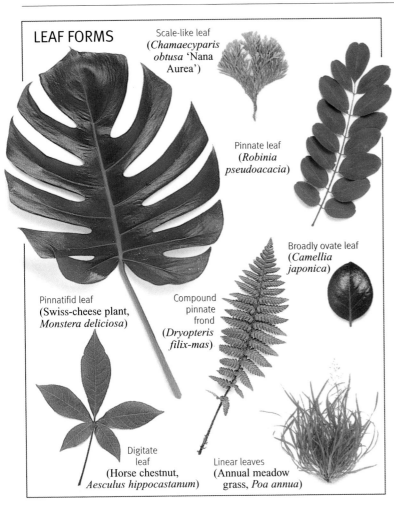

Scale-like leaf
(*Chamaecyparis obtusa* 'Nana Aurea')

Pinnate leaf
(*Robinia pseudoacacia*)

Broadly ovate leaf
(*Camellia japonica*)

Pinnatifid leaf
(Swiss-cheese plant, *Monstera deliciosa*)

Compound pinnate frond
(*Dryopteris filix-mas*)

Digitate leaf
(Horse chestnut, *Aesculus hippocastanum*)

Linear leaves
(Annual meadow grass, *Poa annua*)

PHOTOSYNTHESIS

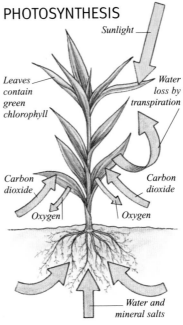

Sunlight

Leaves contain green chlorophyll

Water loss by transpiration

Carbon dioxide

Carbon dioxide

Oxygen

Oxygen

Water and mineral salts

Water and carbon dioxide are converted into carbohydrates and oxygen using the energy of sunlight, which is trapped by the chlorophyll in a plant's leaves.

are directly concerned with the water balance of the cells, and help regulate the passage of substances between cells. They maintain the correct pH for biochemical reactions and are essential components of chlorophyll and enzymes, the biological catalysts of the plant's internal chemistry.

Fruits and seeds

Seeds are a flowering plant's means of reproduction. Each seed develops from a single, fertilized egg and one or more seeds is contained in a fruit. There are many types of fruit that disperse their seeds in various ways. Some seeds germinate rapidly with no special treatment; other seeds may need to undergo specific treatment in cultivation for them to germinate fairly rapidly. (See also PRINCIPLES OF PROPAGATION, "How to overcome dormancy", p.629.)

Pods and capsules are dehiscent fruits, splitting along a regular line or lines to release the seed, as in *Aquilegia*. Indehiscent fruits such as hazel (*Corylus*) do not split; they have a single seed (kernel) enclosed in a tough shell. These large seeds have a high moisture and fat content, and deteriorate quickly unless sown fresh or stored in cool, moist conditions. In roses, many small, indehiscent fruits, each containing one seed, are enclosed in a hollow receptacle – the hip. The individual seeds (strictly, fruits) need to be extracted before sowing.

Succulent fruits, where the seed is enclosed in flesh, include berries (eg bananas, tomatoes, grapes), which have many seeds; drupes (eg plums, cherries, peaches), which typically have one seed in the form of a stone or pip; and pomes (eg apples, pears),

manufactured food (the phloem) from the leaves to all parts of the plant. Stems are often modified for other functions. Corms, rhizomes, and many tubers are swollen, underground stems that are modified for food storage; in cacti, the frequently swollen stems contain water-storage tissue.

Leaves

Leaf form is extremely diverse and may be modified as spines, as in some cacti, or as tendrils, as in the garden pea. Whatever their form, leaves are

the manufacturing centres of a plant. They contain the green pigment chlorophyll, which absorbs the energy of sunlight in order to convert carbon dioxide from the air and water from the soil into carbohydrates by the process known as photosynthesis. The by-product, oxygen, is essential to all life. The energy required to drive the plant's metabolism is produced through respiration, which breaks down carbohydrates to release energy, carbon dioxide, and water.

Leaves present a relatively large surface so that they maximize absorption of light; they are thin

enough for light to penetrate to the cells that contain chlorophyll, and to allow rapid movement of gases to all cells. Their surfaces contain numerous pores (stomata) through which oxygen and carbon dioxide pass in and out of the leaf. The stomata also control water losses through transpiration. A high evaporation of water vapour from the leaves and a lack of water entering through the plant roots is the cause of plants wilting in dry conditions.

Although only 1 per cent of the fresh weight of a plant consists of minerals, they are essential. In solution they

TRANSPIRATION

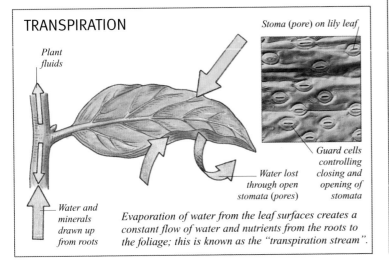

Plant fluids

Stoma (pore) on lily leaf

Guard cells controlling closing and opening of stomata

Water lost through open stomata (pores)

Water and minerals drawn up from roots

Evaporation of water from the leaf surfaces creates a constant flow of water and nutrients from the roots to the foliage; this is known as the "transpiration stream".

FRUIT TYPES

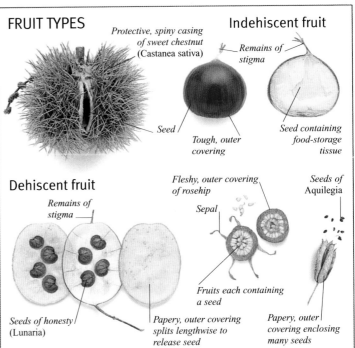

Protective, spiny casing of sweet chestnut (Castanea sativa)

Seed

Indehiscent fruit

Remains of stigma

Tough, outer covering

Seed containing food-storage tissue

Dehiscent fruit

Remains of stigma

Seeds of honesty (Lunaria)

Papery, outer covering splits lengthwise to release seed

Fleshy, outer covering of rosehip

Sepal

Fruits each containing a seed

Seeds of Aquilegia

Papery, outer covering enclosing many seeds

which develop from parts of the flower as well as the ovaries. In all these types of fruit, the seed should be removed from the pulped flesh and cleaned before being sown.

Flowers

Flowers are the fourth basic part of a plant and they show extraordinary diversity in colour, scent, and form, with a wide range of adaptations to ensure that they fulfil their reproductive function. They may be borne as showy, individual flowers (*Hibiscus*, tulips) or in many-flowered spikes (*Kniphofia*), racemes (hyacinth), panicles (*Gypsophila*), umbels (*Agapanthus*), or in heads consisting of numerous small florets such as dahlias in the family Compositae.

A flower has four main parts: petals or tepals, sepals, stamens, and one or more carpels (which are collectively known as the pistil). Most conspicuous are the petals, carried above a whorl of (usually) green sepals. The male reproductive nuclei are carried in pollen grains, enclosed in an anther attached to a stem, the filament – the whole male part being a stamen; these vary greatly in number from three in crocuses to 30 or more in buttercups.

PARTS OF A FLOWER

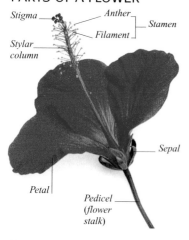

Stigma

Anther

Stylar column

Filament

Stamen

Sepal

Petal

Pedicel (flower stalk)

SEXUALITY IN FLOWERS

Dioecious plants – being either male or female – need a plant of each sex growing close to one another to set seed. Monoecious plants bear separate male and female flowers on the same plant. Bisexual (hermaphrodite) flowers contain both male (stamens) and female (carpels) parts in the same flower.

Female plant

Male plant

Dioecious (*Skimmia japonica*)

Monoecious (*Begonia*)

Male flower (with stamens)

Female flower (without stamens)

Bisexual (*Schlumbergera*)

Stigma (female part)

Stamens (male part)

The carpels enclose the female egg nuclei and have a projecting style, or stylar column, with a stigma at its tip to receive pollen grains. Pollen grains germinate on the stigma and a pollen tube containing the male nuclei grows through the tissue of the style to fuse with the female nuclei (the process of fertilization) eventually forming seeds.

Many plants bear separate female and male (unisexual) flowers on the same plant, for example birch (*Betula*) and hazel (*Corylus*). They are known as monoecious plants. Bisexual, or hermaphrodite, plants have the male and female parts in each flower. A few species bear unisexual and bisexual flowers and are known as polygamous plants. In dioecious plants all the flowers produced are of one sex only; examples are many holly species (*Ilex*),

Garrya, and some *Skimmia* variants. Male and female plants must be grown together if they are to set seed; this is especially important in cases where plants are grown for their ornamental berries, as with many hollies and *Gaultheria* species and cultivars.

Different but related species do not normally interbreed because they often occur in dissimilar habitats, flower at varying times, or possess minor variations in flower characters that prevent successful interbreeding. In cultivation, such barriers can sometimes be overcome, and hybrids are often created by design (see "Producing hybrid plants", p.630).

Angiosperms and gymnosperms

Flowering plants of the division Angiospermae produce seeds that are enclosed in an ovary. The Gymnospermae (literally "naked seeds"), comprise non-flowering plants that produce seed that is only partly enclosed by tissues of the parent plant. Conifers (Coniferae) form the largest gymnosperm family and include many evergreen genera, such as pine (*Pinus*) and cedar (*Cedrus*), as well as some deciduous ones, such as larch (*Larix*), maidenhair tree (*Ginkgo*), and dawn redwood (*Metasequoia*). Also included in the gymnosperms are the cycads – ancient, slow-growing plants with handsome, evergreen, palm-like foliage – such as the genus *Encephalartos*.

CLASSES OF FLOWER

Flowering plants are grouped into two classes: monocotyledons and dicotyledons

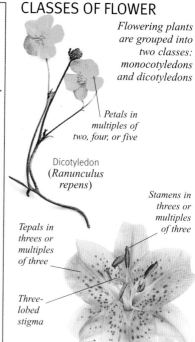

Petals in multiples of two, four, or five

Dicotyledon (*Ranunculus repens*)

Stamens in threes or multiples of three

Tepals in threes or multiples of three

Three-lobed stigma

Monocotyledon (*Lilium*)

LEAF VEINS

Monocotyledon

Dicotyledon

Leaf vein patterns in monocotyledons (here Curculigo capitulata*) are usually parallel; those in dicotyledons (here primula) generally form a network.*

Angiosperms are divided into monocotyledons and dicotyledons, based on the number of "seed leaves" (cotyledons) within the seed itself. Monocotyledons have a single seed leaf, and mature leaves with (usually) parallel veins; also usually relatively slender, non-woody stems. Their flower parts are in threes or multiples thereof, and the sepals and petals are often very similar in shape. Irises, daffodils, all grasses including bamboos, and palms are all monocotyledons. Dicotyledons have leaves with a broad network of veins; the flower parts are in multiples of two, four, or five (occasionally, seven or more) and normally the sepals and petals differ markedly in size and colour from each other. Dicotyledons are very diverse in habit, varying from broadleaved trees, such as oak (*Quercus*), to herbaceous plants such as peonies (*Paeonia*).

Mutation

A mutation, also known as a sport, is a genetic change in a plant, either natural or induced, that may be exploited horticulturally by propagating the mutated material in order to introduce a new cultivar. Mutations may occur in all parts of the plant but those of horticultural interest are mainly colour mutants or doubled flowers and variegated shoots that occur on a normally green-leaved plant.

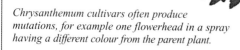

Chrysanthemum cultivars often produce mutations, for example one flowerhead in a spray having a different colour from the parent plant.

White cultivar with yellow sport

Plant names

In general plants are referred to by their botanical names throughout the *RHS Encyclopedia of Gardening*. However, for some plants, including vegetables, fruits, and herbs, the common names have been used in preference to their botanical one. To find out the botanical names of these plants, consult the index, which includes both common and botanical names for all plants mentioned in the book. The botanical name of a plant is based on a hierarchical system of classification and Linnaeus's binomial approach (genus followed by a specific epithet).

Classification and nomenclature

Plants are referred to scientifically by two names, generally written in italics. The first name, which always has its initial letter capitalized, is the genus, the second is the species name, or specific epithet: for example, *Rosa canina*. In nature, species often show minor variations in character; they are then given a third name, prefixed by "subsp." (subspecies), "var." (varietas), or "f." (forma): thus *Rhododendron rex* subsp. *fictolacteum* and *Daboecia cantabrica* f. *alba*. Sexual crosses between botanically distinct species or genera are known as hybrids and are indicated by a multiplication sign: thus *Epimedium* x *rubrum*. Non-sexual crosses – created through grafting plant tissues so they merge together – are known as graft-hybrids and are indicated by a cross sign: thus + *Laburnocytisus* 'Adamii'. Here, *Laburnum* and *Chamaecytisus* species have been combined to form the graft hybrid.

A cultivar (cultivated variety) is one that has been selected or artificially raised either from the wild or from gardens and grown in cultivation, and whose characteristics are preserved by some means of controlled propagation. The name of such a plant is written in Roman script with an initial capital letter and in single quotation marks: thus *Calluna vulgaris* 'Firefly'.

When plant breeders raise a new cultivar, it is given a code-name to ensure its formal identification: this may be different from the name under which the plant is sold. For example, the rose selling under the trade designation Queen Mother also has the code-name of 'Korquemu'; in this *Encyclopedia*, both names are cited in all but captions, and are styled thus: *Rosa* QUEEN MOTHER ('Korquemu'). To safeguard ownership of a cultivar, plant breeders may apply for Plant Breeder's Rights (PBR), which are granted using the code-name.

GLOSSARY

The glossary explains horticultural terms that are used in this book. Words in italic in a definition have a separate entry. Fuller explanations and illustrations may be found elsewhere by looking up the term in the index.

Acid (of soil). With a *pH* value of less than 7. (Cf *Alkaline* and *Neutral*.)
Adventitious. Arising from places where growths do not normally occur; for example, adventitious roots may arise from stems.
Adventitious bud. See *Bud*.
Aerate (of soil). Loosen by mechanical means in order to allow air (oxygen and carbon dioxide) to enter; for example, using a spiked roller to aerate a lawn.
Aerial root. A plant root growing above ground to provide anchorage and, on an *epiphyte*, to absorb atmospheric moisture.
Air layering. See *Layering*.
Alkaline (of soil). With a *pH* value of more than 7. (Cf *Acid* and *Neutral*.)
Alpine. A plant that grows above the tree line in mountainous areas; loosely applied to rock garden plants that may be grown at relatively low altitudes.
Alpine house. An unheated, well-ventilated greenhouse used for cultivating *alpine* and bulbous plants.
Alternate (of leaves). Occurring successively at different levels on opposite sides of a stem. (Cf *Opposite*.)
Anemone-centred (of flowers). Flowers or flowerheads in which the central petals or flowers (modified *stamens*) form a cushion-like mound and the outer rim of petals or ray florets are flat and spreading, as in some chrysanthemums.
Annual. A plant that completes its life cycle (*germination*–flowering–seeding–dying) in one growing season.
Anther. The part of a *stamen* that produces *pollen*; usually borne on a *filament*.

Apical. See *Terminal*. **Apical bud**: see *Bud*.
Apical-wedge grafting. See *Grafting*.
Aquatic. Any plant that grows in water; it may be free-floating, totally submerged, or rooted on the pond bottom with leaves and flowers above the water surface.
Asexual reproduction. A form of reproduction not involving *fertilization* and in propagation often involving mechanical methods (see *Vegetative propagation*).
Auxins. Naturally occurring or artificially synthesized plant growth substances controlling shoot growth, root formation, and other physiological processes in plants.
Awn. A sharp point or bristle, commonly found on a glume of a grass *inflorescence*.
Axil. The upper angle between a leaf and a stem, between a main stem and a lateral branch, or between a stem and a bract. (See also *Bud: Axillary bud*.)
Axillary bud. See *Bud*.
Back-bulb (of orchids). A dormant, old *pseudobulb* without leaves.
Ball. See *Root ball*.
Balled. 1) Of trees and shrubs that have been lifted and had their *root ball* wrapped in hessian or other material to keep it intact during *transplanting*. 2) Of a flower that does not open properly and rots when still in bud.
Bare-root. Of plants sold with their roots bare of soil.
Bark-ringing. The removal of a ring of bark from the trunk or branches of certain fruit trees, to reduce vigorous growth and to encourage fruit cropping. Also known as "girdling".
Basal plate. A compressed *stem*, part of a *bulb*.
Basal stem cutting. See *Cutting*.
Base dressing. An application of fertilizer or humus (manure, compost, etc.) applied to or dug into the soil prior to sowing or planting.
Bastard trenching. See *Double digging*.
Bed system. A method of planting vegetable crops in closely spaced rows, often in blocks or narrow beds for easy access.
Bedding plants. Annuals and biennials (or plants grown as such) raised almost to maturity and then planted out, "bedded out", often in large blocks for temporary display.
Biennial. A plant that flowers and dies in the second growing season after *germination*.
Blanch. To exclude light from developing leaves or stems in order to keep the plant tissue soft and palatable.
Bleed. To lose *sap* through a cut or wound.
Blind. Of a plant that fails to produce flowers, or a stem in which the growing point has been damaged.
Bloom. 1) A flower or blossom. 2) A waxy, white or bluish-white coating on a stem, leaf, or fruit.
Blown. Of flowers or hearted vegetables that are past full maturity and are fading.
Bog plant. A plant whose natural habitat is soil that is permanently damp, or one that thrives in such conditions.
Bole. The *trunk* of a tree from ground level to the first major branch.
Bolt. To produce flowers and seed prematurely.
Bract. A modified, often protective, leaf at the base of a flower or flower cluster. Bracts may resemble normal leaves, or be small and scale-like, or large and brightly coloured.
Branch. A shoot arising from the main stem or trunk of a woody plant.
Brassica. A member of the cabbage *family*.
Break. A *shoot* growing from an *axillary bud*.

Broadcasting. Scattering seed or fertilizer evenly over the ground, rather than in furrows or *drills*.
Broadleaved. Of trees or shrubs that bear broad, flat leaves rather than needle-like foliage.
Bromeliad. A member of the *family* Bromeliaceae.
Bud. A rudimentary or condensed shoot containing an embryonic leaf, leaf cluster, or flower. **Adventitious bud**: one produced abnormally, for example from the stem instead of from a leaf *axil*. **Apical** (or **terminal**) **bud**: the topmost bud on a stem. **Axillary bud**: one that occurs in an *axil*. **Crown bud**: a flower bud at the shoot tip, surrounded by other, usually smaller, flower buds. **Fruit bud**: one from which leaves and flowers (followed by fruits) develop. **Growth bud**: one from which only leaves or a shoot develop.
Bud union. The point at which the *scion* bud unites with the *rootstock*.
Budding. Bud-grafting, a form of *grafting*.
Budding tape. See *Grafting tape*.
Bud-grafting. See *Grafting*.
Budwood. A shoot cut from a tree to provide a *scion* for bud-grafting.
Bulb. A modified *stem* acting as a storage organ and consisting mainly of fleshy, more or less separate or tightly packed, scale leaves (a modified *bud*) on a much reduced stem (basal plate).
Bulb fibre. A mixture of *peat*, oystershell, and charcoal, in which *bulbs* are grown in containers, often without drainage holes.
Bulbil. A small *bulb*-like organ, often borne in a leaf *axil*, occasionally on a stem or in a *flowerhead*. (Cf *Bulblet*.)
Bulblet. A small developing *bulb* produced from the *basal plate* of a mature bulb outside the *tunic*. (Cf *Bulbil* and *Offset*.)

Bush. 1) A small shrub. 2) An open-centre fruit tree with a *trunk* of 90cm (36in) or less. **Bush fruit**: used of soft fruit bushes such as blackcurrants and gooseberries.

Cactus. A member of the *family* Cactaceae, characterized by fleshy, water-storing tissue in the stems and areoles (specialized groups of cells) from which spines, flowers, and shoots develop.

Calcicole. *Lime*-loving; a plant that thrives in *alkaline* soil.

Calcifuge. *Lime*-hating; a plant that will not grow in *alkaline* soil.

Callus. Protective tissue formed by plants over a wounded surface, particularly in *woody* plants but also at the base of cuttings.

Calyx (pl. **calyces**). The collective name for the *sepals*, the outer *whorl* of, usually green, segments that enclose the flower in bud.

Cambium. A layer of meristematic tissue capable of producing new cells to increase the girth of stems and roots. (See also *Meristem.*)

Capillary matting. Matting made of synthetic fibre that is used to draw water upwards by capillary action to irrigate pot plants on capillary beds or benches.

Capping. A crust that forms on the surface of soil damaged by compaction, heavy rain, or watering. (Cf *Pan.*)

Carpel. The female part of the flower of flowering plants that contains the *ovules*; several carpels in a flower are collectively known as the *pistil*.

Carpet bedding. The use of groups of closely planted, low-growing, colourful *bedding plants* in various designs.

Catkin. A racemose (see *Raceme*) flower spike, or a spike-like *inflorescence*, with conspicuous *bracts* and small, often unisexual flowers lacking petals.

Central leader. The central, usually upright stem of a *tree*.

Certified stock. Plants certified by the Department of Environment, Food & Rural Affairs (USDA in the USA) as free from certain pests and diseases.

Chilling requirement. The requirement of plants for a specific period of dormancy below a particular temperature in order for them to initiate flowering.

Chinese layering. An alternative name for air layering; see *Layering.*

Chip-budding. See *Grafting.*

Chlorophyll. The green plant pigment that is mainly responsible for light absorption and hence *photosynthesis* in plants.

Clamp. A method for storing root crops outdoors. The crops are heaped up and protected against frost by layers of straw and soil; a "chimney" hole filled with straw provides ventilation.

Climber. A plant that climbs using other plants or objects as support: **self-clinging climbers** by means of supporting, *adventitious*, *aerial roots* or adhesive tendril tips; **tendril climbers** by coiling their leaf stalks, leaf *tendrils*, or modified *terminal* shoots; **twining climbers** by coiling their *stems*. **Scandent, scrambling,** and

trailing climbers produce long, usually flexuous, stems that grow over or through plants or other supports; they attach themselves only loosely, if at all, to the support.

Cloche. A small, usually portable, structure made of clear plastic or glass, normally in a metal framework; used to protect early crops on open ground and to warm the soil before planting. (See also *Floating cloche.*)

Clone. 1) A group of genetically identical plants produced by *vegetative propagation* or *asexual reproduction*. 2) An individual plant in such a group.

Cold frame. A glazed, box-like, unheated structure, made from brick, wood, or glass, with a hinged or removable glass or clear plastic *light*, used to protect plants from excessive cold.

Collar. 1) The part of a plant where the roots meet the stem; also known as the "neck". 2) The part of a *tree* where a main branch meets the *trunk* (or a side branch meets a main branch).

Companion planting. Positioning plants together that are reputed to have a beneficial effect on neighbouring plants by discouraging pests and diseases or improving growth.

Compositae. The daisy *family*.

Compost. 1) A potting medium comprising a mixture of *loam, sand, peat, leaf mould*, or other ingredients. 2) An organic material, rich in *humus*, formed by decomposed plant remains, and other *organic* matter, used as a soil improver or *mulch*.

Compound. Divided into two or more subsidiary parts, for example a leaf divided into two or more *leaflets*. (Cf *Simple.*)

Cone. The densely clustered *bracts* and flowers of *conifers* and some flowering plants, often developing into a woody, seed-bearing structure as in the familiar pine cone.

Conifer. Gymnosperms, usually evergreen trees and shrubs that are distinguished from flowering plants (Angiosperms) by the naked *ovules* that are not enclosed in an *ovary* but are often borne in *cones*.

Contact action. The action of a *pesticide* or weedkiller that kills or damages the pest or weed by direct contact.

Coppicing. The annual pruning back of trees or shrubs close to ground level to produce vigorous, usually decorative, *shoots*.

Cordon. A trained plant (usually a fruit tree) generally restricted to one main stem by rigorous pruning. A **single cordon** has one main stem, a **double**, or **"U", cordon** has two, and a **multiple cordon**, three or more stems.

Corm. A *bulb*-like, underground, swollen *stem* or stem base, often surrounded by a papery *tunic*. A corm is replaced annually by a new corm that develops from a *terminal*, or *lateral*, *bud*.

Cormel. A small *corm* developing around a mature corm, usually outside the main corm *tunic*, as in *Gladiolus*.

Cormlet. A small *corm* arising at the base (and usually within the old *tunic*) of a mature one. (See also *Offset.*)

Corolla. The interior *whorl* of the *perianth* of a flower, comprising several free or fused *petals*.

Cotyledon. A seed leaf; the first leaf or leaves to emerge from the seed after *germination*, often markedly different from mature leaves. Flowering plants (Angiosperms) are classified into *monocotyledons* (one) and *dicotyledons* (two) depending on how many cotyledons are contained in the mature seed. In Gymnosperms (*conifers*) they are often produced in *whorls*.

Crocks. Broken pieces of clay pot, used to cover the drainage holes of pots in order to provide free drainage and air circulation to the root system and to prevent the growing medium from escaping from or blocking the drainage holes.

Crop rotation. A system in which vegetable crops are grown on different sections of a plot on a three- or four-year cycle to minimize the build-up of soil-borne pests and diseases in one section.

Cross-fertilization. The *fertilization* of the *ovules* of a flower as a result of *cross-pollination*.

Cross-pollination. The transfer of pollen from the *anther* of a flower on one plant to the *stigma* of a flower on another plant; the term is often loosely applied to *cross-fertilization*. (Cf *Self-pollination.*)

Crown. 1) The basal part at soil level of a *herbaceous* plant where roots and stems join and from where new shoots are produced. 2) The upper, branched part of a tree above the *bole*.

Crown bud. See *Bud.*

Culm. The usually hollow stem of a grass or bamboo.

Cultivar. A contraction of "cultivated variety" (abbreviated to cv.); a group (or one among such a group) of cultivated plants clearly distinguished by one or more characteristics and which retains these characteristics when propagated either asexually or sexually. (Cf *Variety.*)

Cutting. A portion of a plant (a leaf, shoot, root, or bud) that is cut off to be used for *propagation*. **Basal stem cutting**: one taken from the base of a (usually *herbaceous*) plant as it begins to produce growth in spring. **Greenwood cutting**: one taken from the soft tips of young growth after the spring growth flush has slowed down; slightly harder and woodier stems than are used for softwood cuttings. **Hardwood cutting**: one taken from mature wood of both deciduous and evergreen plants at the end of the growing season. **Heel cutting**: one taken with a portion of the bark or mature wood at the base. **Internodal cutting**: one in which the basal cut is made between two *nodes* or growth buds. **Leaf cutting**: one taken from a detached leaf or part of a leaf. **Leaf-bud cutting**: one consisting of a short section of stem and a single or double pair of buds or leaves. **Nodal cutting**: one trimmed at the base just below a growth bud or *node*. **Ripewood cutting**: one taken from ripened wood,

usually of evergreens, during the growing season. **Root cutting**: one taken from part of a semi-mature or mature root. **Semi-ripe cutting**: one taken from half-ripened wood during the growing season. **Softwood cutting**: one taken from young, immature growth during the growing season. **Stem cutting**: one taken from any portion of a plant stem. **Stem tip cutting**: any cutting taken from the tip of a shoot; sometimes applied to softwood and greenwood cuttings.

Cyme. A usually flat-topped, *determinate inflorescence* in which the central or *terminal* flower opens first.

Damping down. Wetting greenhouse floors and staging with water to increase humidity, particularly in very hot weather.

Dead-heading. The removal of *spent* flowers or *flowerheads*.

Deciduous. Of plants that shed leaves at the end of the growing season and renew them at the beginning of the next; **semi-deciduous** plants lose only some of their leaves at the end of the growing season.

Degradable pot. A pot made from degradable material such as compressed peat or paper.

Dehiscence. Term used of *fruits* (usually capsules) and *anthers* to describe the process of opening at maturity to release their contents.

Dehiscent. Of a *fruit*, usually a capsule, or an *anther* that splits along definite lines to release seeds or pollen.

Determinate. 1) Used of *inflorescences* where the central or terminal flower opens first so that the main axis cannot extend further. (Cf *Cyme.*) 2) Used of bushy or dwarf tomatoes. (Cf *Indeterminate; Semi-determinate.*)

Dibber. A tool used for making holes in soil or potting compost into which seedlings or cuttings are inserted.

Dicotyledon. A flowering plant that usually has two *cotyledons* or seed leaves in the seed; it is also characterized by the (usually) net-veined leaves, the *petals* and *sepals* in multiples of two, four, or five, and by the presence of a *cambium*. (Cf *Monocotyledon.*)

Die-back. The death of tips of shoots as a result of damage or disease.

Dioecious. Bearing male and female reproductive organs on separate plants.

Disbudding. The removal of surplus *buds* to promote the production of high-quality flowers or fruits.

Distal end (of *cuttings*). The end that was originally farthest from the *crown* of the parent plant. (Cf *Proximal end.*)

Division. A method of increasing plants by dividing them into pieces, each with a root system and one or more shoots (or dormant buds).

Dormancy. The state of temporary cessation of growth and slowing down of other activities in whole plants, usually during the winter; **seed dormancy**: non-*germination* of seed when placed in conditions suitable for germination due to physical, chemical, or other factors inherent in the seed; **double (seed) dormancy**: non-germination of seeds due to two dormancy factors in the seed.

Double (of a flower). See *Flower*.

Double cordon. See *Cordon*.

Double digging. A cultivation technique in which the soil is worked to a depth of two *spits*. Also known as "trench digging" or "bastard trenching".

Drainage. The passage of excess water through soil; the term is also applied to systems of drainage used to remove excess water.

Drill. A narrow, straight furrow in the soil in which seeds are sown or seedlings planted.

Drupes. See *Stone fruits*.

Earthing up. Drawing up soil around the base of a plant to help prevent *wind-rock*, to *blanch* the *stems*, or to encourage stem rooting.

Epicormic shoots. Shoots that develop from latent or *adventitious* buds on or from the *trunk* of a tree or shrub. (See also *Water shoots*.)

Epigeal. Type of seed *germination* in which the seed is pushed above soil level by elongation of the *hypocotyl*. (Cf *Hypogeal*.)

Epiphyte. A plant that grows on another plant without being parasitic, and obtains moisture and nutrients from the atmosphere without rooting into the soil.

Ericaceous. 1) Term describing plants of the *family* Ericaceae, usually *lime*-hating and requiring soils of pH6.5 or less (see also *Calcifuge*). 2) Of compost, with an appropriate *pH* or acidity for growing ericaceous plants.

Espalier. A plant trained with the main stem vertical and (usually) three or more tiers of branches horizontally placed on either side in a single plane; often applied to fruit trees.

Evergreen. Of plants that retain their foliage for more than one growing season; **semi-evergreen** plants retain only a small proportion of their leaves for more than one season.

Eye. 1) A dormant or latent growth *bud*, such as the eye of a potato or dahlia tuber. 2) The centre of a flower, especially if different in colour from the petals.

F1 hybrids. First-generation plants obtained from crossing two selected pure-breeding parents to produce uniform, vigorous, and high-yielding offspring. Seed from F1 hybrids does not come *true*. **F2 hybrids**: plants that result from *self-* or *cross-fertilization* of F1 hybrids; they are less uniform than their parents.

Falls. The pendent or horizontally placed *tepals* or *petals* of irises and some related plants.

Family. A category in plant classification, a grouping together of related *genera*, for example the family Rosaceae includes the genera *Rosa*, *Sorbus*, *Rubus*, *Prunus*, and *Pyracantha*.

Fastigiate. With the branches (usually of trees and shrubs) growing vertically and almost parallel with the main stem.

Feathered. Of *maiden* trees that have several *lateral* branches ("feathers").

Fertile (of plants). Producing viable

seed; shoots bearing flowers are also said to be fertile shoots as opposed to non-flowering (sterile) shoots.

Fertilization. The fusion of a *pollen* grain nucleus (male) with an *ovule* (female) to form a fertile seed.

Fibrous. 1) Of roots, fine and often branching and dense. 2) Of loam, containing fibre derived from (dead) grass roots.

Filament. The *stalk* of the *stamen* which bears the *anther*.

Fimbriate. Of part of a plant that has a fringed margin. Plant organs with a fringe of hairs are said to be ciliate.

Flat. An American term for a shallow seed-box or container.

Flat grafting. See *Grafting*.

Floating cloche. Lightweight sheet, usually of woven polypropylene (fibre fleece), placed over a crop, which is lifted up by the plants as they grow. It provides some frost protection while allowing water and light penetration. Also known as floating mulch. (See also *Cloche*.)

Floret. A (generally) small flower in a *flowerhead* consisting of many flowers.

Flower. The part of the plant containing the reproductive organs usually surrounded by *sepals* and *petals*. The basic flower forms are: **single**, with one row of usually four to six petals; **semi-double**, with two or three times the normal number of petals usually in two or three rows; **double**, with more than the normal number of petals in several rows with few or no *stamens* produced; **fully double**, flowers usually rounded in shape, with densely packed petals and with the stamens obscured or absent. (Cf *Flowerhead*.)

Flowerhead. A mass of small *flowers* or *florets* that together appear to form a single flower as in members of the family Compositae.

Force. To induce plant growth, usually of flowers or fruit by control of the environment, normally by increasing the temperature.

Forma (f.). A variant within a *species* usually distinguished only by minor characteristics. *Clematis montana* f. *grandiflora* is a larger-flowered, more vigorous form of *C. montana*; also loosely used for any variant of a species.

Formative pruning. A method of pruning that is carried out on young trees and shrubs to develop the basic branch structure of the desired form or shape.

Foundation planting. The basic, and usually permanent, structural and shelter planting of trees and shrubs in a garden.

Frame. See *Cold frame*.

Framework. The permanent branch structure of a tree or shrub; the main branches that determine its ultimate shape. **Framework plants**: the plants in a garden that form the basis or structure of the design. (Cf *Foundation planting*.)

Frame-working (of fruit trees). Pruning back all side growths to the main framework and grafting *scions* of a different *cultivar* onto each main framework branch.

French layering. See *Layering*.

Friable (of soil). Of a good, crumbly texture; capable of forming a *tilth* that can be worked easily.

Frond. 1) The *leaf*-like organ of a fern. Some ferns produce both barren and *fertile* fronds, the latter bearing *spores*. 2) Loosely applied to large, usually *compound* leaves such as those of palms.

Frost hardy. See *Hardy*.

Frost pocket. A site, often a hollow, where cold air gathers, that is subject to severe and often prolonged frosts.

Frost tender. See *Tender*.

Fruit. The fertilized, ripe *ovary* of a plant containing one to many seeds, for example, berries, hips, capsules, and nuts; the term is also used of edible fruits.

Fruit bud. See *Bud*.

Fruit set. The successful development of fruits after *pollination* and *fertilization*.

Fully double. See *Flower*.

Fully reflexed. See *Reflexed*.

Fungicide. A chemical that kills fungi, especially those responsible for various plant diseases.

Genus (pl. **genera**). A category in plant classification ranked between *family* and *species*. A group of related species linked by a range of common characters; for example, all species of horse chestnut are grouped under the genus *Aesculus*. (See also *Cultivar*, *Family*, *Forma*, *Hybrid*, *Subspecies*, and *Variety*.)

Germination. The physical and chemical changes that take place as a seed starts to grow and develop into a plant.

Girdling. 1) The removal of bark all round a stem or branch caused by animal or physical damage or by a constricting tie that prevents the flow of water and *nutrients* to the upper part of the plant, eventually causing the death of all tissue above the girdled trunk or branch. 2) See *Bark-ringing*.

Glaucous. With a blue-green, blue-grey, grey, or white bloom.

Graft. To join artificially one or more plant parts to another.

Graft union. The point at which *scion* and *rootstock* are joined.

Grafting. A method of *propagation* by which an artificial union is made between the *scion* of one plant and the *rootstock* of another so that they eventually function as one plant. Methods include apical-wedge grafting; bud-grafting (including chip-budding and T-budding); flat grafting; saddle grafting; side grafting (see CACTI AND OTHER SUCCULENTS, "Side grafting", p.351); side-wedge grafting; spliced side grafting; spliced side-veneer grafting; whip (or splice) grafting; and whip-and-tongue grafting. (For details see PRINCIPLES OF PROPAGATION, "Grafting and budding", pp.635–636.)

Grafting tape. Tape used to protect a *graft union* during healing.

Green manure. A quick-maturing, leafy crop such as mustard that is grown specifically to be dug back into, and thereby enrich, the soil.

Greenwood cutting. See *Cutting*.

Ground colour. Main (background)

colour of petals.

Ground cover. Usually low-growing plants that quickly cover the soil surface and suppress weeds.

Growth bud. See *Bud*.

Half hardy. Used of a plant not tolerating frost in a given climatic zone. The term generally implies an ability to withstand lower temperatures than *tender*.

Half standard. A tree or shrub that has a clear stem of 1–1.5m (3–5ft) between ground level and the lowest branches.

Hardening off. Gradually acclimatizing plants that have been raised under cover to cooler, outdoor conditions.

Hardpan. See *Pan*.

Hardwood cutting. See *Cutting*.

Hardy. Able to withstand year-round climatic conditions, including frost, without protection.

Haulm. The top-growth of plants such as potatoes and legumes.

Head. 1) The part of a tree above a clear *trunk*. 2) A dense *inflorescence*.

Head back. To prune back the main branches of trees or shrubs by half or more.

Heading. See *Heart up*.

Heart up. The stage at which vegetables such as lettuces or cabbages begin to produce tight "hearts" or "heads" of inner leaves.

Heavy (of soil). Having a high proportion of clay.

Heel. A small piece or strip of bark or wood that is retained at the base of a *cutting* when it is pulled away from a main stem.

Heel cutting. See *Cutting*.

Heeling in. Temporary planting until a plant can be placed in its permanent position.

Herb. 1) A plant grown for its medicinal or flavouring properties or for its scented foliage. 2) Botanically, a *herbaceous* plant.

Herbaceous. A non-*woody* plant in which the upper parts die down to a rootstock at the end of the growing season. It is chiefly applied to *perennials*, although botanically it also applies to *annuals* and *biennials*.

Herbicide. A chemical used to control or kill weeds.

Humus. The chemically complex, organic residue of decayed vegetable matter in soil. Also often used to describe partly decayed matter such as *leaf mould* or *compost*.

Hybrid. The offspring of genetically different parents usually of distinct taxa (see *Taxon*). Hybrids between species of the same *genus* are known as interspecific hybrids. Those between different but usually closely related *genera* are known as intergeneric hybrids. (See also *F1 hybrids* and *F2 hybrids*.)

Hybrid vigour. An improvement in growth and yield shown by some hybrids.

Hybridization. The process by which *hybrids* are formed.

Hydroculture. The cultivation of plants in nutrient-rich water, sometimes with sterile aggregates. (See also *Hydroponics*.)

Hydroponics. Growing plants in dilute solutions of nutrients. Applied loosely to any form of soilless culture.

Hypocotyl. The portion of a *seed* or *seedling* just below the *cotyledons*.

Hypogeal. Type of seed *germination* in which the *seed* and *cotyledons* remain below the soil surface while the young shoot (plumule) emerges above soil level.

Incurved. Applied to petals of flowers and *florets* that curve inwards to form a compact, rounded shape. **Incurving** flowerheads are less compact with more loosely arranged but still incurved florets.

Indehiscent. Of a *fruit* that does not split open to release its seeds. (Cf *Dehiscent*.)

Indeterminate. 1) Used of an *inflorescence* not terminated by a single flower, in which the primary axis (stem) continues to develop as the lower flowers open (e.g. a *raceme* as in delphiniums). 2) Used of tall or *cordon* tomatoes, which, in a suitable climate, can grow to an indefinite length. (Cf *Determinate*; *Semi-determinate*.)

Inflorescence. A group of flowers borne on a single axis (stem); for example, *racemes*, *panicles*, and *cymes*.

Informal. Applied to some cultivars of chrysanthemums, dahlias, and other flowers with irregular flower formation.

Inorganic. Of a chemical compound, one that does not contain carbon. Inorganic fertilizers are refined from naturally occurring chemicals or produced artificially. (Cf *Organic*.)

Insecticide. A *pesticide* used to control or kill insects.

Intercropping. The growing of quick-maturing vegetable crops between slower-growing crops to make maximum use of the available space.

Intergeneric hybrid. See *Hybrid*.

Intermediate. 1) A term applied to chrysanthemums with flowerheads intermediate in shape between *reflexed* and *incurved*. 2) A hybrid with characters intermediate between its two parents.

Internodal cutting. See *Cutting*.

Internode. The portion of stem between two *nodes*.

Interplanting. 1) The planting of fast-maturing plants between slower-growing plants to provide a display while they mature. 2) The planting of two or more types of plants together to provide a display of different colours or textures (e.g. tulips among wallflowers). Often used in relation to bedding.

Interspecific hybrid. See *Hybrid*.

Irrigation. 1) General term for watering. 2) The use of a system of basins, channels, or sprinkler systems to provide a controlled supply of water to plants.

John Innes compost. *Loam*-based *composts* devised by the John Innes Horticultural Institute in Norwich, UK, and made to a standard formula.

Knot garden. Beds laid out in a formal, often complex, pattern, formed from dwarf hedges or clipped herbs.

Lateral. A side growth that arises from a shoot or root.

Layer planting. A form of *interplanting* in which groups of plants flower in succession having been planted closely together.

Layering. A method of *propagation* by which a *shoot* is induced to *root* while still attached to the parent plant. The basic form is self layering, which occurs naturally in some plants. Methods include: air layering (also known as Chinese layering or *marcottage*), French layering, mound layering (see THE HERB GARDEN, "Mound layering", p.414), serpentine layering, simple layering, stooling, tip layering, and trench layering. (For details, see PRINCIPLES OF PROPAGATION, "Layering", p.631.)

Leaching. The loss from the topsoil of soluble *nutrients* by downward drainage.

Leader. 1) The main, usually central, stem of a plant. 2) The *terminal* shoot of a main branch.

Leaf. A plant organ, variable in shape and colour but often flattened and green, borne on the stem, that performs the functions of *photosynthesis*, *respiration*, and *transpiration*.

Leaf cutting. See *Cutting*.

Leaf mould. Fibrous, flaky material derived from decomposed leaves, used as an ingredient in potting media and as a soil improver.

Leaf-bud cutting. See *Cutting*.

Leaflet. One of the subdivisions of a *compound* leaf.

Legume. A one-celled, *dehiscent fruit* splitting at maturity into two, belonging to the *family* Leguminosae.

Light. 1) The movable cover of a *cold frame*. 2) Of soil, with a high proportion of sand and little clay.

Lime. Loosely, a number of compounds of calcium; the amount of lime in soil determines whether it is *alkaline*, *acid*, or *neutral*.

Line out. To plant out young plants or insert cuttings in lines in a nursery bed or frame.

Lithophyte. A plant naturally growing on rocks (or in very stony soil) and usually obtaining most of its nutrients and water from the atmosphere.

Loam. A term used for soil of medium texture, often easily worked, that contains more or less equal parts of sand, silt, and clay, and is usually rich in humus. If the proportion of one ingredient is high, the term may be qualified as silt-loam, clay-loam, or sandy loam.

Lute. A piece of equipment used for working (luting) top-dressings into lawns.

Maiden. A *grafted* tree in its first year. (See also *Whip*.)

Maincrop (of vegetables). Those cultivars that produce crops throughout the main growing season, doing so over a longer period than either early or late cultivars.

Marcottage. An alternative name for air layering; see *Layering*.

Marginal water plant. A plant that grows partially submerged in shallow water or in constantly moist soil at the edge of a pond or stream.

Medium. 1) A *compost*, growing mixture, or other material in which

plants may be propagated or grown. 2) Applied to those soils that are intermediate in character between *heavy* and *light*. (See also *Loam*.)

Meristem. Plant tissue that is able to divide to produce new cells. Shoot or root tips contain meristematic tissue and may be used for *micropropagation*.

Micronutrients. Chemical elements essential to plants but needed only in very small quantities, also known as trace elements. (See also *Nutrients*.)

Micropropagation. Propagation of plants by *tissue culture*.

Midrib. The primary, usually central vein of a leaf or leaflet.

Module. Applied to various types of container, particularly those used in multiples for sowing seed and pricking out seedlings.

Monocarpic. Flowering and fruiting only once before dying; such plants may take several years to reach flowering size.

Monocotyledon. A flowering plant that has only one *cotyledon* or seed leaf in the seed; it is also characterized by narrow, parallel-veined *leaves*, and parts of the flower in threes or multiples of three.

Monoecious. Bearing separate male and female reproductive organs on the same plant.

Monopodial. Growing indefinitely from an apical or *terminal bud* on a stem. (Cf *Sympodial*.)

Moss peat. See *Peat*.

Mound layering. See *Layering*.

Mulch. A material applied in a layer to the soil surface to suppress weeds, conserve moisture, and maintain a preferably cool, even root temperature.

Multiple cordon. See *Cordon*.

Mutation. An induced or spontaneous genetic change, often resulting in shoots with variegated foliage or flowers of a different colour from the parent plant. A mutation is also known as a sport.

Mycorrhizae. Soil fungi that live in beneficial association with plant roots.

Naturalize. To establish and grow as if in the wild.

Neck. See *Collar*.

Nectar. Sugary liquid secreted from a *nectary*; often attractive to pollinating insects.

Nectary. Glandular tissue usually found in the flower, but sometimes found on the leaves or stems, that secretes *nectar*.

Neutral (of soil). With a *pH* value of 7, i.e. neither *acid* nor *alkaline*.

Nodal cutting. See *Cutting*.

Node. The point on a stem from which one or more leaves, shoots, branches, or flowers arise.

Non-remontant. Flowering or fruiting only once in a single flush. (Cf *Remontant*.)

Nursery bed. An area used for germinating seeds or growing on young plants before planting them out in their permanent positions.

Nut. A one-seeded, *indehiscent fruit* with a tough or woody coat, for example an acorn. Less specifically, all fruits and seeds with woody or leathery coats.

Nutrients. Minerals (mineral ions) used to develop proteins and other compounds required for plant growth.

Offset. A young plant that arises by natural, vegetative reproduction, usually at the base of the parent plant; in bulbs, offsets are initially formed within the bulb *tunic* but later separate out. Also known as offshoots.

Offshoot. See *Offset*.

Open-pollination. Natural pollination. (See also *Pollination*.)

Opposite. Term describing two leaves or other plant organs, at the same level on opposite sides of a stem or other axis. (Cf *Alternate*.)

Organic. 1) Chemically, referring to compounds containing carbon derived from decomposed plant or animal organisms. 2) Loosely, applied to mulches, composts, or similar materials derived from plant materials. 3) Also applied to crop production and gardening without the use of synthetic or non-organic materials.

Ovary. The basal part of the pistil of a flower, containing one or more *ovules*; it may develop into a *fruit* after *fertilization*. (See also *Carpel*.)

Ovule. The part of the *ovary* that develops into the *seed* after *pollination* and *fertilization*.

Oxygenator. Submerged aquatic plant that releases oxygen into the water.

Packs. Compartmented trays in which individual seeds or seedlings are grown.

Pan. 1) A shallow, earthenware or plastic pot that is much wider than it is deep. 2) A layer of soil that is impermeable to water and oxygen and impedes root growth and drainage. Some pans (hardpans) occur naturally on clay or iron-rich soils. Soils capped (see *Capping*) by heavy rain or excess watering, or by continuous use of cultivation machinery, are also known as pans or hardpans.

Panicle. An *indeterminate*, branched *inflorescence* often consisting of several racemose branches (see *Raceme*). Also loosely used to describe any branching inflorescence.

Parterre. A level area containing ornamental beds, often with low-growing plants and enclosed in dwarf hedges. (Cf *Knot garden*.)

Parthenocarpic. The production of fruit without *fertilization* having taken place.

Pathogens. Micro-organisms that cause disease.

Pathovar (pvar.). A subdivision of several bacterial species.

Peat. Partially decayed, humus-rich vegetation formed on the surface of waterlogged soils. **Moss** or **sphagnum peat** is largely derived from partially decayed sphagnum moss and is used in potting composts. **Sedge peat** is derived from sedges, mosses, and heathers; it is coarser than moss peat and less suitable for potting composts.

Peat bed. Beds usually built from *peat* blocks and filled with very peaty soil; used to grow acid-loving plants, particularly in soils with a high *pH*.

Peat blocks. Blocks of peat cut from natural peat deposits.

Peat substitute. A term applied to a number of different organic materials – such as coconut fibre – used in place of peat for potting composts and soil improvers.

Peduncle. The *stalk* of a *flower*.

Peltate (of leaves). A leaf with the stalk usually attached centrally beneath the leaf blade; sometimes the stalk may be off-centre within the leaf margin.

Perennial. Strictly, any plant living for at least three seasons; commonly applied to *herbaceous* plants and *woody* perennials (i.e. trees and shrubs).

Perianth. The collective term for the *calyx* and the *corolla*, particularly when they are very similar in form, as in many bulb flowers.

Perianth segment. One portion of a *perianth*, usually resembling a *petal* and sometimes known as a *tepal*.

Perlite. Small granules of expanded, volcanic minerals added to growing media to improve aeration.

Perpetual. Of plants that bloom more or less continuously throughout the growing season or over long periods of time.

Pesticide. A chemical substance, usually manufactured, that is used to kill pests including insects (*insecticide*), mites (acaricide), and nematodes (nematicide).

Petal. A modified leaf, often brightly coloured; one part of the *corolla* usually of a *dicotyledonous* flower. (Cf *Tepal*.)

Petiole. The *stalk* of a *leaf*.

pH. A measure of alkalinity or acidity, used horticulturally to refer to soils. The scale measures from 1 to 14; pH7 is neutral, above 7 is alkaline, and below 7 acid. (See also *Acid*, *Alkaline*, and *Neutral*.)

Photosynthesis. The production of organic compounds required for growth in plants by a complex process involving *chlorophyll*, light energy, carbon dioxide, and water.

Picotee. A term describing *petals* with a narrow margin of a contrasting colour.

Pinching out. The removal of the growing tip of a plant (by finger and thumb) to induce the production of *sideshoots* or the formation of flower buds. Also known as "stopping".

Pistil. See *Carpel*.

Pith (of stems). The soft plant tissue in the central part of a stem.

Pleaching. A technique whereby branches from a row of trees are woven together and trained to form a wall or canopy of foliage.

Plumule. See *Hypogeal*.

Plunge. To sink a pot up to its rim in a bed of ashes, peat, sand, or soil to protect the roots of the plant or plants in the pot from extremes of temperature.

Pod. An ill-defined term generally applied to any dry, *dehiscent fruit*; it is particularly used for peas and beans.

Pollarding. The regular pruning back of the main branches of a tree to the main stem or trunk, or to a short branch framework, usually to a height of about 2m (6ft). (Cf *Coppicing*.)

Pollen. The male cells of a plant, formed in the *anther*.

Pollination. The transfer of *pollen* from *anthers* to *stigmas*. (See also *Cross-pollination*, *Open-pollination*, and *Self-pollination*.)

Pollinator. 1) The agent or means by which *pollination* is carried out (e.g. insects, wind). 2) Used in fruit growing to describe a *cultivar* required to ensure fruit set on another self- or partially *self-sterile* cultivar.

Polyembryonic. Containing more than one embryo in an *ovule* or *seed*.

Pome fruit. A firm, fleshy *fruit* formed by the fusion of the *ovary* and the hypanthium (the fused base of *calyx* and *corolla*); for example an apple or pear.

Pompon. Usually small, almost globular *flowerheads* made up of numerous *florets*.

Potting compost (also potting mix or potting medium). A mixture of *loam*, *peat substitute* (or *peat*), sand, and *nutrients* in varying proportions. Soilless *composts* contain no loam and mainly comprise peat with nutrients added.

Potting on. Transferring a plant from one pot to a larger one.

Potting up. Transferring seedlings into individual pots of compost.

Pricking out. The transferring of young seedlings from where they have germinated in beds or containers to positions where they have room to grow on.

Propagation. The increase of plants by *seed* (usually sexual) or *vegetative* (asexual) means.

Propagator. A structure that provides a humid atmosphere for raising seedlings, rooting cuttings, or other plants being propagated.

Proximal end (of *cuttings*). The end that was originally nearest to the *crown* of the parent plant. (Cf *Distal end*.)

Pseudobulb. The thickened, *bulb*-like *stem* of a *sympodial* orchid arising from a (sometimes very short) *rhizome*.

Quartered rosette. A rosetted flower with the petals arranged in four, more or less equal, sections.

Raceme. An *indeterminate*, unbranched *inflorescence* with usually many stalked flowers borne on an elongated axis (stem).

Radicle. A young root.

Rain shadow. An area of ground next to a wall or fence that is sheltered from prevailing winds and therefore receives less rain than open ground.

Rambler. A trailing *climber*.

Ray flower (or floret). Small flower with a tubular *corolla*, as borne in the outermost ring of a *Compositae* flowerhead.

Recurved. Applied to petals of flowers and florets that curve backwards.

Reflexed. Applied to petals of flowers and florets that bend sharply backwards at an angle of more than 90°. They are sometimes called fully reflexed. Also loosely applied to any flower in which the petals or *perianth segments* are recurved.

Remontant. Of a plant that flowers more than once during the growing season (often applied to roses and strawberries). (Cf *Non-remontant*.)

Renewal pruning. A system in which the *laterals* are constantly cut back to be replaced by young laterals stimulated by pruning.

Respiration. The release of energy from complex *organic* molecules as a result of chemical changes.

Revert. To return to an original state, for example when a variegated plant produces a plain green leaf.

Rhizome. A specialized, usually horizontally creeping, swollen or slender, underground *stem* that acts as a storage organ and produces aerial shoots at its apex and along its length.

Rib. Radiating branch on a fan-trained tree.

Rind. The outer bark of a shrub or tree outside the *cambium* layer.

Ripewood cutting. See *Cutting*.

Root. The part of a plant, normally underground, that anchors it and through which water and *nutrients* are absorbed. (See also *Aerial root*.)

Root ball. The roots and accompanying soil or *compost* visible when a plant is removed from a container or lifted from the open ground.

Root cutting. See *Cutting*.

Root run. The area of soil into which a plant's roots may extend.

Root trainers. Long, flexible, bottomless pots used commerically to grow deep-rooted seedling trees. They encourage long, fibrous root systems to develop, which helps seedlings to establish quickly after planting out.

Rooting. The production of roots, usually from cuttings.

Rooting hormone. A chemical compound synthesized in powder or liquid form and used at low concentrations to encourage root production.

Rootstock. A plant used to provide the root system for a *grafted* plant.

Rose (of a watering can). A perforated nozzle that diffuses and regulates the flow of water.

Rosette. 1) A cluster of leaves radiating from approximately the same point, often borne at ground level at the base of a very short stem. 2) A more or less circular arrangement of petals.

Rotation. See *Crop rotation*.

Rounded. Regularly curved, as in a circle.

Runner. A horizontally spreading, usually slender, stem that runs above ground and roots at the *nodes* to form new plants. Often confused with *stolon*.

Saddle grafting. See *Grafting*.

Sap. The juice of a plant contained in the cells and vascular tissue.

Sapling. A young tree; a seedling or any young tree before the wood hardens.

Scandent. Ascending or loosely climbing. (See also *Climber*.)

Scarification. 1) Abrasion or chemical treatment of a seed coat in order to speed up water intake and induce germination. 2) Removing moss and thatch from a lawn using a scarifier or rake.

Scion. A *shoot* or *bud* cut from one plant to *graft* onto a *rootstock* (stock) of another.

Scrambling climber. See *Climber*.

Scree. A slope comprising rock fragments formed by the weathering of rock faces: simulated in gardens as scree beds, in which high-altitude *alpines* that need excellent *drainage* may be grown.

Sedge peat. See *Peat*.

Seed. The ripened, fertilized *ovule* containing a dormant embryo capable of developing into an adult plant.

Seed dormancy. See *Dormancy*.

Seed leaf. See *Cotyledon*.

Seedhead. Any *fruit* that contains ripe seeds.

Seedling. A young plant that has developed from a seed.

Selection. A plant selected for particular characteristics and usually propagated to retain the same characteristics.

Self layering. See *Layering*.

Self-clinging climber. See *Climber*.

Self-fertile. Of a plant that produces viable *seed* when fertilized with its own *pollen*. (See also *Fertilization*, *Pollination*, *Self-pollination*, and *Self-sterile*.)

Self-incompatible. See *Self-sterile*.

Self-pollination. The transfer of *pollen* from the *anthers* to the *stigma* of the same *flower*, or alternatively to another flower on the same plant. (Cf *Cross-pollination*.)

Self-seed. To shed fertile seeds that produce *seedlings* around the parent plant.

Self-sterile. A plant unable to produce viable *seed* after self-fertilization, and requiring a different *pollinator* in order for fertilization to occur. Also known as "self-incompatible" – incapable of self-fertilization.

Semi-deciduous. See *Deciduous*.

Semi-determinate. Used of tall or *cordon* tomatoes that will only grow to 1–1.2m (3–4ft) long. (Cf *Determinate*; *Indeterminate*.)

Semi-double. See *Flower*.

Semi-evergreen. See *Evergreen*.

Semi-ripe cutting. See *Cutting*.

Sepal. The outer *whorl* of the *perianth* of a flower, usually small and green, but sometimes coloured and *petal*-like.

Serpentine layering. See *Layering*.

Set. 1) A small onion, shallot bulb, or potato *tuber*, selected for planting. 2) A term describing flowers that have been successfully fertilized and have produced small *fruits*.

Sexual reproduction. A form of reproduction involving *fertilization*, giving rise to *seed* or *spores*.

Sheet mulch. A *mulch* using an artificially produced material (e.g. plastic).

Shoot. A branch, stem, or twig.

Shrub. A woody-stemmed plant, usually branched from or near the base, lacking a single *trunk*.

Side grafting. See *Grafting*.

Sideshoot. A stem that arises from the side of a main *shoot*.

Side-wedge grafting. See *Grafting*.

Simple (mainly of leaves). Undivided. (Cf *Compound*.)

Simple layering. See *Layering*.

Single. See *Flower*.

Single cordon. See *Cordon*.

Single digging. A method of digging in which only the topsoil is turned over to a depth of one *spit*.

Snag. A short stub or frayed end left after incorrect pruning.

Softwood cutting. See *Cutting*.

Soil mark. The usually noticeable point on a plant's stem that shows the original soil level before the plant was lifted.

Species. A category in plant classification, the lowest principal rank below *genus* containing closely related, very similar individuals.

Specimen plant. A striking plant, usually a tree or shrub in prime condition, grown where it can be seen clearly.

Spent (of flowers). Dying or dead.

Spike. A racemose (see *Raceme*) and hence *indeterminate inflorescence* that bears unstalked flowers along a common axis (stem).

Spikelet. A small spike, forming part of a compound *inflorescence*; often applied to grasses where the flowerhead consists of several flowers with basal *bracts*.

Spit. The depth of a spade's blade, usually 25–30cm (10–12in).

Splice grafting. An alternative name for whip grafting, see *Grafting*.

Spliced side grafting. See *Grafting*.

Spliced side-veneer grafting. See *Grafting*.

Sporangium. A body that produces *spores* on a fern.

Spore. The minute, reproductive structure of flowerless plants, such as ferns, fungi, and mosses.

Sport. See *Mutation*.

Spray. A group of *flowers* or *flowerheads* on a single, branching stem, such as occurs on many chrysanthemums and carnations.

Spur. 1) A hollow projection from a petal, often producing *nectar*. 2) A short branch or branchlet bearing flower buds, as on fruit trees.

Stalk. A general term describing the stem of a leaf or flower (e.g. petiole, peduncle).

Stamen. The male reproductive organ in a plant, comprising the pollen-producing *anther* and usually its supporting *filament* or *stalk*.

Standard. 1) A tree with at least 2m (6ft) of stem below the first branches (see also *Half-standard*). 2) A shrub trained so that it has a clear length of stem below the branches (1–1.2m/3–4ft for roses). 3) One of the three inner and often erect *perianth segments* of the iris flower. 4) The largest, usually uppermost petal of a flower in the *subfamily* Papilionoideae (peas and beans) of the *family* Leguminosae.

Station sow. To sow seed individually or in small groups at fixed intervals along a row or *drill*.

Stem. The main axis of a plant, usually above ground and supporting leaves, flowers, and fruits.

Stem cutting. See *Cutting*.

Stem tip cutting. See *Cutting*.

Sterile. 1) Not producing flowers or viable seed. (Cf *Fertile*.) 2) Of flowers without functional *anthers* and pistils (see *Carpel*).

Stigma. The apical portion of a *carpel*, usually borne at the tip of a *style*, which receives *pollen* prior to *fertilization*.

Stock. See *Rootstock*.

Stock plant. A plant used to obtain propagating material, whether seed or vegetative material.

Stolon. A horizontally spreading or arching stem, usually above ground, which roots at its tip to produce a new plant. Often confused with *runner*.

Stone fruits. Fruits, also known as "drupes", with one or more seeds ("stones") surrounded by fleshy, usually edible tissue. They are common in the genus *Prunus* (e.g. apricots, plums, cherries) and some other plants, such as mangos, that produce *indehiscent*, woody fruits.

Stool. A number of shoots arising, more or less uniformly, from the base of an individual plant, for example some shrubs cut back regularly to produce propagating material and also chrysanthemums.

Stooling. 1) See *Layering*. 2) The routine pruning back of woody plants by *coppicing*.

Stopping. See *Pinching out*.

Strain. A loose, undefined term sometimes applied to races of seed-raised plants; not a term accepted under the International Code for the Nomenclature of Cultivated Plants because of its imprecise definition.

Stratification. Storage of seed in warm or cold conditions to overcome *dormancy* and aid *germination*.

Stylar column. *Styles* fused together.

Style. The usually elongated part of a *carpel* between the *ovary* and *stigma*, not always present.

Subfamily. A category in plant classification, a division within the *family*.

Sub-lateral. A sideshoot originating from a *lateral* shoot or branch.

Subshrub. 1) A low-growing plant that is entirely *woody*. 2) A plant that is woody at the base but has soft, usually *herbaceous*, growth above.

Subsoil. The layers of soil beneath the *topsoil*; these are usually less fertile and of poorer texture and structure than the topsoil.

Subspecies. A subdivision of a *species*, higher in rank than varietas (see *Variety*) or *forma*.

Succulent (of plants). A plant with thick, fleshy leaves and/or stems adapted to store water. All cacti are succulents.

Sucker. 1) A shoot that arises below ground from a plant's roots or under-ground stem. 2) On *grafted* plants, a sucker is any shoot that arises below the *graft union*.

Sympodial. Definite growth of a *shoot* terminating in an *inflorescence* or dying; growth is continued by *lateral* buds. (Cf *Monopodial*.)

Systemic. Term describing a *pesticide* or *fungicide* that is absorbed and distributed through a plant when applied to the soil or foliage.

Tap root. The primary, downward-growing *root* of a plant (especially a tree); also applied loosely to any strong, downward-growing root.

Taxon (pl. **taxa**). A group of living organisms at any rank; applied to groups of plants or entities that share distinct, defined characters.

T-budding. See *Grafting*.

Tender. Of a plant that is vulnerable to frost damage.

Tendril. A modified leaf, branch, or stem, usually filiform (long and slender) and capable of attaching itself to a support. (See also *Climber*.)

Tepal. A single segment of a perianth that cannot be distinguished either as a sepal or petal, as in *Crocus* or *Lilium*. (See also *Perianth segment*.)

Terminal. At the tip of a stem or branch; usually refers to a bud or flower.

Terminal bud. See *Bud*.

Terrarium. An enclosed container made of glass or plastic in which plants are grown.

Terrestrial. Growing in the soil; a land plant. (Cf *Epiphyte* and *Aquatic*.)

Thatch. A layer of dead, *organic* matter intermingled with living stems that accumulates on the soil surface in lawns.

Thin (of soil). Used loosely of poor soil, prone to *capping* and drought.

Thinning. The removal of seedlings, shoots, flowers, or fruit buds to improve the growth and quality of the remainder.

Tilth. A fine, crumbly, surface layer of soil produced by cultivation.

Tip layering. See *Layering*.

Tip prune. To cut back the growing tip of a shoot to encourage sideshoots or to remove damaged growth.

Tissue culture (of plants). The growing of plant tissue under sterile conditions in artificial media.

Top-dressing. 1) An application of soluble fertilizers, fresh soil, or *compost* to the soil surface around a plant or to lawns to replenish nutrients. 2) A decorative dressing applied to the soil surface around a plant.

Topiary. The art of clipping and training trees and shrubs into various, usually intricate, geometric or free shapes.

Topsoil. The uppermost, normally fertile, layer of soil.

Trace element. See *Micronutrients*.

Trailing climber. See *Climber*.

Translocated (of dissolved nutrients or weedkillers). Moving within the vascular system (conducting tissues) of a plant.

Transpiration. The loss of water by evaporation from the leaves and stems of plants.

Transplanting. Moving a plant from one position to another.

Tree. A *woody*, perennial plant usually with a well-defined *trunk* or stem with a *head* or *crown* of branches above.

Trench digging. See *Double digging*.

Trench layering. See *Layering*.

True (True-breeding). Of plants that when self-pollinated (see *Self-pollination*) give rise to offspring similar to their parents.

Trunk. The thickened, woody, main stem of a tree.

Truss. A compact cluster of flowers or fruits.

Tuber. A swollen, usually under-ground, organ derived from a stem or root, used for food storage.

Tufa. Porous limestone rock that absorbs and retains moisture; used for cultivating alpine plants difficult to grow in garden soil.

Tunic. The fibrous membranes or papery outer skin of *bulbs* or corms.

Tunicate. Enclosed in a *tunic*.

Turion. 1) A detached, overwintering, usually fleshy, *bud* produced by certain water plants. 2) A term sometimes applied to an *adventitious* shoot or *sucker*.

Twining climber. See *Climber*.

"U" cordon. A double *cordon*.

Underplanting. Low-growing plants planted beneath larger plants.

Union. See *Graft union*.

Upright. Term describing the habit of a plant with vertical or semi-vertical, main branches. (Cf *Fastigiate*.)

Urn-shaped (of flowers). Globose to cylindrical in shape with a somewhat constricted mouth; "U"-shaped.

Variable. Varying in character from the type; particularly of seed-raised plants that vary in character from the parent.

Variegated. Marked with various colours in an irregular pattern; particularly used for leaves patterned with white and yellow markings but not confined to these colours.

Variety. 1) Botanically, a naturally occurring variant (varietas - var.) of a wild *species*, between the rank of *subspecies* and *forma*. 2) Also commonly but imprecisely used to describe any variant of a plant. (Cf *Cultivar*.)

Vegetative growth. Non-flowering, usually leafy growth.

Vegetative propagation. The increase of plants by asexual methods normally resulting in genetically identical individuals.

Vermiculite. A lightweight, mica-like mineral allowing good water retention and aeration when used in cutting compost and other potting media.

Water shoots. Applied usually to *epicormic shoots* that frequently arise close to pruning wounds on tree trunks or branches.

Whip. A young seedling or grafted tree without *lateral* branches.

Whip grafting. See *Grafting*.

Whip-and-tongue grafting. See *Grafting*.

Whorl. The arrangement of three or more organs arising from the same point.

Widger. A spatula-shaped tool used for transplanting or *pricking out* seedlings.

Windbreak. Any structure but often a hedge, fence, or wall that shelters plants and filters strong winds.

Wind-rock. The destabilizing of a plant's roots by strong wind.

Winter wet. Excessive amounts of water that accumulate in the soil during the winter months.

Woody. Ligneous, a term describing stems or trunks that are hard and thickened rather than soft and pliable. (Cf *Herbaceous*.)

Wound. A cut or broken area in a plant.

Wound paint. A specialized paint that used to be applied to a cut surface of a plant after pruning.

INDEX

Page numbers given in *italics* refer to pages on which there are relevant illustrations. In plant entries topics of general information relating to the main entries appear first; subentries for species and cultivars always follow the general subentries.

A

Abelia
soft/greenwood cuttings 111
suggestions for use 95
floribunda, conditions preferred 91, 95
Abeliophyllum distichum, scent 95
Abelmoschus esculentus see Okra
Abies
pests 654
propagation, spliced side grafting 82
soil preferred 65
training 73
grandis, soil preferred 66
magnifica, suggestions for use 59
procera, suggestions for use 59
Abromeitiella see Deuterocohnia
Abutilon
conditions preferred 95
in containers 319
in garden room *354*
greenhouse conditions required 361
propagation
soft/greenwood cuttings 111
softwood cuttings 380
pruning 105, 376
suggestions for use 95, 318
Abyssinian banana *see Ensete ventricosum*
Acacia
seed scarification 80
baileyana
and climate change 91
seasonal interest 95
suggestions for use 59
dealbata
pruning 73
scent 56
seasonal interest 59
soil preferred 66
suggestions for use 59, 95
pravissima 91
Acaena
height 172
caesiiglauca, soil type preferred 261
microphylla
companion plant for 177
soil type preferred 261
'Kupferteppich' 179
saccaticupola 'Blue Haze', companion plant for 177
Acalypha, softwood cuttings 380
Acantholimon glumaceum, suggestions for use 258, 259

Acanthus
root cuttings 203, *203*
for seedheads 181
hungaricus, architectural form 181
mollis
architectural form 181
conditions tolerated 181
methods of spreading 180
propagation, root cuttings *633*
suggestions for use 61
spinosus
soil type preferred 184
soil type tolerated 185
as specimen plant 179
Acer
diseases 654, 661, 665
foliage 57
grouping 56
informal arrangement *54*
pests 652
physiological disorders 653
propagation, spliced side grafting 82
pruning 71
seasonal interest 50
seed germination 81
soil type preferred 325
stem structure *674*
campestre
to attract wildlife 22
soil type tolerated 65
capillipes
bark *57*
seasonal interest 59
suggestions for use 59
cappadocicum, softwood cuttings 79
x *conspicuuum* 'Silver Vein'
seasonal interest 59
suggestions for use 59
davidii
seasonal interest 59
'Serpentine', seasonal interest 59
griseum
bark *49, 57*
seasonal interest 59
suggestions for use 59
grosseri var. *hersii*, seasonal interest 59
japonicum
in containers 319
pruning 103
lobelii, soil type tolerated 65
negundo
seasonal interest 59
soil preferred 66
soil type tolerated 65
palmatum 312
conditions preferred 95
in containers 94, 319
foliage 317
germination 115
leaf shapes *46*
propagation, spliced side-veneer grafting 119
pruning 103
suggestions for use 55, 59, 307, 317
in water garden *283*
'Dissectum Atropurpureum', in trough *58*
'Sango-kaku'
seasonal interest 59
suggestions for use 59
pensylvanicum
bark *57*
seasonal interest 59
suggestions for use 59
'Erythrocladum', seasonal interest 59

Acer (cont.)
platanoides
conditions tolerated 67
soil types tolerated 65, 66
pseudoplatanus
conditions tolerated 67
and leaf mould 63
resistance to storm damage 68
suggestions for use 59
'Brilliantissimum', suggestions for use 59
rubrum
suggestions for use 59
'Columnare' *55*
saccharinum, conditions tolerated 67
Aceria (mites) 652
genistae 655
Achillea 15
conditions tolerated 181
dividing 201
for drying 181
seedheads 172
decorative plants providing 181
soil type preferred 184
ageratifolia
division 275
"Irishman's" cuttings 275
clavennae, foliage 256
filipendulina 172
'Gold Plate'
flower form *47*
growth rate 181
soil type tolerated 185
grandifolia, growth rate 181
x *kellereri*, soil type preferred 261
millefolium 672
'Moonshine', form 175
Summer Pastels Group 213
'Terracotta', in perennial border *172*
Achimenes
greenhouse conditions required 361
in containers 319
pests 656
Acid soil
climbers requiring 131
deficiencies 617
effect of fertilizers on 100
effects on minerals 637
improving 390
liming 616
mineral deficiency in 651
perennials requiring 185
raised beds to contain 599
rock plants requiring 260
shrubs requiring 91, 99
trees preferring 65
Acid-loving plants
beds for 269, *269*
siting 269
problems 624
soil for 262, 621
Acidic-humus beds 269, *269*
siting 269
Aconite, winter *see Eranthis hyemalis*
Aconitum
dividing 201
seed germination 198
soil type tolerated 185
carmichaelii
companion plant for 177
conditions tolerated 181
napellus, conditions tolerated 181
Acorus
calamus
rootstock division 302, *302*

Acorus calamus (cont.)
site in water garden 285
suggestions for use 284
'Variegatus', position in water garden 285
gramineus
in container water garden *331*
position in water garden 285
'Ogon', suggestions for use 331
var. *pusillus*, suggestions for use 366
'Variegatus'
position in water garden 285
suggestions for use 331
Acrylic sheets, for greenhouse glazing 571
Actaea
podocarpa see Cimicifuga americana
racemosa see Cimicifuga racemosa
Actinidia
propagation
semi-ripe cuttings 142
simple layering 145
pruning 135
deliciosa
edible *see* Kiwi fruits
obtaining seed from 141
vigour 130
kolomikta 143
foliage 127, *128*
propagation, hardwood cuttings 143
soil type tolerated 132
suggestions for use 125
Additives for soil 621, *621*
Adelgids *654*
symptoms and control 654
Adenium obesum
succulent type 338
suggestions for use 342
Adenophora
division 201
softwood cuttings 273
Adiantum
conditions preferred indoors 361
in containers 319
greenhouse conditions required 361
propagation, rootstock 378
watering 194
capillus-veneris, care during absence 374
pedatum, conditions tolerated 181
raddianum
suggestions for use 366
'Fritz Lüthi', propagation *195*
Adlumia fungosa, soil type tolerated 131
Adonis
seed germination 198
amurensis
conditions preferred 259
seed germination 198
Adromischus
stem cuttings 348
cooperi, leaf cuttings 347
Adventitious growth, propagation by *370, 371*
Adventitious roots 632, *632, 633*
Adventitious stem buds 632
Aechmea
conditions preferred indoors 361

Aechmea (cont.)
conditions required 363
displaying 362
greenhouse conditions required 361
as pot plant 362
propagation, division of offsets *363*
fasciata 362
Aegopodium podagraria as weed *see* Ground elder
'Variegatum', suggestions for use 179
Aeonium
stem cuttings 348
arboreum
propagation, leaf cuttings 347
suggestions for use 342
nobile, suggestions for use 342
'Zwartkopf', in containers outdoors 340
Aeration of soil, improving 621
Aerators
hollow-tined *559*
lawn 398, 559, *559*
scarifying rake 398, *398, 559*
star-wheeled slitter *559*
Aerial roots *see* Roots, aerial
Aeschynanthus
greenhouse conditions required 361
softwood cuttings 380
Aesculus
for avenues 58
flowers 57
propagation
apical wedge grafting 82
sowing in containers 80
pruning 71
renovating 74
soil type tolerated 65
californica, suggestions for use 59
hippocastanum
conditions tolerated 67
leaf form *675*
suggestions for use 59
indica 'Sydney Pearce' *82*
parviflora
in informal shrub grouping *90*
propagation, root cuttings 114
Aethionema
soil type tolerated 261
grandiflorum, suggestions for use 259
'Warley Rose'
soil type preferred 261
suggestions for use 259
African Bermuda grass *see Cynodon transvaalensis*
African lily *see Agapanthus*
African marigold *see Tagetes erecta*
African spinach *see Amaranthus*
African violet *see Saintpaulia*
Agapanthus 46, 319
architectural shape 172
conditions preferred 231
in containers *318*, 319
for cutting 231
flowers *676*
in garden room *354*
greenhouse conditions required 361
in greenhouse garden *360*
lawn as foil to *386*
suggestions for use 229
Headbourne Hybrids with bulbs, formal bedding 227

Agapetes
conditions tolerated 129
propagation, semi-ripe
cuttings 142
pruning 376
soil type required 130, 131, 325
Agar jelly, seeds sown on 216
Agastache aurantiaca 213
Agavaceae, dying after flowering 339
Agave
architectural 95
conditions tolerated 339
handling 341
propagation
division of offsets 349
division of rootstock 350
pruning 108
soil type preferred 325
americana 61
conditions tolerated 342
hardiness 339
in succulent group *339*
suggestions for use 318
'Marginata', in succulent
group *338*
'Mediopicta', in indoor
bed *341*
attenuata
conditions tolerated 342
containers for 340
in succulent group *338*
filifera 339
hardiness 339
in mixed succulent
planting *340*
suggestions for use 342
lophantha, conditions
tolerated 342
parryi
conditions tolerated 342
in containers outdoors 340
parviflora, conditions
tolerated 342
stricta, suggestions for use 342
utahensis, conditions tolerated
342
victoriae-reginae, suggestions
for use 342
Ageratum
architectural plant 210
in containers 319
for drying 213
position in border 209
houstonianum, soil type
tolerated 216
Aggregate, definition 591
Aglaonema
care during absence *374*
greenhouse conditions
required 361
Agonis flexuosa, soil preferred 66
Agriotes 662
Agrobacterium tumefaciens 655,
661
Agropyron cristatum, for lawns
389
Agrostemma
self-seeding 218
sowing 217
githago 'Milas', for cutting
213
Agrostis
for lawn 388, 389
sowing rate 394
for meadow garden 401
in turf 392
castellana, for lawns 388
stolonifera, propagation 394
tenuis, for lawns 388
Agrotis caterpillars 655, 660
Ailanthus, propagation by root
cuttings 633
altissima, regeneration 68
Air layering
indoor plants 383, *383*
method 631, *631*
shrubs 116, *117*
plants propagated by 117

Air layering (*cont.*)
trees 81
trees suitable for 81
Air pollution
climbers tolerant of 129
rock plants tolerant of 259
shrubs tolerant of 95
trees tolerant of 67
Air temperature 607
Air-drying herbs 415, *415*
Aira elegantissima, for drying
212
Aizoaceae, division of rootstock
350
Ajuga
dividing 193
pyramidalis, conditions
tolerated 259
reptans
conditions preferred 181
conditions tolerated 259
as ground cover 176, *180*
'Catlins Giant', as ground
cover 180
'Braunherz' *180*
Akebia
climbing method *130*
propagation
semi-ripe cuttings 142
simple layering 145
quinata
conditions tolerated 129
fruit 127
propagation, simple
layering *145*
soil type tolerated 132
vigour 130
Albizia julibrissin, suggestions
for use 59
Albuca
suggestions for use 231
humilis, suggestions for use
231
Albugo candida 646
Alcea 153
cutting down 223
position in border 209
staking 222
'Majorette' 213
rosea (syn. *Althaea rosea*)
architectural plant 213
Summer Carnival Group
213
Alchemilla
in containers 319
flowering time from seed 198
soil type preferred 184
alpina, division 275
ellenbeckii, division 275
mollis 151
in border 174
for cutting 181
for drying 181
foliage 176
softening lines of path *593*
under specimen plant 179
Alder see *Alnus*
Alecost see *Tanacetum balsamita*
Aleyrodes proletella 646
Algae
on lawn *667*
symptoms and control 667
in pond 623
avoiding introduction of
297
control 284, 300, *301*,
673
discouraging 298, 303
encouraging 299
green water caused by 300
Ali Baba jars 307
Alisma
lanceolatum, position in water
garden 285
plantago-aquatica
position in water garden
285
var. *parviflorum*, position
in water garden 285

Alkaline soil
acid-loving plants on 651
annuals tolerating 216
biennials tolerating 216
climbers tolerating 132
deficiencies 617
effects on minerals 637
perennials tolerating 185
problems 667
rock plants tolerating 261
shrubs tolerating 91, 99
trees tolerating 65
Allamanda 129
softwood cuttings 142
cathartica 129
pruning 135, 137
'Hendersonii' *142*
pruning 376
Allium
avoiding in rock garden 260
for cutting 181, 231
dead-heading *242*
edible, in crop rotation 498
germination 630
propagation
bulblets 245
offsets 245
aflatunense, in mixed border
228
cepa see Onions, bulb
cepa Aggregatum Group *see*
Shallots
cristophii, architectural plant
231
dwarf, suggestions for use 231
fistulosum see Onions, Welsh
giganteum 230
architectural plant 231
moly, suggestions for use 239
porrum see Leeks
sativum see Garlic
schoenoprasum see Chives
sikkimense, division 275
tuberosum 407
in herb garden *412*
Allolobophora 668
Alloplectus, softwood cuttings 380
Alluaudiopsis, flat grafting 351
Almonds 488, *489*
diseases, fungal 651
bird damage 657
chilling requirement 489
conditions required 489
diseases 489
in garden 488
harvesting 489
as ornamentals 489
plant type 419
planting 489
pollination 489
propagation 489
pruning 489
recommended cultivars 489
rootstocks 489
routine care 489
site 489
spacing 489
storing 489
training 489
tree size 489
'Balatoni' 489
'Ferragnes' 489
'Ingrid' 489
'Macrocarpa' 489
'Titan' 489
Alnus
conditions tolerated 613
cordata
conditions tolerated 67
suggestions for use 59
glutinosa
conditions tolerated 67
resistance to storm
damage 68
suggestions for use 285
'Aurea', seasonal interest
59
incana, suggestions for use
285

Aloe
conditions tolerated 339
handling 341
propagation
division of offsets 349
division of rootstock 350
in succulent group *339*
succulent type 338
arborescens
conditions tolerated 342
repotting *345*
aristata, conditions tolerated
342
'Black Gem', in bowl *344*
brevifolia, conditions
tolerated 342
ciliaris, suggestions for use
339
distans, conditions tolerated
342
humilis, suggestions for use
342
longistyla, suggestions for use
342
rauhii, suggestions for use 342
variegata 350
conditions tolerated 342
vera
conditions tolerated 342
in containers outdoors 340
Aloinopsis, division of offsets
349
Alonsoa, from seed 379
Aloysia
pruning 105
softwood cuttings 111
triphylla see Lemon verbena
Alpha naphthalene acetic acid
484
Alpine house 258, 277–9, 360,
569, *569*
beds in 278–9
bulbs for 230, 231
damping down 279
display in *277*
displaying plants in 277, *277*
heating 279
natural display in *25*
raised beds in 578
routine maintenance 279
shading 279
siting *23*, 277
using 277, *277*
ventilation 279
watering 267, 567
Alpine strawberries see
Strawberries, alpine
Alpines
acid-loving 257
compost for 262
adapting to conditions 254
bulbs with 229, *229*
buying 260
care after flowering *277*
characteristics 254
choosing 260, *260*
composts for 261–2, 278, 279,
306, 323, *323*
conditions required 255, 256
in containers 258, *258*, 266–7
containers for 321
cutting back after flowering
271, *271*
definition 254
diseases 271
exhibiting 279, *279*
feeding 270
filling gaps between 211
germination 272
in greenhouse 359
greenhouse for 573
growing under cover
feeding 279
routine care 279
shading 279
watering 279
habitats 254
hygiene 279
mulches for 323

Alpines (*cont.*)
pests 271
planting 262, 263–4
in beds 278–9
in crevices *263*, 264, *268*
in dry-stone walls 268,
268
in raised beds 269
in scree bed 264
in troughs 267, *267*
plunging after flowering 277,
277
in pots 278
potting up 272
pricking out 272
propagation 272–6
basal cuttings 274, *274*
cuttings 273–4, *273–4*,
275–6
selecting material for
274, *274*
division 275, *275*
time for 275
greenwood cuttings 273
"Irishman's cuttings" 275,
275
leaf cuttings 274
ripewood cuttings 274
root cuttings 275–6, *276*
rosettes 274
scooping rosettes 276, *276*
from seed 272, *272*
sowing when fresh
272
semi-ripe cuttings 273,
274
softwood cuttings 273,
273
protecting 269, 271
from birds 264
under cover 277, *277*
pruning 270–1, *270*
in raised beds 257–8, *257*,
269
raised beds for, in alpine
house 578
in raised island beds 173
range of plants 254
removing dead leaves 279, *279*
removing dead rosettes 271,
271
repotting 278, *278*
in rock garden 254, 256
routine care 270–1
in scree beds 256–7
seed
collecting 272
pre-sowing treatment 272
storage 272
self-seeding 256
soil requirements 261–2
suggestions for use 255–8
top-dressing 269, 270, *270*,
278, *626*
trimming 270–1
in troughs 258, *258*
in walls 258
watering 270
weeding 270, *270*
winter care 279
Alps, precipitation 609
Alstroemeria
conditions preferred 231
for cutting 181, 231
propagation, division of
offsets 245
seed germination 247
Ligtu Hybrids *230*, 231
Althaea rosea see *Alcea rosea*
Altitude
effect on air temperature 607
effect on temperature 609
Aluminium
excess of 617
for greenhouses 570–1, *570*
markers in 564
Aluminium ammonium sulphate
657, 666, 667
sprays based on 645

Aluminium sulphate-based
  pesticides 644
Aluminium sulphate-based slug
  killers 668
Alyssum
  diseases 646
  from seed 216
  germination 630
  soil type tolerated 261
  montanum, suggestions for
    use 259
Alyssum, sweet *see Lobularia
  maritima*
Amaranths *see Amaranthus*
Amaranthus 515
  conditions required 515
  culinary uses 515
  diseases 515
  for drying 213
  as edible crop 515
  feeding 515
  foliage 209
  growing under cover 515
  harvesting 515
  mulching 515
  nitrogen requirement 504, 515
  pests 515
  pinching out 515
  position in border 209
  propagation from seed 515
  protecting seedlings 515
  routine care 515
  size of plant 515
  soil required 515
  spacing 515
  storing 515
  thinning seedlings 515
  watering 515
  caudatus
    architectural plant 213
    for drying 212
    foliage 515
    in mixed border 210
  cruentus 515
    foliage 515
    cultivars 515
  edible cultivars 515
  tricolor 515
    architectural plant 213
    foliage 515
    cultivars 515
Amaryllis
  from seed 247
  belladonna
    conditions preferred 231
    in containers 319
    for cutting 231
    in mixed border 228
Amberboa moschata, for
  fragrance 213
Amblyseius 656
  as biological pest control
    642
  degenerans 647
Amelanchier
  bird damage 657
  germination 115
  propagation, stooling 117
  pruning 105
  soil type tolerated 97
  canadensis, propagation,
    division of suckers 118
  lamarckii
    seasonal interest 59
    suggestions for use 59
American broccoli *see* Calabrese
Amitrole 671, 673
Ammobium alatum, for drying
  213
Ammonia 621, 625, 628
Ammonium nitrate 426, 503
Ammonium sulphamate 69, 671,
  673
Ammonium sulphate 444, 456,
  503
  nutrient content 624
Ampelopsis 129
  semi-ripe cuttings 142
  serpentine layering 145

Ampelopsis (*cont.*)
  brevipedunculata var.
    maximowiczii (syn. *A.
    glandulosa*)
    growing through trees 127
    soil type tolerated 132
    suggestions for use 127
Amphibians
  attracting 22, 295
  providing conditions for 284
Anacyclus pyrethrum var.
  depressus, propagation, root
    cuttings 275
Ananas 362
  conditions preferred indoors
    361
  propagation 363
  bracteatus 'Tricolor' *362*
  comosus
    as fruit *see* Pineapples
    var. *variegatus*, conditions
      preferred 355
Anaphalis
  conditions tolerated 181
  for drying 181
  nepalensis var. *monocephala*
    (syn. *A. nubigena*) 150
  triplinervis, as ground cover
    180
  'Sommerschnee', ornamental
    ground cover *180*
Anatomy 674
Anchoring bolts 572, *572*
Anchusa
  root cuttings 203
  soil type tolerated 185
  azurea
    to attract wildlife 178
    root cuttings 203
  capensis
    soil type preferred 216
    sowing 217
  cespitosa
    propagation, greenwood
      cuttings 273
    suggestions for use 256,
      259
Andromeda
  propagation
    division of suckers 118
    layering 116
    semi-ripe cuttings 113
  soil type required 99, 325
Androsace
  compost for 278
  conditions required 255, 262
  rosette cuttings 274
  soil type required 262
  suggestions for use 259
  carnea subsp. *laggeri*, self-
    seeding 256
  chamaejasme, suggestions for
    use 258
  lanuginosa 259
    suggestions for use 259
  pubescens, in trough *267*
  sarmentosa, suggestions for
    use 259
  sempervivoides, suggestions
    for use 259
Anemone
  to attract wildlife 178
  conditions tolerated 231
  diseases
    affecting flowers 657
    fungal 652
  flowering time from seed 198
  greenhouse conditions
    required 361
  sowing 272
  suggestions for use 228, 231
  apennina
    conditions preferred 231
    suggestions for use 239
  biflora, resting 240
  blanda
    conditions preferred 231
    in containers 319
    in mixed border 227

Anemone blanda (*cont.*)
  rhizomes 227
  suggestions for use 239
  coronaria
    in containers 319
    St Bridgid Group, for
      cutting 231
    De Caen Series, for cutting 231
  x *fulgens*, in containers 319
  hupehensis
    conditions tolerated 181
    dividing 201
    root cuttings 203
    soil type tolerated 185
  x *hybrida*
    conditions tolerated 181
    pests 647
    root cuttings 203
    seasonal interest 50
    soil type tolerated 185
  multifida, soil type tolerated
    261
  nemorosa
    conditions tolerated 231
    rhizomes 227
    storing 236
    suggestions for use 179
    in woodland 178
  pavonina, suggestions for use
    239
  ranunculoides
    choosing healthy bulbs
      236
    conditions preferred 231
  rivularis, suggestions for use
    285
  tschernjaewii, resting 240
Anemopaegma 129
  semi-ripe cuttings 142
  softwood cuttings 142
Anethum graveolens see Dill
Angelica
  to attract insects 172
  archangelica 407, *407*
    architectural form 181
    conditions tolerated 405
    culinary uses 404, 407
    dead-heading 413
    foliage 407
    harvesting 407
    propagation
      from seed 407, 414
      self-seeding 413
    storing 407
    suggestions for use 309
    thinning out seedlings 414
  gigas 181
Angelica (herb) *see Angelica
  archangelica*
Angels' trumpets *see Brugmansia*
Angiospermae (Angiosperms)
  classes 676
  seed production 676
Anigozanthos manglesii 185
  soil type required 185
Animal manures *see* Manure
Animals
  beneficial 641, *641*
  protecting trees from 67, *67*
  protection from, netting 564
Aniseed 409, *409*
  conditions required 409
  culinary uses 409
  flowers 409
  foliage 409
  harvesting 409
  propagation from seed 409
Anisodontea
  overwintering 335
  capensis, in containers 319
Annual meadow grass *see Poa
  annua*
Annuals 208–23
  architectural 210–11, 213
  for balconies 313
  borders of 208–11, *209*
    colour effects 208
    form and texture in 208–9
    grouping plants 209

Annuals (*cont.*)
  buying
    for bedding 221, *221*
    pot-grown *221*
  characteristics 674
  clearing at end of season 223,
    223
  climbers 128, 129, 211–12
    planting 221
    from seed 141
    supporting 221, 222, *222*
  in containers 212
    plants suitable for 213,
      315, 319
    seasonal display 212, 310,
      326–8
    with trees 58
  crop rotation for disease
    control 640
  cucumbers 525
  for cutting 212, 213, 222
  dahlias 234, *235*
  dead-heading 223, *223*
  definition 208
  designing with 208–12
  Dianthus 196, *196*
  diseases 223
    affecting flowers 656
    bacterial 648, 655, 665
    fungal 646, 648, 654, 656,
      658, 661
  for dry shade 213
  for drying 212, 213, 222, *222*
  effects of high temperatures
    on 650
  effects of low temperatures on
    650, 664
  for exposed sites 213
  F1 hybrids from seed 379
  feeding 222
  as fillers 211
  for foliage 209
  in formal bedding 210–11
  fuchsias 120m 121
  as gap filler in borders 405
  grasses 209–10
  as green manure 625
  in greenhouse 360
  for ground cover 211, *211*
  grouping 209
  half-hardy
    conditions tolerated 220
    definition 208
    hardening off 219–20, *220*
    planting out 220, *220*
    sowing 217, *219*
  hardening off 219–20, *220*
  hardy
    definition 208
    sowing 216–17
  herbs 404
    propagation from seed 414
  mineral deficiency 650–1
  in mixed borders *210*, 210–11
  for moist shade 213
  perennials grown as *208*, 213
  pests 223, 654, 655, 660, 662,
    666
    affecting flowers 657
    damaging leaves 644, 645,
      646, 647, 648, 651
  pinching out 220
  planter's guide 213
  planting to design 221, *221*
  planting out 220, *220*
  potting up 220
  pricking out 219, *219*
  problems
    affecting growth 655
    affecting stems and leaf
      buds 653, 654
  rotation plan 640
  routine care 222–3
  for sandy soil 216
  for scent 213
  seasonal display 210
  from seed 216–21
  seed
    buying 216

Annuals, seed (*cont.*)
  collecting 223, *223*
    with special needs 219
    viability 216
  seedlings
    buying 216, *216*
    protecting 218, *218*
    supporting 218, *218*
    self-seeding 210, 218, 223
      controlling 222
  in shrub border 92
  sowing
    in open ground 217–18,
      217
    in pots or trays 218–20,
      219
    in situ, varieties for 217
    for succession 379
  staking 218, 222, *222*
  stopping 220
  suggestions for use 208–12
  summer-flowering *208*
  thinning 218, *218*
  tolerating alkaline soil 216
  trailing 211–12
    for containers 213
  watering 222
  weeding 222
  weeds 669, *669*, 671
Anomatheca
  suggestions for use 231
  laxa, conditions preferred 231
Anredera 129
  cordifolia 129
    for fragrance 129
    pruning 135, 137
    softwood cuttings 142
    soil type tolerated 131
Antennaria
  dioica
    conditions tolerated 259
    division 275
    'Minima', suggestions for
      use 258, 259
Anthemis 47
  softwood cuttings 273
  tinctoria
    basal stem cuttings 202
    'E.C. Buxton' *202*
Anther 347, 676, *676*
Anthericum liliago 176
Antheridum 195
Anthracnose *666*
  symptoms and control 666
Anthriscus cerefolium see Chervil
Anthurium
  greenhouse conditions
    required 361
  hydroculture 361
  propagation, rootstock 378
Anthyllis
  seed germination 198
  soil type tolerated 185
Antifreeze, for concrete 586
Antigonon
  softwood cuttings 142
  leptopus 129
    pruning 135, 137
Antirrhinum
  clearing at end of season 223
  colours 213
  for cutting 212, 213
  diseases, fungal 666
  dwarf, in containers 319
  flowering shoots 219
  in formal bedding 210
  greenhouse conditions
    required 361
  overwintering 335
  as pot plant 213
  hispanicum (syn. *A.
    glutinosum*), suggestions
    for use 259
  majus
    soil type tolerated 216
    in annual bedding 208
  molle, suggestions for use 259
  sempervirens, suggestions for
    use 259

Ants 271, *668*
　benefits of 641
　deterring 641
　on lawn 668
　symptoms and control 666,
　　668
Aphanomyces euteiches 661
Aphelanchoides 647
Aphelandra, greenhouse
　conditions required 361
Aphelen 647
Aphidius spp. 646
Aphidoletes aphidimyza, as
　biological pest control 642, 646
Aphids 96, 160, 271, *651*
　catching 504
　conifer, woolly *see* Adelgids
　control 646, 668
　　biological 583, 642, 643
　　by companion planting 641
　diseases transmitted by 639,
　　649, 656
　effects of global warming on
　　607
　predators for 641, *641*
　problems caused by 244, 333,
　　646, *646*, 651
　root, symptoms and control
　　661
　types
　　blackfly *646*
　　lettuce root, resistance to
　　　640
　　woolly beech 646
　virus disease carried by 251
　on water plants 301
　woolly *654*
　　control 654
　　plants affected by 654
　　symptoms 654
Apical-wedge grafting 83, 119,
　119, 635
　cacti *350*, 351
　trees suitable for 82
Apium
　graveolens see Celery
　graveolens var. *rapaceum, see*
　　Celeriac
Apocynaceae 338
Aponogeton
　depth of water for 284
　value in water garden 284
　distachyos
　　planting *299*
　　position in water garden
　　　285
　　propagation, division of
　　　tubers 302
　　from seed 303
　undulatus, propagation by
　　plantlets 303
Aporocactus
　stem cuttings 348
　flagelliformis 351
　　flowers 342
　　in hanging baskets 341
　　propagation, side grafting
　　　351
　　suggestions for use 342
x *Aporophyllum*, in greenhouse
　display *360*
Apple cucumbers *see* Cucumbers,
　apple
Apple leaf-mining moth 647
Apple sawfly *659*
　symptoms and control 659
Apple sucker *656*
　symptoms and control 656
Apples 435–43
　arcure 420
　bare-root planting 435
　bark-ringing 430, 437, *437*
　biennial bearing
　　correcting 436
　　cultivars prone to 436, 437
　bitter pit *640*
　bitter pit, susceptible cultivars
　　436
　blossom thinning 436

Apples (*cont.*)
　bush
　　planting distances 436
　　pruning
　　　formative 439
　　　renewal 439, *439*
　　　routine 439
　　　spur pruning 439, *439*
　　　winter 439, *439*
　canker-susceptible cultivars
　　436, 437, 664
　chilling requirement 435
　conditions required 435
　container-grown planting 435
　in containers 319
　cordons 420, *420*
　　double, training 441, *441*
　　planting distances 436
　　pruning
　　　formative 441, *441*
　　　routine 441, *441*
　　　summer 441, *441*
　　　winter 440–1, *441*
　　training 440
　crop timing 423
　cross-pollination 420, 424
　culinary
　　for flavour 437
　　fruit spacing 436
　　recommended cultivars 437
　curbing excessive growth 430
　　by bark-ringing 437, *437*
　dessert
　　fruit spacing 436
　　recommended cultivars
　　　436
　diploids 435
　diseases 436, 649
　　bacterial 665
　　fungal 654, 658, 664
　double cordon, training 441,
　　441
　drying 431
　dwarf pyramid
　　planting distances 436
　　pruning 443
　　staking 443
　encouraging fruit set 437
　espaliers 58, 420
　　planting distances 436
　　pruning
　　　formative 442, *442*
　　　routine 442–3
　　　summer 442, *442*
　　　winter 442, *442*
　　as screen *421*
　　training 442, *442*
　"family" trees 420
　fans
　　planting distances 436
　　pruning 442
　　space required 422
　　training 441–2
　feathered maidens
　　training
　　　as bush 439, *439*
　　　as double cordon 441
　　　as spindlebush 440,
　　　　440
　feeding 436
　for flavour 436, 437
　flowering, temperature
　　required 435
　forms 435
　frame working 443
　freezing 431
　fruit *435*
　　thinning 436, *436*
　　type 419, 435
　fruit buds 437, *437*
　fruit type 675–6
　grafting over 443
　growing against supports 422
　growing in containers 318
　growth buds 437, *437*
　half-standard
　　planting distances 436
　　pruning 439–40
　harvesting 431, 443, *443*

Apples (*cont.*)
　June drop 436
　"King" fruit 436
　late-ripening 421
　maiden whip
　　training
　　　as bush 439
　　　as double cordon
　　　　441, *441*
　　　as espalier 442, *442*
　mineral deficiencies 650, 656,
　　658
　mulching 436
　nicking 437, *437*, 439
　notching 437, *437*
　pests 436, 654, 657, 659
　　damaging flowers 656
　　damaging leaves 646,
　　　647
　　damaging stems 654
　physiological disorders 658
　planting 435
　　distances 435, 436
　pollination compatibility 423
　pollination groups 435
　propagation 443
　　grafting 635
　pruning 437–43
　　Full Lorette System 439
　　Modified Lorette System
　　　438–9, *438*
　　regulated 438, *438*
　　renewal 438, *438*
　　renovative 430
　　spur pruning 438, *438*
　　spur thinning 438, *438*
　　summer 437, 438–9, *438*
　　untrained trees 437
　　winter 428, 438, *438*
　rind grafting 443, *443*
　rootstocks 420, 423, 435, *435*
　routine care 436
　scab-resistant cultivars 436,
　　437
　scab-susceptible cultivars
　　436, 437
　scorch damage to fruits 650
　self-sterile 421, 424
　siting 420–1, 435
　as specimen trees 439
　spindlebush
　　planting distances 436
　　pruning 438
　　　formative 440, *440*
　　　routine 440, *440*
　　　summer 440, *440*
　　　winter 440, *440*
　　training 440, *440*
　spur-bearers 436, 437
　　training 437
　staking 436
　standard
　　planting distances 436
　　pruning 439–40
　storing 421, 423, 431, *431*, 443
　testing for ripeness 431
　thinning fruit 426
　tip-bearers 436, 437
　　training 437
　top working 443, *443*
　training 420, 435, 437–43
　triploids 435
　　pruning 438
　　recommended cultivars
　　　436, 437
　tying 436
　wall-trained 418
　watering 436
　'Alkmene' 436
　'Annie Elizabeth' 437
　'Arthur Turner' 437
　　blossom 418
　'Ashmead's Kernel' 436
　　blossom 418
　　in large fruit garden *421*
　Ballerina 318
　'Blenheim Orange' 437
　　pruning 438
　'Bountiful' 437

Apples (*cont.*)
　'Bramley's Seedling' 437
　　blossom 418
　　cross-pollination 423
　　on "family" tree 420
　　pruning 438
　'Charles Ross' 436
　　on "family" tree 420
　'Cornish Gillyflower' 436
　'Cox's Orange Pippin' 436,
　　664
　　cross-pollination 423, 435
　　in large fruit garden *421*
　'Cox's Pomona' 437
　'Crawley Beauty' 437
　'D'Arcy Spice' 436
　'Delbarestivale' 436
　'Discovery' 436
　　on "family" tree 420
　　in large fruit garden *421*
　'Dumelow's Seedling' 437
　'Early Victoria' 437
　'Edward VII' 437, *437*
　'Egremont Russet' 436
　　on "family" tree 420
　'Ellison's Orange' 436
　'Encore' 437
　'Epicure' 436
　　in large fruit garden *421*
　　in small fruit garden *422*
　'Falstaff', on "family" tree
　　420, 436
　'Fiesta' 436
　'Fortune' 436
　'George Cave' 436, *436*
　'George Neal' 437
　'Golden Delicious' 436
　'Golden Noble' 437
　'Greensleeves' 436
　'Grenadier' 437
　'Howgate Wonder' 437
　'Irish Peach' 436
　'James Grieve' 436, 664
　　on "family" tree 420
　'Jester' 436
　'Jonagold' 436
　　pruning 438
　'Jupiter' 436
　'Katy' 436
　'Kidd's Orange Red' 436, 435
　'King of the Pippins' 436
　'Lane's Prince Albert' 437
　'Lord Derby' 437
　'Lord Lambourne' 436
　　cross-pollination 423
　　in small fruit garden *422*
　'Lord Suffield' 437
　'Monarch' 437
　'Mother' 436
　'Newton Wonder' 437
　'Norfolk Beauty' 437
　'Orleans Reinette' 436
　'Peasgood Nonsuch' 437
　'Pixie' 436
　'Red Pippin (Fiesta)', on
　　"family" tree 420
　'Rev. W. Wilks' 437, *437*
　'Ribston Pippin' 436
　'Rosemary Russet' 436
　'Royal Jubilee' 437
　'St Edmund's Pippin' 436
　　in large fruit garden *421*
　'Saturn' 436
　'Spartan' 436
　'Sturmer Pippin' 436
　'Sunset' 436
　　on "family" tree 420
　　in large fruit garden *421*
　　in small fruit garden *422*
　'Suntan' 436, 435
　'Tydeman's Early Worcester'
　　436
　'Warner's King' 437
　'Winston' 436
　'Winter Gem' 436
　'Worcester Pearmain' 436,
　　436, 664
Apricots 454–5
　biennial bearing 455

Apricots (*cont.*)
　bush, pruning 455
　chilling requirement 454
　conditions required 454
　in cool climates 454
　die-back 454, 455
　diseases 455
　drying 431
　fan 454
　　pruning 455, *455*
　　　after fruiting 455, *455*
　　　thinning 455, *455*
　for flavour 455
　freezing 431
　fruit type 435
　growing under cover 454
　harvesting 455
　pests 455
　　affecting flowers 657
　　eating leaves 644
　planting 454
　　distances 455
　pollination by hand 454
　preserving 431
　propagation 455
　pruning 428, 455, *455*
　recommended cultivars 455
　rootstocks 454
　routine care 455
　site 454
　soil for 454
　staking 454
　storing 431
　thinning blossom 455
　thinning fruit 455
　training 455
　'Alfred' 455
　'Breda' 455
　'Delicot' 455
　'Early Moorpark' 455
　'Farmingdale' 455
　'Flavercot' 455
　'Hemskerk' 455, *455*
　'Moorpark' 455
　'New Large Early' 455
　'St Julien A' 454
　'Shipley's' 455
　'Tomcot' 455
　'Torinel' 454
Aquatics *see* Water plants
Aquilegia
　for cutting 181
　flowering time from seed 198
　fruit type 675
　seeds *675*
　self-sown seedlings 185
　in woodland garden *178*
　chrysantha, in mixed border
　　176
　discolor, suggestions for use
　　259
　flabellata
　　flowers 258
　　suggestions for use 259
　vulgaris, conditions tolerated
　　181
Arabis
　to attract insects 264
　diseases 646
　pruning 271
　procurrens 'Variegata', soil
　　type preferred 261
Arachis hypogaea see Peanuts
Aralia
　propagation, root cuttings 114
　soil type tolerated 97
　elata
　　architectural form 46
　　suggestions for use 61
　　'Aureovariegata'
　　　architectural form 95
　　　spliced side-veneer
　　　　grafting 119
Araucaria heterophylla,
　suggestions for use 59
Araujia 129
　semi-ripe cuttings 142
　sericifera, flowers 127
Arboretum 24

Arbours
  clematis on 138
  climbers on 126
  roses clothing 152–3, *152*
Arbutus
  fruit 56
  germination 115
  soil type required 99
  x *andrachnoides*
    seasonal interest 59
    suggestions for use 59
  menziesii
    seasonal interest 59
    soil preferred 65
  unedo
    seasonal interest 95
    spliced side-veneer
      grafting 119
Archegonium 195
Arches
  Bougainvillea on *124*
  in cottage gardens 178
  existing design and 31
  fruit cordons on *423*
  grape vines on 422
  growing fruit on 422
  of living willow 87
  roses on *152*
    suitable varieties 155
    training 164
  rustic 604
    uses 584
  of trees over walkway 58, *58*
Architectural plants *16*
  annuals 210–11, 213
  biennials 210–11, 213
  bulbs 231
  designing with 46
  as focal points 309
  herbs 405
  indoors 354
  perennials 179, 181
  shrubs 95
Archontophoenix alexandrae 55
Arctostaphylos
  propagation, semi-ripe
    cuttings 113
  soil type required 99, 257,
    325
  alpina, soil type required 260
  uva-ursi, conditions tolerated
    95
Arctotis
  stem tip cuttings 202
  venusta, suggestions for use
    213
Ardisia
  conditions preferred 95
  japonica, seasonal interest 95
Areca palm *see Dypsis lutescens*
Arenaria
  montana
    propagation
      division 275
      "Irishman's" cuttings
        275
    soil type preferred 261
  purpurascens
    "Irishman's" cuttings 275
    suggestions for use 259
Areoles 338
Argemone mexicana, soil type
  preferred 216
Argyranthemum
  in containers 319
  in mixed border 177
  overwintering 335
  propagation
    stem tip cuttings 202
    treating as biennials 217
  standards 326
  suggestions for use 309
  frutescens (syn. *Chry-
    santhemum frutescens*), in
    containers *386*
Argyreia 129
Argyroderma, division of
  rootstock 350
Arion 644

Arisaema, conditions preferred
  231
Arisarum proboscideum, as
  ground cover 180
Aristolochia
  propagation, semi-ripe
    cuttings 142
  pruning 135, 137
  littoralis (syn. *A. elegans*) 129
  macrophylla (syn. *A. durior*),
    soil type tolerated 131
Armadillidium spp. 644
Armeria
  soil type preferred 184, 325
  suggestions for use 257
  juniperifolia
    propagation, rosette
      cuttings 274
    soil type preferred 261
    suggestions for use 259
  maritima 151
    conditions tolerated 181
    habitat 254
Armillaria 661, 665
  control 618
  mellea 661, 665
Armoracia rusticana see
  Horseradish
Arnebia, root cuttings 203
Aronia
  division of suckers 118
  pruning 105
  arbutifolia, soil type tolerated
    97
Arris rails
  repair 602
  securing 602, *602*
Artemisia
  soil type required 325
  abrotanum 407
    benefit to other plants 405
    foliage 407
    harvesting 407
    in herb garden *412*
    propagation
      hardwood cuttings
        407
      mound layering 414
      semi-ripe heel
        cuttings 407
      softwood cuttings 407
    in scented preparations 407
    storing 407
    suggestions for use 407
  absinthium 407
    companion plants 405
    conditions tolerated 181
    decorative uses 407
    foliage 407
    harvesting 407
    in herb garden *412*
    propagation
      mound layering 414
      semi-ripe heel
        cuttings 407
      softwood cuttings 407
    pruning 407
    storing 407
    'Lambrook Silver' 407
  dracunculus see Tarragon,
    French
  dracunculus subsp.
    dracunculoides see
      Tarragon, Russian
  frigida 152
  glacialis, foliage 256
  lactiflora Guizhou Group,
    growth rate 181
  ludoviciana 152
  'Powis Castle', planting in
    container *185*
  schmidtiana 'Nana'
    division 275
    soil type preferred 261
Arthropodium, dividing 200
Artichokes
  globe *see* Globe artichokes
  Jerusalem *see* Jerusalem
    artichokes

Arum
  propagation
    division 201
    offsets 245
  seed germination 198
  suggestions for use 231
  italicum
    conditions preferred 231
    'Marmoratum'
      conditions tolerated
        231
      winter interest 181
Arum lily *see Zantedeschia
  aethiopica*
Aruncus dioicus
  for drying 181
  pests 645
  soil type tolerated 184
  'Kneiffii', suggestions for use
    285
Arundo donax
  suggestions for use 61
  'Macrophylla', growth rate 181
  'Variegata'
    architectural form 181
    suggestions for use 285
Asarina 213
  propagation, softwood
    cuttings 142
  suggestions for use 213
  procumbens, suggestions for
    use 258
Asarum europaeum
  conditions tolerated 181
  as ground cover 180
Asclepiadaceae (Asclepiads) 338
  Arabian, grafting 351
  grafting 350, 351
  latex produced 348
  Madagascan, grafting 351
Ash, *see Fraxinus*
Asparagus, vegetable 535, 539–40
  beds for 535, 539
  conditions preferred 539
  culinary uses 539
  cutting back 540, *540*
  diseases 540
    fungal 661
  F1 hybrids 539
  freezing 506
  harvesting 540, *540*
  intercropping 494
  life of plants 539
  male and female plants 539
  nitrogen requirement 504
  pests 540, 644
  planting out 539–40
  propagation
    planting crowns 539, *539*
    from seed 539
  protecting from frost 613
  recommended cultivars 539
  routine cultivation 540
  site 494, 539
  size of plants 539
  soil preparation for 539
  soil types tolerated 539
  spacing 539, *539*
  storing 540
  weeding 540
  'Backlim' 539
  'Cito' 539
  'Connover's Colossal' 539
  'Dariana' F1 539
  'Franklim' F1 539
  'Gijnlim' 539
  'Grolim' 539
  'Jersey Knight' improved F1
    539
  'Lucullus' 539
  'Pacific' F1 539
Asparagus
  greenhouse conditions
    required 361
  propagation, shoot-axil buds
    635
  densiflorus 'Sprengeri'
    suggestions for use 366
    in terrarium *366*, *374*

Asparagus (*cont.*)
  officinalis see Asparagus,
    vegetable
Asparagus beetle *644*
  control 644
  damage done by 644
Aspect, effect on soil temperature
  607
Asperula
  odorata see Galium odoratum
  suberosa, suggestions for use
    259
Asphalt
  for drives and paths 593
  edging 593
  laying 593
Asphodeline lutea, soil type
  preferred 184
Aspidistra
  conditions preferred indoors
    361
  conditions tolerated 355
  greenhouse conditions
    required 361
  propagation, rootstock 378
Asplenium
  conditions preferred indoors
    361
  conditions tolerated 181
  in winter 194
  bulbiferum, propagation *194*,
    195
  nidus
    in bottle garden *367*
    suggestions for use 366
  scolopendrium, in containers
    319
Astelis chathamica
  suggestions for use 61
Aster
  to attract insects 178, 181
  basal cuttings 202
  dividing 200, 201
  flowering time from seed 198
  in mixed border 177
  in naturalistic setting 178
  pests 657
  planting depth *184*
  staking *192*
  stopping *191*
  thinning 191
  albescens, division of suckers
    118
  amellus, pest resistance 657
  dahlias 235, *235*
  divaricatus, flowers 179
  novae-angliae
    pest resistance 657
    'Harrington's Pink' *201*
  novi-belgii
    diseases 193
    pests 657
    seasonal interest 50
  x *pringlei* 'Monte Cassino'
    175
    dividing *183*
Asteranthera 129
  propagation
    self layering 145
    semi-ripe cuttings 142
  suggestions for use 129
  ovata
    conditions tolerated 129
    soil type required 131, 325
Astilbe
  in border *174*
  in border of mixed textures
    175
  as companion plant 186
  conditions preferred 284
  in containers *315*, 319
  dividing 201
  for drying 181
  in island bed *175*
  soil type tolerated 184
  x *arendsii*, suggestions for use
    285
  chinensis, suggestions for use
    285

Astilbe (*cont.*)
  simplicifolia
    conditions preferred 181
    suggestions for use 285
Astilboides tabularis, suggestions
  for use 285
Astrantia
  for cutting 181
  dividing 201
  flowering time from seed 198
  major, conditions preferred
    181
Astrophytum
  flat grafting 351
  myriostigma *342*
    flowers 342
    suggestions for use 342
  ornatum, suggestions for use
    342
Asyneuma, softwood cuttings 273
Athelia rolfsii (syn. *Corticium
  rolfsii*) 654
Athyrium
  in containers 319
  in winter 194
  niponicum var. *pictum*, as
    companion plant 186
Atmospheric conditions,
  problems caused by 639
Atriplex halimus, hardwood
  cuttings 114
Aubergines *522*, 528–9, *529*
  conditions required 528
  in crop rotation 498
  culinary uses 528
  diseases 529
  feeding 529
  freezing 506
  fruits 528
  growing below wall 493
  growing in containers 318, 501
  growing under cover 529
  harvesting 506, 529, *529*
  mulching 529
  nitrogen requirement 504, 528
  origins 522
  pests 529
  pinching out 528–9
  planting out 528
  potting up 529
  pricking out 528
  pruning 529
  recommended cultivars 528
  ripening under cover 505
  routine cultivation 529
  size of plant 528
  soil type required 528
  sowing 528
  spacing 528
  staking 529
  storing 506, 529
  thinning fruits 529
  watering 529
  'Black Beauty' F1 528
  'Black Enorma' 528
  'Bonica' 528
  'Ghost Buster' F1 528
  'Mohican' F1 528
  'Moneymaker' 528
  'Rosanna' F1 528
Aubrieta
  to attract insects 264
  conditions tolerated 259
  propagation
    greenwood cuttings 273
    softwood cuttings 273
  pruning 271
  soil type tolerated 261
  suggestions for use 255
  x *cultorum*
    'Argenteovariegata' *273*
  deltoidea
    suggestions for use 259
Aucuba
  conditions preferred 95
  conditions tolerated 95
  propagation
    hardwood cuttings 114
    layering 116

Aucuba (cont.)
semi-ripe cuttings with heel 113
pruning 107
soil type tolerated 97
japonica
soil type tolerated 99
'Variegata', in hydroculture display *375*
Auger 622
Auricula primroses *see Primula auricula*
Aurinia
greenwood cuttings 273
pruning 271
saxatilis
conditions tolerated 259
suggestions for use 259
'Citrina', suggestions for use 259
Austrocactus, flat grafting 351
Austrocedrus, semi-ripe cuttings 79
Austrocylindropuntia subulata (syn. *Opuntia exaltata*), conditions tolerated 342
Autovent openers 575, *575*
Autumn
climbers for colour in 128, *128*
colour in 50, *51*
mixed plantings for 228
perennials for 177, 178
shrubs for interest in 91, 95
trees for interest in 57
Autumn crocus *see Colchicum autumnale*
Auxins 632
Avena sterilis, for drying 213
Avenues
formal 58, *58*
informal 58, *58*
paired containers marking *308*, 309
trees for 58
Avocado pears 479, 485–6
choosing plants 486
conditions tolerated 485
diseases 486
feeding 486
fruit 485
ripe *486*
growing under cover 486
feeding 486
pots for 486
watering 486
mulching 486
pests 486
pollination 486
propagation
grafting 486
from seed 486, *486*, 434
protecting from wind 485
pruning 486
recommended cultivars 485
routine care 486
site 485
soil preferred 485
soils tolerated 485–6
training 486
tree *486*
tree size 485
types 485
watering 486
'Ettinger' 485
'Fuerte' 485
'Hass' 485
'Lula' 485, *485*
'Nabal' 485
'Pollock' 485
'Zutano' 485
Axonopus
for lawn 388
sowing rate 394
Azalea *see Rhododendron*
Azalea gall *652*
symptoms and control 652
Azara
semi-ripe cuttings with heel 113
suggestions for use 95

Azolla
control 673
filiculoides (syn. *A. caroliniana*) 285
dangers of 298
propagation, by plantlets 303
suggestions for use 331
value in water garden 284
Azorella trifurcata, rosette cuttings 274
Aztekium, flat grafting 351

B

Babiana, suggestions for use 231
Back-bulbs (orchid), potting up 369
Backfilling around pond or watercourse 289, *289*
Bacopa monnieri, cuttings 302
Bacteria
beneficial 617
colonizing plants 653
Bacterial canker
control 448
plants affected by 426
symptoms and control 665
Bacterial controls 645
Bacterial diseases 639
affecting bulbs 663
affecting leaves 648, 649, 651
affecting roots and tubers 661, 662
affecting stems 655
affecting whole plant 664, 665
as biological pest control 642, 645
Bacterial leaf spots (blotches) *648*
symptoms and control 648
Bacterial rotting of potatoes 662
symptoms and control 662
Badgers, damage caused 667
Bags
carrying 562, *562*
plastic 562
Bahia grass *see Paspalum notatum*
Balconies
annuals to use vertical space 212
containers on 312–13, *312*, *313*
choosing 312
flooring 312
herbs in containers 405
perennials in containers 179
planting on 313
privacy on 313, *313*
problems 312
railings 312
safety 312
screens on *312*, 313, *313*
watering plants on 312
Baldellia ranunculoides, propagation, by plantlets 303
Ballast, definition 591
Ballota pseudodictamnus, soil type preferred 261
Bamboo canes *see* Canes
Bamboo palm *see Chamaedorea selfrizii*
Bamboo spider mite 96
Bamboos 96
in container *307*, 319
cultivation 96
diseases 96
dividing rhizomes 96, *96*, 201
as hedge 85
maturity, time required 96
as partition *92*
pests 96

Bamboos (cont.)
pollution-absorbing 358
pruning 96
restricting growth 96, *96*
suggestions for use 96, 318
texture 48
thinning 96, *96*
Bananas 60–1, *60*
fruit type 675
germination 379
winter protection *61*
Banks
climbers on 124, 127
dwarf conifers for 62
ground cover on 93, 101
lawn on 386
retaining walls on 598
roses on 151, 153
Banksia
conditions preferred 95
serrata, soil preferred 66
Baptisia, seed germination 198
Barbarea verna see Land cress
Bark
for colour, trees for 56, 57, *57*
formation *674*
fungal disease 654
growing orchids on 369, *369*
ornamental
shrubs for 94
winter trees for 59
on poles for rustic work 604
Bark (organic material)
chippings
as mulch 100, 101, *133*, 159, *334*
on plastic 670
as plunge material 365
coarse, as mulch 626
in cuttings compost 565
mulching with 323, 503
as peat alternative 257
in potting composts 322, *322*
as protection for plants in store *193*
pulverized as mulch *98*
as soil additive 621
Bark-ringing 430, 437, *437*
danger to stone fruits 370
Barn cloche *see* Cloches
Barrels *see* Containers
Basal cuttings *see* Cuttings, basal
Basal-whip grafting 636
Base-dressing 503
Basella alba see Ceylon spinach
Basil 409, *409*
conditions required 409
culinary uses 404, 409, 415
foliage 409
freeze-drying 415
as gap filler in border 405
harvesting 409
in herb garden *412*
planting out 414
preserving in oil 415
pricking out 414
propagation from seed 409, 414
related species 409
storing 409
variants 409
Baskets 562
bulb *565*
Bassia (syn. *Kochia*) *scoparia* f. *trichophylla*
architectural plant 213
foliage 209
Bathrooms, plants for 355
Batter board 598
Batteries, rechargeable 556
Bay *see Laurus nobilis*
Bay sucker 647
Beams, joints for 604, *604*
Bean seed fly 666
symptoms and control 666
Bean sprouts, beans suitable for 531, 532
Beans
bird damage 657

Beans (cont.)
climbing, positioning 493
damage caused by mice, rats and voles 662
diseases 654, 661
dwarf, starting under cloches 505
effect of daylength on 495
growing in containers 318, 328
nitrogen requirement 504
pests 645, 646, 661
seed viability 216
sowing 500
sowing depth 499
watering, critical periods 502
Beans, broad 530, 534, *534*
bird damage 659
conditions required 534
conditions tolerated 534
in crop rotation 498
culinary uses 534
diseases 534, 649, 661
earthing up 534
freezing 506
germination 534
growing in containers *501*
harvesting 534
nitrogen requirement 534
overwintering 534
pests 534
pinching out 534, *534*
plant size 534
pods 534
protecting 534
recommended cultivars 534
rotation 534
routine cultivation 534
site 534
sowing 534
spacing 534
storing 534
supporting 534
watering 534
'Aquadulce Claudia' 534
'Express' 534
'Imperial Green Longpod' 534
'Jubilee Hysor' 534
'Masterpiece Green Longpod' 534
'Medes' 534
'The Sutton' 534
'Witkiem Manita' 533
Beans, dolichos 531, *531*
as bean sprouts 531
conditions required 531
in crop rotation 498
culinary uses 531
daylength requirement 531
diseases 531
feeding 531
freezing 506
growing under cover 531
harvesting 531
nitrogen requirement 531
pests 531
pinching out 531
pollination 531
propagation
from seed 531
softwood cuttings 531
protecting 531
routine cultivation 531
size of plants 531
soil for 531
spacing 531
storing 531
supporting 531
training 531
transplanting 531
watering 531
Beans, French 530, 532–3
conditions preferred 532
conditions required 532
in crop rotation 498
culinary uses 532
diseases 533, 661
dried *530*
drying *533*

Beans, French (cont.)
earthing up 533, *533*
freezing 506
growing under cover 533
harvesting 533
mulching 533
nitrogen requirement 533
pests 533, 666
pods 532
pre-germinating *533*
protecting 533
recommended cultivars 533
rotation 533
routine cultivation 53
seed dressing 533
size of plants 532
soil preparation for 532
sowing 533
spacing 533
storing 533
supporting 533
toxins in 532
watering 533
'Barletta Lingua-de-Fuoco' 533
'Canadian Wonder' 533
'Cantare' 533
'Cobra' 533
'Cropper Teepee' 533
'Delinel' 533
'Dutch Brown' 533
'Eva' 533
'Goldukat' 533
'Hunter' 533
'Kingston Gold' 533
'Purple Queen' 533
'Purple Tepee' 533
'Safari' 533
'Sonesta' F1 533
'Sprite' 533
'Sultana' 533
'Tendergrass' 533
Beans, kidney *see* Beans, French
Beans, Lima 532, *532*
as bean sprouts 532
conditions required 532
in crop rotation 498
culinary uses 532
daylength requirement 532
diseases 532
freezing 506
harvesting 532
nitrogen requirement 532
pests 532
plant types 532
planting 532
protecting 532
recommended cultivars 532
routine cultivation 532
size of plants 532
soil type preferred 532
sowing 532
storing 532
'Christmas Pole' 532
'Fordhook 242' 532
'Henderson' 532
'King of Garden Pole' 532
Beans, runner, *see* Beans, scarlet runner
Beans, scarlet runner 530, 531–2, *531*
conditions required 531
converting climbing form to bushes 532
in crop rotation 498
culinary uses 531
diseases 532
effect of frost on 607
flowers 531
freezing 506
germination 532
growing herbs with *495*
harvesting 532
mulching *502*
nitrogen requirement 531
pests 532, 557, 666
pollination 531
positioning *493*
protecting 532

Beans, scarlet runner (*cont.*)
recommended cultivars 531
rotation 531
routine cultivation 532
as screen 212
size of plants 531
soil preparation for 531
sowing 532
spacing 532
storing 532
supports for 531–2, *532*
watering 532, 614
'Celebration' 531
'Enorma' 531
'Gulliver' 531
'Lady Di' 531
'Liberty' 531
'Pickwick' 531
'Polestar' 531
'Red Rum' 531
'White Emergo' 531
'White Lady' 531
'Wisley Magic' 531
Beaumontia 129
propagation
semi-ripe cuttings 142
simple layering 145
pruning 135
grandiflora
for scent 128, 129
soil type required 131, 325
vigour 130
Beauty products, herbs used for 404
Bed system, growing vegetables in 494, 496–7
Bedding
formal schemes 210
semi-permanent *210*
Bedding mortar 591
mixes for 586
Bedding plants
annuals and tender perennials *208*
buying 221, *221*
diseases 654, 661
effect of frost on 607
mixing with bulbs 328
planting to design 221, *221*
on roof garden 313
spacing 45
Bedeguar galls 652
Beds
for acid-loving perennials 185
alpine
outdoors 255
renovating *271*
routine care 270–1
top-dressing 270, *270*
in alpine house 277, *277*, 278–9
bench, preparing 367, *367*
cartwheel, herbs in *405*, 406
colour schemes 176–7
in conservatory 357, *357*
preparing 367
containers in 309
cultivation 497
deep 497
designing 174–8
formal bulbs in 227, *227*
in greenhouse, preparing 367
height of plants 175
herbs in 405
indoor, for cacti 341, *341*
island *175*
herbaceous 173
mixed 173
positioning plants 174
shrubs in 92
in lawn 387
outdoors, planting cacti in *343*
perennials planted in groups *174*, 175–6
plunge, bulbs in 241, *241*
in pond planting 297–8
raised
advantages of 22, *23*, 497, 611, *611*

Beds, raised (*cont.*)
for alpines 255, 269, 278–9
watering 270
alpines for 257
brick 599, *599*
built of sawn logs 599
built of sleepers 599, *599*
for bulbs 230
care 243
for cacti and succulents 340
construction *343*
planting 343
circular 599
concrete block 599
in conservatory 357, *357*
construction 185, 269
design 269
designing with 599
drainage 257
dwarf conifers for 62
as focal point 599
in greenhouse 359, 578
growing vegetables in 496, *496*
herbs in 405
linking 599
making *496*
materials for 269, 599, *599*
natural stone 599
for perennials 173, 185
planting 269
rock plants for 257–8, *257*, 259
shrubs in 93
siting 269
soil in 599
succulents in, planting 343
uses 599
watering 599
rose
colour grouping 150
designing 150
edging 150
terraced 152
underplanting 150
shapes 174
size 175
sloping, advantages of 611
terraced, for roses 152
types 497
in vegetable garden *494*
weeding 191
Beech *see* Fagus
Beech leaf-mining weevil 647
Bees
attracting 22, 178
flowers for 101
leaf-cutting 645, *645*
plants attracting *20*, 172
wild flowers for 401, *401*
Beetles
beneficial *617*
control 504, 643, 668
ground, benefits of 641
Beetroot 542, *542*
bolt-resistant cultivars 542
bolting 542
conditions preferred 542
in crop rotation 498
culinary uses 542
diseases 542
edible parts 542
feeding 542
freezing 506
germination 542
growing in containers 501
harvesting 542, *542*
mineral deficiencies 662
nitrogen requirement 504, 542
pests 542
recommended cultivars 542
roots
colours 542
shapes 542
routine cultivation 542
seed 542
site 542
size of plants 542
soil preparation 542

Beetroot (*cont.*)
sowing 542
spacing 542
storing 506, 542
successional sowings 542
thinning seedlings 542, *542*
watering 542
critical periods 502
'Albina Vereduna' 542
'Alto' F1 542
'Bolthardy' 542
'Bull's Blood' 542
'Burpee's Golden' 542
'Cheltenham Green Top' 542
'Chioggia' 542
'Forono' 542
'Pablo' F1 542
'Pronto' 542
'Red Ace' F1 542
'Regala' 542
'Solo' F1 542
'Wodan' F1 542
Begonia
buying seedlings 216
conditions preferred 355
in container grouping *315*
flower sexuality *676*
germination 219, 630
greenhouse conditions required 361
in indoor plant group *372*
lifting after bedding 223
in mixed border 210
overwintering 230
pests 660, 666
propagation
leaf cuttings *633*
leaf sections 381–2, *382*
sowing 218
in windowbox 212, *328*
fibrous-rooted
foliage 209
from seed 379
natalensis, propagation, division of offsets 349
Panorama Series, suggestions for use 213
peltata, leaf cuttings 347
rex
conditions preferred 355
conditions required 364
greenhouse conditions required 361
leaf sections *382*
Rex Group
in containers 319
leaf cuttings 381
rhizomatous, leaf cuttings 381
semperflorens, as pot plants 213
sheperdii, propagation, division of offsets 349
'Tiger Paws', suggestions for use 366
tuberous
in containers 319
propagation 382, 635
basal cuttings 382, *382*
division of tubers 382, *382*
from seed 379
storing 382, *382*
venosa, leaf cuttings 347
Belamcanda chinensis, conditions preferred 231
"Belgian" blocks 590
Bell peppers *see* Peppers, sweet
Bellevalia
resting 240
suggestions for use 231
Bellflower *see* Campanula
Bellflower, clustered, *see* Campanula glomerata
Bellis
seasonal display 210
perennis
in containers 319
control 400, 672, 673

Bellis perennis (*cont.*)
flowers 209
in formal bedding 210
in mixed border *422*
suggestions for use 178, 308, 315
in turf 392
Pomponette Series, suggestions for use 315
Bench beds, preparing 367, *367*
Benches, cleaning 637
Bendiocarb 644, 659, 666, 668
Benlate 249
Bent *see* Agrostis
Bentomat 295
Bentonite 295
Berberidopsis 129
semi-ripe cuttings 142
corallina
conditions tolerated 129
soil type required 131, 325
Berberis 47
conditions tolerated 95
propagation
heel cuttings 113
mallet cuttings 113
semi-ripe cuttings with heel 113
seed stratification 629
soil type tolerated 97
buxifolia, division of suckers 118
darwinii
as hedge 85
pruning 107
soil type tolerated 99
empetrifolia, soil type preferred 97
x *stenophylla* 'Corallina Compacta' 259
temolaica, seasonal interest 95
thunbergii, as hedge 84, 85
Berchemia, semi-ripe cuttings 142
Bergamot *see* Monarda didyma
Bergenia
in containers 319
planting in groups 176
propagation, division 201
soil type tolerated 185
suggestions for use 175, 179, 285, 316
'Abendglut', as ground cover 180
'Ballawley', winter interest 181
cordifolia
as ground cover 180
winter interest 181
cultivars in container *193*
purpurascens
in containers 179
foliage 175
suggestions for use 179
Bergerocactus
stem cuttings 348
emoryi, flowers 342
Berkheya, soil type tolerated 185
Bermuda grass *see* Cynodon
Berries
fruits producing 675
ornamental trees for 56–7
problems 658–9
shrubs for 94
Beschorneria
conditions preferred 95
yuccoides 339
hardiness 339
suggestions for use 61
Besoms 559, *559*
Beta vulgaris
'Bright Lights', stalks 209
'Bright Yellow', stalks 209
subsp. *cicla* var. *flavescens* see Spinach beet; Swiss chard
'Ruby Chard', stalks 209
subsp. *vulgaris* see Beetroot
Betula
bark colour 48, 316

Betula (*cont.*)
diseases 655
flowers, unisexual 676
perennials with 178
propagation
softwood cuttings 79
spliced side grafting 82
pruning 71
renovating 74
seed germination 81
silver, suggestions for use 54
soil type indicated by 617
albosinensis
var. *septentrionalis*
seasonal interest 59
suggestions for use 59, 316
dahurica seasonal interest 59
ermanii
seasonal interest 59
suggestions for use 59
'Jermyns'
seasonal interest 59
suggestions for use 59
nana 259
pendula
bark 50
conditions tolerated 67
grouping 56
seasonal interest 59
soil preferred 66
suggestions for use 59
'Dalecarlica', suggestions for use 59
pubescens, conditions tolerated 67
utilis var. *jacquemontii*
bark and stem interest 56, 57, *57*
seasonal interest 59
suggestions for use 59
Biarum, suggestions for use 231
Bidens
in containers 319
ferulifolia, suggestions for use 213
Biennials 208–23
architectural 210–11, 213
for balconies 313
characteristics 674
clearing at end of season 223
climbing 211–12
in cold greenhouse 360
collecting seed from 223, *223*
in containers
plants suitable for 213, 315, 319
seasonal display 310, 327
controlling self-seeding 222
for cut flowers 213, 222
dead-heading 223, *223*
definition 208
designing with 208–12
diseases 223
for dried flowers 213, 222
for dry shade 213
for exposed sites 213
F1 hybrids from seed 379
feeding 222
as fillers 211
first-year growth *220*
in formal bedding 210
for ground cover 211
half-hardy, sowing 217
hardy, sowing 216–17
herbs, propagation from seed 414
in mixed borders *210*, 210–11
for moist shade 213
pests 223
planter's guide 213
propagation
from seed 216–20
in open ground 217–18
self-seeding 210, 218, 223
routine care 222–3
for sandy soil 216
for scent 213

Biennials (cont.)
seed
buying 216
viability 216
seedlings, buying 216, 216
suggestions for use 208–12
supporting 222
thinning 218, 218
trailing 211–12, 213
weeding 222
Bifenthrin 644, 645, 646, 647, 648, 652, 654, 656, 657, 658, 659, 661, 668
Big bud mites 655
symptoms and control 655
Bignonia
propagation, softwood cuttings 142
pruning 135
capreolata, climbing method 124
Billardiera
semi-ripe cuttings 142
soil type required 131, 325
longiflora
fruit 127
pruning 135
Billbergia
conditions preferred indoors 361
as pot plant 362
nutans, propagation 363
Bindweed
field *see* Convolvulus
hedge *see* Calystegia sepium
Bins, compost 562
leaf mould 628, 628
worm compost 628, 628
Biodiversity, and lawns 387
Biological control 357, 504, 583, 642–3, 642
Birch, *see* Betula
Birch leaf-mining sawfly 647
Birds 271
attracting 15, 22, 126, 295, 641
benefits of 641
control 645, 657
damage caused 645, 657, 657, 659, 659, 667
deterring 504, 642
feeders and bird tables 22
food for 20, 22
habitats for 22, 284
plants attracting 22, 173
protecting alpines from 264
protecting fruit from 421, 422, 427, 427, 448, 468
protecting vegetables from 504
protection from netting for 564
repelling 642
water for 22
Bisexual plants 676, 676
Bitter pit 640, 658
symptoms and control 658
Bittercress *see* Cardamine
Bittercress, hairy *see* Cardamine hirsuta
Black frost 607
Black spot 156, 160, 642
natural prevention for 159
Blackberries 468, 470–2
choosing healthy plants 470, 470
conditions required 470
diseases 427, 471, 653
freezing 431
harvesting 431, 471
in fedges 126
pests 471, 658
plant type 419, 468
planting 470
times for 470
preserving 431
propagation
layering 434
leaf-bud cuttings 434, 472, 472
tip layering 471, 472, 631, 631

Blackberries (cont.)
pruning
after fruiting 471, 471
after planting 470
frost-damaged stems 471, 471
rampant growth 471
recommended cultivars 471
routine care 471
site 470
preparation 470
spacing 470
storing 471
supporting 470
training 471, 471
alternate bay 471, 471
fan 471, 471
rope 471, 471
weaving 471, 471
'Ashton Cross' 471
'Bedford Giant' 471, 471
'Fantasia' 471
'Helen' 471
'Himalaya Giant' 471
'Loch Ness' 471
'Merton Early', in large fruit garden 421
'Merton Thornless' 471
'Oregon Thornless' 471
'Sylvan' 471
'Thornfree' 471
thornless, vigour 470
'Waldo' 471
Blackbirds
damage caused
to flowers 657
to fruit, berries, and seeds 659, 659
Blackcurrant gall midge 652
Blackcurrants *see* Currants, black
Blackfly *see* Aphids
Blackleg
on cuttings 664
symptoms and control 664
on potatoes 664
symptoms and control 664
Blackthorn *see* Prunus spinosa
Blanching
chicory 517, 517
dandelion 521, 521
endives 516, 517
Blaniulus guttatus 644
Blanket, propagating 580
Blanketweed control 300, 300, 673
Blechnum
conditions required 194
in containers 319
in island bed 173
chilense in hanging box 365
suggestions for use 61
Blennocampa phyllocolpa 652
Blessed Mary's thistle *see* Silybum marianum
Bletilla
suggestions for use 368
temperature required 368
Blight
chrysanthemum petal 657
symptoms and control 657
potato 649
symptoms and control 649
seedling, symptoms and control 654
tomato 649
symptoms and control 649, 658, 658
Blind shoots on roses 160, 160
Blinds
for conservatory 357, 357
for greenhouse 576, 576
Block splitters 590
Blocks
concrete, raised beds of 599
patterns 597
pre-cast concrete 596
rock-faced concrete 596
screenwall, using 505
smooth 596

Blood, dried 503
in cuttings compost 565
Blood, fish, and bone 503, 624
amount required compared to other fertilizers 624
for fruit trees 426
nutrient content 624
Bloomeria crocea, conditions preferred 231
Blossfeldia, flat grafting 351
Blossom end rot 658
symptoms and control 658
Blossom wilt 656
symptoms and control 656
Blowers, leaf 559, 559
Blue Douglas fir, *see* Pseudotsuga menziesii var. glauca
Blue grass *see* Poa
Blue hesper *see* Brahea armata
Blue mould on citrus, symptoms and control 658
Bluebell *see* Hyacinthoides
Bluebell, English *see* Hyacinthoides non-scriptus
Blueberries 468
autumn colour 478
bush 478
chilling requirement 478
compost for 478
conditions required 478
conditions tolerated 478
in containers 319, 478
cropping 478
feeding 478
flavour 478
freezing 431
harvesting 478
height 478
mulching 478
plant type 468
planting 478
pollination 478
propagation
hardwood cuttings 434
softwood cuttings 434, 478, 478
pruning 428, 478, 478
recommended cultivars 478
routine care 478
site 478
preparation 478
soil type required 424, 478
spacing 478
storing 478
training 478
'Berkeley' 478
'Bluecrop' 478
'Bluetta' 478, 478
'Chandler' 478
'Coville' 478
'Goldtraube 71' 478
'Grover' 478
'Herbert' 478
highbush 478
'Ivanhoe' 478
'Jersey' 478
rabbit-eye 478
Bog garden 283, 284, 611, 611
creating 298
beside pond 295, 295
irises for 182
planting 298, 298
Bog plants 284, 285
conditions tolerated 623
planting 298, 298
Bolax gummifera
cuttings 274
suggestions for use 259
Bomarea
andimarcana, soil type tolerated 131
caldasii 129
suggestions for use 129
Bone meal 650
nutrient content 624
Bongardia
resting 240
chrysogonum, suggestions for use 231

Bonsai hydroculture 375
Borage (herb) *see* Borago officinalis
Borago officinalis 407
companion plants 405
conditions tolerated 213
culinary uses 404, 407
dead-heading 413
flowers 405, 407
foliage 407
freezing flowers in ice 415, 415
as gap filler in border 405
as green manure 625
harvesting 407
in herb garden 412
propagation
from seed 407, 414
self-seeding 218, 407
sowing 217
storing 407
'Alba' 407
Borax 662
Bordeaux mixture 648, 649, 668
Borders
annual 208–11, 209
colour effects 208
form and texture 208–9
grouping plants 209
marking out 217, 218
bulbs in, care 242–3
colour schemes 176–7
in conservatory, preparing 367
containers in 309
designing 174–8
size and scale 45
existing design and 32
in greenhouse 570, 578
preparing 578
height of plants 175
herbaceous 24, 44, 172, 173
formal 173
herbs in 405
hot 25, 49
mixed 24, 92, 172, 173, 174, 186, 210
annuals in 210–11, 210
bulbs in 226
fruit in 422
roses for 155
seasonal interest 177–8
specimen tree in 56
perennials planted in groups 174, 175–6
positioning plants 174–5
of self-supporting plants 25
shapes 174
shrub 92
size 175
weeding 191
Boron 484, 637
deficiency, symptoms and control 617, 654, 654, 662
plant requirements 624
Boronia, semi-ripe cuttings with heel 113
Boston fern *see* Nephrolepis exalta 'Bostoniensis'
Botany, basic 674–6
Botrytis (grey mould) 251, 653, 656
causes 610
conditions encouraging 576
control 120, 462, 653, 656
damage caused by 646
plants affected by 646
symptoms 653, 656, 658, 658
allii 663
cinerea 333, 653, 656, 657
elliptica 649
fabae 649
galanthina 653, 656
paeoniae 665
tulipae 327, 649, 656
Bottle gardens 358
care 373–4
condensation 373
planting 367, 367
tools for 367

Bougainvillea
on archways 124
climbing method 124, 130
conditions preferred indoors 361
in containers 128, 319
greenhouse conditions required 361
indoors 354
propagation
hardwood cuttings 143
semi-ripe cuttings 142
softwood cuttings 380
pruning 135, 136, 136, 376
soil type preferred 325
suggestions for use 129, 318
vigour 130
'Miss Manila' 135
Boundaries
adjoining highways, laws on 602
containers marking 308
evergreen ground cover on 101
existing design and 31
fences 600
walls 596
Bouvardia, conditions preferred 95
Bow saw *see* Saws
Bowl gardens for succulents 341
Bowles' mint *see* Mentha x villosa var. alopecuroides
Bowling green 389
mowing 395
Bowls *see* Containers
Box *see* Buxus
Box, Christmas *see* Sarcococca confusa
Box sucker 647
Boysenberries 468, 470, 471
Braces, corner 604
Brachydesmus 644
Brachyglottis
conditions preferred 95
semi-ripe cuttings 113
Brachyscome
in containers 319
iberidifolia
soil type preferred 216
suggestions for use 213
Bracken
protecting plants with 612, 613
protecting trees and shrubs with 612
Bradley Bermuda grass *see* Cynodon incompletus var. hirsutus
Bradysia spp. 666
Brahea armata, hardiness 60
Bramble *see* Rubus fruticosus
Branches *see* Stems
Brassia
suggestions for use 368
temperature required 368
Brassica
juncea see Mustards, Oriental
napus see Salad rape
napus Napobrassica Group see Swedes
oleracea
Acephala Group see Kales
Botrytis Group see Cauliflowers
Capitata Group see Cabbages
as foliage plants 209
Gemmifera Group see Brussels sprouts
Gongylodes Group see Kohl rabi
Italica Group see Calabrese; Sprouting Broccoli
ornamental cultivars 319
Osaka Series 213
'Redbor' 209
'Tokyo' 213
rapa
var. *alboglabra* see Chinese broccoli

Brassica rapa (*cont.*)
  var. *chinensis see* Pak choi
  var. *nipposinica see*
    Mizuna greens
  var. *pekinensis see*
    Chinese cabbages
  var. *perviridis see*
    Komatsuna
  Rapifera Group *see* Turnip
    tops; Turnips
  Utilis Group *see* Broccoli
    raab
Brassicas 507–14
  alternating with lettuces *493*
  in crop rotation 498
  diseases 646, *646*, 649, 660
  freezing 506
  intercropping 494
  mineral deficiencies 652
  Oriental 513–14
    bolting 513
    conditions preferred 513
    conditions tolerated 513
    cultivation 513
    diseases 513
    harvesting 513
    as intercrop 513
    nitrogen requirements 513
    pests 513
    range of plants 513
    soil requirements 513
    sowing 513
    storing 513
    watering 513
    winter cropping under
      cover 505
  pests 498, 504, 644, 645, 660
  sowing depth 499
  storing 506
  temperature requirements 495
  watering critical periods 502
  Western 507–12
    base-dressing 507
    collared seedlings *507*
    conditions preferred 507
    conditions required 507
    conditions tolerated 507
    cultivated as annuals 507
    cultivated as biennials 507
    cultivation 507
    diseases 507
    feeding 507
    intercropping 507
    manuring, problems of 507
    mulching 507
    nitrogen requirements 507
    pests 507
    planting 507
    range of plants 507
    rotation 507
    site 507
    soil type required 507
    sowing 507
      in modules 507
    spacing 507
    supporting 507
    top-heavy
      planting 507
      supporting 507
    watering 507
  winter intercropping 494
Bremia 646
Bricks
  bonding patterns 597, *597*
  buying 589
  choosing 589
  cutting 590
  laying 589, *589*
    patterns for *589*
  paths of 593, *593*
    construction 593
  paving, laying 589, *589*
  raised beds of 497, 599, *599*
  retaining walls of,
    constructing 598, *598*
  types 589
    cored *589*
    engineering *589*, 596
    facing *589*

Bricks, types (*cont.*)
    frogged *589*
    mottled engineering *596*
    smooth-textured *596*
    stock *589*
  for walls 596, *596*
Brickwork
  attaching beams to 604, *604*
  mortar mix for 586
  weeding 673
British Isles, influences on
  climate 606
Briza
  self-sown seedlings 222
  maxima
    for drying 213
    ornamental value 209
  minor, for drying 213
Broccoletti see Broccoli raab
Broccoli
  American *see* Calabrese
  Chinese *see* Chinese broccoli
  Italian *see* Calabrese
  sprouting *see* Sprouting
    broccoli
Broccoli raab 512, *512*
  conditions preferred 512
  culinary uses 512
  freezing 506
  harvesting 512
  nitrogen requirements 504,
    512
  size of plant 512
  sowing 512
  thinning 512
Brodiaea
  corm 227
  suggestions for use 230, 231
  laxa see Triteleia laxa
Brodifacoum 662
Bromelia balansae 362
Bromeliad trees 362
Bromeliads 362–3
  conditions preferred indoors
    361
  dividing rootstocks 363, *363*
  epiphytic
    displaying 362, *362*
    feeding 363
    mist-spraying 363
  feeding 363
  forms 354, 362
  in greenhouse 360
  greenhouse conditions
    required 361
  propagation 363, *363*
    offsets 363, *363*
    from seed 363, *363*
  routine care 363
  seed viability 363
  suitable for indoors *362*
  terrestrial
    growing 362–3
    temperature requirements
      362
  "urn" plants 363
  watering 363
Bronze fennel *see Foeniculum
  vulgare* 'Purpureum'
Broom *see Cytisus*; Genista
Browallia
  conditions preferred indoors
    361
  greenhouse conditions
    required 361
  from seed 379
Brown, Lancelot 'Capability' 56
Brown core, primula *661*
  symptoms and control 661
Brown heart 662
Brown rot, symptoms and control
  658, *658*
Brown scale 648
Brown tail moth caterpillar 647
Browntop bent *see Agrostis tenuis*
Brugmansia
  in containers 319, 324
  greenhouse conditions
    required 361

Brugmansia (*cont.*)
  standards 326
  suggestions for use 318
Brunfelsia
  in greenhouse 360
  greenhouse conditions
    required 361
  pinching out 376
  pauciflora 380
    softwood cuttings 380
Brunnera
  soil type tolerated 185
  macrophylla, conditions
    preferred 181
Brushwood cutters 554, 556, *556*
Brussels sprouts 507, 510–11
  base-dressing 510
  conditions tolerated 510
  in crop rotation 498
  culinary uses 510
  digging up 511
  disease-resistant 646
  diseases 511, 649, 660
  dwarf plant *510*
  earthing up *510*, 511
  F1 cultivars 510, *511*
  feeding 511
  foliage 209
  freezing 506
    varieties suitable for 511
  harvesting 511
  intercropping 511
  manuring, problems of 510
  nitrogen requirements 504, 510
  open-pollinated cultivars 510,
    511
  pests 511, 645, 660
  planting 507, 511
  recommended cultivars 511
  red 510
  removing leaves 511, *511*
  routine cultivation 511
  size of plant 510
  sowing 510
  spacing 511
  storing 511
  thinning out 510
  transplanting 510–11
  types 510
  watering 511
  'Bosworth' F1 511
  'Cascade' F1 511
  'Cromwell' F1 511
  'Diablo' F1 511
  'Montgomery' F1 511
  'Nelson' F1 511
  'Oliver' F1 511
  'Peer Gynt' F1 511
  'Romulus' F1 511
  'Wellington' F1 511
Brutting 489, *489*
Bryonia dioica 671
Bubble fountain *see* Fountains
Buckler-leaf sorrel 410
  in herb garden *412*
Bud eelworms
  control 647
  damage caused by 647, *647*
Bud-grafting
  chip-budding 83, *83*, 432, *432*
    fruit trees 432, *432*
    method 636, *636*
    time for 635
    trees suitable for 82
  double budding 446, *446*
  fruit trees 432–3, *432*, *433*
  roses 156, 166–7, *166*
  T-budding 433, *433*
    method 636, *636*
    time for 635
  tools for 167, *555*
Bud-stripping, protecting fruit
  from 427, *427*
Budding *see* Bud-grafting
Buddleja
  as food source for wildlife 22
  hardwood cuttings 114
  alternifolia
    pruning 106

Buddleja alternifolia (*cont.*)
    scent 95
    training as standard 109
  crispa
    suggestions for use 95
    as wall shrub 93
  davidii
    conditions tolerated 95
    pruning 104, 105, *105*
    soil type tolerated 99
  globosa, pruning 105
Budsticks for grafting 432, *432*
Builder's square *585*
Buildings
  clematis on 138
  climbers on 125
  existing design and 31
  trees near 63, 70
  wisteria on *47*
Bulb basket *565*
Bulb fibre compost 323
Bulb flies 663
Bulb frames 230
Bulb planters *238*, 239, 563, *563*
Bulb scale mites *652*
  symptoms and control 652
Bulb vegetables 535–41
  storing 506
  temperature requirements 495
Bulbils, propagation by 302, 634,
  634
  bulbs 245
  ferns *194*, 195
  indoor plants 379
Bulbine
  frutescens, conditions
    tolerated 342
  latifolia, conditions tolerated
    342
  mesembryanthemoides,
    conditions tolerated 342
Bulblets
  potting 243, 244
  propagation by 245, 634, *634*
    plants suitable for 245
Bulbocodium vernum,
  suggestions for use 231
Bulbs (bulbous plants) 226–51
  in alpine house 231, 258
  with alpines 229, *229*
  architectural 231
  for autumn colour 50
  autumn-flowering 228
    planting time 236
  blind, causes 244
  in borders, care 242–3
  breaking dormancy 607
  bulblets, potting 243, 244
  buying 228, 236, *236*
    responsible 228
  care after flowering 242
  characteristics 226, 227
  choosing 228, 236, *236*
  composts for 240, 323
  conditions preferred 231,
    236–7
  conditions required 226
  conditions tolerated 226, 231,
    237, 256
  conservation 228, 236
  in containers
    layered planting 327–8
    outdoors 229, *229*, 241
      care 243
    plants suitable for 316,
      319
    seasonal display 327–8
    for successional interest
      241
    under cover 230
  in cottage garden 227
  crop rotation for disease
    control 640
  for cut flowers 230, *230*, 231
  cutting, simple 250
  cutting down 242, *242*
  dead-heading 242, *242*
  definition 227
  designing with 226–31

Bulbs (*cont.*)
  diseases 244, 646, 656, 663,
    665
    bacterial 648
    fungal 648
  dormant in frames 277
  drainage for 237
  dry 236
  for dry shade 231
  drying 243, *243*
  dwarf, care 243
  early season 226
  effect of contact weedkillers
    on 650
  effect of high temperatures on
    650
  effect of low temperatures on
    650, 664
  for exposed sites 231
  feeding 242, 243, 244
  as fillers 210
  forced as house plant 355
  forcing 226, 231, 241, *241*
    care 244
    planting out after 244
  in formal bedding 227, *227*
  in frames, care 243
  in grass
    care 242
    dead-heading 242, *242*
    feeding 242
  in greenhouse 360
  ground cover with 180
  group planting 226
  growing with succulents
    339–40
  hydroculture 375
  lifting 226, 243, *243*
  for meadows 401
  mineral deficiency 650–1
  miniature
    alpines with 258
    habitats 254
  in mixed borders 173, 177,
    226, 227–8, *228*
  in mixed island beds 173
  mixing with bedding plants
    328
  for moist shade 231
  naturalized in grass *21*, *389*
  naturalizing 228, *228*, 229,
    238–9
    ground cover with 101
    planting 238–9, *238*, *239*
  non-scaly (tunicate) *634*
  offsets, planting 243
  origins 226, 228, 236
  pests 244, 660, 662, 663, 666
    damaging leaves 644, 646,
      647, 648, 651
  photosynthesis 242
  planter's guide 231
  planting 236–41
    depth 237, *237*
    in grass 238–9, *238*
    in the green 237
    in open 237, *237*
    in pots 240–1, *240*
    time for 237
  pot-grown 236
    planting 237
  in pots
    choosing pots for 240
    compost for 240
    planting 240, *240*
    in plunge bed 241, *241*
    plunging after flowering
      277
    renewing compost 244
    under cover 240
      care 244
      drying off 244
      feeding 244
      watering 244
  problems 244, 653, 663
  propagation 245–50, 634, *634*
    basal cuttings 250
    bulbils 245, *634*
    bulblets 245, 634, *634*

Bulbs, propagation (*cont.*)
chipping 249, *249*, 634, *634*
cutting into sections 249–50, *249*
cutting up with growing points 249, *249*
division 245, *245*
clumps 243, *243*
plants suitable for 245
offsets 245, *245*, 634, *634*
scaling 245, 248–9, *248*, 634, *634*
scooping 245, 250, *250*
scoring 250, *250*, 634, *634*
sectioning 249, *249*
from seed 246–7, *246*, 245
compost for 246
spacing 246
simple cutting 250
twin-scaling 634, *634*
protecting roots of tender climbers 125
in raised beds under cover 243
removing dead leaves 242
replanting after division 243
repotting 244, *244*
resting period, plants requiring 240
in rock garden 231, 255–6
rotation plan 640
routine care 242–4
scaly *634*
scented 229
seasons of interest 50, 226
seed
collecting 246
germination 247
harvesting 242, *242*
storing 246
seedlings
care 246
feeding 246
planting out 246, *247*
potting up 246, *247*
shy-flowering 244
sites 226
small, planting in grass *239*
soil preparation 237
soil types preferred 236–7
soil types tolerated 237
spacing 237
with specimen trees 228
spring-flowering 50, 227–8
staking 242, *242*
storage rots 663, *663*
storing 243, *243*
structure *674*
for successional display 316
suggestions for use 179, 226–31
summer-flowering 228
planting out 613
tender
from seed 247
seedlings 247
to grow beside wall 231
types 227, *227*, *634*
under cover 230–1
care 243
underplanting roses 151
for water gardens 229
watering 242
in the wild 228
in woodland 179
care 242
"woodland"
planting out *247*
from seed 246
soil for 237
Bullaces 447–50
Bullfinches, damage caused 657
Buphthalmum, dividing 201
Bupleurum
semi-ripe cuttings with heel 113
fruticosum, conditions tolerated 95
Bush basil *see Ocimum minimum*

Bush fruits *see* Fruit, soft
Busy Lizzie *see Impatiens*
Butia capitata, hardiness 60
Butomus
soil type tolerated 184
umbellatus
position in water garden 285
propagation
bulbils 302
division of rootstock 302
Butter beans *see* Beans, Lima
Buttercup *see Ranunculus*
Buttercup, creeping *see Ranunculus repens*
Butterflies
flowers for 101
plants attracting *20*, 172
wild flowers for 401, *401*
Butts, water 283, 357, 560, 561, 614–15
linking 28, 614, 615
positioning 614
siting 615
Butyl rubber
as pond liner 288
repairing 300, *300*
Buxus
in bedding scheme *210*
in container *321*
with ferns *195*
hedge for rosebeds 150
in knots and parterres *18*, 210
pests 647, 651
propagation
hardwood cuttings 114
semi-ripe cuttings 113
pruning 107
soil type tolerated 99
suggestions for use 307, 406
in windowbox *316*
balearica, in containers 319
microphylla, in containers 319
sempervirens
as architectural plants *16*
in containers 319
conditions preferred 95
as edging 405
as hedge 84
propagation, division of suckers 118
standards 326
suggestions for use 309, 311, 313, 314, 317
for topiary *18*, 76
'Suffruticosa', as hedge 84
Byturus tomentosus 658

C

Cabbage caterpillars *645*
control 640
symptoms and control 640, 645
Cabbage root fly
collar protection for brassicas *507*
deterring 504, 642
symptoms and control 660
Cabbages 509–11
architectural plants 213
collaring seedlings 509
colours 509
conditions required 509
in crop rotation 498
culinary uses 509
diseases 510, 649, 654, 660
earthing up 510
feeding 510
freezing 506
groups 509
growing in windowbox *495*

Cabbages (*cont.*)
harvesting 510, *510*
head
shape 509
size 509
nitrogen requirements 504, 509
pests 510, 640, 645, 660
plant size 509
planting out 509
protecting from cabbage root fly 509
recommended cultivars 509
routine cultivation 510
second crop on 510, *510*
soil type required 509
sowing 509
spacing 509
storing 510, *510*
transplanting seedlings 500
watering 510
winter sowing 498
'Advantage' F1 509
'Autoro' F1 509
autumn 509
'Castello' 509
'Celtic' F1 509
'Charmant' F1 509
Chinese *see* Chinese cabbages
'Derby Day' 509
'Duncan' F1 509
'Durham Early' 509
'Elisa' F1 509
'First Early Market' 509
'Greensleeves' 509
'Greyhound' 509
'Hidena' 509
'Hispi' F1 509
'January King Hardy Late Stock 3' 509
'Marabel' F1 509
'Marathon' F1 509
'Minicole' F1 509
'Myatt's Offenham Compacta' 509
ornamental 209, *504*
architectural role 211
colour combinations 48
in containers 319
in cottage garden *21*
foliage 209
'Pixie' 509
'Protovoy' F1 509
'Pyramid' F1 509
'Quickstep' 509
red
storing *506*
summer *509*
'Rodeo' 509
'Ruby Ball' 509
Savoy *507*, 509
'Shelta' F1 509
'Sherwood' F1 509
spring 509, *509*
feeding 510
harvesting 510, *510*
protecting 510
top-dressing 510
types to grow 509
'Tarvoy' F1 509
'Winnigstadt' 509
winter *507*
winter storing 506
Cabomba caroliniana cuttings 302
Cacoecimorpha pronubana 648
Cacti 336–51
in greenhouse 359
adapted to drought 609
buying 343, *343*
characteristics 338
choosing healthy plants 343, *343*
climate suited to 339, 606
collecting from the wild 228
composts for 323, 343, 344
conditions required 339, 341, 345, 364, 576
conditions tolerated 338, 339
in containers 318, 342
indoors 341

Cacti, in containers (*cont.*)
outdoors 340, *340*
planting 344, *344*
containers for 340
cross-pollination 347, *347*
day-flowering 342
in desert gardens 340, *340*
designing with 338–41
diseases 345
disorders 648
distinguishing from other succulents 338
dwarf, in containers outdoors 340
dying after flowering 339
environment 339, 345
epiphytic 338
conditions required 341
flowers 339
feeding 345
flowering 339, 342
flowers 338
form 338–9
in greenhouse display *360*
habit 338–9
habitats 338
half-hardy, conditions required 339
handling 341, *343*
in hanging baskets 341
plants suitable for 342
hybridizing 347, *347*
hydroculture 375
hygiene 345
indoor display 340–1
light requirement 341
night-flowering 342
outdoor display 339–40
pad sections 348
pests 345, 646, 648, 653
planting
in desert garden 343
in outdoor bed *343*
in raised bed 343
pots for 344
pricking out 346, *346*
propagation 346–51
cuttings 346
division 346
of offsets 349, *349*
of rootstock 350, *350*
grafting 346, 350–1, *350–1*
apical-wedge *350*, 351
flat 351, *351*
side 351, *351*
varieties suitable for 351
hybridization 347, *347*
leaf cuttings 347, *347*
pad sections 348
from seed 346–7, *346*
stem cuttings 348, *348*
stem sections 348, *348*
purpose of swollen stems 675
repotting 345
routine care 345
scented 339
seedlings pricking out 346, *346*
shading 345
shapes 338
spines 675
spraying 345
succulent type 338
suggestions for use 338–41
temperatures for 339, 345
for troughs 342
ventilation 345
water-storage 338
watering 345
Caesalpinia pulcherrima
germination 379
Calabrese *507*, 512
disease-resistant cultivars 649
bolting 512
conditions required 512
conditions tolerated 512
in crop rotation 498
culinary uses 512
diseases 512

Calabrese (*cont.*)
feeding 512
freezing 506
harvesting 512, *512*
nitrogen requirements 504, 512
pests 512
recommended cultivars 512
routine cultivation 512
size of plant 512
sowing 512
spacing 512
storing 506
top-dressing 512
transplanting 512
types 512
watering 512
'Arcadia' F1 512
'Belstar' F1 512
'Corvet' F1 512
'Decathlon' 512
'Fiesta' F1 512
'Green Comet' F1 512
'Hydra' F1 512
'Kabuki' F1 512
'Marathon' F1 512
'Trixie' 649
Caladium, conditions preferred indoors 361
Calamagrostis x *acutiflora* 'Karl Foerster' 175
conditions tolerated 181
in naturalistic planting *177*
Calamondin orange *see* x *Citrofortunella microcarpa*
Calandrinia, for dry conditions 211
Calanthe, suggestions for use 230
Calathea
conditions preferred 361
foliage 354
greenhouse conditions required 361
propagation
division *378*
rootstock 378
louisae, grouping plants *365*
makoyana, pollution absorbing 358
picturata, grouping plants *365*
zebrina, grouping plants *365*
Calceolaria
germination 640
greenhouse conditions required 361
integrifolia
in containers 319
stem tip cuttings 202
'Sunshine', in conservatory *359*
pavonii 129
Calcicoles *see* Lime lovers
Calcifuges *see* Lime haters
Calcium 637
deficiency
symptoms and control 658, *658*
symptoms of *640*
plant requirements 624
in soil 617
Calcium carbonate 625
in cuttings compost 565
Calcium hydroxide 625
Calcium nitrate 658
Calcium oxide 625
Calendula
attracting beneficial insects 641
colour combinations 48
conditions tolerated 213
in cottage garden *21*
for cutting 213
for drying 213
in mixed border *210*
self-sown 223
soil type preferred 325
officinalis 408
companion plants 405
in containers 319
cosmetic uses 404

Calendula officinalis (*cont.*)
culinary uses 404, 408
flowers 405, 408
harvesting 408
in herb garden *412*
in pot-pourri 408
propagation
from seed 408, 414
self-seeding 218
soil type preferred 216
soil type tolerated 216
storing 408
suggestions for use 408
variants 408
Calibrachoa
in containers 212
suggestions for use 213
Californian poppy *see*
Eschscholzia californica
Caliroa cerasi 647
Calla palustris 285
division of rootstock 302
position in water garden 285
Callianthemum anemonoides,
suggestions for use 259
Callisia
softwood cuttings 380
suggestions for use 366
Callistemon
greenhouse conditions
required 361
semi-ripe cuttings with heel
113
suggestions for use 95
citrinus 'Splendens', in
conservatory *359*
Callistephus
for cutting 213
diseases 654, 661, 662
chinensis, soil type tolerated
216
Callitriche hermaphroditica (syn.
C. autumnalis) 285
cuttings 302
Calluna
clematis growing through 138
dwarf conifers with 62
as ground cover 93
propagation
dropping 116
soft/greenwood cuttings
111
pruning 107
soil type indicated by 617
soil type required 99
suggestions for use 93
vulgaris
conditions tolerated 95
in containers 319
soil type preferred 97
soil type required 325
suggestions for use 317
Callus pads 632, *632*
Calocedrus, semi-ripe cuttings 79
Calochone 129
Calochortus
propagation, bulbils 245
resting 240
suggestions for use 230, 231
luteus 240
tolmiei, seedlings *247*
Calomeria
amaranthoides
for fragrance 213
as pot plants 213
soil type tolerated 216
Caltha
conditions tolerated 284
position in pond *295*
soil type tolerated 184
leptosepala, position in water
garden 285
palustris
choosing healthy plants *297*
planting *298*
position in water garden
285
propagation, division of
rootstock 302

Caltha palustris (*cont.*)
suggestions for use 285
var. *alba*, position in
water garden 285
'Flore Pleno' *302*
position in water
garden 285
Calycanthus
pruning 106
occidentalis, seasonal interest
95
Calystegia sepium 670
Calyx bands 196, 197, *197*
Camassia
for cutting 231
suggestions for use 239
leichtlinii
in mixed border 228
in wild-flower garden 401
quamash, in wild-flower
garden 401
Cambium 632, *635*, 676
activity of in grafting 635
joining layers in grafting 119,
119
matching layers in chip-
budding *83*
revealing *143, 432,* 633, *633*
Camellia
compost for 364
conditions preferred 310
in containers 94, 319
top-dressing 334
diseases, fungal 654
effect of drought on 657, 664
germination 115
greenhouse conditions
required 361
overwintering 102
pests damaging leaves 645
physiological disorders 651
propagation
leaf bud cutting 113, *632*
semi-ripe cuttings 113, *632*
pruning 108
soil type required 99, 325
standards 326
suggestions for use 95, 317
watering 357
japonica
conditions preferred 95
conditions tolerated 95
in conservatory *359*
leaf form *675*
propagation, leaf-bud
cuttings *113*
reticulata, spliced side-veneer
grafting 119
sasanqua
scent 95
spliced side-veneer
grafting 119
x *williamsii*
'Donation' *91*
as specimen 93
'Wilber Foss' *99*
Camissonia cheiranthifolia, soil
type preferred 216
Campanula
to attract insects 178, 264
in containers 319
flowering time from seed 198
planting in crevice *268*
propagation
division 201
root cuttings 203
from seed 379, *379*
softwood cuttings 273
with roses 151
seasonal interest 50
seed germination 198
soil type tolerated 261
carpatica, division 275
chamissonis, removing dead
leaves *279*
cochleariifolia
division 275
flowers 256
suggestions for use 259

Campanula (*cont.*)
garganica, conditions
tolerated 259
glomerata 401
isophylla
conditions preferred
indoors 361
in conservatory *359*
lactiflora, soil type tolerated
185
medium
architectural plants 213
first-year growth *220*
sowing 217
piperi, suggestions for use 259
portenschlagiana
conditions tolerated 259
suggestions for use 259
poscharskyana, conditions
tolerated 259
pyramidalis, as pot plants 213
raineri, suggestions for use
259
trachelium, conditions
tolerated 181
zoysii
pests 271
suggestions for use 258, 259
Campion *see* Lychnis
Campsis
propagation
semi-ripe cuttings 142
serpentine layering 145
pruning 135
soil type tolerated 131
arborescens
spliced side-veneer
grafting 119
standards 326
'Walker', apical-wedge
grafting 119
radicans
conditions tolerated 129
flowers 127
x *tagliabuana*
pruning 137
'Madame Galen', soil type
tolerated 132
Canal, constructing with concrete
293, *293*
Canarina canariensis 129
Candytuft *see* Iberis
Cane blight *653*
symptoms and control 653
Cane fruits *see* Fruit, soft
Canes
bamboo 317, 564, *564*
ring of 192, *192*
single 192, *192*
split *564*
supporting annuals with 222,
222
training sweet peas on 215, *215*
wigwam *214*
Canker *430*, 649
anthracnose 666
bacterial
control 448
plants affected by 426
symptoms and control 665
causes 430
Nectria 426, *664*
causes 428
symptoms and control 664
parsnip, symptoms and
control 661, *661*
Seiridium 664
symptoms and control
664–5
Canna
architectural plants 213, 231
in containers 319
in hot border *25*
in mixed border 173, 177
overwintering 230
in tropical planting *60*
'Rosamond Coles' *61*
Cantaloupe melons *see* Melons,
cantaloupe
Canterbury bells *see* Campanula
medium
Cantua, semi-ripe cuttings with
heel 113
Capillary action, movement of
water in soil by 622

Capillary matting 334–5, 374,
374, 577, *577,* 637
Capillary pores 622
Capillary watering 374, *374,* 577,
577
Capping 621, *621*
Capsella bursa-pastoris see
Shepherd's purse
Capsicum
conditions preferred indoors
361
diseases, virus 662
annuum
Grossum Group *see*
Peppers, sweet
Longum Group *see*
Peppers, chilli
frutescens see Peppers, hot
ornamental, as pot plants 213
Capsicums *see* Peppers, sweet
Capsid bugs 645, *657*
symptoms and control 645, 657
Capsules *675*
Captan 637
Caragana
germination 115
propagation
apical-wedge grafting 119
spliced side-veneer
grafting 119
pruning 105
arborescens
spliced side-veneer
grafting 119
standards 326
'Walker', apical-wedge
grafting 119
Caralluma
division of rootstock 350
stem cuttings 348
europaea, conditions tolerated
342
Caraway 408, *408*
culinary uses 408
flowers 408
foliage 408
harvesting 408
propagation, from seed 408,
414
storing 408
thinning out seedlings 414
Carbohydrates
breaking down 675
converting carbon dioxide
into 675, *675*
Carbon dioxide, converting into
carbohydrates 675, *675*
Cardamine
hirsuta 260, *669*
pratensis
soil type tolerated 184
suggestions for use 285
Cardamon, suggestions for use 405
Cardiocrinum
conditions preferred 231
dying after flowering 246
from seed 246
propagation, division of
offsets 245
giganteum, architectural plant
231
Carduncellus rhaponticoides,
root cuttings 275
Carex
as companion plant 186
conditions preferred 181
in containers 319
dividing 201
position in pond *295*
comans
winter interest 181
'Frosted Curls', as
specimen plant *172*
elata 'Aurea'
place in water garden 285
suggestions for use 285
pendula
place in water garden 285
suggestions for use 285

Carex (*cont.*)
riparia, position in water
garden 285
Carica papaya see Papayas
Carlina acaulis, conditions
tolerated 259
Carmichaelia, semi-ripe cuttings
with heel 113
Carnation *see* Dianthus
Carnivorous plants in greenhouse
359
Carpels 676
Carpenteria
layering 116
semi-ripe cuttings with heel
113
californica 94
Carpet grass *see* Axonopus
Carpeting plants
herbs 405
methods of spreading 180
Carpinus
diseases, fungal 655
as hedge, renovation 86
for leaf mould 63
pleaching 58, 75
propagation, spliced side
grafting 82
shaping *86*
betulus
conditions tolerated 67
as hedge 84
pleaching 18
resistance to storm
damage 68
soil type tolerated 65
suggestions for use 316
'Fastigiata' *55*
Carpobrotus
division of rootstock 350
acinaciformis, conditions
tolerated 342
edulis
conditions tolerated 342
habit 339
Carrot flies 544
control 504
deterring 641
larvae *660*
symptoms and control 660, *660*
Carrots *504*, 542, 544
conditions tolerated 544
in crop rotation 498
culinary uses 544
diseases 544, 661
freezing 506
harvesting 506, 544, *544*
mineral deficiencies 662
nitrogen requirement 504, 544
overwatering 502
pest-resistant cultivars 660
pests 544, 660, 661
protecting from carrot fly 544,
544
recommended cultivars 544
roots 674, *674*
shape 544
size 544
rotation 544
routine cultivation 544
site 544
size of plants 544
soil preparation for 544
soil type preferred 544
sowing 544, *544*
in wide drills 500
sowing *in situ* 499
spacing 544
storing 506, 544, *544*
transplanting 544
watering 544
critical periods 502
weeding 544
'Adelaide' F1 544
'Amsterdam Forcing 2 –
Sweetheart' 544
'Autumn King – Vita Longa'
544
'Autumn King 2' 544

Carrots (*cont.*)
  'Berlicum – Berjo' 544
  'Camberley' 544
  'Chantenay Red Cored 2' 544
  'Flyaway' F1 544, 660
  'Kingston' F1 544
  'Maestro' 544
  'Nairobi' F1 544
  'Nandor' F1 544
  'New Red Intermediate' 544
  'Newmarket' F1 544
  'Parabell' 544
  'Parmex' 544
  'Sugarsnax' 544
  'Sytan' 544. 660
  'Yellow Stone'' 544
Carruanthus, division of offsets 349
Carrying bag 562, *562*
Carrying sheet 562, *562*
Carts, garden 562
Cartwheel bed, herbs in *405*, 406
Carum carvi see Caraway
Carya
  seed germination 81
  illinoinensis see Pecan nuts
Caryopteris
  pests 645
    affecting flowers 657
  propagation, softwood cuttings 111
  scent 95
  x *clandonensis*
    pruning 105
    with roses 151
Casaba melons *see* Melons, winter
Cascade, construction *292*
Cassinia
  propagation, semi-ripe cuttings 273
    with heel 113
  leptophylla subsp. *fulvida*, conditions tolerated 95
Cassiope
  conditions preferred 259
  propagation
    greenwood cuttings 273
    layering 116
    semi-ripe cuttings with heel 113
    softwood cuttings 273
  soil type required 257, 260
  hypnoides, division of suckers 118
Castanea sativa
  bark 48
  fruit type 675, *675*
  nuts *see* Sweet chestnuts
  soil preferred 66
Castanospermum australe, soil type tolerated 66
Castor oil plant *see Ricinus communis*
Catalpa
  apical wedge grafting 82
  softwood cuttings 79
  bignonioides 57
    conditions tolerated 67
    seasonal interest 59
    'Aurea', suggestions for use 59
Catananche
  for drying 181
  flowering time from seed 198
  soil type tolerated 185
  caerulea
    root cuttings 203
    'Major' *203*
Caterpillars
  brown tail moth 647
  cabbage *645*
    symptoms and control 640, 645
  cabbage white, control 640
  control 504, 643, 645
  cutworms 660
  damage done by 645
  hawthorn webber moth 647

Caterpillars (*cont.*)
  juniper webber moth 647
  lackey moth 647
  small ermine moth 647
  tortrix moth *648*
    symptoms and control 648
  webber moth *647*
    symptoms and control 647
  winter moth *645*
    symptoms and control 645
Catharanthus
  greenhouse conditions required 361
  softwood cuttings 380
  roseus, in containers 319
Catmint *see Nepeta*
Cats
  control 667
  damage to lawn 667
  repelling 642
Cattleya
  method of growth 368
  propagation 371
  suggestions for use 368
  temperature required 368
  bowringiana 368
Caudex 338
Cauliflowers *507*, 508
  conditions required 508
  in crop rotation 498
  culinary uses 508
  curds failing to grow 504
  diseases 508
  feeding 508
  freezing 506
  germination 508
  harvesting 508
  mineral deficiencies 504, 652
  mini 508, *508*
  nitrogen requirements 504, 508
  overwintering 508
  pests 508, 645, 660
  planting time for 508
  protecting curds 508, *508*
  purple-headed *508*
  recommended cultivars 508
  routine care 508
  size
    of head 508
    of plant 508
  sowing 508
  spacing 508
  storing 506, 508
  successional cropping 508
  types 508
  watering 508
  'Alverda' 508
  'Autumn Glory' 508
  'Aviso' 508
  'Beauty' F1 508
  'Galleon' 508
  'Graffiti' 508
  'Gypsy' 508
  'Idol' 508
  'Kestrel' 508
  'Minaret' 508
  'Moby Dick' 508
  'Nautilus' 508
  'Pavilion' 508
  'Patriot' 508
  'Penduick' 508
  'Plana' F1 508
  'Prestige' 508
  'Purple Cape' 508
  'Romanesco Veronica' 508
  'Vilna' 508
  'Violet Queen' 508
  'Walcheren Winter 3-Armado' 508
  'White Excel' 508
Cayenne peppers *see* Peppers, hot
Ceanothus
  colour combinations 48
  deciduous
    propagation
      semi-ripe cuttings with heel 113
      soft/greenwood cuttings 111

Ceanothus, deciduous (*cont.*)
    pruning 105
  evergreen
    training 109
    as wall shrub 109
  flowers 94
  formality 43
  propagation
    semi-ripe cuttings with heel 113
    soft/greenwood cuttings 111
  pruning 104, *109*
  suggestions for use 95
  training 109, *109*
  x *delileanus*, pruning 105
  thyrsiflorus, soil preferred 97
Cecidophyopsis
  psilaspis 655
  ribis 655
Cedar *see Cedrus*
Cedar, Japanese, *see Cryptomeria*
Cedrus
  extracting seed 80
  propagation, spliced side grafting 82
  shape 55
  suggestions for use 59
  atlantica f. *glauca*, seasonal interest 59
  libani, soil type tolerated 65
Celandine, lesser *see Ranunculus ficaria*
Celastrus
  propagation
    obtaining seed from 141
    root cuttings 141, 144
    self layering 145
    semi-ripe cuttings 142
    serpentine layering 145
  renovating *137*
  suggestions for use 126, 129
  for winter interest 126
  orbiculatus
    fruit 127
    renovating *137*
    root cuttings *144*
  scandens, soil types tolerated 131, 132
Celeriac 535, *539*
  conditions tolerated 539
  in crop rotation 498
  culinary uses 539
  diseases 539
  exposing crowns 539, *539*
  germination 539
  harvesting 539
  mulching 539
  nitrogen requirement 504
  pests 539
  planting out from module 539, *539*
  protecting 539, *539*
  recommended cultivars 539
  routine cultivation 539
  size of plant 539
  soil type required 539
  sowing 539
  spacing 539
  storing 539
  'Balder' 539
  'Diamant' 539
  'Ibis' 539
  'Monarch' 539
  'Prinz' 539
Celery 535, 538, *538*
  blanching 538, *538*
  bolting 538
  conditions preferred 538
  in crop rotation 498
  culinary uses 538
  diseases 538, 661
  earthing up 538
  feeding 538
  freezing 506
  germination 538
  harvesting 538
  lifting 538, *538*
  mineral deficiency 654

Celery (*cont.*)
  nitrogen requirement 504, 538
  pests 538, 647, 660
  planting in blocks 538, *538*
  recommended cultivars 538
  rotation 538
  routine cultivation 538
  seed treated 538
  seedlings in block 538, *538*
  self-blanching
    colour 538
    planting 538
    sweetening 538
  site 538
  size of plants 538
  soil preparation for 538
  soil type required 538
  sowing 538
  spacing 538
  storing 538
  thinning out 538
  trench
    colour 538
    planting 538
    soil preparation 538
  watering 538
  'Galaxy' 538
  'Giant Pink' 538
  'Golden' 538
  'Hopkins Fenlander' 538
  'Ideal' 538
  'Loretta' 538
  'Tango' F1 538
  'Victoria' F1 538
Celery fly 538
Celery leaf miner 647
Celmisia coriacea, in rock garden 256
Celosia
  in containers 319
  for drying 213
  cristata
    flowers 209
    'Childsii' (*C. plumosa*), flowers 209
Celtis
  australis, soil preferred 66
  occidentalis, softwood cuttings 79
Cement
  definition 591
  masonry, definition 591
  Portland, definition 591
Cement blocks, raised beds of 497
Centaurea
  for cutting 181
  for drying 181
  flowering time from seed 198
  staking 92
  cyanus
    conditions preferred 401
    conditions tolerated 213
    for cutting 212, 213
    for drying 213
    in mixed border *210*
    propagation
      self-seeding 218, 222
      sowing 217
    soil type preferred 216
    sowing 216
  dealbata
    conditions tolerated 181
    dividing 201
  hypoleuca, conditions tolerated 181
  macrocephala, growth rate 181
  moschata 213
    sowing 217
  pindicola, root cuttings 275
Centipede grass *see Eremochloa ophiuroides*
Centipedes *617*
  benefits of 641
  distinguishing from millipedes 641, 644
  recognizing 641
  types
    flat *641*
    snake *641*

Centradenia
  pinching out 376
Centranthus
  soil type tolerated 185
  ruber
    conditions tolerated 181
    soil type preferred 184
    'Albus', white border *176*
Cephalaria
  for cutting 181
  gigantea, growth rate 181
Cephalocereus
  in bowl garden 341
  stem cuttings 348
  senilis
    in desert garden 340
    flowers 342
    suggestions for use 342
Ceramic tiles *see* Tiles
Ceramics, as material for containers 320
Cerastium
  fontanum (syn. *C. vulgatum*) 672
  tomentosum, as weed *669*
Ceratophyllum demersum 297
  cuttings 302
  position in water garden 285
Ceratopteris
  cornuta, propagation by plantlets 303
  pteridioides 285
  thalictroides, position in water garden 285
Ceratostigma
  softwood cuttings 111
  plumbaginoides, division of suckers 118
  willmottianum, pruning 105
Cercidiphyllum
  · layering 81
  japonicum
    soil preferred 65
    suggestions for use 59
Cercis
  apical wedge grafting 82
  siliquastrum 57
    soil preferred 66
    soil type tolerated 65
    suggestions for use 59
Cereus
  stem cuttings 348
  aethiops (syn. *C. chalybaeus*), conditions tolerated 342
  jamacaru, conditions tolerated 342
  uruguayanus (syn. *C. peruvianus*)
    in bowl *344*
    suggestions for use 342
  validus, suggestions for use 342
Cerinthe 213
Ceropegia
  propagation
    offsets 349
    softwood cuttings 142
    stem cuttings 348
  as rootstock 351
  soil type tolerated 131
  haygarthii, suggestions for use 342
  linearis subsp. *woodii*
    form 339
    in conservatory *359*
    suggestions for use 342
  sandersonii, climbing method 124
  woodii
    propagation, division of offsets *349*
Cestrum
  greenhouse conditions required 361
  propagation, softwood cuttings 111
  pruning 109
  suggestions for use 95

Cestrum (*cont.*)
  elegans
    training 109
    as wall shrub 109
Ceterach officinarum, in rock
  crevice *194*
Ceylon spinach 515–16
  conditions required 515
  culinary uses 515
  diseases 516
  feeding 515
  growing under cover 516
  harvesting 516
  mulching 515
  nitrogen requirement 504, 515
  pests 516
  propagation
    cuttings 516
    sowing 515
  removing flowering shoots 516
  removing growing point 516
  routine cultivation 515
  size of plant 515
  soil type required 515
  spacing 515
  storing 516
  supporting 515, *515*
  transplanting 515
  varieties 515
  watering 515
Chaenomeles
  pests damaging leaves 647
  propagation
    layering 116
    stooling 117
  pruning 106
  suggestions for use 95
  as wall shrub 93
  japonica, form 90
  x *superba*
    soil type tolerated 97
    'Nicoline' *97*
Chafer grubs, control 668
Chafer larvae *660*
  control 643, 660, 668
    biological 642
  symptoms 660, 667–8
Chain link fences 600, *600*
Chainsaws 556, *556*
  safety 550
Chalky soil
  effect on pears 444
  growing fruit on 424
  growing peaches on 451
  growing plums on 447
  and naturalistic plantings 183
  structure 616, *616*, 617
Chamaecyparis
  semi-ripe cuttings 79
  lawsoniana
    diseases 654, 661
    as hedge 84
    soil type tolerated 65
    'Ellwoodii'
      seasonal interest 59
      suggestions for use
      316
    'Lanei Aurea', seasonal
      interest 59
    'Pembury Blue', seasonal
      interest 59
    'Stewartii', seasonal
      interest 59
    'Winston Churchill',
      seasonal interest 59
  obtusa
    'Intermedia' 259
    'Nana Aurea' *62*
      leaf form *675*
      semi-ripe cuttings *79*
    'Nana Pyramidalis'
      in rock garden 256
      suggestions for use
      258
Chamaedorea
  conditions preferred indoors
    361
  conditions tolerated 355
  in containers 319

Chamaedorea (*cont.*)
  greenhouse conditions
    required 361
  hydroculture 361
  elegans
    in hydroculture display *375*
    suggestions for use 366
  seifrizii, pollution absorbing
    358
Chamaemelum nobile 393, *408*
  benefit to other plants 405
  cosmetic uses 404
  culinary uses 408
  foliage 408
  harvesting 408
  in herb garden *412*
  for lawn 386, 387, 389, *389*
    establishing 393, *393*
  in pot-pourri 408
  propagation
    cuttings of sideshoots 408
    division 408
  scent 404
  storing 408
  suggestions for use 408
  'Flore Pleno' 408
  'Treneague' 389, 408
    propagation
      cuttings 414
      division 414
    suggestions for use 405
Chamaerops
  architectural 95
  in containers 319
  soil type tolerated 99
  humilis *60*
    in container 94
    hardiness 60
Chamomile *see Chamaemelum
nobile*
Charcoal *346*, *366*, *367*, *368*
Chard *see* Swiss chard
Charlock 649
  spreading disease 660
Cheiranthus see Erysimum
Chemical control 643
Chemical inhibitors, use after
  pruning 430
Chemicals
  adverse reactions to 643
  clearing overgrown site with
    618, *618*
  for disease control 643
  formulation of preparations
    643
  fungicide damage 650
  insecticide damage 650
  leaching into pond 282
  for organic pest and disease
    control 642
  for pest control 643
  safety in use 643
  for soil sterilization 619
  storage 643
  types available 668
  use in integrated control 640
  using safely 643
  weedkillers
    damage caused 650
    lawn 673
    range 671
Chenopodium album 390
Cherries 455–8, for ornamental
  varieties, *see Prunus*
  acid 457–8
    bush pruning 458, *458*
    chilling requirement 457
    conditions required 457
    conditions tolerated 457
    diseases 457
    fan
      pruning
        spring 457, *457*
        summer 457, *457*
        training 457
    feeding 457
    freezing 431
    fruiting habit 457
    harvesting 458, *458*

Cherries, acid (*cont.*)
  pests 457
  planting distances 457
  propagation 458
  protecting from birds 457
  pruning 429, 457, *457*
  recommended cultivars 457
  rootstocks 457
  routine care 457
  self-fertile cultivars 457
  soil for 457
  training 457
  watering 457
  'Montmorency' 457
  'Morello' 457, *457*
    in large fruit garden
    421
    in small fruit garden
    422
  'Nabella' 457
  bird damage 657
  bottling 431
  diseases 647, 648, 665
  fans, space required 422
  fruit type 419, 435, 675
  harvesting 431
  pests 647
  pruning 428
  seed stratification 629
  sweet 455–6
    aspect 456
    chilling requirement 455
    choosing cultivars 455
    conditions required 455–6
    cross-pollination 421, 424
    diseases 456
    dwarfing 456
    fan, pruning
      after fruiting 456, *456*
      spring 456
      summer 456, *456*
      supporting 456
      training 456
    feathered maiden, training
      as fan 456
    feeding 456
    freezing 431, 456
    harvesting 456
    mulching 456
    pests 456
    planting 456
    pollination 456
      compatibility 423
    propagation 456
    protecting from birds 456
    pruning 429, 456, *456*
    recommended cultivars 456
    rootstocks 456, *456*
    routine care 456
    self-fertile cultivars 456
    self-sterile 421, 424
    self-sterile cultivars 456
    site 455–6
    siting 421
    size of trees 455
    storing 456
    watering 456
    'Early Rivers' 456
    'Hertford' 456
    'Lapins' 456
    'Merton Glory' 456
    'Napoleon Bigarreau' 456
    'Noir de Guben' 456
    'Penny' 456
    'Regina' 456
    'Stella' 456, *456*
      in large fruit garden
      421
      in small fruit garden
      422
    'Summer Sun' 456
    'Sunburst' 456
    'Sweetheart' 456
  'Camil' as rootstock 456
  'Colt' as rootstock 456, *456*
  Duke 455
    rootstocks 457
  'Gisela 5' in a small garden
    422

Cherries, rootstock (*cont.*)
  'Inmil' as rootstock 456
  'Malling F12/1' as rootstock
    456, *456*
Cherry plums *see* Plums, cherry
Cherry slugworm *647*
  symptoms and control 647
Chervil 407, *407*
  conditions tolerated 405
  culinary uses 407
  foliage 407
  harvesting 407
  in herb garden *412*
  propagation from seed 407,
    414
  protecting for winter use 411
  storing 407
  suggestions for use 318, 405
Cheshunt compound 637, 668
Chestnuts
  Spanish *see* Sweet chestnuts
  sweet *see* Sweet chestnuts
Chewing's fescue *see Festuca
rubra* var. *commutata*
Chiastophyllum oppositifolium
  conditions tolerated 259
  division 275
Chicken manure, pelleted
  for fruit trees 426
  nutrient content 624
Chicken wire 564
Chickweed *see Stellaria media*
Chickweed, common mouse-ear
  see Cerastium fontanum
Chicons *515*, 517
Chicory 517–18
  forcing *517*
  nitrogen requirement 504, 517
  recommended cultivars 517
  types 517
  'Bianca di Milano' 517
  'Bondissima di Trieste' 517
  'Indigo' Fi 517
  'Pain de Sucre' 517
  'Palla Rossa' 517
  red
    conditions tolerated 518
    culinary uses 518
    F1 hybrids 518
    forcing 518
    form 518
    harvesting 518
    recommended cultivars 517
    sowing 518
    spacing 518
  'Rossa di Treviso' 517
  'Rossa di Verona' 517
  sugar loaf *518*
    as cut-and-come-again
      crop 506
    form 518
    harvesting 518
    recommended cultivars 517
    sowing 518
    spacing 518
    storing 518
  Witlof (Belgian)
    chicons *515*
    conditions preferred 517
    culinary uses 517
    forcing 505, 517, *517*
    form 518
    harvesting 517
    recommended cultivars 517
    sowing 517
    spacing 517
    storing chicons 517
    storing roots 517
    watering 517
  'Zoom' F1 517
Children
  safety during chemical use 643
  water in garden for *23*, 282,
    283, 284, *284*
Chilli peppers *see* Peppers, chilli
Chimney-pots 306
  rock plants in 258
Chimonanthus
  pruning 105

Chimonanthus (*cont.*)
  praecox
    in mixed border 176
    seasonal interest 50
    'Luteus', scent 95
China aster *see Callistephus*
Chinese broccoli *513*
  conditions tolerated 513
  in crop rotation 498
  freezing 506
  harvesting 513
  nitrogen requirement 504
  size of plant 513
  sowing 513
  spacing 513
  for winter crop 513
Chinese cabbages 514
  bolting 514
  colours 514
  conditions preferred 514
  in crop rotation 498
  culinary uses 514
  flavour 514
  freezing 506
  harvesting 514, *514*
  head forms 514
  loose-leaved *513*
  nitrogen requirement 504
  pests 514
  recommended cultivars 514
  sowing 514
  tight-headed *513*
  'Harmony' 649
Chinese chives 407
  in herb garden *412*
Chinese dogwood *see Cornus
kousa* var. *chinensis*
Chinese gooseberries *see* Kiwi
  fruits
Chinese hat 154, *154*
Chinese kale *see* Chinese broccoli
Chinese layering *see* Air layering
Chinese privet *see Ligustrum
lucidum*
Chinese spinach *see Amaranthus
tricolor*
Chionanthus
  layering 116
  retusus, layering 81
Chionochloa rubra, as specimen
  plant 172, *179*
Chionodoxa 151
  conditions tolerated 231
  in containers 319
  in mixed border 227
  suggestions for use 228
  forbesii, suggestions for use
    239
Chip-budding 83, *83*
  fruit trees 432, *432*
  method 636, *636*
  time for 635
  trees suitable for 82
Chipping
  bulbs suitable for 249
  indoor plant, seed 379
  propagation by 249, *249*, 634,
    634
Chisels, bolster 588, *588*
Chives *407*
  conditions tolerated 405
  culinary uses 404, 407
  as edging *495*
  flowers 407
    use 413
  forcing 411, *411*
  freezing in ice 415
  harvesting 407, 415
  in herb garden *412*
  propagation
    division 407
    from seed 407
  related species 407
  storing 407
  suggestions for use 405, 407
  variants 407
  in vegetable garden *495*
Chloride salts, sensitivity to 624
Chlorine, plant requirements 624

Chlorophyll 675, *675*
Chlorophytum
  conditions preferred indoors
    361
  conditions tolerated 355
  division of plantlets/runners
    378
  greenhouse conditions
    required 361
  comosum (syn. *C. capense* of
    gardens), in conservatory
    359
Chlorosis 424
  causes 357, 444
  interveinal 651
  lime-induced 451, 472
Chocolate spot *649*
  symptoms and control 649
Choisya
  semi-ripe cuttings 113
  'Aztec Pearl', scent 95
  ternata
    callus on stem cutting *632*
    form 46
    pruning 107
    scent 95
    soil type tolerated 99
    SUNDANCE *47*
      foliage 94
Chondrostereum purpureum 647
Christmas box *see Sarcococca
  confusa*
Christmas cactus *see
  Schlumbergera* x *buckleyi*
Chromatomyia syngenesiae 647
Chromosomes 168
Chrysanthemum
  basal stem cuttings *202*
  in containers 319
  diseases 655, 657
  effect of frost on 607
  florets
    blooms, "paintbrush"
      stage *190*
    forms *188*
  florists' 188–90
    advancing flowering time
      190
    apical buds 189, *189*
    classification 188, *188*
    conditions required 188
    disbudded types 188, *188*
    disbudding 189, *189*
    early-flowering 188–9
      feeding 189
      overwintering 189,
        189
      planting 189
      routine care 189
      soil preparation 188
      staking 188
      stopping 189, *189*
    for exhibition
      growing for 190
      preparing blooms 190
      protecting blooms
        190, *190*
      retarding flowering
        time 190
    flowerhead shapes 188, *188*
      anemone-centred *188*
      fully reflexed *188*
      incurved *188*
      intermediate *188*
      pompon *188*
      quill *188*
      reflexed *188*
      single *188*
      spider *188*
      spoon *188*
    late-flowering 188,
      189–90
      feeding 190
      overwintering 190
      planting 189
      routine care 190
      stopping 190
      propagation, cuttings 189,
        190

Chrysanthemum, florists' (*cont.*)
  removing excess laterals
    189
  spray types 188, *189*
    creating 189
  in greenhouse 360
    conditions required 361
  as houseplant 355
  mineral deficiency 651
  in mixed border 177
  mutation *676*
  pests 645, 647, 657
  pollution-absorbing 358
  propagation
    basal stem cuttings 202
    cuttings of plants infected
      with eelworms 647
  *balsamita see Tanacetum
    balsamita*
  'Beacon' *188*
  'Brietner' *188*
  charm 190, *190*
    feeding 190
    overwintering 190
    propagation, cuttings 190
    stopping 190
  'George Griffiths' *188*
  'Golden Woolman's Glory'
    188
  'Honeycomb' *188*
  'Morning Star' *190*
  'Muxton Plume' *188*
  *parthenium see Tanacetum
    parthenium*
  'Pennine Alfie' *188*
  'Pennine Oriel' *188*
  'Pin Nu Rosemary' *189*
  'Primrose West Bromwich'
    188
  'Salmon Fairie' *188*
  'Yellow John Hughes' *188*
Chrysanthemum leaf miner 647
Chrysanthemum petal blight *657*
  symptoms and control 657
Chrysanthemum white rust 648
Chusan palm *see Trachycarpus
  fortunei*
Cichorium
  endivia see Endive
  intybus see Chicory
Cime di rapa *see* Broccoli raab
Cimicifuga
  americana (syn. *Actaea
    podocarpa*), suggestions
    for use 285
  racemosa (syn. *Actaea
    racemosa*), suggestions for
    use 285
Cinnamomum
  semi-ripe cuttings 79
  camphora, suggestions for
    use 59
Cirsium arvense 670
Cissus 129
  conditions preferred indoors
    361
  hydroculture 361
  propagation
    semi-ripe cuttings 142
    simple layering 145
    softwood cuttings 380
  pruning 376
  vigour 130
  antarctica
    conditions tolerated 355
    training indoors 355
  discolor, suggestions for use
    366
  rhombifolia, greenhouse
    conditions required 361
Cistus
  conditions preferred 91
  conditions tolerated 95, 622
  dwarf conifers with 62
  soil type tolerated 99
  x *cyprius* 97
    soil type preferred 97
  x *hybridus*, as ground cover
    101

Cistus (*cont.*)
  x *skanbergii*, as ground cover
    101
CITES *see* Convention on
  International Trade in
  Endangered Species
Citrange, Troyer, as rootstock 480
x *Citrofortunella*
  greenhouse conditions
    required 361
  standards 326
  microcarpa (syn. *Citrus mitis*)
    482
    in conservatory *359*
    in garden room *358*
    suggestions for use 319,
      326
Citrons 431–2
  stem pitting 481
  conditions required 481
  fruits 481
  peel 481
Citrullus lanatus see
  Watermelons
Citrus (for edible varieties *see*
  Citrus fruits; also individual
  fruits by name)
  conditions preferred 95
  in containers 319
  diseases 658
  flanking avenue *308, 309*
  fruit 57
  pests 46
  propagation, air layering 117
  pruning 107
  suggestions for use 309
  watering 357
  aurantiifolia see Limes
  aurantium see Oranges, sour
    (Seville)
  limon see Lemons
  medica
    fruit *see* Citrons
    suggestions for use 59
  'Meyer' (syn. 'Meyer's
    Lemon'), seasonal interest
    95
  mitis see x *Citrofortunella
    microcarpa*
  x *paradisi see* Grapefruits
  reticulata see Mandarins;
    Tangerines
  sinensis see Oranges, sweet
  x *tangelo see* Tangelo; Ugli
    fruits
Citrus fruits 420–2, 480–2
  *see also individual fruits by
    name*
  bottling 431
  conditions required 419, 480
  conditions tolerated 480
  in containers 481
    moving under cover 427
  diseases 481
  feeding 480
  flowering 480
  growing under cover 481
  harvesting 481
  mulching 480
  on patio 418
  pests 481
  planting 480–1
  pollination 480
  in pots 423
  preserving peel 431
  propagation
    from seed 481
    T-budding 481
  protecting 480
  pruning 481
  recommended cultivars 481
  ripening 481
  rootstocks 480
  routine care 481
  site 480
  soil for 480
  spacing 480
  species 481–2
  storing 481

Citrus fruits (*cont.*)
  uses 479
  watering 481
Citrus scab 649
Cladding for sheds *605*
Cladrastis lutea, seasonal interest
  59
Clamps
  storing vegetables in 506
  for swedes *543*
Clarkia (syn. *Godetia*)
  conditions tolerated 213
  for drying 213
  in mixed border 210
  sowing 217
  amoena
    propagation, self-seeding
      218
    soil type preferred 216
Classification *677*
Clasterosporium carpophilum 648
Clay, adding to soils 621
Clay pellets/granules 375, 565
  as plunge material 365
Clay pots *see* Pots
Clay soil
  building wall footings on 597
  climbers tolerating 131
  drainage for lawn 390
  effect of frost on 609
  feeding lawn on 396
  foundations for structures on
    585
  growing fruit on 424
  identifying *617, 617*
  improving 621
  lime required to alter pH 625
  mineral deficiency in 650
  perennials for 184
  planting shrubs in 98–9
  preparing for lawn 390
  shrubs tolerant of 97
  structure *616, 616*
  temperature 607
  water in 622
  water table 622
Claytonia
  as herb *see* Winter purslane
  semi-ripe cuttings 273
Cleft chestnut paling *600, 600*
Cleistocactus
  in bowl garden 341
  stem cuttings 348
  strausii
    in desert garden 340
    flowers 342
    form 338
    suggestions for use 342
Clematis 138–40
  climbing method 124, *130*
  combining with other
    climbers *127*
  conditions required 139
  conditions tolerated 129, 138
  container-grown pruning 326
  for containers 129, 138, 319
  diseases 139, 665
  diversity of habits 138
  evergreen, conditions required
    139
  fast-growing 129
  in hedges 126
  flower
    colour 138
    forms 138
  group 1, early-flowering spp.
    and cvs 138, 309
    pruning 139, *139*
  group 2, early large-flowered
    cvs 138, 140
    pruning 140, *140*
  group 3, late-flowering spp
    and cvs 138, 140
    pruning 140, *140*
  groups 138
  growing on host plant 127,
    138
    pruning 140
  growing with roses 152

Clematis (*cont.*)
  growing through ground
    cover, pruning 140
  herbaceous, dividing 201
  mulching 139
  pests 139, 644, 657
  physiological disorders 653
  planting 132, 139, *139*
  propagation 140
    division 201
    internodal cuttings 140,
      140
    layering *631*
    from seed 140
      sowing 141, *141*
    semi-ripe cuttings 140, 143
    serpentine layering 145
    softwood cuttings 140, *142*
  pruning 135, 137, 139–40,
    139, 140, 326
  routine care 139
  scented 129
  as screen 125
  seasonal interest 50
  seed preparation 141
  seedheads 138
  siting 139
  soil preparation 138–9
  soil type preferred 325
  soil types tolerated 130, 131,
    132, 185
  suggestions for use 125, 129,
    138, 307–8, 311
  supports for 138
  tender 138
  training 139–40
  on trees 56
  watering 139
  'Abundance', as ground cover
    127
  alpina
    in containers 319
    propagation, semi-ripe
      cuttings 273
    pruning 139
    suggestions for use 129
  Alpina Group 138
  ANNA LOUISE ('Evithree'),
    pruning 140
  ARCTIC QUEEN ('Evitwo'),
    pruning 140
  armandii 139
    conditions preferred 138
    for fragrance 129
    pruning 139
    suggestions for use 125
  'Barbara Jackman', pruning
    140
  'Carnaby', pruning 140
  x *cartmanii* 'Joe', semi-ripe
    cuttings 273
  cirrhosa
    conditions preferred 138
    pruning 139
    as screen 125
    seasons of interest 128
  'Comtesse de Bouchaud',
    pruning 140
  'Daniel Deronda', pruning
    140
  'Duchess of Albany', pruning
    140
  'Duchess of Edinburgh',
    pruning 140
  'Edith', suggestions for use
    138
  'Elsa Späth' *129*
    pruning 140
  'Ernest Markham' *138*
    as ground cover *127*
  'Etoile Violette'
    flowers *127*
    as ground cover *127*
    pruning 140
  florida, pruning 140
  'Frances Rivis' *138*
    suggestions for use 317
  'Général Sikorski', pruning
    140

Clematis (cont.)
‘Gipsy Queen’, pruning 140
‘Hagley Hybrid’, pruning 140
‘Henryi’ 138
heracleifolia
soil type tolerated 185
var. davidiana,
suggestions for use 138
‘Huldine’, pruning 140
integrifolia 138
suggestions for use 138
‘Jackmanii’ 138, 138
diseases 665
as ground cover 127
‘Jackmanii’ hybrids,
suggestions for use 138
x jouiniana 138
suggestions for use 138
‘Lady Betty Balfour’, pruning
140
‘Lasurstern’, pruning 140
‘Lincoln Star’, pruning 140
macropetala
in containers 128, 319
pruning 139
seasons of interest 127
suggestions for use 129
Macropetala Group 138
‘Madame Julia Correvon’ 138
‘Marie Boisselot’, pruning 140
‘Markham’s Pink’ 138
‘Miss Bateman’, suggestions
for use 317
montana
as cover for wildlife 128
for fragrance 129
growing through trees 127
propagation, internodal
cuttings 633
pruning 135, 139
as screen 125
suggestions for use 127
vigour 130
var. grandiflora, pruning
139
var. rubens 138
pruning 139
‘Elizabeth’ 127
Montana Group 138
‘Mrs N.Thompson’, pruning
140
‘Nelly Moser’ 138
‘Niobe’, pruning 140
orientalis
conditions required 139
suggestions for use 138
‘Perle d’Azur’ 140
pruning 140
PETIT FAUCON (‘Evisix’),
pruning 140
‘Proteus’, flowers 138
recta
soil type tolerated 185
rehderiana, flowers 138
‘Star of India’, pruning 140
tangutica
conditions required 139
flowers 138
pruning 140
suggestions for use 138
texensis, suggestions for use
138
‘The President’ 138
‘Venosa Violacea’, growing
through juniper 139
‘Ville de Lyon’, pruning 140
viticella
cutting back 130
flowers 138
in mixed border 176
pruning 140
suggestions for use 126,
138
‘Vyvyan Pennell’ 140
flowers 138
pruning 140
Clematis wilt 665
cause 139
symptoms and control 665

Clementines see Mandarins
Cleome
architectural role 210
for dry conditions 211
hassleriana, architectural
plant 213
Clerodendrum
root cuttings 114
softwood cuttings 142
bungei
division of suckers 118
seasonal interest 50
splendens 129
thomsoniae 129
in containers 319
conditions tolerated 129
pruning 135, 137, 375
Clethra
pruning 105
soil type required 99
alnifolia
soil type tolerated 97
‘Paniculata’, scent 95
Clianthus
propagation, semi-ripe
cuttings 143
pruning 135
puniceus, soil type tolerated
131
Click beetles 662
Climate 606–13
recent changes 68, 91, 211,
256, 339, 405
desert 606
elements of 607–11
of Europe 608–9, 609
geographical influences on 606
global warming effects 607,
650, 659
lawn grass, choice for 388
Mediterranean 606
microclimate 495
polar 606
regional 606
subtropical 606
temperate 606
tropical 606
zones 606
selecting plants for 61
Climbers 124–45
for acid soil 131
for alkaline soil 132
annual 128, 129, 211–12
planting 221
supporting 221, 222, 222
aspect for 125
to attract wildlife 22
biennial 211–12
on buildings 125
choosing 131, 131
for clay soil 131
climbing methods 124–5, 130,
130
colour combinations 127, 127
colourful 127
conditions required 130
conditions tolerated 125, 130
in conservatory 357
in containers 128, 129, 307–8,
317
care 133
plants suitable for 317, 319
pruning 326
repotting 133
top-dressing 133, 133
training 317, 325, 326,
326, 333
cutting back 133
dead-heading 133
designing with 124–8
diseases 133, 661, 665
evergreen 129
pruning 136
as screen 125
existing design and 28, 32
as food source for wildlife 22,
128
for exposed sites 125
fast-growing 129

Climbers (cont.)
feeding 133
flowering on current season’s
growth 135
flowering on previous
season’s growth 135
foliage for effect 127, 128
frost damage to 607
fruiting 127, 419
as ground cover 127, 129
growing on host plants 126–7
plants suitable for 129
growing under cover
plants suitable for 376
pruning 376–7, 376
autumn 376
time for 376
support framework for
376, 376
training 376
herbaceous 129
indoors, supports for 364, 364
for interest through seasons
127–8
in mixed borders 173
mulching 132
neglected, renovating 137, 137
for north-facing walls 125
on pergolas 126
pests 133
damaging leaves 644, 651
on pillars 126
planter’s guide 129
planting
against wall 132
distances from supports
131
method 132
outdoors 131–2
planting out 141
positioning indoors 355
pot-bound 133
pricking out 141, 141
propagation 141–5
cuttings, compost for 142
hardwood cuttings 143, 143
root cuttings 144, 144
from seed 141
sowing 141, 141
self-layering 141, 144,
144, 145
semi-ripe cuttings 142–3,
143
with heel 143, 143
serpentine layering 145,
145
simple layering 145, 145
softwood cuttings 142, 142
protecting 133, 613
pruning 134–7, 326
after flowering 135, 135,
376
autumn 376
cutting down to ground 137
formative 134, 134
principles 134
spring 134, 134
to restrict growth 376, 376
under cover 376, 376
winter 136, 136
renovating 137, 137
repotting 133
routine care 100
for sandy soil 131
scented 128, 129
screening with 125
seedlings, planting out 141
self-clinging 124
self-layering 141, 144, 144
for shade 129
site 125
siting 131
in soil beds under cover 367
soil preparation 130, 132
on south-facing walls 611
standard
plants suitable for 326
pruning 326
suggestions for use 124–8

Climbers (cont.)
supports for 124, 130, 132,
357
tender
protecting 133
protecting flower buds
125
protecting roots 125
site for 125
tendril climbers 124
tolerant of air pollution 129
training 134–7
formative 134, 134
under cover 376
on trees 56
twining 124
tying in 133
under cover, training and
pruning 376
vigorous 130
watering 133
after planting 132
and wildlife 128
for winter interest 126
Clitoria
from seed 379
softwood cuttings 142
Clivia
conditions preferred indoors
361
in containers 319
for cutting 231
growing with succulents
339–40
Cloches 581, 582
barn 582, 582
dome-shaped 582
end pieces for 582
floating 582
growing vegetables under 505
hardening off in 220, 220
individual 582, 582
as pest deterrent 642
maintenance 583
materials for 582
microclimates in 611
for propagation 637
self-watering 582, 582
tent 582, 582
tunnel 505, 582, 582
growing vegetables in 505
walk-in, growing
vegetables in 505
types 582, 582
uses 566
wall-of-water 582
winter protection with 613
Closeboard fencing 600, 600
erecting 602
Clothing, protective
for disinfectants 583
for power tool use 550, 550,
556
Clover
common white see Trifolium
repens
diseases 652
soil type indicated by 617
Clubroot 617, 623, 649, 660
causes 649
control 504, 649, 660
life in soil 498
preventing 507
rotating crops to avoid 498
symptoms 649, 660
Clustered bellflower see
Campanula glomerata
Clytostoma 129
propagation, semi-ripe
cuttings 143
pruning 135
calystegioides 129
pruning 137
Coastal sites
choosing site for trees 63
salt spray 612
shrubs tolerant of 91, 95
trees tolerant of 67
wind in 611

Cobaea
from seed 141, 379
scandens 129
in containers 319
pruning 376
suggestions for use 212
f. alba 129
Cobble fountain see Fountains
Cobbles 590, 591
buying 265
Cobnuts 488–9, 488
see also Corylus avellana
chilling requirement 488
conditions required 488
feeding 489
harvesting 489
husks 488
mulching 489
pests 489
plant type 419
pollination 488
propagation
from seed 434
suckers 434
pruning 489
brutting 489, 489
recommended cultivars 488
routine care 489
self-fertile cultivars 488–9
site 489
storing 489
training 489
tree size 488
watering 489
‘Cosford’ 489
‘Nottingham’ (syn. ‘Pearson’s
Prolific’) 489
Coccus hesperidum 648
Cock chafers 660
Cocoa shells
amount required compared to
other fertilizers 624
as mulch 133, 159
nutrient content 624
Coconut fibre
as peat alternative 257
as plunge material 365
as soil additive 621, 621
Cocos
architectural 95
in containers 319
Cocoyams 543–4, 544
conditions required 543
conditions tolerated 543
in crop rotation 498
culinary uses 543
daylength requirement 543
diseases 543
earthing up 543
edible parts 542
feeding 543
growing under cover 544
harvesting 544
mulching 543
nitrogen requirement 504, 543
pests 543
plant 543
propagation
tuber cuttings 543
tubers 543
routine cultivation 543
size of plant 543
soil type required 543
spacing 543
storing 544
watering 543
Codiaeum
conditions preferred indoors
361
greenhouse conditions
required 361
hydroculture 361
softwood cuttings 380
suggestions for use 366
variegatum var. pictum, in
containers 319
Codling moth 659
symptoms and control 659, 659
trapping 641, 641

Codonopsis
softwood cuttings 142
sowing 272
convolvulacea 129
Coelogyne
suggestions for use 368
temperature required 368
Coir
as liner for basket 329, *329,
330*
in potting composts 322, *322*
storing tubers in 235, *235*
Colanders, use as container 321,
321
Colchicum
in alpine house *25*
conditions tolerated 231
corm 227
in grass, mowing 242
planting time 236
resting 240
seasonal interest 50
suggestions for use 231
autumnale
in meadows 401
suggestions for use 239
speciosum, suggestions for
use 239
Cold areas, wall footing in 597
Cold frames *see* Frames
Coleocephalocereus, flat grafting
351
Collards 507
Collars for brassica seedlings *507*
Colletia
semi-ripe cuttings with heel
113
hystrix 'Rosea' (syn. *C.
armata* 'Rosea'), scent 95
Colletotrichum 666
Collinsia
self-sown seedlings 222
bicolor
self-seeding 218
sowing 217
Colocasia esculenta
division of tubers 302
position in water garden 285
as vegetable *see* Cocoyams
Colorado beetles 504, 665
Colour
blocks of *48*
combining 48
distance and 48
effect of light on 48, *177*
mutation 676, *676*
planting for 48, *48, 49*
use of greens 48, *48*
Colour schemes
for container plantings 308
foliage colours in 176–7
perennial beds and borders
176–7
suiting conditions 177
Colquhounia
pruning 105
suggestions for use 95
Coltsfoot *see Tussilago farfara*
Columba palumbus 645
Columbine *see Aquilegia*
Columnea
greenhouse conditions
required 361
softwood cuttings 380
Combretum grandiflorum 129
Comfrey *see Symphytum
officinale*
Common Bermuda grass *see
Cynodon dactylon*
Common elder *see Sambucus
nigra*
Common jasmine *see Jasminum
officinale*
Common passion flower *see
Passiflora caerulea*
Common potato scab *662*
symptoms and control 662
Common spotted orchid *see
Dactylorhiza fuchsii*

Common thyme *see Thymus
vulgaris*
Compact marjoram *see Origanum
vulgare* 'Compactum'
Compaction of soil *621*
Compositae
diseases 657
flowers 676
Compost bins 562
making *627*
twin-bin composting system
627
using *627*
Compost heap
making 627–8
materials to avoid in 621, 628
size 627
Compost shredders 562, *562*
Composts
additives 323, *323*
for alpines 261–2, 278, 279,
306, 323, *323*
for aquatics 297, 323
for bulbs in pots 240
for cacti 323, 343, 344
for containers 322–3
for cuttings 142
standard 565
ericaceous 99, 306, 322, *322,*
364
plants requiring 325
for ferns 194
garden 627–8
adding to soil 621, *621*
additives 627
amount required
compared to other
fertilizers *624*
composting process 627
for indoor plants 372
improving soil fertility
with 494
maintaining nutrient levels
with 503
making 110, 627
materials for 110, 627
materials to avoid in 621,
628
as mulch 98, 502, 626
municipal 628
nutrient content 624
as protection for plants in
store *193*
slow composting 628
smell 627
as top-dressing *626*
for houseplants 364
for indoor plants 367
John Innes 322, 323
for lime-haters 99, 306, 322,
322, 364
plants requiring 325
loam-based 322, 364, 367
organic 323
loamless 322–3
nutrients in 332
organic 323
making 110, 323, 628
for orchids 323, *368*, 369
organic 323
peat/peat substitute-based 364
potting 627, 630
ingredients 322, *322,* 323
loamless 322–3
disadvantages 322
organic 323, 372
pH range 637
soil-less *see* loamless
propagation 565, 627
moisture 637
standard cuttings 565
standard seed 565
for rock garden 261–2
for rooting cuttings 633
for scree bed 262
seed 630
for bulbs 246
firming 637, *637*
standard 565

Composts (*cont.*)
for shrubs 99
for succulents 343, 344
water-retention 323, *323*
worm 628, *628*
Concrete
blocks
constructing retaining
walls of 598, *598*
raised beds of 599
for walls 596
canal or rill, constructing 293,
293
casing for metal uprights *604*
colouring 594
containers of 307, 321
definition 591
dye for 588
fence posts in 600
erecting *601*
fences of 600, *600*
for greenhouse foundations *571*
laying 586, *586*
mixes 586
mixing 586
ordering 586
paths of 594
laying 594
making curves 594
preparing base 594
pavers 589, *590*
paving slabs 587–8
colours 587
cutting 588, *588*
laying 587, *587*
paths of 594
pointing *587*, 588
quantities 587
shapes 587, *587*
sizes 587
styles *587*
pond of
constructing 290, *290, 291*
repairing 300, *300*
post spurs 602
reinforcing 564
retardants for 586
sheds of 605
spurs for fence posts 600, *601*
surface finish 594
textured finishes 594, *594*
Cones, extracting seed from 80
Conifer woolly aphids *see*
Adelgids
Conifers
annuals climbing through 212
for avenues 58
buying 63, 64
chemical damage to 651
contrasting with deciduous
trees *56*
cuttings 79
diseases 664
dwarf 62
in alpine house 258
alpines with *257*
associating with other
plants 62
colours 62
in containers 94
designing with 62
forms 62
as ground cover 62
group planting 62
growth rate 54
with heathers *62*
selecting 62
size 54
specimen plants 62, *62*
suggestions for use 62
in troughs 258
grafting 82
as hedges 85
shaping 86
hormone weedkiller damage
655
pests 654
eating leaves 645
pruning 73

Conifers (*cont.*)
in restricted colour border *92*
winter colour 57
Conophytum, division of offsets
349
Conservation
bulbs in the wild 228, 236
of energy, greenhouse for
569, *569*
Conservatories 356–7, 358–9
beds in 357, *357*
preparing 367
borders in 367
cacti for 341
climbers in 357
composts 367
cool, plant arrangement in *359*
damping down 357
displaying plants in 357
furniture in *356*
heating 357
humidity 357
materials for 356
orientation 356
plant health in 357
shading 357, *357*
siting 356
succulents for 341
ventilation 356–7, *356*
watering plants in 357
Consolida
architectural plants 213
for cutting 212
protecting seedlings *218*
thinning *218*
ajacis Giant Imperial Series
210
ambigua
architectural plant 210
for cutting 213
for drying 213
sowing 217
Imperial Series 210
Sublime Series 210
Container gardens 304–35
specialized 318
subtropical 318
Container-grown plants
checking roots 334
dead-heading 332, 333, *333*
diseases 333, 654
fungal 333, 654, 661
emergency revival methods
335
faded, replacing 333, *333*
feeding 332, 624
organic 332
grooming 332–3
hardening off 335
holiday care 334–5
organic composts for 323
overwintering 335, *335*
pests 333, 660, 666
pinching back 333
pruning 326, 333
replacing 333, *333*
root pruning 334, *334*
routine care 332–5
security 335
staking 325
top-dressing 325, *334*
training 326, *326*
water problems 650, 651
watering 308, 310, 332, 614
holiday arrangements
334–5
methods 331, *332*
waterlogging 664
winter protection 335, *335*
Containers (for clay and plastic
pots *see* Pots)
accessories *321*
adapting 321, *321*
advantages of 306
alpines in 255, 258, *258,*
266–7
planting 267, *267*
siting 267
watering 270

Containers (*cont.*)
annuals in 212, 315
climbers 212
for aquatics 297, *297*
auriculas in *24*
on balconies 312–13, *312, 313*
in beds and borders 309
biennials for 315
bulbs in
outdoors 229, *229*, 241
care 243
plants suitable for 316
under cover 230, 240–1
cacti in
indoors 341
outdoors 340, *340*
planting 344, *344*
plants suitable for 342
ceramic 320
choosing 307, 310, 320–1,
320, 324
clematis in 138
climbers in 128, 129, *317*
plants suitable for 317,
319
colour themes in 308
composts for 322–3, 324, 333
of concrete 307, 321
crocks for 325
daffodils in 233
defining accents 308
designing with 306–18
drainage materials for *323*
dwarf conifers for 62
fibreglass 307, 321
flanking avenue *308*
as focal points 212, 306,
308–9, *309*
formal arrangements 306, 308
fruit in 423
fuchsias in 121
grouping *310*, 311
hygiene 311
growing vegetables in,
drainage 501
hanging 314–15
hanging baskets *see* Hanging
baskets
herbs in 405, *405*, 413
for indoor plants 358
informal arrangements 306
informal groupings 311
of marble 321
marking boundary 308
marking changes of level 309,
309
marking transition 309
materials for 307, 320–1
metal 321
mixed plantings in 308, *327*
mulches for 323
for office plants 358
ornamental terracotta *565*
paired *308, 309*
in paved gardens 310–11
arranging 310
plants for 310
pelargoniums in *204*
perennials in 179, *179*, 185
care 193, *193*
plants suitable for 315–16
planting
herbs 411
large and long-term plants
324–5
perennials 185, *185*
seasonal displays 327–8
plants for 315–17
selecting 324, *324*
plastic 320–1
adding weight 369
preparing 324–5
raised 22
replacing faded plants 333, *333*
rock plants in 258, *258*, 266–7
planting 267, *267*
siting 267
on roof gardens 312–13, *312,
313*

Containers (cont.)
  roses in 153
    planting 158
  scale 307
  security 308
  for seed sowing 218
  self-watering 374
  shape 307
  shrubs in 93, 94
    care 100
    planting 99, 99
    plants suitable for 94,
      316–17, 319
    root pruning 110
  siting 308–9
  size 307
  sowing tree seed in 80, 80, 81
  for sowing vegetables 501
  specimen plants in 307–8
  stands for 311
  of stone 321
  stylized display 26
  successional displays in 310
  succulents in
    indoors 341
    outdoors 340, 340
    planting 344, 344
    plants suitable for 342
  suggestions for use 306–18
  terracotta 306, 307, 310, 311,
    320, 321
  trailing plants for annuals and
    biennials 213
  for trees 58
  trees in 58, 58, 59
    plants suitable for 316
  tulips in 232
  types 307
  vegetables in 494, 501, 501
    changing compost 503
    compost 501
    plants to avoid 501
    preparing containers 501
    routine cultivation 503
    siting 501
    top-dressing 503
    types suitable for 501
  wall-mounted 314–15
  for water garden 284
  water garden in 284, 318,
    331, 331
    choosing plants 331
    planting 331, 331
    siting 331
  of wood 307, 321, 321
Contarinia
  pyrivora 658
  quinquenotata 657
Convallaria majalis 181
  scent 172
  suggestions for use 172, 178,
    228
Convention on International
  Trade in Endangered Species,
  and bulbs 228
Convolvulaceae 338
Convolvulus
  softwood cuttings 142
  soil type preferred 325
  arvensis 670
    control 670, 673
  boissieri, semi-ripe cuttings
    273
  cneorum
    seasonal interest 95
    suggestions for use 257
  sabatius
    overwintering 335
    semi-ripe cuttings 273
    in containers 319
  tricolor 129
    as ground cover 211
    suggestions for use 213
Copiapoa, division of offsets 349
Coping finishes for walls 598, 598
Copper
  deficiency 426
  plant requirements 624
Copper band, as slug deterrent 333

Copper oxychloride 648, 668
Copper-based fungicides 648,
  649, 651, 660, 662, 665, 668
Copper-based insecticides,
  organic 642
Coppicing 46, 58, 73–4, 73
  shrubs 107, 107
  trees suited to 74
Coprinus 668
Coprosma
  conditions preferred 95
  semi-ripe cuttings with heel
    113
Coral spot 665
  symptoms and control 665
Cordons
  on arches 423
  form 419, 419
  grapes, pruning 462–3, 462–3
  planting
    against fence 425
    in open ground 425
  soft fruit
    pruning 476, 476
    training 476, 476
  tomatoes 527
    training 527, 527
  training 419–20
  tree fruit
    pruning 440–1, 441, 444
    space required 422
    training 440, 444
Cordyline
  architectural 95
  conditions tolerated 95
  in containers 318
  in greenhouse garden 360
  propagation, hardwood
    cuttings 79
  pruning 108
  australis
    germination 379
    suggestions for use 59, 307
Coreopsis
  grandiflora 'Early Sunrise'
    for cutting 213
    growing as annual 213
  tinctoria, soil type preferred
    216
  verticillata
    dividing 201
    foliage 175
Coriander 408, 408
  culinary uses 408
  flowers 408
  foliage 408
  harvesting 408
  propagation from seed 408, 414
  protecting for winter use 411
  smell of plant 408
  storing 408
Coriandrum sativum see
  Coriander
Corky scab 648
  symptoms and control 648
Cormels
  propagation by 245, 245
  raising 634
Corms 634
  choosing 236
  definition 227
  division 245, 245
  planting 238
    depth 238
    in root growth 238
  propagation 634–5, 634
  purpose 675
  spacing 238
  storage rots 663
Corn poppy see Papaver rhoeas
Corn salad 521
  growing under cover 521
  harvesting 521
  large-leaved 521
  soil types tolerated 521
  sowing 521
  spacing 521
  suggestions for use 521
  types 521

Corners, containers in 310, 311
Cornfields 401
Cornflower see Centaurea cyanus
Cornus
  bark 50, 94
  conditions preferred 91
  coppicing 46
  disease-resistance 661, 665
  in fedges 126
  propagation, stooling 117
  alba 94
    coppicing 107
    for cutting 22
    propagation
      division of suckers
        118
      French layering 117
      hardwood cuttings
        114
    suggestions for use 285
    'Aurea', coppicing 107
    'Elegantissima', coppicing
      107
    'Kesselringii', coppicing
      107
    'Sibirica'
      bark 94
      coppicing 107
      soil type tolerated 97
    'Spaethii', coppicing 107
    'Variegata', coppicing 107
  alternifolia 'Argentea',
    pruning 105
  canadensis 118
    conditions preferred 95
    conditions tolerated 95
    as ground cover 180
    propagation, division of
      suckers 118
    soil type required 99
  controversa
    architectural form 46
    'Variegata' 17
  'Eddie's White Wonder',
    seasonal interest 95
  florida, diseases 666
  kousa
    diseases 666
    seasonal interest 59
    suggestions for use 59
    var. chinensis
      seasonal interest 59
      as specimen tree 55
  mas 'Variegata', seasonal
    interest 95
  nuttallii
    diseases 666
    soil preferred 65
  sericea
    conditions tolerated 95
    propagation
      hardwood cuttings
        114
      division of suckers
        118
      French layering 117
    'Flaviramea'
      coppicing 107
      seasonal interest 92
Corokia
  pruning 105
  semi-ripe cuttings with heel
    113
Coronilla
  germination 115
  pruning 376
  varia, soil type tolerated 185
Correa backhouseana 91
  pulchella in conservatory 359
Cortaderia selloana, architectural
  form 181
  'Pumila', in a border 179
Corticium rolfsii see Athelia
  rolfsii
Corydalis
  conditions preferred 231
  planting 237
  propagation, sowing 272
  resting 240

Corydalis (cont.)
  seed collecting 246
  suggestions for use 231
  tubers 227
  cashmeriana, soil type
    required 260
  flexuosa, soil type required 260
  lutea, soil type tolerated 185
  solida, choosing healthy bulbs
    236
Corylopsis
  layering 116
  in mixed border 227
  pruning 105
  soil type required 99
Corylus
  for coppicing 74
  flowers, unisexual 676
  fruit type 675
  pests 655
  propagation, layering 81
  suggestions for use 54
  avellana
    fruit see Cobnuts
    as hedge 85
    'Contorta'
      seasonal interest 95
      stems 94
      suggestions for use 74
  colurna, conditions tolerated
    67
  maxima
    fruit see Filberts
    'Purpurea' 107
      coppicing 107
Corynebacterium sepedonicum 662
Coryphantha, division of offsets
  349
Cosmetics, herbs used for 404
Cosmos 213
  for cutting 213
  for dry conditions 211
  in mixed border 210, 210
  soil type tolerated 216
  atrosanguineus, for fragrance
    181
Cotinus
  pruning 105
  soil type tolerated 97
  coggygria
    coppicing 107
    propagation
      French layering 117
      softwood cuttings 79
      stooling 117
    seasonal interest 92
    'Flame', seasonal interest 95
    'Grace', coppicing 107
    'Royal Purple', autumn
      interest 177
Cotoneaster
  for autumn colour 57
  conditions tolerated 95
  deciduous
    pruning 106
    soft/greenwood cuttings
      111
  diseases 649, 665
  dwarf
    conditions tolerated 95
    pruning 106
  dwarf conifers with 62
  germination 115
  pests 647, 654
  propagation
    semi-ripe cuttings with
      heel 113
    soft/greenwood cuttings
      111
  pruning 106
    to attract wildlife 103
  seed stratification 629
  soil type tolerated 97, 99
  conspicuus
    as ground cover 101
    seasonal interest 95
  'Cornubia', seasonal interest
    92
  dammeri, as ground cover 101

Cotoneaster (cont.)
  horizontalis, conditions
    tolerated 95
  'Hybridus Pendulus', spliced
    side-veneer grafting 119
  ignescens (syn. C. bullatus
    'Firebird') 113
  lacteus, as hedge 85
  'Rothschildianus', berries 94
  salicifolius 'Gnom', size 90
  x watereri, hardwood cuttings
    114
Cottage garden 15, 20, 21, 210
  bulbs in 227
  colour combinations 49
  planning 43
  plants for 178
  on roof garden 313
  roses in 153
Cotton lavender see Santolina
Cotula
  for lawns 389
  coronopifolia, position in
    water garden 285
Cotyledon
  stem cuttings 348
  campanulata, suggestions for
    use 342
  ladismithensis, leaf cuttings
    347
  orbiculata
    var. oblonga, leaf cuttings
      347
    var. orbiculata (syn. C.
      undulata), suggestions
      for use 342
Cotyledons (seed leaves) 630,
  630, 676
Couch grass 627, 670
  control 619
  eradicating 390, 411
  in lawns 389
  removing from pond site 298
Coumatetralyl 662
Courgettes 522
  conditions required 526
  conditions tolerated 526
  diseases 526
  flowers
    distinguishing female
      from male 526, 526
    harvesting 526
  freezing 506
  fruits 526
  growing in containers 318, 328
  growing under cover 526
  habit 526
  harvesting 526, 526
  nitrogen requirements 504, 526
  pests 526
  pollinating by hand 526, 526
  protecting 526
  recommended cultivars 526
  routine cultivation 526
  soil type required 526
  sowing 526
  spacing 526
  training 526
  watering 614
    critical periods 502
  'Badger Cross' F1 526
  'Bambino' F1 526
  'Blyton Belle' 526
  'Clarion' F1 526
  'Defender' F1 526
  'Eight Ball' 526
  'Hasta la Pasta' 526
  'Jemmer' 526
  'Minipak' 526
  'Parador' 526
  'Patty Pan' 526
  'Pyjamas' 526
  'Rondo di Nice' 526
  'Sunburst' 526
  'Table Dainty' 526
  'Tiger Cross' F1 526
  'Tivoli' 526
  'Vegetable Spaghetti' 526
  'Venus' 526

Courtyards
  containers in 310–11
  perennials in containers 179
Cowslip see Primula veris
Crab apples ornamental, see Malus
Crambe
  cordifolia 181
    division 201
    form 175
    with roses 151
  maritima, conditions tolerated 181
Crane fly larvae 660
  on lawns 667
Cranesbill, meadow see Geranium pratense
Crassula
  conditions preferred indoors 361
  in greenhouse display 341
  hardiness 339
  propagation
    division of offsets 349
    leaf cuttings 347
    softwood cuttings 380
    stem cuttings 348
  arborescens, leaf cuttings 347
  helmsii (syn. Tillaea recurva)
    cuttings 302
    dangers of 298
    position in water garden 285
  ovata (syn. C. portulacea)
    in bowl garden 341
    choosing healthy plant 343
    in bowl 344
    leaf cuttings 347
    suggestions for use 342
  perfoliata
    leaf cuttings 347
    var. minor (syn. C. falcata)
      in containers outdoors 340
      suggestions for use 342
  perforata, division of offsets 349
  rupestris, suggestions for use 342
  sarcocaulis, conditions tolerated 342
  sarmentosa, conditions tolerated 342
  socialis
    division of offsets 349
    leaf cuttings 347
    suggestions for use 342
Crataegus
  for autumn colour 57
  conditions tolerated 67
  disadvantages 57
  diseases 649, 664
  in fedges 126
  as food source for wildlife 22
  pests 647, 652
  propagation, chip budding 82
  shaping 86
  soil type tolerated 65
  laciniata, suggestions for use 59
  laevigata
    soil type tolerated 66
    'Paul's Scarlet'
      suggestions for use 59
    'Rosea Flore Plena', as specimen tree 55
  x lavallei
    conditions tolerated 67
    'Carrierei'
      berries 57
      seasonal interest 59
      suggestions for use 59
  monogyna
    conditions tolerated 67, 613
    as hedge 15, 84, 85
    as security measure 15

Crazy paving see Paving
Creeping bentgrass see Agrostis stolonifera
Creeping savory
  in herb garden 412
  suggestions for use 405, 410
Creeping thistle see Cirsium arvense
Creosote as wood preservative 602
Crepis incana, conditions tolerated 259
Cress 520
  conditions preferred 520
  culinary uses 520
  growing with mustard 520
  harvesting 506, 520
  sowing 520
  suggestions for use 520
  broadleaved 520, 520
  creeping yellow see Rorippa sylvestris
  land see Land cress
  upland see Land cress
Crevices
  planting in 263, 264, 268, 268
  plants suitable for 259, 263
  weeds in, control 673
Crinum
  for cutting 231
  overwintering 230
  propagation, division of offsets 245, 245
  x powellii
    architectural plant 231
    in mixed border 227
    suggestions for use 229
Crioceris asparagi 644
Crithmum maritimum, conditions tolerated 342
Crocosmia 50
  in border 172, 174
  in containers 319
  for cutting 181, 231
  diseases, fungal 663
  in mixed border 228
  propagation, cutting up with growing points 249
  seasonal interest 50
  'Lucifer' 230
    as specimen plant 179
Crocus 226
  to attract insects 264
  bird damage 657
  conditions tolerated 231
  in containers 241, 319
  corm 227
  damage caused by mice, rats, and voles 662
  forcing 231
  greenhouse conditions required 361
  in ground cover 180
  increase 226
  naturalized 229
  planting
    depth 239
    in grass 239
  in pots under cover, watering 244
  propagation, division of offsets 245
  resting 240
  seasonal interest 50
  seed collecting 246
  seedlings 246
  stamens 676
  suggestions for use 228, 230–1, 308, 316
  transplanting from pots 243
  in woodland 228
  autumn-flowering
    in mixed border 228
    planting time 236
  biflorus, suggestions for use 239
  chrysanthus
    suggestions for use 239
    in wild-flower garden 401

Crocus (cont.)
  Dutch Hybrids, suggestions for use 239
  flavus, suggestions for use 239
  laevigatus, in rock garden 255
  nudiflorus, suggestions for use 239
  ochroleucus, suggestions for use 239
  pulchellus 239
    suggestions for use 239
  speciosus
    suggestions for use 239
    in wild-flower garden 401
  tommasinianus
    suggestions for use 228, 239
    in wild-flower garden 401
  vernus, in wild-flower garden 401
Crocus, autumn see Colchicum autumnale
Crooknecks squashes see Marrows, crookneck squashes
Crop rotation see Rotation of crops
Croquet lawn 389
  mowing 395
Cross-pollination 629
  cacti and succulents 347, 347
  fruit 423, 424, 444, 482
  of GM plants 638
  herbs 407
Crossandra, softwood cuttings 380
Crown gall 655, 661
  symptoms and control 655, 661
Crown rot 187, 665
  symptoms and control 665
Cruciferae (Crucifers) see Brassicas
Cryptanthus
  conditions preferred indoors 361
  displaying 362
  propagation, division of plantlets/runners 378
  acaulis, suggestions for use 366
  bivittatus 362
    suggestions for use 366
  bromelioides, suggestions for use 366
  zonatus, suggestions for use 366
Cryptocereus anthonyanus see Selenicereus anthonyanus
Cryptocoryne beckettii var. ciliata, division of rootstock 302
Cryptogramma
  conditions required 194
  in winter 194
Cryptolaemus montrouzieri, as biological pest control 642, 646
Cryptomeria
  soil preferred 65
  japonica
    winter colour 57
    'Vilmoriniana' 259
Cryptostegia, softwood cuttings 142
Ctenanthe amabilis (syn. Stromanthe amabilis)
  suggestions for use 366
  in terrarium 366
Cuckoo spit see Froghoppers
Cucumber mosaic virus 467, 638, 659
Cucumbers 524–5
  conditions preferred 524
  conditions required 524
  culinary uses 524
  diseases 525, 654, 661
  feeding 524–5
  germination 524
  greenhouse 522
  growing under cover 525
  harvesting 506, 524, 525

Cucumbers (cont.)
  nitrogen requirement 504, 524
  pests 525
    damaging leaves 646
  planting out 524, 524
  recommended cultivars 525
  routine cultivation 524
  site 524
  soil type preferred 524
  sowing 524, 524
  spacing 524
  stopping 525
  storing 506
  watering 525
    critical periods 502
  all-female cultivars 524
  apple, fruit 524
  'Burpless Tasty Green' F1 525
  bush 525
  'Bush Champion' F1 525
  'Carmen' F1 525
  climbing 525
  European see greenhouse
  'Flamingo' F1 525
  greenhouse
    bitter flavour 524
    conditions required 524
    fruit 524
  lemon, fruit 524
  'Marketmore' 525
  'Petita' 525
  ridge (outdoor)
    conditions tolerated 524
    flower production 524
    fruit 524
  'Tokyo Slicer' F1 525
  trailing types
    pinching out growing point 524
    training 524
  'Zeine' F1 525
Cucumis melo see Melons
Cucumis sativas see Cucumbers
Cucurbita
  maxima see Pumpkins
  moschata see Pumpkins
  pepo see Courgettes; Marrows; Pumpkins
Cucurbitaceae (Cucurbits) 338
  diseases, virus 659
Cultivars
  definition 677
  names 677
Cultivation tools for 551–3, 551–3
Cultivators
  five-tined 553, 553
  manual 553, 553
  powered 553, 553
  removing prongs 553
  star-wheeled 553, 553
Cumin 408, 408
  conditions required 408
  culinary uses 408
  flowers 408
  foliage 408
  harvesting 408
  propagation from seed 408
Cuminum cyminum see Cumin
Cuphea
  in containers 319
  flowering time from seed 198
  greenhouse conditions required 361
  overwintering 335
  propagation, stem tip cuttings 202
  from seed 379
x Cupressocyparis
  as hedge 84
  semi-ripe cuttings 79
  leylandii
    conditions tolerated 67, 613
    disease resistance 654
    diseases 664
    as hedge 84, 85, 85
    resistance to storm damage 68
    root-balled 63

x Cupressocyparis leylandii (cont.)
  soil type tolerated 65
  'Castlewellan', seasonal interest 59
  'Robinson's Gold', seasonal interest 59
Cupressus
  semi-ripe cuttings 79
  spliced side grafting 82
  arizonica 'Pyramidalis', seasonal interest 59
  glabra
    soil preferred 66
    soil type tolerated 65
    'Pyramidalis', seasonal interest 59
  macrocarpa
    diseases, fungal 664
    'Goldcrest'
      seasonal interest 59
      suggestions for use 59
  sempervirens
    diseases fungal 664
    suggestions for use 59
    for topiary 76
    'Swane's Gold', seasonal interest 59
Curculigo capitulata (syn. C. recurvata), leaf vein patterns 676
Curly kale see Kales, curly
Currant galls 652
Currants
  diseases 665
  freezing 431
  mineral deficiencies 650, 656
  pests 645
  pruning 428
Currants, black 474–5
  big bud mite resistant cultivars 655
  certification schemes 474
  conditions required 474
  conditions tolerated 474
  diseases 427, 474, 655
  feeding 474
  freezing 431
  harvesting 475
  mulching 474
  pests 474, 645, 652, 655
  plant type 419, 468
  planting 474
    time for 474
  propagation, hardwood cuttings 434, 475
  pruning 474, 474–5
    after fruiting 475
    after planting 474
    for rejuvenation 474
    winter 428, 474, 474
  recommended cultivars 475
  rejuvenating 474
  routine care 474
  shoots, new and fruited 474
  site 474
  site preparation 474
  soil types for 474
  spacing 474
  storing 475
  watering 474
  'Baldwin' 475
  'Ben Alder' 475
  'Ben Connan' 475
  'Ben Gairn' 475
  'Ben Hope' 475
  'Ben Lomond' 475, 475
    in large fruit garden 421
  'Ben More' 475
  'Ben Nevis' 475
  'Ben Sarek' 475, 475
    in large fruit garden 421
    in small fruit garden 422
  'Ben Tirran' 475
  'Big Ben' 475
  'Boskoop Giant', in large fruit garden 421, 475
  'Wellington XX' 475
Currants, red 468, 475–6
  conditions required 475

Currants, red (*cont.*)
conditions tolerated 475
cordons 420
pruning 476, *476*
training 476, *476*
diseases 475
feeding 475
freezing 431
harvesting 476
mineral sensitivity 624–5
netting 475
pests 475
plant type 419, 468
planting 475
potash requirements 421
propagation, hardwood
cuttings 434, 476, *476*
protecting from wind 475
pruning
bush 475, *475*
cordon 476, *476*
fan 476
winter 428
recommended cultivars 476
routine care 475
site 475
soil for 475
spacing 475
storing 476
training
as cordon 476, *476*
in small garden 421–2
'Jonkheer van Tets' 476,
476
'Laxton's No.1' 476
'Red Lake' 476
in large fruit garden *421*
in small fruit garden *422*
'Redstart' 476
'Redpoll' 475
'Rondom' 476
'Stanza' 476
Currants, white 475–6
conditions required 475
conditions tolerated 475
cordons 420
pruning 476, *476*
training 476, *476*
diseases 475
feeding 475
freezing 431
harvesting 476
netting 475
pests 475
plant type 419, 468
planting 475
propagation, hardwood
cuttings 434, 476, *476*
protecting from wind 475
pruning
bush 475, *475*
cordon 476, *476*
winter 428
recommended cultivars 476
routine care 475
site 475
soil for 475
spacing 475
storing 476
training as cordon 476, *476*
'Blanka' 475
'White Dutch' 476
'White Grape' 476, *476*
in small fruit garden *422*
Custard marrows *see* Marrows,
custard
Cut flowers *see* Flowers
Cut-and-come-again crops
harvesting 506
lettuce 518, 519
seedlings 500, 516
Cutting, tools for 554–6
maintenance 554
Cuttings
adventitious growth *370*
alpines 273–4, *273–4*, *274*,
275–6, *275*, *276*
plants propagated by 273,
274

Cuttings (*cont.*)
basal 235, *235*, 632
alpines 274
begonias 382, *382*
bulbs 250
dahlias 235, *235*
basal stem, perennials 202–3,
202
blackleg on *664*
symptoms and control 664
bud 287, *287*
cacti 346
climbers 141
composts for 565, 633
cut leaves 381–2, *382*
environment for 633, *633*
fruit 432, 434, *434*
fuchsias 120–1, *120*
greenwood 111–12, *111*, 632
alpines 273
selecting material for 274,
274
shrubs propagated by 111
hardwood 121
climbers 141, 143, *143*
fruit 434, *434*
method 632, *632*
preparing 633, *633*
roses 165, *165*
shrubs 113–14, *114*
shrubs propagated by 114
trees 78–9, *78*
planting depth *78*
trees propagated by 79
truncheons 460
heel 633
climbers 143, *143*
shrubs 112, 113, *113*
trees 79
internodal 140, *140*, 633, *633*
"Irishman's" alpines 275, *275*
leaf 632, 633, *633*
alpines 274
indoor plants 38–2, *381*
large leaves *633*
selecting material for 274,
274
small leaves *633*
succulents 347, *347*
leaf sections 382, *382*
leaf-bud 380, 632, *632*
blackberries 472, *472*
fruit 434
hybrid berries 472, *472*
shrubs 113, *113*
leafy, protecting 636, *636*
mallet 113, *113*
methods 632–3
nodal *632*, 633
shrubs 112
trees 79
pad sections, cacti and
succulents *348*
pests 666
ripewood
see also hardwood
alpines 274
selecting material for 274,
274
root 141, 632, 633, *633*
alpines 275–6, *276*
climbers 144, *144*
perennials 203, *203*
perennials propagated by
203
scooping rosettes 276, *276*
shrub 114
rosette, selecting material for
274, *274*
scored leaves 381–2, *382*
selecting material for 274,
274
semi-ripe 632, *632*
alpines 274
climbers 141, 142–3, *143*
indoor shrubs 380
overwintering 112
preparing 633, *633*
roses 165

Cuttings (*cont.*)
selecting material for 274,
274
shrubs 112–13, *112*
shrubs propagated by 113
trees 79, *79*
compost for 79
trees propagated by 79
shrubs 111–14, *111–14*
softwood 120, 141, 632, *632*
alpines 273, *273*
aquatics *302*, 303
climbers 142, *142*
compost for 142
fruit 434
indoor plants 380–1, *380*
in water 381, *381*
indoor plants propagated
by 380
perennials propagated by
202
protection for 636
shrubs 111, *111*
shrubs propagated by 111
trees 79
trees propagated by 79
stem *370*
perennials suitable for 202
preparing 632–3, *633*
succulents 348, *348*
types 632–3, *632–3*
stem sections, cacti and
succulents 348, *348*
stem tip, perennials 202, *202*
succulents 346
time to take 632
tip *120*, 632
trees 78–9, *78*, *79*
trees suitable for 79
wounding 633, *633*
Cutworms *655*
symptoms and control 504,
655, 660
Cyananthus, soil type required 260
Cyathea medullaris, hardiness 60
Cycas revoluta
architectural 95
in containers 319
suggestions for use 61
Cyclamen 226
choosing healthy plants 236
collecting from the wild 228
conditions preferred indoors
361
conditions tolerated 226, 228,
231
in containers 319
greenhouse conditions
required 361
pests 656, 660, 666
planting 237, 238, *238*
propagation
from seed 247, 379
sowing 272
resting 240, 373, *373*
seasonal interest 50
seed harvesting *247*
suggestions for use 179, 228,
229, 231
tubers 227
watering 372
alpine, sowing 272
coum
conditions tolerated 231
suggestions for use 226
in woodland *228*
hardy, suggestions for use 231
hederifolium
choosing healthy bulbs
236
conditions preferred 259
conditions tolerated 231
propagation, cutting up
with growing points 249,
249
in rock garden 256
persicum, indoors 354
purpurascens, conditions
preferred 259

Cyclamen (*cont.*)
repandum, conditions
tolerated 231
rohlfsianum, cutting up with
growing points 249
Cydia
funebrana 659
nigricana 659
pomonella 659
Cydonia
oblonga
fruit *see* Quinces
suggestions for use 59
Cylindroiulus 644
Cymbidium
in greenhouse 360
propagating 371, *371*
suggestions for use 368
temperature required 368
Strath Kanaid *368*
Cynara
architectural form 181
for drying 181
seedheads 177
cardunculus 181
scolymus as vegetable *see*
Globe artichokes
Cynipid wasps *652*
symptoms 652
Cynodon
for lawns 388, 389
dactylon 388
for lawn, sowing rate 394
incompletus var. *hirsutus* 388
x *magennisii* 388
transvaalensis 388
Cynoglossum amabile, sowing 217
Cyperus
indoors 355
propagation, rootstock 378
involucratus, position in
water garden 285
longus, position in water
garden 285
papyrus
position in water garden
285
'Nanus' (syn. 'Viviparus')
propagation 303
position in water
garden 285
suggestions for use
331
Cyphomandra betacea (syn. *C.
crassicaulis, Solanum
betaceum*) *see* Tamarillos
Cypress *see* Cupressus
Cypress
Lawson's *see* Chamaecyparis
lawsoniana
Leyland, *see*
x *Cupressocyparis leylandii*
Cypripedium
suggestions for use 368
reginae, soil type required 185
Cyrtanthus
conditions preferred indoors
361
growing with succulents
339–40
purpureus, pests 663
Cyrtomium, in winter 194
Cysts 666
Cytisus
conditions preferred 91
dwarf conifers with 62
flowers 94
germination 115
pests 655
propagation
semi-ripe cuttings with
heel 113
soft/greenwood cuttings
111
soil type tolerated 99
battandieri, scent 95
x *beanii*, soil type preferred 261
scoparius, soil type preferred
97

D

Daboecia
clematis growing through 138
dwarf conifers with 62
propagation
dropping 116
soft/greenwood cuttings
111
pruning 107
soil type indicated by 617
soil type required 325
suggestions for use 93
Dactylopsis, division of offsets 349
Dactylorhiza
suggestions for use 228
tubers 227
fuchsii
conditions preferred 401
suggestions for use 239
maculata, suggestions for use
239
Daddy-long-legs *see* Crane fly
Daffodil *see* Narcissus
Dahlia 234–5
classification 34
conditions required 234
in containers 319
cultivation 234–5
for cutting 181
disbudding 235, *235*
diseases 655
effect of frost on 607
exhibiting 235
for exhibition, cultivation 235
feeding 234, 235
flowers 676
types *234*
lifting 235
in mixed border 173, 177
mulching 234
pests 235, 645
affecting flowers 657
eating leaves 644
planting 234, *234*
time 234
propagation 235, *235*
basal cuttings 235, *235*
division of tubers 235, *235*
site 234
soil preparation 234
stopping 235, *235*
storing 235, *235*
tubers 227, *635*
planting 234, *234*
wing buds 235
coccinea, suggestions for use
61
'Comet' 234
'Easter Sunday' 234
'Frank Hornsey' 234
imperialis, suggestions for
use 61
'Monk Marc' *227*
'Pearl of Heemstede' 234
'Shirley Alliance' *234*
'Small World' 234
'So Dainty' *234*
'Wootton Cupid' *234*
'Yellow Hammer' *234*
'Zorro' *230*
Daikon *see* Mooli
Daisy *see* Bellis perennis
Michaelmas *see* Aster
ox-eye *see* Leucanthemum
vulgare
shasta *see* Leucanthemum x
superbum
Daisy grubber 553, *553*
Damasonium alisma, division of
rootstock 302
Damp sites
bulbs for 229
succulents tolerating 342
wild flowers for 401

Damping down 357, 576
Damping off diseases 223, 394,
504, 637, *637*, 654
symptoms and control 660,
660, 664, *664*
Damsons 447–50
conditions preferred 447
forms 447
freezing 431
preserving 431
recommended cultivars 449
rootstocks 447
'Bradley's King' 449
'Farleigh' 449
'Frogmore Damson' 449
'Merryweather' 449
'Prune' 449, *449*
in large fruit garden *421*
Danäe racemosa, division of
suckers 118
Dandelion 670
as edible plant 521
blanching 521, *521*
harvesting 521
sowing 521
eradicating 193, 390
as lawn weed 672
soil types tolerated 521
spread of plant 521
Daphne
fasciation 657
propagation, semi-ripe
cuttings 113, 273
pruning 105
seasonal interest 50
sowing 115
suggestions for use 259
arbuscula
propagation, apical-wedge
grafting 119
suggestions for use 259
bholua
scent 95
spliced side-veneer
grafting 119
suggestions for use 95
blagayana
conditions preferred 259
layering 116
scent 95
'Bramdean', suggestions for
use 93
x *burkwoodii*
soft/greenwood cuttings
111
'Somerset' *255*
seasonal interest 91
cneorum
to attract insects 264
scent 95
suggestions for use 259
collina, to attract insects
264
x *hendersonii*, to attract
insects 264
jasminea, softwood cuttings
273
laureola
conditions preferred 95
conditions tolerated 95
mezereum 105
odora, scent 95
petraea
spliced side-veneer
grafting 119
'Grandiflora', suggestions
for use 259
retusa 259
sericea 259
semi-ripe cuttings 112
x *susannae*
'Cheriton', suggestions for
use 259
'Tichborne', suggestions
for use 259
x *whiteorum* 'Beauworth',
suggestions for use 259
Darlingtonia, soil type required
185

Darmera peltata (syn.
Peltiphyllum peltatum)
conditions preferred 181
division of rootstock 303
soil type tolerated 184
suggestions for use 285
Dasineura
affinis 652
gleditchiae 652
tetensi 652
Date palm *see* *Phoenix
canariensis*
dwarf *see* *Phoenix roebelenii*
Datura
conditions preferred 95
as pot plants 213
pruning 105
Daucus carota see Carrots
Davallia, in containers 319
Davidia, layering 81
Dawn redwood *see Metasequoia
glyptostroboides*
Daylength 495, 610
increasing with growing
lamps 577
manipulating artificially 610
variations in, effects on
strawberry flowering 468
Daylength neutral plants 495
Daylily *see Hemerocallis*
Dead-heading 133, 191–2
annuals 223, *223*
biennials 223, *223*
bulbs in grass 242, *242*
container-grown plants 332,
333, *333*
herbs 413
perennials 191–2
shrubs 100, *100*
Deadman's handle *553, 557, 557*
Deadnettle *see* Lamium
Decabelone *see* Tavatesia
Decaisnea, pruning 105
Deciduous plants
climate suited to 606
composting prunings 110
Decking 591–2
building regulations
concerning 591
disguising drainage system
313
parquet 591, 592
on roof garden *313*
slatted construction 592
stepping stones of *592*
on terrace *312*
timber
choice for 592
patterns 592, *592*
support for 592, *592*
waterside
construction 296, *296*
flexible liner for 296, *296*
foundations 296, *296*
Decodon verticillatus
position in water garden 285
propagation
cuttings 302
division of rootstock 302
Decumaria
semi-ripe cuttings 143
sinensis 129
pruning 135
Deer
control 666
damage caused 645, 666, *666*
deterring 642
protection from 504
Dehiscent fruit 675, *675*
Delairea odorata see Senecio
mikanioides
Delia
antiqua 663
platura 666
radicum see Cabbage root fly
Delosperma
conditions tolerated 342
division of offsets 459
division of rootstock 350

Delphinium 15
in border 174
for cutting 181
cutting back 192, *192*
diseases, bacterial 648, *648*
fasciation 657
flowering time from seed 198
form 176
germination 630
propagation, basal stem
cuttings 202, 203
with roses 151
seasonal interest 50
staking 192, *192*
suggestions for use 173, 178
thinning 191
'Blue Nile', companion plant
for 177
Centurion Series 213
Dendrobium
method of growth 368
propagation
adventitious growth 370
stem cuttings *370*
stem cuttings 371
suggestions for use 368
temperature required 368
Happiness, growing on bark
369
nobile 368
Dendromecon rigida, conditions
preferred 95
Deroceras 644
Derris *see* Rotenone
Deschampsia cespitosa, in
containers 319
Desert climate 606
Desert gardens 340, *340*
planting 343
Desfontainia spinosa, soil type
required 99
Design *see* Planning and design
Deuterocohnia (syn.
Abromeitiella) 362
Deutzia
propagation, semi-ripe
cuttings 113
pruning 106
renovation *110*
seasonal interest 50
soft/greenwood cuttings 111
soil for 91
soil type tolerated 97, 99
x *elegantissima* 'Rosealind'
hardwood cuttings 114
longifolia
hardwood cuttings 114
'Veitchii' *114*
x *rosea*, hardwood cuttings 114
scabra hardwood cuttings 114
Devil's coach-horse beetles *617*
Dianthus 196–7
to attract insects 264
breeding 178
in containers 319
in cottage gardens 177
for cutting 181, 213
for fragrance 181
pests 661
propagation 197
from cuttings 197
softwood cuttings 273
stem tip cuttings 202
in rock garden 254, *255*
scent 172
soil type preferred 184, 216,
325
soil type tolerated 185, 216,
261
suggestions for use 172, 255,
259
supports for 325
alpinus
conditions suitable for 255
flowers 255
suggestions for use 258,
259
anatolicus, suggestions for
use 259

Dianthus (cont.)
barbatus
conditions tolerated 213
in containers 319
for cutting 213
thinning *218*
'Bombardier' suggestions for
use 258
'Bookham Fancy' *196*
border carnations *196*
buying plants 196
conditions preferred 196
cultivation 196
description 196
disbudding 196
flowers *196*
growing for exhibition 197
planting 196
preparing bed for 196
propagation
for exhibition 197
layering 197, *197*
site 196
soil type preferred 196
spacing 196
watering 196
carnations 196–7
diseases 197, 654, 661
flower types
fancy 196
picotee 196
self 196
flowers 196
groups 196
growing for exhibition
197, *197*
feeding 197
good blooms for *197*
protecting buds with
calyx bands 197, *197*
mineral deficiency 654
pests 197
propagation 197, *197*
types 196
carthusianorum
conditions tolerated 259
soil type preferred 261
'Cartouche' *196*
'Champion', growing as
annual 213
chinensis 196
conditions tolerated 213
in containers 319
scent 213
'Clara' *196*
deltoides
conditions tolerated 259
soil type preferred 261
suggestions for use 258
'Doris' *196*
erinaceus, suggestions for use
259
'Floristan', growing as annual
213
freynii, suggestions for use 259
Giant Chabaud Series
for cutting 213
scent 213
glacialis, suggestions for use
259
'Grey Dove' *197*
haematocalyx, conditions
preferred 256
'Hannah Louise' *197*
Knight Series, for cutting 213
'La Bourboule', in trough *267*
Malmaison carnations *196*
description 196
'Mars' *255*
microlepis, suggestions for
use 258
modern pinks *196*
'Musgrave's Pink' *196*
old-fashioned pinks *196*
pinching out 196
perpetual-flowering
carnations *196*
breaking 196, *196*
buying 196

Dianthus, perpetual-flowering
carnations (*cont.*)
compost becoming sour
196
cultivation 196
description 196
disbudding 196, *196*
feeding 196
flowering 196
in greenhouse 360
propagation, cuttings 197,
197
repotting 196
stopping 196, *196*
watering 196
pinks 196
buying plants 196
conditions preferred 196
cultivation 196
description 196
diseases 197
exhibiting 197, *197*
good blooms for *197*
flower types
bicolour 196
fancy 196
laced 196
self 196
flowers 196
groups 196
growing for exhibition
197, *197*
feeding 197
protecting buds with
calyx bands 197, *197*
modern flowering 196
pests 197
pinching out 196
planting 196
propagation 197
cuttings 197, *197*
site 196
soil type preferred 196
spacing 196
types 196
'Souvenir de la Malmaison'
196
spray carnations *196*
description 196
disbudding 196, *196*
propagation, cuttings 197
stopping 196
Diascia
grown as annuals 213
in containers 319
overwintering 335
semi-ripe cuttings 273
stem tip cuttings 202
barberae
'Fisher's Flora' (syn. *D.
cordata* of gardens),
conditions tolerated 259
'Ruby Field', conditions
tolerated 259
Dibbers 219, *219*, *379, 563, 563*
Dicamba 673
Dicentra
conditions tolerated 181
for cutting 181
greenhouse conditions
required 361
spectabilis 'Alba' 48
Dichlobenil 671, 673
Dichomeris marginella 647
Dichondra
conditions required 389
micrantha, for lawns 389
Dicksonia 60
antarctica
buying 60
in containers 319
planting 60
trunk 60
fibrosa, hardiness 60
squarrosa, hardiness 60
Dicotyledons
flower forms 676, *676*
leaf veins 676, *676*
stems 676

Dictamnus albus, for fragrance 181
Didiscus coeruleus see Trachymene coerulea
Didymella applanata 653
Die-back 160, 640, 654, 655
  in alpines, cutting back *270*
  causes 427, 428, 454, 650, 653, 654
  in evergreens 77
  rose *156*
    symptoms and control *161*, 665, *665*
Dieffenbachia
  conditions preferred indoors 361
  greenhouse conditions required 361
  hydroculture 361
  indoors *355*
  seguine 'Exotica', pollution-absorbing 358
Dierama
  for cutting 231
  pendulum, suggestions for use 229
Diervilla lonicera, division of suckers 118
Difenacoum 662
Digging 619–20
  correct position *550*
  cultivators for 553, *553*
  disadvantages 619
  double 620, *620*, 621
    to improve drainage 390
  simple 619, *619*
  single 619, *619*
  time for 619
  tools for 551, *551*, 552, *552*
Digitalis 49
  to attract insects 181
  in mixed border 210
  in naturalistic planting schemes 197
  self-sown seedlings 185
  soil type indicated by 617
  in woodland garden 179
  grandiflora, conditions tolerated 181
  lutea, conditions tolerated 181
  purpurea
    conditions tolerated 213
    propagation, self-seeding 218
    with roses 151
    Excelsior Group
      architectural plant 210, 213
      self-sown 223
Dill 407, *407*
  cross-pollination with fennel 407
  culinary uses 407
  flowers 407
  foliage 407
  growing with vegetables *495*
  harvesting 407
  propagation from seed 407, 414
  storing 407
  suggestions for use 405
Dinteranthus, division of offsets 349
Dioecious plants 676, *676*
Dionysia
  plunging after flowering *277*
  softwood cuttings 273
  aretioides, preparing for exhibition *279*
Dioscorea
  semi-ripe cuttings 143
  discolor 129
Diospyros
  kaki see Persimmons
  virginiana, as rootstock 458
Dipelta
  pruning 106
  yunnanensis, seasonal interest 95

Diploids 435
Diprion 645
Dipteronia, layering 81
Diquat 671, 673
Disabled
  access to greenhouse 570, *570*
  aids for 599
  gardening for 405
Disanthus
  layering 116
  pruning 105
Discocactus, flat grafting 351
Discula destructiva 666
Diseases
  affecting bark 654
  affecting bulbs 663
  affecting flowers 656–7
    discolouration 656
    distorted and eaten 657
  affecting fruit, berries, and seeds 658–9
  affecting lawns 667
  affecting leaf buds 653–4
  affecting leaves 646, 647, 648–50, 651, 652, 654
  affecting roots and tubers 660–2
  affecting stems 653–5
  affecting whole plant 664–6
  in biological pest control 642
  in greenhouses 583
  breeding resistance to 638
  chemical control 643
  definition 639
  diagnosing problems caused by 639, *639*
  effect of pH on 617
  encouraged by growing conditions 641
  global warming effects 607, 659
  government regulations for 655
  identifying method 639
  integrated control 640
  notifiable 654, 665
  organic control 640, 641–2, *641*
    companion planting 641
    traps 641–2
    treatments 642
  plants resistant to 640
  prevention 640
  prevention of build-up 640, *640*
  spread by insects 639
Dishing 622
Disocactus
  apical-wedge grafting 351
  side grafting 351
  stem cuttings 348
  suggestions for use 342
  flagelliformis 351
Disorders
  affecting flowers 656, 657
  affecting fruit, berries, and seeds 658–9
  affecting lawns 667
  affecting leaves 648, 650–1
  affecting roots and tubers 660, 662
  affecting stems and leaf buds 653, 654, 655
  affecting whole plant 664, 665
  causes 639
  cultural 640–1
    symptoms *640*
  diagnosing problems caused by 639, *639*
  method of identifying problem 639
Distictis 129
  propagation
    semi-ripe cuttings 143
    softwood cuttings 142
  pruning 135
  soil type tolerated 131
  buccinatoria 130
    pruning 137, 376
    vigour 130

Ditylenchus dipsaci 652, 663
Dividers, fruit as 422
Division
  alpines 275, *275*
  cacti 346
  indoor plants 378–9, *378*
  of offsets
    cacti 349, *349*
    cacti propagated by 349
    succulents 349, *349*
    succulents propagated by 349
  perennials 193, 200–1, *200–1*
  perennials suitable for 201
  rhizomes, water plants 302, *302*
  of rootstock
    cacti 350, *350*
    succulents 350, *350*
  roses 167, *167*
  shrubs 118, *118*
  shrubs propagated by 118
  succulents 346
  of tubers 382, *382*
  of water plants 301, 302, *302*, 303
Dock *671*
  eradicating 390
  soil type indicated by 617
  broadleaded 670
Dodecatheon
  soil type tolerated 184
  sowing 272
Dog lichens *667*
  symptoms and control 667
Dog rose *see Rosa canina*
Dogs
  control 667
  damage to lawn *667*
Dog's-tooth violet *see Erythronium dens-canis*
Dogwood, *see Cornus*
Dolichos beans *see* Beans, dolichos
Dollar spot *667*
  symptoms and control 667
Dolomitic lime, in cuttings compost 565
Doors, containers framing *311*
Dormancy
  breaking 80, 115, 141, 198, 629–30
  double 198
  factors affecting 607
  high temperature 518
  plant mechanisms for 629
  reasons for 607
Doronicum
  for cutting 181
  division 201
  in mixed border 176
  soil type tolerated 185
  winter interest 181
  orientale 172
    conditions tolerated 180
Dorotheanthus
  for dry conditions 211
  soil type preferred 325
Dorycnium hirsutum see Lotus hirsutus
Double budding 446, *446*
Double grafting 446, *446*
Double-working 446, *446*
Douglas fir, *see Pseudotsuga*
Downy mildew 646
  global warming effects 659
  symptoms and control 193, 646
Draba
  propagation
    rosette cuttings 274
    softwood cuttings 273
  soil type tolerated 261
  aizoides, in trough *267*
  mollissima, suggestions for use 259
  polytricha, suggestions for use 259
  rigida var. *bryoides*, suggestions for use 259

Dracaena
  architectural 95
  conditions preferred indoors 361
  in containers 319
  greenhouse conditions required 361
  hydroculture 361
  in terrarium *374*
  draco, suggestions for use 59
  fragrans
    Deremensis Group, pollution-absorbing 358
    'Lemon and Lime' *365*
    'Warneckei', potting *373*
  sanderiana
    in bottle garden *367*
    suggestions for use 366
Dracophilus, division of offsets 349
Dragonflies, attracting 22
Drainage
  ditches 623, *623*
  in frames *581*
  French drains 623
  improving 616, 621, 623, *623*
  installing *391*, 623, *623*
  for lawn 390
  for patios 585, *585*
  for perennials 183
  poor, testing for 623
  for retaining walls 598
  rock garden 262, *263*
  soakaways 623, *623*
  tile drainage system 623, *623*
  top-dressings as 626, *626*
Draw hoe 552, *552*
Dregea (syn. *Wattakaka*)
  propagation, semi-ripe cuttings 143
  suggestions for use 129
  sinensis, suggestions for use 129
Dribble bars for watering cans 560
Dried flowers, perennials suitable for 181
Drills
  sowing annuals and biennials in 217, *217*
  sowing vegetables in 499–500, *499*
    in dry conditions 499–500, *499*
    in wet conditions 499, *499*
Drimys
  semi-ripe cuttings 113
  winteri, semi-ripe cuttings 79
Drip feed irrigation systems 561, *561*
Drives
  concrete 586
  foundations 585, *585*
    concrete mix for 586
  materials for 593
  paving slabs 587–8
  preparing sub-base 585, *585*
  weedkillers for 671
Dropping shrubs 116–17
Drosera, soil type required 185
Drought 622
  damage to plants 650, *650*
  effects of global warming on 607, 650
  effect on lawn 396, 667
    control 667
  plants adapted to 609
  plants resistant to 256, 614
  plants tolerant of 622–3
  problems of 609–10
  symptoms and control 657, 664
  water conservation and recycling 614–15, *614–15*
Drupes 675
Dry areas, lawns for 389
Dry shade
  annuals tolerant of 213
  biennials tolerant of 213
  bulbous plants tolerant of 231

Dry shade (*cont.*)
  perennials tolerant of 181
  rock plants tolerant of 259
  shrubs tolerant of 95
Dry-stone wall *see* Walls
Dryas
  ripewood cuttings 274
  octopetala 274
    conditions tolerated 259
    ripewood cuttings *274*
    'Minor', suggestions for use 259
Drying
  flowers 222, *222*
  herbs
    air- 415, *415*
    freeze- 415
    microwave 415
    roots 415
  seedheads 415, *415*
Dryopteris
  conditions tolerated 194
  in winter 194
  filix-mas, leaf form *675*
Duckweed *see Lemna*
Dudleya, leaf cuttings 347
Dutch elm disease, symptoms and control 653–4, *653*
Dutch hoe 552, *552*
Duvalia
  division of offsets 349
  division of rootstock 350
  flat grafting 351
Dyckia 362
Dyes for concrete 594
Dypsis lutescens, pollution-absorbing 358

E

Ear protectors *556*
Earth leakage circuit breaker 550
Earthworms 617, *617*, 668
  encouraging 621, 624
  improving soil structure 617
  in lawn 395, 396, 400, 668
    worm casts 400
  protecting pots from 325
  soil rich in 493, 497
  symptoms and control 668
  working mulch into soil 503
  working organic matter into soil 494
Earwigs *644*
  control 643, 644, 657
  damage caused by 644, *644*
  trapping 641, *641*, 657
Eau-de-cologne mint *see Mentha x piperita* f. *citrata*
Ebracteola, division of offsets 349
Eccremocarpus scaber 129
  in containers 319
  on host plant 212
  pruning 135
  soil type tolerated 132
  suggestions for use 128
  survival 223
Echeveria
  in bowl garden 341
  conditions preferred indoors 361
  conditions tolerated outdoors 339
  form 338
  in greenhouse display *341*
  in mixed succulent planting *340*
  propagation
    leaf cuttings 347
    stem cuttings 348
  in raised bed 340
  succulent type 338

Echeveria (cont.)
  agavoides
    division of offsets 349
    leaf cuttings 347
    suggestions for use 342
  coccinea, conditions tolerated
    342
  cuspidata, conditions
    tolerated 342
  derenbergii
    division of offsets 349
    suggestions for use 342
  elegans
    conditions tolerated 342
    division of offsets 349
    leaf cuttings 347
  gibbiflora, conditions
    tolerated 342
  pilosa, suggestions for use
    342
  setosa, division of offsets 349
Echidnopsis, division of offsets
  349
Echinacea purpurea
  to attract insects 181
  in mixed border 177
Echinocactus
  form 338
  in greenhouse display *341*
  grusonii
    flowers 342
    form 339
Echinocereus
  conditions tolerated 339
  containers for 344
  division of offsets 349
  side grafting 351
  berlandieri, suggestions for
    use 342
  *chloranthus see Eviridiflorus
    chloranthus*
  engelmannii, flowers 342
  enneacanthus, conditions
    tolerated 342
  pentalophus 342
    conditions tolerated 342
    suggestions for use 342
  triglochidiatus, flowers 342
  viridiflorus
    conditions tolerated 342
    in containers outdoors
      340
Echinops
  flat grafting 351
  root cuttings 203
  soil type preferred 184
  bannaticus, for drying 181
  ritro
    for drying 181
    'Veitch's Blue' *184*
Echinopsis
  division of offsets 349
  as rootstock 351
  atacamensis subsp. *pasacana*,
    suggestions for use 342
  aurea
    flowers 342
    suggestions for use 342
  chamaecereus (syn. *Lobivia
    silvestrii*)
    conditions tolerated 342
    in containers outdoors 340
    flat grafting 351
    suggestions for use 342
  deserticola, flowers 342
  eyriesii, suggestions for use
    342
  famatimensis (syn. *Lobivia
    famatimensis*), flowers 342
  haematantha (syn. *E.
    kuehnrichii*), suggestions
    for use 342
  hybrids, suggestions for use
    341
  mamillosa (syn. *E.
    kermesina*), flowers 342
  marsoneri, suggestions for
    use 342
  mirabilis, flowers 342

Echniopsis (cont.)
  oxygona
    flowers 342
    suggestions for use 342
  pachanoi, suggestions for use
    342
  pentlandii, suggestions for
    use 342
  spachiana
    flowers 342
    suggestions for use 342
  terscheckii, flowers 342
  viridiflorus subsp.
    chloranthus 342
Echium vulgare, conditions
  tolerated 213
  candicans, suggestions for
    use 61
  pininana, suggestions for use
    61
Edelweiss *see Leontopodium
  alpinum*
Edgers, half-moon 396, 399, *399,
  400, 558*
Edging
  for crazy paving, defining 588
  fruit as 422
  for herb garden 405
  herbs as 405, *495*
  lawn 387–8
    materials for 558
    repairing 399, *399*
    shaping 393, *393*
    tools for 558, *558*
  materials for 591
  for paths 412, 497, 594
  for paving 588, *588*, 590, *590*
  for ponds 291, *291*
  in rose garden 150
  for watercourse 293
Edging boards 638, *638*
Edible landscaping 494
Edithcolea
  flat grafting 351
  grafting 350
Edraianthus
  dinaricus, suggestions for use
    259
  graminifolius, suggestions for
    use 259
  pumilio, suggestions for use
    259
Edwardsiana rosae 647
Eelworms (nematodes) 617, 639,
  652
  as biological control 642, 644,
    645, 660, 666, 668
  bud
    control 647
    damage caused by 647, *647*
  control 618, 652
  damage caused by 652
  diseases transmitted by 649,
    656
  leaf
    control 647
    damage caused by 647, *647*
    plants affected by 647
  narcissus 663
  potato cyst, symptoms and
    control 666, 668
  root-knot 451, 660
  rotating crops to avoid 498
  taking cuttings of plants
    infected with 203, 647
  in vegetable garden 504
  viruses spread by 662
Egeria densa 285
  cuttings 302
Eggplant *see* Aubergines
Eichhornia
  azurea 285
  crassipes 282, 285
    dangers of 298
    propagation
      offsets 303, *303*
      plantlets 303
    suggestions for use 318,
      331

Elaeagnus
  conditions tolerated 95
  diseases, fungal 665
  propagation, semi-ripe
    cuttings with heel 113
  scent 95
  angustifolia, conditions
    tolerated 95
  commutata, layering 116
  x *ebbingei* 'Gilt Edge',
    seasonal interest 95
Elatostema (syn. *Pellionia*)
  softwood cuttings 380
  repens (syn. *Pellionia
    daveauana*), suggestions
    for use 366
Elder *see Sambucus*
Elder, ground *see* Ground elder
Elderly
  aids for 599
  gardening for 405
  raised beds for 173
Electricity
  compared to petrol 556, 557,
    558
  in greenhouse, installing 572
  for greenhouse heating 574
  safety 550, 556
    screened cables 580
  supply to greenhouse 567
Eleocharis acicularis,
  suggestions for use 331
Elettaria cardamomum,
  suggestions for use 405
Elm *see Ulmus*
Elm bark beetles 654
Elodea
  canadensis, cuttings 303
  crispa see Lagarosiphon major
Elsinoe fawcettii 649
Elymus
  repens see Couch grass
  smithii (syn. *Agropyron
    smithii*), for lawns 389
Embothrium coccineum, soil
  preferred 65
Encarsia formosa as biological
  pest control 642, *642*, 646
Endive 516–17
  bitterness 516
  blanching 516, *517*
  bolting 516
  conditions preferred 515
  conditions tolerated 516
  culinary uses 516
  curled, recommended
    cultivars 516
  as cut-and-come-again
    seedling crop 506
  diseases 517
  escarole, recommended
    cultivars 516
  forcing 505
  growing under cover 517
  harvesting 517
  nitrogen requirement 504, 516
  overwintering 517
    cultivars for 516
  pests 517
  recommended cultivars 516
  routine cultivation 516
  sowing 516
  spacing 516
  thinning out 516
  types 516
  'Blond Full Heart' 516
  'Full Heart Italian' 516
  'Grobo' 516
  'Jeti' 516
  'Moss Curled' 516
  'Pancaliere' 516
  'Wallone' 516
English bluebell *see
  Hyacinthoides non-scripta*
Enkianthus
  propagation, soft/greenwood
    cuttings 111
  pruning 105
  soil type required 99

Ensete 61
  protection for 61
  site for 61
  ventricosum, in containers 319
Environmental concerns 15
Enzymes 675
Eomecon, soil type tolerated 184
Epicormic shoots *see* Water shoots
Epidendrum, propagation by stem
  cuttings 371
Epidermis *674*
Epigaea
  layering 116
  gaultherioides, soil type
    required 260
  repens, soil type required 260
Epigeal germination 630, *630*
Epilobium 670
  dividing 201
  angustifolium f. *album*, as
    ground cover 180
Epimedium
  conditions tolerated 181
  cutting back 180
  as ground cover 180
  winter interest 181
Epiphyllum
  conditions preferred indoors
    361
  disorders 648
  in greenhouse display *360*
  propagation
    leaf sections 382
    softwood cuttings 380
    stem cuttings 348
  anguliger, flowers 342
  cartagense, flowers 342
  crenatum, flowers 342
  hybrids, suggestions for use
    341
  'Oakwood', propagation by
    stem section *348*
  oxypetalum
    conditions tolerated 342
    suggestions for use 342
Epiphytes
  bromeliads
    displaying 362, *362*
    feeding 363
    mist-spraying 363
  cacti 338
    apical-wedge grafting 351
    conditions required 341
    flowers 339
    watering 345
  indoors 358
  offsets, propagation by 363, *363*
  orchids
    compost *368, 369*
    conditions preferred 355
    cultivaton 368
    growing without pots 369
    habitats 368
    methods of growth 368
    monopodial 368
    potting 369
    sympodial 368
  succulents
    conditions required 341
    watering 345
Epipremnum 129
  conditions preferred indoors
    361
  softwood cuttings 380
  aureum 129
Episcia
  conditions preferred indoors
    361
  conditions tolerated 355
  propagation by runners 378
  suggestions for use 366
Epithelantha
  division of offsets 349
  flat grafting 351
Epsom salts 426, 651
Equipment 550–65
  see also Tools
  general garden 562–4, *562–4*
  for watering 560–1, *560–1*

Equisetum
  control 670, 673
  arvense 670
Eranthis
  conditions preferred 231
  hyemalis
    diseases 652
    in mixed border 177, 227
    seasonal interest 50, 176
    suggestions for use 179,
      239
Erepsia, division of offsets 349
Ercilla
  semi-ripe cuttings 143
  simple layering 145
  volubilis, soil type tolerated
    131
Eremochloa ophiuroides
  for lawn 388
    sowing rate 394
Eremurus
  form 175
  soil type tolerated 185
Erica
  clematis growing through 138
  in containers 319
  dwarf conifers with 62
  greenhouse conditions
    required 361
  as ground cover 93
    with clematis *127*
  propagation
    division of suckers 118
    dropping 116
    layering 116
    semi-ripe cuttings 113, 273
    soft/greenwood cuttings
      111
  pruning 107
  soil type indicated by 617
  soil type required 99, 325
  suggestions for use 93
  arborea, soil type preferred 97
  carnea
    conditions tolerated 95
    mulching *101*
  cinerea, soil type preferred 97
  lusitanica, scent 95
  x *williamsii* 'P.D. Williams' *91*
Ericaceous plants *see* Lime haters
Erigeron
  for cutting 181
  in mixed border 177
  karvinskianus, conditions
    tolerated 181
Erinacea anthyllis
  semi-ripe cuttings 273
  suggestions for use 259
Erinus alpinus
  conditions tolerated 259
  suggestions for use 259
  'Dr Hähnle', suggestions for
    use 258
Eriobotrya japonica
  architectural 95
  as fruit *see* Loquats
  suggestions for use 59
Eriogonum ovalifolium, softwood
  cuttings 273
Eriophorum
  angustifolium
    division of rootstock 302
    position in water garden
      285
  latifolium, position in water
    garden 285
Eriophyllum lanatum, softwood
  cuttings 273
Eriosoma lanigerum 654
Ermine moth caterpillar, small 647
Erodium
  greenwood cuttings 273, *274*
  root cuttings 203
  reichardii (syn. *E.
    chamaedryoides*),
    suggestions for use 259
  guttatum
    conditions tolerated 259
    soil type preferred 261

Erosion on slopes 493
Eruca vesicaria subsp. *sativa*
see Salad rocket
Erugala *see* Salad rocket
Erwinia
amylovora 649
carotovora var. atroseptica
664
carotovora var. carotovora
663
Eryngium
conditions tolerated 259
foliage 176
root cuttings 203
for seedheads 181
soil type tolerated 185
agavifolium, suggestions for
use 61
x tripartitum, soil type
preferred 184
variifolium, conditions
tolerated 181
Erysimum
with bulbs in formal bedding
227
clearing at end of season 223
conditions tolerated 213
in containers 212, 319
diseases 649, 660
as fillers 211
greenhouse conditions
required 361
in mixed border 173
pests 644
seasonal display 210
soil type preferred 325
stem tip cuttings 202
suggestions for use 328
cheiri
for cutting 213
soil type tolerated 216
suggestions for use 315
Fair Lady Series,
suggestions for use 309
helveticum, soil type tolerated
261
Erysiphe 646
Erythronium
conditions preferred 231
propagation
chipping 249
from seed 246
seedlings 246
planting out 246, 247
storing 236
suggestions for use 178, 229
in woodland 179
californicum 'White Beauty',
suggestions for use 239
dens-canis 401
conditions preferred 401
suggestions for use 239
oregonum, choosing healthy
bulbs 236
revolutum, suggestions for
use 239
Escallonia
conditions tolerated 91, 95,
613
as hedge 84, 85
propagation, semi-ripe
cuttings with heel 113
pruning 108
'Donard Seedling', pruning 107
'Langleyensis' 84
Eschscholzia
conditions tolerated 213
as ground cover 210
in a dry garden 211
in mixed border 210
propagation, self-sown 223
protecting seedlings 218
self-sown seedlings 222
soil type preferred 325
californica 217
for dry conditions 211
self-seeding 218
soil type preferred 216
sowing 217

Escobaria, division of offsets
349
Espalier-trained trees
form 419, 419
pruning 73, 420, 442–3, 442
fruit 442–3, 442, 444
spacing 436
training 73, 420, 442, 442
Espostoa
lanata
flowers 342
planting 343
suggestions for use 342
melanostele, flowers 342
Essential oils from herbs 405
Etiolation, symptoms and control
655
Eucalyptus
bark 54
container-grown 64
for coppicing and pollarding
74
physiological disorders 651
pollarding 107, 107
scent 56
coccifera
seasonal interest 59
suggestions for use 59
dalrympleana
bark 57
seasonal interest 59
suggestions for use 59, 74
ficifolia
seasonal interest 59
soil preferred 66
globulus, suggestions for use
74
gunnii
conditions tolerated 67
suggestions for use 74
pauciflora
conditions tolerated 67
seasonal interest 59
suggestions for use 74, 74
subsp. niphophila
bark 57
seasonal interest 59
suggestions for use
59
Eucomis
conditions preferred 231
in greenhouse garden 360
in mixed border 228
suggestions for use 230
Eucryphia
layering 81
pruning 105
glutinosa, seasonal interest 59
lucida, softwood cuttings 79
milliganii 91
x nymansensis 57
'Nymansay' 79
semi-ripe cuttings 79
Eumerus 663
Euleia heraclei 647
Euonymus
to attract wildlife 103
germination 115
greenhouse conditions
required 361
pests 647
damaging leaves 645
propagation, semi-ripe
cuttings 143
seasonal interest 50
soil type tolerated 99
alatus
in informal shrub
grouping 90
seasonal interest 91
suggestions for use 46
fortunei 94
conditions preferred 95
conditions tolerated 93,
95, 129
in containers 319
propagation, division of
suckers 118
pruning 107

Euonymus fortunei (cont.)
'Emerald Gaiety'
reverted shoot 100
suggestions for use
317
'Emerald 'n' Gold' non-
variegated shoot 100
'Gold Spot' 101
'Silver Queen'
contrasting with
climber 126
foliage 94
soil type tolerated
131
japonicus
conditions preferred 95
conditions tolerated 95
pruning 107
phellomanus bark 48
Eupatorium purpureum
suggestions for use 285
subsp. maculatum
'Atropurpureum'
architectural form 181
growth rate 181
Euphorbia
conditions tolerated 259, 339
latex produced 348
mass planting 26
propagation, stem cuttings 348
in restricted colour border 92
seed germination 198
succulent groups 338
amygdaloides var. robbiae,
winter interest 181
canariensis, in succulent
group 338
candelabrum, in desert garden
340, 340
characias
conditions tolerated 181
winter interest 50, 181
subsp. wulfenii
in mixed border 174
as specimen plant 179
cyparissias
as ground cover 180
'Fens Ruby', method of
spreading 180
flanaganii, suggestions for
use 342
fulgens, greenhouse
conditions required 361
griffithii, as ground cover 180
mellifera 61, 94
milii
hydroculture 361
in hydroculture display
375
suggestions for use 342
myrsinites
conditions tolerated 259
as ground cover 180
obesa, suggestions for use
342
palustris, suggestions for use
285
pulcherrima
conditions preferred 361
greenhouse conditions
required 361
indoors 358
propagation, softwood
cuttings 380
pruning, sap from wound
376
Euphorbiaceae 338
Euproctis chrysorrhoea 647
Europe
average annual rainfall 609,
609
average minimum
temperatures 609, 609
climate 608–9, 609
influences on climate 606
European fan palm *see*
Chamaerops humilis
European Welsh onions *see*
Onions, Welsh

Euryale ferox
position in water garden 285
from seed 303
Euryops
acraeus 259
seasonal interest 95
pectinatus, conditions
preferred 91, 95
Evening, climbers for 126
Evergreens
as backdrop 46
buying 64
climate suited to 606
climbing 129
planting 131
pruning 136
as screen 125
for winter interest 126
winter interest 128
combining with deciduous
trees 57
in containers 315
die-back 77
feeding after pruning 108
as ground cover 101
as hedge 84, 85
shaping 86
mulching 108
perennials 179
planting time 65
propagation
cuttings, preparing 633
hardwood cuttings 632
protecting from frost and
wind 67
pruning 71
and compost 110
established 73
formative 72
in rock garden 256
scorch 77
shrubs
in containers 94
pruning 103, 107–8, 108
renovation 110
tolerating severe pruning
108
snow damage to 609
for topiary 76
Everlasting flowers
annuals to dry as 212
drying 222, 222
harvesting 222, 222
Exacum
conditions preferred indoors
361
greenhouse conditions
required 361
affine
for fragrance 213
as pot plants 213, 319
from seed 379
Exhibition
alpines 279, 279
carnations 197, 197
dahlias 235
equipment for 154
growing roses for 154
preparing for 154
staging blooms 154
Exobasidium vaccinii var.
japonicum 652
Exochorda, pruning 106
Exotic plants 60–1
Exposed sites
annuals and biennials for
213
bulbs for 231
climbers for 125
perennials for 181
rock plants for 259
shrubs for 95
trees for 67
Extractor fans 575
Eyesores
blocking out 313
camouflaging 138
ground-cover plants on 153
trees to screen 58

F

F1 hybrids
method of producing 630
qualities 212, 216, 315
from seed 379
F2 hybrids
method of producing 630
qualities 212, 216, 315
Fagus
for avenues 58
clumps as focal point 56
copper, suggestions for use 54
disease-resistance 661, 665
diseases 664, 665
for leaf mould 63
pests 652
pleaching 58
propagation
apical wedge grafting 82
spliced side grafting 82
seed germination 81
soil type indicated by 617
grandifolia, soil preferred 65
sylvatica
as hedge 84
soil type tolerated 65
'Dawyck Gold'
seasonal interest 59
suggestions for use 59
Fairway crested wheatgrass *see*
Agropyron cristatum
Fairy rings 668
Fallopia (syn. *Bilderdykia*,
Polygonum, Reynoutria) 129
propagation
semi-ripe cuttings 143
serpentine layering 145
baldschuanica
as cover for wildlife 128
pruning 135, 137
soil type tolerated 132
training 134
vigour 125, 130
as weed 669
japonica (syn. *Polygonum
cuspidatum*) 671
False acacia *see* *Robinia
pseudoacacia*
Family garden 22, 22, 23
Fan palm, European *see*
Chamaerops humilis
Fan-training
form 419, 420
shrubs 108, 108
trees, pruning 73
Fargesia
murielae
in containers 319
suggestions for use 318
nitida, in containers 319
Fasciation 657, 657
Fascicularia bicolor, temperature
for 362
Fat-hen *see* *Chenopodium album*
x *Fatshedera*
conditions preferred indoors
361
lizei, in containers 319
Fatsia
conditions preferred indoors
361
greenhouse conditions
required 361
japonica
conditions preferred 95
conditions tolerated 95, 355
in containers 319
foliage 90, 94, 354
form 311
indoors 355
suggestions for use 61, 318
'Variegata'
as ground cover 101
Fatty acids 648, 668

Faucaria
division of offsets 349
division of rootstock 350
felina, suggestions for use 342
Fava beans *see* Beans, broad
Fedges 126
Felicia
stem tip cuttings 202
amelloides
in containers 319
overwintering 335
'Variegata', in hanging basket *330*
bergeriana, suggestions for use 313
Fences 600–3
arris rails
repair 602
securing 602, *602*
chain link 600, *600*
cleft chestnut paling 600, *600*
clematis on 138
climbers on 125
positioning 131
closeboard 600, *600*
erecting 602
concrete 600, *600*
conditions on each side 611
existing design and 31
frost pockets beside *607*
fruit trees against, positioning 425
growing fruit on 422
interference 600, *600*
interwoven 600, *600*
lattice 600, *600*
legal requirements 600, 602
maintenance 602
making decorative 600
metal post supports 601, *601*
panel 600–1, *600*
erecting 600–1, *601*
picket 600, *600*
post and chain 600, *600*
post and rail 600, *600*
posts for 600
concrete 600
erecting *601*
repairs 602
timber 600, *601*
ranch-style 600, *600*
roses for 153, 155
shingle 600, *600*
on sloping ground 602, *602*
south-facing, plants for 611
stepped 602, *602*
timber preservatives for 602
types 600, *600*
uses 584, 600
waney-edged 600, *600*
wattle hurdles 600, *600*
welded wire 600, *600*
as windbreaks 493, 495, 611, *611*
Fenestraria, division of rootstock 350
Fennel, Florence 408, 535, *535*, 540–1, *540*
bolting 540
bulb 540
conditions tolerated 540
culinary uses 540
diseases 541
disorders 541
earthing up 540
foliage 540
harvesting 541, *541*
mulching 540
nitrogen requirement 504, 540
pests 541
protecting 540
recommended cultivars 541
routine cultivation 540
size of plant 540
soil types required 540
sowing 540
spacing 540
transplanting 540
watering 540

Fennel Florence (*cont.*)
weeding 540
'Amigo' 541
'Pronto' 541
'Romanesco' 541
'Rudy' 541
'Selma' 541
'Victoria' 541
'Zefa Fino' 541
Fennel, ornamental *see Foeniculum vulgare*
Fennel, sweet *see* Fennel, Florence
Fenusa pusilla 47
Ferns 194–5
in greenhouse 359
in alpine house 258, 279
compost for 367
conditions preferred 610
in greenhouse 576
conditions required 194
conditions tolerated 194, 355
in containers 315
plants suitable for 319
cultivation 194
hardy 194
indoors 355, 358
in natural planting 24
neglected, renovating 372
propagation 194–5, *194*, *195*
bulbils *194*, 195
spores 195, *195*
suggestions for use 228, 283, 315
tender tropical 194
compost for 194
conditions required 194
potting up 194
suggestions for use 194
watering 194
tree 60, *60*
in water garden *282*
in woodland garden *178*, 179
Ferocactus
handling *343*
cylindraceus, suggestions for use 342
latispinus, suggestions for use 342
Ferric phosphate 644, 668
Ferrous sulphate 479, 673
Fertilization 676
Fertilizers 624–5
adding to peat 323
amount required compared to other fertilizers *624*
applying 503, 625, *625*
broadcast 625, *625*
foliar 625
liquid 625
placement 625, *625*
quantities 625
bulky organic 624
comparing *624*
concentrated 624
foliar 625
sprayers for 560, *560*
forms available 503
for hydroculture 375
inorganic
applying 624
compared to manure 624
nutrient content 624
slow-release 323, 624
soluble 624–5
amount required compared to other fertilizers *624*
for lawns 396
application 396–7, *397*
liquid 625
homemade 332, 372, 625
organic 332, 372, 625
as mulch 68
nutrient content 624
organic 332, 625
"home-grown" 332
nutrient content 624
for tree fruit 426

Fertilizers (*cont.*)
slow-release 100, 323, *323*, 625
advantages 625
methods of working 625, *625*
nutrient content 624
soluble 624–5
speed of action 100
sprayers for 560, *560*
spreaders 559, *559*
for trees 68
types 624–5
Ferula communis, growth rate 181
Fescue *see* Festuca
Chewing's *see Festuca rubra* var. *commutata*
red *see Festuca rubra* var. *rubra*
Festuca
diseases 667
for lawn 388, 389
sowing rate 394
for meadow garden 401
in turf 392
glauca 181
rubra
var. *commutata* 389
for lawn 388
var. *rubra*
for lawn 388
sowing rate 394
Feverfew *see Tanacetum parthenium*
Fibre fleece *see* Fleece
Fibreglass, containers of 307, 321
Fibrous films *see* Fleece
Ficus
fruit 57
greenhouse conditions required 361
for office 358
propagation
air layering 81, 117
hardwood cuttings 79
leaf-bud cuttings 380
semi-ripe cuttings 632
benjamina
hydroculture 361
propagation, softwood cuttings 380
in soil bench *367*
pollution-absorbing 358
suggestions for use 59
'Variegata' *59*
supporting *364*
carica see Figs
deltoidea, suggestions for use 358
elastica
air layering 383, *383*, 631
cleaning foliage 372, *372*
foliage 354
pruning, sap from wound 376
'Robusta', pollution-absorbing 358
lyrata, suggestions for use 358
pumila
propagation, self-layering 145
suggestions for use 366
'Variegata'
in hanging box *365*
care during absence *374*
in terrarium 366, *374*
Field maple *see Acer campestre*
Field scabious *see Knautia arvensis*
Field woodrush *see Luzula campestris*
Figs 459–60, for ornamental varieties *see Ficus*
bush
pruning
spring 459, *459*
summer 459, *459*
chilling requirement 459
conditions required 459

Figs (*cont.*)
in containers 318, 319, 423, 459
repotting 459
root-pruning 459
cropping 459
diseases 459
drying 431
fan, pruning
spring 459–60, *460*
summer 460, *460*
feeding 459
for flavour 459
fruit placement 459, *459*
fruit type 419
in greenhouse 418
growing under cover 459
harvesting 460
mulching 459
pests 459, 657
planting 459
propagation 460
cuttings 432
hardwood cuttings 434, *434*, 460
suckers 434, 460
protecting 459
pruning 459–60, *459*, *460*
recommended cultivars 459
restricting root system 459
routine care 459
site 459
for small gardens 57
soil type preferred 459
spacing 459
standards 326
storing 431, 460
suggestions for use 318
training 459
watering 459
'Black Ischia' 459
'Brown Turkey' 459, *459*
in large fruit garden *421*
'Brunswick' 459
'Negro Largo' 459
'St John's' 459
'White Marseilles' 459
Filament 676, *676*
Filberts 488–9, *488*
see also Corylus maxima
chilling requirement 488
conditions required 488
feeding 489
frizzled 488
harvesting 489
husks 488
mulching 489
pests 489
pollination 488
propagation
from seed 434
suckers 434
pruning 489
brutting 489
recommended cultivars 489
routine care 489
self-fertile cultivar 489
site 489
storing 489
training 489
tree size 488
watering 489
'Butler' 489
'Ennis' 489
'Gunslebert' 489
'Kentish Cob' 489
Filipendula 173
palmata
in border of mixed textures *175*
rubra, suggestions for use 285
ulmaria
conditions preferred 401
for fragrance 181
suggestions for use 285
'Aurea', soil type tolerated 184
Fir *see Abies*
Fir, Douglas, *see Pseudotsuga*

Fireblight 649
symptoms and control 649
Fireplace, plants in 355
Fish
affecting water balance 298, 300
conditions for 284, 298
conditions required 285
in container pond 318
depth of pond for 290, 298
feeding 298, 301
introducing into pond 299, *299*
number for pond 299
oxygen for 283
stocking pond with 299
usefulness in pond 301
in water garden 285
in winter 301
Fish, blood, and bone *see* Blood, fish, and bone
Fittonia
conditions preferred indoors 361
in containers 319
greenhouse conditions required 361
softwood cuttings 380
albivenis Verschaffeltii Group 366
suggestions for use 366
in terrarium *374*
Argyroneura Group (syn. *F. argyroneura*), in soil bench *367*
Flea beetle 644
control 504, 644
damage done by 644
Fleece
as floating mulch 505, *505*
as mulch 582
as pest deterrent 641
protecting plants with 335, *335*, 613
on raised beds *496*
warming soil with 500, *613*
Flint in walls 596
Floating aquatics 282, 284, 285
choosing healthy plants 297
for containers 318, 331
control 673
introducing into pond *298*
species to avoid 298
Floating mulches 626
types 505, *505*
using *505*
Florence fennel *see* Fennel, Florence
Florets 676
shapes, chrysanthemums *188*
Flower gatherers 554, *554*
Flowering vegetables 522–9
Flowers
bisexual 676, *676*
classes 676, *676*
collecting for preserving 415
cut
annuals for 212, 213, 222
bed for *23*
biennials for 213
bulbs for 230, *230*, 231
perennials for 181
removing pollen beetles 657
shrubs for 22
discolouration, causes and treatments 656
distorted and eaten 657
diversity 676
double, as result of mutation 676
drying
annuals 212, 222, *222*
annuals and biennials for 213
fasciation 657
florets 676
forms 676
growing vegetables with 494, *495*

Flowers (*cont.*)
importance of water to 609
individual 676
panicles 676
parts 676, *676*
proliferation 657
racemes 676
reproductive parts 629, *629*
spikes 676
squirrel damage 659
sunlight affecting opening 610
trees for 56, *56*
types 676
umbels 676
unisexual 676, *676*
wild *see* Wild flowers
Flowers of sulphur 249, 478
Fluorescent lamps as growing
lamps 577
Fly larva predators as biological
pest control 642
Foam as liner for basket 329, *329*
Focal points
beside pond *182*
containers as 212, 306, 308–9
dwarf conifers as 62, *62*
framed by climbers *125*
grass as *47*
hanging baskets 314
in indoor plant groups 354
leading eye to *19*, 38
perennials as 179
pond as 283
raised beds as 599
on roof garden *312*
shrubs in containers 94
specimen roses as 152, *152*
specimen shrubs as 92–3
specimen trees as 55–6, *55*
trailing annuals as *211*
Foeniculum
seedheads 172
vulgare 408
architectural form 181
to attract insects 181
cross-pollination with dill
407
culinary uses 408
flowers 408
foliage 172, 175, 408
harvesting 408
in herb garden *404*
propagation
division 408
from seed 408
scent 404
for seedheads 181
var. *dulce see* Florence
fennel
'Purpureum' 408
companion plants 405
in herb garden *412*
Foliage, *see* Leaves
Foliar feeds 332, 503, 625
Fontinalis antipyretica 285
suggestions for use 331
Foot rots 640, *654*, *661*
symptoms and control 654, 661
"Footprinting" 396
Forcing
bulbs 226, 231, 241
care 244
planting out after 244
chicory *517*, 518
herbs 411
Forficula auricularia see
Earwigs
Forget-me-not *see Myosotis*
Forking 619, *619*
Forks 551, *551*
hilts 551, *551*
"D"-type *551*
"T"-type *551*
"Y"-type *551*
shafts 551
size 551
types
border 551, *551*
hand 552, *552*

Forks, types (*cont.*)
potato 551, *551*
standard 551, *551*
Formal gardens 18, *19*, 42–3, *42*
containers in 308
Formica 666
Forsythia
bird damage 657
for cutting 22
disease 655
fasciation 657
flowers 94
as hedge 85
in mixed border 227
propagation
hardwood cuttings 114
soft/greenwood cuttings 111
pruning 105
seasonal interest 50
soil type tolerated 97, 99
x *intermedia* 'Spectabilis', as
hedge 85
suspensa, as wall shrub 93
Forsythia gall *655*
symptoms and control 655
Fortunella
japonica see Kumquats
margarita see Kumquats
Fothergilla
layering 116
pruning 105
soil type required 99
Fountains *23*, 283
bubble (cobble) 282, 283,
284, 294
installing 294, *294*
millstone *284*
wall 284, 294
mounting *294*
Fox tails *see Setaria italica*
Foxes, damage caused 667
Foxglove *see Digitalis*
Fragaria
x *ananassa see* Strawberries
vesca
as ground cover 180
'Semperflorens' *see*
Strawberries, alpine
Fragrance *see* Scent
Frailea, flat grafting 351
Frame-working 443
Frames 566, 581
alpines in 277
bulb 230
cleaning 583
disinfecting 583
drainage *581*
efficient water use 567
glazing 581
growing vegetables in 505
hardening off in 220, *220*
insulation 581
maintenance 583
materials for 581
microclimates in 611
orientation 493
planting in *581*
positioning 493, *493*
for propagation 637
protecting crops with *581*
siting 581
sizes 581
types 581
uses 566, 581, *581*
ventilation 581, *581*
Frangipani *see Plumeria*
Frankliniella occidentalis 647, 656
Fraxinus
buying 64
conditions tolerated 67
propagation
spliced side grafting 82
whip-and-tongue grafting
82
soil type indicated by 617
soil type tolerated 66
angustifolia RAYWOOD
('Flame') suggestions for
use 59

Fraxinus (*cont.*)
excelsior
conditions tolerated 67
soil type tolerated 65
'Pendula' formation 73
ornus soil type tolerated 65
Freesia
in containers 319
for cutting 230, 231
greenhouse conditions
required 361
'Everett' 230
'Oberon' *230*
Freeze-drying herbs 415
Freezing
fruit method 431
fruit suitable for 431
herbs in ice 415, *415*
Fremontodendron, suggestions
for use 95
French beans *see* Beans, French
French drains 623
French lavender *see Lavandula*
stoechas
French layering 631, *631*
shrubs 117–18
French marigold *see Tagetes*
patula
French sorrel *see* Buckler-leaf
sorrel
French tarragon *see* Tarragon,
French
Friends and foes *641*
Fringe cups *see Tellima*
grandiflora
Frithia, division of rootstock 350
Fritillaria
bulb 227
in mixed border 227–8
pests 644
propagation
chipping 249
scaling 248, 634
from seed 246
seed
germination 247
harvesting *242*
suggestions for use 231
acmopetala
division of bulblets 245
in alpine garden *229*
camschatcensis, conditions
preferred 231
cirrhosa, conditions preferred
231
crassifolia, division of
bulblets 245
dwarf, conditions tolerated
231
imperialis
architectural plant 231
in mixed border 228
'Maxima Lutea', colour
combinations 48
meleagris
propagation from seed *246*
suggestions for use 228,
229, 239
in wild-flower garden 401
michailovskyi, suggestions for
use 229
persica
conditions preferred 231
in mixed border 227
pudica, division of bulblets 245
pyrenaica, suggestions for use
239
raddeana, seedlings, potting
up *247*
recurva
division of bulblets 245
flowering problems 244
thunbergii
division of bulblets 245
flowering problems 244
uva-vulpis, transporting for
exhibition 279
whittallii, suggestions for use
229

Frizzled filberts *see* Filberts
Frogbit *see Hydrocharis morsus-*
ranae
Froghoppers *654*
symptoms and control 654
Frogs
benefits of 641
habitats for 284
Fronds
bulbils on *194*, 195
sporangia on 195, *195*
Frost
as aid to cultivation 609
areas susceptible to 422
damage caused 607–8, 664
by cold winds 611
to flowers 657
to fruit 422
to leaves 650
danger of thaw after 607–8
duration 608
effect on soil 411
forms 607
global warming effects 650
occurrence 607
plants covered in *177*
plants lifted by 607–8, 613
ponds in areas of 282
preventive measures 612–13
protecting container-grown
plants from 335, *335*
protecting fruit from 422,
427
protecting herbs from 411
protecting shrubs from 102
protecting tender climbers
from 125
protecting trees from 69
protection from 612, *612–13*,
613
in cold greenhouses 375
floating mulches *505*
insulation *612*, 613
mounding *612*, 613
under cover 613, *613*
in spring *606*, 608
trees tolerating 63
value to soil 609
wall footings in areas of 597
Frost alarm 574, *574*
Frost pockets 607, *607*, 612
causes 607
Fruit
see also Fruit, soft; Fruit,
tender; Fruit, tree;
individual fruits by name
biennial bearing 426
in border *422*
botany 675–6
bottling 431
bush, pests 645
cane, diseases, bacterial 661
choosing cultivars 424
choosing plants 422, *423*
in cold greenhouse 360
conditions preferred 418, 610
conditions required 424
conditions suitable for 422
in containers 318, 418, 423
feeding 426
plants suitable for 319, 328
repotting 426
routine care 426
top-dressing 426
under cover 423
watering 426
crop size 423
crop succession 423
crop timing 423
dehiscent 675, *675*
diseases 427
affecting flowers 656
bacterial 648, 665
fungal 646, 648, 654, 656,
661
drainage problems 424
effect of drought on 62
effect of high temperatures on
650

Fruit (*cont.*)
effect of low temperatures on
650, 664
enhancing flavour 638
forms for small garden 421–2
freezing 431
varieties suitable for 431
fruiting habits, pruning
depending on 429
growing against supports 422
growing organically 422
growing under cover 422–3
pruning 427
routine care 427
harvesting 431
importance of water to 609
improving soil for 424
indehiscent 675, *675*
integrating into garden plan
420–1
mineral deficiencies 424
mineral deficiency 650–1
in mixed planting 422
mulching 424
ornamental trees for 56–7
pests 427, 648
damaging leaves 645, 646,
647, 651
plant types 418–19
planting depth *424*, 425, *425*
pollination compatibility 423
preserving 431
problems 658–9
affecting stems and leaf
buds 653, 654, 655
propagation 432–4, *432–4*
cuttings 434, *434*
hardwood cuttings 434,
434
layering 432, 434, 631
leaf-bud cuttings 434
runners 432, 434
from seed 434
softwood cuttings 434
suckers 432, 434
protecting 418
from birds and animals
421, 422, 427, *427*, 468
from frost 422, 427
netting for 564
from wind 421, 422, 427
pruning
depending on fruiting
habits 429
under glass 427
rootstocks for small garden
421
routine care 426–7
seed dispersal 675, *675*
self-fertile 424
self-sterile 421, 424
site preparation 424
siting 421, 422
in small garden 421–2
soil pH level 424
soil types, effect on quality 424
spacing 421
spraying near ornamentals 422
squirrel damage 659
storing 431, *431*
damage caused by mice,
rats, and voles 662
successional planting 421
succulent 675
suggestions for use 418–23
supports for under cover 427
tender, in greenhouse 418
training for small garden 421–2
tree, pruning for fruitfulness
429, *430*
tropical pests 646
types 675, *675*
weed control 427
Fruit, soft 468–78
see also individual fruits by
name
bush
bird damage 657, 659
pests 657

Fruit, soft (*cont.*)
plant types 419
planting 425, *425*
protecting 468. 613
pruning 428–30
range of fruits 419, 468
training 419, 428–30
cane
bird damage 657, 659
hybrid, pests 658
pests 657
planting 425
protecting 468
propagation, suckers 434
range of fruits 419, 468
suckers 434
training for small garden 421–2
type of growth 419
choosing cultivars 424
conditions tolerated 468
diseases 658
freezing 431, *431*
growing against supports 422
harvesting 431
improving soil for 424
mulching 426
physiological disorders 658
preserving 431
propagation, cuttings 432
pruning 468
range of fruits 419, 468
routine care 426
self-fertile 424
soil type required 468
soil type tolerated 468
storing 431
Fruit, subtropical pests 659
Fruit, tender 479–87
feeding 479
growing under cover 423, 435
origins 479
as ornamental trees 479
overwintering 427
propagation from seed 432, 434
pruning 428
range of fruits 419
routine care 427
site preparation 479
Fruit, tree 435–60
see also individual fruits by name
arcure 420
bare-root
buying 424, *424*
planting 425
bark splitting 427
bird damage 657, 659
bush 419, *419*
buying 424–5, *424*
age to choose 425
categories 418, 435
choosing healthy plants 424, *424*
container-grown
buying 424, *424*
planting 425
cordon arch *423*
cordons 419
double (U) 420
multiple *419*, 420
planting 420
against fence *425*
in open ground *425*
space required 422
stepover *419*, 420
suggestions for use 418
training 419–20
triple 420
types 420
cross-pollination 422, 424, 435
diseases 665
dwarf, staking 425
dwarf pyramid *419*, 420, 421
effect of nitrogen on 426
espalier *419*
space required 422

Fruit, tree, espalier (*cont.*)
suggestions for use 418
training 420
"family" trees 420, *420*
fan *419*
space required 422
suggestions for use 418
training 420
feathered maidens 425
pruning 429
feeding 426, *426*
foliar feeds 625
organic 426
forms 419–20, *419*, 435
trained 419–20, *419*
unrestricted 419, *419*
goblet 420
grafted, planting *424*
in grass 426
growing against support, positioning 425
growing under cover, pruning 430
half-standard 419, *419*
improving fruiting
by root pruning *430*
by training 429
maiden, training 419, 420
maiden whip 425
training for shape 429, *429*
manuring, dangers of 424
mineral deficiencies 426
mulching 426
palmette *419*, 420
pests 657, 660
physiological disorders 658
planting
in containers 425
in open ground 425, *425*
position of graft union *424*, 425
preserving 431
propagation
bud-grafting 432–3, *432*, *433*
chip-budding 432, *432*
grafting 432, 433–4, *433*
T-budding 433, *433*
whip-and-tongue grafting 433–4, *433*
protecting 613
protecting from animals 425, 435
protecting blossom *612*
pruning 428–30, *428*, *429*
aims of 428
curbing excessive vigour 430
formative 428
method 428–9, *428*
over-pruning 428, *428*
removing branch 428, *429*
renovation 430, *430*
spur thinning 430
time for 428
under-pruning 428, *428*
pyramid *419*, 420
range of fruits 419
renovation 430, *430*
root pruning 430, *430*
rootstocks 423
selecting 424
seasonal water requirements 622
self-fertile 424, 435
self-sterile 421, 424, 435
siting for cross-pollination 421
size 423
on south-facing walls 611
spindlebush 419, *419*
staking 425, *425*, 426
standard 419, *419*
supporting branches 426–7, *426*
supports for 376
preparing 424
tender 419
thinning fruit 426, *426*
trained, pruning 428

Fruit, tree (*cont.*)
training 428–30
on canes 429, *429*
for fruitfulness 429
for shape 428, *429*
tying 426
to stake 425, *425*
wall-trained 419
watering 426
Fruit, tropical pests 659
Fruit buds, apples 437, *437*
Fruit cage *427*
Fruit garden 416–89
existing design and 33
grouping plants in 420–1
large, plan *421*
planning 418–23
small *422*
Fruit rot of kiwi fruits 467
Fruiting vegetables 522–9
growing in containers 501
storing 506
watering, critical periods 502
Fuchsia 120–1
bush training *120*, 121
care 120
in containers 121, 319
with trees 58
diseases 120
feeding 120
in greenhouse 359
greenhouse conditions required 361
in greenhouse garden *360*
growing with succulents 340
in hanging baskets 120, *330*
hardy
overwintering 121, *121*
pruning 105
in indoor hanging basket 358
non-hardy, overwintering 121
overwintering 121, *121*, 335
pests 120, 645, 657, 660, 666
pinch pruning 377
pinching out 120, *120*, 121, *121*
propagation 120–1, *120*
hardwood cuttings 120
soft/greenwood cuttings 111
softwood cuttings 120–1, *120*
requirements 120
standards 326
training 109, 121, *121*, 326
stopping 120, 121
suggestions for use 309, 314, 317
training 90, *120*, 121, *121*
'Celia Smedley' *120*
'Checkerboard' 121
'Estelle Marie' *120*
fulgens 120
'Heidi Weiss' *120*
'Lady Thumb' *120*, 317
magellanica 84, 95
conditions tolerated 95
soil type preferred 97
as hedge 85
'Mrs Popple' 121
'Royal Velvet' 121
'Thalia' *120*
Fulvia fulva (syn. *Cladosporium fulvum*) 648
Fumigation 375, 583
Fungal brackets 655, *661*
symptoms and control 661
Fungal diseases
affecting bark 654
affecting bulbs 663
affecting flowers 656, 657
affecting fruit, berries, and seeds 658
affecting lawns 667
affecting leaves 646, 647, 648–9, 651, 652
affecting roots and tubers 660–2
affecting stems, branches, and leaf buds 653–4

Fungal diseases (*cont.*)
affecting whole plant 664–6
discouraging 197
mist propagation and 580
spread 639
in vegetable garden 495
on water plants 301
Fungal leaf spots *648*
symptoms and control 648
Fungi
beneficial 617
colonizing plants 653
fungicide-resistant strains 643
systemic control 643
on timber 592
Fungicides
adverse reactions to 643
damage from 650, *650*
forms available 643
types 643
contact 643
systemic 643
types available 668
use when scooping rosettes 276
Fungus gnats *666*
biological control 642
symptoms and control 666
Furrows for seeds *217*
Fusarium
nivale see *Monographella nivalis*
oxysporum 654
f. *narcissi* 663
solani 661
Fusarium patch 396, 400, *667*
symptoms and control 667
Fusarium wilt 467
symptoms and control 654, 661

G

Gagea, suggestions for use 231
Gages 447–50
freezing 431
pollination 447
recommended cultivars 448
'Bryanston Gage' 448
'Cambridge Gage' 448, *448*
'Count Althann's Gage' 448
'Early Transparent Gage' 448
'Laxton's Gage' 448
'Old Greengage' 448
'Oullin's Gage' 448
'Reine Claude Violette' (syn. 'Purple Gage') 448
Gaillardia
flowers 209
root cuttings 203
x *grandiflora* cvs, soil type preferred 184
pulchella, for cutting 213
Galanthus
buying 236
collecting from the wild 228
companion plants for 177
conditions preferred 231
conditions tolerated 231
diseases 653
flowers 48
in ground cover 180
increase 226
in mixed border 177, 227
in natural planting 24
naturalized *229*
pests 663
planting *37*, 237
propagation
chipping 249, 634, *634*
division of offsets 245
twin-scaling 249, 634

Galanthus (*cont.*)
seasonal interest 50, 176, 178
suggestions for use 228, 231, 316
underplanting roses 151
in woodland 179
elwesii, suggestions for use 239
nivalis
conditions preferred 401
conditions tolerated 231
suggestions for use 239
'Flore Pleno' *401*
plicatus, suggestions for use 239
Galax
urceolata (syn. *G. aphylla*)
conditions preferred 259
soil type required 260
Galega
division 201
seed germination 198
soil type tolerated 185
Gales, damage done by 611
Galium
odoratum (syn. *Asperula odorata*) 408, *408*
conditions suitable for 408
conditions tolerated 292
culinary uses 408
flowers 408
for fragrance 181
harvesting 408
in herb garden *412*
planting to restrict spread 411
propagation, division 408
in scented preparations 408
storing 408
suggestions for use 408
propagation from seed 408
verum, conditions preferred 401
Gall midges 52
Hemerocallis 657
symptoms and control 657
symptoms and control 652
Gall mites, symptoms and control 652, *652*
Gall wasps 652
symptoms 652
Galls 639
azalea *652*
cause 652
control 652
plants affected by 652
symptoms 652
crown *655*, *661*
symptoms and control 655, 661
forsythia *655*
symptoms and control 655
leafy *655*
symptoms and control 655
pineapple 654
Galtonia
buying 236
for cutting 231
in formal bedding 227
growing in pots 244
routine care 244
Games, lawn for 388–9, *388*
Ganoderma 661
Garden carts 562
Garden centres, trees from 54
Garden chafers 660, 668
Garden compost see Compost
Garden egg see Aubergines
Garden lines 563, *563*
Garden rooms *17*, *22*, *310*, *354*
Gardenia
in containers 319
softwood cuttings 380
soil type required 325
watering 357
jasminoides
standards 326

Gardens
  family 22, *22, 23*
  formal 18, *19*, 42–3, *42*
    containers in 308
  informal 20, *20, 21*, 42, 43
  planning and design 12–51
  plant-oriented 24, *24, 25*
  small trees for 59
  stylized 26, *26, 27*
  town 26
  types and styles 16–17
  without plants 26
Garlic *535*, 537–8
  bulb size 537
  conditions tolerated 537
  in crop rotation 498
  culinary uses 537
  diseases 538, 663
  harvesting 538
  intercropping 494
  nitrogen requirement 503, 537
  pests 538, 663
  planting 537–8
  planting in modules *538*
  propagation, division of
    cloves 537, *538*
  repelling pests 641
  routine cultivation 538
  site 537
  size of plants 537
  soil type preferred 537
  spacing 537–8
  storing 506, 537, 538, *538*
  weeding 538
  'Elephant' 537
  'Germidour' 537
  'Purple Wight' 537
  'Solent Wight' 537
  'Wight Cristo' 537
Garlic chives 407
Garrya
  conditions tolerated 95
  flower sexuality 676
  propagation, semi-ripe
    cuttings with heel 113
  soil type tolerated 97
  elliptica
    as hedge 85
    'James Roof' *84*
Gas
  in greenhouse, installing 572
  for greenhouse heating 574
    circulated hot water
      system 574
Gasteria
  division of offsets 349
  angulata, conditions tolerated
    342
  batesiana
    leaf cuttings 347
    suggestions for use 342
  bicolor var. *liliputana*,
    suggestions for use 342
  carinata, conditions tolerated
    342
    var. *verrucosa*, conditions
      tolerated 342
  disticha 342
Gates adjoining highways, laws
  on 602
Gaultheria (syn. *Pernettya*)
  division of suckers 118
  flower sexuality 676
  layering 116
  propagation, division of
    suckers 118
  soil type required 99, 260, 325
  mucronata
    'Sea Shell', berries 94
    'Wintertime' *91*
  shallon 91
    conditions tolerated 95
    propagation, division of
      suckers *118*
Gaura, flowering time from seed
  198
Gazania
  in containers 212, 319
  flowering time from seed 198

Gazania (*cont.*)
  growing with succulents 339
  self-sown seedlings 222
  sowing 217
  suggestions for use 230
  treating as annuals 217
Gelatinous lichens on lawn 667,
  667
Gels, water-retaining 621
Genetic modification 638
Genista
  conditions tolerated 91, 95
  dwarf conifers with 62
  flowers 94
  germination 630
  heel cuttings 113
  propagation, soft/greenwood
    cuttings 111
  soil for 91
  delphinensis 259
  lydia, in rock garden *254*
  sagittalis, conditions tolerated
    259
  tinctoria, soil type preferred
    97
Gentiana
  seed sowing 198
  soil type required 257
  acaulis
    propagation
      division 275, *275*
      "Irishman's" cuttings
        275
    suggestions for use 259
  asclepiadea, seed germination
    198
  lutea, root cuttings 275
  saxosa, suggestions for use
    259
  sino-ornata 275
    division 275
    soil type required 260
  verna
    conditions preferred 255
    propagation, "Irishman's"
      cuttings 275
    subsp. *angulosa*,
      suggestions for use 259
Genus, botanical name 677
Geotextile fabric as weed
  suppressant 265, *265*
Geotextile matting as natural
  pond liner 295, *295*
Geranium
  to attract wildlife 178
  conditions tolerated 181
  as edging 150
  as ground cover 176, 180
  in mixed border *174*, 177
  propagation
    division 201
    greenwood cuttings 273
    root cuttings 203
  underplanting roses 151
  farreri, soil type tolerated 261
  macrorrhizum, as ground
    cover 180
  phaeum, in border 175
  pratense 401
    soil type tolerated 185
  sanguineum
    var. *striatum*
      planting in container
        185
      suggestions for use
        259
  sylvaticum conditions
    preferred 181
  'Tiny Monster', as ground
    cover 180
Geranium (tender) as common
  name for *Pelargonium* 204
Gerbera
  conditions preferred indoors
    361
  grrenhouse conditions
    required 361
Germander *see Teucrium*
Gesneriaceae, leaf sections 382

Geum
  to attract wildlife 178
  pests 645
Gherkins 524–5
  culinary uses 524
  fruits 524
  harvesting 525
  nitrogen requirement 504
  plant *524*
  recommended cultivars 525
  'Diamant' F1 525
  'Venlo Pickling' 525
Ghost spots 658
Giant redwood *see
  Sequoiadendron giganteum*
Gibbaeum album, conditions
  tolerated 342
Gilia
  self-sown seedlings 222
  capitata
    for cutting 213
    for dry conditions 211
    sowing 217
Ginger 410, *410*
  culinary uses 410
  foliage 410
  habit 410
  harvesting 410
  propagation, division of
    rhizomes 410
  storing 410
  suggestions for use 405
Ginkgo
  spliced side grafting 82
  biloba
    conditions tolerated 67
    softwood cuttings 79
Girasoles *see* Jerusalem artichokes
Girdling *see* Bark-ringing
Gladiolus
  buying 236
  corm 227, *634*
  for cut flowers 230
  diseases, virus 662
  for cutting 231
  in mixed border 228
  pests 656
  propagation
    cormels 245, *245*
    cutting up with growing
      points 249
  resting 240
  staking *242*
  suggestions for use 230
  tender, conditions preferred
    231
  Butterfly Group, in formal
    bedding 227
  callianthus 227
  communis subsp. *byzantinus*,
    suggestions for use 239
  'Deliverance' *245*
  Primulinus Group, in formal
    bedding 227
  'Tesoro' *230*
Gladiolus thrips 656
Glass for greenhouses *570*, 571
Glass-fibre sheds of 605
Glasshouse leafhopper 647
Glaucidium palmatum, soil type
  required 260
Glaucium flavum 213
  conditions tolerated 213
  soil type preferred 216
  suggestions for use 257
Glazing bars 572, *572*
Glazing clips 572, *572*
Glechoma hederacea 'Variegata',
  in containers 319
Gleditsia
  conditions tolerated 67
  pests damaging leaves 652
  propagation
    spliced side grafting 82
    whip-and-tongue grafting
      82
  for small gardens 58
  triacanthos
    soil preferred 66

Gleditsia tricanthos (*cont.*)
  'Sunburst'
    foliage 56
    suggestions for use 59
Gleditsia gall midge 652
Gleying 623
Global warming
  benefits 91, 256, 339, 607
  drawbacks 396, 405, 607
Globe artichokes 526–7, *527*
  conditions preferred 526
  culinary uses 526
  cultivar 526
  earthing up 527
  flowers 526
  foliage 526
  harvesting 527
  intercropping 494
  nitrogen requirement 504, 526
  pests 527
  propagation
    division of offsets 527
    division of roots 526, *527*
    from seed 526
  routine cultivation 527
  site 494
  size of plant 526
  soil preferred 526
  storing 527
  watering 527
Globodera
  pallida 666
  rostochiensis 666
Globularia
  soil type preferred 184
  cordifolia, suggestions for use
    259
  meridionalis, suggestions for
    use 259
  repens, suggestions for use 259
Gloriosa
  suggestions for use 230
  superba, soil type tolerated 131
Glory flower *see Clerodendrum
  bungei*
Glottiphyllum
  division of offsets 349
  division of rootstock 350
  linguiforme, suggestions for
    use 342
Gloves
  gardening 563, *563*
  protective 562, 563, *563*
Glufosinate ammonium 671, 673
Glyceria maxima 'Variegata',
  position in water garden 285
Glyphosate 671, 673
Gnats, fungus, biological control
  642
Goggles, safety 556, 558
Golden cyst eelworm 666
Golden feverfew *see Tanacetum
  parthenium* 'Aureum'
Golden lemon balm *see Melissa
  officinalis* 'Aurea'
Golden marjoram *see Origanum
  vulgare* 'Aureum'
Golden rod *see Solidago*
Golf putting greens 389
  mowing 395
Gomphrena globosa
  for cutting 213
  for drying 213
  soil type tolerated 216
Gooseberries 476–7
  bush, pruning 477, *477*
  conditions required 476
  cordon, pruning 477
  disease-resistant 658
  diseases 477, 658
  fan, pruning 477
  feeding 476
  freezing 431
  harvesting 477
  mildew-resistant 477
  pests 476–7, 645
  plant type 419, 468
  planting 476
  potash requirements 421

Gooseberries (*cont.*)
  propagation, hardwood
    cuttings 477, *477*
  protecting from wind 476
  pruning
    regulated 477, *477*
    spur 477, *477*
    summer 428
    winter 428, 477, *477*
  recommended cultivars 477
  routine care 476
  site 476
  spacing 476
  standard
    pruning 477
    rootstocks 477
  storing 477
  thornless cultivars 477
  training in small garden
    421–2
  'Captivator' 477
  'Careless' 477
    in large fruit garden *421*
  Chinese *see* Kiwi fruits
  'Golden Drop' 477
  'Greenfinch' 477, 658
  'Hinonmäki' 477
  'Invicta' 477, *477*, 658
    in small fruit garden *422*
  'Keepsake' 477
  'Lancashire Lad' 477
  'Lancer' 477
  'Langley Gage' 477
  'Leveller' 477
    in large fruit garden *421*
    in small fruit garden *422*
  'London' 477
  'May Duke' 477
  'Pax' 477
  'Rokula' 477
  'Whinham's Industry' 477,
    477
  'White Lion' 477
  'Whitesmith' 477
Gordonia, semi-ripe cuttings with
  heel 113
Gorse *see Ulex*
Grafting
  aftercare 83
  apical-wedge 84, 119, *119*, 636
    cacti *350*, 351
    shrubs suitable for 119
    trees suitable for 82
  apples, grafting over 443
  approach 48
  basal whip 636
  bud-grafting
    fruit trees 432–3, *432, 433*
    roses 156, 166–7, *166*
  cacti 346, 350–1, *350–1*
  chip-budding *83*
    method 636, *636*
    time for 35
    trees suitable for 82
  double budding 446, *446*
  double grafting 446, *446*
  double-working 446, *446*
  flat 351, *351*, 636
    cacti 351
    succulents 351
  frame-working 443
  fruits 432
  hot-pipe callusing 637, *637*
  methods 635–6, *636*
  preparing rootstock 118, 119,
    119
  rind 443, *443*
  rootstocks 635
    influence 635
  saddle 636
    shrubs 118, *119*
    shrubs suitable for 119
  scions
    in cold storage 607
    influence 635
    selecting 118, *119*
  shrubs 118–19, *119*
  side, cacti and succulents 351,
    351

Grafting (*cont.*)
side-veneer
method 636
succulents 351, *351*
side-wedge 636, *636*
splice *see* basal-whip grafting
spliced side 82–3, *82*
trees suitable for 82
spliced side-veneer 118–19
shrubs 118–19
succulents 346, 350–1, *350–1*
T-budding
fruit trees 433, *433*
method 636, *636*
time for 635
time for 635
tools for *555*
top-working
tree fruits 443, *443*
weeping standards 73
whip-and-tongue 636, *636*
fruit trees 433–4, *433*
trees suitable for 82
Grafting over apples 443
Granite chippings as mulch 323
Granite setts *590*, 591
imitation *590*
Grape hyacinth *see* Muscari
Grapefruits
conditions required 482
in containers 319
fruits 482
propagation 482
recommended cultivars 481
spacing 482
stem pitting 481
types 482
'Foster' 481
'Marsh Seedless' 481
'Red Blush' 481, *481*
'Star Ruby' 481
Grapes (*Vitis vinifera*) 461–6
on arches 422
black *461*
chemical damage to 651
conditions required 461
diseases 658
fast-growing 129
freezing 431
fruit type 675
in greenhouse 418
growing under cover 422
harvesting 431
hormone weedkiller damage 655
on pergolas 418, 422
pests 659
damaging leves 645
plant type 419
planting 425
preserving 431
propagation, hardwood cuttings 434
pruning 461
ripening, removing foliage for 464, *466*
shanking 658, *658*
supports 461
under glass *423*
white *461*
'Alicante' 462, *462*
American 461
'Appley Towers' 462
'Bacchus' 464
'Black Frontignan' 462
'Black Hamburgh', in large fruit garden *421*
'Black Monukka' 462
'Canon Hall Muscat' 462
'Cardinal' 462
'Chardonnay' 464
'Chasselas Rose' 462
'Chasselas Vibert' 462
'Chenin Blanc' 464
'Ciotat' 462
dessert 461–4
conditions required 461
double cordon, pruning 463
drainage for 461

Grapes, dessert (*cont.*)
feeding 461
groups 461
growing under cover 461–2
pollination by hand 461
ripening 462
soil replacement 462
training 461
ventilation 462
watering 462
harvesting *463*, 464
mulching 461
multiple cordon, pruning 463, *463*
muscat 461
recommended cultivars 462
sweetwater 461
recommended cultivars 462
vinous 461
recommended cultivars 462
pests 461
planting 461
pollination 461
propagation 464
pruning 461, 462–4, *462–4*
spur 462–4, *462–3*
recommended cultivars 462, 464
ripening, removing foliage for 464, *466*
rootstocks 461
routine care 461
single cordon, pruning
routine 463, *463*
spring 463, *463*
summer 462–3, *462–3*
winter 462–3, *462–3*
site 461
soil preparation 461
soil type required 461
spacing 461
storing 464
supporting 461
thinning bunches 461
thinning fruits 461, *461*
training 462–4, *462–4*
wall cultivation 461
watering 461
wine grapes suitable for 464
'Dornfelder' 464
'Dunkelfelder' 464
European 461
'Foster's Seedling' 462, *462*
'Gagarin Blue' 462
'Gewürztraminer' 464
'Himrod Seedless' 462
'Huxelrebe' 464
'Kernling' 464
'King's Ruby' 462
'Lady Hastings' 462
'Léon Millot' 464
'Madeleine Angevine 7972' 464
'Madeleine Sylvaner' 464
'Madeline Royale' 462
'Madresfield Court' 462
'Mrs Prince's Black Muscat' 462
'Müller Thurgau' 464, *464*
'Muscat of Alexandria' 462, *462*
'Muscat Bleu' 462
'Muscat Hamburgh' 462
'New York Muscat' 462
'Oliver Irsay' 462
'Orion' 464
'Ortega' 464
'Perle de Czaba' 462
'Pinot Gris' 464
'Pinot Meunier' 464
'Pinot Noir' 464
'Phönix' 464
'Précoce de Malingre' 464
'Primavis Frontignan' 462

Grapes (*cont.*)
'Purpurea', suggestions for use 126
'Regent' 464
'Reichensteiner' 464
'Reine Olga' 462
'Riesling' 464
'Roem van Boskoop' 462
'Rondo' 464
'Royale Muscadine' 462
'St Laurent' 462
'Sauvignon Blanc' 464
'Scheurebe' 464
'Schönburger' 464
'Schuyler' 464
'Seibel' 464
'Seyval Blanc' 464
'Siegerrebe' *464*
'Thompson's Seedless' 462
'Trebbiano' 462
'Triomphe d'Alsace' 464
wine 464–6
conditions required 464
harvesting 466, *466*
planting 464–5
propagation
hardwood cuttings 466, *466*
two-bud cuttings 466, *466*
pruning 461, 464–5, 465–6
double Guyot system 464–5, 465–6
Guyot system 465–6
routine 465, 466
summer 464–5, 466
winter 464–5, 466
recommended cultivars 464
removing foliage for ripening *466*
rootstocks 464
site 464
soil type suitable 464
suitable for dessert use 464
supporting 464
Graphocephala fennahi 647, 656
Graptopetalum, leaf cuttings 347
Grasses
border of *44*, *47*
conditions tolerated 623
in container arrangement *307*
in containers 307, 319
cool-season 388, 389
for drying 212
forms 46
indoors 355
for lawns 386–7
cultivars to choose 389
games and sports areas 388, *388*
groups 388
high-quality 388, *388*
selecting 388–9
utility 388, *388*
vegetative propagation 392, 394
for meadow garden 401
naturalizing bulbs in 228, *233*
ornamental
annual 209–10
in contrasting foliage group *175*
foliage forms 176
in naturalistic plantings 178
as specimen plants 179
in winter 192
paths of 387, *387*, 594
pH levels for 390
planting with perennials *47*
propagation, vegetative 392, 394
selecting for lawns 388–9
warm-season 388, 389
Grassland
see also Meadow gardens
flower-rich 389, *389*
path through 387

Grassland (*cont.*)
planting wild flowers in 401
preparations for 183, 401
unmown *21*, 386
Gravel
improving drainage with 621
as mulch 323
for paths 150
paths of
edging 412
laying 594, *594*
planting in 256, *265*
raked *27*
in rose garden 150, *151*
setting pavers in 265
specimen trees in 56
steps of timber and *595*
as top-dressing 626, *626*
top-dressing with 264–5
Gravel beds 256–7
weed suppression 265
Gravel boards 601, 602
Grecian saw *see* Saws
Green manuring 494, 625, *625*
Greenfly *see* Aphids
"Greenhouse effect" *573*
Greenhouses 566–83
see also Alpine house
access 567
anchoring *570*, 572, *572*
annuals for pot plants in 213
base cladding 574
base for *570*
building 571, *571*
bed, raised 578
construction 578
beds and borders, preparing 367
bench beds, preparing 367, *367*
biological controls in 583
borders 570, 578
infected soil in 578
bulbs for 230
buying, checklist 567, *570*
cacti for 341
care of plants in 374–5
choosing 568–71
cleaning 375, 583
cold
balancing environment in 573
frost protection 375
plants for 360, 361
temperature in 360
temperature range 573
uses 573
composts 367
conservation 569, *569*
construction materials for 570–1, *570*
conventional designs 568, *568*
cool/frost-free
balancing environment in 573
multi-level display in 359
plants for 360, 361
temperature range 573
temperatures in 360
uses 573
creating microclimates in 611, *611*
damping down 374, 576
as decorative feature 567
diseases 375
disinfecting 583
displaying plants in 578, 579, *579*
dome-shaped 569, *569*
door *570*
downpipes 567, *570*
maintenance 583
Dutch light 568, *568*
electricity, installing 572
environment 355–60
balancing 573
creating 573–7
erecting 571–2, *571–2*
existing design and 31
foundations, laying 571, *571*

Greenhouses (*cont.*)
framework
maintenance 583
materials for 570–1, *570*
free-standing, siting 567
fruit in 422–3
routine care 427
fumigation 375, 583
in garden 360
gas, installing 572
glazing *570*, 571, *571*, 583
cleaning 583
double- 574
repairing 583
grape vines in *423*
growing bags in 578, *578*
growing peaches in 452
growing plants in 359–60
growing tomatoes in 528
growing vegetables in 505
gutters 567, *570*
maintenance 583
headroom *570*
heat loss *570*
heated uses 566
heating *574*
types 574
humidity 374, 573
measuring 576
plant requirements 576
providing 576
insulation 573
methods 574, *574*
integrated into garden 566
layout 359
lean-to 568, *568*
displaying plants in 359
siting 567
lighting 573, 577, *577*
mains services 567
installing 572
maintenance 583, *583*
mansard 568, *568*
materials for 570–1, *570*
metal
erecting 572, *572*
glazing 572, *572*
ventilators 572
mini 569, *569*
organization 578–9, *578–9*
orientation 493, 567, 567
ornamental displays in 359
paths to 593
pests 375, 646, 647, 648
biological pest control 583, 642–3
trapping 641
planting 367
plants in, care 374–5
plastic-covered frame 567
polygonal 569, *569*
polytunnel 569, *569*
positioning 493, *493*
propagation, aids for 580, *580*
propagation in 636–7
raised beds in 359
ridge height 570, *570*
shading 359, 636
methods 576, *576*
netting for 564, *564*
shelves *578*, 579
site preparation 571
siting 567, *567*
size 570
specialist 569, *569*
staging 359, 578, 579, *579*
disinfecting 583
fitting 572
resting plants beneath *578*, 579, *579*
succulents for 341
temperate
balancing environment in 573
plants for 360, 361
temperature range 573
temperatures in 360
uses 573
temperature 573

Greenhouses (*cont.*)
temperature regulation 375
thermal screens 574, *574*
three-quarter span 568, *568*
traditional span 568, *568*
traditional wood *566*
types 359, 568–9, *568–9*
unheated uses 566
uses 359
ventilation 374, 375, *570*, 573
maintenance 583
methods 575, *575*
principles 575, *575*
warm
balancing environment in 573
plants for 360, 361
temperature range 573
temperatures in 360
uses 573
water, installing 28, 567, 572
watering plants in 374, 567
watering systems 567, 577, *577*
automatic 573
wheelchair access 570, *570*
wooden
erecting 571–2
glazing 571
Greenovia
division of offsets 349
propagation, stem cuttings 348
Grevillea
conditions preferred indoors 361
semi-ripe cuttings 79
with heel 113
robusta, suggestions for use 59
Grey mould *see Botrytis*
Grey squirrels, damage caused 659, *659*
Grey-leaved plants
conditions preferred 355
conditions tolerated 622
as foil for colours 308
herbs 405
mulching 413
trees for winter 59
Griselinia
conditions tolerated 95
semi-ripe cuttings with heel 113
Grit
Cornish, as top-dressing *626*
as mulch 323, *333*, *334*
paths of edging 412
in potting composts 322, *322*, 323
as top-dressing 240, *240*, 626, *626*
top-dressing with 264–5
Ground beetles *617*
Ground cover
annuals for 211, *211*
benefits of 101
biennials for 211
with bulbs in mixed border 227
clematis for 138
climbers for 124, 127, 129
combining plants for 176
dwarf conifers for 62
hostas for 186, *187*
for lawns 389
methods of spreading 180
mixing plants 180
mulching 101, 180
ornamental plants *180*
perennials for 180
planting 101, 180
through black plastic 101
pruning 101, *101*
roses as 149, 153, *153*
cultivars suitable for 155
selecting plants for 101
in shrub border 92
shrubs for 93, *93*, 101
pruning 107
soil for 180
spacing 101

Ground cover (*cont.*)
specimen plants in 179
specimen trees in 56
under roses 151
uses 101
watering 180
weed control with 101, 127, 180, 670
for woodland 179
Ground elder 627, 670, *670*, 671
variegated, suggestions for use 179
Ground frost 607
Groundnuts *see* Peanuts
Groundsel 669
Grout 589
Growing bags 321
growing tomatoes in *528*
preparing 501
use in greenhouse 578, *578*
Growing lamps 355, 577, *577*
Growing media
see also Composts
inert 565
Growmore, nutrient content 624
Growth buds, apples 437, *437*
Growth regulators, damage from 655
Grubs in soil 504
Guavas 486–7
conditions preferred 486
in containers, moving under cover 427
diseases 487
feeding 486
fruit 486, *486*
growing under cover 487
compost for 487
feeding 487
pollination 487
harvesting 487
mulching 486
pests 486
planting 486
propagation 487
chip-budding 487
from seed 434, 487
softwood cuttings 487
pruning 487
recommended cultivars 487
routine care 486
site 486
soil type preferred 486
spacing 486
staking 486
storing 487
training 487
tree *487*
tree size 486
'Apple' 487
'Beaumont' 487
'Malherbe' 487
'Miami White' 487
'Parker's White' 487, *487*
'Patillo' 487
'Patnagola' 487
'Pink Acid' 487
'Red Indian' 487
'Ruby' 487
'Supreme' 487
Gumming 448, 654
Guelder rose *see Viburnum opulus*
Gunnera
manicata
architectural form 181
in border 175
growth rate 181
soil type tolerated 184
as specimen plant 179
suggestions for use 48, 284, 285
tinctoria (syn. *G. chilensis*), suggestions for use 61, 285
Guy ropes for trees 64
Guzmania
displaying 362
lingulata
care during absence *374*
var. *minor 362*

Gymnocalycium
in containers outdoors 340
division of offsets 349
division of rootstock 350
baldianum, suggestions for use 342
bruchii, flowers 342
gibbosum, suggestions for use 342
mihanovichii
flat grafting 351
suggestions for use 342
'Red Head' *351*
Gymnospermae (Gymnosperms), seed production 676
Gynandriris sisyrinchium, conditions preferred 231
Gynura 129
softwood cuttings 380
aurantiaca
foliage 354
propagation, softwood cuttings *380*
pruning 376
suggestions for use 129
Gypsophila
in border 174
for cutting 181, 212
for drying 181
flowers 676
root cuttings 203
sowing 217
aretioides
softwood cuttings 273
suggestions for use 259
elegans
for cutting 213
sowing 217
paniculata
to attract wildlife 178
form 175
soil type tolerated 185
repens
conditions tolerated 259
propagation, softwood cuttings 273, *273*
soil type preferred 261
soil type tolerated 261
suggestions for use 258
'Dubia', conditions tolerated 259
Gypsum 615

H

Haageocereus
side grafting 351
acranthus (syn. *H. limensis*), flowers 342
pseudomelanostele (syn. *H. setosus*), flowers 342
versicolor, flowers 342
Haberlea
compost for 278
leaf cuttings 274
rhodopensis
flowers 258
soil type required 260
suggestions for use 259
Habranthus
conditions preferred 231
suggestions for use 231
Haemanthus, greenhouse conditions required 361
Hairy bittercress *see Cardamine hirsuta*
Hakea
soil type required 99, 325
lissosperma, soil preferred 97
Hakonechloa macra
in containers 319
'Aureola', suggestions for use 307

Halesia
greenwood cuttings 111
layering 81
softwood cuttings 79, 111
Halide lamps as growing lamps 577
Halimodendron halodendron
conditions tolerated 95
soil type preferred 97
Halo blight 648
Hamamelis
in mixed border 227
propagation
air layering 117
spliced side-veneer grafting 119
pruning *104*
sucker removal *100*
x *intermedia*
'Diane', seasonal interest 92
'Pallida', scent 95
Hammers, club 588, *588*, 590, *590*, 591
Hand-pollination 451, *451*
Hanging baskets
annuals in 212, *212*
arrangements of 314
cacti in 340, 341, 342
as focal point 314
feeding 332
fuchsias in 121
height adjustments 332, *332*
indoors 355, 358, *358*
care 373
choosing 358
feeding 373
planting 365–6
plants for 358
positioning 358
watering 373
liners for 329, *329*, 330
materials for 321
orchids in 369, *369*
planting 329, *330*
plants for 314
reducing water requirements 614
siting 314
succulents in 340, 341, *341*, 342
planting 344, *344*
supports for 314, 329, *329*, 358, 366
types 314, 329
for indoors 358
watering *330*, *332*
Hanging boxes
planting 365–6
slatted, wooden, making *365*
Hardcore
definition 591
for foundations 585, *585*, *586*
Hardenbergia 129
propagation, semi-ripe cuttings 143
seed preparation 141
comptoniana, in containers 128
Hardening off 637
container-grown plants 335
cuttings 79
seedlings 214, 219–20, *220*
vegetables 501
Hardpan 621, 623
drainage system on 623
Hardwood cuttings *see* Cuttings, hardwood
Hardy plants, damage of frost and thaw to 607
Hares
control 666
damage caused 666, *666*
Hare's tail *see Lagurus ovatus*
Haricots 530
Harrisia
as rootstock 351
gracilis, flowers 342
pomanensis (syn. *H. bonplandii*), flowers 342

Hatiora
apical-wedge grafting 351
side grafting 351
gaertneri
conditions tolerated 342
flowers 342
in hanging basket 341
propagation, softwood cuttings 380
suggestions for use 342
rosea
conditions tolerated 342
flowers 342
propagation, softwood cuttings 380
suggestions for use 341
salicornioides
flowers 342
suggestions for use 342
Hauptidia maroccana 647
Hawkweed mouse-ear *see Pilosella officinarum*
Haworthia
division of offsets 349
in bowl garden 341
propagation, division of plantlets/runners 378
in raised bed 340
cooperi, suggestions for use 342
cymbiformis, division of offsets 349
limifolia, suggestions for use 342
reinwardtii, suggestions for use 342
Hawthorn, *see Crataegus*
Hawthorn webber moth caterpillar 647
Hayracks 329
fixtures *329*
planting *329*
Hazel, *see Corylus*
Hazel nuts *see* Cobnuts
Hazelnut weevils 489
Health
buying plants for 640
government plant regulations 655
Heart-rot of pineapples 479
Heather gardens, dwarf conifers for 62
Heathers
see also Calluna; Daboecia; Erica
clematis growing through 138
compost for 367
diseases 654, 661
dropping 116
dwarf conifers with *62*
as ground cover 93, *93*
pruning 107
soil type indicated by 617
suggestions for use 308
Heating
in conservatory 357
in greenhouse 573, 574
circulated hot water 574
electric 574
gas 574
paraffin 574
types 574
siting 358
trench 357
underfloor 357
Heavy soil, improving 621
Hebe
conditions tolerated 95, 259
in containers 319
disease-resistance 661, 665
propagation, semi-ripe cuttings 273
with roses 151
soil type tolerated 99
suggestions for use 93, 314
buchananii 'Minor' 259
in rock garden 256
buxifolia, suggestions for use 46

Hebe (cont.)
  cupressoides 'Boughton
    Dome', suggestions for use
    317
  dwarf, pruning 108
  pinguifolia 'Pagei', in rock
    garden *255*
  topiaria, suggestions for use
    46
Hechtia 362
  propagation 363
Hedera
  annuals climbing through 212
  climbing method 124, *130*
  conditions preferred 610
    indoors 361
  conditions required in
    greenhouse 361
  conditions tolerated 95, 125,
    129, 355
  in containers 128
    with trees 58
  for exposed sites 125
  in fedges 126
  foliage 127
  in greenhouse display *359*
  as ground cover, specimen
    tree in 56
  hydroculture 361
  indoors *355*
  miniature, suggestions for use
    366
  in natural planting *24*
  propagation
    self layering 145
    semi-ripe cuttings 143
    softwood cuttings 142
  as screen 125
  soil types tolerated 131, 132
  suggestions for use 125, 126,
    129, 230
  for topiary 76
  training indoors 355
  variegated 127
  in water garden *283*
  in windowbox *212*, *316*
  for winter interest 126, 128
  canariensis, as cover for
    wildlife 128
  colchica
    as cover for wildlife 128
    'Sulphur Heart', cutting
      back *133*
  helix
    in containers 319
    as foil for colours 308
    overwintering 335
    pollution-absorbing 358
    propagation, self layering
     144
    suggestions for use 129,
     307, 311, 313, 316, 317
    as weed 670
    'Atropurpurea' *145*
    'Buttercup', winter
     interest 128
    'Eva', in bottle garden *367*
    'Goldheart' (syn. *H. helix*
     'Oro di Bogliasco'),
     winter interest 128
    'Ivalace', for topiary 76
    'Parsley Crested', winter
     interest 128
    'Pedata', winter interest
     128
Hedgehogs 641, *641*
  attracting 126
Hedges 84–6
  to attract wildlife 22
  choosing plants for 85
  conditions on each side 611
  double planting 85
  dwarf 85
    in herb garden *404*, 406
    herbs for 406
  existing design and 31
  fedges 126
  feeding *86*
  flowering plants for 85

Hedges *(cont.)*
  as food source for wildlife 22
  formal
    plants for 84
    trimming 84, 86
  frost pockets beside 607, *607*
  informal
    plants for 84–5, *84*, *85*
    pruning 86
  low, hostas for 186
  mosaic 84
  mulching *86*
  ornamental 84–5
  planting 85
  pruning 85, 86, 103
  renovating 86
  roses for 153, *153*, 157, *157*
  as screens 58
  shaping 86, *86*
    to prevent snow collecting
     609
  single planting 85
  snow damage to *609*
  soil preparation 85
  spacing plants 84, 85
  tapestry 84
  topiary 76
  training 85–6, *86*
  trimming 86, *86*
    tools for
     hand 555, *555*
     powered 556, *556*
  uses 84
  wind reduction 84
  as windbreaks 493, *493*, 495,
    613
  of woven willow 87, *87*
Hedgetrimmers 556, *556*
  battery-powered 556
  cutting hedge with *86*
  petrol and electric compared
    556
  protective clothing for *556*
  rechargeable 556
  safety 556
Hedychium 61
Heel cuttings *see* Cuttings
Heeling in 157
  trees 65
Helenium
  to attract insects 178, 181
  for cutting 181
  dividing 201
  in naturalistic planting *177*
  in mixed border 177
  soil type tolerated 185
  stopping 191
  'Moerheim Beauty', in
    naturalistic planting *177*
Helianthemum 271
  to attract insects 264
  conditions tolerated 259
  cultivars, suggestions for use
    93
  cutting back 271, *271*
  propagation, semi-ripe
    cuttings 273
  in rock garden *254*, *255*
  soil type preferred 97, 261, 325
  soil type tolerated 261
  'Fire Dragon' *273*
  oelandicum
    suggestions for use 259
    subsp. *alpestre*, in trough
     267
Helianthus
  in annual border 209
  for dry conditions 211
  as food source for wildlife 22
  in mixed border 177, *210*
  propagation, division *200*,
    201
  staking 222
  annuus
    architectural plant 213
    for cutting 213
    flowers 209
    Colour Fashion Series, for
     cutting 213

Helianthus (cont.)
  salicifolius
    architectural form 181
    height 172
  tuberosus see Jerusalem
    artichokes
Helichrysum
  for drying 222
  pinch pruning 377
  soil type preferred 97
  bracteatum see Xerochrysum
    bracteatum
  coralloides see Ozothamnus
    coralloides
  milfordiae, rosette cuttings
    274
  petiolare
    in containers 319
    cuttings, overwintering
     335
    overwintering 335
    suggestions for use 308
    pinching back *333*
    tying in 333
  selago see Ozothamnus
    selago
Helicobasidium brebissonii 661
Helictotrichon sempervirens,
  suggestions for use 46
Heliocereus
  in greenhouse display *360*
  propagation, stem cuttings
    348
  suggestions for use 342
  hybrids, suggestions for use
    341
  speciosus var. *superbus*,
    flowers 342
Heliophila self-sown seedlings
  222
Heliotrope *see* Heliotropium
Heliotropium
  in containers *308*, 319
  overwintering 335
  scent 213
  standards 326
  suggestions for use 213
  arborescens, suggestions for
    use 309
Helipterum
  for cutting 213, 222
  for drying 213, 222
Helix aspersa 644
Helleborus
  to attract wildlife 178
  conditions tolerated 259
  in island bed *175*
  in mixed border 177
  seasonal interest 50
  seed germination 198
  soil type tolerated 185
  suggestions for use 228
  transplanting 199
  winter interest 181
  argutifolius, architectural
    form 181
  foetidus
    conditions tolerated 181
    seasonal interest 172
  orientalis 201
    conditions tolerated 181
    division 201
    seasonal interest 172
Helxine soleirolii see Soleirolia
  soleirolii
Hemerocallis
  conditions preferred 181
  for fragrance 181
  as ground cover 180
  pests 657
  propagation, division *200*,
    201
  soil type tolerated 184
  suggestions for use 285, 316
  'Marion Vaughn' *181*
  'Stella de Oro' 316
Hemerocallis gall midge 657
  symptoms and control 657
Hemispherical scale 653

Hepatica
  sowing 272
  nobilis, conditions preferred
    259
  transsilvanica, conditions
    preferred 259
Herb garden 404–15, *404*
  attractions of 404
  designing 405, 406
  edging 405
  existing design and 33
  focal point in 309
  formal 406, *406*
  geometric designs 406, *406*
  informal 406
  laying paths in 412
  plans for drawing up 406
  planting to design 412, *412*
  roses in 153
Herb pillows 404
Herbaceous borders *see* Borders
Herbaceous perennials *see*
  Perennials
Herbs
  air-drying 415, *415*
  annuals, sowing 414
  architectural 405
  aromatic, handling 415
  autumn clearance 413
  in beds 405
  benefits to other plants 405
  biennials, sowing 414
  in borders 405
  as carpet 405
  in cartwheel bed *405*
  and climate change 405
  coloured-leaved, suggestions
    for use 406
  companion planting 405
  conditions preferred 405, 411
  conditions tolerated 405
  container-grown planting 411
  in containers 318, 328, 405,
    405, 406, 413
    feeding 413
    protecting from cold 413
    repotting 413
    top-dressing 413
    watering 413
  cosmetic uses 404
  in cottage garden *21*
  culinary, siting 405
  culinary uses 404
  cultivars 404
    propagation 414
  cutting back 413
  dead-heading 413
  definition 404
  designing with 404–6
  drying 415
  for dwarf hedges 406
  for edging 405
  evergreen, harvesting in
    winter 411, 415
  flavour, conditions affecting
    415
  flavouring oil with 415
  flavouring vinegar with 415
  flowers 405
    collecting 415
  as focal points 405
  foliage 405
  forcing 411
    compost for 411
    planting out after 411
  in formal herb garden *406*
  in formal planting 18
  freeze-drying 415
  freezing in ice 415, *415*
  in garden 404–6
  grey-leaved 405
    mulching 413
  growing for winter use *411*
  handling 415
  hardening off 411
  hardiness 413
  harvesting 415
    time for 415
  in home 404

Herbs *(cont.)*
  indoors 355
  invasive
    dividing 411
    planting 411, *411*
    removing runners 413
  medicinal uses 404
  in Mediterranean-style
    planting *264*
  microwave drying 415
  mulching 413
  origins 405
  on patio 405
  in patio garden *406*
  in paving 405, *406*
  perennial, propagation from
    seed 414
  pinching out after planting 411
  plant types producing 404
  planting
    container-grown 411
    to restrict spread 411, *411*
  preserving 415
  propagation 414
    cuttings 414
    from seed 414
  pruning 413
  in raised beds 405
  repotting 413
  for rock garden 405
  on roof garden 313
  roots
    collecting 415
    drying 415
  routine care 413
  scent 404, 405
  seed collecting 415
  seedheads drying 415, *415*
  shrubby
    propagation, mound
     layering 414, *414*
    trimming after planting
     411
  site preparation 411
  siting 405
  soil preferred 411
  soil preparation 411
  soil tolerated 411
  storing 415
  in strawberry planter,
    replanting *413*
  suggestions for use 404–6,
    405–6
  tender
    in containers 405
    cutting back 413
    propagation, cuttings 413
    protection in winter 413
  tidying up in winter 413
  underplanting roses *151*, 152
  use after chemical treatment
    413
  uses 404
    in home 404
  variegated
    removing plain shoots 413
    suggestions for use 406
  in vegetable garden 405, *495*
  watering after planting 411
  for winter use 411
Hermaphrodite plants 676, *676*
Hesperis matronalis
  for fragrance 181
  self-seeding 218
Hessian
  clearing dew from lawn with
    395
  protecting plants with 335,
    335, *612*, 613
  protecting trees and shrubs
    with *612*
Heterorhabditis megidis 642,
  645, 660, 666
Heuchera
  in containers 319
  division 201
  as ground cover 180
  soil type tolerated 185
  suggestions for use 316

Heuchera (*cont.*)
'Chocolate Ruffles', winter interest 181
micrantha var. *diversifolia*
'Palace Purple'
foliage 316
planting in container *185*
'Pewter Moon', winter interest 181
Hibbertia
softwood cuttings 142
scandens 129
Hibiscus
flowers 676
propagation
apical-wedge grafting 119
softwood cuttings 380
pruning 376
soil type preferred 325
soil type tolerated 99
rosa-sinensis
conditions preferred indoors 361
in containers 319
greenhouse conditions required 361
propagation, semi-ripe cuttings 113
pruning 107
standards 326
'The President' *380*
schizopetalus 61
sinosyriacus 'Lilac Queen' *119*
syriacus, pruning 105
trionum, retaining seedheads 223
Hieracium pilosella see *Pilosella officinarum*
High-maintenance garden 17
Highland bent see *Agrostis castellana*
Highways, boundaries fronting, laws on 602
Hill-top sites, wind on 611
Himalayacalamus falconeri, in containers 319
Hippeastrum
conditions preferred indoors 361
in containers 319
dwarf, suggestions for use 231
forcing 231, 241
care 244
germination 630
greenhouse conditions required 361
light requirements 355
pests 663
damaging leaves 652
propagation
chipping *249*, 299
from seed 247
root restriction 373
seed germination 247
advenum see *Rhodophiala advena*
'Striped' *249*
Hippophäe
germination 115
soil type preferred 97
soil type tolerated 97
rhamnoides 95
Hire of tools 550
Hoar frost 607
Hoeing
correct position *550*
time for 502
for weed control 618, 671
Hoes 552, *552*
draw *500*
heads 552
shafts 552
types
combination *552*
digging *552*
draw *552*
Dutch 552, *552*
onion *552*
triangular *552*

Hoheria
semi-ripe cuttings 79
deciduous, pruning 105
lyallii
layering 81
suggestions for use 59
Holboellia 129
serpentine layering 145
Holcus lanatus 672
Hole borer *600*
Holiday care 334–5, 374, *374*
Hollows frost pockets in 607, *607*
Holly see *Ilex*
Hollyhocks see *Alcea*
Holodiscus discolor, pruning 106
Honesty see *Lunaria*
Honey fungus 69
control 618, 661, 665
fruiting bodies *665*
mycelium under bark *665*
symptoms 661, 665
Honeydew 58, 333, 646, 647, 648
Honeydew melons see Melons, honeydew
Honeysuckle see *Lonicera*
Hoodia flat grafting 351
x *Hoodiapelia*, flat grafting 351
Hoof and horn 503
in cuttings compost 565
for fruit trees 426
nutrient content 624
Hoops, training houseplants on *364, 364*
Hoplia philanthus 668
Hoplocampa testudinea 659
Hordeum jubatum
for drying 213
in naturalistic planting 177
Hormone rooting products *112,* 143, 632
Hormone weedkillers
damage caused 659, *659*
damage caused by 651, *651*
damage from 655
Hornbeam see *Carpinus*
Horse chestnut see *Aesculus*
Horse chestnut scale 648
Horseradish 407, *407*
culinary uses 407
harvesting 407
propagation
division 407
root cuttings 407
from seed 407
storing 407
Horsetail see *Equisetum*
Hosepipes 560, *560*
double-walled 560
drip feed system 561, *561*
hose-end attachments *560*
porous 561
on reel 560, *560*
reinforced 560
seep 561, 567, 577, 614, *615*
watering vegetables with 502, *502*
spray attachments *560*
timers for 561, *561*
trickle system 561, *561*, 567, 614
Hosta 186–7
classification 186
as companion plants 186
conditions preferred 181, 183, 186
in containers 186, *193, 307,* 315, 319
cultivation 187
diseases 187
feeding 187, 191
flowers 186
foliage *172,* 186, 316
for fragrance 186
for ground cover 186, *187*
as hedge 186
maturity 187
miniature 186
mulching 187
pests 187, *333*

Hosta (*cont.*)
planting 187
depth *184*, 187
time 184
position in pond *295*
propagation
division 187, 200–1, 201
"topping" 187, *187*
routine care 187
for seedheads 181
soil type preferred 187
soil type required 325
soil type tolerated 184, 187
suggestions for use 186–7, 285, 315
top-dressing 187
watering 187
'August Moon' *186*
'Blue Angel' *186*
decorata 186
fortunei var. 'Albomarginata'
'Gold Standard' *186*
'Green Piecrust' *186*
'Ground Master' *186*
'Halcyon' *186*
'Honeybells' *186*
'June' *186*
'Krossa Regal' *186*
lancifolia 186
montana 'Aureomarginata' *186*
'Patriot' *186*
'Pearl Lake' *186*
plantaginea 186
flowers 186
suggestions for use 186
var. *grandiflora*, for fragrance 181
'Richland Gold' *186*
'Shining Tot' *186*
sieboldiana
suggestions for use 285
var. *elegans 186*
architectural form 181
foliage *175,* 319
'So Sweet' *186*
'Sugar and Cream' *186*
'Sum and Substance' 187
tokudama f. *aureonebulosa 186*
undulata
var. *albomarginata* 187
var. *erromena* 187
ventricosa 186
var. *aureomaculata 186*
venusta, suggestions for use 186
Hot peppers see Peppers, hot
Hot-air callusing 637, *637*
Hottonia palustris
position in water garden 285
propagation
by plantlets 303
by turions 303
House sparrows, damage done 657
Houseleek see *Sempervivum*
Houseplants see Indoor plants
Houses
garden enhancing 17
light variations within room 355, *355*
temperature fluctuations 355
Houttuynia
soil type tolerated 184
cordata
in containers 179
position in water garden 285
suggestions for use 179
'Chameleon' (syn. *H. cordata* 'Tricolor') 179
position in water garden 285
in containers 319
'Flore Pleno' (syn. *H. cordata* 'Plena'), position in water garden 285
Hoverflies, attracting 22, 641, *641*

Howea
architectural 95
conditions preferred indoors 361
in containers 319
as specimen tree 55
Hoya 129
compost for 344
greenhouse conditions required 361
propagation
leaf-bud cuttings 380
self layering 145
semi-ripe cuttings 143
softwood cuttings 380
pruning 135, 376
australis
conditions tolerated 342
for fragrance 129
suggestions for use 342
carnosa
conditions preferred 355
conditions tolerated 342
for fragrance 129
suggestions for use 342
lanceolata
greenhouse conditions required 361
subsp. *bella*, suggestions for use 342
linearis, suggestions for use 342
polyneura, suggestions for use 342
Huernia
division of offsets 349
division of rootstock 350
stem cuttings 348
Humidifiers 576
Humidity
in conservatory 357
effects of 610
excessive dangers of 576
factors determining 610
in greenhouse 573
measuring 576
plant requirements 576
high
plants thriving in 610
problems 610
for houseplants 365
indoor pond providing 359
methods of providing 370
for pot plants 372, *372*
relative 576, 610
Humulus
simple layering 145
lupulus 129
'Aureus'
combining with other climbers *127*
foliage *127*
framing statuary *125*
soil type tolerated 131
Humus 183, 616
sources of 63, 628
Hurdles, as windbreaks 493, *613*
Hyacinth see *Hyacinthus*
Hyacinth, water, see *Eichhornia crassipes*
Hyacinth beans see Beans, dolichos
Hyacinthoides
diseases, fungal *648*
in ground cover 180
x *massartiana* (syn. *H. hispanica* of gardens) 227
suggestions for use 228, 239
non-scripta (syn. *Scilla non-scripta*)
conditions tolerated 231
pests 663
suggestions for use 56, 228
Hyacinthus 226
choosing healthy bulbs *236*
conditions preferred indoors 361

Hyacinthus (*cont.*)
in containers 319
diseases 662
flowers 676
forcing 231
in fibre 241, *241*
in water 41, *241*
in formal bedding 227
greenhouse conditions required 361
grouping 354
interplanting 211
propagation
chipping 249
scooping 250, *250*, 634
scoring 634, *634*
twin-scaling 249
suggestions for use 229, 316
transplanting from pots 243
Hybrid berries 470–2
choosing healthy plants 470
conditions required 470
diseases 471
freezing 431
harvesting 431, 471
origins 470
pests 471
plant type *419, 468*
planting 470
times for 470
propagation
layering 434
leaf-bud cuttings 434
tip layering *471, 472*
pruning
after fruiting 471, *471*
after planting 470
frost-damaged stems 471, *471*
rampant growth 471
recommended hybrids 471
routine care 471
site 470
preparation 470
spacing 470
storing 471
supporting 470
training 471, *471*
alternate bay 471, *471*
fan 471, *471*
rope 471, *471*
weaving 471, *471*
thornless, vigour 470
Hybridizing 677
method 630
roses 168–9, *168*
pollinating 169, *169*
preparing pollen parent 169, *169*
preparing seed parent *168,* 169
selecting parents 168
selection 169
Hydrangea
blue, compost for 99
compost for 367
in containers, pruning 326
flower colour 367
pests eating leaves 645
propagation
self layering 145
softwood cuttings 111, 142
pruning 105, *105,* 135, 326
anomala subsp. *petiolaris*
conditions tolerated 129
soil types tolerated 131, 132
suggestions for use 125
arborescens, stooling 117
aspera
pruning 105
subsp. *sargentiana*, bark 48
macrophylla
in containers 319
flowers 317
form 311
propagation, softwood cuttings *111, 632*
pruning 105, *105*
suggestions for use 317

Hydrangea (*cont.*)
  paniculata
    in containers 319
    propagation
      nodal cutting *632*
      stooling 117
    pruning 105
    'Floribunda', coppicing 107
    'Grandiflora', coppicing 107
    'Unique', coppicing 107
  quercifolia 'Snowflake'
    in containers 319
    seasonal interest 95
Hydrated lime 625
Hydrilla verticillata, cuttings 302
Hydrocharis
  propagation, turions 635, *635*
  morsus-ranae 282, 285
  propagation
    offsets 303
    turions 303, *635*
Hydrocleys
  nymphoides 285
    position in water garden 285
  parviflora 285
    cuttings 302
Hydroculture 375
  feeding plants 375
  fertilizers 375
  planting 375
  plants for 361
  preparing plants for 375
Hydroponics 375
  hyacinths 241, *241*
Hygiene
  greenhouse 375
  in integrated pest and disease control 640
  for pest and disease control 640
Hygrometers 576
Hygrophila polysperma, cuttings 302
Hylocereus
  hybrids, conditions preferred 341
  as rootstock 351
  suggestions for use 339, 341
  ocamponis, flowers 342
Hylomecon japonica, conditions preferred 259
Hypericum
  pruning 105
  soil for 91
  soil type tolerated 99
  calycinum, pruning 101, *101*
  x *moserianum*, hardwood cuttings 114
Hypertufa
  covering sink with 266, *266*
  making trough of 266, *266*
Hypoaspis miles 642, 666
Hypoestes
  conditions preferred indoors 361
  in greenhouse display *359*
  phyllostachya
    suggestions for use 366
    'Purpuriana', in bottle garden *367*
    'Splash'
      in bottle garden *367*
      in terrarium *374*
Hypogeal germination 630, *630*
Hyssop *see Hyssopus*
Hyssopus
  suggestions for use 406
  officinalis 408, *408*
    culinary uses 408
    as edging 405
    flowers 408
    harvesting 408
    in herb garden *412*
    propagation
      mound layering 414
      from seed 408
      softwood cuttings 408

Hyssopus officinalis (*cont.*)
    suggestions for use 313, 408
    variants 408
    subsp. *aristatus*
      suggestions for use 405
    f. *roseus*, in herb garden *412*

I

Iberis
  to attract insects 264
  conditions preferred 211
  diseases 649, 660
  as ground cover 211
  amara, conditions tolerated 213
  saxatilis, soil type preferred 261
  umbellata, conditions tolerated 213
Ice on pond, making hole in 301, *301*
Iceland poppy *see Papaver croceum*
Iceplants 521, *521*
  conditions required 521
  culinary uses 521
  flavour 521
  form 521
  habit 521
  harvesting 521
  pests 521
  propagation, stem tip cuttings 521
  sowing 521
  spacing 521
  storing 521
Ilex
  composting prunings 110
  conditions tolerated 613
  disadvantages 57
  flower sexuality 676
  fruiting 57
  in fedges 126
  pests damaging leaves 647
  propagation
    cuttings 632
    semi-ripe cuttings 79, 113
  suggestions for use 55
  for topiary 76
  x *altaclerensis*
    conditions tolerated 67, 95
    pruning 107
    for topiary 76
    'Golden King'
      seasonal interest 59
      semi-ripe cuttings *112*
  aquifolium
    conditions preferred 95
    conditions tolerated 95
    as hedge 15, 84, 85
    in informal shrub grouping *90*
    pruning 107
    resistance to storm damage 68
    as topiary 18
    as security measure 15
    'Golden Milkboy', transplanting *102*
    'Madame Briot' *84*
  crenata 'Mariesii' 259
Illicium, layering 116
Imidacloprid 643, 644, 645, 646, 648, 654, 656, 661, 666, 667, 668
Impatiens
  choosing healthy plants, pot-grown *221*
  conditions preferred 211

Impatiens (*cont.*)
  in containers 212, 319
  germination 219
  greenhouse conditions required 361
  in greenhouse display *359*
  as ground cover 211, *211*
  overwintering 335
  pests 660, 666
  from seed 379
  sowing 217
  suggestions for use 209
  treating as annuals 217
  in windowbox *328*
  cultivars, lifting after bedding 223
  Novette Series 'Red Star' *361*
  repens, softwood cuttings 380
  tinctoria, suggestions for use 61
  walleriana
    conditions preferred 213
    in containers 319
    as pot plants 213
    suggestions for use 213
Imperata cylindrica 'Rubra', in containers 319
Incinerators 562
Indehiscent fruit 675, *675*
India azalea *see Rhododendron simsii*
India rubber tree *see Ficus elastica* 'Robusta'
Indian azalea *see Rhododendron simsii*
Indian shot plant *see Canna*
Indian spinach *see Ceylon spinach*
Indigofera, pruning 105
Indocalamus tessellatus, in containers 319
Indoor garden 352–83
  displaying plants 354–5, 358–60
  environment 355
  foliage plants 354
  grouping plants 354
  light levels 355, *355*
  lighting 358
  positioning plants 355
  range of plants 354
  temperature fluctuations 355
Indoor plants
  cacti 340–1
  care during absence 374, *374*
  choosing 364, *364*
  composts for 323, 364, 367
  diseases 375
    affecting flowers 656
    bacterial 648, 665
    fungal 646, 648, 656, 658
    effect of low temperatures on 650, 664
  feeding 367, 372
    organic 332, 372
  foliage, cleaning 372, *372*
  germination 379
  grouping 354, 364–5
  humidity for 358, 365, 372, *372*, 374, *374*
  hygiene 372, *372*
  mineral deficiency 650–1
  mist-spraying 372
  neglected, renovating 372
  organic 332, 372
  pests 375, 646, 648, 660, 666
    damaging leaves 647
    damaging stems 653
  pinch pruning 377
  pinching out 372
  planting 367
  plunging in large container 365, *365*
  pollution-absorbing 358
  positioning 355, 364
  potting on 372–3, *373*
  preferring direct light 361
  preferring indirect light 361
  pricking out 379–80

Indoor plants (*cont.*)
  problems affecting stems and leaf buds 653
  propagation 378–83
    air layering 383, *383*
    bulbils 379
    cuttings 378, 380–1, *380*, *381*
    division 378–9, *378*
    layering 378, 383, *383*
    leaf cuttings 381, *381*
    leaf sections 381–2, *381*
    leaf-bud cuttings 380
    offsets 378–9
    plantlets 378
    runners 378, *378*
    from seed 378, 379–80, *379*
    sowing 379, *379*
    semi-ripe cuttings 380
    simple layering 383, *383*
    softwood cuttings 380, *380*
      in water 381, *391*
  resting 373, *373*
  routine care 372–5
  soil preparation 367
  stopping 372
  succulents 340–1
  supports for 364, *364*
  top-dressing 372, *372*, 373
  training, pinch pruning 377, *377*
  watering 372
    during absence 374, *374*
  winter-flowering, plunging outdoors 373, *373*
Informal garden 20, *42*, 43
  styles 20, *20*, *21*
Inorganic material, adding to soil 621
Insecticidal fatty acids (soaps) 668
Insecticides *see Pesticides*
Insects
  beneficial 641
  in fedges 126
  lawns attracting 387
  pests 639
  plants attracting 20, 22, 128, 172–3, 178, 181, 264
Inspection covers, treatment in paving 586
Insulation
  of frames 581
  greenhouse 573
    methods 574, *574*
  for plants in winter *612*, 613
Intercropping 498
Interference fencing 600, *600*
Internal rust spot *662*
  symptoms and control 662
Interwoven fencing 600, *600*
Inula magnifica 181
Ipheion
  conditions tolerated 231
  suggestions for use 231
  uniflorum, conditions preferred 231
Ipomoea 129
  propagation, softwood cuttings 142
  pruning 135
  soil type tolerated 131
  suggestions for use 212
  batatas see Sweet potatoes
  hederacea, supports for 130
  horsfalliae
    pruning 376
    vigour 130
  tricolor, in containers, training 317
Ipomopsis, self-sown seedlings 222
Iresine
  in containers 319
  softwood cuttings 380
Iridaceae
  corms 227
  rhizomes 227

Iris
  classification 182
  conditions required 182
  conditions tolerated 182
  in containers 319
  edging pool *49*
  foliage 172
  in mixed border 177
  position in pond 295
  in pots, plunging after flowering *277*
  propagation 182
    chipping 249
    division 201, *201*, 302
  rhizomes 227, *635*
  for seedheads 181
  suggestions for use 229, 283, 308, 316
  aucheri, choosing healthy bulbs *236*
  bearded 182
    rhizomes *674*
  beardless 182
  'Bold Print' *182*
  bucharica 182, *182*
  bulbous 182
    diseases, fungal 663
  'Caprician Butterfly' 182
  'Carnaby' *182*
  chrysographes 182
  clarkei 182
  confusa 182
  crested 182
  cristata 182, 271
    conditions preferred 259
  danfordiae flowering problems 244
  Dutch Hybrids 182
    for cutting 231
  dwarf, suggestions for use 231
  English 182
  ensata (syn. *I. kaempferi*) 182
    suggestions for use 229, 285
  Evansia 182
  foetidissima
    conditions tolerated 181
    'Variegata', winter interest 181
  forrestii 182
  fulva 182
  x *fulvala* 182
  'Geisha Gown' (= 'Caprican Butterfly') 229
  germanica 'Florentina' (syn. *I. florentina*) *see* Orris
  gracilipes 182
  graminea 182
    for fragrance 181
  histrioides 'Major'
    in rock garden 255
    suggestions for use 226
  hoogiana 182
  innominata 182, *182*
  japonica 182
  'Joyce' *182*
  Juno Group 182
    bulb 227
    buying 236
    division of offsets 245
    seed germination 247
    suggestions for use 231
  kaempferi see Iris ensata
  laevigata 182
    in bog garden *284*
    position in water garden 285
    'Variegata', in water garden 284
  latifolia, for cutting 231
  lazica, winter interest 181
  magnifica 182
  missouriensis 181
  Oncocyclus Group 182
    resting 240
  orientalis 182
  Pacific Coast 182
  prismatica 182

Iris (cont.)
  pseudacorus 182
    by pool *182*
    place in water garden 285
    repotting *301*
    in water garden *282*
  Regelia 182
  Regeliocyclus 182
  reticulata, conditions
    tolerated 231
  Reticulata Group 182
    bulb 227
    in container *321*, 319
    diseases 244
    in mixed border 227
    propagation, division of
      bulblets 245
    seed collecting 246
    suggestions for use 231
  rhizomatous 182
    diseases, bacterial 663
    division 201, *201*, 302
    suggestions for use 229
  setosa 182
  Siberian 182
    by pool *182*
  sibirica 182
    seedheads 172
    suggestions for use 285
  Spanish 182
  spuria 182
  Spuria Group 182
  tenax 182
  unguicularis
    seasonal interest 172
    winter interest 181
  verna 182
  versicolor 182
    position in water garden
      285
    water 182
  'White City' *227*
  xiphium, for cutting 231
  Xiphium Group 182
Iris rhizome rot 663
"Irishman's" cuttings, alpines
  275, *275*
Iron 637
  chelated 444
  deficiency 424, 426, 444, 451,
    479, 624, 651
  for lawn 396
  plant requirements 624
  sequestered 424
Irrigation *see* Watering
Island beds *see* Beds
Isotoma 213
Italian broccoli *see* Calabrese
Italian ryegrass *see* Lolium
  multiflorum
Itea
  ilicifolia
    semi-ripe cuttings with
      heel 113
    suggestions for use 95
  virginica, division of suckers
    118
Itersonilia
  pastinaceae 661
  perplexans 657
Ivy *see* Hedera
Ixia 226
  conditions preferred 231
  in containers 319
  for cutting 231
Ixora coccinea, softwood cuttings
  380

J

Jacaranda
  in greenhouse 360
  greenhouse conditions
    required 361

Jacaranda (cont.)
  mimosifolia
    from seed 379
    suggestions for use 59
Jacquemontia 129
  propagation, cuttings 143
Jancaea (syn. *Jankaea*), leaf
  cuttings 274
Japanese anemone *see* Anemone x
  hybrida
Japanese carpet grass *see* Zoysia
  matrella
Japanese cedar *see* Cryptomeria
Japanese knotweed *see* Fallopia
  japonica
Japanese lawn grass *see* Zoysia
  japonica
Japanese maple *see* Acer
  japonicum; *A. palmatum*
Japanese painted fern *see* Athyrium
  niponicum var. *pictum*
Jasmine *see* Jasminum
Jasmine, winter *see* Jasminum
  nudiflorum
Jasminum
  conditions preferred indoors
    361
  in containers 319
  greenhouse conditions
    required 361
  propagation, semi-ripe
    cuttings 143
  pruning 135, 376
  scent 128
  beesianum, pruning *135*
  humile, pruning 106
  mesnyi
    planting *132*
    pruning, formative *134*
    softwood cuttings 380
  nudiflorum
    climbing method 124
    winter interest 128
  officinale
    for fragrance 129
    soil type tolerated 132
    suggestions for use 126,
      129
    training on wire hoop *364*
  polyanthum
    for fragrance 129
    indoors 358
    soil type tolerated 132
    suggestions for use 129
    winter interest 128
Jatropha podagrica, suggestions
  for use 342
Jays, damage caused *659*
  to flowers 657
  to fruit, berries and seeds 659
Jekyll, Gertrude 176
Jelly palm *see* Butia capitata
Jerusalem artichokes *542*, 545
  conditions preferred 545
  culinary uses 545
  cutting down 545, *545*
  earthing up 545
  harvesting 545
  knobbly tuber *545*
  nitrogen requirement 504, 545
  pests 661
  planting tubers 545, *545*
  propagation, tubers 545
  routine cultivation 545
  size of plants 545
  smooth 'Fuseau' tuber *545*
  spacing 545
  storing 545
  tubers *635*
  as windbreak screen 545
Jigger *587*
Joints
  for beams and uprights 604,
    604
  bird's mouth 604, *604*
  dowel *604*
  half-lap 604, *604*
  notched 604, *604*
Joist shoe 604, *604*

Jovibarba, rosette cuttings 274
Jubaea
  architectural 95
  in containers 319
Judas tree, *see* Cercis
  siliquastrum
Juglans
  pruning 71
  nigra
    as rootstock 489
    soil type tolerated 66
  regia see Walnuts
Juncus
  effusus
    position in water garden
      285
    f. *spiralis*
      position in water
        garden 285
      suggestions for use
        318, 331
    'Vittatus', position in
      water garden 285
  ensifolius, position in water
    garden 285
Juniper *see* Juniperus
Juniper webber moth caterpillar
  647
Juniperus
  diseases, fungal 653
  pests damaging leaves 647
  propagation, semi-ripe
    cuttings 79
  protecting from snow *613*
  soil preferred 66, 325
  soil type tolerated 65
  chinensis 'Aurea', seasonal
    interest 59
  communis
    'Compressa' 259
      propagation, ripe-
        wood cuttings 274
      in rock garden 256
      suggestions for use
        62, 258, 311
    horizontalis, as ground cover
      62
    x *pfitzeriana* (syn. *J.* x *media*),
      as ground cover 62
    sabina 'Tamariscifolia',
      clematis growing through
      139
    scopulorum 'Skyrocket' *62*
      suggestions for use 59
    squamata
      'Blue Carpet'
        form 90
        as ground cover 101,
          101
      'Blue Star' *62*
Justicia
  conditions preferred indoors
    361
  greenhouse conditions
    required 361
  in greenhouse garden *360*
  propagation, softwood
    cuttings 380
Juttadinteria, division of offsets
  349

K

Kadsura japonica, conditions
  tolerated 129
Kakothrips pisivorus 647, 659
Kalanchoe
  conditions preferred indoors
    361
  in hanging baskets 341
  propagation
    softwood cuttings 380
    stem cuttings 348

Kalanchoe (cont.)
  beharensis, leaf cuttings 347
  blossfeldiana, suggestions for
    use 342
  daigremontiana, leaf cuttings
    347
  delagoensis *342*
    conditions tolerated 342
  jongsmanii, suggestions for
    use 342
  manginii
    in hanging basket *341*
    suggestions for use 342
  marmorata, conditions
    tolerated 342
  pumila, suggestions for use
    342
  tomentosa, leaf cuttings 347
  'Wendy' *348*
    stem cuttings *348*
Kales 507
  American 507
  broadleaded 507
  Chinese *see* Chinese broccoli
  conditions tolerated 507
  in crop rotation 498
  culinary uses 507
  curly 507, *507*
  curly-broad hybrids 507
  diseases 507
  freezing 506
  growing under cover 507
  harvesting 507
  nitrogen requirements 504, 507
  ornamental *507*
    in containers 319
  ornamental foliage 209
  pests 507
  plain 507
  routine care 507
  sizes 507
  soil preferred 507
  sowing 507
  spacing 507
  storing 507
  top-dressing 507
  types 507
  'Redbor' 209
  'Tall Green Curled' 649
Kalmia
  dead-heading 100
  propagation
    layering 116
    sowing 115
  soil type required 99
  angustifolia, soil type
    required 260
  latifolia 116
    propagation, air layering
      117
    soil type tolerated 97
  microphylla (syn. *K. polifolia*
    var. *microphylla*), soil type
    required 260
Keikis 371
Kennedia 129
  propagation
    semi-ripe cuttings 143
    serpentine layering 145
  soil type required 131, 325
  rubicunda 129, *131*
    pruning 376
    soil type tolerated 131
Kentish rag, for rock garden *261*
Kentucky blue grass *see* Poa
  pratensis
Kerria
  division of suckers 118
  pruning *106*
Kidney beans *see* Beans, French
Kilmarnock willow *see* Salix
  caprea 'Kilmarnock'
King palm *see* Archontophoenix
  alexandrae
Kingfisher daisy *see* Felicia
  bergeriana
Kirengeshoma palmata
  conditions preferred 181
  flowers 179

Kirengeshoma palmata (cont.)
  as ground cover 180
  suggestions for use 179
Kitchen garden *see* Vegetable
  garden
Kitchen waste
  adding to compost heap 627,
    627
  use in worm compost 628, *628*
Kitchens, plants for 355
Kiwi fruits 461, 466–7
  chilling requirement 466
  conditions preferred 466
  conditions required 461
  conditions tolerated 466
  diseases 466
  feeding 466
  female cultivars 466
  fruit 466
  fruit production 467
  fruit rot 467
  growing under cover 467
  harvesting 467
  length of growth 466
  male cultivars 466
  mulching 466
  pests 467
  plant type 419
  planting 466
  pollination 466
  propagation
    grafting 467
    hardwood cuttings 467
    softwood cuttings 467
  protecting 467
  pruning 467
  recommended cultivars 466
  routine care 466
  soil type required 466
  storing 467
  supporting *467*
  training 467, *467*
  watering 466
  'Abbot' 466
  'Allison' 466
  'Bruno' *466*
  'Hayward' 466
  'Jenny' 466
  'Montgomery' 466
  'Tomuri' 466
Knautia
  arvensis, conditions preferred
    401
  macedonica 49
Knee pads 562, *562*
Kneelers 562, *562*
Kniphofia
  for cutting 181
  dividing 201
  flowers 676
  in mixed border 177
  in perennial border *172*
  planting time 184
  soil type tolerated 185
  transplanting 192
  caulescens, planting in groups
    175
Knives
  budding 167, *555*
  garden 555, *555*
  general-purpose *555*
  grafting *555*
  multi-purpose *555*
  pruning *555*
Knopper galls 652
Knot gardens 18, 43
  annuals in 210–11
  hedges for 84, 85
Knotweed, Japanese, *see* Fallopia
  japonica
Kochia see Bassia
Koelreuteria paniculata,
  softwood cuttings 79
Kohl rabi 535, 540
  bolting 540
  conditions preferred 540
  in crop rotation 498
  culinary uses 50
  diseases 540

Kohl rabi (cont.)
edible part 540
freezing 506
green *540*
harvesting 540
nitrogen requirement 504
pests 540
planting out 540
protecting 540
recommended cultivars 540
routine cultivation 540
size of plants 540
soil type preferred 540
nitrogen requirement 540
sowing 540
spacing 540
storing 540
'Green Vienna' 540
'Kolibri' F1 540
'Korist' F1 540
'Lanro' F1 540
'Purple Danube' F1 540
'Quickstar' F1 540
Kohleria
conditions preferred indoors 361
greenhouse conditions required 361
Kolkwitzia
pruning 106
soft/greenwood cuttings 111
Komatsuna 514, *514*
conditions tolerated 514
in crop rotation 498
culinary uses 514
flavour 514
hardiness 513
harvesting 514
nitrogen requirement 504
sowing 514
spacing 514
types 514
as winter crop 514
Kumquats
in containers 319, 481
conditions tolerated 482
fruits 482
growing under cover 481
hybrid with mandarin 482
propagation 482

L

Labels 564, *564*
Lablab purpureus 129
edible *see* Beans, dolichos
growing on tree *128*
'Ruby Moon', suggestions for use 212
Lablab beans *see* Beans, dolichos
Laburnum 57
propagation, chip budding 82
x *watereri* 'Vossii', suggestions for use 59
Lacewings
larvae, benefits of 641
as predator 646
Lachenalia
in containers 319
diseases, fungal 663
greenhouse conditions required 361
Lackey moth caterpillar 647
Lactuca sativa see Lettuces
Lady palm *see Rhapis excelsa*
Ladybirds
benefits of 641
as biological pest control 642, 646
encouraging 641
Lady's bedstraw *see Galium verum*
Lady's fingers *see* Okra

Lady's mantle *see Alchemilla mollis*
Laelia
conditions required 370
suggestions for use 368
temperature required 368
Laetisaria fuciformis 667
Lagarosiphon major (syn. *Elodea crispa* of gardens) 284, 285, *298, 299*
cuttings 302
Lagerstroemia
softwood cuttings 79, 111
indica
standards 326
suggestions for use 59
Lagurus ovatus
for drying 213
ornamental value 209
self-sown seedlings 222
Lamb's lettuce *see* Corn salad
Lamium maculatum
conditions tolerated 259
in containers 319
'Beacon Silver'
as ground cover 180
winter interest 181
GOLDEN ANNIVERSARY ('Dellam'), winter interest 181
'White Nancy' winter interest 181
Lampranthus
growing outdoors 340
habit 339
stem cuttings 348
falcatus, conditions tolerated 342
roseus, conditions tolerated 342
Lamps, growing 577, *577*
Land cress 520, *520*
conditions preferred 520
culinary uses 520
flavour 520
harvesting 520
pests 520
self-seeding 520
soil type required 520
sowing 520
spacing 520
spread of plant 520
suggestions for use 520
Landscape, incorporating *14*
Landscape fabric
as mulch 626
use in raised beds 497, *497*
Lantana
in containers 319
greenhouse conditions required 361
overwintering 335
softwood cuttings 111
Lapageria 124, 129
greenhouse conditions required 361
propagation, simple layering 145
pruning 135
seed preparation 141
rosea
site for 125
soil type required 131, 325
suggestions for use 129
Larch *see Larix*
Lardizabala 129
biternata
soil type required 131
suggestions for use 126
Larix
pests 654
spliced side grafting 82
decidua, soil preferred 66
Larkspur *see Consolida*
Lasius 666
flavus 668
Lathyrus
seed germination 198
grandiflorus 129, *132*
soil type tolerated 132

Lathyrus grandiflorus (cont.)
supports for 130
latifolius 129
soil types tolerated 131, 132
supports for 130
'Blushing Bride', from seed 198
odoratus 129, 212, 214–15
bush, supports for *214, 215*
climbing method 124
in containers, training 317, 319
cordon
layering *25*, 215
supports for 215, *215*
training 215, *215*
for cutting 212, 213
dead-heading 214
diseases, fungal 654, 661
dwarf 214, *214*
feeding 214
for fragrance 129
hardening off 214
netting for 564
old-fashioned 214, *214*
overwintering 214
pests 657
pinching out 214
planting *131*, 214
potting on 214
propagation from seed 214
scent 128, 213
seed germination 214
suggestions for use 125
supports for *214*, 215, 564
types 214, *214*
virus diseases 656
Bijou Group 214
Grandiflora cultivars 214
Knee-hi Group 214
Patio Mixed 214
'Pink Cupid' 214
Snoopea Group 214
Spencer cultivars 214
vernus
conditions tolerated 181
winter interest 181
Lattice fences 600, *600*
Lattice pots 240, *240*, 565, *565*
Laurel *see Prunus laurocerasus*
Laurus
layering 81, 116
pests damaging leaves 651
nobilis
culinary uses 408
foliage 408
for topiary 76
greenhouse conditions required 361
harvesting 408
pests damaging leaves 647
propagation
layering 408
semi-ripe heel cuttings 408
protecting 408
as specimen plant 405
standards 326
storing 408
suggestions for use 59, 316, 408
'Aurea' 408
Lavandula
to attract insects 22, 264
in bedding scheme *210*
conditions preferred 91
conditions tolerated 622
in containers 319
as edging 150, 405
as ground cover 101
pruning 107
hardiness 413
as hedge 84, 85
in knots and parterres 210
propagation
mound layering 414
semi-ripe cuttings 113

Lavandula (cont.)
protecting from frost 335
pruning 107, 413, *413*
with roses 151
soil type preferred 97, 325
steeping in oil or vinegar 415
suggestions for use 318, 406
angustifolia 408–9, *408*
conditions preferred 411
culinary uses 408
flowers 408
foliage 408
harvesting 408
propagation
mound layering 414
semi-ripe cuttings 408
related species 408–9
in scented preparations 408
storing 408
suggestions for use 408
'Hidcote' 409
'Loddon Pink', in herb garden *412*
'Nana Alba' 409
stoechas 325
flowers 409
propagation, mound layering 414
seasonal interest 95
Lavatera
conditions tolerated 95
propagation, softwood cuttings 111
pruning 105
seasonal interest 50
assurgentiflora 105
maritima, conditions tolerated 181
thuringiaca, conditions tolerated 181
trimestris
conditions tolerated 213
soil type preferred 216
'Silver Cup' *216*
soil type tolerated 216
Lavender *see Lavandula*
Lavender, cotton *see Santolina chamaecyparissus*
Lawn 384–400
aerating 397–8, *398*, 559, *559*
annual programme 397
algae on 667
annual maintenance programme 397–8
and droughts 396
ants on 668
to attract wildlife 387
base dressing 391, *391*
biodiversity in 387
brushing away dew 395, *395*
for children 22
clippings 395
coarse grasses 672
conditions tolerated 396, 623
coring *see* hollow tining
creating 386–9
design functions 387
diseases 396, 400
control, annual programme 397
fungal 667–8
drainage 390, *391*
earthworms in 668
edges
mowing 591
repairing 399, *399*
shaping 393, *393*
trimming 396, *396*
edging 387–8, 591
materials for 558
tools for 558, *558*
effects of drought on 667
establishing 392–4
existing design and 30
feeding 396–7
annual programme 397
before seeding or turfing 391, *391*
method 286–7, *397*

Lawn (cont.)
fertilizers for 396
uneven distribution *397*
firming ground for 391, *391*
"footprinting" 396
formal 386, *386*
games areas 388–9, *388*
grass 386–7
climatic considerations 388, 396
cultivars to choose 389
high-quality 388, *388*
hollow tining 397, 398, *398*
informal *387*, 389
leaves on, removing 396, *396*
levelling humps or hollows 400, *400*
levelling site for 390–1, *390, 391*
lichens on 667
liming 390
problems 667
mole damage 668
moss 400
control 672
annual programme 397
preventing 672
moulds on 667
mowing 395–6
after seeding 394, *394*
annual programme 397
clippings 395, 400
in drought conditions 395
edge 591
frequency 395
height of cut 387, 395
for renovation 399
stripes 395, *395*
tools for 557, *557*
neglected, renovating 399
non-grass 389, *389*
establishing 393, *393*
ornamental 386, 389
herbs for 408
paths in 38
stepping stone 593
pests 400, 667–8
control, annual programme 397
pH levels for 390
plants suitable for 386
play areas *23*, 388, *388*
plugging 394
position 387
problem areas 389
problems 667–8
raking 396, *396*, 559, *559*, 672
raking ground for 391, *391*
reducing water requirements 614
renovating 399
repairing 399–400, *399, 400*
rolling 399, 558
routine care 395–400
scarifying 398, *398*, 559, *559*
annual programme 397
seed spreaders 559, *559*
seeding 392, 394, *394*
rates 394
sowing methods 394, *394*
selecting grass for 388–9
shape 387
shaping edge 393, *393*
site preparation 390–1, *390, 391*
slitting 398, *398*
soil
preparation 390, *391*
requirements 390
specimen plants in 179
fruit trees 422
trees 56, 418
spiking 398, *398*
sports areas 388–9
sprigging 394
sprinkler systems for 561, *561*
starvation 667
stolonizing 394

Lawn (cont.)
surrounding tree 387
sweeping tools for 559, 559
tapestry 389
textural contrast in 387, 387
thatch 392, 395, 397, 559, 667
toadstools on 668
tools for 558–9, 558–9
top-dressing 392, 398, 398,
626, 626
treatment during drought 396
trimming, tools for 558, 558
trimming long grass, tools for
555, 555
turf
buying 392
sizes 392
types 392
turfing 392–3
method 392, 393
types 386
unmown 386
utility 386, 388, 388
mowing 396
vegetative propagation 392,
394
watering 396, 396, 623
after seeding 394, 394
after turfing 393
annual programme 397
sprinkler systems 561, 561
weed control, annual
programme 397
weed and feed compounds
396, 400
weeding, tools for 553, 553
weedkillers 672
applying 673
buying 673
range 673
weeds 400, 672–3, 672
control 672
creeping 672
discouraging 395
preventing 672
where grass is long 389
Lawn chamomile see
Chamaemelum nobile
'Treneague'
Lawn mowings, mulching with
502
Lawn sand 396, 672, 673
Lawnmowers 557, 557
blades 557
choosing 557, 557
maintenance 557
manual 557, 557
petrol and electricity
compared 557
power source 557
powered 557, 557
rollers on 557, 557
safety 557
types 395, 557, 557
cylinder 557, 557
hover 557, 557
rotary 394, 557, 557
Laws on fences 600, 602
Lawson's cypress see
Chamaecyparis lawsoniana
Layered planting 20
in container 327–8, 327
using containers 311
Layering
air
indoor plants 383, 383
method 631, 631
shrubs 116
trees 81
Chinese see air
climbers 141, 145, 145
continuous see French
dropping 116–17
French 117–18, 631, 631
indoor plants 383, 383
methods 631, 631
mound, shrubby herbs 414, 414
natural, from runners, method
631, 631

Layering (cont.)
propagation of fruit by 434
roses 167, 167
self-layering climbers 141,
144, 144
serpentine
climbers 145, 145
method 631, 631
shrubs 116–18, 116–17
simple 116, 116, 383, 383
method 631, 631
shrubs propagated by 116
stooling 117, 117
method 631, 631
sweet peas 215, 215
tip
blackberries 471, 472
hybrid berries 471, 472
method 631, 631
shrubs 116
trees 81, 81
trees suitable for 81
trench method 631, 631
Leaching 617, 624, 625
Leaf blotches see Leaf spots
Leaf blowers 559, 559
Leaf buds, problems 653–4
Leaf cuttings 632, 633, 633
alpines 274
indoor plants 381–2, 381
succulents 347, 347
Leaf eelworms
control 647
damage caused by 647, 647
Leaf miners
control 647
damage caused by 647, 647
Leaf mould 63, 628, 628
high-nutrient 625
as peat alternative 257
in potting composts 63, 322,
322, 323
Leaf scorch 576
Leaf sections, propagation by
381–2, 381
Leaf shine 372
Leaf spots
bacterial 648
symptoms and control 648
fungal 648
symptoms and control 648
Leaf sweeper 559, 559
Leaf-bud cuttings 632, 632
blackberries 472, 472
fruit 434
hybrid berries 472, 472
indoor plants 380
shrubs 113, 113
Leaf-cutting bees 645
symptoms and control 645
Leaf-mould beds, bulbs in 229
Leaf-rolling sawfly, rose 652
symptoms and control 652
Leafhoppers 647
control 647
damage caused by 647, 647
disease spread by 652, 656
Leafy galls 655
symptoms and control 655
Leafy vegetables 515–19
growing in containers 328, 501
storing 506, 515
for succession 515
watering, critical periods 502
Leatherjackets 617, 660
biological control 642
control 643, 668
symptoms and control 660, 667
Leaves (foliage)
adapted to drought 609
annuals for 209
broadly ovate 675
browning 624
colour, trees for 56, 56
colours in perennial beds and
borders 176–7
compound pinnate frond 675
contrasting forms in
perennials 175, 176

Leaves (cont.)
digitate 675
discolouration 624, 639
pests and diseases causing
646–51
distorted, problems causing
651–2
eaten
diagnosing symptoms 639
pests and diseases causing
644–5
forms 675, 675
golden in winter, trees for 59
grey in winter, trees for 59
importance of water to 609
impressions in concrete 594
indoor plants for 354
as insulating material 613
linear 675
ornamental, perennials for 172
pinnate 675
pinnatifid 675
plants for greenhouse 361
problems, avoiding when
buying plants 640
purpose 675
scale-like 675
scented shrubs 95
seed (cotyledons) 630, 630, 676
shrubs 93–4
as soil additive, problems 621
structure 675
texture
annuals for 208–9
trees for 56, 56
variegated, light requirements
355
wind-tolerant, types 613
Leeks 535, 537, 537
blanching 537
conditions preferred 537
conditions tolerated 537
in crop rotation 498
culinary uses 537
diseases 537, 663
earthing up 537
harvesting 537
heeling in 537, 537
mulching 537
nitrogen required 504, 537
pests 537, 663
planting 537
pot 537
recommended cultivars 537
routine cultivation 537
site 537
size of plants 537
soil preparation for 537
soil type required 537
sowing 537
in module 37, 537
sowing in modules 501
spacing 537
transplanting 37, 537
watering 537
'Autumn Mammoth –
Argenta' 537
'Autumn Mammoth –
Goliath' 537
'Jolant' 537
'Kayak' 537
'Longbow' 537
'Mammoth Blanch' 537
'Oarsman' F1 537
'Porvite' 537
'Swiss Giant – Pancho' 537
'Toledo' 537
'Welsh Seedling' 537
Legumes
in crop rotation 498
nitrogen-fixing 498, 625
Leiophyllum buxifolium, soil type
required 260
Lemna
control 673
trisulca 285
as weed 297
Lemon balm see Melissa
officinalis

Lemon cucumbers see
Cucumbers, lemon
Lemon thyme see Thymus x
citriodorus
Lemon verbena 407, 407
in containers 405
culinary uses 407
harvesting 407
propagation, softwood
cuttings 407
scent 407
storing 407
suggestions for 310
use for scent 407
Lemons 319, 479, 481
in border 422
conditions required 481
in containers 319, 481
fruit 57
growing under cover 481
recommended cultivars 481
storing 431
suggestions for use 318, 405
'Garey's Eureka' 481
'Genoa' 481
'Lisbon' 481
'Meyer's Lemon' 481
rough, as rootstock 480
'Villa Franca' 481
Lenophyllum
pusillum, leaf cuttings 347
texanum, leaf cuttings 347
Leontice
resting 240
suggestions for use 231
Leontopodium alpinum
conserving moisture 254
soil type tolerated 261
suggestions for use 259
subsp. nivale, suggestions for
use 259
Lepidium
nanum, semi-ripe cuttings 274
sativum see Cress
Lepidosaphes ulmi 648
Lepismium, side grafting 351
Leptosiphon self-sown seedlings
222
Leptospermum
semi-ripe cuttings with heel
113
scoparium, standards 326
Leptosphaeria coniothyrium 653
Lettuce root aphid 640
Lettuces 518–19
alternating with brassicas 493
bolting 518
butterhead 640
conditions preferred 518
conditions required 518
in crop rotation 498
culinary uses 518
as cut-and-come-again crop
506, 519
diseases 519
fungal 646
effect of rainfall on 495
feeding 519
genetic modification 638
germination 499
growing below wall 493
growing in containers 318,
501, 501
growing under cover 519
under perforated film 519
harvesting 518, 519
high temperature dormancy
518
intercropping 494, 494
mineral deficiency 654
mulching 519
nitrogen requirement 504, 518
overwintering 519
under cover cultivars for
518
pest resistance 640
pests 519, 640, 655, 660, 661
recommended cultivars 518
rotating crop 518

Lettuces (cont.)
routine cultivation 519
site 518
size 518
sowing 518, 519
spacing 496, 519
storing 519
successional cropping 500, 518
transplanting 519
seedlings 500
types 518
watering 519
critical periods 502
winter cropping under cover
505
butterhead 515, 518
harvesting 519
pest resistance 640
'Cassandra' 518
'Clarion' 518
'Cocarde' 518
'Corsair' 518
cos 515, 518
harvesting 519
crispheads 518
harvesting 519
'Diana' 518
'Dickinson' 518
'Green Salad Bowl' 518
icebergs 518
'Jewel' 518
'Lakeland' 518
'Little Gem' 518
'Little Gem Pearl' 518
'Little Leprechaun' 518
'Lobjoits Green Cos' 518
'Lollo Rossa' 518
loose-leaf 51, 515
harvesting 518
'Minigreen' 518
'Nymans' 518
'Pinokkio' 518
'Red Salad Bowl' 518
'Robinson' 518
'Rusty' 518
"Salad Bowl" types 518
growing with herbs 495
harvesting 518
'Saladin' 518
semi-cos 518
'Sunny' 518
'Valdor' 518
'Winter Density' 518
Leucanthemum
conditions preferred 401
x superbum 'Snow Lady'
(syn. Chrysanthemum x
superbum 'Snow Lady'),
growing as annual 213
vulgare 401
Leucocoryne
resting 240
suggestions for use 231
Leucojum
division of offsets 245
suggestions for use 231
aestivum
conditions preferred 231
suggestions for use 228,
229, 239, 285
vernum
conditions preferred 231
suggestions for use 239
Leucopogon fraseri, soil type
required 260
Leucothöe
semi-ripe cuttings with heel
113
soil type required 99
keiskei, soil type required 260
Levelling
humps and hollows in lawns
400, 400
site 390–1, 390, 391
Levisticum officinale see Lovage
Lewisia
in containers outdoors 340
propagation
leaf cuttings 274

Lewisia, propagation (*cont.*)
semi-ripe cuttings 274
sowing *272*
suggestions for use 258, 259
Cotyledon Hybrids *261*
conditions tolerated 342
suggestions for use 259
conditions preferred 255–6
soil type preferred 261
leeana, conditions tolerated 342
tweedyi, suggestions for use 259
Leycesteria
conditions tolerated 95
pruning 105
Leyland cypress *see* x *Cupressocyparis leylandii*
Liatris, dividing 201
spicata, to attract wildlife 178
Lice, plant *see* Aphids
Lichens
dog *667*
symptoms and control 667
gelatinous
on lawn *667*
symptoms and control 667
Light
deprivation, symptoms of 355
direct, indoor plants preferring 361
indirect, indoor plants preferring 361
influence on colour 48
manipulating artificially 610
plants growing towards 610
plants' requirements 355
requirements for seed germination 630
variations within room 355, *355*
Light meters 577
Lighting
in greenhouse 573, 577, *577*
growing lamps 577, *577*
ornamental 22
Lightning, damage caused by 655, *655*
Lignin 674
Ligularia
in border *174*
conditions preferred 284
position in pond *295*
dentata (syn. *L. clivorum*)
in contrasting foliage group *175*
suggestions for use 285
'Othello', architectural form *181*
przewalskii
conditions preferred 181
suggestions for use 285
stenocephala, in border of mixed textures *175*
Ligusticum levisticum see Lovage
Ligustrum
conditions tolerated 95
diseases, fungal 661, 665
as hedge 84
shaping 86
soil type tolerated 99
standards 326
japonicum, pruning 107
lucidum
for avenue 58
semi-ripe cuttings 79
'Excelsum Superbum', foliage 56
ovalifolium
hardwood cuttings 114
for topiary 76
Lilac *see Syringa*
Liliaceae
corms 227
rhizomes 227
Lilioceris lilii 645
Lilium
architectural plant 231
bulb 227

Lilium (*cont.*)
care 251
classification 251
compost for 328, 367
conditions preferred 231
conditions required 251
in containers 319, 328
diseases 251
fungal 649
feeding 328
after flowering 243
flowers
form *676*
shapes *251*
for cutting 231
in containers *22*, 229
in mixed border 228
pests 251, 644
planting 251
in containers 328
depth 251, 328
propagation 251, *251*
bulblets 251, *251*, *634*
offsets 245
rhizomes 245
scaling 248–9, *248*, 634, *634*
from seed 247
feeding 247
stem bulbils 245, 251, *251*, *634*
repotting 243
seed germination 247
seedlings 247
sites suitable for 251
soil type required 325
staking *242*
suggestions for use 229, 316
American 251
Aurelian hybrids 251, *251*
'Bright Star' 251
bulbiferum, propagation 251
candidum 251
diseases, fungal 649
planting 251
suggestions for use 178
cernuum 251
chalcedonicum 251
'Connecticut King' *251*
davidii 251
'Enchantment' *230*
formosanum 251
hansonii 231, 251
henryi 251
lancifolium (syn. *L. tigrinum*)
disease carrier 251
propagation 251
bulbils *634*
longiflorum 251
propagation, bulblets *634*
Madonna *see Lilium candidum*
martagon 251, *251*
Oriental hybrids 251, *251*
pardalinum, propagation 251
parryi 251
regale 251
in pots *229*
with roses 151
'Scheherazade' *251*
x *testaceum*, diseases fungal 649
tigrinum see L. lancifolium
Lily *see Lilium*
Lily, arum *see Zantedeschia aethiopica*
Lily beetle 251
red *644*
control 645
damage done by 644
Lily disease *649*
symptoms and control 649
Lily-of-the-valley *see Convallaria*
Lima beans, *see* Beans, Lima
Lime
adding to compost heap 627
amounts required to alter pH levels 625
applying 625, *625*

Lime (*cont.*)
dolomitic, in cuttings compost 565
effect on soil 616, 617
improving soil with 390
as lawn weedkiller 673
reaction with manure 625
as soil additive 621, *621*
types 625
as weed deterrent 670
Lime, tree *see Tilia*
Lime haters 325
alpine 257
beds for 257
compost for 99, 306, 322, *322*, 364
mulches for 323
pH range 617
raised beds for 599
shrubs, suggestions for use 229
watering 332, 372
Lime lovers, pH range 617
Limes *479*
in containers 319, 481
groups 481
growing under cover 481
propagation 481
recommended cultivars 481
stem pitting 481
'Persian' 481, *481*
'West Indian' 481
Limestone
ground
in JI potting composts 565
in seed compost 565
for fruit trees 426
for rock garden 261, *261*
Limestone chippings, as mulch 323
Limestone soil *see* Chalky soil
Liming 424, 625, *625*
benefits of 641
Limnanthemum lacunosum 285
propagation, offsets 303
Limnanthes
conditions tolerated 213
for dry conditions 211
self-sown seedlings 222
douglasii
flowers 209
propagation
self-seeding 218
sowing 217
soil type preferred 216
Limnobium
spongia 285
stoloniferum 285
propagation, offsets 303
Limnophila heterophylla
propagation, cuttings 302
Limonium
for drying 181, 212, 222
suggestions for use 257
bellidifolium, conditions tolerated 259
platyphyllum (syn. *L. latifolium*)
conditions tolerated 181
root cuttings 203
soil type preferred 184
sinuatum
for cutting 213, 222
for drying 213, 222
soil type preferred 216
soil type tolerated 216
Linaria
flowering time from seed 198
alpina
soil type tolerated 261
suggestions for use 259
maroccana
propagation
self-seeding 218
sowing 217
soil type preferred 216
purpurea
growing as annual 213
soil type tolerated 185
Lindera, pruning 105

Lines, garden 563, *563*
Link stakes 192, *192*, 564
Linnaea borealis, soil type required 260
Linum
arboreum, semi-ripe cuttings 274
grandiflorum
conditions tolerated 213
sowing 217
narbonense, soil type tolerated 185
suffruticosum
soil type preferred 261
subsp. *salsoloides*
'Nanum', suggestions for use 259
Liquidambar styraciflua
softwood cuttings 79
suggestions for use 59
'Lane Roberts', suggestions for use 59
Liriodendron
conditions tolerated 67
tulipifera 59
seasonal interest 59
suggestions for use 59
Liriope muscari
in containers 179
seasonal interest 172
suggestions for use 179
'Variegata', winter interest 181
Lithodora
soil type required 325
diffusa
semi-ripe cuttings 274
soil type required 260
Lithophytes 368, 369
Lithops
division of offsets 349
form 354
succulent type 338
dorotheae, suggestions for use 342
karasmontana 349
subsp. *bella*, suggestions for use 342
pseudotruncatella
var. *dendritica* (syn. *L. pseudotruncatella* var. *pulmonuncula*) *339*
Liverwort on compost of purchased plants 183
Livistona, suggestions for use 59
Loam
friable 493
in JI potting composts 565
lime required to alter pH 625
in potting composts 322, *322*
qualities of 493
in seed compost 565
structure 616
water in 622
Lobelia
flowering time from seed 198
in formal bedding 210
in island bed 173
growing as annual 213
sowing 217
suggestions for use 314
treating as annuals 217
in windowbox 328
cardinalis (syn. *L. fulgens*)
dividing 201
planting time 184
soil type tolerated 184
stem tip cuttings 202
suggestions for use 285
erinus
for containers 212, 319
as filler 210, 211
suggestions for use 213
Cascade Series 213
for containers 212
Fountain Series 213
Regatta Series 213
for containers 212
paludosa, position in water garden 285

Lobelia (*cont.*)
x *speciosa*
Compliment Series 213
Fan Series 213
trailing, in windowbox *212*
Lobivia see Echinopsis
Lobularia maritima
conditions tolerated 213
in formal bedding 210
as ground cover 211
position in border 209
propagation, self-seeding 218, 223
scent 213
soil type preferred 216
soil type tolerated 216
suggestions for use 213
Trailing Series 213
'Wandering Star' 213
Loganberries 470, 471
diseases, fungal 427, 653
pests 658
plant type 419
thornless, in large fruit garden *421*
Logs
sawn
as edging 599
raised beds of 599
stepping stones of 593, *593*
Lolium
multiflorum, for lawn 389
perenne
as green manure 625
for lawn 388
sowing rate 394
in meadow garden 401
Lombardy poplar *see Populus nigra* 'Italica'
Lonas, for drying 213
London pride *see Saxifraga* x *urbium*
Long-day plants 495
Lonicera
choosing *131*
climbing
pruning 137, *137*
renovating 137, *137*
conditions tolerated 125
as food source for wildlife 22
for fragrance 129
as hedge, renovation 86
in fedges 126
propagation
hardwood cuttings 143
semi-ripe cuttings 143, *143*
simple layering 145
softwood cuttings 142
pruning 135, 137
repotting *133*
soil types tolerated 97, 99, 131, 132
standards 326
suggestions for use 129
x *americana* *145*
conditions tolerated 129
suggestions for use 125
x *brownii*, conditions tolerated 129
x *heckrottii*, conditions tolerated 129
korolkowii, seasonal interest 95
nitida
as hedge 84
pruning 107
formative *86*
texture 48
for topiary 76
clipping 77
periclymenum 124
climbing method 124
'Graham Thomas', suggestions for use 126
'Serotina', seasons of interest 127
pileata
conditions preferred 95
conditions tolerated 95
pruning 107

Lonicera (*cont.*)
x *purpusii*
in mixed border 176
seasonal interest 50
'Winter Beauty', scent 95
sempervirens, conditions
tolerated 129
standishii, scent 95
x *tellmanniana*, conditions
tolerated 129
Loosestrife *see Lysimachia*
Lophophora, flat grafting 351
Lophospermum
soil type tolerated 131
erubescens 129
pruning 376
Loppers 73, 74, 554, *554*
maintenance 554
Loquats 482–3
diseases, fungal 649
conditions required 482
conditions tolerated 482
feeding 483
fruits 482
ripe *483*
growing under cover 482, 483
compost for 483
harvesting 483
mulching 483
pests 483
pollination 482
propagation 483
from seed 483
protecting from wind 482
pruning 483
rootstocks 482
routine care 483
site 482
size of tree 482
soil for 482
spacing 482
storing 483
thinning fruits 483
tree *483*
watering 483
Lotus
berthelotii
in containers 319
overwintering 335
stem tip cuttings 202
corniculatus, control 673
hirsutus (syn. *Dorycnium*
hirsutum) 259
maculatus
in containers 319
overwintering 335
Lovage 409, *409*
blanching for use as vegetable
409
conditions tolerated 405
culinary uses 409
flavour 409
flowers 409
foliage 409
harvesting 409
propagation
division 409
from seed 409
suggestions for use 409
Love-in-a-mist *see Nigella*
Low maintenance garden 17, 256
Luculia gratissima, scent 95
Ludwigia arcuata, cuttings 302
Luma apiculata, seasonal interest
59
Lunaria
collecting seed 223
conditions tolerated 213
diseases 646
for drying 212
fruit type *675*
retaining seedheads 223
thinning 218
annua
for cutting 213
self-seeding 218
rediviva for seedheads 181
Lupinus 47
annual, as green manure 625

Lupinus (*cont.*)
in border 174
choosing healthy plant *183*
companion plant for 177
cutting back 192
in mixed border 177
propagation, basal stem
cuttings 202, 203
seasonal interest 50
seed germination 198
seed scarification *630*
suggestions for use 173, 178
'The Chatelaine' *198*
Luzula
campestris 670, 672, *672*
control 673
sylvatica
as ground cover 180
'Marginata', conditions
tolerated 181
Lychnis
dividing 201
flowering time from seed 198
self-sown seedlings 222
chalcedonica, soil type
tolerated 185
coronaria, foliage 176
flos-cuculi, conditions
preferred 401
Lycopersicon (*Solanum*)
esculentum see Tomatoes
pimpinellifolium see
Tomatoes, currant
Lycoris squamigera, conditions
preferred 231
Lygocoris pabulinus 645
Lygus rugulipennis 645
Lyonetia clerkella 647
Lysichiton
conditions tolerated 284
division of rootstock 303
in moist woodland *178*
position in pond *295*
soil type tolerated 184
americanus
architectural form 181
position in water garden
285
camtschatcensis 303
position in water garden
285
Lysimachia
propagation, division 201
soil type tolerated 184
clethroides
as ground cover 180
methods of spreading 180
nummularia
in windowbox *212*
'Aurea', in containers 319
Lythrum
dividing 201
soil type tolerated 184
salicaria, suggestions for use
285
virgatum, in border of mixed
textures *175*

M

Maackia amurensis, suggestions
for use 59
Macfadyena 129
semi-ripe cuttings 143
unguis-cati 129
pruning 137
Mâche *see* Corn salad
Macleaya
architectural form 181
cordata
growth rate 181
suggestions for use 46
Macronutrients 624

Madonna lily *see Lilium*
candidum
Magennis Bermuda grass *see*
Cynodon x *magennisii*
Magnesium 637
deficiency 426, 651, *651*
plant requirements 624
Magnolia
air layering 631
bulbs under 228
container-grown 64
diseases, fungal 665
propagation
air layering 117
chip-budding 82, 83
layering 116, *631*
spliced side grafting 82
spliced side-veneer
grafting 119
pruning 105
seed pods 57
suggestions for use 54
acuminata, soil preferred 65
campbellii 65
propagation, layering 81
soil preferred 65
suggestions for use 59
'Charles Raffill'
seasonal interest 59
suggestions for use
59
subsp. *mollicomata 56*
'Elizabeth', suggestions for
use 59
'Galaxy', suggestions for use
59
grandiflora
conditions tolerated 63,
67, 95
propagation
air layering 81
layering 81
semi-ripe cuttings 79
with heel 113
pruning 73
seasonal interest 59
'Galissonnière',
suggestions for use 59
x *loebneri* 'Merrill',
suggestions for use 59
obovata 81
layering 81
scent 56
'Pinkie' 94
sieboldii, scent 95
x *soulangeana*, pruning 106
sprengeri, seasonal interest 59
'Star Wars'
propagation, air layering 81
seasonal interest 59
stellata, pruning 106
x *thompsoniana*, scent 95
tree, resistance to storm
damage 68
Mahonia
as food source for wildlife 22
for cutting 22
leaf-bud cuttings 113
propagation, semi-ripe
cuttings 113
aquifolium
conditions preferred 95
conditions tolerated 95
japonica
scent 95
seasonal interest 92
x *media*
form 90
soil type tolerated 97
repens
conditions tolerated 93
division of suckers 118
Maihuenia
flat grafting 351
poeppigii 339
conditions tolerated 342
Maintenance, design and 17
Maize, ornamental *see Zea mays*
Malacosoma neustria 647

Malcolmia
conditions tolerated 213
self-seeding 218
maritima, sowing 217
Mallet cuttings 113, *113*
Malope trifida
conditions tolerated 213
sowing 217
Malus
for autumn colour 57
buying 64
conditions tolerated 67
diseases, fungal 649, 664
extracting seed 80
features 54
pests 658
propagation, chip-budding 82,
83, *83*
soil type tolerated 65, 66
'Cowichan' *66*
'Dartmouth', suggestions for
use 59
domestica see Apples
'Evereste'
seasonal interest 59
suggestions for use 59
floribunda
as specimen tree 57
suggestions for use 59
'Golden Hornet'
fruit 56–7
seasonal interest 59
suggestions for use 59
'Magdeburgensis' 55
'Red Jade', suggestions for
use 316
tschonoskii, suggestions for
use 55, 59
Malva
flowering time from seed
198
alcea var. *fastigiata*, growth
rate 181
Mamestra brassicae 645
Mammals *see* Animals
Mammillaria
in bowl garden 341
in containers outdoors 340
in greenhouse display *341*
propagation
division of offsets 349
division of rootstock 350
flat grafting 351
in raised bed 340
blossfeldiana, flowers 342
bocasana
flowers 342
suggestions for use 342
compressa, suggestions for
use 342
gracilis, suggestions for use
342
grahamii (syn. *M. milleri*),
flowers 342
hahniana
flowers 342
suggestions for use 342
herrerae, flat grafting *351*
muehlenpfordtii, in bowl
344
mystax, suggestions for use
342
polythele, in bowl *344*
rhodantha, suggestions for
use 342
spinosissima
flowers 342
suggestions for use 342
zeilmanniana
flowers 342
suggestions for use 342
Mancozeb 648, 649, 662, 668
Mandarins
conditions required 482
in containers 319
cross-pollination 482
recommended cultivars 481
size of trees 482
'Clementine' 481, *481*

Mandarins (*cont.*)
Cleopatra Group 482
as rootstock 480
'Encore' 481
hybrid with kumquats 482
'King' 481
'Miyagowa' 481
Satsuma Group, fruits 482
Mandevilla 129
conditions preferred indoors
361
propagation
semi-ripe cuttings 143
simple layering 145
pruning 135
vigour 130
x *amabilis 143*
splendens 376
cuttings 380
pruning 376
Manettia
semi-ripe cuttings 143
softwood cuttings 142
cordifolia, pruning 137
luteorubra (syn. *M. inflata*)
climbing method 124
pruning 137
Manganese 637
deficiency 424, 426, 444, 451,
617, 624, 651
excess of 617
plant requirements 624
Mangers, planting 329
Mangifera indica see Mangoes
Mangoes 479, 483–4
choosing plants 483
conditions required 483
diseases 483
dwarf 483
feeding 483
flowering, promoting 483
fruit 483, *483*
growing under cover 483–4
feeding 484
watering 484
harvesting 431, 484
mulching 483
pests 483
pollination 483
polyembryonic seedlings 483,
484
propagation 484
approach grafting 484
from seed 484
protecting from wind 483
pruning 484
recommended cultivars 484
rootstocks 483
routine care 483
seed 483
germination 484
site 483
soil type required 483
spacing 483
storing 484
training 484
transplanting budded plants
483
tree *483*
tree size 483
watering 483
'Alphonso' 484
'Haden' 484
'Keith' 484
'Kensington' 484
'Kent' 484
'Palmer' 484
'Tommy Atkins' 484, *484*
'Zill' 484
Manila grass *see Zoysia*
matrella
Manure 650
adding to compost heap 627,
627
adding to soil 621, *621*
as additive, problems 621
advantages 624
content 494
green *see* Green manuring

Manure (*cont.*)
  improving soil fertility with 494
  improving water-retention with 621
  liquid, painting hypertufa with 266, *266*
  maintaining nutrient levels with 503
  as mulch 159, 502
  nutrient content 624
  reaction of lime on 625
  as soil additive 621, *621*
  use for bulbs 237
  for water retention *614*
Maple *see Acer*
Maple, red, *see Acer rubrum*
Maranta
  conditions preferred indoors 361
  greenhouse conditions required 361
  leuconeura
    propagation, rootstock 378
    'Kerchoveana' (syn. *M. kerchoviana*) *378*
Marasmius oreades 668
Marble, containers of 321
Marble galls 652
Marcottage see Air layering
Marginal plants *282*, 284, *285*, *331*
  choosing healthy plants *297*
  constructing shelves for *288*, 289
  for containers 318, 331
  cuttings 303
  planting 298, *299*
  preformed shelves for 289, *289*
  repotting *301*
  in water garden *282*
Marguerite *see Argyranthemum*
Marigold *see Calendula*
Marigold
  African *see Tagetes erecta*
  French *see Tagetes patula*
  marsh *see Caltha palustris*
Marjoram *see Origanum vulgare*
Markers 564, *564*
Marling 621
Marrows *522*, 526
  conditions required 526
  conditions tolerated 526
  culinary uses 526
  cultivation 522
  curing 506
  diseases 526
  flowers
    distinguishing female from male 526, *526*
    harvesting 526
  freezing 506
  fruit 526
  growing with flowers *495*
  growing under cover 526
  habit 526
  harvesting 526
  nitrogen requirements 504, 526
  pests 526, 657
  pollinating by hand 526, *526*
  protecting 526
  recommended cultivars 526
  routine cultivation 526
  soil type required 526
  sowing 500, 526
  spacing 526
  storing 506
  training 526
  bush *526*
  crookneck squashes, fruit 526
  custard fruits 526
  spaghetti 526
  trailing types, training 526
Marsh marigold *see Caltha palustris*
Marsilea quadrifolia
  dangers of 298
  propagation by offsets 303
Marssonina salicicola 666

Mascarene grass *see Zoysia tenuifolia*
Masonry mortar, mix for 586
Masonry cement, definition 591
Matteuccia
  conditions tolerated 181
  by stream *194*
  struthiopteris
    in formal planting *195*
    suggestions for use 48, 284
Matthiola
  for cutting 212, 213
  diseases 649, 660
    fungal 646
  flowering shoots 220
  pests 644
  for scent 213
  Brompton Series
    in containers 319
    for cutting 213
    scent 213
    soil type tolerated 216
  East Lothian Series
    in containers 319
    for cutting 213
    scent 213
  incana
    for cutting 213
    soil type tolerated 216
  Ten Week Mixed
    for cutting 213
    scent 213
  longipetala subsp. *bicornis*
    conditions preferred 213
    conditions tolerated 213
Matucana aureiflora, flowers 342
Maurandella antirrhiniflora, soil type tolerated 132
Maurandya, soil type tolerated 131
Maypoling 427
MCPA 673
Meadow cranesbill *see Geranium pratense*
Meadow gardens 20, *20*
  see also Grassland
  bulbs for 228
  collecting seed from 401, *401*
  controlling self-seeding 222
  grasses for 401
  maintenance 401
  mowing 242, 401
  planting 401
  seasonal interest 401
  site 401
  soil for 401
  soil preparation 183, 401
  sowing 401
  types 401
  weeding 401
  wild flowers for *401*
Meadow grass *see Poa*
Meadow turf 392
Meadows *see* Meadow gardens
Meadowsweet *see Filipendula ulmaria*
Mealybugs *646*
  control 646
    biological 583, 642
  damage done by 646
Mechanical wounding 655
Meconopsis
  flowering time from seed 198
  propagation
    division 275
    sowing 272
    seed collecting *198*
    seed germination 198
  cambrica, conditions preferred 259
  delavayi, root cuttings 275
  grandis 198
Mecoprop-p 673
Medinilla, greenhouse conditions required 361
Mediterranean rocket *see* Salad rocket
Mediterranean-style planting *264*

Medlar
  fruit *435*
  as rootstock for loquats 482
  conditions required 447
  conditions tolerated 447
  diseases 447
  fruit 447, *447*
  fruit type 419
  harvesting 447
  pests 447
  planting 447
  propagation 447
  pruning 447
    winter 428
  ripening *447*
  rootstocks 447
  routine care 447
  siting 447
  soil types tolerated 447
  storing 447
  training 447
  tree forms 447
  'Dutch' 447
  'Nottingham' 447
  'Large Russian' 447
Megachile 645
Melia azedarach
  soil preferred 66
  suggestions for use 59
Melianthus major
  architectural form 46, 181
  as specimen plant 179
Meligethes spp. 657
Melissa officinalis 409
  conditions preferred 405
  conditions tolerated 405
  culinary uses 404, 409
  foliage 409
  harvesting 409
  propagation
    division 409
    from seed 409
  scent 404
  storing 409
  variegated, cutting back 413
  variegated cultivars, conditions required 409
  'All Gold' conditions tolerated 405
  'Aurea' (syn. *M. officinalis* 'Variegata' of gardens) 409
    conditions tolerated 405
    in herb garden *412*
Meloidogyne 660
Melolontha melolontha 660
Melons 523–4
  conditions required 523
  diseases 524
    fungal 661
  feeding 523, 524
  fruits 523
  growing under cover 524
    conditions required 524
    pinching out 524
    planting 524
    spacing 524
    supporting fruit 524
    training 524
  harvesting 524
  nitrogen requirement 504, 523
  origins 522
  pests 524
    damaging leaves 646
  pinching out 524
  planting through plastic mulch 503
  planting out 523
  pollination 524
  protecting fruit 524
  protecting from weather 523
  recommended cultivars 523
  ripening under cloches 505
  routine cultivation 523
  soil type required 523
  sowing 523
  spacing 523
  spread of plant 523
  stopping 524, *524*
  storing 524

Melons (*cont.*)
  thinning fruit 524
  training 524
  types 523
  watering 524
  'Blenheim Orange' 523
  cantaloupe, fruit 523
  casaba *see* winter
  'Castella' 523
  'Durandal' F1 523
  'Edonis' F1 523
  'Galia' 523
  Honeydew *522*, 523
  'Minnesota Midget' 523
  Musk *522*, *523*
    fruit 523
  'Ogen' 523
  sweet 523–4
  'Sweetheart' 523
  winter fruit 523
Mentha
  conditions tolerated 405
  cosmetic uses 404
  culinary uses 404
  diseases, fungal 653
  forcing 411
  freezing leaves in ice 415, *415*
  medicinal uses 404
  mulching 413
  planting to restrict spread 411, *411*
  repelling pests 641
  variegated, cutting back 413
  aquatica
    position in water garden 285
    propagation
      division of rootstock 303
      softwood cuttings 303
    value in water garden 284
  cervina position in water garden 285
  x *piperita*
    culinary uses 404, 409
    foliage 409
    f. *citrata*, foliage 409
  requienii, suggestions for use 259
  spicata 409
    culinary uses 409
    flowers 409
    harvesting 409
    propagation
      division 409
      softwood cuttings 409
    related species 409
    storing 409
  suaveolens 'Variegata'
    conditions preferred 405
    foliage 409
    in herb garden *412*
  x *villosa* var. *alopecuroides*
    flowers 409
    foliage 409
    scent 409
Mentzelia lindleyi
  soil type preferred 216
  sowing 217
Menyanthes trifoliata, division of rootstock 303
Menziesia
  soil type required 99
  ciliicalyx
    division of suckers 118
    soil type required 260
Mercury fluorescent lamps 577
Mercury vapour lamps 577
Merendera
  resting 240
  suggestions for use 231
Meripilus 661
Meristem culture, orchids 371, *371*
Merodon equestris 663
Merremia 129
  tuberosa, soil type tolerated 131
Mertensia, root cuttings 203

Mesembryanthemaceae, flowers 339
Mesembryanthemum, for dry conditions 211
  crystallinum see Iceplants
Mesh, for shading greenhouse 576, *576*
Mespilus germanica
  fruit *see* Medlar
  suggestions for use 59
Metabolism
  energy for 675
  of plants 674
Metal
  containers of 321
  sheds of 605
Metal halide lamps 577
Metaldehyde 644, 662, 668
Metaphycus helvolus 648
  as biological pest control 642
Metasequoia
  hardwood cuttings 78, *78*
  glyptostroboides
    suggestions for use 59
    propagation
      hardwood cuttings 79
      softwood cuttings 79
    soil type tolerated 66
Methiocarb 534, 646
Metrosideros
  excelsa, semi-ripe cuttings 79
  robusta, semi-ripe cuttings 79
  umbellata, semi-ripe cuttings 79
Meyerophytum, division of offsets 349
Mice
  control 662
  damage caused 662, *662*
  protection from 504
Michaelmas daisy *see Aster*
Michaelmas daisy mite, symptoms and control 657, *657*
Michelia
  semi-ripe cuttings 79
  soil preferred 65
Micro-organisms, soil rich in 493
Microclimate
  exploiting 611
  factors producing 611
  in garden 611, *611*
  improving 495
Microlepia strigosa, propagation, rootstock 378
Micronutrients *see* Trace elements
Micropropagation 638, *638*
Microwave, drying herbs in 415
Mikania
  propagation, softwood cuttings 142
  pruning 135
Mila, flat grafting 351
Milax 644
Mildew 193
  conditions encouraging 576
  control 452, 462
  downy *646*
    symptoms and control 193, 646
  powdery 640, *646*
    natural prevention for 159
    symptoms and control 193, 646, 658, *658*
  on roses 153, 160
Mile-a-minute vine *see Fallopia baldschuanica*
Milium effusum 'Aureum'
  conditions preferred 181
  in woodland garden *178*
Miller *see* Star-wheeled cultivator
Millipedes 639, 641, *641*, *644*
  control 644
  damage caused by 644
  distinguishing from centipedes 641, 644
  types
    black 644
    flat 644
    spotted snake 644

Millstone fountain *284*
Miltonia candida 368
Mimulus
  in containers 319
  cardinalis
    position in water garden
    285
    suggestions for use 285
  cupreus, position in water
    garden 285
  guttatus
    position in water garden
    285
    soil type tolerated 184
  x *hybridus*
    'Calypso', conditions
    preferred 213
    Magic Series, conditions
    preferred 213
  luteus, suggestions for use 285
  Malibu Series, conditions
    preferred 213
  ringens, position in water
    garden 285
Minerals
  deficiencies
    causes 623
    correcting 625
    problems caused by 639
  importance of 675
Miner's lettuce *see* Winter purslane
Mini-onions *see* Onions, pickling
Mint *see* Mentha
Mirabelles 447
Miscanthus
  dividing 201
  for seedheads 181
  sinensis
    architectural form 46, 181
    'Grosse Fontäne', as
    specimen plant 179
    'Malepartus', foliage form
    175
Mist propagating unit 580
Mist propagation 636
Mist sprayers 560, 576
Mist-spraying
  for bromeliads 363
  for grapes 462
  for pot plants 372
Mitchella repens, soil type
  required 260
Mites 639
  importance to soil 617
  predatory 646, 666
  as biological pest control
    642
Mitraria
  propagation
    self layering 145
    semi-ripe cuttings 143
  coccinea
    conditions tolerated 129
    soil type required 131,
    301, 325
Mizuna greens 514, *514*
  appearance 514
  bolting 514
  conditions tolerated 514
  in crop rotation 498
  culinary uses 514
  harvesting 514
  as intercrop 514
  leaves 513
  nitrogen requirement 504
  sowing 514
  spacing 514
  suggestions for use 514
  for winter crop 514
Modules
  pricking out seedlings into
    219, *219*
  for seed sowing 565, *565*
  sowing seeds in 218
  sowing vegetables in 501, *501*
  types 501
Moist shade
  annuals and biennials
    preferring 213

Moist shade (*cont.*)
  bulbs preferring 231
  herbs tolerant of 405
  perennials preferring 181
  rock plants preferring 259
  shrubs tolerant of 95
  woodland garden *178*
Moisture-loving plants 284,
  285
  planting 298
Moles
  in lawn 668
  protection from 504
  repelling 642
  symptoms and control 668,
  668
Molinia 181
  caerulea subsp. *arundinacea*
    'Karl Foerster' *179*
    'Transparent' *175*
Moluccella
  germination 219
  laevis
    for cutting 213
    for drying 213
Molybdenum
  deficiency
    cause 652
    control 652
    plants affected by 652
    symptoms *52*, 652
  plant requirements 624
Monarda
  for cutting 181
  propagation, basal stem
    cuttings 202
  didyma 409
    in border 405
    conditions preferred 409
    culinary uses 409
    flowers 409
    harvesting 409
    in herb garden *412*
    mulching 413
    propagation
      division 409
      from seed 409
      stem cuttings 409
    related species 409
    storing 409
    variants 409
  fistulosa, flowers 409
Monkeynuts *see* Peanuts
Monilinia 656
  fructigena 658
  laxa 658
Monocarpic plants, cacti 339
Monocotyledons
  flower forms 676, *676*
  leaf veins 676, *676*
  stems 676
Monoecious plants 676, *676*
Monographella nivalis (syn.
  Fusarium nivale) 667
Monstera 129
  conditions preferred indoors
    361
  hydroculture 361
  simple layering 145
  deliciosa 129
    foliage 354
    growth rate 358
    leaf form *675*
    propagation, self layering
    145
Montia perfoliata see Winter
  purslane
Mooli
  conditions tolerated 546
  recommended cultivars 546
  sowing 546
Mop-top virus 662
Moraceae 459, 460
Moraea
  resting 240
  suggestions for use 231
  huttonii 231
  spathulata, conditions
    preferred 231

Morisia
  root cuttings 203
  monanthos, propagation by
    root cuttings 275
Morphology 674
Mortar
  bedding 591
  definition 591
  dry 591
  laying for paving 587, *587*
  mixes 586
  repairing pond cracks with
    300, *300*
  retardants for 586
Morus
  diseases, fungal 664
  propagation, hardwood
    cuttings 79
  alba
    height 460
    'Laciniata' *79*
  nigra see Mulberries
Mosaics 649
Moss
  on compost round bought
    plants 183, *183*
  conditions preferred 610
  and waterlogging 623
  in lawn 400
    control 672, 673
      annual programme
      397
    preventing 672
  lawn of 389
  sphagnum
    in bottle garden *367*
    for bromeliads *362, 363*
    in composts 323
    lining hanging basket with
    344, *344*
    use in air layering 631
    watering 363
Moss pillar, growing houseplants
  on *364, 364*
Moths
  apple leaf-mining 647
  attracting 22, 178
  codling
    symptoms and control
    659, *659*
    trapping 641, *641*
  pea *659*
    symptoms and control 659
  plum *659*
    symptoms and control 659
Mottles 649
Mould, blue on citrus, symptoms
  and control 658
Mound layering herbs 414, *414*
Mounding
  with earth *612*, 613
  with mulch 613
Mounding up, roses *612*
Mountain ash *see Sorbus
  aucuparia*
Mouse-ear chickweed, common
  see Cerastium vulgatum
Mouse-ear hawkweed *see
  Hieracium pilosella*
Mousetail plant *see Arisarum
  proboscideum*
Mucuna, simple layering 145
Mulberries
  black (*Morus nigra*) 460, *460*
    bleeding 460
    harvesting 460
    height 460
    mulching 460
    planting 460
    propagation 460
    pruning 460
    routine care 460
    site 460
    soil type preferred 460
    soil type tolerated 65
    spacing 460
    storing 460
    training 460
    watering 460

Mulberries (*cont.*)
  diseases, fungal 664
  fruit type 419, 435
  white *see Morus alba*
Mulches
  after planting 132
  applying 626
  area to cover *626*
  between ground-cover plants
    101, *101*
  on chalk soil 424
  conserving moisture 622, 650,
    651, 653
  for containers 323
  fertilizers as 68
  floating 582, 626
    types 505
  inorganic 626
  loose 626, *626*
  organic 494, 502–3, 626
  for perennials 191, *191*
    in containers 193
  plastic, planting strawberries
    under *468*, 469
  plastic film 503, *503*
  protecting roots with 613
  protective 99, *333*
  sheet 626, *626*
    planting through *614*
  for shrubs *98*, 100
  for trees 68
    after planting *66*
  uses 616, 626
  for vegetables 502–3, *502*
  as weed suppressant 670
Muriate of potash 475
Musa
  conditions tolerated 61
  growth rate 61
  protecting in winter 61
  basjoo
    conditions preferred 95
    in containers 319
    protecting in winter 61
    suggestions for use 318
  lasiocarpa
    conditions tolerated 61
    flowers 61
    size 61
Muscari
  to attract insects 264
  conditions tolerated 231
  in container 319, *320*
  in mixed border 176
  propagation, division of
    bulblets 245
  suggestions for use 228, 231,
    239, 316
Mushroom compost
  amount required compared to
    other fertilizers *624*
  effect on soil 617
  improving soil fertility with
    494
  mulching with 502
  nutrient content 624
  as soil additive 621, *621*
Musk melons *see* Melons, musk
Mussaenda 129
Mussel scale 648, *653*
Mussels in pond 299
Mustard(s) 520, *520*
  culinary uses 520
  flavour 520
  growing with cress 520
  growing under cover 520
  growing without soil 520
  harvesting 520
  sowing 520
  Oriental 513
    conditions tolerated 513
    cooking 513
    in crop rotation 498
    culinary uses 513
    flavour 513
    hardiness 513
    harvesting 513
    leaf textures 513
    nitrogen requirement 504

Mustard, Oriental (*cont.*)
    purple-leaved *513*
    sowing 513
    spacing 513
    spinach *see* Komatsuna
Mutation 676, *676*
  causes 655
  in shrubs 100
Mutisia 129
  propagation
    from seed 141
    semi-ripe cuttings 143
    simple layering 145
  soil type required 131, 325
  decurrens, pruning 135
  oligodon, soil type tolerated
    131
Mycena 668
Myclobutanil 646, 648, 649, 653,
  668
Mycorrhizae 617
Myosotis
  in bedding scheme *210*
  with bulbs in formal bedding
    227
  colour combinations 48
  propagation
    self-seeding 218, 223
    sowing 217
  seasonal display 210
  self-sown seedlings 222
  suggestions for use 328
  thinning 218
  alpestris (syn. *M. rupicola*),
    suggestions for use 256, 259
  scorpioides
    position in water garden
    285
    propagation
      division of rootstock
      303
      softwood cuttings 303
    soil type tolerated 184
    suggestions for use 285,
    331
    'Mermaid' position in
    water garden 285
  sylvatica suggestions for use
    308
Myrica root cuttings 114
Myriophyllum 284
  cuttings 302
  dangers of 298
  propagation, turions 635
  softwood cuttings *302*
  aquaticum (syn. *M.
    proserpinacoides*) 285, 298
    planting *331*
    suggestions for use 331
  papillosum 298
  spicatum 298
  verticillatum 298
    suggestions for use 318
Myrrhis odorata
  conditions preferred 181
  as herb *see* Sweet cicely
Myrtle *see* Myrtus
Myrtus
  as wall shrub 93
  communis 95
    in containers 405
    seasonal interest 95
    suggestions for use 310
    subsp. *tarentina*, seasonal
    interest 95
Mystrosporium adustum 663

N

Nails for wall fixings 564, *564*
Naphthalene 667
Narcissus 226
  bulb 227

Narcissus (*cont.*)
bulb structure *674*
care after flowering 242
choosing healthy bulbs *236*
collecting from the wild 228
conditions preferred 233
in containers 233, 319
temperatures for 233
cultivation 233, 242
for cutting 230, 231
diseases, fungal 663
dwarf
conditions tolerated 231
suggestions for use 231, 233
flower forms 233, *233*
forcing 241
in grass
care 242
feeding 242
greenhouse conditions
required 361
in ground cover 101, 180
groups 233
growing with tulips *233*
increase 226
in informal planting *387*
interplanting 211
in mixed border 177, 227
naturalizing 233
cutting foliage 233, 242
in grass *233*
plants suitable for 239
pests 233, 244, 657, 663
damaging leaves 652
planting
in grass *238*
in pots *240*
propagation 233
chipping 249
division of offsets 245, *634*
from seed 246
twin-scaling *248*, 249,
634, *634*
repotting *244*
scented 233
seasonal interest 50
starting growth 236
suggestions for use 56, 228,
231, 232, 233, 309, 316
transplanting from pots 243
types 233, *233*
underplanting roses 151
'Ambergate' *233*
asturiensis, suggestions for
use 233
atlanticus, resting 240
bulbocodium, suggestions for
use 239
cantabricus
resting 240
suggestions for use 230,
233
'Cheerfulness' *230*
cyclamineus
conditions preferred 231
naturalizing 233
suggestions for use 228,
239
Cyclamineus hybrids 233, *233*
'Fortune' *233*, 239
'Irene Copeland' *233*
'Jumblie' *233*
minor
naturalizing 233
suggestions for use 239
obvallaris, suggestions for
use 239
papyraceus (syn. *N.* 'Paper
White'), forcing 231, 241
'Passionale' *233*
poeticus
in meadows 401
suggestions for use 239
'Pride of Cornwall' *233*
pseudonarcissus
in meadows 401
suggestions for use 239
pumilis, suggestions for use
239

Narcissus (*cont.*)
romieuxii 233
resting 240
suggestions for use 233
rupicola
resting 240
subsp. *marvieri*, resting
240
subsp. *watieri* 240
resting 240
'Tahiti' *233*
Tazetta, suggestions for use
229, 233
'Tête-à-tête', suggestions for
use 233
triandrus 233
conditions preferred
231
suggestions for use 239
Narcissus basal rot 663
Narcissus bulb flies 663
Narcissus eelworm 663
Nasturtium see *Tropaeolum*
Nasturtium officinale see
Watercress
Naturalizing
bulbs 228, *228*, *229*
care 242
dead-heading 242
feeding 242
in grass 233, *233*
varieties suitable for 239
Nectarines 451–4
bud types 452
bush, pruning
spring *452*, 453
summer *452*, 453
training *452*, 453
chilling requirement 451
conditions required 451
in containers 423
diseases 452
fungal 648, 651, 658
fan, pruning
after fruiting 453, *454*
formative 453, *453*
routine 453, *454*
spring 453, *453*, *454*
summer 453, *453–4*
training 453, *453*
feathered maiden, training
as bush 453
as fan 453
for flavour 452
freezing 431
fruiting 452
in greenhouse 418
growing under cover 422
harvesting 454
pests 452
propagation 454
pruning 428, 452–4, *452–4*
recommended cultivars 452
storing 454
training 452–4, *452–4*
'Early Rivers' 452
'Elruge' 452, *452*
'Humboldt' 452
'John Rivers' 452
'Lord Napier' 452
'Nectarella' 452
'Pineapple' 452
Nectria
cinnabarina 665
galligena 664
Nectria canker *664*
causes 428
plants affected by 426
symptoms and control 664
Neglected garden
clearing 18, 618, *618*
lawn renovation 399
weeding 673
Neglected fruit trees, renovation
430, *430*
Neillia
pruning 106
thibetica *106*
seasonal interest 95

Nelumbo
suggestions for use 331
lutea, position in water garden
285
nucifera
division of tubers 302
'Alba Grandiflora',
position in water garden
285
'Alba Striata', position in
water garden 285
'Rosea Plena', position in
water garden 285
'Pygmaea Alba', suggestions
for use 331
Nematodes see Eelworms
Nemesia, self-sown seedlings 222
Nematus 645
Neolloydia, flat grafting 351
Neoregelia
conditions preferred indoors
361
conditions required 363
in conservatory *357*
displaying 362
as pot plant 362
carolinae f. *tricolor* 362
Nepenthes, soil type required
185
Nepeta
to attract insects 181
conditions tolerated 181
in containers 319
dividing 201
as edging 150
x *faassenii*, soil type preferred
184
Nephrolepis
conditions tolerated 355
in containers 319
hydroculture 361
watering 194
exaltata, removing dead
leaves *372*
'Bostoniensis', pollution-
absorbing 358
Nerine
conditions preferred indoors
361
in containers 319
for cutting 231
planting depth 243
propagation
chipping 249
division of clump *243*
division of offsets 245
suggestions for use 230
bowdenii 230
conditions preferred 231
in formal bedding 227
Nerium
conditions preferred 95
greenhouse conditions
required 361
growing with succulents 340
propagation, semi-ripe
cuttings with heel 113
oleander
in container 94, 319
pruning 107
soil type tolerated 99
standards 326
suggestions for use 318,
356
Nertera granadensis, suggestions
for use 366
Netting 564, *564*
plastic 564, *564*
protecting fruit with 427, *427*
protecting plants with *612*,
613
for reinforcing concrete 564
securing to pillars 604
for shade 564, *564*
as windbreak 493
windbreak made of *613*
wire 564, *564*
Netting films as floating mulch
505, *505*

Nettle
annual *669*
soil type indicated by 617
stinging 670, *671*
eradicating 390
as a liquid feed 332, 372
New Zealand cabbage palm see
Cordyline australis
New Zealand flax see *Phormium*
New Zealand spinach 519
bolting 519
conditions tolerated 519
freezing 506
germination 519
harvesting 519, *519*
nitrogen requirement 504, 519
soil type preferred 519
sowing 519
spacing 519
storing 519
Newspaper
protecting plants with *613*
use on compost heap 627
use in worm compost 628, *628*
Newts, habitats for 284
Nicking apple trees 437, *437*, 439
Nicotiana
in containers 319
diseases 646, 662
seasonal interest 50
suggestions for use 209
alata, scent 213
langsdorffii, self-seeding 218
x *sanderae*
in mixed border 210
scent 213
Nidularium
conditions required 363
displaying 362
as pot plant 362
regelioides 362
Nierembergia scoparia 'Purple
Robe', in conservatory *359*
Nigella
collecting seed 223, *223*
for dry conditions 211
for drying 212, 213
foliage 209
germination 630
sowing 216
damascena
for cutting 213
in mixed border 210
self-seeding 218
Nitrate of potash 503
Nitrochalk 650
Nitrogen 257, 332, 461
adding to compost heap 627
applying 503
content of fertilizers 624
deficiency 396, 426, 621, 623,
624, 650, *650*
effects of 279, 377
fixing in soil 498
from green manure 625
for lawn 396
life in soil 503
mulches using up 503
nitrogen-fixing root nodules
533
plant requirements 624
providing 444
release to plants 503
requirements of vegetables 503
sources of 503, 625
value of 624
"No-dig" system *581*
for vegetables 497, *497*
Noctua caterpillars 655, 660
Nodal cuttings *632*
Nodes 632
Noise, hedges reducing 84
Nomenclature 677
Nomocharis, conditions preferred
231
Nopalxochia
propagation
flat grafting 351
stem cuttings 348

Nopalxochia (*cont.*)
hybrids, suggestions for use
341
phyllanthoides, flowers 342
North American continent,
influences on climate 606
North-facing sites, climbers for
125, 129
Notching apple trees 437, *437*
Nothofagus
alpina, suggestions for use 59
dombeyi, semi-ripe cuttings
79
obliqua, soil preferred 66
Notholirion, conditions preferred
231
Notocactus see *Parodia*
Nuphar
advena
position in water garden
285
propagation by plantlets
303
lutea
division of rootstock 303
position in water garden
285
pumila, suggestions for use
331
Nurseries, trees from 54
Nursery beds
outdoors 637–8, *638*
raised-edge 638, *638*
sand 638, *638*
water-permeable fabric
637–8, *638*
Nutrients
comparative content of
fertilizers 624
composition 624
deficiencies 624, 639
plant requirements 624
for vegetables 503
Nuts 488–9
definition 419
propagation
from seed 432
suckers 434
squirrel damage 659
storing 431
suggestions for use 488
suitable for gardens 488
Nylon-line trimmers see
Trimmers, nylon-line
Nymphaea 286–7
care 286–7
conditions required 286
containers for 286
depth of water for 284, 286
feeding 286
flower forms 286
flowering time 286
foliage 286
in formal pool *283*
hardy 286
numbers required 297, 331
pests 301
planting 286, *286*, 298
in containers *331*
time for 297
position in pond 295
position in water garden 285
propagation 287, *287*
bud cuttings 287, *287*
cuttings 303
division 287, *287*
plantlets 287, 303
from seed 287
scent 286
seed germination 287
tropical 286, *286*
feeding 286
from seed 303
value in water garden 284, 298
alba, suggestions for use 284
'American Star' *286*
'Attraction' *286*
'Aurora', suggestions for use
331

Nymphaea (cont.)
 'Blue Beauty' 286
 candida, suggestions for use
  331
 'Carnea' (syn. *N.* 'Marliacea
  Carnea') 286
 'Chromatella' (syn. *N.*
  'Marliacea Chromatella')
  286
 'Ellisiana', suggestions for
  use 331
 'Escarboucle' 286
 'Fire Crest' 286
 'Laydekeri Lilacea',
  suggestions for use 331
 'Laydekeri Purpurata',
  suggestions for use 331
 'Laydekeri Rosea Prolifera',
  suggestions for use 331
 'Missouri' 286
 odorata
  rhizomes 286
  seed 287
  var. *minor*, suggestions for
   use 331
 'Pygmaea Helvola' 318
  suggestions for use 331
 'Red Flare' 286
 tetragona
  seed 287
  suggestions for use 331
 'Helvola' 286
 tuberosa, rhizomes 286
 'Virginia' 286
Nymphoides
 indica, position in water
  garden 285
 peltata
  position in water garden
   285
  thinning 295
Nyssa
 conditions tolerated 67
 sylvatica, suggestions for use
  59

Oak *see Quercus*
Oak apples 52
Obelisks, as support for climbers
 317
Ocimum
 basilicum 409
  conditions required 409
  culinary uses 404, 409,
   415
  foliage 409
  freeze-drying 415
  harvesting 409
  planting out 414
  preserving in oil 415
  pricking out 414
  propagation from seed
   409, 414
  related species 409
  storing 409
  variants 409
  'Green Ruffles' 409
  var. *purpurascens* 409
   in herb garden 412
   as gap filler in border
    405
 minimum 409
Odontoglossum
 method of growth 368
 propagation by division 371
 suggestions for use 368
 temperature required 368
Oedema, symptoms and control
 651, *651*
Oenothera
 to attract insects 181

Oenothera (cont.)
 biennis
  conditions preferred 213
  conditions tolerated 213
  self-seeding 218
  soil type preferred 216
 fruticosa, dividing 201
 macrocarpa (syn. *O.
  missouriensis*), stem tip
  cuttings 202
 odorata, for fragrance 181
Office, plants for 358
Offsets
 bulbs
  planting 243
  propagation by 245, *245*,
   634, *634*
   plants suitable for 245
 propagation by 363, *363*
  cacti 349, *349*
  indoor plants 378–9
  succulents 349, *349*
   plants suitable for 349
 of tubers, propagation from
  succulents 349, *349*
 water plants, propagation by
  303
Oidium 646
Oil for greenhouse heating 574
Oil seed rape 657
Oils, herb-making 415
Okra 530, *530*
 conditions required 530
 in crop rotation 498
 culinary uses 530
 daylength requirement 530
 diseases 530
 feeding 530
 freezing 506
 germination 530
 growing under cover 530
 harvesting 530
 mulching 530
 nitrogen requirement 504, 530
 pests 530
 pinching out 530
 pods 530
 protecting 530
 recommended cultivars 530
 ripening under cover 505
 routine cultivation 530
 size of plants 530
 soil for 530
 sowing 530
 spacing 530
 staking 530
 storing 530
 watering 530
Old horse bone *see Tufa*
Old man's beard *see Clematis*
Olea europaea
 for fruit *see Olives*
 suggestions for use 59, 318
Oleander *see Nerium oleander*
Olearia
 conditions tolerated 95
 propagation, semi-ripe
  cuttings with heel 113
 soil type preferred 97
 phlogopappa 113
Olives 484–5
 biennial bearing 484
 conditions required 484
 in containers, moving under
  cover 427
 eating 479
 feeding 484
 fruit 484, *484*
  black, table *484*
 growing under cover 484
 harvesting 424–5
 mulching 484
 as ornamentals 484
 pollination 484
 propagation 485
  hardwood cuttings 485
  semi-ripe cuttings 485
 pruning 484
 recommended cultivars 484

Olives (cont.)
 routine care 484
 site 484
 soils suitable for 484
 spacing 484
 staking 484
 storing 485
 suggestions for use 318
 thinning fruit 484
 training 484
 tree *484*
 tree size 484
 under cover 423
 watering 484
 'Aglandau' 484
 'Allegra' 484
 'Bouteilau' 484
 'El Greco' 484
 'Manzanillo' 484
 'Oblonga' 484
Omphalodes
 linifolia, self-seeding 218
 luciliae, suggestions for use
  259
Oncidium
 suggestions for use 368
 temperature required 368
Onion family, rotation 535
Onion fly 663
Onion hoe 552, *552*
Onion neck rot 663
Onion white rot 663
 rotating crops to avoid 498
Onions
 pests 652
 in crop rotation 498
 diseases, fungal 663
 effect of daylength on 495
 intercropping 494
 nitrogen requirement 504
 ornamental *see Allium*
 pests 663
 sowing depth 499
 sowing in modules 501
 storing 506, *506*
 transplanting seedlings 500
Onions, bulb 535–6, *535*
 bulb types 535
 bull-necked *535*
 conditions required 535
 conditions tolerated 535
 in crop rotation 498
 culinary uses 535
 daylength requirement 535
 daylengths required 535
 diseases 535
 feeding 535
 hardening off 345
 harvesting 535
 nitrogen requirement 535
 overwintering 535
 pests 535
 planting 535
 propagation
  from seed 535
  from sets 535
 recommended cultivars
  535
 routine cultivation 535
 soil for 535
 soil preparation 535
 spacing 535
 storing 535, *535*
 watering 535
 weeding 535
 'Brown Pickling' 535
 'Centurion' F1 535
 'Express Yellow' 535
 'Giant Fed Globe' 535
 'Golden Bear' 535
 'Hi Keeper' F1 535
 Japanese overwintering
  recommended cultivars 535
  sowing 535
 'Kelsae' 535
 'Long Red Florence' 535
 'Mammoth' 535
 red, recommended cultivars
  535

Onions, bulb (cont.)
 'Red Pearl' 535
 'Reliance' 535
 'Rijnsburger Robusta' 535
 'Sonic' 535
 'Sturon' 535
 'SY300' 535
 'Tasco' 535
Onions, European Welsh *see*
 Onions, Welsh
Onions, Oriental bunching 536
 in crop rotation 498
 earthing up 536
 edible parts 536
 harvesting 536
 recommended cultivars 536
 soil type required 536
 sowing 536
 spacing 536
 thinning 536
Onions, pickling 535, 536
 conditions required 536
 in crop rotation 498
 culinary uses 536
 diseases 536
 harvesting 536
 pests 536
 recommended cultivars 536
 routine cultivation 536
 soil preferred 536
 soil tolerated 536
 sowing 536
 spacing 536
 storing 536
 thinning 536
Onions, spring 535, *536*
 conditions required 536
 in crop rotation 498
 diseases 536
 freezing 506
 harvesting 536
 overwintering 536
 pests 536
 protecting 536
 recommended cultivars 536
 soil preparation for 536
 soil type required 536
 sowing 536
  in situ 499
 thinning *536*
 using bulb onions as 535
 watering 536
Onions, Welsh 536, *536*
 conditions required 536
 conditions tolerated 536
 in crop rotation 498
 culinary uses 536
 diseases 536
 harvesting 536
 pests 536
 plant form 536
 propagation
  division of clumps 536
  from seed 536
 routine cultivation 536
 soil type required 536
 spacing 536
 thinning 536
Oniscus 644
Onopordum
 acanthium
  architectural plant 210,
   213
  self-seeding 218
 nervosum (syn. *O. arabicum*)
  architectural plant 213
  self-seeding 218
Onosma
 alborosea, suggestions for use
  259
 echioides
  soil type preferred 261
  suggestions for use 259
 taurica
  soil type preferred 261
  suggestions for use 259
Opal basil *see Ocimum basilicum*
 var. *purpurascens*
Operophtera brumata 645

Ophiopogon
 conditions tolerated 181
 dividing 201
 planiscapus 'Nigrescens'
  bulbs with 177
  foliage 177
  winter interest 181
Ophiostoma novo-ulmi 654
Opium poppy *see Papaver
 somniferum*
Opuntia
 conditions preferred indoors
  361
 conditions tolerated 339
 disorders 648
 form 339
 germination 346
 handling 341
 propagation
  division of offsets 349
  stem cuttings 348
 erinacea, conditions tolerated
  342
 *exaltata see
  Austrocylindropuntia
  subulata*
 ficus-indica (syn. *O.
  compressa*) 339
  conditions tolerated 342
  as fruit *see* Prickly pears
 fragilis, conditions tolerated
  342
 humifusa, hardiness 339
 lanceolata, flowers 342
 microdasys, suggestions for
  use 342
 paraguayensis, flowers 342
 polyacantha
  conditions tolerated 342
  in containers outdoors 340
 robusta, conditions tolerated
  342
 subulata, conditions tolerated
  342
Oranges *420*
 in containers 319
 diseases, fungal 58
 sour (Seville)
  fruits 481
  growing under cover 481
  growth habit 481
  ornamental use 481
  as rootstock 480, 481
 sweet *479*
  in containers 481
  fruits 482
  growing under cover 481
  propagation 482
  recommended cultivars 481
  ripe *481*
  as rootstock 480, 482
  spacing 482
  Blood Group 482
  'Jaffa' 481, *481*
  Navel Group 482
  tree *480*
  Valencia (Common)
   Group 482
 'Bouquet de Fleurs' 481
 'Chinotto' 481
 'Jaffa' 481, *481*
 'Malta Blood' 481
 'Moro Blood' 481
 'Ruby' 481
 'Sanguinelli' 481
 'Shamouti' 481
 'Trovita' 481
 'Valencia' 481
 'Washington' 481
Orbea
 flat grafting 351
 variegata, suggestions for use
  342
Orchids 368–71
 in greenhouse 359
 back-bulbs, potting up 369
 choosing plants 368
 collecting from the wild 228
 composts for 323, 364

Orchids (*cont.*)
conditions required 368, 369–70
in containers 369, *369*
epiphytic
compost *368*, 369
conditions preferred 355
cultivation 368
display methods *369*
growing on bark 369, *369*
growing without pots 369
habitats 368
in hanging basket 369, *369*
methods of growth 368
potting 369
feeding 370
in greenhouse 360
humidity required 370
hydroculture 375
in meadow, mowing 242
monopodial 368
numbers 368
potting 369
propagation 370–1, *370–1*
adventitious growth *370*, 371
back-bulbs 371, *371*
commercial techniques 371, *371*
division 371, *371*
in flasks 371, *371*
meristem culture 371, *371*
stem cuttings *370*, 371
pseudobulbs 368
potting 369
propagation by 371, *371*
recommended *368*
resting 370
routine care 369–70
from seed 371
shading 370
staking 369
sympodial 368
back-bulbs 369
propagation by 371, *371*
potting 369
temperatures required 368
terrestrial
compost 369
conditions required 368
habitats 368
roots 674
tuberous 227
ventilation for 370
watering 369–70
when resting 370
Oregano *see Origanum vulgare*
Oreocereus, stem cuttings 348
Organic gardening
reasons for 492
growing fruit 422
growing roses 159
indoor plants 372
liquid feeds 332
vegetable growing 494
weed control 502
Organic matter
adding to soil 493–4, 496, 497
annual application 494
digging in 494
forms of 494
improving drainage with 616
improving soil structure with 621, *621*
in lawn, preparation 390
as mulch 494
protecting roots with 613
for vegetables 502–3
in potting compost 323
for water retention 614, *614*
Organisms in soil 17
Oriental brassicas *see* Brassicas, Oriental
Oriental bunching onions *see* Onions, Oriental bunching
Oriental garden
container in *307*
designs 18, *27*

Oriental greens as cut-and-come-again crop 506
Oriental mustards *see* Mustards, Oriental
Oriental poppy *see Papaver orientale*
Origanum
soil type tolerated 261
suggestions for use 259
amanum
to attract insects 264
semi-ripe cuttings 274
'Kent Beauty' *261*
to attract insects 264
majorana, in herb garden *412*
rotundifolium, semi-ripe cuttings 274
vulgare 409
conditions preferred 411
conditions required 409
culinary uses 409
flowers 409
use 413
harvesting 409
in herb garden *412*
propagation
division 409
root cuttings 409
from seed 409
stem cuttings 409
steeping in oil or vinegar 415
storing 409
variants 409
variegated, cutting back 413
'Aureum' 409
in herb garden *404*
soil type preferred 184
suggestions for use 406
'Compactum' 409
in herb garden *412*
suggestions for use 405
Ornamental plants, pests 660
Ornaments, existing design and 33
Ornithogalum
conditions tolerated 231
dwarf, suggestions for use 231
for cutting 231
propagation, division of offsets 245
nutans, suggestions for use 239
umbellatum, light affecting flower opening 610
Orontium
depth of water for 284
aquaticum
position in water garden 285
from seed 303
Orostachys
division of offsets 349
chanetii
conditions tolerated 342
in indoor bed *341*
propagation, leaf cuttings 347
spinosa, conditions tolerated 342
Oroya peruviana 339
Orris 408, *408*
conditions required 408
flowers 408
foliage 408
harvesting 408
in herb garden *412*
propagation, division of rhizomes 408
related species 508
rhizomes 408
in scented preparations 408
storing 408
Oscularia, stem cuttings 348

Osmanthus
conditions preferred 95
conditions tolerated 95
layering 116
pruning 107
x *burkwoodii*, suggestions for use 317
delavayi
scent 95
for topiary 76
Osmunda
in winter 194
regalis, suggestions for use 285
Osteospermum
in containers 319
flowering time from seed 198
in mixed border 177
overwintering 335
as pot plants 213
propagation
stem tip cuttings 202
treating as biennials 217
self-sown seedlings 222
suggestions for use 230
'Buttermilk' *202*
Ostrich-feather fern *see Matteuccia struthiopteris*
Ostrya
for containers 318
carpinifolia, soil type tolerated 65
Othonna dentata, leaf cuttings 347
Ourisia
caespitosa, soil type required 260
coccinea, soil type required 260
'Loch Ewe', soil type required 260
Overgrown garden *see* Neglected garden
Overwatering, rescuing pot plant after 372
Ox-eye daisy *see Leucanthemum vulgare*
Oxalis
conditions tolerated 231
control 670
propagation, division of offsets 245
suggestions for use 231
adenophylla, suggestions for use 259
corymbosa 671
depressa 231
enneaphylla
suggestions for use 259
'Minutifolia', in trough *267*
'Ione Hecker'
suggestions for use 259
in trough *267*
latifolia 671, 680
Oxydendrum arboreum, soil preferred 65
Oxygen, as product of photosynthesis 675, *675*
Oxygenating plants 284, 285
choosing 298
healthy plants 297, *297*
conditions tolerated 290
in containers 331
cuttings 303
numbers required 297
planting 297, 299, *299*
species to avoid 298
thinning out 301, *301*
in water features 283
Oyster plant *see* Salsify
Ozothamnus
conditions tolerated 95
soil type preferred 97
coralloides (syn. *Helichrysum coralloides*) 259, *259*
ledifolius, seasonal interest 95
selago (syn. *Helichrysum selago*), semi-ripe cuttings 274

P

Pachycereus
stem cuttings 348
pringlei, flowers 342
Pachyphytum
leaf cuttings 347
stem cuttings 458
oviferum 347
Pachypodium
geayi, suggestions for use 342
lamerei, suggestions for use 342
Pachysandra
conditions tolerated 95
terminalis, in container *193*
Pachystachys
greenhouse conditions required 361
softwood cuttings 380
Pad sections, propagation, cacti and succulents by *348*
Paederia, semi-ripe cuttings 143
Paeonia
for cutting 181
diseases, fungal 665
germination 115, 272
mass planting 26
in mixed border 177
mulching *191*
propagation
division 201, *201*
from seed 199
seasonal interest 50
seed germination 198
soil type tolerated 185
staking 192, *192*
suggestions for use 178
transplanting 193
delavayi var. *delavayi* f. *lutea*, seed scarification *630*
lactiflora
for fragrance 181
'Sarah Bernhardt', as specimen plant 179
suffruticosa, flowers 48, 94
Painted fern, Japanese, *see Athyrium niponicum* var. *pictum*
Pak choi 513, 514, *514*
for autumn crop 514
bolting 514
conditions preferred 514
conditions tolerated 514
in crop rotation 498
culinary uses 514
harvesting 514
head forms 514
leaves 513
nitrogen requirement 504
sowing 514
spacing 514
types 514
Palms 60–1, *61*
buying 63, 64
in containers, suitable varieties 319
cultivation 61
greenhouse conditions required 361
grouping 56
hardiness 60
hardy 60–1
conditions preferred 60
protecting in winter *61*
pruning 73
as screen 55
as specimen trees 55
suggestions for use 55
Pampas grass *see Cortaderia*
Pancratium
resting 240
suggestions for use 231
Pandanus, architectural 95

Pandorea 129
semi-ripe cuttings 143
jasminoides, pruning 135, 376
Panel fences 600–1, *600*
erecting 600–1, *601*
Panicles 676
Panicum miliaceum 'Violaceum', for drying 213
Pans 565, *565*
drainage 141
Pansy *see Viola* x *wittrockiana*
Pansy sickness, crop rotation to avoid 640
Papaver
dead-heading 223
flowering time from seed 198
as gap filler in border 405
self-sown seedlings 222
sowing 216, 217
burseri
soil type tolerated 261
suggestions for use 259
croceum (syn. *P. nudicaule* of gardens) 213
for dry conditions 211
'Summer Breeze', for cutting 213
fauriei (syn. *P. miyabeanum* of gardens)
soil type tolerated 261
suggestions for use 259
lateritium, root cuttings 275
nudicaule 222
orientale
to attract wildlife 178
in mixed border 177
root cuttings 203
for seedheads 181
soil type preferred 184
suggestions for use 178, 309
rhaeticum, suggestions for use 259
rhoeas
soil type preferred 216
conditions preferred 401
conditions tolerated 213
as ground cover 211
in mixed border 210
propagation
self-seeding 218
sowing 217
Shirley Series *216*
somniferum
conditions tolerated 213
self-seeding 218
soil type preferred 216
sowing 217
Papayas
conditions required 480
conditions tolerated 480
dioecious cultivars 480
diseases 480
drainage 480
feeding 480
fruits 480
growing under cover 480
compost for 480
feeding 480
planting 480
harvesting 480
hermaphrodite cultivars 480
mulching 480
pests 480
pollination 480
propagation
cuttings 480
from seed 434, 480
pruning 480
recommended cultivars 480
replacing plants 480
routine care 480
site 480
soil type required 480
storing 480
training 480
tree *480*
trees, size 480
watering 480

Papayas (*cont.*)
'Graeme' 480
'Guinea Gold' 480
'Higgins' 480, *480*
'Honey Gold' 480
'Hortus Gold' 480
'Improved Petersen' 480
'Solo' 480
'Sunnybank' 480
'Sunrise' 480
Paper
as mulch 626
recycled, as liner for basket 329, *329*
Paper reed *see Cyperus papyrus*
Paphiopedilum
conditions required 370
habitat 368
suggestions for use 368
temperature required 368
callosum 368
Paraffin, for greenhouse heating 574
Parahebe
stem tip cuttings 202
catarractae, semi-ripe cuttings 274
Paraquat 671, 673
Paraquilegia anemonoides, suggestions for use 259
Parasites as biological control, temperatures required 642
Paris polyphylla, soil type required 260
Parnassia palustris, suggestions for use 285
Parodia
in bowl garden 341
division of offsets 349
flat grafting 351
brevihamata, flowers 342
chrysacanthion 339
erinacea 349
erubescens (syn. *Notocactus schlosseri*), pricking out seedlings *346*
graessneri, flowers 342
haselbergii, flowers 342
leninghausii
flowers 342
suggestions for use 342
mammulosa, flowers 342
mutabilis
flowers 342
suggestions for use 342
Paronychia chionaea (syn. *P. kapela* subsp. *chionaea*), cutting back 271
Parquet decking 591, *592*
Parrotia persica, seasonal interest 50
Parsley 409, *409*
conditions tolerated 405
culinary uses 409
as edging *495*
flowers 409
foliage 409
freeze-drying 415
freezing in ice *415*
harvesting 409, 415
in herb garden *412*
pests 660
pricking out *414*
propagation
from seed 409, 414
sowing in containers *414*
protecting for winter use 411
storing 409
suggestions for use 318, 405
variants 409
in vegetable garden *495*
Parsnip canker *661*
symptoms and control 661
Parsnips 542, 546
conditions preferred 546
in crop rotation 498
disease-resistant cultivars 661
diseases 546
fungal 661

Parsnips (*cont.*)
freezing 506
harvesting 546
intersowing 546, *546*
mineral deficiencies 662
nitrogen requirement 504, 546
pests 546, 660, 661
protecting 546, *546*
root size 546
rotation 546
routine cultivation 546
size of plants 546
soil preparation for 546
soil type preferred 546
sowing 498, 546
in situ 499
spacing 546
storing 506, 546
watering 546
weeding 546
'Avonresister' 661
'Countess' F1 546
'Dagger' F1 546
'Gladiator' F1 546, 661
'Javelin' 546
'Tender and True' 546
Parterres 18, *18*, 43
annuals in 210–11
hedges for 84, 85
Parthenocarpic fruits 444
Parthenocissus 46, 124
climbing methods 124
conditions tolerated 125, 129
as ground cover 127
propagation
hardwood cuttings 143
self layering 145
serpentine layering 145
softwood cuttings 142
pruning 135
soil types tolerated 131
suggestions for use 129
quinquefolia
climbing method 124
vigour 130
tricuspidata 145
autumn display 127, *128*
conditions tolerated 129
soil type tolerated 132
vigour 130
'Lowii' *131*
Parthenolecanium corni 648
Paspalum notatum
for lawn 388
sowing rate 394
Passiflora 124 (for edible varieties *see* Passion fruits)
climbing method 124, *130*
in containers 319
greenhouse conditions required 361
propagation
semi-ripe cuttings 143
simple layering 145
softwood cuttings 380
pruning 135, 137, 376
soil types tolerated 131
suggestions for use 126
vigour 130
caerulea 61, 129
site for 125
soil type tolerated 132
x *caponii* 'John Innes' *137*
edulis see Passion fruits
edulis f. *flavicarpa see* Passion fruits
manicata 129
Passion flower *see Passiflora*
Passion fruits 467
compost for 467
conditions required 461, 467
conditions tolerated 467
feeding 467
fruit 467
growing under cover 467
harvesting 467
mulching 467
pests 467
planting 467

Passion fruits (*cont.*)
pollination 467
propagation
bud-grafting 467
cuttings 467
from seed 467
pruning 467
routine care 467
site 467
spacing 467
storing 467
supporting 467
training 467
watering 467
woodiness 467
Pastinaca sativa see Parsnips
Pathogens 639
Paths 593–4
asphalt 593
beside house, containers for 311
brick 589, 593, *593*
construction 593
concrete 586, 594
laying 594
making curves 594
preparing base 594
concrete paving slabs 594
crazy paving 588
design 593
edging 497, 501, *591*
existing design and 29, 30
focal points on 309
foundations 585, *585*
of grass 387, *387*
grass 594
mowing 497
gravel, laying 594, *594*
in lawn 387
making between beds 497, *497*
materials for 593
natural stone 588
pavers 593
paving slabs 587–8
preparing sub-base 585, *585*
in rose garden 150
stepping stone 593
stone *593*
timber 593
uses 584, *584*, 593
in vegetable garden 492, 496, *497*
weeding 673
weedkillers for 671
width 593
Patio weeder 553, *553*
Patios 585–91
annuals for 212
annuals to use vertical space 211
brick surfaces 589
cacti on 340
clematis on 138
concrete 586
containers on 310–11
crazy paving 588
drainage slope 585, *585*
existing design and 30
foundations 585, *585*
fruit in 418
in containers 423
herbs on 405, *406*
hostas for 186
natural stone 588
paving, choosing 585
paving slabs 587–8
perennials in containers 179
plants on, reducing water requirements 614
preparing sub-base 585, *585*
roses on 153
screening 585
site 585
size 585
succulents on 340
surfaces
choosing 585
textures 585
tile surfaces 588–9

Patios (*cont.*)
trees beside, disadvantages of 585
uses 584
wooden *591*
Paved gardens
containers in 310–11
arranging 310–11
choosing 310
formal arrangements 310–11
Pavers
clay 589, *590*
wire-cut *590*
concrete 589
cutting 590
imitation granite *590*
laying 590–1, *590*
paths of 593
construction 593
Paving
brick 589
combining materials *591*
concrete mix for 586
concrete slabs 587–8
colours 587
cutting 588, *588*
laying 587, *587*
pointing 588, *588*
quantities 587
shapes 587, *587*
sizes 587
styles *587*
crazy paving
defining edges 588
laying 588, *588*
natural stone 588
edging 588, *588*, 590, *590*, 591
flexible 590
laying 590, *590*
herbs in 405, *406*
sowing 414
laying in herb garden 412
mortar mix for 586
natural stone 588
planting 256–7
rock plants for 259
in rose garden 150
timber decking 591–2
types *590*
weedkillers for 671
Paving stone weeder 553
Paw-paws *see* Papayas
Paxistima, division of suckers 118
Pea moth *659*
symptoms and control 659
Pea root rot 661
Pea shingle 265
Pea thrips, symptoms and control 659, *659*
Peach leaf curl 451, *451*, 651
symptoms and control 651
Peaches 451–4
bud types 452
bush
pruning
spring *452*, 453
summer *452*, 453
training *452*, 453
chilling requirement 451, 452
cling 451
conditions required 451
in containers 319, 423
diseases 452
fungal 648, 651, 658
fan 451
protecting *451*
pruning
after fruiting 453, *454*
formative 453, *453*
routine 453, *454*
spring 453, *453*, *454*
summer 453, *453–4*
space required 422
training 453, *453*
on wall *418*
feathered maiden, training
as bush 453
as fan 453

Peaches (*cont.*)
feeding 452
for flavour 451, 452
forms 451
freestone 451
freezing 431
fruit
thinning 451, *451*
type 419, 675
fruiting 452
genetic dwarf cultivars 451
in greenhouse 418
growing under cover 422, 451, 452
fruit thinning 452
supporting 452
syringing foliage 452
temperatures for 452
ventilation 452
harvesting 454
mulching 451–2
ornamental *see Prunus persica*
pests 452
affecting flowers 657
eating leaves 644
planting 451
distances 451
pollination by hand 451, *451*
propagation 454
protecting 451, *451*
pruning 428, 452–4, *452–4*
recommended cultivars 451
as rootstock
for almonds 489
for apricots 454
rootstocks for 451
routine care 451
site 451
soil type preferred 451
staking 451
storing 454
training 452–4, *452–4*
types 451
wall-trained *418*, 419
watering 451
'Amsden June' 451
'Bellegarde' 451
'Bonanza' 451
'Duke of York' 451
'Dymond' 451
'Garden Lady' 451
'Hale's Early' 451
'Kestrel' 451
'Peregrine' 451
in large fruit garden *421*
'Rochester' 451
in small fruit garden *422*
'Royal George' 451
'Saturn' 451
'Terrace Amber' 451
Peacock plant *see Calathea makoyana*
Peanuts 530–1, *530*
conditions required 530
culinary uses 530
diseases 530–1, 654, 661
earthing up 530
growing under cover 531
growth of pods 530
harvesting 531
nitrogen requirement 504, 530
pests 530
pods *531*
pollination 530
protecting 530
routine cultivation 530
shelled *530*
size of plants 530
soil type preferred 530
sowing 530
spacing 530
storing 531
transplanting 530
watering 530
Spanish-Valencia types 530, *530*
Virginia types 530, 531
Peace lily *see Spathiphyllum*
Pear leaf blister mites 444

Pear midge *658*
  symptoms and control 658, *658*
Pear slugworm *647*
  symptoms and control 647
Pear stony pit virus 659
Pear sucker 647
Pearlwort *see Sagina procumbens*
Pears 444–6
  arcure 420
  bark-ringing 430, 437, *437*
  biennial cropping, cultivars prone to 444
  bush
    pruning 444
    training 444
  chilling requirement 444
  conditioning 446
  conditions required 444
  conditions tolerated 444
  cordons 420
    pruning 444
    training 444
  crop timing 423
  cross-pollination 421, 424, 444
  culinary, recommended cultivars 445
  curbing excessive growth 430
    by bark-ringing 437, *437*
  diseases 444, 649
    bacterial 665
    fungal 649, 658
    viral 659
  dwarf pyramid
    pruning 445–6, *445*
      summer 445–6, *445*
      winter 445, 446
    training 445, *445*
  espalier
    pruning 444
    training 444
  espaliers 58, 420
  "family" trees 420
  fan
    pruning 444
    space required 422
    training 444
  feathered maiden, training as dwarf pyramid 445, *445*
  feeding 444
  for flavour 444, 445
  flowering time 444
  forms 444
  frame-working 443
  fruit *435*
    thinning 444
    type 419, *435*
  fruit type 675–6
  fruiting 444
  grafting over 443, *443*
  growing against supports 422
  harvesting 431, 446
  late-ripening 421
  mineral deficiencies 650, 654, 656
  mulching 444
  parthenocarpic fruits 444
  pests 444, 658, 659
    damaging leaves 647, 652
  planting
    distances 444
    time for 444
  pollination compatibility 423
  propagation
    double budding 446, *446*
    double grafting 446, *446*
    grafting 446, 635
      incompatible cultivars 446
    pruning 444–6, *445*
      renovative 430
      spur thinning 446
      winter 428
    rind grafting 443, *443*
    rootstocks 420, 444, *444*
    routine care 444
    scab-resistant cultivars 444
    scab-susceptible cultivars 444
    self-sterile 421, 424

Pears (*cont.*)
  siting 420–1, 444
  "sleepy" 446
  soil types, effect on fruit 444
  soil unsuitable for 424
  spur thinning 444
  spur-bearers 444, 445
  storing 421, 423, 431, 446
  testing for ripeness 431, 446
  thinning fruit 426
  tip-bearers 444, 445
  top-working 443, *443*
  training 420, 444
  triploids 444, 445
  wall-trained 418
  watering 444
  'Abbé Fetel' 444
  'Belle Guerandaise' 444
  'Belle Julie' 444
  'Bellissime d'Hiver' 445
  'Bergamotte d'Espéren' 445
  'Beth' 444, *444*
    on "family" tree 420
    in small fruit garden *422*
  'Beurré Clairgeau' 445
  'Beurré d'Amanlis' 444
    as interstock 446
  'Beurré d'Anjou' 445
  'Beurré Hardy' 444
    as interstock 446
  'Beurré Superfin' 444
  'Bristol Cross' 444
  'Calebasse Bosc' 444
  'Catillac' 445, *445*
  'Clapp's Favourite' 444
  'Comte de Lamy' 444
  'Concorde' 444
    on "family" tree 420
    in large fruit garden *421*
    in small fruit garden *422*
  'Conference' 444, *444*
    on "family" tree 420
  'Cosica' 444
  dessert, recommended cultivars 444, 445
  'Double de Guerre' 445
  'Doyenné d'Eté' 444
  'Doyenné du Comice' 444
    on "family" tree 420
    in large fruit garden *421*
    pruning 444
    in small fruit garden *422*
  'Dr Jules Guyot' 444, 446
  'Easter Beurré' 445
  'Fertility' 444
  'Fondante d'Automne' 444
  'Glou Morceau' 445
  'Jargonelle' 444
    pruning 444
  'Joséphine de Malines' 445, *445*
    in large fruit garden *421*
    pruning 444
  'Louise Bonne of Jersey' 444
  'Marguerite Marillat' 446
  'Marie Louise' 444, 446
  'Merton Pride' 444
  'Olivier de Serres' 445
  'Onward' 444
    in large fruit garden *421*
  'Packham's Triumph' 445, 446
  'Passe Crasanne' 445
  'Pitmaston Duchess' 445
    as interstock 446
  'Santa Claus' 445
  'Seckle' 445
  'Souvenir de Congrès' 446
  'Thompson's' 445, 446
  'Uvedale's St Germain' 445
  'Vicar of Winkfield' 445
    as interstock 446
  'Williams' Bon Chrétien' 444, 446
    on "family" tree 420
  'Winter Nelis' 445
Peas *530*, 533–4
  bird damage 57, 659
  conditions preferred 533
  in crop rotation 498

Peas (*cont.*)
  culinary uses 533
  damage caused by mice, rats and voles 662
  diseases 534
    fungal 654, 661
  effect of rainfall on 495
  freezing 506
  germination 533
  groups 533
  growing below wall 493
  growing in containers 318, *501*
  growing under cover 534
  harvesting 534
  mulching 534
  nitrogen requirement 504, 533
  overwintering 533
  pests 533, 534, 645, 659
  plant size 533
  recommended cultivars 534
  routine cultivation 533
  seed viability 216
  soil preparation for 533
  soil type preferred 533
  sowing 533
    depth 499
    in wide drills 500
  spacing 533
  storing 534
  supporting 533, *534*
  tendrils 675
  types 533
  watering 534
    critical periods 502
  winter cropping under cover 505
  'Ambassador' 534
  'Cavalier' 534
  'Douce Provence' 534
  dwarf, supporting 534
  'Early Onward' 534
  edible-podded
    harvesting 534
    types 533
  'Feltham First' 534
  'Hurst Greenshaft' 534
  'Kelvedon Wonder' 534
  mangetout *530*, 533
    'Delikata' 534
    'Delikett' 534
    'Norli' 534
    'Sugar Ann' 534
    'Sugar Lord' 534
  'Misty' 534
  'Onward' 534
  petit pois 533
  'Rondo' 534
  semi-leafless *533*
    supporting 533–4
  shelled-pea types 533
    harvesting 534
  'Show Perfection' 534
  sugar *530*, 533
  sugar snap harvesting 534
  wrinkle-seeded cultivars 533
Peasticks
  for seedlings 218, *218*
  for sweet peas *214*
Peat
  alternatives to 257, 323
  characteristics 257
  in cuttings compost 565
  formation 616
  improving water-retention with 621
  as mulch 626
  nutrients in 323
  overwatering 365
  as plunge material 365
  pots made of 565
  in potting composts 322, *322*
  in seed compost 565
  as top-dressing 398, 626
Peat beds, siting 269
Peat pellets 565
Peat pots *see* Pots
Peat soil
  foundations for structures on 585

Peat soil (*cont.*)
  mineral deficiency in 650
  pH level 617
  structure *616*, 617
Peat substitutes
  in cuttings compost 565
  improving water-retention with 621
  as mulch 626
  in seed compost 565
  as soil additives 621
  as top-dressing 398
Pebbles, buying 265
Pecan nuts *488*
  chilling requirement 488
  conditions required 488
  conditions tolerated 488
  diseases 488
  feeding 488
  harvesting 488
  pests 488
  plant type 419
  planting 488
  pollination 488
  propagation 488
  pruning 488
  recommended cultivars 488
  rootstocks, growing seedlings for 488
  routine care 488
  site 488
  soil for 488
  spacing 488
  storing 488
  training 488
  tree size 488
  watering 488
  'Desirable' 488
  'Elisabeth' 488
  'Elliot' 488
  'Mohawk' 488
  'Moore' 488
  'Moreland' 488
Pedicel *676*
Pedilanthus, stem cuttings 348
Pediocactus, flat grafting 315
Pelargonium 204–5
  blackleg 664
  conditions preferred 355
    indoors 361
  in containers 204, 205, 311, 319
  diseases, bacterial 655
  distinguishing from geranium 204
  feeding 204
  in formal bedding 210
  germination 219
  greenhouse conditions required 361
  in greenhouse garden *360*
  in hanging baskets *330*
  in mixed border 210
  overwintering 204–5, *205*, 335
  pests 656
    damaging leaves 647
  physiological disorders 651
  pinch pruning 377
  as pot plants 213
  propagation 205, *205*
    cuttings 205, *205*
    from seed 205, 379
    softwood cuttings 380
    stem cuttings 348
  storing 204–5, *205*
  suggestions for use 314, 315–16
    standards 326
  types 204, *204*
  watering 204
  in windowbox *315*
  acetosum, conditions tolerated 342
  AMETHYST ('Fisdel') *204*
  'Caligula' *361*
  'Copthorne' 316
  'Dolly Varden' *204*
  dwarf zonal 204, *204*

Pelargonium (*cont.*)
  echinatum, conditions tolerated 342
  endlicherianum 204
  F1 hybrids 204
    overwintering 223
    from seed 205
  F2 hybrids 204
    overwintering 223
    from seed 205
  'Frank Headley' *204*
  graveolens, in containers 405
  ivy-leaved 204, *204*
    conditions tolerated 313
    for containers *212*
    in containers *205*
    suggestions for use 313, 316
  'Lady Plymouth' *204*, 316
  Mini Cascade, in conservatory *359*
  miniature zonal 204
  'Mrs Quilter' *204*
  Multibloom Series, suggestions for use 213
  'Purple Emperor' *204*
  regal 204, *204*
    cuttings 205
  'Royal Oak' *204*
  scented-leaved 204, *204*
    suggestions for use 316
    in containers *204*
    cuttings 205
    in greenhouse display *359*
  'Summer Showers', suggestions for use 213
  tetragonum, conditions tolerated 342
  'Timothy Clifford' *204*
  trailing
    for hanging baskets and windowboxes 212
    suggestions for use 213
  zonal 204, *204*
    suggestions for use 316
    in containers *204*
    in greenhouse 360
    in soil bench 367
Pelecyphora, flat grafting 351
Pellaea
  in greenhouse display *359*
  rotundifolia, suggestions for use 366
Pellets, peat 565
Pellionia see Elatostema
Peltandra sagittifolia (syn. *P. alba*), position in water garden 285
Peltigera canina 667
Peltiphyllum peltatum see Darmera peltata
Pemphigus bursarius 661
Penconazole 646, 648, 649, 653
Penicillium italicum 658
Pennisetum
  alopecuroides
    in a border *179*
    in containers 319
  setaceum, for drying 212
  villosum, for drying 213
Penstemon
  cutting back 192
  pests 647
  propagation
    softwood cuttings 273
    stem tip cuttings 202, *202*
  seasonal interest 50
  newberryi f. *humilior*
    flowers 258
    suggestions for use 258
  pinifolius, in trough 267
  'Rich Ruby', planting in container *185*
  Tubular Bells Series 213
Pentas lanceolata, softwood cuttings 380
Peony *see Paeonia*
Peony wilt 665
  symptoms and control 665

Peperomia
conditions preferred indoors 361
in containers 319
greenhouse conditions required 361
propagation
leaf cuttings 633, *633*
softwood cuttings 380
caperata, suggestions for use 366
dolabriformis, leaf cuttings 347
Pepper dust 666, 667
Peppercress *see* Cress
Peppermint
culinary uses 404, 409
foliage 409
Peppers
genetic modification 638
growing below wall 495
growing in containers 318, 501
origins 522
watering, critical periods 502
Peppers, cayenne *see* Peppers, hot
Peppers, chilli 522, *522*
conditions tolerated 522
cultivars 522
flavour 522
fruits 522
harvesting 522
nitrogen requirement 504
pungency 522
ripening *522*
routine cultivation 522
Peppers, hot 523, *523*
conditions required 523
culinary uses 523
freezing 506
fruit 523
harvesting 523
nitrogen requirement 504
recommended cultivars 523
spacing 523
storing 523
'Filius Blue' 523
'Fuego' 523
'Habanero' 523
'Hungarian Hot Wax' 523
'Prairie Fire' 523
'Red Cherry' 523
'Red Cayenne' 523
'Super Chilli' 523
'Tabasco' 523
'Yellow Cayenne' 523
Peppers, sweet 522, *522*
conditions required 522
in crop rotation 498
culinary uses 522
diseases 522
feeding 522
freezing 506
fruit
colour 522
colour changes when ripening 522, *522*
size 522
growing under cover 522
harvesting 522, *522*
mineral deficiency 658
mulching 522
nitrogen required 504, 522
pests 522
pinching out 522
planting out 522
potting up 522
pricking out 522
protecting 522
recommended cultivars 522
ripening *522*
routine cultivation 522
size of plant 522
soil type required 522
sowing 522
spacing 522
staking 522
storing 506
watering 522
'Ace' F1 522
'Ariane' F1 522

Peppers, sweet (*cont.*)
'Bell Boy' F1 522
'Bendigo' F1 522
'Gourmet' 522
'Gypsy' F1 522
'Luteus' 522
'Mavras' F1 522
'Mohawk' 522
'Redskin' 522
'Topgirl' 522
'Unicorn' F1 522
Perennials 172–205
for acid soil 185
for alkaline soil 185
alpine, repotting 278
architectural 179, 181
aspect 183
to attract wildlife 22, 178
attractive to insects 181
autumn interest 192, *192*
with bulbs in mixed border *226*
characteristics 674
choosing 172–3, 183, *183*
for clay soil 184
colour 176–7
in containers 179, *179*, 185
care 193, *193*
plants suitable for 315–16, 319
repotting 193, *193*
in cottage gardens 178
cutting back 192, *192*
dead-heading 191–2, *193*
decorative seedheads 181
diseases 193
affecting flowers 656
bacterial 648, 655, 665
fungal 646, 648, 654, 656, 658, 661
for dry shade 181
effects of high temperatures on 650
effects of low temperatures on 650, 664
evergreen 179
existing, incorporating in design 32
as food source for wildlife 22
for exposed sites 181
F1 hybrids from seed 379
fast-growing 181
feeding 191
fibrous-rooted, division 200, *200*
fleshy-rooted, division 200, *200*
flowering, improving 191–2
flowers
for cutting 181
for drying 181
foliage 172
yellowing 191
forms, contrasting *175*, 176
for fragrant flowers 181
for the garden 172–9
for ground cover 180
ground-cover 179
growing as annuals 213
moving at end of season 223
height range 172
herbaceous
climbing
planting 131
from seed 141
deer damage to 666
diseases 665
pests damaging leaves 644, 645, 646, 647
protecting crown 613
protecting from frost *613*
protecting roots of tender climbers 125
in herbaceous borders *172*, 173, *173*
herbs 404
from seed 414
in island beds 173
lifting 193

Perennials (*cont.*)
low-growing, pests 655, 666
mineral deficiency 650–1
in mixed borders 92, 173, *210*, 210–11
for moist shade 181
moisture-loving 284
mulching 191, *191*
and naturalistic gardening 197
pests 193, 654, 655, 660, 662, 666
affecting flowers 657
damaging leaves 647, 648, 651
planted with grasses 47
planting 184–5, *184*
in containers 185, *185*
depth 184, *184*
in groups *174*, 175–6
time for 184
pricking out 199, *199*
problems affecting stems and leaf buds 653, 654, 655
propagation 198–203
basal stem cuttings 202–3, *202*
cuttings 202–3, *202–3*
division 193, 200–1, *200–1*
of large plants 183, *183*
root cuttings 203, *203*
from seed 198–9, *199*
sowing for chilling *199*
sowing in containers 198–9, *199*
sowing outside 199
varieties flowering within two years 198
stem tip cuttings 202, *202*
in raised beds 173, *173*, 185
rhizomatous, division 201, *201*
roses with *148*, 151, *151*
routine care 191–3
in naturalistic planting schemes 197
for sandy soil 184
for seasonal interest 50, 177–8
seed
collecting 198, *198*
germination 198, 199
storing 198
seedheads 172–3
seedlings, pricking out 199, *199*
self-sown seedlings
transplanting 185, *185*
short-lived, cutting down 223, *223*
in shrub border, temporary planting 92
shrubby
cutting back roots 193
cutting back to improve flowering 192
shrubs with 176–7
silhouettes 176
site 183
site clearance for 183
soil preparation 183
specimen planting 179
staking 173, 191, 192, *192*
stopping 191, *191*
storing 193, *193*
suggestions for use 172–205
tender, lifting after bedding 223
textures harmonizing *175*, 176
thinning 191, *191*
top-dressing 191
in containers *193*
transplanting 192–3
during growing season 193
self-sown seedlings 185, *185*
watering 191
weeding 191

Perennials (*cont.*)
weeds 670–1
control 193, 671, 673
types 670
for winter interest 181
in woodland gardens 178–9, *178*
woody
diseases
bacterial 661
fungal 654, 655, 661, 664, 665
physiological disorders 653
pruning, bad 664
Pereskia, stem cuttings 348
Pereskiopsis, as rootstock 351
Perforated plastic films, as floating mulch 505, *505*
Perfumery, herbs used in 404
Pergolas
attaching to brickwork 604, *604*
benefits of 22, *22*
brick and wood *604*
clematis on 138
climbers on 126, *126*
training 136, *136*
construction 603–4
existing design and 31
grape vines on 422
growing fruit on 422
height 603
over timber decking *591*
roses for 152–3
roses to grow on 155
rustic work 603
screening patio 585
single-sided *604*
training roses on 164
uses 584
wooden 603, *603*, 604
Pericallis
in containers 319
x *hybrida*
as pot plants 213
from seed 379
Periploca 129
self layering 145
softwood cuttings 142
graeca, soil type tolerated 131
Periwinkle *see* Vinca
Perlite
in cuttings compost 565
in potting composts 322, *322*, 323
Permanganate of potash, painting hypertufa with 266
Pernettya see Gaultheria
Peronospora 646
Perovskia
pruning 104, 105
softwood cuttings 111
atriplicifolia, with roses 151
Persea americana see Avocado pears
Persicaria 184
as ground cover 180
affinis 'Donald Lowndes' (syn. *Polygonum affine* 'Donald Lowndes'), conditions preferred 255
amphibia, position in water garden 285
amplexicaulis
suggestions for use 285
'Firetail', for drying 181
bistorta
suggestions for use 285
'Superba', conditions preferred 181
campanulata, suggestions for use 285
peltatum, conditions preferred 181
polymorpha
architectural form 181
as ground cover 180
growth rate 181

Persimmons
chilling requirement 458
compost for 458
conditions preferred 458
conditions required 458
in containers 458
diseases 458
feeding 458
fruit type 419, 435
growing under cover 458
harvesting 458
mulching 458
pests 458
planting 458
pollination 458
propagation 458
from seed 458
softwood cuttings 458
suckers 458
pruning 458
recommended cultivars 458
rootstocks 458
routine care 458
site 458
size of tree 458
soil type required 458
storing 458
training 458
watering 458
'Fuyu' 458
'Gailey' 458
'Hachiya' 458
'Hanafuyu' 458, *458*
'Hayakume' 458
'Jiro' 458
'Tamopan' 458
'Zenjimaru' 458
Pesticides
adverse reactions to 643
damage from 650, *650*
forms available 643
for organic treatments 642
organic versus inorganic 642
sprayers for 560, *560*
spraying 643
statutory regulations 668
types 643
contact 643
systemic 643
types available 668
use with biological control 643
Pesticides Safety Directorate 668
Pests
biological control 642–3
in greenhouses 583
breeding resistance to 638
damage caused 639
to bulbs 663
to flowers 656–7
to fruit, berries, and seeds 658, 659
to lawns 667–8
to leaves 644–52
to roots and tubers 660, 662
to stems and leaf buds 653–4
to whole plant 666
definition 639
diagnosing problems caused by 639, *639*
diseases spread by 639
effect of pH on 617
encouraged by growing conditions 641
feeding methods 639
global warming effects 607, 659
government regulations for 655
integrated control 640
method of identifying problem 639
notifiable 654, 665
organic control 640, 641–2, *641*
companion planting 641, *641*
traps 641–2, *641*
treatments 642

Pests (*cont.*)
  pesticide-resistant strains 643
  plants resistant to 640, 641
  predators attracting 641
  prevention 640
  refuge for in bark of poles
    604
  repellents 642
Petals 629, *629*, 676, *676*
Petrea
  propagation, cuttings 143
  volubilis
    pruning 137
    soil type tolerated 131
    vigour 130
Petrol compared to electricity
  556, 557, 558
Petrophytum hendersonii,
  suggestions for use 259
Petroselinum
  in herb garden *412*
  crispum 409
    conditions tolerated 405
    culinary uses 409
    flowers 409
    foliage 409
    harvesting 409
    pricking out *414*
    propagation
      from seed 409, 414
      sowing in containers
        414
    protecting for winter use
      411
    storing 409
    suggestions for use 405
    variants 409
    var. *neapolitanum* 409
Pets, safety during chemical use
  643
Petunia 315
  choosing healthy plants for
    bedding *221*
  colour schemes with 210
  conditions tolerated 213
  in containers 212, *308*, 319
    with trees 58
  diseases, fungal 654, 661
  flowers 209
  in hanging baskets *330*
  overwintering 335
  as pot plants 213
  suggestions for use 213, 309,
    314
  in windowbox *315*
pH levels
  adjusting 424
  for biochemical reactions 675
  effect of fertilizers on 100
  effect of 617
  high
    correcting 615
    problems caused by 625
  for lawn 390
  lime required to alter 625
  optimum 617
  of potting composts 637
  scale 617
  testing *617*
  of water in pond 290
    changing 300
Phacelia
  for dry conditions 211
  germination 219
  campanularia, sowing 217
Phalaenopsis
  conditions preferred 355
  propagation, adventitious
    growths 371
  suggestions for use 368
  temperature required 368
Phalaris arundinacea
  suggestions for use 285
  var. *picta*, in containers 319
Phaseolus
  coccineus see Beans, scarlet
    runner
  lunatus see Beans, Lima
  vulgaris see Beans, French

Phasmarhabditis hermaphrodita
  642, 644, 662
Pheromone traps 641, *641*, 648,
  659
Philadelphus
  conditions tolerated 95
  flowers 94
  propagation
    hardwood cuttings 114
    semi-ripe cuttings 113
    soft/greenwood cuttings
      111, *111*
  pruning 106
    formative *104*
  scent 95
  seasonal interest 50
  soil for 91
  soil type tolerated 97, 99
  'Dame Blanche' *99*
Philaenus spumarius 654
Philesia magellanica, soil type
  required 99
Phillyrea
  pruning 107
  latifolia, soil type tolerated 65
Philodendron
  conditions preferred indoors
    361
  conditions tolerated 129
  greenhouse conditions
    required 361
  propagation, self layering 145
  suggestions for use 129, 358
  erubescens, pollution-
    absorbing 358
  hederaceum (syn. *P.
    scandens*) 129
    simple layering *383*
    suggestions for use 355
    supports for *364*
    training indoors 355
Phlebodium aureum,
  propagation, rootstock 378
Phleum pratense subsp.
  bertolonii, for lawns 389
Phloem 675
Phlomis
  conditions preferred 91
  conditions tolerated 622
  soil type preferred 97
  chrysophylla, seasonal
    interest 95
  fruticosa, soil type tolerated 99
  russeliana, conditions
    tolerated 181
  tuberosa 'Amazone', for
    cutting 181
Phlox
  dwarf, in containers 319
  for cutting 181
  cutting back *192*
  eelworm-free 652
  germination 630
  in mixed border 177
  pests 203, 652
  propagation
    root cuttings 203
    semi-ripe cuttings *274*
    softwood cuttings 273
  suggestions for use 173, 178,
    255
  thinning 191
  bifida, soil type preferred 261
  'Chattahoochee', semi-ripe
    cuttings *274*
  douglasii, in trough *267*
  drummondii, position in
    border 209
  nana subsp. *ensifolia* (syn. *P.
    mesoleuca*), root cuttings
    275
  paniculata
    basal stem cuttings 202
    for fragrance 181
    root cuttings 203
  subulata
    root cuttings 203
    semi-ripe cuttings *274*
    suggestions for use 259

Phoenix
  architectural 95
  in containers 319
  foliage 56
  pollution-absorbing 358
  as specimen tree 55
  suggestions for use 59
  canariensis
    hardiness 60
    soil preferred 66
  dactylifera, suggestions for
    use 59
  roebelenii
    hardiness 60
    pollution-absorbing 358
Phoma clematidina 665
Phormium
  architectural 95
  in a border *179*
  conditions tolerated 95, *312*
  in containers 319
  dividing 201
  as focal point *312*
  greenhouse conditions
    required 361
  in greenhouse garden *360*
  pruning 108
  soil type preferred 97
  soil type tolerated 184
  suggestions for use 61, 257,
    318
  winter interest 181
  tenax
    growth rate 181
    as specimen plant 179
Phosphorus (phosphates) 332, 637
  applying 503, 625
  content of fertilizers 624
  deficiency 62, 426, 617, 624,
    650, *650*
  for lawn 396
  maintaining levels 503
  plant requirements 624
  sources of 503, 625
  uses 391
  value of 624
Photinia
  semi-ripe cuttings with heel
    113
  sol type tolerated 99
  villosa, pruning 106
Photographs, use in design 29
Photosynthesis 242, 298, 299,
  609, 633, 675, *675*
  and bulb leaves 242
  leaves for *674*
Phragmites australis (syn. *P.
  communis*)
  position in water garden 285
  'Variegatus', position in
    water garden 285
Phygelius, suggestions for use 309
Phyllodoce
  caerulea, soil type required
    260
  nipponica, soil type required
    260
Phyllody disease 652, 656
Phyllopertha horticola 660, 668
Phyllostachys
  suggestions for use 61
  aurea, in containers 319
  flexuosa, in containers 319
  nigra, in containers 319
Phyllotreta spp. 644
Phylloxera 432, 461
Phymatocera aterrima 645
Phytonemus pallidus 657
Physalis alkekengi, for seedheads
  181
Physiological disorders *see*
  Disorders
Physiology *674*
Physoplexis comosa, suggestions
  for use 259
Physostegia
  basal stem cuttings 202
  companion plant for 177
  dividing 201

Phytophthora 660, 664
  global warming effects 607,
    659
  cinnamoni 479
  infestans 649, 662
  kernoviae 654, 665
  parasitica 479
  primulae 661
  ramorum 654, 665
Phytophthora root rots *654*
  symptoms and control 654,
    661
Phytoplasmas, symptoms and
  control 651–2, 656, *656*
Phytoptus avellanae 655
Phytoseiulus persimilis 642, 646
Phytotoxicity 643
Picea
  extracting seed 80
  pests 654
  propagation, spliced side
    grafting 82
  soil preferred 65
  training 73
  abies
    conditions tolerated 67
    'Clanbrassiliana' 259
    'Gregoryana' 259
  breweriana, suggestions for
    use 59
  glauca var. *albertiana*
    'Conica' 259
  omorika, suggestions for use
    59
  pungens 'Montgomery' *62*
  sitchensis, conditions
    tolerated 67
Picket fences 600, *600*
Pickling onions *see* Onions,
  pickling
Pieris
  diseases, fungal 654
  foliage 94
  propagation, heel cuttings 113
  soil type required 99, 325
  'Forest Flame', seasonal
    interest 95
  nana, soil type required 260
Pieris (butterfly)
  brassicae 645
  rapae 645
Pig wire *222*, 564
Pigeons
  protection from 504
  wood *645*
    control 645
    damage caused 645, 657
Pilea
  conditions preferred indoors
    361
  conditions tolerated 355
  softwood cuttings 380
  cadierei 361
    in indoor plant group *372*
    suggestions for use 366
  involucrata
    foliage 354
    suggestions for use 366
    'Norfolk', in hydroculture
      display *375*
Pileostegia 129
  propagation
    semi-ripe cuttings 143
    simple layering 145
  pruning 135
  suggestions for use 129
  viburnoides
    conditions tolerated 129
    pruning 135
Pill bugs *see* Woodlice
Pillars
  climbers on 126
    training 136, *136*
  climbing roses on 153
  constructing 604
  moss, growing houseplants on
    364, *364*
  roses to grow on 155
  securing netting to 604

Pillars (*cont.*)
  siting 126
  training roses on 164
Pilosella officinarum (syn.
  Hieracium pilosella) *672*
Pimpinella anisum see Aniseed
Pinching out annuals 220
Pine *see Pinus*
Pine, Scots *see Pinus sylvestris*
Pine needles as mulch 323
Pineapple galls 654
Pineapple mint *see Mentha
  suaveolens* 'Variegata'
Pineapple sage *see Salvia elegans*
  'Scarlet Pineapple'
Pineapples *479*
  bottling 431
  conditions required 419, 479
  diseases 479
  feeding 479
  flavour 479
  fruits 479
  growing under cover 479
  harvesting 479
  mineral deficiencies 479
  mulching 479
  pests 479
  planting 479
  propagating
    crown shoot 479, *479*
    slips 479
    suckers 479, *479*
  recommended cultivars 479
  routine care 479
  site 479
  soil for 479
  spacing 479
  storing 479
  watering 479
  'Baronne de Rothschild' 479
  Cayenne Group 479
  'Cayenne Lissa' 479
  'Natal Queen' 479
  Queen Group 479
  'Red Spanish' 479
  'Ripley Queen' 479
  'Singapore Spanish' 479
  'Smooth Cayenne' 479
  Spanish Group 479
Pinellia, suggestions for use 231
Pinguicula, soil type required 185
Pink *see Dianthus*
Pinus
  extracting seed 80
  pests 654
  propagation, spliced side
    grafting 82
  training 73
  bungeana, seasonal interest
    59
  contorta, conditions tolerated
    67
  halepensis, suggestions for
    use 59
  nigra
    conditions tolerated 67
    soil type tolerated 65
    suggestions for use 59
  pinaster, soil preferred 66
  radiata
    conditions tolerated 67
    soil preferred 66
    suggestions for use 59
  sylvestris
    conditions tolerated 67
    suggestions for use 59
    'Aurea', seasonal interest
      59
    'Gold Coin' *62*
  wallichiana, suggestions for
    use 59
Pistacia, softwood cuttings 79
Pistia stratiotes 285, *285*
  in container water garden *331*
  dangers of 298
  propagation, offsets 303
  suggestions for use 318, 331
Pistils *629*, 676
Pisum sativum see Peas

Pittosporum
  germination 115
  semi-ripe cuttings 113
  eugenioides 'Variegatum',
    spliced side-veneer grafting
    119
  'Garnettii', as specimen 93
  tobira, scent 95
Plane *see Platanus*
Planning and design
  annuals and biennials 208–12
  assessing existing features
    28–9
  bedding 221, *221*
  with bulbous plants 226–31
  cacti and succulents 338–41
  changing existing garden 30–3
  climbers 124–8
  container gardening 306–18
  fruit garden 418–23
    large *421*
  herb garden 404–6, *406*
    planting to design 412, *412*
  high-maintenance garden 17
  importance of 16
  indoor garden 354–5, 358–60
  informal 20, *20*, *21*, *42*, *43*
  lawns 386–9
  low-maintenance garden 17
  perennials 172–205
  planting
    for colour and texture 48,
      48, *49*
    plans 44–5
    principles of 42–5
    for seasonal and year-
      round interest 50, *50*, *51*
    for structure, shape and
      form 46, *46*, *47*
    styles 42–3, *42*
  rock garden 254–8
  with roses 148–53
  shrubs 90–1
  size and scale *45*
  structures and surfaces 584
  with trees 54–8
  vegetable garden 492–8
  water garden 282–5
Planococcus 646
Plans, drawing up
  of existing plot 34–7
  for collecting water 28
  for herb garden 406
  for new garden design 28,
    38–9
Plant associations, climbers
  combined 125
  growing through other plants
    126, *126*
Plant diversity 674
Plant Health and Seeds
  Inspectorate 655
Plant lice *see* Aphids
Plant oils 668
  winter wash 668
Plant problems 639–73
  diagnosing symptoms 639,
    639
  method of identifying 639
  prevention 640
Plant rings 564, *564*
Plantago
  control 400, 672, 673
  major 672
Plantain *see Plantago*
Planters
  bulb 563, *563*
  seed 563
Planting
  for colour and texture 48, *48*,
    49
  containers 324–5
    for seasonal displays 326–7
  design 42–3
  distances 45
  naturalistic 183
  principles of 42–5
  rock garden 262, 263–4
  roses 157, *157*, *158*

Planting (*cont.*)
  for seasonal and year-round
    interest 50, *50*, *51*, 327–8
  for structure, shape and form
    46, *46*, *47*
  to avoid problems 641
  tools for 563, *563*
Plantlets
  propagation by
    indoor plants 378
    water plants 303, *303*
Plants
  basic parts 674–6, *674–6*
  bisexual 676, *676*
  buying to avoid problems 640
  collecting 24
  dioecious 676, *676*
  existing design and 32–3
  grouping, principles of 45
  hermaphrodite 676, *676*
  monoecious 676, *676*
  polygamous 676
  as sculptural forms *26*
  statutory regulations for 665
Plashing *see* Pleaching
Plasmodiophora brassicae 649,
  660
Plastic
  black
    as mulch 503
    planting ground cover
      through 101
    as weed suppressant 670
  for cloches 582
  containers of 307, 320–1
  as floating mulch 582
  glazing greenhouse with 571,
    571
  insulating greenhouse with
    574, *574*
  for labels 564
  as liner for basket 329
  as mulch 626, *626*
    planting strawberries
      under *468*, 469
    for vegetables 503, *503*
  perforated, as floating mulch
    505, *505*
  polytunnel of 569, *569*
  shading greenhouse with 576
  for ties 564, *564*
  transparent as mulch 503
  white, as mulch 503
Plastic film *see* Plastic
Plastic netting *see* Netting
Plastic pots *see* Pots
Plastic sheet *see* Plastic
Platanus
  conditions tolerated 67
  pleaching 58
  pollarding 46
  propagation, hardwood
    cuttings 79
  x *hispanica*, suggestions for
    use 59
Plate compactor 585, *585*, 590, 591
Platycerium
  conditions preferred indoors
    361
  in containers 319
  bifurcatum, indoors *355*
Platycladus orientalis 'Aurea
  Nana' 62
Platystemon californicus
  self-seeding 218
  soil type preferred 216
Play areas 22
  lawn for *23*, 388, *388*
Pleaching 18, 58, *58*
  annual maintenance 75, *75*
  establishing framework 75, *75*
  training, initial 75, *75*
Plecostachys serpyllifolia,
  overwintering 335
Plectranthus
  in containers 319
  overwintering 335
  oertendahlii, suggestions for
    use 366

Pleioblastus
  variegatus, in containers 319
  viridistriatus (syn. *P.
    auricomus*), in containers
    319
Pleione
  suggestions for use 368
  temperature required 368
Pleiospilos, division of offsets 349
Plugging, establishing lawn by
  394
Plum moth 659
  symptoms and control 659
Plum pox 448
Plumbago
  greenhouse conditions
    required 361
  in greenhouse display 359
  indoors *355*
  propagation, semi-ripe
    cuttings 143
  pruning 135
  auriculata 129
    in conservatory *359*
    softwood cuttings 380
Plumeria rubra var. *acutifolia*,
  scent 56
Plums 447–50
  bush
    pruning 448–9, *448*
    training 448, *448*
  chilling requirement 447
  conditions preferred 447
  conditions required 447
  cross-pollination 421, 424
  diseases 448
    bacterial 648, 665
    fungal 647, 648, 658
  dwarf bush 447
  fan
    pruning
      after fruiting *449*, 450
      spring *449*, 450
      summer *449*, 450
    training 449, *449*
  fans 447
    space required 422
  feathered maiden, training
    as bush 448–9, *448*
    as half-standard 449
    as pyramid 450
  feeding 448
  for flavour 448, 449
  flowering time 447
  forms 447
  freezing 431
  fruit thinning 448
  fruit type 419, *675*
  fruiting habit *448*
  gumming 448
  half-standard, pruning 449
  harvesting 450
  maiden whip, pruning 449
  mineral deficiency 654
  mulching 448
  pests 448, 647, 659
    damaging leaves 646, 652
  physiological disorders 448
  planting 447–8
    distances 447
  pollination 447
    compatibility 423
  propagation 450
  protecting
    from birds 448
    from frost 448
  pruning 428, 448–50, *448–50*
  pyramid 447
    pruning
      spring *450*, 450
      summer *450*, 450
    training 450, *450*
  rootstocks 447, *447*
  routine care 448
  self-fertile 448, 449
  self-sterile 421, 424, 448, 449
  sheltering from wind 447
  silver leaf, susceptible
    cultivars 449

Plums (*cont.*)
  site 447
  siting 420–1
  soil types tolerated 447
  spindlebush
    pruning 449
    training 449
  split skins 450
  staking 447
  storing 450
  suckers 447
  thinning fruit 426
  training 448–50, *448–50*
  watering 448
  'Angelina Burdett' 448
  'Anna Späth' 448
  'Ariel' 448
  'Avalon' 448
  'Belle de Louvain' 449
  'Blue Rock' 448
  'Bluetit' 448
  'Brompton'
    as rootstock 447, *447*
    for peaches 451, *451*
  'Cambridge Gage' 448, *448*
  cherry
    flowering time 447
    self-fertility 447
  'Coe's Golden Drop' 448, *448*
  'Cox's Emperor' 449
  culinary recommended
    cultivars 448, 449
  'Czar' 449
    in large fruit garden *421*
  'Demiston's Superb' 448
  dessert, recommended
    cultivars 448
  'Early Laxton' 448
  'Early Rivers' 449
  'Edda' 448
  European
    chilling requirement 447
    pollination 447
  'Excalibur' 448
  'Giant Prune' 449
  'Golden Transparent' 448
  'Goldfinch' 448
  Japanese 447, 448
    chilling requirement 447
    conditions preferred 447
    flowering time 447
    pollination 447
    rootstocks for 447
  'Jefferson' 448
  'Kirke's' 448
  'Late Muscatelle' 448
  'Late Transparent' 448
  'Laxton's Delight' 448
  'Marianna' as rootstock 447
  'Marjorie's Seedling' 449, *449*
  'Merton Gem' 448
  'Myrobalan B' as rootstock
    447, *447*
  'Ontario' 448
  'Opal' 448, *448*
  'Pershore' 449
  'Pixy', as rootstock 447, *447*,
    450
  'Purple Pershore' 449
  'Reine Claude de Bavay' 448
  'Reine Claude Violette' (syn.
    'Purple Gage') 448
  'Royale de Vilvoorde' 448
  'St Julien' A
    as rootstock 447, *447*, 450
    for apricots 454
    for peaches 451, *451*
  'Sanctus Hubertus' 448, 449
  'Severn Cross' 448
  'Utility' 448
  'Victoria' 448, *448*
    in large fruit garden *421*
    pollination 447
    in small fruit garden *422*
    thinning fruit 448
  'Warwickshire Drooper' 449
  'Washington' 448
Plunge bed, bulbs in 241, *241*
Plungers (seed sowers) 563

Plunging alpines after flowering
  277, *277*
Poa
  for lawns 388
  annua 669, 672
    diseases fungal 556
    in lawns 388
    leaf form *675*
    turf free of 392
  nemoralis, for lawn 389
  pratensis, for lawn 388
    sowing rate 394
  trivialis, for lawn 389
Poached-egg plant *see*
  Limnanthes
Podded vegetables 540–4
  conditions required 530
  in crop rotation 498
  storing 530
  suggestions for use 530
Podocarpus, semi-ripe cuttings
  79
Podranea 129
  propagation
    semi-ripe cuttings 143
    simple layering 145
  pruning 135
Pods, fruit type *675*
Poinsettia *see Euphorbia
  pulcherrima*
Polar climate 606
Polemonium
  to attract wildlife 178
  dividing 201
  flowering time from seed 198
  pulcherrimum, suggestions
    for use 259
Poles for rustic work 604
Pollarding 58, 73
  pruning after 74, *74*
  shrubs 107, *107*
  trees suited to 74
Pollen 629, *629*
  dispersal by wind 610
  in flower 676
Pollen beetles *657*
  symptoms and control 657
Pollination
  cross- 629
    of GM plants 638
  hand- 451, *451*
  methods 629
  self- 629
Pollution, air
  climbers tolerant of 129
  rock plants tolerant of 259
  shrubs tolerant of 95
  trees tolerant of 67
Polyanthus *see Primula*,
  Polyanthus Group
Polycarbonate
  for cloches 582
  for greenhouse glazing 571,
    571
  for shading greenhouse 576
Polyembryonic seed 481
Polyester fabric, as frost
  protection 427
Polyester matting, as liner for
  pond or watercourse 289, *292*,
  293
Polyethylene glycol 638
Polygala
  division of suckers 118
  semi-ripe cuttings 274
  softwood cuttings 273
  calcarea 'Bulley's Form' 256
  chamaebuxus 274
    soil type required 260
  x *dalmaisiana* (syn.
    P. myrtifolia 'Grandiflora'),
    in conservatory *359*
  vayredae, soil type required
    260
Polygamous plants 676
Polygonatum
  in island bed *173*
  planting depth *184*
  suggestions for use 178

Polygonum
  affine 'Donald Lowndes' *see*
    Persicaria affinis 'Donald
    Lowndes'
  aubertii see Fallopia
    baldschuanica
  baldschuanicum see Fallopia
    baldschuanica
  cuspidatum see Fallopia
    japonica
Polypodium
  in containers 319
  in winter 194
Polypropylene
  for cloches 582
  for pots 565
  sheets, as frost protection 427
  for ties 564
Polyscias, softwood cuttings 380
Polystichum
  in containers 319
  in winter 194
Polythene
  as pond liner 288, 295
  pots made of 565
  as protection from pests 660
Polytunnels 569, *569*
  fruit in 427
  low, winter protection in *613*
  for propagation 637
Pome fruits, diseases, bacterial 665
Pomegranates
  conditions required 419, 487
  conditions tolerated 487
  dwarf form 487
  feeding 487
  flowers *487*
  fruit 487, *487*
  fruiting 487
  growing under cover 487
  harvesting 487
  mulching 487
  pests 487
  planting 487
  propagation
    hardwood cuttings 487
    root suckers 487
    from seed 487
    softwood cuttings 487
  pruning 487
  recommended cultivars 487
  routine care 487
  site 487
  soil type suitable for 487
  storing 487
  suckers, cutting out 487
  training 487
  tree *487*
  tree size 487
  under cover 423
  watering 487
  'Papershell' 487
  'Ruby' 487
  'Spanish' 487
  'Wonderful' 487, *487*
Pomes
  see also Fruit, tree; individual
    fruits by name
  definition 419, 435
  fruit type 675–6
  pruning, renovative 430
Poncirus, pruning 105
Ponds
  algae in 623
    control 300, *300*
  autumn maintenance 301
  blanketweed control 300, *300*
  bulbs for margins of 229
  chemicals leaching into 282
  circulating water 292, *292*
  cleaning 301
  concrete, construction 290,
    290, 291
  constructing 288–91, *288–91*
    reinforcing 564
  in containers 318
  containers round 308
  creating balanced ecosystem
    298

Ponds (*cont.*)
  decking stepping stones in *592*
  diverting water to 615
  edging 291, *291*, 615
  existing design and 33
  filtration 292
  fish in 283, 284, 285
  flexible liner
    installing 288–9, *288*
    repairing 300, *300*
  formal *19*, 283, *283*
  ice on, making hole in 301,
    301
  indoors 359
  informal *21*, 282–3
  irises for edge of 182
  marginal shelves
    constructing
      in concrete pond *291*
      in flexible-liner pond
        289, *289*
      in preformed pond 289,
        289
  microclimate in *611*
  miniature 284, *331*
  natural 295
    lining 295
    plants in 295
  pests 301
  pH level of water 290
    changing 300
  planting beds in 291
  plants beside *49*
  preformed moulds
    installation 289, *289*
    repairing 300
  raised
    construction 290–1
    lining 291
  repairing 300, *300*
  roses round 153
  routine care 300–1
  sediment in 623
  silting up 623
  siting 282, 298
  structural repairs 300, *300*
  on terrace *17*
  water quality 298, 300–1
  as water storage area 623
  weeds, control *673*
  for wildlife 284
    creating habitats 295, *295*
    planting 295, *295*
    siting 295
  winter care 301
Pontederia
  soil type tolerated 184
  cordata
    division of rootstock 303
    position in water garden
      285
    var. *lancifolia* (syn. *P.*
      lanceolata), position in
      water garden 285
Pools *see* Ponds
Poplar *see Populus*
  Lombardy *see Populus nigra*
    var. *italica*
Poppy
  corn *see Papaver rhoeas*
  Iceland *see Papaver croceum*
  opium *see Papaver*
    somniferum
  oriental *see Papaver orientale*
Populus
  buying 64
  conditions tolerated 67
  for coppicing and pollarding
    74
  diseases, fungal 664
  growth rate 54
  propagation, hardwood
    cuttings 79
  root suckers 69
  roots, damage from 63
  soil type tolerated 66
  alba, soil type tolerated 65
  x *canadensis* 'Aurea',
    suggestions for use 74

Populus (*cont.*)
  x *jackii* 'Aurora' 67
    suggestions for use 74
  nigra 'Italica', as screen 58
Porcellio 644
Pores in soil 622
Portea 362
Portland cement, definition 591
Portulaca
  as filler 211
  grandiflora
    for dry conditions 211
    growing with succulents
      340
    soil type preferred 216
  oleracea see Summer purslane
Post and chain fencing 600, *600*
Post and rail fencing 600, *600*
Posts
  fence 600
    metal supports for 601, *601*
    repair 602
    spurs for 600, *601*, 602
Pot leeks *see* Leeks
Pot plants
  see also Indoor plants
  annuals as 220
  annuals and biennials for 213
  bulbs under cover 240
  diseases 375
  epiphytes as 362
  feeding 372
  in greenhouse
    care 374–5
    frost protection 375
    watering 374
  humidity for 372, *372*
  neglected, renovating 372
  pests 375
  potting on 372–3, *373*
  top-dressing 372, *372*, 373
  watering 372, 577, *577*
  winter-flowering, plunging
    outdoors 373, *373*
Pot-pourri 404, 407, 408
Potager gardening 26, 494, *495*
Potamogeton crispus 285
  choosing healthy plant *297*
  cuttings 302
  softwood cuttings 303
Potash *see* Potassium
Potassium chloride, sensitivity to
  625
Potassium nitrate 483, 638
  in cuttings compost 565
Potassium (potash) 242, 461, 484,
  650
  applying 503
  deficiency 426, 624, 650, *650*,
    656, 662
  effect on magnesium 651
  effects of 204, 243, 377
  for lawn 396
  life in soil 503
  maintaining levels 503
  plant requirements 624
  sources of 323, 503, 625
  uses 235
  value of 624
Potassium sulphate 426, 475,
  503
  in cuttings compost 565
  nutrient content 624
Potato blight 649, 662
  global warming effects 659
  symptoms and control 649,
    662
Potato cyst eelworm
  rotating crops to avoid 498
  symptoms and control 666,
    666
Potato fork 551, *551*
Potato lifter *553*
Potato mop-top virus 662
Potato scab 617
  common *662*
    symptoms and control 662
Potato spraing *662*
  symptoms and control 662

Potatoes 542, 547–8
  blackleg on *664*
    symptoms and control 664
  cleaning ground with 670
  conditions preferred 547
  conditions required 547
  in crop rotation 498
  disease-resistance 662
  disease-resistant cultivars 649
  diseases 547, 548
    affecting tubers 662
    bacterial 662, 664
    fungal 649, 661, 662
    virus 662
  disorders 662
  earthing up 548, *548*, 662
  feeding 548
  freezing 506
  frost damage 548
  groups 547
  growing in containers 501
  growing under black film 503
  harvesting 506, 548, *548*
  nitrogen requirement 504, 547
  "no-dig" cultivation 497, *497*
  pest-resistant varieties 666
  pests 504, 547, 548, 666
    affecting tubers 662
    eating leaves 644
    of tubers 644
  planting 547–8, *548*
    under black plastic film
      548, *548*
    under floating film mulch
      548
  propagation
    by seed potatoes 547–8
    from eyes 548
    from plantlets 548
    from seedlings 548
    sprouting seed potatoes
      547, *547*
  protecting 548, 613
  protecting from frost *613*
  recommended cultivars 548
  rotation 547
  routine cultivation 548
  site 547
  size of plants 547
  soil preparation 547
  soil type required 547
  spacing 548
  starting under cloches 505
  storage 548
  storing 506
  top-dressing 548
  tubers 635
    colours 547
    problems 662
    size 547
  water requirements 622
  watering 548, 614, 662
  for winter harvesting 548
  'Accent' 548, 666
  'Anya' 548
  'Arran Piper' 548
  'Cara' 548, 649, 662, 666
  'Charlotte' 548
  'Concorde' 548
  'Desirée' 548, 662
  'Estima' 548
  'Foremost' 548
  'Kestrel' 548, 644
  'King Edward' 662
  'Kondor' 548, 649, 662
  'Lady Christl' 548
  'Maris Bard' 548
  'Maris Piper' 548, 662, 666
  'Maxine' 548, 666
  'Mimi' 548
  'Nadine' 548
  'Navan' 548
  'Nicola' 548
  'Pentland Crown' 548
  'Pentland Javelin' 548, 666
  'Picasso' 548, 666
  'Pink Fir Apple' 548
  'Ratte' 548
  'Red Duke of York' 548

Potatoes (*cont.*)
  'Rocket' 666
  'Romano' 548, 649, 662
  'Roseval' 548
  'Sante' 548, 644, 666
  'Stemster' 666
  'Swift' 666
  'Valor' 666
  'Wilja' 548, 649, 662
  'Winston' 548
Potatoes, sweet, *see* Sweet
  potatoes
Potential evapotranspiration 622
Potentilla
  propagation, soft/greenwood
    cuttings 111
  in rock garden 254
  shrubby, soil type tolerated 99
  soil type tolerated 97
  fruticosa, as hedge 85
    'Elizabeth', seasonal
      interest 91
    'Nana Argentea' 259
  nitida, suggestions for use
    259
Pots
  see also Containers
  for aquatics 565, *565*
  clay
    capillary watering 577
    cleaning 279
    compared to plastic 278,
      344
    drainage 141
    preparing for bulbs 240,
      240
    preparing for sowing seed
      246
  degradable *199*, 565, *565*
    making 565
    sowing annuals in 218
  drainage 141
  half 565, *565*
  lattice 240, *240*, 565, *565*
  long Toms 565, *565*
  ornamental *see* Containers
  plastic compared to clay 278,
    344
  removing plants from 220
  for seed sowing 218
  self-watering 374
  shapes 565
  sizes 565
  standard 565, *565*
  sweet pea tubes 565, *565*
  types 565, *565*
  watering, capillary system
    577, *577*
  whalehide ring pots 565, *565*
Potting composts *see* Composts,
  potting
Powdery mildew 642, *646*
  global warming effects 659
  symptoms and control 193,
    646, 658, *658*
Powered tools *see* Tools
Pratia pedunculata, suggestions
  for use 259
Predators, in biological pest
  control 159, 642–3
  temperatures required 642
Preserving fruit 431
Presser boards *219*, 637
Pricking out 637
  alpines 272
  annuals 219, *219*
  cacti 346, *346*
  indoor plants 379–80
  into modules *219*
  perennials 199
  seedlings 115, *115*
Prickly pears
  conditions required 419, 485
  conditions tolerated 485
  diseases 485
  fruits 485, *485*
  growing under cover 485
  harvesting 485
  planting 485

Prickly pears (*cont.*)
propagation, stem segments 485, *485*
routine care 485
site 485
size of plants 485
soil type preferred 485
spacing 485
stems 485
storing 485
Primrose *see Primula vulgaris*
Primula
conditions preferred 259
diseases, fungal 650, 661
flowering time from seed 198
germination 219
greenhouse conditions required 361
leaf vein patterns *676*
pests 660, 666
damaging leaves 647
propagation
division 275
from seed 272
softwood cuttings 273
scent 213
seed germination 198
soil type tolerated 216
suggestions for use 178, 179, 228, 308
in water garden *283*
allionii, division 275
alpicola, suggestions for use 285
alpine, sowing 272
auricula
breeding 178
in container display *24*
in a cottage garden *177*
in greenhouse *359*
pests 661
propagation, "Irishman's" cuttings 275
suggestions for use 259
boothii, soil type required 260
bulleyana *184*
in bog garden *284*
conditions preferred 181
soil type tolerated 184
Candelabra hybrids
conditions preferred 282
in woodland garden *178*
denticulata
root cuttings 203, 275, *276*
scooping rosettes 276, *276*
suggestions for use 285
farinosa, suggestions for use 259
florindae
conditions preferred 181, *284*
soil type tolerated 184
suggestions for use 285
gracilipes
propagation, leaf cuttings 274
soil type required 260
japonica
conditions preferred 181
suggestions for use 285
kewensis, from seed 379
malacoides 379
compost for 364
conditions preferred indoors 361
as pot plants 213
from seed 379
marginata
propagation
basal cuttings 274, *274*
"Irishman's" cuttings 275
suggestions for use 259
nana, soil type required 260
obconica
conditions preferred indoors 361
pests 656

Primula obconica (*cont.*)
as pot plants 213
from seed 379
Polyanthus Group
basic parts of plant *674*
bird damage 657
conditions preferred 213
in containers 212, 319
interplanting 211
lifting after bedding 223
pests 660, 666
seasonal group 210
suggestions for use 308, 315
prolifera (syn. *P. helodoxa*), suggestions for use 285
pulverulenta
conditions preferred 181
suggestions for use 285
rosea
soil type tolerated 184
suggestions for use 285
scotica, suggestions for use 258
secundiflora, suggestions for use 285
sikkimensis, suggestions for use 285
sinensis
as pot plants 213
from seed 379
sonchifolia, soil type required 260
veris *401*
vulgaris
bird damage 657
conditions preferred 213
in containers 212, 319
as fillers 211
in mixed border *176*
seasonal display 210
suggestions for use 56, 315
in woodland *178*
'Double Sulphur', suggestions for use 315
'Miss Indigo', suggestions for use 315
Primula brown core *661*
symptoms and control 650, 661
Pristiphora 645
Pritzelago alpina, suggestions for use 259
Privacy
on balcony 313, *313*
of garden *14*, 18
structures to provide 584
Privet *see Ligustrum*
Chinese *see Ligustrum lucidum*
Problems 639–73
diagnosing symptoms 639, *639*
integrated control 640
method of identifying 639
prevention 640
Proliferation 657, *657*
Propagating blanket 580
Propagating units *see* Propagators
Propagation
advanced techniques 629, 638
bottom heat for 636
by bud cuttings 287, *287*
cacti 346–51
care of propagated plant 637–8
feeding during training 637
climbers 141–5
dahlias 235, *235*
environment for 636–7
fruit 432–4, *432–4*
fuchsias 120–1, *120*
in greenhouse, aids for 580, *580*
herbs 414, *414*
hygiene 637
indoor plants 378–83
principles 629–38
roses 165–9, *165–9*
shrubs 111–10
succulents 346–51

Propagation (*cont.*)
"topping" 187, *187*
trees 78–83
water plants 302–3, *302–3*
Propagators
bottom heat 636
germinating seed in 379
heated 578, 580, *580*, 637
mist units 580, 636
rigid-topped 636, *636*
rooting grafted shrubs in 119, *119*
for windowsill 580, *580*
Propane gas 574
Prostanthera
in greenhouse 360
scent 95
cuneata, choosing healthy plant *97*
rotundifolia, in conservatory *359*
Protection
for alpines 269
for hardening off 220
for leafy cuttings 636, *636*
netting for 564
for shrubs newly planted 99
Protective clothing *see* Clothing
Prothalli 195
Prunella
as ground cover 180
in lawns 387
'Pagoda' 213
vulgaris *672*
Pruners
anvil 554, *554*
long-handled 554, *554*
maintenance 554
tree 555, *555*
Pruning
aims 103
bad, symptoms and control 664, *664*
branched-head standards 72, *72*
brutting 489, *489*
central-leader standards 72, *72*
climbers 134–7
after flowering 135, *135*
formative 134, *134*
principles 134
spring 134, *134*
under cover 376
winter 136, *136*
and composting 110
coppicing 107, *107*
cutting methods 376
double Guyot system 464–5, 465–6
effects 103
espaliers 73
fan-trained trees 73
feathered trees 72, *72*
formative 72–3, *72*
fruit trees and bushes 428–30, *428, 429, 430*
Full Lorette System 439
ground-cover plants 101, *101*
hard 103
honeysuckle 137, *137*
light 103
Modified Lorette System 438–9, *438*
pinch pruning 377, *377*
feeding during training 377
pollarding 107, *107*
renovative, fruit trees 430, *430*
root 73
fruit trees 430, *430*
shrubs 110
roses 161–4, *161–4*
into shapes 46
shrubs 103–10
after planting 98
aims 103
to attract wildlife 103
deciduous 104–6, *104–6*
effects 103
formative 103–4, *104*

Pruning, shrubs (*cont.*)
hard in spring *104*, 105
minimal *104*, 105, 106
principles 103, *103*
standards 109
suckering habit 106, *106*
summer 106, *106*
wall 108–9, *109*
tools for 134, 550, 554–6
maintenance 554
for topiary *76*
trees 71–5
established 73
formative 72–3, *72*
principles 71, *71*
weeping standards 73
weeping trees 72
Wisteria 135, *135*
Pruning loppers 73, 74, 554, *554*
maintenance 554
Pruning saws 555, *555*
bow *555*
double-edged *555*
folding *555*
general-purpose *555*
Grecian 555, *555*
Prunus
as arch over walkway *58*
bird damage 657
bulbs under 228
diseases
bacterial 665
fungal 648
evergreen, semi-ripe cuttings with heel 113
flowers 57
form 55
pests damaging leaves 647
propagation
chip budding 82
softwood cuttings 79
spliced side grafting 82
pruning 71, 72
renovating 74
root suckers 69
for small gardens 59
as specimen tree 55
underplanting 58
'Accolade', seasonal interest 59
americana 55
'Amanogawa', suggestions for use 59
armeniaca see Apricots
avium
edible varieties *see* Cherries, sweet
'Plena', soil type tolerated 65
cerasifera see Plums, cherry
cerasus see Cherries, acid
x *domestica see* Gages; Plums
dulcis see Almonds
glandulosa
spliced side-veneer grafting 119
stooling 117
incisa seasonal interest 59
insititia see Bullaces; Damsons; Mirabelles
'Kanzan', shape 55
'Kiku-shidare-zakura' (syn. *P.* 'Cheal's Weeping'), suggestions for use 59
laurocerasus
in containers 319
diseases fungal 648
as hedge 108
pruning 107, 110
and compost 110
'Otto Luyken', as ground cover 101
'Schipkaensis', heel cuttings *113*
lusitanica
propagation, semi-ripe cuttings 79
pruning 107, *108*

Prunus (*cont.*)
maackii 'Amber Beauty', seasonal interest 59
mume
seasonal interest 59
'Beni-chidori', training *108*
'Okame'
seasonal interest 59
suggestions for use 59
'Pandora', suggestions for use 59
persica
edible *see* Peaches
'Klara Mayer', training 108
var. *nectarina see* Nectarines
salicina (syn. *P. triflora*) *see* Plums, Japanese
sargentii 65
seasonal interest 59
soil type tolerated 65
serrula
bark 57, *57*
seasonal interest 59
spinosa
conditions tolerated 95
cultivars as hedge 85
in fedges 126
'Spire' (syn. x *hillieri* 'Spire'), suggestions for use 59
x *subhirtella*
suggestions for use 59
'Autumnalis' *57*
fasciation 657
seasonal interest 59
'Autumnalis Rosea', seasonal interest 59
triflora (syn. *P. salicina*) *see* Plums, Japanese
triloba, pruning 104, 105
virginiana 'Schubert', foliage 56
x *yedoensis*, suggestions for use 59
Pseudobulbs
orchids with 368
potting 369
propagation by 371, *371*
Pseudococcus 646
Pseudolarix amabilis, soil preferred 65
Pseudolithos
flat grafting 315
grafting 350
Pseudomonas syringae
pv. *morsprunorum* 648, 665
pv. *syringae* 665
Pseudotsuga
soil preferred 65
menziesii
pests 654
var. *glauca* 55
Psidium guajava see Guavas
Psila rosae see Carrot fly
Psylla
buxi 647
mali, nymphs 656
pyricola 647
Psyllids *see* Suckers (psyllids)
Psylliostachys suworowii
for cutting 213
as pot plants 213
Ptelea pruning 105
Pteris
conditions preferred indoors 361
cretica
propagation, rootstock 378
suggestions for use 366
Pterocactus, division of offsets 349
Pterocarya fraxinifolia, soil type tolerated 66
Pterocephalus perennis, conditions tolerated 259
Pterostyrax, pruning 105
Puccinia 648

Puddling 622
Pueraria lobata, suggestions for use 128
Pulmonaria
   dividing 201
   as ground cover 180
   in mixed border 176
   seasonal interest 172
   suggestions for use 178
   winter interest 181
   angustifolia subs. *azurea*, ornamental ground cover *180*
   'Sissinghurst White', conditions tolerated 180
Pulsatilla
   propagation
      root cuttings 275
      sowing 272
   in rock garden 256
   soil type tolerated 261
   vulgaris, root cuttings 203
Pulvinaria regalis 648
Pumpkins 525
   culinary uses 525
   cultivation 522
   curing 525, *525*
   diseases, fungal 661
   feeding 525
   freezing 506
   fruit 525
   germination 525
   habit 525
   harvesting 525
   nitrogen requirements 504, 525
   planting 525
   pollination by hand 525
   recommended cultivars 525
   routine cultivation 525
   sowing 500, 525
   spacing 525
   storing 525
   training 525
   on tripod *525*
   watering 525
   'Baby Bear' 525
   'Butternut' 525
   'Crown Prince' 525
   'Dills Atlantic Giant' 525
   'Gem' 525
   'Ghost' F1 525
   'Harrier' F1 525
   'Hooligan' 525
   'Kabocha' 525
   'Mars' 525
   'Queensland Blue' 525
   'Rouge Vif D'Etamp' 525
   'Small Sugar' 525
   'Table Ace' 525
   'Triple Treat' 525
   'Turk's Turban' 525
   'Uchiki Kuri' 525
Pumps
   cleaning 301
   submersible 615
   sump 615
   for water garden 292, *292*
Punica
   granatum see Pomegranates
   granatum var. *nana see* Pomegranates, dwarf
Purple sage *see Salvia officinalis* 'Purpurascens'
Purslane
   summer *see* Summer purslane
   winter *see* Winter purslane
Puschkinia
   suggestions for use 231, 316
   scilloides, suggestions for use 239
Putting greens 389
   mowing 395
Puya 462
   alpestris, form 362
PVC
   for cloches 582
   as pond liner 288, 295
Pycnostysanus azaleae 656
Pygmaeocereus, flat grafting 315

Pygmy palm *see Phoenix roebelenii*
Pyracantha
   berries 90, 94
   conditions tolerated 95
   diseases, fungal 649
   as hedge 15, 85
   pests 654, 658
      damaging stems 654
   planting beside wall *98*
   propagation, semi-ripe cuttings 113
   pruning 109
      to attract wildlife 103
   seasonal interest 95
   as security measure 15
   seed, extracting from berries *114*
   soil type tolerated 97
   suggestions for use 95
   training *109*
      on wall 93, *93*, 109, 130
   'Golden Charmer' *84*
   'Golden Dome', seasonal interest 92
Pyrenees, precipitation 609
Pyrethrum cinerariifolium see Tanacetum cinerariifolium
Pyrola rotundifolia, soil type required 260
Pyrostegia 129
   semi-ripe cuttings 143
   venusta 129
      pruning 135, 137
Pyrrhalta viburni 644
Pyrus
   conditions tolerated 67
   propagation, chip budding 82
   soil type tolerated 65
   calleryana 'Chanticleer' *59*
      soil type tolerated 66
      suggestions for use 59
   communis var. *sativa see* Pears
   pashia, seasonal interest 59
   salicifolia 'Pendula'
      for small garden 57
      suggestions for use 59
Pythium 661, 664
   ultimum 660, 664

Q

Quackgrass *see* Couch grass
Quaking grass *see Briza*
Quamash *see Camassia*
Quarry tiles *see* Tiles
Queen of the Night *see Selenicereus grandiflorus*
Queensland umbrella tree *see Schefflera actinophylla*
Quercus
   clumps as focal point 56
   diseases, fungal 654
   galls 652
   for leaf mould 63
   propagation
      from seed *81*
      sowing in containers 80
   root system *674*
   seed scarification 80
   x *hispanica*, conditions tolerated 67
   ilex
      conditions tolerated 67
      semi-ripe cuttings 79
      soil preferred 66
      as topiary 18
   myrsinifolia, semi-ripe cuttings 79
   palustris, soil type tolerated 66

Quercus (cont.)
   robur
      conditions tolerated 67
      soil type tolerated 66
   semecarpifolia, semi-ripe cuttings 79
   x *turneri*, conditions tolerated 67
Quick decline viruses 480
Quicklime 625
Quinces *446*
   chilling requirement 446
   conditions required 446
   cultivars grown 444
   diseases 446
   feeding 446
   fruit *435*
   harvesting 446
   mulching 446
   planting 446
   pollination 446
   propagation 446
   pruning 446
      winter 428
   as rootstock
      for loquats 482
      for pears 444, *444*
   rootstocks for 446
   routine care 446
   soil type preferred 446
   storing 446
   temperatures required for flowering 446
   training 446
   cultivars grown 446
Quisqualis
   semi-ripe cuttings 143
   indica 129
      climbing method 124
      for fragrance 129
      pruning 137

R

Rabbits 96, 639
   control 666
   damage caused 645, 666, *666*
   deterring 642
   protection from 435, 504, 564
Racemes 676
Radishes 546–7
   bolting 546
   conditions tolerated 546
   in crop rotation 498
   culinary uses 546
   as cut-and-come-again seedling crop 546
   diseases 649, 660
   edible parts 542, 546
   growing in containers 318, 501
   growing under cover 546
   harvesting *546*, 547
   harvesting seed 547
   as intercrop 507, 546
   intersowing 494
   nitrogen requirement 504, 546
   pests 547, 644, 660
   recommended cultivars 546
   roots
      colours 546
      sizes 546
   rotation 546
   routine cultivation 546–7
   size of plants 546
   soil type preferred 546
   sowing 546
      in situ 499
   spacing 546
   storing 547
   successional sowing 546
   types 546
   watering 546–7
      critical periods 502

Radishes (cont.)
   'April Cross' F1 546
   'Black Spanish Round' 546
   'Cherry Belle' 546
   'Flamboyant Sabina' 546
   'French Breakfast' 546
   'Mantang Hong' F1 546
   'Marabelle' 546
   'Minowase Summer Cross' F1 546
   'Mirabeau' 546
   oriental *see* Mooli
   overwintering types
      recommended cultivars 546
      sowing 546
   'Rougette' 546
   'Rudi' 546
   'Saxa' 546
   'Scarlet Globe' 546
   'Sparkler' 546
Raffia, for ties 564
Ragged robin *see Lychnis flos-cuculi*
Railway sleepers *see* Sleepers
Rain gauges 563, *563*
Rain shadow 63, 310, 332, 610, *610*
Rainfall 608–10
   average annual, in Europe 609, *609*
   effects of global warming on 607
   effect on vegetables 495
   measurements of 622
   torrential, damage from 610
   trees' requirements 63
Rainwater
   collecting 357, 614–15
   diverters 585, 615
Raised beds *see* Beds, raised
Rakes 552, *552*
   heads 552
   shafts 552
   types
      bolstered *552*
      flat-tined lawn *559*
      garden 552, *552*
      lawn *398*, 559, *559*
      powered lawn 559, *559*
      scarifying *398*, 559
      spring-tined lawn *398*, *559*
Raking, correct position for *550*
Ramonda
   compost for 278
   propagation, leaf cuttings 274
   suggestions for use 258
   myconi 271
      suggestions for use 259
Ranch-style fencing 600, *600*
Ranunculus
   in grass *389*
   sowing 272
   stamens 676
   alpine sowing 272
   aquatilis 298
   asiaticus
      for cutting 231
      resting 240
      tubers 227
   ficaria 671
      conditions tolerated 231
      soil type tolerated 184
   flammula, soil type tolerated 184
   lingua
      division of rootstock 303
      'Grandiflora', position in water garden 285
   repens 671
      flower form *676*
      in naturalistic planting schemes 197
Rape seed oil, for pest and disease control 642
Raphanus
   sativus see Radishes
   sativus Longipinnatus Group *see* Mooli

Rapini see Broccoli raab
Raspberries *468*, 472–4
   conditions tolerated 472
   diseases 473
      fungal 427, 653, 654, 658, 661
      virus 659
   feeding 426
   for flavour 473
   freezing 431, *431*
   harvesting 431, 473
   mulching 473
   pests 473, 658
   plant type 419, *468*
   planting 472–3, *472*
   propagation
      by suckers 474, *474*
      suckers 434
   pruning 473, *473*
      after planting 472, *473*
      first season 473, *473*
   recommended cultivars 473
   routine care 473
   site 472
   site preparation 472
   soil type required 472
   soil unsuitable for 424
   spacing 472, *472*
   storing 473
   suckers
      digging up *473*
      removing 434, 473
   supporting 472, *472*
   training
      Scandinavian system 472, *472*
   types 472
   virus-susceptible cultivars 473
   watering 473
   weedkiller danger to 671
   yellow *468*
   'All Gold' 473
   American, crosses with 472
   'Autumn Bliss' 473, *473*
      in large fruit garden *421*
      in small fruit garden *422*
   autumn-fruiting
      cropping 472
      pruning 473, 474, *474*
      recommended cultivars 473
      site 474
   'Glen Ample' 473
   'Glen Clova' 473
   'Glen Lyon' 473
   'Glen Magna' 473
   'Glen Moy' 473
   'Glen Prosen' 473
   'Joan J' 473
   'Leo' 473
   'Malling Admiral' 473
   'Malling Jewel' 473
      in large fruit garden *421*
   'Malling Promise' 473, *473*
   North American black, crosses with 472
   'Octavia' 473
   'Polka' 473
   'Southland' 473
   summer-fruiting
      cropping 472
      pruning
         after fruiting 473, *473*
         spring 473, *473*
      recommended cultivars 473
   'Sumner' 473
   'Tulameen' 473
      in small fruit garden *422*
   'Valentina' 473
Raspberry beetle *658*
   symptoms and control 658, *658*
Rats
   control 662
   damage caused 662, *662*
Rattan, for furniture *356*
Rebutia
   choosing healthy plant *343*
   in containers outdoors 340

Rebutia (cont.)
flat grafting 351
propagation
division of offsets 349
division of rootstock 350
albiflora, suggestions for use 342
arenacea (syn. *R. glomeriseta*)
flowers 342
suggestions for use 342
aureiflora
flowers 342
suggestions for use 342
fiebrigii 339
heliosa, suggestions for use 342
marsoneri
flowers 342
suggestions for use 342
minuscula, suggestions for use 342
neocumingii, flowers 342
senilis
flowers 342
suggestions for use 342
steinbachii subsp. *steinbachii*, suggestions for use 342
Red chicory *see* Chicory, red
Red core 469
Red fescue *see Festuca rubra* var. *rubra*
Red hot poker *see Kniphofia*
Red lily beetle *644*
symptoms and control 644
Red maple *see Acer rubrum*
Red plum maggots 659
Red spider mite 96, 244, 375, *646*
control 452, 462, 646
biological 583, 642
damage caused by 646
deterring 504
global warming effects 659
immunity to pesticides 643
Red thread *667*
symptoms and control 667
Redcurrants *see* Currants, red
Redwood, *see Sequoia*
Rehmannia
growing with succulents 339
elata, in conservatory *359*
Reinwardtia, pruning 376
Renovation
alpine beds *271*
climbers 137, *137*
fruit trees 430, *430*
hedges 86
indoor plants 372
lawns 399
shrubs
drastic 110, *110*
gradual 110, *110*
topiary 77
trees 74, *74*
Replant disease 156, 640
symptoms and control 665, *665*
Reseda odorata, scent 213
Residual current device 550
Respiration 609, 675
Reversion of variegated shrubs 100, *100*
Reversion disease 655
Rhamnus
deciduous, pruning 105
alaternus, conditions tolerated 95
Rhaphiolepis
spliced side-veneer grafting 119
excelsa, pollution-absorbing 358
Rhapis in containers 319
excelsa, pollution-absorbing 358
Rheum
dividing 200, 201
feeding 191
soil type tolerated 184

Rheum (cont.)
alexandrae, suggestions for use 285
x *cultorum see* Rhubarb
palmatum
in contrasting foliage group *175*
suggestions for use 61, 283, 285
'Atrosanguineum'
architectural form 181
form 175
growth rate 181
suggestions for use 179, 285
Rhinanthus minor 183
Rhipsalis
compost for 344
conditions required 341
form 339
propagation
side grafting 351
softwood cuttings 380
stem cuttings 348
cereuscula, suggestions for use 342
mesembryanthemoides, suggestions for use 342
pachyptera, suggestions for use 342
Rhizobium granules 533
Rhizoctonia 664
Rhizoecus sp. 646
Rhizomes 635, *635*
definition 227
growth habit *674*
problems 663
propagation
division 201, *201*
scooping 250, *250*
scoring 250, *250*
purpose *674, 675*
weeds with *670*
Rhizomorphs 665
Rhodanthemum hosmariense, soil type tolerated 261
Rhodiola wallichiana (syn. *R. crassipes*), conditions tolerated 342
Rhodochiton atrosanguineus
in containers 319
suggestions for use 212, 317
supports for 325
Rhodococcus fascians 655
Rhododendron
avenue of *91*
and climate change 405
compost for 99, 306, 322, *322*
conditions preferred 310, 610
in containers 94, 319
top-dressing 334, *334*
dead-heading 100, *100*
diseases, fungal 646, 654, 656, 661, 665
dwarf, soil type required 260
effect of drought on 657, 664
galls 652
pests
damaging leaves 647
eating leaves 645
propagation
air layering 117, *117*, 631
cuttings 632
dropping 116
preparing cuttings *633*
saddle grafting 118, 119, *119*
semi-ripe cuttings 274
with heel 113
simple layering 116
pollution-absorbing 358
pruning 106, 108
size 90
soil type indicated by 617
soil type required 91, 99, 260, 325
sowing 115
suckers 100
suggestions for use 317

Rhododendron (cont.)
in water garden *282*
watering 332
auriculatum, scent 95
azaleas
breaking dormancy 607
compost for 306, 322, *322*
diseases, fungal 656
greenhouse conditions required 361
indoors *358*
propagation, heel cuttings 113
resting outdoors *373*
'Cunningham's White', as rootstock 118
edgeworthii, scent 95
'Fragrantissimum', scent 95
Ghent hybrids, scent 95
'Hinode-giri', flowers 94
'Homebush' *91*
Loderi Group, scent 95
luteum 95
scent 95
maddenii, conditions preferred 95
occidentale, scent 95
'Polar Bear', scent 95
ponticum
conditions tolerated 95
pruning 107
as rootstock 118
Rustica hybrids, scent 95
Section Vireya, conditions preferred 95
simsii
galls 652
pollution-absorbing 358
Subsection Triflora, pruning 107
viscosum, scent 95
'Vuyk's Scarlet' *325*
wardii 91
yakushimanum 319
foliage 37
Rhododendron bud blast 647
symptoms and control 656, *656*
Rhododendron leafhopper 647
disease spread by 656
Rhodohypoxis
suggestions for use 229, 231
baurii, in trough *267*
Rhodoleia championii, soil preferred 65
Rhodophiala advena (syn. *Hippeastrum advenum*), conditions preferred 231
Rhoicissus 129
conditions preferred indoors 361
greenhouse conditions required 361
capensis, softwood cuttings 380
Rhombophyllum, division of offsets 349
Rhubarb 541
beds for *535*
conditions tolerated 541
in containers *318*
culinary uses 541
diseases 541
feeding 541
forcing 541, *541*
freezing 506
harvesting 541, *541*
intercropping 494
mulching 541
nitrogen requirement 51, 504
planting out 541
planting sets 541
propagation
division of sets 541, *541*
from seed 541
recommended cultivars 541
removing flower stems 51
routine cultivation 541
site 494

Rhubarb *(cont.)*
size of plant 541
soil preparation for 541
soil types required 541
top-dressing 541
watering 541
Rhus
division of suckers 118
root cuttings 114
typhina
form 55
for small garden 57
Rhynchaenus fagi 647
Ribes
hardwood cuttings 114
stooling 117
divaricatum
edible *see* Worcesterberry
as gooseberry rootstock 477
nigrum see Currants, black
odoratum, as gooseberry rootstock 477
sanguineum 117
pruning 106
'King Edward VII', as hedge 85
silvestre (syn. *R. sativum*) *see* Currants, red; Currants, white
speciosum, as wall shrub 93
uva-crispa see Gooseberries
Riccia fluitans 285
Ricinus
greenhouse conditions required 361
communis
architectural plant 213
architectural role 211
in containers 319
foliage 208, 209
suggestions for use 213, *213*, 318
in tropical planting *60*
'Zanzibarensis' *61*
'Impala' *211*
Rill, formal, construction with concrete 293, *293*
Rind grafting tree fruits 443, *443*
Ring culture 528
Ring rot, symptoms and control 662
Ring stakes 192, *192*, 564
Rings, plant 564, *564*
Ringspots 649
Robinia
conditions tolerated 67
propagation
spliced side grafting 82
whip-and-tongue grafting 82
seed scarification 80
for small gardens 58
soil type tolerated 65
pseudoacacia
leaf form *675*
regeneration 68
'Frisia' *57, 82*
suggestions for use *59*
Robin's pincushions 652
Rock garden 254–79
aspect 255
attracting wildlife 264
bulbs for 231
bulbs in 229
care 243
buying plants for 360
care 270–1
choosing plants for 255–6
and climate change 256
compost for 261–2
constructing 262–3
designing 254–8
drainage 262, *263*
dwarf conifers for 62
miniature, in alpine house 277
placing stone 263
planning 255
planter's guide 259

Rock garden *(cont.)*
planting 262, 263–4
planting bulbs in 237
site 255
site preparation 262–3
siting 260–1, *260*
soil for 261–2
soil preparation for bulbs 237
stone for 261, *261*
top-dressing 264–5, 270, *270*
Rock garden hoe *see* Hoes, onion
Rock gardens, herbs for 405
Rock hyssop *see Hyssopus officinalis* subsp. *aristatus*
Rock phosphate, nutrient content 624
Rock plants
acid-loving compost for 262
for alkaline soil 261
characteristics 254
composts for 261–2
in containers 258, *258*, 266–7
cutting back after flowering 271, *271*
diseases 271
feeding 270
filling gaps between 211
germination 272
habitats 254
in peat beds 269, *269*
pests 271
planter's guide 259
planting 262, 263–4
in crevices 264, *268*
in dry-stone walls 268, *268*
in raised beds 269
potting up 272
pricking out 272
propagation 272–6
cuttings 273–4, *273–4*, 275–6
basal 274, *274*
greenwood 273
"Irishman's" 275, *275*
leaf 274
ripewood 274
root 275–6, *276*
scooping rosettes 276, *276*
selecting material for 274, *274*
semi-ripe 273, 274
softwood 273, *273*
division 275, *275*
time for 275
rosettes 274
from seed 272, *272*
sowing when fresh 272
protecting 271
pruning 270–1, *270*
in raised beds 257–8, 269
range of plants 254
removing dead leaves 279, *279*
requiring acid soil 260
roses with 151
routine care 270–1
for sandy soil 261
seed
collecting 272
pre-sowing treatment 272
storage 272
shrubs and conifers with *257*
soil requirements 261–2
suggestions for use 255–8
trimming 270–1
in troughs 258, *258*
watering 270
weeding 270, *270*
Rock rose *see Helianthemum*
Rocks
see also Stone
artificial 261
natural stratum lines 261, *261*
sedimentary 261, *261*
Rockwool 565

Rodgersia
  architectural form 181, *194*
  in contrasting foliage group *175*
  for drying 181
  soil type tolerated 184
  aesculifolia
    conditions preferred 181
    suggestions for use 285
  pinnata
    conditions preferred 181
    suggestions for use 285
  podophylla, suggestions for use 285
Rollers
  garden 558
  for lawn *392*
  on lawnmowers 557, *557*
Romneya
  root cuttings 203
  coulteri
    growth rate 181
    mass planting 26
    soil type preferred 184
Romulea
  corm 227
  resting 240
  suggestions for use 231
Roof gardens
  containers on 312–13, *312, 313*
    choosing 312
  flooring 312
  formal *313*
  perennials in containers 179
  planting on 313
  plants for *43*
  problems 312
  railings 312
  roses on 153
  safety 312
  screens on *312*
  watering plants on 312
Root aphids, symptoms and control 661
Root cuttings 632, 633, *633*
  alpines 275–6, *276*
  climbers 141, 144, *144*
  distinguishing ends of roots 633, *633*
  perennials 203, *203*
  scooping rosettes 276, *276*
  shrub 114
Root hairs 609, 674
Root nodules 625
Root pruning
  fruit trees 430, *430*
  shrubs 110
Root rots 654, *661*
  pea 661
  Phytophthora 654
    symptoms and control 654, 661
  symptoms and control 654, 661
  tropical, symptoms and control 661
  violet *661*
    symptoms and control 661
Root tubers 635, *635*
  propagation 635
Root vegetables 542–8
  in crop rotation 498
  mounding 613
  overwatering 502
  pests 655, 660, 662
  storing 506, 542
  for successional crops 542
  transplanting 500
  watering, critical periods 502
Root-knot nematodes 451, 467
  symptoms and control 660
Rooting hormones 668
Roots
  adventitious 632, *632, 633*
  aerial, as climbing method 124, *130*
  collecting for preserving 415
  drying 415

Roots (*cont.*)
  fleshy weeds with *671*
  frost and thaw damage to 607
  importance of water to 609
  modified to form storage organs 674
  problems 660–2
  protecting 613
  pruning 73
  purpose 674, *674*
  tap roots, swollen 674, *674*
  types 674
    fibrous *63*, 674, *674*
    "hockey-stick" *63*, 64
    tap 674, *674*
    "water" 375
Rootstocks
  for acid charries 257, *257*
  for apples 435, *435*
  for apricots 454
  fruit 423
  for fruit trees 424, *424*
  influence of 635
  for medlars 447
  for nectarines 451, *451*
  for peaches 451, *451*
  for pears 444, *444*
  for persimmons 458
  for plums 447, *447*
  preparing for grafting 82
  for quinces 446
  rose 166
  selecting 635
Roquette *see* Salad rocket
Rorippa
  nasturtium-aquaticum see Watercress
  sylvestris 670
Rosa
  on arbour *152*
  on arch *152*
  for arches and pillars 155
  balling 650
  bare-root
    planting 157, *157*
    selecting 156, *156*
  bedding spacing 157
  blind shoots 160, *160*
  breeding 149, 168–9, *168, 169*
  buying 131
  categories 149
  chemical damage to 651
  choosing 148, 156, *156*
  chromosomes 168
  conditions preferred 610
  conditions required 156
  conditions tolerated 148
  container-grown, selecting 156, *156*
  in containers 153, *317*
    feeding 159
    planting 157, 158
    pruning 326
    varieties suitable for 317
  cutting back in autumn 160, *160*
  dead-heading 160, *160*, 333
  decorative hips 155
  deer damage to 666
  designing with 148–53
  die-back *156*, 161, 665
  disbudding 154, *154*
  disease-resistant 155, 159
  diseases 160, 665
    bacterial 648, 661
    fungal 653
  exhibiting 154
    cultivation for 154
    equipment for *154*
    selecting blooms 154
    staging 154
  feeding 159, 613
  flowers
    colour 148, 150
    in dry conditions 159
    feeding for 159
    protecting for exhibition 154, *154*

Rosa, flowers (*cont.*)
    reproductive parts 629
    shapes 148, *149*
  foliage colour 150
    varieties recommended for 155
  formal plantings 150
  fruit type 675, *675*
  galls 652
  grafting 156, 166–7, *166*
  for ground cover 155
  ground-cover 153, *153*
    description 149
    layering 167
    pruning 163, *163*
    suggestions for use 151, 152
  growing clematis with 138
  growing organically 159
  growing into trees, varieties recommended for 155
  hardiness 160
  healthy, choosing *156*, 157
  as hedge 85
  hedges 153, *153*
    spacing 157
  heeling in 157
  hips *151*, 160, 675, *675*
    ornamental 150
  hormone weedkiller damage 655
  hybridizing 168–9, *168*
    pollinating 169, *169*
    preparing pollen parent 169, *169*
    preparing seed parent *168*, 169
    selection 169
  hybrids 149
    propagation 168
  hygiene 159
  informal plantings 151, *151*
  mildew 153
  mineral deficiency 651
  in mixed borders *422*
    varieties recommended for 155
  in mixed plantings 151, *151*
  mounding earth round *612*, 613
  moving 160
  mulching 159
  nutrients required 159
  pegging down 163, *163*
  with perennials *148*
  for pergolas 155
  pests 159, 160, 656, 661
    affecting flowers 657
    damaging leaves 647
    eating leaves 645
  pH requirements 156
  planting 157, *157*
    distances 157, *157*
    time for 157
  precautions against frost 613
  pricking out 168, *168*
  proliferation 657
  propagation 165–9, *165–9*
    bud grafting 156, 166–7, *166*
    division 167, *167*
    hardwood cuttings 165, *165*
    layering 167, *167*
    ripewood cuttings 274
    from seed 168, *168*
    semi-ripe cuttings 165
  protection 160
  pruning 161–4, *161–4*, 326
    after planting 161, *161*
    basic principles 161, *161*
    for exhibition 154
    late summer *163*
    time for 161
    tools 161
  rootstocks 156, 166
    planting 166
  routine care 159–60

Rosa (*cont.*)
  scented 148–50
    varieties recommended for 155
  as screen 153
  seasonal interest 50
  seed
    extraction 168
    germination 168
  site 156
  societies 148
  soil preparation 156
  soil type required 325
  spacing 157, *157*
  specimen planting 152
  as specimen plants 155
  stakes for *564*
  staking 158
  standards 326
  suckers 158
    propagation from 167, *167*
    recognising 159
    removing 159, *159*
  suggestions for use 150–3
  supports for 564, *564*
  temperatures withstood 160
  on terraces 152
  thorns, ornamental 150
  top-dressing 159
  transplanting 160
  trenching *612*, 613
  underplanting 150, *151*, 151, 157, 159
  on wall 130
  watering 159
  weed control 159, 671
  winter protection 160
  Alba Group
    foliage colour 150
    description 149
    layering 167
    pruning 163, *163*
    temperatures withstood 160
  'Albéric Barbier' 155
  'Albertine' 155
  ALEC'S RED ('Cored') 155
  ALEXANDER ('Harlex') 155, 157
  'Alister Stella Gray' 155
  'Aloha' 153, 155
  'Alpine Sunset' *149*
  ALTISSIMO ('Delmur') 155
  AMBER QUEEN ('Harroony'), in formal rose garden *150*
  ANNA LIVIA ('Kormetter') 155
  ANNE HARKNESS ('Harkaramel') 153, 155
  ANTIQUE ('Kordalen') 155
  ARMADA ('Haruseful') 155
  'Arthur Bell' 155
  AVON ('Poulmulti') 153, 155
  BABY LOVE ('Scrivluv') 155
  'Ballerina' 155
  'Bantry Bay' 155
  BERKSHIRE ('Korpinka') 155
  BETTY HARKNESS ('Harette') 155
  blanda, temperatures withstood 160
  'Blue Parfum' 150
  'Blush Rambler' 155
  'Bobbie James' 153, 155
  BONICA ('Meidomonac') 155
  Bourbon
    as climber 164
    as climbers 152
    description 149
    layering 167
    pegging down 163
    pruning 163
    temperatures withstood 160
  Boursault
    description 149
    pruning 164
  BREATH OF LIFE ('Harquanne') 155

Rosa (*cont.*)
  BRIDGE OF SIGHS ('Harglowing') 155
  brunonii, as cover for wildlife 128
  'Buff Beauty' 153, 155, 159
  bush
    bud-grafting 166, 167
    planting 157, *157*
  californica, temperatures withstood 160
  canina
    conditions tolerated 156
    diseases 665
    in fedges 126
    as rootstock 166, 167
    temperatures withstood 160
  'Céleste' *148*
  x *centifolia* 155
  Centifolia (Provence)
    description 149
    hybridizing 169
    layering 167
    pruning 163, *163*
    temperatures withstood 160
  'Cerise Bouquet' *148*, 155
  'Charles de Mills' 153, 159
  CHATSWORTH ('Tanotax') 155
  China
    description 149
    in mixed planting 151
    pruning 162
    temperatures withstood 160
  'Chinatown' 152, 155
  chinensis 149
  CITY GIRL ('Harzorba') 155, *155*
  CLAIR MATIN ('Meimont') 155
  climbing
    buying 131
    climbing method 124
    combined with other climbers 125
    in containers 153
    description 149
    layering 167
    planting 158, *158*
    pruning 158, 164, *164*
    as screen 153
    shrubs to grow with 152
    as standards 152
    structures to grow on 152, 153
    thornless 153
    training 153, 157, 158, 164, *164*
    on trees 56
    on vertical support *125*
  'Climbing Cécile Brünner' 155
  'Climbing Etoile de Hollande' 155
  climbing miniature
    description 149
    pruning 164
  climbing sports, pruning 164
  'Compassion' 155
  'Complicata' 151, 155
  'Constance Spry' *148*
  'Cornelia' 155
  CRIMSON CASCADE ('Fryclimbdown') 155
  Damask
    description 149
    layering 167
    in mixed planting 151
    pruning 163, *163*
    shrubs with 151
    temperatures withstood 160
  'Danse du Feu' 155
  'Dortmund' 155
  DOUBLE DELIGHT ('Andeli') 155

Rosa (*cont.*)
'Dr Huey' (*R.* 'Shafter'), as rootstock 166
'Dream Time', exhibition blooms *154*
'Dreaming Spires' 155
hardwood cuttings *165*
DUBLIN BAY ('Macdub') 155
'Easlea's Golden Rambler' 155
ELINA ('Dicjana') 155
preparing for hybridization *169*
'Emily Gray' 155
ESCAPADE ('Harpade') 155
'Fantin-Latour' 155
fedtschenkoana 155
'Felicia' 155
'Félicité Perpétue' 155
FELLOWSHIP ('Harwelcome') 155
filipes
'Kiftsgate' 155, *159*
as cover for wildlife 128
growing through trees 127
suggestions for use 127
Floribunda
cutting back in autumn 160, *160*
dead-heading *160*
description 149
disbudding 154, *154*
exhibition blooms *154*
as hedge 153
propagation 167
pruning 162, *162*
temperatures withstood 160
'Flower Carpet' 155
foetida, temperatures withstood 160
FRAGRANT CLOUD ('Tanellis') 155, *155*
'François Juranville' 155
FRIEND FOR LIFE ('Cocnanne') 155
'Fritz Nobis' 155, *159*
'Fru Dagmar Hastrup' 155
seasonal interest 95
'Frühlingsgold' *152*
FULTON MACKAY ('Cocdana') 156
gallica
var. *officinalis 153*
'Versicolor' (syn. *R. mundi*) *153*, 155
Gallica Group
description 149
propagation 167
pruning 163, *163*
shrubs with 151
temperatures withstood 160
Garnette 149
'Geranium' 155
GERTRUDE JEKYLL ('Ausbord') 155, *155*
glauca 155
foliage 150
from seed 165
temperatures withstood 160
'Gloire de Dijon' *149*
'Golden Showers' 155, 164
in formal rose garden *150*
'Golden Wings' 155, *157*
'Goldfinch' 155
GOOD AS GOLD ('Chewsunbeam') 155
GORDON'S COLLEGE ('Cocjabby') 155
GRAHAM THOMAS ('Ausmas') 155
ground-cover, suggestions for use 317, 319

Rosa (*cont.*)
GROUSE ('Korimro') 153
layering 167
gymnocarpa var. *willmottiae* 155
'Hakuun', in formal rose garden *150*
HANNAH GORDON ('Korweiso'), exhibition blooms *154*
HERITAGE ('Ausblush') 155
HERTFORDSHIRE ('Kortenay') 155
HIGH HOPES ('Haryup') 155
Hybrid Musk
description 149
pruning 162, 164
as screen 153
training 164
Hybrid Perpetual
description 149
pegging down 163
pruning 163
hybrid shrub, as hedge 85
Hybrid Tea
cutting back in autumn 160, *160*
cuttings 165
dead-heading *160*
description 149
disbudding 154, *154*
exhibition blooms *154*
propagation 167
pruning 161, *161*
temperatures withstood 160
ICEBERG ('Korbin') 155
JACQUELINE DU PRÉ ('Harwanna') 155
'Joseph's Coat' 164
'Just Joey' 156
KENT ('Poulcov') 155
'Korresia' 155
in formal rose garden *150*
L'AIMANT ('Harzola') 155
LAURA FORD ('Chewarvel') 155
laxa as rootstock 156, 166
'Leverkusen' 155
LITTLE BO PEEP ('Poullen') 317
LOVELY LADY ('Dicjubell') 155
'Madame Alfred Carrière' 155
suggestions for use 126
'Madame Grégoire Staechelin' 155
'Madame Hardy' 155
'Madame Isaac Pereire' 155
MAGIC CARPET ('Jaclover') 317
'Maigold' 155, *159*, 640
disease resistance 640
MARGARET MERRIL ('Harkuly') 155
in formal rose garden *150*
'Marguerite Hilling' 155
MARJORIE FAIR ('Harhero') 155
propagation 167
'Mevrouw Nathalie Nypels' 155
miniature
in containers 319
cuttings 165
description 149
as edging to rosebeds 150
pruning 162, *162*
climbers 164
with rock plants 151
spacing 157
suggestions for use 152, 311, 317
MISTRESS QUICKLY ('Ausky') 155
modern 148
categories 149
pruning 161

Rosa (*cont.*)
'Morning Jewel' 155
moschata 149
Moss
description 149
pruning 163, *163*
mounding up *612*
moyesii 'Geranium' *149*
seasonal interest 95
mulliganii 155
multiflora 149
as rootstock 166
'Nevada' 152, 155
as hedge 85
'New Dawn' 155
as screen 125
NEW ZEALAND ('Macgenev') 155
NIPPER ('Hareco') 153
nitida 155
Noisette
description 149
pruning 163
old 148
categories 149
pruning 162
to attract wildlife 103
OPEN ARMS ('Chewpixcel') 155
palustris, temperatures withstood 160
Patio
in containers *317, 319*
description 149
pruning 162
suggestions for use 317
'Paul's Himalayan Musk' 155
'Penelope' 155
in mixed planting *151*
spread 157
PENNY LANE ('Hardwell') 155
PERCEPTION ('Harzippee') 155
PHEASANT ('Kordapt') 121, 153
layering 167
'Phyllis Bide' 155
pimpinellifolia 149
propagation 167
soil preferred 156
PINK BELLS ('Poulbells') *149*, 317
Polyantha description 149
Portland
description 149
pruning 163, *163*
shrubs with 151
POUR TOI ('Para Ti') 317
PRETTY POLLY ('Meitonje') 317
'Prima Ballerina' 155
primula 155
PRINCESS MICHAEL OF KENT ('Harlightly'), hybridizing *168*
PRINCESS OF WALES ('Hardinkum') 155
'Prosperity' 155
protecting *612*
Provence *see* Centifolia
QUEEN MOTHER ('Korquemu') 155
propagation 167
ramblers *21*
climbing shrubs to grow with 152
cuttings 165
description 149
as ground-cover 153
layering 167
planting 158
by tree 158
pruning 164, *164*
scent 150
as screen 153
with shrubs 151
structures to grow on 152–3
suggestions for use 152
training 153, 158
'Rambling Rector' 155

Rosa (*cont.*)
RED BLANKET ('Intercell') 155
remontant 148, 149, 152
pruning 162
ROSALIE CORAL ('Chewallop') 155
'Rosa Mundi' 153
'Rose de Rescht' 155
ROSE GAUJARD ('Gaumo') 155
ROSEMARY HARKNESS ('Harrowbond') 155
'Roseraie de l'Haÿ' *83*, 152, 155
as hedge 85
ROSY CUSHION ('Interall') 155
rubiginosa (syn. *R. eglanteria*) 149
rugosa 149, 155
as hedge 153
hybrids, pruning 163
propagation, hardwood cuttings 114
as rootstock 158, 159, 167
soil preferred 156
soil type tolerated 99
temperatures withstood 160
'Alba' 155
'Rosea' *149*
'Rubra' 155
Rugosa Group
description 149
foliage 150
pruning 162
'Sally Holmes' 152, 155
pruning 163
'Sander's White Rambler' 155
SAVOY HOTEL ('Harvintage') 155, 156
'Scabrosa' 155
SCEPTER'D ISLE ('Ausland') 155
'Scharlachglut' 151
Scots (Scotch) 149
pruning 163
'Seagull' 155
'Sealing Wax' 155
sempervirens
description 149
pruning 163
sericea subsp. *omeiensis* f. *pteracantha 150*, 155
'Shafter' *see R.* 'Dr Huey'
shrub *148*
description 149
layering 167
pruning 162
shrubs with 151
as specimen plants 152
'Silver Jubilee' *149*
SIMBA ('Korbelana') *149*
soulieana 155
species
description 149
flowering 152
as hedge 85
layering 167
pruning 162, 163
to attract wildlife 103
from seed 168
shrubs with 151
standard 326
bud grafting 166, 167
in formal rose garden *150*
placing 150
planting 158, *158*
pruning 162, *162*
rootstocks 166
selecting *156*, 157
staking 158, *158*
suckers 158
removing 159, *159*
weeping
forming 152
pruning 162
as specimen 152

Rosa, standard (*cont.*)
'SUFFOLK' ('Kormixal') in formal rose garden 150
SUMA ('Harsuma') 153
SUMMER WINE ('Korizont') 155
SURREY ('Korlanum') 153, 155, *317*
SWANY ('Meiburenac') 155
in formal rose garden *150*
Sweet Briar
description 149
pruning 163
SWEET DREAM ('Fryminicot') 317
'Sympathie' 155
Tea
description 149
pruning 162
'The Fairy' 155
THE TIMES ROSE ('Korpeahn') 155
conditions tolerated 156
TOP MARKS ('Fryministar') 317
'Tour de Malakoff' 149
trailing, in formal rose garden *150*
'Treasure Trove' 155
VALENTINE HEART ('Dicogle') 155
'Veilchenblau' 155
virginiana 155
foliage 150
temperatures withstood 160
WARM WELCOME ('Chewizz') 155
weeping standard
forming 152
pruning 162
as specimen 152
'Wendy Cussons' 155
WESTERLAND ('Korwest') 155
'White Cockade' 155
'White Pet' *152*
wichurana
pruning 163
temperatures withstood 160
wild, to attract wildlife 22
WINE AND DINE ('Dicuncle') 155
xanthina 'Canary Bird' 155
'Zéphirine Drouhin' 153
Rosaceae, diseases 649
bacterial 665
fungal 647
Roscoea cautleyoides, root cuttings 275
Rose *see Rosa*
Rose die-back, symptoms and control 665, *665*
Rose garden 148–68
designing 150
formal 150, *150*
miniature in terraced beds 152
setting 150
sunken 152, 153
Rose leaf-rolling sawfly *652*
symptoms and control 52
Rose leafhopper 647
Rose rust, natural prevention for 159
Rose sickness 156
Rose stakes *564*
Rose thrips 656
Rose ties *564*
Rose-scented geranium *see Pelargonium graveolens*
Rosemary *see Rosmarinus*
Rosemary as herb *see Rosmarinus officinalis*
Rosemary beetle 659
Roses for watering cans 560, *560*
Rosette cuttings, rock plants propagated by 274
Rosettes, of alpines
removing when dead 271, *271*
scooping 276, *276*

Rosmarinus
as ground cover 101
harvesting in winter 411
soil type preferred 325
soil type tolerated 99
officinalis 409–10, *409*
conditions preferred 411
cosmetic uses 404, 410
culinary uses 410
flowers 409
foliage 409
harvesting 410
as herb, culinary uses 404
in herb garden *412*
propagation
layering 410
mound layering 414
from seed 410
semi-ripe cuttings 410
protecting from frost 335
as specimen plant 405
standards 326
storing 410
suggestions for use 318,
409–10
variants 410
'Miss Jessopp's Upright',
suggestions for use 410
'Prostratus', propagation
by mound layering 414
'Severn Sea' 410
Rotation of crops 494, *494, 498,*
660, 661, 664, 666
advantages 494, 498
drawbacks 498
for pest and disease control
640
planning for 498
Rotavation (rotary cultivation)
to clear neglected site 618,
618
for weed control 671, 673
Rotenone 642, 645, 646, 647,
658, 666, 668
Rots
basal 663
blossom end *658*
symptoms and control 658
brown, symptoms and control
645, *658*
crown 187, *665*
symptoms and control 665
foot *654, 661*
symptoms and control
654, 661
in fruit 431
onion neck 663
onion white 663
rotating crops to avoid
498
ring, symptoms and control
662
root 540, *654, 661*
symptoms and control
654, 661
storage, bulbs 663, *663*
white 498
Rough-stalked meadow grass *see*
Poa trivialis
Rowan *see Sorbus aucuparia*
Roystonea, suggestions for use 59
Rubber plant *see Ficus elastica*
Rubus
climbing method 124
layering 116
propagation, hardwood
cuttings 114
biflorus
bark 90, 94
coppicing 107
cockburnianus, coppicing 107
deliciosus, pruning 106
fruticosus
as weed 670, 671, *671,*
673
as fruit *see* Blackberries
idaeus see Raspberries
var. *strigosus see*
Raspberries, American

Rubus (cont.)
occidentalis see Raspberries,
North American black
thibetanus, coppicing 107
tricolor, conditions preferred
95
'Tridel', pruning 106
Rucola *see* Salad rocket
Rudbeckia
to attract wildlife 178
for cutting 181
cutting down *192*
dividing 201
in mixed border 177
stopping 191
hirta
conditions tolerated 213
in containers 319
for cutting 213
soil type preferred 216
laciniata 'Goldquelle',
growth rate 181
Rue *see Ruta*
Ruellia
greenhouse conditions
required 361
softwood cuttings 380
Rumex
preventing 673
as weed *671, 672, 672*
see also Dock
acetosa see Sorrel (herb)
acetosella 672
obtusifolius 670
scutatus 410
in herb garden *412*
Runner beans *see* Beans, scarlet
runner
Runners
layering, natural 631, *631*
propagation by
fruit 434
indoor plants 378, *378*
strawberries *470*
water plants 303, *303*
Ruschia
habit 339
propagation
division of rootstock 350
stem cuttings 348
Ruscus
dividing 118
aculeatus, division of suckers
118
Rushes
and waterlogging 623
in water garden 282
Russian tarragon *see* Tarragon,
Russian
Russian vine *see Fallopia*
baldschuanica
Rustic work 604
joints for 604, *604*
Rusts 160, 639, 642, *648,* 653
internal rust spot *662*
symptoms and control 662
symptoms and control 648,
648, 653
Ruta
as herb 410
graveolens 410
allergy to 410
in border 405
culinary uses 410
foliage 410
harvesting 410
propagation
hardwood cuttings
114
from seed 410
semi-ripe cuttings of
sideshoots 410
scent 95
suggestions for use 410
variants 410
'Jackman's Blue' 410
'Variegata' 410
propagation, seed 414
Ryegrass *see Lolium*

S

Sabal
architectural 95
in containers 319
Saddle grafting 118, *119,* 636
Safety
chemical use 643
compost shredders *562*
electricity 550, 556
screened cables 580
hand tools 550
of home 15
lawnmowers 557
powered tools 550, *550,* 556,
556
weedkiller use 651, 671
equipment for 560
windowboxes 328, *328*
Sage (herb) *see Salvia officinalis*
Sagina
procumbens 260, *672*
subulata 'Aurea' (syn. *S.*
glabra 'Aurea'), division
275
Sagittaria
soil type tolerated 184
graminea, propagation by
offsets 303
latifolia, position in water
garden 285
sagittifolia
division of rootstock 303
position in water garden
285
'Flore Pleno'
position in water
garden 285
propagation by
offsets 303
Sahne farinacea, for dry
conditions 211
St Augustine grass *see*
Stenotaphrum secundatum
Saintpaulia
in bottle garden *367*
conditions preferred indoors
361
greenhouse conditions
required 361
hydroculture 361
in indoor plant group *372*
leaf cuttings 381, *381*
light requirements 355
miniatures, suggestions for
use 366
pests 656
propagation, leaf cuttings 633
Salad crops
in mixed border 210
successional crops 500
Salad rape 520
conditions tolerated 520
culinary uses 520
harvesting 506, 520, *520*
sowing 520
Salad rocket 520, *520*
conditions preferred 520
culinary uses 520
harvesting 506, 520
pests 520
sowing 520
Salad vegetables 515–21
as intercrop 498, 507
minor 520–1
conditions tolerated 520
growing under cover 520
nitrogen requirement 520
overwintering under cloches
505
storing 515
for succession 515
watering, critical periods 502
Salicine plums *see* Plums,
Japanese

Salicornia europaea, conditions
tolerated 342
Salix
adapting to waterlogging 609
conditions preferred 91
conditions tolerated 67, 95,
613
coppicing 46, 58
varieties recommended for
74
cuttings 87
diseases, fungal 666
pests
damaging leaves 647
eating leaves 645
pollarding 58
varieties recommended for
74
propagation
hardwood cuttings 78, 79,
114
internodal cuttings 633
ripewood cuttings 274
stooling 117
regeneration 68
roots, damage from 63
soil type tolerated 66
weaving 87
weaving screens of 87, *87*
acutifolia
pollarding 107
'Blue Streak'
seasonal interest 59
suggestions for use 74
alba 87
conditions tolerated 67
propagation, hardwood
cuttings *632*
suggestions for use 285
var. *sericea*, suggestions
for use 74
var. *vitellina*
bark 57
pollarded pruning *74*
suggestions for use 74
'Britzensis' (syn.
S. alba
'Chermesina')
bark 57
coppicing 107
seasonal
interest 59
suggestions for
use 74
babylonica
suggestions for use 285
var. *pekinensis* 'Tortuosa'
(syn. *S. matsudana*
'Tortuosa') suggestions
for use 55, 285
x *boydii* (syn. *S.* 'Boydii') 259
caprea
soil type tolerated 97
'Kilmarnock' *55*
formation 73
suggestions for use
59, 316
standards 326
daphnoides
coppicing 107
seasonal interest 59
suggestions for use 285
'Aglaia'
seasonal interest 59
suggestions for use 74
elaeagnos, seasonal interest 59
'Erythroflexuosa'
stems 94
seasonal interest 59
suggestions for use 74
exigua, seasonal interest 59
fragilis 87
hastata 'Wehrhahnii',
seasonal interest 91
irrorata
coppicing 107
seasonal interest 95
stems 94
suggestions for use 74

Salix (cont.)
x *sepulcralis* var. *chrysocoma*
diseases, fungal 666
as specimen tree 55
suggestions for use 59
viminalis, as hedge 84
Salpiglossis
as pot plants 213
from seed 379
supporting *222*
Salsify 547
in crop rotation 498
culinary uses 547
flower buds *547*
harvesting 547
nitrogen requirement 504
overwintering 542
roots *547*
storage 547
Salt, in wind on coast 612
Salts, inorganic, harmful effects
of 625
Salvia
to attract insects 22, 178, 181
flowering time from seed 198
overwintering 335
propagation, stem tip cuttings
202
soil type preferred 325
underplanting roses 152
coccinea, in containers 319
discolor, in containers 319
elegans 'Scarlet Pineapple',
supports for 325
farinacea, in containers 319
lavandulifolia, propagation by
mound layering 414
nemorosa
dividing 201
soil type tolerated 185
officinalis 410, *414*
conditions preferred 411
culinary uses 410
flowers 410
foliage 410
hardiness 413
harvesting 410
propagation
mound layering 414
from seed 410
semi-ripe heel
cuttings 410
softwood cuttings 410
stooling 631
storing 410
suggestions for use 410
'Icterina', in herb garden
412
'Purpurascens' 410
in herb garden *412*
suggestions for use
405, 406
'Tricolor' 410
patens, in containers 319
pratensis, dividing 201
sclarea var. *sclarea*,
architectural plant 213
splendens
in containers 319
flowers 173
form 209
in formal bedding 210
planting out 220
uliginosa
in containers 319
growth rate 181
viridis (syn. *S. horminum*)
in containers 319
conditions tolerated 213
for cutting 213
for drying 213
soil type tolerated 216
Salvinia
auriculata 285, *303*
dangers of 298
propagation by offsets
303
natans 285
propagation by offsets 303

Sambucus
  cosmetic uses 404
  culinary uses 404
  propagation
    hardwood cuttings 114
    heel cuttings 113
  in restricted colour border *92*
  as weed 670, 673
  nigra
    conditions tolerated 405, 613
    as weed 670
    'Aurea', conditions tolerated 405
    'Marginata', conditions tolerated 405
  racemosa
    soil type tolerated 97
    'Plumosa Aurea'
      coppicing 107
      pruning 107
Sand
  as additive, problems 621
  for building work 591
  in cuttings compost 565
  improving drainage with 621
  in potting composts 322, *322*
  in seed compost 565
  as top-dressing *398*, 626, *626*
Sand beds 638, *638*
Sandstone
  for paving 588
  for rock garden 261, *261*
Sandy soil
  adding clay to 621
  annuals for 216
  biennials for 216
  climbers tolerating 131
  controlling self-seeding 222
  effect on pears 444
  feeding lawn on 396
  growing fruit on 424
  growing peaches on 451
  growing plums on 447
  identifying 617, *617*
  improving 621
  improving for lawn 390
  improving water-retention 621
  lime required to alter pH 625
  and naturalistic plantings 183
  perennials for 184
  planting shrubs in 99
  rock plants preferring 261
  shrubs preferring 97
  structure 616, *616*
  temperature 607
  water in 622
  water table 622
  weedkillers on 618
Sanguinaria canadensis
  conditions preferred 259
  f. *multiplex*, soil type required 260
Sansevieria
  conditions preferred indoors 361
  conditions tolerated 355
  propagation
    division of rootstock 350
    leaf sections 382
    rootstock 378
  trifasciata
    division of rootstock *350*
    'Hahnii', suggestions for use 342, 366
    'Laurentii', suggestions for use 342
Santolina
  in bedding scheme *210*
  in containers 319
  as hedge 84
  pruning 101, *101*, 107
  scent 95
  soil type preferred 325
  chamaecyparissus 410
    for decoration 410
    flowers 410

Santolina chamaecyparissus (*cont.*)
    foliage 410
    as ground cover, pruning 107
    harvesting 410
    in herb garden *412*
    in pot-pourri 410
    propagation
      mound layering 414
      semi-ripe cuttings of sideshoots 410
    storing 410
    suggestions for use 410
    underplanting roses 152
    'Lemon Queen' *412*
  pinnata, propagation by mound layering 414
  rosmarinifolia, propagation by mound layering 414
Sanvitalia procumbens, suggestions for use 213
Saponaria
  dividing 201
  soil type tolerated 185
  ocymoides
    conditions tolerated 259
    soil type preferred 261
    soil type tolerated 261
    suggestions for use 258
Sarcocaulon, stem cuttings 348
Sarcococca
  conditions preferred 95
  flowers 94
  propagation, division of suckers 118
  pruning 103
  scent 95
  confusa, seasonal interest 50
  hookeriana var. *digyna* 95
  humilis (syn. *S. hookeriana* var. *humilis*), pruning 107
Sarmienta
  semi-ripe cuttings 143
  serpentine layering 145
Sarracenia flava, soil type required 185
Sasa veitchii, suggestions for use 318
Satsumas *see* Mandarins, Satsuma Group
Satureja
  hortensis see Summer savory
  montana see Winter savory
  spicigera see Creeping savory
Saururus cernuus
  division of rootstock 303
  position in water garden 285
Savory
  creeping *see* Creeping savory
  summer *see* Summer savory
  winter *see* Winter savory
Savoy cabbage *see* Cabbage, Savoy
Sawdust, mulching with 503
Sawflies
  apple, symptoms and control 659, *659*
  birch leaf-mining 647
  larvae *645*
    symptoms and control 645, *645*
  rose leaf-rolling *652*
    symptoms and control 652
  Solomon's seal 645
Saws
  bow *555*
  chain 556, *556*
  double-edged pruning *555*
  folding *555*
  general-purpose pruning *555*
  Grecian 555, *555*
  pruning 555, *555*
Saxifraga
  choosing healthy plant 260
  conditions required 255, 262
  in dry-stone wall *268*
  plunging after flowering 277

Saxifraga (*cont.*)
  propagation, rosette cuttings 274, *274*
  removing dead rosettes 271, *271*
  repotting *278*
  in rock garden 254
  soil type tolerated 261
  suggestions for use 258, 259
  callosa, suggestions for use 259
  cochlearis
    suggestions for use 259
    'Minor', in trough *267*
  cotyledon
    suggestions for use 259
    in trough *267*
  granulata, propagation by shoot-axil buds 635
  Kabschias, suggestions for use 259
  longifolia, suggestions for use 259
  paniculata
    suggestions for use 259
    in trough *267*
  sancta 259
  stolonifera (syn. *S. sarmentosa*)
    propagation by rooting runners *378*
    propagation, division of plantlets/runners 378
    'Tricolor' (syn. *S. stolonifera* 'Magic Carpet'), in conservatory *359*
  'Tumbling Waters'
    conditions preferred 255–6
    suggestions for use 259
  umbrosa, conditions tolerated 181
  x *urbium*
    conditions tolerated 181
    planting in groups 175
Scab *649*
  symptoms and control 649, *649*, *658*, *658*
Scabiosa
  for cutting 181
  flowering time from seed 198
  in mixed border 177
  soil type tolerated 185
  atropurpurea, sowing 217
  caucasica
    dividing 201
    planting time 184
    'Clive Greaves' *185*
  graminifolia, suggestions for use 259
Scabious, field, *see Knautia arvensis*
Scaevola
  in container grouping *313*, 319
  overwintering 335
Scaffold poles, joints with beams 604, *604*
Scale insects 648, 653
  in greenhouses 583
  symptoms and control 648, 653
Scaling
  propagation by 248–9, *248*, 634, *634*
  bulbs 245
  twin- *248*, 249, 634, *634*
Scarification 80, 115, 198, 629–30, *630*
  alpines 272
  annuals and biennials 219
  perennials requiring 198
  shrub seed requiring 115
Scarifying rake *see* Rakes, scarifying
Scarlet runner beans *see* Beans, scarlet runner

Scent
  annuals and biennials for 213
  climbers for 128, 129
  flowering trees for 56
  for outdoor room 22, *22*
  perennials for 181
  roses for 148–50, 155
  shrubs for 94, 95
  tree foliage for 56
Schefflera
  conditions preferred indoors 361
  hydroculture 361
  semi-ripe cuttings 79
  actinophylla pollution-absorbing 358
  elegantissima, suggestions for use 366
Schinus molle, soil preferred 66
Schisandra
  semi-ripe cuttings 143
  serpentine layering 145
  softwood cuttings 142
  glaucescens, pruning *136*
Schizanthus
  greenhouse conditions required 361
  as pot plants 213, *220*
  from seed 379
  soil type preferred 216
  pinnatus, in containers 319
Schizophragma
  conditions tolerated 125
  propagation
    semi-ripe cuttings 143
    simple layering 145
    softwood cuttings 142
  pruning 135
  hydrangeoides, growing through trees 127
  integrifolium
    soil type tolerated 132
    suggestions for use 125
Schizostylis
  dividing 201
  in mixed border 228
  planting time 184
  coccinea 'Sunrise' *230*
Schlumbergera
  compost for 344
  flower sexuality *676*
  form 339
  greenhouse conditions required 361
  in hanging basket 341
    planting *344*
  propagation
    apical-wedge grafting 315, *350*
    softwood cuttings 380
    stem cuttings 348
  x *buckleyi* (syn. *S. bridgesii*)
    conditions tolerated 342
    flowers 342
    in hanging basket 358
    suggestions for use 341, 342
  'Gold Charm' *351*
  truncata
    conditions tolerated 342
    flowers 342
    suggestions for use 342
Schoenoplectus lacustris
  position in water garden 285
  subsp. *tabernaemontani*
    'Albescens', position in water garden 285
    'Zebrinus', position in water garden 285
Sciadopitys verticillata, soil preferred 65
Sciarid fly 666
  symptoms and control 666
Scilla
  conditions tolerated 231
  in containers 319
  propagation, chipping 249
  suggestions for use 228, 231, 316, 328

Scilla (*cont.*)
  bifolia
    conditions preferred 231
    in mixed border 227
    suggestions for use 239
  peruviana, conditions preferred 231
  siberica, suggestions for use 239
Scindapsus, self layering 145
Sclerotia 649, 653, 656, 665
  survival in soil 663
Sclerotinia homeocarpa 667
Sclerotium cepivorum 663
Scooping, propagation by
  bulbs 245, 250, *250*, 634
  rhizomes 250, *250*
  rosettes 276, *276*
Scorch
  causes 610, 611, 650
  control 650, 658
  in evergreens 77
  from sun 462
  symptoms 650, *650*, 658, *658*
Scoring, propagation by 250, *250*, 634, *634*
Scorzonera 547
  chards 547
  in crop rotation 498
  culinary uses 547
  feeding 547
  flower buds 547
  flowers 547
  harvesting 547
  nitrogen requirement 504, 547
  overwintering 542
  plant *547*
  root size 547
  roots *547*
  routine cultivation 547
  size of plant 547
  soil type required 547
  sowing 547
  spacing 547
  storing 547
  watering 547
Scorzonera hispanica see Scorzonera
Scotch thistle *see Onopordum acanthium*
Scots pine *see Pinus sylvestris*
Scree beds 256–7, *256*
  and climate change 256
  constructing 264
  planting 264
  rock plants for 259
  siting 260–1
  soil for 262
  soils for 261–2
  top-dressing 264–5
Screens
  annual climbers as 211
  apples as *421*
  on balconies *312*, 313, *313*
  climbers as 125
  fruit as 422
  hedges as 84–6
  indoor plants as 355
  of living willow 87, *87*
  palms as 55
  for patio 585
  protecting shrubs with 99
  on roof gardens *312*, 313
  roses as 153
  rustic work 604
  thermal 574, *574*
  trees as 58
  of walling blocks building 597
  as wind protection 495
  as windbreaks 611, *611*
Scrophularia auriculata
  propagation, stem tip cuttings 202
  soil type tolerated 184
  'Variegata', suggestions for use 285

Sculptural plants
  perennials 179
  set off by lawn 387
Sculpture
  contemporary 26
  of living willow 87, *87*
Scythropia crataegella 647
Sea-marsh turf 392
Seagrass *356*
Seakale beet *see* Swiss chard
Seaside *see* Coastal sites
Seaweed
  for fruit trees 426
  improving soil fertility with
    494
  in liquid feed 332, 372, 503
  mulching with 502
  use on compost heap 627
Seaweed meal, nutrient content 624
Secateurs 73, 74, 550, 554, *554*
  blades 554
  by-pass 554, *554*
  handles 554
  maintenance 554
  safety catch 554, *554*
  types
    anvil 554, *554*
    parrot-beak 554, *554*
    ratchet system 554, *554*
Security of plants 335
Sedges as indication of
  waterlogging 623
Sedum 49
  to attract insects 181, 264
  basal stem cuttings 202
  conditions preferred 183
  conditions tolerated 259
  in containers outdoors 340
  as ground cover 180
  hardiness 339
  pests 660, 666
  propagation
    division of offsets 349
    leaf cuttings 274, *274*
    stem cuttings 348
  seedheads 172
  for seedheads 181
  soil type preferred 184, 261
  soil type tolerated 261
  succulent type 338
  suggestions for use 258
  anglicum, conditions tolerated
    342
  'Autumn Joy', in a border *179*
  cauticola
    as ground cover 180
    suggestions for use 259
  cyaneum, conditions tolerated
    342
  dasyphyllum, conditions
    tolerated 342
  formosanum, conditions
    tolerated 342
  'Herbstfreude', in border *174*
  hintonii, leaf cuttings 347
  hispanicum, conditions
    tolerated 342
  lanceolatum, conditions
    tolerated 342
  morganianum
    in conservatory *359*
    in hanging basket 341
    suggestions for use 342
  rupestre, conditions tolerated
    342
  sediforme, conditions
    tolerated 342
  sempervivoides, leaf cuttings
    347
  spathulifolium
    as ground cover 180
    'Cape Blanco', in tree
      trunk *258*
  spectabile
    to attract insects 172
    conditions tolerated 181,
      342
    for cutting 181
    dividing 201

Sedum spectabile (*cont.*)
    for drying 181
    foliage 175
    in formal border *173*
    stem structure *674*
    in winter 192
    winter interest *176*
  spurium
    as ground cover 180
    in rock garden *255*
    'Schorbuser Blut',
      ornamental ground cover
      180
  telephium 172
    conditions tolerated 181
    for cutting 181
    for drying 181
    'Matrona'
      architectural form 181
      form 175
  ternatum, conditions tolerated
    342
  villosum, conditions tolerated
    342
Seed
  artificially produced 638
  botany 675–6
  bulbs from 246–7
  buying 216
  cacti from 346–7, *346*
  chilling 198, *199*
  chipping 379
  chitted 499
  cleaning 115
  climbers from 141, *141*
  collecting 223, *223*, 629
    from bulbs 246
    perennials 198, *198*
    for preserving 415
    from shrubs *114*, 115
  development 629, 675
  dispersal by wind 610
  dormancy
    breaking 80, 115, 141,
      198, 629–30
    double 198
    plant mechanisms for 629
  extracting from hips 168
  fine sowing 218, 379, *379*
  fleshy, cleaning 80, *80*
  fluid drilling 638
  formation by fertilization 675
  in gel 499
  gels 216
  germination 141, 609,
    629–30, *630*, 675
    bulbs 247
    epigeal 630, *630*
    erratic 247
    factors affecting 607
    hypogeal 630, *630*
    indoor plants 379
    light requirements 630
    in plastic bags 247
    requirements for 630
    signs of 630, *630*
    temperatures for 379
    temperatures required 630
  harvesting from bulbs 242, *242*
  herbs from 414
  high temperature dormancy
    518
  large, sowing 218
  lawn
    sowing by hand 394, *394*
    sowing by machine 394,
      394
  naked 499
  pelleted 216, 638
    sowing *217*
    sowing in pots 218
    of vegetables 499
  perennials from 198–9
  polyembryonic 481
  pre-germinated 499
  pre-germination 198
    method 499
  prepared, of vegetables 499
  primed 216, 638

Seed (*cont.*)
  problems 658–9
  propagation from
    advances in 638
    principles 629–30
    purpose 675
  rose, sowing 168, *168*
  scarification 80, 198, 219,
    629–30, *630*
    alpines 272
    perennials requiring 198
  scarifying 115
  shrubs from 114–15, *115*
  small, sowing 218
  soaking 115, 198, 379
  sowing
    broadcast 217, *217*
    compost for 630
    composts for 565
    in drills 217–18, *217*
    pots and pans for 565, *565*
    preparations for 637
  sowing in pots and trays
    218–19
  storing 115, 629
    damage caused by mice,
      rats, and voles 662
  stratification 80, 115, 168,
    219, 629
    alpines 272
    cold 630
    perennials requiring 198
    warm 630
  succulents from 346–7
  tapes 216
  in tapes or sheets 499
  tree
    extracting 80
    soaking 80, *80*
    sowing
      in containers 80–1,
        80, *81*
      outdoors 81
    storing 80
  trees from 80–1, *80*, *81*
  viability 115, 216, 629
Seed drills 217, *217*
Seed pans 565, *565*
  drainage 141
Seed planters 563
Seed pods, ornamental trees for
  56–7
Seed sowers 563, *563*
  wheeled 563, *563*
Seed trays 565, *565*
  drainage 141
  removing plants from 220
Seed-bearing plants, number of
  species 674
Seed-tray sowers 563
Seedbeds
  preparing 217
    tools for 553, *553*
  stale seedbed technique 502,
    620, *620*
Seedheads
  decorative perennials for 181
  drying 415, *415*
  in frost *177*
Seedling blight, symptoms and
  control 654
Seedling crops
  cut-and-come-again sowing
    500
  growing in containers 501
  harvesting 506
  sowing in wide drills 500
Seedlings
  in agar jelly 216
  bulb care 246
  climbers
    planting out 141
    pricking out 141, *144*
  damage caused
    by dogs and cats 667
    by mice, rats, and voles
      662
  damping off 223, *660*
    symptoms and control 660

Seedlings (*cont.*)
  diseases 219
    fungal 646
  disorders 655
  effects of high temperatures
    on 650
  effects of low temperatures on
    650, 664
  growth *630*
  hardening off 219–20, *220*,
    505
  healthy *630*
  mole damage to 668
  netting for 564
  pests 662, 666
    eating leaves 644
  planting depth, vegetables
    500
  planting out 220, *220*, 613
  in plugs 216, *216*
  pricking out 141, *141*, 219,
    219, 379, *379*, 630, 637
    alpines 272
    cacti 346, *346*
    into modules 219
    shrubs 115
  protecting 218, *218*
    netting for 564
    in winter *613*
  seasonal water requirements
    622
  self-sown
    annuals 223
    biennials 223
    controlling 222
    transplanting 185, *185*
  separating 220
  shrub, protecting 115
  small, buying 216, *216*
  supporting 218, *218*
  thinning
    annuals and biennials 218,
      218
    vegetables 500, *500*
  transplanting vegetables
    500–1, *500*
  trees 64–5
    pricking out 80, 81
  unhealthy *630*
  vegetable, mulching 503
Seep hoses *see* Hosepipes
Seiridium canker 664
  symptoms and control 664–5
Seiridium cardinale 665
Selaginella
  suggestions for use 366
  kraussiana
    in bottle garden *367*
    'Aurea', in terrarium *366*,
      374
  martensii, in terrarium 366,
    374
Selenicereus
  apical-wedge grafting 351
  conditions preferred 341
  propagation, stem cuttings
    348
  as rootstock 351
  side grafting 351
  suggestions for use 339, 342
  anthonyanus (syn.
    Cryptocereus
    anthonyanus), flowers 342
  grandiflorus
    conditions preferred 341
    flowers 342
  macdonaldiae, flowers 342
Self-layering climbers 141, 144,
  144, 145
Self-heal *see* Prunella
Self-pollination 629
Semele 129
Sempervivum
  conditions tolerated 259, 342
  conserving moisture 254
  in containers outdoors 340
  in dry-stone wall *268*
  foliage 254
  hardiness 339

Sempervivum (*cont.*)
  propagation
    division of offsets 349
    rosette cuttings 274
  soil type preferred 184, 261,
    325
  soil type tolerated 261
  suggestions for use 258, 259,
    318
  arachnoideum
    conditions tolerated 342
    suggestions for use 258
    in trough *267*
  montanum 339
  ruthenicum, conditions
    tolerated 342
  tectorum 274
Senecio
  conditions preferred indoors
    361
  conditions tolerated 95
  greenhouse conditions
    required 361
  lawn as foil to *386*
  propagation
    semi-ripe cuttings 143
    softwood cuttings 142
    stem cuttings 348
  pruning 376
  soil type tolerated 99
  in succulent group *339*
  suggestions for use 129
  articulatus 'Variegatus' *361*
  cineraria (syn. *S. maritimus*)
    in container grouping *313*,
      319
    foliage 209
    overwintering 335
  confusus 129
  haworthii, conditions
    tolerated 342
  macroglossus 129
    conditions tolerated 342
    'Variegatus' *142*
      in containers 128
      suggestions for use
        129
  mikanioides (syn. *Delairea*
    odorata) 129
  smithii, suggestions for use
    285
  tamoides 129
  vulgaris 669
Sepals 676, *676*
Sequoia, size 54
Sequoiadendron giganteum
  resistance to storm damage 68
  suggestions for use 55, 59
Serpentine layering
  climbers 145, *145*
  method 631, *631*
Setaria
  glauca, for drying 213
  italica, ornamental value 210
Seville oranges *see* Oranges, sour
  (Seville)
Shade
  bulbs tolerant of 226
  cacti requiring 341
  climbers providing 126
  climbers tolerant of 129
  dry
    annuals and biennials
      tolerant of 213
    bulbs tolerant of 231
    perennials tolerant of 181
    rock plants tolerant of
      259
  ground cover in 211, *211*
  lawns in 388, 389
  moist
    annuals and biennials
      preferring 213
    bulbs preferring 231
    herbs tolerating 405
    perennials preferring 181
    rock plants preferring 259
    woodland garden in *178*
  netting to provide 564, *564*

Shade (*cont.*)
  for outdoor room 22, *22*
  on patio, providing 585
  perennials for 179, 183, *186*
  plants for 611
  plants preferring 610
  shrubs tolerant of 91, 93, 95
  succulents requiring 341
  succulents tolerant of 342
  tender bulbs for 230
  wild flowers for 401
Shade cloth, shading greenhouse 636
Shading
  blinds for 357, *357*, 576, *576*, *578*
  in conservatory 357, *357*
  flexible mesh 576, *576*
  in greenhouse 573, 636
    methods 576, *576*
  netting for 564, *564*
  washes for 576, *576*
Shakers (seed sowers) 563
Shallots *536*
  conditions required 536
  in crop rotation 498
  culinary uses 536
  diseases 536, 663
  harvesting 536
  intercropping 494
  pests 536, 663
  planting sets 536, *536*
  routine cultivation 536
  soil type required 536
  spacing 536
  storing 506, 536
  'Golden Gourmet' 536
  'Jermor' 536
  'Pikant' 536
  'Santé' 536
Shanking of vines, symptoms and control 658, *658*
Sharka *see* Plum pox
Shasta daisy *see Leucanthemum* x *superbum*
Shears
  garden *393*, 555, *555*
  half-moon edger 558, *558*
  lawn 558, *558*
  lawn edging 558, *558*
  long-handled edging 558, *558*
  long-handled lawn 558, *558*
  single-handed *555*
  standard *555*
  trimming hedge with *86*
Sheds 605
  concrete 605
  designs 605
  glass-fibre 605
  materials for 605
  metal 605
  paths to 593
  timber 605
    choosing *605*
    cladding *605*
  and water collection 28
Sheep's sorrel *672*
Sheet mulches 626, *626*
Sheets, carrying 562, *562*
Shelter
  hedges as 84
  trees to provide 58
Sheltered sites, shrubs preferring 95
Shelving
  for greenhouse *578*, 579
  tiered 311
Shepherd's purse 649, 669, *669*
  control 390
  spreading disease 660
Shibataea kumasasa, in containers 319
Shield sorrel *see* Buckler-leaf sorrel
Shim 585
Shingle areas, planting 256–7
Shingle fencing 600, *600*
Shoots, importance of water to 609

Short-day plants 495
Shortia
  soldanelloides, soil type required *260*
  uniflora, conditions preferred 259
Shothole *648*
  symptoms and control 648
Shredders 550, 562, *562*
Shrew, benefits of 641
Shrubs 90–121
  for acid soil 91, *91*, 99
  for alkaline soil 99
  alpine, repotting 278
  alpines with *257*
  anti-transpirant spray for 99
  architectural 95
  aspect 91
  to attract wildlife 22
  bare-root
    buying 97
    planting 98
  bark 94
  berries 94
  bird damage 657
  borders of 92
  buying 97
  choosing 90, 97, *97*, 324, *324*
  climate suitable for 91, 256
  climbers growing through 127
  clipping for topiary 77, *77*
  in cold greenhouse 360
  in cold storage 607
  conditions tolerated 91, 256
  container-grown
    buying healthy plants *324*, 640
    planting 98, *98*
  in containers 94
    buying 97, *97*
    care 100
    compost for 99
    feeding 99
    maintaining 334
    planting 99, *99*
    plants suitable for 94, 316–17, 319
    pruning 326
    root pruning 110
    training 326
  coppicing 107, *107*
  damage caused by mice, rats, and voles 662
  dead-heading 100, *100*
  deciduous
    interest 90
    pruning 104–6, *104–6*
      hard, in spring *104*, 105
      minimal 104, *104*, 105
      in spring 104
      summer 106, *106*
    renovation 110
  deer damage to 666
  definition 90
  as design features 90–1
  designing with 90–4
  diseases 102
    affecting flowers 656
    bacterial 648, 655, 661, 665
    fungal 47, 646, 648, 654, 655, 656, 658, 661, 664, 665
  distinguishing from trees 54, 90
  dwarf 93, 259
    in alpine house 258
    pruning 270–1, *270*
    in rock garden 254, 256
    in troughs 258, *258*
  effects of high temperatures on 650
  effects of low temperatures on 650, 664
  evergreen
    interest 90–1
    pruning 103, 107–8, *108*

Shrubs, evergreen (*cont.*)
    renovation 110
    snow damage to *609*
    tolerating severe pruning 108
  existing design and *28*, 32
  fan-training 108, *108*
  fast-growing in borders 92
  feeding 100
  flower scent 94
  flowers 94
  as food source for wildlife 22
  foliage 93–4
  form 90
  as foundation planting 90–1
  frost damage to 91, 607
  ground-cover 93, *93*, 101
    pruning 101, *101*, 107
  growing clematis on 138
  guarantees on 97
  hardiness 91
  hardy, for wall-training 108
  herbs 404
  indoor cuttings 380
  informal planting *90*
  in informal planting *387*
  in island beds 92
  male and female 94
  mineral deficiency 650–1
  in mixed borders 92, 173, 177–8, 210–11
  in mixed island beds 173
  mulching 100
  needing minimal pruning 104, 105
  neglected, pruning 103
  non-variegated shoots, removing *100*
  pests 102, 654, 660, 666
    affecting flowers 657
    damaging leaves 644, 645, 646, 647, 648, 651, 652
  physical damage 102
  pinch pruning 376
  planter's guide 95
  planting *98*
    in clay soil 98–9
    in containers *324*
    time for 98
  pollarding 107, *107*
  pricking out 115, *115*
  problems 102
    affecting stems and leaf buds 653–4
  propagation 111–10
    air layering 116, *117*
      plants propagated by 117
    cuttings 79, 111–14, *111–14*
      greenwood 111–12, *111*
        plants propagated by 111
      hardwood 113–14, *114*
        plants propagated by 114
      heel 112, 113, *113*
      leaf-bud 113, *113*
      mallet 113, *113*
      nodal 112
      root 114
      semi-ripe 112–13, *112*
        feeding 112
        overwintering 112
        plants propagated by 113
      softwood 111, *111*
        plants propagated by 111
    division 111, 118, *118*
      plants suitable for 118
    dropping 116–17

Shrubs, propagation (*cont.*)
    grafting 111, 118–19, *119*
      apical-wedge 119, *119*
        plants suitable for 119
      saddle 118, *119*
      spliced side-veneer 118–19
    layering 111, 116–18, *116–17*
      dropping 116–17
      French 117–18
      simple 116, *116*
        plants propagated by 116
      stooling 117, *117*
      mound layering 414, *414*
    from seed 111, 114–15, *115*
      sowing
        in containers 115, *115*
        outdoors 115
      stooling 117, *117*
        plants suitable for 117
    suckering
      division 118, *118*
        plants suitable for 118
    tip layering 116
  protecting newly planted 99
  pruning 103–10, 326
    after planting *98*
    aims 103
    to attract wildlife 103
    bad 664
    coppicing 107, *107*
    effects 103
    formative 103–4, *104*
    hard, in spring *104*, 105
    minimal *104*, 105, 106
    pollarding 107, *107*
    principles 103, *103*
    root 110
    in spring 104
    suckering habit 106, *106*
    summer 106, *106*
    in summer after flowering 106
    wall 108–9, *109*
  renovation 110, *110*
    drastic 110, *110*
    gradual 110, *110*
  repotting 334, *334*
  reversion 100, *100*
    removing reverted shoots *100*
  in rock garden 254
  root pruning 110
  root-balled
    buying 97, *97*
    planting 98
  root-balling 102, *102*
  roses with 151
  routine care 100, 102
  for sandy sol 97
  scented 94, 95
  scrambling, training 109
  for seasonal interest 50, 95
  seedlings, protecting 115
  for shade 93, 95
  size 90
  small, protecting *612*, 613
  in soil beds under cover 367
  soil for 91
  soil preparation 97, 98
  on south-facing walls 611
  specimen 92–3, *93*
    siting 93
  staking 99, *99*
  standard
    plants suitable for 326
    pruning 326
    staking 99, *99*
    training and pruning 109
  stem structure *674*

Shrubs (*cont.*)
  stems 94, *94*
  successional interest 91–2
  suckers, removing 100, *100*
  suggestions for use 90–4
  suiting to site 91
  on supports, training 103
  tender, training 109
  testing for live wood 107
  tolerant of clay soil 97
  tolerant of wind 613
  topiary 76–7
  training 103–10
    principles 103
    for topiary 76–7
  transplanting 102, *102*
  under-canopy below trees 101
  variegated, reversion 100, *100*
  wall 93, *93*, 95
    effect of sun on 610
    planting 98, 99
    protecting *612*, 613
    pruning 108–9, *109*
    with roses 152
    training 109, *109*
  watering 100
  weed control round 671, 673
  weeding 100
  winter protecting 102
  young, protecting from frost *613*
Shuttering for concrete 290, *291*
Shuttlecock fern *see Matteuccia struthiopteris*
Sidalcea
  to attract wildlife 178
  dividing 201
  flowering time from seed 198
  soil type tolerated 185
Side-veneer grafting 636
  spliced 118–19
  succulents 351, *351*
Sieves 563, *563*
Silene
  flowering time from seed 198
  propagation, "Irishman's" cuttings 275
  acaulis
    propagation, softwood cuttings 273
    suggestions for use 259
  armeria, self-seeding 218
  coeli-rosa, sowing 217
  schafta
    soil type tolerated 261
    suggestions for use 258
  uniflora
    conditions tolerated 259
    'Robin Whitebreast', suggestions for use 259
Silt
  capping 621, *621*
  improving texture 621
  structure 616, *616*
  water table 622
Silver birch *see Betula pendula*
Silver fir *see Abies*
Silver leaf 74, 428, *647*
  reducing risk of 457
  symptoms and control 448, 647
Silver-leaved plants
  conditions tolerated 622
  for greenhouse 230
  underplanting roses 152
Silybum marianum
  architectural plant 213
  for dry conditions 211
  self-seeding 218
Sinapis alba see Mustards
Sink gardens, dwarf conifers for 62
Sinks
  alpines in 255, 258, 266–7
    care 270–1
    planting 267
  covering with hypertufa 266, *266*
  rock plants in 266–7
    planting 267

Sinningia
  conditions preferred indoors
    361
  greenhouse conditions
    required 361
  pests 656
  propagation, leaf cuttings 633
    from seed 379
  'Red Flicker' *361*
  speciosa, leaf cuttings 381
Siphons 615
Sisyrinchium
  soil type preferred 184
  'E.K. Balls', in trough *267*
  striatum 'Aunt May', planting
    depth *184*
Site
  clearing 183
  levelling 390–1, *390*, *391*
  neglected, weeding 673
  overgrown, clearing 618, *618*
  uncultivated, clearing 673
  weed clearance 618, *618*, 670
Skimmia
  conditions preferred 95
  flower sexuality 676
  propagation
    layering 116
    semi-ripe cuttings with
      heel 113
  suggestions for use 316
  x *confusa*, scent 95
  japonica
    in containers 319
    flower sexuality 676, *676*
    seasonal interest 50
Slaked lime 625
Slaters *see* Woodlice
Sleepers
  cutting 599
  raised beds of 497, 599, *599*
  steps of gravel and *595*
Slender speedwell *see Veronica*
  filiformis
Slime flux 653, 655
  symptoms and control 653
Slime moulds 649, 660, *667*
  symptoms and control 667
Slipper orchid *see Paphiopedilum*
Slitter, star-wheeled *559*
Slopes
  building steps into 595, *595*
  creating 391, *391*
  decking for 592
  dwarf conifers for 62
  erecting fences on 602, *602*
  existing design and 30
  growing vegetables on 493,
    495
  lawn on 386
  Mediterranean-style planting
    on *264*
  retaining walls on 598, *598*
  trees for 63
Slugs 271, 639
  control *333*, 504, 641, 642,
    644, 662, 668
  damage caused by 333, 644,
    644, 662, *662*
  predators 641
  trapping 643
  under plastic film 503
  underground, control 643
    biological 642
Slugworm
  cherry *647*
    symptoms and control 647
  pear *647*
    symptoms and control
      647
Small gardens
  fruit in 418, 419–20, *422*
  fruit tree forms for 419, *419*
  herbs in 405
  trees for 59
Smilacina (syn. *Maianthemum*),
  dividing 201
Smithiantha, greenhouse
  conditions required 361

Smuts *652*
  symptoms and control 652
Snails 271, 639
  checking aquatics for eggs of
    297
  control 504, 641, 642, 644,
    668
  damage caused by 333, 644,
    644
  in pond 299
  predators 641
  ramshorn 299
  trapping 643
Snake's-head fritillary *see*
  Fritillaria meleagris
Snap beans *see* Beans, French
Snow
  damage caused by 335, 609,
    609
  protection from 99
    for topiary 77
  protection provided by 609,
    609
Snow mould *see Fusarium* patch
Snow-in-summer *see Cerastium*
  tomentosum
Snowdrop *see Galanthus*
Snowflake *see Leucojum*
Soakaways 623, *623*
Soaps
  insecticidal 646, 668
    use with biological control
      643
  pest and disease control 642
Sodium 615
Sodium chloride 638
Soft fruit *see* Fruit, soft
Soft scale 648, *648*
Soft scale insects, biological
  control 642
Softwood cuttings *see* Cuttings,
  softwood
Soil 616–28
  acid *see* Acid soil
  acidity
    altering 156
    deficiencies caused by 617
    effect of fertilizers on 100
  additives 621, *621*
    benefits 621
    problems with 621
    top-dressings as 626, *626*
  aeration, improving 621
  alkaline *see* Alkaline soil
  alkalinity
    deficiencies caused by 617
    increasing 617, 625
  blue mottling *621*
  calcium in 617
  capillary pores 622
  capping 621, *621*
  characteristics 616
  chemical clearance 618, *618*
  compacted *621*
    additives for 621
  conditioning 670
  conserving moisture 502, *502*
  crumb formation 621, *621*
  cultivation 618–21
  damaging physical structure
    of 494
  diseases 617
  drainage 183, 616
    improving 623, *623*
    installing 623, *623*
    testing 623
  effect of frost on 411, 609
  effect on health of plant 640
  enhancing water retention
    614, *614*
  erosion
    caused by wind 611
    on slopes 493
  fertility, organisms important
    to 617
  good 621
  in greenhouse borders,
    becoming infected 578
  grubs in 504

Soil (*cont.*)
  hardpan *621*
  heavy
    controlling self-seeding
      222
    cultivating in wet weather
      621
  improving 91, 183, 616
    drainage 621
    for lawn 390
    for roses 156
    structure 63, *620*, 621
  increasing water available in
    609
  layers 617, *617*
  liming 625, *625*
  maintaining fertility 493–4
  moisture take-up 622
  nutrients 503, 616, 624–5
  organisms 617
    beneficial 617, *617*
  pests 617
  pH level 617
    adjusting 424
    effect of fertilizers on 100
    effect of 617
    high, problems caused by
      625
    for lawn 390
    optimum 617
    scale 617
    testing *617*
  poor *621*
  poorly structured 621
  pores 622
  preparing for
    lawn 390
    naturalistic plantings 183
  preserving structure 494
  problems *621*
  problems caused by 639
  profile 617, *617*
  reducing fertility 183, 401
  for rock garden 261–2
  rose-sick 156
  rotavating
    to clear overgrown site
      618, *618*
    for weed control 671, 673
  for scree bed 262
  sterilizing 323, 618–19, *618*
  structure 616–17
    improving *620*, 621
    water content and 620–1
  subsoil in soil profile 617,
    617
  temperature 499
    importance of 607
  testing 183
    thermometer for 563
  tilth forming 620, *620*
  topsoil in soil profile 617, *617*
  types 493, 616
    identifying 617, *617*
  using organic matter on
    493–4, 496, 497
  walking on 496
  warming 500, *613*
  water content 620–1, 622
  water retention 621, 622
    improving 621
    as pot plant 213
  waterlogged 621, *621*, 651
    damage to plants 609
    indications of 623
    perennials tolerant of 184
    plants adapted to 609
    problems 623
    symptoms 660, *660*, 664,
      664
    treatment for 622, 623,
      623, 664
    vulnerable areas 623
  well-structured *621*
Soil blocks, sowing seed in 501
Soil sickness, symptoms and
  control 665, *665*
Soil-warming cables 580, *580*
Solanaceous crops in crop
  rotation 498

Solandra 129
  semi-ripe cuttings 143
  maxima
    for fragrance 129
    pruning 135, 137
    vigour 130
Solanum
  propagation
    root cuttings 144
    semi-ripe cuttings
      143
    simple layering 145
    softwood cuttings 142
  pruning 137
  betaceum see Tamarillos
  x *burbankii see*
    Wonderberries
  capsicastrum
    conditions preferred
      indoors 361
    in containers 319
  crispum 135
    cuttings, softwood *142*
    planting 131
    pruning 135
      spring *134*
    soil type tolerated 132
    'Glasnevin', suggestions
      for use 95
  laxum (syn. *S. jasminoides*)
    planting 131
    pruning 135
    suggestions for use 95
  melongena see Aubergines
  pseudocapsicum
    in containers 319
    indoors 354
  rantonnetii, in containers 319
  tuberosum see Potatoes
  wendlandii
    pruning 376
    soil type tolerated 131
    vigour 130
Soldanella
  alpina, suggestions for use
    259
  montana, suggestions for use
    259
  villosa, soil type required
    260
Soleirolia
  soleirolii (syn. *Helxine*
    soleirolii) 672
    foliage 354
    in terrarium *366*
    suggestions for use 27,
      366
Solenostemon
  choosing healthy plant *364*
  conditions preferred indoors
    361
  in containers 319
  cuttings 380
  foliage 209
  germination 219
  greenhouse conditions
    required 361
  overwintering 335
  pinch pruning 377
    fan shape *377*
  as pot plant 213
  propagation, softwood
    cuttings *381*
  standards 326
  suggestions for use 61
Solid fuel, for greenhouse heating
  574
Solidago
  for cutting 181
  dividing 201
  for drying 181
  canadensis, growth rate 181
Sollya, softwood cuttings 142
Solomon's seal *see Polygonatum*
Solomon's seal sawfly 645
Somatic embryogenesis 638
Sonerila, softwood cuttings 380
Sooty moulds 333, 639, 646, 647,
  648

Sophora japonica, conditions
  tolerated 67
Sorbaria, pruning 105
Sorbus
  for autumn colour 57
  diseases 649
    fungal 664
  extracting seed 80
  leaf shapes *46*
  pricking out *80*
  propagation
    chip budding 82
    sowing in containers 80,
      80
    spliced side grafting 82
  seed germination 81
  aria
    for avenues 58
    conditions tolerated 67
    soil type tolerated 65
    suggestions for use 59
    'Lutescens'
      foliage 57
      seasonal interest 59
  aucuparia
    berries 57
    conditions tolerated 67,
      613
    pests damaging leaves 652
    suggestions for use 55, 59
  cashmiriana
    seasonal interest 59
    suggestions for use 59,
      316
  commixta 'Embley'
    seasonal interest 59
    suggestions for use 59
  intermedia, conditions
    tolerated 67
  reducta 259
  vilmorinii, suggestions for use
    59
Sorrel (herb) 410, *410*
  conditions tolerated 405
  culinary uses 410
  foliage 410
  harvesting 410
  in herb garden *412*
  propagation
    division 410
    from seed 410
  protection for winter 410
  related species 410
  removing flowering stems
    413
  storing 410
Sorrel (weed) *672*
Southernwood *see Artemisia*
  abrotanum
Sowing, tools for 563, *563*
Spades 551, *551*
  blades 551, *551*
  hilts 551, *551*
    "D"-type *551*
    "T"-type *551*
    "Y"-type *551*
  shafts 551
  size 551
  types
    automatic *551*
    border 551, *551*
    standard digging 551, *551*
Spaghetti marrows *see* Marrows,
  spaghetti
Spanish chestnuts *see* Sweet
  chestnuts
Sparaxis 226
  conditions preferred 231
  for cutting 231
Sparganium
  erectum (syn. *S. ramosum*),
    position in water garden
    285
  natans, position in water
    garden 285
Sparmannia
  conditions preferred indoors
    361
  softwood cuttings 380

Spartium
conditions tolerated 95
junceum, soil type preferred 97
Spathiphyllum
conditions preferred 355
conditions preferred indoors 361
greenhouse conditions required 361
hybrids, pollution-absorbing 358
hydroculture 361
Species, botanical names 677
Specimen plants
apples as 439
architectural perennials for 181
backdrop to 179
bulbs with 228
in containers 307–8
dwarf conifers as 62
fruit trees as 418, 422
herbs as 405
indoors 354
in lawn 46, 387
perennials 179
roses 152, 155
shrubs 92–3
in containers 94
trees to use 59
Speedwell *see Veronica*
Speedwell, slender *see Veronica filiformis*
Spent mushroom compost *see* Mushroom compost
Sphaeralcea, stem tip cuttings 202
Sphaerotheca 646
Sphagnum moss *see* Moss, sphagnum
Spickels 652
Spider plant *see Cleome*
Spiders
benefits of 641
garden *641*
Spikes (flowers) 676
Spilocaea
eriobotryae 649
pyracanthae 649
Spinach *515*, 519, *519*
bolting 519
as catch crop 494
Chinese *see Amaranthus tricolor*
conditions preferred 519
conditions tolerated 519
in crop rotation 498
as cut-and-come again crop 519
daylength requirement 519
freezing 506
germination 519
harvesting 519
nitrogen requirement 504, 519
recommended cultivars 519
size of plant 519
sowing 519
spacing 519
storing 519
watering, critical periods 502
winter cropping under cover 505
African *see Amaranthus*
Ceylon *see* Ceylon spinach
Indian *see* Ceylon spinach
New Zealand *see* New Zealand spinach
vine *see* Ceylon spinach
Spinach beet 516
conditions tolerated 516
culinary uses 516
diseases 516
feeding 516
freezing 506
growing in containers 501
harvesting 516
leaf size 516
mulching 516

Spinach beet (*cont.*)
nitrogen requirements 504, 516
pests 516
routine cultivation 516
soil types suitable 516
sowing 516
spacing 516
storing 516
Spinach mustard *see* Komatsuna
Spinacia oleracea see Spinach
Spiraea
conditions tolerated 95
propagation
hardwood cuttings 114
mallet cuttings 113
soil type tolerated 97
'Arguta', pruning 106
douglasii, pruning 105
japonica
division of suckers 118
pruning *104*, 105
'Goldflame'
in mixed border *174*
in container 94
prunifolia, pruning 106
thunbergii, pruning 106
Spirit level *390*, 391, *391*, 585, *585*, *586*, 587, *587*
Spirogyra, control 300, *300*
Spittlebugs *see* Froghoppers
Spores, fern, propagation by 195, *195*
Sport, lawn for 388–9
mowing 395
Sports 676, *676*
reverting to type 100
Spotted orchid, common, *see* *Dactylorhiza fuchsii*
Spraing *662*
symptoms and control 662
Sprayers 560, *560*
compression types 560, *560*
trigger-pump 560
Spraying chemicals, safety precautions 643
Spreaders, fertilizer 559, *559*
Sprekelia
greenhouse conditions required 361
growing with succulents 339–40
pests 663
Sprigging, establishing lawn by 394
Spring
annuals for containers 212
annuals for 210
climbers for colour in 128
colour in 50, *51*
mixed plantings for 227–8
perennials for 177–8
shrubs flowering in 91
shrubs for interest in 50, 95
trees for interest in 57
Spring onions *see* Onions, spring
Sprinklers 561, *561*
oscillating 561, *561*
pulse-jet 561, *561*
rotating 561, *561*
static 561, *561*
travelling 561
underground 396, 561
Sprouting broccoli 511
conditions required 511
conditions tolerated 511
culinary uses 511
diseases 511
freezing 506
harvesting 511
mineral deficiencies 652
nitrogen requirements 504, 511
pests 511
planting 507
protecting from pigeons 511
purple *511*
in crop rotation 498
recommended cultivars 511
size of plant 511

Sprouting broccoli (*cont.*)
sowing 511
spacing 511
staking 511
storing 511
transplanting 511
'Claret' F1 511
'Red Arrow' 511
'Redhead' 511
'Rudolph' 511
'White Sprouting' 511
Spruce *see Picea*
Spur blight *653*
symptoms and control 653
Squashes
curing 506
storing 506
crookneck *see* Marrows, crookneck squashes
summer *see* Marrows
winter *see* Pumpkins
Squirrels 96
grey damage caused 659, *659*
Stachys
dividing 193
as ground cover 180
soil type tolerated 185
byzantina (syn. *S. lanata*) 152
conditions tolerated 181
dividing 201
'Silver Carpet', winter interest 181
Stachyurus, layering 116
Staging
for greenhouse
positioning 579
types 578, 579, *579*
Stains, applying to timber decking 592
Stakes 564, *564*
link 192, *192*, 564
preserving 158
ring 192, *192*, 564
Staking 564, *564*
annuals 222, *222*
climbing annuals 221, 222, *222*
framework for climbers under cover 376, *376*
houseplants 364, *364*
link stake 192, *192*
perennials 192, *192*
ring of canes 192, *192*
ring stake 192, *192*
shrubs 99, *99*
single cane 192, *192*
supports for climbers 124, 130
trees 64, *64*
twigs 192
Stale seedbed technique 502, 620, *620*
Stamens 629, *629*, 676, *676*
Stanhopea
flowering 369
in hanging basket 369
tigrina, in hanging basket *369*
Stapelia 345
propagation
division of offsets 349
division of rootstock 350
stem cuttings 348
as rootstock 351
Staples
fastening layers with *145*
"U"- 440
Star-wheeled cultivator 553, *553*
Star-wheeled slitter 559
Starlings
damage caused
to flowers 657
to fruit, berries, and seeds 659, *659*
Starvation of lawn, symptoms and control 667
Statice *see Limonium*
Statues
as focal point *19*
framed by climbers *125*
in lawn 387

Stauntonia 129
semi-ripe cuttings 143
Steel
for greenhouses *570*, 571
for tools 551
Steinernema
feltiae 642, 660
kraussei 642, 645, 660, 666
Stellaria media 669, *669*
Stem cuttings
succulents 348, *348*
types 632–3, *632–3*
Stem sections, propagation by, succulents 348, *348*
Stem tubers 635, *635*
propagation 635
Stem vegetables 535–41
temperature requirements 495
Stem wilt 639
Stems
abnormal growth 655
cell types in 674
discolouration 640
problems causing 653–4
distortion 655
herbaceous
strengthening tissue in 674
structure 674
modified 675
as bulb structure 674
ornamental in winter 91
purpose 674–5
types 674
woody 674
structure 674
Steneotarsonemus laticeps 652
Stenocereus, flowers 342
Stenotaphrum secundatum, for lawns 388, 389
Stephanandra
pruning 106
stooling 117
Stephanotis 129
conditions preferred indoors 361
in containers 319
propagation
semi-ripe cuttings 143
softwood cuttings 380
pruning 135
floribunda 129
for fragrance 129
pruning 376
suggestions for use 129
Stepping stones
of decking 592
paths of 593
Steps
building 595
into bank 595
calculating number needed 595
containers on 309, *309*
existing design and 30
materials for 593
tread to riser ratio 595, *595*
uses 593
Sterilization of soil 618–19, *618*
Sternbergia
collecting from the wild 228
propagation
chipping 249
division of offsets 245
suggestions for use 231
lutea
conditions preferred 231
conditions tolerated 231
in mixed border 228
in rock garden 256
suggestions for use 231
sicula
conditions preferred 231
in mixed border 228
suggestions for use 231
Stewartia
soil preferred 65
pseudocamellia
seasonal interest 59
suggestions for use 59

Stigma 347, *347*, 629, *629*, 676, *676*
Stigmaphyllon 129
semi-ripe cuttings 143
ciliatum 129
pruning 137
Stinging nettle *see* Nettle, stinging
Stipa
gigantea
architectural form 175, 181
growth rate 181
as specimen plant 179
suggestions for use 46
pennata, for drying 213
tenuissima, in perennial border *172*
Stock *see Matthiola*
Stolonizing, establishing lawn by 394
Stolons, weeds with *670*
Stomata 609, 675, *675*
Stomatium, division of offsets 349
Stone
containers of 321
dressed 588
natural
for paving 588
raised beds of 599
natural strata 261, *261*
paths of 593
for rock garden 261, *261*
stylized arrangement with gravel *27*
Stone chippings as top-dressing 265, 626
Stone fruits
see also Fruit, tree; individual fruits by name
bottling 431
definition 419, 435
propagation, grafting 635
renovation 430
seed stratification 629
Stooling 414
method 631, *631*
shrubs 117, *117*
Stools, kneeling 562, *562*
Stopping
annuals 220
chrysanthemums 189, *189*, 190
Dianthus 196, *196*
fuchsias 120, 121
indoor plants 372
melons 524, *524*
perennials 191, *191*
Storage
bulbs 243, *243*
chemicals 643
fruit 431, *431*
tree seed 80
of turf 392, *392*
Storage organs, propagation 634–5
Storage rots 663, *663*
Stratification 80, 115, 168, 629
alpines 272
annuals and biennials 219
cold 630
perennials 198
shrubs 115
tree seed requiring 81
warm 630
Stratiotes aloides 285
choosing healthy plants *297*
introducing into pond *298*
propagation by offsets 303
Straw
as additive, problems 621
protecting plants with *612*, 613
protecting trees and shrubs with *612*
Strawberries 468–70, *468*
advancing ripening 469
bird damage 657, 659

Strawberries (cont.)
choosing cultivars 468
clearing foliage after
harvesting 470, *470*
compost for 328
in containers 319
diseases 468
affecting flowers 656
damaging leaves 651
fungal 427, 658
virus 659
drainage 468
feeding 426, 470
flavour
cultivars recommended 469
enhancing 469
of fruit under cover 469
freezing 431, 470
growing in containers 328
growing under cloches 469
growing under cover 422, 469
damping down 469
flavour
compared to outdoors
469
enhancing 469
improving fruit size 469
pests 469
pollination 469
temperatures for 469
ventilation 469
growing under polytunnels 469
growing vertically 422
growing in windowbox *495*
harvesting *406*, 431, 469
keeping fruits clean 469, *469*
mineral deficiency 654
natural layering 631, *631*
netting *427*
pests 469, 660, 666
damaging fruit 644
eating leaves 644, *645*
plant type 419
planting 468
in raised beds 468
in matted rows 468
time for 468
under plastic mulch *468*,
469, *470*
pollination 468
in pots under cover 423
propagation 470, *470*
by runners *470*
runners 434
protecting 613
from pests and diseases
640
protecting from frost 427, *613*
recommended cultivars 469
replacing plants 468
rotating crop 468
routine care 469
runners
growing plants from 469
removing 469, *469*
site 468
soil types for 468
spacing 468
storing 469
suggestions for use 318
transplanting *421*
types 468
watering 469
weeding 469
windbreaks for 611
'Alexandra' 469
'Alice' 469
alpine *420*
conditions tolerated 470
cropping 468
edging bed *418*
flavour 470
as ground cover 180
in herb garden *404*
propagation from seed
434, 470, *470*
recommended cultivars 469
suggestions for use 328,
422, 470

Strawberries (cont.)
'Alpine Yellow' 469
'Aromel' 469
'Baron Solemacher' 328, 469
'Bogota' 469
'Bolero' 469
'Calypso' 469
'Cambridge Favourite' 469
'Cambridge Late Pine' 469
'Cambridge Vigour' 469
'Challenger' 469
'Elsanta' 469, *469*
in large fruit garden *421*
'Elvira' 469, *469*
'Eros' 469
ever-bearing *see* perpetual-
fruiting
'Florence' 469
'Hapil' 469
'Honeoye' 469
'Mae' 469
'Mara des Bois' 469
'Pandora' 468
'Pegasus' 469
perpetual-fruiting
recommended cultivars 469
cropping 468
'Red Gauntlet' 469
'Rhapsody Sophie' 469
'Rosie' 469
'Royal Sovereign' 469
summer-fruiting, cropping 468
'Symphony' 469
'Tamella' 469
Strawberry beetles 469
Strawberry green petal 651
Strawberry mats 469, *469*
Strawberry planters 328, 405, 423
herbs in, replanting *413*
Streams 283
informal *282*
Strelitzia
in greenhouse 360
greenhouse conditions
required 361
Streptocarpus
conditions preferred indoors
361
in garden room *354*
in greenhouse 359
conditions required 361
in greenhouse display *359*
hydroculture 361
in indoor plant group *372*
pests 656
propagation
leaf cuttings 633
leaf sections *381*, 382
in soil bench *367*
'Heidi', in conservatory *359*
saxorum, leaf cuttings 347
Streptomyces scabies 662
Streptosolen
greenhouse conditions
required 361
propagation, softwood
cuttings 30, 142
pruning 135
jamesonii
pruning 135
soil type tolerated 131
suggestions for use 129
Stress, water 614
String for ties 564
String beans *see* Beans, French
Strobilanthes dyeriana,
suggestions for use 366
Stromanthe
propagation, rootstock 378
*amabilis see Ctenanthe
amabilis*
Strombocactus disciformis 339
Strongylodon 129
propagation
semi-ripe cuttings 143
simple layering 145
pruning 135
macrobotrys 129
pruning 137

Structures 584–605
designing with 584
selecting materials for 584
sequence of projects 584
Stylar column *676*
Stylophorum diphyllum,
conditions preferred 259
Styrax
japonicus, soil preferred 65
officinalis, soil type required
99
Suaeda
maritima, conditions tolerated
342
vera (syn. *S. fruticosa*),
conditions tolerated 342
Subsoil *see* Soil
Subtropical plants
in containers 318
flowering, conditions required
364
foliage, conditions tolerated
364
Succulents 336–51
adapted to drought 609
annual 211
for bowls and troughs 342
buying 343, *343*
caudiciform 338
characteristics 338
choosing 343, *343*
compatible non-succulents
339–40
compost for 306, 343, 344
conditions preferred 355
conditions required 339,
345
conditions tolerated 338,
339
in containers 318
indoors 341
outdoors 340, *340*
planting 344, *344*
containers for 340
cross-pollination 347, *347*
cuttings
leaf 347, *347*
stem 348, *348*
in desert gardens 340, *340*
designing with 338–41
diseases 345
disorders 648
distinguishing from cacti 338
division
of offsets 349, *349*
of rootstock 350, *350*
environment 339, 345
epiphytic, conditions required
341
feeding 345
flowering 339, *339*
flowers 338
form 338–9, *339*
grafting 350–1, *350–1*
side-veneer 351, *351*
varieties suitable for 351
in greenhouse, conditions
required 576
group *338*
groups 338
habit 338–9
habitats 338
half-hardy *339*
conditions required 339
in hanging baskets 341, *341*
planting 344, *344*
plants recommended for
342
hardy *339*
hybridizing 347, *347*
hygiene 345
indoor display 340–1
leaf succulents 338
light requirement 341
offset tubers 349, *349*
offsets, propagation from 349,
349
outdoor display 339–40
pad sections *348*

Succulents (cont.)
pests 345, 646
damaging leaves 646, 648
damaging stems 653
physiological disorders 651
planter's guide 342
planting
in desert garden 343
in outdoor bed *343*
in raised bed 343
pots for 344
propagation 346–51
division of offsets 349,
349
division of rootstock 350,
350
grafting 350–1, *350–1*
hybridization 347, *347*
leaf cuttings 347, *347*
pad sections 348
from seed 346–7, *346*
stem cuttings 348, *348*
stem sections 348, *348*
repotting 345, *345*
routine care 345
scented 339
shading 345
shapes 338
stem sections 348, *348*
stem succulents 338
suggestions for use 338–41
temperatures for 339, 345
tolerant of damp conditions
342
tolerant of low temperatures
342
tolerant of shade 342
trailing 339
ventilation 345
water storage 338
watering 345
Suckers
propagation by
fruit 434
raspberries 474, *474*
recognizing *100*
rose 158
propagation from 167, *167*
recognising 159
removing 159, *159*
shrubs
plants suitable for
propagation by 118
propagating by 118, *118*
of shrubs, removing 100, *100*
tree 74
removing 69, *69*
Suckers (psyllids) *647*
symptoms and control 647,
651
Sudden oak death 654
Sugar loaf chicory *see* Chicory,
sugar loaf
Sugar peas *see* Peas, sugar
Sulphate of ammonia 650
adjusting pH level 424
Sulphate of potash 159, 650, 656
Sulphur 646, 649, 656, 668
as fungicide 663
plant requirements 624
Sulphur dust 642
Summer
annuals for containers 212
annuals for *208*
climbers for colour in 128
colour in 50, *50, 51*
mixed plantings for 228
perennials for 177
shrubs flowering in 91
shrubs for interest in 95
trees for interest in 57
Summer purslane 521
conditions required 521
culinary uses 521
golden *521*
harvesting 521
pests 521
sowing 521
types 521

Summer savory
flavour 410
flowers 410
in herb garden *412*
Summer snowflake *see Leucojum
aestivum*
Summer squash *see* Marrows
Sun
cacti for containers in 342
ground cover in 211
houseplants for 355
perennials for 183
scorch from 462
shrubs for 91
succulents for containers in
342
Sun plant *see Portulaca
grandiflora*
Sun rooms 358–9, *358*
Sunberries *see* Wonderberries
Sunchokes *see* Jerusalem
artichokes
Sundial beside pool *283*
Sunflower *see Helianthus*
Sunken gardens
for roses 152
terraced surround for 152
roses for 153
Sunlight
excessive problems of 610
importance to plants 607
plants growing towards 610
plants thriving in 610
value of 610
Superphosphate 426, 503, 650
nutrient content 624
Superphosphate of lime
in cuttings compost 565
in seed compost 565
Supports
see also Staking
arches, constructing 604
pergolas, constructing 603
permanent 604
pillars, constructing 604
preparing, for fruit trees 424
tripods, constructing 604
Surface floaters *see* Floating
aquatics
Surfaces 584–605
concrete 586
crazy paving 588
designing with 584
load-bearing foundations 586
natural stone 588
paving slabs 587–8
selecting materials for 584
tile 588–9
Swedes 542–3, *542*
in crop rotation 498
culinary uses 542
diseases 543, 649, 660
fungal 661
freezing 506
harvesting 543
mineral deficiencies 662
nitrogen requirement 504, 542
pests 543, 644, 660
recommended cultivars 542
root colours 542
root size 542
routine cultivation 543
size of plant 542
soil type preferred 542
sowing 542
spacing 542
storing 543
watering 543
weeding 543
'Brora' 542
'Magres' 542
'Marian' 542, 649
'Ruby' 542
Sweepers, lawn 559, *559*
Sweet alyssum *see Lobularia*
Sweet bay *see Laurus nobilis*
Sweet chestnuts *488*
conditions required 488
fruit type 675, *675*

Sweet chestnuts (*cont.*)
harvesting 488
planting 488
pollination 488
propagation 488
from seed 434
site 488
storing 488
tree size 488
Sweet cicely 409, *409*
conditions tolerated 405
culinary uses 409
flavour 409
flowers 409
foliage 409
harvesting 409
in herb garden *412*
propagation from seed 409
self-seeding 409
storing 409
Sweet corn 522, *529*
conditions required 529
cultivation 522
description 529
earthing up 529
freezing 506
germination 529
growing below wall 495
harvesting 529
hoeing 529
intercropping 494, *494*
mini-corn 529
mulching 529
nitrogen requirement 504, 529
ornamental *see* Zea mays
pests 529
planting herbs with *495*
planting out 529
pollination 529
protecting 529
recommended cultivars 529
routine cultivation 529
soil requirements 529
sowing 529
through plastic film 503
sowing depth 499
spacing 529
storing 529
testing for ripeness *529*
watering 529
'Earlibird' F1 529
'Golden Bantam' 529
'Lark' F1 529
'Northern Extra Sweet' 529
'Ovation' 529
'Sundance' F1 529
'Swallow' F1 529
'Swift' F1 529
Sweet fennel *see* Fennel,
Florence
Sweet marjoram *see* Origanum
majorana
Sweet melons *see* Melons
Sweet pea *see* Lathyrus odoratus
Sweet pea tubes 214, 565, *565*
Sweet peppers *see* Peppers, sweet
Sweet potatoes *542*, 545, *545*
conditions required 545
in crop rotation 498
culinary uses 545
curing 545
daylength requirement 545
diseases 545
fungal 654
feeding 545
growing under cover 545
harvesting 545
mulching 545
nitrogen requirement 504, 545
pests 545
planting tubers 545
propagation
from seed 545
stem cuttings 545, *545*
tubers 545
protecting 545
recommended cultivars 545
removing growing points 545
routine cultivation 545

Sweet potatoes (*cont.*)
size of plant 545
soil type required 545
storing 545
training 545
watering 545
'Beauregard' 545
'Bunch Porto Rico' 545
'Gold-rush' 545
'New Jewel' 545
'Vardaman' 545
'White Delight' 545
Swiss chard 516
conditions tolerated 516
culinary uses 516
as cut-and-come-again crop
506
diseases 516
feeding 516
freezing 506
growing in containers 328
harvesting 516
leaf colour 516
leaf size 516
mulching 516
nitrogen requirements 504, 516
pests 516
red-stemmed *516*
routine cultivation 516
soil types suitable 516
sowing 516
spacing 516
storing 516
watering, critical periods 502
white-stemmed *516*
Swiss-cheese plant *see* Monstera
deliciosa
Sycamore *see* Acer
pseudoplatanus
Symphoricarpos, hardwood
cuttings 114
Symphytum
dividing 201
as ground cover 180
'Goldsmith', ornamental
ground cover *180*
grandiflorum, conditions
tolerated 181
officinale
as green manure 625
as leaf mould 323, 625
as a liquid feed 332, 372,
625
in naturalistic planting
schemes 197
x uplandicum 'Bocking 14',
as green manure 625
Syngonium 129
conditions preferred indoors
361
softwood cuttings 380
hoffmannii, suggestions for
use 366
podophyllum
conditions tolerated 129
in hydroculture display
375
'Albolineatum', care
during absence *374*
Syringa
dead-heading 100
flowers 94
pests damaging leaves 647
propagation
air layering 117
apical-wedge grafting 119
layering 116
root cuttings 633
stooling 117
pruning 106
renovation 110, *110*
scent 90
size 54
soil type tolerated 99
meyeri 'Palibin', as standard
326
pubescens subsp. microphylla
'Superba', seasonal interest
91

T

T-budding
fruit trees 433, *433*
method 636, *636*
time for 635
Tabebuia chrysotricha 66
soil preferred 66
Tagetes
in containers 319
flower variety 210
hardening off *220*
planting out *220*
pricking out into pack *219*
soil type preferred 216
soil type tolerated 216
erecta
architectural plant 213
flowers 210
patula
attracting beneficial
insects *641*
flowers 210
colours 210
interplanting tomatoes
with 528
tenuifolia
conditions tolerated 213
flowers 210
Talinum okanoganense in trough
267
Talpa europaea *see* Moles
Tamarillos *482*
conditions preferred 482
conditions required 419,
482
diseases 482
feeding 482
fruits 482
growing under cover 482
harvesting 482
mulching 482
pests 482
propagation 482
pruning 482
ripe fruit *482*
routine care 482
site 482
size of tree 482
spacing 482
storing 482
training 482
under cover 423
watering 482
Tamarix
conditions tolerated 95
propagation, hardwood
cuttings 114
soil type preferred 97
ramosissima, pruning 105
Tamper 367
Tanacetum
balsamita (syn.
Chrysanthemum balsamita)
410
flowers 410
foliage 410
harvesting 410
in herb garden *412*
scent 410
storing 410
subsp. balsamitoides 410
propagation, division 410
cinerariifolium (syn.
Pyrethrum cinerariifolium)
668
coccineum, dividing 201
parthenium (syn.
Chrysanthemum
parthenium) *218*, 410
conditions preferred 405
conditions tolerated 405
flowers 410
foliage 209, 410
harvesting 410

Tanacetum parthenium (*cont.*)
propagation
cuttings 410
division 410
from seed 410
self-seeding 218
in scented preparations 410
storing 410
suggestions for use 410
variants 410
'Aureum' 410, *412*
conditions tolerated
405
'Snowball', flowers 209
ptarmiciflorum, foliage 209
vulgare
conditions tolerated 405
planting to restrict spread
411
Tanakaea radicans, soil type
required 260
Tangelos 482
recommended cultivars 481
'Minneola' 481
'Ugli' 481
Tangerines
conditions required 482
in containers 481
cross-pollination 482
growing under cover 481
size of trees 482
Tanks, water 614–15
Tansy *see* Tanacetum vulgare
Taphrina deformans 651
Taraxacum officinale *see*
Dandelion
Taro *see* Cocoyams
Tarragon
French 407, *407*
culinary uses 407
forcing 407, 411
harvesting 407
in herb garden *412*
propagation
division of rhizomes
407
softwood cuttings 407
related species 407
steeping in oil or vinegar
415
storing 407
Russian 407
Tavatesia (syn. Decabelone), flat
grafting 351
Taxodium distichum
adapting to waterlogging 609
soil type tolerated 66
suggestions for use 285
Taxonomy 674
Taxus
diseases, fungal 654, 661
pruning 107
semi-ripe cuttings 79
soil type tolerated 97
for texture 48
for topiary clipping 77, *77*
baccata
conditions tolerated 67
disease-resistance 661, 665
diseases, fungal 654
hedge 84
as background 55
informal 43
renovation 86
in rose garden *150*
shaping *86*
supporting climber
126
pests 655
resistance to storm
damage 68
soil type tolerated 65
suggestions for use 311
for topiary 18, *19*, 76
'Aurea', as focal point *62*
'Standishii', suggestions
for use 59
x media, conditions tolerated
67

Tayberries 471, *471*
in large fruit garden *421*
Tecoma (syn. Tecomaria) 129
propagation
self layering 145
semi-ripe cuttings 143
suggestions for use 129
Tecomanthe 129
semi-ripe cuttings 143
simple layering 145
Tecomaria 129
semi-ripe cuttings 143
self layering 145
Tecophilaea
suggestions for use 231
cyanocrocus
resting 240
suggestions for use 230
Tellima
as ground cover 180
grandiflora 'Forest Fire'
in container arrangement
307
Rubra Group (syn. *T.
grandiflora* 'Purpurea'),
conditions tolerated 181
Telopea speciosissima, soil type
required 99
Temperate climate 606
Temperatures
air 607
average minimum in Europe
609, *609*
effect of altitude on 607
high
damage from 650, *650*
global warming 607
symptoms and control
658, *658*
importance to plants 607
inappropriate, problems
caused by 639
low
damage caused by 650,
650, 653, *653*
succulents tolerant of 342
symptoms 664
problems for indoor plants
355
range tolerated 607
for seed germination 630
soil 607
Tender fruits *see* Fruit, tender
Tender plants
in cool greenhouse 360
frost and thaw damage to
607
protecting from wind 613
protection from frost 607
Tendrils
climbers supported by 124
as climbing method *130*
Tennis courts 389
Tent cloche *see* Cloches
Tepals *676*
Terraces 585–91
see also Patios
clematis on 138
containers on 310–11, *312*
definition 585
existing design and 29, 30
grouping plants on *312*
microclimate on *611*
roses on 152
size 585
uses 584
Terracotta
granules 375
as material for containers *306,
307, 310*, 311, *320*, *321*
Terracotta tiles *see* Tiles
Terrarium 358
care 373–4
compost for 366
condensation on 366, 373
drainage 366
planting 366, *366*
plants for 366
replanting *374*

Tetragonia tetragonioides (syn. *T. expansa*) see New Zealand spinach
Tetranychus urticae 646
Tetrastigma 129
   voinierianum 129
      vigour 130
Teucrium x *lucidrys*, suggestions for use 406
Textures
   harmonizing perennials *175, 176*
   planting for 48, *48, 49*
Thalia
   dealbata
      division of rootstock 303
      position in water garden 285
   geniculata, position in water garden 285
Thalictrum
   conditions preferred 181
   dividing 201
   in mixed border 176
   rochebruneanum, growth rate 181
Thanatephorus cucumis 661
Thaw, dangers of 607
Thecabius auriculae 661
Theft of plants 335
Thelocactus
   division of offsets 349
   bicolor 342
      flowers 342
      suggestions for use 342
   rinconensis, suggestions for use 342
   setispinus 339
Thelypteris, conditions required 194
Thermal screens 574, *574*
Thermometers
   greenhouse 563, *578*
   maximum/minimum 563, *563*
      in greenhouse 574
   soil 563
   wet and dry bulb 576
Thiacloprid 643, 666, 668
Thielaviopsis basicola 661
Thiram 467
Thistle
   creeping see *Cirsium arvense*
   Scotch see *Onopordum acanthium*
Thladiantha
   propagation, softwood cuttings 142
   pruning 135
   from seed 141
   dubia 129
Thompsonella platyphylla, leaf cuttings 347
Thornless berries 471
Thrips 504
   causes 656
   control 647, 656
      biological 642
   damage caused by 647
   pea, symptoms and control 659, *659*
   symptoms 656, *656*
Thrips
   fuscipennis 656
   simplex 647, 656
   tabaci 647
Thuja
   semi-ripe cuttings 79
   soil type tolerated 65
   occidentalis
      soil preferred 66
      'Caespitosa' *62*
   plicata
      'Fastigiata', as hedge 84
      'Zebrina', seasonal interest 59
Thujopsis, semi-ripe cuttings 79
Thunbergia
   conditions preferred indoors 361

Thunbergia (*cont.*)
   propagation
      semi-ripe cuttings 143
      simple layering 145
      softwood cuttings 142
   pruning 137, 376
   from seed 379
   alata 129
      in containers 319
      germination 219
      as pot plants 213
      suggestions for use 129, 212
   gregorii, pruning 135
Thunderflies see Thrips
Thyme see *Thymus*
Thymus
   autumn clearance 413
   cosmetic uses 404
   in knots and parterres 210
   propagation, mound layering 414, *414*
   pruning 413
   soil type preferred 325
   steeping in oil or vinegar 415
   stooling 631
   suggestions for use 259, 316, 405
   for tapestry lawn 389
   underplanting roses 152
   caespititius
      for lawn 389
      soil type tolerated 261
         suggestions for use 259
   cilicicus, propagation by mound layering 414
   x *citriodorus*
      flowers 410
      in herb garden *412*
      propagation, mound layering 414
      scent 410
      Coccineus Group
         flowers 410
         for lawn 389
      'Doone Valley'
         foliage 410
         for lawn 389
      harvesting in winter 411
   polytrichus subsp.
      britannicus, for lawns 389
   praecox, in wildlife garden 101
   serpyllum
      flowers 410
      habit 410
      in herb garden *412*
      suggestions for use 308, 405
      'Minus', suggestions for use 259
      'Snowdrift', flowers 410
   vulgaris 410
      conditions preferred 411
      culinary uses 410
      flowers 410
      foliage 410
      harvesting 410
      in herb garden *412*
      propagation
         division 410
         layering 410
         mound layering 414
         from seed 410
         semi-ripe heel cuttings 410
      related species 410
      storing 410
      suggestions for use 318, 410
      variants 410
      woody cultivars
         propagation, mound layering 414
      'Silver Posie'
         foliage 410
         in herb garden *412*
Tiarella
   in containers 319
   as ground cover 180

Tiarella (*cont.*)
   cordifolia 180
   polyphylla, winter interest 181
Tibouchina
   in containers 319
   greenhouse conditions required 361
   pruning 376
   softwood cuttings 380
   urvilleana 61
Tiered planting see Layered planting
Ties 564, *564*
   general 564, *564*
   plastic 564, *564*
   rose *564*
   tree 65, *65*, 564, *564*
Tigridia 226
   buying 236
   resting 240
Tiles
   glazed ceramic 588, 589
   laying 589
   for patios and paths 588–9
   quarry 588, 589
   terracotta *590*
Tilia
   for coppicing and pollarding 74
   disadvantages 58
   pests damaging leaves 652
   pleached *19*, 75
      suggestions for use 54
   pleaching 18, 58, *58*
   pollarding 46
   cordata 'Winter Orange'
      seasonal interest 59
      pleaching 75
   x *euchlora*
      conditions tolerated 67
      pleaching 75
   x *europaea*
      conditions tolerated 67
   'Petiolaris'
      seasonal interest 59
      suggestions for use 59
   platyphyllos
      conditions tolerated 67
      pleaching 75
      suggestions for use 59, 74
   tomentosa, soil type tolerated 65
Tillaea see *Crassula*
Tillandsia
   conditions required 363
   displaying 362, *362*
   from seed 363, *363*
   caput-medusae 362
   latifolia, displaying *362*
   stricta 362
   usneoides, form *362*
Timber
   containers of 307, 321, *321*
   decking of 591–2, *591*
      patterns 592, *592*
   for edging paths 594
   for edging paving 590
   fence posts in 600, *601*
   fittings for 592
   fungus growths on 592
   for greenhouses 570, *570*
   maintenance 592
   paths of 593
   preservatives for 602
   rot-resisting 602
   for sheds 605
   staining 592
   steps of gravel and *595*
Timberwork
   attaching to brickwork 604, *604*
   joints for beams and uprights 604, *604*
Timers, hose 561, *561*
Tip layering 116
   blackberries *471*, 472
   hybrid berries *471*, 472
   method 631, *631*
   shrubs 116

Tipula 660, 667
Titanopsis, division of rootstock 350
Toads, benefits of 641
Toadstools *668*
   on lawn 668
   symptoms and control 668
Tobacco, genetic modification 638
Tobacco plant see *Nicotiana*
Tobacco rattle virus 662
Toiletries, herbs used for 404
Tolmiea
   greenhouse conditions required 361
   in greenhouse display *359*
   menziesii, in containers 319
Tomato blight 649
   symptoms and control 649, 658, *658*
Tomato eelworm, rotating crops to avoid 498
Tomato leaf mould 640, *648*
   symptoms and control 648
Tomatoes 527–8
   base fertilizer for 527
   chemical damage to 651
   conditions preferred 356, 527
   conditions tolerated 527
   in crop rotation 498
   disease resistance 640, 648
   diseases 505, 528, 658
      fungal 649, 654, 658, 661, 662
      viral 659
   effect of drought on 622
   effect of frost on 607
   feeding 527
   "home-grown" 332
   freezing 506
   fruit 527
      ripening under cloches 527, *528*
      type 675
   genetic modification 638
   ghost spots 658
   greenhouse diseases, fungal 648
   in growing bags 321, *528*
   growing below wall 493, 495
   growing in containers 318, 501, 527
   growing under cover 528
      diseases 505
      feeding 528
      preventing diseases 528
   growing in windowbox 495
   hardening off 527
   harvesting 506, 528
   hormone damage to 655, 659
   as houseplants 355
   indoor, supporting 376
   intercropping 494
   interplanting to deter pests 528
   mineral deficiency 651, 654, 658
   mulching 527
   nitrogen requirements 504, 527
   origins 522
   overwatering 502
   pests 528
      damaging leaves 647
   phosphorus requirements 527
   physiological disorders 658
   planting through plastic mulch 503, *503*
   potting up 527
   recommended cultivars 527
   ring culture 528
      pots for 565, *565*
   routine cultivation 527
   size of plants 527
   soil preparation for 527
   soil types tolerated 527
   sowing 527
   spacing 527
   storing 506, 528

Tomatoes (*cont.*)
   temperature requirements 495
   types 527
   watering 527, 614
      critical periods 502
   'Alicante' 527
   'Balconi Red' 527
   'Balconi Yellow' 527
   beefsteak 527
   bush *527*
      mulching 527
   cherry *522*, 527
   cordons
      recommended cultivars 527
      ripening fruit 527
      spacing 527
      training 527, *527*
   'Crystal' F1 527
   currant 527
   determinates 527
   dwarf, spacing 27
   'Golden Sunrise' 527
   'Grenadier' 648
   'Ildi' 527
   indeterminates 527
      training as cordons 527
   'Legend' 527
   Marmande 527
   'M.M. Super' 648
   'Olivade' 527
   plum *522*
   'Roma' 527
   semi-determinates 527
      training as cordons 527
   'Shirley' 527, 648
   'Sun Baby' F1 527
   'Sungold' 527
   'Tumbler' 527
Tomatoes, tree, see Tamarillos
Tools 550–65
   see also Equipment
   blades 551, *551*
   for bottle garden 367
   buying 550
   cleaning 550, 637
   for cultivation 551–3, *551–3*
   for cutting 554–6
   hiring 550
   for lawns 557–9, *557–9*
   maintenance 550
   metal for 551
   for planting 563, *563*
   powered
      hiring 550
      petrol and electricity compared 556, 557, 558
      rechargeable 556
      safety 550, *550*
   for pruning 134, 550, 554–6
      maintenance 554
   safety in use 550, *550*
   for sowing 563, *563*
   storing 550
   use 550, *550*
Toona sinensis 'Flamingo', suggestions for use 74
Top fruits see Fruit, tree
Top-dressings 503
   as additives 626, *626*
   alpines 270, *270*
   climbers in containers 133, *133*
   decorative 626, *626*
   fruit in containers 426
   for fruit trees 426
   indoor plants 372
   materials used as 626, *626*
   rock plants 264–5
   use of term 626
   uses 616, 626
Top-grafting see Top-working
Top-working
   apples 443, *443*
   weeping standards 73
Topiary 18, *19*, 43, 76–7
   care 77
   clipping 77
      frequency 77

Topiary (*cont.*)
in containers 307
pruning 326
creating complex design 77
creating shape 76–7, *76*
creating simple design 76
designing with 76
designs 76, *76*, *77*
die-back 77
feeding 77
plants for 76
pruning 103, 326
renovation 77
repairs 77
scorch 77
shaping bird *76*
winter care 77
Topography, effects on wind
611
"Topping" 187, *187*
Topsoil *see* Soil
Torenia
from seed 379
fournieri, as pot plants
213
Tortrix moth caterpillars *648*
symptoms and control 648
Town gardens 26
Trace elements 332, 624, 651,
662
Trachelium caeruleum, as pot
plants 213
Trachelospermum 129
in containers 319
for fragrance 129
propagation
self layering 145
semi-ripe cuttings 143
suggestions for use 129
jasminoides
soil type tolerated 132
supporting *364*
Trachycarpus 29
hardiness 60
fortunei 60
conditions tolerated 60
in containers 319
suggestions for use 59,
318
wagnerianus, conditions
tolerated 60
Trachymene coerulea (syn.
Didiscus coeruleus), as pot
plants 213
Tradescantia
conditions preferred indoors
361
greenhouse conditions
required 361
softwood cuttings 380
stem tip cuttings 202
Andersoniana Group, dividing
201
cerinthoides, suggestions for
use 366
fluminensis, suggestions for
use 319, 366
spathacea, suggestions for
use 366
zebrina, suggestions for use
314, 319
Tragopogon porrifolius see
Salsify
Trailing plants
annual 211–12, *211*
for balconies 313
biennials 211–12
in containers 308, 317
annuals and biennials for
213
pinching back 333
tying in 333
containers for 307
for hanging baskets, annuals
212, *212*
indoors 355
pinching out 372
positioning 355
supports for 364, *364*

Training
climbers under cover 376
shrubs 103–10
fan-training *108*
principles 103
standards 109
wall 108–9, *109*
Transpiration 609, 675, *675*
in dry conditions 576
parts of plant for *674*
reducing 614
reducing in drought 609
reducing water loss by 610
water loss by 622
Transpiration stream *675*
Transplanting shrubs 102, *102*
Transplants, trees 64–5
Trapa natans 285
dangers of 298
from seed 303
softwood cuttings 302
value in water garden 284
Trays, seed, *see* Seed trays
Tree felling, tools for 556, *556*
Tree ferns 60, *60*, 61
Tree fruits *see* Fruit, tree
Tree of heaven *see Ailanthus
altissima*
Tree peony *see Paeonia
suffruticosa*
Tree Preservation Orders 69
Tree pruners 555, *555*
Tree stakes 64, *64*, 564
Tree surgeons 74
Tree surgery, tools for 556, *556*
Tree ties 65, *65*
Tree tomatoes *see* Tamarillos
Tree trunks, rock plants in *258*
Trees
for acid soil 65
for alkaline soil 65
arching 55, *55*
for autumn colour 50
for avenues 58
bare-root
choosing 63, *63*, 64
planting 67
planting time 65
for bark 48, *56*, 57, *57*
bark splitting 427
bird damage 657
as boundary 55
branched-head standard
pruning 72, *72*
training 72, *72*
broadleaded, diseases, fungal
665
care after planting 67
central-leader standard
pruning 72, *72*
training 72, *72*
chip-budding 83, *83*
choosing 54, 63, *63*, 324
climbers on 56, 127
clipping for topiary 77, *77*
collection of 24
columnar *55*
conditions required 65
conditions tolerated 63, 65,
66, 68
conical 55, *55*
container-grown
buying healthy plants 640
choosing 63, *63*, 64
compost for 64
planting 66–7, *66*
planting time 65
in containers 58, *58*, 59
care 68
feeding 68
maintaining 334
mulching 68
plants suitable 316, 319
pruning 68, 73, 326
repotting 68, *68*
root pruning 68, *68*
top-dressing 68, *68*
training 326
watering 68

Trees (*cont.*)
coppicing 58, 73–4, *73*
for coppicing 74
cutting down 69, *69*
damage caused by roots of
63
damage caused to
by climate change 68
by deer 435, 666
by lightning 655, *655*
by mice, rats, and voles
662
by rabbits and hares 435,
666
deciduous
established pruning 73
planting time 65
as design elements 54–5, *54*
diseases 69
affecting flowers 656
bacterial 648, 655, 661,
665
fungal 646, 647, 648, 654,
655, 656, 661, 664, 665
distinction between shrubs
and 54, 90
"drip line" 68
dwarf
in rock garden 256
in troughs 258, *258*
effects of high temperatures
on 650
effects of low temperatures on
650, 664
espalier, pruning 73
evergreen *see* Evergreens
existing design and 29, *29*, 32
for exposed sites 67, 68
fan-trained, pruning 73
feathered 65
pruning 72, *72*
training 72
feeding 68
felling 69, *69*
flowering 56
forms 55
as framework of design 54, *54*
framing door *311*
frost damage to 607
frost pockets beside 607
fruit, buying 64
fruiting, diseases, fungal 658
grafting 78, 82–3, *82*, *83*
aftercare 83
apical-wedge 83
chip-budding 83, *83*
spliced side 82–3, *82*
grouping 56
growing clematis on 138
growth rates 54
guy ropes for 64
half-standard 65
heeling in 65, *65*
herbs 404
lack of vigour 69
large 65
lawn round 387
mineral deficiency 650–1
in mixed borders 173
mulching 68
after planting *66*
neglected, renovating 74, *74*
ornamental 54–87
buying 54
choosing 54
features 54, 56–7
foliage 56, *56*
in garden design 54–7
patio beside, disadvantages of
585
perennials with 178–9
pests 69, 654, 657, 666
damaging leaves 645, 646,
647, 648, 651, 652
planter's guide 59
planting 66–7, *66*, *67*
spacing 56
time for 65
planting roses by 158

Trees (*cont.*)
pleached 58, *58*, 75
establishing framework
75, *75*
pruning, winter 75
training 75, *75*
pollarding 58, 73
plants suitable for 74
pruning after 74, *74*
pricking out *80*, 81
problems 69
affecting stems and leaf
buds 653–4
propagation 78–83
air-layering 81
cuttings
aftercare 79
hardwood 78–9, *78*
heel 79
nodal 79
planting depth *78*
semi-ripe 79, *79*
compost for 79
hardening off 79
softwood 79
suitable varieties
for 79
layering 78, 81, *81*
varieties suitable
for 81
from seed 78, 80–1, *80*, *91*
sowing
in containers 80–1,
80, *91*
outdoors 81
protecting
from animals 67, *67*
from frost and wind 67,
69
pruning 71–5, *71–5*
after planting 67
bad 664
established trees 73
formative 72–3, *72*
"haircut" pruned
renovating 74
principles 71, *71*
removing branches 71, *71*
removing competing
leader 73, *73*
roots 73
time for 71
pyramidal 55, *55*
renovating 74, *74*
"haircut" pruned 74
repotting 68, *68*
for rock garden 254
root pruning 73
root-balled
choosing 63, *63*, 64
planting 67, *67*
planting time 65
roots, damage from 70
roses to grow into 155
round-headed 55, *55*
routine care 68–70
for sandy soil 66
for screens 58
seasonal water requirements
622
seed
breaking dormancy 80
extracting 80
fleshy, cleaning 80, *80*
requiring scarification 81
scarification 80
soaking 80, *80*
storing 80
stratification 80
seedlings 64–5
control 671
shade from 183
shapes 55, *55*
as shelter belt 58
shrubs to grow beneath 93
silhouettes *56*, 57
site preparation 65
siting 54, 63
size range 54

Trees (*cont.*)
small
cutting down 69, *69*
protecting *612*, 613
for small gardens 57–8, *57*, 59
snow damage to *609*
soil depth required 65
soil preparation 63–5
specimen
bulbs with 228
as focal points 55–6, *55*
suggestions for use 46,
55–6
varieties to use 59
spreading 55, *55*
squirrel damage 659
stakes for *564*
staking 64, *64*, 66, *66*, 67
standards 65
containers for 326
pruning 72, *72*, 326
stem structure *674*
for stems 56, 57
for structure *46*
stumps, treatment 69, *69*
for successional interest 57
suckers 74
damage from 70
removing 69, *69*
suggestions for use 54, 54–6
ties for 564, *564*
tolerant of wind 68, 613
top-dressing 68, *68*
topiary 76–7
training 71–5
new leader 73, *73*
training roses on 164
transplanting 70, *70*
transplants 64–5
transportation 65
for two or more seasons of
interest 59
undercutting 65
underplanting 58
on walls, protecting *612*, 613
water shoots 74
removing 69, *69*
watering 63, 67, 68
seasonal requirements 622
weed control round 673
weeding 68–9
weeping 55, *55*
pruning *72*
training *72*
weeping standards
forming 73
pruning 73
whips 64–5
wind scorch 610
as windbreaks 493, 611, *611*
for windy sites 67, 68
for winter interest 59
Trefoil *see* Trifolium
lesser yellow *see Trifolium
dubium*
Trellis
attaching to wall 130, *130*
clematis on 138
for climbers 130
in pots 325, *325*
designs 603, *603*
erecting 603
of living willow 87, *87*
screening patio 585
timber for 603
uses 584, 603
Trench layering 631, *631*
Trenching *612*, 613
roses *612*
Trialeurodes vaporariorum 646
Trichocaulon, flat grafting 351
Trickle irrigation systems 577,
577
Trifolium
control 672, 673
dubium 672
pratense, stem tip cuttings
202
repens 672

Trillium
  conditions preferred 231, 259
  germination 272
  propagation 250, *250*
    scooping 250, *250*
    scoring 250, *250*
  seed germination 198
  seedlings 246
    planting out 246
  soil type required 185
  storing 236
  suggestions for use 229
  grandiflorum, conditions
    preferred 181
  rivale, suggestions for use
    230
  sessile, conditions preferred
    181
Trimmers, nylon-line *393*, 550,
  558, *558*
Trioza alacris 647
Triple superphosphate 503
Triploids 435
Tripods
  bamboo, for houseplants *364*
  constructing 604
Tripterygium
  self layering 145
  semi-ripe cuttings 143
Tristeza viruses 480, 481
Triteleia
  conditions tolerated 231
  suggestions for use 230
  laxa (syn. *Brodiaea laxa*), in
    mixed border 228
Trochodendron aralioides, semi-
  ripe cuttings 79
Trollius
  diseases, fungal 652
  dividing 201
  root cuttings 203
  soil type tolerated 184
  chinensis (syn. *T. ledebourii*
    of gardens), suggestions for
    use 285
  x *cultorum*, suggestions for
    use 285
  europaeus 285
    suggestions for use 285
Tropaeolum
  climbing 212
  climbing method 124
  in containers *318*
    with trees 58
  in cottage garden *21*
  as ground cover 211
  growing with marrows *495*
  as host plant for pests 641
  overwintering 335
  pests 645
  propagation, softwood
    cuttings 142
  seedling growth *630*
  soil type tolerated 216
  majus
    in containers 319
    self-seeding 218
    'Empress of India',
      suggestions for use 213
    Gleam Series, suggestions
      for use 213
    'Hermine Grashoff' as
      focal point *211*
    semi-trailing, suggestions
      for use 213
    Whirlybird Series,
      suggestions for use 213
  peregrinum 129
    on host plant 212
  speciosum 129
    as ground cover 127
    growing through shrubs
      126
    in mixed border 176
    suggestions for use 127,
      129
    on yew *126*
  tricolor 129
  tuberosum 129

Tropical climate 606
Tropical plants 60–1
  compost for 367
  flowering, conditions required
    364
  foliage, conditions tolerated
    364
  humidity requirements 576
  propagator for 580
Tropical root rots, symptoms and
  control 661
Tropical trees, pruning 72
Troughs
  alpines in 255, 258, *258*,
    266–7
    care 270–1
    planting 267, *267*
    replanting 271, *271*
  bulbs and alpines in 229
  cacti in 340
  dwarf conifers for 62
  farmyard, drinking 306
  hypertufa, making 266, *266*
  planting in scale with 307
  rock plants in 258, *258*, 259,
    266–7
    planting 267, *267*
  siting *23*
  stone *316*
  succulents in 340
Trowels 552, *552*
  narrow-bladed *552*
  rock garden *552*
  transplanting *552*
  wide-bladed *552*
Trugs 562, *562*
Truncheons 460
Tsuga
  semi-ripe cuttings 79
  heterophylla
    disease resistance 654
    soil preferred 65
    suggestions for use 59
  mertensiana
    f. *argentea*, seasonal
      interest 59
    'Glauca', seasonal interest
      59
Tuberous vegetables 542–8
  in crop rotation 498
Tubers
  basal cuttings 235, *235*
  characteristics 227
  choosing 236
  definition 227
  division, begonias 382, *382*
  planting 238
    depth 238
    in root growth 238
  planting out 613
  problems 660–2
  purpose 675
  root 635, *635*
    propagation 635
  spacing 238
  stem 635, *635*
    propagation 635
  weeds with *671*
Tubs *see* Containers
Tufa 258, 279
  placing 267
  planting alpines in 267, *267*
  for rock garden 261, *261*
  rock plants for 259
Tulbaghia, conditions preferred
  231
Tulip fire *649*, 656
  crop rotation to avoid
    640
  preventing 327, 640
  symptoms and control 649,
    656
Tulipa 226
  in border *232*
  bulb 227
  buying 236
  choosing healthy bulbs
    236
  colour combinations 48

Tulipa (cont.)
  in containers 319
    with crocuses *241*
    with Muscari *320*
    seasonal display 327–8
  cultivation 232–3
  diseases 233
    fungal 649
    virus 662
  drying *243*
  flowers 676
    types 232, *232*
  for cutting 231
  forcing 231
  in formal bedding 227, *227*
  groups 232
  growing with daffodils *233*
  interplanting 211
  lifting *243*
  in mixed border *174*, 177, *228*
  naturalized in grass 389
  planting 237
  propagation 233
    division of offsets 245
    from seed 246
  seasonal interest 50
  seed germination 247
  storing *243*
  suggestions for use 231, 232,
    308, 309, 316, 328
  in trough *316*
  'Angélique', suggestions for
    use 309
  'Clara Butt' 230
  Darwin hybrids 232, *232*
  'Dawnglow' *232*
  Double Late Group (peony-
    flowered) 232
  'Dreamboat' *232*
  dwarf
    conditions preferred 233
    conditions tolerated 231
    species and hybrids 232,
      232
    suggestions for use 231
  early 232
  'Estella Rijnveld' *232*
  Fosteriana hybrids 232
  'Giuseppe Verdi' *324*
  Greigii hybrids 232, *232*
  'Greuze' *232*
  Kaufmanniana hybrids 232,
    232
  late 232
  mid-season 232
  Parrot 232, *232*
  'Peach Blossom' *232*
  'Queen of Night' *232*
  Rembrandt 232
  sprengeri
    conditions tolerated 232
    in mixed border 228
    suggestions for use 239
  'Spring Green' *232*
  sylvestris
    conditions preferred 231
    conditions tolerated 232
  tarda 232
  Triumph Group 232
  turkestanica 151
  Viridiflora 232, *232*
  'West Point', in containers
    232
Tunnel cloche *see* Cloches
Tunnels, of living willow 87
Turf
  laying *392*, 393
  lifting 393, *393*
    trimming after 393, *393*
  meadow 392
  moving 393, *393*
  purpose-grown 392
  sea-marsh 392
  shaping edge 393, *393*
  sizes 392
  storing 392, *392*
  types 392
Turf timothy *see* *Phleum*
  pratense subsp. *bertolonii*

Turgor, supporting stem *674*
Turions, propagation by 303, 635,
  635
Turnip gall weevils 543
Turnip rape *see* Broccoli raab
Turnip tops 512, *512*
  conditions preferred 512
  culinary uses 512
  harvesting 512
  nitrogen requirements 504, 512
  size of plant 512
  sowing 512
  thinning 512
Turnips 542, 543
  bolting 543
  conditions preferred 543
  conditions tolerated 543
  in crop rotation 498
  culinary uses 543
  diseases 543
    fungal 661
  edible parts 542, 543
  freezing 506
  harvesting 543
  mineral deficiencies 662
  nitrogen requirement 504, 543
  pests 543, 643, 660
  recommended cultivars 543
  roots
    colours 543
    size 543
  routine cultivation 543
  size of plant 543
  soil type required 543
  sowing 543
  spacing 543
  storage 543
  watering 543
  'Atlantic' 543
  'Golden Ball' 543
  'Green Top Stone' 543
  'Ivory' 543
  'Market Express' F1 543
  'Oasis' 543
  'Purple Top Milan' 543
  'Tokyo Cross' F1 543
Tussilago farfara 670
Tweezers 279
Twin-scaling, propagation by
  248, 249, 634, *634*
Twine
  garden 564, *564*
  tar-impregnated 564
  for ties 564, *564*
Twining as climbing method 124,
  130
2,4-D 673
Typha
  angustifolia, position in water
    garden 285
  latifolia
    division of rootstock 302,
      303
    'Variegata', position in
      water garden 285
  laxmannii (syn.
    T. stenophylla), position in
    water garden 285
  minima
    position in water garden
      285
    suggestions for use *318*,
      331

Ulmus
  diseases, fungal 653–4, 665
  in fedges 126
  pests damaging leaves 652
  propagation, softwood
    cuttings 79
  parvifolia 'Geisha',
    suggestions for use 258
Ultrasonic devices 667, 668
  as pest repellent 642
Umbelliferae (Umbellifers)
  to attract insects 172
  herbs, sowing 414
Umbels 676
Umbilicus
  conditions tolerated 342
  hardiness 339
  chloranthus, leaf cuttings 347
  horizontalis var. *intermedius*,
    conditions tolerated 342
  rupestris, conditions tolerated
    342
Uncinula 646
Unisexual plants
  obtaining seed from 141
  sexing 141
Upland cress *see* Land cress
Uprights
  concrete casing for *604*
  joints for 604, *604*
Urea 257
Urocystis 652
Ursinia anthemoides, soil type
  tolerated 216
Urtica
  dioica see Nettle, stinging
  urens see Nettle, annual
Ustilago 652
Utricularia
  gibba (syn. *U. exoleta*),
    propagation by plantlets
    303
  minor 285
  vulgaris 285
Uvularia, soil type required
  185

V

"V" clips 215, *215*
Vaccaria hispanica
  conditions tolerated 213
  self-seeding 218
Vaccinium
  soil type required 99, 257,
    325
  ashei see Blueberries, rabbit-
    eye
  corymbosum
    layering 116
    as fruit *see* Blueberries
  delavayi, soil type required
    260
  myrtillus, soil type required
    260
  parvifolium 91
  uliginosum, soil type required
    260
Valerianella locusta see Corn
  salad
Valleys, frost pockets in 607, *607*
Vanda
  method of growth 368
  suggestions for use 368
  temperature required 368
  Rothschildiana 368
Variegated plants
  light requirements 355
  reversion 100, *100*
Variegated sage *see* *Salvia*
  officinalis 'Icterina'
Variegation, as result of mutation
  676

U

Uebelmannia, flat grafting 351
Ugli fruits 482
Ulex
  conditions tolerated 95
  europaeus
    soil type indicated by 167
    soil type preferred 97

Vegetable garden 492–548
  allocating space in 493
  aspect 492, 492
  beds in 494, 494
    making paths in 497, 497
  chemical controls in 504
  decorative 26
  designing 492–8
  existing design and 33
  healthy practices 504, 504
  herbs in 405
  keeping records 498
  layout 494
    planning 498
  maximizing space 494–5
  month-by-month planning 498
  neglected, weed clearance 673
  paths in 492
  planning 22
  protecting from animals and
    birds 504
  weed suppression 497
  well-designed 492
Vegetable marrows see Marrows
Vegetable oils 648
  as insecticides 646
Vegetable oyster see Salsify
Vegetables
  alternating rows 493
  aspect 495
  aspect for 607
  bird damage 657
  bolting 504
  brassicas
    Oriental 513–14
    Western 507–12
  bulb 535–41
    storing 506
    temperature needs 495
  catch crops 494
  climatic requirements 495
  in cold greenhouse 360
  conditions preferred 492, 610
  conditions required 495
  conserving moisture 502, 502
  in containers 328
  crop rotation for pest and
    disease control 494, 640
  cut-and-come-again crops,
    sowing 500
  daylength requirements 495
  diseases 503–4
    bacterial 648, 665
    fungal 646, 648, 654, 656,
      661
    preventive measures 504
  effect of drought on 622
  effect of high temperatures on
    650
  effect of low temperatures on
    650, 664
  feeding 493, 495, 503
  in flower beds 494–5, 495
  flowering 522–9
  in frames 581
  freezing 506
  fruit set 504
  fruiting 522–9
    growing in containers 501
    storing 506
    watering, critical periods
      502
  germination 499
  green manuring between
    crops 494
  growing
    in bed system 496–7
    organically 494
    in rows 496
  growing in containers 318,
    494, 501, 501
    changing compost 503
    compost for 501
    drainage 501
    plants to avoid 501
    preparing containers 501
    routine cultivation 503
    siting 501
    top-dressing 503

Vegetables (cont.)
  growing days required 495
  growing under cover 495, 505
    hardening off 505
    mulching 505
    watering 505
  growing in windowbox 495
  hardening off 501, 505
  harvesting 506
  herbs with 495
  improving drainage for 494
  improving soil for 493
  influence of temperature on
    495
  intercropping 498
  leafy 515–19
    pests 644
    storing 506
    watering, critical periods
      502
  liming soil for 625
  mineral deficiency 650–1
  in mixed border 210
  mulching 495, 502–3, 502
    organic 502–3
    plastic film 503, 503
  nitrogen requirements 503, 504
  "no-dig" system 497
  organic 494
  ornamental 209
  perennial 494
    site 498
  pests 503–4, 660
    damaging leaves 644, 645,
      646, 647, 651
  physiological disorders 504
  planting 500–1
    in beds 497
    depth 500
    through plastic mulch 503,
      503
  podded 530–4
    conditions required 530
    in crop rotation 498
    storing 530
    suggestions for use 530
  positioning 493
  problems affecting stems and
    leaf buds 653, 654, 655
  propagation
    from seed 499–501
      covering soil 499–500
      soil preparation 499
      sowing broadcast
        500, 500
      sowing depth 499
      sowing in drill
        499–500, 499
      sowing in situ 499
      sowing indoors 501,
        501
      sowing large seed
        500
      sowing in modules
        501, 501
      sowing outdoors
        499–501
      sowing in seed trays
        501
      sowing in small
        containers 501
      sowing in wide drill
        500, 500
      stale seedbed
        technique 502
      watering 502
    vegetative 501
  protecting 496
    from wind 492–3, 495
  protecting seeds 500
  protection, netting for 564
  reasons for growing 492
  on roof garden 313
  root 542–8
    in crop rotation 498
    mounding 613
    overwatering 502
    pests 655, 660, 662
    storing 506

Vegetables, root (cont.)
  for successional crops 542
  transplanting 500
  watering, critical periods
    502
  rotation 498, 498
    advantages 494, 498
    drawbacks 498
    planning for 498
    to prevent problems 640
  routine cultivation 502–4
  salad 515–21
    minor 520–1
    watering, critical periods
      502
  seed
    buying 499
    chitted 499
    in gel 499
    naked 499
    pelleted 499
    pre-germinated 499
    pre-germinating, method
      499
    prepared 499
    in tapes or sheets 499
    viability 499
  seedling crops
    sowing as cut-and-come-
      again crop 500
    sowing in wide drills
      500
  seedlings, watering 502
  site 492–3
  soil types preferred 493
  spacing 496, 501
    in bed system 496
    in drought areas 502
    equidistant 501, 502
  in square beds 494
  stem 535–41
    temperature requirements
      495
  storing 506
    damage caused by mice,
      rats, and voles 662
  successional crops 500
  suggestions for use in garden
    494–5
  tender, climbing, supporting
    505
  thinning seedlings 500, 500
  transplanting, watering after
    502
  transplanting seedlings 500–1,
    500
  tuberous 542–8
    in crop rotation 498
  watering 495, 502, 614
    by irrigation system 496
    critical periods 502
    equipment for 502
    methods 502
    minimizing need 502
    with seep hose 502, 502
    time for 502
  weed control 502
    by mulching 502
    minimizing growth 502
  weeding 671
  windbreaks for 611
Veltheimia
  conditions preferred indoors
    361
  greenhouse conditions
    required 361
  suggestions for use 230
Ventilation
  alpine house 279
  automatic vent openers 575,
    575
  chimney effect 575, 575
  of cold frames 581, 581
  fan 575, 575
  greenhouse 573
    maintenance 583
    methods 575, 575
    principles 575, 575
  wind 575, 575

Venturi
  inaequalis 649
  pirina 649
Verandah, wooden 591
Veratrum nigrum, leaves 49
Verbascum
  to attract insects 181
  in containers 309
  flowering time from seed 198
  in mixed border 210, 210
  root cuttings 203
  self-seeding 218
  soil type tolerated 185
  bombyciferum
    architectural plant 213
    soil type preferred 216
    as specimen plant 179
  densiflorum, architectural
    plant 213
  'Letitia', suggestions for use
    259
  olympicum
    architectural form 181
    as specimen plant 179
Verbena
  in containers 319
  in mixed border 210
  overwintering 335
  propagation, stem tip cuttings
    202
  bonariensis 47, 175
    to attract wildlife 178
    for dry conditions 211
  x hybrida
    for containers 212
    suggestions for use 213,
      314
Vermiculite 565
  in potting composts 322, 322,
    323
  storing tubers in 235, 235
Vernonia crinita, growth rate 181
Veronica
  in border 174
  for cutting 181
  propagation
    division 201
    "Irishman's" cuttings 275
    semi-ripe cuttings 274
    suggestions for use 255
  beccabunga, value in water
    garden 284
  filiformis 672
    control 672
    in lawn 400
  longifolia, to attract insects
    178
  peduncularis, "Irishman's"
    cuttings 275
  'Sightseeing' 213
  spicata
    conditions tolerated 259
    soil type tolerated 185
Veronicastrum
  in border 174
  virginicum, growth rate 181
Versailles tubs 307, 321, 321
Verticillium wilt 653
  symptoms and control 653,
    661
Viburnum
  conditions tolerated 95
  deciduous
    hardwood cuttings 114
    soft/greenwood cuttings
      111
  diseases, fungal 654
  germination 115
  pests 644
  planting 98
  propagation
    hardwood cuttings 114
    semi-ripe cuttings 113
    soft/greenwood cuttings
      111
  pruning 105
    to attract wildlife 103
  scent 95
  seasonal interest 50

Viburnum (cont.)
  x bodnantense, seasonal
    interest 50, 92
  x burkwoodii, propagation by
    spliced side-veneer grafting
    118
  davidii, in containers 319
  farreri, choosing healthy
    plant 97
  x globosum 'Jermyns Globe',
    form 46
  opulus
    berries 94
    in fedges 126
    soil type tolerated 97
  plicatum
    suggestions for use 46
    f. tomentosum 'Mariesii',
      as specimen 93
  tinus
    in containers 319
    pruning 107
    renovation 110
    seasonal interest 50
    soil type tolerated 99
    standards 326
Viburnum beetle 644
  symptoms and control 644
Vicia faba see Beans, broad
Victoria amazonica (syn. V.
  regia), position in water garden
  285
Vigna
  self layering 145
  caracalla, pruning 135
Vinca
  conditions preferred 95, 610
  pruning 101
  specimen tree growing in 56
  winter interest 181
  minor, conditions tolerated
    181
Vine eyes 130, 376, 376, 564,
  564
Vine spinach see Ceylon spinach
Vine weevils
  adult 645
    control 645
    damage done by 333, 645
  control 583, 643, 668
  larvae 375, 666
    biological control 642
    symptoms and control
      333, 660, 666
Vinegars, herb, making 415
Vines
  climbing methods 124
  fruits growing on 461–7
  propagation
    cuttings 432
    hardwood cuttings 434
  supports for 376
  training 419
  use of term 419
Viola
  breeding 178
  with bulbs in formal bedding
    227
  diseases, fungal 652
  fruit type 675
  germination 219
  pests damaging leaves 652
  propagation
    self-seeding 218
    softwood cuttings 273
    stem tip cuttings 202
  soil type required 325
  suggestions for use 308
  underplanting roses 151
  cazorlensis, suggestions for
    use 259
  cornuta
    division 275
    for fragrance 181
    "Irishman's" cuttings 275
    'Minor', suggestions for
      use 259
  delphinantha, suggestions for
    use 259

Viola (cont.)
  'Jackanapes' *273*
  jooi, suggestions for use 259
  odorata
    conditions tolerated 180, 181
    for fragrance 181
    as ground cover 180
  riviniana
    conditions tolerated 181
    'Purpurea'(syn. *V. labradorica* var. *purpurea* of gardens), as ground cover 180
  tricolor
    as filler 211
  x *wittrockiana*
    colours 208
    conditions preferred 213
    in containers 319
    in cottage gardens 177
    dead-heading *223*
    as fillers 211
    germination 219
    lifting after bedding 223
    in mixed container planting *327*
    scent 213
    seasonal display 210
    suggestions for use 230, 310, 313, 315, 316, 328
    in windowbox *212*
    winter-flowering, in containers 212
    Princess Series *319*
    Splendid Series 213
    Universal Series, suggestions for use 309
Violet *see Viola*
Violet gall midge 652
Violet root rot 540, *661*
  symptoms and control 661
Virginia creeper *see Parthenocissus quinquefolia*
Virus diseases, quick decline 480
Viruses 656
  affecting bulbs 665
  breeding resistance to 638
  carriers 244
  causes 649
  pests spreading 639, 646
  symptoms and control 333, 649, *649*, 656, 659, *659*
Vitaliana primuliflora, suggestions for use 256, 259
Vitex agnus-castus
  soil type tolerated 99
  suggestions for use 59
Vitis
  conditions tolerated 129
  in containers, training 317
  pests 646
    damaging leaves 652
  propagation
    hardwood cuttings 141, 143, *633*
    simple layering 145
  pruning 135, 136
  soil type tolerated 132
  training, as standard 326, *326*
  amurensis, simple layering 145
  coignetiae 124
    autumn display *128*
    conditions tolerated 129
    as cover for wildlife 128
    in contrasting grouping *126*
    propagation
      hardwood cuttings *143*
      simple layering 145
    seasonal interest 50
    soil type tolerated 131
    suggestions for use 126, 129
    vigour 130
  labrusca 461
    supports for 376
  vinifera see Grapes

Voles 655
  control 662
  damage caused *662*, 663
"Volunteer" seedlings *see* Seedlings, self-sown
Vriesea
  conditions required 363
  displaying 362
  as pot plant 362
  splendens 362

Waldsteinia ternata 259
  conditions tolerated 259
Wall fixings 564, *564*
Wall-of-water cloche *see* Cloches
Wallflower *see Erysimum*
Walls 596–8
  adjoining highways, laws on 602
  alpines in 258
  apples on 435
  attaching climber supports to 130, *130*
  boundary 596
  brick types for *589*
  bulbs needing protection of 231
  clematis on 138
  climbers on 125, *127*
    positioning 131
  climbers trailing over 127
  constructing concrete footings for 596–7, *596*
  containers near 310, 311
  coping 598, *598*
  deflecting wind 310
  dry-stone
    alpines in 258
      planting 268, *268*
    constructing 598
    retaining wall, building *268*
    rock plants in 258
  existing design and 30
  fixing support wires on 424
  footings, concrete mix for 586
  frost pockets beside 607, *607*
  fruit trees against, positioning 425
  fruit trees trained on 419
  growing fruit on 422
  growing plants beside, effect of sun on 610
  height 596
  of living willow 87
  low, building *597*
  materials for 596, *596*
    mixing 596, *596*
  mounting containers on 311
  north-facing
    climbers for 125, 129
    growing vegetables on 493
  painting 596
  peaches trained on *418*, 419
  protecting plants on *612*, 613
  protection for tender climbers 125
  raised beds against 406
  retaining
    building 598, *598*
    drainage for 598
  rock plants for crevices in 259
  rock plants in 258
    planting 268, *268*
  roses climbing on 152–3
  roses recommended for 155
  roses on top of 153
  of screening blocks, building 597

Walls (*cont.*)
  shrubs against 93, *93*
    pruning 108–9, *109*
    training 108–9, *109*
    varieties suitable 95
  shrubs beside, planting *98*, 99
  softening with plants *598*
  south-facing
    growing vegetables on 493, 495
    plants for 611
  strengthening piers for 596
  trees near 63
  uses 584
Walnuts (*Juglans*) 488, 489
  chilling requirement 489
  choosing plants 489
  diseases 489
  harvesting 489
  pests damaging leaves 652
  planting 489
  pollination 489
  propagation 489
    chip-budding 489
    from seed 434
  pruning 71, 489
  recommended cultivars 489
  site 489
  soil for 489
  soil type preferred 489
  spacing 489
  storing 489
  training 489
  tree size 488, 489
  American black (*Juglans nigra*)
    as rootstock 489
    soil type tolerated 66
  'Broadview' 489
  'Buccaneer' 489
  English 489
  'Franquette' 489
  'Lara' 489
  'Mayette' 489
  'Parisienne' 489
  Persian 489
Waney-edged fencing 600, *600*
Washingtonia, in containers 319
Wasps
  benefits of 547, 641
  cynipid *652*
    symptoms 652
  gall *652*
    symptoms 652
  parasitic, as biological pest control 642, *642*, 646
Water 622–3
  bulbs for margins of 229
  circulating in watercourses 292, *292*
  collecting 561, 567, 585, 614–15, *615*
  conserving 28, 614–15, *614*, *615*, 622
  conversion during photosynthesis 675, *675*
  deficiency 622–3
  diverting 28, 585, 615
  domestic waste 615, *615*
  "grey" 283, 615, *615*
    and indoor plants 372
  high dependency, reducing 614
  importance of 622
    to plant 609
    oxygen 283
  irises to grow beside 182
  plants' seasonal needs 622
  recycling 615, *615*, 623
  retention in soil 621, 622
  safety for children 23, 282, 283, 284, *284*
  in soil 622
    in relation to structure 620–1
  storage areas 28, 567, 585, 623
Water butts *see* Butts, water

Water features
  existing design and 33
  reducing water requirements 614
  maintaining water quality 283
Water forget-me-not *see Myosotis scorpioides*
Water fringe *see Nymphoides peltata*
Water garden 282–303
  attracting wildlife 295
  buying plants for 297, *297*
  circulation of water 292, *292*
  in containers 284, 318, 331, *331*
    choosing plants 331
    number of plants 331
    planting 331, *331*
    siting 331
  creating balanced ecosystem 298
  designing 282–5
  features 282
    and water conservation 283
  filtration 292
  indoors 359
  informal *282*
  plant associations 284–5
  planting 297–9
  plants for 282, 284–5
  routine care 300–1
Water hyacinth *see Eichhornia crassipes*
Water lettuce *see Pistia stratiotes*
Water lily *see Nymphaea*
Water plants
  associations 284–5
  baskets for planting 297, *297*
  bog plants 282, 284, 285
    planting 298, *298*
  buying 297, *297*
  care 301
  categories 284
  choosing 297, *297*
  composts for 297, 323
  in containers
    number required 331
    plants suitable for 331
  deep-water 284, 285
    planting 299, *299*
  diseases 301
  floating 282, 284, 285
    control 298, *673*
    introducing into pond *298*
    species to avoid 298
  health 283
  marginals *282*, 284, 285, *331*
    adapting to waterlogging 609
    for containers 318, 331
    cuttings 303
    planting 298, *299*
    repotting *301*
  moisture-loving 284, 285
    planting 298
  oxygenators 284, 285, 298
    choosing 297, *297*, 298
    conditions tolerated 290
    in containers 331
    cuttings 303
    numbers required 297
    planting 299, *299*
    species to avoid 298
    thinning out 301, *301*
  pests 301
  planter's guide 285
  planting 297–9, *298–9*
    depths 298, *299*
  pots for 565
  propagation 302–3
    cuttings *302*, 303
    division 301, 302, *302*
      plants suitable for 302, 303
    runners 303, *303*
    from seed 303, *303*
    turions 303, 635, *635*
  tender, protecting 301
  thinning out 301, *301*

"Water roots" 375
Water shoots
  inhibiting growth 430
  trees 74
  removing 69, *69*
Water softeners 357
Water spouts 283, *283*
Water stress 614
Water supply
  in greenhouse 567
    installing 572
  irregular
    damage caused by 651, 653
    symptoms and control 659
Water table 622
  high, installing drainage system for 623
Water-permeable fabric beds 638, *638*
Watercourses 283, *283*, 292–4
  circulating water 292, *292*
  construction
    with flexible liner 292–3, *292*
    with rigid units 293, *293*
  edging 293
  filtration 292
  repairing 300
  structural repairs 300
Watercress 521
  conditions required 521
  culinary uses 521
  growing in pot 521, *521*
  habitat 521
  harvesting 521
  propagation, cuttings 521
Waterfalls 283
  construction 292
Watering
  basin watering (dishing) 622, *622*
  capillary systems 374, 384, 567, 577, *577*
  in conservatory 357
  drip feed system 561, *561*
  equipment for 560–1, *560–1*
  in greenhouse
    automatic 573
    systems 567, 577, *577*
  holiday arrangements 334–5, 374, *374*
  indoor plants 372
    during absence 374, *374*
  lawns
    during drought 396
    when newly made 396
  mistakes, rescuing pot plants after 372
  moisture take-up 622
  overhead systems 577
  pot watering 622, *622*
  principles of 561, 614
  seep hoses 561, 567, 577
  sprinkler systems 561, 396
  techniques 622, *622*
    bad *622*
    good 561, 567
  testing requirements 332
  time for 614
  trickle system 561, *561*
    in greenhouse 577, *577*
Watering cans *332*, 560, *560*
  dribble bar for 560
  garden *560*
  greenhouse *560*
  indoor *560*
  roses for 560, *560*
Waterlogged soil 621, *621*, 651
  damage to plants 609
  effects of global warming on 607, 650
  indications of 623
  perennials tolerant of 184
  plants adapted to 609
  problems 623
  symptoms 660, *660*, 664, *664*
  treatment for 622, 623, *623*, 664
  vulnerable areas 623

Watermelons 523, *523*
  conditions required 523
  diseases 523
  feeding 523
  fruit 523
  growing under cover 523
  harvesting 523
  mulching 523
  nitrogen requirement 504, 523
  pests 523
  pinching out 523
  planting out 523
  pollination by hand 523
  protecting fruits 523
  protecting from weather 523
  recommended cultivars 523
  routine cultivation 523
  soil type required 523
  spacing 523
  storing 523
  training 523
  way of eating 523
  'Charleston Grey' 523
  'Crimson Sweet' 523
  'Moon and Stars' 523
  'Sugar Baby' 523
  'Yellow Baby' 523
Watsonia
  conditions preferred 231
  corm 227
  for cutting 231
  suggestions for use 230
Wattakaka see Dregea
Wattle hurdles 600, *600*
Weather
  disorders affected by 640
  plant responses to 606
  problems caused by 639
Weatherboarding *605*
Webber moth caterpillars *647*
  symptoms and control 647
Webbing, for windbreaks 564
Weberocereus, side grafting 351
Weeders 553, *553*
Weeding
  by hand 618, *618*, 671
  lawns 672
  to conserve water 622
  tools for 552, *552*, 553, *553*
Weedkillers
  application 671
  clearing overgrown site with 618, *618*
  contact 618, 671, 673
    damage from 650, *650*
  foliage-acting 671
  hormone
    damage caused 659, *659*
    damage caused by 651, *651*, 655
  lawn 672
    applying 673
    buying 673
  for perennial weeds 670, 671
  residual 671
  safety 651, 671
    equipment for 560
  selective 671
    for lawns 672
  soil-acting 671, 673
  sprayers for 560, *560*
  spreaders 559, *559*
  translocated 618, 671, 673
Weeds
  annual 669, *669*
    control 183, 390, 502, 671
  in beds and borders, control 191
  categorizing 669
  clearing from site 262
  control 618, *618*, 669, 671
    organic 502
    ground cover for 127, 180
    stale seedbed technique 502, 620, *620*
    in vegetable garden 502
  in cracks and crevices 673
  cultivated plants as 669, *669*

Weeds (*cont.*)
  effects of global warming on 607
  indicating soil type 167
  lawn 400, 672–3, *672*
    annual control programme 397
  perennial 669, 670–1
    clearing before mulching 626
    control 191, 502, 671, 673
    eradicating 183, 262, 390
    in meadow garden 401
    rhizomes and stolons *670*
    types 670
  pond, control *673*
  preventing 670
  spot treatment 673
  suppressing 265, *265*, 497
  tubers and fleshy roots *671*
  use on compost heap 627
  woody control 671
Weeping fig *see Ficus benjamina*
Weevils, hazelnut 489
Weigela
  propagation
    hardwood cuttings 114
    semi-ripe cuttings 113, *632*
  pruning 106, *106*
  soft/greenwood cuttings 111
  soil type tolerated 97, 99
Weinmannia, semi-ripe cuttings 79
Welded wire fencing 600, *600*
Weldenia candida, root cuttings 275
Welsh chafer 668
Welsh onions *see Onions, Welsh*
Western brassicas *see Brassicas, Western*
Western flower thrips 656
Western wheatgrass *see Elymus smithii*
Wet areas, lawns for 389
Wet wood *653*
  symptoms and control 653
Wetlands 401
Wheatgrass *see Agropyron*
Wheelbarrows 562, *562*
  ball-wheeled 562, *562*
  garden carts 562
  traditional *562*
Wheelchair users
  access to greenhouse 570, *570*
  raised beds for 599
Whip-and-tongue grafting 636, *636*
  fruit trees 433–4, *433*
  trees suitable for 82
Whips, trees 64–5
Whiptail, symptoms and control 652, *652*
White colour scheme, for perennials 176
White blister *646*
  symptoms and control 646
White cyst eelworm 666
White rots, life in soil 498
Whitebeam, *see Sorbus aria*
Whitecurrants *see Currants, white*
Whiteflies 96
  adult *646*
  control 646, 668
    biological 583, 642, *642*
  damage caused by 646
  deterring 504, 641
  nymph *646*
  pesticide-resistant 643, 646
  plants affected by 646
  trapping 641
  types
    cabbage 646
    glasshouse 646
Whitewash, shading greenhouse with 636
Wick watering systems 335
Wicker for furniture *356*
Widgers *194*, *195*, *268*, 367, 563, *563*

Wigwams, as support
  for beans 531, *532*
  for climbers in pots 317, *317*, 325
Wild cherry *see Prunus avium*
Wild flowers
  in cottage gardens 178
  planting in grassland 401
  suggestions for use 178
Wild gardens 20
Wild thyme *see Thymus serpyllum*
Wild-flower gardens/meadows 20, *20*, 43
  bulbs in 228
  establishing 401
  mowing 242
  site 401
  types 401
Wildlife, attracting 15, 22, 43, 264, 295
  with climbers 22, 128
  with fedges 126
  in a lawn 387
  with perennials 22, 178
  with shrubs 22, 103
  to rock gardens 264
  water for 22
Wildlife gardens
  climbers for 128
  ground cover in 101
  perennials for 178
  pond
    creating habitats 295, *295*
    design 295
    planting 295
    siting 295
  water in 282, 283, 284
Willow *see Salix*
Willow herb *see Epilobium*
Wilt
  clematis 665
    symptoms and control 665
  Fusarium 467
  peony 665
    symptoms and control 665
  stem 639
Wilting
  cause 675
  caused by drought 609
Wind 610–11
  annuals and biennials tolerant of 213
  on balconies 313
  bulbs tolerating 231
  damage done by 610–11, 612
  damage to fruit 422
  effects of topography on 611
  funnelling 610, 611
  problems caused by 610–11
  protection from 612, *612–13*, 613
    floating mulches 505, *505*
    for fruit 421, 422, 427
    for shrubs 102
    for trees 69
    for vegetables 492–3, 495
  rock plants tolerant of 259
  on roof gardens 312, *312*
  shelter from 611
  shelter provided by hedge 84
  shrubs tolerant of 95
  strong 611
  trees tolerating 67
  turbulence *610*
    areas of 611, *611*
  value of 610
Wind funnel 493, *567*
Windbreaks
  conditions on each side 611
  conserving soil moisture with 502
  effect of 611, *611*
  fences as 600
  for fruit 427
  hedges as 84, 493, *493*
  height 611
  making *613*
  netting for 564

Windbreaks (*cont.*)
  positioning 611, *611*
  proprietary *613*
  as protection from wind funnelling 610, 611
  shelter provided by 68, 493
  siting 611
  solid, problems caused by 611, *611*
  trees as 58, 63, 68
  for vegetable garden 493
  webbing for 564
Windmill palm *see Trachycarpus fortunei*
Windowboxes
  annuals in 212, *212*
  arrangements in *315*, *316*
  bulbs in 229, 230
  materials for 314
  planting *328*
  plants for 314
  securing 328, *328*
  trailing plants for, annuals 212
  vegetables in *495*
  watering 332, *332*
  wedging on sloping sill 328, *328*
Windowsills
  herbs on 405
  problems for plants on 355, *355*
  propagator for use on 580, *580*
Wing buds 235
Winter
  climbers for interest in 126, 128
  colour in 50, *50*, 177–8
  perennials for interest in 181
  plants for interest in 50
  protecting alpines in 269, 271
  protecting container-grown plants 335, *335*
  shrubs for interest in 91–2, 95
  trees flowering in 59
  trees for interest in 57
  weed clearance 673
Winter aconite *see Eranthis hyemalis*
Winter jasmine *see Jasminum nudiflorum*
Winter melons *see Melons, winter*
Winter moth caterpillars *645*
  symptoms and control 645
Winter purslane 521, *521*
  conditions preferred 521
  conditions tolerated 521
  culinary uses 521
  harvesting 521
  self-seeding 521
  sowing 521
Winter savory 410, *410*
  conditions preferred 411
  culinary uses 410
  flowers 410
  foliage 410
  harvesting 410
    in winter 411
  propagation
    division 410
    mound layering 414
    from seed 410
    softwood cuttings 410
  related species 410
  storing 410
  suggestions for use 406
Winter squash *see Pumpkins*
Winter sweet *see Chimonanthus praecox*
Wire
  chicken *564*
  for climbers 130–1
  pegging layers down with 145, *145*
  pig *222*, *564*
  plastic-coated, for ties 564
  welded, fences of 600, *600*

Wire netting *see Netting*
Wireworms 617, *662*
  symptoms and control 662
  trapping 641
Wisteria
  in containers 128
    training 317
  diseases, fungal 661, 665
  form 46, *47*
  for fragrance 129
  planting 132
  propagation
    grafting 141
    simple layering 145
    softwood cuttings 142
  pruning 135, *135*
  soil type tolerated 131
  standards 326
  suggestions for use 42, 126, 129
  for winter interest 126
  sinensis
    climbing method 124
    soil type tolerated 132
    suggestions for use 129
    vigour 130
    'Alba', on pergola 126, *126*
Witch hazel *see Hamamelis*
Witches' brooms *655*
  symptoms and control 655
Witloof chicory *see Chicory, Witloof*
Wolffia arrhiza 285
  suggestions for use 331
Wonderberries 528, *528*
  berries 528
  conditions required 528
  in crop rotation 498
  culinary uses 528
  feeding 528
  foliage 528
  freezing 506
  growing under cover 528
  harvesting 528
  mulching 528
  nitrogen requirement 504
  pests 528
  pinching out 528
  planting out 528
  poison in 528
  pricking out 528
  routine cultivation 528
  size of plants 528
  soil type required 528
  sowing 528
  spacing 528
  staking 528
  storing 528
  transplanting 528
  watering 528
Wood *see Timber*
Wood anemone *see Anemone nemorosa*
Wood ash
  for fruit trees 426
  nutrient content 624
Wood meadow grass *see Poa nemoralis*
Wood pigeons *645*
  control 645
  damage caused 645, 657
Wood preservatives 321, 583, 602
Wood stains 602
Woodland 401
  ground cover for *180*
Woodland garden 20, *20*, 43
  bulbs in 228, *228*
    care 242
  and climate change 405
  perennials for 178–9, *178*
  stepping stones in *593*
  steps in 593
  trees for 56
Woodlice 639, *644*
  control 644
  damage caused by 644
Woodruff *see Galium odoratum*

Woodrush *see Luzula*
Woodrush, field *see Luzula campestris*
Woody plants, types included as 674
Wool, as liner for basket 329, *329*
Woolly aphids *654*
    symptoms and control 654
Woolly aphids, conifer *see* Adelgids
Woolly beech aphid 646
Worm casts 400
Worm compost 323, 372, 628, *628*
Wormeries 628
Worms *see* Earthworms
Wormwood *see Artemisia absinthium*
Worcesterberry 476
Wounding 633, *633*

X

Xanthophthalmum carinatum (syn. *Chrysanthemum carinatum*) 213
    coronarium 213
    segetum 213
        self-seeding 218
Xanthorhiza simplicissima, root cuttings 114
Xeranthemum
    drying 222
    harvesting 222
    annuum
        for cutting 213
        soil type tolerated 216
Xerochrysum bracteatum (syn. *Helichrysum bracteatum*)
    for drying 212
    soil type preferred 216
Xerophytes 622
Xylem 674

Y

Yarrow *see Achillea millefolium*
Yeasts, colonizing plants 653
Yellow cress, creeping, *see Rorippa sylvestris*
Yellow-rattle *see Rhinanthus minor*
Yew *see Taxus*
Yponomeuta 647
Yucca
    architectural 95
    conditions tolerated 95
    in containers 319
    as focal point *46*
    pruning 108
    soil type preferred 325
    suggestions for use 307, 318
    aloifolia, soil type tolerated 99
    filamentosa, conditions tolerated 181
    flaccida, conditions tolerated 181
    gloriosa
        form 90
        soil type preferred 97

Z

Zantedeschia
    for cutting 231
    division of tubers 302
    greenhouse conditions required 361
    aethiopica
        indoors 354
        suggestions for use 229
        'Crowborough' *230*
            in water garden 285
Zauschneria
    pruning 105
    californicum subsp. *cana*, stem tip cuttings 202
Zea mays (for edible varieties *see* Sweet corn)
    retaining seedheads 223
    'Quadricolor'
        architectural plant 213
        ornamental value 209
Zelkova
    diseases, fungal 653–4
    carpinifolia, suggestions for use 59
Zenobia
    pruning 105
    pulverulenta 91
        soil type required 99
Zephyranthes
    greenhouse conditions required 361
    suggestions for use 231
    candida
        conditions preferred 231
        suggestions for use 231
Zigadenus, suggestions for use 231
Zinc
    containers of 307
    deficiency 426, 479
    plant requirements 624
Zinc sulphate 479
Zingiber officinale see Ginger
Zinnia
    in containers 212, 319
    for cutting 213
    in formal bedding 210
    soil type tolerated 216
Zizania aquatica 285
Zoysia
    for lawns 388, 389
    japonica 388
    matrella 388
    tenuifolia 388
Zoysia grass *see Zoysia*
Zygopetalum mackaii 369
Zygote 195

ACKNOWLEDGEMENTS

Photography credits

The position on the page is given from top to bottom and across the page from left to right. The photographs in plant portrait boxes are numbered sequentially from left to right across the rows and from the top row to the bottom row. Where the picture is in a step-by-step sequence it is given the number of its caption.

ADAS Crown ©: 621 bottom 1–6, 660 centre left
Alamy Images: Keith M Law 8 left
Ted Andrews: 214 centre left
Heather Angel: 641 bottom left
Jane Aspden: 92 bottom, 338, 339 top left
A–Z Collection: 484 centre left, 488 centre left
Harry Baker: 420 bottom, 488 bottom left and right
B & B Photographs: 652 bottom centre above, 660 bottom right, 662 bottom left
Caryl Baron: AGS/Pershore, Worcs. 263 top right
Gillian Beckett: 232 portrait box 1 and 8
Birmingham Botanical Gardens: 482 left
Boys Syndication: 125 top left, 497 bottom left
Nicola Browne Design: Craig Bergmann 327 top right
W. Atlee Burpee & Co.: 532 top
Prof. Chin: 479 centre right, inset, and bottom left, 486 bottom, 487 top left, centre, and bottom left, 522 bottom right, 523 top, 530 centre left, bottom right, and inset
Trevor Cole: 261 top
Eric Crichton: 93 bottom left and right, 126 bottom, 151 bottom right, 152 top and bottom, 173 top, 175 top, 194 bottom left, 227 box 3, 228, 232 top left and top right, 233 top left and top right, 234 portrait box 2, 254, 258 top, 387 top right, 388 bottom, 389 top and bottom, 404, 494, 495 top, 598 top right
Geoff Dann: 258 bottom
Dr Nigel Dunnett: 8–9
Jack Elliott: 229 bottom left, 255 top
Raymond Evison: 127 top, 138 portrait box 7, 139 bottom left
Forestry Commission: 653 bottom left, 655 centre right
John Galbally: 196 centre centre, 197 top centre, top right, bottom left above and bottom far right
GAP Photos Ltd: Jo Whitworth/The Garden House, Devon 7 bottom; Rob Whitworth/Beth Chatto Garden, Essex 2–3
The Garden Collection: Liz Eddison/Designer: Julian Dowle. RHS Chelsea Flower Show 2005 4 bottom; Jonathan Buckley/West Dean Garden 226; Derek Harris 6 left; Andrew Lawson 61 bottom centre; Nicola Stocken Tomkins 314
Garden Picture Library: 152 bottom left, 210 top, 211 top right, 227 box 4, 257 top, 283 top right and bottom, 340 bottom left, 359 top right; Linda Burgess 146; Christopher Fairweather 206; John Ferro Sims 27 bottom right; John Glover 35 bottom left, 47 bottom left, 173 bottom, 208; Georgia Glynn-Smith 46 right, 615 top centre; Gil Hanly 34 bottom right; Carole Hellman 209 bottom; Michael Howes 17 top; Zara McCallmont 35 bottom right; Clive Nichols 42 bottom left; Lorraine Pullin 23 centre left; Howard Rice 20 bottom left, 47 bottom centre; J.S. Sira 46 left, 256, 336, 46l; Graham Strong 327 top centre; Ron Sutherland 28 bottom right, Tresco Abbey Gardens 61 top right; Brigitte Thomas 23 centre, 34 top; Mel Watson 615 top right; Steve Wooster 43 top right

Will Giles: 60 bottom left, 356 top right, 357 bottom right
John Glover: 94 bottom left, 282, 566, 567 top
Jerry Harpur: 21 top right, 25 top left, 26 top, 34 bottom left, 55 top left, 58 top and bottom left, 124, 126 top left, 151 bottom left, 178 top, 182 bottom, 196 centre right, 257 bottom, 280, 307 top, 312 bottom left and bottom right, 313 top right, 354, 386, 401 top right, 420 top right, 422 bottom, 423 bottom, 492, 493 top, 593 top; Jon Calderwood 22; Beth Chatto 178 bottom; Sir Terence Conran 356 top centre; Simon Fraser 28 top; Marcus Harper Gorse Hill Abbey Farm 47 top right, 122; Helmingham Hall 15 bottom left; Arabella Lennox 26 bottom left; HMP Leyhill/The Garden of Eden 490; Valerie Murray 92 top; Old Rectory, Billingford 48 left; Piet Oudolf 47 centre left, 174 bottom; Park Farm 177 top; Pettifers, Oxon 172; Roford Manor, Oxford 17 bottom; Diana Ross 23 centre right; Xa Tollemache 25 bottom left; Terry Welch 27 top left; Gordon White 176 top; Wollerton Hall, Shropshire 25 top right, 48 top right
Holt Studios International: 648 bottom right, 650 centre, centre left, centre right above, centre right below, and bottom right, 656 bottom right, 658 top left, 662 bottom centre, 664 top centre and bottom centre, 666 centre left above, 667 centre right and bottom left, 671 bottom left, 672 top centre left
Horticulture Research International, Kirton: 250 top sequence 3, 650 bottom centre, 654 right, 661 bottom left
D. Hurst/Alamy: 4 top right
ICI Agrochemicals: 649 top right
Clive Innes: 340 top
Andrew Lawson: 15 top, 16 top, 21 top left, centre left, bottom right, and centre centre, 23 bottom, 24 top, 29 bottom, 41 top centre, 47 top left, 49 centre, bottom left, bottom centre, and right, 50 top left, 51 top left, top right, bottom left and bottom right, 55 top right, 77 top left and top right, 125 bottom, 151 top, 153 top and bottom, 174 left, 180 top right; 210 bottom, 229 top left, 284 bottom right, 306, 307 bottom, 308 bottom and top, 310 top left, 311 bottom, 312 top, 315 top, 316 top, 352, 360 top, 402, 416, 493 bottom; Bosvigo House, Cornwall 40 top; Cothay Manor, Somerset 47 bottom right; Ann and Charles Fraser 18; The Garden House, Devon 20 bottom right; Lady Farm, Somerset 49 bottom right; Pettifers, Oxon 14; The Priory, Kemerton 49 top centre; G. Robb/Hampton Court Show 1999 27 top right; Roford Manor, Oxford 16 bottom; Whichford Pottery 304, 327 top left; Wollerton Hall, Shropshire 49 top left
Elvin McDonald: 340 bottom right, 458 bottom, 531 centre left and inset, 538 centre right
MAFF Crown ©: 657 centre, 664 centre
Marianne Majerus Photography: 229 bottom right
Marston & Langinger Ltd: 356 bottom centre and bottom left, 357 top right; Halpern Associates 357 top left
Silvia Martin: 591 bottom

S & O Mathews Photography: Private Garden, Morrinsville, New Zealand 313 bottom
John Mattock: Mr and Mrs J.S. Mattock 166 centre right
Tania Midgley: 421 top
J. Nicholas: 638 bottom
Clive Nichols: 50 bottom, 88; Architectural Plants, Sussex 29 top right; Jill Billington 19 top right; Eastgrove Cottage 170; Lady Farm, Somerset 177 bottom; Mr and Mrs D. Terry 23 top, 36; The Old Vicarage, Norfolk 179 bottom
Wiert Nieuman: 263 bottom right
Oxford Scientific Films: 126 top right, 665 bottom left, 668 left
Park Seeds: 532 bottom left and right
Photos Horticultural: 423 top, 660 top left, 665 top centre and centre right
Michael Pollock: RHS Wisley 614 top left
Royal Botanic Gardens, Kew: 483 centre
Royal Horticultural Society, Wisley: 496 bottom, 645 top right, 649 bottom left and right, 652 bottom and centre, 653 top right and bottom centre, 654 centre and centre left below, 655 bottom left, 656 centre and bottom centre, 659 top right, centre left above, centre right, and bottom right, 661 top right, 662 top left and centre right above, 663 centre, centre right, and bottom right, 666 top left, top right, centre left bottom, bottom centre, and bottom right
Harry Smith Horticultural Photographic Collection: 58 bottom right, 85, 209 top left, 341 top left, 360 bottom, 480 top, 483 top left, 484 centre right, 489 centre, 523 centre left, 667 centre left
Sports Turf Research Institute: 667 centre right above
Lauren Springer: 55 portrait box 1
Prof. H.D. Tindall: 467 bottom, 480 bottom, 481 top, 483 top right and bottom, 486 top left and right, 515 centre left and bottom right, 543 bottom, 545 centre
Isabelle van Groenihagen: 179 top
Elizabeth Whiting Associates: 54, 57 bottom, 91 top, 255 bottom, 283 top left, 290 bottom right, 406 bottom left
Steve Wooster: 90, 128 bottom left, 148, 175 bottom, 194 top, 584, 593 bottom left, 595 bottom left, 606
Tom Wright: 127 bottom, 211 bottom

Additional photography by:
Jane Burton, Peter Chadwick, Eric Crichton, Geoff Dann, John Glover, Jerry Harpur, Neil Holmes, Jacqui Hurst, Dave King, Andrew McRobb, Andrew Lawson, Andrew de Lory, Tim Ridley, Karl Shone, and Gerry Young

Front cover: Peter Anderson/DK

Back cover: far left, D. Hurst/Alamy; left, Andrew Lawson Photography/Whichford Pottery; centre, Roger Smith/DK; far right, Peter Anderson/DK

Every effort has been made to trace the copyright holders. The publisher apologizes for any unintentional omissions and would be pleased, in such cases, to place an acknowledgement in futre editions of this book.

All other images ©Dorling Kindersley
For further information see: www.dkimages.com

Dorling Kindersley would like to thank the following for:

Specialist advice
Mr Ted Andrews (sweet peas); Peter and Fiona Bainbridge (landscape design and construction); Harry Baker (fruit); Graham Davis (Water Regulations Advisory Scheme); Dr Bob Ellis (vegetable cultivar lists); Dennis Gobbee (rose hybridizing); Patrick Goldsworthy, British Agrochemical Association (chemical controls); Ken Grapes, Royal National Rose Society; Tony Hender (Seedlings); Peter Orme (rock garden design and construction); Terence and Judy Read (grape cultivar lists); Prof. S. Sansavini (fruit cultivar lists); Pham van Tha (fruit cultivar lists); and in particular the many staff at the RHS Garden, Wisley, who so patiently and freely gave of their time to advise on horticultural techniques throughout this project.

Providing plants or locations for photographs
Mrs Joy Bishop; Brickwall House School, Northiam; Brinkman Brothers Ltd, Walton Farm Nurseries, Bosham; Denbies Wine Estate, Dorking; Mrs Donnithorne; Martin Double; J.W. Elliott & Sons (West End) Limited, Fenns Lane Nursery, Woking; Elsoms Seeds Ltd, Spalding; Mrs Randi Evans; Adrian Hall Ltd, Putney Garden Centre, London; Mr & Mrs R.D. Hendriksen, Hill Park Nurseries, Surbiton; The Herb and Heather Centre, West Haddlesey; Hilliers Nurseries (Winchester) Ltd, Romsey; Holly Gate International Ltd, Ashington; John Humphries, Sutton Place Foundation, Guildford; Iden Croft Herbs, Staplehurst; Mr de Jager; Nicolette John; David Knuckey,

Burncoose Nursery; Mr & Mrs John Land; Sarah Martin; Frank P. Matthews Ltd, Tenbury Wells; Mr & Mrs Mead; Anthony Noel, Fulham Park Gardens, London; Andrew Norfield; Notcutts Garden Centre, Bagshot; Bridget Quest-Ritson; Royal Botanic Gardens, Kew; Royal Horticultural Society Enterprises; Lynn and Danny Reynolds, Surrey Water Gardens, West Clandon; Rolawn, Elvington; Mrs Rudd; Miss Skilton; Carole Starr; Mr & Mrs Wagstaff; Mrs Wye.

Tools for demonstration photographs
Spear and Jackson Products Ltd, Wednesbury, West Midlands; Felco secateurs supplied by Burton McCall Group, Leicester.

Supplying equipment
Agralan, Ashton Keynes; Bob Andrews Ltd, Bracknell; Black and Decker Europe, Slough; Blagdon Water Garden Products PLC, Highbridge; Bloomingdales Garden Centre, Laleham; Bulldog Tools Ltd, Wigan; Butterley Brick Ltd, London; CEKA Works Ltd, Pwllheli; Challenge Fencing, Cobham; J. B. Corrie & Co Ltd, Petersfield; Dalfords (London) Ltd, Staines; Diplex Ltd, Watford; Direct Wire Ties Ltd, Hull; Robert Dyas (Ltd), Guildford; Fishtique, Sunbury-on-Thames; Fluid Drilling Ltd, Stratford-upon-Avon; Gardena UK Ltd, Letchworth Garden City; Gloucesters Wholesales Ltd, Woking; Harcros, Walton-on-Thames; Haws Elliott Ltd, Warley; Honda UK Ltd, London; Hozelock Ltd, Birmingham; ICI Garden Products, Haslemere; LBS Polythene, Colne;

Merck Ltd, Poole; Neal Street East, London; Parkers, Worcester Park; Pinks Hill Landscape Merchants Ltd, Guildford; Qualcast Garden Products, Stowmarket; Rapitest, Corwen; Seymours, Ewell; Shoosmith & Lee Ltd, Cobham; SISIS Equipment Ltd, Macclesfield; Thermoforce Ltd, Maldon.

Additional assistance
Sarah Ashun, Jennifer Bagg, Kathryn Bradley-Hole, Lynn Bresler, Diana Brinton, Kim Bryan, Susan Conder, Jeannette Cossar, Diana Craig, Penny David, Paul Docherty, Howard Farrell, Roseanne Hooper, David Joyce, Steve Knowlden, Mary Lambert, Claire Lebas, Margaret Little, Louise McConnell, Caroline Macy, Eunice Martins,

Ruth Midgley, Peter Moloney, Sarah Moule, Fergus Muir, Chez Picthall, Sandra Schneider, Janet Smy, Mary Staples, Tina Tiffin, Roger Tritton, Anne de Verteuil, John Walker.

Design assistance: Murdo Culver, Gadi Farfour, Alison Shackleton, Nicola Erdpresser, Rachael Smith, Aparna Sharma, Kavita Dutta.

Editorial assistance: Fiona Wild, Aakriti Singhal.

Special thanks to the staff at Wisley and Vincent Square, in particular Susannah Charlton, Simon Maughan, Chris Prior, Andrew Halstead, Guy Barter, Jim Arbury, Jim England, and Paul Alexander.

Abbreviations

C	centigrade	ml	millilitre(s)
cf	compare	mm	millimetre(s)
cm	centimetre(s)	oz	ounce(s)
cv(s)	cultivar(s)	p(p).	page(s)
F	fahrenheit	pl.	plural
f.	forma	pv.	pathovar
fl oz	fluid ounce(s)	sp.	species
ft	foot, feet	spp.	species (pl.)
g	gram(s)	sq	square
in	inch(es)	subsp.	subspecies
kg	kilogram(s)	syn.	synonym(s)
lb	pound(s)	var.	varietas
m	metre(s)	yd	yard(s)

Note: The generic and species names of plants are abbreviated to their initial letters after their first full mention in a sentence or a list.